Rating system

★★★★★ Excellent

★★★★ Very Good

★★★ Good

★★ Fair

★ Poor

Turkey

Also by Mick Martin & Marsha Porter, with Ed Remitz
Published by Ballantine Books:

VIDEO MOVIE GUIDE FOR KIDS: A BOOK FOR PARENTS

VIDEO MOVIE GUIDE 1988

Mick Martin
& Marsha Porter

Consulting Editor:
Ed Remitz

BALLANTINE BOOKS • NEW YORK

 Published in the United States of America by Ballantine Books, a division of Random House, Inc., New York, and simultaneously in Canada by Random House of Canada Limited, Toronto.

Library of Congress Catalog Card Number: 87-91525

ISBN 0-345-34925-3

Manufactured in the United States of America

First Edition: December 1987

CONTENTS

CHIEF CONTRIBUTORS

Derrick Bang
Rich Garrison
Phil Hoover
Jack Keaton
Richard Leathers
Greg Leis
Bill McLeod
Don Norris
Dennis Rood
Lisa Smith-Youngs
Jimmy Summers
Tom Tolley
Wendy Welker
Robert Young, Jr.

FOREWORD

They say the third time's the charm, and in the case of *Video Movie Guide 1988*, it happens to be true. Now bulging with over 5,700 reviews, it is the most comprehensive critical guide to video available today.

As in the past, we have covered all of the major video releases currently in stores as well as included several months' worth of upcoming titles. The difference this time is that we have gone backward as well as forward in our coverage.

Our newly added entries include vintage films as well—early sound films, silents, and serials available on video from numerous sources. Add to this greater in-depth collections of foreign films, B westerns, documentaries, made-for-video releases, made-for-television movies, and TV series—and you have what we trust is the most informative and helpful guide to the world of video viewing.

For your convenience, we have created a chapter on foreign language films. Previously, imports were scattered throughout the book in genres such as comedy and drama. During personal appearances, we were shocked to discover that some people assumed we had ignored foreign films altogether. This seemed to indicate to us that it would be wise to collect them and put them in a section of their own, thus making them easier to find.

You will also notice that the Children's Viewing chapter is

now co-titled Family Films. This is just a gentle reminder that many of the films in this section, as elsewhere in the book, are appropriate for all ages.

The comedy chapter now includes a greatly increased number of made-for-video and concert releases. When you walk into a video store in the mood for a few laughs, we want to guide you to the best. Previously, we concentrated on theatrical releases, but now the emphasis has been put where we believe it belongs: on what is available on video.

Not all of the video releases reviewed in this book will be available for rental at your neighborhood outlet. This is especially true of the early sound, silent, and foreign films. But most of these can be ordered by mail.

In the last edition, we included a list of mail-order houses and asked readers to rate the various companies. Thanks to your kind and helpful responses, we have now trimmed down the list to those that you have recommended.

The best source for foreign films is Facets Multimedia, Inc. (1517 Fullerton Avenue, Chicago, IL 60614). Its catalogue (which costs $2) has the most complete list of foreign language movies on video we've ever seen—and it keeps growing. Some hard-to-find American films from the 1920s, '30s, '40s, and '50s are available through this company as well.

Vintage motion pictures are also available through Movies Unlimited (6736 Castor Avenue, Philadelphia, PA 19149); Video Yesteryear (Box C, Sandy Hook, CT 06482); Blackhawk Films (1 Old Eagle Brewery, P.O. Box 3990, Davenport, ID 52808); and Shokus Video (P.O. Box 8434, Van Nuys, CA 91409). According to our readers, these are the places to contact when you want silents, serials, B westerns, and early sound-era releases.

Movies Unlimited (6736 Castor Avenue, Philadelphia, PA 19149) has a large quantity of movies, but you must buy a catalogue for $7.95 to find out what they have. Both Discount Video (3711 Clarke Avenue, Suite B, Burbank, CA 91505) and Budget Video (1534 N. Highland, Los Angeles, CA 90028) have inventory that goes beyond what is generally available. But these are public domain titles and the video versions are not always of pristine-picture or perfect-sound quality. However, they are the only source for some B westerns and other collectors' favorites.

In a similar sense, Kartes Video Communications (7225 Woodland Drive, Indianapolis, IN 46278) has the market cornered on other titles. Its inventory of American and foreign films from the 1930s, '40s, '50s, and '60s is seldom available for rental but can be found for sale in many book and video stores.

Not all of the movies contained in *Video Movie Guide 1988* are still available for sale. Some are out of print. Even the major distributors take some titles out of circulation. So if you try to buy a certain movie through your local video outlet, which is the first place you should check, and find that it is out of print, we apologize in advance. But this is primarily a viewing and renting guide. There is no way for us to know what your local dealer has on the shelves, so we have attempted to include everything that has come out on video with the usual exceptions of adult films, rock videos, and kung-fu imports.

Last, we'd like to thank those readers who have written in with suggestions, comments, and criticisms. You have played a vital role in the growth of *Video Movie Guide* and will find most of your revision requests reflected in this volume. Please do not hesitate to write us. This is your book in an even greater sense than it is ours. Please send all comments to *Video Movie Guide 1988*, P.O. Box 814, El Sobrante, California 94803. We'd love to hear from you. In the meantime, happy viewing!

INTRODUCTION

In creating the *Video Movie Guide* we have attempted to give you the most up-to-the-minute book, with a clear rating system and easy access to the titles covered. Only movies that had been scheduled for release as videos at the time of publication are included in this edition. You will find movies listed in alphabetical order at the beginning of the book and then discussed in depth in their respective genres:

- Action/Mystery/Adventure
- Children's Viewing/Family Films
- Comedy
- Drama
- Foreign Language
- Horror/Suspense
- Musicals
- Science-Fiction/Fantasy
- Westerns

In addition, you will find indexes on pages 1201–1453, organized by directors and performers, as well as a list of films recommended for family viewing.

The rating system runs from five stars to a turkey. We feel a five-star film is a must; a four-star rating means it's well worth watching. The desirability of a film with a lesser rating depends on your liking for a particular type of film or a movie star. A turkey by any other name is still a bad movie. If a film is particularly offensive, even though it has a big-name star, we want you to know why. Likewise, if a little-known gem has special attributes, we've done our best to call your attention to them.

Certain kinds of movies have been purposely ignored. For example, we do not feel that hardcore sex films have a place in a book of this kind.

We've included kung fu movies featuring well-known stars such as Bruce Lee and Chuck Norris. However, the all-the-same Chinese imports with lots of bang-pow fist-and-foot action but no plot don't vary much above mediocre in quality. So we've left them out.

We have, however, been more lenient about the inclusion of horror films. Since there is a huge audience for them and they are readily available, we've attempted to include even the lowest of the low to help prevent you from getting stuck with a turkey.

When a film has been rated G, PG, PG-13, R, or X by the Motion Picture Association of America, we have noted it. Only theatrically released films distributed after November 1967 were considered by the MPAA ratings board, so we have attempted to indicate the potentially objectionable content in films released before then, as well as in made-for-cable and video-only products. Even the MPAA ratings are confusing at times, so, wherever appropriate, we have explained these as well.

Overall, we feel this is the most practical guide to what's available on video. We hope you agree.

ACKNOWLEDGMENTS

Video Movie Guide came into being as the result of a phone call. Cary Nosler, better known as the multimedia health adviser Captain Carrot to thousands of Northern Californians, called film critic Mick Martin at the *Sacramento Union* newspaper.

"Why don't you write a book on videos?" he asked. "I'm sick and tired of getting stuck with bad movies."

It sounded like a great idea, so Martin went to the powers that be at the *Sacramento Union* and secured their cooperation in the development of the book. His reviews from 12 years of writing for the paper formed its basis.

In addition, the writings on the subject by past and present staff and free-lance writers of the *Sacramento Union* also were made available. We would like to thank Twila J. Walker, Peter Anderson, Jim Carnes, Richard Simon, Cathy Cassinos, Alison ApRoberts, Ana Sandoval, Lou Thelen, Steve Connell, Mark Halverson, Kevin Valine, and Tom Miner for permission to use their past writings.

To create a comprehensive guide, Martin joined forces with co-author Marsha Porter and writer/publisher Ed Remitz to form Static Studios. It was through their company that the various activities involved were coordinated.

Although Porter and Martin wrote most of the material, other writers were invaluable in covering the field. Paul Freeman, Rich Garrison and Robert Young Jr. wrote about Hollywood classics, Derrick Bang, Phil Hoover, Jack Keaton, Greg Leis, Bill McLeod, Don Norris, Bob Shaw, Lisa Smith-Youngs, Tom Tolley and Wendy Welker covered a wide variety of films, Richard Leathers specialized in the action-adventure category, and Dennis Rood split his time between horror and comedy. All are ongoing contributors to *Video Movie Guide*.

In addition, Jimmy Summers, Roy Engoron, Gary Zilaff, Tim Eldred, David Linck, Linda Rajotte, Ethan Aronson, Bill Webb, Holly Johnson, Susanne Kocher, Linda Logsden, Ed Slofkosky, Del Forsythe, Gerry D. Watt, Paul C. Plain, Ross Woodbury, J. Douglas Halford, Bill Smith, Jack Schwab, Mitchell Cohen, Mike Antonaros, Sherry Kramer, Jan Patrick, Matias Bombal, Mark Steensland, Fritz Rodrigues, Vicki and Marc Sazaki, and Mary Scott wrote reviews on movies in their particular fields of interest and expertise.

Video Movie Guide began as a Sacramento-released pamphlet called "The Video Rental Guide." It was printed by U.S. Mailist, which is operated by Lyle, Marty, and Linda Hintz. Thanks also go to Robert W. Schmidt, Wade M. Kent, Dennis Rood and the Sazaki family for research.

Others who made this book possible include: Bob Badgley, Marilyn Abraham, Sheila Curry, Joe Blades, Stan Goman, Russ Solomon, Rob Heidt, Walter and Pat Rice, Bob Kronenberg, Paul Hodgkins, Jerry Pompei, Mike Farrace, Linda Phillips, Eric Sakach, Steve Johnson, Ron and Steve Pacheco, Mark Brown, Carol Johnson, Linda Forsythe, Greg Guertin, Eileen and Chuck Porter, Phyllis Donovan, Hope Svrcek, Diane, Hada and Francesca Martin, Matt and Norma Condo, Heidi Keller, Jon Souza, Marcia Raphael, Jeff Kepley, Kris Sazaki, Neil Matsuoka, Duncan Mandrill, John Sudman, Jim Dixon, Cynthia Wright, Catherine Coulter, Robert J. Kantor, Shannon Bryony, Don Besse, Les and Eliza Rosen, Patricia Pausner, and Dr. Patrick O'Donoghue, M.D., PhD..

ACE DRUMMOND

★★½

DIRECTORS: Ford Beebe, Cliff Smith

CAST: John King, Jean Rogers, Noah Beery Jr., Guy Bates Post, Arthur Loft, Chester Gan, Jackie Morrow, Montague Shaw, Lon Chaney Jr., Robert Warwick

An archvillain known as The Dragon has thwarted every effort by an international group attempting to establish a round-the-world airline service. Aviation whiz Ace Drummond jumps from the Sunday funnies to the silver screen in this thirteen-episode Universal serial and, while helping pretty Jean Rogers find her father, he searches for a mountain filled with jade. Sounds like a tall order, but Ace is up to the task, especially with assistance from Noah Beery Jr., a serial star in his own right. Plenty of familiar faces in this one, including an early appearance by future Universal horror film star Lon Chaney Jr. Laughable in many respects, this is a pretty good serial and the only filming of this character's adventures.

1936 B & W 250 minutes

ACROSS 110TH STREET

★★★½

DIRECTOR: Barry Shear

CAST: Anthony Quinn, Yaphet Kotto, Anthony Franciosa, Richard Ward

This one is a real sleeper! An action-packed, extremely violent film concerning gang warfare between the Mafia and their black counterparts. Entire cast is very good, as are the action scenes. Rated R for violence, language.

1972 102 minutes

ACTION IN ARABIA

★★½

DIRECTOR: Leonide Moguy

CAST: George Sanders, Virginia Bruce, Gene Lockhart, Robert Armstrong, Michael Ansara

George Sanders fights against time and Nazi agents as he attempts to inform the Allied authorities about German plans for a pact with the Arabs in this wartime romance-adventure. The love of a woman helps to turn the tide for the western powers in this sandy adventure, but the cost of victory is dear for hero Sanders and the object of his affections (Virginia Bruce). A pretty good adventure film, it is typical of the wartime features that were produced by all the major and minor studios in Hollywood at the time.

1944 B & W 75 minutes

ADVENTURES OF CAPTAIN MARVEL, THE

★★★★

DIRECTORS: William Witney, John English

CAST: Tom Tyler, Frank Coghlan Jr., William Benedict, Louise Currie

Fawcett Comics Captain Marvel is splendidly brought to life by Republic Studios in what is generally regarded as the best serial of all time, certainly the best superhero chapter play ever produced. An expedition seeking relics and information on the lost Scorpion cult is trapped in a tomb in remote Siam. The members are eventually rescued by assistant radio operator Billy Batson in the guise of Captain Marvel, champion of truth and justice, who can be summoned by the magic word "Shazam." Sincerely acted by all involved, this serial set the standards for flying stunts for years to come and still contains some of the best flying scenes ever recorded on film. If you've never seen a serial, watch this one.

1941 B & W 12 chapters

ADVENTURES OF CAPTAIN FABIAN

DIRECTOR: William Marshall

CAST: Errol Flynn, Vincent Price, Agnes Moorehead

The career of Errol Flynn was a roller-coaster ride to be sure, but seldom did it get as low as this turkey. Flynn doesn't have the heart needed to rise above this lackluster swashbuckler. A sad sight for fans of the genre and Errol Flynn alike.

1951 100 minutes

ADVENTURES OF DON JUAN, THE

★★★★

DIRECTOR: Vincent Sherman

CAST: Errol Flynn, Viveca Lindfors, Robert Douglas, Alan Hale, Romney Brent, Ann Rutherford, Robert Warwick, Jerry Austin, Douglas Kennedy, Una O'Connor

Despite the obvious use of footage from *The Adventures of Robin Hood* and *The Private Lives of Elizabeth and Essex*, this is a solid swashbuckler. It was star Errol Fynn's last memorable film in the genre he dominated during the heyday of Hollywood. Paired with his best on-screen buddy, Alan Hale, Flynn plays the great lover and swordsman of the title with tongue planted firmly in cheek. The years of drinking were beginning to show on his once boyishly handsome face. Yet this is quite appropriate to his portrayal of the famous libertine, who comes to the aid of a queen (Viveca Lindfors) in his later years.

1949 110 minutes

ADVENTURES OF TARTU

★★½

DIRECTOR: Harold S. Bucquet

CAST: Robert Donat, Valerie Hobson, Glynis Johns, Walter Rilla, Phyllis Morris

Robert Donat steals the show as a British spy entrusted with the crippling of a poison gas factory behind enemy lines. He is joined in this blend of comedy and suspense by lovely Valerie Hobson and perky Glynis Johns. Nothing really special about this one, but it's fun.

1943 B & W 103 minutes

ADVENTURES OF TARZAN, THE

★★½

DIRECTOR: Robert F. Hill

CAST: Elmo Lincoln, Louise Lorraine, Percy Pembroke, Frank Whitson, James Inslee, Lillian Worth, Frank Merrill, Joe Martin, George Momberg

Early action star Elmo Lincoln dons a wig for the third time to portray the Lord of the Jungle in this ambitious chapter play. Lincoln, a former D. W. Griffith character actor and star of *Elmo the Mighty*, *Elmo the Fearless*, and the first two Tarzan pictures, finds himself fighting unscrupulous Bolsheviks, wild animals, a claimant to his family name, and the hordes of the lost city of Opar. Loosely adapted from two Tarzan novels, this was one of the most popular releases of 1921–1922 and was to be the last Tarzan film until 1927, when Joseph Kennedy's FBO made *Tarzan and the Golden Lion*. Beefy Elmo Lincoln was doubled by a fellow performer named Frank Merrill, who later went on to make two Tarzan serials for Universal in the late 1920s, ultimately introducing both the vine-swinging and the yell that MGM used so effectively for their series with Johnny Weissmuller. Although originally released as a fifteen-chapter serial, Lincoln's final appearance as the ape-man was reedited into a ten-chapter version and released with sound effects in 1928 and played all over the world in various forms for years. Silent.

1921 B & W 15 chapters

ADVENTURES OF THE FLYING CADETS

★★

DIRECTORS: Ray Taylor, Lewis D. Collins

CAST: Johnny Downs, Bobby Jordan, Ward Wood, Billy Benedict, Eduardo Ciannelli, Regis Toomey, Robert Armstrong

A mysterious figure known as the Black Hangman has located a secret deposit of helium in Africa and plans to sell it to the Nazis. The young Flying Cadets (including future announcer Johnny Downs and Dead End Kid Bobby Jordan) have been falsely implicated in a series of murders and set out to clear their names and bring the traitorous agent (actually an American engineer) to justice. The breezy and likable Robert Armstrong plays the two-faced villain in this serial, while character actor Eduardo Ciannelli plays another memorable baddie. Regis Toomey rounds out the cast as stalwart Captain Ralph Carson, the Allied leader who believes in the young cadets and assists them in bringing their quarry to justice. Not a great serial, but even an excess of stock footage is offset by a good cast and some thrilling action sequences.

1943 B & W 13 chapters

ADVENTURES OF ROBIN HOOD, THE

★★★★★

DIRECTOR: Michael Curtiz

CAST: Errol Flynn, Basil Rathbone, Ian Hunter, Olivia De Havilland, Claude Rains, Alan Hale, Eugene Pallette, Montagu Love

This classic presents Errol Flynn at his swashbuckling best. He is backed up in this color spectacular by a perfect cast of supporting actors. Olivia De Havilland is

Maid Marian. Alan Hale and Eugene Pallette are Little John and Friar Tuck. The bad guys are also at their evil best, as played by Basil Rathbone and Claude Rains. Even the smallest roles are colorfully represented. Lavish sets and a stirring musical score help place *Robin Hood* among the very best adventure films.

1938 106 minutes

ADVENTURES OF SHERLOCK HOLMES, THE

★★★★½

DIRECTOR: Alfred Werker
CAST: Basil Rathbone, Nigel Bruce, Ida Lupino, George Zucco

The best of all the Basil Rathbone–Nigel Bruce Sherlock Holmes movies, this pits the great detective against his arch-nemesis, Dr. Moriarty (played by George Zucco). The period setting, atmospheric photography, and the spirited performances of the cast (which includes a young Ida Lupino as Holmes's client) make this a must-see for mystery fans.

1939 B & W 85 minutes

ADVENTURES OF SHERLOCK HOLMES: A SCANDAL IN BOHEMIA

★★★★½

DIRECTOR: Paul Annett
CAST: Jeremy Brett, David Burke, Gayle Hunnicutt, Wolf Kahler, Michael Carter, Max Faulkner, Tim Pearce, Rosalie Williams

The supremely independent Sherlock Holmes falters in this episode of the popular series and almost succumbs to the charms of a female temptress, one Irene Adler, who also happens to be a clever crook. Holmes and Watson come to the aid of the king of Bohemia (who is being blackmailed) and encounter the delightfully unscrupulous Miss Adler, who turns out to be directly involved in the crime. Finely played by all involved, this is one of the best of the series and offers a rare chance to see Sherlock Holmes emotionally involved in a case. Terrific show.

1984 52 minutes

ADVENTURES OF SHERLOCK HOLMES: THE BLUE CARBUNCLE

★★★★

DIRECTOR: David Carson
CAST: Jeremy Brett, David Burke, Rosalind Knight, Ros Simmons, Ken Campbell, Desmond McNamara, Amelda Brown, Brian Miller, Rosalie Williams, Frank Mills

Sherlock Holmes delves into the darkest corners of London's slums in order to solve the mystery of a fabulous gem and save a man's life. Aidec by his friend and colleague, Dr. John Watson, the seemingly supernatural Holmes braves danger from all sides and tenaciously follows the clues until he has solved the problem. Splendidly done (as are all of the stories in this series), this episode captures the flavor of Victorian London and gives the viewer the sense of being involved in the dark doings. Jeremy Brett and David Burke as Holmes and Watson are perhaps the finest team to essay the roles, and the adaptations are the most authentic versions of the original stories ever filmed.

1984 52 minutes

ADVENTURES OF SHERLOCK HOLMES: THE COPPER BEECHES

★★★★

DIRECTOR: Paul Annett
CAST: Jeremy Brett, David Burke, Joss Ackland, Natasha Richardson, Lottie Ward, Patience Collier, Angela Browne, Peter Jonfield

In this exquisitely crafted BBC series of adaptations of Sir Arthur Conan Doyle's celebrated detective stories, Jeremy Brett, as Sherlock Holmes, and David Burke, as his faithful biographer John H. Watson, M.D., transcend all who have gone before. While Basil Rathbone and Nigel Bruce may be the quintessential Holmes and Watson to many movie buffs, Brett and Burke get much closer to the original characters. The result is an authenticity that should please even the most discriminating Sherlockian. In this one, the world's most famous consulting detective comes to the aid of a young governess (Natasha Richardson) who suspects her employer (Joss Ackland) is up to something sinister.

1985 54 minutes

ADVENTURES OF SHERLOCK HOLMES: THE CROOKED MAN

★★★★

DIRECTOR: Alan Grint

CAST: Jeremy Brett, David Burke, Norman Jones, Lisa Daniely, Denys Hawthorne, Fiona Shaw, Paul Chapman

Jeremy Brett stars in another entry in the British television series. This time, he and Dr. Watson (David Burke) must solve an apparent murder/suicide, which (naturally) turns out to have hidden complexities—most notably the muddy, oddly shaped footprints left at the scene of the crime. Although this case does not suitably tax the master sleuth's investigative mind, Brett is—as always—a thrill to watch.

1983 52 minutes

ADVENTURES OF SHERLOCK HOLMES: THE DANCING MEN

★★★★

DIRECTOR: John Bruce

CAST: Jeremy Brett, David Burke, Tenniel Evans, Betsy Brantley, David Ross, Eugene Lupinski, Lorraine Peters, Wendy Jane Walker

An innocent-looking group of stick-figure drawings puzzles Sherlock Holmes and Scotland Yard until the great sleuth uncovers nefarious underworld goings-on and plunges himself and his companion in adventure, Dr. Watson, into deadly danger. Carefully crafted after the original short story by Conan Doyle, this ingenious episode is one of thirteen complete tales of the Baker Street detective currently available on video. There are no weak entries in this popular series, and Holmes and his chronicler Dr. Watson are perfectly portrayed by Jeremy Brett and David Burke.

1984 52 minutes

ADVENTURES OF SHERLOCK HOLMES: THE FINAL PROBLEM

★★★★

DIRECTOR: Alan Grint

CAST: Jeremy Brett, David Burke, Eric Porter, Rosalie Williams, Olivier-Pierre, Claude Le Sache, Michael Goldie, Robert Henderson

Sherlock Holmes is pursued by murderers after he exposes a gang of art forgers led by his rival, Professor Moriarty. After thwarting Moriarty's plans to sell perfect duplicates of the *Mona Lisa*, Holmes meets him face-to-face, and the two engage in a deadly game that traps Moriarty's gang behind bars, but leaves the evil genius loose to pursue his persecutor. The thrilling climax to this fast-moving story takes place in the picturesque Alps, where the two foes square off and fight to the death. Imaginative, exciting, and blessed with a surprise ending, this entry in the popular series first broadcast on public television is perhaps the finest of them all.

1985 52 minutes

ADVENTURES OF SHERLOCK HOLMES: THE GREEK INTERPRETER

★★★★

DIRECTOR: Derek Marlowe

CAST: Jeremy Brett, David Burke, Charles Gray, Alkis Kritikos, George Costigan, Nick Field, Anton Alexander, Victoria Harwood

This complex, tragic story pits Sherlock Holmes, Dr. Watson, and Holmes's brother Mycroft against vicious killers who have kidnapped a Greek national and tortured him into signing some important documents against his will. The interpreter hired by the criminals is the man who brings the story to the sleuth, and he very nearly loses his life to a diabolical fiend before justice is done. A fickle woman, a chuckling murderer, and an exciting climax aboard a speeding train highlight this dark story, but it's Charles Gray as Sherlock's brother Mycroft who steals the show and finally traps the murderer with his quick mind and deft actions.

1985 52 minutes

ADVENTURES OF SHERLOCK HOLMES: THE NAVAL TREATY

★★★★

DIRECTOR: Alan Grint

CAST: Jeremy Brett, David Burke, David Gwillim, Gareth Thomas, Alison Skilbeck, Ronald Russell, Nicholas Geake, Pamela Pitchford, John Malcolm

An old friend of Dr. Watson's is on the verge of being implicated in a treasonous case of espionage, and Sherlock Holmes comes to the aid of friend and country. Cleverly constructed and steeped in the atmosphere of Conan Doyle's London, this episode of the original six-part series was first telecast in this country on PBS's *Mystery* in 1984 and has taken its place with the others as perhaps the best translation of Holmes to the screen. Jeremy Brett seems the personification of the constantly alert Holmes, while David Burke's humorous, dependable Watson is yet another welcome step away from the bumbling image that Nigel Bruce left after so many films with Basil Rathbone.

1984 52 minutes

ADVENTURES OF SHERLOCK HOLMES: THE NORWOOD BUILDER

★★★½

DIRECTOR: Ken Grieve

CAST: Jeremy Brett, David Burke, Rosalie Crutchley, Colin Jeavons, Helen Ryan, Jonathan Adams, Matthew Solon, Anthony Langdon

Holmes and Watson become involved in murder when a young solicitor seeks their help after being accused of doing away with a wealthy recluse. Holmes concentrates on his own powers of deduction and re-creates the crime after disguising himself as a vagrant and uncovering a damning piece of evidence. With enough plot twists to hold the attention of even the most jaded viewer, this episode is highly entertaining and supplies the necessary thrills as Holmes literally smokes the killer out of hiding.

1985 52 minutes

ADVENTURES OF SHERLOCK HOLMES: THE RED-HEADED LEAGUE

★★★½

DIRECTOR: John Bruce

CAST: Jeremy Brett, David Burke, Roger Hammond, Richard Wilson, Tim McInnerty, Bruce Dukov, John Woodnutt, John Labonowski, Eric Porter, Rog Stuart

Holmes is given a three-pipe

problem as he endeavors to unravel an intricate plot that involves a red-headed man, an underpaid employee, a bogus organization, and a bank full of gold. Holmes's malevolent nemesis Professor Moriarty is at the bottom of it all and learns a new respect (and hatred) for his clever antagonist. Jeremy Brett and David Burke make a fine Holmes and Watson. These episodes crackle with excitement and suspense as well as humor and irony.

1985 52 minutes

ADVENTURES OF SHERLOCK HOLMES: THE RESIDENT PATIENT

★★★½

DIRECTOR: David Carson

CAST: Jeremy Brett, David Burke, Nicholas Clay, Patrick Newell, Tim Barlow, Brett Forrest, Charles Cork, John Ringham, David Squire

This grim murder mystery begins as Holmes and Watson are recruited by a young medical man to come to the aid of his benefactor, a secretive man who has reinforced his home with steel bars and lives in constant fear of intruders. After refusing to level with the famous detective and his chronicler, the patron (Mr. Blessington) is found hanged, and the police are prepared to write off his death as suicide until Holmes comes up with a deadly scenario of premeditated, brutal murder. Clever storytelling, engrossing and highly enjoyable.

1985 52 minutes

ADVENTURES OF SHERLOCK HOLMES: THE SOLITARY CYCLIST

★★★★

DIRECTOR: Paul Annett

CAST: Jeremy Brett, David Burke, Barbara Wilshere, John Castle, Michael Siberry, Ellis Dale, Sarah Aitchinson, Simon Bleackley

Intricately woven plot finds Holmes and Watson coming to the aid of a woman who is being mysteriously followed by a man on a bicycle! But, of course, there's more going on than meets the eye, and the world's foremost consulting detective is just the chap to discover it. Atmospheric and exciting.

1984 52 minutes

ADVENTURES OF SHERLOCK HOLMES: THE SPECKLED BAND

★★★★½

DIRECTOR: John Bruce

CAST: Jeremy Brett, David Burke, Jeremy Kemp, Rosalyn Landor, Denise Armon, John Gill, Rosalie Williams

This addition to the Sherlock Holmes saga is one of the most remarkable of Conan Doyle's marvelous stories. Holmes is engaged by a woman who fears for her life after her sister dies mysteriously and horribly in a room that no one has entered. Holmes and Watson uncover the motive and the party responsible, but it's up to Sherlock to offer himself as bait and discover the method of murder. Grim yet fascinating, this is one of the best remembered of these tales and perhaps the finest crafted of them all. Topnotch.

1984 52 minutes

AFRICA—TEXAS STYLE!

★★

DIRECTOR: Andrew Marton

CAST: Hugh O'Brian, John Mills, Tom Nardini

The idea of a movie about cowboys rounding up animals in Africa must have sounded good in theory. But in practice, it's pretty dull going. Even the location photography doesn't help. Give us *Hatari!* any day.

1966 106 minutes

AFTER THE THIN MAN

★★★★½

DIRECTOR: W. S. Van Dyke II
CAST: William Powell, Myrna Loy, James Stewart, Elissa Landi, Joseph Calleia, Sam Levene

Second of the six wonderful *Thin Man* films made with William Powell and Myrna Loy, following on the heels of 1934's *The Thin Man*. Powell, Loy, and Asta, the incorrigible terrier, trade quips and drinks in this decent murder mystery. Rising star James Stewart merely adds to the fun. The dialogue is fast-paced and quite droll, and Powell and Loy demonstrate a chemistry that explains the dozen hits they had together. Not to be missed. Followed, in 1939, by *Another Thin Man*.

1936 B & W 113 minutes

AGAINST ALL FLAGS

★★★

DIRECTOR: George Sherman
CAST: Errol Flynn, Maureen O'Hara, Anthony Quinn, Mildred Natwick

Though Errol Flynn's energy and attractiveness had seriously ebbed by this time, he still possessed the panache to make this simple swashbuckler fun to watch. He portrays a dashing British soldier who infiltrates a pirate stronghold, pausing only to romance the fiery Maureen O'Hara.

1952 83 minutes

AGENT ON ICE

★★★½

DIRECTOR: Clark Worswick
CAST: Tom Ormeny, Clifford David, Louis Pastore, Matt Craven

This exciting action film features Tom Ormeny as John Pope, a former CIA agent who has become a target for both the CIA and the Mafia. Clifford David plays the corrupt CIA official who has been laundering money for Mafia leader Frank Matera (Louis Pastore). Pope must first discover who's after him and destroy them before they find him. Matt Craven plays Matera's trigger-happy little brother, Joey. Rated R for violence and obscenities.

1985 96 minutes

AIR FORCE

★★★★

DIRECTOR: Howard Hawks
CAST: John Garfield, John Ridgely, Gig Young, Charles Drake

This is essentially wartime propaganda about a flying fortress and its crew taking on the enemy at Pearl Harbor, Manila, and the Coral Sea. However, the direction by Howard Hawks puts the film head and shoulders above similar motion pictures. It has an impressive supporting cast, including Harry Carey, Arthur Kennedy, George Tobias, and Edward Brophy. Essentially a character study, it gives each of the players time to bring his role alive.

1943 B & W 124 minutes

AIRPORT

★★★★

DIRECTOR: George Seaton
CAST: Burt Lancaster, Dean Martin, Helen Hayes, Jacqueline Bisset, Van Heflin, Jean Seberg

The daddy of them all, this *Grand Hotel* in the air is slick, enjoyable entertainment. Taking place on a fateful winter night, it miraculously rises above some stiff performances and an often hackneyed plot. Rated G.

1970 137 minutes

AL CAPONE

★★★½

DIRECTOR: Richard Wilson
CAST: Rod Steiger, Fay Spain, James Gregory, Martin Balsam, Nehemiah Persoff

Rod Steiger is mesmerizing as Al

Capone in this perceptive portrait of the legendary Chicago gangster. The film covers Capone's life from his first job for seventy-five dollars a week to his ultimate fate behind prison walls. Filmed in black and white with a documentary-style narrative, which heighten the quality of this film. The supporting cast—Fay Spain in particular—is just right.

1959 B & W 104 minutes

ALAN QUARTERMAIN AND THE LOST CITY OF GOLD

DIRECTOR: Gary Nelson
CAST: Richard Chamberlain, Sharon Stone, James Earl Jones, Henry Silva, Robert Donner, Cassandra Peterson

As if they weren't bad enough in the original, Richard Chamberlain and Sharon Stone reprise their roles from the tongue-in-beak turkey, *King Solomon's Mines*. This equally awful sequel also wastes the considerable talents of James Earl Jones. Rated PG.

1987 95 minutes

ALL QUIET ON THE WESTERN FRONT

★★★★★

DIRECTOR: Lewis Milestone
CAST: Lew Ayres, Louis Wolheim

Despite some dated moments and an "old movie" look, this film still stands as a powerful statement against war and man's inhumanity to man. Lew Ayres and Louis Wolheim star in this story, set during World War I, which follows several young men into battle, examining their disillusionment and eventual death.

1930 B & W 155 minutes

ALOHA, BOBBY AND ROSE

★★

DIRECTOR: Floyd Mutrux
CAST: Paul LeMat, Diane Hull, Tim McIntire

B-movie treatment of two kids on the lam for a murder they didn't mean to commit. Paul LeMat's first starring role after *American Graffiti*. He is interesting, but the film is downbeat and uninspired. Rated R.

1975 88 minutes

AMAZONS

DIRECTOR: Alex Sessa
CAST: Windsor Taylor Randolph, Penelope Reed, Joseph Whipp, Danitza Kingsley, Willie Nelson

The ridiculousness of the fight scenes in this film rivals that of the worst kung-fu flick. Two Amazon warriors (Windsor Taylor Randolph and Penelope Reed) must recover an ancient sword to defeat the evil Kalungo (Joseph Whipp), who is threatening their people. Willie Nelson plays the Amazons' wizard. Not much acting, but plenty of female bondage. This silly film is rated R for nudity, violence, and sex.

1986 76 minutes

AMBUSHERS, THE

★

DIRECTOR: Henry Levin
CAST: Dean Martin, Senta Berger, Janice Rule, James Gregory, Albert Salmi, Kurt Kasznar, Beverly Adams

Only hardcore Dean Martin fans will want to bother with this one, the third movie in the Matt Helm secret-agent series. The weak story has America's first flying saucer in danger of being sabotaged by enemy agents. There are lots of beautiful women running around, but not much else worth looking at.

1968 102 minutes

AMERICAN NINJA

★

DIRECTOR: Sam Firstenberg
CAST: Michael Dudikoff, Guich Koock, Judie Aronson, Steve James, John Fujioka

Dumb, dumb comic book–style adventure film about an American soldier (Michael Dudikoff) who single-handedly takes on an army of martial arts mercenaries in the Philippines. Chuck Norris does it better. Rated R for profanity and violence.

1985 95 minutes

AMERICAN NINJA II

★★

DIRECTOR: Sam Firstenberg
CAST: Michael Dudikoff, Steve James, Larry Poindexter, Gary Conway

Michael Dudikoff continues to set new standards for nonacting in this mindless but enjoyable-for-fans martial arts movie. Dudikoff and Steve James, who is as watchable as ever, play army rangers who come to the aid of the marines and wipe out a passel of heroin dealers. Rated R.

1987 96 minutes

AMSTERDAM KILL, THE

★

DIRECTOR: Robert Clouse
CAST: Robert Mitchum, Bradford Dillman, Richard Egan, Leslie Nielsen, Keye Luke

Fresh from his successes in *Farewell My Lovely* and *The Yakuza*, Robert Mitchum dived into this dud about an international drug conspiracy. He's a retired narcotics agent who comes to the aid of an old buddy accused of smuggling. It sounds exciting, but it's terribly dull, and just more proof that director Robert Clouse must have had a rare, rare good day when he made *Enter the Dragon*. Rated R.

1977 90 minutes

ANDERSON TAPES, THE

★★★★

DIRECTOR: Sidney Lumet
CAST: Martin Balsam, Sean Connery, Dyan Cannon, Ralph Meeker, Margaret Hamilton

Sean Connery is perfectly cast in this exciting film about an ex-con under surveillance who wants to pull off the Big Heist. Slickly done, with tight editing and direction to keep the viewer totally involved, it holds up extremely well on video. Rated PG.

1972 98 minutes

ANGEL

DIRECTOR: Robert Vincent O'Neil
CAST: Cliff Gorman, Susan Tyrrell, Dick Shawn, Donna Wilkes

Bad, low-budget flick about a 15-year-old who moonlights as a Hollywood Boulevard hooker and is menaced by a psychotic killer. Rated R for nudity, violence, suggested sex and profanity.

1983 94 minutes

ANGEL OF H.E.A.T.

DIRECTOR: Myrl A. Schreibman
CAST: Marilyn Chambers, Dan Jesse, Mary Woronov, Stephen Johnson

Marilyn Chambers should stick with what she knows best . . . and this isn't it. Porn queen Chambers appears as Angel Harmony, head of Harmony's Elite Attack Team . . . which should be renamed Hardly Ever Any Talent. Not enough sex and skin for the hardcore crowd, and not enough plot, good acting, or production values for the spy flick lovers. Projects like this, which attempt to cross genres, usually fail in both; *Angel of H.E.A.T.* is no exception. Very anticlimactic. Rated R—considerable nudity and sexual situations.

1982 93 minutes

ANGELS DIE HARD

★★

DIRECTOR: Richard Compton
CAST: William Smith, Tom Baker, R. G. Armstrong, Dan Haggerty

The bikers turn out to help a community during a mining disaster. Less ridiculous than most of its predecessors and contemporaries. Look for Dan Haggerty in an early role. Violence; adult situations. Rated R.

1970 86 minutes

ANGELS WITH DIRTY FACES

★★★★½

DIRECTOR: Michael Curtiz
CAST: James Cagney, Pat O'Brien, Humphrey Bogart, Ann Sheridan, George Bancroft, Bobby Jordan

This is thoroughly enjoyable entertainment—thanks primarily to its stars and director. Certainly, the tale is anything but new and wasn't even new when the movie was released. The plot is that old Hollywood standby about two childhood friends, the one who goes bad (James Cagney) and the other who follows the right path (Pat O'Brien, as the priest), and the conflict between them. Yet, as directed by Warner Bros.' stalwart Michael Curtiz (*Casablanca*; *Captain Blood*), it often seems surprisingly fresh. There's not a wasted moment on the screen. Everything works, making it one of Cagney's best starring vehicles.

1938 B & W 97 minutes

ANGKOR: CAMBODIA EXPRESS

★

DIRECTOR: Alex King
CAST: Robert Walker, Christopher George, Woody Strode, Nancy Kwan

In this subpar variation on *The Killing Fields*, Robert Walker plays an American journalist who leaves his girlfriend (Nancy Kwan) behind in Cambodia as its government falls to the Khmer Rouge. Unable to live without Kwan, Walker returns to Cambodia to bring her out. He joins a small commando unit led by Christopher George, and the bullets start to fly.

1985 86 minutes

ANNIHILATORS, THE

★

DIRECTOR: Charles E. Sellier Jr.
CAST: Christopher Stone, Andy Wood, Lawrence Hilton-Jacobs, Jim Antonio, Gerrit Graham

Another film in which Vietnam veterans reunite, organize a vigilante group, annihilate the sadistic gangs, and return to their normal lives. The only difference this time is that not all of the "heroes" survive. Christopher Stone stars in the Chuck Norris–style lead role. Rated R for grotesque violence and language.

1985 87 minutes

ANOTHER THIN MAN

★★★★

DIRECTOR: W. S. Van Dyke II
CAST: William Powell, Myrna Loy, Virginia Grey, Otto Kruger, C. Aubrey Smith, Ruth Hussey, Nat Pendleton, Tom Neal

The major factor contributing to the gradual decline of this series appeared in this (third) entry, namely the birth of Nick Jr. (the second "Thin Man" of the title).

How could Nick and Nora Charles (William Powell and Myrna Loy) flirt, drink incredible quantities of alcohol, and endanger their lives, with a child in the house? Fortunately, the charming banter remained, along with the always-amusing antics of canine co-star Asta. This time out, Nick and Nora must contend with a gentleman who dreams about catastrophes before they take place. As usual, the plot is secondary to the interaction between the two leads. Follows *After the Thin Man* (1936) and precedes *Shadow of the Thin Man* (1941). Suitable for family viewing.

1939 B & W 105 minutes

ANZIO

★★

DIRECTOR: Edward Dmytryk
CAST: Robert Mitchum, Peter Falk, Robert Ryan, Earl Holliman, Arthur Kennedy, Patrick Magee, Mark Damon, Reni Santoni

Would-be blockbuster about the Allied invasion of Italy during World War II doesn't make the grade as either history or spectacle and ultimately wastes the talents of a great cast and an often inspired director. Sometimes bigger can be better (*A Bridge Too Far* and *The Longest Day* are examples), but this mediocre big-budget bust never pulls things together enough to rise above endless shots of troops, tanks, smoke, and amphibious landings.

1968 117 minutes

APOCALYPSE NOW

★★★★

DIRECTOR: Francis Ford Coppola
CAST: Marlon Brando, Martin Sheen, Robert Duvall, Harrison Ford

An exceptional war film in every sense, this work pulsates with artistic ambition. It reaches for truth, struggles for greatness—and almost succeeds. The central character, Captain Willard (Martin Sheen), tells the story of his slow progress toward a fateful meeting with a man named Kurtz, a highly decorated officer who the army contends has gone mad. To reach Kurtz, Willard must endure a danger-filled journey through the jungle on a Navy patrol boat. During this time, Willard reads the file on Kurtz and begins to doubt the logic of his superiors. Kurtz is doing what they apparently cannot. He's winning. Rated R.

1979 153 minutes

APPOINTMENT IN HONDURAS

★★½

DIRECTOR: Jacques Tourneur
CAST: Glenn Ford, Ann Sheridan, Zachary Scott, Jack Elam

Good cast helps this far-fetched story of an idealistic American (Glenn Ford) helping local misfits free their country from political tyranny. Actors do their level best, but rather silly material gets in their way. Plot and dialogue are somewhat laughable. Ann Sheridan is highly watchable, as usual.

1953 79 minutes

ARABESQUE

★★★

DIRECTOR: Stanley Donen
CAST: Gregory Peck, Sophia Loren, Kieron Moore, Alan Badel, Carl Duering, George Coulouris

Fast-paced espionage adventure about college professor Gregory Peck and his nightmarish involvement with death-dealing secret agents is an entertaining "chase" film and a conscious effort to capture the "now" look of the 1960s. Beautiful Sophia Loren keeps Peck company as they alternate chasing and being pursued by tough-looking men in trench coats across picturesque parts of the world. Entertaining and clever at times, but basically a hollow and calculated attempt to cash in on the Continental spy trend of the time, this film is vague enough to relax the viewers and run its course without causing undue concern about the consequences of all this violence to the characters on the screen. Worth the cost of the rental just for the close-up of Loren's lips.

1966 118 minutes

ARK OF THE SUN GOD... TEMPLE OF HELL, THE

DIRECTOR: Anthony M. Dawson
CAST: David Warbeck, John Steiner, Susie Sudlow, Alan Collins, Riccardo Palacio

Gosh, where did they get the name from? Some people have no shame. A big-time thief is commissioned to steal an ancient artifact from an ark buried thousands of years ago. Not only are the title and story a ripoff of *Raiders of the Lost Ark*, we are also subject to anti-Arabic sentiment and a hero who mutters pseudocool 007-style wisecracks. On top of all this, the video box is a lie, promising Nazis and an all-out war that never materialize in the flick. The film takes place in Turkey. How appropriate. Not rated; violence.

1986 92 minutes

ARMED RESPONSE

★½

DIRECTOR: Fred Olen Ray
CAST: David Carradine, Lee Van Cleef, Mako, Lois Hamilton, Ross Hagen, Brent Huff, Laurene Landon

In Los Angeles's Chinatown, a Vietnam vet and his family fight a Japanese mob for possession of a jade statue. *Armed Response* starts out parodying the action-adventure genre, but it loses its sense of humor in the middle and bogs down for too long, becoming boring and jingoistic. Rated R.

1986 86 minutes

AROUND THE WORLD UNDER THE SEA

★★

DIRECTOR: Andrew Marton
CAST: Lloyd Bridges, Shirley Eaton, David McCallum, Brian Kelly, Keenan Wynn, Marshall Thompson

Volcanoes, a giant eel, a submarine, scuba gear, and a quarrel over who's in charge make this lackluster, harmless viewing. Shirley Eaton was in *Goldfinger*, in case you're a James Bond fan.

1966 117 minutes

ARREST BULLDOG DRUMMOND

★★½

DIRECTOR: James Hogan
CAST: John Howard, Heather Angel, George Zucco, H. B. Warner, E. E. Clive, Reginald Denny, John Sutton

Bulldog Drummond and his cronies pursue a murderer to a tropical island where he has taken refuge along with a death ray he has stolen. The boys have a tough time subduing menacing George Zucco and his allies, but they get the job done. Enjoyable film despite the rear-projected background footage common with all B films set in exotic locales. Fifth in the popular series featuring John Howard. Available on a double-bill video with *Bulldog Drummond in Africa*.

1938 B & W 57 minutes

ASHANTI

★★½

DIRECTOR: Richard Fleischer
CAST: Michael Caine, Peter Ustinov, Beverly Johnson, William Holden, Omar Sharif, Rex Harrison, Kabir Bedi

A shopping trip turns into a tale of horror when the black wife (Beverly Johnson) of a white doctor (Michael Caine) in Africa is kidnapped and turned over to a slave trader (Peter Ustinov). Thus begins a fairly exciting chase across various exotic locales. A good cast adds zest to Richard Fleischer's less-than-inspired direction. Rated R.

1979 118 minutes

ASSASSINATION

★

DIRECTOR: Peter Hunt
CAST: Charles Bronson, Jill Ireland, Stephen Elliott, Jan Gan Boyd, Randy Brooks, Michael Ansara

In this predictable, poorly written action flick, Charles Bronson plays a seasoned secret service agent who is called upon to guard the first lady (Jill Ireland) after several mysterious "accidents" have nearly taken her life. Because the president is impotent (an old war wound, we are told), the agent and the lady fall in love. Give yourself extra points for not gagging on the insipid storyline or, better yet, leave this one on the shelf. Even hard-core Bronson fans are certain to be disappointed. Rated R for profanity and violence.

1987 105 minutes

ASSAULT ON PRECINCT 13

★★★★½

DIRECTOR: John Carpenter
CAST: Austin Stoker, Laurie Zimmer, Tony Burton, Nancy Loomis, Darwin Joston

Here's director John Carpenter's (*Halloween*) riveting movie about a nearly deserted L.A. police station that finds itself under siege by a youth gang. It's a modern-day version of Howard Hawks's *Rio Bravo*, with exceptional performances by its entire cast. Rated R.

1976 90 minutes

ASSISI UNDERGROUND, THE

★★

DIRECTOR: Alexander Ramati
CAST: Ben Cross, James Mason, Irene Papas, Maximilian Schell, Karl Heinz Hackl, Delia Boccardo, Edmund Purdom

There is very little suspense in this melodrama tracing the activities of a Franciscan monastery as part of the Jewish liberation network in World War II Italy. Ben Cross struggles valiantly to bring some life to this dreary fact-based tale; hard work considering the poor dialogue and unrealistic behavior of the Jews he is trying to help escape from Europe. Rated PG.

1985 115 minutes

AT SWORD'S POINT

★★½

DIRECTOR: Lewis Allen
CAST: Cornel Wilde, Maureen O'Hara, Alan Hale Jr., Dan O'Herlihy, Blanche Yurka, Robert Douglas

Colorful story of the offspring of the Three Musketeers joining forces to rid the country of villainy is familiar but harmless. Cornel Wilde displays his Olympic-caliber skill with the sword and Maureen O'Hara is as beautiful and feisty as ever, but this time she backs it up with swordplay. Typical of the mindless sort of historical and costume epics that Hollywood kept churning out in the late 1940s and into the middle 1950s—pleasant but not really memorable.

1952 81 minutes

ATTACK FORCE Z

★★

DIRECTOR: Tim Burstall
CAST: John Phillip Law, Sam Neill, Mel Gibson, Chris Haywood, John Waters

Okay Australian film concerning a group of commandos on a secret mission against the Japanese in World War II. Most notable is a young Mel Gibson as the leader of the commandos. Unrated.

1981 84 minutes

AVALANCHE

DIRECTOR: Corey Allen
CAST: Rock Hudson, Mia Farrow, Robert Forster, Jeanette Nolan

It's movies like this bomb that gave disaster pictures a bad name. Rock Hudson, Mia Farrow, Robert Forster, and Jeanette Nolan are among those fooling around and fighting before the catastrophe of the title. Their performances are so bad, you're glad to see them go. Rated PG.

1978 91 minutes

AVENGERS, THE (TELEVISION SERIES) (overall rating)

★★★

DIRECTORS: Don Leaver, Robert Day
CAST: Patrick Macnee, Diana Rigg, Linda Thorson

What can be said about the finest British secret-agent series ever created, except that it's about time some episodes made it to the home-video market? Patrick Macnee stars as the quintessential agent, the dapper John Steed, a role he perfected for several years before the program was aired in this country. (One of his earlier partners was Cathy Gale, played by Honor Blackman, who rose in the ranks to become a Bond femme fatale in *Goldfinger.*) Diana Rigg replaced Blackman for two years as the rugged, leather-garbed Emma Peel (and these were the first episodes seen in the States); she was followed by Linda Thorson's Tara King for the program's final year. The show borders on science fiction, with outlandish gadgets killing off key British operatives. Of the episodes available on video, the best is "The House That Jack Built," wherein Mrs. Peel gets trapped in a mansion with a mind of its own . . . so to speak. Charming, witty, and absolutely ageless, this program will remain loved for generations to come. Suitable for family viewing.

1965–1969 52 minutes each

AVENGING ANGEL

DIRECTOR: Robert Vincent O'Neil
CAST: Betsy Russell, Rory Calhoun, Susan Tyrrell, Ossie Davis

Remember *Angel*, the high-school student who doubled as a Hollywood hooker? Well, she's back. Only this time our heroine is out to avenge the murder of the cop who acted as her mentor. Dumb. Rated R for nudity, profanity, and violence.

1985 96 minutes

AVENGING FORCE

★★★

DIRECTOR: Saul Firstenberg
CAST: Michael Dudikoff, Steve James, James Booth, Bill Wallace, John P. Ryan, Karl Johnson, Marc Alaimo

A better-than-average action-adventure flick about a former secret service agent forced out of retirement when his best friend, a black southern politician, is involved in an assassination attempt in which his son is killed. The two go after the killers, who turn out to be working for a right-wing extremist group called the Pentacle. This group eventually kills the politician and the rest of his family, leaving our hero alive to participate in a macabre death hunt with himself as the hunted. The acting is admittedly dry, but the action is topnotch, with plenty of opportunity to cheer for the hero. Rated R for violence and profanity.

1986 104 minutes

AWAY ALL BOATS

★½

DIRECTOR: Joseph Pevney
CAST: Jeff Chandler, George Nader, Julie Adams, Lex Barker, Keith Andes, Richard Boone, Jock Mahoney, William Reynolds, Charles McGraw, John McIntire

In this war film, Jeff Chandler plays Captain Hanks, commander of an attack transport unit in the South Pacific during World War II. We follow Chandler and his men, as they train for heavy combat awaiting them. Julie Adams is thrown in for love interest. As the film progresses, we see Japanese kamikaze attacks, huge assaults on Japanese strongholds, and submarine attacks. But the film never really adds up to much. Too many preposterous acts of heroism and routine performances combine with a lackluster script and direction to make it a throwaway.

1956 B & W 114 minutes

BACK TO BATAAN

★★★

DIRECTOR: Edward Dmytryk
CAST: John Wayne, Anthony Quinn, Richard Loo, Beulah Bondi

A fun World War II action film with John Wayne at his two-fisted best. Good script, photography, acting, and battle action make this film well worth your time. Video quality is quite good.

1945 B & W 95 minutes

BAD GUYS

★★

DIRECTOR: Joel Silberg
CAST: Adam Baldwin, Mike Jolly, Michelle Nicastro, Ruth Buzzi, Sgt. Slaughter

A somewhat contrived story about two police officers who are suspended indefinitely, without pay. After having no luck with interim jobs, they decide to become professional wrestlers. They achieve moderate success, then decide to become "bad guys" to further their popularity. They soon find themselves opposing the world tag-team champs. That leads to a no-holds-barred, slugfest finish. Although sophomoric, this film should be great fun for youngsters and wrestling fans. Rated PG.

1985 87 minutes

BADGE 373

★½

DIRECTOR: Howard W. Koch
CAST: Robert Duvall, Verna Bloom, Eddie Egan, Henry Darrow

This very low-rent police drama casts Robert Duvall as a cop out to nab his partner's killer and break the mob in New York City. Pretty routine stuff is thrown together in a even more routine fashion. For hard-core fans of the genre only. Rated R.

1973 116 minutes

BAND OF THE HAND

★★½

DIRECTOR: Paul Michael Glaser
CAST: Stephen Lang, Michael Carmine, Lauren Holly, John Cameron Mitchell, Daniele Quinn, Leon Robinson, James Remar

Executive-produced by Michael

Miami Vice Mann, this is like an episode of the popular television series without Don Johnson or Edward James Olmos. It has the car chases, shootouts, and drug scenes from the TV show combined with an even more lightweight plot than usual. This concerns a Vietnam vet (Stephen Lang) who takes a group of incorrigible Florida teens and turns them into an anti-drug squad. That's right, it's *Mod Squad* for the 1980s and just as silly as it sounds. Rated R for profanity, brief nudity, cocaine use, and violence.

1986 109 minutes

BARE KNUCKLES

★★★

DIRECTOR: Don Edmonds
CAST: Robert Viharo, Sherry Jackson, Michael Heit, Gloria Hendry, John Daniels

A fun martial arts thriller, about a modern-day bounty hunter on the trail of a vicious killer stalking women on the streets of the city. During the course of the manhunt, we are introduced to some sleazy characters (both likable and unlikable), funny and tense situations, great one-liners, and fun fight scenes. With a bigger budget, this could have been a great action-suspense movie. But as it is, it's a fun little escapist adventure. Rated R for brief nudity, violence, and adult language.

1984 90 minutes

BATAAN

★★★★½

DIRECTOR: Tay Garnett
CAST: Robert Taylor, George Murphy, Thomas Mitchell, Lloyd Nolan, Robert Walker, Desi Arnaz, Barry Nelson

One of the best films about World War II chronicles the exploits of an army patrol attempting to stall the Japanese onslaught in the Philippines. Good sets, a fine cast, and exciting battle scenes add to the overall effect. It's a must for fans of the genre. No rating; has violence.

1943 B & W 114 minutes

BATTLE BENEATH THE EARTH

★★½

DIRECTOR: Montgomery Tully
CAST: Kerwin Mathews, Robert Ayres, Martin Benson, Viviane Ventura, Bessie Love

Stalwart Kerwin Mathews leads the fight against the Chinese hordes who intend to invade the United States via underground tunnels. Pretty good adventure fantasy in the comic book/pulp magazine tradition. Silent star Bessie Love, who starred in 1925's *The Lost World*, has a small role.

1967 91 minutes

BATTLE CRY

★★★

DIRECTOR: Raoul Walsh
CAST: Van Heflin, Tab Hunter, Dorothy Malone, Anne Francis

A platoon of marines is followed into battle during World War II. The conflicts they face on the islands of the Pacific are contrasted to the emotional conflicts faced by their girlfriends at home. All in all, it is a successful piece of wartime fluff.

1955 149 minutes

BATTLE FORCE

★★

DIRECTOR: Humphrey Longon
CAST: Henry Fonda, John Huston, Stacy Keach, Helmut Berger, Samantha Eggar

The effect of war on the lives and destinies of two families, one American, the other German, is chronicled in this passable World War II adventure.

1976 92 minutes

BATTLE OF EL ALAMEIN, THE

★★★

DIRECTOR: Calvin Jackson Padget
CAST: Michael Rennie, Robert Hossein, Frederick Stafford, Ettore Manni, George Hilton

A re-creation of the famous twelve-day 1942 turning point clash between the artillery, tanks, and infantry of the British Eighth Army under General Montgomery and the German army's fabled Afrika Korps commanded by Field Marshal Rommel in the windswept Libyan Desert southwest of Alexandria. We know the outcome, but getting there makes for exciting watching. Rated PG.

1968 96 minutes

BATTLE OF THE BULGE

★★

DIRECTOR: Ken Annakin
CAST: Henry Fonda, Robert Shaw, Robert Ryan, Dana Andrews

This is a fairly decent war film. It has solid acting and exciting battle sequences but suffers on video for two reasons: the small screen hurts the epic scale and 23 minutes are cut from the original print, with some important footage missing. It has good acting and battle sequences but a poor script and historical inaccuracies. Worth a look if you like war films.

1965 140 minutes

BATTLE OF THE COMMANDOS

★

DIRECTOR: Umberto Lenzi
CAST: Jack Palance, Curt Jurgens, Tomas Hunter, Diana Largo, Wolfgang Preirs

Jack Palance stars in this boring World War II adventure of commandos attacking the Germans on the eve of D-Day. Lots of phony battle scenes, bad acting, and poor script all add up to a big bomb.

1969 94 minutes

BEDROOM EYES

★★★

DIRECTOR: William Fruet
CAST: Kenneth Gilman, Dayle Haddon, Barbara Law, Christine Cattel

A young stockbroker peers into a window one evening and sees a woman so tantalizing he feels compelled to return every night. When the object of his voyeurism is murdered, the man must try to prove his innocence, with the help of a female psychologist. A silly but undeniably erotic mystery with high production values and an attractive, likable cast. It's no classic, but it will hold your attention. Rated R for language, nudity, and sex.

1986 90 minutes

BEHIND THE RISING SUN

★★½

DIRECTOR: Edward Dmytryk
CAST: Margo, Tom Neal, J. Carrol Naish, Robert Ryan

The versatile J. Carrol Naish plays a Japanese publisher whose political views bring him into conflict with his son, educated in the U.S. It all takes place when Japan was fighting China, not long before World War II.

1943 B & W 89 minutes

BELARUS FILE, THE

★★½

DIRECTOR: Robert Markowitz
CAST: Telly Savalas, Suzanne Pleshette, Max von Sydow, Herbert Berghof, George Savalas

Telly Savalas returns as the lollipop-sucking police detective Kojak in this made-for-television movie about a maniac murdering Russian survivors of a Nazi concentration camp. Our hero's investigation into the killings turns up some damaging information on

an old friend (Max von Sydow) who may be one of the murderer's targets. For fans of the series only.
1986 95 minutes

BENEATH THE 12-MILE REEF

★★★

DIRECTOR: Ted Post
CAST: Robert Wagner, Gilbert Roland, Terry Moore, Richard Boone

Here is some good old-fashioned Hollywood entertainment that requires nothing more from the viewer than to sit back, relax, and enjoy. Film deals with sponge divers off the Florida coast. Beautiful scenery keeps viewers' attention away from the lack of plot. Light, enjoyable fluff.
1953 102 minutes

BEN-HUR

★★★★★

DIRECTOR: William Wyler
CAST: Charlton Heston, Jack Hawkins, Sam Jaffe

In this film, which won eleven Oscars, a wealthy Jewish nobleman during the time of Christ incurs the hostility of the Roman military governor, who was his childhood friend. He is reduced to manning an oar on a slave galley, and his family is sent to prison. Years later he returns to seek vengeance upon his Roman tormentor. This culminates in a spectacular chariot race. Charlton Heston won an Oscar for his first-rate performance in the title role.
1959 211 minutes

BERLIN TUNNEL 21

★★

DIRECTOR: Richard Michaels
CAST: Richard Thomas, Horst Buchholz, José Ferrer, Jacques Breuer, Nicolas Farrell, Ken Griffith, Ute Christensen

Richard Thomas stars as an American soldier in Berlin in 1961. His girlfriend cannot leave the eastern section of Berlin to join him. The solution: sneak her out of East Berlin with the help of Horst Buchholz, an engineer who also has loved ones trapped in the East. Predictable, but fairly well done.
1981 141 minutes

BEST REVENGE

★★½

DIRECTOR: John Trent
CAST: John Heard, Levon Helm, Alberta Watson, John Rhys-Davies

Granger (John Heard), masquerading as an American tourist, has come to Spain to team up with Bo (Levon Helm), who has promised him the contacts for a $4 million hashish deal. Granger will make money on the deal, but his real reason for participating is that his best friend is being tortured by the gangster who set up the deal. This fast-moving action adventure has some good acting, but fails to rise above its pedestrian plot.
1984 92 minutes

BEVERLY HILLS COP II

★★★

DIRECTOR: Tony Scott
CAST: Eddie Murphy, Judge Reinhold, Jürgen Prochnow, Ronny Cox, John Ashton, Brigitte Nielsen, Allen Garfield, Dean Stockwell

This sequel to *Beverly Hills Cop* lacks most of the charm and freshness of the first film, choosing instead to unwind as a thunderous, pounding assault on the senses. *Cop II* comes from the same producers (Don Simpson and Jerry Bruckheimer) and director (Tony Scott) responsible for *Top Gun*, and the style hasn't been altered a jot; the aerial dogfights have been replaced with shrieking tires and blasting handguns, but the action is just as mindless. Forget about following the story, which concerns a series of high-tech heists dubbed "The Alphabet Crimes," because the purpose behind these capers seems to change at the turn of a page in the script. Star Eddie Murphy needs all his considerable talent to enliven this confusing mess, and he just manages to pull it off, comporting himself far better than he did in the lamentable *Golden Child*. The talented supporting cast—particularly Jürgen Prochnow and Dean Stockwell—is given very little to do; this is Murphy's show first, last, and always. Rated R for profanity and brief nudity.

1987 102 minutes

BEYOND ATLANTIS

★★

DIRECTOR: Eddie Romero
CAST: Patrick Wayne, John Ashley, Leigh Christian, Sid Haig

Unexciting movie about a motley bunch of adventurers looking for a fabulous treasure on an uncharted isle. They get more than they bargained for from the ancient race of amphibious humans there who don't exactly welcome the intrusion. Nice location photography, but good scenery can't overcome the wooden acting, inane dialogue, and repetitious music, which'll have you climbing the walls. Rated PG for mild violence.

1973 89 minutes

BEYOND THE POSEIDON ADVENTURE

★

DIRECTOR: Irwin Allen
CAST: Michael Caine, Sally Field, Telly Savalas, Jack Warden, Peter Boyle

Probably one of the weakest ideas yet for a sequel. Michael Caine heads one of two salvage crews (his being the good one, of course) that race each other and time to probe the upside-down wreck of the *Poseidon*. Naturally, our heroes get stuck in the old tub, and disaster-flick king Irwin Allen knocks 'em off, one by one. An incredible waste of a talented cast, most notably Sally Field, who got trapped in this mess the same year she won an Oscar for *Norma Rae*! Rated PG for mild violence and language.

1979 114 minutes

BIG BAD MAMA

★★

DIRECTOR: Steve Carver
CAST: Angie Dickinson, Tom Skerritt, William Shatner, Joan Prather

Here's an okay film concerning a mother (Angie Dickinson), sort of a second-rate Ma Barker, leading her daughters on a robbery spree during the Depression. It's not a classic by any means, but the action keeps things moving along. Rated R for violence, nudity, and sex.

1974 83 minutes

BIG BRAWL, THE

★★★

DIRECTOR: Robert Clouse
CAST: Jackie Chan, José Ferrer, Kristine DeBell, Mako

Director Robert Clouse again fails to reach the heights attained with his *Enter the Dragon*. Nevertheless, this kung-fu comedy has its moments—most provided by its agile star, Jackie Chan. Still, one wonders what a martial arts hero is doing in the 1930s taking on snarling gangsters. If you like fist-and-foot action, however, it's fun. Rated R.

1980 95 minutes

BIG BUST OUT, THE

DIRECTOR: Richard Jackson
CAST: Vonetta McGee, Karen Carter, Linda Fox, Monica Taylor

Four female convicts escape from a prison somewhere in the Middle East when they are sent to do janitorial work at a convent. While this film does deal with escapees, one can't help overlooking the double meaning in the title when these women start peeling off their shirts. If you are tired of women being exploited in the cinema and hate poorly dubbed audio, avoid this one. Not rated, but has sex, violence, and profanity.

1973 75 minutes

BIG CAT, THE

★★★

DIRECTOR: Phil Karlson
CAST: Lon McCallister, Preston Foster, Forrest Tucker

A marauding mountain lion complicates feuding between high country ranchers in this enjoyable adventure film.

1949 75 minutes

BIG COMBO, THE

★★★

DIRECTOR: Joseph H. Lewis
CAST: Cornel Wilde, Jean Wallace, Richard Conte

A classic American gangster film done in the *film noir* style. Cornel Wilde has the starring role as a half-crazed policeman who is after gangsters and will do whatever is necessary to get them. Quite violent for its time and very well photographed, with an exciting climax.

1955 B & W 89 minutes

BIG EASY, THE

★★★★

DIRECTOR: Jim McBride
CAST: Dennis Quaid, Ellen Barkin, Ned Beatty, John Goodman, Charles Ludlam

A snazzy, jazzy thriller set in Cajun country. Dennis Quaid, who performs as if there's a continuous Cajun tune running through his head, gives an ingratiating performance as a slightly crooked cop. And the romantic pairing with his co-star Ellen Barkin is surprisingly steamy. Unfortunately, the mystery plot is sometimes difficult to follow. But because the other elements are so entertaining, ignoring the plot altogether becomes simple. It's rated R for language, violence, and sexual situations.

1987 108 minutes

BIG FIX, THE

★★★½

DIRECTOR: Jeremy Paul Kagan
CAST: Richard Dreyfuss, Susan Anspach, Bonnie Bedelia

Novelist Roger Simon's laid-back detective, Moses Wine, comes to the screen in this flawed thriller. Richard Dreyfuss sleepwalks as the private dick, forcing the picture to survive in spite of his lethargic performance. The setting—which harkens back to the revolutionary 1960s—has become dated, but a murder mystery of any stripe is still suspenseful. And Wine *really* knows how to have fun with the board game *Clue*. Rated PG.

1978 108 minutes

BIG HEAT, THE

★★★★

DIRECTOR: Fritz Lang
CAST: Glenn Ford, Lee Marvin, Gloria Grahame, Carolyn Jones

If you are looking for a first-rate

cop film, look no further than this one. Film deals with a cop's vengeance against the criminals who murdered his wife. Extremely well made. Scene of Lee Marvin throwing coffee into the face of Gloria Grahame is considered a classic. Glenn Ford has never been better.

1953 B & W 90 minutes

BIG RED ONE, THE

★★★★½

DIRECTOR: Samuel Fuller
CAST: Lee Marvin, Mark Hamill, Robert Carradine, Bobby Di-Cicco

This release gave Lee Marvin his best role in years. As a grizzled sergeant leading a platoon of "wetnoses" into the dangers of battle, he's excellent. In fact, he's better than excellent. He's perfect. Marvin is to the war film what John Wayne was to the western and James Cagney was to the gangster picture. *The Big Red One* is based on writer-director Sam Fuller's personal reminiscences of World War II. It's a terrific war movie. Rated PG.

1980 113 minutes

BIG SCORE, THE

★★½

DIRECTOR: Fred Williamson
CAST: Fred Williamson, John Saxon, Richard Roundtree, Nancy Wilson, Ed Lauter, Joe Spinell, Michael Dante

Dirty Harry (Fred Williamson) breaks all the rules in going after drug king Joe Spinell. Wait a minute, you say? Williamson doesn't play Dirty Harry? Well, in this screenplay, originally written for the San Francisco–set detective series—but rejected by Clint Eastwood—Williamson, the actor, does everything but squint his eyes like you-know-who. Unfortunately, Williamson, the director, doesn't make the story move fast enough. We guess you could call this doing yourself in. Rated R for violence and profanity.

1983 85 minutes

BIG SLEEP, THE (ORIGINAL)

★★★★½

DIRECTOR: Howard Hawks
CAST: Humphrey Bogart, Lauren Bacall, Martha Vickers, Bob Steele, Elisha Cook Jr., Dorothy Malone

Raymond Chandler's fans couldn't complain about this moody, atmospheric rendition of Philip Marlowe's most bizarre case. Bogart's gritty interpretation of the tough-talking P.I. is a high point in his glorious career, and sultry Lauren Bacall throws in enough spark to ignite several city blocks. The story concerns a society dame (Bacall) and her addled sister (Martha Vickers). *Film noir* took on new meaning with this picture, since action is almost always secondary to effect. The script passed through many hands, including those of William Faulkner; the result is a plot almost impossible to follow. No matter; the main attractions in this classic lie elsewhere. Be sure not to confuse this—the original—version with the witless remake. Unrated; adult themes and violence.

1946 B & W 114 minutes

BIG SLEEP, THE (Remake)

DIRECTOR: Michael Winner
CAST: Robert Mitchum, James Stewart, Sarah Miles, Oliver Reed, Candy Clark, Edward Fox

Director Michael Winner came up with a loser in this remake of the classic screen detective yarn. Even the considerable talents of Robert Mitchum (repeating the interpretation of the Philip Marlowe created in *Farewell My*

Lovely), James Stewart, and Oliver Reed can't raise this travesty above the threshold of pain. Rated R for violence, profanity, and nudity.

1978 100 minutes

BIG STEAL, THE

★★★

DIRECTOR: Don Siegel

CAST: Robert Mitchum, Jane Greer, William Bendix, Ramon Novarro, Patric Knowles

Four sets of desperate and disparate characters chase each other over bumpy roads in the Southwest and Mexico following a robbery. Robert Mitchum ogles Jane Greer while zeroing in on the baddies. An intriguing film, somewhat difficult to follow but fun to watch.

1949 B & W 71 minutes

BIG TREES, THE

★★½

DIRECTOR: Felix Feist

CAST: Kirk Douglas, Eve Miller, Patrice Wymore, Edgar Buchanan, John Archer, Alan Hale

Lumberman Kirk Douglas wants the redwoods on homesteaders' land in this colorful adventure set in northwest California in 1900. Eve Miller is the passive Quakerlike girl who wins his heart; Patrice Wymore is the obligatory saloon singer who, as usual, gets jilted. A remake of 1938's *Valley of the Giants*.

1952 89 minutes

BIG TROUBLE IN LITTLE CHINA

★★★½

DIRECTOR: John Carpenter

CAST: Kurt Russell, Kim Cattrall, Dennis Dun, James Hong, Victor Wong, Kate Burton, Donald Li, Carter Wong

An adventure fantasy with Kurt Russell as a pig trucker unwittingly swept into a mystical world underneath San Francisco's Chinatown. It's an empire ruled by a sinister 2,000-year-old ghost who must marry a green-eyed woman to restore his youth. The movie is a lighthearted special-effects showcase designed to look a bit silly, in the style of old serials, thriller comics, and Saturday morning cartoon shows. Rated PG-13.

1986 99 minutes

BILLY JACK

★★½

DIRECTOR: Tom Laughlin

CAST: Tom Laughlin, Delores Taylor, Clark Howat, Bert Freed, Julie Webb

A film that seems to suggest that a good kick in the groin will bring "peace and love," *Billy Jack* was a box-office sensation. The star, Tom Laughlin, and his wife, Delores Taylor (who plays the schoolteacher), produced and directed both this film and its prequel, *Born Losers*. They saturated television with advertising, rented local theaters outright, and made a bundle. Neither film can be called art. Laughlin is superb, but the rest can be called mediocre at best. Rated PG.

1971 114 minutes

BIRD OF PARADISE

★★½

DIRECTOR: King Vidor

CAST: Joel McCrea, Dolores Del Rio, John Halliday, Skeets Gallagher, Lon Chaney Jr.

Even the reliable Joel McCrea can't save this bit of South Sea island silliness. Amid sacrifices and angry volcano gods, the seafaring McCrea attempts to woo native princess Dolores Del Rio. This kind of thing was fairly typical (and popular) in the 1930s, but it looks awfully dumb today.

1932 B & W 80 minutes

BIRDS OF PREY

★★★★

DIRECTOR: William Graham
CAST: David Janssen, Ralph Meeker, Elayne Heilveil

Ex–World War II fighter pilot turned peacetime Salt Lake City traffic helicopter jockey (David Janssen) hears the siren song of war anew when he witnesses a bank heist in progress and chases the robbers, who make their getaway in their own 'copter. An aerial battle of wits follows. Terrific flying sequences. There is an atmosphere and quality about this made-for-TV film that makes it one to savor and think about.

1973 81 minutes

BLACK ARROW, THE

★★★½

DIRECTOR: Gordon Douglas
CAST: Louis Hayward, George Macready, Janet Blair, Edgar Buchanan

Hero Louis Hayward is in fine form as he fights the evil George Macready in this highly enjoyable entry into the swashbuckler genre. Some fine action scenes, with a slam-bang finale.

1948 B & W 76 minutes

BLACK BELT JONES

★★★

DIRECTOR: Robert Clouse
CAST: Jim Kelly, Scatman Crothers, Gloria Hendry

A likable kung-fu action film about a self-defense school in Watts combatting a "mafioso"-type group. Not a classic film, but an easy pace and good humor make this a good action movie. Rated PG for violence.

1974 87 minutes

BLACK JACK

★★★

DIRECTOR: Julien Duvivier
CAST: George Sanders, Herbert Marshall, Agnes Moorehead, Patricia Roc, Marcel Dalio

George Sanders is soldier of fortune Michael Alexander who has a drug-smuggling scheme in Tangiers aboard his yacht, the *Black Jack*. Patricia Roc plays his less-than-passionate love interest, Ingrid Decker. More interesting than the principal couple may be Agnes Moorehead as the rich widow, Mrs. Burke, and Herbert Marshall as Michael Alexander's war buddy in their supporting roles. Despite the initial feeling that this is a dated film, the twists in plot will hold viewers' attention.

1949 B & W 103 minutes

BLACK MOON RISING

★★

DIRECTOR: Harley Cokliss
CAST: Tommy Lee Jones, Linda Hamilton, Robert Vaughn, Richard Jaeckel, Lee Ving, Bubba Smith

The only redeeming point of this little car theft number is its occasional accent on humor. Unfortunately, the lighter moments are few and far between. The cast is topnotch, but the material is mostly pedestrian. Rated R for language, nudity, sex, and some rather gruesome scenes of violence.

1986 93 minutes

BLACK PIRATE, THE

★★★½

DIRECTOR: Albert Parker
CAST: Douglas Fairbanks Sr., Donald Crisp, Billie Dove, Anders Randolph, Sam De Grasse, Tempe Pigott, Charles Stevens, Charles Belcher

One of superstar Douglas Fairbanks's most popular films, this early color production packs enough thrills and exciting situations for a dozen pictures. Written by Fairbanks, *Pirate* contains bits of business to be found in dozens of previous and subsequent films, including a duel to the death with cutlasses on the beach, a daring underwater raid on a pirate ship, and one of the most famous of all movie stunts: Fairbanks's ride down the ship's sail on a knife, cleverly achieved with an apparatus hidden from the camera. The use of two-tone Technicolor heightened specific scenes for effect, although today no print of the film in color is known to exist. Silent.

1926 B & W 122 minutes

BLACK SUNDAY

★★★

DIRECTOR: John Frankenheimer
CAST: Robert Shaw, Bruce Dern, Marthe Keller, Fritz Weaver

This film is about an Arab terrorist group attempting to blow up the president. It features an exciting chase involving the Goodyear blimp and police helicopters over the skies of a Superbowl in Miami's Orange Bowl. Tension is maintained throughout. Rated R.

1977 143 minutes

BLACK WINDMILL, THE

★★★½

DIRECTOR: Don Siegel
CAST: Michael Caine, Joseph O'Conor, Donald Pleasence, John Vernon, Janet Suzman, Delphine Seyrig

Straightforward story is enhanced by Don Siegel's razor-sharp direction and Michael Caine's engrossing performance as an intelligence agent whose son has been kidnapped. The suspense builds carefully to a satisfying climax. Rated R.

1974 106 minutes

BLACKOUT

★★★

DIRECTOR: Eddy Matalon
CAST: Jim Mitchum, Robert Carradine, Belinda Montgomery, June Allyson, Jean-Pierre Aumont, Ray Milland

At times, this movie, about a New York City apartment building attacked by a gang of escaped criminals during a blackout, reeks of a disaster film. There's the establishing of cardboard characters, the setup for the unfolding drama, and some pretty wooden acting. Still, there are good action scenes and enough drama to make you almost forget the shortcomings. Rated R for violence.

1978 86 minutes

BLADE MASTER, THE

★

DIRECTOR: David Hills
CAST: Miles O'Keeffe, Lisa Foster

This is one of those action-packed slice-and-dice adventures that may entertain if not taken seriously. Muscleman Miles O'Keeffe, along with his small band of followers, chops his way across the countryside battling nasty sorcerers and spirits in a quest to conquer evil. Rated PG.

1984 92 minutes

BLAKE OF SCOTLAND YARD

★★½

DIRECTOR: Robert Hill
CAST: Ralph Byrd, Lloyd Hughes, Joan Barclay, Herbert Rawlinson, Dickie Jones, Bob Terry, Nick Stuart

Former Scotland Yard inspector Sir James Blake has perfected a death ray, which he demonstrates, firing the greed of munitions maker Count Basil Zegelloff. The power-mad count offers a king's ransom to the man who helps him to obtain the death-dealing device, and a mysterious cloaked character called The Scorpion begins a reign of terror in his campaign to secure the weapon. The Scorpion, wearing heavy make-up and sporting a large right hand similar to a lobster's claw, puts sturdy Ralph Byrd (soon to be famous as the definitive Dick Tracy in serials and movies) through his paces. As the fifteen chapters unwind, one suspect after another is eliminated until the hero finally tricks the evil Scorpion into exposing his true identity. Made by Victory Pictures, a bargain-basement independent producer, this cliffhanger lacks the values that Universal or Republic put into their product, but it's still fun. This serial was also released as a seventy-minute feature film.

1937 B & W 15 chapters

BLASTFIGHTER

🦃

DIRECTOR: John Old Jr.
CAST: Michael Sopkiw, Valerie Blake, George Eastman, Mike Miller

Michael Sopkiw (of *After the Fall of New York* infamy) is Jake "Tiger" Sharp, a rather dull ex-convict who returns to his hometown in the Appalachians, where he becomes a Rambo trying to clean up an immoral populous intent on killing all the little forest critters. Of course, there's violent conflict here when the whole town shows up to kill ol' Tiger. But, with a gun the size of a tree trunk and enough ammo to supply the Russian army, there are enough fireworks and carnage to satisfy the chronically bloodthirsty. We can't figure out what's worse here—the acting, the screenplay, the directing, or the rather low view this piece of sludge holds of southern backwoods people. Not rated, but contains violence.

1984 93 minutes

BLIND RAGE

★

DIRECTOR: Efren C. Pinion
CAST: D'Urville Martin, Leo Fong, Tony Ferrer, Dick Adair, Darnell Garcia, Charlie Davao, Leila Hermosa, Fred Williamson, Jessie Crowder

If you really believe that four blind men could rob a bank during business hours, you deserve this film. The crooks are chosen because they have experience in the various talents it takes to pull off a bank job and also because they are blind so they cannot finger the big shots who designed the heist. Fred Williamson fans, beware; his appearance is very brief. Rated R for violence and profanity.

1978 81 minutes

BLOOD IN THE STREETS

★★

DIRECTOR: Sergio Sollima
CAST: Oliver Reed, Fabio Testi, Agostine Belli

In this French-Italian film, a prison warden (Oliver Reed) is forced to release a prisoner as ransom for his kidnapped wife. When he realizes that the prisoner will be killed when he's turned over to these underworld figures, he has second thoughts about making the trade. There are some exciting chase scenes in this overall so-so film. Rated R for sex, nudity, language, and violence.

1974 111 minutes

BLOOD ON THE SUN

★★★½

DIRECTOR: Frank Lloyd
CAST: James Cagney, Robert Armstrong, Wallace Ford, Sylvia Sidney

This hard-hitting action drama finds James Cagney fighting Japanese military and government men in Japan during World War II. An unusual plot and good pace make this worth watching.

1945 B & W 98 minutes

BLOOD SIMPLE

★★★★½

DIRECTOR: Joel Coen
CAST: John Getz, Frances McDormand, Don Hedaya, M. Emmet Walsh, Samm-Art Williams

"In Russia, they've got it mapped out," intones the narrator (a sleazy private eye played to perfection by character actor M. Emmet Walsh). "Everyone pulls for everyone else. That's the theory, anyway. What I know is Texas. Down here, you're on your own." What follows is a slyly suspenseful, exciting (and sometimes agonizing) edge-of-your-seat story of how a bar owner named Julian Marty (Don Hedaya) hires the private eye to follow his wife, Abby (Frances McDormand), to find out if she's cheating on him. She is—with bartender Ray (John Getz), who works at Marty's club, the Neon Boot. So Marty hires the detective (who remains nameless) to kill them both. Thus begins a series of inventive twists and turns based on the title, *Blood Simple*, which is defined as a "state of confusion that follows the commission of a murder, i.e., 'He's gone blood simple.' " This state of mind, first described by hardboiled detective fiction great Dashiell Hammett (*The Maltese Falcon*; *Red Harvest*), makes the perfect murder impossible. Yet all of the major characters in this terrific film think they have done so at least once during its running time. Rated R for suggested sex, violence, and profanity.

1984 96 minutes

BLOODY MAMA

★★½

DIRECTOR: Roger Corman
CAST: Shelley Winters, Don Stroud, Pat Hingle, Robert Walden, Bruce Dern

Shelley Winters plays Ma Barker in this gangster flick. Her four sons share her notoriety as Depression-era bandits. Rated R.

1970 90 minutes

BLOWING WILD

★

DIRECTOR: Hugo Fregonese
CAST: Gary Cooper, Barbara Stanwyck, Anthony Quinn, Ruth Roman, Ward Bond

Wildcat Barbara Stanwyck lusts almost in vain for Gary Cooper in this foul tale of bandits in the Mexican oilfields. An exceptionally poor script brings a good cast to its knees.

1953 90 minutes

BLUE CITY

DIRECTOR: Michelle Manning
CAST: Judd Nelson, Ally Sheedy, David Caruso, Paul Winfield, Scott Wilson, Anita Morris

Probably one of the worst adaptations of a solid thriller ever made. Ross Macdonald must be rolling over in his grave. Estranged son Judd Nelson returns to his hometown and learns that his father, previously the mayor, has been killed. Determined to avenge this murder, Nelson goes on a ludicrous destructive spree against the local crime lord. All of the characters act like puppets on strings, with no motivation for their actions. The script makes no sense, and first-time director Michelle Manning shouldn't be let out without a leash. The biggest mistake was in updating the story from its 1946 setting to the 1980s;

World War II–era tough-guy tales simply don't play outside that setting. Rated R for language and violence.

1986 83 minutes

BLUE MAX, THE

★★★

DIRECTOR: John Guillermin

CAST: George Peppard, James Mason, Ursula Andress, Jeremy Kemp, Carl Schell

George Peppard (*The A-Team*) stars in this passable treatment of World War I flying aces.

1966 156 minutes

BLUE SUNSHINE

★★½

DIRECTOR: Jeff Lieberman

CAST: Zalman King, Deborah Winters, Mark Goddard, Robert Walden, Charles Siebert

Oddball mystery-thriller dealing with a series of random killings committed by former college students suffering the side effects of a drug taken ten years previously. Low-budget film is both ridiculous and terrifying at the same time. Not for all tastes, but worth a look. Rated PG for mild language and violence.

1976 97 minutes

BLUE THUNDER

★★★★½

DIRECTOR: John Badham

CAST: Roy Scheider, Malcolm McDowell, Candy Clark, Warren Oates

A state-of-the-art helicopter is the centerpiece of this action-paced police melodrama. Piloted by Roy Scheider, the craft—a.k.a. "Blue Thunder"—battles combat jets commanded by villain Malcolm McDowell high above the crowded streets of downtown Los Angeles. The result is a gripping and immensely entertaining—if somewhat implausible—adventure thriller. Rated R for violence, nudity, and profanity.

1983 109 minutes

BOBBIE JO AND THE OUTLAW

★½

DIRECTOR: Mark L. Lester

CAST: Marjoe Gortner, Lynda Carter, Jesse Vint, Merrie Lynn Ross, Belinda Belaski, Gerrit Graham

This one is criminal, indeed. Lynda Carter, hungry for excitement, tags along with Marjoe Gortner and his gang. An orgy of murders and robberies ensues. Lots of violence, little credibility. Unless you're burning to see Wonder Woman seminude for a few seconds, skip it. Rated R for nudity, violence, and profanity.

1976 89 minutes

BOMBARDIER

★★★½

DIRECTOR: Richard Wallace

CAST: Pat O'Brien, Randolph Scott, Eddie Albert, Robert Ryan, Anne Shirley, Barton MacLane

This is a solid action film dealing with the training of flyers during World War II. There is nothing new in the familiar formula of this film, but a good cast and fast pace make it enjoyable.

1943 B & W 99 minutes

BONNIE AND CLYDE

★★★★★

DIRECTOR: Arthur Penn

CAST: Warren Beatty, Faye Dunaway, Gene Hackman, Estelle Parsons, Michael J. Pollard, Gene Wilder

This still fresh and innovative gangster film was one of the first to depict graphic violence, turning the genre inside-out, combining comedy, bloodshed, pathos, and social commentary with fascinating results.

1967 111 minutes

BONNIE'S KIDS

★★½

DIRECTOR: Arthur Marks

CAST: Tiffany Bolling, Steve Sandor, Robin Mattson, Scott Brady

Although this film has no redeeming social value, you can't really call it boring. In it, two amoral girls molested by their stepfather kill him and move in with their criminal uncle. They plan to rob their uncle but are pursued by thugs. Lots of action, but it's all rather pointless. Rated R for simulated sex, nudity, adult themes, and violence.

1982 105 minutes

BORDER, THE

★★★½

DIRECTOR: Tony Richardson

CAST: Jack Nicholson, Harvey Keitel, Valerie Perrine, Warren Oates, Elpidia Carrillo

Jack Nicholson stars in this often effective drama about a border patrol officer who rebels against the corruption in his department and the rampant greed of his wife, Valerie Perrine. This film features what was Nicholson's best major role in years (we're not counting his supporting bits in *Reds* or *Terms of Endearment* here). In addition, Harvey Keitel, Perrine, and Warren Oates give outstanding support. Rated R.

1982 107 minutes

BORDERLINE

★★★½

DIRECTOR: Jerrold Freedman

CAST: Charles Bronson, Bruno Kirby, Bert Remsen, Ed Harris

Old Stone Face Charles Bronson gives one of his better, more committed recent screen portrayals in this release, which got the jump on the similar *The Border*, with Jack Nicholson, by nearly two years (because of the latter's story problems). As in the latter film, the central character—a border guard—becomes involved with the problems of an illegal alien and her child. The result is a watchable action film. Rated R.

1980 105 minutes

BORN AMERICAN

★

DIRECTOR: Renny Harlin

CAST: Mike Norris, Steve Durham, David Coburn, Albert Salmi, Thalmus Rasulala

This low-budget film features a mostly ridiculous and sometimes morbid story in the tradition of *Red Dawn*. It involves three high-school buddies who cross the Russian border while on summer vacation in Lapland. Their drunken exploit lands them in a Russian prison where the guards play a game of chess with live pieces, and the stakes are high! Sadly enough, this might have been a better film if it weren't for the highly unbelievable action sequences. Rated R for sex and violence.

1986 103 minutes

BORN LOSERS

★★★

DIRECTOR: T. C. Frank

CAST: Tom Laughlin, Elizabeth James, Jeremy Slate, William Wellman Jr., Robert Tessier

This biker exploitation movie is better than the celebrated *Billy Jack*, which also starred Tom Laughlin. Granted, we still have to sit through scenes with terrible amateur actors, both kids and adults, but at least there is no girl singing off-key about her brother being dead.

1967 112 minutes

BOTANY BAY

★★★

DIRECTOR: John Farrow

CAST: Alan Ladd, James Mason, Sir Cedric Hardwicke, Patricia Medina, Murray Matheson

It is the 1790s, England still rules the waves, maritime officers are still sadistic, and the innocent are still punished. At least, until the last reel. In this picturesque action tale, Alan Ladd is a wrongly convicted student being transported to penal Australia. James Mason is the captain of the outward-bound convict ship, keelhauling and flogging his cargo of human flotsam with heinous delight. He has eyes for beauteous Patricia Medina, but she is interested in another Ladd. The color is nice.

1953 94 minutes

BOUNTY, THE

★★★★

DIRECTOR: Roger Donaldson

CAST: Mel Gibson, Anthony Hopkins, Laurence Olivier, Edward Fox

Mel Gibson (*Road Warrior*) is Fletcher Christian, and Anthony Hopkins is Captain William Bligh in this, the fourth and most satisfying screen version of *The Mutiny on the Bounty.* The 1935 original, with Clark Gable and Charles Laughton, is undeniably one of the screen's finest adventure films, just as the 1962 remake with Marlon Brando and Trevor Howard was a multimillion-dollar mistake. This sweeping seafaring epic from the director of *Smash Palace* is the first movie to present the historic events accurately—and to do so fascinatingly. Rated PG for nudity and violence.

1984 132 minutes

BOXCAR BERTHA

★★½

DIRECTOR: Martin Scorsese

CAST: David Carradine, Barbara Hershey, Barry Primus, Bernie Casey, John Carradine

Small-town girl (Barbara Hershey) hooks up with a gang of train robbers (led by David Carradine) in this *Bonnie and Clyde* coattailer. Martin Scorsese buffs will be disappointed. Rated R.

1972 97 minutes

BOYS IN COMPANY C, THE

★★★

DIRECTOR: Sidney J. Furie

CAST: Stan Shaw, Andrew Stevens, James Canning, James Whitmore Jr.

The film opens with the arrival of various draftees in the Marine Corps induction center and comes close, at times, to being the powerful film the subject of the Vietnam war suggests. The combat scenes are particularly effective, and the deaths of soldiers are gory without being overdone. Rated R for violence.

1978 127 minutes

BRADY'S ESCAPE

★★★

DIRECTOR: Pal Gabor

CAST: John Savage, Kelly Reno

A minor HBO-produced film concerning an American attempting to escape the Nazis in Europe during WWII. Nothing original is added to the familiar plot.

1984 96 minutes

BRANNIGAN

★★½

DIRECTOR: Douglas Hickox

CAST: John Wayne, Richard Attenborough, Judy Geeson, Mel Ferrer, Ralph Meeker, John Vernon

An aging John Wayne travels to

London to bring back a fugitive in this cops-and-robbers chase film that is long on just about everything but plot and credibility. It's kind of fun to see the Duke in jolly old England and the cast is outstanding, but the film is flat and slow and doesn't deliver the excitement or impact one expects from one of the world's greatest stars. Rated PG.

1975 111 minutes

BRASS TARGET

★★

DIRECTOR: John Hough

CAST: Sophia Loren, George Kennedy, John Cassavetes, Robert Vaughn, Max von Sydow, Bruce Davison

Pure Hollywood hokum at its most ridiculous would ask us to believe that Gen. George Patton (George Kennedy) was murdered after World War II because of a large gold robbery committed by his staff. Not much to recommend this boring film. Rated PG for moderate language and violence.

1978 111 minutes

BREAKER! BREAKER!

DIRECTOR: Don Hulette

CAST: Chuck Norris, George Murdock, Terry O'Connor, Don Gentry

A quickie thrown together to cash in on the CB craze, this Chuck Norris flick promises, but does not deliver, a slam-bang ending. Rated PG.

1977 86 minutes

BREAKER MORANT

★★★★★

DIRECTOR: Bruce Beresford

CAST: Edward Woodward, Jack Thompson, John Waters, Bryan Brown

This is one motion picture you won't want to miss. Imagine the high adventure of the original *Gunga Din*, the wisecracking humor of *To Have and Have Not*, and the character drama of *The Caine Mutiny* all rolled into one super movie and you'll have an idea of just how good *Breaker Morant* is. Edward Woodward (*The Wicker Man*) stars in this film about the court-martial of three soldiers during the Boer War. Rated PG.

1979 107 minutes

BREAKOUT

★★★

DIRECTOR: Tom Gries

CAST: Charles Bronson, Robert Duvall, Jill Ireland, John Huston, Sheree North, Randy Quaid

While not exactly Charles Bronson at his best, this action-adventure film does have its moments as the star, playing a devil-may-care helicopter pilot, rescues Robert Duvall, an American businessman framed for murder and held captive in a Mexican jail. Director-turned-actor John Huston also adds some class to this production, which suffers equally from a featured role played by the untalented Jill Ireland (Mrs. Bronson). In all, *Breakout* is a basically entertaining time-passer. Rated PG.

1975 96 minutes

BREAKTHROUGH

DIRECTOR: Andrew V. McLaglen

CAST: Richard Burton, Robert Mitchum, Rod Steiger, Curt Jurgens

This dull war film—a sequel to Sam Peckinpah's *Cross of Iron*—stars Richard Burton as Sergeant Steiner, a heroic German officer who saves the life of an American colonel (Robert Mitchum) after the Nazis thwart an attempt on Hitler's life. The Allies are placed in danger by their agreement to a discussion of surrender by the conspirators. Rated PG.

1978 115 minutes

BREED APART, A

★★★½

DIRECTOR: Philippe Mora
CAST: Rutger Hauer, Kathleen Turner, Powers Boothe, Donald Pleasence

When a billionaire collector hires an adventurous mountain climber to steal the eggs of an endangered pair of nesting eagles, the result is a nicely paced film that manages to combine drama, suspense, romance, and even a touch of post-Vietnam commentary. Rutger Hauer plays the strange recluse who lives in a tent-palace in the loneliest reaches of the Blue Ridge Mountains, where he protects the fragile birds of the region. Rated R for sex, nudity, and violence.

1984 95 minutes

BRIDGE ON THE RIVER KWAI, THE

★★★★★

DIRECTOR: David Lean
CAST: William Holden, Alec Guinness, Jack Hawkins, Sessue Hayakawa, James Donald

Considered by many to be David Lean's greatest work, this war epic brought the British director his first Oscar. The powerful, dramatic story centers around the construction of a bridge by British and American prisoners of war under the command of Japanese colonel Sessue Hayakawa. Alec Guinness, a Lean semiregular since *Great Expectations*, is the stiff-upper-lipped British commander who uses the task as a way of proving British superiority. William Holden is the American soldier escapee who must return to the camp and, with the aid of British commando Jack Hawkins, blow the bridge up.

1957 161 minutes

BRIDGE TOO FAR, A

★★★½

DIRECTOR: Richard Attenborough
CAST: Dirk Bogarde, James Caan, Michael Caine, Sean Connery, Laurence Olivier, Robert Redford

Here's another story of a famous battle with the traditional all-star cast. In this case it's World War II's "Operation Market Garden," a disastrous Allied push to get troops behind German lines and capture an early bridgehead on the Rhine. Rated PG.

1977 175 minutes

BUCCANEER, THE

DIRECTOR: Anthony Quinn
CAST: Yul Brynner, Charlton Heston, Claire Bloom, Charles Boyer, Douglass Dumbrille, Lorne Greene, Ted de Corsia

Studio-bound remake of C. B. De Mille's 1938 romance of pirate Jean Lafitte and his involvement in the War of 1812 boasts a cast capable of hamming *and* acting, but that's not enough to make this stiff color creaker come alive.

1958 121 minutes

BULLDOG DRUMMOND

★★★

DIRECTOR: F. Richard Jones
CAST: Ronald Colman, Joan Bennett, Lilyan Tashman, Montagu Love, Lawrence Grant, Claud Allister, Tetsu Komai

Ronald Colman smoothly segued from silent to sound films playing the title's ex–British army officer adventurer in this exciting, witty, definitive first stanza of what became a popular series.

1929 B & W 89 minutes

BULLDOG DRUMMOND COMES BACK

★★★

DIRECTOR: Louis King

CAST: John Howard, John Barrymore, Louis Campbell, E. E. Clive, Reginald Denny, J. Carrol Naish, John Sutton, Helen Freeman

The first of seven films starring John Howard as the adventurer-sleuth is an atmospheric tale of revenge. The crazed widow of one of Bulldog Drummond's former enemies makes off with our hero's girl, Phyllis. Full of fog-draped streets, clever clues, and John Barrymore as Colonel Neilson, this gem from Paramount maintains a degree of intelligence. Even though John Barrymore was in decline, he gives hints of the tremendous talent he possessed in his prime. Available on tape with *Bulldog Drummond Escapes*.

1937 B & W 59 minutes

BULLDOG DRUMMOND ESCAPES

★★

DIRECTOR: James Hogan

CAST: Ray Milland, Guy Standing, Heather Angel, Porter Hall, Reginald Denny, E. E. Clive, Fay Holden, Clyde Cook, Walter Kingsford

Famed ex–British army officer Bulldog Drummond comes to the aid of his ladylove when she becomes embroiled in an international espionage ring. Young Ray Milland stars in his only outing as the World War I hero in this okay series entry. Most detective and action buffs prefer the two earlier Ronald Colman epics and the later John Howard–John Barrymore series, although this one has an exemplary cast of stiff-upper-lip types and a beautiful young Heather Angel. Paired on tape with *Bulldog Drummond Comes Back*.

1937 B & W 65 minutes

BULLDOG DRUMMOND IN AFRICA

★★½

DIRECTOR: Louis King

CAST: John Howard, Heather Angel, J. Carrol Naish, H. B. Warner, Anthony Quinn, Michael Brooke

An international spy ring has struck again. This time they've kidnapped Colonel Neilson and hidden him somewhere in North Africa, and Hugh "Bulldog" Drummond isn't going to stand for it. He and his friends attempt to rescue their friend from the violence-prone spies and man-eating lions. Veteran character actor J. Carrol Naish and newcomer Anthony Quinn make this enjoyable mystery-adventure even more so. Double-billed with *Arrest Bulldog Drummond* on tape.

1938 B & W 58 minutes

BULLDOG DRUMMOND'S PERIL

★★★

DIRECTOR: James Hogan

CAST: John Howard, John Barrymore, Louise Campbell, H. B. Warner, Reginald Denny, Elizabeth Patterson, Porter Hall, Nydia Westman

Bulldog Drummond has a personal stake in a chase that takes him from London to Switzerland —the synthetic diamond that was stolen is a wedding gift intended for our hero and his patient fiancée, Phyllis. Full of close calls, witty dialogue, and an injection of controlled lunacy by the great John Barrymore, this third film in Paramount's series with John Howard shows just how good the program films of the late 1930s could be. Modern movies will never be able to duplicate the caliber and cast of these second-string productions; the budget of the entire Bulldog Drummond series was probably less than the cost of a made-for-TV pilot today. On tape with *Bulldog Drummond's Revenge*.

1938 B & W 66 minutes

BULLDOG DRUMMOND'S BRIDE

★★½

DIRECTOR: James Hogan

CAST: John Howard, Heather Angel, Reginald Denny, H. B. Warner, Eduardo Ciannelli, Elizabeth Patterson

The last of Paramount's Bulldog Drummond series finds John Howard combating evil close at hand when a crack bank robber uses Drummond's honeymoon flat as a hideout for himself and his explosives. The amateur investigator jeopardizes his life and his wedding plans as he takes on "one more case" for Scotland Yard, a move that nearly proves fatal for him and his long-suffering fiancée, Phyllis. Not the best of the series, but it's still a rousing adventure. Eduardo Ciannelli makes a fascinating and diabolical villain. On tape with *Bulldog Drummond's Secret Police*.

1939 B & W 56 minutes

BULLDOG DRUMMOND'S REVENGE

★★★

DIRECTOR: Louis King

CAST: John Howard, John Barrymore, Louise Campbell, Reginald Denny, E. E. Clive, Nydia Westman, Lucien Littlefield, John Sutton, Frank Puglia

The second film in Paramount's Drummond series featuring John Howard, this entry focuses on the hero's attempts to recover a powerful explosive and to bring to justice the people responsible for stealing it. Aided by the colorful Colonel Neilson (John Barrymore at his most enjoyable), Drummond fights evildoers at every turn. Why are these old series films so much fun? They have good production values, the stories are based on Bulldog Drummond novels, the pacing is quick, and the cast of characters is hand-picked. Today's filmmaking precludes the possibility of lavishing so much time and effort on any film that was used primarily as the second half of a double bill. Released on a double bill with *Bulldog Drummond's Peril*.

1937 B & W 55 minutes

BULLDOG DRUMMOND'S SECRET POLICE

★★½

DIRECTOR: James Hogan

CAST: John Howard, Heather Angel, Reginald Denny, Leo G. Carroll, H. B. Warner, Elizabeth Patterson

Stylish entry in the long-running series finds gentleman adventurer Bulldog Drummond searching a forbidding castle for hidden treasure while matching wits with a crazed murderer. Not quite as much fun as the entries with John Barrymore, but good production values and a fine cast of series regulars make this unpretentious programmer good entertainment for all crime enthusiasts. This is the second film version of *Temple Tower* and the sixth of seven adventures featuring John Howard as H. C. McNeile's hero. Double billed with *Bulldog Drummond's Bride* on videotape.

1939 B & W 54 minutes

BULLFIGHTER AND THE LADY, THE

★★★★

DIRECTOR: Budd Boetticher

CAST: Robert Stack, Joy Page, Gilbert Roland, Katy Jurado

Many of the themes explored in the superb series of low-budget westerns director Budd Boetticher later made with Randolph Scott (*Decision at Sundown*; *The Tall T*) are evident in this first-rate drama. A skeet-shooting champ (Robert Stack) decides to become a bullfighter and enlists the aid of a top professional (Gilbert Roland). This is the finest film on the subject.

1951 B & W 87 minutes

BULLITT

★★★★

DIRECTOR: Peter Yates
CAST: Steve McQueen, Robert Vaughn, Jacqueline Bisset, Norman Fell, Don Gordon

Although a bit dated now, this police drama directed by Peter Yates (*Breaking Away*) still features one of star Steve McQueen's best screen performances. Costarring Robert Vaughn and Jacqueline Bisset, it features McQueen as a "Dirty Harry"–type renegade cop who smells a rat when his efforts to guard government witnesses are suspiciously thwarted. The San Francisco car-chase sequence is still a corker.

1968 113 minutes

BUNCO

★★½

DIRECTOR: Alexander Singer
CAST: Robert Urich, Tom Selleck, Donna Mills, Michael Sacks, Will Geer, Arte Johnson, James Hampton, Bobby Van

Passable made-for-television crime thriller has Robert Urich and Tom Selleck, sans mustache, as a pair of police detectives out to bust a confidence ring. They enlist the aid of a female undercover cop (Donna Mills), who soon finds herself paired with a psycho (Michael Sacks) and her life in danger. Typical TV fare.

1985 90 minutes

BUSHIDO BLADE

DIRECTOR: Tom Kotani
CAST: Richard Boone, Frank Converse, James Earl Jones, Toshiro Mifune, Mako, Sonny Chiba, Laura Gemser

Top-billed Richard Boone gives an outrageously hammy performance in this Japanese-made answer to *Shogun* as Commander Matthew Perry, whose mission is to find a valuable sword. Gesturing with no regard to believable movement or character, Boone is embarrassingly bad in his last film. The all-star cast of Frank Converse (in the action-hero role), James Earl Jones, Toshiro Mifune (as, what else, a shogun), and Mako (from the *Conan* series and *The Sand Pebbles*) fare little better in this poorly directed adventure. Rated R for violence.

1979 104 minutes

CABO BLANCO

DIRECTOR: J. Lee Thompson
CAST: Charles Bronson, Dominique Sanda, Jason Robards Jr.

When will they ever learn? This is a miserable suspense-thriller remake of *Casablanca*. As good as he can be when he wants to, Charles Bronson is no Humphrey Bogart. And we shouldn't expect him to be. So why is he playing a nightclub owner saving a damsel in distress (Dominique Sanda) from a modern-day Nazi (Jason Robards Jr.)? We don't know—and neither will you. Rated R.

1982 87 minutes

CALL OF THE WILD

★★★½

DIRECTOR: Ken Annakin
CAST: Charlton Heston, Michele Mercier, Maria Rohm, Rik Battaglia

Charlton Heston stars in this adaptation of Jack London's famous novel. This one is a real tear-jerker. A domesticated dog is stolen and forced to pull a snow sled in Alaska as John (Charlton Heston) searches for gold. Some profanity and violence. Rated PG.

1972 100 minutes

CAME A HOT FRIDAY

★★

DIRECTOR: Ian Mune

CAST: Peter Bland, Philip Gordon, Billy T. James, Michael Lawrence, Marshall Napier, Erna Larsen, Patricia Philips, Don Selwyn

Mildly amusing film set in 1949 New Zealand, where two con men make their fortune cheating bookmakers all across the country. Their luck runs out when they reach a small town—the locals turn the tables on them and take the money. So our two "heroes," with the help of the local nut-case, go all out to get the money back. Rated PG for language and adult situations.

1985 101 minutes

CANNONBALL

★½

DIRECTOR: Paul Bartel

CAST: David Carradine, Veronica Hamel, Gerrit Graham, Sylvester Stallone, Robert Carradine, Carl Gottlieb, Belinda Balaski

Before writer-director Paul Bartel got involved with original notions, such as *Eating Raoul*, he was busily copying other successful concepts. This plays like a poor man's *Cannonball Run* or *Gumball Rally*, executed by somebody having neither the skill nor the understanding of complex vehicular stunts. As usual, David Carradine plays an unpleasant antihero out to beat the rest of the cast in an exotic race. Look for cameos by directors Roger Corman, Joe Dante, and Martin Scorsese. Rated R for violence.

1976 93 minutes

CAPTAIN BLOOD

★★★★½

DIRECTOR: Michael Curtiz

CAST: Errol Flynn, Olivia De Havilland, Basil Rathbone, Lionel Atwill, Ross Alexander, Guy Kibbee, Henry Stephenson

Errol Flynn's youthful enthusiasm, great character actors, realistic miniature work, and Erich Wolfgang Korngold's score all meld together under Michael Curtiz's direction and provide audiences with perhaps the best pirate film of all time. Flynn and Basil Rathbone's climactic duel resembles and surpasses Douglas Fairbanks's knife fight in *The Black Pirate* (1926), which was filmed on almost exactly the same section of Malibu Beach. Twenty-six-year-old Errol Flynn was an afterthought for the role of physician Peter Blood—the part had originally been intended for British actor Robert Donat, who suffered from asthma and was not able to fill the bill; so underpaid contract player Flynn assumed the lead and his place in the hearts of adventure fans the world over. This is an infectious film and one of Flynn's best.

1935 B & W 95 minutes

CAPTAIN CAUTION

★★

DIRECTOR: Richard Wallace

CAST: Victor Mature, Louise Platt, Bruce Cabot, Leo Carrillo, Vivienne Osborne, El Brendel, Robert Barrat, Miles Mander, Roscoe Ates

In command of a ship during the War of 1812 with England, Victor Mature, in the title role, is taken for a coward when he urges prudence. Louise Platt, spunky daughter of the vessel's owner, grabs the helm and commands it into victorious battle. Captain Caution proves himself against the enemy and reveals Bruce Cabot to be a traitor. As comic relief, Leo Carrillo and El Brendel fall short. Richard Wallace's fast-paced, cannon-bellowing direction quells all restlessness, however.

1940 B & W 85 minutes

CAPTAIN KIDD

DIRECTOR: Rowland V. Lee
CAST: Charles Laughton, Randolph Scott, Reginald Owen, John Carradine, Sheldon Leonard, Barbara Britton, Gilbert Roland

Not even Charles Laughton's mugging and posturing can redeem this swashbuckling yarn about the pirate whose treasure is still being sought. Great cast, from whom more should have been expected.

1945 89 minutes

CAST A GIANT SHADOW

DIRECTOR: Melville Shavelson
CAST: Kirk Douglas, Senta Berger, Angie Dickinson

The early history of Israel is told through the fictionalized biography of American Col. Mickie Marcus (Kirk Douglas). Marcus, an expatriate army officer, is cajoled into aiding Israel in its impending war to wrest independence from its hostile Arab neighbors. It is a highly romanticized piece of historical fluff. Frank Sinatra, John Wayne, and Yul Brynner make cameo appearances.

1966 142 minutes

CATCH ME A SPY

★★★

DIRECTOR: Dick Clement
CAST: Kirk Douglas, Marlene Jobert, Trevor Howard

This is a good suspense thriller with, surprisingly, a few laughs. The story is built around an East-West espionage theme in which both sides trade for their captured spies. Unfortunately, the West loses its hostage in an accident and is forced to scramble to find new barterable material. This yarn is interesting, suspenseful, and humorous. Rated PG.

1971 93 minutes

C.C. & COMPANY

★★½

DIRECTOR: Seymour Robbie
CAST: Joe Namath, Ann-Margret, William Smith, Sid Haig, Jennifer Billingsley, Greg Mullavey

Basically idiotic action film has Broadway Joe Namath (in his first feature) cast as C.C. Ryder, misfit member of a rowdy biker gang, attempting to "split" when he falls for top fashion photographer Ann-Margret. It's not that easy. Joe's acting is stiff and unnatural, William Smith is good as the gang leader, and cronies Sid Haig and Greg Mullavey handle the comic relief with a certain zeal. Rated R for mild language and nudity.

1970 90 minutes

CERTAIN FURY

DIRECTOR: Stephen Gullenhaal
CAST: Tatum O'Neal, Irene Cara, Nicholas Campbell, George Murdock, Moses Gunn, Peter Fonda

Somebody certainly should be furious about this tasteless, stupid movie. It's a vicious, gratuitously violent film with lots of guns and blood and fire and action—with no purpose. Tatum O'Neal is Scarlet ("Scar")—a dumb white street woman; Irene Cara is Tracy—a dumb pampered black woman. They're thrown together in an opening-scene bloodbath and through the rest of the movie run for their lives from police and drug dealers. Rated R for violence.

1985 87 minutes

CHAIN REACTION

★★★

DIRECTORS: Ian Barry, George Miller

CAST: Steve Bisley, Anna-Maria Winchester, Ross Thompson, Ralph Cotterill, Patrick Ward

This slick and stylish Australian political thriller, co-directed by George Miller before he hit it big with the *Mad Max* films, is a brilliantly photographed, generally engrossing drama following a nuclear power plant employee (Ross Thompson) accidentally exposed to a lethal dose of radiation during a near meltdown. Determined to let the public know of the disaster (which the utility company wants to keep under wraps), he makes a mad dash for the nearest city, with the authorities in hot pursuit. The first half is a scathing political exposé (à la *The China Syndrome*), while the second half regresses to a series of high-powered chase scenes (à la *Mad Max*), but the whole film is involving and visually enticing. Don't blink or you'll miss Mel Gibson in an unbilled cameo. Rated R. Some explicit sex, nudity, and violence.

1980 87 minutes

CHAINED HEAT

★

DIRECTOR: Paul Nicolas

CAST: Linda Blair, John Vernon, Nita Talbot, Stella Stevens, Sybil Danning, Tamara Dobson

The story of women in prison, this cheapo offers few surprises. It's just another visit to the snake pit, with a few lines of phenomenally bad—therefore funny—dialogue. Only those who like cheap laughs, nudity, sex, violence, profanity, and bad acting will enjoy this exploitation flick. Rated R.

1983 95 minutes

CHALLENGE, THE

★★★½

DIRECTOR: John Frankenheimer

CAST: Scott Glenn, Toshiro Mifune, Calvin Young

An American (Scott Glenn, the charismatic bad guy of *Urban Cowboy*) gets caught in the middle of a decades-old private war between two brothers in modern-day Japan. This movie has ample rewards for both samurai film aficionados and regular moviegoers. Sharing top billing and right in the thick of the action is Toshiro Mifune (*The Seven Samurai*; *Shogun*), the greatest Japanese screen actor of them all. Rated R for profanity and violence.

1982 112 minutes

CHARADE

★★★★½

DIRECTOR: Stanley Donen

CAST: Cary Grant, Audrey Hepburn, Walter Matthau, James Coburn, George Kennedy

A comedy-mystery directed in the Alfred Hitchcock suspense style by Stanley Donen (*Singin' in the Rain*; *Blame It on Rio*), this features the ever-suave Cary Grant helping widow Audrey Hepburn find the fortune stashed by her late husband. Walter Matthau, George Kennedy, and James Coburn are the baddies attempting to get to the loot first.

1963 114 minutes

CHARGE OF THE LIGHT BRIGADE, THE

★★★★

DIRECTOR: Michael Curtiz

CAST: Errol Flynn, Olivia De Havilland, Patric Knowles, Donald Crisp, David Niven, Henry Stephenson

October 25, 1854: Balaclava, the Crimea; military minds blunder, and six hundred gallant Britishers, sabers flashing, ride to their deaths. The film, which climaxes with one of the most dramatic cavalry charges in history, is based on Tennyson's famous poem. Errol Flynn and Olivia De Havilland are star-crossed lovers. Donald Crisp and Henry Stephenson are superbly English, as always. Good show!

1936 B & W 116 minutes

CHARLEY VARRICK

★★★★

DIRECTOR: Don Siegel

CAST: Walter Matthau, Joe Don Baker, Felicia Farr, Andy Robinson, John Vernon

Still on a roll after *Dirty Harry*, director Don Siegel turns into a classic this story about a bank robber (Walter Matthau) who accidentally steals money from the mob (he hits a bank where its ill-gotten gains are laundered). Matthau is superb as Varrick, the "last of the independents," and Joe Don Baker sends chills up the spine as the hit man relentlessly pursuing him. Rated PG.

1973 111 minutes

CHESTY ANDERSON, U.S. NAVY

DIRECTOR: Ed Forsyth

CAST: Shari Eubank, Scatman Crothers, Fred Willard, Frank Campanella, Dorri Thompson, Rosanne Katon, Marcie Barkin

This dated, low-budget, tasteless crime thriller features Shari Eubank as the title character. When her sister disappears, she (accompanied by her WAVE friends) becomes involved with a crooked senator and the Mafia. Tacky is the word for *Chesty*. Scatman Crothers has a cameo role as a pool hustler. Rated R for nudity, obscenities, and violence.

1975 83 minutes

CHINA SEAS

★★★½

DIRECTOR: Tay Garnett

CAST: Clark Gable, Jean Harlow, Wallace Beery, Lewis Stone

MGM boasted that it once had all the stars that were in the heavens. *China Seas* brings an element of truth to the boast. The all-star adventure drama reteams Clark Gable and Jean Harlow in roles very similar to those in their popular *Red Dust*. Gable is the captain of a Chinese river steamer in pirate-infested waters. Harlow is once again the lady with a spotted past, who we all know is the perfect mate for Gable if he'd only realize it himself. Wallace Beery, Rosalind Russell, and Lewis Stone are also along on what becomes an enjoyable screen romp.

1935 B & W 90 minutes

CHINATOWN

★★★★½

DIRECTOR: Roman Polanski

CAST: Jack Nicholson, Faye Dunaway, John Huston, Perry Lopez, Diane Ladd

One of the great detective films, this stars Jack Nicholson as a 1940s Los Angeles private eye who stumbles on to a crooked land deal as well as a murder. Faye Dunaway, John Huston, and Perry Lopez offer standout support. Director Roman Polanski has a cameo as a knife-wielding hood. Rated R for language, violence, nudity.

1974 131 minutes

CHINESE CONNECTION, THE

★★★

DIRECTOR: Lo Wei
CAST: Bruce Lee, Miao Ker Hsio

This action-packed import, in which Bruce Lee plays a martial arts expert out to avenge the death of his mentor, is good, watchable fare. But be forewarned: It's dubbed, and not all that expertly. Rated R.

1979 107 minutes

CHOKE CANYON

★

DIRECTOR: Chuck Bail
CAST: Stephen Collins, Janet Julian, Lance Henriksen, Bo Svenson

A two-fisted physicist (Stephen Collins) takes on an evil industrialist in this absurd action-adventure movie. Even the superb stunt work and spectacular scenery do not make up for the lack of a believable story. Rated PG.

1986 96 minutes

CHRISTINA

★★

DIRECTOR: Paul Krasny
CAST: Barbara Parkins, Peter Haskell, James McEachin, Marlyn Mason

Unbelievable mystery film about a wealthy foreigner (Barbara Parkins) who pays an unemployed aircraft engineer (Peter Haskell) twenty-five thousand dollars to marry her so she can acquire a U.S. passport . . . or so we think. The story begins to unfold as the man falls in love with the millionaire. Mildly interesting, but still a bit too contrived to recommend.

1974 95 minutes

CINCINNATI KID, THE

★★★★

DIRECTOR: Norman Jewison
CAST: Steve McQueen, Ann-Margret, Edward G. Robinson, Karl Malden

Steve McQueen had one of his earliest acting challenges in this study of a determined young poker player on his way to the big time. He lets nothing stand in his way, especially not the reigning king of the card tables, Edward G. Robinson. The film is made more interesting by some delicious performances in supporting roles. Most notable are Karl Malden as McQueen's teacher and Joan Blondell as a has-been whose nerves and pocketbook can't stand the strain of the "big games" anymore. Tuesday Weld and Ann-Margret try to provide McQueen with a little feminine distraction from his relentless quest, but it's not in the cards.

1965 113 minutes

CIRCLE OF IRON

★★★

DIRECTOR: Richard Moore
CAST: David Carradine, Jeff Cooper, Christopher Lee, Roddy McDowall, Eli Wallach, Erica Creer

Bruce Lee was preparing the screenplay for this film shortly before he died as the follow-up to his tremendously successful first American film *Enter the Dragon*. Ironically, the lead role fell to David Carradine, who had also been chosen over Lee for the lead in the television series *Kung Fu*. This is a highly satisfying adventure movie about a seeker (Jeff Cooper) who encounters four mysterious martial arts masters (all played by Carradine). Fans of the genre will love it. Rated R for violence.

1979 102 minutes

CLEOPATRA JONES

DIRECTOR: Jack Starrett
CAST: Tamara Dobson, Shelley Winters, Bernie Casey, Brenda Sykes

Secret agent Cleopatra Jones returns from an overseas assignment to save her old neighborhood, including a halfway house run by her ex-boyfriend, from an evil drug queen gang leader (Shelley Winters) known as "Mommy." Rated PG for violence.

1973 80 minutes

CLOAK AND DAGGER

★★★★

DIRECTOR: Richard Franklin
CAST: Henry Thomas, Dabney Coleman, Michael Murphy, John McIntire

A highly imaginative boy (Henry Thomas, of *E.T.*) who often plays pretend games of espionage with his fantasy friend, Jack Flack (Dabney Coleman, who also plays Thomas's father), finds himself involved in a real life-and-death situation when he stumbles on to the evil doings of a group of spies (led by Michael Murphy). Directed by Richard Franklin (*Psycho II*), this movie offers the best of all possible worlds for young and old viewers alike. It's suspenseful and fast-paced enough to keep adults interested and entertained, but not so scary and violent as to upset the kiddies. Rated PG.

1984 101 minutes

CLOUD DANCER

★★★½

DIRECTOR: Barry Brown
CAST: David Carradine, Jennifer O'Neill, Joseph Bottoms, Colleen Camp

A story about competing stunt flyers, this film features one of David Carradine's best performances (right up there with those he gave in *Bound for Glory* and *The Long Riders*). As the king of daredevil pilots, he struggles to keep ahead of his ambitious protégé (Joseph Bottoms) as well as fighting his love for Jennifer O'Neill (in one of her few effective portrayals). His brother (brilliantly played by Albert Salmi) is simple-minded, so Carradine refuses to marry and have children. Yet, unbeknownst to him, he is the father of a perfectly normal child—an element of just one of the films highly effecuive subplots. It's a touching and exciting sleeper. Rated PG.

1980 108 minutes

COBRA

★★

DIRECTOR: George Cosmatos
CAST: Sylvester Stallone, Brigitte Nielsen, Reni Santoni, Andrew Robinson, Art Le Fleur, Val Avery, Bert Williams

Sylvester Stallone comes back for more *Rambo*-like action as a tough city cop on the trail of a serial killer in this unrelentingly grim and gruesome thriller. It is packed with action and violence, but there is so much of it that the effect is numbing rather than exhilarating. In fact, it is more like a slasher flick or a *Death Wish* sequel than the *Dirty Harry* detective movies it seeks to emulate. Rated R for violence, gore, and profanity.

1986 95 minutes

COCKFIGHTER

★★

DIRECTOR: Monte Hellman
CAST: Warren Oates, Harry Dean Stanton, Richard B. Shull, Troy Donahue, Millie Perkins

Title says it all. Warren Oates and Harry Dean Stanton can't breathe life into this simplistic look at the illegal sport of cockfighting. For Oates fans only. Rated R.

1974 83 minutes

CODE NAME: EMERALD

★★★★

DIRECTOR: Jonathan Sanger

CAST: Ed Harris, Max von Sydow, Horst Buchholz, Helmut Berger, Cyrielle Claire, Eric Stoltz

Better-than-average World War II espionage film about a double agent (Ed Harris) who attempts to rescue a U.S. Army officer (Eric Stoltz) held for interrogation in a French prison because he knows the details of the planned Allied invasion at Normandy. Like the best spy thrillers, the plot moves along at a good clip despite the lack of action—and when the action does pick up in the last ten minutes, it proves to be worth the wait. Harris' performance is inconsistent, however; his subtle machismo occasionally hampers his ability to evoke a mood. Still, most of the time he is believable, and Max von Sydow's performance is up to his usual high standard. Rated PG for violence and sex.

1985 95 minutes

CODE NAME: WILD GEESE

★½

DIRECTOR: Anthony M. Dawson

CAST: Lewis Collins, Lee Van Cleef, Ernest Borgnine, Mimsy Farmer, Klaus Kinski

Marginal action-adventure is set in the Golden Triangle of Asia. A group of mercenaries hire out as a task force to destroy the opium trade for the Drug Enforcement Administration. The group knows that the government will deny any involvement in the operation and that they are not to take prisoners. Rated R.

1984 101 minutes

CODE OF SILENCE

★★★★

DIRECTOR: Andy Davis

CAST: Chuck Norris, Henry Silva, Bert Remsen, Mike Genovese, Ralph Foody, Nathan Davis

With this film, Chuck Norris proved himself the heir to Charles Bronson as the king of the no-nonsense action movie. In *Code of Silence*, the star gives a right-on-target performance as tough cop Sgt. Eddie Cusack, who takes on warring mob families and corrupt police officers. This one's a treat for Norris fans and nonfans alike. Rated R for violence and profanity.

1985 102 minutes

COLD SWEAT

★

DIRECTOR: Terence Young

CAST: Charles Bronson, Liv Ullmann, Jill Ireland, James Mason, Gabriele Ferzetti, Michel Constantin

Some old Charles Bronson movies are more comic than action-packed. Watching him develop his vigilante personality is laughable, not heroic. *Cold Sweat*, a dated, offensively sexist piece of machismo, has Charlie shooting his way through an irrelevant plot and yelling at his whining wife to do what he commands. Rated R.

1970 94 minutes

COME AND GET IT

★★★

DIRECTORS: Howard Hawks, William Wyler

CAST: Edward Arnold, Joel McCrea, Frances Farmer, Walter Brennan

Based on Edna Ferber's novel, this involving film depicts life in Wisconsin's lumber country. It captures the robust, resilient nature of the denizens. Edward Arnold is perfectly cast as the grasping capitalist who needs to have his eyes opened. Walter Brennan's performance earned an Oscar for best supporting actor.

1936 B & W 105 minutes

COMMANDO

★★★★

DIRECTOR: Mark L. Lester

CAST: Arnold Schwarzenegger, Rae Dawn Chong, Dan Hedaya, James Olson, Alyssa Milano

"Commando" John Matrix makes Rambo look like a wimp. As played by big, beefy Arnold Schwarzenegger, he "eats Green Berets for breakfast." When we first see him, Big John is making like Paul Bunyan, carrying a tree he has chopped down near his mountain home. This, we know immediately, is one tough guy (and a very silly movie). He soon goes on the warpath when his 11-year-old daughter is kidnapped by a South American dictator (Dan Hedaya) he once helped depose. Matrix is supposed to put the evil guy back in power, but opts instead to put him out of commission. The result is the most outrageously action-packed (and therefore funniest) comic-book-style adventure film of the 1980s. Rated R for violence and profanity.

1986 90 minutes

COMMANDOS

★½

DIRECTOR: Armando Crispino

CAST: Lee Van Cleef, Jack Kelly, Marino Mase, Giampiero Albertini

Italian World War II film with dubbed English and not enough action to make it worth looking in on. Jack Kelly and Lee Van Cleef lead a small special force into North Africa to spy on the German army. Rated PG for violence and sex.

1968 89 minutes

CONQUEROR, THE

DIRECTOR: Dick Powell

CAST: John Wayne, Susan Hayward, Pedro Armendariz, Agnes Moorehead

John Wayne plays Genghis Khan, and the results are unintentionally hilarious as the Duke spouts stilted, clichéd barbarian dialogue in his familiar drawling fashion. *The Conqueror* was perhaps the most tragic motion picture ever made. Unbeknownst to the cast and crew of this period adventure, eleven atomic bombs had been exploded at the U.S. government's testing ground in Yucca Flat, Nevada—just 137 miles from the location. The largest of these was four times the size of the one dropped on Hiroshima. As a possible result, all of the principal actors (Wayne, Susan Hayward, Pedro Armendariz, and Agnes Moorehead), director Dick Powell, and nearly forty crew members died of cancer.

1956 111 minutes

CONVOY

★★

DIRECTOR: Sam Peckinpah

CAST: Kris Kristofferson, Ali MacGraw, Ernest Borgnine, Madge Sinclair, Burt Young

This Sam Peckinpah action film will not be remembered as one of the director's best. Yet the film does possess the crisp editing, accent on action, and exciting photography that we associate with all of Peckinpah's movies. The story concerns some truckers, led by Kris Kristofferson, who go on a tri-state protest over police brutality, high gas prices, and other complaints. An uneven script and just fair acting certainly mar this picture. Rated PG.

1978 110 minutes

COOGAN'S BLUFF

★★★★

DIRECTOR: Don Siegel

CAST: Clint Eastwood, Lee J. Cobb, Susan Clark, Tisha Sterling, Don Stroud, Betty Field, Tom Tully

This modern-day-cowboy-in-the-big-city adventure provided the basis for the *McCloud* TV series, starring Dennis Weaver. Film star Clint Eastwood and director Don Siegel, in their first collaboration, proved they could handle the theme much better with the squinty-eyed star hunting down a murderous fugitive (Don Stroud) in the asphalt jungle. Lee J. Cobb is also memorable as a hard-bitten New York detective. Rated PG.

1968 100 minutes

COOL HAND LUKE

★★★★★

DIRECTOR: Stuart Rosenberg

CAST: Paul Newman, George Kennedy, J. D. Cannon, Lou Antonio, Robert Drivas, Strother Martin

One of Paul Newman's greatest creations is the irrepressible Luke. Luke is a prisoner on a southern chain gang and not even the deprivations of these subhuman conditions will break his spirit. He even manages to win the admiration of his rival on the chain gang, George Kennedy. Kennedy's performance was equally memorable and won him a supporting Oscar.

1967 126 minutes

COP IN BLUE JEANS, THE

★

DIRECTOR: Bruno Corbucci

CAST: Thomas Milian, Jack Palance, Maria Rosaria Omaggio, Guido Mannari, Jack La Cayennie, Raf Luca, Benito Stefanelli

This film about an undercover cop (Thomas Milian) trying to take out an underworld boss (Jack Palance) has plenty of action scenes. But after enduring the shoddy voice dubbing and the poorly developed characters, the viewer is all too relieved to push the rewind button. Not rated; contains violence.

1978 92 minutes

CORNERED

★★★

DIRECTOR: Edward Dmytryk

CAST: Dick Powell, Walter Slezak, Micheline Cheirel, Luther Adler, Morris Carnovsky, Edgar Barrier, Steven Geray

Fresh from his success as hard-boiled sleuth Philip Marlowe in *Murder, My Sweet*, former song-and-dance man Dick Powell continued to score as a dramatic actor in this thriller about a discharged Canadian airman on the trail of Nazi collaborators who murdered his French wife. The hunt takes him from France to Switzerland to Argentina and a rendezvous within a nest of corrupt Europeans.

1946 B & W 102 minutes

CORRUPT ONES, THE

★★★

DIRECTOR: James Hill

CAST: Robert Stack, Nancy Kwan, Elke Sommer, Werner Peters

Robert Stack plays a photographer who receives the key to a Chinese treasure. Not surprisingly, he soon finds that he's not alone in his search for the goodies. This is a good—but not great—adventure film.

1966 92 minutes

CORSICAN BROTHERS, THE

★★★½

DIRECTOR: Gregory Ratoff

CAST: Douglas Fairbanks Jr., Ruth Warrick, J. Carrol Naish, Akim Tamiroff, H. B. Warner, Henry Wilcoxon

Alexandre Dumas's classic story of twins who remain spiritually tied, though separated, crackles in this lavish old Hollywood production. Intrigue and swordplay abound. Douglas Fairbanks Jr. is fine, backed by two of the best supporting players ever: J. Carrol Naish and Akim Tamiroff.

1941 B & W 112 minutes

CORVETTE SUMMER

★

DIRECTOR: Matthew Roberts

CAST: Mark Hamill, Kim Melford, Annie Potts

This mindless car-chase film finds Mark Hamill in Las Vegas hunting car thieves who have ripped off his Corvette. This film is not even up to par with *Cannonball Run*. Rated PG.

1978 105 minutes

COTTON CLUB, THE

★★★★½

DIRECTOR: Francis Ford Coppola

CAST: Richard Gere, Diane Lane, James Remar, Gregory Hines, Lonette McKee

Despite all the scandal, an inflated budget of more than $50 million, and some ragged last-minute trimming, *The Cotton Club* is a winner. The story about two pairs of brothers, one black and one white, is set at Harlem's most famous nightclub. Cornet player Gere and moll Diane Lane make love while gangster James Remar (as Dutch Schultz) fumes, and Gregory Hines dances his way into the heart of songbird Lonette McKee in this flawed but brilliant film. Rated R for violence, nudity, profanity, and suggested sex.

1984 128 minutes

COUNT OF MONTE CRISTO, THE (ORIGINAL)

★★★★

DIRECTOR: Rowland V. Lee

CAST: Robert Donat, Elissa Landi, Irene Hervey, Louis Calhern, Sidney Blackmer, Raymond Walburn, O. P. Heggie

In the title role, Robert Donat heads a superb, fine-tuned cast in this now classic film of Dumas's great story. Innocent sailor Edmond Dantes, falsely accused of aiding the exiled Napoleon and infamously imprisoned for fifteen years, escapes to levy revenge on those who framed him. A secret cache of treasure makes it all very sweet.

1934 B & W 119 minutes

COUNT OF MONTE CRISTO, THE (REMAKE)

★★★½

DIRECTOR: David Greene

CAST: Richard Chamberlain, Tony Curtis, Louis Jourdan, Donald Pleasence, Taryn Power

Solid TV adaptation of the Alexandre Dumas classic. Richard Chamberlain cuts a dashing figure as the persecuted Edmond Dantes. The casting of Tony Curtis as the evil Mondego works surprisingly well.

1975 100 minutes

CRAZY MAMA

★★★

DIRECTOR: Jonathan Demme

CAST: Stuart Whitman, Cloris Leachman, Ann Sothern, Jim Backus

Vibrant film blends crime, comedy, and finely drawn characterizations in this story of three women on a crime spree from California to Arkansas and their experiences with the various men they pick up along the way. Successful mixture of music and atmosphere of the 1950s, coupled with a 1970s attitude, makes this an enjoyable film. Rated PG.

1975 82 minutes

CRIMSON PIRATE, THE

★★★★½

DIRECTOR: Robert Siodmak

CAST: Burt Lancaster, Nick Cravat, Eva Bartok, Torin Thatcher, Christopher Lee

One of the all-time great swashbucklers, this follow-up to *The Flame and the Arrow* features the incredibly agile Burt Lancaster besting villains and winning fair maids in high style. Lancaster's partner from his circus days, Nick Cravat, joins in for some rousing action scenes. It's part adventure story, part spoof, and always entertaining.

1952 104 minutes

CROSS OF IRON

★★★

DIRECTOR: Sam Peckinpah

CAST: James Coburn, Maximilian Schell, James Mason, David Warner

With this action-packed war film, director Sam Peckinpah proved that he hadn't lost the touch that made *Ride the High Country* and *The Wild Bunch* such memorable movies. Still, *Cross of Iron* did not receive much acclaim when released. Perhaps it was the theme: the heroics and humanism of weary German soldiers in World War II. A precursor of *Das Boot*, this film couldn't be called great, but it is certainly an interesting work done by one of Hollywood's more original directors. Rated R.

1977 119 minutes

CRY OF BATTLE

★½

DIRECTOR: Irving Lerner

CAST: James MacArthur, Van Heflin, Rita Moreno, Leopoldo Salcedo, Sidney Clute

The son (James MacArthur) of a wealthy businessman gets caught in the Philippines during the Japanese occupation and has to resort to guerrilla warfare. Poorly directed, but does address the ethical questions of racism and the conduct of war. Not rated; with violence.

1957 B & W 99 minutes

CRY OF THE INNOCENT

★★★½

DIRECTOR: Michael O'Herlihy

CAST: Rod Taylor, Joanna Pettet, Nigel Davenport, Cyril Cusack, Jim Norton, Alexander Knox

This made-for-TV suspense thriller has Rod Taylor playing the grieving husband and father who loses his wife and children when a plane crashes into their summer home in Ireland. When a Dublin detective tells Taylor the crash was no accident, Taylor is determined to find out who planted the bomb in the plane. Joanna Pettet has two parts, first as Taylor's sweet Irish wife and then as a writer who has a theory about corporate espionage that may have led to the crash. This film lacks no excitement as the corporate plot unfolds.

1980 93 minutes

CUBA

★★★

DIRECTOR: Richard Lester

CAST: Sean Connery, Brooke Adams, Jack Weston, Hector Elizondo, Denholm Elliott, Chris Sarandon, Lonette McKee

A thinly veiled remake of *Casa-*

blanca, this Richard Lester film is nonetheless far superior to J. Lee Thompson's similar *Cabo Blanco* (which starred Charles Bronson). Sean Connery and Brooke Adams play one-time lovers renewing their passion amid the dangerous doings during the fall of Batista in 1959. As usual, Lester invests his tale with memorable bits. Rated R.

1979 121 minutes

DAIN CURSE, THE

★

DIRECTOR: E. W. Swackhamer
CAST: James Coburn, Hector Elizondo, Jason Miller, Jean Simmons

A poor, two-hour version of a just passable TV miniseries based on the Dashiell Hammett mystery classic. James Coburn is fine as the dapper detective hero but is thwarted by a muddled screenplay. Unrated.

1978 123 minutes

DAM BUSTERS, THE

★★★★½

DIRECTOR: Michael Anderson
CAST: Richard Todd, Michael Redgrave, Ursula Jeans, Basil Sydney

Richard Todd and Michael Redgrave star in this British film about the development and use of a specially designed bomb to destroy a dam in Germany during World War II. An outstanding cast and great script make this one of the finer World War II films.

1954 102 minutes

DANGER MAN (TELEVISION SERIES) (Overall rating)

★★★

DIRECTOR: Various
CAST: Patrick McGoohan

Needing something with which to replace Steve McQueen's *Wanted: Dead or Alive* series, CBS-TV imported the British-produced *Danger Man*, the first of the three spy-flavored dramas to star Patrick McGoohan. (See additional entries under *Secret Agent* and *The Prisoner*.) This series debuted in May, 1961, and quietly went off the air in September, after an undistinguished run of twenty-four weeks. About twice that many episodes were produced, but the rest never aired in the United States, much to the regret of the small but appreciative group of fans. Creator and executive producer Ralph Smart wrote many of the taut, half-hour thrillers; others came from the pen of Brian Clemens, soon to be famous for his association with *The Avengers*. McGoohan starred as the "danger man," a free-lancer named John Drake, who worked as a security investigator in affiliation with NATO and journeyed around the world searching for wrongs to right. Episodes include "The Key," in which Drake races to find the source of an information leak from the American embassy in Vienna; and "The View from the Villa," which involves a murdered banker and a missing gold shipment. A bit violent, but suitable for family viewing.

1961 B & W 110 minutes

DAREDEVILS OF THE RED CIRCLE

★★★

DIRECTORS: William Witney, John English
CAST: Charles Quigley, Herman Brix, David Sharpe, Carole Landis

One of the most action-packed serials of all time pits three college athletes (including former Tarzan Herman Brix and ace stunt man David Sharpe) against the evil 39013, a former convict who disguises himself in order to gain power and exact vengeance on the society that imprisoned him. Malevolently brought to life by Charles Middleton (Ming the Merciless from *Flash Gordon*), convict 39013 and his gang use every dirty trick in the book to destroy the three friends and their damsel in distress, lovely Carole Landis. But they are always outwitted by the quick thinking and athletic prowess of the trio. Fast-paced and well-acted, this is one of the satisfying and fondly remembered of the pre–World War II serials.

1939 B & W 12 chapters

DARING DOBERMANS, THE

★★½

DIRECTOR: Byron Chudnow
CAST: Charles Knox Robinson, Tim Considine, David Moses, Joan Caulfield

Fun sequel to *The Doberman Gang* is a little more kiddy-oriented, but it's still okay, featuring another well-planned caper for the canine stars. Rated PG for very light violence and language.

1973 90 minutes

DARK PASSAGE

★★★

DIRECTOR: Delmar Daves
CAST: Humphrey Bogart, Lauren Bacall, Bruce Bennett, Agnes Moorehead

This is an okay Humphrey Bogart vehicle in which the star plays an escaped convict who hides out at Lauren Bacall's apartment while undergoing a face change. The stars are watchable, but the uninspired direction (including some disconcerting subjective camera scenes) and the outlandish plot keep the movie from being a real winner.

1947 B & W 106 minutes

DAWN PATROL, THE

★★★★

DIRECTOR: Edmund Goulding
CAST: Errol Flynn, Basil Rathbone, David Niven, Melville Cooper, Barry Fitzgerald, Donald Crisp

This film is what is meant when someone says, "They don't make 'em like that anymore." It has a taut story, a superb cast, and emotionally charged action. Basil Rathbone is excellent as a commanding officer of a frontline British squadron during World War I who has no choice but to order raw replacements into the air against veteran Germans. Errol Flynn and David Niven shine as gentlemen at war. As always, Donald Crisp, one of old Hollywood's best, is superb. Aged it may be, but this is a fine film.

1938 B & W 103 minutes

DAY OF THE ASSASSIN

★

DIRECTORS: Brian Trenchard Smith, Carlos Vasallo
CAST: Chuck Connors, Glenn Ford, Richard Roundtree, Jorge Rivero, Susana Dosamantes, Henry Silva, Andres Garcia

Chuck Connors plays a James Bond–type hero in this dull action film. The shah of Iran's yacht blows up and sinks in a South American bay. In its hull is the exiled leader's treasure—thus sparking international interest in the booty. *Day of the Assassin* is remarkable for its poor plot and bad acting. Not rated; contains violence and profanity.

1979 94 minutes

DAY OF THE JACKAL, THE

★★★★

DIRECTOR: Fred Zinnemann
CAST: Edward Fox, Alan Badel, Tony Britton, Cyril Cusack

Edward Fox is a cunning assassin roaming Europe in hopes of a crack at General Charles de Gaulle. High suspense and a marvelous performance by Fox underscore a strong storyline. Rated PG.

1973 141 minutes

DAYTON'S DEVILS

★½

DIRECTOR: Jack Shea

CAST: Leslie Nielsen, Rory Calhoun, Lainie Kazan, Barry Sadler, Georg Stanford Brown, Hans Gudegast, Pat Renella, Rigg Kennedy

Leslie Nielsen leads a group of has-beens and ex-cons—or, as the video box says, "a melting pot of losers"—in a robbery of an Air Force base bank. Sixties sexpot Lainie Kazan plays Nielsen's lover and sings an absolutely dreadful version of "Sunny."

1968 107 minutes

DEADLY VENGEANCE

DIRECTOR: A. C. Qamar

CAST: Arthur Roberts, Alan Marlowe, Bob Holden, Betty Harrison, Joe Moreno, Grace Jones

The poor acting, editing, and lighting in this insipid film make one wonder if it was planned by a couple of beginning film students over a keg of beer. Betty (Betty Harrison) takes revenge on Big Mike (Joe Moreno) after he murders her boyfriend. Grace Jones appears for about ten minutes in a borderline pornographic sex scene. This film appears to have been made in the 1960s and released only now to cash in on Jones's name. It's unrated, most likely because no one could bear to watch it. Contains obscenities, simulated sex scenes, and violence.

1985 84 minutes

DEADLY FORCE

★★★

DIRECTOR: Paul Aaron

CAST: Wings Hauser, Joyce Ingalls, Paul Shenar, Al Ruscio

The best way to describe this release is *Dirty Harry* meets *Death Wish*. Wings Hauser (*Vice Squad*) plays "Stony" Jackson Cooper, an ex-cop who returns to his old Los Angeles stomping grounds to stomp people until he finds the maniac who stomped a buddy's daughter to death. Unlike *Sudden Impact*, it won't make your day. But you won't be bored. Rated R for violence, nudity, and profanity.

1983 95 minutes

DEATH BEFORE DISHONOR

DIRECTOR: Terry Leonard

CAST: Fred Dryer, Brian Keith, Joanna Pacula, Paul Winfield

Grade Z war film has Fred Dryer as a Marine Corps sergeant in an unnamed Middle Eastern country. His commanding officer, Brian Keith, is kidnapped by Arab terrorists and most of his men are killed. So Dryer is out for revenge. Lots of Arab blood is spilled as he sets things right. Paul Winfield plays the United States ambassador in the middle of all the action. Rated R for violence and profanity.

1986 112 minutes

DEATH HUNT

★★★½

DIRECTOR: Peter R. Hunt

CAST: Charles Bronson, Lee Marvin, Andrew Stevens, Angie Dickinson, Carl Weathers, Ed Lauter

Based on the true story of a hazardous manhunt in the Canadian Rockies, *Death Hunt* pits trapper Charles Bronson against Mountie

Lee Marvin. This gritty adventure film, directed by Peter Hunt, also features vicious dogfights and bloody shootouts set against the spectacular scenery of the Yukon Territory. Rated R.

1981 97 minutes

DEATH KISS, THE

★★★

DIRECTOR: Edwin L. Marin
CAST: Bela Lugosi, David Manners, Adrienne Ames, John Wray, Vince Barnett, Edward Van Sloan

Entertaining movie-within-a-movie whodunit is a treat for fans of early 1930s films and a pretty well-paced mystery to boot as Bela Lugosi (in fine, hammy form) is embroiled in the investigation of a murder that took place during filming. Familiar faces from the past pop in and out of this little thriller, and Lugosi is reunited with Edward Van Sloan (Dr. Van Helsing to his Dracula), a man who distinguished many classic horror films of that golden age.

1933 B & W 75 minutes

DEATH ON THE NILE

★★★½

DIRECTOR: John Guillermin
CAST: Peter Ustinov, Bette Davis, David Niven, Mia Farrow, Angela Lansbury, George Kennedy, Jack Warden

The second in the series of films based on the Hercule Poirot mysteries, written by Agatha Christie, is good, but nothing special. Peter Ustinov stars as the fussy Belgian detective adrift in Africa with a set of murder suspects well played by Bette Davis, Angela Lansbury, Jack Warden, Maggie Smith, David Niven, Mia Farrow, and George Kennedy. Even though it features an all-star cast, lavish sets and settings, and a better-than-average Christie plot, this film, directed by John Guillermin (*The Towering Inferno*) tends to sag here and there. While it never becomes boring, it's never really riveting, either. Rated PG.

1978 140 minutes

DEATH SQUAD, THE

★★

DIRECTOR: Harry Falk
CAST: Robert Forster, Michelle Phillips, Claude Akins, Melvyn Douglas

A self-appointed coterie of cops is rubbing out criminals beating the rap on legal technicalities. A former officer is given the job of finding out who's doing it and cleaning house. Clint Eastwood did it all infinitely better in *Magnum Force*. Made for television.

1974 78 minutes

DEATH WISH

★★★★

DIRECTOR: Michael Winner
CAST: Charles Bronson, Hope Lange, Vincent Gardenia, Jeff Goldblum

Charles Bronson gives an excellent performance as Paul Kersey, a mild-mannered New Yorker moved to violence when his daughter is raped and his wife killed by sleazy muggers. It's a gripping story of one man's revenge. Rated R because of nudity and violence (includes a graphic rape scene).

1974 93 minutes

DEATH WISH II

★★

DIRECTOR: Michael Winner
CAST: Charles Bronson, Jill Ireland, Vincent Gardenia, J. D. Cannon, Anthony Franciosa, Ben Frank

This carbon-copy sequel to the successful *Death Wish* is best described as a revolting, violent crime chiller. Picking up where the first left off, Paul Kersey (Charles Bronson) now lives in Los Angeles, where his daughter and his housekeeper (instead of his wife, as in the first *Death Wish*) are murdered. Once again Kersey metes out his own justice. Rated R because of nudity and violence.

1982 93 minutes

DEATH WISH III

DIRECTOR: Michael Winner

CAST: Charles Bronson, Deborah Raffin, Ed Lauter, Martin Balsam

Michael Winner is one of those filmmakers who packs his works with the most revolting scenes imaginable and cloaks them in a phony perspective of righteousness. The *Death Wish* films are the best examples of this. Winner has a hero, Paul Kersey (Charles Bronson), who becomes a bloodthirsty maniac in reaction to the scum around him. We are supposed to cheer him on, but he's as big a puke as the villains he dispatches by the truckload. The formula, now growing very tired, is always the same: Kersey loses a loved one and then goes on a rampage. Someone should go on a rampage and destroy all the copies of this piece of trash. Rated R for violence, profanity, drug use, nudity, and sex.

1985 99 minutes

DEEP, THE

★★

DIRECTOR: Peter Yates

CAST: Robert Shaw, Jacqueline Bisset, Nick Nolte, Louis Gossett Jr., Eli Wallach, Robert Tessier

The success of *Jaws* prompted this screen adaptation of another Benchley novel, but the results weren't nearly as satisfying. A good cast flounders in this waterlogged tale of treasure-hunting. Rated PG.

1977 123 minutes

DEFIANCE

★★★

DIRECTOR: John Flynn

CAST: Jan-Michael Vincent, Art Carney, Theresa Saldana, Danny Aiello, Fernando Lopez

Potent story depicts savage New York street gang terrorizing helpless neighborhood. Outsider Jan-Michael Vincent reluctantly gets involved. This well-directed film packs quite a wallop. Rated R for violence and profanity.

1980 102 minutes

DELIVERANCE

★★★★★

DIRECTOR: John Boorman

CAST: Jon Voight, Burt Reynolds, Ned Beatty, Ronny Cox, James Dickey

Jon Voight, Burt Reynolds, and Ned Beatty are superb in this first-rate film about a canoe trip down a dangerous river that begins as a holiday but soon turns into a weekend of sheer horror. Based on the novel by James Dickey. Rated R for profanity, sex, and violence.

1972 109 minutes

DELTA FORCE, THE

★★

DIRECTOR: Menahem Golan

CAST: Chuck Norris, Lee Marvin, Martin Balsam, Joey Bishop, Robert Forster, Lainie Kazan, George Kennedy, Hanna Schygulla, Susan Strasberg, Bo Svenson, Robert Vaughn, Shelley Winters

In this disappointing action film, which is perhaps best described as "The Dirty Dozen at the Airport," Chuck Norris and Lee Marvin are leaders of an anti-terrorist group charged with saving the passengers on a hijacked airliner. Director Menahem Golan makes some events in this re-creation of the 1985 hijacking of TWA flight 847 in Athens a bit too realistic and thus works against the comic-book-style heroism of the bulk of the movie. Rated R for profanity and violence.

1986 126 minutes

DESERT FOX, THE

★★★★

DIRECTOR: Henry Hathaway
CAST: James Mason, Jessica Tandy, Sir Cedric Hardwicke, Luther Adler, Desmond Young

A tour-de-force performance by James Mason marks this film biography of German Field Marshal Rommel. Rommel is treated with great sympathy in this historically accurate depiction of America's one-time enemy. His military exploits are glossed over in favor of the human story of the disillusionment and eventual involvement in the plot to assassinate Hitler.

1951 B & W 88 minutes

DIAMONDS

★★★

DIRECTOR: Menahem Golan
CAST: Robert Shaw, Richard Roundtree, Barbara Seagull, Shelley Winters

Well-planned plot and good chemistry between Robert Shaw and Richard Roundtree make this an enjoyable film of action and intrigue. When a British entrepreneur (whose twin brother just so happens to design high-tech security systems) hires an ex-con and his girlfriend to assist him in a $100 million diamond heist, it sets the stage for an amazing number of plot twists, filmed in the blazing landscapes of Israel.

1975 108 minutes

DIAMONDS ARE FOREVER

★★★★

DIRECTOR: Guy Hamilton
CAST: Sean Connery, Jill St. John, Charles Gray, Bruce Cabot

This release was supposed to be Sean Connery's last appearance as James Bond before he decided to *Never Say Never Again*. It's good fun for 007 fans and far superior to the Roger Moore films that followed it. Rated PG.

1971 119 minutes

DICK TRACY

★★★

DIRECTORS: Ray Taylor, Alan James
CAST: Ralph Byrd, Kay Hughes, Smiley Burnette, Lee Van Atta, John Piccori, Carlton Young, Francis X. Bushman, Buddy Roosevelt

Chester Gould's comic-strip detective Dick Tracy became an FBI operative in four serials released by Republic Studios from 1937–1941 starring Ralph Byrd as the granite-jawed manhunter, and they are considered (along with the *Flash Gordon* serials) the best series of all time. Determined Ralph Byrd chases a mysterious criminal known as The Spider who has kidnapped his brother and turned him into a slave. The Spider operates out of an advanced aircraft known as the *Flying Wing* and uses his sonic vibrator in an attempt to cripple America and take his place as rightful ruler, but Tracy and his loyal companions impede his progress at every opportunity. Great stunts and plenty of action in this one.

1937 B & W 15 chapters

DICK TRACY, DETECTIVE

★½

DIRECTOR: William Berke

CAST: Morgan Conway, Anne Jeffreys, Mike Mazurki, Jane Greer

Standard second-feature fare with Morgan Conway as an unconvincing Dick Tracy tangling with the denizens of the underworld. Mike Mazurki, fresh from his role as Moose Malloy in Raymond Chandler's *Murder My Sweet*, provides all the color as the man Dick Tracy has to deal with. Ralph Byrd, who created the role of Dick Tracy in the serials and continued on into feature films and television, is sorely needed to make this one work.

1945 B & W 62 minutes

DICK TRACY MEETS GRUESOME

★★½

DIRECTOR: John Rawlins

CAST: Ralph Byrd, Boris Karloff, Anne Gwynne, Edward Ashley, June Clayworth

Everybody's favorite Dick Tracy, Ralph Byrd, returns to the role he originated in serials for Republic Studios just in time to do battle with Gruesome, played with his usual style by the great Boris Karloff. Although ten years older than when he started the series, Byrd, like Buster Crabbe in the Flash Gordon serials, brings a conviction to his character that redeems the slim storyline and often meager production values and effects. As usual, Boris Karloff is eminently watchable and makes a fine addition to Chester Gould's gallery of bizarre villains.

1947 B & W 65 minutes

DICK TRACY RETURNS

★★★

DIRECTORS: William Witney, John English

CAST: Ralph Byrd, Lynn Roberts, Charles Middleton, David Sharpe, Jerry Tucker, Lee Ford, Michael Kent, John Merton, Ned Glass, Jack Ingram, Jack Roberts

Ralph Byrd's second outing as comic-strip detective Dick Tracy finds the unbeatable G-man hot on the trail of the murderous Stark gang, an evil family that has killed one of Tracy's men. Led by the malevolent Charles Middleton, the wicked Starks practice robbery, extortion, and sabotage with equal finesse until the forces of law and order slowly whittle down their number in one bullet-riddled encounter after another. Determined Dick Tracy and menacing Pa Stark have their final date with destiny onboard a plane filled with nitroglycerine, and any child with the price of matinee admission during Depression-era 1937 could tell you who the victor would be. Since there were two more Tracy serials released by Republic Studios in the next few years, the secret seems to be out: Dick Tracy made it!

1938 B & W 15 chapters

DICK TRACY VERSUS CUEBALL

★½

DIRECTOR: Gordon Douglas

CAST: Morgan Conway, Anne Jeffreys, Lyle Latell, Rita Corday, Dick Wessel, Douglas Walton, Ian Keith

Dick Tracy chases a bald strangler who made off with a fortune in jewelry in this low-budget feature film. Morgan Conway's anemic Dick Tracy holds this one back, but the supporting cast and Dick Wessel as Cueball pep up this modest programmer. Veteran performer Ralph Byrd was wisely chosen to play Dick Tracy in the last two entries in the series, a role he created in the serials in 1937.

1946 B & W 62 minutes

DICK TRACY VS. CRIME INC.

★★★

DIRECTORS: William Witney, John English

CAST: Ralph Byrd, Michael Owen, Jan Wiley, John Davidson, Ralph Morgan, Kenneth Harlan, Robert Frazier, Jack Mulhall, Anthony Ward, Chuck Morrison

Dick Tracy is called in to help stop the mysterious "Ghost," a ruthless member of the Council of Eight, a group of influential citizens attempting to rid the city of crime. Aided by the inventions of the fanatical Lucifer, an evil genius capable of rendering his master invisible, the "Ghost" does his level best to destroy the harbor, melt buildings, and kill Tracy and his henchmen in a dozen different ways. The forces of law and order eventually prevail and the invisible evildoer is electrocuted, slowly returning to human shape and revealed as . . . But why give the ending away? Watch this one for yourself and see what a really topnotch serial is like. This was the fourth and final appearance of Ralph Byrd as Dick Tracy in the serials, but he was to return to play the famous investigator in two feature films and an early television show. They are all worth watching, perhaps twice.

1941 B & W 15 chapters

DICK TRACY'S DILEMMA

★★½

DIRECTOR: John Rawlins

CAST: Ralph Byrd, Lyle Latell, Kay Christopher, Jack Lambert, Ian Keith

Two-fisted detective Dick Tracy returns to the screen in the guise of Ralph Byrd, the no-nonsense action star who first essayed the role ten years before. Tracy finds himself up against a maniacal killer with an iron hook. Heavy Jack Lambert plays one of his great psycho roles and Ralph Byrd still packs plenty of punch as the hard-hitting nemesis of crime. Byrd was one of those rare actors who could imbue a one-dimensional character like Tracy with vitality and believability

1947 B & W 60 minutes

DICK TRACY'S G-MEN

★★★

DIRECTORS: William Witney, John English

CAST: Ralph Byrd, Irving Pichel, Ted Pearson, Phyllis Isley, Walter Miller, George Douglas, Kenneth Harlan, Robert Carson, Ted Mapes

FBI agent Dick Tracy is forced to pursue the evil Zarnoff, the head of an international spy ring, after already capturing him and witnessing his execution. The ruthless spy lord is revived by drugs and redoubles his efforts at sabotage, putting Tracy and his men in one tight spot after another. Byrd gives his usual solid portrayal of Tracy, and actor-director Irving Pichel makes a truly impressive heavy as the cold, superior Zarnoff. Phyllis Isley plays the G-men's office girl Owen; by the time Ralph Byrd played Dick Tracy in feature films in the 1940s, she would be a star with a new name: Jennifer Jones, David O. Selznick's protégée and wife.

1939 B & W 15 chapters

DILLINGER

★★★

DIRECTOR: Max Nosseck

CAST: Edmund Lowe, Anne Jeffreys, Lawrence Tierney,

Eduardo Ciannelli, Marc Lawrence, Elisha Cook Jr.

A genre film, this look at the life and style of archetypal American gangster-antihero John Dillinger bids fair to be rated a *film noir*. Tough guy off-screen Lawrence Tierney is perfect in the title role. Baddy lovers will be delighted by old pros Eduardo Ciannelli, Marc Lawrence, and Elisha Cook, Gutman's boy Wilmer in *The Maltese Falcon*. Remade in color in 1973.

1945 B & W 89 minutes

DILLINGER

★★★★

DIRECTOR: John Milius

CAST: Warren Oates, Ben Johnson, Cloris Leachman, Michelle Phillips, Richard Dreyfuss, Harry Dean Stanton, Geoffrey Lewis, Steve Kanaly, Frank McRae

John Milius made an explosive directorial debut with this rip-roaring gangster film featuring Warren Oates in his best starring role. As a jaunty John Dillinger, he has all the charisma of a Cagney or a Bogart. In many ways, this is a gangster version of Sam Peckinpah's *The Wild Bunch*, with a superb supporting cast energizing every scene. It's the mobster as mythological hero, with Oates gallantly opposing Ben Johnson's Melvis Purvis. Harry Dean Stanton has a stand-out sequence, and the bit in which Oates's Dillinger slaps around Richard Dreyfuss's mouthy Baby Face Nelson is a cinematic high point. Rated R for profanity and violence.

1973 96 minutes

DINNER AT THE RITZ

★★½

DIRECTOR: Harold Schuster

CAST: David Niven, Paul Lukas, Annabella, Romney Brent

Good cast makes British whodunit about Annabella seeking her father's murderer an enjoyable diversion. Well-produced, with just a light enough touch to balance out all the familiar elements of crime melodrama. Early David Niven effort displays his unique qualities at comedy and light drama.

1937 B & W 77 minutes

DIRTY DOZEN, THE

★★★★½

DIRECTOR: Robert Aldrich

CAST: Lee Marvin, Ernest Borgnine, Charles Bronson, Jim Brown, John Cassavetes, Donald Sutherland, Clint Walker

Lee Marvin is assigned to take a group of military prisoners behind German lines and strike a blow for the Allies. It's a terrific entertainment—funny, star-studded, suspenseful, and even touching. In short, a real winner.

1967 145 minutes

DIRTY HARRY

★★★★½

DIRECTOR: Don Siegel

CAST: Clint Eastwood, Harry Guardino, John Mitchum, Reni Santoni, Andy Robinson

This is the original and still the best screen adventure of Clint Eastwood's maverick San Francisco detective. Outfoxed by a maniacal killer (Andy Robinson), "Dirty Harry" Callahan finally decides to deal out justice in his own inimitable and controversial fashion for an exciting, edge-of-your-seat climax. Rated R.

1971 102 minutes

DIRTY MARY, CRAZY LARRY

★★★

DIRECTOR: John Hough

CAST: Peter Fonda, Susan George, Vic Morrow, Adam Roarke, Roddy McDowall

Race-car driver Peter Fonda and

his two accomplices lead Vic Morrow and a small army of law enforcement officers on a frantic, nonstop chase in this satisfying low-budget action film. Intended as a drive-in programmer, the movie gained a considerable reputation among aficionados and remains a minor cult favorite. Marred by an unsatisfactory twist ending, the story is fast-paced and entertaining and a good example of what can be done with limited funds and a talented crew. Similar in some respects to Monte Hellman's muddled *Two Lane Blacktop*, this tire-squealer is one of the best of a seldom-explored subculture. Rated R for language, violence.

1974 93 minutes

DISAPPEARANCE, THE

★★★★

DIRECTOR: Stuart Cooper
CAST: Donald Sutherland, Francine Racete, David Hemmings, John Hurt, Christopher Plummer

This exciting film has Donald Sutherland portraying a professional hit man who can't do his job properly after his wife disappears. He pursues a top man in the organization (Christopher Plummer) because he believes that he is responsible for his wife's disappearance. The ironic ending only adds to the many twists and turns throughout this very watchable film. Rated R for sex and violence.

1977 80 minutes

DISTANT DRUMS

★★

DIRECTOR: Raoul Walsh
CAST: Gary Cooper, Mari Aldon, Richard Webb, Ray Teal, Arthur Hunnicutt, Robert Barrat, Clancy Cooper

Good old laconic Gary Cooper tracks down gun smugglers who are selling firesticks to renegade Seminole Indians in the Everglades. A tired story and screenplay manage to get by on Cooper, good photography, and music.

1951 101 minutes

DOBERMAN GANG, THE

★★½

DIRECTOR: Byron Chudnow
CAST: Byron Mabe, Julie Parrish, Simmy Bow, Hal Reed

A vicious pack of Doberman pinschers are trained as bank robbers in this implausible but well-made action tale. Rated PG for language, mild violence.

1972 87 minutes

DR. KILDARE'S STRANGE CASE

★★★

DIRECTOR: Harold S. Bucquet
CAST: Lew Ayres, Lionel Barrymore, Laraine Day, Nat Pendleton, Samuel S. Hinds, Emma Dunn

Friendly old Dr. Gillespie and his medical whiz junior, Dr. Kildare, are featured in this tale of the deranged. Lew Ayres deals with a cuckoo. Nurse Laraine Day provides love interest; Lionel Barrymore is at the ready to counsel as Dr. Gillespie. This is one of the best of the Kildare series.

1940 B & W 76 minutes

DR. NO

★★★★

DIRECTOR: Terence Young
CAST: Sean Connery, Ursula Andress, Jack Lord, Bernard Lee

The first of the James Bond movie sensations, it was in this film that Sean Connery began his ascent to stardom as the indomitable British secret agent 007. Bond is sent to Jamaica to confront the evil Dr. No, a villain bent on world domination. Ursula Andress was the first of the (now traditional) sensual Bond heroines. As with most of the series films, there is a blend of nonstop action and tongue-in-cheek humor.

1962 111 minutes

DR. SYN

★★½

DIRECTOR: Roy William Neill

CAST: George Arliss, Margaret Lockwood, John Loder, Roy Emerton, Graham Moffatt

Master character actor George Arliss's final film has him playing a traditional English vicar who blossoms into a pirate when the sun goes down. Nothing earth-shaking here, but direction and rich atmosphere make it all palatable.

1937 B & W 80 minutes

DOGS OF WAR, THE

★★

DIRECTOR: John Irvin

CAST: Christopher Walken, Tom Berenger, Colin Blakely, Hugh Millais

A graphic account of the coup d'etat of a West African dictatorship (starring Christopher Walken as the leader of a band of mercenaries), this film depicts a senseless act of violence totally motivated by the lust for wealth and power. Unfortunately, this movie doesn't quite hold together. With a more carefully drawn script and more skillful direction, *Dogs of War* could have been a very powerful film. Instead, we are presented with a sometimes fascinating and sometimes dull entertainment, which is worth watching only if you have nothing better to do. Rated R for violence.

1980 102 minutes

$ (DOLLARS)

★★★★★

DIRECTOR: Richard Brooks

CAST: Warren Beatty, Goldie Hawn, Gert Fröbe, Robert Webber

Simply one of the best heist capers ever filmed. Warren Beatty, bank employee, teams with Goldie Hawn, hooker, to duplicate critical safe deposit keys for a cool $1.5 million. Intriguing concept, deftly directed in a fashion that reveals continuous unexpected plot twists. Gert Fröbe is a great villain, in his best part since *Goldfinger*. The picture concludes with a harrowing chase that lasts nearly half an hour. Don't miss this one. Rated R for violence and sexual situations.

1972 119 minutes

DON IS DEAD, THE

★★★½

DIRECTOR: Richard Fleischer

CAST: Anthony Quinn, Frederic Forrest, Robert Forster, Al Lettieri, Angel Tompkins, Charles Cioffi

Director Richard Fleisher (*Boston Strangler; Mr. Majestyk*) gives us yet another story of a Mafia family struggling for control of Las Vegas interest (à la *The Godfather*). Well-acted performances make for better-than-average viewing in this movie about the code of honor among thieves. Rated R for violence.

1973 115 minutes

DONOVAN'S REEF

★★★

DIRECTOR: John Ford

CAST: John Wayne, Lee Marvin, Elizabeth Allen, Jack Warden, Dorothy Lamour

Director John Ford's low, knockabout style of comedy prevails in this tale of two old drinking, seafaring buddies—John Wayne and Lee Marvin—forced to set aside their playful head-knocking to aid another pal, Jack Warden, in putting on an air of respectability to impress the latter's visiting daughter (Elizabeth Allen).

1963 109 minutes

DOOMED TO DIE

★★

DIRECTOR: William Nigh
CAST: Boris Karloff, Grant Withers, Marjorie Reynolds, Melvin Lang, Guy Usher

Monogram's popular series about the aged Chinese detective, Mr. Wong, was running out of steam by the time this film, the fourth in the series, was released, but even uninspired Boris Karloff is better than most other character actors' work, so this medium-budget effort is worth a look. The venerable Mr. Wong is called in by hard-boiled homicide captain Grant Withers after a millionaire is murdered and his ship, which is carrying a fortune in negotiable bonds, is sunk.

1940 B & W 68 minutes

DRAGNET

★★★★

DIRECTOR: Jack Webb
CAST: Jack Webb, Ben Alexander, Richard Boone, Ann Robinson, Dennis Weaver

Dragnet is the feature-length (color!) version of the popular detective series with director-star Jack Webb as the no-nonsense Sgt. Joe Friday, and Ben Alexander as his original partner, Frank Smith. In the story, based as always on a true case, Friday and Smith are assigned to solve the murder of a mobster. All clues seem to lead to his former associates.

1954 89 minutes

DRESSED TO KILL

★★★

DIRECTOR: Roy William Neill
CAST: Basil Rathbone, Nigel Bruce, Patricia Morison, Edmund Breon, Frederic Worlock, Harry Cording

Final entry in Universal's popular Rathbone/Bruce Sherlock Holmes series. This one involves counterfeiting, specifically a Bank of England plate hidden in one of three music boxes. Even in this, his fourteenth outing as the master sleuth, Basil Rathbone retains all the dramatic integrity for which his portrayal is known. After filming was completed, Rathbone—fearing typecasting—had had enough; his concerns clearly were genuine, as he did not work again for nearly nine years. Unrated—suitable for family viewing.

1946 B & W 72 minutes

DRIVER, THE

★★★★

DIRECTOR: Walter Hill
CAST: Ryan O'Neal, Bruce Dern, Isabelle Adjani, Ronee Blakley, Matt Clark

High-energy crime drama focuses on a professional getaway driver (Ryan O'Neal) and his police pursuer (Bruce Dern). Walter Hill's breakneck pacing and spectacular chase scenes make up for the lack of plot or character development. It's an action movie pure and simple. Rated R for violence and profanity.

1978 90 minutes

DROWNING POOL, THE

★★½

DIRECTOR: Stuart Rosenberg
CAST: Paul Newman, Joanne Woodward, Anthony Franciosa, Richard Jaeckel, Murray Hamilton, Melanie Griffith, Gail Strickland, Linda Haynes

Poor follow-up to *Harper*, with Paul Newman re-creating the title role. Director Stuart Rosenberg (*Brubaker*) doesn't come up with anything fresh in this stale entry into the detective genre. Rated PG—violence.

1976 108 minutes

DRUMS

★★★½

DIRECTOR: Zoltán Korda
CAST: Sabu, Raymond Massey, Valerie Hobson, Roger Livesey, David Tree

Stiff-upper-lip British Empire epic starts slow but builds to an exciting climax as soldiers of the queen aid young Prince Sabu in his struggle against usurping uncle Raymond Massey. Early Technicolor adds to the overall tone of this action drama, one of nearly a dozen pro-British war spectacles made in the magic era between 1935 and 1940. Massey as the crazed pretender to the throne is a standout and young Sabu is at his beguiling best, while Valerie Hobson (better known as Henry Frankenstein's wife in *Bride of Frankenstein*) is a beautiful addition to any film.

1938 99 minutes

DUELLISTS, THE

★★★★

DIRECTOR: Ridley Scott
CAST: Keith Carradine, Harvey Keitel, Albert Finney, Edward Fox, Cristina Raines, Robert Stephens, Tom Conti

The Duellists traces a long and seemingly meaningless feud between two soldiers in the Napoleonic Wars. This fascinating study of honor among men is full of irony and heroism. Keith Carradine plays Armand D'Hubert, a young Hussar who is sent by his general to arrest a hotheaded officer, Gabriel Feraud (Harvey Keitel), for dueling. In the process, D'Hubert finds himself challenged by Feraud to a swordfight. Reluctantly, he obliges and wounds his opponent. But that is not the end of it. Rated R.

1977 101 minutes

EAGLE HAS LANDED, THE

★★★

DIRECTOR: John Sturges
CAST: Michael Caine, Donald Sutherland, Robert Duvall

Michael Caine is a Nazi agent who is given orders to plan and carry out the kidnapping or murder of Prime Minister Churchill. This movie gets started on a promising note, but it is sabotaged by a weak, contrived ending. Rated PG.

1977 123 minutes

EARTHLING, THE

★★★½

DIRECTOR: Peter Collinson
CAST: William Holden, Ricky Schroder, Jack Thompson, Olivia Hamnett, Alwyn Kurts

A dying man (William Holden) and an orphaned boy (Ricky Schroder) meet in the Australian wilderness in this surprisingly absorbing family film. Despite some glaring flaws, this is an extremely enjoyable piece of entertainment for young and old, thanks primarily to the direction of Peter Collinson and the magnificent photography of Don McAlpine. A warning to parents: There is a minor amount of profanity, and a scene in which the boy's mother and father are killed may be too shocking for small children. Rated PG.

1980 102 minutes

EARTHQUAKE

★

DIRECTOR: Mark Robson
CAST: Charlton Heston, Genevieve Bujold, Lorne Greene, Ava Gardner, Walter Matthau, George Kennedy

Once you get past the special-effects mastery of seeing Los Angeles destroyed, you've got a pretty weak film on your hands. The old classic *San Francisco* did it better. Acting honors go to Walter Matthau, who plays a drunk. Everyone else looks as though they really are in the middle of a week-long bender. If they weren't, they should have been, especially Lorne Greene and Ava Gardner. Rated PG.

1974 129 minutes

EAST OF BORNEO

★★★

DIRECTOR: George Melford
CAST: Rose Hobart, Charles Bickford, Georges Renavent, Lupita Tovar, Noble Johnson

Intrepid and tenacious Rose Hobart searches the teeming Borneo jungle for her supposedly lost doctor husband Charles Bickford, who isn't lost at all but living it up as personal physician to native prince Georges Renavent. Filled with wildlife, this jungle adventure is lots of fun and ends with a bang.

1931 B & W 77 minutes

EAT MY DUST

DIRECTOR: Charles Griffith
CAST: Ron Howard, Christopher Norris, Dave Madden, Warren Kemmerling

A low-budget 1976 race yarn notable only for the fact that it gave Ron Howard the power to direct his next starring vehicle, *Grand Theft Auto*, which, in turn, led to such treats as *Night Shift* and *Splash*. Rated PG.

1976 90 minutes

EDDIE MACON'S RUN

★★½

DIRECTOR: Jeff Kanew
CAST: John Schneider, Kirk Douglas, Lee Purcell, Leah Ayres

John Schneider, of television's *Dukes of Hazard*, makes his silver screen debut as a prison escapee who manages to stay one step ahead of the law. Kirk Douglas co-stars as the hard-nosed policeman on his trail. It's a predictable, lightweight movie obviously tailored for *Dukes* watchers. The results are nothing to write home about, yet it is rarely boring. Rated PG for vulgar language and violence.

1983 95 minutes

EDGE OF DARKNESS

★★★★½

DIRECTOR: Martin Campbell
CAST: Bob Peck, Joe Don Baker, Jack Woodson, John Woodvine, Joanne Whalley, Charles Kay, Ian McNeice, Tim McInnerny, Zoe Wanamaker

A complex mystery produced as a miniseries for British television. The story revolves around a nuclear processing plant and its covert government relations. Bob Peck offers an intense portrayal of a British police detective who, step by step, uncovers the truth as he investigates the murder of his daughter. Though the first hour is rather slow and confusing, this miniseries is highly rewarding. It went on to win six British Academy Awards—and deservedly so.

1986 307 minutes

EIGER SANCTION, THE

★★½

DIRECTOR: Clint Eastwood
CAST: Clint Eastwood, George Kennedy, Jack Cassidy, Thayer David, Vonette McGee

Laughable but entertaining adaptation of Trevanian's equally laughable but entertaining novel. Clint Eastwood is a college professor by day (named Hemlock, no less) and supersecret agent by night sent to expose a killer during a dangerous mountain climb. Outrageously overblown characters with silly names—a woman called "Buns," for example—and

plenty of opportunities for Eastwood to strut his macho stuff, but it's all in good fun. A good soundtrack by John Williams, which helps relieve the picture's length. Hardly a classic, but who cares? Rated R for violence and sex.
1975 128 minutes

8 MILLION WAYS TO DIE

★★

DIRECTOR: Hal Ashby
CAST: Jeff Bridges, Rosanna Arquette, Alexandra Paul, Andy Garcia

An alcoholic ex-cop, Jeff Bridges, attempts to help a high-priced L.A. prostitute get away from her boss and crazed Colombian coke dealer boyfriend, Andy Garcia. This only leads to her death and sends him into the nether world of cocaine dealers and expensive hookers. Considering the talent involved, this one should have been a real killer, but there are too many holes in the script and several dead spots throughout. Bridges and Garcia walk off with the acting honors while director Hal Ashby fails to capture the fire of his earlier works—such as *Shampoo* and *Harold and Maude*. Rated R for violence, nudity, and language.
1986 115 minutes

EL CID

★★★

DIRECTOR: Anthony Mann
CAST: Charlton Heston, Sophia Loren, Raf Vallone, Hurd Hatfield

Some of the best battle action scenes ever filmed are included in this 1961 spectacle about the medieval Spanish hero El Cid. Unfortunately, on smaller home screens much of the splendor will be lost. You will be left with the wooden Charlton Heston and the beautiful Sophia Loren in a love story that was underdeveloped due to the movie's emphasis on spectacle.
1961 184 minutes

ELEPHANT BOY

★★★

DIRECTORS: Robert Flaherty, Zoltán Korda
CAST: Sabu, W. E. Holloway, Walter Hudd, Bruce Gordon

Sabu, in later years the butt of many cheap jokes, made his film debut and became a star in this drama about a boy who claims to know where elephants go to die. Robert Flaherty's co-direction gives the film a travelogue quality, but it interests and delights just the same. The Indian atmosphere and backgrounds are true and authentic. A Rudyard Kipling story provided the plot.
1937 B & W 80 minutes

11 HARROWHOUSE

★★½

DIRECTOR: Aram Avakian
CAST: Charles Grodin, Candice Bergen, James Mason, John Gielgud

Confused heist caper which vacillates too wildly between straight drama and dark comedy. Diamond salesman Charles Grodin is talked into stealing valuable gems. Too farfetched to be taken seriously, yet that seems to be the intent. An excellent cast goes to waste. Rated PG—mild sexual overtones.
1974 95 minutes

EMERALD FOREST, THE

★★★★

DIRECTOR: John Boorman
CAST: Powers Boothe, Meg Foster, Charley Boorman

In this riveting adventure film based on a true story, Powers Boothe stars as Bill Markham, an American engineer who, with his family, goes to the Amazon jungle to build a dam. There, his 5-year-old son is stolen by a native tribe known as the Invisible People. Markham spends the next ten years trying to find his son. Rated R for nudity, suggested sex, profanity, and violence.

1985 110 minutes

ENDLESS SUMMER, THE

★★★★

DIRECTOR: Bruce Brown
CAST: Mike Hynson, Robert August

The only surfing documentary ever to gain an audience outside the "Beach Boy" set, this is an imaginatively photographed travelogue that captures the joy, danger, and humor of two youths searching worldwide for the perfect wave. Much of the success is attributable to the whimsical narration. You don't have to be a surfer to enjoy this picture.

1966 95 minutes

ENFORCER, THE

★★★★

DIRECTOR: James Fargo
CAST: Clint Eastwood, Tyne Daly, Harry Guardino, Bradford Dillman, John Mitchum

A step up from the muddled *Magnum Force* and a nice companion piece to *Dirty Harry*, this third entry in the popular series has detective Harry Callahan grudgingly team with a female cop (Tyne Daly) during his pursuit of a band of terrorists. John Mitchum gives a standout performance in his final series bow as tough cop Frank DiGeorgio. It'll make your day. Rated R.

1976 96 minutes

ENFORCER, THE

★★★½

DIRECTOR: Bretaigne Windust
CAST: Humphrey Bogart, Zero Mostel, Everett Sloane, Ted de Corsia, Roy Roberts

A big-city district attorney, Humphrey Bogart, attempts to break up the mob in this effective crime drama. At under ninety minutes, it moves like lightning and is refreshingly devoid of most of the standard clichés of the genre. Not to be confused with the Clint Eastwood film of the same title.

1951 B & W 87 minutes

ENIGMA

★★

DIRECTOR: Jeannot Szwarc
CAST: Martin Sheen, Brigitte Fossey, Sam Neill, Derek Jacobi, Michael Lonsdale, Frank Finlay

Espionage yarn succumbs to lethargy. The KGB sics an elite group of assassins on five Soviet dissidents. A CIA agent (Martin Sheen) attempts to thwart the insidious scheme by entangling his former lover with the top Russian agent. Uninteresting intrigue. Rated PG.

1982 101 minutes

ENTER THE DRAGON

★★★★

DIRECTOR: Robert Clouse
CAST: Bruce Lee, John Saxon, Jim Kelly, Ahna Capri, Yang Tse, Angela Mao

Bruce Lee soared to international superstardom with this fast-paced, tongue-in-cheek kung-fu film. A big-budget American version of the popular Chinese genre, it has a good plot and strong performances—from Lee, John Saxon, and Jim Kelly. In short, it's highly enjoyable and highly recommended. Rated R, due to violence.

1973 97 minutes

ENTER THE NINJA

★★

DIRECTOR: Menahem Golan
CAST: Franco Nero, Susan George, Sho Kosugi, Alex Courtney

A passable martial arts adventure about practitioners of an ancient Oriental art of killing. Rated R.

1981 94 minutes

ESCAPE FROM ALCATRAZ

★★★★

DIRECTOR: Don Siegel
CAST: Clint Eastwood, Patrick McGoohan, Roberts Blossom, Jack Thibeau

Any movie that combines the talents of star Clint Eastwood and director Don Siegel is more than watchable. This is a gripping and believable film about the 1962 breakout from the supposedly perfect prison. Patrick McGoohan is also excellent as the neurotic warden. Rated PG.

1979 112 minutes

ESCAPE FROM NEW YORK

★★★½

DIRECTOR: John Carpenter
CAST: Kurt Russell, Lee Van Cleef, Ernest Borgnine, Donald Pleasence, Adrienne Barbeau

The year is 1997. *Air Force One*—with the president (Donald Pleasence) onboard—is hijacked by a group of revolutionaries and sent crashing into the middle of Manhattan, which has been turned into a top-security prison. It's up to Snake Plissken (Kurt Russell), a former war hero gone renegade, to get him out in twenty-four hours. That's the premise of this science-fiction–adventure film by director John Carpenter. Like *Halloween* and *The Fog*, Carpenter's previous films, it's fun, surprise-filled entertainment from beginning to end. Rated R.

1981 99 minutes

ESCAPE TO ATHENA

★★★

DIRECTOR: George Pan Cosmatos
CAST: Roger Moore, Telly Savalas, David Niven, Claudia Cardinale, Stephanie Powers, Richard Roundtree, Elliott Gould, Sonny Bono

Roger Moore as a Nazi officer? Sonny Bono as a member of the Italian Resistance? Elliott Gould as a hippie in a World War II concentration camp? Sound ridiculous? It is. *Escape to Athena* is a silly, improbable movie. It's a *Hogan's Heroes* for the big screen but, in a dumb sort of way, entertaining. Rated PG.

1979 101 minutes

EVEL KNIEVEL

★★½

DIRECTOR: Marvin C. Homsky
CAST: George Hamilton, Sue Lyon, Rod Cameron

Autobiography of motorcycle stunt man Evel Knievel. George Hamilton is surprisingly good as Knievel. Some nice stunts. Rated PG.

1972 90 minutes

EVIL THAT MEN DO, THE

★½

DIRECTOR: J. Lee Thompson
CAST: Charles Bronson, Theresa Saldana, José Ferrer, Joseph Maher

Believe it or not, Charles Bronson has made a watchable film for a change. This revenge film à la *Death Wish* is not classic, mind you. But it is definitely much better than the sort of junk Bronson has been associated with in the last few years. In it, Bronson plays a professional killer who comes out of retirement to avenge the brutal murder of an old friend. Rated R for violence and profanity.

1984 90 minutes

EVIL UNDER THE SUN

★★★★

DIRECTOR: Guy Hamilton
CAST: Peter Ustinov, Jane Birkin, Colin Blakely, James Mason,

Roddy McDowall, Diana Rigg, Maggie Smith, Nicholas Clay

This highly entertaining mystery, starring Peter Ustinov as Agatha Christie's Belgian detective Hercule Poirot, is set on a remote island in the Adriatic Sea where a privileged group gathers at a luxury hotel. Of course, someone is murdered and Poirot cracks the case. Rated PG because of a scene involving a dead rabbit.

1982 102 minutes

EXTERMINATOR, THE

★★

DIRECTOR: James Glickenhaus
CAST: Christopher George, Samantha Eggar, Robert Ginty, Steve James, Tony DiBenedetto

The Exterminator is a low-budget, extraordinarily violent film. It's the story of a vigilante who takes the law into his own hands when the law refuses to punish the gang members who made a cripple of his best friend during a mugging. The hero runs down the guilty gang and wipes them out, thereby doing the community a favor. He becomes a media hero, and the cops look the other way as he wages his one-man war on crime. Rated R.

1980 101 minutes

EXTERMINATOR 2, THE

DIRECTOR: Mark Buntzman
CAST: Robert Ginty, Deborah Geffner, Frankie Faison, Mario Van Peebles

In this disgusting cheapo, Robert Ginty returns as the one-man vigilante force set on cleaning up New York City à la *Death Wish*. He's just another Vietnam vet who's sick and tired of all the funny-looking people who rule the midnight streets of the Big Apple and make life miserable for law-abiding taxpayers. This time, though, our "hero" has graduated from using a gun to using a blowtorch. Rated R for violence, nudity, and profanity.

1984 104 minutes

EXTREME PREJUDICE

★★★★

DIRECTOR: Walter Hill
CAST: Nick Nolte, Powers Boothe, Maria Conchita Alonso, Michael Ironside, Rip Torn, Clancy Brown, William Forsythe

Nick Nolte is in peak form in this modern-day western as a two-fisted Texas Ranger whose boyhood friend, Powers Boothe, has become a drug kingpin across the border in Mexico. Maria Conchita Alonso is the woman who loves them both. The two men reach an agreement to leave each other alone, but this is upset when the federal government sends six high-tech agents to nail Boothe with "extreme prejudice." Walter Hill was born to direct westerns, and he takes full advantage of his opportunity here. The result is a pastiche of *Rio Bravo*, *The Wild Bunch*, and *The Dirty Dozen* that should delight fans of hard-hitting action movies. Rated R for profanity, drug use, nudity, and violence.

1987 96 minutes

EYE FOR AN EYE

★★½

DIRECTOR: Steve Carver
CAST: Chuck Norris, Christopher Lee, Richard Roundtree, Matt Clark, Maggie Cooper

This surprisingly entertaining kung-fu movie features Chuck Norris as a human weapon battling a variety of bullies. Shawn Kane (Norris) is an ex-cop trying to crack a narcotics-smuggling ring. With the help of a lovely news editor (Maggie Cooper) and a martial arts master (Matt Clark) who doubles as a walking fortune cookie, Kane confronts a sinister Christopher Lee and, finally, a human tank called The Professor. This fist-and-foot opera features some passable acting, good action sequences, and even some intended laughs. Rated R.

1981 106 minutes

EYE OF THE NEEDLE

★★★½

DIRECTOR: Richard Marquand

CAST: Donald Sutherland, Ian Bannen, Kate Nelligan, Christopher Cazenove

Never read the book before you see the movie. That way, there's less chance of being disappointed—as we were with this screen version of Ken Follett's enthralling suspense novel. Donald Sutherland stars as the deadly Nazi agent who discovers a ruse by the Allies during World War II and attempts to get the information to his superiors. Sutherland is excellent. The rest of the film, however, suffers because the novel's hero (played by Ian Bannen) has been all but eliminated. That throws the screen version of *Eye of the Needle* a bit off balance. Nevertheless, it does have plenty of suspense and thrills for those new to the story. Rated R because of nudity, sex, and violence.

1981 112 minutes

EYE OF THE TIGER

★★★

DIRECTOR: Richard Sarafian

CAST: Gary Busey, Yaphet Kotto, Seymour Cassel

Buck Mathews (Gary Busey) stands up against a motorcycle gang and the corrupt law enforcement that have plagued a small town in Texas. When the motorcycle gang kills Mathews's wife, he takes revenge. Busey and Yaphet Kotto give quality performances that save this formula vengeance film. Rated R for violence and language.

1986 90 minutes

F/X

★★★½

DIRECTOR: Robert Mandel

CAST: Bryan Brown, Brian Dennehy, Diane Venora, Cliff De Young, Mason Adams, Jerry Orbach

In this fast-paced, well-acted suspense thriller, Bryan Brown (*Breaker Morant*) plays special effects wizard Rollie Tyler, who accepts thirty thousand dollars from the Justice Department's Witness Relocation Program to stage the fake assassination of a mob figure who has agreed to name names. After he successfully fulfills his assignment, Tyler is double-crossed and must use his wits and movie magic to survive. Rated R for profanity, suggested sex, and violence.

1986 110 minutes

FALCON IN MEXICO, THE

★★

DIRECTOR: William Berke

CAST: Tom Conway, Mona Maris, Nestor Paiva, Bryant Washburn, Emory Parnell, Martha Vickers, Mary Currier, Pedro de Cordoba, George Lewis

The ninth film in the long-running series finds the suave sleuth south of the border as he tries to recover a woman's portrait. The owner of the gallery where the painting was displayed has been murdered and the artist responsible for the painting was reportedly killed fifteen years earlier, but Tom Conway as the smooth Falcon untangles the mystery. This entry was about halfway through the nine-year series and it retains the gloss that even the B pictures of major studios radiated

during the 1930s and early 1940s.
1944 B & W 70 minutes

FALCON TAKES OVER, THE

★★★

DIRECTOR: Irving Reis
CAST: George Sanders, James Gleason, Ward Bond, Hans Conried, Lynn Bari

Early entry in the popular *Falcon* mystery film series sets star George Sanders in a search for a missing woman. During the course of this search he encounters a good many of Hollywood's favorite character actors and actresses as well as much of the plot from Raymond Chandler's *Farewell My Lovely*, of which this is the first filmed version. Well-acted, entertaining, and a gem for lovers of mystery fiction.
1942 B & W 63 minutes

FALCON'S BROTHER, THE

★★★

DIRECTOR: Stanley Logan
CAST: George Sanders, Tom Conway, Don Barclay, Jane Randolph, Amanda Varela, George Lewis, Gwili Andre, Edward Gargan, Cliff Clark, James Newill

The sophisticated Falcon (played by former Saint George Sanders) has decoded a Nazi spy message and races against time to prevent the assassination of a South American diplomat. Aided by his brother (in fact Sanders's real-life brother, Tom Conway), the Falcon realizes his goal but pays with his life at the end. Brother Tom vows to bring the guilty to justice and to continue the work his martyred sibling has left undone. This well-made, nicely acted little detective film is a true oddity—the hero actually dies and passes the mantle to a relative, common enough in fiction but scarce on the screen. George Sanders had played The Saint in five films before RKO began The Falcon series, basically a continuation of the same character using the name of an adventurer created by Michael Arlen years before. Like all the earlier entries, this one contains just about the perfect blend of adventure and comedy.
1942 B & W 63 minutes

FAMILY, THE

★★★

DIRECTOR: Sergio Sollima
CAST: Charles Bronson, Jill Ireland, Telly Savalas, Michael Constantine, George Savalas

Charles Bronson is mad. Some creep framed him and, what's worse, stole his girl! Bronson is out for revenge. This film has plenty of action, but nothing new to offer. Rated R.
1970 100 minutes

FAREWELL MY LOVELY

★★★★½

DIRECTOR: Dick Richards
CAST: Robert Mitchum, Charlotte Rampling, John Ireland, Sylvia Miles, Harry Dean Stanton, Jack O'Halloran

This superb film adaptation of Raymond Chandler's celebrated mystery novel stands as a tribute to the talents of actor Robert Mitchum. In director Dick Richards's brooding classic of *film noir*, Mitchum makes a perfect, world-weary Philip Marlowe, private eye. The detective's search for the long-lost love of gangster Moose Malloy (Jack O'Halloran) takes us into the nether world of pre–World War II Los Angeles for a fast-paced, fascinating period piece. Rated R.
1975 97 minutes

FAST MONEY

DIRECTOR: Douglas Holloway
CAST: Sammy Allred, Sonny Carl Davis, Lou Perry, Marshall Ford, Doris Hargrave

This low-quality bore introduces us to a group of young men who are getting high and smuggling drugs from Mexico—while being pursued by a sheriff and his undercover agents. Sadly, these miscreants are supposed to be the heroes. Things pick up a little when the smugglers begin to have trouble with their girlfriends, the law, and each other. By this time, most viewers are hoping they'll get busted. Sybil Danning introduces the feature as part of her Adventure Video series. She outlines ten important points for a good video—unfortunately, this film meets none of them. Rated R for obscenities, drug use, and lawlessness.

1985 92 minutes

FASTER PUSSYCAT! KILL! KILL!

★★★½

DIRECTOR: Russ Meyer
CAST: Tura Satana, Haji, Jori Williams, Juan Bernard

This movie has everything you could want from a Russ Meyer film. Beautiful girls, fast-paced action, and lots of wild and wacky humor. In its day it was considered fairly hard-core, yet today it could even be shown on late-night television. For fans of the unusual and the bizarre.

1962 B & W 83 minutes

FEAR CITY

★★

DIRECTOR: Abel Ferrara
CAST: Tom Berenger, Billy Dee Williams, Rae Dawn Chong, Melanie Griffith, Rossano Brazzi, Jack Scalia

After a promising directorial debut with *Ms. 45*, Abel Ferrara backslid with this all-too-familiar tale about a psychopath killing prostitutes in New York City. Some good performances and action sequences still can't save this one. Rated R for violence, nudity, and profanity.

1985 93 minutes

FFOLKES

★★★

DIRECTOR: Andrew V. McLaglen
CAST: Roger Moore, James Mason, Anthony Perkins, Michael Parks, David Hedison

Of course, no movie with Roger Moore is a classic, but this tongue-in-cheek spy thriller with the actor playing against his James Bond stereotype provides some good, campy entertainment. This film features Moore as a woman-hating, but cat-loving, gun for hire who takes on a band of terrorists. Rated PG.

1980 99 minutes

FIFTH MUSKETEER, THE

★★

DIRECTOR: Ken Annakin
CAST: Beau Bridges, Sylvia Kristel, Ursula Andress, Cornel Wilde, Olivia De Havilland, José Ferrer, Rex Harrison, Lloyd Bridges, Alan Hale

You really can't blame filmmakers for taking advantage of the popularity of Richard Lester's two superb swashbucklers, *The Three Musketeers* and *The Four Musketeers*, can you? You can if it's as bad as this uninspired retelling of *The Man in the Iron Mask*. Beau Bridges is watchable enough as King Louis XIV and his twin brother, Philipe, who was raised as a peasant by D'Artagnan (Cornel Wilde) and the three musketeers (Lloyd Bridges, José Ferrer, and Alan Hale). It sounds promising. However, the film never springs to life. Rated PG.

1979 103 minutes

FIGHTING BACK

★★★

DIRECTOR: Lewis Teague
CAST: Tom Skerritt, Patti LuPone, Michael Sarrazin, Yaphet

Kotto, David Rashe, Ted Ross, Pat Cooper

It may not be totally realistic, but this film is so action-packed that you'll be captivated throughout. A deli owner decides to organize a neighborhood committee against crime after his wife and mother are victims of violence. Unfortunately, his emotionalism gets in the way of his professionalism, but he still makes his mark—and you can't help but cheer him on. A rapid succession of violent acts, lots of profanity, and occasional nudity make this R-rated film questionable for young audiences.

1982 98 minutes

FIGHTING MARINES, THE

★★

DIRECTORS: Joseph Kane, B. Reeves "Breezy" Eason

CAST: Grant Withers, Adrian Morris, Ann Rutherford, Jason Robards Sr., Pat O'Malley

A detachment of U.S. Marines runs up against the sabotage of a modern-day pirate when it tries to establish a landing field on Halfway Island in the Pacific. The plot's thin, the acting forced, but the special effects are remarkable. Pieced together from twelve serial chapters.

1936 B & W 69 minutes

FIGHTING SEABEES, THE

★★★

DIRECTOR: Edward Ludwig

CAST: John Wayne, Dennis O'Keefe, Susan Hayward, William Frawley, Duncan Renaldo

John Wayne and Dennis O'Keefe are construction workers fighting the Japanese in their own way while each attempts to woo Susan Hayward away from the other. This 1944 war film, which co-stars William Frawley, is actually better than it sounds.

1944 B & W 100 minutes

FINAL CHAPTER—WALKING TALL

★

DIRECTOR: Jack Starrett

CAST: Bo Svenson, Margaret Blye, Forrest Tucker, Lurene Tuttle, Morgan Woodward, Libby Boone

The original *Walking Tall* surprised everyone by becoming a big box-office success. It was a cheaply made, often amateurish film with only graphic violence, a basis in truth, and a powerful performance by Joe Don Baker. Apparently that was enough. The film spawned many imitators, some starring Baker, and two sequels that, oddly enough, did not. The last one is titled *Final Chapter*. While it is not as bad technically as the first, which included an outdoor scene with a boom microphone in plain view, it is flawed just the same, because the script has nothing new to tell us about the life of the protagonist, Buford T. Pusser (Bo Svenson). Rated R for violence.

1977 112 minutes

FINAL JUSTICE

[turkey]

DIRECTOR: Greydon Clark

CAST: Joe Don Baker, Venantino Venantini, Helena Abella, Bill McKinney

In this incoherent ripoff of the Clint Eastwood cops-and-robbers film *Coogan's Bluff*, Joe Don Baker plays a rural sheriff who travels to Italy to take on the Mafia and halt criminal activities. Poor dubbing and mindless violence make this a repelling movie. Rated R for nudity, violence, and language.

1984 90 minutes

FINAL MISSION

DIRECTOR: Cirio Santiago
CAST: Richard Young, John Dresden, Kaz Garaz, Christine Tudor

In this stupid *First Blood* ripoff, a Vietnam veteran comes back to the States to become a cop and fight the American traitor he had to deal with back in Southeast Asia. The final scene is a blatant copy of the Sly Stallone film. Not rated, but with profanity, violence, and nudity.

1984 101 minutes

FINAL OPTION, THE

★★★★

DIRECTOR: Ian Sharp
CAST: Judy Davis, Lewis Collins, Richard Widmark, Robert Webber, Edward Woodard

Judy Davis stars in this first-rate British-made suspense thriller as the leader of a fanatical anti-nuclear group that takes a group of U.S. and British officials hostage and demands that a nuclear missile be launched at a U.S. base in Scotland. If not, the hostages—who include the American secretary of state (Richard Widmark) and chief of the U.S. Strategic Air Command (Robert Webber)—will die. And it's up to Special Air Services undercover agent Peter Skellen (Lewis Collins) to save their lives. The result is a terrific movie with a hold-your-breath, thrill-a-minute conclusion. Rated R for violence and profanity.

1982 125 minutes

FIRE OVER ENGLAND

★★★

DIRECTOR: Alexander Korda
CAST: Laurence Olivier, Vivien Leigh, Flora Robson

A swashbuckling adventure of Elizabethan England's outnumbered stand against the Spanish Armada. Made in the 1930s, it wasn't released in this country until 1941, in order to evoke American support and sympathy for Britain's plight against the Nazi juggernaut during its darkest days. This is only one of the two films that united husband and wife, Laurence Olivier and Vivien Leigh, as co-stars. They play lovers and courtiers to the queen who fight Spanish treachery within the English court.

1936 B & W 92 minutes

FIREFOX

★★★½

DIRECTOR: Clint Eastwood
CAST: Clint Eastwood, Freddie Jones, David Huffman, Warren Clarke, Ronald Lacey, Stephan Schnabel

Clint Eastwood doffs his contemporary cowboy garb to direct, produce, and star in this action-adventure film about an American fighter pilot assigned to steal a sophisticated Russian aircraft. The film takes a while to take off, but when it does, it's good, action-packed fun. Rated PG for violence.

1982 124 minutes

FIREPOWER

★★

DIRECTOR: Michael Winner
CAST: Sophia Loren, James Coburn, O. J. Simpson, Eli Wallach, Vincent Gardenia, Anthony Franciosa

Chalk up another loser for director Michael Winner. *Firepower* is a muddled, mindless mess. The film opens with typical Winner violence. A research chemist is blown up by a letter bomb while his wife, Adele Tasca (Sophia Loren), watches helplessly. The chemist was about to prove to the world that a company owned by the third-richest man in the world, Carl Stegner (George Touliatos), has been distributing contaminated drugs responsible for causing the cancerous deaths of a great many people. The widow joins Justice Department agent James Coburn in trying to bring Stegner out of seclusion to face, among other things, charges of tax evasion. Rated R.

1979 104 minutes

FIREWALKER

★★

DIRECTOR: J. Lee Thompson
CAST: Chuck Norris, Louis Gossett Jr., Melody Anderson, John Rhys-Davies

Two soldiers of fortune search for hidden treasure and end up in a Mayan temple of doom. Along the way, they murder Native Americans trying to protect sacred Indian burial grounds. Believe it or not, we're supposed to root for these pinheads. A misguided attempt at humor by Chuck Norris. Loud and silly, with an unexciting conclusion. The only thing funny or scary about the movie is that they left room for a sequel. Rated PG.

1986 96 minutes

FIRST BLOOD

★★★½

DIRECTOR: Ted Kotcheff
CAST: Sylvester Stallone, Richard Crenna, Brian Dennehy, David Caruso, Jack Starrett

Sylvester Stallone is topnotch as a former Green Beret who is forced to defend himself from a redneck cop (Brian Dennehy) in the Oregon mountains. The action never lets up. A winner for fans. Rated R for violence and profanity.

1982 97 minutes

FIRST DEADLY SIN, THE

★★

DIRECTOR: Brian Hutton
CAST: Frank Sinatra, Faye Dunaway, James Whitmore, David Dukes, Brenda Vaccaro, Martin Gabel, Anthony Zerbe

Lawrence Sanders's excellent mystery is turned into a so-so cop flick with Frank Sinatra looking bored as aging Detective Edward X. Delaney, who is on the trail of a murdering maniac (David Dukes). He, however, fares much better than co-star Faye Dunaway, who spends the entire picture flat on her back in a hospital bed. It's pretty dreary stuff. Rated R.

1980 112 minutes

FIRST YANK INTO TOKYO

★½

DIRECTOR: Gordon Douglas
CAST: Tom Neal, Barbara Hale, Richard Loo, Keye Luke, Benson Fong

Tom Neal has plastic surgery so he can pose as a Japanese soldier and help an American POW escape. As usual, Hollywood casts some fine Asian actors as sinister types. This low-budget melodrama is not worth the time.

1945 B & W 82 minutes

FISTS OF FURY

★★★

DIRECTOR: Lo Wei
CAST: Bruce Lee, Maria Yi, James Tien, Nora Miao

Bruce Lee's first chop-socky movie (made in Hong Kong) is corny, action-filled, and violent. It's no *Enter the Dragon*, but his fans—who have so few films to choose from—undoubtedly will want to see it again. Rated R.

1972 102 minutes

FIVE FOR HELL

DIRECTOR: Frank Kramer
CAST: Klaus Kinski, John Garko, Margaret Lee, Nick Jordan, Sal Borgese, Luciano Rosi, Sam Burke

In this Italian-made World War II bomb, a special unit of American soldiers goes behind enemy lines to copy the plans of an all-out German offensive. The gimmick in this film is that every soldier has an expertise in one thing or another—none of them having anything to do with combat. One guy is an acrobat who takes a trampoline with him so he can do flips over electrified fences. Another soldier is a baseball player who keeps a hardball with him so he can knock out the guards with his pinpoint pitches. If this sounds ridiculous, that's because it is. Not rated; has sex and violence.

1985 88 minutes

FIVE WEEKS IN A BALLOON

★★★

DIRECTOR: Irwin Allen

CAST: Red Buttons, Barbara Eden, Fabian, Cedric Hardwicke, Peter Lorre, Herbert Marshall, Billy Gilbert, Reginald Owen, Henry Daniell, Barbara Luna, Richard Haydn

Up, up, and away on a balloon expedition to Africa, or, Kenya here we come! Author Jules Verne wrote the story. Nothing heavy here, just good, clean fun and adventure in the mold of *Around the World in Eighty Days*.

1962 101 minutes

FLAME AND THE ARROW, THE

★★★★

DIRECTOR: Jacques Tourneur

CAST: Burt Lancaster, Virginia Mayo, Nick Cravat

Burt Lancaster is at his acrobatic, tongue-in-cheek best in this film as a Robin Hood–like hero in Italy leading his oppressed countrymen to victory. It's a rousing swashbuckler.

1950 88 minutes

FLAME OF THE BARBARY COAST

★★½

DIRECTOR: Joseph Kane

CAST: John Wayne, Ann Dvorak, William Frawley, Joseph Schildkraut

John Wayne plays a Montana rancher who fights with a saloon owner (Joseph Schildkraut) over the affections of a dance hall girl (Ann Dvorak). This romantic triangle takes place against the backdrop of the San Francisco earthquake. It's watchable, nothing more.

1945 B & W 91 minutes

FLASH AND THE FIRECAT

★

DIRECTOR: Ferd and Beverly Sebastian

CAST: Richard Kiel, Roger Davis, Tricia Sembera

Flash (Roger Davis) and Firecat (Tricia Sembera) blaze across the California beaches, stealing cars and robbing banks and doing other dumb things. Nevertheless, surprisingly, they outwit the authorities and eventually get away with their crime spree, proving once again that crime pays—but only in trashy movies like this one.

1975 94 minutes

FLASHPOINT

★★★½

DIRECTOR: William Tannen

CAST: Kris Kristofferson, Treat Williams, Rip Torn, Kevin Conway, Tess Harper

Kris Kristofferson and Treat Williams star in this taut, suspenseful, and action-filled thriller as two Texas border officers who accidentally uncover an abandoned jeep containing a skeleton, a rifle, and $800,000 in cash—a discovery that puts their lives in danger.

Rated PG-13 for profanity and violence.

1984 95 minutes

FLAT TOP

★★

DIRECTOR: Lesley Selander

CAST: Richard Carlson, Sterling Hayden, Keith Larsen, Bill Phillips

A mediocre World War II action film following the exploits of an aircraft carrier battling the Japanese forces in the Pacific. Most of the battle scenes are taken from actual combat footage.

1952 B & W 83 minutes

FLESH AND BLOOD

★★★½

DIRECTOR: Paul Verhoeven

CAST: Rutger Hauer, Jennifer Jason Leigh, Tom Burlinson, Susan Tyrrel, Ronald Lacey, Jack Thompson

Set in medieval Europe, *Flesh and Blood* follows the lives of two men—mercenary soldier Rutger Hauer and the son of a feudal lord (Tom Burlinson)—and their love for the same woman (Jennifer Jason Leigh). Like most films by Paul Verhoeven (*Soldier of Orange; Spetters; The Fourth Man*), the dialogue is awkward, but this weak point is more than made up for by the Dutch director's keen eye for the visceral and erotic. The cast is stellar, the sets are lavish, and the plot turns will keep the viewer guessing, but not in the dark. Rated R for violence, sex, nudity, profanity.

1985 126 minutes

FLETCH

★★★★

DIRECTOR: Michael Ritchie

CAST: Chevy Chase, Joe Don Baker, Tim Matheson, Dana Wheeler-Nicholson, Richard Libertini, M. Emmet Walsh

After seven years and seven disappointing movie performances, Chevy Chase proved that he could be a big-screen presence with this *Beverly Hills Cop*–style cops-and-comedy caper. Chase plays Gregory Mcdonald's wisecracking reporter, I. M. "Fletch" Fletcher, who starts out doing what seems to be a fairly simple exposé of drug dealing in Los Angeles and ends up taking on a corrupt cop (Joe Don Baker), a tough managing editor (Richard Libertini), and a powerful millionaire (Tim Matheson) who wants Fletch to kill him. The laughs are plenty and the action almost nonstop in director Michael Ritchie's best film since *The Bad News Bears*. Rated PG for violence and profanity.

1985 96 minutes

FLIGHT OF THE PHOENIX, THE

★★★★

DIRECTOR: Robert Aldrich

CAST: James Stewart, Richard Attenborough, Peter Finch, Ernest Borgnine, Hardy Kruger, Ronald Fraser, Christian Marquand, Richard Jaeckel, Ian Bannen, George Kennedy, Dan Duryea

An all-star international cast shines in this gripping adventure about the desert crash of a small plane and the grueling efforts of the meager band of passengers to rebuild and repair it against impossible odds, not the least of which are starvation and/or heat prostration. Tension mounts as the determined bunch begins to realize the futility of their task under the blazing Arabian sun . . . and their own well-fueled tempers. Directed with style by veteran Robert Aldrich in the rugged area near Yuma, Arizona, with stalwart performances by all. Watch this movie by all means, but keep a water cooler handy!

1965 147 minutes

FLYING LEATHERNECKS, THE

★★★½

DIRECTOR: Nicholas Ray
CAST: John Wayne, Robert Ryan, Jay C. Flippen

John Wayne is the apparently heartless commander of an airborne fighting squad, and Robert Ryan is the caring officer who questions his decisions in this well-acted war film from 1951. The stars play off each other surprisingly well, and it's a shame they didn't do more films together.

1951 102 minutes

FLYING TIGERS, THE

★★½

DIRECTOR: David Miller
CAST: John Wayne, Mae Clarke, Gordon Jones

Exciting dogfight action scenes make this low-budget John Wayne World War II vehicle watchable, but the story sags a bit.

1942 B & W 102 minutes

FOLLOW THAT CAR

★

DIRECTOR: Daniel Haller
CAST: Dirk Benedict, Tanya Tucker, Teri Nunn

Typical good-ol'-boy action-adventure with our three stars, Dirk Benedict, Tanya Tucker, and Teri Nunn, joining forces with Uncle Sam to get bad guys who are running booze and tobacco without paying any taxes. Lots of singing for Tucker fans and car chases and corny dialogue for the *Cannonball Run* crowd. Nothing new here. Rated PG for language and violence.

1980 96 minutes

FOR YOUR EYES ONLY

★★★★

DIRECTOR: John Glen
CAST: Roger Moore, Carol Bouqete, Lynn-Holly Johnson, Topol

For the first time since Roger Moore took over the role of 007 from Sean Connery, we have a film in the style that made the best Bond films—*From Russia with Love* and *Goldfinger*—so enjoyable. Gone are the outrageous gadgets and campy humor; instead, *For Your Eyes Only* is genuine spy adventure, closer in spirit to the novels by Ian Fleming. Rated PG.

1981 127 minutes

FORCE FIVE

★★

DIRECTOR: Walter Grauman
CAST: Gerald Gordon, Nick Pryor, Bradford Dillman

In this action-packed but predictable martial arts film, a soldier of fortune and his four buddies rescue a woman held against her will by an evil cult leader on a remote island. Rated R for violence, nudity, and profanity.

1975 78 minutes

FORCE OF ONE

★★★

DIRECTOR: Paul Aaron
CAST: Chuck Norris, Jennifer O'Neill, James Whitmore, Pepe Serna

This is the sequel to *Good Guys Wear Black*. In this karate film, Chuck Norris cleans up a California town that has drug problems. As always, it only takes one good guy (Norris) to kick and/or punch some sense into the bad guys. Rated PG.

1979 90 minutes

FORCE TEN FROM NAVARONE

★

DIRECTOR: Guy Hamilton
CAST: Robert Shaw, Harrison Ford, Edward Fox, Franco Nero, Barbara Bach, Carl Weathers, Richard Kiel

This is a really bad film and poor sequel to the classic *Guns of Na-*

varone. Decent acting is the only good thing you can say about this World War II film about a commando group out to destroy a bridge.

1978 118 minutes

FORCED VENGEANCE

★★½

DIRECTOR: James Fargo
CAST: Chuck Norris, Mary Louise Weller, Camilla Griggs, Michael Cavanaugh, David Opatoshu, Seiji Sakaguchi

Even pacing and a somewhat suspenseful plot are not enough to make this film a must-see—unless you're a die-hard Chuck Norris fan, that is. This time, our martial arts master plays an ex–Vietnam vet turned casino security chief living in the Far East who gets vengeance on an underworld crime syndicate. Rated R for violence, nudity, and profanity.

1982 90 minutes

FOUR DEUCES, THE

★★

DIRECTOR: William H. Bushnell Jr.
CAST: Jack Palance, Carol Lynley, Warren Berlinger, Adam Roarke, Gianni Russo, H. B. Haggerty, John Haymer, Martin Kove, E. J. Peaker

Jack Palance (*Shane;* the *Ripley's Believe It or Not* TV show) is a gang leader during Prohibition times in this high-camp action film about gangsters. Adam Roarke (*The Stunt Man*) plays a reporter who is allowed to follow the boss around and get exclusives on gangland activities. Palance's performance is excellent, but the movie is poorly conceived, with an odd mixture of blood and spoof. Not a black comedy; not a serious drama, either. *The Four Deuces* does not have an MPAA rating, but it contains sex, nudity, violence, and profanity.

1975 87 minutes

FOUR FEATHERS, THE

★★★★

DIRECTOR: Zoltán Korda
CAST: Ralph Richardson, John Clements, June Duprez, C. Aubrey Smith

A young man (John Clements) from a military background is branded a coward when he forsakes military duty for a home and family during time of war. Rejected by his family, friends, and fiancée, he sets out to prove his manhood. This motion picture was one of the few English productions of its era to gain wide acceptance. It still holds up well today.

1939 115 minutes

FOUR HORSEMEN OF THE APOCALYPSE

★★

DIRECTOR: Vincente Minnelli
CAST: Glenn Ford, Ingrid Thulin, Charles Boyer, Lee J. Cobb, Paul Henreid, Paul Lukas

The 1921 silent version of this complex anti-war tale of two brothers who fight on opposite sides during World War I is still the best. When Rudolph Valentino played Julio, you cared. This one, updated to World War II, falls flat, despite a fine cast.

1961 153 minutes

FOUR MUSKETEERS, THE

★★★★★

DIRECTOR: Richard Lester
CAST: Oliver Reed, Raquel Welch, Richard Chamberlain, Frank Finlay, Michael York, Christopher Lee, Faye Dunaway, Charlton Heston

In this superb sequel to Richard Lester's *The Three Musketeers*, the all-star cast is remarkably good, and the director is at the peak of his form. The final duel between Michael York and Christopher Lee is a stunner. Watched together, the two splendid swashbucklers make a memorable evening of entertainment. If only they made movies this well more often. Rated PG.

1975 108 minutes

FRAMED

★

DIRECTOR: Phil Karlson

CAST: Joe Don Baker, Conny Van Dyke, Gabriel Dell, Brock Peters, John Marley

Thoroughly nauseating and graphically violent story of a man (John Don Baker) framed for a crime he did not commit, and the outrageous lengths to which he resorts in order to clear his name. This is little more than an attempt to capitalize on the success of *Walking Tall* and deserves to stay buried. Rated R for gory violence and language.

1975 106 minutes

FRENCH CONNECTION, THE

★★★★★

DIRECTOR: William Friedkin

CAST: Gene Hackman, Fernando Rey, Roy Scheider, Eddie Egan, Sonny Gross

Gene Hackman is an unorthodox New York narcotics cop in this Oscar-winning performance. He and his partner (Roy Scheider) are investigating the flow of heroin coming into the city from France. The climactic chase is the best in movie history. Hackman's pursuit of the bad guy in a subway train, his car, and finally by foot is as exciting a scene as Hollywood has ever turned out. Rated R.

1971 104 minutes

FROM HELL TO BORNEO

★★

DIRECTOR: George Montgomery

CAST: George Montgomery, Torin Thatcher, Julie Gregg, Lisa Moreno

George Montgomery owns an island. Crooks and smugglers want in. He defends it. Sweat and jungle.

1964 96 minutes

FROM RUSSIA WITH LOVE

★★★★½

DIRECTOR: Terence Young

CAST: Sean Connery, Lotte Lenya, Robert Shaw, Daniela Bianchi

The definitive James Bond movie. Sean Connery's second portrayal of Agent 007 is right on target. Lots of action, beautiful women, and great villains. Connery's fight aboard a passenger train with baddy Robert Shaw is as good as they come.

1963 118 minutes

FUNERAL IN BERLIN

★★★½

DIRECTOR: Guy Hamilton

CAST: Michael Caine, Oscar Homolka, Eva Renzi, Paul Hubschmid, Guy Doleman

Second in Michael Caine's series of three "Harry Palmer" films, following *The Ipcress File* and preceding *The Billion-Dollar Brain*. This time, working-class spy Palmer assists in the possible defection of a top Russian security chief (Oscar Homolka). Director Guy Hamilton abandons his usually light touch for this more somber examination of cold war relationships. As usual, Caine can do no wrong; his brittle performance and the authentic footage of the Berlin Wall add considerably to the film's bleak tone. The other, more intriguing, side of James Bond–type secret agents. Unrated; suitable for family viewing.

1967 102 minutes

GAME OF DEATH

DIRECTOR: Robert Clouse

CAST: Bruce Lee, Kareem Abdul-Jabbar, Danny Inosanto, Gig

Young, Hugh O'Brian, Colleen Camp, Dean Jagger, Chuck Norris

The climactic twenty minutes of Bruce Lee in action fighting Kareem Abdul-Jabbar and Danny Inosanto are thrilling. It's too bad the rest of the film is not. Though top-billed, Lee only appears in those few scenes. He died shortly after their completion. It was left to film producer Raymond Chow and his associates to build a film around them to capitalize on Lee's popularity. The story, designed by Jan Spears to fit the final scenes, is schlocky and inept. Plus, the phony Bruce Lees look nothing like the original. Rated R.

1979 102 minutes

GANGSTER WARS

★★½

DIRECTOR: Richard C. Sarafian
CAST: Michael Nouri, Brian Benben, Joe Penny

This movie traces the lives of mobsters "Lucky" Luciano, "Bugsy" Siegel, and Meyer Lansky from their childhood friendship to becoming the most powerful leaders in organized crime during the 1920s. This is an action-packed gangster movie, which at times is difficult to follow and tends to lead the viewer down some dead ends. Rated PG for violence.

1981 121 minutes

GATOR

★★

DIRECTOR: Burt Reynolds
CAST: Burt Reynolds, Jack Weston, Lauren Hutton, Jerry Reed, Alice Ghostley, Mike Douglas, Dub Taylor

Burt Reynolds directed this mildly entertaining sequel to *White Lightning*. In it, Burt plays an ex-con out to get revenge—with the help of undercover agent Jack Weston—on some nasty southern politicians. Rated PG.

1976 116 minutes

GAUNTLET, THE

★½

DIRECTOR: Clint Eastwood
CAST: Clint Eastwood, Sondra Locke, Pat Hingle, William Prince

One of actor-director Clint Eastwood's few failures, this release features the squinty-eyed star as an alcoholic, barely capable cop assigned to bring a prostitute (Sondra Locke) to trial. Corrupt officials do everything they can to stop him, which leads to a completely preposterous and violent showdown. Rated R.

1977 109 minutes

GETAWAY, THE

★★★★

DIRECTOR: Sam Peckinpah
CAST: Steve McQueen, Ali MacGraw, Ben Johnson, Sally Struthers

Topnotch adventure and excitement occur when convict Steve McQueen has his wife seduce the Texas Parole Board chairman (Ben Johnson) in exchange for his early freedom. McQueen becomes jealous and resentful after the deal is consummated and kills the chairman, setting off a shotgun-charged chase. High-quality acting and exciting gunfire exchanges orchestrated by master director Sam Peckinpah make this film. Rated PG.

1972 122 minutes

GETTING EVEN

★½

DIRECTOR: Dwight H. Little
CAST: Edward Albert, Audrey Landers, Joe Don Baker

This is a fast-paced but unspectacular action-adventure film. The hero is a wealthy industrialist with a passion for danger. Fighting terrorism for the U.S. government, he attempts to stop a rival from killing the people of Texas with nerve gas. Rated R for violence and nudity.

1986 89 minutes

GHOST PATROL

★★

DIRECTOR: Sam Newfield

CAST: Tim McCoy, Claudia Dell, Walter Miller, Wheeler Oakman, Lloyd Ingraham, Dick Curtis, Slim Whitaker, Jim Burtis, Jack Casey

Colonel Tim McCoy, western historian and lifelong advocate of the American Indian and the pioneer spirit, takes a commanding lead in this low-budget film about a government agent investigating the strange crashes of airplanes carrying top-secret information. McCoy carries himself with authority whether on horseback or behind the controls of a plane. This pseudoscience-fiction story appears to have been an effort to cash in on the unexpected success of Gene Autry's *Phantom Empire* and Tom Mix's *Miracle Rider*.

1936 B & W 57 minutes

GHOST WARRIOR

★★

DIRECTOR: Larry Carbol

CAST: Hiroshi Fujioka, John Calvin, Janet Julian, Charles Lampkin, Frank Schuller, Andy Wood

In Japan, two skiers exploring a cave find a four-hundred-year-old samurai warrior entombed in ice. He is taken to the United States in a hush-hush operation and revived. All goes well until an unscrupulous hospital orderly, aware of the value of the samurai's ancient weaponry, tries to steal his sword. The samurai, trying to protect himself and his property, kills the orderly and escapes from the hospital. On the streets he confronts an alien modern world. Although slow at times and obviously derivative of the film *Iceman*, *Ghost Warrior* is an entertaining, though violent, diversion. Rated R for violence.

1984 86 minutes

GLITTER DOME, THE

★★½

DIRECTOR: Stuart Margolin

CAST: James Garner, Margot Kidder, John Lithgow, Colleen Dewhurst, John Marley

Made-for-HBO cable television version of Joseph Wambaugh's depressingly downbeat story concerning two police detectives in Los Angeles, James Garner and John Lithgow, out to solve a murder. Both cops appear on the edge of losing control. This one will not go down as one of the better Wambaugh adaptations. Check out *The Onion Field* or *The Black Marble* for the author at his best.

1985 90 minutes

GLORIA

★★★½

DIRECTOR: John Cassavetes

CAST: Gena Rowlands, Buck Henry, John Adames, Julie Carmen, Lupe Guarnica

After his family is executed by the Mafia, a little boy hides out with a female neighbor. Together they must flee or be killed. Gena Rowlands is very good in the title role as the streetwise Gloria, whose savvy and brains keep the two alive. Rated R—language, violence.

1980 121 minutes

GO FOR IT

★★

DIRECTOR: Paul Rapp

CAST: Documentary

Go For It is just like those documentary shorts that sometimes precede a first-run film in order to fill out the program. The only difference is that this is ninety minutes long and repetitious. We see all sorts of leisure sports. Included are snow skiing, surfing, mountain climbing, rafting, hang gliding, and skateboarding. Director Paul Rapp attempts to break the monotony by switching from one sport to another. The result is that the audience keeps expecting the film to end. Rated PG for nudity.

1978 90 minutes

GO TELL THE SPARTANS

★★★★

DIRECTOR: Ted Post
CAST: Burt Lancaster, Craig Wasson, Marc Singer

In one of the best Vietnam war films, Burt Lancaster is as a commander who begins to wonder "what we're doing over there." It's a very honest portrayal of America's early days in Vietnam, with Lancaster giving an excellent performance. Ted Post's direction has never been better. Rated R.

1978 114 minutes

GOLDEN CHILD, THE

★★

DIRECTOR: Michael Ritchie
CAST: Eddie Murphy, Charlotte Lewis, Charles Dance, Randall "Tex" Cobb, Victor Wong, James Hong

Ever wonder what it would be like to see Eddie Murphy in a cheapo fantasy film with kung-fu fight scenes? Neither did we, but this is essentially what you get in *The Golden Child*, a movie whose success at the box office remains singularly baffling. Murphy stars as a Los Angeles social worker who is stunned when members of a religious sect call him "The Chosen One" and expect him to save a magical child from the forces of evil. You'll be even more stunned when you watch this cheesy comedy-adventure and realize it was one of the biggest hits of its year. Rated PG-13 for violence and profanity.

1986 96 minutes

GOLDFINGER

★★★★

DIRECTOR: Guy Hamilton
CAST: Sean Connery, Gert Fröbe, Honor Blackman, Harold Sakata

Goldfinger is so enjoyable to watch that it's easy to forget the influence of the film on the spy-adventure genre. From the pre-credits sequence (cut out of most TV versions) to the final spectacular fight with Goldfinger's superhuman henchman, Oddjob (Harold Sakata), the film firmly establishes characters and situations that measured not only future Bond films but all spy films to follow. Sean Connery is the ultimate 007, John Barry's music is unforgettable, and Oddjob made bowler hats fashionable for heavies.

1964 108 minutes

GOLIATH AND THE BARBARIANS

★★

DIRECTOR: Carlo Campogalliani
CAST: Steve Reeves, Bruce Cabot, Giulia Rubini, Chelo Alonso

Steve Reeves plays Goliath in this so-so Italian action film. In this episode, he saves Italy from invading barbaric tribes. As in many of Reeves's films, the only object of interest is the flexing of his muscles.

1960 86 minutes

GONE IN 60 SECONDS

★

DIRECTOR: H. B. Halicki
CAST: H. B. Halicki, Marion Busia, George Cole, James McIntyre, Jerry Daugirda

Stuntman-turned-film-auteur H. B. Halicki can wreck a bunch of cars faster than you can say Hal Needham, but when it comes to making a watchable action film, George Miller he ain't. This movie, about a ring of car thieves working under the front of an insurance adjustment firm, is bone dull except for the forty-minute car chase finale, which is twenty minutes too long. Rated PG for violence.

1974 97 minutes

GOOD GUYS WEAR BLACK

★★

DIRECTOR: Ted Post

CAST: Chuck Norris, Anne Archer, James Franciscus, Lloyd Haynes, Jim Backus, Dana Andrews

This Chuck Norris action film starts out well but quickly dissolves into a routine political action-thriller that really goes nowhere. Lightweight entertainment. Rated PG.

1979 96 minutes

GOONIES, THE

★★★

DIRECTOR: Richard Donner

CAST: Sean Astin, Josh Brolin, Jeff Cohen, Corey Feldman, Kerri Green, Martha Plimpton, Ke Huy-Quan

This "Steven Spielberg production" is a mess. But it's sometimes an entertaining mess. Directed in jerky style by Richard Donner (*Superman—The Movie*) from a quirky screenplay by Chris Columbus, it's a grab bag of good and bad. One minute it's frustratingly weird and inane; the next minute something utterly delightful happens. The screenplay, taken from a story by Spielberg, concerns a feisty group of underprivileged kids—whose housing project is about to be destroyed—spending one last adventure-filled Saturday afternoon together. This happens after they find a treasure map, which could be the solution to all their problems. Rated PG for profanity.

1985 111 minutes

GORKY PARK

★★½

DIRECTOR: Michael Apted

CAST: William Hurt, Lee Marvin, Joanna Pacula, Brian Dennehy, Ian Bannen, Alexander Knox

In this maddeningly uninvolving screen version of Martin Cruz Smith's best-selling mystery novel, three mutilated bodies are found in the Moscow park, and it's up to Russian policeman Arkady Renko (a miscast William Hurt) to find the maniacal killer. Lee Marvin is quite good as a suave bad guy, as are Joanna Pacula and Brian Dennehy in their supporting roles. Still, there's something missing in this release, directed by Michael Apted (*Coal Miner's Daughter*). It's a thriller that isn't all that thrilling. Rated R for nudity, sex, violence, and profanity.

1983 128 minutes

GOTCHA!

★★★★

DIRECTOR: Jeff Kanew

CAST: Anthony Edwards, Linda Fiorentino, Alex Rocco, Nick Carri, Marla Adams, Klaus Loewitsch

In this wonderfully entertaining mixture of the coming-of-age comedy and the suspense thriller, a college boy (Anthony Edwards from *Revenge of the Nerds*) goes to Paris in search of romance and adventure. He gets both when he meets a beautiful, mysterious woman (Linda Fiorentino, of *Vision Quest*) who puts both of their lives in danger. When you're not laughing, you're on the edge of your seat. That's what entertainment is all about. Rated PG-13 for slight nudity, suggested sex, profanity, and violence.

1985 97 minutes

GRAND THEFT AUTO

★★½

DIRECTOR: Ron Howard

CAST: Ron Howard, Nancy Morgan

The basic plot of *It's a Mad Mad Mad Mad World* is given a retread by first-time director—and star—Ron Howard in this frantic 1977 car-chase comedy. Sadly, little of the style that made *Night Shift* and *Splash* such treats is evident here. Rated PG.

1977 89 minutes

GRAY LADY DOWN

★★★½

DIRECTOR: David Greene

CAST: Charlton Heston, David Carradine, Stacy Keach, Ned Beatty, Ronny Cox, Rosemary Forsyth

This adventure film starring Charlton Heston is action-packed and well-acted. The story concerns a two-man rescue operation of a sunken nuclear sub that has accidentally collided with a freighter. Beautiful photography and special effects highlight the drama pitting man and machine against time and underwater dangers.

1977 111 minutes

GREASED LIGHTNING

★★★

DIRECTOR: Michael Schultz

CAST: Richard Pryor, Pam Grier, Beau Bridges, Cleavon Little, Richie Havens

Greased Lightning is a funny and exciting film. Richard Pryor is a knockout in the lead role, and the film is a real audience pleaser. Because the story is true, it carries a punch even *Rocky* couldn't match. Comparisons of the two films are inevitable, as both center on the ambitions of sports hopefuls and feature slam-bang endings that bring the audience to its feet rooting for the hero. While Rocky Balboa remains a stirring character of fiction, Wendell Scott's story is the more dramatic of the two. Scott was the first black man to win a NASCAR Grand National stock car race. Rated PG.

1977 96 minutes

GREAT CHASE, THE

★★★★

NARRATED BY: Frank Gallop

CAST: Buster Keaton, Douglas Fairbanks Sr., Lillian Gish, Pearl White

Silent film chases from several classics comprise the bulk of this compilation, including the running acrobatics of Douglas Fairbanks in *The Mark of Zorro*, the escape of Lillian Gish over the ice floes in *Way Down East*, and car chases and stunts of all descriptions from silent comedies. A large part of the film is devoted to Buster Keaton's locomotive chase from *The General*.

1963 B & W 79 minutes

GREAT ESCAPE, THE

★★★★★

DIRECTOR: John Sturges

CAST: Steve McQueen, James Garner, Charles Bronson, Richard Attenborough, James Coburn

If ever there was a movie that could be called pure cheer-the-heroes entertainment, it's *The Great Escape*. The plot centers around a German prison camp in World War II. The commandant has received the assignment of housing all the escape-minded Allied prisoners, or, as he puts it, "putting all the rotten eggs in one basket." The Germans are obviously playing with fire with this all-star group, and, sure enough, all hell breaks loose with excitement galore.

1963 168 minutes

GREAT RIVIERA BANK ROBBERY, THE

★★★½

DIRECTOR: Francis Megahy
CAST: Ian McShane, Warren Clarke, Stephen Greif, Christopher Malcolm

In 1976, a group of French right-wing terrorists called "The Chain," with the assistance of a gang of thieves, pulled off one of the largest heists in history. The step-by-step illustration of this bold operation proves to be interesting, and the fact that this incident really happened makes this film all the more enjoyable.

1979 98 minutes

GREAT SMOKEY ROADBLOCK, THE

★★½

DIRECTOR: John Leone
CAST: Henry Fonda, Eileen Brennan, John Byner, Dub Taylor, Susan Sarandon, Austin Pendleton

Entertaining if somewhat hokey comedy-drama casts Henry Fonda as a trucker on the verge of losing his rig, when along comes a homeless entourage of prostitutes (led by Eileen Brennan), who persuade Henry to take them for a ride. Good-natured film is a good time-passer. Rated PG for language.

1976 84 minutes

GREAT TEXAS DYNAMITE CHASE, THE

★½

DIRECTOR: Michael Pressman
CAST: Claudia Jennings, Jocelyn Jones, Johnny Crawford, Chris Pennock

Bullets and bodies fly in this low-budget cult film about two female bank robbers who blast their way across the countryside. Former Playmate Claudia Jennings adds the extra zest to this otherwise routine drive-in feature. Look for Johnny Crawford, of *The Rifleman* fame, in a featured role. Violence, some nudity, suggestive scenes. Rated R.

1977 90 minutes

GREAT TRAIN ROBBERY, THE

★★★★

DIRECTOR: Michael Crichton
CAST: Sean Connery, Lesley-Anne Down, Donald Sutherland, Alan Webb

Michael Crichton's film version of *The Great Train Robbery* is just as entertaining as his novel of the same name. Based on a true incident, this suspense-filled caper has plenty of hooks to keep you interested. But the title may be misleading; it is not a remake of the famous silent western. In fact, the story takes place in Victorian England. The cast is superb. Sean Connery is dashing and convincing as mastermind Edward Pierce. Lesley-Anne Down is stunning as his mistress, accomplice, and disguise expert. Add a pinch of Donald Sutherland as a boastful pickpocket and cracksman and you have a trio of crooks that can steal your heart. Rated PG.

1979 111 minutes

GREAT WALDO PEPPER, THE

★★★

DIRECTOR: George Roy Hill
CAST: Robert Redford, Bo Svenson, Susan Sarandon, Bo Boundin

The daredevil barnstorming pilots of the era between the world wars are sent a pleasant valentine by director George Roy Hill in this flying film. Robert Redford, in a satisfying low-key performance, is Waldo Pepper, a barnstormer who yearns for the action of the World War I dogfights. The flight scenes are topnotch. Only the script leaves the audience wanting more. It just isn't meaty enough

to hold the interest of those who aren't flying buffs. Rated PG.
1975 108 minutes

GREEN ARCHER

★★

DIRECTOR: James W. Horne
CAST: Victor Jory, Iris Meredith, James Craven, Robert Fiske, Dorothy Fay, Forrest Taylor, Jack Ingram, Fred Kelsey, Joseph W. Girard, Kit Guard

Detective Spike Holland tries to unravel the mystery of Garr Castle after he is called in to investigate the disappearance of Valerie Howett's sister, Elaine. A jealous claimant to the castle as well as a gang of jewel thieves thicken the plot in this venerable old Edgar Wallace story. Faithfully remade for Columbia as a fifteen-episode serial, this story was originally filmed by Pathé Studios in 1925 with the popular team of Allene Ray and Walter Miller. Lots of sliding panels and silhouettes of the phantom bowman in this slow-moving chapter play. Fine character actor Victor Jory (who also played The Shadow in a serial) is wasted in his role although he gives it what he can.
1940 B & W 15 chapters

GREEN BERETS, THE

★★★½

DIRECTORS: John Wayne, Ray Kellogg
CAST: John Wayne, David Janssen, Jim Hutton, Aldo Ray, Raymond St. Jacques, Bruce Cabot, Jack Soo, George Takei, Patrick Wayne

John Wayne's Vietnam war movie is much better than its reputation would suggest. We were fully prepared to hate the film after having avoided it when originally released. However, it turned out to be an exciting and enjoyable (albeit typical) Wayne vehicle. Although somewhat simplistic politically, it fits in well with such contemporary releases as *Uncommon Valor* and *Missing in Action*. Rated G.
1968 141 minutes

GREEN ICE

★½

DIRECTOR: Ernest Day
CAST: Ryan O'Neal, Anne Archer, Omar Sharif

Unconvincing tale of an emerald theft in Colombia. Ryan O'Neal engineers the robbery. Rated PG.
1981 115 minutes

GREYSTOKE: THE LEGEND OF TARZAN, LORD OF THE APES

★★★½

DIRECTOR: Hugh Hudson
CAST: Christopher Lambert, Andie McDowell, Ian Holm, Ralph Richardson, James Fox, Cheryl Campbell

Director Hugh Hudson, whose uplifting *Chariots of Fire* swept the Oscars in 1982, made one of the few Tarzan movies to remain faithful to the books and original character created by Edgar Rice Burroughs. For those unacquainted with the ape-man made famous—or infamous, depending on whether you're a Burroughs purist or not—by the barely verbal Johnny Weissmuller, Tarzan is a half-savage survivor of the jungle. Here, in one dramatic leap, he goes from the dank, dangerous rain forests of West Africa to claim his rightful heritage—a baronial mansion in Scotland and a title as the seventh Earl of Greystoke. Rated PG for nudity and violence.
1984 129 minutes

GUMBALL RALLY, THE

★★½

DIRECTOR: Chuck Bail
CAST: Michael Sarrazin, Gary Busey, Tim McIntire, Raul Julia, Normann Burton

First film based on an anything-goes cross-country road race. Featuring some excellent stunt driving, with occasional laughs, it's much better than *Cannonball Run*. Rated PG for language.
1976 107 minutes

GUNG HO!

★★½

DIRECTOR: Ray Enright
CAST: Randolph Scott, Grace McDonald, Alan Curtis, Noah Beery Jr., J. Carrol Naish, David Bruce, Robert Mitchum, Sam Levene

Although not meant to be funny, this ultrapatriotic war film has its truly outrageous moments. It must have been a real booster for wartime film-goers in America. Today it's almost embarrassing—particularly during the scene in which a recruit is accepted into a special team of commandos simply because he "hates Japs."
1943 B & W 88 minutes

GUNGA DIN

★★★★★

DIRECTOR: George Stevens
CAST: Cary Grant, Victor McLaglen, Douglas Fairbanks Jr., Joan Fontaine, Sam Jaffe, Eduardo Ciannelli

An acknowledged classic, this release has it all: laughs, thrills, and chills. Howard Hawks was originally set to direct it and played a large part in its creation. That explains why it is so unlike the rest of director George (*Shane*; *Giant*) Stevens's other films. For sheer entertainment, regardless of who directed it, *Gunga Din* is tops. Plot: Three soldiers in nineteenth-century India put down a native uprising with the help of an Indian water carrier.
1939 B & W 117 minutes

GUNS OF NAVARONE, THE

★★★★

DIRECTOR: J. Lee Thompson
CAST: Gregory Peck, David Niven, Anthony Quinn, Stanley Baker, Anthony Quayle, James Darren

Along with *The Great Escape*, this film is one of the best World War II adventure yarns. Gregory Peck, David Niven, and Anthony Quinn are part of a multinational task force that is sent to Greece with a mission to destroy two huge German batteries that threaten a fleet of Allied troop transports. Their attempt to land undetected and blow up the guns from under the Nazis' noses keeps you on the edge of your seat from start to finish.
1961 157 minutes

GYMKATA

★

DIRECTOR: Robert Clouse
CAST: Kurt Thomas, Tetchie Agbayani, Richard Norton, Edward Bell, John Barrett

Gold medal–winning World Champion gymnast Kurt Thomas stars in this disappointing fist-and-foot actioner as a secret agent who must compete in a deadly athletics competition to retrieve U.S. secrets. If the plot sounds suspiciously familiar to *Enter the Dragon*, it should. Director Robert Clouse and producer Fred Weintraub scored their biggest commercial and artistic success with that classic adventure film starring Bruce Lee. *Gymkata* not only doesn't come close to the latter; it's an insult to its star. Rated R for violence.
1985 90 minutes

HAMMETT

★

DIRECTOR: Wim Wenders
CAST: Frederic Forrest, Peter Boyle, Marilu Henner, Elisha Cook Jr., R. G. Armstrong

A disappointing homage to mystery writer Dashiell Hammett, this Wim Wenders–directed and Francis Ford Coppola–meddled production was two years in the making and hardly seems worth it. The plot is nearly incomprehensible, something that could never be said of the real-life Hammett's works (*The Maltese Falcon*; *The Thin Man*; etc.). Rated PG.

1982 97 minutes

HARD COUNTRY

★★★½

DIRECTOR: David Greene
CAST: Jan-Michael Vincent, Michael Parks, Kim Basinger, Gailard Sartain, Tanya Tucker, Ted Neeley

Though it tries to make a statement about the contemporary cowboy lost in the modern world and feminism in the boondocks, this is really just light-hearted entertainment. It's full of barroom brawls, beer-chugging contests, and hillbilly jokes. It's a lot like a Clint Eastwood comedy; a rockabilly love story of the macho man (Jan-Michael Vincent) versus the liberated woman (Kim Basinger). The foot-stomping soundtrack is by Tanya Tucker and Michael Martin Murphey, with his Great American Honky Tonk Band. Rated PG.

1981 104 minutes

HARD TIMES

★★★★½

DIRECTOR: Walter Hill
CAST: Charles Bronson, James Coburn, Jill Ireland, Strother Martin

This release is far and away one of Charles Bronson's best starring vehicles. In it he plays a bare-knuckles fighter who teams up with a couple of hustlers, James Coburn and Strother Martin, to "sting" some local hoods. Bronson's wife, Jill Ireland, is surprisingly good as the love interest. Rated PG.

1975 97 minutes

HARD WAY, THE

★★

DIRECTOR: Michael Dryhurst
CAST: Patrick McGoohan, Lee Van Cleef, Donal McCann, Edna O'Brien, Michael Muldoon

Patrick McGoohan is an international terrorist who wants out of the business. His wife has taken the children, so he decides to quit before he loses his freedom or his life. Unfortunately for him, a former associate (Lee Van Cleef) wants him to do one more job and will have him killed if he doesn't.

1979 88 minutes

HARPER

★★★★½

DIRECTOR: Jack Smight
CAST: Paul Newman, Lauren Bacall, Shelley Winters, Arthur Hill, Julie Harris, Janet Leigh, Robert Wagner

Ross MacDonald's detective, Lew Archer, undergoes a name change but still survives as a memorable screen character in the capable hands of Paul Newman. This one ranks right up there with *The Maltese Falcon*, *The Big Sleep* (the Humphrey Bogart version), *Farewell My Lovely*, and *The Long Goodbye* as one of the best of its type. The story, in which Harper is hired to find a missing husband, has its dated moments, but the impressive all-star cast more than pulls it through.

1966 121 minutes

HATARI!

★★★

DIRECTOR: Howard Hawks
CAST: John Wayne, Elsa Martinelli, Red Buttons, Hardy Krüger

If only Howard Hawks had been able to do as he wanted and cast Clark Gable along with John Wayne in this story of zoo-supplying animal hunters in Africa, this could have been a great film. As it is, it's still enjoyable, with a fine blend of action, romance, and comedy.

1962 159 minutes

HAWK THE SLAYER

★★★

DIRECTOR: Terry Marcel
CAST: Jack Palance, John Terry

In this sword-and-sorcery adventure, John Terry plays the good Hawk, who, with his band of warriors—a dwarf and an elf among them—fights Jack Palance, his evil older brother. Palance's performance saves the film from mediocrity. Not rated; has violence.

1980 90 minutes

HEARTBREAK RIDGE

★★★

DIRECTOR: Clint Eastwood
CAST: Clint Eastwood, Marsha Mason, Everett McGill, Bo Svenson, Mario Van Peebles, Moses Gunn

Whoever thought Grenada would be the subject of cinematic war heroics? Though the film could use some trimming, the story of a hard-nosed marine sergeant whipping a hopeless-looking unit into a crack fighting team is still compelling. Actually, the most intriguing element of the movie is the rocky romance between Clint Eastwood and Marsha Mason, who plays his skeptical ex-wife. Eastwood is both amusing and touching as a macho military dinosaur trying to be a sensitive, '80s kind of guy. Rated R.

1986 126 minutes

HEART LIKE A WHEEL

★★★★

DIRECTOR: Jonathan Kaplan
CAST: Bonnie Bedelia, Beau Bridges, Leo Rossi, Hoyt Axton, Bill McKinney, Dean Paul Martin, Dick Miller

A first-rate film biography of racing champion Shirley Muldowney, this features a marvelous performance by Bonnie Bedelia as the first woman to crack the National Hot Rod Association's embargo against female competitors. When the NHRA won't let her race, veteran drivers "Big Daddy" Garlitts (Bill McKinney) and Connie Kalitta (Beau Bridges) take the lead in trying to get her on the track. It's an emotionally involving, thrilling tale of success and heartache. Rated PG for language.

1983 113 minutes

HEARTS AND ARMOUR

★★½

DIRECTOR: Giacomo Battiato
CAST: Zenda Araya, Barbara de Rossi, Rick Edwards, Ron Moss, Maurizio Nichetti, Tanya Roberts, Giovanni Vesentin, Tony Vogel

Warrior Orlando (Rick Edwards) seeks victory over the Moors and the rescue of his love (Tanya Roberts), while his female comrade-in-arms, Bradamante (Barbara de Rossi), falls in love with Ruggero (Ron Moss), the Moor whom Orlando is fated to kill. This film is loosely based on the legend of Orlando Furioso, and attempts to do for that story what *Excalibur* did for the Arthurian legends. Unfortunately, the script is not strong enough to do justice to the complex plot. Entertaining, but not extraordinary. Not rated; has violence and nudity.

1983 101 minutes

HEAT

★★½

DIRECTOR: Dick Richards
CAST: Burt Reynolds, Karen Young, Peter MacNicol, Howard Hesseman, Neill Barry, Diana Scarwid

A good try at an action thriller that doesn't succeed because of awkward pacing, uneven direction, and a mood that swings wildly from raw violence to good-buddy playfulness. Novelist-screenwriter William Goldman adapted his own book, keeping the story's thin shell but stripping away the meat that made it such a gutsy read. Burt Reynolds is a Las Vegas–based troubleshooter with two problems: an old girlfriend who craves revenge after being ill-treated by slimy syndicate types, and a mousy young executive (Peter MacNicol, stealing every scene he shared with Reynolds) who craves the ability to protect himself. Although a few attempts are made at deeper characterization, mostly with MacNicol, the film quickly degenerates into a slo-mo loner-against-many melodrama. Too bad, because it had genuine potential. Rated R for language and violence.

1987 101 minutes

HELL ON FRISCO BAY

★★★

DIRECTOR: Frank Tuttle
CAST: Alan Ladd, Joanne Dru, Edward G. Robinson, William Demarest, Fay Wray

A 1930s-type hardboiled crime story of a framed cop who does his time, is released from prison, and goes after the bigwig gangster who set him up. Lots of action on San Francisco's streets and its famous bay.

1955 98 minutes

HELL SQUAD

DIRECTOR: Kenneth Hartford
CAST: Bainbridge Scott, Glen Hartford, Tina Lederman, William Bryant, Marvin Miller

Low-budget, poorly acted action film concerns a group of Las Vegas showgirls who are recruited by the CIA. Their mission: rescue an American kidnapped by Arab terrorists. The nine women who make up the squad are nice to look at as they destroy a small army, fight wild animals, and battle the natural elements of the desert. But you can't say the same thing about this whole silly mess. Rated R for nudity and gore.

1985 88 minutes

HELLCATS OF THE NAVY

★★★

DIRECTOR: Nathan Juran
CAST: Ronald Reagan, Nancy Davis, Arthur Franz, Harry Lauter

This none-too-exciting 1957 drama has one thing to attract viewers: President Ronald Reagan and First Lady Nancy co-star.

1957 B & W 82 minutes

HELLFIGHTERS

★★

DIRECTOR: Andrew V. McLaglen
CAST: John Wayne, Katharine Ross, Vera Miles, Jim Hutton, Bruce Cabot

Once again the talents of John Wayne have been squandered. The Duke is cast as a high-priced fireman sent around the world to put out dangerous oil rig fires. Even hard-core Wayne fans will wince at this one. Rated PG.

1969 121 minutes

HELL'S ANGELS ON WHEELS

★★½

DIRECTOR: Richard Rush

CAST: Adam Roarke, Jack Nicholson, Sabrina Scharf, John Garwood, Jana Taylor

This film is one of the better 1960s biker films, most notably because Jack Nicholson has a big role in it. Not a great film by any means, but if you like biker films . . .

1967 95 minutes

HELL'S BRIGADE

★

DIRECTOR: Henry Mankiewirk

CAST: Jack Palance, John Douglas

Fairly rotten film concerning a commando raid on Hitler's Germany during World War II. Low budget, poorly acted.

1980 99 minutes

HELL'S HOUSE

★★

DIRECTOR: Howard Higgin

CAST: Junior Durkin, Bette Davis, Pat O'Brien, Junior Coghlan, Charley Grapewin, Emma Dunn

Gangster and prison films in the 1930s had their junior counterparts. In this barely so-so example, an innocent boy does time in a harsh reformatory because he won't rat on an adult crook friend. Junior Durkin is the poor kid, Pat O'Brien is the crook—a bootlegger, and Bette Davis is his girl. All hot stuff in Big Al's time.

1932 B & W 72 minutes

HERCULES

★★½

DIRECTOR: Pietro Francisci

CAST: Steve Reeves, Sylva Koscina, Ivo Garrani

The first and still the best of the Italian-made epics based on the mythical superhero. Steve Reeves looks perfect in the part as Hercules out to win over his true love, the ravishing Sylva Koscina. Some nice action scenes.

1959 107 minutes

HEROES IN HELL

DIRECTOR: Michael Wotruba

CAST: Klaus Kinski, Stan Simon, Lars Block, George Manes, Carlos Ewing, Luis Joyce, Rosemary Lindt

Lame World War II battle picture has captured Allied prisoners of war escaping from a Nazi POW camp, joining a group of partisans, and taking on the Germans. Klaus Kinski has a small role as the leader of the SS whose job is to destroy the partisans. Poorly done combat scenes and terrible acting make this a trite, boring mess. Unrated, but PG for violence would be proper.

1974 90 minutes

HIGH-BALLIN'

★★

DIRECTOR: Peter Carter

CAST: Peter Fonda, Jerry Reed, Helen Shaver, Chris Wiggins, David Ferry

Peter Fonda and Jerry Reed are good old boys squaring off against the bad boss of a rival trucking company. The film has enough action and humor to make it a passable entertainment. Helen Shaver is its most provocative element. Rated PG.

1978 100 minutes

HIGH COMMAND, THE

★★★

DIRECTOR: Thorold Dickinson

CAST: Lionel Atwill, Lucie Mannheim, James Mason

Rebellion, a new murder, and a 16-year-old killing absorb the interest of officers and men at an isolated British outpost on an island off the coast of Africa.

Honor, integrity, and the tradition of the Colonial Service are at stake in this adventure during the fading days of the British empire.
1937 B & W 84 minutes

HIGH CRIME

★★

DIRECTOR: Enzo G. Castellari
CAST: Franco Nero, James Whitmore, Fernando Rey

Narcotics cop vs. Mafia kingpin in the picturesque Italian seaport of Genoa. Full of action, but no surprises. Rated PG.
1973 100 minutes

HIGH RISK

★★½

DIRECTOR: Stewart Raffill
CAST: James Brolin, Cleavon Little, Bruce Davison, Chick Vennera, Anthony Quinn, James Coburn, Ernest Borgnine, Lindsay Wagner

While snatching $5 million from a South American drug smuggler (James Coburn), four amateur conspirators (James Brolin, Cleavon Little, Bruce Davison, and Chick Vennera) blaze their way through numerous shootouts, crossing paths with a sleazy bandit leader (Anthony Quinn), hordes of Colombian soldiers, and plenty of riotous trouble. Alternately hysterically funny, exciting, hokey, crass, and tacky, this preposterous comic-strip adventure offers diversion, but a lot of it is just plain awful. Rated R.
1981 94 minutes

HIGH ROAD TO CHINA

★★★

DIRECTOR: Brian G. Hutton
CAST: Tom Selleck, Bess Armstrong, Jack Weston, Wilford Brimley, Robert Morley, Brian Blessed

Old-fashioned movie fun is yours in this adventure film. Tom Selleck (of television's *Magnum P.I.*) stars as a World War I flying ace who, with the aid of his sidekick/mechanic, Jack Weston, helps a spoiled heiress (Bess Armstrong) track down her missing father (Wilford Brimley). Directed by Brian Hutton (*Kelly's Heroes*), it's just like the B movies of yesteryear: predictable, silly, and fun. Rated PG for violence.
1983 120 minutes

HIGH ROLLING

[turkey]

DIRECTOR: Igor Auzins
CAST: Joseph Bottoms, Grigor Taylor, Sandy Hughs, Judy Davis, John Clayton

Two out-of-work carnival workers hitchhike through Australia until they are picked up by a drug runner. They end up stealing the runner's dope, money, and his car—a hot Corvette. They soon find a young girl who joins them in their outrageous criminal adventures. One such adventure is the hijacking of a bus. Rated PG for profanity and brief nudity, this feature is a big disappointment.
1977 88 minutes

HIGH SIERRA

★★★★½

DIRECTOR: Raoul Walsh
CAST: Humphrey Bogart, Ida Lupino, Alan Curtis, Arthur Kennedy, Joan Leslie, Henry Hull

Humphrey Bogart is at his best as a bad guy with a heart of gold in this 1941 gangster film. Bogart pays for the operation that corrects pretty Joan Leslie's crippled foot, but he finds his love is misplaced. The film's mountaintop finale—as well as several scenes involving co-stars Ida Lupino, Arthur Kennedy, and Henry Hull—make it one of the finest of the Warner Bros. genre entries.
1941 B & W 100 minutes

HIGH VOLTAGE

★★½

DIRECTOR: Howard Higgin

CAST: William Boyd, Carole Lombard, Owen Moore, Diane Ellis, Billy Bevan, Phillips Smalley

Elements of *Stagecoach* are evident in this early Pathé sound film (made ten years before John Ford's classic) that teams a pre–Hopalong Cassidy William Boyd and a lovely, young Carole Lombard as a world-wise couple who fall for each other while snowbound during a bus trip in California's Sierra Nevada Mountains. Silent film star Owen Moore (first husband of Mary Pickford) plays a hardboiled detective bringing wisecracking Carole Lombard to justice on the ill-fated bus. Boyd plays a fugitive who falls for the tough but touching Carole and decides to return to civilization and face the music. There's even a comic bus driver and a crooked banker who's absconded with a satchel full of money and securities. Sound familiar? This film was co-scripted by James Gleason, who went from a distinguished career as a writer to greater recognition as the lean, tough, sardonic manager-detective-newsman of countless films of the 1930s and 1940s. Young Lombard gives a performance full of fire and frailty—her irreplaceable humor and charm are readily evident in this obscure little film. Worth a try.

1929 B & W 57 minutes

HIGHEST HONOR, THE

★★★★★

DIRECTOR: Peter Maxwell

CAST: John Howard, Atsuo Nakamura, Stuart Wilson

A story of a unique friendship between two enemies: Captain Robert Page, a young World War II U.S. Army officer, and Winoyu Tamiya, a security officer in the Japanese army. After being captured for attempting to raid Japanese ships, Page is imprisoned in Singapore and befriends Tamiya as he waits for his trial for spying. This great war film, packed with high adventure and warm human drama, is also a true story. Rated R.

1984 99 minutes

HIS KIND OF WOMAN

★★★½

DIRECTOR: John Farrow

CAST: Robert Mitchum, Jane Russell, Vincent Price, Tim Holt, Charles McGraw, Raymond Burr, Jim Backus, Marjorie Reynolds

Entertaining chase film is an adventure to watch and figure out as two-fisted gambler Robert Mitchum breezes down to South America to pick up fifty thousand dollars only to find out he's being set up for the kill. Jane Russell is in fine shape as the worldly-looking gal with a good heart, and Vincent Price steals the show as a hammy Hollywood actor who is thrilled to be involved in *real* danger and intrigue. A *Who's Who* of character actors and B-movie leads, this film is a successful blend of comedy, romance, and excitement, and in style and attitude is still superior to current color productions cut from the same cloth.

1951 B & W 120 minutes

HIT, THE

★★★★

DIRECTOR: Stephen Frears

CAST: John Hurt, Terence Stamp, Tim Roth, Fernando Rey, Laura Del Sol, Bill Hunter

The British seem to have latched on to the gangster film with a vengeance. First, they made the superb film *The Long Good Friday*, and now they've scored again with this gripping character study. John Hurt gives an unusually restrained (and highly effective) performance as a hit man assigned to take care of a squealer (Terence Stamp) who has been hiding in Spain after testifying against the mob. Hurt finds his prey full of surprises and his contract more difficult to fulfill than he might have imagined. Rated R for violence.

1984 97 minutes

HITLER'S CHILDREN

★★★★

DIRECTORS: Edward Dmytryk, Irving Reis

CAST: Tim Holt, Bonita Granville, Kent Smith, Otto Kruger

A great love story is created with the horror of Nazi Germany as a background. This film shows a young German boy who falls in love with an American girl. The boy gets caught up in Hitler's enticing web of propaganda, while his girlfriend resists all of Hitler's ideas. When the government decides to severely punish her for her resistance, her boyfriend comes to her aid.

1942 B & W 83 minutes

HOLCROFT COVENANT, THE

★★

DIRECTOR: John Frankenheimer

CAST: Michael Caine, Anthony Andrews, Victoria Tennant, Mario Adorf, Lilli Palmer

In the closing days of World War II, three infamous Nazi officers deposit a large sum of money into a Swiss bank account to be withdrawn years later by their children. The three then kill themselves to hide their secret from all but their heirs. Years later the offspring must sign a covenant before withdrawing the fortune, then use it for reparations to those who suffered during the war. But people begin to be eliminated and Michael Caine unravels a plot to use the money to establish an international terrorist network that would send the world crashing into anarchy and out of which will arise a "Fourth Reich." This slow but intriguing film, based on the novel by Robert Ludlum, will undoubtedly please spy film enthusiasts, although others may find it tedious and contrived. Rated R for adult situations.

1985 105 minutes

HOLLYWOOD VICE SQUAD

★

DIRECTOR: Penelope Spheeris

CAST: Ronny Cox, Frank Gorshin, Leon Isaac Kennedy, Trish Van de Veer, Carrie Fisher

Despite a name cast and a director—Penelope Spheeris (*Suburbia*)—who once showed promise, this semisequel to *Vice Squad* lacks even the raw energy of its predecessor. Instead, it's a tepid affair about a woman (Trish Van Devere) who goes searching for her runaway daughter in the sleazoid areas of Hollywood. Her fear is that the teenager may have becomed involved in porno or prostitution—just like George C. Scott's daughter in *Hardcore*. This similarity brings the movie's only point of interest: Van Devere and Scott are married. Big deal that they made essentially the same film, right? Right. Rated R for nudity, profanity, and violence.

1986 93 minutes

HONOR AMONG THIEVES

★★½

DIRECTOR: Jean Herman

CAST: Charles Bronson, Alain Delon, Brigitte Fossey

Charles Bronson plays a mercenary who is locked in a French bank over the weekend with Alain Delon, a doctor. Bronson is there to rob the bank of its 200 million francs, while Delon is there to replace some misappropriated securities. The two men are in constant conflict but find that they must work together. In the end, they discover they have been betrayed in a web of murder and intrigue. This is a little different type of picture for Bronson—a bit more subtle, a little slower-paced, and with more dialogue than action. Rated R.

1983 93 minutes

HOPSCOTCH

★★★★

DIRECTOR: Ronald Neame
CAST: Walter Matthau, Ned Beatty, Glenda Jackson

Walter Matthau is wonderful in this fast-paced and funny film as a spy who decides to extract a little revenge on the pompous supervisor (Ned Beatty) who demoted him. Glenda Jackson has a nice bit as Matthau's romantic interest. Rated R.

1980 104 minutes

HOT ROCK, THE

★★★★

DIRECTOR: Peter Yates
CAST: Robert Redford, George Segal, Ron Leibman, Paul Sand, Zero Mostel, Moses Gunn, William Redfield, Charlotte Rae

A neatly planned jewelry heist goes awry and the fun begins. Peter Yates's direction is razor sharp. The cast is absolutely perfect. This movie is a crowd-pleasing blend of action, humor, and suspense. It's the best caper film imaginable. Rated PG.

1972 105 minutes

HOUND OF THE BASKERVILLES, THE (ORIGINAL)

★★★★

DIRECTOR: Sidney Lanfield
CAST: Basil Rathbone, Nigel Bruce, John Carradine, Lionel Atwill, Mary Gordon, E. E. Clive, Richard Greene

The second best of the Basil Rathbone–Nigel Bruce Sherlock Holmes movies, this 1939 release marked the stars' debut in the roles for which they would forever be known. While *The Adventures of Sherlock Holmes*, which was made the same year, featured the on-screen detective team at its peak, this 20th Century Fox–produced adaptation of Sir Arthur Conan Doyle's most famous mystery novel still can be called a classic. For those unfamiliar with the story, Holmes and Watson are called upon by Henry Baskerville (Richard Greene) to save him from a curse—in the form of a hound from hell—that has plagued his family for centuries.

1939 B & W 84 minutes

HOUND OF THE BASKERVILLES, THE (REMAKE)

★★★★

DIRECTOR: Terence Fisher
CAST: Peter Cushing, Christopher Lee, André Morell, Marla Landi, Miles Malleson

One of the better adaptations of A. Conan Doyle's moody novel, and particularly enjoyable for its presentation of Peter Cushing (as Sherlock Holmes) and Christopher Lee together in non-horror roles. This British entry (from the Hammer House of Horror) caught more of the murky atmosphere than any other version of any other Holmes tale. Intelligent scripting, compelling acting, and spooky cinematography. Doyle would have been pleased.

1959 84 minutes

HOUR OF THE ASSASSIN

★½

DIRECTOR: Luis Llosa
CAST: Erik Estrada, Robert Vaughn

Action thriller set in the fictional South American country of San

Pedro where Erik Estrada has been hired by the military forces to kill the president. Robert Vaughn plays the CIA agent who has to stop him. Although this film has its share of car crashes, gunfire, and explosions, it lacks any real suspense. Rated R.

1986 96 minutes

HUNTER

★★½

DIRECTOR: Leonard Horn
CAST: John Vernon, Steve Ihnat, Fritz Weaver, Edward Binns

A brainwashed agent is programmed to release a deadly virus. The scheme is discovered, and a good guy takes his place to catch the bad guys. Made for television.

1971 73 minutes

HUNTER, THE

★★

DIRECTOR: Buzz Kulik
CAST: Steve McQueen, Eli Wallach, LeVar Burton, Ben Johnson, Kathryn Harrold

The Hunter, an uneven action film, focuses on a modern-day bounty hunter. Steve McQueen plays real-life troubleshooter Ralph "Papa" Thorson. Though old and a bit awkward, Thorson leads—at least on screen—a dangerous, action-filled life. Traveling from one state to another in pursuit of fugitives, he is constantly putting his life on the line. Rated PG.

1980 97 minutes

HURRICANE

DIRECTOR: Jan Troell
CAST: Jason Robards, Mia Farrow, Dayton Ka'ne, Max von Sydow, Trevor Howard

Another Dino de Laurentiis misfire, this remake of the John Ford classic details a love affair between Charlotte Bruckner (Mia Farrow), daughter of the governor (Jason Robards) of Pago Pago, and the young native chief, Matangi (Dayton Ka'ne). Charlotte, recently returned to the lush tropic isle, is at first courted by Ensign Jack Sanford (Timothy Bottoms, in an absolutely awful portrayal), but she is ultimately drawn to the intelligent and willful young leader. Though Matangi is betrothed to a young native girl, he falls in love with Charlotte and the groans build like the storm of the title. Rated PG.

1979 119 minutes

HURRICANE EXPRESS

★★

DIRECTORS: Armand Schaefer, J. P. McGowan
CAST: John Wayne, Tully Marshall, Conway Tearle, Shirley Gray

Big John Wayne stars in his second serial for Mascot Pictures and plays an aviator on the trail of the mysterious "Wrecker," who has been wreaking havoc with the local trains and is responsible for the death of his father. This feature, edited down from a twelve-chapter serial, features many famous western character actors and stunt men as the villains' sidekicks and henchmen. Even in this somewhat confused state it is fun and displays a high level of energy and excitement, a great deal of it as a direct result of young Wayne's wholehearted involvement in this basically simple chase film. Although the production values are missing, this vigorous outing has as much to offer as any of the famed serials from Universal and Republic.

1932 B & W 80 minutes

HUSTLE, THE

★★½

DIRECTOR: Robert Aldrich
CAST: Burt Reynolds, Eddie Albert, Ernest Borgnine, Jack Carter,

Ben Johnson

The Hustle reteams director Robert Aldrich and actor Burt Reynolds after their box-office success with *The Longest Yard*. Fine character performances from Eddie Albert, Ernest Borgnine, and Jack Carter help to elevate the macho/action yarn, but it is Academy Award–winner Ben Johnson who provides the real show. Rated R.

1975 120 minutes

I COVER THE WATERFRONT

★★★

DIRECTOR: James Cruze
CAST: Claudette Colbert, Ernest Torrence, Ben Lyon, Wilfred Lucas, George Humbert

One, and one of the better, of a spate of newspaper stories that vied with gangster films on 1930s screens. In this one, a ruthless fisherman who smuggles Chinese into the United States doesn't think twice about pushing them overboard when approached by the Coast Guard. Claudette Colbert is his innocent daughter. Ace reporter Ben Lyon courts her in an effort to get at the truth. A great moment takes place when the daughter chats with a cathouse madam while waiting to take her drunken father home.

1933 B & W 70 minutes

I, THE JURY

★

DIRECTOR: Richard T. Heffron
CAST: Armand Assante, Barbara Carrera, Alan King

In the mid-1940s, Mickey Spillane wrote *I, the Jury*, introducing Mike Hammer, his no-nonsense private eye. For this updated version, Spillane's basic plot—Hammer out to find the killer of his old army buddy—has been kept intact. However, the film is a disappointing and sleazy hybrid of James Bond and *Death Wish II*, in which there is one man against a mean, globally involved system. Rated R.

1982 111 minutes

ICE STATION ZEBRA

★★★

DIRECTOR: John Sturges
CAST: Rock Hudson, Ernest Borgnine, Patrick McGoohan, Jim Brown, Tony Bill, Lloyd Nolan

This long cold war cliff-hanger about a submarine skipper awaiting orders while cruising to the North Pole under the ice was eccentric billionaire Howard Hughes's favorite film. The suspense comes with a British agent's hunt for the usual Russian spy. Rated G.

1968 148 minutes

INSIDE OUT

★★★

DIRECTOR: Peter Duffell
CAST: Telly Savalas, Robert Culp, James Mason, Aldo Ray

An unlikely trio (Telly Savalas, Robert Culp, and James Mason) band together to recover $6 million in gold that Hitler had hidden. Only one man knows where the gold is, so the trio must get this ex-Nazi out of a maximum-security prison so that he can lead them to it. The action and suspense in this film should hold most viewers' attention. Rated PG.

1975 98 minutes

INSTANT JUSTICE

🦃

DIRECTOR: Craig T. Rumar
CAST: Michael Pare, Tawny Kitaen, Peter Crook, Eddie Avoth, Charles Napier

Instant Justice is the worst of the one-man-army movies. Michael Pare plays marine Sergeant Youngblood, an overblown Stallone/Eastwood/Bronson amalgam who has a penchant for head-butting. When on leave in Madrid to visit his sister, he finds she's been murdered by drug dealers. He then goes on a vengeful rampage. This is sexist, jingoistic movie-making. Pare and Tawny Kitaen (she looks and acts like her name) are equally vapid characters. *Instant Justice* is instant garbage, no need to add water. Rated R.

1986 101 minutes

INVASION U.S.A.

★★★½

DIRECTOR: Joseph Zito
CAST: Chuck Norris, Richard Lynch, Melissa Prophet

There is no question that Chuck Norris is the new king of the action movie. As star and co-screenwriter of this preposterous but enjoyable film about America being invaded by terrorists, he's sculpted a story around his ever-growing talents. His fans will have to content themselves with silly B-style movies like this, in which Norris plays a one-man army (as always) who comes to the rescue of the good ol' U.S.A. and pummels the minions of psychotic spy Richard Lynch. Rated R for violence, gore, and profanity.

1985 107 minutes

IRON EAGLE

★★

DIRECTOR: Sidney J. Furie
CAST: Louis Gossett Jr., Jason Gedrick, Tim Thomerson, David Suchet

A better name for this modern war movie might have been *Ramboy*, so shamelessly does it attempt to be a *Rambo* for the teen-age set. Jason Gedrick stars as an 18-year-old would-be pilot who steals an F-16 fighter plane to rescue his father (Tim Thomerson), a prisoner of war in the Middle East. Louis Gossett plays a retired colonel who aids the young man on his dangerous, improbable mission. Comparing *Iron Eagle* with *Rambo* may be unfair in a way. Love him or hate him, Sylvester Stallone knows how to make a movie move. *Iron Eagle* director Sidney J. Furie, on the other hand, can only make one crawl. His film, therefore, is a terminally dull fantasy of blood-lust. Furie intended for viewers to cheer on his hero, but all one can muster during this movie's nearly two hours of painful predictability is an occasional groan. Rated PG-13 for violence and profanity.

1986 115 minutes

IRON MASK, THE

★★★½

DIRECTOR: Allan Dwan
CAST: Douglas Fairbanks Sr., Nigel de Brulier, Marguerite de la Motte, Dorothy Revier, Vera Lewis, William Bakewell, Ullrich Haupt

The last of Douglas Fairbanks's truly memorable series of historical adventures is a rousing version of the Dumas story of the later adventures of D'Artagnan and his efforts to restore the rightful king to the throne of France. One by one the famous "Three Musketeers" fail in their valiant quest, leaving only the ever-agile Fairbanks to uncover the secret of the iron mask. Well-budgeted and full of good stunts and deadly encounters, this film was released with sound effects and a synchronized score. It was Fairbanks's final outing as a romantic hero of literature.

1929 B & W 87 minutes

ISLAND TRADER

★★

DIRECTOR: Howard Rubie
CAST: John Ewart, Ruth Cracknell, Eric Oldfield

A young boy on an island finds a wrecked airplane laden with gold bullion. He is then pursued by a dangerous criminal and a tugboat skipper, both of whom want the treasure. All three are soon involved in a chase through shark-infested waters and dense jungle. This potentially exciting adventure film is marred by amateurish direction, a low budget, and uninspired acting.

1970 95 minutes

IVANHOE

★★★★

DIRECTOR: Richard Thorpe

CAST: Robert Taylor, Elizabeth Taylor, Joan Fontaine, George Sanders, Sebastian Cabot

Robert Taylor stars as Sir Walter Scott's dashing knight Ivanhoe. His mission is to secure the ransom for King Richard the Lionhearted, who has been captured while returning from the Crusades. Action and swordplay abound as Ivanhoe strives for Richard's release and protects two very fair maidens (Elizabeth Taylor and Joan Fontaine) from the lecherous grasp of archvillain George Sanders.

1952 106 minutes

JACKSON COUNTY JAIL

★★★½

DIRECTOR: Michael Miller

CAST: Yvette Mimieux, Tommy Lee Jones, Robert Carradine

This chase film is pretty good. Yvette Mimieux escapes from jail with fellow inmate Tommy Lee Jones. Audiences can't help but sympathize with Mimieux, because she was unfairly arrested and then raped by her jailer. Rated R.

1976 89 minutes

JAKE SPEED

★★★½

DIRECTOR: Andrew Lane

CAST: Wayne Crawford, Dennis Christopher, Karen Kopins, John Hurt, Leon Ames, Donna Pescow, Roy London, Barry Primus, Monte Markham

This quirky little adventure thriller, from the folks involved with the equally deft *Night of the Comet*, postulates that the book adventures of a pulp hero named Jake Speed actually are biographical chapters in the life of a real person. When Karen Kopins's younger sister is kidnapped and threatened with white slavery by John Hurt's delightfully oily villain, Speed (Wayne Crawford) and his associate Remo (Dennis Christopher) materialize and offer to help. What follows is paced a bit too slowly and demonstrates questionable taste by using an African civil war as a backdrop, but the droll premise remains quite intriguing. Things pick up when Hurt appears; it's a shame he couldn't have arrived sooner. The dialogue occasionally is inspired, as when Kopins sarcastically asks if other pulp heroes will show up to assist, and Christopher calmly replies that they "work for another publisher." Rated PG for mild violence.

1986 100 minutes

JEWEL OF THE NILE, THE

★★★½

DIRECTOR: Lewis Teague

CAST: Michael Douglas, Kathleen Turner, Danny DeVito, Spiros Focas, Avner Eisenberg, the Flying Karamazov Brothers

This sequel to *Romancing the Stone* details the further adventures of novelist Joan Wilder (Kathleen Turner) and soldier of fortune Jack Colton (Michael Douglas) in the deserts of North Africa. Joan is asked by an Arab leader, Omar (Spiros Focas), to write his life story. She accepts and then discovers too late that Omar is a rather nasty fellow. So it's up to Jack—with the jewel-crazy Ralph (Danny DeVito) watching his every move—to save the day. The story seems to come to a logical conclusion three-quarters of the way through, and the viewer must endure a rather protracted build-up to the exciting climax. That said, *Jewel of the Nile* will not displease those seeking fun video fare. Turner and Douglas make appealing protagonists, and delightful comedy bits by the wisecracking DeVito (who wrote many of his lines) and Avner Eisenberg (as an impossibly cheerful guru) come at just the right moments. Therefore, those who loved the original will find much to like in this sequel. Rated PG.

1985 106 minutes

JOHNNY ANGEL

★★★

DIRECTOR: Edwin L. Marin

CAST: George Raft, Claire Trevor, Signe Hasso, Hoagy Carmichael

Above-average gangster film provides some nice moments. George Raft seeks the killer of his father while busting up the mob. Nothing special, but fun to watch.

1945 B & W 79 minutes

JUGGERNAUT

★★★★½

DIRECTOR: Richard Lester

CAST: Richard Harris, Omar Sharif, David Hemmings, Anthony Hopkins, Shirley Knight, Ian Holm, Roy Kinnear

Here's a first-rate, suspenseful thriller about demolitions expert Richard Harris attempting to deactivate a bomb aboard a luxury liner. Richard Lester elevates the familiar plot line with inspired direction, and Lester regular Roy Kinnear is on hand to add some deft bits of comedy. Rated PG.

1974 109 minutes

JUNGLE HEAT

★½

DIRECTOR: Gus Trikonis

CAST: Peter Fonda, Deborah Raffin, John Amos, Carlos Palomino

Although this film is considered to be an adventure tale, it tries to please everyone with a little horror and romance thrown in. Unfortunately, it fails to use any of these elements effectively. Dr. Evelyn Howard (Deborah Raffin), an anthropologist from L.A., hires an alcoholic ex–Vietnam vet (Peter Fonda) to fly her into the jungles of South America. There she looks for an ancient tribe of pygmies but finds instead monsters that greatly resemble the Creature from the Black Lagoon. Rated PG for language and gore.

1984 93 minutes

JUNGLE MASTER, THE

DIRECTOR: Miles Deem

CAST: Johnny Kissmuller, Simone Blondell, Edward Mann, Jerry Ross

An expedition journeys to Africa in search of the legendary ape-man, Karzan, no, not Tarzan—Karzan. Somebody must have been sued for this movie, if not for copyright infringement, then bad film-making. Obviously foreign, the dubbing is exceptionally bad. Parents who watch any of their children's cartoons may hear some familiar voices. If you've sharp eyes, watch the wildlife scenes. You'll catch some of the footage used in the credits of *Wild Kingdom*. This movie is not a total loss, though; there is quite a bit of unintentional humor. In fact, this film would have been a turkey if it weren't so funny. A gem for bad film buffs.

1985 90 minutes

JUNGLE WARRIORS

★★★

DIRECTOR: Ernst R. von Theumer
CAST: Sybil Danning, Marjoe Gortner, Nina Van Pallandt, Paul Smith, John Vernon, Alex Cord, Woody Strode, Kai Wulfe, Dana Elcar

The idea of a group of female models in Peru for a shoot in the jungle is quite absurd. If you can overlook the premise, though, this action film about a cocaine producer and his perverted sister is modestly satisfying. It's rather like an episode of *Miami Vice* but with scantily dressed women packing machine guns. Rated R for violence, profanity, and nudity.

1983 96 minutes

JUNKMAN, THE

★

DIRECTOR: H. B. Halecki
CAST: Christopher Stone, Susan Shaw, Lang Jeffries, Lynda Day George

From the makers of *Gone in 60 Seconds*, this sequel is tagged as the "chase film for the '80s." What this story lacks in plot and acting, it makes up for in action. More than 150 cars, trucks, and airplanes were destroyed in this "wall-to-wall" chase movie. There are so many crash scenes that it actually becomes boring. The story is about a junk dealer–turned–millionaire–turned–filmmaker being chased by a gang of thugs hired by his advertising agent to kill him. The ad agent seeks to reap the publicity benefits from his boss's death in order to promote the film our star is making. Thin. Rated PG.

1982 99 minutes

KARATE KID, PART 2, THE

★★★½

DIRECTOR: John G. Avildsen
CAST: Ralph Macchio, Noriyuki "Pat" Morita, Danny Kamekona, Nobu McCarthy, Tamlyn Tomita, Yuji Okumoto, Martin Kove, William Zabka

This second in the *Karate Kid* series begins moments after the conclusion of the first film. Mr. Miyagi (Noriyuki "Pat" Morita) receives word that his father, residing in Okinawa, is dying, so he drops everything and heads for home, with young Daniel (Ralph Macchio) along for the ride. Once in Okinawa, Miyagi encounters an old rival and an old love, while Daniel makes a new enemy and a new love; the latter is quite well played by newcomer Tamlyn Tomita. The film runs a bit long, and Miyagi's little philosophies aren't quite as well integrated as they were in the first film, but this new installment still is quite pleasant for all ages. As was true in the first film, the show belongs to Morita. Rated PG for mild violence.

1986 113 minutes

KASHMIRI RUN, THE

DIRECTOR: John Peyser
CAST: Pernell Roberts, Alexandra Gasteda, Julian Mateos, Gloria Camara

Pernell Roberts is an American adventurer in the Far East who is commissioned to take two scientists to India and bring back a load of yak skins. On the way he faces communist Chinese soldiers, bandits, and wild animals. If you can watch further than this, you have the world's strongest stomach. Roberts must have nightmares about this film, it's so bad. The only redeeming quality is

some beautiful scenery.
1969 93 minutes

KEEPING TRACK

★★★½

DIRECTOR: Robin Spry
CAST: Michael Sarrazin, Margot Kidder, Alan Scarfe, Ken Pogue

Superior action thriller follows Michael Sarrazin and Margot Kidder as two innocent bystanders who witness a murder and a robbery. Once they find the five million dollars, they must learn to trust one another because everyone is after them, including the CIA and Russian spies. This one will keep you guessing. Rated R.
1985 102 minutes

KELLY'S HEROES

★★★

DIRECTOR: Brian G. Hutton
CAST: Clint Eastwood, Telly Savalas, Donald Sutherland, Don Rickles, Gavin MacLeod, Carroll O'Connor

An amiable ripoff of *The Dirty Dozen*, this 1970 war comedy was funnier at the time of its original release. Stoic Clint Eastwood is stuck with a bunch of goof-offs (Telly Savalas, Donald Sutherland, Don Rickles, and Gavin McLeod) as he searches for Nazi treasure. Sutherland's World War II hippie ("Give me those positive waves, man") is a little tough to take these days, but this caper picture still has its moments. Rated PG.
1970 145 minutes

KENNEL MURDER CASE, THE

★★★★

DIRECTOR: Michael Curtiz
CAST: William Powell, Mary Astor, Eugene Pallette, Ralph Morgan, Jack LaRue

A classic detective thriller, this features William Powell as the dapper Philo Vance solving a locked-door murder. The supporting players complement his suave characterization perfectly. Dated, but good.
1933 B & W 73 minutes

KEY LARGO

★★★★

DIRECTOR: John Huston
CAST: Humphrey Bogart, Lauren Bacall, Edward G. Robinson, Claire Trevor, Lionel Barrymore

Humphrey Bogart is one of a group of dissimilar individuals held in a run-down Florida Keys hotel by a band of hoodlums on the lam. Lauren Bacall looks to him as her white knight, but as a disillusioned war vet he has had enough violence. That is, until a crime kingpin (Edward G. Robinson) pushes things a little too far.
1948 B & W 101 minutes

KIDNAPPED

★★★

DIRECTOR: Robert Stevenson
CAST: James MacArthur, Peter Finch

Walt Disney takes a shot at filming this Robert Louis Stevenson eighteenth-century adventure. A young man (James MacArthur) is spirited away to sea just as he is about to inherit his family's estate. Plenty of swashbuckling swordplay for children of all ages.
1960 94 minutes

KILL AND KILL AGAIN

★★

DIRECTOR: Ivan Hall
CAST: James Ryan, Anneline Kriel

Kung-fu champ James Ryan repeats his starring role from *Kill or Be Killed* in this sequel to that box-office winner. This time, martial arts master Steve Chase (Ryan) has been hired to rescue a Nobel Prize–winning chemist from the clutches of a demented billionaire who wants his victim's formula for synthetic fuel. Rated R.

1981 100 minutes

KILL CASTRO

🦃

DIRECTOR: Peter Barton

CAST: Stuart Whitman, Caren Kaye, Robert Vaughn, Woody Strode, Albert Salmi, Michael Gazzo, Sybil Danning, Raymond St. Jacques

Espionage and murder are the formulas for this implausible adventure yarn. Captain Tony (Stuart Whitman) is a Key West boat skipper who is "blackmailed" into helping a CIA agent named Hud (Robert Vaughn) carry out an assassination plot against Fidel Castro. The CIA is helping the Mafia bring drugs into Cuba in return for help in carrying out its murder plot. If Castro were to see this turkey, he would probably die—laughing. Rated R for violence, profanity, and incompetence.

1978 90 minutes

KILL OR BE KILLED

★½

DIRECTOR: Ivan Hall

CAST: James Ryan, Norman Combes, Charlotte Michelle, Danie DuPlessis

A former Nazi pits himself against the Japanese master who defeated him in an important tournament during World War II. Run-of-the-mill martial arts nonsense. James Ryan shows a glimmer of personality to go with his physical prowess. Rated PG.

1980 90 minutes

KILL POINT

★

DIRECTOR: Frank Harris

CAST: Leo Fong, Richard Roundtree, Cameron Mitchell, Stark Pierce, Hope Holiday

Incredibly bloody tale of gang warfare, revenge, and justice in L.A. Leo Fong plays a police detective whose brother is murdered by a gang of hoods. Fong is out to get the killers, who have also robbed a National Guard armory and are passing out weapons to all the scum in L.A. Weak performances and gratuitous violence mar this low-budget thriller. Rated R for violence and language.

1984 89 minutes

KILLER ELITE, THE

★★½

DIRECTOR: Sam Peckinpah

CAST: James Caan, Robert Duvall, Arthur Hill, Bo Hopkins, Mako, Burt Young, Gig Young

Secret service agent James Caan is double-crossed by his partner (Robert Duvall) while guarding a witness. Disabled by a bullet wound, he has to begin a long process of recovery. He wants revenge. The story seems to have a lot of promise, but this is never realized. There are some good action scenes. However, considering all the top-flight talent involved, it is a major disappointment. Rated PG.

1975 120 minutes

KILLERS, THE

★★★★

DIRECTOR: Robert Siodmak

CAST: Burt Lancaster, Ava Gardner, Edmond O'Brien, Albert Dekker, Sam Levene

Burt Lancaster made an impressive film debut in this *film noir* masterwork directed by Robert Siodmak. *Film noir*, for those who aren't movie buffs, is a particular style of film story-telling bathed in light and shadow and dealing with the darker doings of mankind. Based on an Ernest Hemingway story, the plot concerns the murder of an ex-fighter (Lancaster) and the subsequent investigation into the circumstances that led to his death.

1946 B & W 105 minutes

KIM

★★★½

DIRECTOR: Victor Saville

CAST: Errol Flynn, Dean Stockwell, Paul Lukas, Thomas Gomez, Cecil Kellaway

Rudyard Kipling's India comes to life in this colorful story of the young son of a soldier and his adventures with a dashing secret operative in defense of queen and country. Dean Stockwell is one of the finest and most believable of child stars, and the great Errol Flynn is still capable of personifying the spirit of adventure and romance in this one-dimensional but entertaining story. Good supporting cast, beautiful photography, and exotic settings help to make this film fun for the whole family.

1951 113 minutes

KING ARTHUR, THE YOUNG WARLORD

★½

DIRECTORS: Sidney Hayers, Patrick Jackson, Peter Sasdy

CAST: Oliver Tobias, Michael Gothard, Jack Watson, Brian Blessed, Peter Firth

King Arthur, the Young Warlord follows the English legend in his early years through subplots that lead nowhere. Some of these vignettes promise some kind of conclusion and build upon opening narration (which sets the stage for the unification of the English tribes into a nation led by Arthur), but in the end none of the stories deliver the goods. The acting is second-rate, and while some of the action scenes are good, it must be noted that the violence displayed may not be some people's idea of good ol' G-rated fun despite the MPAA approval.

1975 96 minutes

KING OF THE KONGO

★★

DIRECTOR: Richard Thorpe

CAST: Walter Miller, Jacqueline Logan, Richard Tucker, Boris Karloff, Larry Steers, Harry Todd, Lafe McKee, Richard Neil

Historically important as the first serial released in both silent and sound versions, this early Mascot serial features veteran chapterplay hero Walter Miller as a secret service agent searching both for his brother and for the secret of a temple's treasure. Boris Karloff is a stand-out as the heavy. This is about as primitive as early talkies get, but at the time the sound effects and disc-recorded dialogue was considered exciting.

1929 B & W 10 chapters

KING SOLOMON'S MINES

★★★★★

DIRECTORS: Compton Bennett, Andrew Martins

CAST: Stewart Granger, Deborah Kerr, Hugo Haas

The "great white hunter" genre of adventure films has been a movie staple for ages, yet only one rates as a cinema classic. That picture is the rousing adventure *King Solomon's Mines*. Stewart Granger guides a party through darkest Africa in search of a lady's husband. Don't let this surprise you, but on the way, the hunter and the lady (Deborah Kerr) become fast friends. Sounds like a pretty basic plot, doesn't it? Why, then, has it stood the test of time where other jungle safari pics have faded? The seemingly routine script is actually an exceptional blend of action and suspense. The brilliant location photography has never been excelled, and the acting is first-rate.

1950 102 minutes

KING SOLOMON'S MINES (1985)

DIRECTOR: J. Lee Thompson
CAST: Richard Chamberlain, Sharon Stone, John Rhys-Davies, Herbert Lom, Ken Gampu

A bad movie may not be a crime against nature, but this film is definitely a crime against H. Rider Haggard's classic adventure novel. The previous film versions in 1937 and 1950 were rousing entertainment, whereas this one is nothing more than a blatant ripoff of *Raiders of the Lost Ark*. Starring Richard Chamberlain as Allan Quartermain, the film is an embarrassment—a compedium of cornball clichés and stupid slapstick. Rated PG for violence.

1985 100 minutes

KING SOLOMON'S TREASURE

★

DIRECTOR: Alvin Rakoff
CAST: David McCallum, Britt Ekland, Patrick Macnee, John Colicos

This mindless adventure features John Colicos, Patrick Macnee, and a stuttering David McCallum pursuing treasure in Africa's Forbidden City. Britt Ekland makes a silly Phoenician queen. No need to rent this one, folks!

1976 90 minutes

KNIGHTRIDERS

★★★

DIRECTOR: George A. Romero
CAST: Ed Harris, Tom Savini, Amy Ingersoll

What was supposed to be a modern-day look at the lost Code of Honor comes across on screen as a bunch of weirdos dressed in armor riding motorcycles in a traveling circus. At a length of almost two-and-a-half hours, there isn't enough to hold the viewer's interest. A novel idea, but it wears thin in a very short while. Rated PG.

1981 145 minutes

KNIGHTS OF THE ROUND TABLE

★★½

DIRECTOR: Richard Thorpe
CAST: Robert Taylor, Ava Gardner, Mel Ferrer, Stanley Baker, Felix Aylmer, Robert Urquhart

Colorful wide-screen epic of King Arthur's court is long on pageantry but lacks the spirit required to make this type of film work well. MGM mainstay Robert Taylor plays another of his one-dimensional storybook heroes against a backdrop of real English hills, meadows, and castles. Able-bodied assistance is offered in the form of Stanley Baker and Mel Ferrer, and Ava Gardner is as lovely as ever, but this tale of Camelot is not as fondly remembered as other films of its ilk.

1953 115 minutes

KUNG FU

★★★

DIRECTOR: Jerry Thorpe
CAST: David Carradine, Keye Luke, Philip Ahn, Keith Carradine, Barry Sullivan

The pilot of the 1970s television series starring David Carradine has its moments for those who fondly remember the show. Carradine plays a Buddhist monk roaming the Old West. When his wisdom fails to mollify the bad guys, he is forced to use martial arts to see justice done.

1971 75 minutes

LADY FROM SHANGHAI

★★★½

DIRECTOR: Orson Welles
CAST: Rita Hayworth, Orson Welles, Everett Sloane,

Glenn Anders, Erskine Sanford, Ted De Corsia, Gus Schilling

Orson Welles and Rita Hayworth were husband and wife when they made this taut, surprising thriller about a beautiful, amoral woman, her crippled, repulsive lawyer husband, his partner, and a somewhat naive Irish sailor made cat's-paw in a murder scheme. Under Welles's inventive direction, Everett Sloane and the camera steal the show with a climactic scene in the hall of mirrors at San Francisco's old oceanfront Playland.

1948 B & W 87 minutes

LADY IN RED

★★★½

DIRECTOR: Lewis Teague

CAST: Pamela Sue Martin, Robert Conrad, Robert Forster, Louise Fletcher, Robert Hogan, Laurie Heineman, Glenn Withrow, Christopher Lloyd, Dick Miller

A splendid screenplay by John Sayles energizes this telling of the Dillinger story from the distaff side, with Pamela Sue Martin as the gangster's moll enduring the results of a life of crime. Director Lewis Teague keeps things moving right along, and the cast members seem blissfully unaware that they are in a low-budget exploitation flick. The result is a little gem sure to please fans of the action genre. Rated R for profanity, nudity, and violence.

1979 93 minutes

LADY OF BURLESQUE

★★★

DIRECTOR: William Wellman

CAST: Barbara Stanwyck, Michael O'Shea, J. Edward Bromberg, Iris Adrian, Pinky Lee

Slick and amusing adaptation of Gypsy Rose Lee's clever mystery novel of top bananas, blackouts, and strippers, *The G-String Murder*. Interesting look into an aspect of show business that now exists only in fading memories. "Slowly I turned. . . ."

1943 B & W 91 minutes

LADY SCARFACE

★★½

DIRECTOR: Frank Woodruff

CAST: Judith Anderson, Dennis O'Keefe, Frances Neal, Eric Blore, Marc Lawrence, Mildred Coles

Role reversal is the order of the day for this story of a hardened dame who spits lead and asks questions later, ruling her gang with a velvet glove and leading the police and authorities on a grim chase. Atmospheric but pretentious, this offbeat attempt to inject new life into a basic crime story isn't as good as it could have been despite the presence of classy Judith Anderson and character greats Eric Blore and Marc Lawrence.

1941 B & W 66 minutes

LADYHAWKE

★★★½

DIRECTOR: Richard Donner

CAST: Matthew Broderick, Rutger Hauer, Michelle Pfeiffer, Leo McKern, John Wood

In this seven-hundred-year-old legend of love and honor, Rutger Hauer and Michelle Pfeiffer are lovers separated by an evil curse. Hauer, a valiant knight, is aided by a wisecracking thief, Matthew Broderick, in his quest to break the spell by destroying its creator. This is a lush and lavish fantasy that will please the young and the young at heart. Rated PG-13 for violence.

1985 124 minutes

LASSITER

★★★

DIRECTOR: Roger Young

CAST: Tom Selleck, Jane Seymour, Lauren Hutton, Bob Hoskins

Tom Selleck (of television's *Magnum P.I.* and *High Road to China*) stars in yet another period adventure film as a jewel thief in the 1930s who attempts to steal a cache of uncut diamonds from the Nazis. This could be called good-but-not-great entertainment. Rated R for nudity, suggested sex, violence, and profanity.

1984 100 minutes

LAST AMERICAN HERO, THE

★★★★

DIRECTOR: Lamont Johnson
CAST: Jeff Bridges, Valerie Perrine, Geraldine Fitzgerald, Ned Beatty, Gary Busey, Art Lund, Ed Lauter, William Smith II

Hollywood took a lot of the bite out of the Tom Wolfe article this movie was based on, but *The Last American Hero* holds up as an entertaining action film about the famous whiskey runner from North Carolina who becomes a legend when he proves himself a great stock-car driver. Jeff Bridges's portrait of the rebel Johnson is engaging, but Art Lund steals the show as Johnson's bootlegger father. Rated PG for profanity and sex.

1973 95 minutes

LAST CONTRACT, THE

★★

DIRECTOR: Allan A. Buckhantz
CAST: Jack Palance, Rod Steiger, Bo Svenson, Richard Roundtree, Ann Turkel

In this violent film, Jack Palance stars as an artist and a hit man who is hired to kill his best friend. Unable to do it, he is ordered to assassinate a rival crime lord. When he kills the wrong man, the deadly game of hit and counterhit gets out of hand. Rated R.

1986 85 minutes

LAST DAYS OF POMPEII

★★

DIRECTOR: Mario Bonnard
CAST: Steve Reeves, Fernando Rey, Cristine Kauffman, Barbara Carroll, Anne Marie Baumann, Mimmo Palmara, Guillerma Marin, Angel Aranda

A different scenario than the 1935 original. Steve Reeves plays a hero in the Roman army stationed in Greece who tries to save a group of Christians that has been jailed and condemned to death. The story is interesting, but the action scenes are rather dumb.

1960 93 minutes

LAST DRAGON, THE

★★★½

DIRECTOR: Michael Schultz
CAST: Taimak, Vanity, Chris Murney

Produced by Motown Records man Berry Gordy, this is lively, unpretentious nonsense about a shy karate champ (Taimak) fending off villains threatening a disc jockey (Vanity). A combined music video and comic strip, it's good, silly fun. Rated PG-13 for violence.

1985 109 minutes

LAST EMBRACE, THE

★★★½

DIRECTOR: Jonathan Demme
CAST: Roy Scheider, Janet Margolin, Sam Levene, Marcia Rodd, Christopher Walken, John Glover, Charles Napier

A CIA agent must track down an obsessed, methodical killer. A complex, intellegent thriller in the Hitchcock style with skilled performances, a lush music score, and a cliff-hanging climax at Niagara Falls. Rated R for nudity and violence.

1979 102 minutes

LAST OF SHEILA, THE

★★★★

DIRECTOR: Herbert Ross
CAST: James Coburn, Dyan Cannon, James Mason, Raquel Welch, Richard Benjamin

A cleverly planned, very watchable whodunit. Because of some unusual camera angles and subtle dialogue, the audience is drawn into active participation in the mystery. A sundry collection of Hollywood types are invited on a yachting cruise by James Coburn. It seems one of them has been involved in the murder of Coburn's wife. Rated PG.

1973 120 minutes

LAST PLANE OUT

[turkey symbol]

DIRECTOR: David Nelson
CAST: Jan-Michael Vincent, Lloyd Batista, Julie Carmen

Poor ripoff of *Under Fire*, with Jan-Michael Vincent playing a news reporter in Nicaragua during the final days of the Somoza regime in 1979. Bad acting, a poor script, and historical inaccuracies all add up to a big bomb. Not hard to understand why this film was not released in the cinema. Unrated.

1983 98 minutes

LATE SHOW, THE

★★★★½

DIRECTOR: Robert Benton
CAST: Art Carney, Howard Duff, Lily Tomlin, Bill Macy, John Considine

Just prior to directing *Kramer vs. Kramer*, Robert Benton created this little gem. It stars Art Carney as an aging private eye out to avenge the death of his partner (Howard Duff) with the unwanted help of wacky Lily Tomlin. Loosely lifted from Sam Peckinpah's *Ride the High Country* and John Huston's *The Maltese Falcon*, this detective story is a bittersweet, sometimes tragic, takeoff on the genre. That it works so well is a credit to all involved. Rated PG.

1977 94 minutes

LAUGHING POLICEMAN, THE

★★★½

DIRECTOR: Stuart Rosenberg
CAST: Walter Matthau, Bruce Dern, Louis Gossett, Albert Paulsen, Cathy Lee Crosby, Anthony Zerbe

Little-known police thriller that deserved far better than it got at the box office. Walter Matthau and Bruce Dern are a pair of cops seeking a mass murderer who preys on bus passengers. Taut drama, taken from the superb thriller by Maj Sjowall and Per Wahloo . . . although characterization suffers a bit in the transition from book to screen. Rated R for violence.

1974 111 minutes

LAURA

★★★★★

DIRECTOR: Otto Preminger
CAST: Gene Tierney, Dana Andrews, Vincent Price, Judith Anderson, Clifton Webb

A lovely socialite (Gene Tierney) is apparently murdered, and the police detective (Dana Andrews) assigned to the case is up to his neck in likely suspects. To compound matters, he has developed a strange attraction for the deceased woman through her portrait. So starts one of the most original mysteries ever to come from Hollywood. Vincent Price and Judith Anderson highlight an excellent supporting cast, but the role still remembered today belongs to Clifton Webb. With his superb performance as the acid-tongued columnist, he stole the show from this talented cast. A haunting music score also contributes to this fast-paced classic, which has always delighted audiences.

1944 B & W 88 minutes

LAWRENCE OF ARABIA

★★★★★

DIRECTOR: David Lean
CAST: Peter O'Toole, Alec Guinness, Anthony Quinn, Arthur Kennedy, Omar Sharif

Director David Lean brings us an expansive screen biography of T. E. Lawrence, the complex English leader of the Arab revolt against Turkey in World War I. This is a tremendous accomplishment in every respect. Peter O'Toole is stunning in his motion picture debut as Lawrence. The supporting cast is superb. The cinematography captures the beauty of the desert as never before. Maurice Jarré has added a stirring musical score. A definite thinking person's spectacle.

1962 222 minutes

LEFT HAND OF GOD, THE

★★★½

DIRECTOR: Edward Dmytryk
CAST: Humphrey Bogart, Lee J. Cobb, Gene Tierney, Agnes Moorehead

This 1955 release features Humphrey Bogart as an American forced to pose as a priest while on the run from a renegade Chinese warlord (Lee J. Cobb). It's not the fastest-moving adventure story, but Bogart and Cobb are quite good, and Gene Tierney is an effective heroine. The result is worthy entertainment.

1955 87 minutes

LEGAL EAGLES

★★★½

DIRECTOR: Ivan Reitman
CAST: Robert Redford, Debra Winger, Daryl Hannah, Brian Dennehy, Terence Stamp, Steven Hill, Jennie Dundas, Roscoe Lee Browne

This droll courtroom comedy succeeds due to the engaging presence of Robert Redford as a assistant district attorney and Debra Winger as a defense attorney. The two become uneasy partners in a complex case involving art theft and a loopy performance artist, played by Daryl Hannah. A charming subplot involves Redford's daughter (nicely played by Jennie Dundas) who visits when his ex-wife permits. The story doesn't bear close examination, but Redford and Winger keep things moving with energy and charisma. Rated PG for mild adult situations.

1986 114 minutes

LEGEND OF BILLY JEAN, THE

★

DIRECTOR: Matthew Robbins
CAST: Helen Slater, Keith Gordon, Christian Slater, Peter Coyote

Another one of those teen rebel flicks. This one is about a girl from Texas (*Supergirl*'s Helen Slater) who becomes an outlaw and ends up with all the youths in Corpus Christi backing her up. There are few subtleties here and the obvious is exploited for the dim of wit. Rated PG-13 for language and (only a little) violence.

1985 92 minutes

LEPKE

★★★

DIRECTOR: Menahem Golan
CAST: Tony Curtis, Anjanette Comer, Michael Callan, Warren Berlinger, Milton Berle, Vic Tayback

Tony Curtis gives an effective performance in the lead role of this gangster drama. He's the head of Murder Inc. The story sticks close to the facts. It's no classic, but watchable. Rated R.

1975 110 minutes

LETHAL WEAPON

★★★★

DIRECTOR: Richard Donner
CAST: Mel Gibson, Danny Glover, Gary Busey, Mitchell Ryan, Tom Atkins, Darlene Love, Traci Wolfe

This fast, frantic, and wholly improbable police thriller owes its success to the chemistry between the two leads. Mel Gibson is fine as the cop on the edge, the human killing machine (the weapon of the title) who might possess a death wish because of his wife's recent death. Danny Glover is equally good as the careful company man, the methodical worker who has just turned 50 and would like to live to see 51. They run afoul of deadly drug smugglers, and Glover rapidly loses his ability to play a complacent game. Shane Black's script contains considerable humor, and he never loses track of his protagonists' humanity—although the villains are strictly two-dimensional bad guys. Richard Donner directs with a lot of zip, and the result is a lot of fun. Rated R for violence.

1987 105 minutes

LION AND THE HAWK, THE

★★★

DIRECTOR: Peter Ustinov
CAST: Peter Ustinov, Herbert Lom, Simon Dutton, Leonie Mellinger, Denis Quilley, Michael Elphick

Turkey in 1923, with its social, religious, and economic revolution picking up steam, is the backdrop for this film about a young rebel (Simon Dutton) who defies cultural tradition and runs off with a woman betrothed to a powerful regional governor's nephew. Peter Ustinov is excellent as the governor, who seeks revenge on the young Turk. *The Lion and the Hawk* is entertaining but lacks definition: the viewer may watch the film from start to finish and never really get the point. Not rated; has sex, nudity, and violence.

1983 105 minutes

LION OF THE DESERT

★★★½

DIRECTOR: Moustapha Akkad
CAST: Anthony Quinn, Oliver Reed, Rod Steiger

This epic motion picture gives an absorbing portrait of the 1929–31 war in the North African deserts of Libya when Bedouin troops on horseback faced the tanks and mechanized armies of Mussolini. Anthony Quinn is Omar Mukhtar, the desert lion who became a nationalist and a warrior at the age of 52 and fought the Italians until they captured and hanged him twenty years later. Rated PG.

1981 162 minutes

LISBON

★★

DIRECTOR: Ray Milland
CAST: Ray Milland, Claude Rains, Maureen O'Hara, Francis Lederer, Percy Marmont

Maureen O'Hara's husband is in a communist prison. International gentleman thief Claude Rains hires Ray Milland to rescue him. Not James Bond caliber. Not *To Catch a Thief* classy. Not really worth much.

1956 90 minutes

LIST OF ADRIAN MESSENGER, THE

★★★★½

DIRECTOR: John Huston
CAST: George C. Scott, Dana Wynter, Clive Brook, Herbert Marshall

Excellent suspenser has a mysterious stranger visiting an English estate and the puzzling series of murders that coincide with his arrival. Crisp acting, coupled with John Huston's taut direction, makes this crackerjack entertainment. Superb finale involving a fox hunt is not to be missed. With cameo appearances by Kirk Douglas, Tony Curtis, Burt Lancaster, Robert Mitchum, Frank Sinatra. Rated PG.

1963 B & W 98 minutes

LITTLE CAESAR

★★★

DIRECTOR: Mervyn LeRoy

CAST: Edward G. Robinson, Douglas Fairbanks Jr.

Historically, this is an important film. Made in 1930, it started the whole genre of gangster films. As entertainment, this veiled biography of Al Capone is terribly dated. Edward G. Robinson's performance is like a Warner Bros. cartoon in places, but one has to remember this is the original; the rest are imitators.

1930 B & W 80 minutes

LITTLE DRUMMER GIRL, THE

★★½

DIRECTOR: George Roy Hill

CAST: Diane Keaton, Yorgo Voyagis, Klaus Kinski

Director George Roy Hill (*Butch Cassidy and the Sundance Kid*) did everything he could to make this adaptation of John Le Carré's bestseller a fast-paced, involving political thriller. However, his work is thwarted by an unconvincing lead performance by Diane Keaton, who plays an actress recruited by an Israeli general (Klaus Kinski) to help trap a Palestinian terrorist. Even though the movie has its moments, Keaton's poor acting eventually does it in. Rated R for violence, profanity, suggested sex, and nudity.

1984 130 minutes

LITTLE LAURA AND BIG JOHN

DIRECTORS: Luke Moberly, Bob Woodburn

CAST: Karen Black, Fabian Forte, Ivy Thayer, Ken Miller, Paul Gleason, Jerry Albert, Lee Warren, Ben Rossi

A very cheap response to the popular outlaw films of the late 1960s (*Bonnie and Clyde; Butch Cassidy and the Sundance Kid;* etc.). *Little Laura and Big John* is about the Ashley Gang, a bunch of losers who can put you to sleep by just saying "Stick 'em up." The acting is bad enough, but what really stands out here is the canned dialogue, or at least the poorly handled on-the-set-audio—everyone sounds like they're in a wind tunnel. If you dare to rent this, you'll be amazed how boring the Roaring Twenties seemed to this team of directors. Rated R for violence, nudity, and profanity.

1972 82 minutes

LITTLE TREASURE

★★★

DIRECTOR: Alan Sharp

CAST: Margot Kidder, Ted Danson, Burt Lancaster

While the synopsis on the back of the box may give one the impression this release is a ripoff of *Romancing the Stone*, only the rough outline of the story is lifted from the 1984 hit. The Margot Kidder/Ted Danson team is not a copy of the Kathleen Turner/Michael Douglas couple; these characters are more down-home. And the concentration on domestic drama almost fills the gap left by the absence of action. Plodding at times, but generally satisfying. Rated R for nudity and language.

1985 95 minutes

LIVE AND LET DIE

★★

DIRECTOR: Guy Hamilton
CAST: Roger Moore, Jane Seymour, Yaphet Kotto, Geoffrey Holder

The first Roger Moore (as James Bond) adventure is a hodgepodge of the surrealistic and the slick that doesn't quite live up to its Sean Connery–powered predecessors. The chase-and-suspense formula wears thin in this series entry. Rated PG.

1973 121 minutes

LIVES OF A BENGAL LANCER, THE

★★★★½

DIRECTOR: Henry Hathaway
CAST: Gary Cooper, Franchot Tone, Richard Cromwell, Sir Guy Standing, C. Aubrey Smith, Monte Blue, Kathleen Burke

One of the great adventure films, this action-packed epic stars Gary Cooper and Franchot Tone as fearless friends in the famed British regiment. Their lives become complicated when they take the commander's son (Richard Cromwell) under their wings and he turns out to be less than a model soldier.

1935 B & W 109 minutes

LIVING DAYLIGHTS, THE

★★★★

DIRECTOR: John Glen
CAST: Timothy Dalton, Maryam d'Abo, Jeroen Krabbé, Joe Don Baker, John Rhys-Davies, Art Malik, Desmond Llewelyn

Even more effective than *For Your Eyes Only, The Living Daylights* is a welcome return to the no-nonsense style of the classic James Bond films starring Sean Connery. Timothy Dalton adds a dimension of humanity to Ian Fleming's famous creation in his screen bow as the ultimate spy hero. The silly set pieces and gimmicks that marred even the best Roger Moore entries in the series are gone. Instead, director John Glen and screenwriters Richard Maibaum and Michael Wilson have opted for a strong plot about a phony KGB defector (Jeroen Krabbé) and a renegade arms dealer (Joe Don Baker) who wreak all sorts of havoc until 007 steps in. Rated PG.

1987 130 minutes

LOADED GUNS

DIRECTOR: Fernando Di Leo
CAST: Ursula Andress, Woody Strode, Isabella Biagin, Lino Banfi, Aldo Giuffre, Maurizio Arena

Thoroughly stupid espionage flick from Italy that tries to be comical when it's not and is a laugh riot when it's supposed to be serious. Ursula Andress (*Dr. No; What's New Pussycat?*) is a spy who tries to bust up a cocaine-smuggling ring. For those who couldn't care less about the story or the dubbed dialogue, Ursula does walk around naked a lot. Not rated, but would be an R by MPAA standards due to sex, nudity, violence, and profanity.

1975 90 minutes

LONE WOLF MCQUADE

★★★½

DIRECTOR: Steve Carver
CAST: Chuck Norris, L. Q. Jones, R. G. Armstrong, David Carradine, Barbara Carrera

Chuck Norris plays a maverick Texas ranger who forgets the rules in his zeal to punish the bad guys. Norris still isn't a great actor, but director Steve Carver compensates by surrounding him with a quality supporting cast and by meticulously setting up and pacing the film. As McQuade, Norris meets his match in David Carradine (who starred in TV's *Kung Fu*), the ruthless leader of a gun-smuggling ring. The worth-waiting-for climax is a martial arts battle between the two. Rated PG for violence and profanity.

1983 107 minutes

LONG GOOD FRIDAY, THE

★★★★★

DIRECTOR: John MacKenzie
CAST: Bob Hoskins, Helen Mirren, Pierce Brosnan

This superb British film depicts the struggle of an underworld boss (Bob Hoskins, in a brilliant performance) to hold on to his territory. It's a classic in the genre on a par with *The Godfather*, *The Public Enemy*, and *High Sierra*. Rated R for nudity, profanity, and violence.

1980 114 minutes

LONG JOHN SILVER

★★★

DIRECTOR: Byron Haskin
CAST: Robert Newton, Connie Gilchrist, Kit Taylor, Grant Taylor

Avast me hearties, Robert Newton is at his scene-chewing best in this otherwise unexceptional (and unofficial) sequel to Disney's *Treasure Island*.

1954 109 minutes

LONGEST DAY, THE

★★★★★

DIRECTORS: Ken Annakin, Andrew Marton, Bernhard Wicki
CAST: John Wayne, Robert Mitchum, Henry Fonda, Richard Burton, Rod Steiger, Sean Connery, Robert Wagner

A magnificent re-creation of the Allied invasion of Normandy in June of 1944 with an all-star cast, this epic war film succeeds where others may fail—*Midway* and *Tora! Tora! Tora!*, for example. A big-budget film that shows you where the money was spent, it's first-rate in all respects.

1963 B & W 180 minutes

LONGEST YARD, THE

★★★★½

DIRECTOR: Robert Aldrich
CAST: Burt Reynolds, Eddie Albert, Michael Conrad, Bernadette Peters, Ed Lauter

An ex–professional football quarterback (Burt Reynolds) is sent to a Florida prison for stealing his girlfriend's car. The warden (Eddie Albert) forces Reynolds to put together a prisoner team to play his semipro team made up of guards. Great audience participation film with the last third dedicated to the game. Very funny, with some truly touching moments. Rated R for language and violence.

1974 123 minutes

LORD JIM

★★★★

DIRECTOR: Richard Brooks
CAST: Peter O'Toole, James Mason, Eli Wallach

Joseph Conrad's complex novel of human weakness has been simplified for easier appreciation and brought to the screen in a lavish visual style. Peter O'Toole is Jim, a sailor in Southeast Asia who is adopted by a suppressed village as its leader in spite of a past clouded by allegations of cowardice. The belief shown in him by the native villagers is put to the test by a group of European thugs.

1965 154 minutes

LOST CITY OF THE JUNGLE

★½

DIRECTORS: Ray Taylor, Lewis D. Collins
CAST: Russell Hayden, Lionel Atwill, Jane Adams, Keye

Luke, Helen Bennett, Ted Hecht, John Eldredge, John Miljan, Ralph Lewis

Sir Eric Hazarias (Lionel Atwill) wants to rule the world and he thinks he's discovered the way with Meteorium 245, the only defense against the atomic bomb. The United Peace Foundation sends their ace operative, Rod Stanton, to deal with the doctor and all the diabolical plots he concocts during the interminable thirteen episodes that this Universal serial runs. Phony temples, stock footage, familiar car chases, and cheating chapter endings are common to this minor chapter play—the only outstanding thing about it is the presence of Lionel Atwill in his last screen role. Atwill had once been among the greatest of character actors, highly regarded and eagerly sought by the industry's top talents. But after the disclosure of a scandalous party he had given and a publicized trial, he was no longer in demand.

1946 B & W 13 chapters

LOST EMPIRE, THE

★½

DIRECTOR: Jim Wynorski

CAST: Melanie Vincz, Raven De La Croix, Angela Aames, Paul Coufos, Bob Tessier, Angus Scrimm, Kenneth Tobey, Tom Rettig

Inept, hokey film about busty gals who infiltrate the island stronghold of a mysterious and powerful ruler is just one excuse for the female leads to model skimpy outfits. Mud fights, women with whips, baldheaded men, snakes—this film has it all. There's even a bumbling boyfriend to come to the rescue, and the inevitable confrontation and escape from destruction. The character actors are the real (and only) stars in this slap-dash production, so be on the lookout for former film and TV owner Tommy Rettig, horror-film favorite Angus Scrimm, and one of the truly menacing men of cinema, Bob Tessier (*Hard Times; The Longest Yard*). Rated R for some nudity, violence.

1983 86 minutes

LOST PATROL, THE

★★★★

DIRECTOR: John Ford

CAST: Victor McLaglen, Boris Karloff, Wallace Ford, Reginald Denny, Alan Hale, J. M. Kerrigan, Billy Bevan

An intrepid band of British cavalrymen lost in the Mesopotamian desert are picked off by the Arabs, one by one. Brisk direction and topnotch characterizations make this a winner—though it is grim. Stout heart, forever England, and all that.

1934 B & W 65 minutes

LOST SQUADRON

★★★

DIRECTOR: George Archainbaud

CAST: Richard Dix, Mary Astor, Erich Von Stroheim, Joel McCrea, Dorothy Jordan, Robert Armstrong

Mystery-adventure about the "accidental" deaths of former World War I pilots engaged as stunt fliers for the movies is unique. Movie good guys Richard Dix, Joel McCrea, and Robert Armstrong play the likes of Frank Clarke, Al Wilson, Paul Mantz, and other daredevils who provided most of the thrills in dozens of aviation epics and potboilers for years; Erich Von Stroheim plays an uneasy caricature of himself as a fanatical director who might be responsible for the fatal accidents that have plagued production of his current film. Full of industry "in-jokes," breezy dialogue, and good stunts, this is a fun film—especially for anyone with an interest in stunt flying or aviation in general.

1932 B & W 79 minutes

LOVE AND BULLETS

★½

DIRECTOR: Stuart Rosenberg

CAST: Charles Bronson, Rod Steiger, Strother Martin, Bradford Dillman, Henry Silva, Jill Ireland

Incredibly dull Charles Bronson thriller marred by Jill Ireland. Bronson is hired to snatch Ireland from crime lord Rod Steiger. An absolute waste of a good cast and completely lacking the savage bite that powered earlier Bronson vehicles, such as *The Mechanic*. Don't bother. Rated PG for violence.

1979 103 minutes

LOVE SPELL

★

DIRECTOR: Tom Donavan

CAST: Richard Burton, Kate Mulgrew, Nicholas Clay, Cyril Cusack, Kathryn Dowlin

In this film based on the legend of Tristan and Isolde and their doomed love, Richard Burton portrays Mark, king of Cornwall, who sends his nephew, Tristan, to fetch Mark's intended bride. Unfortunately, the two fall in love, creating the most difficult of triangles. The chase and battle scenes are unimaginatively filmed, and most of the acting mediocre. Burton, however, does his best with the material at hand. Hopeless romantics may find some entertainment here, but others will find this grand-legend-turned-soap-opera a bore.

1979 90 minutes

LUCKY LUCIANO

DIRECTOR: Francesco Rosi

CAST: Gian Maria Volonte, Rod Steiger, Edmond O'Brien, Vincent Gardenia, Charles Cioffi

This U.S.-Franco-Italian production deals with the last years of one of crimeland's most "influential" bosses. The film started out to be an important one for Francesco Rosi, but the distributors ot the English edition went in for the sensationalism with too graphic subtitles and/or dubbing, depending on the version. Not a bad film if you know Italian. If you don't, stick with *The Godfather*. Rated R for profanity and violence.

1974 110 minutes

MACAO

★★

DIRECTOR: Josef von Sternberg

CAST: Jane Russell, Robert Mitchum, William Bendix, Gloria Grahame, Thomas Gomez

Jane Russell is a singer in the fabled Oriental port and gambling heaven of Macao, across the bay from Hong Kong. She's in love with Robert Mitchum, a good guy caught in a web of circumstance. La Russell is the only thing about this film that isn't flat.

1952 B & W 80 minutes

MACKINTOSH MAN, THE

★★★

DIRECTOR: John Huston

CAST: Paul Newman, James Mason, Dominique Sanda, Ian Bannen, Nigel Patrick

A cold war spy thriller with all the edge-of-seat trimmings: car chases, beatings, escapes, and captures. Trouble is, it has been done before, before, and before. Paul Newman is the agent; wily and wonderful James Mason is the communist spy he must catch. Rated PG.

1973 98 minutes

MACON COUNTY LINE

★★★

DIRECTOR: Richard Compton
CAST: Alan Vint, Max Baer Jr., Geoffrey Lewis

A very effective little thriller based on a true incident. Set in Georgia in the 1950s, the story concerns three youths hunted by the law for a murder they did not commit. Producer Max Baer Jr. has a good eye for detail and the flavor of the times. Rated R.

1974 89 minutes

MAD DOG MORGAN

★★½

DIRECTOR: Philippe Mora
CAST: Dennis Hopper, Jack Thompson, David Gulpilil, Michael Pate

Dennis Hopper plays an Australian bush ranger in this familiar tale of a man forced into a life of crime. Good support from aborigine David Gulpilil and Australian actor Jack Thompson help this visually stimulating film, but Hopper's excesses and a muddled ending weigh against it. Early prison sequences and scattered scenes are brutal. Violence, brutality, and offensive scenes. Rated R.

1976 102 minutes

MADIGAN

★★★½

DIRECTOR: Don Siegel
CAST: Richard Widmark, Henry Fonda, Harry Guardino, James Whitmore, Inger Stevens, Michael Dunn, Steve Ihnat, Sheree North

Well-acted, atmospheric police adventure-drama pits tough Brooklyn cop Richard Widmark and New York's finest against a crazed escaped murderer. Veteran Henry Fonda and a fine cast of character actors and actresses breathe life into this taut pre–*Dirty Harry* outing by director Don Siegel, and location shooting adds to the authentic, gritty tone of this film. Realistic and exciting, this is still one of the best of the "behind-the-scenes" police films and topflight entertainment. Tame by today's standards, this is still not ideal fare for young children.

1968 101 minutes

MAGNUM FORCE

★★★

DIRECTOR: Ted Post
CAST: Clint Eastwood, Hal Holbrook, David Soul, Tim Matheson, Robert Urich

This is the second and least enjoyable of the four Dirty Harry films. Harry (Clint Eastwood) must deal with vigilante cops as well as the usual big-city scum. Body count is way up there, Clint is iron-jawed and athletic, but the film still lacks something. Rated R for language, violence, nudity, and gore.

1973 124 minutes

MALONE

★★★★

DIRECTOR: Harley Cokliss
CAST: Burt Reynolds, Cliff Robertson, Kenneth McMillan, Scott Wilson, Lauren Hutton, Cynthia Gibb

In this modern-day western, Burt Reynolds is in top form as Malone, an ex-CIA hit man on the run. When his car breaks down in a small Oregon town, Malone finds himself the only hope of citizens beset by the murderous minions of a ruthless millionaire (Cliff Robertson). Underneath all the car chases, big-bang explosions, and the blitz fire of automatic weapons is the simplest of all B-western plots—in which a former gunfighter is forced out of retirement by the plight of settlers forced off their land by black-hatted villains. Director Harley Cokliss handles the story (based on William Wingate's Hard-acre novel, *Shotgun*) so well, however, that one doesn't mind its basic familiarity. Rated R for profanity, violence, and suggested sex.

1987 92 minutes

MALTESE FALCON, THE

★★★★★

DIRECTOR: John Huston

CAST: Humphrey Bogart, Mary Astor, Sydney Greenstreet, Peter Lorre, Elisha Cook Jr., Ward Bond

One of the all-time great movies, John Huston's first effort as a director is the definitive screen version of Dashiell Hammett's crime story. In a maze of double-crosses and back-stabbing, Humphrey Bogart, as Sam Spade, fights to get hold of a black bird, "the stuff that dreams are made of." One of the greatest casts of supporting heavies fits perfectly into the Hammett characterizations. Sydney Greenstreet, in his first movie, is especially memorable as Kasper Gutman, the "Fat Man" behind the search for the falcon. Mary Astor, Peter Lorre, and Elisha Cook Jr. complete this perfect rogues gallery.

1941 B & W 100 minutes

MAN, A WOMAN AND A BANK, A

★★

DIRECTOR: Noel Black

CAST: Donald Sutherland, Brooke Adams, Paul Mazursky

An odd little caper flick which never quite gets off the ground. A couple of guys decide to rob a bank via computer, and—of course—things don't work out as planned. Donald Sutherland and Paul Mazursky (usually on the other side of the camera) are quite charming, and Brooke Adams delightfuly appealing, but these characters can't rise above the weak plot. Could (and should) have been much better. Rated PG.

1979 100 minutes

MAN FROM SNOWY RIVER, THE

★★★★

DIRECTOR: George Miller

CAST: Tom Burlinson, Kirk Douglas, Jack Thompson, Bruce Kerr

If you've been looking for an adventure film for the whole family, this Australian western about the coming of age of a mountain man (Tom Burlinson) is it. Like a first-rate Disney movie from the 1950s, sometimes it's corny and a little too cutesy. But it's just right for folks who are tired of all the cussing, nudity, and gore that seem to pervade most modern so-called family films. Rated PG, the film has no objectionable material.

1982 115 minutes

MAN IN THE IRON MASK, THE (ORIGINAL)

★★★

DIRECTOR: James Whale

CAST: Louis Hayward, Joan Bennett, Warren William, Alan Hale, Joseph Schildkraut, Marion Martin, Walter Kingsford

Louis Hayward plays twin brothers—a fop and a swashbuckler—in this first sound version of Dumas's classic novel of malice, mayhem, intrigue, and ironic revenge in eighteenth-century France. Separated at birth, one brother becomes the king of France, the other a sword-wielding cohort of the Three Musketeers. Their clash makes for great romantic adventure.

1939 B & W 110 minutes

MAN IN THE IRON MASK, THE (REMAKE)

★★★

DIRECTOR: Mike Newell

CAST: Richard Chamberlain, Patrick McGoohan, Louis Jourdan, Jenny Agutter, Ralph Richardson

This is the Alexandre Dumas tale of twin brothers, separated at birth. One becomes the wicked king of France, the other, a heroic peasant. The story receives a top-drawer treatment in this classy TV movie. Richard Chamberlain proves he's the most appealing swashbuckler since Errol Flynn retired his sword.

1977 100 minutes

MAN INSIDE, THE

★★½

DIRECTOR: Gerald Mayer
CAST: James Franciscus, Stefanie Powers, Jacques Godin, Len Birman, Donald Davis, Allan Royale

In this so-so film, James Franciscus is a Canadian vice squad agent who works his way into the organization of a major heroin dealer. In the course of his assignment he has the opportunity to split with $2 million, and is tempted to do so. This would provide the means for a new way of life, which his girlfriend (Stefanie Powers) is demanding. It would also put a heroin dealer out of business for good. This Canadian film is unrated.

1984 96 minutes

MAN WHO WOULD BE KING, THE

★★★★½

DIRECTOR: John Huston
CAST: Sean Connery, Michael Caine, Christopher Plummer

A superb screen adventure, this is loosely based on Rudyard Kipling's story and was made at the same time Sean Connery and John Huston starred in the other sand-and-camel flick, the excellent *The Wind and the Lion*. Both are classics in the adventure genre. Rated PG.

1975 129 minutes

MAN WITH BOGART'S FACE, THE

★★½

DIRECTOR: Robert Day
CAST: Robert Sacchi, Michelle Phillips, Olivia Hussey, Franco Nero, Misty Rowe, Victor Buono, Herbert Lom, Sybil Danning, George Raft, Mike Mazurki

A modern-day Humphrey Bogart–type mystery. Film has fun with the genre while avoiding outright parody. A warm-hearted homage. Enjoyable, but of no great importance. Rated PG.

1980 106 minutes

MAN WITH THE GOLDEN GUN, THE

★½

DIRECTOR: Guy Hamilton
CAST: Roger Moore, Christopher Lee, Britt Ekland, Maud Adams, Herve Villechaize, Bernard Lee, Lois Maxwell

In spite of the potentially sinister presence of Christopher Lee as the head baddie, this is the most poorly constructed of all the Bond films. Roger Moore sleepwalks through the entire picture, and the plot tosses in every cliché, including the (then) obligatory nod to kung fu. Even John Barry's score is less spirited than usual, and Britt Ekland represents a low in leading ladies... even in *this series*. Sorry 'bout that, James. Rated PG—some violence.

1974 125 minutes

MANHUNT IN THE AFRICAN JUNGLE (SECRET SERVICE IN DARKEST AFRICA)

★★

DIRECTOR: Spencer Bennet
CAST: Rod Cameron, Joan Marsh, Duncan Renaldo, Lionel Royce

American undercover agent Rod Cameron, posing as a Nazi, joins forces with United Nations agent Joan Marsh, posing as a journalist, to defeat the Axis in North Africa, which is headed by Lionel Royce, who in turn is disguised as an Arab leader. Duncan Renaldo (*The Cisco Kid*) as a French officer comes along to help and takes his turn in being pummeled, conked on the head, and tied up in true serial fashion. The good guys naturally win in the end, although they make a pretty bland bunch compared with Nazis Kurt Kreuger and Kurt Katch. Not the most thrill-laden of serials.

1943 B & W 15 chapters

MANHUNTER

★★★★½

DIRECTOR: Michael Mann
CAST: William Petersen, Kim Greist, Brian Cox, Dennis Farina, Joan Allen, Chris Elliot

Thoroughly engrossing tale of an FBI man (William Petersen of *To Live and Die in L.A.*) following a trail of blood through the Southeast left by a ruthless, calculating psychopath known only as "The Tooth Fairy," for reasons made shockingly clear. This genuine edge-of-your-seat nail-biter from *Miami Vice* creator and producer Michael Mann must be viewed very attentively if one is to catch all the details and motives in the intricate plot. Produced with the utmost care and skill, *Manhunter* also features tight performances and some beautiful imagery in the best *Vice* tradition, with Iron Butterfly's classic "In-a-gadda-da-vida" used to create maximum impact at the jarring climax. A certified winner, intense and compelling from beginning to end. Rated R for violence and various adult contents.

1986 118 minutes

MARATHON MAN

★★★★

DIRECTOR: John Schlesinger
CAST: Dustin Hoffman, Laurence Olivier, Roy Scheider, William Devane, Marthe Keller

A young student (Dustin Hoffman) unwittingly becomes involved in the pursuit of an ex–Nazi war criminal (Laurence Olivier) in this chase-thriller. The action holds your interest throughout. Most chilling is the scene where Olivier makes use of his ex-profession of dentistry to persuade Hoffman to share some information. A few of the more violent moments may be too excessive for some viewers' tastes. Rated R.

1976 125 minutes

MASKED MARVEL, THE

★★½

DIRECTOR: Spencer Bennet
CAST: William Forrest, Louise Currie, Johnny Arthur, David Bacon

The mysterious Masked Marvel comes to the aid of the World-Wide Insurance Company to battle the evil Sakima, a former Japanese envoy, and his gang of saboteurs, who are threatening the security of America. The Masked Marvel finally triumphs after dodging bombs, bullets, falls, and runaway vehicles of all kinds. He keeps his identity a secret, too, ready to emerge again when America needs a champion. Practically nonstop action and top stunt work highlight this wartime Republic serial, which is about as patriotic as a serial can be.

1943 B & W 12 chapters

MATA HARI

★★

DIRECTOR: Curtis Harrington
CAST: Sylvia Kristel, Christopher Cazenove, Oliver Tobias, Gaye Brown

Liberally sprinkled with action, erotica, and existentialism, *Mata Hari* is one of Sylvia (*Emmanuelle*) Kristel's better works. A departure from the more familiar tales of Mata Hari, this story traces the erotic dancer from Indonesia as she unwittingly becomes the tool of the German government during World War II. Naturally, she does it all for love —and lust! Rated R for sex and nudity.

1985 103 minutes

MCQ

★★★½

DIRECTOR: John Sturges
CAST: John Wayne, Al Lettieri, Eddie Albert, Diana Muldaur, Clu Gulager, Colleen Dewhurst

The success of *Dirty Harry* and the slow death of the western prompted John Wayne to shed his Stetson and six guns for cop clothes. While this John Sturges film doesn't quite match the Clint Eastwood–Don Siegel production that inspired it, there are some good scenes and suspense. The best moment comes when Big John bangs around bad guy Al Lettieri in a men's room. Recommended for fans of the Duke only. Rated PG.

1974 116 minutes

MEAN JOHNNY BARROWS

🦃

DIRECTOR: Fred Williamson
CAST: Fred Williamson, Roddy McDowall, Stuart Whitman, Elliott Gould, Jenny Sherman

Fred Williamson plays Johnny Barrows, a Vietnam war hero, dishonorably discharged for striking an officer. Trying to make it as a civilian, he becomes involved in a gang war, bad acting, and horrible music. This is one of the *Shaft*-inspired black exploitation films, and like too many of them, it's a waste of time. Rated R.

1976 80 minutes

MEAN SEASON, THE

★★★½

DIRECTOR: Phillip Borsos
CAST: Kurt Russell, Richard Jordan, Mariel Hemingway, Richard Masur

Miami crime reporter Kurt Russell finds himself the unwilling confidant of a maniacal killer in this exciting thriller. The film occasionally relies on stock shocks. Still, it is fast-paced and inventive enough to overcome the clichés. Mariel Hemingway is featured as the journalist's imperiled girlfriend, with Richard Jordan effective in a change-of-pace role as the villain. Rated R for violence.

1985 109 minutes

MECHANIC, THE

★★½

DIRECTOR: Michael Winner
CAST: Charles Bronson, Jan-Michael Vincent, Jill Ireland, Keenan Wynn

A professional hit man (Charles Bronson) teaches his craft to a young student (Jan-Michael Vincent). Slow-moving for the most part, with a few good action scenes. The ending has a nice twist to it, but the film is generally much ado about nothing. Rated R for violence and language.

1972 100 minutes

MEN IN WAR

★★★★

DIRECTOR: Anthony Mann
CAST: Robert Ryan, Aldo Ray, Vic Morrow

This outstanding Korean War action film with Robert Ryan and Aldo Ray fighting the Chinese and each other is one of the very best "war is hell" films. Battle scenes are first-rate, thanks to

Anthony Mann's crisp and uncompromising direction.
1957 B & W 104 minutes

MIAMI VICE

★★★★

DIRECTOR: Thomas Carter
CAST: Don Johnson, Philip Michael Thomas, Saundra Santiago, Michael Talbott, John Diehl, Gregory Sierra, Bill Smitrovich, Belinda Montgomery, Martin Ferrero, Mykel T. Williamson, Olivia Brown, Miguel Pinero

This pilot for the popular NBC series is slam-bang entertainment. A New York City cop (Philip Michael Thomas) on the trail of the powerful drug kingpin who killed his brother traces him to Miami, running into a vice cop (Don Johnson) who's after the same guy. All the trademarks of the series are here: great music, rapid-fire editing, gritty low-key performances, and bursts of sporadic violence. Combine these elements with a superb video transfer (far better than network TV), and you have a dynamite action show outdone only by its sequel episode, "The Return of Calderone." The only real flaw in this tape is the sound quality, which, even in hi-fi stereo, is muffled.
1984 97 minutes

MIAMI VICE: "THE PRODIGAL SON"

★★★

DIRECTOR: Paul Michael Glaser
CAST: Don Johnson, Philip Michael Thomas, Edward James Olmos, Olivia Brown, Penn Jilette, Pam Grier

The pastel duo, Crockett (Don Johnson) and Tubbs (Philip Michael Thomas), trek up to New York in search of the bad guys in this second-season opener. Out of Miami and into the Big Apple's glitz, Crockett falls in love with a criminal's girlfriend and almost gets killed.The bad guys turn out to be good guys, and everyone is running through the crowded streets of the city with Uzis, pistols, and shotguns blaring, without ever once seeing a uniformed cop.
1985 99 minutes

MIDNIGHT LACE

★★★

DIRECTOR: David Miller
CAST: Doris Day, Rex Harrison, John Gavin, Myrna Loy, Roddy McDowall, Herbert Marshall, Natasha Perry

A fine mystery with a cast that makes the most of it. Doris Day is an American living in London and married to successful businessman Rex Harrison. She soon finds her life in danger. Some viewers may find it less sophisticated than present-day thrillers, but there's plenty of suspense and plot twists to recommend it.
1960 100 minutes

MIDWAY

★★★

DIRECTOR: Jack Smight
CAST: Henry Fonda, Charlton Heston, Robert Mitchum, Hal Holbrook, Edward Albert, Cliff Robertson

An all-star cast was assembled to bring to the screen this famous sea battle of World War II. Midway became famous as the site of the overwhelming victory of American carrier forces, which shifted the balance of power in the Pacific. As a historical drama, this film is accurate and maintains interest. However, a subplot involving Charlton Heston's son (Edward Albert) and his romance with a Japanese girl is totally out of place. Rated PG.
1976 132 minutes

MIRROR CRACK'D, THE

★½

DIRECTOR: Guy Hamilton
CAST: Elizabeth Taylor, Kim Novak, Tony Curtis, Angela Lansbury, Edward Fox, Rock Hudson

Elizabeth Taylor, Kim Novak, and Tony Curtis seem to be vying to see who can turn in the worst performance in this tepid adaptation of the Agatha Christie murder mystery. Angela Lansbury makes an excellent Miss Marple, and Edward Fox is topnotch as her Scotland Yard inspector nephew. But overall this film—awkwardly directed by James Bond specialist Guy Hamilton (*Goldfinger*; *The Man with the Golden Gun*)—is a definite step down from the other Christie films, such as *Murder on the Orient Express* and *Death on the Nile*. Rated PG.

1980 105 minutes

MISSING IN ACTION

★★★½

DIRECTOR: Joseph Zito
CAST: Chuck Norris, M. Emmet Walsh, Lenore Kasdorf, James Hong

Chuck Norris is a one-man army in this Vietnam-based action film. Anyone else might be laughable in such a role. But the former karate star makes it work, resulting in the best film he'd made to date. The story focuses on an attempt by Col. James Braddock (Norris), a former Vietnam prisoner of war, to free the other Americans he believes are still there. Rated R for profanity, violence, and brief nudity.

1984 101 minutes

MISSING IN ACTION 2: THE BEGINNING

★★½

DIRECTOR: Lance Hool
CAST: Chuck Norris, Cosie Costa, Soon-Teck Oh, Steven Williams, Bennett Ohta

Following on the heels of the previous year's surprise hit, this "prequel" is really the same movie, only it tells the story of how Colonel Braddock (Chuck Norris) and his men escaped their Vietnam prison camp after ten years of torture. The acting is nonexistent, the action predictable and violent. Soon-Teck Oh (from television's *East of Eden*) stars as the sadistic camp commandant and prime enemy in this martial arts/action drama. Rated R for violence.

1985 95 minutes

MR. ACE

★½

DIRECTOR: Edwin L. Marin
CAST: George Raft, Sylvia Sidney, Stanley Ridges, Sara Haden, Jerome Cowan

Studio potboiler about spoiled society woman (Sylvia Sidney) who uses gangster (George Raft) to win congressional election goes through the motions but very little else. Raft, an interesting nonactor at best, seems to be in this film simply because he fills the part; he never brings the kind of excitement or character that a Lloyd Nolan could have breathed into it. The acting is okay, but the story is too familiar and the ending too trite to be taken seriously. Basically a programmer and a vehicle for the two aging stars, this film never really takes off and offers a pretty low-priority rental choice when compared with the better films in which these actors and actresses appeared.

1946 B & W 84 minutes

MR. BILLION

★★½

DIRECTOR: Jonathan Kaplan
CAST: Terence Hill, Valerie Perrine, Jackie Gleason, Slim Pickens, William Redfield, Chill Wills, Dick Miller

Sappy but seductive story about a humble Italian mechanic (Terence Hill) who will inherit a financial empire if he can get to the signing-over of his uncle's will before a gang of kidnappers or the corporation's chairman (Jackie Gleason) gets to him first. Valerie Perrine plays a call girl who is hired to seduce the benefactor and get him to sign over his inheritance. While this all sounds like heavy drama, there are enough car chases and fist fights to earn this one a place in the action category. Rated PG for violence and sex.

1977 89 minutes

MR. INSIDE/MR. OUTSIDE

★★

DIRECTOR: William Graham
CAST: Hal Linden, Tony LoBianco, Phil Bruns, Paul Benjamin, Stefan Schnabel

Hal Linden and Tony LoBianco are fine in this made-for-television cop thriller as two New York City detectives attempting to foil a smuggling ring. Director William Graham's pacing makes you forget how much this movie is like so many other works created for TV.

1973 74 minutes

MR. LUCKY

★★★

DIRECTOR: H. C. Potter
CAST: Cary Grant, Laraine Day

Cary Grant is a gambler attempting to bilk money from a charity relief program. He changes his tune when he falls for a wealthy society girl, Laraine Day. This is a slick piece of wartime fluff. The plot has nothing you haven't seen before, but the charm of Grant makes it watchable.

1943 B & W 100 minutes

MR. MAJESTYK

★★★½

DIRECTOR: Richard Fleischer
CAST: Charles Bronson, Al Lettieri, Linda Cristal, Lee Purcell, Paul Koslo

In this better-than-average Charles Bronson vehicle, he's a watermelon grower (!) coming up against gangster Al Lettieri (in a first-rate performance). If you like Chuck, you'll love this one. Rated R.

1974 103 minutes

MR. MOTO'S LAST WARNING

★★★

DIRECTOR: Norman Foster
CAST: Peter Lorre, Ricardo Cortez, Virginia Field, John Carradine, George Sanders

One of the last in the low-budget series that produced eight films in less than three years. This time out, the detective gets involved with terrorist spies intent on blowing up the French fleet in the Suez Canal. Enjoyable, quaint entertainment with a good supporting cast.

1939 B & W 71 minutes

MR. ROBINSON CRUSOE

★★★

DIRECTOR: Edward Sutherland
CAST: Douglas Fairbanks Sr., William Farnum, Maria Alba

Dashing Douglas Fairbanks Sr. bets he can survive like Crusoe on a South Sea island. Just how he does it makes for great fun. Fairbanks was just short of 50 when he made this film, but he was still the agile, athletic swashbuckler whose wholesome charm made him the idol of millions.

1932 B & W 76 minutes

MR. WONG, DETECTIVE

★★★

DIRECTOR: William Nigh
CAST: Boris Karloff, Grant Withers, Evelyn Brent, Maxine Jennings, Lucien Prival

First of five Mr. Wong films starring Boris Karloff as Hugh Wiley's black-suited sleuth is a notch above most of Mascot Pictures programmers. Mr. Wong (with the dubious assistance of Captain Street of Homicide) attempts to solve the deaths of three industrialists, which have baffled the authorities and have the government and media in an uproar. The great Karloff is always a treat to watch and this series marked his only continuing character that wasn't a monster or villain of some sort. Fun for mystery and detective fans and a nice complement to the other Oriental sleuths of the 1930s, Charlie Chan and Mr. Moto.

1938 B & W 69 minutes

MIXED BLOOD

★★★½

DIRECTOR: Paul Morrissey
CAST: Marilia Pera, Richard Ulacia, Linda Kerridge, Geraldine Smith, Angel David, Ulrich Berr, Rodney Harvey

Paul Morrissey, the same man who brought you Andy Warhol's versions of *Frankenstein* and *Dracula*, has made a serious film about the Alphabet City drug subculture and its inherent violent nature. *Mixed Blood* is actually a mixed bag. Morrissey's choice of actors hasn't changed; they all read their lines devoid of emotion. While this detracts from the story most of the time, there are moments when this makes complete sense. The film is similar to Penelope Spheeris's *Suburbia*. The lack of emotion in the characters shifts the focus from the actor to the landscape to which he or she is reacting. Here the surroundings are brutal and unforgiving, and the cheap film stock gives the movie a newsreel feeling. Not rated, but contains an abundance of violence and profanity.

1985 98 minutes

MOBY DICK

★★★★½

DIRECTOR: John Huston
CAST: Gregory Peck, Richard Basehart, Leo Genn, Orson Welles

Director John Huston's brilliant adaptation of Herman Melville's classic novel features Gregory Peck in one of his best performances as the driven Captain Ahab. Richard Basehart, Leo Genn, and Orson Welles lend fine support. The final action scenes are pure Hollywood magic. No rating, with some violence, but all right for the family.

1956 116 minutes

MOGAMBO

★★★

DIRECTOR: John Ford
CAST: Clark Gable, Grace Kelly, Ava Gardner

This remake of the film classic *Red Dust* stars Clark Gable as the great white hunter who dallies with a sophisticated married woman (Grace Kelly), only to return to the arms of a jaded lady (Ava Gardner, who is quite good in the role of the woman with a past). It's not great John Ford, but it'll do.

1953 115 minutes

MOONLIGHTING

★★★★

DIRECTOR: Robert Butler
CAST: Cybill Shepherd, Bruce Willis, Allyce Beasley

This is the pilot film for the delightfully offbeat ABC series. Maddie, a supersuccessful model, suddenly finds herself facing poverty, thanks to an embezzler. She decides to sell off all her assets, including a money-losing detective agency. David, a fast-talking, irresistible eccentric, tries to talk her into making a career of sleuthing instead. Bruce Willis is dazzling as David. And the chemistry beween Willis and Cybill Shepherd heats up to just the right temperature. The pilot displays a degree of wit and style rarely seen in a TV movie.

1985 97 minutes

MOONRAKER

DIRECTOR: Lewis Gilbert

CAST: Roger Moore, Lois Chiles, Michael Lonsdale

The James Bond series hit absolute rock bottom in 1979 with this outer-space adventure featuring Roger Moore as the famed secret agent. It's a groaner for 007 fans and nonfans alike. Rated PG.

1979 126 minutes

MOONSHINE COUNTY EXPRESS

★★

DIRECTOR: Gus Trikonis

CAST: John Saxon, Susan Howard, William Conrad, Dub Taylor

In this bogus action flick, William Conrad has his hands full with the three vengeful daughters of a man he just murdered. Rated PG for mild language and violence.

1977 95 minutes

MORGAN THE PIRATE

★★★

DIRECTORS: André de Toth, Primo Zeglio

CAST: Steve Reeves, Valerie Lagrange, Ivo Garbani, Lidia Alfonsi, Giulio Bosetti, Angelo Zanolli

This fictionalized account of the adventures of the historical Henry Morgan (with muscleman Steve Reeves in the title role) is perhaps the most entertaining of that actor's many Italian-made features. Even by current standards, there is plenty of action and romance.

1961 93 minutes

MOTHER LODE

★★

DIRECTOR: Charlton Heston

CAST: Charlton Heston, John Marley, Nick Mancuso, Kim Basinger

Although this modern-day adventure yarn about a search for gold boasts a feasible plot and fine acting by Charlton Heston (who also directed) and John Marley, its liabilities far outweigh its assets. It is uneven, lacks character development, and the performances of Nick Mancuso and Kim Basinger leave much to be desired. Despite a good deal of suspense in the second half, it remains a mediocre piece of escapism. Rated PG, the film contains occasional obscenities and violence.

1982 101 minutes

MS. .45

★★★★

DIRECTOR: Abel Ferrara

CAST: Zoe Tamerlis

An attractive mute woman is raped and beaten twice in the same evening. She slips into madness and seeks revenge with a .45 pistol. A female version of *Death Wish* with an ending at a Halloween costume party that will knock your socks off. Not for all tastes. Rated R for violence, nudity, rape, language, and gore.

1981 90 minutes

MURDER BY DECREE

★★★½

DIRECTOR: Bob Clark

CAST: Christopher Plummer, James Mason, Donald Sutherland, Genevieve Bujold, Susan Clark, David Hemmings,

John Gielgud, Anthony Quayle

Excellent cast stylishly serves up this Sherlock Holmes mystery. Christopher Plummer and James Mason are well suited to the roles of Holmes and Dr. Watson. The murky story deals with Jack the Ripper. Rated R for violence and gore.

1979 121 minutes

MURDER MY SWEET

★★★★

DIRECTOR: Edward Dmytryk
CAST: Dick Powell, Claire Trevor, Anne Shirley

In the mid-1940s, Dick Powell decided to change his clean-cut crooner image by playing Raymond Chandler's hard-boiled detective, Philip Marlowe. It worked marvelously, with Powell making a fine white knight in tarnished armor on the trail of killers and blackmailers.

1944 B & W 95 minutes

MURDER ON THE ORIENT EXPRESS

★★★★½

DIRECTOR: Sidney Lumet
CAST: Albert Finney, Ingrid Bergman, Lauren Bacall, Sean Connery, Vanessa Redgrave, Michael York, Jacqueline Bisset

Belgian detective Hercule Poirot solves a murder on a train in this stylish prestige picture based on the Agatha Christie mystery. Albert Finney is terrific as the detective and is supported by an all-star cast. Rated PG.

1974 127 minutes

MURDERERS' ROW

★★½

DIRECTOR: Henry Levin
CAST: Dean Martin, Ann-Margret, Karl Malden, James Gregory

This entry into the Matt Helm secret-agent series is pretty dismal. Dean Martin has been much better in other films. The Matt Helm series was an attempt to grab the Bond and Flint audience, but Martin just couldn't cut it as a superspy.

1966 108 minutes

MURPH THE SURF

★★½

DIRECTOR: Marvin Chomsky
CAST: Robert Conrad, Don Stroud, Donna Mills, Luther Adler

In this based-on-real-life thriller, two Florida beachniks connive to do the impossible: steal the fabled 564-carat Star of India sapphire out of New York's American Museum of Natural History. Re-creation of the 1964 crime induces sweat, along with a good speedboat chase, but the picture never really catches a wave.

1975 101 minutes

MURPHY'S LAW

★

DIRECTOR: J. Lee Thompson
CAST: Charles Bronson, Carrie Snodgress, Kathleen Wilhoite

Guess what! Charles Bronson plays a tough guy! He's a cop framed for the murder of his ex-wife, who escapes from jail handcuffed to the teenage girl who stole his car. It's a plot line used before in *The Defiant Ones*, *The Gauntlet*, and *48 Hrs*, all of which are better films. The movie suffers from a complete lack of subtlety. The bad guys are snarling Neanderthals, the good guys are honest to a fault, and Bronson's young cohort (Kathleen Wilhoite) is so relentlessly spunky, she makes you want to retch. The only thing *Murphy's Law* does well is prove Murphy's Law. Rated R.

1986 101 minutes

MURPHY'S WAR

★★★

DIRECTOR: Peter Yates

CAST: Peter O'Toole, Sian Phillips, Horst Janson, Philippe Noiret, John Hallam

World War II sea drama follows British seaman, sole survivor of a brutal massacre of his ship's crew by a German U-boat, as he seeks revenge. Peter O'Toole gives a hard-hitting, no-holds-barred performance as the outraged, bloodthirsty Murphy. This film is something of a psychological study. Action sequences are great, but talky scenes tend to slow things to a bore. Well done nonetheless. Rated PG.

1971 108 minutes

MUTINY ON THE BOUNTY (ORIGINAL)

★★★★

DIRECTOR: Frank Lloyd

CAST: Charles Laughton, Clark Gable, Franchot Tone, Dudley Digges, Eddie Quillan, Donald Crisp, Henry Stephenson, Spring Byington, Herbert Mundin, Douglas Walton, Ian Wolfe

The first and best known of three versions of the now classic account of mutiny against the tyranny of Captain William Bligh during a worldwide British naval expedition in 1789. Charles Laughton is superb as the merciless Bligh, Clark Gable unquestionably fine as the leader of the mutiny, Fletcher Christian. The film won an Oscar for best picture and still entertains today.

1935 B & W 132 minutes

MUTINY ON THE BOUNTY (REMAKE)

★★

DIRECTOR: Lewis Milestone

CAST: Marlon Brando, Trevor Howard, Richard Harris, Hugh Griffith, Richard Haydn, Gordon Jackson

This years-later remake hits the South Seas with a gigantic belly flop. The color is beautiful, Trevor Howard is commanding as the tyrannical Captain Bligh, but Marlon Brando as mutiny leader Fletcher Christian? Yucko!

1962 179 minutes

NAKED AND THE DEAD, THE

★★★

DIRECTOR: Raoul Walsh

CAST: Aldo Ray, Joey Bishop, Cliff Robertson, Raymond Massey

This action-packed World War II film is based on Norman Mailer's famous book. Not nearly as good as the book, nevertheless the film is still quite powerful and exciting. Worth a watch. Bernard Herrmann did the film score.

1958 131 minutes

NAKED PREY, THE

★★★½

DIRECTOR: Cornel Wilde

CAST: Cornel Wilde, Gert Van Den Bergh, Ken Gampu

An African safari takes a disastrous turn and Cornel Wilde winds up running naked and unarmed through the searing jungle as a large band of native warriors keeps on his heels, determined to finish him off. This is an amazingly intense adventure of man versus man and man verus nature. Wilde does a remarkable job, both as star and director.

1966 94 minutes

NAME OF THE ROSE, THE

★★★

DIRECTOR: Jean-Jacques Annaud

CAST: Sean Connery, F. Murray Abraham, Christian Slater, Elya Baskin, Feodor Chaliapin Jr., William Hickey, Michael Lonsdale, Ron Perlman

In this passable screen adaptation of Umberto Eco's bestseller, Sean Connery stars as a monkish Sherlock Holmes trying to solve a series of murders in a fourteenth-century monastery. Connery is fun to watch, but the plot is rather feeble. Rated R for nudity, simulated sex, and violence.

1986 118 minutes

NATE AND HAYES

★★★

DIRECTOR: Ferdinand Fairfax
CAST: Tommy Lee Jones, Michael O'Keefe, Max Phipps

Tommy Lee Jones as a good pirate, Michael O'Keefe as his missionary accomplice, and Max Phipps as their cutthroat nemesis make this a jolly movie. Set in the South Seas of the late nineteenth century, it's unpretentious, old-fashioned movie fun. Rated PG for violence.

1983 100 minutes

NEVER CRY WOLF

★★★★★

DIRECTOR: Carroll Ballard
CAST: Charles Martin Smith, Brian Dennehy

Carroll Ballard (*The Black Stallion*) made this breathtakingly beautiful, richly rewarding Disney feature about a lone biologist (Charles Martin Smith, of *American Graffiti*) learning firsthand about the white wolves of the Yukon by living with them. It's an extraordinary motion picture in every sense of the word. Not only is it the kind of movie the whole family can enjoy, but it's also a state-of-the-art cinematic creation. Rated PG for brief nudity.

1983 105 minutes

NEVER SAY NEVER AGAIN

★★★★½

DIRECTOR: Irvin Kershner
CAST: Sean Connery, Klaus Maria Brandauer, Barbara Carrera, Max von Sydow, Kim Basinger, Bernie Casey

In the battle of the Bonds, Sean Connery wins over Roger Moore by a hair—or is that hairpiece? (Sorry, Sean.) All kidding aside, it's great to see Connery back in the role he made—and that made him—famous. Although *Never Say Never Again* is essentially a remake of *Thunderball*, it is a far superior film; much funnier, sexier, and more action-filled than its predecessor. Rated PG for violence, suggested sex, and nudity.

1983 137 minutes

NEVER TOO YOUNG TO DIE

★

DIRECTOR: Gil Bettman
CAST: John Stamos, Vanity, Gene Simmons, George Lazenby

A really rotten film that steals everything it can from the James Bond and *Road Warrior* series. John Stamos plays the son of George Lazenby, an American secret agent who is murdered by a gang of crazies, led by Gene Simmons. The gang's plan is to poison the water supply of Los Angeles if $50 million ransom isn't paid to them. Unbelievably bad dialogue, and boring action scenes make this a real bomb, with only Vanity's good looks and charm left for enjoyment. Rated R for language, sex, and violence.

1986 90 minutes

NEW ADVENTURES OF TARZAN

★★½

DIRECTORS: Edward Kull, W. F. McGaugh
CAST: Herman Brix (Bruce Bennett), Ula Holt, Frank Baker, Dale Walsh, Harry Ernest, Don Castello, Lewis Sargent

For the first time on film, Edgar Rice Burroughs's immortal jungle lord spoke and behaved the way he had been created. This twelve-episode chapter play wove a complex story about a search for Tarzan's missing friend and a treacherous agent intent on stealing an ancient Mayan stone. Tarzan breaks ropes with his chest, survives a plunge over a waterfall, and throws numerous small South American natives about. Location footage with the cast was intercut with film from the Dearholt-Stout expedition; unfortunately, this extensive footage also slowed down the pace. This serial proved a bonanza, and the twelve chapters were cut into two feature-length films: *Tarzan's New Adventure* and *Tarzan and the Green Goddess*. Herman Brix went on to star in several good serials and, as Bruce Bennett, appeared in a number of A productions, among them *Sahara* and *The Treasure of the Sierra Madre*.

1935 B & W 12 chapters

NEWMAN'S LAW

★

DIRECTOR: Richard Heffron

CAST: George Peppard, Roger Robinson, Abe Vigoda, Eugene Roche

George Peppard plays a good cop accused of corruption and suspended from the force, who privately pursues the case he is on. Sound familiar? It is, with all the clichés intact. Rated PG for violence.

1974 98 minutes

NIGHT CROSSING

★★★½

DIRECTOR: Delbert Mann

CAST: John Hurt, Jane Alexander, Beau Bridges, Ian Bannen

This Disney film is about a real-life escape from East Germany by two families in a gas-filled balloon. The performances by John Hurt, Jane Alexander, Beau Bridges, and Ian Bannen are excellent, and director Delbert Mann makes the most of the possibilities for suspense. Unfortunately, minor flaws, such as mismatched accents and Americanized situations, prevent it from being a total success. Rated PG for violence.

1981 106 minutes

NIGHT MOVES

★★★★

DIRECTOR: Arthur Penn

CAST: Gene Hackman, Susan Clark, Melanie Griffith

A dark and disturbing detective study with Gene Hackman superb as the private eye trying to solve a baffling mystery. This release was unfairly overlooked when in theaters—but you don't have to miss it now. Rated R.

1975 95 minutes

NIGHT OF THE GENERALS

★

DIRECTOR: Anatole Litvak

CAST: Peter O'Toole, Omar Sharif, Tom Courtenay, Donald Pleasence, Joanna Pettet, Christopher Plummer

This lurid WWII murder mystery, revolving around a group of Nazi generals, has very little to offer. It will leave you bored, confused, and slightly repulsed.

1967 148 minutes

NIGHT OF THE JUGGLER

★★

DIRECTOR: Robert Butler

CAST: James Brolin, Cliff Gorman, Richard Castellano, Abby Bluestone, Linda G. Miller, Mandy Patinkin

Psychopath kidnaps little girl for ransom. It's the wrong little girl. Her daddy's an ex-cop with no money and lots of rage. The movie, buoyed by James Brolin's potent performance, initially grabs viewers' attention. Eventually, a cruel streak undermines the drama as it wheezes to a predictable conclusion. Rated R.

1980 101 minutes

NIGHTHAWKS

★★★★½

DIRECTOR: Bruce Malmuth
CAST: Sylvester Stallone, Billy Dee Williams, Rutger Hauer, Lindsay Wagner

From its explosive first scene to the breathtakingly suspenseful denouement, *Nighthawks*, about a police detective hunting a wily terrorist, is a thoroughly enjoyable, supercharged action film. Rated R for violence, nudity, and profanity.

1981 99 minutes

NIGHTKILL

★★★

DIRECTOR: Ted Post
CAST: Jaclyn Smith, Robert Mitchum, James Franciscus

Largely unreleased in theaters, this is a tidy little cat-and-mouse thriller with former Charlie's Angel Jaclyn Smith as a conniving widow and Mitchum as the world-weary investigator who gets caught up in her scheme. Smith and Mitchum are very good. Despite some inept direction, the last half-hour is a nail-biter, particularly scenes in a bathroom shower. Financed by a German company and filmed with a German crew by director Post. Rated R for violence, nudity, and profanity.

1983 97 minutes

NINE DEATHS OF THE NINJA

DIRECTOR: Emmet Alston
CAST: Sho Kosugi, Brent Huff, Emilia Lesniak, Blackie Dammett

Sho Kosugi (*Enter the Ninja*) stars in yet another grunt-and-groan, low-budget martial arts mess. This time, he attempts to rescue a congressman who has been kidnapped by terrorists. You'll need chopsticks to keep your eyes open, and a good kick in the head to find it enjoyable. Rated R.

1985 94 minutes

99 AND 44/100 PERCENT DEAD

★

DIRECTOR: John Frankenheimer
CAST: Richard Harris, Chuck Connors, Edmond O'Brien, Bradford Dillman, Ann Turkel

A hit man is hired to rub out a gangland boss. The first five minutes are stylish, and Bradford Dillman's impersonation of Elmer Fudd is sort of fun, but the rest of the film is a bore. If you are forced to watch it, try to entertain yourself by counting how many times the cast says "Hello, Harry." (Or in Dillman's case, "Hewwo, Hawwy.") Rated PG for violence.

1974 98 minutes

NINJA III: THE DOMINATION

DIRECTOR: Sam Firstenberg
CAST: Lucinda Dickey, Sho Kosugi

Now that *Ghostbusters* has spoofed the whole demonic-possession genre out of existence, it's only natural that the quick-buck moviemakers of the Cannon Group would come up with a completely idiotic film of that kind. Best described as *The Exorcist* meets *Enter the Dragon*, this turkey stars Lucinda Dickey (*Breakin'*) as a young woman possessed by the spirit of an evil revenge-seeking Ninja. And only Sho Kosugi (*Enter the Ninja* and *Revenge of the Ninja*) can bring her bloody rampage to an end. Even its many moments of unintentional humor don't make this pathetic picture worth watching. Avoid it at all costs. Rated R for violence and profanity.

1984 95 minutes

NO MERCY

★½

DIRECTOR: Richard Pearce

CAST: Richard Gere, Kim Basinger, Jeroen Krabbé, George Dzundza, William Atherton, Terry Kinney, Bruce McGill, Ray Sharkey, Gary Basaraba

No Mercy is a predictable, rapid-paced thriller about a Chicago cop (Richard Gere) who travels to New Orleans to avenge the murder of his partner. Kim Basinger is the Cajun woman who is Gere's link to the villain. Dutch actor Jeroen Krabbé is the big baddie from the bayou, but he seems to be in the wrong movie. With his stylishKarl Lagerfeld ponytail, he could have stepped off the set of *Blade Runner*. The cops in this movie go around slapping women and firing off multiple gutter-side metaphors and similes, which are supposed to make them sound tough but really make you ache for a better scriptwriter. Gere plays his cop Eddie Jillette with little or no shading; his performance is a catalogue of souped-up mannerisms. Basinger, exuding an uncharacteristic innocence, is more interesting. She doesn't have much of a role, however, so she does a lot of screaming from the sidelines. Because of this movie's staleness, so do we. Rated R for violence, language, and sexual situations.

1986 107 minutes

NO RETREAT, NO SURRENDER

DIRECTOR: Corey Yuen

CAST: Kurt McKinney, J. W. Fails, Ron Pohnel, Kathie Sileno, Peter "Sugarfoot" Cunningham, Kent Lipham, Jean Claude Van Damme

An uninspired cross between *The Karate Kid* and *Rocky IV* about a teenager who keeps getting beaten up by kung-fu students. Tired of bloody noses, this living punching bag finds an instructor, but instead of being taught by a karate expert from Okinawa, his teacher is the ghost of Bruce Lee. After he becomes a martial arts master, he battles an evil Russian in a karate competition. Some scenes are so stupid, they are beyond belief. Breakdancing and rapping during workouts. Family turmoil for no reason. This and rotten acting sends this ripoff down for the count.

1985 85 minutes

NORSEMAN, THE

DIRECTOR: Charles B. Pierce

CAST: Lee Majors, Charles B. Pierce Jr., Cornel Wilde, Mel Ferrer

This low-budget story of the Vikings landing in America in A.D. 1022 is so full of stupid historical errors and unbelievable elements that it should never have been released. Star Lee Majors, in addition to a performance so wooden it is almost petrified, speaks with a southern accent. Who ever heard of a Viking with a southern accent? Writer-producer-director Charles B. Pierce committed the worst kind of nepotism by casting his untalented son, Charles B. Pierce Jr., as one of the Vikings. Rated PG.

1978 90 minutes

NORTH STAR, THE

★★★★

DIRECTOR: Lewis Milestone

CAST: Ruth Gordon, Walter Huston, Anne Baxter, Dana Andrews

This is a well-done World War II film about Russian peasants battling Nazi invaders during the early days of the German invasion of Russia in 1941. This film was reedited in the early 1950s, during the McCarthy witch-hunt days, and released as *Armored Attack*. The reedited version became an anti-Soviet, incoherent mess. Thanks to home video, we can now see the original. It's a bit corny and sentimental in places, but the battle scenes have the usual Milestone high-quality excitement. The cast does an excellent job.

1943 B & W 105 minutes

NORTHEAST OF SEOUL

★½

DIRECTOR: David Lowell Rich

CAST: Anita Ekberg, John Ireland, Victor Buono, Irvan Stansby, Yung Kyeon Sin, Chi-He Choi

In this movie, a 1972 version of what used to be called a B picture, three unlikely down-and-outers join forces and end up double-crossing each other in their pursuit of an ancient mystical sword that promises wealth and power to the owner. This poorly dubbed movie is very routine. Rated PG for violence.

1972 84 minutes

NORTHERN PURSUIT

★★★

DIRECTOR: Raoul Walsh

CAST: Errol Flynn, Julie Bishop, Tom Tully

This was the first picture made by Errol Flynn for Warner Bros. following his rape trial. Its uninspired plot and low budget seem to bespeak a certain lack of confidence in the star on the part of the studio. Despite Raoul Walsh's capable direction, this film, about a German heritage Canadian Mountie (Flynn) who feigns defection and guides a party of Nazi saboteurs to their secret base, is pure claptrap. It marked the beginning of Flynn's slow descent into obscurity and, eventually, illness.

1943 B & W 94 minutes

NYOKA AND THE TIGER MEN (PERILS OF NYOKA)

★★½

DIRECTOR: William Witney

CAST: Kay Aldrige, Clayton Moore, William Benedict, Lorna Gray

Nyoka, the Jungle Girl, aids archeologist Clayton Moore (*The Lone Ranger*) in saving and deciphering the long-lost Tablets of Hippocrates, which contain the medical knowledge of the ancient Greeks. The evil Vultura, ruler of a band of ruthless desert no-goods who hang out in a temple with a giant gorilla named Satan, covets the same tablets, and does everything possible to obtain them and do away with her competitors. It's one chase after another as the players scramble all over one another to secure the tablets, which only Nyoka can read. Plenty of stunts and familiar heavies Charles Middleton and Tristram Coffin make this an enjoyable afternoon diversion.

1942 B & W 15 chapters

OCEAN'S ELEVEN

★★★

DIRECTOR: Lewis Milestone

CAST: Frank Sinatra, Dean Martin, Sammy Davis Jr., Peter Lawford, Angie Dickinson, Cesar Romero

A twist ending, several stars, and good production values save this tale of an attempted robbery in Las Vegas. Frank Sinatra is the leader of the gang, and his now-famous "rat pack" are the gang members. Lightweight but pleasant.

1960 127 minutes

OCTAGON, THE

★★

DIRECTOR: Eric Karson

CAST: Chuck Norris, Karen Carlson, Lee Van Cleef, Jack Carter

This "kung-fu" flick stars Chuck Norris as a bodyguard for Karen Carlson. Norris naturally takes on multiple opponents and beats them easily. Rated R.

1980 103 minutes

OCTOPUSSY

★★★★

DIRECTOR: John Glen

CAST: Roger Moore, Maud Adams, Louis Jourdan

Roger Moore returns as James Bond in the thirteenth screen adventure of Ian Fleming's superspy. It's like an adult-oriented *Raiders of the Lost Ark*: light, fast-paced, funny, and almost over before you know it—almost, because the film tends to overstay its welcome just a bit. The ending, though full of the usual thrills and chills, could have been shorter. Rated PG for violence and suggested sex.

1983 130 minutes

ODESSA FILE, THE

★½

DIRECTOR: Ronald Neame

CAST: Jon Voight, Maximilian Schell, Derek Jacobi, Maria Schell

Frederick Forsyth wrote the best-selling novel, but little of the zip remains in this weary film adaptation. German journalist Jon Voight learns of a secret file that may expose some former Nazis. That's about all there is to tell. Rated PG for violence.

1974 128 minutes

OLD IRONSIDES

★

DIRECTOR: James Cruze

CAST: Charles Farrell, Esther Ralson, Wallace Beery, George Bancroft, Fred Kohler, Boris Karloff

This big-budget, action-packed yarn of wooden ships and iron men besting pirates in the Mediterranean has a big director, big stars, big scenes, and was ballyhooed at its premiere, but it was scuttled by a lackluster script. Far from a golden silent, it bombed at the box office. If you can read lips, the dialogue will surprise and amaze you. Silent.

1926 B & W 88 minutes

OMEGA SYNDROME

★★

DIRECTOR: Joseph Manduke

CAST: Ken Wahl, George DiCenzo, Doug McClure, Ron Kuhlman, Patti Tippo

Ken Wahl is a single parent who teams up with his old Vietnam war buddy (Doug DiCenzo) to track down his daughter's abductors. They find that a white supremist group is behind the kidnapping. A very manipulative screenplay makes the film hard to take seriously. Rated R for violence and profanity.

1986 90 minutes

ON HER MAJESTY'S SECRET SERVICE

★★★★

DIRECTOR: Peter Hunt

CAST: George Lazenby, Diana Rigg, Telly Savalas

With Sean Connery temporarily out of the James Bond series, Australian actor George Lazenby stepped into the 007 part for this entry—and did remarkably well. While not as charismatic as Connery, he carries himself well and fights convincingly. Director Peter Hunt keeps this moving at an incredibly fast pace, and this story about everyone's favorite superspy falling in love with an heiress (Diana Rigg) is one of author Ian Fleming's best. Rated PG.

1969 140 minutes

ONCE UPON A TIME IN AMERICA (LONG VERSION)

★★★★

DIRECTOR: Sergio Leone
CAST: Robert DeNiro, James Woods, Elizabeth McGovern, Tuesday Weld, Treat Williams, Burt Young

Italian director Sergio Leone's richly rewarding gangster epic; a $30 million production starring Robert DeNiro in a forty-five-year saga of Jewish gangsters in New York City. Leone is best known for his spaghetti westerns *A Fistful of Dollars*, *The Good, the Bad and the Ugly*, and *Once upon a Time in the West*. This release culminates ten years of planning and false starts by the filmmaker. It was well worth the wait. Rated R for profanity, nudity, suggested sex, and violence.

1984 225 minutes

ONE BODY TOO MANY

★★½

DIRECTOR: Frank McDonald
CAST: Bela Lugosi, Jack Haley, Jean Parker, Blanche Yurka, Lyle Talbot, Douglas Fowley

Snappy dialogue and a memorable cast of good performers make this fast-paced whodunit worth a watch. Wise-cracking Jack Haley is mistaken for a private investigator and finds himself in the thick of murder and intrigue. Bela Lugosi is again typecast as a menace, but this caricature role isn't nearly as offensive as many he was forced into in the 1940s. Nothing special, but not too bad for a low-budget programmer.

1944 B & W 75 minutes

ONE DOWN, TWO TO GO

★★

DIRECTOR: Fred Williamson
CAST: Fred Williamson, Jim Brown, Jim Kelly, Richard Roundtree

Kung-fu fighter (Jim Kelly) suspects a tournament is fixed and calls on his buddies (Jim Brown and director Fred Williamson) for help in this low-budget, theatrically unreleased sequel to *Three the Hard Way*. This time, Richard Roundtree (*Shaft*) joins in the action. Some actors are hopelessly amateurish, and the story is a mere sketch. Considering all the talent involved, it's a major disappointment. Unrated, the film has violence.

1983 84 minutes

ONE SHOE MAKES IT MURDER

★★½

DIRECTOR: William Hale
CAST: Robert Mitchum, Angie Dickinson, Mel Ferrer, Jose Perez, John Harkins, Howard Hesseman

In this made-for-television movie, reminiscent in plot of *Out of the Past*, Robert Mitchum plays a world-weary detective who is hired by a crime boss (Mel Ferrer) to find his wayward wife (Angie Dickinson). Mitchum is watchable in a variation on his Philip Marlowe characterization from *Farewell My Lovely*, but the story and direction never achieve a level of intensity.

1982 97 minutes

OPERATION C.I.A.

★★½

DIRECTOR: Christian Nyby
CAST: Burt Reynolds, Kieu Chinh, Danielle Aubry, John Hoyt, Cyril Collack

Political intrigue in Vietnam before the United States' full involvement finds a youthful Burt Reynolds at his physical peak as an agent assigned to derail an assassination attempt. Good location photography and Reynolds's enthusiasm and believability mark this film and the first few films he starred in as minor action classics and the best chase films of the mid-1960s. Look for a U.S. world in the Far East that doesn't exist anymore and was on its way out then.

1965 B & W 90 minutes

OPERATION THUNDERBOLT

★½

DIRECTOR: Menahem Golan
CAST: Yehoram Gaon, Klaus Kinski, Assaf Dayan

Another film, like *The Raid on Entebbe*, dealing with the Israeli commando raid in Uganda in 1976 to free 104 hijacked airline passengers. Overly sentimental, with poor performances and rather routine action sequences. No MPAA rating.

1977 125 minutes

OPPOSING FORCE

★★½

DIRECTOR: Eric Karson
CAST: Tom Skerritt, Lisa Eichhorn, Richard Roundtree, Anthony Zerbe

Action-adventure film about a group of military personnel who have signed up for the air force's elite Reconnaissance/Escape program. After being parachuted onto a Pacific island, their mission is to avoid being captured by the "enemy." The game gets completely out of control when the commanding officer goes insane. Rated R for language, sex, and violence.

1986 99 minutes

ORDEAL BY INNOCENCE

★★

DIRECTOR: Desmond Davis
CAST: Donald Sutherland, Sarah Miles, Christopher Plummer, Ian McShane, Diana Quick, Faye Dunaway

In this production of yet another Agatha Christie novel, the cast may be stellar, but the performances are almost all phoned in. Donald Sutherland plays a man who is certain that justice has been ill served in a small British community. Half of the film is disjointed flashbacks and echoed voices of conversations long over. Dave Brubeck provides the mood music. And while his groove is good on record, it's hardly the proper soundtrack for a murder mystery set in Great Britain. Rated PG-13 for language and nudity.

1984 91 minutes

ORGANIZATION, THE

★★★

DIRECTOR: Don Medford
CAST: Sidney Poitier, Barbara McNair, Raul Julia, Sheree North

This is the third and last installment of the Virgil Tibbs series based on the character Sidney Poitier originated in *In the Heat of the Night*. Tibbs is out to break up a ring of dope smugglers. A pretty good cop film, with some exciting action scenes. Rated PG; some strong stuff for the kids.

1971 107 minutes

OSTERMAN WEEKEND, THE

★★★

DIRECTOR: Sam Peckinpah
CAST: Rutger Hauer, John Hurt, Burt Lancaster, Dennis Hopper, Chris Sarandon, Meg Foster

When a brilliant but erratic director makes his first film after a five-year absence, the first question is: Is it a classic? In the case of *The Osterman Weekend*, Sam Peckinpah's last, the answer is no. That, however, does not make it a bad picture. *The Osterman Weekend* is, in fact, a good action movie, with many viewing rewards for the filmmaker's fans. But you have to pay attention. Based on Robert Ludlum's novel, it tells a complicated and convoluted story of espionage, revenge, and duplicity. Rated R for profanity, nudity, sex, and violence.

1983 102 minutes

OUT OF BOUNDS

★½

DIRECTOR: Richard Tuggle
CAST: Anthony Michael Hall, Jenny Wright, Jeff Kober, Glynn Turman, Raymond J. Barry

Teen star Anthony Michael Hall, seeking a more mature role, took a wrong turn and wound up in this incomprehensible thriller. He plays a naïve Iowa boy who journeys to Los Angeles and accidentally switches luggage with a nasty heroin smuggler. Tony Kayden's script assumes lunatic proportions: the story progresses only because every character behaves like a total idiot at all times. It remains barely watchable thanks to Richard Tuggle's dark and moody direction, a style he use with Clint Eastwood in *Tightrope*. *Out of Bounds*, however, is out of control. Rated R for extreme violence.

1986 93 minutes

OUT OF THE PAST

★★★★½

DIRECTOR: Jacques Tourneur
CAST: Robert Mitchum, Jane Greer, Kirk Douglas, Richard Webb, Rhonda Fleming, Dickie Moore, Steve Brodie

This film, which stars Robert Mitchum, is perhaps the quintessential example of *film noir*. *Film noir*, which translates roughly as "dark film," is a phrase the French coined to describe a popular style of European-influenced film-making in Hollywood in the 1940s. Bathed in darkness and shadow, the characters in these movies are inevitably doomed as they cross, double-cross, and triple-cross each other. In *Out of the Past*, a private eye (Mitchum, in a role intended for Bogart) allows himself to be duped by the beautiful but two-faced mistress (Jane Greer) of a big-time gangster (Kirk Douglas). It's a forgotten masterwork.

1947 B & W 97 minutes

P.O.W.: THE ESCAPE

★★½

DIRECTOR: Gideon Amir
CAST: David Carradine, Mako, Charles R. Floyd, Steve James

David Carradine's considerable acting talents are wasted once again in this *Rambo* ripoff that is missing everything but action. Carradine plays battle-hardened vet Col. Jim Cooper, who leads a group of POWs through enemy lines to freedom during the closing days of the Vietnam war. For Carradine at his best, try *Bound for Glory*, *The Long Riders*, or his self-directed *Americana*. Rated R for profanity and violence.

1986 90 minutes

PAPER TIGER

★★

DIRECTOR: Ken Annakin
CAST: David Niven, Toshiro Mifune, Ando, Hardy Krüger

Stiffly British David Niven is tutor to the son (Ando) of a Japanese ambassador (Toshiro Mifune). He and his young charge are kidnapped by terrorists for political reasons. Derring-do follows, but it's all lukewarm and paplike. Rated PG.

1976 99 minutes

PAPILLON

★★★★½

DIRECTOR: Frank Schaffner
CAST: Steve McQueen, Dustin Hoffman, Victor Jory, Don Gordon

Unfairly criticized, this is a truly exceptional film biography of the man who escaped from Devil's Island. Steve McQueen gives an excellent performance, and Dustin Hoffman is once again a chameleon. Director Frank Schaffner invests the same gusto here as he did in *Patton*. Rated PG.

1973 150 minutes

PARADISE

★½

DIRECTOR: Stuart Gillard

CAST: Willie Aames, Phoebe Cates, Tuvia Tavi

Willie Aames (of television's *Eight Is Enough*) and Phoebe Cates star as two teenagers who, as members of a caravan traveling from Bagdad to Damascus in the nineteenth century, escape a surprise attack by a sheik intent on adding Cates to his harem. While fleeing the villain and looking for help, they have time to diddle à la Brooke Shields and Christopher Atkins in *Blue Lagoon*. It's just as dumb and unoriginal as it sounds. Rated R for frontal male and female nudity and graphic sexual treatment.

1982 100 minutes

PARTNERS IN CRIME—THE SECRET ADVERSARY

★★★

DIRECTOR: Tony Wharmby

CAST: James Warwick, Francesca Annis, George Baker, Peter Barkworth, Honor Blackman, John Fraser, Toria Fuller, Donald Houston, Alec McCowen, Gavan O'Herlihy

Originally broadcast on PBS, this film serves to introduce the *Partners in Crime* series, based on Agatha Christie's mysteries. Tommy Beresford (James Warwick), recently discharged from World War I, meets Tuppence Cowley, the girl who nursed him when he was wounded. Together they look for work and are offered a job that leads them in a race to find a secret treaty which, in the wrong hands, could overthrow the British government. Set in the 1920s, the film maintains high production values, and the characters are charming if at times too whimsically British.

1983 120 minutes

PASSAGE TO MARSEILLES

★★★

DIRECTOR: Michael Curtiz

CAST: Humphrey Bogart, Claude Rains, Sydney Greenstreet, Peter Lorre

The performances of Humphrey Bogart, Claude Rains, Sydney Greenstreet, and Peter Lorre are all that's good about this muddled film about an escape from Devil's Island during World War II. Directed by Michael Curtiz, its flashback-within-flashback scenes all but totally confuse the viewer.

1944 B & W 110 minutes

PASSION

★★

DIRECTOR: Allan Dwan

CAST: Cornel Wilde, Yvonne DeCarlo, Raymond Burr, Lon Chaney Jr., John Qualen

Colorful hokum about a hot-blooded adventurer (Cornel Wilde) and his quest for vengeance in old California. Directed by veteran filmmaker Allan Dwan, this okay adventure boast a nice cast of character actors and some nice scenery, but it's little more than adequate. Wilde, however, is dashing.

1954 84 minutes

PATRIOT

DIRECTOR: Frank Harris

CAST: Gregg Henry, Simone Griffeth, Michael J. Pollard, Jeff Conaway, Stack Pierce, Leslie Nielsen

Underwater commandos fighting

terrorists over nuclear weapons sounds like a good idea for an action-adventure film, but you wouldn't know it from watching this one. Rated R for nudity and violence.

1986 90 minutes

PENDULUM

★★

DIRECTOR: George Schaefer
CAST: George Peppard, Richard Kiley, Jean Seberg, Charles McGraw

In this rather confusing mystery, police captain George Peppard must acquit himself of a murder charge and catch the real culprit. One of the most oft-used plots in detective films doesn't get any special treatment here. A good cast perks things up some, but the story is too full of holes to be taken seriously. Some violence, adult situations. Rated PG.

1969 106 minutes

PENITENTIARY I AND II

★★

DIRECTOR: Jamaa Fanaka
CAST: Leon Isaac Kennedy

Leon Isaac Kennedy dons boxing gloves as the black Rocky to triumph over pure evil in these lurid, but entertaining, movies. Rated R.

1979 202 minutes

PERILS OF GWENDOLINE, THE

★

DIRECTOR: Just Jaeckin
CAST: Tawny Kitaen, Brent Huff

Adapting this film from the 1940s comic strip "The Adventures of Sweet Gwendoline," Just Jaeckin, who is also responsible for *Emmanuelle* and *The Story of O*, claims to have made a sexy comedy adventure. What he's made instead is a poorly acted escapade that tries to titillate through glorification of sadomasochistic forays into sex. This partly dubbed fiasco will probably develop a cult following. Stars Tawny Kitaen (*Bachelor Party*) in the role of the young heroine searching for her explorer father in the land of Yik-Yak. Yuck! Rated R for violence, profanity, and sexual content.

1985 96 minutes

PERILS OF PAULINE, THE

★½

DIRECTOR: Ray Taylor
CAST: Evalyn Knapp, Robert Allen, James Durkin, John Davidson, Sonny Ray, Frank Lackteen, William Desmond, Pat O'Malley, Adolph Muller

Sound serial version of the famous Pearl White cliffhanger retains only the original title. The daughter of a prominent scientist and her companion struggle to keep the formula for a deadly gas out of the hands of evil Dr. Bashan and his slimy assistant Fang. Spunky Pauline and her boyfriend Robert defy efforts to blow them up as they face danger from all directions, including hordes of the inevitable murderous natives. The two leads are secondary to great character villain John Davidson and the equally menacing Frank Lackteen as the boys who want that poison gas formula and eventually die trying to get it. Not as well known as its silent namesake or the 1947 Betty Hutton version, this so-so serial lacks the charisma of later efforts from Universal Studios, especially their magnificent *Flash Gordon* serials.

1933 B & W 12 chapters

PERMISSION TO KILL

★★

DIRECTOR: Cyril Frankel
CAST: Dirk Bogarde, Ava Gardner, Bekim Fehmiu, Timothy Dalton, Nicole Calfan, Frederic Forrest

An exiled politician (Bekim Fehmiu) from an Eastern bloc nation living in Austria decides to return to his native country. A Western intelligence agent (Dirk Bogarde) must stop him. He uses extortion to persuade four people with personal or professional connections to the politician to try to prevent him from returning. Ava Gardner is the ex-lover who trys to speak to his heart, Frederic Forrest is the reporter and buddy giving friendly advice, Timothy Dalton is the financial secretary giving him money to call off the trip. And if all else fails, the politician is to be assassinated by another blackmail victim (Nicole Calfan). With a lineup like this, it's shocking to find that only Bogarde and Dalton are believable. *Permission to Kill* has some interesting things to say about international politics vis-à-vis personal freedom, but the screenplay and the acting make the film hard to take seriously. Rated PG for violence, profanity, and nudity.

1975 96 minutes

PERSUADERS, THE (TELEVISION SERIES)

★★★

DIRECTORS: Basil Deardon, Val Guest

CAST: Roger Moore, Tony Curtis, Laurence Naismith

This tongue-in-cheek adventure series lasted just one season on ABC, but it offers a fair bit of action, humor, and style. Set in the glamor spots of Europe, the show follows two dashing playboys: Brett Sinclair (Roger Moore), a British lord, and Daniel Wilde (Tony Curis), a self-made millionaire from the Bronx. A retired judge has tricked them into joining forces and fighting for justice. Moore and Curtis are fun to watch in these tailor-made roles, smoothly handling the roughhousing, rivalry, and romance. The first two episodes to be released on tape are "Overture," guest starring Imogen Hassal, and "Five Miles to Midnight," with Joan Collins.

1972 60 minutes

PHANTOM EMPIRE

★★★

DIRECTORS: Otto Brewer, B. Reeves "Breezy" Eason

CAST: Gene Autry, Franie Darro, Betsy King Ross, "Smiley" Burnette

Gene Autry, with the aid of Frankie Darro, champion rider Betsy King Ross, and the Junior Thunder Riders, overcomes threats from above ground (greedy crooks who want his radium-riddled Radio Ranch and do their best to interrupt his frequent radio broadcasts) and the deadly threat of Murania, the futuristic city twenty thousand feet beneath the ground. Ruled by the statuesque Queen Tika (played to the hilt by Dorothy Christy), Murania is on the verge of a revolt when Gene and the other "surface dwellers" enter and throw a monkey wrench into their plan of surface domination. Plenty of action, the wonders of the "city of the future," and good special effects (including a death ray) make this one of Mascot Films's best serials before they merged the next year to form Republic Pictures, producers of the best chapter plays of the 1930s and 1940s.

1935 B & W 12 chapters

PHANTOM EXPRESS

★★

DIRECTOR: Emory Johnson

CAST: J. Farrell MacDonald, Sally Blane, William Collier Jr., Hobart Bosworth

J. Farrell MacDonald loses his job and his pension with the railroad after his own engine is ruined in a wreck with a mysterious train. Shunned by his friends and co-workers, the salty old engineer decides to bring the villains to justice himself and does so with the help of young Sally Blane. Nothing new here, but former silent star Hobart Bosworth plays a meaty role and the vintage trains are a treat to look at.

1932 B & W 65 minutes

PHILIP MARLOWE, PRIVATE EYE: FINGER MAN

★★★★

DIRECTOR: Sidney Hayers

CAST: Powers Boothe, William Kearns, Gayle Hunnicutt, Ed Bishop, William Hootkins, David Baxt

Another installment in the HBO series featuring Powers Boothe's delicious interpretation of Raymond Chandler's square-jawed detective. This time out, Philip Marlowe has his own life to worry about, as the sole witness to the killing of a government investigator who was poking into mob activities. Marlowe has to make it through a long weekend so that he can testify before a grand jury on Monday; needless to say, quite a few folks would like to see him miss that appointment. The usual crisp writing from scripter Jo Eisinger, along with John Cameron's mood-setting music. Chandler would have been pleased. Unrated; brief violence.

1983 55 minutes

PHILIP MARLOWE, PRIVATE EYE: THE PENCIL

★★★★

DIRECTOR: Peter Hunt

CAST: Powers Boothe, William Kearns, Kathryn Leigh Scott, David Healy, Stephen Davies

First in the series of absolutely gorgeous made-for-cable adaptations of Raymond Chandler's famed detective. Production values are superb, from the meticulous attention paid to period authenticity, to the mournful wail of John Cameron's music. (The glitzy opening credits from James Bond title designer Maurice Binder also set an appropriate mood.) Powers Boothe is perfect as the cynical, world-weary, hard-boiled dick who usually manages to solve a case minutes before losing his license (again). In this episode, Marlowe is hired to protect a stoolie who's been sent a pencil by the mob (signaling their intention to kill him). Boothe is masterful and his voice-over commentary deftly captures the beat of Chandler's original stories. A must for mystery fans. Unrated; brief violence.

1983 55 minutes

PIMPERNEL SMITH

★★★

DIRECTOR: Leslie Howard

CAST: Leslie Howard, David Tomlinson, Philip Friend, Hugh McDermott, Mary Morris, Peter Gawthorne, Francis L. Sullivan, A. E. Matthews

Star Leslie Howard, who also produced, brought his 1934 role in *The Scarlet Pimpernel* up to modern times in this anti-Nazi thriller involving a daring rescue of important scientists from prison.

1942 B & W 122 minutes

POSEIDON ADVENTURE, THE

★★★

DIRECTOR: Ronald Neame

CAST: Gene Hackman, Ernest Borgnine, Shelley Winters, Roddy McDowall, Red Buttons, Stella Stevens

It's New Year's Eve on the passenger liner *Poseidon*. A tidal wave overturns the ship, and from here on out the all-star cast, special effects, and imaginative sets take over. It's a fairly watchable disaster flick, nothing more. Rated PG.

1972 117 minutes

PRIME CUT

★★

DIRECTOR: Michael Ritchie

CAST: Lee Marvin, Gene Hackman, Angel Tompkins, Gregory Walcott, Sissy Spacek

Sissy Spacek made her film debut in this sleazy but energetic crime thriller about big-time gangsters and the slaughterhouse they use to convert their enemies into sausage. The talents of Lee Marvin and Gene Hackman elevate this essentially tasteless offering. Rated R for nudity, gore, and violence.

1972 86 minutes

PRIME RISK

★★★½

DIRECTOR: Michael Frakas

CAST: Lee Montgomery, Samuel Bottoms, Toni Hudson, Keenan Wynn, Clu Gulager, John Lykes, Roy Stuart

Two frustrated young people (Lee Montgomery and Samuel Bottoms) devise a scheme to rip off automatic-teller machines. Trouble arises when they stumble on to a greater conspiracy involving foreign agents planning to sabotage the Federal Reserve System. There is nonstop action in this entertaining thriller, with Keenan Wynn as a suitable villain. Rated PG-13 for mature situations and language.

1984 98 minutes

PRISONER OF ZENDA, THE

★★★

DIRECTOR: Richard Thorpe

CAST: Stewart Granger, Deborah Kerr, Jane Greer, Louis Calhern, James Mason, Lewis Stone

An innocent traveler in a small European country is the exact double of its king and gets involved in a murder plot. This is a flashy Technicolor remake of the famous 1937 Ronald Colman version.

1952 101 minutes

PRIVATE INVESTIGATIONS

DIRECTOR: Nigel Dick

CAST: Clayton Rohner, Ray Sharkey, Paul LeMat, Talia Balsam, Anthony Zerbe

One more time with an overworked plot: a young Los Angeles architect is chased around town by bad guys who think he knows something that could expose their schemes. The details rely on foolish coincidences, and the leading man, Clayton Rohner, is extremely uncharismatic. A pointless use of film stock. It's rated R for language and violence.

1987 91 minutes

PRIVATE LIFE OF SHERLOCK HOLMES, THE

★★★★½

DIRECTOR: Billy Wilder

CAST: Robert Stephens, Colin Blakely, Genevieve Page, Christopher Lee, Irene Handl, Clive Revill, Stanley Holloway

Director Billy Wilder's affectionately satirical pastiche of the Conan Doyle stories reveals the "secrets" allegedly shared by Sherlock Holmes (Robert Stephens) and Dr. John H. Watson (Colin Blakely). It does so with wit, humor, taste, and even suspense. Originally made as a 3½-hour road-show production, *The Private Life of Sherlock Holmes* was trimmed nearly by half before its release. While what remains is eminently satisfying and memorable, after seeing it, one can only hope Wilder's unique and highly personal film will one day be available in its entirety. For now, we can enjoy the performances of Stephens (as a wonderfully droll and sometimes sad Holmes), Blakely (as his too earnest helpmate), Genevieve Page (as a client with a special appeal), and Christopher Lee (as Mycroft Holmes); the funny and quotable screenplay by Wilder and I.A.L. Diamond; and two adventures (including an encounter with the Loch Ness Monster) that are more than worthy of the Great Detective. Rated PG.

1970 125 minutes

PROFESSIONALS, THE

★★★★½

DIRECTOR: Richard Brooks
CAST: Lee Marvin, Burt Lancaster, Robert Ryan, Woody Strode, Claudia Cardinale, Ralph Bellamy

A rip-snorting adventure film with Lee Marvin, Burt Lancaster, Robert Ryan, and Woody Strode as the title characters out to rescue the wife (Claudia Cardinale) of a wealthy industrialist (Ralph Bellamy) from the clutches of a Mexican bandit (Jack Palance) who allegedly kidnapped her. Directed with a fine eye for character and action by Richard Brooks.

1966 117 minutes

PROTECTOR, THE

★★½

DIRECTOR: James Glickenhaus
CAST: Jackie Chan, Danny Aiello, Roy Chiao, Victor Arnold, Kim Bass, Richard Clark

Standard kung-fu film distinguished by nicely photographed action sequences and a sense of humor. Story has Jackie Chan as an undercover New York cop traveling to Hong Kong to break up a big heoin ring that is shipping its goods to New York City. Rated R for violence, nudity, and language.

1985 94 minutes

PUBLIC ENEMY, THE

★★★★½

DIRECTOR: William A. Wellman
CAST: James Cagney, Jean Harlow, Mae Clarke, Eddie Woods, Beryl Mercer

Public Enemy, with a snarling, unredeemable James Cagney in the title role, is still a highly watchable gangster film. William A. Wellman directed this fast-paced and unpretentious portrait of the rise and fall of a vicious hoodlum. Jean Harlow and Mae Clarke play the women in Cagney's life. Audiences will always remember Miss Clarke as the target of Cagney's grapefruit in one of the truly classic scenes in movie history.

1931 B & W 84 minutes

PURSUIT OF D. B. COOPER

★★½

DIRECTOR: Roger Spottiswoode
CAST: Treat Williams, Robert Duvall, Kathryn Harrold, Ed Flanders, Paul Gleason, R. G. Armstrong

The famous skyjacker is turned into a fun-loving good old boy in this hit-and-miss comedy starring Treat Williams, Robert Duvall, and Kathryn Harrold. If you liked *Smokey and the Bandit*, you'll probably enjoy this. Otherwise, avoid it. Rated PG because of minimal violence and sexuality.

1981 100 minutes

PURSUIT TO ALGIERS

★★★

DIRECTOR: Roy William Neill
CAST: Basil Rathbone, Nigel Bruce, John Abbott, Marjorie Riordan, Martin Kosleck, Gerald Hamer, Rosalind Ivan, Rex Evans

Basil Rathbone's Holmes and Nigel Bruce's Watson become bodyguards accompanying the young heir to a royal throne on a hazardous sea voyage. Their client disguises himself as Watson's nephew, which makes for some droll dialogue. One of the few Rathbon/Bruce films that borrows nothing from the book canon. Unrated—suitable for family viewing.

1945 B & W 65 minutes

QUIET COOL

★

DIRECTOR: Clay Borris

CAST: James Remar, Adam Coleman Howard, Daphne Ashbrook, Jared Martin, Nick Cassavettes, Fran Ryan

This amateurishly directed action-adventure film casts veteran heavy James Remar as a New York cop who journeys to the Pacific Northwest to take on the maniacal marijuana growers who have killed the parents of sweet-natured Joshua (Adam Coleman Howard). The setting is beautiful; the story, ludicrous. Rated R.

1986 80 minutes

QUIET MAN, THE

★★★★★

DIRECTOR: John Ford

CAST: John Wayne, Maureen O'Hara, Victor McLaglen, Barry Fitzgerald, Mildred Natwick, Arthur Shields, Ward Bond, Jack MacGowran

As with many Irish-Americans, John Ford held a very romanticized love of his ancestral home. *The Quiet Man* is Ford's easygoing and marvelously entertaining tribute to the people and the land of Ireland. He was to win a best-director Oscar for his efforts. The story centers around an American ex-boxer (John Wayne) who returns to his native land, his efforts to understand the culture and people of a rural village, and especially his interest in taming a spirited colleen (Maureen O'Hara) in spite of the disapproval of her brother (Victor McLaglen). Nearly every Irish character actor makes an appearance in this wonderful film.

1952 129 minutes

QUILLER MEMORANDUM, THE

★★★½

DIRECTOR: Michael Anderson

CAST: George Segal, Alec Guinness, Max von Sydow, George Sanders, Senta Berger, Robert Helpmann

First-rate espionage film abandons the gadgets and gimmickry that marked most of the spy movies of the 1960s and concentrates on Harold Pinter's intelligent script. An American secret agent (George Segal) goes undercover to shatter a neo-Nazi hate organization that is gaining strength in Berlin. Full of suspense and convoluted plot twists, this thriller is well executed and finely acted by an international cast that includes Alec Guinness, Max von Sydow, and perennial favorite George Sanders in one of his last roles. Not rated, this film features some adult situations and violence, but nothing compared to current films.

1966 105 minutes

RACKETEER

★★½

DIRECTOR: Howard Higgin

CAST: Robert Armstrong, Carole Lombard, Roland Drew, Jeanette Loff, John Loder, Paul Hurst, Hedda Hopper

This early sound gangster film finds gang leader Robert Armstrong involved in the familiar eternal triangle as he falls for Carole Lombard. She, in turn, pines for ailing concert violinist

Roland Drew. Just when it looks as if Armstrong will have a chance with beautiful Carole, a gang war breaks out and the picture changes. Though the story has been done with some variations dozens of times, this primitive talkie has some snappy dialogue and features lively performances from pugnacious Armstrong and world-weary Lombard, still a few years away from major success as everyone's favorite screwball comedienne.

1930 B & W 68 minutes

RAD

★★½

DIRECTOR: Hal Needham
CAST: Bill Allen, Lori Laughlin, Talia Shire, Ray Walston, Jack Weston, Bart Connor

Staunch character players Talia Shire, Ray Walston, and Jack Weston support a cast of youthful actors in this film about a daredevil bicyclist (Bill Allen) who competes to win a thousand dollars at Hell Track, "the most dangerous bicycle race in the world." Although the direction is unimpressive and the story predictable, *Rad* turns out to be fairly entertaining, thanks to the exciting race sequences. Rated PG.

1986 95 minutes

RADAR MEN FROM THE MOON

★★

DIRECTOR: Fred Brannon
CAST: George Wallace, Aline Towne, Roy Barcroft, William Blakewell

Commando Cody, Sky Marshal of the Universe and inventor of a flying suit and a rocket ship, uses all the means at his disposal to aid America in combating Retik, the ruler of the moon, who is bent on (what else?) invading the Earth. The bullet-headed hero chases villains on land, in the air, and all the way to the moon and back and gets his fair share of abuse along the way. Shrinking serial budgets are evident from sparse sets and unimaginative props and special effects. Clayton Moore moonlights from "The Lone Ranger" to play Graber, one of the heavies. Lots of fisticuffs and stock footage.

1952 B & W 12 chapters

RAID ON ROMMEL

★

DIRECTOR: Henry Hathaway
CAST: Richard Burton, John Colicos, Clinton Greyn, Wolfgang Preiss, Danielle Demetz

Veteran director Henry Hathaway must have had his mind somewhere else when he was making this substandard war film. Richard Burton plays a British Intelligence officer who leads a small group of Allied POWs behind enemy lines in North Africa. His mission: destroy the big guns at Tobruk before the British invasion fleet lands. During the course of this mission, Burton must match wits with General Erwin Rommel (poorly played by Wolfgang Preiss). Of course, our hero outsmarts Rommel at every turn. Rated PG for violence.

1971 98 minutes

RAISE THE TITANIC

★

DIRECTOR: Jerry Jameson
CAST: Jason Robards, David Selby, Richard Jordan, Anne Archer, Alec Guinness, J. D. Cannon

In this disastrously dull disaster flick, a marine research foundation headed by Jason Robards has developed a laser protective screen that could be installed around the perimeter of the United States to make it impregnable to missile attack. But to power the screen, the government needs byzanium, a precious radioactive metal whose only known world supply reportedly went down as contraband aboard the *Titanic*. The bulk of this boring movie surrounds plans to locate and raise the big ship and recover the metal. Rated PG.

1980 112 minutes

RAMBO: FIRST BLOOD II

★★★

DIRECTOR: George P. Cosmatos
CAST: Sylvester Stallone, Richard Crenna, Charles Napier, Steven Berkoff, Julia Nickson, Martin Kove

Rambo is an old-fashioned war movie. Its hero is larger than life, and the villains are pure mule-mean. In other words, it's an action fan's delight. Sylvester Stallone returns as Johnny Rambo, the disillusioned but not-to-be-messed-with ex–Green Beret who all but wiped out an unfriendly Oregon town singlehandedly in *First Blood*. This time, he follows in the footsteps of Gene Hackman (in *Uncommon Valor*) and Chuck Norris (in *Missing in Action*) by going back to Vietnam to rescue American prisoners of war. Hold on to your seat—this is an exciting, involving, and explosive entertainment. Rated R.

1985 94 minutes

RANSOM

★★½

DIRECTOR: Richard Compton
CAST: Oliver Reed, Stuart Whitman, Deborah Raffin, John Ireland, Jim Mitchum, Paul Koslo

When a psycho begins killing people in a small town and refuses to stop until he receives a $4 million ransom, Stuart Whitman (the richest man in town) hires a mercenary (Oliver Reed) to kill the extortionist. Reed manages to find time for a pretty reporter (Deborah Raffin), while the chief of police (John Ireland) frowns at his tactics. There are some slow moments, but worse than these are the unanswered questions about why the murderer dresses like an American Indian and what his motive really is. Rated PG for violence.

1977 90 minutes

RAW COURAGE

★★★★

DIRECTOR: Robert L. Rosen
CAST: Ronny Cox, Tim Maier, Art Hindle, M. Emmet Walsh, William Russ, Lisa Sutton, Lois Chiles

Three cross-country runners must fend for themselves when they run into a group of weekend warriors in the Colorado desert lands. Ronny Cox is excellent as one of the runners. His performance here is equal to his fine job in *Deliverance*. However, Cox, who wrote the screenplay, has taken a few too many pages from James Dickey's survival-horror story. Still, *Raw Courage* has enough white-knuckle moments to make you forget about the lack of originality. Rated R for violence and profanity.

1983 90 minutes

RAW DEAL

★★★½

DIRECTOR: John Irvin
CAST: Arnold Schwarzenegger, Kathryn Harrold, Darren McGavin, Sam Wanamaker, Paul Shenar, Steven Hill, Joe Regalbuto, Ed Lauter, Robert Davi

Big Arnold Schwarzenegger stars in this fast-paced action film as a former FBI agent who is recruited by his former boss (Darren McGavin) to infiltrate the Chicago mob as an act of revenge. It's predictable, even formula. But the formula works because we like Schwarzenegger's character and hate the bad guys—well played by Sam Wanamaker, Paul Shenar, Robert Davi, and Joe Regalbuto. Director John Irvin (*Turtle Diary*) keeps things moving so fast the viewer forgets about everything except what is happening at the moment on-screen. That's entertainment. Rated R for profanity and violence.

1986 97 minutes

REBEL ROUSERS

★★

DIRECTOR: Martin B. Cohen
CAST: Cameron Mitchell, Jack Nicholson, Bruce Dern, Diane Ladd, Harry Dean Stanton

This drive-in biker film from the late 1960s would barely rate a second look if it weren't for a crop of future big-name stars and character performers who inhabit it. This low-budget programmer seems light-years away from the triumphs Jack Nicholson, Bruce Dern, and Harry Dean Stanton later scored, but it was this exposure in the last studio-style training ground—American-International-Pictures—that got them to where they are today. The ill-mannered-youth-on-motorcycles-versus-uptight-establishment-straights story takes a backseat to flamboyant characterizations in this one.

1967 78 minutes

RED DAWN

★★★½

DIRECTOR: John Milius
CAST: Patrick Swayze, C. Thomas Howell, Ron O'Neal, Lea Thompson, Ben Johnson, Harry Dean Stanton, William Smith, Powers Boothe

Some viewers undoubtedly will feel that right-wing writer-director John Milius (*The Wind and the Lion* and *Conan the Barbarian*) has gone too far with this tale of the Russians invading a small American town. But we took this film as a simple "what if?" entertainment and, perhaps because we happen to like war movies anyway, really enjoyed it. Rated PG-13 for violence and profanity.

1984 114 minutes

RED FLAG: THE ULTIMATE GAME

★★½

DIRECTOR: Don Taylor
CAST: Barry Bostwick, Joan Van Ark, Fred McCarren, Debra Fever, George Coe, Linden Chiles, Arlen Dean Synder, William Devane

The air force has a jet-fighter combat course located near Las Vegas that over the years has fine-tuned thousands of the best pilots in the air force. The combat game is called Red Flag. It's an older and weaker version of *Top Gun* and suffers by comparison. Unrated.

1981 90 minutes

RED SONJA

DIRECTOR: Richard Fleischer
CAST: Arnold Schwarzenegger, Brigitte Nielsen, Sandahl Bergman, Paul Smith, Ernie Reyes Jr.

Agony, agoneee . . . this dreadful sword-and-sorcery film introduces us to Red Sonja (Brigitte Nielsen), pulp author Robert E. Howard's female counterpart to Conan. With the help of super-swordsman Kalifor (Arnold Schwarzenegger), our heroine takes on the evil minions of cruel Queen Gedren (Sandahl Bergman). It's all to save the world from a powerful green light bulb. Although there are some unintended laughs, the groans in this movie greatly outnumber them. Unlike *Conan the Destroyer*, which also was directed by Richard Fleischer, it is not a good bad movie . . . it's just plain bad. Rated PG-13 for violence.

1985 89 minutes

REFORM SCHOOL GIRLS

★★

DIRECTOR: Tom DeSimone

CAST: Wendy O. Williams, Sybil Danning, Pat Ast, Linda Carol

"So young. So bad. So what?" That was the promo line for this spoof of the women-in-prison genre. Writer-director Tom DeSimone manages to get in the usual exploitative ingredients—women taking showers, etc.—while simultaneously making fun of them. No, this is not a good movie. But it does have its moments, many of which are provided by Pat Ast as a campy heir to the prison matron so chillingly played by Hope Emerson in *Caged*. Rated R for violence, profanity, nudity, and simulated sex.

1986 94 minutes

REHEARSAL FOR MURDER

★★★½

DIRECTOR: David Greene

CAST: Robert Preston, Lynn Redgrave, Jeff Goldblum, Patrick MacNee, William Daniels, Lawrence Pressman

Richard Levinson and William Link, those clever fellows behind the creation of "Columbo," occasionally stray into the realm of made-for-television movies; this is one of the best. Robert Preston leads his stage friends through the reading of a "play" designed to ferret out the killer of star Lynn Redgrave. "The play's the thing," as Shakespeare would have said; this technique for trapping the guilty party goes all the way back to Alfred Hitchcock's *Murder*, made in 1930. The excellent cast does a fine job with the witty material, and Levinson and Link deliver another of their surprise conclusions.

1982 100 minutes

REMO WILLIAMS: THE ADVENTURE BEGINS

★★★

DIRECTOR: Guy Hamilton

CAST: Fred Ward, Joel Grey, Wilford Brimley, J. A. Preston, George Coe, Charles Cioffi, Kate Mulgrew

Directed by Guy Hamilton (*Goldfinger*) and scripted by Christopher Wood (*The Spy Who Loved Me*), this adaptation of the *Destroyer* novels is like a second-rate James Bond adventure. It offers pleasant diversion and nothing more. Fred Ward is fine as the hero of the title and Joel Grey is a kick as his Asian martial arts mentor, but the film takes too much time establishing the characters and too little giving us the adventure promised in the title. Rated PG-13 for violence and profanity.

1985 121 minutes

RETURN OF CHANDU

★★½

DIRECTOR: Ray Taylor

CAST: Bela Lugosi, Maria Alba, Clara Kimball Young, Lucien Prival, Dean Benton, Bryant Washburn, Phyllis Ludwig, Dick Botellier

Enjoyable Saturday afternoon matinee hokum has hammy Bela Lugosi at his best as Frank Chandler, known to the world as Chandu the Magician, who risks strange supernatural powers to best the evil cult that has kidnapped his friend and plans to sacrifice her. In the best serial tradition, Lugosi faces twelve episodes of pulse-pounding excitement. This was one of the best liked of early sound serials and it was also released in two feature versions. Chandu was a radio hero of the day, one of a number of magicians whose adventures were featured in comic strips and pulps during the 1930s.

1934 B & W 12 chapters

RETURN OF THE DRAGON

★★★½

DIRECTOR: Bruce Lee

CAST: Bruce Lee, Chuck Norris, Nora Miao

After seeing *Return of the Dragon*, we have no doubt that Bruce Lee, not Robert Clouse, directed *Enter the Dragon*. Lee was credited with staging the fight scenes, but our guess is that he was well aware of the latter film's possible impact and exercised control over the creative nonacting facets of the film whenever he could. *Return of the Dragon* was made before *Enter*, and it shows Lee's considerable directorial talent, although he did not think it would be popular with western audiences. On the contrary, it is a delightful film, brim-full of comedy, action, and the superb physical (including facial) acrobatics of the unmatchable Bruce Lee. Even the fight scenes have comedy interwoven, and it works marvelously. Rated R.

1973 91 minutes

RETURN OF THE MAN FROM U.N.C.L.E., THE

★★★

DIRECTOR: Ray Austin

CAST: Robert Vaughn, David McCallum, Patrick MacNee, Tom Mason, Gayle Hunnicutt, Geoffrey Lewis, Anthony Zerbe, Keenan Wynn, George Lazenby

Secret agents Napoleon Solo (Robert Vaugh) and Illya Kuryakin (David McCallum) are called out of a fifteen-year retirement by U.N.C.L.E. to battle their nemesis Justin Sepheran (Anthony Zerbe) and the evil organization T.H.R.U.S.H. Half the fun of this TV reunion is seeing so many actors known for their secret-agent roles from film and television. Patrick MacNee, star of the smash series *The Avengers*, portrays Mother, leader of U.N.C.L.E. (a role originally played by Leo G. Carroll), and in a hilarious chase scene, former James Bond, George Lazenby (*On Her Majesty's Secret Service*) drives a specially equipped Aston Martin. Fans of the original series will find this light-hearted spy adventure especially entertaining. Not rated, but suitable for all family members.

1983 109 minutes

RETURN TO MACON COUNTY

★

DIRECTOR: Richard Compton

CAST: Don Johnson, Nick Nolte, Robin Mattson

Two fun-loving boneheads run afoul of the law in the rural south. No style or substance. A lame sequel to the surprisingly good thriller *Macon County Line*. Interesting only to see Nick Nolte in his first film and Don Johnson before *A Boy and His Dog* and *Miami Vice*. Rated PG.

1975 104 minutes

REVENGE OF THE NINJA

DIRECTOR: Sam Firstenberg

CAST: Sho Kosugi, Keith Vitali, Arthur Roberts, Mario Gallo

Japanese karate experts take on the mob in this kung-fu flick, which is a cut or so above most of the Hong Kong–made martial arts junk. Rated R for violence and nudity.

1983 88 minutes

RIDDLE OF THE SANDS

★★★★

DIRECTOR: Tony Maylam
CAST: Michael York, Jenny Agutter, Simon MacCorkindale

Based on the spy novel by Erskine Childers, this is the story of two young Englishmen (Michael York, Simon MacCorkindale) who set sail on a holiday just prior to World War I and stumble upon political intrigue and adventure in the North Sea. The result is an absorbing adventure film. Rated PG for slight violence and profanity.

1984 102 minutes

RIDER ON THE RAIN

★★★★

DIRECTOR: Rene Clement
CAST: Charles Bronson, Marlene Jobert, Jill Ireland

Charles Bronson gives one of his finest screen performances in this gripping, Hitchcock-style thriller made in France. The story deals with the plight of a woman (Marlene Jobert) who kills an unhinged rapist and dumps his body into the sea. She is soon pursued by a mysterious American (Bronson). Thus begins a fascinating game of cat and mouse. Rated R for violence.

1970 115 minutes

RIFIFI

★★★★

DIRECTOR: Jules Dassin
CAST: Jean Servais, Carl Mohner, Perlo Vita, Robert Manuel, Magali Noel

A milestone that begat a continuing breed of films hinging on the big, carefully planned robbery that falls apart—usually just as the criminals and the audience are convinced of success. This one is sure to have you pumping adrenaline from start to finish, especially during the brilliant twenty-minutes silent robbery sequence that is its selling point, and the falling out of thieves which follows.

1955 B & W 115 minutes

RIOT IN CELL BLOCK ELEVEN

★★★

DIRECTOR: Don Siegel
CAST: Neville Brand, Leo Gordon, Emile Meyer, Frank Faylen

This taut prison drama with a message depicts an aborted prison escape that ends with the convicts barricaded and demanding to be heard. Made at the height of the "exposé" and true-crime wave in the mid-fifties, this film avoids the sensational and documentary style of its contemporaries and focuses on the action and the characterizations of the convicts, the prison staff, and the media. The message gets a bit heavy, but a good cast and quick pacing make this one of the best of its kind.

1954 B & W 80 minutes

ROADHOUSE 66

★★★½

DIRECTOR: John Mark Robinson
CAST: Willem Dafoe, Judge Reinhold, Kaaren Lee, Kate Vernon, Stephen Elliott, Alan Autry, Kevyn Major Howard, Peter Van Norden, Erica Yohn

As teen exploitation films go, this one is pretty good. Judge Reinhold plays a yuppie stuck in a small New Mexico town with car trouble. Willem Dafoe is an ex-rock-and-roller and all-around tough guy who helps the young executive in dealing with the existential crisis. The film drags a bit and Dafoe overplays his role, but there are some good moments to be had. Rated R for sex, nudity, violence, and profanity.

1984 94 minutes

ROARING TWENTIES, THE

★★★★½

DIRECTOR: Raoul Walsh

CAST: James Cagney, Humphrey Bogart, Priscilla Lane, Gladys George, Jeffrey Lynn, Frank McHugh, Joe Sawyer

James Cagney and Humphrey Bogart star in this superb Warner Bros. gangster entry. Produced by Mark Hellinger and directed by Raoul Walsh (*White Heat*), it's one of the best of its kind, with Cagney featured as a World War I veteran who comes back to no job and no future after fighting for his country. Embittered by all this, he turns to crime.

1939 B & W 104 minutes

ROBBERS OF THE SACRED MOUNTAIN

★★

DIRECTOR: Bob Schulz

CAST: John Marley, Simon MacCorkindale, Louise Vallance, George Touliatos, Blanca Guerra

This action-adventure film could have been another *Raiders of the Lost Ark*. Unfortunately, poor acting and choppy editing leave it in the mediocre range. Simon MacCorkindale does, however, stand out as a determined British reporter who wants to interview a famous anthropologist (John Marley). MacCorkindale becomes part of an expedition seeking lost Indian treasure after he's kidnapped with Marley's granddaughter (Louise Vallance). George Touliatos plays Murdock, a ruthless millionaire, who is determined to use the treasure to rule the world. Rated R for sex, nudity, and violence.

1982 90 minutes

ROBIN AND MARIAN

★★★★½

DIRECTOR: Richard Lester

CAST: Sean Connery, Audrey Hepburn, Richard Harris, Ian Holm, Robert Shaw, Nicol Williamson, Denholm Elliott, Kenneth Haigh

Take the best director of swashbucklers, Richard Lester; add the foremost adventure film actor, Sean Connery; mix well with a fine actress with haunting presence, Audrey Hepburn; and finish off with some of the choicest character actors: You get *Robin and Marian*, a triumph for everyone involved. Rated PG.

1976 112 minutes

ROBIN HOOD AND THE SORCERER

★★★★½

DIRECTOR: Ian Sharp

CAST: Michael Praed, Anthony Valentine, Nickolas Grace, Clive Mantle, Peter Williams, Phil Rose, Judi Trott, Phillip Jackson

While the telling of the Robin Hood legend in this film may be less straightforward than most, the added element of the mysticism enhances the all-too-familiar story and gives the dusty old characters new life. Michael Praed (best known for his work on the TV series *Dynasty*) plays the legendary English outlaw with conviction. Great performances are given by Anthony Valentine as the evil Simon De Belleme and Nickolas Grace as the scheming sheriff of Nottingham. The story has a natural drama to it that will entertain adults as well as youngsters. *Robin Hood and the Sorcerer* is the first episode in a video series called *Robin Hood . . . The Legend*, released by Playhouse Video. Not rated. Contains violence.

1983 115 minutes

ROLLING THUNDER

★★★★

DIRECTOR: John Flynn

CAST: William Devane, Tommy Lee Jones, Linda Haynes, James Best, Dabney Coleman, Lisa Richards, Luke Askew

William Devane delivers a fine performance as a Vietnam POW returned home to a small town in Texas. For his courage and endurance under torture, he is honored with two thousand silver dollars by the local merchants. (A dollar for every day served as a POW.) A gang of vicious killers attempts to rob him, but his conditioning to pain under the Vietnamese will not let him tell them where the silver is, even when they begin to torture him. They then threaten to kill his family. He reveals the whereabouts of the money; they kill his family anyway. After some hospitalization, Devane recruits his Vietnam buddy (played superbly by Tommy Lee Jones) and the hunt is violently and realistically played out. Rated R.

1977 99 minutes

ROMANCING THE STONE

★★★★½

DIRECTOR: Robert Zemeckis

CAST: Kathleen Turner, Michael Douglas, Danny DeVito, Alfonso Arau, Zack Norman

A rip-snorting adventure film that combines action, a love story, suspense, and plenty of laughs, this movie stars Kathleen Turner (*Body Heat*) as a timid romance novelist who becomes involved in a situation more dangerous, exciting, and romantic than anything she could ever dream up. Michael Douglas plays the shotgun-wielding soldier of fortune who comes to her aid while Danny DeVito (*Taxi*), Alfonso Arau (*The Wild Bunch*), and Zack Norman add delightful bits of comedy. Director Robert Zemeckis keeps the film interesting. Whenever the romantic angle becomes a little too much, he throws in some humor or an action sequence, helping to make this movie a feast of fun. Rated PG for violence, nudity, and profanity.

1984 105 minutes

ROUGH CUT

★★★

DIRECTOR: Don Siegel

CAST: Burt Reynolds, Lesley-Anne Down, David Niven, Patrick Magee

The screenplay, by Francis Burns, is a welcome return to the stylish romantic comedies of the 1930s and 1940s with the accent on witty dialogue, action, and suspense. Burt Reynolds and Lesley-Anne Down are a perfect screen combination. As two sophisticated jewel thieves who plot to steal $30 million in uncut diamonds, they exchange quips, become romantically entwined, and are delightful. Rated R.

1980 112 minutes

RUCKUS

★★★½

DIRECTOR: Max Kleven

CAST: Dirk Benedict, Linda Blair, Ben Johnson, Richard Farnsworth, Matt Clark

This light-hearted adventure film is like *Rambo* without the killing. There's lots of action, chases, explosions, and outright destruction, but nobody dies. That's one of the appealing things about this tale of a Vietnam soldier, Dirk Benedict (of TV's *A-Team*), who escapes from an army psycho ward in Mobile and ends up in a little southern town where he is harassed by the locals—but not for long. An impressive supporting cast features Richard Farnsworth as the sheriff, Ben Johnson as the town's kingpin, and Linda Blair as the hero's helper. Comic relief is provided by a cowardly country bumpkin played by veteran character actor Matt Clark. Willie Nelson, Hank Cochran, and Janie Fricke provide the music for some surprisingly good fun. A PG for violence and language.

1984 91 minutes

RUMOR OF WAR, A

★★★

DIRECTOR: Richard T. Heffron

CAST: Brad Davis, Keith Carradine, Stacy Keach, Michael O'Keefe

A well-made television movie about a marine combat unit in Vietnam. Brad Davis plays a young officer who bravely leads his men into combat. He eventually gets charged with murder. The video version is about an hour and a half shorter than the original television print. Too bad.

1980 105 minutes

RUN SILENT, RUN DEEP

★★★★

DIRECTOR: Robert Wise

CAST: Clark Gable, Burt Lancaster, Jack Warden, Don Rickles

Clark Gable becomes the captain of a submarine that Burt Lancaster was to command. Although he resents his new boss, Lancaster stays on. Tensions rise among Lancaster, Gable, and the crew as they set out from Pearl Harbor to destroy a Japanese cruiser. This film is noted as one of the finest World War II submarine movies.

1958 B & W 93 minutes

RUNAWAY TRAIN

★★★★

DIRECTOR: Andrei Konchalovsky

CAST: Jon Voight, Eric Roberts, Rebecca DeMornay, John P. Ryan, Kenneth McMillan, Kyle T. Heffner, T. K. Carter

In this riveting, pulse-pounding adventure movie, based on a screenplay by Akira Kurosawa, two convicts escape from prison and, accompanied by a hostage (Rebecca DeMornay), make the mistake of hopping a train speeding straight for disaster. While the story gets a bit too allegorical and philosophical for its own good on occasion, the film's unrelenting intensity more than makes up for it. In addition, Roberts is hilarious as the young, terminally dumb prisoner who tags along with wild man Voight (in a performance that just skirts parody) and lives long enough to whine about it. Rated R for violence, gore, and profanity.

1986 112 minutes

RUNNING SCARED (1980)

★★★

DIRECTOR: Paul Glicker

CAST: Ken Wahl, Judge Reinhold, Bradford Dillman, Pat Hingle, Lonny Chapman, John Saxon

Ken Wahl and Judge Reinhold are servicemen returning home after two years in the Panama Canal Zone. Reinhold has appropriated some military property, including cameras and guns. He takes an aerial photo to check out the camera. Unknowingly, he has filmed a secret base that is to be used in the Bay of Pigs operation. When their plane lands, authorities find negatives and the chase is on. Lonny Chapman picks up the hitchhiking Wahl and becomes an unsuspecting accomplice. Pursuit in the Florida Everglades adds to the adventure. Unrated.

1980 82 minutes

RUNNING SCARED (1986)

★★★★

DIRECTOR: Peter Hyams

CAST: Gregory Hines, Billy Crystal, Steven Bauer, Darlanne Fluegel, Joe Pantoliano, Dan Hedaya, Jimmy Smits, Jonathan Gries, Tracy Reed

Fast, funny, and exciting, this *Beverly Hills Cop*–style comedy-cop thriller features inspired on-screen teamwork from Gregory Hines and Billy Crystal as a pair of wisecracking detectives on the trail of a devious drug dealer. For his film-making debut in 1973, director Peter Hyams made an underrated action-comedy called *Busting*, which starred the perfect team of Elliott Gould and Robert Blake. *Running Scared* is just a tad better than its predecessor, which makes it one of the best films of its kind. Rated R for violence, nudity, and profanity.

1986 107 minutes

SAHARA

★★★½

DIRECTOR: Zoltán Korda

CAST: Humphrey Bogart, Bruce Bennett, Lloyd Bridges, Dan Duryea, J. Carrol Naish

One of the better war films, this production contains plenty of action, suspense, and characterization. Humphrey Bogart plays the head of a British-American unit stranded in the desert. The soldiers must keep the ever-present Nazi forces at bay while searching for the precious water they need to stay alive. It's a down-to-the-bone, exciting World War II drama.

1943 B & W 97 minutes

SAHARA

🦃

DIRECTOR: Andrew V. McLaglen

CAST: Brooke Shields, Lambert Wilson, Horst Buchholz, John Rhys-Davies, John Mills

Brooke Shields (*Blue Lagoon* and *Endless Love*) stars in this turkey of an adventure picture as a young heiress who, in order to fulfill a promise to her dying father, enters "the world's most treacherous auto race" (across the Sahara Desert), gets kidnapped by an Arab sheik (Lambert Wilson), and eventually falls in love with him. Sound awful? It is! Rated PG for violence and profanity.

1984 104 minutes

SAINT, THE (TELEVISION SERIES)

★★ (OVERALL RATING)

DIRECTORS: Roy Baker, Leslie Norman

CAST: Roger Moore, Winsley Pithey, Norman Pitt, Ivor Dean, Percy Herbert, Ronald Radd, Lois Maxwell, Suzanne Lloyd

Before essaying the role of James Bond, Roger Moore honed his suavity in the series *The Saint*. He sparkled as international adventurer Simon Templar, a connoisseur of fine wine and women. The devilishly daring troubleshooter continually aided the police, who considered him a foe. Made in England, the production could usually be relied on to provide intriguing mysteries, witty dialogue, and solid action. Two episodes per tape.

1963–1969 100 minutes

SAINT IN LONDON, THE

★★★

DIRECTOR: John Paddy Carstairs

CAST: George Sanders, Sally Gray, David Burns, Henry Oscar, Ralph Truman, Norah Howard, Carl Jaffe

George Sanders as the Saint is up to his halo in spies, murder, and intrigue in this entertaining series entry, the second to star Sanders as Simon Templar. Entrusted to protect a foreign ambassador from hired killers, the Saint fails and feels honor-bound to track down the culprits. Based on a short story by Leslie Charteris, this handsome programmer is fun to watch and features a charming and witty lead in Sanders.

1939 B & W 72 minutes

SAINT IN NEW YORK, THE

★★★

DIRECTOR: Ben Holmes
CAST: Louis Hayward, Kay Sutton, Jonathon Hale, Jack Carson, Sig Ruman

The first of Leslie Charteris's popular crime novels to hit the screen, this smooth adventure features Louis Hayward as the Saint, gentleman crimefighter, and his efforts to clean up the city. Simon Templar has been called in by concerned citizens who want him to put an end to six gangsters who have been plaguing their metropolis. Hayward is fine in the title role of the continental adventurer, but George Sanders is the man most associated with the Saint on film.

1938 B & W 71 minutes

ST. IVES

★★★½

DIRECTOR: J. Lee Thompson
CAST: Charles Bronson, Jacqueline Bisset, John Houseman, Maximilian Schell, Harry Guardino, Dana Elcar, Dick O'Neill, Elisha Cook Jr.

This is a good Charles Bronson film about a former police reporter who becomes involved in a murder. Director J. Lee Thompson pulls an understated and believable performance out of the star and the added treat of excellent support from John Houseman, Jacqueline Bisset, Maximilian Schell, Harry Guardino, Dana Elcar, Dick O'Neill, and Elisha Cook make this actioner one of Bronson's memorable films. Rated PG.

1976 93 minutes

SAINT STRIKES BACK, THE

★★★

DIRECTOR: John Farrow
CAST: George Sanders, Wendy Barrie, Jonathon Hale, Jerome Cowan, Neil Hamilton, Barry Fitzgerald, Edward Gargan

A good cast, a good story, and a charming performance by George Sanders as Simon Templar, debonair crimefighter, make this one of the best of a very pleasant series. Sanders, in his first appearance as the suave adventurer, pulls out all the stops in his efforts to clear the name of a dead policeman and straighten out his wayward daughter. These modestly budgeted detective adventures were some of the best ever put on film, and Sanders is the principal reason.

1939 B & W 67 minutes

ST. VALENTINE'S DAY MASSACRE, THE

★★

DIRECTOR: Roger Corman
CAST: Jason Robards Jr., George Segal, Ralph Meeker, Jean Hale, Frank Silvera, Joseph Campanella, Bruce Dern

Watching the leads ham it up provides sporadic fun, but this gaudy gangster picture is long on violence and short on dramatic impact. The massacre itself has been depicted in more exciting style in other films. Where's Eliot Ness when you need him?

1967 100 minutes

SAINT'S VACATION, THE

★★

DIRECTOR: Leslie Fenton
CAST: Hugh Sinclair, Sally Gray, Arthur Macrae, Cecil Parker, Gordon McLeod

Simon Templar finds mystery and adventure instead of peace and quiet when he encounters spies and intrigue on his vacation attempt. Hugh Sinclair plays the sophisticated Saint for the first time in this programmer filmed in England with a British cast. Passable, but not up to the earlier entries in the series.

1941 B & W 60 minutes

SALZBURG CONNECTION, THE

★

DIRECTOR: Lee H. Katzin

CAST: Barry Newman, Anna Karina, Joe Maross, Wolfgang Preiss, Helmut Schmid, Udo Kier, Michael Haussermann, Raoul Retzer, Elisabeth Flechner, Whit Bissel, Klaus Maria Brandauer

This incredibly bad spy film set in Europe has Barry Newman playing an American lawyer on vacation who gets mixed up with Nazi spies, double agents, and a pretty girl (Anna Karina). The story is almost incoherent, with acting to match. Rated PG for violence and language.

1972 93 minutes

SAND PEBBLES, THE

★★★½

DIRECTOR: Robert Wise

CAST: Steve McQueen, Richard Crenna, Richard Attenborough, Candice Bergen, Mako, Simon Oakland, Gavin MacLeod

In Robert Wise's thoughtful film *The Sand Pebbles*, Steve McQueen gives his most compelling performance as Hollman, an ordinary seaman on an American warship stationed off China in the early 1930s. He prefers to remain below deck with his only love, the ship's engines. That way he avoids involvement or decisions, and as long as he obeys orders his life will flow smoothly, yet uneventfully, along. In many ways, China in 1930 was just like Hollman. It was sleeping quietly after years of foreign domination, but events were happening that would bring about revolution. Hollman is forced by these changes in China to become involved with the world outside his engine room. The result is an enjoyable, sweeping epic with unforgettable characters.

1966 179 minutes

SANDERS OF THE RIVER

★★½

DIRECTOR: Zoltán Korda

CAST: Paul Robeson, Leslie Banks, Nina Mae McKinney, Robert Cochran

"Sandy the lawgiver" is the heavy right hand of the British Empire in this action drama of colonialism in darkest Africa. Famed actor and singer Paul Robeson rises above demeaning circumstances and fills the screen with his commanding presence. Great footage of the people and terrain of Africa add to the mood of this adventure and give it an aura lacking in many jungle films. The theme music as sung by Robeson is reprised throughout the film and stays with you, but his other songs tend to pad and interrupt the flow of the film. Leslie Banks as the unyielding, godlike Sanders is condescending and aloof, a man who has learned the language of the Congo and knows its history and secrets, yet remains the classic embodiment of British imperialism. Overall a pretty enjoyable film, but the racial overtones of another age might disturb today's audiences.

1935 B & W 98 minutes

SANDS OF IWO JIMA

★★★★½

DIRECTOR: Allan Dwan

CAST: John Wayne, John Agar, Forrest Tucker, Richard Jaeckel, Arthur Franz

Every time some misguided soul opines that John Wayne can't act, after letting out a hearty derisive laugh, we instruct him or her to watch one of three movies: *The Quiet Man*, *She Wore a Yellow*

Ribbon, and this superb war film. The Duke was never better than as the haunted Sergeant Stryker, a man hated by his men (with a few exceptions) for his unyielding toughness, but it is by that attitude that he hopes to keep them alive in combat. Watch it and see how good the Duke really was.

1949 B & W 110 minutes

SATAN'S SATELLITES

★½

DIRECTOR: Fred C. Brannon
CAST: Judd Holdren, Aline Towne, Wilson Wood, Lane Bradford, John Crawford, Craig Kelly, Leonard Nimoy, Ray Boyle

Heroic Judd Holdren of the Inter-Planetary Patrol, aided by his two assistants and his flying suit, battles otherworldly villains Lans Bradford and Leonard Nimoy, who want to blow the Earth out of its orbit. Originally released by Republic Studios as a twevle-episode serial entitled *Zombies of the Stratosphere*, this sequel to *Radar Men from the Moon* is a cheaply done paste-up job that uses stock footage from previous serials and forgotten feature films of the 1930s and 1940s. Condensed from over three hours into its present length, this hodgepodge of absurdities has only Leonard Nimoy's presence as an alien with a change of heart to recommend it.

1958 B & W 70 minutes

SAVAGE STREETS

DIRECTOR: Danny Steinmann
CAST: Linda Blair, Robert Dryer, Sal Landi, John Vernon, Johnny Venocur, Scott Mayer

That *Exorcist* kid, Linda Blair, is at it again. Only instead of throwing up because she's possessed by the devil, she's making us sick to our stomachs with another violent exploitation film. This time, she's the tough leader of a street gang that stops terrorizing tourists and senior citizens when her sister is raped by a rival gang. Poor sis is a deaf-mute, which makes it all the more disgusting a scene, and Blair decides "this means war." But it really means bore. Rated R for everything imaginable.

1985 90 minutes

SCARFACE (ORIGINAL)

★★★★½

DIRECTOR: Howard Hawks
CAST: Paul Muni, Ann Dvorak, George Raft, Boris Karloff, Osgood Perkins

Subtitled "Shame of the Nation" when released in the 1930s, this thinly veiled account of the rise and fall (the latter being fictional) of Al Capone easily ranks as one of the very best films in the gangster genre—right up there with *The Public Enemy*, *The Roaring Twenties*, *High Sierra*, and *White Heat*. Paul Muni is first-rate as the Chicago gangster and receives excellent support from Ann Dvorak, George Raft, and, outstanding as a rival gangster, Boris Karloff. See it.

1932 B & W 93 minutes

SCARFACE (REMAKE)

★★★★½

DIRECTOR: Brian De Palma
CAST: Al Pacino, Steven Bauer, Robert Loggia, Paul Shenar

One-time "Godfather" Al Pacino returns to his screen beginnings with a bravura performance in the title role of this updating of Howard Hawks's 1932 gangster classic. Rather than bootleg gin as Paul Muni did in the original, Pacino imports and sells cocaine. Directed by Brian De Palma (*Carrie* and *Dressed to Kill*), it's the most violent, thrilling, revolting, surprising, and gruesome gangster movie ever made. Although it runs nearly three hours, you hardly notice the time. What's more, you can't take your eyes off the screen. Rated R for nudity, violence, sex, and profanity.

1983 170 minutes

SCARLET AND THE BLACK, THE

★★★

DIRECTOR: Jerry London
CAST: Gregory Peck, Christopher Plummer, John Gielgud

The action in this film is centered around the Vatican during the time of the German occupation of Rome in 1943. Based on a story entitled "The Scarlet Pimpernel of the Vatican," it chronicles the adventures of an Irish priest who manages to elude the German captors in true Pimpernel fashion. Moderately entertaining.

1983 143 minutes

SCARLET PIMPERNEL, THE (ORIGINAL)

★★★

DIRECTOR: Harold Young
CAST: Leslie Howard, Raymond Massey, Merle Oberon, Nigel Bruce

Leslie Howard plays Sir Percy, an English aristocrat engaged in the underground effort to snatch out from under the blade of the guillotine Frenchmen caught in the Reign of Terror. In the tradition of many swashbucklers, he hides his activities under the guise of a fop. His ruse may throw off the French authorities, as ably represented by a sinister Raymond Massey, but he is also turning off his beautiful wife, Merle Oberon.

1934 B & W 95 minutes

SCARLET PIMPERNEL, THE (REMAKE)

★★★½

DIRECTOR: Clive Donner
CAST: Anthony Andrews, Jane Seymour, Ian McKellen, James Villiers, Elinore David, Michael Jamieson

This is the made-for-TV version of the much-filmed (seven times) adventure classic. Anthony Andrews (*Brideshead Revisited*) makes a dashing hero leading a double life aiding French revolutionaries while posing as a foppish member of British society. Jane Seymour is breathtakingly beautiful as his ladylove. This lavish production proves that remakes, even for television, can be worthwhile.

1982 150 minutes

SCENES FROM A MURDER

DIRECTOR: Alberto De Martino
CAST: Telly Savalas, Anne Heywood, Giorio Piazza, Osvaldo Rugger

This slow-moving Italian suspense tale features Telly Savalas as a killer hired to eliminate a beautiful actress. Savalas is either flicking his stiletto or furtively following his victim throughout the film. The conclusion is plain ridiculous. Unrated, but with nudity and violence.

1974 92 minutes

SCORCHY

★

DIRECTOR: Hinket Avedis
CAST: Connie Stevens, Cesare Danova, William Smith, Marlene Schmidt, Normann Burton, Joyce Jameson

Connie Stevens is an undercover cop trying to bust a major drug ring. You won't check this out for its acting ability, so you won't be surprised. However, you will get some action and lots of gratuitous gore. Rated R.

1976 99 minutes

SCORPION

DIRECTOR: William Riead
CAST: Tonny Tulleners, Don Murray

Dimwitted martial arts film stars nonactor Tonny Tulleners, who is famous for defeating Chuck Norris three times in karate contests. He plays a two-fisted and -footed hero who takes on a band of terrorists. But his dreadful performance is only one of the dismal ingredients in this grade-Z gobbler. Rated R.

1987 98 minutes

SEA DEVILS

★★

DIRECTOR: Ben Stoloff
CAST: Victor McLaglen, Preston Foster, Ida Lupino, Donald Woods

Victor McLaglen and Ida Lupino play father and daughter in this soggy tale of Coast Guard trial and tribulation. McLaglen and Preston Foster are service rivals given to settling problems with their fists. Unfortunately, the audience can't fight back.

1937 B & W 88 minutes

SEA HAWK, THE

★★★★

DIRECTOR: Michael Curtiz
CAST: Errol Flynn, Flora Robson, Claude Rains, Donald Crisp, Alan Hale, Henry Daniell, Gilbert Roland

Errol Flynn was the best of the screen's costumed adventurers. *The Sea Hawk* shows him at his swashbuckling peak. He plays a buccaneer sea captain who is given tacit approval by Queen Elizabeth I (Flora Robson) to wreak havoc on the Spanish fleet and their cities in the New World. It is a fun-packed adventure for the whole family.

1940 B & W 109 minutes

SEA SHALL NOT HAVE THEM, THE

★★½

DIRECTOR: Lewis Gilbert
CAST: Michael Redgrave, Dirk Bogarde, John Mitchell

Nicely done World War II film about British air rescue operations. Main story follows an RAF bomber crew shot down over the North Sea and their rescue from the ocean. This film could have used more action scenes and a faster pace, but it is worth watching if you like war films.

1955 B & W 92 minutes

SEA WOLVES, THE

★★★

DIRECTOR: Andrew V. McLaglen
CAST: Gregory Peck, Roger Moore, David Niven, Trevor Howard, Barbara Kellerman, Patrick MacNee, Kenneth Griffith

A World War II version of *The Over the Hill Gang*. Gregory Peck and Roger Moore play two British officers who recruit a bunch of Boer War veterans now in their autumn years to do some espionage against the Germans along the coast of India. While the film relies too heavily on comedy that doesn't work, the last twenty minutes has enough spirit to redeem it. The film is based on a true story. Rated PG for violence and sex.

1980 120 minutes

SEARCH AND DESTROY

★½

DIRECTOR: William Fruet
CAST: Perry King, Don Stroud, Tisa Farrow, George Kennedy, Park Jong Soo

Though *Search and Destroy* is a pain to watch—the continuity problems are so serious that the viewer may get a headache by watching the camera's subject jump from one side of the screen to the other—the film illuminates a curious phenomenon evident in American cinema since the Tet offensive in Vietnam. With the rise of the *Dirty Harry* films as well as Charles Bronson's antihero flicks, one can see the people's lack of confidence in law enforcement and the judicial system and a swing to a more anarchistic form of crime deterrence. Perry King is an American Vietnam veteran who is being chased by a Vietnamese villain seeking revenge. Of course, the cops are ineffectual and even a little hostile to the ex-soldier, so he has to face the bad guy alone. Not rated, the film has violence and profanity.

1981 93 minutes

SECOND CHANCE

★★½

DIRECTOR: Rudolph Mate

CAST: Robert Mitchum, Linda Darnell, Jack Palance, Reginald Sheffield, Roy Roberts

Robert Mitchum plays protector to a former gangster's girlfriend (Linda Darnell) as they are pursued through South America by hit man Jack Palance. This passable chase melodrama was Howard Hughes's first excursion into wide screen, and the often-imitated climax aboard the gondola cars suspended above a deep chasm is the centerpiece of the film. Robert Mitchum is breezy and believable; Palance is at his cool, methodical best; and Linda Darnell, finally beyond the virginal young leads she is best remembered for, does a creditable job as the tough-talking, vulnerable target.

1953 82 minutes

SECRET AGENT (TELEVISION SERIES)

★★★½ (OVERALL RATING)

DIRECTORS: Don Chaffey, Peter Maxwell, Michael Truman, etc.

CAST: Patrick McGoohan, Peter Madden

The suave, debonair, and resourceful John Drake (Patrick McGoohan) turned out to have more than one life; after the limited success of his 1961 series, *Danger Man*, he returned in 1965 with the far more flamboyant—and popular—*Secret Agent*. In spite of a faithful following, the new show disappeared after forty-five episodes had been aired. (But Drake would appear again—in a sense—as *The Prisoner*.) Creator and executive producer Ralph Smart, who wore the same hats during *Danger Man*, changed the format a bit for this second outing; now Drake worked for the specifically British agency known as M.I.9 and took orders from an "M"-like figure named Hobbs (Peter Madden). Drake still hated guns, preferring to rely on his own fists and a grand series of gadgets. (The miniature tape recorder hidden in his electric shaver was an oft-seen toy.) The hour-length dramas, many written by Smart, were far grittier and more realistic than their American counterparts. Available episodes include "Battle of the Cameras," which concerns chemical warfare (and was the first aired in this country, and "A Room in the Basement," highly reminiscent of *Mission: Impossible*. The slick title theme, written by Phil Sloan and Steve Barri, became a Top-10 hit and made a star of singer Johnny Rivers. The series, which has not dated in the slightest, is suitable for family viewing.

1965–1966 B & W 53 minutes

SECRET AGENT, THE

★★★

DIRECTOR: Alfred Hitchcock

CAST: John Gielgud, Madeleine Carroll, Robert Young, Peter Lorre, Percy Marmont, Lilli Palmer

Off-beat espionage film by the master of suspense contains many typical Alfred Hitchcock touches, but lacks the pacing and characterizations that set his best efforts apart from those of his contemporaries. Great collection of fine performers and familiar faces still comes short of making this one of the master's better-known classics, although Peter Lorre's portrayal of the murderous spy is one of his most memorable. Alternately grim and humorous, this uneven film (based on a novel by Somerset Maugham) is still watchable and comparable with many of the best films in the genre.

1936 B & W 93 minutes

SERGEANT YORK

★★★

DIRECTOR: Howard Hawks

CAST: Gary Cooper, Walter Brennan, George Tobias, Ward Bond, Noah Beery Jr., June Lockhart

A World War II morale booster that succeeded beyond mere propaganda and is still good entertainment today. Gary Cooper got an Academy Award as the deeply religious young farmer from backwoods Tennessee who tries to avoid service in World War I because of his religious convictions only to become the war's most decorated American hero!

1941 B & W 134 minutes

SEVEN-PER-CENT SOLUTION, THE

★★★★

DIRECTOR: Herbert Ross

CAST: Nicol Williamson, Alan Arkin, Robert Duvall, Laurence Olivier, Vanessa Redgrave, Joel Grey

Sherlock Holmes (Nicol Williamson) attempts to get rid of his cocaine addiction by getting treatment from Sigmund Freud (Alan Arkin). This is a fast-paced adventure with touches of humor. Robert Duvall's portrayal of Dr. Watson nearly steals the show. Great fun. Rated PG; okay for everyone.

1976 113 minutes

SEVEN-UPS, THE

★★½

DIRECTOR: Philip D'Antoni

CAST: Roy Scheider, Tony LoBianco, Richard Lynch

Hoping to cash in on the popularity of *The French Connection*, the producer of that film directs this slam-bang action flick in an intellectual vacuum. All that's missing are William Friedkin, Gene Hackman, and an intelligent story . . . but what the hey, we've got a better car chase! Roy Scheider is, as always, quite appealing, but he can't make something out of this nothing. Only for those who prefer form over content. Rated PG for violence.

1973 103 minutes

SHADOW OF THE EAGLE

★★½

DIRECTOR: Ford Beebe

CAST: John Wayne, Dorothy Gulliver, Walter Miller, Kenneth Harlan, Yakima Canutt, Roy D'Arcy

John Wayne's second serial for Mascot Pictures is another one of those stolen inventions–kidnapped scientist affairs, this time masterminded by a mysterious criminal known as The Eagle, who likes to write his threats in the sky with an airplane. Although a bit creaky, this is fun to watch and the cast includes many silent serial players in character roles. This film marked the first time Wayne and Yakima Canutt, dean of all stuntmen, worked together—they would fight it out dozens of times in as many films over the next seven years, until *Stagecoach* made Wayne a star and Canutt a legend.

1932 B & W 12 chapters

SHADOW OF THE THIN MAN

★★★★

DIRECTOR: W. S. Van Dyke II
CAST: William Powell, Myrna Loy, Sam Levene, Donna Reed, Barry Nelson

Fourth in the series, with sleuths Nick and Nora Charles (William Powell and Myrna Loy) dividing their time between mysteries, Asta the wonder dog, and a stroller-bound Nick Jr. (who arrived in the previous film). Barry Nelson and Donna Reed are among the innocents this time around, and the story concerns dire deeds at the local race track. Another sumptuous serving of sophisticated fun.

1941 B & W 97 minutes

SHADOW STRIKES, THE

★½

DIRECTOR: Lynn Shores
CAST: Rod La Rocque, Lynn Anders, Norman Ainsley

Loosely based on *The Ghost of the Manor*, one of hundreds of stories featuring the mysterious Shadow written by Walter Gibson under the name of Maxwell Grant, this lackluster effort finds Rod La Rocque on the trail of a gang of crooks who have murdered his father, a prominent attorney. This anemic whodunit is a big disappointment for fans of the radio and pulp-magazine hero and ignores most of his strange powers, as well as girl Friday, Margo Lane.

1937 B & W 61 minutes

SHAFT

★★★

DIRECTOR: Gordon Parks
CAST: Richard Roundtree, Charles Cioffi, Moses Gunn

One of the best black films from the late 1960s and early 1970s. There is plenty of action and raw energy as private eye Shaft (Richard Roundtree) battles the bad guys in order to rescue a kidnapped woman. Great musical score by Isaac Hayes. Rated PG for violence.

1971 100 minutes

SHAKER RUN

★½

DIRECTOR: Bruce Morrison
CAST: Cliff Robertson, Leif Garrett, Lisa Harrow, Shane Briant, Ian Mune, Peter Rowell, Peter Hayden, Bruce Phillips

A New Zealand laboratory accidentally creates a deadly virus that the military wants as a weapon. But the culture is lifted by a conscientious doctor (Lisa Harrow) who commissions a daredevil driver and his mechanic (Cliff Robertson and Leif Garrett, respectively) to transport it across the country. Yes, folks, another car flick, and like most of its kind, it lacks credibility: on more than one occasion, a wall of secret service men with automatic weapons can't seem to shoot out the tires of the hot rod; the bad guys are reduced to pure evil icons so they are easy to identify; and our hero is an ex—if that really matters here—but ex-teen idol Garrett is just awful. Not rated, but the equivalent of a PG for violence and profanity.

1985 91 minutes

SHAMUS

★★½

DIRECTOR: Buzz Kulik
CAST: Burt Reynolds, Dyan Cannon, John Ryan, Joe Santos

An okay detective thriller, with Burt playing Burt. Nothing new to add to the genre, but lots of action keeps things moving along in this story of a private eye investigating a weapons-smuggling ring. Rated PG.

1973 106 minutes

SHANGHAI SURPRISE

★★½

DIRECTOR: Jim Goddard
CAST: Sean Penn, Madonna, Paul Freeman, Richard Griffiths, Phillip Sayer, Victor Wong

The only surprise here is the amount of money poured into this silly farce. Madonna plays an uptight missionary in Shanghai, 1938. She recruits a con artist (Sean Penn) to help her recover eleven hundred pounds of opium to ease the pain of the suffering. The plot thickens when others search for "Faraday's Flowers." Madonna comes off looking good despite the silly dialogue, but Penn would have helped his career by passing this one up. The scenery and songs by George Harrison help this otherwise hopeless film a bit. The few comic moments don't really classify this romantic adventure as a comedy. Rated PG for occasional obscenities and partial nudity.

1986 93 minutes

SHAOLIN TEMPLE

★★★★

DIRECTOR: Chang Hsin Yen
CAST: Li Lin Jei, Yue Chen Wei, Yue Hai, Din Nan

The best kung-fu film since *Enter the Dragon*, this period piece, set in seventh-century China, traces the history of the Shaolin Temple. It stars the country's top martial arts experts, yet characterization and plot are not slighted. The hokey camera tricks and dumb sound effects so common to the kung-fu genre are absent in this Hong Kong production, which was filmed on location. As always in films of this kind, the accent is on nonstop action. Unrated, the film has violence. In Chinese, with English subtitles.

1982 111 minutes

SHARK! (AKA MANEATERS!)

★

DIRECTOR: Samuel Fuller
CAST: Burt Reynolds, Barry Sullivan, Arthur Kennedy, Sylvia Pinal, Enrique Lucero

Waterlogged undersea adventure about Burt Reynolds and the boys braving man(and ham)-eating sharks to retrieve sunken loot is nothing new and loaded with scenic and stock footage to pad out the tired storyline. Not as good as the adventure films Reynolds was making prior to this weak entry. Director Samuel Fuller disavowed his association with this joint Mexico-U.S. production. Rated PG.

1969 92 minutes

SHARK HUNTER, THE

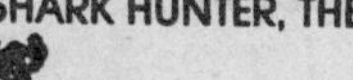

DIRECTOR: Enzo G. Castellari
CAST: Franco Nero, Jorge Luke, Mike Forrest, Eduardo Fajardo

Franco Nero (*Force Ten from Navarone; Enter the Ninja*) stars as a Caribbean island recluse who beats up sharks and searches for buried treasure. Good for a laugh, thanks to the lame voice dubbing. Otherwise, feed this one to the you-know-what. Not rated, but the equivalent of a PG for violence and brief nudity.

1984 92 minutes

SHARK'S TREASURE

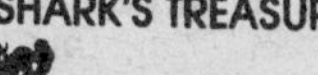

DIRECTOR: Cornel Wilde
CAST: Cornel Wilde, Yaphet Kotto, John Neilson, Cliff Osmond

Good guys and bad guys search for sunken treasure while Cornel Wilde and tiger sharks mete out justice. This was the first film to cash in on the success of *Jaws*, though these sharks look downright anemic. Silly and pompous, with jarring homosexual overtones. A complete embarrassment. Rated PG for violence.

1975 95 minutes

SHARKY'S MACHINE

★★★★½

DIRECTOR: Burt Reynolds
CAST: Burt Reynolds, Rachel Ward, Brian Keith, Bernie Casey, Vittorio Gassman, Charles Durning

This is one of the best cop thrillers ever made. It's exciting, suspenseful, funny, and intelligent, so good it joins *48 Hrs*, *Dirty Harry*, and *Tightrope* as the best of the genre. Burt Reynolds stars under his own direction as an undercover cop who has a compulsion to crack down on a new wave of crime in his city. He does so by turning a crew of vice cops into a personal police machine. Rated R because of violence and profanity.

1981 119 minutes

S.H.E.

★★★

DIRECTOR: Robert Lewis
CAST: Omar Sharif, Cornelia Sharpe, Robert Lansing, Anita Ekberg

This average made-for-TV spy/action thriller has one twist . . . a female James Bond. Beautiful Cornelia Sharpe is S.H.E. (Security Hazards Expert). She pursues Robert Lansing, the U.S. syndicate boss, throughout Europe. Omar Sharif makes an appearance as a wine baron. The beautiful sights (both Sharpe and Europe) make the film more than watchable.

1979 105 minutes

SHEENA

★

DIRECTOR: John Guillermin
CAST: Tanya Roberts, Ted Wass, Donovan Scott

Tanya Roberts (of *Beastmaster* and TV's *Charlie's Angels*) stars as the comic book heroine Sheena, Queen of the Jungle. In this adventure film, an evil African prince tries to take over his brother's kingdom while our heroine, with the help of reporters Ted Wass and Donovan Scott, attempts to stop him. Rated PG.

1984 117 minutes

SHERLOCK HOLMES AND THE SECRET WEAPON

★★★

DIRECTOR: Roy William Neill
CAST: Basil Rathbone, Nigel Bruce, Lionel Atwill, Karen Verne, Dennis Hoey, Mary Gordon

Although the contemporary (1940s) setting makes the Baker Street sleuth seem oddly out of place, Basil Rathbone remains one of the definitive Holmeses. In this case, he once again faces the ruthless Professor Moriarty (Lionel Atwill), who tries to torture a scientist into revealing the plans of a revolutionary bombsight. A code that appears in this film is borrowed from *The Adventure of the Dancing Man*. This also is the first Rathbone Holmes to be rereleased in color, a dubious distinction that won't improve it a bit; these films were made for the shadowy world of black and white.

1942 68 minutes

SHOGUN (SHORT VERSION)

★★

DIRECTOR: Jerry London
CAST: Richard Chamberlain, Toshiro Mifune, John Rhys-Davies

This is a confusing, lackluster condensation of writer James Clavell's epic twelve-hour TV miniseries about an English seaman's experiences in feudal Japan.

1980 125 minutes

SHOGUN (FULL-LENGTH VERSION)

★★★★

DIRECTOR: Jerry London
CAST: Richard Chamberlain, Toshiro Mifune, Yoko Shimada, Damien Thomas

Forget about the shortened version that is also out on video; this ten-hour original is the only one that does justice to James Clavell's sweeping novel. Richard Chamberlain began his reign as king of the miniseries with his portrayal of Blackthorne, the English sailor shipwrecked among the feudal Japanese. Rarely has television been the original home for a program of this epic scope, and it all works, from the breathtaking cinematography to the superb acting by the entire cast. The stranger-in-a-strange-land feeling is heightened by the on-screen use of Japanese dialogue; if you recall being confused the first time around, though, don't fret, because subtitles have now been added.

1980 600 minutes

SHOOT

★★★½

DIRECTOR: Harvey Hart
CAST: Cliff Robertson, Ernest Borgnine, Henry Silva

A group of buddies spending a weekend hunting are attacked by another group of hunters who are after game more interesting than deer. When one of their party is wounded, the attacked hunters, led by Cliff Robertson and Ernest Borgnine, want revenge and mount a military-style campaign to get it. Robertson and Borgnine give us fine portrayals as the hunters go from frightened to angry and vengeful in this better-than-average action adventure. Rated R for violence and profanity.

1976 98 minutes

SHOUT AT THE DEVIL

★★

DIRECTOR: Peter Hunt
CAST: Lee Marvin, Roger Moore, Barbara Parkins, Ian Holm

Good action scenes elevate this otherwise distasteful and overly complicated film about a hard-drinking American adventurer (Lee Marvin) and an upper-crust Englishman (Roger Moore) who join forces to blow up a German battleship before the breakout of World War I. Rated PG.

1976 119 minutes

SHRIEK IN THE NIGHT, A

★★★

DIRECTOR: Albert Ray
CAST: Ginger Rogers, Lyle Talbot, Arthur Hoyt, Purnell Pratt, Harvey Clark

Ginger Rogers and Lyle Talbot play two fast-talking reporters competing for a juicy scoop on a murder case in this entertaining low-budget whodunit. Full of mysterious goings-on and creaking doors, this tidy thriller makes up for its lack of production quality by the spunky, enthusiastic performances by the two leads. A good example of the classic old-dark-house murder-mystery from the 1920s and 1930s.

1933 B & W 66 minutes

SIDEWINDER 1

★★

DIRECTOR: Earl Bellamy
CAST: Marjoe Gortner, Michael Parks, Susan Howard, Alex Cord

Michael Parks (*The Bible*) is a quiet, reclusive motocross racer who becomes a partner in developing a new dirt bike. *Sidewinder 1* has good racing scenes—motocross fans will love them—but the story is studded with sexist remarks and attitudes about women as sex objects and professional women as frigid and misguided. Rated PG.

1977 97 minutes

SILENT RAGE

★

DIRECTOR: Michael Miller
CAST: Chuck Norris, Ron Silver, Stephen Furst

A Texas sheriff is pitted against a psychotic killer who has become virtually indestructible through genetic engineering in this karate-horror-thriller-western. Rated R for nudity, profanity, sex, and violence.

1982 105 minutes

SILVER BLAZE

★★★

DIRECTOR: Thomas Bentley
CAST: Arthur Wontner, Ian Fleming, Lyn Harding, John Turnbull, Robert Horton, Lawrence Grossmith, Judy Gunn, Arthur Goulet

In the 1930s, noted Sherlockian Vincent Starrett proclaimed, "No better Sherlock Holmes than Arthur Wontner is likely to be seen and heard in pictures in our time. His detective is the veritable fathomer of Baker Street in person." This tall, gaunt British actor was the living image of the Sidney Paget illustrations that graced Conan Doyle's mystery stories in *Strand* magazine. Beginning with *Sherlock Holmes' Fatal Hour*, in 1931, Wontner starred as Holmes in five handsome but low-budget films, of which *Silver Blaze* was the last. Ironically, the latter movie was not released in America until after the 1939 *Hound of the Baskervilles* introduced Basil Rathbone as the screen's most famous detective. So impressive was Rathbone's debut as Holmes, the American distributor retitled *Silver Blaze* as *Murder at the Baskervilles*. Indeed, Sir Henry Baskerville himself pops up in this loose adaptation of the original story about the disappearance of a prized racehorse. In a further variation, Professor Moriarty (Lyn Harding) and Colonel Moran (Arthur Goulet) are behind the nefarious goings-on. It may not be faithful, but *Silver Blaze* is fun for mystery fans even though it shows its age. Most of all, it is a treat to have Arthur Wontner's seldom-seen interpretation of Sherlock Holmes on video.

1937 B & W 60 minutes

SINBAD THE SAILOR

★★★

DIRECTOR: Richard Wallace
CAST: Douglas Fairbanks Jr., Walter Slezak, Maureen O'Hara, Jane Greer, Anthony Quinn, Sheldon Leonard

Ho for the Bounding Main and strange doings in exotic lands! Aping his father, Douglas Fairbanks Jr., as Sinbad, sails forth in search of Alexander the Great's fabled treasure and hits a variety of reefs. Unfortunately, the plot not only thickens but gets murky, to boot. Some say it's all tongue-in-cheek, but it's really more foot-in-mouth. Pictorially lavish and impressive, but definitely not steak. Nonetheless, it is fun.

1947 117 minutes

SIROCCO

★★★

DIRECTOR: Curtis Bernhardt
CAST: Humphrey Bogart, Marta Toren, Lee J. Cobb, Everett Sloane, Zero Mostel

This gritty, low-key later effort by Humphrey Bogart doesn't have the reputation of his more popular films, but his sleazy, self-serving gunrunner seems to be the logical evolution of the cynical, idealistic Rick Blaine in *Casablanca*. Bogart plays a successful crook operating in postwar Syria. He is forced to intercede in a terrorist-police situation and gets himself in trouble with both factions. Deceit and complicity are the order of the day in troubled Sirocco as Bogart reluctantly aids his decent rival, the French commandant (Lee J. Cobb), while berating and using his hangers-on and associates. One of Bogart's best later works and a representative sample of the darker side of romance and intrigue, poles apart from but structurally related to films like *Casablanca* and *Beat the Devil*. Give it a try.

1951 B & W 98 minutes

SKY BANDITS

DIRECTOR: Zoran Perisic
CAST: Scott McGinnis, Jeff Osterhage, Ronald Lacey, Miles Anderson, Nicholas Lyndhurst

An uninspired mixing of *Butch Cassidy and the Sundance Kid* and *The Blue Max*, this British production features Scott McGinnis and Jeff Osterhage as outlaws from the Old West who end up as flying aces in World War I. It isn't worth the price of an off-night video rental. Rated PG for violence.

1986 95 minutes

SLAUGHTER IN SAN FRANCISCO

DIRECTOR: William Lowe
CAST: Chuck Norris, Robert Jones, Daniel Ivan, Bob Talbert, Robert J. Herguth, Jame Ecomomides, Chuck Boyde, Don Wong, Sylvia Channing

Another abysmal martial arts chop-socky fest. All voices are dubbed and all sounds of fists and feet hitting flesh boom like slamming doors. All fights are one on ten, and each of the ten attack the solitary opponent one at a time so that he can win. Everyone has guns, but nobody uses them, etc., etc..... A police officer tries to uncover the killers of his fellow cop and finds a crime ring along the way. Thoroughly stupid. Top-billed Chuck Norris appears only briefly. Rated R for violence and profanity.

1974 87 minutes

SLAVE OF THE CANNIBAL GOD

DIRECTOR: Sergio Martino
CAST: Stacy Keach, Ursula Andress

A woman (Ursula Andress) encounters a cult of flesh-eaters while attempting to find her missing husband in New Guinea. Her resourceful guide (Stacy Keach) helps her through one close call after another as they are pursued by a helicopter full of bad guys. The low, low budget and inept production team—look for the occasional intrusion of a boom mike in the dialogue scenes—offer a few laughs, but the groans greatly outnumber them. Rated R for violence and nudity.

1979 87 minutes

SLEEPING DOGS

★★½

DIRECTOR: Roger Donaldson
CAST: Sam Neill, Warren Oates, Nevan Rowe, Ian Mune

Here's a "what if?" film set in New Zealand during a time of economic crisis. Sam Neill plays a husband and father who discovers his wife is having an affair, so he goes off to live by himself for a while. Meanwhile, a group of government agents manufacture a revolution by killing innocent bystanders during demonstrations and making it look like the work of the protesters. Neill's wife and her boyfriend accidentally get caught up in an encounter between police and revolutionaries and are pegged as conspirators. Soon he, too, is a wanted man, the so-called mastermind behind the phony revolt. No MPAA rating.

1977 107 minutes

SLOANE

DIRECTOR: Dan Rosenthal
CAST: Robert Resnik, Debra Blee, Raul Aragon, Ann Milhench, Carissa Carbs, Charles Black

On the box of this video, the sales pitch begins: "In the action-packed tradition of *Rambo*..." But Stallone never looked as wimpy as Robert Resnik, who stars in this dreadful film about organized crime in Manila. Wholly unbelievable, even without the cannibalistic pygmies. Not rated, but has plenty of sex, violence, and profanity.

1984 95 minutes

SMALL TOWN IN TEXAS, A

★★

DIRECTOR: Jack Starrett
CAST: Timothy Bottoms, Susan George, Bo Hopkins, Art Hindle, Morgan Woodward

Fairly effective B picture pits a revenge-lusting Timothy Bottoms against the crooked sheriff (Bo Hopkins) who framed him in a drug bust and stole his wife (Susan George). Car crashes, fights, and even a little suspense. Rated R.

1976 95 minutes

SOLDIER, THE

DIRECTOR: James Glickenhaus
CAST: Ken Wahl, Klaus Kinski, William Prince

In this boring, stupid, and disgusting "thriller" by writer-director James Glickenhaus (*The Exterminator*), Russian agents pretending to be a terrorist group steal enough plutonium for a large nuclear explosion, and it is up to the soldier (Ken Wahl, of *The Wanderers*) to sabotage their plan without the official sanction or support of the United States government. It's all about as thrilling as a traffic jam. Rated R for blood, gore, violence, and profanity.

1982 96 minutes

SOLDIER'S STORY, A

★★★★★

DIRECTOR: Norman Jewison
CAST: Howard E. Rollins Jr., Adolph Caesar

A murder mystery, a character study, and a deeply affecting drama rolled into one, *A Soldier's Story*, based on Charles Fuller's 1981 Pulitzer Prize–winning play, is an unforgettable viewing experience. This riveting movie examines man's inhumanity to man in one of its most venal forms: racial hatred. Rated PG for violence and profanity.

1984 102 minutes

SOMETHING OF VALUE

★★★

DIRECTOR: Richard Brooks
CAST: Rock Hudson, Dana Wynter, Sidney Poitier, Wendy Hiller, Frederick O'Neal, Juano Hernandez, William Marshall, Michael Pate

White settlers in Kenya are preyed upon by bloodthirsty Mau Mau tribesmen sick of oppression in this often too-graphic drama, which opens with a specially filmed foreword from Winston Churchill.

1957 B & W 113 minutes

SON OF MONTE CRISTO, THE

★★★

DIRECTOR: Rowland V. Lee
CAST: Joan Bennett, Louis Hayward, George Sanders, Florence Bates, Montagu Love, Ian Wolfe, Clayton Moore, Ralph Byrd

True to established swashbuckler form, masked avenging hero Louis Hayward crosses wits, then swords, with would-be dictator George Sanders. Honoring tradition, he then frees imprisoned fair lady Joan Bennett from the villain's clutches.

1941 B & W 102 minutes

SON OF THE SHEIK

★★½

DIRECTOR: George Fitzmaurice
CAST: Rudolph Valentino, Vilma Banky, Agnes Ayres, Bull Montana, Montague Love, George Fawcett, Karl Dane, William Donovan

This sequel to the 1921 adventure *The Sheik*, proved to be bedroom-eyed, ex-gardener Rudolph Valentino's final film. Made shortly before his death at age 31, it was released to coincide with his funeral and was an immediate hit. In the title role, the legendary Valentino acquitted himself with confidence and flair, foiling his enemies and winning the heart of nomadic dancer Vilma Banky. Silent.

1926 B & W 62 minutes

SONG OF THE THIN MAN

★★★½

DIRECTOR: Edward Buzzell
CAST: William Powell, Myrna Loy, Keenan Wynn, Dean Stockwell, Gloria Grahame, Patricia Morison

Sixth and final entry in the series, a cut above the previous one because of its involvement in jazz music circles. Nick and Nora Charles (William Powell and Myrna Loy) match wits with a murderer this time out, and the setting helps their dialogue regain its crisp sparkle. Nick Jr. isn't around as much; his absence also keeps things moving. All in all, a worthy effort with which to conclude things.

1947 B & W 86 minutes

SOUTH OF PAGO PAGO

★★

DIRECTOR: Alfred E. Green
CAST: Victor McLaglen, Jon Hall, Frances Farmer, Olympe Bradna, Gene Lockhart

A good title is wasted on this so-so action tale of pirates heisting native-harvested pearls and being pursued and engaged by the locals. Typical South Sea fare.

1940 B & W 98 minutes

SOUTHERN COMFORT

★★★★

DIRECTOR: Walter Hill
CAST: Keith Carradine, Powers Boothe, Fred Ward, Byron James

Director Walter (*48 HRS*) Hill's 1981 "war" film focuses on the plight of a National Guard unit lost in Cajun country while on routine training maneuvers. Armed only with M-16 rifles loaded with blanks, the soldiers (who include Keith Carradine and Powers Boothe) find themselves ill-equipped to deal with the hostile locals—and an edge-of-your-seat entertainment is the result. Rated R for violence.

1981 106 minutes

SPARTACUS

★★★★½

DIRECTOR: Stanley Kubrick
CAST: Kirk Douglas, Jean Simmons, Laurence Olivier, Peter Ustinov, Charles Laughton, Tony Curtis

One of the more rewarding big-budget epics that marked the late 1950s and 1960s. Even though this fictional story of an actual slave revolt against the Roman Empire is large-scale in every detail, it never lets the human drama get lost in favor of spectacle. Except for an inept effort by Tony Curtis, the large cast of movie luminaries excel in their many fine roles.

1960 196 minutes

SPY SMASHER

★★★

DIRECTOR: William Witney

CAST: Kane Richmond, Sam Flint, Marguerite Chapman, Hans Schumm, Tristram Coffin

The costumed radio hero (Kane Richmond) takes on the Nazis in this fun-for-fans cliff-hanger serial.

1942 B & W 12 chapters

SPY WHO LOVED ME, THE

★★★★

DIRECTOR: Lewis Gilbert

CAST: Roger Moore, Barbara Bach, Curt Jurgens, Richard Kiel, Bernard Lee, Lois Maxwell, Desmond Llewellyn, Caroline Munro

This, the tenth James Bond epic, is Roger Moore's third, and he finally hits his stride. Directed with a blend of excitement and tongue-in-cheek humor, the film teams Bond with Russian agent XXX (Barbara Bach) in an effort to stop an industrialist (Curt Jurgens) from destroying the surface world so he can rule an undersea kingdom. This marked the first appearance by Richard Kiel's "Jaws," and he's menacing indeed. Bach has an equally good part, a strong female lead in a series famous for its lack thereof. The music, by Marvin Hamlisch, lacks the bite of series regular John Barry, but Carly Simon's rendition of the title theme is excellent. Rated PG for violence, sexual situations.

1977 125 minutes

SQUIZZY TAYLOR

★★½

DIRECTOR: Kevin Dobson

CAST: David Atkins, Jacki Weaver, Alan Cassell, Michael Long, Robert Hughes

Fairly interesting film about the notorious Australian gangster of the 1920s who rose to fame in Melbourne because of his keen wit and flamboyant style. David Atkins gives a convincing performance. But the story begins to lose its edge after a while. Not rated. Has sex, nudity, and violence.

1983 103 minutes

STAKEOUT

★★★★½

DIRECTOR: John Badham

CAST: Richard Dreyfuss, Emilio Estevez, Aidan Quinn, Madeline Stowe, Dan Lauria, Forest Whitaker, Ian Tracy

Topnotch thriller offers memorable moments of comedy, romance, and suspense as two detectives (Richard Dreyfuss and Emilio Estevez) wait for a psychotic escaped convict (Aidan Quinn) to show up at the home of his ex-girlfriend (Madeline Stowe). In the process, Dreyfuss falls in love with Stowe, thus putting his career on the line and both of their lives in danger. Director John Badham expertly handles the various elements. Rated R for violence, profanity, nudity, and simulated sex.

1987 118 minutes

STALAG 17

★★★★★

DIRECTOR: Billy Wilder

CAST: William Holden, Robert Strauss, Peter Graves, Otto Preminger

Many critics felt William Holden's Academy Award for *Stalag 17* was a gift for failing to give him proper recognition in *Sunset Boulevard*. Those critics should view this prison camp comedy-drama again. This film still holds up brilliantly today. Billy Wilder successfully alternated between suspense and comedy in this story of a World War II prison camp. It seems all of the prisoners' activities are being reported to their German commandant. Holden plays an opportunistic and cynical sergeant whose actions make him a natural suspect as the spy in the POWs' midst.

1953 B & W 120 minutes

STAR OF MIDNIGHT

★★½

DIRECTOR: Stephen Roberts

CAST: William Powell, Ginger Rogers, Paul Kelly, Gene Lockhart, Ralph Morgan

William Powell, in a role cloned from his *Thin Man* series, is a debonair, urbane lawyer accused of murder. Abetted by Ginger Rogers, he sallies forth, repartee in mouth, to catch the real culprit. The police and gangsters alike make it difficult. Not bad.

1935 B & W 90 minutes

STEEL

★★★

DIRECTOR: Steve Carver

CAST: Lee Majors, Jennifer O'Neill, Art Carney, George Kennedy, Harris Yulin, Terry Kiser, Richard Lynch, Roger E. Mosley, Albert Salmi, R. G. Armstrong

Plenty of action and stunts keep this minor film popping along surprisingly well. Mr. Wooden himself, Lee Majors, stars as the head of a construction crew struggling to complete a skyscraper on schedule. Majors is almost convincing, and a strong cast of character actors are great fun to watch. George Kennedy gets one of his rare juicy roles and does a bang-up job with it. Rated R.

1980 99 minutes

STEELE JUSTICE

★

DIRECTOR: Robert Boris

CAST: Martin Kove, Sela Ward, Ronny Cox, Bernie Casey, Joseph Campanella, Sarah Douglas, Soon-Teck Oh

One-man-army Martin Kove is hired to wipe out the Vietnamese mafia in Los Angeles. He succeeds, of course. The film doesn't. Rated R for profanity and violence.

1987 94 minutes

STICK

★★★

DIRECTOR: Burt Reynolds

CAST: Burt Reynolds, Charles Durning, George Segal, Candice Bergen, Castulo Guerra

Directed by and starring Burt Reynolds, *Stick* is an odd mixture of comedy and violence that more than once strains the viewer's suspension of disbelief. Fans of the original novel, by Elmore Leonard, will be shocked at how far Reynolds's film strays from its source. Leonard's hardened criminal—who in the story gets out of prison only to find himself right back on the wrong side of the law and on the bad side of some ruthless gangsters—is turned by Reynolds into a variation of his *Smokey and the Bandit* good ol' boy. What should have been a tough, lean, and mean movie contains a surprising amount of clowning by its stars. Despite all this, it has enough action and genuine laughs to please Reynolds's fans. It's no critic's movie, but you could do worse. Rated R for profanity and violence.

1985 109 minutes

STILETTO

★½

DIRECTOR: Bernard Kowalski
CAST: Alex Cord, Britt Ekland, Patrick O'Neal, Barbara McNair

Alex Cord has the starring role in this weak picture about a rich jet-setter who also happens to be a professional killer who decides to quit his job. The Mafia doesn't like that idea, so they decide to kill him. Lots of violent action and sexy situations, but it all adds up to a disappointment. Harold Robbins wrote the story. Rated R.

1969 98 minutes

STING, THE

★★★★½

DIRECTOR: George Roy Hill
CAST: Paul Newman, Robert Redford, Robert Shaw, Charles Durning, Ray Walston, Eileen Brennan, Harold Gould, Dana Elcar

Those *Butch Cassidy and the Sundance Kid* stars, Paul Newman and Robert Redford, were reunited for this fast-paced entertainment as two con men who outcon a con. Winner of seven Academy Awards—including best picture—this film, directed by George Roy Hill (*A Little Romance* and *Butch Cassidy*) revived Scott Joplin's music. For that, and the more obvious reasons, it is not to be missed. Rated PG.

1973 129 minutes

STING II, THE

★★★

DIRECTOR: Jeremy Paul Kagan
CAST: Jackie Gleason, Mac Davis, Teri Garr, Karl Malden, Oliver Reed, Bert Remsen

You could hardly expect a sequel to such a joyously entertaining film as *The Sting* to measure up. True to those expectations, this film, starring Jackie Gleason, Mac Davis, Teri Garr, and Karl Malden, doesn't come close. What it lacks, of course, is Paul Newman and Robert Redford. But then, comparisons are odious and, in this case especially, perhaps unfair. There is much to enjoy in this comedy if taken on its own terms . . . so enjoy. Rated PG for violence.

1983 102 minutes

STONE COLD DEAD

★★

DIRECTOR: George Mendeluk
CAST: Richard Crenna, Belinda J. Montgomery, Paul Williams, Linda Sorenson

This fair film, based on the novel *Sin Sniper* by Hugh Garner, centers on the investigation by Sergeant Boyd (Richard Crenna) into a bizarre series of prostitute killings. The murderer photographs his victims at the moment of death with a camera mounted on a high-powered rifle. Sandy McCauley (Belinda Montgomery), an undercover agent, is also assigned to the case. In addition to posing as a prostitute and acting as bait for the murderer, Boyd wants her to help him get incriminating evidence on Julius Kurtz (Paul Williams), the city's biggest dope trafficker and an occasional pimp. Rated R.

1980 97 minutes

STONE KILLER, THE

★★★½

DIRECTOR: Michael Winner
CAST: Charles Bronson, Martin Balsam, David Sheiner, Norman Fell, Ralph Waite

A *Dirty Harry*–style cop thriller, this casts Charles Bronson as a no-nonsense New York cop who gets transferred to Los Angeles because of his direct way of dealing with gun-toting criminals . . . he shoots them. Called even more violent than the Eastwood original by critics of the time, *The Stone Killer* looks pretty mild today—even in the uncut video version (which is far superior to the TV print). It still packs enough of a wallop to make it a good bet for action fans. Rated R.

1973 95 minutes

STOPOVER TOKYO

★★

DIRECTOR: Richard L. Breen
CAST: Robert Wagner, Edmond O'Brien, Joan Collins, Ken Scott

Based on a story by John P. Marquand, this ho-hum espionage tale has an American spy (Robert Wagner) chasing a communist undercover agent all over Tokyo, making this a combination spy/travelogue movie. Wagner is earnest, as usual, but even the cast's enthusiasm can't put life into this one. Joan Collins is worth watching, as always.

1957 100 minutes

STRANGER ON THE THIRD FLOOR

★★★★

DIRECTOR: Boris Ingster
CAST: Peter Lorre, John McGuire, Elisha Cook Jr., Margaret Tallichet, Charles Waldron

This intriguing film from RKO is a gem that transcends its potboiler storyline (innocent man accused of murder) and predates the later more highly acclaimed *film noir* favorites of the mid to late 1940s. Peter Lorre gives yet another singular performance as a disinterested murderer, a character truly alien yet strangely sympathetic. A great hallucination sequence and good performances all the way around make this a compelling treat.

1940 B & W 64 minutes

STREETHAWK

★

DIRECTOR: Virgil W. Vogel
CAST: Rex Smith, Jayne Modean, Christopher Lloyd, Richard Venture, Joe Regalbuto, Lawrence Pressman, Robert Beltran

Only kiddies—and fans of the short-lived television series, if there are any—will find much to enjoy in this story of a police officer (Rex Smith) left for dead by drug dealers. He is "resurrected" by the FBI to become a black-costumed, undercover crime fighter who rides a souped-up motorcycle. This two-wheeled retread of TV's *Knight Rider* could have been worse, but its only real asset is a score by Tangerine Dream.

1986 60 minutes

STREETS OF FIRE

★★★

DIRECTOR: Walter Hill
CAST: Diane Lane, Michael Pare, Rick Moranis, Amy Madigan, Willem DaFoe

Directed by Walter Hill (*48 HRS*), this is a self-proclaimed "rock 'n' roll fable" that takes place in "another time, another place." Those expecting any more than that will undoubtedly be disappointed. Yet taken on its own terms, this comic book–style movie is a diverting compendium of nonstop action and stylized storytelling set to a rocking backbeat. In it a famous rock singer (played by Diane Lane, of *The Outsiders* and *A Little Romance*) is captured by a motorcycle gang in Hill's mythic world, which combines 1950s attitudes and styles with a futuristic feel. It's up to her two-fisted former boyfriend, Tom Cady (Michael Pare, of *Eddie and the Cruisers*), to save her. Rated R for profanity and violence.

1984 93 minutes

STRIKE FORCE

★★

DIRECTOR: Barry Shear
CAST: Richard Gere, Cliff Gorman, Donald Blakely, Edward Grover, Joe Spinell

A *French Connection* rehash, this made-for-television movie stars Richard Gere as a cop out to make a big drug bust. Lots of action, not much story.

1975 74 minutes

STRIPPED TO KILL

★★★

DIRECTOR: Katt Shea Ruben
CAST: Kay Lenz, Greg Evigan, Norman Fell, Tracy Crowder, Debbie Nassar, Pia Kamakahi

This generally impressive terror film has nearly an hour of tense excitement but wastes thirty minutes on strip tease acts. Two undercover cops (Kay Lenz and Greg Evigan) investigate the murder of a young stripper. Norman Fell plays the jaded strip joint owner. Rated R for excessive nudity, erotic dancing, and violence.

1987 83 minutes

STUDY IN SCARLET, A

★

DIRECTOR: Edward L. Marin
CAST: Reginald Owen, Anna May Wong, Alan Dinehart, June Clyde, Alan Mowbray

Bearing absolutely no resemblance to the first of Arthur Conan Doyle's Sherlock Holmes stories, this low-budget entry from a poverty-row producer is perhaps the most lackluster of all the sound Holmes films. Reginald Owen plays Holmes as a portly gadfly, drawing conclusions that can't possibly be explained through the action (or lack of it) in the film. Most of Holmes's companions and foils are barely recognizable (Alan Mowbray is completely wasted as Lestrade), and Owen's self-created dialogue is stilted and absurd. Owen has the distinction of having played both the famous sleuth *and* Dr. Watson (to Clive Brook in Fox's *Sherlock Holmes*). Slow and creaky, this is of interest *only* as a seldom-seen title. If you're not a Holmes enthusiast (and a completist at that), you might think twice about renting or buying this one.

1933 B & W 70 minutes

STUDY IN TERROR, A

★★★★

DIRECTOR: James Hill
CAST: John Neville, Donald Houston, Georgia Brown, John Fraser, Anthony Quayle, Barbara Windsor, Robert Morley, Cecil Parker

This superior Sherlock Holmes adventure pits "the original caped crusader," as the ads called him, against Jack the Ripper. John Neville is an excellent Holmes. And Donald Houston is perhaps the screen's finest Dr. John Watson. His performance is a rarity, one faithful to the novels by Sir Arthur Conan Doyle. Always exciting, this undeservedly neglected film has something to offer Sherlockians, mystery fans, and even casual movie-watchers.

1965 94 minutes

SUDDEN DEATH

DIRECTOR: Sig Shore
CAST: Denise Coward, Frank Runyeon, Jaime Tinelli, Robert Trumbell

While on her way to meet her fiancé, a woman is kidnapped by two men in a stolen cab, brutally beaten, raped, and left for dead. With the police unable to apprehend the criminals and with her fiancé shunning her, she buys a gun and begins to deal out her own justice. Cheaply made rehash of *Death Wish* and *Ms. 45*. Predictable, exploitative trash. Rated R.

1986 93 minutes

SUDDEN IMPACT

★★★★

DIRECTOR: Clint Eastwood
CAST: Clint Eastwood, Sondra Locke, Pat Hingle, Bradford Dillman

"Dirty Harry" Callahan (Clint Eastwood) is back, and he's meaner, nastier, and—surprise!—funnier than ever in this, his fourth screen adventure. In the story, a killer (Sondra Locke, in a rare, effective performance) is methodically extracting bloody revenge on the sickos who raped her and a younger sister. It becomes Harry's job to track her down, but not until he's done away with a half-dozen villains and delivered twice as many quips including, "Go ahead, make my day." Rated R for violence and profanity.

1983 117 minutes

SUMMER CITY

★★

DIRECTOR: Christopher Fraser
CAST: Mel Gibson, Phil Avalon, Steve Bisley, John Jarrat, Debbie Forman, James Elliot

Mel Gibson (the *Mad Max* films) stars in this Australian teen rebel flick that lacks a fresh approach to one of the oldest stories in film: four wild and crazy teens go on a surfing weekend at a sleepy little seaside community only to find trouble when one of the delinquents messes around with a local's daughter. A few intense moments, and the acting is not bad, but even some of the dialogue is indistinguishable in the muddy audio, and the Aussie vulgate only aggravates the problem. Not rated, but the equivalent of PG for some sex, partial nudity, and violence.

1976 83 minutes

SUMMERTIME KILLER, THE

★★½

DIRECTOR: Antonio Isasi
CAST: Christopher Mitchum, Karl Malden, Olivia Hussey, Raf Vallone, Claudine Auger, Gerard Tichy

A 6-year-old boy witnesses the beating and drowning of his father by a gang of hoods. Twenty years pass, and we follow the grown-up son (Christopher Mitchum) as he systematically pursues and kills these men in New York, Rome, and Portugal. While a police detective (Karl Malden) is investigating one of the murders, a Mafia boss hires him to privately track down the killer. There are some exciting motorcycle pursuits along the way before the ending takes a slight twist. Rated R for violence and language.

1972 100 minutes

SUNBURN

★

DIRECTOR: Richard C. Sarafian
CAST: Farrah Fawcett-Majors, Charles Grodin, Art Carney, William Daniels, Joan Collins

Farrah Fawcett-Majors's second feature film is worse than her first (*Somebody Killed Her Husband*). This time she pretends to be the wife of insurance investigator Charles Grodin to get the real scoop on a suicide case in Acapulco. Breathy acting and ham-handed scripting do not help the paper-thin plot. Rated PG.

1979 94 minutes

SUPERFLY

★★★

DIRECTOR: Gordon Parks Jr.

CAST: Ron O'Neal, Carl Lee, Sheila Frazier, Julius W. Harris, Charles McGregor

This exciting film follows a Harlem drug dealer's last big sale before he attempts to leave the drug world for a normal life. Rated R.

1972 96 minutes

SURFACING

★

DIRECTOR: Claude Jutra

CAST: Joseph Bottoms, Kathleen Beller, R. H. Thompson

This adventure film is essentially *Deliverance* stirred with pyschological mumbo jumbo and kinky sex. The result is unsavory and illogical. Kathleen Beller and friends search for traces of her father and an ancient Indian civilization in a beautiful but brutal wilderness. You'll root for Mother Nature. Rated R.

1984 90 minutes

SWASHBUCKLER, THE

DIRECTOR: Jean-Paul Rappeneau

CAST: Jean-Paul Belmond, Marlene Jobert, Laura Antonelli, Michel Auclair, Julien Guiomar

Stupid story about a naturalized American who gets caught up in the French Revolution while delivering grain and seeking a divorce from his wife. This is not the Robert Shaw movie of the same name, but a French export that has been dubbed in English. Beware!

1984 100 minutes

SWEET SIXTEEN

★½

CAST: Aliesa Shirley, Bo Hopkins, Patrick Macnee, Susan Strasberg, Don Stroud

In this static mystery, which is surprisingly "clean" by today's mad-slasher movie standards, a young woman (Aliesa Shirley) from the big city reluctantly spends her summer—and her sixteenth birthday—in a small Texas town and becomes the chief suspect in a series of murders. Rated R for profanity and partial nudity.

1984 96 minutes

SWEET SWEETBACK'S BAADASSSSS SONG

★★★½

DIRECTOR: Melvin Van Peebles

CAST: Melvin Van Peebles, Rhetta Hughes, Simon Chuckster, John Amos

Minor cult black film about a man running from racist white police forces. Melvin Van Peebles plays the title character, who will do anything to stay free. Very controversial when released in 1971. Lots of sex and violence gave this an X rating at the time. Probably the best of the black-produced and -directed films of the early 1970s. Rated R.

1971 97 minutes

SWORD OF LANCELOT

★★★

DIRECTOR: Cornel Wilde

CAST: Cornel Wilde, Jean Wallace, Brian Aherne, George Baker

Colorful production and location photography highlight this pre-*Camelot* version of life at the court of King Arthur and the forbidden love between Lancelot and Queen Guinevere (Mr. and Mrs. Cornel Wilde in real life). Long on pageantry, action, and chivalrous acts of derring-do, this is a "fun" film in the same vein as *Ivanhoe* and *The Vikings*, and glosses over the serious overtones that made the better-known version a popular tragedy.

1963 116 minutes

TAI-PAN

★★

DIRECTOR: Daryl Duke

CAST: Bryan Brown, John Stanton, Joan Chen, Tim Guinee, Bill Leadbitter

Pretentious, overblown adaptation of James Clavell's bestseller, this disjointed mess plays like a television miniseries chopped from eight hours to two. Time is compressed at the worst of moments, and some of the best scenes are those (sadly) left to the imagination. The story suggests that all grand, historical, behind-the-scenes maneuvers were made in brothels; even if that's true, this tale could have been related with more panache. Bryan Brown is properly stoic as the "Tai-Pan," chief trader, who dreams of establishing a colony of commerce to be named Hong Kong. Joan Chen is ludicrous as his concubine, a woman given to superlatives such as "fantastical-good" and "terrifical-bad." Afternoon soap-opera addicts may enjoy this; other movie lovers are advised to read the book. Rated R for brief nudity and violence.

1986 127 minutes

TAKING OF PELHAM ONE TWO THREE, THE

★★★★

DIRECTOR: Joseph Sargent

CAST: Walter Matthau, Robert Shaw, Martin Balsam, Tony Roberts

Walter Matthau is at his growling, grumbling, gum-chewing best in this film. He plays the chief detective of security on the New York subway who must deal with the unthinkable: the hijacking of a commuter train by four men (with a fine Robert Shaw as their leader) and a demand by them for a $1 million ransom to prevent their killing the passengers one by one. It was at this time that Matthau made two similar films, *Charley Varrick* and *The Laughing Policeman*, and the three pictures stand out as prime examples of the actor at his dramatic (as opposed to comedic) best. The story and direction in this motion picture are also topnotch, making for a fine edge-of-your-seat entertainment. Rated PG.

1974 104 minutes

TAMARIND SEED, THE

★★★

DIRECTOR: Blake Edwards

CAST: Omar Sharif, Julie Andrews, Anthony Quayle

A sudsy melodrama in the old tradition, but still a lot of fun. Julie Andrews falls in love with a foreign emissary played by Omar Sharif, only to be told (by her own State Department) to stay away from him. The cold war intrigue seems pretty absurd these days, but Andrews and Sharif generate a playful chemistry that overlooks many sins. A trifle overlong, but worth more than the obscurity granted it by most critics. Rated PG.

1974 123 minutes

TANK

★★½

DIRECTOR: Marvin J. Chomsky

CAST: James Garner, Shirley Jones, C. Thomas Howell, G. D. Spradlin

The always likeable James Garner plays Sgt. Maj. Zack Carey, an army career soldier who has to use his privately owned Sherman tank to rescue his family (Shirley Jones and C. Thomas Howell) from the clutches of a mean country sheriff (G. D. Spradlin). It's all a bunch of hokum, but a sure audience pleaser. Rated PG.

1984 113 minutes

TARGET

★★★

DIRECTOR: Arthur Penn

CAST: Gene Hackman, Matt Dillon, Gayle Hunnicutt, Josef Sommer, Victoria Fyodora, Herbert Berghof

In this fast-paced, entertaining suspense-thriller directed by Arthur Penn (*Bonnie and Clyde*), a father (Gene Hackman) and son (Matt Dillon) put aside their differences when they become the targets of an international spy ring. *Target* is a tad predictable, but it is the kind of predictability that adds to the viewer's enjoyment rather than detracting from it. Rated R for violence, profanity, and nudity.

1985 117 minutes

TARGET EAGLE

★½

DIRECTOR: J. Anthony Loma

CAST: George Rivero, Maud Adams, George Peppard, Max von Sydow, Susana Dosamantes, Chuck Connors

A man and a woman are sent to infiltrate a big heroin ring. What ensues is a European mishmash of spies, crooks, drugs, and murder. Interesting scenery and a strong cast are not enough to counterbalance the glaring weaknesses in this mediocre action-thriller. Unrated.

1984 100 minutes

TARZAN AND THE TRAPPERS

★½

DIRECTOR: H. Bruce Humberstone

CAST: Gordon Scott, Eve Brent, Rickie Sorenson, Leslie Bradly, Maurice Marsac

This oddity is actually three television pilots that producer Sol Lesser was unable to sell to networks back in 1958 (they were shown on TV for the first time in 1966). Using the same performers from the previous Tarzan entry, *Tarzan's Fight for Life*, Lesser hoped to extend his long association with the character by giving him back a family and selling Tarzan to television as a prime-time show. The trappers of the title are poachers that Tarzan deals with during the first episode. This is pretty ordinary, uninspired stuff, but it's a one-of-a-kind Tarzan film, unavailable for years.

1958 B & W 74 minutes

TARZAN OF THE APES

★★★½

DIRECTOR: Scott Sidney

CAST: Elmo Lincoln, Enid Markey, George French, Colin Kenny, Thomas Jefferson, True Boardman, Kathleen Kirkham, Gordon Griffith (as young Tarzan)

The first filmed version of Edgar Rice Burroughs's classic jungle story adheres closely to the original book-length novel first published in a pulp magazine in 1912. It's one of the first silent feature-length films to earn over $1 million. Heavily advertised and widely seen upon initial release, this blockbuster tells the story of Lord and Lady Greystoke, their shipwreck and abandonment on the African coast, and the fate of their boy child, John. Raised by Kala the she-ape, infant John becomes Tarzan of the Apes. The upbringing and education of the young man-ape are creatively filmed (even though gymnasts in monkey suits play all the apes in the film), and the major changes in plot don't really affect the movie itself. Barrel-chested Elmo Lincoln (who changed his name from Otto Linkenhelt) portrayed Tarzan as an adult and actually killed the lion he fights in one of the film's more exciting moments. Enhanced with a synchronized musical score, this silent extravaganza is well worth the watch. Silent.

1918 B & W 130 minutes

TARZAN THE APE MAN (ORIGINAL)

★★★½

DIRECTOR: W. S. Van Dyke

CAST: Johnny Weissmuller, Maureen O'Sullivan, Neil Hamilton

Tarzan the Ape Man is the film that made Johnny Weissmuller a star and Tarzan an idiot. That classic "Me Tarzan, you Jane" blasphemy is here in its original splendor. Maureen O'Sullivan seduces the dumb beast, and it's all great fun. Hollywood at its peak . . . but no relation to Edgar Rice Burroughs's hero.

1932 B & W 99 minutes

TARZAN THE APE MAN (REMAKE)

DIRECTOR: John Derek

CAST: Bo Derek, Richard Harris, Miles O'Keeffe, John Phillip Law

One suggestion for anyone planning to watch this movie: grab a book. That way, you'll have something interesting to do while it's on the screen. Even counting the lowest of the low-budget Tarzan flicks, this one, with Bo Derek, Richard Harris, and Miles O'Keeffe (in the title role), is the absolute worst. Rated R for profanity, sex, and nudity.

1981 112 minutes

TARZAN THE FEARLESS

★

DIRECTOR: Robert Hill

CAST: Buster Crabbe, Jacqueline Wells, E. Alyn Warren, Edward Woods

Buster Crabbe stars as the Lord of the Jungle in this low, low-budget feature. Johnny Weissmuller he ain't. Crabbe fared much better in the now campy "Flash Gordon" and "Buck Rogers" serials. Leave this one on the vine.

1933 B & W 85 minutes

TARZAN'S REVENGE

★

DIRECTOR: Ross Lederman

CAST: Glenn Morris, Eleanor Holm, George Barbier, C. Henry Gordon, Hedda Hopper, George Meeker

Back-lot nonsense with Olympic champions Glenn Morris as the Lord of the Jungle and Eleanor Holm as his Jane gives the hammy supporting actors (including gossip queen Hedda Hopper and slimy villain C. Henry Gordon) plenty of opportunity to chew on the scenery. The 1930s saw four screen Tarzans, but Sol Lesser's choice of Morris as the fourth wasn't exactly inspired. He made much less of an impression (and money) than did his illustrious predecessors, Johnny Weissmuller, Buster Crabbe, and Herman Brix.

1938 B & W 70 minutes

TELEFON

★★★½

DIRECTOR: Don Siegel

CAST: Charles Bronson, Lee Remick, Donald Pleasence, John Mitchum, Patrick Magee

Charles Bronson is a KGB agent who, with the help of the CIA's Lee Remick, is out to stop some preprogrammed Soviet spies from blowing up the United States. Donald Pleasence (*Halloween*) shines as an unhinged maniac, and John Mitchum (*The Enforcer*) has a nice bit as a car mechanic who starts the show off with a bang. Rated PG.

1977 102 minutes

TEN LITTLE INDIANS

DIRECTOR: Peter Collinson
CAST: Oliver Reed, Richard Attenborough, Elke Sommer, Herbert Lom, Gert Frobe

Absolutely dismal third version of the Agatha Christie classic. This one completely mucks up the plot, switching from an isolated island mansion to a hotel deep in the Iranian desert(!). The entire cast overacts abysmally, and the script must have been written with a purple pen. The plot concerns an unseen killer who sequentially knocks off the visitors. Avoid at all costs and stick with the original, 1945's *And Then There Were None*. Rated PG—mild violence.

1975 98 minutes

TEN TO MIDNIGHT

★

DIRECTOR: J. Lee Thompson
CAST: Charles Bronson, Andrew Stevens, Lisa Eilbacher, Cosie Costa

They might as well have titled this one *Charles Bronson Meets the Slasher*. Old "Death Wish" himself goes up against a *Friday the 13th*–type killer in this disappointing action film. It's all rather disgusting, and Bronson looks bored. Rated R for sex, nudity, profanity, and violence.

1983 101 minutes

TENNESSEE STALLION

★★★

DIRECTOR: Don Hulette
CAST: Audrey Landers, Judy Landers, Jimmy Van Patten, Reid Smith, Frederick Cole

Interesting background, beautiful photography, and more than competent acting save this otherwise ordinary action-adventure film set in the world of the Tennessee walking horse show circuit. Jimmy Van Patten is excellent as a man from the wrong circles of society who makes it to the big time with his outstanding horse and the help of the woman who loves him.

1978 87 minutes

TERMINAL ISLAND

DIRECTOR: Stephanie Rothman
CAST: Phyllis Davis, Tom Selleck, Don Marshall, Ena Hartman, Marta Kristen

Don't be fooled by the fact that Tom Selleck's name has been moved up in the credits. He has very little to do in this trite piece of exploitation, made very early in his career. No matter. It's an awful movie, anyway, one of those would-be titillating flicks about two groups of male prisoners fighting over the favors of the only females on an island penal colony. It'll titillate you right over to the rewind button. Rated R.

1977 88 minutes

TERROR BY NIGHT

★★★

DIRECTOR: Roy William Neill
CAST: Basil Rathbone, Nigel Bruce, Alan Mowbray, Renee Godfrey, Billy Bevan, Dennis Hoey

Penultimate entry in the Rathbone/Bruce Sherlock Holmes series, with the master sleuth and his loyal companion up against a series of murders on a train bound from London to Edinburgh. The culprit ultimately turns out to be Col. Sebastian Moran, but you'll have to watch the film to discover which of the passengers he impersonates!

1946 B & W 69 minutes

TERRORISTS, THE

★★★★

DIRECTOR: Caspar Wrede
CAST: Sean Connery, Ian McShane, James Maxwell, Isabel

Dean, Jeffrey Wickham, John Quentin, Robert Harris

Solid suspense thriller has Sean Connery as the bullheaded commander of Norway's national security force, which is galvanized into action when a group of English terrorists takes over the British embassy. In the process, they endanger an airliner full of passengers, something that Connery's far-from-diplomatic troubleshooter doesn't like at all. This puts him at odds with politicians and political criminals alike. The result? A very enjoyable motion picture. Rated PG for violence.

1975 100 minutes

THEY CALL ME MISTER TIBBS

★★★

DIRECTOR: Gordon Douglas
CAST: Sidney Poitier, Barbara McNair, Martin Landau

An inferior follow-up, this contains the further adventures of the character Sidney Poitier created for the film *In the Heat of the Night*. Detective Virgil Tibbs is again investigating a murder and trying to clear his friend, as well. Rated PG—contains strong language and some violence.

1970 108 minutes

THEY DRIVE BY NIGHT

★★★★

DIRECTOR: Raoul Walsh
CAST: Geroge Raft, Humphrey Bogart, Ann Sheridan, Ida Lupino

Here's a Warner Bros. gem! George Raft and Humphrey Bogart star as truck-driving brothers who cope with crooked bosses while wooing Ann Sheridan and Ida Lupino. The dialogue is terrific, and the direction by Raoul Walsh is crisp.

1940 B & W 93 minutes

THEY WERE EXPENDABLE

★★★★½

DIRECTOR: John Ford
CAST: John Wayne, Robert Montgomery, Donna Reed, Jack Holt, Ward Bond, Marshall Thompson, Louis Jean Heydt

First-rate action drama about American PT boat crews fighting a losing battle against advancing Japanese forces in the Philippines. Director John Ford based this film, his most personal, on his war experiences and the people he knew in the conflict. No phony heroics or glory here, but a realistic, bleak, and ultimately inspiring picture of men in war. John Wayne gives an uncharacteristically restrained performance as Rusty Ryan, second in command to John Brickly (Robert Montgomery), who reluctantly leads his men on a suicide mission. Donna Reed plays Sandy Davis, a navy nurse who falls in love with Wayne.

1945 B & W 136 minutes

THIEF

★★★★

DIRECTOR: Michael Mann
CAST: James Caan, Tuesday Weld, Jim Belushi, Willie Nelson

James Caan stars in this superb study of a jewel thief. Caan's character tries desperately to create the life he visualized while in prison—one complete with a car, money, house, wife, and kids. But as soon as he manages to acquire these things, they start slipping away. It's an interesting plot, and Michael Mann's direction gives it a sense of realism. Visually stunning, with a great score by Tangerine Dream. Rated R for violence, language, and brief nudity.

1981 122 minutes

THIN MAN, THE

★★★★½

DIRECTOR: W. S. Van Dyke
CAST: William Powell, Myrna Loy, Edward S. Brophy, Porter Hall, Maureen O'Sullivan, Asta

Viewers and critics alike were captivated by William Powell and Myrna Loy in this first (and best) of a series based on Dashiell Hammett's mystery novel about his "other" detective and wife, Nick and Nora Charles. The thin man is a murder victim. But never mind. The delight of this fun film is the banter between its stars. You'll like their little dog, too.

1934 B & W 89 minutes

THIN MAN GOES HOME, THE

★★½

DIRECTOR: Richard Thorpe
CAST: William Powell, Myrna Loy, Lucile Watson, Gloria DeHaven, Anne Revere, Helen Vinson, Henry Davenport, Leon Ames, Donald Meek, Edward Brophy

Fifth and weakest entry in the series. Nick Charles (William Powell) returns to his old hometown, accompanied by Nora (Myrna Loy) and young Nick Jr. The mystery this time around just doesn't have the same spark, and the witty dialogue sounds a bit wilted. Part of the problem may be young Nick; the casual consumption of alcohol—one of this series' trademarks—just doesn't feel right with a small child in the wings. Still entertaining, but a lesser effort.

1944 B & W 101 minutes

13 RUE MADELEINE

★★★

DIRECTOR: Henry Hathaway
CAST: James Cagney, Annabella, Watler Abel, Frank Latimore, Melville Cooper, E. G. Marshall, Red Buttons, Karl Malden, Sam Jaffe, Richard Conte

Espionage thriller, inspired by *March of Time* series, shot in semidocumentary style. James Cagney is OSS chief who goes to France to complete a mission when one of his men is killed.

1946 B & W 95 minutes

THIRTY SECONDS OVER TOKYO

★★★★

DIRECTOR: Mervyn LeRoy
CAST: Spencer Tracy, Van Johnson, Robert Walker, Phyllis Thaxter, Scott McKay, Robert Mitchum, Stephen McNally, Louis Jean Heydt, Paul Langton, Leon Ames

Spencer Tracy is in top form as General Doolittle, who led the first bombing attack on Tokyo during World War II. Robert Mitchum and Van Johnson give effective supporting performances as air crew chiefs. We follow Doolittle and his men as they train for the big mission, bomb Tokyo, and make their way home on foot through China. A true-life adventure that, despite its length, never bogs down.

1944 B & W 138 minutes

THIRTY-NINE STEPS, THE (SECOND REMAKE)

★★★½

DIRECTOR: Don Sharp
CAST: Robert Powell, David Warner, Eric Porter, Karen Dotrice, John Mills

An innocent man stumbles on to a spy plot in pre-WWI London. Hunted by enemy agents who think he has intercepted an important communiqué, and civil authorities who believe he is a murderer, the man has nowhere to turn. The best of several Hitchcock remakes in the 1970s. It can't compete with the original, of course, but the cast is good. The script is witty, and the climax atop Big Ben is exciting. Rated PG.

1978 102 minutes

THIS GUN FOR HIRE

★★★★

DIRECTOR: Frank Tuttle
CAST: Alan Ladd, Robert Preston, Veronica Lake

Alan Ladd made his first big impression in this 1942 gangster film as a bad guy who turns good guy in the end. Robert Preston and Veronica Lake co-star in this still enjoyable revenge film.

1942 B & W 80 minutes

THOMAS CROWN AFFAIR, THE

★★★★

DIRECTOR: Norman Jewison
CAST: Steve McQueen, Faye Dunaway, Paul Burke

Combine an engrossing bank-heist caper with an offbeat romance and you have the ingredients for a fun-filled movie. Steve McQueen and Faye Dunaway are at their best as the sophisticated bank robber and unscrupulous insurance investigator who happens to be tracking him. The emotional tricks and verbal sparring between these two are a joy. This is one of the few films where the split-screen technique really moves the story along.

1968 102 minutes

THREE DAYS OF THE CONDOR

★★★★

DIRECTOR: Sydney Pollack
CAST: Robert Redford, Cliff Robertson, Max von Sydow, Faye Dunaway, John Houseman

Robert Redford is a CIA information researcher who is forced to flee for his life when his New York cover operation is blown and all of his co-workers brutally murdered. What seems at first to be a standard man-on-the-run drama gradually deepens into an engrossing mystery as to who is chasing him and why. Faye Dunaway expertly handles a vignette as the stranger Redford uses to avoid capture. Rated R.

1975 117 minutes

THREE MUSKETEERS, THE (1948)

★★

DIRECTOR: George Sidney
CAST: Gene Kelly, Lana Turner, June Allyson, Van Heflin, Vincent Price, Gig Young, Angela Lansbury, Keenan Wynn

MGM's all-star version of the classic swashbuckler by Alexandre Dumas gets its swords crossed up. This is primarily due to some blatant miscasting. Gene Kelly as D'Artagnan and his co-star June Allyson playing the queen's seamstress are never convincing as French citizens during the reign of Louis XIII. The production has lots of energy, but little substance. Fans of Lana Turner may find the movie worthwhile, because hidden in this fluff is one of her finest performances as the villainous Lady DeWinter.

1948 B & W 128 minutes

THREE MUSKETEERS, THE (1973)

★★★★★

DIRECTOR: Richard Lester
CAST: Michael York, Oliver Reed, Raquel Welch, Richard Chamberlain, Faye Dunaway, Charlton Heston

Alexandre Dumas's oft-filmed swashbuckler classic—there may have been as many as ten previous versions—finally came to full life with this 1973 release, directed by Richard Lester (*Superman II*). It is a superb adventure romp with scrumptious moments of comedy, character, and action. There's never a dull moment. Throughout, Lester injects throwaway bits of slapstick and wordplay—you have to pay careful attention to catch them, and it's well worth it. Rated PG.

1973 105 minutes

THREE THE HARD WAY

★★★

DIRECTOR: Gordon Parks Jr.
CAST: Fred Williamson, Jim Brown, Jim Kelly, Sheila Frazier, Jay Robinson

A white supremacist (Jay Robinson) attempts to wipe out the black race by putting a deadly serum in the country's water supply. Fred Williamson, Jim Brown (*The Dirty Dozen*), and Jim Kelly (*Enter the Dragon*) team up to stop him in this action-packed movie. Rated PG for violence.

1974 93 minutes

THUNDER AND LIGHTNING

★★

DIRECTOR: Corey Allen
CAST: David Carradine, Kate Jackson, Roger C. Carmel, Sterling Holloway, Ed Barth

Weak "action film" about moonshiners and their misadventures. Stars David Carradine and Kate Jackson are watchable enough, but a few touches of originality wouldn't have hurt. Rated PG for profanity and violence.

1977 95 minutes

THUNDER BAY

★★★½

DIRECTOR: Anthony Mann
CAST: James Stewart, Dan Duryea, Joanne Dru, Jay C. Flippen, Gilbert Roland

Star James Stewart and director Anthony Mann teamed up for a series of memorable westerns in the 1950s, *The Man from Laramie*, *The Far Country*, and *Bend of the River* among them. But they also made some nonwesterns together, arguably the best of which was this release. In it, Stewart plays an oil driller forced to take on a nasty group of Louisiana shrimp fishermen. The story is full of action and fine characterizations from a talented cast.

1953 102 minutes

THUNDER RUN

DIRECTOR: Gary Hudson
CAST: Forrest Tucker, John Ireland, John Shepherd, Jill Whitlow, Wally Ward, Cheryl M. Lynn, Marilyn O'Connor

Forrest Tucker stars in this grade Z action flick as a truck driver who is persuaded by an old army pal (John Ireland) to act as bait in a scheme to catch terrorists. He is to haul plutonium so they can be caught trying to steal it. Therefore, this movie is a bomb in more ways than one. Rated R for nudity, profanity, suggested sex, and violence.

1986 89 minutes

THUNDER WARRIOR II

DIRECTOR: Larry Ludman
CAST: Mark Gregory, Karen Reel, Bo Svenson

This hokum about a small-town crooked cop is set in the present-day Southwest. The hero is an American Indian who joins the police force and is discriminated against, set up, falsely imprisoned, and generally abused. Surviving against all odds, he fights back.

1985 88 minutes

THUNDERBALL

★★★

DIRECTOR: Terence Young
CAST: Sean Connery, Claudine Auger, Adolfo Celi

When originally released in 1965, this fourth entry in the James Bond series suffered from comparison to its two admittedly superior predecessors, *From Russia with Love* and *Goldfinger*. However, time has proved it to be one of the more watchable movies based on the books by Ian Fleming, with Sean Connery in top form as 007 and assured direction by Terence Young.

1965 129 minutes

THUNDERBOLT AND LIGHTFOOT

★★★★

DIRECTOR: Michael Cimino

CAST: Clint Eastwood, Jeff Bridges, George Kennedy, Geoffrey Lewis, Gary Busey

Clint Eastwood's right-on-target performance is equaled by those of co-stars Jeff Bridges, George Kennedy, and Geoffrey Lewis in this decidedly offbeat caper picture. The stoic top-lined actor plays an ex-con who hooks up with petty thief Bridges to hunt down the hidden spoils of a heist committed several years before. The only problem is that his ex-partners in the crime, Kennedy and Lewis, have the same idea, but no intention of sharing the loot. *Thunderbolt and Lightfoot* is a little-known action gem that proved a little too offbeat for Clint's fans when originally released in 1974. However, movie buffs have since proclaimed it a cinematic gem, a reputation it deserves. Look for Gary Busey (*The Buddy Holly Story* and *Barbarosa*) in a brief supporting role. Rated R.

1974 114 minutes

TIMERIDER

DIRECTOR: William Dear

CAST: Fred Ward, Belinda Bauer, Peter Coyote, L. Q. Jones, Ed Lauter

There are the films that just sort of sit there, never achieving anything. This is one of those films. A motorcycle rider and his motorcycle break the time barrier and end up being chased by cowboys in the Old West. It sounds far more interesting than it is. If you're having difficulty sleeping, this is the cure. Rated PG.

1983 94 minutes

TO HAVE AND HAVE NOT

★★★★½

DIRECTOR: Howard Hawks

CAST: Humphrey Bogart, Lauren Bacall, Walter Brennan

Director Howard Hawks once bet Ernest Hemingway he could make a good film from one of the author's worst books. Needless to say, he won the bet with this exquisite entertainment, which teamed Humphrey Bogart and Lauren Bacall for the first time. The story takes place before the events of the book and concerns the decision of an apathetic soldier of fortune (Bogart) to fight the Nazis.

1944 B & W 100 minutes

TO HELL AND BACK

★★½

DIRECTOR: Jesse Hibbs

CAST: Audie Murphy, Marshall Thompson, Charles Drake, Gregg Palmer, Jack Kelly, Paul Picerni, Susan Kohner, David Janssen

Real-life war hero Audie Murphy plays himself in this sprawling World War II action film. We follow Audie Murphy and his buddies (Marshall Thompson, Jack Kelly, and David Janssen) from North Africa to Berlin. Murphy received twenty-four medals, including the Congressional Medal of Honor, which made him the most decorated soldier in World War II. But the price of war is high, as most of Murphy's friends were killed, along with countless Germans and other Americans. Good performances and true-life drama make up for a static script and rather routine battle sequences.

1955 106 minutes

TO LIVE AND DIE IN L.A.

DIRECTOR: William Friedkin
CAST: William L. Petersen, Willem Dafoe, John Pankow, Dean Stockwell, Debra Feuer, John Turturro, Darlanne Fluegel

This vile and violent exercise in bloody self-indulgence is one of the bleakest cinema statements mankind ever produced. There is no way to distinguish bad from good; every character is equally insensitive, manipulative, and emotionally bankrupt. Director William Friedkin clearly wanted a hit thriller to re-create his success with *The French Connection*. What he made, with co-scripter and ex–secret service agent Gerald Petievich (on whose book the film is based), is an overly violent account of lone wolf William L. Petersen's attempt to shut down counterfeiter Willem DaFoe. This film goes so far overboard that it's only for the *Friday the 13th* gore crowd. Rated R for sex, nudity, and excessive violence.

1985 114 minutes

TOBRUK
★★★

DIRECTOR: Arthur Hiller
CAST: Rock Hudson, George Peppard, Guy Stockwell, Nigel Green

Rock Hudson, Nigel Green, and George Peppard lead a ragtag group of British soldiers and homeless Jews against the Nazi and Italian armies in the North African desert during World War II. To do so, they must sneak through Axis lines disguised as German soldiers escorting Allied prisoners through the desert. Their mission is to blow up the big guns at Tobruk before the British invasion fleet lands. Along the way our heroes encounter hostile Arabs, spies, beautiful women, and much more. An exciting climax, beautiful photography, and good performances help offset a farfetched script.

1966 110 minutes

TOMBOY

DIRECTOR: Herb Freed
CAST: Betsy Russell, Kristi Somers, Jerry Dinome

Mindless nonsense (with plenty of skin) about a female race car driver named Tommy (Betsy Russell) who takes on the man of her dreams (Jerry Dinome) on and off the track. Rated R.

1985 91 minutes

TOP GUN
★★★½

DIRECTOR: Tony Scott
CAST: Tom Cruise, Kelly McGillis, Val Kilmer, Anthony Edwards, Tom Skerritt, Michael Ironside, John Stockwell, Rick Rossovich, Barry Tubb, Whip Hubley

Tom Cruise stars as a student at the navy's Fighter Weapons School, where fliers are turned into crack fighter pilots. While competing for the title of Top Gun there, he falls in love with an instructor (Kelly McGillis of *Witness*). Because the film moves like a supersonic bullet for most of its running time, one is inclined to forgive most of its eyebrow-raising "commercial elements" and the fact that its story is merely a thinly veiled rewrite of *An Officer and a Gentleman*. Rated PG for light profanity, suggested sex, and violence.

1986 118 minutes

TOPKAPI
★★★★★

DIRECTOR: Jules Dassin
CAST: Peter Ustinov, Melina Mercouri, Maximilian Schell

This is one of the finest and funniest of the "big heist" genre. Director Jules Dassin assembled a highly talented international cast. They are members of a charming group of jewel thieves whose target is a priceless jeweled dagger in a Turkish museum. The execution of their clever plan is both humorous and exciting.

1964 120 minutes

TORA! TORA! TORA!

★★★★

DIRECTORS: Richard Fleischer, Toshio Masuda, Kinji Fakasaku

CAST: Jason Robards, Martin Balsam, James Whitmore, Joseph Cotten, So Yamamura

An American-Japanese cooperative venture reenacts the events up to and including the December 7 attack on Pearl Harbor. Although many well-known actors contribute their skills, they are overshadowed by the technical brilliance of the realistic re-creation of the climactic attack. Rated G.

1970 143 minutes

TOUGH ENOUGH

★★½

DIRECTOR: Richard Fleischer

CAST: Dennis Quaid, Warren Oates, Stan Shaw, Pam Grier, Wilford Brimley

Dennis Quaid plays the "Country-and-Western Warrior," a singer-fighter who slugs his way through taxing "Toughman" contests from Fort Worth to Detroit in a quest for fame and fortune. It's *Rocky* meets *Honeysuckle Rose*, yet still mildly enjoyable. The main reason for that is the watchability of stars Quaid, the late Warrren Oates, Stan Shaw, Pam Grier, and Wilford Brimley, with screenwriter John Leone's nice touches of humor coming in a close second. Rated PG for profanity and violence.

1983 106 minutes

TOWERING INFERNO, THE

★★★★

DIRECTORS: John Guillermin, Irwin Allen

CAST: Steve McQueen, Paul Newman, William Holden, Faye Dunaway, Fred Astaire, Richard Chamberlain

This is the undisputed king of the disaster movies of the 1970s. An all-star cast came together for this big-budget thriller about a newly constructed San Francisco high-rise hotel and office building that is set ablaze due to substandard materials. The action is nonstop as fire chief Steve McQueen and architect Paul Newman combine their efforts to free a score of big-name stars who become trapped in its penthouse restaurant. Rated PG.

1974 165 minutes

TOY SOLDIERS

★

DIRECTOR: David Fisher

CAST: Jason Miller, Cleavon Little, Rodolfo DeAnda

This is an inept and poorly acted film about a group of vacationing college students in Latin America. As the unconvincing story unfolds, we find our young heroes attempting to rescue a captured friend. Rated R.

1983 85 minutes

TRAIN, THE

★★★★

DIRECTOR: John Frankenheimer

CAST: Burt Lancaster, Paul Scofield, Michel Simon, Jeanne Moreau

A suspenseful World War II adventure about the French Resistance's attempt to stop a train loaded with fine art, seized from French museums, from reaching its destination in Nazi Germany. Burt Lancaster is fine as the head of the French railway system, but

he is far outclassed by the performance of Paul Scofield as the unrelenting German commander.
1965 B & W 113 minutes

TREASURE OF THE FOUR CROWNS

DIRECTORS: Ferdinando Baldi
CAST: Tony Anthony, Ana Obregon, Gene Quintano

In this ripoff of *Raiders of the Lost Ark* by the folks who created the dreadful *Comin' at Ya*, a group of adventurers attempt to steal invaluable Visigoth treasures from a crazed cult leader. The story is boring. The acting is pitiful. Rated PG for violence and gore.
1983 97 minutes

TREASURE OF THE SIERRA MADRE, THE

★★★★★

DIRECTOR: John Huston
CAST: Humphrey Bogart, Tim Holt, Walter Huston, Bruce Bennett

Humphrey Bogart gives a brilliant performance in this study of greed. The setting is rugged mountains in Mexico where Bogart, with Tim Holt and a grizzled prospector, played marvelously by Walter Huston, set out to make a fortune in gold prospecting. They do, with their troubles getting worse. Seamless script and magnificent performances add up to a classic. Witness Bogart's amazing portrayal of creeping dementia, and listen for one of moviedom's most famous lines, "Badges . . . ."
1948 B & W 126 minutes

TRIUMPH OF SHERLOCK HOLMES, THE

★★★½

DIRECTOR: Leslie S. Hiscott
CAST: Arthur Wontner, Ian Fleming, Lyn Harding, Leslie Perrins, Jane Carr, Charles Mortimer, Minnie Raynor, Ben Welden, Michael Shepley

A candle is the clue that unlocks the secret of a murder in this superior Sherlock Holmes film featuring Arthur Wontner and Ian Fleming as the infallible consulting detective and his friend and assistant Dr. John Watson. Made by an independent production company on a limited budget, this rendering of Conan Doyle's "Valley of Fear" retains much of the story's original dialogue and ranks with the first two Basil Rathbone films for Twentieth Century Fox and Hammer's *Hound of the Baskervilles* as the best movie versions of Doyle's tales. Wontner looks very much like Sydney Paget's original illustrations of Holmes for *The Strand* magazine. Wontner made five films as Sherlock Holmes—*Silver Blaze* (aka *Murder at the Baskervilles*) is the only other title currently available on videocassette, but if you are a fan, you'll want to see them all, because Wontner brings the same energy and quality to the role that Basil Rathbone and contemporary actor Jeremy Brett do. Topnotch.
1935 B & W 75 minutes

TWELVE O'CLOCK HIGH

★★★★

DIRECTOR: Henry King
CAST: Gregory Peck, Dean Jagger, Gary Merrill, Hugh Marlowe

Gregory Peck is the flight commander who takes over an England-based bomber squadron during World War II. He begins to feel the strain of leadership and becomes too involved with the men in his command. This is a well-produced and well-acted film. The compassion Peck shows in his role is superb, and it helped assure him a place in Hollywood immortality. Dean Jagger won an

Oscar for supporting actor for his fine performance.

1950 B & W 132 minutes

20,000 LEAGUES UNDER THE SEA

★★★★

DIRECTOR: Richard Fleischer
CAST: Kirk Douglas, James Mason, Paul Lukas, Peter Lorre

In this Disney version of the famous Jules Verne adventure-fantasy, a sailor (Kirk Douglas) and a scientist (Paul Lukas) get thoroughly involved with Captain Nemo, played by James Mason, and his fascinating submarine of the future. The cast is great, the action sequences ditto. Good popcorn pic.

1954 127 minutes

TWILIGHT'S LAST GLEAMING

★★★

DIRECTOR: Robert Aldrich
CAST: Burt Lancaster, Paul Winfield, Burt Young, William Smith, Charles Durning, Richard Widmark, Melvyn Douglas, Joseph Cotten

Although this is another maniac-at-the-button doomsday chronicle, it is so convincing that it makes the well-worn premise seem new. From the moment a group of ex-cons (Burt Lancaster, Paul Winfield, Burt Young, and William Smith) seize control of an air force pickup truck, it becomes obvious the audience is in the front seat of a nonstop roller coaster. Lancaster and his henchmen take over an atomic missile station and exploit his knowledge as a former general and designer of the Titan base to force the President (Charles Durning) to become their hostage in order to compel him to reveal the "truth" about Vietnam. Rated R for violence and profanity.

1977 146 minutes

TWO LOST WORLDS

½

DIRECTOR: Norman Dawn
CAST: James Arness, Laura Elliot, Bill Kennedy, Gloria Petroff, Tom Hubbard, Pierre Watkin, James Guilfoyle

Pointless story involving pirates and kidnapping, shipwreck and rescue. This is one of half a dozen or so films from the early 1950s that rented stock footage from Hal Roach's *One Million B.C.* and built a loose story around prehistoric lizards and erupting volcanoes. This one was a dud when it was released, and time hasn't done it any favors.

1950 B & W 61 minutes

TYCOON

★

DIRECTOR: Richard Wallace
CAST: John Wayne, Laraine Day, Cedric Hardwicke, Judith Anderson, Anthony Quinn, James Gleason

A would-be epic about the building of a railroad through the Andes. John Wayne stinks as the headstrong and reckless engineer who feuds with tycoon Cedric Hardwicke while listlessly romancing his daughter, Laraine Day. It's all overblown, ridiculous, and unconvincing.

1947 128 minutes

ULYSSES

★★

DIRECTOR: Mario Camerini
CAST: Kirk Douglas, Silvana Mangano, Anthony Quinn, Rossana Podesta, Sylvie

One of Kirk Douglas's least successful independent productions, this heavily dubbed Italian epic emphasizes dialogue over thrills —although it did spark American interest in myths and legends and eventually resulted in Ray Harryhausen's spectacular special effects films of the 1950s and 1960s. Kirk Douglas does his best, but he gets mired down in this slow retelling of Ulysses's long voyage home after the Trojan War. Anthony Quinn is in good form, but a lot of the performances are laughable, especially the overacting by the shaggy Cyclops. Pretty tame stuff for today's audiences, but fun to watch if you aren't expecting much.

1955 104 minutes

UNCOMMON VALOR

★★★★

DIRECTOR: Ted Kotcheff

CAST: Gene Hackman, Fred Ward, Reb Brown, Randall "Tex" Cobb, Harold Sylvester, Robert Stack

In this action-packed adventure film, directed by Ted Kotcheff (*First Blood*), retired marine Gene Hackman learns that his son may still be alive in a Vietnamese prison camp ten years after being listed as missing in action. He decides to go in after him. Rated R for profanity and violence.

1983 105 minutes

UNDER FIRE

★★½

DIRECTOR: Roger Spottiswoode

CAST: Nick Nolte, Gene Hackman, Joanna Cassidy, Ed Harris, Jean-Louis Trintignant

Take a little *Missing*, mix it with a generous portion of *The Year of Living Dangerously*, and add a dash of *Reds* and you have this release. Sound awful? Actually, passable is a more accurate appraisal of this movie, starring Nick Nolte, Gene Hackman, and Joanna Cassidy as journalists covering political upheaval in Central America circa 1979. While *Under Fire* has its moments (found primarily in the superb supporting performances of Ed Harris and French actor Jean-Louis Trintignant), you have to wade through a bit of sludge to get to them. Rated R for profanity, violence, and gore.

1983 128 minutes

UNTOUCHABLES, THE

★★★★½

DIRECTOR: Brian De Palma

CAST: Kevin Costner, Sean Connery, Robert De Niro, Charles Martin Smith, Andy Garcia, Billy Drago, Richard Bradford

An absolutely superb retelling of the events made famous by the beloved television series, with director Brian De Palma working his stylish magic in tandem with a deft script from Pulitzer-winning playwright David Mamet (*Sexual Perversity in Chicago*). This battle between archetypes concerns a different sort of perversity, and Prohibition-era Chicago has been beautifully re-created to emphasize big-city decadence. Al Capone (a grand seriocomic performance by Robert De Niro) was the populist hero for providing alcohol for the masses; Eliot Ness was the arrow-straight federal agent who rose to the challenge. Kevin Costner plays Ness as the ultimate *naif* who fails miserably untiltaken under the protective wing of an honest beat cop (Sean Connery, in the performance of his career). De Palma's shining moment is one of pure film majesty: a train station confrontation that hearkens back to the famed Odessa steps sequence in Eisenstein's 1925 *Battleship Potemkin*. Rated R for language and extreme violence.

1987 119 minutes

UNTOUCHABLES: SCARFACE MOB, THE

★★★

DIRECTOR: Phil Karlson

CAST: Robert Stack, Keenan Wynn, Barbara Nichols, Pat Crowley, Neville Brand, Bruce Gordon, Jerry Paris, Anthony George, Abel Fernandez, Nick Giorgiade

This violence-ridden film was released theatrically in 1962 but was actually the original two-part pilot for this popular series, first telecast in 1959. Steely-eyed Robert Stack as Eliot Ness gets the government's go-ahead to form his own special team of uncorruptible agents and leads them in forays against the enemy: bootleggers, racketeers, and especially the minions of kingpin Al "Scarface" Capone and his enforcer, Frank Nitti, played to perfection by Neville Brand and the incomparable Bruce Gordon. Veteran actor Keenan Wynn is the bad apple in the Ness organization, and the bullets, booze, and blood flow freely in this hard-hitting, enormously popular effort by Phil Karlson, one of the gritty, realistic directors who made their mark in American films of the 1950s. This is a tough movie, full of heroics and retribution. This still seems like strong fare, even for today's gore-saturated audiences. Narrated by often caricatured Walter Winchell.

1962 B & W 90 minutes

UTU

★★★★★

DIRECTOR: Geoff Murphy
CAST: Anzac Wallace, Bruno Lawrence, Kelly Johnson, Tim Elliot

This stunner from New Zealand contains all the action of the great American westerns, but with a moral message that leaves most of that genre's best in the dust. Anzac Wallace plays Te Wheke, a Maori corporal in the nineteenth-century British army who finds his family slaughtered by his own army. It is there at his burning village that he vows "utu" (Maori for revenge) and goes on a march with fellow Maori rebels to rid his land of white people. This moral tale is not as simple as retribution, however. The story masterfully introduces and develops many characters along the way; Bruno Lawrence is brilliant as a white settler who seeks his own revenge on Wheke, and Kelly Johnson is convincing as an aspiring soldier in the British army who develops personal reasons for wanting Wheke's capture. Rated R for violence.

1985 100 minutes

VANISHING POINT

★★½

DIRECTOR: Richard C. Sarafian
CAST: Cleavon Little, Barry Newman, Dean Jagger

Interesting story of a marathon car chase through Colorado and California. Cleavon Little gives a standout performance as the disc jockey who helps a driver (Barry Newman) elude the police. Richard Sarafian's direction is competent, but the story eventually runs out of gas before the film ends. Rated PG.

1971 107 minutes

VEGA$

★★½

DIRECTOR: Richard Lang
CAST: Robert Urich, Judy Landers, Tony Curtis, Will Sampson, Greg Morris

A few days in the life of a high-flying, T-Bird-driving private eye whose beat is highways, byways, and gambling casinos of Las Vegas. Robert Urich, an ex-cop, is hired to find a runaway teenage girl who's gotten in too deep with the sleazy side of Fortune Town.

1978 104 minutes

VENDETTA

🦃

DIRECTOR: Bruce Logan
CAST: Karen Chase, Sandy Martin, Roberta Collins, Kin Shriner

This is a laughably bad women's prison flick. *Vendetta* is the story of a stuntwoman who purposely commits several crimes so that she'll be thrown in the slammer—the same one her younger sister was unjustly put in—where she can then avenge the death of that sister, who was murdered by a jail gang. Pure low-budget slime. There is one classic line in this wretched excuse for a movie. When asked what she's doing time for, an older inmate says, "I killed my husband and his mother. They deserved it and I enjoyed it." John Waters would love this movie. Rated R.

1985 89 minutes

VENGEANCE

🦃

DIRECTOR: Antonio Isasi
CAST: Jason Miller, Lea Massari, Marisa Peredes, Manuel DeBlas, Aldo Sambrell, Yolanda Farr, Francisco Casares

What can you say about a film in which the most compelling actor is a German shepherd? That's the problem with this dull account of an escape from a Latin American prison camp. Jason Miller stars as a political prisoner whose flight to freedom begins when the man he's chained to is run over by a truck. Miller escapes into the swamps and kills the guard sent to pursue him. The guard's last words are a command for the dog to follow and kill, thus setting the stage for a seemingly endless number of bloody and violent attacks by the dog, who always seems to miss his target. Unrated, the film has graphic violence and sex.

1987 114 minutes

VENUS IN FURS

★

DIRECTOR: Jess Franco
CAST: James Darren, Barbara McNair, Klaus Kinski, Dennis Price

British, Italian, and German talents joined to make this pitifully poor mystery involving a musician and a mutilated woman who washes ashore. Almost, but not quite, a turkey. Rated R.

1970 86 minutes

VICE SQUAD

★★★½

DIRECTOR: Gary A. Sherman
CAST: Season Hubley, Wings Hauser, Gary Swanson, Beverly Todd

Slick, fast-paced thriller set in the seamy world of pimps and prostitutes. Season Hubley is an adorable mom by day and a smart-mouthed hooker by night forced to help cop Gary Swanson capture a sicko killer, played with frightening intensity by Wings Hauser. The police get their man, but he breaks away—after learning that Hubley set him up—and then the fun *really* begins. A total fairy tale, but it moves quickly enough to mask improbabilities. Hauser's one of the best psycho nutcases since *Dirty Harry*'s Andy Robinson. Not for the squeamish. Rated R.

1982 97 minutes

VICTORY

★★★

DIRECTOR: John Huston
CAST: Sylvester Stallone, Michael Caine, Pelé, Max von Sydow

Sylvester Stallone and Michael Caine star in this entertaining but predictable World War II drama about a soccer game between Allied prisoners of war and the Nazis. Germany intends to cheat. But our boys want to strike a blow for democracy. With a title like *Victory*, guess who wins. A hokey ending—in which the prisoners forgo certain escape to win the game—destroys the film's credibility. Rated PG.

1981 110 minutes

VIEW TO A KILL, A

★★★

DIRECTOR: John Glen
CAST: Roger Moore, Tanya Roberts, Christopher Walken, Grace Jones

Despite a spectacular opening sequence and some dandy little moments along the way, the James Bond series is starting to look a little old and tired—just like its star, Roger Moore. Christopher Walken co-stars as the maniacal villain who plans to corner the world's microchip market by flooding the San Andreas Fault. Good for fans only. Rated PG for violence and suggested sex.

1985 131 minutes

VIKINGS, THE

★★★½

DIRECTOR: Richard Fleischer
CAST: Kirk Douglas, Tony Curtis, Ernest Borgnine, Janet Leigh

Well-done action film following the exploits of a group of Vikings (led by Tony Curtis and Kirk Douglas). Many good battle scenes and beautiful photography and locations make the picture a standout. Ernest Borgnine gives a great performance. Don't miss it.

1958 114 minutes

VILLAIN STILL PURSUED HER, THE

★

DIRECTOR: Edward F. Cline
CAST: Anita Louise, Richard Cromwell, Hugh Herbert, Alan Mowbray, Buster Keaton, Billy Gilbert, Margaret Hamilton

Dull, old-fashioned melodrama is pretty thick sledding even with a veteran crew of character actors and actresses to break the monotony. Buster Keaton adds a little pep to this otherwise tired production, but the overall tone of this movie is that of tedium.

1940 B & W 66 minutes

VIOLENT BREED, THE

[turkey]

DIRECTORS: Fernando DiLeo
CAST: Henry Silva, Harrison Muller, Woody Strode, Carole Andre, Debora Keith, Danika

The CIA goes into Vietnam to stop a guerrilla gang that is importing drugs to America. Impossible situations, terrible acting, rotten dubbing, gratuitous nudity, and violence galore.

1983 91 minutes

VIVA KNIEVEL

★

DIRECTOR: Gordon Douglas
CAST: Evel Knievel, Marjoe Gortner, Leslie Nielsen, Gene Kelly, Lauren Hutton

Despite a healthy budget, this film is highly reminiscent of the old Republic Studio cheapie cliffhangers complete with goody good guys, nasty bad guys, stereotyped supporting characters, and lots of action. The film is too corny for adults, but still too complex for the kiddies, which leaves it in a state of limbo as far as audience appeal is concerned. The story has Evel Knievel (playing himself) being duped by a former buddy, Jessie (Marjoe Gortner), into doing a stunt tour of Mexico. What Evel doesn't know is that Jessie's boss, Stanley Millard (Leslie Nielsen), plans to murder him during the climax of one of his feats of daring. Rated PG, the film has no profanity, sex, or nudity, and very little violence.

1977 106 minutes

VON RYAN'S EXPRESS

★★★★

DIRECTOR: Mark Robson

CAST: Frank Sinatra, Trevor Howard, Edward Mulhare, James Brolin, Luther Adler

This is a World War II tale of escape from a prisoner-of-war camp aboard a German train to neutral Switzerland. Trevor Howard is the officer in charge until a feisty Frank Sinatra takes over the escape plan. This is a great action story, with Sinatra playing the hero's role perfectly. The antagonism between Howard, as the "safety of the men first" commander, and Sinatra, as the "escape at any cost" colonel, is well acted and believable.

1965 117 minutes

WAKE ISLAND

★★★★

DIRECTOR: John Farrow

CAST: Brian Donlevy, Macdonald Carey, Robert Preston, Albert Dekker, William Bendix, Walter Abel

Hard-hitting tale of a small gallant detachment of U.S. marines holding out against attack after attack by the Japanese army, navy, and air force. A true story from the early dark days of World War II when there had been no American victories. These marines held out for sixteen days while all of America held its breath. Brian Donlevy commands the troops, and William Bendix and Robert Preston fight each other as much as they fight the Japanese. *Wake Island* received four Academy Award nominations and was the first realistic American film made about World War II.

1942 B & W 88 minutes

WAKE OF THE RED WITCH

★★★★

DIRECTOR: Edward Ludwig

CAST: John Wayne, Gail Russell, Gig Young, Luther Adler

Good, seafaring adventure tale with John Wayne outstanding as a wronged ship's captain seeking justice and battling an octopus for sunken treasure.

1948 B & W 106 minutes

WALKING TALL

★★½

DIRECTOR: Phil Karlson

CAST: Joe Don Baker, Elizabeth Hartman, Noah Beery, Rosemary Murphy

Poor Joe Don Baker never outran his one-note performance as Buford Pusser, the baseball bat–toting southern sheriff who decided to take the law into his own hands in his fight against the cancerous scum of society. Unpleasantly brutal and difficult to enjoy for any reason; good guy Baker is almost worse than the outrageously stereotyped baddies he reduces to pulp. Talented Elizabeth Hartman is completely wasted. Not a family picture. Rated R.

1973 125 minutes

WALKING TALL PART II

★½

DIRECTOR: Earl Bellamy

CAST: Bo Svenson, Luke Askew, Richard Jaeckel, Noah Beery Jr.

In this sequel, there is more baseball than justice from Sheriff Buford T. Pusser (Bo Svenson). This follow-up to the successful *Walking Tall* proves that sequels are better off not being made at all. This storyline gives Svenson a chance to flex his muscles and look mean, but that's about it. Rated R for violence and language.

1975 109 minutes

WANTED: DEAD OR ALIVE

★★★

DIRECTOR: Gary Sherman

CAST: Rutger Hauer, Gene Simmons, Robert Guillaume, Mel Harris, William Russ

In this lean and mean action thriller, Rutger Hauer stars as Nick Randall, the great-grandson of Old West bounty hunter Josh Randall (who was played by Steve McQueen in the *Wanted: Dead or Alive* television series). Nick is a former CIA agent who is brought out of retirement by the company when an international terrorist (Gene Simmons) begins leaving a bloody trail across Los Angeles. Hauer is supposed to trap Simmons, but what our hero doesn't know is that some agency higher-ups have laid a trap of their own —with Hauer as bait. Rated R for profanity and violence.

1987 104 minutes

WARBUS

★★

DIRECTOR: Ted Kaplan

CAST: Daniel Stephen, Rom Kristoff, Urs Althaus, Gwendoline Cook, Ernie Zarte, Don Gordon, Josephine Sylva, Steve Eliott

A Vietnam adventure about a motley crew fleeing a mission in a school bus, heading south during the closing days of the war. On the way, they run into the remnants of a U.S. military unit that is cut off and trying to get to the nearest American-held military base. On the way, the two groups run into traps, POW camps, and enemy soldiers. Hardly a realistic portrayal of the war, this film is obviously an attempt to capitalize on the success of *Rambo*. The acting and the photography are somewhat stiff, but the characters are likable and the action is tightly paced. This film may not be everyone's cup of tea, but fans of mindless action films should find this one an entertaining diversion. Rated R for violence and profanity.

1985 90 minutes

WARNING, THE

DIRECTOR: Damiano Damiani

CAST: Martin Balsam, Giuliano Gemma, Giancarlo Zanetti, Guido Leontini, Marcello Mando

Convoluted dirty-cop flick from Italy. The folks who dubbed this thing must not have been up on the really emotionally loaded colloquialisms of modern English—to be really insulted in this flick is to be called a "turd." Martin Balsam's performance is pure paycheck and everyone else takes the whole affair far too seriously. Not rated, but probably equal to an R for violence, profanity, and nudity.

1985 101 minutes

WARRIORS, THE

★★★★

DIRECTOR: Walter Hill

CAST: Michael Beck, James Remar, Thomas Waites

Comic book–style violence and sensibilities made this Walter Hill film an unworthy target for those worried about its prompting real-life gang wars. It's just meant for fun, and mostly it is, as a group of kids try to make their way home through the territories of other, less-understanding gangs in a surrealistic New York. Rated R.

1979 94 minutes

WE OF THE NEVER NEVER

★★★★½

DIRECTOR: Igor Auzins

CAST: Angela Punch McGregor, Arthur Dignam, Tony Barry

The compelling story of a woman's year in the Australian Outback, where she learns about aborigines and they learn about her, is based on a true-life account written by Jeannie Gunn and published in 1908. Angela Punch McGregor stars in this first-rate import from Down Under. Rated G.

1983 132 minutes

WHEELS OF FIRE

DIRECTOR: Cirio Santiago

CAST: Gary Watkins, Laura Banks, Lynda Wiesmeiser, Linda Grovenor

Shameless ripoff of *The Road Warrior* lacks the taste of most of the films that have come in the wake of George Miller's action masterpiece. Nudity, violence, and rape dominate this story about a gang of nomadic bad guys with a leader named Scourge. If you can handle the misogyny, this one might be good for the mistaken humor: the cast members talk like high-school teenagers—*Frankie and Annette Meet Mad Max*? Rated R for sex, nudity, violence, and profanity.

1984 81 minutes

WHERE EAGLES DARE

★★★

DIRECTOR: Brian G. Hutton

CAST: Richard Burton, Clint Eastwood, Mary Ure, Michael Hordern, Patrick Wymark, Anton Diffring, Robert Beatty, Donald Houston, Ingrid Pitt

Clint Eastwood and Richard Burton portray Allied commandos in this World War II adventure film which is short on realism. Instead we have far-fetched but exciting shootouts, explosions, and mass slaughter. Our heroes must break out an American general being held captive in a heavily fortified German castle before the Nazis can get highly secret information out of him. Basically a spaghetti western set during World War II, this movie should please most action-adventure buffs.

1969 158 minutes

WHILE THE CITY SLEEPS

★★½

DIRECTOR: Fritz Lang

CAST: Dana Andrews, Ida Lupino, Rhonda Fleming, George Sanders, Vincent Price, John Drew Barrymore, Thomas Mitchell, Howard Duff, Mae Marsh

An impressive cast and the talents of director Fritz Lang can't transform this standard newspaper-crime story into a great film, although so many of the necessary elements seem to be present. Rival newspaper executives compete with each other and the police in an effort to come up with the identity of a mad killer who has been stalking the city, but this convoluted gabfest quickly bogs down and wastes the considerable acting talents involved. Slow moving despite the cross-cutting of different stories, this project remains an interesting but unsatisfactory entry in Lang's portfolio.

1956 B & W 100 minutes

WHITE DAWN, THE

★★★★

DIRECTOR: Phil Kaufman

CAST: Warren Oates, Louis Gossett Jr., Timothy Bottoms, Simonie Kopapik, Joanasie Salomonie

This is a gripping and thought-provoking adventure film. Three whalers (Warren Oates, Louis Gossett Jr., and Timothy Bottoms) get lost in the Arctic and are rescued by Eskimos, whom they end up exploiting. Rated PG.

1974 109 minutes

WHITE HEAT

★★★★½

DIRECTOR: Raoul Walsh
CAST: James Cagney, Margaret Wycherly, Virginia Mayo, Edmond O'Brien, Steve Cochran

James Cagney gives one of his greatest screen performances as a totally insane mama's boy and gangster, Cody Jarrett, in this film. Margaret Wycherly is chillingly effective as the evil mom, and Virginia Mayo is uncommonly outstanding as the badman's moll. But it is Cagney's picture pure and simple as he ironically makes it to "the top of the world, Ma!"

1949 B & W 114 minutes

WHITE LIGHTNING

★★

DIRECTOR: Joseph Sargent
CAST: Burt Reynolds, Jennifer Billingsley, Ned Beatty, Bo Hopkins, Matt Clark, Louise Latham, Diane Ladd

Good old boy Burt Reynolds as a speed-loving moonshiner fights the inevitable mean and inept cops and revenue agents in this comic-book chase and retribution film. A good cast of character actors make this stock drive-in movie entertaining, and there's plenty of mindless action to keep your eyes on the screen, but this throwback to Robert Mitchum's *Thunder Road* is just like the majority of Burt Reynolds's car films —gimmicky and predictable. Not bad if you consider a VCR as something to keep you company rather than to enlighten and inform, but basically a longer episode of *The Dukes of Hazzard*. Rated PG.

1973 101 minutes

WHITE LINE FEVER

★★★

DIRECTOR: Jonathan Kaplan
CAST: Jan-Michael Vincent, Kay Lenz, Slim Pickens, L. Q. Jones, Leigh French, Don Porter

Jan-Michael Vincent plays an incorruptible young trucker in this film. He is angered when forced to smuggle goods in his truck. He fights back after he and his pregnant wife (Kay Lenz) are attacked. Rated PG.

1975 92 minutes

WHITEWATER SAM

★★½

DIRECTOR: Keith Larsen
CAST: Keith Larsen

Keith Larsen wrote, directed, coproduced, and stars in this family film of a wilderness adventure. He plays the legendary Whitewater Sam, the first white man to survive the harsh Rocky Mountain winters. The real star, however, seems to be his darling, intelligent dog, Sybar. The beautiful scenery makes this film more than watchable. Rated PG for violence.

1978 85 minutes

WHO'LL STOP THE RAIN

★★★★½

DIRECTOR: Karel Reisz
CAST: Nick Nolte, Michael Moriarty, Tuesday Weld, Anthony Zerbe, Richard Masur, Ray Sharkey, David Opatoshu, Gail Strickland

In this brilliant film, Nick Nolte gives one of his finest performances as a hardened vet who agrees to smuggle drugs for a buddy (the always effective Michael Moriarty). What neither of them knows is that it's a setup, so Nolte and Moriarty's neurotic wife, played to perfection by Tuesday Weld, have to hide out from the baddies (Anthony Zerbe, Richard Masur, and Ray Sharkey) who want to steal their stash and then kill them. Directed by Karel Riesz, this gripping and suspenseful film builds to a powerful climax that's reminiscent of Raoul Walsh's classic *High Sierra*. Rated R.

1978 126 minutes

WICKED LADY, THE

DIRECTOR: Michael Winner
CAST: Faye Dunaway, Alan Bates, John Gielgud, Denholm Elliott, Prunella Scales, Oliver Tobias, Glynis Barber

An absolutely awful swashbuckler directed by Michael Winner (*Death Wish*), this wastes the talents of stars Faye Dunaway and Alan Bates. Despite the presence of two such high-powered acting talents, this period adventure film about an aristocrat who gets her kicks robbing travelers is a real groaner, and it's easy to see why the production company (Cannon Films) decided not to release it to the theaters. Rated R.

1983 98 minutes

WILD ANGELS, THE

★★

DIRECTOR: Roger Corman
CAST: Peter Fonda, Nancy Sinatra, Bruce Dern, Michael J. Pollard, Diane Ladd, Gayle Hunnicutt

It's 1960s hip, low-budget Hollywood style. If they gave Oscars for cool, Peter Fonda—in shades, three-day growth of beard, and leather—would win for sure. This cool motorcycle gang leader needs a hot mama. Unfortunately, he has to make do with Nancy ("These Boots Are Made for Walkin") Sinatra. It's always fun to watch Bruce Dern doing his psychotic biker routine. But the movie's greatest asset is "Blue's Theme," which revs up the proceedings with wonderfully tacky fuzz-tone guitar.

1966 93 minutes

WILD GEESE, THE

★★★

DIRECTOR: Andrew V. McLaglen
CAST: Richard Burton, Roger More, Richard Harris, Stewart Granger, Hardy Kruger, Jack Watson, Frank Finlay, Jeff Wrey, Winston Ntshona

The Wild Geese features the unlikely combination of Richard Burton, Roger Moore, and Richard Harris as three mercenaries hired by a rich British industrialist (Stewart Granger) to go into Rhodesia and free a captured humanist leader so the millionaire's company can again have the copper rights to the country. Burton is first-rate. His usual overblown, theatrical approach is subdued, making this one of the most effective film performances he ever achieved. He is perfect as the cool-headed leader. Moore is acceptable as the roguish part-time crook. Harris adds humanity as the brilliant strategist and loving father who reluctantly joins the mission because of his political beliefs. The battle scenes are some of the best ever. Rated R.

1978 134 minutes

WILD GEESE II

★

DIRECTOR: Peter Hunt
CAST: Scott Glenn, Barbara Carrera, Edward Fox, Laurence Olivier, Stratford Johns

In this contrived and vastly inferior sequel to the adventure film that starred Richard Burton, Richard Harris, and Roger Moore, a new group of mercenaries attempt to break into a Berlin prison to free Nazi war criminal Rudolf Hess. Even more ludicrous, this operation is backed by an American television network. Gone from this film are the earlier film's believable situations and three-dimensional characters. Here, the characters, dialogue, and violence are straight out of a comic book. The actors do their best, but even Olivier can't turn in a decent performance with this script. Rated R for violence and language.

1985 118 minutes

WILD ONE, THE

★★★½

DIRECTOR: Laslo Benedek
CAST: Marlon Brando, Mary Murphy, Robert Keith, Lee Marvin, Jay C. Flippen, Jerry Paris, Alvy Moore, Gil Stratton

This classic film (based loosely on a real event in Hollister, California) about rival motorcycle gangs taking over a small town is pretty tame stuff these days and provides more laughs than thrills. Producer Stanley Kramer's heavy-handed moralizing and the incredible dialogue mark this as one of the first of the "phony" teen films, where young people were played by actors in their twenties and thirties, and the slang and "hip-talk" were made up on the spot. Marlon Brando and his brooding Johnny are at the heart of this film's popularity; that coupled with the theme of motorcycle nomads have assured the film a cult following.

1953 B & W 79 minutes

WIND AND THE LION, THE

★★★★

DIRECTOR: John Milius
CAST: Sean Connery, Brian Keith, Candice Bergen, John Huston, Geoffrey Lewis, Steve Kanaly, Vladek Sheybal

In the 1970s, Sean Connery made a trio of memorable adventure movies, one being this release, directed by John Milius (*Conan the Barbarian*). As in the other two films—*The Man Who Would Be King* and *Robin and Marian*—*The Wind and the Lion*, in which Connery plays a dashing Arab chieftain, is a thoroughly satisfying motion picture. Rated PG.

1975 119 minutes

WINGS

★★★★

DIRECTOR: William Wellman
CAST: Clara Bow, Charles Rogers, Richard Arlen, Jobyna Ralston, Gary Cooper, Arlette Marchal, El Brendel

The first recipient of the Academy Award for best picture, this is a silent film with organ music in the background. The story concerns two buddies who join the Air Corps in World War I and go to France to battle the Germans. War scenes are excellent, even by today's standards. Anti-war message is well done, although the love story tends to bog the film down a bit. Look for a young Gary Cooper. Much of the story rings true.

1927 B & W 139 minutes

WINNING

★★★½

DIRECTOR: James Goldstone
CAST: Paul Newman, Joanne Woodward, Robert Wagner, Richard Thomas

Paul Newman is very good as a race car driver who puts winning above all else, including his family. Some very good racing sequences and fine support from Joanne Woodward and Richard Thomas. Rated PG.

1969 123 minutes

WISDOM

★

DIRECTOR: Emilio Estevez
CAST: Emilio Estevez, Demi Moore, Tom Skerritt, Veronica Cartwright, William Allen Young

Writer-director Emilio Estevez plays a modern-day Robin Hood who comes to the aid of America's farmers in a bank-robbing spree with girlfriend Demi Moore. *Wisdom* is at its best when played as a light-hearted, tongue-in-cheek romp. Too bad Estevez, who wrote an outstanding screenplay for *That Was Then—This Is Now*, is unable to maintain this tone throughout. Instead, he assaults the viewer with violence, angst, and overlong mood shots of scenery and lovemaking. Rated R for violence, profanity, and sex.

1986 109 minutes

WITNESS

★★★★½

DIRECTOR: Peter Weir
CAST: Harrison Ford, Kelly McGillis, Josef Summer, Lukas Haas, Alexander Godunov, Danny Glover

This is three terrific movies in one: an exciting cop thriller, a touching romance, and a fascinating screen study of a modern-day clash of cultures. Harrison Ford is superb in the starring role as a police captain who must protect an 8-year-old boy, the only witness to a drug-related murder. The policeman's attentions are welcomed (in more than one way) by the boy's mother (Kelly McGillis). However, both are thwarted by her friends and family—being Amish, they shun the devices and denizens of the modern world. Nevertheless, everyone is endangered when the murderer turns out to be a corrupt cop. Rated R for violence, profanity, and nudity.

1985 112 minutes

WOMAN IN GREEN, THE

★★★

DIRECTOR: Roy William Neill
CAST: Basil Rathbone, Nigel Bruce, Hillary Brooke, Henry Daniell, Paul Cavanagh, Matthew Boulton

This is a grisly little entry in the Rathbone/Bruce Sherlock Holmes series, with the master sleuth investigating a series of severed fingers sent to Scotland Yard. The culprit is, once again, Professor Moriarty (Henry Daniell), this time masterminding a hypnosis-blackmail-murder scheme. Careful viewers will detect moments from *The Adventure of the Empty House*.

1945 B & W 68 minutes

YAKUZA, THE

★★★★★

DIRECTOR: Sydney Pollack
CAST: Robert Mitchum, Brian Keith, Ken Takakura, Herb Edelman, Richard Jordan, Kishi Keiko

This superb blending of the American gangster and Japanese samurai genres was directed by Sydney Pollack (*Tootsie*). In the screenplay by Paul Schrader and Robert Towne, Robert Mitchum plays Harry Kilmer, an ex-G.I. who returns to Japan to do a dangerous favor for a friend, George Tanner (Brian Keith). The latter's daughter has been kidnapped by a Japanese gangster—a Yakuza—who is holding her for ransom. This forces Kilmer to call on Tanaka (Ken Takakura), a one-time enemy who owes him a debt. Thus begins a clash of cultures and a web of intrigue that keep the viewers on the edge of their seats. Rated R.

1975 112 minutes

YANKEE CLIPPER

★★½

DIRECTOR: Rupert Julian

CAST: William Boyd, Elinor Fair, Junior Coghlan, John Miljan, Walter Long, Louis Payne, Burr McIntosh, George Ovey, Zack Williams

Future Hopalong Cassidy William Boyd plays a tough seadog determined to win a race against a British ship as they sail from China to Boston. Plenty of good sea footage is interspersed with a sticky love story between Boyd and an English girl, Elinor Fair, but a near mutiny and Walter Long as the villainous Iron-Head Joe help offset the mush. Silent, with soundtrack.

1927 B & W 51 minutes

YEAR OF LIVING DANGEROUSLY, THE

★★★★½

DIRECTOR: Peter Weir

CAST: Mel Gibson, Sigourney Weaver, Linda Hunt, Michael Murphy, Bill Kerr, Noel Ferrier

The Year of Living Dangerously is set in 1965 Indonesia when the Sukarno regime was toppling from pressures left and right. As in his previous efforts, Weir creates so much atmosphere that it seems to fill your nostrils at times. Mel Gibson and Sigourney Weaver star as an Australian journalist and a British diplomatic attaché, respectively. The film, however, belongs to Linda Hunt, in her Academy Award–winning role as free-lance photographer Billy Kwan. Rated R for profanity, nudity, and violence.

1983 115 minutes

YEAR OF THE DRAGON

★

DIRECTOR: Michael Cimino

CAST: Mickey Rourke, John Lone, Ariane, Leonard Termo, Ray Barry

This film about the attempts of a New York police officer (Mickey Rourke) to stop the violence caused by youth gangs in Chinatown has some exciting and effectively dramatic moments. Overall, however, it's racist, sexist, foul-mouthed, overly violent, and just plain disgusting, another study in excess from director Michael Cimino. As with the overly praised *The Deer Hunter* and the overly criticized *Heaven's Gate*, *Year of the Dragon* sometimes fascinates and thrills. Its better moments come wrapped in a decidedly distasteful package. Rated R for violence, profanity, gore, simulated sex, and nudity.

1985 136 minutes

YOU ONLY LIVE TWICE

★★★

DIRECTOR: Lewis Gilbert

CAST: Sean Connery, Akiko Wakabayashi, Tetsuro Tamba, Mie Hama, Karin Dor, Bernard Lee, Lois Maxwell, Desmond Llewellyn, Donald Pleasence

Sean Connery as James Bond—who could expect more, especially in these days of cheap imitations? Well, a better plot and more believable cliff-hanger situations come to mind. Still, this entry isn't a bad 007, and it does star the best Bond.

1967 116 minutes

YOUNG AND INNOCENT

★★★

DIRECTOR: Alfred Hitchcock

CAST: Derrek de Marney, Nova Pilbeam, Percy Marmont, Edward Rigby, Mary Clare, Basil Radford

Reputedly director Alfred Hitchcock's favorite of the films he made in Great Britain, this chase-within-a-chase film employs one of his favorite devices, that of an innocent man avoiding the police while attempting to catch the real criminal and prove his innocence. Convincingly played against a series of different backdrops and settings by a cast of players all but unknown to contemporary American audiences, this neat little thriller (based on Josephine Tey's first mystery novel) is a skillful blend of comedy and suspense and boasts one of Hitchcock's best touches, an elaborate soundstage-length moving close-up that reveals the real murderer to the audience as a member of a performing band. Not as well known as many of his other films, this seldom-seen movie is vintage Hitchcock and on a par with much of his best work.

1937 B & W 80 minutes

YOUNG SHERLOCK HOLMES

★★½

DIRECTOR: Barry Levinson
CAST: Nicholas Rowe, Alan Cox, Sophie Ward, Anthony Higgins, Freddie Jones

This disappointingly derivative Steven Spielberg production speculates on what might have happened if Sherlock Holmes (Nicholas Rowe) and Dr. John H. Watson (Alan Cox) had met during their student days in 1870 England. A better name for it might be *Sherlock Holmes and the Temple of Doom*. While youngsters are likely to enjoy it, most adults—especially frequent filmgoers or video viewers—are cautioned to avoid it. Rated PG-13 for violence and scary stuff.

1985 115 minutes

ZOMBIES OF THE STRATOSPHERE (SATAN'S SATELLITES)

★★

DIRECTOR: Fred Brannon
CAST: Judd Holdren, Aline Towne, Wilson Wood, Lane Bradford

Judd Holdren, representing the Inter-Planetary Patrol, dons a flying suit and tracks down part-human zombies who have enlisted the aid of a renegade scientist to construct a hydrogen bomb that will blow Earth off its orbit and enable them to conquer what's left of the world. Balsa wood rocket ships and stock footage from the other "Rocket Man" serials make this one of the more ludicrous entries from Republic Studios in the last years of the movie serial. Enjoy the stunts in this one and skip the story.

1952 B & W 12 chapters

ZULU

★★★★½

DIRECTOR: Cy Endfield
CAST: Stanley Baker, Michael Caine, Jack Hawkins, Nigel Green

Several films have been made about the British army and its exploits in Africa during the nineteenth century. *Zulu* ranks with the finest. A stellar cast headed by Stanley Baker and Michael Caine charged through this story of an outmanned British garrison laid to siege by several thousand Zulu warriors. Based on fact, this one delivers the goods for action and tension.

1964 138 minutes

ZULU DAWN

★★★

DIRECTOR: Douglas Hickox
CAST: Burt Lancaster, Peter O'Toole, Simon Ward, John Mills, Nigel Davenport

This prequel to the film *Zulu*, which was made fifteen years earlier, seems quite pale when compared with the first. Based on the crushing defeat to the British army at the hands of the Zulu warriors, *Zulu Dawn* depicts the events leading up to the confrontation portrayed in *Zulu*. Considering all involved, this is a disappointment. Rated PG for violence.

1979 121 minutes

ABSENT-MINDED PROFESSOR, THE

★★★★

DIRECTOR: Robert Stevenson
CAST: Fred MacMurray, Nancy Olson, Tommy Kirk, Ed Wynn, Keenan Wynn

One of Disney's best live-action comedies, this stars Fred MacMurray in the title role of a scientist who discovers "flubber" (flying rubber). Only trouble is, no one will believe him—except Keenan Wynn, who tries to steal his invention.

1961 B & W 104 minutes

ACROSS THE GREAT DIVIDE

★★

DIRECTOR: Stewart Raffill
CAST: Robert Logan, George Flower, Heather Rattray, Mark Edward Hall

Across the Great Divide is family entertainment at its most unchallenging. Two kids (Heather Rattray and Mark Hall) meet up with a shifty gambler (Robert Logan), and the three eventually unite for safety on their monotonous trek through valleys, mountains, and rivers. There are some bright spots. The dog, Chastity, humorously romps with a playful beaver. An attack by mountain lions and another by wolves are both suspenseful. The Indians are well played and sensitively presented. Rated G.

1976 89 minutes

ADVENTURES OF AN AMERICAN RABBIT, THE

★★★

DIRECTOR: Steward Moskowitz
CAST: Animated

In this enjoyable-for-kids feature-length cartoon, mild-mannered and sweet-natured Rob Rabbit becomes the heir to the Legacy, which magically transforms him into the star-spangled protector of all animalkind, the American Rabbit. Rated G.

1986 85 minutes

ADVENTURES OF BULLWHIP GRIFFIN, THE

★★

DIRECTOR: James Neilson
CAST: Roddy McDowall, Suzanne Pleshette, Karl Malden, Harry Guardino, Richard Haydn, Hermione Baddeley, Cecil Kellaway

Typical, flyweight Disney comedy, this ripoff of *Ruggles of Red Gap* is textured with unique character performers, such as Richard Haydn and Karl Malden, but fails to offer anything original. Roddy McDowall plays a proper English butler who finds himself smack-dab in the wilds of California during the Gold Rush and helps save the day for his young "master," Brian Russell. Okay for the kids but not much to recommend for a discriminating audience.

1966 110 minutes

ADVENTURES OF DROOPY

★★½

DIRECTOR: Tex Avery
CAST: Animated

Next to Tom and Jerry, Droopy was MGM's most famous cartoon character. The sad-eyed dog could best any foe. Nothing seemed to faze him and he magically recovered from any attack. As a result, he wasn't—and still isn't—the most exciting animated hero. Even though his cartoons were crafted by Tex Avery, one of the greatest cartoon directors, his stoic nature tended to be a one-joke premise that made seeing him more than twice a letdown. Although enjoyable, this six-cartoon collection suffers from this redundancy. Any one of the cartoons—"Dumb-hounded," "Wags to Riches," "The Shooting of Dan McGoo," "Droopy's Good Deed," "Dragalong Droopy," and "Deputy Droopy"—would be a fine addition to a collection of Avery's work. But as a program, they leave the viewer almost as impassive as Droopy.

1985 53 minutes

ADVENTURES OF HUCKLEBERRY FINN, THE

★★

DIRECTOR: Jack B. Hively
CAST: Forrest Tucker, Larry Storch, Brock Peters

This drawn-out version of Mark Twain's classic has its moments but lacks continuous action. In it, young Huck fakes his own drowning to avoid attendance of a proper eastern school for boys. When his friend, the slave Jim (Brock Peters), is accused of his murder, he must devise a plan to free him. Huck and Jim find themselves rafting down the Mississippi with two likable con artists (Larry Storch and Forrest Tucker).

1978 97 minutes

ADVENTURES OF THE WILDERNESS FAMILY

★★★½

DIRECTOR: Stuart Raffill
CAST: Robert Logan, Susan D. Shaw, Ham Larsen, Heather Rattray, George (Buck) Flower, Hollye Holmes, William Cornford

This is a variation on the Swiss Family Robinson story. A family (oddly enough named Robinson) moves to the Rocky Mountains to escape the frustrations and congestion of life in Los Angeles. They're sick of smog, hassles, and crime. And, more important, the daughter, Jenny (Heather Rattray), has a serious respiratory problem that only fresh, clean air can rectify. They build a cabin and brave the dangers of the wild. Rated G.

1975 100 minutes

ADVENTURES OF TOM SAWYER, THE

★★★★

DIRECTOR: Norman Taurog
CAST: Tommy Kelly, Jackie Moran, Victor Jory, May Robson, Walter Brennan, Ann Gillis

One of the better screen adaptations of Mark Twain's works. Tommy Kelly is a perfect Tom Sawyer, but it's Victor Jory as the villainous Indian Joe who steals the show. Good sets and beautiful cinematography make this one work. Fine family entertainment for the young and old.

1938 B & W 93 minutes

ALADDIN AND HIS WONDERFUL LAMP

★★★½

DIRECTOR: Tim Burtin
CAST: Valerie Bertinelli, Robert Carradine, James Earl Jones, Leonard Nimoy

This *Faerie Tale Theatre* interpretation of the classic Arabian Nights tale adds a few twists. One is the offer of the genie (James Earl Jones) to rearrange Aladdin's (Robert Carradine) face when Aladdin makes demands on him. The second surprise is the TV the genie produces to satisfy the sultan and win the princess (Valerie Bertinelli) for Aladdin. Leonard Nimoy is good as the manipulative wizard who entices Aladdin into retrieving the magic lamp from a dangerous and spooky cave. The whole family can enjoy this one.

1985 60 minutes

ALICE IN WONDERLAND

★★★½

DIRECTORS: Clyde Geronimi, Hamilton Luske, Wilfred Jackson
CAST: Animated

The magic of the Walt Disney Studio animators is applied to Lewis Carroll's classic in this feature-length cartoon with mostly entertaining results. As with the book, the film is episodic and lacking the customary Disney warmth. But a few absolutely wonderful sequences—like the Mad Hatter's tea party and the appearances of the Cheshire cat—make it worth seeing. Rated G.

1951 75 minutes

ALICE'S ADVENTURES IN WONDERLAND

★★

DIRECTOR: William Sterling
CAST: Fiona Fullerton, Dudley Moore, Peter Sellers, Sir Ralph Richardson, Spike Milligan

This British live-action version of Lewis Carroll's classic tale is too long and boring. It is a musical that employs an endless array of silly songs, dances, and riddles. Although it sticks closely to the book, it's not as entertaining as Disney's fast-paced animated version of 1951. Fiona Fullerton stars as Alice. Dudley Moore is featured as the Dormouse, Peter Sellers plays the March Hare, and Sir Ralph Richardson is the caterpillar. Children between 5 and 10 may enjoy this, but parents will undoubtedly fall asleep. Rated G.

1973 97 minutes

ALL CREATURES GREAT AND SMALL

★★★½

DIRECTOR: Terence Dudley
CAST: Christopher Timothy, Robert Hardy, Peter Davison, Carol Drinkwater

This feature-length film picks up where the popular British television series left off, with veterinarian James Herriot (Christopher Timothy) returning to his home and practice after having served in World War II. Although he has been away for years, things quickly settle into a comfortable routine; irascible Siegfried Farnon (superbly played by Robert Hardy) still squabbles constantly with younger brother Tristan (Peter Davison), with Herriot's wife, Helen (Carol Drinkwater) using her considerable charm to keep peace in their extended family. The animal stories are lifted from Dr. Herriot's poignant, bittersweet books, with a few moments likely to require a hanky or two. This film hasn't received the exposure granted the series, so many fans are in for a pleasant surprise. Unrated; absolutely appropriate for family viewing.

1986 94 minutes

ALMOST ANGELS

★★½

DIRECTOR: Steve Previn
CAST: Peter Weck, Hans Holt, Fritz Eckhardt, Bruni Lobel, Sean Scully

Schmaltzy film focusing on the Vienna Boys' Choir and the problems one boy encounters when his voice cracks and he can no longer sing in the choir. Rated G.

1962 93 minutes

AMAZING DOBERMANS

★★

DIRECTORS: David and Byron Chudnow
CAST: James Franciscus, Barbara Eden, Fred Astaire, Jack Carter

Third in a series of films about do-gooder dogs pits a treasury agent (James Franciscus) against inept crooks who can dodge the long arm of the law but can't compete with the dogged determination of the Dobermans. This odd film not only features Fred Astaire as the colorful top-dog of the canine corps but throws in everyone's favorite midget, Billy Barty, as a special bonus. Harmless but hardly inspired. Rated G.

1976 94 minutes

AMAZING MR. BLUNDEN, THE

★★★

DIRECTOR: Lionel Jeffries
CAST: Laurence Naismith, Lynne Frederick, Garry Miller, Dorothy Alison, Diana Dors

Neat little ghost story about children from the 20th century (Lynne Frederick, Garry Miller) helping right a wrong done 100 years previously. Laurence Naismith is the mysterious (and amazing) Mr. Blunden, a 19th-century lawyer who is at home in the 20th. The children seem a little old to be involved in this type of adventure, but on the whole the story is delightful. Rated PG.

1972 100 minutes

AMERICAN TAIL, AN

★★★

DIRECTOR: Don Bluth
CAST: Dom De Luise, Phillip Glasser, Madeline Kahn, Nehemiah Persoff, Christopher Plummer (voices)

Don Bluth, the renegade Disney animator who formed his own company and released *The Secret of NIMH* in 1982, returns with this charming tale. An immigrant mouse becomes separated from his family while voyaging to the United States. The execution and lavish animation make up for the trite and predictable story, which sends little Fievel Mousekewitz on a series of near misses with the family that searches so hard for him. Film picks up steam with the introduction of Dom De Luise, as a vegetarian cat. Good family viewing . Rated G.

1986 82 minutes

ANIMALS ARE BEAUTIFUL PEOPLE

★★★½

DIRECTOR: Jamie Uys
CAST: Documentary

South African filmmaker Jamie Uys takes a pixilated perspective on wildlife documentaries in this sporadically hilarious film. Some viewers might complain that he relies a bit too much on editing tricks to get laughs, but we found this forgivable. Youngsters especially will love it and learn something while they are giggling. The sequence on the Bushmen of the Kalahari Desert was obviously the inspiration for Uys's worldwide smash hit, *The Gods Must Be Crazy*. Rated G.

1974 92 minutes

ANNIE OAKLEY

★★★

DIRECTOR: Michael Lindsay-Hogg

CAST: Jamie Lee Curtis, Brian Dennehy, Cliff DeYoung, Nick Ramus, Joyce Van Patten

This first episode of Shelley Duvall's new series, *Tall Tales and Legends*, deals with true-life character Annie Oakley. Jamie Lee Curtis convincingly plays the sharp-shooting Annie with Brian Dennehy as her Wild West show boss, Buffalo Bill. She struggles with the pressures of fame, but Chief Sitting Bull (Nick Ramus) persuades her that the struggle is worth it. At times, the pace is slow, but the 1903 footage taken by Thomas Edison, as well as the sepia-toned posters of Curtis as Annie, grant authenticity to the legend.

1985 52 minutes

APPLE DUMPLING GANG, THE

★★

DIRECTOR: Norman Tokar

CAST: Bill Bixby, Tim Conway, Don Knotts, Susan Clark, David Wayne, Slim Pickens, Harry Morgan

A gambler (Bill Bixby) inherits three children who find a huge gold nugget in a supposedly played-out mine in 1870. Tim Conway and Don Knotts trip and foul up as left-footed bad guys. The best word for this is "innocuous." Good, clean, unoriginal, predictable fare from Disney. The kids will love it. Rated G.

1975 100 minutes

APPLE DUMPLING GANG RIDES AGAIN, THE

★½

DIRECTOR: Vincent McEveety

CAST: Tim Conway, Don Knotts, Harry Morgan, Jack Elam, Kenneth Mars, Ruth Buzzi, Robert Pine

A cast composed of comic actors, each of whom is topnotch in solo spots, is no guarantee of hilarious ensemble playing. In this sequel to the 1975 original, Tim Conway and Don Knotts again play bumbling, inept outlaws in the Old West. Not quite a turkey, but close! Even so, the kids will enjoy it—once. Rated G.

1979 88 minutes

BABES IN TOYLAND

DIRECTOR: Jack Donohue

CAST: Ray Bolger, Tommy Sands, Ed Wynn, Annette Funicello, Tommy Kirk

A disappointing Disney version of the Victor Herbert operetta. In Mother Goose Land, Barnaby (Ray Bolger) kidnaps Tom the Piper's Son (Tommy Sands) in order to marry Mary (Annette Funicello). The Toymaker (Ed Wynn) and his assistant (Tommy Kirk) eventually provide the means for Tom to save the day. Despite a good Disney cast, this film never jells. Rated G.

1961 105 minutes

BAREFOOT EXECUTIVE, THE

★★

DIRECTOR: Robert Butler

CAST: Kurt Russell, Joe Flynn, Harry Morgan, Wally Cox, Heather North, Alan Hewitt, John Ritter

Mild Disney comedy about an individual (Kurt Russell) who finds a chimpanzee that can select top television shows. Based on the chimp's selections, a network moves to the top of the ratings charts, and Russell becomes a vice president in charge of programming. The usual confusions come about as Russell tries to explain that the monkey did the selecting. Rated G.

1971 92 minutes

BATMAN

★★★

DIRECTOR: Leslie Martinson

CAST: Adam West, Burt Ward, Frank Gorshin, Burgess Meredith, Lee Meriwether, Cesar Romero

Holy success story! The caped crusader and his youthful sidekick jump from their popular mid-1960s television series into a full-length feature film. Adam West and Burt Ward keep quip in cheek as they battle the Fearsome Foursome: the Riddler (Frank Gorshin), the Penguin (Burgess Meredith), the Catwoman (Lee Meriwether), and the Joker (Cesar Romero). Even summer isn't this camp. The plot, a thin excuse for a series of exciting bat-chases and clever bat-traps, concerns a plot to transform United Nations delegates into small piles of dust. Very silly material played with ludicrous seriousness, resulting in a lot of fun. Pretty bat-ty.

1966 105 minutes

BEAUTY AND THE BEAST

★★★★

DIRECTOR: Roger Vadim

CAST: Klaus Kinski, Susan Sarandon

A merchant's daughter takes her father's place as the prisoner of a melancholy beast and finds that love can change all things. Klaus Kinski is marvelous as the Beast and Susan Sarandon a fine Beauty in this Faerie Tale Theatre production.

1983 52 minutes

BEDKNOBS AND BROOMSTICKS

★★★½

DIRECTOR: Robert Stevenson

CAST: Angela Lansbury, David Tomlinson, Roddy McDowall

Angela Lansbury is a witch who uses her powers to aid the Allies against the Nazis during World War II. She transports two children to faraway and strange locales during which they meet and play soccer with talking animals, among other things. This Disney film is an effective combination of special effects, animation, and live action. While some may consider it a weaker version of *Mary Poppins*, it has plenty of what it takes to stand on its own. Rated G.

1971 117 minutes

BENJI

★★★★

DIRECTOR: Joe Camp

CAST: Peter Breck, Deborah Walley, Edgar Buchanan, Frances Bavier, Patsy Garrett

Benji parallels *Lassie* and *Rin Tin Tin* by intuitively doing the right thing at the right time. In this film, a dog saves two children who get kidnapped. Unlike Lassie or Rin Tin Tin, Benji is a small, unassuming mutt, which makes him all the more endearing. Deborah Walley and Edgar Buchanan costar with Benji (who played Higgins on television's "Petticoat Junction"), but the lovable mutt is the real star in this one. Rated G.

1974 86 minutes

BENJI THE HUNTED

★★★

DIRECTOR: Joe Camp

CAST: Benji

Most kids will love this adventure

featuring everyone's favorite sweet-faced mutt slogging his poor little lost way through the wilderness of the Pacific Northwest to civilization. Along the way, he has time to save some cute cougar cubs—say "aaaah." Adults may find it all a little too much, but the absence of dialogue makes it the perfect background for a good read while the kiddies get their video fix. Rated G.

1987 90 minutes

BEST OF BUGS BUNNY AND FRIENDS, THE

★★★★

DIRECTORS: Tex Avery, Bob Clampett, Arthur Davis, Friz Freleng, Chuck Jones

CAST: Animated

Some of the best pre-1947 Warner Bros. cartoons have been collected for this long overdue package. Highlights include Bob Clampett's "What's Cookin' Doc?" (in which Bugs Bunny campaigns shamelessly for an Oscar) and Friz Freleng's Oscar-winning "Tweetie Pie," as well as Chuck Jones's touching and clever "Bedtime for Sniffles." The directors are not listed on each cartoon, which is our only complaint. Otherwise, this collection—which also features Freleng's "Duck Soup to Nuts," Tex Avery's "A Feud There Was," Arthur Davis' "Nothing But the Tooth" and Jones's "The Little Lion Hunter" —is a real treasure for fans of classic cartoons. For all ages.

1986 53 minutes

BIG RED

★★★

DIRECTOR: Norman Tokar

CAST: Walter Pidgeon, Gilles Payant, Emile Genest, Janette Bertrand

This pleasant family film drawn from the beloved children's book of the same title features Walter Pidgeon as the owner of a sleek Irish setter named Big Red, which spends its formative years in loving companionship with young Gilles Payant. When the dog grows older and is groomed for professional shows, it escapes and tries to find its youthful friend.

1962 89 minutes

BLACK ARROW

★★★½

DIRECTOR: John Hough

CAST: Oliver Reed, Georgia Slowe, Benedict Taylor, Fernando Rey, Stephen Chase, Donald Pleasence

In this enjoyable Disney adventure film, Sir Daniel Brackley (Oliver Reed), a corrupt and wealthy landowner, is robbed by the Black Arrow, an outlaw. He then conceives of a plan to marry his ward, Joanna (Georgia Slowe), and send his nephew (Benedict Taylor) to his death. The tide turns when his nephew and the Black Arrow combine forces to rescue Joanna.

1984 93 minutes

BLACK STALLION, THE

★★★★★

DIRECTOR: Carroll Ballard

CAST: Kelly Reno, Mickey Rooney, Teri Garr, Hoyt Axton, Clarence Muse

Before taking our breath away with the superb *Never Cry Wolf*, director Carroll Ballard made an impressive directorial debut with this gorgeous screen version of the well-known children's story. Kelly Reno plays the young boy stranded on a deserted island with "The Black," a wild, but very intelligent, horse who comes to be his best friend. The scenes in the first half of the film are absolutely hypnotic. Even small children are transfixed by the story, told only via director of photography Caleb Deschanel's images and composer

Carmine Coppola's music. It's a treat the whole family can enjoy. Rated G.

1979 118 minutes

BLACK STALLION RETURNS, THE

★★★★

DIRECTOR: Robert Dalva

CAST: Kelly Reno, Vincent Spano, Teri Garr, Allen Goorwitz, Woody Strode

A sequel to the 1979 film *The Black Stallion*, this is first-rate fare for the young and the young at heart. The story, based on the novel by Walter Farley, picks up where the first film left off. Alec Ramsey (Kelly Reno) is a little older and a little taller, but he still loves his horse, The Black. And this time, Alec must journey halfway around the world to find the stallion, which has been stolen by an Arab chieftain. Rated PG for slight violence.

1983 93 minutes

BLACKBEARD'S GHOST

★★★

DIRECTOR: Robert Stevenson

CAST: Peter Ustinov, Dean Jones, Suzanne Pleshette, Elsa Lanchester

This fun Disney comedy has Peter Ustinov playing a ghost who must prevent his ancestors' home from becoming a gambling casino.

1968 107 minutes

BLUE FIN

★★

DIRECTOR: Carl Schultz

CAST: Hardy Kruger, Greg Rowe, John Jarratt, Liddy Clark, Hugh Keays-Byrne, Alfred Bell, Elspeth Ballantyne, Ralph Cotterill

The son of a commercial fisherman finds that growing up is hard to do, especially when he has to do so before he's ready. On a fishing trip with his father, the boy is caught in a storm. With the fishing boat nearly destroyed and his father seriously injured, the young hero must act responsibly for the first time in his life.

1977 93 minutes

BLUE FIRE LADY

★★½

DIRECTOR: Ross Dimsey

CAST: Cathryn Harrison, Mark Holden, Peter Cummins

The story of racetracks and horse racing, the trust and love between an animal and a person are well handled in this family film. It chronicles the story of Jenny (Cathryn Harrison) and her love for horses, which endures despite her father's disapproval.

1983 96 minutes

BLUE YONDER, THE

★★★½

DIRECTOR: Mark Rosman

CAST: Peter Coyote, Huckleberry Fox, Art Carney, Dennis Lipscomb, Joe Flood, Mittie Smith, Frank Simons

Heartfelt tale of a boy (Huckleberry Fox) who goes back in time in a time machine to warn his late grandfather (Peter Coyote) of his unsuccessful attempt at a nonstop transatlantic flight. Good performances keep the creaky plot airborne.

1985 89 minutes

BOATNIKS, THE

★★½

DIRECTOR: Norman Tokar

CAST: Stephanie Powers, Phil Silvers, Norman Fell, Robert Morse, Mickey Shaughnessy

Disney comedy in which Robert Morse plays a heroic Coast Guard officer who manages a romantic relationship with Stephanie Powers while pursuing bumbling thieves (Phil Silvers, Norman Fell, and Mickey Shaughnessy). Rated G.

1970 99 minutes

BON VOYAGE, CHARLIE BROWN

★★★

DIRECTOR: Bill Melendez
CAST: Animated

An animated film starring the "Peanuts" gang, this is well suited for the viewing of the younger generation. It's basically a "Peanuts" guide to world travel. *Bon Voyage*... begins as Charlie Brown, Linus, Marcie, and Peppermint Patty discover themselves headed toward France as part of a student-exchange program. Of course, Snoopy and Woodstock must come along for the ride. Although much of the film chronicles their travels through England and France, the emphasis is on their stay in a small French village where Charlie and Linus find themselves invited to a dark, scary castle in which no one seems to live. Rated G.

1980 75 minutes

BORN FREE

★★★★★

DIRECTOR: James Hill
CAST: Virginia McKenna, Bill Travers, Geoffrey Keen, Peter Lukoye

An established family classic, this is the tale of Elsa the lioness and her relationship with an African game warden and his wife. Not since *The Yearling* and *National Velvet* has such compassion been given to the interaction between people and the animals they love and eventually lose. A brilliant film.

1966 96 minutes

BOY NAMED CHARLIE BROWN, A

★★★★

DIRECTOR: Bill Melendez
CAST: Animated

Charles Schulz's "Peanuts" gang jumps to the big screen in this delightful, wistful tale of Charlie Brown's shot at fame in a national spelling bee. Great jazzy piano score by the incomparable Vince Guaraldi brings life to great sequences, such as Snoopy's ice skating debut. Lucy and her girl gang are a bit hard on ol' Chuck at times, and things definitely pick up when Charlie Brown, Linus, and Snoopy are off on their own. Good songs, including a poignant title tune by Rod McKuen. Rated G.

1969 85 minutes

BOY WHO LEFT HOME TO FIND OUT ABOUT THE SHIVERS, THE

★★★½

DIRECTOR: Graeme Clifford
CAST: Peter MacNicol, Dana Hill, Christopher Lee, David Warner, Frank Zappa, Jeff Corey

In this *Faerie Tale Theatre* production narrated by Vincent Price, a boy (Peter MacNicol, of *Sophie's Choice*) goes off to a Transylvanian castle (operated by Christopher Lee, no less) to find out about fear. Good moments overcome a rather protracted midsection where our hero does a bit too much goofing around with ghosts. Not for young children.

1985 54 minutes

BROTHERS LIONHEART, THE

★★½

DIRECTOR: Olle Hellbom
CAST: Staffan Gotestam, Lars Soderdahl, Allan Edwall, Gunn Wallgren

This slow-moving children's fantasy was filmed in Sweden, Denmark, and Finland. Two brothers are reunited after death in a medieval world where they fight dragons and villains in an attempt to free their war leader, Ulva, who will rid the country of tyrants. If you don't fall asleep within the first forty-five minutes, you will be rewarded with a fine fairy tale. Rated G.

1977 108 minutes

BUGS BUNNY CARTOON FESTIVAL FEATURING "HOLD THE LION PLEASE"

★★★★

DIRECTORS: Bob Clampett, Friz Freleng, Chuck Jones

CAST: Animated

While everyone's favorite rabbit is better represented in other collections of cartoons, this release is a thousand times better than the Looney Tune Video Shows of a few years back. One of the selections, Friz Freleng's "Racketeer Rabbit," in which Bugs befuddles baddies Edward G. Robinson and Peter Lorre, is a bona-fide cartoon classic. The others—Bob Clampett's "Buckaroo Bugs" and Chuck Jones's "Super Rabbit" and "Hold the Lion Please"—are worth a chuckle or two.

1942–1946 34 minutes

BUGS BUNNY AND ELMER FUDD CARTOON FESTIVAL FEATURING "WABBIT TWOUBLE"

★★★★

DIRECTORS: Tex Avery, Bob Clampett, Friz Freleng

CAST: Animated

Another winning collection of vintage Warner Bros. cartoons, this tape features some real classics. For example, Bob Clampett's "The Big Snooze" has Elmer Fudd, like James Cagney and Oliva de Havilland before him, quitting the studio because of a contract dispute. He's sick of Bugs always winning their contests. Nevertheless, that wascally wabbit follows him everywhere—even in his dreams. It's a riot. So is Clampett's "The Old Grey Hare," in which aged versions of the animated antagonists reminisce over their years of combat. Good, too, are Friz Freleng's "Slick Hare," in which tough-guy Humphrey Bogart demands a rabbit dinner from restaurateur Elmer, and "Stage Door Cartoon." Clampett's "Wabbit Twouble," which features an early, chubbier version of Elmer, and Tex Avery's seminal "Wild Hare," generally considered the first bona-fide Bugs cartoon, are more interesting for their historical significance than their laugh quota. It all adds up to a first-class collection.

1940–1946 54 minutes

BUGS BUNNY/ROAD RUNNER MOVIE, THE

★★★★

DIRECTORS: Chuck Jones, Phil Monroe

CAST: Animated

Classic cartoons made by Chuck Jones for Warner Bros. are interwoven into this laugh fest; the first and best of the 1970s and '80s feature-length compilations. Includes such winners as "Duck Amuck" and "What's Opera, Doc?" Rated G.

1979 92 minutes

BUGS BUNNY'S WACKY ADVENTURES

★★★★

DIRECTORS: Friz Freleng, Chuck Jones

CAST: Animated

Warner Home Video pulled out all the stops on its Golden Jubilee 14-Karat Collection, and this release featuring that wascally wabbit is one of the best. Included are such Chuck Jones–directed classics as "Duck! Rabbit! Duck!," "Ali Baba Bunny," "Bunny Hugged," and "Long-Haired Hare." The package also includes Friz Freleng's "Hare Do," "Roman Legion Hare," and "The Grey Hounded Hare." This is cartoon fun for all ages.

1985 59 minutes

BUGSY MALONE

★★★½

DIRECTOR: Alan Parker

CAST: Scott Baio, Florrie Augger, Jodie Foster, John Cassisi, Martin Lev

The 1920s gangsters weren't really as cute as these children, who run around shooting whipping cream out of their pistols. But if you can forget that, this British musical provides light diversion. Rated G.

1976 93 minutes

C.H.O.M.P.S.

★★

DIRECTOR: Don Chaffey

CAST: Wesley Eure, Valerie Bertinelli, Conrad Bain, Chuck McCann, Red Buttons, Jim Backus

A small-town enterprise is saved from bankruptcy when a young engineer (Wesley Eure) designs a computer-controlled watchdog. *C.H.O.M.P.S*, which stands for *C*anine *HOM*e *P*rotection *S*ystem, has a lot of the absurdity of a cartoon (Joseph Barbera, of Hanna-Barbera fame, conceived and produced the film). And while a little terrier knocking over a speeding van is acceptable in animation, it does nothing for the viewer's suspension of disbelief in this outing. Kids under twelve may enjoy it, but the profanity thrown in for the PG rating is purely gratuitous.

1979 90 minutes

CANDLESHOE

★★½

DIRECTOR: Norman Tokar

CAST: David Niven, Helen Hayes, Jodie Foster, Leo McKern, Vivian Pickles

Confused Disney comedy about a street kid (Jodie Foster) duped by shady Leo McKern into posing as an heir to Helen Hayes. All the better to swipe your estate, my dear. David Niven is an identity-laden butler whose smugness, for once, becomes tiresome. Marred by typically excessive Disney physical "humor" (read: slapstick). Average for younger folks. Rated G.

1977 101 minutes

CARE BEARS MOVIE, THE

★★★

DIRECTOR: Aran Selznick

CAST: Mickey Rooney, Georgia Engel (voices)

Poor animation mars this children's movie about bears who cheer up a pair of kids. However, the music of John Sebastian keeps things hopping along, and adults don't have to worry about letting the kiddies watch it (unless they can't afford to buy the stuffed versions of the title characters). Rated G, no objectionable material.

1985 80 minutes

CASEY AT THE BAT

★★½

DIRECTOR: David Steinberg

CAST: Elliott Gould, Bill Macy, Hamilton Camp, Carol Kane, Howard Cosell

One of Shelley Duvall's *Tall Tales and Legends*. Howard Cosell narrates this embellishment of the Casey legend, with Elliott Gould's Casey as the father of baseball and Hamilton Camp as Boss Undercrawl, the evil landowner out to destroy the national pastime. Carol Kane is Casey's loving fiancée, and Bill Macy is the man behind Casey's confidence. Fairly imaginative.

1986 52 minutes

CASEY'S SHADOW

★★½

DIRECTOR: Martin Ritt

CAST: Walter Matthau, Alexis Smith, Robert Webber, Murray Hamilton

Only the droll playing of star Walter Matthau makes this family film watchable. Matthau is a horse trainer deserted by his wife and left to raise three sons. It lopes along at a slow pace, and only the star's fans will want to ride it out. Rated PG.

1978 116 minutes

CASTAWAY COWBOY, THE

★★★½

DIRECTOR: Vincent McEveety
CAST: James Garner, Vera Miles, Robert Culp, Eric Shea

James Garner plays a Texas cowboy in Hawaii during the 1850s. There he helps a lovely widow (Vera Miles) start a cattle ranch despite problems created by a land-grabbing enemy (played by Robert Culp). Good family entertainment. Rated G.

1974 91 minutes

CAT FROM OUTER SPACE, THE

★★½

DIRECTOR: Norman Tokar
CAST: Ken Berry, Sandy Duncan, Harry Morgan, Roddy McDowall

Disney comedy/sci-fi about a cat from outer space with a magical collar. The cat needs United States help to return to its planet. Rated G.

1978 103 minutes

CHALLENGE TO BE FREE

★★

DIRECTORS: Tay Garnett, Ford Beebe
CAST: Mike Mazurki, Vic Christy, Jimmy Kane, Fritz Ford

Originally entitled *Mad Trapper of the Yukon*, this forgettable film features a fur trapper being chased across one thousand miles of frozen Arctic wasteland by twelve men and one hundred dogs. Resort to this one only when desperate! Rated G.

1974 88 minutes

CHARLIE AND THE ANGEL

★★

DIRECTOR: Vincent McEveety
CAST: Fred MacMurray, Cloris Leachman, Harry Morgan, Kurt Russell, Vincent Van Patten, Kathleen Cody

Time-worn plot about a guardian angel who teaches an exacting man (Fred MacMurray) a few lessons in kindness and humility before his time on Earth is up is reminiscent of many better, more sincere films. Harry Morgan is okay as the angel, and the rest of the cast is competent enough, but one gets the impression that everyone is just going through the motions in this lesser effort from Walt Disney Productions. The kids won't mind, but chances are you've seen a better version already.

1973 93 minutes

CHARLIE, THE LONESOME COUGAR

★★★

DIRECTOR: Not Credited
CAST: Ron Brown, Brian Russell, Linda Wallace, Jim Wilson, Rex Allen (narrator)

A misunderstood cougar comes into a lumber camp in search of food and companionship. After adopting the animal, the men are not certain whether it will adapt back to its wild habitat, or even if they want it to. This entertaining Disney animal film is more believable than the storyline would suggest. Rated G.

1968 75 minutes

CHARLOTTE'S WEB

★★

DIRECTORS: Charles A. Nichols, Iwao Takamoto
CAST: Debbie Reynolds, Paul Lynde, Henry Gibson (voices)

Absolutely wretched adaptation of E. B. White's beloved children's book. Charlotte the spider, Wilbur the pig, and Templeton the rat lose all their charm and turn into simpering participants in a vacuous musical. Blocky animation, typical of Hanna-Barbera's Saturday-morning drivel, and insipid songs. Only for those under age four. Rated G.

1973 85 minutes

CHIPMUNK ADVENTURE, THE

★★

DIRECTOR: Janice Karman
CAST: Animated

Alvin, Simon, and Theodore go on a round-the-world adventure in this uninspired feature-length cartoon. Ross Bagdasarian Jr. took over the chipmunks and allowed them to be redesigned by someone named Sandra. They look awfully cute—as do their new female counterparts, the Chipettes. Of course, what made the original, scruffy chipmunks so appealing is missing, replaced by a sort of ersatz Disney plot about jewel-smuggling villains. The kids may get a kick out of this, but anyone over the age of nine is advised to find something else to do. Rated G.

1987 76 minutes

CHITTY CHITTY BANG BANG

★★½

DIRECTOR: Ken Hughes
CAST: Dick Van Dyke, Sally Ann Howes, Anna Quayle, Lionel Jeffries, Benny Hill

This musical extravaganza, based on a book by Ian Fleming, is aimed at a children's audience. In it, a car flies, but the flat jokes and songs leave adult viewers a bit seasick as they hope for a quick finale. However, the kiddies will like it. Rated G.

1968 142 minutes

CHRISTMAS CAROL, A

★★★★★

DIRECTOR: Brian Desmond Hurst
CAST: Alastair Sim, Kathleen Harrison, Jack Warner, Michael Hordern

Starring Alastair Sim as Ebenezer Scrooge, the meanest miser in all of London, this is a wondrously uplifting story—as only Charles Dickens could craft one. Recommended for the whole family, *A Christmas Carol* is sure to bring a tear to your eye and joy to your heart.

1951 B & W 86 minutes

CHRISTMAS STORY, A

★★★★

DIRECTOR: Bob Clark
CAST: Peter Billingsley, Darren McGavin, Melinda Dillon, Ian Petrella

Both heartwarming and hilarious, this is humorist Jean Shepherd's wacky recollections of being a kid in the 1940s and the monumental Christmas that brought the ultimate longing—for a regulation Red Ryder air rifle. Problem is, his parents don't think it's such a good idea. But our hero isn't about to give up. Peter Billingsley is marvelous as the kid. Melinda Dillon (*Close Encounters of the Third Kind*) and Darren McGavin also shine as the put-upon parents. A delight for young and old.

1983 98 minutes

CINDERELLA

★★★★

DIRECTOR: Mark Cullingham
CAST: Jennifer Beals, Matthew Broderick, Jean Stapleton, Eve Arden, Jane Alden, Edie McClurg

This is one of the most entertaining of producer Shelley Duvall's Faerie Tale Theatre entries. Jennifer Beals is a shy, considerate, and absolutely gorgeous Cinderella; Matthew Broderick does his aw-shucks best as the smitten Prince Henry. The dialogue is wonderful: "It's hard to be anonymous when your face is on all the money," Henry confesses. Nicely wacky Fairy Godmother by Jean Stapleton, and delightfully shrewish stepmother and stepdaughters by Eve Arden, Jane Alden, and Edie McClurg. Sweetly romantic, a treat for all. Unrated—family fare.

1985 60 minutes

COLD RIVER

★★★★

DIRECTOR: Fred G. Sullivan
CAST: Suzanna Weber, Pete Teterson, Richard Jaeckel

In the autumn of 1932, an experienced guide takes his 14-year-old daughter and his 12-year-old stepson on an extended camping trip. Far out in the wilderness, the father dies of a heart attack, and the children must survive a blizzard, starvation, and an encounter with a wild mountain man. This wonderful family movie is rated PG but should be seen by all.

1981 94 minutes

COMPUTER WORE TENNIS SHOES, THE

★★

DIRECTOR: Robert Butler
CAST: Kurt Russell, Cesar Romero, Joe Flynn, William Schallert

In the late 1960s and early 1970s, it was the practice of the Disney Studios to produce and distribute low-budget comedies at the beginning of each year. Medfield College was often the locale. This was the first production to star Kurt Russell in the college comedies, after Fred MacMurray (*The Absent-Minded Professor* and *Son of Flubber*) and Tommy Kirk left the fold. The flimsy premise is that a student accidentally becomes a genius after being short-circuited with a computer. The movie is weak, with the "excitement" provided by a group of mobsters and gamblers which attempts to use the student for its nefarious purposes. Not rated.

1969 87 minutes

CONDORMAN

★½

DIRECTOR: Charles Jarrot
CAST: Michael Crawford, Oliver Reed, James Hampton, Barbara Carrera

This Disney film has everything you've ever seen in a spy film—but it was better the first time. A comic book writer (Michael Crawford) gets his chance to become a spy when he goes after a beautiful Russian defector (Barbara Carrera). Despite all the ridiculous gadgetry and car wrecks, there's very little excitement to the action, and even less humor. The best thing that can be said is that it's a watchable film that you can show your kids. Rated PG.

1981 90 minutes

DAFFY DUCK: THE NUTTINESS CONTINUES

★★★★½

DIRECTORS: Tex Avery, Bob Clampett, Chuck Jones
CAST: Animated

Chuck Jones's superb "Duck Amuck," in which the vain and selfish Daffy Duck gets more than his just deserts from an animated witch with a rather wicked sense of humor, is but one of many treats in this absolutely first-rate cartoon collection. Real Warner Bros. buffs will be delighted by the inclusion of Bob Clampett's "The Daffy Doc" and Tex Avery's "Porky's Duck Hunt," two classic black-and-white cartoons by the men who shaped and defined the studio's most enduring characters. Jones equals them in every respect with his clever and hilarious "Rabbit Fire!," "Deduce You Say" (with Daffy as Dorlock Homes), "Beanstalk Bunny" (with Daffy as a rude and rather greedy Jack), "Drip-Along Daffy," and "The Scarlet Pumpernickle." Uproarious fun.

1985 59 minutes

DAFFY DUCK CARTOON FESTIVAL

★★★½

DIRECTORS: Bob Clampett, Friz Freleng, Chuck Jones, Robert McKimson

CAST: Animated

A perfect companion to Warner Bros. "*Daffy Duck: The Nuttiness Continues.*" Featured are some prime 1940s cartoons directed by Bob Clampett, Chuck Jones, Friz Freleng, and Robert McKimson. The titles include: "Ain't That Ducky," "Daffy Duck Slept Here," "Conrad the Sailor," "Hollywood Daffy," and "The Wise Quacking Duck."

1986 35 minutes

DAFFY DUCK'S MOVIE: FANTASTIC ISLAND

★★

DIRECTOR: Friz Freleng

CAST: Animated

This pedestrian compilation is for Warner Brothers cartoon fanatics and toddlers only. Chunks of fairly funny shorts are strung together with a weak, dated parody of TV's *Fantasy Island.* Daffy deserved better. Rated G.

1983 78 minutes

DANCING PRINCESSES, THE

★★★★

DIRECTOR: Peter Medak

CAST: Lesley Ann Warren, Peter Weller, Roy Dotrice

This enchanting *Faerie Tale Theatre* production features Roy Dotrice as an overprotective king who locks his daughters in their room each night. When the shoe cobbler insists the princesses are wearing out a pair of dancing slippers each day, the king offers one of his daughters to any man who can discover where the girls go each night. Lesley Ann Warren plays the eldest and cleverest princess, Janetta. Peter Weller is the dashing soldier who discovers their secret. There is a wonderful absence of violence in this charming tale, which is suitable for the entire family.

1984 50 minutes

DANNY

★★★

DIRECTOR: Gene Feldman

CAST: Rebecca Page, Janet Zarish, Barbara Jean Ehrhardt, George Luce, Gloria Maddox, Michael Coerver

A warm, touching, predictable story of an unhappy little girl who obtains a horse that has been injured and then sold off by the spoiled daughter of the wealthy stable owners. A fine family film. Rated G.

1977 90 minutes

DARBY O'GILL AND THE LITTLE PEOPLE

★★★½

DIRECTOR: Robert Stevenson

CAST: Albert Sharpe, Janet Munro, Sean Connery, Jimmy O'Dea

Darby O'Gill is an Irish storyteller who becomes involved with some of the very things he talks about, namely leprechauns, the banshee, and other Irish folk characters. Darby tricks the leprechaun king into granting him three wishes but soon regrets his trickery. This wonderful tale is one of Disney's best films and a delightful fantasy film in its own right. It features a young and relatively unknown Sean Connery as Darby's future son-in-law.

1959 93 minutes

DAVY CROCKETT AND THE RIVER PIRATES

★★★

DIRECTOR: Norman Foster
CAST: Fess Parker, Buddy Ebsen, Kenneth Tobey, Jeff York

Fess Parker, as idealized Davy Crockett, takes on Big Mike Fink (Jeff York) in a keelboat race and tangles with Indians in the second Walt Disney–produced Davy Crockett feature composed of two television episodes. Thoroughly enjoyable and full of the kind of boyhood images that Disney productions evoked so successfully in the late 1940s and '50s. Fun for the whole family.

1956 81 minutes

DAVY CROCKETT (KING OF THE WILD FRONTIER)

★★★½

DIRECTOR: Norman Foster
CAST: Fess Parker, Buddy Ebsen, Hans Conried, Kenneth Tobey

One of Walt Disney's most unexpected surprises of the 1950s was this colorful, history-bending saga of frontier hero Davy Crockett and his irascible but capable sidekick, Georgie Russell, and their adventures in the early part of the nineteenth century. Finely played by all involved, this is actually a compilation of three episodes that appeared originally on television and were then released theatrically. Davy's journeys take him to the swamps of the South, where he fights Indians and helps restore peace; to the halls of Congress, where he fights politicians and tries to restore peace. His last and most famous journey is, of course, to Texas and the Alamo mission where he and the other gallant defenders laid down their lives for their land and their beliefs, joined by that other frontier legend, Jim Bowie (ruggedly played by Kenneth Tobey). Fine family fare.

1955 88 minutes

DAYDREAMER, THE

★★★

DIRECTOR: Jules Bass
CAST: Paul O'Keefe, Burl Ives, Tallulah Bankhead, Terry-Thomas, Victor Borge, Ed Wynn, Patty Duke, Boris Karloff, Ray Bolger, Hayley Mills, Jack Gilford, Margaret Hamilton

This "Children's Treasure" presentation combines live action with puppetry to bring a young Hans Christian Andersen and his tales to life. Paul O'Keefe plays the young Andersen and Jack Gilford plays his shoemaker father. Young Andersen prefers daydreaming to his studies as he takes us with him into his fantasy world. In "The Little Mermaid," Hayley Mills provides the voice for the generous mermaid who saves his life. Burl Ives is her Father. Next, young Chris Andersen becomes an apprentice to two shady tailors in "The Emperor's New Clothes." Finally, Patty Duke gives voice to Thumbelina and Boris Karloff speaks for the evil Rat who captures Chris and Thumbelina. The characters occasionally burst into song to convey their feelings but not so much as to intrude on the story.

1966 80 minutes

DIRT BIKE KID, THE

DIRECTOR: Hoite C. Caston
CAST: Peter Billingsley, Stuart Pankin, Anne Bloom, Patrick Collins, Sage Parker, Danny Breen, Chad Sheets

A ridiculous story about a boy who buys an old dirt bike that turns out to have a life of its own.

The tale soon becomes a contrived adventure as people try to steal, wreck, own, or control the motorcycle. All the characters are cardboard cutouts: nasty bikers, a crooked bank president, and childern who are vulgar and rude. The family life of the main character is almost a direct ripoff of *E.T.* (divorced mother and fatherless child trying to make ends meet). This film even goes so far as to have the bike fly the boy across the moon and starscape. Youngsters may like this film but almost everyone else will absolutely hate it. Rated PG for vulgarity.

1985 91 minutes

DOCTOR DOLITTLE

★★½

DIRECTOR: Richard Fleischer
CAST: Rex Harrison, Samantha Eggar, Anthony Newley, Richard Attenborough

Rex Harrison plays the title role in this children's tale, about a man who finds more satisfaction being around animals than people. Children may find this film amusing, but for the most part, the acting is weak, and any real script is nonexistent. This film almost broke Fox Studios, even though it did gain an Oscar nomination for best picture.

1967 152 minutes

DR. SYN, ALIAS THE SCARECROW

★★½

DIRECTOR: James Neilson
CAST: Patrick McGoohan, George Cole, Tony Britton, Geoffrey Keen, Kay Walsh

Showcased in America as a three-part television program in 1964, this colorful tale of a man who poses as a minister by day and a champion of the oppressed by night is a variation on Disney's popular *Zorro* show of the late 1950s. Patrick McGoohan brings style and substance to the legendary Dr. Syn, a role essayed in 1937 by George Arliss and again in 1962 by Peter Cushing in *Night Creatures* (although Cushing's minister hid his secret identity as a former pirate and rum runner). A bit long but fun viewing for the entire family. Originally released as a feature in Europe in 1962.

1962 129 minutes

DOG OF FLANDERS, A

★★★★

DIRECTOR: James B. Clark
CAST: David Ladd, Donald Crisp, Theodore Bikel

Ouida's world-famous 1872 tear-jerking novel about a boy and his dog and their devotion to each other tastefully filmed in its European locale. Nello (David Ladd) delivers milk from a cart pulled by the dog Patrasche. Donald Crisp and Theodore Bikel shine in character roles, but the picture belongs to Ladd and the scene-stealing mutt fans will recall from *Old Yeller*. Have Kleenex handy.

1960 96 minutes

DUMBO

★★★★

DIRECTOR: Ben Sharpstein
CAST: Animated

Disney's cartoon favorite about the outcast circus elephant with the big ears is a family classic. It has everything: personable animals, a poignant story, and a happy ending. It is good fun and can still invoke a tear or two in the right places.

1941 64 minutes

DUSTY

★★★

DIRECTOR: John Richardson
CAST: Bill Kerr, Noel Trevarthen, Carol Burns, Nicholas Holland, John Stanton

An emotional story of a retired, lonely shepherd in Australia who is adopted by Dusty, a stray sheepdog of undetermined breeding. Dusty yields to the call of the hunt and is sentenced to death by local ranchers.

1985 89 minutes

ELMER FUDD CARTOON FESTIVAL

★★★½

DIRECTORS: Bob Clampett, Friz Freleng, Chuck Jones

CAST: Animated

This is an enjoyable collection of the Warner Bros. Studio's pre-1947 cartoons. Mr. Fudd (whose voice is supplied by Arthur Q. Bryan, not Mel Blanc) is featured in Bob Clampett's "An Itch in Time," Friz Freleng's "The Hardship of Miles Standish," Chuck Jones's "Elmer's Pet Rabbit" (an early Bugs Bunny), and —the collection's real classic— Freleng's "Back Alley Oproar" in which a pesky Sylvester the Cat serenades a sleepy, frustrated Elmer to the point of all-out war.

1940s 33 minutes

ELMER FUDD'S COMEDY CAPERS

★★★★

DIRECTORS: Friz Freleng, Chuck Jones, Robert McKimson

CAST: Animated

An outstanding collection of Warner Bros. cartoons, this set is highlighted by a quartet of Chuck Jones gems: "The Rabbit of Seville," a spoof of Rossini's opera; "Bugs' Bonnets," in which Bugs and Elmer undergo a personality change as they switch from one hat to another; "What's Opera, Doc?," the classic cartoon version of the Wagnerian opera, *Ride of the Valkyries*; and "Rabbit Seasoning," in which Daffy Duck joins the duo for some "pronoun trouble" and genuine belly laughs. Rounding out the program are "Hare Brush" (Friz Freleng), "What's Up, Doc?" (Robert McKimson), "Design for Leaving" (McKimson), and a Chuck Jones ditty, "Cat Feud," featuring Marc Anthony, the dog, and two cats, Claude and Pussyfoot.

1950–1957 57 minutes

EMIL AND THE DETECTIVES

★★★½

DIRECTOR: Peter Tewksbury

CAST: Roger Moseby, Walter Slezak, Bryan Russell, Heinz Schubert

Another of the excellent live-action adventures made by the Disney Studios in the early 1960s, this grand little tale follows the escapades of a young boy who hires a gang of young, amateur sleuths after he's been robbed. Wholly improbable, but neatly constructed from the classic children's novel by Erich Kastner. The premise is impossible to resist, and the talented cast makes it work. Perfect for the entire family.

1964 99 minutes

ENCHANTED FOREST, THE

★★★

DIRECTOR: Lew Landers

CAST: Edmund Lowe, Harry Davenport, Brenda Joyce, Billy Severn, John Litel

Pleasant fantasy about an old hermit who teaches a young boy to love the forest and its creatures is one of the best films to come out of bargain-basement PRC Films as well as being the best surviving example of the Cinecolor process. Veteran actors Edmund Lowe and Harry Davenport provide the solid support this simple story needs, and Billy Severn as the lost boy is engaging. This long-neglected little gem lacks a big-studio budget but is fine family fare.

1945 77 minutes

ESCAPADE IN FLORENCE

★½

DIRECTOR: Steve Previn

CAST: Ivan Desny, Tommy Kirk, Annette Alliotto, Nino Castelnuovo

Uninspired story about two young men and their misadventures in picturesque Italy contains the obligatory chases and seemingly perilous situations that seem to be a prerequisite for movies about art theft and forgery. Walt Disney star Tommy Kirk is pleasant enough, but this film is routine. Too bad Tommy Kirk didn't have Annette Funicello along on this one.

1962 80 minutes

ESCAPADE IN JAPAN

★★★½

DIRECTOR: Arthur Lubin

CAST: Jon Provost, Roger Nakagawa, Cameron Mitchell, Teresa Wright

Little Jon Provost, his friend Roger Nakagawa, and Japan itself are the stars of this charming film about a young boy who survives an airplane crash in Japan and is taken in by a family of isolated fishers. The American boy and his Japanese counterpart misinterpret attempts by police to locate the missing boy, and the two decide to run away. Their wanderings provide us with a loving portrait of the country and a vibrant sense of metropolitan Japan. This is one of the all-time best kids-on-the-run films.

1957 93 minutes

ESCAPE ARTIST, THE

★★

DIRECTOR: Caleb Deschanel

CAST: Griffin O'Neal, Raul Julia, Teri Garr, Joan Hackett, Desi Arnaz Sr.

Annoying little adventure film from producer Francis Ford Coppola which feels like it was re-edited and dumped on the market. Confusing, rambling account of a boy (Griffin O'Neal, who might be appealing with better material) who uses a love of magic and escape artistry to frame the city politicos responsible for killing his father. What's left makes little sense, although it is composed beautifully by Caleb Deschanel, better known for *The Black Stallion*. Don't expect much. Rated PG—mild violence and profanity.

1982 96 minutes

ESCAPE TO WITCH MOUNTAIN

★★★½

DIRECTOR: John Hough

CAST: Eddie Albert, Ray Milland, Kim Richards, Ike Eisenmann

In this engaging Disney mystery/fantasy, two children with strange powers are pursued by men who want to use them for evil purposes. It's good! Rated G.

1975 97 minutes

FATTY FINN

★★★

DIRECTOR: Maurice Murphy

CAST: Ben Oxenbould, Bert Newton, Noni Haglehurst

This film seems to borrow from the Little Rascals comedy series. In it, young Fatty Finn is desperately trying to earn money to buy a radio. But every time he tries, the neighborhood bully and his gang sabotage Fatty's efforts. The happy ending makes up for all the hardships 10-year-old Fatty has endured along the way.

1984 91 minutes

FIGHTING PRINCE OF DONEGAL, THE

★★½

DIRECTOR: Michael O'Herlihy

CAST: Peter McEnery, Susan Hampshire, Tom Adams, Gordon Jackson

A rousing adventure-action film set in sixteenth-century Ireland. When Peter McEnery succeeds to the title of Prince of Donegal, the Irish clans are ready to fight English troops to make Ireland free. McEnery convinces them to let him try and negotiate a treaty first. He is captured, imprisoned, and tortured, but finally escapes to lead the Irish clans in defeating the English and rescuing his castle, lady love, and country's freedom. This is a Disney British endeavor that is often overlooked but definitely worth watching.

1966 110 minutes

FLIGHT OF DRAGONS, THE

★★★

DIRECTORS: Arthur Rankin Jr., Jules Bass

CAST: Animated

This animated film features a modern young man named Peter (John Ritter's voice) called back in time to stop the evil Red Wizard. There are plenty of dragons around, but the real problem is the Red Crown of Ommadon—with the power to destroy nature. As long as it's in the Red Wizard's possession, the world is not safe. The animation isn't the greatest, but children under twelve should still be entertained by it.

1982 98 minutes

FOGHORN LEGHORN'S FRACTURED FUNNIES

★★★½

DIRECTOR: Robert McKimson

CAST: Animated

Warner Bros. director Robert McKimson made some hilarious Bugs Bunny, Daffy Duck, and Porky Pig cartoons, but his best work was to be found in a series that featured a cantankerous country rooster and a young Hawk with the mannerisms of a big-city kid. Lest we forget, Foghorn's nemesis, the barnyard dog, provides his share of chuckles as well. The earliest of these minor animation classics is "The Foghorn Leghorn" (1948), in which Henery Hawk and his dad encounter the "loud-mouthed schnook" for the first time. Other titles include: "Lovelorn Leghorn," "Plop Goes the Weasel," "The Leghorn Blows at Midnight," "Leghorn Swoggled," "A Fractured Leghorn," and a Claude Cat entry by Chuck Jones, "The Hypochondri-Cat."

1948–1955 58 minutes

FOLLOW ME BOYS!

★★★½

DIRECTOR: Norman Tokar

CAST: Vera Miles, Fred MacMurray, Lillian Gish, Kurt Russell

Heartwarming Disney film in which Fred MacMurray plays the new Boy Scout leader in a small 1930s town.

1966 131 minutes

FOR THE LOVE OF BENJI

★★★½

DIRECTOR: Joe Camp

CAST: Benji, Patsy Garrett, Cynthia Smith, Allen Fuizat, Ed Nelson

The adorable mutt cleverly saves the day again when he takes on a spy ring in Athens. Ed Nelson plays the villain who attaches microfilm to Benji's paw. As in all Benji flicks, the rest of the cast plays second string to his darling and daring antics. The whole family can enjoy this one together. Rated G.

1977 85 minutes

FREAKY FRIDAY

★★★½

DIRECTOR: Gary Nelson

CAST: Jodie Foster, Barbara Harris, John Astin, Ruth Buzzi, Kaye Ballard

One of Disney's better comedies from the 1970s, this perceptive fantasy allows mom Barbara Harris and daughter Jodie Foster to share a role-reversing out-of-body experience. Harris, due to her experience, does better mixing with school traumas than Foster does figuring out how to wash clothes and cook dinners. Husband/father John Astin has a lot of fun trying to make sense of the situation. Adapted with wit by Mary Rodgers from her own book. This is a good family conversation-starter, although such lofty intentions are nearly sabotaged by the slapstick conclusion. Rated G.

1977 95 minutes

FUN AND FANCY FREE

★★★½

DIRECTOR: Walt Disney
CAST: Edgar Bergen, Charlie McCarthy, Mortimer Snerd, Luana Patten, Dinah Shore

The first segment of this Disney feature is the story of Bongo, a circus bear who runs off into the forest and falls for a female bear. It's a moderately entertaining tale. When Edgar Bergen narrates the clever version of "Jack and the Beanstalk," pitting Mickey, Donald, and Goofy against Willie the Giant, things pick up considerably. Although *Fun and Fancy Free* certainly isn't one of Disney's classic features, it will keep the kids amused.

1947 96 minutes

GIRL WHO SPELLED FREEDOM, THE

★★★★½

DIRECTOR: Simon Wincer
CAST: Wayne Rogers, Mary Kay Place, Jade Chinn, Kathleen Sisk

Disney does an excellent job of adapting the Yann family's true story, dramatizing their flight from Cambodia to find refuge with a Tennessee family. The story concentrates on little Linn Yann's struggle to learn English and to succeed in America. Jade Chinn is darling as the determined Linn. Wayne Rogers plays the ever-optimistic sponsor opposite his, at first, apprehensive wife (Mary Kay Place). Made for TV, this fine film is unrated.

1985 90 minutes

GNOME-MOBILE, THE

★★½

DIRECTOR: Robert Stevenson
CAST: Walter Brennan, Ed Wynn, Mathew Garber, Karen Dotrice

This one is kid city. From Disney, of course. Walter Brennan doubles as a wealthy businessman and a gnome who must find a wife for his grandson-gnome. The Gnome-Mobile is one fancy Rolls-Royce.

1967 104 minutes

GOLDEN SEAL, THE

★★★½

DIRECTOR: Frank Zuniga
CAST: Torquil Campbell, Steven Railsback, Penelope Milford

A young boy (Torquil Campbell) living with his parents (Steven Railsback and Penelope Milford) on the Aleutian Islands makes friends with a rare golden seal and her pup, and tries to protect them from fur hunters. It's a good story, predictably told. Rated PG.

1983 95 minutes

GOLDILOCKS AND THE THREE BEARS

★

DIRECTOR: Gilbert Cates
CAST: Tatum O'Neal, Hoyt Axton, Alex Karras, John Lithgow, Brandis Kemp, Carole King, Donovan Scott

Although it features a well-known and talented cast, this Faerie Tale Theatre production is a lifeless adaptation of the story about a little girl who trespasses into the home of three bears and creates havoc. Its attempts at humor fall flat. In addition, the characters are hardly memorable, with the bears being too nerdish and Goldilocks far from lovable. Read the story to your child instead.

1982 51 minutes

GREAT LOCOMOTIVE CHASE, THE

★★★½

DIRECTOR: Francis D. Lyon

CAST: Fess Parker, Jeffrey Hunter, Jeff York, John Lupton

This film is the true story of Andrew's Raiders during the Civil War. Fess Parker and his band of spies infiltrate the South and abscond with a railroad train. Jeffrey Hunter is the conductor who chases them to regain possession of the train. This is a straightforward telling of the events, emphasizing action and suspense. All cast members fit their roles except for Jeff York, who is woefully out of character as a spy. Buster Keaton told the story comically in his *The General*, but this version is very effective on its own.

1956 85 minutes

GREAT MUPPET CAPER, THE

★★★★

DIRECTOR: Jim Henson

CAST: Muppets, Diana Rigg, Charles Grodin, Peter Falk, Peter Ustinov, Jack Warden, Robert Morley

Miss Piggy, Kermit the Frog, Fozzie Bear, and the Great Gonzo attempt to solve the mysterious theft of the fabulous Baseball Diamond in this, the second feature-length motion picture Muppet outing. From the disarmingly funny opening credits to its gangbusters conclusion, this film, directed by Muppet creator Jim Henson, is a significant improvement over *The Muppet Movie*, which was pretty darn good to begin with. Rated G.

1981 95 minutes

GREENSTONE, THE

★★★

DIRECTOR: Kevin Irvine

CAST: Joseph Corey, John Riley, Kathleen Irvine, Jack Mauck

A young boy and his family live on the edge of an enchanted forest. But the forest and the Greenstone inside call to the young boy. Despite his family's warnings, he goes into the forest and finds the stone, which transports him to a magical fantasy world. A good family film for all ages. Rated G.

1985 48 minutes

GREYFRIARS BOBBY

★★★

DIRECTOR: Don Chaffey

CAST: Donald Crisp, Laurence Naismith, Alex Mackenzie, Kay Walsh

Somewhat lethargic tale of a dog that is befriended by an entire town after his owner dies. The plot drags, but the cast and the atmosphere of the settings make it worth watching. A Disney British import.

1961 91 minutes

GULLIVER'S TRAVELS

★★½

DIRECTOR: Dave Fleischer

CAST: Lanny Ross and Jessica Dragonette (voices)

Made and issued as an answer to Disney's *Snow White and the Seven Dwarfs*, this full-length cartoon of the famous Jonathan Swift satire about an English sailor who falls among tiny people in a land called Lilliput is just so-so. Strictly for kids.

1939 74 minutes

GUS

★★★½

DIRECTOR: Vincent McEveety

CAST: Edward Asner, Don Knotts, Gary Grimes, Dick Van Patten

This Disney comedy has a mule named Gus delivering the winning kicks for a losing football team. Naturally, the rival team kidnaps the mule before the big game, and the search is on. Lots of slapstick comedy for the kids to enjoy in this one. Rated G.

1976 96 minutes

HANS BRINKER

★★★

DIRECTOR: Robert Scheerer

CAST: Robin Askwith, Eleanor Parker, Richard Basehart, Roberta Torey, John Gregson, Cyril Ritchard

This is the well-known tale of Hans Brinker and his silver skates. Made this time as a musical, it stars Robin Askwith as Hans with Eleanor Parker and Richard Basehart as his mother and invalid father. Cyril Ritchard has a cameo musical number, and there are some pleasant skating sequences. This film would make particularly good family viewing for the holidays. It is not rated, but would be considered a G.

1979 103 minutes

HANSEL AND GRETEL

★★★

DIRECTOR: James Frawley

CAST: Joan Collins, Ricky Schroder, Paul Dooley, Bridgette Anderson

Joan Collins is a perfectly wicked stepmother-cum-witch in this *Faerie Tale Theatre* production of the classic tale of two children (Ricky Schroder and Bridgette Anderson) who learn a valuable lesson when they take candy from a stranger.

1982 51 minutes

HAPPIEST MILLIONAIRE, THE

★★★

DIRECTOR: Norman Tokar

CAST: Fred MacMurray, Tommy Steele, Greer Garson, Geraldine Page, Gladys Cooper

The Disney version of a factual memoir of life in the Philadelphia household of eccentric millionaire Anthony J. Drexel Biddle. Lively light entertainment that hops along between musical numbers.

1967 118 minutes

HEARTBEEPS

★★★

DIRECTOR: Alan Arkush

CAST: Andy Kaufman, Bernadette Peters, Dennis Quaid

Andy Kaufman and Bernadette Peters play robots who fall in love, leave a factory, and decide to explore the world around them. It's a good family film by director Alan Arkush, and the kids will probably love it. Rated PG.

1981 79 minutes

HEATHCLIFF—THE MOVIE

★

DIRECTOR: Bruno Bianchi

CAST: Animated

An example of everything that is wrong with cartoons today, this release is sloppily drawn, poorly scripted, and generally pointless. What's worse, its main character (whose voice is provided by Mel Blanc) is a mean-spirited cat who likes nothing better than to cause trouble—and this is a children's movie! Rated G.

1986 89 minutes

HEIDI

★★★★

DIRECTOR: Allan Dwan

CAST: Shirley Temple, Jean Hersholt, Arthur Treacher

This classic stars a spunky Shirley Temple as the girl who is taken away from her kind and loving grandfather's home in the Swiss Alps and forced to live with her cruel aunt. Love triumphs when Heidi finds a way to return to her grandfather. Lots of touching scenes, so have plenty of Kleenex on hand. Children will especially love this one.

1937 B & W 88 minutes

HEIDI'S SONG

★½

DIRECTOR: Robert Taylor
CAST: Animated

Only those 5 years old and younger will enjoy this feature-length cartoon adaptation of Johanna Spyri's classic children's tale. The producers, William Hanna and Joseph Barbera, made what many aficionados consider to be the best "Tom and Jerry" shorts for MGM. But they are best known as the creators of *Yogi Bear* and *The Flintstones*, TV shows that ushered in the age of limited (as in cheap and unconvincing) animation. It is the latter style that pervades and—along with a mediocre screenplay and musical score—ultimately ruins *Heidi's Song*. Rated G.

1982 94 minutes

HERBIE GOES BANANAS

★★½

DIRECTOR: Vincent McEveety
CAST: Cloris Leachman, Charles Martin Smith, John Vernon, Stephan W. Burns, Harvey Korman

This is the corniest and least funny of Disney's "Love Bug" series. This time Herbie is headed for Brazil to compete in the Grand Primio. He is waylaid in Panama after a small Mexican boy named Paco is found stowed away in Herbie's trunk. Cloris Leachman plays an eccentric aunt who is willing to bail Herbie out if Herbie's owner will woo her homely, intellectual niece. Rated G.

1980 93 minutes

HERBIE GOES TO MONTE CARLO

★★★½

DIRECTOR: Vincent McEveety
CAST: Dean Jones, Don Knotts, Julie Sommars, Eric Braeden, Roy Kinnear, Jacque Marin

Herbie the VW stars in this Walt Disney comedy. This time he falls in love with a sports car as they compete in a race from Paris to Monte Carlo. Don Knotts plays Herbie's mechanic, and Dean Jones is his owner. Complications arise when jewel thieves hide a $6 million diamond in Herbie's gas tank. Julie Sommars co-stars as Jones's love interest, while Eric Braeden plays his racetrack rival. There are lots of laughs in this one. Rated G.

1977 104 minutes

HERBIE RIDES AGAIN

★★★½

DIRECTOR: Robert Stevenson
CAST: Helen Hayes, Ken Berry, Stephanie Powers, Keenan Wynn

This Disney comedy/adventure is a sequel to *The Love Bug*. This time, Helen Hayes, Ken Berry, and Stephanie Powers depend on Herbie, the magical Volkswagen, to save them from an evil Keenan Wynn. Rated G.

1974 88 minutes

HERE COMES SANTA CLAUS

[turkey symbol]

DIRECTOR: Christian Gion
CAST: Karen Cheryl, Armand Meffre, Little Alexia, Emeric Chapuis

This dud is not even adequate for small children. Two kids visit Santa at the North Pole to make a personal plea for the return of the boy's parents on Christmas. Santa looks all right, but doesn't say

Santa-like things, and gets into some ridiculous situations with African rebels. *Miracle on 34th Street* is safe as the ultimate Christmas movie.

1984 78 minutes

HEY THERE, IT'S YOGI BEAR

★★★

DIRECTORS: William Hanna, Joseph Barbera

CAST: Mel Blanc, J. Pat O'Malley, Julie Bennett, Daws Butler, and Don Messick (voices)

With this movie, Hanna-Barbera Studios made the jump from TV to feature-length cartoon. The result is consistently pleasant. The animation is limited, the songs are forgettable, and the humor is mild, but the characters are likable, and kids under 9 should find the movie quite entertaining. Rated G.

1964 89 minutes

HORSE IN THE GRAY FLANNEL SUIT, THE

★★

DIRECTOR: Norman Tokar

CAST: Dean Jones, Diane Baker, Lloyd Bochner, Fred Clark, Kurt Russell

This Disney film takes you back to America's early awareness of Madison Avenue and the many games and gimmicks it devises to get the almighty dollar. Dean Jones is an ad executive who develops an ad campaign around his daughter's devotion to horses. The gray flannel suit refers to the typical businessman's apparel of the period.

1968 113 minutes

HORSEMASTERS

★★

DIRECTOR: Bill Fairchild

CAST: Annette Funicello, Janet Munro, Tommy Kirk, Donald Pleasence, Tony Britton

Annette and Tommy team up once again in this average story about young Americans pursuing their careers in horse training among the great riding academies of Europe. Shot on location for *Walt Disney Presents*, this two-part episode was released later as a feature. Lots of beautiful horses on display for all the horse fanciers in the audience. Fine character actor Donald Pleasence makes an early film appearance in this one.

1961 77 minutes

HOT LEAD AND COLD FEET

★★

DIRECTOR: Robert Butler

CAST: Jim Dale, Karen Valentine, Don Knotts, Jack Elam, Darren McGavin

This predictable, occasionally funny western stars Jim Dale as twin brothers who are forced to race to determine which will receive their father's legacy of a town; one is a drunk who terrorizes the town and the other a missionary. Darren McGavin schemes to help the drunk win. Karen Valentine befriends the missionary. Don Knotts is the town's inept sheriff, mostly engaged in a feud with Jack Elam. Rated G.

1978 89 minutes

IN SEARCH OF THE CASTAWAYS

★★★★

DIRECTOR: Robert Stevenson

CAST: Hayley Mills, Maurice Chevalier, George Sanders, Wilfrid Hyde-White, Michael Anderson Jr.

Director Robert Stevenson gives a Disney interpretation of this Jules Verne adventure tale. A young Hayley Mills plays the kidnapped daughter of a sea captain (Maurice Chevalier). There are lots of great special effects depicting natural disasters for them to overcome.

1962 100 minutes

INCREDIBLE JOURNEY, THE

★★★★½

DIRECTOR: Fletcher Markle

CAST: Emile Genest, John Drainie

This live-action Walt Disney film, narrated by Rex Allen, is the story of two dogs and a cat that make a treacherous journey across Canada to find their home and family. The distinct personalities given to the Labrador retriever, the bull terrier, and the Siamese cat carry the film, making it a delight for viewers. It's impossible to dislike this heart-warming tale.

1963 80 minutes

INTERNATIONAL VELVET

★★

DIRECTOR: Bryan Forbes

CAST: Tatum O'Neal, Christopher Plummer, Anthony Hopkins

A disappointing sequel to *National Velvet* (1944), with Tatum O'Neal only passable as the young horsewoman who rides to victory. Fine supporting performances by Anthony Hopkins and Christopher Plummer help raise this family film to the level of watchability. Rated PG.

1978 127 minutes

IT'S AN ADVENTURE, CHARLIE BROWN

★★★★

DIRECTOR: Bill Melendez

CAST: Animated

This made-for-television program was the first "Peanuts" special to present short sketches and blackouts taken directly from the material in Charles Schulz's newspaper strip. With no central theme, each segment runs only as long as it needs to. By far the best—and one of the most poignant tales ever constructed within the strip—is "Sack," wherein Charlie Brown goes to summer camp with a bag over his head and becomes a hero. A masterful and entertaining package, in a style that later was used for the Saturday-morning *Charlie Brown and Snoopy Show.* Unrated this is family fare.

1983 50 minutes

JACK AND THE BEANSTALK

★★★

DIRECTOR: Lamont Johnson

CAST: Dennis Christopher, Elliott Gould, Jean Stapleton, Mark Blankfield, Katherine Helmond

This *Faerie Tale Theatre* production sticks more to the original story than most. Katherine Helmond plays Jack's complaining mom. Jean Stapleton plays a kind giantess, while Elliott Gould is a very dumb giant. Jack sells the family cow (named Spot) for five magic beans and manages to acquire great wealth while learning about his past.

1982 60 minutes

JIMMY THE KID

★★

DIRECTOR: Gary Nelson

CAST: Paul Le Mat, Gary Coleman, Cleavon Little, Fay Hauser, Dee Wallace

Paul Le Mat (of *American Graffiti*) leads a band of bungling criminals in an attempt to kidnap the precocious son (Gary Coleman) of some extremely wealthy country-western singers (Cleavon Little and Fay Hauser). To everyone's surprise, Jimmy doesn't mind being kidnapped; in fact, he sort of likes it. Yawn. This is the kind of silly film the Walt Disney studios stopped making. Rated PG.

1983 85 minutes

JOHNNY TREMAIN

★★★½

DIRECTOR: Robert Stevenson
CAST: Hal Stalmaster, Luana Patten, Sebastian Cabot, Richard Beymer

Colorful Walt Disney Revolutionary War entry is a perfect blend of schoolboy heroics and Hollywood history, with young Johnny Tremain an apprentice silversmith caught up in the brewing American Revolution. Heavy on the patriotism, with picture-book tableaus of the Boston Tea Party, Paul Revere's ride, and the battles at Concord. Infectious score throughout.

1957 80 minutes

JOURNEY BACK TO OZ

★★½

DIRECTOR: Hal Sutherland
CAST: Liza Minnelli, Milton Berle, Paul Lynde, Ethel Merman, Mickey Rooney, Danny Thomas (voices)

This cartoon version sequel to *The Wizard of Oz* leaves the Wizard out. The voices of famous stars help maintain adult interest. Ironically, Liza Minnelli plays Dorothy (as her mother did in the original *Oz*). Milton Berle, Paul Lynde, Ethel Merman, Mickey Rooney, and Danny Thomas provide other voices. Rated G.

1974 90 minutes

JOURNEY OF NATTY GANN, THE

★★★★★

DIRECTOR: Jeremy Paul Kagan
CAST: Meredith Salenger, Ray Wise, John Cusack, Lainie Kazan, Scatman Crothers

With this superb film, the Disney Studios returned triumphantly to the genre of family films. It is a wonderful movie for all ages. Not since *E.T.—The Extraterrestrial* has there been such a touching and involving wide-audience movie. Meredith Salenger stars as Natty, a 14-year-old street urchin who must ride the rails from Chicago to Seattle during the Depression to find her father (Ray Wise). Do not miss this one. Rated PG for light violence.

1985 101 minutes

JUNGLE BOOK

★★★★

DIRECTOR: Zoltán Korda
CAST: Sabu, Joseph Calleia, John Qualen

This one's for fantasy fans of all ages. Sabu stars in Rudyard Kipling's tale of a boy raised by wolves in the jungle of India. Beautiful color presentation holds the viewer from start to finish. Rated G.

1942 109 minutes

JUNGLE CAT

★★★★

DIRECTOR: James Algar
CAST: Documentary

This Disney True Life Adventure won the best feature documentary award at the Berlin International Film Festival in 1960. It follows the life of a spotted female jaguar in a South American jungle from her loner, highly territorial days to her courtship, mating, and motherhood with a sleek black jaguar. In addition to the excellent footage of her daily life, we also get an armchair tour of the beautiful rain forests of Brazil and Argentina. We meet the other inhabitants of the jungle: mischievous monkeys, slow-moving sloths, multicolored birds, anteaters, snakes, etc. Fascinating and educational.

1960 69 minutes

KAVIK THE WOLF DOG

★★★

DIRECTOR: Peter Carter
CAST: Ronny Cox, John Ireland, Linda Sorenson, Andrew Ian McMillan, Chris Wiggins

This average made-for-TV movie was originally titled *The Courage of Kavik, The Wolf Dog*. It is the story of Kavik, a brave sled dog who journeys back to the boy he loves when a ruthless, wealthy man transports him from Alaska to Seattle. Defying all odds, the determined canine travels two thousand miles back to his young master. This heartwarming tale is rated G.

1980 104 minutes

KID FROM LEFT FIELD, THE

★★★

DIRECTOR: Adell Aldrich

CAST: Gary Coleman, Tab Hunter, Gary Collins, Ed McMahon

Gary Coleman plays a batboy who leads the San Diego Padres to victory through the advice of his father (a former baseball great). Ed McMahon co-stars in this remake of the 1953 Dan Dailey version. Made for TV.

1979 100 minutes

KID WITH THE 200 I.Q., THE

★★

DIRECTOR: Leslie Martinson

CAST: Gary Coleman, Robert Guillaume, Dean Butler, Kari Michaelson, Harriet Nelson

In this predictable TV movie, Gary Coleman plays a 13-year-old genius who enters college. Academics present no problem. Social life does. It's mildly amusing at best.

1983 96 minutes

KING OF THE GRIZZLIES

★★½

DIRECTOR: Ron Kelly

CAST: Wahb, John Yesno, Chris Wiggins, Hug Webster, Jack Van Evera

Wahb, a grizzly cub, loses his mother and sister to cattlemen protecting their herd. He quickly gets into trouble but is rescued by John Yesño, a Cree Indian. Descended from the Indian Clan of the Bear, Yesno feels a mystical attachment to Wahb and risks his job with the cattlemen to take Wahb to safety. Wahb grows up to be the largest grizzly and eventually returns to wreak havoc on the cattlemen's ranch. Yesno is the only person who can stop him, and he must rely upon that mystical attachment he felt. Average animal adventure film in the Disney mold. Rated G.

1969 93 minutes

LADY AND THE TRAMP

★★★★

DIRECTORS: Hamilton Luske, Clyde Geronimi, Wilfred Jackson

CAST: Animated

One of the sweetest animated tales from the Disney canon, this fantasy concerns a high-bred cocker spaniel (Lady) and the adventures she has with a raffish mongrel stray (The Tramp). While it's not love at first sight, Lady eventually comes around, right about the point they share a plate of spaghetti in the alley behind Tony's Restaurant (while Tony croons "Bella Notte" in the background). All the songs are better than average, with the highlight taking place when Lady is caught and thrown into the dog pound: one of the other "residents" is the tartish Peg (voiced by Peggy Lee), who rumbles through the signature tune, "He's a Tramp." Since Disney originally had the film released in CinemaScope, more attention has been given to the lush backgrounds. Unrated; suitable for family viewing.

1955 75 minutes

LAST FLIGHT OF NOAH'S ARK

★★★

DIRECTOR: Charles Jarrott
CAST: Elliott Gould, Genevieve Bujold, Ricky Schroder, Vincent Gardenia

This is the story of an unemployed pilot (Elliott Gould) who, against his better judgment, agrees to fly a plane full of farm animals to a Pacific island for a young missionary (Genevieve Bujold). The plane, a converted B-29, is forced down by a storm on an out-of-the-way island and Gould, Bujold, and Ricky Schroder are put upon to rescue themselves from the island. This film, while not one of Disney's best, does offer clean, wholesome fun for the younger (and young-at-heart) audience. Rated G.

1980 97 minutes

LEGEND OF LOBO, THE

★★★

DIRECTOR: Not credited
CAST: Documentary

An animal adventure film told from the perspective of Lobo, a wolf, this is one of the excellent nature films produced by Disney in the 1950s and 1960s. The film follows Lobo as he grows from infant to adult, with episodes showing the challenges he must meet along the way—being orphaned, having to battle his way into acceptance with a new pack, and rescuing his mate from a hunter. Although the story is highly fictionalized to create dramatic impact, this is an entertaining film.

1962 67 minutes

LEGEND OF SLEEPY HOLLOW, THE

★★★★

DIRECTORS: Jack Kinney, Clyde Geronimi, James Algar
CAST: Animated

One of the finest of the Disney "novelette" cartoons, this adaptation of the spooky Washington Irving tale is given a properly sepulchral tone by narrator Bing Crosby. Reasonably scary, particularly for small fry, who might get pretty nervous during poor Ichabod Crane's final, fateful ride. The tape includes two cartoon shorts, "Lonesome Ghosts" (1937) and "Trick or Treat" (1952); the former is a classic haunted house story starring Mickey Mouse, Donald Duck, and Goofy, the latter a weak entry featuring Donald and his three nephews. Unrated—family fare.

1949 49 minutes

LT. ROBIN CRUSOE, U.S.N.

★

DIRECTOR: Byron Paul
CAST: Dick Van Dyke, Nancy Kwan, Akim Tamiroff

Modern-day story of Robinson Crusoe, poorly done and with few laughs. Dick Van Dyke is stranded on a tropical island and gets involved with a female revolt against the island's male chauvinist ruler. Van Dyke's talents are totally wasted in a film that started with an idea by Walt Disney and ended without a decent script. Rated G.

1966 113 minutes

LIFE AND TIMES OF GRIZZLY ADAMS, THE

★½

DIRECTOR: Richard Friedenberg
CAST: Dan Haggerty, Don Shanks, Lisa Jones, Marjory Harper, Bozo

The big question is: Which one is Bozo? It seems that everyone connected with this sloppy, syrupy movie must have been a bozo. Fur trapper Dan Haggerty heads for the hills when he's unjustly accused of a crime. There he befriends an oversize bear and they live happily ever after. This film inspired (?) the TV series. Rated G.

1976 93 minutes

LIGHT IN THE FOREST, THE

★★½

DIRECTOR: Herschel Daugherty

CAST: James MacArthur, Fess Parker, Wendell Corey, Joanne Dru, Carol Lynley

James MacArthur stars as a young man who had been captured and raised by the Delaware Indians. When a treaty forces the Indians to release all of their white captives, he is returned to the family he doesn't know. He considers himself to be an Indian and rebels at having to conform to white ways. Generally a good story with adequate acting, the ending is much too contrived and trite.

1958 92 minutes

LIGHTNING, THE WHITE STALLION

★

DIRECTOR: William A. Levey

CAST: Mickey Rooney, Susan George, Isavel Lorca

In this disappointing family film, Mickey Rooney plays a down-on-his-luck gambler who owns a white stallion that is a champion jumper. The horse is stolen. With the aid of two young people, he recovers the horse for one last make-or-break race. Rated PG.

1986 93 minutes

LITTLE LORD FAUNTLEROY (REMAKE)

★★★★

DIRECTOR: Jack Gold

CAST: Ricky Schroder, Alec Guinness, Eric Porter, Colin Blakely, Connie Booth

This is the made-for-television version of the heartwarming classic about a poor young boy (Ricky Schroder) whose life is dramatically changed when his wealthy grandfather (Alec Guinness) takes him in. Well done.

1980 120 minutes

LITTLE MATCH GIRL, THE

★★

DIRECTORS: Mark Hoeger, Wally Broodbent

CAST: Monica McSwain, Nancy Duncan, Matt McKim, Dan Hays

This "Children's Treasures" production was originally a stage play. Unfortunately, the pageantry and emotion of the live-action production are lost in the video translation. The song-and-dance routines throughout the film grow tiresome. The topic of this play seems much too somber and mature for children to handle. In it, a poor girl's grandmother, about to die, reveals a magic in the matches that they sell. After the grandmother's death, the girl (Monica McSwain) gets so caught up in the magic that she neglects to sell her wares. The story takes place in Russia just before the revolution and she is able to befriend the young, sickly prince before his family is killed. *Not advised for children under 10.*

1983 54 minutes

LITTLE MERMAID, THE

★★★½

DIRECTOR: Robert Iscove

CAST: Pam Dawber, Karen Black, Treat Williams, Brian Dennehy, Helen Mirren

In this segment of Shelley Duvall's Faerie Tale Theatre, Pam Dawber plays Pearl, a mermaid daughter of King Neptune. She falls hopelessly in love with a human and sacrifices all to win his love. Although this is a low-budget production, it still manages to keep its viewers entertained.

1984 50 minutes

LITTLE MISS MARKER (Original)

★★★★

DIRECTOR: Alexander Hall

CAST: Adolphe Menjou, Shirley Temple, Dorothy Dell, Charles Bickford, Lynne Overman

Delightful Shirley Temple vehicle has our little heroine left as an I.O.U. on a gambling debt and charming hard-hearted racetrack denizens into becoming better people. This is the best of the screen adaptations of Damon Runyon's story.

1934 B & W 88 minutes

LITTLE MISS MARKER (Remake)

★★

DIRECTOR: Walter Bernstein

CAST: Walter Matthau, Julie Andrews, Tony Curtis, Bob Newhart, Sara Stimson, Lee Grant

Even the star power of Walter Matthau, Julie Andrews, and Bob Newhart can't save this turgid remake of the 1934 Shirley Temple classic. Sara Stimson is cute, and the stars try hard, but this one never leaves the gate. Rated PG.

1980 103 minutes

LITTLE ORPHAN ANNIE

★★½

DIRECTOR: John S. Robertson

CAST: Mitzie Green, Edgar Kennedy, Buster Phelps, May Robson, Matt Moore, Kate Lawson, Sidney Bracy

The first sound version featuring the adventures of Harold Gray's pupilless, precocious adolescent is practically forgotten today, but it proved to be a winner at the box office when first released. Cute Mitzie Green got plenty of opportunity to say "leaping lizards" and show her spunk while comedian Edgar Kennedy played a firm but fun-loving Daddy Warbucks. A good cast and engaging score by Max Steiner add to the charm of this undeservedly neglected comic strip adaptation.

1932 B & W 60 minutes

LITTLE PRINCESS, THE

★★★½

DIRECTOR: Walter Lang

CAST: Shirley Temple, Richard Greene, Anita Louise, Ian Hunter, Cesar Romero, Arthur Treacher

The 1930s supertyke Shirley Temple had one of her very best vehicles in this Victorian era tearjerker. In it, she's a sweet-natured child who is mistreated at a strict boarding school when her father disappears during the Boer War. Get out your handkerchiefs.

1939 B & W 93 minutes

LITTLE RED RIDING HOOD

★★★★

DIRECTOR: Graeme Clifford

CAST: Mary Steenburgen, Malcolm McDowell, Frances Bay, Darrell Larson

Malcolm McDowell plays a brazenly wicked wolf to a perky Red Riding Hood (Mary Steenburgen). Frances Bay makes for a rather zany grandmother. Although this production is highly entertaining, don't expect it to stick to the tale as most would remember it.

1983 51 minutes

LITTLE TWEETY AND LITTLE INKI CARTOON FESTIVAL

★★★★

DIRECTORS: Bob Clampett, Friz Freleng, Chuck Jones

CAST: Animated

Bob Clampett brought the feisty yellow canary, alternately known as Tweety Pie and Tweety Bird, to life in "A Tale of Two Kitties," in which the little champ fought off two felines who bore more than a passing resemblance to

Bud Abbott and Lou Costello. Sadly, this classic is not included here (although Tweety does take on a Jimmy Durante–type cat in "Gruesome Twosome"). Still, the birdy's cartoons, which also include Clampett's "Birdy and the Beast" and Friz Freleng's "I Taw a Putty Tat," are fun to watch. However, the real gem in this collection is Chuck Jones's "Inki and the Lion," which also features the superb animation of Shamus Culhane (on the lion). For those who don't remember him, Inki is the youthful African warrior whose exploits are thwarted by the surprise appearances of a strange black bird who periodically hops onscreen to the strains of Mendelssohn's overture from "Fingal's Cave." The two adversaries are also featured in "The Little Lion Hunter" and "Inki at the Circus," but the Jones-Culhane collaboration is the classic.

1939–1948 50 minutes

LITTLEST HORSE THIEVES, THE

★★★

DIRECTOR: Charles Jarrott
CAST: Alastair Sim, Peter Barkworth, Maurice Colbourne, Susan Tebbs, Andrew Harrison, Chloe Franks

At the turn of the century, some children become alarmed when they learn that the pit ponies working in the coal mines are to be destroyed. To prevent the deaths, the children decide to steal the ponies. Rather predictable but with good characterizations and a solid period atmosphere. Rated G.

1976 104 minutes

LITTLEST OUTLAW, THE

★★★

DIRECTOR: Roberto Gavaldon
CAST: Pedro Armendariz, Joseph Calleia, Rodolfo Acosta, Andres Velasquez

This Walt Disney import from Mexico tells a familiar but pleasant story of a young boy who befriends a renegade horse and saves him from destruction. Nicely photographed and lovingly handled, this film ranks with the best of the animal pictures of the 1950s and succeeds where more ambitious efforts from the Disney studios have failed. Andres Velasquez made his debut as the young boy with spirit and is ably assisted by character favorites Pedro Armendariz and Joseph Calleia. The kids should like it, and this one will appeal to the adults as well.

1954 73 minutes

LOONEY, LOONEY, LOONEY BUGS BUNNY MOVIE

★★★½

DIRECTOR: Friz Freleng
CAST: Animated

This followup to the *Bugs Bunny/Road Runner Movie* lacks the earlier film's inventiveness, but then Chuck Jones was always the most cerebral of the Warner Bros. cartoon directors. Friz Freleng, on the other hand, only tried to make people laugh. This collection of his cartoons—which feature Daffy Duck, Porky Pig, Tweety Pie, and Yosemite Sam, among others, in addition to Bugs—does just that with general efficiency. Rated G.

1981 79 minutes

LOVE BUG, THE

★★★½

DIRECTOR: Robert Stevenson
CAST: Michele Lee, Dean Jones, Buddy Hackett, Joe Flynn

This is a delightful Disney comedy. A family film about a Volkswagen with a mind of its own and some special talents as well, it was the first of the four "Herbie" films. Rated G.

1969 107 minutes

MAD MONSTER PARTY

★★½

DIRECTOR: Jules Bass

CAST: Boris Karloff, Phyllis Diller, Ethel Ennis, Gale Garnett (voices)

An amusing little puppet film; a lot more fun for genre buffs who will understand all the references made to classic horror films. All the beloved monsters (led by a Dr. Frankenstein given voice by Boris Karloff) gather for a great bash . . . sort of a *Thank God It's Friday* for the Transylvania set. Wry little script, co-written by Harvey Kurtzman of *Mad Magazine* fame. Worth seeing once, as a novelty.

1967 94 minutes

MAGIC OF LASSIE, THE

★★½

DIRECTOR: Don Chaffey

CAST: James Stewart, Mickey Rooney, Pernell Roberts, Stephanie Zimbalist, Michael Sharrett, Alice Faye, Gene Evans, Lane Davies, Mike Mazurki, Lassie

Like the Disney live-action films of yore, *The Magic of Lassie* tries to incorporate a little of everything: heartwarming drama, suspense, comedy and even music (by the Mike Curb Congregation). But here the formula is bland. There's Grandpa (James Stewart) and the cute little boy (Michael Sharrett), the villain (Pernell Roberts) who tries to take Lassie away, and the kind people (Mickey Rooney, Mike Mazurki) who help Lassie on her way home while providing comedy relief. Stewart can make just about anything palatable—and this syrupy concoction definitely benefits from his measured delivery and mastery of pathos. The story is okay, as far as cute kids pining for their dogs go, but it is all too long. To make things worse, screenwriters Robert B. Sherman and Richard M. Sherman also added a bunch of awful songs. Rated G.

1978 100 minutes

MAGIC SWORD, THE

★★

DIRECTOR: Bert I. Gordon

CAST: Gary Lockwood, Anne Helm, Basil Rathbone, Estelle Winwood, Liam Sullivan

Fanciful juvenile adventure from low-budget film czar Bert I. Gordon is long on imagination but short on the props and effects necessary to pull a film like this off. Young Gary Lockwood is on a quest to free an imprisoned princess and fights his way through an ogre, dragon, and other uninspired monsters with the help of the witch in the family, Estelle Winwood. It's Basil Rathbone who makes the show work, and he makes a fine old evil sorcerer, relishing his foul deeds and eagerly planning new transgressions. The kids might like it, but compared with Ray Harryhausen's efforts of that period and the phenomenal special effects of the past decade, it's laughable.

1962 80 minutes

MARY POPPINS

★★★★★

DIRECTOR: Robert Stevenson

CAST: Julie Andrews, Dick Van Dyke, David Tomlinson, Glynis Johns, Karen Dotrice, Matthew Garber, Jane Darwell, Ed Wynn, Arthur Treacher, Hermione Baddeley

Here's Julie Andrews in her screen debut. She plays a nanny who believes that "a spoonful of sugar makes the medicine go down." Andrews is great in the role and sings ever so sweetly. The song and dance numbers are attractively laid on, with Dick Van Dyke, as Mary's Cockney beau, giving an amusing performance. Rated G.

1964 140 minutes

MICKEY'S CHRISTMAS CAROL

★★★★

DIRECTOR: Burney Matinson
CAST: Animated

Mickey Mouse plays Bob Cratchit in this adaptation of the Dickens classic. A pleasant animated feature with cameos by Donald Duck, Jimminy Cricket, Goofy, and other Disney characters. Rated G.

1984 26 minutes

MILLION DOLLAR DUCK, THE

★★

DIRECTOR: Vincent McEveety
CAST: Dean Jones, Sandy Duncan, Joe Flynn, Tony Roberts

A duck is accidentally given a dose of radiation that makes it produce eggs with solid gold yolks. Dean Jones and Sandy Duncan, as the owners of the duck, use the yolks to pay off bills until the Treasury Department gets wise. Mildly entertaining comedy in the Disney tradition. Rated G.

1971 92 minutes

MINOR MIRACLE, A

★★½

DIRECTOR: Raoul Lomas
CAST: John Huston, Pele, Peter Fox

A heartwarming story about a group of orphaned children and their devoted guardian (John Huston), who band together to save the St. Francis School for Boys. If you liked *Going My Way* and *Oh God!* you'll like this G-rated movie.

1983 100 minutes

MIRACLE OF THE WHITE STALLIONS

★★

DIRECTOR: Arthur Hiller
CAST: Robert Taylor, Lilli Palmer, Curt Jurgens, Eddie Albert, James Franciscus, John Larch

True story of the evacuation of the famed Lipizzan stallions from war-torn Vienna doesn't pack much of a wallop, but the kids and horse fans should enjoy it. The director of the Spanish Riding School (former matinee idol Robert Taylor) fights against bombs, the enemy, and time in his efforts to move his four-legged charges to the safety of a secluded chateau. Curt Jurgens plays yet another Nazi officer, and Eddie Albert and James Franciscus play U.S. Army officers who give the school and its supporters a hand. Plenty of nice horses to look at.

1963 92 minutes

MIRACLE ON 34TH STREET

★★★★★

DIRECTOR: George Seaton
CAST: Natalie Wood, Edmund Gwenn, Maureen O'Hara

In this, one of Hollywood's most delightful fantasies, the spirit of Christmas is rekindled in a young girl (Natalie Wood) by a department store Santa. Edmund Gwenn is perfect as the endearing Macy's employee who causes a furor when he claims to be the real Kris Kringle. Is he or isn't he? That is for you to decide in this heartwarming family classic.

1947 B & W 96 minutes

MISADVENTURES OF MERLIN JONES, THE

★★½

DIRECTOR: Robert Stevenson
CAST: Tommy Kirk, Annette Funicello, Leon Ames, Stuart Erwin, Alan Hewitt

Tommy Kirk stars in this Disney family programmer as a boy genius whose talents for mind reading and hypnotism land him in all sorts of trouble. Annette Funicello is on hand for some overly wholesome romantic fun. Entertaining for the young or indiscriminate; pretty bland for everybody else.

1964 88 minutes

MONKEY'S UNCLE, THE

★★

DIRECTOR: Robert Stevenson

CAST: Tommy Kirk, Annette Funicello, Leon Ames, Arthur O'Connell, Frank Faylen

This sequel to *The Misadventures of Merlin Jones* finds whiz kid Tommy Kirk up to no good with a flying machine and a sleep-learning technique employed on a monkey. More of the same from Disney, really: bumbling scientific high-jinks, mild slapstick, and G-rated romance with Annette Funicello. For young minds only.

1965 87 minutes

MONKEYS GO HOME

★½

DIRECTOR: Andrew V. McLaglen

CAST: Maurice Chevalier, Dean Jones, Yvette Mimieux, Bernard Woringer

Stupid even for a Walt Disney film (and that covers a lot of territory), this is a low-water mark for action director Andrew McLaglen. Disney regular Dean Jones plays an American who inherits an olive farm in France and is stymied in his attempts to pick the delicate fruit until he hits on the idea of using "retired" air force test chimps! More of a fleshed-out fourth-grade-level short story than creative film-making, this ridiculous entry in a never-ending stream of inane Disney releases on video wouldn't be considered suitable adult viewing if it weren't for the locations, beautiful Yvette Mimieux, and French institution Maurice Chevalier (in his last role). Not the worst available from Disney, but pretty bad. Rated G.

1966 89 minutes

MOON PILOT

★★★½

DIRECTOR: James Neilson

CAST: Tom Tryon, Brian Keith, Edmond O'Brien, Dany Saval

Tom Tryon gets volunteered to become the first astronaut to circle the moon. A mysterious woman appears and seemingly breaches the confidentiality surrounding the mission. The FBI is called in, and the launch takes place on schedule. The woman appears in the capsule, however, and love blooms between her and the astronaut. Good script, with satire and laughs in ample quantities. Rated G.

1962 98 minutes

MOONCUSSERS

★★½

DIRECTOR: James Neilson

CAST: Oscar Homolka, Kevin Corcoran, Robert Emhardt, Rian Garrick, Joan Freeman

Kevin Corcoran stars as a boy who discovers the secrets of the Mooncussers—pirates who work on moonless nights to draw ships to their doom by means of false signal lamps on shore. After the ships are wrecked, the Mooncussers plunder the cargo and kill the crew. The ship owners try to investigate the cause of the wreck but are unsuccessful until Corcoran helps them with his knowledge and daring.

1962 85 minutes

MOONSPINNERS, THE

★★★

DIRECTOR: James Neilson
CAST: Hayley Mills, Eli Wallach, Pola Negri, Peter McEnery, Joan Greenwood

A young girl (Hayley Mills) becomes involved in a jewel theft in Crete. A young man is accused of the theft and has to work with the girl to prove his innocence. The best features of this film are the appearance of a "grown-up" Hayley Mills and the return to the screen of Pola Negri. The film is essentially a lightweight melodrama in the Hitchcock mold.

1964 118 minutes

MOUNTAIN FAMILY ROBINSON

★★½

DIRECTOR: John Cotter
CAST: Robert Logan, Susan D. Shaw, Heather Rattray, Ham Larsen

Though it could just as easily have been titled *Wilderness Family, Part 3,* the sum of this Pacific International Enterprises, Inc., film is that its simplicity is its merit. *Mountain Family Robinson* delivers exactly what it set out to achieve. It does not purport to have any other message than that of the value of familial love, understanding, and togetherness. Predictable and a bit corny. Robert Logan, Susan Shaw, Heather Rattray, and Ham Larsen display an affability that should charm the children and make this film a relaxing, easy time-passer for parents as well. Rated G.

1979 100 minutes

MUPPET MOVIE, THE

★★★½

DIRECTOR: James Frawley
CAST: Muppets, Edgar Bergen, Charlie McCarthy, Milton Berle, Mel Brooks, James Coburn, Dom De Luise, Elliott Gould, Bob Hope, Madeline Kahn, Carol Kane, Cloris Leachman, Steve Martin, Richard Pryor, Telly Savalas, Orson Welles, Paul Williams

Though there is a huge all-star guest cast, the Muppets are the real stars of this superior family film in which the characters trek to Hollywood in search of stardom. Rated G.

1979 94 minutes

MUPPETS TAKE MANHATTAN, THE

★★★

DIRECTOR: Frank Oz
CAST: Muppets, Art Carney, Dabney Coleman, Joan Rivers, Elliott Gould, Liza Minnelli, Brooke Shields

Jim Henson's popular puppets take a bite of the Big Apple in their third and least effective screen romp. The screenplay, by director Frank Oz, Tom Patchett, and Jay Tarses, is of the old "let's put on a show" genre, with playwright Kermit and his pals trying to get their musical on the Broadway stage. It's hackneyed and unnecessarily padded, but occasionally fun even for adults—thanks to a number of plot digressions. Surprisingly, the best of these have nothing to do with the cameo appearances. So what are we to make of *The Muppets Take Manhattan*? An excellent show for the kiddies, that's what. And there's nothing wrong with that. Rated G.

1984 94 minutes

MY LITTLE PONY: THE MOVIE

★★★

DIRECTOR: Michael Joens
CAST: Danny DeVito, Madeline Kahn, Cloris Leachman, Rhea Perlman, Tony Randall (voices)

Darling ponies are threatened by the evil witch family (Cloris Leachman, Madeline Kahn, and

Rhea Perlman) who live in the Volcano of Gloom. When the witches release the purple, lava-like "smooze," it destroys the contryside as well as the ponies' Dream Castle. Before this catastrophe, one proud baby pony, Lickety-split, runs away from home, followed by the dragon baby, Spike. Trapped by smooze, they meet the troll-like Grundles. Danny DeVito, the Grundle King, helps them escape. It takes the magic of the flutter ponies to reverse the damage caused by the witches and their smooze. The brilliant colors soften most of the potentially frightening scenes. All subplots reaffirm that everybody needs a friend. Children under 7 should enjoy this, but older children and adults may feel it's too long. Rated G.

1986 85 minutes

MYSTERY ISLAND

★★★

DIRECTOR: Gene Scott

CAST: Jayson Duncan, Niklas Juhlin

When four children whose boat has run out of gas discover what appears to be a deserted island, they promptly name it Mystery Island. There is actually an old pirate who lives there. The children find a case of counterfeit money which belongs to villains, who later return to the island for it. The old pirate's timely intervention saves the kids. The best part about this children's film is the beautiful underwater photography.

1981 75 minutes

MYSTERY MANSION

★

DIRECTOR: David F. Jackson

CAST: Dallas McKennon, Greg Wynne, Jane Ferguson, Barry Hostetler, Joseph D. Savery

An absolutely unremarkable film about a girl with strange but true dreams, two escaped convicts, a harried father in danger of losing his land to an evil tycoon, and hidden treasure—all involved with an old Victorian mystery house. It's all been done before, and better, in countless other films. Rated G.

1986 95 minutes

NAPOLEON AND SAMANTHA

★★★½

DIRECTOR: Bernard McEveety

CAST: Johnny Whitaker, Jodie Foster, Michael Douglas, Will Geer, Arch Johnson, Henry Jones, Major the Lion

This Disney film features Johnny Whitaker as Napoleon, an orphan who decides to hide his grandpa's body when the old man dies and care for their pet lion, Major. When a college student/goat herder named Danny (Michael Douglas) helps bury Grandpa, Napoleon decides to follow him to his flock. Samantha (Jodie Foster) joins him and the lion as they cross mountains and streams and face the dangers of a fierce mountain lion and a bear. Rated G.

1972 91 minutes

NATIONAL VELVET

★★★★

DIRECTOR: Clarence Brown

CAST: Mickey Rooney, Elizabeth Taylor, Donald Crisp, Anne Revere, Angela Lansbury, Reginald Owen

This heartwarming tale of two youngsters determined to train a beloved horse to win the famed Grand National Race is good for the whole family, and especially good for little girls who love horses and sentimentalists who fondly recall Elizabeth Taylor when she was young, innocent, and adorable. Have Kleenex on hand.

1944 125 minutes

NEVER A DULL MOMENT

½

DIRECTOR: Jerry Paris

CAST: Dick Van Dyke, Edward G. Robinson, Dorothy Provine, Henry Silva

Undoubtedly one of the weakest of all Disney feature films, this dismal effort has all the finesse one would expect from Dick Van Dyke doing his sophisticated version of Jerry Lewis at his worst. Hackneyed, boring, and inane are the adjectives that come to mind in discussing this film. Not even Edward G. Robinson and the character actors can save this one. Rated G.

1968 100 minutes

NIGHTINGALE, THE

★★★½

DIRECTOR: Ivan Passer

CAST: Mick Jagger, Bud Cort, Barbara Hershey, Edward James Olmos

An emperor (Mick Jagger) survives court intrigue to discover true friendship from a lowly maid (Barbara Hershey) with the help of a nightingale in this *Faerie Tale Theatre* production. Some of the best-designed sets in the series provide lovely backdrops for the acting—most of it serene and heartfelt. Jagger makes a superb emperor (although Rolling Stones fans may be disappointed with his passiveness), and the corny humor found in other films in the series is happily absent. This one is made especially for children under 10, so older viewers may find it slow moving. One concession made to the younger viewers is that the traditional imperial converted to "A punch in your stomach."

1983 51 minutes

NIKKI, WILD DOG OF THE NORTH

★★★

DIRECTOR: Jack Couffer

CAST: Don Haldane, Jean Coutu, Emile Genest, Uriel Luft, Robert Rivarol

The rugged wilderness of northern Canada provides the backdrop to this story of a dog that is separated from his owner. Based on the perennial favorite by James Oliver Curwood, this French-Canadian production is beautifully photographed and contains some of the best live-action animal footage ever incorporated into a Walt Disney film. Released theatrically in 1961, Nikki was televised in two parts in 1964. Narration is by Jacques Fanteux and Dwight Hauser.

1961 73 minutes

NO DEPOSIT, NO RETURN

★★

DIRECTOR: Norman Tokar

CAST: David Niven, Don Knotts, Darren McGavin, Herschel Bernardi, Barbara Feldon

Two kids decide to escape from their multimillionaire grandfather (David Niven) and visit their mother in Hong Kong. On their way to the airport, they end up in a getaway car with two incompetent safe-crackers with (surprise!) a soft spot in their hearts for kids. The kids end up taking over the hideout and engineer their own "kidnapping"—demanding ransom from their grandfather for the fare to Hong Kong. The attempt backfires, and the movie degenerates into a cops-and-robbers chase scene. It is typical of

the Disney movie products of the mid-1970s with Ron Miller as producer: unrealistic and not very believable, with occasional bits of real entertainment. Rated G.
1976 115 minutes

NORTH AVENUE IRREGULARS, THE

★★½

DIRECTOR: Bruce Bilson
CAST: Edward Herrmann, Barbara Harris, Cloris Leachman, Susan Clark, Karen Valentine, Michael Constantine, Patsy Kelly, Virginia Capers

Average Disney film about a young priest (Edward Herrmann) who wants to do something about crime. He enlists a group of churchgoing, do-good women to work with him. Quality cast is wasted on marginal script. Rated G.
1979 100 minutes

NOW YOU SEE HIM, NOW YOU DON'T

★★

DIRECTOR: Robert Butler
CAST: Kurt Russell, Joe Flynn, Jim Backus, Cesar Romero, William Windom

Medfield College, the campus of Fred MacMurray in *The Absent-Minded Professor* and *Son of Flubber*, is once again host to college high-jinks. This is the second of the Kurt Russell films which followed the tradition of the MacMurray and Tommy Kirk college films. In this one, Russell discovers a formula that will make a person or item invisible. Bad guy Cesar Romero attempts to hijack the discovery for nefarious purposes, which leads to disastrous results. Rated G.
1972 85 minutes

OH, HEAVENLY DOG!

★

DIRECTOR: Joe Camp
CAST: Benji, Chevy Chase, Jane Seymour, Omar Sharif, Robert Morley

Chevy Chase should have known better. This movie is an overly silly cutesy about a private eye (Chase) who is murdered and then comes back as a dog (Benji) to trap his killers. Kids, however, should enjoy it. Rated PG.
1980 103 minutes

OLD YELLER

★★★★

DIRECTOR: Robert Stevenson
CAST: Dorothy McGuire, Fess Parker, Tommy Kirk, Chuck Connors

Here's a live-action Walt Disney favorite. A big yellow mongrel is taken in by a Southwestern family. The warm attachment and numerous adventures of the dog and the two boys of the family are sure to endear this old mutt to your heart. A few tears are guaranteed to fall at the conclusion, so you'd best bring a hankie.
1957 83 minutes

ONE AND ONLY, GENUINE, ORIGINAL FAMILY BAND, THE

★★½

DIRECTOR: Michael O'Herlihy
CAST: Walter Brennan, Buddy Ebsen, Lesley Ann Warren, John Davidson, Goldie Hawn

This period comedy, set in the Dakota territories, features Walter Brennan–who struggles to keep his family's band together in order to get invited to the Democratic convention in St. Louis. Lesley Ann Warren and John Davidson play the love interest. The Sherman brothers (of *Mary Poppins* fame) contribute several songs. This is a lightweight movie made shortly after Walt Disney's death. It misses his touch but is, nonetheless, moderately enjoyable for the whole family. Rated G.

1967 110 minutes

ONE OF OUR DINOSAURS IS MISSING

★★½

DIRECTOR: Robert Stevenson
CAST: Peter Ustinov, Helen Hayes, Derek Nimmo, Clive Revill

In this moderately entertaining comedy spy film, Peter Ustinov plays a Chinese intelligence agent attempting to recover some stolen microfilm. Helen Hayes plays a nanny who becomes involved in trying to get the film to the British authorities. The film is in a dinosaur skeleton that Hayes and other nannies take to the streets of London. Rated G.

1975 101 minutes

1001 RABBIT TALES

★★★★

DIRECTORS: Friz Freleng, Chuck Jones
CAST: Animated

Fourteen classic cartoons are interwoven with new footage to make another feature-length film out of the well-known Warner Brothers characters. This time the theme is fairy tales. Bugs and the gang spoof "Goldilocks and the Three Bears," "Jack and the Bean Stalk,"and "Little Red Riding Hood," among others. This one also contains Chuck Jones's "One Froggy Evening," one of the greatest cartoons ever! Rated G.

1982 76 minutes

ON THE RIGHT TRACK

★★

DIRECTOR: Lee Philips
CAST: Gary Coleman, Maureen Stapleton, Michael Lembeck, Norman Fell

Gary Coleman (of television's "Diff'rent Strokes") plays a tyke who sets up residence in a railroad station to escape the hustle and bustle of the city. Once the word gets around that he has a talent for picking the winners in horse races, his life becomes complicated all over again. Without Coleman, this would be an awful movie. Even with him, it is nothing to shout about. At best it has a kind of cornball charm—like an old-style Disney movie with a little extra zing—but at other times it lulls you to sleep. Rated PG.

1981 98 minutes

PACKIN' IT IN

★★★½

DIRECTOR: Jud Taylor
CAST: Richard Benjamin, Paula Prentiss, Molly Ringwald, Tony Roberts, Andrea Marcovicci

When Gary and Dianna Webber (Richard Benjamin and Paula Prentiss) flee from the pollution ad crime of Los Angeles, they find themselves living among survivalists in Woodcrest, Oregon. The laughs begin as these city folks, including their punked-out daughter (played by Molly Ringwald), try to adjust to life in the wilderness. Tony Roberts co-stars as an old friend who encouraged them to leave L.A. for the "good life." Unrated, it is fine for the whole family.

1982 92 minutes

PARENT TRAP, THE

★★★★

DIRECTOR: David Swift
CAST: Hayley Mills, Brian Keith, Maureen O'Hara, Joanna Barnes

Walt Disney doubled the fun in this comedy when he had Hayley Mills play twins. Mills plays sisters who meet for the first time at summer camp and decide to reunite their divorced parents (Brian Keith and Maureen O'Hara).

1961 124 minutes

PEANUT BUTTER SOLUTION, THE

★★½

DIRECTOR: Michael Rubbo

CAST: Mathew Mackay, Siluk Saysanasy, Alison Rodbrey, Michael Hogan, Michael Maillot, Helen Hughes

Remember sitting around a campfire when you were a kid and creating a story that just went on and on? This is a campfire movie. Part of the *Tales for All* series, it combines old houses, ghosts, an evil madman, enforced child labor, and a main character with a real hairy problem, all mixed together in sort of a story. The child actors (Mathew Mackay, Siluk Saysanasy, and Alison Rodbrey) are excellent and really support the film through its story lapses.

1985 96 minutes

PECK'S BAD BOY

★★★

DIRECTOR: Sam Wood

CAST: Jackie Coogan, Wheeler Oakman, Doris May, Raymond Hatton, Lillian Leighton

Jackie Coogan shines as the mischievous scamp who commits all manner of mayhem upon anyone who happens to cross his path, yet miraculously escapes the lethal designs his victims must harbor. A popular old stage play that perpetuates the lazy attitude that "boys will be boys," this box-office smash helped to launch director Sam Wood's career. Silent.

1921 B & W 54 minutes

PECK'S BAD BOY WITH THE CIRCUS

★★

DIRECTOR: Edward Cline

CAST: Tommy Kelly, Ann Gillis, Edgar Kennedy, Billy Gilbert, Benita Hume, Spanky MacFarland, Grant Mitchell

After tackling the leading role in *The Adventures of Tom Sawyer*, young Tommy Kelly played another time-tested character out of a boy's book, the mischievous Peck's Bad Boy, but with less success. Kelly and his ragamuffin gang of troublemakers (including an aging Spanky MacFarland) wreak havoc around the circus and cause all manner of juvenile mayhem on the unsuspecting carnival folk. Comedy greats Edgar Kennedy and Billy Gilbert are the best part of this kids' film.

1938 B & W 78 minutes

PEPE LE PEW'S SKUNK TALES

★★★

DIRECTORS: Chuck Jones, Arthur Davis, Abe Levitow

CAST: Animated

Once again, Warner Bros. director Chuck Jones takes top honors in a Warner Bros. cartoon release. His 1949 Oscar-winning "For Scent-imental Reasons" features the amorous skunk, Pepe Le Pew, at his cat-wooing best. Other Jones gems include "Scent-imental Romeo," "Past Perfumance," "Really Scent" (with Abe Levitow), "Who Scent You?," and "The Cat's Bah." Arthur Davis is represented with "Odor of the Day," an early Pepe in which he fights for shelter with an odor-sensitive shaggy dog. Rounding out the package is Jones's "Much Ado About Nutting," in which a determined squirrel gets a surprise when he cracks a rather special nut. For all ages.

1948–1960 56 minutes

PETE'S DRAGON

★★½

DIRECTOR: Don Chaffey

CAST: Mickey Rooney, Jim Dale, Helen Reddy, Red Buttons, Jim Backus, Sean Marshall

Only the kiddies will get a kick out of this Disney feature, which combines live action featuring stars such as Mickey Rooney, Jim Dale, Helen Reddy, Red Buttons, and Jim (Mr. Magoo) Backus, with animation. The story takes place in Maine circa 1908 when a 9-year-old boy (Sean Marshall) escapes his overbearing foster parents with the aid of the pet dragon that only he can see. Sort of a children's version of *Harvey*, it's generally lackluster and uninspired. But, again, most children will probably enjoy it. Parents, on the other hand, may want to read a book while the film is running. Rated G.

1977 134 minutes

PETRONELLA

★★★★

DIRECTOR: Rick Locke

CAST: Sylvia, Mayf Nutter, James Arrington, Jerry Maren, David Jensen, David E. Morgan

This live-action production of "Enchanted Musical Playhouse" stars the lovely country-pop singer Sylvia as a liberated princess who sets out to rescue an imprisoned prince. When her two elder brothers set out to seek their fortunes, she insists that she will do the same rather than wait for a prince to find her. When she encounters Albion the Enchantor, superbly played by Mayf Nutter, she agrees to spend three nights with some vicious animals—a dog, a horse, and a falcon—in order to free an imprisoned prince. After successfully performing her three tasks, she rides off with the reluctant prince only to find out he hadn't been a prisoner at all. Happiness reigns in the surprise ending when the spunky princess finds her true love. The whole family can enjoy this delightful tale with its cheerful songs and humorous moments.

1985 30 minutes

PIED PIPER OF HAMELIN, THE

★★★★★

DIRECTOR: Nicholas Meyer

CAST: Eric Idle, Tony Van Bridge, Keram Malicki-Sanchez, Peter Blaise

Nicholas Meyer, who also directed *The Day After* and *Star Trek III*, does a terrific job of adapting Robert Browning's eerie poem for this Faerie Tale Theatre episode. Eric Idle does remarkably well with his two major parts: as poet Robert Browning and the medieval piper. As the piper, he agrees to rid Hamelin of its rats if the mayor will pay him his fee. When the mayor refuses, the piper spirits the town's children away, as well. Because the dialogue is totally done in rhyming couplets (sticking closely to Browning's original style), it may be difficult for children under 8 to follow. Also, the close-ups of huge, ugly rats should be considered before showing this to the wee ones. Otherwise, the cast, costumes, sets, and production are outstanding and should entertain the whole family.

1985 60 minutes

PINOCCHIO

★★★★★

DIRECTOR: Walt Disney

CAST: Animated

In this timeless Walt Disney animated classic, a puppet made by a lonely old man gets the chance to become a real boy. *Pinocchio* is one of those rare motion pictures that can be enjoyed over and over again by adults as well as children. If you remember it as a "kid's show," watch it again. You'll be surprised at how wonderfully entertaining it is. Rated G.

1940 87 minutes

PINOCCHIO

★★★★

DIRECTOR: Peter Medak

CAST: James Coburn, Carl Reiner, Paul Reubens, Jim Belushi, Lainie Kazan, Don Novello (narrating as Father Guido Sarducci)

An excellent adaptation of the classic tale about the adventures of a wooden puppet who turns into a real boy. This Faerie Tale Theatre production, as with most of the others, will be best appreciated—and understood—by adults. It's blessed with just the right touch of humor, and Lainie Kazan is wonderful as the "Italian" fairy godmother.

1983 51 minutes

POLLYANNA

★★★½

DIRECTOR: David Swift

CAST: Hayley Mills, Jane Wyman, Agnes Moorehead, Adolphe Menjou, Karl Malden, Nancy Olson

Walt Disney's version of this classic childhood book is good entertainment for the whole family. Hayley Mills is the energetic and optimistic young girl who improves the lives of everyone she meets. Jane Wyman, Agnes Moorehead, and Adolphe Menjou head an exceptional supporting cast for this film.

1960 134 minutes

POPEYE

★★★

DIRECTOR: Robert Altman

CAST: Robin Williams, Shelley Duvall, Ray Walston, Paul Smith, Paul Dooley, Richard Libertini, Wesley Ivan Hurt

This adaptation of the famous comic strip by director Robert Altman (*A Wedding*) is the cinematic equivalent of the old "good news, bad news" routine. The good news is that the casting, dialogue, and sets are superb. Robin Williams makes a terrific Popeye, and Shelley Duvall was born to play Olive Oyl. The bad news is it's often boring. And the songs (by Harry Nilsson) seem to go on forever. Still, it's hard to really dislike *Popeye*—it's so wonderfully weird to look at and so much fun at times. Rated PG.

1980 114 minutes

POPEYE CARTOONS

★★★★

DIRECTOR: Dave Fleischer

CAST: Animated

Popeye the Sailor Man gets his finest treatment in this trio of classic big-screen cartoons from Max and Dave Fleischer: "Popeye Meets Sindbad," "Aladdin and His Wonderful Lamp," and "Popeye Meets Ali Baba." Unfortunately, several of the companies that released these animated works on video haven't been as respectful. Most of the copies we've seen have had at least a few scratches on the prints. But if you can overlook such matters, Popeye, Olive Oyl, Bluto, and Wimpy have never been better.

1930s–1940s 56 minutes

PORKY PIG CARTOON FESTIVAL FEATURING "NOTHING BUT THE TOOTH"

★★★

DIRECTORS: Bob Clampett, Arthur Davis, Chuck Jones, Frank Tashlin

CAST: Animated

There are some great Porky Pig cartoons in the MGM/UA vaults. Too bad none of them are included in this repetitive but still watchable collection. In three out of the five selections, Porky battles mice and mousers: Bob Clampett's "Kitty Kornered" and "Mouse Menace" and Arthur Davis's "Nothing But the Tooth." These cartoons might have been more enjoyable if they had been spread out amongst several packages. Oh, well, they're still fun—as are Chuck Jones's "Trap Happy Daffy" and Frank Tashlin's "Swooner Crooner," in which farmer Porky uses roosters resembling Bing Crosby and Frank Sinatra to move a group of hens to complete eggs-haustion.

1938–1946 36 minutes

PORKY PIG AND DAFFY DUCK CARTOON FESTIVAL FEATURING "TICK TOCK TUCKERED"

★★★★

DIRECTORS: Bob Clampett, Chuck Jones, Robert McKimson

CAST: Animated

Porky Pig was always better when teamed with the unpredictable Daffy Duck than by himself—and this delightful cartoon collection provides ample proof of this. Once again, Bob Clampett takes the top prizes for the sheer hilarity of his contributions: "Baby Bottleneck," in which Porky and Daffy go boom in the baby boom; "Wagon Heels"; and "Tick Tock Tuckered," in which our guys play Beat the Clock. Robert McKimson's "Daffy Doodles," in which Daffy becomes the ultimate graffiti gagster with policeman Porky hot on his trail, is very much in Clampett's high-flying style. Wild and wacky, each is a classic. More chuckles can be found in McKimson's "One Meat Brawl" and a pair by Chuck Jones: "My Favorite Duck" and "Tom Turk and Daffy." It's a cartoonaholic's dream come true.

1943–1947 57 minutes

PORKY PIG'S SCREWBALL COMEDIES

★★★

DIRECTORS: Friz Freleng, Chuck Jones, Robert McKimson

CAST: Animated

Why Bob Clampett's superb "Porky in Wackyland" was not included in this collection is anyone's guess. It was Clampett who made most of Porky's starring classics in the 1930s and 1940s. That omission overlooked, this is a fun collection with two delightful Friz Freleng–directed cartoons the standouts: "You Ought to Be in Pictures," in which Porky lets Daffy Duck talk him into quitting cartoons for feature films; and "Dough for the Do-Do," in which Porky goes after the priceless dodo in Africa amidst surreal backgrounds. The set also includes "Cracked Quack," "Curtain Razor," "Often an Orphan," "Wearing of the Grin," "Boobs in the Woods," and "Mouse Wreckers," the latter starring Hubie and Bertie, rodent versions of Leo Gorcey and Huntz Hall.

1985 59 minutes

PRINCE AND THE PAUPER, THE (ORIGINAL)

★★★★½

DIRECTOR: William Keighley

CAST: Errol Flynn, Claude Rains, Barton MacLane, Alan Hale, Billy and Bobby Mauch

Exciting story of the young Prince of England trading places with his identical look-alike, a street beggar. One of Errol Flynn's lesser-known films but still one of his best. This film captures the flavor of the times. Erich Wolfgang Korngold wrote the music.

1937 B & W 120 minutes

PRINCE AND THE PAUPER, THE (REMAKE)

★★★½

DIRECTOR: Richard Fleischer
CAST: Charlton Heston, Oliver Reed, George C. Scott, Rex Harrison, Mark Lester

An all-star cast brings Mark Twain's novel of mistaken identity in not-so-jolly old England to life. Edward, the only son of King Henry VIII (Charlton Heston), trades places with his double, a child from the London slums. The young prince has trouble reclaiming his crown even with the aid of a swashbuckling soldier-of-fortune (Oliver Reed). Nothing pretentious here, just a costumed adventure that should satisfy young and old. Rated PG.

1978 113 minutes

PRINCE OF CENTRAL PARK, THE

★★

DIRECTOR: Harvey Hart
CAST: T. J. Hargrave, Lisa Richards, Ruth Gordon, Marc Vahanian

Ruth Gordon is, as usual, a bright spot in this made-for-TV children's film about an orphaned brother and sister who flee their foster home for a tree house in Central Park. The script is a bit cynical for a story aimed at children, but Gordon's charm serves to turn that around to her benefit.

1976 76 minutes

PRINCESS AND THE PEA, THE

★★★½

DIRECTOR: Tony Bill
CAST: Liza Minnelli, Tom Conti, Beatrice Straight, Tim Kazurinsky

One of the most interesting Faerie Tale Theatre productions, this film features fine performances from Liza Minnelli and Tom Conti. In a way, it's sort of a take-off on *Arthur*, in which Minnelli starred with Dudley Moore. The actress delivers some rather familiar lines of dialogue as she plays a princess tested for her royal qualities, which include a special kind of sensitivity.

1983 53 minutes

PRINCESS WHO HAD NEVER LAUGHED, THE

★★★★

DIRECTOR: Mark Cullingham
CAST: Howie Mandel, Ellen Barkin, Howard Hesseman

In this funny Grimm's fairy tale, laughter does prove to be the best medicine for the forlorn princess (Ellen Barkin). Growing up with her father (Howard Hesseman), who prefers to be called "Your Seriousness," she has never had a happy or amusing moment. When she locks herself in her room, her father decrees a Royal Laugh-off to make his daughter happy. At this point Howie Mandel appears as Weinerhead Waldo and the fun begins.

1984 51 minutes

PRIZEFIGHTER, THE

★★½

DIRECTOR: Michael Preece
CAST: Tim Conway, Don Knotts, David Wayne

In addition to starring in this goofy comedy, Tim Conway wrote the story. In it, we get a glimpse of 1930s boxing, with Conway playing a stupid boxer who has Don Knotts for his manager. Children may find the corny gags amusing, but most adults will be disappointed. Rated PG.

1979 99 minutes

PUSS IN BOOTS

★★★★

DIRECTOR: Robert Iscove
CAST: Ben Vereen, Gregory Hines, George Kirby, Brock Peters, Alfre Woodard

To ensure himself an easy life, a wily feline carries out a plan to turn his impoverished master into a rich marquis by winning him an ogre's castle and the hand of the king's daughter in marriage. Ben Vereen is purringly convincing as the cat and Brock Peters a standout as the ogre in this Faerie Tale Theatre production.

1984 53 minutes

RACE FOR YOUR LIFE, CHARLIE BROWN

★★★

DIRECTOR: Bill Melendez
CAST: Animated

Third entry in the "Peanuts" film series has moved further away from the poignant sophistication of *A Boy Named Charlie Brown* and closer to the mindless pap of Saturday-morning cartoon fare. The gang travels to summer camp and gets involved in a river-rafting race, which gives the film its title. The story lies dead in the water most of the time, with the tedium relieved only by the far better—and quite recognizable—echoes from Charles Schulz's newspaper strip. Rated G.

1977 75 minutes

RAINBOW BRITE AND THE STAR STEALER

★★★

DIRECTORS: Bernard Deyries, Kimio Yabuki
CAST: Animated

When the Dark Princess tries to steal Spectra (the world's light source), Rainbow Brite teams up with a chauvinistic, but admittedly brave, little boy named Krys to prevent the theft. Rainbow Brite teaches Krys that girls are as smart and brave as boys, and their bond helps them overcome the evil of the princess. This is Rainbow Brite's first feature-length film, and should continue to thrill the little girls who tend to be her most avid fans.

1985 85 minutes

RAPUNZEL

★★★½

DIRECTOR: Gilbert Cates
CAST: Jeff Bridges, Shelley Duvall, Gena Rowlands

A pregnant woman's desire for radishes results in her having to give her baby daughter to the witch who owns the radish garden. Shelley Duvall is amusing as both the mother and a grown Rapunzel. Jeff Bridges makes a fine, put-upon husband and a handsome prince who must rescue Rapunzel from the man-hating witch, delightfully played by Gena Rowlands. Another *Faerie Tale Theatre* production.

1982 51 minutes

RED BALLOON, THE

★★★★★

DIRECTOR: Albert Lamorisse
CAST: Pascal Lamorisse, Georges Sellier, Wladimir Popof, Renee Marion

This fanciful, endearing tale of a giant balloon that befriends a small boy in Paris is a delight for children and adults alike. Outside of a catchable word or two here and there, the film is without dialogue. The story is crystal clear in the visual telling, punctuated by an engaging musical score. A unique film, in 1956 it won a Golden Palm at the Cannes Film Festival, the Gold Medal of the French Cinema, and, in Hollywood, an Oscar for best original screenplay.

1956 34 minutes

RED PONY, THE

★★

DIRECTOR: Lewis Milestone
CAST: Myrna Loy, Robert Mitchum, Peter Miles, Louis Calhern,

Shepperd Strudwick, Margaret Hamilton

It is very hard to make a dull movie from a John Steinbeck novel. This rendition manages to accomplish that. Myrna Loy and Robert Mitchum are wasted in this story of a young Northern California boy who is given a colt, which runs away.

1948 89 minutes

RETURN FROM WITCH MOUNTAIN

★★

DIRECTOR: John Hough

CAST: Bette Davis, Christopher Lee, Kim Richards, Ike Eisenmann

Christopher Lee and Bette Davis capture Ike Eisenmann to use his supernatural powers to accomplish their own purposes. Sequel to *Escape to Witch Mountain*, in which Eisenmann and Kim Richards discover their powers and the effect they can have on humans. Lee wants to conquer the world, while Davis just wants to get rich. A good children's film, but weak Disney. Rated G.

1978 93 minutes

RETURN TO OZ

★★★★½

DIRECTOR: Walter Murch

CAST: Fairuza Balk, Nicol Williamson, Jean Marsh, Piper Laurie, Matt Clark

In this semi-sequel to *The Wizard of Oz*, viewers will hear no songs nor see any Munchkins. It is a very different, but equally enjoyable, trip down the Yellow Brick Road, with young star Fairuza Balk outstanding as Dorothy. It gets pretty scary at times and isn't all fluff and wonder like the Oz of yore. However, this is nevertheless a magical film for the child in everyone. Rated PG for scary stuff.

1985 110 minutes

RETURN TO TREASURE ISLAND

★★★½

DIRECTOR: Piers Haggard

CAST: Brian Blessed, Christopher Guard, Reiner Schone, Ken Colley

This five-tape series was produced for the Disney Channel. It is a sequel to Disney's 1950 film *Treasure Island*, based on Robert Louis Stevenson's classic novel. The action here takes place ten years later with young Jim Hawkins (Christopher Guard) now an educated young man being reunited with the scheming Long John (Brian Blessed). They find themselves on the same ship—Long John as a prisoner and Jim as a privileged passenger. Guard makes a very handsome, gullible Jim, but Blessed is almost too soft-spoken and polite to be believable as Long John. The scenery (filmed in Spain, Jamaica, and Wales) is magnificent. Overall, these tapes make fine family entertainment. But it would be best to watch the original *Treasure Island* first in order to understand who is who and why they are the way they are.

1985 101 minutes per tape

ROAD RUNNER VS. WILE E. COYOTE: THE CLASSIC CHASE

★★★★

DIRECTOR: Chuck Jones

CAST: Animated

Although Chuck Jones deserves credit for some of the funniest Bugs Bunny/Daffy Duck cartoons and for creating Pepe Le Pew, for many, the cliff-hanging (and falling) attempts of Wile E. Coyote to catch the uncatchable Road Runner stand as his greatest achievements. This first-rate collection includes: "Fast and Furry-ous," "Hook, Line and Stinker," "Zip n' Snort," "To Beep Beep or Not to Beep Beep," and "Beep

Beep." Wile E. pursues Bugs Bunny in "Operation Rabbit" and the very similar Wolf character takes on the ever-vigilant Sheepdog in "Ready, Woolen and Able."

1985 54 minutes

ROB ROY, THE HIGHLAND ROGUE

★★

DIRECTOR: Harold French

CAST: Richard Todd, Glynis Johns, James Robertson Justice, Michael Gough, Finlay Currie, Jean Taylor-Smith

Slow-moving historical saga is not up to the usual Walt Disney adventure film and is perhaps the weakest of the three films made in England with sturdy Richard Todd as the heroic lead. The few battle scenes are enjoyable enough and the scenery is lovely, but the pace is erratic and there is just too much dead time. This one is for Richard Todd fans only.

1954 85 minutes

ROBIN HOOD

★★★

DIRECTOR: Wolfgang Reitherman

CAST: Animated

A feature-length cartoon featuring the adventures of Robin Hood and his gang, this is one of the lesser animated works from the Walt Disney Studios, but still good entertainment for the kiddies. Rated G.

1973 83 minutes

RUMPELSTILTSKIN

★★★½

DIRECTOR: Emile Andolino

CAST: Herve Villechaize, Shelley Duvall, Ned Beatty, Jack Fletcher, Bud Cort

In this *Faerie Tale Theatre* production, a poor miller's daughter (Shelley Duvall, the series' executive producer) becomes a queen by outwitting a dwarf (Herve Villechaize) and fulfilling her boastful father's promise that she can spin straw into gold. Villechaize is great as a rather unsavory Rumpelstiltskin, and Ned Beatty is convincing as the selfish king who learns to think about others as well as himself. The sets are especially beautiful.

1982 53 minutes

RUMPELSTILTSKIN

★★★½

DIRECTOR: David Irving

CAST: Amy Irving, Billy Barty, Clive Revill, Priscilla Pointer, John Moulder-Brown

This musical, based on the Brothers Grimm fairy tale, will delight most viewers under the age of 12. In it, Amy Irving plays a poor daydreamer who wishes she could marry a prince. When her father brags that everything she touches turns to gold, she is summoned by the greedy king (Clive Revill) to spin straw into gold. Rumpelstiltskin (Billy Barty) rescues her from this impossible task but expects her to repay him with her firstborn child. The scenery is lavish, but the songs grow tiresome. Priscilla Pointer is very convincing as the scheming queen. Rated G.

1987 85 minutes

RUN FOR THE ROSES

★★½

DIRECTOR: Henry Levin

CAST: Vera Miles, Stuart Whitman, Sam Groom, Panchito Gomez

Originally titled *Thoroughbred*, this is a *Rocky*-ish saga about a horse that eventually competes in the Kentucky Derby. A Puerto Rican boy, staying with his stepfather, devotes himself to making the nearly lame horse a winner. Rated PG.

1978 93 minutes

RUN, REBECCA, RUN

★★★★

DIRECTOR: Peter Maxwell

CAST: Henri Szeps, Simone Buchanan, John Stanton

This action-filled adventure finds a brave young girl captured by an illegal alien on an Australian island. Her fear of him soon dissolves as she helps him face the Australian authorities in order to be legally admitted to their country.

1983 81 minutes

SALUTE TO CHUCK JONES, A

★★★★½

DIRECTOR: Chuck Jones

CAST: Animated

Along with Tex Avery and Bob Clampett, Chuck Jones was the most inventive of the Warner Bros. cartoons creators. With writer Michael Maltese, he crafted some of the cleverest and funniest animated shorts ever made. This terrific package includes "One Froggy Evening" (perhaps the best cartoon of all time), along with "Duck Dodgers in the 25½ Century" (*Star Wars* creator George Lucas's favorite), "What's Opera, Doc?" (a superb Wagnerian takeoff), the Oscar-winning "For Scent-imental Reasons," "Rabbit Seasoning" (with Bugs, Daffy Duck, and Elmer Fudd in one of their immortal clashes), "Feed the Kitty," "Zoom and Bored" (with the Road Runner), and "High Note."

1985 56 minutes

SALUTE TO FRIZ FRELENG, A

★★★½

DIRECTOR: Friz Freleng

CAST: Animated

Three Academy Award–winning shorts—"Knighty Knight Bugs," "Speedy Gonzales," and "Birds Anonymous" (with Sylvester and Tweety Pie)—highlight this tribute to Friz Freleng, who went on to direct Pink Panther cartoons after leaving Warner Bros. Also included are "High Diving Hare," "Bunker Hill Bunny," "Show Biz Bugs," "Greedy for Tweety," and "A Mouse Divided."

1985 57 minutes

SALUTE TO MEL BLANC, A

★★★★

DIRECTORS: Friz Freleng, Chuck Jones, Robert McKimson

CAST: Animated

The main voice behind the Warner Bros. cartoons gets a fitting tribute in this superb collection of animated shorts. His vast repertoire of character voices is highlighted in Friz Freleng's "Bad Ol' Puddy Tat" (with Sylvester and Tweety Pie) and "Ballot Box Bunny" (with Bugs Bunny and Yosemite Sam, the latter being the most difficult voice Blanc had to do); Robert McKimson's "Who's Kitten Who?," "Bedeviled Rabbit" (with Bugs and the Tasmanian Devil), and "Little Boy Boo" (with Foghorn Leghorn); and Chuck Jones's "The Rabbit of Seville" (with Bugs and Elmer Fudd, whose voice was supplied by the late Arthur Q. Bryan), "Past Perfumance" (with Pepe Le Pew), and "Robin Hood Daffy," in which Blanc supplies an infectious laugh scene for Porky Pig as Friar Tuck.

1985 58 minutes

SAMMY, THE WAY-OUT SEAL

★★½

DIRECTOR: Norman Tokar

CAST: Jack Carson, Robert Culp, Patricia Barry, Billy Mumy,

Ann Jillian, Michael McGreevey, Elisabeth Fraser

Better than the title would imply. This series of misadventures involves two young brothers and the seal they attempt to keep as a pet. The film moves along briskly and features larger-than-life comic Jack Carson in one of his last performances. Long-suffering Robert Culp and the young culprits do a credible job with a tired old situation. Look for Ann Jillian in an early role. Originally aired as a two-part television program, this Disney production was released in Europe as a feature film.

1962 89 minutes

SANTA CLAUS—THE MOVIE

★★★★

DIRECTOR: Jeannot Szwarc

CAST: Dudley Moore, John Lithgow, David Huddleston, Burgess Meredith, Judy Cornwell, Christian Fitzpatrick, Carrie Kei Heim

In this enjoyable family film, one of Santa's helpers, an elf named Patch (Dudley Moore), visits Earth and innocently joins forces with an evil toy manufacturer (delightfully played by John Lithgow). It is up to Santa (David Huddleston) to save him—and the spirit of Christmas in children everywhere. Rated PG for light profanity and adult themes.

1985 105 minutes

SAVAGE SAM

★★½

DIRECTOR: Norman Tokar

CAST: Brian Keith, Tommy Kirk, Kevin Corcoran, Dewey Martin, Jeff York, Marta Kristen

Officially a sequel to *Old Yeller*, the film has little in common with its predecessor, except for some of the character names. Captured by Indians, the only hope of rescue for three children lies with Savage Sam, Old Yeller's son. This is an entertaining action film, albeit without the characterizations and depth of its predecessor. Not rated.

1963 103 minutes

SAVANNAH SMILES

★★★½

DIRECTOR: Pierre DeMoro

CAST: Bridgette Anderson, Mark Miller, Donovan Scott, Peter Graves, Chris Robinson, Michael Parks

In this surprisingly good, independently made family film, a 6-year-old runaway named Savannah (Bridgette Anderson) accidentally hides in the backseat of a car operated by two small-time crooks, Alvie (Mark Miller) and Boots (Donovan Scott). It's love at first sight for the trio, who decide to try to be a real family. The authorities, however, have other ideas. Rated G.

1982 107 minutes

SAVE THE LADY

★★★

DIRECTOR: Leon Thau

CAST: Matthew Excell, Robert Clarkson, Miranda Cartledge, Kim Clifford

Four kids set out to fight City Hall after a bureaucrat orders the historic *Lady Hope* steam ferry to be destroyed. The kids rescue *Lady Hope*'s former skipper from a retirement home. Together with an expert engineer, the team valiantly repairs and repaints the boat. The action picks up when the ferry must elude a fleet of police boats.

1981 76 minutes

SCANDALOUS JOHN

★★★

DIRECTOR: Robert Butler

CAST: Brian Keith, Alfonso Arau, Michele Carey, Rick Lenz,

Harry Morgan, Simon Oakland

Brian Keith stars as an eccentric ranch owner fighting to maintain his way of life. In his world, a cattle drive consists of one steer, and gunfights are practiced in the house with live ammunition. He must battle with the law, the world in general, and reality to keep his ranch and the life he loves. Laughs and poignancy are combined in this movie. Rated G.

1971 113 minutes

SEA GYPSIES, THE

★★★

DIRECTOR: Stewart Raffill

CAST: Robert Logan, Mikki Jamison-Olsen, Heather Rattray, Shanon Saylor

Director Stewart Raffill, who gave us the *Wilderness Family* films, also wrote this adventure movie. It was filmed in Alaska and Canada and tells of five castaways in the Pacific who end up on a remote Aleutian island. This Disney-style tale takes the survivors through many difficulties and is climaxed by a race against the approaching Alaskan winter to build a makeshift escape craft.

1978 102 minutes

SECRET OF NIMH, THE

★★★★★

DIRECTOR: Don Bluth

CAST: Dom De Luise, Peter Strauss, John Carradine (voices)

Lovers of classic screen animation, rejoice! Don Bluth's *The Secret of Nimh* is the best feature-length cartoon to be released since the golden age of Walt Disney. This movie, about the adventures of a widow mouse, is more than just a children's tale. Adults will enjoy it, too. Indeed, it deserves to be considered a classic. Don't miss it. Rated G.

1982 82 minutes

SECRET OF THE SWORD, THE

★

DIRECTORS: Bill Reed, Gwen Wetzler, Ed Friedman, Lou Kachivas, Marsh Lamore

CAST: Animated

Characters from the television series "He-Man and the Masters of the Universe" are featured in this poorly animated, ineptly written feature-length cartoon. Rated G.

1985 90 minutes

SESAME STREET PRESENTS FOLLOW THAT BIRD

★★★★

DIRECTOR: Ken Kwapis

CAST: Sandra Bernhard, Chevy Chase, John Candy, Dave Thomas, Joe Flaherty, Waylon Jennings

Although this kiddie film has an impressive "guest cast," the real stars are *Sesame Street* TV show regulars Big Bird, the Cookie Monster, Oscar the Grouch, Count von Count, the Telly Monster, etc. Children will love this story about Big Bird being evicted from Sesame Street. Rated G.

1985 88 minutes

SHAGGY D.A., THE

★

DIRECTOR: Robert Stevenson

CAST: Dean Jones, Tim Conway, Suzanne Pleshette

Feeble sequel to Disney's far superior *The Shaggy Dog*, this retread stars Dean Jones as the victim of an ancient curse that turns him into a canine at the worst of moments. This entry is a pointless example of Disney slapstick at its worst, with no attention to the character interaction that made the original so charming. A real dog. Rated G.

1976 91 minutes

SHAGGY DOG, THE

★★★½

DIRECTOR: Charles Barton
CAST: Fred MacMurray, Jean Hagen, Tommy Kirk, Annette Funicello

An ancient spell turns a boy into a sheepdog, and the fur flies in this slapstick Disney fantasy. Many of the gags are good, but the film sometimes drags.

1959 104 minutes

SHERLOCK HOLMES AND THE BASKERVILLE CURSE

★★

DIRECTOR: Eddy Graham
CAST: Animated

We weren't very impressed by this feature-length cartoon version of Sir Arthur Conan Doyle's oft-filmed "The Hound of the Baskervilles." The animation is way below par, and the story trifled with a bit too much for our tastes. It may be an effective introduction for youngsters to the joys of the canon. Rated G.

1984 60 minutes

SIGN OF ZORRO, THE

★★½

DIRECTORS: Norman Foster, Lewis R. Foster
CAST: Guy Williams, Henry Calvin, Gene Sheldon, Britt Lomond, George J. Lewis, Lisa Gaye

Baby boomers, beware. If you have fond memories of this swashbuckling Disney television series about the Z-slashing Robin Hood of Old Mexico, you might want to skip this uneven feature compilation of original episodes. It's still fine for the kiddies, however.

1960 B & W 91 minutes

SLEEPING BEAUTY

★★★★½

DIRECTOR: Clyde Geronimi
CAST: Animated

This Disney adaptation of Charles Perrault's seventeenth-century version of the famous fairy tale features distinctive animation that may surprise those accustomed to the softer style of the studio's other feature-length cartoons. Nevertheless, it is the last genre classic to be supervised by Walt Disney himself and belongs in any list of the best children's films (while having the added asset of being enjoyable for adults, as well). Rated G.

1959 75 minutes

SLEEPING BEAUTY

★★★★

DIRECTOR: Jeremy Kagan
CAST: Beverly D'Angelo, Bernadette Peters, Christopher Reeve, Sally Kellerman

This is one of the funniest *Faerie Tale Theatre* episodes. The sets may not be as spectacular as most in the series, but the cast makes up for it. Viewers should not expect to see much of the original tale because a lot of time is spent on the prince's past and his quest for the perfect woman. Christopher Reeve is excellent as the handsome prince, and Bernadette Peters makes a sweet and pretty princess. Sally Kellerman is wonderful as the queen.

1983 60 minutes

SMURFS AND THE MAGIC FLUTE, THE

★

DIRECTOR: John Rust
CAST: Animated

Those little blue people from the popular Saturday-morning television cartoon show are featured in their first movie. Oily McCreep steals the musical instrument of the title—which causes anyone who hears it to dance until they collapse from exhaustion—and uses it to steal all the wealth from an ancient kingdom until the

Smurfs intervene. The kiddies will probably love it, but parents should read a book. Rated G.

1983 80 minutes

SNIFFLES THE MOUSE CARTOON FESTIVAL FEATURING "SNIFFLES BELLS THE CAT"

★★★★

DIRECTOR: Chuck Jones

CAST: Animated

The achievements of Porky, Bugs, Daffy, and the other, more flamboyant Warner Bros. cartoon characters have tended to overshadow the simple charm of another of the studio's creations: the sweet-natured Sniffles the Mouse, as directed by Chuck Jones. But now that wrong has been righted with the release of this excellent collection of animated shorts. Coming from the acclaimed cartoon director's Disneyesque period, three of these—"Sniffles Bells the Cat," "The Brave Little Bat," and "Toy Trouble"—feature exquisite animation. Indeed, Sniffles owes quite a bit to another mouse named Mickey and the big-screen cartoon features he spawned, such as *Pinocchio* and *Bambi*.

1940–1944 36 minutes

SNOOPY, COME HOME

★★★½

DIRECTOR: Bill Melendez

CAST: Animated

Charming second entry in the "Peanuts" film series doesn't contain the childhood *angst* of the first but maintains the irreverent view of life found in the best of Charles Schulz's comic strips. Snoopy decides life at home ain't all it's cracked up to be, so he and Woodstock set off to find America. Needless to say, there's no place like home. Rated G.

1972 70 minutes

SNOW QUEEN

★★

DIRECTOR: Peter Medak

CAST: Melissa Gilbert, Lance Kerwin, Lee Remick, Lauren Hutton, Linda Manz, David Hemmings

This film is an exceedingly dull Faerie Tale Theatre tale of the Snow Queen (played by Lee Remick), who teaches an unruly boy a valuable lesson. The sets and special effects are second only to the actors' lines for their banality.

1983 48 minutes

SNOW WHITE AND THE SEVEN DWARFS

★★★★

DIRECTOR: Peter Medak

CAST: Elizabeth McGovern, Vanessa Redgrave, Vincent Price, Rex Smith

Both Vincent Price and Vanessa Redgrave are wickedly wonderful in this splendid adaptation of this Grimm's tale. Price plays the evil queen's (Redgrave) advising mirror. Lovely Elizabeth McGovern plays a sweet Snow White.

1983 51 minutes

SNOW WHITE AND THE THREE STOOGES

DIRECTOR: Walter Lang

CAST: The Three Stooges, Patricia Medina, Carol Heiss, Guy Rolfe, Buddy Baer, Edgar Barrier

Just about as bad as a film can be, this sad entry from what was left of the Three Stooges just lumbers on like a bad grammar-school play done on movie sets. Former temptress Patricia Medina as the wicked queen has every right to succeed in her efforts to eradicate ice-skating nonactress Carol Heiss as Snow White, but those darn Stooges keep upsetting her plans. This one is for Three Stooges completists *only*—the kids will hold it against you if you rent them this one.

1961 107 minutes

SNOWBALL EXPRESS

★★

DIRECTOR: Norman Tokar

CAST: Dean Jones, Nancy Olson, Harry Morgan, Keenan Wynn, Johnny Whitaker

This formula comedy stars the Disney stable of players from the 1960s and 1970s. Dean Jones inherits a run-down hotel and attempts to turn it into a ski resort. This is standard family viewing with a ski chase to help the pace and provide some laughs. Rated G.

1972 99 minutes

SO DEAR TO MY HEART

★★★★

DIRECTOR: Harold Schuster

CAST: Burl Ives, Beulah Bondi, Harry Carey, Luana Patten, Bobby Driscoll, Raymond Bond, Walter Soderling, Matt Willis, Spelman B. Collins

One of the finest of all feature-length Walt Disney films, this loving re-creation of small-town life in the early years of this century is wonderful entertainment for the whole family and a pure piece of Americana that mirrors simpler and much more pleasant times. Young Bobby Driscoll (one of the finest of all child actors) has taken a notion to enter his black lamb Danny in the county fair. A singing blacksmith (Burl Ives in his film debut) encourages him in his dreams. Sprinkled with lovely animated lead-ins and filmed in Sequoia National Park and Visalia, California, this gentle film presents a beautiful evocation of a time that has passed, and is loaded with love, goodwill, and sentiment. "Lavender Blue (Dilly Dilly)" was one of six new songs that debuted in this film.

1949 84 minutes

SOMEWHERE, TOMORROW

★★★

DIRECTOR: Robert Weimer

CAST: Sarah Jessica Parker, Nancy Addison, Tom Shea, Rick Weber

The Ghost and Mrs. Muir for a teen audience, this film is about a girl, played by Sarah Jessica Parker, who learns how to deal with her father's death by falling in love with the ghost of a teenage boy. The result is good family entertainment. Parker brings her usual solid competence to the role, and Tom Shea, as the ghost, is fine. Only a rather contrived happy ending dims the charm.

1986 91 minutes

SON OF FLUBBER

★★★½

DIRECTOR: Robert Stevenson

CAST: Fred MacMurray, Nancy Olson, Keenan Wynn, Tommy Kirk, William Demarest, Paul Lynde

This Disney sequel to *The Absent-Minded Professor* once again stars Fred MacMurray as the inventor of Flubber. Two new discoveries are featured: "dry rain" and "flubbergas." A multitude of character actors, including Keenan Wynn, William Demarest, and Paul Lynde, star in the supporting roles. While not as good as the original "Flubber" film, it does have some moments reminiscent of the original.

1963 B & W 100 minutes

STORY OF ROBIN HOOD, THE

★★★

DIRECTOR: Ken Annakin

CAST: Richard Todd, Joan Rice, Peter Finch, James Hayter, James Robertson Justice, Michael Hordern

This is Disney's live-action version of the Robin Hood legend, and it is much better than the later cartoon effort. The story holds to the well-known legend of the outlaw of Sherwood Forest but has elements that give the movie its own identity. One nice touch is the use of a wandering minstrel, who draws the story together. Richard Todd is a most appealing Robin Hood, while James Robertson Justice, as Little John, and Peter Finch, as the Sheriff of Nottingham, are first-rate. A fine cast, lush British settings, and imaginative touches added to the story make this movie most entertaining.

1952 83 minutes

SUMMER MAGIC

★★½

DIRECTOR: James Neilson

CAST: Hayley Mills, Burl Ives, Dorothy McGuire, Deborah Walley, Eddie Hodges, Peter Brown

Dorothy McGuire is a recent widow who finds out she has no money available. She moves her family to Maine, where they live in a fixer-upper house but are charged no rent by Burl Ives. Deborah Walley, a snobbish cousin, comes to visit and causes trouble. The house belongs to Peter Brown, who unexpectedly arrives home from Europe. Musical numbers by the Sherman brothers enliven the film, which is lightweight and enjoyable. Rated G.

1963 100 minutes

SUPERDAD

★★½

DIRECTOR: Vincent McEveety

CAST: Bob Crane, Barbara Rush, Kurt Russell, Joe Flynn

Bob Crane doesn't approve of his daughter's boyfriend (Kurt Russell) or the crowd she runs with. She claims that he just doesn't understand them. He decides to find out about the kids first-hand and to prove to his daughter that he's not hopelessly behind the times. His subsequent misadventures include beach football, surfing, and waterskiing. Rated G.

1973 94 minutes

SUPERMAN CARTOONS

★★★★

DIRECTORS: Dave Fleischer, Seymour Kneitel, I. Sparber

CAST: Animated

All other superhero cartoons pale in comparison to this collection of excellent Man of Steel shorts from the Max Fleischer Studios. Made between 1941 and 1943, these actually constitute the company's finest work, its "Popeye" cartoons notwithstanding. Included are "Superman," "The Bulleteers," "The Magnetic Telescope," "Mechanical Monsters," "The Mummy Strikes," "Jungle Drums," "Volcano," "Terror on the Midway," and "The Japoteurs." Because these cartoons are in the public domain, they have been collected by other companies on cassettes entitled "Superman," "Superman—The Cartoons," "The Color Adventures of Superman," etc.

1941–1943 75 minutes

SWISS FAMILY ROBINSON, THE

★★★½

DIRECTOR: Ken Annakin

CAST: John Mills, Dorothy McGuire, James MacArthur, Tommy Kirk, Sessue Hayakawa

Walt Disney's classic comedy-adventure film, adapted from the classic children's story by Johann

Wyss about a family shipwrecked on a desert island.

1960 128 minutes

SWORD AND THE ROSE, THE

★★½

DIRECTOR: Ken Annakin

CAST: Richard Todd, Glynis Johns, James Robertson Justice, Michael Gough

Romance, intrigue, and heroic acts of derring-do are the order of the day in this colorful Walt Disney adaptation of *When Knighthood Was in Flower*, filmed in England as one of a series of historical adventures that Disney would continue making in America during the fifties. Richard Todd is adept with both the lance and the ladies and makes an ideal lead (as he does in Disney's *Rob Roy* and *Robin Hood*), and Michael Gough is a truly malevolent heavy. The rest of the cast is on the mark and makes this film fun for everyone. The England of Henry VIII never looked so good.

1953 93 minutes

SWORD IN THE STONE

★★★½

DIRECTOR: Wolfgang Reitherman

CAST: Animated

The legend of King Arthur provided the storyline for this animated feature film from the Walt Disney studios. Although not up to the film company's highest standards, it still provides fine entertainment for the young and the young at heart. Rated G.

1963 80 minutes

SWORD OF THE VALIANT

★★★½

DIRECTOR: Stephen Weeks

CAST: Miles O'Keeffe, Sean Connery, Trevor Howard

The Old English tale of Sir Gawain and the Green Knight is brought to the screen with an appealing blend of action-adventure and tongue-in-cheek humor. Miles O'Keeffe (Bo Derek's "Tarzan the Ape Man") plays Sir Gawain, a rookie knight in the court of King Arthur. He is sent out on a quest brought on by a challenge issued by the magical Green Knight (Sean Connery). His knightly concept of medieval chivalry is often in contrast to the modernistic collection of bad guys and alluring ladies Gawain meets on his quest. Rated PG.

1984 162 minutes

SYLVESTER AND TWEETY'S CRAZY CAPERS

★★★

DIRECTORS: Friz Freleng, Robert McKimson

CAST: Animated

More Warner Bros. madness with that "bad old puddy tat" and the ready-for-anything little birdy. Directed by Friz Freleng and Robert McKimson, the titles include "The Last Hungry Cat," "Tweet and Lovely," "Tweety and the Beanstalk," "Tree for Two," "Tweety's S.O.S.," "Canned Feud," and "Hide and Go Tweet." Sylvester goes solo in "Mouse-Taken Identity," but those cartoons pitting him against Tweety Pie are the best. For all ages.

1985 54 minutes

TALE OF THE FROG PRINCE

★★★★

DIRECTOR: Eric Idle

CAST: Robin Williams, Teri Garr, Rene Auberjonois, Candy Clark

Perhaps the best of the Faerie Tale Theatre presentations, this story about a slighted fairy godmother who exacts revenge by turning a prince (Robin Williams) into a frog was inventively written and directed by Eric Idle, of

Monty Python fame. It's witty and well-acted.

1982 51 minutes

TEN WHO DARED

★

DIRECTOR: William Beaudine

CAST: Brian Keith, John Beal, James Drury, David Stollery

In 1869, Major John Wesley Powell and nine other explorers set out to explore the wild Colorado River. This movie is based on Major Powell's journal of that trip, but reading the journal would be more worthwhile and entertaining. An unbelievable and poorly crafted script, one-dimensional characters, and obvious studio and matte shots make this a movie to be missed by the entire family.

1960 92 minutes

THAT DARN CAT

★★½

DIRECTOR: Robert Stevenson

CAST: Dean Jones, Hayley Mills, Dorothy Provine, Roddy McDowall, Elsa Lanchester, Neville Brand, William Demarest, Ed Wynn, Frank Gorshin

Trust Disney to take a great book —*Undercover Cat*, by Gordon and Mildred Gordon—and turn it into a moronic slapstick farce. Hayley Mills and Dorothy Provine are a bit long in the tooth as the youthful (?) owners of a fulsome feline christened "DC" (for Darn Cat). One evening DC returns from his nightly rounds with an unusual collar: a watch belonging to a woman taken hostage in a recent bank robbery. Enter Dean Jones as an aelurophobic FBI agent who, with the stumble-footed assistance of his men, attempts to tail DC. The great supporting cast includes Roddy McDowall as a duck-hunting neighbor, Elsa Lanchester as the local snoop, and a pre-Riddler Frank Gorshin as one of the hoods.

1965 116 minutes

THEY WENT THAT-A-WAY AND THAT-A-WAY

★★

DIRECTORS: Edward Montagne, Stuart E. McGowan

CAST: Tim Conway, Chuck McCann, Reni Santoni, Richard Kiel, Lenny Montana, Dub Taylor

Tim Conway wrote and stars in this prison-escape comedy. He plays a small-town deputy who follows the governor's orders by being secretly placed in a maximum-security prison as an undercover agent posing as a hardened criminal. Fellow deputy (Chuck McCann) is his partner on the mission. When the governor suddenly dies, the two must escape from the prison. There are some silly gags, but this film does provide fair entertainment if you are looking for a few laughs and no deep plots. Rated PG.

1978 106 minutes

THIRD MAN ON THE MOUNTAIN

★★★

DIRECTOR: Ken Annakin

CAST: Michael Rennie, James MacArthur, Janet Munro, Herbert Lom

James MacArthur stars as a young man whose father was killed in a climbing accident. He wants badly to get into climbing, but his mother forbids it. He still sneaks practice and develops his skills. The Citadel (actually the Matterhorn) has never been scaled, and the boy's father died in an attempt. Several groups decide to try the climb independently, and MacArthur is among them. Miraculously, he finds the secret passage his father had been seeking. Breath-taking scenery and an excellent script make this film an excellent adventure story for the family. Not rated.

1959 106 minutes

THOSE CALLOWAYS

★★★★

DIRECTOR: Norman Tokar
CAST: Brian Keith, Vera Miles, Brandon de Wilde, Linda Evans

Sensitive, sentimental film about a family in New England. Man battles townspeople and nature to preserve a safe haven for geese. Marvelous scenes of life in a small town and the love between individuals. Rated G.

1965 131 minutes

THREE CABALLEROS, THE

★★★

DIRECTOR: Walt Disney
CAST: Animated

In Walt Disney's first attempt at combining animation and live action, Donald Duck is joined by two Latin feathered friends for a trip down to Rio. Originally, this cartoon travelogue was designed as a World War II propaganda piece promoting inter-American unity. It still holds up well today and remains a timeless learning experience for the kids.

1942 72 minutes

THREE LITTLE PIGS, THE

★★★★

DIRECTOR: Howard Storm
CAST: Billy Crystal, Jeff Goldblum, Valerie Perrine

Billy Crystal plays the industrious little pig who proves that "haste makes waste" when he takes his time building a sturdy house to keep the big, bad wolf away. The twist in this Faerie Tale Theatre version is that they've added a female companion (Valerie Perrine) who flees from the wolf with Crystal. Jeff Goldblum makes a hilarious, cigar-chomping wolf.

1984 51 minutes

THREE LIVES OF THOMASINA, THE

★★★★

DIRECTOR: Don Chaffey
CAST: Patrick McGoohan, Susan Hampshire, Karen Dotrice, Vincent Winter

An excellent cast and innovative ways of telling the story highlight this tale of love and caring. A young girl's cat is brought back to life by a woman who also teaches the girl's father to let others into his life. The cat's trip to cat heaven is outstandingly executed.

1964 97 minutes

THUMBELINA

★★★★

DIRECTOR: Michael Lindsay-Hogg
CAST: Carrie Fisher, William Katt, Burgess Meredith, narration by David Hemmings

This is an *Alice in Wonderland*–type tale of a thumb-size girl (Carrie Fisher) and her adventures as she tries to find her way home. The creatures she meets along the way are well characterized. This is one of the more rewarding Faerie Tale Theatre productions.

1983 48 minutes

TIGER TOWN

★★½

DIRECTOR: Alan Shapiro
CAST: Roy Scheider, Justin Henry

In this passable movie, made for the Disney Channel, Roy Scheider stars as a legendary baseball player whose final year with the Detroit Tigers looks dismal until a young boy (Justin Henry) "wishes" him to success. At least, that's what the. boy believes. Both Scheider and Henry give good performances, but the overall effect is not as impressive as it could have been. Rated G.

1984 76 minutes

TIGER WALKS, A

★★½

DIRECTOR: Norman Tokar
CAST: Brian Keith, Vera Miles, Pamela Franklin, Sabu, Kevin Corcoran, Peter Brown, Una Merkel, Frank McHugh

This Disney drama about an escaped circus tiger and the impact his fate has on a small town boasts a good cast of veteran film personalities as well as a jaundiced view of politics and mass hysteria. In the best Walt Disney tradition, the youths and cooler heads in the community fight an uphill battle to capture the runaway tiger (aided by former child star Sabu), only to be thwarted at every turn by the fearful majority who want to shoot the animal on sight. Brian Keith is at his solid best as the sheriff who refuses to be intimidated by the scared citizens and does his best to bring the beast to bay without hurting it. Look for Frank McHugh, friend and foil of James Cagney in many films, in one of his last roles. Released theatrically, this drama also showed up as a two-part show on television in the mid-1960s.

1964 88 minutes

TOBY TYLER

★★★½

DIRECTOR: Charles Barton
CAST: Kevin Corcoran, Henry Calvin, Gene Sheldon, Bob Sweeney, Mr. Stubbs, James Drury

Disney version of the popular juvenile book about a young runaway and his adventures with the circus is breezy entertainment and a showcase for young Kevin Corcoran (Moochie of many Disney television shows and the *Mickey Mouse Club*). The animals are charming, Mr. Stubbs the chimpanzee provides laughs and tears, young Corcoran is effective, and the recreated small towns of early twentieth-century America are reminiscent of old photographs and book illustrations of the period. Good entertainment for the family but certainly not the best of Disney's period films. Originally made as a silent film starring Jackie Coogan.

1960 96 minutes

TOM EDISON—THE BOY WHO LIT UP THE WORLD

★★★★

DIRECTOR: Henning Schellerup
CAST: David Huffman, Adam Arkin, Michael Callan, Rosemary DeCamp, James Griffith

A fine cast makes this film enjoyable. Tom Edison (David Huffman) and Cole Bogardis (Adam Arkin) begin working for the telegraph company at the same time. In Tom's spare time, he works on an assortment of inventions, including a cockroach electrocutor and a direct telegraph machine. Mr. Craner (Michael Callan) is threatened by Edison's inventiveness and tries to sabotage his efforts.

1983 49 minutes

TOM SAWYER

★★

DIRECTOR: James Nielson
CAST: Josh Albee, Jeff Tyler, Jane Wyatt, Buddy Ebsen, Vic Morrow, John McGiver

Mark Twain's classic story loses its satirical edge in this homogenized made-for-television production about the adventures of Tom Sawyer (Josh Albee) and Huckleberry Finn (Jeff Tyler). The kids may enjoy it, but adults will want to reread the book. Better yet, read the book to your kids. Rated G.

1973 78 minutes

TOM THUMB

★★★½

DIRECTOR: George Pal

CAST: Russ Tamblyn, June Thorburn, Peter Sellers, Terry-Thomas, Alan Young, Jessie Matthews, Bernard Miles

This underrated George Pal fantasy is a treat for young and old viewers. Good effects, pleasant tunes, and a distinguished cast of veteran British performers combine with Russ Tamblyn's infectious lead to make this a surefire choice for the VCR when the kids demand colorful entertainment and the adults don't want to watch another minute of "Rainbow Brite" or "The Care Bears." Worth a try.

1958 98 minutes

TONKA

★★★

DIRECTOR: Lewis R. Foster

CAST: Sal Mineo, Philip Carey, Jerome Courtland

Sal Mineo is White Bull, a Sioux Indian who captures and tames a wild stallion and names it Tonka Wakan—The Great One. Tribal law requires him to give the horse to his older Indian cousin, a bully who would mistreat the animal. Rather than do so, Mineo frees the horse. The horse is captured again and sold to the U.S. cavalry. Mineo tracks down the horse and finds it being gently handled by a captain. The cavalry is ordered to join Custer at the Little Big Horn, and Tonka, White Bull, and the captain face each other on the battlefield.

1958 97 minutes

TRANSFORMERS, THE MOVIE

DIRECTOR: Nelson Shin

CAST: Animated

In this animated vehicle for violence and destruction, the "good" autobots (who convert or transform into cars) and the dinobots (who change into dinosaurs) must battle the evil forces of Unicrom (Orson Welles) and Megatron (who later becomes Galvatron). There are endless shootouts and bombings between the two groups but in case that's not enough, other villains (such as the savage Octogons) wreak havoc as well. Throughout the film the heavy metal music proves to be distracting. The animation is sketchy and for non-Transformer fans it's impossible to keep track of who's good and who's bad. Rated PG for violence and occasional obscenities, and we do not recommend it for children under 12.

1986 80 minutes

TREASURE ISLAND (Original)

★★★★

DIRECTOR: Victor Fleming

CAST: Wallace Beery, Lionel Barrymore, Jackie Cooper, Lewis Stone

This is an MGM all-star presentation of Robert Louis Stevenson's children's classic of a young boy's adventure with pirates, buried treasure, and that delightful rogue of fiction Long John Silver. It seems all the great character actors of the 1930s put in an appearance, including Wallace Beery, as Silver, and Lionel Barrymore, as Billy Bones.

1934 B & W 105 minutes

TREASURE ISLAND (Remake)

★★★★

DIRECTOR: Byron Haskin

CAST: Robert Newton, Bobby Driscoll, Basil Sydney

Disney remake of the Robert Louis Stevenson pirate adventure is powered by a memorable Robert Newton as Long John Silver.

1950 87 minutes

UGLY DACHSHUND, THE

★★

DIRECTOR: Norman Tokar
CAST: Dean Jones, Suzanne Pleshette, Charlie Ruggles, Parley Baer, Kelly Thordsen

In this Disney movie, Dean Jones and Suzanne Pleshette are husband and wife; she loves dachshunds and owns a number of puppies. Charlie Ruggles convinces Jones to take a Great Dane puppy to raise. Since all of its peers are dachshunds, the Great Dane assumes it is one, too, and tries to act like them. The disparity in size causes various misfortunes and calamities. Finally, the Dane gets recognized on his own merits after winning a dog show. Somewhat entertaining along the lines of a made-for-TV-movie. Not rated.

1966 93 minutes

UNDERGRADS, THE

★★★½

DIRECTOR: Steven H. Stern
CAST: Art Carney, Chris Makepeace, Jackie Burroughs, Len Birman, Alfie Scopp

Billed as a comedy, this made-for-cable Disney film has only sporadic funny moments. Instead, it underlines the depression and loneliness of the elderly. Art Carney plays a spunky senior citizen whose son would like to put him into a rest home. Chris Makepeace (Carney's movie grandson) refuses to allow this. Instead, he and his grandfather become college roommates. A good film with a message, this one has some heavy moments. Unrated, but suitable for family viewing.

1984 102 minutes

UNIDENTIFIED FLYING ODDBALL

★★½

DIRECTOR: Russ Mayberry
CAST: Dennis Dugan, Jim Dale, Ron Moody, Kenneth More

Inept astronaut is transported to the court of King Arthur in his spacecraft. Once there, he discovers that Merlin and a knight are plotting against the king and sets out to expose them with his modern technology. Uneven script with situations not fully developed or explored hampers this Disney trifle. Rated G.

1979 92 minutes

WALTZ KING, THE

★★½

DIRECTOR: Steve Previn
CAST: Kerwin Mathews, Brian Aherne, Senta Berger, Peter Kraus, Fritz Eckhardt

The wonderful music of Johann Strauss Jr. is the real star of this Walt Disney biography filmed on location in Vienna. It stars earnest Kerwin Mathews as the famous composer and Senta Berger as the woman of his dreams. A treat to the eyes and ears, this is a good family film. Kerwin Mathews is better known for his fantasy and adventure films (especially Ray Harryhausen's classic *The Seventh Voyage of Sinbad*), but he's just as solid playing a piano as he is in dueling with a skeleton. Originally shown as a two-part television program on *Walt Disney's Wonderful World of Color*.

1963 94 minutes

WESTWARD HO THE WAGONS

★★½

DIRECTOR: William Beaudine
CAST: Fess Parker, Kathleen Crowley, Jeff York, David Stollery, Sebastian Cabot, George Reeves

Episodic film about a wagon train

traveling west. Vignettes include children being captured by Indians, an Indian attack on the wagon train, and an Indian boy being medically saved by a combination of Indian and white man's medicine. The basic appeal is seeing Fess Parker in another Davy Crockett–type role and four of the Mouseketeers as children in the train. Devoid of a real beginning or end, this movie just rambles along for its entire running time. Not rated.

1956 90 minutes

WHERE THE RED FERN GROWS

★★★★

DIRECTOR: Norman Tokar
CAST: James Whitmore, Beverly Garland, Jack Ging, Lonnie Chapman, Stewart Peterson

Fine family fare about a boy's love for two hunting dogs and his coming of age in Oklahoma in the 1930s. Rated G.

1974 90 minutes

WHISTLE DOWN THE WIND

★★★½

DIRECTOR: Bryan Forbes
CAST: Hayley Mills, Alan Bates, Bernard Lee, Norman Bird, Elsie Wagstaff

Bryan Forbes's first film is a thoughtful, allegorical tale about three children who encounter an accused murderer hiding in a barn and take him to be a Christ figure fleeing from his persecutors. Alan Bates as the fugitive and Hayley Mills as the oldest child bring the touchy subject beautifully to life in this warm, thought-provoking story. Based on Mary Hayley Bell's popular novel, this is one of the best films ever made dealing with the fragile nature of childhood trust and beliefs. This would be an interesting film to juxtapose with *Night of the Hunter* or *The Window*, where the children are potential victims of a murderer rather than his self-appointed salvation. Good family entertainment for all.

1962 B & W 99 minutes

WHITE FANG AND THE HUNTER

★★

DIRECTOR: Alfonso Brescia
CAST: Robert Wood, Pedro Sanchez

A dog, White Fang, and his master, Daniel (Robert Wood), are attacked by wolves, and only White Fang's protection saves Daniel. They are taken in by a young widow who is being forced to marry. So Daniel and the dog come to her aid. Poor acting and directing hamper this familiar story. Rated G.

1985 87 minutes

WILBUR AND ORVILLE: THE FIRST TO FLY

★★★★

DIRECTOR: Henning Schellerup
CAST: James Carroll Jordon, Chris Beaumont, John Randolph, Louise Latham, Edward Andrews

This entertaining biography of the Wright brothers shows their determination in the face of ridicule and harassment. In their early years, their experiments with flying machines cause some damage to their hometown and earn them the scorn of the townspeople. In an attempt to lead respectable lives, they begin working at a bicycle repair shop. Not surprisingly, they decide to use a bike for the next flying machine. The moral of this delightful film lies in sticking to something when you know you're right.

1973 47 minutes

WILDERNESS FAMILY, PART 2, THE

★★★

DIRECTOR: Frank Zuniga
CAST: Robert Logan, Susan D. Shaw, Heather Rattray, Ham

Larsen, George (Buck) Flower, Brian Cutler

Taken on its own terms, *The Wilderness Family, Part 2* isn't a bad motion picture. It's certainly one of the best of its kind. Film fans who want thrills and chills or something challenging to the mind should skip it; however, for pleasant family entertainment that will entrance the kiddies and mildly divert the adults, you could do a whole lot worse. Rated G.

1978 105 minutes

WILLY WONKA AND THE CHOCOLATE FACTORY

★★★

DIRECTOR: Mel Stuart

CAST: Gene Wilder, Jack Albertson, Peter Ostrum, Roy Kinnear, Aubrey Woods, Michael Bollner, Ursula Reit

Gene Wilder plays a candy company owner who allows some lucky kids to tour the facility. However, a few of his guests get sticky fingers (pun intended) and suffer the consequences. This essentially entertaining movie has its memorable moments—as well as bad. Its biggest problem is the Oompa Loompas, not-so-cuddly dwarfs who were supposed to delight kids but, instead, scared most of them. Rated G.

1971 98 minutes

WIND IN THE WILLOWS, THE

★★★★★

DIRECTOR: Wolfgang Reitherman

CAST: Animated

One of Disney's finest. This adaptation of Kenneth Grahame's classic deals with the adventures of J. Thaddeus Toad and his friends Cyril, Mole, Rat, and Mac Badger. Basil Rathbone narrates this classic short (which was originally released with *The Legend of Sleepy Hollow*). Disney artists on this project included Ollie Johnston, Frank Thomas, Ward Kimball, and Wolfgang Reitherman.

1949 75 minutes

WORLD'S GREATEST ATHLETE, THE

★★★

DIRECTOR: Robert Scheerer

CAST: Jan-Michael Vincent, John Amos, Tim Conway, Roscoe Lee Browne

John Amos is the athletics instructor at Merrivale College and has the misfortune to coach a large group of bumblers and incompetents. He and his assistant, Tim Conway, travel to Africa to get away from their toubles and come across Nanu (Jan-Michael Vincent), the greatest natural athlete in the world. To save their careers and give the college a winning team, they trick Nanu into coming to the United States and enroll him at the college. Some laughs take place as they introduce him to the various sports and develop a love interest for him. The big finale is the NCAA track-and-field championship, where Nanu singlehandedly takes on the other teams. The final sequence is improved by a young Howard Cosell as the announcer. One of the better Disney college films. Rated G.

1973 89 minutes

YEARLING, THE

★★★★½

DIRECTOR: Clarence Brown

CAST: Gregory Peck, Jane Wyman, Claude Jarman Jr., Chill Wills

A beautiful film version of Marjorie Kinnan Rawlings's sensitive story of a young boy's love for a pet fawn that his father must destroy. Simply told, this emotionally charged drama has been rated one of the finest films ever made.

1946 134 minutes

COMEDY

ABBOTT AND COSTELLO IN HOLLYWOOD

★★

DIRECTOR: S. Sylvan Simon
CAST: Bud Abbott, Lou Costello, Frances Rafferty, Robert Stanton

Lesser Abbott and Costello effort has Bud and Lou trying to make it big as movie stars. Best scenes occur early in the film, with Lou playing a barber.

1945 B & W 83 minutes

ABBOTT AND COSTELLO MEET CAPTAIN KIDD

★½

DIRECTOR: Charles Lamont
CAST: Bud Abbott, Lou Costello, Charles Laughton, Hillary Brooke, Leif Erickson

One of Abbott and Costello's few color films, this is strictly preschooler fare. As the title suggests, the boys play a pair of jerks who get chased around uncharted islands, pirate ships, etc., by the infamous Captain Kidd, as portrayed by Charles Laughton, who makes every effort to retain his dignity. Only worthwhile aspect of the film is the rare opportunity to see the comedy team in living color.

1952 70 minutes

ABBOTT AND COSTELLO MEET DR. JEKYLL AND MR. HYDE

★★★½

DIRECTOR: Charles Lamont
CAST: Bud Abbott, Lou Costello, Boris Karloff

Fun mixture of comedy and horror has the team up against the smooth Dr. Jekyll and the maniacal Mr. Hyde. The laughs come fast and furious in this, one of the boys' better films of the 1950s. Boris Karloff is in top form in the dual role, and don't miss the hilarious scene in which Lou is turned into a mouse!

1953 B & W 77 minutes

ABBOTT AND COSTELLO MEET FRANKENSTEIN

★★★★

DIRECTOR: Charles Barton
CAST: Bud Abbott, Lou Costello, Lon Chaney Jr., Bela Lugosi

Whenever someone writes about the Universal horror classics, they always cite this film as evidence of how the series fell into decline. Likewise, screen historians call it the beginning of the end for the comedy team. It deserves neither rap. For Bud Abbott and Lou Costello, it meant a resurgence of popularity after a slow fall from favor as the 1940s box-office champs. Yet it never compromises the characters of Dracula (Bela Lugosi), the Wolfman (Lon Chaney), or the Frankenstein monster (Glenn Strange). Director Charles Barton mixes fright and fun without sacrificing either.

1948 B & W 83 minutes

ADAM'S RIB

★★★★½

DIRECTOR: George Cukor

CAST: Spencer Tracy, Katharine Hepburn, Judy Holliday, Tom Ewell, David Wayne

The screen team of Spencer Tracy and Katharine Hepburn was always watchable, but never more so than in this comedy, directed by George Cukor. As husband-and-wife lawyers on opposing sides of the same case, they remind us of what movie magic is really all about. The supporting performances by Judy Holliday, Tom Ewell, David Wayne, and Jean Hagen greatly add to the fun.

1949 B & W 101 minutes

ADVENTURES IN BABYSITTING

★★★½

DIRECTOR: Chris Columbus

CAST: Elisabeth Shue, Keith Coogan, Anthony Rapp, Maia Brewton, Penelope Ann Miller, Vincent D'Onofrio

A sort of *After Hours* for the teen crowd, this is a surprisingly entertaining film about what happens when 17-year-old Chris Parker (Elisabeth Shue) accepts a babysitting assignment in the *Twilight Zone*. Actually, Chris doesn't really enter another dimension, it just seems like it after she gets a call from a runaway girlfriend (Penelope Ann Miller) who is stranded in the bus station in downtown Chicago. Once Chris loads up her charges (Keith Coogan, Anthony Rapp, and Maia Brewton), they face one potentially nightmarish situation after another. Since this is a comedy, things never become too frightening and there are a number of hilarious moments—our favorite being a sequence in a blues club presided over by superguitarist Albert Collins. Rated PG-13 for profanity and violence.

1987 100 minutes

ADVENTURES OF SHERLOCK HOLMES' SMARTER BROTHER, THE

★★½

DIRECTOR: Gene Wilder

CAST: Gene Wilder, Madeline Kahn, Marty Feldman, Dom De Luise

Even discounting the effrontery of writer-director-star Gene Wilder's creating a smarter sibling, Sigerson Holmes (Gene Wilder), one is still left with a less-than-hilarious, highly uneven romp. There are a few laughs, but you have to wait patiently for them. In the story, Sigerson falls in love with a dance hall damsel in distress (Madeline Kahn) and finds himself pursued by the baddies (Leo McKern and Roy Kinnear). Though the principals—who also include Marty Feldman and Dom De Luise—try hard, the film's soggy structure (and Wilder's poor research into the canon) plunge the whole thing into mediocrity. Rated PG.

1975 91 minutes

ADVENTURES OF OZZIE AND HARRIET, THE (TELEVISION SERIES)

★★★★

DIRECTOR: Ozzie Nelson

CAST: Ozzie Nelson, Harriet Nelson, Ricky Nelson, David Nelson, Kris Nelson, June Nelson, Don DeFore, Lyle Talbot, Mary Jane Croft, Parley Baer, Frank Cady, Skip Young, James Stacy, Kent McCord, Barry Livingston

This is the prototypical family sitcom. Though it's primarily remembered for its all-American wholesomeness, the show was genuinely funny on a consistent basis for 14 years. That remarkable accomplishment must be primarily credited to Ozzie Nelson, who produced, directed, and co-wrote, as well as starred as the earnest father who could create chaos out of the simplest situations. Real-life wife Harriet and sons Ricky and David added warmth and naturalness. In later episodes, Ricky's wife Kris and David's wife June appeared. By the last season, when the show had gone to color, the plots seemed stale. But, of the more than 400 episodes produced, the vast majority are well worth repeat viewing. Best bets are shows from 1951 to 1954, when the boys were at their most precocious and the series had an irresistible vitality and then from 1957–61, when Rick helped to popularize rock-'n-roll and planted the seeds of MTV. On the show, he introduced such hits as "Believe What You Say," "Lonesome Town," "Travelin' Man," and "Hello Mary Lou."

1952–1966 B & W 60 minutes

ADVENTURES OF TOPPER, THE

★★★

DIRECTOR: Philip Rapp

CAST: Anne Jeffreys, Robert Sterling, Leo G. Carroll, Lee Patrick, Thurston Hall, Kathleen Freeman

This television comedy, based on the film classic, ran on both NBC and ABC. It consistently earned chuckles, if not an abundance of belly laughs as this video compilation attests. Leo G. Carroll is delightful as Cosmo Topper, the henpecked bank vice-president who is the only one who can see a trio of ghosts—Marion Kirby (Anne Jeffreys), her husband George (Robert Sterling), "That most sporting spirit," and their booze-swilling Saint Bernard, Neil.

1953 93 minutes

AFRICA SCREAMS

★★

DIRECTOR: Charles Barton

CAST: Bud Abbott, Lou Costello, Hillary Brooke, Shemp Howard, Max Baer, Clyde Beatty, Frank Buck

Bud and Lou are joined by circus great Clyde Beatty and Frank (*Bring 'Em Back Alive*) Buck in this thin but enjoyable comedy, one of their last feature films. Most of the jungle and safari clichés are evident in this fast-paced, oddball film but they work acceptably, especially with plenty of familiar and capable players in support. Fun for the kids as well as the adults.

1949 B & W 79 minutes

AFTER HOURS

★★★★

DIRECTOR: Martin Scorsese

CAST: Griffin Dunne, Rosanna Arquette, Teri Garr, John Heard, Linda Fiorentino, Richard "Cheech" Marin,

Tommy Chong, Catherine O'Hara, Verna Bloom

Watching *After Hours* is not unlike listening to someone tell very funny jokes while scraping his fingers across a blackboard. If you can survive the agony, the laughs are well worth it. It is the most brutal and bizarre black (as in dark) comedy we are ever likely to see—a mixture of guffaws and goose pimples. Griffin Dunne, who was so ghoulishly hilarious as the decaying friend of wolfman David Naughton in *An American Werewolf in London*, stars as a computer operator who unwillingly spends a night in the SoHo area of downtown Manhattan. A trio of strange women (played by Rosanna Arquette, Teri Garr, and Linda Fiorentino) mystify, seduce, and horrify our hapless hero, and his life soon becomes a total nightmare. Director Martin Scorsese has never been better, and a topflight cast (which also includes John Heard, Cheech & Chong, and Catherine O'Hara) is wonderful to watch. Rated R for profanity, nudity, violence, and general weirdness.

1985 94 minutes

AFTER THE FOX

★

DIRECTOR: Vittorio De Sica

CAST: Peter Sellers, Victor Mature, Britt Ekland, Martin Balsam

Peter Sellers is at his worst, playing an Italian movie director in this flat farce. Victor Mature gives an amusing portrayal of a leading man whose ego remains mammoth, though his screen popularity is declining rapidly. The script for this fiasco was written by none other than Neil Simon.

1966 103 minutes

AIRPLANE!

★★★★

DIRECTORS: Jim Abrahams, David and Jerry Zucker

CAST: Robert Hays, Julie Hagerty, Leslie Nielsen, Kareem Abdul Jabbar, Lloyd Bridges, Peter Graves, Robert Stack

This is a hilarious spoof of the *Airport* series—and movies in general. While the jokes don't always work, there are so many of them that this comedy ends up with enough laughs for three movies. Rated PG.

1980 88 minutes

AIRPLANE II: THE SEQUEL

★★★½

DIRECTOR: Ken Finkleman

CAST: Robert Hays, Julie Hagerty, Peter Graves, William Shatner

Viewers who laughed uncontrollably through *Airplane!* will find much to like about this sequel. The stars of the original are back, with silly jokes and sight gags galore. However, those who thought the original was more stupid than funny undoubtedly will mutter the same about the sequel. Rated PG for occasional adult content.

1982 85 minutes

ALFIE

★★★★

DIRECTOR: Lewis Gilbert

CAST: Michael Caine, Shelley Winters, Millicent Martin, Julia Foster, Shirley Anne Field

Wild and ribald comedy about a Cockney playboy (Michael Caine) who finds "birds" irresistible. Full of sex and delightful charm, this quick-moving film also tells the poignant tragedy of a man uncertain about his lifestyle. Nominated for five Oscars, including best picture and best actor.

1966 113 minutes

ALL OF ME

★★★★½

DIRECTOR: Carl Reiner

CAST: Steve Martin, Lily Tomlin, Victoria Tennant, Richard Libertini

Steve Martin finds himself haunted from within by the soul of a recently deceased Lily Tomlin when an attempt to put her spirit in another woman's body backfires. This delightful comedy is directed by Carl Reiner (*Where's Poppa?*; *The Man with Two Brains*) and gives its two stars the best showcase for their talents to date. Rated PG for suggested sex, violence, and profanity.

1984 93 minutes

ALL THE MARBLES

DIRECTOR: Robert Aldrich

CAST: Peter Falk, Vicki Frederick, Laurene Landon, Burt Young, Tracy Reed, Ursalin Bryant-King

Peter Falk stars as the unscrupulous manager of two female wrestlers in this dreadful movie, directed by Robert Aldrich (*The Dirty Dozen*). Bad taste . . . total waste. Rated R because of nudity, violence, and profanity.

1981 113 minutes

ALLNIGHTER, THE

DIRECTOR: Tamar Simon Hoffs

CAST: Susanne Hoffs, John Terlesky, Joan Cusack, Dedee Pfeiffer, James Anthony Shanta, Janielle Brady

Rock star Susanna Hoffs (of the Bangles) stars in this terminally dumb 1980s beach movie as a college student who goes on one last fling before graduating. After about 10 minutes, you'll want to fling the tape out the window. This, by the way, was a family affair. Director Tamar Simon Hoffs is the star's mother. What some parents do to their kids! Rated PG.

1987 90 minutes

ALMOST PERFECT AFFAIR, AN

★★★

DIRECTOR: Michael Ritchie

CAST: Keith Carradine, Monica Vitti, Raf Vallone

A very human love triangle evolves amidst the frenzy of film politics that surrounds the Cannes Film Festival. This romantic comedy about a young American filmmaker and the worldly but lovable wife of a powerful Italian film mogul is slow to start, but leaves you with a warm feeling. Aside from being an enjoyable story, it takes the time to look with perspective at the difference between European and American values. Rated PG with suggested sex and partial nudity.

1979 92 minutes

ALMOST YOU

★★★★

DIRECTOR: Adam Books

CAST: Brooke Adams, Griffin Dunne, Karen Young, Marty Watt

Brooke Adams and Griffin Dunne give excellent performances in this film about a restless husband and his down-to-earth wife. Dunne, who displayed similar characteristics in Martin Scorsese's *After Hours*, perfectly emulates the frustrated over-30 businessman and husband with comic results. Adams plays his wife, who is recovering from a car accident that gives her a new perspective on life. Rated R for language, sex, and nudity.

1985 91 minutes

ALWAYS

★★★

DIRECTOR: Henry Jaglom
CAST: Henry Jaglom, Patrice Townsend, Joanna Frank, Alan Rachins, Jonathan Kaufer, Melissa Leo

Largely autobiographical, *Always* follows Henry Jaglom and Patrice Townsend through their breakup and their reckoning of the relationship. The film's centerpiece is a party where the individual members bare their souls, revealing their insecurities in dealing with love and life. *Always* has a bittersweet feeling that is reminiscent of some of Woody Allen's films dealing with romance. Unfortunately, the movie doesn't have the laughs that Allen provides, so the melancholy moments seem a bit long. Rated R for profanity and nudity.

1984 105 minutes

AMAZING ADVENTURE

★★★

DIRECTOR: Alfred Zeisler
CAST: Cary Grant, Mary Brian, Peter Gawthorne, Henry Kendall, Leon M. Lion

Feeling guilty after inheriting a fortune, Cary Grant sets out to earn his living in this comedy of stout hearts among the poor-but-honest in England during the Depression.

1936 B & W 70 minutes

AMERICAN DREAMER

★★★½

DIRECTOR: Rick Rosenthal
CAST: JoBeth Williams, Tom Conti, Giancarlo Giannini

JoBeth Williams (*The Big Chill*) plays Cathy Palmer, a would-be novelist who, in a short story contest, successfully captures the style of a series of adventure stories that feature a superspy named Rebecca Ryan and thereby wins a trip to Paris. But once there, Palmer is hit by a car and wakes up believing she is the fictional character. That's when she starts causing all sorts of trouble for a hapless fellow she thinks is her sidekick (Tom Conti, of *Reuben, Reuben*) and a French diplomat (Giancarlo Giannini) whose life she fears is in danger. The picture is sort of a *Romancing the Stone II*, but never quite shines as brightly as one expects. Rated PG for violence.

1984 105 minutes

AMERICAN GRAFFITI

★★★★½

DIRECTOR: George Lucas
CAST: Richard Dreyfuss, Ron Howard, Paul LeMat, Cindy Williams, Candy Clark, Mackenzie Phillips, Wolfman Jack, Harrison Ford, Bo Hopkins, Suzanne Somers, Charles Martin Smith

Star Wars creator George Lucas discovered his talent for creating light-hearted, likable entertainment with this film about the coming of age of a group of high-school students in Northern California. Blessed with a superb rock-'n-roll score and fine performances by Richard Dreyfuss, Ron Howard, Paul LeMat, Cindy Williams, Charles Martin Smith, and Candy Clark, it's the best of its kind and inspired the long-running television series *Happy Days*. Rated PG.

1973 110 minutes

AMERICATHON

DIRECTOR: Neal Israel
CAST: John Ritter, Harvey Korman, Nancy Morgan, Peter Riegert, Zane Buzby, Fred Willard, Chief Dan George

Before managing to entertain audiences with such questionable movies as *Bachelor Party* and *Moving Violations*, director Neal Israel made this absolutely abysmal comedy about a bankrupt American government staging a telethon to save itself. Rated R for profanity and sleaze.

1979 86 minutes

AND NOW FOR SOMETHING COMPLETELY DIFFERENT

★★★½

DIRECTOR: Ian McNaughton
CAST: John Cleese, Eric Idle, Terry Jones, Michael Palin, Graham Chapman, Terry Gilliam

Fitfully funny but still a treat for their fans, this was the first screen outing of the Monty Python comedy troupe. It's a collection of the best bits from the team's television series. With delightful ditties, such as "The Lumberjack Song," how can you go wrong? Rated PG.

1972 89 minutes

ANIMAL CRACKERS

★★★★

DIRECTOR: Victor Heerman
CAST: The Marx Brothers, Margaret Dumont, Lillian Roth, Robert Greig, Hal Thompson, Louis Sorin

Animal Crackers is pure Marx Brothers, a total farce loosely based on a hit play by George S. Kaufman. Highlights include Groucho's African lecture—"One morning I shot an elephant in my pajamas. How he got into my pajamas, I'll never know"—and the uproariously funny card game with Harpo, Chico, and the ever-put-upon Margaret Dumont.

1930 B & W 98 minutes

ANIMAL HOUSE

★★★★½

DIRECTOR: John Landis
CAST: John Belushi, Tim Matheson, Karen Allen, Peter Riegert, John Vernon

Although it has spawned a seemingly relentless onslaught of inferior carbon copies, this comedy is still one of the funniest movies ever made. If you're into rock-'n-roll, partying, and general craziness, this picture—directed by John Landis (*The Blues Brothers*)—is for you. We gave it a 95, because it has a good beat and you can dance to it. The late John Belushi, Tim Matheson, Karen Allen (*Raiders of the Lost Ark*), Peter Riegert (*Local Hero*), and John Vernon all are terrific in this story of a wild college fraternity that gets put on "double secret probation" and, of course, blows it. But guess who gets the last laugh. Rated R.

1978 109 minutes

ANNIE HALL

★★★★★

DIRECTOR: Woody Allen
CAST: Woody Allen, Diane Keaton, Tony Roberts, Paul Simon, Shelley Duvall, Carol Kane

Woody Allen's exquisite romantic comedy won the 1977 Academy Awards for best picture, actress (Diane Keaton), director (Allen), and screenplay (Allen and Marshall Brickman)—and deserved every one of them. This delightful semiautobiographical romp features Allen as Alvy Singer, a more assured version of Alan Felix, from *Play It Again, Sam*, who falls in love (again) with Keaton (in the title role), proving that a kiss is still just a kiss—and wonderfully entertaining when in a classic motion picture. Rated PG for profanity and bedroom scenes.

1977 94 minutes

ANY WHICH WAY YOU CAN

★

DIRECTOR: Buddy Van Horn
CAST: Clint Eastwood, Sondra Locke, Geoffrey Lewis, William Smith, Ruth Gordon

Another comedy clinker from Clint Eastwood and company, this features the same cast and story (about the adventures of a streetfighter and his pet orangutan) from *Every Which Way But Loose*, a movie that wasn't very good to begin with. Aside from a few funny moments provided by Clyde (the orangutan), it's a waste. Rated PG.

1980 116 minutes

APARTMENT, THE

★★★★★

DIRECTOR: Billy Wilder
CAST: Jack Lemmon, Shirley MacLaine, Fred MacMurray, Ray Walston, Jack Kruschen, Edie Adams

Rarely have comedy and drama been satisfyingly blended into a cohesive whole. Director Billy Wilder does it masterfully in this film. With career advancement in mind, Jack Lemmon permits his boss (Fred MacMurray) to use his apartment for illicit love affairs. Then he gets involved with the boss's emotionally distraught girlfriend (Shirley MacLaine). Lemmon sparkles. MacLaine is irresistible. And MacMurray, playing a heel, is a revelation. Beautifully balancing wit and pathos, the film bears repeated viewing.

1960 B & W 125 minutes

APRIL FOOLS, THE

DIRECTOR: Stuart Rosenberg
CAST: Jack Lemmon, Catherine Deneuve, Peter Lawford, Sally Kellerman, Myrna Loy, Charles Boyer

A failed attempt at a serious romantic comedy that veers too often into awkward slapstick. This is the sort of film best left to the French; director Stuart Rosenberg just doesn't know what to make of the genre. Jack Lemmon falls in love with his boss's wife . . . and that's it. An excellent—and completely wasted—supporting cast cannot disguise the thin script, and the obligatory, last-minute happy ending doesn't fit at all. This isn't even up to the standards of most made-for-television features. Rated PG for adult situations.

1969 95 minutes

ARMED AND DANGEROUS

DIRECTOR: Mark L. Lester
CAST: John Candy, Eugene Levy, Robert Loggia, Kenneth McMillan, Meg Ryan, Jonathan Banks, Brion James

Comedy fizzle from two talented SCTV graduates whose theatrical films have consistently fallen short of their usually hilarious TV sketches and bits. The story concerns fired cop Frank Dooley (John Candy) and former lawyer Norman Kane (Eugene Levy), who meet and become partners at their new jobs as private security guards for a firm known as Guard Dog. When Dooley uncovers an embezzling plot by the owner of the company (Robert Loggia), the pair find themselves in a real mess. There are a few comedic gems, to be sure, but most of the gags are just rehashed from countless other films of this sort, and the obligatory slapstick chase finale in which numerous perfectly good cars are demolished is simply too much. Rated PG-13 for language.

1986 89 minutes

ARMY BRATS

DIRECTOR: Ruud van Hemert
CAST: Frank Schaafsma, Geert DeJong, Akemay, Peter Faber, Rijk De Gooher

This ridiculous comedy centers around the war taking place within the Gisbert family. Mr. Gisbert has been the paranoid commander at his home while his apathetic wife amused herself with her tennis coach. Meanwhile, their four children have armed themselves to battle and overthrow their less-than-ideal parents. Foreign, it is dubbed and unrated. The obscene language and nudity make it comparable with an R.

1984 103 minutes

AROUND THE WORLD IN 80 DAYS

★★★

DIRECTOR: Michael Anderson
CAST: David Niven, Cantinflas, Shirley MacLaine, Marlene Dietrich, Robert Newton

An all-star spectacular with David Niven, Cantinflas, and Shirley MacLaine in the pivotal roles, this inflated travelogue was a spectacular success when originally released. However, it seems hopelessly dated today and loses all too much on the small screen. Even picking out the dozens of stars in cameo roles doesn't yield as much joy under the plodding direction of Michael Anderson as it could have. It's a curiosity at best.

1956 167 minutes

ARSENIC AND OLD LACE

★★★★½

DIRECTOR: Frank Capra
CAST: Cary Grant, Priscilla Lane, Jack Carson, James Gleason, Peter Lorre, Raymond Massey, Jean Adair, Josephine Hull

Two sweet old ladies have found a solution for the loneliness of elderly men with no family or friends—they poison them! Then they give them a proper Christian burial in their basement. Their nephew, Mortimer (Cary Grant), an obvious party pooper, finds out and wants them to stop. This delightful comedy is crammed with sparkling performances. Jean Adair and Josephine Hull recreate their Broadway roles as the daffy sisters. Peter Lorre, Raymond Massey, and Jack Carson also add some memorable characterizations to this screen version of the Joseph Kesselring play.

1944 B & W 118 minutes

ARTHUR

★★★★

DIRECTOR: Steve Gordon
CAST: Dudley Moore, Liza Minnelli, Stephen Elliott, John Gielgud

Dudley Moore is Arthur, the world's richest (and obviously happiest) alcoholic. But all is not well in his pickled paradise. Arthur will lose access to the family's great wealth if he doesn't marry the uptight debutante picked out for him by his parents. He doesn't love her . . . in fact, he doesn't even like her. And what's worse, he's in love with a wacky shoplifter (Liza Minnelli). Most of the time, it's hilarious, with John Gielgud as a sharp-tongued butler providing the majority of the laughs. Rated PG because of profanity.

1981 97 minutes

AS YOU LIKE IT

★★★

DIRECTOR: Paul Czinner
CAST: Elisabeth Bergner, Laurence Olivier, Felix Aylmer, Leon Quartermaine

Laurence Olivier is commanding

as Orlando to beautiful Elisabeth Bergner's stylized Rosalind in this early filming of Shakespeare's delightful comedy. Lovers of the Bard will be pleased.

1936 B & W 96 minutes

AT THE CIRCUS

★★★½

DIRECTOR: Edward Buzzell

CAST: The Marx Brothers, Margaret Dumont, Kenny Baker, Eve Arden

The Marx Brothers were running out of steam as a comedy team by the time of this film. Still, any film with Groucho, Harpo, and Chico is worth watching, although you'll probably feel like punching the comedy's "hero" (or is that a zero?), Kenny Baker, when he sings that highly forgettable ditty "Step Up, Take a Bow."

1939 B & W 87 minutes

AT WAR WITH THE ARMY

★★★★

DIRECTOR: Hal Walker

CAST: Dean Martin, Jerry Lewis, Polly Bergen, Angela Greene, Mike Kellin

Dean Martin and Jerry Lewis were still fresh and funny at the time of this comedy release, but a classic it isn't (though some scenes are gems).

1950 B & W 93 minutes

ATOLL K (UTOPIA)

DIRECTOR: Léo Joannon

CAST: Stan Laurel, Oliver Hardy

The final screen outing of the great comedy team of Stan Laurel and Oliver Hardy is a keen disappointment. Laurel became ill during its making and looks just awful (making his crying scenes more sad than funny). It's a regrettable final bow for two of the screen's greatest clowns.

1950 B & W 80 minutes

ATTACK OF THE KILLER TOMATOES

T

DIRECTOR: John De Bello

CAST: David Miller, Sharon Taylor, George Wilson, Jack Riley

In this campy cult film, the tomatoes are funnier than the actors, most of whom are rank amateurs. Jack Riley, of the first Bob Newhart television show, supplies the few moments of subtle comic timing as an agriculture department official. Unfortunately for him and the viewers, he is killed by thousands of squished tomatoes. George Wilson, as presidential aide Jim Richardson, is not bad either. There is little that they can do to soften the bludgeoning sophomoric comedy of the screenplay. The plot? Killer tomatoes begin terrorizing the western United States while the military plans inept strategies. Rated PG.

1980 87 minutes

AUDIENCE WITH MEL BROOKS, AN

★★★½

DIRECTOR: Mel Brooks

CAST: Mel Brooks

This is a reserved, delightfully anecdotal evening with the comic genius. Filmed in England, it features Brooks answering questions from the audience about his career, life, and famous collaborators. There are a few clips from his version of *To Be or Not To Be*, which smacks a little too much of self-promotion. However, it's one of the better comedy videos, primarily because it features the master of the ad-lib at his funniest. Unrated.

1984 55 minutes

AUNTIE MAME

★★★½

DIRECTOR: Morton Da Costa
CAST: Rosalind Russell, Forrest Tucker, Coral Browne, Fred Clark

Rosalind Russell, in the title role, plays a free-thinking eccentric woman whose young nephew is placed in her care. Russell created the role on the stage; it was a once-in-a-lifetime showcase that she made uniquely her own.

1958 143 minutes

AUTHOR! AUTHOR!

★★★

DIRECTOR: Arthur Hiller
CAST: Al Pacino, Dyan Cannon, Alan King, Tuesday Weld

Al Pacino stars as a playwright whose wife (Tuesday Weld) leaves him with five kids (not all his) to raise in this nicely done bittersweet comedy. Dyan Cannon plays the actress with whom he falls in love. Rated PG for brief profanity.

1982 110 minutes

AWFUL TRUTH, THE

★★★★

DIRECTOR: Leo McCarey
CAST: Irene Dunne, Cary Grant, Ralph Bellamy, Molly Lamont, Cecil Cunningham, Mary Forbes

Irene Dunne and Cary Grant divorce so that they can marry others. Then they do their best to spoil one another's plans. Leo McCarey won an Oscar for directing this prime example of the screwball comedies that made viewing such a delight in the 1930s. Grant—a master of timing—is in top form, as is co-star Dunne. It's hilarious all the way.

1937 B & W 92 minutes

BACHELOR AND THE BOBBY-SOXER, THE

★★½

DIRECTOR: Irving Reis
CAST: Cary Grant, Myrna Loy, Shirley Temple, Rudy Vallee

Lady judge Myrna Loy cleverly sentences playboy Cary Grant to baby-sit Shirley Temple, her sister, a panting nubile teenager with a crush on him. There are some hilarious moments, but the comedy gets thin as Loy's lesson begins to cloy. Best bit is the play on words about the Man with the Power, Voodoo and Youdo.

1947 B & W 95 minutes

BACHELOR MOTHER

★★★

DIRECTOR: Garson Kanin
CAST: Ginger Rogers, David Niven, Charles Coburn, Frank Albertson, Ernest Truex

The old story about a single woman who finds a baby on a doorstep and is mistaken for its mother has never been funnier than in this witty film by writer-director Garson Kanin. Ginger Rogers as the shop girl who finds her job in jeopardy and her whole life upside-down as a result of the confusion shows her considerable skill for comedy. David Niven, in an early starring role, is just great as the store owner's son who attempts to "rehabilitate" the fallen Rogers and ends up falling for her and the baby. The entire film benefits from a brisk pace. A lot of the action takes place in a department store at Christmas and the counters are *filled* with Donald Duck dolls and toys of all descriptions—in fact, Donald Duck plays an important part in the eventual romance between Rogers and Niven. This film is fun for everyone.

1939 B & W 82 minutes

BACHELOR PARTY

★★

DIRECTOR: Neil Israel
CAST: Tom Hanks, Tawny Kitaen, Adrian Zmed, George Grizzard, Robert Prescott

Even Tom Hanks (of *Splash*) can't save this "wild" escapade into degradation when a carefree bus driver who has decided to get married is given an all-out bachelor party by his friends. Rated R for profanity and nudity.

1984 106 minutes

BACK TO SCHOOL

★★★½

DIRECTOR: Alan Metter
CAST: Rodney Dangerfield, Sally Kellerman, Burt Young, Keith Gordon, Robert Downey Jr., Ned Beatty, M. Emmet Walsh, Adrienne Barbeau, William Zabka, Severn Darden

A true surprise from the usually acerbic Rodney Dangerfield, who sheds his lewd-'n-crude image in favor of one more sympathetic and controlled. He stars as the self-made owner of a chain of "Tall and Fat" stores who decides to return to college for a never-achieved diploma. He selects the college attended by his son in order to spend more time with the boy (well played, with eyes that frequently roll heavenward, by Keith Gordon). The story then focuses on their differing approaches to life: Gordon wants his own victories or failures, but Dangerfield prefers to buy his way through life. He even hires Kurt Vonnegut (who appears as himself) to write an English report, which is rejected for being an obvious crib job by "somebody who knows nothing about the author." Rated PG-13 for occasionally vulgar humor.

1986 96 minutes

BAD MEDICINE

★★★½

DIRECTOR: Harvey Miller
CAST: Steve Guttenberg, Julie Hagerty, Alan Arkin, Bill Macy, Curtis Armstrong, Julie Kavner, Joe Grifasi, Robert Romanus, Taylor Negron

Steve Guttenburg (*Cocoon, Diner*) and Julie Hagerty (*Lost in America*, the *Airplane* movies) play students attending a "Mickey Mouse" med school in Central America. When they find the health conditions in a nearby village unacceptable, they set up a medical clinic, stealing the needed drugs from the school's pharmacy. The all-star cast does not disappoint. Alan Arkin's role as the owner of the school is especially fine. Rated PG-13 for profanity, sex, and adult situations.

1985 97 minutes

BAD NEWS BEARS, THE

★★★★★

DIRECTOR: Michael Ritchie
CAST: Walter Matthau, Tatum O'Neal, Vic Morrow, Alfred Lutter, Jackie Earle Haley

An utterly hilarious comedy directed by Michael Ritchie, this film focuses on the antics of some foul-mouthed Little Leaguers, their beer-guzzling coach (Walter Matthau), and girl pitcher (Tatum O'Neal). But be forewarned, the sequels, *Breaking Training* and *The Bad News Bears Go to Japan*, are strictly no-hitters. Rated PG.

1976 102 minutes

BAD NEWS BEARS GO TO JAPAN, THE

DIRECTOR: John Berry
CAST: Tony Curtis, Jackie Earle Haley, Tomisaburo Wakayama, George Wyner, Lonnie Chapman

Worst of the *Bad News Bears* trio of films, this features Tony Curtis as a small-time promoter with big ideas, which involve taking the unpredictable (but now sanitized) pint-size ball team to Japan. Unfunny and too cutesy, it was their last screen romp. Rated PG.

1978 91 minutes

BAD NEWS BEARS IN BREAKING TRAINING, THE

★★

DIRECTOR: Michael Pressman
CAST: William Devane, Jackie Earle Haley, Clifton James

Without Walter Matthau, Tatum O'Neal, and director Michael Ritchie, this sequel to *The Bad News Bears* truly is bad news . . . and rather idiotic. How many kids do *you* know who'd be allowed to hop into a minibus and drive to Houston *sans* adult supervision? Jackie Earle Haley returns as the team star, and William Devane has a reasonable part as Haley's footloose father. Don't expect much. Rated PG for mild language.

1977 100 minutes

minutes

BALL OF FIRE

★★★½

DIRECTOR: Howard Hawks
CAST: Gary Cooper, Barbara Stanwyck, Dana Andrews, Oscar Homolka, S. Z. Sakall, Richard Haydn, Henry Travers, Tully Marshall, Leonid Kinskey, Allen Jenkins, Aubrey Mather

Stuffy linguistics professor Gary Cooper meets hotch-cha dancer Barbara Stanwyck. He and seven lovable colleagues are putting together an encyclopedia. She's recruited to fill them in on slanguage. She does this, and more! Gangster Dana Andrews and motor-mouthed garbage man Allen Jenkins add to the madcap antics in what has been dubbed the last of the prewar screwball comedies. Good show!

1941 B & W 111 minutes

BALLOONATIC, THE/ONE WEEK

★★★

DIRECTORS: Buster Keaton, Eddie Cline
CAST: Buster Keaton, Phyllis Haver, Sybil Seely

The comedic invention and physical stamina of the Great Stone Face, as Buster Keaton was called, are shown to perfect advantage in these early 1920s silent shorts. In *The Balloonatic* Buster is "skyjacked" by a runaway balloon and dropped into the wilderness. In *One Week* he constructs a kit house from fouled-up assembly plans. An ample demonstration of why Keaton was one of the great silent comics. Silent.

1920–1923 B & W 48 minutes

BALTIMORE BULLET, THE

★★½

DIRECTOR: Robert Ellis Miller
CAST: James Coburn, Bruce Boxleitner, Omar Sharif, Ronee Blakley

In this tale of big-league pool hustling, clever cuesters James Coburn and Bruce Boxleitner carefully build up to scoring big in a nail-biting shootout with suave Omar Sharif. Rated PG.

1980 103 minutes

BANANAS

★★★★

DIRECTOR: Woody Allen
CAST: Woody Allen, Louise Lasser, Carlos Montalban, Howard Cosell

Before he started making classic comedies, such as *Annie Hall*, *Zelig*, and *Broadway Danny Rose*, writer-director-star Woody Allen made some pretty wild—

though generally uneven—wacky movies. This 1971 comedy, with Woody's hapless hero becoming involved in a South American revolution, does have its share of hilarious moments. It is, in fact, one of the better examples of Allen's early experiments in laugh-getting and film-making. Rated PG.

1971 82 minutes

BANANAS BOAT, THE

DIRECTOR: Sidney Hayers
CAST: Doug McClure, Hayley Mills, Lionel Jeffries, Warren Mitchell

Often a film comes along that raises important questions, such as "Why was it made?" This purported comedy has no plot, no acting, and no laughs, unless old men getting beat up and Doug McClure's bare rear end are considered funny. The music is stupid, too. McClure plays an American loser caught up with a crazy Englishman in a typical revolution-torn South American nation. Rated PG for naughty language and nudity.

1987 91 minutes

BANK DICK, THE

★★★★★

DIRECTOR: Eddie Cline
CAST: W. C. Fields, Cora Witherspoon, Una Merkel, Shemp Howard

W. C. Fields is at his best in this laugh-filled comedy. In it, Fields plays a drunkard who becomes a hero. But the story is just an excuse for the moments of hilarity —of which there are many.

1940 B & W 74 minutes

BAREFOOT IN THE PARK

★★★★½

DIRECTOR: Gene Saks
CAST: Robert Redford, Jane Fonda, Charles Boyer, Mildred Natwick, Herb Edelman

A young Robert Redford and Jane Fonda team up as newlyweds in this adaptation of Neil Simon's Broadway play. The comedy focuses on the adjustments of married life. Ethel Banks and Mildred Natwick play the mothers-in-law, and Charles Boyer is a daffy, unconventional neighbor.

1967 105 minutes

BASIC TRAINING

★½

DIRECTOR: Andrew Sugerman
CAST: Ann Dusenberry, Rhonda Shear, Angela Aames, Walter Gotell

A small-town girl with the mission of cleaning up our government ends up at the Pentagon. Rooming with two other girls in Washington, D.C., she manages to become involved in endless hijinks. This movie is intermittently tasteless, and the attempts at comedy are old and tired. It ends up being mainly a vehicle for T&A. Rated R for sex and language.

1984 86 minutes

BAWDY ADVENTURES OF TOM JONES, THE

★

DIRECTOR: Cliff Owen
CAST: Nick Henson, Trevor Howard, Joan Collins, Arthur Lowe, Georgia Brown, Madeline Smith, Jeremy Lloyd

This ridiculous romp features Trevor Howard as the leacherous Squire Western. Young Tom Jones (played by an innocent-looking Nick Henson), an outcast due to his illegitimate birth, is in love with Western's daughter and spends the entire film hoping to win her hand. Along the way he is "forced" to cavort with an assortment of other ladies. Joan Collins plays a highway bandit who fancies Tom as well. Although this is a comedy, there are several occasions during which the cast bursts out in song to explain what is going on . . . strange! Rated R for nudity and a multitude of sexual situations.

1976 89 minutes

BEACH GIRLS, THE

★½

DIRECTOR: Pat Townsend
CAST: Debra Blee, Val Kline, Jeana Tomasina

Dumb sex comedy about a couple of teen-age girls who throw a big party at their uncle's Malibu beach house while he's away. Typical unrealistic nonsense. Rated R for nudity.

1982 91 minutes

BEAT THE DEVIL

★★★★

DIRECTOR: John Huston
CAST: Humphrey Bogart, Robert Morley, Peter Lorre, Jennifer Jones, Gina Lollobrigida, Edward Underdown, Ivor Bernard, Marco Tulli

Because it's all played straight, critics and audiences alike didn't know what to make of this delightful though at times baffling satire of films in the vein of *The Maltese Falcon* and *Key Largo* when it first hit screens. Sadly, some still do not. Nonetheless, this droll comedy, cobbled on location in Italy by John Huston and Truman Capote, is a twenty-four-cara gem. It has everything: a once rich, now broke fortune hunter; four disparate and desperate international crooks; a paranoiac hit man; a chronic liar; an airheaded fake British peer; and assorted accented characters. Steadily mounting appreciation has made this a solidly statured cult film. Humphrey Bogart said "only the phonies" liked it, but cynicism isn't criticism. In a unique context, "Try posting" is one of filmdom's all-time hilarious great lines.

1954 B & W 93 minutes

BEDAZZLED

★★★★

DIRECTOR: Stanley Donen
CAST: Peter Cook, Dudley Moore, Raquel Welch, Eleanor Bron

A cult favorite, this British comedy stars Dudley Moore as a fry cook tempted by the devil (played by his one-time comedy partner, Peter Cook). Co-starring Raquel Welch, it's an often-hilarious updating of the Faust legend.

1967 107 minutes

BEDTIME FOR BONZO

★★★

DIRECTOR: Frederick De Cordova
CAST: Ronald Reagan, Diana Lynn, Walter Slezak, Jesse White, Lucille Barkley

This film is worth watching just to look at Ronald Reagan before his political career began. He plays a young college professor who uses a chimpanzee to prove that environment, not heredity, determines a person's moral fiber. He hires a young woman (Diana Lynn) to pose as the chimp's mom while he plays father to it. Not surprisingly, Mom and Dad fall in love. Walter Slezak adds some funny moments with his mispronunciations and comic expressions.

1951 B & W 83 minutes

BEER

★★★★

DIRECTOR: Patrick Kelly
CAST: Loretta Swit, Rip Torn, Kenneth Mars, David Alan Grier, William Russ, Saul Stein, Peter Michael Goetz, Dick Shawn

Hilarious comedy that examines the seamy side of the advertising industry. Loretta Swit plays a cold-blooded advertising agent who tries to turn three ordinary guys (David Alan Grier, William Russ, and Saul Stein) into beer-drinking American heroes. The plan works, and soon they are the talk of the country. If you think the beer commercials on television are sexist and macho, wait until you see this. The controversy over the regressive attitudes in these ads is central to the film's theme. Rip Torn is excellent as the alcoholic director of the commercials. Dick Shawn's impression of Phil Donahue must be seen to be believed. Rated R for profanity, sex,and adult subject matter.

1985 83 minutes

BEING THERE

★★★★½

DIRECTOR: Hal Ashby
CAST: Peter Sellers, Shirley MacLaine, Melvyn Douglas, Jack Warden

This sublimely funny and bitingly satiric comedy features Peter Sellers's last great screen performance. It's too bad that it, rather than the abysmal *Fiendish Plot of Dr. Fu Manchu*, will not be remembered as his final bow. His portrayal of a simple-minded gardener—who knows only what he sees on television yet rises to great political heights—is a classic. Shirley MacLaine and Melvyn Douglas are also excellent in this memorable film, directed by Hal Ashby (*Harold and Maude*). Rated PG.

1979 130 minutes

BELL, BOOK AND CANDLE

★★★½

DIRECTOR: Richard Quine
CAST: James Stewart, Kim Novak, Jack Lemmon, Ernie Kovacs

A modestly entertaining bit of whimsy about a beautiful witch (Kim Novak) who works her magic on an unsuspecting publisher (James Stewart). Although the performances (including those in support by Jack Lemmon, Ernie Kovacs, and Hermione Gingold) are fine, this comedy is only mildly diverting.

1958 103 minutes

BELLBOY, THE

★★

DIRECTOR: Jerry Lewis
CAST: Jerry Lewis, Alex Gerry, Sonny Sands

A typical hour-plus of Jerry Lewis mugging and antics so dear to those who find him funny. This time around, Jerry is a bellboy at a swank Miami Beach hotel. Years ago, "Fatty" Arbuckle made a film of the same name that was funny. This, unfortunately, is plotless drivel seasoned with guest appearances by Milton Berle and Walter Winchell. Rated G when rereleased in 1972.

1960 B & W 72 minutes

BELLES OF ST. TRINIAN'S, THE

★★★½

DIRECTOR: Frank Launder
CAST: Alastair Sim, Joyce Grenfell, Hermione Baddeley, George Cole

Alastair Sim doubles as the dotty headmistress of a bonkers school for girls and her crafty bookie brother, who wants to use the place as a cover for his nefarious operations. Joyce Grenfell adds to the hilarity in this British comedy based on English cartoonist Ronald Searle's schoolgirls with a genius for mischief.

1955 B & W 90 minutes

BERNICE BOBS HER HAIR

★★★½

DIRECTOR: Joan Micklin Silver
CAST: Shelley Duvall, Veronica Cartwright, Bud Cort, Dennis Christopher, Polly Holliday, Mark La Mura

Shelley Duvall stars in this careful adaptation of F. Scott Fitzgerald's classic 1920 short story. Bernice is a shy, ugly girl who flouts convention by having her long hair bobbed, only to see her blow for independence backfire. Highly recommended.

1977 B & W 49 minutes

BEST DEFENSE

★★★

DIRECTOR: Willard Huyck

CAST: Dudley Moore, Eddie Murphy, Kate Capshaw, George Dzundza, Helen Shaver

Any movie that features the combined talents of Dudley Moore and Eddie Murphy has to be funny. Sometimes, however, laughs aren't enough. It's very easy to get confused, as the story jumps back and forth between the 1982 segments, featuring Moore as the inept inventor of a malfunctioning piece of defense equipment, and the 1984 footage, with Murphy as the hapless soldier forced to cope with it. Another minus is that the stars never have a scene together. Still, *Best Defense* works fairly often, although the liberal use of profanity and several sex scenes make this R-rated romp unfit for youngsters.

1984 94 minutes

BEST FRIENDS

★★

DIRECTOR: Norman Jewison

CAST: Burt Reynolds, Goldie Hawn, Ron Silver, Jessica Tandy

Burt Reynolds and Goldie Hawn star in this disappointingly tepid romantic comedy as a pair of successful screenwriters who decide to marry—thus destroying their profitable working relationship. A mess. Rated PG for profanity and adult situations.

1982 116 minutes

BEST OF COMIC RELIEF, THE

★★

DIRECTORS: John Moffitt, Pat Tourk Lee, Bob Zmuda

CAST: Billy Crystal, Whoopi Goldberg, Robin Williams, Martin Short, Harold Ramis, Sid Caesar, Carl Reiner, Jerry Lewis, Minnie Pearl

On March 29, 1986, over thirty comedians assembled to produce a show to help raise money for the homeless. But if this is the *best,* we can only cringe at how boring the other six hours must have been. Also, many of the stars who do their things here are old-timers (Carl Reiner, Sid Caesar, Minnie Pearl, Jerry Lewis) performing overfamiliar acts, while the material from the new comedians (Martin Short, Harold Ramis, and our hosts Billy Crystal, Whoopi Goldberg, and Robin Williams) isn't good enough to pick up the slack. Not rated, but contains some profanity.

1986 120 minutes

BEST OF DAN AYKROYD, THE

★★★★

DIRECTOR: Lorne Michaels

CAST: Dan Aykroyd, John Belushi, Chevy Chase, Jane Curtin, Garrett Morris, Bill Murray, Laraine Newman, Gilda Radner, Shelley Duvall, Madeline Kahn, Margot Kidder, Steve Martin

The title notwithstanding, this is a collaborative effort; some of the best skits of *Saturday Night Live* from 1975 to 1979. And as in *The Best of John Belushi,* the namesake is not always the center of attention. Also, some of these pieces ("The Two Wild and Crazy Guys: the Festrunk Brothers" and "The Final Days of the Nixon

Presidency") haven't worn well over the last half-decade. Even so, the shortcomings really don't matter when you are rolling on the floor over such great skits as "Fred Garvin: Male Prostitute," "Consumer Probe Interviews Entrepreneur Irwin Mainway," and "Julia Child."

1986 56 minutes

BEST OF JOHN BELUSHI, THE

★★★½

DIRECTOR: Lorne Michaels

CAST: John Belushi, Dan Aykroyd, Chevy Chase, Jane Curtin, Garrett Morris, Bill Murray, Laraine Newman, Gilda Radner, Elliott Gould, Buck Henry, Robert Klein, Rob Reiner

A collection of skits from *Saturday Night Live* shows between 1975 and 1979. From "Samurai Delicatessen" to his hilarious Joe Cocker impression, this is John Belushi at his best. The tape ends with Tom Schiller's short subject "Don't Look Back in Anger," the now-ironic piece that is set in the future where Belushi visits the graves of his fellow Not Ready for Prime Time Players who he "outlived."

1985 60 minutes

BEST OF SPIKE JONES, VOLUMES 1 & 2, THE

★★★

DIRECTOR: Bud Yorkin

CAST: Spike Jones & His City Slickers, Earl Bennett, Billy Barty

Compilations from Jones's 1954 TV show, these tapes are a nostalgic record of the star's manic comedy style. There are truly funny, if sporadic, moments. Jones's humor derived from comedically destroying a well-known piece of music with outrageous sight and sound gags. He and his band, the City Slickers, had a successful live show in the early 1940s, as well as a hit radio show, which produced two memorable songs: "Der Fuehrer's Face"(1942) and "Cocktails for Two" (1944).

1954 B & W 51 and 53 minutes

BEST OF TIMES, THE

★★★

DIRECTOR: Roger Spottiswoode

CAST: Robin Williams, Kurt Russell, Pamela Reed, Holly Palance, Donald Moffat, Margaret Whitton, M. Emmet Walsh, R. G. Armstrong, Dub Taylor

This comedy starts off well, then continues to lose momentum right up to the *Rocky*-style ending. That said, it is an amiable enough little movie which benefits from likable performances by its lead players. Robin Williams and Kurt Russell star as two former football players who dropped the ball when their moment for hometown glory came and went. But they get a second chance to win one for the folks in Taft (formerly Moron), California. Rated PG-13 for profanity and suggested sex.

1986 100 minutes

BETTER LATE THAN NEVER

★★½

DIRECTOR: Richard Crenna

CAST: Harold Gould, Larry Storch, Strother Martin, Tyne Daly, Harry Morgan, Victor Buono, George Gobel, Donald Pleasence, Lou Jacobi

Your average made-for-television comedy about a motley mixture of nursing home inhabitants who revolt against house rules that limit their freedom. The premise is good, the execution so-so. Theft of a train is a nice touch. Rated PG.

1979 100 minutes

BETTER OFF DEAD

★★

DIRECTOR: Savage Steve Holland
CAST: John Cusack, David Ogden Stiers, Diane Franklin, Kim Darby, Amanda Wyss

A mixture of clever ideas and awfully silly ones, this comedy focuses on the plight of teen-age Everyman, Lance Meyer (John Cusack), who finds his world shattered when the love of his life, Beth (Amanda Wyss), takes up with a conceited jock. Lance figures he is "Better Off Dead" than Beth-less. The film is at its best when writer-director Savage Steve Holland throws in little sketches that stand out from the familiar plot. For some of these, he uses animation in highly original ways. *Better Off Dead* is sometimes gross and predictable, but there are some little gems of hilarity scattered throughout. Rated PG for profanity.

1985 97 minutes

BEVERLY HILLS COP

★★★★

DIRECTOR: Martin Brest
CAST: Eddie Murphy, Lisa Eilbacher, Judge Reinhold, John Ashton

In this highly entertaining cops-and-comedy caper, Eddie Murphy plays a street-wise policeman from the East Coast who takes a leave of absence to track down the men who killed his best friend. This quest takes him to the unfamiliar hills of ritzy Southern California, where he's greeted as anything but a hero. Rated R for violence and profanity.

1984 105 minutes

BEYOND THERAPY

★★

DIRECTOR: Robert Altman
CAST: Julie Hagerty, Jeff Goldblum, Glenda Jackson, Tom Conti, Christopher Guest Chris Campion

Robert Altman is a hit-and-miss director and his *Beyond Therapy* (adapted from Christopher Durang's play) qualifies as a miss. The movie, which pokes fun at psychiatrists and their patients, really is a mess filled with unconnected episodes. Most of the performances and much of the dialogue are salvageable and hilarious, however. Most notable are Tom Conti and, as a bizarre psychiatrist, Glenda Jackson. Chris Campion as a brooding, ponytailed waiter is humorous in a sensually mysterious way. Rated R.

1987 93 minutes

BIG BUS, THE

★★★

DIRECTOR: James Frawley
CAST: Joseph Bologna, Stockard Channing, John Beck, Lynn Redgrave, José Ferrer, Ruth Gordon, Richard B. Shull, Sally Kellerman, Ned Beatty, Richard Mulligan, Larry Hagman, Howard Hesseman, Harold Gould

A super-luxurious nuclear-powered bus runs into trouble while carrying a group of misfits from New York to Denver. This spoof of disaster movies appeared four years before *Airplane!*. It's not as funny or as tightly paced, but it does have a silly and sarcastic playfulness that grows on you. One of those few films that work better on the small screen. Rated PG.

1976 88 minutes

BIG CITY COMEDY

★★

DIRECTOR: Mark Warren
CAST: John Candy, Billy Crystal, McLean Stevenson, Martin Mull, Tim Kazurinsky, Fred Willard

This is a compilation of skits from a 1980 John Candy syndicated TV series. Even with funny guys Billy Crystal, Martin Mull, and Tim Kazurinsky on hand as guests, this is a disappointing tape. Candy can be very funny but, unfortunately, not here. He is quite a sight to behold as Queen Victoria, but you can see that on the cassette box.

1986 56 minutes

BIG TROUBLE

★★

DIRECTOR: John Cassavetes
CAST: Peter Falk, Alan Arkin, Beverly D'Angelo, Charles Durning, Robert Stack, Paul Dooley, Valerie Curtin, Richard Libertinti

While this movie may be a major disappointment, this is so only because we expect more of the outstanding cast. *Big Trouble* has its moments, but alas, they are few and far between. Alan Arkin is an honest insurance salesman trying to put his three talented sons through Yale. When he meets up with a rich married woman (Beverly D'Angelo), the two plot against her husband (Peter Falk). Crazy plots twists abound, but none of them are all that funny. Director John Cassavetes tries to create a comic mood similar to director Arthur Hiller's *The In-Laws,* in which Falk and Arkin also starred. But he never comes close. Rated R for profanity and adult subject matter.

1985 93 minutes

BILL COSBY—HIMSELF

★★★★

DIRECTOR: William H. Cosby Jr.
CAST: Bill Cosby

The wit and wisdom of Bill Cosby on the subjects of childbirth, raising a family (and being raised), going to the dentist, taking drugs and drinking, and life in general provide laughs and food for thought in this excellent comedy video. One can see how the hugely successful television series "The Cosby Show" evolved from his family and observations of their behavior. Rated G.

1985 104 minutes

BILLY CRYSTAL: A COMIC'S LINE

★★★★

DIRECTOR: Bruce Gower
CAST: Billy Crystal

This HBO special released on tape features an innovative and very funny performance by Billy Crystal. Using the premise of a Broadway musical audition, he presents various characters trying out for the part. There is also an amusing yet wonderfully warm sequence with Crystal as a small boy being left at home for the first time. He shows much more than just a flair for comedy and timing.

1984 59 minutes

BILLY CRYSTAL: DON'T GET ME STARTED

★★★

DIRECTORS: Paul Flaherty, Billy Crystal
CAST: Billy Crystal, Rob Reiner, Christopher Guest, Eugene Levy, Brother Theodore

In the first part of this video, Rob Reiner takes the role of interviewer in a "yockumentary" on the making of a Billy Crystal special. Eugene Levy is manager and promoter, and Crystal shows up as Sammy Davis Jr., Whoopi Goldberg, and himself as they attempt to show us what happens behind the scenes prior to showtime. The second half is the actual live performance with Crystal inviting Fernando ("You look mahvelous!") to the stage.

1986 60 minutes

BINGO LONG TRAVELING ALL-STARS AND MOTOR KINGS, THE

★★★

DIRECTOR: John Badham
CAST: Billy Dee Williams, James Earl Jones, Richard Pryor, Ted Ross

This is a comedy-adventure of a barnstorming group of black baseball players as they tour rural America in the late 1930s. Billy Dee Williams, Richard Pryor, and James Earl Jones are three of the team's players and must resort to conniving, clowning, and conning to ensure their team's survival. Only the lack of a cohesive script keeps this from receiving a few more stars. Rated PG.

1976 110 minutes

BIRDS AND THE BEES, THE

★★

DIRECTOR: Norman Taurog
CAST: George Gobel, Mitzi Gaynor, David Niven

This poor remake of the 1941 Barbara Stanwyck–Henry Fonda comedy hit, *The Lady Eve*, has military cardsharp David Niven setting daughter Mitzi Gaynor on playboy millionaire George Gobel in hopes of getting rich from the marriage. "Lonesome George" wiggles free, but falls for her anyway. Don't settle for imitations. Insist on the original.

1956 94 minutes

BISHOP'S WIFE, THE

★★★

DIRECTOR: Henry Koster
CAST: Cary Grant, Loretta Young, David Niven, James Gleason

Harmless story of debonair angel (Cary Grant) sent to Earth to aid a bishop (David Niven) in his quest for a new church. The kind of film they just don't make anymore. No rating, but okay for the whole family.

1947 B & W 108 minutes

BLACK BIRD, THE

★★★

DIRECTOR: David Giler
CAST: George Segal, Stéphane Audran, Lionel Stander, Lee Patrick

Surprisingly enjoyable comedy produced by and starring George Segal as Sam Spade Jr. The visual gags abound, and an air of authenticity is added by the performances of 1940s detective film regulars Lionel Stander, Elisha Cook, and Lee Patrick. The latter two co-starred with Humphrey Bogart in *The Maltese Falcon*, on which the film is based. It's funny, with a strong performance from Segal. This film continues the pursuit of the multi-jeweled prize bird. Rated PG.

1975 98 minutes

BLACKSMITH, THE/ COPS

★★★½

DIRECTOR: Buster Keaton
CAST: Buster Keaton, Virginia Fox

Two shining examples of deadpan silent comedian Buster Keaton at his best. What he does to a white luxury limo in *The Blacksmith* is a hilarious crime. His antics in *Cops* bid fair to prove him Chaplin's master. The chase scene is a classic of timing and invention. Silent.

1922 B & W 38 minutes

BLAME IT ON RIO

★★½

DIRECTOR: Stanley Donen
CAST: Michael Caine, Joseph Bologna, Valerie Harper, Michelle Johnson

A middle-aged male sex fantasy directed by Stanley Donen (*Lucky Lady*; *Charade*), this film —which equally combines both good and bad elements—features Michael Caine as a befuddled fellow who finds himself involved in an affair with the teen-age daughter (Michelle Johnson) of his best friend (Joseph Bologna). Although essentially in bad taste, *Blame It on Rio* does have a number of very funny moments. Rated R for nudity, profanity, and suggested sex.

1984 110 minutes

BLAZING SADDLES

★★★½

DIRECTOR: Mel Brooks

CAST: Cleavon Little, Gene Wilder, Harvey Korman, Madeline Kahn, Mel Brooks, Slim Pickens

Mel Brooks directed this sometimes hilarious, mostly crude spoof of westerns. The jokes come with machine-gun rapidity, and the stars race around like maniacs. If it weren't in such bad taste, it would be perfect for the kiddies. Rated R.

1974 93 minutes

BLIND DATE

DIRECTOR: Blake Edwards

CAST: Bruce Willis, Kim Basinger, John Larroquette, William Daniels, George Coe, Mark Blum, Phil Hartman

A tasteless exercise in slapstick that sends Bruce Willis (in his film debut) on a last-minute blind date with Kim Basinger, an attractively gift-wrapped bundle that comes with one explicit instruction: Do not let her drink. Naturally, Willis can't wait to pour champagne down her throat, which shows considerable sensitivity for somebody who might—as far as he knows, at this point—be an alcoholic. By way of retribution, Willis loses his job, his car, and his self-esteem, and we lose our patience with the forced, mind-numbing attempts at physical humor. Was it *ever* funny to watch a car crash into a paint store and get covered with gallons of exterior high-gloss? Unbelievably, this crass attempt at humor comes from screen-writer Dale Launer, responsible for the manic and inventive *Ruthless People*. Undoubtedly, everybody is entitled to an off day. Rated PG-13 for adult situations.

1987 93 minutes

BLISS

★★★★

DIRECTOR: Ray Lawrence

CAST: Barry Otto, Lynette Curran, Helen Jones, Jeff Truman

In this biting black comedy from Australia, a business executive (Barry Otto) nearly dies from a heart attack. By managing to survive, he finds himself in a hellish version of the life he once had. Not everyone will appreciate this nightmarish vision of modern life, but it is one of the most original motion pictures of recent years. Rated R.

1986 93 minutes

BLOCK-HEADS

★★★★

DIRECTOR: John G. Blystone

CAST: Stan Laurel, Oliver Hardy, Patricia Ellis, Minna Gombell, Billy Gilbert, James Finlayson

Twenty years after the end of World War I, Stan Laurel is discovered still guarding a bunker. He returns to a veterans' home, where Oliver Hardy comes to visit and take him to dinner. A well-crafted script provides the perfect setting for the boys' escapades. Their characters have seldom been used as well in feature films.

1938 B & W 55 minutes

BLOODBATH AT THE HOUSE OF DEATH

★★

DIRECTOR: Ray Cameron

CAST: Vincent Price, Kenny Everett, Pamela Stephenson, Gareth Hunt, Don Warrington, John Fortune, Sheila Steafel

Although advertised as one, this British movie is not all that much of a spoof on horror films. There is realistic gore (especially in the opening scene, where the film lives up to its not-so-ironic title), and near the film's end the camp antics turn serious. In the story, a team of paranormal specialists investigates a house that was the scene of a mysterious massacre. Vincent Price plays a nutty devil worshiper who plots to get rid of the snoopy scientists who are inhabiting this house of Satan. As in most good parodies, the film draws liberally from the genre it's poking fun at. (Scenes from *Carrie*, *Poltergeist*, and *Alien* are used.) Science fiction is also spoofed (*Star Wars*). But borrowing shticks from Mel Brooks and the *Airplane* films is no fair. Not rated, but equivalent to an R for violence, gore, sex, nudity, and profanity.

1985 92 minutes

BLUE MONEY

★★★

DIRECTOR: Colin Bucksey
CAST: Tim Curry, Debby Bishop, Billy Connolly, Dermot Crowley, Frances Tomelty, George Irving, John Bind

Larry Gormley (Tim Curry) discovers a suitcase with half a million dollars in his cab. The money turns out to belong to the mob, and they want it back. Not a very original idea, but well written, acted, and directed, this comedy provides plenty of fast-moving fun. Made for British television.

1984 82 minutes

BLUES BROTHERS, THE

★★★½

DIRECTOR: John Landis
CAST: John Belushi, Dan Aykroyd, John Candy, Carrie Fisher

Director John Landis attempted to film an epic comedy and came pretty darn close. In it, the musicians of the title, John Belushi and Dan Aykroyd, attempt to save an orphanage. The movie's excesses—too many car crashes and chases—are offset by Belushi and Aykroyd as the Laurel and Hardy of backbeat; the musical turns of Aretha Franklin, James Brown, and Ray Charles; and Landis's flair for comic timing. Rated R.

1980 132 minutes

BOB & CAROL & TED & ALICE

★★★★½

DIRECTOR: Paul Mazursky
CAST: Natalie Wood, Robert Culp, Elliott Gould, Dyan Cannon

In this comedy, Natalie Wood and Robert Culp (Carol and Bob) play a modern couple who believe in open marriage, pot-smoking, etc. Their friends, conservative Elliott Gould and Dyan Cannon (Ted and Alice), are shocked by Bob and Carol's behavior. Meanwhile, Bob and Carol try to liven up Ted and Alice's marriage by introducing them to their way of life. Lots of funny moments. Rated R.

1969 104 minutes

BOB & RAY, JANE, LARAINE & GILDA

★★★

DIRECTOR: Dave Wilson
CAST: Bob Elliott, Ray Goulding, Jane Curtin, Laraine Newman, Gilda Radner, Willie Nelson

The low-key humor of Bob & Ray takes center-stage in this summer replacement special from the *Saturday Night Live* folks. As far as these two fellows are concerned, you either love 'em or hate 'em. If routines like "House of Toast," in which Bob & Ray introduce a restaurant that specializes in you-know-what, or a deadpan reading of the lyrics of Rod Stewart's "If You Think I'm Sexy" by the middle-aged humorists sound like fun to you, this is the tape you've been waiting for. Other folks might want to enjoy the appearances of Not Ready for Prime Time Players Jane Curtin, Laraine Newman, and Gilda Radner–or tap their feet to the tunes of guest star Willie Nelson.

1979 75 minutes

BOBO, THE

★

DIRECTOR: Robert Parrish
CAST: Peter Sellers, Britt Ekland, Rossano Brazzi

A bumbling matador (Peter Sellers) has to seduce a high-priced courtesan (Britt Ekland) in order to get employment as a singer. If this plot sounds stupid, then you have reached the core of this hopeless movie.

1967 105 minutes

BOHEMIAN GIRL, THE

★★★

DIRECTORS: James W. Horne, Charles R. Rogers
CAST: Stan Laurel, Oliver Hardy, Thelma Todd, Antonio Moreno

Laurel and Hardy portray gypsies in this typical tale of the gypsy band versus the country officials. A variety of misadventures occur, and the film is entertaining, especially with the hilarious scene of Stan attempting to fill wine bottles and becoming more and more inebriated.

1936 B & W 70 minutes

BONNIE SCOTLAND

★★★

DIRECTOR: James W. Horne
CAST: Stan Laurel, Oliver Hardy, James Finlayson, June Vlasek (June Lang), William Janney

Stan Laurel and Oliver Hardy venture to Scotland so that Stan can reap a "major" inheritance—which turns out to be merely bagpipes and a snuffbox. By mistake, they join the army and are sent to India, where they help to quell a native uprising. An average Laurel and Hardy offering, the thin plot offers the boys an opportunity to play off each other's strengths: Ollie's reactions and Stan's fantasy world that keeps becoming reality.

1935 B & W 80 minutes

BORN YESTERDAY

★★★★½

DIRECTOR: George Cukor
CAST: Judy Holliday, William Holden, Broderick Crawford, Howard St. John

Judy Holliday is simply delightful as a dizzy dame who isn't as dizzy as everyone thinks she is, in this comedy directed by George Cukor. William Holden is the professor hired by a junk-dealer-made-good (Broderick Crawford) to give Holliday lessons in how to be "high-toned." The results are highly entertaining—and very funny.

1950 B & W 103 minutes

BOSS' WIFE, THE

★★★½

DIRECTOR: Ziggy Steinberg
CAST: Daniel Stern, Christopher Plummer, Arielle Dombasle, Fisher Stevens, Melanie Mayron, Martin Mull

After the first twenty minutes, this comedy starts rolling. Daniel Stern and Melanie Mayron play Joel and Janet, a two-career couple trying to make time for a baby. When Joel's boss (Christopher Plummer) finally notices him, he expects Joel to spend the weekend at the company resort where he will compete with slick, sleazy Tony (Martin Mull) for a coveted promotion. Laughs abound when Joel is pursued by the boss's nymphomaniac wife (beautiful Arielle Dombasle), as well as his own wife and her photographer colleague, Carlos (hilariously played by Fisher Stevens). Rated R for nudity, obscenities and sexual situations.

1986 83 minutes

BOY, DID I GET A WRONG NUMBER!

DIRECTOR: George Marshall
CAST: Bob Hope, Elke Sommer, Phyllis Diller

When you get a wrong number, hang up and dial again. Too bad the cast and director didn't. This one is a bomb!

1966 99 minutes

BRAZIL

★★★★

DIRECTOR: Terry Gilliam
CAST: Jonathan Pryce, Robert De Niro, Katherine Helmond, Ian Holm, Bob Hoskins, Michael Palin, Ian Richardson

A savage blend of *1984* and *The Time Bandits* from Monty Python director Terry Gilliam. Jonathan Pryce stars as a bemused paper shuffler in a red tape–choked future society at the brink of collapsing under its own bureaucracy. Content to remain anonymous until he glimpses the woman of his dreams, he enters a bizarre world of renegade service technicians and bomb-toting terrorists bent on overthrowing the government. Definitely not for all tastes, but a treat for those with an appreciation for social satire. Were it not for a chaotic conclusion and slightly overlong running time, this would be a perfect picture. Rated R for language and adult situations.

1985 131 minutes

BREAKFAST CLUB, THE

★★★★

DIRECTOR: John Hughes
CAST: Emilio Estevez, Molly Ringwald, Paul Gleason, Anthony Michael Hall, Ally Sheedy

A group of assorted high-school misfits get to be friends while serving weekend detention, in this comedy, directed by John Hughes (*Sixteen Candles*). Molly Ringwald, Anthony Michael Hall (both from *Sixteen Candles*), Emilio Estevez (*Repo Man*), Ally Sheedy (*War Games*), and Judd Nelson (*St. Elmo's Fire*) portray the teens. Rated R.

1985 100 minutes

BREAKING AWAY

★★★★★

DIRECTOR: Peter Yates
CAST: Dennis Christopher, Dennis Quaid, Daniel Stern, Jackie Earle Haley

There comes a time in every young man's life when he must loose the ties of home, family, and friends and test his mettle. Dennis Christopher is the young man who retains an innocence we too often mistake for naïveté; Paul Dooley and Barbara Barrie are the often humorously confused parents who offer subtle, sure guidance. This is a warm portrayal of family life and love, of friendships, of growing up and growing away. Rated PG for brief profanity.

1979 100 minutes

BREATH OF SCANDAL, A

★★

DIRECTOR: Michael Curtiz
CAST: Sophia Loren, John Gavin, Maurice Chevalier, Angela Lansbury

This intended high-style romantic comedy set in Austria in the gossip-rife court of Franz Joseph has little going for it. Beautiful princess scorns mama's wish she marry a prince. Instead, encouraged by papa, she conveniently opts for a visiting American mining engineer. The script, taken from the Molnar play that poor John Gilbert adapted for his disastrous first talkie, is uninspired. The casting is uninspired. The directing is uninspired. But the scenery and costumes are nice.

1960 98 minutes

BREWSTER MCCLOUD

★★★

DIRECTOR: Robert Altman
CAST: Bud Cort, Sally Kellerman

If you liked Robert Altman's *M*A*S*H* (the movie) and *Harold and Maude*, and your humor lies a few degrees off-center, you'll enjoy this "flight of fantasy" about a boy (Bud Cort) who wants to make like a bird. Rated R.

1970 104 minutes

BREWSTER'S MILLIONS (1945)

★★½

DIRECTOR: Allan Dwan
CAST: Dennis O'Keefe, Helen Walker, June Havoc, Mischa Auer, Eddie "Rochester" Anderson, Gail Patrick

This is the fifth of seven film versions of the 1902 novel and stage success about a young man who will inherit millions if he is able to spend $1 million quickly and quietly within a set period of time. Dennis O'Keefe and company perform this Tinsel-town stalwart in fine fashion, making for a bright, entertaining comic romp. As always, Mischa Auer does one of his delightful noble idiot characterizations without flaw. Fun to watch. Curiously, this version is not listed in the recent history of Paramount Studios' 2,805 films.

1945 B & W 79 minutes

BREWSTER'S MILLIONS (1985)

★★★

DIRECTOR: Walter Hill
CAST: Richard Pryor, John Candy, Lonette McKee, Stephen Collins, Pat Hingle, Tovah Feldshuh, Hume Cronyn

It took director Walter Hill to bring Richard Pryor out of his movie slump with this unspectacular, but still entertaining, comedy about a minor-league baseball player who stands to inherit $300 million if he can fulfill the provisions of a rather daffy will. As Hill did with Eddie Murphy in *48 HRS.*, the filmmaker brings out the best in Pryor and gives him some fine supporting actors (with John Candy as the standout). It's no classic, but still much, much better than *The Toy* or *Superman III*. Rated PG for profanity.

1985 97 minutes

BRIGHTON BEACH MEMOIRS

★★★½

DIRECTOR: Gene Saks
CAST: Jonathan Silverman, Blythe Danner, Bob Dishy, Brian Brillinger, Stacey Glick, Judith Ivey, Lisa Waltz

Neil Simon's reminiscences of his adolescence make for genuinely enjoyable viewing. Refreshingly free of Simon's often too-clever dialogue, it aims for the heart and, more often than not, hits its mark. Rated PG-13 for sexual references.

1986 110 minutes

BRINGING UP BABY

★★★★★

DIRECTOR: Howard Hawks
CAST: Cary Grant, Katharine Hepburn, Charlie Ruggles, May Robson

Howard Hawks's *Bringing Up Baby* is a must-see. Starring Cary Grant and Katharine Hepburn, this screwball comedy has lost none of its punch. Hepburn plays a daffy rich girl who gets an absent-minded professor (Grant), who also happens to be engaged, into all sorts of trouble. It doesn't sound like much, but *Bringing Up Baby* is guaranteed to have you falling out of your seat in helpless laughter.

1938 B & W 102 minutes

BRINKS JOB, THE

★★★½

DIRECTOR: William Friedkin

CAST: Peter Falk, Peter Boyle, Allen Goorwitz, Warren Oates, Paul Sorvino, Gena Rowlands

Peter Falk stars in this enjoyable release in which a gang of klutzy crooks pulls off "the crime of the century." It's a breezy caper film reminiscent of George Roy Hill's *Butch Cassidy and the Sundance Kid* and *The Sting*. The cast is superb. Falk, who plays the wacky ringleader, gets strong support from Allen Goorwitz, Paul Sorvino, Gena Rowlands, and Peter Boyle. But the film's best performance comes from the late Warren Oates as the gang member who turns stool pigeon. He should have won an Oscar for it. Rated PG.

1978 103 minutes

BRITANNIA HOSPITAL

★★★

DIRECTOR: Lindsay Anderson

CAST: Leonard Rossiter, Graham Crowden, Malcolm McDowell, Joan Plowright

A wildly inadequate hospital serves as a metaphor for a sick society in this okay black comedy by British director Lindsay Anderson (*If; O Lucky Man*). Rated R.

1982 115 minutes

BROADWAY DANNY ROSE

★★★★½

DIRECTOR: Woody Allen

CAST: Woody Allen, Mia Farrow, Milton Berle, Sandy Baron

The legendary talent agent Broadway Danny Rose (Woody Allen) takes on an alcoholic crooner (Nick Apollo Forte) and carefully nurtures him to the brink of stardom, in this hilarious comedy, also written and directed by Allen. Mia Farrow is delightful as a blond gangster's moll who inadvertently gets Rose in big trouble. Rated PG for brief violence.

1984 B & W 86 minutes

BUCK PRIVATES

★★★★

DIRECTOR: Arthur Lubin

CAST: Bud Abbott, Lou Costello, Lee Bowman, Alan Curtis, Jane Frazee

Abbott and Costello are at their best in their first starring film, but it's still no classic.

1941 B & W 82 minutes

BUDDY, BUDDY

★★

DIRECTOR: Billy Wilder

CAST: Jack Lemmon, Walter Matthau, Paula Prentiss, Klaus Kinski

Jack Lemmon is a clumsy would-be suicide who decides to end it all in a hotel. Walter Matthau is a hit man who rents the room next door and finds the filling of his contract difficult. The results are less than hilarious but do provoke a few smiles. Rated R because of profanity and brief nudity.

1981 96 minutes

BULLFIGHTERS, THE

★★★

DIRECTOR: Malcolm St. Clair

CAST: Stan Laurel, Oliver Hardy, Margo Woode, Richard Lane, Carol Andrews

While not a classic, this latter-day Laurel and Hardy film is surprisingly good—especially when you consider that the boys had lost all control over the making of their pictures by this time. The story has Laurel resembling a famous bullfighter, and, of course, this leads to chaos in the ring.

1945 B & W 61 minutes

BULLSHOT

★★½

DIRECTOR: Dick Clement

CAST: Alan Shearman, Diz White, Ron House, Frances Tomelty, Michael Aldridge

Sometimes amovie can be fun for a while, then overstay its welcome. Such is the case with this spoof of Herman Cyril "Scapper" McNiele's *Bulldog Drummond* mystery/spy adventures. Written by stars Alan Shearman, Diz White, and Ron House, the screenplay has Capt. Hugh "Bullshot Crummond" (Shearman), a former RAF pilot, once again confronting his wartime nemesis, Count Otto von Bruno (House), who recalls Snoopy's foe, the Red Baron. The film presents a kind of British comedy rarely seen in this country. As opposed to the dry, droll humor of the Monty Python troupe and the classic Ealing comedies starring Alec Guinness, for example, it is a very broad form of slapstick not unlike that perpetrated by Jerry Lewis. The stars mug shamelessly. Everything is played to the hilt, and the characters go beyond stereotypes to become caricatures. Although this is occasionally irritating, the star-screenwriters do create some funny moments. But you have to wade through an enormous amount of sludge to get to them. Rated PG for profanity, sex, and violence.

1985 95 minutes

BURGLAR

★★★

DIRECTOR: Hugh Wilson

CAST: Whoopi Goldberg, Bobcat Goldthwait, G. W. Bailey, Lesley Ann Warren

Whoopi Goldberg stars in this amiable but unspectacular caper comedy as a retired cat burglar forced back into a life of crime by a crooked cop (G. W. Bailey) who is blackmailing her. In doing his bidding, she ends up the prime suspect in a rather messy murder case. Goldberg does well in a role originally written for Bruce Willis, but one wishes she would find a comedy script tailored for her impressive talents. Rated R for profanity and violence.

1987 91 minutes

BUS STOP

★★★★½

DIRECTOR: Joshua Logan

CAST: Marilyn Monroe, Don Murray, Arthur O'Connell, Betty Field, Casey Adams

Marilyn Monroe plays a distraught showgirl who is endlessly pursued by an oaf of a cowboy named Bo (Don Murray). He even kidnaps her when she refuses to marry him. Lots of laughs as Bo mistreats his newly found "angel." Arthur O'Connell is excellent as Verg, Bo's older and wiser friend who advises Bo on the way to treat women.

1956 96 minutes

BUSTIN' LOOSE

★★½

DIRECTOR: Oz Scott

CAST: Richard Pryor, Cicely Tyson, Robert Christian, Alphonso Alexander, Janet Wong

You take super-bad ex-con Richard Pryor, stick him on a school bus with goody-two-shoes teacher Cicely Tyson and eight ornery schoolchildren, and what have you got? A nonstop, cross-country, comic odyssey called *Bustin' Loose*. It's a hilarious comedy as long as the bus is rolling and Pryor is up to his madcap antics. But *Bustin' Loose* bogs down in its last half-hour. Rated R for profanity and violence.

1981 94 minutes

CACTUS FLOWER

★★★

DIRECTOR: Gene Saks

CAST: Walter Matthau, Ingrid Bergman, Goldie Hawn

Watch this one for Goldie Hawn's film debut, a poignant and charming performance that earned her an Academy Award as best supporting actress. She's the slightly wonky girlfriend of dentist Walter Matthau, who actually loves his nurse (Ingrid Bergman). Although adapted from a hit Broadway play by Abe Burrows, this film version is pretty short on laughs. Ingrid Bergman is far too serious in her role, and Matthau simply doesn't make a credible dentist. Without Hawn, this would have been a below-average comedy, but she makes the experience worthwhile. Rated PG for adult situations.

1969 103 minutes

CADDYSHACK

★★

DIRECTOR: Harold Ramis

CAST: Chevy Chase, Rodney Dangerfield, Ted Knight, Michael O'Keefe, Bill Murray

Only Rodney Dangerfield, as an obnoxious refugee from a leisure-suit collectors' convention, offers anything of value in this rip-off of the *Animal House* formula. Chevy Chase and Bill Murray sleepwalk through their poorly written roles, and Ted Knight looks a little weary of imitating his Ted Baxter routine from *The Mary Tyler Moore Show*. The few laughs in this golf comedy are all but obliterated by the yawns. Rated R for nudity and sex.

1980 99 minutes

CALIFORNIA SUITE

★★★½

DIRECTOR: Herbert Ross

CAST: Jane Fonda, Alan Alda, Maggie Smith, Richard Pryor, Bill Cosby

This adaptation of the Neil Simon play features multiple stars, including Jane Fonda, Alan Alda, Maggie Smith, Michael Caine, Walter Matthau, Richard Pryor, and Bill Cosby. The action revolves around the various inhabitants of a Beverly Hills hotel room. We are allowed to enter and observe the private lives of the various guests in the room, in the four short stories within this watchable film. Rated PG.

1978 103 minutes

CAMPUS MAN

★★

DIRECTOR: Ron Casden

CAST: John Dye, Kim Delaney, Kathleen Wilhoite, Steve Lyon, Morgan Fairchild, Miles O'Keeffe

In this well-intended and generally watchable movie, a college student (John Dye) produces and markets an all-male, pinup calendar and strikes it rich. His roommate (Steve Lyon) agrees to be one of the hunks of the month and ends up becoming a celebrity. Rated PG.

1987 95 minutes

CAN I DO IT 'TIL I NEED GLASSES?

DIRECTOR: I. Robert Levy

CAST: Robin Williams, Roger Behr, Debra Klose, Moose Carlson, Walter Olkewicz

A follow-up to *If You Don't Stop, You'll Go Blind.* A trash-heap of prehistoric naughty jokes acted out by hopped-up extras in need of a buck. Robin Williams appears for all of a minute, enough for the filmmakers to cash in on his success. Williams sued to keep his name as small as possible in the credits. May this serve as a lesson to all struggling actors. Rated R for nudity and profanity.
1980 72 minutes

CANNERY ROW

★★★½

DIRECTOR: Davis S. Ward
CAST: Nick Nolte, Debra Winger, Audra Lindley, M. Emmet Walsh, Frank McRae

It's hard to really dislike this film, starring Nick Nolte and Debra Winger, even though it has so many problems. Despite its artificiality, halting pace, and general unevenness, there are so many marvelous moments—most provided by character actor Frank McRae as the lovable simpleton Hazel—that you don't regret having seen it. Rated PG for slight nudity, profanity, and violence.
1982 120 minutes

CANNONBALL RUN

★

DIRECTOR: Hal Needham
CAST: Burt Reynolds, Roger Moore, Farrah Fawcett, Dom De Luise, Dean Martin, Sammy Davis Jr.

This star-studded bore is the story of an unsanctioned, totally illegal cross-country car race in which there are no rules and few survivors. Director Hal Needham (*Smokey and the Bandit*; *Smokey and the Bandit II*) and writer Brock Yates team up once again with Burt Reynolds to make another action-comedy, but laughs have never been so rare nor stunts so unspectacular. Rated PG for profanity.
1981 95 minutes

CANNONBALL RUN II

DIRECTOR: Hal Needham
CAST: Burt Reynolds, Dom De Luise, Shirley MacLaine, Marilu Henner, Telly Savalas, Dean Martin, Sammy Davis Jr., Frank Sinatra

Take an Arab fortune, a pair of bogus nuns, inept underworld warfare, and a bunch of crazies willing to risk their necks in a mad cross-country race with no rules or regulations, and you have the starting line-up for this typically awful Hal Needham rehash of *Cannonball Run*. What a waste of talent. Rated PG for simulated violence and profanity.
1984 108 minutes

CAN SHE BAKE A CHERRY PIE?

★★★

DIRECTOR: Henry Jaglom
CAST: Karen Black, Michael Emil

Can She Bake a Cherry Pie?, while often quite crude, has its revelations. One of those is the performance of Karen Black. She plays a woman whose first name apparently is Zee and whose husband leaves her before she has fully awakened one morning. She meets Eli, played by Michael Emil, a balding character actor whose body is slowly sliding into his knees. They're both a little neurotic, and pretty dippy in the bargain. Thus begins a nearly plotless amble through the lives of Zee and Eli as they parry and thrust and decide to be in love with each other. This is a small film, and its appeal is quiet. It also is an example of what can be right with American movie-making, even when the money isn't

there. No rating, but considerable vulgar language, sexual situations.
1984 90 minutes

CAPTAIN'S PARADISE, THE

★★★★

DIRECTOR: Anthony Kimmins
CAST: Alec Guinness, Celia Johnson, Yvonne de Carlo, Bill Fraser

From the opening shot, in which he is "shot," Alec Guinness displays the seemingly artless comedy form that marked him for stardom. He plays the bigamist skipper of a ferry, a wife in each port, flirting with delicious danger. Timing is all, and close shaves—including a chance meeting of the wives—yields edge of seat entertainment. Lotsa fun.
1953 B & W 77 minutes

CARBON COPY

★★★½

DIRECTOR: Michael Schultz
CAST: George Segal, Susan Saint James, Jack Warden, Dick Martin

This amiable, lightweight comedy of racial manners stars George Segal as a white corporation executive who suddenly discovers he has a teen-age black son just itching to be adopted in lily-white San Marino, California. Rated PG.
1981 92 minutes

CARLIN AT CARNEGIE

★★★½

DIRECTOR: Steven J. Santos
CAST: George Carlin

This Home Box Office–backed video may not be as consistently funny as other comedy videos, but it has that special quality of having come from the heart—as well as hard-earned experience and deep thought. It's funny and sad at the same time. Carlin has found that you can't always have a nice day and does a very funny, brilliant routine on how being told to have one can be irritating. And, as always, Carlin uses the English language—and our taboos on certain parts of it—against itself in several bits. No one else can reduce us to tears of laughter by simply reading a list of words. Unrated, the film has profanity.
1983 60 minutes

CARRY ON COWBOY

★★½

DIRECTOR: Gerald Thomas
CAST: Sidney James, Kenneth Williams, Joan Sims, Angela Douglas, Jim Dale

Another in a very long, and weakening, line of British farces—*Carry on Doctor, Carry On Nurse*—many of them spoofs of highly popular films. Replete with the usual double-entendre jokes and sight gags, this one sends up *High Noon*.
1966 91 minutes

CARRY ON NURSE

★★★

DIRECTOR: Gerald Thomas
CAST: Kenneth Connor, Kenneth Williams, Charles Hawtrey, Terence Longden

Daffy struggle between patients and hospital staff. It's one of the most consistently amusing entries in this distinctive British comedy series.
1960 90 minutes

CARTIER AFFAIR, THE

★½

DIRECTOR: Rob Holcomb
CAST: Joan Collins, David Hasselhoff, Telly Savalas, Jay Gerber, Hilly Hicks

Less than funny comic romance that involves a male secretary (David Hasselhoff) falling in love with his soap-opera-legend boss (Joan Collins). The twist is that he's actually an ex-con planted in her employ to set up a heist of her fabulous jewels. Telly Savalas has a minor role as a prison boss who expects Hasselhoff to repay him for protecting him while he was in prison. Basically boring, unbelievable story with uninspired acting. Don't waste your time.

1985 96 minutes

CAR WASH

★★★½

DIRECTOR: Michael Schultz

CAST: Richard Pryor, Franklin Ajaye, Sully Boyar, Ivan Dixon

With *D.C. Cab*, writer-director Joel Schumacher attempted to recreate the success he achieved with his screenplay for this effective comedy-drama. This is an ensemble film that features memorable bits from Richard Pryor, George Carlin, Franklin Ajaye, Ivan Dixon, and the Pointer Sisters. There are plenty of laughs, music, and even a moral in this fine low-budget production. Rated PG.

1976 97 minutes

CASANOVA'S BIG NIGHT

★★½

DIRECTOR: Norman Z. McLeod

CAST: Bob Hope, Joan Fontaine, Basil Rathbone, Audrey Dalton, Freida Inescort, Hope Emerson, Hugh Marlowe, John Carradine, John Hoyt, Robert Hutton, Raymond Burr, Lon Chaney Jr.

The evergreen Bob Hope is a lowly tailor's assistant masquerading as the great lover Casanova in this costume comedy set in plot-and-intrigue-ridden Venice. Old Ski Nose is irrepressible, as always, sets are sumptuous, and costumes lavish, but the script and direction don't measure up. Funny, but not *that* funny.

1954 86 minutes

CASINO ROYALE

★★

DIRECTORS: John Huston, Ken Hughes, Robert Parrish, Joe McGrath, Val Guest

CAST: Peter Sellers, Ursula Andress, David Niven, Orson Welles, Joanna Pettet, Woody Allen, Deborah Kerr, William Holden, Charles Boyer, John Huston, George Raft, Jean-Paul Belmondo

What do you get when you combine the talents of this all-star ensemble? Not much. This is the black sheep of the James Bond family of films. The rights to *Casino Royale* weren't part of the Ian Fleming package. Not wanting to compete with the Sean Connery vehicles, this film was intended to be a stylish spoof. It's only sporadically amusing. For the most part, it's an overblown bore.

1967 130 minutes

CATCH-22

★★★

DIRECTOR: Mike Nichols

CAST: Alan Arkin, Martin Balsam, Richard Benjamin, Anthony Perkins, Art Garfunkel

This release stars Alan Arkin as a soldier in World War II most interested in avoiding the insanity of combat. Its sarcasm alone is enough to sustain interest. Rated R.

1970 121 minutes

CAVEMAN

★

DIRECTOR: Carl Gottlieb

CAST: Ringo Starr, Barbara Bach, John Matuszak, Shelley Long

Ex-Beatle Ringo Starr plays the prehistoric hero in this silly, vulgar, and sometimes outright stupid spoof of *One Million Years B.C.* Because of the amount of sexual innuendo, it is definitely not recommended for kids, although they are perhaps the only people who would really think it was funny. Rated PG.

1981 92 minutes

CHAMPAGNE FOR CAESAR

★★★★

DIRECTOR: Richard Whorf

CAST: Ronald Colman, Celeste Holm, Vincent Price, Barbara Britton, Art Linkletter

Satire of early television and the concept of game shows is funnier now than when it was originally released. A treasure trove of trivia and great one-liners, this intelligent spoof features classic actor Ronald Colman as Beauregarde Bottomley, self-proclaimed genius and scholar who exacts his revenge on soap tycoon Vincent Price by appearing on his quiz show and attempting to bankrupt his company by winning all their assets. Art Linkletter is great as the inane game show host, Colman is in top comedic form as a man of humor and integrity, and Vincent Price gives the comedy performance of his career. Bogged down with the love story between Colman and Celeste Holm (as Flame O'Neill!) and some needless physical humor, this gem is still solid entertainment and will please anyone who questions the mindless direction commercial television has taken since its inception.

1950 B & W 99 minutes

CHANGE OF SEASONS, A

DIRECTOR: Richard Lang

CAST: Shirley MacLaine, Anthony Hopkins, Bo Derek, Michael Brandon

Poor Shirley MacLaine. She seems destined to make the same movie over and over again. The only difference between this film and *Loving Couples*, which closely followed it into release, is that Anthony Hopkins and Bo Derek co-star as the ultramodern mate-swappers who discover the real meaning of love just in the nick of time, instead of James Coburn and Susan Sarandon. It's pure corn, with a little nudity thrown in; another example of the "commercial" package at its worst. Miss it. Rated R.

1980 102 minutes

CHAPLIN REVUE, THE

★★★★

DIRECTOR: Charles Chaplin

CAST: Charlie Chaplin, Edna Purviance, Tom Wilson, Sydney Chaplin, Henry Bergman, Chuck Riesner, Bud Jamison, Jack Wilson, John Rand, Park Jones, Kitty Bradbury, Mack Swain, Tom Murray, Monta Bell, May Wells, Raymond Lee, Florence Latimer, Dinky Dean

Assembled and scored by Charlie Chaplin for release in 1959, this revue is composed of three of his longer, more complex and polished films: *A Dog's Life*, (1918) which established Chaplin's, reputation as a satirist; *Shoulder Arms*, a model for *The Great Dictator*; and *The Pilgrim* (1923), in which escaped convict Chaplin assumes the garb of a minister.

1959 B & W 121 minutes

CHARLIE CHAN AND THE CURSE OF THE DRAGON QUEEN

★★

DIRECTOR: Clive Donner

CAST: Peter Ustinov, Lee Grant, Angie Dickinson, Richard Hatch

Although there are moments in this tongue-in-cheek send-up of the 1930s Charlie Chan mystery series that recapture the fun of yesteryear, overall it's just not a very good movie. The only thing that saves this film is that the stars—Peter Ustinov (who plays Chan), Lee Grant, Angie Dickinson, Brian Keith, Roddy McDowall, Rachel Roberts, and Richard Hatch—seem to be having so much fun it's hard not to get caught up in it, even though afterward you sometimes regret laughing. Besides, the Oriental sleuth belongs to another, less-aware age, which is perhaps where he should remain. Rated PG.

1981 97 minutes

CHARLIE CHAPLIN CARNIVAL

★★★

DIRECTOR: Charles Chaplin

CAST: Charlie Chaplin, Edna Purviance, Eric Campbell, Lloyd Bacon, Henry Bergman, Leo White, Albert Austin, James T. Kelly, Leota Bryan, Loyal Underwood

One of a number of anthologies made up of two-reel Chaplin films, this one is composed of *The Vagabond*, *The Count*, *Behind the Screen*, and *The Fireman*. Charlie Chaplin, Edna Purviance (his forever leading lady), and the giant Eric Campbell provide most of the hilarious, romantic, touching moments. Bedrock fans will find *The Vagabond* a study for the longer films that followed in the 1920s—*The Kid*, in particular.

1916 B & W 80 minutes

CHARLIE CHAPLIN CAVALCADE

★★★

DIRECTOR: Charles Chaplin

CAST: Charlie Chaplin, Henry Bergman, Edna Purviance, John Rand, Wesley Ruggles, Frank J. Coleman, Albert Austin, Eric Campbell, Lloyd Bacon, Leo White

Another in a series of anthologies spliced up out of two- and three-reel Chaplin comedies. This features four of his best: *One A. M.*, *The Pawnshop*, *The Floorwalker*, *The Rink*. As in most of Chaplin's short comedies, the sidesplitting action results mainly from underdog Chaplin clashing with the short-fused giant Eric Campbell.

1916 B & W 81 minutes

CHARLIE CHAPLIN FESTIVAL

★★★

DIRECTOR: Charles Chaplin

CAST: Charlie Chaplin, Eric Campbell, Edna Purviance, Albert Austin, Henry Bergman, Loyal Underwood, Charlotte Mineau, Janet Miller Sully, John Rand, Tom Wood, James T. Kelly, Kitty Bradbury, Frank J. Coleman, Marta Golden, Kono, May White, Phyllis Allen

The third in a number of Chaplin film anthologies. Featuring *Easy Street*, one of his best-known hits, this group contains *The Cure*, *The Adventurer*, and *The Immigrant*, and gives viewers the full gamut of famous Chaplin emotional expressions. The coin sequence in the latter is sight-gag ingenuity at its best.

1917 B & W 80 minutes

CHARLIE CHAPLIN—THE EARLY YEARS, VOL. 1

★★★★★

DIRECTOR: Charlie Chaplin

CAST: Charlie Chaplin, Edna Purviance, Eric Campbell, Albert Austin

In this collection of early Charlie Chaplin shorts, we get three outstanding stories. *The Immigrant* finds Charlie, who meets Edna Purviance on the boat to America, in love and broke. The story is how they survive in the land of dreams. *The Count* has Charlie trying to lead the high life with no money. *Easy Street* finds Charlie "saved" by missionary Purviance and out to save everyone else. All three episodes are quite funny and heartwarming. If you like old silent comedies, you'll love these.

1917 B & W 62 minutes

CHARLIE CHAPLIN—THE EARLY YEARS, VOL. 2

★★★★★

DIRECTOR: Charlie Chaplin
CAST: Charlie Chaplin, Edna Purviance, Eric Campbell, Albert Austin

Volume Two of the Charlie Chaplin series presents three more classic shorts. The first is *The Pawnbroker,* with Charlie running a pawnshop. As you might expect, nothing is quite normal in this pawnshop. The second feature is called *The Adventure,* as Charlie plays an escaped con who gets mistaken for a high-society man and finds himself in the middle of wealthy society. And *One A.M.* ends the collection as Charlie tries desperately to get some sleep after a long night of boozing it up. Everything in his room keeps moving. A must for Chaplin fans.

1916 B & W 61 minutes

CHARLIE CHAPLIN, THE EARLY YEARS, VOL. 3

★★★★★

DIRECTOR: Charlie Chaplin
CAST: Charlie Chaplin, Edna Purviance, Eric Campbell, Henry Bergman

In Volume Three of this great series, we get three more classic Chaplin shorts. First off is *The Cure,* where Charlie plays a drunk who goes to a health spa to dry out. He also happens to bring a trunkload of booze with him; the result is a spa full of smashed people. Next Charlie shows up as *The Floorwalker* in a large department store who catches his boss trying to make off with the store money. Last Charlie is *The Vagabond,* a wandering violinist who saves a young girl's life and also falls in love with her. Unfortunately for Charlie, her mother takes her away from him. Don't miss these wonderful treasures from the past.

1917 B & W 64 minutes

CHARLIE CHAPLIN—THE EARLY YEARS, VOL. 4

★★★★★

DIRECTOR: Charlie Chaplin
CAST: Charlie Chaplin, Edna Purviance, Eric Campbell, Albert Austin, Lloyd Bacon, Charlotte Mineau, James T. Kelly, Leo White

In Volume Four of the Charlie Chaplin series, we start out with *Behind The Screen,* as Charlie plays a movie studio stagehand who goes crazy from being overworked. The final pie-throwing clash is a classic. Next is *The Fireman,* with Charlie a brave firefighter who must rescue Edna Purviance, his girlfriend, from a fire. The final story is *The Ring,* with Charlie playing a bumbling waiter in a high-class restaurant. All three stories are in the great Chaplin tradition.

1916 B & W 63 minutes

CHATTANOOGA CHOO CHOO

★★★

DIRECTOR: Bruce Bilson
CAST: George Kennedy, Barbara Eden, Joe Namath, Melissa Sue Anderson

A sillier and cornier movie you'll probably never see, yet *Chattanooga Choo Choo* fills a longtime void in screen entertainment. It's a family-oriented picture that's just a little naughtier than the live-action releases the Disney Studios used to make in the 1950s and 1960s and most likely will appeal to those filmgoers who enjoyed *Smokey and the Bandit* and *Every Which Way but Loose*. The story deals with a bet to make a New York–to–Chattanooga train trip within a deadline. George Kennedy plays the comedy villain and owner of a football team on which Joe Namath is the coach. Barbara Eden starts out as Kennedy's girlfriend but soon falls in love with the "good guy"—Namath. Rated PG for mild profanity.

1984 102 minutes

CHEAPER TO KEEP HER

★

DIRECTOR: Ken Annakin
CAST: Mac Davis, Tovah Feldshuh, Art Metrano, Ian McShane

Mac Davis (*North Dallas Forty*) plays a sexist private detective whose investigations are confined to tracking down ex-husbands who haven't paid their alimony. Despite an advertising claim that it's about women's rights, this film cares as little about women as it does about good comedy. This insult to one's intelligence is simply a waste of time. Rated R.

1980 92 minutes

CHECK AND DOUBLE CHECK

★

DIRECTOR: Melville Brown
CAST: Freeman Gosden, Charles Correll, Sue Carol, Charles Norton, Ralf Harolde, Irene Rich, Duke Ellington and His Orchestra

This sad comedy starring radio's Amos 'n Andy in blackface was RKO's biggest hit for the 1930 season and made Freeman Gosden and Charles Correll the top stars for that year—but by that time they weren't even with the studio anymore and never made another film. Very popular in the Midwest and the South when it was first released, this clinker looks its age and then some. Early footage of Duke Ellington and His Orchestra and the chance to see early radio at work on the screen are the main incentives for sitting through this one.

1930 B & W 80 minutes

CHECK IS IN THE MAIL, THE

DIRECTOR: Joan Darling
CAST: Brian Dennehy, Anne Archer, Hallie Todd, Chris Herbert, Michael Bowen, Dick Shawn, Beau Starr

This unfunny comedy tells the lamentable story of a man (Brian Dennehy) who is tired of the capitalist system. A hard-luck case, he decides to rebel, all the while not realizing that he is part of the same system he so disdains. The humor in this film relies on putting the characters through embarrassing and bad-luck situations, techniques commonly used in slapstick comedy, few of which work here. The acting isn't bad. In fact, Dennehy is as good as ever, but nothing can save this film and its overused storyline. All in all, it is just a boorish mess. Rated R for profanity and adult situations.

1986 83 minutes

CHEECH AND CHONG'S NEXT MOVIE

★★

DIRECTOR: Thomas Chong
CAST: Cheech and Chong, Evelyn Guerrero, Betty Kennedy

This is Cheech and Chong's (Richard Marin and Thomas Chong) in-between movie—in between *Up in Smoke*, their first, and *Nice Dreams*, number three. If you liked either of the other two, you'll like *Next Movie*. But if you didn't care for the duo's brand of humor there, you won't in this one either. Rated R for nudity and profanity.

1980 99 minutes

CHICKEN CHRONICLES, THE

★

DIRECTOR: Francis Simon
CAST: Steven Guttenberg, Ed Lauter, Lisa Reeves, Meredith Baer, Phil Silvers

This witless comedy centers on the carnal pursuits of Steve (*Police Academy*) Guttenberg, a charmless high school senior. Even Phil Silvers can't scare up many laughs in this one. Rated PG.

1977 95 minutes

CHRISTMAS IN JULY

★★★½

DIRECTOR: Preston Sturges
CAST: Dick Powell, Ellen Drew, Raymond Walburn, William Demarest, Ernest Truex, Franklin Pangborn

Touching, insightful comedy-drama about a young couple's dreams and aspirations was yet another coup for writer-producer-director Preston Sturges, one of Hollywood's true creative geniuses and Paramount's most valuable asset during the early 1940s. Partly based on a play Sturges had written in the 1930s, this story of a young office worker who enters slogan-writing contests and optimistically plans on success being right around the corner is every bit as valid and meaningful today. Dick Powell is fine as the enthusiastic young man who mistakenly believes that he has won a contest and finds all doors opening to him—until the error is discovered. Director Sturges peopled this film (as he did all his films) with some of the greatest character actors ever assembled, and the ensemble clicks. This one is a treat for all audiences. Once you've seen it, you'll want to see all of Preston Sturges's films. Fortunately, most of them are available on cassette.

1940 B & W 67 minutes

CHU CHU AND THE PHILLY FLASH

★★

DIRECTOR: David Lowell Rich
CAST: Alan Arkin, Carol Burnett, Jack Warden, Ruth Buzzi

This is another bittersweet comedy about a couple of losers. It's supposed to be funny. It isn't. The stars, Alan Arkin and Carol Burnett, do manage to invest it with a certain wacky charm, but that isn't enough to make up for its shortcomings. Rated PG.

1981 100 minutes

CHUMP AT OXFORD, A

★★★

DIRECTOR: Alfred Goulding
CAST: Stan Laurel, Oliver Hardy, Wilfred Lucas, Forrester Harvey, James Finlayson, Anita Garvin

Stan Laurel receives a scholarship to Oxford, and Oliver Hardy accompanies him. Not accepted by the other students, they are the butt of pranks and jokes until Stan receives a blow on the head and becomes a reincarnation of a college hero. A fair script, but the Stan and Ollie characters never seem to fit well into it.

1940 B & W 63 minutes

CIRCUS/A DAY'S PLEASURE, THE

★★★

DIRECTOR: Charles Chaplin
CAST: Charlie Chaplin, Allan Garcia, Merna Kennedy, Harry Crocker, Betty Morrisey, George Davis, Henry Bergman

This double feature admirably showcases Charlie Chaplin's world-famous gifts for comedy and pathos. In the first, vagabond Charlie hooks up with a traveling circus and falls for the bareback rider, who loves a muscle-bound trapeze artist. The film earned

Chaplin a special Oscar at the first Academy Awards ceremony for writing, acting, directing, and producing. In the second feature, Charlie and his family try in vain to have Sunday fun. Silent.

1928 B & W 105 minutes

CITY HEAT

★★★

DIRECTOR: Richard Benjamin

CAST: Clint Eastwood, Burt Reynolds, Jane Alexander, Madeline Kahn, Irene Cara, Richard Roundtree, Rip Torn, Tony Lo Bianco

Clint Eastwood and Burt Reynolds portray a cop and a private eye, respectively, in this enjoyable action comedy, directed by Richard Benjamin (*My Favorite Year*). Despite a few clashes while pursuing gangsters, the two have a "grudging mutual respect," according to the filmmakers. It's fun for fans of the stars. Rated PG for violence.

1984 94 minutes

CITY LIGHTS

★★★★★

DIRECTOR: Charles Chaplin

CAST: Charlie Chaplin, Virginia Cherrill, Harry Myers, Hank Mann

In his finest film, Charlie Chaplin's little tramp befriends a blind flower-seller, providing her with every kindness he can afford. Charlie develops a friendship with a drunken millionaire and takes advantage of it to help the girl even more. Taking money from the millionaire so the girl can have an eye operation, he is arrested and sent to jail. His release from jail and the subsequent reunion with the girl may well be the most poignant ending of all his films.

1931 B & W 81 minutes

CLASS

DIRECTOR: Lewis John Carlino

CAST: Rob Lowe, Jacqueline Bisset, Andrew McCarthy, Stuart Margolin

This is a generally unfunny and offensive comedy about two preppies, one of whom unwittingly falls in love with the other's alcoholic mother (Jacqueline Bisset). Rated R for nudity, profanity, sex, and violence.

1983 98 minutes

CLASS REUNION

DIRECTOR: Michael Miller

CAST: Gerrit Graham, Stephen Furst, Zane Buzby, Michael Lerner

The graduating class of 1972 returns to wreak havoc on its alma mater, Lizzie Borden High School, in this awful *Animal House*–style comedy. Gerrit Graham (who played Beef in *Phantom of the Paradise*), Stephen Furst (Flounder from *Animal House*), and Zane Buzby (the pill freak from *Up in Smoke*) are bound to have nightmares about appearing in this moronic mess. Avoid it. Rated R for nudity, leering sexual references, profanity, and drug-taking.

1982 84 minutes

CLOCKWISE

★★★½

DIRECTOR: Christopher Morahan

CAST: John Cleese, Penelope Wilton, Alison Steadman, Stephen Moore, Sharon Maiden, Joan Hickson

No one plays a pillar of pomposity better than John Cleese. In *Clockwise*, written expressly for Cleese, he gets a perfect role for his patented persona. Brian Stimpson, a headmaster, runs everything by the clock—in the extreme. However, his complete control is soon shattered by a misunderstanding—and hilarity is the result. Rated PG.

1987 96 minutes

CLUB PARADISE

DIRECTOR: Harold Ramis

CAST: Robin Williams, Peter O'Toole, Jimmy Cliff, Twiggy, Rick Moranis, Adolph Caesar, Eugene Levy, Joanna Cassidy

Lame, witless, boring, and offensive attempt to use adult stars in a concept overdone by moronic teen comedies. Robin Williams and Jimmy Cliff start their own little Club Med-style resort; other cast members play tourists who arrive for a vacation. This is filmmaking at the top of its lungs, everybody shouts and screams. The tasteless and sexist humor includes potshots at women, and drugs. A civil war is thrown in for good measure. Rarely have so many labored so long and delivered so little. Rated PG-13 for language and drug humor.

1986 104 minutes

CLUE

★★½

DIRECTOR: Jonathan Lynn

CAST: Eileen Brennan, Tim Curry, Madeline Kahn, Christopher Lloyd, Michael McKean, Martin Mull, Lesley Ann Warren

Inspired by the popular board game, the movie is a pleasant spoof of whodunits. The delightful ensemble establishes a suitably breezy style. Silliness eventually overwhelms the proceedings. As a gimmick, the film was originally shown in theatres with three different endings. All versions are included on the videocassette. Rated PG-13.

1985 100 minutes

COAST TO COAST

DIRECTOR: Joseph Sargent

CAST: Dyan Cannon, Robert Blake, Quinn Redeker, Michael Lerner, Maxine Stuart, Bill Lucking

Dyan Cannon stars as a wacko blonde who's been railroaded into a mental hospital by her husband. He has had her declared insane so he can avoid an expensive divorce. Cannon escapes by bopping her psychiatrist over the head with a bust of Freud, and the chase is on. Trucker Charlie Calahan (Robert Blake) gives Cannon a lift, and they romp from Pennsylvania to California with a couple of private detectives and a thug who's trying to repossess Calahan's truck shadowing their journey. The abundance of their expletives may discourage some parents from making *Coast to Coast* a family outing, but Blake fans will find him as loose and energetic as always, and scrappy enough to be amusing. Rated PG.

1980 95 minutes

COCA COLA KID, THE

★★★

DIRECTOR: Dusan Makavejev

CAST: Eric Roberts, Greta Scacchi, Bill Kerr

A nude scene between Eric Roberts and Greta Scacchi in a bed covered with feathers is enough to make anyone's temperature rise, but as a whole this little film doesn't have enough bite to it. Roberts plays a gung-ho troubleshooter from the popular beverage company who comes to Australia to sell the drink to a hard-nosed businessman (Bill Kerr) who has a monopoly on a stretch of land with his own soft drink. Worth a look. Rated R for nudity.

1985 90 minutes

COLLEGE

★★★½

DIRECTOR: James W. Horne
CAST: Buster Keaton, Anne Cornwall, Flora Bramley, Harold Goodwin, Grant Winters, Snitz Edwards

An anti-athletics bookworm, Buster Keaton, goes to college with a scholarship. His girl falls for a jock, and Keaton decides to prove he can succeed in athletics to win her back. He fails hilariously in every attempt, but finally rescues her from the evil-intentioned jock by unwittingly using every athletic skill. Lack of a solid, complete script keeps the film from attaining the excellence of *Steamboat Bill, Jr.*

1927 B & W 65 minutes

COLONEL EFFINGHAM'S RAID

★★½

DIRECTOR: Irving Pichel
CAST: Charles Coburn, Joan Bennett, William Eythe, Allyn Joslyn, Elizabeth Patterson, Donald Meek

Slight small-town story about Charles Coburn's efforts to preserve a local monument and save the community's pride is pleasant enough and has marvelous characters like Donald Meek populating it. Similar in tone and story to several American productions of the same vintage, this entertaining little film, while espousing the values of wartime movies, shifts the emphasis from overseas to hometown America and pits the war veteran against a new and increasingly insidious enemy facing postwar America, the creeping rise of indifferent government bureaucracy. Not a great film, but harmless fun and at times thought-provoking.

1945 B & W 70 minutes

COMFORT AND JOY

★★★★½

DIRECTOR: Bill Forsyth
CAST: Bill Paterson, Eleanor David, C. P. Grogan, Alex Norton

Scottish filmmaker Bill Forsyth (*Local Hero*; *Gregory's Girl*) scores again with this delightful tale of a disc jockey (Bill Paterson) whose life is falling apart. His girlfriend walks out on him, taking nearly everything he owns. Birds seem to like decorating his pride and joy: a red BMW. And what's worse, he gets involved in a gangland war over—are you ready for this?—the control of ice cream manufacturing and sales. It's one you'll want to see. Rated PG.

1984 90 minutes

COMIC CABBY

DIRECTOR: Carl Lindahl
CAST: Bill McLaughlin, Al Lewis, Frank Guy, Scott Johnson, Tom Reid

This has to be one of the worst hours of video you could rent. Based on Jim Pietsch's book *The New York City Cab Driver's Joke Book*, it's an extended skit that dramatizes a day in the life of a rookie cabby. The jokes are bad and the acting worse. You'll want to take the bus from now on.

1986 60 minutes

COMMIES ARE COMING, THE COMMIES ARE COMING, THE

★★

DIRECTOR: George Waggner
CAST: Jack Kelly, Jean Cooper, Peter Brown, Patricia Woodell, Andrew Duggan, Robert Conrad

Jack Webb narrates this 1950s anti-communist pseudodocumentary about what would happen if the Russians captured the United

States. It's easy to laugh at this silly film. Unrated.

1984 B & W 60 minutes

COMPLEAT "WEIRD AL" YANKOVIC, THE

★★½

DIRECTORS: Jay Levey, Robert K. Weiss

CAST: "Weird Al" Yankovic

This is all that you ever wanted to know about "Weird Al" Yankovic. At 100 minutes, it's probably more than most people want to know. Filmed in documentary fashion, it traces Al's birth on October 23, 1959, through school, early jobs, and finally his entertainment career. In the process, eight of his videos are shown, including *Eat It*, *I Love Rocky Road*, *I Lost on Jeopardy*, and *Like a Surgeon*. The two best sequences show Al going to Michael Jackson for permission to do a parody of *Beat It* and a Devo send-up entitled *Dare to Be Stupid*. Weird Al—the man, the myth, the legend? You decide.

1985 100 minutes

COMPROMISING POSITIONS

★★

DIRECTOR: Frank Perry

CAST: Susan Sarandon, Raul Julia, Edward Herrmann, Judith Ivey, Mary Beth Hurt, Anne DeSalvo, Josh Mostel

In the first half-hour, this is a hilarious and innovative takeoff on murder mysteries and a devastatingly witty send-up of suburban life. However, it soon descends into the clichés of the mystery genre. That's too bad, because the plot, about an overly amorous dentist who is murdered, has great possibilities. Old Doc was given to taking pictures of his many sexual conquests . . . all female patients, many of whom are married. This brings many delightfully bitchy encounters as the women bemoan their respective fates. But it eventually collapses into a not-very-suspenseful whodunit. Rated R for nudity, profanity, and violence.

1985 98 minutes

CONNECTICUT YANKEE IN KING ARTHUR'S COURT, A

★★★

DIRECTOR: Tay Garnett

CAST: Bing Crosby, Rhonda Fleming, Sir Cedric Hardwicke, William Bendix, Henry Wilcoxon, Murvyn Vye

The third film version of Mark Twain's intriguing social satire, this costly but profitable production presents Bing Crosby as the blacksmith who dreams himself back to Camelot and is proclaimed a wizard because of his modern knowledge. It's good, clean, happy fun for all.

1948 107 minutes

CONTEMPT

★★★½

DIRECTOR: Jean-Luc Godard

CAST: Brigitte Bardot, Jack Palance, Fritz Lang, Jean-Luc Godard, Michel Piccoli

A cult film to be, if it isn't already, this one takes a tongue-in-cheek, raised-eyebrow look at European moviemaking. Jack Palance is a vulgar producer; Fritz Lang, playing himself, is his director; Jean-Luc Godard plays Lang's assistant, and in directing this film turned it into an inside joke—in real (not reel) life, he held the film's producer Joseph E. Levine in contempt.

1963 103 minutes

CONTINENTAL DIVIDE

★★★½

DIRECTOR: Michael Apted

CAST: John Belushi, Blair Brown, Allen Goorwitz, Carlin Glynn

As light-hearted romantic comedies go, this one is tops. John Belushi stars as Ernie Souchak, a Chicago newspaper columnist unexpectedly sent into the Rockies to write a story about an ornithologist (Blair Brown). Just as unexpectedly, they fall in love. Rated PG because of slight amounts of nudity.

1981 103 minutes

COPACABANA

★

DIRECTOR: Alfred E. Green

CAST: Groucho Marx, Carmen Miranda, Andy Russell, Steve Cochran, Abel Green

Not even Groucho Marx can save this slight comedy about the problems caused by a woman applying for two jobs at the same nightclub. Carmen Miranda does her "banana hat bit" and the viewer eventually falls asleep.

1947 B & W 92 minutes

CORSICAN BROTHERS, THE

DIRECTOR: Thomas Chong

CAST: Cheech and Chong, Roy Dotrice

The comedy team of Cheech and Chong apparently enjoyed working on the Monty Python–powered period pirate comedy *Yellowbeard* so much they decided to do a silly swashbuckler of their own. Loosely based on the book by Alexandre Dumas, this forgettable film features Tommy Chong and Richard "Cheech" Marin as twins dueling to the death with dastardly villains. Rated R.

1984 90 minutes

COUNTRY GENTLEMEN

★★

DIRECTOR: Ralph Staub

CAST: Ole Olson, Chic Johnson, Joyce Compton, Lila Lee

Fast-talking confidence men Ole Olson and Chic Johnson sell shares in a worthless oil field to a group of World War I veterans, then learn thar's oil in them thar hills! Humorous, but what a weary plot! This flick did little for the comic duo, who always fared better on the stage.

1936 B & W 54 minutes

COURT JESTER, THE

★★★

DIRECTORS: Norman Panama, Melvin Frank

CAST: Danny Kaye, Glynis Johns, Basil Rathbone, Angela Lansbury, Mildred Natwick, Robert Middleton

Romance, court intrigue, a joust, and in the middle of it all the one and only Danny Kaye as a phony court jester full of double-takes and double-talk. This is one funny film of clever and complicated comic situations superbly brought off.

1956 101 minutes

CRACKERS

★½

DIRECTOR: Louis Malle

CAST: Donald Sutherland, Jack Warden, Sean Penn, Wallace Shawn

Crackers is a nearly unwatchable film directed by Louis Malle (*Atlantic City*; *My Dinner with Andre*). It isn't often Malle comes up with a turkey, but when he does, it comes complete with all the trimmings. Even the high-powered talents of stars Donald Sutherland, Sean Penn (*Bad Boys*; *The Falcon and the Snowman*), and Jack Warden can't lift this caper "comedy" above mediocrity. It's about a bunch of down-and-out San Franciscans who decide to turn to crime in order to survive. Rated PG.

1984 92 minutes

CRACKING UP

DIRECTOR: Jerry Lewis
CAST: Jerry Lewis, Herb Edelman, Zane Buzby, Dick Butkus, Milton Berle

A relatively new Jerry Lewis comedy. Translation: No laughs here. Rated R.

1983 83 minutes

CRIME & PASSION

★★

DIRECTOR: Ivan Passer
CAST: Omar Sharif, Karen Black, Joseph Bottoms, Bernhard Wicki

Except for Karen Black, *Crime & Passion* is a weak comedy of sex and money that gives us Omar Sharif as a rich businessman who becomes sexually aroused when bad things happen to him. Karen Black provides the zany aggressive sexuality that makes some moments zing with her particular brand of oddness. Her seduction of Joseph Bottoms is a classic. Weird and wild. Rated R.

1975 92 minutes

CRIMES OF THE HEART

★★★★½

DIRECTOR: Bruce Beresford
CAST: Diane Keaton, Jessica Lange, Sissy Spacek, Sam Shepard, Tess Harper, David Carpenter, Hurd Hatfield

In this superb screen adaptation of Beth Henley's Pulitzer Prize–winning play, Diane Keaton, Jessica Lange, and Sissy Spacek star as three eccentric sisters who stick together despite an onslaught of extraordinary problems. It is a film of many joys. Not the least of which are the performances of the stars, fine bits by Sam Shepard and Tess Harper in support, the biting humor, and the overall intelligence. Rated PG-13 for subject matter.

1986 105 minutes

CRITICAL CONDITION

★★½

DIRECTOR: Michael Apted
CAST: Richard Pryor, Rachel Ticotin, Rubén Blades, Joe Mantegna, Bob Dishy, Joe Dallesandro, Garrett Morris, Randall "Tex" Cob

Mishmash of a comedy has some funny moments but ultimately tests the viewer's patience. Richard Pryor stars as a hustler who runs afoul of the law and the mob. He must feign insanity to stay out of prison, where the crime kingpins have arranged for his instant demise. While under observation in a psychiatric ward of a big hospital, Pryor finds himself in charge of the institution when a failed escape during a power failure traps him in the guise of a surgeon. The star has some good moments, which mostly comes in tandem with *Saturday Night Live* original Garrett Morris and character actor Randall "Tex" Cobb. Rated R for profanity, violence, and scatological humor.

1987 105 minutes

"CROCODILE" DUNDEE

★★★★½

DIRECTOR: Peter Faiman
CAST: Paul Hogan, Linda Kozlowski, John Meillen, Mark Blum, David Gulpilil, Michael Lombard

Those folks who moan that they don't make movies like they used to will be delighted by this hilarious Australian import. Not only is it made the old-fashioned way, it also has the most heartwarming laughs of any film of recent memory. Paul Hogan plays the title character, a hunter who allegedly crawled several miles for help after a king-size crocodile gnawed off a leg. This slight exaggeration is enough to persuade an American newspaper reporter (Linda Kozlowski) to seek him out and persuade him to join her on a trip to New York, where the naïve outbacker faces a new set of perils (and deals with them in high comic style). Rated PG-13 for profanity and violence.

1986 98 minutes

CURSE OF THE PINK PANTHER, THE

★★★

DIRECTOR: Blake Edwards

CAST: Ted Wass, David Niven, Robert Wagner, Harvey Korman, Herbert Lom

No, this isn't another trashy compilation of outtakes featuring the late Peter Sellers. Instead, series producer-writer-director Blake Edwards has hired Ted Wass (of TV's *Soap*) to play a bumbling American detective searching for the still-missing Jacques Clouseau, and he's a delight. The movie isn't always good. However, when Wass is featured, *Curse* is fresh and diverting—and, on a couple of memorable occasions, it's hilarious. Rated PG for nudity, profanity, violence, and scatological humor.

1983 109 minutes

DAY AT THE RACES, A

★★★½

DIRECTOR: Sam Wood

CAST: The Marx Brothers, Allan Jones, Maureen O'Sullivan, Margaret Dumont

The Marx Brothers—Groucho, Harpo, and Chico, that is—were still at the peak of their fame in this MGM musical-comedy. Though not as unrelentingly hilarious and outrageous as the films they made at Paramount with Zeppo, it is nonetheless an enjoyable film. The first to follow *A Night at the Opera*, their biggest hit, and use a variation on its formula, it works very well—which, sadly, did not prove to be the case with most of the Marx Brothers movies that followed.

1937 B & W 111 minutes

D.C. CAB

DIRECTOR: Joel Schumacher

CAST: Gary Busey, Mr. T, Adam Baldwin, Charlie Barnett, Max Gail

A mindless "madcap" comedy with Gary Busey and Mr. T. Don't pay the fare. Rated R.

1983 99 minutes

DEAD MEN DON'T WEAR PLAID

★★★★

DIRECTOR: Carl Reiner

CAST: Steve Martin, Rachel Ward, Reni Santoni, Carl Reiner, George Gaynes, Frank McCarthy

In this often hilarious and always entertaining comedy, Steve Martin plays a private eye who confronts the suspicious likes of Humphrey Bogart, Burt Lancaster, Alan Ladd, Bette Davis, and other stars of Hollywood's golden age, with the help of tricky editing and writer-director Carl Reiner. Rachel Ward co-stars as Martin's sexy client. Rated PG for adult themes.

1982 B & W 89 minutes

DEAL OF THE CENTURY

DIRECTOR: William Friedkin

CAST: Chevy Chase, Sigourney Weaver, Gregory Hines, Vince Edwards

A two-bit arms hustler (Chevy Chase) peddles an ultrasophisticated superweapon to a Central American dictator. This black comedy has its good moments. Unfortunately, it also has its bad moments and, as a result, ends up in that nether world of the near misses. Rated PG for violence and profanity.

1983 99 minutes

DEAR WIFE

★★½

DIRECTOR: Richard Haydn
CAST: Joan Caulfield, William Holden, Mona Freeman, Edward Arnold, Billy DeWolfe

The second of three amusing films involving the same cast of characters, and mostly the same players. This sequel to *Dear Ruth* has fresh-faced younger sister (to Joan Caulfield) Mona Freeman conniving to elect heartthrob William Holden to the state senate seat sought by her politician father Edward Arnold. Billy DeWolfe fills it all out with his peculiar brand of haughty humor. William Holden had yet to break the boy-next-door mold when this was made. *Stalag 17* and *Picnic* were years in the future; *The Wild Bunch* and *Network* not even motes in the eyes of destiny.

1949 B & W 88 minutes

DECAMERON NIGHTS

★★★

DIRECTOR: Hugo Fregonese
CAST: Joan Fontaine, Louis Jourdan, Joan Collins, Binnie Barnes, Marjorie Rhodes, Godfrey Tearle

Louis Jourdan is Boccaccio, the poet, story-teller, and humanist best known for *The Decameron*. Three of his tales are told within the overall frame of his trying to win the love of a recent widow (Joan Fontaine). Each story features the cast members as various characters. The sets and costumes add greatly to this period comedy.

1953 75 minutes

DELIVERY BOYS

★★½

DIRECTOR: Ken Handler
CAST: Jody Olivery, Joss Marcano, Mario Van Peebles

This average teen comedy features pizza delivery boys who breakdance during their time off. They plan to compete in a breakdance contest that offers a $10,000 prize but encounter problems in getting there on time. Rated R.

1984 94 minutes

DENTIST, THE

★★★½

DIRECTOR: Leslie Pearce
CAST: W. C. Fields, Babe Kane, Elise Cavanna, Zedna Farley, Bud Jamison, Dorothy Granger

The first (and possibly best) of four comedy shorts starring the incomparable W. C. Fields and produced by Mack Sennett from vaudeville material in Fields's files. Most of the film has dentist Fields dealing with a parade of patients. The highlight is his monumental tooth-pulling sequence with leggy foil Elise Cavanna, certain phases of which had to be deleted before American television audiences could see it.

1932 B & W 20 minutes

DESPERATE LIVING

🦃

DIRECTOR: John Waters
CAST: Mink Stole, Edith Massey, Jean Hill, Liz Renay, Susan Lowe

A "monstrous fairy tale," director John Waters calls it. And that may be an understatement. This story about a murderess (played by Mink Stole) and her escapades through a village of criminals who are ruled by a demented queen (Edith Massey) is a bit redundant. But various scenes provide enough humor and wit for anyone with a taste for the perverse and a yen for some good old-fashioned misanthropy. This is unrated, but it is the equivalent of an X, due to violence, nudity, and unbridled gore.

1977 95 minutes

DESPERATELY SEEKING SUSAN

★★★★½

DIRECTOR: Susan Siedelman

CAST: Rosanna Arquette, Madonna, Robert Joy, Mark Blum, Laurie Metcalf

Even the clichés in this film seem fresh. It's a delightfully daffy, smart, and intriguing comedy made from a feminine perspective. Rosanna Arquette stars as a bored housewife who adds spice to her life by following the personal column love adventures of the mysterious Susan (Madonna). One day, Susan is to meet someone close by, so our heroine decides to catch a glimpse of her idol and, through a set of unlikely but easy-to-take plot convolutions, ends up switching places with her. After this, it's nothing but amusing and watchable. Rated PG-13 for violence.

1985 104 minutes

DETECTIVE SCHOOL DROPOUTS

★★★★

DIRECTOR: Filippo Ottoni

CAST: David Landsberg, Lorin Dreyfuss, Christian De Sica, Valeria Golina, George Eastman

David Landsberg and Lorin Dreyfuss co-star in this hilarious comedy. (The two wrote the screenplay as well.) Landsberg plays Wilson, whose obsession with detective stories loses him a string of jobs. Finally, he goes to P.I. Miller (Dreyfuss) for lessons in investigation. The two accidentally become involved in an intrigue with star-crossed lovers (Christian De Sica and Valeria Golina). The chase scenes and slapstick gags are great. Rated PG for obscenities.

1985 92 minutes

DEVIL AND MAX DEVLIN, THE

★★

DIRECTOR: Steven Hillard Stern

CAST: Elliott Gould, Bill Cosby, Susan Anspach, Adam Rich

This is visible proof that it takes more than just a few talented people to create quality entertainment. Despite Elliott Gould, Bill Cosby, and Susan Anspach, this Disney production—another take-off on the Faustian theme of a pact made with the devil—offers little more than mediocre fare. It's basically a waste of fine talent. Rated PG.

1981 96 minutes

DEVIL AND MISS JONES, THE

★★★★

DIRECTOR: Sam Wood

CAST: Jean Arthur, Robert Cummings, Charles Coburn, Spring Byington, S. Z. Sakall, William Demarest

One of those wonderful comedies Hollywood used to make. Witty, sophisticated, poignant, and breezy, this one has millionaire Charles Coburn going undercover as a clerk in his own department store in order to probe employee complaints and unrest. Delightful doings.

1941 B & W 92 minutes

DIARY OF A YOUNG COMIC

★★½

DIRECTOR: Gary Weis

CAST: Richard Lewis, Stacy Keach, Dom De Luise, Nina Van Pallandt, Bill Macy, George Jessel

This low-budget comedy follows the adventures of a young New York comic, Richard Lewis, who thinks that by moving to Hollywood he'll be an instant hit. Along the way we are given vignettes as he finds an apartment, encounters an agent, gets a booking, takes odd jobs, and finally performs at the Improvisation in

Los Angeles. We found this more interesting and enjoyable the second time around. Since it's a short film, and has some fun cameo roles, it may be worth your time for something different in video viewing.

1979 67 minutes

DIE LAUGHING

DIRECTOR: Jeff Werner
CAST: Robby Benson, Linda Grovernor, Charles Durning, Bud Cort

Robby Benson stars as Pinsky, a young cabbie with aspirations of becoming a rock recording star. He gets mixed up in a conspiracy that involves the changing of nuclear waste into weapons-grade plutonium. It's neither very funny nor exciting. Rated PG.

1980 108 minutes

DINER

★★★★½

DIRECTOR: Barry Levinson
CAST: Steven Guttenberg, Daniel Stern, Mickey Rourke, Kevin Bacon, Ellen Barkin

Writer-director Barry Levinson's much-acclaimed bittersweet tale of growing up in the late 1950s, unlike *American Graffiti*, is never cute or idealized. Instead, it combines insight, sensitive drama, and low-key humor. Rated R for profanity and adult themes.

1982 110 minutes

DINNER AT EIGHT

★★★★★

DIRECTOR: George Cukor
CAST: John Barrymore, Jean Harlow, Marie Dressler, Billie Burke, Wallace Beery

A sparkling, sophisticated, and witty comedy of character written by George S. Kaufman and Edna Ferber for the Broadway stage, this motion picture has a terrific all-star cast and lots of laughs. It's an all-time movie classic.

1933 B & W 113 minutes

DIRTY TRICKS

DIRECTOR: Alvin Rakoff
CAST: Elliott Gould, Kate Jackson, Rich Little, Arthur Hill, Nick Campbell

The makers of this film couldn't have picked a more appropriate title. People who pay to see it will undoubtedly feel that they've been the victims of a dirty trick. This Canadian-made movie brings the comedy-thriller genre to an all-time low. The story is ridiculous, the dialogue insipid, and the characters unappealing. Worse than that, this movie is incredibly dull. Rated PG.

1980 91 minutes

DISORDERLY ORDERLY, THE

★★★

DIRECTOR: Frank Tashlin
CAST: Jerry Lewis, Glenda Farrell, Susan Oliver, Everett Sloane, Jack E. Leonard, Kathleen Freeman

Jerry Lewis is out of control at a nursing home in a good solo effort directed by comedy veteran Frank Tashlin, who reached his peak here. Comic gems abound in this film, which isn't just for fans. In fact, if you've never been one of Jerry's faithful, give this one a try to see if you can't be swayed. You just might be surprised. Fine supporting cast adds to the fun.

1964 90 minutes

DIVORCE OF LADY X, THE

★★★★

DIRECTOR: Tim Whelan
CAST: Merle Oberon, Laurence Olivier, Binnie Barnes, Ralph Richardson

In this British comedy, Laurence Olivier plays a lawyer who allows

Merle Oberon to spend the night at his place. Although nothing actually happened that night, Olivier finds himself branded "the other man" in her divorce. A series of hilarious misunderstandings are the result.

1938 90 minutes

DIXIE CHANGING HABITS

★★★½

DIRECTOR: George Englund
CAST: Suzanne Pleshette, Cloris Leachman, Kenneth McMillan, John Considine

Suzanne Pleshette plays Dixie, who runs a highly successful prostitution ring. When she's busted, she must spend time in a convent directed by Cloris Leachman as the Mother Superior. The sisters learn about business and making a profit, and Dixie learns to respect herself. All in all, this made-for-TV comedy is highly entertaining.

1982 96 minutes

DOCTOR AT LARGE

★★★

DIRECTOR: Ralph Thomas
CAST: Dirk Bogarde, James Robertson Justice, Shirley Eaton

Young Dr. Simon Sparrow wants to join the hospital staff, but the grumpy superintendent isn't buying. Comic conniving ensues as Sparrow seeks a place. Third in a series of six films featuring Dr. Sparrow.

1957 98 minutes

DOCTOR AT SEA

★★★

DIRECTOR: Ralph Thomas
CAST: Dirk Bogarde, Brigitte Bardot, Brenda de Banzie, James Robertson Justice

Fed up with the myriad complications of London life and romance, young, handsome Dr. Simon Sparrow seeks a rugged man's world by signing on a passenger-carrying freighter as ship's doctor. He goes from the frying pan into the fire when he meets Brigitte Bardot on the high seas! Second in the highly successful British comedy series.

1955 92 minutes

DOCTOR DETROIT

★★½

DIRECTOR: Michael Pressman
CAST: Dan Aykroyd, Howard Hessman, Nan Martin, T. K. Carter

Dan Aykroyd (*Trading Places*; *The Blues Brothers*) stars in this comedy as a soft-spoken Chicago English professor who becomes a comic book–style pimp and takes on the local mob. Aykroyd has some genuinely funny moments, but the movie is uneven overall. Rated R for profanity, nudity, and violence.

1983 89 minutes

DOCTOR IN DISTRESS

★★★

DIRECTOR: Ralph Thomas
CAST: Dirk Bogarde, Samantha Eggar, James Robertson Justice

In this high jinks–jammed British comedy of medical student and young physician trials and tribulations, head of hospital Sir Lancelot Spratt reveals he is human when he falls in love. Hero Dr. Simon Sparrow has trouble romancing a beautiful model. It's all fast-pace and very funny. Fourth in a series of six that began with *Doctor in the House*.

1963 B & W 103 minutes

DR. OTTO AND THE RIDDLE OF THE GLOOM BEAM

★★★

DIRECTOR: John R. Cherry III
CAST: Jim Varney

A fun and wacky journey into the mind of Jim Varney. Dr. Otto has a deranged plan for taking over the world and Lance Sterling is the only person who can stop him. Varney plays both Otto and Sterling and most of the other leading roles in this refreshingly strange comedy. Another must for Varney fans. Rated PG.

1986 97 minutes

DR. STRANGELOVE OR HOW I LEARNED TO STOP WORRYING AND LOVE THE BOMB

★★★★★

DIRECTOR: Stanley Kubrick
CAST: Peter Sellers, Sterling Hayden, George C. Scott, Slim Pickens, Keenan Wynn

Stanley Kubrick's black comedy masterpiece about the dropping of the "bomb." Great performances from an all-star cast, including Peter Sellers in three hilarious roles. Don't miss it.

1964 B & W 93 minutes

DOGPOUND SHUFFLE

★

DIRECTOR: Jeffery Bloom
CAST: Ron Moody, David Soul, Raymond Sutton, Pamela McMyler, Ray Sticklyn

Movies don't get much worse than this piece of sentimental slop. Story has Ron Moody and David Soul as two drifters who rescue a dog from the pound and spend the rest of the movie working up a song-and-dance team with their four-legged friend. Even kids will be bored with this mess. Rated PG for language.

1974 98 minutes

DOIN' TIME

★

DIRECTOR: George Mendeluk
CAST: Jeff Altman, Dey Young, Richard Mulligan, John Vernon, Judy Landers, Colleen Camp, Melanie Chartoff, Graham Jarvis, Pat McCormick, Eddie Velez, Jimmie Walker

Doin' Time is a bum rap: It resorts to the worst toilet humor and uses physical comedy that was rendered trite years ago. A pie fight within the first 15 minutes of this film should be an effective "we told you so" if you decide to ignore this review. We must admit, however, that there are some funny moments—like flotsam in a swamp of bad taste. Rated R for profanity and sex.

1984 84 minutes

DON RICKLES: BUY THIS TAPE YOU HOCKEY PUCK

★½

DIRECTOR: Barry Shear
CAST: Don Rickles, Jack Klugman, Don Adams, Michele Lee, James Caan, Michael Caine, Jose Ferrer, Arthur Godfrey, Elliott Gould

With Don Rickles cracking the same tired jokes in a Las Vegas lounge setting, one may ask: Why has he put out this video of his 1975 television special? Besides the obvious monetary reason, there is another. When the camera is not on Rickles insulting his audience, it is used to showcase the comedian's talent as an actor. There are scenes of him impersonating Dustin Hoffman's Ratso from *Midnight Cowboy* and an excellent reenactment of a scene from the Lee–Lawrence play *Inherit the Wind*. But the segment with Michele Lee is a shameless Las Vegas commercial.

1975 51 minutes

DON'S PARTY

★★★½

DIRECTOR: Bruce Beresford
CAST: John Hargreaves, Pat Bishop, Graham Kennedy, Veronica Lang

Directed by Australian Bruce Beresford (*Breaker Morant*),

Don's Party is a hilarious, and at times vulgar, adult comedy. Like the characters in *Who's Afraid of Virginia Woolf?*, the eleven revelers at Don's party lose all control, and the evening climaxes in bitter hostilities and humiliating confessions. With no MPAA rating, the film has nudity and profanity.

1976 91 minutes

DON'T DRINK THE WATER

★★★★½

DIRECTOR: Howard Morris

CAST: Jackie Gleason, Estelle Parsons, Ted Bessell, Joan Delaney, Michael Constantine, Howard St. John, Danny Meehan, Richard Libertini

Jackie Gleason plays a caterer on a vacation with his wife (Estelle Parsons) and daughter (Joan Delaney). When the plane taking them to Greece is hijacked behind the Iron Curtain, Gleason is accused of spying and finds asylum in the U.S. embassy. Gleason's cranky *Honeymooners* attitude is perfectly balanced by Parsons's bubbleheaded comments. Time hasn't worn the screenplay, based on Woody Allen's wacky play, too much; the cold war cracks and global political humor are just as funny today as they were back in the 1960s. Rated G.

1969 100 minutes

DON'T RAISE THE BRIDGE, LOWER THE RIVER

★

DIRECTOR: Jerry Paris

CAST: Jerry Lewis, Terry-Thomas, Jacqueline Pearce, Bernard Cribbins

Weak vehicle for Jerry Lewis concerns the once-outstanding comedian's efforts to keep his marriage alive, even as everything seems to be going against him. This just isn't funny. Rated G.

1968 99 minutes

DOUGH AND DYNAMITE/ KNOCKOUT, THE

★★★

DIRECTORS: Mack Sennett, Charles Chaplin

CAST: Roscoe Arbuckle, Charlie Chaplin, Chester Conklin, Fritz Schade, Phyllis Allen, Charlie Chase, Slim Summerville, Edgar Kennedy, Minta Durfee, Hank Mann, Mack Swain, Al St. John, Mack Sennett, Joe Bordeaux, Eddie Cline, The Keystone Cops

Two of the best slapstick two-reelers Mack Sennett's famous Keystone Studios churned out during the heyday of fast-and-furious, rough-and-tumble comedies. *The Knockout*, actually a Fatty Arbuckle film, has Charlie Chaplin playing the referee, the third man in the ring, in a fight sequence between behemoths (to him) Edgar Kennedy and Arbuckle. *Dough and Dynamite* is set in a French restaurant. Chaplin and Chester Conklin are waiters who take over the baking during a strike. Mayhem follows when the strikers put dynamite in the bread dough.

1914 B & W 54 minutes

DOWN AMONG THE "Z" MEN

★

DIRECTOR: Maclean Rogers

CAST: Peter Sellers, Harry Secombe, Michael Bentine, Spike Milligan, Carol Carr

Before there was a Monty Python there were the Goons, a British comedy team that featured Peter Sellers, among others (see cast). This comedy troupe was not all that funny, as this film so vividly illustrates. An absentminded professor misplaces his formula for a special combat gas. What follows is a madcap and tired race between the professor, the military, and a couple of crooks to find the secret formula.

1961 B & W 82 minutes

DOWN AND OUT IN BEVERLY HILLS

★★★½

DIRECTOR: Paul Mazursky

CAST: Nick Nolte, Bette Midler, Richard Dreyfuss, Little Richard, Tracy Nelson, Elizabeth Pena, Evan Richards

When a Los Angeles bum (Nick Nolte) loses his dog to a happy home, he decides to commit suicide in a Beverly Hills swimming pool. The pool's owner (Richard Dreyfuss) saves the seedy-looking character's life and thereby sets in motion a chain of events that threatens to destroy his family's rarefied existence. The result is an uneven but often funny and always outrageous adult sex comedy. Based on Jean Renoir's 1932 film, *Boudu Saved From Drowning*, this is not a film for everyone. Some people will love it and others will hate it. Rated R for profanity, violence, nudity, and simulated sex.

1986 102 minutes

DOWN BY LAW

★★★★½

DIRECTOR: Jim Jarmusch

CAST: John Lurie, Tom Waits, Roberto Benigni, Ellen Barkin

Stranger Than Paradise director Jim Jarmusch improves on his static deadpan style by allowing his *Down by Law* characters a bit more life. In fact, he appears to be leaning more optimistically toward activity. He gives the film an energetic Italian comedian (Roberto Benigni), who looks like a dark-haired Kewpie doll. This lively imp inspires his lethargic companions (John Lurie, Tom Waits) to speak, sing, and generally loosen up a little. The three meet in the same jail cell and eventually end up escaping together. Lurie plays a variation of his *Stranger Than Paradise* role, characteristically selfish and isolated. Singer Tom Waits is the real jewel. There's subtle grace and charm under his bum exterior. *Down by Law* will probably stand as one of the decade's best comedies. Rated R for nudity and profanity.

1986 90 minutes

DRAGNET

★★½

DIRECTOR: Tom Mankiewicz

CAST: Dan Aykroyd, Tom Hanks, Alexandra Paul, Harry Morgan, Christopher Plummer, Dabney Coleman, Elizabeth Ashley, Jack O'Halloran, Kathleen Freeman

Dan Aykroyd's deliriously funny impersonation of Jack Webb can only carry this comedy so far. While Tom Hanks adds some funny moments of his own, the contrived screenplay about political double-dealing in Los Angeles tends to bog down. That said, this is a perfect VCR movie. One can glance at a magazine during the dull spots and look up in time to savor its funnier bits. Rated PG-13 for profanity and violence.

1987 120 minutes

DUCK SOUP

★★★★★

DIRECTOR: Leo McCarey

CAST: The Marx Brothers, Margaret Dumont, Louis Calhern, Raquel Torres, Edgar Kennedy

Groucho, Harpo, Chico, and Zeppo in their best film: an anti-establishment comedy that failed miserably at the box office at the time of its release. Today, this Leo McCarey–directed romp has achieved its proper reputation as the quintessential Marx Brothers classic.

1933 B & W 70 minutes

EAGLE, THE

★★★

DIRECTOR: Clarence Brown
CAST: Rudolph Valentino, Vilma Banky, Louise Dresser, James Marcus, Clark Ward, Spottiswoode Aitken

Produced to boost the legendary Rudolph Valentino's then-sagging popularity, this satirical romantic story of a Russian Cossack lieutenant who masquerades as a do-gooder bandit to avenge his father's death proved a box-office winner for the star. Valentino is at his romantic, swoon-inducing, self-mocking best in the title role. Silent.

1925 B & W 72 minutes

EASY MONEY

★½

DIRECTOR: James Signorelli
CAST: Rodney Dangerfield, Joe Pesci, Geraldine Fitzgerald, Candy Azzara

Nothing is worse than an unfunny comedy—except maybe an unfunny comedy with someone who is ordinarily hilarious. So it is with this film, starring Rodney Dangerfield as a high-living, good-time guy who has to give up all his vices or forfeit a $10 million inheritance. After seeing it, you understand how the comic put-upon stage character feels; in the case of *Easy Money*, it's viewers who get no respect. Rated R for profanity and suggested sex.

1983 95 minutes

EAT OR BE EATEN

★★★

DIRECTOR: Phil Austin
CAST: Firesign Theatre Players

This spoof centers around newscasters Haryll Hee and Sharyll Shee as they cover the crisis in Labyrinth County. There, the deadly Koodzoo threatens to cover the city with its vine if a virgin is not sacrificed to him. Between news coverage, we see clever commercials that poke fun at those we normally see, as well as takeoffs on TV evangelists and sitcoms. This one has nonstop laughs. Unrated, it deals with adult topics and is comparable with a PG.

1985 30 minutes

EATING RAOUL

★★★★

DIRECTOR: Paul Bartel
CAST: Paul Bartel, Mary Woronov, Robert Beltran, Susan Saiger

A hilarious black comedy co-written and directed by Paul Bartel (*Death Race 2000*), this low-budget film presents an inventive but rather bizarre solution to the recession. When Mary Bland (Mary Woronov) is saved by her frying-pan-wielding husband, Paul (Bartel), from a would-be rapist, the happily married couple happily discover that the now-deceased attacker was rolling in dough—so they roll him and hit on a way to end their economic woes. Rated R for nudity, profanity, sexual situations, and violence.

1982 83 minutes

EDDIE MURPHY—DELIRIOUS

★★★

DIRECTOR: Bruce Gowers
CAST: Eddie Murphy, The Bus Boys

Stand-up comedy performance by the superstar at Constitution Hall, Washington, D.C., runs more hot than cold, as Eddie hurls barbs at gays, Michael Jackson, Ralph Kramden and Ed Norton of *The Honeymooners,* his parents, Mr. T, etc. Most of the gags are obscene and often hilarious, but there are also occasional stretches of boredom as the show progresses. Very entertaining overall, though, with Eddie showing flashes of true inspiration every now and then. Be forewarned: contains strong language.

1983 70 minutes

EDUCATING RITA

★★★★½

DIRECTOR: Lewis Gilbert

CAST: Michael Caine, Julie Walters, Michael Williams

A boozing, depressed English professor (Michael Caine) takes on a sharp-witted, eager-to-learn hairdresser (Julie Walters) for Open University tutorials and each educates the other, in this delightful romantic comedy based on a London hit play. Rated PG for profanity.

1983 110 minutes

EGG AND I, THE

★★★

DIRECTOR: Chester Erskine

CAST: Claudette Colbert, Fred MacMurray, Louise Allbritton, Marjorie Main, Percy Kilbride, Billy House, Donald MacBride, Samuel S. Hinds, Fuzzy Knight, Elisabeth Risdon

Hayseed Fred MacMurray spirits his finishing-school bride Claudette Colbert away from the snooty atmosphere of Boston to cope with chicken farming in the rural Pacific Northwest. Everything goes wrong. Marjorie Main and Percy Kilbride as Ma and Pa Kettle made comic marks bright enough to earn them their own film series. Not a laugh riot, but above-average funny.

1947 B & W 108 minutes

ELECTRIC DREAMS

★★★

DIRECTOR: Steve Barron

CAST: Lenny Von Dohlen, Virginia Madsen, Bud Cort (voice)

An ingenious blending of the motion picture with the rock music video, this release deals with the complications that arise when an absentminded architect, Miles (Lenny Von Dohlen), buys his first home computer. It's a wonderful convenience—at least at first. But it isn't long before the computer (the voice for which is supplied by Bud Cort, of *Harold and Maude* fame) begins to develop a rather feisty personality and even starts wooing Miles's cellist girlfriend, Madeline (Virginia Madsen). Rated PG for profanity.

1984 96 minutes

EMANON

★

DIRECTOR: Stuart Paul

CAST: Stuart Paul, Cheryl M. Lynn, Jeremy Miller, Patrick Wright, B. J. Garrett, Robert Hackman, Tallie Cochrane

The Messiah comes to New York City. He wears rags and lives among the bums, and "respectable" people ignore him until a crippled boy (Jeremy Miller) discovers that Emanon (no name, spelled backwards), played by writer-director Stuart Paul, can perform miracles. So the boy asks Emanon to help his mother's floundering dress business. The poor script, unbelievable dialogue, and talentless actors destroy the potential concept and transform a spiritual drama into a bad comedy. Rated PG-13 for minor obscenities.

1986 98 minutes

END, THE

★★★

DIRECTOR: Burt Reynolds

CAST: Burt Reynolds, Sally Field, Dom De Luise, Joanne Woodward, David Steinberg, Pat O'Brien, Myrna Loy, Kristy McNichol, Robby Benson

The blackest of black comedies, this stars Burt Reynolds (who also directed) as an unfortunate fellow who is informed he's dying of a rare disease. Poor Burt can hardly believe it. What's worse, his friends and family don't seem to care. So he decides to end it all. In the process, he meets a maniac (Dom De Luise) who is more than willing to lend a hand. This is when Burt realizes he'd prefer to enjoy whatever time he has left. But De Luise doesn't believe him. It's surprisingly funny. Rated R.

1978 100 minutes

ENSIGN PULVER

DIRECTOR: Joshua Logan
CAST: Robert Walker Jr., Burl Ives, Walter Matthau, Tommy Sands, Millie Perkins, Kay Medford, Larry Hagman, Jack Nicholson

This sequel to *Mr. Roberts* doesn't quite measure up. The comedy, which takes place aboard a World War II cargo ship, can't stay afloat despite the large and impressive cast. Robert Walker Jr. is no match for Jack Lemmon, who played the original Ensign Pulver in 1955.

1964 104 minutes

ENTER LAUGHING

★★½

DIRECTOR: Carl Reiner
CAST: Reni Santoni, José Ferrer, Shelley Winters, Elaine May, Jack Gilford, Janet Margolin, Michael J. Pollard, Don Rickles, Rob Reiner, Nancy Kovack

Carl Reiner's semiautobiographical comedy, about a young man who shucks his training and ambitions as a pharmacist to become a comedian, is studded with familiar faces and peopled by engaging personalities—but doesn't really leave a lasting memory. There are more than a few genuinely funny scenes, but overall the film is bland. Much of this material might have worked better on television, where gags don't have to extend too long and commercials save scenes from becoming stale.

1967 112 minutes

ERNEST FILM FESTIVAL

★★

DIRECTOR: John R. Cherry III
CAST: Jim Varney

This appears to be a promo tape used to secure future commercials for Jim Varney's character, Ernest. On it you will see, if you can stand it, 101 commercials and bloopers of the Ernest and Vern variety. He sells everything from cars to eggs using his country-hick lingo. Only the staunchest Ernest fans will continue chuckling after the first fifty commericials.

1986 55 minutes

ERNEST GOES TO CAMP

★

DIRECTOR: John R. Cherry III
CAST: Jim Varney, Victoria Racimo, John Vernon, Iron Eyes Cody, Lyle Alzado, Patrick Day

Ernest P. Worrell (Jim Varney) gets his first big-screen introduction in this comedy. Fans of the many commercials starring Ernest (Hey, Vern!) will enjoy some of Varney's comedy antics, but the film could have been called *Meatballs XI* for all the originality it contains. The story revolves around a dim-witted groundskeeper (Varney) who becomes the counselor for a group of juvenile delinquents being given a second chance by attending a posh summer camp. A subplot has veteran nasty John Vernon as an industrialist out to steal the camp's land from a couple of Indians (Victoria Racimo, Iron Eyes Cody). We've seen it all before—and better. Rated PG for profanity and scatological humor.

1987 95 minutes

ERNIE KOVACS: TELEVISION'S ORIGINAL GENIUS

★★★★

DIRECTOR: Keith Burns
CAST: Ernie Kovacs, Edie Adams, Jack Lemmon, Steve Allen, Chevy Chase, John Barbour

This tribute to the late Ernie Kovacs was produced for cable television. It is a series of clips from Kovacs's television career along with comments from friends (Jack Lemmon and Steve Allen) and family (wife Edie Adams and daughter). Narration is provided by John Barbour of *Real People*. Those familiar with Kovacs's work will fondly remember his innovative creations: Percy Dovetonsils, Eugene, and the Nairobi Trio. For others, this serves as an introduction to Kovacs's comic genuis.

1982 86 minutes

ERRAND BOY, THE

★★★

DIRECTOR: Jerry Lewis
CAST: Jerry Lewis, Brian Donlevy, Sig Ruman

One of Jerry Lewis's better solo efforts, as he proceeds (in his own inimitable style) to make a shambles of the Hollywood movie studio where he is employed as the local gofer. Very funny. Watch for Howard McNear, best remembered as Floyd, the barber on *The Andy Griffith Show.*

1961 B & W 92 minutes

EUROPEAN VACATION

DIRECTOR: Amy Heckerling
CAST: Chevy Chase, Beverly D'Angelo, Dana Hill, Jason Lively, Eric Idle, Victor Lanoux, John Astin

The sappy sequel to *Vacation*, this moronic mess has three laughs. Two of them are provided by Eric Idle as a veddy, veddy polite British bicyclist mangled by the vacationing Griswalds (Chevy Chase, Beverly D'Angelo, Dana Hill, and Jason Lively). They win an all-expense (but decidedly low-budget) European vacation grand prize on the television game show *Pig in a Poke*. It was—surprisingly—written by John Hughes (*Weird Science*; *The Breakfast Club*) and directed —not surprisingly—by Amy Heckerling (*Johnny Dangerously*; *Fast Times at Ridgemont High*). Rated PG-13 for nudity, violence, and profanity.

1985 95 minutes

EVENING WITH ROBIN WILLIAMS, AN

★★★★

DIRECTOR: Don Mischer
CAST: Robin Williams

Here's a remarkably good comedy video with Robin Williams going back to his stand-up comedy roots. He's totally unpredictable when improvising on stage, and this adds to his charm. Filmed at San Francisco's Great American Music Hall, it provides ample proof why Williams was considered one of the finest live comedians of his era before scoring on television (with *Mork and Mindy*) and the movies. Unrated, it has profanity.

1983 60 minutes

EVERY GIRL SHOULD BE MARRIED

★★½

DIRECTOR: Don Hartman
CAST: Cary Grant, Betsy Drake, Franchot Tone, Diana Lynn, Alan Mowbray

A bit of light comedy froth balanced mostly on Cary Grant's charm and polish. He plays a baby doctor. Betsy Drake, who later got him off-screen, plays a salesgirl bent on leading him to the altar. The title is irksome, but the picture's diverting, innocent fun.

1948 B & W 85 minutes

EVERY WHICH WAY BUT LOOSE

★★★

DIRECTOR: James Fargo
CAST: Clint Eastwood, Sondra Locke, Geoffrey Lewis, Clyde (the ape), Ruth Gordon

After *Smokey and the Bandit* cleaned up at the box office, Clint Eastwood decided to make his own modern-day cowboy movie. This 1978 release proved to be one of the squinty-eyed star's biggest moneymakers. The film is far superior to its sequel, *Any Which Way You Can*. Rated R.

1978 114 minutes

EVERYTHING YOU ALWAYS WANTED TO KNOW ABOUT SEX BUT WERE AFRAID TO ASK

★★★★

DIRECTOR: Woody Allen
CAST: John Carradine, Woody Allen, Lou Jacobi, Louise Lasser, Anthony Quayle, Lynn Redgrave, Tony Randall, Burt Reynolds, Gene Wilder

Everything You Always Wanted to Know about Sex But Were Afraid to Ask gave Woody Allen, scriptwriter, star, and director, an opportunity to stretch out without having to supply all the talent himself. Several sequences do not feature Woody at all. As the film is broken up into vignettes supposedly relating to questions asked, it was possible for him to direct and concentrate on the strengths of his stars without the obvious strain of having to turn in a strong performance himself. Rated R.

1972 87 minutes

EXPERIENCE PREFERRED...BUT NOT ESSENTIAL

★★★★★

DIRECTOR: Peter Duffell
CAST: Elizabeth Edmonds, Sue Wallace, Geraldine Griffith, Karen Meagher, Ron Bain, Alun Lewis, Robert Blythe

This delightful British import, which is somewhat reminiscent of Scottish director Bill Forsyth's *Gregory's Girl* and *Local Hero*, follows the awkward and amusing adventures of a young woman during her first summer job at a Welsh coastal resort in 1962. She comes to town insecure and frumpy and leaves at the end of the summer pretty, sexy, and confident. Can you guess why? Right! Rated PG for language.

1983 80 minutes

FALLING IN LOVE AGAIN

★★½

DIRECTOR: Steven Paul
CAST: Elliott Gould, Susannah York, Michelle Pfeiffer, Stuart Paul

Elliott Gould stars as a middle-aged dreamer who is obsessed with his younger days in the Bronx. Gould and wife (Susannah York) are on vacation and headed east to recapture the past. The film suffers from countless long flashbacks of his youth and romance with WASP princess (Michelle Pfeiffer) and is a poor attempt at romantic comedy. Rated R.

1980 103 minutes

FANDANGO

★★

DIRECTOR: Kevin Reynolds
CAST: Kevin Costner, Judd Nelson, Sam Robards, Chuck Bush, Brian Cesak

This is an unfunny comedy about a group of college chums (led by Kevin Costner of *Silverado* and Judd Nelson of *St. Elmo's Fire*) going on one last romp together before being inducted into the army—or running away from the draft—in 1971. Slow-going and a bit too angst-ridden, *Fandango* seems as if it's going to get better any minute, but it doesn't. Rated PG for profanity.

1984 91 minutes

FARMER'S DAUGHTER, THE

★★★

DIRECTOR: H. C. Potter

CAST: Loretta Young, Joseph Cotten, Ethel Barrymore, Charles Bickford, Lex Barker, Keith Andes, James Arness

Loretta Young won the best actress Oscar for her delightful performance in this charming comedy about a Swedish woman who clashes with the man she loves over a congressional election.

1947 B & W 97 minutes

FARMER'S OTHER DAUGHTER, THE

DIRECTOR: John Patrick Hayes

CAST: Judy Pennebaker, Bill Michael, Ernest Ashworth, William Guhl, Harry Lovejoy, Jean Bennett, Norman Hartweg, Janice Evan

Incredibly lame film about a family trying to save their farm from the mean old banker who wants to foreclose on the place. Totally insufferable.

1965 84 minutes

FAST TIMES AT RIDGEMONT HIGH

★★½

DIRECTOR: Amy Heckerling

CAST: Sean Penn, Jennifer Jason Leigh, Judge Reinhold, Brian Backer, Phoebe Cates, Ray Walston

In 1979, Cameron Crow went back to high school to discover what today's teens are up to and wrote about his experiences. From his excellent book, they've made a kind of *Animal House* of the teen-age set. Youngsters will love it, but adults will probably want to skip the movie and read the book. Rated R for nudity, profanity, and simulated sex.

1982 92 minutes

FASTBREAK

★★½

DIRECTOR: Jack Smight

CAST: Gabriel Kaplan, Harold Sylvester, Mike Warren, Bernard King, Reb Brown

As a basketball coach, Gabe Kaplan resurrects some of the laughs he got with his sweathogs on *Welcome Back, Kotter.* Kaplan plays a New York deli worker who quits to coach a college basketball team in Nevada. He brings four blacks from his New York ghetto to help the team, and one turns out to be a girl. Kaplan must beat a tough rival team in order to get a $30,000-a-year contract at the university, so he whips the unpromising team into shape. Rated PG.

1979 107 minutes

FATAL GLASS OF BEER, A/POOL SHARKS

★★★

DIRECTORS: Clyde Bruckman, Edwin Middleton

CAST: W. C. Fields, George Chandler, Rosemary Theby, Bud Ross

This pairing brings together two distinct examples of the unique comedy of W. C. Fields. The first, produced by Mack Sennett, finds Fields practicing his peculiar art in the frozen North, complete with snow on cue and misplaced Indians. *Pool Sharks*, made 18 years earlier, is the comedian's first distributed film. In it, he is pitted against Bud Ross in the pool game of all pool games—played for the love of a mutually sought girl. Fields's bizarre brand of humor highlights both.

1915–1933 B & W 60 minutes

FATHER GOOSE

★★★

DIRECTOR: Ralph Nelson
CAST: Cary Grant, Leslie Caron

A bedraggled, unshaven, and unsophisticated Cary Grant is worth watching even in a mediocre comedy. Grant plays a hard-drinking Australian coast watcher during the height of World War II. His reclusive lifestyle on a remote Pacific island is interrupted when he is forced to play nursemaid to a group of adolescent schoolgirls and their prudish teacher (Leslie Caron).

1964 115 minutes

FATHER GUIDO SARDUCCI GOES TO COLLEGE

★★

DIRECTOR: Steve Binder
CAST: Don Novello, Father Billy Vera, The Beaters

Don Novello re-creates his *Saturday Night Live* character of Father Guido Sarducci during a live concert at U.C. Santa Barbara. He touches on birthdays, life insurance, his years at DooDa U., and President Reagan. His priestly character is sometimes lost in his more worldly comments. We guess you had to be there to really enjoy it.

1985 59 minutes

FATHER'S LITTLE DIVIDEND

★★★

DIRECTOR: Vincente Minnelli
CAST: Spencer Tracy, Elizabeth Taylor, Joan Bennett, Don Taylor, Billie Burke

In *Father of the Bride*, the marriage of daughter Elizabeth Taylor to Don Taylor made a wreck out of Spencer Tracy. Now, in the sequel, she's expecting, and Tracy is not exactly overjoyed at the prospect of being a grandfather. This play off of a winner doesn't measure up to the original, but it's entertaining fare anyway. Spencer Tracy could bluster and be flustered with the best.

1951 82 minutes

FATTY AND MABEL ADRIFT/ MABEL, FATTY AND THE LAW

★★★

DIRECTOR: Roscoe Arbuckle
CAST: Fatty Arbuckle, Mabel Normand, Frank Hayes, May Wells, Al St. John, Wayland Trask, James Bryant, Joe Bordeau, Glen Cavender, Luke the dog, Minta Durfee, Harry Gribbon

Solo and as a duet, Fatty Arbuckle and Mabel Normand were near peerless in the halcyon days of silent comedies. These two Mack Sennett features are outstanding examples of why the public held them both in admiration. The kiss-good-night sequence in *Fatty and Mabel Adrift* is reason enough to see the film.

1915–1916 B & W 40 minutes

FATTY'S TIN-TYPE TANGLE / OUR CONGRESSMAN

★★★

DIRECTORS: Roscoe Arbuckle, Rob Wagner
CAST: Fatty Arbuckle, Mabel Norman, Al St. John, Will Rogers, Mollie Thompson, Sammy Brooks, Chet Brandberg

This is a curious pairing of a Mack Sennett Keystone comedy and a Hal Roach satire made a decade apart and totally unrelated in subject matter. In the first, Fatty gets Mabel's goat by making goo-goo eyes at the maid. In the second, newly elected congressman Will Rogers, straight from the sticks, bombs in Washington society.

1915–1924 B & W 44 minutes

FAWLTY TOWERS

★★★★

DIRECTORS: John Cleese, Connie Booth

CAST: John Cleese, Prunella Scales, Connie Booth

This British television series is a true comedy classic. Written by Monty Python's John Cleese and his ex-wife Connie Booth, the show is a situation comedy about the problems of running a small seaside inn. The characters are typical (harried husband, shrewish wife, incompetent help) and the storylines mundane (guest loses money; fire drill; restaurant critics arrive), but in the hands of Cleese and company, each episode is a near-perfect ballet of escalating frustration. For Basil Fawlty, friends turn into enemies, the smallest annoyances are disastrous, and every touch of good luck becomes a curse. But Fawlty is so nasty he deserves everything he gets, and the results are hysterical. For sheer, double-over belly laughs, this series has never been equalled. Years later, ABC tried to remake the show as *Amanda's* starring Bea Arthur. It was awful.

1975 75 minutes

FEEL MY PULSE

★★½

DIRECTOR: Gregory La Cava

CAST: Bebe Daniels, Richard Arlen, William Powell

Silent screwball comedy boasts a hypochondriac heiress who inherits a sanitarium that is used by bootleggers as a front and a hideout. Bebe Daniels, armed with a stethoscope to keep track of her heartbeat, does a fine job as the germ-wary, sheltered young girl who encounters a life she didn't dream existed. Silent.

1928 B & W 86 minutes

FEMALE TROUBLE

DIRECTOR: John Waters

CAST: Divine, Edith Massey, Cookie Mueller, David Lochary, Mink Stole, Michael Potter

The story of Dawn Davenport (Divine) from her days as a teenage belligerent through her rise to fame as a criminal and then to her death as a convicted murderer. As in other films by Waters, the theme here is the Jean Genet–like credo "crime equals beauty." Also, as in other films by the enfant terrible from Baltimore, *Female Trouble* will offend just about anyone who takes the bourgeois life, with its voyeurlike view on fame, too seriously. He sees the status quo as something far sicker than his films. Though it is unrated, this film is the equivalent of an X, due to sex, nudity, and violence.

1973 90 minutes

FERRIS BUELLER'S DAY OFF

★★★★

DIRECTOR: John Hughes

CAST: Matthew Broderick, Alan Ruck, Mia Sara, Jeffrey Jones, Jennifer Grey, Charlie Sheen, Cindy Pickett, Lyman Ward

Writer-director John Hughes strikes again, this time with a charming tale of a high-school legend in his own time (Matthew Broderick, playing the title character) who pretends to be ill in order to have a day away from school. After Ferris springs his girlfriend (sloe-eyed Mia Sara) and best friend (Alan Ruck, who makes a good nebbish), the trio heads into the Big City for eight hours of excitement. The dangerous thrill of breaking the rules transforms each event into an exciting challenge. The expressive Broderick owns the film, although he receives heavy competition from Jeffrey Jones, whose broadly played dean of students has been trying to nail Ferris Bueller for months. One subplot, involving an expensive car owned by Ferris's friend's father, is too uncomfortable to be funny, but the rest of the film succeeds on all accounts. Rated PG-13 for mild profanity.

1986 104 minutes

FIENDISH PLOT OF DR. FU MANCHU, THE

DIRECTOR: Piers Haggard
CAST: Peter Sellers, Helen Mirren, Sid Caesar, David Tomlinson

Peter Sellers plays a dual role of "insidious Oriental villain" Fu Manchu, who is out to rule the world, and his arch-enemy, the Holmes-like Nayland Smith of Scotland Yard. It's unfunny, racist, and just plain awful. Sellers's last movie. Rated PG.

1980 108 minutes

FIFTH AVENUE GIRL

★★

DIRECTOR: Gregory La Cava
CAST: Ginger Rogers, Walter Connolly, Verree Teasdale, Tim Holt, James Ellison, Kathryn Adams

Limp social comedy features Ginger Rogers as a homeless but levelheaded young lady who is taken in by Walter Connolly, one of those unhappy movieland millionaires who are just dying to find someone to lavish gifts on. Director La Cava, responsible for some of the brightest comedies of all time, stubs his toe on this feature. This isn't a terrible film, it just doesn't work as well as it should, and the premise is threadbare.

1939 B & W 83 minutes

FIND THE LADY

★★★

DIRECTOR: John Trent
CAST: John Candy, Mickey Rooney, Peter Cook, Lawrence Dane, Alexandra Bastedo

In this slapstick rendition of a cops-and-robbers spoof, John Candy, as the cop, and Mickey Rooney, as a kidnapper, create lots of laughs. The story is filled with car crashes, disasters on the pistol range, and every kind of general catastrophe on the way to a very funny finish.

1986 90 minutes

FINDERS KEEPERS

★★½

DIRECTOR: Richard Lester
CAST: Louis Gossett Jr., Michael O'Keefe, Beverly D'Angelo

Director Richard Lester (*A Hard Day's Night*; *Superman II*) went back to his comedy roots with this disappointingly uneven slapstick chase film, which stars Louis Gossett Jr. (*An Officer and a Gentleman*), Michael O'Keefe (*The Great Santini*), and Beverly D'Angelo (*Vacation*) as a trio of wacky characters. The story deals with a missing $5 million and a wild train ride at the end of which the winner takes all. Rated PG for profanity and violence.

1983 96 minutes

FINE MADNESS, A

★★★

DIRECTOR: Irvin Kershner
CAST: Sean Connery, Joanne Woodward, Jean Seberg

Whimsical story of a daffy, radical poet, well portrayed by Sean Connery (proving that, even in the 1960s, he could stretch further than James Bond). Many of the laughs come from his well-developed relationship with wife Joanne Woodward, although the film occasionally lapses into lurid slapstick. A late-era screwball comedy, similar in tone to those made in the 1930s and 1940s. Unrated; adult themes.

1966 104 minutes

FINE MESS, A

★

DIRECTOR: Blake Edwards
CAST: Ted Danson, Howie Mandel, Richard Mulligan, Stuart Margolin, Maria Conchita Alonso, Jennifer Edwards, Paul Sorvino

Blake Edwards deserves a heavy fine for inflicting this mess on an unsuspecting public. Supposedly inspired by the Laurel and Hardy classic, *The Music Box*, this movie is totally lacking in originality. The illogical plot has Ted Danson and Howie Mandel winning a bundle on a fixed horse race and spending the rest of the picture running from gangster Paul Sorvino's henchmen. The pace is that of an old gray mare on Quaaludes. Gag after gag falls embarrassingly flat. The cast works hard to no avail. Rated PG.

1986 100 minutes

FINNEGAN BEGIN AGAIN

★★★★

DIRECTOR: Joan Micklin Silver
CAST: Mary Tyler Moore, Robert Preston, Sam Waterston, Sylvia Sidney

In this endearing romance, Robert Preston plays Michael Finnegan, an eccentric retired advice columnist who befriends schoolteacher Elizabeth (Mary Tyler Moore) after learning of her secret affair with a married undertaker (Sam Waterston). Their eventual romance becomes a warm, funny, and tender portrayal of love blossoming in later life. Made for cable.

1985 97 minutes

FIRST FAMILY

DIRECTOR: Buck Henry
CAST: Bob Newhart, Gilda Radner, Madeline Kahn, Richard Benjamin, Harvey Korman, Bob Dishy, Rip Torn

The superior comic talents of Bob Newhart, Madeline Kahn, Gilda Radner, Richard Benjamin, and Harvey Korman are totally wasted in this unfunny farce about an inept president, his family, and his aides, written and directed by Buck Henry. Watching it, you get the impression that Henry had a vague idea of what he wanted to do but was never quite able to make up his mind. It's a mess. Rated R.

1980 104 minutes

FIRST HOWIE MANDEL SPECIAL, THE

★★½

DIRECTOR: Maurice Abraham
CAST: Howie Mandel

This Howie Mandel concert was filmed live in Toronto, Canada. Mandel is from Canada and his countrypeople give him a surprisingly lukewarm reception. They seem to like his comedy, but they are reluctant to participate in the performance. This makes for strained viewing—something you don't need in comedy. If you like Mandel's screaming, his nervous off-the-wall delivery, and X-rated material meant to shock, you'll enjoy this one.

1983 57 minutes

FISH THAT SAVED PITTSBURGH, THE

★★½

DIRECTOR: Gilbert Moses
CAST: Stockard Channing, Flip Wilson, Jonathan Winters, Julius Irving

Curious mixture of disco, astrology, and comedy. A failing basketball team turns to a rather eccentric medium for help, and the resulting confusion makes for a few amusing moments. Features a veritable smorgasbord of second-rate actors, from Jonathan Winters to basketball great Julius Irving (Dr. J.). Proceed at your own risk. Rated PG for profanity.

1979 102 minutes

FLAMINGO KID, THE

★★★½

DIRECTOR: Garry Marshall

CAST: Matt Dillon, Richard Crenna, Jessica Walter, Janet Jones, Hector Elizondo

A teen comedy-drama with more on its mind than stale sex jokes. Matt Dillon stars as Jeffrey Willis, a Brooklyn kid who discovers how the other half lives when he takes a summer job at a beach resort. A good story which explores the things (and people) that shape our values as we reach adulthood. Dillon's clashes with his poor-but-proud-of-it parents are a bit difficult to swallow, but the rest of the film rings quite clearly, particularly Richard Crenna's smooth-talking wheeler-dealer. A genuine pleasure, and you'll be glad you tried it. Rated PG-13 for frank sexual situations.

1984 100 minutes

FLASK OF FIELDS, A

★★★★½

DIRECTORS: Monte Brice, Clyde Bruckman, Leslie Pearce

CAST: W. C. Fields, Rosemary Theby, George Chandler, Elise Cavanna, Bud Jamison, Babe Kane, Zedna Farley

The Golf Specialist, *A Fatal Glass of Beer*, and *The Dentist*—three short comedy gems—amply display the matchless talents of W. C. Fields. This is an entertaining tribute. Don't be misled by the credits; Fields directed himself. Hilarious. Bawdy is the only word for the tooth-pulling sequence in *The Dentist*.

1930–1933 B & W 61 minutes

FLICKS

★½

DIRECTOR: Peter Winograd

CAST: Pamela Sue Martin, Joan Hackett, Martin Mull, Richard Belzer, Betty Kennedy

Aside from "Cat and Mouse," a hilarious cartoon about a retirement home for elderly cartoon characters, *Flicks* is a structureless string of movie parodies that's long on mediocre satire and short on laughs. Rated R.

1985 79 minutes

FLYING DEUCES

★★★

DIRECTOR: Edward Sutherland

CAST: Stan Laurel, Oliver Hardy, Jean Parker

Stan Laurel and Oliver Hardy join the Foreign Legion to help Ollie forget his troubled romantic past. Their attempts at adjusting to Legion life provide many laugh-filled situations, although the script has weak areas and the movie occasionally drags.

1939 B & W 65 minutes

FOLLOW THAT CAMEL

★★★½

DIRECTOR: Gerald Thomas

CAST: Phil Silvers, Jim Dale, Peter Butterworth, Charles Hawtrey, Anita Harris, Joan Sims, Kenneth Williams

This British comedy, part of the *Carry On* series, features Phil Silvers as the conniving Sgt. Knockers. Lots of laughs, mostly derived from puns and sexist jokes. Some dialogue is a bit racy for young children. Unrated.

1967 91 minutes

FOLLOW THAT DREAM

★★★½

DIRECTOR: Gordon Douglas
CAST: Elvis Presley, Arthur O'Connell, Joanne Moore, Anne Helm, Jack Kruschen

Elvis is almost too sweet as the naïve hillbilly who, along with his family, moves to a Florida beach. Some laughs result from their inability to fit in and the reactions of the local folk to them. The story is based on Richard Powell's novel *Pioneer Go Home*. Unrated, but contains no objectionable material.

1962 110 minutes

FOOLIN' AROUND

★★★

DIRECTOR: Richard T. Heffron
CAST: Gary Busey, Annette O'Toole, John Calvin, Eddie Albert, Cloris Leachman, Tony Randall

Gary Busey went from his acclaimed title performance in *The Buddy Holly Story* to starring in this amiable rip-off of *The Graduate* and *The Heartbreak Kid*. Still, Busey, as a working-class boy who falls in love with rich girl Annette O'Toole, is always watchable. He and O'Toole make an appealing screen team, and this makes the movie's lack of originality easier to take. Rated PG.

1980 111 minutes

FOR LOVE OF IVY

★★★★

DIRECTOR: Daniel Mann
CAST: Sidney Poitier, Abbey Lincoln, Beau Bridges, Nan Martin, Carroll O'Connor, Lauri Peters

Sidney Poitier delivers a terrific performance as Jack Parks, trucking company owner by day and gambling operator by night. Ivy (Abbey Lincoln) is a maid for a wealthy family. When she decides to leave their employ, the family's children (Beau Bridges and Lauri Peters) connive to get Parks to take her out and make her happy. Carroll O'Connor and Nan Martin play Ivy's employers. This is a fine comedy-drama with a wonderful ending.

1968 101 minutes

FOR PETE'S SAKE

★★★

DIRECTOR: Peter Yates
CAST: Barbra Streisand, Michael Sarrazin, Estelle Parsons, Molly Picon

Lightweight comedy vehicle tailor-made to fit the talents of Barbra Streisand. In this one she plays the wife of cab driver Michael Sarrazin, trying to raise money for him while becoming involved with underworld thugs. Strictly for Streisand fans. Rated PG.

1974 90 minutes

FOR THE LOVE OF IT

★★½

DIRECTOR: Hal Kantor
CAST: Don Rickles, Deborah Raffin, Jeff Conaway, Tom Bosley, Henry Gibson, Barbi Benton, Adam West, Norman Fell, Pat Morita

This would-be wacky comedy is so confusing you'll find yourself absorbed in figuring out who's chasing who and why. Don Rickles wants the Russians' secret plans to take over the Middle East to create a new video game called "Doom's Day," but the CIA and FBI are also interested in them. Barbi Benton drags her friend (Deborah Raffin) into the chase, and Raffin convinces three parking-lot attendants to help. Some of the chase scenes become so involved that the viewer forgets this is a comedy. Rated PG for violence and adult themes.

1980 98 minutes

FORTUNE COOKIE, THE

★★★★½

DIRECTOR: Billy Wilder
CAST: Jack Lemmon, Walter Matthau, Ron Rich, Cliff Osmond

Jack Lemmon is accidently injured by a player while filming a football game from the sidelines. His brother-in-law, Walter Matthau, sees this as an ideal attempt to make some lawsuit money. So starts the first of the usually delightful Lemon-Matthau comedies. Matthau is at his scene-stealing best in this Oscar-winning role.

1966 B & W 125 minutes

FORTY CARATS

★★★½

DIRECTOR: Milton Katselas
CAST: Liv Ullmann, Edward Albert, Gene Kelly, Nancy Walker, Deborah Raffin

This comedy has Liv Ullmann playing a 40-year-old divorcée being pursued by a rich 22-year-old, Edward Albert. Laughs come in as Ullmann's grown daughter (Deborah Raffin) and ex-husband (Gene Kelly) react to her latest suitor. Rated PG.

1973 110 minutes

48 HRS.

★★★★½

DIRECTOR: Walter Hill
CAST: Eddie Murphy, Nick Nolte, Annette O'Toole, Frank McRae, James Remar, David Patrick Kelly

Add *48 Hrs.* to the list of the best cops-and-robbers movies ever made. It's so action-packed, it'll keep you on the edge of your seat from beginning to end. There's more good news: It's funny too. In the story, a cop (Nick Nolte) goes looking for a psychotic prison escapee (James Remar) with the help of a fast-talking con man (Eddie Murphy). It's a dangerous mission, and there's never a dull moment. Rated R for violence, profanity, and nudity.

1982 96 minutes

FOUL PLAY

★★★

DIRECTOR: Colin Higgins
CAST: Goldie Hawn, Chevy Chase, Dudley Moore, Burgess Meredith, Marilyn Sokol

Gloria Mundy (Goldie Hawn) accidentally becomes involved in a plot to assassinate the Pope. Detective Tony Carlson (Chevy Chase) tries to protect and seduce her. Hawn is good as the damsel in distress, but Chase is hardly the Cary Grant type. Rated PG. Still, it's fun.

1978 116 minutes

FRANCIS, THE TALKING MULE

★★★½

DIRECTOR: Arthur Lubin
CAST: Donald O'Connor, Patricia Medina, Zasu Pitts, Tony Curtis, Ray Collins, voice of Chill Wills

First in a series from Universal, this well-known comedy tells the story of how a dimwitted student at West Point (Donald O'Connor) first met up with the famous talking mule of the title. The gags really fly as Francis proceeds to get O'Connor in all sorts of outrageous predicaments, consistently pulling him out just in the nick of time. Some screamingly funny scenes. Followed by six sequels.

1950 B & W 91 minutes

FRANKEN AND DAVIS AT STOCKTON STATE

★★★

DIRECTOR: Randy Cohen
CAST: Al Franken, Tom Davis

The weird, cerebral humor of Al Franken and Tom Davis is undoubtedly an acquired taste. Those who enjoyed their occasional stints—with "The Franken and Davis Show"—on the original *Saturday Night Live* will find much to appreciate in this live comedy concert, taped at Stockon College in New Jersey. Others may be a little perplexed by what they see at first. But we suggest you stick it out; there are some gems here.

1984 55 minutes

FRATERNITY VACATION

DIRECTOR: James Frawley
CAST: Stephen Geoffreys, Sheree Wilson, Cameron Dye, Leigh McCloskey

A teen-lust comedy with no laughs, no imagination, and no point in existing, *Fraternity Vacation* stars Stephen Geoffreys as a world-class nerd who somehow scores during vacation time in Palm Springs. He scores and the viewer snores. Rated R for profanity and nudity.

1985 95 minutes

FREEBIE AND THE BEAN

★★★

DIRECTOR: Richard Rush
CAST: Alan Arkin, James Caan, Valerie Harper, Loretta Swit

Before astounding filmgoers with the outrageous black comedy *The Stunt Man*, director Richard Rush twisted the cop genre around with this watchable (but not spectacular) release. James Caan and Alan Arkin play San Francisco detectives who wreak havoc while on the trail of gangster Jack Kruschen. Rated R.

1974 113 minutes

FRENCH LESSONS

★★★½

DIRECTOR: Brian Gilbert
CAST: Jane Snowden, Diana Blackburn, Françoise Brion, Raoul Delfosse

Romantic comedy about an English teenager who goes to Paris to study French for the summer. She is determined to fall in love and learns more out of the classroom than in. Rated PG.

1986 90 minutes

FRENCH POSTCARDS

★★★½

DIRECTOR: Willard Huyck
CAST: David Marshall Grant, Blanche Baker, Miles Chapin, Debra Winger

Written, produced, and directed by the couple who gave us *American Graffiti*, Gloria Katz and Willard Huyck, this film benefits greatly from the skillful supporting performances by two noted French film stars, Marie-France Pisier (*Love on the Run*) and Jean Rochefort (*Till Marriage Do Us Part*). The younger set of characters are well played by David Marshall Grant, Miles Chapin, Valerie Quennessen, and Blanche Baker. *French Postcards* is an enjoyable way to spend a couple of hours. Rated PG.

1979 92 minutes

FRITZ THE CAT

★★★

DIRECTOR: Ralph Bakshi
CAST: Animated

This is an X-rated rendition of Robert Crumb's revolutionary feline and it's the most outrageous cartoon ever produced. Fritz the Cat has appeared in Zap Comix and Head Comix, as well as in other underground mags. It's sometimes funny and sometimes gross, but mostly just so-so.

1972 77 minutes

FROM THE HIP

★★★

DIRECTOR: Bob Clark
CAST: Judd Nelson, Elizabeth Perkins, John Hurt, Ray Walston, Darren McGavin

Thoroughly unrealistic but nonetheless entertaining courtroom comedy that works in spite of director Bob Clark's tendency to forget that he's no longer making *Porky's*. Judd Nelson stars as a brash young attorney (Robin "Stormy" Weathers, no less) whose histrionic flair nets him the opportunity to defend John Hurt, a man accused of murder. Hurt delivers a particularly fine, high-powered performance as a ruthless egomaniac who considers himself better than the rest of humanity. Rated PG for language.

1987 111 minutes

FRONT PAGE, THE

★★★★

DIRECTOR: Lewis Milestone
CAST: Pat O'Brien, Adolphe Menjou, Mary Brian, Edward Everett Horton

A newspaper editor and his ace reporter do battle with civic corruption and each other in the first version of this oft-filmed hit comedy. The fast-paced, sparkling dialogue and the performances of the Warner Bros. stable of character actors have not aged after more than fifty years. This classic movie retains a great deal of charm.

1931 B & W 99 minutes

FULLER BRUSH GIRL, THE

★★★

DIRECTOR: Lloyd Bacon
CAST: Lucille Ball, Eddie Albert, Jerome Cowan, Lee Patrick

Lucy's in typical form as a dizzy cosmetics salesgirl up to her mascara in murder and hoodlums. Wisecracking dialogue and familiar character faces help this one out. Harmless fun.

1950 B & W 85 minutes

FULLER BRUSH MAN, THE

★★★

DIRECTOR: S. Sylvan Simon
CAST: Red Skelton, Janet Blair, Don McGuire, Adele Jergens, Buster Keaton

Red Skelton slapsticks along his route as a door-to-door salesman and gets involved with murder. Sadly, unsung master gagster Buster Keaton deserves a lot of credit for the humor he adds to many other Skelton films.

1948 B & W 93 minutes

FUN WITH DICK AND JANE

★★★★

DIRECTOR: Ted Kotcheff
CAST: Jane Fonda, George Segal, Ed McMahon

How does one maintain one's lifestyle after a sacking from a highly paid aerospace position? George Segal and Jane Fonda have a unique solution. They steal. This comedy caper is well named, because once they begin their career in crime, some quality fun is in store for the audience. Rated PG.

1977 95 minutes

FUNNY THING HAPPENED ON THE WAY TO THE FORUM, A

★★★★

DIRECTOR: Richard Lester
CAST: Zero Mostel, Phil Silvers, Jack Gilford, Michael Crawford, Buster Keaton

Ancient Rome is the setting for this fast-paced musical comedy. Zero Mostel is a never-ending source of zany plots to gain his freedom and line his toga with loot as a cunning slave. He is ably assisted by Phil Silvers and Jack Gilford in this bawdy romp through classic times. Look for Buster Keaton in a nice cameo.

1966 99 minutes

FUZZ

★★★

DIRECTOR: Richard A. Colla
CAST: Raquel Welch, Burt Reynolds, Yul Brynner, Tom Skerritt

Raquel Welch and Burt Reynolds star as police in this comedy-drama. Yul Brynner plays a bomb-happy villain. It has a few good moments, but you'd have to be a member of the Burt Reynolds fan club to really love it. Rated PG.

1972 92 minutes

GALLAGHER—MELON CRAZY

★★★★

DIRECTOR: Joe Hostettler

CAST: Gallagher, Bill Kirchenbauer

Mr. Smash and Splash considers his favorite fruit in all its various incarnations. Things get as wild as three-piece melon suits, melon blimps, and giant, 30-foot melons. All this is climaxed by a Super-Sledge-o-Matic smashing spree. In addition to Gallagher's bit, there's a "guest appearance" by Bill Kirchenbauer, who played Tony Roletti on *Fernwood Tonight*, doing his impressions of Xerox machines. It's funny stuff.

1984 58 minutes

GALLAGHER—OVER YOUR HEAD

★★★★

DIRECTOR: Joe Hostettler

CAST: Gallagher

Gallagher performs in the Lone Star state. The Texas audience goes wild when he enters wearing a 20-gallon hat and carrying a pistol with a 10-foot barrel. It gets better from there. He takes sarcastic swipes at politicians, ancient history, and gun control. There's also an enjoyable warm commentary on child rearing.

1984 58 minutes

GALLAGHER—STUCK IN THE 60S

★★★★

DIRECTOR: Wayne Orr

CAST: Gallagher

If you're a product of the 1960s, and even if you're not, you'll love this hilarious comedy video. Gallagher takes it all into account—the 1960s tendency toward militance; he asks why aren't we doing anything about the things that are wrong today, and offers some unique and inane suggestions. He looks at the things that matter to the 1960s generation today—like ugly bathrobes and fuzzy slippers! It's all playfully honest and enjoyably silly.

1983 58 minutes

GALLAGHER—THE BOOKEEPER

★★★★

DIRECTOR: Joe Hostettler

CAST: Gallagher

Gallagher takes a potshot at what seems to matter most in our society: the almighty dollar. In this concert performance, he whimsically attacks the IRS, banking, and what we spent our money on. There's a delightful twist when he shows off a new invention: the invisible elephant diving platform (the audience is sprayed with water when the phantom pachyderm takes the plunge). And, of course, be prepared for the Sledge-o-Matic!

1985 58 minutes

GALLAGHER—THE MADDEST

★★★½

DIRECTOR: Wayne Orr

CAST: Gallagher

Here's more inspired Gallagher-style madness for comedy fans. Bits include the introduction of a mutant sofa, a treatise on hats with and without handles, and, of course, everything ends with the gush of Gallagher's Sledge-o-Matic. Filmed live in concert.

1984 59 minutes

GAMBIT

★★★½

DIRECTOR: Ronald Neame

CAST: Michael Caine, Shirley MacLaine, Herbert Lom

An engaging caper comedy that teams Michael Caine's inventive but unlucky thief with Shirley MacLaine's mute and mysterious woman of the world . . . or *is* she?

The target is a valuable art treasure, jealously guarded by ruthless owner Herbert Lom, and Caine's plan is—to say the least—unusual. Naturally, things don't work out as expected, and that's when the fun begins. Caine and MacLaine make a grand pair; it's a shame they didn't get together for another film of this sort. Pay close attention, because the story contains one *major* surprise. Unrated; suitable for family viewing.

1966 108 minutes

GARBO TALKS

★★★★

DIRECTOR: Sidney Lumet
CAST: Anne Bancroft, Ron Silver, Carrie Fisher, Howard Da Silva, Dorothy Loudon, Hermione Gingold

In this often funny and touching contemporary comedy, Anne Bancroft is delightful as an outspoken crusader against the small injustices in the world. But she has her fantasies, too, and enlists the aid of her son (Ron Silver) in finding Greta Garbo, who at age 79 can occasionally be spotted walking around New York. Rated PG for profanity.

1984 103 minutes

GARRY SHANDLING SHOW, THE

★★★

DIRECTOR: Tom Trbovich
CAST: Garry Shandling, Paul Willson, Rose Marie, Doug McClure, Donny Osmond, Johnny Carson

Garry Shandling spoofs late-night talk shows, specifically Johnny Carson's anniversary shows. He looks back over the last twenty-five years of this mock variety show, with clips featuring Mr. Ed, the world's fattest man, and some very funny bits about the Beatles. Zany comedy abounds with guest stars coming out of the walls. If you're a fan of *The Tonight Show*, then you'll love this. Even if you're not, you'll find this a fun hour of smiles.

1985 60 minutes

GAS

[turkey]

DIRECTOR: Les Rose
CAST: Sterling Hayden, Peter Aykroyd, Susan Anspach, Donald Sutherland, Howie Mandel, Sanee Currie, Helen Shaver

America's past petroleum shortages (whether real or conspiratorial) have not been laughing matters, and neither is this tasteless, tedious comedy about an artificial gas-crisis in a Midwest city. More frenetic than funny and overstuffed with offensive ethnic stereotyping, car chases, and stale humor, it's generally a moronic mess. Rated R because of sex and rough language.

1981 94 minutes

GAS PUMP GIRLS

★

DIRECTOR: Joel Bender
CAST: Kirsten Baker, Dennis Bowen, Huntz Hall, Sandy Johnson, Leslie King, Linda Lawrence, Rikki Marin

This teen comedy features four beautifual girls who take on the big oil company across the street in an all-out gas war. The little gas station picks up business when the sexy girls offer service with a smile. Rated PG for nudity.

1978 102 minutes

GENERAL, THE

★★★★★

DIRECTOR: Buster Keaton
CAST: Buster Keaton, Marion Mack, Glen Cavender, Jim Farley, Joseph Keaton

The General is a film based on an incident in the Civil War. Buster

Keaton is an engineer determined to recapture his stolen locomotive. Magnificent battle scenes are mere backdrops for Keaton's inspired acrobatics and comedy. Solid scripting, meticulous attention to detail, and ingenious stunt work make this picture excellent.

1927 B & W 74 minutes

GENEVIEVE

★★★½

DIRECTOR: Henry Cornelius
CAST: Kenneth More, Kay Kendall, Dinah Sheridan, John Gregson, Arthur Wontner

Captivating, low-key comedy about friendly rivals who engage in a race after finishing a sports car rally in England. No pretenses or false claims in this charming, film, just great performances, beautiful countryside, and a spirit of fun and cameraderie. Originally shown as the second half of a double bill in America, this stylish feature gave Kenneth More one of his best roles and showcased the charm and comedy flair of Kay Kendall, one Britain's top talents.

1954 86 minutes

GENTLEMEN PREFER BLONDES

★★

DIRECTOR: Howard Hawks
CAST: Jane Russell, Marilyn Monroe, Charles Coburn, Tony Noonan, Elliott Reid, George Winslow

Howard Hawks gets surprisingly good performances from his stars, Jane Russell and Marilyn Monroe, in this 1953 musical comedy. As usual, Hawks does his best to make good scenes, but this time the silly plot—about two women searching for husbands—thwarts his esteemable talents.

1953 91 minutes

GEORGE BURNS AND GRACIE ALLEN SHOW, THE (TELEVISION SERIES)

★★★½

DIRECTOR: Ralph Levy
CAST: George Burns, Gracie Allen, Harry Von Zell, Ronnie Burns, Bea Benaderet, Hal March, Bob Sweeney, Fred Clark, Larry Keating

In this classic series, George Burns plays a nearly imperturbable entertainer, married to madcap Gracie Allen. Allen turns everyday life into a nonstop adventure by innocently causing a whirlwind of confusion. She's endlessly endearing. Burns is dryly delightful, puffing on his cigar and looking into the camera, commenting on the developing plot. In many episodes, George and Gracie's son Ronnie plays himself as a well-adjusted young ladies' man. Harry Von Zell is George's announcer. Colorful support is provided by the comic involvement of the neighbors, the Mortons—Blanche (played by Bea Benaderet) and Harry, played by a succession of character actors: Hal March, Bob Sweeney, Fred Clark, and Larry Keating.

1950–1958 B & W 120 minutes

GEORGE BURNS IN CONCERT

★★★★

DIRECTOR: Jim Shaw
CAST: George Burns

George Burns is at his funniest in this live, onstage performance produced for Home Box Office. It's all standup jokes and stories that Burns aims at himself. He spends a lot of time talking in a hilarious fashion about his part in the film *Oh, God* and of his extraodinary lifespan. Combined with a number of delightfully silly songs that sound suspiciously like vaudeville, *George Burns in Con-*

cert makes for thoroughly enjoyable entertainment.

1982 55 minutes

GEORGE CARLIN—PLAYIN' WITH YOUR HEAD

★★

DIRECTOR: Rocco Urbishi

CAST: George Carlin, Vic Tayback

There's little of the classic Carlin character to be seen in this comedy video. The one redeeming factor is a black-and-white short at the beginning—"The Envelope," in which Carlin plays a Sam Spade character named Mike Holder. Vic Tayback co-stars as the ringleader of a bunch of hooligans. No rating, but there's an ample helping of raw language.

1986 58 minutes

GEORGY GIRL

★★★½

DIRECTOR: Silvio Narizzano

CAST: Lynn Redgrave, James Mason, Alan Bates, Charlotte Rampling

Generations clash as suave, patient fairy-godfather James Mason works to make chubby London mod girl Lynn Redgrave his mistress in this totally engaging British comedy. Charlotte Rampling is a standout as the chubby's tough-bitch roommate. Mason, of course, gives another of his flawless characterizations.

1966 B & W 100 minutes

GET CRAZY

★★★½

DIRECTOR: Allan Arkush

CAST: Malcolm McDowell, Allen Goorwitz, Daniel Stern, Ed Begley Jr., Miles Chapin, Lou Reed, Stacey Nelkin, Bill Henderson, Franklin Ajaye, Bobby Sherman, Fabian Forte

Here's the wildest, weirdest, and most outrageous rock 'n' roll comedy any of us is likely to see. It's a story about a rock concert on New Year's Eve, during which everything that can go wrong does. It is basically a jumping-off point for sight gags, low humor, high humor, and general nuttiness. You're never bored. Malcolm McDowell plays a Mick Jagger–style rock singer, Allen Goorwitz is a Bill Graham–ish promoter, and Daniel Stern is his lovesick stage manager. Rated R for nudity, profanity, violence, and suggested sex.

1983 92 minutes

GET OUT OF MY ROOM

★

DIRECTOR: Richard "Cheech" Marin

CAST: Cheech and Chong, John Paragon, Elvira, Jan-Michael Vincent

The only good thing about this tape is Cheech's "Born in East L.A." musical video, featuring Elvira and Jan Michael Vincent. Unfortunately, the rest of the tape is boring. Cheech and Chong talk about how to make videos and decide that the main thing to do is to hire lots of beautiful girls. Other songs include: "Get Out of My Room," "I'm Not Home Right Now," and "Love Is Strange."

1985 53 minutes

GHOST GOES WEST, THE

★★★★

DIRECTOR: René Clair

CAST: Robert Donat, Jean Parker

A millionaire buys a Scottish castle and transports it stone by stone to America only to discover that it comes complete with a ghost. Robert Donat gives a memorable performance in this bit of whimsy.

1935 B & W 100 minutes

GHOST IN THE NOONDAY SUN

★½

DIRECTOR: Peter Medak

CAST: Peter Sellers, Anthony Franciosa, Peter Boyle, Spike Milligan, Clive Revill

Too silly pirate parody features a Peter Sellers so demented that his dialogue is almost indistinguishable. Sellers and his fellow pirates go searching for lost treasure and are haunted by a ghost. Not rated. Appropriate for children.

1974 90 minutes

GHOSTBUSTERS

★★★★

DIRECTOR: Ivan Reitman

CAST: Bill Murray, Dan Aykroyd, Sigourney Weaver, Harold Ramis, Annie Potts, Ernie Hudson, William Atherton, Rick Moranis

Bill Murray, Dan Aykroyd, Sigourney Weaver, and Harold Ramis (*Stripes*) are terrific in this very funny and often frightening comedy-horror film about a special organization that fights evil spirits. Is it *The Exorcist* meets *Saturday Night Live*? That's pretty close—but it's better. This big-budget horror-comedy delivers a bellyful of laughs as well as lots of unexpected shocks and excitement. Even little kids might enjoy it. There are some really scary scenes, but because the whole thing is done in a comedic vein, children just might be able to see it without having nightmares. Rated PG for profanity and scary scenes.

1984 107 minutes

GHOSTS ON THE LOOSE

★½

DIRECTOR: William Beaudine

CAST: The East Side Kids, Bela Lugosi, Ava Gardner, Rick Vallin

Silly movie pits Monogram's moronic East Side Kids against a bored Bela Lugosi and his German henchmen in this pallid variation on the "old haunted house" theme. No real thrills, no real laughs in this tired creaker. Even a youthful Ava Gardner can't perk this pooch up, and one wonders why on Earth it was even packaged for the video market. This is the kind of movie you turn off when it's on TV, so why would you go out and spend money just so you can do the same thing?

1943 B & W 65 minutes

GIDGET

★★½

DIRECTOR: Paul Wendkos

CAST: Sandra Dee, James Darren, Arthur O'Connell, Cliff Robertson, Doug McClure

The eternal beach bunny, Gidget (Sandra Dee), becomes involved with Cliff Robertson in order to make the man she's infatuated with (James Darren) notice her. This is the first and the best of a sub-par surfer series.

1959 95 minutes

GIDGET GOES HAWAIIAN

★★

DIRECTOR: Paul Wendkos

CAST: Deborah Walley, James Darren, Michael Callan, Carl Reiner, Peggy Cass, Eddie Foy Jr.

Everyone's favorite "girl-midget" (played here by Deborah Walley, taking over from Sandra Dee) returns to the screen in this inoffensive, brainless sequel to the 1959 box-office hit. This time around, she's off to Waikiki with her family for another series of romantic misadventures amid songs, surfing, and other adolescent fluff that movie producers in the early 1960s apparently thought teenagers were obsessed with. Some picturesque Hawaiian locations (all of which you've already seen in other, better movies) and a bright supporting cast are the main assets.

1961 102 minutes

GIDGET GOES TO ROME

★½

DIRECTOR: Paul Wendkos
CAST: Cindy Carol, James Darren, Jeff Donnell, Jessie Royce Landis

Glendon Swarthout's irrepressible beach bunny presses onward, if not upward, in this below-average sequel to *Gidget*. Strictly a time-passer.

1963 101 minutes

GIG, THE

★★★

DIRECTOR: Frank D. Gilroy
CAST: Wayne Rogers, Cleavon Little, Joe Silver, Andrew Duncan, Daniel Nalbach

Very nicely done comedy-drama concerning a group of men who get together once a week to play Dixieland jazz and their reactions to being hired for a two-week stint at a resort in the Catskill Mountains of New York. Film admirably avoids the clichés associated with this type of buddy film. Nice ensemble acting, with Cleavon Little and Joe Silver leading the way. Give this one a try.

1985 92 minutes

GILDA LIVE

★★

DIRECTOR: Mike Nichols
CAST: Gilda Radner, Don Novello, Paul Shaffer, Candy Slice

We've always loved Gilda Radner's characters from *Saturday Night Live*, and they're all represented in *Gilda Live*. But something is missing in her live show. The result is very few laughs. Rated R.

1980 96 minutes

GIRL CAN'T HELP IT, THE

★★★

DIRECTOR: Frank Tashlin
CAST: Tom Ewell, Jayne Mansfield, Edmond O'Brien, Julie London, Henry Jones, Fats Domino, The Platters, The Treniers, Little Richard, Gene Vincent and His Blue Caps, Eddie Cochran, Barry Gordon, Ray Anthony, Nino Tempo, The Chuckles, Abby Lincoln

Twentieth Century Fox decided to pull out all the stops in 1957 and make *the* comedy-exploitation-ripoff film of the year when they starred Tom Ewell (Marilyn Monroe's foil in *The Seven Year Itch*), Jayne Mansfield (thrust upon breast-crazy America as a Marilyn substitute and a rival to Anita Ekberg), and a bevy of rock-'n-roll performers in this cluttered film. Tom Ewell is given the task of turning squealing Jayne Mansfield into a singer on the clear understanding that he keep his hands to himself, a tough request when faced with the would-be singer's winning ways and obvious charms. Great rock-'n-roll by some of its premier interpreters is the real reason for watching this film, although the subject matter mirrors the infamous payola scandals that were shocking the nation. Don't miss Gene Vincent and His Blue Caps—this type of footage is rare in color.

1957 99 minutes

GIRL IN EVERY PORT, A

★½

DIRECTOR: Chester Erskine
CAST: Groucho Marx, William Bendix, Marie Wilson, Don DeFore, Gene Lockhart

Silly film about sailors involved in horse-racing scheme milks the old hide-the-horse-on-the-ship gag for all that it's worth (which isn't much) and then some. Only the presence of Groucho Marx makes this tired story worthy of note, and he, like the other fine character players stuck in this vacuum, can't do a thing with laughs that just aren't there. The kids might like it, but don't plan it for the evening's entertainment.

1952 B & W 86 minutes

GIRL IN THE PICTURE, THE

★★★

DIRECTOR: Cary Parker
CAST: John Gordon-Sinclair, Irina Brook, David McKay, Gregor Fisher, Paul Young, Rikki Fulton

The Girl in the Picture is a slight but very charming movie from Scotland. John Gordon-Sinclair (*Gregory's Girl*) plays a Glasgow photographer who's feeling stagnant in his relationship with his live-in design-student girlfriend. The film charts their breakup and what ensues because of it. The problems they face are never dealt with, but it doesn't seem to matter because the going is so enjoyable. The lovers are an amusing pair—Gordon-Sinclair, with his trademark understated manner and Irina Brook, with her intelligence and graceful strength. Rated PG.

1985 90 minutes

GIRLS JUST WANT TO HAVE FUN

DIRECTOR: Alan Metter
CAST: Sarah Jessica Parker, Lee Montgomery, Morgan Woodward, Jonathan Silverman

Sarah Jessica Parker (*Footloose*) stars as a young woman whose family moves to Chicago, where the popular television show *Dance TV* is filmed. She just lovvves to dance, and it just so happens the show is holding auditions for new dancers. She's going to give it a try, but will she be picked? This is a predictable, boring, and dumb movie. Rated PG for profanity.

1985 90 minutes

GIZMO!

★★★★½

DIRECTOR: Howard Smith
CAST: Documentary

A collection of short films from daredevils, flying machines, and enthusiastic inventors demonstrating their questionable benefits to mankind. It's up to the audience to decide whether these people were complete morons or just ahead of their time. A delightful, often hysterical celebration of the American spirit. Rated G.

1977 B & W 77 minutes

GO WEST

★★★½

DIRECTOR: Edward Buzzell
CAST: The Marx Brothers, John Carroll, Diana Lewis, Walter Woolf King

Far from prime-screen Marx Brothers, this is still one of their best MGM movies and a treat for their fans. Good comedy bits combine with a rip-roaring climax (stolen by screenwriter Buster Keaton from *The General*) for a highly watchable star comedy.

1940 B & W 81 minutes

GODS MUST BE CRAZY, THE

★★★★★

DIRECTOR: Jamie Uys
CAST: Marius Meyers, Sandra Prinsloo

This work, by South African filmmaker Jamie Uys, is a hilarious, poignant, exciting, thought-provoking, violent, and slapstick concoction that involves three separate stories. One is about a Bushman whose tribe selects him to get rid of an evil thing sent by the gods: a Coke bottle. The second features the awkward love affair of a teacher and a klutzy scientist. The last involves a band of terrorists fleeing for their lives. These all come together for a surprising and satisfying climax. Unrated, the film has violence.

1980 109 minutes

GOING APE!

★

DIRECTOR: Jeremy Jue Kronsberg
CAST: Tony Danza, Jessica Walter, Stacey Nelkin, Danny DeVito, Art Metrano, Joseph Maher

If one orangutan can help Clint Eastwood rack up millions at the box office, then three should make motion picture history, right? Wrong. There's nothing very original here. Tony Danza plays the heir to a million-dollar fortune-with-a-catch: In order to get the money, he has to care for three unpredictable simians. Because the film is padded with all-too-familiar material, very little fun shines through. Rated PG.

1981 87 minutes

GOING BERSERK

★

DIRECTOR: David Steinberg
CAST: John Candy, Joe Flaherty, Eugene Levy, Alley Mills, Pat Hingle, Richard Libertini

This is an unfunny comedy starring former SCTV regulars John Candy, Joe Flaherty, and Eugene Levy. Written and directed by David Steinberg (a former stand-up comedian who made his film-making debut with *Paternity*, starring Burt Reynolds), it never really goes anywhere, and its collection of supposedly "zany" bits just isn't funny. Rated R.

1983 85 minutes

GOING IN STYLE

★★★★

DIRECTOR: Martin Brest
CAST: George Burns, Art Carney, Lee Strasberg, Charles Hallahan, Pamela Payton-Wright

Three retirees who gather daily on a park bench need to add some spice to their empty existence. One of their sons needs help in paying his bills, so they decide to pitch in by robbing a bank. This crime caper has some unexpected plot twists mixed with a perfect sprinkling of humor. It is a delight throughout. Rated PG.

1979 96 minutes

GOLD RUSH, THE

★★★★★

DIRECTOR: Charles Chaplin
CAST: Charlie Chaplin, Mack Swain, Tom Murray, Georgia Hale

Charlie Chaplin's classic comedy is immortal for the scrumptious supper of a boiled boot, the teetering Klondike cabin, and the dance of the dinner rolls. Some parts are very sentimental, but these give the viewer time to catch his or her breath after laughing so much.

1925 B & W 100 minutes

GOLDEN AGE OF COMEDY, THE

★★★★

DIRECTOR: Robert Youngson
CAST: Laurel and Hardy, Will Rogers, Harry Langdon, Ben Turpin, Carole Lombard, Snub Pollard

First and most popular of Robert Youngson's tributes to silent film comedy, this compilation of highlights introduced new generations of moviegoers to the great years of silent comedy and continues to do so. Many of the shorts with Laurel and Hardy (including the classics "Two Tars") will be familiar to viewers due to their popularity and availability, but the segments with Will Rogers spoofing silent film greats Douglas Fairbanks and Tom Mix, and the footage with Harry Langdon (who was at one time considered a comedic equal to Charlie Chaplin, Buster Keaton, and Harold Lloyd) are seldom seen and worth the wait. Future star Carole Lombard shows her form rather than her famous screwball style in a Mack Sennett short, and the Keystone Kops go through their paces. Fun for everyone, but it's a shame all these films aren't available in their entirety on video.

1957 B & W 78 minutes

GONE ARE THE DAYS

★★★

DIRECTOR: Gabrielle Beaumont
CAST: Harvey Korman, Susan Anspach, Robert Hogan

After witnessing a gangland-style shooting, the Daye family is assigned to a witness relocation agent (Harvey Korman), who is creatively unsuccessful in a long-distance game of hide-and-seek. This wacky comedy is pleasantly acted and well photographed. Some fairly clever situations arise from an otherwise predictable premise. A Disney made-for-cable production. Good fun for the family.

1984 90 minutes

GOOD NEIGHBOR SAM

★★★

DIRECTOR: David Swift
CAST: Jack Lemmon, Romy Schneider, Dorothy Provine, Edward G. Robinson

This comedy is similar to many of the lightweight pot-boilers given to Jack Lemmon in the 1960s. He is a likable average American forced by circumstances beyond his control to bumble his way out of misadventures. *Good Neighbor Sam* makes only marginal use of Lemmon's comic gifts. It is an overlong farce about a married advertising designer who pretends marriage to his foreign neighbor next door so she can secure an inheritance. He must continue the charade to avoid offending his firm's puritanical client who chanced to see them together.

1964 130 minutes

GOOD SAM

★★

DIRECTOR: Leo McCarey
CAST: Gary Cooper, Ann Sheridan, Edmund Lowe

Gary Cooper plays a guy who can't say no in this barely watchable "comedy." He's Mr. Nice-Guy to everyone but his own family and feels he has to help everyone. So he lends all his money to "friends" and the "needy." Unfortunately, when it comes to buying things for his family (such as a house) he has no money left.

1948 B & W 114 minutes

GOODBYE COLUMBUS

★★★★

DIRECTOR: Larry Peerce
CAST: Richard Benjamin, Ali MacGraw, Jack Klugman

This film marked the start of Ali McGraw's and Richard Benjamin's movie careers. Ali plays a rich, spoiled Jewish-American princess who meets college dropout (Benjamin) at her country club. They have an affair, and we get to see her flaws through his "average guy" eyes. Rated R.

1969 105 minutes

GOODBYE GIRL, THE

★★★★½

DIRECTOR: Herbert Ross
CAST: Richard Dreyfuss, Marsha Mason, Quinn Cummings

Neil Simon's sparkling screenplay and the acting of Marsha Mason and Richard Dreyfuss combine to produce one of the best pure comedies since Hollywood's golden '30s. Mason and Dreyfuss are a mismatched pair of New Yorkers forced into becoming roommates. Rated PG.

1977 110 minutes

GOODBYE NEW YORK

★★★★

DIRECTOR: Amos Kollek

CAST: Julie Hagerty, Amos Kollek, David Topaz, Shmuel Shiloh, Christopher Goutman

An insurance salesperson (Julie Hagerty) becomes fed up with her job and husband and leaves for Paris. After falling asleep on the plane, she wakes up in Israel with no money and no luggage. This is similar to *Lost in America*, a comedy about survival in which she also starred, only this one is more like *Lost in the Middle East*. The film showcases Hagerty's talents without treating the film as merely a vehicle for the star. Rated R for language and very brief nudity.

1984 90 minutes

GORILLA, THE

★★

DIRECTOR: Allan Dwan

CAST: The Ritz Brothers, Bela Lugosi, Lionel Atwill

This is another one of those horror comedies that takes place in an old mansion and again wastes poor Bela Lugosi's acting talents. The Ritz Brothers were an acquired taste, to be sure, and this is not their best vehicle by any stretch of the imagination.

1939 B & W 66 minutes

GOSPEL ACCORDING TO VIC, THE

★★★½

DIRECTOR: Charles Gormley

CAST: Tom Conti, Helen Mirren, David Hayman, Brian Pettifer, Jennifer Black, David Anderson, Tom Busby

In this delightful comedy from Scotland, a teacher (Tom Conti) at a Glasgow parochial school finds that he can create miracles—even though he doesn't believe in them. Those who have reveled in the subtle, sly humor of *Gregory's Girl*, *Local Hero*, and other Scottish films will find similar joys in this. Some viewers, however, may find it offensive, even though the tone is essentially sweet-natured and warmly human. Rated PG-13 for adult content.

1986 92 minutes

GRACE QUIGLEY

★★½

DIRECTOR: Anthony Harvey

CAST: Katharine Hepburn, Nick Nolte, Elizabeth Wilson, Chip Zien, Christopher Murney, Kit Le Fever

After witnessing the murder of her landlord, spinster Katharine Hepburn enlists the aid of freelance hit man Nick Nolte. Hepburn wants Nolte to end her life, but not before he puts to rest some of her elderly friends who feel it is time for them to die. Extremely black comedy doesn't have enough humor and warmth to rise above its gruesome subject matter. Not for all tastes, to be sure, although Nolte and Hepburn work well together. Rated R.

1985 87 minutes

GRASS IS ALWAYS GREENER OVER THE SEPTIC TANK, THE

★★★½

DIRECTOR: Robert Day

CAST: Carol Burnett, Charles Grodin, Alex Rocco, Linda Gray

Carol Burnett and Charles Grodin shine in this tale of the domestic horrors of suburban life taken from Erma Bombeck's bestseller. The comedy doesn't always work, but when it does it rivals Grodin's *The Heartbreak Kid* and some of the best moments of Burnett's TV show. No rating, but the equivalent of a PG for language.

1978 98 minutes

GRASS IS GREENER, THE

★★★½

DIRECTOR: Stanley Donen
CAST: Cary Grant, Deborah Kerr, Jean Simmons, Robert Mitchum

Cary Grant and Deborah Kerr star as a married couple experimenting with extramarital affairs in this comedy. Jean Simmons plays Grant's girlfriend, while Robert Mitchum courts Kerr. Some funny moments, but it's not hilarious.

1960 105 minutes

GREAT BANK HOAX, THE

★★½

DIRECTOR: Joseph Jacoby
CAST: Richard Basehart, Burgess Meredith, Paul Sand, Ned Beatty, Michael Murphy, Arthur Godfrey

It is doubtful that viewers today will think of Watergate when watching this comedy caper, but it was originally intended as a parable. When the pillars of the community find out that the bank has been embezzled they decide to rob it. Great characterizations by all-star cast. Rated PG.

1977 89 minutes

GREAT DICTATOR, THE

★★★★★

DIRECTOR: Charles Chaplin
CAST: Charlie Chaplin, Jack Oakie, Paulette Goddard

Charlie Chaplin stars in and directed this devastating lampoon of the Third Reich. The celebrated clown's first all-talking picture, it casts him in two roles—as his famous Little Tramp and as Adenoid Hynkel, the Hitler-like ruler of Tomania. As with the similarly themed *Duck Soup*, starring the Marx Brothers, the comedy was a little too whimsical for wartime audiences. But it has to be regarded as a classic.

1940 B & W 128 minutes

GREAT GUNS

★★

DIRECTOR: Monty Banks
CAST: Stan Laurel, Oliver Hardy, Sheila Ryan, Dick Nelson

Although it's a cut below their classics, Sons of the Desert will love it, and so will most—especially the young. Stan and Ollie have jobs guarding a rich man's playboy son, Dick Nelson. He gets drafted; the fellows join up to continue their work. The playboy gets along just fine in khaki. The boys get up to their ears in trouble with an archetypical sergeant.

1941 B & W 74 minutes

GREAT RACE, THE

★★★½

DIRECTOR: Blake Edwards
CAST: Tony Curtis, Natalie Wood, Jack Lemmon, Peter Falk, Keenan Wynn, Larry Storch, Arthur O'Connell, Vivian Vance

Set in the early 1900s, this film comically traces the daily events of the first New York–to–Paris car race. Unfortunately, two-and-a-half hours of silly spoofs will have even the most avid film fan yawning.

1965 150 minutes

GREAT WALL, A

★★★½

DIRECTOR: Peter Wang
CAST: Peter Wang, Sharon Iwai, Kelvin Han Yee, Li Qinqin, Hu Xiao-guang, Shen Guanglan, Wang Xiao

A Great Wall is not a documentary about the 1,500-mile structure that rolls wavelike through northern China. Instead, it is a warm comedy about the clash of cultures that results when a Chinese-American family returns to its homeland. It is also the first American movie to be made in the People's Republic of China. As such, it gives some fascinating insights into Chinese culture and often does so in a marvelously entertaining way. Rated PG.

1986 100 minutes

GREGORY'S GIRL

★★★★½

DIRECTOR: Bill Forsyth
CAST: Gordon John Sinclair, Dee Hepburn, Chic Murray, Jake D'Arcy, Alex Norton, John Bett, Clare Grogan

In this utterly delightful movie from Scotland, a gangly, good-natured kid named Gregory—who has just gone through a five-inch growth spurt that has left him with the physical grace of a drunken stilt walker and made him a problem player on the school's winless soccer team—falls in love with the team's newest and best player: a girl named Dorothy. Unrated, the film has no objectionable content.

1981 91 minutes

GROOVE TUBE, THE

★★½

DIRECTOR: Ken Shapiro
CAST: Ken Shapiro, Lane Sarasohn, Chevy Chase, Richard Belzer, Mary Mendham, Bill Kemmill

A sometimes funny and most times just silly—or gross—1974 takeoff on television by writer-director Ken Shapiro. The V.D. commercial is a classic, however. Look for Chevy Chase in his first, brief screen appearance. Rated R.

1974 75 minutes

GUIDE FOR THE MARRIED MAN, A

★★★½

DIRECTOR: Gene Kelly
CAST: Walter Matthau, Inger Stevens, Robert Morse, Sue Ane Langdon, Lucille Ball, Jack Benny, Joey Bishop, Art Carney, Jayne Mansfield, Carl Reiner, Sid Caesar, Phil Silvers, Jeffrey Hunter, Sam Jaffe

Worldly Robert Morse tries to teach reluctant Walter Matthau the fundamentals of adultery. His lessons are acted out by a dazzling roster of top comedy stars. This episodic film provides a steady stream of laughs. The bit in which Joey Bishop is caught red-handed and practices the "deny, deny, deny" technique is a classic.

1967 89 minutes

GUMSHOE

★★★½

DIRECTOR: Stephen Frears
CAST: Albert Finney, Billie Whitelaw, Frank Finlay, Janice Rule, Caroline Seymour

Every hard-bitten private-eye film and film noir is saluted in this crime-edged comedy. Liverpool bingo caller Albert Finney finds himself in deep, murky water when he tries to live his fantasy of being a Humphrey Bogart–type shamus. Raymond Chandler and Dashiell Hammett fans will love every frame. Rated PG.

1972 88 minutes

GUNG HO

★★★★

DIRECTOR: Ron Howard
CAST: Michael Keaton, Gedde Watanabe, George Wendt, Mimi Rogers, John Turturro, Sab Shimono, Clint Howard

Another winner from director Ron Howard and writers Lowell Ganz and Babaloo Mandel, who previously teamed on *Night Shift* and *Splash*. This is a pointed and relevant study of the cultural chaos that occurs when small-town Hadleyville's automobile plant is rescued from closure by imported Japanese management. Michael Keaton holds things together as the fast-talking liaison between employees and management; he squares off against baby-faced Gedde Watanabe, as the exec who must look good to the big bosses back in Japan. Extremely unflattering in its portrait of the "ugly American," the script bravely suggests that we could learn a thing or two from other cultures. Rated PG-13 for language.

1985 111 minutes

HAMBURGER—THE MOTION PICTURE

DIRECTOR: Mike Marvin
CAST: Leigh McCloskey, Sandy Hackett, Randi Brooks, Charles Tyner, Chuck McCann, Dick Butkus

A very funny comedy could be made about the fast-food industry, but this isn't it. From the beginning of this insipid and achingly predictable movie, it is obvious the viewer is in trouble. In short order, we are introduced to a dopey nun (whose job, it seems, is to be bashed about whenever the filmmakers need a cheap laugh), a fat man (who jolts himself with electricity to stay on his diet), and a slobbering nerd (who prefers radio commercials to real music). The story involves a promiscuous fellow (Leigh McCloskey) who has to clean up his act or lose a $250,000 inheritance. We are supposed to care about this, but McCloskey's character is so one-dimensional we can hardly stand him. In fact, all the characters in *Hamburger* are lifeless jokes. Put this one on the back burner. Rated R for profanity, nudity, suggested sex, and violence.

1986 90 minutes

HANKY PANKY

DIRECTOR: Sidney Poitier
CAST: Gene Wilder, Gilda Radner, Richard Widmark, Kathleen Quinlan, Robert Prosky

In an obvious takeoff on the Hitchcock suspense formula, this seldom funny comedy features Gene Wilder as an innocent man caught up in international intrigue and murder. Gilda Radner is Wilder's confused helpmate, and Richard Widmark leads the baddies in this ultimately disappointing and, in the last half, boring film, directed by Sidney Poitier (*Stir Crazy*). Rated PG for violence and gore.

1982 110 minutes

HANNAH AND HER SISTERS

★★★★★

DIRECTOR: Woody Allen
CAST: Woody Allen, Michael Caine, Mia Farrow, Carrie Fisher, Barbara Hershey, Maureen O'Sullivan, Dianne Wiest, Max Von Sydow, Daniel Stern, Lloyd Nolan, Sam Waterston

One of Woody Allen's very best, a two-year study of a family held together by house-mother Mia Farrow. Hannah is best friend, trusted confidante, and sympathetic peacemaker for sisters Barbara Hershey and Dianne Wiest, husband Michael Caine, and parents Maureen O'Sullivan and Lloyd Nolan. Woody's along for a glib part as a hypochondriac who may get his fondest wish: a fatal disease. Farrow is superb as the woman in control of everything and everybody, until she snaps upon realizing the others may not *want* her ever-vigilant assistance. A change for Woody, because the film—and, most important, its conclusion—remains optimistic. Rated PG-13 for sexual situations.

1986 106 minutes

HAPPY HOOKER, THE

★★★

DIRECTOR: Nicholas Sgarro
CAST: Lynn Redgrave, Jean-Pierre Aumont, Elizabeth Wilson,

Tom Poston, Lovelady Powell, Nicholas Pryor

After Xaviera Hollander's novel became a bestseller, Lynn Redgrave was cast as Hollander in this offbeat comedy. Redgrave adds a wry touch as she recounts Hollander's rise from free-lance prostitute to one of New York's most infamous madams. Additionally, viewers get a peek at the kinky scenes one gets into when they play the sex-for-hire game. Rated R for nudity and sex.

1975 96 minutes

HAPPY HOOKER GOES TO WASHINGTON, THE

DIRECTOR: William A. Levey
CAST: Joey Heatherton, George Hamilton, Ray Walston, Jack Carter

Xaviera Hollander (Joey Heatherton) is innocently pursuing her career as a madam when she is surprised by a process server and called to Washington. Once there, she is forced to give testimony to a Senate committee sworn to uphold the morals of America. Naturally, she finds that all the senators use call girls and are unfit to judge her. But not before this soft-core sex film features plenty of nudity and profanity. Rated R for profanity, nudity, and sex.

1977 89 minutes

HARDBODIES

DIRECTOR: Mark Griffith
CAST: Grant Cramer, Teal Roberts, Gary Wood, Michael Rappaport, Roberta Collins

In this disgusting, insulting, and degrading-to-women sexploitation flick, three middle-aged, successful, but far-from-sexy men rent a summer beach house in hopes of seducing teen-age girls. They have no luck until Scotty Palmer (Grant Cramer), "the hottest guy on the beach," according to the press kit, decides to help them score. A few years ago, this piece of trash would have been considered hard-core pornography. The "target audience" (in film industry jargon) of this release is teenagers. We find that depressing. Rated R for nudity, simulated sex, and profanity.

1984 90 minutes

HARDLY WORKING

DIRECTOR: Jerry Lewis
CAST: Jerry Lewis, Susan Oliver, Roger C. Carmel, Deanna Lund, Harold J. Stone, Steve Franken

Jerry Lewis's 1980s screen comeback is passable family fare. As a middle-aged, out-of-work clown, he tries his hand at a number of jobs and flubs them all. As a gas station attendant, he nearly blows a service station sky-high. As a bartender in a strip joint, he gets bounced for handling the help. As a teriyaki chef, he fends off disgruntled customers with verbal karate: "I have a black and blue belt." His fans will love it; others need not apply. Rated PG.

1981 91 minutes

HAROLD AND MAUDE

★★★★★

DIRECTOR: Hal Ashby
CAST: Bud Cort, Vivian Pickles, Ruth Gordon, Cyril Cusack, Charles Tyner, Ellen Geer

Hal Ashby (*Coming Home*; *Shampoo*) directed this delightful black comedy about an odd young man named Harold (Bud Cort) who devises some rather elaborate fake deaths to jar his snooty, manipulative mother (Vivian Pickles). Soon his attention turns to an octogenarian named Maude (Ruth Gordon), with whom he falls in love. Featuring a superb soundtrack of songs by Cat Stevens, this is one of the original cult classics—and deservedly so. Rated PG.

1972 90 minutes

HARPER VALLEY P.T.A.

★

DIRECTOR: Richard Bennett
CAST: Barbara Eden, Ronny Cox, Nanette Fabray, Susan Swift, Ron Masak

Based on the popular country song, this silly piece of fluff features Barbara Eden as the sexy woman who gives her gossiping neighbors their proper comeuppance. Rated PG.

1978 102 minutes

HARRY AND WALTER GO TO NEW YORK

★★½

DIRECTOR: Mark Rydell
CAST: James Caan, Elliott Gould, Michael Caine, Diane Keaton, Charles Durning

Harry and Walter Go to New York looks as if it were fun for the principals to make. James Caan and Elliott Gould appear to be having the time of their lives portraying two inept con men. Michael Caine and Diane Keaton are, as always, excellent. Mark Rydell directs this unusually light film with an invisible touch. *Harry and Walter* is sort of like Chinese food—an hour later, you feel as if you haven't had anything. Rated PG.

1976 123 minutes

HARRY'S WAR

★½

DIRECTOR: Keith Merrill
CAST: Edward Herrmann, Geraldine Page, Karen Grassle, David Ogden Stiers, Salome Jens, Elisha Cook Jr.

In this cornball comedy, Harry Johnson (Edward Herrmann) takes on the Internal Revenue Service, which made a mistake on his return. As a result, Harry is left homeless and broke. Unfortunately, the script is more dumb than funny. And the constant sniping at the IRS will bore the kids. It does have a few bright moments—most of them provided by character actor Elisha Cook Jr. Rated PG.

1981 98 minutes

HAUNTED HONEYMOON

★

DIRECTOR: Gene Wilder
CAST: Gene Wilder, Gilda Radner, Dom De Luise, Jonathan Pryce, Paul L. Smith, Peter Vaughan, Bryan Pringle, Jim Carter, Eve Ferret

Writer-director-star Gene Wilder fails to scare up a single solid laugh in this sadly limp chiller spoof. He once again squanders the talents of his wife, Gilda Radner. They play 40s radio stars who plan to wed at an ominous family estate, which is populated by loonies, werewolves, and transvestites. Even Dom De Luise, improbably cast as Wilder's elderly aunt, fails to amuse. The movie drags on interminably. Rated PG.

1986 90 minutes

HAVING IT ALL

★★★

DIRECTOR: Edward Zwick
CAST: Dyan Cannon, Hart Bochner, Barry Newman, Sylvia Sidney, Melanie Chartoff

Dyan Cannon makes up for any script deficiencies with sheer exuberance. In this remake of Alec Guiness's *The Captain's Paradise*, the roles are reversed, and it is Cannon who plays the bigamist. As a fashion designer, she is constantly traveling between New York and Los Angeles. She has a home and husband in each of the two cities and manages to juggle the two. Despite Cannon's hilarious bustling, her assistant (Melanie Chartoff) manages to steal the spotlight from her in more than one scene. Made for TV, this is unrated.

1982 100 minutes

HAVING WONDERFUL TIME

DIRECTOR: Alfred Santell
CAST: Ginger Rogers, Douglas Fairbanks Jr., Red Skelton, Lucille Ball, Eve Arden, Lee Bowman, Jack Carson, Peggy Conklin, Grady Sutton, Dorothy Tree, Clarence H. Brown

Based on a Broadway stage hit, this was supposed to be romance and comedy at a famed Catskills resort hotel. It proved to be a big waste of a big cast that produced a big loss ($276,000) while misusing and abusing some great talent. Not the best way to remember Red Skelton's screen debut.

1938 B & W 71 minutes

HAWMPS!

DIRECTOR: Joe Camp
CAST: James Hampton, Christopher Connelly, Slim Pickens, Denver Pyle, Jack Elam

An extremely unfunny movie from the director of *Benji*, centering on an Old West cavalry unit that uses camels instead of horses. The cast is made up of familiar faces who appear uninspired. A very dumb film. Rated G.

1976 120 minutes

HEAD OFFICE

★

DIRECTOR: Ken Finkleman
CAST: Judge Reinhold, Lori-Nan Engler, Eddie Albert, Merritt Butrick, Ron Frazier, Richard Masur, Rick Moranis, Jane Seymour, Danny DeVito

A sometimes funny but mostly silly comedy, about the son of an influential politician who upon graduating from college gets a high-paying job with a major corporation. He then begins scaling the business ladder at an incredible rate, no matter how badly he fouls up. As it turns out, the owner of the company is hoping to get preferential political treatment from the man's father. A few laughs, but what is unforgivable is the advertising of major stars, almost all of whom are onscreen for about five minutes. This movie does contain some harsh language but should be suitable for more mature teen-age audiences. Rated PG-13.

1985 90 minutes

HEARTBREAK KID, THE

★★★★

DIRECTOR: Elaine May
CAST: Charles Grodin, Cybill Shepherd, Jeannie Berlin, Eddie Albert, Audra Lindley

The lack of care or commitment in the modern marriage is satirized in this comedy. Charles Grodin plays a young man who's grown tired of his wife while driving to their honeymoon in Florida. By the time he sees beautiful Cybil Shepherd on the beach, his marriage has totally disintegrated. Jeannie Berlin, director Elaine May's daughter, is the big scene stealer as Grodin's whining bride. Rated PG.

1972 104 minutes

HEARTBURN

★★★

DIRECTOR: Mike Nichols
CAST: Meryl Streep, Jack Nicholson, Jeff Daniels, Maureen Stapleton, Stockard Channing, Richard Masur, Catherine O'Hara, Milos Forman

Uneven adaptation of Nora Ephron's novel (she also wrote

the screenplay) and a thinly disguised account of her own separation from Watergate journalist Carl Bernstein. Jack Nicholson and Meryl Streep, both veterans of previous relationships, meet, fall in love, get married, and drift apart. Little explanation is given for this eventual drift, which is the film's weakness; its strength, on the other hand, comes from the superb performances by the stars and an incredible supporting cast. At times quite funny, such as during the wedding itself, or later, when Streep's character announces her pregnancy. Needlessly rated R for language.

1986 108 minutes

HEARTS OF THE WEST

★★★

DIRECTOR: Howard Zieff

CAST: Jeff Bridges, Alan Arkin, Blythe Danner, Andy Griffith

Pleasant little comedy-drama about an aspiring writer from Iowa (Jeff Bridges) who, determined to pen masterful westerns, winds up in Hollywood as a most reluctant cowboy. The setting is the early 1920s, and the story playfully explodes many of those classic western myths—such as the notion that a cowboy could leap from a second-story balcony onto his horse and then ride off into the sunset. Bridge's attempt at that bit of derring-do is the funniest moment in an always amusing picture. Rated PG.

1975 103 minutes

HEAVEN CAN WAIT

★★★★½

DIRECTOR: Warren Beatty, Buck Henry

CAST: Warren Beatty, Julie Christie, Jack Warden, Dyan Cannon, Charles Grodin, James Mason, Buck Henry, Vincent Gardenia

In this charming, thoroughly entertaining remake of *Here Comes Mr. Jordan* (1941), Warren Beatty stars as quarterback Joe Pendleton, who meets a premature demise when an overzealous angel (Buck Henry) takes the athlete's spirit out of his body after an accident. As it turns out, it wasn't Joe's time to die. However, in the intrim, his body is cremated. Thus begins a quest by Joe, the angel, and his superior (James Mason) to find a proper earthly replacement. This, of course, brings a number of humorous and touching complications. Rated PG.

1978 100 minutes

HEAVEN HELP US

★

DIRECTOR: Michael Dinner

CAST: Andrew McCarthy, Kevin Dillon, Malcolm Dunarie, Stephen Geoffreys, Donald Sutherland, John Heard, Wallace Shawn, Kate Reid

Donald Sutherland, John Heard, Wallace Shawn, and Kate Reid support the youthful cast of this generally unfunny and often repulsive comedy about a group of schoolboys (played by Andrew McCarthy, Kevin Dillon, Malcolm Danarie, and Stephen Geoffreys) discovering the opposite sex and other adolescent pursuits. Rated R.

1985 90 minutes

HEAVENLY BODIES

★½

DIRECTOR: Lawrence Dane

CAST: Cynthia Dale, Richard Rebiere, Laura Henry, Walter George Alton

More sweaty dancing bodies à la *Flashdance* are featured in this low-budget release about a secretary who is tired of her nine-to-five existence and opens her own aerobics exercise club in a warehouse. With at least five credited production companies mentioned —one of them being Playboy Enterprises—before they even get to the title, you'd figure this film would have something going for it. Unfortunately, the only thing going here is the audience moving for the exits. Rated R for nudity, profanity, and sexual innuendo.

1985 90 minutes

HEAVENLY KID, THE

★★

DIRECTOR: Cary Medoway
CAST: Lewis Smith, Jason Gedrick, Jane Kaczmarek, Richard Mulligan, Nancy Valen, Anne Sawyer

Despite a wee bit of physical humor, marginally amusing dope jokes, and an unobstructed shot of teen-throb Jason Gedrick's well-muscled backside, *The Heavenly Kid* is earthbound with lead in its black engineer boots. Cocky Bobby Fontana (Lewis Smith) bit the big one in a chicken race seventeen years ago: which would make it 1968, but the soundtrack and the wardrobe are definitely 1955—a basic problem rendering this otherwise simply stupid film completely unintelligible. To get out of limbo (a subway train to nowhere, no less) and into heaven, angel Bobby needs a special project. Spazzola Lenny Barnes (Gedrick) is the lucky guy. And if you hadn't guessed by now, Bobby left behind a pregnant girlfriend, making him you-know-who's daddy-o. Richard Mulligan has a thankless role as a grizzled, motorcycle-riding archangel. Rated PG-13 for language, situations, and bare body parts.

1985 90 minutes

HEAVENS ABOVE

★★★

DIRECTORS: John Boulting, Roy Boulting
CAST: Peter Sellers, Cecil Parker, Isabel Jeans, Eric Sykes

Another low-key gem from the late Peter Sellers, this irreverent story of a clergyman with the common touch spoofs just about everything within reach, some of it brilliantly. Sellers shows his congregation the error of their selfish ways and engages them in some odd charities, often with hilarious results. Not as successful as other British comedies of this period, this slightly overblown romp is still intelligently crafted and has the laughs and witty dialogue to hold the viewer's attention.

1963 B & W 105 minutes

HERE COMES MR. JORDAN

★★★★★

DIRECTOR: Alexander Hall
CAST: Robert Montgomery, Evelyn Keyes, Claude Rains, Rita Johnson, Edward Everett Horton, James Gleason, John Emery

We all know that bureaucracy can botch up almost anything. Well, the bureaucrats of heaven can really throw a lulu at boxer Joe Pendleton (Robert Montgomery). The heavenly administrators have called Joe up before his time, and they've got to set things straight. That's the basis for the delightful fantasy *Here Comes Mr. Jordan*. A sequel was made with Rita

Hayworth in 1947, and Warren Beatty recycled the whole thing in 1978's *Heaven Can Wait*. Excellent supporting performances are given by Claude Rains and Edward Everett Horton in the air and Evelyn Keyes and James Gleason on the ground in this comedy classic.

1941 B & W 93 minutes

HERO AT LARGE

★★★½

DIRECTOR: Martin Davidson
CAST: John Ritter, Anne Archer, Bert Convy, Kevin McCarthy

In this enjoyably lightweight film, John Ritter plays Steve Nichols, an out-of-work actor who takes a part-time job to promote a movie about a crusading superhero, *Captain Avenger.* Along with thirty or so other young men, he dresses up like the film's title character and signs autographs for youngsters who see the movie. Unlike the other impersonators, who grumble about how degrading the job is, Nichols finds pleasure in representing, if only in the minds of children, the powers of justice. Shortly, he saves an old couple and becomes a real hero. Rated PG.

1980 98 minutes

HEY ABBOTT!

★★★★

DIRECTOR: Jim Gates
CAST: Bud Abbott, Lou Costello, Joe Besser, Phil Silvers, Steve Allen

This is a hilarious anthology of high points from Abbott and Costello television programs. Narrated by Milton Berle, the distillation includes the now-legendary duo's classic routines: "Who's on First?," "Oyster Stew," "Floogle Street," and "The Birthday Party."

1978 B & W 76 minutes

HIGH ANXIETY

★★★

DIRECTOR: Mel Brooks
CAST: Mel Brooks, Madeline Kahn, Cloris Leachman, Harvey Korman, Dick Van Patten, Ron Carey

Mel Brooks successfully spoofed the horror film with *Young Frankenstein* and the western with *Blazing Saddles*. However, this takeoff of the Alfred Hitchcock suspense movies falls miserably flat. Rated PG.

1977 94 minutes

HIGH POINT

★★

DIRECTOR: Peter Carter
CAST: Christopher Plummer, Richard Harris

The only high point in this movie is the ending. Christopher Plummer and Richard Harris co-star in this would-be comedy. The CIA pays to eliminate a king, but when the king flees on his own, they want their money back. Rated PG for violence.

1984 91 minutes

HIGH SCHOOL, USA

★★

DIRECTOR: Rod Amateau
CAST: Michael J. Fox, Dwayne Hickman, Angela Cartwright

The fact that the dancing robot is the best actor in this film should tell you something. This made-for-TV feature is your typical teen flick, which is exceptional only because it doesn't rely on nudity and foul language to hold its audience's attention. Michael J. Fox and his pals fight back against the rich preppies who run the school. Fox races his car against Beau's (the preppy leader) and wins both the race and Beau's girlfriend. Subplots include a romance between Dwayne Hickman and Angela Cartwright, who play teachers; the school genius's creation of a robot; and the contest for teacher of the year. The thing that makes this film fun to watch is that almost everyone in it is a recognizable star from a TV sitcom. Most viewers will forget about the lack of plot as they identify the shows these people come from. Trivial pursuit fans should find this "name-that-show" game the film's one redeeming aspect.

1983 96 minutes

HILLBILLYS IN A HAUNTED HOUSE

★

DIRECTOR: Jean Yarbrough
CAST: Ferlin Husky, Joi Lansing, Don Bowman, John Carradine, Lon Chaney Jr., Basil Rathbone, Molly Bee, Merle Haggard, Sonny James

Unbelievably bad mishmash of country corn and horror humor is an insult to both genres and deserves its star only because of the appearance of great horror film veterans (including Basil Rathbone's last film role). The acting, story, and songs are inane and make director Jean Yarbrough's earlier efforts *King of the Zombies* and *Devil Bat* look like classics. Except for the cameos by the stars, and the thrill of seeing country and western stars acting like morons, there is little excuse for watching this film and one questions the advisability of even making it available on video. Rent at your own risk.

1967 88 minutes

HIPS, HIPS, HOORAY

★★★

DIRECTOR: Mark Sandrich
CAST: Bert Wheeler, Robert Woolsey, Thelma Todd, Ruth Etting, George Meeker, Dorothy Lee

Clowns Bert Wheeler and Robert Woolsey liven up this early, somewhat blue, musical. The pair play havoc as they invade Thelma Todd's ailing cosmetic business.

1934 B & W 68 minutes

HIS DOUBLE LIFE

★★★

DIRECTORS: Arthur Hopkins, William C. de Mille
CAST: Lillian Gish, Roland Young

Edwardian novelist Arnold Bennett's comedy about a wealthy recluse who finds a better life by becoming a valet when his valet dies and is buried under his name. Remade with Monty Woolley and Gracie Fields as *Holy Matrimony* in 1943.

1933 B & W 67 minutes

HIS GIRL FRIDAY

★★★★

DIRECTOR: Howard Hawks
CAST: Cary Grant, Rosalind Russell, Ralph Bellamy, Gene Lockhart, Helen Mack, Ernest Truex

Based on Ben Hecht and Charles MacArthur's *The Front Page*, which was filmed on two other occasions, this is undoubtedly the best of Howard Hawks's comedies. Originally with two male leads, Hawks converted this gentle spoof of newspapers and reporters into a hilarious battle of the sexes. Rosalind Russell is the reporter bent on retirement, and Cary Grant is the editor bent on maneuvering her out of it—and winning her heart in the process. The dialogue comes fast, funny, and furious, and there's never a dull moment.

1940 B & W 92 minutes

HIS ROYAL SLYNESS/HAUNTED SPOOKS

★★★½

DIRECTORS: Hal Roach, Alf Goulding

CAST: Harold Lloyd, Mildred Davis, Harry Pollard, Wallace Howe, Gaylord Lloyd

Silent comedy star Harold Lloyd spreads his considerable talent in this pair of bellybusters from Hal Roach's fun factory. In the first, Lloyd impersonates the king of a small monarchy; in the second, he is maneuvered into living in a haunted mansion. Sight gags and double takes highlight both these shorts. Silent, with music.

1920 B & W 52 minutes

HISTORY OF THE WORLD, PART ONE, THE

DIRECTOR: Mel Brooks

CAST: Mel Brooks, Dom De Luise, Madeline Kahn, Harvey Korman, Gregory Hines, Cloris Leachman

Without the thematic unity of *Blazing Saddles* or *Young Frankenstein*, Mel Brooks is lost in this collection of bits that emerge like unused footage from *Monty Python's The Meaning of Life*. Brooks apparently feels that five-year-old "poo-poo jokes" are the height of humor, but their frequent overuse does not mask the complete absence of witty material in this episodic glance at life in ancient Rome, during the French Revolution, and other noteworthy (?) stops along the way. A big-budget, high-tech, multicolored flop. Rated R for crude language.

1981 86 minutes

HISTORY OF WHITE PEOPLE IN AMERICA, THE

★★★½

DIRECTOR: Harry Shearer

CAST: Martin Mull, Mary Kay Place, Fred Willard, Steve Martin

Martin Mull narrates this hilarious spoof documentary on white heritage, current hobbies, and food preferences. He takes us to the Institute for White Studies and into the home of a very white family. We get to know the Harrison family (with Mary Kay Place and Fred Willard as Mom and Dad). Made for cable TV, this is unrated, but it contains obscenities and sexual topics.

1985 48 minutes

HISTORY OF WHITE PEOPLE IN AMERICA, THE (VOLUME II)

★★★½

DIRECTOR: Harry Shearer

CAST: Fred Willard, Mary Kay Place, Martin Mull, Michael McKean, Amy Lynn , George Gobel, Christian Jacobs, Eileen Brennan, Stella Stevens

Martin Mull returns in four hilarious new episodes with the very white Harrison family. In "White Religion," Mr. and Mrs. Harrison (Fred Willard and Mary Kay Place) must deal with their daughter's teen pregnancy. They turn to their pastor (Michael McKean) for guidance. "White Stress" features Mr. Harrison coming unglued, seeing a psychiatrist, and trying to relax. In "White Politics," Mr. Harrison runs for water commissioner because their water is polluted. The last episode, "White Crime," finds Mr. Harrison, his son, and Martin Mull in court with Eileen Brennan as the judge. These are wonderful tongue-in-cheek spoofs with the cast managing to keep straight faces while doing or saying the silliest things. Unrated, this does contain obscenities.

1986 100 minutes

HIT THE ICE

★★★

DIRECTOR: Charles Lamont

CAST: Bud Abbott, Lou Costello, Patric Knowles, Elyse Knox

Abbott and Costello play a pair of photographers in this outing, eluding assorted crooks. Gags abound, but so do musical numbers, which always seem to grind these films to a halt. On a par with most of their other efforts, it guarantees a great time for A & C fans.

1943 B & W 82 minutes

HOBSON'S CHOICE

★★★★★

DIRECTOR: David Lean

CAST: Charles Laughton, John Mills, Brenda de Banzie, Daphne Anderson

Charles Laughton gives one of his most brilliant performances as a turn-of-the-century London shoemaker whose love for the status quo and his whiskey is shattered by the determination of his daughter to wed. This is the original 1954 movie version of the British comedy. Laughton is expertly supported by John Mills and Brenda de Banzie as the two who wish to marry.

1954 B & W 107 minutes

HOLD THAT GHOST

★★★½

DIRECTOR: Arthur Lubin

CAST: Bud Abbott, Lou Costello, Richard Carlson, Joan Davis

Abbott and Costello score in this super comedy about two goofs (guess who) inheriting a haunted house where all kinds of bizarre events occur. You may have to watch this one a few times to catch all the gags.

1941 B & W 86 minutes

HOLIDAY

★★★★½

DIRECTOR: George Cukor

CAST: Katharine Hepburn, Cary Grant, Doris Nolan, Lew Ayres, Edward Everett Horton, Binnie Barnes, Henry Daniell

This delightful film was adapted from the Broadway play by Phillip (*The Philadelphia Story*) Barry and features Cary Grant as a nonconformist, who, for love's sake, must confront New York City's upper-class society. Indeed, he must make the ultimate sacrifice to please his fiancée (Doris Nolan) and join her father's banking firm. Only her sister (Katharine Hepburn) seems to understand Grant's need to live a different kind of life. It's a charming story wonderfully told and acted.

1938 B & W 93 minutes

HOLLYWOOD BOULEVARD

★★★

DIRECTORS: Joe Dante, Allan Arkush

CAST: Candice Rialson, Mary Woronov, Rita George, Jeffrey Kramer, Dick Miller, Paul Bartel

A would-be actress goes to work for inept movie-makers in this comedy. This is the first film that Joe Dante (*Gremlins*) directed. Rated R.

1976 83 minutes

HOLLYWOOD HOT TUBS

[turkey]

DIRECTOR: Chuck Vincent

CAST: Paul Gunning, Donna McDaniel, Michael Andrew

In this ludicrous video a young man wangles a job at a local hot tub firm in L.A. Lots of imbecilic jokes, naked girls, and a frenetic climax all help *not* to distinguish this quickie from the rest of the

crowd. Somebody pull the drain plug, please. Rated R for nudity.
1984 103 minutes

HOLLYWOOD OR BUST

★★½

DIRECTOR: Frank Tashlin
CAST: Jerry Lewis, Dean Martin, Pat Crowley, Anita Ekberg

One of Dean Martin and Jerry Lewis's lesser efforts concerns the boys' misadventures on a trip to Hollywood where movie nut Jerry hopes to meet his dream girl, Anita Ekberg (who plays herself). Starts off well, but stalls as soon as Dean meets Pat Crowley and the musical interludes begin. Still, there are some choice moments, including Jerry's Great Dane, Mr. Bascom, speeding off at the wheel of a car. The final teaming of Martin and Lewis.
1956 95 minutes

HOLLYWOOD OUTTAKES

★★½

DIRECTOR: Bruce Goldstein
CAST: Humphrey Bogart, Bette Davis, Errol Flynn, George Raft, James Cagney, Judy Garland, Mickey Rooney

This is a sometimes terrific, most times passable, collection of blooper and newsreel footage from the 1930s, 1940s, and 1950s. No MPAA rating.
1984 90 minutes

HOLLYWOOD SHUFFLE

★★★½

DIRECTOR: Robert Townsend
CAST: Robert Townsend, Anne-Marie Johnson, Starletta Dupois, Helen Martin, Craigus T. Johnson, Paul Mooney

In the style of *Kentucky Fried Movie*, writer-director-star Robert Townsend lampoons Hollywood's perception of blacks—and racial stereotypes in general. It's not always funny, but some scenes are hilarious. A private-eye spoof called "Death of a Break Dancer," a parody of television movie-review shows called "Sneakin' into the Movies," and something entitled "Black Acting School" are the standouts, in this mixed bag of skits held together by the quest for big-screen success by Bobby Taylor (Townsend). It's uneven but worth the watch. Rated R for profanity and adult content.
1987 82 minutes

HOME MOVIES

★★

DIRECTOR: Brian De Palma
CAST: Nancy Allen, Keith Gordon, Kirk Douglas, Gerrit Graham, Vincent Gardenia

A little film produced with the help of Brian De Palma's filmmaking students at Sarah Lawrence College. A director, played by Kirk Douglas, gives "star therapy" to a young man who feels he is a mere extra in his own life. The film is quirky and fun at times, but more often it's simply pointless. Interesting as an experiment by an established talent, but as entertainment, it's quite tedious. Rated PG.
1980 90 minutes

HONKY TONK FREEWAY

★★★

DIRECTOR: John Schlesinger
CAST: William Devane, Beverly D'Angelo, Beau Bridges, Geraldine Page, Teri Garr

Director John Schlesinger captures the comedy of modern American life in a small Florida town. The stars keep you laughing. Rated R.
1981 107 minutes

HOOPER

★★★★

DIRECTOR: Hal Needham
CAST: Burt Reynolds, Sally Field, Jan-Michael Vincent, Brian Keith

Fresh from their success with *Smokey and the Bandit*, director Hal Needham and stars Burt Reynolds and Sally Field are reunited for this humorous, knockabout comedy about Hollywood stuntmen. Jan-Michael Vincent adds to the film's impact as an up-and-coming fall guy out to best top-of-the-heap Reynolds. Good fun. Rated PG.

1978 99 minutes

HORSE'S MOUTH, THE

★★★½

DIRECTOR: Ronald Neame
CAST: Alec Guinness, Kay Walsh, Renee Houston, Michael Gough

Star Alec Guinness, who also penned the script, romps in high comic style through this film version of Joyce Cary's mocking novel about an eccentric painter.

1958 93 minutes

HOSPITAL, THE

★★★★½

DIRECTOR: Arthur Hiller
CAST: George C. Scott, Diana Rigg, Barnard Hughes

You definitely don't want to check in. But if you like to laugh, you'll want to check it out. This 1971 black comedy did for the medical profession what . . . *And Justice for All* did for our court system and *Network* did for television. Paddy Cheyefsky's Oscar-winning screenplay casts George C. Scott as an embittered doctor battling against the outrageous goings-on at the institution of the title. Rated PG.

1971 103 minutes

HOT DOG...THE MOVIE

★★

DIRECTOR: Peter Markle
CAST: David Naughton, Patrick Houser, Shannon Tweed

He may no longer be a Pepper, but David Naughton (*An American Werewolf in London*) co-stars with one-time Playboy Playmate of the Year Shannon Tweed in this comedy about high jinks on the ski slopes that will no doubt delight its youthful target audience. *Hot Dog* is another one of those made-to-order teen flicks and is a first-rate example of its genre. Rated R for nudity, profanity, and suggested sex.

1984 96 minutes

HOT MOVES

DIRECTOR: Jim Sotos
CAST: Michael Zorek, Adam Blair, Jeff Fishman, Johnny Timko

Here's another rip-off of *Animal House*; a teen lust comedy with little lust and less laughs. Rated R.

1985 80 minutes

HOT STUFF

★★★½

DIRECTOR: Dom De Luise
CAST: Dom De Luise, Jerry Reed, Suzanne Pleshette, Ossie Davis

Movie fans who love to laugh will appreciate *Hot Stuff*. It's an entertaining, old-fashioned comedy that whips right along. Director-star Dom De Luise makes the most of his dual role. His is a good-natured kind of comedy. You like all of the characters, even the bad guys. The story concerns a government fencing operation for capturing crooks. And the results are humorous. Rated PG.

1979 87 minutes

HOUSE CALLS

★★★★½

DIRECTOR: Howard Zieff

CAST: Walter Matthau, Glenda Jackson, Richard Benjamin, Art Carney

Here's a romantic comedy reminiscent of films Spencer Tracy and Katharine Hepburn made together in the 1940s and 1950s, mostly because of the teaming of Walter Matthau and Glenda Jackson. A recently widowed doctor (Matthau) finds his bachelor spree cut short by a romantic encounter with a nurse (Jackson) who refuses to be just another conquest. It is a bit more risqué than the ones from that earlier period. But it still is a delightful battle of the sexes with two equally matched opponents. Rated PG.

1978 96 minutes

HOUSEBOAT

★★★

DIRECTOR: Melville Shavelson

CAST: Cary Grant, Sophia Loren, Martha Hyer, Harry Guardino

A minor entry in Cary Grant's *oeuvre* of romantic fluff, largely unremarkable because of its ho-hum script. With this sort of insubstantial material coming his way, it's little wonder Grant chose to retire eight years later. He lives on a houseboat *sans* wife; Sophia Loren is the housekeeper-maid with whom he falls in love. Although Grant and Loren share a pleasant chemistry, such charm cannot successfully rise above the weak script. Unrated; suitable for family viewing.

1958 110 minutes

HOW I WON THE WAR

★★★½

DIRECTOR: Richard Lester

CAST: Michael Crawford, John Lennon, Michael Hordern, Jack MacGowran

John Lennon had his only solo screen turn (away from the Beatles) in this often hilarious war spoof. Directed by Richard Lester (*A Hard Day's Night*; *Superman II*), it features Michael Crawford as a military man who has a wacky way of distorting the truth as he reminisces about his adventures in battle.

1967 109 minutes

HOW TO BEAT THE HIGH CO$T OF LIVING

★★

DIRECTOR: Robert Scheerer

CAST: Jessica Lange, Susan Saint James, Jane Curtin, Richard Benjamin, Fred Willard, Dabney Coleman

A great cast all dressed up with no place to go . . . except Jane Curtin, whose shopping-mall strip-tease is a marginal high point in a caper comedy not even up to the substandards of an average made-for-television movie. Curtin, Jessica Lange, and Susan Saint James are a trio of housewives who decide to heist a large display of cash in order to meet the grocery payments. Tiresome and taxing; rarely have so many labored to produce so little. Rated PG.

1980 110 minutes

HOW TO BREAK UP A HAPPY DIVORCE

★★★

DIRECTOR: Jerry Paris

CAST: Hal Linden, Barbara Eden, Harold Gould

Ex-wife Barbara Eden wants ex-husband Hal Linden back. To make him jealous, she dates a well-known playboy. Comic mayhem follows. Lots of sight gags. This is an unrated TV movie.

1976 78 minutes

HOW TO MARRY A MILLIONAIRE

★★★

DIRECTOR: Jean Negulesco
CAST: Lauren Bacall, Marilyn Monroe, Betty Grable, William Powell, Cameron Mitchell, David Wayne, Rory Calhoun

The stars, Marilyn Monroe, Lauren Bacall, and Betty Grable, are fun to watch in this comedy. However, director Jean Negulesco doesn't do much to keep our interest. The story in this slight romp is all in the title—with William Powell giving the girls a run for his money.

1953 96 minutes

HOWIE MANDEL'S NORTH AMERICAN WATUSI TOUR

★★★½

DIRECTOR: Jerry Kramer
CAST: Howie Mandel

This Howie Mandel concert was filmed in Chicago and shows how much he has improved in his timing and delivery since his first special in 1983. His screaming and sight-gag props are still here, but his improvisation and interplay with the audience are now the highlights of his act. This group of fans really gets into the performance and you will, too.

1986 52 minutes

HUNK

DIRECTOR: Lawrence Bassoff
CAST: John Allen Nelson, Steve Levitt, Rebeccah Bush, Robert Morse, James Coco, Avery Schreiber, Deborah Shelton

A social outcast (John Allen Nelson) makes a deal with the devil (James Coco) to get a sexy, muscular body and then has to suffer the consequences in this dull, unfunny comedy. Rated PG.

1987 90 minutes

HYSTERICAL

★½

DIRECTOR: Chris Bearde
CAST: William, Mark, and Brett Hudson, Cindy Pickett, Richard Kiel, Julie Newmar, Bud Cort, Robert Donner, Murray Hamilton, Clint Walker, Franklin Ajaye, Charlie Callas, Keenan Wynn, Gary Owens

Zany horror spoof generates only a sprinkling of laughs as the bulk of its off-the-wall humor thuds embarrassingly. This movie was supposed to make the Hudson Brothers the Marx Brothers of the 1980s. The Hudsons have an undeniable charm, but their film debut is more like chicken poop than *Duck Soup*. Rated PG.

1983 87 minutes

I LOVE MY WIFE

★½

DIRECTOR: Mel Stuart
CAST: Elliott Gould, Brenda Vaccaro, Angel Tompkins, Dabney Coleman, Joan Tompkins

Barely laughable sex comedy dealing with the problems of an upper-class couple (Elliott Gould, Brenda Vaccaro) and their ridiculous attempts to solve them. Rather daring for the time and far too tame for today's audiences, this film would have been silly no matter when it was released. This a classic example of the way Elliott Gould was overexpose into near oblivion by a host of stupid exploitative films after his great success with *M*A*S*H*. This pointless film seems to go on and on. Rated PG.

1970 95 minutes

I LOVE YOU ALICE B. TOKLAS!

★★★

DIRECTOR: Hy Averback
CAST: Peter Sellers, Leigh Taylor-Young, Jo Van Fleet

Peter Sellers plays a lawyer-cum-hippie in this far-out comedy about middle-age crisis. Rated PG.

1968 93 minutes

I OUGHT TO BE IN PICTURES

★★★★

DIRECTOR: Herbert Ross
CAST: Walter Matthau, Ann-Margret, Dinah Manoff

Neil Simon's best work since *The Goodbye Girl*, this heartwarming story stars Walter Matthau as a father who deserts his Brooklyn family. Dinah Manoff is the daughter who wants to be a movie star, and Ann-Margret is the woman who brings the two together. Rated PG for mild profanity and brief nudity.

1982 107 minutes

I WILL, I WILL... FOR NOW

½

DIRECTOR: Norman Panama
CAST: Elliott Gould, Diane Keaton, Paul Sorvino, Victoria Principal, Robert Alda, Warren Berlinger

This is one of those mid-1970s trashers complete with mistaken-identity plot and a Santa Barbara sex clinic where "nothing is unnatural." Diane Keaton is the only one who comes out of this mess without looking ridiculous. Half a star for her ability to float above the wreckage. Rated R.

1976 96 minutes

IF...

★★★★

DIRECTOR: Lindsay Anderson
CAST: Malcolm McDowell, David Wood, Richard Warwick

This is British director Lindsay Anderson's black comedy about English private schools and the revolt against its strict code of behavior taken to the farthest limits of the imagination. Malcolm McDowell's movie debut. Rated R.

1969 111 minutes

I'M ALL RIGHT JACK

★★★½

DIRECTOR: John Boulting
CAST: Peter Sellers, Terry-Thomas, Ian Carmichael

British comedies can be marvelously entertaining, especially when they star Peter Sellers, as in this witty spoof of the absurdities of the labor movement carried to its ultimate extreme. This is humor at its best.

1960 B & W 101 minutes

IMPROPER CHANNELS

★

DIRECTOR: Eric Till
CAST: Alan Arkin, Mariette Hartley, Sarah Stevens, Monica Parker

Is this comedy... or bureaucratic nightmare? The two should mix, but unfortunately don't, in this story of an overeager social worker who accuses a father (Alan Arkin) of child abuse. Only the child (Sarah Stevens) is more than passably likable. The cheap cliché treatment of the doctors, nurses, policemen, lawyers, social workers, etc., is deplorable; and ethnic slurs abound. Rated PG for language.

1981 92 minutes

INCREDIBLE ROCKY MOUNTAIN RACE, THE

★★★

DIRECTOR: James L. Conway
CAST: Christopher Connelly, Forrest Tucker, Larry Storch, Jack Kruschen, Mike Mazurki

This western with a comic touch is about a race used by townspeople to get rid of two troublemakers. These troublemakers include

Mark Twain (Christopher Connelly) and his arch enemy, Mike Fink (Forrest Tucker). They are to race to the West Coast and retrieve five rare relics. There is more comedy as the snags increase and the problems get out of hand. Rated G.

1985 97 minutes

INCREDIBLE SHRINKING WOMAN, THE

★★

DIRECTOR: Joel Schumacher
CAST: Lily Tomlin, Ned Beatty, Henry Gibson, Elizabeth Wilson, Charles Grodin, Pamela Bellwood, Mike Douglas, Mark Blankfield

The great temptation in reviewing this comedy, starring Lily Tomlin, is to say that it falls prey to the law of diminishing returns—because it, like that assessment, all too often relies on bad puns and clichés. But to simply dismiss it as a failure would be inaccurate and unfair. This comic adaptation of Richard Matheson's classic science-fiction novel (*The Shrinking Man*) is not a bad movie. It's more like . . . well . . . the perfect old-fashioned Disney movie—a little corny and strained at times but not a total loss. Rated PG.

1981 88 minutes

INDISCREET

★

DIRECTOR: Leo McCarey
CAST: Gloria Swanson, Ben Lyon, Arthur Lake

Near-boring comedy-drama in which Gloria Swanson spends most of her time trying to conceal her questionable past from Ben Lyon. That she sings three songs does not help things a bit. Not to be confused with 1958's fine film of same title starring Ingrid Bergman and Cary Grant.

1931 B & W 92 minutes

IN-LAWS, THE

★★★★

DIRECTOR: Arthur Hiller
CAST: Peter Falk, Alan Arkin, Penny Peyser, Michael Lembeck

This delightful caper comedy mixes mystery and action with the fun. Vince Ricardo (Peter Falk) is the mastermind behind a bold theft of engravings of U.S. currency from a Treasury Department armored car. The caper is finished just in time for him to attend a dinner. His son, Tommy (Michael Lembeck), is to be married on Saturday, and Vince is to meet the parents of the bride (Penny Peyser). Her father, Sheldon Kornpett (Alan Arkin), is a slightly neurotic dentist. After just a few minutes with Vince, he is convinced the man is completely out of his mind, and soon they're off on a perilous mission. Falk and Arkin make a great team, playing off each other brilliantly. Rated PG.

1979 103 minutes

INSPECTOR GENERAL, THE

★★★★

DIRECTOR: Henry Koster
CAST: Danny Kaye, Walter Slezak, Elsa Lanchester

In this classic comedy set in Russia of the 1800s, Danny Kaye is the town fool who is mistaken for a confidant of Napoleon. The laughs come when Danny is caught up in court intrigue and really has no idea what is going on. Kaye's talents are showcased in this film.

1949 102 minutes

INTERNATIONAL HOUSE

★★★½

DIRECTOR: A. Edward Sutherland
CAST: W. C. Fields, Peggy Hopkins Joyce, Baby Rose Marie, Cab Calloway, Stu Erwin, George Burns and Gracie Allen, Bela Lugosi, Franklin

Pangborn, Edmund Breese, Sterling Holloway, Lumsden Hare

An offbeat, must-see film involving a melting pot of characters gathered at the luxurious International House Hotel to bid on the rights to the radioscope, an early version of television. As usual, a Russian muddies the waters with cunning and craft, while an American bumbles to the rescue. W. C. Fields and Burns and Allen are in rare form throughout, with Fields slipping through lines censors still find objectionable. The sight gags, too, are priceless. Among guest stars insinuated into scenes, look for Rudy Vallee and Colonel Stoopnagle and Bud.

1933 B & W 70 minutes

INVITATION TO THE WEDDING

★★

DIRECTOR: Joseph Brooks
CAST: John Gielgud, Ralph Richardson, Paul Nicholas, Elizabeth Shepherd

A feeble little British tale about a young American college student who falls in love with his best friend's sister, who just so happens to be engaged to an English war hero. The student is invited to the wedding in England, and during the rehearsal he's accidentally married to the girl by her bungling uncle, the village vicar (played with great style by Ralph Richardson). John Gielgud offers the only comic relief in this film as an Englishman-turned-Southern evangelist.

1973 89 minutes

IRMA LA DOUCE

★★★

DIRECTOR: Billy Wilder
CAST: Shirley MacLaine, Jack Lemmon, Lou Jacobi, Herschel Bernardi

Gendarme Jack Lemmon gets involved with prostitute Shirley MacLaine in what director Billy Wilder hoped would be another MacLaine/Lemmon hit like *The Apartment*. It isn't. It's raw humor in glorious color. Send the "Silver Spoons" set off to bed before you screen this one.

1963 142 minutes

ISHTAR

★★½

DIRECTOR: Elaine May
CAST: Warren Beatty, Dustin Hoffman, Isabelle Adjani, Charles Grodin, Jack Weston, Tess Harper, Carol Kane

A bloated, disjointed, and ponderous megabuck vanity production that might have been satisfying as a smaller film but sinks under its own weight. Warren Beatty and Dustin Hoffman star as a pair of inept, would-be singer-songwriters—named Rogers and Clarke, no less—who travel all the way to north Africa to get a booking. Once there, this latter-day *Road* picture completely derails, and our heroes wind up stranded in the Sahara Desert with a blind camel. Charles Grodin, as an unscrupulous CIA operative, outperforms everybody (except, perhaps, that poor camel); Tess Harper and Carol Kane fare less well during their all-too-brief screen time. Aside from Grodin, the film's only other highlights are the deliciously dreadful songs performed by Rogers and Clarke, all actually written by accomplished tunesmith Paul Williams. Rated PG-13 for language and brief nudity.

1987 107 minutes

IT

★★★

DIRECTOR: Clarence Badger
CAST: Clara Bow, Antonio Moreno, William Austin, Lloyd Corrigan, Jacqueline Gadsden, Gary Cooper

Advance promotion about *It* (read: sex appeal) made this clever little comedy about shopgirl Clara Bow chasing and catching her boss Antonio Moreno a solid hit. It also boosted redhaired Brooklyn bombshell Clara to superstardom. Rising star Gary Cooper appears only briefly. Silent.

1927 B & W 71 minutes

IT CAME FROM HOLLYWOOD

★★★

DIRECTORS: Malcolm Leo, Andrew Solt

CAST: Dan Aykroyd, John Candy, Cheech and Chong, Gilda Radner

Dan Aykroyd, John Candy, Cheech and Chong, and Gilda Radner appear in comedy vignettes as the hosts of this watchable *That's Entertainment*–style compilation of the worst all-time (but hilarious) losers such as *Plan 9 from Outer Space, Robot Monster, Batmen of Africa,* and *Untamed Women.* The *Star Wars* generation may not understand what's so funny about all this, but those who grew up in the 1950s and 1960s, when flying saucers were often hubcaps tossed into the air and monsters were guys in gorilla suits, are sure to get a kick out of it. Rated PG for sexual references and scatological humor.

1982 80 minutes

IT HAPPENED ONE NIGHT

★★★★★

DIRECTOR: Frank Capra

CAST: Clark Gable, Claudette Colbert, Ward Bond

Prior to *One Flew over the Cuckoo's Nest*, this 1934 comedy was the only film to capture all the major Academy Awards. Clark Gable stars as a cynical reporter on the trail of a runaway heiress, Claudette Colbert. They fall in love, of course, and the result is vintage movie magic.

1934 B & W 105 minutes

IT SHOULD HAPPEN TO YOU

★★½

DIRECTOR: George Cukor

CAST: Judy Holliday, Peter Lawford, Jack Lemmon, Michael O'Shea, Vaughn Taylor

Judy Holliday plays an actress who's desperate to garner publicity and hopes splashing her name across billboards all over New York City will ignite her career. The movie provides a steady stream of chuckles. Jack Lemmon makes an amusing screen debut. Holliday is hard to resist.

1954 B & W 81 minutes

IT'S A GIFT

★★★★

DIRECTOR: Norman Z. McLeod

CAST: W. C. Fileds, Kathleen Howard, Baby LeRoy, Julian Madison, Jean Rouverol, Tommy Bupp, Tammany Young, T. Roy Barnes

It's a treat for everyone to have the great W. C. Fields's best Paramount film available on videotape. In a class with the best of the comedies of the 1930s (including *Duck Soup*, *I'm No Angel*, *My Man Godfrey*), this classic was produced during the peak of Fields's association with Paramount Studios and is his archetypal vehicle, peopled with characters whose sole purpose in life seems to be to annoy the long-suffering Harold Bissonette. Originally titled *The Back Porch* and assembled from some of his vaudeville sketches as well as parts of his silent film *It's the Old Army Game*, this gem combines many of the elements Fields used in his short subjects and subsequent feature films (including *The Pharmacist* and *The Bank Dick*) and blends them into a side-splitting series of visual delights punctuated by the great comedian's verbal observations and dark mutterings.

1934 B & W 73 minutes

IT'S A MAD MAD MAD MAD WORLD

★★★★

DIRECTOR: Stanley Kramer

CAST: Spencer Tracy, Milton Berle, Jonathan Winters, Buddy Hackett, Sid Caesar, Phil Silvers, Mickey Rooney, Peter Falk, Dick Shawn, Ethel Merman, Buster Keaton, Jimmy Durante, Edie Adams, Dorothy Provine, Terry-Thomas, William Demarest, Andy Devine

Spencer Tracy and a cast made up of "Who's Who of American Comedy" are combined in this wacky chase movie to end all chase movies. Tracy is the crafty police captain who is following the progress of various money-mad citizens out to beat one another in discovering the buried hiding place of 350,000 stolen dollars.

1963 154 minutes

IT'S IN THE BAG

★★★

DIRECTOR: Richard Wallace

CAST: Fred Allen, Jack Benny, Binnie Barnes, Robert Benchley, Victor Moore, Sidney Toler, Rudy Vallee, William Bendix, Don Ameche

The plot (if there ever was one) derives from the Russian fable about an impoverished nobleman on a treasure hunt. Continuity soon goes out the window, however, when the cast starts winging it in one hilarious episode after another. This is Fred Allen, acerbic and nasal as always, in his best screen comedy. Those who yearn for the return of vaudeville and radio as it once was will love this wacky romp. A high point is an encounter between Fred and Jack that's bound to stir a lot of memories.

1945 B & W 87 minutes

IZZY & MOE

★★★½

DIRECTOR: Jackie Cooper

CAST: Jackie Gleason, Art Carney, Cynthia Harris, Zohra Lampert, Drew Snyder

Together for the last time, Jackie Gleason and Art Carney are near perfect as two ex-vaudevillians who become New York Prohibition agents in this made-for-TV movie based on actual characters. The two stars still work beautifully together after all these years. This is not as hilarious as you might expect, but there are plenty of amusing scenes, and it is fun to watch these two pros perform.

1985 100 minutes

JABBERWOCKY

★★½

DIRECTOR: Terry Gilliam

CAST: Michael Palin, Max Wall, Deborah Fallender, Annette Badland

Monty Python fans will be disappointed to see only one group member, Michael Palin, in this British film. Palin plays a dim-witted peasant during the Dark Ages. A monster called Jabberwocky is destroying villages all over the countryside, so Palin tries to destroy the monster. There are some funny moments but nothing in comparison with true Python films. No MPAA rating.

1977 100 minutes

JACK BENNY PROGRAM, THE (TELEVISION SERIES)

★★★★

DIRECTOR: Fred De Cordova

CAST: Jack Benny, Mary Livingstone, Eddie "Rochester" Anderson, Dennis Day, Don Wilson, Mel Blanc

Following the formula that had made him a smash on radio, Jack Benny became a fixture on TV. His show ran from 1950—1964 on CBS, plus a season on NBC. Bolstered by the topnotch character actors who popped up on the show, Benny held the spotlight with a pregnant pause, a hand on the chin, or a shift of the eyes. Comic bits frequently revolved around Benny's stinginess and deadly violin playing. A host of stars visited the show over the years, appearing in songs and/or sketches. The roster on video includes Ernie Kovacs, Jayne Mansfield, Johnny Carson, Connie Francis, The Smothers Brothers, George Burns, Humphrey Bogart, Kirk Douglas, Fred Allen, Ann-Margret, and Bob Hope.

1950–1965 B & W 30 minutes

JAY LENO'S AMERICAN DREAM

★★★½

DIRECTOR: Ira Wohl
CAST: Jay Leno

Talented comedian Jay Leno takes an irreverent look at all that is Americana as he saunters through much of this video in a glossy silver sports coat. His commentary is salty and enjoyable because it hits all too close to home. One particularly funny segment finds Leno in the hubof U.S. quality workmanship:an economy car factory. What's the catch? They manufacture toy cars! This comedy video is recommended for those who don't have a hard time laughing at themselves, because sooner or later you're likely to find the finger pointed at you.

1986 49 minutes

JEKYLL & HYDE—TOGETHER AGAIN

★★★

DIRECTOR: Jerry Belson
CAST: Mark Blankfield, Bess Armstrong, Krista Erickson

If you like offbeat, crude, and timely humor, you'll enjoy this 1980s-style version of Robert Louis Stevenson's horror classic. Though the film needs some editing, Mark Blankfield is a riot as the mad scientist who can't snort enough of the powdery white stuff he's invented. Rated R for heavy doses of vulgarity and sexual innuendo.

1982 87 minutes

JERK, THE

★★★★

DIRECTOR: Carl Reiner
CAST: Steve Martin, Bernadette Peters, Bill Macy, Jackie Mason

Steve Martin made a very funny film debut in this wacky comedy. Nonfans probably won't like it, but then Martin has always had limited appeal. For those who think he's hilarious, the laughs just keep on coming. Rated R.

1979 94 minutes

JERRY LEWIS LIVE

DIRECTOR: Arthur Forrest
CAST: Jerry Lewis

One of the worst stand-up comedy tapes we've viewed so far. Jerry Lewis's comedy is dull and pointless. His pantomime is poor and his singing even worse. Lewis is straining to prove himself—as if we didn't know who he is. And when he caps almost every shtick with an obnoxious cackle and a comment on how dumb his jokes are, the viewer is only too aware of how miserable an unfunny comedian can be.

1984 73 minutes

JINXED

★★★

DIRECTOR: Don Siegel
CAST: Bette Midler, Ken Wahl, Rip Torn, Benson Fong

Bette Midler is in peak form as a would-be cabaret singer who enlists the aid of a blackjack dealer (Ken Wahl) in a plot to murder her gambler boyfriend (Rip Torn) in this often funny black comedy, directed by Don Siegel (*Dirty Harry*; *Invasion of the Body Snatchers*). If it weren't for Midler, you'd notice how silly and unbelievable it all is. However, she's so watchable you don't mind suspending your disbelief. Rated R for profanity and sexual situations.

1982 103 minutes

JOCKS

DIRECTOR: Steve Carver
CAST: Scott Strader, Perry Lang, Mariska Hargitay, Richard Roundtree, Christopher Lee

Discounting Christopher Lee's brief appearance in this stupid film, Richard Roundtree is the only one with true acting ability. Roundtree plays a tennis coach at L.A. College, who must make his goofy team champions in order to keep his job. Scott Strader plays Kid, the ace tennis player and chief party organizer. The tennis match is in the background as the team concentrates on getting drunk and finding women. Rated R for nudity and obscenities.

1986 90 minutes

JOE PISCOPO VIDEO, THE

★★½

DIRECTOR: Jay Dubin
CAST: Joe Piscopo, Eddie Murphy, Joseph Bologna, Jan Hooks

This HBO special has some funny moments, most deriving from Joe Piscopo's impressions. But aside from a Frank Sinatra look-alike singing in a heavy-metal rock band and a "Thriller" spinoff where the ghouls popping up out of the graveyard are Jerry Lewis clones *à la The Nutty Professor*, the moments are delivered in a quick montage and then disappear for good. Most of the video centers on Piscopo's stand-up comedy act. Eddie Murphy puts in a guest appearance, but even he is not all that funny here. Not rated, but has profanity.

1984 60 minutes

JOHNNY DANGEROUSLY

★

DIRECTOR: Amy Heckerling
CAST: Michael Keaton, Joe Piscopo, Marilu Henner, Maureen Stapleton

In this fitfully funny spoof of 1930s gangster movies, Michael Keaton (*Mr. Mom*) and Joe Piscopo (*Saturday Night Live*) play rival crime lords. Directed by Amy Heckerling (*Fast Times at Ridgemont High*), it leaves the viewer with genuinely mixed feelings. That's because many of its gags rely on shock laughs (such as when Maureen Stapleton confesses to Marilu Henner that she "goes both ways"—sick!) and others never seem to make it to the punchline. Rated PG-13 for violence and profanity.

1984 90 minutes

JOSEPH ANDREWS

★★

DIRECTOR: Tony Richardson
CAST: Ann-Margret, Peter Firth, Beryl Reid, Michael Hordern, Jim Dale, John Gielgud, Hugh Griffith, Wendy Craig, Peggy Ashcroft

Follows the adventures of Joseph Andrews (Peter Firth) as he rises from lowly servant to personal footman and becomes the fancy of Lady Boaby (Ann-Margret). This is director Tony Richardson's second attempt to transform a Henry Fielding novel to film. Unfortunately, the first-rate cast cannot save this ill-fated attempt to restage *Tom Jones*. Rated R for sex and profanity.

1977 99 minutes

JOSHUA THEN AND NOW

★★★★½

DIRECTOR: Ted Kotcheff

CAST: James Woods, Alan Arkin, Gabrielle Lazure, Michael Sarrazin, Linda Sorensen

Based by screenwriter Mordecai Richler (*The Apprenticeship of Duddy Kravitz*) on his autobiographical novel of the same name, this little-known gem is blessed with humor, poignancy, and insight. James Woods, is wonderful as Jewish writer Joshua Shapiro, whose life seems to be in shambles at the beginning of the picture. But, as we see in flashbacks, he is a hard guy to keep down. Surviving an embarrassing upbringing by a gangster father (Alan Arkin in his funniest performance ever) and a would-be entertainer mother (Linda Sorensen), who as a special treat strips at his bar mitzvah, Joshua nearly meets his match in the snobbish high society of his WASP wife (Gabrielle Lazure). Although *Joshua Then and Now* may occasionally be a bit too raw for some viewers, its unerring sense of humanity and humor should put aside all objections. Rated R for profanity, nudity, suggested sex, and adult themes.

1985 118 minutes

JOY OF SEX, THE

★★

DIRECTOR: Martha Coolidge

CAST: Michelle Meyrink, Cameron Dye, Lisa Langlois

You have to give credit to director Martha Coolidge (*Valley Girl*) for trying to do something different with *The Joy of Sex*. With a title like that, you'd expect it to be another teen lust movie with lots of topless young women, boys leering and drooling after girls, and gross humor. This comedy, about the plight of two virgins, male and female, unhappy with their status in a sex-crazy age, has very few such offensive elements. But there is one problem: It isn't funny. Rated R for profanity, suggested sex, and scatological humor.

1984 93 minutes

JOY STICKS

DIRECTOR: Greydon Clark

CAST: Joe Don Baker, Leif Green, Logan Ramsey

The alleged story in *Joy Sticks* is that a wealthy businessman (Joe Don Baker) wants to shut down the local video gameroom frequented by his teen-age daughter. Little of interest happens. Rated R.

1983 88 minutes

JUMPIN' JACK FLASH

★★½

DIRECTOR: Penny Marshall

CAST: Whoopi Goldberg, Stephen Collins, John Wood, Carol Kane, Jim Belushi, Annie Potts, Peter Michael Goetz, Roscoe Lee Browne, Jeroen Krabbe, Jonathan Pryce

Comedienne Whoopi Goldberg's inspired clowning is the only worthwhile element in her first big-screen comedy. She plays a computer operator who breaks the monotony of her job by sending personal messages. Then she gets one from an endangered undercover agent and finds herself involved in international intrigue. The film is worth watching if only for the hilarious scene in which Goldberg attempts to decipher the lyrics to the title song by the

Rolling Stones. Rated R for profanity and violence.

1986 100 minutes

JUST ONE OF THE GUYS

★★★

DIRECTOR: Lisa Gottlieb

CAST: Joyce Hyser, Clayton Rohner, Billy Jacoby, Toni Hudson

A sort of reverse *Tootsie*, this surprisingly restrained and humanistic teen-lust comedy stars Joyce Hyser as Terry Griffith, an attractive young woman who switches high schools and sexes to overcome an imagined prejudice against her writing and win a journalism prize. The premise is flimsy and forced, but director Lisa Gottlieb and her cast do a wonderful job of keeping the viewer interested and entertained. Rated PG-13 for nudity, violence, and profanity.

1985 88 minutes

JUST TELL ME WHAT YOU WANT

★½

DIRECTOR: Sidney Lumet

CAST: Alan King, Ali MacGraw, Peter Weller, Myrna Loy, Keenan Wynn, Tony Roberts, Dina Merrill

Alan King gives a fine performance in this otherwise forgettable film as an executive who attempts to get his mistress (Ali MacGraw) back. She's in love with a younger man (Peter Weller), and King will do anything to get her back. She's not interested, and the viewer is soon fast asleep. Rated R.

1980 112 minutes

JUST YOU AND ME, KID

★★

DIRECTOR: Leonard Stern

CAST: George Burns, Brooke Shields, Ray Bolger, Lorraine Gary, Burl Ives

The delights of George Burns as an ex–vaudeville performer do not mask the worthless plot in this tale of Burns's attempt to hide a young runaway (Brooke Shields) fleeing a drug dealer. Shields's inability to move with Burns's rhythm rapidly becomes annoying. It all plays like a subpar made-for-TV movie, which is no surprise since director-co-writer Leonard Stern made this his feature-film debut after years of work in television. Rated PG for mild language and brief nudity.

1979 93 minutes

KENTUCKY FRIED MOVIE

★★★

DIRECTOR: John Landis

CAST: Evan Kim, Master Bong Soo-Han, Bill Bixby, Donald Sutherland

The first film outing of the creators of *Airplane!* is an on-again, off-again collection of comedy skits. Directed by John Landis, the best bits involve a Bruce Lee takeoff and a surprise appearance by Wally and the Beaver. Rated R.

1977 78 minutes

KEYSTONE COMEDIES, VOL. 1

★★★

DIRECTOR: Roscoe Arbuckle

CAST: Roscoe Arbuckle, Minta Durfee, Al St. John, Louise Fazenda, Edgar Kennedy, Joe Bordeaux

Fatty's Faithful Fido, Fatty's Tintype Tangle, and *Fatty's New Role* —three fast-moving bop-and-bash comedies in the celebrated Fatty series produced by Mack Sennett at Keystone Studios in 1915—compose this first of five volumes devoted to the famed silent comedian's artistry. *Fatty's Faithful Fido* is a comedy action gem. The dog comes close to stealing the show. Slapstick humor in the classic mold.

1915 B & W 46 minutes

KEYSTONE COMEDIES, VOL. 2

★★★

DIRECTOR: Roscoe Arbuckle

CAST: Roscoe Arbuckle, Mabel Normand, Minta Durfee, Al St. John, Alice Davenport, Joe Bordeaux

Mack Sennett hit real reel paydirt when he teamed rotund comic Roscoe Arbuckle and elfin comedienne Mabel Normand in a film series. These three examples—*Fatty and Mabel at the San Diego Exposition, Fatty and Mabel's Simple Life,* and *Mabel's Washday*—amply show why. Classic double-take slapstick silent comedy.

1915 B & W 42 minutes

KEYSTONE COMEDIES, VOL. 3

★★★

DIRECTOR: Roscoe Arbuckle

CAST: Roscoe Arbuckle, Mabel Normand, Minta Durfee, Dora Rogers, Alice Davenport, Al St. John, Owen Moore

Four more stanzas in the screen lives of two of silent film's great comedic performers: Roscoe Arbuckle and Mabel Normand. They're all "watch springs and elastic" as they create marvelous mayhem in *Mabel Lost and Won Wished on Mabel, Mabel, Fatty and the Law* and *Fatty's Plucky Pup*. This quartet from Mack Sennett's legendary film fun factory can't help but raise laughter.

1915 B & W 58 minutes

KEYSTONE COMEDIES: VOL. 4

★★★

DIRECTOR: Roscoe Arbuckle

CAST: Roscoe Arbuckle, Mabel Normand, Edgar Kennedy, Glenn Cavender, Ford Sterling, Mae Busch, Al St. John, Alice Davenport

Three stanzas in the sidesplitting Fatty-and-Mabel slapstick series Mack Sennett connived and contrived between 1912 and 1916: *Mabel's Willful Way, That Little Band of Gold*, and *Mabel and Fatty's Married Life*. Mayhem and mirth only past masters of the double take and pratfall can muster. Roscoe Arbuckle and Mabel Normand are marvelous in these comedy capers from days long gone.

1915 B & W 44 minutes

KEYSTONE COMEDIES: VOL. 5

★★★

DIRECTOR: Roscoe Arbuckle

CAST: Roscoe Arbuckle, Bill Bennett, Walter Reed, Edgar Kennedy, Harold Lloyd, Joe Bordeaux, Minta Durfee, Ford Sterling, Charles Arling, Joe Swickard, Dora Rogers, Nick Cogley, Charles Chase, W. C. Hauber

Fabled Mack Sennett's madcap mob of laugh-catchers dish up three more hilarious happy helpings of classic silent comedy: *Miss Fatty's Seaside Lovers, Court House Crooks,* and *Love Loot and Crash.* Keystone Studio's pride, roly-poly Roscoe Arbuckle, is a tubby terror in drag. Here's slapstick comedy in the sea and off the wall in days of yore.

1915 B & W 45 minutes

KID FROM BROOKLYN, THE

★★★

DIRECTOR: Norman Z. McLeod

CAST: Danny Kaye, Virginia Mayo, Vera-Ellen, Steve Cochran, Eve Arden

Danny Kaye is fine as the comedy lead in this remake of Harold Lloyd's *The Milky Way.* He plays the milkman who becomes a prizefighter. Good family entertainment.

1946 104 minutes

KIND HEARTS AND CORONETS

★★★★

DIRECTOR: Robert Hamer
CAST: Dennis Price, Alec Guinness, Valerie Hobson

A young man (Dennis Price) thinks up a novel way to speed up his inheritance—by killing off all the other heirs. This is the central premise of this arresting black comedy, which manages to poke fun at mass murder and get away with it. Alec Guinness plays all eight of his victims.

1949 104 minutes

KING IN NEW YORK, A

★★½

DIRECTOR: Charles Chaplin
CAST: Charlie Chaplin, Dawn Addams, Michael Chaplin

Supposedly anti-American, this 1957 film by Charles Chaplin, not seen in the United States until 1973, was a big let-down to his fans, who had built their worship on *Easy Street*, *City Lights*, *Modern Times*, and *The Great Dictator*. It pokes fun at the 1950s, with its witch hunts and burgeoning post-war technology. It is not the Chaplin of old, but just old Chaplin, and too much of him.

1957 B & W 105 minutes

KISS ME GOODBYE

★★★

DIRECTOR: Robert Mulligan
CAST: Sally Field, James Caan, Jeff Bridges, Claire Trevor

Sally Field plays a widow of three years who has just fallen in love again. Her first husband was an electrifying Broadway choreographer named Jolly (James Caan). Her husband-to-be is a slightly stuffy Egyptologist (Jeff Bridges). Before her wedding day she receives a visit from Jolly's ghost, who is apparently upset about the approaching wedding. Rated PG for profanity and sexual situations.

1982 101 minutes

KNOWHUTIMEAN?

★★★

DIRECTOR: John R. Cherry III
CAST: Jim Varney

A fun, if slightly repetitive, collection of Ernest commercials followed by a series of skits featuring Varney as a variety of Ernest's colorful ancestors. A must for Jim Varney fans.

1983 57 minutes

KOTCH

★★★★

DIRECTOR: Jack Lemmon
CAST: Walter Matthau, Deborah Winters, Felicia Farr

Walter Matthau gives an affecting performance in this heartwarming film. He plays a senior citizen who has a lot more smarts than anyone gives him credit for and a lot more heart than anyone around him deserves. It's a splendid motion picture the whole family will love. Rated PG.

1971 113 minutes

LADY EVE, THE

★★★★

DIRECTOR: Preston Sturges
CAST: Barbara Stanwyck, Henry Fonda, Charles Coburn, William Demarest

Barbara Stanwyck, Henry Fonda, and Charles Coburn are first-rate in this romantic comedy, which was brilliantly written and directed by Preston Sturges. Fonda is a rather simple-minded millionaire, and Stanwyck is the conniving woman who seeks to snare him. The results are hilarious.

1941 B & W 94 minutes

LADYKILLERS, THE

★★★★½

DIRECTOR: Alexander Mackendrick

CAST: Alec Guinness, Peter Sellers, Cecil Parker

England had a golden decade of great comedies during the 1950s. *The Ladykillers* is one of the best. Alec Guinness and Peter Sellers are teamed as a couple of small-time criminals who have devised what they believe to be the perfect crime. Unfortunately, their plans are thwarted by the sweetest, most innocent little old landlady you'd ever want to meet. Great fun!

1955 87 minutes

LAST AMERICAN VIRGIN, THE

★

DIRECTOR: Boaz Davidson

CAST: Lawrence Monoson, Diane Franklin, Steve Antin, Joe Rubbo, Louisa Moritz

Tawdry teen-sex flick with one of the worst morals ever captured on film: don't bother to help a friend, 'cause he (or she) will burn you every time. Writer director Boaz Davidson must have led one miserable childhood. Lawrence Monoson, Steve Antin, and Joe Rubbo are three buddies in search of the usual sexual thrills; the lame comedy of the premise is offset by the graphic cruelty of the encounters. Most ludicrous is a scene where two of our heroes start getting hot with a couple of curvaceous cuties, only to discover distinctly male genitals on their "women." Diane Franklin, a charming young actress, has what must be the meanest part ever written. Only for masochists. Rated R for sex.

1982 92 minutes

LAST MARRIED COUPLE IN AMERICA, THE

★★

DIRECTOR: Gilbert Cates

CAST: Natalie Wood, George Segal, Arlene Golonka, Bob Dishy, Priscilla Barnes, Dom De Luise, Valerie Harper

Lamebrained little sex farce about one perfect couple's struggle to hold their own marriage together amid the divorces and separations around them. The cast includes Dom De Luise as a plumber–turned–porn star and Valerie Harper as a seductress in a blond wig. Tries desperately to be hip but ends up as nothing more than a smutty little dirty joke with a lot of very annoying characters. Redeemed only by the incandescent Natalie Wood. Rated R for profanity and nudity.

1980 103 minutes

LAST OF THE RED HOT LOVERS

★½

DIRECTOR: Gene Saks

CAST: Alan Arkin, Paula Prentiss, Sally Kellerman

Alan Arkin plays a married man trying to sneak around, in this 1972 comedy. He uses his mother's apartment for his rendezvous and cracks us up with his unsuave manner. Rated PG.

1972 98 minutes

LAST POLKA, THE

★★★★

DIRECTOR: John Blanchard

CAST: John Candy, Eugene Levy, Catherine O'Hara, Rick Moranis

This made-for-HBO special features the unique Second City comedy of Yosh (John Candy) and Stan (Eugene Levy) Schmenge, a delightful pair of polka bandleaders, as they reminisce about their checkered musical careers. Fellow SCTV troupe members Catherine O'Hara and Rick Moranis add to the hilarity in this adept send-up of *The Last Waltz*, Martin Scorsese's documentary chronicling the final concert of real-life rock legends The Band.

1984 60 minutes

LAST REMAKE OF BEAU GESTE, THE

★

DIRECTOR: Marty Feldman
CAST: Marty Feldman, Michael York, Ann-Margret, Trevor Howard

We have Marty Feldman's success in *Young Frankenstein* to thank for this vapid Foreign Legion comedy, Feldman's first (and last) attempt at the triple crown of writing, directing, and starring. Most of the desert hijinks play like television outtakes, and the good supporting cast is given little to do. If you try for the long haul, watch for Feldman's sequence with "co-star" Gary Cooper in footage intercut from the 1939 classic. Overall, this is pretty dry stuff. Rated PG—sexual situations.

1977 84 minutes

LAST RESORT

★★½

DIRECTOR: Zane Buzby
CAST: Charles Grodin, Jon Lovitz, Robin Pearson Rose, Megan Mullally, John Ashton

Charles Grodin and family are off on vacation to Club Sand, which turns out to be Army cots, marauding armed guerrillas, and horny club counselors. Amid slapstick jokes and Grodin's exasperated yelling is an intermittently entertaining movie. Rated R for sex and language.

1985 80 minutes

LAUREL AND HARDY CLASSICS, VOLUME 1

★★★

DIRECTORS: James Parrott, Charles Rogers
CAST: Stan Laurel, Oliver Hardy, Billy Gilbert, Charlie Hall

This collection contains *The Music Box*, *County Hospital*, *The Live Ghost*, and *Twice Two*. *The Music Box* won an Oscar as the Best Short of 1932. In it, Stan Laurel and Oliver Hardy attempt to deliver a piano up a long flight of stairs to the home of Theodore Swarzenhoffen (Billy Gilbert), a man who is crazy about pianos. Other than that outstanding offering, this is a mediocre collection of L&H comedy.

1930s B & W 90 minutes

LAUREL AND HARDY CLASSICS, VOLUME 2

★★★★★

DIRECTORS: James Parrott, George Marshall
CAST: Stan Laurel, Oliver Hardy, Stanley Sanford, Charlie Hall

Packed with laughs in every minute, this collection contains *Blotto*, *Towed in a Hole*, *Brats*, and *Hog Wild*, four of the best short comedies produced by this classic team. While some of the situations might seem dated (sneaking out to drink booze during Prohibition and putting up a radio antenna), the development of the plots is flawless and transcends time. The plots and laughs proceed relentlessly, wrapping the viewer in an insane logic that cannot be stopped. *Brats* features the team as their own children, revealing the childlike appeal of the adult characters by juxtaposition. This is the best of the short-subject collections.

1930s B & W 80 minutes

LAUREL AND HARDY CLASSICS, VOLUME 3

★★½

DIRECTORS: Lloyd French, George Marshall

CAST: Stan Laurel, Oliver Hardy, Mae Busch, Charlie Hall

Four more Laurel and Hardy short subjects: *Oliver the Eighth*, *Busy Bodies*, *Their First Mistake*, and *Dirty Work*. *Busy Bodies* is by far the best of the bunch, with a lumber-factory setting. *Dirty Work* has the team cleaning the chimney of a mad scientist who invents a youth potion—with Ollie getting a dose and returning to his Darwinian beginnings.

1930s B & W 80 minutes

LAUREL AND HARDY CLASSICS, VOLUME 4

★★★

DIRECTORS: James W. Horne, James Parrott

CAST: Stan Laurel, Oliver Hardy, Charlie Hall, James Finlayson, Walter Long, Mae Busch

In *Another Fine Mess*, Stan Laurel and Oliver Hardy are trapped in a house when escaping from the police. The house is for rent, and they are mistaken for the owner and his servants by prospective renters. Stan plays both male and female servants, while Ollie bluffs his way through the house's merits ("Now, where did I put that billiard room?"). James Finlayson, the rightful owner, returns for a rousing finale. *Laughing Gray* has Stan and Ollie attempting to hide a forbidden dog in their room on a freezing winter's night. *Come Clean* starts with a simple trip for ice cream, but after saving Mae Busch's life, Stan and Ollie can't get rid of her. *Any Old Port* pits them against Walter Long twice; once as the manager of a hotel and again as a boxer. This collection contains a consistently entertaining group of short subjects.

1930s B & W 90 minutes

LAUREL AND HARDY CLASSICS, VOLUME 5

★★★

DIRECTOR: James Parrott

CAST: Stan Laurel, Oliver Hardy, Edgar Kennedy, Anita Garvin

Two good and two moderate comedies—*Perfect Day*, *Helpmates*, *Be Big*, and *Night Owls*, respectively—make up this tape. *Perfect Day* is an example of how an idea can generate ideas and laughs spontaneously; the film was originally supposed to include another sequence, but Stan Laurel and Oliver Hardy created new ideas on the spot and generated laughs as the cameras rolled to fill up the film's running time. In *Helpmates*, the action develops from a simple idea: Ollie has to clean up the house so that his wife won't know he's hosted a party in her absence. From this simple beginning, laughs are many and well earned. The two other films are not top-rated L&H.

1930s B & W 80 minutes

LAUREL AND HARDY CLASSICS, VOLUME 6

★★★★

DIRECTORS: James W. Horne, Charles Rogers

CAST: Stan Laurel, Oliver Hardy, Mae Busch, Charlie Hall

A collection of topnotch comedies all: *Our Wife*, *The Fixer-Uppers*, *Them Thar Hills*, and *Tit for Tat*. *Them Thar Hills* is a marvelous blend of logic and silliness, with Stan and Ollie going to the mountains for Ollie's health and ending up in a tit-for-tat duel with Charlie Hall. The duel is resumed in

Tit for Tat, the only sequel ever made by L&H. The boys unknowingly open an electrical store next to Hall's grocery, and the tit-for-tat continues unabated from the previous encounter. (Ollie delivers a nicely risqué line, often unheard amidst the laughs in movie houses, as he emerges from Hall's upstairs with Mrs. Hall.) *The Fixer-Uppers* has Stan and Ollie selling greeting cards for all occasions. And *Our Wife*, the weakest of the group, has a scene that forecasts the stateroom sequence in the Marx Brothers' *A Night at the Opera*.

1930s B & W 80 minutes

LAUREL AND HARDY CLASSICS, VOLUME 7

★★½

DIRECTORS: James Parrott, James W. Horne, Lloyd French, Charles Rogers

CAST: Stan Laurel, Oliver Hardy, Charlie Hall, James Finlayson

A collection of two moderately funny films, *Thicker Than Water* and *Midnight Patrol*, and two well-done films, *Below Zero* and *Me and My Pal*. *Me and My Pal* is an excruciatingly funny story of obsession and dedication to a single purpose—in this case, completing a jigsaw puzzle. *Below Zero* is a tale of lost-and-found opportunities, and the moral is that some opportunities are better left for someone else! *Water* pits Stan and Ollie, once again, against Ollie's wife. *Patrol* places Stan and Ollie in the police force. It may bear the distinction of having the most gruesome ending of any of their films.

1930s B & W 80 minutes

LAUREL AND HARDY CLASSICS, VOLUME 8

★★

DIRECTORS: Lewis Foster, James W. Horne, James Parrott

CAST: Stan Laurel, Oliver Hardy, Stanley Sanford, Billy Gilbert

Men o' War is the standout of this collection. As sailors on leave, Laurel and Hardy attempt to impress two young ladies in Los Angeles' MacArthur Park. Ice cream doesn't seem to work, so they rent a boat to demonstrate their nautical prowess—and end up in a free-for-all in the middle of the lake with other boaters. *One Good Turn* has them attempting to help an older woman save her home. *The Laurel and Hardy Murder Case*, the weakest film here, is a parody of murder mysteries.

1930s B & W 70 minutes

LAVENDER HILL MOB, THE

★★★★★

DIRECTOR: Charles Crichton

CAST: Alec Guinness, Stanley Holloway, Sidney James, Alfie Bass

Fun, fun, and more fun from this 1951 most celebrated British comedy. Alec Guinness is a mousy bank clerk. He has a plan for intercepting the bank's armored-car shipment. With the aid of a few friends he forms an amateur robbery squad. Lo and behold, they escape with the loot. After all, the plan was foolproof. Or was it? Be sure to see the outcome for yourself.

1951 B & W 82 minutes

LEMON DROP KID, THE

★★★

DIRECTOR: Sidney Lanfield

CAST: Bob Hope, Marilyn Maxwell, Lloyd Nolan, Jane Darwell, Andrea King, Fred Clark,

Jay C. Flippen, William Frawley

Great group of character actors makes this Damon Runyon story of an incompetent bookie, who has to cough up some money quick or breathe his last, work like a charm. Fast-talking Bob Hope has the tailor-made leading role, and the fast patter and scene-stealing that goes on with pros like Jay C. Flippen and William Frawley is a treat to watch. Deadly Lloyd Nolan plays the guy putting the screws to Hope, and Marilyn Maxwell plays the girl caught in the middle. Jane Darwell rounds out an impeccable cast.

1951 B & W 91 minutes

LET'S DO IT AGAIN

★★★½

DIRECTOR: Sidney Poitier

CAST: Sidney Poitier, Bill Cosby, Jimmie Walker, Calvin Lockhart, John Amos

After scoring with *Uptown Saturday Night*, Sidney Poiter and Bill Cosby decided to reteam for another enjoyable comedy in 1975. Jimmie Walker, Calvin Lockhart, and John Amos are also on hand to add to the fun in this tale of a couple of lodge brothers taking on the gangsters. Rated PG.

1975 112 minutes

LETTER TO BREZHNEV

★★★½

DIRECTOR: Chris Bernard

CAST: Alexandra Pigg, Alfred Molina, Peter Firth, Margi Clarke

This wistful, spunky little movie presents two young women of Liverpool who decide to forgo their usual night out at the local Kirby disco in favor of a night in town, where they befriend a couple of Russian sailors. Teresa (played by Liverpool's stand-up comedienne Margi Clarke) is just after some fun, but Elaine (Alexandra Pigg) falls in love with her sailor. The men have to return to Russia the next day, but Elaine is determined to keep the relationship. Peter Firth plays Elaine's love and he's the quintessence of sweetness. With his little bulb of a nose and blond curls, he's a cherub in a sailor suit. Alexandra Pigg gives the film some street-talking sass and Firth imbues it with adorable innocence.

1985 95 minutes

LIBELED LADY

★★★★★

DIRECTOR: Jack Conway

CAST: William Powell, Myrna Loy, Spencer Tracy, Jean Harlow

Their fame as Nick and Nora Charles in the *Thin Man* series notwithstanding, this is the finest film to have paired William Powell and Myrna Loy. They take part in a deliciously funny tale of a newspaper that, when faced with a libel suit from an angered woman, attempts to turn the libel into irrefutable fact. Spencer Tracy and Jean Harlow lend their considerable support, and the result is a delight from start to finish. In spite of its age, the story remains fresh; if anything, it takes on even more meaning during these times of litigation run amok.

1936 98 minutes

LIFE OF BRIAN

★★★★

DIRECTOR: Terry Jones

CAST: Terry Jones, John Cleese, Eric Idle, Michael Palin, Terry Gilliam, Graham Chapman

Religious fanaticism gets a real drubbing in this irreverent and often sidesplitting comedy, which features and was created by those Monty Python crazies. Graham Chapman plays the title role of a reluctant "savior" born in a manger just down the street from Jesus Christ's. Rated R for nudity and profanity.

1979 93 minutes

LIFE WITH FATHER

★★★★

DIRECTOR: Michael Curtiz
CAST: William Powell, Irene Dunne, Edmund Gwenn, ZaSu Pitts, Jimmy Lydon, Elizabeth Taylor, Martin Milner

A warm, witty, charming, nostalgic memoir of life and the coming of age of author Clarence Day in turn-of-the-century New York City. Centering on his staid, eccentric father (William Powell), the film is a 100 percent delight. Based on the long-running Broadway play.

1947 118 minutes

LI'L ABNER

★½

DIRECTOR: Albert S. Rogell
CAST: Granville Owen, Martha Driscoll, Buster Keaton, Mona Ray, Johnnie Morris, Kay Sutton, Edgar Kennedy, Chester Conklin, Billy Bevan, Al St. John

The first of two filmed versions of Al Capp's popular comic strip boasts a great cast of silent film's best clowns but comes across with a thud—no timing, no suspense, no laughs. The bizarre make-up and outlandish costumes alone are almost enough to recommend this oddity, one of a handful of movies based on the Sunday pages and aimed at general audiences. All the actors have fared much better in other ventures. This would be an interesting double bill with 1932's *Little Orphan Annie*, also featuring Edgar Kennedy.

1940 B & W 78 minutes

LILY IN LOVE

★★★★

DIRECTOR: Karoly Makk
CAST: Christopher Plummer, Maggie Smith, Elke Sommer, Adolph Green

Christopher Plummer is superb as an aging, egocentric actor who disguises himself as a younger man in an attempt to snag a plum role in a film written by his wife (Maggie Smith), and succeeds all too well. *Lily in Love* is a marvelously warm and witty adult comedy. That's adult as in appealing to mature audiences rather than steeped in sex and nudity. There are no teenagers, special effects, sex scenes, or acts of violence. It is simply a very fine motion picture that dares to do something different, and does it extremely well. Unrated, the film has some profanity.

1985 105 minutes

LIMELIGHT

★★★½

DIRECTOR: Charles Chaplin
CAST: Charlie Chaplin, Claire Bloom, Buster Keaton, Sydney Chaplin, Nigel Bruce

Too long and too much Charlie Chaplin (who trimmed Buster Keaton's part when it became obvious he was stealing the film), this is nevertheless a poignant excursion. Chaplin is an aging music hall comic on the skids who saves a ballerina (Claire Bloom) from suicide and, while bolstering her hopes, regains his confidence. The comedy skit with Chaplin and Keaton is a "keeper." The score, by Chaplin, is haunting.

1952 B & W 145 minutes

LISTEN TO YOUR HEART

★★★

DIRECTOR: Don Taylor
CAST: Kate Jackson, Tim Matheson, Cassie Yates, George Coe, Will Nye, Tony Plana

This cute but predictable romatic comedy features a book editor (Tim Matheson) falling in love with his art director (Kate Jackson). Naturally, problems and embarrassing situations arise when co-workers realize that they're having an affair. Made for TV, this is unrated.

1983 104 minutes

LITTLE DARLINGS

★★★

DIRECTOR: Ronald F. Maxwell
CAST: Tatum O'Neal, Kristy McNichol, Matt Dillon

A story of the trials and tribulations of teen-age virginity, this film too often lapses into chronic cuteness, with characters more darling than realistic. *Little Darlings* follows the antics of two 15-year-old outcasts—rich, sophisticated Ferris Whitney (Tatum O'Neal) and poor, belligerent Angel Bright (Kristy McNichol)—as they spend their summer at Camp Little Wolf and compete to "score" with a boy first. Rated R.

1980 95 minutes

LITTLE ROMANCE, A

★★★★½

DIRECTOR: George Roy Hill
CAST: Thelonious Bernard, Diane Lane, Laurence Olivier, Sally Kellerman; Broderick Crawford, David Dukes

Everyone needs *A Little Romance* in their life. This absolutely enchanting film by director George Roy Hill (*Butch Cassidy and the Sundance Kid*; *The Sting*) has something for everyone. Its story of two appealing youngsters (Thelonious Bernard and Diane Lane) who fall in love in Paris is full of surprises, laughs, and uplifting moments. Supporting cast adds to the fun. Rated PG.

1979 108 minutes

LITTLE SEX, A

★½

DIRECTOR: Bruce Paltrow
CAST: Tim Matheson, Kate Capshaw, Edward Herrmann

A New York director of television commercials can't keep his hands off his actresses, even though he's married to a beautiful, intelligent woman. This is a tepid romantic comedy. Rated R.

1982 95 minutes

LITTLE TOUGH GUYS

★★

DIRECTOR: Harold Young
CAST: Bill Halop, Huntz Hall, Gabriel Dell, Bernard Punsley, David Gorcey, Hally Chester, Helen Parrish, Robert Wilcox, Marjorie Main, Jackie Searl

Offshoot of the popular Dead End Kids films for Warner Bros., this was the first in a series for Universal that would eventually redefine the gang's hard edges and turn them into the bumbling East Side Kids and finally the hopelessly inept Bowery Boys. Most of the original crew is on hand for this routine programmer, including the marvelous Marjorie Main, fresh from her standout performance in *Dead End* and years away from her best-remembered role as Ma Kettle. Not as good as the earlier entries, this film is still far superior to the treatment the boys would receive from Monogram Pictures in the years ahead.

1938 B & W 63 minutes

LIVE AT HARRAH'S

★★

DIRECTOR: Greg Stevens
CAST: Bill Cosby, Rip Taylor, Elaine Boozler, Dick Shawn, Sammy King, The One Step Ahead Dancers

Rip Taylor is the host for the on- and off-stage routines of Bill

Cosby, Elaine Boozler, Dick Shawn and Sammy King. This is a curiously uneven selection of material. Boozler and Shawn deliver adult humor and then Cosby comes onstage with an overly long routine with kids from the audience. This is not a good representation of any of these comedians' best work, and Cosby is particularly disappointing.

1981 60 minutes

LOCAL HERO

★★★★½

DIRECTOR: Bill Forsyth

CAST: Burt Lancaster, Peter Riegert, Fulton MacKay

A wonderfully offbeat comedy by Bill Forsyth (*Gregory's Girl*). Burt Lancaster plays a Houston oil baron who sends Peter Riegert (*Animal House*) to the west coast of Scotland to negotiate with the natives for North Sea oil rights. As with *Gregory's Girl*, which was about a gangly, good-natured boy's first crush, this film is blessed with sparkling little moments of humor, unforgettable characters, and a warmly human story. Rated PG for language.

1983 111 minutes

LONELY GUY, THE

★★★½

DIRECTOR: Arthur Hiller

CAST: Steve Martin, Robyn Douglass, Charles Grodin, Merv Griffin, Dr. Joyce Brothers

Steve Martin stars in this okay comedy as a struggling young writer who makes his living working for a greeting card company. One day he comes home to find his live-in mate (Robyn Douglass) in bed with another man and becomes the "Lonely Guy" of the title. Only recommended for Steve Martin fans. Rated R for brief nudity and profanity.

1984 90 minutes

LOOKIN' TO GET OUT

★★★

DIRECTOR: Hal Ashby

CAST: Jon Voight, Burt Young, Ann-Margret, Bert Remsen

This off-beat comedy stars Jon Voight and Burt Young as a couple of compulsive gamblers out to hit the fabled "big score" in Las Vegas. It'll keep you interested for most of its running time, although it does drag a bit in the middle. However, the first hour zips by before you know it, and the ending is a humdinger. Rated R for violence and profanity.

1982 104 minutes

LOOSE SHOES

★

DIRECTOR: Ira Miller

CAST: Buddy Hackett, Howard Hesseman, Bill Murray, Susan Tyrrell, Avery Schreiber

Failed attempt to spoof B movies. The successful gags are very few and the whole outing reeks of a *Kentucky Fried Movie* ripoff. At least with that film the sex, nudity, and profanity were used to poke fun at sexploitation flicks. Here, these qualities are exposed simply for the drive-in audience's satisfaction. Rated R.

1977 73 minutes

LOSIN' IT

★★★

DIRECTOR: Curtis Hanson

CAST: Tom Cruise, Shelley Long, Jackie Earle Haley, John Stockwell

Better-than-average teen exploitation flick, this one has four boys off to Tijuana for a good time. Shelley Long ("Cheers") adds interest as a runaway wife who joins them on their journey. Rated R.

1982 104 minutes

LOST AND FOUND

★

DIRECTOR: Melvin Frank
CAST: Glenda Jackson, George Segal, Maureen Stapleton

After teaming up successfully for *A Touch of Class*, writer-director Melvin Frank and his stars, Glenda Jackson and George Segal, tried again. But the result was an unfunny comedy about two bickering, cardboard characters. Rated PG.

1979 112 minutes

LOST IN AMERICA

★★★★½

DIRECTOR: Albert Brooks
CAST: Albert Brooks, Julie Hagerty, Garry Marshall

Writer-director-star Albert Brooks is one of America's great natural comedic resources. *Lost in America* is his funniest film to date. Some viewers may be driven to distraction by Brooks's all-too-true study of what happens when a "successful" and "responsible" married couple chucks it all and goes out on an *Easy Rider*–style trip across the country. Brooks makes movies about the things most adults would consider their worst nightmare. He cuts close to the bone and makes us laugh at ourselves in a very original way. If you can stand the pain, the pleasure is well worth it. Rated R for profanity and adult situations.

1985 92 minutes

LOVE AND DEATH

★★★★

DIRECTOR: Woody Allen
CAST: Woody Allen, Diane Keaton, Harold Gould, Alfred Lutter, Zvee Scooler

This comedy set in 1812 Russia is one of Woody Allen's funniest films. Diane Keaton is the high-minded Russian with assassination (of Napoleon) in mind. Allen is her cowardly accomplice with sex on the brain. The movie satirizes not only love and death, but politics, classic Russian literature (Tolstoy's *War and Peace*), and foreign films, as well. Use of Prokofiev music enhances the piece. Rated PG.

1975 82 minutes

LOVE AT FIRST BITE

★★★★

DIRECTOR: Stan Dragoti
CAST: George Hamilton, Susan Saint James, Richard Benjamin, Dick Shawn, Arte Johnson

The Dracula legend is given the comedy treatment in this amusing parody of horror films. George Hamilton plays the campy Count, who has an unorthodox way with the ladies. (In this case, it's Susan Saint James, much to the chagrin of her boyfriend, Richard Benjamin.) Even though the humor is heavy-handed in parts, you find yourself chuckling continually in spite of yourself. Rated PG.

1979 96 minutes

LOVE HAPPY

★★

DIRECTOR: David Miller
CAST: The Marx Brothers, Marilyn Monroe, Raymond Burr

The last Marx Brothers movie, this 1949 production was originally set to star only Harpo, but Chico and, later, Groucho were brought in to beef up its box-office potential. They should've known better. This "Let's put on a show" retread doesn't even come close to their lesser works at MGM. Only Groucho's ogling of then-screen-newcomer Marilyn Monroe makes it interesting for movie buffs.

1949 B & W 91 minutes

LOVE IN THE AFTERNOON

★★★★

DIRECTOR: Billy Wilder
CAST: Gary Cooper, Audrey Hepburn, Maurice Chevalier, John McGiver, Van Doude, Lise Bourdin, Olga Valery

This witty romantic farce sports timeless allure under the direction of the immortal Billy Wilder. Audrey Hepburn shares fantastic chemistry with both Maurice Chevalier and Gary Cooper in this film classic, which explores the love interests of an American entrepreneur and his lopsided involvement with a young French ingenue. When her doting father (a detective) is asked to investigate the American's love life, it makes for a touching, charming bit of entertainment that never loses its appeal.

1957 130 minutes

LOVE LAUGHS AT ANDY HARDY

★★

DIRECTOR: Willis Goldbeck
CAST: Mickey Rooney, Lewis Stone, Fay Holden, Sara Haden, Bonita Granville

America's all-American, lovable, irritating, well-meaning wimp comes home from World War II and plunges back into the same adolescent rut of agonizing young love. The change of times has made this cookie-cutter film very predictable. But it's fun anyway.

1946 B & W 93 minutes

LOVELINES

DIRECTOR: Rod Amateau
CAST: Michael Winslow, Greg Bradford, Mary Beth Evans

Michael Winslow, the sound-effects cop in *Police Academy*, is the only recognizable face in this dreadful teen comedy. The film is supposed to be about a teen telephone service and an all-girl rock band attempting to break into the big time. But there are so many plot digressions, it ends up being about how not to make a movie. The point seems to be sex and laughs at any cost. Yet the sex is just a tease, and the humor is all but nonexistent. Rated R for nudity, suggested sex, violence, and profanity.

1984 93 minutes

LOVER COME BACK

★★★★

DIRECTOR: Delbert Mann
CAST: Rock Hudson, Doris Day, Tony Randall, Edie Adams, Jack Oakie, Jack Kruschen, Ann B. Davis, Joe Flynn, Jack Albertson

Rock Hudson and Doris Day are rival advertising executives battling professionally, psychologically, and sexually. A bright comedy that builds nicely. One of their best. Silly, innocent fun with a great supporting cast.

1961 107 minutes

LOVERS AND LIARS

★★½

DIRECTOR: Mario Monicelli
CAST: Goldie Hawn, Giancarlo Giannini, Laura Betti

The first thing that occurs to you while watching this film is a question: What's Goldie Hawn doing in a dubbed Italian sex comedy? It was obviously released to take advantage of her box-office success at the time with films like *Private Benjamin* and *Seems like Old Times*. But we doubt it will prove very popular on video—especially when people discover it is anything but a typical Goldie Hawn comedy. Co-starring Giancarlo Giannini (*Swept Away*), it is a modestly entertaining piece of fluff tailored primarily for European tastes and, therefore, will probably disappoint most of Hawn's fans. Rated R.

1979 96 minutes

LOVERS AND OTHER STRANGERS

★★★½

DIRECTOR: Cy Howard

CAST: Gig Young, Diane Keaton, Bea Arthur, Bonnie Bedelia, Anne Jackson, Harry Guardino, Richard Castellano, Michael Brandon, Cloris Leachman, Anne Meara

A very funny and memorable film about young love, marriage, and their many side effects on others. Marks Diane Keaton's debut in pictures. The late Gig Young is a delight.

1970 106 minutes

LOVES AND TIMES OF SCARAMOUCHE, THE

★

DIRECTOR: Enzo G. Castellari

CAST: Michael Sarrazin, Ursula Andress, Aldo Maccioni, Gian Carlo Prete, Michael Forest, Sal Borgese

Michael Sarrazin, as Scaramouche, stumbles through this ridiculous swashbuckler in the tradition of *The Three Musketeers*. Scaramouche is a young Lothario who unwittingly becomes a draftee in Napoleon's army while fleeing from the irate husband of one of his many loves. Of course, Napoleon's true love also has an eye on him, which only makes matters worse. This silly romantic farce has few redeeming points—even the comic love scenes between Ursula Andress and Sarrazin are hard to endure.

1976 92 minutes

LOVESICK

★★★½

DIRECTOR: Marshall Brickman

CAST: Dudley Moore, Elizabeth McGovern, Alec Guinness, John Huston

This is a sweet romantic comedy that tugs at your heart as it tickles your funnybone. You won't fall out of your seat laughing or grab a tissue to dab away the tears. But this movie, about a psychiatrist's (Dudley Moore) obsession with his patient (Elizabeth McGovern), does have its moments. Rated PG.

1983 95 minutes

LOVING COUPLES

★★★

DIRECTOR: Jack Smight

CAST: Shirley MacLaine, James Coburn, Susan Sarandon, Stephen Collins

Can a film be both entertaining and boring? If the film is *Loving Couples*, the answer is yes. This romantic comedy can have you roaring with laughter one minute and yawning the next. The good moments outnumber the bad. But after it's over, you can't decide whether it was worth seeing or not. The plot is that old and tired one, about two couples who swap partners for a temporary fling only to reunite by film's end happier and wiser for the experience. It's a premise that's been worn thin by filmmakers and especially television since the swinging 1960s and badly in need of retirement. Rated PG.

1980 97 minutes

LUST IN THE DUST

★★★

DIRECTOR: Paul Bartel

CAST: Tab Hunter, Divine, Lainie Kazan, Geoffrey Lewis, Henry Silva, Cesar Romero

Tab Hunter and female impersonator Divine (who's anything but), who first teamed in *Polyester*, star in this so-so spoof of spaghetti westerns, directed by Paul Bartel (*Eating Raoul*). The ad blurb tells all: "He rode the West. The girls rode the rest. Together they ravaged the land." Rated R for nudity, suggested sex, and violence.

1985 86 minutes

LUV

★★

DIRECTOR: Clive Donner

CAST: Jack Lemmon, Elaine May, Peter Falk, Severn Darden

When talent the caliber of Jack Lemmon, Peter Falk, and Elaine May cannot breathe life into a film, then nothing can. The plot concerns three New York intellectuals and their tribulations through life. Who cares?

1967 95 minutes

MACARONI

★★★★½

DIRECTOR: Ettore Scola

CAST: Jack Lemmon, Marcello Mastroianni, Daria Nicolodi, Isa Danieli, Maria Luisa Santella, Patrizia Sacchi

Wonderful Italian comedy-drama from the director of *A Special Day* and *Le Bal*. This one concerns an American executive (Jack Lemmon) who returns to Naples for a business meeting forty years after his stay there with the army. He is visited by an old friend (Marcello Mastroianni). *Macaroni* addresses the ideals of friendship with a fresh approach that defies clichés and gives sentimentality a more intelligent definition. Both Lemmon and Mastroianni deliver brilliant performances. Rated PG for profanity.

1985 104 minutes

MAD MISS MANTON, THE

★★★

DIRECTOR: Leigh Jason

CAST: Barbara Stanwyck, Henry Fonda, Sam Levene, Frances Mercer, Stanley Ridges, Whitney Bourne, Leona Maricle, James Burke, Penny Singleton

A group of high-society ladies led by Miss Manton (Barbara Stanwyck) help solve a murder mystery with comic results—sometimes. The humor is pretty outdated, and the brand of romanticism, while being in step with the 1930s, comes off rather silly in the latter part of the twentieth century. Henry Fonda plays a newspaper editor who falls in love with the mad Miss Manton.

1938 B & W 80 minutes

MAD WEDNESDAY

★★½

DIRECTOR: Preston Sturges

CAST: Harold Lloyd, Frances Ramsden, Jimmy Conlin, Raymond Walburn, Arline Judge, Lionel Stander, Rudy Vallee, Edgar Kennedy

The great silent comedian Harold Lloyd stars in an update of his famous brash, go-getting 1920s straw-hatted, black-rimmed-glasses character. A good, but not well executed, idea. Lloyd never really successfully shifted his brand of comedy to sound. Fortunately, his silents made him many times a millionaire. Originally issued in 1947 as *The Sin of Harold Diddlebrock* in the director's version. This was producer Howard Hughes's "improved" version.

1950 B & W 90 minutes

MADE FOR EACH OTHER

★★★★

DIRECTOR: John Cromwell

CAST: Carole Lombard, James Stewart, Charles Coburn, Lucile Watson, Harry Davenport

This is a highly appealing comedy-drama centering on the rocky first years of a marriage. The young couple (Carole Lombard and James Stewart) must do battle with interfering in-laws, inept servants, and the consequences of childbirth. The real strength of this film lies in the screenplay, by Jo Swerling. It gives viewers a thoughtful and tasteful picture of events that we can all relate to.

1939 B & W 100 minutes

MADIGAN'S MILLIONS

DIRECTOR: Stanley Prager
CAST: Dustin Hoffman, Elsa Martinelli, Cesar Romero

Only the most fanatical Dustin Hoffman fans need bother with this tedious spy farce. Hoffman plays a buffoonish treasury agent sent to recover some dirty money in Italy. This clumsy film offers neither laughs nor suspense. It was filmed before *The Graduate* but not released until well after Hoffman's success was established. You'll have to look hard to find any glimmer of star potential here.

1967 86 minutes

MAGIC CHRISTIAN, THE

★★★

DIRECTOR: Joseph McGrath
CAST: Peter Sellers, Ringo Starr, Christopher Lee, Raquel Welch, Richard Attenborough, Yul Brynner

A now-dated comedy about the world's wealthiest man (Peter Sellers) and his adopted son (Ringo Starr) testing the depths of degradation to which people will plunge themselves for money still has some funny scenes and outrageous cameos by Christopher Lee (as Dracula), Raquel Welch, and Richard Attenborough. Rated PG.

1970 93 minutes

MAIN EVENT, THE

★

DIRECTOR: Howard Zieff
CAST: Barbra Streisand, Ryan O'Neal, Paul Sand

A limp boxing comedy that tried unsuccessfully to reunite the stars of *What's Up Doc?*, Barbra Streisand and Ryan O'Neal. This movie will put you to sleep the hard way. Rated PG.

1979 112 minutes

MAJOR BARBARA

★★★½

DIRECTOR: Gabriel Pascal
CAST: Wendy Hiller, Rex Harrison, Robert Morley, Robert Newton, Emlyn Williams, Sybil Thorndike, Deborah Kerr, David Tree, Penelope Dudley-Ward, Marie Lohr

In the title role as a Salvation Army officer, Wendy Hiller heads a matchless cast in this thoughtful film of George Bernard Shaw's comedy about the power of money and the evils of poverty. Rex Harrison, as her fiancé, and Robert Newton, as a hardcase with doubts about the honesty and motives of do-gooders, are excellent.

1941 B & W 136 minutes

MAKE A MILLION

★★★

DIRECTOR: Lewis Collins
CAST: Charles Starrett, Pauline Brooks

In this Depression comedy, college economics professor Charles Starrett's radical ideas for sharing the wealth get him fired. He develops a plan that soon has him rolling in money—and attracting a greedy banker and others bent on getting in on the gravy. The student whose lies got him fired, the daughter of the banker, switches sides to help him carry the day against the power of position and wealth.

1935 B & W 66 minutes

MAKE MINE MINK

★★★★

DIRECTOR: Robert Asher
CAST: Terry-Thomas, Athene Seyler, Billie Whitelaw

Bright dialogue and clever situations make this crazy comedy from Britain highly enjoyable. An ex-officer, a dowager, and a motley crew of fur thieves team to commit larceny for charity. Gap-toothed Terry-Thomas is in top form in this one.

1960 100 minutes

MAKING MR. RIGHT

★★½

DIRECTOR: Susan Seidelman
CAST: John Malkovich, Ann Magnuson, Ben Masters, Glenne Headly, Laurie Metcalf, Polly Bergen, Hart Bochner

This mild satire, about a female image consultant who falls for the android she's supposed to be promoting, doesn't come close to the energy level of director Susan Seidelman's *Desperately Seeking Susan*. The juicy possibilities inherent in giving a modern woman the opportunity to program her ideal mate are largely ignored. John Malkovich shows impressive comedic dexterity in the dual role of the ingenuous android and the antisocial scientist who created him. Rated PG-13.

1987 98 minutes

MAKING THE GRADE

★★½

DIRECTOR: Dorian Walker
CAST: Judd Nelson, Jonna Lee, Carey Scott

A rich kid pays a surrogate to attend prep school for him. Typical teen-exploitation fare. Rated R.

1984 105 minutes

MALCOLM

★★★★½

DIRECTOR: Nadia Tess
CAST: Colin Friels, John Hargreaves, Lindy Davies, Chris Haywood

An absolutely charming Australian entry that swept that country's Oscars the year it was released. Colin Friels has the title role as an emotionally immature young man who, after he loses his job with a local rapid-transit company (for building his own tram with company parts), must take in boarders to make ends meet. His new roomies turn out to be John Hargreaves, an embittered ex-con with no shortage of plans for knocking over banks, and his earthy lady friend (Lindy Davies), whose tendency to wander about half-dressed badly upsets Malcolm's delicate sensibilities. The story picks up when Malcolm—who's actually a genius with mechanical contrivances and other gadgets—decides to abet his tenants in their unlawful careers. Friels is nothing less than stunning as the doe-eyed innocent, but he's almost upstaged by his numerous inventions. A delight for the entire family. Unrated.

1986 90 minutes

MALIBU EXPRESS

🦃

DIRECTOR: Andy Sidaris
CAST: Darby Hinton, Sybil Danning, Shelley Taylor Morgan, Brett Clark, Art Metrano

Darby Hinton plays Cody, a millionaire turned private eye. He narrates the events *à la Magnum, P.I.*, but the similarities between this film and any decent movie or TV show end there. His latest case is to find out who's selling computer secrets to the Russians. He soon becomes involved in numerous contrived situations with four *Playboy* playmates and several massive bodybuilders. The amazing thing about this film is how it managed to get an R rating when it is clearly soft porn. It contains obscenities, violence, and an overdose of nudity and sex. Not recommended for anyone!

1984 101 minutes

MAN IN THE WHITE SUIT, THE

★★★★★

DIRECTOR: Alexander Mackendrick
CAST: Alec Guinness, Joan Greenwood, Cecil Parker

In *The Man in the White Suit*, Alec Guinness is the perfect choice to play an unassuming scientist who invents a fabric that can't be torn, frayed, or stained! Can you imagine the furor this causes in the textile industry? This uniquely original script pokes fun at big business and big labor as they try to suppress his discovery. Joan Greenwood is a treasure in a supporting role.

1952 B & W 84 minutes

MAN OF FLOWERS

★★★★★

DIRECTOR: Paul Cox
CAST: Norman Kaye, Alyson Best, Chris Haywood, Werner Herzog

Kinky, humorous, and touching, this winner from Australia affirms Paul Cox (of *Lonely Hearts* fame) as one of the wittiest and most sensitive directors from Down Under. Norman Kaye is terrific as an eccentric old man who collects art and flowers and watches pretty women undress. To him these are things of beauty that he can observe but either can't touch or can't participate in, thanks to an oppressive upbringing. The story moves slyly from the funny to the erotic to the macabre without warning. Rated R for nudity.

1984 90 minutes

MAN WHO LOVED WOMEN, THE

★★★

DIRECTOR: Blake Edwards
CAST: Burt Reynolds, Julie Andrews, Marilu Henner, Kim Basinger, Barry Corbin

The first screen collaboration of Burt Reynolds, Julie Andrews, and her director hubby, Blake Edwards (*The Pink Panther; S.O.B.*), didn't sound like the kind of thing that would make screen history. And it isn't. But, surprise of surprises, it is a pleasantly entertaining—and sometimes uproariously funny—adult sex comedy. The always likable Reynolds plays a guy who just can't say no to the opposite sex, and Andrews is the pyschiatrist who wants him to try. Rated R for nudity and profanity.

1983 110 minutes

MAN WHO WASN'T THERE, THE

DIRECTOR: Bruce Malmuth
CAST: Steve Guttenberg, Jeffrey Tambor, Lisa Langlois, Art Hindle, Vincent Baggetta

Clumsy comedy involves Steve Guttenberg in espionage and invisibility. This was originally released in 3-D, but the characters are barely one-dimensional. The film disappeared quickly from movie theaters, making it *The Movie That Wasn't There*. Rated R for nudity, language.

1983 111 minutes

MAN WITH ONE RED SHOE, THE

★★★½

DIRECTOR: Stan Dragoti
CAST: Tom Hanks, Dabney Coleman, Charles Durning, Lori Singer, Jim Belushi, Carrie Fisher, Edward Herrmann

An American remake of the French comedy *The Tall Blond Man with One Black Shoe*, this casts Tom Hanks (*Splash*) as a concert violinist who is pursued by a group of spies led by Dabney Coleman. It's all because Edward Herrmann, assistant to head of the CIA Charles Durning, picked Hanks as a decoy to confuse the power-hungry Coleman. Sound complicated? It is—but fun, too. Hanks is nearly the whole show. However, Jim Belushi (as his practical-joke-loving buddy) and Carrie Fisher (as an overly amorous flute player) also provide some hearty laughs. And Lori Singer (*Footloose*) makes a very sexy spy. Rated PG for profanity and violence.

1985 96 minutes

MAN WITH TWO BRAINS, THE

★★★★

DIRECTOR: Carl Reiner

CAST: Steve Martin, Kathleen Turner, David Warner, Paul Benedict

Steve Martin stars in this generally amusing takeoff of 1950s horror-sci-fi flicks as a scientist involved with two women: a nasty wife (Kathleen Turner, of *Body Heat*) and a sweet patient (the voice of Sissy Spacek). There's only one problem in his relationship with the latter: All that's left of her is her brain. While those who aren't partial to Martin's silly brand of humor are likely to remain so, fans of the wild and crazy guy will no doubt think this is his funniest film yet. Rated R for nudity, profanity, and violence.

1983 93 minutes

MAN'S FAVORITE SPORT?

★★★

DIRECTOR: Howard Hawks

CAST: Rock Hudson, Paula Prentiss, John McGiver, Roscoe Karns, Maria Perschy, Charlene Holt

Comedy about a nonfishing outdoor-sports columnist who finds himself entered in an anglers' contest is fast and funny and provides Rock Hudson with one of his best roles. Screwball Paula Prentiss spends most of her time gumming up the works for poor Rock. The situations and dialogue are clever and breezy, employing director Howard Hawks's famous overlapping dialogue to maximum advantage. Keep an eye out for some familiar character faces and some pretty inventive bits. This was Hawks's final comedy and runs a long two hours.

1964 120 minutes

MANHATTAN

★★★★★

DIRECTOR: Woody Allen

CAST: Diane Keaton, Woody Allen, Michael Murphy, Mariel Hemingway, Meryl Streep

Reworking the same themes he explored in *Play It Again, Sam* and *Annie Hall*, Woody Allen again comes up with a masterpiece in this film—perhaps his greatest. Diane Keaton returns as the object of his awkward but well-meaning affections. It's heartwarming, insightful, screamingly funny, and a feast for the eyes. The black-and-white cinematography of long-time Allen collaborator Gordon Willis recalls the great visuals of *Citizen Kane* and *The Third Man*. In short, it's wonderful. Rated R.

1979 B & W 96 minutes

MANNEQUIN

DIRECTOR: Michael Gottlieb

CAST: Andrew McCarthy, Kim Cattrall, Estelle Getty, G. W. Bailey

Mannequin is a boy-meets-girl film with a twist: it's actually boy makes girl. Andrew McCarthy plays a sensitive window shop dresser who builds a mannequin that comes to life only around him. Actually, she's an Egyptian princess who's been reincarnated through the ages and deposits herself into McCarthy's inanimate creation. *Mannequin* is a very stupid, unfunny film that is a boring mixture of MTV glitz and worn-out comedy bits. It's disheartening to see the charming McCarthy laden with this schlock (without him this movie is a walk-out). Kim Cattrall as the dream girl shamelessly overacts, making her inexhaustible spunk thoroughly obnoxious. Rated PG.

1987 90 minutes

MARATHON

★★½

DIRECTOR: Jackie Cooper

CAST: Bob Newhart, Herb Edelman, Dick Gautier, Anita Gillette, Leigh Taylor-Young, John Hillerman

In this comic examination of midlife crisis, Bob Newhart becomes enamored with a woman he sees at a local running event. With his wife busy with her career, he eventually travels to the New York marathon, only to discover his true feelings. The uninspired direction and screenplay weaken the efforts of a veteran cast. Rated PG for mild language.

1985 97 minutes

MARCH OF THE WOODEN SOLDIERS

★★★★

DIRECTOR: Gus Meins

CAST: Stan Laurel, Oliver Hardy, Charlotte Henry

Originally titled *Babes in Toyland*, this film features Stan Laurel and Oliver Hardy as the toymaker's assistants in the land of Old King Cole. Utterly forgettable songs slow down an otherwise enjoyable fantasy film. Stan and Ollie are integrated well into the storyline, finally saving the town from the attack of the boogeymen.

1934 B & W 73 minutes

MARY HARTMAN, MARY HARTMAN (TELEVISION SERIES)

★★★★

DIRECTORS: Joan Darling, Jim Drake

CAST: Louise Lasser, Greg Mullavey, Mary Kay Place, Graham Jarvis, Victor Kilian, Debralee Scott, Martin Mull

This series was too off-the-wall for the networks, so producer Norman Lear sold it in syndication. It was seen five nights a week, usually in late-night slots. Full of whimsy and satire, the show plunged into subjects considered taboo by normal sitcoms, such as impotence and marijuana, not to mention waxy yellow buildup. Conceived as a spoof of soap operas, this series became just as habit-forming. Beneath the drollery was rare pathos. Louise Lasser, as Mary, fashioned a unique character with which a wide audience empathized. As her blue-collar husband, Greg Mullavey was always likeable and believable. Adorable Mary Kay Place provided many high spots as a would-be country singing star. Volumes I and II deal with such provocative and hilarious storylines as the search for the Fernwood Flasher. This series is definitely worth another look.

1976 70 minutes

M*A*S*H

★★★★½

DIRECTOR: Robert Altman

CAST: Elliott Gould, Donald Sutherland, Sally Kellerman, Tom Skerritt, Robert Duvall, JoAnn Pflug, Bud Cort

Fans of the television series of the same name and *Trapper John, M.D.* may have a bit of trouble recognizing their favorite characters, but this is the original. One of eccentric film director Robert Altman's few true artistic successes, this release is outrageous good fun. Rated PG.

1970 116 minutes

M*A*S*H: GOODBYE, FAREWELL, AMEN

★★★★

DIRECTOR: Alan Alda
CAST: Alan Alda, Henry Morgan, Loretta Swit, Jamie Farr

A beautiful send-off to one of the great television series. Alan Alda and company have finally seen the end of the Korean War and are headed home. This last episode is handled with the usual excellence that one has come to associate with the series. A must for "M*A*S*H" fans and those who think there is nothing worth watching on television.

1983 120 minutes

MATILDA

★★★½

DIRECTOR: Daniel Mann
CAST: Elliott Gould, Robert Mitchum, Clive Revill, Harry Guardino, Roy Clark, Lionel Stander, Art Metrano, Karen Carlson, Robert Mitchum

A cute comedy about a boxing kangaroo who becomes a legend in the sport. Elliott Gould plays a small-time booking agent who becomes the manager of the heavyweight marsupial. Despite some problems in the directing, the film is watchable and humorous. Sentimental at times and a bit corny, too, but worth the time. Recommended for family viewing. Rated G.

1978 105 minutes

MAXIE

★★

DIRECTOR: Paul Aaron
CAST: Glenn Close, Mandy Patinkin, Ruth Gordon, Barnard Hughes, Valerie Curtin

Cute but not particularly impressive fantasy about a conservative secretary (Glenn Close) who becomes possessed by the spirit of a flamboyant flapper (Close, too). The star is wonderful, but the predictable plot and the uninspired direction let her—and the viewer—down. Few laughs and no surprises. Rated PG for suggested sex.

1985 98 minutes

MEATBALLS

★★★½

DIRECTOR: Ivan Reitman
CAST: Bill Murray, Harvey Atkin, Kate Lynch, Chris Makepeace

Somehow, this *Animal House*–style comedy's disjointedness is easier to swallow than it should be. Elmer Bernstein's music gets sentimental in the right places, and star Bill Murray is fun to watch. Rated PG.

1979 92 minutes

MEATBALLS PART II

🦃

DIRECTOR: Ken Weiderhorn
CAST: Richard Mulligan, Kim Richards, John Mengatti, Misty Rowe

This lame sequel to *Meatballs* should never have been made. Pitifully unfunny high jinks at summer camp, with an alien getting in on the action this time. In fact, he has all three of the good lines. Rated PG for sexual references.

1984 87 minutes

MEATBALLS III

★

DIRECTOR: George Mendeluk
CAST: Sally Kellerman, Patrick Dempsey, Al Waxman, Isabelle Mejias, Shannon Tweed

Poor Sally Kellerman. She deserves better than this lousy sex comedy. Bearing little relationship to the Bill Murray charmer and its dreadful follow-up, this yawner cast Kellerman as the ghost of a porno star who has to do a good deed in order to get into heaven. So she sets about trying to get the nerdy Patrick Dempsey laid. No more *Meatballs*, please. Rated R for nudity, profanity, and suggested sex.

1987 94 minutes

MELVIN AND HOWARD

★★★★★

DIRECTOR: Jonathan Demme

CAST: Paul LeMat, Jason Robards, Mary Steenburgen

This brilliantly directed slice-of-life film works marvelously well . . . on two levels. On the surface, it's the entertaining tale of how Melvin Dummar (Paul LeMat) met Howard Hughes (Jason Robards)—or did he? Underneath, it's a hilarious spoof of our society. Mary Steenburgen co-stars in this triumph of American filmmaking, a rare gem that deserves to be seen and talked about. Rated R.

1980 95 minutes

MICKI & MAUDE

★★★★½

DIRECTOR: Blake Edwards

CAST: Dudley Moore, Amy Irving, Ann Reinking, George Gaynes, Wallace Shawn

In this hysterically funny comedy Dudley Moore stars as a television personality who tries to juggle marriages to two women, Amy Irving and Ann Reinking. Directed by Blake Edwards (*10*), it's a triumph for filmmaker and cast alike: One of the funniest films of its year. Rated PG-13 for profanity and suggested sex.

1984 96 minutes

MIDNIGHT MADNESS

DIRECTORS: David Wechter, Michael Nankin

CAST: David Naughton, Debra Clinger, Eddie Deezen, Stephen Furst

Absolutely awful post–*Animal House* Disney production about a bunch of teen-age idiots going on a midnight scavenger hunt. Rated PG.

1980 110 minutes

MIDSUMMER NIGHT'S SEX COMEDY, A

★★½

DIRECTOR: Woody Allen

CAST: Woody Allen, Mia Farrow, José Ferrer, Julie Hagerty, Tony Roberts, Mary Steenburgen

Woody Allen's sometimes dull cinematic treatise—albeit sweet-natured, and beautifully photographed by Gordon Willis—on the star-writer-director's favorite subjects: sex and death. That's not to say *A Midsummer Night's Sex Comedy* doesn't have its humorous moments. Allen's fans will undoubtedly enjoy it. But, like *Stardust Memories*, it isn't really a comedy, and viewers expecting one will be disappointed. Rated PG for adult themes.

1982 88 minutes

MIKEY AND NICKY

★★★

DIRECTOR: Elaine May

CAST: Peter Falk, John Cassavetes, Ned Beatty, Joyce Van Patten, Rose Arrick, Carol Grace

The story of a fateful day and the relationship of two small-time crooks who have considered each other best friends since childhood. This hauntingly funny film slowly builds to its climax in the Elaine May tradition. Great acting from Peter Falk and John Cassavetes. Rated R for profanity.

1976 119 minutes

MILKY WAY, THE

★★★★

DIRECTOR: Leo McCarey

CAST: Harold Lloyd, Adolphe Menjou, Helen Mack

In this superb compendium of gags flowing from his character of a milkman who innocently decks the champion during a brawl, the great Harold Lloyd amply proves why he was such a success. It's all carefully thought out and planned (a switch from his old silent days when off the cuff was good enough), but highly entertaining just the same. Harold Lloyd was a master comic craftsman. This is the finest of his few talking films.

1936 B & W 83 minutes

MIRACLES

★★½

DIRECTOR: Jim Kouf
CAST: Tom Conti, Teri Garr, Paul Rodriguez, Christopher Lloyd

This film involves a sick little girl in a remote Mexican jungle, a doctor and his recently divorced wife in L.A., and a bungling burglar. The story revolves around the sometimes funny circumstances that bring all these characters together. This film verges on being good but falls short. Garr and Rodriguez carry most of the humor while Conti yells a lot. Rated PG for language and mild violence.

1986 90 minutes

MISCHIEF

★★★

DIRECTOR: Mel Damski
CAST: Doug McKeon, Catherine Mary Stewart, Chris Nash, Kelly Preston, D. W. Brown

In this disarming coming-of-age comedy, Doug McKeon (*On Golden Pond*) plays Jonathan, whose hopes of romance are thwarted until Gene (Chris Nash, in an impressive debut), a kid from the big city, shows him how. Rated R for violence, profanity, nudity, and simulated sex.

1985 93 minutes

MISSIONARY, THE

★★★½

DIRECTOR: Richard Loncraine
CAST: Michael Palin, Maggie Smith, Denholm Elliott, Trevor Howard, Michael Hordern

Monty Python's Michael Palin, who also wrote the script, plays a well-meaning American minister assigned the task of saving the souls of London's fallen women. Those familiar with its British-style comedy, and even those who are not, will probably get most of the jokes. It is not a nonstop, gag-filled descent into absurdity like the Monty Python movies. It is, instead, a warm-hearted spoof with the accent on character and very sparing but effective in its humor. Rated R.

1982 90 minutes

MR. AND MRS. SMITH

★★★★

DIRECTOR: Alfred Hitchcock
CAST: Carole Lombard, Robert Montgomery, Gene Raymond, Jack Carson

This film deals with the love-hate-love relationship of Carole Lombard and Robert Montgomery, who play a couple who discover their marriage isn't legal. The bouncy dialogue by Norman Krasna is justly famous and includes some of the most classic comedy scenes ever to come out of this screwball gender of films. Directing this enjoyable farce, in his only pure comedy, is Alfred Hitchcock.

1941 B & W 95 minutes

MR. BILL LOOKS BACK

★★★

DIRECTOR: Walter Williams
CAST: Animated

This is a collection of shorts taken from *Saturday Night Live* episodes. In each, Mr. Bill and his dog Spot are tormented by Mr. Hands and the evil Sluggo. Bill's adventures take him to Coney Island, Skid Row, a psychiatrist's office, the police station, and Sing Sing. There are some hilarious moments, but they're all a result of violent acts against our heroes.

1980 30 minutes

MR. BILL'S REAL LIFE ADVENTURES

★★½

DIRECTOR: Jim Drake

CAST: Peter Scolari, Valerie Mahaffey, Lenore Kasdorf, Michael McAnus

The hilarity of the clay figure's misfortunes doesn't quite translate with real-life characters. Peter Scolari as Mr. Bill, however, is terrific. Mr. Bill, his sweet wife Sally (Valerie Mahaffey), their son Billy, and dog Spot are tiny people who must battle not only the huge world around them but also their neighbors. Mr. Sluggo (Michael McAnus), his sexy wife, Dutchess (Lenore Kasdorf), and their daughter (who strongly resembles the little girl in *The Bad Seed*) constantly complicate the otherwise ideal life of Bill's family.

1986 43 minutes

MR. BLANDINGS BUILDS HIS DREAM HOUSE

★★★★

DIRECTOR: H. C. Potter

CAST: Cary Grant, Myrna Loy, Melvyn Douglas

In this screwball comedy, Cary Grant plays a man tired of the hustle and bustle of city life. He decides to move to the country, construct his private Shangri-La, and settle back into what he feels will be a serene rural lifestyle. His fantasy and reality come into comic conflict. Myrna Loy is cast as his ever-patient wife in this very fine film.

1948 B & W 94 minutes

MR. MIKE'S MONDO VIDEO

★★★

DIRECTOR: Michael O'Donoghue

CAST: Michael O'Donoghue, Dan Aykroyd, Jane Curtin, Carrie Fisher, Teri Garr, Deborah Harry, Margot Kidder, Bill Murray, Laraine Newman, Gilda Radner, Julius LaRosa, Paul Schaeffer, Sid Vicious

This comedy special by former *Saturday Night Live* writer Michael O'Donoghue was originally slated to run on late-night network television, but NBC decided it was too outrageous—even offensive in some parts—to be broadcast. *Mr. Mike's Mondo Video* was then briefly released to theaters where it did little box-office and received negative reviews. We don't think it's as bad as all that. In fact, it is kind of a time capsule of comedy and pop figures from the 1970s. It may make you groan as often as laugh, but it stands as a reminder of how far-out comedy got on television after years of safe, insipid sitcoms.

1979 75 minutes

MR. MOM

★★★★

DIRECTOR: Stan Dragoti

CAST: Michael Keaton, Teri Garr, Ann Jillian, Martin Mull

Michael Keaton is hilarious as an engineer who loses his job at an automobile manufacturing plant and, when wife Teri Garr gets a high-paying job at an advertising agency, becomes a hopelessly inept househusband. The story is familiar and the events somewhat predictable, but Keaton's off-the-wall antics and boyish charm make it all seem fresh and lively. In addition, Garr is perfect as the wife, and there's fine support from Ann Jillian and Martin Mull. Rated PG for light profanity.

1983 91 minutes

MR. PEABODY AND THE MERMAID

★★

DIRECTOR: Irving Pichel
CAST: William Powell, Ann Blyth, Irene Hervey

This is *Splash*, 1940s-style. A married New Englander (William Powell) snags an amorous mermaid while fishing and transfers her to his swimming pool, with the expected results.

1948 B & W 89 minutes

MR. ROBERTS

★★★★½

DIRECTORS: John Ford, Mervyn LeRoy
CAST: Henry Fonda, James Cagney, Jack Lemmon, William Powell, Ward Bond

A Navy cargo ship well outside the World War II battle zone is the setting for this hit comedy-drama. Henry Fonda is Lieutenant Roberts, the first officer who helps the crew battle their ceaseless boredom and tyrannical captain (James Cagney). Jack Lemmon began his road to stardom with his sparkling performance as the irrepressible conman Ensign Pulver.

1955 123 minutes

MR. WINKLE GOES TO WAR

★★★

DIRECTOR: Alfred E. Green
CAST: Edward G. Robinson, Ruth Warrick, Richard Lane, Robert Armstrong, Richard Gaines

Edward G. Robinson is a henpecked bookkeeper who gets drafted into the army during World War II. As the saying goes, the army makes a man out of him. Like so many films of its time, *Mr. Winkle Goes to War* was part of the war effort and as such hasn't worn very well; what was considered heartfelt or patriotic back in the 1940s is now rendered maudlin or just corny. Still, the acting is excellent.

1944 B & W 80 minutes

MODERN GIRLS

★★★

DIRECTOR: Jerry Kramer
CAST: Cynthia Gibb, Virginia Madsen, Daphne Zuniga, Clayton Rohner, Steve Shellen, Chris Nash

Cynthia Gibb, Virginia Madsen, and Daphne Zuniga turn in fine individual performances as the *Modern Girls*, but this well-edited and visually striking film has some slow scenes among the funny. This teen comedy about a night in L.A.'s rock clubs begins better than it ends. However, younger viewers should find it enjoyable overall. Rated PG-13 for profanity and sexual situations.

1987 82 minutes

MODERN PROBLEMS

★★

DIRECTOR: Ken Shapiro
CAST: Chevy Chase, Patti D'Arbanville, Mary Kay Place

In this passable comedy, directed by Ken (*The Groove Tube*) Shapiro, Chevy Chase plays an air traffic controller who may be permanently out to lunch. His girlfriend has left him, and a freak nuclear accident has endowed him with telekinetic powers. Rated PG because of its brief nudity and sexual theme.

1981 91 minutes

MODERN ROMANCE

★★★★

DIRECTOR: Albert Brooks
CAST: Albert Brooks, Kathryn Harrold, Bruno Kirby

Love may be a many-splendored thing for some people, but it's sheer torture for Robert Cole (Albert Brooks) in this contemporary comedy. Brooks wrote, directed, and starred in this very entertaining, often hilarious story about a self-indulgent, narcissistic Hollywood film editor whose love life has the stability of Mount St. Helens. Offbeat lunacy, wit, and insight give this rethrashing of the old "you can't live with 'em and you can't live without 'em" axiom a full sail of wind. Kathryn Harrold co-stars as the intelligent and beautiful recipient of Cole's compulsively jealous affections. Rated R.

1981 93 minutes

MODERN TIMES

★★★★

DIRECTOR: Charles Chaplin
CAST: Charlie Chaplin, Paulette Goddard

Charlie Chaplin must have had a crystal ball when he created *Modern Times*. His satire of life in an industrial society has more relevance today than when it was made. Primarily it is still pure Chaplin, with his perfectly timed and edited sight gags. The story finds the Little Tramp confronting all the dehumanizing inventions of a futuristic manufacturing plant. Especially delightful is the sequence in which Chaplin is used as a guinea pig for an automatic feeding machine that goes berserk. Paulette Goddard plays the beautiful waif the tramp befriends during his adventures.

1936 B & W 89 minutes

MONDO TRASHO

DIRECTOR: John Waters
CAST: Divine, Mary Vivian Pearce, Mink Stole, David Lochary

Director John Waters's longest film—and you can feel every minute of it. This is not a sync-sound movie, and the 1950s rock-'n-roll, along with the occasional wild dubbed-over dialogue, gets tiresome after twenty minutes. The images do not reveal anything visionary or even vaguely humorous. Waters put it best—this is a "gutter film." Unrated, but this is equivalent to an X for violence, gore, and sex.

1971 130 minutes

MONKEY BUSINESS

★★★★½

DIRECTOR: Norman Z. McLeod
CAST: The Marx Brothers, Thelma Todd, Ruth Hall

The Marx Brothers are stowaways on a cruise ship, deflating pomposity and confusing authority. This movie dispenses with needless subplots and stagy musical numbers. It's undiluted Marx zaniness, and one of the team's best films.

1931 B & W 77 minutes

MONSIEUR VERDOUX

★★★★

DIRECTOR: Charles Chaplin
CAST: Charlie Chaplin, Martha Raye, Isobel Elsom, Marilyn Nash, William Frawley

A trend-setting black comedy in which a dandified Parisian Bluebeard murders wives for their money. Wry humor abounds. Charlie Chaplin is superb in the title role. But it's Martha Raye who steals the film—most decidedly in the rowboat scene. The genius that made Charles Spencer Chaplin famous the world over shows throughout.

1947 B & W 123 minutes

MONTY PYTHON AND THE HOLY GRAIL

★★★½

DIRECTOR: Terry Gilliam
CAST: Terry Jones, Graham Chapman, John Cleese, Terry Gilliam, Terry Jones, Michael Palin

The Monty Python gang assault the legend of King Arthur and his knights in this often uproariously funny, sometimes tedious, movie. Rated PG.

1974 90 minutes

MONTY PYTHON LIVE AT THE HOLLYWOOD BOWL

★★★★

DIRECTOR: Terry Hughes
CAST: John Cleese, Eric Idle, Graham Chapman, Terry Jones, Michael Palin, Terry Gilliam

Hold on to your sides! Those Monty Python crazies are back with more unbridled hilarity. The first thirty minutes of this 73-minute concert film nearly had us on the floor. After that, we either had most of the laughs out of our systems or the material was not as funny. Either way, we were never bored—which is a lot more than you can say for most comedies these days. Rated R for profanity, nudity, and the best in bad taste.

1982 73 minutes

MONTY PYTHON'S THE MEANING OF LIFE

★★★★

DIRECTOR: Terry Jones
CAST: John Cleese, Eric Idle, Graham Chapman, Terry Jones, Terry Gilliam

Those Monty Python goons perform a series of sketches on the important issues of life. According to Michael Palin, the film "ranges from philosophy to history to medicine to halibut—especially halibut." It's the English troupe's finest feature film to date—a heady mixture of satiric and surreal bits about the life cycle from birth to death. It may prove offensive to some and a sheer delight to others. Rated R for all manner of offensive goings-on.

1983 103 minutes

MONTY PYTHON'S FLYING CIRCUS (TELEVISION SERIES)

★★★★

DIRECTOR: Ian MacNaughton
CAST: Graham Chapman, John Cleese, Terry Gilliam, Eric Idle, Terry Jones, Michael Palin

This is a series of videos featuring highlights from the popular English TV show of the early 1970s. All the madcap characters remain intact along with the innovative and trendsetting animation by Terry Gilliam. You don't have to be British to enjoy the various political asides and lampoons. You do have to like fast-paced, off-the-wall craziness. The talented cast also conceived and wrote all of the material.

1970–1972 60 minutes each

MOON IS BLUE, THE

★★

DIRECTOR: Otto Preminger
CAST: William Holden, David Niven, Maggie McNamara, Tom Tully, Dawn Addams

It's hard to believe this comedy, based on a stage hit, was once considered highly controversial. We doubt that even your grandmother would be offended by the sexual innuendos in this very moral film. The thin plot concerns a young woman who fends off two slightly aging playboys by repeatedly vowing to remain a virgin until married. The laughs are few in this stagnant piece. It's fun to watch such smooth performers as William Holden and David Niven, but the material betrays them. Today, racier dialogue can be found on any TV sit-com.

1953 B & W 95 minutes

MORGAN

★★★★

DIRECTOR: Karel Reisz

CAST: Vanessa Redgrave, David Warner, Robert Stephens, Irene Handl

In this cult favorite, Vanessa Redgrave decides to leave her wacky husband (David Warner). He's a wild man who has a thing for gorillas (this brings scenes from *King Kong*). Nevertheless, he tries to win her back in an increasingly unorthodox manner. Deeply imbedded in the 1960s, this film still brings quite a few laughs.

1966 B & W 97 minutes

MORGAN STEWART'S COMING HOME

★

DIRECTOR: Alan Smithee

CAST: Jon Cryer, Lynn Redgrave, Viveka Davis, Paul Gleason, Nicholas Pryor

Made before *Pretty in Pink* but released after it to take advantage of the impression Jon Cryer made in that John Hughes teen comedy. The young actor stars in this tepid comedy as a preppie who tries to reorder his family's priorities. Cryer has some good moments, and Lynn Redgrave is topnotch as his mom, but the laughs just aren't there. Rated PG-13.

1987 92 minutes

MORONS FROM OUTER SPACE

★★½

DIRECTOR: Mike Hodges

CAST: Griff Rhys Jones, Mel Smith, James B. Sikking, Dindsdale Landen, Jimmy Nail, Joanne Pearce, Paul Brown

Four aliens from a distant planet crash-land on Earth, but unlike most of the recent films dealing with this idea, their arrival is not a secret and they soon become international celebrities. The comedy comes from the fact that they're idiots and act accordingly. Unfortunately, the morons are not as funny as the viewer would hope. Some good gags and a cohesive plot that hits the corporate world's exploitation of popular culture heroes where it hurts, but on the whole, not enough laughs to deem it a good comedy. Rated PG for language.

1985 78 minutes

MOSCOW ON THE HUDSON

★★★★½

DIRECTOR: Paul Mazursky

CAST: Robin Williams, Maria Conchita Alonso, Cleavant Derricks

Robin Williams stars in this sweet, funny, sad, and sexy comedy as a Russian circus performer who, while on tour in the United States, decides to defect after experiencing the wonders of Bloomingdale's department store in New York. Paul Mazursky (*An Unmarried Woman*; *Blume in Love*) cowrote and directed this touching character study, which features Williams's best screen performance and impressive American screen bows by Maria Conchita Alonso and Cleavant Derricks. Rated R for profanity, nudity, suggested sex, and violence.

1984 115 minutes

MOUSE THAT ROARED, THE

★★★★

DIRECTOR: Jack Arnold

CAST: Peter Sellers, Jean Seberg, Leo McKern

Any film that combines the comic talents of Peter Sellers at his peak can't help but be funny. In this British movie, a tiny European nation devises a foolproof method of filling its depleted treasury. It declares war on the United States, then loses and collects war reparations from the generous Americans. Even foolproof plans don't always go as expected . . . in this case with hilarious results.

1958 83 minutes

MOVERS AND SHAKERS

★★★

DIRECTOR: William Asher

CAST: Walter Matthau, Charles Grodin, Vincent Gardenia, Tyne Daly, Bill Macy, Gilda Radner, Steve Martin, Penny Marshall

This star-studded film starts off well but quickly falls apart. Walter Matthau plays a Hollywood producer who, through loyalty to an old friend and business associate, begins work on a movie project with only the title, *Love in Sex*, to start with. Charles Grodin plays the screenwriter who is commissioned to write the script, which is intended as a tribute to love. But with serious marital problems, Grodin is hardly the proper candidate. Bill Macy is the hack director who is looking for the inspiration to pull off the project. All performances are good, which makes the weak plot more bearable. Rated PG for profanity.

1985 80 minutes

MOVIE MOVIE

★★

DIRECTOR: Stanley Donen

CAST: George C. Scott, Trish Van Devere, Eli Wallach, Red Buttons, Barry Bostwick, Harry Hamlin, Barbara Harris, Art Carney, Ann Reinking, Kathleen Beller

Clever, affectionate spoof of 1930s pictures presents a double feature: *Dynamite Hands* is a black-and-white boxing story; *Baxter's Beauties of 1933* is a lavish, Busby Berkeley–type extravaganza. The nostalgic package even includes a preview of coming attractions. Rated PG.

1978 107 minutes

MOVIE STRUCK (aka pick a star)

★★

DIRECTOR: Edward Sedgewick

CAST: Stan Laurel, Oliver Hardy, Jack Haley, Patsy Kelly, Rosina Lawrence

Typical story about a young girl trying to break into pictures is brightened by a brief appearance by Stan Laurel and Oliver Hardy, who demonstrate the effectiveness of breakaway glass during a barroom confrontation with a tough. Strange musical numbers and some witty dialogue buoy this thin story a little, but Stan and Ollie are still the main reasons to catch this one—and there just isn't that much of them.

1937 B & W 70 minutes

MOVING VIOLATIONS

★★

DIRECTOR: Neal Israel

CAST: John Murray, Jennifer Tilly, James Keach, Wendy Jo Sperber, Sally Kellerman, Fred Willard

Neal Israel and Pat Proft, who brought us *Police Academy* and *Bachelor Party*, writhe again with another "subject" comedy—this time about traffic school. The team has come up with more laughs than usual, and star John Murray does a reasonable job of imitating his older brother, Bill. Definitely a beer-and-popcorn time-passer. Rated PG-13 for profanity and suggested sex.

1985 90 minutes

MURDER BY DEATH

★★★★

DIRECTOR: Robert Moore

CAST: Peter Sellers, Peter Falk, David Niven, Maggie Smith, James Coco, Alec Guinness

Mystery buffs will get a big kick out of this spoof of the genre, penned by Neil Simon. Peter

Sellers, Peter Falk, David Niven, Maggie Smith, and James Coco play thinly disguised send-ups of famed fictional detectives who are invited to the home of Truman Capote to solve a baffling murder. Rated PG.

1976 94 minutes

MY AMERICAN COUSIN

★★★★

DIRECTOR: Sandy Wilson

CAST: Margaret Langrick, John Wildman, Richard Donat, Jane Mortifee, T. J. Scott

This delightful Canadian comedy-drama focuses on what happens when the dull life of 12-year-old Sandra (played by feisty newcomer Margaret Langrick) is invaded by her high-spirited 17-year-old relative, Butch (John Wildman), from California. A warm character study with a number of funny moments, this is a refreshing antidote to the mindless teen flicks so common today. Rated PG for mild sexuality.

1986 110 minutes

MY BEST GIRL

★★½

DIRECTOR: Sam Taylor

CAST: Mary Pickford, Charles "Buddy" Rogers, Lucien Littlefield, Sunshine Hart, Carmelita Geraghty, Hobart Bosworth, Mark Swain, Evelyn Hall

Typical sweet, sunshiny Mary Pickford fare, this is a small-town romantic comedy about a tried-and-true shop girl who falls in love with the new clerk. He's really the boss's son. Virtue is rewarded, of course. Silent.

1927 B & W 60 minutes

MY BREAKFAST WITH BLASSIE

★½

DIRECTORS: Johnny Legend, Linda Lautrec

CAST: Andy Kaufman, Fred Blassie

Former professional wrestling champion Fred Blassie and protegé Andy Kaufman discuss life, breakfast, and various ways of insulting people during a breakfast at a Southern California coffee shop. Spoof on *My Dinner with Andre* is mildly amusing at first and the concept is reasonably clever, but even fans of the two performers will find the film tedious. This one gets a passing grade (barely) for effort, but it really doesn't go anywhere.

1983 60 minutes

MY CHAUFFEUR

★★½

DIRECTOR: David Beaird

CAST: Deborah Foreman, Sam Jones, Howard Hesseman, E. G. Marshall, Sean McClory, John O'Leary

In this better-than-average (for the genre) softcore sex comedy, an aggressive, slightly kooky young woman (Deborah Foreman of *Valley Girl*) upsets things at an all-male limousine company. Rated R for oodles of nudity, leering dirty old men by the truckload, suggested sex, and profanity. Don't let the kids rent this while you're out playing poker.

1986 97 minutes

MY DEAR SECRETARY

★★½

DIRECTOR: Charles Martin

CAST: Laraine Day, Kirk Douglas, Helen Walker, Keenan Wynn, Alan Mowbray

A comedy battle of quips and wits between writer Kirk Douglas and best-selling author Laraine Day. Both lose the picture to Keenan Wynn, who is a droll delight.

1948 B & W 94 minutes

MY DEMON LOVER

★★★½

DIRECTOR: Charlie Loventhal

CAST: Scott Valentine, Michelle Little, Robert Trebor, Gina Gallego, Alan Fudge, Arnold Johnson

Scott Valentine is delightful as a lovable bum who is possessed by the devil. His infatuation with a very gullible Denny (Michelle Little) becomes complicated when he is transformed into a demon every time he gets amorous. Denny stands by him as they seek a solution to his problem. A spoof on horror flicks, *My Demon Lover* contains several hilarious moments. The special effects are also good. Rated PG for simulated sex and mild gore.

1987 87 minutes

MY FAVORITE BRUNETTE

★★★★½

DIRECTOR: Elliott Nugent
CAST: Bob Hope, Dorothy Lamour, Peter Lorre, Lon Chaney Jr., John Hoyt

Classic Bob Hope comedy with Bob as a photographer who, thanks to a case of mistaken identity, makes No. 1 on the death list of a gang of thugs, played beautifully by Peter Lorre, Lon Chaney, John Hoyt, and Elisha Cook Jr. The gags fly one after another as Bob tries every trick in the book to save his neck, as well as Dorothy Lamour's. A scream!

1947 B & W 87 minutes

MY FAVORITE WIFE

★★★★★

DIRECTOR: Garson Kanin
CAST: Cary Grant, Irene Dunne, Randolph Scott

Cary Grant and Irene Dunne teamed up for many hilarious films, but the best is this often-copied comedy. Grant is a widower about to be remarried when his long-lost and presumed-dead wife (Dunne) is rescued after years on an island with a handsome young scientist (Randolph Scott). The delightful complications that result make this one of the 1940s' best comedies.

1940 B & W 88 minutes

MY FAVORITE YEAR

★★★★½

DIRECTOR: Richard Benjamin
CAST: Peter O'Toole, Joseph Bologna, Lainie Kazan, Bill Macy

This warm-hearted, hilarious comedy is an affectionate tribute to the frenzied Golden Age of television, that period when uninhibited comics like Sid Caesar faced the added pressure of performing live. With superb performances all around and on-the-money direction by Richard Benjamin, it's a real treasure. Rated PG for slight profanity and sexual situations.

1982 92 minutes

MY LITTLE CHICKADEE

★★★★★

DIRECTOR: Edward Kline
CAST: W. C. Fields, Mae West, Dick Foran, Joseph Calleia

W. C. Fields and Mae West enter a marriage of convenience in the Old West. It seems the card sharp (Fields) and the tainted lady (West) need to create an aura of respectability before they descend upon an unsuspecting town. That indicates trouble ahead for the town, and lots of fun for viewers.

1940 B & W 83 minutes

MY LOVE FOR YOURS

★★★

DIRECTOR: Edward H. Griffith
CAST: Madeleine Carroll, Fred MacMurray, Allan Jones, Helen Broderick, Akim Tamiroff, Osa Massen, John Qualen

An eager cast and a witty script make a passable entertainment of this otherwise trite story of a cool, self-assured career girl thawed by love. It's also known as *Honeymoon in Bali*.

1939 B & W 99 minutes

MY MAN GODFREY

★★★★★

DIRECTOR: Gregory La Cava
CAST: Carole Lombard, William Powell, Gail Patrick, Alice Brady, Eugene Pallette

My Man Godfrey is one of the great screwball comedies of the 1930s. The standard formula for a screwball comedy is quite simple. You take a wacky family, preferably rich, and add one relatively sane individual loosely sprinkled in their midst. Then mix thoroughly until all the craziness boils to the surface. In *My Man Godfrey*, Carole Lombard plays the most eccentric member of an eccentric family. William Powell is the relatively sane portion of the formula. Carole finds him when she is sent to find a "lost man." Powell seems to fit the bill, since he's living a hobo's life on the wrong side of the tracks. She brings him home to act as the umpteenth butler the family has employed. Most seem to last only a few days in this nuthouse, but Powell has some surprises in store for the family.

1936 B & W 95 minutes

MY TUTOR

★

DIRECTOR: George Bowers
CAST: Matt Lattanzi, Caren Kaye, Kevin McCarthy

It looks like a dumb exploitation movie. It sounds like a ripoff of *Private Lessons*. It's advertised like a sleazoid trash. Put it all together and that's exactly what this film—in which a young man (Matt Lattanzi) gets an education in more than just reading, writing, and 'rithmetic from his warm and willing tutor, Caren Kaye—is. Beware. Rated R for nudity and implied sex.

1983 97 minutes

NASTY HABITS

★★

DIRECTOR: Michael Lindsay-Hogg
CAST: Glenda Jackson, Sandy Dennis, Susan Penhaligon, Edith Evans, Melina Mercouri

Nasty Habits promises much more than it delivers. As a satire of the Watergate conspiracy placed in a convent, it relies too heavily on the true incident for its punch. Philadelphia is the setting for the confrontation between Alexandra (Glenda Jackson) and Felicity (Susan Penhaligon), who are vying for the position of abbess after the sudden death of the incumbent, Hildegarde (Edith Evans). Because the script only superficially exploits the potential of the theme, it falls to the performers to supply the film's high points, which they do admirably. In the end, however, the film surpasses neither *Network* as a biting satire of American culture nor *All the President's Men* as an indictment of our country's political practices. Rated PG, with some profanity.

1977 96 minutes

NEIGHBORS

★★★½

DIRECTOR: John G. Avildsen
CAST: John Belushi, Dan Aykroyd, Cathy Moriarty, Kathryn Walker, Tim Kazkurinsky

This is a strange movie. John Belushi plays a suburban homeowner whose peaceful existence is threatened when his new neighbors (played by Dan Aykroyd and Cathy Moriarty of *Raging Bull*) turn out to be complete wackos. It isn't a laugh-a-minute farce, but there are numerous chuckles and a few guffaws along the way. It's never boring.... You're always wondering what outrageous thing will happen next. Rated R because of profanity and sexual content.

1981 94 minutes

NEVER GIVE A SUCKER AN EVEN BREAK

★★★★

DIRECTOR: Edward Cline
CAST: W. C. Fields, Gloria Jean, Leon Errol

This is a wild and wooly pastiche of hilarious gags and bizarre comedy routines revolving around W. C. Fields's attempt to sell an outlandish script to a movie studio. Some of the jokes misfire, but the absurdity of the situations makes up for the weak spots.

1941 B & W 71 minutes

NEW LEAF, A

★★★★

DIRECTOR: Elaine May
CAST: Walter Matthau, Elaine May, Jack Weston, James Coco, William Redfield

A rare (and wonderful) triple play from an American female talent: writer-director-star Elaine May makes an impressive mark with this latter-day screwball comedy, about a bankrupt rogue (Walter Matthau) who must find a rich woman to marry—within six weeks. His target turns out to be a clumsy botanist (May) seeking immortality by finding a new specimen of plant life (hence one element of the title). Matthau is at his sly best, and May demonstrates timing so splendid it's a shame she chooses not to appear on screen more often. A true find, not to be missed. Rated PG for adult situations.

1971 102 minutes

NEW WAVE COMEDY

★

DIRECTOR: Michael Kriegman
CAST: Mark Weiner, Eric Bogosian, Margaret Smith, John Kassir, Wayne Federman, Patty Rosborough, Jefferey Essman, Steve Sweeny

A comical hodgepodge offering everything from breakdancing hand puppets to an overly worldly Barbie Doll impersonation. The only familiar faces in this eight-part comedy tape are those of Mark Weiner (*Saturday Night Live*), Margaret Smith, a deadpan stand-up comic who frequents the David Letterman set, and John Kassir, the 1985 comedy champ from *Star Search*. Strong language.

1986 60 minutes

NICE DREAMS

★★★

DIRECTOR: Thomas Chong
CAST: Cheech and Chong, Evelyn Guerrero, Paul Reubens, Stacy Keach

Cheech and Chong, the counterculture kings of drug-oriented comedy, haven't run out of steam yet. Their third feature film doesn't have quite as many classic comic gems as its predecessors, but it's more consistently entertaining. Rated R for nudity and profanity.

1981 87 minutes

NICK DANGER IN THE CASE OF THE MISSING YOLK

🦃

DIRECTOR: William Dear
CAST: Firesign Theatre Players, Wendy Cutler, Christy Kaatz

The usually funny Firesign Theatre Players (Phil Austin, Peter Berman, and Phil Proctor) don't quite make it with this one. A hillbilly family, the Yolks, are transported to a futuristic home with multiple gadgets and begin to realize that their poor, simple lifestyle was not so bad after all. Private eye Nick Danger becomes involved with the family when their son runs away with a TV commercial star and both are kidnapped. All we can say for this not-quite-funny spoof is that it'll provide a speedy cure to insomnia.

1983 60 minutes

NIGHT AT THE OPERA, A

★★★★★

DIRECTOR: Sam Wood
CAST: The Marx Brothers, Margaret Dumont, Kitty Carlisle, Allan Jones, Sigfried Ruman

Despite the songs and sappy love story, the Marx Brothers (minus Zeppo) are in peak form in this classical musical comedy, which co-stars the legendary Margaret Dumont.

1935 B & W 92 minutes

NIGHT IN CASABLANCA, A

★★★

DIRECTOR: Archie L. Mayo
CAST: The Marx Brothers, Charles Drake, Lisette Verea, Dan Seymour, Lois Collier

Although the Marx Brothers' formula was wearing thin by 1946, Groucho's wisecracks and the incomparable antics of Chico and Harpo still carry the film. Joining forces to foil Nazi treasure thieves in post-WWII Casablanca, the brothers anarchize the staid Hotel Casablanca, insulting the guests and wooing the beautiful but evil Beatrice (Lisette Verea).

1946 B & W 85 minutes

NIGHT PATROL

★

DIRECTOR: Jackie Kong
CAST: Linda Blair, Pat Paulsen, Jaye P. Morgan, Jack Riley, Billy Barty, Murray Langston

In this dumb variation on *Police Academy*, screenwriter Murray Langston plays a bumbling rookie policeman who doubles at night as "The Unknown Comic," cracking jokes in Los Angeles comedy clubs while wearing a paper bag over his head. The jokes often are offensive and the plot even worse. Even the few laughs it contains doesn't make this cheapo release worth sitting through. Miss it. Rated R for the usual garbage.

1985 84 minutes

NIGHT SHIFT

★★★★

DIRECTOR: Ron Howard
CAST: Henry Winkler, Shelley Long, Michael Keaton

When a nerdish morgue attendant (Henry Winkler) gets talked into becoming a pimp by a sweet hooker (Shelley Long) and his crazed co-worker (Michael Keaton), the result is uproarious comedy. While the concept is a little weird, director Ron Howard (Winkler's co-star in the old *Happy Days* television series) packs it with so many laughs and such appealing characters that you can't help but like it. Rated R for nudity, profanity, sex, and violence.

1982 105 minutes

NIGHT THEY RAIDED MINSKY'S, THE

★★★½

DIRECTOR: William Friedkin
CAST: Britt Ekland, Jason Robards Jr., Elliott Gould

Director William Friedkin's (*The French Connection*) tale of a religious girl's (Britt Ekland) involvement, much to her father's dismay, with a burlesque comic (Jason Robards). It's a nice look at what early burlesque was like, with good performances by all. Rated PG.

1968 99 minutes

1941

DIRECTOR: Steven Spielberg
CAST: John Belushi, Dan Aykroyd, Toshiro Mifune, Christopher Lee, Slim Pickens, Ned Beatty, John Candy, Nancy Allen, Tim Matheson, Murray Hamilton, Treat Williams

Steven Spielberg laid his first and (so far) only multimillion-dollar egg with this unfunny what-if comedy about the Japanese attacking Los Angeles during World War II. An all-star cast is all but completely wasted in this—pardon the pun—bomb. Rated PG.

1979 118 minutes

NINE TO FIVE

★★★★

DIRECTOR: Colin Higgins
CAST: Jane Fonda, Lily Tomlin, Dolly Parton, Dabney Coleman

In this delightful comedy, Jane Fonda almost ends up playing third fiddle to two marvelous comediennes, Lily Tomlin and Dolly Parton. (That's right, Dolly Parton!) The gifted singer-songwriter makes one of the brightest acting debuts ever in this hilarious farce about three secretaries who decide to get revenge on their sexist, egomaniacal boss (Dabney Coleman). Rated PG.

1980 110 minutes

92 IN THE SHADE

★★★

DIRECTOR: Thomas McGuane
CAST: Peter Fonda, Warren Oates, Margot Kidder, Harry Dean Stanton, Burgess Meredith, Elizabeth Ashley, Sylvia Miles

This wild and hilarious adaptation of first-time director Thomas McGuane's prize-winning novel concerns rival fishing-boat captains in Florida. Entire cast is first-rate in this sleeper from the summer of 1975. Take a chance on this one. Rated R.

1975 93 minutes

NINOTCHKA

★★★★★

DIRECTOR: Ernst Lubitsch
CAST: Greta Garbo, Melvyn Douglas, Bela Lugosi

"Garbo laughs," proclaimed the ads of its day; and so will you in this classic screen comedy. Greta Garbo is a soviet commissar sent to Paris to check on the lack of progress of three bumbling trade envoys who have been seduced by the decadent trappings of capitalism. Melvyn Douglas, as a Parisian playboy, meets Garbo at the Eiffel Tower and plans a seduction of his own, in this most joyous of Hollywood comedies.

1939 B & W 110 minutes

NO MAN OF HER OWN

★★★★

DIRECTOR: Wesley Ruggles
CAST: Clark Gable, Carole Lombard

A big-time gambler marries a local girl on a bet and tries to keep her innocent of his activities. This vintage film has everything the average film fan looks for—drama, romance, and comedy.

1932 B & W 85 minutes

NO SMALL AFFAIR

★★½

DIRECTOR: Jerry Schatzberg
CAST: Jon Cryer, Demi Moore

A 16-year-old amateur photographer named Charles Cummings (Jon Cryer) falls in love with an up-and-coming 23-year-old rock singer, Laura Victor (Demi Moore), and his passion for her eventually leads to the performer's big break. A mixture of delightfully clever and unabashedly stupid elements, *No Small Affair* ultimately fails as a screen entertainment. That's really too bad. In the first half-hour, it seems to be adding up to a little comic gem. Yet it goes on to prompt extreme disbelief and disappointment. Rated R for nudity, violence, and profanity.

1984 102 minutes

NO TIME FOR SERGEANTS

★★★★

DIRECTOR: Mervyn LeRoy

CAST: Andy Griffith, Nick Adams, Myron McCormick, Murray Hamilton, Don Knotts

In this hilarious film version of the Broadway play by Ira Levin, young Andy Griffith is superb as a country boy drafted into the service. You'll scream with laughter as good-natured Will Stockdale (as portrayed by Andy on stage as well as here) proceeds to make a complete shambles of the U.S. Air Force through nothing more than sheer ignorance. This is film comedy at its best. One criticism: Don Knotts's only scene is way too short, though it alone is worth the price of a rental.

1957 B & W 119 minutes

NOBODY'S FOOL

★

DIRECTOR: Evelyn Purcell

CAST: Rosanna Arquette, Eric Roberts, Mare Winningham, Jim Youngs, Louise Fletcher, Charlie Barnett

Despite its pedigree—a screenplay by playwright Beth Henley *(Crimes of the Heart)*—this film is a real disappointment that wastes the talents of its stars, Rosanna Arquette and Eric Roberts. The only thing it has going for it is a kind of sustained wackiness, and this is not enough to keep the viewer entertained for its nearly two hour running time. It is, one guesses, supposed to be a black comedy, but, if so, it is never funny or gruesome enough. Arquette plays a small-town klutz who is fated to fall in love with the lighting director (Roberts) of a traveling theatrical company. Because both characters are such oddballs, we couldn't care less whether they get together or not. As a result, *Nobody's Fool* is darn near nobody's movie. Rated PG-13 for mild violence.

1986 107 minutes

NOBODY'S PERFEKT

★

DIRECTOR: Peter Bonerz

CAST: Gabe Kaplan, Alex Karras, Robert Klein, Susan Clark, Paul Stewart, Alex Rocco

Three friends all undergoing psychoanalysis (Gabe Kaplan, Robert Klein, and Alex Karras) decide to extort $650.00 from the city of Miami to pay for their car, which was totaled because they ran into a large pothole. Along the way, they become heroes by capturing armored-car robbers. This unfunny comedy is one embarrassing flat joke after another. Klein is especially bad as a split personality whose other personas are James Cagney and Bette Davis.

1981 96 minutes

NORMAN CONQUESTS, THE Episode 1: *Table Manners*

★★★½

DIRECTOR: Herbert Wise

CAST: Richard Briers, Penelope Keith, Tom Conti, David Troughton, Fiona Walker, Penelope Wilton

Alan Ayckbourn's clever trilogy is set in a family home in a small English town. The three segments each take place in a different part of the house but encompass the same span of time. Furthermore, each part is complete in itself, but blends with the others for a delightful experience. In the dining room, Norman (Tom Conti) tries to seduce his two sisters-in-law and draws the rest of the family into the tangle with surprising results. Sara (Penelope Keith) is a treat as she tries to organize meals and control the others.

1980 108 minutes

NORMAN CONQUESTS, THE Episode 2: *Living Together*

★★★½

DIRECTOR: Herbert Wise
CAST: Richard Briers, Penelope Keith, Tom Conti, David Troughton, Fiona Walker, Penelope Wilton

The parlor is the setting as the family gathers for the weekend. Norman (Tom Conti) keeps everyone on the run as he drinks, manipulates, and seduces.

1980 93 minutes

NORMAN CONQUESTS, THE Episode 3: *Round and Round the Garden*

★★★½

DIRECTOR: Herbert Wise
CAST: Richard Briers, Penelope Keith, Tom Conti, David Troughton, Fiona Walker, Penelope Wilton

A garden setting rounds out a zany weekend at an English house. As Norman (Tom Conti) pursues his wife's sister and sister-in-law, Tom (David Troughton), the visiting vet, misinterprets the goings-on and embarrasses himself in the bargain.

1980 106 minutes

NORMAN LOVES ROSE

★★★½

DIRECTOR: Henry Safran
CAST: Carol Kane, Tony Owen, Warren Mitchell, Myra de-Groot, David Downer

In this Australian-made comedy, Tony Owen plays a love-struck teenager who is enamored of his sister-in-law, Carol Kane. When she gets pregnant, the question of paternity arises. Lots of laughs in this one! Rated R.

1982 98 minutes

NOT FOR PUBLICATION

★★½

DIRECTOR: Paul Bartel
CAST: Nancy Allen, David Naughton, Lawrence Luckinbill

A writer and a photographer attempt to break out of sleazy tabloid journalism by doing an investigative piece about high-level corruption. Amusing story starts off well but loses momentum. Playful, but not as distinctive as Paul Bartel's other works, such as *Eating Raoul* and *Lust in the Dust*. Rated PG for profanity.

1984 87 minutes

NOTHING PERSONAL

DIRECTOR: George Bloomfield
CAST: Donald Sutherland, Suzanne Somers, Lawrence Dane, Roscoe Lee Browne, Dabney Coleman, Saul Rubinek, John Dehner

A romantic comedy about the fight to stop the slaughter of baby seals? This is how Suzanne Somers decided to launch her motion picture career? Sure, Donald Sutherland is a dependable leading man, but even he looks silly in this mishmash of message and entertainment. It should have been called *Nothing Playing*. Rated PG.

1980 97 minutes

NOTHING SACRED

★★★★

DIRECTOR: William Wellman
CAST: Carole Lombard, Fredric March, Walter Connolly, Charles Winninger, Frank Fay

Ace scriptwriter Ben Hecht's cynical mixture of slapstick and bitterness perfectly performed by Fredric March and Carole Lombard makes this satirical comedy a real winner. Vermont innocent Lombard is mistakenly thought to be dying of a rare disease. Goaded by his editor, Walter Connolly, a crack New York reporter (March) pulls out all the stops in exploiting her to near national sainthood. The boy-bites-man scene is priceless.

1937 75 minutes

NUMBER ONE OF THE SECRET SERVICE

★★★

DIRECTOR: Lindsay Shonteff
CAST: Nicky Henson, Richard Todd, Aimi MacDonald, Geoffrey Keen, Sue Lloyd, Dudley Sutton, Jon Pertwee, Milton Reid

In this enjoyable spoof of James Bond films, secret agent Charles Blind attempts to stop evil Arthur Loveday from killing prominent international financiers. Rated PG.

1970 87 minutes

NUTCASE

DIRECTOR: Roger Donaldson
CAST: Nevan Rowe, Ian Watkin, Michael Wilson, Ian Mune, Melissa Donaldson, Peter Shand, Aaron Donaldson

The kids are the only ones who aren't complete idiots in this silly movie. The plot, which is extremely far-fetched, has a group of wacky villains threatening to blow up New Zealand's volcanoes if they don't receive $5 million. The bumbling police department gets even worse when their coffee is laced with laughing powder. Only the children can stop the villains by using the anti-gravity device that young Jamie has invented. The show is both bizarre and low-budget. The villains, the police, and even the garbage men sing weird tunes at strange times. This show is not recommended for anyone, but 8- to 12-year-olds—and anyone who enjoys the Keystone Kops—may find it mildly amusing.

1983 49 minutes

NUTTY PROFESSOR, THE

★★★★

DIRECTOR: Jerry Lewis
CAST: Jerry Lewis, Stella Stevens, Kathleen Freeman

Jerry Lewis's funniest self-directed comedy, this release—a take-off on Robert Louis Stevenson's *Dr. Jekyll and Mr. Hyde*—is about a klutz who becomes a smoothie when he drinks a magic formula. Reportedly, this was Lewis's put-down of former partner Dean Martin.

1963 107 minutes

ODD COUPLE, THE

★★★★

DIRECTOR: Gene Saks
CAST: Walter Matthau, Jack Lemmon, John Fiedler, Herb Edelman

Walter Matthau as Oscar Madison and Jack Lemmon as Felix Unger bring Neil Simon's delightful stage play to life in this comedy. They play two divorced men who try living together. Felix has just split up with his wife of twelve years and is going through an emotional crisis. The biggest laughs come from the fact that Felix is "Mr. Clean" and Oscar is a total slob—they're constantly getting on each other's nerves. Rated G.

1968 105 minutes

ODDBALLS

DIRECTOR: Miklos Lente
CAST: Foster Brooks, Michael Macdonald, Konnie Krome

Beefing up character actor Foster Brooks's role might have saved this confusing comedy, but we doubt it. Brooks plays the alcoholic owner of a boys' summer camp. Naturally, his camp is directly across from Camp Bountiful, which is a retreat for sexy young women. The plot (?!) thickens when Brooks agrees to sell his camp to a man who'd like to use it for a shopping mall. Many strange, unbelievable, unrelated bits are thrown in. Rated PG for obscenities and sexual situations.

1984 92 minutes

OFF BEAT

★★★

DIRECTOR: Michael Dinner
CAST: Meg Tilly, Judge Reinhold, Cleavant Derricks, Harvey Keitel

This attempt at an old-fashioned romantic comedy succeeds as a romance, but as a comedy, it elicits only an occasional chuckle. One gains instant sympathy for captivating Meg Tilly's vulnerable big-city police officer. She finds herself falling for her partner, Judge Reinhold, while trying out for a mixed precinct police dance program. The humor was intended to be generated from the fact that Reinhold is only masquerading as a cop; he's actually a shy, fumbling librarian. As much as we like the Tilly-Reinhold pairing, the script leaves them with nothing unpredictable or interesting to do. Rated PG.

1986 100 minutes

OFF LIMITS

★½

DIRECTOR: George Marshall
CAST: Bob Hope, Mickey Rooney, Marilyn Maxwell, Marvin Miller

Marilyn Maxwell adds a little "oomph" to this otherwise silly story of two army buddies and their inane and seldom hilarious antics. Yet another of those limp comedies about an ineffectual loser who winds up a boxing contender; the concept was stale years before this dud was filmed, having been done by most of the comedy greats and not-so-greats as well as comedy teams. Only the presence of Bob Hope and Mickey Rooney makes this film worth watching, and both are represented on video in much better films. Basically lightweight filler and a source of much-needed revenue for Mickey Rooney in those lean years following his departure from the protection of the MGM fold.

1953 B & W 89 minutes

OFF THE WALL

[turkey]

DIRECTOR: Rick Friedberg
CAST: Paul Sorvino, Patrick Cassidy, Rosanna Arquette, Billy Hufsey, Mickey Gilley, Ralph Wilcox, Monte Markham

A Tennessee speed demon (Rosanna Arquette) picks up two handsome hitchhikers (Billy Hufsey and Patrick Cassidy) and leaves them to take the rap for her joyriding. When they're sentenced to six months in Snake Canyon Prison, they must deal with the wacky warden (Paul Sorvino), hardened criminals, and Arquette's attempts to rescue them. This low-budget farce would be best forgotten. Rated R.

1982 86 minutes

OH DAD, POOR DAD—MAMA'S HUNG YOU IN THE CLOSET AND I'M FEELING SO SAD

★★★½

DIRECTOR: Richard Quine
CAST: Rosalind Russell, Robert Morse, Barbara Harris, Jonathan Winters, Lionel Jeffries

A cult favorite, and deservedly so. The plot has something to do with an odd young man (Robert

Morse) whose mother (Rosalind Russell) drags him off on a vacation in the tropics with the boy's dead father. Morse excels in this unique, well-written, often hilarious film.

1967 86 minutes

OH GOD!

★★★★

DIRECTOR: Carl Reiner

CAST: George Burns, John Denver, Teri Garr, Ralph Bellamy

God is made visible to a supermarket manager in this modern-day fantasy. The complications that result make for some predictable humor, but the story is kept flowing by some inspired casting. Ageless George Burns is a perfect vision of a God for Everyman in his tennis shoes and golf hat. John Denver exudes the right degree of naivete as the put-upon grocer. Rated PG.

1977 104 minutes

OH, GOD! BOOK II

★★

DIRECTOR: Gilbert Cates

CAST: George Burns, Suzanne Pleshette, David Birney, Louanne, Howard Duff

George Burns, as God, returns in this fair sequel and enters a little girl's life, assigning her the task of coming up with a slogan that will revive interest in him. So she comes up with "Think God" and begins her campaign. It's passable family fare. Rated PG.

1980 94 minutes

OH GOD, YOU DEVIL!

★★★★½

DIRECTOR: Paul Bogart

CAST: George Burns, Ted Wass, Roxanne Hart, Ron Silver, Eugene Roche

George Burns is back as the wisecracking, cigar-smoking deity. Only this time he plays a dual role—appearing as the devil. Ted Wass (*Curse of the Pink Panther*) is the songwriter who strikes a Faustian bargain with Burns's bad side. This delightful comedy-with-a-moral is guaranteed to lift your spirits and make the whole world seem brighter. It's as emotionally moving as Frank Capra's *It's a Wonderful Life* and as funny as anything ever made by Hollywood's greatest clowns—the Marx Brothers, W. C. Fields, Laurel and Hardy, Mae West... you name it. Rated PG for suggested sex and profanity.

1984 96 minutes

OKLAHOMA ANNIE

★

DIRECTOR: R. G. Springsteen

CAST: Judy Canova, John Russell, Grant Withers, Allen Jenkins, Almira Sessions, Minerva Urecal

This moronic movie is little more than an excuse for Judy Canova to ham it up and inflict a few tunes on the audience as she chases the varmints out of town and brings decency to her community. Mercifully, this was one of the last films Canova made America suffer through and is almost redeemed by a great cast of familiar character actors.

1952 90 minutes

ON APPROVAL

★★★

DIRECTOR: Clive Brook

CAST: Beatrice Lillie, Clive Brook, Googie Withers, Roland Culver

Former Sherlock Holmes Clive Brook displays a confident hand at directing in this enjoyable farce about women who exchange boyfriends. Fun and breezy with terrific performances by some of England's best talents, this film gave beloved Beatrice Lillie one of her best screen roles and proved popular on both sides of the Atlantic. Just as funny now as when it was originally released.

1943 B & W 80 minutes

ONCE BITTEN

★★★

DIRECTOR: Howard Storm
CAST: Lauren Hutton, Jim Carrey, Karen Kopins, Cleavon Little

Sly little vampire film about an ancient bloodsucker (Lauren Hutton) who can remain young and beautiful only by periodically supping on youthful male virgins. Likable Jim Carrey is her latest target, and their first few encounters (three's the magic number) leave him with an appetite for raw hamburgers and a tendency to sleep during the day so as to avoid sunlight. Girlfriend Karen Kopins enters the picture and faces a climactic decision: Is her virtue more important than Carrey's life? Cleavon Little has a droll supporting part as Hutton's prim and proper personal servant. A tasty little treat. Rated PG-13 for sexual situations.

1985 92 minutes

ONCE UPON A HONEYMOON

★★½

DIRECTOR: Leo McCarey
CAST: Ginger Rogers, Cary Grant, Walter Slezak, Albert Dekker, Albert Bassermann, Ferike Boros, Harry Shannon, Natasha Lytess, John Banner

In this travesty, one Cary Grant preferred to forget, he plays a newspaperman trying to get innocent stripteaser Ginger Rogers out of Europe as the German army advances. Complicating matters is her marriage to Nazi officer Walter Slezak. This amusing adventure-comedy is a bit dated, but Grant fans won't mind.

1942 B & W 117 minutes

ONE CRAZY SUMMER

★★½

DIRECTOR: Savage Steve Holland
CAST: John Cusack, Demi Moore, Curtis Armstrong, Bobcat Goldthwait, Joel Murray, Joe Flaherty, Tom Villard, Kimberly Foster

Star John Cusack and writer-director Savage Steve Holland of *Better Off Dead* are reunited in this weird, slightly sick, and sometimes stupidly funny comedy about a college hopeful (Cusack) who must learn about love to gain entrance to an institute of higher learning. Say what? If you accept that silly premise, then you may get a few laughs out of *One Crazy Summer*. But we make no guarantee. Rated PG.

1986 94 minutes

ONE MORE SATURDAY NIGHT

★★★½

DIRECTOR: Dennis Klein
CAST: Al Franken, Tom Davis, Moira Harris, Frank Howard, Bess Meyer, Dave Reynolds, Chelcie Ross, Nan Woods, Eric Saiet, Jessica Schwartz

Al Franken and Tom Davis, who were writers and semiregulars on the original *Saturday Night Live* TV show, star in this enjoyable comedy, which they also wrote, about the problems encountered by adults and teenagers when trying to get a date on the most important night of the week. In its humane and decidedly offbeat way, *One More Saturday Night* is about the human condition in all its funny/sad complexity. Rated R for profanity and simulated sex.

1986 95 minutes

ONE RAINY AFTERNOON

★★

DIRECTOR: Rowland V. Lee
CAST: Francis Lederer, Ida Lupino, Roland Young, Hugh Her-

bert, Erik Rhodes, Mischa Auer

Silly movie about a young man who causes a furor when he kisses the wrong girl during a performance in the theater. It's a pretty slight premise to builda film on, but under the skillful hands of director Rowland V. Lee (*The Count of Monte Cristo*, *Son of Frankenstein*), it becomes entertaining fare. A fine supporting cast helps flesh out the thin story, and a young Ida Lupino makes for a lovely leading lady.

1936 B & W 79 minutes

ONE TOUCH OF VENUS

★★

DIRECTOR: William Seiter

CAST: Robert Walker, Ava Gardner

The Pygmalion myth gets the Hollywood treatment, long before *My Fair Lady*, although this is a wee bit diluted. Robert Walker plays a department store window decorator who becomes smitten, predictably, when a display statue of Venus comes to life in the form of Ava Gardner. The potentially entertaining premise is left flat by a script that lacks originality and wit.

1948 B & W 90 minutes

ONE, TWO, THREE

★★★½

DIRECTOR: Billy Wilder

CAST: James Cagney, Arlene Francis, Horst Buchholz, Pamela Tiffin, Lilo Pulver, Howard St. John, Hanns Lothar, Leon Askin, Red Buttons

James Cagney's "retirement" film (and his only movie with famed director Billy Wilder) is a nonstop, madcap assault on the audience. Dialogue and one-liners are thrown and caught by the principals with the timing of a professional sports team, but whether this is amusing or annoying is an individual choice. A throwback to the mayhem and wacky antics of the silent comedians coupled with the clever situations and biting repartee of the great screwball comedies of the mid to late 1930s, this is Cagney's movie and could only have succeeded with him in the lead. Wilder's questionable humor and odd plot about the clash between capitalism and communism and its effect on a young couple could have spelled catastrophe for any other leading man, but veteran Cagney pulls it off with style and leaes the audience wishing that he hadn't stopped making films for twenty years when he was so desperately needed.

1961 B & W 108 minutes

OPERATION PETTICOAT

★★★★

DIRECTOR: Blake Edwards

CAST: Cary Grant, Tony Curtis, Dina Merrill, Gene Evans, Arthur O'Connell, Richard Sargent

The ageless Cary Grant stars with Tony Curtis in this wacky service comedy. They are captain and first officer of a submarine that undergoes a madcap series of misadventures during World War II. Their voyage across the Pacific is further complicated when a group of Navy women is forced to join the crew.

1959 124 minutes

OUR RELATIONS

★★★½

DIRECTOR: Harry Lachman

CAST: Stan Laurel, Oliver Hardy, James Finlayson, Alan Hale, Sidney Toler

Stan Laurel and Oliver Hardy play two sets of twins. One set are sailors; the other are happily married civilians. When the boys' ship docks in the same city, a hilarious case of mistaken identity occurs. Highly enjoyable, the film doesn't lag at all. It features excellent performances by James Finlayson, Alan Hale, and Sidney Toler.

1936 B & W 74 minutes

OUT OF CONTROL

DIRECTOR: Allan Holzman

CAST: Martin Hewitt, Betsy Russell, Jim Youngs

Filmed in Yugoslavia and the USA, this movie seems unable to decide whether it should be a comedy, a romance, or a thriller. A group of teenagers take off for an exciting weekend on a private island. When their plane crashes, they must survive on a seemingly deserted island. The plot thickens when they're discovered by violent smugglers. One of the teenagers, the token nerd named Elliott, offers misplaced Woody Allen–type dialogue throughout. Except for the street-wise cowboy, the teenagers are as helpless as kittens, but not nearly as intelligent. This forgettable film is rated R for obscenities, nudity, and violence.

1984 78 minutes

OUT OF THE BLUE

★★★

DIRECTOR: Leigh Jason

CAST: George Brent, Virginia Mayo, Ann Dvorak, Turhan Bey, Carole Landis, Hadda Brooks

A not very innocent young woman passes out in a naïvely married man's apartment, making all sorts of trouble in this entertaining romantic comedy of errors and such.

1947 B & W 84 minutes

OUT OF TOWNERS, THE

★★★

DIRECTOR: Arthur Hiller

CAST: Jack Lemmon, Sandy Dennis, Sandy Baron, Anne Meara, Billy Dee Williams

Jack Lemmon and Sandy Dennis star in this Neil Simon comedy of a New York City vacation gone awry. It's a good idea that doesn't come off as well as one would have hoped. Rated PG for language.

1970 97 minutes

OUTLAW BLUES

★★½

DIRECTOR: Richard Heffron

CAST: Peter Fonda, Susan Saint James, James Callahan, Michael Lerner

Yet another of Peter Fonda's harmless but rather bland light comedies. He's an ex-con with a talent for song-writing but little in the way of industry smarts; he naively allows established country-western star James Callahan to make off with a few hits. Aided by backup singer Susan Saint James, in a charming little part, Fonda figures out how to outfox the Establishment and succeed on his own. Would have made a good television film, but it's too understated for the big screen. Rated PG for light violence and brief nudity.

1977 100 minutes

OUTRAGEOUS

★★★★

DIRECTOR: Richard Benner

CAST: Craig Russell, Hollis McLaren, Richard Easley

A very offbeat and original comedy drama concerning a gay nightclub performer's relationship with a pregnant mental patient. A different kind of love story, told with taste and compassion. Female impersonator Craig Russell steals the show. Take a chance on this one. Rated R.

1977 100 minutes

OUTRAGEOUS FORTUNE

★★★★

DIRECTOR: Arthur Hiller
CAST: Bette Midler, Shelley Long, Peter Coyote, Robert Prosky, John Schuck, George Carlin

Yet another delightfully inventive adult comedy from Disney's Touchstone arm, highlighted by a show-stealing performance by the Mae West of the 1980s: Bette Midler. Her strutting, strident would-be actress is a scream, a word that also describes the level at which she delivers her rapid-fire dialogue. (Why speak a line when it can be hurled?) Shelley Long, the personification of grace under fire, is the straight (wo)man in this rarest of film commodities: a buddy comedy starring two women. Of course, the two hate each other on sight, but quickly form an uneasy alliance when they discover that both have developed passionate romances with the same man—who is presumed dead after being blown up in a flower shop (!). Nobody is what he appears to be in Leslie Dixon's sly, witty script, least of all Peter Coyote, as the object of both women's affections. The laughs are fast and furious in this one, and you'll have a wonderful time. Rated R for profanity.

1987 100 minutes

OVER THE BROOKLYN BRIDGE

★★½

DIRECTOR: Menahem Golan
CAST: Elliott Gould, Shelley Winters, Sid Caesar, Carol Kane, Burt Young, Margaux Hemingway

Elliott Gould stars in this occasionally interesting but mostly uneven slice-of-life story about a slovenly, diabetic Jewish luncheonette owner who dreams of getting out by buying a restaurant in downtown Manhattan. Standing in the way are his strict but loony relatives and his chic fashion-model girlfriend, who isn't Jewish. Full of eccentric characters, including Sid Caesar as Gould's uncle and Shelley Winters in her umpteenth Jewish-mother turn. Marred by poor direction and some extremely crude and unnecessary scenes. Rated R for nudity and profanity.

1983 108 minutes

OWL AND THE PUSSYCAT, THE

★★★★

DIRECTOR: Herbert Ross
CAST: Barbra Streisand, George Segal, Robert Klein

Barbra Streisand plays a street-smart but undereducated prostitute who teams up with intellectual snob and bookstore clerk George Segal. The laughs abound as the two express themselves, with numerous debates, in this comedy. Rated R.

1970 95 minutes

PACK UP YOUR TROUBLES

★★★

DIRECTOR: George Marshall
CAST: Stan Laurel, Oliver Hardy

Stan Laurel and Oliver Hardy join the army in World War I, with the usual disastrous results. After being discharged, they assume responsibility for a fallen comrade's young daughter and search for her grandparents. The plot line and scripting aren't as solid as in other films, but the boys squeeze out every laugh possible.

1932 B & W 68 minutes

PADDY

★★½

DIRECTOR: Daniel Haller
CAST: Des Cave, Milo O'Shea, Dearbha Molloy, Peggy Cass

Excellent performances by all the actors, especially Des Cave in the title role, cannot save this rather confused coming-of-age comedy.

Despite moments of true hilarity, the film remains at best mildly amusing.

1969 97 minutes

PALEFACE, THE

★★★★½

DIRECTOR: Norman McLeod

CAST: Bob Hope, Jane Russell, Robert Armstrong

When most people think of Bob Hope comedies, they tend to remember his perfectly putrid pictures from the 1960s and 1970s. But there was a time—in the 1930s, 1940s, and early 1950s—that the name Hope on a theater marquee meant marvelous movie merriment. Take this delightful 1948 western spoof, for example. Hope stars as a cowardly dentist who marries Calamity Jane (Jane Russell in rare form) and becomes, thanks to her quick draw, a celebrated gunslinger. It inspired a sequel, *Son of Paleface*, and a remake, *The Shakiest Gun in the West*, with Don Knotts, but the original is still tops.

1948 91 minutes

PALM BEACH STORY, THE

★★★★

DIRECTOR: Preston Sturges

CAST: Claudette Colbert, Joel McCrea, Rudy Vallee, Mary Astor, Sig Arno, William Demarest, Robert Dudley, Jack Norton, Franklin Pangborn, Jimmy Conlin

Preston Sturges was perhaps the greatest of all American writer-directors. This light story of an engineer's wife (Claudette Colbert) who takes a vacation from marriage in sunny Florida and encounters one of the oddest groupings of talented characters ever assembled may well be his best film. Sturges was a master at turning inconsequential stories and situations into complex, multilayered personality studies. A near-perfect cast of his Paramount stable of actors textures this terrific film and justifies Sturges's reputation as one of American cinema's top talents.

1942 B & W 90 minutes

PANAMA LADY

★★

DIRECTOR: Jack Hively

CAST: Lucille Ball, Allan Lane, Donald Briggs, Evelyn Brent, Steffi Duna, Abner Biberman, William Pawley

Lucille Ball does her best to liven up this tired story about a saloon dancer stuck in the tropics with her pick of the local sweat-soaked swains. Future Saturday-matinee cowboy favorite Allan "Rocky" Lane plays the two-fisted hombre who whisks everybody's favorite redhead off to the romantic oil fields in the jungle that he calls home and shows her the joys of primitive life. This is a remake of *Panama Flo* (1932).

1939 B & W 65 minutes

PANDEMONIUM

★★★

DIRECTOR: Alfred Sole

CAST: Carol Kane, Tom Smothers, Debralee Scott, Candy Azzara, Paul Reubens (Pee-Wee Herman), Miles Chapin, Tab Hunter

After a mass murder of cheerleaders in 1962 and continued attacks on cheerleading camps across the nation, there is only one place left to learn—Bambi's Cheerleading School. Candy Azzara plays Bambi, a former would-be cheerleader. Her 1980 cheerleading camp is small, with an enrollment of only three girls and three boys. They manage to become romantically involved with one another before the killer strikes again. In this parody of slasher movies, Carol Kane steals the show as Candy, a girl with supernatural powers who just wants to have fun and fit in. Tom Smothers is a displaced Canadian Mountie; Paul Reubens (currently Pee-Wee Herman) plays his assistant. Rated PG for obscenities.

1980 82 minutes

PAPER MOON

★★★★★

DIRECTOR: Peter Bogdanovich
CAST: Ryan O'Neal, Tatum O'Neal, Madeline Kahn, John Hillerman

Critic-turned-director Peter Bogdanovich ended his four-film winning streak—which included *Targets*, *The Last Picture Show*, and *What's Up Doc?*—with this comedy, starring Ryan O'Neal and Tatum O'Neal as a con man and a kid in the 1930s who get involved in some pretty wild predicaments and meet up with a variety of wacky characters. It's a delightful entertainment from beginning to end. Rated PG.

1973 B & W 102 minutes

PARADISE MOTEL

★★★

DIRECTOR: Cary Medoway
CAST: Gary Hershberger, Robert Krantz, Joanna Leigh Stack, Bob Basso, Dena Tencate, Rick Gibbs, Laurie Gold

Another teen romp, but with a surprise: the appealing cast can act. Gary Hershberger is a student whose father keeps moving the family around in pursuit of his get-rich schemes. The latest venture is the Paradise Motel. To gain acceptance quickly at his new school, Hershberger loans out one of the rooms to the class stud. All goes well until the girl of his dreams is taken there and then it's time to take a stand. Rated R for language and nudity.

1985 87 minutes

PARAMOUNT COMEDY THEATRE, VOL. 1: WELL DEVELOPED

★★★★

DIRECTOR: Joe Hostettler
CAST: Howie Mandel, Bob Saget, Judy Carter, Philip Wellford, Bruce Mahler

Howie Mandel hosts this very funny comic review filmed live at the Magic Club in Hermosa Beach, California. A big plus is that the material is new, and in many cases it is quite hilarious. Bob Saget is very funny with a fast-paced off-the-wall delivery. Judy Carter combines magic and comedy. Bruce Mahler uses an accordion and piano effectively and has actually put words to "Flight of the Bumble Bee." He also does a hilarious routine as a Jewish ventriloquist whose dummy is a fresh, skinned chicken. Our favorite is Philip Wellford, whose juggling and unicycle skills are perfect complements for his witty delivery. His Adam and Eve routine won an Emmy, and it is easy to see why. There is some adult-oriented material in the first two acts, but the remainder can be seen by the entire family.

1986 65 minutes

PARAMOUNT COMEDY THEATRE, VOL. 2: DECENT EXPOSURES

★★★

DIRECTOR: Joe Hostettler
CAST: Howie Mandel, Marsha Warfield, Doug Ferrari, Paul Feig, Joe Alaskey

Howie Mandel once again hosts live performances by four up-and-coming comedians. Marsha Warfield, from the *Night Court* cast, is a standout. Doug Ferrari makes a couple of good observations on modern hangups. Paul Feig comes off as a well-dressed Pee Wee Herman. The best performance is by Joe Alaskey. His impressions of Don Knotts as Abe Lincoln and Jack Nicholson as Eddie Haskell from *Leave It to Beaver* are very skillful. This is not as good as Volume 1, but it is better than many comedy videos and feature films.

1987 67 minutes

PARDON US

★★★★

DIRECTOR: James Parrott

CAST: Stan Laurel, Oliver Hardy, Wilfred Lucas

Stan Laurel and Oliver Hardy are sent to prison for selling home-brewed beer. They encounter all the usual prison stereotypical characters and play off them to delightful comedy effect. During an escape, they put on black faces and pick cotton along with blacks and Ollie sings "Lazy Moon." Always amusing, this film has few slow or weak spots.

1931 B & W 55 minutes

PARIS HOLIDAY

★★

DIRECTOR: Gerd Oswald

CAST: Bob Hope, Fernandel, Anita Ekberg, Martha Hyer, Preston Sturges

Film-within-a-film show business story featuring Bob Hope and French comic Fernandel never gets off the ground. Statuesque Anita Ekberg succeeds in diverting attention from the two uncomfortable comedians and the hokey subplot involving a gang of counterfeiters, but the real highlight of this film for movie buffs is the appearance of legendary writer-director-producer Preston Sturges in a small role.

1957 101 minutes

PARIS WHEN IT SIZZLES

★★★

DIRECTOR: Richard Quine

CAST: William Holden, Audrey Hepburn, Noel Coward, Gregoire Aslan, Marlene Dietrich

Uneven story-within-a-story about a screenwriter (William Holden) who "creates" a Parisian fantasy-land for himself and the assistant (Audrey Hepburn) with whom he's fallen in love. As the story progresses, they—and the viewer—have an increasingly difficult time distinguishing fact from scripted fiction. Even a brief (don't blink!) appearance by Marlene Dietrich doesn't help matters. As is often the case, this Hollywood-style remake of an enchanting French film (Julien Duvivier's inventive *Holiday for Henrietta*) loses everything in the translation. Unrated; suitable for family viewing.

1954 110 minutes

PARLOR, BEDROOM AND BATH

★★★

DIRECTOR: Edward Sedgwick

CAST: Buster Keaton, Charlotte Greenwood, Reginald Denny, Cliff Edwards, Dorothy Christy, Joan Peers, Sally Eilers, Natalie Moorhead, Edward Brophy

Some genuine belly laughs buoy this slight comedy about a bewildered bumpkin (Buster Keaton) at the mercy of some society wackos. Charlotte Greenwood works well with the Great Stone Face, but it is not the kind of film Keaton did best. Even so, he gave his all in this MGM comedy and created quite a few memorable moments.

1932 B & W 75 minutes

PARTNERS

★★★

DIRECTOR: James Burrows

CAST: Ryan O'Neal, John Hurt

Ryan O'Neal and John Hurt are two undercover detectives assigned to pose as lovers in order to track down the murderer of a gay in this warm, funny, and suspenseful comedy-drama written by Francis Veber (*La Cage aux*

Folles). Rated R for nudity, profanity, violence, and adult themes.

1982 98 minutes

PARTY ANIMAL

DIRECTOR: Havey Hart

CAST: Mathew Causey, Robin Harlan, Tim Carhart, Jerry Jones, Luci Roucis

Not even a great rock soundtrack can save this despicable piece of sludge. Another one of those sex-crazed frat-boy films—a genre that could use a moratorium. Rated R for sex, nudity, and profanity.

1983 78 minutes

PASSPORT TO PIMLICO

★★★½

DIRECTOR: Henry Cornelius

CAST: Margaret Rutherford, Stanley Holloway, Hermione Baddeley, Basil Radford, Naunton Wayne

One of a number of first-rate comedies turned out by Britian in the wake of World War II. A salty group of characters raise hob when they invoke an ancient treaty giving them the right to form their own self-governing enclave smack in the middle of London. Sly Margaret Rutherford and Stanley Holloway divide comedy chores with cricket-crazy Basil Radford and Naunton Wayne.

1948 B & W 85 minutes

PATERNITY

★★★½

DIRECTOR: David Steinberg

CAST: Burt Reynolds, Beverly D'Angelo, Norman Fell, Elizabeth Ashley, Lauren Hutton

Buddy Evans (Burt Reynolds) decides to have a son—without the commitment of marriage—and recruits a music student working as a waitress (Beverly D'Angelo) to bear his child in this adult comedy. The first two-thirds provide belly laughs and chuckles. The problem comes with the unoriginal and predictable romantic ending. But it's still mostly fun. Rated PG because of dialogue involving sex and childbirth.

1981 94 minutes

PATSY, THE

★★½

DIRECTOR: Jerry Lewis

CAST: Jerry Lewis, Everett Sloane, Ina Balin, Keenan Wynn, Peter Lorre, John Carradine

A very minor Jerry Lewis comedy, though the stellar supporting cast is fun to watch. This one is for Lewis fans only; new viewers to Jerry's type of comedy should take in *The Errand Boy* or *The Nutty Professor* first.

1964 101 minutes

PEE WEE HERMAN SHOW, THE

★★½

DIRECTOR: Marty Callner

CAST: Pee-Wee Herman, Phil Hartman, Brian Seft

Adult fans of Pee-Wee Herman will fit right into his childish but risqué playhouse. Others will no doubt wonder what planet he's from. This live comedy-variety show has Pee-Wee entertaining a host of friends: Mailman Mike, Hammie and Susan, Captain Carl, Hermit Annie, and a sexy singer. In addition to these humans, he also converses with a variety of puppets. He sings a semiserious medley of Sly and the Family Stone hits, which is the best part of the program. Unrated, but some of the humor is sexual in nature.

1981 58 minutes

PEE-WEE'S BIG ADVENTURE

★★★½

DIRECTOR: Tim Burton

CAST: Pee-Wee Herman, Elizabeth Daily, Mark Holton, Diane Salinger, Judd Omen

You want weird? Here it is. Pee-Wee Herman, best known for his appearances on *Late Night with David Letterman*, makes the jump from television to feature films with this totally bizarre movie about a man-size petulant 12-year-old goofball (Herman) going on a big adventure after his most prized possession—a bicycle—is stolen by some nasties. The film has some terrific sequences—don't miss the appearance of Large Marge—but overall, it seems more likely to please Herman's fans and his fans alone. Rated PG for a scary scene and some daffy violence.

1985 90 minutes

PEGGY SUE GOT MARRIED

★★★★½

DIRECTOR: Francis Coppola

CAST: Kathleen Turner, Nicolas Cage, Barry Miller, Catherine Hicks, Joan Allen, Kevin J. O'Connor, Lisa Jane Persky, Barbara Harris, Don Murray, Maureen O'Sullivan, Leon Ames, John Carradine

Some have called this film a *Back to the Future* for adults. This description is fine as far as it goes, but there is much more to the film. It has an emotional power that makes it more than just simple entertainment. Wistful, touching, and often joyously funny, it features Kathleen Turner as Peggy, a 43-year-old mother of two who is facing divorce. When she attends her twenty-fifth annual high-school reunion, she is thrust back in time and gets a chance to change the course of her life. Rated PG-13 for profanity and suggested sex.

1986 103 minutes

PERFECT FURLOUGH

★★

DIRECTOR: Blake Edwards

CAST: Tony Curtis, Janet Leigh, Keenan Wynn, Linda Cristal, Elaine Stritch, Troy Donahue

Perfectly forgettable fluff about soldier Tony Curtis (who is taking the leave for his entire unit, which is stationed in the Arctic) and his "perfect" vacation in Paris. The usual setbacks and misunderstandings plague poor Tony's furlough, but at least he gets to meet and eventually win Janet Leigh (Mrs. Tony Curtis at that time) two years before her fatal rendezvous with Norman Bates's mother in a shower stall. An early Blake Edwards film, this harmless escapism typifies American film farces of the late 1950s.

1958 93 minutes

PERILS OF PAULINE, THE

★★★

DIRECTOR: George Marshall

CAST: Betty Hutton, John Lund, Billy de Wolfe, William Demarest, Constance Collier, Frank Faylen

Betty Hutton plays Pearl White, the queen of the silent serials, in this agreeable little movie. The old-style chase scenes and cliff-hanger situations make up for the overdose of sentimentality.

1947 96 minutes

PERSONAL SERVICES

★★★

DIRECTOR: Terry Jones

CAST: Julie Walters, Alec McCowen, Shirley Stelfox

The true-life story of Christine Painter, a British waitress who happened into a very successful career as a brothel madam, catering to gentlemen with kinky interests. Julie Walters gives an all-out performance that's fascinating, but the movie's overall bluntness about its subject matter may be offputting to most American viewers. It's rated R for language.

1987 105 minutes

PHILADELPHIA STORY, THE

★★★★★

DIRECTOR: George Cukor

CAST: Katharine Hepburn, Cary Grant, Jimmy Stewart, Ruth Hussey, John Howard

This is one of the best comedies to come out of Hollywood. From the first scene, where Tracy Lord (Katharine Hepburn) deposits her ex-husband's (Cary Grant) golf clubs in a heap at her front door and in return Grant deposits Hepburn in a heap right next to the clubs, the 1940s version of *The Taming of the Shrew* proceeds at a blistering pace. The scene shifts to the Lord estate, where all is in readiness for Hepburn's second marriage to a stuffy businessman. Some uninvited guests arrive, namely her "ex" and two reporters from a gossip magazine (Ruth Hussey and Jimmy Stewart). Needless to say, this wedding is headed for chaos for Hepburn and grand entertainment for you.

1940 B & W 112 minutes

PIECE OF THE ACTION, A

★★★

DIRECTOR: Sidney Poitier

CAST: Sidney Poitier, Bill Cosby, Denise Nicholas, James Earl Jones, Hope Clark

Third entry in the Bill Cosby–Sidney Poitier partnership (after *Uptown Saturday Night* and *Let's Do It Again*), this one showing Poitier's greater comfort on both sides of the camera. The story concerns a pair of rascals given one of Life's Awful Choices: prison, or a team-up with some social workers to help a group of ghetto kids. It's all been done before, but the material is handled adequately, and Bill Cosby gets his usual chances to mug. A heavy-handed moral, but what else can one expect from such stories? Rated PG.

1977 135 minutes

PILLOW TALK

★★★★

DIRECTOR: Michael Gordon

CAST: Doris Day, Rock Hudson, Tony Randall, Thelma Ritter

If you like the fluffy light comedy of Doris Day and Rock Hudson, this is their best effort. The ever-virginal Miss Day is keeping the wolves at bay. In the tradition of Ralph Bellamy and Gig Young, Tony Randall is excellent as the suitor who never wins the girl.

1959 105 minutes

PINK FLAMINGOS

DIRECTOR: John Waters

CAST: Divine, Mink Stole, David Lochary, Mary Vivian Pearce, Edith Massey, Danny Mills, Channing Wilroy

One of the most infamous films of all times is also an acute study of the seamy underbelly of the bourgeois. *Pink Flamingos* is the story of Babs Johnson (Divine), the "filthiest person alive," and Connie and Raymond Marble (Mink Stole and David Lochary), two challengers who are jealous of Babs's notoriety. The film is shot in cheap 16mm cheesy color, which adds to the sleaziness. As in all of Waters's films, don't look for brilliant acting or sophisticated plot turns—the point here is to shock. If this doesn't, nothing will. Not for the faint at heart. Due to violence, nudity, and very poor taste, we'd rate this one an X.

1972 95 minutes

PINK PANTHER, THE

★★★½

DIRECTOR: Blake Edwards
CAST: Peter Sellers, David Niven, Capucine, Claudia Cardinale, Robert Wagner

Peter Sellers is featured in his first bow as Inspector Jacques Clouseau, the inept French detective, on the trail of a jewel thief known as the Phantom in this, the original *Pink Panther*. This release has some good—and even hilarious—moments. But the sequel, *A Shot in the Dark*, is better.

1964 113 minutes

PINK PANTHER STRIKES AGAIN, THE

★★★½

DIRECTOR: Blake Edwards
CAST: Peter Sellers, Herbert Lom, Lesley-Anne Down, Burt Kwouk, Colin Blakely

Peter Sellers's fourth time out as the clumsy Inspector Clouseau. Clouseau's former supervisor, Herbert Lom, cracks up and tries to destroy the world with a superlaser. Meanwhile, he's hired a team of international killers to do away with Clouseau. One turns out to be Lesley-Anne Down, who falls in love with the diminutive Frenchman . . . the result of which is a surprisingly erotic bedroom scene. Henry Mancini recycles his famous theme yet again; the opening credits, by the Richard Williams Studios, are the best in the series. Rated PG.

1976 103 minutes

PIRATES

DIRECTOR: Roman Polanski
CAST: Walter Matthau, Cris Campion, Charlotte Lewis, Roy Kinnear

A turgid, overblown mess which doesn't even succeed as the pirate comedy it's intended to be. Walter Matthau is horribly miscast as Captain Red, a luckless scoundrel. He sets his eyes on a golden throne and spends most of this interminable picture trying to steal it. Nothing much happens, because the camera's too busy making love with the re-created Spanish galleon (costing eight of the picture's thirty million bucks). Director and co-scripter Roman Polanski has no business even attempting this genre, and the performers should strike it from their résumés. Rated PG-13 for vulgarity.

1986 117 minutes

PLAY IT AGAIN SAM

★★★★½

DIRECTOR: Herbert Ross
CAST: Woody Allen, Diane Keaton, Tony Roberts, Jerry Lacy, Susan Anspach

Woody Allen plays a movie columnist and feature writer who lives his life watching movies. Humphrey Bogart is his idol, and the film commences with the final scenes from *Casablanca*. Allen's wife leaves him for a life of adventure, and the film revolves around some unsuccessful attempts by his friends (Diane Keaton and Tony Roberts) to set him up with a girl. What evolves from that synopsis is a procession of pointed, sometimes ironic, and generally humorous stabs at stereotypes and "manufactured" images. In an age when funny movies may make you smile at best, this is an oasis of sidesplitting humor. Rated PG.

1972 87 minutes

PLAYING FOR KEEPS

DIRECTORS: Bob Weinstein, Harvey Weinstein
CAST: Daniel Jordano, Matthew Penn, Leon W. Grant, Harold Gould, Mary B. Ward, Marisa Tomei, Jimmy Baio

In this achingly familiar movie, a group of teenagers inherit a dilapidated hotel and attempt to turn it into a rock-'n-roll resort for kids. However, a chemical company wants the property for waste dumping and pulls every dirty trick possible to get it. After an interesting fifteen-minute sequence that takes place on the streets of New York and introduces the characters, the film slips into cornball cliché, with very little respite. Rated PG-13 for profanity, violence, nudity, and suggested sex.

1986 103 minutes

PLAZA SUITE

★★★★½

DIRECTOR: Arthur Hiller

CAST: Walter Matthau, Maureen Stapleton, Barbara Harris, Lee Grant

Walter Matthau is at his comic best as he re-creates three separate roles from Neil Simon's stage comedy. The movie is actually three tales of what goes on in a particular suite. Rated PG.

1971 115 minutes

POLICE ACADEMY

★

DIRECTOR: Hugh Wilson

CAST: Steve Guttenberg, George Gaynes, Kim Cattrall, Bubba Smith, Michael Winslow, Andrew Rubin

Here's another *Animal House*–style comedy that tries very hard to be funny. Sometimes it is, and sometimes it isn't. But overall, it's highly forgettable. Director Hugh Wilson created, wrote, produced, and directed the television situation comedy *WKRP in Cincinnati*. And whether he realizes it or not, Wilson is still doing TV comedy —all that's missing in *Police Academy* is the laugh track. Or is it just the laughs? Steve Guttenberg (*The Man Who Wasn't There*) and George Gaynes (*Tootsie*) star. Rated R for nudity, violence, and profanity.

1984 95 minutes

POLICE ACADEMY II: THEIR FIRST ASSIGNMENT

★★

DIRECTOR: Jerry Paris

CAST: Steve Guttenberg, Bubba Smith, David Graf, Michael Winslow, Bruce Mahler, Colleen Camp, Marion Ramsey, Howard Hesseman, George Gaynes

Those inept would-be police officers from Hugh Wilson's *Police Academy* (which was written by Neal Israel and Pat Proft, of *Bachelor Party*) return in this less funny but still box office–potent production. Episodic and silly, it has no story to speak of, just more mindless high jinks with the boys in blue. Rated PG-13 for profanity.

1985 90 minutes

POLICE ACADEMY III: BACK IN TRAINING

DIRECTOR: Jerry Paris

CAST: Steve Guttenberg, Bubba Smith, David Graf, Michael Winslow, Marion Ramsey, Leslie Easterbrook, Art Metrano, Tim Kazurinsky, Bobcat Goldthwait, George Gaynes

The graduates from the original *Police Academy* return to their alma mater to aid their muddleheaded mentor (George Gaynes), who is engaged in a pitched battle with his rival (Art Metrano). The governor has decided to close one of the state's two police academies, and which one survives depends on results. So Steve Guttenberg, Bubba Smith, Michael Winslow, and others come back to take on the training of a new gang of nerds. This, of course, brings one moronic joke after another in a nearly plotless and poorly edited series of set pieces. Rated PG for silly violence and references to body parts.

1986 90 minutes

POLICE ACADEMY 4: CITIZENS ON PATROL

★½

DIRECTOR: Jim Drake

CAST: Steve Guttenberg, Bubba Smith, Michael Winslow, David Graf, Tim Kazurinsky, Sharon Stone, G. W. Bailey, Bobcat Goldthwait

It's like a curse. Each spring a new *Police Academy* movie is released. And each year, for several weeks, it becomes the number-one film in America. Let's just say that if you liked the first three, there's no reason you shouldn't like the fourth—because it's exactly the same. The same unrestrained cast, the same tired lines, the same absence of creativity. Gags that weren't funny before are shamelessly repeated in this one. The best thing you can say about these movies is, believe it or not, they could be worse. Just think: If anything happens to Steve Guttenburg, the star of this series will be . . . Bubba Smith. Rated PG for mild profanity.

1987 87 minutes

POLICE SQUAD!

★★★★

DIRECTORS: Jim Abrahams, David Zucker, Jerry Zucker, Joe Dante, Reza S. Badiyi

CAST: Leslie Nielsen, Alan North

Originally a 1982 summer TV show, with only six episodes aired, this is now a minor cult classic. The folks who made *Airplane!* went all out on this. Each one of the episodes is hilarious, much funnier than the popular film *Police Academy.*

1982 75 minutes

POLYESTER

DIRECTOR: John Waters

CAST: Divine, Tab Hunter, Edith Massey, Mary Garlington, Ken King

Anyone for bad taste? Female impersonator Divine and 1950s heartthrob Tab Hunter play lovers in this film by writer-producer-director John Waters (*Pink Flamingos*). A special gimmick called "Odorama" allows viewers to experience the story's various smells via a scratch-and-sniff card. That's just one reason why *Polyester* really stinks, and it's all intentional. Rated R for bad taste.

1981 86 minutes

POOR LITTLE RICH GIRL, THE

★★★

DIRECTOR: Maurice Tourneur

CAST: Mary Pickford

Mary Pickford's main claim to fame was her uncanny ability to portray convincingly females many years her junior. She stunted her range by doing so again and again, but the public loved it and willingly paid for it. She earned high critical acclaim demonstrating her range in this sentimental comedy-drama. One critic said that she was 8 years old, then a haughty 16, with no warning or motivation for the mercurial change. Silent, with organ music.

1917 B & W 64 minutes

PORKY'S

★½

DIRECTOR: Bob Clark

CAST: Dan Monahan, Mark Herrier, Wyatt Knight, Roger Wilson, Kim Cattrall, Scott Colomby

The ads lied when they called this the "funniest movie about growing up ever made." Dumbest is a better description. Bob Clark (*Tribute*) wrote and directed this "comedy" about teenagers in the 1950s whose hormones and hot tempers lead them into all kinds of strange situations, including a fateful trip to a redneck dive called Porky's. Rated R for vulgarity, nudity, and adult themes.

1981 94 minutes

PORKY'S II: THE NEXT DAY

DIRECTOR: Bob Clark
CAST: Dan Monahan, Wyatt Knight, Mark Herrier, Roger Wilson, Kaki Hunter, Scott Colomby, Nancy Parsons, Edward Winter

Bob Clark (*Tribute*) wrote and directed this sequel to his hit comedy. This time, the lustful kids of Angel Beach High battle with the Ku Klux Klan, which is trying to prevent (of all things) a Shakespeare festival. Dumb. Rated R for the usual garbage.

1983 95 minutes

PORKY'S REVENGE

DIRECTOR: James Komack
CAST: Dan Monahan, Wyatt Knight, Tony Ganios, Mark Herrier, Kaki Hunter, Scott Colomby

James Komack (creator of TV's *Chico and the Man*) took over the directorial reins from creator Bob Clark for the third installment in this teen-lust comedy series. You'd think this switch would bring an improvement, but no-o-o! It's just more of the same stupidity. This time, the owner of the redneck dive that gave the series its name attempts to get even with the goons from Angel Beach High. This turkey gives new meaning to the word *sleeper*. Rated R for profanity, suggested sex, and nudity.

1985 90 minutes

PREPPIES

DIRECTOR: Chuck Vincent
CAST: Nitchie Barrett, Dennis Drake, Steven Holt, Jo-Ann Marshall, Peter Brady Reardon, Katt Shea

Adult movie king Chuck Vincent, with the assistance of Playboy Enterprises, attempted to make the minor leap from porno to R-rated sexploitation flicks with this teen sex comedy. He didn't make it. The performances he elicits from his cast are embarrassingly amateurish. The screenplay he co-authored with Rick Marx about three women of easy virtue who are hired to prevent a trio of college students from passing an important final exam (thus making it possible for a cousin of one of the victims to inherit the family fortune) is just as insipid as those normally found in the substandard explicit sex films with which Vincent made his reputation. Rated R for nudity, simulated sex, and profanity.

1984 90 minutes

PRESIDENT'S ANALYST, THE

★★★★

DIRECTOR: Theodore J. Flicker
CAST: James Coburn, Godfrey Cambridge, Pat Harrington, Will Geer

Vastly underappreciated satire from writer-director Theodore J. Flicker, who concocts a wild tale concerning a psychiatrist (James Coburn) selected to be our president's "secret shrink." Coburn walks away with the picture, his wicked smile and piercing eyes becoming more and more suspicious as he falls prey to the paranoia of his elite assignment. Inevitably, events get beyond his control, and he hurtles through a series of chases, assassination attempts, and kidnappings. Flicker runs out of steam in the last act, although the conclusion may be quite satisfying for those who have always suspected there's more to Ma Bell than meets the eye. Unrated; adult themes.

1967 104 minutes

PRINCE AND THE SHOWGIRL, THE

★★½

DIRECTOR: Laurence Olivier
CAST: Laurence Olivier, Marilyn Monroe, Sybil Thorndike, Jeremy Spencer

In a romantic comedy about the attraction of a nobleman for an American showgirl, you'd want to stress the attraction of opposites. Marilyn Monroe and Laurence Olivier's acting talents are in full flower, and they are fun to watch; however, they are so dissimilar that they never click.

1957 117 minutes

PRINCESS AND THE PIRATE, THE

★★★

DIRECTOR: David Butler
CAST: Bob Hope, Virginia Mayo, Victor McLaglen, Walter Brennan, Walter Selzak

A happy, hilarious Bob Hope howler. He and the beautiful Virginia Mayo are pursued by pirates and trapped by potentate Walter Slezak. Victor McLaglen is properly menacing as a buccaneer bent on their destruction. Walter Brennan is something else—a pirate? This one's lots of fun for all!

1944 94 minutes

PRISONER OF SECOND AVENUE, THE

★★★★

DIRECTOR: Melvin Frank
CAST: Neil Simon, Jack Lemmon, Anne Bancroft, Gene Saks, Elizabeth Wilson, Florence Stanley

Neil Simon blends laughter with tears in this film about an executive (Jack Lemmon) who loses his job and has a nervous breakdown. Anne Bancroft plays Lemmon's wife. Rated PG.

1975 105 minutes

PRISONER OF ZENDA, THE

★★★½

DIRECTOR: Richard Quine
CAST: Peter Sellers, Lionel Jeffries, Elke Sommer, Lynne Frederick

Zany rendition of the classic tale of a look-alike commoner who stands in for the endangered king of Ruritania. A warm and hilarious film despite the lack of critical acclaim. Rated PG for language.

1979 108 minutes

PRIVATE BENJAMIN

★★★★

DIRECTOR: Howard Zieff
CAST: Goldie Hawn, Eileen Brennan, Armand Assante, Robert Webber, Sam Wanamaker

Here's an upbeat, delightful comedy with a gentle message. The movie is at its best in the first half, when Goldie Hawn, as a spoiled Jewish princess, joins the army after the surprise termination of her second marriage. Thanks to the sales pitch of a double-crossing army recruiter, she expects her hitch to be like a vacation in the Bahamas. Of course, it isn't—and that's where most of the fun comes in. The last part of the movie gets a little heavy on the message end, but Hawn's buoyant personality makes it easy to take. Rated R for profanity, nudity, and implicit sex.

1980 110 minutes

PRIVATE EYES, THE

★

DIRECTOR: Lang Elliott
CAST: Tim Conway, Don Knotts, Trisha Noble, Bernard Fox, John Fujioka

If Tim Conway and Don Knotts had depended on movies like this to make it in show business, they could easily have wound up on unemployment rather than television. This Holmes and Watson send-up, directed by Lang Elliott (*The Prize Fighter*), is neither consistently funny nor engaging. In short, a waste of time. Rated PG.

1980 91 minutes

PRIVATE FUNCTION, A

★★★★

DIRECTOR: Malcolm Mowbray
CAST: Michael Palin, Maggie Smith, Denholm Elliott, Richard Griffiths, Tony Haygarth, Bill Paterson, John Normington, Liz Smith, Alison Steadman

The Michael Palin/Maggie Smith team repeat the success of *The Missionary* with this hilarious film about a meek foot doctor and his socially aspiring wife who become involved with the black market during the food rationing days of post–World War II England when they acquire an unlicensed pig. The humor is open to those who like Monty Python, but is also accessible to audiences who do not find that brand of humor funny. Rated R.

1985 96 minutes

PRIVATE LESSONS

★

DIRECTOR: Alan Myerson
CAST: Sylvia Kristel, Howard Hesseman, Eric Brown, Pamela Bryant

This soft-porn comedy, about a wealthy, virginal teen-age boy being seduced by his sexy, conniving 30-year-old housekeeper, is a seedy movie, run through with amateurish acting, cheap production values, and silly dialogue. Rated R because of nudity and sexual content.

1981 87 minutes

PRIVATE POPSICLE

★

DIRECTOR: Boaz Davidson
CAST: Yftach Katzur, Zachi Noy, Jonathan Segall, Bea Fiedler, Dietmar Siegert

In this fourth film featuring the Lemon Popsicle gang, a popular comedy team in Europe, we find the trio joining the Israeli army. But all three of the lads are more interested in the opposite sex than they are in military training or discipline. The attempts at comedy fall flat throughout, from the characters' attempts at sneaking into the female barracks to the impersonation of women officers. The inept dubbing just makes it all the worse. The picture is unrated, but there is much nudity and sex in it.

1982 100 minutes

PRIVATE RESORT

★★

DIRECTOR: George Bowers
CAST: Rob Morror, Johnny Debb, Karyn O'Bryan, Emily Longstretch, Tony Azito, Dody Goodman, Hector Elizondo

This teen comedy features two young men (Rob Morror and Johnny Debb) seeking romance and excitement at a luxurious resort. Morror falls for a cocktail waitress (Emily Longstretch) and must deal with her jealous boss. Debb falls for a wealthy girl (Karyn O'Bryan). Her grandmother's diamond necklace leads to a wild chase when the thief (Hector Elizondo) and the house detective (Tony Azito) go round and round with them. The few funny moments come from these slapstick chases and Three Stooges–type routines. Rated R for nudity, obscenities, and sexual situations.

1985 82 minutes

PRIVATE SCHOOL

🦃

DIRECTOR: Noel Black
CAST: Phoebe Cates, Martin Mull, Sylvia Kristel, Ray Walston, Julie Payne, Fran Ryan, Michael Zorek

If *Porky's*, *Porky's II*, *Bachelor Party*, *Class*, etc., haven't sated your appetite for slobbering sexploitation comedies geared to adolescents, this awful film with Phoebe Cates, Martin Mull (uncredited), Sylvia Kristel (*Emmanuelle*), and Ray Walston offers more of the same: skin, stupidity, and more skin. Enroll at your own risk. Rated R for nudity and profanity.

1983 97 minutes

PRIVATES ON PARADE

★★★½

DIRECTOR: Michael Blakemore
CAST: John Cleese, Denis Quilley, Michael Elphick, Simon Jones, Joe Melia, John Standing, Nicola Pagett

While this story of a gay USO-type unit in the British army is a comedy, it has its serious moments. These come when the unit accidentally runs into a gang of gunrunners. John Cleese is hilarious as the pathetic army major who's ignorant of the foul play that goes on under his nose. Those who dislike Monty Python need not worry—most of the comedy in this film is universal. Rated PG-13 for adult situations and profanity.

1983 107 minutes

PRODUCERS, THE

★★★★

DIRECTOR: Mel Brooks
CAST: Zero Mostel, Gene Wilder, Kenneth Mars, Dick Shawn, Lee Meredith, Christopher Hewett

Mel Brooks's first film as a director remains a laugh-filled winner. Zero Mostel stars as a sleazy Broadway promoter who, with the help of a neurotic accountant (Gene Wilder), comes up with a scheme to produce an intentional flop titled *Springtime for Hitler* and bilk its backers. The plan backfires, and the disappointed duo ends up with a hit and more troubles than before. Rated PG.

1968 88 minutes

PROJECTIONIST, THE

★★

DIRECTOR: Harry Hurwitz
CAST: Chuck McCann, Ina Balin, Rodney Dangerfield

A projectionist in a New York movie palace escapes his drab life by creating fantasies, casting himself as the hero in various films. The movie intercuts new footage into old classics, a technique used later by Steve Martin in *Dead Men Don't Wear Plaid*. While interesting as a low-budget experiment, the film has surprisingly little entertainment value. Rodney Dangerfield plays the gruff theater manager, but don't expect the Rodney we know today. Rated R for profanity and partial nudity.

1970 85 minutes

PROTOCOL

★★★½

DIRECTOR: Herbert Ross
CAST: Goldie Hawn, Chris Sarandon, Richard Romanus, Cliff DeYoung, Gail Strickland

In this film, directed by Herbert Ross, Goldie Hawn is a lovable airhead who goes through a startling metamorphosis to become a true individual. Sound a little like *Private Benjamin*? You bet your blond movie actress. As unoriginal as it is, this comedy-with-a-message works surprisingly well. It's no classic. However, viewers could do a lot worse. Rated PG for violence, partial nudity, and adult situations.

1984 96 minutes

PURPLE ROSE OF CAIRO, THE

★★★★

DIRECTOR: Woody Allen

CAST: Mia Farrow, Jeff Daniels, Danny Aiello, Edward Herrmann, John Wood

Woody Allen's clever screen creation recalls his story for *Play It Again Sam*. The latter had Allen's character interacting with the specter of Humphrey Bogart, who sagely advised him on his love life. In *The Purple Rose of Cairo*, Mia Farrow is a Depression-era housewife who finds her dreary day-to-day existence enlivened when a dashing, romantic hero walks off the screen and sweeps her off her feet. The film becomes even more outlandish and delightful by the minute. It's not a laugh-a-minute farce. Like Allen's other recent films, *Zelig* and *Broadway Danny Rose*, it mixes humor with very human situations. The result, as in the two previous cases, is a very satisfying work of celluloid. Rated PG for violence.

1985 85 minutes

PUTNEY SWOPE

★★★★

DIRECTOR: Robert Downey

CAST: Alan Abel, Mel Brooks, Allen Garfield, Arnold Johnson, Pepi Hermine, Ruth Hermine, Antonio Fargas

This wildly funny film concerns a black man who takes over a Madison Avenue advertising firm. Alan Abel, Mel Brooks, and Allen Garfield appear in this zany parody of American lifestyles. Rated R.

1969 88 minutes

PYGMALION

★★★★½

DIRECTORS: Anthony Asquith, Leslie Howard

CAST: Leslie Howard, Wendy Hiller, Wilfrid Lawson, Marie Lohr, David Tree

This is an impeccable adaptation of George Bernard Shaw's classic play. The comedy is deliciously sophisticated. The performances are exquisite, particularly that of Leslie Howard, who'll make you forget Rex Harrison's Henry Higgins in an instant. As the professor's feisty Cockney pupil, Wendy Hiller is a delight. This urbane battle of the sexes is irresistible.

1938 B & W 95 minutes

RABBIT TEST

DIRECTOR: Joan Rivers

CAST: Billy Crystal, Roddy McDowall, Joan Prather

Horrible comedy about the world's first pregnant man. Joan Rivers borrows her leaden stage persona for her directing debut, and even the occasionally talented Billy Crystal can't do anything with this wretched material. Too awful, even, to be viewed as camp. A miscarriage of cinema. Rated R—profanity.

1978 84 minutes

RADIO DAYS

★★★

DIRECTOR: Woody Allen

CAST: Mia Farrow, Seth Green, Julie Kavner, Josh Mostel, Michael Tucker, Dianne Wiest

One of writer-director Woody Allen's gentler fables, a pleasant little fantasy about people whose lives revolved around the radio during the days prior to World War II. This affectionate overview does for radio what *The Purple Rose of Cairo* did for the movies; unfortunately, Allen's intentions in *Radio Days* are a bit *too* ambitious. Many of the characters in his large ensemble cast get lost, and too much time is spent with others. Although Allen does not appear in this film, his off-screen narration blends nicely with the antics of his younger alter-ego, played disarmingly by Seth Green. The saddest realization about this film is an echo from the radio stars who wonder, wistfully, during a New Year's Eve party, if anybody will remember them decades into the future. We, on the other side of the screen, know the answer—and the same fate probably awaits *Radio Days*. Rated PG.

1987 85 minutes

RAFFERTY AND THE GOLD DUST TWINS

★★½

DIRECTOR: Dick Richards

CAST: Sally Kellerman, Mackenzie Phillips, Alan Arkin, Alex Rocco, Charlie Martin Smith, Harry Dean Stanton

Amusing and entertaining little film with Sally Kellerman and Mackenzie Phillips kidnapping a hapless Alan Arkin and forcing him to drive them to New Orleans from California. Good cast and pacing make up for simple plot. Rated PG for profanity.

1975 92 minutes

RAGE OF PARIS, THE

★★½

DIRECTOR: Henry Koster

CAST: Danielle Darrieux, Douglas Fairbanks Jr., Mischa Auer, Helen Broderick, Glenda Farrell, Louis Hayward, Harry Davenport, Samuel S. Hinds

Famed French star Danielle Darrieux made her U.S. film debut in this airy romantic comedy about mistaken identity and artful conniving for the sake of love and money. Deft direction steered the excellent cast through an engaging script. Good, clean fun all around.

1938 B & W 78 minutes

RAISING ARIZONA

★★★★

DIRECTOR: Joel Coen

CAST: Nicolas Cage, Holly Hunter, Randall "Tex" Cobb, Trey Wilson, John Goodman, William Forsythe

An almost indescribable lunatic comedy from the makers of *Blood Simple*. Nicolas Cage plays an ex-convict married to policewoman Holly Hunter. Both want children but cannot have any. So they decide to help themselves to one. What follows is a delightful, offbeat comedy that is extremely fast-paced, with eye-popping cinematography and decidedly different characters. A real gem. Rated PG-13.

1987 94 minutes

RAVISHING IDIOT, THE

DIRECTOR: Edouard Molinaro

CAST: Anthony Perkins, Brigitte Bardot

A big bomb of a comedy that can be recommended only for insomniacs. Thin plot concerns a spy out to steal NATO plans of ship movements. Skip it.

1965 B & W 110 minutes

REACHING FOR THE MOON

★★★

DIRECTOR: Edmund Goulding

CAST: Douglas Fairbanks, Bebe Daniels, Edward Everett Horton

Robust and energetic Douglas Fairbanks plays a financier on

whom liquor has an interesting effect. Edward Everett Horton is his valet and Bebe Daniels is the girl.

1931 B & W 62 minutes

REAL GENIUS

★★★

DIRECTOR: Martha Coolidge

CAST: Val Kilmer, Gabe Jarret, Michelle Meyrink, William Atherton, Ed Lauter

This is a mildly amusing but predictable comedy about a group of science prodigies (led by Val Kilmer, of *Top Secret!*) who decide to thwart the plans of their egomaniacal mentor (William Atherton) who is secretly using their research to build a rather nasty little laser weapon for the CIA. Screenwriters Neal Israel and Pat Proft throw in a few witty lines and silly—but effective—slapstick situations here and there, yet overall the film comes off rather flat. Director Martha Coolidge does her best to keep things interesting, but she can't overcome the predictability of the climax. Rated PG for profanity.

1985 105 minutes

REAL LIFE

★★★

DIRECTOR: Albert Brooks

CAST: Albert Brooks, Charles Grodin, Frances Lee McCain, J. A. Preston, Matthew Tobin

Albert Brooks's fans will eat up this tasty satire parodying an unrelenting PBS series that put the day-to-day life of an American family under the microscope. In Brooks's film the typical family comes hilariously unglued under the omnipresent eye of the camera. The script (written by Brooks) eventually falters, but not before a healthy number of intelligent laughs are produced. Rated PG.

1979 99 minutes

RECRUITS

DIRECTOR: Rafal Zielinski

CAST: Alan Deveau, Annie McAuley, Lolita David

In this dismal, low-budget takeoff on the *Police Academy* movies, which were bad enough to begin with, a sheriff hires hookers, thieves, and bums as deputies. That's when the "fun" starts. Save us. Rated R.

1987 90 minutes

REEFER MADNESS

★★½

DIRECTOR: Louis J. Gasnier

CAST: Dave O'Brien, Dorothy Short, Warren McCollum, Lillian Miles, Carleton Young, Thelma White

This 1930s anti-marijuana film is very silly, and sometimes funny. It's a cult film that really isn't as good as its reputation suggests.

1936 B & W 67 minutes

REIVERS, THE

★★★★

DIRECTOR: Mark Rydell

CAST: Steve McQueen, Rupert Crosse, Will Geer, Sharon Farrell, Mitch Vogel, Michael Constantine

Grand adaptation of the William Faulkner tale concerning a young boy (Mitch Vogel) who, with the help of his mischievous older friends (Steve McQueen and Rupert Crosse), "borrows" an automobile and heads for fun and excitement in 1905 Mississippi. The charming vignettes include a stopover in a brothel and a climactic horse race that could spell doom for the adventurers. Good period soundtrack by John Williams. Lots of fun for everybody; don't miss it. Rated PG.

1969 107 minutes

REPO MAN

★★★½

DIRECTOR: Alex Cox

CAST: Emilio Estevez, Harry Dean Stanton, Vonetta McGee, Olivia Barash, Sy Richardson, Tracey Walter

Wild, weird, and unpredictable, this film stars Emilio Estevez as a young man who gets into the repossession racket. Under the tutelage of Harry Dean Stanton (in a typically terrific performance), Estevez learns how to steal cars from people who haven't kept up their payments. Meanwhile, a succession of increasingly bizarre events lead them to an encounter with what may be beings from space. Sound weird? You bet. *Repo Man* is not for every taste. However, those who occasionally like to watch something different will enjoy it. Rated R.

1984 92 minutes

RETURN OF THE PINK PANTHER, THE

★★★★

DIRECTOR: Blake Edwards

CAST: Peter Sellers, Christopher Plummer, Herbert Lom, Catherine Schell, Burt Kwouk, Peter Arne, Gregoire Aslan, Andre Maranne, Victor Spinetti

Writer-director Blake Edwards and star Peter Sellers revived their Inspector Clouseau character for a new series of comic adventures beginning with this slapstick classic. There are many funny scenes as Sellers attempts to track down the Phantom (Christopher Plummer) while making life intolerable for the chief inspector (Herbert Lom). Rated PG.

1975 113 minutes

RETURN OF THE SECAUCUS 7

★★★★½

DIRECTOR: John Sayles

CAST: Mark Arnott, Gordon Clapp, Maggie Cousineau, Adam Lefevre, Bruce MacDonald, Jean Passanante, Maggie Renzl

Here's an absolute gem of a movie. Written, produced, and directed by John Sayles, it's a story about the reunion of seven friends ten years after they were wrongfully busted in Secaucus, New Jersey, while on their way to the last demonstration against the Vietnam war in Washington, D.C. It is a delicious blend of characterization, humor, and insight. No MPAA rating, but *Secaucus 7* has nudity, profanity, and implicit sex.

1980 100 minutes

REUBEN, REUBEN

★★★★½

DIRECTOR: Robert Ellis Miller

CAST: Tom Conti, Kelly McGillis, Roberts Blossom, Cynthia Harris, E. Katherine Kerr, Joel Fabiani, Kara Wilson, Lois Smith

A funny, touching, and memorable character study about an irascible Scottish poet, this film, directed by Robert Ellis Miller (*The Heart Is a Lonely Hunter*) and written by Julius J. Epstein (*Casablanca*), ranges from romantic to ribald, and from low-key believability to blistering black comedy. In short, it's a rare cinematic treat. First and foremost among the picture's assets is a superb leading performance by Tom Conti. Rated R for profanity and suggested sex.

1983 101 minutes

REVENGE OF THE NERDS

★★★½

DIRECTOR: Jeff Kanew

CAST: Robert Carradine, Anthony Edwards, Julie Montgomery,

Curtis Armstrong, Ted McGinley, Michelle Meyrink, James Cromwell, Bernie Casey, Timothy Busfield

The title characters, Lewis (Robert Carradine) and Gilbert (Anthony Edwards), strike back at the jocks who torment them in this watchable, fitfully funny comedy. Rated R.

1984 90 minutes

REVENGE OF THE NERDS II: NERDS IN PARADISE

★½

DIRECTOR: Joe Roth

CAST: Robert Carradine, Timothy Busfield, Curtis Armstrong, Larry B. Scott, Courtney Thorne-Smith, Andrew Cassese, Anthony Edwards, Ed Lauter

With this sequel, one assumes that the filmmakers were out for revenge against their audience. The story is lame, and the direction is perfunctory at best. Only the leads—Robert Carradine, Timothy Busfield, and Curtis Armstrong—seem to know what they're supposed to be doing and provide some real laughs. The story has the Tri-Lambs being harassed by the jocks of the Alpha fraternity at a conference in Fort Lauderdale, Florida. Prepare to groan when Anthony Edwards, in a cameo role, gives Carradine a win-one-for-the-Gipper speech. In fact, prepare to groan and gag throughout this testament to bad taste. Rated PG for profanity and brief nudity.

1987 95 minutes

REVENGE OF THE PINK PANTHER, THE

★★★★½

DIRECTOR: Blake Edwards

CAST: Peter Sellers, Dyan Cannon, Robert Webber, Marc Lawrence, Herbert Lom, Burt Kwouk, Robert Loggia, Paul Stewart, Andre Maranne, Graham Stark, Ferdy Mayne

This is arguably the best of the slapstick series about an inept French police inspector. It contains inspired bits penned by director Blake Edwards and played to perfection by Peter Sellers. Rated PG.

1978 99 minutes

RHINESTONE

★½

DIRECTOR: Bob Clark

CAST: Sylvester Stallone, Dolly Parton, Richard Farnsworth, Ron Liebman

It was hard enough to believe Clint Eastwood as a country singer in *Honkytonk Man*. But Sylvester Stallone? Forget it. In the screenplay, by Phil Alden Robinson and Stallone, Dolly Parton plays Jake (Jacqueline) Ferris, a country singer who bets her lascivious manager that she can take an average guy off the street and turn him into a country star in two weeks. What she gets stuck with is a New York cabbie named Nick Martinelli (Stallone), who, when she first meets him, can't carry a tune in a bag. While the film does have its moments of laugh-getting comedy and deft characterization, the hokey premise eventually does it in. If judged on its overall effectiveness, *Rhinestone* goes out with a whimper instead of the intended bang. Rated PG for profanity, sexual innuendo, and violence.

1984 111 minutes

RICH HALL'S VANISHING AMERICA

★★★

DIRECTOR: Steve Rash

CAST: Rich Hall, M. Emmet Walsh, Peter Isacksen, Harry Anderson, Wilt Chamberlain, Charles Lane, Kyle Petty

Rich Hall, a *Saturday Night Live* alumnus, goes in search of the Junior Seed Sales Club. (When he was 8, he joined the club. He sold the seeds, but never got his prize of a Wilt Chamberlain basketball and hoop.) In his quest, he meets various characters. A number of guest stars are on hand for this look at a nostalgic era—a vanishing America. This enjoyable film was made for cable and is recommended for general audience viewing.

1986 50 minutes

RICHARD PRYOR—HERE AND NOW

★★★★½

DIRECTOR: Richard Pryor
CAST: Richard Pryor

The popular comedian doing what he does best, stand-up comedy. Rated R for profanity.

1983 83 minutes

RICHARD PRYOR—LIVE AND SMOKIN'

★★½

DIRECTOR: Michael Blum
CAST: Richard Pryor

The title of this never-before-released, disappointing comedy concert film featuring Richard Pryor must refer to the star's frequent smoking of cigarettes. Certainly, there's nothing smokin' in this film. It's not boring, but Pryor is clearly unnerved by the presence of the film crew. He refers to the fact that he's nervous often and can't seem to get his routines moving with any kind of comedic rhythm. While there are some nice bits, the laughs are few. Pryor's re-creations of ghetto life are poignant. However, those looking for hilarity will want to try his other tapes. Unrated, the film has profanity.

1985 45 minutes

RICHARD PRYOR—LIVE IN CONCERT

★★★★★

DIRECTOR: Jeff Margolis
CAST: Richard Pryor

Comedian–movie star Richard Pryor's first live comedy performance film is still the best. Life has never been so sad and funny at the same time. You'll be exhausted from laughter by its end and be left with a lot to think about. Rated R for profanity.

1979 78 minutes

RICHARD PRYOR LIVE ON THE SUNSET STRIP

★★★

DIRECTOR: Joe Layton
CAST: Richard Pryor

Richard Pryor's second concert film (and first film after his accidental burning) is highly watchable. *Richard Pryor—Live in Concert* and *Richard Pryor—Here and Now*, however, are superior. Rated R for nonstop profanity and vulgarity.

1982 82 minutes

RIDING ON AIR

★★★

DIRECTOR: Edward Sedgwick
CAST: Joe E. Brown, Florence Rice, Vinton Haworth, Guy Kibbee, Clem Bevans

Lots of thrills and laughs in this topically dated comedy adventure about two small-town newspaper correspondents vying for the same girl and the scoop on a story involving aerial smugglers and a device for flying airplanes by a remote control radio beam—a reality today, but not when the film was made. Joe E. Brown is, as always, warm, winning, and wholesome. Guy Kibbee plays a stinker.

1937 B & W 58 minutes

RISKY BUSINESS

★★★★

DIRECTOR: Paul Brickman

CAST: Tom Cruise, Rebecca DeMornay, Curtis Armstrong, Bronson Pinchot, Raphael Sbarge, Joe Pantoliano, Nicholas Pryor, Janet Carroll, Richard Masur

An ordinarily well-behaved boy (Tom Cruise) goes wild when his parents are on vacation. His troubles begin when a gorgeous hooker (Rebecca DeMornay) who doesn't exactly have a heart of gold makes a house call at his request and he doesn't have enough in his piggy bank to cover the cost of her services. It's stylish, funny, and sexy—everything, in fact, that most movies of this kind generally are not. Rated R for nudity, profanity, and suggested sex.

1983 99 minutes

RITZ, THE

★★★★

DIRECTOR: Richard Lester

CAST: Jack Weston, Rita Moreno, Jerry Stiller, Kaye Ballard, F. Murray Abraham, Treat Williams, Paul Price, George Coulouris, Bessie Love

This film is brimful of belly laughs that will leave you exhausted. Richard Lester is at his best directing comedy, and this film tops his celebrated success with the Beatles in *A Hard Day's Night* and 1974's popular *The Three Musketeers*. One reason is the story. After the death of his father-in-law, Jack Weston (as Geatano Proclo) flees Cleveland. His brother-in-law has put out a contract on him to prevent his inheriting any part of the family garbage business. His escape takes him to New York City and, by accident, a gay hotel called The Ritz. The confusion that results will have you gasping for air. Rated R for profanity.

1976 91 minutes

ROAD TO BALI

★★★½

DIRECTOR: Hal Walker

CAST: Bob Hope, Bing Crosby, Dorothy Lamour, Murvyn Vye

Excellent entry in the Bob Hope/Bing Crosby *Road* series is the only one to make it to video as yet. In this one the boys play a pair of vaudeville performers in competition for Dorothy Lamour, pursuing her to the South Seas island of Bali, where they must contend with all sorts of jungle dangers, from cannibalistic natives to various Hollywood stars who appear in hilarious (though very brief) cameos. The Humphrey Bogart scene is a classic.

1952 90 minutes

ROBIN WILLIAMS LIVE

★★★½

DIRECTOR: Bruce Cowers

CAST: Robin Williams

An always funny and sometimes hilarious live performance by one of comedy's premier talents. Irreverent and vulgar, Williams doesn't so much shock as he carefully picks sensitive factors of the human condition. He will then immediately switch to impressions of Jack Nicholson debating Clint Eastwood. In the funniest portion of the show, he attacks our sexual practices and mocks radio sex therapists. Although not as funny as Williams's first live tape, it comes very close. Not rated, but contains profanity and many sexual references. Recommended for adult audiences.

1986 65 minutes

ROCK 'N' ROLL HIGH SCHOOL

★★★½

DIRECTOR: Allan Arkush

CAST: P. J. Soles, Vincent Van Patten, Clint Howard, Dey Young, The Ramones

The stern new principal tries to turn a school into a concentration camp. The popular Riff (P. J. Soles) goes against the principal by playing loud Ramones music all the time. Meanwhile, boring Tom (Vincent Van Patten) has a crush on Riff. The film includes lots of laughs and good rock-'n'-roll music—a cult favorite. Rated PG.

1979 93 minutes

ROCK 'N ROLL WRESTLING WOMEN VS. THE AZTEC MUMMY

DIRECTORS: René Cardona, Manuel San Fernando

CAST: Lorena Velazquez, Armand Silvestre, Elizabeth Campbell, Eugenia Saint Martin, Chucho Salinas, Raymond Bugarini, Victor Velazques

Some folks found this old Mexican horror flick and attempted to turn it into a comedy by redubbing the dialogue, giving it a comical rock-'n-roll soundtrack, and retitling it. Two female wrestlers assist an archeologist in foiling a madman's plans of ruling the world by possessing the secrets of an ancient mummy's tomb. What these revisers didn't realize is that this film would have been more entertaining if left alone. It could have been another *Plan 9 From Outer Space*. Not rated; has violence.

1986 B & W 88 minutes

ROMANCE WITH A DOUBLE BASS

★★★½

DIRECTOR: Robert Young

CAST: John Cleese, Connie Booth, Graham Crowden, Desmond Jones, Freddie Jones, Johnathan Lynn, Andrew Sachs, Denis Ramsden

Monty Python madman John Cleese stars in this delightfully silly vignette about a double-bass player and a princess who are caught naked in a pond when a thief makes off with their clothes. The ensuing romance will tickle and charm most adult viewers with its refreshing subtlety, but a word of caution for parents: This short will not win any awards for costume design.

1974 40 minutes

ROMANTIC COMEDY

★★★

DIRECTOR: Arthur Hiller

CAST: Dudley Moore, Mary Steenburgen, Frances Sternhagen, Janet Eilber, Robyn Douglass, Ron Liebman

In this enjoyable comedy, based on the 1979 Broadway play, Dudley Moore and Mary Steenburgen star as two collaborating playwrights who, during their long association, suffer from "unsynchronized passion." Rated PG for profanity and suggested sex.

1983 103 minutes

ROOM SERVICE

★★★

DIRECTOR: William A. Seiter

CAST: The Marx Brothers, Lucille Ball, Ann Miller

After leaving his brothers (Groucho, Harpo, and Chico) to try movie producing, Zeppo Marx came up with this Broadway play about a foundering stage production and attempted to have it rewritten to suit his siblings' talents. He wasn't completely successful, but this romp does have its moments. Look for Lucille Ball and Ann Miller in early supporting roles.

1938 B & W 78 minutes

ROSEBUD BEACH HOTEL, THE

DIRECTOR: Harry Hurwitz

CAST: Colleen Camp, Peter Scolari, Christopher Lee, Hamilton Camp, Eddie Deezen, Chuck McCann, Hank Garrett

An absolutely awful attempt to combine comedy with soft-core porn. Colleen Camp and Peter Scolari take over her father's failing hotel and hire prostitutes as bellgirls to improve business. Scolari rips off Chevy Chase at every turn. Poor Christopher Lee, as Camp's father, looks as though he wishes he were back making Dracula movies for Hammer Films. Stay away from this mess. Rated R.

1985 82 minutes

ROXANNE

★★★★½

DIRECTOR: Fred Schepisi

CAST: Steve Martin, Daryl Hannah, Shelley Duvall, Rick Rossovich, Michael J. Pollard, Fred Willard, Shandra Beri

Steve Martin's most effective and rewarding comedy since *All of Me*, *Roxanne* seems destined to be regarded as a classic. Like his other screen triumph, which costarred Lily Tomlin, this modern-day version of Edmond Rostand's *Cyrano de Bergerac* is loaded with comic gems. Martin, who wrote the screenplay, plays the big-nosed fire chief of a small town who befriends a professional firefighter (Rick Rossovich) who has come to help train the inept local firemen. While doing so, he meets and falls in love with the title character (Daryl Hannah) and soon enlists Martin's aid in wooing her with words. When the letter-writing Martin falls in love with Hannah, the famous love triangle takes flight. Rated PG for profanity and suggested sex.

1987 107 minutes

RSVP

★★★

DIRECTORS: John Almo, Lem Almo

CAST: Ray Colbert, Veronica Hart, Carey Hayes, Lola Mason, Adam Mills, Steve Nave, Robert Pinkerton, Harry Reems, Katt Shea, Allene Simmons, Arlene Steger, Dustin Stevens, Lynda Weismeier

This is an out-and-out sex comedy with lots of nudity and sexual situations. The plot concerns an author who has written a novel that turns out to be based on fact. The people who inspired the "characters" have been invited to a Hollywood party to celebrate the making of a movie from the book and discover the truth. The writing is lively, and the puns and gags are funny. For those who enjoy a sex comedy, this one has beautiful bodies and funny lines. Rated R for sexual situations and language that will be offensive to some.

1984 87 minutes

RULING CLASS, THE

★★★★

DIRECTOR: Peter Medak

CAST: Peter O'Toole, Alastair Sim, Arthur Lowe, Harry Andrews, Coral Browne

Superbly irreverent satire about upper-crust British eccentricities. Peter O'Toole plays the heir to a peerage who proves problematic because of his insane belief that he is Jesus Christ. Rated PG.

1972 154 minutes

RUSSIANS ARE COMING, THE RUSSIANS ARE COMING, THE

★★★½

DIRECTOR: Norman Jewison
CAST: Alan Arkin, Carl Reiner, Paul Ford, Theodore Bikel, Brian Keith, Jonathan Winters, Eva Marie Saint

A Russian submarine runs aground off Nantucket Island, and the townspeople go gaga, not knowing what to do first, get guns or pour vodka. Cued by Alan Arkin's engaging portrayal of an out-of-his-depth Russian sailor, the cast delivers a solid comedy as cultures clash. With Jonathan Winters aboard, think wacky.

1966 120 minutes

RUSTLER'S RHAPSODY

★★★

DIRECTOR: Hugh Wilson
CAST: Tom Berenger, G. W. Bailey, Marilu Henner, Andy Griffith, Fernando Rey, Patrick Wayne

In this fun spoof of the singing cowboy movies of the 1930s, 1940s, and 1950s, Tom Berenger plays the "greatest" horseback crooner of them all, Rex O'Herlihan, who must face his greatest challenge. Thanks to a rather unkind narrator (G. W. Bailey, who also plays Rex's sidekick), our hero finds himself in a modern western, with nastier villains than he's ever encountered before, women who won't take no for an answer, and a character who questions his confidence as a heterosexual. (Rex, like most of his ilk, wears rather bright, fringy clothes and seems to prefer his horse to the fairer sex.) It's all quite tastefully done by writer-director Hugh Wilson (*Police Academy*). There's only one problem: Viewers need to be familiar with the old B westerns to get the jokes. If you are, it's a hoot. Rated PG for mild violence and slight profanity.

1985 88 minutes

RUTHLESS PEOPLE

★★★★½

DIRECTORS: Jim Abrahams, David Zucker, Jerry Zucker
CAST: Danny DeVito, Bette Midler, Judge Reinhold, Helen Slater, Anita Morris

Hollywood's only three-man directing team comes up with another comedy classic. Danny DeVito portrays a man who decides to murder his obnoxious but rich wife, played by Bette Midler. But when he arrives home to carry out the deed, he discovers she has been abducted. The kidnappers demand fifty thousand dollars "or else." *Or else* is exactly what DeVito has in mind, so he refuses to pay a cent. As the ransom drops, tempers flare, and DeVito does all he can to ensure his wife's demise. Everyone in the film is selfish and evil except the kidnappers, who haven't the heart to carry out their threat and are hopelessly victimized by their victim. A hilarious black comedy from the makers of *Airplane!* An excellent example of ensemble acting, comic timing, and snowballing confusion, with a brilliantly intricate script by first-time screen writer Dale Launer. Rated R for nudity and profanity.

1986 90 minutes

SALLY OF THE SAWDUST

★★★

DIRECTOR: D. W. Griffith
CAST: Carol Dempster, W. C. Fields, Alfred Lunt, Effie Shannon, Elville Alderson, Tammany Young, Glenn Anders

Carol Dempster plays Sally and W. C. Fields her corner-cutting, larcenous foster father in this comedy set in a traveling circus a century ago. Unfortunately, inept editing ruined a lot of Fields's clever turns and timing. However, flaws and all, the film is something of a minor classic. Silent. (*Poppy*, a sound version with Fields, was made in 1936.)

1925 B & W 124 minutes

SAME TIME NEXT YEAR

★★★★

DIRECTOR: Robert Mulligan
CAST: Ellen Burstyn, Alan Alda

Funny, touching film begins with an accidental meeting in 1951 between two married strangers at a rural California inn. Doris (Ellen Burstyn) is a young housewife from California, and George (Alan Alda) an accountant from New Jersey. At first, as they begin their romance, it's awkward and very funny. But later, they realize they truly care for each other. Their meetings become an annual event. And through them, we see the changes in America and its people as we return to the same cottage every five years until 1977. Rated PG.

1978 117 minutes

SAPS AT SEA

★★★

DIRECTOR: Gordon Douglas
CAST: Oliver Hardy, Stan Laurel, Ben Turpin

Oliver Hardy contracts "hornophobia," and the only cure is rest and sea air. The boys rent a houseboat, but an escaped killer strands them all at sea to avoid the police. Comedy timing is off and some of the jokes misfire, but enough of them work to make the movie enjoyable.

1940 B & W 57 minutes

SATURDAY NIGHT LIVE

DIRECTOR: Dave Wilson
CAST: John Belushi, Chevy Chase, Dan Aykroyd, Bill Murray, Gilda Radner, Jane Curtin, Laraine Newman, Garrett Morris, Steve Martin, Lily Tomlin, George Carlin, Richard Pryor, Ray Charles, Rodney Dangerfield

Saturday Night Live was to the 1970s what *Your Show of Shows* was to 1950s and *Rowan & Martin's Laugh-In* to the 1960s—a hit comedy-variety show that reflected the times. Its nucleus was The Not Ready For Prime Time Players, a group of talented yet struggling comedians assembled by producer Lorne Michaels. Virtually all of the Players went on to increased stardom in the entertainment world. John Belushi, Chevy Chase, Dan Aykroyd, Bill Murray, and Jane Curtin all based successful careers on their initial fame earned on the show. *Saturday Night Live* was also very helpful to its guest hosts. Among those represented on these tapes are Lily Tomlin, Steve Martin, Richard Pryor, and George Carlin. (The latter hosted the first show in 1975.) The real stars of the show, however, were The Not Ready For Prime Time Players and the characters they created. The Killer Bees, The Coneheads,Chevy Chase's Weekend Update— they're all here.

1980 64–120 minutes

SAVING GRACE

★★★★

DIRECTOR: Robert M. Young
CAST: Tom Conti, Fernando Rey, Edward James Olmos, Patricia Mauceri, Giancarlo Giannini, Erland Josephson

The pope (Tom Conti), frustrated with his lack of freedom, finds himself in the small, depressed Italian village of Montepetra where he gets back to helping people on a one-on-one basis. All this is done with only a couple of people knowing who he really is. In the village he finds that some of the people have given up hope and resorted to crime and deception to survive. Though this film is billed as a comedy, it has few laughs. As a drama, *Saving Grace* is very good, showing moments of conflict with the human element exposed in all its emotions. Rated PG for violence and profanity.

1986 112 minutes

SAY YES

★★

DIRECTOR: Larry Yust
CAST: Art Hindle, Lissa Layng, Logan Ramsey, Jonathan Winters, Maryedith Burrell, Jensen Collier, Jaque Lynn Colton, Devon Ericson, Art La Fleur, John Milford, Laurie Prange, Anne Ramsey

A multimillionaire (Jonathan Winters) dies, leaving his estate to his son (Art Hindle) on the condition that he marries before his thirty-fifth birthday—only a day away. When his first, hastily picked bride backs out at the altar, the birthday boy runs into a country girl (Lissa Layng) who has just arrived in the big city. It is with her that he finds true love. The comedy doesn't work most of the time, but the story is cute enough to tolerate. Rated PG-13 for sex, nudity, and profanity.

1986 87 minutes

SCANDALOUS

DIRECTOR: Rob Byrum
CAST: Robert Hays, Pamela Stephenson, John Gielgud, Jim Dale, M. Emmet Walsh, Bow Wow Wow

The star of *Airplane* takes a nosedive in this inept attempt at a spy thriller. Robert Hays plays an investigative reporter who gets mixed up with spies, con men, and murder in London. The cast, who seem to be working at feverish pitch to keep things interesting, includes Pamela Stephenson (from *Saturday Night Live*) and John Gielgud, as a pair of con artists, and a casual concert appearance by Bow Wow Wow. Gielgud seems to be having a grand old time playing everything from an old Chinese man to the world's oldest punk rocker, while Jim Dale is embarrassing as an eccentric detective chasing Hays. Rated PG for profanity, nudity, and brief violence.

1983 93 minutes

SCAVENGER HUNT

DIRECTOR: Michael Schultz
CAST: Richard Benjamin, James Coco, Scatman Crothers, Ruth Gordon, Cloris Leachman, Roddy McDowall, Cleavon Little, Robert Morley, Richard Mulligan, Tony Randall, Vincent Price

It's a Mad Mad Mad Mad World writhes again as a bunch of wackos run hither, thither, and yawn to reap a dead man's inheritance in this "comedy." Rated PG.

1979 117 minutes

SCHLOCK

DIRECTOR: John Landis
CAST: John Landis, Saul Kahan, Joseph Piantadosi

Directed by and starring John Landis (*Thriller*; *An American Werewolf in London*; et al.), this film is a spoof of not only "missing link" monster movies but other types of horror and science-fiction films. It involves the discovery of a prehistoric man (still alive) and his "rampages" in the world of modern man. This is Landis's first film, and while it doesn't have the laughs of his later effort *Animal House*, it does include some chuckles of its own. Rated PG.

1971 80 minutes

SCHOOL SPIRIT

DIRECTOR: Alan Holleb

CAST: Tom Nolan, Elizabeth Foxx, Larry Linville, Roberta Collins, Daniele Arnaud, Nick Segal, Toni Hudson, Frank Mugavero, John Finnegan

Stupid high-school flick about an obnoxious libido case (Tom Nolan) who dies in an auto accident and returns as a ghost. Now he can see all the naked girls he wants, and director Alan Holleb doesn't pull the punches in that department. Come back, *Heavenly Kid*, all is forgiven! Not rated, but an easy R for sex, nudity, and profanity.

1985 90 minutes

SCREEN TEST

DIRECTOR: Sam Auster

CAST: Michael Allan Bloom, Robert Bundy, Paul Leuken, David Simpatico, Cynthia Kahn, Mari Laskarin

Unfunny "naughty" comedy about a group of teen-age boys who pose as film producers in order to audition beautiful women nude for a bogus sex comedy. When one of their "stars" turns out to be the daughter of a big-time gangster, they have to come up with a real movie or else. It's as stupid and tasteless as it sounds. Rated R.

1986 84 minutes

SCREWBALLS

DIRECTOR: Rafal Zielinski

CAST: Peter Keleghan, Linda Speciale, Linda Shayne

Set in 1965, this dreadful teen-lust comedy takes place at Taft and Adams Educational Center, otherwise know as "T&A High." (Get it?) The ads say it features "the nuts who always score" in the game of getting girls. It should have been rained out. Rated R for nudity, sex, and profanity.

1983 80 minutes

SECRET ADMIRER

★★½

DIRECTOR: David Greenwalt

CAST: C. Thomas Howell, Lori Laughlin, Kelly Preston, Dee Wallace Stone, Cliff DeYoung, Fred Ward, Leigh Taylor-Young

A sweet-natured sex comedy that suffers from predictability, this stars teen heartthrob C. Thomas Howell as a 16-year-old who, on the last day of school before summer vacation, receives an anonymous letter from a female who swears undying love. He hopes it's from the girl of his dreams (Kelly Preston) and decides to find out. Meanwhile, the letter falls into a number of other hands, the owners of which each interpret the letter differently. This causes all sorts of problems. Rated R for nudity, light violence, and profanity.

1985 100 minutes

SECRET DIARY OF SIGMUND FREUD, THE

★★★½

DIRECTOR: Danford B. Greene

CAST: Bud Cort, Carol Kane, Klaus Kinski, Marisa Berenson, Carroll Baker, Ferdinand Mayne, Dick Shawn

The Secret Diary of Sigmund Freud is a consistently humorous satire on the early life of Sigmund Freud. Everyone in the cast looks to be having a swell time. Carroll Baker, Klaus Kinski, Marisa Berenson, Carol Kane, Dick Shawn, and Bud (*Harold and Maude*) Cort as Freud all have their share of wildly comic moments. Needless to say, sexual and psychological jokes abound. That they are flamboyantly funny is no small feat. Rated PG.

1984 129 minutes

SECRET LIFE OF AN AMERICAN WIFE, THE

★★

DIRECTOR: George Axelrod

CAST: Walter Matthau, Anne Jackson, Patrick O'Neal, Edy Williams, Richard Bull, Paul Napier, Gary Brown

To see if she still has sex appeal, bored wife Anne Jackson decides to moonlight as a call girl. Her first client is her husband's employer. Husband walks in on wife and employer, etc. Director and writer George Axelrod had a cute idea, but it really doesn't jell.

1968 93 minutes

SECRET LIFE OF WALTER MITTY, THE

★★★★

DIRECTOR: Norman Z. McLeod

CAST: Danny Kaye, Virginia Mayo, Boris Karloff, Reginald Denny, Florence Bates, Ann Rutherford, Thurston Hall

This is a comedy fit for the whole family. Based on James Thurber's story, this film presents Danny Kaye as a timid man who dreams of being a brave, glory-bound hero. This film provides plenty of laughs and enjoyable moments.

1947 105 minutes

SECRET OF MY SUCCESS, THE

★★★½

DIRECTOR: Herbert Ross

CAST: Michael J. Fox, Helen Slater, Margaret Whitton, Richard Jordan, Christopher Murney, John Pankow, Fred Gwynne

The secret of this movie's success can be found in its ingredients: a witty script, vibrant direction, bouncy pop score, ingratiating star, and gifted supporting cast. Michael J. Fox is terrifically likable as a wildly ambitious Kansas lad who heads for New York City with plans to conquer the corporate world overnight. This is a slick, 1980s version of a Molière-style farce. Margaret Whitton, as the married woman who lusts after Fox, is hilarious. Rated PG-13.

1987 110 minutes

SECRET POLICEMAN'S PRIVATE PARTS, THE

★★★

DIRECTORS: Roger Graef, Julian Temple

CAST: John Cleese, Michael Palin, Terry Jones, Graham Chapman, Peter Cook, Terry Gilliam, Pete Townshend, Phil Collins, Donovan, Bob Geldof

Monty Python fans will find some of their favorite sketches in this Amnesty International production, but they have been executed elsewhere in better form. The whole film seems lackluster, with so-so performances by the musical guests. If you are a fan, you probably will enjoy it, but if you're less of an enthusiast, you might check out *Monty Python Live at the Hollywood Bowl* first. *Bowl* has the team in fine form and is technically superior as well. The chuckles, guffaws, and quirky surprises are here, too, though, so you could do worse. Rated R.

1984 77 minutes

SECRET POLICEMEN'S OTHER BALL, THE

★★★★

DIRECTORS: Julian Temple, Roger Graef

CAST: John Cleese, Graham Chapman, Michael Palin, Terry Jones, Eric Clapton, Jeff Beck, Pete Townshend, Peter Cook

British comedians John Cleese, Graham Chapman, Michael Palin, and Terry Jones (of Monty Python) join with rock performers Sting (of the Police), Eric Clapton, Jeff Beck, and Pete Townshend (of the Who) in a live performance to benefit Amnesty International. The comedy bits—which also feature Dudley Moore's former partner, Peter Cook—go from funny to hilarious, and the music is surprisingly effective. *Ball* jumps from comedy to rock and back again somewhat erratically, but the material included makes it well worth watching. Rated R for profanity and adult themes.

1982 91 minutes

SECRET WAR OF HARRY FRIGG, THE

★★

DIRECTOR: Jack Smight
CAST: Paul Newman, Sylva Koscina, Andrew Duggan, James Gregory

A group of Allied generals has been captured by the Italians. Strangely, they make no attempt to escape. In their vast wisdom, the high command chooses a disgruntled private (Paul Newman) to go behind the lines and free them if possible. This is a very basic comedy, with few original laughs. Sylva Koscina is on hand to provide Newman with some female diversion. Rated PG.

1968 110 minutes

SEEMS LIKE OLD TIMES

★★★

DIRECTOR: Jay Sandrich
CAST: Goldie Hawn, Chevy Chase, Charles Grodin, Robert Guillaume, Harold Gould

This slick, commercial package is much better than it deserves to be. It's another predictable Neil Simon sit-com packed with one-liners. But at least it's funny most of the time, which is more than you can say for some of his films. Rated PG.

1980 121 minutes

SEMI-TOUGH

★★★

DIRECTOR: Michael Ritchie
CAST: Burt Reynolds, Jill Clayburgh, Kris Kristofferson, Robert Preston, Bert Convy, Lotte Lenya

Semihumorous love triangle set in a professional football background is just not as funny as it should be. Some inspired moments and very funny scenes make it a highly watchable film (especially Lotte Lenya's guest bit as an untemptable masseuse), and the character actors are fine, but the film is mean-spirited at times and much of the humor relies on profanity and cruel situations the female pawns in the story are subjected to. About as much fun as watching a guy eat glass can be. Burt Reynolds hams it up as usual, Kris Kristofferson doesn't say much, and Jill Clayburgh is the rather unbelievable object of their passions and eventual competition. Rated R.

1977 108 minutes

SENATOR WAS INDISCREET, THE

★★★

DIRECTOR: George S. Kaufman
CAST: William Powell, Ella Raines, Peter Lind Hayes, Arleen Whelan, Hans Conried

A staid and unreproachable U.S. senator's diary disclosures cause considerable embarrassment in this satire. Urbane and suave as always, William Powell is perfect in the title role.

1947 B & W 81 minutes

SEND ME NO FLOWERS

★★★

DIRECTOR: Norman Jewison
CAST: Rock Hudson, Doris Day, Tony Randall, Paul Lynde, Clint Walker, Hal March, Edward Andrews

Typically bright and bubbly Doris Day vehicle has Rock Hudson as her hypochondriacal hubby, who, believing he is dying, keeps trying to find a mate for his increasingly flustered wife. This is a light, frothy comedy that asks for no more than a smile. It also provokes some solid chuckles, thanks to the two leads and Tony Randall's supporting turn.

1964 100 minutes

SEPARATE VACATIONS

★★★½

DIRECTOR: Michael Anderson
CAST: David Naughton, Jennifer Dale, Mark Keyloun, Lally Cadeau, Tony Rosato, Blanca Guerra, Laurie Holden

This comedy about Richard, a bored husband (David Naughton of *An American Werewolf in London*) suddenly seeking romance outside his marriage, has some hilarious, if contrived, moments. When Richard goes to Mexico alone, he constantly strikes out with the beautiful women he meets. His wife Sarah (played by Jennifer Dale) is pursued by a determined ski instructor when she takes the kids to the snow. Both have flashbacks on their courtship and prekids days that make them wonder why their own romance disappeared. Well worth watching but definitely *not* family viewing. Rated R for nudity and sexual situations.

1985 92 minutes

SERIAL

★★★½

DIRECTOR: Bill Persky
CAST: Martin Mull, Tuesday Weld, Jennifer McAlister, Bill Macy, Tom Smothers, Christopher Lee

Perhaps the best-known California joke is Cyra McFadden's best-selling novel *The Serial*, which mercilessly pokes fun at the laid-back, trendy lifestyle of a group of "average" affluent Marin County residents. At the center of this farce is the Holroyd family. Harvey Holroyd (Martin Mull) finds it difficult to go with the flow, especially when he finds out his wife, Kate (Tuesday Weld), is having an affair with a Cuban poodle-groomer while his daughter, Joan (Jennifer McAlister), has joined a religious cult. That's when the problems really begin. Rated R.

1980 86 minutes

SEVEN LITTLE FOYS, THE

★★★

DIRECTOR: Melville Shavelson
CAST: Bob Hope, Milly Vitale, George Tobias, Billy Gray, James Cagney, Angela Clark

Deftly tailored to Bob Hope, this biography of famed vaudevillian Eddie Foy and his performing offspring is gag-filled entertainment until death makes him a widower at odds with his talented brood. A classic scene with James Cagney as George M. Cohan has Hope dancing on a tabletop. All's well that ends well—in church!

1955 95 minutes

SEVEN MINUTES IN HEAVEN

★★½

DIRECTOR: Linda Feferman
CAST: Jennifer Connelly, Byron Thames, Maddie Corman, Michael Zaslow, Polly Draper, Alan Boyce, Billy Wirth

When her only parent leaves town on business, 15-year-old Natalie (Jennifer Connelly) allows classmate Jeff (Byron Thames) to move into her home. Their relationship is purely platonic, but no one will believe them. Average but well-meant teen comedy. Rated PG for tastefully suggested sex.

1986 95 minutes

SEVEN YEAR ITCH, THE

★★★★

DIRECTOR: Billy Wilder

CAST: Tom Ewell, Marilyn Monroe, Oscar Homolka, Carolyn Jones

This movie is Marilyn Monroe's most enjoyable comedy—she plays the innocent "dumb blonde" to perfection. Marilyn lives upstairs from average American Tom Ewell. It seems his wife has escaped the heat of their New York home by going on vacation. This leaves Tom alone and unprotected, and one visit from luscious neighbor Marilyn leads him on a Walter Mitty–style adventure that is a joy to behold.

1957 105 minutes

SEX WITH A SMILE

★½

DIRECTOR: Sergio Martino

CAST: Marty Feldman, Edwige Fenech, Sydne Rome, Barbara Bouchet, Dayle Haddon

Silly, badly dubbed Italian film featuring five short stories on sexual misunderstandings. Marty Feldman's section produces some laughs, but the film is too broad and too dependent on sexism Italian-style. Rated R for nudity and sex.

1976 100 minutes

SEXTETTE

★

DIRECTORS: Ken Hughes, Irving Rapper

CAST: Mae West, Timothy Dalton, Dom De Luise, Tony Curtis, Ringo Starr, George Hamilton, George Raft

A dreadful movie only *barely* worth a viewing on fast-forward to witness the vulgar campiness of the nearly 80-year-old Mae West barely able to move through a bevy of barely clad beefcake—and certainly unable to shock or amuse. Her famous way with innuendo, her sexy purr, her let's-see-if-whatcha-got-measures-up and come-hither-with-it look—the whole package is decades past its expiration date. This is the vanity production that really led people to suspect that Mae West was a drag queen with one helluva secret. Rated R.

1978 91 minutes

SHANGHAI SURPRISE

★★½

DIRECTOR: Jim Goddard

CAST: Sean Penn, Madonna, Paul Freeman, Richard Griffiths, Phillip Sayer, Victor Wong

The only surprise here is the amount of money poured into this silly farce. Madonna plays an uptight missionary in Shanghai, 1938. She recruits a con artist (Sean Penn) to help her recover eleven hundred pounds of opium to ease the pain of the suffering. The plot thickens when others search for "Faraday's Flowers." Madonna comes off looking good despite the silly dialogue, but Penn would have helped his career by passing this one up. The scenery and songs by George Harrison help this otherwise hopeless film a bit. The few comic moments don't really classify this romantic adventure as a comedy.

Rated PG for occasional obscenities and partial nudity.

1986 93 minutes

SHE'S GOTTA HAVE IT

★★★★

DIRECTOR: Spike Lee
CAST: Tracy Camilla Johns, Redmond Hicks, John Terrell, Spike Lee

Here in the late 1980s a movie about a randy young woman who's "gotta have it" might seem a bit iffy. But independent filmmaker Spike Lee—who wrote, directed, and edited this unique narrative-quasidocumentary—set up the challenge for himself and then set out to succeed *con gusto*. The beautiful lady in question, Nola Darling, is played by Tracy Camilla Johns, who infuses her character with intriguing charm and plenty of push-pull ambiguity, keeping us interested in her affairs and in her choosing not to make a choice. The perplexed beaux who cannot get enough of her sweets (and sours) are played by Redmond Hicks (Mr. Sensitive), John Terrell (Mr. GQ), and Lee himself (Mr. Hip-Hop). Ernest Dickerson's Super-16 black-and-white photography is terrific, and this whimsical and topical production is an uncommon treat. Rated R for language and nudity.

1986 B & W 100 minutes

SHOCK TREATMENT

DIRECTOR: Jim Sharman
CAST: Jessica Harper, Cliff De-Young, Richard O'Brien, Ruby Wax

Forgettable sequel to *The Rocky Horror Picture Show* that bombed out even with the rabid *Rocky Horror* crowd. Plot concerns two heroes, Janet and Brad, going on a TV game show and ending up trying to escape from it. Avoid this one at all costs. Rated PG.

1981 94 minutes

SHOOT LOUD, LOUDER... I DON'T UNDERSTAND

★½

DIRECTOR: Eduardo De Filippo
CAST: Marcello Mastroianni, Raquel Welch, Guido Alberti, Leopoldo Trieste

The last part of the title is indicative of this confusing jumble, which is alternately surreal and pedestrian as antique dealer Marcello Mastroianni confronts wooden Raquel Welch and inept gunmen. This film was released at a time when American audiences were receptive to all types of foreign films—from spy spoofs and adventures to incomprehensible gibberish. This one falls in the latter category. Italy's most popular actor scored many solid hits with international audiences, but this hodgepodge lacks pace and cohesiveness. Unrated, this film contains some violence and adult situations, and even at 100 minutes it runs too long.

1966 100 minutes

SHOT IN THE DARK, A

★★★★

DIRECTOR: Blake Edwards
CAST: Peter Sellers, Elke Sommer, George Sanders, Burt Kwouk, Herbert Lom, Graham Stark

A Shot in the Dark is a one-man show, with Peter Sellers outdoing himself as the character he later reprised in *The Return of the Pink Panther*, *The Pink Panther Strikes Back*, and *The Revenge of the Pink Panther*. In this slapstick delight, Clouseau attempts to discover whether or not a woman (Elke Sommer) is guilty of murdering her lover.

1964 101 minutes

SILENT MOVIE

★★★½

DIRECTOR: Mel Brooks
CAST: Mel Brooks, Marty Feldman, Dom De Luise, Bernadette Peters, Sid Caesar, James Caan, Burt Reynolds, Paul Newman, Liza Minnelli, Anne Bancroft, Marcel Marceau, Harry Ritz, Ron Carey

Mel Brooks's *Silent Movie* is another kitchen-sink affair, with Brooks going from the ridiculous to the sublime with a beautiful idea that bears more exploring. Silent films were the best for comedy, and Brooks, along with co-stars Marty Feldman, Dom De Luise, and Sid Caesar, supplies numerous funny moments. The biggest surprises are the guest stars, who make the film thrilling, each in his own talented way. *Silent Movie* is well worth seeing for the laughs among the clutter. Rated PG.

1976 86 minutes

SILVER BEARS

★★

DIRECTOR: Ivan Passer
CAST: Michael Caine, Cybill Shepherd, Louis Jourdan, Martin Balsam, Stéphane Audran, Tommy Smothers, David Warner

If *Silver Bears* was meant to be a comedy, it isn't funny. If it was meant to be a drama, it isn't gripping. It's boring. Michael Caine stars as a Mafia henchman sent to Switzerland to buy a bank for a Las Vegas gambler (Martin Balsam). He's swindled and ends up buying two rooms over a pizza parlor. It's all he can do to evade the gangsters on his trail. It's all the viewer can do to stay awake. Rated PG.

1978 113 minutes

SILVER STREAK

★★★★½

DIRECTOR: Arthur Hiller
CAST: Gene Wilder, Jill Clayburgh, Richard Pryor, Patrick McGoohan, Ray Walston, Ned Beatty, Richard Kiel

Films with a slam-bang finish have long had one problem: What do you do to fill up the time it takes to get to that half-hour thrill? All you need is a fast-paced, action story laced with comedy and stars such as Gene Wilder, Jill Clayburgh, and Richard Pryor. It will have you cheering, laughing, gasping, and jumping. *Streak* pits neurotic Wilder, sexy Clayburgh, and shifty Pryor against cool millionaire villain Patrick McGoohan and his evil henchman, Ray Walston, in a wild high-speed chase that brings back the train as a modern-day source for good thrillers. Rated PG.

1976 113 minutes

SIMON

★★

DIRECTOR: Marshall Brickman
CAST: Alan Arkin, Madeline Kahn, Austin Pendleton, William Finley, Fred Gwynne

Weird, weird comedy about an average guy (Alan Arkin) who is brainwashed into thinking he's a visitor from outer space. The film has some funny moments, as well as a few interesting things to say, but it just doesn't work as a whole. Rated PG.

1980 97 minutes

SIN OF HAROLD DIDDLEBOCK (aka mad wednesday)

★★★½

DIRECTOR: Preston Sturges
CAST: Harold Lloyd, Frances Ramsden, Jimmy Conlin, Raymond Walburn, Edgar Kennedy, Arline Judge, Lionel Stander, Margaret Hamilton, Rudy Vallee

The result of a disastrous joint effort of director Preston Sturges, silent-screen great Harold Lloyd, and backer Howard Hughes is a much better film than popular Hollywood legend implies and is a bonus addition to anyone's library or viewing experience. This story about a middle-aged man fired from his job and set adrift with nothing but unfulfilled potential doesn't sound like a scream. However, Lloyd's bizarre antics when under-the-influence redeem the character, who has let life slip by, and makes a positive statement about dealing with life's futilities. A great roster of veteran character actors and actresses and some outstanding gags make this one of the most enjoyable "comeback" comedies of all time and on a par with any of the comedies made by the still-active comedy greats or teams of the 1940s. All of the principals disagreed about the film upon its completion and distribution was spotty. Hughes rereleased it in 1950 as *Mad Wednesday* and edited it down to seventy-nine minutes. Lloyd wears the best zoot suit in films.

1947 B & W 90 minutes

SIX PACK

★

DIRECTOR: Daniel Petrie
CAST: Kenny Rogers, Diane Lane, Erin Gray, Barry Corbin

In this unimaginative retread of *Rocky, Smokey and the Bandit*, and every bachelor-father comedy ever made, country crossover king Kenny Rogers plays a footloose stock-car racer who is latched on to by six homeless, sticky-fingered kids ranging in age from 7 to 16. In his feature-film debut, Rogers is wooden and unconvincing, but then so is the whole movie. Rated PG for profanity.

1982 110 minutes

SIXTEEN CANDLES

★★★★

DIRECTOR: John Hughes
CAST: Molly Ringwald, Paul Dooley, Blanche Baker, Edward Andrews, Anthony Michael Hall, Billie Bird

Molly Ringwald stars in this fast and funny teen comedy as a high-school student who is crushed when the whole family forgets her sixteenth birthday. Things, it seems to her, go downhill from there—that is, until the boy of her dreams suddenly starts showing some interest. Sort of the female flip side of *Risky Business*, this work was written and directed by John Hughes (screenwriter of *Mr. Mom* and *Vacation*). Rated PG for profanity.

1984 93 minutes

SKYLINE

★★★

DIRECTOR: Fernando Colombo
CAST: Antonio Resines, Susana Ocana

Although there are a few laughs in this film, it—while billed as one—could hardly be called a comedy. Antonio Resines plays a Spanish photographer named Gustavo who comes to New York seeking international fame. Once there, he struggles to learn English, find work, and pursue friendship and romance. In Spanish and English, with subtitles it would be excellent for bilingual viewers. The twist ending really gives one a jolt. We'd rate it PG for slight profanity and because most children would not appreciate or understand it.

1984 84 minutes

SLAP SHOT

★★★★

DIRECTOR: George Roy Hill
CAST: Paul Newman, Strother Martin, Jennifer Warren, Lindsay Crouse, Melinda Dillon

When released in 1977, this comedy about a down-and-out hockey team was criticized for its liberal use of profanity. The controversy tended to obscure the fact that *Slap Shot* is a very funny, marvelously acted movie. Paul Newman, as an aging player-coach who's a loser in love and on the ice until he instructs the members of his team to behave like animals during their matches, has never been better. The marvelous Strother Martin still manages to steal half the film from him. Rated R.

1977 122 minutes

SLAPSTICK OF ANOTHER KIND

🦃

DIRECTOR: Steven Paul

CAST: Jerry Lewis, Madeline Kahn, Marty Feldman

Jerry Lewis hasn't made a funny film in years, and this sci-fi spoof is no exception. The gags are old, predictable, and forced. It seems the harder Jerry tries, the fewer laughs he generates. All of the elaborate costumes and props and the help of the usually funny Marty Feldman and Madeline Kahn cannot save this turkey based on a Kurt Vonnegut story. Rated PG.

1983 85 minutes

SLEEPER

★★★★

DIRECTOR: Woody Allen

CAST: Woody Allen, Diane Keaton, John McLiam, John Beck

Writer-star-director Woody Allen finally exhibited some true filmmaking talent with this 1973 sci-fi spoof. The frenetic gag-a-minute comedy style of Allen's earlier films (*Take the Money and Run*; *Bananas*; and *Everything You Always Wanted to Know About Sex*) was replaced by some nice bits of character comedy. This makes *Sleeper* the most enjoyable of Allen's pre–*Annie Hall* creations. Rated PG.

1973 88 minutes

SLIGHTLY HONORABLE

★★★

DIRECTOR: Tay Garnett

CAST: Pat O'Brien, Edward Arnold, Broderick Crawford, Evelyn Keyes, Phyllis Brooks, Eve Arden, Alan Dinehart, Ruth Terry, Douglas Fowley, Willie Best, Janet Beecher, Clarie Dodd

Wisecracks and red herrings provide the drawing cards in this fast-paced comedy-thriller. The plot's muddy, but basically it concerns a lawyer, Pat O'Brien, set up for a murder by crooked politician Edward Arnold, clearing himself and netting the real killer in the bargain.

1939 B & W 85 minutes

SLUGGER'S WIFE, THE

★★

DIRECTOR: Hal Ashby

CAST: Michael O'Keefe, Rebecca DeMornay, Martin Ritt, Randy Quaid, Cleavant Derricks

The most shallow of Neil Simon's works to date, this is bad television situation comedy blown up to big-screen size. Darryl Palmer (Michael O'Keefe, the son in *The Great Santini*) is a self-centered baseball player who bullies his way into the affections of Debby Palmer (Rebecca DeMornay, from *Risky Business*), a would-be rock star. O'Keefe's Darryl is essentially a jerk, and Debby winds up with guilt by association, because we can't believe she could fall in love with such an egotist. Rated PG-13 for nudity and profanity.

1985 105 minutes

SMOKEY AND THE BANDIT

★★★½

DIRECTOR: Hal Needham
CAST: Burt Reynolds, Pat McCormick, Jerry Reed, Sally Field, Mike Henry, Jackie Gleason, Paul Williams

Smokey and the Bandit may strain credibility, but it never stops being fun. The Bandit (Burt Reynolds) is an infamous independent trucker who is hired to transport four hundred cases of Coors beer from Texarkana, Texas, where it is legal, to Atlanta, Georgia, where it is not, for the reward of eighty thousand dollars. With his buddy, the Snowman (Jerry Reed), the Bandit picks up the beer and something he didn't expect, a girl in a wedding gown (Sally Field). What she doesn't tell him is that she is jilting the son (Mike Henry) of Texarkana's sheriff, Buford T. Justice (Jackie Gleason), who is in hot pursuit. Hold on to your hat. Rated PG for profanity.

1977 97 minutes

SMOKEY AND THE BANDIT II

★★

DIRECTOR: Hal Needham
CAST: Burt Reynolds, Jerry Reed, Pat McCormick, Paul Williams, Mike Henry, Jackie Gleason, Dom De Luise

Smokey II is just more proof that "sequels aren't equal." But it isn't a total loss. If you find yourself sitting through this pale imitation, don't turn it off until the credits roll (although you may want to fast-forward). Outtakes featuring the stars flubbing their lines are spliced together at the end, and they're hilarious. If only the movie had been that good . . . Rated PG.

1980 101 minutes

SMOKEY AND THE BANDIT III

DIRECTOR: Dick Lowry
CAST: Jerry Reed, Jackie Gleason, Paul Williams, Pat McCormick

The Bandit may be back, but it ain't Burt. Instead, Jerry Reed, who played Reynolds's buddy Cletus in the first two films, takes over that half of the title roles, with Jackie Gleason returning for the other as Sheriff Buford T. Justice. You can easily see why Reynolds decided to pass—it's an embarrassing waste of celluloid and money. Avoid it. Rated PG for nudity, profanity, and scatological humor.

1983 86 minutes

SMOKEY BITES THE DUST

★★½

DIRECTOR: Charles B. Griffith
CAST: Jimmy McNichol, Walter Barnes, Patrick Campbell, Karie Lizer, John Blythe Barrymore, William Forsythe

Jimmy McNichol stars as a mischievous teenager who takes great delight in stealing cars and making buffoons out of the sheriff and his deputies. To make matters worse, he takes the sheriff's daughter along for the ride. This is pretty standard car-chase action, but it does move along and there are some laughs along the way, particularly for the younger viewers. Rated PG.

1981 85 minutes

S.O.B.

★★★

DIRECTOR: Blake Edwards
CAST: Julie Andrews, William Holden, Robert Preston, Richard Mulligan, Robert Vaughn, Loretta Swit, Larry Hagman, Craig Stevens, Shelley Winters, Rosanna Arquette

Director Blake Edwards vents his resentment over Hollywood's treatment of him in the early 1970s in this failed attempt at satire. There are some good moments, but they are too few to make this potent satire. Self-indulgent, but frequently on target. Rated R.

1981 121 minutes

SO FINE

DIRECTOR: Andrew Bergman

CAST: Ryan O'Neal, Jack Warden, Richard Kiel, Fred Gwynne, Mike Kellin, David Rounds

This so-called sex comedy—about a fashion house (run by Ryan O'Neal and Jack Warden) that introduces a new line of designer jeans with see-through plastic inserts in the seat—is little more than a television situation comedy with leers, skin, and foul language. It's amazing that it's even watchable. But it is. Just barely. Rated R because of nudity and brief profanity.

1981 91 minutes

SOME KIND OF HERO

★½

DIRECTOR: Michael Pressman

CAST: Richard Pryor, Margot Kidder, Ronny Cox, Olivia Cole

This Richard Pryor movie can't decide whether it should tell the story of a Vietnam prisoner of war and his problems returning to American society or be another comedy caper film. As a result, it's neither very funny nor worth thinking about. Rated R for profanity, nudity, and violence.

1982 97 minutes

SOME KIND OF WONDERFUL

★★★★

DIRECTOR: Howard Deutch

CAST: Eric Stoltz, Mary Stuart Masterson, Lea Thompson, Craig Sheffer, John Ashton

This rather transparent remake of *Pretty in Pink*—also from the team of writer-producer John Hughes and director Howard Deutch—actually improves on that earlier effort, most notably with a conclusion that makes thematic sense. Eric Stoltz (*Mask*) stars as an affable, talented, intelligent high-school lad with drop-dead good looks who can't seem to make any headway with women (remember, this is a fantasy). Unaware of the deep affection hurled in his direction by constant companion Mary Stuart Masterson (who all but steals the show), Stoltz sets his sights high, on Lea Thompson, who mingles with the school's upper-echelon social caste. Once again, Hughes has constructed a tale of love between the haves and have-nots, and it's a story he tells quite well. As usual, his scripts are leagues above the hormone sagas of most mindless teen-oriented films. Perceptive, thoughtful viewing for the entire family. Rated PG-13 for mature situations.

1987 93 minutes

SOME LIKE IT HOT

★★★★★

DIRECTOR: Billy Wilder

CAST: Marilyn Monroe, Jack Lemmon, Tony Curtis, Joe E. Brown, George Raft, Pat O'Brien, Nehemiah Persoff, Mike Mazurki

Billy Wilder's *Some Like It Hot* is the outlandish story of two men (Jack Lemmon and Tony Curtis) who accidentally witness a gangland slaying. They pose as members of an all-girl band in order to avoid the gangsters, who are now trying to silence them permanently. Marilyn Monroe is at her sensual best as the band's singer. Joe E. Brown is also hilarious as a wealthy playboy who develops an attraction for an obviously bewildered Lemmon.

1959 B & W 119 minutes

SOMETHING SHORT OF PARADISE

★★★

DIRECTOR: David Helpern Jr.
CAST: Susan Sarandon, David Steinberg, Marilyn Sokol, Jean-Pierre Aumont

This romantic comedy is something short of perfect but still manages to entertain. Two New Yorkers (Susan Sarandon and David Steinberg) manage to find love and happiness together despite distractions from other conniving singles. Marilyn Sokol is great as one of the obstacles. Rated PG.

1979 91 minutes

SOMETHING SPECIAL

★★★

DIRECTOR: Paul Schneider
CAST: Patty Duke, Pamela Segall, Eric Gurry, Mary Tanner, John Glover, Seth Green, John David Cullum

Offbeat but surprisingly pleasant comedy about a 15-year-old girl named Milly (Pamela Segall) who is convinced that life would be easier if she were a boy. With the help of a magical potion and a solar eclipse, she manages to grow a penis. Forced to choose between the sexes, she changes her name to Willy to please her father and to satisfy her own curiosity. Rated PG-13.

1987 90 minutes

SOMETHING WILD

★★★★½

DIRECTOR: Jonathan Demme
CAST: Jeff Daniels, Melanie Griffith, Ray Liotta, Margaret Colin, Tracey Walter

If unexpected plot twists are the key to successful suspense, then this is one of the most absorbing suspense films ever lensed. Jeff Daniels stars as a desk-bound investment type whose idea of yuppie rebellion is stiffing a local diner for the price of a lunch. This petty larceny is observed by a mysterious woman in black (Melanie Griffith) who, to Daniels's relief and surprise, takes him not to the local police but to a seedy motel, where they share an afternoon that justifies the film's R rating. When Daniels next comes up for air, Griffith has transformed into a blonde beauty (who looks strikingly like her mother, actress Tippi Hedren), and they're at her high-school reunion—with him posing as her husband. Then her *real* husband (a strikingly evil performance from newcomer Ray Liotta) shows up, and the picture kicks into high gear. This moves from humble beginnings to true edge-of-the-seat terror, with quite a few amusing stops along the way.

1986 113 minutes

SON OF PALEFACE

★★★½

DIRECTOR: Frank Tashlin
CAST: Bob Hope, Jane Russell, Roy Rogers, Douglas Dumbrille, Bill Williams, Harry Von Zell, Iron Eyes Cody

This is one of those rare instances when the sequel is actually better than the original. Bob Hope is in top shape as he matches wits with smooth villain Douglas Dumbrille and consistently loses, only to be aided by gun-totin' Jane Russell and government agent Roy Rogers. Roy and Trigger are an extra bonus in this solid comedy. It's too bad they didn't grace more big-budget films away from the B western with ranch hands and perpetual songs. Lots of familiar faces are found in this comedy, and it's fun for the whole family.

1952 95 minutes

SONS OF THE DESERT

★★★★★

DIRECTOR: William A. Seiter
CAST: Stan Laurel, Oliver Hardy, Charley Chase

In *Sons of the Desert*, Stan Laurel and Oliver Hardy scheme to get away from their wives and attend a lodge convention in Chicago. After persuading the wives that Ollie needs to sail to Honolulu for his health, they go off to Chicago. The boat sinks on the way back from Hawaii, and the boys end up having to explain how they got home a day earlier than the other survivors (they ship-hiked). This film has no flaws.

1933 B & W 69 minutes

SOUL MAN

★★★

DIRECTOR: Steve Miner
CAST: C. Thomas Howell, Rae Dawn Chong, James Earl Jones, Arye Gross, James B. Sikking, Leslie Nielsen

Soul Man is a well-meant, often funny comedy that manages to surmount its ridiculous premise and even deliver a humanistic message. It is a rarity: a teen comedy that isn't completely mindless. Not that its story is one bit believable. It concerns a Los Angeles preppie, Mark Watson (C. Thomas Howell), who masquerades as a needy black to gain entrance to Harvard Law School. Director Steve Miner keeps things moving so fast one doesn't have time to consider how silly it all is, and the capable supporting performances by Rae Dawn Chong and James Earl Jones help a sincere Howell make the grade. Rated PG-13 for profanity, suggested sex, and violence.

1986 101 minutes

SOUP FOR ONE

★★★

DIRECTOR: Jonathan Kaufer
CAST: Saul Rubinek, Marcia Strassman, Teddy Pendergrass

Marcia Strassman (formerly the wife on *Welcome Back Kotter*) stars as the dream girl to an often disappointed lover. When he finds her, he tries to persuade her to marry him. Although there are a few slow-moving parts, it is a generally enjoyable comedy. Rated R for sexual themes.

1982 87 minutes

SPACEBALLS

★★½

DIRECTOR: Mel Brooks
CAST: Mel Brooks, John Candy, Rick Moranis, Bill Pullman, Daphne Zuniga, Dick Van Patten, George Wyner, Michael Winslow, Lorene Yarnell

Had this film appeared years earlier, it might be recognized as the definitive spoof of the *Star Wars* genre, but too many other efforts have established claims on that territory. For once, Brooks has attacked a style that already has a tongue planted rather firmly in its alien cheek, and the result is occasionally similar to the fate that befell *Casino Royale* (which attempted to spoof the already whimsical James Bond series). The visual humor works best in *Spaceballs*, such as the first appearance of the *incredibly* long flagship of the evil Spaceball fleet. The plot loosely concerns planet Spaceball's attempt to "steal" the atmosphere from neighbor Druidia by kidnapping and ransoming off the royally spoiled Princess Vespa (a Druish princess, of course). The wacky Dark Helmet (Rick Moranis) is responsible for this dastardly plot, and he is opposed by rogue trader Lone Starr

(Bill Pullman) and his human-canine sidekick, John Candy's Barf the Mawg ("I'm my own best friend"). Watch for a surprise cameo by John Hurt, whose strangled cry of "Oh, no . . . not again!" should warn you of events to come. Rated PG for mild profanity.

1987 96 minutes

SPACED OUT

★★★

DIRECTOR: Norman Warren
CAST: Barry Stokes, Tony Maiden, Glory Annen, Michael Rowlatt, Kate Ferguson, Lynne Ross, Ava Cadell

In this spoof of science-fiction films, the Earth is visited by an all-female crew on a broken-down spaceship. Three men and a woman are taken hostage. The testing of these hostages and the discovery of the differences between men and women make for a watchable but raunchy comedy. This film is rated R for nudity and implied sex.

1985 85 minutes

SPACESHIP

DIRECTOR: Bruce Kimmel
CAST: Cindy Williams, Bruce Kimmel, Leslie Nielsen, Gerrit Graham

This "comedy" is all about an unwanted alien tagging along on a rocket full of idiots. Tries to be another *Airplane!*, even going as far as to steal that film's co-star (Leslie Nielsen), but there's not one funny moment in this dud. A complete failure. Original title: *The Creature Wasn't Nice*. Rated PG.

1981 88 minutes

SPIES LIKE US

★★½

DIRECTOR: John Landis
CAST: Chevy Chase, Dan Aykroyd, Bruce Davison, William Prince, Steve Forrest, Bernie Casey, Donna Dixon

Chevy Chase and Dan Aykroyd, who were co-stars on the original *Saturday Night Live* television show, appeared together on the big screen for the first time in this generally enjoyable comedy about two inept recruits in a U.S. intelligence organization's counterespionage mission. The stars are fun to watch even though the movie only occasionally elicits laughter. Rated PG for violence and profanity.

1985 104 minutes

SPLASH

★★★★★

DIRECTOR: Ron Howard
CAST: Tom Hanks, Daryl Hannah, John Candy, Eugene Levy, Dody Goodman, Richard B. Shull

If you split your sides laughing at actor-turned-director Ron Howard's *Night Shift*, get ready for another achingly funny screen treat. Howard, co-star of *The Shootist* and one-time regular on TV's *The Andy Griffith Show* and *Happy Days,* helmed this uproarious comedy about a young man (Tom Hanks) who unknowingly falls in love with a mermaid (Daryl Hannah, of *Reckless* and *Blade Runner*). Former SCTV regulars John Candy and Eugene Levy add some marvelous bits of comedy. Rated PG for profanity and brief nudity.

1984 111 minutes

SPOOKS RUN WILD

★½

DIRECTOR: Phil Rosen
CAST: Bela Lugosi, East Side Kids, Dave O'Brien, Dennis Moore

Bottom-of-the-barrel "entertainment" from Poverty Row film-grinders Monogram Studios wastes a rapidly deteriorating Bela Lugosi in another silly role that gives the aging East Side Kids a chance to humiliate him on-screen. Inane, laughless, and overlong at sixty-nine minutes, this film fails on all levels, and only the presence of Lugosi and energetic Dave O'Brien lend it any value at all. Made before the equally dreadful *Ghosts on the Loose*, this film joins the growing list of video releases that should always be on the "bargain" table at any sales or rental outlet. The kids might like it, but don't count on it as a baby-sitter substitute.

1941 B & W 69 minutes

SPRING BREAK

★

DIRECTOR: Sean S. Cunningham

CAST: David Knell, Steve Bassett, Perry Lang, Paul Land

Here's a numbingly stupid movie about four guys on the make in Fort Lauderdale. It's reminiscent of the old "Beach Party" films, with one major exception—Annette Funicello never took off her top. Parents of the teenagers it's directed at may be shocked by the nudity, implied sex, and profanity that rightfully earned *Spring Break* its R rating.

1983 101 minutes

SPRING FEVER

DIRECTOR: Joseph L. Scanlan

CAST: Jessica Walter, Susan Anton, Frank Converse, Carling Bassett, Stephen Young

In spite of an advertising come-on that promised another beach romp in the tradition of *Where the Boys Are*, this limp Canadian production is an unbelievably dull story about a rising young tennis star (Carling Bassett). Susan Anton has neither the screen time nor the skill to be a successful vamp. Even the tennis sequences are boring, making the film seem to run an hour too long. Rated PG.

1983 100 minutes

SPY WITH A COLD NOSE, THE

★★★

DIRECTOR: Daniel Petrie

CAST: Laurence Harvey, Daliah Lavi, Lionel Jeffries, Eric Sykes, Paul Ford

This cute British spy spoof features Lionel Jeffries as an un-Bond-like counterintelligence agent. His plan to implant a microphone in the goodwill gift to the Soviets goes awry. The gift, a bulldog, may require an operation, and then the Soviets would be outraged. Thus, our agent seeks the help of a womanizing vet (Laurence Harvey). They go to Moscow to remove the microphone.

1966 113 minutes

SQUEEZE, THE

★

DIRECTOR: Roger Young

CAST: Michael Keaton, Rae Dawn Chong, Meat Loaf, Liane Langland

Michael Keaton can always be counted on for at least a few laughs, but a few laughs is about all you get in this dreary comedy-thriller. Keaton is an urban wiseguy, Rae Dawn Chong is a bill collector, and together they try to stop a plot to defraud the New York lottery. The story looks like something that was made up on the set, the violence is painfully real for a supposed comedy, and Chong's performance is grating. It's rated PG-13 for language and violence.

1987 101 minutes

STAGE DOOR

★★★★

DIRECTOR: Gregory La Cava
CAST: Katharine Hepburn, Ginger Rogers, Eve Arden, Lucille Ball, Ann Miller

A funny and tender taste of New York theatrical life. Katharine Hepburn and Ginger Rogers are two aspiring actresses who undergo the stifling yet stimulating life of a lodging house that caters to a vast array of prospective actresses trying any avenue to break into the big time. Eve Arden, Lucille Ball, and Ann Miller also take residence in this overcrowded and active boardinghouse.

1937 B & W 92 minutes

STAND-IN

★★★

DIRECTOR: Tay Garnett
CAST: Leslie Howard, Humphrey Bogart, Joan Blondell, Jack Carson, Alan Mowbray

This send-up of Hollywood rubbed more than one Tinsel Town mogul the wrong way by satirizing front office studio manipulators. Eastern financial genius Leslie Howard is sent west to "stand in" for stockholders and find out why Colossal Pictures is heading for skidsville. Ignorant of film-making, he gets a lot of smoke until star stand-in Joan Blondell takes him in hand, and he links with lush producer Humphrey Bogart to salvage a turkey. The relish with which Howard and Bogart play their parts strongly suggests they thoroughly enjoyed biting the hands that fed them. Alan Mowbray's performance is a fine burlesque of the stripe of foreign-born director that inhabited sound stages in the 1920s and 1930s.

1937 B & W 91 minutes

STARDUST MEMORIES

★

DIRECTOR: Woody Allen
CAST: Woody Allen, Charlotte Rampling, Jessica Harper, Marie-Christine Barrault

Absolutely unwatchable Woody Allen film, his most chaotic and Bergmanesque attempt to claim that he can't stand his fans. Boring, self-indulgent, and completely lacking the charm and perception of Allen's other films. And if this all was intended, as he has claimed, then he should be smacked for maiming the hand that feeds him. Rated PG—profanity.

1980 88 minutes

START THE REVOLUTION WITHOUT ME

★★★★

DIRECTOR: Bud Yorkin
CAST: Gene Wilder, Donald Sutherland, Hugh Griffith, Jack MacGowran

Gene Wilder and Donald Sutherland star in this hilarious comedy as two sets of twins who meet just before the French Revolution. Cheech and Chong's *The Corsican Brothers* covered pretty much the same ground. Only trouble was, it wasn't funny. If you want to see the story done right, check this one out. Rated PG.

1970 98 minutes

STARTING OVER

★★★★

DIRECTOR: Alan Pakula
CAST: Burt Reynolds, Jill Clayburgh, Candice Bergen, Charles Durning, Frances Sternhagen

Burt Reynolds and Jill Clayburgh are delightful in this Alan Pakula film about two lonely hearts trying to find romance in a cynical world. Candice Bergen is superb as Reynolds's off-key singer/ex-wife, whom he has trouble trying to forget in this winner. Rated R.

1979 106 minutes

STEAGLE, THE

★★★

DIRECTOR: Paul Sylbert

CAST: Richard Benjamin, Cloris Leachman, Chill Wills, Susan Tyrrell, Jean Allison, Suzanne Charny, Ivor Francis, Jack Bernard, Susan Kussman, Peter Hobbs

Black comedy about how a daydreaming college professor (Richard Benjamin) deals with his mortality during the Cuban missile crisis. The week-long living spree he goes on over the fear that it might be his last has some hilarious consequences, but the screenplay is not handled very well despite the excellent cast. Rated PG for profanity and sex.

1971 94 minutes

STEAMBOAT BILL JR.

★★★★½

DIRECTOR: Charles F. Reisner

CAST: Buster Keaton, Ernest Torrence, Marion Byron, Tom Lewis, Tom McGuire

Buster Keaton is at his comedic-genius best in this delightful silent film as an accident-prone college student who is forced to take over his father's old Mississippi steamboat. The climax features spectacular stunts by Keaton. It is truly something to behold—and to laugh with. Silent.

1928 B & W 71 minutes

STEELYARD BLUES

★★★½

DIRECTOR: Alan Meyerson

CAST: Jane Fonda, Donald Sutherland, Peter Boyle, Alan Myerson, Gary Goodrow

This is a quirky little film about a group of social misfits who band together to help one of their own against his government-employed brother. Jane Fonda, Donald Sutherland, and Peter Boyle seem to have fun playing the misfits. This movie has its ups and downs, with Boyle's imitation of Marlon Brando a highlight. Rated PG for language.

1973 93 minutes

STEVE MARTIN LIVE

★★★½

DIRECTORS: Carl Gottlieb, Gary Weis

CAST: Steve Martin, Buck Henry, Teri Garr, David Letterman, Paul Simon, Alan King, Henny Youngman, Henry Winkler

Though the bulk of this video offers a 1979 live performance that you've probably already seen in part on television, there are a number of reasons you'll enjoy this comedy video. If you're a fan of Martin's on-stage bits, such as "King Tut" (with a cameo by Henry Winkler) and "Happy Feet," the live segment is for you. Viewers are also offered a tasty heaping of Martin's satirical wit in his comedic short, *The Absent Minded Waiter*, which was nominated for an Academy Award. David Letterman guests in a skit where Martin offers tips to a number of name comedians—plus Paul Simon—who hang on his every word.

1986 60 minutes

STILL SMOKIN

🦃

DIRECTOR: Thomas Chong

CAST: Cheech and Chong, Hansman In't Veld, Carol Van Herwijnen

Richard "Cheech" Marin and Thomas Chong, who also directed, hit rock bottom with this humorless shambles about a film festival in Amsterdam, Holland. It seems to indicate Cheech and Chong's disrespect for their audience. Rated R for nudity and scatological humor.

1983 91 minutes

STIR CRAZY

★★★½

DIRECTOR: Sidney Poitier

CAST: Richard Pryor, Gene Wilder, Georg Stanford Brown, JoBeth Williams

Richard Pryor and Gene Wilder work something close to a miracle in this comedy, making something out of nothing or, at least, close to nothing. It's a simple-minded spoof of crime and prison movies with, of all things, a little *Urban Cowboy* thrown in. You've seen it all before, but you have so much fun watching the stars, you don't mind. You're too busy laughing. Rated R.

1980 111 minutes

STITCHES

🦃

DIRECTOR: Alan Smithee

CAST: Parker Stevenson, Geoffrey Lewis, Eddie Albert

Stitches is a formula bomb in which three med school students spend 92 minutes playing pranks on classmates and teachers. The humor isn't as aggressive or mean-spirited as in other *Porky's*-style movies, but a turkey by any other name is still a turkey. Rated R.

1985 92 minutes

STORM IN A TEACUP

★★★

DIRECTORS: Victor Saville, Ian Dalrymple

CAST: Vivien Leigh, Rex Harrison, Cecil Parker, Sara Allgood

The refusal of an old lady to pay for a dog license touches off this amusing farrago on love, politics, and life. Rex Harrison is, of course, smashing. The dialogue is the thing.

1937 B & W 87 minutes

STRANGE BREW

★★★½

DIRECTORS: Dave Thomas, Rick Moranis

CAST: Rick Moranis, Dave Thomas, Max von Sydow, Paul Dooley, Lynne Griffin

Okay, all you hosers and hoseheads, here come those SCTV superstars from the Great White North, Bob and Doug McKenzie (Rick Moranis and Dave Thomas) in their first feature film. Beauty, eh? A mad scientist employed by a brewery controls a group of mental patients by feeding them beer laced with a mind-controlling drug. Rated PG.

1983 90 minutes

STRANGER THAN PARADISE

★★★★½

DIRECTOR: Jim Jarmusch

CAST: John Lurie, Richard Edson, Eszter Balint

In this superb independently made comedy, three oddball characters go on a spontaneous road trip through the United States, where they encounter boredom, routine problems, bad luck, and outrageous good fortune. The film, which won acclaim at the Cannes and New York film festivals, plays a lot like a Woody Allen comedy. It's a silly film for smart people—and marvelously entertaining because of it. Rated R for profanity.

1985 B & W 90 minutes

STRIKE UP THE BAND

★★★

DIRECTOR: Busby Berkeley

CAST: Mickey Rooney, Judy Garland, June Preisser, Paul Whiteman

This encore to *Babes in Arms* has ever-exuberant Mickey Rooney leading a high-school band that would shade Glenn Miller's going for the gold in a nationwide radio contest hosted by Paul Whiteman.

Second banana Judy Garland sings. "Come on, kids, let's put on a show" in a different setting.

1940 B & W 120 minutes

STRIPES

★★★★

DIRECTOR: Ivan Reitman

CAST: Bill Murray, Harold Ramis, John Candy, Warren Oates, P. J. Soles, Sean Young, John Larroquette

It's laughs aplenty when *Saturday Night Live* graduate Bill Murray enlists in the army. But hey, as Murray might say, after a guy loses his job, his car, and his girl all in the same day, what else is he supposed to do? Thanks to Murray, Harold Ramis, and John Candy, the U.S. Army may never be the same—or at least our perception of it. The late Warren Oates also is in top form as the boys' no-nonsense sergeant. Rated R.

1981 105 minutes

STROKER ACE

★★★

DIRECTOR: Hal Needham

CAST: Burt Reynolds, Ned Beatty, Jim Nabors, Loni Anderson, Parker Stevenson

Film critics all over the country jumped on this, Burt Reynolds's latest car - crash - and - cornpone comedy, with both feet. That doesn't seem quite fair, so we'll only use one foot. Besides, it's not all that bad. About an egotistical, woman-chasing race-car driver (Reynolds, of course) who gets himself tangled up with a nasty fast-food-chain owner (Ned Beatty), it's the same old predictable nonsense. Yet it's certain to please the audience it was intended for, and, after all, isn't that what movies are all about? Rated PG for sexual innuendo and violence.

1983 96 minutes

STUCK ON YOU

★½

DIRECTORS: Michael Herz, Samuel Weil

CAST: Professor Irwin Corey, Virginia Penta, Mark Mikulski

A dewinged Angel Gabriel (Professor Irwin Corey) is sent to Earth to help bring a couple back together. Gabriel becomes the judge in their palimony case and relates all their problems to events in history. The best and funniest parts of the film are when Carol (Virginia Penta) and Bill (Mark Mikulski) discuss their early relationship. The history bits with cavemen, Adam and Eve, Christopher Columbus, and so on seem to be senseless time-fillers. Rated R for nudity, obscenities, and simulated sex.

1982 86 minutes

SUMMER RENTAL

★★½

DIRECTOR: Carl Reiner

CAST: John Candy, Richard Crenna, Karen Austin, Rip Torn, Kerri Green, Joey Lawrence, Aubrey Jene

John Candy is watchable in his first film as star. Unfortunately, the film itself does not live up to his talents. It starts off well enough—with air traffic controller Candy exhibiting the kind of stress that causes his superiors to suggest a vacation—but after a fairly funny first hour, it sinks into the mire of plot resolution as our hero decides to take up sailing and take on snobbish Richard Crenna. After Candy hooks up with sailing expert Rip Torn, the film rarely provides a chuckle. Rated PG for profanity.

1985 88 minutes

SUMMER SCHOOL

★★★★

DIRECTOR: Carl Reiner

CAST: Mark Harmon, Kirstie Alley, Nels Van Patton, Carl Reiner, Courtney Thorne-Smith, Lucy Lee Flippin, Robin Thomas, Dean Cameron, Kelly Minter, Frank McCarthy, Shawnee Smith

This teen comedy does something almost unheard of for its genre—it bridges the generation gap and entertains young and old alike. Director Carl Reiner knows how to milk every scene for a laugh. Mark Harmon stars as a P.E. coach forced to teach remedial English in summer school. He has no idea how to teach his less than angelic students, so he makes contracts with them to encourage them to learn. After school he becomes a chauffeur, driving instructor, workout partner, Lamaze coach, etc. Among teen films, this is one of the best. Rated PG-13 for obsenities and gore.

1987 95 minutes

SUNSHINE BOYS, THE

★★★★

DIRECTOR: Herbert Ross

CAST: Walter Matthau, Richard Benjamin, George Burns, Lee Meredith, Carol Arthur, Howard Hesseman, Ron Rifkin

The Sunshine Boys tells the story of two feuding ex–vaudeville stars who make a TV special. Walter Matthau, Richard Benjamin, and (especially) George Burns give memorable performances. Director Herbert Ross (*Play It Again Sam*) turns this adaptation of the successful Broadway play by Neil Simon into a celluloid winner. Rated PG.

1975 111 minutes

SUPPOSE THEY GAVE A WAR AND NOBODY CAME?

★★

DIRECTOR: Hy Averback

CAST: Brian Keith, Ernest Borgnine, Suzanne Pleshette, Tom Ewell, Tony Curtis, Bradford Dillman, Ivan Dixon, Arthur O'Connell, Don Ameche

In this comedy involving a confrontation between a rural town and a nearby military base, Brian Keith, Tony Curtis, and Ivan Dixon play three army buddies who take it upon themselves to stop the fighting. Ernest Borgnine plays a nasty police chief. Some funny moments and good acting. Rated PG for adult themes.

1970 113 minutes

SURE THING, THE

★★★½

DIRECTOR: Rob Reiner

CAST: John Cusack, Daphne Zuniga, Anthony Edwards, Boyd Gaines, Lisa Jane Persky

This enjoyable romantic comedy, about two college freshmen who discover themselves and each other through a series of misadventures on the road, is more or less director Rob Reiner's updating of Frank Capra's *It Happened One Night*. John Cusack and Daphne Zuniga star as the unlikely protagonists. Rated PG-13 for profanity and suggested sex.

1985 100 minutes

SURVIVORS, THE

★★★½

DIRECTOR: Michael Ritchie

CAST: Robin Williams, Walter Matthau, Jerry Reed, James Wainwright, Kristen Vigard

This is an often funny movie about a goofy "survivalist" (Robin Williams), who is "adopted" by a service station owner (Walter

Matthau) and pursued by a friendly but determined hit man (Jerry Reed). Generally a black comedy, this movie features a variety of comedic styles, and they all work. Rated R for vulgar language and violence.

1983 102 minutes

SUSAN SLEPT HERE

★★½

DIRECTOR: Frank Tashlin

CAST: Dick Powell, Debbie Reynolds, Anne Francis, Glenda Farrell

Screenwriter Dick Powell must keep a tight leash on the ultra-high-spirited vagrant teenager he protects and falls for in the course of researching a script on juvenile delinquency. Amusing dialogue and lots of innuendo mark this otherwise pedestrian sex comedy.

1954 98 minutes

SWEATER GIRLS

★

DIRECTOR: Don Jones

CAST: Harry Moses, Meegan King, Noelle North, Kate Sarchet, Michael Goodron, Charlene Tilton

One of the silliest of the teen sexcapade movies, this concerns a club called "Sweater Girls" that Meegan King and Noelle North decide to form because they are fed up with their drinking, pawing boyfriends. Charlene Tilton, who is featured on the box, does appear in a sweater in the final five minutes of the film. We give it a D, but not for cup size. Rated R for sex and language.

1984 84 minutes

SWEET LIBERTY

★★★★

DIRECTOR: Alan Alda

CAST: Alan Alda, Michael Caine, Michelle Pfeiffer, Bob Hoskins, Lise Hilboldt, Lillian Gish, Saul Rubinek, Lois Chiles, Linda Thorson

Writer-director-star Alan Alda strikes again, this time with the story of a small-town historian (Alda) whose prize-winning saga of the Revolutionary War is optioned by Hollywood and turned into a movie. When the film crew descends on Alda's hometown for location shooting, predictable chaos erupts. Star Elliot James (Michael Caine, in a droll portrayal) struggles to have his way with all the local women, including the historian's girlfriend, played by Lise Hilboldt. Alda, meanwhile, is concerned that his scholarly tome has been turned into mass-market junk food by a young turk director (Saul Rubinek) with three ingredients for movie success: characters must 1. defy authority, 2. destroy property, and 3. remove their clothes. Alda's attempts, with screenwriter Stanley Gould (the always excellent Bob Hoskins), to retain some of his book's substance makes up the bulk of this quite entertaining picture. Rated PG for mild sexual situations.

1986 107 minutes

SWIMMING TO CAMBODIA

★★★★

DIRECTOR: Jonathan Demme

CAST: Spalding Gray

This low-budget movie consists of nothing more than actor-monologist Spalding Gray sitting at a desk while he tells about his experiences as a supporting actor in *The Killing Fields*. But seldom has so much come from so little. Gray is an excellent storyteller and his extended anecdotes—covering the political history of Cambodia, the filming of the movie, the sex and drugs available in Southeast Asia, and life in New York City—are often hilarious. If you enjoy good storytelling and can connect with Gray's occasionally surreal ideas, this simple little monologue can be more entertaining than any big-budget extravaganza. Unrated.

1987 87 minutes

SWING HIGH, SWING LOW

★★½

DIRECTOR: Mitchell Leisen

CAST: Carole Lombard, Fred MacMurray, Dorothy Lamour, Charles Butterworth, Franklin Pangborn, Anthony Quinn, Jean Dixon

Entertainers Carole Lombard and Fred MacMurray, stranded in Panama, get married, split, and fight ennui and a variety of troubles. This is a slanted-for-comedy remake of 1929's highly successful tearjerking backstage drama, *The Dance of Life*.

1937 B & W 95 minutes

SWINGIN' SUMMER, A

★

DIRECTOR: Robert Sparr

CAST: Raquel Welch, James Stacy, William A. Wellman Jr., Quinn O'Hara, Martin West

This is one of those swingin' sixties flicks where three swingin' teens move to a swingin' summer resort for a swingin' vacation. They start up their own swingin' dance concert schedule and book big-name acts like Gary and the Playboys, the Rip Tides, and the Righteous Brothers. Raquel Welch debuts here and also sings. It's good for a few laughs.

1965 82 minutes

SWISS MISS

★★★

DIRECTOR: John Blystone

CAST: Stan Laurel, Oliver Hardy, Della Lind, Walter Woolf King, Eric Blore, Adia Kuznetzof

Here we have Stan Laurel and Oliver Hardy in the Swiss Alps. A weak and uneven script is overcome by the stars, who seize several opportunities for brilliant comedy. For the most part, however, the film is mediocre.

1938 B & W 72 minutes

TAKE DOWN

★★½

DIRECTOR: Keith Merrill

CAST: Edward Herrmann, Kathleen Lloyd, Lorenzo Lamas, Maureen McCormick, Kevin Hooks, Stephen Furst

Earnest comedy-drama set in the arena of high-school wrestling. It centers on two initially reluctant participants: an intellectual teacher-turned-coach and a fiery student. The movie has enough heart to carry it to victory. Rated PG.

1978 107 minutes

TAKE THE MONEY AND RUN

★★★★

DIRECTOR: Woody Allen

CAST: Woody Allen, Janet Margolin, Marcel Hillaire

Woody Allen's first original feature is still a laugh-filled delight as the star-director plays an inept criminal in a story told in pseudo-documentary-style (à la *Zelig*). It's hilarious. Rated PG.

1969 85 minutes

TAKE THIS JOB AND SHOVE IT

★★★½

DIRECTOR: Gus Trikonis

CAST: Robert Hays, Art Carney, Barbara Hershey, Martin Mull, Eddie Albert

Robert Hays (*Airplane!*) stars as a rising corporate executive who returns, after a ten-year absence, to his hometown to take charge of a brewery where he once worked, and winds up organizing a revolt among his fellow employees. The serious side of this contemporary comedy-drama is shallow, but it isn't meant to be a landmark statement concerning labor strife or moral dilemmas. It's out to raise one's spirits, and it does just that. Rated PG.

1981 100 minutes

TALK OF THE TOWN, THE

★★★★

DIRECTOR: George Stevens

CAST: Ronald Colman, Jean Arthur, Cary Grant, Edgar Buchanan, Glenda Farrell, Emma Dunn, Charles Dingle, Leonide Kinsky, Tom Tyler, Don Beddoe, Rex Ingram

Falsely accused of arson and murder, parlor radical Cary Grant escapes jail and holes up in a country house Jean Arthur is readying for law professor Ronald Colman. The radical and the egghead take to one another. From the former, the latter learns there is more to the law than the inflexibility of Blackstone. Enlightened, Colman provides Grant with the winning defense that the rigid establishment, blindly intent on enforcing the rules, would have denied him. Gifted direction and a brilliant cast make this intelligent comedy topflight entertainment.

1942 B & W 118 minutes

TAMING OF THE SHREW, THE (ORIGINAL)

★★★

DIRECTOR: Sam Taylor

CAST: Mary Pickford, Douglas Fairbanks, Edwin Maxwell, Clyde Cook, Joseph Cawthorn, Geoffrey Wardwell, Dorothy Jordon

The first royal couple of Hollywood co-starred in this film while under the duress of a failing marriage. Mary Pickford is properly shrewish as Katharina; Douglas Fairbanks is smug, commanding, and virile as Petruchio. Critics liked it and the public flocked to see the famous duo have at the Bard. Director Sam Taylor gave Hollywood one of its enduring anecdotes by taking screen credit for additional dialogue.

1929 B & W 66 minutes

TAMING OF THE SHREW, THE

★★★★½

DIRECTOR: Franco Zeffirelli

CAST: Richard Burton, Elizabeth Taylor, Cyril Cusack, Michael York

As in his *Romeo and Juliet* (1968), director Franco Zeffirelli shows his unique knack for bringing Shakespeare vividly to life. This is a beautifully mounted comedy of the battle of the sexes. Petruchio (Richard Burton), a spirited minor nobleman of the Italian Renaissance, pits his wits against the man-hating Kate (Elizabeth Taylor) in order to win her hand. The zest with which this famous play is transferred to the screen can be enjoyed even by those who feel intimidated by Shakespeare.

1966 126 minutes

TEACHER'S PET

★★★

DIRECTOR: George Seaton

CAST: Clark Gable, Doris Day, Gig Young, Mamie Van Doren, Nick Adams, Jack Albertson, Marion Ross

Winsome journalism instructor Doris Day fascinates and charms hard-boiled city editor Clark Gable in this near plotless but most diverting comedy of incidents. The two are terrific, but Gig Young, as the teacher's erudite but liquor-logged boyfriend, is the one to watch. His near picture-stealing performance earned him an Academy Award nomination. Slug this: Clever, cute, coy film fun.

1958 B & W 120 minutes

TEACHERS

★★

DIRECTOR: Arthur Hiller
CAST: Nick Nolte, JoBeth Williams, Judd Hirsch, Richard Mulligan, Ralph Macchio

This satirical look at a contemporary urban high school flunks as a film. Students will hate it because it's not serious enough; teachers will hate it because it's just terrible. It promised to "do for high school what *Network* did for television." Actually, it's no more interesting than a dull day in high school. Rated R for sexual innuendo, violence, and profanity.

1984 106 minutes

10

★★★½

DIRECTOR: Blake Edwards
CAST: Dudley Moore, Bo Derek, Julie Andrews, Robert Webber, Dee Wallace

Ravel's "Bolero" enjoyed a renewed popularity, and Bo Derek rocketed to stardom because of this uneven but generally entertaining sex comedy, directed by Blake Edwards (*The Pink Panther*). Most of the film's funny moments come from the deftly timed physical antics of Dudley Moore, who plays a just-turned-40 songwriter who at long last meets the girl (Bo Derek) of his dreams—on her wedding day. Rated R.

1979 122 minutes

10 FROM YOUR SHOW OF SHOWS

★★★★

DIRECTOR: Max Liebman
CAST: Sid Caesar, Imogene Coca, Carl Reiner, Howard Morris, Louis Nye

Ten skits from the early 1950s television program that set the pace for all variety shows. Granted, the style is dated and far from subtle, but as a joyful look at television's formative years, it can't be beat. Unrated.

1973 B & W 92 minutes

THAT LUCKY TOUCH

★★★

DIRECTOR: Christopher Miles
CAST: Roger Moore, Susannah York, Shelley Winters, Lee J. Cobb, Sydne Rome

This romantic comedy features unlikely neighbors falling in love. Roger Moore plays Michael Scott, a weapons merchant who wheels and deals with everyone from Arabs to NATO. Susannah York, on the other hand, is an antimilitary writer. Shelley Winters provides a few laughs as the airhead wife of a NATO general (Lee J. Cobb). Comparable with a PG, but basically pretty tame.

1975 93 minutes

THAT SINKING FEELING

★★★★

DIRECTOR: Bill Forsyth
CAST: Robert Buchanan, Billy Greenlees, John Hughes

This is the first film by Scottish filmmaker Bill Forsyth (*Local Hero*; *Gregory's Girl*), and with it you can easily see the promise the young talent has proved in his later works. Shot on a shoestring budget, utilizing many of the Glasgow youths seen in *Gregory's Girl*, it's a delightful tale of a group of young men who decide to take their unemployment situation in hand in a most unusual way. Suffice it to say it has something to do with stainless-steel sinks. No MPAA rating; no objectionable material.

1979 82 minutes

THAT TOUCH OF MINK

★★★½

DIRECTOR: Delbert Mann

CAST: Doris Day, Cary Grant, Gig Young, Audrey Meadows, John Astin

This 1962 romantic comedy is enjoyable, but only as escapist fare. Doris Day stars as an unemployed girl pursued by a wealthy businessman (Cary Grant).

1962 99 minutes

THAT UNCERTAIN FEELING

★★½

DIRECTOR: Ernst Lubitsch

CAST: Merle Oberon, Melvyn Douglas, Alan Mowbray, Burgess Meredith, Eve Arden, Sig Rumann

This is an amusing film about marital unrest until somewhere around the midpoint, when the time-tried romantic triangle plot thins rather than thickens. Burgess Meredith all but filches the film in a supporting role. Merle Oberon is devastatingly beautiful, even when she has the hiccups—an important plot device.

1941 B & W 86 minutes

THAT'S LIFE

★★★

DIRECTOR: Blake Edwards

CAST: Julie Andrews, Jack Lemmon, Sally Kellerman, Robert Loggia, Jennifer Edwards, Chris Lemmon, Emma Walton

That's Life is a perfect title for writer-director Blake Edwards's semi-autobiographical movie. It gets as close to real life as any motion picture can and still remain entertaining. Jack Lemmon and Julie Andrews play a married couple enduring a torrent of personal and family crises during one fateful weekend. The film is a mixture of good and bad, funny and sad, tasteful and tasteless, boring and fascinating. That it ends up on the plus side is more to the credit of its lead players than to its theme or handling. Rated PG-13 for profanity and scatological humor.

1986 102 minutes

THERE'S A GIRL IN MY SOUP

★★½

DIRECTOR: Roy Boulting

CAST: Peter Sellers, Goldie Hawn, Diana Dors, Tony Britton

Goldie Hawn hadn't completely shed her *Laugh-In* image when this British sex farce came out, and it didn't do her career any good. Quite a letdown, after her Oscar-winning performance in *Cactus Flower*. Peter Sellers is a middle-aged boob who falls in lust with flower-child Hawn. Very few laughs; would have been far better if made in France . . . they understand the genre much better. A low point for all concerned. Rated R.

1970 95 minutes

THEY ALL LAUGHED

★★★★

DIRECTOR: Peter Bogdanovich

CAST: Audrey Hepburn, Ben Gazzara, John Ritter, Dorothy Stratten

This is director Peter Bogdanovich at his best. A very offbeat comedy that looks at four New York private eyes' adventures and love lives. Final film of ex–Playboy bunny Dorothy Stratten. Worth a look. Rated PG.

1981 115 minutes

THEY CALL ME BRUCE?

★★

DIRECTOR: Elliot Hong

CAST: Johnny Yune, Ralph Mauro, Margaux Hemingway, Pam Huntington

In this unsophisticated kung-fu comedy, Johnny Yune portrays an Asian immigrant who, because of his "resemblance" to Bruce Lee and an accidental exhibition of craziness (misinterpreted as martial arts expertise), gets a reputation as a mean man with fists and feet. But it is Ralph Mauro, playing Bruce's chauffeur, who steals the show. Margaux Hemingway appears in a supporting role. Rated PG.

1982 88 minutes

THEY GOT ME COVERED

★★½

DIRECTOR: David Butler

CAST: Bob Hope, Dorothy Lamour, Lenore Aubert, Otto Preminger, Eduardo Ciannelli, Marion Martin, Donald MacBride, Walter Catlett, Donald Meek, Philip Ahn

Typical Bob Hope vehicle of the 1940s is full of gals, gags, goofy situations, snappy dialogue, and one-line zingers, and boasts an incredible supporting cast of great character actors and actresses. Thin story about spy nonsense in Washington, D.C., is secondary to the zany antics of Paramount's ski-nosed comedian before he became an American institution by sheer longevity if nothing else. Not a comedy classic, but harmless fun and clever to boot. This is basically *the* Bob Hope movie, which he continued to make, with varying degrees of success, for the next twenty-five years.

1943 B & W 95 minutes

THEY STILL CALL ME BRUCE

DIRECTORS: Johnny Yune, James Orr

CAST: Johnny Yune, David Mendenhall, Joey Travolta, Bethany Wright, Carl Bensen

Perhaps one of the least-anticipated sequels ever, this attempt by Korean comic Johnny Yune to follow up his 1982 nonhit *They Call Me Bruce?* is completely hopeless. Yune plays an Asian immigrant who arrives in Houston and becomes involved with gangsters, street vigilantes, a runaway prostitute, and a sad little orphan boy. The jokes aren't funny, the drama is maudlin, and the production values are almost nil. It's rated PG for Yune's occasionally off-color humor.

1987 91 minutes

THIEF WHO CAME TO DINNER, THE

★★★

DIRECTOR: Bud Yorkin

CAST: Ryan O'Neal, Jacqueline Bisset, Warren Oates, Jill Clayburgh, Charles Cioffi, Ned Beatty

Silly stuff about Ryan O'Neal leading a double life: as a bookish computer programmer by day and a jewel thief by night. Jacqueline Bisset is, as always, highly watchable—as is the great character actor Warren Oates. The film's most interesting performance comes from Jill Clayburgh in an early screen role. It's mindless fluff and inoffensive. Rated PG.

1973 102 minutes

THINGS ARE TOUGH ALL OVER

★

DIRECTOR: Tom Avildsen

CAST: Cheech and Chong, Rikki Marin, Rip Taylor

If cheap laughs are worthless, then so is this romp starring Cheech and Chong. Not that it isn't amusing—it has a number of funny moments—unfortunately, they're mostly from the toilet. This time around, Richard "Cheech" Marin and Tommy Chong play dual roles: as their usual spaced-out characters, plus two Arab brothers up to no good. But you've seen most of the comedy bits before, in the team's previous pictures. Rated R for profanity and scatological humor.

1982 92 minutes

THINGS WE DID LAST SUMMER

★★½

DIRECTOR: Gary Weis

CAST: John Belushi, Dan Aykroyd, Bill Murray, Gilda Radner, Garrett Morris, Laraine Newman

A mixed bag used to supplement *Saturday Night Live* episodes in the show's first golden era, this features some of The Not Ready For Prime Time Players in skits of varying quality. The highlights are provided by John Belushi and Dan Aykroyd performing live in concert as the Blues Brothers.

1977 50 minutes

30 FOOT BRIDE OF CANDY ROCK, THE

★★

DIRECTOR: Sidney Miller

CAST: Lou Costello, Dorothy Provine, Gale Gordon, Charles Lane, Doodles Weaver

A nebbish inventor turns his girlfriend into a giant. A mild comedy with a certain amount of charm, this was the last film made by Columbia's B-picture unit, and Lou Costello's only feature film after breaking up with Bud Abbott. Although he proved to be an effective dramatic actor in television work during his later years, here he plays his usual bumbling character. But it's difficult to laugh at the movie due to a lame script and Costello's ill health. He died before the film was released.

1959 B & W 75 minutes

30 IS A DANGEROUS AGE, CYNTHIA

★½

DIRECTOR: Joseph McGrath

CAST: Dudley Moore, Suzy Kendall, Eddie Fox Jr., John Bird, Patricia Routledge

Dated British comedy features Dudley Moore as a pianist-composer who intends to find a bride and write a musical before he turns 30. Unfortunately, he has only six weeks. Much of the action takes place in Moore's fantasies about his success and happiness. Suzy Kendall plays the object of his affections. A few chuckles here, but not enough.

1967 83 minutes

THIS HAPPY FEELING

★★

DIRECTOR: Blake Edwards

CAST: Debbie Reynolds, Curt Jurgens, John Saxon, Alexis Smith, Mary Astor, Estelle Winwood, Troy Donahue, Hayden Rourke

Curt Jurgens is an aging actor, Debbie Reynolds is the young girl who develops a crush on him, and John Saxon is Jurgens's handsome young neighbor who falls hard for Reynolds. The film is truly reflective of the 1950s, with its unreal colors and a musical score inundating every scene. Jurgens is uncomfortable in the leading role; Reynolds's character is not up to expectations; and Blake Edwards had not yet hit his comedic stride. Alexis Smith as "the other woman" is enjoyable.

1958 92 minutes

THIS IS SPINAL TAP

★★★★½

DIRECTOR: Rob Reiner

CAST: Michael McKean, Christopher Guest, Harry Shearer, Rob Reiner

This is one of the funniest movies ever made about rock-'n-roll. Not since Monty Python member Eric Idle's spoof of the Beatles (*The Rutles*) has there been such an irreverently humorous look at the world of pop music. Directed by Rob Reiner, son of Carl and a one-time regular (Meathead) on

All in the Family, this is a satire of rock documentaries that tells the story of Spinal Tap, an over-the-hill British heavy-metal rock group that's fast rocketing to the bottom of the charts. *This Is Spinal Tap* isn't consistently funny, but does it ever have its moments. Some of the song lyrics are hysterical, and the performances are perfect. In fact, the actors are so good some younger film-goers in San Francisco reportedly took them for the real thing. Rated R for profanity.

1984 82 minutes

THOSE ENDEARING YOUNG CHARMS

★★★

DIRECTOR: Lewis Allen

CAST: Robert Young, Laraine Day, Bill Williams, Ann Harding, Anne Jeffreys, Lawrence Tierney, Marc Cramer

Heroine Laraine Day brings smoothie Robert Young to bay and then to heel in this cliché-plotted, but sprightly played, romantic comedy. Public hunger for wholesome laughter and sentimental tears as World War II wound down made this a box-office bonanza. Ann Harding is perfect as the wise mother.

1945 B & W 82 minutes

THOSE MAGNIFICENT MEN IN THEIR FLYING MACHINES

★★★★

DIRECTOR: Ken Annakin

CAST: Terry-Thomas, Stuart Whitman, Sarah Miles, Gert Frobe

Here is some fun, just plain fun, for the family. An air race between London and Paris in the early days of flight is this comedy's centerpiece. Around it hang an enjoyable number of rib-tickling vignettes. A large international cast each get their chance to shine as the contest's zany participants. Terry-Thomas stands out as the hapless villain. He reminds one of the coyote in the Road Runner cartoons. His ingenious evil schemes continually go wrong, with hilarious results.

1965 132 minutes

THOUSAND CLOWNS, A

★★★★

DIRECTOR: Fred Coe

CAST: Jason Robards, Barry Gordon, Barbara Harris, Martin Balsam, Gene Saks, William Daniels

Famous Broadway play comes to the screen with memorable performances by all the principals and standout jobs by Jason Robards as a talented nonconformist and Barry Gordon as his precocious ward, who struggle against welfare bureaucracy in order to stay together. Very funny in spots and equally poignant at others, this well-written story about the loss of innocence and coming of age of the main characters has something to say to everyone about losing sight of early goals and conforming to an uncaring world. Gene Saks as the neurotic Chuckles the Chipmunk is just great, as are Martin Balsam as Robards's successful brother and William Daniels as the unyielding welfare investigator who realizes he is not "one of the warm ones." Barbara Harris (in the role Sandy Dennis originated on-stage) is the weakest of the characters, but her role is central to the success of the story, so it's a necessary evil. Good on many levels.

1965 B & W 118 minutes

THREE AMIGOS

★★½

DIRECTOR: John Landis

CAST: Steve Martin, Chevy Chase, Martin Short, Alfonso Arau, Patrice Martinez, Joe Mantegna, Jon Lovitz, Fred Asparagus

In this send-up of *The Magnificent Seven*, Steve Martin, Chevy Chase, and Martin Short play three silent-screen cowboys who attempt to save a Mexican village from bloodthirsty banditos. Steve Martin, in particular, has some very funny moments. Overall, it's pleasant — even amusing — but nothing more. Rated PG.

1986 105 minutes

THREE FOR THE ROAD

★

DIRECTOR: B. W. L. Norton

CAST: Charlie Sheen, Kerri Green, Adam Ruck, Sally Kellerman, Blair Tefkin, Alexa Hamilton, James Avery

Dull comedy about a senator's aide (Charlie Sheen) who is assigned to take his employer's difficult daughter (Kerri Green) to a reform school. The cast tries hard, but the result is an amiable, yet generally tedious, rehash of all the road movies that have gone before. Rated PG.

1987 95 minutes

THREE STOOGES, THE (VOLUMES 1-10)

★★★★

DIRECTOR: (Various)

CAST: Moe Howard, Curly (Jerry) Howard, Larry Fine

The Three Stooges made 190 two-reel short subjects between 1934 and 1959, making them the most prolific comedy team of all time. For over fifty years, people have either loved them or hated them. Those in the latter category should, of course, avoid these tapes. But if you are a fan, you'll find these collections the answer to a knucklehead's dream. Each cassette features three shorts of impeccable quality, transferred from brand-new, complete 35-mm prints. After years of scratchy, poorly edited television prints, it's like seeing them for the first time. All of the films are from the classic "Curly" period, when the team was at the peak of its energy and originality. One note of caution: These shorts have been completely restored. Since they were made in less enlightened times, they occasionally display some unfortunate examples of racist comedy.

1934 B & W 60 minutes

TIGHT LITTLE ISLAND

★★★★

DIRECTOR: Alexander Mackendrick

CAST: Basil Radford, Joan Greenwood, James Robertson Justice, Gordon Jackson, Wylie Watson

A World War II transport laden with whiskey founders just off the shore of a Scottish island. Hilarious hell breaks loose as dram-delirious lads and lassies seek to salvage the water of life before authorities can claim it and put it under government control. One of the great comedies that revived the British film industry after the war.

1949 B & W 82 minutes

TILT

🦃

DIRECTOR: Rudy Durand

CAST: Brooke Shields, Ken Marshall, Charles Durning, Geoffrey Lewis

Brooke Shields's third movie (after *Alice Sweet Alice* and *Pretty Baby*) is a mess. Co-starring Ken Marshall (*Krull*), Charles Durning, and Geoffrey Lewis, this film (written and directed by Rudy Durand) is pitiful at best and unbearable at worst. The dialogue is laughable, and the performances are generally putrid. Rated PG.

1978 104 minutes

TIN MEN

★★★★

DIRECTOR: Barry Levinson
CAST: Richard Dreyfuss, Danny DeVito, Barbara Hershey

Writer-director Barry Levinson takes a simple subject—the vendetta between two aluminum-siding salesmen in the 1950s—and fashions it into an insightful, witty comedy. The tone is similar to Levinson's earlier *Diner*. He has elicited topnotch performances from his trio of stars. Richard Dreyfuss and Danny DeVito are absolutely perfect. Barbara Hershey is convincing as she transforms her character from mousy pawn to attractive, assertive woman. Rated R.

1987 110 minutes

TO BE OR NOT TO BE (ORIGINAL)

★★★★½

DIRECTOR: Ernst Lubitsch
CAST: Carole Lombard, Jack Benny, Robert Stack

After gaining early stardom in *Twentieth Century*, Carole Lombard returned to another black comedy and another role as an oddball theater performer, for the last film of her life. One of Hollywood's premier comedy directors, Ernst Lubitsch, coached excellent performances from Carole Lombard and co-star Jack Benny, in this hilarious farce about a theater couple who outwit the Nazis.

1942 B & W 99 minutes

TO BE OR NOT TO BE (REMAKE)

★★★★

DIRECTOR: Alan Johnson
CAST: Mel Brooks, Anne Bancroft, Charles Durning, Tim Matheson

In this hilarious remake of the Jack Benny–Carole Lombard classic from 1942, Mel Brooks and Anne Bancroft are Polish actors who foil the Nazis at the outbreak of World War II. Charles Durning's Gestapo officer alone is worth the price of the rental of this delightful comedy-melodrama. It's producer-star Brooks's best film since *Young Frankenstein* and was directed by Alan Johnson, who choreographed *Springtime for Hitler* for Brooks's first film, *The Producers*. Rated PG, the film has no objectionable material.

1983 108 minutes

TOM JONES

★★★★★

DIRECTOR: Tony Richardson
CAST: Albert Finney, Susannah York, Hugh Griffith, Edith Evans

Rarely has a movie captured the spirit and flavor of its times or the novel on which it was based. This is a rambunctious, witty, and often bawdy tale of a youth's misadventures in eighteenth-century England. Albert Finney is a perfect rascal as Tom. We joyously follow him through all levels of British society as he tries to make his fortune and win the lovely Sophie (Susannah York). The entire cast is brilliant.

1963 129 minutes

TOOTSIE

★★★★★

DIRECTOR: Sydney Pollack
CAST: Dustin Hoffman, Bill Murray, Jessica Lange, Teri Garr, Dabney Coleman, Sydney Pollack

Dustin Hoffman is Michael Dorsey, an out-of-work actor who disguises himself as a woman—Dorothy Michaels—to get a job and becomes a big star on a popular television soap opera. An absolute delight, *Tootsie* is hilarious, touching, and marvelously acted. Rated PG for adult content.

1982 119 minutes

TO PARIS WITH LOVE

★★½

DIRECTOR: Robert Hamer
CAST: Alec Guinness, Odile Versois, Austin Trevor, Vernon Gray

Alec Guinness stands out like a pumpkin in a pea patch in this average comedy about a rich and indulgent father who takes his son to gay Paree to learn the facts of life.

1955 78 minutes

TOP SECRET

★★½

DIRECTORS: Jim Abrahams, David Zucker, Jerry Zucker
CAST: Val Kilmer, Omar Sharif, Peter Cushing, Lucy Gutteridge

By the makers of *Airplane!*, this film makes up for its flimsy plot with one gag after another. Nick Rivers (Val Kilmer) is the main character who, as a rock-'n-roll star, visits East Germany. There he falls in love with Hilary and becomes involved in the plot to free her scientist father. The soundtrack features lots of lively old Beach Boys and Elvis Presley tunes. Omar Sharif makes a cameo appearance as a much-abused spy. Rated PG for some profanity and sexually oriented gags.

1984 90 minutes

TOPPER

★★★★

DIRECTOR: Norman Z. McLeod
CAST: Cary Grant, Constance Bennett, Roland Young, Billie Burke

This is the original feature of what became a delightful fantasy movie series and television series. Cary Grant and Constance Bennett are the Kirbys, a duo of social high livers who, due to an unfortunate auto accident, become ghosts. They now want to transfer their spirit of living the good life to a rather stodgy banker, the fellow they are now haunting, one Cosmo Topper (Roland Young). Good fun all around.

1937 B & W 97 minutes

TOPPER RETURNS

★★★

DIRECTOR: Roy Del Ruth
CAST: Roland Young, Joan Blondell, Eddie Anderson, Carole Landis, Dennis O'Keefe, H. B. Warner

Cary Grant and Constance Bennett have gone on to their heavenly rewards, but Roland Young, as Cosmo Topper, is still seeing ghosts. This time the spooky personage is that of Joan Blondell, who helps our hero solve a murder in this entertaining comedy.

1941 B & W 87 minutes

TOPPER TAKES A TRIP

★★★

DIRECTOR: Norman Z. McLeod
CAST: Constance Bennett, Roland Young, Billie Burke, Alan Mowbray, Franklin Pangborn, Cary Grant (in flashback)

Second film in the original series finds Cosmo and Henrietta Topper on the French Riviera accompanied by their ghostly friend Marion Kirby, portrayed by the star of the original film, Constance Bennett. Topper and Marion pool forces to stop Mrs. Topper from being victimized by a smooth-talking confidence man (Alan Mowbray), and overcome all obstacles with the special effects and sleight of hand that highlight the series. Marion's new companion is a pet dog, but Cary Grant makes a brief appearance in a flashback sequence. Harmless fun.

1939 B & W 85 minutes

TO SEE SUCH FUN

DIRECTOR: Jon Scoffield
CAST: Peter Sellers, Marty Feldman, Benny Hill, Eric Idle, Margaret Rutherford, Alec Guinness, Dirk Bogarde, Spike Milligan, Norman Wisdom

This is a compilation of a vast number of comedy film clips from 1930 to 1970. Many of the clips illustrate the British love of puns, rhymes, and slapstick. Included are many phone gags, famous recurring lines, men in drag, student and teacher skits, wild car rides, and male-female conflicts. Viewers hoping to see a lot of Peter Sellers, Benny Hill, and Marty Feldman clips will be disappointed because most of the footage comes from films of the 1930s and 1940s. Unless you're a British film buff, you'll probably miss the point on many of the bits because they're too short to really figure out.

1977 90 minutes

TOUCH AND GO

★★½

DIRECTOR: Robert Mandel
CAST: Michael Keaton, Maria Conchita Alonso, Ajay Naido

A comedy that sat on the shelf for two years. Chicago hockey player falls in love with the mother of a young delinquent who mugged him. Michael Keaton is appealing, Maria Conchita Alonso is fiery, and the script contains sharp dialogue, a few good laughs, and a number of sweet moments. But the ending is cheap, nasty, and insulting to the characters. Rated PG for profanity.

1984 101 minutes

TOUCH OF CLASS, A

★★★★★

DIRECTOR: Melvin Frank
CAST: George Segal, Glenda Jackson, Paul Sorvino, Hildegard Neil

In one of the best romantic comedies of recent years, George Segal and Glenda Jackson are marvelously paired as a sometimes loving — sometimes bickering — couple who struggle through an extramarital affair. They begin their oddball romance when he runs over one of her children while chasing a fly ball in a baseball game. Fine acting and witty dialogue carry the film from this auspicious beginning. Rated PG.

1972 105 minutes

TOUGH GUYS

★★★

DIRECTOR: Jeff Kanew
CAST: Burt Lancaster, Kirk Douglas, Charles Durning, Alexis Smith, Dana Carvey, Darlanne Fleugel, Eli Wallach

This enjoyable movie features Burt Lancaster and Kirk Douglas as two flamboyant train robbers who are released from prison after thirty years to find they have no place in society. Angered by being relegated to the nonperson status suffered by many older people, they decide to strike back by doing what they do best. It's featherweight, but the stars make it fun. Rated PG for light profanity, suggested sex, and mild violence.

1986 103 minutes

TOY, THE

★★

DIRECTOR: Richard Donner
CAST: Richard Pryor, Jackie Gleason, Scott Schwartz, Ned Beatty

You would think any comedy that combines the talents of Richard

Pryor and Jackie Gleason would have to be exceptionally good, to say nothing of funny. But that's simply not true of this movie, about a spoiled rich kid (Scott Schwartz) whose father (Gleason) allows him to buy the ultimate toy (Pryor). Not that it isn't watchable. How could any picture with Pryor be otherwise? Rated PG for profanity and adult themes.

1982 99 minutes

TRADING PLACES

★★★★

DIRECTOR: John Landis

CAST: Dan Aykroyd, Eddie Murphy, Ralph Bellamy, Don Ameche, Jamie Lee Curtis

Here's an uproarious comedy about what happens when uptight Philadelphia broker (Dan Aykroyd) and dynamic black street hustler (Eddie Murphy) change places. *Trading Places* was directed by John Landis (*Animal House*; *The Blues Brothers*), who is undoubtedly the best director of comedies today. His sense of timing is exquisite—he knows how to milk every bit of mirth out of any situation. The stars share his expertise, and the result is a treat for those who love to laugh. Rated R for nudity and profanity.

1983 117 minutes

TRAIL OF THE PINK PANTHER, THE

★★½

DIRECTOR: Blake Edwards

CAST: Peter Sellers, David Niven, Herbert Lom, Capucine, Robert Wagner

Through the magic of editing, the late Peter Sellers "stars" as the bumbling Inspector Clouseau, in this late entry in the comedy series. Writer-director Blake Edwards uses outtakes of Sellers from previous films and combines them with new footage featuring David Niven, Herbert Lom, and Capucine. The results are disappointing. After Edwards runs out of never-before-seen Sellers scenes, the movie goes decidedly downhill. He should have left well enough alone. Rated PG for nudity and scatological humor.

1982 97 minutes

TRANSYLVANIA 6-5000

★★

DIRECTOR: Rudy DeLuca

CAST: Jeff Goldblum, Ed Begley Jr., Joseph Bologna, Carol Kane, Jeffrey Jones, John Byner, Michael Richards, Geena Davis, Teresa Ganzel, Norman Fell

Sometimes amusing but ultimately silly horror spoof focusing on an inept pair of tabloid reporters (Jeff Goldblum and Ed Begley Jr.) sent to Transylvania to investigate the possible resurgence of the Frankenstein monster. They soon find themselves up to their idiotic necks in trouble. The large cast does its best with what may generously be referred to as weak material, which the director hoped to compensate for by having everyone scream their lines and run around frantically throughout most of the film. Still, there are a few bright spots, most notably Michael Richards (of TV's *Fridays*) as a loosely wound butler, and a video transfer that ranks with the best. Rated PG for mild profanity.

1985 93 minutes

TRENCHCOAT

★½

DIRECTOR: Michael Tuchner

CAST: Margot Kidder, Robert Hays, Daniel Faraldo

No one is what he appears to be in this inept spoof of the detective genre. Margot Kidder plays Mickey Raymond, a would-be writer of hard-boiled detective fiction who is ensnared in a scheme that involves drugs (perhaps), stolen plutonium (most likely), and murder (definitely). While there are moments that will evoke some chuckles, *Trenchcoat* rarely hits the mark as being the spontaneous, unpredictable madcap chase film it was meant to be. Rated PG.

1983 91 minutes

TROUBLE IN THE GLEN

★★

DIRECTOR: Herbert Wilcox

CAST: Orson Welles, Margaret Lockwood, Victor McLaglen, Forrest Tucker

A white-haired, cigar-chomping Orson Welles in Scots kilts is farfetched, to say the least. The film turns on a feud over a closed road. What was projected as a Highland comedy is thoroughly scotched by poor pacing and a script that misses the mark. Deep-dyed Welles fans will like it.

1953 91 minutes

TROUBLE WITH ANGELS, THE

★★★

DIRECTOR: Ida Lupino

CAST: Rosalind Russell, Hayley Mills, June Harding

Rosalind Russell stars as the Mother Superior at the St. Francis Academy for Girls. Her serenity and the educational pursuits of the institution are coming apart at the seams due to the pranks of two rambunctious teenagers, Hayley Mills and June Harding. This comedy's humor is uninspired, but the warmth and humanity of the entire production make it worthwhile family viewing.

1966 112 minutes

TROUBLE WITH HARRY, THE

★★★★

DIRECTOR: Alfred Hitchcock

CAST: John Forsythe, Edmund Gwenn, Shirley MacLaine, Mildred Natwick, Jerry Mathers

Shirley MacLaine made her film debut in this wickedly funny black comedy, directed by Alfred Hitchcock. This is the last of long-unseen screen works by the master of suspense to be rereleased, and the most unusual, because the accent is on humor instead of tension-filled drama. In it, a murdered man causes no end of problems for his neighbors in a peaceful New England community. Rated PG when it was rereleased.

1955 100 minutes

TRUE STORIES

★★½

DIRECTOR: David Byrne

CAST: David Byrne, John Goodman, Annie McEnroe, Swoosie Kurtz, Spalding Gray, Pops Staples, Tito Lavviva

True Stories is Talking Heads leader David Byrne's satirical look at the imaginary town of Virgil, Texas. It's a mixture of *The National Enquirer* and deadpan cinematic humor. Some of the bits are truly funny, but the lethargic tone becomes an aggravating artistic conceit. Rated PG.

1986 89 minutes

TUNNELVISION

★★½

DIRECTORS: Neal Israel, Brad Swirnoff

CAST: Chevy Chase, Howard Hesseman, Betty Thomas, Laraine Newman

Here is a lightweight spoof of television. Sometimes it is funny, and other times it is just gross. The "stars," like Chevy Chase, have small bits, and it is not at all what one would expect from the billing. Still, there are some funny moments. *Tunnelvision* is like *The Groove Tube* in most respects, the good equally in proportion to the bad. Rated R.

1976 67 minutes

TURTLE DIARY

★★★★½

DIRECTOR: John Irvin

CAST: Glenda Jackson, Ben Kingsley, Richard Johnson, Michael Gambon, Rosemary Leach, Eleanor Bron, Harriet Walker, Jeroen Krabbé

Glenda Jackson and Ben Kingsley are absolutely delightful in this deliciously offbeat bit of British whimsy about urban life—of people living side by side but rarely touching. Jackson is Neaera Duncan, an author of children's books, while Kingsley is William Snow, a bookstore assistant. Both share an obsession for turtles and devise a plan to kidnap the shelled creatures, who are imprisoned in a nearby zoo, and release them into their natural habitat. The result is a thinking person's comedy that should please all but the *Porky's* and *Police Academy* crowd. Rated PG for nudity.

1986 97 minutes

TUTTLES OF TAHITI, THE

★★★

DIRECTOR: Charles Vidor

CAST: Charles Laughton, Jon Hall, Peggy Drake, Mala, Florence Bates, Alma Ross, Victor Francen, Curt Bois, Gene Reynolds

Captain Bligh goes native in this comedy of arch indolence and planned sloth in beautiful, bountiful Tahiti. Impoverished Charles Laughton and Florence Bates are rivals whose son Jon Hall and daughter Peggy Drake fall in love. A good-natured, congenial film of leisure life in which worries and woes include cockfights and a lack of gasoline.

1942 B & W 91 minutes

TWELVE CHAIRS, THE

★★★

DIRECTOR: Mel Brooks

CAST: Mel Brooks, Dom De Luise, Frank Langella, Ron Moody

Based on a Russian comedy-fable about an impoverished nobleman seeking jewels secreted in one of a dozen fancy dining room chairs. Ron Moody is the anguished Russian, Dom De Luise his chief rival in the hunt. Mel Brooks's direction keeps things moving with laughs. Rated G.

1970 94 minutes

TWO OF A KIND

★★

DIRECTOR: John Herzfeld

CAST: John Travolta, Olivia Newton-John, Charles Durning

John Travolta and Olivia Newton-John, who first teamed on screen in the box-office smash *Grease*, are reunited in this 1980s-style screwball comedy, which mixes clever ideas with incredibly stupid ones. The result is a movie the young viewers it was made for probably won't rave about, but neither will they be too disappointed. Others, however, should stay away. Rated PG for profanity and violence.

1983 87 minutes

UFORIA

★★★★

DIRECTOR: John Binder

CAST: Cindy Williams, Harry Dean Stanton, Fred Ward, Harry Carey Jr., Beverly Hope Atkinson, Robert Gray, Darrell Larson

Like *Repo Man* and *Stranger Than Paradise,* this low-budget American film deserved better treatment than the limited theatrical release it was given. Cindy Williams (TV's *Laverne and Shirley*) is hilarious as a born-again Christian who believes that salvation will come to Earth in the form of a flying saucer. Fred Ward *(The Right Stuff; Remo Williams)* is equally humorous as a truck-driving Waylon Jennings look-alike. Harry Dean Stanton plays a crooked evangelist who exploits the Jesus-in-a-spaceship concept for every penny he can get. Rated PG for profanity.

1984 100 minutes

UNDER THE RAINBOW

★★½

DIRECTOR: Steve Rash
CAST: Chevy Chase, Carrie Fisher, Eve Arden, Joseph Maher

While this comedy is not quite jam-packed with laughs, it certainly keeps your interest. Set in 1938, the improbable story centers around the making of *The Wizard of Oz*, assassination attempts on a duke and duchess, the nefarious doings of Nazi and Japanese spies prior to World War II, and the lifespan of a dog named Streudel. *Rainbow* is fun—though not always in the best of taste (some of the jokes border on crude). Director Steve Rash (*The Buddy Holly Story*) keeps things popping at a good rate. Rated PG because of slight nudity and suggestive dialogue.

1981 98 minutes

UNDERGROUND ACES

DIRECTOR: Robert Butler
CAST: Dirk Benedict, Melanie Griffith, Rick Podell, Kario Salem, Robert Hegyes, Audrey Landers, Mimi Maynard, Frank Gorshin

In this stupid comedy à la *Car Wash*, a bunch of obnoxious big-city hotel parking attendants run amok. They don't spend much time parking cars, because that would be boring. So they do a lot of wild and crazy things like wrecking the customers' vehicles, having sex, and poking fun at the hotel management. Rated PG for profanity and nudity.

1980 93 minutes

UNFAITHFULLY YOURS (ORIGINAL)

★★★

DIRECTOR: Preston Sturges
CAST: Rex Harrison, Linda Darnell, Kurt Kreuger, Barbara Lawrence, Rudy Vallee, Lionel Stander

Symphony conductor Rex Harrison suspects his wife of infidelity and contemplates several solutions to his "problem." This film follows all the prerequisites of screwball comedies—mistaken identities, misinterpreted remarks—but the humor seems forced and dated. Particularly tiresome are Harrison's endless fantasies, which seem to drag on forever. (The 1984 remake, whatever its other faults, used only one fantasy.) Harrison has fun as a sort of manic Henry Higgins, but his energy cannot sustain a film that runs about fifteen minutes too long. Unrated—family fare.

1948 B & W 105 minutes

UNFAITHFULLY YOURS (REMAKE)

★★★

DIRECTOR: Howard Zieff
CAST: Dudley Moore, Nastassja Kinski, Armand Assante, Albert Brooks

In this entertaining and sometimes hilarious remake of Preston Sturges's 1948 comedy, Dudley Moore plays a symphony orchestra conductor who suspects his wife (Nastassja Kinski) of fooling around with a violinist (Armand Assante) and decides to get revenge. Rated PG for nudity and profanity.

1984 96 minutes

UNKISSED BRIDE

🦃

DIRECTOR: Jack H. Harris
CAST: Tom Kirk, Danica d'Hondt, Anne Helm, Jacques Bergerac, Robert Ball, Joe Pyne

The theme song of this forgettable comedy is "Mother Goose A-Go-Go." That should tell you something! Tom Kirk plays the groom who passes out every time he and his wife (Anne Helm) contemplate lovemaking. His beautiful psychiatrist (played by Danica d'Hondt) says he has a hangup about the tales of Mother Goose as she uses a psychedelic drug to take him back to his childhood. Though this is unrated, the use of drugs and alcohol, as well as the sexual topic, should make this one a no-no for children. The fact that it is stupid should make it a no-no for adults.

1966 82 minutes

UPHILL ALL THE WAY

★

DIRECTOR: Frank Q. Dobbs
CAST: Roy Clark, Mel Tillis, Glen Campbell

Ridiculous film concerns two down-and-outers, Roy Clark and Mel Tillis, mistaken for bank robbers. The standard clichés are all here, and they have been done better so many times before. A good lesson here: Keep the boys playin' guitars instead of trying to be movie stars. Rated PG.

1985 86 minutes

UP IN SMOKE

★★★★

DIRECTOR: Lou Adler
CAST: Cheech and Chong, Strother Martin, Stacy Keach, Edie Adams, Tom Skerritt

This is Cheech and Chong's first, and best, film. Forget about any plot as Cheech and Chong go on the hunt for good weed, rock-'n-roll, and good times. Several truly hysterical moments, with Stacy Keach's spaced-out cop almost stealing the show. Rated R for language, nudity, and general raunchiness.

1978 87 minutes

UP THE ACADEMY

★½

DIRECTOR: Robert Downey
CAST: Ron Liebman, Wendell Brown, Ralph Macchio, Tom Citera, Tom Poston, Stacey Nelkin, Barbara Bach

This was *MAD* magazine's first and only attempt to emulate *National Lampoon*'s film success. Set in a strict military academy, the movie holds promise but is quickly done in by tasteless gags and gross over acting. Ron Liebman, who had his name taken off the credits, is the best thing about it. The film originally ran 96 minutes, but various people have been hacking it up over the years. Even *MAD* has disowned it. Rated R for profanity and general disgustingness.

1980 88 minutes

UP THE CREEK

★★★

DIRECTOR: Robert Butler
CAST: Tim Matheson, Stephen Furst, Dan Monahan, John Hillerman, James B. Sikking

Two stars from *Animal House*, Tim Matheson ("Otter") and Stephen Furst ("Flounder"), are reunited in this mostly entertaining raft-race comedy. It doesn't beg you to laugh at it the way *Police Academy* does. Matheson is charismatic enough—in his own audacious way—to carry the film. Dan Monahan (*Porky's*), John Hillerman (of television's *Magnum, P.I.*), and James Sikking (*Hill Street Blues*) co-star. Rated R for nudity, profanity, suggested sex, scatological humor, and violence.

1984 95 minutes

UP THE SANDBOX

★

DIRECTOR: Irvin Kershner
CAST: Barbra Streisand, David Selby, Jane Hoffman

A weird, uneven comedy about a neglected housewife (Barbra Streisand). Its fantasy sequences are among the strangest ever put on film. Rated R.

1972 97 minutes

UPTOWN SATURDAY NIGHT

★★★½

DIRECTOR: Sidney Poitier
CAST: Sidney Poitier, Bill Cosby, Harry Belafonte, Richard Pryor, Flip Wilson

Sidney Poitier (who also directed), Bill Cosby, Harry Belafonte, Richard Pryor, and Flip Wilson head an all-star cast in this enjoyable comedy about a couple of buddies (Poitier and Cosby) who get into all sorts of trouble during a night on the town. Rated PG.

1974 104 minutes

UP YOUR ANCHOR

★

DIRECTOR: Dan Wolman
CAST: Yftach Katzur, Zachi Nay, Joseph Shiloah, Deborah Keidar, Alexandra Kaster, Yehuda Efroni

Ever wonder what one of the beach films of the 1960s or *Love Boat* would be like with nudity and rampant sexual encounters? Pick up this video and find out. This is the story of three friends of indeterminate age—Benji, Huey, and Froggy. Benji is the good kid who only wants to find his one true love. Huey is overweight and oversexed. He will attack anyone of the opposite sex. Froggy is the nerd who has trouble getting to first base with a girl. Unrated, this Israeli film would be comparable with an R.

1985 89 minutes

USED CARS

★★★★

DIRECTOR: Robert Zemeckis
CAST: Jack Warden, Kurt Russell, Frank McRae, Gerrit Graham, Deborah Harmon

This is a riotous account of two feuding used-car businesses. Jack Warden and Kurt Russell are both excellent in this overlooked comedy. Fine support is offered by Frank McRae, Gerritt Graham, and Deborah Harmon. Rated R for language, nudity, and some violence.

1980 111 minutes

UTILITIES

★★★½

DIRECTOR: Harvey Hart
CAST: Robert Hays, Brooke Adams, John Marley, James Blendick, Helen Burns, Benjamin Gordon

Despite some rather crude humor once in a while, this modest comedy has a lot of charm and the heart of a Frank Capra film. Robert Hays (the *Airplane* films) plays a fed-up social worker who turns vigilante against the public utility companies. Brooke Adams (*Days of Heaven*; *Almost You*) is a cop who is torn between her job as a peace officer and her feelings for Hays. Rated PG for profanity and sex.

1983 94 minutes

VACATION

(turkey)

DIRECTOR: Harold Ramis
CAST: Chevy Chase, Beverly D'Angelo, Anthony Michael Hall, Dana Barron, Christie Brinkley, John Candy

One of the unfunniest comedies ever made, *Vacation* contains one laugh. Count 'em . . . one. That's when Clark Griswold (Chevy Chase), who goes on a disastrous vacation with his wife, Ellen (Beverly D'Angelo), and kids, Rusty (Anthony Michael Hall) and Audrey (Dana Barron), falls asleep at the wheel and the family station wagon careens hilariously out of control. Otherwise, no laughs—only yawns. Rated R for nudity and profanity.

1983 98 minutes

VALLEY GIRL

★★★½

DIRECTOR: Martha Coolidge

CAST: Nicolas Cage, Deborah Foreman, Colleen Camp

The story of a romance between a San Francisco valley girl and a Hollywood punker, *Valley Girl* claims the distinction of being one of the few teen movies directed by a woman: Martha Coolidge. And, perhaps for that reason, it's a little treasure; a funny, sexy, appealing story that makes fun of no one but contains something for nearly everyone. Rated R.

1983 95 minutes

VASECTOMY

★★½

DIRECTOR: Robert Burge

CAST: Paul Sorvino, Abe Vigoda, Cassandra Edwards, Lorne Greene

A bank vice-president (Paul Sorvino) is having plenty of family problems. After bearing their eighth child, his wife urges him to have a vasectomy while other family members are stealing from his bank. He hires a detective (Abe Vigoda) to stop his family's pilfering while overcoming his fear of the operation. This comedy is rated R for nudity and obscenities.

1986 92 minutes

VICTOR/VICTORIA

★★★★

DIRECTOR: Blake Edwards

CAST: Julie Andrews, James Garner, Robert Preston, Lesley Ann Warren

Director Blake Edwards takes us on a funny, off-the-wall romp through 1930s Paris. Julie Andrews plays a down-on-her-luck singer who poses as a gay Polish count to make ends meet. Rated PG because of adult situations.

1982 133 minutes

VIVA MAX!

★★★

DIRECTOR: Jerry Paris

CAST: Peter Ustinov, Jonathan Winters, Keenan Wynn, Pamela Tiffin

Skip credibility and enjoy. Peter Ustinov is a contemporary Mexican general who leads his men across the border to reclaim the Alamo as a tourist attraction. Jonathan Winters all but steals this romp, playing a bumbling, confused National Guard officer in the face of an audacious "enemy." Rated G.

1969 92 minutes

VIVACIOUS LADY

★★★

DIRECTOR: George Stevens

CAST: Ginger Rogers, James Stewart, Charles Coburn, Frances Mercer, James Ellison, Beulah Bondi, Franklin Pangborn, Grady Sutton, Jack Carson, Willie Best

Cultures clash when small-town college botany professor James Stewart impulsively weds New York nightclub singer Ginger Rogers, brings her back to the campus, and cannot find the time or the words to tell his father, upright and stuffy college president Charles Coburn, who the new lady is. Compounding things is an ex-sweetheart with whom the bride tangles in one of the screen's best broad brawls. A great supporting cast, headed by Franklin Pangborn, adds further luster to this slapstick riot.

1938 B & W 90 minutes

VOLUNTEERS

★★

DIRECTOR: Nicholas Meyer
CAST: Tom Hanks, John Candy, Rita Wilson, Tim Thomerson, Gedde Watanabe

At first glance, this comedy seems to have everything going for it: It reunites Tom Hanks and John Candy, who were so marvelously funny together in Ron Howard's *Splash*, and was directed by Nicholas Meyer, who made the first good *Star Trek* movie (*Star Trek II: The Wrath of Khan*). In truth, however, this film about high jinks in the Peace Corps in Thailand circa 1962 has very little going for it. Hanks and Candy do their best, but the laughs are far and few between. Rated R for profanity, violence, and sexual innuendo.

1985 105 minutes

WACKIEST SHIP IN THE ARMY, THE

★★★

DIRECTOR: Richard Murphy
CAST: Jack Lemmon, Ricky Nelson, John Lund, Chips Rafferty, Tom Tully, Joby Baker, Warren Berlinger

A battered ship becomes an unlikely implement for World War II heroism. The situation is played mostly for laughs, but dramatic moments are smoothly included. Jack Lemmon sets his performance at just the right pitch. Ricky Nelson is amiable and amusing. He even gets to sing "Do You Know What It Means to Miss New Orleans?"

1960 99 minutes

WALTZ OF THE TOREADORS

★★★★

DIRECTOR: John Guillermin
CAST: Peter Sellers, Margaret Leighton, Dany Robin

The unique Peter Sellers is superb as a retired military officer who can't subdue his roving eye. Margaret Leighton is fine, as always. Dany Robin is adorable. It's saucy and sex-shot, but intellectually stimulating nonetheless. A charming film, and not just for Sellers's fans.

1962 105 minutes

WATER

★★★

DIRECTOR: Dick Clement
CAST: Michael Caine, Brenda Vaccaro, Valerie Perrine, Billy Connelly, Fred Gwynne, George Harrison, Ringo Starr, Eric Clapton, Eddy Grant

In this delightful British comedy, Michael Caine is the governor of the small English colony located on the island of Cascara. The governor's wife (Brenda Vaccaro) is bored with life on Cascara (the Spanish word for rind!) until an oil company headed by Fred Gwynne sends out a famous actor to film a commercial. No one seems to notice that the oil company is using the commercial as a cover-up for actual oil drilling. The madness begins when instead of hitting oil, they hit Perrier! The oil company wants the rights to the water, as do the governments of several nations, a group of island rebels (headed by Billy Connelly), and a conservationist (Valerie Perrine), who turns out to be the daughter of the head of the oil company. What ensues is pleasant craziness accompanied by a great soundtrack featuring the music of Eddy Grant, and a jam session with Ringo Starr,

George Harrison, and Eric Clapton. Rated PG-13.

1986 91 minutes

WATERMELON MAN

★★★

DIRECTOR: Melvin Van Peebles

CAST: Godfrey Cambridge, Estelle Parsons

The life of a bigoted white man is turned inside-out when he wakes up one morning and finds himself black. Using the late, great black comedian Godfrey Cambridge in the title role shows that someone in production had his head on right. The film makes a statement. Trouble is, it makes it over and over and over again. Rated R.

1970 97 minutes

WAY OUT WEST

★★★★★

DIRECTOR: James W. Horne

CAST: Stan Laurel, Oliver Hardy, Sharon Lynn

Stan Laurel and Oliver Hardy travel west to deliver a gold mine map to the daughter of a friend. The map is given to an imposter, and the boys have to retrieve it and ensure correct delivery. A delightful, marvelous film that demonstrates the team's mastery of timing and characterization.

1937 B & W 65 minutes

WEDDING, A

★★★

DIRECTOR: Robert Altman

CAST: Carol Burnett, Desi Arnaz Jr., Geraldine Chaplin, Amy Stryker, Vittorio Gassman, Lillian Gish, Lauren Hutton, Paul Dooley, Howard Duff, Pam Dawber, Dina Merrill, John Considine

This is one of those *almost* movies—one that has enough good things about it to recommend, but that could have been so much better. During the late 1970s, director Robert Altman's films had begun to lose their focus, and any kind of coherence had largely disappeared, as this film demonstrates. The story deals with a wedding between two relatively wealthy families and the comic implications that follow. Fine acting keeps things afloat, but this one is a disappointment. Rated PG.

1978 125 minutes

WEEKEND PASS

★

DIRECTOR: Lawrence Bassoff

CAST: D. W. Brown, Peter Ellenstein, Patrick Hauser, Chip McAllister

A quartet of stupid sailors on shore leave cavorts uncomically in Los Angeles, in this tired and lewd low-budget sex comedy. Rated R.

1984 92 minutes

WEIRD SCIENCE

★★★

DIRECTOR: John Hughes

CAST: Anthony Michael Hall, Kelly LeBrock, Ilan Mitchell-Smith

In this wacky comedy by writer-director John Hughes (*16 Candles*; *The Breakfast Club*), two put-upon nerds (Anthony Michael Hall and Ilan Mitchell-Smith), desperate for a date, cop an idea from James Whale's *Frankenstein* (which is playing on television) and create a sexy woman via computer. Once brought to life (after the boys have fed *Penthouse* and *Playboy* centerfolds and a picture of Albert Einstein into the machine), she says, "Well, what do you little maniacs want to do first?" Thus begins a roller coaster ride of hit-and-miss humor as the nerds get class fast. Rated PG-13 for slight violence, partial nudity, and profanity.

1985 94 minutes

WELCOME TO 18

DIRECTOR: Terry Carr
CAST: Mariska Hargitay, Courtney Thorne-Smith, Jo Ann Willette, E. Erich Anderson

This low-budget film's only point of interest is that it marks the big-screen debut of Mariska Hargitay, the daughter of Jayne Mansfield—and she can't act. Otherwise, it's an unrelentingly awful movie about three typically pert female high-school graduates who take summer jobs at a Lake Tahoe dude ranch and soon find themselves at the mercy of a drug-dealing pimp. Rated PG-13 for profanity and nudity.

1986 91 minutes

WE'RE NO ANGELS

★★½

DIRECTOR: Michael Curtiz
CAST: Humphrey Bogart, Peter Ustinov, Aldo Ray, Basil Rathbone, Joan Bennett, Leo G. Carroll

The *New York Times* dubbed this "a slow, talky reprise of the delightful stage comedy" and was right. Three Devil's Island convicts "adopt" an island family and protect it against an uncle it can do without. There is a roguishness about the trio that almost makes them endearing, and there is humor, but the film does drag.

1955 106 minutes

WHAT DO YOU SAY TO A NAKED LADY?

DIRECTOR: Allen Funt
CAST: Allen Funt, Richard Roundtree

Allen Funt's R-rated version of *Candid Camera* is a bust from the start. Imagine the same candid camera gags only with naked women and you've pretty well figured this dud out. Pass on this one. Rated R for nudity.

1970 90 minutes

WHAT PRICE GLORY

★★★

DIRECTOR: John Ford
CAST: James Cagney, Dan Dailey, Corinne Calvet, William Demarest, Robert Wagner, Marisa Pavan, James Gleason, Wally Vernon

James Cagney is Captain Flagg, Dan Dailey is Sergeant Quirt in this rough-and-tumble tale of rivalry in romance set against the sobering background of World War I in France. The feisty pair of marines vies for the affections of adorable Charmaine (Corinne Calvet). Between quarrels, they fight in the trenches. John Ford's direction stresses the comedy aspects of the hard-drinking, brawling duo's conflict. The film is based upon the Broadway stage hit by Laurence Stallings and Maxwell Anderson. From it, the line "Hey, wait for baby!" passed permanently into the language.

1952 109 minutes

WHAT'S NEW PUSSYCAT?

★★★

DIRECTOR: Clive Donner
CAST: Peter Sellers, Peter O'Toole, Woody Allen, Ursula Andress, Romy Schneider, Capucine, Paula Prentiss

Peter O'Toole is a fashion editor who can't stop becoming romantically involved with his models. In spite of a strong supporting cast, this dated 1960s "hip" comedy has few genuine laughs. Mostly, it's just silly.

1965 108 minutes

WHAT'S UP DOC?

★★★★

DIRECTOR: Peter Bogdanovich
CAST: Ryan O'Neal, Barbra Streisand, Kenneth Mars, Austin Pendleton

A virtual remake of Howard Hawks's classic *Bringing Up Baby*, with Ryan O'Neal and Barbra Streisand representing the Cary Grant and Katharine Hepburn roles, this manages to recapture much of the madcap charm and nonstop action of the original story. O'Neal is the studious scientist delightfully led astray by a dizzy Streisand, who keeps forcing herself into his life. The zany final chase through the streets of San Francisco is one of filmdom's best. Rated G.

1972 94 minutes

WHAT'S UP TIGER LILY?

★★★

DIRECTOR: Woody Allen
CAST: Tatsuya Mihashi, Miya Hana, Woody Allen

A dreadful Japanese spy movie has been given a zany English-language soundtrack by Woody Allen in one of his earliest movie productions. You are left with an offbeat spoof of the whole genre of spy films. The results are often amusing, but its one-joke premise gets rather tedious before it's over.

1966 80 minutes

WHEN THINGS WERE ROTTEN

★★★

DIRECTORS: Coby Ruskin, Marty Feldman, Peter Bonerz
CAST: Dick Gautier, Dick Van Patten, Bernie Kopell, Richard Dimitri, Henry Polic II, Misty Rowe, David Sabin

This compilation of three episodes from the short-lived television series of the same name is sure to please fans of *Blazing Saddles*–style humor. Dick Gautier's nearly serious portrayal of Robin Hood is a perfect foil for the slapstick antics of the rest of the cast.

1975 78 minutes

WHERE THE BOYS ARE

★★★

DIRECTOR: Henry Levin
CAST: Dolores Hart, George Hamilton, Yvette Mimieux, Jim Hutton, Barbara Nichols, Connie Francis

Connie Francis warbled the title tune and made her movie debut in this frothy, mildly entertaining film about teenagers doing what's natural during Easter vacation in Fort Lauderdale. It's miles ahead of the idiotic remake.

1960 99 minutes

WHERE THE BOYS ARE '84

DIRECTOR: Hy Averback
CAST: Lisa Hartman, Russell Todd, Lorna Luft, Lynn-Holly Johnson, Wendy Schaal, Howard McGillin, Louise Sorel, Alana Stewart

No, this isn't a rerelease of the 1960 film about teens tearin' it up in Fort Lauderdale, which Connie Francis immortalized in the song of the same name. It's a poorly made remake by Mr. "Can't Stop the Music" himself: producer Allan Carr. Rated R.

1984 96 minutes

WHERE THE BUFFALO ROAM

DIRECTOR: Art Linson
CAST: Bill Murray, Peter Boyle, Bruno Kirby, Rene Auberjonois, R. G. Armstrong, Rafael Campos, Leonard Frey

Director Art Linson's horrendous film about the exploits of gonzo journalist Hunter S. Thompson. Bill Murray turns in one of his few bad performances as the consistently stoned-out writer. Thompson has reportedly sworn "to rip Murray's throat out" if they ever meet. It's our feeling it would have been better if this movie had never been released on video. Rated R.

1980 96 minutes

WHERE'S POPPA?

★★★★

DIRECTOR: Carl Reiner

CAST: George Segal, Ruth Gordon, Trish Van Devere, Ron Liebman, Rae Allen, Vincent Gardenia, Barnard Hughes, Rob Reiner, Garrett Morris

One of George Segal's best comic performances is found in this cult favorite. Ruth Gordon co-stars as the senile mother whom Segal tries to scare into having a cardiac arrest. Director Carl Reiner's son, Rob, makes a short appearance as a fervent draft resister. Rated R.

1970 82 minutes

WHICH WAY IS UP?

★★★★

DIRECTOR: Michael Shultz

CAST: Richard Pryor, Lonette McKee, Margaret Avery, Dolph Sweet, Morgan Woodward

This irreverent, ribald farce reunites the talented comedy team of director Michael Shultz and star Richard Pryor (*Greased Lightning*) for one of the funnier movies of the 1970s. Pryor plays three major roles. His ability to create totally separate and distinctive characters contributes greatly to the success of this oft-tried but rarely believable gimmick. The language and subject matter of this film are not suited for the young, but adults will convulse with laughter at the unexpected and hilarious comedy of *Which Way Is Up?* Rated R.

1977 94 minutes

WHICH WAY TO THE FRONT

DIRECTOR: Jerry Lewis

CAST: Jerry Lewis, John Wood, Jan Murray, Kaye Ballard, Robert Middleton, Paul Winchell, Sidney Miller, Gary Crosby

Mention this film to even the staunchest of Jerry Lewis fans and they're likely to blanch or bristle. Even they usually admit that this is a *bad* film—tasteless in concept, inept and foolish in execution, and devoid of any charm or flavor to elevate it to cult status. Jerry Lewis directs and stars in this pathetic story about a rich 4-F American who enlists other such unfortunates into a military unit to combat Nazi Germany. Worse than it sounds, this ridiculous film might have made it during the second World War, but it fell flat with Vietnam-era audiences and it continues to appall film fans and videophiles today.

1970 96 minutes

WHO AM I THIS TIME?

★★★½

DIRECTOR: Jonathan Demme

CAST: Susan Sarandon, Christopher Walken, Robert Ridgely, Dorothy Patterson

The new girl in town, Helene Shaw (Susan Sarandon), gets a part in the local theater group production of *A Streetcar Named Desire* opposite Harry Nash (Christopher Walken). Dreadfully shy, Harry only comes to life in every part he plays on the stage. Helene, an introvert herself, falls for both sides of his persona and sets out to win him. This is a pleasing Kurt Vonnegut Jr. story played by a capable cast.

1982 60 minutes

WHOLLY MOSES!

★★½

DIRECTOR: Gary Weis
CAST: Dudley Moore, Richard Pryor, Laraine Newman, James Coco, Paul Sand, Jack Gilford, Dom De Luise, John Houseman, Madeline Kahn, David L. Lander, John Ritter

Wholly Moses! pokes fun at Hollywood biblical epics in a rapid-fire fashion. While the film is sometimes very funny, it is also loaded with a fair share of predictable, flat, and corny moments. It's so-so viewing fare. Rated R.

1980 109 minutes

WHOOPEE BOYS, THE

DIRECTOR: John Byrum
CAST: Michael O'Keefe, Paul Rodriguez, Lucinda Jenney, Denholm Elliott, Eddie Deezen

Not since *Mad* magazine's *Up the Academy* has a so-called outrageous comedy been so unrelentingly awful. Stand-up comic Paul Rodriguez seems to have trouble in choosing his film properties. His others, *Quicksilver* and *D.C. Cab*, were just as bad. In this one, Rodriguez teams up with Michael O'Keefe in a clichéd story about a pair of obnoxious—and supposedly lovable—misfits who attempt to save a school for needy children. If the unfunny jokes don't get you, the sickeningly sweet plot twists will. Rated R for profanity.

1986 94 minutes

WHOOPS APOCALYPSE

★★½

DIRECTOR: John Reardon
CAST: John Barron, John Cleese, Richard Griffiths, Peter Jones, Bruce Montague, Barry Morse

This overlong but sometimes rewarding British comedy consists of a news coverage spoof on events leading up to World War III. There are some funny parts as the newscasters interview world leaders. The plot centers around the theft of a U.S. nuclear bomb. Many viewers may get fidgety during the second, less successful half. Unrated, it contains nudity and obscene language.

1981 137 minutes

WHO'S MINDING THE MINT?

★★★½

DIRECTOR: Howard Morris
CAST: Milton Berle, Jim Hutton, Dorothy Provine, Joey Bishop, Walter Brennan, Jamie Farr, Victor Buono

When a U.S. Mint employee (Jim Hutton) accidentally destroys thousands of newly printed bills, a group of misfits bands together to help him out. This film is often hilarious and always enjoyable.

1967 97 minutes

WILDCATS

★★★

DIRECTOR: Michael Ritchie
CAST: Goldie Hawn, Swoosie Kurtz, James Keach, Nipsy Russell, Woody Harrelson, M. Emmet Walsh

Standard Goldie Hawn vehicle, with her playing high-school football coach to a rowdy group of inner-city kids who need to prove their worth as much as she needs to prove her self-esteem and skill to chauvinistic athletic directors. Director Michael Ritchie shows little of the tension he brought to *The Bad News Bears*. Awkward subplot involves Hawn in a custody battle with wimpish James Keach over their two daughters. Another low point is an embarrassingly gratuitous nude shot of Hawn in a bathtub. On the other hand, the film ends on its best note: a spirited rendition of the "Football Rap" by Hawn and her fellas. Rated R for nudity and language.

1986 107 minutes

WILD LIFE, THE

★★

DIRECTOR: Art Linson
CAST: Christopher Penn, Lea Thompson, Rick Moranis, Randy Quaid, Ilan Mitchell Smith

From some of the same people who brought you *Fast Times at Ridgemont High* comes a film set in a world where your "cool" is measured by how many cigarettes you can smoke (and eat) and how many girls you can bed. Christopher Penn offers a believable performance as the leader of a pack of teens trying to grow up too fast. They're not fooling anyone! Amid all this silliness, the movie does take time to make a poignant commentary about Vietnam, when Randy Quaid makes a stirring cameo appearance as a veteran on the skids. Rated R for suggested sex and language.

1984 96 minutes

WIN, PLACE OR STEAL

DIRECTOR: Richard Bailey
CAST: Dean Stockwell, Russ Tamblyn, Alex Karras, McLean Stevenson

Slow, boring comedy about three aging adolescents who prefer playing the ponies to working. Strapped for money, they steal a racetrack betting machine and decide to print their own winning tickets. McLean Stevenson provides a few chuckles. Unrated, it features brief nudity comparable to a PG.

1972 88 minutes

WISE GUYS

★★★½

DIRECTOR: Brian De Palma
CAST: Danny DeVito, Joe Piscopo, Harvey Keitel, Ray Sharkey, Captain Lou Albano, Dan Hedaya

Director Brian De Palma, apparently tired of derivative Hitchcockian thrillers, returned to his roots with this send-up of gangster movies. Danny DeVito and Joe Piscopo play Harry and Moe, a couple of goofball syndicate gofers trusted with little above the boss's laundry. The reason for this becomes obvious when they muck up a bet on the ponies; as punishment, the boss secretly instructs each to kill the other. To make sure everything works out properly, both are watchdogged by "The Fixer," a man-mountain played by pro-wrestler Captain Lou Albano. DeVito's and Piscopo's comedic talents notwithstanding, Albano owns this film; his growling delivery (his bark *and* bite are equally bad) is wonderful. Inexplicably rated R for language.

1986 91 minutes

WITCHES' BREW

★★

DIRECTORS: Richard Shoor, Herbert L. Strock
CAST: Richard Benjamin, Teri Garr, Lana Turner, Kathryn Leigh Scott, Kelly Jean Peters, Jordan Charney

Margret (Teri Garr) and her two girlfriends have been dabbling in witchcraft to help their university professor husbands succeed. When a coveted chairmanship opens up, the two friends use their powers against Margret and her husband Josh (Richard Benjamin). Although this is advertised as a comedy, it just isn't funny. It's supposed to be a horror spoof but turns out to be more of a horror ripoff of *Burn Witch Burn*! Lana Turner has a small role as the witchcraft mentor to the three young women. Rated PG.

1980 98 minutes

WITCHES OF EASTWICK, THE

★★★★½

DIRECTOR: George Miller

CAST: Jack Nicholson, Cher, Susan Sarandon, Michelle Pfeiffer, Veronica Cartwright, Richard Jenkins

In this wickedly funny comedy, Jack Nicholson gives one of his finest—and funniest—performances as a self-described "horny little devil" who comes to a tiny hamlet at the behest of three women (Cher, Susan Sarandon, and Michelle Pfeiffer). Only trouble is, these "witches" have no idea of what they've done until it is very nearly too late. Pulitzer Prize–winning playwright Michael Cristofer's witty screenplay is based on the novel by John Updike. A black comedy on one level, it is also a thought-provoking, biting commentary on man's inhumanity to woman. It's a real treat for open-minded adults. Rated R for profanity and suggested sex.

1987 121 minutes

WITH SIX YOU GET EGGROLL

★★

DIRECTOR: Howard Morris

CAST: Doris Day, Brian Keith, Barbara Hershey

Widow Doris Day has three kids; widower Brian Keith has a daughter. They get together. Awwwww! *Bachelor Father* meets *Mother Knows Best.* The two stars refer to Doris and Brian, neither of whom helped their cause with this turkey. Strictly a picture for the 1960s. Unrated.

1968 99 minutes

WITHNAIL AND I

★★★★

DIRECTOR: Bruce Robinson

CAST: Richard E. Grant, Paul McGann, Richard Griffiths

A funny but sometimes grim comedy set in the Great Britain of the late 1960s. Two friends, whose decadent lifestyle of booze and drugs has hit bottom, try to make a new start by taking a holiday in the country. The vacation, which includes uneasy encounters with crazed poachers, angry bulls, and an elderly homosexual, is a disaster. The performances are excellent, period details are perfect, and the movie is well made. But because the pair's self-destructive behavior veers between funny and appalling, one watches the movie with mixed emotions. Rated R for profanity and adult themes.

1987 110 minutes

WITHOUT RESERVATIONS

★★★

DIRECTOR: Mervyn LeRoy

CAST: John Wayne, Claudette Colbert, Don Defore, Frank Puglia, Anne Triola, Phil Brown, Thurston Hall, Louella Parsons

Wartime comedy about authoress Claudette Colbert and her plan to turn soldier John Wayne into the leading man of her filmed novel is light and enjoyable and sprinkled with guest appearances by Hollywood celebrities. This is hardly the kind of war film in which one would expect to find John Wayne, but the Duke makes the best of a chance to act under top director Mervyn LeRoy (who was in a slump during this period). No telling what the executives at RKO had in mind when they came up with this idea, but after forty years, the idea of John Wayne teaming with Claudette Colbert in a comedy (or any other kind of film) still sounds ridiculous. However, this unlikely combination came out surprisingly well.

1946 B & W 107 minutes

WOMAN IN RED, THE

★★★★

DIRECTOR: Gene Wilder

CAST: Gene Wilder, Charles Grodin, Joseph Bologna, Gilda Radner, Judith Ivey, Michael Huddleston, Kelly Lebrock

Gene Wilder's funniest film in years, this is best described as a bittersweet romantic comedy. Wilder, who also adapted the screenplay and directed, plays an advertising executive and heretofore happily married man who becomes obsessed with a beautiful woman he happens to see one day in a parking garage. The results are hilarious. Rated PG-13 for partial nudity, brief violence, and profanity.

1984 87 minutes

WOMAN OF THE YEAR

★★★★★

DIRECTOR: George Stevens

CAST: Spencer Tracy, Katharine Hepburn, Fay Bainter, Reginald Owen, William Bendix

Ah, you knew it from the very first moments; these two had something. This is the film that first teamed Spencer Tracy and Katharine Hepburn, and it's impossible to imagine anybody else doing a better job. He's a sports reporter; she's a famed political journalist who needs to be reminded of life's simple pleasures. Like baseball . . . and her attempts to learn the game are priceless. The witty script garnered an Oscar for Ring Lardner Jr. and Michael Kanin. A classic in every respect; watch it several times. Unrated—family fare.

1942 B & W 112 minutes

WOMEN, THE

★★★★½

DIRECTOR: George Cukor

CAST: Norma Shearer, Joan Crawford, Rosalind Russell, Joan Fontaine, Paulette Goddard

Director George Cukor and some of Hollywood's finest female stars combine for a winning screen version of Claire Booth's stage hit. This look at the state of matrimony is great entertainment. The script is full of witty, stinging dialogue.

1939 B & W 132 minutes

WONDER MAN

★★★

DIRECTOR: Bruce Humberstone

CAST: Danny Kaye, Vera-Ellen, Virginia Mayo, Donald Woods, S. Z. Sakall, Allen Jenkins, Edward S. Brophy, Otto Kruger, Virginia Gilmore, Natalie Schafer, Huntz Hall

Deftly doubling, Danny Kaye plays identical twins with personalities as far apart as the polar regions. One, Buzzy Bellew, is a brash, irrepressible nightclub comic; his mirror, Edwin Dingle, is a mousy double-dome full of tongue-twisting erudition. Identities are switched, of course. Thin on plot, this is mostly a tailored showcase for Kaye's brilliant talents.

1945 98 minutes

WORLD OF ABBOTT AND COSTELLO, THE

★★★

NARRATED BY: Jack E. Leonard

CAST: Bud Abbott, Lou Costello, various guest stars

Compilation of Abbott and Costello's best film footage is well handled, with many of their classic scenes intact: the frog in the soup, Lou in the wrestling ring, Lou meeting Dracula, and of course "Who's on First?"

Would've been better without the narration, but the film never fails to entertain. Add one star if you're a fan.

1965 B & W 79 minutes

WORLD OF HENRY ORIENT, THE

★★★★

DIRECTOR: George Roy Hill

CAST: Peter Sellers, Paula Prentiss, Angela Lansbury, Phyllis Thaxter

A quirky comedy for the whole family. Peter Sellers is a woman-crazy New York pianist who finds himself being followed by two teen-age girls who have come to idolize him. Loads of fun, with a great performance by Angela Lansbury.

1964 106 minutes

WORLD'S GREATEST LOVER, THE

★★½

DIRECTOR: Gene Wilder

CAST: Gene Wilder, Carol Kane, Dom De Luise, Fritz Feld, Carl Ballantine, Michael Huddleston, Matt Collins, Ronny Graham

Gene Wilder plays a would-be silent-movie star who tests for the part of the "new Valentino" while his wife (Carol Kane) runs off with the real Rudolph. Dom De Luise is around to brighten things up, but writer-director Wilder's ideas of what's funny and well-timed aren't quite right. Rated PG.

1977 89 minutes

WRONG ARM OF THE LAW, THE

★★★★

DIRECTOR: Cliff Owens

CAST: Peter Sellers, Lionel Jeffries, Bernard Cribbins, Davy Kaye, Nanette Newman

Peter Sellers is hilarious as Pearly Gates, the Cockney leader of a group of bandits. Sellers and his gang join forces with police inspector Parker (Lionel Jeffries) after a group of Australians pose as police and capture Sellers's stolen goods. This British comedy contains enough of the wacky zaniness that Sellers built his reputation on to keep most viewers in stitches.

1962 B & W 94 minutes

WRONG BOX, THE

★★★★

DIRECTOR: Bryan Forbes

CAST: John Mills, Ralph Richardson, Dudley Moore, Peter Sellers, Peter Cook, Michael Caine, Nanette Newman, Wilfred Lawson, Tony Hancock

Some of Britain's best-known comics appear in this screwball farce about two zany families who battle over an inheritance in Victorian England. The film borders on black humor as the corpse of a wealthy brother is shuffled all over London by the contending parties—headed by John Mills and Ralph Richardson. Dudley Moore, Peter Sellers, and Peter Cook are just a few of the funnymen who give cameo performances in the delightful comedy.

1966 105 minutes

WRONG IS RIGHT

★★★★

DIRECTOR: Richard Brooks

CAST: Sean Connery, Robert Conrad, George Grizzard, Katherine Ross, G. D. Spradlin, John Saxon, Henry Silva, Leslie Nielsen, Robert Webber, Rosalind Cash, Hardy Krüger, Dean Stockwell, Ron Moody

Sean Connery, as a globe-trotting television reporter, gives what may be the best performance of his career, in this outrageous, thoroughly entertaining end-of-the-world black comedy, written, produced, and directed by Richard Brooks (*The Professionals* and *Bite the Bullet*). It's an updated combination of *Network* and *Dr. Strangelove*, and wickedly funny. Rated R because of profanity and violence.

1982 117 minutes

YELLOWBEARD

★★½

DIRECTOR: Mel Damski

CAST: Graham Chapman, Eric Idle, John Cleese, Peter Cook, Cheech and Chong, Peter Boyle, Madeline Kahn, Marty Feldman, Kenneth Mars

This pirate comedy has a shipload of comedians; unfortunately, it barely contains a boatload of laughs under the directorship of first-timer Mel Damski. Rated PG for profanity, nudity, violence, gore, and scatological humor.

1983 101 minutes

YOU BET YOUR LIFE (TELEVISION SERIES)

★★★½

DIRECTORS: Robert Dwan, Bernie Smith

CAST: Groucho Marx, George Fenneman

Over the years, two different game formats were devised for this show, but it was the interview segment that made the program a winner. In grilling the contestants, who ranged from average folks to celebrities to bizarre characters, Groucho Marx invariably got off a number of clever quips. Among those who tested their knowledge on the show over the years were William Peter Blatty (author of *The Exorcist*), Phyllis Diller, Ronnie Schell, Bobby Van, Johnny Weissmuller, and Melinda Marx (Groucho's daughter) with her little friend, Candice Bergen. Announcer George Fenneman was the target of many of Groucho's barbs. Also attracting attention were the comical duck and the sexy young ladies who appeared when contestants stumbled on the secret word. In syndication, this show is known as *The Best of Groucho*.

1950–1961 B & W 30 minutes

YOUNG DOCTORS IN LOVE

★★★

DIRECTOR: Garry Marshall

CAST: Michael McKean, Sean Young, Harry Dean Stanton, Patrick Macnee, Hector Elizondo, Dabney Coleman, Pamela Reed, Michael Richards, Taylor Negron, Saul Rubinek, Titos Vandis

This comedy attempts to do for medical soap operas what *Airplane!* did for disaster movies—and doesn't quite make it. That said, director Garry Marshall (of television's *Laverne and Shirley*) has nevertheless created an enjoyable movie for open-minded adults. The R-rated film is a bit too raunchy and suggestive for the younger set.

1982 95 minutes

YOUNG FRANKENSTEIN

★★★★½

DIRECTOR: Mel Brooks

CAST: Gene Wilder, Marty Feldman, Peter Boyle, Teri Garr, Madeline Kahn, Cloris Leachman, Kenneth Mars, Richard Haydn

This is one of Mel Brooks's best. *Young Frankenstein* is the story of Dr. Frankenstein's college professor descendant who abhors his family history. This spoof of the old Universal horror films is hilarious from start to finish. Rated PG.

1974 B & W 105 minutes

YOU'RE A BIG BOY NOW

★★★★½

DIRECTOR: Francis Ford Coppola

CAST: Peter Kastner, Elizabeth Hartman, Geraldine Page, Julie Harris, Rip Torn, Michael Dunn, Tony Bill, Karen Black

Francis Ford Coppola not only directed this (his first) film but also wrote the screenplay. Peter Kastner, the product of overprotective parents, learns about life from street-wise go-go dancer Elizabeth Hartman. Fast-paced and very entertaining.

1966 96 minutes

ZAPPED!

★★

DIRECTOR: Robert J. Rosenthal

CAST: Scott Baio, Willie Aames, Felice Schachter, Heather Thomas, Scatman Crothers, Robert Mandan, Greg Bradford

A campy takeoff on high-school movies that doesn't work. *Zapped* is a bore. Rated R for nudity and sexual situations.

1982 96 minutes

ZELIG

★★★★★

DIRECTOR: Woody Allen

CAST: Woody Allen, Mia Farrow

This is Woody Allen's masterpiece. He plays Leonard Zelig, a remarkable man who can fit anywhere in society because he can change his appearance at will. The laughs come fast and furious in this account of his adventures in the 1920s, when he became all the rage and hung out with the likes of F. Scott Fitzgerald, Jack Dempsey, and Babe Ruth. Mia Farrow plays the psychiatrist who tries in vain to figure out the funny little man. Allen seamlessly weds black-and-white newsreel footage with his humorous tale, allowing Zelig to be right in the thick of history. Rated PG.

1984 B & W 79 minutes

ZORRO, THE GAY BLADE

★★★★

DIRECTOR: Peter Medak

CAST: George Hamilton, Lauren Hutton, Brenda Vaccaro, Ron Leibman, Donovan Scott

Here's another delight from (and starring) actor-producer George Hamilton. As with *Love at First Bite*, in which Hamilton played a slightly bent and bewildered Count Dracula to great effect, the accent in *Zorro, the Gay Blade* is on belly-wrenching laughs . . . and there are plenty of them. Director Peter Medak (*The Ruling Class*) blends these elements—along with the supporting performances by Lauren Hutton, Brenda Vaccaro, Ron Liebman, and Donovan Scott—into the most consistently entertaining spoof of a classic movie since Mel Brooks's *Young Frankenstein*. Rated PG because of sexual innuendo.

1981 93 minutes

ZOTZ!

★★★½

DIRECTOR: William Castle

CAST: Tom Poston, Jim Backus, Julia Meade

Charming, underrated little fantasy about a college professor (Tom Poston) who finds a magical coin blessed with three bizarre powers: sudden pain, slow motion, and explosive destruction. Good adaptation of the novel by Walter Karig, and an excellent opportunity for Poston to control a film in one of his rare leading parts. One of the last of William Castle's gimmick films—patrons at the original release were given plastic replicas of the coin. Give this a try; you won't be disappointed.

1962 B & W 87 minutes

DRAMA

ABDUCTION

★★

DIRECTOR: Joseph Zito

CAST: Gregory Rozakis, Leif Erickson, Dorothy Malone, Lawrence Tierney

This film comes across as a cheap exploitation of the Patty Hearst kidnapping. It includes theories and conclusions that may or may not be true. The wealthy but distraught parents of Patty Prescott (Hearst, to us) are played by Dorothy Malone and Leif Erickson. As in the real incident, Patty is kidnapped from the house she shares with her boyfriend. Rated R for profanity, violence, nudity, and sex.

1975 100 minutes

ABE LINCOLN IN ILLINOIS

★★★★

DIRECTOR: John Cromwell

CAST: Raymond Massey, Ruth Gordon, Gene Lockhart, Mary Howard

Based on Sherwood Anderson's Broadway play, this is a reverent look at the early career and loves of the sixteenth president. As contrasted to John Ford's *Young Mr. Lincoln*, this is a more somber, historically accurate, and better-acted version.

1934 B & W 110 minutes

ABOUT LAST NIGHT

★★★★

DIRECTOR: Edward Zwick

CAST: Rob Lowe, Demi Moore, Jim Belushi, Elizabeth Perkins, George DiCenzo, Michael Alldredge

A slick adaptation of David Mamet's play, *Sexual Perversity in Chicago*, which focuses on the difficulties involved in "making a commitment." Demi Moore and Rob Lowe, as the central couple, meet for a one-night stand and then realize they *like* each other. The painful, hesitant steps toward a stable relationship—a shared drawer, living together first as friends, then as lovers—are detailed with excruciating familiarity by director Edward Zwick and screenwriters Tim Kazurinsky and

Denise DeClue. If you haven't known people like this, you've probably *been* people like this. Jim Belushi and Elizabeth Perkins turn in solid performances as respective friends, but the film belongs to Moore, who finally has found a role worthy of her talent. Rated R for nudity and explicit adult situations.

1986 113 minutes

ABRAHAM LINCOLN

★★★★

DIRECTOR: D. W. Griffith
CAST: Walter Huston, Una Merkel, Kay Hammond, Ian Keith, Hobart Bosworth, Jason Robards Sr., Henry B. Walthall

A milestone in many ways, this episodic film is legendary director Griffith's first "talkie," Hollywood's first sound biography of an American, the first attempt to cover Lincoln's life from cradle to grave, and the first about the martyred president to include the Civil War. Walter Huston's peerless performance in the title role dominates throughout. Ian Keith is properly hotheaded and flamboyant as murderer John Wilkes Booth. Una Merkel, later to be typecast as comic support, plays Lincoln's great love, Ann Rutledge; Kay Hammond portrays Mary Todd. The film shows its age, but is well worth the watching, nonetheless. Huston fans will treasure it.

1930 B & W 91 minutes

ABSENCE OF MALICE

★★★★

DIRECTOR: Sydney Pollack
CAST: Paul Newman, Sally Field, Bob Balaban, Melinda Dillon, Wilford Brimley

Sally Field is a Miami reporter who writes a story implicating an innocent man (Paul Newman) in the mysterious disappearance—and possible murder—of a union leader in this taut, thoughtful drama about the ethics of journalism. It's sort of *All the President's Men* turned inside out. Rated PG because of minor violence.

1982 116 minutes

ACCIDENT

★★★★

DIRECTOR: Joseph Losey
CAST: Dirk Bogarde, Stanley Baker, Jacqueline Sassard, Michael York

Harold Pinter's complicated play retains its subtleties in this sometimes baffling film. Dirk Bogarde is excellent as a married professor pursuing an attractive student. There are enough twists and turns in the characters' actual desires to maintain your complete attention. Fascinating character studies abound in this British film.

1967 105 minutes

ACT OF PASSION

★★

DIRECTOR: Simon Langton
CAST: Marlo Thomas, Kris Kristofferson, Jon De Vries, David Rasche, Linda Thorson, Edward Winter, Randy Rocca, George Dzundza

In this made-for-television movie, Marlo Thomas plays a single woman who picks up a stranger (Kris Kristofferson) at a party. She is subsequently subjected to harassment by the police and the press when the man turns out to be a suspected terrorist. The filmmakers attempt to examine the potential for mistreatment of the innocent by law enforcement agencies and the press. While there is good reason to sound such an alarm, the siren here is harsh and blatantly exaggerated. In this movie, the press and the police are too one-dimensional in their ruthlessness. Unrated.

1984 95 minutes

ACTORS AND SIN

★★½

DIRECTORS: Ben Hecht, Lee Garmes

CAST: Edward G. Robinson, Eddie Albert, Marsha Hunt, Alan Reed, Dan O'Herlihy, Tracey Roberts

Actors and Sin is actually two short films. *Actor's Blood* is a drama starring Edward G. Robinson as the devoted father of a successful Broadway actress (Marsha Hunt) whose prima donna attitude earns her a reputation that catches up with her when her talents start to wane. *Woman's Sin* is a comedy starring Eddie Albert as an irrepressible Hollywood agent who finds a winning screenplay but loses its author. When the person who penned the script turns out to be only nine years old, the fireworks start.

1952 B & W 86 minutes

ADAM

★★★★

DIRECTOR: Michael Tuchner

CAST: Daniel J. Travanti, JoBeth Williams, Richard Masur

Daniel J. Travanti (*Hill St. Blues*) and JoBeth Williams (*The Big Chill*, *Poltergeist*) deliver fine performances in this chillingly real account of John and Reve Williams's search for their missing 6-year-old son, Adam. A quite believable picture, detailing the months of uncertainty and anguish that surrounded the child's disappearance from a department store. This ordeal resulted in the formation of the Missing Children's Bureau. Made for television.

1983 97 minutes

ADAM HAD FOUR SONS

★★★★

DIRECTOR: Gregory Ratoff

CAST: Ingrid Bergman, Warner Baxter, Susan Hayward

This classic has it all: good acting, romance, seduction, betrayal, tears, and laughter. Ingrid Bergman plays the good governess, and Susan Hayward plays the seductive hussy who tries to turn brother against brother. Warner Baxter offers a fine performance as Adam, the father.

1941 B & W 81 minutes

ADULTRESS, THE

DIRECTOR: Norbert Meisel

CAST: Tyne Daly, Eric Braeden, Greg Morton, Lynn Roth

Gobble, gobble, gobble . . . this is an abysmal film about an impotent husband (Greg Morton) who hires a gigolo (Eric Braeden) to service his physically deprived wife (Tyne Daly). The only thing more painful to watch than the story in this turkey is the attempt at profundity and art by director Norbert Meisel.

1973 85 minutes

ADVISE AND CONSENT

★★★½

DIRECTOR: Otto Preminger

CAST: Henry Fonda, Don Murray, Charles Laughton, Franchot Tone, Lew Ayres, Walter Pidgeon, Peter Lawford, Paul Ford, Burgess Meredith, Gene Tierney

An engrossing adaptation of Allen Drury's bestseller about behind-the-scenes Washington. Fine performances abound among the familiar faces that populate Otto Preminger's vision of the U.S. Senate as it is called upon to confirm a controversial nominee for Secretary of State (Henry Fonda). Easily the most riveting is

Charles Laughton, at his scene-stealing best, as a smiling old crocodile of a Southern senator. Also worth noting is Don Murray's anguished legislator, whose clouded past holds the key to his pivotal vote.

1962 B & W 140 minutes

AFFAIR, THE

★★★

DIRECTOR: Gilbert Cates

CAST: Natalie Wood, Robert Wagner, Bruce Davison, Kent Smith, Pat Harrington

Touching, honest story of a crippled songwriter (Natalie Wood) tentatively entering into her first love affair—with an attorney (Robert Wagner). This is an unusually well-acted, sensitively told TV movie.

1973 74 minutes

AFRICAN QUEEN, THE

★★★★★

DIRECTOR: John Huston

CAST: Humphrey Bogart, Katharine Hepburn, Peter Bull, Robert Morley, Theodore Bikel

Humphrey Bogart and Katharine Hepburn star in this exciting World War I adventure film. Bogart's a drunkard, and Hepburn's the spinster sister of a murdered missionary. Together they take on the Germans and, in doing so, are surprised to find themselves falling in love.

1951 106 minutes

AGAINST ALL ODDS

★★★½

DIRECTOR: Taylor Hackford

CAST: Jeff Bridges, Rachel Ward, Alex Karras, James Woods

A respectable remake of *Out of the Past*, a 1947 *film noir* classic, this release stars Jeff Bridges as a man hired by a wealthy gangster (James Woods) to track down his girlfriend (Rachel Ward), who allegedly tried to kill him and made off with forty thousand dollars. Bridges finds her, they fall in love, and that's when the plot's twists really begin. Car chase fans will love the hair-raising race at the beginning of the film. Romance fans will find Bridges and Ward convincing as the star-crossed lovers. Thriller buffs will be kept on their seats by the tension-filled ending. Rated R for nudity, suggested sex, violence, and profanity.

1984 128 minutes

AGATHA

★★½

DIRECTOR: Michael Apted

CAST: Dustin Hoffman, Vanessa Redgrave, Cecelia Gregory, Paul Brooks

Supposedly based on a true event in the life of mystery author Agatha Christie (during which she disappeared for eleven days in 1926), this is a moderately effective thriller. Vanessa Redgrave is excellent in the title role, but co-star Dustin Hoffman is miscast as the American detective on her trail. Rated PG.

1979 98 minutes

AGENCY

★★

DIRECTOR: George Kaczender

CAST: Robert Mitchum, Lee Majors, Saul Rubinek, Valerie Perrine

Despite the presence of Robert Mitchum, this Canadian feature about a power struggle in the world of advertising doesn't convince. Nor do the supporting performances by wooden Lee Majors and lovely, but wasted, Valerie Perrine. Rated PG.

1981 94 minutes

AGNES OF GOD

★★★

DIRECTOR: Norman Jewison
CAST: Jane Fonda, Anne Bancroft, Meg Tilly, Anne Pitoniak, Winston Rekert, Gratien Gelinas

This fascinating drama features tour-de-force performances by Jane Fonda, Anne Bancroft, and Meg Tilly. Tilly's character, the childlike novice of an extremely sheltered convent, is discovered one night with the bloodied body of a baby she claims not to recognize. Psychiatrist Fonda is sent to determine Tilly's sanity in anticipation of a court hearing; Bancroft, as the Mother Superior, struggles to prevent the young girl's loss of innocence. John Pielmeier's screenplay, adapted from his stage play, sweeps through Catholic guilt, distrust of contemporary society, and old-fashioned whodunit trappings, all of which allow Fonda and Bancroft to jab each other with sharp verbal barbs. The film is ultimately sabotaged, though, by its own lack of conviction. An intriguing near-miss. Rated PG-13 for subject matter.

1985 101 minutes

AIRPORT 1975

★½

DIRECTOR: Jack Smight
CAST: Charlton Heston, George Kennedy, Karen Black, Sid Caesar, Helen Reddy

Universal waited four years after the release of the original *Airport* but could resist the temptation no longer. Released at the height of the disaster film craze, this second entry in the series profits from a strong performance by Charlton Heston and very little else. Characters get the most trifling introductions in an attempt to create drama, and the trend in supporting casts already was leaning toward a Love Boat-ish opportunity to empty the closets of B and C players. And Helen Reddy, as a (spare us) singing nun? Rated PG—moderate tension.

1974 106 minutes

AIRPORT 77

★

DIRECTOR: Jerry Jameson
CAST: Jack Lemmon, Lee Grant, George Kennedy, Christopher Lee

This movie is, at best, inoffensive diversion and, at worst, a regurgitation of all the clichéd situations and stereotyped characters we have come to expect from a disaster flick. If you've seen one *Airport*, you've seen them all. For those who haven't heard, this film is about a luxury 747 that is skyjacked and crashes in the sea at the Bermuda Triangle. Rated PG for violence.

1977 113 minutes

AIRPORT '79: THE CONCORDE

★

DIRECTOR: David Lowell Rich
CAST: Alain Delon, Robert Wagner, Susan Blakely, George Kennedy, Eddie Albert, Cicely Tyson

This is another in the seemingly endless *Airport* series. Robert Wagner is a ruthless tycoon with a scheme to destroy the aircaft to cover up for some of his dirty business affairs soon to be revealed by another affair, one with his mistress, Susan Blakely, a top newscaster with a hot story. Bring your own air sickness bag. Rated PG.

1979 113 minutes

ALAMO BAY

★★★★

DIRECTOR: Louis Malle
CAST: Ed Harris, Amy Madigan, Ho Nquyen, Donald Moffat

French director Louis Malle (*Atlantic City*) once again looks at the underbelly of the American dream. This time, he takes us to the Gulf Coast of Texas in the late 1970s where Vietnamese refugees arrived, expecting the land of opportunity and came face to face, instead, with the Ku Klux Klan. The immigrants joined the locals in fishing for shrimp and proved to be much better at it. This, in tough economic times, brought resentment—brilliantly brought to the screen by Ed Harris as a once-admirable man turned into a monster by resentment and frustration. Amy Madigan (also superb) is the woman who loves him but cannot condone his twisted attitude and actions. Rated R for nudity, violence, and profanity.

1985 105 minutes

ALEXANDER THE GREAT

★★★½

DIRECTOR: Robert Rossen

CAST: Richard Burton, Fredric March, Claire Bloom, Danielle Darrieux

The strange, enigmatic, self-possessed Macedonian conqueror of Greece and most of the civilized world of his time rides again. Richard Burton, with his enthralling voice and uniquely hypnotic eyes, dominates an outstanding cast in this lavish epic of life and love among the upper crust from 356 to 323 B.C.

1956 141 minutes

ALGIERS

★★★½

DIRECTOR: John Cromwell

CAST: Charles Boyer, Hedy Lamarr, Sigrid Gurie

"Come with me to the Casbah." Charles Boyer set female hearts aflutter in the 1930s with his portrayal of Pepe Le Moko, a gentleman thief on the run from the authorities. It's still fun to watch.

1938 B & W 100 minutes

ALICE ADAMS

★★★★

DIRECTOR: George Stevens

CAST: Katharine Hepburn, Fred MacMurray, Evelyn Venable, Fred Stone, Frank Albertson, Hattie McDaniel, Charley Grapewin, Hedda Hopper

Life and love in a typical mid-American small town when there were still such things as concerts in the park and ice cream socials. Hepburn is a social-climbing girl wistfully seeking love while trying to overcome the stigma of her father's lack of money and ambition. High point of the film is the dinner scene, at once a comic gem and painful insight into character.

1935 B & W 99 minutes

ALICE DOESN'T LIVE HERE ANYMORE

★★★★½

DIRECTOR: Martin Scorsese

CAST: Ellen Burstyn, Kris Kristofferson, Harvey Keitel, Billy Green Bush, Alfred Lutter, Jodie Foster, Vic Tayback

The feature film that spawned the television series "Alice" is a memorable character study about a woman (Ellen Burstyn, who won an Oscar for her performance) attempting to survive after her husband's death has left her penniless and with a young son to support. The hard-edged direction by Martin Scorsese (*Taxi Driver*) adds grit to what might have been a lightweight yarn, and the supporting portrayals add greatly to the film's effectiveness. Rated PG for profanity and violence.

1975 113 minutes

ALICE'S RESTAURANT

★★★½

DIRECTOR: Arthur Penn

CAST: Arlo Guthrie, Pat Quinn, James Broderick, Michael McClanathan, Geoff Outlaw, Tina Chen

This film was based on Arlo Guthrie's hit record of the same name. Some insights into the 1960s counterculture can be found in this story of Guthrie's attempt to stay out of the draft. There is some fine acting by a basically unknown cast. Rated PG for language and some nudity.

1969 111 minutes

ALL ABOUT EVE

★★★★★

DIRECTOR: Joseph L. Mankiewicz

CAST: Bette Davis, Anne Baxter, Marilyn Monroe, George Sanders, Celeste Holm, Gary Merrill

The behind-the-scenes world of the New York theater is the subject of this classic. The picture won several Academy Awards, including best picture, but it is Bette Davis as Margo Channing that most remember. Her characterization is softer and more vulnerable than had been seen in her long stay at Warner Bros. It was also miles away from the assortment of hags she played in her later career. Margo Channing is a woman apparently at the apex of her career, but she's beginning to slide. A conniving Eve (Anne Baxter) is there to give her a push downward as she attempts to take Margo's place. The dialogue sparkles, and the performances are of high caliber.

1950 B & W 138 minutes

ALL GOD'S CHILDREN

★★

DIRECTOR: Jerry Thorpe

CAST: Richard Widmark, Ned Beatty, Ossie Davis, Ruby Dee

Forced busing to achieve educational integration is the crux of this story of two families, one white and one black, whose sons are friends. The cast is excellent, but a wandering script makes comprehension difficult. Rated PG for violence.

1980 107 minutes

ALL NIGHT LONG

★★★

DIRECTOR: Jean-Claude Tramount

CAST: Gene Hackman, Barbra Streisand

Praised by some for its offbeat style and story, this comedy, starring the odd couple of Gene Hackman and Barbra Streisand, is only occasionally convincing. Hackman stars as an executive demoted to the position of managing a twenty-four-hour grocery store. There, he meets a daffy housewife (played by a miscast Streisand) and love blooms. This picture has its partisans (including several top-name critics), but it is still unlikely to satisfy most viewers.

1981 95 minutes

ALL QUIET ON THE WESTERN FRONT

★★★½

DIRECTOR: Delbert Mann

CAST: Richard Thomas, Ernest Borgnine, Donald Pleasence, Ian Holm, Patricia Neal

This is a television remake of the 1930 film, which was taken from Erich Maria Remarque's classic anti-war novel. It attempts to bring back all the horrors of World War I, but even the great detail issued to this film can't hide its TV mentality and melodramatic characters. The characters are exaggerated to promote the difference between good and bad, and while this dichotomy is one of the main points of the material, the viewer may feel a bit patronized. Despite this major flaw, the film is watchable for its rich look and compelling story.

1979 126 minutes

ALL THE KING'S MEN

★★★★

DIRECTOR: Robert Rossen

CAST: Broderick Crawford, Joanne Dru, John Ireland, Mercedes McCambridge, John Derek

Broderick Crawford and Mercedes McCambridge won Academy Awards for their work in this adaptation of Robert Penn Warren's Pulitzer Prize–winning novel about a corrupt politician's ascension to power. Seen today, the film retains its relevance and potency.

1949 B & W 109 minutes

ALL THE PRESIDENT'S MEN

★★★★★

DIRECTOR: Alan J. Pakula

CAST: Dustin Hoffman, Robert Redford, Jason Robards Jr., Jane Alexander, Jack Warden, Martin Balsam

Robert Redford, who also produced, and Dustin Hoffman star in this gripping reenactment of the exposure of the Watergate conspiracy by reporters Bob Woodward and Carl Bernstein. What's so remarkable about this docudrama is, although we know how it eventually comes out, we're on the edge of our seats from beginning to end. That's inspired movie-making. Rated PG.

1976 136 minutes

ALL THE RIGHT MOVES

★★★½

DIRECTOR: Michael Chapman

CAST: Tom Cruise, Craig T. Nelson, Christopher Penn

Tom Cruise (*Risky Business*) stars in this entertaining coming-of-age picture as a blue-collar high-school senior trying to get out of a Pennsylvania mill town by way of a football scholarship. Rated R for profanity, sex, and nudity.

1983 91 minutes

ALL THIS AND HEAVEN TOO

★★★★

DIRECTOR: Anatole Litvak

CAST: Bette Davis, Charles Boyer, Jeffrey Lynn, Barbara O'Neill, Virginia Weidler, Henry Daniell, Ann Todd, June Lockhart, Harry Davenport

Based on a true murder case, this film, set in Paris in 1840, has an outstanding cast. Bette Davis is wonderful as the governess who wins Charles Boyer's heart. Barbara O'Neill is the uncaring mother and obsessed wife who becomes jealous of Davis and the attention given her by both the children and her husband. When she is found murdered, Davis and Boyer become prime suspects. Davis is unjustly put on trial. O'Neill's death scene is typically melodramatic for its time, but this period piece is worthy of its status as a classic and a Bette Davis fan must-see.

1940 B & W 121 minutes

ALLIGATOR SHOES

★★

DIRECTOR: Clay Borris

CAST: Gary Borris, Clay Borris, Ronalda Jones, Rose Mallais-Borris, Len Perry, Simone Champagne

As can be surmised from the cast, this is pretty much a home movie by two brothers, Gary and Clay Borris. Although grownup, they still live at home. When their mentally disturbed aunt (Ronalda Jones) moves in, trouble arises. How each deals with this problem forms the basis for this drama, which becomes strained before its fatal conclusion. This Canadian film is unrated.

1982 98 minutes

ALPHABET CITY

★½

DIRECTOR: Amos Poe

CAST: Vincent Spano, Kate Vernon, Michael Winslow, Zohra Lampert, Raymond Serra

Talented Vincent Spano (*Baby It's You*; *The Black Stallion Returns*) plays a "sympathetic" drug dealer in this pretentious movie set in Manhattan's Lower East Side. Rated R for profanity, sex, nudity, and violence.

1984 98 minutes

AMATEUR, THE

★★★½

DIRECTOR: Charles Jarrott

CAST: John Savage, Christopher Plummer, Marthe Keller, John Marley

A CIA computer technologist (John Savage) blackmails The Company into helping him avenge the terrorist murder of his girlfriend, only to find himself abandoned—and hunted—by the CIA. Rated R because of violence.

1982 111 minutes

AMAZING HOWARD HUGHES, THE

★½

DIRECTOR: William A. Graham

CAST: Tommy Lee Jones, Ed Flanders, Tovah Feldshuh, Sorrell Booke, Lee Purcell, Arthur Franz

Howard Hughes was amazing, but little in this lackluster account of his life and career would so indicate. Best portrayal is Ed Flanders as longtime, finally turned-upon associate Noah Dietrich. An ambitious TV production that falls short of the mark.

1977 215 minutes

AMBASSADOR, THE

★★★½

DIRECTOR: J. Lee Thompson

CAST: Robert Mitchum, Rock Hudson, Ellen Burstyn, Fabio Testi, Donald Pleasence

Even if it simplifies a complex situation, *The Ambassador* confronts the Arab-Israeli conflict with a clear head and an optimistic viewpoint. Robert Mitchum plays the controversial U.S. ambassador to Israel, who tries to solve the Palestinian question while being criticized by all factions. Rock Hudson (in his last big-screen role) is the security officer who works around the clock saving the ambassador's life from KGB assassins and radicals from various camps. Ellen Burstyn plays the ambassador's wife, who complicates the situation when she is caught in an affair with a PLO leader. Rated R for violence, profanity, sex, and nudity.

1984 97 minutes

AMERICAN ANTHEM

★

DIRECTOR: Albert Magnoli

CAST: Mitch Gaylord, Janet Jones, Michelle Phillips

Starring 1984 Olympic gold medal gymnast Mitch Gaylord, and directed by Albert Magnoli (*Purple Rain*), this film features superb gymnastics. Otherwise, it is hard to find anything likable. The screenplay is amateurish, and the acting, except for a few brief moments by Gaylord, is even worse. Poorly executed technical effects simply exacerbate the problems. Rated PG.

1986 100 minutes

AMERICAN FLYERS

★★★½

DIRECTOR: John Badham

CAST: Kevin Costner, David Grant, Rae Dawn Chong, Alexandra Paul, Janice Rule, John Amos

Another bicycle-racing tale from writer Steve Tesich (*Breaking Away*), who correctly decided he could milk that theme at least one more time. Kevin Costner and David Grant star as estranged brothers who get to know and like each other again during their participation in a grueling three-day overland race. The script is best when it concentrates on that major premise, and worst when it lapses into a subplot concerning one brother's impending death from one of those Dread Hollywood Diseases That Always Prove Fatal. Rae Dawn Chong, as Costner's live-in lover, has *never* looked more appealing or seemed more credible. Her presence alone makes the film worthwhile; the excitement of the race is mere icing on the cake. Rated PG-13 for brief nudity and language.

1985 113 minutes

AMERICAN GIGOLO

★★

DIRECTOR: Paul Schrader
CAST: Richard Gere, Lauren Hutton, Hector Elizondo, Nina Van Pallandt

This story of a male hooker, Julian Kay (Richard Gere), who attends to the physical needs of bored, rich, middle-aged women in Beverly Hills, may be something different. But who needs it? This is sensationalism in the guise of social comment. It has some incidental humor (supplied by Hector Elizondo as a disheveled Columbo-like cop who learns about fashion from Kay) that is quite welcome. The performances of Richard Gere in the title role and Lauren Hutton as a nonclient lover are impressive. However, it is steeped in sleaze. Rated R for explicit depictions of a low lifestyle.

1980 117 minutes

AMERICANA

★★½

DIRECTOR: David Carradine
CAST: David Carradine, Barbara Hershey, Michael Greene, Bruce Carradine, John Barrymore III, Fran Ryan

Strange, offbeat film about a Vietnam veteran (director David Carradine) who attempts to rebuild a merry-go-round in a rural Kansas town and meets with hostility from the locals. Carradine attempts to make a statement about rebuilding America and reinstating its simple, honest values, but this gets lost in the impressionistic haze of his film. A noble effort, competently directed and acted (by professionals and nonprofessionals alike), but ultimately unsatisfying. Rated PG for violence and profanity.

1981 90 minutes

AMIN: THE RISE AND FALL

[turkey]

DIRECTOR: Richard Fleischer
CAST: Joseph Olita

Putrid garbage isn't strong enough to adequately describe this awful movie about the atrocities committed by Idi Amin during his reign of terror in Uganda. But it'll have to do. It's exploitation in the worst sense—and boring, to boot. In the title role, Joseph Olita shows all the acting talent of a diseased goat. Rated R for violence, nudity, sex, and profanity.

1981 101 minutes

AMONG THE CINDERS

★★½

DIRECTOR: Rolf Haedrick
CAST: Paul O'Shea, Derek Hardwick, Amanda Jones, Rebecca Gigney, Yvonne Yawley

A teenager (Paul O'Shea) holds himself responsible for the accidental death of a friend, and it takes a trip to the wilds with his grandfather (Derek Hardwick) to pull him out of it. This coming-of-age drama from New Zealand has its good moments, but these are outnumbered by the unremarkable ones. Rated R for nudity, profanity, suggested sex, and brief gore.

1985 105 minutes

ANATOMY OF A MURDER

★★★★

DIRECTOR: Otto Preminger

CAST: James Stewart, Arthur O'Connell, Lee Remick, Ben Gazzara, Eve Arden, Kathryn Grant, George C. Scott, Joseph Welch, Orson Bean, Murray Hamilton

A clever plot, realistic atmosphere, smooth direction, and sterling performances from a top-flight cast make this frank and exciting small-town courtroom drama first-rate fare. For the defense, it's James Stewart at his best vs. prosecuting attorney George C. Scott. Ben Gazzara plays a moody young army officer charged with killing the man who raped his wife, Lee Remick. Real-life lawyer Joseph Welch, of McCarthy hearings fame, plays the judge. Honest realism saturates throughout.

1959 B & W 160 minutes

AND JUSTICE FOR ALL

★★★½

DIRECTOR: Norman Jewison

CAST: Al Pacino, Jack Warden, John Forsythe, Craig T. Nelson

This is a bristling black comedy starring Al Pacino as a lawyer who becomes fed up with the red tape of our country's legal system. It's both heartrending and darkly hilarious—but not for all tastes. Rated R.

1979 117 minutes

AND THEN THERE WERE NONE

★★★★★

DIRECTOR: René Clair

CAST: Barry Fitzgerald, Walter Huston, Richard Haydn, Roland Young, Judith Anderson, Louis Hayward, June Duprez, Aubrey Smith

One of the best screen adaptations of an Agatha Christie mystery. A select group of people is invited to a lonely island and murdered one by one. René Clair's inspired visual style gives this release just the right atmosphere and tension.

1945 B & W 98 minutes

ANDY WARHOL'S BAD

★★★½

DIRECTOR: Jed Johnson

CAST: Carroll Baker, Perry King, Susan Tyrrell

Carroll Baker stars in this nasty and very sick outing from producer Andy Warhol. She plays a tough mama who runs a squad of female hit men out of her cheery suburban home while disguising it as an electrolysis operation. Into this strange company comes Perry King as a mysterious stranger who boards there until he completes his "mission." Full of sick scenes, including a baby being thrown out a window and splatting on the pavement below, and a dog stabbing. Everybody speaks very nasty to everyone else, just like in a John Waters film, which this seems to be emulating. Not for weak stomachs, it includes one of the great actresses of trash cinema, Susan Tyrrell, as a sickly mother with a whining baby. Sick, but you may not be able to take your eyes off it. The film has gore, violence, and nudity.

1977 107 minutes

ANGEL ON MY SHOULDER

★★★★

DIRECTOR: Archie Mayo

CAST: Paul Muni, Anne Baxter, Claude Rains, George Cleveland, Onslow Stevens

In a break from his big-budget prestige screen biographies of the period, Paul Muni stars in this entertaining fantasy as a murdered gangster who makes a deal with the devil. He wants to return to his human form. He gets his wish and spends his time on Earth—as a judge—trying to outwit Satan.

1946 B & W 101 minutes

ANGELO MY LOVE

★★★★

DIRECTOR: Robert Duvall

CAST: Angelo and Michael Evans, Steve and Millie Tsigonoff, Cathy Kitchen

Robert Duvall wrote and directed this loosely scripted, wonderfully different movie about a street-wise 11-year-old gypsy boy. Duvall reportedly conceived the project when he spotted the fast-talking, charismatic Angelo Evans on a New York street and decided he ought to be in pictures. Rated R for profanity.

1983 115 minutes

ANGELS OVER BROADWAY

★★★

DIRECTORS: Ben Hecht, Lee Garmes

CAST: Douglas Fairbanks Jr., Rita Hayworth, Thomas Mitchell, John Qualen, George Watts

Co-directed by legendary newsmen and playwrights Ben Hecht and Lee Garmes, this tale of street-wise Douglas Fairbanks's efforts to save would-be suicide John Qualen and provide him with a reason for living is full of great dialogue and pithy comments on life and the human condition. But it lacks the charm that would mark it as a true classic. Down-at-the-heels showgirl Rita Hayworth and philosophizing drunk Thomas Mitchell follow in the wake of Fairbanks's hustler and contribute a great deal to this pseudofantasy film. Recommended for its dialogue, as well as its odd tone.

1940 B & W 80 minutes

ANIMAL FARM

★★½

DIRECTORS: John Halas, Joy Batchelor

CAST: Animated

Serious, sincere animated adaptation of George Orwell's ingenious satire concerning the follies of government. The treatment would have benefited from greater intensity. The attempt at creating an optimistic ending was ill-advised. Keep in mind the film isn't children's fare.

1954 72 minutes

ANN VICKERS

★★★★

DIRECTOR: John Cromwell

CAST: Irene Dunne, Bruce Cabot, Walter Huston, Conrad Nagel, Edna May Oliver, J. Carrol Naish

Rebuffed by Bruce Cabot, noble and self-sacrificing Irene Dunne scorns all men and turns to social service. Against all odds she seeks penal reform. After writing a book exposing disgraceful prison conditions, she is appointed superintendent of a model women's detention home. Later she learns Walter Huston, a liberal judge, had quietly backed her career. When he is accused of graft, she comes to his aid, but he is convicted anyway. She waits while he serves eight years, and they are finally united. A somewhat unique women's prison film in that the heroine is not a victimized inmate.

1933 B & W 72 minutes

ANNA CHRISTIE

★★★★

DIRECTOR: Clarence Brown

CAST: Greta Garbo, Charles Bickford, Marie Dressler, Lee Phelps, George Marion

Greta Garbo is mesmerizing and Marie Dressler hilariously memorable in this early sound classic adapted from Eugene O'Neill's play. The tag line for it in 1930 was "Garbo speaks!" And speak she does, uttering the famous line "Gif me a viskey, ginger ale on the side, and don't be stingy, baby" while portraying a woman with a shady past.

1930 B & W 90 minutes

ANNA KARENINA

★★★★

DIRECTOR: Clarence Brown

CAST: Greta Garbo, Fredric March, Basil Rathbone, Freddie Bartholomew, Maureen O'Sullivan, Reginald Denny, May Robson, Reginald Owen

The forever fascinating, peerless Greta Garbo, a superb supporting cast headed by Fredric March, and the masterful direction of Clarence Brown make this film one of the actress's greatest, a true film classic. An interesting contrast is *Love*, a version of the Tolstoy novel made by Garbo and Brown in 1927.

1935 B & W 95 minutes

ANNE OF GREEN GABLES

★★★★

DIRECTOR: Kevin Sullivan

CAST: Megan Follows, Richard Farnsworth, Colleen Dewhurst

This delightful film, based on L. M. Montgomery's classic novel, is set in 1908 on Canada's Prince Edward Island. Anne (Megan Follows) is a foster child taken in by Matthew (Richard Farnsworth) and Marilla Cuthbert (Colleen Dewhurst), who mistakenly expects her to be the boy they need for a farmhand. Anne is a nonstop, long-playing record of girltalk, interspersed with unexpected foibles that invariably get her into hot water with the prim, proper, and unbending Marilla. Fortunately, Anne has a staunch supporter in Matthew, who nurtures her spirit and intelligence. This is perfect entertainment with superb performances by all. Unrated; suitable for family viewing.

1985 240 minutes

ANNE OF THE THOUSAND DAYS

★★★

DIRECTOR: Charles Jarrott

CAST: Genevieve Bujold, Richard Burton, Anthony Quayle

The story of Anne Boleyn, Henry VIII's second wife and mother of Queen Elizabeth I, is given the big-budget treatment. Luckily, the tragic tale of a woman who is at first pressured into an unwanted union with England's lusty king, only to fall in love with him and eventually lose her head to court intrigue, is not lost beneath the spectacle. Genevieve Bujold's well-balanced performance of Anne carries the entire production. Richard Burton, however, offers only a hammy Henry. Rated PG.

1969 146 minutes

ANOTHER COUNTRY

★★★½

DIRECTOR: Mark Kanievska

CAST: Rupert Everett, Colin Firth

For this film, directed by Mark Kanievska, Julian Mitchell adapted his stage play about Guy Burgess, an Englishman who became a spy for Russia in the 1930s. Little in this story reportedly was based on fact. Still, Mitchell's postulations provide interesting viewing, and Rupert Everett's lead performance—as Guy "Bennett"—is stunning.

Rated PG for suggested sex and profanity.

1984 90 minutes

ANOTHER TIME, ANOTHER PLACE

★★★

DIRECTOR: Michael Radford
CAST: Phyllis Logan, Paul Young

In this British import set in 1944, a woman named Janie (Phyllis Logan) lives on a small farm in Scotland with her husband, Dongal (Paul Young), fifteen years her senior. As part of a war rehabilitation program, the couple welcomes three Italian POW's onto their place, and Janie, infatuated with their accents and cultural differences, falls in love. Rated PG.

1984 118 minutes

ANOTHER TIME, ANOTHER PLACE

DIRECTOR: Lewis Allen
CAST: Lana Turner, Barry Sullivan, Glynis Johns, Sean Connery, Sidney James

Ho-hum melodrama about American newspaperwoman whose brief affair with British journalist ends in tragedy when he dies during World War II. Flat and unconvincing, this indifferent weeper is notable mainly for the appearance of a young and sturdy-looking Sean Connery and an older, worldly-wise Lana Turner, who would soon face her greatest role as a mother during the trial of her daughter Cheryl, charged with murdering Turner's live-in lover, Johnny Stompanato. Connery gained some distinction and the admiration of the film crew when he flattened the overbearing Stompanato during production, but none of the behind-the-scenes excitement is evident in this dreary love story.

1958 B & W 98 minutes

ANTONY AND CLEOPATRA

★★

DIRECTOR: Charlton Heston
CAST: Charlton Heston, Hildegarde Neil, Eric Porter, Fernando Rey, John Castle

Marginal film interpretation of Shakespeare's play. Obviously a tremendous amount of work on Charlton Heston's part, casting himself as Antony, but the film is lacking in energy. Rated PG.

1973 160 minutes

APPRENTICESHIP OF DUDDY KRAVITZ, THE

★★★

DIRECTOR: Ted Kotcheff
CAST: Richard Dreyfuss, Jack Warden, Micheline Lanctot, Denholm Elliott, Randy Quaid

Richard Dreyfuss, in an early starring role, is the main attraction in this quirky little comedy about the rise of a poor Jewish lad from a Montreal ghetto. The story is full of cruel and smartassed humor, a trait that haunts Dreyfuss to this day. One of the brighter moments is a film-within-the-film, an avant-garde interpretation of a bar mitzvah (one of Duddy's attempts to get rich quick). Another involves the buoyancy of various parts of the anatomy. Ultimately, the film is too long and too shrill. Rated PG for sexual content.

1974 121 minutes

ARCH OF TRIUMPH

★★★

DIRECTOR: Lewis Milestone
CAST: Ingrid Bergman, Charles Boyer, Charles Laughton, Louis Calhern

In Paris before the Nazis arrive, a refugee doctor meets and falls in love with a woman with a past in this long, slow-paced, emotionless drama. It's sad, frustrating, tedious, and sometimes murky, but fans of the principal players will forgive and enjoy.

1948 B & W 120 minutes

ARRANGEMENT, THE

★

DIRECTOR: Elia Kazan

CAST: Kirk Douglas, Deborah Kerr, Faye Dunaway, Richard Boone

The cast is the only real reason for watching this tedious talkfest between Kirk Douglas and whoever will listen after he botches a suicide attempt and reevaluates his life. Very nicely produced, but sets and style contribute only so much to a film. A hook that involves the audience is sadly lacking here. The principal performers deserve better. Rated R for adult themes, language.

1969 127 minutes

ARROWSMITH

★★★★

DIRECTOR: John Ford

CAST: Ronald Colman, Helen Hayes, Richard Bennett, DeWitt Jennings, Beulah Bondi, Myrna Loy

Mellifluous-voiced Ronald Colman is a young, career-dedicated research doctor tempted by the profits of commercialism in this faithful rendering of Sinclair Lewis's noted novel of medicine. Helen Hayes is his first wife—doomed to die before he sees the light. This is the first film to center seriously on a doctor's career and raise the question of professional integrity and morality versus quick money and social status.

1931 B & W 101 minutes

ARRUZA

★★★

DIRECTOR: Budd Boetticher

CAST: Documentary

This labor of love by director Budd Boetticher tells the story of Carlos Arruza, arguably Mexico's greatest bullfighter. After achieving all he could as a matador, Arruza retired in 1953 to raise bulls for the ring. He could not get the ring out of his life, and he returned to fight on horseback as a rejoneador. He conquered this, too, until his untimely death in a car accident on the way home from a successful day in the ring. An often compelling film about bullfighting, this contains several actual contests and follows Arruza's career, as well as shows the breeding and training of the bulls and horses.

1987 91 minutes

ASPHALT JUNGLE, THE

★★★★½

DIRECTOR: John Huston

CAST: Sterling Hayden, Sam Jaffe, Louis Calhern, Marilyn Monroe, Jean Hagen, James Whitmore, Marc Lawrence, Anthony Caruso

One of the greatest crime films of all time. This realistic study of a jewel robbery that sours, lets the audience in early on what the outcome will be while building tension for any unexpected surprises that might pop up. Sterling Hayden and a near-perfect cast charge the film with an electric current that never lets up and only increases in power as they scheme their way closer to their fate. John Huston broke new ground with this landmark drama and provided Marilyn Monroe with a small part that opened the door for her ambitions, but the credit for this materpiece must be shared among the cast and crew as well as with W. R. Burnett's story and Miklos Rozsa's perfectly attuned musical score. This is one of John Huston's ten best films. Definitely a must-see film if you're a fan of crime drama.

1950 B & W 112 minutes

ASSASSIN OF YOUTH (AKA MARIJUANA)

★

DIRECTOR: Elmer Clifton
CAST: Luana Walters, Arthur Gardner, Earl Dwire, Fern Emmett

This silly, low-budget exploitation film tells the story of a courageous young reporter who goes undercover to infiltrate the marijuana cult that has been wreaking havoc with a local town. Cornball humor in the form of "Pop" Brady and the scooter-riding Henrietta Frisbie, the town snoop, gives this an extra edge on most films of this nature, but not much of an edge. Veteran silent film director Elmer Clifton and producer Leo J. McCarthy co-wrote this epic and appear to be responsible for the dialogue and the newspaper headlines which appear like title cards (MARIJUANA CRAZED YOUTH, MARIJUANA DEALS DEATH). Some hardboiled stuff, but not too dynamic.

1936 B & W 67 minutes

AT CLOSE RANGE

★★★★

DIRECTOR: James Foley
CAST: Christopher Walken, Sean Penn, Christopher Penn

A powerful thriller based on true events that occurred in Pennsylvania during the summer of 1978. A rural gang leader returns to the family he abandoned years ago. His two sons try to prove themselves worthy of joining the gang. Events beyond their control lead to a brutal showdown between father and sons. It is a quiet, almost pastoral film with an underlying current of evil that explodes into a shattering climax. Emotionally draining, with many fine, restrained performances. The movie received spotty release, but Madonna's song "Live to Tell" hit number one on the charts. Rated R for violence and profanity.

1986 115 minutes

ATLANTIC CITY

★★★★★

DIRECTOR: Louis Malle
CAST: Burt Lancaster, Susan Sarandon, Kate Reid

This superb motion picture has all of the elements that made the films of Hollywood's golden age great—with a few appropriately modern twists tossed in. The screenplay, by John Guare—about a struggling casino worker (Susan Sarandon) who becomes involved in a drug deal—gives us powerful drama, wonderful characters, memorable dialogue, and delightfully funny situations. And the performances by Burt Lancaster, Sarandon, and Kate Reid, in particular, are topnotch. As a result, every moment is worth savoring. Rated R because of brief nudity and violence.

1981 104 minutes

ATOMIC CAFE, THE

★★

DIRECTORS: Kevin Rafferty, Jayne Loader, Pierce Rafferty
CAST: Documentary

Beyond being an interesting cultural document, this feature-length compilation of post–World War II propaganda, documentary, and newsreel footage on official and unofficial American attitudes toward the atomic bomb has little to offer, especially as entertainment. Advance word was that it was both funny and frightening. Well, it is funny in a very dark, unrelenting sort of way. Overall, however, it's just plain depressing. No MPAA rating. The film has no objectionable material, though some of the footage featuring casualties of atomic bomb explosions is quite graphic.

1982 B & W 88 minutes

AUTOBIOGRAPHY OF MISS JANE PITTMAN, THE

★★★★★

DIRECTOR: John Korty
CAST: Cicely Tyson, Richard Dysart, Odetta, Michael Murphy, Barbara Chuney, Thalmus Rasulala

This terrific television movie traces black history in America from the Civil War years to the turbulent civil rights movement of the 1960s. All this is seen through the eyes of 110-year-old ex-slave Jane Pittman (Cicely Tyson). The entire cast is superb, but Tyson still manages to tower above the others in the title role. This is a real must-see film. There is no rating, but it should be noted that there are some violent scenes.

1974 110 minutes

AUTUMN LEAVES

★★½

DIRECTOR: Robert Aldrich
CAST: Joan Crawford, Cliff Robertson, Vera Miles, Lorne Greene

Troubled middle-aged typist Joan Crawford is further anguished after marrying a younger man (Cliff Robertson) who proves to be mentally disturbed and already married. Run-of-the-mill Crawford fare.

1956 B & W 108 minutes

AVIATOR, THE

★★

DIRECTOR: George Miller
CAST: Christopher Reeve, Rosanna Arquette, Jack Warden, Scott Wilson, Tyne Daly, Sam Wanamaker

This film, about a grumpy flyer (Christopher Reeve) during the 1920s who is forced to take a feisty passenger (Rosanna Arquette) on his mail route, is too similar to *High Road to China*. It has neither the high adventure nor the humor of the latter. What we're left with is a predictable boy-meets-girl drama that takes a left turn into a danger-in-the-wilderness cliché. To the credit of director George Miller, the second half works fairly well. But by that time most viewers will have given up on the movie, something the film company did as well (they put it on the shelf after a brief theatrical release). Rated PG.

1984 102 minutes

BABY DOLL

★★★★

DIRECTOR: Elia Kazan
CAST: Carroll Baker, Eli Wallach, Karl Malden, Mildred Dunnock, Lonnie Chapman, Rip Torn

Set in hot, humid, sleazy Mississippi, this is the story of a child bride (Carroll Baker) who sleeps in a crib, her lusting, short-on-brains husband (Karl Malden), and a scheming business rival (Eli Wallach) determined to use and abuse them both. What else but a Tennessee Williams story? Tepid stuff today, but when first released, the film was condemned by the Legion of Decency. The lead actors, all of whom are identified with the playwright, are excellent. Baker's portrayal gave her a lifetime nickname. Her skimpy pajamas became fashionable.

1956 B & W 114 minutes

BABY THE RAIN MUST FALL

★★½

DIRECTOR: Robert Mulligan
CAST: Steve McQueen, Lee Remick, Don Murray

This confusing character study of a convict who is paroled and reunited with his family raises a lot of questions but answers none of them.

1965 B & W 100 minutes

BACK FROM ETERNITY

★★

DIRECTOR: John Farrow

CAST: Robert Ryan, Anita Ekberg, Rod Steiger, Phyllis Kirk

No surprises in this rehash of similar films about a handful of people who survive a calamity (in this case, an airplane crash) and have to learn to cope with their predicament as well as with each other. Basically a potboiler that depends on stock footage and phony studio sets, this tired story limps along through the jungles of South America and gives Anita Ekberg plenty of opportunity to show off her torn blouse. Rod Steiger gives one of his hammier performances, while reliable Robert Ryan displays his usual strength and integrity of characterization. Nothing here that hasn't been seen many times before.

1956 B & W 97 minutes

BACK ROADS

★★★

DIRECTOR: Martin Ritt

CAST: Sally Field, Tommy Lee Jones, David Keith

Pug (Tommy Lee Jones) and prostitute (Sally Field) hitch and brawl down the back roads of the South in this sometimes raunchy, often hilarious romance-fantasy. Though it drags a bit, the performances by the two stars and an earthy, down-home charm make it worthwhile. Rated R.

1981 94 minutes

BACK STREET

★★★

DIRECTOR: David Miller

CAST: Susan Hayward, John Gavin, Vera Miles

Third version of novelist Fannie Hurst's romantic tearjerker about clandestine love, with Susan Hayward as the noble mistress who sacrifices all and stands by her lover even when he stupidly marries another woman.

1961 107 minutes

BAD BOYS

★★★★½

DIRECTOR: Rick Rosenthal

CAST: Sean Penn, Esai Morales, Reni Santoni, Ally Sheedy, Jim Moody, Eric Gurry

This is a grimly riveting vision of troubled youth. Sean Penn and Esai Morales are featured as Chicago street hoods sworn to kill each other in prison. It's exciting, thought-provoking, and violent, but the violence, for once, is justified and not merely exploitative. Rated R for language, violence, and nudity.

1983 123 minutes

BADLANDS

★★★★

DIRECTOR: Terence Malick

CAST: Martin Sheen, Sissy Spacek, Warren Oates, Ramon Bieri, Alan Vint

Featuring fine performances by Sissy Spacek, Martin Sheen, and Warren Oates, this is a disturbing recreation of the Starkweather-Fugate killing spree of the 1950s. It is undeniably a work of intelligence and fine craftsmanship. However, as with Martin Scorsese's *Taxi Driver* and Bob Fosse's *Star 80*, *Badlands* is not an easy film to watch. Rated PG.

1973 95 minutes

BANG THE DRUM SLOWLY

★★★★

DIRECTOR: John Hancock

CAST: Robert De Niro, Michael Moriarty, Vincent Gardenia

Robert De Niro and Michael Moriarty are given a perfect showcase for their acting talents in this poignant film, and they don't disappoint. The friendship of two baseball players comes alive as the team's star pitcher

(Moriarty) tries to assist journeyman catcher (De Niro) in completing one last season before succumbing to Hodgkin's disease. The story may lead to death, but it is filled with life, hope, and compassion. Rated PG.

1973 98 minutes

BARABBAS

★★½

DIRECTOR: Richard Fleischer
CAST: Anthony Quinn, Jack Palance, Ernest Borgnine, Katy Jurado

Early Dino De Laurentiis opus is long on production, short on credibility. Standard gory religious spectacle follows the life of the thief Barabbas, whom Pilate freed when Jesus was condemned to die. Good cast of veteran character actors attempts to move this epic along, but fails.

1962 144 minutes

BARBARY COAST, THE

★★★½

DIRECTOR: Howard Hawks
CAST: Edward G. Robinson, Miriam Hopkins, Joel McCrea, Walter Brennan, Brian Donlevy, Frank Craven

Big-budget Hollywood hokum drew its inspiration from Herbert Asbury's colorful history of early San Francisco, but tailored the book to fit the unique talents of its great cast. Directed by Howard Hawks in his usual fast-paced style, this story of femme fatale Miriam Hopkins and the men in her life is fun for the whole family and a treat for film buffs who like the look of the past as created on studio backlots. Modern viewers may be hard-pressed to understand why Miriam Hopkins was a top star of her day, but the performances of the other principals (and supporting cast) reaffirm that they don't make 'em like that anymore. Look for David Niven in his first recognizable bit as a drunken tramp who gets thrown out of a tavern into the street.

1935 B & W 90 minutes

BAREFOOT CONTESSA, THE

★★★

DIRECTOR: Joseph L. Mankiewicz
CAST: Humphrey Bogart, Ava Gardner, Edmond O'Brien, Marius Goring, Rossano Brazzi

A gaggle of Hollywood vultures headed by director Humphrey Bogart picks naïve dancer Ava Gardner out of a Madrid nightclub and proceeds to mold her into a film star. A simple unpretentious soul who never really comes to grips with all that transpires, she marries an impotent Italian noblemen (Rossano Brazzi), dies, and is buried by her chief mentor who tells her tragic story in flashback. A cynical, bizarre tale that never delivers what it promises. Edmond O'Brien won a best supporting actor Oscar for his portrayal of a press agent.

1954 128 minutes

BARRY LYNDON

★★★

DIRECTOR: Stanley Kubrick
CAST: Ryan O'Neal, Marisa Berenson, Patrick Magee, Hardy Krüger, Steven Berkoff, Gay Hamilton

This period epic directed by Stanley Kubrick will please only the filmmaker's most fervent admirers and get yawns from most other viewers. Although exquisitely photographed and meticulously designed, this three-hour motion picture adaptation of William Makepeace Thackeray's novel about an eighteenth-century rogue is a flawed masterpiece at best and is far too drawn out. In addition, Ryan O'Neal is a real zero in the title role. However, it is worth watching for the lush cinematography by John Alcott and its memorable moments, of which there are admittedly quite a few. Rated PG for brief nudity and violence.

1975 183 minutes

BAY BOY, THE

★★★★½

DIRECTOR: Daniel Petrie

CAST: Liv Ullmann, Kiefer Sutherland, Robert Taylor, Joe MacPherson, Kevin McKenzie, Iris Currie, Francis MacNeil, Michael Egyes, Mary Mackinnon

The story of a brief period in an adolescent boy's life while growing up in a small mining town on the Nova Scotia coast during the mid-1930s, this film develops the character, including the sexual awakening, guilt, and terror, of Donald Campbell (Kiefer Sutherland). Liv Ullmann is well cast as Donald's mother. Young Donald, an extremely fine student, is encouraged by his mother to enter the priesthood. Donald is much too interested in exploring his growing (yet still quite naive) interest in young ladies. Donald becomes the sole witness to a tragic murder and is forced to endure in silence the knowledge that the murderer is behind virtually every step he takes.

1985 104 minutes

BAYOU ROMANCE

★½

DIRECTOR: Alan Myerson

CAST: Annie Potts, Michael Ansara, Paul Rossill, Barbara Horan, Michael Durrell, Eugene Jackson

Louis Jourdan plays host to this low-budget Romantic Theatre entry. In it, Lily (played by Annie Potts), a successful artist, inherits a Louisiana plantation. There, she is pursued by a handsome, well-educated gypsy (Michael Ansara) as well as a scheming doctor. The sets leave something to be desired but are on par with the plot and dialogue. Avoid if possible! Not rated but has no offensive language or nudity.

1982 105 minutes

BEACHCOMBER, THE

★★★

DIRECTOR: Erich Pommer

CAST: Charles Laughton, Elsa Lanchester, Tyrone Guthrie, Robert Newton

This Somerset Maugham story of a dissolute South Seas beachcomber and the lady missionary who reforms him is sculptor's clay in the expert dramatic hands of Charles Laughton and Elsa Lanchester. He is delightful as the shiftless, conniving bum; she is clever and captivating as his Bible-toting nemesis. There's a scene at a bar that is Charles Laughton at his wily, eye-rolling, blustering best.

1938 B & W 80 minutes

BECKET

★★★★

DIRECTOR: Peter Glenville

CAST: Richard Burton, Peter O'Toole, Martita Hunt, Pamela Brown

Magnificently acted spectacle of the stormy relationship between England's King Henry II (Peter O'Toole) and his friend and nemesis Archbishop Thomas Becket (Richard Burton). This visually stimulating historical pageant, set in twelfth-century England, garnered Oscar nominations for both its protagonists.

1964 148 minutes

BECKY SHARP

★★½

DIRECTOR: Rouben Mamoulian

CAST: Miriam Hopkins, Frances Dee, Cedric Hardwicke, Billie Burke, Alison Skipworth, Nigel Bruce

Well-mounted historical drama of a callous young woman who lives for social success is lovely to look at in its original three-strip Technicolor. Fine performances by a veteran cast bolster this first sound screen adaptation of Thackeray's *Vanity Fair*, and director Rouben Mamoulian shows his famous style and fluidity with the new color cameras. Title player Miriam Hopkins was at this point in her career at the top of the industry and considered by many (especially herself) to be a serious rival to Bette Davis, Katharine Hepburn, etc.

1935 83 minutes

BEDFORD INCIDENT, THE

★★★

DIRECTOR: James B. Harris
CAST: Richard Widmark, Sidney Poitier, Martin Balsam, Wally Cox, Eric Portman

A battle of wits aboard a U.S. destroyer tracking Soviet submarines off Greenland during the Cold War. Richard Widmark is a skipper with an obsession to hunt and hound a particular sub. A conflict develops between the captain and Sidney Poitier, a cocky magazine reporter along for the ride.

1965 B & W 102 minutes

BEGUILED, THE

★★★★

DIRECTOR: Don Siegel
CAST: Clint Eastwood, Geraldine Page, Jo Ann Harris

An atmospheric, daring change of pace for director Don Siegel (*Dirty Harry*) and star Clint Eastwood, this production features the squinty-eyed actor as a wounded Yankee soldier taken in by the head (Geraldine Page) of a girls' school. He becomes the catalyst for incidents of jealousy and hatred among its inhabitants, and this leads to a startling, unpredictable conclusion. Rated R.

1971 109 minutes

BEHOLD A PALE HORSE

★

DIRECTOR: Fred Zinnemann
CAST: Gregory Peck, Anthony Quinn, Omar Sharif

Gregory Peck is miscast in this slow, talky, vague drama of a Loyalist holdout in post–Civil War Spain who continues to harass the Franco regime. Everyone tries hard, but the film steadily sinks.

1963 118 minutes

BELFAST ASSASSIN

★★½

DIRECTOR: Lawrence Gordon Clark
CAST: Derek Thompson, Ray Lonnen, Margaret Shevlin, Gil Brailey, Benjamin Whitrow

This film, about an IRA hit man and a British antiterrorist who is ordered to track down the Irish assassin on his own turf, could have used a clipper-happy editor; the same statement could have been said in much less than two hours plus. The film takes a pro-IRA stand, yet is open-minded enough to see the other side of the story without resorting to self-righteouness. Not rated, but the equivalent of a PG for sex, violence, and profanity.

1982 130 minutes

BELIZAIRE THE CAJUN

★★★★

DIRECTOR: Glen Pitre
CAST: Armand Assante, Gail Youngs, Michael Schoeffling, Stephen McHattie, Will Patton

Belizaire the Cajun is a film that is atmospheric in the best sense of the word. The Louisiana bayou of the 1850s is richly re-created in a cadence of texture and deep, dark swampland colors, along with the rhythms of Cajun accents and full-bodied folk music (score by

Michael Doucet). Armand Assante is Belizaire, an herbal doctor who finds himself in a mess of trouble because of his affection for his childhood sweetheart and his efforts to save a friend from persecution. Assante's Belizaire is an earthy charmer and a bit of a comic, and the actor makes him warm and engaging.

1986 114 minutes

BELL JAR, THE

★★★

DIRECTOR: Larry Peerce
CAST: Marilyn Hassett, Julie Harris, Anne Jackson, Barbara Barrie, Robert Klein, Donna Mitchell

Based on the novel by Sylvia Plath about the mental breakdown of an overachiever in the world of big business in the 1950s, this film has a strong lead performance by Marilyn Hassett and thoughtful direction by her husband, Larry Peerce. But the overriding melancholy of the subject matter makes it difficult to watch. Barbara Barrie is also memorable in a key supporting role. Rated R.

1979 107 minutes

BELLS OF ST. MARY'S, THE

★★★★½

DIRECTOR: Leo McCarey
CAST: Bing Crosby, Ingrid Bergman, Ruth Donnelly

An effective sequel to *Going My Way,* also directed by Leo McCarey, this film has Bing Crosby returning as the modern-minded priest once again up against a headstrong opponent, Mother Superior (played by Ingrid Bergman). While not as memorable as his encounter with hard-headed older priest Barry Fitzgerald in the first film, this relationship—and the movie as a whole—does have its viewing rewards.

1945 B & W 126 minutes

BEST LITTLE GIRL IN THE WORLD, THE

★★★★½

DIRECTOR: Sam O'Steen
CAST: Jennifer Jason Leigh, Charles Durning, Eva Marie Saint, Jason Miller

This gut-wrenching teleplay about a girl, portrayed by Jennifer Jason Leigh (*Fast Times at Ridgemont High, Eyes of a Stranger, Grandview U.S.A.*), who suffers from anorexia nervosa pulls no punches; some of the drama is hard to take, but if you can make it through the film's end, you'll feel rewarded. This was originally an after-school special. The entire cast turn in great performances, especially Leigh, who proves she is better than the teen exploitation films that are (hopefully) behind her. Not rated, but the equivalent of a PG for intense drama.

1986 90 minutes

BEST YEARS OF OUR LIVES, THE

★★★★★

DIRECTOR: William Wyler
CAST: Myrna Loy, Fredric March, Teresa Wright, Dana Andrews, Virginia Mayo, Harold Russell, Cathy O'Donnell

What happens when the fighting ends and warriors return home is the basis of this eloquent, compassionate film. Old master William Wyler takes his time and guides a superb group of players through a tangle of postwar emotional conflicts. Harold Russell's first scene has lost none of its impact. Keep in mind World War II had just ended when this film debuted.

1946 B & W 170 minutes

BETRAYAL

★★★★★

DIRECTOR: David Jones

CAST: Jeremy Irons, Ben Kingsley, Patricia Hodge

Harold Pinter's play about the slow death of a marriage has been turned into an intelligent and innovative film that begins with the affair breaking apart and follows it backward to the beginning. Stars Ben Kingsley (*Gandhi*), Jeremy Irons (*Moonlighting*), and Patricia Hodge are superb. Rated R for profanity.

1983 95 minutes

BETSY, THE

★

DIRECTOR: Daniel Petrie

CAST: Laurence Olivier, Tommy Lee Jones, Robert Duvall, Katharine Ross, Lesley-Anne Down, Jane Alexander

Here is a classic example of how to waste loads of talent and money. The Harold Robbins novel about a wealthy family in the auto manufacturing business was trashy to start with, but after Hollywood gets done with it, not even the likes of Laurence Olivier can save this debacle. The cast is hopelessly lost in this mess. Rated R.

1978 125 minutes

BETWEEN FRIENDS

★★½

DIRECTOR: Lou Antonio

CAST: Elizabeth Taylor, Carol Burnett, Barbara Rush, Stephen Young, Henry Ramer

Two middle-aged divorcées meet and gradually form a life-sustaining friendship. This made-for-cable feature occasionally gets mired in melodramatic tendencies, but the dynamic performances of its two charismatic stars make it well worth watching. Unrated.

1983 100 minutes

BEYOND A REASONABLE DOUBT

★★★

DIRECTOR: Fritz Lang

CAST: Dana Andrews, Joan Fontaine, Sidney Blackmer, Philip Bourneuf, Shepperd Strudwick, Dan Seymour

To reveal the faults of the justice system, novelist Dana Andrews allows himself to be incriminated in a murder. The plan is to reveal his innocence and discredit capital punishment at the last minute. But the one man who can exonerate him is killed. As this plot develops, a variety of submerged elements slowly surfaces to make this film far more than just one of suspense. Don't expect surprise, but shock!

1956 B & W 80 minutes

BEYOND THE LIMIT

★★½

DIRECTOR: John MacKenzie

CAST: Michael Caine, Richard Gere, Bob Hoskins, Elpedia Carrillo

A dull, unconvincing adaptation of *The Honorary Consul*, Graham Greene's novel about love and betrayal in an Argentinian town, stars Michael Caine as a kidnapped diplomat and Richard Gere as the doctor in love with his wife. It'll take you beyond your limit. Rated R.

1983 103 minutes

BEYOND THE VALLEY OF THE DOLLS

DIRECTOR: Russ Meyer

CAST: Dolly Red, Cynthia Myers, Marcia McBroom

Like all other films by Russ Meyer, *Dolls* dabbles in petty political ideas and contains enough

1960s hip talk to make you lose your lunch. The folks down at Fox must have been on mushrooms to back this one; it's like a bad acid trip, man. This was rated X when it came out, but by today's standards it's an R for gratuitous nudity and profanity.

1970 109 minutes

BIBLE, THE

★★★

DIRECTOR: John Huston

CAST: Michael Parks, Ulla Bergryd, Richard Harris, John Huston, Ava Gardner

An overblown all-star treatment of five of the early stories in the Old Testament. Director John Huston gives this movie the feel of a Cecil B. De Mille spectacle, but there is little human touch to any of the stories. This expensively mounted production forgets that in the Bible, individual accomplishments are equally relevant to grandeur.

1966 174 minutes

BIG CHILL, THE

★★★★½

DIRECTOR: Lawrence Kasdan

CAST: Tom Berenger, William Hurt, Glenn Close, Jeff Goldblum, Jo Beth Williams, Kevin Kline, Mary Kay Place, Meg Tilly

As with John Sayles's superb *Return of the Secaucus 7*, this equally impressive and thoroughly enjoyable film by writer-director Lawrence Kasdan (*Body Heat*) concerns a weekend reunion of old friends, all of whom have gone on to varied lifestyles after once being united in the hip, committed 1960s. It features a who's-who of today's hot young stars as the friends who find they must face the maxim "Never trust anyone over thirty" and reassess its validity, especially since they are now in that age bracket. Rated R for nudity and profanity.

1983 103 minutes

BIG WEDNESDAY

★★

DIRECTOR: John Milius

CAST: Jan-Michael Vincent, Gary Busey, William Katt, Lee Purcell, Patti D'Arbanville

Only nostalgic surfers with more than a little patience will enjoy this ode to the beach set and that perfect wave by writer-director John Milius (*Conan the Barbarian*). Rated PG.

1978 120 minutes

BIG WHEEL, THE

★★½

DIRECTOR: Edward Ludwig

CAST: Mickey Rooney, Thomas Mitchell, Spring Byington, Allen Jenkins, Michael O'Shea, Mary Hatcher

Smart-mouthed Mickey Rooney rises from garage mechanic to champion racing-car driver, losing respect and friends along the way in this well-worn story worn thinner by a poor script and poorer direction. Spring Byington is Rooney's anguished mother and Michael O'Shea is the rival whose respect he earns while redeeming himself driving in the Indianapolis 500. Of course he gets the girl! More than 20 of the film's 92 minutes are given over to ear-splitting scenes of high-speed racing.

1949 B & W 92 minutes

BILL

★★★★½

DIRECTOR: Anthony Page

CAST: Mickey Rooney, Dennis Quaid, Largo Woodruff

Extremely moving drama based on the real-life experiences of Bill Sackter, a retarded adult forced to leave the mental institution that has been his home for the past forty-fiveyears. Mickey Rooney won an Emmy for his excellent portrayal of Bill. Dennis Quaid plays a filmmaker who offers kindness and employment to Bill as he tries to cope with life on the "outside." Unrated.

1981 100 minutes

BILL: ON HIS OWN

★★★½

DIRECTOR: Anthony Page
CAST: Mickey Rooney, Helen Hunt, Teresa Wright, Dennis Quaid, Largo Woodruff

This is the sequel to the 1981 drama *Bill*. Mickey Rooney continues his role as Bill Sackter, a mentally retarted adult forced to live on his own after spending forty-six years in an institution. Helen Hunt co-stars as the college student who tutors him. It doesn't quite have the emotional impact that *Bill* carried, but it's still good.

1983 104 minutes

BILLY BUDD

★★★½

DIRECTOR: Peter Ustinov
CAST: Terence Stamp, Robert Ryan, Peter Ustinov

Herman Melville's brooding, allegorical novel of the overpowering of the innocent is set against a backdrop of life on an eighteenth-century British warship. The plight of a young sailor subjected to the treacherous whims of his ship's tyrannical first mate is well-acted throughout. It is powerful filmmaking and succeeds in leaving its audience unsettled and questioning.

1962 B & W 112 minutes

BILLY LIAR

★★★★

DIRECTOR: John Schlesinger
CAST: Tom Courtenay, Julie Christie, Finlay Currie, Ethel Griffies, Mona Washbourne

Poignant slices of English middle-class life are served expertly in this finely played story of a lazy young man who escapes dulling routine by retreating into fantasy. The eleven minutes Julie Christie is on-screen are electric and worth the whole picture.

1963 B & W 96 minutes

BIRDMAN OF ALCATRAZ

★★★★

DIRECTOR: John Frankenheimer
CAST: Burt Lancaster, Karl Malden, Thelma Ritter, Telly Savalas

In one of his best screen performances, Burt Lancaster plays Robert Sroud, the prisoner who became a world-renowned authority on birds.

1962 B & W 143 minutes

BIRDY

★★★★½

DIRECTOR: Alan Parker
CAST: Matthew Modine, Nicolas Cage, John Harkins, Sandy Baron, Karen Young, Bruno Kirby

Matthew Modine and Nicolas Cage give unforgettable performances in this dark, disturbing, yet somehow uplifting study of an odd young man named Birdy (Modine) from South Philadelphia who wants to be a bird. That way he can fly away from all his troubles—which worsen manifold after a traumatic tour of duty in Vietnam. Based on the novel by William Wharton, this is a multi-level and rewarding work directed with uncommon restraint and insight by Alan Parker. Rated R for violence, nudity, and profanity.

1985 120 minutes

BIRTH OF A NATION, THE

★★★★

DIRECTOR: D. W. Griffith
CAST: Lillian Gish, Mae Marsh, Henry B. Walthall, Miriam Cooper

Videotape will probably be the only medium in which you will ever see this landmark silent classic. D. W. Griffith's epic saga of the American Civil War and its aftermath is today considered too racist in its glorification of the Ku Klux Klan ever to be touched by television or revival theaters. This is filmdom's most important milestone (the first to tell a cohesive story) but should only be seen by those emotionally prepared for its disturbing point of view.

1915 B & W 158 minutes

BITCH, THE

DIRECTOR: Gerry O'Hara
CAST: Joan Collins, Kenneth Haigh, Michael Coby

Joan Collins has the title role in this fiasco, an adaptation of sister Jackie Collins's book. Unfortunately, much was lost when transferred to the screen. It's about two "users," Fontaine (Collins) and Niko (Michael Coby), who find each other when she's in need of money because her disco almost goes under and he's fencing stolen jewels for the mob. This film spends too much time showing Joan Collins (and her lady friends) jumping into bed with younger men and then rejecting them. Only worth watching if you want to see Collins in the buff before her "Dynasty" days. Heavy British accents make the dialogue hard to follow. Rated R.

1979 93 minutes

BITTER HARVEST

★★★★

DIRECTOR: Roger Young
CAST: Ron Howard, Art Carney, Richard Dysart

In this made-for-television film based on a true incident, Ron Howard gives an excellent performance as an at-first panicky and then take-charge farmer whose dairy farm herd becomes sick and begins dying. His battle against bureaucracy, as he earnestly tries to find out the cause of the illness (chemicals in the feed), provides for scary, close-to-home drama. Good supporting cast.

1981 104 minutes

BLACK FURY

★★★★

DIRECTOR: Michael Curtiz
CAST: Paul Muni, Karen Morley, William Gargan, Barton MacLane

Paul Muni is excellent as Joe Radek, an apolitical eastern European immigrant coal miner who unwittingly falls into the middle of a labor dispute that ends up leaving the impoverished miners out of work. The acting is good, but the film doen't reach its happy ending in a logical manner, so things just seem to fall into place without any reason.

1935 B & W 95 minutes

BLACK LIKE ME

★★★

DIRECTOR: Carl Lerner
CAST: James Whitmore, Roscoe Lee Browne, Will Geer, Sorrell Booke

Based on the book by John Griffin, this film poses the question: What happens when a white journalist takes a drug that turns his skin black? The interesting premise almost works. James Whitmore plays the reporter, who wishes to experience racism firsthand. Somewhat provocative at its initial release, but by today's standards, a lot of the punch is missing.

1964 B & W 107 minutes

BLACK MAGIC

★★½

DIRECTOR: Gregory Ratoff

CAST: Orson Welles, Akim Tamiroff, Nancy Guild, Raymond Burr, Frank Latimore

Orson Welles revels in the role of famous eighteenth-century charlatan Count Cagliostro—born Joseph Balsamo, a peasant with imagination and a flair for magic, hypnosis, and the power of superstition. The story is of his tempestuous life and career, and Cagliostro's attempt to gain influence and clout in Italy using his strange and sinister talents. The star co-directed (without credit) and enjoyed a busman's holiday performing legerdemain and other magic, an off-screen hobby for which he had considerable ability. Raymond Burr is a long way from Perry Mason in this one. Though a handsome film, under analysis it shakes down to a rather amateurish effort.

1949 B & W 105 minutes

BLACK MARBLE, THE

★★★

DIRECTOR: Harold Becker

CAST: Paula Prentiss, Harry Dean Stanton, Robert Foxworth

A Los Angeles cop (Robert Foxworth) and his new partner (Paula Prentiss) attempt to capture a dog snatcher (Harry Dean Stanton) who is demanding a high ransom from a wealthy dog lover. Along the way, they fall in love. Based on Joseph Wambaugh's novel. Directed by Harold Becker (*The Onion Field*). Overlooked at the time of its release, but well worth the viewer's time. Rated PG—language, some violence.

1980 110 minutes

BLACK NARCISSUS

★★★½

DIRECTOR: Michael Powell

CAST: Deborah Kerr, Jean Simmons, David Farrar, Flora Robson, Sabu

Worldly temptations, including those of the flesh, create many difficulties for a group of nuns starting a mission in the Himalayas. Superb photography makes this early postwar British effort a visual delight. Unfortunately, key plot elements in this unusual drama were cut from the American prints by censors.

1947 99 minutes

BLACKMAIL

★★★

DIRECTOR: Alfred Hitchcock

CAST: Anny Ondra, Sara Allgood, John Longden, Charles Paton, Donald Calthrop, Cyril Ritchard

Hitchock's first sound film stands up well when viewed today and was responsible for pushing Great Britain into the world film market. Many bits of film business that were to become Hitchcock trademarks are evident in this film, including the first of his cameo appearances. Story of a woman who faces the legal system as well as a blackmailer for murdering an attacker in self-defense was originally shot as a silent film but partially reshot and converted into England's first sound release in an effort to compete with American imports. Future Captain Hook Cyril Ritchard essays an early role in this film along with respected stage actress Sara Allgood, still years away from her contract with Twentieth Century Fox and classic films like *How Green Was My Valley* and *The Lodger*.

1929 B & W 86 minutes

BLESS THE BEASTS AND THE CHILDREN

★

DIRECTOR: Stanley Kramer
CAST: Billy Mumy, Barry Robins, Miles Chapin, Ken Swofford, Jesse White, Vanessa Brown

Stanley Kramer's heavy-handed allegory is about as subtle as a brick through a plate-glass window. A group of misfit teenagers (led by Billy Mumy, of "Lost in Space" fame) at a western ranch-resort rebel against their moronic counselors to save a nearby herd of buffalo from being slaughtered. This knee-jerk liberal treatise is a virtual textbook on excess: the kids are all sensitive and thoughtful, the adults all bigoted and brutal, and the storyline consistently overwrought. A major waste of a good cast and an intriguing premise. Rated R for explicit violence.

1972 109 minutes

BLIND HUSBANDS

★★★

DIRECTOR: Erich Von Stroheim
CAST: Sam de Grasse, Francis Billington, Erich Von Stroheim, Gibson Gowland, Fay Holderness

A doctor and his wife are in an Alpine village so that he can do some mountain climbing. His wife falls prey to the attentions of a suave Austrian army officer who seduces her. The doctor and the officer go climbing together. In addition to directing and starring, Erich Von Stroheim adapted the screenplay from his own story and designed the sets. A shocker when first released. Silent.

1919 B & W 98 minutes

BLONDE VENUS

★

DIRECTOR: Josef von Sternberg
CAST: Marlene Dietrich, Cary Grant, Herbert Marshall

This is a rambling, incomprehensible piece of glitzy fluff. Only diehard fans of Marlene Dietrich will find it worth watching. In this, the least interesting of her seven collaborations with director Josef von Sternberg, we witness Miss Dietrich descend from being a loving wife to becoming involved in all sorts of distasteful activities because she is required to pay the medical costs for her sick husband. It is all quite ludicrous.

1932 B & W 90 minutes

BLOOD AND SAND

★★★

DIRECTOR: Rouben Mamoulian
CAST: Tyrone Power, Rita Hayworth, Anthony Quinn, Linda Darnell, Nazimova, John Carradine

The "Moment of Truth" is not always just before the matador places his sword, as Tyrone Power learns in this classic story of a poor boy who rises to fame in the bullring. Linda Darnell loves him, Rita Hayworth leads him on, in this colorful remake of a 1922 Valentino starrer.

1941 B & W 123 minutes

BLOOD TIES

★

DIRECTOR: Giacomo Battiato
CAST: Brad Davis, Tony LoBianco, Vincent Spano, Barbara de Rossi, Ricky Tognazzi, Michael Gazzo

Brad Davis and Tony LoBianco are wasted in this pointless ripoff of *The Godfather*. Davis is an innocent American engineer blackmailed into assassinating his cousin, an anticrime justice in Sicily. Bad writing and bad direction are the culprits, and Davis is not on screen enough to carry the film. Not rated, but contains strong language, violence, and nudity.

1987 98 minutes

BLOODBROTHERS

★★★½

DIRECTOR: Robert Mulligan
CAST: Richard Gere, Paul Sorvino, Tony LoBianco, Marilu Henner

Richard Gere and Marilu Henner take top honors in this drama. Plot revolves around a family of construction workers and the son (Gere) who wants to do something else with his life. Rated R.

1978 116 minutes

BLOODLINE

DIRECTOR: Terence Young
CAST: Audrey Hepburn, Ben Gazzara, James Mason, Omar Sharif

This is an inexcusably repulsive montage of bad taste, predictability, and incoherence. Fans of Audrey Hepburn will be sickened to see her in such a travesty. Rated R for graphic sex scenes.

1979 116 minutes

BLUE COLLAR

★★★★½

DIRECTOR: Paul Schrader
CAST: Richard Pryor, Harvey Keitel, Yaphet Kotto

This film delves into the underbelly of the auto industry by focusing on the fears, frustrations, and suppressed anger of three factory workers, superbly played by Richard Pryor, Harvey Keitel, and Yaphet Kotto. It is the social comment and intense drama that make this a highly effective and memorable film. Good music, too. Rated R for violence, sex, nudity, and profanity.

1978 114 minutes

BLUE LAGOON, THE

★★½

DIRECTOR: Randal Kleiser
CAST: Brooke Shields, Christopher Atkins, Leo McKern, William Daniels

Two things save *The Blue Lagoon* from being a complete waste: Nestor Almendros's beautiful cinematography and the hilarious dialogue. Unfortunately, the laughs are unintentional. The screenplay is a combination of *Swiss Family Robinson* and the story of Adam and Eve, focusing on the growing love and sexuality of two children stranded on a South Sea island. Rated R for nudity and suggested sex.

1980 101 minutes

BLUE SKIES AGAIN

★★

DIRECTOR: Richard Michaels
CAST: Harry Hamlin, Robyn Barto, Mimi Rogers, Kenneth McMillan, Dana Elcar

A sure-fielding, solid-hitting prospect tries to break into the lineup of a minor league team. There's just one problem: The determined ballplayer is a female. This "triumph of the underdog" story, set on a baseball diamond, aims at the skies but is nothing more than a routine grounder. Rated PG.

1983 96 minutes

BLUME IN LOVE

★★★★

DIRECTOR: Paul Mazursky
CAST: George Segal, Susan Anspach, Kris Kristofferson, Marsha Mason, Shelley Winters

Sort of the male version of *An Unmarried Woman*, this Paul Mazursky film is the heartrending, sometimes shocking tale of a lawyer (George Segal) who can't believe his wife (Susan Anspach) doesn't love him anymore. He tries everything to win her back (including rape), and the result is a drama the viewer won't soon forget. Superb performances by Segal, Anspach, and Kris Kristofferson (as the wife's new beau) help immensely. Strong stuff, but memorable. Rated R for suggested sex, profanity, and violence.

1973 117 minutes

BOBBY DEERFIELD

★★★½

DIRECTOR: Sydney Pollack
CAST: Al Pacino, Marthe Keller, Romolo Valli

In this film, a racing driver (Al Pacino) becomes obsessed with the cause of how a competitor was seriously injured in an accident on the track. In a visit to the hospitalized driver, he meets a strange lady (Marthe Keller) and has an affair. Adapted by Oscar winner Alvin Sargent from Erich Remarque's novel *Heaven Has No Favorites*. Rated PG.

1977 124 minutes

BODY AND SOUL (ORIGINAL)

★★★★★

DIRECTOR: Robert Rossen
CAST: John Garfield, Lilli Palmer, Hazel Brooks, Anne Revere, William Conrad

The best boxing film ever, this is an allegorical work that covers everything from the importance of personal honor to corruption in politics. It details the story of a fighter (John Garfield) who'll do anything to get to the top—and does, with tragic results. Great performances, gripping drama, and stark realism make this a must-see.

1947 B & W 104 minutes

BODY AND SOUL (REMAKE)

★★★

DIRECTOR: George Bowers
CAST: Leon Isaac Kennedy, Jayne Kennedy, Perry Lang

Okay remake of the 1947 boxing classic. It's not original, deep, or profound, but entertaining, and for a movie like this, that's enough. However, the original, with John Garfield, is better. Rated R for violence and profanity.

1981 100 minutes

BODY HEAT

★★★★½

DIRECTOR: Lawrence Kasdan
CAST: William Hurt, Kathleen Turner, Richard Crenna, Mickey Rourke

This is a classic piece of *film noir*; full of suspense, characterization, atmosphere, and sexuality. Lawrence Kasdan (*Raiders of the Lost Ark* screenwriter) makes his directorial debut with this top-flight 1940s-style entertainment about a lustful romance between an attorney (William Hurt) and a married woman (Kathleen Turner) that leads to murder. Rated R because of nudity, sex, and murder.

1981 113 minutes

BOGIE

★★½

DIRECTOR: Vincent Sherman
CAST: Kevin O'Connor, Kathryn Harrold, Ann Wedgeworth, Patricia Barry

Boring biography of Humphrey Bogart unconvincingly enacted by Bogie and Bacall look-alikes. Too much time is spent on the drinking and temper problems of Bogie's third wife, Mayo Methot, and not enough time is spent on Lauren Bacall. Kathryn Harrold, as Bacall, is so bad, however, that it's probably a blessing her part is small.

1980 100 minutes

BOLERO

DIRECTOR: John Derek
CAST: Bo Derek, George Kennedy, Andrea Occhipinti, Ana Obregon, Olivia D'Abo, Greg Benson

Bo Derek stars in this simply awful soft-core porno flick as an American heiress in the 1920s who goes to Morocco in search of a real-life version of the passionate sheiks played by Rudolph Valentino in order to lose her virginity. She finds one, but he turns out to be a little lacking in the passion department. Next stop, Spain, and the bed of a sensitive bullfighter. What follows is indeed a lot of bull—it's stupid, boring, and amateurish. Unrated, the film has explicit sex, profanity, and nudity.

1984 106 minutes

BORN INNOCENT

★★★

DIRECTOR: Donald Wyre
CAST: Linda Blair, Kim Hunter, Joanna Miles

Rape with a broomstick marked this made-for-television film a shocker when first aired. The scene has been toned down, but the picture still penetrates with its searing story of cruelty in a juvenile detention home. Linda Blair does well as the runaway teenager. Joanna Miles is excellent as a compassionate teacher whose heart lies with her charges. It's strong stuff.

1974 100 minutes

BORN TO KILL

★★★½

DIRECTOR: Robert Wise
CAST: Lawrence Tierney, Claire Trevor, Walter Slezak, Elisha Cook Jr., Audrey Long, Phillip Terry

Tough film about two bad apples whose star-crossed love brings them both nothing but grief is one of the best examples of American *film noir*. Lawrence Tierney's aggressive pursuit of his wife's sister (Claire Trevor) defies description. And his buddy Elisha Cook Jr. is no slouch either, especially when he sidles up to one of his intended victims, grins ingratiatingly, and remarks, "I'm a bad boy." Filled with location shots of San Francisco and the Bay Area, this hardboiled crime melodrama is an early surprise from director Robert Wise. It rates with low-budget classics like *Detour*, *Gun Crazy*, and *Dillinger* as the best of the no-way-out films so popular during the mid-1940s to the 1950s.

1947 B & W 97 minutes

BOSTONIANS, THE

★★★

DIRECTOR: James Ivory
CAST: Christopher Reeve, Vanessa Redgrave, Jessica Tandy, Madeleine Potter, Nancy Marchand, Wesley Addy, Barbara Bryne, Linda Hunt, Charles McCaughan, Nancy New, John Van Ness, Wallace Shawn

A visually striking but dry production from Merchant Ivory Productions. Most of the sparks of conflict come not from the tortured love affair between Christopher Reeve and Madeleine Potter or the main theme of women's fight for equality, but from the few scenes of direct confrontation between Reeve and Vanessa Redgrave. Redgrave delivers another fascinating character study that draws you to the screen. Costumes and settings are, as always in these productions, lavish and rich. The setting is Boston during the Centennial.

A good "quiet-evening-at-home-by-the-fire-type" movie.
1984 120 minutes

BOUND FOR GLORY

★★★★

DIRECTOR: Hal Ashby
CAST: David Carradine, Ronny Cox, Melinda Dillon, Randy Quaid, Gail Strickland, Ji-Tu Cumbuka, John Lehne

David Carradine had one of the best roles of his career as singer-composer Woody Guthrie. Film focuses on the depression years when Guthrie rode the rails across America. Director Hal Ashby explores the lives of those hit hardest during those times. Haskell Wexler won the Oscar for his beautiful cinematography. Rated PG.
1976 147 minutes

BOY IN BLUE, THE

★★★

DIRECTOR: Charles Jarrott
CAST: Nicolas Cage, Christopher Plummer, Cynthia Dale, David Naughton

Nice little screen biography of Ned Hanlan (Nicolas Cage), the famed Canadian lad who owned the sport of international sculling (rowing) for ten years during the end of the nineteenth century. Although the picture plays like a thin retread of *Rocky*—particularly with respect to its music—the result is no less inspirational. Cage makes Hanlan larger than life, which is appropriate for legends, and Cynthia Dale is quite appealing as his upper-class lover. Christopher Plummer, who has made a career of oily villains, makes a suitably sinister foil. Inexplicably rated R for very brief nudity and coarse language.
1986 97 minutes

BOY IN THE PLASTIC BUBBLE, THE

★

DIRECTOR: Randal Kleiser
CAST: John Travolta, Glynnis O'Connor, Ralph Bellamy, Robert Reed, Diana Hyland, Buzz Aldrin

John Travolta has his hands full in this significantly altered television adaptation of the boy who, because of an immunity deficiency, must spend every breathing moment in a sealed environment. Vapid stuff needlessly mired with sci-fi jargon and an embarrassing romance with Glynnis O'Connor. Considering the heroic struggles of the true David (who was much younger), this film is a grotesque insult. Unrated.
1976 100 minutes

BOY WHO COULD FLY, THE

★★★★

DIRECTOR: Nick Castle
CAST: Lucy Deakins, Jay Underwood, Bonnie Bedelia, Fred Savage, Colleen Dewhurst, Fred Gwynne, Mindy Cohn

Writer-director Nick Castle has created a marvelous motion picture which speaks to the dreamer in all of us. His heroine, Milly (Lucy Deakins), is a newcomer to a small town where her neighbor, Eric (Jay Underwood), neither speaks nor responds to other people. All he does is sit on his roof and pretend to fly. The authorities want to put him away, but Milly has other ideas. How these two outsiders overcome all odds is a story the entire family can enjoy. The performances are wonderful and the film leaves one feeling lighter than air—just like the title character. Rated PG for dramatic intensity.
1986 114 minutes

BOY WITH GREEN HAIR, THE

★★★

DIRECTOR: Joseph Losey
CAST: Dean Stockwell, Robert Ryan, Barbara Hale, Pat O'Brien

A young war orphan's hair changes color, makes him a social outcast, and brings a variety of bigots and narrow minds out of the woodwork in this food-for-thought fable. The medium is the message in this one.

1948 82 minutes

BOYS IN THE BAND, THE

★★★

DIRECTOR: William Friedkin
CAST: Kenneth Nelson, Peter White, Leonard Frey, Cliff Gorman

Widely acclaimed film about nine men who attend a birthday party and end up exposing their lives and feelings to one another in the course of the night. Eight of the men are gay; one is straight. One of the first American films to deal honestly with the subject of homosexuality. Sort of a large-scale *My Dinner with André* with the whole film shot on one set. Rated R.

1970 119 minutes

BOYS NEXT DOOR, THE

★★★

DIRECTOR: Penelope Spheeris
CAST: Charlie Sheen, Maxwell Caulfield, Hank Garrett, Patti D'Arbanville, Christopher McDonald, Moon Zappa

This story of two alienated teenage youths, Charlie Sheen and Maxwell Caulfield, going on a killing spree in Los Angeles, makes for some tense film as filmgoing viewing. Having been rejected by their peers, Sheen and Caulfield decide to go to L.A. for the weekend before graduation. Once in the city, things turn ugly as one violent encounter spawns another. Beware: This one is extremely graphic in its depiction of violence. Rated R.

1985 88 minutes

BREAKFAST AT TIFFANY'S

★★★★

DIRECTOR: Blake Edwards
CAST: Audrey Hepburn, George Peppard, Patricia Neal, Buddy Ebsen, Mickey Rooney, Martin Balsam

An offbeat yet tender love story of a New York writer and a fey party girl. Strong performances are turned in by George Peppard and Audrey Hepburn. Hepburn's Holly Golightly is a masterful creation that blends the sophistication of her job as a Manhattan "escort" with the childish country girl of her roots. Henry Mancini's score is justly famous, as it creates much of the mood for this wistful story.

1961 115 minutes

BREATHLESS (REMAKE)

DIRECTOR: Jim McBride
CAST: Richard Gere, Valerie Kaprisky, Art Metrano, John P. Ryan

In this rambling, repulsive remake of Jean-Luc Godard's 1961 French film classic, Richard Gere plays a car thief hunted by police, and Valerie Kaprisky is the college student who is both attracted and repelled by the danger he represents. Watching these two aimless, amoral jerks fooling around for nearly two hours is not the proverbial good time at the movies. It's boring. Rated R for sex, nudity, profanity, and violence.

1983 100 minutes

BRIAN'S SONG

★★★★★

DIRECTOR: Buzz Kulik

CAST: James Caan, Billy Dee Williams, Jack Warden, Judy Pace, Shelley Fabares

This is one of the best movies ever made originally for television. James Caan is Brian Piccolo, a running back for football's Chicago Bears. His friendship for superstar Gale Sayers (Billy Dee Williams) becomes a mutually stimulating rivalry on the field and inspirational strength when Brian is felled by cancer. As with any quality film that deals with death, this movie is buoyant with life and warmth. Rated G.

1970 73 minutes

BRIDGE OF SAN LUIS REY, THE

★★½

DIRECTOR: Rowland V. Lee

CAST: Lynn Bari, Nazimova, Louis Calhern, Akim Tamiroff, Francis Lederer, Blanche Yurka, Donald Woods

Five people meet death when an old Peruvian rope bridge collapses. This snail's-pace, moody version of Thornton Wilder's fatalistic 1920s novel traces their lives. Not too hot, and neither was the 1929 version.

1944 B & W 85 minutes

BRIDGE TO NOWHERE

★★½

DIRECTOR: Ian Mune

CAST: Bruno Lawrence, Alison Routledge, Margaret Umbers, Philip Gordon

When five street-wise city kids head to the rough-and-rugged country for a fun-filled weekend, they are not prepared to end up fighting for their lives. Once they trespass on the land of an extremely vicious and violent man (Bruno Lawrence), they are forced to fight for survival. Made in the tradition of *Deliverance* and *Southern Comfort*. Parental discretion advised.

1986 87 minutes

BROKEN BLOSSOMS

★★★½

DIRECTOR: D. W. Griffith

CAST: Lillian Gish, Richard Barthelmess, Donald Crisp, Edmund Peil, Arthur Howard, George Beranger, Norman Selby "Kid McCoy"

The tragic story of a young Chinese boy's unselfish love for a cruelly mistreated white girl. Lillian Gish is heart-twisting as the girl; Richard Barthelmess's portrayal of the Chinese boy made him an overnight star. Donald Crisp, later famous in warm and sympathetic roles, is the unfortunate girl's evil tormentor. Also starring is the then-new soft-focus cinematography, scenes shot in mood-setting mist and fog, and the use of close-ups for emphasis and suspense. Trivia note: This is the first film made and released by United Artists. Silent.

1919 B & W 68 minutes

BROTHER SUN, SISTER MOON

★★★★

DIRECTOR: Franco Zeffirelli

CAST: Graham Faulkner, Judi Bowker, Alec Guinness

Alec Guinness stars as the Pope in this movie about religious reformation. This film shows a young Francis of Assisi starting his own church. He confronts the Pope and rejects the extravagant and pompous ceremonies of the Catholic Church, preferring simple religious practices. Rated PG.

1973 121 minutes

BROTHERS KARAMAZOV, THE

★★★

DIRECTOR: Richard Brooks

CAST: Yul Brynner, Claire Bloom, Lee J. Cobb, Maria Schell,

Richard Basehart, William Shatner, Albert Salmi

Director Richard Brooks, who also scripted, and a fine cast work hard to give life to Russian novelist Fyodor Dostoyevsky's turgid account of the effect of the death of a domineering father on his disparate sons: a fun lover, a scholar, a religious zealot, and an epileptic. Studio promotion called it absorbing and exciting. It is, but only in flashes. In the long haul, it's like a train trip across Kansas at night.

1957 146 minutes

BRUBAKER

★★★½

DIRECTOR: Stuart Rosenberg
CAST: Robert Redford, Yaphet Kotto, Jane Alexander, Murray Hamilton

Robert Redford stars as Henry Brubaker, a reform-minded penologist who takes over a decrepit Ohio prison, only to discover the state prison system is even more rotten than its facilities. The film begins dramatically enough, with Redford arriving undercover at the prison, masquerading as one of the convicts. He witnesses cruel and unusual punishments, the wholesale theft of prison food, and the rape of a new inmate. After that, its dramatic impact lessens. Rated R.

1980 132 minutes

BUDDY SYSTEM, THE

★★

DIRECTOR: Glenn Jordan
CAST: Richard Dreyfuss, Susan Sarandon, Nancy Allen, Wil Weaton

In the middle of this movie, the would-be novelist (Richard Dreyfuss) takes his unbound manuscripts to the edge of the sea and lets the wind blow the pages away. He should have done the same thing with the screenplay for this mediocre romantic comedy. Dreyfuss is too good for this kind of slush. Perhaps because he won the best actor Oscar in 1977 for a similar kind of role (a would-be actor) in Neil Simon's *The Goodbye Girl*, the star thought he could repeat his success. Doesn't the poor guy know lightning rarely strikes twice in the same place? The plot is that old chestnut about a fatherless little kid (Wil Wheaton) who helps his mom (Susan Sarandon) and an eligible man (Dreyfuss) get together. Are you yawning yet? Rated PG for profanity.

1984 110 minutes

BURKE AND WILLS

★★

DIRECTOR: Grame Clifford
CAST: Jack Thompson, Nigel Travers, Greta Scacchi

Like most Australian period movies, this historical drama about a failed attempt to travel through the uncharted interior of 19th century Australia is meticulously produced. But the story follows the trip through the desert with numbling detail and it ends up being more exhausting than entertaining. It's also about 45 minutes too long. It's rated PG-13 for language and brief nudity.

1987 140 minutes

BURN!

★★★★

DIRECTOR: Gillo Pontecorvo
CAST: Marlon Brando, Evaristo Marquez, Renato Salvatori, Tom Lyons, Norman Hill

Marlon Brando's performance alone makes *Burn*! worth watching. Seldom has a star so vividly and memorably lived up to his promise as an acting great, and that's what makes this film, directed by Gillo Pontecarvo (*The Battle of Algiers*), a must-see. Brando plays Sir William Walker, an egotistical mercenary sent by the British to instigate a slave revolt on a Portuguese-controlled sugar-producing island. He succeeds all too well by turning José Dolores (Evaristo Marquez) into a powerful leader and soon finds himself back on the island, plotting the downfall of his Frankenstein monster. Rated PG.

1969 112 minutes

BURNING BED, THE

★★★★

DIRECTOR: Robert Greenwald

CAST: Farrah Fawcett, Paul LeMat, Richard Masur, Grace Zabriskie

Farrah Fawcett is remarkably good in this made-for-TV film based on a true story. She plays a woman reaching the breaking point with her abusive and brutish husband, well played by Paul LeMat. Fawcett not only proves she can act, but that she has the capacity to pull off a multilayered role. Believable from start to finish, this is a superior television film.

1985 105 minutes

BUS IS COMING, THE

★★★

DIRECTOR: Wendell J. Franklin

CAST: Mike Sims, Stephanie Faulkner, Burl Bullock, Sandra Reed

The message of this production is: racism (both black and white) is wrong. In this film, Billy Mitchell (Mike Sims) is a young black soldier who returns to his hometown after his brother is murdered. Billy's white friend encourages him to nonviolently investigate the death of his brother, while his black friends want to use the death as an excuse to tear the town down. The bigoted white sheriff is the counterpart to the black radicals. The acting is not the greatest, but the film does succeed in making its point. Rated PG for violence.

1971 102 minutes

BUSTER AND BILLIE

★★

DIRECTOR: Daniel Petrie

CAST: Jan-Michael Vincent, Joan Goodfellow, Pamela Sue Martin, Clifton James

A handsome high-school boy falls in love with a homely but loving girl in rural South. Set in the 1940s, the film has an innocent, sweet quality until it abruptly shifts tone and turns into a mean-spirited revenge picture. Rated R for violence and nudity.

1974 100 minutes

BUTTERFLIES ARE FREE

★★★★

DIRECTOR: Milton Katselas

CAST: Goldie Hawn, Edward Albert, Eileen Heckart, Mike Warren

Edward Albert is a blind youth determined to be self-sufficient in spite of his overbearing mother and the distraction of his will-o'-the-wisp next-door neighbor (Goldie Hawn). This fast-paced comedy benefits from some outstanding performances. None is better than that by Eileen Heckart. Her concerned, protective, and sometimes overloving mother is a treasure to behold. Rated PG.

1972 109 minutes

BUTTERFLY

★★

DIRECTOR: Matt Climber

CAST: Pia Zadora, Stacy Keach, Orson Welles, Lois Nettleton

Sex symbol Pia Zadora starts an incestuous relationship with her father (played by Stacy Keach). Orson Welles, as a judge, is the best thing about this film. Rated R.

1982 107 minutes

CABIN IN THE SKY

★★★

DIRECTOR: Vincente Minnelli
CAST: Eddie Anderson, Lena Horne, Ethel Waters, Rex Ingram, Louis Armstrong

One of Hollywood's first general-release black films and Vincente Minnelli's first feature. Eddie Anderson shows acting skill that was sadly and too long diluted by his playing foil for Jack Benny. Ethel Waters, as always, is superb. The film is a shade racist, but bear in mind that it was made in 1943, when Tinsel Town still thought blacks did nothing but sing, dance, and love watermelon.

1943 B & W 100 minutes

CADDIE

★★★★

DIRECTOR: Donald Crombie
CAST: Helen Morse, Takis Emmanuel, Jack Thompson, Jacki Weaver, Melissa Jaffer

This is an absorbing character study of a woman (Helen Morse, of *A Town like Alice*) who struggles to support herself and her children in Australia in the 1920s. Thanks greatly to the star's performance, it is yet another winner from Down Under. MPAA unrated, but contains mild sexual situations.

1976 107 minutes

CAESAR AND CLEOPATRA

★½

DIRECTOR: Gabriel Pascal
CAST: Claude Rains, Vivien Leigh, Stewart Granger, Francis L. Sullivan, Flora Robson

George Bernard Shaw's wordy play about Rome's titanic leader and Egypt's young queen. Claude Rains and Vivien Leigh are brilliant, but talk alone does not save the film from slowly sinking into the sands surrounding the Sphinx.

1946 127 minutes

CAINE MUTINY, THE

★★★★

DIRECTOR: Edward Dmytryk
CAST: Humphrey Bogart, José Ferrer, Van Johnson, Robert Francis, Fred MacMurray

Superb performances by Humphrey Bogart, Van Johnson, José Ferrer, and Fred MacMurray, among others, make this adaptation of Herman Wouk's classic novel an absolute must-see. This brilliant film concerns the hard-nosed Captain Queeg (Bogart), who may or may not be slightly unhinged, and the subsequent mutiny by his first officer and crew, who are certain he is. Beautifully done, a terrific movie.

1954 125 minutes

CAL

★★★★

DIRECTOR: Pat O'Connor
CAST: Helen Mirren, John Lynch, Danal McCann, Kitty Gibson

This superb Irish film, which focuses on "the troubles" in Northern Ireland, stars newcomer John Lynch as Cal, a teenaged boy who wants to sever his ties with the IRA. This turns out to be anything but easy, as the leader of the group tells him, "Not to act is to act." In other words, if he isn't for them, he's against them. Cal hides out at the home of local librarian Marcella (Helen Mirren, in a knockout of a performance). She's the widow of a policeman he helped murder. Nevertheless, Cal falls in love with her, and she, eventually, with him. But their idyllic love affair is ill-fated. Not only does she not know of Cal's involvement in her husband's death, but the IRA has no intention of letting him slip out of their grasp. Rated R for sex, nudity, profanity, and violence.

1984 102 minutes

CALIFORNIA DREAMING

★★

DIRECTOR: John Hancock

CAST: Glynnis O'Connor, Seymour Cassel, Dennis Christopher, Tanya Roberts

Wimpy film about a dork from Chicago trying to fit into the California lifestyle. The cast is good, but the story is maudlin and slow-moving. Rated R for partial nudity.

1979 93 minutes

CALIGULA

DIRECTOR: Tinto Brass

CAST: Malcolm McDowell, Peter O'Toole, Teresa Ann Savoy, Helen Mirren

A $15 million porno flick with big stars, this is a disgusting historical piece that follows the ruthless Roman ruler through an endless series of decapitations and disembowelments. Not satisfied with the amount of nudity and sex put into the film by director Tinto Brass, *Penthouse* magazine publisher and film producer Bob Guccione inserted scenes of homosexuality and other sex acts. This release is a waste of celluloid and filmgoers' time. Rated X for every excess imaginable.

1980 156 minutes

CALL IT MURDER

★★★

DIRECTOR: Chester Erskine

CAST: Sidney Fox, Humphrey Bogart, Lynne Overman, Henry Hull, O. P. Heggie, Margaret Wycherly, Henry O'Neill, Richard Whorf

An inflexible jury foreman casts the vote that sends a young girl to her death in the electric chair. Hounded by the press, he nevertheless says he would do it again—even if a loved one were involved. Then he learns his daughter has committed murder under the same circumstances. As was usual in his early films, Bogie gets blasted in this one, originally released under the title *Midnight*.

1934 B & W 73 minutes

CALL TO GLORY

★★★½

DIRECTOR: Thomas Carter

CAST: Craig T. Nelson, Cindy Pickett, Keenan Wynn, Elisabeth Shue, David Hollander

Engrossing pilot episode for what was to be a short-lived TV series. Set in the early 1960s, it follows an Air Force officer's family through the events of the Kennedy presidency. The taut script ably balances the story of their struggle to deal with military life and still retains the flavor of a historical chronicle of the times. This uniformly well-acted and -directed opening show promised much quality that was unfortunately unfulfilled in later episodes.

1984 97 minutes

CAMILLE

★★★★

DIRECTOR: George Cukor

CAST: Greta Garbo, Robert Taylor, Lionel Barrymore, Henry Daniell, Laura Hope Crews, Elizabeth Allan, Lenore Ulric, Jessie Ralph

Metro-Goldwyn-Mayer's lavish production of the Dumas classic provided screen goddess Greta Garbo with one of her last unqualified successes and remains the consummate adaptation of this popular weeper. The combined magic of the studio and Garbo's presence legitimized this archaic creaker about a dying woman and her love affair with a younger man (Robert Taylor, soon to be one of MGM's biggest stars). This is still a classic of its kind as well as being a thoughtful and beautifully produced movie graced with the distant, vulnerable quality that only Garbo could bring to a role. This is a richly textured film made as only MGM could, transforming accepted masterpieces into celluloid facsimiles that audiences could understand and appreciate without having to read. If you've never seen Garbo, watch this or *Ninotchka.*

1936 B & W 108 minutes

CAN YOU HEAR THE LAUGHTER? THE STORY OF FREDDIE PRINZE

★★½

DIRECTOR: Burt Brinckerhoff
CAST: Ira Angustain, Kevin Hooks, Randee Heller, Devon Ericson, Julie Carmen

Freddie Prinze was a Puerto Rican comedian who rose from the barrio to television superstardom in a relatively brief time. His premiere achievement was a starring role in *Chico and The Man,* with Jack Albertson. This is a sympathetic handling of his story, but no punches are pulled on the facts surrounding his death.

1979 106 minutes

CANDIDATE, THE

★★★½

DIRECTOR: Michael Ritchie
CAST: Robert Redford, Peter Boyle, Don Porter, Allen Garfield

Michael Ritchie expertly directed this release, an incisive look at a political hopeful (Robert Redford) and the obstacles and truths he must confront on the campaign trail. Rated PG.

1972 109 minutes

CAPTAIN NEWMAN, M.D.

★★★

DIRECTOR: David Miller
CAST: Gregory Peck, Angie Dickinson, Tony Curtis, Eddie Albert, Jane Withers, Bobby Darin, Larry Storch

The movie fluctuates between meaningful laughter and heavy drama. An excellent ensemble neatly maintains the balance. Gregory Peck is at his noble best as a sympathetic army psychiatrist. The film's most gripping performance comes from Bobby Darin, who plays a psychotic.

1963 126 minutes

CAPTAINS COURAGEOUS

★★★★★

DIRECTOR: Victor Fleming
CAST: Spencer Tracy, Freddie Bartholomew, Lionel Barrymore, Melvyn Douglas, Mickey Rooney

This is an exquisite adaptation of Rudyard Kipling's story about a spoiled rich kid who falls from an ocean liner and is rescued by fishermen. Through them, the lad learns about the rewards of hard work and genuine friendship. Spencer Tracy won a well-deserved best-actor Oscar for his performance as the fatherly fisherman.

1937 B & W 116 minutes

CAREFUL HE MIGHT HEAR YOU

★★★★½

DIRECTOR: Carl Schultz
CAST: Robyn Nevin, Nicholas Gledhill, Wendy Hughes, John Hargreaves, Geraldine Turner

A child's-eye view of the harsh realities of life, this Australian import is a poignant, heartwarming, sad, and sometimes frightening motion picture. A young boy named P.S. (played by 7-year-old Nicholas Gledhill) gets caught up in a bitter custody fight between his two aunts. While the movie does tend to become a tearjerker on occasion, it does so without putting off the viewer. The situations are always invested with an edge of realism. Rated PG for suggested sex and violence.

1983 116 minutes

CARNAL KNOWLEDGE

★★★★

DIRECTOR: Mike Nichols

CAST: Jack Nicholson, Candice Bergen, Art Garfunkel, Ann-Margret

The sexual dilemmas of the modern American are analyzed and come up short in this thoughtful film. Jack Nicholson and singer Art Garfunkel are college roommates whose lives are followed through varied relationships with the opposite sex. Nicholson is somewhat of a stinker, and one finds oneself more in sympathy with the women in the cast. Rated R.

1971 96 minutes

CARNIVAL STORY

★½

DIRECTOR: Kurt Neumann

CAST: Anne Baxter, Steve Cochran, Jay C. Flippen, George Nader

Familiar story of rivalry between circus performers over the affections of the girl they both love. No real surprises in this production, which was filmed in Germany on a limited budget, with the cast simply going through the motions. Star Anne Baxter gives it a try, but it's pretty tough sledding for her.

1954 95 minutes

CARNY

★★★★

DIRECTOR: Robert Kaylor

CAST: Gary Busey, Jodie Foster, Robbie Robertson, Meg Foster, Bert Remsen

This film takes us behind the bright lights, shouting barkers, and games of chance into the netherworld of the "carnies," people who spend their lives cheating, lying, and stealing from others yet consider themselves superior to their victims. Gary Busey (*The Buddy Holly Story*), Jodie Foster, Robbie Robertson (former singer/songwriter/guitarist from the Band in his acting debut), and veteran character actor Elisha Cook are all outstanding. The accent in *Carny* is on realism. The characters aren't the typical motion-picture heroes and heroines. Instead, they're disenchanted losers who live only from day to day. Rated R.

1980 107 minutes

CARPETBAGGERS, THE

★★★

DIRECTOR: Edward Dmytryk

CAST: George Peppard, Alan Ladd, Audrey Totter, Carroll Baker, Bob Cummings, Lew Ayres, Martin Balsam, Archie Moore

Howard Hughes–like millionaire George Peppard makes movies, love, and enemies in the Hollywood of the 1920s and 1930s. Alan Ladd, as a Tom Mix clone, helps in this, his last picture. Carroll Baker is steamy. Very tame compared with the porno-edged Harold Robbins novel. Insights into early Hollywood are interesting.

1964 150 minutes

CARRINGTON, V. C.

★★★

DIRECTOR: Anthony Asquith

CAST: David Niven, Margaret Leighton, Noelle Middleton, Laurence Naismith, Victor Maddern, Maurice Denham

Everybody's Englishman David Niven gives one of the finest performances of his long film career in this story of a stalwart British army officer, accused of stealing military funds, who undertakes to conduct his own defense at court-martial proceedings. This is a solid, engrossing drama, but suffers from sticking too close to its confining stage origin. Filmed in England and released heavily cut in the United States under the title *Court Martial*.

1955 B & W 105 minutes

CASABLANCA

★★★★★

DIRECTOR: Michael Curtiz

CAST: Humphrey Bogart, Ingrid Bergman, Claude Rains, Paul Henreid, Peter Lorre, Sydney Greenstreet

A kiss may be just a kiss and a sigh just a sigh, but there is only one *Casablanca*. Some misguided souls tried to remake this classic in 1980 as *Caboblanco*, with Charles Bronson, Jason Robards, and Dominique Sanda, but film lovers are well advised to accept no substitutes. The original feast of romance and pre–World War II intrigue is still the best. Superb performances by Humphrey Bogart and Ingrid Bergman, Paul Henreid, Claude Rains, Peter Lorre, and Sydney Greenstreet, and the fluid direction of Michael Curtiz combined to make it an all-time classic.

1942 B & W 102 minutes

CASE OF LIBEL, A

★★★★★

DIRECTOR: Eric Till

CAST: Edward Asner, Daniel J. Travanti, Gordon Pinsent, Lawrence Dane

Slick, superb made-for-cable adaptation of Henry Denker's famed Broadway play, which itself is taken from the first portion of Louis Nizer's excellent biography, *My Life in Court*. The story closely follows the legendary Westbrook Pegler–Quentin Reynolds libel suit, wherein columnist Pegler had attempted to smear Reynolds's reputation with a series of vicious lies. Ed Asner plays the lawyer and Daniel Travanti the columnist, and the verbal give-and-take ranks with the finest courtroom dramas on film. Travanti is perfect for the part: stiff, unyielding, and charming. Asner, in contrast, is languid, flexible, and deadly. The final outcome proves once again that truth is always stranger than fiction. Unrated.

1984 92 minutes

CASSANDRA CROSSING, THE

DIRECTOR: George Pan Cosmatos

CAST: Richard Harris, Sophia Loren, Burt Lancaster, Ava Gardner, Martin Sheen

One of the worst all-star disaster pictures, this involves a plague-infested train heading for a weakened bridge. The star power of Burt Lancaster, Sophia Loren, Richard Harris, Martin Sheen, and Ava Gardner, among others, does little to relieve its boredom. Rated PG.

1977 127 minutes

CAT ON A HOT TIN ROOF (ORIGINAL)

★★★★

DIRECTOR: Richard Brooks

CAST: Elizabeth Taylor, Paul Newman, Burl Ives, Jack Carson

This heavy drama stars Elizabeth Taylor as the frustrated Maggie and Paul Newman as her alcoholic, ex-athlete husband. They've returned to his father's (Big Daddy, played by Burl Ives) home upon hearing he's dying. They are joined by Newman's brother, Gooper, and his wife, May, and their many obnoxious children. Maggie struggles against May and Gooper to get a larger share in Big Daddy's will.

1958 108 minutes

CAT ON A HOT TIN ROOF (REMAKE)

★★★½

DIRECTOR: Jack Hofsiss

CAST: Jessica Lange, Tommy Lee Jones, Rip Torn, Kim Stanley, David Dukes, Penny Fuller

Updated rendition of the famed Tennessee Williams play strikes to the core in most scenes but remains oddly distanced in others. The story itself is just as powerful as it must have been in 1955, with its acute examination of a family under stress and the things that bother us all: mendacity and "little no-neck monsters" (certainly one of the best ways yet to describe bratty children). Jessica Lange is far too melodramatic as Maggie the Cat; it's impossible to forget that she's acting. Things really come alive, though, when Big Daddy (Rip Torn) and Brick (Tommy Lee Jones) square off. The play ends on what is for Williams an uncharacteristically optimistic note. A near miss. Unrated—sexual situations.

1985 140 minutes

CATHERINE THE GREAT

★★

DIRECTOR: Paul Czinner

CAST: Elisabeth Bergner, Douglas Fairbanks Jr., Flora Robson, Joan Gardner, Gerald Du Maurier

Stodgy spectacle from Great Britain is sumptuously mounted but takes its own time in telling the story of the famed czarina of Russia and her (toned-down) love life. Elisabeth Bergner in the title role lacks a real star personality, and dashing Douglas Fairbanks Jr. and sage Flora Robson provide the only screen charisma evident. Pretty fair for a historical romance of this period, but it won't keep you on the edge of your seat.

1934 B & W 92 minutes

CATHOLICS

★★★★½

DIRECTOR: Jack Gold

CAST: Trevor Howard, Martin Sheen, Raf Vallone, Andrew Keir

This film has Martin Sheen playing the representative of the Father General (the Pope). He comes to Ireland to persuade the Catholic priests there to conform to the "new" teachings of the Catholic Church. The Irish priests and monks refuse to discard traditional ways and beliefs. Trevor Howard is excellent as the rebellious Irish abbot.

1973 78 minutes

CAUGHT

★★★

DIRECTOR: Max Ophuls

CAST: Robert Ryan, Barbara Bel Geddes, James Mason, Natalie Schafer, Ruth Brady, Curt Bois, Frank Ferguson

Starry-eyed model Barbara Bel Geddes marries neurotic millionaire Robert Ryan, who proceeds to make her life miserable. His treatment drives her away and into the arms of young doctor James Mason. Upon learning she is pregnant, she returns to her husband, who refuses to give her a divorce unless she gives him the child.

1949 B & W 88 minutes

CEASE FIRE

★★★½

DIRECTOR: David Nutter

CAST: Don Johnson, Lisa Blount, Robert F. Lyons, Richard Chaves, Rick Richards, Chris Noel, Jorge Gil

An answer to the comic book–style heroism of *Rambo* and the *Missing in Action* movies, *Cease Fire* is a heartfelt, well-acted, and touching drama about the aftereffects of Vietnam and the battle still being fought by some veterans. Don Johnson ("Miami Vice") stars as Tim Murphy, a veteran whose life begins to crumble after fifteen years of valiant effort at fitting back into society. It is the story of one man's personal hell and how he triumphs over it. While director David Nutter has problems with pace, he does well with actors. Johnson, Lisa Blount (*An Officer and a Gentleman*) as his wife, and Robert F. Lyons as his even-more-troubled buddy give outstanding performances. And because the film is a tribute to those men and women who fought for their country overseas only to come home and fight an equally tough battle, we cannot help but cheer them (and the film) on. Rated R for profanity and violence.

1985 97 minutes

CERTAIN SACRIFICE, A

DIRECTOR: Stephen Jon Lewicki
CAST: Jeremy Pattnosh, Madonna

Avoid this one at all costs. A thoroughly inept film about two drifters who fall in love, are assaulted by a bigot, and then get revenge on him. The camera work is terrible, and while director Stephen Jon Lewicki attempts the avant-garde, he ends up making us all nauseous. The dialogue follows suit; favorite nonironic line by Madonna: "Do you think any lover of mine could be tamed?" Rated R for language, sex, nudity, violence.

1985 58 minutes

CHAMP, THE (ORIGINAL)

★★★★

DIRECTOR: King Vidor
CAST: Wallace Beery, Jackie Cooper, Irene Rich

Wallace Beery is at his absolute best in the Oscar-winning title role of this tearjerker, about a washed-up fighter and his adoring son (Jackie Cooper) who are separated against their will. King Vidor manages to make even the hokiest bits of hokum work in this four-hankie feast of sentimentality.

1931 B & W 87 minutes

CHAMP, THE (REMAKE)

★★★½

DIRECTOR: Franco Zeffirelli
CAST: Jon Voight, Faye Dunaway, Ricky Schroder, Jack Warden

This remake is a first-class tearjerker. The main reason for this is Ricky Schroder. This little actor projects joy, fear, and innocence equally well. Schroder and Jon Voight, as son and father, may do more for family relations in America than all the counseling agencies put together. Billy Flynn (Voight), a former boxing champion, works in the back-stretch at Hialeah when not drinking or gambling away his money. His son, T.J. (Schroder), calls him "Champ" and tells all his friends about his father's comeback, which never seems to happen. Flynn was badly injured in his last bout, his only loss, and fear prevents him from going back into the ring. Rated PG.

1979 121 minutes

CHAMPION

★★★★

DIRECTOR: Stanley Kramer
CAST: Kirk Douglas, Arthur Kennedy, Ruth Roman

One of Hollywood's better efforts about the fight game. Kirk Douglas is a young boxer whose climb to the top is accomplished while forsaking his friends and family. He gives one of his best performances in an unsympathetic role.

1949 B & W 100 minutes

CHAMPIONS

★★★★

DIRECTOR: John Irvin
CAST: John Hurt, Edward Woodward, Jan Francis, Ben Johnson

The touching true story of English steeplechase jockey Bob Champion (John Hurt), who fought a desperate battle against cancer through chemotherapy to win the 1981 Grand National. Rated PG.

1984 113 minutes

CHANEL SOLITAIRE

★★

DIRECTOR: George Kaczender
CAST: Marie-France Pisier, Timothy Dalton, Rutger Hauer, Karen Black, Brigitte Fossey

This half-hearted rendering of the rise to prominence of French designer Coco Chanel (played by fragile Marie-France Pisier) is long on sap and short on plot. Timothy Dalton and Rutger Hauer, as two of Coco's well-heeled suitors, fare best; Miss Pisier wears a sour pout throughout. For the terminally romantic only. Rated R.

1981 120 minutes

CHANGE OF HABIT

DIRECTOR: William Graham
CAST: Elvis Presley, Mary Tyler Moore, Barbara McNair, Jane Elliot, Edward Asner

In direct contrast to the many comedy/musicals that Elvis Presley starred in, this drama offers a more substantial plot. Elvis plays a doctor helping the poor in his clinic. Mary Tyler Moore plays a nun who is tempted to leave the order to be with Elvis. Rated G.

1970 93 minutes

CHAPTER TWO

★★★½

DIRECTOR: Robert Moore
CAST: James Caan, Marsha Mason, Valerie Harper, Joseph Bologna

In *Chapter Two*, writer Neil Simon examines the problems that arise when a recently widowed author courts and marries a recently divorced actress. George Schneider (James Caan) is recovering from the death of his wife when he strikes up a whirlwind courtship with actress Jennie MacLaine (Marsha Mason). They get married, but George is tormented by the memory of his first, beloved wife. An idyllic honeymoon shifts from newlywed bliss to emotional misery for George, and his mental distress threatens to destroy his marriage to Jennie just as it's getting started. Rated PG.

1979 124 minutes

CHARIOTS OF FIRE

★★★★★

DIRECTOR: Hugh Hudson
CAST: Ben Cross, Ian Charleson, Nigel Havers, Nick Farrell, Alice Krige

Made in England, this is the beautifully told and inspiring story of two runners (Ian Charleson and Ben Cross) who competed for England in the 1924 Olympics. An all-star supporting cast—Ian Holm, John Gielgud, Dennis Christopher (*Breaking Away*), Brad Davis (*Midnight Express*), and Nigel Davenport—and taut direction by Hugh Hudson help make this a must-see motion picture. Rated PG, the film has no objectionable content.

1981 123 minutes

CHASE, THE

★★½

DIRECTOR: Arthur Penn
CAST: Robert Redford, Jane Fonda, Marlon Brando, Angie Dick-

inson, Janice Rule, James Fox, Robert Duvall, E. G. Marshall, Miriam Hopkins, Martha Hyer

Convoluted tale of prison escapee (Robert Redford) who returns to the turmoil of his Texas hometown. The exceptional cast provides flashes of brilliance, but overall, the film is rather dull. Redford definitely showed signs of his superstar potential here.

1966 135 minutes

CHEERS FOR MISS BISHOP

★★★

DIRECTOR: Tay Garnett

CAST: Martha Scott, William Gargan, Edmund Gwenn, Sterling Holloway, Mary Anderson, Sidney Blackmer

Nostalgic, poignant story of a schoolteacher in a midwestern town who devotes her life to teaching. A warm reassuring film in the tradition of *Miss Dove* and *Mr. Chips*.

1941 B & W 95 minutes

CHIEFS

★★★★

DIRECTOR: Jerry London

CAST: Charlton Heston, Wayne Rogers, Billy Dee Williams, Brad Davis, Keith Carradine, Stephen Collins, Tess Harper, Paul Sorvino, Victoria Tennant

An impressive cast turns in some excellent performances in this, one of the better TV miniseries. A string of unsolved murders in 1920 in a small southern town is at the base of this engrossing suspense drama. The story follows the various police chiefs from the time of the murders to 1962 when Billy Dee Williams, the town's first black police chief, is intrigued by the case and the spell it casts over the town and its political boss (Charlton Heston). Despite threats, he continues to delve into the mystery until its climactic conclusion. Some material not suitable for children.

1985 200 minutes

CHILDREN OF A LESSER GOD

★★★★★

DIRECTOR: Randa Haines

CAST: William Hurt, Marlee Matlin, Piper Laurie, Phillip Bosco

Based on the Tony Award–winning play by Mark Medoff, this superb film concerns the love that grows between a teacher (William Hurt) for the hearing-impaired and a deaf woman (Oscar-winner Marlee Matlin). The performances are impeccable, the direction inspired, and the story unforgettable. Considering the problems inherent in telling its tale, this represents a phenomenal achievement for first-time film director Randa Haines. Rated R for suggested sex, profanity, and adult themes.

1986 118 minutes

CHILDREN OF SANCHEZ, THE

★★★

DIRECTOR: Hall Bartlett

CAST: Anthony Quinn, Dolores Del Rio

Anthony Quinn stars as a poor Mexican worker who tries to keep his large family together. This well-intentioned film is slightly boring. Rated PG.

1978 126 minutes

CHILLY SCENES OF WINTER

★★★★

DIRECTOR: Joan Micklin Silver

CAST: John Heard, Mary Beth Hurt, Peter Riegert, Kenneth McMillan, Gloria Grahame

You'll probably find this excellent little film in the comedy section of your local video store, but don't be fooled; it's funny all right, but it has some scenes that evoke the true pain of love. John Heard plays a man in love with a married woman (Mary Beth Hurt). She also loves him, but is still attached to her husband. Rated PG for language and sex.

1979 96 minutes

CHINA SYNDROME, THE

★★★★★

DIRECTOR: James Bridges
CAST: Jane Fonda, Jack Lemmon, Michael Douglas, Scott Brady

This taut thriller, about an accident at a nuclear power plant, has no real competition. It's superb entertainment with a timely message. Rated PG.

1979 123 minutes

CHOOSE ME

★★★★

DIRECTOR: Alan Rudolph
CAST: Lesley Ann Warren, Keith Carradine, Genevieve Bujold

A feast of fine acting and deliciously different situations, this stylish independent film works on every level and proves that inventive, non-mainstream entertainment is still a viable form. Written and directed by Alan Rudolph (*Welcome to L.A.*; *Remember My Name*), *Choose Me* is a funny, quirky, suspenseful, and surprising essay on love, sex, and the wacky state of male-female relationships in the 1980s. Rated R for violence and profanity.

1984 110 minutes

CHOSEN, THE

★★★★★

DIRECTOR: Jeremy Paul Kagan
CAST: Robby Benson, Rod Steiger, Maximilian Schell

The Chosen is a flawless, arresting drama illustrating the conflict between friendship and family loyalty. Based on the novel of the same name by Chaim Potok, the story, centering on Jewish issues, transcends its setting to attain universal impact. Rated G.

1978 105 minutes

CHRISTMAS TO REMEMBER, A

★★★★

DIRECTOR: George Englund
CAST: Jason Robards, Eva Marie Saint, Joanne Woodward

Grandpa Larson (Jason Robards), who never got over his son's death, resents his grandson's visit. His unkind manner toward the boy convinces the youngster that he must run away. Eva Marie Saint plays Grandma Larson, who rebuffs her husband for his cruelty. Joanne Woodward makes a cameo appearance as the boy's impoverished mom. Unrated, this provides fine family entertainment comparable with a G rating.

1979 96 minutes

CHRISTOPHER STRONG

★★½

DIRECTOR: Dorothy Arzner
CAST: Katharine Hepburn, Colin Clive, Billie Burke, Helen Chandler, Jack LaRue, Ralph Forbes

Katharine Hepburn's second film, this one gave her her first starring role. She is a record-breaking flyer who falls passionately in love with a married man she cannot have. Pregnancy complicates things further. High-plane soap opera. Kate's legions of fans will love it, however.

1933 B & W 77 minutes

CIAO! MANHATTAN

(turkey)

DIRECTORS: John Palmer, David Weisman
CAST: Edie Sedgwick, Isabel Jewell, Baby Jane Holzer, Roger Vadim, Viva, Paul America

Far more pornographic than any skin flick, this sleazy, low-budget release features Edie Sedgwick, a one-time Andy Warhol "superstar," in a grotesque parody of her life. Sedgwick, who, at the age of 28, died shortly after the film's completion, is most often topless and slurs her way through this near-documentary of the last days of an aimless self-indulgent young woman. While watching *Ciao! Manhattan*, the viewer can't help but feel a morbid fascination. But afterward, you feel like you need a bath and reassurance that there is some hope in life. No MPAA rating, but rife with objectionable material.

1983 84 minutes

CIRCLE OF TWO

★½

DIRECTOR: Jules Dassin

CAST: Richard Burton, Tatum O'Neal, Kate Reid, Robin Gammell

Thoroughly ludicrous tale of an eccentric artist (Richard Burton) who develops a romantic—but somehow platonic—relationship with a teen-age girl (Tatum O'Neal). Laughable dialogue throughout, punctuated by heavy sighs and fluttering eyelashes. O'Neal has a painfully embarrassing nude scene that is out of place in this story with its gentle tone. Rated PG for nudity.

1980 105 minutes

CITADEL, THE

★★★½

DIRECTOR: King Vidor

CAST: Robert Donat, Rosalind Russell, Ralph Richardson, Rex Harrison, Emlyn Williams, Penelope Dudley-Ward, Francis L. Sullivan, Felix Aylmer, Mary Clare, Cecil Parker

Superb acting by a fine cast marks this adaptation of novelist A. J. Cronin's story of an impoverished doctor who temporarily forsakes his ideals but comes to his senses when tragedy strikes. Their performances were strong career boosters for both Robert Donat and Rosalind Russell.

1938 B & W 112 minutes

CITIZEN KANE

★★★★★

DIRECTOR: Orson Welles

CAST: Orson Welles, Joseph Cotten, Everett Sloane, Agnes Moorehead, Ray Collins, George Colouris, Ruth Chatterton

What can you say about the film considered by many to be the finest picture ever made in America? The story of a reporter's quest to find the "truth" about the life of a dead newspaper tycoon closely parallels the life of William Randolph Hearst. To 1940s audiences, the plot may have seemed obscured by flashbacks, unusual camera angles, and lens distortion. After forty years, however, most of these film tricks are now commonplace, but the story, the acting of the Mercury Company cast, Gregg Toland's camera work, and Bernard Herrmann's score haven't aged a bit. This picture is still a very enjoyable experience for first-time viewers, as well as for those who have seen it ten times.

1941 B & W 119 minutes

CLASH BY NIGHT

★★★½

DIRECTOR: Fritz Lang

CAST: Barbara Stanwyck, Paul Douglas, Robert Ryan, Marilyn Monroe, Keith Andes, J. Carrol Naish

Intense, adult story is a dramatist's dream but not entertainment for the masses. Barbara Stanwyck gives another of her strong characterizations as a woman with a past who marries amiable Paul Douglas only to find herself gravitating toward tough but sensual Robert Ryan. Gritty realism of fishing village locale adds to the strong mood of this somber love triangle, and outstanding performances by all the principals (including a young Marilyn Monroe and master character actor J. Carrol Naish) make this a slice-of-life tragedy that lingers in the memory. This film is justly remembered as one of the highlights of Hollywood's efforts of the early 1950s.

1952 B & W 105 minutes

CLASS OF '44

★★★

DIRECTOR: Paul Bogart
CAST: Gary Grimes, Jerry Houser, William Atherton, Deborah Winters

Sequel to the very popular *Summer of '42* proves once again it's tough to top the original. Gary Grimes and Jerry Houser are back again. This time we follow the two through college romances. No new ground broken, but Grimes is very watchable. Rated PG.

1973 95 minutes

CLASS OF MISS MACMICHAEL, THE

★★

DIRECTOR: Silvio Narizzano
CAST: Glenda Jackson, Oliver Reed, Michael Murphy

British film about obnoxious students battling obnoxious teachers. Mixes *The Blackboard Jungle*, *To Sir with Love*, and *Teachers* without expanding on them. Loud and angry, but doesn't say much. Rated R for profanity.

1978 91 minutes

CLEOPATRA

★★★★

DIRECTOR: Joseph L. Mankiewicz
CAST: Elizabeth Taylor, Richard Burton, Rex Harrison, Roddy McDowall, Pamela Brown

This multimillion-dollar, four-hour-long extravaganza created quite a sensation when released. Its all-star cast includes Elizabeth Taylor (as Cleopatra), Richard Burton (as Marc Antony), Rex Harrison (as Julius Caesar), Martin Landau (as Rufio), Roddy McDowall (as Octavian), and Carroll O'Connor (as Casca). The story begins when Caesar meets Cleopatra in her native Egypt and she has his son. Later she comes to Rome to join Caesar when he becomes the lifetime dictator of Rome. Marc Antony gets into the act as Cleopatra's Roman lover. It created quite a stir in 1963, but there is actually minimal sex and nudity by today's standards.

1963 243 minutes

CLOCK AND DAGGER

★★½

DIRECTOR: Fritz Lang
CAST: Gary Cooper, Lilli Palmer, Robert Alda, James Flavin, J. Edward Bromberg, Helen Thimig, Marc Lawrence

Director Fritz Lang wanted to make *Clock and Dagger* as a warning about the dangers of the atomic age. But Warner Bros. reedited the film into a standard spy melodrama. The story has American scientist Gary Cooper, working for the OSS, sneaking into Nazi Germany to grab an Italian scientist who is helping the Nazis build the atom bomb. Lilli Palmer, in her first American film, is a German woman who falls for Cooper. Considering the talent involved, *Clock and Dagger* is a disappointment.

1946 B & W 106 minutes

CLOUDS OVER EUROPE

★★½

DIRECTOR: Tim Whelan
CAST: Laurence Olivier, Valerie Hobson, Ralph Richardson

Handsome test pilot Laurence Olivier teams up with a man from Scotland Yard to discover why new bombers are disappearing in this on-the-verge-of-war thriller.

1939 B & W 82 minutes

COCAINE FIENDS

★½

DIRECTOR: William A. O'Connor
CAST: Lois January, Sheila Manners, Noel Madison, Dean Benton, Lois Lindsay

Grim drama about drug addiction follows two women down their path to dependency. One is lured from her home by a smooth-talking hoodlum who gives her a taste of "headache medicine;" the other turns her boyfriend into a user as well. Better acted than most cheap morality tales, this one even uses symbolism to convey the heroines' tragedy. Although cocaine is referred to often (as *snow, joy powder,* etc.), it is never actually shown, and the paraphernalia and ingestion of drugs are never depicted. Melodramatic, yes, but not as funny as *Reefer Madness* and some of the more outlandish exploitation films that went for bawdier, more sensational footage.

1936 B & W 74 minutes

COCAINE: ONE MAN'S SEDUCTION

★★★½

DIRECTOR: Paul Wendkos
CAST: Dennis Weaver, Karen Grassle, Pamela Bellwood, James Spader, David Ackroyd, Jeffrey Tambor, Richard Venture

Though this is not another *Reefer Madness*, the subject could have been handled a little more subtly. Still, the melodrama is not obtrusive enough to take away from Dennis Weaver's brilliant performance as a real estate salesman who gets hooked on the expensive habit to help cope with the pressure of his work. Not rated, but the equivalent of a PG for adult subject matter.

1983 97 minutes

COLDITZ STORY, THE

★★★½

DIRECTOR: Guy Hamilton
CAST: John Mills, Eric Portman, Lionel Jeffries, Christopher Rhodes, Bryan Forbes, Ian Carmichael, Theodore Bikel, Anton Diffring, Richard Wattis

Tight direction, an intelligent script, and a terrific cast make this one of the most compelling British dramas of the 1950s and one of the best prison films of all time. John Mills is outstanding as the glue that keeps the escape plans together, but the entire crew works well together. None of them, however, can overshadow the story or the prison itself, the real star of this show. Well worth the watch, even if you aren't wild about prison or escape films. Director Guy Hamilton later went on to direct *Goldfinger*, one of the most successful James Bond films.

1957 B & W 97 minutes

COLOR ME DEAD

★★½

DIRECTOR: Eddie Davis
CAST: Tom Tryon, Carolyn Jones, Rick Jason, Patricia Connelly, Tony Ward, Penny Sugg, Reg Gillam

An innocent accountant (Tom Tryon) gets caught in the middle of an illegal uranium robbery and is poisoned with a deadly slow-working drug. With his days numbered, he adopts the methods of a detective and tries to find out why he was murdered. Carolyn Jones is effective as Tryon's girlfriend-secretary and gives the story poignancy; but the screenplay is wanting. Not rated, the film contains violence.

1969 91 minutes

COLOR OF MONEY, THE

★★★★

DIRECTOR: Martin Scorsese

CAST: Paul Newman, Tom Cruise, Mary Elizabeth Mastrantonio, Helen Shaver, John Turturro, Bill Cobbs

A sequel to *The Hustler*, this film features outstanding performances by Paul Newman as the now-aging pool champion and Tom Cruise as his protégé. The story may be predictable, even clichéd but the actors make it worth watching. In addition, there are some fine moments of comedy and suspense, and director Martin Scorsese adds some startling visual touches. The result proves that even a formula film can be memorable when it's made by the right people. Rated R for nudity, profanity, and violence.

1986 117 minutes

COLOR PURPLE, THE

★★★★★

DIRECTOR: Steven Spielberg

CAST: Whoopi Goldberg, Danny Glover, Adolph Caesar, Margaret Avery, Oprah Winfrey, Rae Dawn Chong, Akousa Busia, Willard Pugh

Steven Spielberg's adaptation of Alice Walker's Pulitzer Prize–winning novel about the growth to maturity and independence of a mistreated black woman is one of those rare and wonderful movies that can bring a tear to the eye, a lift to the soul, and joy to the heart. Walker's story, set between 1909 and 1947 in a small town in Georgia, celebrates the qualities of kindness, compassion, and love. Rated PG-13 for violence, profanity, and suggested sex.

1985 130 minutes

COME BACK TO THE FIVE AND DIME, JIMMY DEAN, JIMMY DEAN

★★★½

DIRECTOR: Robert Altman

CAST: Sandy Dennis, Cher, Karen Black, Sudie Bond, Kathy Bates, Marta Heflin

This film adaptation of Ed Graczyk's failed Broadway play concerns the twenty-year reunion of the Disciples of James Dean, a group formed by high-school friends from a small Texas town after *Giant* was filmed on location nearby. Their get-together ends up being a catalyst that forces the members to confront the lies they have been living since those innocent days. Though a surreal work that deals with broken dreams and crippling illusions, *Jimmy Dean* is highlighted by some excellent comedy and dramatic moments as well as a terrific performance by Cher. Unrated, the film contains profanity and mature subject matter.

1982 110 minutes

COMEDIAN, THE

★★★★★

DIRECTOR: John Frankenheimer

CAST: Mickey Rooney, Mel Torme, Edmond O'Brien, Kim Hunter

This gem from the golden age of television proves that they don't make 'em like they used to. Originally aired live as a *Playhouse 90* drama, features Mickey Rooney as Sammy Hogarth, a ruthless, egomaniacal comedy star. His insatiable desire for unconditional adoration and obedience from those closest to him makes life a nightmare for his humilated brother Lester (Mel Torme) and gag writer (Edmond O'Brien). Rod Serling's tight screenplay and the outstanding performances combine to make this an undated classic. Carl Reiner introduces the show with interviews of the cast and director today.

1957 B & W 90 minutes

COMEDIANS, THE

★★

DIRECTOR: Peter Glenville

CAST: Elizabeth Taylor, Richard Burton, Alec Guinness, Peter Ustinov, Paul Ford, Lillian Gish, James Earl Jones, Cicely Tyson

In this drama, Elizabeth Taylor and Richard Burton inadvertently become involved in the political violence and unrest of Haiti under Papa Doc Duvalier. The all-star cast does little to improve an average script—based on Graham Greene's novel.

1967 160 minutes

COMIC, THE

★★★★

DIRECTOR: Carl Reiner

CAST: Dick Van Dyke, Mickey Rooney, Michele Lee, Cornel Wilde, Nina Wayne, Pert Kelton, Jeannine Riley

There's a bit of every famous silent film funny man—Chaplin, Keaton, Arbuckle, Langdon, and Lloyd—in this engrossing account of a beloved reel comedian who's an egocentric heel in real life. Dick Van Dyke is peerless in the title character. Well planned and executed, this is a gem of its genre. Beautiflly handled, the closing minutes alone are worth the entire film. Rated PG.

1969 96 minutes

COMING HOME

★★★★½

DIRECTOR: Hal Ashby

CAST: Jane Fonda, Jon Voight, Bruce Dern, Robert Carradine, Robert Ginty, Penelope Milford

Jane Fonda, Jon Voight, and Bruce Dern give superb performances in this thought-provoking drama about the effect the Vietnam War has on three people. Directed by Hal Ashby (*Harold and Maude*; *The Last Detail*), it features a romantic triangle with a twist: Fonda, the wife of a gung-ho officer, Dern, finds real love when she becomes an aide at a veteran's hospital and meets a bitter but sensitive paraplegic, Voight. This release does have a few false moments, but overall, it's a movie with a message that still manages to entertain. What more could you ask? Rated R.

1978 127 minutes

COMING OUT OF THE ICE

★★★½

DIRECTOR: Waris Hussein

CAST: John Savage, Willie Nelson, Ben Cross, Francesca Annis

An engrossing made-for-television movie based on a true story. An American spends thirty-eight years in a Soviet prison camp for not renouncing his American citizenship. He is jailed and then banished to a remote northern village where he learns the meaning of freedom and finally is allowed to go home.

1987 97 minutes

COMPETITION, THE

★★★½

DIRECTOR: Joel Oliansky

CAST: Richard Dreyfuss, Amy Irving, Lee Remick, Sam Wanamaker

Richard Dreyfuss and Amy Irving star in this exquisitely crafted and completely enjoyable romance about two classical pianists who, while competing for top honors in a recital program, fall in love. Lee Remick and Sam Wanamaker add excellent support. Watch it with someone you love. Rated PG.

1980 129 minutes

CONCRETE JUNGLE, THE (AKA THE CRIMINAL)

★★★

DIRECTOR: Joseph Losey

CAST: Stanley Baker, Margit Saad, Sam Wanamaker, Gregoire Aslan, Jill Bennett, Laurence Naismith, Edward Judd

Grim, claustrophobic prison drama is tightly directed and well acted (especially by the underrated Stanley Baker), and remains one of the best films of its kind as well as one of director Joseph Losey's most satisfying works. Often referred to in filmographies as *The Criminal*, this uncompromising look at life inside the concrete walls of confinement boasts gutsy, believable performances by a fine crew of veteran British character actors and convincingly conveys the hopelessness and despair of forced isolation.

1962 B & W 86 minutes

CONFESSIONS OF A POLICE CAPTAIN

★½

DIRECTOR: Damiano Damiani

CAST: Martin Balsam, Franco Nero, Marilu Tolo

Heavy-handed melodrama wastes a fine performance by Martin Balsam as a good cop trying to close a tough case amid an avalanche of bureaucratic corruption. This Italian-made film is given to excess, and the confusing story fails to sustain interest. Rated PG.

1971 102 minutes

CONFESSIONS OF A VICE BARON

★

DIRECTOR: Harvey Thew

CAST: Willy Castello

Fly-by-night film chronicling the rise and fall of vice baron Lombardo isn't quite as bad as it could have been. The shoddy production values of this basement opus don't get in the way of the sleazy story of Lombardo's world of flesh peddling and illegal operations (not to mention dope!) that fell apart when he went sappy and fell in love. In classic exploitation style, Lombardo wants to bare his soul and "tell all" in order to save future victims of the vice rackets before he walks "the last mile". Some nudity thrown in, but overall pretty tame. Last part of tape features previews of other exploitation titles.

1942 B & W 70 minutes

CONRACK

★★★★

DIRECTOR: Martin Ritt

CAST: Jon Voight, Paul Winfield, Hume Cronyn, Madge Sinclair

In this sleeper, based on a true story, Jon Voight plays a dedicated white teacher determined to bring the joys of education to deprived blacks inhabiting an island off the coast of South Carolina. Rated PG.

1974 107 minutes

CONVERSATION, THE

★★★★★

DIRECTOR: Francis Ford Coppola

CAST: Gene Hackman, John Cazale, Allen Garfield, Cindy Williams, Harrison Ford

Following his box-office and artistic triumph with *The Godfather*, director Francis Ford Coppola made this absorbing character study about a bugging-device expert (Gene Hackman) who lives only for his work but finds himself developing a conscience. Although not a box-office hit when originally released, this is a fine little film. Rated PG.

1974 113 minutes

CORN IS GREEN, THE

★★★½

DIRECTOR: George Cukor

CAST: Katharine Hepburn, Ian Saynor, Bill Fraser, Patricia Hayes, Anna Massey

Based on Emlyn Williams's play and directed by George Cukor (*The Philadelphia Story*), this telefilm stars Katharine Hepburn. She gives a tour-de-force performance as the eccentric spinster-teacher who helps a gifted young man discover the joys of learning.

1979 100 minutes

CORNBREAD, EARL, AND ME

★★½

DIRECTOR: Joe Manduke

CAST: Moses Gunn, Bernie Casey, Rosalind Cash, Madge Sinclair, Keith Wilkes, Tierre Turner

A fine cast of black performers is ill served by this overdone drama about racism. A gifted basketball player is mistakenly killed by the police. It's a familiar plot directed with little inspiration by Joe Manduke. Rated R.

1975 95 minutes

COUNTDOWN

★★★

DIRECTOR: Robert Altman

CAST: James Caan, Robert Duvall, Charles Aidman

This lesser-known Robert Altman film finds James Caan and Robert Duvall as American astronauts preparing for a moonshot. The realistic scenes and great acting raise this film high above most films of this kind—well worth watching. Unrated.

1968 101 minutes

COUNTRY

★★★★

DIRECTOR: Richard Pearce

CAST: Jessica Lange, Sam Shepard, Wilford Brimley, Matt Clark

A quietly powerful movie about the plight of farmers struggling to hold on while the government and financial institutions seem intent on fostering their failure. Directed by Richard Pearce (*Heartland*), *Country* teams Jessica Lange and Sam Shepard on screen for the first time since the Oscar-nominated *Frances* in a film as topical as today's headlines. Rated PG.

1984 109 minutes

COUNTRY GIRL, THE

★★★★½

DIRECTOR: George Seaton

CAST: Bing Crosby, Grace Kelly, William Holden, Anthony Ross

Bing Crosby and Grace Kelly give terrific performances in this little-seen production. Crosby plays an alcoholic singer who wallows in self-pity until he seizes a chance to make a comeback. Kelly won an Oscar for her sensitive portrayal of his wife.

1954 B & W 104 minutes

COUNTRYMAN

★★★½

DIRECTOR: Dickie Jobson

CAST: "Countryman" Hiram Keller, Kristian Sinclair

A strange and fun film following the adventures of a young marijuana-smuggling woman (Kristian Sinclair) whose airplane crash-lands in Jamaica. She is rescued by Countryman and led to safety from the police and the army who are closing in on the two. Lots of Rasta humor and supernatural happenings keep the viewer entertained. *Countryman* also has a great reggae music soundtrack with sounds by Bob Marley, Steel Pulse, and Toots and the Maytals. Rated R for nudity and adult themes.

1984 103 minutes

COWARD OF THE COUNTY

★★★

DIRECTOR: Dick Lowry
CAST: Kenny Rogers, Frederic Lehne, Largo Woodruff, Mariclare Costello, Ana Alicia

This made-for-TV film is based on Kenny Rogers's hit song. He plays a World War II Georgia preacher with a pacifist nephew. When the nephew's girlfriend is raped, he's put to the ultimate test of his nonviolent beliefs. The acting and setting are believable, making this a film worth viewing.

1981 110 minutes

CRACKER FACTORY

★★★★

DIRECTOR: Burt Brinckerhoff
CAST: Natalie Wood, Peter Haskell, Shelley Long, Vivian Blaine, Perry King

This made-for-TV drama features Natalie Wood as Cassie Barrett, an alcoholic housewife who loses her grip on reality. Her long-suffering husband, Charlie (Peter Haskell), silently offers support while she spends her rehabilitation in the Cracker Factory, a mental institution. Perry King plays the handsome psychiatrist that fellow patient Cara (Shelley Long) falls in love with. The destructive effects of alcohol on Cassie and her family are well presented. Unrated, but the mature topic warrants parental discretion.

1979 95 minutes

CRAIG'S WIFE

★★★

DIRECTOR: Dorothy Arzner
CAST: Rosalind Russell, John Boles, Billie Burke, Jane Darwell, Thomas Mitchell, Alma Kruger, Dorothy Wilson

In her first film success, Rosalind Russell is brilliant as Harriet Craig, the wife of the title, a heartless domestic tyrant whose neurotic preference for material concerns over human feelings alienates all around her. John Boles is her long-suffering, slow-to-see-the-light husband. Note: In what hindsight pegs as plus-perfect typecasting, Joan Crawford plays the title role in *Harriet Craig*, the 1948 remake.

1936 B & W 75 minutes

CREATOR

★★

DIRECTOR: Ivan Passer
CAST: Peter O'Toole, Mariel Hemingway, Vincent Spano, Virginia Madsen, David Ogden Stiers, John Dehner

This film, about a scientist (Peter O'Toole) who is attempting to bring back to life the wife who died thirty years before during childbirth, is, at first, a very witty and occasionally heart-tugging comedy. However, in its last third, it turns into a sort of second-rate tearjerker. As a result, the movie —to say nothing of the viewer— suffers. Rated R for nudity, profanity, and simulated sex.

1985 108 minutes

CRIMES OF PASSION

DIRECTOR: Ken Russell
CAST: Kathleen Turner, Anthony Perkins, John Laughlin

Kathleen Turner (*Romancing the Stone*) stars in director Ken Russell's disgusting and perverse sex film as Joanna Crane, a woman who leads a double life. By day she's a highly paid fashion designer; by night, a kinky high-priced hooker called China Blue. Anthony Perkins (in a role reminiscent of his famous *Psycho* turn) is a sleazy street-corner preacher who becomes obsessed with her. His plans are complicated when an investigator (John Laughlin) discovers her secret and, because of a sexless marriage, finds himself drawn to Joanna's erotic alter ego. That's when things really get ugly. You'd have to dig pretty deep to find a more disgusting, pretentious, and ludicrous motion picture. Rated R for nudity, suggested sex, profanity, and violence.

1984 107 minutes

CRIMINAL CODE, THE

★★★★

DIRECTOR: Howard Hawks
CAST: Boris Karloff, Walter Huston, Phillips Holmes

A powerful performance by Boris Karloff as a revenge-minded convict elevates this Howard Hawks release from interesting to memorable. It's a lost classic that deserves its release on video. The story involves a district attorney (impressively played by Walter Huston) who overzealously pursues his job, with the result that an innocent man (Phillips Holmes) is sent to prison. When the ex-D.A. becomes warden at the institution where the young man is incarcerated, he has the chance to right this wrong.

1931 B & W 83 minutes

CROMWELL

★★

DIRECTOR: Ken Hughes
CAST: Richard Harris, Alec Guinness, Robert Morley, Frank Finlay, Dorothy Tutin, Timothy Dalton, Patrick Magee

Richard Harris hams it up again in this overblown historical melodrama. A fine cast founders amid tradition-soaked locations and beautiful backgrounds. The accoutrements and design are splendid, but the story is lacking and Harris's performance is inept. This film will not please most history buffs and will bore and confuse anyone attempting to gain any insight into Cromwell or his times. On top of all that, it's loooonnnggg!

1970 145 minutes

CROSS COUNTRY

★★

DIRECTOR: Paul Lynch
CAST: Richard Beymer, Nina Axelrod, Michael Ironside, Brent Carver

Michael Ironside plays Detective Ed Roersch, who pursues Richard Beymer following the murder of an expensive call girl. Although this movie involves prostitution, blackmail, murder, and deceit, it still manages to bore. Rated R for nudity, sex, profanity, and violence.

1983 95 minutes

CROSS CREEK

★★★½

DIRECTOR: Martin Ritt
CAST: Mary Steenburgen, Rip Torn, Peter Coyote, Dana Hill

About the life of 1930s author Marjorie Kinnan Rawlings (Mary Steenburgen), this watchable release illustrates how Rawlings's relationships with backwoods folks inspired her novels, particularly *The Yearling* and *Jacob's Ladder.* Rated PG for brief violence.

1983 122 minutes

CROSSFIRE

★★★½

DIRECTOR: Edward Dmytryk
CAST: Robert Ryan, Robert Mitchum, Robert Young, Sam Levene, George Cooper, Gloria Grahame, Paul Kelly, Steve Brodie, Jacqueline White

While on leave from the army, psychopathic bigot Robert Ryan meets Sam Levene in a nightclub and later murders him during an argument. An army buddy is blamed; another is also murdered. Ryan is arrested after being cleverly tricked by police detective Robert Young, who is aided by yet another army pal, Robert Mitchum. Often billed as a *film noir*, this interesting film is more of a message indicting anti-Semitism, and was the first major Hollywood picture to explore racial bigotry.

1947 B & W 86 minutes

CRUEL SEA, THE

★★★½

DIRECTOR: Charles Frend
CAST: Jack Hawkins, Virginia MacKenna, Stanley Baker, Donald Sinden

The ever-changing and unpredictable wind-lashed sea is the star of this gripping documentary-style adventure about a stalwart British warship and its crew during World War II.

1953 B & W 121 minutes

CRUISING

★★

DIRECTOR: William Friedkin
CAST: Al Pacino, Paul Sorvino, Karen Allen, Richard Cox, Don Scardino

Writer-director William Friedkin went on to make a movie more horrifying than his big blockbuster, *The Exorcist*, but *Cruising*, which was based on a series of brutal murders in New York City between 1962 and 1979, is horror in the real sense of the word. It is repulsive, sickening, and almost unbearable to watch. Friedkin throws in everything you can think of to make it a grisly ordeal for the viewer: dismembered body parts, graphic stabbing scenes, and the like. Scenes of men pawing, clawing, and gnawing at each other are interspersed throughout. The film begins when the skipper of a tugboat finds a rotted, bloated forearm floating in the East River. The police captain, Edelson (Paul Sorvino), believes it's part of a series of brutal killings that have taken place in the homosexual community. Because all the known victims have had a general similarity, he offers the chance to become a detective to a patrolman, Steve Burns (Al Pacino), who bears a resemblance to the killer's targets. All Burns has to do is act as bait. Rated R.

1980 106 minutes

CRYSTAL HEART

DIRECTOR: Gil Bettman
CAST: Tawny Kitaen, Lee Curreri, Lloyd Bochner, Simon Andreu, May Heatherly

A young man with a rare illness falls in love with an aspiring rock singer in this brainless weeper with awful music video sequences. The viewer suffers more than the characters. Avoid this preposterous tearjerker. Rated R.

1987 103 minutes

CUT AND RUN

DIRECTOR: Ruggero Deodato
CAST: Lisa Blount, Leonard Mann, Willie Aames, Richard Lynch, Richard Bright, Michael Berryman, Valentina Forte, John Steiner, Karen Black

Lisa Blount plays a television journalist in search of the ultimate scoop. She finds it in South America, while covering a bloody cocaine war. She finally encounters the conquering army led by one of Jim Jones's hit men. It is quite difficult to like anyone or anything in this miserable outing. Karen Black puts in a brief appearance as a TV anchorwoman. Rated R for violence, profanity, sex, and nudity.

1985 87 minutes

CUTTER'S WAY

★★★★

DIRECTOR: Ivan Passer
CAST: Jeff Bridges, John Heard, Lisa Eichhorn, Ann Dusenberry

Director Ivan Passer must be praised for attempting to create more than just mindless movie mush. *Cutter's Way* comes very close to being a masterpiece. It's hokey sometimes and some of its elements are clichéd, but, surprisingly, Passer manages to turn this to his advantage. The screenplay, by Jeffrey Alan Fiskin, adapted from the novel *Cutter and Bone*, by Newton Thornburg, is a murder mystery. The three lead performances (John Heard, Jeff Bridges, and Lisa Eichhorn) are first-rate. *Cutter's Way* is certainly not what anyone would call a commercial film—it's too tough and uncompromising for that—but there is still an audience for it, one composed of viewers who prefer pictures that aspire to greatness. Rated R because of violence, nudity, and profanity.

1981 105 minutes

CYRANO DE BERGERAC

★★★★

DIRECTOR: Michael Gordon
CAST: José Ferrer, Mala Powers, William Prince

Charming, touching story of steadfast devotion and unrequited love done with brilliance and panache. As the fearless soldier of the large nose, José Ferrer superbly dominates this fine film. Mala Powers is beautiful as his beloved Roxanne. William Prince, who now often plays heavies, makes Christian a proper handsome, unimaginative nerd.

1950 B & W 112 minutes

D-DAY THE SIXTH OF JUNE

★½

DIRECTOR: Henry Koster
CAST: Robert Taylor, Richard Todd, Dana Wynter, Edmond O'Brien

Slow-moving account of the Normandy invasion in World War II. Story concentrates on Allied officers Robert Taylor's and Richard Todd's romantic and professional problems. The actual invasion scenes are good, but come way too late to save this poor excuse for a war film.

1956 106 minutes

D.I., THE

★★★

DIRECTOR: Jack Webb
CAST: Jack Webb, Don Dubbins, Lin McCarthy, Monica Lewis, Jackie Loughery, Virginia Gregg, Barbara Pepper

Jack Webb embodies the tough, no-nonsense drill instructor so commonly associated with the Marine Corps in this straightforward story of basic training and the men that it makes (or breaks). Don Dubbins plays the troublesome recruit who makes life miserable for Webb; many other roles are played by real-life members of the armed services. Webb brings his usual intensity and attention to detail to this film, one of a handful of highly individual films he co-produced, directed, and starred in during the 1950s. "Cause If'n You Don't, Somebody Else Will" is one of the most memorable tunes of this (or any other) film of the era.

1957 B & W 106 minutes

D.O.A.

★★★½

DIRECTOR: Rudolph Maté
CAST: Edmond O'Brien, Pamela Britton, Luther Adler, Lynne Baggett, Neville Brand

CPA Edmond O'Brien, slowly dying from radiation poisoning, seeks those responsible in this fast-paced, stylized *film noir* thriller. Most unusual is the device of having the victim play detective and hunt his killers as time runs out. Neville Brand takes honors as a psychopath who tries to turn the tables on the victim before he can inform the police.

1949 B & W 83 minutes

D. W. GRIFFITH TRIPLE FEATURE

★★★

DIRECTOR: D. W. Griffith
CAST: Mae Marsh, Lillian Gish, Charles West, Blanche Sweet, Mary Pickford

Kentucky dreamer and failed playwright David Wark Griffith was the American film industry's first great mover and shaker. Three fine examples of his early short films make up this feature: *The Battle of Elderbush Gulch, Iola's Promise,* and *The Goddess of Sagebrush Gulch*. Silent.

1912–1922 B & W 50 minutes

DAISY MILLER

★

DIRECTOR: Peter Bogdanovich
CAST: Cybill Shepherd, Barry Brown, Cloris Leachman, Mildred Natwick, Eileen Brennan, Duilio Del Prete

Even a world-class director has a bad outing now and then. Peter Bogdanovich, who has made such great films as *Targets*, *The Last Picture Show*, and *Mask*, seemed to have lost his edge on this effort. This limp screen adaptation of a story by the great novelist Henry James is more a study on rambling dialogue than on the clashing of two cultures. Cybill Shepherd (of *The Last Picture Show* and TV's *Moonlighting*) plays a young American visiting Europe in the 1880s who sets the Victorian high society on its ear with her gauche behavior. She babbles her way through the film without really saying anything. Cloris Leachman and Eileen Brennan's talents are wasted in this exercise in vapid verbosity. Rated G.

1974 93 minutes

DANCE HALL RACKET

★½

DIRECTOR: Phil Tucker
CAST: Lenny Bruce

Inane dance scenes, cheap sets, and ham acting take up a lot of this film, and screenplay writer Lenny Bruce takes up the rest of the scenes. Bruce plays creepy killer Vincent, bodyguard to a vice lord who enjoys hurting women and saying things like "Big deal, I killed a guy. That makes me a criminal?" The comedy relief is too bad to believe and most of the cast look like they'd rather be doing something else, but this is a genuine sleazy exploitation film from the 1950s underground and it has a nasty feeling all its own, aided by the score by Charles Ruddy. Bruce gives an uneven performance but goes out in glory at the end. Last part of the tape features trailers for *Racket Girls* and a women's wrestling film featuring the fabulous Peaches Page!

1953 B & W 60 minutes

DANCE WITH A STRANGER

★★★★½

DIRECTOR: Mike Newell
CAST: Miranda Richardson, Rupert Everett, Ian Holm, Matthew Carroll, Tom Chadbon, Jane Bertish

A superbly acted, solidly directed import, this British drama is a completely convincing tale of tragic love. It is not unlike a British version of *The Postman Always Rings Twice*, but it has none of the heavy breathing and melodramatic style found in the two screen versions of James M. Cain's celebrated novel of murder and unbridled lust. Newcomer Miranda Richardson makes a stunning film debut as the platinum-blonde hostess in a working-class night club who falls in love with a self-indulgent, upperclass snob (Rupert Everett). The screen play was based on the true story of Ruth Ellis, who, on July 13, 1955, was hanged at London's Holloway prison for shooting her lover outside a pub. She was the last woman to be so executed in Britain, and her story provides gripping screen fare. Rated R for profanity, nudity, sex, and violence.

1985 102 minutes

DANCING IN THE DARK

★★½

DIRECTOR: Leon Marr

CAST: Martha Henry, Neil Munro, Rosemary Dunsmore, Richard Monette

Interesting drama about Edna Cormick (Martha Henry) who—after twenty years of being the ideal housewife, always faithful to her husband and willing to please—finds her life torn apart in a few short hours. From her hospital bed, Edna reconstructs the events that led up to her act of vengeance. Although this film is extremely slow-moving, feminists are likely to appreciate it. Rated PG-13.

1986 93 minutes

DANGER LIGHTS

★★★

DIRECTOR: George B. Seitz

CAST: Louis Wolheim, Jean Arthur, Robert Armstrong, Hugh Herbert

Louis Wolheim plays a tough-as-nails rail-yard boss who befriends hobo Robert Armstrong and jeopardizes his chances with a young Jean Arthur, who is "almost" a fiancée. This story, done many times before and since, works well against the backdrop of a railroad world that is now largely gone. Wolheim was a standout in an era when ugly men and women (notably Wallace Beery and Marie Dressler) were among the top box-office draws, but he died within a year after completing this film and deprived the rest of the 1930s of a fine character star.

1930 B & W 73 minutes

DANGEROUS SUMMER, A

★★

DIRECTOR: Quentin Masters

CAST: James Mason, Tom Skerritt, Ian Gilmour, Wendy Hughes

Set in Australia, this film deals with a posh resort—owned in part by American Howard Anderson (Tom Skerritt)—damaged by fire and the subsequent investigation by insurance troubleshooter George Engels (James Mason), sent by Lloyds of London to discover whether the incident was an accident or arson. The film was cheaply made, unimaginatively photographed, and poorly directed. Only the actors seem to know what they're doing, but, unfortunately, they aren't encouraged to do anything near their best. Even Mason's staunchest fans will be disappointed. Unrated, the film has violence and profanity.

1984 100 minutes

DANIEL

★★½

DIRECTOR: Sidney Lumet

CAST: Timothy Hutton, Mandy Patinkin, Lindsay Crouse, Edward Asner, Amanda Plummer

Sidney Lumet (*The Verdict*) directed this disappointing and ultimately depressing screen version of E. L. Doctorow's thinly veiled account of the Rosenberg case of thirty years ago, in which the parents of two young children were electrocuted as spies. If it weren't for Timothy Hutton's superb performance in the title role (as one of the children), *Daniel* would be much less effective. As it is, the film is powerful but frustrating, posing questions about the guilt of the Rosenbergs and then dodging them by dealing with a fictional family called the Isaacsons (with Mandy Patinkin and Lindsay Crouse excellent as the accused traitors) and then refusing to draw any conclusions. Rated R for profanity and violence.

1983 130 minutes

DANNY BOY

★★★★

DIRECTOR: Neil Jordan
CAST: Stephen Rea, Marie Kean, Ray McAnally, Donal McCann, Honor Heffernan

A young saxophone player witnesses the brutal murder of two people and becomes obsessed with understanding the act. Set in Ireland, this movie is enhanced by haunting musical interludes that highlight the drama of the people caught up in the Irish "troubles." The combination of the music, scenery, characters, and atmosphere creates an undeniably powerful experience. There are flaws, most notably in some of the coincidences, but the overall effect is mesmerizing. Rated R.

1982 92 minutes

DARK JOURNEY

★★★

DIRECTOR: Victor Saville
CAST: Vivien Leigh, Conrad Veidt, Joan Gardner, Anthony Bushell

Espionage with a twist. A British and a German spy fall in love in Stockholm during World War I.

1937 B & W 82 minutes

DARK VICTORY

★★★★

DIRECTOR: Edmund Goulding
CAST: Bette Davis, George Brent, Humphrey Bogart, Ronald Reagan, Geraldine Fitzgerald

This Warner Bros. release gave Bette Davis one of her best roles, as a headstrong heiress who discovers she has a brain tumor. A successful operation leads to a love affair with her doctor (George Brent). In the midst of all this bliss, Davis learns the tragic truth: surgery was only a halfway measure, and she will die in a year. Sure it's corny. But director Edmund Goulding, Davis, and her co-stars make it work. The only sour note comes from the miscasting of Humphrey Bogart as an Irish (!) stablehand.

1939 B & W 106 minutes

DARK WATERS

★★½

DIRECTOR: André de Toth
CAST: Merle Oberon, Franchot Tone, Thomas Mitchell, Fay Bainter, Rex Ingram, John Qualen, Elisha Cook Jr.

Muddled story of orphaned girl(?) Merle Oberon and her strange and terrifying experiences with her aunt and uncle in the bayou backwaters of Louisiana is atmospheric and properly chilling at times, but fails to deliver enough of a story to justify its moody build-up. This has the potential to be a first-rated thriller à la Hitchcock or Val Lewton and boasts one of the finest character casts of any film of the 1940s (including the powerful Rex Ingram and the wonderfully odd Elisha Cook Jr.), but never quite succeeds on any level. The leads are all right, but the supporting players (along with the misty bogs) really carry the ball in this film.

1944 B & W 90 minutes

DARLING

★★★★

DIRECTOR: John Schlesinger
CAST: Julie Christie, Dirk Bogarde, Laurence Harvey, Jose Luis de Villalonga

John Schlesinger's direction is first-rate, and Julie Christie gives an Oscar-winning portrayal of a ruthless model who bullies, bluffs, and claws her way to social success, only to find life at the top depressing and meaningless.

1965 B & W 122 minutes

DAVID AND LISA

★★★½

DIRECTOR: Frank Perry
CAST: Keir Dullea, Janet Margolin, Howard Da Silva, Neva Patterson, Clifton James

Mentally disturbed teenagers (Keir Dullea and Janet Margolin) meet and develop a sensitive emotional attachment while institutionalized. "A courageous and appealing little drama," said the *New York Times*. Indeed it is. Abetted by Howard Da Silva as their understanding doctor, Dullea and Margolin make this study highly watchable. Independently produced, this one was a sleeper.

1962 B & W 94 minutes

DAVID COPPERFIELD

★★★★½

DIRECTOR: George Cukor
CAST: Freddie Bartholomew, Frank Lawton, Lionel Barrymore, W. C. Fields, Edna May Oliver, Basil Rathbone

A first-rate production of Charles Dickens's rambling novel about a young man's adventures in nineteenth-century England. W. C. Fields and Edna May Oliver are standouts in an all-star cast.

1935 B & W 100 minutes

DAY OF THE LOCUST, THE

★★★★½

DIRECTOR: John Schlesinger
CAST: Donald Sutherland, Karen Black, Burgess Meredith, Bo Hopkins

This drama is both extremely depressing and spellbinding. It shows the unglamorous side of Hollywood in the 1930s. The people who don't succeed in the entertainment capital are the focus of the film. Rated R.

1975 144 minutes

DAYS OF HEAVEN

★★★★½

DIRECTOR: Terence Malick
CAST: Richard Gere, Brooke Adams, Sam Shepard, Linda Manz

Each frame of *Days of Heaven* looks like a page torn from an exquisitely beautiful picture book. The film begins in the slums of Chicago, where Bill (Richard Gere) works in a steel mill. He's hot-tempered, and a fight with the superintendent at the mill leaves him jobless. He decides to take Abby (Brooke Adams), his girl, and Linda (Linda Manz), his young sister, to the Texas Panhandle to work in the wheat fields at harvest time. "Bill and Abby told everybody they was brother and sister," explains narrator Manz in a heavy New York accent. "You know how people are. You tell 'em something and pretty soon they start talking." The owner of the farm (Sam Shepard) falls in love with Abby. Bill accidentally overhears a doctor tell the farmer he has a short time to live. Tired of seeing Abby work herself to exhaustion every day in the fields, Bill encourages her to respond to the farmer's attentions. That's the beginning of an idyllic year that ends in tragedy. Rated PG.

1978 95 minutes

DAYS OF WINE AND ROSES

★★★½

DIRECTOR: Blake Edwards
CAST: Jack Lemmon, Lee Remick, Charles Bickford, Jack Klugman

In this saddening film, Jack Lemmon and Lee Remick shatter the misconceptions about middle-class alcoholism.

1962 B & W 117 minutes

DEAD EASY

★★½

DIRECTOR: Bert Diling
CAST: Scott Burgess, Rosemary Paul, Tim McKenzie

George, Alexa, and Armstrong are three friends who try to break into the big-city night life. In doing so they anger a crime boss whose overreaction sets off a chain of events that results in every small-time hood and paid killer chasing them. Well-done contemporary crime thriller. Rated R for nudity, violence, language.

1978 90 minutes

DEAD END

★★★

DIRECTOR: William Wyler
CAST: Humphrey Bogart, Sylvia Sidney, Joel McCrea, Claire Trevor

Many famous names combined to film this story of people trying to escape their oppressive slum environment. Humphrey Bogart is cast in one of his many gangster roles from the 1930s. Joel McCrea conforms to his Hollywood stereotype by playing the "nice guy" architect, who dreams of rebuilding New York's waterfront.

1937 B & W 93 minutes

DEADLINE USA

★★★★

DIRECTOR: Richard Brooks
CAST: Humphrey Bogart, Kim Hunter, Ethel Barrymore

In this hard-hitting newspaper drama, Humphrey Bogart plays an editor who has to fight the city's underworld while keeping the publisher (superbly portrayed by Ethel Barrymore) from giving in to pressure and closing the paper down. While Kim Hunter is wasted in the small role as Bogart's ex-wife, the picture has much to recommend it. The scenes featuring Bogart and Barrymore together are absolutely electric.

1952 B & W 87 minutes

DEATH IN VENICE

★★★

DIRECTOR: Luchino Visconti
CAST: Dirk Bogarde, Marisa Berenson, Mark Burns, Silvana Mangano

This slow, studied film based on Thomas Mann's classic novel is about an artist's life and quest for beauty and perfection. The good cast seems to move through this movie without communicating with one another or the audience. Visually absorbing, but lifeless; seems longer than its 130-minute running time. Adult language, adult situations throughout. Rated PG.

1971 130 minutes

DEATH OF A CENTERFOLD

★★

DIRECTOR: Gabrielle Beaumont
CAST: Jamie Lee Curtis, Robert Reed, Bruce Weitz

This made-for-TV film chronicles the brutal murder of Playboy playmate Dorothy Stratten. Bob Fosse's *Star 80* does a much better job of getting inside the characters of Stratten and her power-crazy husband. Unrated.

1981 100 minutes

DEATH OF A SCOUNDREL

★★★

DIRECTOR: Charles Martin
CAST: George Sanders, Zsa Zsa Gabor, Tom Conway, Yvonne DeCarlo, Lisa Farraday, Nancy Gates, Coleen Grey, Victor Jory, John Hoyt

If anyone could portray a suave, debonair, conniving, ruthlessly charming, amoral, despicable, notorious, manipulating cad, it was George Sanders. He does so to a *T* in this portrait of the compleat rake—based on the life of financier Serge Rubenstein. Sadly, the film—while replete with seduction, suicide, murder, betrayal, and thievery—is mainly banal trash made palatable now and then by touches of comedy. However, if you would like to see Sanders cavort with his real-life ex-wife, Zsa Zsa, and stab his real-life brother Tom Conway in the back....

1956 119 minutes

DEATH OF A SOLDIER

★★½

DIRECTOR: Philippe Mora
CAST: James Coburn, Bill Hunter, Reb Brown, Maurie Fields

Based on a true story that changed the procedures of military court-martial. In 1942 an American GI stationed in Australia murders three Melbourne women. The incident aggravates U.S.-Australian relations, and General MacArthur orders the execution of the serviceman to firm up Allied unity. James Coburn plays a major who believes the GI isn't sane enough to stand trial. While the movie is well-acted and technically slick, the script is surprisingly dull and uninvolving. Rated R for profanity, violence, and nudity.

1985 93 minutes

DEATHTRAP

★★★

DIRECTOR: Sidney Lumet
CAST: Michael Caine, Christopher Reeve, Dyan Cannon, Irene Worth, Henry Jones

An enjoyable mystery-comedy based on the long-running Broadway play, this Sidney Lumet film stars Michael Caine, Christopher Reeve, and Dyan Cannon. Caine plays a once-successful playwright who decides to steal a brilliant murder mystery just written by one of his drama students (Reeve), claim it as his own, murder the student, and collect the royalties. Rated PG for violence and adult themes.

1982 116 minutes

DEER HUNTER, THE

★★★★★

DIRECTOR: Michael Cimino
CAST: Robert De Niro, John Cazale, John Savage, Meryl Streep, Christopher Walken

Five friends—Michael (Robert De Niro), Stan (John Cazale), Nick (Christopher Walken), Steven (John Savage), and Axel (Chuck Aspergen)—work at the dangerous blast furnace in a steel mill of a dingy Midwestern industrial town in 1968. At quitting time, they make their way to their favorite local bar to drink away the pressures of the day. For Michael, Nick, and Steven it is the last participation in the ritual. In a few days, they leave for Vietnam, where they find horror and death. What follows is a gripping study of heroism and the meaning of friendship. Rated R for profanity and violence.

1978 183 minutes

DEFENSE OF THE REALM

★★★★

DIRECTOR: David Drury
CAST: Gabriel Byrne, Greta Scacchi, Denholm Elliott, Ian Bannen, Bill Paterson, Fulton MacKay

In London, two reporters (Gabriel Byrne and Denholm Elliott) become convinced that a scandal involving a government official (Ian Bannen) may be a sinister coverup. Acting on this belief puts both their lives in danger. *Defense of the Realm* is a tough-minded British thriller that asks some thought-provoking questions about what the public has a right to know. Rated PG for suspense.

1986 96 minutes

DEFIANT ONES, THE

★★★★

DIRECTOR: Stanley Kramer
CAST: Tony Curtis, Sidney Poitier, Theodore Bikel, Charles McGraw, Lon Chaney Jr.

Director Stanley Kramer (*Inherit the Wind*) scored one of his few artistic successes with this compelling story about two escaped convicts (Tony Curtis and Sidney Poitier) shackled together—and coping with mutual hatred—as they run from the authorities in the South.

1958 B & W 97 minutes

DEJA VU

★

DIRECTOR: Anthony Richmond
CAST: Jaclyn Smith, Shelley Winters, Claire Bloom, Nigel Terry, Richard Kay, Frank Gatliff

Jaclyn Smith (of TV *Charlie's Angels* fame) and Nigel Terry (*Excalibur*) put in equally lame performances in this stupid story about reincarnation. Shelley Winters's portrayal of a stereotypical Russian gypsy is so bad it's laughable. The film's one and only good point is Claire Bloom, whose performance is so convincing that one wonders whether her scenes were not meant for this lamentable affair. Rated R for some sex, nudity, and violence.

1984 91 minutes

DESERT BLOOM

★★★

DIRECTOR: Eugene Corr
CAST: Jon Voight, JoBeth Williams, Ellen Barkin, Allen Garfield, Annabeth Gish

This poignant study of awakening adolescence and family turmoil is effectively set against a backdrop of 1950 Las Vegas, as the atomic age dawns. The story unfolds slowly but sensitively. The cast is superb. Thirteen-year-old Annabeth Gish gives a remarkably complex performance as a brilliant girl who must cope with an abusive stepfather, an ineffectual mother, and a sexpot aunt. Rated PG.

1986 106 minutes

DESERT HEARTS

★★★½

DIRECTOR: Donna Deitch
CAST: Helen Shaver, Patricia Charbonneau, Audra Lindley, Andra Akers, Gwen Welles, Dean Butler, James Stanley

A sensitive portrayal of the evolving relationship between a young, openly lesbian woman and a quiet university professor ten years her senior. Set on a Reno "divorce ranch" in 1959. The excellent acting by Patricia Charbonneau and Helen Shaver superbly sets off the development of their individual and joint characters. Audra Lindley adds a welcome touch as the grumbling stepmother. Some may find the explicit love scenes upsetting, but the humor and characterization entirely overrule any objection on this basis, and the bonus of 1950s props and sets is a treat. Rated R for profanity and sex.

1986 90 minutes

DESIRE UNDER THE ELMS

★★

DIRECTOR: Delbert Mann

CAST: Sophia Loren, Anthony Perkins, Burl Ives, Frank Overton

There is not much to recommend in this adaptation of Eugene O'Neill's play. Burl Ives brings home a new wife, Sophia Loren, and sparks are supposed to ignite with the stepson, Anthony Perkins. But this film merely proves that good actors, when miscast, make for tedious viewing and disappointment.

1958 114 minutes

DETECTIVE, THE

★★★

DIRECTOR: Gordon Douglas

CAST: Frank Sinatra, Lee Remick, Al Freeman, Jacqueline Bisset, Ralph Meeker, Jack Klugman, Robert Duvall, William Windom

A disgusted NYPD detective (Frank Sinatra), carrying an overload of both professional and personal problems, railroads the wrong man into the electric chair while seeking a homosexual's killer. He loses his job and leaves his nympho wife (Lee Remick). Filmed on location in New York, this is one of the first hard-look-at-a-cop's life films.

1968 114 minutes

DETOUR

★★★

DIRECTOR: Edgar G. Ulmer

CAST: Tom Neal, Ann Savage, Claudia Drake, Edmund MacDonald, Tim Ryan, Esther Howard

This routine story about a drifter enticed into crime is skillfully constructed, economically produced, and competently acted; it has long been considered one of the best (if not *the* best) low-budget film ever made. German director Edgar G. Ulmer took the best that PRC (Producer's Releasing Corporation) had to offer him in the way of budget and resources and made the most acclaimed film PRC ever released. Ann Savage as the beguiling, destructive enchantress playing off Tom Neal's infatuation rings just as true in this bargain-basement production as it does in the highly acclaimed adult crime dramas produced by the major studios.

1945 B & W 69 minutes

DEVIL AND DANIEL WEBSTER, THE

★★★★

DIRECTOR: William Dieterle

CAST: Edward Arnold, Walter Huston, James Craig, Anne Shirley, Jane Darwell, Simone Simon, Gene Lockhart

This wickedly witty tale, based on a Stephen Vincent Benét story, delivers some potent messages. But the moralizing never interferes with the sparkling quality of the entertainment. Edward Arnold, so often cast as a despicable villain, is riveting as the noble Webster. This eloquent hero must defend ingenuous James Craig in a bizarre courtroom. Both of their immortal souls are at stake. And the jury is straight from hell. Opposing Webster is Mr. Scratch, also known as the Devil. Walter Huston gives a dazzling performance in the role.

1941 B & W 85 minutes

DEVIL AT 4 O'CLOCK, THE

★★★

DIRECTOR: Mervyn LeRoy

CAST: Spencer Tracy, Frank Sinatra, Kerwin Mathews, Jean-Pierre Aumont

This script may be weak and predictable, but the acting of Spencer Tracy and Frank Sinatra make this a watchable motion picture. Tracy is a priest who is in charge of an orphanage. When their island home is endangered by an impending volcanic eruption, he seeks the aid of a group of convicts headed by Sinatra.

1961 126 minutes

DEVILS, THE

★★★★

DIRECTOR: Ken Russell
CAST: Oliver Reed, Vanessa Redgrave, Dudley Sutton, Max Adrian, Gemma Jones

Next to *Women in Love*, this is director Ken Russell's best film. Exploring witchcraft and politics in France during the seventeenth century, it's a mad mixture of drama, horror, camp, and comedy. Ugly for the most part (with several truly unsettling scenes), it is still fascinating. Rated R.

1971 109 minutes

DIAMOND HEAD

★★

DIRECTOR: Guy Green
CAST: Charlton Heston, Yvette Mimieux, George Chakiris, France Nuyen, James Darren

Domineering Hawaiian plantation boss Charlton Heston comes close to ruining his family with his dictatorial ways. For openers, he snobbishly considers his sister Yvette Mimieux's suitor his social inferior and thus beneath contempt. Sex kitten Yvette reacts accordingly. The lush scenery is the only credible thing in this pineapple opera.

1963 107 minutes

DIARY OF A MAD HOUSEWIFE

★★★

DIRECTOR: Frank Perry
CAST: Richard Benjamin, Carrie Snodgress, Frank Langella

Most women will detest Jonathan (Richard Benjamin), the self-centered, social climber husband of Tina (Carrie Snodgress). He has had an affair and also lost all their savings in a bad investment. Tina, a college graduate, has been unhappily stuck at home for years with their two children. She finally finds happiness in an affair with George (Frank Langella). Profanity, sex, and nudity are included in this film.

1970 94 minutes

DIARY OF ANNE FRANK, THE

★★★★½

DIRECTOR: George Stevens
CAST: Millie Perkins, Joseph Schildkraut, Shelley Winters

Excellent adaptation of the Broadway play dealing with the terror Jews felt during the Nazi raids of World War II. Two families are forced to hide in a Jewish sympathizer's attic to avoid capture by the Nazis. Anne (Millie Perkins) is the teen-age girl who doesn't stop dreaming of a better future. Shelley Winters won an Oscar for her role as the hysterical Mrs. Van Daan, who shares sparse food and space with the Frank family.

1959 B & W 170 minutes

DIFFERENT STORY, A

★★★½

DIRECTOR: Paul Aaron
CAST: Perry King, Meg Foster, Valerie Curtin, Peter Donat

Perry King and Meg Foster play homosexuals who realize their romances are just not clicking. They fall in love with each other, marry, grow rich, and, eventually, dissatisfied. To be fair, this is not a boring film. King and Foster are genuinely funny and appealing as the most modern of young adult couples. The screenplay, however, lets them down on more than one occasion, and whoever came up with the King character's voice and movement should be given a manual on why caricatures of humans sometimes fail to win an audience. Taken strictly as an entertainment, it works. Rated PG.

1979 107 minutes

DIM SUM: A LITTLE BIT OF HEART

★★★★

DIRECTOR: Wayne Wang

CAST: Laureen Chew, Kim Chew, Victor Wong, Ida F. O. Chung, Cora Miao

Dim Sum is an independently made American movie about the tension and affection between a Chinese mother and daughter living in San Francisco's Chinatown. The film moves quietly, but contains many moments of humor. The restraint of the mother, who wants her daughter to marry, and the frustration of the daughter, who wants to live her life as she chooses, are beautifully conveyed by real-life mother and daughter Laureen and Kim Chew. Victor Wong, as a rambunctious uncle, is a gas. Rated PG.

1985 88 minutes

DINO

★★½

DIRECTOR: Thomas Carr

CAST: Sal Mineo, Brian Keith, Susan Kohner, Joe De Santis

In this okay story of a wayward young man who comes to grips with his life and environment as a result of assistance from social worker Brian Keith and girlfriend Susan Kohner, Sal Mineo takes his place along with James Dean, James MacArthur, Paul Newman, and Steve McQueen as rebellious, troubled youths of the 1950s. Nothing new, but interestingly done.

1957 B & W 94 minutes

DIVORCE HIS: DIVORCE HERS

★★½

DIRECTOR: Waris Hussein

CAST: Richard Burton, Elizabeth Taylor, Carrie Nye, Barry Foster, Gabriele Ferzetti

This less-than-exceptional TV movie follows the breakup of a marriage in which both partners are allowed to explain what they think led to the failure of their marriage. Although its soap-opera format is mildly interesting, the talents of Elizabeth Taylor and Richard Burton are barely tapped.

1972 144 minutes

DOCKS OF NEW YORK, THE

★★★★

DIRECTOR: Josef von Sternberg

CAST: George Bancroft, Betty Compson, Olga Baclanova, Mitchell Lewis, Clyde Cook

A solid drama of love and death on a big-city waterfront. Rough-edged George Bancroft rescues would-be suicide Betty Compson, marries her, clears her of a murder charge, and goes to jail for her. The direction is masterful, the camerawork and lighting superb in this, one of the last silent films to be released.

1928 B & W 60 minutes

DOCTOR FAUSTUS

★

DIRECTORS: Richard Burton, Neville Coghill

CAST: Richard Burton, Andreas Teuber, Ian Marter, Elizabeth Donovan, Elizabeth Taylor

The best performance in this laughable variation on Christopher Marlowe's timeless story is by Andreas Teuber, a member of the Oxford University Dramatic Society. That wouldn't be so outrageous a claim if it weren't for the fact that this artsy little film stars the world's highest paid acting team, Richard Burton and

Elizabeth Taylor. Taylor actually gives one of her better performances from this period in her career—she has no dialogue and appears on screen as the silent embodiment of the female characters in the story, most notably Helen of Troy and a silver-coated lover of Alexander the Great. Pretentious and dull, this failed effort is no worse than some of the famous couple's better-known flops, and it cost a lot less to can this ham than it did to bring in *The Comedians* or *Boom*!

1968 93 minutes

DR. ZHIVAGO

★★★★

DIRECTOR: David Lean
CAST: Omar Sharif, Julie Christie, Geraldine Chaplin, Rod Steiger, Alec Guinness

An epic treatment was given to Boris Pasternak's novel of romance and revolution in this film. Omar Sharif is Zhivago, a Russian doctor and poet whose personal life is ripped apart by the upheaval of the Russian Revolution. The screenplay is choppy and overlong and is often sacrificed to the spectacle of vast panoramas, detailed sets, and impressive costumes. These artistic elements, along with a beautiful musical score, make for cinema on a grand scale, and it remains a most watchable movie.

1965 197 minutes

DODSWORTH

★★★★

DIRECTOR: William Wyler
CAST: Walter Huston, Ruth Chatterton, Mary Astor, David Niven, Spring Byington, Paul Lukas, John Payne, Maria Ouspenskaya

Walter Huston, in the title role, heads an all-star cast in this outstanding adaptation of the Sinclair Lewis novel. Auto tycoon Samuel Dodsworth is the epitome of the classic American self-made man. His wife is an appearance-conscious *nouveau riche* snob who goes European during a vacation trip over the water. Suddenly Dodsworth's values are rustic, and he is a bumpkin. But for an idyllic affair in Italy, he comes close to losing the peace and contentment he believes he has achieved through hard work and adherence to basic ideals. An intelligent, mature script, excellent characterizations, and sensitive cinematography make this film a modern classic.

1936 B & W 101 minutes

DOG DAY AFTERNOON

★★★★½

DIRECTOR: Sidney Lumet
CAST: Al Pacino, John Cazale, Charles Durning, Carol Kane

Dog Day Afternoon is a masterpiece of contemporary commentary. Al Pacino once again proves himself to be in the front rank of America's finest actors. Director Sidney Lumet (*Murder on the Orient Express*; *Serpico*; etc.) scores high with masterful pacing and real suspense. This is an offbeat drama about a gay man who's involved in bank-robbing. Highly recommended. Rated R.

1975 130 minutes

DOLL'S HOUSE, A

★★★

DIRECTOR: Joseph Losey
CAST: Jane Fonda, David Warner, Trevor Howard

Jane Fonda is quite good in this screen version of Henrik Ibsen's play about a liberated woman in the nineteenth century, and her struggles to maintain her freedom. Pacing is a problem at times, but first-class acting and beautiful sets keep the viewer interested.

1973 103 minutes

DOLLMAKER, THE

★★★★

DIRECTOR: Daniel Petrie

CAST: Jane Fonda, Levon Helm, Amanda Plummer, Susan Kingsley, Ann Hearn, Geraldine Page

Jane Fonda won an Emmy for her intensely quiet portrayal of a mother of five in 1940s Kentucky. As a devoted mother, her only personal happiness is sculpting dolls out of wood. When her husband is forced to take work in Detroit, their relocation causes many personal hardships and setbacks. The story is beautifully told. This made-for-TV movie is unrated, but it provides excellent family entertainment.

1984 140 minutes

DOMINO PRINCIPLE, THE

★

DIRECTOR: Stanley Kramer

CAST: Gene Hackman, Richard Widmark, Candice Bergen, Eli Wallach, Mickey Rooney

Never have so many been wasted on so little. The only true victims in this assassination/double-cross/conspiracy thriller are the viewers tricked into watching it. Even Gene Hackman can't do anything as a confused convict busted out of prison with the intent to kill somebody. Nothing makes sense in this mess, and the book from which it is taken is no better. Rated R for violence.

1977 100 minutes

DON'T CRY, IT'S ONLY THUNDER

★★★★

DIRECTOR: Peter Werner

CAST: Dennis Christopher, Susan Saint James

Here is one of those "little" movies that slipped by without much notice yet are so satisfying when discovered by adventurous video renters. A black market wheeler-dealer (Dennis Christopher, from *Breaking Away*) lining his pockets behind the lines during the Vietnam War is forced to aid some Asian nuns and their ever-increasing group of Saigon street orphans. The results are predictably heartwarming and occasionally heartbreaking, but the film never drifts off into sentimental melodrama. Rated PG.

1982 108 minutes

DOOMSDAY FLIGHT, THE

★★★

DIRECTOR: William Graham

CAST: Jack Lord, Edmond O'Brien, Van Johnson, John Saxon, Michael Sarrazin

Rod Serling wrote the script for this made-for-television movie, the first to depict the hijacking of an airliner. A distraught Edmond O'Brien blackmails an airline company by planting a bomb aboard a passenger plane. *The Doomsday Flight* offered good suspense at the time, but may not be as provocative today. Still, good acting is on hand as the search for the bomb is carried out.

1966 100 minutes

DOUBLE LIFE, A

★★★★

DIRECTOR: George Cukor

CAST: Ronald Colman, Edmond O'Brien, Shelley Winters, Ray Collins

Ronald Colman gives an Oscar-winning performance as a famous actor whose stage life begins to take over his personality and private life, forcing him to revert to stage characters, including Othello, to cope with everyday situations. Clever, brilliantly written by Garson Kanin and Ruth Gordon, and impressively acted by a stand-out cast of top character actors and actresses. Top treatment of a fine story.

1947 B & W 104 minutes

DOWN TO THE SEA IN SHIPS

★★★

DIRECTOR: Elmer Clifton

CAST: William Walcott, Marguerite Courtot, Clara Bow, Raymond McKee

The plot involving a romantic conflict within a family of whalers has a beard, but vivid scenes filmed at sea aboard real New England whalers out of Bedford make it worth while.

1922 B & W 83 minutes

DOWNHILL RACER

★★★½

DIRECTOR: Michael Ritchie

CAST: Robert Redford, Gene Hackman, Camilla Sparv

Robert Redford struggles with an unappealing character, in this study of an Olympic skier. But Gene Hackman is excellent as the coach who tries to turn him around, and the exciting scenes of this snow sport hold the film together. Rated PG.

1969 101 minutes

DRAGON SEED

★★½

DIRECTORS: Jack Conway, Harold S. Bucquet

CAST: Katharine Hepburn, Walter Huston, Turhan Bey, Hurd Hatfield

This study of a Chinese town torn asunder by Japanese occupation is taken from the novel by Nobel Prize winner Pearl S. Buck. It's occasionally gripping but in general too long.

1944 B & W 145 minutes

DREAM OF PASSION, A

★★★½

DIRECTOR: Jules Dassin

CAST: Melina Mercouri, Ellen Burstyn, Andreas Voutsinas, Despo Diamantidou, Dimitris Papamichael

Melina Mercouri plays a Greek actress who is preparing to play Medea. As a publicity stunt, she goes to a prison to meet a real-life Medea. Ellen Burstyn is brilliant as the American prisoner who has killed her three children in order to take revenge on her husband. Rated R.

1978 106 minutes

DREAM STREET

★★

DIRECTOR: D. W. Griffith

CAST: Carol Dempster, Charles Emmett Mack, Ralph Graves, Edward Peil, Tyrone Power Sr., Morgan Wallace

Good struggles with evil in this sentimental morality tale of London's infamous Limehouse slum. Two brothers, in love with the same girl, vie for her attentions while a wily, blackmailing Chinese gambler plans to take her by force. Good eventually wins, but a weak plot, undermined by lackluster acting and preposterous resolution, induces sleep. Silent.

1921 B & W 138 minutes

DRESSER, THE

★★★★★

DIRECTOR: Peter Yates

CAST: Albert Finney, Tom Courtenay, Edward Fox, Zena Walker

Peter Yates (*Breaking Away*; *Bullitt*) directed this superb screen treatment of Ronald Harwood's play about an eccentric stage actor (Albert Finney) in wartime England and the loyal valet (Tom Courtenay) who cares for him, sharing his triumphs and tragedies. Rated PG for language.

1983 118 minutes

DUET FOR ONE

★★★

DIRECTOR: Andrei Konchalovsky
CAST: Julie Andrews, Alan Bates, Max von Sydow, Rupert Everett

As an English virtuoso violinist with multiple sclerosis, Julie Andrews gives an outstanding performance in this high-class tearjerker. Alan Bates is her sympathetic but philandering husband. Max von Sydow is the psychiatrist who atttempts to help her. And Rupert Everett plays her protégé who shuns the classical world for big time showbiz. Rated R.

1987 110 minutes

EARLY FROST, AN

★★★★½

DIRECTOR: John Erman
CAST: Gena Rowlands, Ben Gazzara, Aidan Quinn, Sylvia Sidney, John Glover

This timely, extremely effective drama focuses on a family's attempt to come to grips with the fact that their son is not only gay but has AIDS as well. Gena Rowlands, one of Hollywood's most neglected actresses, and Aidan Quinn take the acting honors as mother and son. One of those rare television movies that works on all levels, it is highly recommended.

1985 100 minutes

EAST OF EDEN (ORIGINAL)

★★★★★

DIRECTOR: Elia Kazan
CAST: James Dean, Jo Van Fleet, Julie Harris, Raymond Massey, Burl Ives

The final portion of John Steinbeck's renowned novel of miscommunication and conflict between a father and son was transformed into a powerful, emotional movie. James Dean burst onto the screen as the rebellious son in his first starring role. Jo Van Fleet received an Oscar for her role as Kate, a bordello madam and Dean's long-forgotten mother.

1955 115 minutes

EAST OF EDEN (REMAKE)

★★★½

DIRECTOR: Harvey Hart
CAST: Jane Seymour, Timothy Bottoms, Bruce Boxleitner, Warren Oates, Anne Baxter, Lloyd Bridges, Howard Duff

This above-average television miniseries maintains the integrity of the source material by John Steinbeck without dipping too far into bathos. One major change: the focus shifts from the two sons —Timothy Bottoms and Bruce Boxleitner—who crave Papa's affection, to the deliciously evil woman—Jane Seymour—who twists them all around her little finger. Excellent supporting cast tries to follow the script while Seymour chews up the scenery. Ponderous and overlong; although the tone is conserved with no commercial interruptions, it's a bit much for one sitting. Stick with the 1955 film version. Unrated.

1982 240 minutes

EAST OF ELEPHANT ROCK

★★

DIRECTOR: Don Boyd
CAST: John Hurt, Jeremy Kemp, Judi Bowker

This story of the 1948 British struggle to maintain a Far Eastern colony focuses on a new governor general's takeover after his predecessor is murdered by terrorists. The film is slow-paced and burdened with soap-opera overtones. Rated R.

1981 93 minutes

EASY RIDER

★★★½

DIRECTOR: Dennis Hopper
CAST: Peter Fonda, Dennis Hopper, Jack Nicholson, Karen Black, Luana Anders

Time has not been kind to this 1969 release, about two drifters (Peter Fonda and Dennis Hopper) motorcycling their way across the country only to be confronted with violence and bigotry. Jack Nicholson's keystone performance, however, still makes it worth watching. Rated R.

1969 94 minutes

ECHO PARK

★★★

DIRECTOR: Robert Dornhelm
CAST: Susan Dey, Thomas Hulce, Michael Bowen, Christopher Walker, Shirley Jo Finney, Heinrich Schweiger, John Paragon, Richard "Cheech" Marin, Cassandra Peterson

Tom Hulce (*Amadeus*, *Animal House*), Susan Dey (formerly of TV's *The Partridge Family*), and Michael Bowen, half-brother of David Carradine, star as three young show-biz hopefuls living in one of Los Angeles's seedier neighborhoods and waiting for stardom to strike. Director Robert Dornhelm and screenwriter Michael Ventura have some interesting things to say about the quest for fame, and the stars provide some memorable moments. But these are wrapped up in a meandering, espisodic, and sometimes off-putting package. Overall, it is a watchable "little" film that should please those with a taste for something different. Rated R for nudity, profanity, and violence.

1986 93 minutes

EIGHTY BLOCKS FROM TIFFANY'S

★★★½

DIRECTOR: Gary Weis
CAST: Documentary

An incredibly candid look at the society of inner-city gang members and their outlook at life. Directed by Gary Weis, who produced a number of film shorts for *Saturday Night Live*, this documentary allows the participants to speak for themselves, without much commentary by the filmmaker. Everyone appears up front and unaffected by the presence of the film crew, which leaves the viewer pitying these people who can't see beyond the few city blocks that make up their world. No rating, but some very rough language.

1979 72 minutes

84 CHARING CROSS ROAD

★★½

DIRECTOR: David Jones
CAST: Anne Bancroft, Anthony Hopkins, Judi Dench, Maurice Denham

Anne Bancroft manages to act manic even while reading books in this true story based on the life of Helene Hanff, a writer and reader who begins a twenty-year correspondance with a London bookseller (Anthony Hopkins). Along with her orders for first editions, Hanff sends witty letters and care packages to the employees during the hard postwar times. Hanff and the bookseller begin to rely on the correspondence, yet never get to meet. Columbia released this "specialty product" film without much fanfare. Rated PG for language.

1986 99 minutes

ELECTRIC HORSEMAN, THE

★★★

DIRECTOR: Sydney Pollack
CAST: Robert Redford, Jane Fonda, Valerie Perrine, Willie Nelson, John Saxon, Nicolas Coster

Directed by Sydney Pollack (*Tootsie*), *The Electric Horseman* brought the third teaming of Jane Fonda and Robert Redford on the screen. The result is a winsome piece of light entertainment. *The Electric Horseman* explores themes like the importance of individual integrity and the dangers of manipulation by the rich. Redford plays Sonny Steele, a former rodeo star who has become the unhappy spokesman for Ranch Breakfast, a brand of cereal. He's always in trouble and in danger of blowing the job—until he decides to rebel. Fonda is the TV reporter who covers his story. Rated PG.

1979 120 minutes

ELENI

★★★

DIRECTOR: Peter Yates
CAST: Kate Nelligan, John Malkovich, Linda Hunt

Interesting film adaptation of Nicholas Gage's factual book *Eleni*. In 1948, during the civil war in Greece, a small mountain village is terrorized by a group of communist guerrillas. Eleni Gatzoyiannis (Kate Nelligan) defies the communists and their attempts to abduct her children to send them to prison camps behind the Iron Curtain, and is subsequently held captive, tortured, and eventually executed in cold blood. Eleni's son Nicholas Gage (John Malkovich) returns to Greece after many years as a reporter for the *New York Times*, devoting his life there to discovering the facts surrounding his mother's death while trying to unmask her killers. Rated PG for language and violence.

1985 116 minutes

ELEPHANT MAN, THE

★★★★

DIRECTOR: David Lynch
CAST: Anthony Hopkins, John Hurt, Anne Bancroft, Wendy Hiller, Freddie Jones

Though it has its flaws, this film is a fascinating and heartbreaking study of the life of John Merrick, a hopelessly deformed but kind and intelligent man who struggles for dignity. John Hurt is magnificent in the title role. Rated PG.

1980 B & W 125 minutes

ELLIS ISLAND

★★★

DIRECTOR: Jerry London
CAST: Richard Burton, Faye Dunaway, Ben Vereen, Melba Moore, Ann Jillian, Greg Martyn, Peter Riegert

This TV miniseries, of the soap-opera variety, follows the lives of three immigrants who come to the United States at the turn of the century. All struggle to find acceptance, happiness, and success in the promised land.

1984 310 minutes

ELMER GANTRY

★★★★

DIRECTOR: Richard Brooks
CAST: Burt Lancaster, Jean Simmons, Dean Jagger, Arthur Kennedy, Shirley Jones

Burt Lancaster gives one of his most memorable performances in this release as a phony evangelist who, along with Jean Simmons, exploits the faithful with his fire-and-brimstone sermons. Arthur Kennedy is the reporter out to expose their operation in this screen version of Sinclair Lewis's story set in the Midwest of the 1920s.

1960 145 minutes

EMILY

★★

DIRECTOR: Henry Herbert
CAST: Koo Stark

This British film was Koo Stark's premiere in soft-core porn. She plays a teenager returning home from boarding school who finds out that her mother is a well-paid prostitute. This bit of news upsets Emily momentarily, but she manages to create her own sexual world with a female painter, the painter's husband, and her boyfriend, James. Lots of nudity and sex, but it still manages to be boring. Rated R.

1982 87 minutes

EMPEROR JONES, THE

★★★½

DIRECTOR: Dudley Murphy
CAST: Paul Robeson, Dudley Digges, Frank Wilson, Ruby Elzy, Fredi Washington

This liberal version of Eugene O'Neill's prize-winning play invents entire sections that were written to capitalize on star Paul Robeson's fame as a singer as well as an introductory piece that provides a background for Robeson's character, the doomed Jones. This is still an interesting and sometimes strong film despite the drastic changes. Watching and listening to Robeson is always a treat. This was considered a lost film for years. Surviving prints that have been transferred to tape are not always in the best of condition, so quality will vary on this title.

1933 B & W 72 minutes

END OF THE ROAD

★★

DIRECTOR: Aram Avakian
CAST: Stacy Keach, Harris Yulin, Dorothy Tristan, James Earl Jones

As daring as this film is, it remains almost unwatchable as a general form of entertainment and at times a bit boring as an experiment. Stacy Keach plays a college graduate who falls out of society, receives help from an unorthodox psychotherapist named Doctor D (James Earl Jones), then becomes intimately involved with a married couple. The imagery can be compelling at times, but the finale is too graphic for the eyes. Graded leniently for sheer nerve. Rated X (by 1960s standards) but more like a hard R for sex, nudity, and adult themes.

1969 110 minutes

ENDLESS LOVE

★★

DIRECTOR: Franco Zeffirelli
CAST: Brooke Shields, Martin Hewitt, Shirley Knight, Don Murray

Though this story of a teen-age love affair has all the elements of a great romance, it is marred by implausibility and inconsistency. The film improves as it progresses and even offers some compelling moments, but not enough to compensate for its flaws. It's unfortunate that director Franco Zeffirelli didn't do more with this modern-day *Romeo and Juliet*. Rated R because of sex and nudity.

1981 115 minutes

ENOLA GAY: THE MEN, THE MISSION, THE ATOMIC BOMB

★★★

DIRECTOR: David Lowell Rich
CAST: Billy Crystal, Kim Darby, Patrick Duffy, Gary Frank, Gregory Harrison

In this made-for-TV drama, Patrick Duffy plays Paul Tibbets, the man in charge of the plane that dropped the atomic bomb over Hiroshima. The film delves into the lives and reactions of the crew members in a fairly effective manner.

1980 150 minutes

EQUUS

★★★★

DIRECTOR: Sidney Lumet

CAST: Richard Burton, Peter Firth, Colin Blakely, Joan Plowright, Harry Andrews, Eileen Atkins, Jenny Agutter

Peter Firth plays a stableboy whose mysterious fascination with horses results in an act of meaningless cruelty and violence. Richard Burton plays the psychiatrist brought in to uncover Firth's hidden hostilities. The expanding of Peter Shaffer's play leaves the film somewhat unfocused but the scenes between Burton and Firth are intense, riveting, and beautifully acted. This was Burton's last quality film role; he was nominated for best actor. Rated R for profanity and nudity.

1977 137 minutes

ERIC

★★★★

DIRECTOR: James Goldstone

CAST: Patricia Neal, John Savage, Claude Akins, Sian Barbara Allen, Mark Hamill, Nehemiah Persoff

This made-for-TV movie is the true story of Eric Lund, a teenager with a promising athletic future who becomes terminally ill. John Savage, in the title role, gives a meaningful portrayal of a young man who refuses to give up. Patricia Neal, as the mother, gives the kind of warm, sensitive performance she is noted for, and there is a fine supporting cast. This is not just another disease-of-the-week tearjerker.

1975 100 minutes

ESCAPE TO BURMA

★

DIRECTOR: Allan Dwan

CAST: Barbara Stanwyck, Robert Ryan, David Farrar, Murvyn Vye

This features a tea plantation, wild animals, and a hunted man seeking refuge. Every great star makes a turkey, and this is Barbara Stanwyck's. But some films are so bad they are good. This may be one.

1955 B & W 87 minutes

ESCAPE TO THE SUN

★★★

DIRECTOR: Menahem Golan

CAST: Laurence Harvey, Josephine Chaplin, John Ireland, Jack Hawkins

Two young university students try to escape from the oppressive Soviet Union under the watchful eyes of the KGB. They try first for an exit visa; only one visa is issued, and one of the students is taken into custody. The two are forced to make a heroic escape to the West. Rated PG for violence.

1984 94 minutes

ESCAPIST, THE

DIRECTOR: Eddie Beverly Jr.

CAST: Bill Shirk, Peter Lupus, Milbourne Christopher, Dick the Bruiser, Gary Todd, Cynthia Johns, Terri Mann

Real-life escape artist, Bill Shirk, plays himself in this exhibition of his talents through multiple escapes. The thin plot encasing his feats has him as a radio station owner threatened by a big-business takeover. To keep his station known, he performs stunts for publicity. He acquires a mentor, Mr. Weiss (Harry Houdini's real name), to help him improve before the frightening climax. Many of the players, including Shirk, have limited acting ablility. The script and dialogue lack a slick professional touch. Unrated, the film contains nudity and simulated sex.

1983 87 minutes

ETERNALLY YOURS

★★★

DIRECTOR: Tay Garnett

CAST: Loretta Young, David Niven, C. Aubrey Smith, ZaSu Pitts, Billie Burke, Eve Arden, Hugh Herbert, Broderick Crawford

A stellar cast of accomplished scene-stealers deftly brings off this iffy story of a magician (David Niven) and his wife (Loretta Young), who thinks his tricks are overshadowing their marital happiness.

1939 B & W 95 minutes

EUREKA

★★★★½

DIRECTOR: Nicolas Roeg

CAST: Gene Hackman, Theresa Russell, Rutger Hauer, Jane Lapotaire, Mickey Rourke, Ed Lauter, Joe Pesci

Another stunner from one of the greatest living directors, Nicolas Roeg (*Don't Look Now, Insignificance*). *Eureka* is about an ambitious gold miner (Gene Hackman) who makes his fortune in the snowbound Canadian wilderness, then retires to his very own Caribbean island. It is some twenty years after he struck it rich that he finds himself up against some prospectors of a different type: a fortune-hunting gigolo (Rutger Hauer) who wants to marry his daughter (Theresa Russell), and the mob, who want to purchase his island and build a casino. All of this expressed by Roeg's visionary cinematic eye with attention to irony and biting wit. Rated R for sex, nudity, violence, and profanity.

1983 130 minutes

EUROPEANS, THE

★★★★

DIRECTOR: James Ivory

CAST: Lee Remick, Robin Ellis, Wesley Addy, Tim Choate, Lisa Eichhorn, Tim Woodward, Kristin Griffith

This intelligent, involving adaptation of the Henry James novel is another wonder from director James Ivory (*A Room with a View*). Lee Remick is one of two free-thinking, outspoken foreigners who descend on their Puritan relatives in nineteenth-century New England. The result is a character-rich study of a clash of cultures. Rated PG.

1979 90 minutes

EVERYTIME WE SAY GOODBYE

★★★

DIRECTOR: Moshe Mizrahi

CAST: Tom Hanks, Cristina Marsillach, Benedict Taylor, Anat Atzman, Monny Moshonov, Gila Almagor

A change-of-pace role for Tom Hanks, who stars as an American pilot in WWII Jerusalem who falls in love with a young Jewish girl. The Jewish girl's family are dead set against a gentile-Jew match. Hanks brings a certain well-rounded realism to this dramatic part, injecting the seriousness with humor, and Cristian Marshillach is very subtle as the Jewish girl. Rated PG-13 for mild profanity, brief nudity, and mature themes.

1987 97 minutes

EXECUTION, THE

★★

DIRECTOR: Paul Wendkos

CAST: Jessica Walter, Barbara Barrie, Sandy Dennis, Valerie Harper, Michael Lerner, Robert Hooks

Five women survivors of the Holocaust, now living in Los Angeles, have a chance meeting with a former Nazi doctor from their camp. They plot to seduce and then kill him. There is some suspense in this made-for-TV movie, but it is too melodramatic to be believable.

1985 100 minutes

EXECUTIONER'S SONG, THE

★★★½

DIRECTOR: Lawrence Schiller

CAST: Tommy Lee Jones, Rosanna Arquette, Christine Lahti, Eli Wallach

Pulitzer Prize novelist Norman Mailer's made-for-television adaptation of his engrossing account of convicted killer Gary Gilmore's fight to get Utah to carry out his death sentence. The performances of Tommy Lee Jones and Rosanna Arquette are electrifying. Unrated.

1982 200 minutes

EXECUTIVE ACTION

★★★★

DIRECTOR: David Miller

CAST: Burt Lancaster, Robert Ryan, Will Geer, Gilbert Green, John Anderson

This forceful film, based on Mark Lane's book *Rush to Judgment*, features a fascinating look at possible reasons for the assassination of John F. Kennedy. Rated PG.

1973 91 minutes

EXODUS

★★½

DIRECTOR: Otto Preminger

CAST: Paul Newman, Eva Marie Saint, Ralph Richardson, Peter Lawford, Lee J. Cobb, Sal Mineo

The early days of Israel are seen through the eyes of various characters, in this epic, adapted from the novel by Leon Uris. Directed by the heavy-handed Otto Preminger, its length and plodding pace caused comic Mort Sahl to quip, "Otto, let my people go," at a preview. Paul Newman simply called it "chilly."

1960 213 minutes

EXTREMITIES

★★½

DIRECTOR: Robert M. Young

CAST: Farrah Fawcett, James Russo, Diana Scarwid, Alfre Woodard

This well-meant but difficult-to-watch thriller casts Farrah Fawcett (in a first-rate performance) as a single woman who is brutalized and terrorized in her own home by a homicidal maniac (James Russo). When she manages to outwit her attacker and render him helpless, she must decide between bloody revenge and human compassion. Robert M. Young directs this adaptation by William Mastrosimone of his play with authority and realism, which makes it almost unendurable during the first hour. Nevertheless, the second part contains some fine moments of drama. Rated R for violence.

1986 100 minutes

F.I.S.T.

★★★

DIRECTOR: Norman Jewison

CAST: Sylvester Stallone, Rod Steiger, Peter Boyle, Melinda Dillon, David Huffman, Tony LoBianco

It's too bad that *F.I.S.T.* is so predictable and cliché-ridden, because Sylvester Stallone gives a fine performance. As Johnny Kovak, organizer and later leader of the Federation of Interstate Truckers, he creates an even more human and poignant character than his Rocky Balboa. It is ironic that Stallone, after being favorably compared with Marlon Brando, should end up in a film so similar to *On the Waterfront* . . . and with Rod Steiger yet! The story is a composite of *Waterfront*, *The Godfather*, and the Warner Bros. melodramas of the 1930s and '40s. Rated PG.

1978 145 minutes

FACE IN THE CROWD, A

★★★★

DIRECTOR: Elia Kazan

CAST: Andy Griffith, Patricia Neal, Lee Remick, Anthony Franciosa, Walter Matthau, Kay Medford

A sow's ear is turned into a silk purse in this Budd Shulberg story, scripted by the author, of a television executive who discovers gold in a winsome hobo she molds into a tube star. But all that glitters is not gold. A fine cast makes this a winning film, which brought Andy Griffith and Lee Remick to the screen for the first time.

1957 B & W 125 minutes

FACES OF DEATH I & II

CAST: Documentary

These two gruesome video programs are the ultimate in tasteless exploitation. Both feature graphic, uncensored footage of death—autopsies, suicides, executions, and the brutal slaughter of animals. You'll have to have a strong stomach to sit through it, and even would-be thrill seekers may find they get more than they bargain for.

1985 88 + 84 minutes

FAILSAFE

★★★★

DIRECTOR: Sidney Lumet

CAST: Henry Fonda, Walter Matthau, Fritz Weaver, Larry Hagman, Dom De Luise, Frank Overton

In this gripping film, a United States aircraft is mistakenly assigned to drop the big one on Russia, and the leaders of the two countries grapple for some kind of solution as time runs out.

1964 B & W 111 minutes

FALCON AND THE SNOWMAN, THE

★★★★★

DIRECTOR: John Schlesinger

CAST: Timothy Hutton, Sean Penn, Pat Hingle, Lori Singer, Richard Dysart

In this powerful motion picture, directed by John Schlesinger (*Midnight Cowboy*), Timothy Hutton and Sean Penn give stunning performances as two childhood friends who decide to sell United States secrets to the Russians. Based on a true incident, this release—to its credit—makes no judgments. The viewer is left to decide what's right and wrong, and whether Boyce met with justice. It is not an easy decision to make. We suspect most viewers will feel sorry for the two misguided youths and stunned and riveted by their story. Rated R for violence and profanity.

1985 131 minutes

FALL OF THE ROMAN EMPIRE, THE

★★★★

DIRECTOR: Anthony Mann

CAST: Sophia Loren, James Mason, Stephen Boyd, Alec Guinness, Christopher Plummer, John Ireland, Mel Ferrer

During the early and mid-1960s, Hollywood looked to the history books for many of its films. Director Anthony Mann was involved with two of the best within the genre, *El Cid* and *The Fall of the Roman Empire*. Having the advantage of a brilliant cast and an intelligent script, Mann has fashioned an epic that is a feast for the eyes and does not insult the viewers' intelligence. Like Stanley Kubrick's earlier film *Spartacus*, *The Fall of the Roman Empire* has thrilling moments of action and characters the viewer cares about. Though running over two and a half hours, this one is well worth it.

1964 149 minutes

FALLEN ANGEL

★★★½

DIRECTOR: Robert Lewis

CAST: Dana Hill, Richard Masur, Melinda Dillon, Ronny Cox, David Hayward

This made-for-television drama deals with the controversial topic of child pornography. A young girl, Jennifer (played by Dana Hill), is pushed into pornography by a so-called adult friend, Howard (played by Richard Masur). Jennifer sees no hope of getting out of her predicament, because she can't communicate with her mother (played by Melinda Dillon). Very timely topic!

1981 100 minutes

FALLEN IDOL, THE

★★★★

DIRECTOR: Carol Reed

CAST: Ralph Richardson, Michele Morgan, Bobby Henrey, Jack Hawkins, Bernard Lee

A small boy hero-worships a household servant suspected of murdering his wife in this quiet Graham Greene thriller. Largely told from the child's point of view, this one is pulse-raising. As always, the late Ralph Richardson is great. Bernard Lee later became "M" in the Bond films.

1948 B & W 94 minutes

FALLEN SPARROW, THE

★★★

DIRECTOR: Richard Wallace

CAST: John Garfield, Maureen O'Hara, Walter Slezak, Patricia Morison, Martha O'Driscoll, Bruce Edwards, John Banner

In this sometimes confusing but generally engrossing film, John Garfield is a veteran of the Spanish Civil War whose wartime buddy is later murdered by Fascists in New York City. Maureen O'Hara is Garfield's girlfriend. Walter Slezak is the head Fascist out to get Garfield. Many powerful scenes and strong performances make this one of Garfield's best films.

1943 94 minutes

FALLING IN LOVE

★★★

DIRECTOR: Ulu Grosbard

CAST: Robert De Niro, Meryl Streep, Harvey Keitel

Robert De Niro and Meryl Streep are fine as star-crossed lovers who risk their marriages for a moment of passion. Thanks to the uenven direction of Ulu Grosbard and an unbelievable story by Michael Cristofer, the stars' performances are the only outstanding features in this watchable love story. Rated PG for profanity and adult situations.

1984 107 minutes

FAMILY UPSIDE DOWN, A

★★★

DIRECTOR: David Lowell Rich

CAST: Helen Hayes, Fred Astaire, Efrem Zimbalist Jr., Patty Duke Astin

A touching, all too real drama about a previously self-sufficient couple whose age makes them dependent on their grown children. Hayes, Astin, and Zimbalist were nominated, and Astaire won an Emmy for this affecting made-for-television film.

1978 100 minutes

FANNY

★★★★

DIRECTOR: Joshua Logan

CAST: Leslie Caron, Maurice Chevalier, Charles Boyer, Horst

Buchholz, Baccaloni, Lionel Jeffries

Leslie Caron is a beautiful and lively Fanny in this 1961 film. She plays a young girl seeking romance with the boy she grew up with. Unfortunately, he leaves her pregnant as he pursues a life at sea.

1961 133 minutes

FANTASIES

DIRECTOR: John Derek

CAST: Bo Derek, Peter Hotten, Anna Alexiadis, Nicos Paschalidis

Bo Derek stars in this ridiculous story of the adopted sister of a well-to-do orphan in Greece. Derek lives her life like a female Walter Mitty, always lost in a fantasy world. This has to be one of the worst films ever made, though it does have one merit: director John Derek's gorgeous cinematography. Rated R for brief nudity and adult situations.

1984 81 minutes

FAR PAVILIONS, THE

★★★

DIRECTOR: Peter Duffell

CAST: Ben Cross, Amy Irving, Omar Sharif, Christopher Lee, Benedict Taylor, Rossano Brazzi

In this romantic adventure, based on a novel by M. M. Kaye, Ben Cross plays Ash, a young British officer in Imperial India. Oddly enough, he had been raised as an Indian until he was eleven. As an adult, he is reunited with his childhood friend the Princess Anjuli (played by Amy Irving). Despite her impending marriage to the elderly Rajaha (Rossano Brazzi), Ash and Anjuli fall in love. Although this is a watchable film, there is an overabundance of meaningful glances, which fail to take the place of dialogue and action. Rated PG for sex and violence.

1983 108 minutes

FAREWELL TO ARMS, A

★★★★

DIRECTOR: Frank Borzage

CAST: Helen Hayes, Gary Cooper, Adolphe Menjou, Mary Philips, Jack LaRue

Macho author Ernest Hemingway's well-crafted story of doomed love between a wounded ambulance driver and a nurse in Italy during World War I. Adolphe Menjou is peerless as the Italian army officer, Helen Hayes dies touchingly, and Gary Cooper strides away in the rain.

1932 B & W 78 minutes

FAST-WALKING

★★★½

DIRECTOR: James B. Harris

CAST: James Woods, Kay Lenz, Tim McIntire, Robert Hooks, Susan Tyrrell

This one is definitely not for everyone, but if you are adventurous, it may surprise you. James Woods plays a prison guard whose yearning for the good life leads him into a jail-break scheme. Film plays for black comedy and generally succeeds. Some very good acting and nice plot twists make this one worth your time. Rated R for violence, language, nudity.

1983 116 minutes

FATAL VISION

★★★★½

DIRECTOR: David Green

CAST: Karl Malden, Gary Cole, Eva Marie Saint, Gary Grubbs, Mitchell Ryan, Andy Griffith

This excellent TV miniseries is based on the actual case of convicted murderer, Dr. Jeffrey MacDonald. In 1970, MacDonald (Gary Cole) murdered his pregnant wife and two daughters. Although he denies the charges, his father-in-law (Karl Malden) becomes suspicious and helps to convict him.

1984 198 minutes

FEVER PITCH

DIRECTOR: Richard Brooks
CAST: Ryan O'Neal, Catharine Hicks, Giancarlo Giannini, Bridgette Anderson, Chad Everett, John Saxon, William Smith

Ryan O'Neal plays a sports journalist writing about gambling. To research his story, O'Neal becomes a gambler, living on the edge. He loses his wife, endangers his job, and becomes involved with a sleazy bookie. Discovering he's a compulsive gambler, he tries to help professional athletes beat the gambling bug, even though he can't help himself. The film is predictable because we've seen this all before, and done better. O'Neal is stiff and uninspired. Chad Everett is fine as a major gambling bookie with a mean streak, but no one lifts this film off the ground. What we get are too many shots of gambling in casinos and not enough about the characters. A real disappointment. Rated R for profanity and violence.

1985 95 minutes

55 DAYS AT PEKING

★★

DIRECTOR: Nicholas Ray
CAST: Charlton Heston, Ava Gardner, David Niven, John Ireland

A lackluster big-screen adventure about the Boxer Revolt in 1900. The story about a group of multinational embassy officials who become besieged within the Peking embassy compound takes no time to develop any rounded characterizations. Charlton Heston, David Niven, and the rest of the large cast seem made of wood.

1963 150 minutes

52 PICK-UP

★½

DIRECTOR: John Frankenheimer
CAST: Roy Scheider, Ann-Margret, Vanity, John Glover, Clarence Williams III, Kelly Preston

Generally unentertaining tale of money, blackmail, and pornography, as adapted from Elmore Leonard's story. Roy Scheider's secret fling with Kelly Preston (he thought it was secret!) leads to big-time blackmail and murder. It's more cards than Scheider could ever pick up, and a more mean and nasty movie than most people will want to watch. Leonard was reportedly pleased with the results, but as the screenwriter he may have been too close to the project to see how sleazy and unbelievable it turned out. Rated R for nudity, profanity, simulated sex, and violence.

1986 111 minutes

FINGERS

★★★★

DIRECTOR: James Toback
CAST: Harvey Keitel, Jim Brown, Tisa Farrow, Michael V. Gazzo

Harvey Keitel gives an electric performance as a would-be concert pianist who is also a death-dealing collector for his loan-sharking dad. Film is extremely violent and not for all tastes, but there is an undeniable fascination one feels toward the Keitel character and his tortured life. Rated R.

1978 91 minutes

FIRE DOWN BELOW

★★★

DIRECTOR: Robert Parrish

CAST: Rita Hayworth, Robert Mitchum, Jack Lemmon, Herbert Lom, Anthony Newley

Rita Hayworth is a lady of dubious background and virtue on a voyage between islands aboard a tramp steamer owned by adventurers Robert Mitchum and Jack Lemmon, both of whom chase her. A below-decks explosion traps one of the partners. The other comes to his rescue while Rita and the audience hold their breaths. The plot is familiar, contrived, but entertaining just the same.

1957 116 minutes

FIRE WITH FIRE

★★

DIRECTOR: Duncan Gibbins

CAST: Craig Sheffer, Virginia Madsen, Jon Polito, Jeffrey Jay Cohen, Kate Reid, Jean Smart

What hath Shakespeare wrought? The true story of a girl's Catholic school that invited the residents of a neighboring boy's reform school to a dance has been turned into another of those good girl/bad boy melodramas wherein misunderstood teens triumph against all odds. Craig Sheffer and Virginia Madsen are very appealing newcomers whose shared scenes generate pleasant chemistry, but the plot is laughable. Jon Polito has a thankless part as a gun-crazy reform boss, and a book could be filled with the dangling questions left unresolved at film's end. It even swipes that great plunge into the river made by Paul Newman and Robert Redford in *Butch Cassidy and the Sundance Kid*. Rated PG-13 for mild sex and language.

1986 103 minutes

FIRST BORN

★★★★

DIRECTOR: Michael Apted

CAST: Teri Garr, Peter Weller

An emotionally charged screen drama that deftly examines some topical, thought-provoking themes, this stars Teri Garr (*Mr. Mom*) as a divorced woman who gets involved with the wrong man (Peter Weller) to the horror of her two sons. "It's about the world of adults seen through the eyes of a kid," says screenwriter Ron Koslow. And it works. Rated PG for profanity and violence.

1984 100 minutes

FIRST MONDAY IN OCTOBER

★★★

DIRECTOR: Ronald Neame

CAST: Walter Matthau, Jill Clayburgh, Barnard Hughes, Jan Sterling

This enjoyable, old-fashioned entertainment is reminiscent of the days when people went to see "a Humphrey Bogart picture" or "a Clark Gable picture." It's a Walter Matthau picture, with all the joys that implies. As he did in *Hopscotch*, director Ronald Neame allows Matthau, who plays a crusty Supreme Court justice, to make the most of every screen moment. *The First Monday in October* also had the advantage of perfect timing: Jill Clayburgh plays the first woman appointed to the Supreme Court (mirrored in real life the same year by the appointment of Sandra Day O'Connor). Rated R for nudity and profanity.

1981 98 minutes

FIVE CAME BACK

★★★

DIRECTOR: John Farrow

CAST: Chester Morris, Wendy Barrie, John Carradine, Allen Jenkins, Joseph Calleia, C.

Aubrey Smith, Patric Knowles, Lucille Ball

A plane carrying the usual mixed bag of passengers goes down in the jungle. Only five of the group will survive. The cast, fine character players all, makes this melodrama worthwhile, though it shows its age.

1939 B & W 75 minutes

FIVE DAYS ONE SUMMER

★★★

DIRECTOR: Fred Zinnemann
CAST: Sean Connery, Anna Massey, Betsy Brantley, Lambert Wilson

This is an old-fashioned romance, with Sean Connery as a mountain climber caught in a triangle involving his lovely niece and a handsome young guide. Two handkerchiefs and a liking for soap opera are suggested. Rated PG for adult situations.

1983 108 minutes

FLASH OF GREEN, A

★★★½

DIRECTOR: Victor Nunez
CAST: Ed Harris, Blair Brown, Richard Jordan, George Coe, Isa Thomas, William Mooney, Joan Goodfellow, Helen Stenborg, John Glover

This is a compelling adaptation of John D. MacDonald's novel about a small-town Florida reporter (Ed Harris) whose boredom, lust, and curiosity lead him into helping an ambitious, amoral county official (Richard Jordan) win approval for a controversial housing project. Their tactics of deceit, blackmail, and coercion soon grow uglier than they expected. The acting is superb. The story is disturbing and thought-provoking.

1984 118 minutes

FLIM-FLAM MAN, THE

★★★

DIRECTOR: Irvin Kershner
CAST: George C. Scott, Michael Sarrazin, Sue Lyon, Harry Morgan, Jack Albertson

A con man (George C. Scott) teaches an army deserter (Michael Sarrazin) the art of fleecing yokels. Scott is an altogether charming, wry, winning rascal in this improbable, clever film, which is highlighted by a spectacular car-chase scene.

1967 104 minutes

FOOL FOR LOVE

★★★½

DIRECTOR: Robert Altman
CAST: Sam Shepard, Kim Basinger, Harry Dean Stanton, Randy Quaid

Writer-star Sam Shepard's disturbing, thought-provoking screenplay is about people who, as one of his characters comments, "can't help themselves." Shepard plays a cowboy-stuntman who is continuing his romantic pursuit of Kim Basinger in spite of her objections. A dark secret they share with a mysterious observer (Harry Dean Stanton) keeps them from finding contentment in each other's arms. *Fool for Love* deals with the anger, lies, and hurtful words that come from people who go on believing they are good or right or honest—like most of us. It does not depict any of these things graphically. Instead, it insinuates and teases until it makes the viewers feel a little dirty and a little sad. For open-minded adults who appreciate daring, original works. Rated R for profanity and violence.

1986 107 minutes

FOOLISH WIVES

★★★★

DIRECTOR: Erich Von Stroheim

CAST: Erich Von Stroheim, Maude George, Mae Busch, Miss DuPont, Rudolph Christians, Dale Fuller, Ceasare Gravina, Malvine Polo

Anticipating Orson Welles by two decades, director and star Erich Von Stroheim also wrote, produced, codesigned, and cocostumed this stark and unsettling account of a sleazy rogue's depraved use of women to achieve his aims. Von Stroheim is brilliant as the oily, morally corrupt, bogus nobleman plying his confidence game against the naïve rich in post–World War I Monaco and Monte Carlo. Even by current standards, this film is shocking. The final scene is a masterful simile. Silent.

1921–1922 B & W 107 minutes

FORBIDDEN

★★★

DIRECTOR: Anthony Page

CAST: Jacqueline Bisset, Jurgen Prochnow, Irene Worth, Peter Vaughan

Made-for-cable film about a gentile woman who falls in love with a Jewish man during World War II: a crime in Hitler Germany. Enough suspense here to keep the viewer attentive, but not enough atmosphere to make it as intense as the melodramatic soundtrack assumes it to be. Not rated, but the equivalent of a PG for some violence and light sex.

1984 114 minutes

FORCE OF EVIL

★★★

DIRECTOR: Abraham Polonsky

CAST: John Garfield, Thomas Gomez, Roy Roberts, Marie Windsor

A lawyer (John Garfield) abandons his principles and goes to work for a racketeer in this somber, downbeat story of corruption and loss of values. Compelling story and acting compensate for some of the heavy-handedness of the approach. A good study of ambition and the different paths it leads the characters on.

1948 B & W 78 minutes

FOREVER YOUNG

★★

DIRECTOR: David Drury

CAST: James Aubrey, Nicholas Gecks, Alec McCowen, Karen Archer, Liam Holt

This slow-moving British soap opera features a handsome priest who is idolized by a lonely boy. When the priest's old friend returns, the viewer learns (through black-and-white flashbacks) that the priest had betrayed his friend. The plot thickens when the friend decides to take revenge on the priest. Just when it starts to get interesting, the movie ends inconclusively. Unrated, but brief nudity and mature themes would make it comparable with a PG.

1983 85 minutes

FORMULA, THE

★★

DIRECTOR: John G. Avildsen

CAST: George C. Scott, Marlon Brando, Marthe Keller, John Gielgud, G. D. Spradlin

Take a plot to conceal a method producing enough synthetic fuel to take care of the current oil shortage and add two superstars like George C. Scott and Marlon Brando. Sounds like the formula for a real blockbuster, doesn't it? Unfortunately, it turns out to be the formula for a major disappointment. Rated R.

1980 117 minutes

FORT APACHE—THE BRONX

★★★½

DIRECTOR: Daniel Petrie
CAST: Paul Newman, Ken Wahl, Edward Asner, Kathleen Beller, Rachel Ticotin

Jarring violence surfaces throughout this story about New York's crime-besieged South Bronx, but absorbing dramatic elements give this routine cops-and-criminals format gutsy substance. Paul Newman, as an idealistic police veteran, proves his screen magnetism hasn't withered with time. The supporting cast is topnotch. Rated R for violence, profanity, and sexual references.

1981 125 minutes

FORTRESS

★★½

DIRECTOR: Arch Nicholson
CAST: Rachel Ward, Sean Garlick, Rebecca Rigg

In this drawn-out story of a mass kidnapping in the Australian Outback, Rachel Ward is passable as a teacher in a one-room school. She is abducted along with her students, ranging in age from about six to fourteen. The story centers around their attempts to escape.

1985 90 minutes

49TH PARALLEL, THE

★★★★

DIRECTOR: Michael Powell
CAST: Laurence Olivier, Anton Wallbrook, Eric Portman, Leslie Howard, Raymond Massey, Finlay Currie, Glynis Johns

Rich suspense drama about a World War II German U-boat sunk off the coast of Canada whose crew makes it to shore and tries to reach safety in neutral territory. The cast is first-rate, the characterizations outstanding. Original story won an Oscar.

1941 B & W 105 minutes

FOUNTAINHEAD, THE

★★½

DIRECTOR: King Vidor
CAST: Gary Cooper, Patricia Neal, Raymond Massey, Kent Smith, Robert Douglas

Gary Cooper tries his best in this Ayn Rand novel, brought to the screen without any of the book's vitality or character development. "Coop" is cast as Howard Roark a Frank Lloyd Wright-type architect whose creations are ahead of their time and therefore go unappreciated. Patricia Neal is the love interest.

1949 B & W 114 minutes

FOUR FRIENDS

★★

DIRECTOR: Arthur Penn
CAST: Craig Wasson, James Leo Herlihy, Jodi Thelen

Arthur Penn (*Bonnie and Clyde*) directed and Steve Tesich (*Breaking Away*) wrote this interesting but ultimately disappointing film about America as seen through the eyes of a young immigrant (Craig Wasson) and the love he shares with two friends for a free-thinking young woman (Jodi Thelen). What could have been an arresting story of growing up in the 1960s and '70s is ruined by excessive, implausible sequences. Rated R because of violence, nudity, and profanity.

1981 114 minutes

FOUR SEASONS, THE

★★★½

DIRECTOR: Alan Alda
CAST: Alan Alda, Carol Burnett, Len Cariou, Sandy Dennis, Rita Moreno, Jack Weston

Written and directed by Alan Alda, this film focuses on the pains and joys of friendship shared by three couples who are vacationing together. Despite a flawed and uneven script, the characters have been skillfully drawn by Alda and convincingly played by an excellent cast. *Four Seasons* is by no means a perfect film, yet it is an appealing, uplifting piece of entertainment. Rated PG.

1981 117 minutes

FOXES

★★★

DIRECTOR: Adrian Lyne

CAST: Jodie Foster, Sally Kellerman, Cherie Currie, Randy Quaid, Scott Baio

Adrian Lyne (*Flashdance*) directed this fitfully interesting film, about four young women who share an apartment in Los Angeles. The cast is good and the film has some interesting things to say about young society, but somehow it all falls flat. Rated R.

1980 106 minutes

FOXTROT

★★½

DIRECTOR: Arturo Ripstein

CAST: Peter O'Toole, Charlotte Rampling, Max von Sydow, Jorge Luke, Helena Rojo, Claudio Brook, Anne Porterfield

Peter O'Toole plays a European aristocrat who escapes World War II when he takes a yacht to a deserted island in the Black Sea and sets up residence with his wife (Charlotte Rampling), his ship's captain (Max von Sydow), and his servant (Jorge Luke). Tension builds when visiting aristocrats hunt down all the wild game on the island purely for sport. *Foxtrot* centers on the wastes of the leisure class even in a time of war. Some of the actions of the characters are unbelievable at times. Rated R for sex, nudity, and violence.

1975 91 minutes

FRANCES

★★★★½

DIRECTOR: Graeme Clifford

CAST: Jessica Lange, Kim Stanley, Sam Shepard, Jeffrey DeMunn, Jordan Charney

Director Howard Hawks called Frances Farmer "the best actress I ever worked with." However, the Seattle-born free-thinker was never allowed to reign as a star in Hollywood. This chilling, poignant motion picture explains why. Jessica Lange is superb as the starlet who snubs the power structure at every turn and pays a horrifying price for it. Kim Stanley is also impressive as Frances's mother, a money- and fame-hungry hag who uses her daughter. Sam Shepard is the one person who loves Frances for who and what she really is. An unforgettable film. Rated R.

1982 139 minutes

FRENCH CONNECTION II, THE

★★

DIRECTOR: John Frankenheimer

CAST: Gene Hackman, Fernando Rey, Bernard Fresson, Jean-Pierre Castaldi, Charles Milot

Disappointing sequel to the 1971 winner for best picture has none of the thrills, chills, and action of the original. Instead, New York detective Popeye Doyle (Gene Hackman), who has journeyed to Paris to track the drug trafficker who eluded him in the States, finds himself addicted to heroin and suffering withdrawal. He isn't the only one who suffers. There's the viewer, too. Rated R.

1975 119 minutes

FRENCH LIEUTENANT'S WOMAN, THE

★★★★★

DIRECTOR: Karel Reisz
CAST: Meryl Streep, Jeremy Irons, Leo McKern, Hilton McRae, Emily Morgan

A brilliant adaptation of John Fowles's bestseller, starring Meryl Streep as the enigmatic title heroine and Jeremy Irons as her obsessed lover. Victorian and modern attitudes on love are contrasted in this intellectually and emotionally engrossing film. Rated R because of sexual references and sex scenes.

1981 123 minutes

FRIENDLY PERSUASION

★★★★

DIRECTOR: William Wyler
CAST: Gary Cooper, Dorothy McGuire, Marjorie Main, Anthony Perkins, Robert Middleton, Richard Eyer, Phyllis Love, Walter Catlett

Jessamyn West's finely crafted novel of a Quaker family beset by the realities of the Civil War in southern Indiana is superbly transferred to film by an outstanding cast guided by gifted direction. "Thou swell," said the *New York Times* when it debuted.

1956 140 minutes

FRINGE DWELLERS, THE

★★★★

DIRECTOR: Bruce Beresford
CAST: Justine Saunders, Kristina Nehm, Bob Maza

Bruce Beresford, the Austrialian filmmaker who directed *Breaker Morant* and *Tender Mercies*, has a tendency to make movies that have rambling stories but fascinating characters and rich performances. That description fits this Australian production, which follows the domestic problems of a family of Aborigines who move from a shantytown to a clean and proper suburban neighborhood. The story is told from the point of view of the family's ambitious daughter, who instigates the attempt at upward mobility and has no patience for her irresponsible father, socially awkward mother, and their swarm of freeloading relatives. It's an intriguing, touching, but nonsentimental look at a race of people unfamiliar to most Americans. It's rated PG for language.

1987 98 minutes

FROM HERE TO ETERNITY

★★★★★

DIRECTOR: Fred Zinnemann
CAST: Burt Lancaster, Montgomery Clift, Deborah Kerr, Frank Sinatra, Donna Reed, Ernest Borgnine

This smoldering drama, depicting the demands of military life just before America's involvement in World War II, earned the Academy Award for best picture of 1953. This riveting classic includes the historic on-the-beach love scene that turned a few heads during its time. And no wonder! Director Fred Zinnemann took chances with this realistic portrait of the U.S. military. In all, the film garnered eight Oscars, including those for supporting players Donna Reed and Frank Sinatra.

1953 B & W 118 minutes

FRONT, THE

★★★★

DIRECTOR: Martin Ritt
CAST: Woody Allen, Zero Mostel, Andrea Marcovicci, Joshua Shelley, Georgann Johnson

Focusing on the horrendous blacklist of entertainers in the 1950s, this film manages to drive its point home with wit and poignance. Joseph McCarthy started finding communists under every bush right after World War II and, by manipulating media, was able to destroy careers. Instead of defending their friends, people were frightened into silence. This film is about writers who find a man to submit their scripts to after they have been blacklisted. Woody Allen plays the title role. Rated PG.

1976 94 minutes

FULL METAL JACKET

★★★★

DIRECTOR: Stanley Kubrick

CAST: Matthew Modine, Adam Baldwin, Vincent D'Onofrio, Lee Ermey, Dorian Harewood, Arliss Howard, Kevyn Major Howard, Ed O'Ross

Stanley Kubrick and Vietnam? How can that combination miss? Well, it does and it doesn't. It doesn't have the impact one might expect from the director of *2001: A Space Odyssey*, *A Clockwork Orange*, and the film many people were hoping *Jacket* would imitate: *Doctor Strangelove*. Kubrick scores higher in smaller moments than in scenes seemingly intended to be climactic. Don't be surprised if days later fragments of what you saw and heard are still with you. Particularly memorable is Lee Ermey as Gunnery Sgt. Hartman. Rated R for violence and some inventive and colorful profanity.

1987 120 minutes

GALLIPOLI

★★★★½

DIRECTOR: Peter Weir

CAST: Mark Lee, Mel Gibson, Robert Grubb, Tim McKenzie, David Argue

Add this to the list of outstanding motion pictures from Australia and the very best films about war. Directed by Peter Weir (*The Last Wave*), this appealing character study, which is set during World War I, manages to say more about life on the battlefront than many of the more straightforward pictures in the genre. Rated PG because of violence.

1981 110 minutes

GAMBLER, THE

★★★½

DIRECTOR: Karel Reisz

CAST: James Caan, Paul Sorvino, Lauren Hutton, Jacqueline Brooks, Morris Carnovsky

This gritty film features James Caan in one of his best screen portrayals as a compulsive, self-destructive gambler. Director Karel Reisz (*The French Lieutenant's Woman*) keeps the atmosphere thick with tension. Always thinking he's on the edge of a big score, Caan's otherwise intelligent college professor character gets himself deeper and deeper into trouble. It's a downer, but still worth watching. Rated R.

1974 111 minutes

GANDHI

★★★★★

DIRECTOR: Richard Attenborough

CAST: Ben Kingsley, Candice Bergen, Edward Fox, John Gielgud, Martin Sheen, John Mills, Trevor Howard, Saeed Jaffrey, Roshan Seth

One of the finest screen biographies in the history of motion pictures, this film, by Richard Attenborough, chronicles the life of the deceased Indian leader (Ben Kingsley). Running three hours, it is an old-style "big" picture, with spectacle, great drama, superb performances, and, as they used to say, a cast of thousands. Yet for all its hugeness, *Gandhi* achieves a remarkable intimacy. Afterward, viewers feel as if they have actually known—and, more important, been touched by—the man Indians called the "Great Soul." Rated PG for violence.

1982 188 minutes

GANGSTER'S LAW

★

DIRECTOR: Siro Marcellini
CAST: Klaus Kinski, Maurice Poli, Susy Andersen, Max Delys

This is a routine Mafia story filmed in Italy. Klaus Kinski, who is sometimes in interesting and distinguished films, is reduced to playing a con man double-crossing another bank-robbing gang. The subplot has the head of the family, Maurice Poli, grooming a young boy in the laws and practices of gangster operations. The acting is poor. Dubbed.

1986 89 minutes

GARDEN OF ALLAH, THE

★★

DIRECTOR: Richard Boleslawski
CAST: Marlene Dietrich, Charles Boyer, Tilly Losch, John Carradine, Basil Rathbone, Joseph Schildkraut

Gloriously photographed, yawnable yarn of romance in the Algerian boondocks. Tepid, silly, and full of clichéd dialogue. However, the early Technicolor—which won a special Oscar—is outstanding. Could be retitled: *Marlene's Manhunt*.

1936 80 minutes

GARDENS OF STONE

★★★½

DIRECTOR: Francis Coppola
CAST: James Caan, Anjelica Huston, James Earl Jones, D. B. Sweeney, Dean Stockwell, Mary Stuart Masterson, Dick Anthony Williams, Lonette McKee, Sam Bottoms

A poignant drama examining the self-described toy soldiers of the Old Guard—those who officiate at military funerals at Virginia's Fort Myer, adjacent to Arlington National Cemetery. The setting is the Vietnam 1960s, and James Caan (after a five-year screen absence) stars as a disillusioned sergeant who'd rather be training recruits. Caan eloquently expresses the pain of his profession. "We're told that the business of war is killing," he explains, "and business is good. Well, our business is burial . . . and our business is *better*." D. B . Sweeney is excellent as the young recruit who is taken under Caan's wing, and Mary Stuart Masterson is superb as the young man's childhood sweetheart, but James Earl Jones walks away with his every scene as the poetically foul-mouthed Sergeant Major "Goody" Nelson. Rated R for profanity.

1987 111 minutes

GATHERING STORM

★

DIRECTOR: Herbert Wise
CAST: Richard Burton, Virginia McKenna, Robert Hardy, Ian Bannen

Richard Burton tries his best to bring some life to this dull movie, which covers Winston Churchill's life from 1937 to the start of World War II. Filmed almost entirely on a few indoor stages, this film plays more like an episode of *Masterpiece Theater* than a motion picture. Only for Churchill buffs.

1974 72 minutes

GENTLEMAN JIM

★★★★½

DIRECTOR: Raoul Walsh
CAST: Errol Flynn, Jack Carson, Alan Hale, Alexis Smith

Errol Flynn has a field day in this beautifully filmed biography of heavyweight champion Jim Corbett. Always cocky and light on his feet, Flynn is a joy to behold and will make those who considered him a star instead of a actor think twice. Ward Bond is equally fine as John L. Sullivan. Said to have been Flynn's favorite role.

1942 B & W 104 minutes

GEORGIA, GEORGIA

★★

DIRECTOR: Stig Bjorknan

CAST: Diana Sands, Dirk Benedict, Minnie Gentry, Roger Furman

This film, adapted by Maya Angelou from one of her stories, is a dated but fairly interesting study of racism. The story centers around the relationship between a white photographer and a black singer, whose motherly touring companion is adamantly anti-white. If you get mildly involved with this movie, stay with it. Rated R.

1972 91 minutes

GETTING OF WISDOM, THE

★★★★

DIRECTOR: Bruce Beresford

CAST: Susannah Fowle, Sheila Helpmann, Patricia Kennedy, Hilary Ryan

Out of Australia, this better-than-average rites-of-passage story of an unrefined country girl (Susannah Fowle) who gets sent off to school in the city displays all the qualities of topnotch directing. (Beresford also did *Breaker Morant* and *Don's Party.*) Being from a remote area of the country, the girl is easy prey for her more sophisticated, yet equally immature classmates. Hilary Ryan is excellent as an older student who befriends her. The story takes place in the mid-1800s and is taken from the classic Australian novel by Henry Handel Richardson. Not rated but the equivalent of a G.

1980 100 minutes

GETTING STRAIGHT

★★½

DIRECTOR: Richard Rush

CAST: Elliott Gould, Candice Bergen, Max Julien, Jeff Corey, Robert F. Lyons

During the campus riots of the 1960s, Hollywood jumped on the bandwagon with such forgettable films as *The Strawberry Statement* and *R.P.M.* Add *Getting Straight* to the list. Elliott Gould plays a "hip" graduate student caught up in campus unrest. Somewhat effective during its initial release, it now seems like an odd curio. Rated PG.

1970 124 minutes

GIANT

★★★½

DIRECTOR: George Stevens

CAST: James Dean, Rock Hudson, Elizabeth Taylor, Carroll Baker, Dennis Hopper

The third part of director George Stevens's American Trilogy, which also included *Shane* and *A Place in the Sun*, this 1956 release traces the life of a cattle rancher through two generations. Although the lead performances by Elizabeth Taylor, Rock Hudson, and James Dean are unconvincing when the stars are poorly "aged" with make-up, *Giant* is still a stylish, if overlong movie that lives up to its title.

1956 198 minutes

GIDEON'S TRUMPET

★★★★

DIRECTOR: Robert Collins

CAST: Henry Fonda, John Houseman, José Ferrer

Henry Fonda is the chief delight in this factual account of Clarence Earl Gideon, who was thrown into prison in the early 1960s for a minor crime—and denied a legal counsel because he could not afford to pay for one. Gideon viewed his "enforced vacation" as an opportunity to bone up on the laws of our land, and he concluded that everybody was entitled to a lawyer's advice—whether or not such advice was affordable. This made-for-TV movie accurately follows Anthony Lewis's source book, which chronicled Gideon's quest to, and eventual hearing before, the Supreme Court. Powerful, stirring drama that reveals how law must always be tempered with justice. Unrated; suitable for family viewing.

1980 104 minutes

GILDA

★★★★

DIRECTOR: Charles Vidor
CAST: Glenn Ford, Rita Hayworth, George Macready, Joseph Calleia, Steven Geray

Glenn Ford plays a small-time gambler, who goes to work for a South American casino owner and his beautiful wife, Gilda (Rita Hayworth). When the casino owner disappears and is presumed dead, Ford marries Hayworth and they run the casino together. All goes well until the husband returns, seeking revenge against them. There is some violence in this film.

1946 B & W 110 minutes

GINGER IN THE MORNING

★★½

DIRECTOR: Gordon Wiles
CAST: Sissy Spacek, Monte Markham, Slim Pickens, Susan Oliver, Mark Miller.

A lonely salesman, Monte Markham, picks up a hitchhiker, Sissy Spacek, and romance blossoms in this okay romantic comedy. No great revelations about human nature will be found in this one, just harmless fluff that will be forgotten soon after it's been viewed.

1973 89 minutes

GIRL FROM PETROVKA, THE

★★★

DIRECTOR: Robert Ellis Miller
CAST: Goldie Hawn, Hal Holbrook, Anthony Hopkins

American journalist Hal Holbrook falls in love with Russian Goldie Hawn while on assignment in the Soviet Union. Hawn's accent leaves much to be desired, and the manipulative script often becomes overly melodramatic, but the film still works as an effective tearjerker. Something about Hawn's guileless, resourceful character is impossible to resist, and the story's conclusion packs a surprising punch. Perhaps this film deserves to be recognized as a guilty pleasure; it's too contrived to take seriously, but it proves to be oddly poignant. Rated PG for adult situations.

1974 104 minutes

GIRLFRIENDS

★★★★

DIRECTOR: Claudia Weill
CAST: Melanie Mayron, Anita Skinner, Eli Wallach, Christopher Guest, Viveca Lindfors

Realistic film about a young Jewish woman who learns to make it on her own after her best friend/roommate leaves to get married. Melanie Mayron's performance is the highlight of this touching and offbeat comic-drama. Rated PG.

1978 88 minutes

GIVE 'EM HELL HARRY!

★★★★

DIRECTOR: Steve Binder
CAST: James Whitmore

This is the film version of James Whitmore's wonderful portrayal of President Harry S. Truman. Taken from the stage production, the film is a magnificent tribute and entertainment. Rated PG.

1975 102 minutes

GLASS HOUSE, THE

★★★★

DIRECTOR: Tom Gries
CAST: Vic Morrow, Clu Gulager, Billy Dee Williams, Dean Jagger, Alan Alda

This powerful prison drama is based on a story by Truman Capote. An idealistic new prison guard (Clu Gulager) is overwhelmed by the gang violence within the prison. Alan Alda plays a new prisoner who becomes the target of a violent gang leader (Vic Morrow). Dean Jagger plays the burnt-out warden who can offer no solutions for his prison's problems. This film is a powerful protest against our current prison system. Rated R for sex and violence.

1972 89 minutes

GLEN OR GLENDA

DIRECTOR: Edward D. Wood Jr.
CAST: Bela Lugosi, Dolores Fuller, Daniel Davis (director Ed Wood Jr.), Lyle Talbot, Timothy Farrell, George Weiss

Incredible film by the incomparably *inept* Edward D. Wood Jr., tells the powerful story of a young man who finally summons up the courage to come out of the closet and ask his fiancée if he can wear her sweater. Aided by some bizarre footage with Bela Lugosi as some sort of a mumbo jumbo artist and a pseudoscientific documentary approach, our hero/heroine (played by director Wood) takes us through the transvestite's world and gives us a soul-searching look at the problems they face daily. Sincere but cheaply done and hopelessly inept. Wood's films (including *Plan 9 from Outer Space* and *Bride of the Monster*) are all kitsch classics and have an outré charm of their own.

1953 B & W 67 minutes

GOD'S LITTLE ACRE

★★★★

DIRECTOR: Anthony Mann
CAST: Robert Ryan, Aldo Ray, Tina Louise, Jack Lord, Fay Spain, Buddy Hackett

This is a terrific little film focusing on poor Georgia farmers. Robert Ryan gives one of his best performances as an itinerant farmer. Aldo Ray, Jack Lord, and Buddy Hackett lend good support.

1958 B & W 110 minutes

GODDESS, THE

★★★

DIRECTOR: John Cromwell
CAST: Kim Stanley, Lloyd Bridges, Betty Lou Holland, Joyce Van Patten, Steven Hill

A lonely girl working in a Maryland five-and-dime dreams of film stardom, goes to Hollywood, clicks in a minor role, and makes the bigtime, only to find it all bittersweet. Stage star Kim Stanley, largely ignored by Hollywood, does well in the title role, though she was far from suited for it. Paddy Chayefsky supposedly based his screenplay on Marilyn Monroe.

1958 B & W 105 minutes

GODFATHER, THE

★★★★

DIRECTOR: Francis Ford Coppola
CAST: Marlon Brando, Al Pacino, James Caan, Richard Castellano, John Cazale, Diane Keaton, Talia Shire, Robert Duvall, Sterling Hayden, John Marley, Richard Conte, Al Lettieri, Al Martino

Mario Puzo's incredibly popular novel comes to life in artful fashion. Filmed in foreboding tones, the movie takes us into the lurid world of the Mafia. Jarring scenes of violence don't overshadow the fascinating relationships among Don Corleone and his family. Marlon Brando, with stuffed cheeks, won an Oscar for his performance, but it's Al Pacino who grabs your attention with an unnerving intensity. Rated R.

1972 175 minutes

GODFATHER, THE, PART II

★★★★

DIRECTOR: Francis Ford Coppola
CAST: Al Pacino, Robert Duvall, Diane Keaton, Robert DeNiro, John Cazale, Talia Shire, Lee Strasberg, Michael V. Gazzo

This is a sequel that equals the quality of the original, an almost unheard-of circumstance in Hollywood. Director Francis Ford Coppola skillfully meshes past and present, intercutting the story of young Don Corleone (Robert DeNiro), an ambitious, immoral immigrant, and his son Michael (Al Pacino), who lives up to his father's expectations, turning the family's crime organization into a sleek, cold, modern operation. This gripping film won seven Academy Awards. Rated R.

1974 200 minutes

GODFATHER EPIC, THE

★★★★★

DIRECTOR: Francis Ford Coppola
CAST: Marlon Brando, Talia Shire, James Caan, Robert Duvall, John Cazale, Al Pacino, Diane Keaton, Robert De Niro

Few screen creations qualify as first-class entertainment and cinematic art. Francis Ford Coppola's *The Godfather* series unquestionably belongs in that category. Yet as good as *The Godfather* and *The Godfather, Part II* are, they are no match for *The Godfather Epic*. A compilation of the two films with extra scenes added, it is nothing less than a masterwork. By editing the two films together in chronological order, for the videotape release of *The Godfather Epic*, Coppola has created a work greater than the sum of its parts. See it! Rated R.

1977 450 minutes

GOING MY WAY

★★★★½

DIRECTOR: Leo McCarey
CAST: Bing Crosby, Barry Fitzgerald, Rise Stevens, Gene Lockhart, Frank McHugh

Bing Crosby won the best-actor Oscar in 1944 for his delightful portrayal of the easygoing priest who finally wins over his strict superior (Barry Fitzgerald, who also won an Oscar for his supporting role). Leo McCarey (*Duck Soup*) wrote and directed this funny, heartwarming character study and netted two Academy Awards for his efforts, as well as crafting the year's Oscar-winning best picture.

1944 B & W 130 minutes

GOLDEN BOY

★★★★

DIRECTOR: Rouben Mamoulian
CAST: William Holden, Barbara Stanwyck, Adolphe Menjou, Lee J. Cobb

William Holden made a strong starring debut in this screen adaptation of Clifford Odets's, play about a musician who becomes a boxer. Though a bit dated today, Holden and co-star Barbara Stanwyck still shine.

1939 B & W 100 minutes

GONE WITH THE WIND

★★★★★

DIRECTOR: Victor Fleming
CAST: Clark Gable, Vivien Leigh, Leslie Howard, Olivia De Havilland, Thomas Mitchell, Hattie McDaniel

The all-time movie classic with Clark Gable and Vivien Leigh as Margaret Mitchell's star-crossed lovers in the final days of the Old South. Need we say more?

1939 222 minutes

GOOD EARTH, THE

★★★★

DIRECTOR: Sidney Franklin
CAST: Paul Muni, Luise Rainer, Keye Luke, Walter Connolly, Jessie Ralph

Nobel Prize novelist Pearl Buck's engrossing, richly detailed story of a simple Chinese farm couple whose lives are ruined by greed is impressively brought to life in this milestone film. Luise Rainer won the second of her back-to-back best-actress Oscars for her portrayal of the ever-patient wife. The photography and special effects are outstanding.

1937 B & W 138 minutes

GOOD FATHER, THE

★★★★½

DIRECTOR: Mike Newell
CAST: Anthony Hopkins, Jim Broadbent, Harriet Walker, Fanny Viner, Simon Callow, Joanne Whalley, Miriam Margoyles, Michael Byrne

In this brilliant British import, Anthony Hopkins is a walking time bomb. A separation from his wife has left him on the outside of his son's life. Hopkins's reaction is so extreme that he is haunted by nightmares. Director Mike Newell lays on the suspense artfully with this device while detailing the revenge Hopkins plots against the wife of a friend who is in similar circumstances. *The Good Father* is astonishing in its ability to capture real emotions. It is also that rare film that uses suspense but still plays fair with its characters and the viewer. There are surprises in the story, but one never feels cheated by them. Instead, they make the experience of watching the film all the richer. Rated R for profanity, suggested sex, and stylized violence.

1986 90 minutes

GOOD MORNING, BABYLON

★★★

DIRECTORS: Paolo Taviani, Vittorio Taviani
CAST: Vincent Spano, Joaquim de Almeida, Greta Scacchi, Desiree Becker, Charles Dance

Admirers of Italian filmmakers Paolo and Vittorio Taviani will want to check out their first attempt at an English-language production. It follows the misadventures of two brothers who come to America to find their fortunes as artists and find jobs on the production of D. W. Griffith's silent classic, *Intolerance*. The movie has moments of lyrical beauty and its story is sweet. But the dialogue has been translated into English in an occasionally awkward fashion and the younger actors don't seem entirely comfortable performing in the Tavianis' operatic style. Rated PG-13 for nudity and profanity.

1987 115 minutes

GOOD WIFE, THE

★

DIRECTOR: Ken Cameron
CAST: Rachel Ward, Bryan Brown, Sam Neill, Steven Vidler

The Good Wife is about one woman's yearning for sexual fulfillment. Unfortunately, like many films with this subject, the woman is made to pay for her desires. Women in these films are usually destined for insanity, suicide, or speeches where they declare themselves unworthy of honest love. Rachel Ward as the wife seeking sexual excitement is given to obsessive behavior and made to humble herself before her husband, whom she must say is too good for her. This tremendous oversight of the central problem is bad enough, but the film has a bigger problem because Ward lacks the tension of repressed lust. When the movie has

Ward bed her husband's brother (with hubby's consent), and then set her sights on the town Casanova, who is totally loathsome and unappealing, the story's logic completely disintegrates. Rated R.

1987 97 minutes

GOODBYE, MR. CHIPS

★★★★½

DIRECTOR: Sam Wood
CAST: Robert Donat, Greer Garson, John Mills

Robert Donat creates one of filmdom's most heartwarming roles as Chips, the Latin teacher of an English boys' school. The poignant movie follows Chips from his first bumbling, early teaching days until he becomes a beloved school institution. Greer Garson was introduced to American audiences in the rewarding role of Chips's loving wife.

1939 B & W 114 minutes

GOODBYE PEOPLE, THE

★★★★

DIRECTOR: Herb Gardner
CAST: Judd Hirsch, Martin Balsam, Pamela Reed, Ron Silver, Michael Tucker, Gene Saks

This unashamedly sentimental film is a delight. Martin Balsam is memorable as a man attempting to realize the dream of many years by rebuilding his Coney Island hot-dog stand. Pamela Reed and Judd Hirsch, as the young people who help him, turn in outstanding performances, and the hot-dog stand itself is a fantastic structure.

1984 104 minutes

GRADUATE, THE

★★★★½

DIRECTOR: Mike Nichols
CAST: Dustin Hoffman, Anne Bancroft, Katharine Ross

Director Mike Nichols won an Academy Award for his direction of this touching, funny, unsettling, and unforgettable release about a young man (Dustin Hoffman, in his first major role) attempting to chart his future and develop his own set of values (as opposed to those of the swimming-pool-and-sun set). He falls in love with Katharine Ross, but finds himself seduced by her wily, sexy mother, Anne Bancroft (as Mrs. Robinson). Don't forget the superb soundtrack of songs by Paul Simon and Art Garfunkel. A superb coming-of-age film.

1967 105 minutes

GRAND HOTEL

★★★★

DIRECTOR: Edmund Goulding
CAST: John Barrymore, Greta Garbo, Wallace Beery, Joan Crawford, Lionel Barrymore, Lewis Stone

World War I is over. Life in the fast lane has returned to Berlin's Grand Hotel, crossroads of a thousand lives, backdrop to as many stories. This anthology of life at various levels won an Oscar for best picture. John Barrymore is a suave jewel thief, Greta Garbo is a world-weary ballerina, Lionel Barrymore is dying but making the most of living it up under the eye of boss Wallace Beery, a jaded industrialist bent on making it with stenographer Joan Crawford. A sage selection of others people the suites and salons.

1932 B & W 113 minutes

GRAND PRIX

★★½

DIRECTOR: John Frankenheimer
CAST: James Garner, Eva Marie Saint, Yves Montand, Toshiro Mifune, Brian Bedford, Jessica Walter, Antonio Sabato, Adolfo Celi

The cars, the drivers, and the race itself are the real stars of this international epic, beautifully filmed on locations in France, England, Belgium, and other countries that host the world's most famous automobile competition. The four inter-related stories of professional adversaries and their personal lives intrude on the exciting footage of the real thing. Yves Montand does a credible job in what is basically a big-budget soap-opera with oil stains. Toshiro Mifune was probably seen by a wider Western audience in this film than any of his previous classics with director Akira Kurosawa (*Rashomon*, *The Seven Samurai*, *Yojimbo*) but his role and the story he's forced into is strictly paint-by-numbers stuff.

1966 179 minutes

GRANDVIEW, U.S.A

★

DIRECTOR: Randal Kleiser

CAST: Jamie Lee Curtis, C. Thomas Howell, Patrick Swayze, Jennifer Jason Leigh, Ramon Bieri, Carole Cook, Troy Donahue, William Windom

Jamie Lee Curtis is one of the finest actresses in movies today. Therefore, to see her talents wasted in *Grandview, U.S.A.*, another of director Randal Kleiser's (*Blue Lagoon*; *Summer Lovers*) blatantly commercial, light-headed entertainments, made our blood boil. *Grandview, U.S.A.* is a coming-of-age study totally lacking in depth and characterization. Rated R for nudity, violence, and profanity.

1984 97 minutes

GRAPES OF WRATH, THE

★★★★★

DIRECTOR: John Ford

CAST: Henry Fonda, John Carradine, Jane Darwell, Russell Simpson, Charley Grapewin, John Qualen

Henry Fonda stars in this superb screen adaptation of the John Steinbeck novel about farmers from Oklahoma fleeing the Dust Bowl and poverty of their home state only to be confronted by prejudice and violence in California. Directed by John Ford (*Young Mr. Lincoln* and *The Searchers*), it's a compelling drama beautifully acted by the director's stock company.

1940 B & W 129 minutes

GREAT DAN PATCH, THE

★★★

DIRECTOR: Joseph M. Newman

CAST: Dennis O'Keefe, Gail Russell, Ruth Warrick, Charlotte Greenwood

The story of the greatest trotting horse of them all. Good racing scenes. An opera for horse lovers.

1949 B & W 94 minutes

GREAT GABBO, THE

★★★½

DIRECTOR: James Cruze

CAST: Erich Von Stroheim, Betty Compson, Don Douglas, Margie Kane

Cinema giant Erich Von Stroheim gives a tour de force performance as a brilliant but cold ventriloquist whose disregard for the feelings of others comes back to haunt him when he realizes that he has lost the affection of a girl he has come to love. Von Stroheim and his little wooden pal are a compelling couple—this is a film that lingers in the memory and rates with other fine films about ventgriloquism like *Dead Of Night* and *Magic*. Silent film director James Cruze seems to have pulled this effective drama out of a hat, but the sound seems smooth and realistic for a film of this vintage.

1929 B & W 89 minutes

GREAT GATSBY, THE

★★★

DIRECTOR: Jack Clayton
CAST: Robert Redford, Mia Farrow, Karen Black, Sam Waterston, Bruce Dern

This is a well-mounted, well-acted film that is, perhaps, a bit overlong. However, Robert Redford, the mysterious title character, is marvelous as Gatsby. Bruce Dern is equally memorable as the man who always has been rich and selfish. He emits an animal brutality that acts as a perfect contrast to Mia Farrow's fragility as Daisy (Gatsby's love) and to Redford's grace and poise. Rated PG.

1974 144 minutes

GREAT GUY

★★

DIRECTOR: John G. Blystone
CAST: James Cagney, Mae Clarke, Edward Brophy

Depression film about a feisty inspector crusading against corruption in the meat-packing business. Not vintage James Cagney . . . but okay.

1936 B & W 75 minutes

GREAT SANTINI, THE

★★★★

DIRECTOR: Lewis J. Carlino
CAST: Robert Duvall, Blythe Danner, Michael O'Keefe

Robert Duvall's superb performance in the title role is the most outstanding feature of this fine "little" film. The story of a troubled family and its unpredictable patriarch (Duvall), it was released briefly in early 1980 as *The Ace* and then disappeared. But thanks to the efforts of the New York film critics, it was re-released with appropriate hoopla and did well at the box office. Rated PG for profanity and violence.

1979 116 minutes

GREAT WALLENDAS, THE

★★★

DIRECTOR: Larry Elikann
CAST: Lloyd Bridges, Britt Ekland, Taina Elg, John van Dreelen, Cathy Rigby, Michael McGuire

In this made-for-television movie, Lloyd Bridges stars as the head of the Wallenda family of high-wire artists. Bridges gives one of his most convincing performances as he keeps the spirit and determination of the family alive through their many tragedies. The viewer shares the excitement of their hard-won achievement in the creation of the legendary seven-person pyramid. A good family film.

1978 104 minutes

GREATEST, THE

★★

DIRECTOR: Tom Gries
CAST: Muhammad Ali, Ernest Borgnine, John Marley, Robert Duvall, James Earl Jones, Roger E. Mosley

Muhammad Ali plays himself in this disjointed screen biography, which is poorly directed by Tom Gries. Even the supporting performances of Robert Duvall, Ernest Borgnine, Ben Johnson, James Earl Jones, and John Marley don't help much. Only "Magnum, P.I." regular Roger E. Mosley shines, as Sonny Liston—and steals the movie from its star. Rated PG.

1977 101 minutes

GREATEST SHOW ON EARTH, THE

★★★★

DIRECTOR: Cecil B. De Mille
CAST: Betty Hutton, James Stewart, Charlton Heston, Cornel Wilde, Dorothy Lamour, Gloria Grahame

The 1952 Oscar winner for best picture succeeds in the same manner as its subject, the circus; it's enjoyable family entertainment. Three major stories of backstage circus life all work well and blend in well in this film.

1952 153 minutes

GREATEST STORY EVER TOLD, THE

★★★

DIRECTOR: George Stevens

CAST: Max von Sydow, Charlton Heston, Carroll Baker, Angela Lansbury, Sidney Poitier, Telly Savalas, José Ferrer, Van Heflin, Dorothy McGuire, John Wayne, Ed Wynn, Shelley Winters

Although this well-meant movie is accurate to the story of Jesus, the viewer tends to be distracted by its long-running time and the appearance of Hollywood stars in unexpected roles.

1965 141 minutes

GREEK TYCOON, THE

★★½

DIRECTOR: J. Lee Thompson

CAST: Anthony Quinn, Jacqueline Bisset, Raf Vallone, Edward Albert, Charles Durning, Camilla Sparv, James Franciscus

When this film was first shown, it stimulated much controversy and interest, because it promised to tell all about the Aristotle Onassis and Jackie Kennedy romance. Anthony Quinn borrows from his *Zorba the Greek* role to be a convincingly macho and callous Greek shipping tycoon. Jacqueline Bisset makes a beautiful Jackie O. Unfortunately, the plot was neglected and the story comes across as grade-B soap. Rated R.

1978 106 minutes

GREEN DOLPHIN STREET

★★½

DIRECTOR: Victor Saville

CAST: Lana Turner, Donna Reed, Van Heflin, Edmund Gwenn, Frank Morgan, Richard Hart

Tedious, plodding drama about two sisters, Lana Turner and Donna Reed, in romantic pursuit of the same man, Van Heflin, in nineteenth-century New Zealand. Special effects, including a whopper of an earthquake, won an Oscar, but do not a film make.

1947 B & W 141 minutes

GREEN PASTURES, THE

★★★★

DIRECTORS: William Keighley, Marc Connelly

CAST: Rex Ingram, Oscar Polk, Eddie Anderson, Frank Wilson, George Reed

Now recognized as a classic, this was Hollywood's first all-black film given general release, and only the second made between 1929 and 1942. Based on Marc Connelly's play and true to the source, it retells stories from the Old Testament as they might be told in a black Sunday-school class in the Deep South. Rex Ingram is superb as "de Lawd," who is depicted as a dignified gray-haired patient and kind minister.

1936 B & W 90 minutes

GREEN PROMISE, THE

★★★

DIRECTOR: William D. Russell

CAST: Marguerite Chapman, Walter Brennan, Robert Paige, Natalie Wood

The hard life of farmers and their families is explored in this surprisingly involving and well-acted film. Walter Brennan gives his usual first-rate performance as the patriarch who toils over and tills the land.

1949 B & W 93 minutes

GROUP, THE

★★★

DIRECTOR: Sidney Lumet
CAST: Joan Hackett, Elizabeth Hartman, Shirley Knight, Joanna Pettet, Jessica Walter, James Broderick, Larry Hagman, Richard Mulligan, Hal Holbrook

Based on the book by Mary McCarthy about the lives and loves of eight female college friends. Overlong, convoluted semi-sleazy fun. The impressive cast almost makes you forget it's just a catty soap opera. So watch it anyway.

1966 150 minutes

GUARDIAN, THE

★★★½

DIRECTOR: David Green
CAST: Martin Sheen, Louis Gossett Jr., Arthur Hill

When the tenants of an upper-class New York City apartment house become fed up with the violence of the streets intruding on their building, they hire a live-in guard (Louis Gossett Jr.). While he does manage to rid the building of lawbreakers, some begin to question his methods. This HBO made-for-cable film is notches above most cable fare. Profanity and violence.

1984 102 minutes

GUESS WHO'S COMING TO DINNER

★★★½

DIRECTOR: Stanley Kramer
CAST: Spencer Tracy, Katharine Hepburn, Sidney Poitier, Katharine Houghton, Cecil Kellaway, Beah Richards, Roy E. Glenn Sr., Virginia Christine

This final film pairing of Spencer Tracy and Katharine Hepburn was also one of the first to deal with interracial marriage. Though quite daring at the time of its original release, this movie, directed by the heavy-handed Stanley Kramer, seems rather quaint today. Still, Tracy and Hepburn are fun to watch, and Sidney Poitier and Katharine Houghton (Hepburn's niece) make an appealing young couple.

1967 108 minutes

GULAG

★★½

DIRECTOR: Roger Young
CAST: David Keith, Malcolm McDowell

This engrossing tale of an American athlete shipped to a Soviet prison camp works at odd moments in spite of a preposterous script. No viewer will swallow the notion of a multi–Olympic gold winner being carted off without so much as a by-your-leave. On the other hand, the escape sequence is clever and quite exciting. Needlessly violent, it also contains a laughably gratuitous skin shot of a minor actress. David Keith's final line of dialogue is a good reflection of viewer sentiment by the time it's all over.

1985 120 minutes

HALF-MOON STREET

★★

DIRECTOR: Bob Swaim
CAST: Sigourney Weaver, Michael Caine, Patrick Kavanagh, Faith Kent, Ram John Holder

Half-baked adaptation of Paul Theroux's *Doctor Slaughter*, which was equally flawed as a novel. Sigourney Weaver stars as an American abroad who decides to supplement her academic (but low-paid) government position by moonlighting as a sophisticated "escort." The story goes out of its way to establish the sophistication and intelligence of the protagonist and then forces her to behave like a naïve twit when things get nasty. Michael Caine is charming as the member of the House of Lords who falls in love with the enigmatic lady, but his character is badly underdeveloped. Rated R for nudity and sexual themes.

1986 90 minutes

HAMBONE AND HILLIE

★★★

DIRECTOR: Roy Watts

CAST: Lillian Gish, Timothy Bottoms, Candy Clark, O. J. Simpson, Robert Walker

A delightful story of love and loyalty between an old woman (Lillian Gish) and her dog and constant companion, Hambone. While boarding a flight in New York to return to Los Angeles, Hambone is accidentally set loose from his travel cage and becomes lost. And so begins a three-thousand-mile cross-country trip filled with perilous freeways, wicked humans, and dangerous animals. Helped along the way by a friendly trucker and a streetwise stray mutt, Hambone captures your heart and tickles your funny bone. A fun and touching family movie. Rated PG.

1984 97 minutes

HAMLET

★★★★★

DIRECTOR: Laurence Olivier

CAST: Laurence Olivier, Basil Sydney, Eileen Herlie, Jean Simmons, Felix Aylmer, Terence Morgan, Norman Wooland, Peter Cushing, Esmond Knight, Stanley Holloway

In every way a brilliant presentation of Shakespeare's best-known play masterminded by England's foremost player. Superb in the title role, Laurence Olivier won the 1948 Oscar for best actor, and (as producer) for best picture. Then an 18-year-old newcomer, Jean Simmons was nominated for best supporting actress. A high point among many is Stanley Holloway's droll performance as the First Gravedigger.

1948 B & W 150 minutes

HANOI HILTON

★

DIRECTOR: Lionel Chetwynd

CAST: Michael Moriarty, Paul LeMat, David Soul, Jeffrey Jones, Lawrence Pressman, Gloria Carlin

This overly long, poorly directed and acted drama is set in a prisoner-of-war camp during the Vietnam war. We witness eight long years of torture and confinement suffered by American prisoners at the hands of the enemy. Halfway through, the viewer begins to feel as victimized as the U.S. soldiers. Rated R for profanity and extreme violence.

1987 130 minutes

HANOVER STREET

DIRECTOR: Peter Hyams

CAST: Harrison Ford, Lesley-Anne Down, Christopher Plummer, Alec McCowen

This inept story of a romance during World War II features Harrison Ford as an American soldier and Lesley-Anne Down as a British nurse who meet by accident and fall in love. There are complications. She won't tell him her name. Later we find that she's married to a British intelligence officer (Christopher Plummer) and has a little girl (Patsy Kensit). Naturally, Plummer and Ford end up on a secret mission behind German lines, becoming friends while they fend off bullets and tanks. Dumb. Rated PG.

1979 109 minutes

HARDCORE

DIRECTOR: Paul Schrader

CAST: George C. Scott, Ilah Davis, Peter Boyle, Season Hubley,

Dick Sargent, Leonard Gaines, David Nichols

This film stars George C. Scott as Jake Van Dorn, whose family leads a church-oriented life in their home in Grand Rapids, Michigan. When the church sponsors a youth trip to California, Van Dorn's daughter Kristen (Ilah Davis) is allowed to go. She disappears, so Van Dorn goes to Los Angeles to find her. Once there, he sees a cheaply made skin flick that features a girl seduced by two men. It's Kristen. *Hardcore* is rated R but is closer to an X. Even though it's cloaked in righteous respectability, it makes the most of its subject matter. It is rather reminiscent of those old porn films that were advertised as sex-education films. Who's kidding whom?

1979 108 minutes

HARDER THEY FALL, THE

★★★½

DIRECTOR: Mark Robson

CAST: Humphrey Bogart, Rod Steiger, Jan Sterling, Mike Lane, Max Baer, Jersey Joe Walcott

This boxing drama is as mean and brutal as they come. A gentle giant is built up, set up, and brought down by a collection of human vultures while sports writer Humphrey Bogart flip-flops on the moral issues. The ring photography is spectacular. Don't expect anything like *Rocky*.

1956 B & W 109 minutes

HARDHAT AND LEGS

★★★

DIRECTOR: Lee Philips

CAST: Kevin Dobson, Sharon Gless

The scene is New York City. Kevin Dobson is a horse-playing Italian construction worker who whistles at nice gams. Sharon Gless is democratic upper-class. The twain meet, and sparks fly as he tries to make it work despite educational and cultural differences. It's all cheerful and upbeat and works because of first-rate acting. Made for television.

1980 104 minutes

HARLAN COUNTY, U.S.A.

★★★★½

DIRECTOR: Barbara Kopple

CAST: Documentary

This Oscar-winning documentary concerning Kentucky coal miners is both tragic and riveting. Its grippping scenes draw the audience into the world of miners and their families. Superior from start to finish. Rated PG.

1977 103 minutes

HARLOW

★★

DIRECTOR: Gordon Douglas

CAST: Carroll Baker, Peter Lawford, Red Buttons, Michael Connors, Raf Vallone, Angela Lansbury, Martin Balsam, Leslie Nielsen

One of two films made in 1965 that dealt with the life of the late film star and sex goddess Jean Harlow. Carroll Baker simply is not the actress to play Harlow, and the whole thing is a trashy mess, with the emphasis on Harlow's sexual encounters. A cheap shot all around.

1965 125 minutes

HARRAD EXPERIMENT, THE

★★

DIRECTOR: Ted Post

CAST: Don Johnson, James Whitmore, Tippi Hedren, B. Kirby Jr., Laurie Walters

Uninvolving adaptation of Robert Rimmer's well-intentioned bestseller about an experimental college that makes exploration of sexual freedom the primary hands-on curriculum of the student body. The film is attractive as a novelty item today because of its erotic scenes between Don Johnson of TV's *Miami Vice* and Lauri Walters of *Eight Is Enough*. Rated R.

1973 88 minutes

HARRY AND SON

★★★

DIRECTOR: Paul Newman

CAST: Paul Newman, Robby Benson, Joanne Woodward, Ellen Barkin, Ossie Davis, Wilford Brimley

A widower (Paul Newman) can land a wrecking ball on a dime but can't seem to make contact with his artistically inclined son, Howard (Robby Benson), in this superb character study. Directed, co-produced, and co-written by Newman, it's sort of a male *Terms of Endearment*. Rated PG for nudity and profanity.

1984 117 minutes

HARRY AND TONTO

★★★★

DIRECTOR: Paul Mazursky

CAST: Art Carney, Ellen Burstyn, Chief Dan George, Geraldine Fitzgerald, Larry Hagman, Arthur Hunnicutt

Art Carney won an Oscar for his tour-de-force performance in this character study, directed by Paul Mazursky (*Moscow on the Hudson*). In a role that's a far cry from his Ed Norton on Jackie Gleason's "The Honeymooners," the star plays an older gentleman who, with his cat, takes a cross-country trip and lives life to the fullest. Rated R.

1974 115 minutes

HAWAII

★★★★

DIRECTOR: George Roy Hill

CAST: Julie Andrews, Max von Sydow, Richard Harris, Gene Hackman, Carroll O'Connor

All-star epic presentation of Part III of James Michener's six-part novel of the same title. Excellent performances by Max von Sydow and Julie Andrews as the early 1800s missionaries to Hawaii, as well as by Richard Harris as the sea captain who tries to woo Andrews away.

1966 171 minutes

HEART BEAT

★★★★

DIRECTOR: John Byrum

CAST: Nick Nolte, Sissy Spacek, John Heard, Ray Sharkey, Ann Dusenberry

Heart Beat is a perfect title for this warm, bittersweet visual poem on the beat generation by writer-director John Byrum. It pulses with life and emotion, intoxicating the viewer with a rhythmic flow of stunning images and superb performances by Nick Nolte, Sissy Spacek, and John Heard. Over the opening montage, Carolyn Cassady (Spacek), wife of Neal (Nolte), reminisces, "After World War II, we all thought we knew who we were and where we were going . . . what each one of us wanted most in the world was a house in the suburbs, two cars and exactly 3.2 children." The story begins with the cross-country adventure that inspired Jack Kerouac's (Heard) *On the Road* and began a time of re-evaluation, introspection, and experimentation. Rated R.

1980 109 minutes

HEART IS A LONELY HUNTER, THE

★★★★

DIRECTOR: Robert Ellis Miller

CAST: Alan Arkin, Sondra Locke, Laurinda Barrett, Stacy Keach, Chuck McCann, Cicely Tyson

This release features Alan Arkin in a superb performance, which won him an Academy Award nomination. In it, he plays a sensitive and compassionate man who is also a deaf-mute. Rated G.

1968 125 minutes

HEART OF THE STAG

★★★★

DIRECTOR: Michael Firth

CAST: Bruno Lawrence, Terence Cooper, Mary Regan, Anne Flannery

The shocking subject matter of *Heart of the Stag*—forced incest—could have resulted in an uncomfortable film to watch. However, New Zealander Michael Firth, who directed the movie and conceived the story, handles it expertly, and the result is a riveting viewing experience. A drifter Peter Daly (powerfully played by Bruno Lawrence, of *Smash Palace*) becomes involved in the lives of a sheep rancher (Terence Cooper) who has made his daughter, Kathy (Mary Regan), into a sexual slave. The mother (Anne Flannery) has had a stroke and, as a result, can only sit in her wheelchair and whimper as her child suffers nightly abuse. The story in *Heart of the Stag* is handled in a thrillerlike fashion. This alleviates some of the natural distress the viewer feels in regard to the subject matter and provides for an exciting and satisfying conclusion. Rated R for violence, profanity, and sexual situations.

1983 94 minutes

HEARTACHES

★★★

DIRECTOR: Donald Shebib

CAST: Robert Carradine, Margot Kidder, Annie Potts, Winston Rekert, George Touliatos, Guy Sanvido

A touching, yet light-hearted, film about love, friendship, and survival, *Heartaches* follows the trials and tribulations of a young pregnant woman (Annie Potts), who is separated from her husband (Robert Carradine), and the kooky girlfriend she meets on the bus (Margot Kidder). Although the two women are total opposites, they wind up rooming together and share a variety of experiences. The Canadian film is rated R for a minimal amount of sex, which is handled discreetly.

1981 93 minutes

HEARTBREAKERS

★★★½

DIRECTOR: Bobby Roth

CAST: Peter Coyote, Nick Mancuso, Max Gail, Kathryn Harrold

Two men in their thirties, Arthur Blue (Peter Coyote) and Eli Kahn (Nick Mancuso), friends since childhood, find their relationship severely tested when each is suddenly caught up in his own fervent drive for success. Rated R for simulated sex and profanity.

1984 106 minutes

HEARTS AND MINDS

★★★★½

DIRECTOR: Peter Davis

CAST: Documentary

The Vietnam War and its effects on America at home are vividly examined in this beautifully done documentary. Much of it is still high-voltage material. Not to be missed. Rated PG for language, riot scenes.

1974 110 minutes

HEAT AND DUST

★★★★

DIRECTOR: James Ivory

CAST: Julie Christie, Greta Scacchi, Shashi Kapoor, Christopher Cazenove, Julian Glover, Susan Fleetwood

Two love stories—one from the 1920s and one from today—are entwined in this classy, thoroughly enjoyable soap opera about two British women who go to India and become involved in its seductive mysteries. Julie Christie stars as a modern woman retracing the steps of her great-aunt (Greta Scacchi), who fell in love with an Indian ruler (played by the celebrated Indian star Shashi Kapoor). Rated R for nudity and brief violence.

1983 130 minutes

HEATWAVE

★★★

DIRECTOR: Phillip Noyce
CAST: Judy Davis, Richard Moir, Chris Haywood, Bill Hunter, John Gregg, Anna Jemison

Judy Davis (*The Final Option*; *My Brilliant Career*) plays an idealistic liberal opposed to proposed real estate developments that will leave some people homeless. In this political thriller, Davis's crusade leads to her involvement in a possible kidnap/murder and a love affair with the young architect of the housing project she's protesting. Unrated.

1983 99 minutes

HEAVY TRAFFIC

★★★

DIRECTOR: Ralph Bakshi
CAST: Animated

Ralph Bakshi's follow-up to *Fritz the Cat* is a mixture of live action and animation. Technically outstanding, but its downbeat look at urban life is rather unpleasant to watch. Rated R for profanity, nudity, and violence.

1973 76 minutes

HEIRESS, THE

★★★★½

DIRECTOR: William Wyler
CAST: Olivia De Havilland, Montgomery Clift, Ralph Richardson, Miriam Hopkins, Vanessa Brown, Mona Freeman, Ray Collins

This moving drama takes place in New York City around 1900. Olivia De Havilland is excellent (she won an Oscar for this performance) as a plain but extraordinarily rich woman who is pursued by a wily gold digger (played by Montgomery Clift). Ralph Richardson is great as her straitlaced father.

1949 B & W 115 minutes

HELL TO ETERNITY

★★★

DIRECTOR: Phil Karlson
CAST: Jeffrey Hunter, David Janssen, Vic Damone, Patricia Owens, Sessue Hayakawa

A trimly told and performed anti-prejudice, anti-war drama based on the life of World War II hero Guy Gabaldon, a Californian raised by Japanese-American parents. Jeffrey Hunter and Sessue Hayakawa share acting honors as the hero and the strong-minded Japanese commander who confronts him in the South Pacific. Lots of battle scenes.

1960 B & W 132 minutes

HELL'S ANGELS FOREVER

★★½

DIRECTOR: Richard Chase
CAST: Documentary

Most of this documentary, produced by and featuring the infamous outlaw motorcycle gang, focuses on the "runs" made by the Angels, trips where the bikers turn out in force to party. During these get-togethers, the Angels talk to the camera, telling their stories and talking about their beliefs. It's when their way of life is explored that the film is at its best. The last third of the movie attempts to prove that the government and law-enforcement agencies tried to destroy the organization by unfair means. At that point, it drags, and the viewer's interest wanes. Rated R for violence, nudity, sex, and profanity.

1983 92 minutes

HELTER SKELTER

★★★★

DIRECTOR: Tom Gries

CAST: George Dicenzo, Steve Railsback, Nancy Wolfe, Marilyn Burns

The story of Charles Manson's 1969 murder spree is vividly retold in this excellent TV movie. Steve Railsback (*The Stunt Man*) is superb as the crazed Manson. Based on prosecutor Vincent Bugliosi's novel, this is high-voltage stuff. Unrated and too intense for the kids.

1976 114 minutes

HEROES

★★★½

DIRECTOR: Jeremy Paul Kagan

CAST: Henry Winkler, Sally Field, Harrison Ford, Val Avery

Henry Winkler is excellent in this compelling story of a confused Vietnam vet traveling cross-country to meet a few of his old war buddies who are planning to start a worm farm in California. Some hilarious scenes are mixed with some strong statements about the war in this first theatrical film for Henry, who's given solid support by Sally Field as his sort-of girlfriend, and a pre-stardom Harrison Ford as his best pal. One important note: MCA Home Video has elected to alter the film's closing theme for this release. Removing the emotionally charged "Carry on Wayward Son" by Kansas in favor of a teary generic tune somewhat diminishes the overall impact of the movie. Rated PG for mild language and violence.

1977 113 minutes

HESTER STREET

★★★★

DIRECTOR: Joan Micklin Silver

CAST: Carol Kane, Steven Keats, Mel Howard

Beautifully filmed look at the Jewish community in nineteenth-century New York City. Film focuses on the relationship of a young couple, he turning his back on the old Jewish ways while she fights to hold on to them. Fine performances and great attention to period detail make this very enjoyable. Rated PG.

1975 B & W 92 minutes

HEY GOOD LOOKIN'

★

DIRECTOR: Ralph Bakshi

CAST: Animated

This boring animated film from the director of *Wizards* follows the street gangs of New York City during the 1950s. It tends to put the viewer to sleep with its poor storyline and lousy animation. Skip it. Rated R.

1983 86 minutes

HIDE IN PLAIN SIGHT

★★★½

DIRECTOR: James Caan

CAST: James Caan, Jill Eikenberry, Robert Viharo, Joe Gripasi, Barbara Rae

James Caan is a tire factory laborer whose former wife marries a two-bit hoodlum who pulls a robbery and gets busted. The hood turns informant and, under the government's Witness Relocation Program, is given a secret identity. Caan's former wife and their two children are spirited off to points unknown. Caan's subsequent quest for his kids becomes a one-man-against-the-system crusade in this watchable movie. Rated PG.

1980 98 minutes

HIGH SCHOOL CONFIDENTIAL!

★★½

DIRECTOR: Jack Arnold

CAST: Russ Tamblyn, Jan Sterling, John Drew Barrymore, Mamie Van Doren

A narcotics officer sneaks into a tough high school to bust hopheads. Incredibly naive treatment of drug scene is bad enough, but it's the actors' desperate attempts to look "hip" that make the film an unintentional laugh riot.

1958 B & W 85 minutes

HINDENBURG, THE

★

DIRECTOR: Robert Wise

CAST: George C. Scott, Anne Bancroft, William Atherton, Roy Thinnes, Burgess Meredith, Charles Durning

Another disaster movie whose major disaster is its own script. It is a fictionalized account of the German airship *Hindenburg*, which exploded over New Jersey in 1937. George C. Scott portrays a German official who suspects sabotage and races against time to prevent a catastrophe. The story drags so much you wish the dirigible never had gotten off the ground. This movie certainly doesn't. Rated PG.

1975 125 minutes

HISTORY IS MADE AT NIGHT

★★★

DIRECTOR: Frank Borzage

CAST: Charles Boyer, Jean Arthur, Colin Clive, Leo Carrillo

A preposterous film, but . . . Colin Clive is a sadistic jealous husband whose wife, Jean Arthur, falls for Parisian headwaiter Charles Boyer. He tries to frame the headwaiter for a murder he himself committed. He fails. Insanely determined to destroy the lovers, he arranges for his superliner to hit an iceberg! The film, once defined as a mixture of farce, melodrama, comedy, and tragedy, made from half a dozen scripts shuffled together, ends with a *Titanic*-like climax. Talk about ways to get rid of the other man!

1937 B & W 97 minutes

HITLER

★★

DIRECTOR: Stuart Heisler

CAST: Richard Basehart, Cordula Trantow, Maria Emo, John Banner, John Mitchum

Richard Basehart plays Adolf Hitler in this rather slow-moving, shallow account of *der Führer*'s last years. You're better off watching a good documentary on the subject.

1962 107 minutes

HITLER, THE LAST TEN DAYS

★★

DIRECTOR: Ennio DeConcini

CAST: Alec Guinness, Simon Ward, Adolfo Celi, Diane Cilento

This film should hold interest only for history buffs. It is a rather dry and tedious account of the desperate closing days of the Third Reich. Alec Guinness gives a capable, yet sometimes overwrought, performance as the Nazi leader from the time he enters his underground bunker in Berlin until his eventual suicide. Rated PG.

1973 108 minutes

HOLD THE DREAM

★★★

DIRECTOR: Don Sharp

CAST: Jenny Seagrove, Deborah Kerr, Stephen Collins, James Brolin

This made-for-TV sequel to *A Woman of Substance* finds an aging Emma Harte (Deborah Kerr) turning over her department-store empire to her granddaughter, Paula (Jenny Seagrove). The rest of the family, in an uproar after being slighted, has plans to steal away much of the business for themselves. Paula's marriage takes a nosedive as she devotes more and more of her time to running "Grandy's" empire. Not as captivating as *Woman of Substance*, this sequel will still manage to entertain patrons of the soaps.

1986 180 minutes

HOME OF THE BRAVE

★★★

DIRECTOR: Mark Robson

CAST: James Edwards, Steve Brodie, Jeff Corey, Douglas Dick

This is one of the first films dealing with blacks serving in the military during World War II. The story finds James Edwards on a mission in the Pacific and deals with the racial abuse that he encounters from his own men. The good plot of this film could use some more "blood and guts"-type action, yet it is still worth watching.

1949 B & W 85 minutes

HOME, SWEET HOME

★★½

DIRECTOR: D. W. Griffith

CAST: Henry B. Walthall, Lillian Gish, Dorothy Gish, Mae Marsh, Spottiswoode Aiken, Miriam Cooper, Robert Harron, Jack Pickford, Donald Crisp, James Kirkwood, Blanche Sweet, Owen Moore

Henry B. Walthall is John Howard Payne in this fanciful biography of the famous composer of the song from which the title is taken. Lillian Gish is his faithful, long-suffering sweetheart. Denied happiness in life, the lovers are united as they "fly" to heaven. Silent.

1914 B & W 80 minutes

HOMECOMING, THE

★★★★

DIRECTOR: Peter Hall

CAST: Cyrill Cusack, Ian Holm, Michael Jayston, Vivien Merchant, Terrence Rigby, Paul Rogers

Michael Jayston brings his wife, Vivien Merchant, home to meet the family after several years of separation. His father and two brothers are no-holds-barred Harold Pinter characters. If you like drama and Pinter, you'll want to check out this American Film Theater production, which has outstanding direction by Peter Hall. The play translates beautifully to the screen and the performances are first-rate, especially Merchant's.

1973 111 minutes

HOMEWORK

🦃

DIRECTOR: James Beshears

CAST: Joan Collins, Shell Kepler, Wings Hauser, Betty Thomas

Terrible film, about a high-school teacher who seduces one of her students, does its best to cash in on the Joan Collins craze, but it's a total ripoff. Since a double was used in Joan's nude scene, the poor sucker watching this trash is left with nothing but horrendous acting by all. Rated R for nudity.

1982 90 minutes

HONKYTONK MAN

★★★★

DIRECTOR: Clint Eastwood

CAST: Clint Eastwood, Kyle Eastwood, John McIntire

Clint Eastwood stars as an alcoholic, tubercular country singer headed for an audition at the Grand Ole Opry during the depths of the Depression. A bittersweet character study, it works remarkably well. You even begin to believe Eastwood in the role. The star's son, Kyle Eastwood, makes an impressive film debut. Rated PG for strong language and sexual content.

1982 122 minutes

HOOSIERS

★★★★½

DIRECTOR: David Anspaugh

CAST: Gene Hackman, Barbara Hershey, Dennis Hopper, Sheb Wooley, Fern Parsons

Hoosiers is the most satisfying high school basketball movie in years. Gene Hackman is the new coach—with a mysterious past—at Hickory High. His unorthodox methods rankle the locals and his fellow teachers (particularly frosty Barbara Hershey), not to mention the undisciplined team members—all five of them. But before you can say hoosiermania, the team is at the 1951 state championships; Coach has a lady friend; and the town rummy (Oscar-nominated Dennis Hopper) is drying out. It doesn't hurt, either, that the realistic script is based on a true Indiana Cinderella story. Rated PG.

1986 114 minutes

HOT SPELL

★★★

DIRECTOR: Daniel Mann

CAST: Shirley Booth, Anthony Quinn, Shirley MacLaine, Earl Holliman, Eileen Heckart

Entertaining thoughts of leaving her for a younger woman, macho husband Anthony Quinn has anguishing housewife Shirley Booth sweating out this and younger-generation problems in this near remake of *Come Back, Little Sheba*. The impact of that film is lost here, however. Booth invokes empathy, Quinn again proves his depth of talent, Shirley MacLaine shows why stardom soon was hers; but a soap opera is a soap opera.

1958 B & W 86 minutes

HOTEL

★★½

DIRECTOR: Richard Quine

CAST: Rod Taylor, Catherine Spaak, Melvyn Douglas, Karl Malden, Richard Conte, Michael Rennie, Merle Oberon, Kevin McCarthy

This film is based on Arthur Hailey's bestseller, which eventually spawned a TV series. In its *Airport*-style story, a number of characters and events unfold against the main theme of Melvyn Douglas's attempt to keep from selling the hotel to a tycoon who would modernize and change the landmark. It's amusing to see Karl Malden as a thief in his pre-traveler's checks days.

1967 125 minutes

HOTEL NEW HAMPSHIRE, THE

★

DIRECTOR: Tony Richardson

CAST: Beau Bridges, Jodie Foster, Rob Lowe, Nastassja Kinski, Amanda Plummer

Based on John (*The World According to Garp*) Irving's novel, this muddled motion picture has its moments, but very few of them. Unlike George Roy Hill's *The World According to Garp*, which had a touching quality about its zaniness, *Hotel* features all of Irving's quirks without any polish. As a result, the story seems to jump from one incident to another in a totally illogical manner. Beau Bridges stars as the head of a family (which includes Jodie Foster and Rob Lowe) that weathers all sorts of disasters—including rape, incest, and death—and keeps going in spite of it all. Rated R for profanity, violence, and sex.

1984 110 minutes

HOUSE ACROSS THE BAY, THE

★★½

DIRECTOR: Archie Mayo

CAST: George Raft, Joan Bennett, Lloyd Nolan, Gladys George, Walter Pidgeon

An airplane designer (Walter Pidgeon) swipes the waiting wife (Joan Bennett) of a gangster (George Raft) while Raft is paying his dues in the joint. Then he gets out.... Classic Raft film. Tense, exciting, but familiar. Lloyd Nolan plays a shyster very well.

1940 B & W 86 minutes

HOWARDS OF VIRGINIA, THE

★★

DIRECTOR: Frank Lloyd

CAST: Cary Grant, Martha Scott, Sir Cedric Hardwicke, Alan Marshall, Richard Carlson, Paul Kelly, Elizabeth Risdon, Anne Revere, Irving Bacon

Tiring, too-long retelling of the Revolutionary War centering on an aristocratic Virginia family. In the Cary Grant filmography, it is just plain awful—especially coming as it did in the wake of *His Girl Friday* and *My Favorite Wife*.

1940 B & W 117 minutes

HUD

★★★★★

DIRECTOR: Martin Ritt

CAST: Paul Newman, Patricia Neal, Melvyn Douglas, Brandon De Wilde

In one of his most memorable performances, Paul Newman stars as the arrogant ne'er-do-well son of a Texas rancher (Melvyn Douglas) who has fallen on hard times. Instead of helping his father, Hud drunkenly pursues the family's housekeeper (Patricia Neal), who wants nothing to do with him. When asked, Newman dubbed this one "pretty good." An understatement.

1963 B & W 112 minutes

HUMAN COMEDY, THE

★★★½

DIRECTOR: Clarence Brown

CAST: Mickey Rooney, Frank Morgan, "Butch" Jenkins, Ray Collins, Darryl Hickman, Marsha Hunt, Fay Bainter, Donna Reed, James Craig, Van Johnson

California author William Saroyan's tender and touching story of life in a small valley town during World War II is a winner all around in this compassionate, now nostalgic film. Mickey Rooney shines as the Western Union messenger verging on manhood. A sentimental slice of life, comic and tragic. Rooney and the film earned Oscar nominations. Saroyan won for best original story.

1943 B & W 118 minutes

HUNTER'S BLOOD

★

DIRECTOR: Robert C. Hughes

CAST: Sam Bottoms, Clu Gulager, Kim Delaney, Mayf Nutter, Ken Swofford, Joey Travolta

This film has an amazing resemblance to *Deliverance*, but without any of that film's tension or acting. Several Yuppie deer hunters from Oklahoma go to Arkansas. Of course, they have a run-in with some backwoods boys, and blood starts flowing. Sam Bottoms sleepwalks through this movie, as does most of the cast. The script is an insult to any intelligent viewer. Rated R for language, violence, and adult content.

1987 101 minutes

HURRICANE, THE (Original)

★★★

DIRECTOR: John Ford

CAST: Jon Hall, Dorothy Lamour, Raymond Massey, Mary Astor

One of early Hollywood's disaster films. The lives and loves of a group of stereotyped characters on a Pacific island are interrupted by the big wind of the title. The sequences involving people are labored, but the special effects of the hurricane make this picture worth watching.

1937 B & W 120 minutes

HUSTLER, THE

★★★★★

DIRECTOR: Robert Rossen

CAST: Paul Newman, Jackie Gleason, Piper Laurie, George C. Scott, Myron McCormick, Murray Hamilton

This film may well contain Paul Newman's best screen performance. As pool shark Eddie Felson, he's magnificent. A two-bit hustler who travels from pool room to pool room taking suckers —whom he allows to win until the stakes get high enough, then wipes them out—Felson decides to take a shot at the big time. He challenges Minnesota Fats (nicely played by Jackie Gleason) to a big money match and almost wins—until overconfidence and booze do him in. The climax, of course, is a rematch—and writer-director Robert Rossen artfully milks it for all it's worth.

1961 B & W 135 minutes

HUSTLING

★★★★

DIRECTOR: Joseph Sargent

CAST: Lee Remick, Jill Clayburgh, Alex Rocco, Monte Markham

An investigative report delves into the world of big city prostitution in this adult TV movie. Fine performances and a good script place this above the average TV film.

1975 100 minutes

I AM A CAMERA

★★★½

DIRECTOR: Henry Cornelius

CAST: Julie Harris, Laurence Harvey, Shelley Winters, Ron Randell, Patrick McGoohan

Julie Harris is perfect as the easy, good-time English bohemian Sally Bowles in this finely honed film clone of the play adapted by John Van Druten from novelist Christopher Isherwood's autobiographical stories about pre–World War II Berlin. The Broadway and screen versions ultimately became the musical *Cabaret*.

1955 98 minutes

I AM A FUGITIVE FROM A CHAIN GANG

★★★★

DIRECTOR: Mervyn LeRoy

CAST: Paul Muni, Glenda Farrell, Helen Vinson, Preston Foster

Dark, disturbing, and effective Paul Muni vehicle. The star plays an innocent man who finds himself convicted of a crime and brutalized by a corrupt court system. An unforgettable film.

1932 B & W 90 minutes

I HEARD THE OWL CALL MY NAME

★★★½

DIRECTOR: Daryl Duke

CAST: Tom Courtenay, Dean Jagger, Paul Stanley, Marianna Jones

In this mystical tale of love and courage, Tom Courtenay beautifully portrays Father Mark Brian, a young Anglican priest bishop, played by Dean Jagger, sends him to make his mark and finds himself among the proud Indians of the Northwest. Rated G.

1973 79 minutes

I NEVER PROMISED YOU A ROSE GARDEN

★★★½

DIRECTOR: Anthony Page

CAST: Bibi Andersson, Kathleen Quinlan, Diane Varsi

Kathleen Quinlan plays a schizophrenic teenager seeking treatment from a dedicated psychiatrist in this well-acted but depressing drama. Rated R.

1977 96 minutes

I REMEMBER MAMA

★★★½

DIRECTOR: George Stevens

CAST: Irene Dunne, Barbara Bel Geddes, Oscar Homolka, Philip Dorn, Ellen Corby

Irene Dunne is Mama in this sentimental drama about an engaging Norwegian family in San Francisco. Definitely a feel-good film for the nostalgic-minded. Hearts of gold all the way!

1948 B & W 148 minutes

I STAND CONDEMNED

★★★

DIRECTOR: Anthony Asquith

CAST: Harry Baur, Laurence Olivier, Penelope Dudley Ward, Robert Cochran

A jealous suitor frames a rival in order to have a clear field for the affections of the woman both love. Not much here, except a young and dashing Laurence Olivier in one of his first films.

1935 B & W 75 minutes

I WANT TO LIVE

★★★

DIRECTOR: Robert Wise

CAST: Susan Hayward, Simon Oakland, Virginia Vincent, Theodore Bikel

Pulling all stops out, Susan Hayward won an Oscar playing antiheroine B-girl Barbara Graham in this shattering real-life drama. Stupidly involved in a robbery-murder, Graham was indicted, railroaded to conviction, and executed at California's infamous San Quentin State Prison in 1955. To sit through this one you have to be steel-nerved or supremely callous, or both. The film is all the more devastating for being based on a true story.

1958 B & W 120 minutes

I'M DANCING AS FAST AS I CAN

★

DIRECTOR: Jack Hofsiss

CAST: Jill Clayburgh, Nicol Williamson, Geraldine Page

When a major motion picture with a top star is quickly stuck on a shelf shortly after a limited run, there's usually a good reason for it. The reason often turns out to be that it just doesn't work. Such is the case with this release, starring Jill Clayburgh. Based on documentary filmmaker Barbara Gordon's best-selling autobiography, which dealt with her valiant—and sometimes horrifying—struggle with Valium addiction, this film seems more like a "Saturday Night Live" parody of the subject than a serious examination of it. It's one movie that belongs on a shelf—permanently. Rated PG for profanity and violence.

1981 107 minutes

ICE CASTLES

★★½

DIRECTOR: Donald Wrye

CAST: Robby Benson, Lynn-Holly Johnson, Colleen Dewhurst, Tom Skerritt

Alexis Wintson (Lynn-Holly Johnson) is a girl from a small Midwestern town who dreams of skating in the Olympics. No matter how fetching and believable Johnson may be, or how accomplished her fellow cast members, nothing can surmount the soggy sentimentality and predictability of this cliché-ridden work. Rated PG.

1979 109 minutes

IDIOT'S DELIGHT

★★★½

DIRECTOR: Clarence Brown

CAST: Clark Gable, Norma Shearer, Edward Arnold, Charles Coburn, Burgess Meredith, Laura Hope Crews, Joseph Schildkraut, Virginia Grey

An all-star cast makes memorable movie history in this, the last antiwar film produced before World War II erupted. Norma Shearer is at her best as a Garbo-like fake-Russian-accented mistress companion of munitions tycoon Edward Arnold. Clark Gable is her ex, a wise-cracking vaudeville hoofer who's slipped while she's climbed. With other types, they are stranded in a European luxury hotel as war looms. It's all a bit dated, but nonetheless well worth the while.

1938 B & W 105 minutes

IF EVER I SEE YOU AGAIN

DIRECTOR: Joe Brooks

CAST: Joe Brooks, Shelley Hack, Jimmy Breslin, Jerry Keller, George Plimpton

This one could be called *The Attack of the Nonactors*. Fresh from his success with *You Light Up My Life*, writer-director-composer Joe Brooks threw together this celluloid love poem to model Shelley Hack. It's blatantly autobiographical and incredibly egotistical. Rated PG.

1978 105 minutes

IF YOU COULD SEE WHAT I HEAR

★

DIRECTOR: Eric Till

CAST: Marc Singer, R. H. Thomson, Sarah Torgov, Shari Belafonte Harper, Douglas Campbell

The film is supposedly the biography of blind singer/composer Tom Sullivan. You'd have to be not only blind but deaf and, most of all, dumb to appreciate this one. Acting, directing, and script are lamentable. The serious moments are sappy. The attempts at humor are insulting . . . to Sullivan and the audience. Rated PG.

1982 103 minutes

ILL MET BY MOONLIGHT

★★★

DIRECTOR: Michael Powell

CAST: Dirk Bogarde, Marius Goring, David Oxley, Cyril Cusack

In 1944 on the island of Crete, the British hatch a plot to kidnap a German general and smuggle him to Cairo. This sets off a manhunt with twenty thousand German troops and airplanes pursuing the partisans through Crete's mountainous terrain.

1957 B & W 105 minutes

IMITATION OF LIFE

★★★½

DIRECTOR: Douglas Sirk

CAST: Lana Turner, John Gavin, Sandra Dee, Dan O'Herlihy,

CAST: Susan Kohner, Troy Donahue, Robert Alda, Juanita Moore

Earnest performances and gifted direction make this soap-operaish, Fannie Hurst tearjerker tolerable viewing. Lana Turner is a fame-greedy actress who neglects her daughter for her career. Juanita Moore is her black friend whose daughter repudiates her heritage and breaks her mother's heart by passing for white. John Gavin is his usual stouthearted, chin-up, starchy self. Prepare to cry, cry, and cry.

1959 124 minutes

IMMORTAL BATTALION, THE (A.K.A THE WAY AHEAD)

★★★½

DIRECTOR: Carol Reed
CAST: David Niven, Stanley Holloway, Raymond Huntley, Penelope Dudley Ward, Peter Ustinov, Trevor Howard, Leo Genn, Billy Hartnell, James Donald

Based on an idea conceived by Lt. Col. David Niven, this highly effective wartime semidocumentary follows his attempts to turn a group of newly activated civilians into a combat team capable of fighting the Germans on any terrain. This gem from Sir Carol Reed skillfully mixes training and combat footage with filmed sequences to create a powerful mood while delicately balancing great performances is one of the most satisfying of all training-for-battle films. Released in Britian as *The Way Ahead*, this stirring movie was originally seen in a version running 116 minutes.

1944 91 minutes

IN COLD BLOOD

★★★★★

DIRECTOR: Richard Brooks
CAST: Robert Blake, Scott Wilson, John Forsythe, Jeff Corey

A chilling documentarylike recreation of the senseless murder of a Kansas farm family. This stark black-and-white drama follows two ex-convicts (Robert Blake and Scott Wilson) from the point at which they hatch their plan until their eventual capture and execution. This is an emotionally powerful film that is not for the faint of heart.

1967 B & W 134 minutes

IN NAME ONLY

★★★½

DIRECTOR: John Cromwell
CAST: Carole Lombard, Cary Grant, Kay Francis, Charles Coburn, Helen Vinson, Peggy Ann Garner

This is a classic soap opera. Cary Grant is desperately in love with sweet and lovely Carole Lombard. Unfortunately, he's married to venomous Kay Francis, who sadistically refuses to give him a divorce. You can't help but get completely wrapped up in the skillfully executed story. The performances are all topnotch.

1939 B & W 102 minutes

IN PRAISE OF OLDER WOMEN

DIRECTOR: George Kaczender
CAST: Tom Berenger, Karen Black, Susan Strasberg, Alexandra Stewart

This dull film about a man's reflections on the past two decades and his various affairs along the way goes nowhere fast with uninteresting characterizations and plot line. Rated R.

1978 108 minutes

IN THE HEAT OF THE NIGHT

★★★★

DIRECTOR: Norman Jewison
CAST: Sidney Poitier, Rod Steiger, Warren Oates, Lee Grant

This film is a rousing murder mystery elevated by the excellent acting of Rod Steiger and Sidney Poitier. Racial tension is created when a rural Southern sheriff (Steiger) and a black Northern detective reluctantly join forces to solve the crime. The picture received Oscars for best picture and Steiger's performance.

1967 109 minutes

IN TROUBLE

DIRECTOR: Gilles Carle
CAST: Julie Lachapelle, Jacques Cohen, Kathrine Mousseall, Daniel Pilon, Andre Gagnon, Jacques Chenail, Susan Kay

An incomprehensible Canadian film, this seems to be about a young woman who finds herself pregnant and unmarried. She wanders aimlessly through lovers and friends, all of whom put down America. Finally, her mob-affiliated brothers come to visit, demanding the identity of the unborn child's father. Since the young mother-to-be has no idea who the father is, she invents one. It's not enough to say that this film is bad. Instead of approaching the sensitive subject of unwed motherhood, the writer brings in stupid characters and unbelievable situations. Not rated but contains brief nudity, adult situations, and profanity.

1967 82 minutes

IN WHICH WE SERVE

★★★★★

DIRECTORS: Noel Coward, David Lean
CAST: Noel Coward, John Mills, Michael Wilding

Noel Coward wrote, produced, directed, and acted in this, one of the most moving wartime portrayals of men at sea. It is not the stirring battle sequences that make this film stand out but the intimate human story of the crew, their families, and the ship they love. A great film in all respects.

1942 B & W 115 minutes

INCREDIBLE JOURNEY OF DR. MEG LAUREL, THE

★★★½

DIRECTOR: Guy Green
CAST: Lindsay Wagner, Jane Wyman, Dorothy McGuire, James Woods, Gary Lockwood, Charles Tyner, Andrew Duggan, Brock Peters, John Reilly

In this made-for-television film, Lindsay Wagner gives her usual solid performance as Meg Laurel. From humble beginnings as an orphan from the Appalachian Mountains, she becomes a doctor through the aid of the head of the orphanage (Dorothy McGuire). After graduating from Harvard Medical School, she sets up practice in 1930s Boston. Wagner is disturbed by repeated nightmares of a childhood illness and the attendance of a healer, which has left her scarred. She decides to return to the mountain people and administer the latest in medical procedures. She meets bitter opposition from the people who are unprepared to give up their antiquated ways and from Granny Arrowroot (Jane Wyman), a third-generation local healer.

1978 150 minutes

INCREDIBLE SARAH, THE

DIRECTOR: Richard Fleischer
CAST: Glenda Jackson, Daniel Massey, Yvonne Mitchell, Douglas Wilmer, David Langdon

As the legendary French actress Sarah Bernhardt—in her time the toast of Paris, London, and New York—Glenda Jackson tears passions to tatters, to very rags. Theater history buffs may like this pseudobiography.

1976 106 minutes

INDEPENDENCE DAY

★★★★

DIRECTOR: Robert Mandel

CAST: David Keith, Kathleen Quinlan, Richard Farnsworth, Frances Sternhagen, Cliff De Young, Dianne Wiest

Excellent little story about a young woman (Kathleen Quinlan) who wants to leave the stifling environment of her home town to become a big-city photographer. She's helped and hindered by a growing attachment to David Keith, a garage mechanic with his own problems. His sister, Dianne Wiest, is the uncomplaining victim of her wife-beating husband, played with unsavory menace by Cliff DeYoung. Both women are fabulous in their respective parts, and the story concludes with pleasant sincerity. A real treat. Rated R for violence and sex.

1983 110 minutes

INDISCRETION OF AN AMERICAN WIFE

★★½

DIRECTOR: Vittorio De Sica

CAST: Jennifer Jones, Montgomery Clift, Gino Cervi, Richard Beymer

One hour and three minutes of emotional turmoil played out against the background of Rome's railway station as adultress Jennifer Jones meets her lover, Montgomery Clift, for the last time. Yuck!

1954 B & W 63 minutes

INFORMER, THE

★★★★

DIRECTOR: John Ford

CAST: Victor McLaglen, Heather Angel, Preston Foster

John Ford's classic about a slow-witted Irish pug (Victor McLaglen) who turns his friend in for money to impress his ladylove and gets his comeuppance from the IRA has lost none of its atmospheric punch over the years. McLaglen is superb, and the movie lingers in your memory long after the credits roll.

1935 B & W 91 minutes

INHERIT THE WIND

★★★★★

DIRECTOR: Stanley Kramer

CAST: Spencer Tracy, Fredric March, Gene Kelly, Dick York, Claude Akins

In this superb film based on the stage play of the notorious Scopes monkey trial, a biology teacher is put on trial for teaching the theory of evolution. The courtroom battle that actually took place between Clarence Darrow and William Jennings Bryan could not have been more powerful or stimulating than the acting battle put on by two of America's most respected actors—Spencer Tracy and Fredric March.

1960 B & W 127 minutes

INN OF THE SIXTH HAPPINESS, THE

★★★★

DIRECTOR: Mark Robson

CAST: Ingrid Bergman, Curt Jurgens, Robert Donat

Superb acting marks this heartwarming biography of China missionary Gladys Aylward (Ingrid Bergman). The movie opens with her determined attempt to enter the missionary sevice and follows her to strife-torn China. The highlight is her cross-country adventure as she leads a group of orphans away from the war zone. Robert Donat is especially moving as a Mandarin lord.

1958 158 minutes

INSERTS

DIRECTOR: John Byrum

CAST: Richard Dreyfuss, Jessica Harper, Bob Hoskins, Veronica Cartwright

Even Richard Dreyfuss can't save this dreary film about a once-great 1930s film director now making porno movies. Rated R.

1976 99 minutes

INSIDE MOVES

DIRECTOR: Richard Donner

CAST: John Savage, David Morse, Amy Wright, Tony Burton

This is a film that grows on you as the heartwarming story unfolds. With a unique blend of humor and insight, director Richard Donner (*Superman*) and screenwriters Valerie Curtin and Barry Levinson (*And Justice for All*) provide a captivating look into a very special friendship. John Savage (*The Deer Hunter*) plays a man who, after failing at suicide, succeeds at life with the help of some disabled friends. Rated PG.

1980 113 minutes

INSIDE THE THIRD REICH

DIRECTOR: Marvin J. Chomsky

CAST: Rutger Hauer, Derek Jacobi, Blythe Danner, John Gielgud, Ian Holm, Elke Sommer, Trevor Howard, Robert Vaughn

This made-for-TV miniseries is based on the autobiography of Albert Speer, the German architect who became Hitler's chief builder. Both Rutger Hauer as Speer and Derek Jacobi as Hitler are very convincing. Hauer portrays Speer as a man obsessed with the opportunity to build extensively while being blissfully unaware of the horrors of war around him.

1982 250 minutes

INSIGNIFICANCE

DIRECTOR: Nicholas Roeg

CAST: Michael Emil, Theresa Russell, Gary Busey, Tony Curtis, Will Sampson

Michael Emil's absolutely wonderful impersonation of Albert Einstein makes this film worth seeing. The movie itself ends up as an inventive idea gone astray. Director Nicholas Roeg has envisioned a night in 1954 New York where Marilyn Monroe comes to visit Einstein in his hotel room to explain the theory of relativity to him. The encounter is a charming one, but it eventually loses its uniqueness as it incorporates disjunctive symbolic flashbacks into the narrative. Also disruptive is Theresa Russell's annoying Monroe impersonation. Rated R.

1985 110 minutes

INTERIORS

★★★★

DIRECTOR: Woody Allen

CAST: Diane Keaton, E. G. Marshall, Geraldine Page, Richard Jordan, Sam Waterston

Woody Allen tips his hat to Swedish director Ingmar Bergman with this very downbeat drama about a family tearing itself apart. Extremely serious stuff, with fine performances by all. Allen shows he can direct more than comedy. Rated R for language.

1978 99 minutes

INTERMEZZO

★★★★

DIRECTOR: Gregory Ratoff
CAST: Leslie Howard, Ingrid Bergman, Cecil Kellaway

A love affair between a married concert violinist and a young woman doesn't stray very far from the standard eternal love triangle. This classic weeper has more renown as the English-language debut of Ingrid Bergman.

1939 B & W 70 minutes

INTO THE NIGHT

★★½

DIRECTOR: John Landis
CAST: Jeff Goldblum, Michelle Pfeiffer, Paul Mazursky, Kathryn Harrold, Richard Farnsworth, Irene Papas, David Bowie, Dan Aykroyd

Packed with cinematic in-jokes and guest appearances by more than a dozen film directors, this is a film fan's dream. Unfortunately, it might also be a casual viewer's nightmare. You need to know quite a bit about motion pictures (to say nothing of filmmakers) to appreciate it. Directed by John Landis, of *Animal House* and *Trading Places* fame, it still has much to offer. In the story two strangers (Jeff Goldblum and Michelle Pfeiffer) stumble into international intrigue and share a bizarre and deadly adventure in the night world of contemporary Los Angeles. Rated R for violence and profanity.

1985 115 minutes

INTOLERANCE

★★★★

DIRECTOR: D. W. Griffith
CAST: Lillian Gish, Bessie Love, Mae Marsh, Elmo Lincoln, Tully Marshall, Eugene Pallette, Tod Browning, Monte Blue, Robert Harron, Miriam Cooper, Constance Talmadge, Erich Von Stroheim

This milestone silent epic tells and blends four stories of injustice, modern and ancient. Gigantic, lavish, spectacular, and monumental are only a few of the adjectives that describe the film's scale, scope, and impact. The sets for the Babylonian sequence were the largest ever built for a film. One scene alone involved 15,000 people and 250 chariots. The acting is dated, but the picture presents a powerful viewing experience. A true classic and must-have for collectors.

1916 B & W 123 minutes

IRON DUKE, THE

★★★★

DIRECTOR: Victor Saville
CAST: George Arliss, A. E. Matthews, Allan Aynesworth, Edmund Willard, Farren Soutar, Emlyn Williams, Felix Aylmer, Gladys Cooper, Ellaline Terris

A thoroughly English stage actor, George Arliss did not make this, his first British film, until late in the decade he spent in the Hollywood studios. His Duke of Wellington, victor over Napoleon at Waterloo, is picture perfect—not the historical public conception of the duke, but real, eloquent, and as fascinating as the real man is said to have been. Buffs will particularly enjoy a younger Felix Aylmer, later Polonius in Laurence Olivier's 1948 *Hamlet*, and Gladys Cooper, David Niven's haughty, heartless scourge in *Separate Tables* in 1958. Of course, Emlyn Williams is, as almost always, matchless.

1936 B & W 88 minutes

IRRECONCILABLE DIFFERENCES

★★½

DIRECTOR: Charles Shyer
CAST: Drew Barrymore, Ryan O'Neal, Shelley Long

Drew Barrymore (*Firestarter*; *E.T.*) plays a little girl who sues her self-centered, career-conscious parents—Ryan O'Neal and Shelley Long (of television's "Cheers")—for divorce. This uneven comedy-drama was written by the creators of *Private Benjamin*, Nancy Meyers and Charles Shyer, who also directed. The laughs are few, but there are some effective scenes of character development. If ever a movie was just so-so, this is it. Rated PG for profanity and nudity.

1984 101 minutes

ISLANDS IN THE STREAM

★★★½

DIRECTOR: Franklin J. Schaffner

CAST: George C. Scott, Julius W. Harris, David Hemmings, Brad Savage, Hart Bochner, Claire Bloom

Islands in the Stream is really two movies in one. The first part is an affecting and effective look at a broken family. The second is a cheap action adventure. Thomas Hudson (George C. Scott), a famous painter and sculptor, lives the life of a recluse in the Bahamas. His only companions are his seagoing crew of Joseph (Julius Harris) and Eddy (David Hemmings). One summer, his three sons Tom (Hart Bochner), Andy (Brad Savage), and Davy (Michael-James Wixted) arrive by plane to see him for the first time in four years. The brooding character of Hudson fits Scott and the slow regeneration of his love for his sons is handled without the maudlin touches one would expect from a self-proclaimed "family picture." Too bad it goes downhill in the final third. Rated PG for violence and profanity.

1977 105 minutes

IT RAINED ALL NIGHT THE DAY I LEFT

★★½

DIRECTOR: Nicolas Gessner

CAST: Louis Gossett Jr., Sally Kellerman, Tony Curtis

Tony Curtis and Louis Gossett Jr. play two small-time weapons salesmen who are ambushed in Africa. They go to work for a recently widowed woman (Sally Kellerman) who controls all the water in this extremely hot and dry region. Because she blames the natives for her husband's death, she rations their water. That leads to trouble. The slow-moving parts to this movie make it just watchable and nothing out of the ordinary. Rated R for sex and violence.

1978 100 minutes

IT'S A WONDERFUL LIFE

★★★★½

DIRECTOR: Frank Capra

CAST: James Stewart, Donna Reed, Lionel Barrymore, Thomas Mitchell, Ward Bond, Henry Travers

Have you ever wished you'd never been born? What if that wish were granted? That's the premise of Frank Capra's heartbreaking, humorous, and ultimately heartwarming *It's a Wonderful Life*. James Stewart was tapped for the lead role right after he left the service at the end of World War II. The story is about a good man who is so busy helping others that life seems to pass him by.

1946 B & W 129 minutes

IT'S MY TURN

★★

DIRECTOR: Claudia Weill

CAST: Jill Clayburgh, Michael Douglas, Beverly Garland, Charles Grodin

Jill Clayburgh is a college professor confused about her relationship with live-in lover Charles Grodin, a Chicago real-estate salesman. Then she meets baseball player Michael Douglas. They fall in love. The viewer yawns. Rated R.

1980 91 minutes

JACK LONDON

DIRECTOR: Alfred Santell

CAST: Michael O'Shea, Susan Hayward, Osa Massen, Harry Davenport, Frank Craven, Virginia Mayo

Episodic, fictionalized account of the life of one of America's most popular authors is entertaining enough, but one wishes that a more accurate, detailed biography of this fabulous man were available on film. Bound by traditional studio restraints and seldom straying from the conventions of biopics of the time, this movie fails to capture the larger-than-life London who was almost as well-known as an adventurer and vagabond as he was a writer of young adult fiction, which is what he is best remembered for today. Heavily influenced by the anti-Japanese sentiment rampant at the time of its release, the colorful and tragic tale of the poor boy from Oakland who gained and alienated the love of America and the world cries out to be remade in today's more permissive and investigative atmosphere.

1943 B & W 94 minutes

JAGGED EDGE

★★★

DIRECTOR: Richard Marquand

CAST: Glenn Close, Jeff Bridges, Peter Coyote, Robert Loggia, Leigh Taylor-Young

A grand roller coaster of a film, pleasing to the eyes and fun to watch, that (alas) falls to pieces when the story is closely scrutinized. The characters behave according to the whims of writer Joe Eszterhas, rather than following the dictates of logic and intelligence. A publishing magnate (Jeff Bridges) is accused of the ritualistic slaying of his wife, who, it turns out, owned him lock, stock, and barrel; an attorney (Glenn Close) is hired to defend him. They fall in love, conduct an affair during the course of the trial(!), which is not noticed by the ambitious prosecutor (Peter Coyote) (!), and generally behave like total fools; during this, we and Close ponder the burning question: Did Bridges do the dirty deed? Excellent cinematography by Matthew F. Leonetti, superb score by John Barry; too bad the story doesn't measure up. Rated R for violence and sexual vulgarity.

1985 108 minutes

JAMAICA INN

DIRECTOR: Alfred Hitchcock

CAST: Charles Laughton, Maureen O'Hara, Leslie Banks, Emlyn Williams, Robert Newton, Mervyn Johns

"Chadwick! Saddle the mares!" is this film's most memorable line, but the film in general is not one of Alfred Hitchcock's best directorial efforts. But the cast makes it, just the same. Charles Laughton is Squire Pengallon, the evil chief of a band of cutthroats who lure ships onto the rocks of the Cornish Coast in Victorian England. Maureen O'Hara is a beautiful damsel in distress who must contend with his madness. The opening of the film sets the tone: a sign half in gloom buffeted by wind and rain.

1939 B & W 98 minutes

JAMES DEAN—A LEGEND IN HIS OWN TIME

★★½

DIRECTOR: Robert Butler
CAST: Michael Brandon, Stephen McHattie, Candy Clark, Amy Irving, Meg Foster, Jayne Meadows, Brooke Adams

Lackluster dramatization of actor James Dean's life as seen through the eyes of a friend. Stephen McHattie qualifies as a James Dean look-alike and gives a solid performance. This film features a fine supporting cast.

1976 99 minutes

JAMES DEAN STORY, THE

★★½

DIRECTORS: George W. George, Robert Altman
CAST: Documentary

Disappointing biographical documentary about instant legend James Dean contains some great footage of film's quintessential rebel (including a chilling traffic safety message he gave while dressed in his outfit from *Giant* shortly before his death in a car crash). Overall, there's too little Dean and too many interludes and interviews. Maverick director Robert Altman cut his teeth on this early job (his second film), but in this episodic tribute there's no hint of the major talent he was to become in the late 1960s. Fans of the irreplaceable James Dean should be interested, but even at the time of its release this film was largely unseen.

1957 B & W 82 minutes

JAMES JOYCE'S WOMEN

★★★★½

DIRECTOR: Michael Pearce
CAST: Fionnula Flanagan, Timothy E. O'Grady, Chris O'Neill

James Joyce's Women is a delicious, verbally erotic movie. With Joyce as the writer and Fionnula Flanagan (writer and producer) as interpreter, things are bound to be intense. The film is virtually a one-woman show, with Flanagan portraying seven different characters from Joyce's life and works. Flanagan's delivery of word and image feels right every step of the way. When her Molly Bloom rolls over in bed accompanied by a lion's roar on the soundtrack, you know you're in the hands of one who knows Joyce. The humor and sensuality will thrill Joyce fans. Rated R for nudity and sexual situations.

1985 89 minutes

JAYNE MANSFIELD STORY, THE

★½

DIRECTOR: Dick Lowry
CAST: Loni Anderson, Arnold Schwarzenegger, Kathleen Lloyd

Loni Anderson gives only an average performance as 1950s blond sex bomb Mansfield. She portrays Mansfield as a ruthless starlet who puts publicity stunts and fame ahead of all other life goals. Arnold Schwarzenegger is more convincing as her bodybuilding mate, Mickey Hargitay. Made for television.

1980 100 minutes

JERICHO MILE, THE

★★★★

DIRECTOR: Michael Mann
CAST: Peter Strauss, Roger E. Mosley, Brian Dennehy, Billy Green Bush, Ed Lauter, Beverly Todd

This tough, inspiring TV movie tells the story of a man, serving a life sentence at Folsom Prison, who dedicates himself to becoming an Olympic-caliber runner. Director Michael Mann (of *Miami Vice* fame) makes sure the film is riveting and realistic at all times. Peter Strauss, in a powerful performance, gives the character an edge, never letting him appear too noble or sympathetic.

1979 100 minutes

JESSIE OWENS STORY, THE

★★★

DIRECTOR: Richard Irving

CAST: Dorian Harewood, Debbi Morgan, George Kennedy, Georg Stanford Brown, Tom Bosley, LeVar Burton

This made-for-TV movie of the Olympic hero provides a provocative insight into the many behind-the-scenes events that plague people who are thrust into public attention and admiration. Dorian Harewood is perfect in his performance of the not-always-admirable hero, a victim both of his own inabilities and of the uncontrollable events surrounding him. This film also holds up a mirror to our society's many embarrassing racial attitudes.

1984 180 minutes

JEWEL IN THE CROWN, THE

★★★★★

DIRECTORS: Christopher Morahan, Jim O'Brien

CAST: Tim Pigott-Smith, Geraldine James, Peggy Ashcroft, Charles Dance, Susan Wooldridge, Art Malik, Judy Parfitt

Based on Paul Scott's *Raj Quartet*, this Emmy Award–winning series first aired on the BBC in fourteen episodes. It is a wonderful epic that depicts Britain's last years of power in India (1942–1947). The story revolves around the love of an Indian man, Hari Kumar (Art Malik), for a white woman, Daphne Manners (Susan Wooldridge), and the repercussions of their forbidden romance. The love-hate relationship of the English and the Indians is well depicted. Fine entertainment!

1984 700 minutes

JEZEBEL

★★★★

DIRECTOR: William Wyler

CAST: Bette Davis, Henry Fonda, George Brent, Spring Byington

Bette Davis gives one of her finest performances as a spoiled Southern belle in this release. Devised by Warner Bros. as a consolation prize for their star, who was turned down when she tried for the role of Scarlett O'Hara, it's not as good a film as *Gone with the Wind*. But then, how many are? Directed by William Wyler, it brought Davis her second Best Actress Oscar—and a well-deserved one at that. She's superb as the self-centered "Jezebel" who takes too long in deciding between a banker (Henry Fonda) and a dandy (George Brent) and loses all.

1938 B & W 103 minutes

JO JO DANCER, YOUR LIFE IS CALLING

★★★★½

DIRECTOR: Richard Pryor

CAST: Richard Pryor, Debbie Allen, Art Evans, Fay Hauser, Barbara Williams, Carmen McRae, Paula Kelly, Diahnne Abbott, Scoey Mitchell, Billy Eckstine, Wings Hauser, Michael Ironside

In this brilliant show-biz biography, Richard Pryor plays Jo Jo Dancer, a well-known entertainer at the peak of his popularity and the depths of self-understanding and love. A drug-related accident puts Jo Jo in the hospital and forces him to reexamine his life. Pryor's best work has always come from his hard-edged, often bitterly honest observations of real life. Even while laughing at his comedy routines, one is always conscious of their sobering truths. *Jo Jo* takes this approach to its zenith. Rated R for profanity, nudity, suggested sex, drug use, violence, and unflinching honesty.

1986 100 minutes

JOAN OF ARC

★★★

DIRECTOR: Victor Fleming
CAST: Ingrid Bergman, Jose Ferrer, Francis L. Sullivan, J. Carrol Naish, Ward Bond

Ingrid Bergman is touching and devout in this by-the-book rendering of Maxwell Anderson's noted play, but too much talk and too little action strain patience and buttocks.

1948 100 minutes

JOE

★★★

DIRECTOR: John G. Avildsen
CAST: Peter Boyle, Dennis Patrick, Susan Sarandon

Peter Boyle stars in this violent film about a bigot who ends up associating much more closely with the people he hates. Falling short in the storytelling, *Joe* is nevertheless helped along by topnotch acting. Rated R.

1970 107 minutes

JOHNNY BELINDA

★★★★

DIRECTOR: Jean Negulesco
CAST: Jane Wyman, Lew Ayres, Charles Bickford, Agnes Moorehead

Jane Wyman won an Oscar for her remarkable performance as a deaf-mute farm girl. Her multidimensional characterization lifts this movie over mere melodrama. The many disasters that befall its put-upon heroine, including rape and trying to raise the resulting offspring in the face of community pressure, would be scoffed at in a lesser actress. Wyman brings off a heartwarming, convincing portrayal.

1948 B & W 103 minutes

JOHNNY GOT HIS GUN

★★½

DIRECTOR: Dalton Trumbo
CAST: Timothy Bottoms, Marsha Hunt, Jason Robards, Donald Sutherland, Diane Varsi, David Soul, Tony Geary

Featuring Timothy Bottoms (*The Last Picture Show*) as an American World War I soldier who loses his legs, eyes, ears, mouth, and nose after a German artillery shell explodes, this is a morbid, depressing anti-war film with flashes of brilliance. The beginning, when we meet Joe Bonham (Bottoms) and experience the tragedy that puts him all but dead in a military hospital, is very powerful. Likewise, the climax, wherein the haunted soldier, whom we see in the hospital hidden by bandages, begs doctors in Morse code to kill him by banging his head, will, indeed, long remain in the memories of those who see it. However, what comes in between is all too often pretentious, boring, and amateurish. Rated PG.

1971 111 minutes

JOHNNY TIGER

★★½

DIRECTOR: Paul Wendkos
CAST: Robert Taylor, Geraldine Brooks, Chad Everett

Chad Everett is a half-breed Seminole, Robert Taylor is a sympathetic teacher, and Geraldine Brooks is a sympathetic doctor, all trying to reach some valid conclusion about the American Indians' role in the modern world. It's nothing to get excited about.

1966 102 minutes

JONATHAN LIVINGSTON SEAGULL

★★

DIRECTOR: Hall Bartlett
CAST: Seagulls

You may have been convinced that a man can fly, but you'll

never believe that a bird can talk. This misfired adaptation of Richard Bach's bestseller used real locations and actual seagulls, rather than infinitely more expressive animated counterparts. Needless to say, seagulls aren't the world's best method actors. Listen carefully for George Takei (Sulu in "Star Trek") as a supporting fowl. Overblown and laughable, in complete contrast to Bach's gentle fable. Catch this only for Neil Diamond's soundtrack; better yet, buy the album and skip the film. Rated G.

1973 120 minutes

JOURNEY INTO FEAR

★★

DIRECTOR: Daniel Mann

CAST: Sam Waterston, Zero Mostel, Yvette Mimieux, Scott Marlowe, Ian McShane, Joseph Wiseman, Shelley Winters, Stanley Holloway, Donald Pleasence, Vincent Price

This Canadian remake of Orson Welles' 1942 spy drama is occasionally intriguing but ultimately ambiguous and lacking in dramatic punch. Sam Waterston's portrayal of a research geologist, and wide-ranging European locations help sustain interest. Rated PG.

1975 103 minutes

JOY HOUSE

★★½

DIRECTOR: Rene Clement

CAST: Jane Fonda, Alain Delon, Lola Albright, Sorrell Booke

Spooky and interesting, but ultimately only mildly rewarding, this film features Jane Fonda in one of her sexy French roles as a free-spirited waif attempting to seduce her cousin's chauffeur (Alain Delon). Meanwhile, said cousin (Lola Albright) tries to help her criminal lover hide from the authorities. You could do worse.

1964 98 minutes

JOYRIDE

★★½

DIRECTOR: Joseph Ruben

CAST: Desi Arnaz Jr., Robert Carradine, Melanie Griffith, Anne Lockhart, Tom Ligon, Cliff Lenz

Four second-generation actors acquit themselves fairly well in this loosely directed drama about a quartet of youngsters who start off in search of adventure and find themselves turning to crime. Rated R.

1977 92 minutes

JUAREZ

★★★★

DIRECTOR: William Dieterle

CAST: Paul Muni, Bette Davis, Brian Aherne, Claude Rains, John Garfield

Warner Bros. in the 1930s and '40s seemed to trot out veteran actor Paul Muni every time they attempted to film a screen biography. This recreation of the life of Mexico's famous peasant leader was no exception. Surrounded by an all-star cast, including Bette Davis and Brian Aherne, this big budget bio is well-mounted and well-intentioned.

1939 B & W 132 minutes

JUDGE PRIEST

★★★½

DIRECTOR: John Ford

CAST: Will Rogers, Anita Louise, Stepin Fetchit, Henry B. Walthall, Tom Brown, Hattie McDaniel

A slice of Americana, and a good one. Life and drama in an old southern town, with all the clichés painted brilliantly. Will Rogers is fine. Stepin Fetchit is properly Uncle Tom. John Ford's sensitive direction makes this film one for the books. A touching, poignant portrait of community life lost and gone forever.

1934 B & W 71 minutes

JUDGMENT AT NUREMBERG

★★★★

DIRECTOR: Stanley Kramer

CAST: Spencer Tracy, Burt Lancaster, Maximilian Schell, Richard Widmark, Marlene Dietrich, Montgomery Clift, Judy Garland

An all-star cast shines in this thoughtful social drama. During the late stages of the Nazi war crimes trial, an American judge (Spencer Tracy) must ponder the issue of how extensive is the responsibility of citizens for carrying out the criminal orders of their governments. Maximilian Schell was to win an Oscar for his role as an impassioned defense attorney.

1961 B & W 178 minutes

JULIA

★★★★½

DIRECTOR: Fred Zinnemann

CAST: Jane Fonda, Vanessa Redgrave, Jason Robards, Maximilian Schell

Alvin Sargent won an Oscar for his taut screen adaptation of the late Lillian Hellman's best-selling memoir *Pentimento*. It's a harrowing tale of Hellman's journey into Germany to locate her childhood friend who has joined in the resistance against the Nazis. Great performances by all cast members. Rated PG.

1977 118 minutes

JUST BETWEEN FRIENDS

★★★½

DIRECTOR: Allan Burns

CAST: Mary Tyler Moore, Christine Lahti, Sam Waterston, Ted Danson, Susan Rinell, Timothy Gibbs, Mark Blum

Mary Tyler Moore stars in this big-screen soap opera as a homemaker happily married to Ted Danson (of television's *Cheers*). One day at an aerobics class, she meets TV news reporter Christine Lahti and they become friends. They have a lot in common—including being in love with the same man. The screenplay by director Allan Burns relies a bit too much on coincidence, and one particular plot twist is hopelessly contrived. Yet Lahti is a terrific actress and Moore nearly matches her scene for scene. Rated PG-13 for profanity and suggested sex.

1986 115 minutes

JUST THE WAY YOU ARE

★★½

DIRECTOR: Edouard Molinaro

CAST: Kristy McNichol, Michael Ontkean, Kaki Hunter

In her first "grown-up" role, Kristy McNichol gives a fine performance as a pretty flautist who cleverly overcomes the need to wear a leg brace—she had something akin to polio as a child—and fulfills her wish to "be like other people." But this deception brings an unexpected moment of truth. Even the plodding direction of Edouard Molinaro (*La Cage aux Folles I* and *II*) can't prevent this well-written work (by Allan Burns, of *A Little Romance*) from occasionally being witty and touching. Rated PG.

1984 95 minutes

KANGAROO

★★★★

DIRECTOR: Tim Burstall

CAST: Colin Friels, Judy Davis, John Walton, Julie Nihill, Hugh Keays-Byrne, Peter Hehir

Real-life husband and wife Colin Friels and Judy Davis give superb performances in this Australian film adaptation of the semiautobiographical novel by D. H. Lawrence. Writer Richard Somers

(Friels), a thinly veiled version of Lawrence, finds himself vilified by critics in his native England for writing sexually suggestive novels and, with his German-born wife Harriet (Davis), journey Down Under in search of a better life and ends up being caught between rival political factions. Director Tim Burstall wisely adds a touch of suspense to Lawrence's slightly self-serving tale, and the actors manage to bring even the most far-fetched moments to life. Friels, by the way, played the title character in the Australian comedy *Malcolm*. Rated R for violence, nudity, and profanity.

1986 100 minutes

KARATE KID, THE

★★★★½

DIRECTOR: John G. Avildsen
CAST: Ralph Macchio, Noriyuki "Pat" Morita, Elizabeth Shue

A heartwarming, sure-fire crowd pleaser, this believable and touching work about the hazards of high-school days and adolescence will have you cheering during its climax and leave you with a smile on your face. You'll find yourself rooting for the put-upon hero, Daniel (Ralph Macchio), and booing the bad guys just as writer Robert Mark Kamen and director John G. Avildsen (*Rocky*) intended. Rated PG for violence and profanity.

1984 126 minutes

KATHERINE

★★★

DIRECTOR: Jeremy Kagan
CAST: Sissy Spacek, Art Carney, Henry Winkler, Jane Wyatt, Julie Kavner

This television movie follows Sissy Spacek from a middle-class young student to a social activist and finally to an underground terrorist. Spacek is very convincing in this demanding role. The movie tends to remind one of the Patty Hearst case and features good, solid storytelling.

1975 100 minutes

KEROUAC

★★★★

DIRECTOR: John Antonelli
CAST: Documentary; Allen Ginsberg, Lawrence Ferlinghetti, Michael McClure, William Burroughs, Carolyn Cassady, Jack Coulter, Peter Coyote (Narrator)

This is an unusually affecting and enlightening documentary on the major voice of the Beat Generation, author Jack Kerouac (*On the Road*). In examining the glory and tragedy of genius, director John Antonelli uses reenactments of events in the author's life (with Jack Coulter as Kerouac) played over passages read from his books, rare television footage, and interviews with the author's friends and contemporaries. The result is a surprisingly intimate portrait of a driven man, illustrating, as Michael McClure quotes, that "poetry is the language of crisis." Unrated, the film has no objectionable material.

1985 73 minutes

KEY EXCHANGE

★★★

DIRECTOR: Barnet Kellman
CAST: Brooke Adams, Ben Masters, Daniel Stern, Danny Aiello, Tony Roberts

This movie, taken from the Kevin Wade play, is a good study of modern-day relationships. Brooke Adams and Ben Masters play a couple who confront the idea of making a firm commitment in their relationship. Daniel Stern is hilarious as a friend of the couple who is going through his own domestic crisis. Masters plays the difficult-to-watch role. Rated R for language, sex, and nudity.

1985 96 minutes

KILLING 'EM SOFTLY

★★

DIRECTOR: Max Fischer

CAST: George Segal, Irene Cara, Joyce Gordon, Andrew Martin Thompson, Barbara Cook, Clark Johnson

George Segal is a down-and-out musician who kills the friend of a young singer (Irene Cara) in an argument over the death of his dog. While attempting to prove that Segal is not the killer, Cara falls in love with him. An interesting and well-acted story bogs down in the attempt to turn this film—billed as a "drama-musical" —into a music video. The music is good, but it overpowers the story and causes the whole to lose focus. Filmed in Canada.

1985 90 minutes

KILLING FIELDS, THE

★★★★★

DIRECTOR: Roland Joffe

CAST: Sam Waterston, Haing S. Ngor, John Malkovich, Julian Sands, Craig T. Nelson

Here's an unforgettable motion picture. Based on the experiences of *New York Times* correspondent Sidney Schanberg during the war in Cambodia and his friendship with Cambodian guide and self-proclaimed journalist Dith Pran (whom Schanberg fights to save from imprisonment), it is a tale of love, loyalty, political intrigue, and horror. The viewer cannot help but be jarred and emotionally moved by it. Rated R for violence.

1984 142 minutes

KILLING HEAT

★★½

DIRECTOR: Michael Raeburn

CAST: Karen Black, John Thaw, John Kani, Patrick Mynhardt

Uneven acting and a general lack of atmosphere hinder the screen adaptation of Doris Lessing's novel *The Grass is Singing*. Karen Black plays a city woman who marries a small-time farmer and slowly goes insane while trying to adapt herself to the rural lifestyle. Black's performance is sometimes unconvincing while at other times riveting. And by film's end there are still questions left unanswered. Set in South Africa in the early 1960s, *Killing Heat* may be interesting for those acutely aware of the civil rights movement in that country. Not rated but contains nudity and violence.

1984 104 minutes

KILLING OF ANGEL STREET, THE

★

DIRECTOR: Donald Crombie

CAST: Liz Alexander, John Hargreaves, Reg Lye, David Downer, Allen Bickford, Alexander Archdale

The misleading title and packaging of *The Killing of Angel Street* makes it look like a teenage slasher flick, but the title refers to an actual street in a neighborhood in Australia. The plot involves the citizens' struggle to keep their homes from demolition by corrupt businessmen. The movie is alternately dull and unbelievable.

1981 100 minutes

KING

★★★★

DIRECTOR: Abby Mann

CAST: Paul Winfield, Cicely Tyson, Ossie Davis, Roscoe Lee Browne, Howard Rollins, Cliff De Young, Dolph Sweet, Lonny Chapman

Paul Winfield and Cicely Tyson star as the Rev. Martin Luther King Jr. and Coretta Scott King in this outstanding docudrama of the martyred civil rights leader's murder-capped battle against segregation and for black human dignity. Director Abby Mann, who also scripted, interpolated actual newsreel footage with restaged confrontation incidents for maximum dramatic impact. Friends and foes alike will learn much from this powerful slice of carefully re-created American history.

1978 272 minutes

KING DAVID

★★★

DIRECTOR: Bruce Beresford

CAST: Richard Gere, Edward Woodward, Alice Krige, Denis Quilley

Only biblical scholars will be able to say whether the makers of *King David* remained faithful to the Old Testament. As a big-screen production, however, it is impressive. Directed by Australian filmmaker Bruce Beresford (*Tender Mercies*), it is one of the few responsible attempts at filming the Bible. Telling the story of David—who slew Goliath, ruled Israel, stole Bathsheba from her husband, and sired Solomon—in a serious and thoughtful manner. Rated PG-13 for nudity and violence.

1985 115 minutes

KING OF COMEDY, THE

★★★★

DIRECTOR: Martin Scorsese

CAST: Robert De Niro, Jerry Lewis, Sandra Bernhard

Director Brian De Palma called this the best film of 1983 in a *Playboy* interview. It's certainly one of the most unusual movies of all time; a sort of black-comedy variation on creator Martin Scorsese's *Taxi Driver*. The star of that film, Robert De Niro, stars as aspiring comic Rupert Pupkin. In order to get his big break on television, Pupkin kidnaps a talk-show host (Jerry Lewis). It's a bizarre look at the price of fame and what some misguided souls are willing to pay for it. Rated PG.

1983 109 minutes

KING OF KINGS, THE

★★★

DIRECTOR: Cecil B. De Mille

CAST: H. B. Warner, Ernest Torrence, Jacqueline Logan, Robert Edeson, William Boyd, Joseph Schildkraut

Cecil B. De Mille was more than ready when he made this one. It's silent, but Hollywood's greatest showman displays his gift for telling a story with required reverence. Naturally, since it's by De Mille, the production is a lavish one.

1927 B & W 115 minutes

KING OF THE GYPSIES

★★★

DIRECTOR: Frank Pierson

CAST: Eric Roberts, Sterling Hayden, Susan Sarandon, Annette O'Toole, Brooke Shields, Shelley Winters

Dave Stepanowicz (Eric Roberts) is the grandson of King Zharko Stepanowicz (Sterling Hayden), the patriarch of a gypsy tribe who is both intelligent and violent. Though Dave renounces his gypsy heritage, he is unable to escape it. The performances are uniformly excellent. Director Frank Pierson is the only one who can be held responsible for the film's lack of power. As with his tragic remake of *A Star Is Born*, the finished product is hackneyed and disjointed. Rated R.

1978 112 minutes

KING OF THE MOUNTAIN

★½

DIRECTOR: Noel Nossack

CAST: Harry Hamlin, Richard Cox, Joseph Bottoms, Dennis Hopper

The quest for success and peer group immortality by a trio of buddies—Harry Hamlin, Richard Cox, and Joseph Bottoms—leads mostly to unexciting night races on Hollywood's winding Mulholland Drive and cliché back-stabbing in the music business. Dennis Hopper provides the film with a few good moments as a spaced-out 1960s has-been trying for a comeback but overall, *King of the Mountain* goes nowhere at low throttle. Rated PG.

1981 90 minutes

KING RAT

★★★★

DIRECTOR: Bryan Forbes
CAST: George Segal, Tom Courtenay, James Fox, John Mills

A Japanese prison camp in World War II is the setting for this stark drama of survival of the fittest, the fittest in this case being "King Rat" (George Segal), the opportunistic head of black market operations within the compound. In this camp the prisoners fight one another for the meager necessities of existence. This is not the traditional "prisoners against the enemy guards" prison camp movie.

1965 B & W 133 minutes

KING'S ROW

★★★★★

DIRECTOR: Sam Wood
CAST: Ann Sheridan, Robert Cummings, Ronald Reagan, Claude Rains, Charles Coburn, Betty Field, Judith Anderson

A small American town at the turn of the century is the setting where two men (Ronald Reagan and Robert Cummings) grow up to experience the corruption and moral decay behind the facade of a peaceful, serene community. This brilliantly photographed drama is close to being a masterpiece, thanks to exceptional performances by many of Hollywood's best character actors.

1941 B & W 127 minutes

KISS OF THE SPIDER WOMAN

★★★★

DIRECTOR: Hector Babenco
CAST: William Hurt, Raul Julia

This first English-language film by Hector Babenco (*Pixote*) is a somber, brilliantly acted tale about a gay window dresser, Molina (William Hurt), and a revolutionary, Valentin (Raul Julia), who slowly begin to care for each other and understand each other's viewpoint while imprisoned together in a South American prison. It is stark, violent, and daring. But its stars are magnificent to watch. Rated R for profanity, violence, and suggested sex.

1985 119 minutes

KITTY FOYLE

★★★★½

DIRECTOR: Sam Wood
CAST: Ginger Rogers, Dennis Morgan, James Craig, Eduardo Ciannelli

Ginger Rogers won an Oscar for her outstanding performance in this drama. She plays a poor girl who falls in love with a wealthy socialite.

1940 B & W 107 minutes

KLUTE

★★★★

DIRECTOR: Alan J. Pakula
CAST: Jane Fonda, Donald Sutherland, Roy Scheider

Jane Fonda dominates every frame in this study of a worldly call girl. Her Oscar-winning performance looks into the hidden sides of a prostitute's lifestyle; the dreams, fears, shame, and loneliness of Klute's world are graphically illustrated. Donald Sutherland co-stars as an out-of-town cop looking for a missing

friend. He feels Fonda holds the key to his whereabouts. Rated R.
1971 114 minutes

KNIGHT WITHOUT ARMOUR

★★★

DIRECTOR: Jacque Feyder
CAST: Robert Donat, Marlene Dietrich, Irene Vanbrugh, Herbert Lomas, Miles Malleson, David Tree

This melodrama, about a British national caught up in the Russian revolution and his attempts to save aristocrat Marlene Dietrich, is filled with beautiful photography and many nice touches but remains basically a curiosity, one of the few American films to depict communism in the 1930s. Robert Donat is an unassuming, gentle hero, and Marlene Dietrich plays the pampered countess with just the right touch of elegant compassion. Two great international stars raise this interesting film to a level that transcends the coincidence-ridden story from which it springs.
1937 B & W 107 minutes

KNOCK ON ANY DOOR

★★★½

DIRECTOR: Nicholas Ray
CAST: John Derek, Humphrey Bogart, Susan Perry, Allene Roberts

Before John Derek became a Svengali for Ursula Andress, Linda Evans, and Bo Derek, he was an actor—and a pretty good one, too, as he proves in this courtroom drama directed by Nicholas Ray. He's a kid who can't help having gotten into trouble, and Humphrey Bogart is the attorney who attempts to explain his plight to the jury.
1949 B & W 100 minutes

KNUTE ROCKNE—ALL AMERICAN

★★★

DIRECTOR: Lloyd Bacon
CAST: Ronald Reagan, Pat O'Brien, Donald Crisp

This is an overly sentimental biography of the famous Notre Dame football coach. But if you like football or you want to see Ronald Reagan show off his moves, it could hold your interest. Pat O'Brien has the cental role, and he plays it with real gusto.
1940 B & W 84 minutes

KRAMER VS. KRAMER

★★★★

DIRECTOR: Robert Benton
CAST: Dustin Hoffman, Meryl Streep, Jane Alexander, Howard Duff, JoBeth Williams

Dustin Hoffman and Meryl Streep star in the Academy Award–winning drama about a couple who separate, leaving their only son in the custody of the father, who is a stranger to his child. Just when the father and son have learned to live with each other, the mother fights for custody of the child. *Kramer vs. Kramer* jerks you from tears to laughs and back again—and all the while you're begging for more. Rated PG.
1979 104 minutes

LADY CHATTERLEY'S LOVER

★

DIRECTOR: Just Jaeckin
CAST: Sylvia Kristel, Nicholas Clay

A beautifully staged, but banal, version of the D. H. Lawrence classic. The sometimes compelling score is the only force to help this creep along. Viewers should compare other, always difficult attempts to portray Lawrence (*Sons and Lovers*, 1963; *Women in Love*, 1970). Rated R.
1981 105 minutes

LADY FOR A NIGHT

★½

DIRECTOR: Leigh Jason
CAST: John Wayne, Joan Blondell, Ray Middleton

John Wayne plays second fiddle to Joan Blondell. She's a saloon singer fighting for a measure of respectability in this release. If you plan to watch it, have some coffee brewed—you'll need it to help you stay awake.

1941 B & W 87 minutes

LADY OF THE HOUSE

★½

DIRECTORS: Ralph Nelson, Vincent Sherman
CAST: Dyan Cannon, Armand Assante, Zohra Lampert, Susan Tyrrell

Dyan Cannon stars in this TV dramatization of the life of Sally Stanford, Mayor of Sausalito, California. Cannon gives a better performance than usual, and Armand Assante is even better. Quite a bit of footage was cut from the original TV broadcast, leaving the audience lost between scenes.

1978 90 minutes

LAST COMMAND, THE

★★★★

DIRECTOR: Josef Von Sternberg
CAST: Emil Jannings, William Powell, Evelyn Brent, Jack Raymond, Nicholas Soussanin, Michael Visaroff

German star Emil Jannings's second U.S. film has him portraying a Czarist army commander who flees the Russian revolution to America. Here, he sinks into poverty and winds up as a Hollywood extra. Art imitates life when he is cast to play a Russian general in a film directed by a former revolutionary (and former rival in love). William Powell plays the director, a stiff, unbending sadist bent upon humiliating Jannings. The film, its scripter Lajos Biro, and its brilliant star were all nominated for the first Academy Awards. An Oscar went to Jannings, whose best-remembered films are *The Blue Angel* and *The Last Laugh*. Silent.

1928 B & W 80 minutes

LAST DAYS OF POMPEII, THE

★★★

DIRECTOR: Ernest B. Schoedsack
CAST: Preston Foster, Basil Rathbone, Dorothy Wilson, David Holt, Alan Hale, Louis Calhern

Roman blacksmith Preston Foster becomes a gladiator after tragedy takes his wife and baby. En route to fortune, he adopts the young son of one of his victims. In Judea, he sees but refuses to help Christ, who cures the boy following serious injury. Like Richard Blaine and Fred C. Dobbs, he sticks his neck out for nobody. Touched by Jesus, the boy grows up to help runaway slaves, a practice that undercuts his fathers's business. Things come to a head when the boy is arrested, faces death, and Vesuvius lets go. Tremendous special effects.

1935 B & W 96 minutes

LAST DETAIL, THE

★★★★

DIRECTOR: Hal Ashby
CAST: Jack Nicholson, Otis Young, Randy Quaid, Michael Moriarty, Nancy Allen

Two veteran Navy men (Jack Nicholson and Otis Young) are assigned to transport a young sailor to the brig for theft. They take pity on the naive loser (Randy Quaid) and decide to show him one last good time. By opening the youngster's eyes to the previously unknown world around him, their kindness is in danger of backfiring in this drama. Rated R.

1973 105 minutes

LAST GAME, THE

★★

DIRECTOR: Martin Beck

CAST: Howard Segal, Ed L. Grady, Terry Alden, Jerry Rushing, Mike Allen, Toby Wallace, Julian Morton, Joan Hotchkis, Bob Supan

Maudlin tale of an attractive and responsible clean-cut college kid who works two jobs, goes to school, and takes care of his blind father while his father dreams that one day his boy will play pro football. In an attempt to spice up the plot, the filmmakers have added a few extra conflicts and miles of football footage, but this only contributes to the film's lack of focus. Video shoppers could do a lot worse, but this movie is just too banal for recommendation. No MPAA rating, but equal to a PG for sex and profanity.

1980 107 minutes

LAST MILE, THE

★★★

DIRECTOR: Sam Bischoff

CAST: Preston Foster, Howard Phillips, George E. Stone, Noel Madison, Alan Roscoe, Paul Fix

No-win prison film (based on a then-current stage play) is a claustrophobic foray into death row, where cons talk tough and the audience better listen. Full of hard-boiled sentiment, off-screen machine-gun bursts, and even a squealer or two, this archetypal prison-break melodrama has a quiet dignity that elevates the dialogue between the inmates to high drama. Preston Foster as Killer Miles plays the toughest con in the block and the leader of the break attempt, a role Clark Gable played on the stage in Los Angeles in 1930, but no longer needed by 1932.

1932 B & W 70 minutes

LAST PICTURE SHOW, THE

★★★★★

DIRECTOR: Peter Bogdanovich

CAST: Timothy Bottoms, Ben Johnson, Jeff Bridges, Cloris Leachman, Cybill Shepherd, Randy Quaid

Outstanding adaptation of Larry McMurtry's novel about a boy's rites of passage in a small Texas town during the 1950s. Virtually all the performances are excellent due to the deft direction of Peter Bogdanovich, who assured his fame with this picture. Ben Johnson, as a pool hall owner, and Cloris Leachman, as a lonely wife, deservedly won Oscars for their supporting performances. Filmed in black and white, which makes the gritty story even more stark, this will leave lasting impressions. An absolute must. Rated R for brief nudity and adult situations.

1971 B & W 118 minutes

LAST SUMMER

★★½

DIRECTOR: Frank Perry

CAST: Richard Thomas, Barbara Hershey, Bruce Davison, Cathy Burns, Ralph Waite, Conrad Bain

Engrossing tale of teen desires, frustrations, and fears, played out in disturbingly dark fashion. Bruce Davison and Cathy Burns are especially memorable in unusual roles. Rated R.

1969 97 minutes

LAST TANGO IN PARIS

★★★

DIRECTOR: Bernardo Bertolucci

CAST: Marlon Brando, Maria Schneider, Jean-Pierre Léaud

A middle-aged man (Marlon Brando) and a young French girl (Maria Schneider) have a doomed love affair. This pretentious sex melodrama was mainly notable for being banned when it first came out. Rated R for sex.

1972 129 minutes

LAST TYCOON, THE

★★★

DIRECTOR: Elia Kazan

CAST: Robert DeNiro, Robert Mitchum, Tony Curtis, Jeanne Moreau, Jack Nicholson, Donald Pleasence, Peter Strauss, Ray Milland, Ingrid Boulting, Dana Andrews, John Carradine

Tantalizing yet frustrating, this slow-moving attempt to film F. Scott Fitzgerald's last (and unfinished) book is a blockbuster conglomeration of talent at all levels, but fails to really capture the imagination of the average filmgoer and appears to be a somewhat confusing collection of scenes and confrontations. Robert DeNiro as Monroe Starr, the sickly motion picture magnate and the "last tycoon" of the story, gives another fine, understated performance, but the film just lacks the form and punch to entertain or inveigle the casual video renter, who knows little about the studio system (and especially MGM, Irving Thalberg, or Louis B. Mayer) and cares less. A satisfying treat for film history buffs and a unique chance to see an incredible collection of great actors and actresses from the old studio days (Ray Milland, Dana Andrews, John Carradine, Robert Mitchum) as well as some of today's finest talent (Jeanne Moreau, Jack Nicholson, Robert DeNiro).

1976 125 minutes

LAST WINTER, THE

DIRECTOR: Riki Shelach

CAST: Kathleen Quinlan, Yona Elian, Stephen Macht, Zipora Peled, Michael Schneider, Brian Aaron

Kathleen Quinlan (*Independence Day, Twilight Zone—The Movie*) and Yona Elian are wives of Israeli soldiers missing in action during the Yom Kippur War of 1973. Over the prospect of both women becoming widows, their friendship grows intense, with hints of homosexuality. This outing had potential, but it was bound for trouble with dialogue like "My body aches for him" and "I want to have his child," and a slow-motion sequence that tries to develop character when the screenwriter has run out of all other types of clichés to use. The entire film has a harsh tone about it that makes it difficult for the viewer to feel any sympathy for the two women. Rated R for sex, nudity, language, and adult situations.

1984 92 minutes

LATINO

★½

DIRECTOR: Haskell Wexler

CAST: Robert Beltran, Annette Cardona, Tony Plana, Ricardo Lopez, Julio Medina, Luiz Torrentes

Master cinematographer Haskell Wexler (*Days of Heaven*, *Bound for Glory*) tries his hand at writing and directing in this story of a Chicago Green Beret who questions the morality of the activities required of him in the Nicaraguan war. This is a fairly routine war story, with the exception of the protagonist being a Latin American. There's a big problem when this Green Beret begins to think about what he's doing and decides to quit the army after his assignment is over. It comes out of left field, and the way Robert Beltran plays the soldier, you don't believe in his enlightenment for a minute.

1985 108 minutes

LEATHER BOYS, THE

★★

DIRECTOR: Sidney J. Furie

CAST: Rita Tushingham, Dudley Sutton, Colin Campbell, Gladys Henson

Considered adult and controversial when first released in England, this slice-of-life drama about teenagers who marry for sex and settle into drab existences doesn't carry the weight it once did. Rita Tushingham, one of Britain's most promising New Wave performers (*A Taste of Honey, The Knack*) finds her marriage devoid of the romance and magic that she envisioned, and her young husband's interest in motorbikes and a homosexual crony leaves her with many lonely hours in squalid surroundings. Rather depressing, this film is an interesting look at life in London in the early 1960s, but it has dated badly.

1963 B & W 108 minutes

LEAVE 'EM LAUGHING

★★★★½

DIRECTOR: Jackie Cooper

CAST: Mickey Rooney, Anne Jackson, Red Buttons, William Windom, Elisha Cook

Mickey Rooney is outstanding portraying real-life Chicago clown Jack Thum. Thum and his wife (played by Anne Jackson) cared for dozens of unwanted children. When Thum realizes he has terminal cancer, he falls apart and his wife must help him regain his inner strength and deal with reality. A real tearjerker! Made for TV, this is unrated.

1981 104 minutes

LEGEND OF VALENTINO, THE

★

DIRECTOR: Graeme Ferguson

CAST: Documentary

This documentary on silent-screen star Rudolph Valentino was produced in 1983 but has the superficial flavor of one made much earlier. It smacks of old newsreel-biography footage. *The Legend of Valentino* does provide interesting early film clips of Valentino as an all-American boy and other types. It relies heavily on scenes from later movies, with extensive footage from *The Son of the Sheik*. The makers of this film don't have anything new to offer on Valentino; they are just riding on his coattails.

1983 72 minutes

LEGEND OF VALENTINO

★★

DIRECTOR: Melville Shavelson

CAST: Franco Nero, Suzanne Pleshette, Judd Hirsch, Lesley Warren, Milton Berle, Yvette Mimieux, Harold Stone

TV movie released close to the fiftieth anniversary of the fabled actor's death adheres to some facts concerning the archetypal Latin lover, but still presents an unsatisfying and incomplete portrait. A good cast eases many of the clichéd plot turns, and Franco Nero does a credible job as a rather confused young god; but this one still has its share of hokum. Better than Anthony Dexter's portrayal in *Valentino* (1951) and more conservative than Ken Russell's incredible version featuring Rudolf Nureyev, this film still leaves too many questions either unanswered or glossed over. Not too bad for a TV movie.

1975 100 minutes

LENNY

★★★★★

DIRECTOR: Bob Fosse

CAST: Dustin Hoffman, Valerie Perrine, Jan Miner

Bob Fosse brilliantly directed this stark biography of self-destructive, controversial persecuted comic talent Lenny Bruce. Dustin

Hoffman captures all those contrary emotions in his portrayal of the late 1950s and '60s stand-up comedian. Valerie Perrine is a treasure in her low-key role as Bruce's stripper wife. Rated R.

1974 B & W 112 minutes

LET'S GET HARRY

★★½

DIRECTOR: Alan Smithee

CAST: Robert Duvall, Gary Busey, Mark Harmon, Glenn Frey, Michael Schoeffling

When an American (Mark Harmon) is kidnapped during a South American revolution, a group of his friends decide that they are going to bring him home. When the government doesn't respond, they hire a soldier of fortune (Robert Duvall) to lead them into the jungles of Colombia where, against all odds, they fight to bring Harry home. Rated R for violence and language.

1986 98 minutes

LETTER, THE

★★★★

DIRECTOR: William Wyler

CAST: Bette Davis, Herbert Marshall, James Stephenson

Bette Davis stars in this screen adaptation of Somerset Maugham's play as the coldly calculating wife of a rubber plantation owner (Herbert Marshall) in Malaya. In a fit of pique, she shoots her lover and concocts an elaborate tissue of lies to protect herself. With tension mounting all the way, we wonder if her evil ways will eventually lead to her downfall.

1940 B & W 95 minutes

LETTER OF INTRODUCTION

★★★★

DIRECTOR: John M. Stahl

CAST: Adolphe Menjou, Andrea Leeds, Edgar Bergen and Charlie McCarthy, George Murphy, Eve Arden, Rita Johnson, Ernest Cossart, Ann Sheridan

An essentially enjoyable melodrama, *Letter of Introduction* is the story of a young actress (Andrea Leeds) who seeks out the advice of an old actor (Adolphe Menjou). The aging star encourages her in her various endeavors. The relationship between the two lead characters is so real, so warm that it carries the film. Look for Ann Sheridan in one of her early roles, along with the antics of Edgar Bergen and Charlie McCarthy.

1938 B & W 100 minutes

LIANNA

★★★★

DIRECTOR: John Sayles

CAST: Linda Griffiths, Jane Halloren, Jon DeVries, Jo Henderson

The problem with most motion pictures about gays is they always seem to be more concerned with sex than love. In comparison, this film, written and directed by John Sayles (*Baby, It's You*; *Return of the Secaucus Seven*) stands as a remarkable achievement. About a married housewife named Lianna (Linda Griffiths) who decides to have an affair with, and eventually move in with, another woman (Jane Halloren), it is a sensitive study of one woman's life and loves. Rated R for nudity, sex, and profanity.

1983 110 minutes

LIAR'S MOON

★★★½

DIRECTOR: David Fisher

CAST: Matt Dillon, Cindy Fisher, Christopher Connelly, Hoyt Axton, Yvonne DeCarlo, Susan Tyrrell

Two young lovers encounter unusually hostile resistance from their parents. Their elopement produces many of the expected problems faced by youths just starting out: limited finances, inexperience and incompatibility. They also must come to grips with a major problem that is totally unexpected. The plight of the couple remains interesting throughout, mostly due to the leads' believable performances. Rated PG for language.

1983 106 minutes

LIBERATION OF L. B. JONES, THE

★

DIRECTOR: William Wyler
CAST: Lola Falana, Roscoe Lee Browne, Lee J. Cobb, Lee Majors, Barbara Hershey

Famed director William Wyler really laid an egg in this uninteresting "message" movie. In what starts as a movie effort to portray race relations gone asunder, all we are given is cardboard cutout stereotypes and a confusing plot. This story, of a wealthy black man who is deluded into divorcing his wife (Lola Falana) because of her believed infidelity with a white cop, never gains our sympathy or interest. Rated R.

1970 102 minutes

LIES

★★★★

DIRECTORS: Ken Wheat, Jim Wheat
CAST: Ann Dusenberry, Gail Strickland, Bruce Davison, Clu Gulager, Terence Knox, Bert Remsen, Stacy Keach Sr., Douglas Leonard

Ann Dusenberry plays a starving actress who gets sucked into a complicated and treacherous plan to gain the inheritance of a rich patient in a mental hospital. The plot is complicated and the good acting balances the intensity. The best part: a great performance by Gail Strickland, who plays a character you'll love to hate. Rated R for violence, sex, nudity, and profanity.

1986 93 minutes

LIFE AND DEATH OF COLONEL BLIMP, THE

★★★★★

DIRECTORS: Michael Powell, Emeric Pressburger
CAST: Roger Livesey, Deborah Kerr, Anton Walbrook

A truly superb film chronicling the life and times of a staunch for-king-and-country British soldier. Sentimentally celebrating the human spirit, it opens during World War II and unfolds through a series of flashbacks that reach as far back as the Boer War. Roger Livesey is excellent in the title role. Deborah Kerr portrays the four women in his life across four decades with charm and insight. Definitely a keeper.

1943 163 minutes

LIFE OF EMILE ZOLA, THE

★★★★

DIRECTOR: William Dieterle
CAST: Paul Muni, Joseph Schildkraut, Gale Sondergaard, Gloria Holden, Donald Crisp, Louis Calhern

Paul Muni is excellent in the title role of the nineteenth-century novelist who championed the cause of the wrongly accused Captain Dreyfus (Joseph Schildkraut). A lavish production!

1937 B & W 93 minutes

LIFEBOAT

★★★½

DIRECTOR: Alfred Hitchcock
CAST: Tallulah Bankhead, John Hodiak, William Bendix, Walter Slezak, Henry Hull, Canada Lee, Hume Cronyn, Heather Angel, Mary Anderson

A microcosm of American society, survivors of a World War II torpedoing, adrift in a lifeboat, nearly come a cropper when they take a Nazi aboard. Dumbly dismissed as an artistic failure by most critics, it has some ridiculous flaws, but is nonetheless an interesting and engrossing film. Said one critic: "John Steinbeck wrote the allegorical story, screenwriter MacKinley Kantor heightened the allegory, screenwriter Jo Swerling provided Hollywood gloss, and Alfred Hitchcock created a thriller." Tunnel-voiced Tallulah Bankhead is tops in this sea-going *Grand Hotel*. Look for Hitchcock's pictorial trademark in a newspaper.

1944 B & W 96 minutes

LIFEGUARD

★★½

DIRECTOR: Daniel Petrie
CAST: Sam Elliott, Anne Archer, Kathleen Quinlan, Parker Stevenson, Stephen Young

Is happiness enough? Don't we have to do something with our lives? After his fifteen-year high-school reunion, Sam Elliott begins to feel twinges of fear and guilt. How long can he go on being a lifeguard? Shouldn't he be making the move into a career with a future? Shouldn't he be chasing the almighty dollar like everyone else? The film is likable and easy-going, like its star. If your interest starts to drift, Elliott's charisma will pull you back. Rated PG.

1976 96 minutes

LIGHT OF DAY

★★½

DIRECTOR: Paul Schrader
CAST: Michael J. Fox, Gena Rowlands, Joan Jett, Jason Miller, Michael McKean, Billy Sullivan

Director Paul Schrader (*Cat People, Hardcore*) tends toward the perverse and seedy, and in *Light of Day* the dregs lure him once again. The object of his obsessive gaze is the dead-end lives of a Cleveland bar band. There's Michael J. Fox as the guitarist willing to compromise in life for some stability. And there's his nihilistic sister (Joan Jett), the leader of the group who says that the beat of the music is all-important. Fox is miscast as a rock-'n-roller. He looks like a regular guy who's living out the fantasy of being a musician. Jett is the one to watch. True, she's playing herself (or a variation on her image), but she's good at selfish anger. She's good behind the mike, too, giving a terrific interpretation of the Bruce Springsteen–penned title song. Rated PG.

1987 107 minutes

LIGHTSHIP, THE

★★

DIRECTOR: Jerzy Skolimowski
CAST: Robert Duvall, Klaus Maria Brandauer, Michael Lyndon

The chief interest in this allegorical suspense drama is in seeing Robert Duvall play an over-the-top villian. It's an effete, simpering, verbose characterization that resembles one of those guest villains on the old *Batman* series, and there are moments when he's a real hoot. But the story itself—a trio of sadistic bank robbers hijack a floating, anchored lighthouse and the ship's pacifist captain (Klaus Maria Brandauer) tries to stop his crew from fighting back—is overloaded with too obvious symbolism and is short on suspense. Rated R.

1986 90 minutes

LILIES OF THE FIELD

★★★★

DIRECTOR: Ralph Nelson
CAST: Sidney Poitier, Lilia Skala

Sidney Poitier won an Academy Award for his portrayal of a handyman who happens upon a group of nuns who have fled from East

Germany and finds himself building a chapel for them. With little or no build-up, the movie went on to become a big hit.

1963 B & W 93 minutes

LILITH

★★

DIRECTOR: Robert Rossen

CAST: Warren Beatty, Jean Seberg, Peter Fonda, Kim Hunter, Anne Meacham, Jessica Walter, Gene Hackman

Producer-director Robert Rossen's adaptation of J. R. Salamanca's cult novel is an intriguing, somber, frequently indecipherable journey into the darker depths of the human psyche. Warren Beatty is a young psychiatric therapist at a mental institute who falls in love with a beautiful schizophrenic patient (Jean Seberg), with tragic results. Visually impressive, with its poetic, dreamlike imagery, it remains dramatically frustrating due to its ambiguous blending of sanity and madness, reality and fantasy. More of a feature-length experiment in mood than a traditional "movie," it's a fascinating film, though not an especially likable one.

1964 B & W 114 minutes

LINDBERGH KIDNAPPING CASE, THE

★★★

DIRECTOR: Buzz Kulik

CAST: Cliff DeYoung, Anthony Hopkins, Joseph Cotten, Denise Alexander, Sian Barbara Allen, Martin Balsam, Peter Donat, Dean Jagger, Walter Pidgeon

Still another look at one of this century's most famous and fascinating tragedies, this made-for-television version is above average. Anthony Hopkins rates four stars as Bruno Hauptmann, the man convicted and executed for the crime.

1976 150 minutes

LION IN WINTER, THE

★★★★½

DIRECTOR: Anthony Harvey

CAST: Katharine Hepburn, Peter O'Toole, Anthony Hopkins, John Castle, Timothy Dalton

Acerbic retelling of the clash of wits between England's King Henry II (Peter O'Toole) and Eleanor of Aquitaine (Katharine Hepburn), adapted by James Goldman from his Broadway play. Hepburn won an Oscar for her part, and it's quite well played. The story's extended power struggle rages back and forth, with Henry and Eleanor striking sparks throughout. Snappy dialogue, flawlessly delivered. O'Toole hasn't had a part this good since *Lawrence of Arabia*. Not at all boring, in spite of its length. Excellent score by John Barry. Rated PG.

1968 135 minutes

LITTLE ANNIE ROONEY

★★★

DIRECTOR: William Beaudine

CAST: Mary Pickford, Spec O'Donnell, Hugh Fay, Walter James, Gordon Griffith, William Haines

The title character is a teen-aged street kid in braids, but America's Sweetheart, Mary Pickford, who played her, was 32 at the time. Pickford gets away with it—as she did in many of her films. As the daughter of a widowed New York cop, Annie keeps house, runs a street gang, and anguishes when her father is killed and her boyfriend is wrongly accused of the crime. Love and justice triumph, however, at fadeout. Corny then and now, but interesting if only for the star's uncanny ability to impersonate a child.

Miss Pickford came to loathe playing such roles, but public demand and great financial rewards kept her at it . Silent.

1925 B & W 60 minutes

LITTLE FOXES, THE

★★★★

DIRECTOR: William Wyler

CAST: Bette Davis, Herbert Marshall, Teresa Wright, Richard Carlson, Dan Duryea

The ever-fascinating, ever-unique Bette Davis dominates this outstanding rendering of controversial playwright Lillian Hellman's drama of amoral family greed and corruption down South. Davis's ruthless matriarch, Regina, is the ultimate Edwardian bitch, for whom murder by inaction is not beyond the pale when it comes to achieving her desires.

1941 B & W 116 minutes

LITTLE LORD FAUNTLEROY

★★★★

DIRECTOR: John Cromwell

CAST: Freddie Bartholomew, C. Aubrey Smith, Dolores Costello, Jessie Ralph, Mickey Rooney, Guy Kibbee

Far from a syrupy-sweet child movie, this is the affecting tale of a long-lost American heir (Freddie Bartholomew) brought to live with a hard-hearted British lord (C. Aubrey Smith) whose icy manner is warmed by the cheerful child.

1936 B & W 98 minutes

LITTLE MEN

★½

DIRECTOR: Norman Z. McLeod

CAST: Jack Oakie, Kay Francis, George Bancroft, Jimmy Lydon, Ann Gillis, Charles Esmond, William Demarest, Sterling Holloway, Isabel Jewell

Louisa May Alcott's classic of childhood turned into a travesty. Poor writing and second-rate histrionic endeavors by mediocre cast stifled the charm and sentiment of the novel, making the production one of cheap jokes and dialogue from the Ice Age. Film was a box-officer loser.

1940 B & W 84 minutes

LITTLE MINISTER, THE

★★★½

DIRECTOR: Richard Wallace

CAST: Katharine Hepburn, Donald Crisp, John Beal, Andy Clyde

An early effort in the career of Katharine Hepburn. This charming story, of a proper Scottish minister who falls in love with what he believes is a gypsy girl, is not only of merit to just Hepburn fans.

1934 B & W 110 minutes

LITTLE WOMEN

★★★★½

DIRECTOR: George Cukor

CAST: Katharine Hepburn, Spring Byington, Joan Bennett, Frances Dee, Jean Parker

George Cukor's *Little Women* is far and away the best of the four film versions of Louisa May Alcott's timeless story of the March family. Katharine Hepburn is excellent as the tomboyish Jo. The remainder of the New England family, which endures the Civil War and grows to maturity, is wonderfully played by Spring Byington, Joan Bennett, Frances Dee, and Jean Parker.

1933 B & W 115 minutes

LOLITA

★★★

DIRECTOR: Stanley Kubrick

CAST: James Mason, Sue Lyon, Shelley Winters, Peter Sellers

A man's unconventional obsession for a "nymphet" is the basis for this bizarre satire. James

Mason and Sue Lyon are the naughty pair in this film, which caused quite a stir in the 1960s but seems fairly tame today.

1962 B & W 152 minutes

LONELY HEARTS

★★★★½

DIRECTOR: Paul Cox

CAST: Norman Kaye, Wendy Hughes, Julia Blake

A funny, touching Australian romantic comedy about two offbeat characters who fall in love. Peter (Norman Kaye) is a 50-year-old mama's boy who doesn't know what to do with his life when his mother dies. Then he meets Patricia (Wendy Hughes), a woman who has never had a life of her own. It's a warmly human delight. Rated R.

1981 95 minutes

LONELY LADY, THE

DIRECTOR: Peter Sasdy

CAST: Pia Zadora, Lloyd Bochner, Bibi Besch

Adapted from the novel by Harold Robbins, this film stars Pia Zadora as Jerilee Randall, an aspiring writer who is used and abused by every man she meets. You never believe it for a moment. As a result, it's often a real hoot; a hilarious mixture of bad dialogue, campy performances, and outrageous situations. Rated R for sex, violence, nudity, and profanity.

1983 92 minutes

LONELYHEARTS

★★

DIRECTOR: Vincent J. Donahue

CAST: Montgomery Clift, Robert Ryan, Myrna Loy, Maureen Stapleton, Frank Maxwell, Dolores Hart, Jackie Coogan, Mike Kellin, Frank Overton, Onslow Stevens

A perfect example of how Hollywood can ruin great material. Montgomery Clift is tortured as only he could be, Robert Ryan is cynical, and Maureen Stapleton is pitifully sex-starved in this disappointing adaptation of Nathaniel West's brilliant novel about an agony columnist who gets too caught up in a correspondent's life. Baloney!

1958 B & W 101 minutes

LONG AGO TOMORROW

★★★

DIRECTOR: Bryan Forbes

CAST: Malcolm McDowell, Nanette Newman, Georgia Brown, Gerald Sim, Bernard Lee, Michael Flanders, Richard Moore

Malcolm McDowell stars in this in-depth story about an arrogant soccer player who is paralyzed by a mysterious disease. In an attempt to escape from the sympathy of friends and family, he admits himself to a countryside home for the disabled, where a pretty young woman who shares the same disability is able to help him adapt. McDowell keeps the plot alive with a very believable performance. Rated PG.

1970 116 minutes

LONG DAY'S JOURNEY INTO NIGHT

★★★★★

DIRECTOR: Sidney Lumet

CAST: Katharine Hepburn, Ralph Richardson, Jason Robards Jr., Dean Stockwell

This superb film was based on Eugene O'Neill's play about a troubled turn-of-the-century New England family. Katharine Hepburn is brilliant as the drug-addict wife. Ralph Richardson is equally good as her husband, a self-centered actor. One of their sons is an alcoholic, while the other is dying of tuberculosis. Although depressing, it is an unforgettable viewing experience.

1962 B & W 136 minutes

LONG VOYAGE HOME, THE

★★★★½

DIRECTOR: John Ford

CAST: John Wayne, Barry Fitzgerald, Thomas Mitchell, Mildred Natwick

Life in the merchant marine as experienced and recalled by Nobel Prize–winning playwright Eugene O'Neill. The hopes and dreams and comradeship of a group of seamen beautifully blended in a gripping, moving account of men, a ship, and the ever-enigmatic sea. The major characters are superbly drawn by those playing them. Definitely a must-see, and see-again, film. Classic.

1940 B & W 105 minutes

LOOK BACK IN ANGER

★★★★½

DIRECTOR: Tony Richardson

CAST: Richard Burton, Claire Bloom

Based on the John Osborne play of the same name, this riveting look into one of the "angry young men" of the 1950s has Richard Burton and Claire Bloom at their best. Burton exposes the torment and frustration these men felt toward their country and private life with more vividness than you may want to deal with, but if you're looking for a realistic recreation of the period, look no further. Ultimately depressing but revealing, it leaves you thoughtful and haunted.

1958 B & W 99 minutes

LOOKING FOR MR. GOODBAR

★

DIRECTOR: Richard Brooks

CAST: Diane Keaton, Tuesday Weld, Richard Gere, LeVar Burton, Richard Kiley

A strong performance by star Diane Keaton can't save this dismal character study about a woman drawn to sleazy sex and lowlifes. Tuesday Weld and Richard Gere also are memorable in support, but director Richard Brooks obviously intended to revolt the audience through the main character's aimless immorality and untimely end—and did so to the detriment of his picture. Rated R.

1977 135 minutes

LOOKING GLASS WAR, THE

★★

DIRECTOR: Frank R. Pierson

CAST: Christopher Jones, Pia Degermark, Ralph Richardson, Anthony Hopkins

This plodding adaptation of John Le Carré's espionage novel about a Pole sent to get the scam on a rocket in East Berlin is replete with spy slang and the usual covert and clandestine operations. But it never gets off the ground. Having actor's actor Ralph Richardson in the cast should have, but did not, help. Most of the acting is as wooden as bleacher seating. Where's Smiley when we need him? Rated PG.

1970 106 minutes

LORD OF THE FLIES

★★★★

DIRECTOR: Peter Brook

CAST: James Aubrey, Hugh Edwards, Tom Chapin

William Golding's grim allegory comes to the screen in a near-perfect adaptation helmed by British stage director Peter Brook. English schoolboys, stranded on an island and left to their own devices, gradually revert to the savage cruelty of wild animals. Visually hypnotic and powerful, something you just can't tear your eyes away from. The cast is outstanding, and what the film fails to take from

Golding's novel—much of the symbolism, for example—it compensates for with raw energy. It'll make you think twice about the little boys who live down the street.

1963 B & W 91 minutes

LORDS OF DISCIPLINE, THE

★★★½

DIRECTOR: Franc Roddam

CAST: David Keith, Robert Prosky, G. D. Spradlin, Rick Rossovich

A thought provoking film, *Lords* contains many emotionally charged and well-played scenes. David Keith (*An Officer and a Gentleman*; *Brubaker*) stars as a student at a military academy who puts his life in danger by helping a black cadet being hazed by The Ten, a secret group of white students dedicated to the "purification" of the campus. Rated R for profanity, nudity, and violence.

1983 102 minutes

LORDS OF FLATBUSH, THE

★★½

DIRECTORS: Stephen F. Verona, Martin Davidson

CAST: Perry King, Sylvester Stallone, Henry Winkler, Paul Mace, Susan Blakely

Of all the leads, only Paul Mace didn't go on to bigger things. A stocky Sylvester Stallone shows promise as a character actor. Perry King is dashing. Susan Blakely is lovely. And Henry Winkler is particularly winning, playing an unexaggerated Fonzie-type character. The film provides a fairly satisfying blend of toughness and sentimentality, humor and pathos, as it tells a story of coming of age in 1950s New York. Rated PG.

1974 88 minutes

LOST HORIZON

★★★★

DIRECTOR: Frank Capra

CAST: Ronald Colman, Jane Wyatt, John Howard, Edward Everett Horton, Margo, Sam Jaffe, Thomas Mitchell, Isabel Jewell, H. B. Warner

Novelist James Hilton's intriguing story of a group of disparate people who survive an air crash and stumble on to a strange and haunting Tibetan land. One of the great classic films of the late 1930s. Long-missing footage has recently been restored, along with so-called lost scenes.

1937 B & W 117 minutes

LOST MOMENT, THE

★★★½

DIRECTOR: Martin Gable

CAST: Robert Cummings, Susan Hayward, Agnes Moorehead, Eduardo Ciannelli

A low-key, dark, offbeat drama based on Henry James's novel *The Aspern Papers*, which was based on the true story of Claire Clairmont, friend of the poet Percy Bysshe Shelley and mother of a love child by George Gordon, Lord Byron. A publisher (Robert Cummings), seeking love letters written by a long-dead great poet, goes to Italy to interview a very old lady and her niece. The old lady is spooky, the niece neurotic, the film fascinating. Those who know Cummings only from his TV series will be pleasantly surprised with his serious acting.

1947 B & W 88 minutes

LOST WEEKEND, THE

★★★★★

DIRECTOR: Billy Wilder

CAST: Ray Milland, Jane Wyman, Philip Terry, Howard DaSilva, Frank Faylen

Gripping, powerful study of alcoholism and its destructive effect on one man's life. Arguably Ray Milland's best performance (he won an Oscar) and undeniably one of the most potent films of all time. Forty years after its release, the movie has lost none of its importance or effectiveness. Additional Oscars for best picture, director, and screenplay. A real gem.

1945 B & W 101 minutes

LOVE CHILD

★★★★

DIRECTOR: Larry Peerce
CAST: Amy Madigan, Beau Bridges, Mackenzie Phillips

Although its ads gave *Love Child* the appearance of a cheapo exploitation flick, this superb prison drama is anything but. Directed by Larry Peerce (*The Other Side of the Mountain*), it is the gripping story of a young woman, Terry Jean Moore (Amy Madigan), who became pregnant by a guard in a women's prison in Florida and fought for the right to keep her baby. Madigan gives a stirring performance. Rated R for profanity, nudity, sex, and violence.

1982 96 minutes

LOVE IS A MANY-SPLENDORED THING

★★★

DIRECTOR: Henry King
CAST: Jennifer Jones, William Holden, Isobel Elsom, Richard Loo

Clichéd story of ill-starred lovers from two different worlds who don't make it. Jennifer Joes is a Eurasian doctor who falls in love with war correspondent William Holden during the Korean conflict. Love does not win out, but the effort is superbly made. The title song was a hit.

1955 102 minutes

LOVE LEADS THE WAY

★★★★

DIRECTOR: Delbert Mann
CAST: Timothy Bottoms, Eva Marie Saint, Arthur Hill, Susan Dey

This Disney TV movie features Timothy Bottoms in the true story of Morris Frank, the first American to train with a seeing-eye dog. Blinded while boxing, Frank at first refuses to accept his handicap and later resents the dog who offers to be his eyes. Fortunately, he adapts and later lobbies for acceptance of seeing-eye dogs throughout the United States. This moving film doesn't gloss over the real frustrations involved. Bottoms turns in an exceptional performance as the struggling Frank.

1984 99 minutes

LOVE LETTERS

★★★★

DIRECTOR: Amy Jones
CAST: Jamie Lee Curtis, Amy Madigan, Bud Cort, James Keach

At one time or another, we've all wondered what our lives would have been like had we taken a radical step in another direction. In this impressive character study, the heroine, played by Jamie Lee Curtis, wonders aloud to her friend (Amy Madigan): "Sometimes it's right to do the wrong thing, isn't it?" But is it? Probing the emotions that lead to infidelity, *Love Letters* is a true adult motion picture. It deals explicitly with themes and ideas from which most movies shy away. This concept is intelligently explored by writer-director Amy Jones in this, her second film. Curtis's remarkable portrayal adds greatly to the believability. The result is resounding screen work that stays with the viewer long after the ending credits have rolled. Rated R for graphic sex.

1983 98 minutes

LOVE STORY

★★★★

DIRECTOR: Arthur Hiller
CAST: Ryan O'Neal, Ali MacGraw, Ray Milland, John Marley

Unabashedly sentimental and manipulative, this film was a box-office smash. Directed by Arthur Hiller (*Silver Streak*; *Making Love*) and adapted by Erich Segal from his best-selling novel, it features Ryan O'Neal and Ali MacGraw as star-crossed lovers who meet, marry, make it, and then discover she is dying. Liking this kind of soap opera means never having to say you're sorry. Rated PG.

1970 99 minutes

LOVE STREAMS

★★

DIRECTOR: John Cassavetes
CAST: John Cassavetes, Gena Rowlands, Diahnne Abbott, Seymour Cassel, Margaret Abbott

A rather depressing story of a writer who involves himself in the lives of lonely women for inspiration, and his emotionally unstable sister, whom he takes in after a difficult divorce has left her without possession of her child. There are some funny moments and some heartfelt scenes, as well, but John Cassavetes's direction, though suggesting more than what Ted Allan's play implies, is awkward. Rated PG-13 for language and adult situations.

1984 122 minutes

LOVE'S SAVAGE FURY

DIRECTOR: Joseph Hardy
CAST: Jennifer O'Neill, Perry King, Robert Reed, Raymond Burr, Connie Stevens

This historical romance was a made-for-TV movie. Jennifer O' Neill plays a Sourthern belle who is forced to come down a peg when thrown into a less than glamorous Union prison camp. There she meets the ever handsome Perry King and they escape together. She has plans to find the gold her father had buried. Overall, this is just a boring soap opera with a Civil War backdrop that employs limited acting ability and fails to draw more than a mild "ho-hum" from its viewers. Avoid if possible.

1979 104 minutes

LOVELESS, THE

★★

DIRECTORS: Kathryn Bigelow, Monty Montgomery
CAST: Willem DaFoe, Robert Gordon, Marin Kanter, Tina L'Hotsky, J. Don Ferguson, Danny Rosen

This could have been called *The Senseless* thanks to its lack of plot and emphasis on violence. It's a biker picture set in the 1950s and stars Willem DaFoe, who gives a good performance with the scant dialogue he's given. Though a poor tribute to *The Wild One*, this film does have a cult following and will probably be found in the midnight movie section if your store has one. Rated R for violence, nudity and sex scenes.

1984 85 minutes

LUCAS

★★★★

DIRECTOR: David Seltzer
CAST: Corey Haim, Kerri Green, Charlie Sheen, Courtney Thorne-Smith, Winona Ryder

Charming tale of young love, leagues above the usual teen-oriented fare due to an intelligent and compassionate script by writer/director David Seltzer.

Corey Haim stars as a 14-year-old whiz kid "accelerated" into high school who falls in love, during the summer between terms, with 16-year-old Kerri Green. They form a budding relationship destined to wilt upon the return to school, when Green shows interest in boys closer to her own age, notably football star Charlie Sheen (another talented son of Martin Sheen). Poignant, powerful, and quite perceptive in its examination of high-school life. Rated PG-13 for language.

1986 100 minutes

MACARTHUR

★★★

DIRECTOR: Joseph Sargent
CAST: Gregory Peck, Dan O'Herlihy, Ed Flanders

Gregory Peck is cast as the famous general during the latter years of his long military career. It begins with his assumption of command of the Philippine garrison in World War II and continues through his sacking by President Truman during the Korean Conflict. The film takes a middle ground in its depiction of this complex man and the controversy that surrounded him. Peck's performance is creditable, but the film remains uneven and flat. Rated PG.

1977 130 minutes

MACBETH

★★★½

DIRECTOR: Roman Polanski
CAST: Jon Finch, Francesca Annis, Martin Shaw, Nicholas Selby, John Stride, Stephan Chase

The violent retelling of this classic story was commissioned and underwritten by publisher Hugh Hefner. Shakespeare's tragedy about a man driven to self-destruction by the forces of evil is vividly brought to life by director Roman Polanski, no stranger to violence and adversity himself. Grim yet compelling, this version of one of our great plays is not for everyone and contains scenes that make it objectionable for children (or sequeamish adults). The star is Jon Finch, perhaps best known as the star of Alfred Hitchcock's black comedy *Frenzy*.

1971 140 minutes

MACBETH

★★★

DIRECTOR: Orson Welles
CAST: Orson Welles, Roddy McDowall, Jeanette Nolan, Edgar Barrier, Dan O'Herlihy

Shakespeare's noted tragedy, filmed according to a script by Orson Welles. Interesting moviemaking on a low budget of $700,000 within a time frame of three weeks. Welles is an intriguing MacBeth, but Jeanette Nolan as his lady is out of her element. Edgar Barrier and Dan O'Herlihy are fine as Banquo and MacDuff. Wear your Kilt. Everybody speaks with a Scottish accent.

1948 B & W 105 minutes

MADAME BOVARY

★★★

DIRECTOR: Vincente Minnelli
CAST: Jennifer Jones, Louis Jourdan, Van Heflin, James Mason

Emma Bovary is an incurable romantic whose affairs of the heart ultimately lead to her destruction. Jennifer Jones is superb as Emma. Louis Jourdan plays her most engaging lover. Van Heflin portrays her betrayed husband. James Mason portrays Gustave Flaubert, on whose classic French novel the film is based.

1949 B & W 115 minutes

MADAME X

★★★

DIRECTOR: David Lowell Rich
CAST: Lana Turner, John Forsythe, Constance Bennett, Ricardo Montalban, Burgess Meredith

In this sentimental old chestnut, filmed six times since 1909, a woman is defended against murder charges by an attorney who is not aware he is her son. Lana Turner is good and is backed by a fine cast, but Technicolor and a big budget make this one of producer Ross Hunter's mistakes. Constance Bennett's last film.

1966 100 minutes

MAGIC TOWN

★★

DIRECTOR: William Wellman
CAST: James Stewart, Jane Wyman, Ned Sparks

After successfully collaborating with Frank Capra on some of his finest films, writer Robert Riskin teamed with director William Wellman for this mildly entertaining but preachy tale. An advertising executive (James Stewart) finds the perfect American community, which is turned topsy-turvy when the secret gets out.

1947 B & W 103 minutes

MAGNIFICENT AMBERSONS, THE

★★★★★

DIRECTOR: Orson Welles
CAST: Joseph Cotten, Tim Holt, Agnes Moorehead

Orson Welles's legendary depiction of the decline of a wealthy Midwestern family and the comeuppance of its youngest member is a definite must-see motion picture. Much has been made about the callous editing of the final print by studio henchmen, but that doesn't change the total impact. It's still a classic. The stars can take bows for their acting. Special notice must be given to Welles and cameraman Stanley Cortez for the artistic, almost portraitlike, look of the film.

1942 B & W 88 minutes

MAGNIFICENT OBSESSION

★★★

DIRECTOR: Douglas Sirk
CAST: Jane Wyman, Rock Hudson, Agnes Moorehead, Otto Kruger

Rock Hudson, a drunken playboy, blinds Jane Wyman in an auto accident. Stricken, he reforms and becomes a doctor in order to restore her sight in this melodramatic tearjerker from the well-known Lloyd C. Douglas novel. First filmed in 1935, with Irene Dunne and Robert Taylor.

1954 108 minutes

MAHLER

★★½

DIRECTOR: Ken Russell
CAST: Robert Powell, Georgina Hale, Richard Morant

Ken Russell's fantasy film about the biography of composer Gustav Mahler. Robert Powell's portrayal of Mahler as a man consumed with passion and ambition is a brilliant one. Georgina Hale as Alma, Mahler's wife, is also well played. Unfortunately, the cast cannot give coherence to the script.

1974 115 minutes

MAHOGANY

★★½

DIRECTOR: Berry Gordy
CAST: Diana Ross, Anthony Perkins, Billy Dee Williams

The highlight of this unimpressive melodrama is Diana Ross's lovely wardrobe. She plays a poor girl who makes it big as a famous model and, later, dress designer after Anthony Perkins discovers her. That's when she leaves boyfriend Billy Dee Williams behind to pursue a world of glamour and success. This one jerks more yawns than tears. Rated PG.

1975 109 minutes

MAKE A WISH

DIRECTOR: Kurt Neumann
CAST: Bobby Breen, Basil Rathbone, Marion Claire, Ralph Forbes, Henry Armetta, Leon Errol, Donald Meek, Leonid Kinsky, Fred Scott

Young Bobby Breen is a prodigy. Basil Rathbone is a jolly good composer. Henry Armetta, Leon Errol, and Donald Meek want to steal Basil's latest operetta. The whole sweet, wholesome thing is enough to curdle milk. Basil probably wished he'd never made it.

1937 B & W 80 minutes

MAKING LOVE

★

DIRECTOR: Arthur Hiller
CAST: Kate Jackson, Michael Ontkean, Harry Hamlin

A wife (Kate Jackson) discovers that her husband (Michael Ontkean) is in love with another . . . man (Harry Hamlin) in this contrived soap opera, directed by Arthur Hiller (*Love Story*; *The In-Laws*). Rated R because of adult subject matter, profanity, and implicit sexual activity.

1982 113 minutes

MALTA STORY, THE

★★★

DIRECTOR: Brian Desmond Hurst
CAST: Alec Guinness, Jack Hawkins, Anthony Steel, Muriel Pavlow

Set in 1942, this is about British pluck on the island of Malta while the British were under siege from the Axis forces and the effect the war has on private lives. Flight Lieutenant Ross's (Alec Guinness) love for a native girl (Muriel Pavlow) goes unrequited when his commanding officer (Anthony Steel) sends him on a dangerous mission.

1953 B & W 103 minutes

MAN FOR ALL SEASONS, A

★★★★★

DIRECTOR: Fred Zinnemann
CAST: Paul Scofield, Wendy Hiller, Robert Shaw, Orson Welles, Susannah York

This splendid film, about Sir Thomas More's heartfelt refusal to help King Henry VIII break with the Catholic Church and form the Church of England, won the best-picture Oscar in 1966. Paul Scofield, who is magnificent in the title role, also won best actor. Directed by Fred Zinnemann and written by Robert Bolt, the picture also benefits from memorable supporting performances by an all-star cast.

1966 120 minutes

MAN IN GREY, THE

★★★

DIRECTOR: Leslie Arliss
CAST: Margaret Lockwood, James Mason, Phyllis Calvert, Stewart Granger, Martita Hunt

A tale of attempted husband-stealing that worked well to make the prey, James Mason, a star. Margaret Lockwood is the love thief who proves to intended victim Phyllis Calvert that with her for a friend she needs no enemies. Mason is a stand-out as the coveted husband.

1943 B & W 116 minutes

MAN WITH THE GOLDEN ARM, THE

★★★

DIRECTOR: Otto Preminger
CAST: Frank Sinatra, Eleanor Parker, Kim Novak, Arnold Stang, Darren McGavin, Robert Strauss, John Conte

This dated film attempts to be *The Lost Weekend* of drug-addiction movies. Frank Sinatra is the loser on the needle and the nod in sleazy Chicago surroundings. Eleanor Parker is his crippled wife. Kim Novak, in an early role, is the girl who saves him. As a study of those who say yes, it carries a small jolt.

1955 B & W 119 minutes

MAN, WOMAN AND CHILD

★★★½

DIRECTOR: Dick Richards
CAST: Martin Sheen, Blythe Danner, Sebastian Dungan

Here's a surprisingly tasteful and well-acted tearjerker directed by Dick Richards (*Farewell My Lovely*) and written by Erich Segal (*Love Story*). Martin Sheen stars as a married college professor who finds out he has a son in France, the result of an affair that took place there ten years before. The boy's mother, who kept their son's existence a secret, is dead—the victim of a car accident. So, with the grudging approval of his wife, Blythe Danner, Sheen decides to bring his son to America, which causes complications for the boy, the couple, and their two daughters. Rated PG for language and adult situations.

1983 99 minutes

MANDINGO

★

DIRECTOR: Richard Fleischer
CAST: James Mason, Susan George, Perry King, Richard Ward, Brenda Sykes

Sick film concerning the southern plantations before the Civil War and the treatment of the black slaves. The top-name cast should have known better. Rated R.

1975 127 minutes

MANSON

★★★

DIRECTOR: Robert Hendrickson
CAST: Documentary

Either the ultimate horror show or a consummate bore. This award-winning documentary chronicles the life and times of Charles Manson's "family." It blends footage of the group at play with near-lucid interviews and comments from the killers and their accomplices into an eerie ode to the insane crimes that shocked the nation. Alternately fascinating and inane, this investigation into the source of the evil that claimed at least ten lives might be hard to handle for many, especially when Manson's female followers line up for the camera with their knives at the ready and try to explain the new order they hope to create and the role violence and fear will play in it. Bizarre and incomprehensible at times, this film is still an important work in the relatively small body of films on real-life murderers, methods, and motivations. Rated R for language and content.

1973 83 minutes

MARIA'S LOVERS

★

DIRECTOR: Andrei Konchalovsky
CAST: Nastassja Kinski, John Savage, Keith Carradine, Robert Mitchum, Vincent Spano, Bud Cort

The story details the unhappy marriage of a former World War II prisoner of war (John Savage) and his loving wife (Nastassja Kinski). Only problem is there isn't too much loving going on. While Savage was in the Japanese P.O.W. camps he fantasized about being married to Kinski and imagined enduring the tortures for her. Once he comes home and actually weds her, all he can think about when they're together are the horrors of imprisonment. Finally, he seeks sexual relief with the town trollop and is caught by Kinski, so she takes up with a traveling troubadour (Keith Carradine). Can their marriage survive this? Who cares? This film, despite all its artistic pretentions, is just another dumb soap opera. Even a fine, understated performance by Robert Mitchum as Savage's father can't save it. Rated R for profanity, nudity, suggested sex, and violence.

1985 105 minutes

MARIE

★★★

DIRECTOR: Roger Donaldson
CAST: Sissy Spacek, Jeff Daniels, Keith Szarabajka, Don Hood, Fred Thompson, Rob Benson, Dawn Carmen, Shane Wexel

Sissy Spacek plays real-life heroine Marie Ragghianti, whose courage and honesty brought about the fall of a corrupt administration in Tennessee. At the beginning of the film, Marie is a battered housewife who leaves her cruel husband. Struggling to raise her three children and get an education at the same time, she works in a bar at night to make ends meet. Upon graduating, she gets a government job and works her way up to becoming the state's first female parole board head, and this is where she discovers some ugly truths. Spacek is typically fine as the title character, and Jeff Daniels does well as her shady mentor. But somehow the movie lacks punch. Rated PG-13 for violence and profanity.

1986 100 minutes

MARJOE

★★★½

DIRECTORS: Howard Smith, Sarah Kernochan
CAST: Marjoe Gortner

The life of evangelist-turned-actor Marjoe Gortner is traced in this entertaining documentary. Film offers the viewer a peek into the world of the traveling evangelist. When Marjoe gets his act going, the movie is at its best. At times a little stagy, but always interesting. Rated PG for language.

1972 88 minutes

MARLENE

★★★★

DIRECTOR: Maximilian Schell
CAST: Marlene Dietrich, Maximilian Schell

In this documentary, director Maximilian Schell pulls off something close to a miracle: He creates an absorbing and entertaining study of Marlene Dietrich without ever having her on camera during the interviews. (She refused to be photographed, claiming, "It's not in my contract.") Instead, we hear her famous husky voice talking about her life, loves, and movies as scenes from the latter—as well as newsreels and TV clips—play onscreen. The result is, by turns, hilarious, nostalgic, and remarkably candid.

1985 95 minutes

MARTY

★★★★★

DIRECTOR: Delbert Mann
CAST: Ernest Borgnine, Betsy Blair, Joe De Santis

This heartwarming "little" movie about a New York butcher captured the Academy Award for best picture and another for Ernest Borgnine's poignant portrayal. In it, two lonely people manage to stumble into romance in spite of their own insecurities and the pressures of others. Based on a television production by author Paddy Chayefsky, this love story of everyday people is much more moving than the perfect

"Barbie and Ken" romances of the "beautiful people" we are accustomed to watching.

1955 B & W 91 minutes

MARVIN AND TIGE

★★★★

DIRECTOR: Eric Weston
CAST: John Cassavetes, Gibran Brown, Billy Dee Williams, Denise Nicholas-Hill, Fay Hauser

Touching story of a runaway (Gibran Brown) who finds a friend in a poor and lonely man (John Cassavetes). Cassavetes' beautiful loser character works so well with Brown's street-wise pomp that the tension created by the clash of personalities makes their eventual deep relationship that much more rewarding for the viewer. Rated PG for a few profane words.

1982 104 minutes

MARY OF SCOTLAND

★★★★

DIRECTOR: John Ford
CAST: Katharine Hepburn, Fredric March, John Carradine

Katharine Hepburn plays one of history's tragic figures in director John Ford's biography of the sixteenth-century queen of Scotland. Fredric March is Bothwell, her supporter (and eventual lover) in her battle for power. The last scene, where Mary confronts her English accusers in court, is so well acted and photographed, it alone is worth the price of the rental.

1936 B & W 123 minutes

MASADA

★★★★

DIRECTOR: Boris Sagal
CAST: Peter O'Toole, Peter Strauss, Barbara Carrera

A spectacular TV movie based on the famous battle of Masada during the Roman domination of the known world. Fine acting, especially by Peter O'Toole, and excellent production values elevate this one far above the average small-screen movie. Unrated.

1984 131 minutes

MASK

★★★★★

DIRECTOR: Peter Bogdanovich
CAST: Cher, Sam Elliott, Eric Stoltz, Laura Dern

They used to call them moving pictures, and few films fit this phrase as well as this one, starring Cher, Sam Elliott, and Eric Stoltz. The story of a teen-age boy coping with a disfiguring disease, it touches the viewer's heart as few movies have ever done. The only releases of recent memory in its class in this respect are *Terms of Endearment* and *E.T.* But even those two mega-hits provide poor comparison. *E.T.* is a lovely fantasy, and *Terms* is essentially a situation comedy with emotional resonance. *Mask*, on the other hand, rises above simple entertainment with its uplifting true-life tale. Rated PG13.

1985 120 minutes

MASS APPEAL

★★★★½

DIRECTOR: Glenn Jordan
CAST: Jack Lemmon, Zeljko Ivanek, Charles Durning, Louise Latham, James Ray

A first-rate discussion of the dichotomy between private conscience and mass appeal, this film finds a mediocre and worldly priest, Father Tim Farley (Jack Lemmon), walking a political tightrope between the young seminarian (Zeljko Ivanek) he has befriended and his superior, Monsignor Burke (Charles Durning). Based on the stage play of the same title and funded as a memorial to Ray Kroc (of MacDonald's hamburger fame) by his widow, there is hardly a false note throughout. Witty, powerful, and at times both comic and tragic, it is not only a fine memorial but also a splendid motion picture. Rated PG.

1984 99 minutes

MASTER RACE, THE

★★★

DIRECTOR: Herbert J. Biberman

CAST: George Coulouris, Stanley Ridges, Osa Massen, Lloyd Bridges

Hitler's Third Reich collapses. A dedicated Nazi officer escapes. His refusal to accept defeat becomes an engrossing study of blind obedience to immorality.

1944 B & W 96 minutes

MATTER OF TIME, A

DIRECTOR: Vincente Minnelli

CAST: Liza Minnelli, Ingrid Bergman, Charles Boyer, Spiro Andros, Isabella Rossellini

A penniless countess takes a country-bumpkin-come-to-the-big-city hotel chambermaid in hand and feeds her dreams of becoming a famous movie star. Skipping between present and past, this is a film of small consequence made palatable by adroit editing. Director Vincente Minnelli should have and could have done far better by daughter Liza in this first collaboration. Ingrid Bergman and Charles Boyer, fading shadows of themselves, are misused. Rated PG.

1976 99 minutes

MAX DUGAN RETURNS

★★½

DIRECTOR: Herbert Ross

CAST: Jason Robards, Marsha Mason, Donald Sutherland

After spending many years in jail and gambling to big winnings, Max Dugan (Jason Robards) seeks his widowed daughter (Marsha Mason) to bestow gifts upon her and her son. Though grateful for her new-found wealth, she finds it difficult to explain to her policeman-boyfriend, Donald Sutherland. The charm of this Neil Simon fable wears thin through repetition. Rated PG.

1983 98 minutes

MCVICAR

★★★

DIRECTOR: Tom Clegg

CAST: Roger Daltrey, Adam Faith, Jeremy Blake

In this interesting British film, Roger Daltrey (lead singer for the Who) portrays John McVicar, whose real-life escape from the high-security wing of a British prison led to him being named "public enemy No. 1." Rated R.

1980 111 minutes

MEAN STREETS

★★★★½

DIRECTOR: Martin Scorsese

CAST: Robert De Niro, Harvey Keitel, Amy Robinson, Robert Carradine, David Carradine

This impressive first film by director Martin Scorsese has criminal realism and explosive violence. Robet De Niro gives a high-energy performance as a ghetto psycho in New York's Little Italy who insults a Mafia loan shark by avoiding payment. He then rips off the friend who tries to save him. This study of street life at its most savage is a cult favorite. Rated R.

1973 110 minutes

MEDIUM COOL

★★★★½

DIRECTOR: Haskell Wexler

CAST: Robert Forster, Verna Bloom, Peter Bonerz

Robert Forster stars as a television news cameraman in Chicago during the 1968 Democratic convention. All the political themes of the 1960s are here—many scenes were filmed during the riots. Cinematographer Haskell Wexler's first try at directing is a winner. Highly recommended. Rated R for nudity and language.

1969 110 minutes

MEET DR. CHRISTIAN

★★

DIRECTOR: Bernard Vorhaus

CAST: Jean Hersholt, Dorothy Lovett, Robert Baldwin, Enid Bennett, Paul Harvey, Marcia Mae Jones, Jackie Moran

Folksy Jean Hersholt enacts the title role, meeting and besting medical crisis after medical crisis, in this first of six films translated from the popular 1930s radio series. He is wise, witty, kindly, and belovedby all, including Dorothy Lovett as his faithful nurse.

1939 B & W 63 minutes

MEET JOHN DOE

★★★★

DIRECTOR: Frank Capra

CAST: Gary Cooper, Barbara Stanwyck, Walter Brennan, Spring Byington

A penniless drifter (Gary Cooper) gets caught up in a newspaper publicity stunt. He is groomed and presented as the spokesman of the common man by powerful men who manipulate his every action for their own purposes. When he finally resists, he is exposed as a fraud. His fellow common men turn against him, or do they? Barbara Stanwyck is the newspaperwoman who first uses him and with whom she predictably falls in love.

1941 B & W 132 minutes

MEN, THE

★★★★

DIRECTOR: Fred Zinnemann

CAST: Marlon Brando, Jack Webb, Teresa Wright

Marlon Brando's first film, this is about a paralyzed World War II vet trying to deal with his injury. A sensitive script and good acting make this film a classic. Better than *Coming Home* in depicting vets' feelings and attitudes about readjusting to society.

1950 B & W 85 minutes

MEN'S CLUB, THE

★★★

DIRECTOR: Peter Medak

CAST: Roy Scheider, Frank Langella, Harvey Keitel, Treat Williams, Richard Jordan, David Dukes, Craig Wasson, Stockard Channing, Ann Wedgeworth, Jennifer Jason Leigh, Cindy Pickett

Fine performances by an all-star cast are the main draw in this offbeat and disturbing film about a boy's night out that is turned into an exploration of men's attitudes toward women by novelist-screenwriter Leonard Michaels. Instead of giving us typical, movie-style "big realizations," Michaels and director Peter Medak have chosen to mirror life. The changes remain inside the characters, although we can guess what has happened to the character by their actions. This kind of storytelling may not please all video viewers, but it wil intrigue those who don't mind thinking about what they see. Rated R for nudity, profanity, suggested sex, and violence.

1986 93 minutes

MERRY CHRISTMAS, MR. LAWRENCE

★★★½

DIRECTOR: Nagisa Oshima

CAST: David Bowie, Ryuichi Sakomoto, Tom Conti

Set in a prisoner-of-war camp in Java in 1942, this film, by Nagisa Oshima (*In the Realm of the Senses*), focuses on a clash of cultures—and wills. Oshima's camera looks on relentlessly as a

British officer (David Bowie), who refuses to cooperate or knuckle under, is beaten and tortured by camp commander Ryuichi Sakomoto. Rated R for violence, strong language, and adult situations.

1983 122 minutes

MESSAGE, THE (MOHAMMAD, MESSENGER OF GOD)

★★½

DIRECTOR: Moustapha Akkad

CAST: Anthony Quinn, Irene Papas, Michael Ansara, Johnny Sekka, Michael Forest, Neville Jason

Viewers expecting to see Mohammad in this three-hour epic will be disappointed.... He never appears on the screen. Instead, we see Anthony Quinn, as Mohammad's uncle, struggling to win religious freedom for Mohammad. The film tends to drag a bit and is definitely overlong. Only those who are truly interested in following the last twenty years of Mohammad's life will be able to sit still to the end of this film. Rated PG.

1977 180 minutes

MIDNIGHT COWBOY

★★★★★

DIRECTOR: John Schlesinger

CAST: Jon Voight, Dustin Hoffman, Sylvia Miles, Barnard Hughes, Brenda Vaccaro

In this tremendous film, about the struggle for existence in the urban nightmare of New York's Forty-second Street area, Jon Voight and Dustin Hoffman deliver brilliant performances. The film won Oscars for best picture, best director (John Schlesinger), and best screenplay. Voight plays handsome Joe Buck, who arrives from Texas to make his mark as a hustler, only to be out-hustled by everyone else, including the crafty, sleazy "Ratso," superbly played by Hoffman. One of the best films of the 1960s, this has a sad but stunning twist ending. Rated R.

1969 113 minutes

MIDNIGHT EXPRESS

★★★★½

DIRECTOR: Alan Parker

CAST: Brad Davis, John Hurt, Randy Quaid

This is the true story of Billy Hayes, who was busted for trying to smuggle hashish out of Turkey and spent five years in the squalor and terror of a Turkish prison. It was brought to the screen with exquisite skill by director Alan Parker and screenwriter Oliver Stone. *Midnight Express* is not an experience easily shaken. After you see this work, the events during Hayes's imprisonment come back to haunt you long afterward. Yet it is a film for our times that teaches a powerful and important lesson. Rated R.

1978 121 minutes

MIKE'S MURDER

★★★

DIRECTOR: James Bridges

CAST: Debra Winger, Mark Keyloun

This could have been an interesting tale of a small-time Los Angeles drug dealer and part-time tennis pro who becomes involved in a drug ripoff. But the confusing plot device of having his one-night stand with Debra Winger lead to her subsequent search into why he was killed doesn't work. A much better film is buried in this unfortunate misfire. Rated R for violence, language, and nudity.

1984 97 minutes

MILDRED PIERCE

★★★★

DIRECTOR: Michael Curtiz

CAST: Joan Crawford, Jack Carson, Zachary Scott, Eve Arden,

Ann Blyth, Bruce Bennett, George Tobias, Lee Patrick, Moroni Olson, Jo Ann Marlowe, Barbara Brown

A hardboiled melodrama of the strictly American *film noir* genre. Bored housewife Joan Crawford parlays waiting tables into a restaurant chain and an infatuation with Zachary Scott. Her spoiled daughter, Ann Blyth, hits on him. Emotions run high and taut as everything unravels in this A-one adaptation of James M. Cain's novel of murder and cheap love. Her performance in the title role won Joan Crawford an Oscar for best actress.

1945 B & W 109 minutes

MILL ON THE FLOSS, THE

★★★½

DIRECTOR: Tim Whelan

CAST: Geraldine Fitzgerald, James Mason

Geraldine Fitzgerald is Maggie and James Mason is Tom Tolliver in this careful and faithful adaptation of novelist George Eliot's story of ill-starred romance in a tradition-bound English village.

1939 B & W 77 minutes

MIN AND BILL

★★★

DIRECTOR: George Hill

CAST: Marie Dressler, Wallace Beery, Dorothy Jordan, Marjorie Rambeau, Frank McGlynn

Their first picture together as a team puts Marie Dressler and Wallace Beery to the test when the future of the waif (Dorothy Jordan) she has reared on the rough-and-tumble waterfront is threatened by the girl's disreputable mother, Marjorie Rambeau. Her emotional portarayal won Marie Dressler an Oscar for best actress and helped make the film the box-office hit of its year.

1931 B & W 70 minutes

MIRACLE OF THE BELLS, THE

★★★

DIRECTOR: Irving Pichel

CAST: Fred MacMurray, Valli, Frank Sinatra, Lee J. Cobb

A miracle takes place when a movie star is buried in her coal-mining hometown. Hard-bitten press agent Fred MacMurray turns mushy to see "the kid" gets the right send-off. The story is trite and its telling too long, but the cast is earnest and the film has a way of clicking.

1948 B & W 120 minutes

MIRACLE WORKER, THE

★★★★½

DIRECTOR: Arthur Penn

CAST: Anne Bancroft, Patty Duke (Astin), Andrew Prine

Anne Bancroft and Patty Duke are superb when re-creating their acclaimed Broadway performances in this production. Patty Duke is the untamed and blind deaf-mute Helen Keller and Bancroft is her equally strong-willed, but compassionate, teacher. Their harrowing fight for power and the ultimately touching first communication make up one of the screen's great sequences.

1962 B & W 107 minutes

MIRAGE

★★★½

DIRECTOR: Edward Dmytryk

CAST: Gregory Peck, Diane Baker, Walter Matthau, Kevin McCarthy, Jack Weston, George Kennedy, Leif Erickson, Walter Abel

Some really fine scenes and top-notch actors enliven this slow but ultimately satisfying mystery thriller. Gregory Peck is David Stillwell, a man who has lost his memory and becomes the victim of numerous murder attempts. The police are unhelpful, but Walter Mattau, a sympathetic and wry private eye, assists David. Diane Baker is the mystery woman. Occasionally snappy dialogue, with an interesting but overdone use of flashbacks.

1965 B & W 108 minutes

MISFITS, THE

★★★

DIRECTOR: John Huston

CAST: Marilyn Monroe, Clark Gable, Montgomery Clift, Thelma Ritter, Eli Wallach, James Barton, Estelle Winwood

Arthur Miller's parable of a hope-stripped divorcee and a gaggle of her boot-shod cowpoke boyfriends shagging wild horses in the Nevada desert, this film was the last hurrah for Marilyn Monroe and Clark Gable. The acting is good, but the storyline is mean.

1961 B & W 124 minutes

MISHIMA: A LIFE IN FOUR CHAPTERS

★★★★

DIRECTOR: Paul Schrader

CAST: Ken Ogata, Ken Swada, Yasusuka Brando, Toshiyuku Nagashimaj

By depicting this enigmatic writer's life through his art, filmmaker Paul Schrader has come close to illustrating the true heart of an artist. This is not a standard narrative biography but a bold attempt to meld an artist's life with his life's work. The movie is, as suggested in the title, divided into four parts: "Beauty," "Art," "Action," and the climactic "A Harmony of Pen and Sword." This film is not for everyone, but literary enthusiasts should appreciate its innovative approach. Rated R for sex, nudity, violence, and adult situations.

1985 121 minutes

MISS SADIE THOMPSON

★★½

DIRECTOR: Curtis Bernhardt

CAST: Rita Hayworth, José Ferrer, Aldo Ray

A remake of *Rain*, the 1932 adaptation of Somerset Maugham's novel with Joan Crawford and Walter Huston, this production (with music) is notable only for the outstanding performance by Rita Hayworth in the title role.

1953 91 minutes

MISSING

★★★★★

DIRECTOR: Constantin Costa-Gavras

CAST: Jack Lemmon, Sissy Spacek, John Shea, Melanie Mayron, Janice Rule, David Clennon

A superb political thriller directed by Costa-Gavras (*Z; State of Siege*), this stars Jack Lemmon and Sissy Spacek as the father and wife of a young American journalist who disappears during a bloody South American coup. Rated R for violence, nudity, and profanity.

1982 122 minutes

MISSION, THE

★★★½

DIRECTOR: Roland Joffe

CAST: Jeremy Irons, Robert De Niro, Philip Bosco, Aidan Quinn

Jeremy Irons plays a Spanish Jesuit who goes into the South American wilderness to build a mission in the hope of converting the barbaric Indians of the region. Robert De Niro plays a slave hunter who is converted and joins Irons in his mission. When Spain sells the colony to Portugal, they are forced to defend all they have built against the Portuguese aggressors. Irons is excellent as the holy man, but while De Niro is very believable as a dealer in human flesh, his portrayal of a born-again Christian is not as convincing. The stunning visuals earned the film an Oscar for best cinematography. Rated PG for violence and sex.

1986 125 minutes

MISSION TO GLORY

★

DIRECTOR: Ken Kennedy
CAST: Ricardo Montalban, Cesar Romero, Rory Calhoun, Michael Ansara, Keenan Wynn, Richard Egan

The true story of Father Francisco Kin, the Spanish padre who helped develop California in the late seventeenth century. This film has all the dullness of one of those elementary-school movies you were forced to suffer through, complete with narrator, soundtrack, and acting that all stoop to the occasion. You'd almost expect a pop quiz after the closing credits. As for Ricardo Montalban, Cesar Romero, and Keenan Wynn, their performances are very brief. For California historians only. Rated PG for violence.

1979 97 minutes

MR. HALPERN AND MR. JOHNSON

★★★

DIRECTOR: Alvin Rakoff
CAST: Laurence Olivier, Jackie Gleason

This one-hour show could be called *My Dinner with Andre (After He Romanced My Wife).* Laurence Olivier plays a recently widowed Jewish manufacturer who, to his surprise, is asked to join a seemingly well-off stranger named Johnson (Jackie Gleason) for a drink after the funeral. It seems that Johnson was once in love with the late Mrs. Halpern. What's more, they carried on a friendship (and monthly platonic get-togethers) for a number of years right up to just before her death. Mr. Halpern is, of course, shocked. And therein lies the drama of this slight tale.

1983 57 minutes

MR. SMITH GOES TO WASHINGTON

★★★★★

DIRECTOR: Frank Capra
CAST: James Stewart, Jean Arthur, Claude Rains

This Frank Capra classic is the story of a naive senator's fight against political corruption. James Stewart stars as Jefferson Smith, the idealistic scoutmaster who is appointed to fill out the term of a dead senator. Upon arriving in the capitol, he begins to get a hint of the corruption in his home state. His passionate filibuster against this corruption remains one of the most emotionally powerful scenes in film history.

1939 B & W 129 minutes

MRS. SOFFEL

★★★

DIRECTOR: Gillian Armstrong
CAST: Diane Keaton, Mel Gibson, Matthew Modine, Edward Herrmann, Trini Alvarado

We assume Australian director Gillian Armstrong's intent was to make more than a simple entertainment of this story about a warden's wife (Diane Keaton) who helps two prisoners (Mel Gibson and Matthew Modine) escape. But in aiming for this, she expands what sounded like promising material into a kind of shapeless "statement" about the plight of women at the turn of the century. Even the stars' excellent performances can't save it. Rated PG-13 for violence, suggested sex, and profanity.

1984 112 minutes

MISUNDERSTOOD

★

DIRECTOR: Jerry Schatzberg

CAST: Gene Hackman, Henry Thomas, Huckleberry Fox

A rich businessman (Gene Hackman) has to cope with the problem of raising two young sons (Henry Thomas of *E.T.*, and Huckleberry Fox, of *Terms of Endearment*) who are traumatized by the sudden death of their mother. This is a dull, almost unbearable, tearjerker. Rated PG for profanity.

1984 91 minutes

MOLLY MAGUIRES, THE

★★★

DIRECTOR: Martin Ritt

CAST: Sean Connery, Richard Harris, Samantha Eggar, Frank Finlay, Art Lund

The Molly Maguires were a group of terrorists in the 1870s who fought for better conditions for the Pennsylvania coal miners. In this dramatization, Sean Connery is their leader and Richard Harris is a Pinkerton detective who infiltrates the group. The film gives a vivid portrayal of the period and the miners' dreadful existence. Performances are first-rate. Unfortunately, more people heard the theme music by Henry Mancini than saw the movie. A little long, but worth checking out.

1970 123 minutes

MOMMIE DEAREST

★★★½

DIRECTOR: Frank Perry

CAST: Faye Dunaway, Diana Scarwid, Steve Forrest

At times this trashy screen version of Christine Crawford's controversial autobiography—which stars Faye Dunaway in an astounding performance as Joan Crawford—is so harrowing and grotesque you're tempted to stop the tape. But it's so morbidly fascinating you can't take your eyes off the screen. Rated PG.

1981 129 minutes

MONA LISA

★★★★½

DIRECTOR: Neil Jordan

CAST: Bob Hoskins, Cathy Tyson, Michael Caine, Robbie Coltrane, Clark Peters, Kate Hardie, Sammi Davies

Bob Hoskins is Britain's answer to Humphrey Bogart and James Cagney. In this crime thriller, which was crafted specifically for its star by director Neil Jordan, Hoskins plays a simple but moral man whose less than honest endeavors have landed him in prison. Upon his release, he goes to his former boss (Michael Caine) in search of a job. He gets one—driving a prostitute (Cathy Tyson) on her nightly rounds. He doesn't like the job, but he likes her. And the more he likes her, the less he can understand why she does what she does. Eventually, his quest for the truth—which comes in the form of a search for her friend, who has been enslaved by a black pimp—leads to a *Taxi Driver*–style conclusion. Hoskins equals his outstanding performance in *The Long Good Friday.* Unrated, the film has profanity, suggested sex, and violence.

1986 100 minutes

MONSIGNOR

★½

DIRECTOR: Frank Perry

CAST: Christopher Reeve, Genevieve Bujold, Fernando Rey, Jason Miller

Christopher Reeve stars in the highly implausible story of a Vatican priest who seduces a student nun and makes deals with the Mafia to help the Church's finances. It's an outrageous melodrama that will have you groaning in no time at all. Rated R for profanity, nudity, sex, and violence.

1982 122 minutes

MONTENEGRO

★★★★

DIRECTOR: Dusan Makavejev

CAST: Susan Anspach, John Zacharias

Susan Anspach stars as a discontented housewife who wanders into a Yugoslavian nightclub, finds herself surrounded by sex and violence, and discovers she rather likes it, in this outlandish, outrageous, and sometimes shocking black comedy. The laughs come with the realization that everyone in this movie is totally bonkers. Rated R because of profanity, nudity, sex, and violence.

1981 981 minutes

MORNING GLORY

★★½

DIRECTOR: Lowell Sherman

CAST: Katharine Hepburn, Adolphe Menjou, Douglas Fairbanks Jr., C. Aubrey Smith, Mary Duncan

A naïve young actress comes to New York to find fame and romance. Based on the Zoe Akins's play, the stagy film version hasn't aged well. The melodrama often creaks. But C. Aubrey Smith adds dignity to the piece in a supporting role and Katharine Hepburn is charismatic as the actress, Eva Lovelace. She won her first Academy Award for this showy performance.

1933 B & W 74 minutes

MOSES

★★★

DIRECTOR: Gianfranco De Bosio

CAST: Burt Lancaster, Anthony Quayle, Irene Papas, Ingrid Thulin, William Lancaster

This biblical screen story of the Hebrew lawgiver is fairly standard as such films go. Burt Lancaster is well-suited to play the stoic Moses. However, in trimming down this six-hour TV miniseries for video release, its makers lost most of the character development in the supporting roles.

1975 141 minutes

MOSQUITO COAST, THE

★★★

DIRECTOR: Peter Weir

CAST: Harrison Ford, Helen Mirren, River Phoenix, Conrad Roberts, Andre Gregory, Martha Plimpton

In spite of the topnotch talent involved—the source novel by Paul Theroux, the reteaming of director Peter Weir and star Harrison Ford, and a superb supporting performance from young River Phoenix—this remains a flawed endeavor. Theroux's Allie Fox (Ford) is a monomaniacal genius who can't bear what he perceives to be the rape of the United States, so he drags his wife and four children on one of the most outrageous picnics of all time, to the untamed wilderness of the Mosquito Coast in a self-indulgent attempt to mimic the Swiss Family Robinson. Alas, Ford's rendition of Fox is strident and unpleasant from the very beginning; it's impossible to empathize with a one-note lunatic when there's no sense of his shifting from a man of rational behavior to one of no rationality all. Rated PG.

1986 117 minutes

MOTHER TERESA

★★★★★

DIRECTORS: Ann Petrie, Jeanette Petrie

CAST: Documentary

Many consider her to be a living saint and her selfless dedication to the world's sick of heart, body, mind, and soul seems to justify that claim. Mother Teresa is, at the very least, a heroic figure who simply believes that "we must all be holy in what we do." Five years in the making, this documentary lets an extraordinary life speak for itself. The result is an unforgettable work that is once heartbreaking and inspiring. Unrated, this film has shocking scenes of poverty and starvation.

1987 83 minutes

MUD HONEY

★★★★

DIRECTOR: Russ Meyer
CAST: Hal Hopper, Antoinette Cristiani, John Furlong

A cult favorite from Russ Meyer about the exploits of some rural folks involved in the pursuit of cheap thrills and the meaning of life. Considered an adults-only film when released, it now seems quite tame. Plot has a local scum (John Furlong) terrorizing Antoinette Cristiani, a deaf-and-dumb beautiful blonde until her rescue by Hal Hopper. Unrated, but an R rating would be in order because of some nudity and adult themes.

1965 B & W 92 minutes

MURDER ELITE

★★

DIRECTOR: Claude Whatham
CAST: Ali MacGraw, Billie Whitelaw, Hywel Bennett, Ray Lonnen, Garfield Morgan, Don Henderson

Ali MacGraw plays a woman who, after losing all her money in America, comes back to her native England to start fresh. She finds that tending to business on her sister's estate is not what she wants to do. Meanwhile, there is a killer on the loose. The two stories ultimately collide, but MacGraw's uninspired acting and the poor direction make the film rather plodding. Not rated.

1985 104 minutes

MURDER IN A COWETA COUNTY

★★★½

DIRECTOR: Gary Nelson
CAST: Andy Griffith, Johnny Cash, June Carter Cash, Earl Hindman

Andy Griffith is outstanding as a Georgia businessman who thinks he can get away with murder. Johnny Cash plays the determined sheriff who's willing to go to any lengths to prove Griffith's guilt. This made-for-TV suspense-drama was based on an actual Georgia murder that took place in 1948.

1983 104 minutes

MURDER: NO APPARENT MOTIVE

★½

DIRECTOR: Imre Horvath
CAST: Documentary

Exploitation: Little Redeeming Value would make a better title for this sometimes fascinating, often ridiculous attempt to explain why people commit mass murder. Gruesome evidence and self-righteous rage from law-enforcement officials and the private sector are edited into with rambling, self-serving monologues by the likes of Ed "Forklift" Kemper, the six-foot-nine-inch necrophile of Santa Cruz who brutally murdered his mother, as well as at least six coeds. An ineffective documentary. Unrated but this should be R for repulsive.

1985 72 minutes

MURPHY'S ROMANCE

★★★★

DIRECTOR: Martin Ritt
CAST: Sally Field, James Garner, Brian Kerwin, Corey Haim

Director Martin Ritt and star Sally Field get together again for this sweet little love story which also marks the finest performance given on film by James Garner. He's a crusty small-town pharmacist, a widower with no shortage of home-cooked meals but little interest in anything more permanent; she's a recently arrived divorcee, complete with son Corey Haim, determined to make a living by boarding and training horses. To complicate matters a little further, her ex (Brian Kerwin) shows up and tries to rekindle the flame. The story's complete inevitability isn't the point here; getting there is all the fun. Garner and Field are great together, and the result is a complete charmer. Rated PG-13.

1985 107 minutes

MURROW

★★★★

DIRECTOR: Jack Gold
CAST: Daniel J. Travanti, Dabney Coleman, Edward Herrmann, John McMartin, David Suchet, Kathryn Leigh Scott

Compassionate film about the famous radio and television journalist Edward R. Murrow, played brilliantly by Daniel Travanti (from *Hill Street Blues*). Travanti expresses Murrow's ambivalence and caution in confronting Joseph McCarthy with a subtlety worthy of an Oscar. The film devotes most of its running time to the journalist's struggle against McCarthyism. While Murrow's battle with McCarthy was, in reality, not as heroic as the filmmakers would have you believe, the drama is seductive enough to make the story very watchable. Perhaps the most fascinating issue that *Murrow* confronts is the conflict between the media's responsibility to the public and the media corporations' profit incentive. The film starts out disjointed and difficult to watch. (The cheap special effects don't help the matter, either.) Still, this is a hard one to pass up.

1985 114 minutes

MUSSOLINI AND I

★★★

DIRECTOR: Alberto Negrin
CAST: Anthony Hopkins, Susan Sarandon, Bob Hoskins, Annie Girardot, Barbara De Rossi, Dietlinde Turban, Vittorio Mezzogiorno, Fabio Testi, Kurt Raab

A weak and confusing narrative hinders this HBO film about the Fascist leader and his family's struggle with power. Bob Hoskins (*The Long Good Friday*) plays the Italian premier with a British accent; ditto for Anthony Hopkins (*The Elephant Man*, *The Bounty*), who portrays Galeazzo Ciano, Italy's minister of foreign affairs and the dictator's brother-in-law. Still, the story is kept interesting despite its length. Not rated, but the equivalent of a PG for violence.

1985 130 minutes

MY BEAUTIFUL LAUNDRETTE

★★★★½

DIRECTOR: Stephen Frears
CAST: Saeed Jaffrey, Roshan Seth, Daniel Day Lewis, Gordon Warnecke, Shirley Anne Field

In modern-day England, a young Pakistani immigrant (Gordon Warnecke) is given a launderette by his rich uncle (Saeed Jaffrey) and, with the help of his punk-rocker boyfriend (Daniel Day Lewis), turns it into a showplace. Everything goes along reasonably well until a racist gang decides to close them down. British director Stephen Frears (*The Hit*) keeps things from becoming too heavy by adding deft touches of comedy in just the right places. The result is an uncommonly satisfying and original film on the subject of human relations. Rated R for profanity, suggested and simulated sex, and violence.

1985 103 minutes

MY BODYGUARD

★★★★★

DIRECTOR: Tony Bill
CAST: Chris Makepeace, Matt Dillon, Martin Mull, Ruth Gordon, Adam Baldwin

This is a wonderfully funny and touching movie. This story (by Alan Ormsby) deals with a situation that all ages can identify with. Fifteen-year-old Clifford Peache (Chris Makepeace) must face the challenges of public high school (in Chicago, no less) after nine years of private education. His classes are easy. It's his schoolmates who cause problems. Specifically, there's Moody (Matt Dillon), a good-looking but nasty young thug who extorts money from the other students. He and his gang terrorize the younger, less aggressive kids unmercifully —until Clifford comes along. Unaccustomed to dealing with hoodlums like Moody, Clifford refuses to pay the protection money demanded by the gang. This attitude threatens Moody's little empire, and Clifford's days at school turn into a continuing nightmare. Rated PG.

1980 96 minutes

MY BRILLIANT CAREER

★★★★½

DIRECTOR: Gillian Armstrong
CAST: Judy Davis, Sam Neill, Wendy Hughes

A superb Australian import, *My Brilliant Career* is about a young woman clearly born before her time. It is the waning years of the nineteenth century, when the only respectable status for a woman is to be married. Sybylla Melvyn (Judy Davis), who lives with her family in the Australian bush, does not want to marry. She has "immortal longings," and—when pressed by her conventional and rather perplexed mother—she reveals, "I want to be a concert pianist." Rated G.

1979 101 minutes

MY DINNER WITH ANDRE

★★★★★

DIRECTOR: Louis Malle
CAST: Andre Gregory, Wallace Shawn

One of the most daring films ever made, this fascinating work consists almost entirely of a dinner conversation between two men. It's a terrific little movie. You'll be surprised how entertaining it is. No MPAA rating. The film has no objectionable material.

1981 110 minutes

MY FIRST WIFE

★★★½

DIRECTOR: Paul Cox
CAST: John Hargreaves, Wendy Hughes

In the tradition of *Ordinary People*, *Kramer vs Kramer*, *Shoot the Moon*, and *Smash Palace* comes another film about the dissolution of a marriage. This film contains scenes that rival some of the best and worst of those movies. The story deals with a classical music programmer/composer who finds that his wife doesn't love him anymore. Unlike some of the other films, this one ends on a positive, albeit somber note. Rated PG for adult situations and language.

1985 95 minutes

MY FORBIDDEN PAST

★★

DIRECTOR: Robert Stevenson
CAST: Robert Mitchum, Ava Gardner, Janis Carter, Melvyn Douglas, Will Wright, Lucille Watson

Set in steamy New Orleans in 1890, this one's about Ava

Gardner's cold-blooded attempts to buy married-man Robert Mitchum's affections with the help of an unexpected inheritance. His wife is killed. He's accused of her murder. La Gardner, revealing her unsavory past in order to save him, wins his love. Being rich doesn't hurt, either.

1951 B & W 81 minutes

MY OLD MAN

★★★★

DIRECTOR: John Erman

CAST: Warren Oates, Kristy McNichol, Eileen Brennan

Excellent made-for-television adaptation of a short story by Ernest Hemingway about a down-on-his-luck horse trainer (Warren Oates) and the daughter (Kristy McNichol) who loves him even more than horses. Oates gives a fabulous performance; certainly one of the best of his too-brief career. Eileen Brennan lends support as a sympathetic waitress. Made once before for the big screen, in 1950, and called *Under My Skin*. A good, solid drama, though filled with Hemingway's characteristically depressing scenarios. Unrated; suitable for family viewing.

1979 104 minutes

MY SWEET CHARLIE

★★★★

DIRECTOR: Lamont Johnson

CAST: Patty Duke, Al Freeman Jr., Ford Rainey, William Hardy

The fine performances of Patty Duke and Al Freeman Jr. make this made-for-TV drama especially watchable. Duke plays a disowned, unwed mom-to-be who meets a black lawyer being pursued by the police. They hit it off and manage to help each other. A must-see for viewers interested in drama with a social comment.

1969 97 minutes

MYSTERY OF THE MARIE CELESTE, THE

★★★

DIRECTOR: John English

CAST: Bela Lugosi, Shirley Grey, Edmund Willard

On December 4, 1872, the brigantine *Marie Celeste*, said to have been jinxed by death, fire, and collision since its launching in 1861, was found moving smoothly under halfsail, completely deserted, east of the Azores. No trace of those who had been aboard was ever found. To this day, what happend remains a true mystery of the sea. This account offers one explanation. Also released as *The Phantom Ship*.

1937 B & W 64 minutes

NAPOLEON

★

DIRECTOR: Sacha Guitry

CAST: Orson Welles, Maria Schell, Yves Montand, Erich von Stroheim

It seems inconceivable that Napoleon, who towered historically over Patton, MacArthur, and Rommel and is equaled only by Attila the Hun and Alexander the Great, could be the subject of such an insignificant little film. This offering mumbles its way from nowhere to nowhere with little along the way. It's boring.

1955 115 minutes

NASHVILLE

★★★★★

DIRECTOR: Robert Altman

CAST: Keith Carradine, Lily Tomlin, Ned Beatty, Henry Gibson, Karen Black, Ronee Blakley

Robert Altman's classic study of American culture is, on the surface, a look into the country-western music business. But underneath, Altman has many things to say about all of us. Great ensemble acting by Keith Carradine, Lily Tomlin, Ned Beatty, and Henry Gibson, to name just a few, makes this one of the great films of the 1970s. Rated R for language and violence.

1975 159 minutes

NATIVE SON

★★½

DIRECTOR: Jerrold Freedman

CAST: Victor Love, Geraldine Page, Elizabeth McGovern, Matt Dillon, Oprah Winfrey, Akousa Busia, Carroll Baker, Art Evans, David Rasche, Lane Smith, John McMartin

In this well-meant but muddled screen adaptation of Richard Wright's 1940 novel, a 19-year-old black youth (Victor Love) takes a job as a chauffeur to a wealthy white couple. His hopes for a brighter future are shattered when a tragic accident leads to the death of their daughter (Elizabeth McGovern) and he is accused of murder. This is an unrelentingly ugly and depressing film that almost defies the viewer to watch it—despite sincere performances by a highly talented cast. Rated R for nudity, suggested sex, violence, and gore.

1986 101 minutes

NATURAL, THE

★★★★

DIRECTOR: Barry Levinson

CAST: Robert Redford, Robert Duvall, Glenn Close, Kim Basinger, Wilford Brimley, Richard Farnsworth, Robert Prosky, Joe Don Baker

A thoroughly rewarding, old-fashioned screen entertainment, this adaptation of Bernard Malamud's novel about an unusually gifted baseball player is a must-see. With its brilliant all-star cast, superb story, unforgettable characters, sumptuous cinematography, and sure-handed direction, this two-and-a-half-hour feast of film-watching recalls the Golden Age of Hollywood at its best. Rated PG for brief violence.

1984 134 minutes

NETWORK

★★★★★

DIRECTOR: Sidney Lumet

CAST: Peter Finch, William Holden, Faye Dunaway, Robert Duvall, Ned Beatty

"I'm mad as hell and I'm not going to take it anymore!" Peter Finch (who won a posthumous Academy Award for best actor), William Holden, Faye Dunaway, Robert Duvall, and Ned Beatty give superb performances in this black comedy about the world of television as penned by Paddy Chayefsky. It's a biting satire on the inner workings of this century's most powerful medium. Rated R.

1976 121 minutes

NEVER LET GO

★★

DIRECTOR: John Guillermin

CAST: Peter Sellers, Richard Todd, Elizabeth Sellars, Carol White, Mervyn Johns

Peter Sellers bombs out in his first dramatic role as a ruthless criminal in this thin story about car stealing. The sure acting of Mervyn Johns, longtime dependable supporting player, helps things but cannot begin to save the film. Nor can Richard Todd's efforts.

1960 B & W 90 minutes

NEVER LOVE A STRANGER

★

DIRECTOR: Robert Stevens

CAST: John Drew Barrymore, Lita Milan, Steve McQueen, Peg Murray

Insulting his theatrical heritage, John Drew Barrymore struggles to portray one of novelist Harold Robbins's sleazy gangster types: a young hustler whose success puts him on a collision course with his old boss and an eager district attorney.

1958 91 minutes

NEVER ON SUNDAY

★★★★

DIRECTOR: Jules Dassin
CAST: Melina Mercouri, Jules Dassin

A wimpy egghead tries to make a lady out of an earthy, fun-loving prostitute. The setting is Greece; the dialogue and situations are delightful. Melina Mercouri is terrific.

1960 91 minutes

NEW CENTURIONS, THE

★★★★

DIRECTOR: Richard Fleischer
CAST: George C. Scott, Stacy Keach, Jane Alexander, Erik Estrada

The New Centurions is a blend of harsh reality and soap opera. The moral seems to be "It is no fun being a cop." Watching George C. Scott and Stacy Keach get their lumps, we have to agree. Rated R.

1972 103 minutes

NEWSFRONT

★★★★

DIRECTOR: Phillip Noyce
CAST: Bill Hunter, Wendy Hughes, Gerald Kennedy

A story of a newsreel company from 1948 until technology brought its existence to an end, this is a warm and wonderful film about real people. It's an insightful glimpse at the early days of the news business, with good character development. Rated PG.

1978 110 minutes

NICHOLAS AND ALEXANDRA

★★

DIRECTOR: Franklin Schaffner
CAST: Michael Jayston, Janet Suzman, Tom Baker, Laurence Olivier, Michael Redgrave

This is an overlong, overdetailed depiction of the events preceding the Russian Revolution until the deaths of Czar Nicholas (Michael Jayston), his wife (Janet Suzman) and family. Some of the performances are outstanding, particularly Suzman's, and the sets and costumes are topnotch. However, the film gets mired in trying to encompass too much historical detail. Rated PG.

1971 183 minutes

NICHOLAS NICKLEBY

★★★½

DIRECTOR: Alberto Cavalcanti
CAST: Derek Bond, Cedric Hardwicke, Sally Ann Howes, Cathleen Nesbitt, Alfred Drayton

Proud but penniless young Nicholas Nickleby struggles to forge a life for himself and his family while contending with a money-mad scheming uncle and lesser villains. Good acting and authentic Victorian settings bring this classic Dickens novel to vivid screen life. Not quite in the mold of *Great Expectations*, but well above average.

1947 B & W 108 minutes

NIGHT AND DAY

★★

DIRECTOR: Michael Curtiz
CAST: Cary Grant, Alexis Smith, Jane Wyman, Monty Woolley, Eve Arden

The life of composer Cole Porter, told with cloying pretension. The story vaguely resembles truth and is mostly song-stuffed baloney. The film is too long, too smug, and too deceiving. Cary Grant sings, Alexis Smith tries, and Monty Woolley is funny now and then.

1946 128 minutes

NIGHT GAMES

DIRECTOR: Don Taylor

CAST: Barry Newman, Susan Howard, Albert Salmi, Luke Askew, Ralph Meeker, Stephanie Powers

This film, which was originally made for television, led to the "Petrocelli" TV series for Barry Newman. He plays a lawyer who defends Stephanie Powers when she's accused of her husband's murder. There's enough intrigue and suspense in this film to capture most viewers' attention. Rated R.

1974 78 minutes

NIGHT IN HEAVEN, A

DIRECTOR: John G. Avildsen

CAST: Lesley Ann Warren, Christopher Atkins, Robert Logan, Carrie Snodgress

As incredible as it may seem, this movie is just as bad and tasteless as it appears to be. Lesley Ann Warren (*Choose Me*) plays a respectable college teacher who falls in lust with student/male stripper Christopher Atkins (*Blue Lagoon*). All in all, it's a movie to forget. Rated R for nudity, slight profanity, and simulated sex.

1983 80 minutes

'NIGHT, MOTHER

★★

DIRECTOR: Tom Moore

CAST: Sissy Spacek, Anne Bancroft

'Night, Mother, playwright Marsha Norman's argument in favor of suicide, is incredibly depressing material. Watching Tom Moore's screen version is like being locked in a room with a bomb and knowing there's no escape. Sissy Spacek plays a woman who has chosen to end her life. She decides to commit the act in her mother's house, with her mother there. We are only shown Spacek's unhappiness, and this limited manipulative view has left us with nothing to do but wait uncomfortably for the outcome. Spacek is competent in the part, but she's not enjoyable to watch. The script only allows for misery. Anne Bancroft as the mother turns in another self-conscious, overacted performance. Check out a suicidal Spacek in the marvelous *Crimes of the Heart* instead. Rated PG-13.

1986 97 minutes

NIGHT OF THE IGUANA, THE

★★★

DIRECTOR: John Huston

CAST: Richard Burton, Ava Gardner, Deborah Kerr, Sue Lyon

Mexico sets the scene for Richard Burton (as Reverend Shannon), Ava Gardner (as Maxine, who runs the hotel), and Deborah Kerr (the unhappy old maid). In this film, based on Tennessee Williams's play, Burton is a former minister trying to be reinstated in his church. Meanwhile, he takes a menial job as a tour guide, from which he gets fired. His attempted suicide is foiled and confusing. Finally, he finds other reasons to continue living. Sound dull? If not for the stars, it would be.

1964 B & W 118 minutes

NIGHT PORTER, THE

★★

DIRECTOR: Liliana Cavani

CAST: Dirk Bogarde, Charlotte Rampling, Philippe Leroy, Gabriele Ferzetti, Isa Miranda

Sordid little outing about a sadomasochistic relationship between an ex-Nazi and the woman he used to abuse sexually in a concentration camp. With the darkly sensual Charlotte Rampling, and the irritating Dirk Bogarde. Lots of kinky scenes, including love-making on broken glass. Rated R for violence, nudity, and profanity.

1974 115 minutes

NIGHT THE LIGHTS WENT OUT IN GEORGIA, THE

★★★½

DIRECTOR: Rowald F. Maxwell
CAST: Kristy McNichol, Mark Hamill, Dennis Quaid, Sunny Johnson, Don Stroud

Gutsy, lusty, and satisfying film about a country singer (Dennis Quaid) with wayward appetites and his level-headed sister-manager (Kristy McNichol) who run into big trouble while working their way to Nashville. The gritty deep-South settings, fine action, a cast of credible extras, some memorable musical moments, and a dramatic script with comic overtones add up to above-average entertainment. Rated PG.

1981 120 minutes

9 1/2 WEEKS

★★

DIRECTOR: Adrian Lyne
CAST: Mickey Rourke, Kim Basinger, Margaret Whitton, David Margulies, David Branski, Karen Young

Adrian Lyne (*Flashdance*) creates some exceptional music video-type sequences in adapting the Elizabeth McNeil book. Somewhere between toning down the bondage and liberating the heroine in this adaptation, the story definitely loses out to the imagery. Mickey Rourke is quite believable in the lead role of the masochistic seducer, but Kim Basinger does little more than look pretty. However, together this couple makes steamy work of simple things like dressing and eating. Rated R for sex and violence.

1986 113 minutes

NINE DAYS A QUEEN

★★★

DIRECTOR: Robert Stevenson
CAST: Cedric Hardwicke, Nova Pilbeam, John Mills, Desmond Tester, Sybil Thorndike, Leslie Perrins, Felix Aylmer, Miles Malleson

This well-acted historical drama picks ups after the death of Henry VIII and follows the frenzied and often lethal scramble for power that went on in the court of England. Lovely Nova Pilbeam plays Lady Jane Grey, the heroine of the title who is taken to the headsman's block by Mary Tudor's armies after a pathetic reign of only nine days. Tragic and moving, this British film was well received by critics when it premiered in October of 1936 but is practically forgotten today. A truly fine cast of topflight actors and actrresses, including great character performer Miles Malleson in an early role, make this worth a watch.

1936 B & W 80 minutes

NINTH CONFIGURATION, THE

★★★★½

DIRECTOR: William Peter Blatty
CAST: Stacy Keach, Scott Wilson, Jason Miller, Ed Flanders, Neville Brand, George Di Dicenzo, Moses Gunn, Robert Loggia, Joe Spinell, Alejandro Rey, Tom Atkins

This terse, intense film is not for everyone; a barroom brawl near the film's close is one of the most uncomfortable scenes in all of flickdom, but the plot, screenplay, and acting are topnotch. Stacy Keach plays a psychiatrist caring for Vietnam War veterans who suffer from acute emotional disorders. The drama is at first light and focuses on the patients but soon shifts to Keach taking on a more serious tone. Any more and we'd be spilling the beans. Rated R for profanity and violence.

1979 115 minutes

NO WAY TO TREAT A LADY

★★★★

DIRECTOR: Jack Smight

CAST: Rod Steiger, George Segal, Lee Remick, Eileen Heckart, Michael Dunn, Murray Hamilton

Excellent thriller with a tour-de-force performance by Rod Steiger, who dons various disguises and personas to strangle women and imprint them with red lipstick lips. Superb script, adapted from William Goldman's novel, and a skilled supporting cast: George Segal as a mothered cop, Eileen Heckart as his delightfully pick-pick-picking mother, and Lee Remick as the attractive love interest. Segal and company get all the good lines, but the show belongs to Steiger; not since Alec Guinness in *Kind Hearts and Coronets* has an actor so successfully taken so many roles in a single picture. Rated PG for violence.

1968 108 minutes

NONE BUT THE LONELY HEART

★★★

DIRECTOR: Clifford Odets

CAST: Cary Grant, Ethel Barrymore, Barry Fitzgerald, Jane Wyatt, June Duprez, Dan Duryea

Old pro Ethel Barrymore won an Oscar for her sympathetic portrayal of moody, whining Cockney Cary Grant's mother Ma Mott in this murky drama of broken dreams, thwarted hopes, and petty crime in the slums of London in the late 1930s. Director Clifford Odets and star Grant never get together, yet the film has a certain appeal. Nothing else like it in the Grant filmography.

1944 B & W 113 minutes

NORMA RAE

★★★★

DIRECTOR: Martin Ritt

CAST: Sally Field, Ron Leibman, Pat Hingle, Beau Bridges

Sally Field won her first Oscar for her outstanding performance as a southern textile worker attempting to unionize the mill with the aid of organizer Ron Leibman. Film is based on a true story and has good eyes and ears for authenticity. Entire cast is first-rate. Rated PG, some language, minor violence.

1979 113 minutes

NORTH DALLAS FORTY

★★★★½

DIRECTOR: Ted Kotcheff

CAST: Nick Nolte, Bo Svenson, G. D. Spradlin, Dayle Haddon, Mac Davis

Remarkably enough, *North Dallas Forty* isn't just another numbingly predictable sports film. It's an offbeat, sometimes brutal, examination of the business of football. Not that it isn't entertaining. Director Ted Kotcheff has a fine feel for the outrageous and genuinely funny and makes the most of it in this picture. Yet the overriding theme is one of exploitation for profit and self-realization. Kotcheff turns it all into a compelling mixture. A first-rate Nick Nolte stars, and the film has other superb performances. Bo Svenson is a knockout as a not-too-bright-but-lethal star player. G. D. Spradlin oozes calculated menace as the coach. Dayle Haddon gives depth to her role as Nolte's concerned lover, and even singer/songwriter Mac Davis is convincing as a laconic, aging quarterback. Rated R.

1979 119 minutes

NOTHING IN COMMON

★★★½

DIRECTOR: Garry Marshall

CAST: Tom Hanks, Jackie Gleason, Eva Marie Saint, Hector Elizondo, Barry Corbin, Bess Armstrong, Sela Ward

In his most impressive performance to date, Tom Hanks plays a hotshot advertising executive who must deal with his increasingly demanding parents, who are divorcing after thirty-four years of marriage. Jackie Gleason gives a subtle, touching portrayal of the father. The film succeeds at making the difficult shift from zany humor to pathos. Rated PG for profanity and suggested sex.

1986 120 minutes

NOW AND FOREVER

★

DIRECTOR: Adrian Carr

CAST: Cheryl Ladd, Robert Coleby, Carmen Duncan

In this sappy romance flick, Cheryl Ladd (formerly one of television's "Charlie's Angels") is a boutique owner who comes back from a clothes-buying trip to New York to find that her husband (Robert Coleby) has been accused of rape. This Australian production has a good first half, with fine acting and strong suspense, and a perfectly awful second half, where drama and logic are abandoned in favor of sequences that look like outtakes from perfume commercials. In other words, it's a mess. Rated R for violence, profanity, and sex.

1983 93 minutes

NOW, VOYAGER

★★★½

DIRECTOR: Irving Rapper

CAST: Bette Davis, Claude Rains, Paul Henreid

"As far as I'm concerned, it's the greatest one of all!" said Bette Davis of this tearjerker. Davis plays a neurotic, unattractive spinster named Charlotte Vail; an ugly duckling, who, of course, blossoms into a beautiful swan. And it's all thanks to the expert counsel of her psychiatrist (Claude Rains) and a shipboard romance with a married man (Paul Henreid). Directed by Irving Rapper, it features the famous cigarette-lighting ritual that set a trend in the 1940s. Davis considers it one of her favorites—primarily because it was one of the few films that came out right during her contract years at Warner Bros. Once again, she had to fight for the role. Originally, Irene Dunne was supposed to star in the film.

1942 B & W 117 minutes

NURSE EDITH CAVELL

★★★

DIRECTOR: Herbert Wilcox

CAST: Anna Neagle, Edna May Oliver, George Sanders, ZaSu Pitts, H. B. Warner, May Robson, Robert Coote, Martin Kosleck, Fritz Leiber, Mary Howard

The story of England's second most famous nurse, who helped transport refugee soldiers out of German-held Belgium during World War I. The film delivered a dramatically satisfying antiwar message just as World War II got under way.

1939 B & W 95 minutes

O LUCKY MAN!

★★★★

DIRECTOR: Lindsay Anderson
CAST: Malcolm McDowell, Rachel Roberts, Ralph Richardson, Alan Price, Lindsay Anderson

Offbeat, often stunning story of a young salesman (Malcolm McDowell) and his efforts and obstacles in reaching the top rung of the success ladder. Allegorical and surrealistic at times, this film takes its own course like a fine piece of music. Great acting by a great cast (many of the principals play multiple roles) makes this a real viewing pleasure. Although it is very long, this film is at once a full course in film-making and a rewarding study of corporate power and control. Some adult situations and language. Rated R.

1973 173 minutes

OCTAVIA

DIRECTOR: David Beaird
CAST: Susan Curtis, Neil Kinsella, Jake Foley, G. B. File, Tom Wagner, James Eric Stinson, John Norman

Octavia is a weird movie. It starts out like a ridiculously sappy fairytale about a girl who buries her heart in the backyard until someone she can love comes along and she can retrieve it. The film quickly falls into an exploitation mode. The girl in the film is blind and her father likes to abuse her. Then a criminal seeks shelter in their yard and the girl instantly falls in love with him. They escape from her father's house, and from then on the movie opts for comedy, until the end when it goes back to exploitation, and then full circle to pure sap. Rated R.

1982 93 minutes

ODD ANGRY SHOT, THE

★★★

DIRECTOR: Tom Jeffrey
CAST: Bryan Brown, John Hargreaves, Graham Kennedy, John Jarratt

This low-key film about Australian soldiers stationed in Vietnam during the undeclared war is a good attempt to make sense out of a senseless situation as Bryan Brown and his comrades attempt to come to grips with the reality and morality of their involvement in a fight they have no heart for. Odd, sometimes highly effective blend of comedy and drama characterize this offbeat war entry. Some violence; adult situations and language.

1979 89 minutes

ODE TO BILLY JOE

★★★

DIRECTOR: Max Baer
CAST: Robby Benson, Glynnis O'Connor, Joan Hotchkis

For those who listened to Bobbie Gentry's hit song and wondered why Billy Joe jumped off the Talahachi Bridge, this movie tries to provide one hypothesis. Robby Benson plays Billy Joe with just the right amount of innocence and confusion to be convincing as a youth who doubts his sexual orientation. Rated PG.

1976 108 minutes

OF HUMAN BONDAGE (ORIGINAL)

★★★★½

DIRECTOR: John Cromwell
CAST: Bette Davis, Leslie Howard, Alan Hale, Frances Dee

A young doctor (Leslie Howard) becomes obsessed with a sluttish waitress (Bette Davis), almost causing his downfall. Fine acting by all, with Davis an absolute knockout. No rating, but still a little adult for the kiddies.

1934 B & W 83 minutes

OF HUMAN BONDAGE (REMAKE)

★★★★½

DIRECTOR: Kenneth Hughes

CAST: Kim Novak, Laurence Harvey, Robert Morley, Siobhan McKenna, Roger Livesey, Jack Hedley, Nanette Newman, Ronald Lacey

Excellent remake of the 1934 film with Bette Davis. This time Kim Novak plays Mildred Rogers, the promiscuous free spirit who becomes the obsession of Philip Carey (Laurence Harvey). Harvey's performance is wonderfully understated, and Novak plays the slut to the hilt without overdoing it. With the attention going to the two main characters, something must be said about Siobhan McKenna, who plays the soft-spoken Nora Nesbitt, who takes in the love-struck Carey for a short period. Her matronlike appearance and disposition give the part she plays the pathos that adds to the complexity of emotions that spill out from W. Somerset Maugham's story of obsession.

1964 B & W 100 minutes

OF MICE AND MEN

★★★½

DIRECTOR: Reza Badiyi

CAST: Robert Blake, Randy Quaid, Lew Ayres, Pat Hingle, Cassie Yates

Robert Blake is George, Randy Quaid is big, dimwitted Lenny in this Blake-produced TV remake of the classic 1939 Burgess Meredith/Lon Chaney Jr. rendition of John Steinbeck's morality tale of migrant-working life on a California ranch during the Depression. While not as sensitive as the original, this version merits attention and appreciation.

1981 125 minutes

OFFICER AND A GENTLEMAN, AN

★★★★½

DIRECTOR: Taylor Hackford

CAST: Richard Gere, Debra Winger, Louis Gossett Jr., David Keith, Harold Sylvester

Soap opera has never been art. However, this funny, touching, corny, and predictable movie, starring Richard Gere and Debra Winger, takes the genre as close to it as any of the old three-handkerchief classics—i.e., *Now Voyager*; *Waterloo Bridge*; *Gone with the Wind*—ever did. Director Taylor Hackford keeps just the right balance between the ridiculous and the sublime, making *An Officer and a Gentleman* one of the best of its kind. Rated R for nudity, profanity, and simulated sex.

1982 125 minutes

OH, ALFIE

★

DIRECTOR: Ken Hughes

CAST: Alan Price, Jill Townsend, Joan Collins, Annie Ross, Sheila White, Rula Lenska, Paul Copley, Hannah Gordon

Alan Price is an uncaring ladies' man who beds every woman he comes in contact with and then goes on to the next conquest. But there's always one who resists, isn't there? This time it's Jill Townsend, a successful businesswoman who seems most unsuited to our trucker Lothario. About the only thing of interest in this cheap sequel to the classic *Alfie* is a nude Joan Collins. Rated R for nudity, language, and sex.

1975 99 minutes

OLD BOYFRIENDS

★½

DIRECTOR: Joan Tewkesbury

CAST: Talia Shire, Richard Jordan, Keith Carradine, John Belushi, John Houseman, Buck Henry

Fresh from her successes in *The Godfather* and *Rocky* series, Talia Shire plunged into this muddled morass about a woman who decides to exact some revenge on those men who made her past miserable. The viewer is miserable, too, within a very few minutes of this picture, which can't be saved even by John Belushi. Rated R for profanity and violence.

1979 103 minutes

OLD ENOUGH

★

DIRECTOR: Marisa Silver

CAST: Sarah Boyd, Rainbow Harvest, Neill Barry, Danny Aiello

A pre-pubescent "coming of age" movie. The two principal characters live on opposite sides of the tracks. It is their curiosity about each other and their radically different lifestyles that spark their friendship, or so we are led to believe. This film, while showing great promise and potential from both the character portrayals and the story, fails to deliver. The picture is plagued with a major problem from start to finish. Sarah Boyd's character, the rich kid, is always trying to please her streetwise friend, while the tough girl (Rainbow Harvest) never really tries to meet her nice friend halfway. There is a vain attempt to pad the script with a little diversion from Danny Aiello, who portrays the rough kid's father, but this also ends up being very narrow and shallow. Rated PG.

1984 91 minutes

OLD SWIMMIN' HOLE, THE

★★

DIRECTOR: Robert McGowan

CAST: Marcia Mae Jones, Jackie Moran, Leatrice Joy, Charles Brown

Easygoing homage to small-town America focuses on young Jackie Moran's plans to become a doctor and his and his mother's life in simpler times. Modest and pleasant enough, this Monogram production came out at the same time as *Our Town* and other films about heartland America and bears some similarities to them.

1940 B & W 78 minutes

OLDEST LIVING GRADUATE, THE

★★★★

DIRECTOR: Jack Hofsiss

CAST: Henry Fonda, George Grizzard, Harry Dean Stanton, Penelope Milford, Cloris Leachman, David Ogden Stiers, Timothy Hutton

The Oldest Living Graduate features a memorable performance by Henry Fonda as the oldest living member of a prestigious Texas military academy. His character is somewhat similar to his role in *On Golden Pond*. Nonetheless, he is more than capable of bringing unique traits to this story. Cloris Leachman shines in her role of the Colonel's daughter-in-law. The final moments of this teleplay are poignantly realistic.

1983 90 minutes

OLIVER TWIST

★★★

DIRECTOR: Frank Lloyd

CAST: Jackie Coogan, Lon Chaney Sr., Gladys Brockwell, George Siegmann, Esther Ralston

Young Jackie Coogan, who Charlie Chaplin made a momentary star in *The Kid* (1921), teamed with the legendary "Man of a

Thousand Faces" Lon Chaney to portray, respectively, abused orphan Oliver Twist and literature's great manipulator of thieving children, Fagin, in this loose adaptation of Charles Dickens's enduring classic. Something of an oddity, this is one of at least eight film versions of the world-famous novel. It's good, but nothing like the entrancing British edition of 1948. Silent.

1922 B & W 77 minutes

OLIVER TWIST

★½

DIRECTOR: William Cowen
CAST: Dickie Moore, Irving Pichel, William "Stage" Boyd, Barbara Kent, Doris Lloyd

Low-budget, forgotten version of the popular Charles Dickens story features some intereting performances and a few effective moments. It was designed as a vehicle for minor-league child star Dickie Moore, an ineffective lead at best. Both David Lean's 1948 version and Carol Reed's musical twenty years later are superior. This is a curiosity for students of literature or early sound film; anyone else might not finish the tape. Print quality is marginal.

1933 B & W 77 minutes

OLIVER TWIST

★★★★

DIRECTOR: David Lean
CAST: Alec Guinness, Robert Newton, John Howard Davies

Alec Guinness and Robert Newton give superb performances as the villains in this David Lean adaptation of the Charles Dickens story about a young boy who is forced into a life of thievery until he's rescued by a kindly old gentleman.

1948 B & W 105 minutes

OLIVER'S STORY

★

DIRECTOR: John Korty
CAST: Ryan O'Neal, Candice Bergen, Nicola Pagett, Edward Binns, Ray Milland

Even if you loved *Love Story* you'll find it difficult to like this lame sequel. O'Neal's character apparently decides money's not so bad after all and courts an heiress. Movies like this mean always having to say you're sorry. Rated PG.

1978 92 minutes

ON ANY SUNDAY

★★★★

DIRECTOR: Bruce Brown
CAST: Documentary

The classic motorcycle racing film with which all others are compared. This documentary follows the careers of racers Mert Lawwill and Malcolm Smith, among others and takes us from the desert to motocross, to hill climbs, to road racing, to dirt tracks. A must-see for racing fans. Rated G.

1971 89 minutes

ON GOLDEN POND

★★★★★

DIRECTOR: Mark Rydell
CAST: Henry Fonda, Katharine Hepburn, Jane Fonda, Doug McKeon

Henry Fonda, Katharine Hepburn, and Jane Fonda are terrific in this warm, funny, and often quite moving film, written by Ernest Thompson, about the conflicts and reconciliations among the members of a family that take place during a fateful summer. Rated PG because of brief profanity.

1981 109 minutes

ON THE EDGE

★★★½

DIRECTOR: Rob Nilsson
CAST: Bruce Dern, Bill Bailey, Jim Haynie, John Marley, Pam Grier

Bruce Dern gives a solid performance as a middle-aged runner hoping to regain the glory that escaped him twenty years earlier when he was disqualified from the 1964 Olympic trials. The race to test his ability is the grueling 14.2-mile annual Cielo Sea Race over California's Mount Tamalpais. The mobile camera action in the training and race sequences is very effective. A "feel good" movie. Rated PG.

1985 95 minutes

ON THE WATERFRONT

★★★★★

DIRECTOR: Elia Kazan
CAST: Marlon Brando, Eva Marie Saint, Karl Malden, Lee J. Cobb, Rod Steiger

Tough, uncompromising look at corruption on the New York waterfront. Marlon Brando is brilliant as Terry Malloy, a one-time fight contender who is now a longshoreman. Led into crime by his older brother (Rod Steiger), Terry is disgusted by the violent tactics of boss Lee J. Cobb. Yet if he should turn against the crooks, it could mean his life. A classic American film with uniformly superb performances.

1954 B & W 108 minutes

ONCE IS NOT ENOUGH

DIRECTOR: Guy Green
CAST: Kirk Douglas, Alexis Smith, David Janssen, Deborah Raffin, George Hamilton, Melina Mercouri, Brenda Vaccaro

Trash based on trash, this film of the late Jacqueline Susann's novel of jet-set sex and shenanigans is still being lived down by all concerned. One viewing is not enough; it's too much. Pass. Rated R.

1975 121 minutes

ONE AND ONLY, THE

★★★

DIRECTOR: Carl Reiner
CAST: Henry Winkler, Kim Darby, Herve Villechaize, Harold Gould, Gene Saks, William Daniels

Writer Steve Gordon (*Arthur*) got started with this tale of an obnoxious college show-off who eventually finds fame as a wrestling showboater. Henry Winkler was still struggling to find a big-screen personality, but his occasional character flaws often are overshadowed by Gordon's deft little script. The material has become more timely, considering the current fascination with big-time wrestling. Rated PG.

1978 98 minutes

ONE FLEW OVER THE CUCKOO'S NEST

★★★★★

DIRECTOR: Milos Forman
CAST: Jack Nicholson, Louise Fletcher, Will Sampson, Danny DeVito, Christopher Lloyd, Scatman Crothers

Not since Capra's *It Happened One Night* had a motion picture swept all the major Academy Awards. This stunning film deserved to become the second picture to receive that honor. Jack Nicholson sparkles as Randall P. McMurphy, a convict who is committed to a northwestern mental institution for examination. While there, he stimulates in each of his ward inmates an awakening spirit of self-worth and frees them from their passive acceptance of the hospital authorities' domination. Louise Fletcher is brilliant as the insensitive head nurse. This film is one of those rarities that get better with each viewing. Rated R.

1975 133 minutes

ONE MAGIC CHRISTMAS

★★★★½

DIRECTOR: Phillip Borsos

CAST: Mary Steenburgen, Harry Dean Stanton, Gary Basaraba, Arthur Hill, Elizabeth Harnois, Robbie Magwood, Ken Pogue

Mary Steenburgen stars in this touching, feel-good movie as a young mother who has lost the spirit of Christmas. She regains it with the help of her 6-year-old daughter (Elizabeth Harnois) and a Christmas angel (played by that terrific character actor Harry Dean Stanton). Rated G.

1985 95 minutes

ONE ON ONE

★★★★

DIRECTOR: Lamont Johnson

CAST: Robby Benson, Annette O'Toole, G. D. Spradlin

The harsh world of big-time college athletics is brought into clearer focus by this unheralded "little film." Robby Benson is a naive small-town basketball star who has his eyes opened when he wins a scholarship to a large western university. He doesn't play up to his coach's expectations, and the pressure is put on to take away his scholarship. Annette O'Toole turns in a winning performance as Benson's helpmate. Rated R.

1980 98 minutes

ONION FIELD, THE

★★★★

DIRECTOR: Harold Becker

CAST: John Savage, James Woods, Franklyn Seales, Ted Danson, Ronny Cox, Dianne Hull

Solid screen version of Joseph Wambaugh's book about a cop (John Savage) who cracks up after his partner is murdered. James Woods and Franklyn Seales are memorable as the criminals. While not for all tastes, this film has a kind of subtle power and an almost documentarylike quality that will please those fascinated by true crime stories. Rated R.

1979 124 minutes

ONLY WHEN I LAUGH

★★★

DIRECTOR: Glenn Jordan

CAST: Marsha Mason, Kristy McNichol, James Coco, Joan Hackett

A brilliant but self-destructive actress (Marsha Mason) and her daughter (Kristy McNichol) reach toward understanding in this sometimes funny, sometimes tearful, but always entertaining adaptation by Neil Simon of his play *The Gingerbread Lady.* Rated R for profanity.

1981 121 minutes

ORDEAL OF DR. MUDD, THE

★★★½

DIRECTOR: Paul Wendkos

CAST: Dennis Weaver, Susan Sullivan, Richard Dysart, Arthur Hill

The true story of Dr. Samuel Mudd, who innocently aided the injured, fleeing John Wilkes Booth following Lincoln's assassination and was sent to prison for alleged participation in the conspiracy. Dennis Weaver's fine portrayal of the ill-fated doctor makes this film well worthwhile. More than a century passed before Mudd was cleared, thanks to the efforts of a descendant, newscaster Roger Mudd. Rated PG.

1980 143 minutes

ORDINARY PEOPLE

★★★★½

DIRECTOR: Robert Redford

CAST: Mary Tyler Moore, Donald Sutherland, Timothy Hutton, Judd Hirsch, Elizabeth McGovern, Dinah Manoff, James B. Sikking

This moving human drama, which won the Academy Award for best picture of 1980, marked the directorial debut of Robert Redford . . . and an auspicious one it is, too. Redford elicits memorable performances from Mary Tyler Moore, Donald Sutherland, Timothy Hutton, and Judd Hirsch and makes the intelligent, powerful script by Alvin Sargent seem even better. Rated R for adult situations.

1980 123 minutes

ORPHANS OF THE STORM

★★★½

DIRECTOR: D. W. Griffith

CAST: Lillian Gish, Dorothy Gish, Sidney Herbert, Sheldon Lewis, Monte Blue, Joseph Schildkraut, Lucille LaVerne, Creighton Hale, Frank Losee, Catherine Emmett, Morgan Wallace, Frank Puglia, Leo Kolmer

Film's first master director blends fact and fiction, mixing the French Revolution with the trials and tribulations of two sisters—one blind and raised by thieves, the other betrayed by self-saving aristocrats. The plot creaks with age, but the settings and action—including a hair's-breadth rescue from the guillotine—spell good entertainment. Historians say this film was D. W. Griffith's last great epic. Lillian and Dorothy Gish play the ill-starred sisters. Silent.

1922 B & W 125 minutes

OSCAR, THE

DIRECTOR: Russell Rouse

CAST: Stephen Boyd, Elke Sommer, Tony Bennett, Eleanor Parker, Ernest Borgnine, Joseph Cotten

Take a trite story of an unscrupulous actor trying to advance his career at the expense of others. Add some acting by the entire cast that is so embarrassing it makes you slump in your seat. Give it a form of anarchy attempting to pass as direction. What you get is a real stinker. And that's what you have here. Avoid this turkey at all costs.

1966 119 minutes

OTHER SIDE OF MIDNIGHT, THE

★½

DIRECTOR: Charles Jarrot

CAST: Marie-France Pisier, John Beck, Susan Sarandon, Raf Vallone, Clu Gulager

Glossy, tasteless soap opera derived from schlockmaster Sidney Sheldon's best-selling novel. The story runs from 1939 to 1947 and the movie seems to last that long. This picture definitely needs an injection of panache. Stick to *Dynasty.* Rated R.

1977 165 minutes

OTHER SIDE OF THE MOUNTAIN, THE

★★★

DIRECTOR: Larry Peerce

CAST: Marilyn Hassett, Beau Bridges

Absolutely heart-wrenching account of Jill Kinmont, an Olympic-bound skier whose career was cut short by a fall that left her paralyzed. Marilyn Hassett, in her film debut, makes Kinmont a fighter whose determination initially backfires and prompts some to have unreasonable expectations of her limited recovery. The accident itself looks horrifyingly authentic, the subsequent therapy grim and uncompromising. Sudsy at times (particularly at the end), but generally a reasonable story about a fighter trying to make the most of her new life. Superior to its sequel. Rated PG.

1975 103 minutes

OTHER SIDE OF THE MOUNTAIN, PART II, THE

★★

DIRECTOR: Larry Peerce

CAST: Marilyn Hassett, Timothy Bottoms, Nan Martin, Belinda J. Montgomery, Gretchen Corbett

A sequel to the modest 1975 hit, the film continues the story of Jill Kinmont, a promising young skier who was paralyzed from the shoulders down in an accident. The tender romance, well played by Hassett and Bottoms, provides some fine moments. Rated PG.

1978 100 minutes

OUR DAILY BREAD

★★½

DIRECTOR: King Vidor

CAST: Tom Keene, Karen Morley, John Qualen, Addison Richards

This vintage Depression social drama about an idealistic man organizing community farms and socialistic society is pretty creaky despite sincere effort by director King Vidor. Lead actor Tom Keene did better in cowboy films, and his appearances detract from the rest of the cast, which is pretty good. Look for John Qualen in a role that's a precursor to his "Muley Jones" from *The Grapes of Wrath*.

1934 B & W 74 minutes

OUR TOWN

★★★★

DIRECTOR: Sam Wood

CAST: Frank Craven, William Holden, Martha Scott, Thomas Mitchell, Fay Bainter

Superb performances from a top-flight cast add zest to this well-done adaptation of Thornton Wilder's play about life in a small town.

1940 B & W 90 minutes

OUT OF AFRICA

★★★★½

DIRECTOR: Sydney Pollack

CAST: Robert Redford, Meryl Streep, Klaus Maria Brandauer, Michael Kitchen, Malick Bowens, Michael Gough, Suzanna Hamilton

Robert Redford and Meryl Streep are at the peaks of their considerable talents in this 1985 Oscar winner for best picture, a grand-scale motion picture also blessed with inspired direction (by Sydney Pollack), gorgeous cinematography, and a haunting score (by John Barry). An epic romance, it was based by Kurt Luedtke (*Absence of Malice*) on the life and works of Isak Dineson and concerns the love of two staunch individualists for each other and the land in which they live. There are so many levels of meaning and so many stunning sequences in *Out of Africa* that it begs to be seen more than once. Rated PG for a discreet sex scene and some moments of suspense.

1985 160 minutes

OUTSIDE THE LAW

★★★

DIRECTOR: Tod Browning

CAST: Priscilla Dean, Lon Chaney Sr., Ralph Lewis, Wheeler Oakman, E. A. Warren

Director Tod Browning's long association with the greatest of all character actors and one of the biggest stars of the silent screen began in 1921 when Lon Chaney supported female star Priscilla Dean in this crime drama. The incomparable Chaney plays Black Mike, the meanest and smarmiest of hoodlums, as well as an old Chinese man, the faithful retainer to Miss Dean. Silent.

1921 B & W 77 minutes

OUTSIDERS, THE

★½

DIRECTOR: Francis Ford Coppola
CAST: C. Thomas Howell, Matt Dillon, Ralph Macchio, Emilio Estevez, Tom Cruise, Leif Garrett

Based on S. E. Hinton's popular novel, which has sold some four million copies, this is a fairly simple—and simplistic—movie about kids from the wrong side of the tracks. The pace is slow, and staying interested while watching it soon becomes a trial—even though it was directed by Francis Ford Coppola. In fact, if it weren't for Coppola's sometimes stunning visuals and some scenes of gang violence, *The Outsiders* would be more suitable as an after-school TV special than as a feature film. Rated PG for profanity and violence.

1983 91 minutes

OVER THE EDGE

★★★★

DIRECTOR: Jonathan Kaplan
CAST: Matt Dillon, Michael Kramer Pamela Ludwig

An explosive commentary on the restlessness of today's youth, this film also serves as an indictment against America's hypocritically permissive society. The violence that was supposedly caused by the release of gang films like *The Warriors*, *Boulevard Nights*, and *The Wanderers* caused the movie's makers to shelve it. However, Matt Dillon, who made his film debut herein, is now a hot property, and that's why this deserving movie is out on video. Rated R.

1979 95 minutes

OVER THE TOP

★★

DIRECTOR: Menahem Golan
CAST: Sylvester Stallone, Robert Loggia, Susan Blakely, Rick Zumwalt, David Mendenhall

Thoroughly silly effort. Sylvester Stallone stars as a compassionate trucker who only wants to spend time with the son (David Mendenhall) whom he left, years before, in the custody of his wife (Susan Blakely, in a thankless role) and her rich, iron-willed father (Robert Loggia, as a one-note villain). Sly's teddy-bear aura is slightly altered by his Rockyish desire to win big at arm wrestling, and the larger-than-life opponents he meets during his quest for gold make the participants in the wrestling field look normal by comparison. Try as he might, Stallone just can't make arm wrestling look very exciting, and the clichéd story has little else of interest. Rated PG for mild violence.

1987 94 minutes

OXFORD BLUES

★★

DIRECTOR: Robert Boris
CAST: Rob Lowe, Amanda Pays

Rob Lowe plays a brash American who attempts to woo the beautiful Lady Victoria (Amanda Pays) while attending England's Oxford University. Writer-director Robert Boris has even worked in the sports angle, by making Lowe a rowing champ who has to prove himself. This, in short, is a formula picture. However, Boris makes it watchable by inserting a few well-placed surprises, nice bits of comedy, and an underlying theme of the importance of personal honor. Rated PG-13.

1984 93 minutes

PALOOKA

★★½

DIRECTOR: Bejamin Stoloff

CAST: Jimmy Durante, Stu Erwin, Lupe Velez, Marjorie Rambeau, Robert Armstrong, William Cagney, Thelma Todd, Mary Carlisle

First filmed version of Ham Fisher's popular *Joe Palooka* is an okay little film about country bumpkin Stu Erwin's rise to the top in the fight game. Jimmy Durante as Palooka's manager is overwhelming (as usual), but he's got some top competition in the forms of spitfire Lupe Velez, boisterous Robert Armstrong, luscious Thelma Todd (the "ice cream blonde"), and tough William Cagney, even tougher James Cagney's brother. This film shares a niche with the other seldom-seen comic-strip film adaptations of the 1930s, including *Little Orphan Annie* and *L'il Abner,* and its availability on video is a pleasant gift to the fan who loves those tough and slightly goofy movies of the early 1930s.

1934 B & W 86 minutes

PAPA'S DELICATE CONDITION

★★½

DIRECTOR: George Marshall

CAST: Jackie Gleason, Glynis Johns, Charlie Ruggles, Laurel Goodwin, Charles Lane, Elisha Cook Jr., Juanita Moore, Murray Hamilton

Somewhat stolid but pleasant enough story of family life in a small Texas town and the sometimes unpleasant notoriety brought to a family by their alcoholic patriarch, Jackie Gleason. Gleason, an audience favorite for years and highly visible on television in the 1950's and early 1960's, opted for drama in this film and imbues his character with a poignant sensitivity reminiscent of Chaplin and Keaton, but the result is uneven and at times saccharine although well-intentioned. Not as good a film as it was considered when released, this is still an enjoyable movie and a good chance to watch "the great one" tackle some serious acting, something he is very good at. Based on the reminiscences of silent film star Corinne Griffith and patterned largely after her father and her own small-town upbringing.

1963 98 minutes

PAPER CHASE, THE

★★★★

DIRECTOR: James Bridges

CAST: Timothy Bottoms, John Houseman, Lindsay Wagner

John Houseman won the Oscar for best actor in a supporting role in 1973 with his first-rate performance in this excellent film. Timothy Bottoms stars as a law student attempting to earn his law degree in spite of a stuffy professor (Houseman). Rated PG.

1973 111 minutes

PARADISE ALLEY

DIRECTOR: Sylvester Stallone

CAST: Sylvester Stallone, Armand Assante, Lee Canalito

Sylvester Stallone wrote, directed (his debut), and starred in this turgid mess about three brothers hoping for a quick ride out of the slums and into high society. The dialogue is infantile, the delivery mawkish, the direction completely inept. Even when on familiar ground—Stallone's character hopes to turn his brother into a champion wrestler—Stallone's guiding hand feels more like a punch in the mouth. Avoid at all costs. Rated PG for violence.

1978 107 minutes

PARALLAX VIEW, THE

★★★★

DIRECTOR: Alan J. Pakula

CAST: Warren Beatty, Paula Prentiss, William Daniels

This fine film offers a fascinating study of a reporter, played by Warren Beatty, trying to penetrate the cover-up of an assassination in which the hunter becomes the hunted. Rated R.

1974 102 minutes

PARIS BLUES

★★★½

DIRECTOR: Martin Ritt

CAST: Paul Newman, Joanne Woodward, Diahann Carroll, Sidney Poitier, Louis Armstrong, Serge Reggiani

Duke Ellington's superb jazz score enhances this boys-meet-girls drama. The action takes place in Paris where two jazz musicians (Paul Newman and Sidney Poitier) fall for two lovely tourists (Joanne Woodward and Diahann Carroll). What the plot lacks in originality is amply made up for by the fine music and outstanding cast.

1961 98 minutes

PARIS, TEXAS

★★★★½

DIRECTOR: Wim Wenders

CAST: Harry Dean Stanton, Nastassja Kinski, Dean Stockwell, Aurore Clement, Hunter Carson

This is a film about disillusionment, isolation, lost love, and the American dream gone bad. Adapted from the story by playwright Sam Shepard by L. M. Kit Carson. *Paris, Texas* is a haunting vision of personal pain and universal suffering, with Harry Dean Stanton impeccable as the weary wanderer who returns after four years to reclaim his son (Hunter Carson) and search for his wife (Nastassja Kinski). It is the kind of motion picture we rarely see, one that attempts to say something about our country and its people—and succeeds. (This is all the more impressive/ironic when you consider that it was directed by German filmmaker Wim Wenders.) For those who want something different and with substance. A thinking person's movie. Rated R for profanity and adult content.

1984 144 minutes

PARK IS MINE, THE

★★½

DIRECTOR: Steven Hilliard Stern

CAST: Tommy Lee Jones, Helen Shaver, Yaphet Kotto

After his friend is killed, unstable Vietnam vet (Tommy Lee Jones) invades New York's Central Park and proclaims it to be his. Using combat tactics, Jones holds off the authorities until the predictable ending. Pretty far-fetched stuff. An HBO Film.

1985 102 minutes

PARTING GLANCES

★★★★

DIRECTOR: Bill Sherwood

CAST: Richard Ganoung, John Bolger, Steve Buscemi, Adam Nathan, Kathy Kinney, Patrick Tull, Yolande Bavan, Richard Wall

Nick (Steve Buscemi), a rock singer, discovers he is dying of AIDS. Writer-director Bill Sherwood charts the effect this discovery has on Nick and his estranged lover, Michael (Richard Ganoung), who now lives with Robert (John Bolger). Subject matter aside, *Parting Glances* has a number of funny moments and is a life-affirming look at the gay lifestyle.

1986 90 minutes

PASSAGE TO INDIA, A

★★★★★

DIRECTOR: David Lean

CAST: Judy Davis, Victor Banerjee, Alec Guinness, Peggy Ashcroft

After an absence from the screen of fourteen years, British director David Lean returned triumphantly, with the brilliant *A Passage to India*. Based on the 1924 novel by E. M. Forster, it is a work that compares favorably with the 76-year-old filmmaker's finest: *Great Expectations*; *Oliver Twist*; *The Bridge on the River Kwai*; and *Lawrence of Arabia*. Ostensibly about the romantic adventures of a young Englishwoman in "the mysterious East" that culminate in a court trial (for attempted rape), it is also a multilayered, symbolic work about, in the words of Forster, "the difficulty of living in the universe." Rated PG.

1984 163 minutes

PASSENGER, THE

★★

DIRECTOR: Michelangelo Antonioni

CAST: Jack Nicholson, Maria Schneider, Jenny Runacre, Ian Hendry, Stephen Berkoff

Billed as a suspense drama, *The Passenger* is a very slow-moving tale about a disillusioned TV reporter (Jack Nicholson) working in Africa. He exchanges identities with a dead Englishman and thereby becomes involved with underworld international arms smugglers. Rated R.

1975 119 minutes

PATHS OF GLORY

★★★★★

DIRECTOR: Stanley Kubrick

CAST: Kirk Douglas, Adolphe Menjou, George Macready, Timothy Carey, Ralph Meeker

A great anti-war movie! Stanley Kubrick gives us a scathing indictment against the staff-officer mentality that cares about promotions more than the men who make those promotions possible. Kirk Douglas plays the compassionate French officer in World War I who must lead his men against insurmountable enemy positions, and then must defend three of them against charges of cowardice when the battle is lost. Adolphe Menjou and George Macready perfectly portray Douglas's monstrous senior officers.

1957 B & W 86 minutes

PATTON

★★★★★

DIRECTOR: Franklin Schaffner

CAST: George C. Scott, Karl Malden, Stephen Young, Tim Considine

Flamboyant, controversial General George S. Patton is the subject of this Oscar-winning picture. George C. Scott is spellbinding in the title role. Scott's brilliant performance manages to bring alive this military hero, who strode a fine line between effective battlefield commander and demigod. Rated PG.

1970 169 minutes

PAWNBROKER, THE

★★★★★

DIRECTOR: Sidney Lumet

CAST: Rod Steiger, Geraldine Fitzgerald, Brock Peters

This is a somber and powerfully acted portrayal of a Jewish man who survived the Nazi holocaust, only to find his spirit still as bleak as the Harlem ghetto in which he operates a pawnshop. Rod Steiger gives a tour-de-force performance as a man with dead emotions who is shocked out of his zombielike existence by confronting the realities of modern urban life.

1965 B & W 116 minutes

PAY OR DIE

★★★½

DIRECTOR: Richard Wilson

CAST: Ernest Borgnine, Zohra Lampert, Al Austin, John Duke, Robert Ellenstein, Franco Corsaro, Mario Siletti

Before *The Godfather* or *The Brotherhood* brought the Mafia back to American movie screens, Ernest Borgnine played the fabled leader of the Italian Squad, New York's crack police detectives who dealt with the turn-of-the-century Black Hand. Borgnine and his fellow Italian-Americans use force and intimidation to combat the savage Mafia-connected hoodlums who extort and murder their own people in Little Italy. An underrated crime film. (Ironically, the policeman that Borgnine portrays was eventually murdered by the criminals he sought to expose and eradicate.)

1960 B & W 110 minutes

PAYDAY

★★★★

DIRECTOR: Daryl Duke

CAST: Rip Torn, Ahna Capri, Elayne Heilveil, Cliff Emmich, Michael C. Gwynne

Bravura performance by Rip Torn as a hard-drinking, ruthless country singer who's bent on destroying himself and everyone around him. Gripping, emotionally draining drama. Rarely seen in theaters, this one is definitely worth viewing on tape. Rated R for language, nudity, sexual situations.

1973 103 minutes

PEARL, THE

★★

DIRECTOR: Emilio Fernandez

CAST: Pedro Armendariz, Maria Elena Marques

John Steinbeck's heavy-handed parable about the true riches in life and the value of wealth when compared with natural treasures is beautifully photographed and effectively presented, but the film suffers from the same shortcoming inherent in the book. The tragic plight of the loving couple and their desperately ill son is relentlessly hammered home as they discover that their poverty bars from help of one kind while the great pearl they find brings them no joy or relief either. Pedro Armendariz does a competent job as the pawn who thinks he has found a way out of his frugal existence —only to be slapped down by fate.

1948 77 minutes

PEARL OF THE SOUTH PACIFIC

★½

DIRECTOR: Allan Dwan

CAST: Virginia Mayo, Dennis Morgan, David Farrar, Murvyn Vye

Allan Dwan guides another one down the tubes. A dull film about murder in the tropics that tries to be intriguing and exotic but fails on both counts.

1955 86 minutes

PEDESTRIAN, THE

★★★½

DIRECTOR: Maximilian Schell

CAST: Gustav Rudolph Sellner, Peter Hall, Alexander May, Elsa Wagner, Gila von Weiterschausen, Maximilian Schell

The directorial debut for Maximilian Schell, this is a disturbing near masterpiece of drama exploring the realm of guilt and self-doubt that surrounds ex–World

War II Nazis. Gustav Rudolph Sellner's haunting and quiet performance as an aging industrialist who is exposed as an ex-Nazi is a little tedious but thought-provoking in the outcome—much like the film itself.

1974 97 minutes

PENNY SERENADE

★★★★

DIRECTOR: George Stevens
CAST: Cary Grant, Irene Dunne, Edgar Buchanan

Cary Grant and Irene Dunne are one of the most fondly remembered comedy teams in films such as *The Awful Truth* and *My Favorite Wife*. This 1941 film is a radical change of pace, for it is a ten-hankie tearjerker about a couple's attempt to have children. They are excellent in this drama far removed from their standard comic fare.

1941 B & W 125 minutes

PERFECT

★½

DIRECTOR: James Bridges
CAST: John Travolta, Jamie Lee Curtis, Jann Wenner, Marilu Henner, Laraine Newman

In this irritatingly uneven and unfocused film, John Travolta stars as a *Rolling Stone* reporter out to do an exposé on the current health-club boom. Jamie Lee Curtis is the uncooperative aerobics instructor he attempts to spotlight in his story. What could have been the *Saturday Night Fever* of the Perrier and pumping iron set turns out to be just another moralizing mess about journalistic ethics. Rated R for profanity, suggested sex, and violence.

1985 120 minutes

PERFORMANCE

★★★★

DIRECTORS: Nicolas Roeg, Donald Cammell
CAST: Mick Jagger, James Fox, Anita Pallenberg

Mick Jagger, the leader of the Rolling Stones rock group, stars in this bizarre film as Turner, a rock singer who decides to switch identities with a hunted hit man (James Fox). Co-directed by Nicolas Roeg (*Don't Look Now*; *The Man Who Fell to Earth*) and Donald Cammell, *Performance* is a chilling, profoundly disturbing cinematic nightmare about the dark side of man's consciousness. Rated R for profanity, nudity, violence, and all manner of perversity and evil.

1970 105 minutes

PERSONAL BEST

★★★★

DIRECTOR: Robert Towne
CAST: Mariel Hemingway, Patrice Donnelly, Scott Glenn

Oscar-winning screenwriter Robert Towne (*Chinatown*) wrote, directed, and produced this tough, honest, and nonexploitive story about two women who are friends, teammates, and sometimes lovers (Mariel Hemingway, Patrice Donnelly) preparing for the 1980 Olympics. Hemingway's and Donnelly's stunning performances make the film an impressive achievement. Rated R for male and female frontal nudity, strong language, and drug use.

1982 124 minutes

PETRIFIED FOREST, THE

★★★★½

DIRECTOR: Archie Mayo
CAST: Humphrey Bogart, Leslie Howard, Bette Davis, Dick Foran

This adaptation of the Robert Sherwood play seems a bit dated at first. It's about a gangster (Humphrey Bogart, in one of his first important screen roles) who holds a writer (Leslie Howard), a waitress (Bette Davis), and others hostage in a diner. The first-rate story, exquisite ensemble acting by the stars, and taut direction by Archie Mayo soon mesmerize the viewer. The result is a memorable movie-watching experience.

1936 B & W 83 minutes

PHAR LAP

★★★★½

DIRECTOR: Simon Wincer
CAST: Tom Burlinson, Ron Leibman, Martin Vaughn

Absolutely chilling (and true) account of the superb Australian racehorse that chewed up the track in the 1920s and early 1930s. Tom Burlinson, remembered as *The Man from Snowy River*, stars as the stableboy who first believed in, and then followed to fame, the indefatigable Phar Lap. This film's indictment of early horse-racing practices will make you shudder; when an animal (such as Phar Lap) did too well, it was weighted down in an attempt to prevent its being able to move at all. Such measures won't stop heroes, though . . . not even the four-legged variety. Keep the Kleenex handy. Rated PG—very intense for younger children.

1984 106 minutes

PIANO FOR MRS. CIMINO, A

★★★★

DIRECTOR: George Schaefer
CAST: Bette Davis, Keenan Wynn, Alexa Kenin, Penny Fuller, Christopher Guest, George Hearn

Blessed with great humor and a terrific performance by Bette Davis, this made-for-television film about growing old with dignity is manipulative at times. In light of all the wonderful moments, however, the contrivances don't seem so bad. Davis plays a widow who is institutionalized for senility. The film follows her through her recovery and her rebirth as a single, self-sufficient woman. Keenan Wynn also puts in a good peformance as an old musician friend.

1982 96 minutes

PILOT, THE

★★½

DIRECTOR: Cliff Robertson
CAST: Cliff Robertson, Frank Converse, Diane Baker, Gordon MacRae, Dana Andrews, Milo O'Shea, Ed Binns

Cliff Robertson directed and starred in this film about an airline pilot's struggle with alcohol. A lot of heart went into this film, and we are glad to announce that despite the all-star cast and the subject matter, this is not a disaster flick. Just the same, Robertson's directing is not as convincing as his acting, and the screenplay is sometimes sickeningly sweet. Rated PG for profanity.

1979 98 minutes

PIPE DREAMS

★

DIRECTOR: Stephen F. Verona
CAST: Gladys Knight, Barry L. Hankerson, Bruce French, Wayne Tippitt, Sherry Bain, Barbara Shaw

While writer/director/producer Stephen F. Verona may have had good intentions, the story is trite, and the poor acting and weak direction only aggravate the problem. Gladys Knight (of Pip fame) plays a wife who moves to Alaska to win back her estranged man who is working on the pipe line. The title pun is a good example of the wit involved here. Rated PG for sex, violence, profanity, and adult subject matter.

1976 89 minutes

PLACE IN THE SUN, A

★★★★

DIRECTOR: George Stevens
CAST: Elizabeth Taylor, Montgomery Clift, Shelley Winters, Keefe Brasselle, Raymond Burr, Anne Revere

Elizabeth Taylor, Montgomery Clift, and Shelley Winters are caught in a tragic love triangle in this picture, based on Theodore Dreiser's *An American Tragedy.* All three artists give first-rate performances. The story of a working-class man who falls for a wealthy girl is a traditional one, yet the eroticism conveyed in the scenes between Taylor and Clift keeps this production well above a standard story of doomed lovers.

1951 B & W 122 minutes

PLACE OF WEEPING

★★★½

DIRECTOR: Darrell Roodt
CAST: James Whylie, Gcina Mhlope, Charles Comyn, Norman Coombes, Michelle Du Toit

The first film about the South African struggle made by South Africans, this drama follows the battle of one woman who, with the help of a white reporter, stands against the system of apartheid. Although this film is a bit slow-moving and obviously made on a low budget, its political importance cannot be denied. Certainly an important film in the history of filmmaking. Rated PG.

1986 88 minutes

PLACES IN THE HEART

★★★★★

DIRECTOR: Robert Benton
CAST: Sally Field, Ed Harris, Lindsay Crouse, John Malkovich, Danny Glover

Writer-director Robert Benton's *Places in the Heart* is a great film. Based on Benton's childhood memories in Waxahachie, Texas, the film stars Sally Field, Ed Harris, Lindsay Crouse, with special performances by John Malkovich and Danny Glover. Field plays Edna Spalding, a mother of two who is suddenly widowed. Almost immediately, she is pressured by the bank to sell her home and the surrounding property. But Edna vows, despite all supposed "logic," to make it on her own. The result is a movie celebrating the human spirit. Rated PG for suggested sex, violence, and profanity.

1984 110 minutes

PLATOON

★★★★★

DIRECTOR: Oliver Stone
CAST: Tom Berenger, Willem DaFoe, Charlie Sheen, Forrest Whitaker, Francesco Quinn, John C. McGinley, Richard Edson

Writer-director Oliver Stone's Oscar-winning work is not just the best film made on the subject of Vietnam; it is a great cinematic work that stands high among the finest films ever made. Charlie Sheen is the well-meaning youth who volunteers for military service to become a real person instead of, in his words, "a fake human being." His parents' middle-class values seem more foreign to him than the jungle he enters on his first day in the war. But it doesn't take long for him to realize how hopelessly out of his element he is. Not only does every step and noise bring the threat of death, but there is an intercompany war going on between the brutal Tom Berenger and the humanistic Willem DaFoe. *Platoon* hits the truth like a rifle butt to the brainpan. It should not be missed. Rated R for profanity, gore, and violence.

1986 111 minutes

PLAYERS

(turkey symbol)

DIRECTOR: Anthony Harvey
CAST: Ali MacGraw, Dean-Paul Martin, Maximilian Schell

It boggles the mind to consider that the man responsible for this unrelenting bomb also directed *The Lion in Winter.* Ali MacGraw is the bored mistress of Maximilian Schell; she falls for tennis pro Dean-Paul Martin. Ludicrous dialogue, banal acting, lethargic directing . . . even the tennis scenes are terrible. Rated PG—sexual situations.

1979 120 minutes

PLEASURE PALACE

★★

DIRECTOR: Walter Grauman
CAST: Omar Sharif, Victoria Principal, Walter Grauman, J. D. Cannon, Gerald S. O'Loughlin, José Ferrer, Hope Lange

No, this is not a porno flick—in fact, the characters in this made-for-TV movie are more like old-fashioned melodrama icons. Hope Lange plays an honest widowed casino owner (yay!) who is afraid she will loose her casino to an influential oil baron (boo!). Omar Sharif portrays a high-rolling international gambler (a similar role to the one he played in *Funny Girl*) who comes to the rescue—gambler's style. Despite the lack of subtlety in characters, some of the gambling scenes have real tension in them. And screenwriter Blanche Hanalis should watch her anti-Arab insults. Not rated, but the equivalent of a PG for violence.

1980 92 minutes

PLENTY

★★★★

DIRECTOR: Fred Schepisi
CAST: Meryl Streep, Charles Dance, Sam Neill, Tracey Ullman, John Gielgud, Sting, Ian McKellen

In this difficult but rewarding film, which is like a great stage production played out with high movie style on screen, Meryl Streep is superb as a former member of the French Resistance who finds life in her native England increasingly maddening during the postwar reconstruction period. Rated R for profanity, suggested sex, and violence.

1985 120 minutes

PLOUGHMAN'S LUNCH, THE

★½

DIRECTOR: Richard Eyre
CAST: Jonathan Pryce, Tim Curry, Rosemary Harris, Frank Finlay, Charlie Dore

The Ploughman's Lunch is a morality piece about opportunism and exploitation portrayed throught the world of journalism. The problem is that almost everyone in the film is a weasel; they're all users. The point is to call attention to this fact, but it doesn't make for very enjoyable movie watching. The cynicism and callousness of the characters override the simplistic message. Rated R.

1984 107 minutes

POCKETFUL OF MIRACLES

★★★

DIRECTOR: Frank Capra
CAST: Bette Davis, Glenn Ford, Ann-Margret, Thomas Mitchell

Frank Capra's last film; Ann-Margret's first. A not-as-good remake of Capra's *Lady for a Day*, with Bette Davis playing Apple Annie, a Damon Runyon Broadway character, whom gangster Glenn Ford turns into a lady. It's sentimental hokum worth watching, but not well worth watching, and it's too long.

1961 136 minutes

POPE OF GREENWICH VILLAGE, THE

★★★½

DIRECTOR: Stuart Rosenberg
CAST: Eric Roberts, Mickey Rourke, Daryl Hannah, Geraldine Page

This watchable film focuses on the hard-edged misadventures of two Italian cousins, Paulie (Eric Roberts) and Charlie (Mickey Rourke). Paulie is a not-so-bright dreamer who's obviously headed for trouble, and Charlie, who is smart enough to know better, always seems to get caught up in the middle of his cousin's half-baked and dangerous ripoff schemes. Rated R for profanity and violence.

1984 120 minutes

PORT OF NEW YORK

★★½

DIRECTOR: Laslo Benedek
CAST: Scott Brady, Richard Rober, K. T. Stevens, Yul Brynner

A female narcotics smuggler decides to play ball with the police and deliver her former colleagues to them. Scott Brady plays the cop eager to make the arrest while protecting his lovely informant. Yul Brynner is the head smuggler who wants to stop the squealing—fast. Gritty and engrossing, this is one of a number of semidocumentary films dealing with all levels of vice that filled the screens of post–World War II America.

1949 B & W 82 minutes

PORTNOY'S COMPLAINT

★

DIRECTOR: Ernest Lehman
CAST: Richard Benjamin, Karen Black, Lee Grant, Jack Somack, Jeannie Berlin, Jill Clayburgh

Amazing that anyone had the nerve to attempt to translate Philip Roth's infamous novel to the screen. The neurotic Jewish boy, who has a strange relationship with his mother and an obsession with sex, should be neutered. Richard Benjamin is at his most annoying in the role. Karen Black's poignant portrayal of "Monkey" provides the only worthwhile moments. It's worth viewing only as a curiosity. Rated R for profanity and sex.

1972 101 minutes

PORTRAIT OF A STRIPPER

★★

DIRECTOR: John A. Alonzo
CAST: Lesley Ann Warren, Edward Herrmann, Vic Tayback, Sheree North

A dancer is forced to strip in order to support her fatherless son, causing the authorities to label her an unfit mother. Since this was originally made for TV, its timid presentation will, no doubt, disappoint many drooling video renters.

1979 100 minutes

POSSESSED

★★★

DIRECTOR: Curtis Bernhardt
CAST: Van Heflin, Joan Crawford, Raymond Massey, Geraldine Brooks, Stanley Ridges

A cold and clinical account of loveless marriage, mysterious suicide, frustrated love for a scoundrel, murder, and schizophrenia. The much-maligned Joan Crawford heads a fine, mature cast and gives one of her finer performances as a mentally troubled nurse whose head and heart problems destroy her life. Extremely watchable. The opening scene is a real grabber.

1947 B & W 108 minutes

POSTMAN ALWAYS RINGS TWICE, THE (ORIGINAL)

★★★

DIRECTOR: Tay Garnett
CAST: John Garfield, Lana Turner, Cecil Kellaway, Hume Cronyn

If you wondered what went wrong in the sometimes steamily sexy and all too often soggy 1981 screen version of James M. Cain's celebrated novel, you need only watch this 1946 adaptation. John Garfield and Lana Turner play the lovers who murder the husband who stands in the way of their lust and suffer the consequences. While not as good as Billy Widler's film of Cain's equally famous *Double Indemnity*, this picture is still superior to the remake.

1946 B & W 113 minutes

POSTMAN ALWAYS RINGS TWICE, THE (REMAKE)

★★★

DIRECTOR: Bob Rafelson
CAST: Jessica Lange, Jack Nicholson, John Colicos, Michael Lerner, John P. Ryan, Anjelica Huston

Jack Nicholson plays the drifter whose lust for a married woman (Jessica Lange) leads to murder in this disappointing remake based on James M. Cain's hard-boiled novel of sex and violence. After an electric first hour, it begins to ramble and ends abruptly, leaving the viewer dissatisfied. Rated R for graphic sex and violence.

1981 123 minutes

POT O' GOLD

DIRECTOR: George Marshall
CAST: James Stewart, Paulette Goddard, Horace Heidt, Charles Winninger, Mary Gordon

An amusing time-passer based on a one-time popular radio show. Obviously a studio effort to use contract talent. The plot concerns an enthusiastic young man's effort to get Horace Heidt and his orchestra on his uncle's radio program. Gee!

1941 B & W 86 minutes

POWER

★★★★

DIRECTOR: Sidney Lumet
CAST: Richard Gere, Julie Christie, Gene Hackman, Kate Capshaw, Denzel Washington, E. G. Marshall, Beatrice Straight

Sidney Lumet, who directed the much-praised black comedy about television, *Network*, once again takes viewers into the bowels of an American institution with this hard-edged study of the manipulation of the political process by market research and advertizing. Richard Gere gives one of his better performances as a ruthless hustler who is given pause when the one politician he believes in (E. G. Marshall) becomes a pawn in the political power trade. Julie Christie is the ex-wife/journalist who helps Gere discover the truth, and Gene Hackman is his former mentor and chief critic. Rated R for profanity, violence, and suggested sex.

1986 111 minutes

PRESENTING LILY MARS

★½

DIRECTOR: Norman Taurog
CAST: Judy Garland, Van Heflin, Richard Carlson, Marta Eggerth, Connie Gilchrist, Fay Bainter, Spring Byington, Leonid Kinsky, Marilyn Maxwell, Tommy Dorsey, Bob Crosby

Stagestruck girl plugs her way to stardom. High points are when

Judy Garland sings and has a nostalgic backstage conversation with has-been actress Connie Gilchrist. The Tommy Dorsey and Bob Crosby bands help keep audiences awake.

1943 B & W 104 minutes

PRESIDENT'S PLANE IS MISSING, THE

★★★

DIRECTOR: Daryl Duke

CAST: Buddy Ebsen, Peter Graves, Arthur Kennedy, Raymond Massey, Mercedes McCambridge, Rip Torn, Dabney Coleman

Crisis after crisis occurs when *Air Force One* disappears with the president on board. This story of indecision and desire for control against a background of international crisis is an engaging suspense yarn. A very good story is helped by a veteran cast.

1971 100 minutes

PRETTY BABY

★★★★

DIRECTOR: Louis Malle

CAST: Brooke Shields, Susan Sarandon, Keith Carradine, Frances Faye, Antonio Fargas, Matthew Anton

Forcing the audience to reexamine many accepted concepts is just one of the effects of this brilliant work by Louis Malle. He is clearly fascinated by Violet (Brooke Shields), the young girl we see growing up in a whorehouse in New Orleans. For Violet, all that goes on around her is normal and quite unshocking. The first scene in the film shows Violet watching as her mother (Susan Sarandon) is gasping and groaning on the bed. We naturally assume that she is with one of her many clients. But as the camera pulls back, we see that she is giving birth, and the first of Malle's searching questions is instilled in the viewer. It is not Violet or her mother who has the dirty mind, but we, the audience. Rated R.

1978 109 minutes

PRETTY IN PINK

★★★★

DIRECTOR: Howard Deutch

CAST: Molly Ringwald, Harry Dean Stanton, Jon Cryer, Andrew McCarthy, Annie Potts, James Spader

Molly Ringwald is wonderful to watch as a young woman "from the poor side of town" who falls in love with rich kid Andrew McCarthy (*St. Elmo's Fire*). The feeling is mutual, but their peers do everything they can to keep them apart. Harry Dean Stanton gives a typically terrific performance as Molly's understanding troubled dad, and Jon Cryer (*No Small Affair*) is a delight as her secret lover. Written by John Hughes (*Sixteen Candles*, *The Breakfast Club*), it is that rare teen-age–oriented release that can be enjoyed by teens and adults. Rated PG-13 for profanity and violence.

1986 96 minutes

PRICK UP YOUR EARS

★★★★

DIRECTOR: Stephen Frears

CAST: Gary Oldman, Alfred Molina, Vanessa Redgrave, Julie Walters, Wallace Shawn

The poignant love story at the center of *Prick Up Your Ears* will be touching to some and shocking to others. But this film about the rise to prominence of British playwright Joe Orton (Gary Oldman) and his relationship with Kenneth Halliwell (Alfred Molina) never fails to fascinate. Often gruesomely funny as only a genuine black comedy can be, *Prick Up* engages all of the viewer's emotions. Screenwriter Alan Bennett adapted his script from the biography of Orton by John Lahr (who is played by Wallace Shawn) and begins, in a sense, at the end —with the playwright's death at the hands of his longtime lover. Rated R for profanity and scenes of graphic sex.

1987 110 minutes

PRIDE AND PREJUDICE

★★★★

DIRECTOR: Robert Z. Leonard
CAST: Greer Garson, Laurence Olivier, Maureen O'Sullivan, Marsha Hunt

This film is an accurate adaptation of Jane Austen's famous novel. The story takes place in nineteenth-century England with five sisters looking for suitable husbands.

1940 B & W 116 minutes

PRIDE AND THE PASSION, THE

★★

DIRECTOR: Stanley Kramer
CAST: Frank Sinatra, Cary Grant, Sophia Loren, Theodore Bikel, John Wengray

Here is a supreme example of how miscasting can ruin a movie's potential. Frank Sinatra is horrible as the Spanish peasant leader of a guerrilla army during the Napoleonic era. He secures the services of a gigantic cannon and a British Navy officer (Cary Grant) to fire it. Sophia Loren is also in the cast, primarily as window dressing. Sinatra treks the cannon and his ragtag army across Spain in order to capture a walled city from the supporters of Napoleon. The idea sounds exciting, but Sinatra's performance makes you want to look away from the screen.

1957 132 minutes

PRIDE OF JESSE HALLMAN, THE

★★

DIRECTOR: Gary Nelson
CAST: Johnny Cash, Brenda Vaccaro, Eli Wallach, Ben Marley, Guy Boyd

This is a well-meant but sluggish account of the quest for literacy by the title character, who is played by country singer–songwriter Johnny Cash. Made for television.

1981 99 minutes

PRIDE OF THE BOWERY

DIRECTOR: Joseph H. Lewis
CAST: Leo Gorcey, Bobby Jordan, Donald Haines, Carleton Young, Kenneth Howell, David Gorcey

This offshoot of the famous Dead-End Kids features Leo Gorcey and Bobby Jordan, two of the original "kids," along with Gorcey's brother David, who continued on and off for the rest of the series. Not quite as bad as their later efforts, this film still needs a dyed-in-the-wool East Side Kids fan to really enjoy it. No surprises in this routine programmer, which is basically the same film these perennial juveniles will make for the next seventeen years.

1940 B & W 63 minutes

PRIDE OF THE YANKEES, THE

★★★★★

DIRECTOR: Sam Wood
CAST: Gary Cooper, Teresa Wright, Babe Ruth, Walter Brennan, Dan Duryea, Ludwig Stossel

Gary Cooper gives one of his finest performances as he captures the courageous spirit of New York Yankee immortal Lou Gehrig. This 1942 drama is a perfect blend of an exciting sports biography and a touching melodrama as we follow Gehrig's baseball career from its earliest playground beginnings until an illness strikes him down in his prime. Teresa Wright is just right in the difficult role of his loving wife.

1942 B & W 127 minutes

PRIEST OF LOVE

★★★★

DIRECTOR: Christopher Miles
CAST: Ian McKellen, Janet Suzman, Ava Gardner, John Gielgud, Penelope Keith, Jorge Rivero, Maurizio Merli

The culmination of a decade-long quest to film the life of D. H. Lawrence (Ian McKellen) by producer-director Christopher Miles, *Priest of Love* is absorbing, brilliantly acted, and stunningly photographed. It deals with Lawrence's exile from his native England, where his books, *Women in Love* and *Sons and Lovers*, were generally reviled; his relationship with wife Frieda (Janet Suzman), whom Miles called the "first hippie;" and their final time together in Italy, where Lawrence wrote *Lady Chatterley's Lover.* Miles takes us deep into Lawrence's life and times, creating believable moments of love, happiness, and torment. Rated R for profanity and sex.

1981 125 minutes

PRINCE OF THE CITY

★★★★

DIRECTOR: Sidney Lumet
CAST: Treat Williams, Jerry Orbach, Richard Foronjy, Don Billet, Kenny Marino

Director Sidney Lumet (*Serpico*; *Dog Day Afternoon*) has created one of the screen's most intense character studies out of the true story of a corrupt New York narcotics cop, played wonderfully by Treat Williams. In becoming a government agent, the cop destroys the lives of his closest friends. Rated R because of violence and strong profanity.

1981 167 minutes

PRIVATE HELL 36

★★½

DIRECTOR: Don Siegel
CAST: Ida Lupino, Steve Cochran, Howard Duff, Dean Jagger, Dorothy Malone

Tight, well-constructed story of two cops who skim money from a haul they have intercepted and have trouble living with it, is nicely acted by veteran performers. Ida Lupino, equally adept on either side of the camera, co-wrote and produced this grim drama. Director Don Siegel was still turning out some of the best low-budget crime fare available on any screen, and this jaundiced look at the human condition reappeared in a few short years when he was to direct one of the most frightening films of all time: *Invasion of the Body Snatchers*.

1954 B & W 81 minutes

PRIVATE LIFE OF DON JUAN, THE

★★

DIRECTOR: Alexander Korda
CAST: Douglas Fairbanks, Merle Oberon, Binnie Barnes, Benita Hume, Joan Gardner, Melville Cooper, Owen Naves

A vehicle for the aging Douglas Fairbanks, his last picture is set in seventeenth-century Spain. A famous lover (Fairbanks) fakes a suicide in order to make a comeback in disguise. To quote Oscar Wilde, "Life imitates art;" this is the case here. It is somewhat tragic that the first great hero of the screen should have ended up in this disappointment. It is better to remember him as *Robin Hood* or *The Black Pirate*. The supporting cast seems idle, as if the whole picture is just a party to humor Fairbanks.

1934 B & W 90 minutes

PRIVATE LIFE OF HENRY THE EIGHTH, THE

★★★★

DIRECTOR: Alexander Korda

CAST: Charles Laughton, Robert Donat, Merle Oberon, Elsa Lanchester, Binnie Barnes

This well-paced historical chronicle of England's bluebeard monarch and his six wives was to be Britain's first successful entry into worldwide movie-making. Charles Laughton's tour-de-force as the notorious king remains one of filmdom's greatest portrayals. The segment dealing with his relationship with Anne of Cleves is the funniest and most rewarding portion of the film. Laughton's real-life spouse, Elsa Lanchester, plays Anne, the fourth wife. She manages to keep her head off the chopping block by humoring the volatile king during a memorable game of cards.

1933 B & W 87 minutes

PRIVATE LIVES OF ELIZABETH AND ESSEX, THE

★★★½

DIRECTOR: Michael Curtiz

CAST: Bette Davis, Errol Flynn, Olivia De Havilland, Vincent Price, Donald Crisp, Nanette Fabray, Henry Daniell, Alan Hale, Robert Warwick, Henry Stephenson

Bette Davis is Queen Elizabeth and Errol Flynn is her dashing suitor in this enjoyable costume drama directed by Michael Curtiz (*Casablanca*).

1939 106 minutes

PRIZZI'S HONOR

★★★★★

DIRECTOR: John Huston

CAST: Jack Nicholson, Kathleen Turner, Robert Loggia, John Randolph, William Hickey, Anjelica Huston

This totally bent black comedy is perhaps best described as *The Godfather* gone stark, raving mad. It is not a film for every taste. Jack Nicholson plays a Mafia hit man who falls in love with a mystery woman (Kathleen Turner), who turns out to be full of surprises. Perhaps the blackest black comedy ever made, *Prizzi's Honor* makes *Being There*, *Harold and Maude*, and even *Dr. Strangelove* seem tame in comparison. In other words, it's a real find for fans of the genre. Rated R for nudity, suggested sex, profanity, and violence.

1985 130 minutes

PROMISES IN THE DARK

★★★½

DIRECTOR: Jerome Hellman

CAST: Marsha Mason, Ned Beatty, Susan Clark, Michael Brandon, Kathleen Beller, Paul Clemens, Donald Moffat

This film is about a young girl dying of cancer. Marsha Mason co-stars as her sympathetic doctor. Good movie, but very depressing! Rated PG.

1979 115 minutes

PROVIDENCE

★★★★

DIRECTOR: Alain Resnais

CAST: Dirk Bogarde, John Gielgud, Ellen Burstyn, David Warner, Elaine Stritch

Director Alain Resnais's first English-language film includes the great cast of Dirk Bogarde, John Gielgud, Ellen Burstyn, and David Warner. An old and dying writer (Gielgud) completing his last novel invites his family up for the weekend. The fast cutting between the writer's imagined thoughts and real life makes this film difficult to follow for some. Rated R.

1977 104 minutes

PT 109

★★½

DIRECTOR: Leslie Martinson

CAST: Cliff Robertson, Robert Culp, Ty Hardin, James Gregory, Robert Blake, Grant Williams

Cliff Robertson is John F. Kennedy in this monument to the former President's war adventures on a World War II PT boat. Robertson is credible, but the story is only interesting because of the famous people and events it represents.

1963 140 minutes

PUBERTY BLUES

★★★½

DIRECTOR: Bruce Beresford

CAST: Nell Schofield, Jad Capelja

This film takes a frank look at the coming of age of two teenagers as they grow up on the beaches of Australia. The two girls become temporary victims of peer group pressure that involves drugs, alcohol, and sex. Unlike many other teen-age films, *Puberty Blues* offers interesting insights into the rite of passage as seen from a female point of view. Rated R.

1981 86 minutes

PUMPING IRON

★★★★

DIRECTORS: George Butler, Robert Fiore

CAST: Arnold Schwarzenegger, Lou Ferrigno, Matty and Victoria Ferrigno, Mike Katz

Very good documentary concerning professional body building. Arnold Schwarzenegger and Lou Ferrigno ("The Hulk") are at the forefront as they prepare for the Mr. Universe contest. Always interesting and at times fascinating. Rated PG for language.

1977 85 minutes

PUMPING IRON II: THE WOMEN

★★★★½

DIRECTOR: George Butler

CAST: Lori Bowen, Carla Dunlap, Bev Francis, Rachel McLish

This documentary on the 1983 Women's World Cup held at Caesar's Palace is more than just beauty and brawn. While it does seem to side with one contestant (and when you see Bev Francis's massive body, you'll know why), the film has all the passion and wit of a first-rate narrative. The movie follows four competitors for the prize from their arrival in Las Vegas, through their workouts, to the moment they've all been waiting for. This picture also gives the viewer an in depth view of these bodybuilders through illuminating interviews. Not rated, but an equivalent of a PG.

1985 107 minutes

PURPLE HEART, THE

★★★★

DIRECTOR: Lewis Milestone

CAST: Dana Andrews, Richard Conte, Farley Granger, Sam Levene, Tala Birell, Nestor Paiva

Dana Andrews and Richard Conte are leaders of a group of American fliers who are captured by the Japanese after they bomb Tokyo and put on trial for war crimes. This fascinating film is a minor classic.

1944 B & W 99 minutes

PURPLE HEARTS

★

DIRECTOR: Sidney J. Furie

CAST: Ken Wahl, Cheryl Ladd

Anyone who can sit all the way through this Vietnam war-film romance deserves a medal. Ken Wahl (*The Wanderers*; *Fort*

Apache—The Bronx) stars as a surgeon in the United States Navy Medical Corps who falls in love with a nurse (Cheryl Ladd, formerly of television's "Charlie's Angels"). Halfway through this film, directed by Sidney J. Furie (*The Boys in Company C*; *The Entity*), there's a natural and satisfying ending. But does it end there? Noooo. There's an additional forty minutes of unnecessary and unoriginal story tacked on. What Furie is going for is a ripoff of *An Officer and a Gentleman*, complete with a teary-eyed ending—and he gets it. But the tears are more from eyestrain than emotional involvement or release. Rated R for nudity, profanity, violence, and gore.

1984 115 minutes

PURPLE TAXI, THE

★★★

DIRECTOR: Yves Boisset

CAST: Fred Astaire, Edward Albert, Philippe Noiret, Peter Ustinov, Charlotte Rampling, Agostine Belli

Fred Astaire, Edward Albert, and Philippe Noiret star in this exploration of angst, love, and friendship in Ireland, where a collection of expatriate characters impaled on memories and self-destructive compulsions work out their kinks before returning to various homelands. Capably supporting are Peter Ustinov, as a tortured and despicable con man, and Charlotte Rampling, as the spoiled and distraught sister of troubled Jerry (Edward Albert). Fine backdrops in Ireland's "curtain of rain" and impressive acting. Rated R.

1977 107 minutes

QB VII

★★★★

DIRECTOR: Tom Gries

CAST: Anthony Hopkins, Ben Gazzara, Leslie Caron, Lee Remick, Anthony Quayle

Leon Uris's hefty bestseller is vividly brought to life in this five-hours-plus made-for-television drama about a Polish expatriate doctor living in England who sues an American writer for libel when the writer accuses him of carrying out criminal medical activities for the Nazis during World War II. Anthony Hopkins is brilliant as the physician, Ben Gazzara outraged and tenacious as the writer. Expect a powerful, engrossing ending.

1974 312 minutes

QUACKSER FORTUNE HAS A COUSIN IN THE BRONX

★★★★

DIRECTOR: Waris Hussein

CAST: Gene Wilder, Margot Kidder, Eileen Colga, Seamus Ford, David Kelly

This movie falls into the category of sleeper. Gene Wilder is delightful as an Irishman who marches to the beat of a different drummer. Margot Kidder is a rich American going to univeristy in Dublin who meets and falls in love with him. Humor and sadness abound in this insightful comedy-drama. Don't be put off by the strange title; it becomes very meaningful. Filmed in Ireland and rated R for nudity and language.

1970 88 minutes

QUARTET

★★

DIRECTOR: James Ivory

CAST: Isabelle Adjani, Alan Bates, Anthony Higgins, Maggie Smith

In terms of acting, this is a first-rate film. If movies are a ninety-percent visual medium, then the scenes of Paris in the 1920s would make this well worthwhile. Unfortunately, the pathetic characters that mope around in this period piece drag down any positive points to the film. Isabelle Adjani plays the wife of a convicted criminal who ends up in a *ménage à trois* with a married couple, played by Alan Bates and Maggie Smith. Rated R for nudity.

1981 101 minutes

QUEEN OF THE STARDUST BALLROOM

★★★★

DIRECTOR: Sam O'Steen
CAST: Maureen Stapleton, Charles Durning, Michael Brandon, Michael Strong

Touching love story about a lonely widow (Maureen Stapleton) who finally finds Mr. Right (Charles Durning). Stapleton is outstanding.

1975 100 minutes

QUICKSILVER

★

DIRECTOR: Tom Donnelly
CAST: Kevin Bacon, Jami Gertz, Paul Rodriguez, Rudy Ramos, Andrew Smith

Wretched mess of a film, which moves in too many directions and succeeds with none. Kevin Bacon stars as a Wall Street wizard who blows it all one day—including his parents' savings account—and then puts his natural talents to work by becoming . . . a bicycle messenger. Nice bicycle-level camera work and a decent performance by Jami Gertz, but the rest is a mess of rock video sequences and weak plot elements: the nasty drug dealer, the independent young girl who gets in over her head, the lad whose idea of American success is opening his own hot dog stand. Puh-*leaze*. Bacon displays none of the talent he's shown in the past. Rated PG for mild violence.

1986 101 minutes

QUO VADIS

★★★

DIRECTOR: Mervyn Leroy
CAST: Robert Taylor, Deborah Kerr, Peter Ustinov, Leo Genn, Finlay Currie, Patricia Laffan, Abraham Sofaer, Felix Aylmer, Marina Berti, Buddy Baer

Colossal is just one of the superlatives trumpeting the size and scope of this mammoth drama about Romans, Christians, lions, pagan rites, rituals, and Nero. Roman soldier Robert Taylor loves and pursues Christian maiden Deborah Kerr. It's Christians versus Nero and the lions in the eternal fight between good and evil. The sets, scenery, and crowd scenes are nearly overwhelming. Peter Ustinov as Nero is priceless.

1951 171 minutes

R.P.M. (REVOLUTIONS PER MINUTE)

★★

DIRECTOR: Stanley Kramer
CAST: Anthony Quinn, Ann-Margret, Gary Lockwood

In this story set on a small-town college campus in the late 1960s, a liberal professor (Anthony Quinn) and his coed mistress (Ann-Margret) become involved in the efforts of a liberal student (Gary Lockwood) to have the professor made president of the university. Good intentions turn into campus unrest and violence. This movie starts out interesting, but as with many of director Stanley Kramer's efforts, it falls short. Rated R for violence.

1970 92 minutes

RABBIT RUN

DIRECTOR: Jack Smight
CAST: James Caan, Carrie Snodgress, Jack Albertson, Henry Jones, Anjanette Comer

John Updike's novel concerning an ex–high school athlete's trouble adjusting to life off the playing field is brought to the screen in a very dull fashion. James Caan has the title role as the lost ex-jock who can't find out why life is so hard. Supporting cast is good, but the script sinks everyone involved.

1970 74 minutes

RACHEL, RACHEL

★★★½

DIRECTOR: Paul Newman

CAST: Joanne Woodward, James Olson, Kate Harrington, Estelle Parsons

Paul Newman's directorial debut focuses on a spinsterish schoolteacher (Joanne Woodward) and her awakening to a world beyond her job and her elderly mother's influence. One of the first and still one of the best modern "women's" films made in America, this bittersweet story is perfectly acted by Woodward, with strong support by James Olson as her short-term lover and Estelle Parsons as her friend. Rewarding on all levels and one of the best "first efforts" by any director. Rated R.

1968 101 minutes

RACING WITH THE MOON

★★★½

DIRECTOR: Richard Benjamin

CAST: Sean Penn, Elizabeth McGovern, Nicolas Cage, John Karlen, Rutianya Alda, Carol Kane

Sean Penn and Elizabeth McGovern star in this entertaining and touching comedy-romance set during World War II. He's just a regular town boy who discovers he's fallen in love with a "Gatsby," one of the area's rich girls. But that doesn't stop him from trying to win her heart. Richard Benjamin does a solid job of directing, balancing moments of romance, comedy, excitement, and suspense. The stars are attractive, believable, and likable. Rated R for nudity, profanity, suggested sex, and brief violence.

1984 108 minutes

RACKET, THE

★★★

DIRECTOR: John Cromwell

CAST: Robert Mitchum, Robert Ryan, Lizabeth Scott, William Talman, Ray Collins, Joyce MacKenzie, Robert Hutton

This pessimistic look at political corruption focuses on the steps honest police captain Robert Mitchum takes in order to bring underworld figure Robert Ryan to justice. Mitchum is a man alone as he confronts seemingly insurmountable opposition from both police and political higher-ups who want to keep things just as crooked as they are. A remake of Howard Hughes's silent hit of the same name, this film was initially based on a popular stage play and veteran tough-guy writer W. R. Burnett (*Little Caesar*, *Scarface*, *of the Sierra Madre*) was called in to tighten up the script.

1951 B & W 88 minutes

RAGE

★★★

DIRECTOR: George C. Scott

CAST: George C. Scott, Martin Sheen, Richard Basehart, Barnard Hughes

This pits a lone man against the impersonal Establishment (in this instance the U.S. Army). This is not a happy film by any means, but it is an interesting one. Making his directorial debut, George C. Scott plays a peaceful sheep rancher whose son is the victim of military chemical testing. Seeking revenge, he sets out to nail those responsible. Rated PG.

1972 104 minutes

RAGING BULL

★★★★½

DIRECTOR: Martin Scorsese

CAST: Robert De Niro, Cathy Moriarty, Joe Pesci, Frank Vincent, Nicholas Colasanto, Theresa Saldana

This is a tough, compelling film . . . in fact, a great one. Directed by Martin Scorsese (*Alice Doesn't Live Here Anymore* and *Taxi Driver*) and starring the incredible Robert De Niro, it's one movie you won't want to miss. In playing prize fighter Jake La Motta from his twenties through to middle age, De Niro undergoes a transformation that takes him from his normal weight of 150 to 212 pounds. That is startling in itself, but the performance he gives is even more startling—see it. Rated R.

1980 B & W 128 minutes

RAGTIME

★★★★½

DIRECTOR: Milos Forman

CAST: James Cagney, Brad Dourif, Pat O'Brien, Donald O'Connor, Elizabeth McGovern, Mary Steenburgen

James Cagney returned to the screen after an absence of twenty years in this brilliant screen adaptation of E. L. Doctorow's best-selling novel about New York City at the turn of the century. It's a bountifully rewarding motion picture. Rated PG because of violence.

1981 155 minutes

RAID ON ENTEBBE

★★★

DIRECTOR: Irvin Kershner

CAST: Peter Finch, Charles Bronson, Horst Buchholz, Martin Balsam, John Saxon, Jack Warden, Yaphet Kotto

Second of three dramas filmed in 1976–1977 about the daring Israeli commando assault on the Entebbe airport in Uganda, this TV movie avoids the soap-opera tone of the earlier *Victory at Entebbe* (also made for TV) and focuses on the action and power struggle between the Israelis and crazed 'president for life', Idi Amin. The cast and script put this above most TV movies; the timeliness of the subject matter made it more effective when it was initially shown, but it's still worth a watch. The story was also filmed for theatrical release as *Operation Thunderbolt*, perhaps the best of the three versions. *Raid on Entebbe* was Peter Finch's last film.

1977 150 minutes

RAILROADED

★★★

DIRECTOR: Anthony Mann

CAST: John Ireland, Sheila Ryan, Hugh Beaumont, Ed Kelly, Jane Randolph, Keefe Brasselle

Future TV father Hugh Beaumont has his hands full as a police detective trying to run interference between gangster John Ireland and his intended victim Sheila Ryan. Tough, tight, and deadly, this early effort from director Anthony Mann oozes suspense and remains a fine example of American *film noir*, modestly budgeted and effectively conveyed. Good work all the way around, with future leading man Keefe Brasselle doing a standout bit in a supporting role. Long before he became forever typed as Ward Cleaver, Beaumont costarred with big names like Alan Ladd and James Cagney in crime dramas and played the lead in the last five films featuring the adventures of Michael Shayne, two-fisted private investigator. Don't tell the Beav, though.

1947 B & W 71 minutes

RAIN

★★★★

DIRECTOR: Lewis Milestone

CAST: Joan Crawford, Walter Huston, William Gargan, Guy Kibbee, Walter Catlett, Beulah Bondi

Joan Crawford plays island hussy Sadie Thompson in this depressing drama. Walter Huston is the preacher who wants to "save" her —for himself.

1932 B & W 93 minutes

RAIN PEOPLE, THE

★★★★

DIRECTOR: Francis Ford Coppola

CAST: James Caan, Shirley Knight, Robert Duvall, Marya Zimmet, Tom Aldredge, Lloyd Crews

James Caan plays a retired football star who is picked up by a bored pregnant woman (played by Shirley Knight). She felt trapped as a housewife and ran away from her husband to be free. Directed by Francis Ford Coppola, this is an interesting, well-acted character study. Rated R.

1969 102 minutes

RAINTREE COUNTY

★★★

DIRECTOR: Edward Dmytryk

CAST: Elizabeth Taylor, Montgomery Clift, Eva Marie Saint, Nigel Patrick, Lee Marvin, Rod Taylor, Agnes Moorehead, Walter Abel, Rhys Williams

Civil War melodrama with Elizabeth Taylor as a southern belle is two and one-half hours of showy tedium that wastes a fine cast and miles of film. Best-selling novel comes to the screen as an extended soap opera with little promise and less results. Beautiful Elizabeth Taylor fiddle-de-dees her way around spectacular settings guided by impressive music, but the whole production is hollow and has no purpose or substance. Montgomery Clift's near-fatal car crash forced production to slow down on this ponderous epic, but even the extra time couldn't produce enough of a story to spark this overblown effort. Clift plays a wary second lead in this film, and his insecurities and physical pain as a result of the accident and subsequent plastic surgery are evident in his lack of success in imbuing this MGM entry with some of his charm and acting skill.

1957 168 minutes

RAISIN IN THE SUN, A

★★★★

DIRECTOR: Daniel Petrie

CAST: Sidney Poitier, Claudia McNeil, Ruby Dee, Diana Sands, Ivan Dixon, John Fiedler, Louis Gossett Jr.

A black family tries to escape from their crowded apartment life by moving to a house in an all-white neighborhood. Sidney Poitier delivers his usual outstanding performance in this film with a message about the limited opportunities open to blacks in the 1950s.

1961 B & W 128 minutes

RATBOY

DIRECTOR: Sondra Locke

CAST: Sondra Locke, Robert Townsend, Louie Anderson, Gerrit Graham, Christopher Hewlett, Larry Hankin, Chris Lassick, Sharon Baird, Bill Bird

Not a horror film but a satirical allegory directed by and starring Sondra Locke. Eugene, a boy with the face of a rat, is torn out of his peaceful existence in a dump by an unemployed window dresser (Locke). She sees him as her ticket to the big time. With her two brothers, she sets out to market the ratboy as a media star. The film is unrelentingly cynical, and none of the characters, save the unfortunate Eugene, is sympathetic. Louie Anderson, the overweight Canadian comic, provides some funny moments as Omer, one of the bumbling brothers. But, on the whole, the satirical bent of the film isn't successfully maintained throughout. Rated PG-13 for profanity and some violence.

1986 104 minutes

RAZOR'S EDGE, THE (ORIGINAL)

★★★★½

DIRECTOR: Edmund Goulding

CAST: Tyrone Power, Gene Tierney, Clifton Webb, Herbert Marshall, Anne Baxter, John Payne, Elsa Lanchester

A long but engrossing presentation of Somerset Maugham's philosophical novel about a young man seeking the goodness in life. Full of memorable characterizations and scenes. Herbert Marshall steers the plot, playing the author. Clifton Webb is brilliant as arch-snob Elliot Templeton; Gene Tierney is beautiful and selfish. Tyrone Power is fine as Larry, who sees more to life than money and social position. Standing out are Anne Baxter as Sophie, whose tragic personal losses drive her to dipsomania, and Elsa Lanchester as a prim social secretary with a soft center.

1946 B & W 146 minutes

RAZOR'S EDGE, THE (REMAKE)

★★★½

DIRECTOR: John Byrum

CAST: Bill Murray, Theresa Russell, Catharine Hicks, James Keach, Brian Doyle-Murray

Bill Murray gives a finely balanced comic and dramatic portrayal as Larry Darrell, a man searching for meaning after World War I in this adaptation of W. Somerset Maugham's novel. The result is a richly rewarding film, which survives the unevenness of John Byrum's direction. Rated PG-13 for suggested sex, violence, and profanity.

1984 128 minutes

REBECCA

★★★★★

DIRECTOR: Alfred Hitchcock

CAST: Laurence Olivier, Joan Fontaine, George Sanders, Nigel Bruce, Reginald Denny, Judith Anderson

Alfred Hitchcock made a very auspicious debut in American films with *Rebecca* which won an Oscar for best picture and nominations for its stars, Laurence Olivier and Joan Fontaine. The popular Daphne du Maurier novel was transferred to the screen by cameraman George Barnes without losing any of its gothic blend of romance and mystery. In it, a shy American (Fontaine) is acting as a conceited woman's traveling companion in Europe. After a whirlwind courtship, she marries the brooding Max de Winter (Olivier). Her chances for happiness with this secretive man hinge on her ability to break through the shroud that envelops his past. Somehow the key to unlocking the mystery lies with his dead first wife, Rebecca. Judith Anderson as the sinister housekeeper is one of the most compelling figures in film history.

1940 B & W 130 minutes

REBECCA OF SUNNYBROOK FARM

★★½

DIRECTOR: Marshall Neilan

CAST: Mary Pickford, Eugene O'Brien, Helen Jerome Eddy,

Charles Ogle, Mayme Kelso, Josephine Crowell

One again, the adult Mary Pickford successfully portrays a saucy teenager who wins love, respect, and prosperity in this rags-to-riches tearjerker based on the famous Kate Douglas Wiggin bestseller. Shirley Temple starred in a talkie version in 1938. Silent.

1917 B & W 77 minutes

REBEL

DIRECTOR: Michael Jenkins
CAST: Matt Dillon, Debbie Byrne, Bryan Brown, Bill Hunter, Ray Barrett, Julie Nihill, John O'May, Kim Deacon

During World War II, a marine sergeant in Australia goes AWOL and falls in love with a nightclub singer. He is torn between trying to get home to the States and staying Down Under. This soap opera quickly gets mired in sludge. The musical numbers are really the only recommendable ingredient (even though the songs are too contemporary to have been composed in the 1940s). Rated R for profanity and adult situations.

1985 93 minutes

REBEL WITHOUT A CAUSE

★★★★★

DIRECTOR: Nicholas Ray
CAST: James Dean, Natalie Wood, Sal Mineo, Jim Backus, Ann Doran, Corey Allen, Edward Platt, Dennis Hopper, Nick Adams

This is the film that made James Dean a legend. Directed by Nicholas Ray, it is undoubtedly the classic film about juvenile delinquency. Featuring fine performances by Dean (in one of only three screen appearances, the others being *East of Eden* and *Giant*), Natalie Wood, and Sal Mineo as the teens in trouble, it has stood up surprisingly well over the years. It and *The Wild One* are the only 1950s "bad youth" movies that still pack a punch today.

1955 111 minutes

RECKLESS

★★

DIRECTOR: James Foley
CAST: Aidan Quinn, Daryl Hannah, Kenneth McMillan, Cliff DeYoung, Lois Smith, Adam Baldwin, Dan Hedaya

A 1980s version of the standard 1950s "angry young man" movie, this features Aidan Quinn as a motorcycle-riding, mumbling (à la James Dean and Marlon Brando) outcast and Daryl Hannah (*Summer Lovers*) as the "good girl." She is the A-student cheerleader both attracted and repelled by the danger he represents. Wait a minute . . . wasn't that the synopsis of *Breathless*? It was, and that should give you an idea of how original this movie is—about as original as the cliché "a stitch in time saves nine." You can save some money if you skip this uninspired release. Rated R for nudity, profanity, violence, and suggested sex.

1984 90 minutes

RED BADGE OF COURAGE, THE

★★★½

DIRECTOR: John Huston
CAST: Audie Murphy, Bill Mauldin, Royal Dano, Arthur Hunnicutt, Douglas Dick

Natural performances mark this realistic treatment of Stephen Crane's famous Civil War novel of a young soldier's initiation to battle. A John Huston classic, and a major film achievement by any standard.

1951 B & W 69 minutes

RED DUST

★★★★

DIRECTOR: Victor Fleming
CAST: Clark Gable, Jean Harlow, Mary Astor, Donald Crisp, Gene Raymond, Tully Marshall, Willie Fung

Red Dust is one of those remarkable films where the performances of its stars propel a movie to classic status despite a rather uninspired story. The erotic chemistry between Clark Gable and Jean Harlow generates much more magic than the hackneyed story of a rubber plantation boss (Gable) who dallies with another man's wife only to return to the arms of a shady lady (Harlow) with the proverbial heart of gold.

1932 B & W 83 minutes

RED KIMONO, THE

★½

DIRECTOR: Walter Lang
CAST: Priscilla Bonner, Nellie Bly Baker, Carl Miller, Mary Carr, Tyrone Power Sr.

The widow of tragic screen favorite Wallace Reid dedicated herself to helping squelch the drug traffic that she felt destroyed her husband. To achieve this goal, she produced moralistic films like *Human Wreckage*, which barnstormed rural America. *Red Kimono* is a tawdry story about a young lady who is abandoned by her philandering husband and forced to become a scarlet woman. When she encounters her former husband in a shop purchasing a wedding ring for his new victim, she reacts in rage and shoots him dead. The story is told in flashbacks as the wretched woman sits on the witness stand. Cheap and corny, this exploitation film exists in versions of different lengths; some versions run as short as seventy-five minutes while other copies are twenty minutes longer. Silent.

1925 B & W 95 minutes

RED LIGHT STING, THE

★★

DIRECTOR: Rod Holcomb
CAST: Farrah Fawcett, Beau Bridges, Harold Gould, Paul Burke, Alex Henteloff, Conrad Janis, Sunny Johnson, James Luisi, Philip Charles MacKenzie

Pale TV film about a young district attorney (Beau Bridges) who is assigned to buy a whorehouse to bring out an elusive big-time crook (Harold Gould). Farrah Fawcett plays a hooker whom Bridges confides in. Very few surprises and the screenplay is pedestrian, but entertaining enough to engage the attention. Not rated, but the equivalent of a PG for adult subject matter.

1984 96 minutes

REDS

★★★★★

DIRECTOR: Warren Beatty
CAST: Warren Beatty, Diane Keaton, Jack Nicholson, Gene Hackman, Edward Herrmann, Maureen Stapleton, Jerzy Kosinski

Warren Beatty produced, directed, co-wrote, and starred in this $33 million American film masterpiece. This three-hour-plus film biography of left-wing American journalist John Reed (Beatty) and Louise Bryant (Diane Keaton) also features brilliant bits from Jack Nicholson, Gene Hackman, Edward Herrmann, Maureen Stapleton, and Jerzy Kosinski (author of *Being There*). Rated PG because of profanity, silhouetted sex scenes, and war scenes.

1981 200 minutes

REFLECTIONS IN A GOLDEN EYE

★★½

DIRECTOR: John Huston
CAST: Marlon Brando, Elizabeth Taylor, Brian Keith, Julie Harris, Robert Forster, Zorro David

Very bizarre film concerning a homosexual army officer (Marlon Brando) stationed in the South. This very strange film very rarely works—despite a high-powered cast.

1967 108 minutes

REMBRANDT

★★★★

DIRECTOR: Alexander Korda
CAST: Charles Laughton, Gertrude Lawrence, Elsa Lanchester

This is one of the few satisfying movie biographies of an artist. The depiction of the famous Dutch painter and his struggle to maintain his artistic integrity is related with respectful restraint and attention to factual detail. Charles Laughton, as Rembrandt, is brilliant in what was for him an atypically low-key performance. More than any of his screen characterizations, this role shows how completely Laughton was a master of his craft. The sets deserve special praise. They capture the feel of Dutch life in the seventeenth century.

1936 B & W 90 minutes

RENO AND THE DOC

★★½

DIRECTOR: Charles Dennis
CAST: Ken Walsh, Henry Ramer, Linda Griffiths, Laura Dickson

Though it has a slow start, this tale of two middle-aged men brought together by mental telepathy soon gains momentum. Ken Walsh plays Reno, a solitary mountain man who is induced by Doc (Henry Ramer) to enter the pro-ski tour. Reno's surprising success leads to his romance with Savannah, a *Sports Illustrated* writer (Linda Griffiths). Mild nudity and obscenities.

1984 88 minutes

REQUIEM FOR A HEAVYWEIGHT

★★★½

DIRECTOR: Ralph Nelson
CAST: Anthony Quinn, Julie Harris, Jackie Gleason, Mickey Rooney, Muhammad Ali

Anthony Quinn, Julie Harris, Jackie Gleason, Mickey Roney, and Muhammad Ali (at that time Cassius Clay) give fine performances in this watchable film about boxing corruption. An over-the-hill boxer (Quinn) receives career counseling from a social worker (Harris).

1962 B & W 100 minutes

RESURRECTION

★★★★½

DIRECTOR: Daniel Petrie
CAST: Ellen Burstyn, Sam Shepard, Richard Farnsworth, Roberts Blossom, Clifford David, Pamela Payton-Wright, Eva LeGallienne

Ellen Burstyn's superb performance is but one of the topflight elements in this emotional powerhouse of a film written by Lewis John Carlino (*Great Santini*) and directed by Daniel Petrie. After Burstyn loses her husband and the use of her legs in a freak automobile accident, she discovers she has the power to heal not only herself but anyone who is sick or crippled. Pulitzer Prize–winning playwright Sam Shepard is also memorable as the young hellraiser who begins to believe she is Jesus reborn. It's strong stuff, intelligently handled. Rated PG.

1980 103 minutes

RETURN OF THE SOLDIER, THE

★★★★★

DIRECTOR: Alan Bridges
CAST: Glenda Jackson, Julie Christie, Ann-Margret, Alan Bates, Ian Holm, Frank Finlay, Jeremy Kemp

During World War I, a soldier (Alan Bates) suffers shell shock and forgets the last twenty years of his life. His doctors must decide whether he should be allowed to enjoy what has resulted in a carefree second youth, or be brought back to real life and the responsibilities—to say nothing of horrifying battle experience memories—that go with it. Glenda Jackson is the childhood sweetheart he longs to hold once again. Julie Christie is the selfish wife who wants him "normal" (and unhappy) again. Ann-Margret is the loving sister who only wishes him happiness. Everyone in the cast is superb. Not rated, the film contains adult situations.

1985 105 minutes

REVOLUTION

★★

DIRECTOR: Hugh Hudson
CAST: Al Pacino, Nastassja Kinski, Donald Sutherland

Director Hugh Hudson must have had good intentions going into this project, examining what it might have been like to be involved in the American Revolution. The sets, costumes, battle scenes, and cinematography are some of the best to be put on film. Unfortunately, his actors are so miscast and the script so ragged that Hudson's project stalls almost before it gets started. Al Pacino and his son become caught up in the frenzy of the early days of the Revolution and soon find themselves facing the British, led by Donald Sutherland. We follow them through several years and historical events for the next two grueling hours. Rated R.

1986 125 minutes

RICH AND FAMOUS

★★★★

DIRECTOR: George Cukor
CAST: Jacqueline Bisset, Candice Bergen, David Selay, Hart Bochner, Steven Hill, Meg Ryan, Matt Lattanzi, Michael Brandon

Jacqueline Bisset and Candice Bergen star in this warm, witty, and involving chronicle of the ups, downs, joys, and heartbreak experienced by two friends during a twenty-year relationship. Hollywood great George Cukor (*The Philadelphia Story*) directed in his inimitable style. Rated R because of profanity and sex.

1981 117 minutes

RICH KIDS

★★

DIRECTOR: Robert M. Young
CAST: Trini Alvarado, Jeremy Levy, John Lithgow, Kathryn Walker, Terry Kiser, Paul Dooley

A poor screenplay (which includes some incredibly bad jokes) plagues this movie about two kids going through puberty at the same time they are experiencing the dissolution of their parents' marriages. A great cast helps. Also, there is an unforgettable heartfelt moment between mother and daughter (Kathryn Walker and Trini Alvarado). Rated PG for language.

1979 97 minutes

RICHARD'S THINGS

★★

DIRECTOR: Anthony Harvey
CAST: Liv Ullmann, Amanda Redman, Elizabeth Spriggs, David Markham

Gloomy drama about a widow who gets seduced by her late husband's girlfriend. Liv Ullmann plays the patsy as if she were on depressants. Promises of the film's premise are never kept.

1980 104 minutes

RICHARD III

★★★★

DIRECTOR: Laurence Olivier
CAST: Laurence Olivier, Ralph Richardson, John Gielgud, Claire Bloom

Once again, as in *Henry V* and *Hamlet*, England's foremost player displays his near-matchless acting and directing skills in bringing Shakespeare to life on film. His royal crookback usurper is beautifully malevolent, a completely intriguing, smiling villain. The film fascinates from first to last.

1955 161 minutes

RIGHT OF WAY

★★★★

DIRECTOR: George Shaefer
CAST: James Stewart, Bette Davis, Melinda Dillon, Priscilla Morrill, John Harkins

This made-for-cable work deals with a rather unusual decision made by an old married couple, Mini and Teddy Dwyer (Bette Davis and James Stewart, respectively), who have decided to commit suicide. Mini has a terminal blood disease and doesn't want to go through the agony of a slow death. And Teddy, who is completely devoted to his lifelong mate, has no desire to go on without her. Thus begins a battle between daughter (Melinda Dillon) and parents: one that grows from a personal dispute to a newspaper scandal. The result is a surprisingly gripping character study. Davis is excellent as the strong-willed, sharp-tongued matriarch. Stewart, of course, is as watchable as always. But it is Dillon who nearly steals the picture, with her affecting portrayal of the confused but concerned daughter.

1983 106 minutes

RIGHT STUFF, THE

★★★★★

DIRECTOR: Phil Kaufman
CAST: Sam Shepard, Scott Glenn, Ed Harris, Dennis Quaid, Barbara Hershey, Fred Ward, Kim Stanley, Veronica Cartwright, Pamela Reed, Donald Moffat, Levon Helm, Scott Wilson, Jeff Goldblum, Harry Shearer

The most impressive American screen drama since *The Godfather*. From Tom Wolfe's bestseller about the early years of the American space program, writer-director Phil Kaufman has created an epic screen tribute to, and examination of, the men (both test pilots and astronauts) who "pushed the outside of the envelope," and the women who watched and waited while the world watched them. Rated PG for profanity.

1983 193 minutes

RITA HAYWORTH: THE LOVE GODDESS

★★½

DIRECTOR: James Goldstone
CAST: Lynda Carter, Michael Lerner, John Considine, Alejandro Rey

This lifeless attempt to recreate pinup queen Rita Hayworth's exciting life falls short of its goal. Beautiful Lynda Carter ("Wonder Woman") as Hayworth, however, keeps the viewer's attention. Made for television.

1983 100 minutes

RIVER, THE

★★★★

DIRECTOR: Pare Lorentz
CAST: Documentary

Blending historical footage, Hollywood film excerpts, and newly shot footage, ace documentary filmmaker Pare Lorentz recounts the story of the gigantic Mississippi River—where it comes from, where it goes, what it means to the nation, and what it has cost—from the Civil War to the 1930s. Truly a cinematic masterpiece, it was denied Academy Award recognition when a jealous Hollywood whined about it having been financed by the federal government.

1937 B & W 32 minutes

RIVER, THE

★★★½

DIRECTOR: Mark Rydell

CAST: Mel Gibson, Sissy Spacek, Scott Glenn

Had it been the first of its kind, this film, starring Mel Gibson, Sissy Spacek, and Scott Glenn, could very well have been heralded as a powerful drama, if not a great motion picture. But following as it does on the heels of two other first-rate farmer films, this work by director Mark Rydell (*On Golden Pond*) often seems hopelessly unoriginal and, as a result, boring. As with *Country*, it deals with a farming family—the Garveys—who must battle a severe storm and foreclosure proceedings. Like Sally Field's character in *Places in the Heart*, the Garveys must resort to extreme methods to survive. *The River* is not a bad film. It is, in fact, a very good one. It simply has little new to say. Rated PG for nudity, violence, and profanity.

1984 122 minutes

RIVER OF UNREST

★★

DIRECTORS: Brian Desmond, Walter Summers

CAST: John Lodge, John Loder, Antoinette Cellier, Niall MacGinnis, Clifford Evans

Melodrama about the Sinn Fein rebellion in Ireland bears a strong resemblance to John Ford's classic *The Informer*, but there's more emphasis on the love story between Antoinette Cellier and the two men in her life. Good performances by a capable cast help this slow-moving story, which was based on a stage play. Filmed in England with a British cast that included John Loder, who made films with some degree of success in America in the 1940s.

1937 B & W 69 minutes

RIVER RAT, THE

★★★½

DIRECTOR: Tom Rickman

CAST: Tommy Lee Jones, Martha Plimpton, Brian Dennehy

Although essentially the story of the growing love between a long-separated father (Tommy Lee Jones), who has been in prison for thirteen years, and daughter (newcomer Martha Plimpton), this release is much more than a simple tearjerker. Writer-director Tom Rickman has invested his story with a grit and realism that set it apart from similar works. As a result, he's created a powerful, thought-provoking motion picture. Rated R for profanity and violence.

1984 109 minutes

RIVER'S EDGE

★★★½

DIRECTOR: Tim Hunter

CAST: Dennis Hopper, Crispin Glover, Keanu Reeves, Ione Skye Leitch, Roxana Zal, Daniel Roebuck, Joshua Miller, Tom Bower, Leo Rossi

This is a deeply disturbing film based by screenwriter Neal Jimenez on a real-life 1980 murder case. The teen-age murderer in *River's Edge* takes his friends to see the corpse of his classmate-victim. The death becomes a secret bond among them until two decent kids (Keanu Reeves, Ione Skye Leitch) decide to do something about it. The movie is hampered by an overly hammy performance by Crispin Glover as the gang leader and Jimenez's device of having Dennis Hopper, as a drug-dealing ex-biker named Feck, tote around a sex doll. Despite these misguided artistic touches, the film packs a punch. Rated R for violence, profanity, nudity, and simulated sex.

1987 99 minutes

ROBE, THE

★★★★

DIRECTOR: Henry Koster
CAST: Richard Burton, Victor Mature, Jean Simmons, Michael Rennie, Richard Boone, Dean Jagger, Dawn Addams, Jan Robinson

Richard Burton is the Roman tribune charged with overseeing the execution of Christ in this story of his involvement with the followers of Christ and the effect the robe of Jesus has on all involved. It is a well-made film, and although it revolves around a religious subject, it is not heavy-handed in its approach. Well-acted performances are turned in by Burton, the tribune who must make a choice, and Victor Mature, as the follower of Christ.

1953 135 minutes

ROCKY

★★★★½

DIRECTOR: John G. Avildsen
CAST: Sylvester Stallone, Talia Shire, Burt Young, Burgess Meredith, Carl Weathers, Thayer David

Despite the spectacular success of *Rocky III*, this initial adventure of Sylvester Stallone's boxing Everyman is still the best. It is a moving portrait of a man's fight to regain his dignity. Rated PG.

1976 119 minutes

ROCKY II

★★

DIRECTOR: Sylvester Stallone
CAST: Sylvester Stallone, Carl Weathers, Talia Shire, Burgess Meredith, Burt Young

The weakest entry in Sylvester Stallone's boxing trilogy, about a down-and-out fighter attempting to prove himself through a rematch with the champ (Carl Weathers). Talia Shire, Burgess Meredith, and Burt Young reprise their series roles in this soaper in the ring. Rated PG.

1979 119 minutes

ROCKY III

★★★

DIRECTOR: Sylvester Stallone
CAST: Sylvester Stallone, Talia Shire, Burgess Meredith, Mr. T, Carl Weathers

Writer-director-star Sylvester Stallone's third entry in the Rocky Balboa series is surprisingly entertaining. Though we've seen it all before, Stallone manages to make it work one more time—and even better than in *Rocky II*. That's no small feat. Rated PG for violence and mild profanity.

1982 99 minutes

ROCKY IV

★★★

DIRECTOR: Sylvester Stallone
CAST: Sylvester Stallone, Talia Shire, Burt Young, Carl Weathers, Brigitte Nielsen, Tony Burton, Michael Pataki, Dolph Lundgren

Sylvester Stallone's Everyman boxing hero returns to take on a massive Russian fighter (Dolph Lundgren) trained via computer and programmed to kill. The result is deliciously corny, enjoyably predictable entertainment. *Rocky IV* is not unlike an old-fashioned chapter serial with its cliffhanger situations, goody good guys, and dastardly villains. Even though we know the *Rocky* formula—an early failure by the good guys, a bit of soul searching by the hero, the training sequence, and the final confrontation—the movie works. Rated PG for violence and profanity.

1985 90 minutes

RODEO GIRL

★★★★

DIRECTOR: Jackie Cooper

CAST: Katharine Ross, Bo Hopkins, Candy Clark, Jacqueline Brookes, Wilford Brimley

Katharine Ross (*The Graduate, Butch Cassidy and the Sundance Kid)* is Sammy, the wife of rodeo champ Will Garrett (Bo Hopkins). When she decides to try her hand at roping and bronco riding, she finds that she has the potential to be a rodeo champ. But complications arise when she discovers she is pregnant. Of course, Will wants Sammy to forget the rodeo circuit, and with Sammy's refusal, the conflict begins. *Rodeo Girl* offers a fresh resolution to an old conflict. Still, the film has its drawbacks: Ross's performance is inconsistent, and Candy Clark (*American Grafitti, Blue Thunder*), who plays Sammy's roping teammate, misses the "good ol' cowgirl" mark by overdoing a southern twang. Based on a true story. Rated G.

1980 92 minutes

ROLLOVER

★★★½

DIRECTOR: Alan J. Pakula

CAST: Jane Fonda, Kris Kristofferson, Hume Cronyn, Josef Sommer, Bob Gunton

Jane Fonda plays an ex–film star who inherits a multimillion-dollar empire when her husband is mysteriously murdered in this gripping, but not great, film. Kris Kristofferson is the financial troubleshooter who joins forces with her to save the company. Soon both their lives are in danger. Rated R because of profanity.

1981 118 minutes

ROMAN HOLIDAY

★★★★★

DIRECTOR: William Wyler

CAST: Gregory Peck, Audrey Hepburn, Eddie Albert

Amid the beauty and mystique of Rome, an American newspaperman (Gregory Peck) is handed a news scoop on the proverbial silver platter. A princess (Audrey Hepburn) has slipped away from her stifling royal lifestyle. In her efforts to hide as one of Rome's common people, she encounters Peck. Their amiable adventures provide the basis for a charming fantasy-romance.

1953 B & W 119 minutes

ROMAN SPRING OF MRS. STONE, THE

★★½

DIRECTOR: Jose Quintero

CAST: Vivien Leigh, Warren Beatty, Lotte Lenya, Jill St. John

A sensitive, elegant middle-aged actress (Vivien Leigh) has retreated to Rome to get a new focus. Warren Beatty plays a sleek, surly, wet-lipped Italian gigolo out for what he can get with the help of a crass, waspish procuress (Lotte Lenya). It's all banal. Based on a Tennessee Williams novel.

1961 104 minutes

ROMANTIC ENGLISHWOMAN, THE

★★★★

DIRECTOR: Joseph Losey

CAST: Glenda Jackson, Michael Caine, Helmut Berger

Though not a completely successful adaptation of Thomas Wiseman's novel (by Wiseman and playwright Tom Stoppard), this is likely to be vastly more engaging than anything on television on any given night. Casual infidelity among the wealthy intelligentsia is always at least voyeuristically satisfying. And here pulp novel writer Michael Caine actually impels his discontented, but presumably faithful, wife Glenda Jackson into an affair with gigolo Helmut Berger. This tragicomedy of manners is scarcely explicit: it is as superficially refined as are its characters—but there is real Continental sleaze lurking beneath the snappy dialogue, the lush scenery, and the impeccably tailored clothes. All the principals are in top form, however Helmut Berger's role fits him like a fine glove. Rated R for language, adult situations.

1975 115 minutes

ROMEO AND JULIET

★★★★½

DIRECTOR: Franco Zeffirelli
CAST: Olivia Hussey, Leonard Whiting, John McEnery, Michael York, Milo O'Shea

Franco Zeffirelli directed this excellent version of *Romeo and Juliet*. When it was filmed, Olivia Hussey was only 15 and Leonard Whiting was only 17, keeping their characters in tune with Shakespeare's hero and heroine. Rated PG.

1968 138 minutes

ROOM WITH A VIEW, A

★★★★★

DIRECTOR: James Ivory
CAST: Maggie Smith, Helena Bonham Carter, Denholm Elliott, Julian Sands, Daniel Day Lewis, Simon Callow, Judi Dench, Rosemary Leach

Adapted from the novel by E. M. Forster, this is a triumph of tasteful, intelligent filmmaking. Director James Ivory (*The Bostonians*) painstakingly re-creates the mood, manners, and milieu of 1908 Edwardian England as he explores the consequence of a tour of Florence, Italy, taken by an innocently curious young woman (Helena Bonham Carter) and her persnickety, meddling aunt (Maggie Smith, in top form). The characters, even down to the smallest supporting bit, are skillfully drawn by screenwriter Ruth Prawer Jhabvala, and the acting is exquisite. *A Room With a View* will especially please those with a fondness for the best in literature, music, and art. Even those with less cultivated tastes may find watching it a rare and wonderful experience. Unrated, the film has one brief scene of violence and some male frontal nudity.

1986 115 minutes

ROSELAND

★★★½

DIRECTOR: James Ivory
CAST: Christopher Walken, Geraldine Chaplin, Teresa Wright, Lou Jacobi, Don DeNatale, Lilia Skala

Protean—and gentleman—filmmaker James Ivory and his collaborators (Ruth Prawer Jhabvala, screenplay, Ismail Merchant, producer) have fashioned a somewhat overly respectful triptych set in the famous, now-tattered, New York dance palace. The three stories about aging people seeking a haven of nostalgia are quietly compelling, but only Christopher Walken (certainly a good enough dancer and showing here a preview of his talents in *Pennies from Heaven*) and Don DeNatale (who was an emcee at Roseland) give the film any vim. It did receive a seven-minute standing ovation at the New York Film Festival; we don't ask that you do the same.

1977 103 minutes

RUBY GENTRY

★★★

DIRECTOR: King Vidor
CAST: Jennifer Jones, Charlton Heston, Karl Malden, Tom Tully

An excellent cast and sensitive direction make this drama of a Carolina swamp girl's social progress better than might be expected. Its focus is the caste system and prejudice in a picturesque region of the great melting pot.

1952 B & W 82 minutes

RUMBLE FISH

★★

DIRECTOR: Francis Ford Coppola
CAST: Christopher Penn, Tom Waites, Matt Dillon, Dennis Hopper, Vincent Spano

Francis Ford Coppola's black-and-white screen portrait of S. E. Hinton's second-rate novel about a teen-age boy (Matt Dillon) seeking to escape his hellish life is a disappointing misfire. Rated R.

1983 B & W 94 minutes

RUNNER STUMBLES, THE

★★★

DIRECTOR: Stanley Kramer
CAST: Dick Van Dyke, Kathleen Quinlan, Maureen Stapleton, Beau Bridges

A good adaptation of Milan Stitt's play, which certainly did not deserve the scorching hatred generated during its brief box-office appearance. Dick Van Dyke plays a priest who falls in love with Kathleen Quinlan's appealing nun. Subsequent thoughts and counterthoughts are talked to death, which betrays the story's origin on-stage, but both leads contribute sensitive performances. The subject may make viewers uneasy, but the film is by no means tacky or exploitative. A near miss, but still worth catching. Rated PG for adult subject matter.

1979 99 minutes

RUNNING BRAVE

★★★★

DIRECTOR: Don Shebib
CAST: Robby Benson, Pat Hingle, Jeff McCracken

Robby Benson stars as Billy Mills, whose winning the ten-thousand meter race in the 1964 Olympics was one of the biggest upsets in sports history. The direction, credited to "D. S. Everett" (a pseudonym for Don Shebib, who demanded his name be taken off the credits after the film was re-edited), is pedestrian at best. But Benson's fine performance and the true-life drama of Mills's determination to set a positive example of achievement for his people—the Sioux and all Native Americans—are affecting enough to carry the film. Rated PG for profanity.

1983 105 minutes

RUNNING HOT

★★★

DIRECTOR: Mark Griffiths
CAST: Eric Stoltz, Stuart Margolin, Monica Carrico, Virgil Frye

Eric Stoltz gives a very good performance as a 17-year-old convicted of killing his father and sentenced to death row. The publicity of his case arouses the interest of 30-year-old Monica Carrico, who sends him love letters in prison. His escape and bizarre affair with her have serious consequences in this fast-paced drama. Through flashbacks we are shown the surprising facts to the crime. Rated R for sex, violence, language, and nudity.

1983 88 minutes

RUNNING WILD

★★

DIRECTOR: Abner Biberman
CAST: William Campbell, Mamie Van Doren, Keenan Wynn, Katherine Case, Jan Merlin, John Saxon

Rookie cop William Campbell pretends to be a young tough in order to go undercover to get the goods on an auto theft gang headed by Keenan Wynn. Made to catch the teen-age rock-'n-roll crowd. Mamie Van Doren sings and twitches as the racy girlfriend of Wynn's lieutenant Jan Merlin. Mixed in is Wynn's hold over Katherine Case; he threatens to blow the whistle on her Nazi-fleeing father's illegal entry into the U.S.

1955 81 minutes

RYAN'S DAUGHTER

★★½

DIRECTOR: David Lean
CAST: Sarah Miles, Christopher Jones, Robert Mitchum, Trevor Howard, John Mills, Leo McKern

Director David Lean, who had been acclaimed for such films as *The Bridge on the River Kwai*, *Lawrence of Arabia*, and *Dr. Zhivago*, took a critical beating with this release, about a spoiled woman (Sarah Miles) who shamelessly lusts after an officer (Christopher Jones). Robert Michum, as Miles's long-suffering husband, is the best thing about this watchable misfire. Rated R.

1970 176 minutes

S.O.S. TITANIC

★★★

DIRECTOR: William Hale
CAST: David Janssen, Cloris Leachman, Susan Saint James, David Warner

The "unsinkable" pride of the Ismay Line once again goes to her watery grave deep beneath the cold Atlantic in this made-for-television docudrama compounded of fiction and fact.

1979 105 minutes

SAILOR WHO FELL FROM GRACE WITH THE SEA, THE

★★

DIRECTOR: Lewis John Carlino
CAST: Sarah Miles, Kris Kristofferson, Margo Cunningham, Earl Rhodes

Much of Japanese culture remains misunderstood, and this inept adaptation of Yukio Mishima's novel is a perfect example. Kris Kristofferson doesn't have to stretch his limited abilities as an amiable sailor who falls in love with Sarah Miles. Her son, unfortunately, views the relationship with less than delight . . . although he views it a lot, through an unseen peephole. Story attempts to turn its audience into voyeurs, like the boy, but the celebrated love scenes are too stiff and artificial. The boy then meets up with a friend who likes to dissect cats; things go downhill from there. Quite dull. Rated R for violence and sex.

1976 104 minutes

ST. BENNY THE DIP

★★

DIRECTOR: Edgar G. Ulmer
CAST: Dick Haymes, Nina Foch, Roland Young, Lionel Stander, Freddie Bartholomew

A good cast is about all that recommends this time-worn story of con artists who disguise their larceny behind clerics' robes and find themselves thinking clearer and walking the straight and narrow as a result of their contact with religion. Director Edgar G. Ulmer was responsible for one of Universal's most stylish horror masterpieces, *The Black Cat*, with Karloff and Lugosi, and he also churned out what is perhaps considered to be the finest low-budget B film of all time *Detour* but this stale vehicle fails to spark any interest. Former child star Freddie Bartholomew makes a rare adult appearance.

1951 B & W 79 minutes

ST. ELMO'S FIRE

★★★

DIRECTOR: Joel Schumacher
CAST: Emilio Estevez, Rob Lowe, Andrew McCarthy, Demi Moore, Judd Nelson, Ally Sheedy, Mare Winningham, Martin Balsam, Andie MacDowell, Joyce Van Patten

Written and directed by Joel Schumacher, this film would have us believe a group of college graduates are, at the age of 22, all suffering from mid-life crises. It's a little hard to believe. However, the fine acting by some of the screen's hottest young stars helps us forgive this off-kilter premise. In addition, Schumacher adds some nice touches of humanity and humor. The result is a good, though not great, movie that succeeds almost in spite of itself. Rated R for suggested sex, violence, nudity, and profanity.

1985 110 minutes

ST. HELENS

★★½

DIRECTOR: Ernest Pintoff
CAST: Art Carney, David Huffman, Cassie Yates, Albert Salmi, Ron O'Neal

Very shallow look at the Mount St. Helens volcanic eruption and the following disasters. Art Carney plays Harry, the old man who refuses to move from his home as the upcoming fiasco is about to take place. Pretty bland stuff. Rated PG for no particular reason.

1981 90 minutes

SAINT JACK

★★★½

DIRECTOR: Peter Bogdanovich
CAST: Ben Gazzara, Denholm Elliott, James Villiers, Joss Ackland, Peter Bogdanovich, George Lazenby

Although an interesting film, *Saint Jack* lacks power and a sense of wholeness. The story has all the right elements, but the treatment by director Peter Bogdanovich is rambling and lacking a specific point of view. Ben Gazzara plays an oddly likable pimp plying his trade in Singapore in the 1970s who wants to become rich and powerful by running the classiest whorehouse in the Far East. Even with its problems, this offbeat character study has its share of memorable moments. Gazzara and Denholm Elliott are first-rate. Rated R.

1979 112 minutes

SAINT JOAN

★★½

DIRECTOR: Otto Preminger
CAST: Jean Seberg, Richard Widmark, Richard Todd, John Gielgud, Anton Walbrook, Harry Andrews, Felix Aylmer

Even a screenplay by Graham Greene can't salvage Otto Preminger's dull screen version of George Bernard Shaw's intriguing play. Jean Seberg seems at a loss to convey the complexity of her character, and the presence of such perfomers as Richard Todd, Richard Widmark, John Gielgud, and Harry Andrews just remind one what a great production this could have been. Downbeat and muddled.

1957 B & W 110 minutes

SAKHAROV

★★★★

DIRECTOR: Jack Gold
CAST: Jason Robards Jr., Glenda Jackson, Michael Bryant, Paul Freeman, Anna Massey, Joe Melia, Lee Montague, Jim Norton

Compassionate story of the nuclear physicist and designer of the H-bomb, Andrei Sakharov (Jason Robards), who won the Nobel Peace Prize after waking up to the global terror of the nuclear gambit and contributing to the budding human rights movement in the Soviet Union during the late 1960s. The story bogs down at times, and while the predominantly British cast puts in fine performances (including Glenda Jackson, who plays Elena Bonner Sakharov, Andrei's brave and headstrong wife and political comrade), the accents do become a bit obtrusive at times.

1984 118 minutes

SALOME

★½

DIRECTOR: Claude D'Anna
CAST: Jo Ciampa, Tomas Milian, Pamela Salem, Tim Woodward, Fabrizio Bentivoglio

This is a strange mixture. It is the story of the famous temptress Salome, but in director Claude D'Anna's version the Roman soldiers are in World War II overcoats, there is an elevator in the palace, and the slaves are listening to portable radios. Whatever he had in mind—maybe Ken Russell is his idol—it doesn't make it. It's too bad, because Tomas Milian as Herod and Pamela Salem as Herodius give interesting performances. Rated R.

1985 105 minutes

SALVADOR

★★★★

DIRECTOR: Oliver Stone
CAST: James Woods, John Savage, Jim Belushi, Michael Murphy, Elpedia Carrillo, Tony Plana, Cynthia Gibb

James Woods (*Joshua Then and Now*) plays screenwriter/photojournalist Richard Boyle in the latter's semiautobiographical account of the events that occurred in El Salvador circa 1980–81. It is a fascinating movie despite its flaws and outrageousness. Overt audience manipulation cannot dull its impact as a gripping thriller or thwart the outstanding performances by Woods, John Savage, Jim Belushi, and Michael Murphy. Oliver Stone directs with uncommon skill. Rated R for profanity, nudity, suggested sex, drug use, and violence.

1986 120 minutes

SAM'S SON

★★★½

DIRECTOR: Michael Landon
CAST: Timothy Patrick Murphy, Eli Wallach, Anne Jackson

Written and directed by Michael Landon, this sweetly nostalgic semiautobiographical family film features Timothy Patrick Murphy as the young Eugene Orowitz (Landon's real name), whose parents, Sam (Eli Wallach) and Harriet (Anne Jackson), seem destined never to realize their fondest dreams until their son takes a hand. Rated PG for brief violence.

1984 104 minutes

SAMSON AND DELILAH

★★★★

DIRECTOR: Cecil B. De Mille
CAST: Hedy Lamarr, Victor Mature, George Sanders, Angela Lansbury

This Cecil B. De Mille extravaganza still looks good today. Hedy Lamarr plays the beautiful vixen Delilah, who robs Samson (Victor Mature) of his incredible strength. Dumb but fun.

1949 128 minutes

SAN FRANCISCO

★★★★

DIRECTOR: W. S. Van Dyke

CAST: Clark Gable, Jeanette MacDonald, Spencer Tracy

In its heyday, MGM boasted it had more stars than were in the heavens, and it made some terrific star-studded movies as a result. Take this 1936 production, starring Clark Gable, Jeanette MacDonald, and Spencer Tracy, for example. It's entertainment of the first order, with special effects—of the San Francisco earthquake—that still stand up today.

1936 B & W 115 minutes

SANDPIPER, THE

★½

DIRECTOR: Vincente Minnelli

CAST: Richard Burton, Elizabeth Taylor, Eva Marie Saint, Charles Bronson

Corny love triangle involves barefoot Elizabeth Taylor, who loves Richard Burton, who is married to Eva Marie Saint. Lots of surf and birds in this so-what star vehicle, which capitalizes on its location shooting off the California coast. Watch for Charles Bronson in his pre-star days.

1965 116 minutes

SAVAGE IS LOOSE, THE

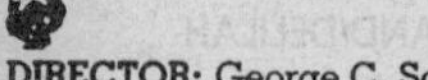

DIRECTOR: George C. Scott

CAST: George C. Scott, Trish Van Devere, John David Carson, Lee H. Montgomery

Kill it before it multiplies. In addition to acting and directing, George C. Scott also produced and distributed this pretentious disaster. The tedious tale strands a young man and his parents on an island for many years. They explore a recreational activity the Swiss Family Robinson never considered: incest. Rated R.

1974 114 minutes

SAVE THE TIGER

★★★

DIRECTOR: John G. Avildsen

CAST: Jack Lemmon, Jack Gilford, Thayer David

Jack Lemmon won the Academy Award for best actor for his portrayal in this 1973 film as a garment manufacturer who is at the end of his professional and emotional rope. His excellent performance helps offset the fact that the picture is essentially a downer. Rated R.

1973 101 minutes

SAYONARA

★★★★

DIRECTOR: Joshua Logan

CAST: Marlon Brando, Red Buttons, Miyoshi Umeki, Ricardo Montalban, James Garner

Marlon Brando is an American airman who engages in a romance with a Japanese actress while stationed in Japan after World War II. His love is put to the test by each culture's misconceptions and prejudices. James A. Michener's thought-provoking tragedy-romance still holds up well. Red Buttons and Miyoshi Umeki deservedly won Oscars for their roles as star-crossed lovers "American Occupation"-style.

1957 147 minutes

SCARECROW

★★★

DIRECTOR: Jerry Schatzberg

CAST: Al Pacino, Gene Hackman, Eileen Brennan, Richard Lynch

A real downer about two losers (Al Pacino and Gene Hackman) trying to make something of themselves, this drama is made watchable by the performances. Rated R.

1973 115 minutes

SCARLET LETTER, THE

★★★

DIRECTOR: Victor Seastrom

CAST: Lillian Gish, Henry B. Walthall, Karl Dane, Lars Hanson, William H. Tooker

Hester Prynne wears the scarlet letter A for adultery. Only her sadistic husband Roger knows that minister Arthur Dimmesdale is the father of her daughter, Pearl. Roger taunts Arthur, who plans to flee with Hester and the child but finally confesses his sin publicly. Silent.

1926 B & W 80 minutes

SCARLET LETTER, THE

★★★

DIRECTOR: Robert Vignola

CAST: Colleen Moore, Hardie Albright, Henry B. Walthall

Twenties flapper star Colleen Moore proved she had acting skill in this second version (first sound) of Nathaniel Hawthorne's great classic of love, hate, jealousy, and emotional blackmail in Puritan New England. Moore is a very creditable Hester Prynne to Hardie Albright's spineless Reverend Dimmesdale. As in the 1926 silent version, D. W. Griffith star Henry B. Walthall portrays the heartless persecutor Roger Chillingworth.

1934 B & W 69 minutes

SCARLET STREET

★★★½

DIRECTOR: Fritz Lang

CAST: Edward G. Robinson, Joan Bennett, Dan Duryea, Margaret Lindsay, Rosalind Ivan

The director (Fritz Lang) and stars (Edward G. Robinson, Joan Bennett, and Dan Duryea) of the excellent *Woman in the Window* reteamed with less spectacular results for this film about a mild-mannered fellow (Robinson) seduced into a life of crime by a temptress (Bennett).

1945 B & W 103 minutes

SCOTT OF THE ANTARCTIC

★½

DIRECTOR: Charles Frend

CAST: John Mills, Derek Bond, Christopher Lee, Kenneth More, James Robertson

This is a plodding, straightforward account of British explorer Robert Scott, complete with fake atmosphere (i.e., painted backdrops). You'd do much better to rent the superior expedition film, *Flight of the Eagle*.

1948 110 minutes

SCROOGE

★★★

DIRECTOR: Henry Edwards

CAST: Sir Seymour Hicks, Donald Calthrop, Robert Cochran, Mary Glynne, Oscar Asche, Maurice Evans

This little-known British version of Charles Dickens's classic *A Christmas Carol* is faithful to the original story and boasts a standout performance by Sir Seymour Hicks, who also cowrote the screenplay. A youthful Maurice Evans plays an early part in this well-acted, heartwarming tale. Effective sets and capable acting make this a truly enjoyable film, unjustly overshadowed by Alistair Sim's bravura performance as Scrooge in the venerated 1951 version. Hicks makes a fine old curmudgeon and breathes life into Ebenezer Scrooge, the man who discovers that it's never too late to repent and join humanity.

1935 B & W 78 minutes

SEA LION, THE

★★½

DIRECTOR: Rowland V. Lee

CAST: Hobart Bosworth, Bessie Love, Richard Morris, Emory Johnson, Charles Clary

Stern sea story with hard-bitten Hobart Bosworth as a tyrannical ship's master who vents his pent-up hatred on the men in his charge. But just when the old boy is really hitting his stride, romance rears its head and we find out that he's not all bad; he was just acting like a sadist because he had a broken heart. Bosworth, a big name in the cinema of the period around WWI, starred in a series of adaptations of Jack London stories, including *The Sea Wolf*, which has some similarities to this film. Silent.

1921 B & W 50 minutes

SECRET CEREMONY

★★½

DIRECTOR: Joseph Losey

CAST: Elizabeth Taylor, Mia Farrow, Robert Mitchum, Peggy Ashcroft, Pamela Brown

Typical Joseph Losey psychodrama about a psychotic girl (Mia Farrow) semikidnapping an aging streetwalker (Elizabeth Taylor) who reminds her of her dead mother. Robert Mitchum plays Farrow's lecherous stepfather who disrupts the relationship. Losey's films speak more to the subconscious than to the realities of the situations presented, which leads to muddled and unreasonable actions. With its strong sexual undertones, this film is not for kids (and probably not for some adults). Luckily, the three stars bring their charisma along, which helps to carry some weaker scenes.

1968 108 minutes

SECRETS

★★

DIRECTOR: Philip Saville

CAST: Jacqueline Bisset, Per Oscarsson, Shirley Knight Hopkins, Robert Powell

Jacqueline Bisset's torrid sex scene is about the only interesting thing in this turgid soap opera about the romantic "secrets" of a husband, wife, and daughter. Rated R for nudity, suggested sex, and profanity.

1971 86 minutes

SECRETS OF THE TITANIC

★★★★

DIRECTORS: Nicolas Noxon, Dr. Robert D. Ballard

CAST: Documentary

For years the tragic sinking of the giant British luxury oceanliner, *Titanic,* has gripped the interest and imagination of millions. In 1986, seventy years after she went down in the icy Atlantic east of Newfoundland, oceanographers found her broken remains two-and-a-half miles deep. Filming from a submersible deep-sea craft named *Alvin* and a manueverable tethered remote camera, incredible pictures were taken of the great shattered hull, her decks, inside, and outside and assembled into this astounding and revealing documentary.

1986 60 minutes

SEDUCTION OF JOE TYNAN, THE

★★★

DIRECTOR: Jerry Schatzberg

CAST: Alan Alda, Barbara Harris, Meryl Streep, Rip Torn, Charles Kimbrough, Melvyn Douglas

Alan Alda plays Senator Joe Tynan in this story of behind-the-scenes romance and political maneuvering in Washington, D.C. Tynan must face moral questions about himself and his job. It's familiar ground for Alda but still entertaining. Rated PG for language, brief nudity.

1979 107 minutes

SEIZE THE DAY

★★★

DIRECTOR: Fielder Cook

CAST: Robin Williams, Joseph Wiseman, Jerry Stiller, Glenne Headley, John Fiedler, Tom Aldredge, Tony Roberts

Robin Williams is watchable in this drama, but like so many comedians who attempt serious acting, he is haunted by his madcap persona. Adapted from Saul Bellow's novel, this PBS *Great Peformances* entry casts Williams as Wilhelm "Tommy" Adler, the Jewish ne'er-do-well son of wealthy, unsympathetic Joseph Wiseman. The story concerns the distintegration of Tommy's life, with con man "Dr." Tamkin (Jerry Stiller) taking Tommy's last cent and driving the final nail into his psychological coffin. Wiseman is excellent as the cold Dr. Adler, and Stiller gives a fine performance as the bombastic Tamkin. Williams and Tom Aldredge as another con man work well together.

1986 87 minutes

SEPARATE TABLES

★★★★★

DIRECTOR: John Schlesinger

CAST: Julie Christie, Alan Bates, Claire Bloom

Adapted from Terence Rattigan's play and directed by veteran John Schlesinger, this is a cable-television remake of the 1958 film with Burt Lancaster and Wendy Hiller. This time the work achieves a remarkable intimacy on tape with a topnotch British cast. Divided into two segments, this is a sort of British *Grand Hotel* room with Alan Bates as a philandering husband and retired colonel with a questionable background and the radiant Julie Christie as his mistress in the first section and a wallflower in the second half. Richly engrossing adult entertainment. Rated PG for adult subject matter.

1983 108 minutes

SERPENT'S EGG, THE

★½

DIRECTOR: Ingmar Bergman

CAST: Liv Ullmann, David Carradine, Gert Frobe, James Whitmore

Two trapeze artists are trapped in Berlin during pre-Nazi Germany. They find work in a strange clinic, where they discover a satanic plot. Director Ingmar Bergman's nightmare vision is disappointing at best. David Carradine gives a poor performance. Sven Nykvist's cinematography is the one redeeming element of this film.

1977 120 minutes

SERPICO

★★★★

DIRECTOR: Sidney Lumet

CAST: Al Pacino, Tony Roberts, John Randolph, Jack Kehoe, Biff McGuire

Al Pacino is magnificent in this poignant story of an honest man who happens to be a cop. The fact that this is a true story of one man's fight against corruption adds even more punch. Rated R.

1973 130 minutes

SERVANT, THE

★★★★

DIRECTOR: Joseph Losey

CAST: Dirk Bogarde, Sarah Miles, James Fox

A conniving manservant (Dirk Bogarde) gradually dominates the life of his spoiled master in this psychological horror story. By preying on his sexual weaknesses, he is able to easily maneuver him to his will. The taut, well-acted adult drama holds your interest throughout, mainly because the shock value is heightened for the audience because of its plausibility.

1963 B & W 115 minutes

SET-UP, THE

★★★★

DIRECTOR: Robert Wise

CAST: Robert Ryan, Audrey Totter, George Tobias, Alan Baxter, James Edwards, Wallace Ford

Taut *film noir* boxing flick takes the simple story of an over-the-hill boxer who refuses to disregard his principles and throw the big fight and elevates it to true tragedy. Robert Ryan as the has-been fighter gives another of the finely drawn and fiercely independent portrayals that marked his illustrious career as one of Hollywood's finest character actors/stars. This claustrophobic but deeply moving picture combines fine acting and personal integrity, which results in one of the best boxing films of all time, right up there with *Body and Soul* and *Raging Bull*. An early coup for famed director Robert Wise.

1949 B & W 72 minutes

SEVEN DAYS IN MAY

★★★★

DIRECTOR: John Frankenheimer

CAST: Burt Lancaster, Fredric March, Kirk Douglas, Ava Gardner, Edmond O'Brien, Martin Balsam

A highly suspenseful account of an attempted military takeover of the U.S. government. After a slow buildup, the movie's tension snowballs toward a thrilling conclusion. This is one of those rare films that treat their audiences with respect. A working knowledge of the political process is helpful for optimum appreciation. Fredric March, as a president under pressure, heads an all-star cast, all of whom give admirable performances.

1964 B & W 120 minutes

SEX MADNESS

★

DIRECTOR: Dwayne Vesper

CAST: Not Credited

"Educational" film about the dangers of syphilis is long on melodrama and morality and surprisingly short on graphic footage of disease victims. Several stories about youth gone wrong tie together in this sometimes hilarious exploitation film, but the exaggerated clichés and inept burlesque scenes can't lighten the heavy-handed story. One young woman contracts a social disease as result of her only affair, and she goes from doctor to doctor seeking help, only to find a quack who takes her money and declares her cured. After she marries her sweetheart and has his child, she discovers that her syhilis had not been arrested and that the baby is afflicted with it. Her husband goes blind and loses his job, and their life becomes one of despair. Corny.

1934 B & W 50 minutes

SHACK-OUT ON 101

★★★½

DIRECTOR: Edward Dein

CAST: Frank Lovejoy, Terry Moore, Lee Marvin, Keenan Wynn, Whit Bissell

This odd blend of character study and espionage thriller, which takes place at a highway hash-house, involves some of the most colorful patrons you'll ever run across. Perky Terry Moore plays the waitress who keeps her eyes open and helps the authorities close in on the men who have sabotage plans for a local chemical plant, and Lee Marvin is his most audacious as Slob, a name he does his best to live up to. More like a play than a movie at times, this is a mirror of the 1950s hysteria over communism. Keenan Wynn runs the diner and veteran character performers Frank Lovejoy and Whit Bissell brighten up the bill of fare.

1955 B & W 80 minutes

SHADES OF LOVE: CHAMPAGNE FOR TWO

★★

DIRECTOR: Lewis Furey

CAST: Nicholas Campbell, Kirsten Bishop

Comedy and romance are blended in this so-so story about a young architect (Kirsten Bishop) who falls in love with her roommate (Nicholas Campbell). This modern romance is complicated by the choice she must make between love and a career.

1987 82 minutes

SHADES OF LOVE: LILAC DREAM

★½

DIRECTOR: Marc Voizard

CAST: Dack Rambo, Susan Almgren

Mystery and romance combine in this tale of a young women left brokenhearted by a former lover. Then a storm leaves a man with no memory on the shore of her island. She nurses him back to health. Gradually, his past comes back to haunt him, and the heroine must decide whether to let him go or to hold on.

1987 83 minutes

SHADES OF LOVE: THE ROSE CAFE

★½

DIRECTOR: Daniele J. Suissa

CAST: Parker Stevenson, Linda Smith, Damir Andrei

Dreams can sometimes hide the truth, and in the case of Courtney Fairchild (Linda Smith), her dream of opening a restaurant has hidden her feelings for the men in her life. When trouble hits her restaurant, Courtney finds she must solve her man problems before she can find happiness.

1987 84 minutes

SHADES OF LOVE: SINCERELY, VIOLET

★½

DIRECTOR: Mort Ransen

CAST: Simon MacCorkindale, Patricia Phillips, Barbara Jones

In this mediocre story of love and romance a professor (Patricia Phillips) becomes a cat burglar named Violet. She is caught in the act of stealing by Mark Janson (Simon MacCorkindale) who tries to reform her. Love conquers all, and the romantic ending is just as we expect it to be.

1987 86 minutes

SHADOWS

★★★

DIRECTOR: Tom Forman

CAST: Lon Chaney Sr., Harrison Ford, Marguerite de la Motte, Walter Long, John Sainpolis, Buddy Messenger

A zealous young minister takes it upon himself to convert the local Chinese laundry men. Lon Chaney as Yen Sin gives a moving performance as the man who must confront the self-righteous churchmen, played by Harrison Ford (no relation to today's star). A colorful cast of good character actors help to make this a thought-provoking film. Silent.

1922 B & W 70 minutes

SHAMING, THE

★★

DIRECTOR: Marvin J. Chomsky

CAST: Anne Heywood, Donald Pleasence, Robert Vaughn, Carolyn Jones, Dorothy Malone, Dana Elcar

A spinster schoolteacher seeks psychiatric help because of extreme emotional problems relating to her virginity. She is then raped by a black janitor and continues to have sex with him until she is exposed and then ostracized by the school. Based on a novel by William Inge. This film is rated R for sex.

1975 90 minutes

SHAMPOO

★★★★

DIRECTOR: Hal Ashby

CAST: Warren Beatty, Julie Christie, Lee Grant, Jack Warden, Goldie Hawn, Carrie Fisher

Star Warren Beatty and Robert Towne co-wrote this perceptive comedy of morals, most of them bad, which focuses on a hedonistic Beverly Hills hairdresser played by Beatty. Although portions come perilously close to slapstick, the balance is an insightful study of the pain caused by people who try for no-strings-attached relationships. Watch for a brief, but potent, appearance by (pre–Princess Leia) Carrie Fisher, as well as cameos by several Hollywood directors. Rated R—sexuality and adult themes.

1975 112 minutes

SHATTERED

★★

DIRECTOR: Alistair Reid

CAST: Peter Finch, Shelley Winters, Colin Blakely, John Stride, Linda Hayden

Peter Finch plays a mild-mannered, neurotic businessman who picks up a hitchhiker (Linda Hayden) only to have her attach herself to him. As a result, he slowly begins to lose his sanity. Shelley Winters plays Finch's obnoxious wife. Like a lot of British thrillers, this one has little action until it explodes in the final fifteen minutes. Rated R for profanity and violence.

1972 100 minutes

SHINING SEASON, A

★★★

DIRECTOR: Stuart Margolin

CAST: Timothy Bottoms, Allyn Ann McLerie, Ed Begley Jr., Rip Torn, Connie Forslund, Mason Adams

Fact-based story of track star and Olympic hopeful John Baker, (Timothy Bottoms) who, when stricken by cancer, devoted his final months to coaching a girls' track team. The film's focus is on the various lives he helped to change and on his own personal courage. This is very familiar territory, but director Stuart Margolin keeps things above water most of the time. Bottoms is an engaging hero-victim. Made for television.

1979 100 minutes

SHIP OF FOOLS

★★★★★

DIRECTOR: Stanley Kramer

CAST: Vivien Leigh, Oskar Werner, Simone Signoret, José Ferrer, Lee Marvin, Jose Greco, George Segal, Michael Dunn, Elizabeth Ashley, Lilia Skala, Charles Korvin

In 1933, a vast and varied group of characters take passage on a German liner sailing from Mexico to Germany amidst impending doom. The all-star cast features most memorable performances by Vivien Leigh (her last film) as the neurotic divorcee, Oskar Werner as the ship's doctor, who has an affair with the despairing Simone Signoret, Lee Marvin as the forceful American baseball player, and Michael Dunn as the wise dwarf. Superb screen adaptation of the Katherine Anne Porter novel of the same name. Ernest Laszlo received an Academy Award for cinematography in this film.

1965 B & W 150 minutes

SHOCK, THE

★★★

DIRECTOR: Lambert Hillyer
CAST: Lon Chaney Sr., Christine Mayo, Virginia Valli

The legendary Lon Chaney Sr. added yet another grotesque character to his growing closet to skeltons when as he played Wilse Dilling. This decent crime melodrama, no different in plot than dozens of other films over the years, has the advantage of Chaney and an exciting climax consisting of a bang-up earthquake. Corny at times, this one is still a good bet if you're interested in silent films and want to try something that hasn't been available for many years. Silent.

1923 B & W 96 minutes

SHOES OF THE FISHERMAN

★½

DIRECTOR: Michael Anderson
CAST: Anthony Quinn, Laurence Olivier, Oskar Werner, David Janssen, Vittorio De Sica, John Gielgud, Leo McKern, Barbara Jefford

A truly memorable cast is about all there is to recommend this improbable and boring film about an enthusiastic pope who singlehandedly attempts to stop nuclear war, starvation, world strife, and people who think that the pontiff should stay in Rome and say Mass. David Janssen plays a journalist with a direct line to the action, but too much of this "topical" film is spent following Janssen as he tries to straighten out his love life. This one's based on a best-selling book by Morris West, but the zip went out of it somewhere along the line. Part of the problem is the film's length—the content of the story just doesn't warrant it. Famed producer-director Vittorio De Sica plays a role.

1968 157 minutes

SHOOT THE MOON

★★

DIRECTOR: Alan Parker
CAST: Albert Finney, Diane Keaton, Karen Allen, Dana Hill, Tracey Gold, Tina Yothers

Why didn't they just call it *Ordinary People Go West*? If we knew it was a sequel, perhaps *Shoot the Moon* wouldn't be such a disappointment. Of course, this film isn't really a sequel to the 1980 Oscar winner for best picture. It's closer to a ripoff; another somber movie about the disintegration of a marriage and a family. Yet it has none of the style, believability, or consistency of its predecessor. A few really good moments are provided by stars Albert Finney and Diane Keaton, but the the farfetched conclusion nearly negates them all. Rated R because of profanity, violence, and adult themes.

1982 123 minutes

SHOOTING PARTY, THE

★★★★

DIRECTOR: Alan Bridges
CAST: James Mason, Edward Fox, Dorthy Tutin, John Gielgud, Gordon Jackson, Cheryl Campbell, Robert Hardy

This meditation on the fading English aristocracy is an acting showcase. All main characters are played with verve, or at least the verve one would expect from English nobility in the years preceding World War I. While nothing much happens here, the rich texture of the characters, the highly stylized sets, and the incidental affairs in the plot are enough to sustain the viewer. Not rated, but equivalent to a PG for partial nudity and sex.

1985 97 minutes

SHORT EYES

★★★★

DIRECTOR: Robert M. Young
CAST: Bruce Davison, Jose Perez

Film version of Miguel Pinero's hard-hitting play about a convicted child molester at the mercy of other prisoners. A brutal and frightening film. Excellent, but difficult to watch. Rated R for violence and profanity.

1977 104 minutes

SID AND NANCY

★★★½

DIRECTOR: Alex Cox

CAST: Gary Oldman, Chloe Webb, Drew Schofield, David Hayman

Leave it to Alex Cox, director of the suburban punk classic *Repo Man*, to try to make sense out of punk rocker Sid Vicious and his girlfriend Nancy Spungen. Cox gives the two a sense of meaning and compassion that was missing from all the news stories. *Sid and Nancy* follows Vicious through his short stint with the Sex Pistols, his even shorter solo career, and his heroin addiction with Spungen. Don't look for many laughs; this rather sober and often repulsive black comedy lacks the humor of *Repo Man*, but its compassionate portrait of the two famed nihilists is a powerful one, which nevertheless is not for everyone. Rated R for violence, sex, nudity, and adult subject matter.

1986 111 minutes

SIDEWALKS OF LONDON

★★★★

DIRECTOR: Tim Whelan

CAST: Vivien Leigh, Charles Laughton, Rex Harrison, Larry Alder, Tyrone Guthrie, Gus McNaughton

Street entertainer Charles Laughton puts pretty petty thief Vivien Leigh in his song-and-dance act, then falls in love with her. Befriended by successful songwriter Rex Harrison, she puts the streets and old friends behind her and rises to stage stardom while her rejected and dejected mentor hits the skids and winds up masquerading as a blind beggar. Vivien Leigh is entrancing, and Charles Laughton is compelling and touching, in this dramatic sojourn in London byways. A British production, originally released as *St. Martin's Lane*.

1940 B & W 85 minutes

SILAS MARNER

★★★★

DIRECTOR: Giles Foster

CAST: Ben Kingsley, Jenny Agutter, Patrick Ryecart, Patsy Kensit, Rosemary Martin, Jonathan Coy

Fate is the strongest character in this BBC-TV adaptation of George Eliot's novel, although Ben Kingsley gives an excellent performance as the cataleptic eighteenth-century English weaver. Betrayed by his closest friend and cast out of the church, Marner disappears into the English countryside and becomes a bitter miser, only to have his life wonderfully changed when fate brings an orphan girl to his hovel. The mathematical precision of the plot twists, coupled with careful scripting and production values make, this gentle drama a pleasure.

1985 97 minutes

SILENCE OF THE NORTH

★★

DIRECTOR: Allan Winton King

CAST: Ellen Burstyn, Tom Skerritt, Gordon Pinsent

There are some of us here at the *Video Movie Guide* who would follow Ellen Burstyn anywhere. Imagine our surprise when *Silence of the North* turned out to be like a movie from the *Wonderful World of Disney* series, minus the mischievous racoon wreaking havoc in the cabin. Now, we've got nothing against Disney productions—indeed, a little of Walt's humor here would've helped—but Burstyn's narration is pure melodrama, and ninety minutes of one catastrophe after the next is more tiring than entertaining. Burstyn portrays a woman who falls in love with a fur trapper, played by Tom Skerritt *(Alien)*, and moves into the Canadian wilderness. Rated PG for violence.

1981 94 minutes

SILENT ENEMY, THE

★★★★

DIRECTOR: H. P. Carver
CAST: Documentary

Haunting silent saga of North America's dwindling Indian population and their perpetual struggle against hunger. This is a powerful, eloquent film shot on location in the wilds of northern Canada in the last part of the 1920s. Unseen in its orginial length for many years, this lost gem was painstakingly tracked down and reassembled by cooperating film archivists and provides an important link between the silent and sound documentary film. Yellow Robe, chief of the featured Ojibwa tribe and a nephew of Sitting Bull, provides the opening sound narration, which he wrote himself, and he tells a sad, prophetic tale of his people and the times facing them. Many of the Indians died of starvation before the film was released and it failed to attract the audience it could have with a soundtrack and publicity campaign. As a result, the film became source of stock shots of Indians and their way of life and found limited play in an abridged form in classrooms and auditoriums across the country. Poignant and dignified, this is one of the great documentary chronicles of a near extinct way of life and is perhaps the finest of all primary-source films on the Indians of the Northwest. Silent.

1930 B & W 110 minutes

SILENT REBELLION

★★½

DIRECTOR: Charles Dubin
CAST: Telly Savalas, Michael Constantine, Keith Gordon, Edye Byrde, Lori-Man Elegler, James Dukas, George Hall

Telly Savalas plays a naturalized American who goes back to his hometown in Greece to visit. He finds that the old ways in the village where he was born are too outdated for him and tries to introduce his kin to the American way of life. The cross-cultural experience is not always pleasant as he finds that he has changed more than he would like to admit since moving to America. Some poignant moments, but lots of dull ones, too. Not rated

1982 90 minutes

SILKWOOD

★★★★

DIRECTOR: Mike Nichols
CAST: Meryl Streep, Kurt Russell, Cher, Craig T. Nelson, Fred Ward, Sudie Bond

At more than two hours, *Silkwood* is a shift-and-squirm movie that's worth shifting and squirming through. While it seems slow and drawn-out at times, the fine portrayals by Meryl Streep, Kurt Russell, and Cher keep the viewer's interest. Based on real events, the story focuses on 28-year-old nuclear worker and union activist Karen Silkwood, who died in a mysterious car crash while she was attempting to expose the alleged dangers in the Oklahoma plutonium plant where she was employed. Director Mike Nichols could have made better use of the suspense elements inherent in the story, but chose instead to make a character study.

As a result, he's given us a very good—but not great—motion picture. Rated R for nudity, sex, and profanity.

1984 128 minutes

SILVER CHALICE, THE

★★

DIRECTOR: Victor Saville

CAST: E. G. Marshall, Jack Palance Joseph Wiseman, Paul Newman, Virginia Mayo, Pier Angeli, Alexander Scourby, Walter Hampden, Natalie Wood, Lorne Greene

Thomas Costain's historical novel about the cup used at the Last Supper comes off third best in this ripe Technicolor presentation. Full of intrigue and togas, this film is notable only for two unnotable screen debuts by Paul Newman and Lorne Greene. The vessel of the title is also known as the Holy Grail.

1954 144 minutes

SILVER DREAM RACER

★★½

DIRECTOR: David Wickes

CAST: David Essex, Beau Bridges, Cristina Raines, Clark Peters, Harry Corbett, Diane Keen, Lee Montague

This so-so British drama features David Essex as a mechanic turned racer. He is determined to win not only the World Motorcycle Championship but another man's girlfriend as well. Rated PG.

1980 110 minutes

SILVER STREAK

★★

DIRECTOR: Thomas Atkins

CAST: Charles Starrett, Sally Blane, Hardie Albright, William Farnum, Irving Pichel, Arthur Lake

Interesting primarily for the vintage locomotives and the railway system as well as a good cast of unique personalities, this slowly paced drama follows a high-speed train on a mission of mercy. Good guy Charles Starrett is the man in charge of delivering iron lungs to the victims of an epidemic and he pours on the coals to do so, but the engine is the only thing that gets hot in this so-so effort.

1934 B & W 72 minutes

SINCERELY YOURS

DIRECTOR: Gordon Douglas

CAST: Liberace, Joanne Dru, Dorothy Malone, William Demarest, Lurene Tuttle, Richard Eyer

Written by Irving Wallace, who should have known better, this tepid, camp remake of George Arliss's classic *The Man Who Played God* may earn cult status because the leading man is Liberace. While supported by an experienced and dependable cast—including William Demarest and Lurene Tuttle (Sam Spade's Effie Perrine on radio)—Mr. Showmanship can't cut it when the stage is small, the camera's close, and the corn syrup's thick and sticky. Ridiculous, sincerely.

1955 115 minutes

SISTER KENNY

DIRECTOR: Dudley Nichols

CAST: Rosalind Russell, Alexander Knox, Dean Jagger, Charles Dingle, Philip Merivale, Beulah Bondi, John Litel

Rosalind Russell is noble, dedicated, self-sacrificing, serious, and sincere in the title role of the Australian nurse who fought polio in the bush. Her pioneering treatment methods finally prevailed over a skeptical, rebuffing medical community jealous of allowing her recognition. But the telling of her life in this dull and slow box-office flop is tiresome.

1946 B & W 116 minutes

SIX WEEKS

★★★½

DIRECTOR: Tony Bill

CAST: Dudley Moore, Mary Tyler Moore, Katherine Healy, Joe Regalbuto

Dudley Moore and Mary Tyler Moore star as two adults trying to make the dreams of a young girl (Katherine Healy)—who has a very short time to live—come true in this tearjerker. Directed by Tony Bill (*My Bodyguard*), it's enjoyable for viewers who like a good cry. Rated PG for strong content.

1982 107 minutes

16 DAYS OF GLORY

★★★★

DIRECTOR: Bud Greenspan

CAST: Documentary

Dramatic retelling of the 1984 Summer Olympics held in Los Angeles. This presentation of the games comes with interesting historical notes, in-depth background information on the athletes (not all of them winners), and no commercials! Particularly exciting are the pieces on swimmer Rowdy Gaines and gymnast Mary Lou Retton. Terrific cinematography. Rated G.

1985 145 minutes

SKAG

★★★½

DIRECTOR: Frank Perry

CAST: Karl Malden, Piper Laurie, Craig Wasson, Peter Gallagher, George Voskovec

Home-ridden to recuperate after being felled by a stroke, veteran steelworker Pete Skagska must deal with family problems, his own poor health, and the chance his illness may leave him impotent. In the title role, Karl Malden gives a towering, hard-driving performance as a man determined to prevail, no matter what the emotional cost. TV movie.

1980 152 minutes

SLAYGROUND

★½

DIRECTOR: Terry Bedford

CAST: Peter Coyote, Billie Whitelaw, Philip Sayer, Bill Luhr

Based on the hard-boiled Parker series of crime novels by Richard Stark (a pseudonym for Donald E. Westlake), *Slayground* will disappoint fans of the books. The character of Parker, a tough, no-nonsense professional criminal who shoots first and walks away, has been softened into a whiny thief named Stone (Peter Coyote). When a heist he masterminds goes awry because of a lead-footed getaway driver, Stone finds himself hunted by a sadistic hit man. Director Terry Bedford has all but trashed the Stark/Weslake story by infusing it with the clichés of a slasher flick. Rated R.

1984 89 minutes

SLEUTH

★★★★★

DIRECTOR: Joseph L. Mankiewicz

CAST: Michael Caine, Laurence Olivier

Michael Caine and Laurence Olivier engage in a heavyweight acting *bataille royal* in this stimulating mystery. Both actors are brilliant as the characters engage in the struggle of one-upmanship and social game-playing. Without giving away the movie's twists and turns, we can let on that the ultimate game is being played on its audience. It is great fun. Rated PG.

1972 138 minutes

SLIGHTLY SCARLET

★½

DIRECTOR: Allan Dwan
CAST: John Payne, Arlene Dahl, Rhonda Fleming, Kent Taylor

Confused blend of romance, crime, and political corruption focuses on good girl falling for gang leader. The fact that she's the mayor's secretary mucks the plot of this one up even further. Based on a book by James Cain and about as muddled as they come. Forget the story. Just watch the character actors and actresses interplay.

1956 99 minutes

SMALL CIRCLE OF FRIENDS, A

★½

DIRECTOR: Rob Cohen
CAST: Karen Allen, Brad Davis, Jameson Parker, Shelley Long, John Friedrich

Despite a solid cast, this story of campus unrest during the 1960s never comes together. As college students at Harvard, Karen Allen, Brad Davis, and Jameson Parker play three inseparable friends living and loving their way through protests and riots. Check out *Medium Cool* for the definitive film on the social unrest of this time period. Rated PG.

1980 112 minutes

SMASH PALACE

★★★★

DIRECTOR: Roger Donaldson
CAST: Bruno Lawrence, Anna Jemison, Greer Robson, Desmond Kelly

A scrap yard of crumpled and rusting automobiles serves as a backdrop to the story of a marriage in an equally deteriorated condition in this well-made, exceptionally acted film from New Zealand. Explicit sex and nude scenes may shock some viewers, yet they are intrinsic to the thrust of the storyline. It's a *Kramer vs. Kramer*, *Ordinary People*–style of movie that builds to a scary, nail-chewing climax. No MPAA rating; this has sex, violence, nudity, and profanity.

1981 100 minutes

SMASH-UP: THE STORY OF A WOMAN

★★★

DIRECTOR: Stuart Heisler
CAST: Susan Hayward, Lee Bowman, Marsha Hunt, Eddie Albert, Carleton Young, Carl Esmond

Night-club songbird Susan Hayward puts her songwriter husband's (Lee Bowman) career first. As he succeeds, she slips. His subsequent neglect and indifference make her a scenery-shedding bottle baby until near tragedy restores her sobriety and his attention. Skoal!

1947 B & W 103 minutes

SMITHEREENS

★★★

DIRECTOR: Susan Siedelman
CAST: Susan Berman, Brad Rinn, Richard Hell, Roger Jett

An independently made feature (its budget was only $100,000), this work by producer-director Susan Siedelman examines the life of an amoral and aimless young woman (Susan Berman) living in New York. Rated R.

1982 90 minutes

SMOOTH TALK

★★★★

DIRECTOR: Joyce Chopra
CAST: Laura Dern, Treat Williams, Mary Kay Place, Elizabeth Berridge, Levon Helm

Coltish Laura Dern owns this film, an uncompromising adaptation of the Joyce Carol Oates short story "Where Are You

Going, Where Have You Been?" Dern hits every note as a sultry woman-child poised on the brink of adulthood and sexual maturity. Mary Kay Place does well as an exasperated mom, and Elizabeth Berridge is a sympathetic older sister. The picture takes an unexpected turn when Dern attracts the attention of Treat Williams, a sinister, sunglassed stranger anxious to cut through the coyness . . . and who may exist only in the girl's mind. Rarely has a film better captured this awkward time of life. Rated PG-13 for language and sexual situations.

1985 92 minutes

SOLDIER IN THE RAIN

★★★

DIRECTOR: Ralph Nelson
CAST: Steve McQueen, Tony Bill, Jackie Gleason, Tuesday Weld, Tom Poston

My Bodyguard director Tony Bill is among the featured performers in this fine combination of sweet drama and rollicking comedy starring Steve McQueen, Jackie Gleason, and Tuesday Weld. The Great One (Gleason) is, well, great as a high-living, worldly master sergeant, and McQueen is equally good as his protégé.

1963 B & W 88 minutes

SOLO

★

DIRECTOR: Tony Williams
CAST: Vincent Gil, Lisa Peer, Perry Armstrong

An uninteresting love story with three forgettable characters. This movie will cure the most serious case of insomnia. Rated PG.

1977 90 minutes

SOLOMON AND SHEBA

★★★

DIRECTOR: King Vidor
CAST: Yul Brynner, Gina Lollobrigida, George Sanders

High times in biblical times as Sheba vamps Solomon. Don't look for too much of a script, because the emphasis is on lavish spectacle. Eyewash, not brain food.

1959 139 minutes

SOME CALL IT LOVING

★

DIRECTOR: James B. Harris
CAST: Zalman King, Carol White, Tisa Farrow, Richard Pryor, Logan Ramsey, Brandy Herrod

Herein lies the bizarre tale of a rich jazz musician, Zalman King, who buys a "Sleeping Beauty" (Carol White) from a circus side show for his own perverse enjoyment. Don't let the Richard Pryor billing draw you in. His performance does nothing for him or the film, which is a rambling, incoherent mess. Rated R for nudity, sex, and language.

1974 103 minutes

SOMETHING FOR EVERYONE

★★★

DIRECTOR: Harold Prince
CAST: Michael York, Angela Lansbury, Anthony Corlan, Heidelinde Weis, Eva-Maria Meineke, Jane Carr

This sleeper about a manipulative, amoral young man (Michael York) and the lengths he goes to in order to advance himself might not be to everyone's tastes. Veteran stage and screen star Angela Lansbury gives one of her best performances as the down-on-her-luck aristocrat who falls victim to York's charms and ends up regretting their association. This seldom-seen adult film was Harold Prince's first film and features the pastoral beauty of the Bavarian countryside where it was shot. Mature themes and situations make this film more suitable for an older audience.

1970 112 minutes

SOMETIMES A GREAT NOTION

★★★

DIRECTOR: Paul Newman

CAST: Paul Newman, Henry Fonda, Lee Remick, Michael Sarrazin, Richard Jaeckel

In the story, adapted from the novel by Ken Kesey (*One Flew over the Cuckoo's Nest*), Paul Newman plays the elder son of an Oregon logging family that refuses to go on strike with the other lumberjacks in the area. The family pays dearly for its unwillingness to go along. One scene in particular, which features Newman aiding Richard Jaeckel, who has been pinned in the water by a fallen tree, is unforgettable. Rated PG.

1971 114 minutes

SONG OF BERNADETTE, THE

★★★★

DIRECTOR: Henry King

CAST: Jennifer Jones, Charles Bickford, William Eythe, Vincent Price, Lee J. Cobb, Gladys Cooper, Anne Revere

Four Oscars, including one to Jennifer Jones for best actress, went to this beautifully filmed story of the simple nineteenth-century French peasant girl, Bernadette Soubirous, who saw a vision of the Virgin Mary in the town of Lourdes.

1943 B & W 156 minutes

SOPHIE'S CHOICE

★★★★★

DIRECTOR: Alan J. Pakula

CAST: Meryl Streep, Kevin Kline, Peter MacNicol

A young, inexperienced southern writer named Stingo (Peter MacNichol) learns about love, life, and death in this absorbing, wonderfully acted, and heartbreaking movie. One summer, while observing the affair between Sophie (Meryl Streep), a victim of a concentration camp, and Nathan (Kevin Kline), a charming, but sometimes explosive biologist, Stingo falls in love with Sophie, a woman with deep, dark secrets. Rated R.

1982 157 minutes

SOUNDER

★★★★★

DIRECTOR: Martin Ritt

CAST: Cicely Tyson, Paul Winfield, Kevin Hooks, Carmen Mathews, Taj Mahal, James Best, Janet Maccachlan

Beautifully made film detailing the struggle of a black sharecropper and his family. Director Martin Ritt (*Norma Rae*; *Cross Creek*) gets outstanding performances from Cicely Tyson and Paul Winfield. When her husband is sent to jail, Tyson must raise her family and run the farm by herself while trying to get the eldest son an education. A truly moving and thought-provoking film. Don't miss this one. Rated G.

1972 105 minutes

SOUTHERNER, THE

★★★★

DIRECTOR: Jean Renoir

CAST: Zachary Scott, Betty Field, J. Carrol Naish

Stark life in the rural South before civil rights. Dirt-poor tenant farmer (Zachary Scott) struggles against insurmountable odds to provide for his family while maintaining his dignity. Visually a beautiful film, but uneven in dramatic continuity. Nonetheless, its high rating is deserved.

1945 B & W 91 minutes

SPARROWS

★★★

DIRECTOR: William Beaudine

CAST: Mary Pickford, Gustav von Seyffertitz, Roy Stewart, Mary Louise Miller

The now legendary Mary Pickford—"Our Mary" to millions during her reign as Queen of Hollywood when this film was made—plays the resolute, intrepid champion of a group of younger orphans besieged by an evil captor. Silent melodrama at its best, folks.

1926 B & W 84 minutes

SPIRIT OF ST. LOUIS, THE

★★★★

DIRECTOR: Billy Wilder

CAST: James Stewart, Patricia Smith, Murray Hamilton, Marc Connelly

Jimmy Stewart always wanted to portray Charles Lindbergh in a recreation of his historic solo flight across the Atlantic. When he finally got his chance, at age 48, many critics felt he was too old to be believable. Stewart did just fine. Within his performance, the actor ensures the quiet courage of one of America's greatest heroes comes through. The action does drag at times, but this remains a quality picture for the whole family.

1957 138 minutes

SPITFIRE

★★★½

DIRECTOR: John Cromwell

CAST: Katharine Hepburn, Robert Young, Ralph Bellamy, Martha Sleeper, Sara Haden, Sidney Toler

A girl (Katharine Hepburn) believes herself to have healing powers and is cast out from her Ozark Mountain home as a result. It's an interesting premise, and well-acted.

1934 B & W 88 minutes

SPLENDOR IN THE GRASS

★★★★

DIRECTOR: Elia Kazan

CAST: Warren Beatty, Natalie Wood, Pat Hingle, Audrey Christie

Warren Beatty made his film debut in this 1961 film, as a popular, rich high-school boy. Natalie Wood plays his less prosperous girlfriend who has a nervous breakdown when he dumps her. A few tears shed by the viewer make this romantic drama all the more intriguing.

1961 124 minutes

SPLIT IMAGE

★★★★

DIRECTOR: Ted Kotcheff

CAST: Peter Fonda, James Woods, Karen Allen, Michael O'Keefe

This is a very interesting, thought-provoking film about religious cults and those who become caught up in them. Michael O'Keefe plays a young man who is drawn into a pseudo-religious organization run by Peter Fonda. The entire cast is good, but Fonda stands out in one of his best roles. Rated R for language and nudity.

1982 113 minutes

SPLIT SECOND

★★★

DIRECTOR: Dick Powell

CAST: Stephen McNally, Alexis Smith, Jan Sterling, Paul Kelly, Richard Egan

Tense film about an escaped convict who holds several people hostage in a deserted town has a lot working for it, including the fact that the place they're holed up in is a nuclear test site. Former crooner Dick Powell found his niche late in his career as a hard-boiled character in films and a talented director on the other side of the camera.

1953 B & W 85 minutes

SPY IN BLACK, THE

★★★

DIRECTOR: Michael Powell

CAST: Conrad Veidt, Valerie Hobson, Sebastian Shaw, June Duprez, Marius Goring

Unusual espionage-cum-romance story of German agent Conrad Veidt and his love affair with British agent Valerie Hobson. British director Michael Powell brings just the right blend of duty and tragedy to this story, set in the turmoil of World War I. June Duprez, soon to star in *The Thief of Baghdad* for the Korda brothers, plays the second lead to Hobson, *true* wife to Frankenstein in *The Bride of Frankenstein*.

1939 B & W 82 minutes

SPY OF NAPOLEON

★★

DIRECTOR: Maurice Elvey

CAST: Richard Barthelmess, Dolly Hass, Francis Sullivan

Heavy-handed historical hokum finds Emperor Napoleon III using his illegitimate daughter to ferret out dissidents and enemies. This harmless fact-bender is amusing enough and stars former silent-screen good guy Richard Barthelmess in a meaty role.

1936 B & W 77 minutes

SQUEEZE, THE

★★½

DIRECTOR: Michael Apted

CAST: Stacy Keach, David Hemmings, Edward Fox, Stephen Boyd, Carol White, Freddie Star

Stacy Keach plays an alcoholic detective whose ex-wife is kidnapped for a large ransom. As he plots to save her from the brutal kidnappers, he is forced to confront his drinking problem. Good performances from the cast unfortunately do not save this mediocre film. Rated R for nudity and language.

1977 106 minutes

STAGE DOOR CANTEEN

★★

DIRECTOR: Frank Borzage

CAST: William Terry, Cheryl Walkers, Katharine Hepburn, Harpo Marx, Helen Hayes, Count Basie, Edgar Bergen

An all-star cast play themselves in this mildly amusing romance about the behind-the-scenes world of Broadway. Unless you enjoy looking at the many stage luminaries during their early years, you will find this entire film to be ordinary, predictable, and uninspired.

1943 B & W 85 minutes

STAGE STRUCK

★★½

DIRECTOR: Sidney Lumet

CAST: Henry Fonda, Susan Strasberg, Joan Greenwood, Herbert Marshall, Christopher Plummer

Despite a fine cast—Susan Strasberg excepted—this rehash of *Morning Glory* is flat and wearisome. You don't really care to pull for the young actress trying to make her mark. The late Joan Greenwood's throaty voice, however, is sheer delight.

1958 95 minutes

STAND BY ME

★★★★½

DIRECTOR: Rob Reiner

CAST: Wil Wheaton, River Phoenix, Corey Feldman, Jerry O'Connell, Kiefer Sutherland, John Cusack, Richard Dreyfuss

Finally, someone has proven that a Stephen King story can be adapted successfully to the screen.

Based on King's novella, *The Body*, the story involves four young boys in the last days of summer and their search for the missing body of a young boy believed hit by a train. Morbid as it may sound, this is not a horror movie. Rather, it is a story of leaving boyhood behind and ascending to manhood. Sometimes sad and often funny, this film, with its rich acting and marvelous direction, is guaranteed to leave you with a feeling that could keep you warm through the coldest winter. Rated R.

1986 90 minutes

STANLEY AND LIVINGSTONE

★★★

DIRECTOR: Henry King

CAST: Spencer Tracy, Cedric Hardwicke, Richard Greene, Nancy Kelly

When Spencer Tracy delivers the historic line, "Doctor Livingstone, I presume," to Cedric Hardwicke in this production, you know why he was such a great screen actor. It is primarily his performance, as a reporter who journeys to Africa in order to find a lost Victorian explorer, that injects life and interest into what could have been just another stodgy prestige picture from the 1930s.

1939 B & W 101 minutes

STAR 80

★★★★

DIRECTOR: Bob Fosse

CAST: Mariel Hemingway, Eric Roberts, Cliff Robertson, Carroll Baker

A depressing, uncompromising, but brilliantly filmed and acted portrait of a tragedy. Mariel Hemingway stars as Dorothy Stratten, the Playboy playmate of the year who was murdered in 1980 by the husband (an equally impressive portrayal by Eric Roberts) she had outgrown. The movie paints a bleak portrait of her life, times, and death. Rated R for nudity, violence, profanity, and sex.

1983 102 minutes

STAR CHAMBER, THE

★★★★

DIRECTOR: Peter Hyams

CAST: Michael Douglas, Hal Holbrook, Yaphet Kotto, Sharon Gless, Jack Kehoe

A model group of Superior Court judges lose faith in the constitutional bylaws that they have sworn to uphold and decide to take the law into their own hands. Michael Douglas (*The China Syndrome*) plays the idealistic young judge who uncovers the organization. Rated PG for profanity and violence.

1983 109 minutes

STAR IS BORN, A (ORIGINAL)

★★★★

DIRECTOR: William Wellman

CAST: Fredric March, Janet Gaynor, Adolphe Menjou, May Robson

The first version of this trice-filmed in-house Hollywood weeper, this is the story of an aging actor (Fredric March) whose career is beginning to go on the skids while his youthful bride's (Janet Gaynor) career is starting to blossom. Great acting and a tight script keep this poignant movie from falling into melodrama.

1937 111 minutes

STAR IS BORN, A (REMAKE)

★★★★½

DIRECTOR: George Cukor

CAST: Judy Garland, James Mason, Charles Bickford, Jack Carson, Tom Noonan

Judy Garland's acting triumph is the highlight of this movie, which is considered to be the best version of this classic romantic tragedy. Newly restored to its original length via long-lost footage, stills, and a complete soundtrack, this one is well worth watching. James Mason is also memorable in the role originated by Fredric March. Be sure to get the full restored version.

1954 154 minutes

STAR IS BORN, A (REMAKE)

★★

DIRECTOR: Frank Pierson
CAST: Barbra Streisand, Kris Kristofferson, Gary Busey, Oliver Clark

The third and by far least watchable version of this venerable Hollywood warhorse has been sloppily crafted into a vehicle for star Barbra Streisand. The rocky romance between a declining star (Kris Kristofferson) and an up-and-coming new talent (Streisand) has been switched from the world of the stage to that of rock 'n' roll. A weak script and uneven direction leaves the viewer with no feeling for the central characters. Even Streisand's fans may find it difficult to watch. Rated R.

1976 140 minutes

STARS LOOK DOWN, THE

★★★★

DIRECTOR: Carol Reed
CAST: Michael Redgrave, Margaret Lockwood, Edward Rigby, Emlyn Williams, Nancy Price, Cecil Parker, Linden Travers

Classic film about a Welsh coal miner and his struggle to rise above his station and maintain his identity and the respect of his community is every bit as good today as it was when released. While lacking the sentimentality of John Ford's *How Green Was My Valley*, this film boasts the same high caliber of acting talent and remains a vital and highly personal look at a conflict that still exists in today's society. A coup for director Carol Reed and another great performance by Michael Redgrave as a man of quiet dignity and determination. Well worth the watching.

1939 B & W 110 minutes

STATE OF THE UNION

★★★

DIRECTOR: Frank Capra
CAST: Spencer Tracy, Katharine Hepburn, Adolphe Menjou, Van Johnson, Angela Lansbury

Combine the acting talents of Spencer Tracy and Katharine Hepburn with the direction of Frank Capra, and you can be guaranteed something of interest will result. In this case, it's a political fable about an American businessman who is encouraged by opportunities to run for the presidency, and leave his integrity behind in the process. Tracy and Hepburn are a joy to watch, as usual. This film loses much of its impact due to the overuse of obvious political stereotypes in its supporting players.

1948 B & W 124 minutes

STAY AS YOU ARE

★★★★

DIRECTOR: Alberto Lattuada
CAST: Nastassja Kinski, Marcello Mastroianni, Francisco Rabal, Monica Randal, Giuliana Cazandra

This film begins conventionally but charmingly as the story of a romance between a 20-year-old girl, Francesca (Nastassja Kinski), and Giulio (Marcello Mastroianni), a man old enough to be her father. It remains charming, but the charm becomes mingled with a controlled anguish when it becomes evident that Giulio may indeed be her father. No MPAA rating.

1978 95 minutes

STAY HUNGRY

★★★★½

DIRECTOR: Bob Rafelson

CAST: Jeff Bridges, Sally Field, R. G. Armstrong, Arnold Schwarzenegger

An underrated film dealing with a young southern aristocrat's (Jeff Bridges) attempt to complete a real estate deal by purchasing a body-building gym. Bridges begins to appreciate those who work and train at the gym as well as getting some insights into his own life. A wonderful film; highly recommended. Rated R for violence, brief nudity, and language.

1976 103 minutes

STEAMING

★½

DIRECTOR: Joseph Losey

CAST: Vanessa Redgrave, Sarah Miles, Diana Dors, Patti Love, Brenda Bruce, Felicity Dean

Nell Dunn's play, *Steaming*, takes place in an English Turkish-style bathhouse where a group of women share their feelings about life. The play has some interesting structural symbolism, but also a lot of stale dialogue, mostly concerning the worthlessness of men. Joseph Losey's film version is minus the connective structure but full of the banal colloquies. Vanessa Redgrave lends some needed reality to this sweaty gabfest. Rated R.

1984 112 minutes

STELLA DALLAS

★★★★

DIRECTOR: King Vidor

CAST: Barbara Stanwyck, Anne Shirley, John Boles, Alan Hale, Tim Holt, Marjorie Main

Barbara Stanwyck's title-role performance as the small-town vulgar innocent who sacrifices everything for her daughter got her a well-deserved Oscar nomination and set the standard for this type of screen character. John Boles is the elegant wealthy heel who does her wrong. Anne Shirley is Laurel, the object of her mother's completely self-effacing conduct. In its time a winner, and still well worth the viewing.

1937 B & W 111 minutes

STERILE CUCKOO, THE

★★★★

DIRECTOR: Alan J. Pakula

CAST: Liza Minnelli, Wendell Burton, Tim McIntire

Painfully poignant story about a dedicated young college lad (Wendell Burton) and the loopy young woman (Liza Minnelli) who, unable to handle people on their own terms, demands too much of those with whom she becomes involved. Minnelli's Pookie Adams won the actress a well-deserved Academy Award nomination. Her character is an uncomfortable blend of free spirits and frightening instability. An excellent directorial debut from Alan J. Pakula. Don't watch this film if you're in the middle of an unpleasant love affair. Rated PG for sexual situations.

1969 107 minutes

STEVIE

★★★★

DIRECTOR: Robert Enders

CAST: Glenda Jackson, Mona Washbourne, Trevor Howard, Alec McCowen

Glenda Jackson gives a brilliant performance (which won her best-actress honors at the Montreal Film Festival in 1978) as reclusive poet Stevie Smith in this stagey, but still interesting, film. Mona Washbourne ("stuff and nonsense") is the film's true delight as Smith's doting—and slightly dotty—aunt. Trevor Howard narrates and co-stars in this British release. Rated PG for brief profanity.

1978 102 minutes

STOCKS AND BLONDES

DIRECTOR: Arthur Greenstands
CAST: Leigh Wood, Veronica Hart, Jamie Kantor, Dick Beil

A female college student researches a term paper on hostile corporate takeovers. Her investigation of one company acquisition soon unearths some dirty work. She zeros in on an affluent businesswoman who has illegally consumed many a business. Soon the student is stalked by a violent stranger bent on keeping her quiet. This is an old pornographic film with all scenes graphically portraying sexual situations cut out. However, the nudity, obscene language, and horrible acting remain intact. Stay away from this trash. Rated R.

1984 79 minutes

STONE BOY, THE

★★★★★

DIRECTOR: Christopher Cain
CAST: Robert Duvall, Frederic Forrest, Glenn Close, Wilford Brimley

A superb ensemble cast elevates this rural *Ordinary People*–style film about a boy who accidentally shoots the older brother he adores and begins losing touch with reality. It's a tough subject, exquisitely handled. For some reason, this fine film was never theatrically released on a wide scale. Thanks to video, it can be seen and appreciated. Rated PG for brief violence and some profanity.

1984 93 minutes

STRAIGHT TIME

★★★★

DIRECTOR: Ulu Gosbard
CAST: Dustin Hoffman, Harry Dean Stanton, Gary Busey, Theresa Russell, M. Emmet Walsh

Well-told story of an ex-convict (Dustin Hoffman) attempting to make good on the outside only to return to crime after a run-in with his parole officer (M. Emmet Walsh). Hoffman's performance is truly chilling, exposing a side of him rarely seen on the screen. Harry Dean Stanton is equally fine as Hoffman's partner in crime. A very grim and powerful film that was sadly overlooked on its initial release. Rated R for violence, nudity, and language.

1978 114 minutes

STRANGE LOVE OF MARTHA IVERS, THE

★★★

DIRECTOR: Lewis Milestone
CAST: Barbara Stanwyck, Van Heflin, Kirk Douglas, Lizabeth Scott, Judith Anderson, Darryl Hickman

Terrible title doesn't do this well-acted drama justice. Woman-with-a-past Barbara Stanwyck excels in this story of a secret that comes back to threaten her now-stable life and the lengths she must go to in order to ensure her securtiy. Full of deep emotions and seething passions this class production boasts a haunting score by great Hollywood composer Miklos Rozsa and a tight story by Robert Rossen. Young Kirk Douglas in his film debut already charges the screen with the electricity that he will continue to discharge for generations to come. A little long, but worth the time.

1946 B & W 117 minutes

STRATEGIC AIR COMMAND

★★½

DIRECTOR: Anthony Mann
CAST: James Stewart, June Allyson, Frank Lovejoy, Barry Sullivan, Bruce Bennett, Rosemary DeCamp

Aviation and sports come together as professional baseball player Jimmy Stewart is called back to active service and forced to leave his career, his teammates, and his wife (June Allyson). Air Force veterans will love the footage and "new" aircraft of the day, and baseball fans will enjoy the all-too-brief glimpses of real games, but, otherwise, this is just routine studio fare. Anthony Mann's best pictures with Jimmy Stewart are his westerns, so try *Bend of the River* or *The Naked Spur*.

1955 114 minutes

STRAWBERRY BLONDE, THE

★★★

DIRECTOR: Raoul Walsh

CAST: James Cagney, Olivia De Havilland, Rita Hayworth, Alan Hale, Jack Carson, George Tobias, Una O'Connor, George Reeves.

Sentimental flashback story of young man's unrequited love for *The Strawbery Blonde* (Rita Hayworth) is a change of pace for dynamic James Cagney and one of the most evocative period pieces produced in America about the innocent "Gay Nineties." Winsome Olivia De Havilland and a great cast of characters (including Alan Hale as Cagney's father) breathe life into this tragicomic tale.

1941 B & W 97 minutes

STRAWBERRY STATEMENT, THE

★½

DIRECTOR: Stuart Hagman

CAST: Kim Darby, Bruce Davison, Bob Balaban, James Kunen

Inane "message" film attempts to make some sense (and money) out of student dissidents and rebellion, focusing on the Columbia University riots of the late 1960s. Some good performances in this hodgepodge of comedy, drama, and youth-authority confrontations and clichés. Halfway serious attempt to study student activists ends up as a safe, establishment movie. Rated R.

1970 103 minutes

STREAMERS

★★★½

DIRECTOR: Robert Altman

CAST: Matthew Modine, Michael Wright

This tense film is about four recruits and two veterans awaiting orders that will send them to Vietnam. The six men are a microcosm of American life in the late 1960s and early 1970s. A powerful, violent drama, this film is not suitable for everyone. Rated R.

1984 118 minutes

STREET SCENE

★★★½

DIRECTOR: King Vidor

CAST: Sylvia Sidney, William Collier Jr., Beulah Bondi, David Landau, Estelle Taylor, Walter Miller

Playwright Elmer Rice wrote the screenplay for this fine film version of his Pulitzer Prize–winning drama of life in the New York tenements and the yearning and anguish of the young and hopeful who are desperate to get out and rise above the mean streets. The cast is excellent, the score classic Alfred Newman, the camera work outstanding. Still under the arcs today, Sylvia Sidney is old big-time Hollywood beside which talentless newcomers pale to oblivion.

1931 B & W 80 minutes

STREET SMART

★★½

DIRECTOR: Jerry Schatzberg

CAST: Christopher Reeve, Kathy Baker, Mimi Rogers, Andre Gregory, Morgan Freeman

Christopher Reeve gives a listless performance as a magazine writer under pressure who fabricates the life story of a New York pimp. Problems arise when parallels with a real pimp under investigation by the D.A. surface. In order not to lose credibility, Reeve must play both sides against the middle. Kathy Baker is the hooker Reeve befriends and beds. Morgan Freeman plays the pimp Fast Black with an electrifying mesh of elegance and sleaze. Director Jerry Schatzberg falls short of expectations since he has proven he knows the streets (*Panic in Needle Park*), but the story idea is quite engaging. Rated R for language and theme.

1986 97 minutes

STREETCAR NAMED DESIRE, A

★★★★★

DIRECTOR: Elia Kazan

CAST: Vivien Leigh, Marlon Brando, Kim Hunter, Karl Malden

Virtuoso acting highlights this powerful and disturbing drama based on the Tennessee Williams play. Vivien Leigh once again is the southern belle. Unlike Scarlett O'Hara, however, her Blanche DuBois is no longer young. She is a sexually disturbed woman who lives in a world of illusion. Her world begins to crumble when she moves in with her sister and brutish brother-in-law (Marlon Brando). Well-deserved Academy Awards were garnered by Leigh, and by Kim Hunter and Karl Malden in supporting roles.

1951 B & W 122 minutes

STREETS OF GOLD

★★★

DIRECTOR: Joe Roth

CAST: Klaus Maria Brandauer, Adrian Pasdar, Wesley Snipes, Angela Molina

Since Sylvester Stallone entered the ring back in 1976, boxing films with other stars haven't fared too well. This one was no exception, which is a shame; it's a pleasant story about an ex-boxer (Klaus Maria Brandauer) who decides to regain his self-worth by passing on his skills to a pair of streetboxers. Brandauer puts a lot of energy into his role, demonstrating shading and character depth far beyond what you'd expect from a routine story. This is a simple fairy-tale, although it brushes against serious topics such as racism and love of country. Inexplicably rated R for mild language and violence.

1986 95 minutes

STREETS OF L.A., THE

★★★½

DIRECTOR: Jerrold Freedman

CAST: Joanne Woodward, Robert Webber, Michael Gwynne, Audrey Christie, Isela Vega, Pepe Serna, Cliff Emmich, Mercedes Aberti, Migeu Pinero, James Victor, Tony Plana

Joanne Woodward plays a struggling real-estate saleswoman who gets her new tires slashed by a group of angry Hispanics and decides to pursue them in the hopes of getting reimbursed for the damage. The acting is quite good even if the film is low-budget production. Despite the video-box art and the action-packed film description, this is not an action film but a sensitive, rather quiet drama. Not rated, but contains violence.

1979 94 minutes

STREETWALKIN'

★

DIRECTOR: Joan Freeman

CAST: Julie Newmar, Melissa Leo, Dale Midkiff, Leon Robinson, Antonio Fargas

As a lesson on why not to become a prostitute, this film has a lot to say. As entertainment, it is unsuccessful. Good acting cannot save an incoherent and pointless script. Too little character development and a heavy reliance on profanity and brutality blunt Melissa Leo's portrayal of Cookie, the runaway-turned-prostitute, and reduce Julie Newmar's soft-hearted madam character to a stereotype. Rated R for simulated sex, profanity, and violence.

1985 84 minutes

STRIPPER, THE

★★½

DIRECTOR: Franklin Schaffner

CAST: Joanne Woodward, Richard Beymer, Claire Trevor, Carol Lynley, Robert Webber, Gypsy Rose Lee, Louis Nye

Somewhat engrossing account of an aging stripper (Joanne Woodward) falling in love with a teenager (Richard Beymer). Good performances by all, but the film tends to drag and become too stagy. Based on William Inge's play.

1963 95 minutes

STUD, THE

DIRECTOR: Quentin Masters

CAST: Joan Collins, Oliver Tobias

Joan Collins reaches new lows in the boring, sordid soft-core porn film concerning a young man's rise to fortune through his various affairs. This one will be tough to get through, even for hardcore Collins fans. Rated R.

1978 95 minutes

STUDS LONIGAN

★★

DIRECTOR: Irving Lerner

CAST: Christopher Knight, Frank Gorshin, Jack Nicholson, Venetia Stevenson, Dick Foran, Jay C. Flippen, Carolyn Craig, Robert Casper

Film version of James T. Farrell's landmark first novel is a major disappointment to those familiar with the *Studs Lonigan* trilogy, and it doesn't offer much for the casual viewer. Depressing tale of a young man's slide into drunkenness and debauchery pulls most of the punches that the books delivered and ends up candy-coating the message and drastically changing the ending to a more conventional Hollywood fadeout. Memorable mainly as a vain effort to bring an unfilmable novel to the screen and for Jack Nicholson, miscast as the coldhearted Weary Reilly, Studs Lonigan's nemesis and one of literature's true badmen. Remade more successfully in the 1970s as a three-part television drama with Harry Hamlin.

1960 B & W 95 minutes

STUNT MAN, THE

★★★★½

DIRECTOR: Richard Rush

CAST: Peter O'Toole, Steven Railsback, Barbara Hershey, Chuck Bail, Allen Goorwitz, Adam Roarke, Alex Rocco

Nothing is ever quite what it seems in this fast-paced, superbly crafted film. It's a Chinese puzzle of a movie and, therefore, may not please all viewers. Nevertheless, this directorial tour de force by Richard Rush has ample thrills, chills, suspense, and surprises for those with a taste for something different. Rated R.

1980 129 minutes

SUBURBIA

★★★

DIRECTOR: Penelope Spheeris

CAST: Chris Pederson, Bill Coyne, Jennifer Clay, Timothy Eric O'Brien

Penelope Spheeris, who directed the punk-rock documentary *Decline of Western Civilization*, did this low-budget film of punk rockers versus local rednecks and townspeople in a small suburban area. Not for all tastes, but a good little film for people who are bored with releases like *Cannonball Run II*. Rated R.

1983 96 minutes

SUDDENLY

★★★★

DIRECTOR: Lewis Allen

CAST: Frank Sinatra, Sterling Hayden, James Gleason, Nancy Gates

Here's topnotch entertainment with Frank Sinatra perfectly cast as a leader of a gang of assassins out to kill the President of the United States. *Suddenly* has gone largely unnoticed over the last few years, but thanks to home video, we can all enjoy this gem of a picture. Reportedly, Sinatra has kept this film out of public circulation for fifteen years, most likely because he plays the role of a psychopath too well.

1954 B & W 77 minutes

SUDDENLY, LAST SUMMER

★★★

DIRECTOR: Joseph L. Mankiewicz

CAST: Elizabeth Taylor, Montgomery Clift, Katharine Hepburn

Another one of those unpleasant but totally intriguing forays of Tennessee Williams. Elizabeth Taylor is a neurotic girl being prodded into madness by the memory of her gay cousin's bizarre death, a memory that Katharine Hepburn, his adoring mother, wants to remain vague if not submerged. She prevails upon Montgomery Clift to make sure it does. Lots of talk in this one leading up to lots more.

1959 B & W 114 minutes

SUGARLAND EXPRESS, THE

★★★★

DIRECTOR: Steven Spielberg

CAST: Goldie Hawn, Ben Johnson, Michael Sacks, William Atherton

A rewarding film in many respects, this was Steven Spielberg's first feature effort. Based on an actual incident in Texas during the late 1960s, a couple released from prison tries to regain custody of their infant child. Their desperation results in a madcap chase across the state with the stolen child and a kidnapped state trooper. Rated PG.

1974 109 minutes

SUMMER HEAT

★

DIRECTOR: Jack Starrett

CAST: Bruce Davison, Susan George, Tony Franciosa

The cover may look sexy, but the film isn't. In fact, most of the time it's just plain silly. Bruce Davison stars as Dolin Pike, a young sheepherder who, upon being sentenced to prison, attempts to escape with his new love, Baby (Susan George). First, they must rob Baby's wealthy gangster exboyfriend, Charlie (Tony Franciosa). Although the acting is fine, as is director Jack Starrett's pacing, the film falls flat due to predictability, implausibility, and corniness. Rated R for violence, profanity, and implied sex.

1983 101 minutes

SUMMER HEAT

★

DIRECTOR: Michie Gleason

CAST: Lori Singer, Bruce Abbott, Anthony Edwards, Clu Gulager, Kathy Bates

This is a barely lukewarm sex-and-soap sizzler about the complications that ensue when plantation wife Lori Singer cheats on husband Anthony Edwards with farmhand Bruce Abbott. They should have called it *Sex with a Yawn*. Rated R.

1987 95 minutes

SUMMER LOVERS

DIRECTOR: Randal Kleiser

CAST: Peter Gallagher, Daryl Hannah, Valerie Quennessen, Barbara Rush, Carole Cook

The director of *Grease* and *Blue Lagoon*, Randal Kleiser, returns with more young lust in this self-penned study of a *ménage à trois* in Greece. *Summer Lovers* is really little more than a two-hour commercial for teen-age promiscuity. When stars Peter Gallagher, Daryl Hannah, and Valerie Quennessen finally end up in bed together, the soundtrack booms the rock song *I'm So Excited*, which is profoundly disturbing. Rated R for nudity, profanity, and implied sex.

1982 98 minutes

SUMMER OF '42

★★★★

DIRECTOR: Robert Mulligan

CAST: Gary Grimes, Jennifer O'Neill, Jerry Houser, Oliver Conant, Katherine Allentuck, Christopher Norris, Lou Frizell

This is one of the more acceptable depictions of the sexual rites of passage of a teen-age boy. Set against the backdrop of a vacationers' resort island off the New England coast during World War II, an inexperienced young man (Gary Grimes) has a crush on the 22-year-old bride (Jennifer O'Neill) of a serviceman. His stumbling attempts to acquire sexual knowledge are handled tenderly and thoughtfully. The climactic scene between the two becomes believable in spite of the audience's initial resistance to such a union. Rated PG.

1971 102 minutes

SUMMER WISHES, WINTER DREAMS

★

DIRECTOR: Gilbert Cates

CAST: Joanne Woodward, Martin Balsam, Sylvia Sydney, Dori Brenner, Ron Richards

This is one of those all-too-well-intentioned films about a Manhattan housewife's depression. The movie feels dated and stale. The character are either screaming at each other ("I may love you, but I don't like you at all!") or reciting banalities ("You are more beautiful now than the day I met you, and I'm not just talking about looks."). Rated PG.

1973 95 minutes

SUMMERTIME

★★★★

DIRECTOR: David Lean

CAST: Katharine Hepburn, Rossano Brazzi, Edward Andrews, Darren McGavin, Isa Miranda

Katharine Hepburn is a sensitive, vulnerable spinster on holiday in Venice. She falls in love with unhappily married shopkeeper Rossano Brazzi, and the romantic idyll is beautiful. David Lean's direction is superb, Jack Hildyard's cinematography excellent. The film has its light moments, but keep the Kleenex handy.

1955 99 minutes

SUNDAY, BLOODY SUNDAY

★★★

DIRECTOR: John Schlesinger

CAST: Peter Finch, Glenda Jackson, Murray Head, Peggy Ashcroft, Maurice Denham

Brilliant performances by Peter Finch and Glenda Jackson are the major reason to watch this very

British three-sided love story; the sides are a bit different, though . . . both love Murray Head. His performance is the film's weak point; it's difficult to imagine anybody falling in love with such a bland, unpleasant person. The script, by Penelope Gilliat, takes a pleasantly intelligent approach to the complexities of the gay relationship. Difficult to watch at times, but intriguing from a historical standpoint. Rated R for sexual situations.

1971 110 minutes

SUNDAY TOO FAR AWAY

★★★½

DIRECTOR: Ken Hannam

CAST: Jack Thompson, Max Cullen, John Ewart, Reg Lye, Lisa Peers

An Australian film about the life and lot of a sheepshearer Down Under circa 1956. The title comes from a piece of verse titled "The Shearer's Wife's Lament" that states: "Friday night, he's too tired, Saturday night too drunk, Sunday too far away." This refers to the many miles traveled to sheep stations by the shearer and the brief weekends he has at home in the city. Jack Thompson stars as Foley, a champion shearer who finds his mantle challenged. Unrated, the film has profanity, nudity, and violence.

1983 100 minutes

SUNDOWN

★★½

DIRECTOR: Henry Hathaway

CAST: Gene Tierney, Bruce Cabot, George Sanders, Harry Carey, Cedric Hardwicke, Joseph Calleia, Reginald Gardiner, Marc Lawrence

Fairly entertaining stiff-upper-lip British drama in Africa features Bruce Cabot as a Canadian and George Sanders as the army officer who replaces him and prepares their desert outpost for action. It seems that the local tribesmen are being armed by the Germans, and native queen Gene Tierney helps the empire locate the gun smugglers and deal with them. Although there are some bursts of energy in this film and the great Miklos Rozsa did the music, it is still slow going.

1941 B & W 90 minutes

SUNDOWNERS, THE

★★★★

DIRECTOR: Fred Zinnemann

CAST: Robert Mitchum, Deborah Kerr, Peter Ustinov, Glynis Johns, Dina Merrill, Chips Rafferty

Robert Mitchum and Deborah Kerr were—like Tracy and Hepburn, Bogart and Bacall, Wayne and O'Hara—one of the great screen teams, and this is our choice as their best film together. The story of Australian sheepherders in the 1920s, it is a character study brought alive by Fred Zinnemann's sensitive direction and attention to detail, as well as by the fine acting of a superb cast. Watching Mitchum in something this good reminds one of what a great screen actor he really is. His obvious affection and respect for Kerr electrifies their scenes together.

1960 113 minutes

SUNRISE AT CAMPOBELLO

★★★★★

DIRECTOR: Vincent J. Donehue

CAST: Ralph Bellamy, Greer Garson, Alan Bunce, Hume Cronyn

Producer/writer Dore Schary's inspiring and heartwarming drama of Franklin Delano Roosevelt's public political battles and private fight against polio. Ralph Bellamy is FDR; Greer Garson is Eleanor. Both are superb. The acting is tops, the entire production sincere. Taken from Schary's impressive stage play, with all the fine qualities intact.

1960 143 minutes

SUNSET BLVD.

★★★★★

DIRECTOR: Billy Wilder
CAST: William Holden, Gloria Swanson, Erich von Stroheim, Fred Clark, Jack Webb, Hedda Hopper, Buster Keaton

Sunset Boulevard is one of Hollywood's strongest indictments against its own excesses. It justly deserves its place among the best films ever made. William Holden plays an out-of-work gigolo-screenwriter who attaches himself to a faded screen star attempting a comeback. Gloria Swanson, in a stunning parody, is brilliant as the tragically deluded Norma Desmond.

1950 B & W 110 minutes

SWIMMER, THE

★★★★

DIRECTOR: Frank Perry
CAST: Burt Lancaster, Janet Landgard, Janice Rule, Joan Rivers, Tony Bickley, Marge Champion, Kim Hunter, Bill Fiore

A middle-aged man in a gray flannel suit who has never achieved his potential swims from neighbor's pool to neighbor's pool on his way home on a hot afternoon in social Connecticut. Each stop brings back memories of what was and what might have been. Burt Lancaster is excellent in the title role. Rated PG.

1968 94 minutes

SWING SHIFT

★½

DIRECTOR: Jonathan Demme
CAST: Goldie Hawn, Kurt Russell, Ed Harris, Fred Ward, Christine Lahti, Sudie Bond

Goldie Hawn stars in this disappointing 1940s-era romance as Kay Walsh, the girl who's left behind when her husband, Jack (Ed Harris), goes off to fight in World War II. With America's work force depleted by the country's need for soldiers, women are needed to replace men on the assembly line. So Kay goes to work and, despite a few misgivings, finds she has all sorts of hidden talents—including an untapped potential for passion, fulfilled by co-worker Lucky Lockhart (Kurt Russell, of *Silkwood*). Rated PG for profanity and suggested sex.

1984 100 minutes

SYBIL

★★★★

DIRECTOR: Daniel Petrie
CAST: Joanne Woodward, Sally Field, William Prince

Sally Field is outstanding in this deeply disturbing but utterly fascinating made-for-TV drama of a young woman whose intense pyschological childhood trauma has given her seventeen distinct personalities. Joanne Woodward is the patient, dedicated psychiatrist who sorts it all out.

1976 116 minutes

SYLVESTER

★★★★

DIRECTOR: Tim Hunter
CAST: Melissa Gilbert, Richard Farnsworth, Michael Schoeffling, Constance Towers, Yankton Hatten, Shane Sherwin

Director Tim Hunter (*Tex*) does an admirable job with this hard-edged *National Velvet*–style drama about a tomboy (Melissa Gilbert) who rides her horse, Sylvester (named after the Italian Stallion himself, Sylvester Stallone), to victory in the Olympics' Three-Day Event in Lexington, Kentucky. Gilbert is first-rate as the aspiring horsewoman, and Richard Farnsworth is his reliable, watchable self as her cantankerous mentor. It's a touching story with the grit and punch of reality. Rated PG-13 for profanity and violence.

1985 109 minutes

SYLVIA

★★

DIRECTOR: Michael Firth

CAST: Eleanor David, Nigel Terry, Tom Wilkinson, Mary Regan

Sylvia is about as underwhelming as a film can get and still have some redeeming qualities. Were it not for the fine performance by Eleanor David in the title role, this film about seminal educator Sylvia Ashton-Warner would be a muddled bore. It jumps from one event to another with little or no buildup or continuity. There is no dramatic tension. Perhaps everyone in New Zealand, where the movie was made, knows of the main character's accomplishments, but the rest of us need a little background and story-telling logic to appreciate a picture about her. Rated PG for graphic descriptions of violence.

1985 97 minutes

T-MEN

★★½

DIRECTOR: Anthony Mann

CAST: Dennis O'Keefe, Alfred Ryder, Mary Meade, Wallace Ford, June Lockhart, Charles McGraw, Jane Randolph, Art Smith, Jim Bannon

Two undercover operatives for the Treasury Department infiltrate a master counterfeiting ring and find themselves on opposite sides when the lead starts to fly. Unable to save the life of his partner without exposing himself, agent Dennis O'Keefe courageously continues the work of both men and sets up the final showdown between the T-men and the counterfeiters. Compact, gritty with few visible ties to anything but his job and his mission. True stories from the files of the U.S. Treasury Department are the basis of this production.

1948 B & W 92 minutes

TABLE FOR FIVE

★★★

DIRECTOR: Robert Lieberman

CAST: Jon Voight, Richard Crenna, Millie Perkins

Had it up to here with *Kramer vs. Kramer* clones about single parents coping with their kids? If you have, you'll probably decide to skip this movie—and that would be a shame, because it's a good one. Jon Voight stars as J. P. Tannen, a divorcé who takes his three youngsters on a Mediterranean cruise in hopes of getting back into their lives full-time. But despite his good intentions, Tannen has never really grown up. If his dream is to come true, that is exactly what he has to do. Rated PG for mature situations.

1983 122 minutes

TALE OF TWO CITIES, A

★★★★★

DIRECTOR: Jack Conway

CAST: Ronald Colman, Basil Rathbone, Edna May Oliver, Elizabeth Allan

A Tale of Two Cities is a satisfactory rendition of Charles Dickens's novel. It is richly acted, with true Dickens flavor. Ronald Colman was ideally cast in the role of Sydney Carton, the English no-account who finds purpose in life amid the turmoil of the French Revolution. The photography in this film is one of its most outstanding features. The dark shadows are in keeping with the spirit of this somber Dickens story.

1935 B & W 121 minutes

TAMMY AND THE BACHELOR

★★★

DIRECTOR: Joseph Pevney
CAST: Debbie Reynolds, Leslie Nielsen, Walter Brennan, Mala Powers, Fay Wray, Sidney Blackmer, Mildred Natwick, Louise Beavers

Like Debbie Reynolds's number-one hit song *Tammy*, the movie is corny but irresistible. Ingenuous country girl Reynolds falls in love with injured pilot Leslie Nielsen and nurses him back to health. The romance and humor are sweet and charming, though predictable. Reynolds and Nielsen have never been more likable, and a crew of classic character actors contribute solid support. The movie's success led to sequels and a TV series.

1957 89 minutes

TAMMY AND THE DOCTOR

★

DIRECTOR: Harry Keller
CAST: Sandra Dee, Peter Fonda, Macdonald Carey, Beulah Bondi, Margaret Lindsay, Reginald Owen, Adam West

There's an audience for this kind of film somewhere, and thanks to the video revolution, closet Sandra Dee fans can enjoy this undemanding fare without the snickers and giggles that would certainly accompany a public screening. Cutesy romance between country gal Sandra Dee and young Peter Fonda is relatively harmless and studded with familiar character faces, but this is definitely an example of a youth film with a limited audience. No muss, no fuss, no rough stuff—in fact, not much of anything at all.

1963 88 minutes

TAPS

★★★½

DIRECTOR: Harold Becker
CAST: George C. Scott, Timothy Hutton, Ronny Cox, Tom Cruise

George C. Scott is an iron-jawed commander of a military academy and Timothy Hutton a gung-ho cadet who leads a student revolt in this often exciting but mostly unbelievable and unnecessarily violent drama. Rated R.

1981 118 minutes

TARTUFFE

★★★

DIRECTOR: Bill Alexander
CAST: Antony Sher, Nigel Hawthorne, Alison Steadman

Let's be upfront about this one: It's a sophisticated version of Molière's play about religious hypocrisy. The satire is funny and biting, but this Royal Shakespeare Company production is not for everyone. The performances, especially Antony Sher's interpretation of Tartuffe, are brilliant in concept, but very subtle.

1984 110 minutes

TATTOO

DIRECTOR: Bob Brooks
CAST: Bruce Dern, Maud Adams, Rikke Borge, John Getz

Simply the most vile, reprehensible, sexist, and misogynistic piece of tripe ever released under the guise of a mainstream film. Bruce Dern is a demented tattoo artist who kidnaps Maud Adams to use as a "living tableau." The film concludes with her scarred for life, and we're supposed to believe it's an upbeat ending. Incredibly, this trash was written by a woman: Joyce Buñuel, daughter-in-law of Luis. Only for demented minds. Rated R for gross violence and kinky sex.

1981 103 minutes

TAXI DRIVER

★★★★★

DIRECTOR: Martin Scorsese
CAST: Robert De Niro, Harvey Keitel, Cybill Shepherd, Jodie Foster, Peter Boyle

Robert De Niro plays an alienated Vietnam-era vet thrust into the nighttime urban sprawl of New York City. In his despair after a romantic rejection by an attractive political campaign aide, he focuses on "freeing" a 12-year-old prostitute by unleashing violent retribution on her pimp. It's unnerving and realistic, with a great twist ending. Rated R for violence and profanity.

1976 113 minutes

TELL ME A RIDDLE

★★★★

DIRECTOR: Lee Grant
CAST: Melvyn Douglas, Lila Kedrova, Brooke Adams, Dolores Dorn, Bob Elross, Joan Harris, Zalman King

Actress Lee Grant directed this genuinely moving, marvelously acted film adaptation of Tillie Olsen's novella about an elderly immigrant couple (Melvyn Douglas and Lila Kedrova) who, after years of quarreling, rediscover the love that originally brought them together. Although it may require concentration and commitment, *Tell Me a Riddle* gives much in return. It defies the traditionally acceptable—and overdone—formulas for moviemaking to become a fresh and rewarding experience. Unrated, the film has profanity.

1980 90 minutes

TEMPEST

★

DIRECTOR: Paul Mazursky
CAST: John Cassavetes, Gena Rowlands, Vittorio Gassman, Molly Ringwald, Susan Sarandon

This isn't a movie; it's an endurance test. About an architect (John Cassavetes) who has prophetic dreams and is going through a mid-life crisis, nothing ever really happens. The only thing that saves it from being a complete bust is the acting. Unfortunately, the cast can't quite make up for the fact that this film, directed by Paul Mazursky (*Willie and Phil*; *An Unmarried Woman*), is just plain boring. Rated PG, the film has nudity and profanity.

1982 140 minutes

TEMPEST

★★½

DIRECTOR: Sam Taylor
CAST: John Barrymore, Camilla Horn, Louis Wolheim, Boris De Fas, George Fawcett

Set during the 1914 Bolshevik uprising in Russia, this richly romantic drama has Army officer John Barrymore stepping out of place to court his aristocratic commandant's daughter. As a result, both are undone and must flee for their lives and love. Silent, with music track.

1928 B & W 105 minutes

TEN COMMANDMENTS, THE (ORIGINAL)

★★★

DIRECTOR: Cecil B. De Mille
CAST: Theodore Roberts, Charles de Roche, Estelle Taylor, James Neill, Noble Johnson, Edythe Chapman, Richard Dix, Rod La Rocque, Leatrice Joy, Nita Naldi, Robert Edeson, Agnes Ayres

Master showman Cecil B. De Mille's monumental two-phase silent version of the Book of Exodus and the application of the Ten Commandments in modern life. Part One, set in ancient times, is in early color; Part Two, set in the modern (1923) period, is in black and white. Impressive special effects, including the parting of the Red Sea. In scope, this is the film that foreshadows De Mille's great spectacles of the sound era.

1923 140 minutes

TEN COMMANDMENTS, THE (REMAKE)

★★★½

DIRECTOR: Cecil B. De Mille

CAST: Charlton Heston, Yul Brynner, Edward G. Robinson, Sir Cedric Hardwicke, John Derek, Anne Baxter

A stylish, visually stunning, epic-scale biblical study as only Cecil B. De Mille could make 'em (until William Wyler came along three years later with *Ben Hur*). Charlton Heston, as Moses, takes charge of "God's people" and wrests them from Egypt's punishing grasp. Heston's utter conviction holds the lengthy film together, sweeping us into the story in spite of the occasionally melodramatic staging and purple dialogue. Then, of course, there's the parting of the Red Sea—an effect that *still* looks great. Unrated; suitable for family viewing.

1956 219 minutes

10 RILLINGTON PLACE

★★★★

DIRECTOR: Richard Fleischer

CAST: Richard Attenborough, Judy Geeson, John Hurt, Gabrielle Daye, Andre Morell

This bleak true-crime drama is based on one of England's most famous murder cases and was actually shot in the house and the neighborhood where the crimes took place. The seamy squalor of the surroundings perfectly mirror the poverty of mind and soul that allowed John Christy to murder and remain undetected for over ten years; the irony that he was a prosecution witness for the feeble-minded man accused of murdering his wife is not wasted on the audience. Brilliantly acted by Richard Attenborough and John Hurt.

1971 111 minutes

TENDER MERCIES

★★★★★

DIRECTOR: Bruce Beresford

CAST: Robert Duvall, Tess Harper, Ellen Barkin

Robert Duvall more than deserved his best-actor Oscar for this superb character study about a down-and-out country singer trying for a comeback. His Mac Sledge is a man who still has songs to sing, but barely the heart to sing them. That is, until he meets up with a sweet-natured widow (Tess Harper) who gives him back the will to live. Rated PG.

1983 89 minutes

TERMS OF ENDEARMENT

★★★★

DIRECTOR: James L. Brooks

CAST: Shirley MacLaine, Debra Winger, Jack Nicholson, Danny DeVito

This stylish soap opera, written, produced, and directed by James L. Brooks, covers thirty years in the lives of a Houston matron, played by Shirley MacLaine, and her daughter, played by Debra Winger, who marries an English teacher with a wandering eye. Jack Nicholson is also on hand, to play MacLaine's neighbor, an astronaut with the wrong stuff. Funny, touching, and unforgettable, it's one of the best of its kind. Rated PG for profanity and suggested sex.

1983 132 minutes

TERRY FOX STORY, THE

★★★

DIRECTOR: Ralph Thomas

CAST: Eric Fryer, Robert Duvall, Chris Makepeace, Rosalind Chao, Michael Zelniker

This made-for-HBO film chronicles the "Marathon of Hope" undertaken by amputee Terry Fox (Eric Fryer), who lost a leg to cancer. Fox jogged 3,000 miles across Canada before collapsing from exhaustion in Ontario. Based on a true story, this uplifting film is helped by solid performances, direction, and writing.

1983 96 minutes

TESS

★★★★½

DIRECTOR: Roman Polanski

CAST: Nastassja Kinski, Peter Firth, John Bett

A hypothetically beautiful adaptation of Thomas Hardy's late-nineteenth-century novel *Tess of the D'Urbervilles*, this is director Roman Polanski's finest artistic achievement. Nastassja Kinski is stunning as the country girl who is "wronged" by a suave aristocrat and the man she marries. The story unfolds at the pace of a lazy afternoon stroll, and the drama is sedated, but Polanski's technical skills and the cinematography are spellbinding. Rated PG.

1979 170 minutes

TEST OF LOVE, A

★★

DIRECTOR: Gil Brealey

CAST: Angela Punch McGregor, Drew Forsythe, Tina Arhondis, Wallas Eaton, Simon Chilvers, Monica Maughan, Mark Butler

This tearjerker, taken from the Australian best-selling novel *Annie's Coming Out*, vividly displays the love and determination a therapist (Angela Punch McGregor) has in fighting for the rights of Anne O'Farrell, a severely disabled teenager who was misdiagnosed as being retarded. In that sense the film is a winner. Yet the makers of this movie lack the finesse it takes to make the antagonists of this story more than one-dimensional. Indeed, with nasty nurses and hostile hospital officials against our heroes, the stacked deck is all too obvious, and the viewer can't help feeling manipulated. All performances are sound, including Tina Arhondis, a disabled 9-year-old who plays the role of Anne. Rated PG for profanity.

1984 93 minutes

TEX

★★★★½

DIRECTOR: Tim Hunter

CAST: Matt Dillon, Jim Metzler, Ben Johnson, Emilio Estevez, Meg Tilly

This adaptation of S. E. Hinton's novel is what Francis Ford Coppola's *The Outsiders*, which was based on another book by Hinton, should have been but wasn't. Matt Dillon, Jim Metzler, and Ben Johnson star in this superb coming-of-age adventure about the struggles and conflicts of two teen-age brothers growing up in the Southwest without parental guidance. Rated PG for violence and mature situations.

1982 103 minutes

THAT CHAMPIONSHIP SEASON

★★★½

DIRECTOR: Jason Miller

CAST: Bruce Dern, Stacy Keach, Martin Sheen, Paul Sorvino, Robert Mitchum

Former high-school basketball stars (Bruce Dern, Stacy Keach, Martin Sheen, and Paul Sorvino) and their coach (Robert Mitchum) get together for the twenty-fourth annual celebration of their championship season. However, it turns out to be a fiasco as the longtime friendships begin disintegrating under the pressure of a mayoral election. While there's nothing wrong with a sobering look at broken dreams and the pain of mid-life crisis, we've seen it all on screen before. And, more to the point, most of us have enough problems of our own without taking on those of a quintet of shallow, self-centered men. Rated R for profanity, racial epithets, violence, and adult content.

1982 110 minutes

THAT COLD DAY IN THE PARK

★★

DIRECTOR: Robert Altman

CAST: Sandy Dennis, Michael Burns, Susanne Benton, John Garfield Jr., Luana Anders, Michael Murphy

Bearing little resemblance to the work that made director Robert Altman one of the darlings of moviegoers in the late 1960s and early 1970s, this claustrophobic study of an emotionally disturbed woman and her obsessive interest in a young man who frequents the park across from her house is just about as strange as they come. It, nonetheless gives gifted Sandy Dennis one of her most memorable roles. This film focuses on repressed sexuality in a style somewhat comparable to Roman Polanski's *Repulsion*, but also hints at incest and other subjects considered taboo when this Canadian-made movie was released. Definitely different, and worth a try, but be forewarned: This is not an ordinary romance.

1969 113 minutes

THAT HAMILTON WOMAN

★★★½

DIRECTOR: Alexander Korda

CAST: Vivien Leigh, Laurence Olivier

The legendary acting duo of Mr. and Mrs. Laurence Olivier recreates one of England's legendary romantic scandals: the love of naval hero Horatio Nelson for the alluring Lady Emma Hamilton. The affair between these two already married lovers caused quite a stir in early nineteenth-century Britain. This was Winston Churchill's favorite movie, no doubt because when it was released in mid World War II, it showed a man choosing duty to country over the attraction of a beautiful woman. With Vivien Leigh looking more striking than in her famous portrayal of Scarlett O'Hara, one has trouble being convinced. The film drags in places, but remains quite watchable.

1941 B & W 128 minutes

THAT WAS THEN . . . THIS IS NOW

★★★★

DIRECTOR: Christopher Cain

CAST: Emilio Estevez, Craig Sheffer, Kim Delaney, Morgan Freeman, Frank Howard, Larry B. Scott, Barbara Babcock

The best film to be adapted from a novel by S. E. Hinton (*The Outsiders; Rumble Fish*), this work, directed by Christopher Cain, has a tough, raw edge and a resounding ring of truth. The cuteness and condescension that mar most coming-of-age films are laudably absent in its tale of two working-class teenagers (Emilio Estevez and Craig Sheffer) coming to grips with adulthood. Cain makes us feel as if we are watching a movie about real kids. Sharing the credit for this is Estevez, who also wrote the screenplay. They have created a work that teens and adults alike can appreciate. Rated R for violence and profanity.

1985 103 minutes

THESE THREE

★★★★

DIRECTOR: William Wyler

CAST: Miriam Hopkins, Merle Oberon, Joel McCrea, Bonita Granville, Marcia Mae Jones

A superb cast brings alive this story of two upright and decent schoolteachers victimized by the lies of a malicious student. Miriam Hopkins and Merle Oberon are the pair brutally slandered; Bonita Granville is the evil liar. Script by Lillian Hellman, loosely based on her play *The Children's Hour*, under which title the film was remade in 1961.

1936 B & W 93 minutes

THEY CAME TO CORDURA

★★

DIRECTOR: Robert Rossen

CAST: Gary Cooper, Rita Hayworth, Van Heflin, Tab Hunter, Richard Conte

This film, which examines the true character of the war hero, is not one of Gary Cooper's best. The story has Cooper in Mexico during World War I as one of six military men returning to base. The hardships they encounter on the way create the drama. The movie has a nice look, but just not enough action.

1959 123 minutes

THEY KNEW WHAT THEY WANTED

★★★

DIRECTOR: Garson Kanin

CAST: Charles Laughton, Carole Lombard, William Gargan, Harry Carey, Frank Fay

This film is a fine example of offbeat casting that somehow succeeds. Charles Laughton and Carole Lombard, two actors noted for their exuberant acting styles, were required to submerge their histrionics in order to bring off a low-key, little tragedy. The story is of the unrequited love of an Italian wine grower for the opportunistic hash house waitress that he marries. Lombard is excellent as the greedy wife, but Laughton's heavily accented performance does not always ring true.

1940 B & W 96 minutes

THEY LIVE BY NIGHT

★★★½

DIRECTOR: Nicholas Ray

CAST: Farley Granger, Cathy O'Donnell, Howard da Silva, Jay C. Flippen, Helen Craig

The first screen version of Edward Anderson's *Thieves Like Us* is a seminal film dealing with youth, alienation, and the concept of the loner who operates outside the confines of conventional behavior and morality. Likened to the true-life odyssey of Clyde Barrow and Bonnie Parker in the 1930s, this postwar crime drama gave American youth a minor cultural folk hero in Farley Granger and began the directing career of young Nicholas Ray, who would in turn provide the world with the ultimate image of teen-age alienation: *Rebel Without a Cause*.

1949 B & W 95 minutes

THEY MADE ME A CRIMINAL

★★★

DIRECTOR: Busby Berkeley

CAST: John Garfield, Claude Rains, Ann Sheridan, Gloria Dickson, The Dead-End Kids, Ward Bond

John Garfield's film persona is a direct result of this Warner Bros. story about the redemption of a loner on the lam from the law for a crime he didn't commit. A great cast (including a young Ann Sheridan, the great Claude Rains, and the Dead-End Kids in their fourth film) still doesn't change the fact that this remake of 1933's *The Life of Jimmy Dolan* is muddled and not too solidly constructed.

This film was director Busby Berkeley's only venture outside the realm of the movie musicals he made for his home studio, but the image of the antihero as epitomized by a defiant John Garfield was the first of a series of young rebels that still scowl out at us from the screen.

1939 B & W 92 minutes

THEY MEET AGAIN

★½

DIRECTOR: Erle C. Kenton

CAST: Jean Hersholt, Robert Baldwin, Neil Hamilton, Dorothy Lovett, Maude Eburne, Anne Bennett, Barton Yarborough, Arthur Hoyt

In this film, the last in the popular Dr. Christian series about a snoopy small-town doctor, genial Jean Hersholt is upset because a man he feels is innocent is serving time in prison. Spurred on by the plight of the convicted man's young daughter, the good doctor finds out who embezzled the missing money and leads the authorities to them. This slice of artificial Americana was directed by Erle C. Kenton, a little-known professional who guided everything from Dracula and Frankenstein to Abbott and Costello but is perhaps best known for one of the truly nightmarish horror films of the early 1930s: *Island of Lost Souls*.

1941 B & W 69 minutes

THEY MIGHT BE GIANTS

★★★★

DIRECTOR: Anthony Harvey

CAST: George C. Scott, Joanne Woodward, Jack Gilford

Stylish and engaging study of a retired judge (George C. Scott) who imagines himself to be Sherlock Holmes. With visions of dollar signs floating before his eyes, the judge's brother hopes to have this ersatz detective committed; to this end, the brother brings in a female psychiatrist whose name happens to be—you guessed it—Watson. This unlikely duo embarks on a series of adventures, real and imagined, with Scott's view of humanity—and this, after all, is the point of James Goldman's deft script—far more compassionate and understanding than that of his "saner" fellow citizens. Although not for all tastes, and cursed with a rather oblique ending, this will be heartily enjoyed by anti-establishment viewers who loved *A Thousand Clowns* and *Harold and Maude*. Rated PG.

1971 88 minutes

THEY SHOOT HORSES, DON'T THEY?

★★★★★

DIRECTOR: Sydney Pollack

CAST: Jane Fonda, Gig Young, Michael Sarrazin

The desperation and hopelessness of the Great Depression is graphically shown in this powerful drama, in a pitiful collection of marathon dancers. Some of the group will endure this physical and mental assault on their human spirit; some will not. Jane Fonda, as a cynical casualty of the Depression, and Gig Young, as the uncaring master of ceremonies, give stunning performances. Rated PG.

1969 121 minutes

THEY WON'T BELIEVE ME

★★★½

DIRECTOR: Irving Pichel

CAST: Robert Young, Susan Hayward, Jane Greer, Rita Johnson, Tom Powers, George Tyne, Don Beddoe, Frank Ferguson

Robert Young is a grade-A stinker in this classic *film noir* of deceit, mistaken murder, suicide, and doomed romance. Rita Johnson is especially fine as the wronged wife.

1947 B & W 95 minutes

THEY'RE PLAYING WITH FIRE

DIRECTOR: Howard Avedis
CAST: Sybil Danning, Eric Brown, Andrew Prine

A high-school student is seduced by his English teacher, who is hatching a plot that will enmesh the student in a plan to defraud an elderly relative of her estate. The scheme turns into murder, with the student suspected of the crime. The movie is punctuated with steamy seduction scenes involving the teacher and the student. In the end, the immoral woman rushes off with the money and the student. Everyone wins, except whoever watches this turkey. Rated R.

1983 96 minutes

THIEF OF HEARTS

★★★

DIRECTOR: Douglas Day Stewart
CAST: Steven Bauer, Barbara Williams

A young, upwardly mobile married woman loses her intimate diary of sexual fantasies to a thief who has broken into her home. In an interesting premise, the woman becomes a willing participant in the thief's sexual manipulations without knowing that he is the man who stole her secrets. Rated R.

1984 100 minutes

THIS LAND IS MINE

★★★

DIRECTOR: Jean Renoir
CAST: Charles Laughton, Maureen O'Hara, George Sanders, Walter Slezak

Charles Laughton in another fine characterization, this time as a timid French teacher who blossoms as a hero when he is incited to vigorous action by the Nazi occupation. Time has dulled the cutting edge of this obviously patriotic wartime film, but the artistry of the director and players remains sharp.

1943 B & W 103 minutes

THIS PROPERTY IS CONDEMNED

★★½

DIRECTOR: Sydney Pollack
CAST: Natalie Wood, Robert Redford, Charles Bronson, Kate Reid, Robert Blake

Marginal film interpretation of Tennessee Williams's play. Owen Legate (Robert Redford) is a stranger in town, there for the purpose of laying off local railroaders. Alva (Natalie Wood) is a flirtatious southern girl who casts her spell of romance on the stranger, who is staying at her mother's boardinghouse. Her vengeful mother is willing to sacrifice her daughter's happiness to soothe her own ego. Co-scripted by Francis Ford Coppola.

1966 109 minutes

THORN BIRDS, THE

★★★

DIRECTOR: Daryl Duke
CAST: Richard Chamberlain, Rachel Ward, Christopher Plummer, Bryan Brown, Barbara Stanwyck, Richard Kiley, Jean Simmons

In this made-for-television miniseries, a handsome and ambitious priest becomes a moral cropper when he falls in love with the nubile promise of an innocent, trusting child, whom he eventually betrays sexually while on his way up the apostolic ladder. It's all played out against shifting backgrounds of outback Australia, Vatican Rome, and idyllic Greece.

1983 500 minutes

THURSDAY'S GAME

★★★

DIRECTOR: Robert Moore

CAST: Gene Wilder, Bob Newhart, Ellen Burstyn, Cloris Leachman, Rob Reiner, Nancy Walker, Valerie Harper

Engaging made-for-television film about two ordinary guys (Gene Wilder and Bob Newhart) who continue to get together on Thursday nights after their weekly poker game collapses. Both have reasons for wanting to leave the house, and both make the most of this small rebellion. The supporting cast is excellent; this is one of those little films that attracted talented performers before they broke loose in their own careers. Newhart is the standout, as a prissy businessman who merely wants more control of his life. Unrated; adult themes.

1974 74 minutes

TICKET TO HEAVEN

★★★

DIRECTOR: Ralph L. Thomas

CAST: Nick Mancuso, Saul Rubinek, Meg Foster, Kim Cattrall, R. H. Thompson

This Canadian film presents a lacerating look at the frightening phenomenon of contemporary religious cults. Nick Mancuso is riveting as the brainwashed victim. Saul Rubinek and Meg Foster are splendid in support. And R. H. Thompson almost steals the show as a painfully pragmatic deprogrammer. Nice touches of humor give the movie balance. Rated PG.

1981 107 minutes

TILL THE END OF TIME

★★★

DIRECTOR: Edward Dmytryk

CAST: Dorothy McGuire, Guy Madison, Robert Mitchum, Jean Porter

Three veterans of World War II come home to find life, in general and how it was when they left, considerably changed. Readjustment is tough, and the love they left has soured. A good drama.

1946 B & W 105 minutes

TIM

★★★★½

DIRECTOR: Michael Pate

CAST: Mel Gibson, Piper Laurie, Alwyn Kurts, Pat Evison

An unforgettable character study from Down Under, this features Mel Gibson in his film debut as a simple-minded young adult and Piper Laurie as the older woman who finds herself falling in love with him. Superb supporting performances by the Australian cast—especially Alwyn Kurts and Pat Evison, as Tim's parents—help make this screen adaptation of the first novel by Colleen McCullough (*The Thorn Birds*) a heartwarming and profoundly moving viewing experience. Rated PG for suggested sex.

1979 108 minutes

TIME TO LOVE AND A TIME TO DIE, A

★★½

DIRECTOR: Douglas Sirk

CAST: John Gavin, Lilo Pulver, Jock Mahoney, Don DeFore, Keenan Wynn, Erich Maria Remarque, Jim Hutton, Klaus Kinski

A well-intentioned but preachy and largely unsatisfying antiwar film adapted from the novel by Erich Maria Remarque (*All Quiet on the Western Front*), who also portrays the Professor. John Gavin is a German soldier who receives a furlough from the Russian front in 1944. He returns home to find his town a bombed-out shell and his parents missing.

Lilo Pulver is the girl he meets and marries while on leave.

1958 133 minutes

TIMES OF HARVEY MILK, THE

★★★★

DIRECTOR: Robert Epstein

CAST: Documentary

This sensitive documentary uses television footage and personal observations from friends, fans, and fellows to follow the political life of slain politician Harvey Milk, from his acknowledgment of his homosexuality at age 14 through his murder at the hands of Dan White in San Francisco. No MPAA rating; no objectionable material.

1985 87 minutes

TO KILL A MOCKINGBIRD

★★★★★

DIRECTOR: Robert Mulligan

CAST: Gregory Peck, Mary Badham, Philip Alford, John Megna

To Kill a Mockingbird is a leisurely paced, flavorful filming of Harper Lee's best-selling novel. Gregory Peck earned an Oscar as a small-town southern lawyer who defends a black man accused of rape. Mary Badham, Philip Alford, and John Megna are superb as Peck's children and a visiting friend who are trying to understand life in a small town.

1962 B & W 129 minutes

TO SIR WITH LOVE

★★★★

DIRECTOR: James Clavell

CAST: Sidney Poitier, Judy Geeson, Christian Roberts, Suzy Kendall, Lulu

A moving, gentle portrait of the influence of a black teacher upon a classroom of poverty-ridden teenagers in London's East End, this stars Sidney Poitier, in one of his finer performances, as the teacher. He instills in his pupils a belief in themselves and respect for one another.

1967 105 minutes

TOAST OF NEW YORK, THE

★★★

DIRECTOR: Rowland V. Lee

CAST: Edward Arnold, Cary Grant, Frances Farmer, Jack Oakie, Donald Meek, Clarence Kolb, Thelma Leeds, Billy Gilbert, Oscar Apfel, Virginia Carroll

Lack of star appeal hindered this semiaccurate biography of legendary post–Civil War Wall Street wheeler-dealer James Fisk. But, even so, it is a good film. Edward Arnold superbly plays Fisk. Jack Oakie does a fine turn. Don't expect the Cary Grant you know and love, however.

1937 B & W 109 minutes

TOL'ABLE DAVID

★★½

DIRECTOR: King Vidor

CAST: Richard Barthelmess, Gladys Hulette, Ernest Torrence, Walter P. Lewis, Warner Richmond

Though it creaks a bit with age, this stalwart tale of good besting evil deserves attention and rewards it. Silent.

1921 B & W 80 minutes

TOM BROWN'S SCHOOL DAYS

★★½

DIRECTOR: Robert Stevenson

CAST: Cedric Hardwicke, Freddie Bartholomew, Gale Storm, Jimmy Lydon, Josephine Hutchinson, Polly Moran, Billy Halop

"Old school tie" story mixes top Hollywood production values and minor classic of British secondary schools into an enjoyable froth filled with all the clichés that have since been completely devalued by constant exposure in ludicrous movie and television treatments.

Everybody's favorite English kid Freddie Bartholomew and veteran Cedric Hardwicke do their duty in the best tradition while blatantly American juveniles recruited from the "East Side Kids" and "Henry Aldrich" series perform surprisingly well in this structured effort. Better than one would think and not the creaky old groaner it could have been.

1940 B & W 86 minutes

TOMORROW

★★★★★

DIRECTOR: Joseph Anthony

CAST: Robert Duvall, Olga Bellin, Sudie Bond, Richard McConnell

Robert Duvall gives yet another sensitive, powerful, and completely convincing performance in this superb black-and-white character study about a caretaker who finds himself caring for—in both senses—a pregnant woman (Olga Bellin) who turns up one day at the lumber mill where he works. Viewers will never forget this simple tale of a brief but devastating episode in one man's life. Rated PG for violence.

1972 B & W 103 minutes

TOMORROW AT SEVEN

★★

DIRECTOR: Ray Enright

CAST: Chester Morris, Vivienne Osborne, Allen Jenkins, Frank McHugh, Henry Stephenson, Grant Mitchell, Oscar Apfel, Charles Middleton, Cornelius Keefe

Obscure murder drama pits crime novelist Chester Morris and bumbling policemen Allen Jenkins and Frank McHugh against the mysterious Ace, who sends his victims a calling card and tells them where to go to die, which they inevitably do. One of the most time-worn of all conventions in mystery drama, the sinister stranger with an axe to grind was pretty threadbare even in the 1930s, and this routine whodunit has little to offer.

1933 B & W 62 minutes

TORCHLIGHT

★½

DIRECTOR: Tom Wright

CAST: Pamela Sue Martin, Steve Railsback, Ian McShane, Al Corley, Rita Taggart

Pamela Sue Martin, of *Nancy Drew* and *Dynasty* TV fame, produced, co-wrote, and starred in this less-than-memorable film. In it, her successful but insecure husband, Jake (Steve Railsback), becomes hopelessly addicted to cocaine. Naturally their marriage suffers as a result of his addiction. Ian McShane plays Sidney, the pusher everyone loves to hate. Although the idea behind this film could have been captivating, nothing can make up for the poor dialogue and acting. If viewers do somehow manage to stay awake until the end of this film, they will be rewarded with Carly Simon's sweet voice as she sings the theme song. Rated R for explicit drug use and sadism.

1985 90 minutes

TORN BETWEEN TWO LOVERS

★★★½

DIRECTOR: Delbert Mann

CAST: Lee Remick, Joseph Bologna, George Peppard, Giorgio Tozzi, Molly Cheek

This made-for-TV romantic triangle features a married Lee Remick who finds herself having an affair with a divorced architect. She must finally tell her husband the truth and choose between the two. Nothing boring about this soap!

1979 100 minutes

TOUCHED

★★★

DIRECTOR: John Flynn
CAST: Robert Hays, Kathleen Beller, Gilbert Lewis, Ned Beatty

This sensitive drama involves the struggle of two young psychiatric patients who try to make it outside the hospital walls. Robert Hays and Kathleen Beller are terrific as the frightened couple who must deal with numerous unforeseen obstacles. Rated R for mature topic.

1982 89 minutes

TOUCHED BY LOVE

★★★

DIRECTOR: Gus Trikonis
CAST: Deborah Raffin, Diane Lane, Michael Learned, Cristina Raines, Mary Wickes, Clu Gulager, John Amos

Strong performances make this affecting sentimental drama about a teen-age cerebral palsy victim given hope through correspondence with singer Elvis Presley. Deborah Raffin is excellent as the nurse who nurtures patient Diane Lane from cripple to functioning teenager. Originally titled *From Elvis with Love*. Rated PG.

1980 95 minutes

TOWN LIKE ALICE, A

★★★★½

DIRECTOR: David Stevens
CAST: Helen Morse, Bryan Brown, Gordon Jackson

This outstanding PBS series is based on a Nevil Shute novel. It is even more enjoyable to watch in one viewing than during a six-week period. It is the story of female British POWs in Malaysia and their incredible struggle. Helen Morse is wonderful as the one who takes charge to help maintain the sanity and welfare of the group. Bryan Brown is the soldier who risks his life to help the women and falls in love with Morse. Another example of an outstanding Australian production by director David Stevens.

1980 301 minutes

TRACKS

DIRECTOR: Henry Jaglom
CAST: Dennis Hopper, Taryn Power, Dean Stockwell, Topo Swope, Michael Emil

Dennis Hopper plays a Vietnam War veteran who escorts his dead buddy on a train across country and goes crazy in the process. Rated R.

1977 90 minutes

TRAIN KILLER, THE

★★

DIRECTOR: Sandor Simo
CAST: Michael Sarrazin, Towje Kleiner, Armin Mueller-Stahl, Ferenc Bacs

The true story of Sylvester Matushka, the Hungarian businessman who was responsible for a number of train wrecks in 1931. What is frustrating about this film is that it prepares the viewer for political intrigue that is never fully explained by the end of the film. Also, Michael Sarrazin *(The Flim-Flam Man; They Shoot Horses, Don't They?)* puts in a trying performance as Matushka. On the other hand, Towje Kleiner is superb as Dr. Epstein, the cool, Hitchcockian character who is the investigator in the train wrecks. *The Train Killer* is not rated, but contains sex, nudity, and violence.

1983 90 minutes

TRAPEZE

★★½

DIRECTOR: Carole Reed
CAST: Burt Lancaster, Tony Curtis, Gina Lollobrigida, Katy Jurado, Thomas Gomez, Johnny Puleo

Overly familiar tale of professional (Burt Lancaster) who takes young protégé (Tony Curtis) under his wing and teaches him all he knows about aerial acrobatics only to have scheming opportunist Gina Lollobrigida come between them is okay but nothing out of the ordinary. Solid performances and competent stunting highlight this international effort set in European circus circuit, but director Carol Reed and a good cast have been involved in better films.

1956 105 minutes

TRIAL, THE

★★★½

DIRECTOR: Orson Welles

CAST: Anthony Perkins, Jeanne Moreau, Romy Schneider, Orson Welles, Elsa Martinelli, Akim Tamiroff

A man in an unnamed country is arrested for an unexplained crime he is never told about. It is never made too clear to the audience, either. Orson Welles's unique staging and direction nevertheless make it all fascinating, if disturbing, entertainment.

1963 B & W 118 minutes

TRIAL OF THE CANTONSVILLE NINE, THE

★

DIRECTOR: Gordon Davidson

CAST: Ed Flanders, Douglass Watson, William Schallert, Peter Strauss, Richard Jordan, Gwen Arner, Barton Heyman

This film is a claustrophobic adaptation of a play about nine Baltimore antiwar protesters (two are priests), who faced trial for burning draft records in 1968. It's high-minded and too self-righteous. William Schallert as the judge is a complete annoyance.

1972 85 minutes

TRIBUTE

★★★½

DIRECTOR: Bob Clark

CAST: Jack Lemmon, Robby Benson, Lee Remick, Colleen Dewhurst, John Marley

A moving portrait of a man in crisis, *Tribute* bestows a unique gift to its audience: the feeling that they have come to know a very special man. Jack Lemmon stars as a Broadway press agent who has contracted a terminal blood disease and is feted by his friends in show business. Though adjusted to his fate, Lemmon finds that he has some unfinished business: to make peace with his son, Robby Benson. Rated PG.

1980 121 minutes

TRIP, THE

★★

DIRECTOR: Roger Corman

CAST: Peter Fonda, Susan Strasberg, Bruce Dern, Dennis Hopper, Dick Miller, Luana Anders, Peter Bogdanovich

Peter Fonda plays a director of TV commercials who discovers the kaleidoscopic pleasures of LSD. This curio of the psychedelic era features outdated special effects and sensibilities. Screenplay by Jack Nicholson.

1967 85 minutes

TRIP TO BOUNTIFUL, THE

★★★★½

DIRECTOR: Peter Masterson

CAST: Geraldine Page, John Heard, Carlin Glynn, Richard Bradford, Rebecca DeMornay, Kevin Cooney

In 1947, an elderly widow (wonderfully played by Oscar-winner Geraldine Page) leaves the cramped apartment where she lives with her loving but weak son (John Heard) and his demanding wife (Carlin Glynn) to return to Bountiful, the small town where she had spent her happy youth ... unaware that it no longer exists. Along the way, she meets a kindred spirit (Rebecca DeMornay) and the film becomes a joyous celebration of life. Rated PG.

1986 105 minutes

TROJAN WOMEN, THE

★½

DIRECTOR: Michael Cacoyannis
CAST: Katharine Hepburn, Vanessa Redgrave, Genevieve Bujold, Irene Papas

This Greek-American film is worth seeing only for the four female leads: Katharine Hepburn, Vanessa Redgrave, Genevieve Bujold, and Irene Papas. Unfortunately, the plot (revolving around the Trojan War and their defeat) is lost, and even the most ardent fans can't find it. Rated PG.

1972 105 minutes

TROUBLE IN MIND

★★★★

DIRECTOR: Alan Rudolph
CAST: Kris Kristofferson, Keith Carradine, Genevieve Bujold, Lori Singer, Joe Morton, Divine

An ex-cop, Kris Kristofferson, is paroled from prison and returns to Rain City, hoping to rekindle his romance with café owner Genevieve Bujold. Once there, he falls in love with the wife (Lori Singer) of a thief (Keith Carradine). Director Alan Rudolph's ultrabizarre, semi-futuristic tale is a free-form character study, an unusual screen experience that almost defies description. Beautiful cinematography (the film was shot in Seattle) and fine acting make up for the lack of a strong plot. Like Rudolph's *Choose Me,* it is not for all tastes. Rated R.

1986 111 minutes

TRUE CONFESSIONS

★★★★½

DIRECTOR: Ulu Grosbard
CAST: Robert De Niro, Robert Duvall, Charles Durning, Burgess Meredith

This is the thoughtful, powerful story of two brothers (Robert De Niro and Robert Duvall)—one a priest, the other a jaded detective —caught in the sordid world of power politics in post–World War II Los Angeles. It's a brilliant and disturbing film. Rated R.

1981 108 minutes

TRUE HEART SUSIE

★★★

DIRECTOR: D. W. Griffith
CAST: Lillian Gish, Robert Herron, Wilbur Higby, Loyola O'Connor, George Fawcett, Clarine Seymour, Kate Bruce, Carol Dempster, Raymond Cannon

Lillian Gish and Robert Herron are sweethearts in a small, rural, bedrock-solid American town in this sentimental silent film account of a young girl's transition from scatterbrained, uninhibited adolescent to dignified, self-assured woman. Sensitive acting and directing make what could have been cloying mush a touching, charming excursion back to what are nostalgically recalled as "the good old days," whether they were or not.

1919 B & W 62 minutes

TUFF TURF

★★

DIRECTOR: Fritz Kiersch
CAST: James Spader, Kim Richards, Paul Mones

"He's always been a rebel—Now, he's about to become a hero." So reads the advertisements for this forgettable movie about young love as the new kid in town falls for a street-wise young woman with a dangerous lover. Featuring music by Southside Johnny, Lene Lovich, Marianne Faithfull, Jim Carroll, Jack Mack and the Heart Attack. Rated R for violence, profanity, and suggested sex.

1984 112 minutes

TULSA

★★½

DIRECTOR: Stuart Heisler

CAST: Susan Hayward, Robert Preston, Pedro Armendariz, Chill Wills, Ed Begley Sr.

Typical pot-boiler has feisty Susan Hayward as a strong-willed woman intent on drilling oil wells on her property no matter who tries to interfere. Standard stock situations made more palatable by fine cast of character actors typify this story of a hard-headed businesswoman humanized during the course of the action.

1949 90 minutes

TUNES OF GLORY

★★★★

DIRECTOR: Ronald Neame

CAST: Alec Guinness, John Mills, Susannah York, Dennis Price, Duncan Macrae, Kay Walsh, Gordon Jackson, John Fraser, Allan Cuthbertson

Gripping drama of rivalry between embittered Alec Guinness and his younger replacement John Mills is a classic study of cruelty as Guinness loses no opportunity to bully and belittle the competent but less aggressive Mills. Superb acting highlights this tragic story, and its universal message could be applied to similar situations in any walk of life. Guinness excels as the cold, calculating old soldier who choreographs the humiliation and downfall of the younger officer, and Mills is superb as the sensitive victim whose self-doubt and insecurities increase with each passing day. Certainly no light entertainment, this strong fare might not qualify as an evening's diversion, but it's an emotional, cathartic experience and one of the finest films of any period.

1960 107 minutes

TURK 182

★★

DIRECTOR: Bob Clark

CAST: Timothy Hutton, Robert Urich, Kim Cattrall, Robert Culp, Darren McGavin, Peter Boyle

Timothy Hutton stars as Jimmy Lynch, a young man who embarks on a personal crusade against injustice. His older brother, Terry (Robert Urich), a fireman, has been denied his pension after being injured while saving a child from a burning building when he was off-duty. So Jimmy decides to right this wrong. *Turk 182* is one of those hollow, manipulative movies obviously thought by their makers to be sure-fire crowd-pleasers. It's anything but. Rated PG-13 for violence, profanity, and suggested sex.

1985 102 minutes

TURNING POINT, THE

★★★★½

DIRECTOR: Herbert Ross

CAST: Anne Bancroft, Shirley MacLaine, Mikhail Baryshnikov, Leslie Browne, Tom Skerritt

Anne Bancroft and Shirley MacLaine have the meaty scenes in this well-crafted drama, as a pair of dancers blessed/cursed with the aftermaths of their own personal turning points. Bancroft, forsaking family and stability, became a ballet star; MacLaine, forsaking fame and personal expression, embraced family and stability. Now, years later, MacLaine's daughter (expressively played by Leslie Browne) is at that same stage of a budding ballet career, and Bancroft wants to sponsor her. The resulting friction between old friends climaxes in several torrential exchanges between the two leads. Blended with the story is a series of beautifully rendered ballet sequences featuring Mikhail Baryshnikov, in his film debut. Great stuff, played with strength and conviction by all concerned. Rated PG for intensity of theme.

1977 119 minutes

12 ANGRY MEN

★★★★★

DIRECTOR: Sidney Lumet
CAST: Henry Fonda, Lee J. Cobb, Ed Begley Sr., E. G. Marshall, Jack Klugman, Jack Warden, Martin Balsam, John Fiedler, Robert Webber, George Voskovec, Edward Binns, Joseph Sweeney

A superb cast under inspired direction makes this film brilliant in every aspect. Henry Fonda is the holdout on a jury who desperately seeks to convince his eleven peers to reconsider their hasty conviction of a boy accused of murdering his father. The struggle behind closed doors is taut, charged, and fascinating.

1957 B & W 95 minutes

TWICE IN A LIFETIME

★★★★★

DIRECTOR: Bud Yorkin
CAST: Gene Hackman, Ann-Margret, Ellen Burstyn, Amy Madigan, Ally Sheedy, Brian Dennehy

Superior slice-of-life drama about a Washington mill worker (Gene Hackman) who reaches a mid-life crisis and decides that he and wife Ellen Burstyn can't sustain the magic anymore. That decision is helped by a sudden interest in local barmaid Ann-Margret, but the script isn't that simplistic. There aren't any "bad guys" and "good guys" . . . just several decent people forced to make painful choices. Oscar-nominated Amy Madigan plays the elder daughter as a firebrand who, fearful of her *own* marriage, takes her anger out on Dad. The cast is uniformly fine, the story poignant without being sugary. Rated R for adult situations.

1985 111 minutes

TWO OF A KIND

★★★★

DIRECTOR: Roger Young
CAST: George Burns, Robby Benson, Cliff Robertson, Barbara Barrie, Ronny Cox

This heartwarming TV film features George Burns as a discarded senior citizen and Robby Benson as his retarded grandson. The two come together when the boy decides to help his seemingly disabled grandpa play golf again. Cliff Robertson and Barbara Barrie play Benson's parents. All in all, this is a fine film with a positive message about family unity.

1982 102 minutes

UGLY AMERICAN, THE

★★½

DIRECTOR: George H. Englund
CAST: Marlon Brando, Pat Hingle, Sandra Church, Arthur Hill, Eiji Okada, Jocelyn Brando

With Marlon Brando playing an American ambassador newly arrived at his Asian post, more is expected of this film than just a routine potboiler. However, the film attempts to focus on the political interworkings of Brando's struggle with rising communist elements, and fails to generate any excitement.

1963 120 minutes

UNAPPROACHABLE, THE

🦃

DIRECTOR: Krzysztof Zanussi
CAST: Leslie Caron, Daniel Webb, Leslie Magon

A completely unwatchable film about a young man obsessed with a reclusive aging starlet. To enter her home, he acts as though he's just been mugged and needs to use the phone. He tries to persuade her that he's an art student who wants to photograph her famous collection of paintings. When this story proves false, he then admits that he's a reporter trying to get an interview. Finally it comes out that he's in love with her and has a fantasy about sleeping with her. By this time, the retired starlet begins playing with his mind and emotions, turning the tables on him. This film is so ridiculous and poorly acted that it's unimaginable how it could ever have been made. Stay away from this one. Not rated, but contains profanity and adult situations.

1982 100 minutes

UNDER CAPRICORN

★★★

DIRECTOR: Alfred Hitchcock
CAST: Michael Wilding, Ingrid Bergman, Joseph Cotten

This film is about a nineteenth-century Australian household that is hiding some dark secrets. Michael Wilding is drawn into solving the family's mystery because of his attraction to the lady of the house, Ingrid Bergman. This is not a typical Alfred Hitchcock movie. It lacks his customary suspense, and its pace could be called leisurely at best.

1949 117 minutes

UNDER MILK WOOD

★★

DIRECTOR: Andrew Sinclair
CAST: Elizabeth Taylor, Richard Burton, Peter O'Toole, Glynis Johns, Vivian Merchant, Sian Phillips

The late, great Welsh poet Dylan Thomas's play loses its charm, vitality, and message in this slow, stuffy, dry, pretentious, image-burdened film version. All the queen's men (Richard Burton and Peter O'Toole), plus the beautiful Elizabeth Taylor, cannot deliver the lusty verve required to infuse it with life. Dull, plodding, murky. A photo buff's picture.

1973 90 minutes

UNDER THE CHERRY MOON

★★

DIRECTOR: Prince
CAST: Prince, Jerome Benton, Steve Berkoff, Alexandra Stewart, Kristin Scott Thomas, Francesca Annis, Emmanuelle Sallet

Although this film is slow moving, it may appeal to teenagers, especially Prince fans. Prince plays a gigolo-type singer who pursues a debutante, Mary (Kristin Scott Thomas), who's due to inherit a huge trust on her twenty-first birthday. Mary's greedy father (Steve Berkoff) has planned a marriage for Mary that will merge two large fortunes. When Mary realizes her dad is using her, she takes off with Prince and his friend Tricky (Jerome Benton). Benton provides the few humorous moments in an otherwise melodramatic film. Viewers will marvel at the bizarre variety of clothes that Prince wears. Rated PG for language and mature theme.

1986 B & W 100 minutes

UNDER THE VOLCANO

★★★★

DIRECTOR: John Huston
CAST: Albert Finney, Jacqueline Bisset, Anthony Andrews

Director John Huston's brilliant, but disturbing, adaptation of the Malcolm Lowry novel about a suicidal, alcoholic British consul in Mexico on the eve of World War II. Albert Finney's performance is superb, as is that by co-star Jacqueline Bisset, who plays Finney's wife. Rated R for suggested sex, violence, and profanity.

1984 109 minutes

UNION CITY

★★★

DIRECTOR: Mark Reichert
CAST: Deborah Harry, Dennis Lipscomb, Irina Maleeva, Pat Benatar

Called the "punk rock *film noir*," *Union City* is a quietly disturbing tale of murder and paranoia circa 1953. Deborah Harry (of the rock group Blondie) stars as a bored housewife; Dennis Lipscomb is her high-strung, paranoid husband. Though the plot of the film isn't especially strong, Mark Reichert's direction is. The mood, tone, and feel of the film are spooky, though it may be too oblique for some. Rated PG for adult themes and violence.

1980 87 minutes

UNMARRIED WOMAN, AN

★★★★★

DIRECTOR: Paul Mazursky
CAST: Jill Clayburgh, Michael Murphy, Alan Bates, Pat Quinn

Jill Clayburgh's Erica starts out as a well-adjusted wife who doesn't mind her part-time job and loves her family. She has settled into a comfortable rut and barely notices it when things begin to go wrong. One day, after lunch with her husband Martin (Michael Murphy), she is shocked by his sobbing admission that he is in love with another woman. Her world is shattered. This first-rate film concerns itself with her attempts to cope with the situation. Rated R for sex, nudity, and profanity.

1978 124 minutes

UNTIL SEPTEMBER

★½

DIRECTOR: Richard Marquand
CAST: Karen Allen, Thierry Lhermitte, Christopher Cazenove

A midwestern divorcée (Karen Allen, of *Raiders of the Lost Ark*) falls in love with a married Parisian banker (Thierry Lhermitte, of *My Best Friend's Girl*) during the summer vacation in this unabashed soap opera. Rated R.

1984 95 minutes

UPTOWN NEW YORK

★★

DIRECTOR: Victor Schertzinger
CAST: Jack Oakie, Shirley Grey

Sobby melodrama about a doctor whose family forces him to jilt the girl he loves and marry for money. She bounces into marriage with a bubble gum machine salesman who nobly offers her a divorce when he learns the truth.

1932 B & W 80 minutes

URBAN COWBOY

★★★

DIRECTOR: James Bridges
CAST: John Travolta, Debra Winger, Scott Glenn, Madolyn Smith, Charlie Daniels Band

The film is a slice-of-life *Saturday Night Fever*–like look at the after-hours life of blue-collar cowboys. Overall, the film works because of excellent directing by James Bridges and the fine acting of John Travolta, Debra Winger, and Scott Glenn. This film had a strong cultural impact, moving country music into the mainstream of American life. Rated PG.

1980 132 minutes

USERS, THE

★★

DIRECTOR: Joseph Hardy
CAST: Jaclyn Smith, Tony Curtis, Joan Fontaine, Red Buttons

Another overbloated TV movie boasts a fine cast and little else. Jaclyn Smith stars as a beautiful girl who plays a major role in the resurgence of a down-and-out movie star's career. Standard "television" production values and "television" dialogue do this one in.

1978 125 minutes

VERDICT, THE

★★★★½

DIRECTOR: Sidney Lumet

CAST: Paul Newman, James Mason, Charlotte Rampling, Jack Warden

In this first-rate drama, Paul Newman brilliantly plays an alcoholic Boston lawyer who redeems himself by taking on slick James Mason in a medical malpractice suit. Rated R for profanity and adult situations.

1982 129 minutes

VIOLETS ARE BLUE

★★★½

DIRECTOR: Jack Fisk

CAST: Sissy Spacek, Kevin Kline, Bonnie Bedelia, John Kellogg, Jim Standiford, Augusta Dabney

In this watchable screen soap opera, former high-school sweethearts Sissy Spacek and Kevin Kline are reunited when she, a successful photojournalist, returns to her hometown after a particularly debilitating assignment in strife-torn Belfast. Their romance is rekindled although he is now married (to Bonnie Bedelia, who is terrific in her all-too-brief onscreen bits) and has a 13-year-old son. Without the occasionally inspired lines of dialogue by screenwriter Naomi Foner, *Violets Are Blue* would be a lightweight star vehicle. Even with them, this romance movie directed by Spacek's husband Jack Fisk falls a bit short. Rated PG for suggested sex and light profanity.

1986 89 minutes

VISION QUEST

★★★½

DIRECTOR: Harold Becker

CAST: Matthew Modine, Linda Fiorentino, Michael Schoeffling, Ronny Cox, Harold Sylvester

Here's yet another movie in which a young athlete makes good against all odds. If you can get past the (over) familiarity of the plot, it isn't bad. It benefits particularly from a charismatic lead performance by Matthew Modine (who played Mel Gibson's brother in *Mrs. Soffel*). He's likeable and, as a result, so is the movie. Rated R for nudity, suggested sex, violence, and profanity.

1985 96 minutes

VIVA ZAPATA!

★★★★½

DIRECTOR: Elia Kazan

CAST: Marlon Brando, Anthony Quinn, Jean Peters, Joseph Wiseman

This film chonicles Mexican revolutionary leader Emiliano Zapata from his peasant upbringings until his death as a weary, disillusioned political liability. Marlon Brando was to win an Oscar nomination for his inciteful portrayal of Zapata. Anthony Quinn, as Zapata's brother, did manage to hold his own against the powerful Brando characterization and was rewarded with a supporting actor Oscar.

1952 B & W 113 minutes

VOICES

★★★

DIRECTOR: Robert Markowitz

CAST: Amy Irving, Michael Ontkean, Herbert Berghof, Viveca Lindfors

A sentimental love story that, while bordering on treacle, manages to maintain a sensitive tone that ultimately proves infectious. Amy Irving stars as a deaf young woman who wants, almost more than life itself, to become a dancer; Michael Ontkean is young man who, trapped in a family business, would rather be a singer. They meet, fall in love, and come to an imaginative and poignant meeting of the minds. The material is sugary, but Irving and Ontkean make it work. Rated PG for language and adult themes.

1979 107 minutes

VOYAGE OF THE DAMNED

★★★★

DIRECTOR: Stuart Rosenberg
CAST: Oskar Werner, Faye Dunaway, Max von Sydow, Orson Welles, Malcolm McDowell, James Mason, Julie Harris, Lee Grant

This fine drama takes place in 1939 as a shipload of Jewish refugees are refused refuge in Havana and are forced to return to Germany for certain imprisonment and/or death. Rated PG.

1976 134 minutes

WAITING FOR THE MOON

★★½

DIRECTOR: Jill Godmilow
CAST: Linda Hunt, Linda Bassett, Bruce McGill, Andrew McGarthy, Bernadette Lafont, Jacques Boudet

Linda Hunt is Alice B. Toklas and Linda Bassett is Gertrude Stein in this idiosyncratic, self-indulgent, and frustrating film. The stars' performances are fine, but the impressionistic style of co-writer-director Jill Godmilow, who plays with the sequence of events in a way that will thoroughly confuse most viewers, tends to be more irritating than artistic. Rated PG-13 for profanity and adult themes.

1987 88 minutes

WANDERERS, THE

★★★★

DIRECTOR: Phil Kaufman
CAST: Ken Wahl, John Friedrich, Karen Allen, Tony Ganios

This enjoyable film is set in the early 1960s and focuses on the world of teenagers. Though it has ample amounts of comedy and excitement, because it deals with life on the streets of the Bronx, there is an atmosphere of ever-present danger and fear. It is the dark side of adolescence, with all the anguish, brutality, and painful reality that comes with survival and growing up. The Wanderers are a gang of Italian-American youths who have banded together for safety and good times. While they are not overt troublemakers, life in the asphalt jungle presents dangers both real and imagined. Rated R.

1979 113 minutes

WAR AND PEACE

★★½

DIRECTOR: King Vidor
CAST: Henry Fonda, Audrey Hepburn, Mel Ferrer, John Mills

Mammoth international effort to film this classic novel results in an overlong, unevenly constructed melodrama. The massive battle scenes and outdoor panoramas are truly impressive, as are the performers on occasion. But the whole production seems to swallow up the principals and the action, leaving a rather lifeless film. An early Dino De Laurentiis coproduction (with Carlo Ponti), and the next-to-last effort of King Vidor, legendary American director.

1956 208 minutes

WAR LOVER, THE

★★½

DIRECTOR: Philip Leacock
CAST: Steve McQueen, Robert Wagner, Shirley Ann Field

This is a very slow-moving account of pilots (Steve McQueen and Robert Wagner) in England during World War II. Both pilots are seeking the affections of the same woman. Nothing in the film raises it above the level of mediocrity.

1962 B & W 105 minutes

WASHINGTON AFFAIR, THE

★★★

DIRECTOR: Victor Stoloff
CAST: Tom Selleck, Barry Sullivan, Carol Lynley, Arlene Banas

Jim Hawley (Tom Selleck) is an incorruptible federal agent who must award a government contract. Walter Nicholson (Barry Sullivan) is a wheeler-dealer who tries to blackmail Hawley into giving him the contract. When Nicholson hires someone to film Hawley in his hotel bedroom, he's shocked to find out that his own wife, Barbara (Carol Lynley), is Hawley's lover. There's enough heavy breathing and surprises in this film to keep most viewers on the edge of their couch wondering what will happen next. Rated R for simulated sex.

1977 104 minutes

WATCH ON THE RHINE

★★★★

DIRECTOR: Herman Shumlin
CAST: Paul Lukas, Bette Davis, Geraldine Fitzgerald

Lillian Hellman's expose of Nazi terrorism was brought from Broadway to the screen in first-rate form. Paul Lukas won a best-actor Oscar for his role of an underground leader who fled Germany for the U.S., only to be hunted down by Nazi agents. Bette Davis is wonderful in what was one of her few small supporting roles.

1943 B & W 114 minutes

WATERLOO BRIDGE

★★★★

DIRECTOR: Mervyn LeRoy
CAST: Vivien Leigh, Robert Taylor, Lucile Watson

A five-hanky romance about the lives of two people caught up in the turmoil of World War II, this is a poignant tale of a beautiful ballerina (Vivien Leigh) who falls in love with a British officer (Robert Taylor) and how her life is altered when he leaves for the battlefields of Europe. This is one of Leigh's best performances, although she rarely gave a bad one.

1941 B & W 103 minutes

WAY DOWN EAST

★★★

DIRECTOR: D. W. Griffith
CAST: Lillian Gish, Richard Barthelmess, Lowell Sherman, Mary Hay

Classic story of a young woman ostracized by her family and community for moral reasons was an audience favorite of the early part of this century but old hat even by 1920, when this melodrama was released. Justly famous for the exciting and dangerous flight of the beautiful Lillian Gish across the ice floes, pursued and eventually rescued by stalwart yet sensitive Richard Barthelmess, this was one of classic director D. W. Griffith's best-remembered films, but was also one of his last solid critical and commercial blockbusters. Although he made films for another ten years with stars ranging from W. C. Fields to Walter Huston, "the Master" was never able to match his earlier successes and gradually made way for newer, less stage-bound film directors. Silent.

1920 B & W 119 minutes

WAY WE WERE, THE

★★★½

DIRECTOR: Sydney Pollack

CAST: Barbra Streisand, Robert Redford, Patrick O'Neal, Viveca Lindfors, Bradford Dillman, Lois Chiles

The popular theme song somewhat obscured the fact this is a rather slow-moving romance about a Jewish girl (Barbra Streisand) who marries a WASPish writer (Robert Redford). The film has its moments, but the portion dealing with the McCarthy communist witch hunt falls flat. Rated PG.

1973 118 minutes

WEDDING IN WHITE

★½

DIRECTOR: William Fruet

CAST: Donald Pleasence, Carol Kane, Doris Petrie, Leo Phillips

It's World War II and Carol Kane is the young naïve daughter of an authoritative father who only shows affection for his son. When Kane becomes pregnant as a result of being raped by her brother's soldier friend, her father sets out to maintain the family honor by destroying his daughter's future. *Wedding in White* is a study of the effects of intolerance that stem from sexual double standards and male pride. The film succeeds in making you feel outrage, but you may also find yourself drowning in the gloom. The movie is unrelentlessly bleak from beginning to end. Right from the start you know the oppressive hold will never lift.

1972 103 minutes

WEDDING MARCH, THE

★★★½

DIRECTOR: Erich Von Stroheim

CAST: Erich Von Stroheim, Fay Wray, ZaSu Pitts, George Fawcett, Dale Fuller, Matthew Betz, Maude George, Cesare Gravina, George Nichols

The story is simple: the corrupt, money-hungry family of an Austrian prince forces him to forsake his true love, a penniless musician, and marry a dull, crippled heiress. The telling is incredibly overblown, lavish, extravagant, tedious, and long beyond belief (thiry-nine hours before editing). Critics and big-city audiences acclaimed this film, but it laid eggs by the gross in the hinterlands. Silent.

1928 B & W 140 minutes

WELCOME TO L.A.

★★★½

DIRECTOR: Alan Rudolph

CAST: Keith Carradine, Geraldine Chaplin, Harvey Keitel, Sally Kellerman, Sissy Spacek, Lauren Hutton

Extremely well made film concerning the disjointed love lives of several Los Angeles nouveaux riches. Film's focal point is songwriter Keith Carradine, whose romantic interludes set the wheels in motion. Entire cast is first-rate, with Richard Baskin's musical score the only drawback. Director Alan Rudolph's prelude to the cult favorite *Choose Me*. Rated R.

1977 106 minutes

WETHERBY

★★½

DIRECTOR: David Hare

CAST: Vanessa Redgrave, Ian Holm, Judi Dench, Marjorie Yates, Joely Richardson, Tom Wilkinson, Tim McInnerny, Stuart Wilson

Buried under *Wetherby*'s dismally portentous attitudes about England and loneliness is a pretty interesting story. It begins with a very unusual suicide and then proceeds to try to figure out the motive. The film unfolds like a thriller, cutting back and forth between past and present, giving us snatches of information along the way. That it doesn't satisfy in the end is what causes the movie to fail as a good sustained piece of work. Vanessa Redgrave in the lead is characteristically excellent. She draws your interest so completely that finding out about her past becomes more involving than the suicide she witnessed.

1985 104 minutes

WHAT COMES AROUND

★★

DIRECTOR: Jerry Reed

CAST: Jerry Reed, Bo Hopkins, Barry Corbin, Arte Johnson

Jerry Reed stars as a world-famous country-western singer who is strung out on booze and pills. Bo Hopkins plays the younger brother who kidnaps Reed to save him from his own self-destruction and the corruption of his manager (Barry Corbin). This all-American action-comedy-drama features the country music of Jerry Reed. A must-see for his fans. Rated PG.

1985 92 minutes

WHAT PRICE HOLLYWOOD?

★★★★

DIRECTOR: George Cukor

CAST: Constance Bennett, Lowell Sherman, Neil Hamilton, Gregory Ratoff, Brooks Benedict

This first production of *A Star Is Born* packs the same punch as the two more famous versions and showcases popular 1930s actress Constance Bennett as a tough but tender girl who wants to reach the top. Lowell Sherman plays the man with the connections who starts Constance on her way, but who eventually becomes a hindrance to her. Witty and caustic, this David O. Selznick production was written by Adela Rogers St. John and gave failing RKO studios a shot in the arm. Bennett seems somehow less martyred and long-suffering than either Janet Gaynor or Judy Garland, and that gives this version an edge that the others lack.

1932 B & W 88 minutes

WHEN WOLVES CRY

★

DIRECTOR: Terence Young

CAST: William Holden, Virna Lisi, Brook Fuller, Bourvil

Poorly directed melodrama about a 10-year-old boy, Pascal, who is diagnosed as being terminally ill. His father, Laurent (William Holden), dedicates himself to indulging his son's every whim—including stealing two wild wolves from the Paris zoo. Originally titled *The Christmas Tree*. Rated G.

1983 108 minutes

WHITE NIGHTS

★★★½

DIRECTOR: Taylor Hackford

CAST: Mikhail Baryshnikov, Gregory Hines, Geraldine Page, Jerzy Skolimowski, Isabella Rosellini

Russian defector and ballet star Mikhail Baryshnikov, finding himself back in the U.S.S.R., joins forces with American defector Gregory Hines to escape to freedom in this soap opera–styled thriller directed by Taylor Hackford (*An Officer and a Gentleman*). The plot is contrived, but the dance sequences featuring the two stars together and separately are spectacular. Rated PG-13 for violence and profanity.

1985 135 minutes

WHO ARE THE DEBOLTS AND WHERE DID THEY GET 19 KIDS?

★★★★★

DIRECTOR: John Korty
CAST: Documentary

This Academy Award–winning documentary features Dorothy and Bob Debolt and their nineteen children—some natural, most adopted. Their family is unique not only for its great size but for the multiple physical disabilities their adopted children have, the positive way these problems are dealt with, and the fantastic organizational system under which their daily lives are run. This film is an eyeopener for adults as well as children and helps us all see our problems in a new perspective. Although there are sad and touching moments, there are also hilarious ones. By the end of the film, you don't pity the disabled kids, you just wish that you could be as strong and "whole" as they are. This is an excellent and inspirational film. Rated G.

1978 73 minutes

WHO IS THE BLACK DAHLIA?

★★★

DIRECTOR: Joseph Pevney
CAST: Lucie Arnaz, Efrem Zimbalist Jr., Ronny Cox, MacDonald Carey, Gloria DeHaven, Tom Bosley, Mercedes McCambridge, Donna Mills, June Lockhart

An above-average semidocumentary crime drama based on one of the Los Angeles Police Department's most famous unsolved cases: the 1947 murder, mutilation, and gruesome dissection of a mysterious young woman whose lifestyle and mode of dress earned her the nickname of Black Dahlia. Though the case is forty years old, the killer is most likely still alive. An excellent cast performs a first-rate script in this gripping film.

1975 100 minutes

WHO'S AFRAID OF VIRGINIA WOOLF?

★★★★★

DIRECTOR: Mike Nichols
CAST: Elizabeth Taylor, Richard Burton, Sandy Dennis, George Segal

Edward Albee's powerful play about the love-hate relationship of a college professor and his bitchy wife was brilliantly transferred to the screen by director Mike Nichols. Elizabeth Taylor gives her best acting performance as Martha, a screeching bitch caught in an unfulfilled marriage. Richard Burton is equally stunning as the quiet, authoritative professor who must decide between abandoning or salvaging their marriage after a night of bitter recriminations and painful revelations. Sandy Dennis and George Segal more than hold their own in support.

1966 B & W 129 minutes

WHOSE LIFE IS IT, ANYWAY?

★★★★

DIRECTOR: John Badham
CAST: Richard Dreyfuss, John Cassavetes, Christine Lahti, Bob Balaban, Kenneth McMillan, Kaki Hunter, Janet Eilber, Thomas Carter

Richard Dreyfuss is superb as a witty and intellectually dynamic sculptor who is paralyzed after an auto accident and fights for his right to be left alone to die. John Cassavetes and Christine Lahti co-star as doctors in this surprisingly upbeat movie. Rated R.

1981 118 minutes

WHY SHOOT THE TEACHER?

★★★

DIRECTOR: Silvio Narizzano
CAST: Bud Cort, Samantha Eggar, Chris Wiggins, Gary Reineke, John Friesen, Michael J. Reynolds

Bud Cort (*Harold and Maude*) stars in this intimate and simple film about a young instructor whose first teaching position lands him in the barren plains of Canada. Lean realism and bright dashes of humor give the picture some memorable moments, but this story of an outsider trying to adapt to the lifestyle of an isolated community develops with a disengaging slowness. This PG-rated project has a warm charm, but not enough grit.

1977 101 minutes

WILD DUCK, THE

★★½

DIRECTOR: Henri Safran
CAST: Liv Ullmann, Jeremy Irons, Lucinda Jones, Arthur Dignam, John Meillon, Michael Pate

Despite the cast, or maybe because of it, this poignant story of love and tragedy falls short of its ambitious mark. Jeremy Irons *(Moonlighting; The French Lieutenant's Woman)* and Liv Ullmann *(Autumn Sonata; Cries and Whispers)* are struggling parents whose child is slowly going blind. An idealistic friend (Arthur Dignam) complicates matters by unearthing truths that were better off buried. The touching story is botched up by an awkward screenplay. Both Ullmann's and Irons's performances are inconsistent, and while there may be some justification for their odd behavior, it is incongruous with the general mood of the plot. Rated PG for profanity.

1983 96 minutes

WILD GUITAR

DIRECTOR: Ray Dennis Steckler
CAST: Arch Hall Jr., Nancy Czar, William Watters (Arch Hall Sr.), Cash Flagg (Ray Dennis Steckler)

Exploitative record company gets their comeuppance from hell-raising Arch Hall Jr., a motorcycle-riding rock-'n-roller who sings up a storm on cue and couldn't act if his life depended on it. This terrible movie is actually the fusion of two near-legendary bad film producers: Ray Dennis Steckler (*Incredibly Strange Creatures Who Stopped Living and Became Mixed-Up Zombies*) and Arch Hall (*Eegah*). Incredibly bad, this film and others of its ilk still have a unique charm because of the sheer audacity displayed by barely talented people who could afford to put themselves and their offspring in the movies and did so.

1962 87 minutes

WILD IN THE COUNTRY

★★★

DIRECTOR: Philip Dunne
CAST: Elvis Presley, Hope Lange, Tuesday Weld, Millie Perkins, John Ireland

Elvis Presley is encouraged to pursue a literary career when counseled during his wayward youth. Most viewers will find it interesting to see Elvis in such a serious role. The supporting cast also has something to add to the okay script.

1961 114 minutes

WILD ORCHIDS

★★★

DIRECTOR: Sidney Franklin
CAST: Greta Garbo, Lewis Stone, Nils Asther

A young Greta Garbo, already on her way to becoming a screen legend after only three years with

Metro-Goldwyn-Mayer, is the highlight of this familiar story of tropic love. Plantation owner Lewis Stone busies himself with overseeing his property in Java, but local prince Nils Asther finds himself overseeing the owner's wife and the usual complications ensue. Pretty standard love-triangle-in-the-tropics story is redeemed by the exotic, mysterious Greta Garbo. Silent.

1928 B & W 103 minutes

WILD PARTY, THE

★★★½

DIRECTOR: James Ivory
CAST: James Coco, Raquel Welch, Perry King, David Dukes

This is a very grim look at how Hollywood treats its fading stars. James Coco plays a one-time comedy star trying to come back with a hit film. Raquel Welch plays Coco's longtime girlfriend who plans a party for Hollywood's elite in order to push his film. Things fall apart during the party. The film is based on the career of Fatty Arbuckle and provides some interesting insights into the Hollywood power structure, with good performances by Coco and Welch. Rated R.

1975 107 minutes

WILD ROSE

★★

DIRECTOR: John Hanson
CAST: Lisa Eichhorn, Tom Bower, James Cada, Cinda Jackson, Dan Nemanick, Lydia Olson

This low-budget film, shot in and around the Wisconsin coal mine fields, floats between being a love story (showing a woman's search for independence) and a social commentary on mining conditions. By trying to cover all the bases, writer-director John Hanson fails to cover even one satisfactorily. Far too many dead spots in the script and the extensive use of nonactors and sparse dialogue sink this one quickly.

1984 96 minutes

WILL, G. GORDON LIDDY

★★★½

DIRECTOR: Robert Leiberman
CAST: Robert Conrad, Katherine Cannon, Gary Bayer, Peter Rattray, James Rebhorn, Red West, Maurice Woods, Danny Lloyd

Robert Conrad (*The Wild Wild West*) is transformed into the fanatic, strong-willed Watergate mastermind Liddy. The first half lacks excitement or revelation for most viewers who remember the Watergate scandal. Liddy's stay in prison, however, is a fascinating study of his personality.

1982 100 minutes

WILMA

★★½

DIRECTOR: Bud Greenspan
CAST: Cicely Tyson, Shirley Jo Finney, Joe Seneca, Jason Bernard

This made-for-TV film chronicles the early years of Olympic star Wilma Rudolph (Cicely Tyson) and follows her career up to her winning the gold. Film fails to do justice to its subject matter. Lackluster production.

1977 100 minutes

WINDOM'S WAY

★★★

DIRECTOR: Ronald Neame
CAST: Peter Finch, Mary Ure, Natasha Parry, Robert Flemyng, Michael Hordern, John Cairney, Marne Maitland, Gregoire Aslan

In this British drama set on an island in the Far East, a struggle ensues between the natives and plantation owners over civil rights. A doctor (Peter Finch) is enlisted as the spokesperson for the natives; he experiences a great deal of social pressure from his countrymen, while simultaneously trying to patch things up with his estranged wife. Set against the backdrop of World War II, and containing a stirring undercurrent of suspense regarding which superpower will eventually dominate the island, *Windom's Way* is enjoyable entertainment.

1957 104 minutes

WINDY CITY

★★★

DIRECTOR: Armyan Bernstein

CAST: John Shea, Kate Capshaw, Josh Mostel, Jim Borrelli, Jeffrey DeMunn, Eric Pierpoint, Lewis J. Stadlen, James Sutorius

Very uneven, very frustrating attempt to chronicle the story of a group of young adults who have known one another since they were kids. Told through the eyes of one of their own, a writer (John Shea), it has the feel of being based on real-life experiences but is embarrassingly true to some of the more rude and off-putting behavior most people would rather have private memories of. It gets three stars for its honesty, the fun of watching Kate Capshaw (who is charming even when given silly things to say) and because we were touched by its idealistic and sentimental view of "friends forever." Rated R.

1984 103 minutes

WINSLOW BOY, THE

★★★★

DIRECTOR: Anthony Asquith

CAST: Robert Donat, Margaret Leighton, Cedric Hardwicke, Basil Radford, Francis X. Sullivan, Frank Lawton, Wilfrid Hyde-White, Neil North

Robert Donat is superb as the proper British barrister defending a young naval cadet, wrongly accused of theft, against the overbearing pomp and indifferent might of the Crown. At stake in this tense Edwardian courtroom melodrama is the long cherished and maintained democratic right to be regarded as innocent until proven guilty by a fair trial. Opposing the boy and his defender are the complacent lethargy of officialdom and the apparent blindness of justice. "Let right be done" is the key line. Playwright Terence Rattigan scripted from his West End and Broadway stage hit, based on an actual 1912 case. The case is excellent, the cause just, the drama and suspense first-rate.

1950 B & W 118 minutes

WINTER KILLS

★★★★

DIRECTOR: William Richert

CAST: Jeff Bridges, John Huston, Belinda Bauer, Richard Boone, Anthony Perkins, Toshiro Mifune, Sterling Hayden, Eli Wallach, Ralph Meeker, Dorothy Malone, Tomas Milian, Elizabeth Taylor

An all-star cast is featured in this sometimes melodramatic, but often wry, account of a presidential assassination. Rated R.

1979 97 minutes

WINTER OF OUR DREAMS

★★

DIRECTOR: John Duigan

CAST: Judy Davis, Bryan Brown, Cathy Downes, Baz Luhrmann, Peter Mochrie, Mervyn Drake

An all-too-typical soaper about a married man (Bryan Brown) who tries to help a lost soul (Judy Davis), this downbeat film has good acting but less-than-adequate direction. Rated R.

1981 90 minutes

WINTERSET

★★½

DIRECTOR: Alfred Santell

CAST: Burgess Meredith, Margo, Eduardo Ciannelli, John Carradine, Paul Guilfoyle, Stanley Ridges, Mischa Auer

Heavy-duty drama of bitter young man's efforts to clear his father's name lacks the punch it must have possessed as a top stage play in the 1930s but boasts a great cast of distinguished character actors and marks the screen debut of the versatile Burgess Meredith. Talkfest is long on moralizing and short on action, but it's a class production and has impressive, if stagy, set of actors and circumstances.

1936 B & W 78 minutes

WISE BLOOD

★★★★

DIRECTOR: John Huston

CAST: Brad Dourif, Harry Dean Stanton, Ned Beatty, Amy Wright, Dan Shor

While there are many laughs in this fascinating black comedy about a slow-witted country boy (Brad Dourif) who decides to become a man of the world, they tend to stick in your throat. Underneath the wryly comic surface is the poignant, often disturbing story of a man's desperate search for something or someone to believe in. Flannery O'Connor wrote the novel on which Benedict Fitzgerald's screenplay was based. As brilliant as it is, this searing satire on southern do-it-yourself religion comes so close to the truth, it is almost painful to watch at times. But you can't take your eyes off the screen as it holds you in a grip of morbid fascination. Rated PG.

1979 108 minutes

WITHOUT A TRACE

★★★½

DIRECTOR: Stanley Jaffe

CAST: Kate Nelligan, Judd Hirsch, David Dukes, Stockard Channing, Jacqueline Brookes, Kathleen Widdoes

A drama about a boy who vanishes and his mother's unrelenting faith that he will return, this is yet another entry in the family-in-trouble movie genre. If you didn't get your fill of that from *Kramer vs. Kramer*, *Ordinary People*, *Shoot the Moon*, and the rest, you might enjoy this well-acted but sometimes overwrought and predictable film. Rated PG for mature content.

1983 120 minutes

WITNESS FOR THE PROSECUTION

★★★★★

DIRECTOR: Billy Wilder

CAST: Tyrone Power, Charles Laughton, Marlene Dietrich, Elsa Lanchester, John Williams, Henry Daniell, Una O'Connor

Superb performances from Tyrone Power, Charles Laughton, and Marlene Dietrich help make this gripping courtroom drama an enduring favorite of film buffs. The screenplay was adapted from a play by mystery novelist Agatha Christie and features Laughton as an aging lawyer called upon to defend an alleged murderer (Power). It is Dietrich, in what is perhaps her greatest screen performance, who nearly steals the show.

1957 B & W 114 minutes

WOMAN CALLED GOLDA, A

★★★½

DIRECTOR: Alan Gibson

CAST: Ingrid Bergman, Judy Davis, Leonard Nimoy

Ingrid Bergman won an Emmy for her outstanding performance as Israeli Prime Minister Golda Meir. Leonard Nimoy co-stars in this highly watchable film, which was originally made for TV.

1982 200 minutes

WOMAN OF PARIS, A

★★★★

DIRECTOR: Charles Chaplin

CAST: Edna Purviance, Adolphe Menjou, Carl Miller, Lydia Knott, Henry Bergman

In this now-classic silent, a simple country girl (Edna Purviance) goes to Paris and becomes the mistress of a wealthy philanderer (Adolphe Menjou). In her wake follow her artist sweetheart and his mother. Resulting complications trigger an engrossing study of human relationships. Director Charles Chaplin surprised everyone with this film by suddenly forsaking, if only momentarily, his Little Tramp comedy for serious caustic drama, auguring what was to ultimately come in *The Great Dictator*, *Monsieur Verdoux*, and *Limelight*.

1923 B & W 112 minutes

WOMAN OF SUBSTANCE, A

★★★½

DIRECTOR: Don Sharp

CAST: Jenny Seagrove, Deborah Kerr, Barry Bostwick, John Mills, Barry Morse

This TV mini-series accurately retells Barbara Taylor Bradford's best-selling novel of love and revenge. Multimillionairess Emma Hart (played by Deborah Kerr) recalls her humble beginnings as a poor servant girl (played by Jenny Seagrove). Due to the length of this film it's broken down into three volumes (tapes), each with its own title. Volume I ("A Nest of Vipers") finds young Emma employed by the wealthy Fairleys. She falls in love with young Master Edwin but must leave when she becomes pregnant. Volume II ("Fighting for the Dream") centers around Emma's struggle to survive in a new city, caring for her baby and building a business for herself. Her driving force is her desire to ruin the Fairley family. In the final volume ("The Secret Is Revealed"), Emma finds the love of her life, Paul McGill (portrayed by Barry Bostwick). Overall, this is fine entertainment.

1984 300 minutes

WOMAN TIMES SEVEN

★★

DIRECTOR: Vittorio De Sica

CAST: Shirley MacLaine, Peter Sellers, Alan Arkin, Rossano Brazzi, Robert Morley, Michael Caine, Vittorio Gassman, Anita Ekberg

Shirley MacLaine essays seven different roles in this episodic stew and is not as good as she could have been in any of them—even when playing opposite Peter Sellers and Michael Caine. There are some funny moments, but they do not a film make. Something better to do? Do it.

1967 99 minutes

WOMAN'S FACE, A

★★★½

DIRECTOR: George Cukor

CAST: Joan Crawford, Conrad Veidt, Melvyn Douglas, Osa Massen, Reginald Owen, Albert Basserman, Marjorie Main, Charles Quigley, Henry Daniell, George Zucco, Robert Warwick

Joan Crawford is the heroine accused of villain Conrad Veidt's murder. Her personality undergoes an amazing transformation following plastic surgery in this taut, strongly plotted melodrama. High production values and impeccable direction combined with fine casting make this film well worth watching.

1941 B & W 105 minutes

WOMEN IN LOVE

★★★★½

DIRECTOR: Ken Russell

CAST: Glenda Jackson, Oliver Reed, Alan Bates, Eleanor Bron, Jennie Linden, Alan Webb

Glenda Jackson won an Oscar for her performance in this British film. Two love affairs are followed simultaneously in this excellent adaptation of D. H. Lawrence's novel. Rated R.

1970 B & W 129 minutes

WOODEN HORSE, THE

★★★

DIRECTOR: Jack Lee

CAST: Leo Genn, David Tomlinson, Anthony Steel, Peter Finch

Good casting and taut direction make this tale of British POWs tunneling out a Nazi prison camp well worth watching. Made when memories were fresh, the film glows with reality as English cunning, grit, and timing vies with Nazi suspicion, assumed superiority, and complacency.

1950 B & W 101 minutes

WORD, THE

★★★

DIRECTOR: Richard Lang

CAST: David Janssen, John Huston, James Whitmore

In a catacomb beneath Ostia, Italy, an archeologist discovers an ancient manuscript that could cause chaos in the Christian world. The manuscript is said to contain the writings of Christ's younger brother, James the Just. The writings contain heretofore unknown fragments of Jesus' life and death, which turns the religious world upside-down and confusion to conflict. A good story, with wonderful actors. Unrated.

1978 188 minutes

WORKING GIRLS

★★★★

DIRECTOR: Lizzie Borden

CAST: Louise Smith, Ellen McElduff

The sex in this feminist docudrama about prostitution is about as appealing as the smell of dirty socks. The story, on the other hand, is compelling, thought-provoking, oddly touching, and often funny. The main character, Molly (Louise Smith), is a Yale graduate who lives with a female lover and is working toward becoming a professional photographer. Twice a week, she clocks in at an upscale New York City brothel and has "sessions" with a steady stream of customers. A note of warning: The film is guaranteed to offend all but the most open-minded adults. Unrated, the film has simulated sex, profanity, nudity, and violence.

1987 90 minutes

WORLD ACCORDING TO GARP, THE

★★★★½

DIRECTOR: George Roy Hill

CAST: Robin Williams, Glenn Close, John Lithgow, Mary Beth Hurt, Hume Cronyn, Jessica Tandy, Swoosie Kurtz, Amanda Plummer

Director George Roy Hill (*Butch Cassidy and the Sundance Kid* and *A Little Romance*) and screenwriter Steven Tesich (*Breaking Away*) have captured the quirky blend of humor and pathos of John Irving's bestseller. The acting is impressive, with first-rate turns by Robin Williams (in the title role), Glenn Close as his mother, Jenny Fields, and John Lithgow as a kindly transsexual. Rated R for nudity, profanity, sexual situations, and violence.

1982 136 minutes

WORLD AT WAR VOL. 1–26

★★★★★

DIRECTOR: John Pett
CAST: Documentary

These twenty-six volumes, approximately one hour each, comprise the best historical account of World War II ever assembled. Made by the Thames company for British and American television, it is topnotch in all respects. Each volume incorporates interviews with former soldiers, civilian accounts, and lots of actual newsreel footage from the war. Highly recommended for anyone interested in the subject. Narrated by Lawrence Olivier.

1980 60 minutes

WUTHERING HEIGHTS

★★★★

DIRECTOR: William Wyler
CAST: Merle Oberon, Laurence Olivier, Flora Robson, David Niven

Time and talk have made this film a classic. Taken from the Emily Brontë novel, this is a haunting, mesmerizing film. Set on the murky, isolated moors, it tells the tale of Heathcliff, a foundling Gypsy boy who loves Cathy, the spoiled daughter of the house. Their affair, born in childhood, is doomed. She dies; he is left to brood and despair. The moors abide in wind and rain and eerie gloom. As the star-crossed lovers, Olivier and Oberon are impressive.

1939 B & W 103 minutes

X, Y AND ZEE

½

DIRECTOR: Brian G. Hutton
CAST: Elizabeth Taylor, Michael Caine, Susannah York, Margaret Leighton, John Standing

Pointless, tasteless tale of sexual and interpersonal relationships between the three principals is aptly described by the last three letters of the alphabet used to name this mess—X for sick sexual content, Y for why was it made, and Z for the sounds of sleep that emanate from any auditorium or living room where this mess is playing. The only way to explain Michael Caine's presence is to recognize that he is a *working* actor who accepts a wide variety of parts and films. He should have skipped this one. Add this to Elizabeth Taylor's alarming number of bargain-basement films and roles that date back to her association with Richard Burton in the mid-1960s. Rated R.

1972 110 minutes

YOLANDA AND THE THIEF

★★

DIRECTOR: Vincente Minnelli
CAST: Fred Astaire, Lucille Bremer, Frank Morgan, Mildred Natwick, Mary Nash, Ludwig Stossel, Leon Ames, Gigi Pereau

An exotic fantasy, staged with near-cloying opulence, and now a cult favorite. Down on his luck con man Fred Astaire finds beautiful, rich, convent-bred Lucille Bremer praying to her guardian angel. His eye on her money, he claims to be the angel come to earth to protect her. While pursuing his swindle, he falls in love with his mark. This film begins with charm, then goes steadily downhill, thanks to a poor screenplay and inappropriate casting. Fred can't play a con man; Lucille is too cool to be sweet, too lofty to be trusting.

1945 108 minutes

YOU LIGHT UP MY LIFE

★★½

DIRECTOR: Joseph Brooks
CAST: Didi Conn, Michael Zaslow, Joe Silver

Pretty weak story concerning a young girl, Didi Conn, trying to make it in show business. Notable for the title song, which was Debbie Boone's only claim to fame. Film proves it's tough to make a hit song stretch into a feature film. Rated PG.

1977 90 minutes

YOU ONLY LIVE ONCE

★★★

DIRECTOR: Fritz Lang
CAST: Henry Fonda, Sylvia Sidney, William Gargan, Barton MacLane, Jean Dixon, Jerome Cowan, Margaret Hamilton, Ward Bond, Guinn Williams

About a three-time loser (Henry Fonda) who can't even be saved by the love of a good woman (Sylvia Sidney) because society won't allow him to go straight, this film is definitely not a light-hearted or even enjoyable entertainment. In fact, it's a real downer—recommended for Fonda fans only.

1937 B & W 86 minutes

YOUNG AND WILLING

★★½

DIRECTOR: Edward H. Griffith
CAST: William Holden, Susan Hayward, Eddie Bracken, Barbara Britton, Robert Benchley

Hope springs eternal in the hearts of a gaggle of show business neophytes living and loving in a New York theatrical boardinghouse. Cute and entertaining, but formula. Summer stock in Manhattan.

1943 B & W 82 minutes

YOUNG LOVE, FIRST LOVE

★★

DIRECTOR: Steven Hilliard Stern
CAST: Valerie Bertinelli, Timothy Hutton

Boy loves girl, girl loves boy. Does girl love boy enough to go all the way? Nothing better to do? Then watch and find out. Valerie Bertinelli is super-cute as the girl in the quandary of whether to or not. Timothy Hutton is wasted as the boy with the sweats. Unrated.

1979 100 minutes

YOUNG PHILADELPHIANS, THE

★★★★

DIRECTOR: Vincent Sherman
CAST: Robert Vaughn, Paul Newman, Barbara Rush, Alexis Smith, Brian Keith, Adam West, Diane Brewster, Billie Burke, John Williams, Otto Kruger

In this excellent film, Robert Vaughn stars as a rich young man framed for murder. Paul Newman, a young lawyer, defends Vaughn while pursuing society girl Barbara Rush.

1959 B & W 136 minutes

YOUNG WINSTON

★★★

DIRECTOR: Richard Attenborough
CAST: Simon Ward, Anne Bancroft, Robert Shaw, John Mills, Jack Hawkins, Robert Flemyng, Patrick Magee, Laurence Naismith

A first-rate cast peoples this rousing and thoroughly entertaining account of this century's man for all seasons, England's indomitable Winston Leonard Spencer Churchill: journalist, politician, historian, prime minister, bricklayer, peer, brandy and cigar expert. The film takes him from his often wretched school days to his beginnings as a journalist of resource and daring in South Africa during the Boer War, up to his first election to Parliament and the start of an incredible career of many turns and hues. Simon Ward is excellent in the title role. History fares quite well, despite ample opportunity and temptation to gilt truth. Rated PG.

1972 145 minutes

YOUNGBLOOD

★½

DIRECTOR: Peter Markle

CAST: Rob Lowe, Patrick Swayze, Cynthia Gibb, Ed Lauter, Jim Youngs, Fionnula Flanagan

Rob Lowe has stated that this *Rocky* ripoff will be the last of his movies "about teenage problems." Good for him. But he could have stopped before making this bit of silliness about a sensitive kid who tries to make it in the world of hockey. Lowe's character can race around anyone to score a goal. The problem is, he lacks the killer instinct this movie would have us believe is an integral part of the game. Some nice character moments help the story along, but writer-director Peter Markle drops the puck when it comes to comedy bits and credibility. Rated R for profanity, nudity, simulated sex, and violence.

1986 110 minutes

YURI NOSENKO, KGB

★★★½

DIRECTOR: Mick Jackson

CAST: Tommy Lee Jones, Josef Sommer, Ed Lauter, Oleg Rudnik

This aptly directed spy drama is based on the transcripts of public hearings, interviews, and published sources relating to the defection of KGB agent Yuri Nosenko in 1962. The filmmakers have filled in the gaps where direct evidence was unavailable. Tommy Lee Jones gives a tremendous performance as CIA agent Steve Daley. Oleg Rudnik is also good as Yuri Nosenko. This film was co-produced by the BBC and is a fascinating real-life drama.

1986 89 minutes

ZABRISKIE POINT

★★½

DIRECTOR: Michelangelo Antonioni

CAST: Mark Freshene, Daria Halprin, Rod Taylor

An interesting but confusing story of a young college radical who shoots a policeman during a campus demonstration in the late 1960s. This film examines subjects such as Vietnam, black power, and government repression but does not really say too much. The finale is quite exciting, but not worth waiting for. Rated R.

1970 112 minutes

ZORBA THE GREEK

★★★★

DIRECTOR: Michael Cacoyannis

CAST: Anthony Quinn, Alan Bates, Irene Papas, Lila Kedrova, George Foundas

A tiny Greek village in Crete is the home of Zorba, a zesty, uncomplicated man whose love of life is a joy to his friends and an eye-opener to a visiting stranger, Alan Bates. Anthony Quinn is a delight as Zorba, a role he has become identified with. Lila Kedrova was to win an Oscar for her poignant role as an aging courtesan in this 1963 drama.

1963 B & W 146 minutes

A COEUR JOIE (HEAD OVER HEELS)

DIRECTOR: Serge Bourguignon
CAST: Brigitte Bardot, Laurent Terzieff

France has produced some of the world's very best movies. On the flip side, a bad French film is about as bad as it gets. The 1960s were not a great time for moviemaking, and *A Coeur Joie* is proof of that. This piece of swinging sixties fluff about a woman torn between two men has plenty of wide belts, black eyeliner, and bad acting by Brigitte Bardot. Original title in its American release: *Two Weeks in September*. In French with English subtitles.

1967 — 89 minutes

A NOS AMOURS

★★★

DIRECTOR: Maurice Pialat
CAST: Sandrine Bonnaire, Dominique Besnehard, Maurice Pialat

Winner of the Cesar (French Oscar) for best film of 1983, *A Nos Amours* examines the life of a working-class girl of 15 (Sandrine Bonnaire) who engages in one sexual relationship after another because, as she says, "I'm only happy when I'm with a guy." Her characters could be easy targets for snap judgments, but she has the ability to make us stave them off and just observe. In French with English subtitles. Rated R for nudity.

1983 — 110 minutes

A NOUS LA LIBERTE

★★½

DIRECTOR: Rene Claire
CAST: Raymond Cordy, Henri Marchand

Louis and Emile are two prisoners who plan an escape. Only Louis gets away and, surprisingly, he becomes a rich, successful businessman. When Emile gets released, he seeks romantic advice from his friend, but trouble arises when other ex-cons threaten to expose Louis. There are some slapstick segments, and many believe that this film was the inspiration for

Charlie Chaplin's *Modern Times*. In French, with English subtitles.

1931 B & W 87 minutes

AFTER THE REHEARSAL

★★★½

DIRECTOR: Ingmar Bergman
CAST: Erland Josephson

This Ingmar Bergman movie—which was originally made for Swedish television—is about a director (Erland Josephson) who is approached by a young actress with a proposition: she wants to have an affair with him. The approach takes place at the end of their rehearsal of his presentation of Strindberg's *Dream Play*, and the director has a rather atypical response to her advances. In Swedish with English subtitles.

1984 72 minutes

AGUIRRE: WRATH OF GOD

★★★★

DIRECTOR: Werner Herzog
CAST: Klaus Kinski, Ruy Guerra, Del Negro, Helena Rojo, Cecilia Rivera, Peter Berling, Danny Ades

Klaus Kinski gives one of his finest screen performances in the title role as the mad, traitorous Spanish conquistador who leads an expedition through the South American wilds in a quest for the lost golden city of El Dorado. That real-life madman, German director Werner Herzog, took his cameras, cast, and crew into the jungles of the Amazon for this spectacular adventure story. In German with English subtitles. Unrated, the film has violence.

1972 90 minutes

ALEXANDER NEVSKY

★★★★

DIRECTOR: Sergei Eisenstein
CAST: Nikolai Cherkassov, Dmitri Orlov, Vassily Novikov

Another classic from the inimitable Russian director Sergei Eisenstein (*Ivan the Terrible*; *Battleship Potemkin*), this film is a Soviet attempt to prepare Russia for the coming conflict with Hitlerian Germany via portrayal of Alexander Nevsky, a thirteenth-century Russian prince, and his victories over the Teutonic knights of that era. As with all state-commissioned art, the situations can be corny, but the direction is superb, and there is the added bonus of an original musical score by Sergei Prokofieff. In Russian with English subtitles.

1938 B & W 105 minutes

ALLEGRO NON TROPPO

★★★★

DIRECTOR: Bruno Bozzetto
CAST: Animated

An animated spoof of Disney's *Fantasia* by Italian filmmaker Bruno Bozzetto, this release entertainingly weds stylish slapstick with the music of Debussy, Ravel, Vivaldi, Stravinsky, Dvorak, and Sibelius. Rated PG.

1976 75 minutes

ALPHAVILLE

★★★

DIRECTOR: Jean-Luc Godard
CAST: Eddie Constantine, Anna Karina, Akim Tamiroff, Howard Vernon, Laszlo Szabo, Michael Delahaye

Eddie Constantine portrays Lemmy Caution, French private eye extraordinaire, who is sent into the future to rescue a trapped scientist. The future is Alphaville, a logic-constricted city run by a computer. It's a Dick Tracy–type of story with sci-fi leanings. Director Jean-Luc Godard has camped it up, stretching rather far for some of his plot points and loading down the comic-book simplicity with literary and cinematic references. In French, with English subtitles.

1965 98 minutes

ALSINO AND THE CONDOR

★★

DIRECTOR: Miguel Littin

CAST: Alan Esquivel, Dean Stockwell, Carmen Bunster, Alejandro Parodi, Delia Casanova

This is an earnest attempt to dramatize the conflict between the Central American governments and the Sandinista rebels in Nicaragua. The film revolves around the story of one young boy caught in the turmoil. Alan Esquivel is Alsino, the boy who escapes into a fantasy world of flight. Esquivel is compelling; his thoughtful, intelligent face bears the mark of heavy circumstance. The movie would have done better to concentrate more intensely on the life of this boy.

1983 90 minutes

AMARCORD

★★★½

DIRECTOR: Federico Fellini

CAST: Magali Noel, Bruno Zanin, Pupella Maggio, Armando Branciia

Another Federico Fellini film that is good if you like Fellini. A Fellini history of the Italy he remembers, with lots of color, humor, and sex . . . in other words, what it's like to be an Italian. In Italian with English subtitles. Rated R.

1973 127 minutes

AMERICAN FRIEND, THE

★★★★½

DIRECTOR: Wim Wenders

CAST: Dennis Hopper, Bruno Ganz, Lisa Kreuzer, Gerard Blain, Jean Eustache

Tense story of an American criminal (Dennis Hopper) in Germany talking a picture framer into murdering a gangster. Extremely well done, with lots of surprises. Cameo appearances by American film directors Sam Fuller and Nicholas Ray. Rated R—language, violence.

1977 127 minutes

AND GOD CREATED WOMAN

★★½

DIRECTOR: Roger Vadim

CAST: Brigitte Bardot, Curt Jurgens, Jean-Louis Trintignant, Christian Marquand

Brigitte Bardot rose to international fame as the loose-moraled coquette who finds it hard to say no to an attractive male, especially a well-heeled one. Shot on location at the beach with as much of Bardot exposed as the law then allowed, this rather slight story works well and is peopled with interesting characters. In French, with English subtitles.

1957 92 minutes

AND NOW, MY LOVE

★★★½

DIRECTOR: Claude Lelouch

CAST: Marthe Keller, André Dussolier, Charles Denner, Gilbert Becaud, Carla Gravina, Gabriele Tinti, Charles Giraud

In biography-documentary style, director Claude Lelouch juxtaposes three generations of a family while depicting the moral, political, and artistic events that shaped the members' lives. All this is wonderfully designed to show how inevitable it is for two young people (played by André Dussolier and Marthe Keller) from different backgrounds to fall in love. This approach telescopes the generations in novel fashion to underscore the historical continuity that reduces the eventual meeting to a simple matter of fate. Yet it is at this crucial juncture that an otherwise scintillating film falls apart. Lelouch wallows around in modern irrelevances so that one begins to wonder if there is indeed any point to his work. However, the first part of the film is so good and original that the drawbacks of the rest are not all that bothersome. Dubbed.

1974 121 minutes

AND THE SHIP SAILS ON

★★

DIRECTOR: Federico Fellini

CAST: Freddie Jones, Barbara Jefford, Victor Poletti

Italian director Federico Fellini's heavily symbolic parable about a luxury liner filled with eccentric beautiful people sailing the Adriatic on the eve of World War I was called by one critic "a spellbinding, often magical tribute to the illusions and delusions of art." That's one way of looking at it. We found it boring. However, Fellini fans and lovers of foreign films may find it rewarding. In Italian with English subtitles.

1984 138 minutes

ANTARCTICA

★

DIRECTOR: Koreyoshi Kurahara

CAST: Ken Takaura, Tsunehiko Watase, Masako Natsume, Keiko Oginome

Antarctica, produced in part by Japanese television, comes across like an episode of *Wild Kingdom*. It is the true story of a 1958 Japan to Antarctica expedition. While in Antarctica, the traveling scientists encounter complications and are forced to return home, leaving their team of dogs behind to fend for themselves. The dogs are pretty good naturalistic actors, but that only goes so far when you have a tepid representation of events. The strong connections between the men and the animals is not established well enough, so their year-long grieving seems overdone. The dogs themselves don't come across as individual personalities. Collectively, they are of some interest but you're not drawn to them as you are to the wolves of Carroll Ballard's *Never Cry Wolf*. Dubbed in English.

1984 112 minutes

ASSASSINS DE L'ORDRE, LES (LAW BREAKERS)

★★

DIRECTOR: Marcel Carné

CAST: Jacques Brel, Catherine Rouvel, Michael Lonsdale, Charles Denner, Didier Haudepin

Marcel Carné, who directed the 1944 classic *Children of Paradise*, slips into innocuousness with this less than riveting tale. Jacques Brel plays a judge who is trying to get to the bottom of corrupt police practices. The present case concerns a burglary suspect who is taken in for routine questioning and winds up dead. The judge is met with great resistance by the community when he declares the incident a case of police brutality. A long suspension of belief is required for this one.

1971 107 minutes

AUTUMN SONATA

★★★★★

DIRECTOR: Ingmar Bergman

CAST: Ingrid Bergman, Liv Ullmann, Lena Nyman

Ingmar Bergman directed this superb Swedish release about the first meeting in seven years of a daughter (Liv Ullmann) with her difficult concert pianist mother (Ingrid Bergman). A great film, without a doubt. In Swedish and English. Rated PG.

1978 97 minutes

AVIATOR'S WIFE, THE

★★★½

DIRECTOR: Eric Rohmer
CAST: Philippe Marlaud, Marie Riviere, Anne-Laure Marie, Matthieu Carriere

Not much happens in a film by French director Eric Rohmer, at least not in the traditional sense. Mostly, there's just talk. Yet, if you pay close attention, a few special things do happen—and they are quite enough. In the story, a young law student named François (Philippe Marlaud) is crushed when he discovers his lover, Anne (Marie Riviere), in the company of another man and decides to spy on them. In French, with English subtitles. Unrated, the film has no objectionable material.

1981 104 minutes

BAKER'S WIFE, THE

★★★★

DIRECTOR: Marcel Pagnol
CAST: Raimu, Ginette Leclerc, Charles Moulin, Robert Battier, Robert Brassac, Charpin

The new baker is coming to a town that has been without fresh-baked goods for too long. With great fanfare, the baker and his new wife arrive, but she has a roving eye for another. Caught in an upheaval of emotions, the baker begins to function badly in his kitchen after his wife leaves. This comedy is a gem of French film-making. In French with English subtitles.

1938 B & W 124 minutes

BALLAD OF A SOLDIER

★★★½

DIRECTOR: Grigori Chukhrai
CAST: Vladimir Ivashov, Shanna Prokhorenko, Antonina Maximova, Nikolai Kruchkov

A soldier finds love and adventure on a ten-day pass to see his mother. This import features excellent cinematography and acting, and despite the always obvious Soviet propaganda, some piercing insights into the Russian soul. In Russian with English subtitles.

1959 B & W 89 minutes

BATTLE OF ALGIERS

★★★★

DIRECTOR: Gillo Pontecorvo
CAST: Yacef Saadi, Jean Martin, Brahim Haggiag, Tomasso Neri, Samia Kerbash

This gut-wrenching Italian-Algerian pseudodocumentary about the war between Algerian citizens and their French "protectors" was released when America's involvement in Vietnam was still to reach its peak, but the parallels between the two stories are obvious. Covering the years from 1954 to 1962, this film is an emotional experience—it is not recommended for the casual viewer and is too strong (and depressing) for children, but if you want to take a look into a world without security and learn some history along the way, *Battle of Algiers* is a good choice.

1965 B & W 123 minutes

BATTLESHIP POTEMKIN, THE

★★★★★

DIRECTOR: Sergei Eisenstein
CAST: Alexander Antonov, Vladimir Barsky, Grigori Alexandrov, Mikhail Goronorov

One of a handful of landmark motion pictures. This silent classic, directed by the legendary Sergei Eisenstein, depicts the mutiny of the crew of a Russian battleship and its aftermath. It was primarily released by the infant Soviet government as propaganda to glorify those who first revolted against the Czar. Its impact far exceeded such narrow boundaries. The photography, editing, and directorial technique expanded the threshold of what was then standard cinema story-telling. The massacre of civilians on the steppes of Odessa remains one of the most powerful scenes in film history. Silent.

1925 B & W 65 minutes

BEAU PERE

★★★★

DIRECTOR: Bernard Blier

CAST: Patrick Dewaere, Ariel Besse, Maurice Ronet, Nicole Garcia

Patrick Dewaere stars again for French director Bernard Blier (*Get Out Your Handkerchiefs*) in this film, about a stepfather who falls in love with his adopted pubescent daughter. It could have been shocking—or just plain perverse. But *Beau Pere* is nothing of the sort. Rather, it is a bittersweet, thoroughly charming motion picture. Blier handles the subject with such wit, humor, and inventiveness that it never descends into the realms of exploitation or bad taste. In French, with English subtitles. Unrated, the film has nudity, profanity, and adult themes.

1982 120 minutes

BEAUTY AND THE BEAST

★★★★★

DIRECTOR: Jean Cocteau

CAST: Josette Day, Jean Marais

This French classic goes far beyond mere retelling of the well-known fairy tale. Its eerie visual beauty and surrealistic atmosphere mark it as a genuine original. The tragic love story between Beauty (Josette Day) and the all-too-human Beast (Jean Marais) resembles a moving painting. Every detail is presented with painstaking care by its innovative director, Jean Cocteau. In French with English subtitles.

1946 B & W 90 minutes

BELLISSIMA

★★★

DIRECTOR: Luchino Visconti

CAST: Anna Magnani, Walter Chairi, Tina Apicella

Luchino Visconti is known for such pioneering works as *Ossessione, La Terra Trema, Rocco and His Brothers, The Dammned,* and *Death in Venice*. As for *Bellissima,* if you are programming an Anna Magnani festival, you might be interested in this oddly and determinedly lightweight comedy. Otherwise, there is not much going for this offbeat trifle. The story is set in the Cinecitta Studios, where a search is on for the prettiest child in Rome. Magnani seems a bit out of place as an earnest neo-realist mother who enters her daughter, only to get trapped in a stampede of hysterical stage mothers and contestants. In Italian with English subtitles.

1951 B & W 95 minutes

BERLIN ALEXANDERPLATZ

★★★½

DIRECTOR: Rainer Werner Fassbinder

CAST: Gunter Lamprecht, Hanna Schygulla, Barbara Sukowa, Gottfried John, Elisabeth Trissenaar

Remember the scene in Stanley Kubrick's *A Clockwork Orange* in which Malcolm McDowell's eyes are wired open and he is forced to watch agonizing hour after agonizing hour of movies? That's how we often felt when wading through the fifteen-and-a-half hours of Rainer Werner Fassbinder's *magnum opus, Berlin Alexanderplatz*. Not that this much-praised German television production doesn't have its moments of interest, fascination, and yes, even genius. But as with all of Fassbinder's other films (*Lili Marleen*; *Veronika Voss*; *The Marriage of Maria Braun*; etc.), *Berlin*

Alexanderplatz also has its excesses and false notes (only there are many more of them than usual, thanks to its length). In German with English subtitles.

1983 930 minutes

BETTY BLUE

★★½

DIRECTOR: Jean-Jacques Beineix
CAST: Jean-Hugues Anglade, Beatrice Dalle

Betty Blue showcases one of those obnoxiously impetuous female characters the French seem to adore. Director Beineix, a wizard of the Luscious Style But Little Content school of movie-making, has himself a pretty lame story. It's about Betty, who is radically spontaneous and a bit wacko (we don't know why), and Zorg, the man she inspires to continue writing. The trick is not to think too much about the ridiculousness of the film (or wonder who these people are and what they're doing here), but instead to bask in Beineix's sensuous visual flair. His films can be a real treat for the senses. He can make a lonely-looking beachfront community oddly fascinating. Jean-Hugues Anglade as Zorg has some lovely moments, and there are ample doses of comedy and uninhibited sex. The sexuality is hearty and natural and grounded in reality—which is more than you can say for Betty. The outstanding musical score is by Gabriel Yared. In French with English subtitles. Rated R.

1986 117 minutes

BEYOND FEAR

★★★

DIRECTOR: Yannick Andrei
CAST: Michel Bouquet, Michel Constantin, Marilu Tolo, Moustache, Paul Crauchet, Gerard Borman

While dubbing foreign-language films with English is a major irritant in so many of the foreign films that come out on video these days, this movie is almost compelling enough to make the viewer forget this problem. Ultimately, his wife and child are taken hostage by the band of outlaws and he must work with the police to ensure the safety of his family. Rated R by mid-1970s standards due to violence and profanity (very little of both, actually).

1975 92 minutes

BICYCLE THIEF, THE

★★★★

DIRECTOR: Vittorio De Sica
CAST: Lamberto Maggiorani, Lianella Carell, Enzo Staiola, Elena Altieri

Considered by critics an all-time classic, this touching, honest, beautifully human film speaks realistically to the heart with simple cinematic eloquence. A bill poster's bicycle, on which his job depends, is stolen. Ignored by the police, who see nothing special in the loss, and by the Church, to which material things are of small consequence, the anguished worker and his young son search Rome for the thief. One of a number of superb films to come out of postwar Italy, this one captured the 1949 Oscar for best foreign film. In Italian with English subtitles.

1949 B & W 90 minutes

BILITIS

★★★★

DIRECTOR: David Hamilton
CAST: Patti D'Arbanville, Bernard Giraudeau, Gillis Kohler, Mona Kristensen, Mathieu Carriere

A surprisingly tasteful and sensitive soft-core sex film, this details the sexual awakening of the title character, a 16-year-old French girl (Mona Kristensen) while she spends the summer with a family friend (Patti D'Arbanville). The two briefly become lovers, but this ends when Bilitis encounters a young man (Bernard Giraudeau) and engages in a sweet summer romance. Rated R for nudity and simulated sex.

1982 93 minutes

BIRGIT HAAS MUST BE KILLED

★★★★★

DIRECTOR: Laurent Heynemann

CAST: Phillippe Noiret, Jean Rochefort, Lisa Kreuzer, Bernard Le Coq

It is hard to imagine a more perfect film than this spellbinding, French thriller-drama. Though its plot revolves around the assassination of a German terrorist (Birgit Haas) by a French counterspy organization, this film says as much about human relationships as it does espionage. And that's what makes it such a thoroughly fulfilling movie experience. Unrated, the film contains well-handled violence and nudity. In French with English subtitles.

1981 105 minutes

BIZET'S CARMEN

★★★★★

DIRECTOR: Francesco Rosi

CAST: Placido Domingo, Julia Migenes-Johnson

Julia Migenes-Johnson and Placido Domingo star in this film adaptation of the opera by Georges Bizet based on the short story by Prosper Mérimée. It is about a poor girl whose fierce independence maddens the men who become obsessed with her. Francesco Rosi directed this, the most satisfying treatment of an opera yet to be done in a big commercial film. In French, with English subtitles. Rated PG for mild violence.

1985 152 minutes

BLACK ORPHEUS

★★★★★

DIRECTOR: Marcel Camus

CAST: Breno Mello, Marpessa Dawn, Lea Garcia, Lourdes de Oliveira

The Greek myth of Orpheus, the unrivaled musician, and his ill-fated love for Eurydice has been updated and set in Rio de Janeiro during carnival for this superb film. A Portuguese-French co-production, it has all the qualities of a genuine classic. Its stunning photography captures both the magical spirit of the original legend and the tawdry yet effervescent spirit of Brazil. Fine acting and a haunting musical round out this splendid viewing treat.

1959 98 minutes

BLACK VENUS

★

DIRECTOR: Claude Mulot

CAST: Josephine Jacqueline Jones, Emiliano Redondo, Jose Antonio Ceinos, Mandy Rice Davies, Karin Schubert

Lavish 19th-century Parisian costumes and settings can't salvage this endless sex romp for the former Miss Bahamas (Josephine Jacqueline Jones, who plays Venus). She becomes involved with a starving artist, Armand (Jose Antonio Ceinos). As a model, she performs many special services for her wealthy clients, which Armand can't handle. He creates a marble statue of her that he can't live without. Very loosely based on stories by French novelist Honoré de Balzac, this European film is poorly dubbed. Rated R.

1983 80 minutes

BLOOD OF A POET

★★½

DIRECTOR: Jean Cocteau
CAST: Jean Cocteau

This pretentious and self-centered first film by France's multitalented Jean Cocteau is also intriguing, provoking, and inventive. Cocteau stars in and narrates this highly personal excursion into a poet's inner life: his fears and obsessions, his relation to the world about him, and the classic poetic preoccupation with death. Filmed in 1930, it was not shown publicly until 1932. In French with English subtitles.

1930 B & W 55 minutes

BLUE ANGEL, THE

★★★★★

DIRECTOR: Joseph von Sternberg
CAST: Emil Jannings, Marlene Dietrich, Kurt Gerron, Hans Albers

This stunning tale about a strait-laced schoolteacher's obsession with a strip-tease dancer in Germany is the subject of many film classes. The photography, set design, and script are all topnotch, and there are spectacular performances by all. Not just to be enjoyed by film students, this classic should sit well with anybody looking for an intelligent evening of entertainment. In German, with English subtitles.

1930 B & W 98 minutes

BLUE COUNTRY

★★★½

DIRECTOR: Jean-Charles Tacchella
CAST: Brigitte Fossey, Jacques Serres, Ginette Garcin, Armand Meffre, Ginett Mathieu

A light-hearted comedy involving a nurse who leaves the city to enjoy a free and independent life in the country. She meets up with a bachelor who equally enjoys his freedom. The womanizing country boy initially finds this strong-willed modern girl hard to handle. Their encounters with the local townspeople provide amusing glimpses of French folk life. In French with English subtitles.

1977 90 minutes

BOAT IS FULL, THE

★★★

DIRECTOR: Markus Imhoof
CAST: Tina Engel, Marin Walz

Markus Imhoof's film about refugees from the Nazis trying to obtain refuge in Switzerland is tragic and extraordinarily effective. It could have been a better movie, but it could hardly have been more heartbreaking. No MPAA rating.

1983 100 minutes

BOB LE FLAMBEUR

★★★★★

DIRECTOR: Jean-Pierre Melville
CAST: Roger Duchesne, Isabel Corey, Daniel Cauchy, Howard Vernon

This is an exquisite example of early French *film noir* (which translates as "dark film" and was a style of movie made predominantly by European directors in Hollywood during the 1940s). Moreover, it is an exquisite example of filmmaking—period. In it are all the trappings of the classic gangster movie—a flamboyant main character, tough cops, tougher gangsters, and the seedy joints where criminal plots are hatched. But there is more to it. The most fascinating element of this import is the title character, Bob Montagne (Roger Duchesne). A one-time bank robber and gang member, he has spent the last twenty years of his life without venturing into crime. All he does is gamble. He hasn't been lucky in a long time, however, and plans to rob a casino of $800 million. But pulling it off isn't as easy as it seems. In French with English subtitles.

1955 B & W 102 minutes

BOCCACCIO 70

★★★★

DIRECTORS: Federico Fellini, Luchino Visconti, Vittorio De Sica

CAST: Anita Ekberg, Sophia Loren, Romy Schneider, Peppino De Filippo, Dante Maggio, Tomas Milian

As with its Renaissance namesake, this film tells stories—three of them, in fact, by three of Italy's greatest directors. Each has a trademark on his entry. Federico Fellini's entry, "The Temptation of Dr. Antonio," showcases Peppino De Filippo as the puritanical bluenose who becomes obsessed with a billboard that comes to life in the voluptuous form of a young Anita Ekberg. The second playlet, by Luchino Visconti, is "The Bet," which features Romy Schneider as a not-so-typical housewife who takes over the position (excuse the expression) of her husband's mistress. A funnier chain of events could not be imagined. The third entry, "The Raffle," by Vittorio De Sica, is pure farce and has wisely been left for last. The treatment of this story is reminiscent of a dirty joke told badly, and it tends to cheapen the panache of the first two. However, any film with Sophia Loren is worth watching, and this one is no exception. In Italian with English subtitles.

1962 165 minutes

BOUDU SAVED FROM DROWNING

★★★★★

DIRECTOR: Jean Renoir

CAST: Michel Simon, Charles Granval, Max Dalban, Jean Daste

This is the original *Down and Out in Beverly Hills,* except that the tramp (the beloved Michel Simon) is saved by an antiquarian bookseller after a suicide attempt in the Seine—down and out in Paris. As in the 1985 version, Boudu is taken into the rescuer's house and seduces the wife and maid. But here he marries the maid, then accidentally falls in the river after the ceremony and rediscovers his own brand of freedom. Unlike the play on which it was based and unlike the Hollywood version—both of which have the bum accept his responsibilities—*Boudu Saved from Drowning* is a celebration of joyful anarchy, and Simon's interpretation of his role is enchanting. A masterpiece. In French, with English subtitles.

1932 B & W 88 minutes

BREATHLESS (ORIGINAL)

★★★★★

DIRECTOR: Jean-Luc Godard

CAST: Jean-Paul Belmondo, Jean Seberg

Richard Gere or Jean-Paul Belmondo? The choice should be easy after you see the Godard version of this story of a carefree crook and his "along for the ride" girlfriend. Jean Seberg is the perfect "American in Paris," and Paris never looked more exotic or beckoning. In case you don't already know, the original screenplay was written by François Truffaut. See it for Belmondo's performance as the continent's most charming crook, but while you're along for the ride, note just how well-made a film can be.

1959 B & W 89 minutes

BYE BYE BRAZIL

★★★½

DIRECTOR: Carlos Diegues

CAST: Joe Wilker, Betty Faria, Fabio Junior, Zaira Zambelli

This is a bawdy, bizarre, satiric, and sometimes even touching film that follows a ramshackle traveling tent show—the Caravana Rolidei—through the cities, jungle, and villages of Brazil. On the dramatic level, it lifts the sparkling veil of illusion that surrounds the "glamorous" world of show business to reveal the threadbare strings of reality. Visually, it gives the audience a fascinating tour of the South American country and a taste of its culture. In Portuguese with English subtitles. Rated R.

1980 110 minutes

CABINET OF DOCTOR CALIGARI, THE

★★★½

DIRECTOR: Robert Wiene
CAST: Werner Krauss, Conrad Veidt, Lil Dagover

A nightmarish story and surrealistic settings are the main ingredients of this early German classic of horror and fantasy. Cesare, a hollow-eyed sleepwalker (Conrad Veidt), commits murder while under the spell of the evil hypnotist Dr. Caligari (Werner Krauss). Ordered to kill Jane, a beautiful girl (Lil Dagover), Cesare defies Caligari, and instead abducts her. The chase that follows takes Cesare to his death. It's all very real and unreal, tricking until the very end. Veidt specialized in horror at the outset of his career following World War I. Nearly half a century later, he was last seen as the suave, ill-fated Nazi Major Strasser of *Casablanca*. Silent.

1919 B & W 51 minutes

CAMILA

★★★½

DIRECTOR: Maria Luisa Bemberg
CAST: Susu Pecoraro, Imanol Arias, Hector Alterio, Mona Maris, Elena Tasisto, Carlos Munoz

A romantic and true story of forbidden love in the classic tradition, as well as a nominee for best foreign film at the 1985 Academy Awards. Susu Pecoraro is Camila O'Gorman, the daughter of a wealthy aristocrat in Buenos Aires in the mid-1800s. Imanol Arias plays Ladislao Gutierrez, a Jesuit priest who falls in love with Camila. The film says nothing that hasn't been said hundreds of times in the past, but the cinematography is superb, and the love scenes are red-hot. Not rated, but with sex, nudity, and violence. In Spanish with English subtitles.

1984 105 minutes

CARNIVAL IN FLANDERS

★★★★

DIRECTOR: Jacques Feyder
CAST: Françoise Rosay, Andre Alerme, Jean Murat, Louis Jouret, Micheline Cheirel, Bernard Lancret, Lynne Clevers

This sly drama about a village that postpones its destruction by collaborating with their conquerors and freely offering them their goods during carnival season was reputed to be one of Joseph Goebbels' favorite films and was considered a poor statement to make to the rest of the world in light of what Nazi Germany and Italy were attempting to do to their neighbors. A clever, subtle work and one of Jacques Feyder's finest achievements, this classic is a conscious effort to re-create on celluloid the great paintings of the masters depicting village life during carnival time. Interesting on many levels, this film poses some intriguing questions, not the least of which is: "To exactly what length did the women of the village collaborate in order to alleviate the threat of destruction?" In French with English subtitles.

1936 B & W 92 minutes

CAT AND MOUSE

★★★★½

DIRECTOR: Claude Lelouch
CAST: Michèle Morgan, Jean-Pierre Aumont, Serge Reggiani, Valerie LaGrangg

Written, produced, and directed by Claude Lelouch, *Cat and Mouse* is a deliciously urbane and witty whodunit guaranteed to charm and deceive while keeping you marvelously entertained. The plot has more twists and turns than a country road, and the characters are . . . well . . . just slightly corrupt and totally fascinating. In French with English subtitles. Rated PG.

1975 107 minutes

CHEATERS, THE

★

DIRECTOR: Sergio Martino
CAST: Dayle Haddon, Luc Merenda, Lino Troisi, Enrico Maria Salerno

From the director of such gems as *Screamers*, *Sex With a Smile*, and *Slave of the Cannibal God* comes another dumb Italian flick. *The Cheaters* is about a topnotch card cheat who makes his way to the top working for a Milan crimelord. He falls in love with the boss's son's girlfriend and the sparks begin to fly. The dubbing is as poor as it gets and the 90-minute running time seems much longer. Rated R for profanity, sex, and violence.

1976 91 minutes

CHILDREN OF PARADISE

★★★★½

DIRECTOR: Marcel Carné
CAST: Jean-Louis Barrault, Arletty, Pierre Brasseur

This classic French film, directed by Marcel Carné, follows the career of a nineteenth-century mime (Jean-Louis Barrault) and his love affair with a beautiful courtesan (Arletty).

1944 B & W 188 minutes

CHRIST STOPPED AT EBOLI

★★

DIRECTOR: Francesco Rosi
CAST: Gian Maria Volonte, Irene Papas, Alain Cuny, Lea Massari, François Simon, Paoblo Bonacelli

Christ Stopped at Eboli is based on a renowned Italian novel about Carlo Levi, a political exile who was punished in 1935 for his antifascist writings and exiled to a village in southern Italy. This is a leisurely film that can drag at times. Irene Papas livens things up with her resounding laugh, but ultimately this quiet tale is forgettable. In Italian with English subtitles.

1983 118 minutes

CHRISTIANE F.

★½

DIRECTOR: Ulrich Edel
CAST: Natja Brunkhorst, Thomas Haustein, Jens Kuphal, Reiner Wolk

Although quite interesting in places, this West German film dealing with young heroin addicts ultimately becomes a bore. Too many repetitive scenes of kids shooting dope, and bad acting, make this rate a yawn. In German with English subtitles.

1981 124 minutes

CLAIRE'S KNEE

★★★★★

DIRECTOR: Eric Rohmer
CAST: Jean-Claude Brialy, Aurora Cornu, Beatrice Romand, Laurence De Monaghan, Michele Montel, Geral Falconetti, Fabrica Luchini

For anyone who thought that an adult comedy about sex and love must be X-rated, *Claire's Knee* is a must. There is no substitute for class, and director Eric Rohmer exhibits a great deal of it in this fifth film in a series entitled *Six Moral Tales*. The plot is simplicity itself. Jerome (Jean-Claude Brialy) is engaged. He awaits his fiancée at Annecy, where he has spent many happy times. He renews his friendship with a writer (Aurora Cornu) who has two daughters; one is Claire. Jerome is intrigued by Claire but is obsessed with her knee—her right knee, to be specific. Rohmer's work is economical but poignant. The denouement is so delicious, it would be folly to recount it here. In French with English subtitles. PG rating.

1971 103 minutes

CLEAN SLATE (COUP DE TORCHON)

★★★★

DIRECTOR: Bertrand Tavernier
CAST: Philippe Noiret, Isabelle Huppert, Stéphane Audran, Irene Skobline

Set during 1938 in a French West African colonial town, this savage and sardonic black comedy (the title of which translates as "Clean Slate") is a study of the circumstances under which racism and fascism flourish. Philippe Noiret stars as a simple-minded sheriff who, though he loves eating, drinking, and taking bribes, decides that it's time to wipe out the corruption that runs rampant in his village. The way he does it is shocking—and often hilarious. In French, with English subtitles. Unrated, the film has nudity, implied sex, violence, profanity, and racial epithets.

1981 128 minutes

CLOSELY WATCHED TRAINS

★★★★½

DIRECTOR: Jiří Menzel
CAST: Vaclav Neckar, Jitka Bendova

A bittersweet coming-of-age comedy-drama against a backdrop of the Nazi occupation of Czechoslovakia. A naive young train dispatcher is forced to grow up quickly when asked to help the Czech underground. This gentle film is one of the more artistic efforts to come from behind the Iron Curtain. Its release coincided with the brief period of relaxed government control before the Soviet crackdown in 1967. This production is unusual because it stresses the development of interpersonal relations among its characters, rather than the traditional heroic aspects of communist war films.

1966 B & W 91 minutes

CLOWNS, THE

★★★★½

DIRECTOR: Federico Fellini
CAST: Mayo Morin, Lima Alberti, Alvaro Vitali, Gasparmo

Psychoautobiographical revelations . . . life as art and art as life . . . transcending the documentary format . . . expressing the spirit and the passing of the Commedia dell'Arte . . . the tragicomic clown as the central metaphor for an existential century. Yes, yes—but good grief! Federico Fellini's television documentary is a three-ring spectacle of fun and silliness, too. Here, style is substance, and the only substance worth noting is the water thrown onto the journalist who asks the cast of circus crazies, "What does it all mean?" It only means that we are all in the predicament of survival, and we had better not take it too seriously. In Italian with English subtitles.

1971 90 minutes

COLONEL REDL

★★★½

DIRECTOR: Istvan Szabo
CAST: Klaus Maria Brandauer, Armin Mueller-Stahl, Gu-

drun Landgrebe, Jan Niklas, Hans Christian Blech

Director Istvan Szabo and star Klaus Maria Brandauer collaborated for the first time on the superb *Mephisto*. Their second teaming, on *Colonel Redl*, despite its Academy Award nomination, brings less felicitous results. Not that it's a bad film. No movie featuring Brandauer could be. However, the ponderous and deliberate nature of *Colonel Redl*, which tells the story of how the title character became a pawn in a struggle for power in the Austro-Hungarian Empire just prior to World War I, keeps it from becoming a fully satisfying film. Rated R for profanity, nudity, simulated sex, and violence. In German with English subtitles.

1985 144 minutes

CONFIDENTIALLY YOURS

★★

DIRECTOR: François Truffaut
CAST: Fanny Arandt, Jean-Louis Trintignant, Jean-Pierre Kalfon, Philippe Laudenbach, Philippe Morier-Genoud

François Truffaut's last film is a stylized murder mystery in the tradition of Hitchcock (whom Truffaut so fervently admired). Truffaut might have had a jolly time making this homage, but it's only a light-hearted soufflé of a film that is too thin to hold its air. The movie tips its hat to good old suspense films without becoming one itself. Jean-Louis Trintignant plays a real estate agent framed for murder. His secretary (Fanny Ardant) helps him solve the case. In French with English subtitles. Rated PG.

1983 B & W 110 minutes

CONFORMIST, THE

★★★★

DIRECTOR: Bernardo Bertolucci
CAST: Jean-Louis Trintignant, Stefania Sandrelli, Dominique Sanda, Pierre Clementi

Fascinating character study of Marcello Clerici (Jean-Louis Trintignant), a young, driven follower of Mussolini. He becomes increasingly obsessed with conformity as he tries to suppress a traumatic homosexual experience suffered as a youth. After a strange series of events, he is forced to prove his loyalty to the fascist state by murdering a former professor who lives in exile. Interesting historical study of a highly decadent society. In French with English subtitles. Rated R for language and subject matter.

1971 107 minutes

CONTEMPT

★½

DIRECTOR: Jean-Luc Godard
CAST: Brigitte Bardot, Michel Piccoli, Jack Palance, Fritz Lang, Giorgia Moll

Jean-Luc Godard parallels Homer's epic of Ulysses and Penelope with the lives of a contemporary French couple. *Contempt* is a symbol-laden semibore that's set in the world of moviemaking in Rome. Veteran film director Fritz Lang plays himself, and Jack Palance gives another creepy impersonation. In French, with English subtitles.

1964 102 minutes

CONTRABAND

★★

DIRECTOR: Lucio Fulci
CAST: Fabio Testi, Ivana Monti, Guido Alberti, Daniele Dublino, Marcel Bozzuffi, Saverio Marconi

A mediocre Italian gangster movie, dubbed into English. This time the main vice is contraband goods rather than hard drugs or prostitution. But the story is the same. Each gang is vying for complete control and is killing and undermining the other's operations. The oldest brother of a powerful family is murdered and revenge is the order of the day.

1987 87 minutes

CONVERSATION PIECE

★

DIRECTOR: Luchino Visconti
CAST: Burt Lancaster, Silvana Mangano, Helmut Berger, Claudia Marsani, Claudia Cardinale

All the talent collected to produce this film can't save it from being mundane, wordy, and phlegmatic. Burt Lancaster portrays a bewildered, reclusive professor whose life changes direction when he encounters a countess and her children who live life for its pleasures rather than its meaning. The countess's lover (Helmut Berger) serves only to complicate and confuse the already ponderous story. In Italian with English subtitles.

1974 122 minutes

COUSIN, COUSINE

★★★½

DIRECTOR: Jean-Charles Tacchella
CAST: Marie-Christine Barrault, Victor Lanoux, Marie-France Pisier, Guy Marchand, Ginette Garcin, Sybil Maas

Marie-Christine Barrault and Victor Lanoux star in this ever-popular French comedy. Both married to others, they become cousins by marriage. Once the kissing starts, their relationship expands beyond the boundaries of convention. In French with English subtitles.

1975 95 minutes

CRAZY RAY, THE

★★★½

DIRECTOR: René Clair
CAST: Henri Rollan, Madeline Rodrigue, Albert Prejean

René Clair's classic fantasy about a scientist's paralyzing ray is basically an experimental film that utilizes camera tricks and location shooting to entertain and amuse the audience. A handful of people who have not been affected by the ray take advantage of the situation and help themselves to whatever they want but eventually begin to fight among themselves. After locating the scientist who has invented the ray, they persuade him to restore things to normal and meet with skepticism from the police when they attempt to explain things. This is more of an experience than a film, but however you want to approach it, it's very entertaining. Clair later edited prints of this film down to thirty-six minutes and declared those to be the film as it should be seen, but many copies run closer to sixty minutes, with many confusing subtitles included.

1923 B & W 60 minutes

CRIES AND WHISPERS

★★★★★

DIRECTOR: Ingmar Bergman
CAST: Harriet Andersson, Liv Ullmann, Ingrid Thulin, Kari Sylwan

Directed and written by Ingmar Bergman and hauntingly photographed by cinematographer Sven Nykvist, this Swedish language film tells a story of a dying woman, her two sisters, and a servant girl. Faultless performances by Liv Ullmann, Ingrid Thulin, and Harriet Andersson make this an unforgettable film experience. Rated R.

1972 106 minutes

DAMNED, THE

★★★½

DIRECTOR: Luchino Visconti

CAST: Dirk Bogarde, Ingrid Thulin, Helmut Griem, Helmut Berger

Deep, heavy drama about a German industrialist family that is destroyed under Nazi power. This film is difficult to watch, as the images are as bleak as the story itself. In German, with English subtitles. Rated R for sex.

1969 155 minutes

DANGEROUS MOVES

★★★★½

DIRECTOR: Richard Dembo

CAST: Michel Piccoli, Leslie Caron, Alexandre Arbatt, Liv Ullmann

Worthy of its Oscar for best foreign film of 1984, this French film about a chess match between two grand masters in Geneva is not just for fans of the game. Indeed, the real intensity that is created here comes from the sidelines: the two masters' camps, the psych-out attempts, the political stakes, and the personal dramas. Rated PG for adult situations and language.

1984 95 minutes

DANTON

★★★½

DIRECTOR: Andrezej Wajda

CAST: Gerard Depardieu, Wojiech Pszoniak, Patrice Chereau

Polish director Andrezej Wajda (*Man of Iron*) takes the French revolutionary figure (well played by Gerard Depardieu) and the events surrounding his execution by one-time comrades and turns it into a parable of modern life. The struggle between the title character and Robespierre is not unlike that of America versus the Soviet Union. It may not be good history, but the film does provide interesting viewing and food for thought. This French film has one more thing going for it: It has been subtitled in English rather than dubbed, a factor that undermined the video version of another Depardieu picture, *The Return of Martin Guerre*. Rated PG.

1982 136 minutes

DAS BOOT (THE BOAT)

★★★★★

DIRECTOR: Wolfgang Petersen

CAST: Jurgen Prochnow, Herbert Grongmeyer, Klaus Wennemann

During World War II, forty thousand young Germans served aboard Nazi submarines. Only ten thousand survived. This magnificent $13 million West German film masterpiece recreates the tension and claustrophobic conditions of forty-three men assigned to a U-boat in 1941. This is the English-dubbed version. Rated R for tense situations, violence, and profanity.

1981 150 minutes

DAY FOR NIGHT

★★★★★

DIRECTOR: François Truffaut

CAST: Jacqueline Bisset, Jean-Pierre Léaud, François Truffaut

One of the best of the film-within-a-film movies ever made, this work by the late François Truffaut captures the poetry and energy of the creative artist at his peak. In French with English subtitles. Rated PG.

1973 120 minutes

DAY OF WRATH

★★★½

DIRECTOR: Carl Dreyer

CAST: Lisbeth Movin, Thorkild Roose, Sigrid Neiiendam, Preben Lerdorff, Olaf Ussing, Anna Svierkier

Slow-moving, intriguing story of a young woman who marries an elderly preacher but falls in love with his son is an allegorical indictment on the appearances of evil. It is reminiscent of Arthur Miller's *The Crucible* in that they both deal with the witch hunts of the Middle Ages, and they present the "pious" folk as being the real blight. Visually effective and well acted by all the principals, this film relies too much on symbolism and implied action but is still worthy as a study in hysteria and the motivations behind the fear. This is one of the last feature films made by internationally renowned director Carl Dreyer, perhaps best known for his *Passion of Joan of Arc*.

1944 B & W 98 minutes

DECLINE OF THE AMERICAN EMPIRE, THE

★★★★

DIRECTOR: Denys Arcand

CAST: Dominique Michel, Dorothee Berryman, Louise Portal, Genevieve Rioux, Pierre Curzi, Remy Girard, Yves Jacques, Daniel Briere, Gabriel Arcand

Forget the title of this French-Canadian import. The phrase comes up during an early scene in which one character interviews another about her new book, *Variations on the Idea of Happiness*. It is her contention that civilizations fall when their citizens become more concerned with fulfillment than survival. In *Decline*, all of the characters are very concerned with personal happiness, which essentially translates as love and sex. Writer-director Denys Arcand focuses on two groups, one male and one female, in the first half of the film. Both reveal intimate secrets about their lives. Then he brings them together for some surprising, funny, and sad encounters. The film is perhaps best described as *The Big Chill* meets *My Dinner with Andre*. It is a thinking person's comedy that leaves one with much to ponder after the rewind button is pushed. Rated R for profanity, nudity, and simulated sex. In French with English subtitles.

1986 101 minutes

DERSU UZALA

★★★★½

DIRECTOR: Akira Kurosawa

CAST: Maxim Munzuk, Yuri Solomin

This epic about the charting of the Siberian wilderness (circa 1900) is surprisingly as intimate in relationships and details as it is grand in vistas and scope. A Japanese-Russian co-production, the second half of this Oscar winner, directed by Akira Kurosawa, is much better than the first. Still, as only a great film can do, it transports viewers to a time and place unknown to any of us, and we emerge exhilarated. The gorgeous photography (wide-screen in the theaters) and Maxim Munzuk's performance as Dersu Uzala, an old native hunter and guide, always carry the film through its occasional sluggish moments. In Russian and Japanese with English subtitles.

1974 140 minutes

DESPAIR

★★★★

DIRECTOR: Rainer Werner Fassbinder

CAST: Dirk Bogarde, Klaus Lowitsch

Karlovich (Dirk Bogarde), a Russian living in Germany in 1930, runs an unsuccessful chocolate factory. The stock market crash in America pushes his business into even deeper trouble, and he begins to lose touch with himself in a major way. Enjoying *Despair* requires a taste for black comedy at its blackest and an appreciation of ingenious film-making. Rated R.

1979 119 minutes

DEVIL'S EYE, THE

★★

DIRECTOR: Ingmar Bergman
CAST: Jarl Kulle, Bibi Andersson, Gunnar Bjornstrand, Nib Poppe

Disappointing comedy based on the Danish radio play *Don Juan Returns*. In order to cure the stye in his eye, the devil sends Don Juan (Jarl Kulle) from hell to breach a woman's chastity. Bibi Andersson plays Britt-Marie, the pastor's virgin daughter. The film is without spark or significance.

1960 90 minutes

DIARY OF A COUNTRY PRIEST

★★★★

DIRECTOR: Robert Bresson
CAST: Claude Laydu, Nicole Ladmiral, Jean Riveyre, Nicole Maurey, André Guibert, Martine Lemaire

The slow pace at the beginning of this tale about a priest trying to minister to his parish might tend to put some viewers off. However, with Bresson's poetic style and camera work, the wait is well worth it. The film flows like a stream rather than roaring like a river, but this only lends to its charm and beauty. In French with English subtitles.

1950 B & W 120 minutes

DISCREET CHARM OF THE BOURGEOISIE, THE

★★★★

DIRECTOR: Luis Buñuel
CAST: Fernando Rey, Delphine Seyrig, Stephane Audran, Bulle Ogier, Jean-Pierre Cassel, Michel Piccoli

Dinner is being served in this Louis Buñuel masterpiece, but the food never gets a chance to arrive at the table. Every time the hosts and guests try to begin the meal, some outside problem rises. Typically French, typically Buñuel, topically hilarious. Winner of the best foreign film Oscar for 1972.

1972 100 minutes

DIVA

★★★★

DIRECTOR: Jean-Jacques Beineix
CAST: Frederic Andrei, Wilhemenia Wiggins Fernandez, Roland Berlin

In this stunningly stylish suspense film by first-time director Jean-Jacques Beineix, a young opera lover unknowingly becomes involved with the underworld. Unbeknownst to him, he's in possession of some very valuable tapes—and the delightful chase is on. In French, with English subtitles. Rated R for profanity, nudity, and violence.

1982 123 minutes

DIVINE NYMPH, THE

★★½

DIRECTOR: Giuseppe Patroni Griffi
CAST: Laura Antonelli, Terence Stamp, Marcello Mastroianni

This story of love and passion resembles an Italian soap opera at best. Laura Antonelli is the young beauty who is unfaithful to her fiancé. She has an affair with Terence Stamp, who coerces her into having another affair with Marcello Mastroianni. In Italian, with English subtitles. Rated R for nudity.

1977 89 minutes

DODES 'KA-DEN

★★★★

DIRECTOR: Akira Kurosawa
CAST: Yoshitaka Zushi, Tomako Yamazaki, Hishashi Akutagawa, Noburu Mitsutahi

Akira Kurosawa's first color film is a spellbinding blend of fantasy and reality. The film chronicles the lives of a group of Tokyo slum dwellers that includes children, alcoholics, and the disabled. Illusion and imagination are their weapons as they fight for survival. This masterpiece is best known for its stellar photography and superb editing. In Japanese with English subtitles.

1970 140 minutes

DONA FLOR AND HER TWO HUSBANDS

★★★★

DIRECTOR: Bruno Barreto
CAST: Sonia Braga, José Wilker, Maura Mendonca, Denorah Billanti

A ribald Brazilian comedy about a woman (Sonia Braga) haunted by the sexy ghost of her first husband (José Wilker), who's anything but happy about her impending remarriage, this film inspired the Sally Field vehicle *Kiss Me Goodbye*. The original is more adult and better all around. In Portuguese, with English subtitles. Unrated, the film has sex and nudity.

1978 106 minutes

DONKEY SKIN

★★★

DIRECTOR: Jacques Demy
CAST: Catherine Deneuve, Jean Marais, Jacques Perrin, Micheline Presle, Delphine Seyrig, Fernand Ledoux, Henri Gremieux

In this cute variation on the Cindralla theme with a number of 20th-century twists, Catherine Deneuve stars as the princess in a tiny fairy-tale kingdom. When the queen's dying request of the king is that he remarry a woman more beautiful than she, the stage is set for some adult humor about the love between father and daughter. Much of this comedy is tongue-in-cheek and characteristically French. In French, with English subtitles.

1971 89 minutes

EARTH

★★★★

DIRECTOR: Alexander Dovzhenko
CAST: Semyon Svashenko, Stephan Shkurat

One of the last classic silent films, this short homage to the spirit of the collective farmer and his intangible ties to the land employs stunning camera shots. After the funeral of his father, a peasant working on one of the new collective farms drives a tractor onto the property of a neighboring Kulak, one of the oppressive landlords of the area. Later in the film, as the peasant is drunkenly walking down a moonlit lane, he is shot dead, and his blood mingles with the soil. Certain scenes from the original print no longer exist, but what remains of this film tells a beautiful, moving story. Russian, silent.

1930 B & W 56 minutes

ECSTASY

★★½

DIRECTOR: Gustav Machaty
CAST: Hedy Kiesler (Lamarr), Aribert Mog, Jaromir Rogoz, Leopold Kramer

Completely overshadowed in the years since its release by the notoriety of Kiesler-Lamarr's nude scenes, this new packaging in video should shift the emphasis back to the film itself, which is basically a romance of illicit love between a married woman and a stranger to whom she is attracted. The justly famous seduction scene has probably received more frame-by-frame exposure in movie books than any other film in history, and the worldwide scandal wrought by young Hedy

Lamarr's husband's efforts to destroy all copies of this movie has made it a cinema curio for over 50 years, a reputation today's jaded audiences will find hard to fathom. Filmed in pre-Hitler Czechoslovakia, this version is subtitled in English.

1933 B & W 88 minutes

EDITH AND MARCEL

★★★★

DIRECTOR: Claude Lelouch

CAST: Evelyn Bouix, Marcel Cerdan Jr., Jacques Villeret, Francis Huster

Based on the real life of famous torch singer Edith Piaf (Evelyn Bouix), this powerful musical-drama follows the passionate affair she had with champion boxer Marcel Cerdan (Marcel Cerdan Jr.). Director Claude Lelouch brings to life the stormy romance that at one time captured the attention of the world. Powerful acting combined with the wealth of Piaf's own recordings add up to quality fare. In French with English subtitles.

1983 170 minutes

8½

★★★

DIRECTOR: Federico Fellini

CAST: Marcello Mastroianni, Claudia Cardinale, Sandra Milo

Federico Fellini is at his most bizarre in telling this story about a filmmaker trying to make a movie and all the strange and weird things that take place within his reality. If you like Fellini, you'll love this; if you don't, forget it.

1963 B & W 135 minutes

EL AMOR BRUJO

★★★

DIRECTOR: Carlos Saura

CAST: Antonio Gades, Christina Hoyos, Laura del Sol, Juan Antonio Jimenez, Emma Penello

This occasionally brilliant big-screen production of Manella de Falla's ballet will appeal primarily to flamenco fans. Unlike *Carmen*, its predecessor and a stunning film capable of pleasing all tastes, *El Amor Brujo* seems slow and padded. No wonder. It was adapted from the 27-minute ballet into a 100-minute drama with dance. The cast is excellent and some of the scenes rivet the viewer, but overall the movie fails to fascinate as it should. In Spanish with English subtitles. Rated PG for brief, stylized violence and references to sex in lyrics.

1986 100 minutes

EL NORTE

★★★★★

DIRECTOR: Gregory Nava

CAST: Aide Silvia Gutierrez, David Villalpando, Ernesto Cruz, Alicia Del Lago

This work, by the husband-wife film-making team of Gregory Nava and Anna Thomas is the kind of movie that will have viewers recommending it to their friends. It is essentially an American-made foreign film. Most of the dialogue is in Spanish. Sound odd? Well, it isn't really. In fact, it may be one of the most memorable movie experiences you'll ever have. A story about two Guatemalans, a young brother and sister, whose American dream takes them on a long trek through Mexico to El Norte—the United States. They end up in Los Angeles in a cheap motel for day laborers and a series of jobs in the illegal job market. This screen work is funny, frightening, poignant, and sobering—a movie that stays with you. Rated R for profanity and violence.

1983 139 minutes

ELUSIVE CORPORAL, THE

★★★★½

DIRECTOR: Jean Renoir
CAST: Jean-Pierre Cassel, Claude Brasseur, Claude Rich

Twenty-five years after he made his greatest masterpiece. *La Grande Illusion,* Renoir reexamines men in war with almost equally satisfying results. This time the soldiers are Frenchmen in a World War II prison camp. *The Elusive Corporal* is a delicate drama infused with considerable wit—mostly derived from fake heroics made all the more sadly comic when juxtaposed with genuine heroism. Good performances and well worth discovering. In French with English subtitles.

1962 108 minutes

ELVIRA MADIGAN

★★★★

DIRECTOR: Bo Widerberg
CAST: Pia Degermark, Thommy Gerggren, Lennart Malmen, Cleo Jensen

This is a simple and tragic story of a young Swedish officer who falls in love with a beautiful circus performer. Outstanding photography makes this film. Try to see the subtitled version.

1967 89 minutes

EMMANUELLE

★★★

DIRECTOR: Just Jaeckin
CAST: Sylvia Kristel, Marika Green, Daniel Sarky, Alain Cuny

Sylvia Kristel (*Private Lessons*) became an international star as a result of this French screen adaptation of Emmanuelle Aran's controversial book about the initiation of a diplomat's young wife into the world of sensuality. In the soft-core sex film genre, this stands out as one of the best. That's not exactly high praise, but it is a movie that open-minded members of both sexes can enjoy. Rated R for nudity and sex.

1974 92 minutes

ENTRE NOUS (BETWEEN US)

★★★★★

DIRECTOR: Diane Kurys
CAST: Miou-Mioû, Isabelle Huppert, Guy Marchand, Jean-Pierre Bacri

This down-to-earth, highly human story by director Diane Kurys concentrates on the friendship between two women, Madeline (Miou-Miou) and Lena (Isabelle Huppert), who find they have more in common with each other than with their husbands. Most of Kurys's works (*Peppermint Soda* and *Cocktail Molotov*, for example) have been autobiographical. *Entre Nous* is the story of her parents and her mother's dearest friend. It is an affecting remembrance the viewer won't soon forget. Rated PG for nudity, suggested sex, and violence.

1983 110 minutes

ERENDIRA

★★½

DIRECTOR: Ruy Guerra
CAST: Irene Papas, Claudia Ohana, Michael Lonsdale, Oliver Wehe

In this disturbing and distasteful black comedy, Irene Papas stars as a wealthy old woman who loses everything in a fire accidentally set by her sleepwalking granddaughter, Erendira (Claudia Ohana). To regain her lost riches, the grandmother turns her charge into a prostitute and insists that she earn back over $1 million by taking on all comers in modern-day Mexico. In Spanish, with English subtitles. Unrated, the film has nudity, profanity, simulated sex, simulated rape, gore, and violence.

1983 103 minutes

EVERY MAN FOR HIMSELF AND GOD AGAINST ALL

★★★★

DIRECTOR: Werner Herzog
CAST: Bruno S., Walter Ladengast, Brigitte Mira

Based on a real incident, the story of Kasper Hauser (Bruno S.) tells of a man who had been kept in confinement since birth. Hauser's appearance in Nuremberg in the 1920s was a mystery. He was a man who tried to adjust to a new society while maintaining his own vision. One of Herzog's best. Also released as *The Mystery of Kasper Hauser.* In German, with English subtitles. No MPAA rating.

1975 110 minutes

EXTERMINATING ANGEL, THE

★★★★★

DIRECTOR: Luis Buñuel
CAST: Silvia Pinal, Enrique Rambal, Jacqueline Andere, Jose Baviera, Augusto Benedico

Luis Buñuel always did love a good dinner party. In *The Discreet Charm of the Bourgeoisie,* the dinner party never could get under way, and here the elite *après-opéra* diners find they cannot escape the host's sumptuous music room. This is a very funny film—in a very black key. *The Exterminating Angel* was made in Mexico, and a Mexican proverb may be one key to Buñuel's intent: "After twenty-four hours, corpses and guests smell bad." That is the satiric surreal side. The more serious allegorical side is Buñuel's reflecting upon the spectre of bourgeois vacuity. A seminal work from the director's middle period. In Spanish with English subtitles.

1962 B & W 95 minutes

EYES, THE MOUTH, THE

★

DIRECTOR: Marco Bellocchio
CAST: Lou Castel, Angela Molina, Emanuelle Riva

This movie presumes to tell the story of a man (Lou Castel) who liberates his soul from the past and embraces life after his twin brother commits suicide. It founders so much that your mind soon drifts from the plot to the face and mannerisms of Castel, who not only looks like Jack Nicholson but mugs like him through the entire film. He even does Nicholson-like things, such as standing upright in a fireplace removing his clothes. Somehow none of this jives. The movie feels like an impostor. In Italian with English subtitles. Rated R for language and nudity.

1983 100 minutes

FANNY AND ALEXANDER

★★★★★

DIRECTOR: Ingmar Bergman
CAST: Pernilla Allwin, Bertil Guve, Gunn Wallgren, Allan Edwall, Ewa Froling, Jan Malmsjo

Set in Sweden around the turn of the century, this movie follows the adventures of two children. Some have called this Ingmar Bergman's first truly accessible work. We wouldn't go quite that far. Viewers still have to work a little to reap its rewards. Still, it is undeniably his most optimistic—and thus most enjoyable—motion picture. In Swedish, with English subtitles. Rated R for profanity and violence.

1983 197 minutes

FEARLESS

DIRECTOR: Stelvio Massi
CAST: Joan Collins, Maurizio Merli, Franco Ressel

This confusing, raunchy Italian film features Joan Collins as a rather inept striptease artist in Vienna. On the side, she induces young girls to meet with her wealthy clients. Maurizio Merli plays the oft-battered Italian detective investigating the disappearance of one girl and the death of another. The only interesting thing here is the laughable dubbing. Unrated, it contains violence and nudity.

1978 89 minutes

FERNANDEL THE DRESSMAKER

★★

DIRECTOR: Jean Boyer
CAST: Fernandel, Suzy Delair, Françoise Fabian, Georges Chamarat

Using Fernandel as the hub, the film is a bit of whimsy about a gentleman's tailor who desires to become a world-famous couturier. Even with a lightweight plot, watching this famous comedian is certainly worth the time and effort to wade through the nonsense. A bit of Red Skelton, a dash of Danny Kaye, and soupçon of Jerry Lewis. No pretense here—just good fun. In French with English subtitles.

1957 B & W 84 minutes

FIRES ON THE PLAIN

★★★★

DIRECTOR: Kon Ichikawa
CAST: Eiji Funakoshi, Osamu Takizawa

Kon Ichikawa's classic uses World War II and malnourished soldiers' cannibalism as symbols for the brutality of man. *Fires on the Plain* is uncomplicated and its emotion intensely focused. It is a stark and disturbing vision. In Japanese with English subtitles.

1959 105 minutes

FITZCARRALDO

★★★½

DIRECTOR: Werner Herzog
CAST: Klaus Kinski, Claudia Cardinale, Paul Hittscher

For German film director Werner Herzog, the making of this film was reportedly quite an ordeal. Watching it may be an ordeal for some viewers as well. In order to bring Caruso, the greatest voice in the world, to the backwater town of Iquitos, the title character (Klaus Kinski) decides to become a rubber baron. A virgin forest that's just waiting to make a man rich is inaccessible by water because of raging rapids. He decides to haul a large boat over a mountain from a good river to a navigable portion of the bad one. The real Fitzcarraldo used a 28-ton boat that was dismantled for the task, but Herzog decided to drag a complete 328-ton steamboat inch-by-inch. As a result, probably only film buffs will enjoy this quirky triumph of a real-life madman. Unrated, this film has profanity. In German, with English subtitles.

1982 157 minutes

FLIGHT OF THE EAGLE

★★★½

DIRECTOR: Jan Troell
CAST: Max von Sydow, Eva Von Hanno

This Swedish production presents the true adventure of three foolhardy 1897 polar explorers (including Max von Sydow) who tried to conquer the Arctic in a balloon. Unrated, the film has some gore. In Swedish with English subtitles.

1982 139 minutes

FORBIDDEN GAMES

★★★★★

DIRECTOR: René Clement
CAST: Brigitte Fossey, Georges Poujouly, Louis Herbert

It has been said that *Forbidden Games* is to World War II what *Grand Illusion* is to World War I. The horror of war has never been more real than as portrayed here against the bucolic surroundings of the French countryside. At the nucleus of the plot is Paulette, played by five-year-old Brigitte Fossey. Witnessing German troops kill her parents and pet dog twists the girl, who acquires an attraction for the symbols of death (much like Emily Dickinson). She and her friend (Georges Poujouly) wander about killing animals so they can give them ceremonial burials next to the dog. The fact that sentimentality is virtually nonexistent makes for a powerful, gut-wrenching film about the tragic follies, foibles, and frailties of mankind. The film is palatable only because of the tasteful artistry of René Clement. A truly tragic, must-see work. In French with English subtitles.

1951 B & W 87 minutes

FORTUNE'S FOOL

★★½

DIRECTOR: Reinhold Schunzel
CAST: Emil Jannings, Daguey Servaes, Reinhold Schunzel

Best known for his dramatic roles, Emil Jannings hams it up in this German-made comedy about a highly successful, profiteering meat-packer and the problems greedy ambition can cause. Jannings was years away from *The Blue Angel* and international stardom when this was filmed, but he displays the gifts that easily made him a dominating screen figure throughout his career. Silent.

1925 B & W 60 minutes

400 BLOWS, THE

★★★★★

DIRECTOR: François Truffaut
CAST: Jean-Pierre Léaud, Patrick Auffay, Claire Maurier, Albert Remy

Poignant story of a boy and the life that seems to be at odds with him is true and touching as few films have ever been. Director François Truffaut's feature film debut is one of those marvelous rarities that on occasion can produce a new creative force as well as an instant screen classic. Powerful, tender, and at times overwhelmingly sad, this great film touches all the right buttons without being exploitative and losing its integrity. If you've never seen a classic foreign subtitled film, start yourself off right and see this one. In French with English subtitles.

1959 B & W 99 minutes

FOURTH MAN, THE

★★★½

DIRECTOR: Paul Verhoeven
CAST: Jeroen Krabbe, Renee Soutenduk, Thom Hoffman

Jeroen Krabbe plays Gerard Reve, a gay alcoholic writer prone to hallucinations. Invited to lecture at a literary society, he meets a mysterious woman (Renee Soutenduk, of *Spetters*), who he becomes convinced intends to kill him or his—and her—lover, Herman (Thom Hoffman). Some filmgoers will be shocked by the explicitness of many of the scenes in this import. Yet with all this, *The Fourth Man* emerges as an atmospheric, highly original chiller, albeit one only for broad-minded adults. In Dutch, with English subtitles. Unrated, the film has full frontal nudity, simulated sex, blood, gore, violence, and profanity.

1984 128 minutes

FRANZ

DIRECTOR: Jacques Brel
CAST: Jacques Brel, Barbara, Daniele Evenou, Francois Cadet, Fernand Fabre, Serge Sauvion, Louis Navarre

Franz is a royal mess. A shy man named Leon falls in love with a woman named Leonie. He is tortured by his oppressive mother and his war memories. Leonie is just aloof and strange-looking, sort of like a mix of the Wicked Witch and Dracula. Jacques Brel and Barbara in the leads are alternately embarrassingly dramatic and grotesque. In French with English subtitles.

1972 88 minutes

FROM THE LIVES OF THE MARIONETTES

★★★★

DIRECTOR: Ingmar Bergman

CAST: Robert Atzorn, Christine Buchegger, Martin Benrath, Rita Russek, Lola Muethel, Heinz Bennent, Walter Schmidinger

This Ingmar Bergman film, which details the vicious sex murder of a prostitute by an outwardly compassionate and intelligent man, is a puzzle that never really resolves itself. Viewers expecting to be entertained will be disappointed. Bergman does not make movies that are intended to help us forget our cares. Instead, he challenges the viewer to think and feel. Because it is told in flashbacks which are not in chronological order, *From the Lives of the Marionettes* is somewhat difficult to follow. Nevertheless, fans of the acclaimed Swedish director's works will no doubt consider it another triumphant essay on the complexities of the human condition, containing the stunning visual imagery and dramatic power for which he's become famous. Rated R.

1980 B & W 104 minutes

FULL MOON IN PARIS

★★

DIRECTOR: Eric Rohmer

CAST: Pascale Ogier, Fabrice Luchini, Tcheky Karyo

This French film from Eric Rohmer, the director of the delightful *My Night at Maud's* and *Pauline at the Beach,* does not sustain its momentum with this tale of a young girl's disillusionment with her live-in lover. Perhaps the problem is her self-absorption and lack of commitment, but you just don't seem to care about what happens. Whatever the reason, it lacks the fun of his earlier films. In French with English subtitles.

1984 102 minutes

FUNNY DIRTY LITTLE WAR (NO HABRA MAS PENSAS NI OLVIDO)

★★★

DIRECTOR: Hector Olivera

CAST: Federico Luppi, Hector Bidonde, Victor Laplace Commissar, Rodolfo Ranni, Miquel Angel Sola, Julio de Grazia

This allegorical, comedic piece begins in the small town of Colonia Vela. The comedy centers around the struggle between the Marxists and the Peronistas in 1974, shortly before the death of Juan Peron. The action quickly builds from a series of foolish misunderstandings to a very funny confrontation. The confrontation then leads to real bullets, the torture of prisoners, and the arrival of newsmen from Buenos Aires to cover the war. The photography, acting, and writing are all above average, but the viewer who is not aware of the history of Juan, Evita, and Isabel Peron may have difficulty following the allegorical line. Not rated. Spanish with English subtitles.

1985 80 minutes

GABRIELA

★★★

DIRECTOR: Bruno Barreto
CAST: Sonia Braga, Marcello Mastroianni, Antonio Cantafora, Ricardo Petraglia

Sexy Sonia Braga is both cook and mistress for bar owner Marcello Mastroianni in this excellent adaptation of Brazilian novelist Jorge Amado's comic romp *Gabriela, Clove and Cinnamon*. In Portuguese, with English subtitles. Rated R.

1983 102 minutes

GAME IS OVER, THE

★★★

DIRECTOR: Roger Vadim
CAST: Jane Fonda, Peter McEnery, Michel Piccoli, Tina Marquand, Jacques Monod

Emile Zola's novel *La Curée* was the basis for this adult story of a young woman who marries an older man but finds herself attracted to (and eventually sharing a bed with) his son. Well-acted and intelligently scripted, this French film by Jane Fonda's then-husband Roger Vadim was considered daring at the time and holds up well for today's audiences. This was one of Fonda's best roles in the days when she was an extension of Vadim's sexual ego; only later did she play women of integrity and conscience. Not as shocking as it was considered on first release, this unrated film contains some nudity and adult situations. In French.

1966 96 minutes

GARDEN OF THE FINZI-CONTINIS, THE

★★★★

DIRECTOR: Vittorio De Sica
CAST: Dominique Sanda, Helmut Berger, Lino Capolicchio, Fabio Testi

Vittorio De Sica's adaptation of a Giorgio Bassani novel views the life of an aristocratic Jewish family's misfortune in fascist Italy. Flawless acting by Dominique Sanda and Helmut Berger. One of De Sica's best. Rated R.

1971 95 minutes

GET OUT YOUR HANDKERCHIEFS

★★★½

DIRECTOR: Bertrand Blier
CAST: Gerard Depardieu, Patrick Dewaere, Carol Laure

Winner of the 1978 Academy Award for best foreign film, this stars Gerard Depardieu as a clumsy husband so desperate to make his melancholic wife happy and pregnant that he provides her with a lover (Patrick Dewaere). A mostly improbable existential drama, what comedy there was in the original version was sacrificed for lip-synchronization in the dubbed version. Nevertheless, this film has a few surprises in store not only for the two male leads but also for the viewer, when young Christian Beloeil (Riton) appears on the scene. Unrated, contains nudity. In French.

1978 108 minutes

GIFT, THE

★★★

DIRECTOR: Michael Lang
CAST: Clio Goldsmith, Pierre Mondy, Claudia Cardinale

A 55-year-old bank worker (Pierre Mondy) decides to take early retirement because he fears stress will kill him. So his co-workers give him an unusual retirement gift, an expensive hooker (Clio Goldsmith), who is asked to seduce him without his knowing her profession. The chuckles in this import do not come fast and furious. Yet it is an amiable sex comedy that most adult viewers will find quite charming and diverting. In French with

English subtitles. Rated R for partial nudity and profanity.

1982 105 minutes

GINGER AND FRED

★★★★

DIRECTOR: Federico Fellini

CAST: Marcello Mastrocianni, Giulietta Masina, Franco Fabrizi, Toto Mingone

Set in the bizarre world of a modern-television supernetwork, this Fellini fantasy presents Giulietta Masina and Marcello Mastroianni as Ginger and Fred—a dance couple of the late forties who copied the style of Fred Astaire and Ginger Rogers. The two are reunited for *Here's to You*, a television extravaganza. The dancers are out of place in this icon of modern life. With the odd mixture of people that populate the studio, they seem to be the last representatives of a simpler time. *Ginger and Fred* is a brillant satire of today's television and modern life. Rated PG-13 for profanity and adult themes.

1986 127 minutes

GOING PLACES

★★

DIRECTOR: Bertrand Blier

CAST: Gerard Depardieu, Patrick Dewaere, Miou-Miou, Jeanne Moreau, Isabelle Huppert, Brigitte Fossey

Memorable only as one of Gerard Depardieu's first screen appearances. He and Patrick Dewaere play a couple of amiable lowlifes who dabble in petty thievery and have their way with all the local women. Contains one of filmdom's most acutely uncomfortable scenes, when one of the young lads gets shot in the testicles. Too unpleasant and chauvinistic for a sex farce, but too unbelievable as straight drama. Don't blink, or you'll miss Jeanne Moreau's brief cameo. In French with English subtitles. Rated R for sex.

1974 117 minutes

GOLDEN DEMON

★★★

DIRECTOR: Koji Shima

CAST: Jun Negami, Fujiko Yamamoto

As a rule, most Japanese love stories are sad. *Golden Demon*, a story of true love broken by pride, tradition, and avarice, is an exception to that rule. The story of a poor young man, in love with his adopted parents' daughter, who loses her to a rich entrepreneur (an arranged marriage), is richly entertaining. Be ready to hurdle a variety of intricate cultural situations that border on the silly for those untutored in Japanese rhetoric. In Japanese, with English subtitles.

1953 91 minutes

THE GOLEM (HOW HE CAME INTO THE WORLD) (DER GOLEM, WIE ER IN DIE WELT KAM)

★★★★

DIRECTOR: Paul Wegener

CAST: Paul Wegener, Albert Steinrück, Lydia Salmonova, Ernst Deutch, Hannes Sturm, Max Kronert, Greta Schroder

Director Paul Wegener plays the lead role as the Golem, an ancient clay figure from Hebrew mythology that is brought to life by Rabbi Loew (Albert Steinrück) by means of an amulet activated by the magic word "Aemaet" (the Hebrew word for truth). The Golem becomes the rabbi's servant but later turns against him. In a story similar to *Frankenstein*, the man of clay roams through medieval Prague in a mystic atmosphere created by the brilliant cameraman Karl Freund. A superb rendition of a classic myth by the German film industry of the 1920s. Silent.

1920 B & W 70 minutes

GRAND ILLUSION

★★★★★

DIRECTOR: Jean Renoir

CAST: Jean Gabin, Pierre Fresnay, Erich von Stroheim, Marcel Dalio, Julien Carette, Dita Parlo, Gaston Modot

Shortly before Hitler plunged Europe into World War II, this monumental French film tried to examine why men submit to warfare's "grand illusions." It brilliantly exposes the romantic notions applied to war: the noble-cause mentality, glorified chivalry, needless nationalism. We are taken to a German prison camp in World War I, where it becomes quite easy to see the hypocrisy of war while watching the day-to-day mini-world of camp life. This classic, by Jean Renoir, has the universal appeal and technical brilliance that makes it one of the world's finest films and a must-see for anyone who appreciates great entertainment.

1937 B & W 74 minutes

GRANDE BOURGEOISE, LA

★½

DIRECTOR: Mauro Bolognini

CAST: Catherine Deneuve, Giancarlo Giannini, Fernando Rey

This should be an impassioned, suspenseful film about a brother who murders his sister's lackluster husband because he believes her true nature is suffocating in marriage. However, the movie's primary concern is with costume and soft-focus lenses so that even the lukewarm emotions are overshadowed. Giancarlo Giannini as the brother tries hard to fire things up, but when Catherine Deneuve is on hand in one of her ice queen performances, sympathizing becomes a difficult thing. She extinguishes all the sparks he sets. Every time she gazes through a veiled hat, her stony perfection deadens the movie a little bit more. In Italian with English subtitles.

1974 115 minutes

GREEN ROOM, THE

★★★

DIRECTOR: François Truffaut

CAST: François Truffaut, Nathalie Baye, Jean Daste, Jean-Paul Moulin

Based on the writings of Henry James, this is a lifeless and disappointing film by François Truffaut about a writer obsessed with death who turns a dilapidated chapel into a memorial for World War I soldiers. Not the French filmmaker at his best. In French, with English subtitles. Rated PG.

1978 93 minutes

HAIL MARY

★★★★

DIRECTOR: Jean-Luc Godard

CAST: Myriem Roussel, Thierry Lacoste, Philippe Lacoste, Manon Anderson, Juliette Binoche, Johann Leysen, Anne Gauthier

This story of the coming of Christ in modern times will offend only the most dogmatic Christians, or narrow-minded religious zealots who have only heard a sketchy outline of the plot. Godard's eye for the aesthetic gives this film a compassionate feel, more so than a lot of the sandal epics that are about the Savior himself. Like many other French films, *Hail Mary* is sensuous yet nonexploitative. *The Book of Mary*, a film by Anne-Marie Mieville, is the prologue and is equally beautiful. In French with English subtitles. Not rated; the equivalent of an R for nudity.

1985 107 minutes

HANNA K.

★½

DIRECTOR: Constantin Costa-Gavras

CAST: Jill Clayburgh, Jean Yanne, Gabriel Byrne, Muhamad Bakri, David Clennon, Oded Kotler

An intriguing premise that fails to live up to its promise. Jill Clayburgh is an Israeli lawyer appointed to defend a man who entered the country illegally in an attempt to reclaim the land where he grew up. Alas, the man is an Arab, which complicates matters between Clayburgh and her Israeli lover . . . not to mention her French Catholic husband. The very talky story never explores the religious dichotomies and degenerates, instead, into a soap opera, all leading to a thoroughly annoying conclusion. Something good must have been in the story by Franco Solinas, but it didn't appear on the screen. Rated R for coarse language.

1984 110 minutes

HAPPY NEW YEAR (LA BONNE ANNEE)

★★★★

DIRECTOR: Claude Lelouch

CAST: Lino Ventura, Francoise Fabian, Charles Gerard

Delightful French crime caper mixed with romance and comedy. As two thieves plot a jewel heist, one (Lino Ventura) also plans a meeting with the lovely antique dealer (Francoise Fabian) who runs the shop next-door to their target. Director Claude Lelouch's film blends suspense with engaging wit. Rated PG for profanity and sex. Available in French version or dubbed.

1974 114 minutes

HEAT OF DESIRE

★★½

DIRECTOR: Luc Beraud

CAST: Patrick Dewaere, Clio Goldsmith, Jeanne Moreau, Guy Marchand

So many sex comedies are about married men who discover adultery brings new vitality, this plot has become a cinematic cliché. But this didn't stop director Luc Beraud from using it again in this disappointing film about a writer (Patrick Dewaere) who dallies with an unpredictable flirt (Clio Goldsmith). This one's only for fans of typical Gallic movies. In French, with English subtitles. Unrated, the film has nudity and suggested sex.

1984 91 minutes

HIDDEN FORTRESS, THE

★★★★★

DIRECTOR: Akira Kurosawa

CAST: Toshiro Mifune, Misa Uehara, Minoru Chiaki, Kamatari Fujiwara

Toshiro Mifune stars in this recently reconstructed, uncut, and immensely entertaining 1958 Japanese period epic directed by Akira Kurosawa (*The Seven Samurai*, *Kagemusha*, *Ran*). George Lucas has openly admitted the film's influence on his *Star Wars* trilogy. *Hidden Fortress* deals with the adventures of a strong-willed princess (à la Carrie Fisher in the space fantasy) and her wise, sword-wielding protector (Mifune in the role adapted for Alec Guinness). There are even a couple of comic characters whose misadventures act as the thread that holds the story together (the same role fulfilled by the robots C3PO and R2D2 in Lucas's work). In Japanese with English subtitles. Unrated, the film has violence.

1958 B & W 126 minutes

HIGH HEELS

★★

DIRECTOR: Claude Chabrol

CAST: Laura Antonelli, Jean-Paul Belmondo, Mia Farrow, Daniel Lecourtois

A French comedy to make you chuckle more often than not. The story involves a medical student who marries the homely daughter of a hospital president to ensure himself of a job after graduation. He soon falls in love with his beautiful sister-in-law and, in some of the film's funniest moments, begins eliminating her suitors. Director Chabrol borrows from Monty Python in a unique dream sequence, which is guaranteed to make you smile. Not rated, but recommended for viewers over 18 years of age. In French with English subtitles.

1980 90 minutes

HIMATSURI

★★★★½

DIRECTOR: Mitsuo Yanaglmachi
CAST: Kinya Kitaoji, Kiwako Taichi, Norihei Miki

Metaphysical story about man's lustful and often destructive relationship with nature. Kinya Kitaoji plays a Hemingway-like lumberjack in a beautiful seaboard wilderness which is about to be marred by the building of a marine park. His struggle to deal with this reality results in dramatic consequences. Japanese director Mitsuo Yanaglimachi has the flair of Peter Weir. Rated R for sex, nudity, and violence.

1985 120 minutes

HIROSHIMA, MON AMOUR

★★★★

DIRECTOR: Alain Resnais
CAST: Emmanuelle Riva, Bernard Fresson, Eiji Okada

A mind-boggling tale about two people: one, a French woman, the other, a male survivor of the blast at Hiroshima. They meet and become lovers. Together they live their pasts, present, and futures in a complex series of dreams, fantasies, and nightmares that always puzzles the viewer. In French, with English subtitles.

1959 B & W 88 minutes

HOLIDAY HOTEL

★★★

DIRECTOR: Michel Lang
CAST: Sophie Barjac, Myrian Bager, Daniel Ceccaldi, Michel Grellier, Bruno Guillain, Francis Lemoire, Robert Lombard, Guy Marchand

It's August, and all of France is going on vacation for the entire month. The cast of this fast-paced comedy is heading toward the Brittany coast. Birds do it, bees do it, and everyone from oldsters to the youngsters are doing it (or trying) in this film. Michel Lang keeps the tempo moving with clever farcical bits and dialogue. Paradoxically, that is one of the weak points. The subtitles come fast and furiously and sometimes prove difficult to read. But the cast has just the right touch to keep the viewer interested. Partially in English, the movie has an R rating due to nudity and profanity.

1978 109 minutes

I AM CURIOUS YELLOW

★½

DIRECTOR: Vilgot Sjoman
CAST: Lena Nyman, Borje Ahlstedt, Peter Lindgren

This Swedish import caused quite an uproar when it was released in the mid-1960s, because of its frontal nudity and sexual content. It seems pretty tame today. There isn't much of a plot built around the escapades of a young Swedish sociologist whose goal in life appears to be having sex in as many weird places as she can. If you want erotica, pass this one by. It was intended to present a good-natured and healthy sexual outlook, but after two hours of viewing, dull is the only word that comes to mind.

1967 B & W 121 minutes

I LOVE YOU (EU TE AMO)

★★★

DIRECTOR: Arnaldo Jabor
CAST: Sonia Braga, Paulo Cesar Pereio

This release, starring Brazilian sexpot Sonia Braga (*Dona Flor and Her Two Husbands*), is a high-class hard-core—though not close-up—sex film with pretensions of being a work of art. And if that turns you on, go for it. Unrated, the film has nudity, profanity, and explicit sex.

1982 104 minutes

I SENT A LETTER TO MY LOVE

★★★

DIRECTOR: Moshe Mizrahi
CAST: Simone Signoret, Jean Rochefort, Delphine Seyrig

Simone Signoret and Jean Rochefort star as sister and brother in this absorbing—often painful—study of love, devotion, loneliness, and frustration. After Signoret places a personal ad (requesting male companionship) in the local paper, Rochefort responds—and they begin a correspondence, via mail, that brings passion and hope to their otherwise empty lives. The plot is twisty and interesting, but does drag a bit at times. It's an intelligent, thought-provoking film, but some may find it maudlin and melancholy. In French with English subtitles.

1981 96 minutes

IKIRU

★★★★½

DIRECTOR: Akira Kurosawa
CAST: Takashi Shimura, Nabuo Kaneko

Ikiru is the Japanese infinitive *to live*. The film opens with a shot of an X-ray; a narrator tells us the man—an Everyman—is dying of cancer. The narrator says the man has actually been "dead" for years, a spiritual victim of bureaucracy and of his job as a petty bureaucrat, of dreams rendered infeasible by the war and by postwar red tape. The man must now face death; he must find what it means to live. His family is cold, his co-workers unavailable; nights of carousing and debauchery just leave him hung over. But a dream flickers to life, and his last years are fulfilled by a lasting accomplishment. *Ikiru* packs a genuine emotional wallop. In Japanese with English subtitles.

1952 B & W 143 minutes

INHERITORS, THE

(turkey symbol)

DIRECTOR: Walter Bannert
CAST: Nicholas Vogel, Rolef Schauer, Wolfgang Casser, Ottwald John, Helmut Kahn

A teen-age boy with a troubled family life stumbles into a Neo-Nazi group, which trains him in the use of weapons and how and who to hate. What could have been a work of some social significance is instead a muddled mess. A German film, the translations seem mismatched with the actions of the performers. The dubbed voices are so bad, one can't help but wince. Overall, this production didn't survive its trip overseas.

1984 90 minutes

INNOCENT, THE

★★★★

DIRECTOR: Luchino Visconti
CAST: Laura Antonelli, Giancarlo Giannini

Some rate this as the most beautiful of all Luchino Visconti's films. Considering his meticulous attention to detail in bringing a time period to life, this should come as no surprise. Set in a nineteenth-century baronial manor, the main characters at first exhibit all the idealism one would expect of youth before their marriage. This is in sharp contrast to the later situation in which responsibilities of the relationship bring about the central conflict. It's the old tale of the real versus the ideal, but beautifully done. This film should not be confused with the 1961 British film *The Innocents*. Rated R due to some explicit scenes. In Italian with English subtitles.

1976 115 minutes

INVITATION AU VOYAGE

★★★½

DIRECTOR: Peter Del Monte

CAST: Laurent Malet, Aurore Clement, Mario Adorf, Nina Scott, Raymond Bussieres

Here is a strange but watchable French import with plenty of suspense and surprises for those willing to give it a chance to work its unusual magic. Peter Del Monte's film is a sometimes demanding and unpredictable work that plays little tricks on the audience. It allows the viewer to make assumptions and then shatters those conceptions with a succession of inventive twists and revelations. In French, with English subtitles. Rated R for adult content.

1982 100 minutes

IPHIGENIA

★★★★★

DIRECTOR: Michael Cacoyannis

CAST: Irene Papas, Tatiana Papamoskou, Costa Kazakos

A stunning film interpretation of the Greek classic *Iphigenia in Aulis*, by Euripedes. Irene Papas (*Electra*; *The Trojan Women*) is brilliant as Clytemnestra, the caring and outraged mother. Tatiana Papamoskou (Iphigenia) gives an intelligent and sensitive performance as the young girl who is sacrificed for man's greed and ambition. Intense score by Mikos Theodorakis. In Greek, with English subtitles. No MPAA rating.

1978 127 minutes

IREZUMI (SPIRIT OF TATTOO)

★★★★½

DIRECTOR: Yoichi Takabayashi

CAST: Masayo Utsunomiya, Tomisaburo Wakayama, Yuhsuke Takita, Masaki Kyomoto

An erotic tale of obsession that calls forth the rebirth of a near-dead art. A woman defies cultural taboos and gets her back elaborately tattooed to fulfill her mate's obsession. The subcult of this form of tattooing is all but dead when this woman approaches an old expert in the art. While the film gives the viewer an idea of how this ancient art applies to the culture and where its place in history belongs, it also shows the tattooing process as an erotic act. Rated R for nudity.

1983 88 minutes

IVAN THE TERRIBLE—PART I & PART II

★★★★★

DIRECTOR: Sergei Mikhailovich Eisenstein

CAST: Nikolai Cherkassov, Ludmila Tselikovskaya

Considered among the classics of world cinema, this certainly is the most impressive film to come out of the Soviet Union. This epic biography of Russia's first tsar was commissioned personally by Joseph Stalin to encourage acceptance of his harsh and historically similar policies. World-renowned director Sergei Eisenstein, instead, transformed what was designed as party propaganda into a panoramic saga of how power corrupts those seeking it. Eisenstein ended up in Stalin's doghouse and was little heard from again, but the world received a sweeping masterpiece.

1945 B & W 188 minutes

JACKO AND LISE

★

DIRECTOR: Walter Bal
CAST: Laurent Malet, Annie Girardot, Michel Montanary, Evelyne Bouix, Françoise Arnoul, Jean Franval

This film should have been called *Jacko and Freddie* because most of it concerns Jacko and his pal Freddie escaping responsibility and adulthood by doing juvenile things. When Jacko finally does meet Lise, the movie tries to sell us the idea that he's maturing because of her. Well, Lise is almost a nonentity. She has zero personality and we have no clue as to what is going on in her head. In the end, Jacko still seems not very enlightened by his experiences. In French. Rated PG.

1975 92 minutes

JE VOUS AIME (I LOVE YOU ALL)

★★★

DIRECTOR: Claude Berri
CAST: Catherine Deneuve, Jean-Louis Trintignant, Serge Gainsbourg

Some films are so complicated and convoluted you feel you need a viewer's guide while watching them. So it is with this flashback-ridden French import directed by Claude Berri. About a 35-year-old woman, Alice (Catherine Deneuve), who finds it impossible to keep a love relationship alive, it hops, skips, and jumps back and forth through her life so confusingly you feel as if you need to stop the show occasionally to figure out what you've just seen. Therefore, even though the performances by Deneuve, Jean-Louis Trintignant, and Serge Gainsbourg are excellent, they get lost in the continual sequential shuffle. No MPAA rating; the film has sexual situations and nudity.

1981 105 minutes

JOKE OF DESTINY

★★

DIRECTOR: Lina Wertmuller
CAST: Ugo Tognazzi, Piera Degli Esposti, Gastone Moschin

Italian audiences may have laughed uproariously at this new film by director Lina Wertmuller (*Swept Away*, *Seven Beauties*). However, American viewers are unlikely to get the joke. It shows what happens to a government official (Ugo Tognazzi of *La Cage aux Folles*) when a computerized car carrying his country's highest official breaks down in front of his house. The problem is, its elements of social satire are unfathomable for those unfamiliar with political events in Italy. Rated PG for profanity. In Italian with English subtitles.

1984 105 minutes

JOUR DE FETE

★★½

DIRECTOR: Jacques Tati
CAST: Jacques Tati, Guy Decomble, Paul Frankeur, Santa Nelli

Jacques Tati is the focal point of this light comedy loosely tied to the arrival of a carnival in a small village. As François, the bumbling postman, Tati sees a film on the heroism of the American postal service and tries to emulate it on his small rural route. Because of the lack of quality of the subtitles and the language and culture barriers, some of the comedy is lost. Tati, however, with his slapstick style, translates well, which leads to some really funny moments. Tati's bicycle does a fine job in a major supporting role. In French, with subtitles.

1949 B & W 81 minutes

JUDEX

★★★½

DIRECTOR: Georges Franju

CAST: Channing Pollock, Jacques Jouanneau, Edith Scob, Michel Vitold, Francine Berge

This funny look at an old serial from the early days of cinema will make you laugh out loud one moment and become misty-eyed with nostalgia the next. Based on an old potboiler serial by Feuillade and Bernede, *Judex* ("the judge") is an enjoyable adventure of a superhero who is lovable, human, and fallible. In French with English subtitles.

1963 B & W 103 minutes

JULES AND JIM

★★★★★

DIRECTOR: François Truffaut

CAST: Oskar Werner, Jeanne Moreau, Henri Serre

Superb character study, which revolves around a bizarre ménage à trois. It is really a film about wanting what you can't have and not wanting what you think you desire once you have it. In French with English subtitles.

1961 B & W 104 minutes

JULIET OF THE SPIRITS

★★★★★

DIRECTOR: Federico Fellini

CAST: Giulietta Masina, Sandra Milo, Mario Pisu, Valentina Cortese, Lou Gilbert, Sylva Koscina

"Are your eyes in good condition, able to encompass and abide some of the liveliest, most rococo resplendence ever fashioned in a fairyland on film . . . and enjoy a game of armchair psychoanalyzing in a spirit of good bawdy fun?" Such was the way Bosley Crowther began his review of *Juliet of the Spirits*. The convoluted plot centers around a wealthy wife suspicious of her cheating husband. Giulietta Masina (in real life, Mrs. Fellini) has never been so tantalizingly innocent with her Bambi eyes. This is Fellini's first attempt with color. It seems obvious that he wants his audience to have as much fun in this surreal world as he had creating it. The results are a feast for the eye, the ear, and the brain. Not too heavy, not too light—just right.

1965 148 minutes

JUPITER'S THIGH

★★★★½

DIRECTOR: Philippe de Broca

CAST: Annie Girardot, Philippe Noiret

The delightful *Dear Inspector* duo is back in this delicious sequel directed by Philippe de Broca (*King of Hearts*). This time, the lady detective (Annie Girardot) and her Greek archeologist lover (Philippe Noiret) get married and honeymoon—where else?—in Greece. But they aren't there long before they find themselves caught up in murder, madness, and mayhem. It's great fun, served up with sophistication. In French with English subtitles.

1983 90 minutes

KAGEMUSHA

★★★★★

DIRECTOR: Akira Kurosawa

CAST: Tatsuya Nakadai, Tsutomo Yamazaki

The 70-year-old Japanese director Akira Kurosawa outdoes himself in this epic masterpiece about honor and illusion. Kurosawa popularized the samurai genre—which has been described as the Japanese equivalent of the western—in America with his breathtaking, action-packed films. *Seven Samurai* (which was adapted by Western filmmakers as *The Magnificent Seven* and *Battle beyond the Stars*), *Yojimbo* (remade by Italian director Sergio Leone as *A Fistful of Dollars*, with Clint Eastwood), *Rashomon*, and *Sanjuro* are perhaps his best-known classics. *Kagemusha* is yet another feast for the eyes, heart, and mind. Rated PG.

1980 159 minutes

KAMERADSCHAFT

★★★½

DIRECTOR: G. W. Pabst

CAST: George Chalia, David Mendaille, Ernest Busch

This film was a milestone for 1931. The fluid camera movements and the spectacular mine-disaster footage would have made Irwin Allen proud. The story development is slow, and the characterizations a little heavy-handed, but the story concept is so strong, and the sense of cross-cultural camaraderie between German and French miners so evident, that the film remains impressive. The story concerns French miners getting trapped by a mine disaster, with German miners attempting a daring rescue. Too old to be rated, parents may want to consider the intensity of the situations and some brief, nonsexual nudity. In German and French, with English subtitles.

1931 B & W 87 minutes

KAOS

★★★½

DIRECTORS: Paolo Taviani, Vittorio Taviani

CAST: Margarita Lovano, Enrica Maria Mudugno, Ciccio Ingrassia, Omero Antonutti, Regina Bianchi, Franco Franchi

Italian writer-director Paolo and Vittorio Taviani adapted four short stories by Luigi Pirandello for this sumptuously photographed film about peasant life in Sicily. For all its beauty and style, this is a disappointing, uneven work. The first two stories are wonderful, but the final pair leave a lot to be desired. Foreign film buffs might want to savor the first two tales and hit the rewind button, thus getting the best of this ambitious production. In Italian, with English subtitles. Rated R for nudity and violence.

1986 188 minutes

KIDNAP SYNDICATE, THE

★

DIRECTOR: Fernando DiLeo

CAST: James Mason, Luc Merenda, Valentina Cortese, Irina Maleva, Marino Mase, Daniele Dublino, Vittorio Caprioli

The dubbing is so poor in this Italian import that even James Mason's voice and mouth are not synchronized. Mason plays a millionaire whose child has been kidnapped. Luc Merenda is the poor father of a child who has been taken along with Mason's. Director Fernando DiLeo tries to juxtapose the irony of the two fathers—Mason, with his riches, trying to bargain with the kidnappers and Merenda, with only pennies, willing to give up all he has for the safety of his son—but it comes off like a trite melodrama with lots of blood spilling and profanity.

1976 105 minutes

KING OF HEARTS

★★★★½

DIRECTOR: Philippe de Broca

CAST: Alan Bates, Genevieve Bujold

Philippe de Broca's wartime fantasy provides delightful insights into human behavior. A World War I Scottish infantryman (Alan Bates) searching for a hidden enemy bunker enters a small town that, after being deserted by its citizens, has been taken over by inmates of an insane asylum. In assuming the characters of the village people and affecting normalcy, the "crazies" emphasize the senselessness of war. In

French, with English subtitles. No MPAA rating.
1966 102 minutes

KNIFE IN THE WATER

★★★★

DIRECTOR: Roman Polanski
CAST: Leon Niemczyk, Jolanta Umecka, Zygmunt Malanowicz

Absolutely fascinating feature-film debut for director Roman Polanski, who immediately demonstrated his strength with character studies. A couple off for a sailing holiday encounters a young hitchhiker and invite him along. The resulting sexual tension is riveting, the outcome impossible to anticipate. In many ways, this remains one of Polanski's finest pictures. In Polish, with English subtitles. Unrated, the film has sexual situations.
1962 B & W 94 minutes

KOJIRO

★★★★

DIRECTOR: Hiroshi Inagaki
CAST: Kikunosuke Onoe, Yuriko Hoshi, Yoko Tsukasa, Tatsuya Nakadai

This first-rate semisequel to director Hiroshi Inagaki's superb *Samurai Trilogy* casts Tatsuya Nakadai as the fabled master swordsman, Musashi Miyamoto, whose exploits made up the three previous films. But he is not the main character here. Instead, the focus is on Kojiro (Kikunosuke Onoe), whose goal is to become the greatest swordsman in all Japan and thus follow the trail blazed by Miyamoto, who was the first to become a respected masterless samurai. This goal puts the younger man on a path that leads to the final, death-dealing duel with his hero. Unrated, the film contains violence. In Japanese with English subtitles.
1967 152 minutes

L'ADDITION

DIRECTOR: Denis Amar
CAST: Richard Berry, Richard Bohringer, Victoria Abril, Fadrid Chopel, Daniel Sarky, Fabrice Eberhard

L'Addition is a formula prison movie about a man accused of a crime he did not commit. This is not even an entertaining routine suspense flick. Richard Berry as the tough but stylish condemned man is like an Al Pacino sucked dry of emotion. Asking us to worry over Berry's fate is asking too much. This movie is a merciless question beggar. We know Berry's character is an actor because we're told he's one. We see nothing of his actor's life. Worse yet is the romantic relationship between Berry and a shoplifter (Victoria Abril). We are even deprived of Richard Bohringer's voice, which would have given the movie some power; unfortunately, *L'Addition* is dubbed. For a terrific, sexy thriller with good jokes and a magnificent Bohringer performance (complete with original voice), rent Michel Deville's *Peril*. *L'Addition* is rated R for language and violence.
1985 85 minutes

L'ODEUR DES FAUVES (SCANDAL MAN)

½

DIRECTOR: Richard Balducci
CAST: Maurice Ronet, Josephine Chaplin, Vittorio De Sica, Francis Blanche, Raymond Pellegrin, Tanya Lopert

This is a real slipshod movie about a hack photographer-reporter who earns his living digging up *National Enquirer*–type stories. He eventually and unintentionally hits on a real scoop involving an affair between a black man and a white woman whose father is a Ku Klux Klan leader.

The film is almost as sensational as its subject matter. The attempts at sarcastic newspaper humor are banal and induce only heavy sighs.

1986 86 minutes

LA BALANCE

★★★★

DIRECTOR: Bob Swaim

CAST: Nathalie Baye, Philippe Léotard, Richard Berry, Maurice Ronet, Christophe Malavoy, Jean-Paul Connart

Early on in this French import directed by American filmmaker Bob Swaim, we see posters of *The Enforcer*, starring Clint Eastwood as "Dirty Harry" Callahan, and *Bullitt*, with Steve McQueen in the title role. Swaim is making it clear that *La Balance* is an homage of sorts to the American cop thriller. He turns the genre inside out, however, by not focusing on the problems of the detective (Richard Berry). Instead, he concentrates on the plights of two unfortunates—a prostitute (Nathalie Baye) and a petty criminal (Philippe Léotard)—who get caught in a vise between the cops and a gangland chief. The result is a first-rate crime story. In French with English subtitles. Rated R for nudity, profanity, and violence.

1982 102 minutes

LA BETE HUMAINE

★★★★½

DIRECTOR: Jean Renoir

CAST: Jean Gabin, Julien Carette, Fernand Ledoux, Jean Renoir, Simone Simon

Remarkable performances by Jean Gabin, Fernand Ledoux, and Simone Simon, along with Jean Renoir's masterful editing and perfectly simple visuals, elevate a middling Emile Zola novel to fine cinema. The story—with a screenplay by Renoir—is a rather grim reworking of the even grimmer Atreus myth: A railway mechanic and hereditary alcoholic (Gabin) is pushed into crime; he becomes a lover to Simon, who wants him to kill her husband (Ledoux), himself a criminal; but he ends by strangling her. The artistry of *La Bête Humaine* more than transcends what, in other hands, could have been a seedy little tale—and becomes an absorbing unity of story and style. In French with English subtitles.

1938 B & W 99 minutes

LA BOUM

★★★

DIRECTOR: Claude Pinoteau

CAST: Sophie Marceau, Brigitte Fossey, Claude Brasseur

A young teenager (Sophie Marceau) discovers a whole new world open to her when her parents move to Paris. Her new set of friends delight in giving "boums"—French slang for big parties. Although this film seems overly long for the subject matter and strains to hang together, many of its scenes are nevertheless tender and lovingly directed by Claude Pinoteau. No MPAA rating. In French with English subtitles.

1980 100 minutes

LA CAGE AUX FOLLES

★★★★½

DIRECTOR: Edouard Molinaro

CAST: Ugo Tognazzi, Michel Serrault

A screamingly funny French comedy and the biggest-grossing foreign-language film ever released in America, this stars Ugo Tognazzi and Michel Serrault as two male lovers who must masquerade as husband and wife so as not to obstruct the marriage of Tognazzi's son to the daughter of a stuffy bureaucrat. In French with English subtitles. Rated PG for mature situations.

1978 110 minutes

LA CAGE AUX FOLLES II

★★

DIRECTOR: Eduoard Molinaro
CAST: Ugo Tognazzi, Michel Serrault

This follow-up to the superb French comedy is just more proof sequels aren't equals. Though it reunites Ugo Tognazzi and Michel Serrault as those crazy "Birds of a Feather," it has little of the original's special charm and unbridled hilarity. In French with English subtitles. Rated PG for mature situations.

1981 101 minutes

LA CAGE AUX FOLLES III, THE WEDDING

DIRECTOR: Georges Lautner
CAST: Michel Serrault, Ugo Tognazzi, Stephane Audran, Michel Galabru

Another pathetic and dreadful sequel to *La Cage Aux Folles (Birds of a Feather)*. The two gay entrepreneurs are back, and in an effort to save their financially failing night club, Renato (Ugo Tognazzi) sends Albin (Michel Serrault) to the reading of a distant relative's will in which he stands to inherit a fortune. One of the stipulations Albin must comply with before he receives the inheritance is that he must get legally married to a woman and have a child by her. Simply put, this movie is preposterous, and an offense to both gay and straight audiences alike. In French with English subtitles. Rated PG-13.

1986 88 minutes

LA DOLCE VITA

★★★½

DIRECTOR: Federico Fellini
CAST: Marcello Mastroianni, Anita Ekberg, Anouk Aimee, Nadia Gray

Mastroianni stars as a journalist who is caught up in the high society of Rome. He is both enchanted and repulsed by his life and the world around him. Entertaining, a trendsetter for the time. Not as complicated as most Fellini films. In Italian, with English subtitles.

1960 B & W 173 minutes

LA MARSEILLAISE

★★★★

DIRECTOR: Jean Renoir
CAST: Pierre Renoir, Louis Jouvet, Julien Carette

Though its plot is somewhat uneven, *La Marseillaise* contains many beautiful sequences, and it is still noted for its appropriate lack of idealizaton and dramatization. This documentarylike story (and Jean Renoir's call to his countrymen to stand fast against the growing threat of Hitler) parallels the rise of the French Revolution with the spread of the new rallying song as 150 revolutionary volunteers from Marseilles march to Paris and join with others to storm the Bastille. Since it was financed by the French trade unions, it is interesting that Louis XVI (played by Renoir's brother) is portrayed as an intelligent and sensible man (albeit a bit distraught) who is overwhelmed by the march of history. In French with English subtitles.

1937 B & W 130 minutes

LA NUIT DE VARENNES

★★½

DIRECTOR: Ettore De Scola
CAST: Marcello Mastroianni, Jean-Louis Barrault, Harvey Keitel

An ambitious and imaginative, but ultimately disappointing, film of King Louis XVI's flight from revolutionary Paris in 1791 as seen through the ideologically opposed sensibilities of Casanova (Marcello Mastroianni), Restif de la Bretonne (Jean-Louis Barrault), and Tom Paine (Harvey Keitel). This French import is a lot like Steve

Allen's PBS series "Meeting of the Minds," with costumes and scenery. All these folks do is talk, talk, talk. Talk about the rights of the individual. Talk about the elegant ways of the aristocracy. Talk about boring! In French, with English subtitles. Rated R for nudity, sex, and profanity.

1983 133 minutes

LA RONDE

★★★

DIRECTOR: Max Ophuls

CAST: Anton Walbrook, Serge Reggiani, Simone Simon, Simone Signoret, Daniel Gelin, Danielle Darrieux, Fernand Gravet, Odette Joyeux, Jean-Louis Barrault, Isa Miranda, Gerard Philippe

It would be hard to imagine any film more like a French farce than *La Ronde*, in spite of its Austrian origins from the play by Arthur Schnitzler. This fast-paced, witty, and sometimes wicked look at amours and indiscretions begins with the soldier (Serge Reggiani) and lady of easy virtue (Simone Signoret). Their assignation starts a chain of events that is charmingly risqué. Unfortunately, the film's release occurred at a time when the world was infested with "commie hunters" and neo-Victorians—and it was heavily criticized. Ultimately, though, *La Ronde* was approved by the Supreme Court of the United States of America and the House of Representatives Committee on Un-American Activities. In French with English subtitles.

1950 B & W 97 minutes

LA STRADA

★★★★★

DIRECTOR: Federico Fellini

CAST: Giulietta Masina, Anthony Quinn, Richard Basehart

This is Fellini's first internationally acclaimed film. Gelsomina (Giulietta Masina), a simple-minded peasant girl, is sold to a circus strongman (Anthony Quinn), and as she follows him on his tour through the countryside, she falls desperately in love with him. She becomes the victim of his constant abuse and brutality until their meeting with an acrobat (Richard Basehart) dramatically changes the course of their lives. Masina's performance is unforgettable. This poetic masterpiece won the Academy Award for best foreign-language film.

1954 B & W 94 minutes

LA TRAVIATA

★★★★

DIRECTOR: Franco Zeffirelli

CAST: Teresa Stratas, Placido Domingo, Cornell McNeill

Director Franco Zeffirelli set out to make an opera film of Verdi's *La Traviata* that would appeal to a general audience as well as opera buffs, and he has handsomely succeeded. He has found the right visual terms for the pathetic romance of a courtesan compelled to give up her aristocratic lover. The score is beautifully sung by Teresa Stratas, as Violetta; Placido Domingo, as Alfredo; and Cornell McNeill, as his stern father, who feels obliged to bring the romance to an end. In Italian, with English subtitles. Rated G.

1982 112 minutes

LA TRUITE (THE TROUT)

★★★½

DIRECTOR: Joseph Losey

CAST: Lissette Malidor, Isabelle Huppert, Jacques Spiesser, Roland Bertin, Daniel Ollrychski

Sometimes disjointed story of a young girl who leaves her rural background and arranged marriage to climb the rocky path to success in both love and business. Although director Joseph Losey generally has the right idea, *La*

Truite, in the end, lacks warmth and a sense of cohesion. Many viewers may find it disappointingly dull and dreary. In French, with English subtitles. Rated R.

1982 100 minutes

LADY ON THE BUS

★★

DIRECTOR: Neville D'Almeida

CAST: Sonia Braga

Story of a shy bride who is frigid on her wedding night. She first turns to her husband's friends and then goes on to sample strangers she meets on buses. Her psychiatrist thinks she is normal, although she is driving her husband mad. Marginal comedy. In Portuguese with English subtitles. Rated R for sex.

1978 102 minutes

LAND WITHOUT BREAD

★★★★½

DIRECTOR: Luis Buñuel

CAST: Documentary

Critics who had been unsympathetic to Luis Buñuel's first two films, the brilliant surrealist manifestos *Un Chien Andalou* and *L'Age d'Or,* were slapped flat by this documentary of the monstrous conditions of life in the poorest district of northern Spain. This "morbid fantasy" dramatizes the harshness of nature and the benign neglect of Christian tradition. Nearly every scene of poverty, disease, and death—as well as marriage and valiant struggle—is indelible. The ironic travelogue-style narration only serves to intensify the image of human degradation. *Land Without Bread* was financed by the twenty thousand pesetas given to Buñuel by an anarchist friend who had won the money in a lottery. It was his last film project without the aggravation of commerical strings attached. No rating, but not for the youngsters. In Spanish with English subtitles.

1932 B & W 27 minutes

LAST LAUGH, THE

★★★★

DIRECTOR: F. W. Murnau

CAST: Emil Jannings, Mary Delshaft, Kurt Hiller

Historically recognized as the first film to exploit the moving camera, this titleless silent classic tells the story of a lordly luxury hotel doorman who is abruptly and callously demoted to the menial status of a washroom attendant. Deprived of his job and uniform, his life slowly disintegrates. Emil Jannings, one of the screen's early character stars in the mold of George Arliss and Paul Muni, gives a brilliant performance as the once-proud major-domo on whom the sin of pride visits cruel retribution. In a questionable effect-destroying epilogue, the old man inherits a fortune, and has *The Last Laugh*.

1924 B & W 74 minutes

LAST METRO, THE

★★★½

DIRECTOR: François Truffaut

CAST: Catherine Deneuve, Gerard Depardieu, Jean Poiret

Catherine Deneuve and Gerard Depardieu star in this drama about a Parisian theatrical company that believes "the show must go on" despite the restrictions and terrors of the Nazis during their World War II occupation of France. This film has several nice moments and surprises that make up for its occasional dull spots and extended running time. Rated PG.

1980 133 minutes

LAST YEAR AT MARIENBAD

★★★

DIRECTOR: Alain Resnais

CAST: Delphine Seyrig, Giorgio Albertazzi, Sacha Pitoeff,

Françoise Bertin, Luce Garcia-Ville

This film provides no middle ground—you either love it or you hate it. The confusing story is about a young man (Giorgio Albertazzi) finding himself in a monstrous, baroque hotel trying to renew his love affair with a woman who seems to have forgotten that there is an affair to renew. The past, present, and future all seem to run parallel, cross over, and converge. Even the hotel loses its baroqueness at times. This has been called a landmark film by some. If that is the case, then it exists in that state for the most esoteric students, directors, and cinematographers. In French with English subtitles.

1962 B & W 93 minutes

LE BAL

★★★★

DIRECTOR: Ettore Scola

European history of the last half-century is reduced to some fifty popular dance tunes—and a variety of very human dancers—in this innovative and entertaining film by Italian director Ettore Scola (*La Nuit de Varennes*). Nominated for the Academy Award for best foreign-language film (it lost to Ingmar Bergman's *Fanny and Alexander*), this unusual import eschews dialogue for tangos, fox trots, and jazz to make its points. Scola chronicles the dramatic changes in political power, social behavior, and fashion trends from the 1930s to the present without ever moving his cameras out of an art deco ballroom. No MPAA rating; the film has brief violence.

1983 109 minutes

LE BEAU MARIAGE

★★★★

DIRECTOR: Eric Rohmer

CAST: Beatrice Romand, Arielle Dombasle, André Dussollier

A young woman decides it is high time she got married. She chooses the man she wants, a busy lawyer, and tells her friends of their coming wedding. He knows nothing of this, but she is confident. After all, is she not beautiful, intelligent, and impossible to resist? That is the premise in this film by French director Eric Rohmer, whose works have always been more concerned with human nature than plot. As a result, we have a character-rich import that will please those with a taste for something different. In French with English subtitles. Rated R.

1982 100 minutes

LE CAVALEUR

★★★★

DIRECTOR: Philippe de Broca

CAST: Jean Rochefort, Annie Giradot

A poignantly philosophical, yet witty and often hilarious, farce about the perils of the middle-aged heartbreak kid. Our cad about town is unerringly portrayed by Jean Rochefort (*French Postcards*; *Till Marriage Do Us Part*) as a classical pianist trying to juggle his art and the many past, present, and possible future women in his life. He does so well he almost loses them all. Annie Giradot warmly plays his ex-wife, and Catherine Le Prince the almost girl of his dreams. Written and directed by Philippe de Broca (*King of Hearts*), this film will be a delight for those who usually eschew foreign films. Nudity but generally innocent adult situations.

1980 106 minutes

LE CHEVRE (THE GOAT)

★★½

DIRECTOR: Francis Veber

CAST: Pierre Richard, Gerard Depardieu, Corynne Charbit, Michel Robin, Andre Valardy, Pedro Armendariz Jr

The stars of *Les Comperes*, Pierre Richard and Gerard Depardieu, romp again in this French comedy as two investigators searching for a missing girl in Mexico. While this import may please staunch fans of the stars, it is far from being a laugh riot. Unrated, the film has profanity and violence. In French with English subtitles.

1981 91 minutes

LE GENTLEMAN D'ESPOM, (DUKE OF THE DERBY)

★★★

DIRECTOR: Jacques Juranville
CAST: Jean Gabin, Madeleine Robinson, Paul Frankeur, Franck Villard, Jean Lefebvre, Louis De Funes

This light-hearted look at the sport of kings gives veteran French film star Jean Gabin ample chance to shine as the title character, an aged, suave snob living by his wits and luck handicapping and soliciting bets from the rich. Everything is fine until, eager to impress an old flame, he passes a bad check. Gabin is at once engaging and impressive. A fine cast supports him, though the plot is thin.

1962 B & W 83 minutes

LE JOUR SE LEVE (DAYBREAK)

★★★

DIRECTOR: Marcel Carne
CAST: Jean Gabin, Jules Berry, Arletty, Jacqueline Laurent

An affecting, atmospheric French melodrama by the director of the classic *Les Enfants du Paradis (Children of Paradise)*. Jean Gabin plays a man provoked to murder his lover's seducer, who then barricades himself in his room through the night. There is some brilliant, sensuous moviemaking here. The poetic realism of this 1939 film puts to shame all the ridiculously prudish American movies of the time. Written by Jacques Prevert. The existing print lacks sufficient subtitling but is still worth viewing.

1939 B & W 85 minutes

LE MILLION

★★★★

DIRECTOR: René Clair
CAST: Annabella, Rene Lefevre, Louis Allibert, Wanda Greville, Paul Olivier

Made more than fifty years ago, this delightful comedy about the efforts of a group of people to retrieve an elusive lottery ticket is more applicable to American audiences of today than it was when originally released. René Clair's classic fantasy-adventure is freewheeling and fun. The plot is secondary to the form in this movie, and the clever camera work and ingenious situations carry the audience along at a dizzying pace. A memorable experience and lots of fun for everyone. Subtitled in English.

1931 B & W 85 minutes

LE REPOS DU GUERRIER (WARRIOR'S REST)

★★★★

DIRECTOR: Roger Vadim
CAST: Brigitte Bardot, Robert Hossein, James Robertson Justice, Jean-Marc Bory

Brigitte Bardot plays a proper French girl who rescues a sociopathic drifter from a suicide attempt. The drifter immediately takes over Bardot's life, ruining her reputation and abusing her verbally and emotionally, yet denying her attempts to form a real relationship. This is a precursor of *The Servant*, *9 1/2 Weeks*, and other frank observations of sexual obsession. Vadim's direction is fine, with lots of interesting camera angles and movements, but the subtitles tend to get in the way, sometimes flashing across the screen almost subliminally. In French.

1962 98 minutes

LEGEND OF THE EIGHT SAMURAI

★★

DIRECTOR: Haruki Kaduwara

CAST: Hiroku Yokoshimaru, Sonny Chiba, Sue Shihomi, Henry Sanada

Shizu (Sue Shihomi) is the warrior princess who, aided by eight loyal samurai, attempts to lift a curse from her clan. She leads her warriors into battle against a giant centipede, ghosts, and the nearly immortal witch who cursed the clan a hundred years ago. This Japanese fantasy features an interesting storyline, but is derivative, slow in spots, badly dubbed, and disappointing. Unrated, has moderate violence.

1984 130 minutes

LES COMPERES

★★★★

DIRECTOR: Bernard Bher

CAST: Pierre Richard, Gerard Depardieu

Pierre Richard and Gerard Depardieu star in this madcap French comedy as two strangers who find themselves on the trail of a runaway teenager. Both think they're the father—it was the only way the boy's mother could think of to enlist their aid. In French with English subtitles. Rated PG for profanity and brief violence.

1984 90 minutes

LES GRANDES GUEULES (JAILBIRDS' VACATION)

★★½

DIRECTOR: Robert Enrico

CAST: Lino Ventura, Bourvil, Marie Dubois, Jean-Claude Rolland

This comedy-drama about parolees working on a backwoods sawmill would be better if it were shorter and the extended fistfight scenes were cut measurăbly. Otherwise, the "jailbirds" are a lively, entertaining bunch. In French with English subtitles.

1965 125 minutes

LESSON IN LOVE, A

★★★

DIRECTOR: Ingmar Bergman

CAST: Gunner Bjo[diaeresis]rnstrand, Eva Dahlbek, Åve Gronberg, Yvonne Lombard, Harriet Andersson

Ingmar Bergman makes films with an eye on the American market, and hence not only are the subtitles carefully done, but the whole film style is more recognizable to American audiences. In this film, Gunnar Björnstrand plays a philandering gynecologist who realizes that his long-suffering wife is the woman he loves the most, and he sets out to win her back. This is a little ponderous for a true light-romantic comedy, but good writing and good acting move the film along well and provide some funny yet realistic situations. In Swedish, with subtitles.

1954 B & W 97 minutes

LOS OLVIDADOS

★★★★★

DIRECTOR: Luis Buñuel

CAST: Alfonso Mejia, Roberto Cobo, Estela Ina, Miguel Inclan

Although its basic plot was taken from police records, this film, which was released in England and the United States as *The Young and the Damned*, is a far cry from the soap opera its title might indicate. Luis Buñuel marks the beginning of his mature style with this film. Hyperpersonal, shocking, erotic, hallucinogenic, and surrealistic images are integrated into naturalistic action: two youths of the Mexican slums venture deeper and deeper into the criminal world until they are beyond redemption. Buñuel's focus is pitiless; his hardened eye and pained soul do not hold with the liberal sociologist's view of violence. His characters alone are responsible for their actions—and their deaths. In Spanish with English subtitles.

1950 B & W 88 minutes

LOST HONOR OF KATHARINA BLUM, THE

★★★

DIRECTOR: Volker Schlondorff
CAST: Angela Winkler

Angela Winkler's performance as Katharina Blum is the central force behind Schlondorff's interpretation of Heinrich Boll's novel. Katharina Blum is a poor, young housekeeper who spends one night with a suspected political terrorist. Her life is thereby ruined by the police and the media. This film dramatizes political statements and is without surprises. In German, with English subtitles. Rated R.

1977 97 minutes

LOVE AND ANARCHY

★★★★★

DIRECTOR: Lina Wertmuller
CAST: Giancarlo Giannini, Mariangela Melato, Eros Pagni, Lina Polito

Giancarlo Giannini gets to eat up the screen with this role. Comic, tragic, and intellectually stimulating, this is Wertmuller's best film. Giannini is bent on assassinating Mussolini right after the rise of Fascism but somehow gets waylaid. Imagine the possibilities and they're probably in the film. A classic. Rated R for sexual situations, language, and some nudity.

1973 117 minutes

LOVE IN GERMANY, A

★★

DIRECTOR: Andrzej Wajda
CAST: Hanna Schygulla, Marie-Christine Barrault, Armin Mueller-Stahl, Elisabeth Trissenaar, Bernhard Wicki

During World War II, the Germans bring in Polish POWs to do menial labor. While Frau Kopp's (Hanna Schygulla) husband is off fighting, she is finding it increasingly difficult to run the family grocery store alone, so she hires a young Polish POW to handle the crates. Eventually the POW's visits to the store bring about an illicit affair. The first half of the film effectively creates the sense of danger and the political consequences of the clandestine affair but the second half receives an excessively sensationalistic treatment, ultimately diminishing the flavor and appeal. In German with English subtitles. Rated R for violence, nudity.

1984 107 minutes

LOVE ON THE RUN

★★★½

DIRECTOR: François Truffaut
CAST: Jean-Pierre Léaud, Claude Jade, Marie-France Pisier

François Truffaut's tribute to himself. *Love on the Run* is the fifth film (*400 Blows*; *Love at Twenty*; *Stolen Kisses*; *Bed & Board*) in the series for character Antoine Doinel (Jean-Pierre Léaud). Now in his thirties and on the eve of divorce, Doinel rediscovers women. Light romantic work filled with humor and compassion. In French, with English subtitles. Rated PG.

1979 93 minutes

LUMIERE

★

DIRECTOR: Jeanne Moreau
CAST: Jeanne Moreau, Francine Racette, Bruno Ganz, Fran-

çois Simon, Caroline Cartier, Lucia Bose, Keith Carradine

The only thing this film illuminates is Jeanne Moreau's pretentiousness. The famed French actress fares poorly behind the camera as writer and director of this self-conscious story about the life of an actress (Moreau herself). The protagonist is presented as a loving, intuitive queen figure, and her self-appointment loses us from the start. In French.

1976 95 minutes

M

★★★★★

DIRECTOR: Fritz Lang

CAST: Peter Lorre, Gustav Grundgens, Ellen Widman, Inge Landgut

A child-killer is chased by police, and by other criminals who would prefer to mete out their own justice. Peter Lorre, in his first film role, gives a striking portrayal of a man driven by uncontrollable forces. Detested by all elements of society, his character is both pitiful and frightening. A classic German film, understated, yet filled with haunting images. Beware of videocassettes containing edited versions of the movie, and badly translated, illegible subtitles. Unrated. In German, with English subtitles.

1931 B & W 99 minutes

MACARTHUR'S CHILDREN

★★

DIRECTOR: Masahiro Shinoda

CAST: Takaya Yamauchi, Yoshiyuki Omori, Shiori Shakura, Masaka Natsume, Shuji Otaki, Haruko Kato, Ken Watanabe

This import deals with effects of Japan's defeat during World War II, and its subsequent occupation by America, on a group of youngsters and adults living on a tiny Japanese island. While there are some brilliant touches by director Masahiro Shinoda, the film as a whole fails to live up to them. It is essentially a collection of vignettes that never quite come together. It results in frustration for the viewer and the feeling of having watched an overlong yet incomplete motion picture. Rated PG for profanity and suggested sex. In Japanese with English subtitles.

1984 120 minutes

MADAME ROSA

★★★★★

DIRECTOR: Moshe Mizrahi

CAST: Simone Signoret, Sammy Den Youb, Claude Dauphin

This superbly moving motion picture features Simone Signoret in one of her greatest roles. It is a simple, human story that takes place six flights up in a dilapidated building where a once-beautiful prostitute and survivor of Nazi concentration camps cares for the children of hookers. In French with English subtitles. No MPAA rating.

1977 105 minutes

MAGICIAN, THE

★★★

DIRECTOR: Ingmar Bergman

CAST: Max von Sydow, Ingrid Thulin, Gunnar Bjorstrand, Bibi Andersson

Dark and somber parable deals with the quest for an afterlife by focusing on confrontation between a mesmerist and a magician and their attempts to show their power over life and death. This shadowy allegory may not be everyone's idea of entertainment, but the richness of ideas and the excellent acting of director Ingmar Bergman's fine stable of dependable actors and actresses make this a compelling film with rewards on all levels. Subtitled in English.

1959 B & W 102 minutes

MAKE ROOM FOR TOMORROW

★★★

DIRECTOR: Peter Kassovitz

CAST: Victor Lanoux, Jane Birkin, Georges Wilson, Henri Cremieux

More a collection of mildly humorous events than an out-and-out comedy. Victor Lanoux plays a father going through a midlife crisis. His wife, Jane Birkin, is separated from him. He is having trouble handling his son. And he is entertaining both his father and grandfather for a week in celebration of his father's birthday. What happens during that week is the subject of this sitcom. Good acting and careful translation from the original French make this film better than the average subtitled venture. Rated R for language and nudity.

1982 104 minutes

MALICIOUS

★★★½

DIRECTOR: Salvatore Samperi

CAST: Laura Antonelli, Turi Ferro, Alessandro Momo, Tina Aumont

Italian beauty Laura Antonelli *(Wifemistress, The Innocent)* is hired as a housekeeper for a widower and his three sons. Not surprisingly, she becomes the object of affection for all four men—particularly 14-year-old Nino. While Papa makes proper and methodical plans to court and marry, Nino ensnares the somewhat willing lady in a compelling game of sexual power. Antonelli is tantalizing, and director Samperi easily traverses moods from amusement with the boy's awakening sexual awareness to sequences of disturbing, slightly dangerous, eroticism. Rated R.

1974 98 minutes

MAN AND A WOMAN: 20 YEARS LATER, A

DIRECTOR: Claude Lelouch

CAST: Anouk Aimee, Jean-Louis Trintignant, Richard Berry, Evelyne Bouix, Robert Hossein, Philippe Leroy-Beaulieu

A Man and a Woman: 20 Years Later may be the most narcissistic bad film ever made. The director of this movie took his 1966 *A Man and a Woman* and, after twenty years, assembled the original lead actors and created a monster. The new film is ruined primarily because it's in love with itself—an excuse to dredge up the memories of the first. The plot has Anouk Aimee, now a film producer, seeking daredevil Jean-Louis Trintignant's permission to make a movie about their personal love story. From then on, it becomes a succession of flashbacks clips from the first film and reenactments of those events by Aimee's film company. *A Man and a Woman: 20 Years Later* is a tedious piece of nostalgic self-admiration. In French. Rated PG.

1986 112 minutes

MARIUS

DIRECTOR: Alexander Korda

CAST: Raimu, Pierre Fresnay, Charpin, Alida Rouffe, Orane Demazis

This French movie is a marvelous view of the working class in Marseilles between the wars. The story revolves around Marius (Pierre Fresnay) and his love for Fanny (Orane Demazis), the daughter of a fish store proprietess. The poetic essence of the film is captured with style as

Marius ships out to sea, unknowingly leaving Fanny with child. The film is based on the play by Marcel Pagnol, which in turn is the basis for the Broadway musical *Fanny* (later filmed as a semi-musical). The excess exposition may make this version turgid to Americans, but the story and peformances (especially Raimu as Marius's father) are worthwhile. In French with English subtitles.

1931 B & W 125 minutes

MARRIAGE OF MARIA BRAUN, THE

★★½

DIRECTOR: Rainer Werner Fassbinder

CAST: Hanna Schygulla, Klaus Lowitsch, Ivan Desny

The Marriage of Maria Braun is probably Rainer Werner Fassbinder's easiest film to take because it's basically straightforward and stars the sensual and comedic Hanna Schygulla. She plays Maria Braun, a tough cookie who marries a Wehrmacht officer whom she loses to the war and then prison. Through her ambition and shrewdness she tries to maintain a standard of life for herself and her husband, when he returns home. The film is full of Fassbinder's overly dramatic, sordid sexual atmosphere. It can be both funny and perverse. In German. Rated R.

1979 120 minutes

MASTER OF THE HOUSE (DU SKAL AERE DIN HUSTRU)

★★★★

DIRECTOR: Carl Dreyer

CAST: Johannes Meyer, Astrid Holm, Karin Nellmose, Mathilde Nielsen

In this funny satire of middle-class life, a wife (played with charm by Karin Nellmose) runs away from her husband (Johannes Meyer), a male chauvinist who treats her brutally. Later, the wife is reunited with her husband after an old nurse has taught him a lesson. These may seem like light themes for the director who later went on to make films like *The Passion of Joan of Arc* and *Vampyr*. However, it is very enjoyable. Silent.

1925 B & W 81 minutes

MAYERLING

★★★

DIRECTOR: Anatole Litvak

CAST: Charles Boyer, Danielle Darrieux, Suzy Prim, Jean Dax, Vladimir Sokoloff

Fine-tuned, convincing performances mark this French-made romantic tragedy based upon one of history's most dramatic personal incidents: Austrian Crown Prince Rudolph's ill-starred clandestine love for court lady-in-waiting Countess Marie Vetsera, in 1889. Mayerling is the royal hunting lodge where it all comes together—and falls apart. Despite a topnotch cast, a 1969 British remake stinks by comparison. In French with English subtitles.

1936 B & W 91 minutes

MELODIE EN SOUS-SOL (THE BIG GRAB)

★★★

DIRECTOR: Henri Verneuil

CAST: Jean Gabin, Alain Delon, Viviane Romance, Carla Marlier, Maurice Biraud, Dora Doll

Fresh from prison, aging gangster Jean Gabin makes intricate and elaborate plans to score big by robbing a major Riviera gambling casino. Alain Delon joins him in conniving their way to the casino vault by seducing a showgirl to gain vital backstage access. Suspense builds as delays threaten the plan. Crime ultimately pays, but a clever twist of fate resolves the usual moral dilemma of right versus wrong. Gabin, as the cool, experienced ex-convict, and Delon, as his young, upstart, eager partner, are part-perfect. In French, with English subtitles. Originally released in U.S. as *Any Number Can Win*.

1963 B & W 118 minutes

MEN...

★★★★

DIRECTOR: Doris Dörrie
CAST: Uwe Ochenknecht, Ulrike Kriener, Heiner Lauterbach

In this delightful, tongue-in-cheek anthropological study of the male animal by German writer-director Doris Dörrie, a hotshot advertising executive, who has been having a fling with his secretary, is outraged to discover that his wife has a lover. Devastated at first, he finally decides to get even, and his revenge is one of the most inventive and hilarious ever to grace the screen. In German with English subtitles. Unrated, the film has profanity.

1985 99 minutes

MENAGE

★★★

DIRECTOR: Bertrand Blier
CAST: Gerard Depardieu, Michel Blanc, Miou-Miou, Bruno Cremer

Two down-and-outers (Michel Blanc and Miou-Miou) are taken in by a flamboyant thief (Gerard Depardieu), who introduces them to a life of crime, luxury, and kinky sex in this alternately hilarious and mean-spirited comedy. The first half of this bizarre work by French writer-director Bertrand Blier is enjoyable, albeit adult-oriented, but the acceptance of the last part will depend on the taste—and tolerance—of the viewer. In French, with English subtitles. Unrated, the film has profanity, violence, nudity, and simulated sex.

1986 84 minutes

MEPHISTO

★★★★★

DIRECTOR: Istvan Szabo
CAST: Klaus Maria Brandauer, Krystyna Janda, Karin Boyd

Winner of the 1981 Academy Award for best foreign-language film, this brilliant movie, by Hungarian writer-director Istvan Szabo, examines the conceits of artists with devastating honesty and insight. Klaus Maria Brandauer, in a stunning performance, plays an actor whose overwhelming desire for artistic success leads to his becoming a puppet of the Nazi government. *Mephisto* is so powerful, so full of truth, it not only merited its Oscar, but should be considered a cinematic work of art. No MPAA rating. The film has nudity and violence. In German, with English subtitles.

1981 135 minutes

MISS MARY

★★★½

DIRECTOR: Maria Luisa Bemberg
CAST: Julie Christie, Nacha Guevara, Tato Pavlovsky, Gerardo Romano, Luisina Brando

A good knowledge of the history of Argentina—specifically between the years 1930 and 1945—will help viewers appreciate this biting black comedy. Julie Christie gives a marvelous performance as a British governess brought to the South American country to work for a wealthy family. Through her eyes, in a series of flashbacks, we see how the corrupt aristocracy slowly falls apart, to be replaced by the Peron regime. Although in both English and Portuguese, this should be considered a foreign film. Rated R for profanity, nudity, and suggested and simulated sex.

1987 100 minutes

MR. HULOT'S HOLIDAY

★★★½

DIRECTOR: Jacques Tati
CAST: Jacques Tati, Nathale Pascaud

A delightfully light-hearted film about the natural comedy to be found in vacationing. Jacques Tati plays the famous Monsieur Hulot, who has some silly adventures at a seaside resort. Although partially dubbed in English, this film has a mime quality that is magical.

1953 B & W 86 minutes

MR. KLEIN

★★★½

DIRECTOR: Jospeh Losey
CAST: Alain Delon, Jeanne Moreau, Juliet Berto, Michel Lonsdale, Jean Bouise, Francine Berge

Dark-sided character study of a Parisian antique dealer who buys artwork and personal treasures from Jews trying to escape Paris in 1942. He (Alain Delon) finds himself mistaken for a missing Jew of the same name. This thriller builds around the search to reveal the identity of the second Mr. Klein. Rated PG. Available in French version.

1976 123 minutes

MON ONCLE D'AMERIQUE

★★★★

DIRECTOR: Alain Resnais
CAST: Gerard Depardieu, Nicole Garcia, Roger Pierre

In this bizarre French comedy, director Alain Resnais works something close to a miracle: He combines intelligence with entertainment. On one level, *Mon Oncle d'Amerique* is a delectable farce with the requisite ironies, surprise complications, and bittersweet truths. Underneath, it is a thought-provoking scientific treatise—by biologist Henri Laborit—on the human condition. That makes it a genuinely human comedy. Rated PG. In French with English subtitles.

1980 123 minutes

MOON IN THE GUTTER, THE

★

DIRECTOR: Jean-Jacques Beineix
CAST: Gerard Depardieu, Nastassja Kinski, Victoria Abril

A pretentious, self-consciously artistic bore that seems to defy any viewer to sit through it. Gerard Depardieu, who co-stars in this piece of directorial meandering with Nastassja Kinski, was openly critical of co-scriptwriter-director Jean-Jacques Beineix, who scored such a critical and commercial success with his first film, *Diva*. Shortly after the film was completed, the prolific French film actor complained the movie didn't make any sense and had serious problems in pacing. He was absolutely right. Rated R for profanity, nudity, and violence. In French with subtitles.

1983 126 minutes

MOONLIGHTING

★★★★½

DIRECTOR: Jerzy Skolimowski
CAST: Jeremy Irons, Eugene Lipinski, Jiri Stanislav, Eugeniusz Haczkiewicz

This film, a political parable criticizing the Soviet Union's suppression of Solidarity in Poland, may sound rather heavy, gloomy, and dull. It isn't. Written and directed by Jerzy Skolimowski, it is a thoroughly entertaining film; funny, suspenseful, thought-provoking, and even exciting. It essentially focuses on four Polish construction workers remodeling a flat in London. Give it a look. In Polish, with English subtitles. Rated PG for very brief nudity.

1983 97 minutes

MOSCOW DOES NOT BELIEVE IN TEARS

★★★★

DIRECTOR: Vladimir Menshov
CAST: Vera Alentova, Irina Muravyova

You wouldn't think it possible. A sensitive, richly rewarding movie from the Soviet Union? But it's true. *Moscow Does Not Believe in Tears*, the 1981 Academy Award winner for best foreign film, is that—and then some. Few movies allow you to know their characters so well and care so much about them. Director Vladimir Menshov achieves this without resorting to the clichés and devices of soap opera. That makes it a very special experience. But for all its rewards, *Moscow Does Not Believe in Tears* requires a bit of patience on the part of the viewer. The first hour of this tragic comedy is almost excruciatingly slow. You're tempted to give up on it and walk out. But once it gets deeper into the story, you're very glad you toughed it out. MPAA unrated, but contains brief nudity and brief violence.

1980 152 minutes

MY LIFE AS A DOG

★★★★★

DIRECTOR: Lasse Hallstro[diaeresis]m
CAST: Anton Glanzelius, Tomas von Bromssen

Swedish movies aren't known for being warm or funny, so this charming, offbeat, and downright lovable import from Sweden is a big surprise. It tells of a young boy in 1950s Sweden who's shipped off to a country village when his mother becomes seriously ill. There, as he tries to come to terms with his new life, he encounters a town filled with colorful eccentrics and a young tomboy who becomes his first love. Among the movie's many virtues is the extraordinary performance by Anton Glanzelius, an 11-year-old charmer with a marvelously expressive face. In Swedish, with English subtitles.

1987 101 minutes

MY NIGHT AT MAUD'S

★★★★

DIRECTOR: Eric Rohmer
CAST: Jean-Louis Trintignant, Françoise Fabian, Marie-Christine Barrault, Antoine Vitez

My Night At Maud's was the first feature by Eric Rohmer to be shown in the United States. It is the third film of the cycle he called *Six Moral Tales*. The premise of the morality is quite simple: A man is in love with a woman, but his eyes wander to another. However, the transgression is only brief, for, according to Rohmer, the only true love is the love ordained by God. Beautifully photographed in black and white, the camera looks the actors straight in the eye and captures every nuance. The acting is sedate and dignified (that is *not* a euphemism for boring), especially the portrayal of Jean-Louis by Jean-Louis Trintignant. This is French cinema at its best. No pretenses, just honest story-telling. In French with English subtitles.

1970 B & W 105 minutes

MY OTHER HUSBAND

★★★★

DIRECTOR: Georges Lautner
CAST: Miou-Miou, Roger Hanin, Eddy Mitchell, Charlotte de Tuckheim, Dominique Lavanant, Rachid Ferrache

At first, this French import starring the marvelous Miou-Miou seems rather like a scatterbrained, faintly funny retread of the old person-with-two-spouses comedy plot (à la *Micki & Maude*, etc.). But it goes on to become an affecting, sweetly sad little treasure. In French with English subtitles. Rated PG-13 for profanity.

1981 110 minutes

MY UNCLE (MON ONCLE)

★★★★

DIRECTOR: Jacques Tati

CAST: Jacques Tati, Jean-Pierre Zola, Adrienne Servantie, Alain Bercourt

The second of Jacques Tati's cinematic romps as Mr. Hulot (the first was the famous *Mr. Hulot's Holiday*), this delightful comedy continues Tati's recurrent theme of the common man confronted with an increasingly mechanized and depersonalized society. (It's also the only Tati film to win the Academy Award for best foreign film.) This time around, the bumbling but lovable Mr. Hulot is taken under the wing of his oh-so-chic Parisian in-laws who live in a sterile, futuristic suburban house dominated by every conceivable form of ridiculous electronic gadget. Needless to say, Hulot's old-world mentality can't easily adapt to this bizarre new environment, and the results are, to put it mildly, catastrophic. Though overlong and occasionally uncentered, this remains one of Tati's most rewarding films, a universally appealing blend of satire, sentiment, and slapstick. (As with all Tati films, there are no subtitles needed, as the minimal dialogue consists of little more than mumbled gibberish.)

1958 116 minutes

NAPOLEON

★★★★★

DIRECTOR: Abel Gance

CAST: Albert Dieudonné, Antonin Artaud

The first film to use the three-screen process, director Abel Gance's 1927 silent epic may be the greatest cinematic event of the century. Over a half century after its debut, *Napoleon* remains a visual wonder, encompassing a number of film-making techniques, some of which still seem revolutionary. The complete film—as pieced together by British film historian Kevin Brownlow over a period of twenty years—is one motion picture event no lover of the art form will want to miss even on the small screen without the full effect of its spectacular three-screen climax.

1927 B & W 235 minutes

NEA (A YOUNG EMMANUELLE)

★★★

DIRECTOR: Nelly Kaplan

CAST: Sammy Frey, Ann Zacharias, Micheline Presle, Francoise Brion, Heinz Bennent

In this French sex comedy, a young girl, Sybille Ashby (Ann Zacharias), stifled by the wealth of her parents turns to anonymously writing erotic literature via first-hand experience. Her anonymity betrayed, she perfects her novel, *Nea*, by the sweetest revenge she can devise. A relatively successful and entertaining film of its kind, this has sex and adult themes. In French, with English subtitles. Rated R.

1978 103 minutes

NEST, THE

★★½

DIRECTOR: Jaime De Arminan

CAST: Hector Alterio, Ana Torrent, Luis Politti, Patricia Adriani, Amparo Baro

The Nest is the story of a tragic relationship between a 60-year-old widower and a 12-year-old girl. The movie takes a far too romantic view of the widower's sacrifices to the friendship, and Ana Torrent is a bit too austere and worldly-wise for her own good. Hector Alterio as the older man has a warm and inviting face and voice. He is the one who enlists our sympathies. In Spanish, with English subtitles.

1981 109 minutes

NIGHT AND FOG, THE

★★★★

DIRECTOR: Alain Resnais
CAST: Documentary

Graphic footage of the Nazi death camps makes this sad, shockingly painful documentary one of the most personal and effective of all studies of Hitler's final solution. Beautifully composed by director Alain Resnais, this film juxtaposes still photographs and Allied footage of gruesome spectacles. Made in 1955 when the wounds were still raw, this controversial look at man's incredible disdain for his own species is ageless and unsettling. Recommended. No rating, but the content may be objectionable to some and it isn't suggested viewing for children. French, subtitled in English.

1955 32 minutes

NIGHT OF THE SHOOTING STARS

★★½

DIRECTORS: Paolo, Vittorio Taviani
CAST: Omero Antonutti, Margarita Lozano

Made by Paolo and Vittorio Taviani (*Padre Padrone*), this Italian import is about the flight of peasants from their mined village in pastoral Tuscany during the waning days of World War II. Despite its subject matter, the horrors of war, it is a strangely unaffecting—and ineffective—motion picture. It has no central character or strong dramatic thrust. Instead, it is a series of vignettes. Consequently, though it runs only 104 minutes, the film seems much longer. In Italian, with English subtitles. Unrated, the film has violence.

1982 116 minutes

NOSFERATU

★★★★

DIRECTOR: F. W. Murnau
CAST: Max Schreck, Gustav von Wagenheim, Greta Schroeder, Alexander Granach

A product of the German expressionist era, *Nosferatu* is a milestone in the history of world cinema. Each shot is a masterpiece of photography. Director F. W. Murnau seems to make the characters jump out at you. With his skeletal frame, rodent face, long nails, and long, pointed ears, Max Schreck is the most terrifying of all screen vampires. Fans of the Dracula myth may be disappointed when Nosferatu's image appears in a mirror, or that his demise is not by the stake. Nevertheless, this picture stands as a tribute to the power of the silent screen.

1922 B & W 63 minutes

NUDO DI DONNA (PORTRAIT OF A WOMAN, NUDE)

★★★

DIRECTOR: Nino Manfredi
CAST: Nino Manfredi, Eleonora Giorgi

Nino Manfredi stars in this Italian comedy as a husband shocked to discover his wife (Eleonora Giorgi) may have posed nude for a painting. Told the model was a hooker, the skeptical Manfredi attempts to discover the truth in this madcap import. In Italian, with English subtitles. Unrated.

1982 112 minutes

OCCURRENCE AT OWL CREEK BRIDGE, AN

★★★½

DIRECTOR: La Riviere du Hibou
CAST: Roger Jacquet, Anne Cornaly

This fascinating French film looks at the last fleeting moments of the life of a man being hanged from the bridge of the title during the American Civil War. This memorable short film works on all levels.

1962 B & W 22 minutes

OFFICIAL STORY, THE

★★★★★

DIRECTOR: Luis Puenzo
CAST: Norma Aleandro, Hector Alterio, Analia Castro, Chunchuna Villafane

This winner of the Oscar for best foreign language film unforgettably details the destruction of a middle-class Argentinian family. The beginning of the end comes when the wife (brilliantly played by Norma Aleandro) suspects that her adopted baby daughter may be the orphan of parents murdered during the "dirty war" of the 1970s. Gripping, superbly acted, and ultimately heartbreaking, this is a must-see motion picture. In Spanish with English subtitles. Unrated, the film has violence.

1985 110 minutes

OLD TESTAMENT, THE

★

DIRECTOR: Gianfranco Parolini
CAST: Susan Paget, Brad Harris, Mara Lane, John Heston, Philippe Hersent, Margaret Taylor, Bridgette Corey

In this boring Italian epic, the Jews of Jerusalem are ruled by cruel Syrians. They flee, gather strength in the desert, and return to reclaim their city. The only mildly interesting parts involve the Jewish leader Simon and his friendship with a Syrian soldier and love for a Syrian princess. What could have been inspirational has been reduced to a viewing sedative. The acting is wooden, the English is poorly dubbed, and the photography is not always sharp or clear. Unrated, this contains violence.

1963 88 minutes

OLYMPIA

★★★★

DIRECTOR: Leni Riefenstahl
CAST: Documentary

The 1936 Olympic Games in Berlin. Leni Riefenstahl's masterpiece is the most massive coverage of any sporting event until recent years and still stands as one of the greatest documentaries of all time. Adolf Hilter gave the young filmmaker carte blanche on available talent and equipment; over forty cameramen are credited with supplying footage. Filmed in two parts with prologues shot in Greece in order to trace the Olympic flame to present-day Germany, the imagery, intensity of concentration, and symmetry of motion captured on film is a tribute to all athletes of all time. Riefenstahl braved Hitler's wrath by including entensive coverage of Jesse Owens, three-time gold medalist and one of the few black Americans who dared to appear in Nazi Germany. A great film on many levels, it's the yardstick by which all other event documentaries are measured by 1.

1936 (edited and released in 1938) B & W 220 minutes

ONE SINGS, THE OTHER DOESN'T

★★½

DIRECTOR: Agnes Varda
CAST: Valerie Mairesse, Thérèse Liotard

Labeled early on as a feminist film, this story is about a friendship between two different types of women spanning 1962 to 1976. When they meet again at a women's rally after ten years, they renew their friendship by discussing events in their lives.

1977 105 minutes

ONE WILD MOMENT

★★★★

DIRECTOR: Claude Berri

CAST: Jean-Pierre Marielle, Victor Lanoux, Agnes Soral, Christine Dejoux, Martine Sarcey

In French director Claude Berri's warm and very sensitive film, a middle-aged man (Jean-Pierre Marielle) is told by his best friend's daughter (Agnes Soral) that she's in love with him. Not knowing whether to tell his friend (Victor Lanoux) about it or not, our hero lets things go a bit too far one night and she seduces him. Enjoy the story (which was adapted by director Stanley Donen for *Blame it on Rio*) as it should be told, as delicately and thoughtfully handled by Berri. In French with English subtitles. Unrated, the film has sex, nudity, and profanity.

1980 90 minutes

OPEN CITY

★★★★½

DIRECTOR: Robert Rossellini

CAST: Aldo Fabrizi, Anna Magnani, Marcello Pagliero, Harry Feist, Vito Annicchiarico, Nando Bruno, Giovanna Galletti

Stunning study of resistance and survival in World War II Italy was the first important film to come out of postwar Europe and has been considered a classic in realism. Co-scripted by a young Federico Fellini, this powerful story traces the threads of people's lives as they interact and eventually entangle and doom themselves in the shadow of their Gestapo-controlled "open city." Anna Magnani became the first of a new breed of international stars as a result of her portrayal of Pina, the young widow whose fiancé is snatched away by the Gestapo, but all the performers are superlative. *Open City* drags the viewer down into the horror of a world controlled by a vengeful enemy. Not the most pleasant of films, but an experience to linger long after more amiable images have faded. In Italian with English subtitles.

1946 B & W 105 minutes

PAIN IN THE A—, A

★★

DIRECTOR: Edouard Molinaro

CAST: Lino Ventura, Jacques Brel, Xavier Depraz

A professional hit man (Lino Ventura) arrives in Montpellier, Italy, to fulfill a contract by killing a government witness (Xavier Depraz) who is set to testify against the mob. While waiting in the squealer's hotel room, the hit man notices something strange through a window. In the next room, a man (Jacques Brel) tries to hang himself but fails. The hit man decides to save the would-be suicide, much to his regret; he has gained an unwanted companion who consistently interferes in the carrying-out of his contract. This unfunny slapstick comedy was adapted by director Billy Wilder for the equally disappointing *Buddy, Buddy* with Jack Lemmon and Walter Matthau. In Italian, with English subtitles. Rated PG for light violence.

1973 90 minutes

PAISAN

★★★½

DIRECTOR: Roberto Rossellini

CAST: Carmela Sazio, Robert Van Loon, Dots Johnson, Alfonsino, Gar Moore, Maria Michi, Harriet White, Renzo Avanzo, Bill Tubbs, Dale Edmonds

Six separate stories of survival are hauntingly presented by writer Federico Fellini and director Roberto Rossellini in this early postwar Italian film. Released the year after the landmark *Open City*, this movie solidified Rossellini's position as the leader in the school of Neo-Realism and reestablished Italy's place in world cinema. Shot on the streets and often improvised, this strong drama exposes the raw nerves brought on by living in a battleground and drags the audience into the lives of these victims. This is compelling adult drama, still powerful today.

1946 B & W 90 minutes

PANDORA'S BOX

★★★★½

DIRECTOR: G. W. Pabst

CAST: Louise Brooks, Fritz Kortner, Franz Lederer, Carl Gotz

Here is a gem from the heyday of German silent screen expressionism. The film follows a winning yet amoral temptress, Lulu (a sparkling performance by largely ignored American actress Louise Brooks). Without concerns or inhibitions, Lulu blissfully ensnares a variety of weak men, only to contribute to their eventual downfall. Brooks plays Lulu, not as the traditional silent screen vamp, but as a freespirited victim of her own sexuality. This movie is primarily a showcase for the beautiful Miss Brooks, but credit must be given to director Pabst's technical innovations, and the originality of its story.

1929 B & W 131 minutes

PANIQUE

★★★½

DIRECTOR: Julien Duvivier

CAST: Michel Simon, Viviane Romance, Paul Bernard

Based on a thriller by Georges Simenon, this gripping story features Michel Simon as a stranger who is framed for murder by a couple covering their own crime. This is a taut film comparable to the best of the chase *noir* genre so prevalent in French and American cinema of the mid-1940s. This is an exciting, involving film. In French, with English subtitles.

1946 B & W 87 minutes

PARDON MON AFFAIRE

★★★★

DIRECTOR: Yves Robert

CAST: Jean Rochefort, Claude Brasseur, Anny Duperey, Guy Bedos, Victor Lanoux

Enjoyable romantic comedy about a middle-class, happily married man (Jean Rochefort) who pursues his fantasy of meeting a beautiful model (Anny Duperey) and having an affair. Later remade in America as *The Woman in Red*. In French with English subtitles. Rated PG.

1976 105 minutes

PARDON MON AFFAIRE, TOO!

★½

DIRECTOR: Yves Robert

CAST: Jean Rochefort, Claude Brasseur, Guy Bedos, Victor Lanoux, Daniele Delorme

Pardon Mon Affaire, Too! is a lukewarm comedy of infidelity and friendship. The focus is on four middle-aged men who share their troubles and feelings about their marriages and sex lives. A sequel to *Pardon Mon Affaire*, the movie elicits occasional smiles and chuckles, but no real laughs. Unless, of course, you guffaw at the idea of husbands, wives, and lovers cheating on each other and merrily getting away with it. In French with English subtitles.

1977 110 minutes

PASSION

★★★

DIRECTOR: Ernst Lubitsch
CAST: Pola Negri, Emil Jannings

Combining realism with spectacle, this account of famous eighteenth-century French courtesan Madame Du Barry was the first German film to earn international acclaim after World War I. As a result, the director and the stars received Hollywood contracts. The film is still recognized as the best of seven made about the subject between 1915 and 1954. Silent.

1919 B & W 134 minutes

PASSION OF JOAN OF ARC, THE

★★★★★

DIRECTOR: Carl Dreyer
CAST: Maria Falconetti, Silvain, Antonin Artaud

This is simply one of the greatest films ever made. Its emotional intensity is unsurpassed. Faces tell the tale of this movie. Maria Falconetti's Joan is unforgettable. *The Passion of Joan of Arc* will break your heart and leave you speechless. Silent

1928 B & W 114 minutes

PASSION OF LOVE

★★★★

DIRECTOR: Ettore Scola
CAST: Valeria D'Obici, Bernard Giraudeau, Laura Antonelli, Bernard Blier, Jean-Louis Trintignant, Massimo Girotti

In 1862 Italy just after the war, a decorated captain (Bernard Giraudeau) has a passionate affair with a beautiful married woman (Laura Antonelli). Giraudeau is transferred to a faraway outpost, where he becomes the love object of his commander's cousin (Valeria D'Obici). What follows is a fascinating study of torment and anguish as the incredibly ugly and illness-plagued D'Obici relentlessly pursues Giraudeau. There are outstanding performances by all. Awards went to D'Obici and the film at the Cannes Film Festival. Dubbed in English and unrated.

1982 117 minutes

PAULINE AT THE BEACH

★★★★

DIRECTOR: Eric Rohmer
CAST: Amanda Langlet, Arielle Dombasle, Pascal Gregory, Feodor Atkine

The screen works of French writer-director Eric Rohmer are decidedly unconventional. Nothing particularly monumental happens in them. All the characters really do is talk, talk, talk. Yet Rohmer's movies still manage to keep the viewer interested, because their creator cares deeply about people and all the underlying quirks and complications that make them who and what they are. In this, the latest in what he calls his "Comedies and Proverbs," the 14-year-old title character (Amanda Langlet) shows herself to have a better sense of self and reality than the adults around her. In French, with English subtitles. Rated R for nudity.

1983 94 minutes

PEPE LE MOKO

★★★½

DIRECTOR: Julien Duvivier
CAST: Jean Gabin, Mireille Balin, Gabriel Gario, Lucas Gridoux, Marcel Dalio

Algiers criminal Pepe Le Moko (Jean Gabin) is safe just as long as he remains in the city's picturesque, squalid native quarter, the Casbah, a sanctuary for fugitives where the police have no power. His passionate infatuation with a beautiful visitor from his beloved Paris, however, spells his doom. His superb performance in this film, *La Grande Illusion,* and *Port of Shadows*—all milestones of French cinema—made Jean Gabin's reputation as a strong, silent, deeply human hero and, often, antihero. *Algiers,* the U.S. remake with suave Charles Boyer and Hedy Lamarr, in her American film debut, is as good, but not better. Knockoffs rarely are. In French with English subtitles.

1937 B & W 93 minutes

PERIL

★★

DIRECTOR: Michel Deville
CAST: Christophe Malavoy, Nicole Garcia, Richard Bohringer, Anemone, Michel Piccoli, Anais Jeanneret

Despite some guitar transcriptions of Brahms and Schubert, the absence of a soundtrack gives this film a harsh and stagnant tone that makes the story difficult to experience. And while there may be some justification for the cold feel, it does nothing for the viewer's patience. Nicole Garcia plays the wife of a wealthy businessman who is having an affair with their daughter's guitar instructor (Christophe Malavoy). From there the story becomes very complex, with possible hidden agendas revealed every twenty minutes or so. Filmmaker Michel Deville aims too high in his direction with French New Wave–like scene cuts; they come off more amateurish than artistic. French cinema enthusiasts will welcome the appearance of Richard Bohringer, the lovable rogue hero from *Diva,* who plays a lovable hit man here. Rated R for sex, nudity, violence, profanity, and adult subject matter. In French with English subtitles.

1985 100 minutes

PETIT CON

★

DIRECTOR: Gerard Lauzier
CAST: Guy Marchand, Caroline Cellier, Bernard Brieux, Souad Amidou

France's equivalent of our American teen-age-boy-in-heat flicks, with a few differences. The film tries for a serious side involving the trauma that Michel (Bernard Brieux) is causing his family. This movie doesn't glorify Michel, as one of our films might. It shows him to be a pain in the neck. The film doesn't get the one-star rating for the failed attempt to bring something more substantial to the storyline. The girls in *Petit Con* are smart and savvy and create situations that are cause for some very funny sexual dialogue that keeps this movie away from the turkey farm–though not by much. Rated R. In French with English subtitles.

1986 90 minutes

PIXOTE

★★★★

DIRECTOR: Hector Babenco
CAST: Fernando Ramos Da Silla, Marilia Pera, Jorge Juliano, Gilberto Moura

In Rio, Brazil, half the population is younger than 18. Kids, only 10- or 12-year-olds, become thieves, beggars, and prostitutes. *Pixote* is the story of one of these unfortunates. For some viewers it may be too powerful and disturbing, yet it is not the least bit exploitative or exaggerated. Though fictional, it is based on fact, and that makes *Pixote* all the more unsettling. Rated R for violence, explicit sex, and nudity.

1981 127 minutes

PLAYTIME

★★★½

DIRECTOR: Jacques Tati

CAST: Jacques Tati, Barbara Denneck, Jacqueline Lecomte, Valerie Camille

Mr. Hulot is back again in this slapstick comedy as he attempts to keep an appointment in the big city. Paris and all of its buildings, automobiles, and population seem to conspire to thwart Mr. Hulot at every turn, and there are plenty of visual gags and situations worthy of the great silent comedians. The subtitled American release version is over thirty minutes shorter than the original French release and it shows in the continuity, but what's left for our viewing is more than enough to provide the laughs.

1967 108 minutes

PORT OF CALL

★★★

DIRECTOR: Ingmar Bergman

CAST: Nine Christine Jonsson, Bengt Eklund

When a seaman begins working on the docks, he falls in love with a suicidal young woman. The woman has had an unhappy childhood and a wild past, which has given her a bad reputation. Their relationship falters when he has trouble loving and accepting her in spite of her past indiscretions. This drama seems dated today. In Swedish with English subtitles.

1948 B & W 100 minutes

QUERELLE

★★½

DIRECTOR: Rainer Werner Fassbinder

CAST: Rainer Werner Fassbinder, Brad Davis, Franco Nero, Jeanne Moreau, Gunther Kaufmann, Hanna Poschl

In what turned out to be his last film, the late German film director Rainer Werner Fassbinder uses Jean Genet's *Querelle de Bres* as a way of confronting his own homosexuality. In this murky, unhappy rendering of Genet's story, Brad Davis (*Midnight Express*) stars in the title role as a young sailor whose good looks set off a chain reaction. As filmed by an obviously enfeebled Fassbinder, who died a drug-related death at 36, this is a disturbing and depressing portrait of terminally unhappy people doomed to destroy either themselves, one another, or both. In German with English subtitles. Rated R for homosexual sex and obscenity.

1982 120 minutes

QUESTION OF SILENCE, A

★★★★½

DIRECTOR: Marleen Gorris

CAST: Cox Habbema, Nelly Frijda, Henriette Tol, Edda Barends

After an unusual murder is committed, three women, all strangers to one another, stand trial for the same crime. A woman psychiatrist is appointed to the case after the three openly display their hostilities toward male-dominated society. The psychiatrist is forced to examine her own nature as her understanding and sympathy for the women evolve. Rated R for profanity. Available in original Dutch or dubbed.

1983 92 minutes

QUI ETES-VOUS MR. SORGE (SOVIET SPY)

½

DIRECTOR: André Girard

CAST: Thomas Holtzman, Keiko Kishi, Hans Otto Meissner, Max Klausen, Anna Klausen

This is a docudrama about the case of Richard Sorge, a German WWII journalist who, records show, was hanged as a Soviet spy in 1944. The movie spends the time offering up differing opinions of various witnesses as to the accuracy of the information. *Qui Etes-Vous Mr. Sorge* is nothing but a treacherously long, very dry film. At times it comes close to accidental self-parody. In French with English subtitles.

1961 130 minutes

RAMPARTS OF CLAY

★★★★

DIRECTOR: Jean-Louis Bertucelli
CAST: Leila Schenna and the villagers of Tehouda, Algeria

Terse but hauntingly beautiful documentary-style film set against the harsh background of a poor North African village. A young woman (Leila Schenna) struggles to free herself from the second-class role imposed on her by the village culture, much as the village tries to liberate itself from subservience to the corporate powers that control its salt mines, the citizens' only means of survival and livelihood. In Arabic, with English subtitles. Rated PG.

1970 87 minutes

RAN

★★★★★

DIRECTOR: Akira Kurosawa
CAST: Tatsuya Nakadai, Akira Terao, Jinpachi Nezu, Daisuke Ryu, Mieko Harada

This superb Japanese historical epic tells the story of a sixteenth-century warlord's time of tragedy. Based on Shakespeare's *King Lear,* this is yet another masterwork from director Akira Kurosawa, a film on a par with D. W. Griffith's *Birth of a Nation,* Abel Gance's *Napoleon*, and Orson Welles' *Citizen Kane* as a triumph of personal artistic vision. It is stunningly photographed and acted, and blessed with touches of great drama, glorious humor, and hair-raising battle sequences. In other words, it is what motion pictures were meant to be but so seldom are. In Japanese with English subtitles. Rated R for violence and suggested sex.

1985 160 minutes

RASCAL, THE

★★★

DIRECTOR: Bernard Revon
CAST: Bernard Brieux, Thomas Chabrol, Pascale Rocard

Two kids (Bernard Brieux and Thomas Chabrol) go through school together trying to beat the system. Taking place in the German-occupied France of 1942, *The Rascals* deals with the coming-of-age themes we have seen many times: cheating on school exams, peer group pressure, sexual curiosity, etc. But the film's nationalistic subtext, which results in a triumphant ending, is, perhaps, a new one. In French, with English subtitles. Rated R for sex and nudity.

1979 93 minutes

RASHOMON

★★★★★

DIRECTOR: Akira Kurosawa
CAST: Toshiro Mifune, Machiko Kyo, Masayuki Mori, Takashi

After a violent murder and rape is committed by a bandit, four people tell their own different versions of what happened. Set in medieval Japan, this examination of truth and guilt is charged with action. The combination of brilliant photography, stellar acting, direction, and script won this Japanese classic the Oscar for best foreign film.

1951 B & W 83 minutes

RED BEARD

★★★★½

DIRECTOR: Akira Kurosawa
CAST: Toshiro Mifune, Yuzo Kayama, Yoshio Tsuchiya

In the early nineteenth-century, a newly graduated doctor, Yasumoto (Yuzo Kayama), hopes to become a society doctor. Instead, he is posted at an impoverished clinic run by Dr. Niide (Toshiro Mifune), whose destitute patients affectionately call him "Red Beard." We are never once fidgety during the three hours. At first we are caught up in the story's soap opera web, and then won by the wisdom of Red Beard's words and ways. Won over, too, of course, is Yasumoto. Mifune is at his most brilliant. Akira Kurosawa, at one of his many directorial pinnacles, describes his film as a "monument to the goodness in man." In Japanese with English subtitles.

1965 B & W 185 minutes

RETURN OF MARTIN GUERRE, THE

★★★★½

DIRECTOR: Daniel Vigne

CAST: Gerard Depardieu, Nathalie Baye, Roger Planchon, Maurice Jaquemont, Bernard Pierre, Donna Dieu

Brilliantly absorbing account of an actual sixteenth-century court case in which a man returns to his family and village after years away at the wars, only to have his identity questioned. Gerard Depardieu and Nathalie Baye give outstanding, carefully restrained performances in this haunting historical drama. In French with English subtitles. No MPAA rating.

1982 111 minutes

RETURN OF THE TALL BLOND MAN WITH ONE BLACK SHOE, THE

★★★½

DIRECTOR: Yves Robert

CAST: Pierre Richard, Mireille Darc, Jean Rochefort

This sequel to the original *Tall Blond Man*... is, unfortunately, inferior. But it's still a delight to watch Pierre Richard go through his comic paces. The plot is, once again, really not important, except that in this case it takes away from the fun instead of adding to it. Once again our hero is caught up in intrigue and derring-do, and his reactions to what he's faced with are the reason to see this or the original. If you haven't seen the original, do. If you have, we might even go so far as to recommend you have a second laugh with it rather than watching this. In French with English subtitles. No MPAA rating.

1974 84 minutes

REVOLT OF JOB, THE

★★★★

DIRECTOR: Imre Gyongyossy

CAST: Fereno Zenthe, Hedi Tenessy, Gabor Feher, Peter Rudolph, Leticia Caro

In this moving account of the Holocaust in rural Hungary, an old Jewish couple awaiting the inevitable Nazi takeover adopt a gentile orphan boy to survive them. Nominated for best foreign-language film in 1983's Academy Awards. In Hungarian, with English subtitles. No rating.

1983 97 minutes

ROBERT ET ROBERT

★★★★½

DIRECTOR: Claude Lelouch

CAST: Charles Denner, Jacques Villeret, Jean-Claude Brialy, Macha Meril, Germaine Montero, Regine

A brilliant French film about two lonely but very different men (Charles Denner and Jacques Villeret) who strike up a tenuous friendship while waiting for their respective computer dates. It is a bittersweet tale of loneliness and compassion, of the painful differences that separate people, and of the dream of discovering full human potential. No MPAA rating.

1978 105 minutes

RULES OF THE GAME, THE

★★★★★

DIRECTOR: Jean Renoir
CAST: Marcel Dalio, Nora Gregor, Mila Parely

This is Jean Renoir's comedy/farce that deftly exposes the moral bankruptcy of the French upper classes. A French manor house is the location for a high livers' party as the shallowness of each partygoer is brilliantly exposed. Some scenes may be a trifle too "French" for American comprehension, but it's a visual feast for the eye and no less than intriguing.

1939 B & W 110 minutes

SACRIFICE, THE

★★★★

DIRECTOR: Andrei Tarkovsky
CAST: Erland Josephson, Susan Fleetwood, Valerie Mairesse, Allan Edwall, Gudrun Gislodotir, Svan Wallter, Flippa Franzen

In this Andrei Tarkovsky film, the actors—particularly Erland Josephson, Susan Fleetwood, and the multitalented Allan Edwall (one of the leads in Ingmar Bergman's *Fanny and Alexander)* —do most of the work that expensive special effects would accomplish in an American film with a similar theme. During an approaching world holocaust, we don't see anything as unsubtle as bombs bursting, bloodshed, or devastation. Rather, the camera carefully records the various emotional reactions of six people in a house in the secluded countryside. Actors' faces and unpredictable actions mirror horror, pathos, and even grim humor as the plot twists in a surprisingly supernatural direction. Like Bergman, Tarkovsky gives his actors time to think on celluloid. In Swedish, with English subtitles. Unrated, the film has suggested sex.

1986 145 minutes

SAMSON

★½

DIRECTOR: Gianfranco Parolini
CAST: Brad Harris, Bridgette Corey

This Italian mini-epic features muscle-bound Brad Harris as Samson. He uses his strength to restore peace in his kingdom. This dubbed film is a yawner.

1960 99 minutes

SAMURAI TRILOGY, THE

★★★★★

DIRECTOR: Hiroshi Inagaki
CAST: Toshiro Mifune, Koji Tsuruta, Rentaro Mikuni, Kaoru Yachigusa, Kuroemon Onoe, Sachio Sakai, Akihiko Hirata, Mariko Okada, Yu Fujiki, Daisuke Kato

This brilliant and cinematically beautiful three-deck epic by director Hiroshi Inagaki tells the story of the legendary Japanese hero Musashi Miyamoto, a sixteenth-century samurai who righted wrongs in the fashion of Robin Hood and Zorro. Toshiro Mifune is impeccable as Miyamoto, whom we follow from his wild youth through spiritual discovery to the final battle with his archenemy, Sasaki Kojiro (Koji Tsuruta). The samurai film, for the uninitiated, is the Japanese equivalent of the American western. It has all of the action, code-of-honor mythic quality, and entertainment value of its counterpart. Hiroshi and Akira Kurosawa (*The Seven Samurai*) have raised the samurai film to the level of high art. The thrills are matched scene for scene with inspired visual moments and riveting characterizations. *The*

Samurai Trilogy is one of the best films in the genre; a perfect introduction to some of the most gratifying experiences in film viewing. In Japanese with English subtitles.

1954 B & W 303 minutes

SANJURO

★★★★½

DIRECTOR: Akira Kurosawa

CAST: Toshiro Mifune, Tatsuya Nakadai, Takashi Shimura, Yuzo Kayama, Reiko Dan

First-rate sequel to *Yojimbo* has the original Man With No Name (Toshiro Mifune) again stirring up trouble in feudal Japan. He is recruited by several young would-be samurai as their teacher and leader in exposing corruption in their clan. In his usual gentle manner, Mifune wreaks all sorts of havoc while occasionally warning, "Watch it, I'm in a bad mood." In Japanese, with English subtitles.

1962 B & W 96 minutes

SAWDUST AND TINSEL

★★★½

DIRECTOR: Ingmar Bergman

CAST: Harriet Andersson, Ake Grönberg, Anders Ek, Gudrun Brost

A traveling circus is the background for this study of love relationships between a circus manager, the woman he loves, and her lover. Director Ingmar Bergman scores some emotional bull's-eyes in this early effort with many haunting scenes. Love triangles lead to powerful climax, somewhat reminiscent of *The Blue Angel*.

1953 B & W 95 minutes

SCENE OF THE CRIME

★★★

DIRECTOR: André Téchiné

CAST: Catherine Deneuve, Danielle Darrieux, Wadeck Stanczak, Victor Lanoux

Scene of the Crime is a romantic thriller with an Oedipal angle. A nightclub owner (Catherine Deneuve) and her son get caught up in an increasingly dangerous attempt to safeguard a criminal. This watchable movie could use fast pacing and less obvious camera pyrotechnics. Made by a French director, this feels like a nontraveled American's view of rural France. Everything is soft-focused in a washed-out way, even Deneuve's face. Deneuve is still an aloof actress, but she's a little more human than usual in this film. In French, with English subtitles.

1987 90 minutes

SCENES FROM A MARRIAGE

★★★★★

DIRECTOR: Ingmar Bergman

CAST: Liv Ullmann, Erland Josephson, Bibi Andersson

Director Ingmar Bergman successfully captures the pain and emotions of a marriage that is disintegrating. Several scenes are extremely hard to watch because there is so much truth to what is being said. Originally a six-part film for Swedish television, the theatrical version was edited by Bergman. Believable throughout, this one packs a real punch. In Swedish. No rating (contains some strong language).

1973 168 minutes

SECRETS OF WOMEN (OR WAITING WOMEN)

★★★½

DIRECTOR: Ingmar Bergman

CAST: Anita Bjork, Jarl Kulle, Eva Dahlbeck, Gunnar Bjornstrand, Maj-Britt Nilsson, Birger Malmsten, Gerd Anderson

Infidelity is the theme of this early Ingmar Bergman film. Three wives (Anita Bjork, Maj-Britt Nilsson, and Eva Dahlbeck) who are staying at a summer house recount adventures from their marriages while they are waiting for their husbands' return. Bergman staged the film in three segments, and although it is often referred to as a comedy, the film is grave. There are amusing moments in the first two segments, but the third is by far the best. Karin (Dahlbeck) and Fredrik (Gunnar Bjornstrand) portray a married couple who are trapped in an elevator. They are forced to talk to each other for the first time in years. Clearly illustrates Bergman's talent for comedy and was his first commercial success.

1952 B & W 107 minutes

SEDUCED AND ABANDONED

★★★

DIRECTOR: Pietro Germi
CAST: Saro Urzi, Stefania Sandrelli, Aldo Puglisi

This raucous Italian film takes wonderfully funny pot shots at Italian life and codes of honor. It centers on a statute of Italian law that absolves a man for the crime of seducing and abandoning a girl if he marries her. This is one of the funniest movies exposing the strategems of saving face. In Italian with English subtitles.

1964 B & W 118 minutes

SEDUCTION OF MIMI, THE

★★★★

DIRECTOR: Lina Wertmuller
CAST: Giancarlo Giannini, Mariangela Melato, Agostina Belli, Elena Fiore

Giancarlo Giannini gives an unforgettable performance as the sad-eyed Mimi, a Sicilian who migrates to the big city as a member of the working class. He soon gets into trouble because of his obstinate character and his simple mind. Like all Wertmuller's films, sex and politics are at the heart of her dark humor. Includes one of the funniest love scenes ever filmed. Rated R for language and sex.

1974 89 minutes

SEVEN BEAUTIES

★★★★★

DIRECTOR: Lina Wertmuller
CAST: Giancarlo Giannini, Fernando Rey, Shirley Stoler

Winner of many international awards, this Italian film classic is not what the title might suggest. *Seven Beauties* is actually the street name for a small-time gangster, played by Giancarlo Giannini. We watch him struggle and survive on the streets and in a World War II German prisoner-of-war camp. Excellent! Rated R.

1976 115 minutes

SEVEN SAMURAI, THE

★★★★★

DIRECTOR: Akira Kurosawa
CAST: Toshiro Mifune, Takoshi Shimura, Yoshio Inaba

This Japanese release—about seven swordsmen coming to the aid of a besieged peasant village—is one of those rare screen wonders that seem to end much too soon. That's because its timeless and appealing story, which served as the basis for *The Magnificent Seven* and other American films, moves so fast it carries the viewer along. How many movies can you say that about? Unrated, the film has violence. In Japanese, with English subtitles.

1954 B & W 141 minutes

SEVENTH SEAL, THE

★★★★

DIRECTOR: Ingmar Bergman
CAST: Max von Sydow, Bibi Andersson, Gunnar Bjornstrand

This is considered by many to be director Ingmar Bergman's masterpiee. It tells the story of a knight coming back from the Crusades. He meets Death, who challenges him to a chess match, the stakes being his life. The knight is brilliantly played by Max von Sydow. In Swedish with English subtitles.

1956 B & W 96 minutes

SEX SHOP, LE

★★★½

DIRECTOR: Claude Berri
CAST: Claude Berri, Juliet Berto, Jean-Pierre Marielle

This French sex comedy stars and was directed by Claude Berri. He plays a bookstore owner struggling to make a living. Unable to make ends meet, he converts his store into a sex shop specializing in pornography and sex gadgets. The laughs begin when he, acting clumsy and nerdlike, tries to get in on the action that his customers are a part of. His wife allows him to realize he's no Romeo. Rated R for nudity and sexual reference.

1974 93 minutes

SHOAH

★★★★★

DIRECTOR: Claude Lanzmann
CAST: Documentary

In this magnificent document, director Claude Lanzmann depicts the horrors of the Holocaust through the eyes of the survivors. Rather than use stock or newsreel footage of concentration camp casualties, Lanzmann opts for capturing the memories and emotions of those who lived through the Nazis' reign of terror. He recreates the past through the voices and scenes from the present. The result is an unforgettable viewing experience.

1985 570 minutes

SHOGUN ASSASSIN

★★★

DIRECTORS: (Japan) Kenji Masuni; (United States) David Weisman and Robert Hous
CAST: Tomisaburo Wakayama, Masahiro Tomikawa

This film will rate a zero for the squeamish and close to five for fans of the nineteen-film "Baby Cart" series, so popular in Japan in the 1970s. The color red predominates in this meticulously reedited, rescripted, rescored (by Mark Lindsay), and English-dubbed version of the original *Baby-Cart at the River Styx*: swords enter bodies at the most imaginative angles; a body-count is impossible; all records are broken for bloodletting. But there is no time to cry over spilled blood for Lone Wolf—a disillusioned samurai (an "official decapitator" for a deranged shogun)—and his 6-year-old son as they wander the back roads of feudal Japan on an odyssey of vengeance. Rated R for the violence, which really is fairly aesthetic.

1980 90 minutes

SHOOT THE PIANO PLAYER

★★★½

DIRECTOR: François Truffaut
CAST: Charles Aznavour, Marie Dubois, Nicole Berger, Michele Mercier

Singer Charles Aznavour plays to perfection the antihero of this minor masterpiece directed by France's late, great François Truffaut. Don't look for plot, unity of theme, or understandable mood transitions. This one's a brilliantly offbeat organization of disorganization, a hyping mix of crime melodrama, romance, and slapstick. Aznavour is a lonely little piano player in a seedy Paris café who rejects involvement, moving through the film as a melancholic character who does not act but is acted upon. Goaded by his well-meaning lover, Marie Dubois, to resume a once-successful concert career, he instead consorts with gangsters and other riffraff. Aznavour catches the character brilliantly. Truffaut, however, the genius behind the camera, dominates throughout with incredible taste, invention, and compassionate understanding of just how disparate real life can be. Fans of Jean-Luc Godard's *Breathless* will delight in this film. In French, with English subtitles.

1962 B & W 85 minutes

SHOP ON MAIN STREET, THE

★★★★

DIRECTOR: Ján Kadár

CAST: Elmar Klos, Josef Kroner, Ida Kaminska, Han Slivkova

This World War II film finds a Jewish woman removed from her small business and portrays her growing relationship with the man who has been put in charge of her shop. Set among the turbulent and depressing days of the Nazi occupation of Czechoslovakia, this tender film depicts the instincts of survival among the innocent pawns of a brutal war and the innate decency that is able to survive in even such a bleak atmosphere. A moving film.

1964 B & W 128 minutes

SIEGFRIED

★★★★

DIRECTOR: Fritz Lang

CAST: Paul Richter, Margarete Schon, Theodor Loos, Bernhrd Goetzke, Gertrude Arnold, Hanna Ralph, Hans Carl Muller, Hans Adalbert von Schlettow

Vivid, spectacular story of young god Siegfried, whose conquests and eventual murder form an intrinsic part of Teutonic legend, this nationalistic triumph for German director Fritz Lang was the most ambitious attempt to transfer folklore to film and proved an international success. Moody sets and photography give this movie an other-worldly feeling and evoke just the right atmosphere for this fantasy-drama. The battle with Fafnir, the giant dragon Lang had built specifically for this superproduction, ranks with some of the finest special-effects work ever done for black-and-white film and proved a monumental achievement in full-scale models. This is the first part of a masterwork entitled *Die Nibelungile*. The sequel was entitled *Kriemheld's Revenge* and was released in 1924. Silent.

1923 B & W 100 minutes

SILENCE, THE

★★

DIRECTOR: Ingmar Bergman

CAST: Ingrid Thulin, Gunnel Lindblom, Hakan Jahnberg, Birger Malmstem

The Silence is one of Ingmar Bergman's more pretentious and claustrophobic films. Typically, Bergman deals in women. In *The Silence*, it's two sisters who are traveling together and stop for a time in a European hotel. The film is laden with heavy-handed symbolism and banal dialogue concerning repression, sexuality, guilt, and hate. Bergman is a superlative stylist, so even amongst the dense ambiguity of the story there are intense, memorable images. In Swedish with English subtitles.

1963 95 minutes

SIMON OF THE DESERT

★★★★½

DIRECTOR: Luis Buñuel

CAST: Claudio Brook, Silvia Pinal, Hortensia Santovena

Even though it won the Special Jury Prize at the 1965 Venice Film Festival and is hailed by some critics (not generally prone to hyperbole) as "the best short film ever made," one still has the feeling that *Simon of the Desert* is a short film because Luis Buñuel simply ran out of money (and tacked on a fairly unsatisfactory ending). It is, however, impossible to deny the sly pleasure we have with St. Simon Stylites, the desert anchorite who spent thirty-seven years atop a sixty-foot column (circa A.D. 400) preaching to Christian flocks and avoiding temptation—particularly with blond knockout Silvia Pinal, as the devil, who comes along to tempt him. (She/he travels in a self-propelled casket!) Good nasty fun for aficionados and novices alike. In Spanish with English subtitles.

1965 B & W 40 minutes

SIMPLE STORY, A

★★★½

DIRECTOR: Claude Sautet

CAST: Romy Schneider, Bruno Cremer, Claude Brasseur, Roger Pigaut

Marie (Romy Schneider) is pregnant and decides to have an abortion. At forty, she is forced to reevaluate her life and her relationships with men. Film is paced very slowly and plot is interwoven with subplots of other characters in distress. One of Romy Schneider's best performances. In French, with English subtitles. No MPAA rating.

1978 110 minutes

SINCERELY CHARLOTTE

★★★

DIRECTOR: Caroline Huppert

CAST: Isabelle Huppert, Neils Arestrup, Christine Pascal, Luc Beraud, Francoise Berleaud

Caroline Huppert directs her sister Isabelle in this intriguing tale of a woman with a shady past. Isabelle finds herself in trouble with the law and seeks the help of her old lover, who's now married. It's the interaction between these three characters that is fun and enticing. In French, with English subtitles.

1986 92 minutes

SLAVE OF LOVE, A

★★★★½

DIRECTOR: Nikita Mikhalkov

CAST: Elena Solovei, Rodion Nakhapetov, Alexandar Kalyagin

Shortly after the Bolshevik revolution, a crew of silent filmmakers attempt to complete a melodrama while fighting the forces of the changing world around them. This examines the role of the Bourgeois as Olga (Elena Solovei) changes from matinee idol to revolutionary. Politically and emotionally charged. In Russian, with English subtitles. Unrated.

1978 94 minutes

SLIGHTLY PREGNANT MAN, A

★★

DIRECTOR: Jacques Demy

CAST: Catherine Deneuve, Marcello Mastroianni, Mireille Mathieu

This French comedy features Marcello Mastroianni as the first pregnant man. His girlfriend (played by Catherine Deneuve) stands by his side when other men reportedly become pregnant also. A male maternity clothes campaign is created with Mastroianni as the model. The reversal of parenting roles provides a few laughs and the surprise ending is worth the wait in an otherwise ho-hum film. Unrated, this film contains adult subject matter and would not be appropriate for young viewers. In French, with subtitles.

1973 92 minutes

SMALL CHANGE

★★★★★

DIRECTOR: François Truffaut
CAST: Geary Desmouceaux, Philippe Goldman, Claudia Deluca

One of François Truffaut's best pictures, this is a charming and perceptive film viewing the joys and sorrows of young children's lives in a small French town. Wonderfully and naturally acted by a cast of young children.

1976 104 minutes

SOFT SKIN, THE

★★★½

DIRECTOR: François Truffaut
CAST: Jean Desailly, Nelly Benedetti, Françoise Dorleac

Up to this point, Truffaut was batting a perfect 1.000: *The 400 Blows, Shoot the Piano Player, Jules and Jim.* For some critics, *The Soft Skin* ranks as one of the New Wave master's worst; for some it remains one of his best. As usual, the truth lies in between. What keeps this from being at least a minor classic is the less-than-fresh plot (eminent literary journalist meets and keeps a lovely, decent stewardess half his age and is murdered by his wife when she learns of the affair) and the fact that by the conclusion of the film, we know scarcely more about the trio than at the beginning. Still, Truffaut suffuses the film with his trademark effortless style, with amusing detail and sensuality. In French with English subtitles.

1964 118 minutes

SOIS BELLE ET TAIS-TOI (JUST ANOTHER PRETTY FACE)

★★★

DIRECTOR: Marc Allegret
CAST: Mylene Demongeot, Henri Vidal, Beatrice Altariba, René Lefévre, Jean-Paul Belmondo, Alain Delon

This French import tries to be a lighthearted, romantic adventure, but doesn't focus itself properly. Mylene Demongeot is Virginie, an 18-year-old orphan who runs away from a reformatory and falls in with a jewel-smuggling gang. Along the way, Virginie falls in love with and marries a policeman, further complicating her life as a smuggler. Jean-Paul Belmondo and Alain Delon, both in their first film roles, are members of the teen-age gang. In French, with English subtitles.

1958 B & W 110 minutes

SOLDIER OF THE NIGHT

DIRECTOR: Dan Wolman
CAST: Iris Kaner, Ze'ev Shimshoni, Hellel Neeman, Yftach Katzur

This Israeli movie about a man who kills soldiers by night while working in a toy store by day has some pyschological thriller elements, but its plodding storyline and poor dubbing make it almost impossible to watch. Not rated, has sex, nudity, violence, and profanity.

1984 89 minutes

SOLDIER OF ORANGE

★★★★★

DIRECTOR: Paul Verhoeven
CAST: Rutger Hauer, Peter Faber, Jeroen Krabbe

Rutger Hauer became an international star thanks to his remarkable performance in this 1979 Dutch release, in which he plays one of four college buddies galvanized into action when the Nazis invade the Netherlands. This is an exceptional work; an exciting, suspenseful, and intelligent war-adventure film that is as rich in character and performance as it is in story and direction. In several languages and subtitled. Rated R for nudity, profanity, implied sex, and violence.

1979 165 minutes

SORROW AND THE PITY, THE

★★★★½

DIRECTOR: Marcel Ophüls
CAST: Documentary

This four-and-a-half-hour documentary about France during the Occupation is more than just cinema. It is a penetrating examination of the human condition. Director Marcel Ophüls edited fifty hours of interviews with people from all walks of life and newsreel footage from Germany, England, and France into a devastating masterpiece. Ophüls does not take a stance in this study of racial prejudice and political ambiguities in war-torn France; rather, he allows his subjects to paint a picture of confusion, commitment, fear, and courage. Instead of presenting a clear political statement, Ophüls makes the viewer painfully aware of the consequences of war by presenting it from all sides. Rated PG.

1970 B & W 260 minutes

SPECIAL DAY, A

★★★★

DIRECTOR: Ettore Scola
CAST: Sophia Loren, Marcello Mastroianni

Antonietta (Sophia Loren), a slovenly housewife, and Gabriele (Marcello Mastroianni), a depressed homosexual, meet in the spring of 1938—the same day Hitler arrives in Rome. Their experience together enriches but does not change the course of their lives. Escapes usual dramatics and contrivance of woman-meets-homosexual plots. In Italian, with English subtitles. No MPAA rating.

1977 106 minutes

SPETTERS

★★★★½

DIRECTOR: Paul Verhoeven
CAST: Hans Van Tongeren, Toon Agterberg, Renee Soutenduk, Marteen Boyer

A study of the dreams, loves, discoveries, and tragedies of six young people in modern-day Holland, this is yet another tough, uncompromising motion picture from Dutch director Paul Verhoeven (*Soldier of Orange*). Though the sex scenes are more graphic than anything we've ever had in a major American movie, *Spetters* is never exploitative. Instead, it captures the attitude of the young toward all aspects of life, resulting in a credible and rewarding film experience for open-minded adults. MPAA-unrated, it contains violence, profanity, nudity, and sex.

1980 115 minutes

SPIES

★★★★

DIRECTOR: Fritz Lang
CAST: Rudolph Klein-Rogge, Gerda Maurus, Willy Fritsch, Lupu Pick, Fritz Rasp

Thrilling, imaginative drama of the underworld and the dark doings of espionage agents is one of the finest of all such films and remains a classic of the genre as well as a terrific adventure movie. The camera moves in and out among the shadowy doings of the spies and their pursuers like a silent spider weaving all the components together. The final chase provides a fitting climax to this topflight entertainment from the great German director Fritz Lang. Silent.

1928 B & W 90 minutes

SPRING SYMPHONY

★

DIRECTOR: Peter Schamoni
CAST: Nastassja Kinski, Herbert Gronemeyer, Rolf Hoppe, Andre Heller, Bernhard Wicki

Spring Symphony is a routine presentation of the lives of German composer Robert Schumann and celebrated pianist Clara Wieck, who wooed and wed despite the objections of Clara's father. The film portrays emotion in fairy-tale fashion, simplistic and overstated. Nastassja Kinski, who has been fascinating in other films, is without intrigue as Clara. The music is the star of this show. Dubbed in English. Rated PG.

1984 102 minutes

STATE OF SEIGE

★★★½

DIRECTOR: Constantin Costa-Gavras
CAST: Yves Montand, O. E. Hasse, Renato Salvatori

This is a highly controversial but brilliant film about the kidnapping of an American A.I.D. official by left-wing guerrillas in Uruguay. The film follows step-by-step how U.S. aid is sent to fascist countries through the pretext of helping the economy and strengthening democracy. Strong action and flashback scenes make this film a winner. No MPAA rating.

1973 120 minutes

STATELINE MOTEL

★★

DIRECTOR: Maurizio Lucidi
CAST: Ursula Andress, Eli Wallach, Barbara Bach, Fabio Testi, Massimo Girotti

This Italian-made film involves a jewelry store robbery by a ruthless killer (Eli Wallach) and his handsome partner, Floyd (Fabio Testi). Floyd later becomes involved with Ursula Andress. When Wallach suspects a double-cross, he goes to the Stateline Motel to collect his jewels. Not much else to the film except the surprise ending featuring Barbara Bach. The film is dubbed and rated R for nudity, violence, sexual situations, and obscenities.

1975 87 minutes

STOLEN KISSES

★★★★★

DIRECTOR: François Truffaut
CAST: Jean-Pierre Leaud, Delphine Seyrig, Michel Lonsdale, Claude Jade, Harry Max, Daniel Ceccaldi

This is François Truffaut's third film in the continuing story about Antoine Doinel (Jean-Pierre Leaud) which began with *400 Blows*. Like the other films in the series, this work resembles Truffaut's autobiography as he romantically captures the awkwardness of Doinel and his encounters with women. This delightful comedy is often considered one of Truffaut's best movies. In French with English subtitles.

1968 90 minutes

STORMY WATERS

★★★

DIRECTOR: Jean Gremillon
CAST: Jean Gabin, Michele Morgan, Madeleine Renaud, Fernand Ledoux

Tough rescue-ship captain Jean Gabin braves stormy waters to save hauntingly beautiful Michele Morgan. They then have a passionate love affair every bit as tempestuous as the circumstances of their meeting. Fate intervenes to compel a poignant, exciting conclusion. This film is a fine example of French cinema at its pre–WWII zenith.

1941 75 minutes

STORY OF ADELE H, THE

★★★

DIRECTOR: François Truffaut

CAST: Isabelle Adjani, Bruce Robinson, Sylvia Marriott, Joseph Blatchley

This basically simple story of author Victor Hugo's daughter, who loves a soldier in vain, is surprisingly textured and intriguing. Slow, exquisite unfolding of many-layered love story is arresting and pictorially beautiful. Nicely done. Some adult situations. In French with English subtitles. Rated PG.

1975 97 minutes

STRIKE

★★★★

DIRECTOR: Sergei Eisenstein

CAST: Grigori Alexandrov, Maxim Strauch, Mikhail Gomarov, Alexander Antonov

Shot in a documentarylike style, this drama about a labor dispute during the czarist era was Russian director Sergei Eisenstein's first feature film. Advanced for its time and using techniques Eisenstein would perfect in his later masterpieces, *Strike* remains a remarkable achievement and still holds one's interest today. Silent.

1924 B & W 82 minutes

STROMBOLI

DIRECTOR: Roberto Rossellini

CAST: Ingrid Bergman, Mario Vitale, Renzo Cesana, Mario Spanza

This potboiler from the director of *Open City* is a brooding, sometimes boring movie about an attractive woman who marries a fisherman and attempts to adjust to the isolation and tedium of the life. Even screen beauty Ingrid Bergman (by this time married to Rossellini) couldn't salvage this film. Watch for the volcanic action at the end if you're still awake. Subtitled.

1950 B & W 81 minutes

SUBWAY

★★

DIRECTOR: Luc Besson

CAST: Isabelle Adjani, Christopher Lambert, Richard Bohringer, Jean-Pierre Bacri, Jean Reno, Michel Galabru, Jean Bouise

The stunning Isabelle Adjani (*The Story of Adele H*, *The Driver*) plays a young wife who becomes involved with a streetwise rogue played by Christopher Lambert (*Greystoke*). The plot is not very clear and the bad jokes don't help. Fast-paced action scenes keep the film interesting, but they all lead to nowhere. In French with English subtitles. Rated R for profanity and violence.

1985 110 minutes

SUGAR CANE ALLEY

★★★★★

DIRECTOR: Euzhan Paloy

CAST: Garry Cadenat, Darling Legitimus, Douta Seck, Joby Bernabe, Franisco Charles

Set in Martinque of the 1930s, this superb French import examines the lives led by black sugar cane plantation workers. Specifically, it focuses on the hopes and dreams of Jose (Garry Cadenat), an 11-year-old orphan with a brilliant mind, which just may be the key to his breaking the bonds of slavery. Lest the reader think *Sugar Cane Alley* is a depressing exposé of man's inhumanity to man, we should mention here that this motion picture, despite its setting, is a joyous celebration of life, love, and courage. In French with English subtitles. Unrated, the film has some scenes of slight violence.

1983 100 minutes

SUMMER

★★★★

DIRECTOR: Eric Rohmer

CAST: Marie Riviere, Lisa Heredia, Beatrice Romand, Rosette, Eric Hamm, Vanessa LeLeu, Vincent Gauthier

French director Eric Rohmer's fifth of his proposed six-part *Comedies and Proverbs*, *Summer* is the slight but emotionally resonant tale of Delphine (Marie Riviere), a Paris secretary whose vacation plans are suddenly ruined. Forced to come up with a quick alternate plan or else spend August in Paris, where only tourists and the very poor can be found, she ends up trying several locations and finally finds a magical truth that turns her disappointing life around. Like the previous films in the series, *Summer* requires a real commitment on the part of the viewer. It even seems boring—especially during the first third of the film when Rohmer is setting up his theme. Ultimately, his story captures your fancy and touches your heart. In French with English subtitles. Rated R for nudity and profanity.

1986 98 minutes

SUNDAY IN THE COUNTRY, A

★★★★

DIRECTOR: Bertrand Tavernier

CAST: Louis Ducreux, Michel Aumont, Sabine Azema, Genevieve Mnich, Monique Chaumette

Filmed like an Impressionist painting, this is a romantic look at French family life in pre-World War II France. Bertrand Tavernier won the best director prize at the 1984 Cannes Film Festival for this delightful drama. In French, with English subtitles. Rated G.

1984 94 minutes

SWANN IN LOVE

★★★★

DIRECTOR: Volker Schlondorff

CAST: Jeremy Irons, Ornella Muti, Alain Delon, Fanny Ardant, Marie-Christine Barrault

Slow-moving but fascinating film portrait of a Jewish aristocrat (Jeremy Irons) totally consumed by his romantic and sexual obsession with an ambitious French courtesan (Ornella Muti). It's definitely not for all tastes. However, those who can remember the overwhelming ache of first love may find it worth watching. Based on the first two volumes of Marcel Proust's *Remembrance of Things Past*. In French with English subtitles. Rated R for nudity and suggested sex.

1985 110 minutes

SWEPT AWAY

★★★

DIRECTOR: Lina Wertmuller

CAST: Giancarlo Giannini, Mariangela Melato

The full title is *Swept Away by an Unusual Destiny in the Blue Sea in August*, and what this Italian import addresses is a condescending, chic goddess who gets hers on a deserted island. In Italian with English subtitles. Rated R.

1975 116 minutes

SWORD OF DOOM

★★★

DIRECTOR: Kihachi Okamoto

CAST: Tatsuya Nakadai, Toshiro Mifune, Michiyo Aratama, Yuzo Kayama, Yoko Naito

Tatsuya Nakadei gives a fascinating performance as a brutal samurai, whose need to kill alienates even his once devoted father. Several stories are interwoven in this film, but, suprisingly, at least two are left unresolved at film's end. This will make it disappointing—and confusing—for all but the most devoted fans of Japanese action movies. And these folks will be pleased by the numerous fight scenes and a strong cameo appearance by Toshiro Mifune. In Japanese with English subtitles (which, for once, are easy to follow).

1967 122 minutes

SYLVIA AND THE PHANTOM

★★★★

DIRECTOR: Claude Autant-Lara
CAST: Odette Joyeux, Francoise Perier, Louise Salon, Julien Carette, Pierre Larquey, Jean Desailly, Jacques Tati, Marguerite Cassan

A delightful story concerning hosts and the fantasies of a young lady living with her family in a castle. As the story begins, we meet Sylvia on the eve of her sixteenth birthday and find that she fantasizes about the portrait of her grandmother's lover and the rumors that he haunts the castle. When her father (who it appears is dealing with dwindling finances) sells the painting to cut his losses, the ghost becomes a stronger presence in the home. In French, with English subtitles.

1950 97 minutes

TALL BLOND MAN WITH ONE BLACK SHOE, THE

★★★★

DIRECTOR: Yves Robert
CAST: Pierre Richard, Bernard Blier, Mireille Darc

If you're looking for an entertaining, easy-to-watch comedy, this is one of the best. Pierre Richard plays the bumbling blond man to hilarious perfection, especially when it comes to physical comedy. The story involves spies, murder, a mysterious sexy woman, and plenty of action. The real fun comes in watching Richard's reactions to it all. Highly recommended, but try to see the original version, with subtitles, not the dubbed version. Rated PG.

1972 90 minutes

TEN DAYS THAT SHOOK THE WORLD (OCTOBER)

★★★★

DIRECTOR: Sergei Eisenstein
CAST: Documentary

A loose depiction of the months between the February 1917 Russian Revolution against the Czar and the eventual triumph of the Bolsheviks in October of that year. This documentarylike film is considered one of the great silent classics by legendary director, Sergei Eisenstein. It lacks the emotional power of his *Strike* and *Battleship Potemkin,* because the narrative is often interrupted by political satire and symbolic imagery that can best be appreciated by those steeped in Russian history. If for no other reason, the stunning re-creation of the storming of the Czar's Winter Palace makes this movie worth watching. Silent.

1928 B & W 92 minutes

TENDRES COUSINES

★★

DIRECTOR: David Hamilton
CAST: Thierry Tevini, Anja Shute

Okay soft-core sex comedy about the amorous adventures of two pubescent cousins. Directed by David Hamilton (*Bilitis*), this film has the problems innate in most movies of this type: It lacks the purpose and power of serious films and the explicit scenes of their hard-core cousins. In French, with English subtitles. Rated R.

1980 90 minutes

THAT OBSCURE OBJECT OF DESIRE

★★★★½

DIRECTOR: Luis Buñuel
CAST: Fernando Rey, Carole Bouquet, Angela Molina, Pieral, Julien Bertheau

Luis Buñuel's last film cunningly combines erotic teasing, wit, and social comment. Mathieu (Fernando Rey) is a 50-year-old man who falls hopelessly in love with a young woman. Buñuel, a master of surrealism, tantalizes the viewer by casting two actresses to play the heroine and a third actress to do the voice of both. Conchita, who is part tramp (Carole Bouquet) and part virgin (Angela Molina) torments and humiliates Mathieu. The entire film is seen in flashbacks as he confesses his dilemma to a dwarf psychologist (Pieral). Rated R for profanity and nudity.

1977 100 minutes

THERESE

★★★★½

DIRECTOR: Alain Cavalier
CAST: Catherine Mouchet, Helene Alexandridis, Aurore Priett, Sylvie Habault, Clemence Massart

French director Alain Cavalier's breathtakingly beautiful *Therese* is the story of St. Theresa of Lisieux, who entered a Carmelite nunnery in the late nineteenth century at the age of 15 and lived there for eight years until she died of tuberculosis. She was declared a saint by Pope Pius XI in 1925, twenty-eight years after her death. Rather than a morose chronicle of her brief life, this exquisite motion picture is a celebration of her overpowering love for Jesus Christ and delight in doing the simplest of tasks. Winner of the jury prize at the 1986 Cannes Film Festival, *Therese* is a true work of art with scenes that look as if they were plucked from superb Renaissance paintings. In French with English subtitles.

1986 90 minutes

THERESE AND ISABELLE

★½

DIRECTOR: Radley Metzger
CAST: Essy Persson, Anna Gael, Barbara Laage, Anne Vernon

Two French schoolgirls keep their growing sexual attraction for each other a secret until they take a holiday together. Considered daring at the time of its release, this adult story takes the form of a flashback as one of the girls revisits the locations where she and her lover met and goes over the actions in her mind. Not too bad, but nothing really new. Unrated, but this might earn an R rating today because of nudity and story content. In French, with English subtitles.

1968 102 minutes

THREE BROTHERS

★★★★★

DIRECTOR: Francesco Rosi
CAST: Philippe Noiret, Michele Placido, Vittorio Mezzogiorno, Charles Vanel

Francesco Rosi (*Eboli*, *Bizet's Carmen*) directed this thoughtful, emotionally powerful movie that details the effect of a mother's recent death on her family. In the press kit for the movie, Rosi states that "through the story of three brothers and their family, I have tried to speak about all of us, our life, death, loneliness, the old and eternal values that we all carry within ourselves and the forces which threaten them; but of our need for hope and trust as well." And he does so eloquently, with great insight and compassion. Philippe Noiret (*Dear Inspector*), Michele Placido, and Vittorio Mezzogiorno play the title roles. Unrated, the film has a few scenes of violence. In Italian with English subtitles.

1980 113 minutes

THREE MEN AND A CRADLE

★★★★

DIRECTOR: Coline Serreau
CAST: Roland Giraud, Michel Boujenah, André Dussolier, Philipe Leroy Beulieu, Gwendoline Mourlet

In this sweet-natured character study from France, three high-living bachelors become the guardians of a baby girl through a series of misunderstandings. In addition to turning their lifestyles inside out, she forces them to confront their values—with heartwarming results. Meanwhile, a favor for a friend puts the trio at madcap odds with crooks and cops. Rated PG for profanity and nudity. In French with English subtitles.

1985 105 minutes

THREEPENNY OPERA, THE

★★★★

DIRECTOR: G. W. Pabst

CAST: Rudolph Forster, Lotte Lenya, Reinhold Schunzel, Carola Neher

Classic gangster musical features mob leader Rudolph Forster (alias Mack the Knife), his moll Lotte Lenya, and the hordes of the underworld as the king of the beggars joins forces with the gang chief to take control of their city and what may lie beyond. Their third partner? The police, of course. This Bertolt Brecht satire (with music by Kurt Weill), although not too popular with the Nazis or their predecessors, is always a favorite with the audience and has been filmed under its original title at least twice and in many subsequent guises.

1931 B & W 113 minutes

THRONE OF BLOOD

★★★★★

DIRECTOR: Akira Kurosawa

CAST: Toshiro Mifune, Isuzu Yamada, Minoru Chiaki, Akira Kubo, Takamoru Sasaki, Yoichi Tachikoiwa, Takashi Shimura

Japanese director Akira Kurosawa's retelling of *Macbeth* may be the best film adaptation of Shakespeare ever made. Kurosawa uses the medium to present Shakespeare's themes in visual images. And what images they are! When Birnam Wood literally comes to Dunsinane, it is a truly great moment you would have believed could only happen in the limitless landscapes of a dream. In Japanese with English subtitles.

1957 B & W 105 minutes

TILL MARRIAGE DO US PART

★★★

DIRECTOR: Luigi Comencini

CAST: Laura Antonelli

Although a slight Italian sex comedy, its star, Laura Antonelli, is as delicious as ever. It's a treat for her fans only. Rated R.

1974 97 minutes

TIME STANDS STILL

★★½

DIRECTOR: Peter Gothar

CAST: Ben Barenholtz, Albert Schwartz, Michael S. Landes, Istvan Znamenak, Henrik Pauer, Sandor Soth, Aniko Ivan, Agi Kakassy, Lajos Oze

This Hungarian export dwells so much on the "art for art's sake" credo that it nearly destroys some of the life the film tries to depict. The cinematography is stunning at first and really drives home what the filmmaker sees as Budapest in the early 1960s, but after a half-hour, the blue-and-red-tinted scenes grow tiresome. *Time Stands Still* is about restless youths at the threshold of adulthood in Hungary. The film is presented in the original language with subtitles. Not rated, but the equivalent of an R for sex, nudity, and language.

1982 99 minutes

TIN DRUM, THE

★★★★½

DIRECTOR: Volker Schlondorff

CAST: David Bennent, Mario Adorf, Angela Winkler, Daniel Olbrychski

This is the film version of Günter Grass's bizarre tale of three-year-old Oskar, who stops growing as the Nazis rise to power in Germany. He expresses his outrage by banging on a tin drum. This unique German film has a disturbing dreamlike quality, while its visuals are alternately startling and haunting. It's fascinating. *The Tin Drum* won an Academy Award for Best Foreign Film. In German, with English subtitles. Rated R for nudity and gore.

1979 142 minutes

TONI

★★★★

DIRECTOR: Jean Renoir
CAST: Charles Blavette, Edouard Delmont, Max Dalban, Jenny Helia

Of the Italian neorealists, only Luchino Visconti is known to have been aware of this film before 1950, but in story, style, and mood, *Toni* anticipates the methods of the future master postwar directors. The film is direct, spare, simple, and touching. A love quadrangle, a murder, a trial, an execution, a confession—these are the everyday elements director Jean Renoir chose to show "without makeup," as objectively as possible. No studio sets were used, and many citizens of the town where *Toni* was shot filled out the cast. Renoir was proud of his film (something of an experiment), and it holds up well. In French with English subtitles.

1934 B & W 90 minutes

TOPSY TURVY

★★

DIRECTOR: Edward Fleming
CAST: Lisbet Dahl, Ebbe Rode, Axel Strobye, Elin Reimer, Lars Bom, Nonny Sand, Thomas Alling

A conservative young man finds his world turned topsy-turvy when a swinging neighbor girl takes him on vacation in this European sex comedy, dubbed into English. The dubbing is fair to good. The humor tends to the European, and some may not find it to their liking. The main subject of the humor is sex. and at times it is very funny. The locations are beautiful, but the acting is uneven. Those who enjoy sex comedies will probably like this film.

1984 90 minutes

TRIUMPH OF THE WILL

★★★★

DIRECTOR: Leni Riefenstahl
CAST: Documentary

World-renowned German documentary of the rise of Hitler's Third Reich is a masterpiece of propaganda and remains a chilling testament to the insanity that can lurk in great art. Director Leni Riefenstahl created a powerful and noble image of a German empire that was already threatening Europe and would eventually engulf the world in a devastating war. Riefenstahl's editing of this massive paean to the grandiose dreams of Adolph Hitler is a textbook lesson to future filmmakers, and the footage used is some of the most stunning political persuasion any power-seeking potentate ever had access to. Along with Riefenstahl's *Olympia*, this film qualifies as an unquestioned classic of its kind.

1935 B & W 110 minutes

TWIST AND SHOUT

★★★★½

DIRECTOR: Bille August
CAST: Adam Tonsberg, Lars Simonsen, Camilla Soeberg, Ulrikke Juul Bondo, Thomas Nielsen, Lane Lindroff, Arne Hansen

Danish director Bille August's *Twist and Shout* could be described as *American Graffiti* meets *Ordinary People*. The film, which was more appropriately titled *Faith, Hope and Love* in its native country, mixes the headiness of first love with the tragedy of growing adult awareness in its coming-of-age story about two friends, Bjorn (Adam Tonsberg), a drummer with a pseudo-Beatles group called the Sea Lions, and Erik (Lars Simonsen), a quiet sort with severe problems at home, circa 1964. Featuring an outstanding supporting performance by Camilla Soeberg, it is a true-to-life movie that will leave no viewer unmoved. Unrated, the film has profanity, nudity, and suggested sex. In Danish with English subtitles.

1986 99 minutes

TWO ENGLISH GIRLS

★★★★½

DIRECTOR: François Truffaut

CAST: Jean-Pierre Léaud, Kiki Markham, Stacey Tendeter

Twenty-two minutes were recently added to make this very civilized and rewarding film actually as long as it always had seemed. Thanks to the skills of a mellowed master director and the cinematography of Nestor Almendros, *Two English Girls* is quite worth the patience sometimes needed. Set in pre–World War I Europe and based on the Henri-Pierre Roché novel (his only other being *Jules et Jim,* the modern flip-side of the arrangement here), Truffaut's studied work has Frenchman Léaud the object of two English sisters' desire. Whereas the *Jules and Jim* ménage à trois explored the intolerable extremes of freedom, *Two English Girls* concentrates on the damage that Victorianism wreaked upon the European spirit, and on the consequences of trying to rid oneself of such stultifying repression. In French with English subtitles.

1972 130 minutes

TWO OF US, THE

★★★½

DIRECTOR: Claude Berri

CAST: Alain Cohen, Michel Simon, Luce Fabiole, Roger Carel

This story of generational and religious differences joins an 8-year-old Jewish boy (Alain Cohen) and an irascible Catholic grandpa (Michel Simon) for some very warm and funny performances. The boy is fleeing Nazi-occupied France in 1944 and comes to live with the anti-Semitic old man who is a family friend's relative. As the boy has difficulties adjusting to school and his new home, a deep relationship develops between the two. Beautifully acted, this is a different kind of movie for the family to enjoy with their older children. In French with English subtitles.

1968 86 minutes

UGETSU

★★★★½

DIRECTOR: Kenji Mizoguchi

CAST: Machiko Kyo, Masayuki Mori, Sakae Ozawa

Set in sixteenth-century Japan, this film follows the lives of two Japanese peasants as their quest for greed and ambition brings disaster upon their families. There is a fine blending of action and comedy in this ghostly tale. In Japanese, with English subtitles.

1953 94 minutes

UMBERTO D

★★★★★

DIRECTOR: Vittorio De Sica

CAST: Carlo Battisti, Maria Pia Casilio, Lina Gennari

With the constant threat of cuts in the Social Security System, *Umberto D* seems to be as poignant now as when it was initially released. Quite simply, the plot centers upon a retired civil servant trying to maintain some sort of dignity and life for himself and his dog on his meager government pension. The film is a sordid, unromanticized view of the human condition in modern Italy. It is agonizingly candid and almost unbearably heartbreaking. This is even more amazing considering the fact that Carlo Battisti (Umberto D) had never acted before. A Vittorio De Sica masterpiece that should be shown to every government employee and should not be missed by anyone. In Italian with English subtitles.

1955 B & W 89 minutes

UMBRELLAS OF CHERBOURG, THE

★★★★

DIRECTOR: Jacques Demy
CAST: Catherine Deneuve, Nino Castelmuovo, Marc Michel, Ellen Farnen

Simply the most romantic film to come from France in the 1960s. Catherine Deneuve made her first popular appearance, and we've been madly in love with her ever since. Simple story—boy meets girl—but played against a luxuriously photographed backdrop. Exquisite score from Michel Legrand. Watch this with somebody you love.

1964 91 minutes

UN SINGE EN HIVER (A MONKEY IN WINTER)

★★½

DIRECTOR: Henri Verneuil
CAST: Jean Gabin, Jean-Paul Belmondo, Suzanne Flon, Paul Frankeur, Noel Roquevert

Alcoholic Jean Gabin vows to swear off if he and his wife survive the bombing of their village during World War II. They do, and he does. Years pass. A young version of Gabin arrives and rekindles the older man's memories of drink and dreams, fostering regret and making him feel he has lost the golden opportunity of his youth. The pair team up to tear up the village on one last binge. Gabin, while past his prime, is nonetheless magnetic and superb. In French, with English subtitles. Originally released in the U.S. as *A Monkey in Winter*. Marred by murky photography.

1962 B & W 105 minutes

VAGABOND

★★★½

DIRECTOR: Agnes Varda
CAST: Sandrine Bonnaire, Macha Meril, Stephane Freiss, Marthe Jarnais

French New Wave writer-director Agnes Varda's dispassionate but beautifully photographed "investigation"—via flashbacks—of a young misfit's meandering trek through the French countryside features a superb performance by Sandrine Bonnaire. Her *Vagabond* is presented as rude, lazy, ungrateful, and therefore unsympathetic, which makes it difficult for the viewer to become completely involved. Yet in some subliminal way the film draws one into the alienation that fuels this outsider's journey into death. Although fictional, the film tends to resemble a documentary. In French with English subtitles. Rated R for profanity and suggested sex.

1986 105 minutes

VAMPYR

★★★★★

DIRECTOR: Carl Dreyer
CAST: Julian West, Sybille Schmitz, Maurice Schultz, Rena Mandel, Jan Hieronimko

Director Carl Dreyer believed that horror is best implied. By relying on the viewer's imagination, he created a classic film. A young man arrives at a very bizarre inn, where he discovers an unconscious woman who had been attacked by a vampire in the form of an old woman. The young man finds a book on vampire legends. By following the instructions in the book, he succeeds in destroying the old woman and her evil assistant. This outstanding film is one of the few serious films of the macabre.

1931 B & W 68 minutes

VARIETY

★★★★★

DIRECTOR: E. A. Dupont

CAST: Emil Jannings, Lya de Putti, Warwick Ward, Maly Delshaft

A milestone of cinema art, this is a brilliant film. It tells a simple, tragic tale of a famous and conceited vaudeville acrobat whose character flaw is cowardice; a clever and entirely unscrupulous girl; and a trusting waterfront circus boss—made a fool of by love—who murders because of that hollow love. The cast is incredible, the cinematography superb. It was from the film, made in post–World War I Germany, that U.S. technicians learned what makes a film art and what can be achieved with camera and lighting. A great film, unjustly left off most top-ten lists. Silent.

1926 B & W 104 minutes

VIRGIN SPRING, THE

★★★★★

DIRECTOR: Ingmar Bergman

CAST: Max von Sydow, Birgitta Pettersson, Gunnel Lindblom, Birgitta Valberg

Ingmar Bergman's scenario is based on a fourteenth-century Swedish legend: Accompanied by her jealous older stepsister, a young girl is raped and killed while on a journey to her church—and the three killers make the mistake of seeking shelter with the parents. Bergman is absolutley masterful in his attention to detail and mood; to the evocation of a long-ago and rather mystical era; to his direction of the innocent girl (Birgitta Pettersson), the evil sister (Gunnel Lindblom), and the grief-stricken and vengeful father (Max von Sydow). Step by step he leads us to accept completely the film's glorious, miraculous finale. Won an Oscar for best foreign language film. In Swedish, with English subtitles.

1960 B & W 87 minutes

VIRIDIANA

★★★★★

DIRECTOR: Luis Buñuel

CAST: Silvia Pinal, Fernando Rey, Francisco Rabal, Margarita Lozano

Angelic Viridiana (Silvia Pinal) visits her uncle (Fernando Rey) prior to taking her religious vows. Uncle Jaime is overcome by her resemblance to his wife, who died on their wedding night, and has his niece drugged. Unable to rape her, he nevertheless tells her he has and then hangs himself with a jump rope. This is just the first reel! The film was an amazing cause célèbre at the time: the script for the first fictional film Buñuel had directed in his native Spain had been approved and the film "in the can" when the authorities got wind of its subversive nature. Despite the government's massive efforts to confiscate all copies of the film, one or two had made their way to France, as had Buñuel, and *Viridiana*—much to Spain's and the Catholic Church's consternation—won the Palme d'Or at Cannes. In Spanish with English subtitles.

1961 B & W 90 minutes

VOLPONE

★★★★

DIRECTOR: Maurice Tourneur

CAST: Harry Baur, Louis Jouvet

Filmed in 1939, this superb screen version of Shakespeare contemporary Ben Jonson's classic play of greed was not released until after World War II, by which time star Harry Baur, a titan of French cinema, was mysteriously dead, having been, it is supposed, erased by the Nazis in 1941. Aided by his avaricious and parasitic servant, Mosca, Volpone, an old Venetian, pretends he is dying and convinces his greedy friends that each of them is his heir. To buy preference, the friends shower the conniving faker with rich gifts. Each expects to get his gift and more back when the will is read. Not satisfied with their success, Volpone and Mosca spin a web of lies until they themselves are caught. In French with English subtitles.

1939 B & W 80 minutes

VOULEZ VOUS DANSER AVEC MOI? (WILL YOU DANCE WITH ME?)

DIRECTOR: Michel Boisrone
CAST: Brigitte Bardot, Henri Vidal, Dawn Addams, Noel Roquevert, Dario Moreno

This is another interminable Brigitte Bardot film, one in which a marital squabble lands her in the center of a murder investigation. It's supposed to be flirtatious, cute, and light-hearted, but it's just junky. Frankie and Annette movies are better than this. In French with English subtitles.

1959 89 minutes

VOYAGE EN BALLON (A.K.A. STOWAWAY TO THE STARS)

★★★

DIRECTOR: Albert Lamorisse
CAST: Andrè Gille, Maurice Baquet, Pascal Lamorisse

This endearing little French film is somewhat of a follow-up to *The Red Balloon* (also directed by Albert Lamorisse and starring son Pascal, this time allowing that small boy genuinely to ascend into the clouds—in the basket of a hot-air balloon). Unfortunately, Lamorisse *père* is a far better director than writer, and this film lacks the drama needed to sustain its greater length. The result resembles a documentary travelogue—all the beautiful sights of France—until the final 15 mintues, when boy and balloon take off without his grandfather's guiding hand at the controls. The amusing antics of co-star Maurice Baquet (somewhat of a French Cantinflas) relieve the tedium somewhat, but youngsters still are apt to get pretty restless. Unrated; suitable for family viewing.

1959 82 minutes

WAGES OF FEAR, THE

★★★★

DIRECTOR: Henri-Georges Clouzot
CAST: Yves Montand, Charles Vanel, Peter Van Eyck, Vera Clouzot, Folco Lulli, William Tubbs

This masterpiece of suspense pits four seedy and destitute men against the challenge of driving two nitroglycerin-laden trucks over crude and treacherous Central American mountain roads to quell a monstrous oil well fire. Incredible risk and numbing fear ride along as the drivers, goaded by high wages, cope with dilemma after dilemma. Be ready to sweat. This one really is a cliff-hanger. In French with English subtitles.

1953 B & W 105 minutes

WANTON CONTESSA, THE

★★★★½

DIRECTOR: Luchino Visconti
CAST: Alida Valli, Farley Granger, Massimo Girotti

Luchino Visconti—aristocrat by birth, Marxist by conviction—offers one of the lushest and most expressive Italian films ever made (known there as *Senso*). The large-budget spectacular is operatic in scope and look. The story, too, is an opera romance. Venice, 1866: Patriots are conspiring against the occupying Austrians; a countess (the alluring Alida Valli) finds herself passionately in love with a young Austrian officer (Farley Granger), forsaking family and patriotic allegiances; but, of course, the officer turns out to be a coward and a cad. Visconti seemed to have turned his back on neorealism, embracing neoromanticism, confounding critics and audiences. But this film's reputation has grown steadily, and it is now something of a classic. Dubbed in English (with dialogue by Tennessee Williams and Paul Bowles).

1954 120 minutes

WHEN FATHER WAS AWAY ON BUSINESS

★★★

DIRECTOR: Emir Kusturica
CAST: Moreno D'e Bartolli, Miki Manojlovic, Mirfana Karanovic

Seen through the eyes of a young boy, the film deals with the sudden disappearance of a father from a family because of a few minor yet commonly held opinions of the party in power and the party in disfavor. Tension mounts when it becomes clear that it is the father's brother-in-law who turned him in and had him sent to a work camp. The story is touchingly realistic and able to carry the audience step by step through this Yugoslavian drama. It is not surprising that the film received the Gold Palm at the 1985 Cannes Film Festival. Rated R for sex and nudity. In Slavic with English subtitles.

1985 144 minutes

WHERE THE GREEN ANTS DREAM

★★★★

DIRECTOR: Werner Herzog
CAST: Bruce Spence, Wandjuk Marika, Roy Marika, Ray Barrett, Norman Kaye, Colleen Clifford, Nicolas Lathouris, Gary Williams, Trevor Orford

Another stark, yet captivating vision from perhaps the most popular director of current German cinema. The film is basically an ecological tug of war between progress and tradition, namely uranium mining interests against aborigines and their practices. The basic theme is nothing new, but Herzog's treatment, and in particular the film's quirky elements, is nothing short of fascinating.

1984 100 minutes

WHITE ROSE, THE

★★

DIRECTOR: Michael Verhoeven
CAST: Lena Stolze, Wulf Kessler, Martin Benrath, Werner Stocke

The White Rose is based on a true story about a group of youths in wartime Germany who revolted against Hitler by printing and distributing subversive leaflets to the public. All of the young actors are good, especially Lena Stolze, who plays the main protagonist. *The White Rose* is a competent thriller, but nothing raises it from the ordinary. In German.

1983 108 minutes

WIFEMISTRESS

★★★½

DIRECTOR: Marco Vicario
CAST: Marcello Mastroianni, Annie Belle, Laura Antonelli, Leonard Mann, Gaston Muschin, William Berger

Marcello Mastroianni stars as a husband in hiding, and Laura Antonelli as his repressed wife. When Mastroianni is falsely accused of murder, he hides out in a building across the street from his own home. His wife, not knowing where he is, begins to relive his sexual escapades. There are some comic moments as the former philandering husband must deal with his wife's new sexual freedom. Nudity and sex are included in this Italian film.

1977 110 minutes

WILD STRAWBERRIES

★★★★

DIRECTOR: Ingmar Bergman

CAST: Victor Sjöström, Ingrid Thulin, Bibi Andersson, Gunner Bjorstrand, Folk Sundquist, Bjorn Bjelvenstam

This film is probably Ingmar Bergman's least ambiguous. Superbly photographed and acted, the film tells the story of an elderly professor facing old age and reviewing his life's disappointments. The use of flashbacks is very effective in this film.

1957 B & W 90 minutes

WINTER LIGHT

★★★

DIRECTOR: Ingmar Bergman

CAST: Ingrid Thulin, Gunnar Bjorstrand, Max von Sydow, Gunnel Lindblom

Second film in director Bergman's "faith" trilogy (it follows *Through a Glass Darkly* and precedes *The Silence*) centers on a disillusioned priest who attempts to come to grips with his religion and his position in the inner workings of the church. Not an easy film to watch. This honest effort to explore the psyche of a cleric and answer the questions that have troubled the "spiritual" side of man for centuries is a thoughtful, incisive drama with great performances that inveigles the audience into participating in this quest for truth and the answers of life. In Swedish with English subtitles.

1962 B & W 80 minutes

WITCHCRAFT THROUGH THE AGES (HAXAN)

★★★½

DIRECTOR: Benjamin Christensen

CAST: Maren Pedersen, Clara Pontoppidan, Elith Pio, Oscar Stribolt, Benjamin Christensen, John Andersen, Astrid Holm, Poul Roumert, Alice O'Fredericks

After almost seventy years of notoriety, this controversial film is still unique as one of the most blasphemous and outrageous movies of all time. Envisioned by director Benjamin Christensen as a study of black magic, witchcraft, and demonology from the Middle Ages to the present, this silent Scandinavian epic fluctuates between lecture material and incredibly vivid footage that gave the censors ulcers back in the early 1920s. This film might not be acceptable to all family members and is not recommended for impressionable children. There is a version available with William Burroughs reading the narration; other prints are captioned and subtitled in English.

1921 B & W 82 minutes

WOMAN IN FLAMES, A

★★★★

DIRECTOR: Robert Van Ackeren

CAST: Gudrun Landgrebe, Mathieu Carriere

A male and a female prostitute fall in love and decide to set up shop in the same household, insisting that their business trysts will not interfere with their personal relationship. They do. At times steamy, intense, and provocative. If erotic drama and bizarre twists are your fancy, this should be your film. Rated R for sexual situations and language.

1984 104 minutes

WOMAN IN THE MOON (A.K.A. GIRL IN THE MOON; BY ROCKET TO THE MOON)

★★★

DIRECTOR: Fritz Lang
CAST: Gerda Maurus, Willy Fritsch, Fritz Rasp, Klaus Pohl, Gustav von Waggenheim

Fritz Lang's last silent film is actually a futuristic melodrama written by his wife and collaborator, Thea von Harbou, and moves along at a slow pace. Although much of the action (what there is of it) takes place on the moon, (and is obviously shot on indoor sets) this film remains stuck to a story that could have taken place just as easily on Earth. Hitler, who greatly admired Fritz Lang's work, was supposed to have studied the rocket designs in this film and incorporated them into his own weapon and flight plans, modeling his "V" rockets after them. Though not as popular as his earlier *Metropolis, Die Frau im Mond* (the original title of this film) has always been admired by science-fiction aficionados for Lang's imaginative visual sense, not the content of the story. German, silent.

1929 B & W 115 minutes

WOMAN NEXT DOOR, THE

★★★★½

DIRECTOR: François Truffaut
CAST: Gerard Depardieu, Fanny Ardant, Henri Garcin, Michele Baumgartner, Veronique Silver

François Truffaut is on record as one of the greatest admirers of Alfred Hitchcock, and the influence shows in his gripping, well-made film about guilt, passion, and the growing influence of a small sin that grows. In French with English subtitles. MPAA unrated but contains nudity and violence.

1981 106 minutes

WORLD OF APU, THE

★★★★

DIRECTOR: Satyajit Ray
CAST: Soumitra Chatterjee, Shamila Tagore, Alok Charkravarty, Swapan Mukherji

This is the concluding part of director Satyajit Ray's famed *Apu* trilogy covering the life and growth of a young man in India. In this last film, Apu marries and helps bring life into the world himself, completing the cycle amid realizations about himself and his limitations in this world. This movie and its predecessors form a beautiful tapestry of existence in a different culture and were among the most influential of all Indian films for many years. In Bengalese, with English subtitles.

1959 B & W 103 minutes

YOJIMBO

★★★★½

DIRECTOR: Akira Kurosawa
CAST: Toshiro Mifune, Eijiro Tono

Viewed from different perspectives, *Yojimbo* ("bodyguard") is: the most devastating comedy ever made; Kurosawa's parody of the American western; or his satire on the United States and Soviet Union's achieving peace through nuclear proliferation. Toshiro Mifune, an unemployed samurai in nineteenth-century Japan, sells his services to two rival merchants, each with killer gangs that are tearing the town apart. Both groups of thugs are efficiently and systematically eliminated. The film is boisterous—*lots* of bones crunching and samurai swords flashing and slashing—and exuberant. It is a rare Japanese film that is accessible to a broad spectrum of Americans. (Remade by Sergio Leone as *A Fistful of Dollars*.) No rating, but very violent.

1961 B & W 110 minutes

YOL

★★★½

DIRECTOR: Serif Goren

CAST: Tarik Akin, Serif Sezer, Halil Ergun, Heral Orhonsoy, Necmettin Cobanoglu

Winner of the Grand Prix at the Cannes Film Festival, this work, by Turkish filmmaker and political prisoner Yilmaz Gurney, follows several inmates of a minimum-security prison who are granted a few days' leave, telling their stories in parallel scenes. Although Gurney—who smuggled instructions out of prison to his trusted assistants, then escaped from prison and edited the film—was hailed at Cannes for creating an eloquent protest against suppression and totalitarian government, *Yol* is more of a study in slavery of the women they dominate, humiliate, torture, and even murder. Unrated, the film has violence and suggested sex.

1982 111 minutes

Z

★★★★

DIRECTOR: Constantin Costa-Gavras

CAST: Yves Montand, Irene Papas, Jean-Louis Trintignant, Charles Denner, Georges Geret, Jacques Perrin, François Périer, Marcel Bozzuffi

Director Costa-Gavras (*Missing*) first explored political corruption in this taut French thriller. Yves Montand plays a political leader who is assassinated. Based on a true story. Academy Award for best foreign film. Well worth a try. No rating, with some violence and coarse language.

1969 127 minutes

ZERO FOR CONDUCT

★★★★½

DIRECTOR: Jean Vigo

CAST: Jean Daste, Robert le Flon, Louis Lefebvre, Constantin Kelber, Gerard De Bedarieux

This unique fantasy about the rebellion of a group of young boys in a French boarding school is told from the point of view of the students and provides perhaps the purest picture in the history of cinema of what authority appears to be to young minds. Shot from the angle that a youth would view things from and slowed down to present a dreamlike picture, this allegorical tale depicts the boys of the school as inmates and incisively illustrates their frustrations and suppression at the hands of the adult schoolmasters, who force them to obey rules and conventions that have no meaning to them. This all too short gem was sadly one of only four films made by terminally ill director Jean Vigo, who was to die the year following its release at the age of 29. Banned across the Continent when first released, this 50-year-old film provided much of the storyline for Lindsay Anderson's 1969 update *If...* starring Malcolm McDowell, and has continued to delight audiences at colleges and film societies. In French with English subtitles.

1933 B & W 44 minutes

ABOMINABLE DR. PHIBES, THE

★★★½

DIRECTOR: Robert Fuest

CAST: Vincent Price, Joseph Cotten, Hugh Griffith, Virginia North, Terry-Thomas

A stylish horror film directed by Robert Fuest, this features Vincent Price in one of his best latter-day roles as a man disfigured in a car wreck taking revenge on those he considers responsible for the death of his wife. Rated PG.

1971 93 minutes

AGAINST ALL ODDS (KISS AND KILL, BLOOD OF FU MANCHU)

★

DIRECTOR: Jess (Jesus) Franco

CAST: Christopher Lee, Richard Greene, Tsai Chin, Shirley Eaton

Next-to-last entry in the low-budget series that got worse with each outing. The evil Fu Manchu hatches another dastardly plan for world domination. This time he saturates ten beautiful slave girls with a deadly poison and sends them out to kiss his enemies to death. The stars of the film disappear for long stretches, no doubt to keep their fees down. A complete bore. Believe it or not, three of these were filmed in one year. The dialogue was postdubbed, so everyone is a bit out of sync. The film print is dirty, scratchy, and fuzzy. Don't be misled by the picture of the topless girl on the cassette box. It was taken from the foreign version of the film, not this one. Rated PG.

1968 93 minutes

ALICE, SWEET ALICE (COMMUNION AND HOLY TERROR)

★★

DIRECTOR: Alfred Sole

CAST: Brooke Shields, Tom Signorelli, Louisa Horton, Paula E. Sheppard, Mildred Clinton, Lillian Roth

A 12-year-old girl goes on a chopping spree. No, it's not Brooke Shields. She only has a small role in this, her first film. But after the success of *Pretty Baby* the following year, the distributor changed the title, gave Brooke top billing, and rereleased this uninteresting thriller. Rated R for violence.

1977 96 minutes

ALIEN PREY

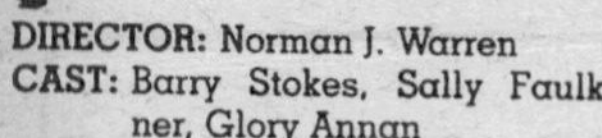

DIRECTOR: Norman J. Warren
CAST: Barry Stokes, Sally Faulkner, Glory Annan

This is not just another science-fiction/horror alien film. This savage alien is on a protein mission. Unfortunately the vegetarian dinner served up by his two lesbian hosts does not satisfy him. This film contains sexual and cannibalistic scenes, making it unsuitable for the squeamish. Unrated.

1984 85 minutes

ALISON'S BIRTHDAY

★★½

DIRECTOR: Ian Coughlan
CAST: Joanne Samuel, Lou Brown, Bunny Brooke, John Bluthal, Vincent Ball

A slow but interesting Australian horror story involving curses and possession. A young girl is told by her father's ghost to leave home before her nineteenth birthday, but as you may guess, she's summoned back days before the big day, and things get nasty. Not only is the acting tight, but if a Gothic setting can be transplanted to suburbia, then it happens here.

1984 99 minutes

ALLIGATOR

★★★½

DIRECTOR: Lewis Teague
CAST: Robert Forster, Michael Gazzo, Robin Riker, Perry Lang, Jack Carter, Bart Braverman, Henry Silva, Dean Jagger

The wild imagination of screenwriter John Sayles (writer-director of *Return of the Secaucus Seven* and *Brother From Another Planet*) invests this comedy-horror film with wit and style. It features Robert Forster as a cop tracking down a giant alligator. It's good, unpretentious fun, but you have to be on your toes to catch all the gags (be sure to read the hilarious graffiti). Rated R.

1980 94 minutes

ALONE IN THE DARK

DIRECTOR: Jack Sholder
CAST: Jack Palance, Donald Pleasence, Martin Landau, Dwight Schultz, Deborah Hedwall, Erland Van Lidth

The inmates of a New Jersey mental institution (played by Jack Palance, Martin Landau, and Erland Van Lidth) break out during a blackout (with a little help from psychiatrist Donald Pleasence) to terrorize a doctor and his family. No matter how quickly they're all killed, it isn't soon enough. Rated R.

1982 92 minutes

AMERICAN WEREWOLF IN LONDON, AN

★★★½

DIRECTOR: John Landis
CAST: David Naughton, Jenny Agutter, Griffin Dunne

This is one of the better horror films to come out in many a moon—pun intended. Director John Landis weaves humor, violence, and the classic horror elements of suspense in the tale of the two American travelers who find more than they bargained for on the English moors. A great soundtrack, featuring Van Morrison and Creedence Clearwater Revival, adds greatly to the total effect. Rated R for violence, nudity, and gore.

1981 97 minutes

AMITYVILLE HORROR, THE

DIRECTOR: Stuart Rosenberg
CAST: James Brolin, Margot Kidder, Rod Steiger

A better title for this turgid mish-mash would be *The Amityville Bore*. Based on a supposedly true story, it's a hackneyed, unbelievable horror flick. Avoid it. Rated R.

1979 117 minutes

AMITYVILLE II: THE POSSESSION

★★½

DIRECTOR: Damiano Damiani
CAST: Burt Young, Rutianya Alda, James Olson, Moses Gunn

Okay, so it's not a horror classic. But thanks to tight pacing, skillful special effects, and fine acting, *Amityville II: The Possession* is a fairly suspenseful flick. And—thank goodness—this "prequel" is much better than *Amityville Horror.* Preceding the events in the latter film, a family of six moves into the eerie Long Island house, and the eldest son winds up being possessed. James Olson (the priest who tries to exorcise the house) and Burt Young (the boy's father) head the cast. Rated R for violence, implied sex, light profanity, and adult themes.

1982 104 minutes

AMITYVILLE III: THE DEMON

★

DIRECTOR: Richard Fleischer
CAST: Tony Roberts, Robert Jay, Candy Clark, Tess Harper, Lori Laughlin, Meg Ryan

In this soggy second sequel to *The Amityville Horror*, one of the worst movies of all time, Tony Roberts (Woody Allen's pal in *Play It Again, Sam* and *Annie Hall*) plays a reporter who, along with photographer Candy Clark (*American Graffiti*), investigates the spooky goings-on at the infamous house in Amityville, New York, and ends up as one of its victims. It's hack horror. Rated PG for violence and gore.

1983 105 minutes

AND NOW THE SCREAMING STARTS

★★★

DIRECTOR: Roy Ward Baker
CAST: Peter Cushing, Stephanie Beacham, Herbert Lom, Patrick Magee, Ian Ogilvy

Frightening British horror film about a young newlywed couple moving into a house haunted by a centuries-old curse on the husband's family. Well done, with a great cast, but occasionally a bit too bloody. Rated R.

1973 87 minutes

ANDY WARHOL'S DRACULA

★

DIRECTOR: Paul Morrissey
CAST: Udo Kier, Joe Dallesandro, Vittorio DeSica, Roman Polanski, Arno Juerging

Companion piece to Andy Warhol's equally revolting version of *Frankenstein*. The "joke" this time is that Dracula (Udo Kier) can survive only on the blood of "were-gins" and vomits that which comes from more experienced ladies. Needless to say, considerable amounts of blood gush into various bathtubs and sinks. Plucky Joe Dallesandro, learning of the Count's weakness, engages in a madcap race to deflower the castle women before Dracula can empty them. The Count gets so upset that he literally goes to pieces. Rated X for excessive violence and kinky sex.

1974 93 minutes

ANDY WARHOL'S FRANKENSTEIN

DIRECTOR: Paul Morrissey
CAST: Joe Dallesandro, Monique Van Vooren, Udo Kier, Srdjan Zelewovic

"Bore, bore, bore," says Kate Hepburn to Jane Fonda during a mother-daughter talk in *On Golden Pond*. She could easily have been critiquing this stupendously awful "horror film" by Warhol's New York Pop Art crowd. Third-rate Marlon Brando imitator Joe Dallesandro meanders around muttering inane dialogue. Blood and gore gush at every opportunity. This turkey should have been left on the shelf. Rated R for obvious reasons.

1974 94 minutes

ANGEL HEART

★★★½

DIRECTOR: Alan Parker
CAST: Mickey Rourke, Lisa Bonet, Robert De Niro, Charlotte Rampling

This first-rate adaptation of William Hjortsberg's *Falling Angel* stars Mickey Rourke as a down-and-out private investigator in New York of the mid-1950s. The P.I. is given a rather bizarre case to solve. The elegant, dapper, and more than slightly sinister Louis Cyphre (Robert De Niro, who blows everybody off the screen during his four brief appearances) wants a missing singer found, in order to settle a vague "debt" between the two. As the investigation proceeds, all of the chief witnesses begin to lose their lives—in grotesquely violent ways that smack of voodoo—and Rourke finds himself the chief suspect. Clever script by director Alan Parker, who builds the story to a striking climax. Absolutely not for the squeamish or for children; rated R for violence, sex, and language.

1987 113 minutes

APE, THE

★★

DIRECTOR: William Nigh
CAST: Boris Karloff, Maris Wrixon, Gertrude Hoffman, Henry Hall, Gene O'Donnell, Philo McCullough, George Cleveland, Jessie Arnold

Boris Karloff finished out his contract with Monogram Studios with this story about a doctor who discovers a cure for polio that requires spinal fluid from a human being. The ape of the title is an escaped circus animal that Karloff kills and then uses as a disguise while obtaining more spinal fluid for his experiments. The master of menace has a heart of gold in this film, going to extremes in order to save never-again-seen starlet Maris Wrixon from a life of paralysis. Not too many thrills, but Karloff is always worth watching.

1940 B & W 61 minutes

APE MAN, THE

★★

DIRECTOR: William Beaudine
CAST: Bela Lugosi, Louise Currie, Wallace Ford, Minerva Urecal

In the 1930s, thanks to the success of *Dracula* at the beginning of the decade, Bela Lugosi was one of the great horror film stars. However, the monster-movie boom stopped short in 1935, leaving the Hungarian actor out of work. When shockers came back in vogue four years later, Lugosi took any and every role he was offered. The result was grade-Z pictures such as this one, about a scientist (Lugosi) attempting to harness the physical power of apes for humankind. Too bad.

1943 B & W 64 minutes

APOLOGY

★★★

DIRECTOR: Robert Bierman
CAST: Lesley Ann Warren, Peter Weller, George Loros, John Glover, Christopher North

This psycho-suspense film features Lesley Ann Warren as a bizarre artist who starts an anonymous phone service to get ideas for her latest project. People call the recording and confess a sin they've committed. All goes well until a caller named Claude falls in love with the confessional idea and begins killing people in order to have something to be sorry for. At this point the police are called in, and Warren falls for the detective (Peter Weller). The storyline is okay, but it seems like the filmmakers had a tight sixty-minute film and decided to inflate it. Made for cable TV, this is unrated but it contains obscenities, gore, and simulated sex.

1986 98 minutes

APPOINTMENT, THE

★

DIRECTOR: Lindsey C. Vickers
CAST: Edward Woodward, Jane Merrow, Samantha Weysom, John Judd

Only the distinguished acting of Edward Woodward, known to television viewers as *The Equalizer* and movie buffs as *Breaker Morant*, prevents this British-made supernatural thriller from being rated as a turkey. Writer-director Lindsey C. Vickers shows very little talent with this story of a father (Woodward) cursed by his evil daughter (Samantha Weysom) because a business meeting prevents him from attending her music recital. We get to see Woodward experience his highway death in dreams. Then his wife (Jane Merrow) sees it in a nightmare as well. And for a conclusion, Vickers has us sit through it all over again. It's boring, insulting to one's intelligence and a low point in Woodward's career. Unrated, the film has some violence.

1982 90 minutes

APRIL FOOL'S DAY

★★★

DIRECTOR: Fred Walton
CAST: Jay Baker, Deborah Foreman, Griffin O'Neal, Amy Steel

A group of college kids on spring break are invited to a mansion on a desolate island by a rich girl named Muffy St. John. They read Milton, quote Boswell, play practical jokes, and get killed off in a nice, orderly fashion. The survivors get anxious, Muffy turns squirrelly, and the party is a total bust. Not really a horror film; more of a mystery à la *Ten Little Indians*. It will probably disappoint fans of gore, naked starlets, and gratuitous stupidity, but it's a pleasant surprise that creates suspense without turning stomachs. Rated R for violence and profanity.

1986 90 minutes

ARNOLD

★½

DIRECTOR: Georg Fenady
CAST: Roddy McDowall, Elsa Lanchester, Stella Stevens, Farley Granger, Victor Buono, John McGiver, Shani Wallis

A delightful cast cannot save this rather muddled mess of murder and mirth. Stella Stevens, married to a corpse, suddenly discovers her co-stars meeting their maker in a variety of strange ways reminiscent of *The Abominable Dr. Phibes*. Unfortunately, director Georg Fenady doesn't display one-tenth of that film's style, and the characters are rather cheerless. Pretty ho-hum. Rated PG for violence.

1973 100 minutes

ASTRO-ZOMBIES

DIRECTOR: Ted V. Mikels
CAST: Wendell Corey, John Carradine, Tom Pace, Joan Patrick, Rafael Campos

A grade-Z horror film that wastes the talent of star John Carradine.

1967 83 minutes

ASYLUM

★★★★

DIRECTOR: Roy Ward Baker
CAST: Barbara Parkins, Sylvia Syms, Peter Cushing, Barry Morse, Richard Todd, Herbert Lom, Patrick Magee

A first-rate horror anthology from England featuring fine performances. Four seemingly unrelated stories of madness are interwoven, leading to a nail-biting climax. Rated PG.

1972 92 minutes

ATOM AGE VAMPIRE

DIRECTOR: Richard McNamara (aka Anton Giulio Masano)
CAST: Alberto Lupo, Susanne Loret

Badly dubbed Italian time waster with cheese-ball special effects and a tired premise. A mad professor restores the face of a scarred accident victim. To keep her beautiful, he must kill other women and swipe their glands. Every so often, just for fun, the doc transforms into something resembling that troll doll your sister used to have.

1961 B & W 87 minutes

ATTACK OF THE CRAB MONSTERS

★★★

DIRECTOR: Roger Corman
CAST: Richard Garland, Pamela Duncan, Mel Welles, Russell Johnson, Leslie Bradley, Ed Nelson

Neat Roger Corman low-budget movie, seemed scarier when you were a kid, but it's still a lot of fun. A remote Pacific atoll is besieged by a horde of giant land crabs that, upon devouring members of a scientific expedition, absorb their brains and acquire the ability to speak in their voices. Though the lack of available funds caused some scenes to be unintentionally funny, the movie has more than its share of chills, along with plenty of eerie atmosphere.

1957 B & W 64 minutes

ATTACK OF THE 50-FOOT WOMAN

★★★

DIRECTOR: Nathan Juran
CAST: Allison Hayes, William Hudson, Yvette Vickers, Roy Gordon

One of the best "schlock" films from the 1950s. Allison Hayes stars as a woman who's kidnapped by a tremendous bald alien and transformed into a giant herself. Duddy special effects only serve to heighten the enjoyment of this kitsch classic.

1958 B & W 66 minutes

ATTACK OF THE SWAMP CREATURE

DIRECTOR: Arnold Stevens
CAST: Frank Crowell, Patricia Robertson, Patrick Allison, Lee Kropiewnicki, David Robertson

In one of Elvira's "thriller Video" movies, we're treated to the story of a mad scientist who turns himself into a giant, man-eating, walking catfish. Need we go further? We'll say one thing for Elvira and her producers: they know how to pick the worst films in the horror genre. This one is so bad, it's not even funny—just boring.

1985 96 minutes

ATTIC, THE

★½

DIRECTOR: George Edwards
CAST: Carrie Snodgress, Ray Milland, Ruth Cox, Francis Bay

Rather slow-moving and routine story concerning a young woman (Carrie Snodgress) fighting to free herself from the clutches of her crippled, almost insane, father. Tries to be deep and psychological and falls flat on its face. Rated PG.

1979 97 minutes

AUDREY ROSE

★

DIRECTOR: Robert Wise
CAST: Marsha Mason, Anthony Hopkins, John Beck

Plodding melodrama about a man (Anthony Hopkins) who constantly annoys a couple by claiming that his dead daughter has been reincarnated as their live one. Bad script is only one problem in one of director Wise's few duds. Rated PG.

1977 113 minutes

AWAKENING, THE

★★½

DIRECTOR: Michael Newell
CAST: Charlton Heston, Susannah York, Jill Townsend, Patrick Drury, Stephanie Zimbalist

In this mediocre horror flick, Charlton Heston plays an Egyptologist who discovers the tomb of a wicked queen. The evil spirit escapes the tomb and is reincarnated in Heston's newborn daughter. Years later Heston's daughter (Stephanie Zimbalist) is possessed. A bit hard to follow the plot. Rated R for gore.

1980 102 minutes

BABY, THE

★★★

DIRECTOR: Ted Post
CAST: Ruth Roman, Mariana Hill, David Manzy

Extremely odd film by veteran director Ted Post about a teenager who has remained an infant all his life (yes, he still lives in his crib) and his insane, overprotective mother. Eerily effective chiller is highly entertaining, though many will undoubtedly find it repulsive and ridiculous. Rated PG.

1974 80 minutes

BABYSITTER, THE

★★★½

DIRECTOR: Peter Medak
CAST: Patty Duke Astin, William Shatner, Quinn Cummings, David Wallace, Stephanie Zimbalist, John Houseman

Outside of some glaring plot flaws, *The Babysitter* is an effectively eerie film. Stephanie Zimbalist is Joanna, a woman hired as a housekeeper (not a babysitter) for the Benedict family (William Shatner, Patty Duke-Astin, and Quinn Cummings). But after a series of mysterious accidents and some rather ominous behavior, we find that Joanna is no Mary Poppins. Not rated; has violence.

1980 96 minutes

BASKET CASE

★★★★

DIRECTOR: Frank Henenlotter
CAST: Kevin Vanhentryck, Terri Susan Smith, Beverly Bonner, Robert Vogel, Diana Browne

Comedy and horror are mixed beautifully in this weird tale of a young man and his deformed Siamese twin out for revenge against the doctors who separated them. Extremely entertaining and highly recommended for shock buffs. Rated R.

1982 91 minutes

BEAR ISLAND

★

DIRECTOR: Don Sharp

CAST: Donald Sutherland, Richard Widmark, Vanessa Redgrave, Christopher Lee, Lloyd Bridges

Alistair MacLean writes some of the best thrillers around; why can't they be turned into better films? This is one of the worst, a pointlessly melodramatic tale mixing gold fever, murder, and other incidental intrigue. Beautiful snowbound setting just emphasizes the empty script. Without question, read the book. Rated PG for mild violence.

1980 118 minutes

BEAST IN THE CELLAR, THE

★½

DIRECTOR: James Kelly

CAST: Beryl Reid, Flora Robson, T. P. McKenna, John Hamill

Boring story about a pair of aging sisters (well played by veterans Beryl Reid and Flora Robson) with something to hide. Only, instead of a skeleton in the closet, they've got a beast in the cellar. More specifically, their deranged, deformed brother is down there, and he wants out! Intriguing idea is given a lackluster treatment here that not even the topflight cast can save. Weak. Rated R.

1971 87 minutes

BEAST MUST DIE, THE

★★

DIRECTOR: Paul Annett

CAST: Calvin Lockhart, Peter Cushing, Marlene Clark, Charles Gray, Anton Diffring

A millionaire hunter invites a group of guests to an isolated mansion. One of them is a werewolf he intends to destroy. This tame, talky reworking of Agatha Christie's *Ten Little Indians* featured a "werewolf break," ostensibly to provide the theatrical audience time to ponder clues and determine the identity of the hairy beast. In practice, however, the gimmick merely resulted in derisive laughter and scattered obscenities. Rated PG.

1974 98 minutes

BEAST WITHIN, THE

★

DIRECTOR: Phillippe Mora

CAST: Ronny Cox, Bibi Besch, Paul Clemens, Don Gordon

This unbelievably gory movie consists mainly of one grisly murder after another. Phillippe Mora, an Australian documentary filmmaker, tries his best to create an atmosphere of intelligent horror (as does top-billed Ronny Cox), but there's no competing with the excessive gore. Rated R for violence, gore, and nudity.

1982 90 minutes

BEDLAM

★★★

DIRECTOR: Mark Robson

CAST: Boris Karloff, Anna Lee, Ian Wolfe, Richard Fraser, Billy House, Jason Robards Sr.

One of the lesser entries in the Val Lewton-produced horror film series at RKO, this release still has its moments as the courageous Anna Lee tries to expose the cruelties and inadequacies of an insane asylum run by Boris Karloff, who is first-rate, as usual.

1946 B & W 79 minutes

BEDROOM WINDOW, THE

★★★

DIRECTOR: Curtis Hanson
CAST: Steve Guttenberg, Elizabeth McGovern, Isabelle Huppert, Paul Shenar, Carl Lumbly, Wallace Shawn, Frederick Coffin, Brad Greenquist

Upwardly mobile architect Steve Guttenberg has it made until his boss's wife (Isabelle Huppert) sees a murder being committed—from his bedroom window. When Guttenberg goes to the police in her place, he becomes the prime suspect. This is a tense thriller that manages to stay interesting despite some wildly unbelievable plot twists. Like a low-budget horror film, it has its characters do some incredibly stupid things, which put their lives in jeopardy. Rated R for profanity, nudity, and violence.

1987 112 minutes

BEES, THE

★½

DIRECTOR: Alfredo Zacharias
CAST: John Saxon, John Carradine, Alicia Encinias

Despite all temptation to label this a honey of a picture, it's a drone that will probably give viewers the hives. Rated PG.

1978 83 minutes

BEFORE I HANG

★★★

DIRECTOR: Nick Grindé
CAST: Boris Karloff, Evelyn Keyes, Bruce Bennett, Pedro de Cordoba, Edward Van Sloan

Neat little thriller has Boris Karloff as a good-hearted doctor who creates an age-retardant serum. Trouble begins when he tests it on himself, with horrible side effects. Nicely done, the film benefits from a good supporting performance by horror veteran Edward Van Sloan.

1940 B & W 71 minutes

BEING, THE

DIRECTOR: Jackie Kong
CAST: Martin Landau, José Ferrer, Dorothy Malone, Ruth Buzzi, Rexx Coltrane (Johnny Commander)

This inept little horror film must have taxed the funds or patience of its producers, since gaping hunks of plot are missing and replaced with laughable narration. Hard to choose between the picture's funniest moments: the *Alien*-esque creature so obviously pushed around on wheels, or Martin Landau saying, with a straight face, that water contaminated with nuclear waste is harmless. This particular batch of water spawned a beast that likes to shove itself *through* people . . . or maybe the monster is the deformed child of Dorothy Malone; the story's that confusing. The creature supposedly melts away in direct light, which allows for dim nighttime shooting that disguises the poor effects. Unwatchable. Rated R for gore and nudity.

1984 82 minutes

BELIEVERS, THE

★★★½

DIRECTOR: John Schlesinger
CAST: Martin Sheen, Helen Shaver, Robert Loggia, Richard Masur, Elizabeth Wilson, Lee Richardson, Harris Yulin, Jimmy Smits

Martin Sheen portrays a recently widowed father whose son is chosen as a sacrifice to a voodoo cult running rampant in New York. Robert Loggia is the politically savvy yet sympathetic police detective investigating the cult's bloody path through the city, and Helen Shaver is the love interest. John Schlesinger is not the best director for a thriller of this type, but in this case the quality of the acting, the snap of the writing, and the strength of the story build the suspense nicely and provide a wonderful climax. Richard Masur is perfectly cast as Sheen's offbeat lawyer. Rater R for language, nudity, and nightmarism.

1987 110 minutes

BEN

★

DIRECTOR: Phil Karlson

CAST: Arthur O'Connell, Lee Harcourt Montgomery, Rosemary Murphy

The only thing going for this silly sequel to *Willard* is an awkwardly charming title song performed by a young Michael Jackson (a love song for a rat, no less). Turgid entry in the beasts-get-even subgenre of horror films. Where's a better rattrap when you need one? Rated PG—violence.

1972 95 minutes

BERSERK

★★★½

DIRECTOR: Jim O'Connolly

CAST: Joan Crawford, Ty Hardin, Michael Gough, Diana Dors, Judy Geeson

Effectively staged thriller stars Joan Crawford as the owner of a once-great circus now on its last legs—until a number of accidental deaths of the performers starts packing 'em in. Joan comes under suspicion immediately when the cops begin counting the box-office receipts. Could she be guilty? Watch and see. Compelling scores by Patrick John Scott, too.

1967 96 minutes

BEST OF SEX AND VIOLENCE

★★

DIRECTOR: Ken Dixon

CAST: Hosted by John Carradine

A quickie video production containing unrelated clips and preview trailers from low-budget exploitation films. John Carradine hosts with a wink, and his sons David and Keith drop by for some ad-lib kidding. A ripoff, to be sure, but not without laughs and a certain sleazy charm. Unrated, the film has profanity, nudity, and, of course, sex and violence.

1981 76 minutes

BEYOND EVIL

★

DIRECTOR: Herb Freed

CAST: John Saxon, Lynda Day George, Michael Dante, Mario Milano, Janice Lynde

Larry Andrews (John Saxon) and his wife, Barbara (Lynda Day George), travel to a tropical island to mix business with their honeymoon. Andrews is to supervise a construction project for Barbara's ex-spouse, and the former husband lodges the newlyweds in a luxurious mansion, which happens to be haunted. The ghost is Alma Martin, a well-to-do lady who was murdered by her husband, and she's out to possess poor Barbara. Rated R.

1980 94 minutes

BEYOND THE DOOR

★

DIRECTOR: Ovidio Assonitis (Oliver Hellman)

CAST: Juliet Mills, Richard Johnson, David Colin Jr.

Sick ripoff of *The Exorcist* has Juliet Mills as a woman possessed by guess what. Or should we say guess who? Disgusting production only serves to induce nausea. Made in Italy. Rated R.

1975 94 minutes

BEYOND THE DOOR 2

★★

DIRECTOR: Mario Bava

CAST: Daria Nicolodi, John Steiner, David Colin Jr.

Why, why, why? Actually, this semi-sequel is much better than the original mainly because its director was the famed Mario Bava (his final film). This time a young boy becomes possessed by the unseen power of Hell, and many die. Alternate title: *Shock*. Rated R.

1979 92 minutes

BIG FOOT

DIRECTOR: Robert Slatzer
CAST: John Carradine, Joi Lansing, John Mitchum, Chris Mitchum, Joy Wilkerson

Legendary monster comes down from the hills and beats the hell out of everybody. Laughable film is worthless, one of John Carradine's worst. Why does he keep makin' 'em? Rated R.

1971 94 minutes

BILLY THE KID VS. DRACULA

★½

DIRECTOR: William Beaudine
CAST: John Carradine, Chuck Courtney, Melinda Plowman, Virginia Christine, Harry Carey Jr.

Hokey horror film casts John Carradine as the famous vampire, on the loose in a small western town. From the director of *Bela Lugosi Meets a Brooklyn Gorilla*, another so-bad-it's-funny film.

1966 95 minutes

BIRD WITH THE CRYSTAL PLUMAGE, THE

★★½

DIRECTOR: Dario Argento
CAST: Tony Musante, Suzy Kendall, Eva Renzi, Enrico Maria Salerno, Renato Romano, Umberto Rano

Stylish thriller weaves a complex story thread in adventure of an American writer who witnesses a murder and is drawn into the web of mystery and violence. Plenty of clues and red herrings, but the story is convoluted and hard to follow at times. Minor cult and detective genre favorite, well photographed and nicely acted by resilient Tony Musante and fashion plate Suzy Kendall. Rated PG.

1969 98 minutes

BIRDS, THE

★★★★

DIRECTOR: Alfred Hitchcock
CAST: Rod Taylor, Tippi Hedren, Suzanne Pleshette, Jessica Tandy

After scaring the socks off filmgoers with *Psycho* in 1960, director Alfred Hitchcock took one more successful slash at the horror genre with this suspenseful shocker.

1963 120 minutes

BLACK CAT, THE

★★★★

DIRECTOR: Edgar G. Ulmer
CAST: Boris Karloff, Bela Lugosi, Jacqueline Wells (aka Julie Bishop)

A surrealistic, strikingly designed horror thriller that has become a cult favorite thanks to its pairing of Boris Karloff and Bela Lugosi (both in *starring* roles; Lugosi usually got the short end of the billing stick). Lugosi has one of his very few good-guy roles as a concerned citizen who gets drawn into a web of evil that surrounds Karloff's black magic. The climax is unusually violent and sadistic for a general-audience programmer; small children are advised to stay away from this one. The delight, for older fans, comes from watching these two horror legends chew up the scenery. Unrated; not recommended for youngsters. Available on a videocassette double feature with *The Raven*.

1934 B & W 70 minutes

BLACK DRAGONS

★

DIRECTOR: William Nigh
CAST: Bela Lugosi, Joan Barclay, Clayton Moore, George Pembroke, Kenneth Harlon

A silly film about Japanese agents who are surgically altered to resemble American businessmen and chiefs of industry, this is a low-budget bore that gives former horror film champion Bela Lugosi little to do but eavesdrop and appear unexpectedly from behind doors. Future Lone Ranger Clayton Moore plays the hero in this bizarre but lifeless film as he attempts to discover why all the bodies are piling up in front of the Japanese embassy. Bargain-basement entertainment with no real pretense—just a low-budget film thrown together in the hopes of turning a buck.

1949 B & W 62 minutes

BLACK SABBATH

★★★½

DIRECTOR: Mario Bava
CAST: Boris Karloff, Mark Damon, Suzy Andersen

Above-average trio of horror tales given wonderful atmosphere by Italian director Mario Bava. Boris Karloff plays host, echoing the function he performed on television's *Thriller*, and stars in the third story, a vampire opus entitled "The Wurdalak." One of the others, "A Drop of Water," is based on a story by Chekhov; the third, "The Telephone," involves disconnected calls of the worst sort. Great fun late at night, and Karloff's narration adds considerable dignity.

1964 99 minutes

BLACK WIDOW

★★★★

DIRECTOR: Bob Rafelson
CAST: Debra Winger, Theresa Russell, Sami Frey, Dennis Hopper, Nicol Williamson, Terry O'Quinn

A superb thriller from director Bob Rafelson that recalls the best of the Bette Davis–Joan Crawford "bad girl" films of earlier decades. Debra Winger stars as an inquisitive federal agent who stumbles upon an odd pattern of deaths by apparently natural causes: the victims are quite wealthy, reclusive, and leave behind a young—and very rich—widow. The more Winger studies the case, the more all those widows begin to look like Theresa Russell. Writer Ronald Bass's script recalls the best manipulative moments from Lawrence Kasdan's *Body Heat*, particularly as Winger's insatiable curiosity—and determination to prove conspiracy in spite of such slight evidence—forces her ever closer to Russell's complex, macabre murderess. In spite of its weak and abrupt conclusion, *Black Widow* is a mesmerizing film. Rated R for nudity, adult situations.

1987 103 minutes

BLACK ROOM, THE

★★★

DIRECTOR: Roy William Neill
CAST: Boris Karloff, Marian Marsh, Robert Allen, Katherine DeMille, Thurston Hall

Boris Karloff is excellent as usual in a dual role of twin brothers with an age-old family curse hanging over their heads and the strange way it affects their lives. Well-handled thriller never stops moving. Also worth noting is the video quality of this tape, which is superb, resulting in a film that looks as if it were shot yesterday. The sound is also exceptionally good, the clearest we've heard from a film of this vintage.

1935 B & W 67 minutes

BLACKENSTEIN

DIRECTOR: William A. Levy
CAST: John Hart, Joe DiSue, Ivory Stone

Tasteless and grotesque entry in the tiny subgenre of "blaxploitation" horror films. Mad doctor John Hart takes a maimed Vietnam veteran (Joe DiSue) and transforms him into a shambling nightmare. Perhaps one of the sickest excuses for a plot ever conceived. All the horror in this film comes from the notion that human beings actually put it together. Rated R for violence and nudity.

1973 92 minutes

BLACULA

★★★½

DIRECTOR: William Crain
CAST: William Marshall, Denise Nicholas, Vonetta McGee, Thalmus Rasulala

An old victim (William Marshall) of Dracula's bite is loose in modern L.A. Surprisingly well-done shocker. Fierce and energetic, with a solid cast. Rated R for violence.

1972 92 minutes

BLOB, THE

★★★

DIRECTOR: Irvin S. Yeaworth Jr.
CAST: Steve McQueen, Aneta Corseaut, Earl Rowe, Olin Howlin

This was Steve McQueen's first starring role. He plays a teenager battling parents and a voracious hunk of protoplasm from outer space. Long surpassed by more sophisticated sci-fi, it's still fun to watch.

1958 86 minutes

BLOOD AND BLACK LACE

★★½

DIRECTOR: Mario Bava
CAST: Cameron Mitchell, Eva Bartok, Mary Arden

This sometimes frightening Italian horror film features a psychotic killer eliminating members of the modeling industry with gusto. Decent entry in the genre from specialist Mario Bava.

1964 88 minutes

BLOOD BEACH

★

DIRECTOR: Jeffrey Bloom
CAST: John Saxon, Mariana Hill, Otis Young

Poor horror story of mysterious forces sucking people down into the sand isn't nearly as fun as it sounds. Bad acting, bad writing, and bad special effects. Rated R.

1981 89 minutes

BLOOD FEAST

★

DIRECTOR: Herschell Gordon Lewis
CAST: Connie Mason, Thomas Wood, Mal Arnold, Lyn Bolton

First and most infamous of the drive-in gore movies bolsters practically nonexistent plot of crazed murderer with gallons of director Herschell Gordon Lewis's patented stage blood as well as props like a sheep's tongue and a power saw. Crude, vulgar, and ineptly acted, this bargain-basement production was one of the low-budget bonanzas of the 1960s and set the tone for dozens of subsequent nauseating hack-and-slash films.

1963 75 minutes

BLOOD LINK

DIRECTOR: Alberto De Martino
CAST: Michael Moriarty, Penelope Milford, Cameron Mitchell, Sarah Langenfeld, Martha Smith, Reinhold K. Olszewski, Geraldine Fitzgerald

All his life, a prominent physician has had strange hallucinations about older women being brutally murdered. But the real problem is that the murderer in his visions looks like him. He discovers that he is seeing through the eyes of his Siamese twin (who was separated from him during infancy) as he kills his victims. The doctor sets off to find his homicidal sibling in hopes of curing him. The film starts off contrived and becomes even more so. Much of it is slow and incomprehensible, padding itself with gratuitous nudity. Even Michael Moriarty's performance as the twins is bland and disappointing. Rated R for nudity and violence.

1983 98 minutes

BLOOD OF DRACULA'S CASTLE

DIRECTORS: Al Adamson, Jean Hewitt
CAST: John Carradine, Paula Raymond, Alex D'Arcy, Robert Dix

Quite possibly the worst Dracula movie ever made. The count and countess spend most of the film sitting around, rambling incoherently, sipping blood cocktails provided by their butler (John Carradine). The film has a werewolf, a hunchback, women in chains, human sacrifices, a laughable script, and a ten-dollar budget. Rated PG.

1967 84 minutes

BLOOD ON SATAN'S CLAW

★★★

DIRECTOR: Piers Haggard
CAST: Patrick Wymark, Barry Andrews, Linda Hayden, Simon Williams

Fun, frightening horror film set in seventeenth-century England. A small farming community is besieged by the devil himself, who succeeds in turning the local children into a coven of witches. Familiar story is presented in a unique manner by director Piers Haggard, helped by excellent period detail and clever effects. Not for the kids, though. Rated R.

1971 93 minutes

BLOOD SISTERS

DIRECTOR: Roberta Findlay
CAST: Amy Brentano, Shannon McMahon, Dan Erickson, Marla Mackart, Elizabeth Rose, Cjerste Thor, Patricia Finneran, Gretchen Kingsley, Brigitte Cossu

Gore fans will be disappointed by the false tag line on the box "Their hazing was a night to dismember." All of the sorority hopefuls who have to spend a night in an old haunted house that was the scene of a murder some years ago—which we get to see in a flashback used over and over again—die. But the big question in this horror flick is not whodunit, but who cares? Rated R for sex, nudity, violence, and profanity.

1986 85 minutes

BLOODBEAT

DIRECTOR: Fabrice A. Zaphiratos
CAST: Helen Benton, Terry Brown, Claudia Peyton, Dana Day, James Fitz Gibbons

If Prokofiev and Vivaldi knew that their music was being used in a death-fest like this film, the masters would be spinning in their crypts like drill bits. This cheap supernatural flick also tries to pass off the idea that a samurai ghost is haunting the backwoods of an American wilderness because of an old war debt—we think. The plot is not at all clear, and the bad acting and poor direction only aggravate the problem. May be of some interest to those fascinated with fifteenth-century Japanese war armor. No MPAA rating, but with sex, nudity, profanity, and a mean samurai ghost loose, it's a sure R rating.

1985 84 minutes

BLOODSUCKERS, THE

★★½

DIRECTOR: David Hewitt
CAST: Lon Chaney Jr., John Carradine

Lots of blood, gory special effects, and some good humor. Not bad for this type of film. Also known as *Return from the Past* and *Dr. Terror's Gallery of Horrors*. Not for the squeamish.

1967 84 minutes

BLOODSUCKING FREAKS AKA THE INCREDIBLE TORTURE SHOW

DIRECTOR: Joel M. Reed
CAST: Seamus O'Brian, Niles McMaster

Any movie with a title this outrageous just has to be fun, right? *Wrong!* This putrid film is an endurance test for even the most hardcore horror buffs. The story is absurd, the performances are hammy, and the stomach-churning effects could make you toss your popcorn. The scene where one of the maniacs sucks a woman's brains out with a straw has to be one of the most repulsive moments ever put on film. We would love to tell you the plot, but we couldn't find one. Rated R for nudity and violence.

1978 89 minutes

BLOODTHIRSTY BUTCHERS

DIRECTOR: Andy Milligan
CAST: John Miranda, Annabella Wood, Berwick Kaler

As the title suggests, an extremely violent series of murders is committed in very gruesome fashion. A dreadful ripoff of *The Demon Barber of Fleet Street*, with Sweeney Todd and his baker friend selling human meat pies. Nothing new here. Rated R.

1970 80 minutes

BLOODTIDE

DIRECTOR: Richard Jeffries
CAST: James Earl Jones, José Ferrer, Lila Kedrova

Cheap horror film that isn't worthy of your time. A dud! Rated R.

1984 82 minutes

BLOW OUT

★★★★

DIRECTOR: Brian De Palma
CAST: John Travolta, Nancy Allen, John Lithgow, Dennis Franz, Peter Boyden

John Travolta and Nancy Allen are terrific in this thriller by director Brian De Palma (*Dressed to Kill*; *Carrie*). The story concerns a motion picture sound man (Travolta) who becomes involved in murder when he rescues a young woman (Allen) from a car that crashes into a river. It's suspenseful, thrill-packed, adult entertainment. Rated R because of sex, nudity, profanity, and violence.

1981 107 minutes

BLOW-UP

★★★★★

DIRECTOR: Michelangelo Antonioni

CAST: Vanessa Redgrave, David Hemmings, Sarah Miles, Jill Kennington

Director Michelangelo Antonioni's first English-language film was this stimulating examination into what is or is not reality. On its surface a photographer (David Hemmings) believes he has taken a snapshot of a murder taking place. Vanessa Redgrave arrives at his studio and tries to seduce him out of the photo. This sometimes baffling film challenges its audience to think.

1966 108 minutes

BLUE VELVET

★★★★½

DIRECTOR: David Lynch

CAST: Kyle MacLachlan, Isabella Rossellini, Dennis Hopper, Laura Dern, Dean Stockwell, George Dickerson, Brad Dourif, Jack Nance

In this brilliant but disturbing film, Kyle MacLachlan and Laura Dern play youngsters who become involved in the mystery surrounding night-club singer Isabella Rossellini. The story seems to take place in the netherworld of daydreams and nightmares, giving only an occasional and unnerving nod to reality. As with writer-director David Lynch's previous films—especially *Eraserhead* and *The Elephant Man*—it seldom lets the viewer off easy, yet it is nevertheless a stunning cinematic work. Rated R for violence, nudity, profanity, and sex.

1986 120 minutes

BLUEBEARD

★★★

DIRECTOR: Edgar G. Ulmer

CAST: John Carradine, Jean Parker, Nils Asther, Ludwig Stossel, Iris Adrian, Emmett Lynn

Atmospheric low-budget thriller by resourceful German director Edgar G. Ulmer gives great character actor John Carradine one of his finest leading roles as a strangler who preys on women. Full of swirling mists, constricted sets, and familiar faces, this film, while initially considered a lesser entry, is on a par with the better known "mist-and-murder" films of the mid-1940s, including *The Lodger*, *Hangover Square*, and *The Picture of Dorian Gray*. Cadaverous Carradine cuts a fine figure as the refined maniac who aims to make lovely Jean Parker his next victim. Make up some popcorn, grab a zombie movie for a second feature, and sit back and enjoy this low-key creeper.

1944 B & W 73 minutes

BLUEBEARD

★★½

DIRECTOR: Edward Dmytryk

CAST: Richard Burton, Raquel Welch, Karin Schubert, Joey Heatherton

Richard Burton stars in *Bluebeard*, a film with its tongue planted firmly in cheek. The legend of the multiple murderer is intermingled with Nazi lore to come out as a reasonably convincing foray into a combination of black comedy and classic horror films. Rated R.

1972 125 minutes

BODY DOUBLE

★★★½

DIRECTOR: Brian De Palma

CAST: Craig Wasson, Melanie Griffith, Gregg Henry, Deborah Shelton

This Brian De Palma (*Carrie*; *Scarface*) thriller, which owes quite a bit to Alfred Hitchcock's *Rear Window* and *Vertigo*, is often gruesome, disgusting, and exploitative. But you can't take your eyes off the screen. Craig Wasson is first-rate as a young actor who witnesses a brutal murder, and Melanie Griffith is often hilarious as the porno star who holds the key to the crime. De Palma experiments with new ways—often tongue-in-cheek—of portraying violence on screen. Some may call it sick and tasteless; others will find it surprisingly entertaining. Rated R for nudity, suggested sex, profanity, gore, and violence.

1984 110 minutes

BODY SNATCHER, THE

★★★★

DIRECTOR: Robert Wise

CAST: Henry Daniell, Boris Karloff, Bela Lugosi, Russell Wade

Boris Karloff gives one of his finest screen performances in the title role of this 1945 Val Lewton production, adapted from the novel by Robert Louis Stevenson. Karloff is a sinister grave robber who provides dead bodies for illegal medical research and then uses his activities as blackmail to form a bond of "friendship" with the doctor he services, Henry Daniell (in an equally impressive turn).

1945 B & W 77 minutes

BOG

[turkey symbol]

DIRECTOR: Don Keeslar

CAST: Gloria Dehaven, Aldo Ray, Marshall Thompson

Extremely low-budget film is entertaining for just that reason. Unlucky group of people on an excursion into the wilderness run into the recently defrosted monster Bog. Needless to say, things go downhill from there. Rated PG.

1983 87 minutes

BOOGEYMAN, THE

★★★½

DIRECTOR: Ulli Lommel

CAST: Suzanna Love, Michael Love, John Carradine, Ron James

Despite the lame title, this is an inventive, atmospheric fright flick about pieces of a broken mirror causing horrifying deaths. Good special effects add to the creepiness. Rated R for violence and gore.

1980 86 minutes

BOOGEYMAN 2, THE

★

DIRECTOR: Bruce Star

CAST: Suzanna Love, Shana Hall, Ulli Lommel

Not nearly as good as *The Boogeyman*, this cheapo sequel uses footage from the original and a substandard plot to cash in on success of its predecessor. Don't be fooled. Rated R for violence and gore.

1983 79 minutes

BOSTON STRANGLER, THE

★★★

DIRECTOR: Richard Fleischer

CAST: Tony Curtis, Henry Fonda, Mike Kellin, Murray Hamilton, Sally Kellerman, Hurd Hatfield, George Kennedy, Jeff Corey

True account, told in semi-documentary-style, of Beantown's notorious deranged murderer, plumber Albert De Salvo. Tony Curtis gives a first-class performance as the woman-killer. Credibility abounds in the portrayals of Henry Fonda, Murray Hamilton, and the rest. Color softens the impact, which would have been far more arresting in black and white.

1968 120 minutes

BOYS FROM BRAZIL, THE

★★½

DIRECTOR: Franklin J. Schaffner
CAST: Gregory Peck, Laurence Olivier, James Mason, Lilli Palmer

In this thriller, Gregory Peck plays an evil Nazi war criminal with farfetched plans to resurrect the Third Reich. Laurence Olivier pursues him throughout as a Jewish Nazi-hunter. Rated R.

1978 123 minutes

BOYS FROM BROOKLYN, THE

DIRECTOR: William Beaudine
CAST: Bela Lugosi, Duke Mitchell, Sammy Petrillo, Ramona the Chimp

Absolutely hilarious bomb with Bela Lugosi as a mad scientist turning people into apes on a forgotten island. Standout performance by Sammy Petrillo as a Jerry Lewis clone will have you rolling in the aisles! Better known as *Bela Lugosi Meets a Brooklyn Gorilla*, a much more appropriate title.

1952 B & W 72 minutes

BRIDE, THE

★½

DIRECTOR: Franc Roddam
CAST: Sting, Jennifer Beals, Geraldine Page, Clancy Brown, Anthony Higgins, David Rappaport

This remake of James Whale's classic 1935 horror comedy of the macabre, *Bride of Frankenstein*, has some laughs. But these, unlike in the original, are unintentional. Rock singer Sting (of the Police) makes a rather stuffy, unsavory Dr. Charles (?!) Frankenstein, and Jennifer Beals (*Flashdance*) is terribly miscast as his second creation. In fact, the film's few good moments come in a subplot about the adventures of the Frankenstein monster (Clancy Brown) and a happy-go-lucky, positive-thinking midget (charismatically portrayed by David Rappaport, of *Time Bandits*). This movie gives new meaning to the word pretentious. Rated PG-13 for violence, suggested sex, and nudity.

1985 119 minutes

BRIDE OF FRANKENSTEIN

★★★★★

DIRECTOR: James Whale
CAST: Boris Karloff, Colin Clive, Valerie Hobson, Dwight Frye, Ernest Thesiger, Elsa Lanchester

This is a first-rate sequel to *Frankenstein*. Many of the cast members from the original—most importantly Boris Karloff, Colin Clive, and Dwight Frye—returned for one of the few follow-ups to outclass its predecessor. Their performances and Whale's bizarre sense of humor make *Bride* a real treat. This time, Henry Frankenstein (Clive) is coerced by the evil Dr. Praetorius (Ernest Thesiger in a delightfully weird and sinister performance) into creating a mate for the monster.

1935 B & W 75 minutes

BRIDE OF THE MONSTER

DIRECTOR: Edward D. Wood Jr.
CAST: Bela Lugosi, Tor Johnson, Tony McCoy, Loretta King

Another incredibly inept but hilarious film from Ed Wood Jr., who brought us *Plan 9 From Outer Space* and *Glen or Glenda?*, this stinker uses most of the mad scientist clichés and uses them poorly as a cadaverous-looking Bela Lugosi tries to do fiendish things to an unconscious (even while alert) Loretta King. This bottom-of-the-barrel independent monstrosity boasts possibly the worst special-effects monster of all time, a rubber octopus that any novelty store would be ashamed to stock.

1955 B & W 69 minutes

BRIGHTON STRANGLER, THE

★★½

DIRECTOR: Max Nosseck

CAST: John Loder, June Duprez, Miles Mander, Michael St. Angel, Rose Hobart, Gilbert Emery, Ian Wolfe

Actor John Loder runs amok after a Nazi bomb destroys the London theatre where he has been playing a murderer in a drama. Stunned in the explosion, he confuses his true identity with the character he has been playing. A chance remark by a stranger sends him off to the seaside resort of Brighton, where he performs his stage role for real!

1945 B & W 67 minutes

BRIMSTONE AND TREACLE

★★★

DIRECTOR: Richard Loncraine

CAST: Denholm Elliott, Joan Plowright, Suzanne Hamilton, Sting

Sting, of the rock group the Police, plays an angelic-diabolic young drifter who insinuates himself into the home lives of respectable Denholm Elliott and Joan Plowright in this British-made shocker. Rated R.

1982 85 minutes

BROOD, THE

★★

DIRECTOR: David Cronenberg

CAST: Oliver Reed, Samantha Eggar, Art Hindle, Cindy Hinds

Fans of director David Cronenberg (*Dead Zone*) will no doubt enjoy this offbeat, grisly horror tale about genetic experiments. Others need not apply. Rated R.

1979 90 minutes

BROTHERHOOD OF SATAN

★

DIRECTOR: Bernard McEveety

CAST: Strother Martin, L. Q. Jones, Charles Bateman, Ahna Capri

Strong cast is wasted in this ridiculous thriller about a small town taken over by witches and devil worshipers, led by maniacal Strother Martin. Boring. Rated PG.

1971 92 minutes

BRUTE MAN, THE

★½

DIRECTOR: Jean Yarbrough

CAST: Tom Neal, Rondo Hatton, Jane Adams

A homicidal maniac escapes from an asylum. Unmemorable, standard B-movie stuff, notable mainly as a showcase for actor Rondo Hatton. Hatton appeared in several low-budget thrillers in the 1940s, usually as a menacing thug. He needed no make-up; he suffered from acromegaly, a genetic disease that causes distortion of the facial features. *The Brute Man* was one of Hatton's last films. He died in the year of its release, at the age of 42.

1946 B & W 60 minutes

BUG

★★½

DIRECTOR: Jeannot Szwarc

CAST: Bradford Dillman, Joanna Miles, Richard Gilliland, Jamie Smith Jackson

Weird horror film with the world, led by Bradford Dillman, staving off masses of giant mutant beetles with the ability to commit arson, setting fire to every living thing they can find. Rated PG for violence.

1975 100 minutes

BULLIES

DIRECTOR: Paul Lynch
CAST: Jonathon Crombie, Janet Laine Green, Stephen B. Hunter, Dehl Berti, Olivia D'Abo, Bill Croft, Bernie Coulson

A frustrating and painful-to-watch film about a family who moves to a small town that happens to be run by a murderous family of moonshiners. The sleazy folks rape, pillage, and kill. When the new citizens of the town stand up for their rights, they gain a perverse sense of respect from the bullies. This respect soon turns to disdain and violence. After a brutal rape scene, the father and son go out to seek their well-deserved revenge. Although not badly acted, the brutality portrayed in this film makes it hard to sit through. If you do make it to the end, the climax is quite satisfying. Rated R for graphic violence and profanity.

1985 96 minutes

BURNING, THE

DIRECTOR: Tony Maylam
CAST: Brian Matthews, Leah Ayres, Brian Backer, Larry Joshua, Lou David, Lee Montgomery, Eileen Heckart

This tedious film is just one more stab at the horror genre that trades surprises and suspense for buckets of blood and severed limbs. Similar to many other blood feasts of late, it's the story of a summer camp custodian who, savagely burned as a result of a teenage prank, comes back years later for revenge. With an excessive amount of blood and absolutely no surprises, you're far more likely to be disgusted than frightened. Rated R.

1981 90 minutes

BURNT OFFERINGS

★½

DIRECTOR: Dan Curtis
CAST: Oliver Reed, Karen Black, Burgess Meredith, Bette Davis, Lee Montgomery, Eileen Heckart

Good acting by Bette Davis, Karen Black, and Oliver Reed cannot save this predictable horror film concerning a haunted house. More of a made-for-television type of film than a true motion picture. Barely watchable. Rated PG.

1976 115 minutes

C.H.U.D.

★

DIRECTOR: Douglas Cheek
CAST: John Heard, Daniel Stern, Christopher Curry

The performances by John Heard and Daniel Stern are all that make this cheapo horror film even barely watchable. *C.H.U.D.* (Cannibalistic Humanoid Underground Dwellers) are New York City bag people who have been exposed to large doses of radiation and start treating the other inhabitants of the city as lunch. Rated R for violence, profanity, and gore.

1984 88 minutes

CAPE FEAR

★★★★

DIRECTOR: J. Lee Thompson
CAST: Gregory Peck, Polly Bergen, Robert Mitchum, Lori Martin, Martin Balsam, Telly Savalas, Jack Kruschen

Great cast in a riveting tale of a lawyer (Gregory Peck) and his family menaced by a vengeful ex-con (Robert Mitchum), who Peck helped to send up the river eight years earlier. Now he's out, with big plans for Peck's wife and, especially, his daughter. High marks in all categories, not the least of which are the cast, the uncompromising script (from John D. MacDonald's novel *The Exterminators*), crisp black and white photography, and an exceptional music score by Bernard Herrmann. A hidden treasure that deserves to be discovered.

1962 B & W 106 minutes

CAPTAIN KRONOS: VAMPIRE HUNTER

★★★½

DIRECTOR: Brian Clemens
CAST: Horst Janson, John David Carson, Caroline Munro, Shane Briant

British film directed by the producer of *The Avengers* television show. It's an unconventional horror tale about a sword-wielding vampire killer. An interesting mix of genres. Good adventure, with high production values. Rated PG for violence.

1974 91 minutes

CARNIVAL OF SOULS

★★★★

DIRECTOR: Herk Harvey
CAST: Candace Hilligoss, Sidney Berger, Francis Feist, Stan Levitt

Creepy film made on shoestring budget in Lawrence, Kansas, concerns a girl who, after a near-fatal car crash, is haunted by a ghoulish, zombielike character. Extremely eerie, with nightmarish black-and-white photography, this little-known gem has a way of getting to you and causing a feeling of uneasiness long after it's over. Better keep the lights on.

1962 B & W 80 minutes

CARPATHIAN EAGLE

★★

DIRECTOR: Francis Meahy
CAST: Anthony Valentine, Suzanne Danielle, Barry Stanton, Sian Phillips

Murdered men begin popping up with their hearts cut out. A police detective scours the town and racks his brain looking for the killer, not realizing how close he is. What all this has to do with the title is never resolved in this addition to Elvira's "Thriller Video." Also, Pierce Brosnan makes a brief cameo appearance.

1982 60 minutes

CARRIE

★★★★½

DIRECTOR: Brian De Palma
CAST: Sissy Spacek, Piper Laurie, John Travolta, Nancy Allen, Amy Irving

Carrie is the ultimate revenge tale for the person who remembers high school as a time of rejection and ridicule. The story follows the strange life of Carrie White (Sissy Spacek), a student severely humiliated by her classmates and stifled by the Puritan beliefs of her mother (Piper Laurie), a religious fanatic who considers adolescence the first step for a woman into a life of sin and degradation. Many of us have wanted to see those cruel, self-important high-school big shots get their just deserts, and *Carrie* does it as completely and frighteningly as only Brian De Palma could envision it. Rated R for nudity, violence, and profanity.

1976 97 minutes

CARS THAT EAT PEOPLE (THE CARS THAT ATE PARIS)

★½

DIRECTOR: Peter Weir
CAST: John Meillen, Terry Camilleri, Kevin Miles

Peter Weir, director of *Witness* and *The Year of Living Dangerously*, had to start somewhere. He began with this fantastic and weird black comedy about an Outback Australian town where motorists and their cars are trapped each night. Rated PG.

1975 90 minutes

CAT AND THE CANARY, THE

★★★½

DIRECTOR: Radley Metzger
CAST: Honor Blackman, Michael Callan, Edward Fox, Wendy Hiller, Carol Lynley, Olivia Hussey

This is a surprisingly entertaining remake of the 1927 period thriller about a group of people trapped in a British mansion and murdered one by one. Rated PG.

1978 90 minutes

CAT PEOPLE (ORIGINAL)

★★★★

DIRECTOR: Jacques Tourneur
CAST: Simone Simon, Kent Smith, Tom Conway

Simone Simon, Kent Smith, and Tom Conway are excellent in this movie about a shy woman (Simon) who believes she carries the curse of the panther. Producer Lewton and director Jacques Tourneur knew the imagination was stronger and more impressive than anything filmmakers could show visually and played on it with impressive results.

1942 B & W 73 minutes

CAT PEOPLE (REMAKE)

★

DIRECTOR: Paul Schrader
CAST: Nastassja Kinski, Malcolm McDowell, John Heard, Annette O'Toole, Scott Paulin, Ed Begley Jr., Ruby Dee

While technically a well-made film, *Cat People* spares the viewer nothing—incest, bondage, fellatio, cunnilingus, bestiality—for no worthy purpose. It makes one yearn for the films of yesteryear, which achieved horror through implication and the viewer's own imagination. Rated R for nudity, profanity, sex, and gore.

1982 118 minutes

CAT'S EYE

★★★½

DIRECTOR: Lewis Teague
CAST: James Woods, Robert Hays, Kenneth McMillan, Drew Barrymore, Candy Clark, Alan King

Writer Stephen King and director Lewis Teague, who brought us *Cujo*, reteam for this even better horror release: a trilogy of terror in the much-missed "Night Gallery" anthology style. In the first story, James Woods plays a poor fellow who wants to quit smoking and goes to a clinic that guarantees results (which he finds, to his horror, will be gotten through the torturing of his wife and child if necessary). It's funny and spooky—the best of the three. In number two, Robert Hays is a tennis bum who takes up with the wrong man's wife and finds himself involved in a deadly wager. The last has Drew Barrymore (*Firestarter*; *E.T.*) as a tyke plagued by a rather nasty troll. It's good, old-fashioned, tell-me-a-scary-story fun. Rated PG-13 for violence and gruesome scenes.

1985 98 minutes

CAULDRON OF BLOOD

★

DIRECTOR: Edward Mann (Santos Alocer)
CAST: Boris Karloff, Viveca Lindfors, Jean-Pierre Aumont

One of several films Boris Karloff made outside the U.S. shortly before his death, this is far from one of his best. Boris plays a blind sculptor who uses the skeletons of women his wife has murdered as the foundations for his projects. Slow going. Unrated.

1968 95 minutes

CHAMBER OF HORRORS

★★½

DIRECTOR: Hy Averback
CAST: Patrick O'Neal, Cesare Danova, Wilfrid Hyde-White, Suzy Parker, Tun Tun, Tony Curtis, Jeanette Nolan

A mad killer stalks 1880s Baltimore. Two wax museum owners attempt to bring him to justice. Originally produced as a television pilot titled *House of Wax*, but it was considered too violent. So extra scenes were shot, and a gimmick was added for theatrical release. Before all of the "shocking" parts, the action freezes while the "fear flasher" and the "horror horn" go off so you can cover your eyes. Don't bother; it's tame stuff. But Patrick O'Neal is deliciously demented as the one-handed killer with a custom-made stump that accommodates an assortment of wild and wicked attachments.

1966 99 minutes

CHANGELING, THE

★★★★

DIRECTOR: Peter Medak
CAST: George C. Scott, Trish Van Devere, Melvyn Douglas, Jean Marsh, Barry Morse

The first film from Canada's production boom to be released in America, this is blessed with everything a good thriller needs: a suspenseful story, excellent performances by a top-name cast, and well-paced solid direction by Peter Medak. The story centers around John Russell (Scott), a composer whose wife and daughter are killed in a tragic auto accident not far from their home in New York City. He decides he must get away from the memories of happier times, which haunt him on every familiar street corner, so he accepts a teaching position in Seattle, where he hopes to build some kind of a life for himself and continue with the only thing he has left: music. But dreams of his family plague his sleep, and strange things begin to happen in the house. Rated R.

1979 109 minutes

CHARLIE BOY

DIRECTOR: Robert Young
CAST: Leigh Lawson, Angela Bruce

Charlie Boy is an African fetish, inherited by a young British couple, that will take care of all your problems—usually by killing them. Unfortunately, the couple curses themselves and races to try to destroy the fetish and break the curse. It sounds interesting enough, but poor acting and bad direction hamper what could have been a worthwhile film.

1982 60 minutes

CHILDREN, THE

DIRECTOR: Max Calmanowicz
CAST: Martin Shaker, Gil Rogers, Gale Garnett, Joy Glacum

This is really a terrible film about kids marked by a radioactive accident while they were on a school bus. The picture should be avoided. Rated R.

1980 89 minutes

CHILDREN OF THE CORN

DIRECTOR: Fritz Kiersch
CAST: Peter Horton, Linda Hamilton, R. G. Armstrong, John Franklin

Yet another adaptation of one of author Stephen (*Carrie*; *Christine*) King's horror novels comes to the screen. This time, it's a total mess. Peter Horton and Linda Hamilton play a young couple who come to a Midwestern farming town where a young preacher with mesmerizing powers has instructed all the children to slaughter adults in order to appease a satanic demon.

The scary and serious parts in this low-budget horror flick are often laughable, but it's not funny enough to rank with *Yor: The Hunter from the Future* or *Plan 9 from Outer Space* as a classic bad movie. In other words, it's just plain bad. Rated R for violence and profanity.

1984 93 minutes

CHILDREN OF THE FULL MOON

DIRECTOR: Tom Clegg
CAST: Christopher Cazenove, Celia Gregory, Diana Dors

Even the curvaceous horror hostess Elvira and her off brand of humor can't salvage this cross between *Rosemary's Baby* and *The Wolfman*. Fans of truly bad films won't want to waste their time on this one.

1982 60 minutes

CHILDREN SHOULDN'T PLAY WITH DEAD THINGS

★

DIRECTOR: Benjamin (Bob) Clark
CAST: Alan Ormsby, Anya Ormsby, Jeffrey Gillen, Valerie Mauches, Jane Daly

If the film were as good as its title, this might have amounted to something; instead, it's notable only as an example of Bob (*Porky's*) Clark's early career. Amazing he survived such beginnings. Typical "evil dead" entry; amateur filmmakers work in a spooky graveyard and make enough noise to, well, wake the dead. Poor, washed-out cinematography and an all-but-unintelligible soundtrack make this more trouble than it's worth. Pretty grave stuff. Rated PG for violence.

1972 85 minutes

CHOPPING MALL

★★½

DIRECTOR: Jim Wynorski
CAST: Kelli Maroney, Tony O'Dell, John Terlesky, Russell Todd, Karrie Emerson, Barbara Crampton, Susie Slater, Nick Segal, Dick Miller

A group of teenagers hold the ultimate office party in the store in which they work in the local shopping mall. However, this mall is in the vanguard of modern security systems. At midnight it is impenetrably sealed and security droids, armed with high-tech weaponry, go on patrol, incapacitating any unauthorized personnel. As you may guess, the kids get trapped in the mall with the robots malfunctioning, killing anyone with whom they come in contact. This film has a good sense of humor and good visual effects. Horror fans should have a good time with it. Rated R for nudity, profanity, and violence.

1986 77 minutes

CHRISTINE

★★★½

DIRECTOR: John Carpenter
CAST: Keith Gordon, John Stockwell, Alexandra Paul, Harry Dean Stanton, Robert Prosky, Christine Belford, Roberts Blossom

Novelist Stephen King (*Carrie*; *Dead Zone*) and director John Carpenter (*Halloween*; *The Thing*) team up for top-flight, tasteful terror with this movie about a 1958 Plymouth Fury with spooky powers. It's scary without being gory; a triumph of suspense and atmosphere. Rated R for profanity and violence.

1983 111 minutes

CHRISTMAS EVIL

★½

DIRECTOR: Lewis Jackson

CAST: Brandon Maggart, Jeffery De Munn

This film about a toy factory employee who goes slowly insane has some great black comedy moments, but not enough to save the rest of the boring narrative from putting the viewer to sleep. Brandon Maggart plays the toy maker who goes over the edge and becomes a sick Santa Claus just in time to reward the nice and do some terrible things to the naughty. A great idea handled poorly. Gore fans will be disappointed by the modest body count. Not rated, but the equivalent of an R rating for sex and violence.

1983 91 minutes

CIRCUS OF HORRORS

★★★

DIRECTOR: Sidney Hayers

CAST: Anton Diffring, Erika Remberg, Yvonne Romain, Donald Pleasence

Lurid British thriller about a renegade plastic surgeon using a circus as a front. After making female criminals gorgeous, he enslaves them in his Temple of Beauty. When they want out, he colorfully offs them. Well made with good performances. This is the more violent European version.

1960 87 minutes

CLASS OF 1984

★★½

DIRECTOR: Mark Lester

CAST: Perry King, Merrie Lynn Ross, Roddy McDowall, Timothy Van Patten

Violent punkers run a school, forcing teachers to arm and security to be hired. A new teacher arrives and tries to change things, but he's beaten, and his pregnant wife is raped. He takes revenge by killing all the punkers. Rated R for violence.

1982 93 minutes

CLASS OF NUKE 'EM HIGH

DIRECTORS: Richard W. Haines, Samuel Weil

CAST: Janelle Brady, Gilbert Brenton, R. E. Ryan, Brad Dunker, James Nugent Vernon, Rick Howard, Mary Taylor

The makers of *The Toxic Avenger* strike again in this black comedy–monster movie. A sloppily managed nuclear power plant is located next door to a high school and begins to have harmful radioactive effects on the students. And what is this effect? Well, they turn into punk rockers and mutated monsters. They commit suicide and become over-sexed. And in a truly nasty scene, one girl gives birth through the mouth to a horrible bloodthirsty beast. The rest of the film highlights the attempts to kill this aberration. As far as being scary, this one fails miserably, and as far as humor, forget it. Rated R for nudity, profanity, and graphic violence.

1987 84 minutes

COLLECTOR, THE

★★★★½

DIRECTOR: William Wyler

CAST: Terence Stamp, Samantha Eggar, Maurice Dallimore, Mona Washbourne

In this chiller, Terence Stamp plays a disturbed young man who, having no friends, collects things. Unfortunately, one of the things he collects is beautiful Samantha Eggar. He keeps her as his prisoner and waits for her to fall in love with him. Extremely interesting profile of a madman but most disturbing to sane viewers.

1965 119 minutes

COLOR ME BLOOD RED

DIRECTOR: Herschell Gordon Lewis
CAST: Don Joseph, Candi Conder

An artist discovers the perfect shade of red for his paintings. (Take a guess.) Another low-budget gore film from the people who brought you *Blood Feast*. Everything about this movie is absolutely awful. Neither as funny nor as sick as Herschell Gordon Lewis's other works. Unrated, the film has violence.

1965 70 minutes

COMA

★★★½

DIRECTOR: Michael Crichton
CAST: Genevieve Bujold, Michael Douglas, Richard Widmark, Rip Torn

A woman doctor (Genevieve Bujold) becomes curious about several deaths at a hospital where patients have all lapsed into comas. Very original melodrama keeps the audience guessing. One of Michael Crichton's better film efforts. Rated PG for brief nudity and violence.

1978 113 minutes

CORPSE VANISHES, THE

★

DIRECTOR: Wallace Fox
CAST: Bela Lugosi, Luana Walters, Tristram Coffin, Minerva Urecal, George Eldredge, Elizabeth Russell

Hokey pseudoscientific thriller about crazed scientist Bela Lugosi and his efforts to keep his elderly wife young through transfusions from young girls. Another cheap quickie rushed through production and made primarily to capitalize on Bela Lugosi's waning popularity at the box office. Look for veteran character actor Tristram Coffin (*King of the Rocketmen*), but don't bother looking for Manton Moreland—he was busy making a zombie movie on Monogram's other soundstage.

1942 B & W 64 minutes

COSMIC MONSTERS, THE

★★

DIRECTOR: Gilbert Gunn
CAST: Forrest Tucker, Gaby André

Low-budget horror from Great Britain. Giant carnivorous insects invade our planet. (Sounds plausible.) No one on Earth can stop them. (I can believe that.) An alien in a flying saucer arrives to save the day. (It could happen.) Forrest Tucker plays a scientist. (Oh, come on! Now you're just getting silly.) The effects are so cheap that the monsters are transparent. But the English accents do give the picture a partial dignity.

1958 B & W 75 minutes

COUNT DRACULA

★★½

DIRECTOR: Jess (Jesus) Franco
CAST: Christopher Lee, Herbert Lom, Klaus Kinski

Christopher Lee dons the cape once again in this mediocre version of the famous tale about the undead fiend terrorizing the countryside. Lee makes a good Count, but the film's few strengths lie in its formidable supporting cast. Rated R.

1970 98 minutes

COUNT YORGA, VAMPIRE

★★★

DIRECTOR: Bob Kelljan
CAST: Robert Quarry, Roger Perry, Donna Anders, Michael Murphy

Contemporary vampire terrorizes Los Angeles. Somewhat dated, but a sharp and powerful thriller. Stars Robert Quarry, an intense, dignified actor who appeared in several horror films in the early

1970s, then abruptly left the genre. Rated R for violence.

1970 91 minutes

CRATER LAKE MONSTER, THE

★

DIRECTOR: William R. Stromberg
CAST: Richard Cardella, Glenn Roberts, Kacey Cobb

Inexpensive, unimpressive film about a prehistoric creature emerging from the usually quiet lake of the title and raising hell. Rated PG.

1977 89 minutes

CRAWLING EYE, THE

★★★

DIRECTOR: Quentin Lawrence
CAST: Forrest Tucker, Janet Munro

Acceptable horror thriller about an unseen menace hiding within the dense fog surrounding a mountaintop. A nice sense of doom builds throughout, and the monster remains unseen (always the best way) until the very end. That public appearance isn't a letdown, either; this is one vile beast. Forrest Tucker is an acceptable hero, but the real star is the picture itself... it delivers a good case of the jitters.

1958 B & W 85 minutes

CRAWLING HAND, THE

½

DIRECTOR: Herbert L. Strock
CAST: Peter Breck, Rod Lauren, Kent Taylor

Low-budget tale of a dismembered hand at large in a small town, killing off the local residents in a psychotic "reign of terror." Goofy film really is as dumb as it sounds.

1963 B & W 89 minutes

CRAZIES, THE

★★

DIRECTOR: George Romero
CAST: Lane Carroll, W. G. McMillan, Harold Wayne Jones, Loyd Hollar, Lynn Lowry, Richard Liberty, Richard France

A military plane carrying an experimental germ warfare virus crashes near a small midwestern town, releasing a plague of murderous madness. A young couple tries to escape infection, evade the crazies, and outrun soldiers sworn to quarantine the town or —failing that—nuke the community in an attempt to burn out the virus before it can spread. Director Romero attempts to make a statement about martial law while trying to capitalize on the success of his cult classic, *Night of the Living Dead*. While not as intense as other Romero movies, this one contains its share of spilt blood, shocks, and chills. Recommended for horror fans. Rated R.

1975 103 minutes

CREATURE FROM BLACK LAKE

★★

DIRECTOR: Joy Houck Jr.
CAST: Jack Elam, Dub Taylor, Dennis Fimple, John David Carson

This is another forgettable, cliché-ridden horror film. The "stars," Jack Elam and Dub Taylor, actually play small supporting roles, while the leads were given to two novices. That's a shame, because Elam and Taylor provide the only relief from a routine and inconsistent script. Dennis Fimple and John David Carson play two college students from Chicago who go to the swamps of Louisiana in search of the missing link. Through the reluctant help of the locals, they come face to face with a man in an ape suit. Rated PG.

1979 97 minutes

CREATURE FROM THE BLACK LAGOON

★★★½

DIRECTOR: Jack Arnold
CAST: Richard Carlson, Julia Adams, Richard Denning, Nestor Paiva, Antonio Moreno, Whit Bissell

In the remote backwaters of the Amazon, members of a scientific expedition run afoul of a vicious prehistoric man-fish inhabiting the area and are forced to fight for their lives. Excellent film (first in a trilogy) features true-to-life performances, a bone-chilling score by Joseph Gershenson, and beautiful, lush photography that unfortunately turns to mud in this murky 3-D video print.

1954 79 minutes

CREEPERS

★★

DIRECTOR: Dario Argento
CAST: Jennifer Connelly, Donald Pleasence, Daria Nicolodi, Dalila Di Lazzaro

Plodding Italian production casts Jennifer Connelly as a young girl with the ability to communicate with, and control, insects (à la Willard and his rats). This unique power comes into play when she must use her little friends to track down the maniac who's been murdering students at the Swiss girl's school she's attending, as bugs are attracted to rotting corpses. Yes, it's all as dumb as it sounds, with numerous close-ups of maggots to make the viewer cringe. Originally released overseas as *Phenomena*, one would hate to have to sit through that version, as it's at least thirty minutes longer. Rated R for gore and slime.

1985 82 minutes

CREEPING FLESH, THE

★★★

DIRECTOR: Freddie Francis
CAST: Peter Cushing, Christopher Lee, Lorna Heilbron, George Benson

Peter Cushing and Christopher Lee are, as always, topnotch, in this creepy tale about an evil entity accidentally brought back to life by an unsuspecting scientist. While not as good as the stars' Hammer Film collaborations (*Horror of Dracula*; *The Mummy*), this will still prove pleasing to their fans. Rated PG.

1972 91 minutes

CREEPSHOW

★★★★

DIRECTOR: George Romero
CAST: Hal Holbrook, Adrienne Barbeau, Fritz Weaver, Leslie Nielsen, Stephen King

Stephen King, the modern master of printed terror, and George Romero, the director who frightened unsuspecting moviegoers out of their wits with *Night of the Living Dead*, teamed for this funny and scary tribute to the E.C. horror comics of the 1950s. Like *Vault of Horror* and *Tales from the Crypt*, two titles from that period, it's an anthology of ghoulish bedtime stories. Rated R for profanity and gore.

1982 120 minutes

CRITTERS

★★★

DIRECTOR: Stephen Hereck
CAST: Dee Wallace Stone, M. Emmet Walsh, Scott Grimes, Don Opper, Terrence Mann

This mild horror film with its hilarious spots could become a cult classic. In it, eight ravenous critters escape from a distant planet and head for earth. Two futuristic bounty hunters pursue them, and the fun begins. The creatures kill a sheriff, then invade a farm to terrorize that family. The comedy begins when the creatures talk and the audience enjoys the subtitles. The bounty hunters also provide some light moments as they drive in reverse all the way to the town and then exhibit their outstanding strength to a "prove-it-to-me" Kansas crowd. These humorous touches set this film apart from the other takeoffs of *E.T.* and *Gremlins* and make it well worth watching. Rated PG for gore and profanity.

1986 90 minutes

CRUCIBLE OF HORROR

★★★½

DIRECTOR: Viktors Ritelis

CAST: Michael Gough, Yvonne Mitchell, Sharon Gurney

Intense story of a violent, domineering man (Michael Gough in one of his better roles) who drives his passive wife (Yvonne Mitchell) and nubile daughter (Sharon Gurney) to murder in this English spine-chiller. The suspense and terror build unrelentingly as the two begin to suspect that their victim may not be as dead as they led themselves to believe, and is now quite possibly stalking *them*! Keep the lights on! Rated R.

1971 91 minutes

CRUISE INTO TERROR

★

DIRECTOR: Bruce Kessler

CAST: Dirk Benedict, John Forsythe, Lynda Day George, Christopher George, Stella Stevens, Ray Milland, Frank Converse, Lee Meriwether, Hugh O'Brian

Dreadful suspense flick made for the tube. When a band of TV actors, old-timers, and hacks assemble on one boat for a cruise, you know something dull is going to take place. This one is about an ancient Egyptian sarcophagus that is haunting the small ocean liner and the poor souls on board. Completely predictable. This made-for-TV movie is not rated, but would be a PG for adult subject matter.

1977 100 minutes

CUJO

★★★½

DIRECTOR: Lewis Teague

CAST: Dee Wallace, Danny Pintauro, Daniel Hugh-Kelly, Christopher Stone

Stephen King's story of a mother and son terrorized by a rabid Saint Bernard results in a movie that keeps viewers on the edge of their seats. Rated R for violence, language.

1983 91 minutes

CURSE OF FRANKENSTEIN, THE

★★★½

DIRECTOR: Terence Fisher

CAST: Peter Cushing, Christopher Lee, Robert Urquhart, Noel Hood

Hammer Films' version of the Frankenstein story about a scientist who creates a living man from the limbs and organs of corpses. Peter Cushing gives a strong performance as the doctor, with Christopher Lee his equal as the sympathetic creature. Some inspired moments are peppered throughout this well-handled horror tale.

1957 83 minutes

CURSE OF KING TUT'S TOMB, THE

★½

DIRECTOR: Philip Leacock

CAST: Eva Marie Saint, Robin Ellis, Raymond Burr, Harry Andrews, Tom Baker

Made-for-TV misfire concerning the mysterious events surrounding the opening of King Tut's tomb. Dumb film made even more ridiculous by Paul Scofield's uninspired narration. Close the lid and bury this one.

1980 100 minutes

CURSE OF THE CAT PEOPLE, THE

★★★

DIRECTORS: Gunther Von Fristch, Robert Wise

CAST: Simone Simon, Kent Smith, Jane Randolph, Elizabeth Russell

When Val Lewton was ordered by the studio to make a sequel to the successful *Cat People*, he came up with this gentle fantasy about a child who is haunted by spirits. Not to be confused with the 1980s version of *Cat People*.

1944 B & W 70 minutes

CURSE OF THE DEMON

★★★★½

DIRECTOR: Jacques Tourneur

CAST: Dana Andrews, Peggy Cummins, Niall MacGinnis, Maurice Denham

Horrifying tale of an American occult expert, Dr. Holden (Dana Andrews), traveling to London to expose a supposed devil cult led by sinister Professor Karswell (Niall MacGinnis). Unfortunately for Holden, Karswell's cult proves to be all too real as a demon from hell is dispatched by the professor to put an end to the annoying investigation. Riveting, electric production is a true classic of the genre, with knockout effects and Clifton Parker's dynamite score adding to the fun. Based on the story "Casting the Runes," by M. R. James.

1958 B & W 96 minutes

CURSE OF THE WEREWOLF, THE

★★★½

DIRECTOR: Terence Fisher

CAST: Oliver Reed, Clifford Evans, Yvonne Romain, Anthony Dawson

After being brutally raped in a castle dungeon by an imprisoned street beggar, a young woman gives birth to a son with a strange appetite for blood. His heritage remains a mystery until adulthood, whereupon he begins transforming into a wolf as the full moon rises. This brooding Hammer Films production builds slowly, hesitant to show its monster before the rousing climax. Oliver Reed is fine in the role of the werewolf, one of his earliest screen performances.

1961 91 minutes

CURTAINS

★

DIRECTOR: Jonathan Stryker

CAST: John Vernon, Samantha Eggar, Linda Thorson, Anne Ditchburn

Samantha Eggar stars in this mediocre splatter flick as a movie actress who, with the help of her director (John Vernon, from *Animal House*), gets herself committed to a mental institution as preparation for an upcoming film. However, she is left in the funny farm while the director and the movie go on without her. She escapes, and, one by one, the actresses trying out for her role are murdered. Watching your clothes toss around in a machine at a coin laundry offers more excitement. Rated R for nudity, profanity, violence, and sex.

1983 89 minutes

CYCLOPS, THE

★★½

DIRECTOR: Bert I. Gordon

CAST: James Craig, Lon Chaney Jr., Gloria Talbott

Low-budget whiz Bert I. Gordon does it again with this cheaply made but effective film about a woman (Gloria Talbott) whose brother is transformed into a big, crazy monster by—what else?—radiation. Neat little movie.

1957 B & W 75 minutes

DAMIEN: OMEN II

★★★½

DIRECTOR: Don Taylor
CAST: William Holden, Lee Grant, Lew Ayres, Sylvia Sidney

In this first sequel to *The Omen*, William Holden plays the world's richest man, Richard Thorn. In the previous picture, Richard's brother Robert (Gregory Peck) is shot by police while attempting to kill his son, who he believed to be the Antichrist, son of Satan. *Damien: Omen II* picks up seven years later and shows Richard and his wife, Ann (Lee Grant), raising Damien (Jonathon Scott-Taylor) as their own son. He and their real son, Mark (Lucas Donat), get along well, and the family is the picture of happiness . . . until Damien reaches puberty. Rated R.

1978 107 minutes

DANGEROUSLY CLOSE

★★

DIRECTOR: Albert Pyun
CAST: John Stockwell, Carey Lowell, Bradford Bancroft, Madison Mason, J. Eddie Peck

In this disappointing modern-day vigilante film, a group of students, led by a Vietnam veteran teacher, tries to purge their school of "undesirable elements" by any means necessary—including murder. Film starts out promising enough but soon loses focus with its rambling script and stereotypical situations. Director Albert Pyun does well in building suspense and evolving characters, but spoils everything by opting for an unimaginative, trite ending. Rated R for profanity, violence, and brief nudity.

1986 95 minutes

DARK, THE

★½

DIRECTOR: John "Bud" Cardos
CAST: William Devane, Cathy Lee Crosby, Richard Jaeckel, Keenan Wynn, Vivian Blaine

If your parents told you there was nothing frightening about the dark, you should have listened to them. This unthrilling thriller pits writer William Devane and TV reporter Cathy Lee Crosby against a deadly alien. Little tension and few surprises. Rated R.

1979 92 minutes

DARK FORCES

★★★

DIRECTOR: Simon Wincer
CAST: Robert Powell, Broderick Crawford, David Hemmings, Carmen Duncan, Alyson Best

Robert Powell plays a modern-day conjurer who gains the confidence of a family by curing their terminally ill son; or does he? The evidence stacks up against Powell as we find he may be a foreign spy and stage magician *extraordinaire*. Twists and turns run rampant in this supernatural thriller. Powell is as intense and flamboyant as he was in any of his previous roles, while Broderick Crawford is two-dimensional and dull. While uneven in pacing at times, this film is decent entertainment. Rated PG for brief nudity and some violence.

1984 96 minutes

DARK MIRROR, THE

★★★½

DIRECTOR: Robert Siodmak
CAST: Olivia De Havilland, Lew Ayres, Thomas Mitchell, Richard Long

Olivia De Havilland, who did this sort of thing extremely well, plays twin sisters—one good, one evil —enmeshed in murder. Lew Ayres is the shrink who must divine who is who as the evil sibling deftly connives to muddy the waters. Good suspense.

1946 B & W 85 minutes

DARK NIGHT OF THE SCARECROW

★★★★

DIRECTOR: Frank di Felitta

CAST: Charles Durning, Tonya Crowe, Jocelyn Brando, Larry Drake

Despite its hasty beginning that fails to set up a strong premise for the pivotal scene of the movie, *Dark Night of the Scarecrows* is a chilling film that mixes the supernatural with a moral message. While the film borrows some ideas from such films as *To Kill a Mockingbird* and *Of Mice and Men*, its overall feel is quite different. Charles Durning plays an uncharacteristic bad guy here that gives this made-for-television film an even more intense edge.

1981 100 minutes

DARK PLACES

★★★½

DIRECTOR: Don Sharp

CAST: Christopher Lee, Joan Collins, Herbert Lom, Robert Hardy, Jane Birkin, Jean Marsh

Better-than-average British haunted house film complete with Mr. Dracula himself—Christopher Lee! The Count and Joan Collins play two fortune hunters trying to scare away the caretaker of a dead man's mansion (Robert Hardy) so they can get to the bundle of cash stashed in the old house. The film has a sophisticated psychological twist to it that is missing in most horror films of late, but the cardboard bats on clearly visible wires have got to go! Rated PG for gore, sex, and profanity.

1973 91 minutes

DARK SECRET OF HARVEST HOME, THE

★★½

DIRECTOR: Leo Penn

CAST: Bette Davis, Rosanna Arquette, David Ackroyd, Michael O'Keefe

Novelist-actor Tom Tryon's bewitching story of creeping horror gets fair treatment in this dark and foreboding film of Janus personalities and incantations in picturesque New England.

1978 118 minutes

DAUGHTER OF DR. JEKYLL

★★

DIRECTOR: Edgar G. Ulmer

CAST: Gloria Talbott, John Agar, Arthur Shields, John Dierkes

Okay horror film about a girl (Gloria Talbott) who thinks she's inherited the famous dual personality after several local citizens turn up dead.

1957 B & W 71 minutes

DAWN OF THE DEAD

★★★★

DIRECTOR: George A. Romero

CAST: David Emge, Ken Foree, Scott Reiniger, Gaylen Ross, Tom Savini

This movie can only be described as hard-core blood and gore. The central characters are three men and one woman who try to escape from man-eating corpses. This film is the sequel to *Night of the Living Dead*. As a horror movie, it's a masterpiece, but if you have a weak stomach, avoid this one. Rated R.

1979 126 minutes

DAY OF THE ANIMALS

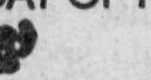

DIRECTOR: William Girdler

CAST: Christopher George, Lynda Day George, Richard Jaeckel, Leslie Nielsen, Michael Ansara, Ruth Roman

Nature goes nuts after being exposed to the sun's radiation when the Earth's ozone layer is destroyed. Another solidly laughable piece of nonsense from the star of *Pieces* and *Grizzly*, Christopher George. Teaming up with his wife, Lynda Day, these two became the Tracy and Hepburn of junk films, and here's an example of their prime. Chock full of the kind of gory violence that action fans crave, *Animals* masquerades as an ecological horror story but is really nothing more than a sick, dull bloodbath. With Leslie Nielsen, who is getting harder to take seriously anyway, and a lot of very talented German shepherds, which do us all a favor by helping their furry friends finish off the cast. Rated R for violence, profanity, and gore.

1977 98 minutes

DAY OF THE DEAD

★½

DIRECTOR: George A. Romero
CAST: Lori Cardille, Terry Alexander, Joe Picato, Richard Liberty

The third film in George A. Romero's *Dead* series doesn't hold up to its predecessors. It takes place some months after *Dawn of the Dead* in an underground military complex. A group of soldiers and civilian scientists, trying to find a way to stop the spread of flesh-eating dead, have lost all contact with the outside world and tempers are flaring. One of the scientists believes the cannibalistic zombies can be domesticated and his experiments only further enrage the already short-tempered soldiers. What ensues is a power struggle between the two factions—with, eventually, a bloody battle with the zombies in the middle. Like earlier films in the series, *Day of the Dead* portrays graphic scenes of cannibalism, dismemberment, and other gory carnage. Unlike the other films this one has no truly likable characters to root for, with the exception of one very funny zombie named Bad. There are quite few scary moments, but after *Night of the Living Dead* and *Dawn of the Dead*, two exciting and truly horrifying films, *Day of the Dead* is a real disappointment. Not rated, but contains scenes of graphic violence.

1985 100 minutes

DEAD AND BURIED

★★

DIRECTOR: Gary A. Sherman
CAST: James Farentino, Melody Anderson, Jack Albertson, Dennis Redfield

Although this cinematic venture by the creators of *Alien* (Ronald Shusett and Dan O'Bannon) is a notch above many science-fiction/horror films, it falls short on intelligence and excitement. The story involves a series of gory murders, and the weird part is that the victims seem to be coming back to life. The puzzle is resolved during the suspenseful, eerie ending—definitely the high point of the movie. James Farentino stars as the sheriff investigating the murders. Jack Albertson, in his last film, is a sinister mortician. Rated R for sex and violence.

1981 92 minutes

DEAD MEN DON'T DIE, THE

★½

DIRECTOR: Curtis Harrington
CAST: Geroge Hamilton, Ray Milland, Joan Blondell, Linda Cristal, Ralph Meeker

This rather unfrightening horror film features George Hamilton, who must take on the Zombie Master in order to clear his dead brother's name. The unbelievable story is set in the 1930s. Made for TV, this film bores more than it entertains.

1975 76 minutes

DEAD MEN WALK

★★

DIRECTOR: Sam Newfield
CAST: George Zucco, Mary Carlisle, Nedrick Young, Dwight Frye

Master character actor George Zucco makes the most of one of his few leading roles, a dual one at that, in this grade-Z cheapie from Hollywood's infamous Poverty Row. Zucco is two brothers, one good, one evil, in this spooky tale about vampires and zombies. Dwight Frye adds to the fun in a supporting role that recalls those he played in *Dracula* and *Frankenstein*. For buffs only.

1943 B & W 67 minutes

DEAD OF NIGHT

★

DIRECTOR: Dan Curtis
CAST: Ed Begley Jr., John Hackett, Patrick MacNee

This trilogy of shockers written by Richard Matheson *(Incredible Shrinking Man)* and directed by Dan Curtis *(Dark Shadows)* has some suspense and interesting twists, but is far inferior to these gentlemen's other achievements. Elvira is host on this, another in her "Thriller Video" series, and offers some light comedy and nice scenery to round out the film.

1977 76 minutes

DEAD OF WINTER

★★★

DIRECTOR: Arthur Penn
CAST: Mary Steenburgen, Roddy McDowall, Jan Rubes, William Russ, Wayne Robson, Ken Pogue

When aspiring actress Mary Steenburgen steps in at the last minute to replace a starring performer who has walked off the set of a film in production, she is certain it is the chance of a lifetime. But once trapped in a remote mansion with the creepy filmmakers (Roddy McDowall and Jan Rubes), she begins to believe it may be the last act of her lifetime. Steenburgen makes the most of a juicy role in this shocker, solidly directed by Arthur Penn. The story is a bit contrived, but one only realizes it after the film is over. Rated R for profanity and violence.

1987 98 minutes

DEAD ZONE, THE

★★★★

DIRECTOR: David Cronenberg
CAST: Christopher Walken, Brooke Adams, Tom Skerritt, Herbert Lom, Martin Sheen

This is an exciting adaptation of the Stephen King suspense novel about a man who uses his psychic powers to solve multiple murders and perhaps prevent the end of the world. Rated R for violence and profanity.

1983 103 minutes

DEADLY BLESSING

★

DIRECTOR: Wes Craven
CAST: Maren Jensen, Susan Buckner, Sharon Strone, Lois Nettleton, Ernest Borgnine, Jeff East

If beautiful women were enough to make a horror film succeed, this one would rate a 10. Unfortunately, that's all this film—about a young woman (Maren Jensen) who marries a member of a strange religious sect and finds herself plagued by strange forces after he is murdered—has going for it. The tactics are, for the most part, obvious, and the story is predictable. Wes Craven (*The Last House on the Left*; *The Hills Have Eyes*) directed. Rated R because of nudity and bloody scenes.

1981 102 minutes

DEADLY EYES

★

DIRECTOR: Robert Clouse
CAST: Sam Groom, Sara Botsford, Scatman Crothers

Grain full of steroids creates rats the size of small dogs in this seemingly familiar horror tale adapted from British author James Herbert's novel *The Rats*. "Character development" is ridiculously slow, making us wait for another rat attack, but those are so silly that the whole film rapidly descends into the sewer. Cast turns in reasonable performances, but the script and direction are both by the numbers. Only for diehard Scatman Crothers fans. This is a B movie, all right—but the B stands for Boring. Rated R for gore, nudity, and simulated sex.

1982 87 minutes

DEADLY FRIEND

★½

DIRECTOR: Wes Craven
CAST: Matthew Laborteaux, Michael Sharrett, Kristy Swanson

A teen-age whiz revives his murdered girlfriend by inserting a computer chip into her brain. The girl becomes a robot-zombie and kills people. This would-be thriller has much in common with its title character. It's cold, mechanical, and brain-dead. Rated R for violence.

1986 99 minutes

DEADLY SANCTUARY

DIRECTOR: Jess (Jesus) Franco
CAST: Sylva Koscina, Mercedes McCambridge, Jack Palance, Klaus Kinski, Akim Tamiroff

Based on the writings of the Marquis de Sade, this poor excuse for a horror film follows the tragic lives of two newly orphaned sisters as they fall prey to prison, prostitution, murder, and a torturous hellfire club led by Jack Palance. All this is framed by sequences of de Sade (Klaus Kinski) wiping the perspiration from his brow, sitting at his writing table . . . and on and on. This film was supposedly banned in Europe because of its violent content, though any graphic violence is limited. Nudity is brief, and scenes of torture are only intimated.

1970 93 minutes

DEADTIME STORIES

DIRECTOR: Jeffrey S. Delman
CAST: Mike Mesmer, Brian DePersia, Scott Valentine

Bizarre, ghoulish versions of fairy tales—including "Little Red Riding Hood" and "Goldilocks and the Three Bears"—make up this low-budget horror anthology. Its framing stories feature a beer-guzzling uncle cajoled into reading bedtime stories to a pesky nephew and the scary twists he puts on each. The score, cinematography, and settings are all pretty tacky, and so, now that we think about it, is everything about this film. Rated R.

1987 89 minutes

DEAR DEAD DELILAH

★

DIRECTOR: John Farris
CAST: Agnes Moorehead, Will Geer, Michael Ansara, Dennis Patrick

Delilah (Agnes Moorehead) is about to die, but there's a fortune buried somewhere on her property that her loony relatives will do anything to get a hold of. Idiotic from the outset, with many well-known stars wasted. Rated R for blood.

1972 90 minutes

DEATH AT LOVE HOUSE

★★

DIRECTOR: E. W. Swackhamer
CAST: Robert Wagner, Kate Jackson, Sylvia Sidney, Joan Blondell, Dorothy Lamour, John Carradine, Bill Macy, Marianna Hill

Much tamer than the lurid title would suggest. Robert Wagner plays a writer who becomes obsessed with a movie queen who died years earlier. He struggles to hang on to his personality and sanity as he investigates the link between her and his own past. This mildly suspenseful hokum is made more palatable by the engaging cast, particularly the veteran performers, who turn in juicy character bits. Made for TV.

1976 78 minutes

DEATH VALLEY

★★

DIRECTOR: Dick Richards
CAST: Paul Le Mat, Catharine Hicks, Stephen McHattie, A. Wilford Brimley

Paul Le Mat (*American Graffiti*) and Catharine Hicks star in this okay horror film about a vacation that turns into a nightmare. Rated R for violence and gore.

1982 87 minutes

DEATHSHIP

★★

DIRECTOR: Alvin Rakoff
CAST: George Kennedy, Richard Crenna, Nick Mancuso, Sally Ann Howes, Kate Reid, Victoria Burgoyne, Jennifer McKinney, Saul Rubinek

This story of a modern-day lost *Dutchman* involves a World War II battleship—haunted by the ghosts of those who died on it. The ship seeks out and destroys any seagoing vessels it can find because it needs blood to continue running. The survivors of an ocean liner board this relic and are immediately possessed or killed off one by one. There are a few chills along the way, but not enough. Rated R for violence and brief nudity.

1980 91 minutes

DEEP END

★★★½

DIRECTOR: Jerzy Skolimowski
CAST: John Moulder-Brown, Jane Asher, Diana Dors

A young man working in a London bath house becomes obsessed with a beautiful female co-worker, which eventually leads to disaster. Offbeat drama with realistic performances by the cast. Rated R.

1970 88 minutes

DEEP RED

★★★

DIRECTOR: Dario Argento
CAST: David Hemmings, Daria Nicolodi, Gabrielle Lavia

Another stylish and brutal horror-mystery from Italian director Dario Argento. His other works include *The Bird with the Crystal Plummage* and *Suspiria*. Like those, this film is slim on plot and a bit too talky, but Argento builds tension beautifully with rich atmosphere and driving electronic music. Rated R for violence.

1975 98 minutes

DEMENTIA 13

★★½

DIRECTOR: Francis Coppola
CAST: William Campbell, Luana Anders, Mary Mitchel, Patrick Magee

Early Francis Ford Coppola film is a low-budget shocker centering on a family plagued by violent ax murders that are somehow connected with the death of the youngest daughter many years before. Acting is standard, but the dreary photography, creepy locations, and weird music are what make this movie click. Produced by Roger Corman.

1963 B & W 75 minutes

DEMON BARBER OF FLEET STREET, THE

★★½

DIRECTOR: George King
CAST: Tod Slaughter, Eve Lister, Bruce Seton, Davina Craig

Long before Vincent Price was the embodiment of evil, there was Tod Slaughter, master of the Grand Guignol school of lip-smacking villainy and star of many bloody thrillers. Partially based on a true occurrence, this popular folk tale tells the story of an amoral barber who cuts the throats of his clients, robs them, and then drops them to his confederate who truns them into meat pies. Seldom seen in America since World War II, this influential film was a great success for the flamboyant Slaughter and provides the basis for the recent musical theater hit.

1936 B & W 76 minutes

DEMON LOVER, THE

DIRECTOR: Donald B. Jackson
CAST: Christmas Robbins, Val Mayeric, Gunnar Hansen, Tom Hutton, Sonny Bell

A bunch of college kids and bikers get involved with a Satanist who raises a demon that tears almost everyone apart. Not only is the acting rotten, but half the incantations are stolen from Robert Howard's Conan stories. A point of interest is that the star, Val Mayeric, is the man who designed the comic-book character Howard the Duck. Only true horror and gore fans will find entertainment here. Rated R for nudity, profanity, and violence.

1976 87 minutes

DEMONS

★★★

DIRECTOR: Lamberto Bava
CAST: Urbano Barberini, Natasha Hovey, Paola Cozza

Selected at random, people on the street are invited to an advance screening of a new horror film. In the lobby of the theatre are statues portraying various demonic figures and scenes of violence. A prostitute pricks her finger on the horn of one of the demonic statues and later, in a shockingly, well-crafted transformation, becomes a demon. In a murderous rage, she tears apart others in the theatre. When the members of the audience try to escape, they find themselves trapped within. Although much of the acting is poor and some story elements are plain stupid, this actually is a very frightening movie. It also sports some of the best special effects you've ever seen and has a soundtrack featuring such heavy metal bands as Billy Idol and Mötley Crüe. Not rated, but features graphic violence and adult language.

1986 89 minutes

DEMONS OF LUDLOW, THE

DIRECTOR: Bill Rebane
CAST: Paul Von Hausen, Shephanie Cushna, James Robinson, Carol Perry, C. Dave Davis, Debra Dulman

Regrettable little horror flick about an eastern seaboard community haunted by an old piano that is possessed. Terrible special effects and an ending that leaves a few questions unanswered. But by that time, will you really care? Not rated, but the equivalent of an R for sex, nudity, profanity, violence, and gore.

1983 83 minutes

DEVIL BAT, THE

★★

DIRECTOR: Jean Yarbrough
CAST: Bela Lugosi, Suzanne Kaaren, Dave O'Brien, Guy Usher, Yolande Mallot, Donald Kerr

Pretty fair thriller from PRC, chief competition to Monogram Studios for the title of Poverty Row King, gives us Bela Lugosi as yet another bloodthirsty mad scientist who trains oversize rubber bats to suck blood from selected victims by use of a scent. Lugosi is as hammy as ever, and popular B star Dave O'Brien (*Captain Midnight*) plays an enthusiastic and resilient hero with conviction. One of director Jean Yarbrough's better efforts, but typical of the kind of roles once-important actor Lugosi reprised for the rest of his career.

1941 B & W 69 minutes

DEVIL BAT'S DAUGHTER

★½

DIRECTOR: Frank Wisbar
CAST: Rosemary La Planche, Michael Hale, John James, Molly Lamont

Unimaginative sequel to *Devil Bat* finds heroine Rosemary La Planche fearing for her sanity as her father spends more and more of his time experimenting with those darn bats . . . . Low-buget bore from PRC offers a pseudo-monster in the form of a giant bat suspected of murdering several locals, but this ploy had been used in many films before this and was old hat by the time this groaner was made.

1946 B & W 66 minutes

DEVIL DOG: THE HOUND OF HELL

(turkey)

DIRECTOR: Curtis Harrington
CAST: Richard Crenna, Yvette Mimieux, Victor Jory, Ken Kercheval

This made-for-television movie is even more ridiculous than the title implies. Richard Crenna tries to save the wife and kids from the family pooch, which is actually a demon in disguise. It gets worse as Crenna uses Indian magic to battle lousy acting and poor special effects.

1976 95 minutes

DEVIL DOLL, THE

★★★½

DIRECTOR: Tod Browning
CAST: Lionel Barrymore, Maureen O'Sullivan, Frank Lawton, Henry B. Walthall

This imaginative fantasy thriller pits crazed Lionel Barrymore and his tiny "devil dolls" against those who have done him wrong. Although not as original an idea now as it was then, the acting, special effects, and director Tod Browning's odd sense of humor make this worth seeing.

1936 B & W 79 minutes

DEVIL GIRL FROM MARS

½

DIRECTOR: David McDonald
CAST: Patricia Laffan, Hazel Court, Hugh McDermott, Peter Reynolds

This oddball British "horror" film must be the overseas answer to *Cat Women of the Moon*, except that it doesn't have the saving grace of Sonny Tufts' presence. This novel story of a lanky messenger (the Devil Girl) sent from her native planet to kidnap Earthmen for reproductive purposes is lacking in thrills, special effects, tension, and just about everything else a good horror film should have—but like its sister entry *Fire Maidens from Outer Space*, it has a certain audacity that earns its half star. If you want to be glued to your seat, pass this one by; if you just want a few laughs or a nondemanding film this might be for you.

1955 B & W 76 minutes

DEVIL'S RAIN, THE

★★½

DIRECTOR: Robert Fuest
CAST: Ernest Borgnine, Ida Lupino, William Shatner, Eddie Albert, Tom Skerritt, Keenan Wynn

Great cast in a fair shocker about a band of devil worshipers at large in a small town. Terrific make-up, especially Ernest Borgnine's! Rated PG for language, violence.

1975 85 minutes

DEVIL'S UNDEAD, THE

★★★½

DIRECTOR: Peter Sasdy
CAST: Christopher Lee, Peter Cushing, Georgia Brown, Diana Dors

A surprisingly entertaining and suspenseful release starring the two kings of British horror, Christopher Lee and Peter Cushing, as a sort of modern-day Holmes and Watson in a tale of demonic possession. Rated PG.

1979 91 minutes

DEVONSVILLE TERROR, THE

★★★

DIRECTOR: Ulli Lommel
CAST: Paul Wilson, Suzanna Love, Donald Pleasence

Three witches are killed in Devonsville in 1683, and one of them places a curse on the townspeople. Flash forward to the present, when three women arrive in Devonsville. Are they, or are they not, the reincarnations of the witches? Although this may sound like pure exploitation, this film is actually a complex psychological text about the difficulties of being a woman. Good performances, high production values, and a competently scary script that is not based on special effects. Rated R for nudity, violence, mild gore.

1983 97 minutes

DIABOLIQUE

★★★★

DIRECTOR: Henri-Georges Clouzot
CAST: Simone Signoret, Vera Clouzot, Charles Vanel, Paul Meurisse

This classic thriller builds slowly but rapidly gathers momentum along the way. Both wife and mistress of a headmaster conspire to kill him. This twisted plot of murder has since been copied many times. In French, with English subtitles.

1955 B & W 107 minutes

DIAL M FOR MURDER

★★★★

DIRECTOR: Alfred Hitchcock
CAST: Grace Kelly, Robert Cummings, Ray Milland, John Williams

Alfred Hitchcock imbues this classic thiller with his well-known touches of sustained suspense and clever camera vantages. Ray Milland is a rather sympathetic villain whose desire to inherit his wife's fortune leads him to one conclusion: murder. His plan for pulling off the "perfect crime" is foiled temporarily. Undaunted, he quickly switches to Plan B, with even more entertaining results.

1954 105 minutes

DIE! DIE! MY DARLING!

★★½

DIRECTOR: Silvio Narizzano
CAST: Tallulah Bankhead, Stephanie Powers, Peter Vaughn, Donald Sutherland

This British thriller was Tallulah

Bankhead's last movie. She plays a crazed woman who kidnaps her late son's fiancée for punishment and salvation. Grisly fun for Bankhead fans, but may be too heavy-handed for others. Unrated, the film has violence.

1965 97 minutes

DIE SCREAMING, MARIANNE

DIRECTOR: Pete Walker
CAST: Susan George, Barry Evans, Chris Sandford

Graphic horror film concerns a young girl (Susan George), pursued by numerous crazies who try their best to prevent her from reaching her twenty-first birthday. Why does trash like this have to be made? Full of clichés and bad acting. Rated R.

1972 99 minutes

DINOSAURUS!

★★½

DIRECTOR: Irvin S. Yeaworth Jr.
CAST: Ward Ramsey, Paul Lukather, Kristina Hanson, Alan Roberts

Workers at a remote construction site accidentally stumble upon a prehistoric brontosaurus, tyrannosaurus rex, and a caveman (all quite alive) while excavating the area. Sure, the monsters look fake, and most of the humor is unintentional, but this film is entertaining nonetheless.

1960 85 minutes

DOCTOR AND THE DEVILS, THE

★★★

DIRECTOR: Freddie Francis
CAST: Timothy Dalton, Jonathan Pryce, Twiggy, Julian Sands, Stephen Rea, Phyllis Logan, Beryl Reid, Sian Phillips

This film, based on a true story, with an original screenplay by Dylan Thomas, is set in England in the 1800s. Dr. Cook (Timothy Dalton) is a professor of anatomy, and his philosophy is, "Anatomy is vital to the progress of medicine, medicine is vital to the progress of mankind, and any end justifies the means to see that I fulfill this." His problem is not having enough corpses to use in class demonstrations. The law provides for only the use of bodies of hanged criminals. Since he has used up this resource, he pays grave robbers for his supply. Enter two of the most ruthless and unsavory murderers in recent film history, Fallon (Jonathan Pryce) and Broom (Stephen Rea). Dr. Murray (Julian Sands), Cook's assistant, who develops a love interest with a local prostitute (Twiggy), discovers and disapproves of Cook's methods. After several encounters, with scenes not for the squeamish, our villains meet an ironic conclusion. Rated R for language, simulated sex, and violence.

1985 93 minutes

DR. JEKYLL AND MR. HYDE

★★★

DIRECTOR: Victor Fleming
CAST: Spencer Tracy, Ingrid Bergman, Lana Turner, Donald Crisp, C. Aubrey Smith, Sara Allgood

A well-done version of Robert Louis Stevenson's classic story about a good doctor who dares to venture into the unknown. The horror of his transformation is played down in favor of the emotional and psychological consequences. Spencer Tracy and Ingrid Bergman are excellent, the production lush.

1941 B & W 114 minutes

DR. PHIBES RISES AGAIN

★★★½

DIRECTOR: Robert Fuest
CAST: Vincent Price, Robert Quarry, Peter Jeffrey, Valli Kemp, Fiona Lewis, Peter

Cushing, Hugh Griffith, Terry-Thomas, Beryl Reid

Good-natured terror abounds in this fun sequel to *The Abominable Dr. Phibes*, with Vincent Price reprising his role as a disfigured doctor desperately searching for a way to restore his dead wife, Victoria, to life. This time there appears to be a slight ray of hope in Egypt, but there's also competition from Robert Quarry's expedition to contend with. So begins Phibes's gradual elimination of his adversaries, with the help of his dedicated assistant, Vulnavia (Valli Kemp), in the ingenious fashion that makes these films so entertaining. Rated PG for mild violence.

1972 89 minutes

DR. TERROR'S HOUSE OF HORRORS

★★★

DIRECTOR: Freddie Francis
CAST: Peter Cushing, Christopher Lee, Ray Castle, Donald Sutherland, Neil McCallum

Good anthology horror entertainment about a fortune-teller (Peter Cushing) who has some frightening revelations for his clients. A top-flight example of British genre movie-making.

1965 98 minutes

DOMINIQUE IS DEAD

★★

DIRECTOR: Michael Anderson
CAST: Cliff Robertson, Jean Simmons, Jenny Agutter, Flora Robson, Judy Geeson

Weird film from England about a greedy man attempting to rid himself of his wife in order to get his hands on her money. Of course, things don't quite work out as planned. Mildly interesting movie has too many dull spots to make it worthwhile. Also known as *Dominique*. Rated PG.

1978 98 minutes

DON'T ANSWER THE PHONE

★★

DIRECTOR: Robert Hammer
CAST: James Westmoreland, Flo Gerrish, Ben Frank, Nicholas Worth

Also known as *The Hollywood Strangler*, this unpleasantly brutal exploitation quickie might have been better in more competent hands. Nicholas Worth is a truly horrific killer in the *Hillside Strangler* mode, and the screenplay is far above average. All the other actors, though, are so wooden they warp. James Westmoreland seems determined to be a poor imitation of James Brolin, as one of the investigative cops, and Flo Gerrish is simply awful as a radio psychologist. The other few high points are marred by lurid and lengthy scenes of the killer as he strangles half-naked women; the first fifteen minutes are the work of a depraved mind. Music by Byron Allred, which is appropriate. Rated R for violence and nudity.

1981 94 minutes

DON'T BE AFRAID OF THE DARK

★★★

DIRECTOR: John Newland
CAST: Kim Darby, Jim Hutton, Pedro Armendariz Jr., Barbara Anderson, William Demarest

Scary TV movie as newlyweds Kim Darby and Jim Hutton move into a weird old house inhabited by eerie little monsters who want Kim for one of their own. The human actors are okay, but the creatures steal the show.

1973 74 minutes

DON'T LOOK NOW

★★★★

DIRECTOR: Nicolas Roeg
CAST: Julie Christie, Donald Sutherland

Excellent psychic thriller about a married couple who, just after the accidental drowning of their young daughter, start having strange occurrences in their lives. Beautifully photographed by director Nicolas Roeg. Strong performances by Julie Christie and Donald Sutherland make this film a must-see. Rated R.

1973 110 minutes

DORIAN GRAY

DIRECTOR: Massimo Dallamano
CAST: Helmut Berger, Richard Todd, Herbert Lom

Horrid updating of the Oscar Wilde classic novel. Helmut Berger plays the title role this time as the man who remains eternally young while a painting of him grows increasingly decrepit. Fascinating story has never been more boring, with some good actors wasted. Alternate title: *The Secret of Dorian Gray.* Rated R.

1970 93 minutes

DORM THAT DRIPPED BLOOD, THE

DIRECTORS: Jeffrey Osbrow, Stephen Carpenter
CAST: Pamela Holland, Stephen Sachs, Laurie Lapinski

The only good thing about this film is the title, and the producers got the idea for it from a memorable genre film starring Christopher Lee and Peter Cushing from the 1970s, *The House That Dripped Blood*. It turns out this mess was originally titled *Pranks*. Whatever they want to call it, this awful, low-budget flick is just another excuse to serve up gratuitous violence with college students—once again—being hacked up at every turn. Don't see it! Rated R for violence.

1981 84 minutes

DOUBLE EXPOSURE

★★★½

DIRECTOR: Wiliam Byron Hillman
CAST: Michael Callan, Joanna Pettet, James Stacy, Pamela Hensley, Cleavon Little, Seymour Cassel, Robert Tessier

This psychological thriller about a photographer (Michael Callan) who has nightmares of murders that come true has some pretty ghoulish scenes, but the tension created here comes more from the element of surprise rather than the fashion of violence displayed. The cast of lesser-known actors puts in solid performances. Not rated, the film contains violence, profanity, nudity, and adult subject matter.

1982 95 minutes

DRACULA (ORIGINAL)

★★★★

DIRECTOR: Tod Browning
CAST: Bela Lugosi, Dwight Frye, David Manners, Helen Chandler, Edward Van Sloan

Bela Lugosi found himself forever typecast after brilliantly bringing to life the bloodthirsty Transylvanian vampire of the title in this 1930 genre classic, directed by Tod Browning. His performance and that of Dwight Frye as the spider-eating Renfield still impress even though this early talkie seems somewhat dated today.

1931 B & W 75 minutes

DRACULA (REMAKE)

★★½

DIRECTOR: John Badham
CAST: Frank Langella, Laurence Olivier, Donald Pleasence, Tony Haygarth, Jan Francis

This *Dracula* is a film of missed opportunities. Not that it doesn't have something to offer—it does—but not enough to make it a fully satisfying experience. Frank Langella makes an excellent Count Dracula. He projects just the right combination of menace, animal appeal, and mystery. His reading of the classic lines, "I never drink . . . wine" and "The children of the night, what music they make," is refreshingly untheatrical and effective. It's a pity he has so little screen time. The story, for the uninitiated, revolves around the activities of a bloodthirsty vampire who leaves his castle in Transylvania for fresh hunting in London. There, he comes up against Professor Van Helsing (Laurence Olivier), whose daughter, Mina (Jan Francis), becomes the first to join his legion of the undead. Rated R.

1979 109 minutes

DRACULA VS. FRANKENSTEIN

½

DIRECTOR: Al Adamson
CAST: J. Carrol Naish, Lon Chaney Jr., Zandor Vorkov, Jim Davis

This dud rates higher than a bomb simply for the presences of J. Carrol Naish and Lon Chaney, but even they can't save this piece of junk about Dracula's eternal search for blood, eventually leading to a showdown with a dumb-looking Frankenstein monster. Pretty bad. Rated R.

1971 90 minutes

DREAM LOVER

★½

DIRECTOR: Alan J. Pakula
CAST: Kristy McNichol, Ben Masters, Paul Shenar, Justin Deas, John McMartin, Gayle Hunnicutt, Joseph Culp

This dull and pretentious psychological thriller presents Kristy McNichol as a struggling musician living alone, in New York City no less, for the first time. After barely escaping from a knife-wielding maniac her first night in a new apartment, she suffers bloodcurdling nightmares. When she turns to a sleep researcher (Ben Masters) for help, the treatment backfires and the dream-created horrors begin taking over her life. Despite the promising premise, things seem to take forever to happen, and when they do, the viewer wishes they had not. As a result, *Dream Lover* is more of an endurance test than an entertainment. Rated R for violence.

1986 104 minutes

DRESSED TO KILL

★★★½

DIRECTOR: Brian De Palma
CAST: Michael Caine, Angie Dickinson, Nancy Allen, Keith Gordon

Director Brian De Palma again borrows heavily from Alfred Hitchcock in this story of sexual frustration, madness, and murder set in New York City. Angie Dickinson plays a sexually active housewife whose affairs lead to an unexpected conclusion. At times it is slow-moving, but De Palma's visual style will keep you interested. The elevator scene will send chills up your spine. Rated R for violence, strong language, nudity, and simulated sex.

1980 105 minutes

DUEL

★★★★★

DIRECTOR: Steven Spielberg
CAST: Dennis Weaver, Eddie Firestone, Tim Herbert

Duel, an early Spielberg film, was originally a 73-minute ABC made-for-TV movie, but this full-length version was released theatrically overseas. The story is a simple one: a mild-mannered businessman (Dennis Weaver) alone on a desolate stretch of highway suddenly finds himself the unwitting prey of the maniacal driver of a big, greasy, oil tanker. Blessed with a heart-pounding music score and some truly odd camera angles, this nonstop thriller never lets go. Based on a real-life situation encountered by author Richard Matheson, who wrote the screenplay, this film established Spielberg as a major new talent in Hollywood.

1971 91 minutes

DUNWICH HORROR, THE

★

DIRECTOR: Daniel Haller

CAST: Sandra Dee, Dean Stockwell, Sam Jaffe, Ed Begley Sr., Talia (Coppola) Shire

Torpid horror thriller made back in the good ol' days when folks didn't know that it's impossible to adapt H. P. Lovecraft. Dean Stockwell foreshadowed his hammy role in *Dune* with this laughable portrayal of a warlock whose talents run more toward hooded expressions than magical incantations. Watch for a quick part by Talia Shire, back when she still shared brother Francis's last name. Epitome of that type of video that, as it's being watched, makes you think, "It can't get worse" . . . and then the conclusion comes along, and it *does* get worse! Rated PG for violence.

1970 90 minutes

EATEN ALIVE

DIRECTOR: Tobe Hooper

CAST: Mel Ferrer, Stuart Whitman, Carolyn Jones, Marilyn Burns

A monster stalks the swamps of Louisiana in this sickening low-budget horror flick. Rated R.

1976 96 minutes

EEGAH!

★

DIRECTOR: Nicholas Merriwether (Arch W. Hall Sr.)

CAST: Arch W. Hall Jr., Richard Kiel, Marilyn Manning, William Watters (Arch W. Hall Sr.)

Teen-age caveman gets the hots for brain-dead babe. A truly wretched film, but it rates one star for unintentional humor. Giant Richard Kiel plays the Neanderthal with disturbing authenticity. The heroine is a real bag of air; she can't even fall down with conviction. And the hero is the kind of oxygen-waster you'd love to beat about the face. He's played by actor-singer Arch W. Hall Jr., a man in whose hands a mere guitar becomes an instrument of horror. (You may never forget the haunting love theme from *Eegah!*) Hall's father wrote, produced, and directed the movie to help get the kid out of the house. You can't blame him.

1962 90 minutes

ENTITY, THE

DIRECTOR: Sidney J. Furie

CAST: Barbara Hershey, Ron Silver, Jacqueline Brooks, David Lablosa

Barbara Hershey (*The Stuntman*) stars in this reprehensible horror flick as a woman who is sexually molested by an invisible, sex-crazed demon. Director Sidney J. Furie (*Lady Sings the Blues*; *The Boys in Company C*) has created what amounts to a two-hour celebration of rape and the degradation of women. Rated R for nudity, profanity, violence, and rape.

1983 115 minutes

EQUINOX (THE BEAST)

DIRECTOR: Jack Woods

CAST: Edward Connell, Barbara Hewitt, Frank Boers Jr., Robin Christopher

Good special effects save this unprofessional movie about college students searching for their archeology professor. On their search, they must face monsters and the occult. Rated PG.

1971 82 minutes

ERASERHEAD

★★★½

DIRECTOR: David Lynch

CAST: John Nance, Charlotte Stewart, Allen Joseph, Jeanne Bates

Weird, weird movie . . . director David Lynch (*Elephant Man*) created this nightmarish film about Henry Spencer (John Nance), who, we assume, lives in the far (possibly post-apocalyptic) future when everyone is given a free lobotomy at birth. Nothing else could explain the bizarre behavior of its characters. Be forewarned: This unrated film has no objectionable elements in the traditional sense, yet still leaves you nauseous.

1978 B & W 90 minutes

EVIL DEAD, THE

★

DIRECTOR: Sam Raimi

CAST: Bruce Campbell, Ellen Sandweiss, Betsy Baker, Hal Delrich, Sarah York

An amateurish horror movie about a handful of college kids trapped in a haunted house, this is all special effects, no plot, no acting, no point. Unrated, the film has violence and gore.

1983 85 minutes

EVIL DEAD II, THE

★★★½

DIRECTOR: Sam Raimi

CAST: Bruce Campbell, Sarah Barry, Dan Hicks, Cassie Wesley, Theodore Raimi, Denise Bixler

More of a remake than a sequel, this film has better effects, acting, and story than its predecessor. The prologue briefly recaps the events of *The Evil Dead I* in which, while camping in an old cabin up in the mountains, some friends find the ancient book of the dead and a tape recording made by an archaeologist who is presumably dead. The friends unleash a horde of ancient demons who possess and kill all but one, Ashley. When he learns, come daylight, that he can't escape from the mountain, he is forced to try to survive another night in the cabin. There're lots of chills, shocks, and even some humor here. One should be warned, though, that there are some very unsettling special effects. Not rated, but contains graphic violence and profanity.

1987 85 minutes

EVIL MIND, THE (AKA THE CLAIRVOYANT)

★★★

DIRECTOR: Maurice Elvey

CAST: Claude Rains, Fay Wray, Jane Baxter, Mary Clare, Athole Stewart

Nicely mounted story of fake mentalist who realizes that his phony predictions are actually coming true. The elegant Claude Rains gives a fine performance as a man who has inexplicably acquired a strange power and finds himself frightened by it. Lovely Fay Wray plays his assistant. Nicely photographed, this British film is one of a handful of psychic films that doesn't cheat on its subject by explaining things away logically. A good minor thriller, interesting and fun.

1934 B & W 80 minutes

EVIL OF FRANKENSTEIN, THE

★★½

DIRECTOR: Freddie Francis

CAST: Peter Cushing, Duncan Lamont, Peter Woodthorpe, Kiwi Kingston

A weaker entry in Hammer Films's popular Frankenstein series pits Dr. Frankenstein (Peter Cushing) against an underhanded hypnotist (Peter Woodthorpe), who is using the monster (Kiwi Kingston) to do his bidding, namely, killing off his enemies. The doctor doesn't take to the idea, so the monster is dispatched to eliminate him. Good production values and handsome set pieces, but the monster make-up is silly and the script convoluted.

1964 98 minutes

EVILSPEAK

DIRECTOR: Eric Weston
CAST: Clint Howard, R. G. Armstrong, Joseph Cortese, Claude Earl Jones

The alleged script centers on a devil-worshiping medieval Spanish priest brought into modern times by a student (Clint Howard) on a computer. Everything goes downhill—three minutes into the story—when the reborn father lops off the head of a topless female. Ick! Rated R for nudity, violence, and a lot of cheap, pointless, and disgusting gore.

1982 89 minutes

EXORCIST, THE

★★★★½

DIRECTOR: William Friedkin
CAST: Ellen Burstyn, Max von Sydow, Linda Blair, Jason Miller, Lee J. Cobb

A sensation at the time of its release, this horror film—directed by William Friedkin (*The French Connection*)—has lost some of its punch because of the numerous imitations it spawned. An awful sequel, *Exorcist II: The Heretic*, didn't help much either. Rated R.

1973 121 minutes

EXORCIST II: THE HERETIC

DIRECTOR: John Boorman
CAST: Richard Burton, Linda Blair, Louise Fletcher, Kitty Winn, James Earl Jones, Max von Sydow

The script is bad, the acting poor, and the direction lacking in pace or conviction. The story concerns a priest, Father Lamount (Richard Burton), assigned by the Vatican to investigate the work of Father Merrin (Max von Sydow), who died freeing Regan MacNeil from possession by the devil. Rated R for violence and profanity.

1977 110 minutes

EXPERIMENT IN TERROR

★★★½

DIRECTOR: Blake Edwards
CAST: Glenn Ford, Lee Remick, Stefanie Powers, Ross Martin, Ned Glass

A sadistic killer (Ross Martin) kidnaps the teenage sister (Stephanie Powers) of a bank teller (Lee Remick). An FBI agent is hot on the trail, fighting the clock. The film crackles with suspense. The acting is uniformly excellent. Martin paints an unnerving portrait of evil.

1962 B & W 123 minutes

EXPOSED

★

DIRECTOR: James Toback
CAST: Nastassja Kinski, Rudolph Nureyev, Harvey Keitel, Ian McShane

Nastassja Kinski stars, in this mediocre and confusing film directed by James Toback (*Fingers*; *Love and Money*), as a high-priced fashion model whose constant exposure in magazines and on television have made her the target for the sometimes dangerous desires of two men. Former ballet star Rudolph Nureyev (*Valentino*) is also featured. Rated R.

1983 100 minutes

EYES OF A STRANGER

★★

DIRECTOR: Ken Weiderhorn
CAST: Lauren Tewes, Jennifer Jason Leigh, John DiSanti, Peter Dupre, Gwen Lewis

"The Love Boat's" Julie, Lauren Tewes, makes an unexpected appearance in this blood-and-guts horror film. She plays a reporter who decides to track down a psychopathic killer. Lots of blood and some sexual molestation. Rated R.

1981 85 minutes

EYES OF LAURA MARS, THE

★★

DIRECTOR: Irvin Kershner
CAST: Faye Dunaway, Tommy Lee Jones, Brad Dourif, René Auberjonois

Laura Mars (Faye Dunaway) is a kinky commercial photographer who is haunted by psychic visions of murder. Her photographs, which are composed of violent scenes, somehow become the blueprints for a series of actual killings. It soon becomes apparent the maniac is really after her. Although well-acted and suspenseful, *The Eyes of Laura Mars* is an unrelentingly cold and gruesome movie. Rated R for the aforementioned content.

1978 103 minutes

EYEWITNESS

★★★★

DIRECTOR: Peter Yates
CAST: William Hurt, Sigourney Weaver, Christopher Plummer, James Woods

Director Peter Yates and screenwriter Steve Tesich (the team that created *Breaking Away*) have done it again. *Eyewitness* has everything: suspense, romance, laughs, thrills, surprises . . . in short, it's a humdinger of a movie. The story is in the Hitchcock vein of mystery and terror. William Hurt (*Gorky Park* and *Altered States*) plays a janitor who, after discovering a murder victim, meets the glamorous television reporter (Sigourney Weaver, of *Alien*) he has admired from afar. In order to prolong their relationship, he pretends to know the killer's identity—and puts both their lives in danger. Rated R for sex, violence, and profanity.

1981 102 minutes

FADE TO BLACK

★★★½

DIRECTOR: Vernon Zimmerman
CAST: Dennis Christopher, Linda Kerridge, Tim Thomerson, Morgan Paull, Marya Small

Movie buffs and horror fans will especially love *Fade to Black*, a funny, suspenseful, and entertaining low-budget film that features Dennis Christopher (the pseudo-Italian bicyclist of *Breaking Away*) in a tour-de-force performance. Christopher plays Eric Binford, an odd young man who spends most of his time absorbing films. He can quote entire passages of dialogue and reel off cast lists for the most obscure B movies. But his talents aren't of much use to him in the real world. His all-night videotaping sessions and movie orgies only make him late for work and out of step with other people his age, and soon Eric goes over the edge. Rated R.

1980 100 minutes

FALL OF THE HOUSE OF USHER, THE

★★★½

DIRECTOR: Roger Corman
CAST: Vincent Price, Mark Damon, Myrna Fahey, Harry Ellerbe

Imagination and a chilling sense of the sinister make this low-budget Roger Corman version of Edgar Allan Poe's famous haunted-house story highly effective. Vincent Price is without peer as Usher.

1960 79 minutes

FALL OF THE HOUSE OF USHER, THE (REMAKE)

★

DIRECTOR: Stephen Lord

CAST: Martin Landau, Robert Hays, Charlene Tolton, Ray Walston, Dimitra Arliss

Despite a name cast, this low-budget remake of the Edgar Allan Poe tale is tacky, inept, and dull. Stick with the Roger Corman version and its delicious performance by Vincent Price. Rated PG.

1979 101 minutes

FAMILY PLOT

★★★★

DIRECTOR: Alfred Hitchcock

CAST: Karen Black, Bruce Dern, Barbara Harris, William Devane, Ed Lauter, Cathleen Nesbitt, Katherine Helmond

Alfred Hitchcock's last film proved to be a winner. He interjects this story with more humor than in his other latter-day films, which emphasized suspense and terror. A seedy medium and her ne'er-do-well boyfriend (Barbara Harris and Bruce Dern) encounter a sinister couple (Karen Black and William Devane) while searching for a missing heir. They all become involved in diamond theft and attempted murder. Rated PG.

1976 120 minutes

FAN, THE

★★★½

DIRECTOR: Edward Bianchi

CAST: Lauren Bacall, James Garner, Maureen Stapleton, Michael Biehn

In this fast-moving suspense yarn, a young fan is obsessed with a famous actress (Lauren Bacall). When his love letters to her are ignored, he embarks on a murder spree. Bacall is superb as the sassy, chain-smoking celebrity; James Garner is her amiable ex-husband and confidant; and Maureen Stapleton almost steals the show as Bacall's all-suffering secretary. *The Fan* is an absorbing thriller. The acting is first-rate, the camera work breathtaking, and the script plausible. Rated R.

1981 95 minutes

FATAL ATTRACTION

★★★½

DIRECTOR: Michael Grant

CAST: Salley Kellerman, Stephen Lack, Lawrence Dane, John Huston

In this suspenseful film, two people get caught up in sexual fantasy games so intense that they begin to act them out—in public. Sally Kellerman plays a jaded child psychotherapist who meets a college professor (Stephen Lack) after the two collide in an automobile accident. *Fatal Attraction* would receive a higher rating if it had a smoother transition from the innocent flirting to the heavy-duty activity that leads to the film's thrilling and ironic close. Rated R for sex, nudity, violence, and profanity.

1985 90 minutes

FATAL GAMES

DIRECTOR: Michael Elliot

CAST: Sally Kirkland, Lynn Banashek, Sean Masterson, Teal Roberts

At first, it's difficult to determine whether or not this one is a comedy or a horror film. Then it becomes evident that this is just another slasher-type flick that is so stupid it's funny. In a school for young athletes, a murderer begins eliminating the students, using a javelin. The film is filled with bad acting and resembles a porno film rather than a slasher flick. Not rated, but contains explicit nudity, profanity, and violence.

1984 88 minutes

FEAR IN THE NIGHT (DYNASTY OF FEAR)

★★★½

DIRECTOR: Jimmy Sangster
CAST: Ralph Bates, Judy Geeson, Peter Cushing, Joan Collins

Effective British shocker about a teacher and his off-balance bride encountering lust, jealousy, and murder at a desolate boys' school. Another suspensful, literate offering from Hammer Films. Following Joan Collins's television success, the film was rereleased on video under the title *Dynasty of Fear,* with altered credits to give her top billing. Rated PG.

1972 94 minutes

FEAR NO EVIL

DIRECTOR: Frank Laloggia
CAST: Stephan Arngrim, Elizabeth Hoffman, Kathleen Rong McAllen, Frank Birney, Daniel Eden

Advertised as an exercise in horrific thrills and special effects, this is no horror movie. It's just plain horrible. The story of the satanic high-school student hell-bent on destroying a senior class, this film tries to be a male *Carrie*, a punk rock *The Exorcist*, and a contemporary *Night of the Living Dead*, all in one. It just doesn't work. Rated R.

1981 96 minutes

FER-DE-LANCE

★★

DIRECTOR: Russ Mayberry
CAST: David Janssen, Hope Lange, Jason Evers, Ivan Dixon

Made-for-TV suspense film is mildly entertaining as a cargo of poisonous snakes escape aboard a crippled submarine at the bottom of the sea, making life unpleasant for all concerned.

1974 100 minutes

FIEND WITHOUT A FACE

★★★½

DIRECTOR: Arthur Crabtree
CAST: Marshall Thompson, Kim Parker, Gil Winfield, Terence Kilburn

Surprisingly effective little horror chiller with slight overtones of the "Id" creature from *Forbidden Planet*. Scientific thought experiment goes awry and creates nasty creatures that look like brains with coiled tails. Naturally, they eat people. Story builds to a great climax as our heroes hole up in a shack and try to fend off an army of the repulsive beasties. Lots of fun.

1958 B & W 74 minutes

FIFTH FLOOR, THE

½

DIRECTOR: Howard Avedis
CAST: Bo Hopkins, Dianne Hull, Patti D'Arbanville, Mel Ferrer, Sharon Farrell

Thoroughly contemptible and completely unbelievable tale of an attractive college lass who is mistakenly popped into an insane asylum. Weak script is a poor excuse for disgusting treatment of women. Even fans of the always intriguing Patti D'Arbanbville will have trouble sitting through this one. Bo Hopkins chews through the scenery in a mad attempt to escape into a better picture. Don't watch this with the woman you love. Rated R for violence and nudity.

1980 90 minutes

FINAL CONFLICT, THE

★★

DIRECTOR: Graham Baker
CAST: Sam Neill, Rossano Brazzi, Don Gordon, Lisa Harrow, Mason Adams

The third and last in the *Omen* trilogy, this disturbing but passionless film concerns the rise to power of the son of Satan, Damien Thorn (Sam Neill, of *My Brilliant Career*), and the second coming of the Saviour. It is a crassly commercialized version of the ultimate clash between good and evil that depends more on shocking spectacle than gripping tension for its impact. It takes more energy and endurance to sit through than it deserves. Rated R.

1981 108 minutes

FINAL EXAM

DIRECTOR: Jimmy Huston
CAST: Celice Bagdadi, Joel S. Rice, Ralph Brown

A mad slasher hacks his way through a college campus in this *Friday the 13th* ripoff; and a bad ripoff it is. Even gore fans will find this film a bore. Rated R.

1981 90 minutes

FINAL TERROR, THE

★½

DIRECTOR: Andrew Davis
CAST: Rachel Ward, Daryl Hannah, John Friedrich, Adrian Zmed

Rachel Ward (*Against All Odds*) and Daryl Hannah (*Splash*) weren't big stars when they made this mediocre low-budget slasher flick for one-time B-movie king Sam Arkoff (*Beach Party*; *The Raven*) and now probably wish they hadn't. Although it's a cut above most films in its genre, *The Final Terror* is nothing special. Rated R for brief nudity and violence.

1981 82 minutes

FIRE!

★★

DIRECTOR: Earl Bellamy
CAST: Ernest Borgnine, Vera Miles, Alex Cord, Donna Mills, Lloyd Nolan, Ty Hardin, Neville Brand, Gene Evans, Erik Estrada

Another of producer Irwin Allen's suspense spectaculars involving an all-star cast caught in a major calamity. This one concerns a mountain town in the path of a forest fire set by an escaped convict. Worth watching once.

1977 100 minutes

FIRESTARTER

★★★½

DIRECTOR: Mark L. Lester
CAST: David Keith, Drew Barrymore, George C. Scott, Martin Sheen, Heather Locklear

Stephen King writhes again. This time, Drew Barrymore (*E.T.*) stars as the gifted (or is that haunted) child of the title, who has the ability—sometimes uncontrollable—to ignite objects around her. David Keith is the father who tries to protect her from the baddies, played by George C. Scott and Martin Sheen. *Firestarter* is an old-fashioned terror movie. It's a suspenseful, poignant, and sometimes frightening entertainment that goes beyond its genre. Rated PG for violence.

1984 115 minutes

FLESHBURN

★★★½

DIRECTOR: George Gage
CAST: Sonny Landham, Steve Kanaly, Karen Carlson, Macon McCalman

An Indian who left five men in the desert to die breaks out of an insane asylum to hunt down and wreak his revenge against the psychiatrists who sentenced him. From the moment the opening credits roll, giving the background on the story, this film promises to be more than exploitation, and it does not let you down. The characters are neatly established before the action begins, and the dialogue has a certain snappiness to it. Sonny Landham's performance as the Indian is chillingly good. Rated R for profanity, violence.

1983 91 minutes

FLOOD!

★★★

DIRECTOR: Earl Bellamy

CAST: Robert Culp, Martin Milner, Barbara Hershey, Richard Basehart, Carol Lynley, Roddy McDowall, Cameron Mitchell, Eric Olson, Teresa Wright

Bureaucratic peevishness is responsible for a small town being caught short when a dam bursts. The resulting flood threatens to wipe out everybody and everything. Slick and predictable, but interesting just the same. If you like this, you'll like its sister film, *Fire!*

1976 100 minutes

FLY, THE (ORIGINAL)

★★★★

DIRECTOR: Kurt Neumann

CAST: Al Hedison, Patricia Owens, Vincent Price, Herbert Marshall

Classic horror film builds slowly but really pays off. A scientist (Al Hedison, soon to become David) experimenting with unknown forces turns himself into the hideous title character. Impressive production with top-notch acting and real neat special effects.

1958 94 minutes

FLY, THE (REMAKE)

★★★½

DIRECTOR: David Cronenberg

CAST: Jeff Goldblum, Geena Davis, John Getz, Joy Boushel, Les Carlson

Promising film from the director of the ever popular *Scanners* and *Videodrome*. It's the story of a brilliant research scientist, Seth Brundle (Jeff Goldblum in the role originated by David Hedison in the 1958 version), who has developed a way to transport matter from one point to another instantaneously by means of molecular breakdown/reconstruction. One night, thoroughly gassed, he decides to test the device on himself. Unfortunately, a pesky housefly finds its way into the chamber with the scientist, causing the confused machine to merge their genes at the receiving end across the room. To say more would surely ruin the film, though it must be stated that this is one of the grossest, most brutally unnerving movies in history as far as the special effects are concerned. It must also be said that this otherwise entertaining update simply falls apart at the conclusion. Rated R for gore and slime.

1986 100 minutes

FOG, THE

★★★

DIRECTOR: John Carpenter

CAST: Adrienne Barbeau, Jamie Lee Curtis, John Houseman, Hal Holbrook, Janet Leigh

This is one of those almost movies. Director John Carpenter is on familiar ground with this story of eighteenth-century pirates back from the dead, terrorizing a modern-day fishing village. There's plenty of blood and gore, but the lack of any real chills or surprises makes this one a nice try but no cigar. Rated R.

1980 91 minutes

FORBIDDEN WORLD

★★

DIRECTOR: Allan Holzman

CAST: Jesse Vint, Dawn Dunlap, June Chadwick, Linden Chiles, Don Olivera, Fox Harris

Jesse Vint was rescued from the obscurity of his deep-space death in *Silent Running*, and his reward was a starring role in this ripoff of *Alien*. Vint is a troubleshooter sent to an isolated science colony where a medical experiment has gone awry; instead of synthesizing a protein foodstuff that would replicate itself at a grand rate, a team of Dedicated Scientists wound up with a monster after implanting a gene-spliced mutant into the womb of a rather dense volunteer. (Well, what did they expect?) Typical acts of lunacy—impassioned idealists who try to communicate with the thing, crew members who persist in wandering around alone, and women who undress in the wrong cubicle—quickly decimate the cast until a truly clever means is discovered to kill the beast. Where was that sort of thinking earlier in the story? Rated R for violence and sex.

1982 77 minutes

FOREIGN CORRESPONDENT

★★★★★

DIRECTOR: Alfred Hitchcock

CAST: Joel McCrea, Laraine Day, Herbert Marshall, George Sanders, Edmund Gwenn

Classic Alfred Hitchcock thriller still stands as one of his most complex and satisfying films. Joel McCrea stars as an American reporter in Europe during the war, caught up in all sorts of intrigue, romance, etc., in his dealings with Nazi spies, hired killers, and the like as he attempts to get the truth to the American public. This truly great movie features many standout scenes, including one where a suspect is lost in a desolate field of windmills, a daring escape along a narrow hotel ledge, and a pilot's-eye view of a plane crash. One of the best. Don't miss it.

1940 B & W 120 minutes

FOREST, THE

★

DIRECTOR: Don Jones

CAST: Dean Russell, Michael Brody, Elaine Warner

This is an extremely amateurish attempt at a horror film. A very low budget coupled with an unprofessional cast makes this film a boorish waste of time. Two of the campers are served in a cannibal feast and the other two campers are left to destroy the evil. Unrated.

1983 90 minutes

FRANKENSTEIN (ORIGINAL)

★★★★

DIRECTOR: James Whale

CAST: Colin Clive, Mae Clarke, Boris Karloff, John Boles

Despite all the padding, grease paint, and restrictive, awkward costuming, Boris Karloff gives a strong, sensitive performance in this 1931 horror classic—with only eyes and an occasional grunt to convey meaning. It still stands as one of the great screen performances.

1931 B & W 71 minutes

FRANKENSTEIN (RESTORED VERSION)

★★★★☆

DIRECTOR: James Whale

CAST: Boris Karloff, Colin Clive, Mae Clarke, Edward Van Sloan, John Boles, Marilyn Harris

The classic adaptation of Mary Shelly's novel about a scientist (Colin Clive) who creates a living man (a then unknown Boris Karloff) from parts of old dead bodies can now be seen in its entirety for the first time in over fifty years, as Universal Pictures has finally unearthed the missing scene where the monster throws a little girl (Marilyn Harris) into a lake in the hope that she will float, just like the flowers they had been tossing together moments before. While the excised footage was very brief, it did change the complexity of the character considerably. In the regular cut version we've all seen a hundred times, the monster is shown to have apparently murdered the child and violently thrown her body into the lake, whereas the complete print tells it like it really was as we see his confusion and panic as the girl drowns before his terrified eyes. The scene was admittedly too strong for audiences of the day, but now at last on video, it serves to make a great film still better. Universal deserves congratulations.

1931 B & W 72 minutes

FRANKENSTEIN (REMAKE)

★★½

DIRECTOR: Glenn Jordan
CAST: Robert Foxworth, Susan Strasberg, Bo Svenson, Willie Aames

Bo Svenson's sympathetic portrayal of the monster is the one saving grace of this essentially average made-for-TV retelling of Mary Wollstonecraft Shelley's horror tale. Because of Svenson's outstanding performance, one is reminded of the original Universal film and Boris Karloff's history-making interpretation. This is not particularly good because this 1973 version, which was produced by Dan Curtis (*The Night Stalker*), has little of the atmosphere which makes director James Whale's 1931 creation worth watching again and again for fans of the horror genre.

1973 130 minutes

FRANKENSTEIN—1970

★

DIRECTOR: Howard W. Koch
CAST: Boris Karloff, Tom Duggan, Jana Lund, Donald Barry

This poor excuse for a movie wastes Boris Karloff as the great-grandson of the famous doctor, attempting to create a monster of his own. Unfortunately, the only ones who succeeded were the producers of this movie. Rates higher than a turkey solely because of Karloff's appearance.

1958 B & W 83 minutes

FRANKENSTEIN ISLAND

DIRECTOR: Jerry Warren
CAST: John Carradine, Robert Clarke, Steve Brodie, Cameron Mitchell, Andrew Duggan, Robert Christopher

A group of men stranded on a remote island stumble upon a colony of young women in leopard-skin bikinis. Sounds like fun until they run up against a relative of the famous doctor, who's creating a monster of his very own. Worse than you'd think. In fact, the best thing about this piece of junk is the cover of the video box, which shows the Frankenstein monster doing a jig. Rated PG.

1981 89 minutes

FRANKENSTEIN MEETS THE WOLF MAN

★★★½

DIRECTOR: Roy William Neill
CAST: Lon Chaney Jr. Patric Knowles, Bela Lugosi, Ilona Massey, Maria Ouspenskaya

As the title suggests, two of Universal's most famous monsters clash in this series horror film. Very atmospheric, with beautiful photography, music, set design, and special effects (especially the miniature work). Only drawback is Bela Lugosi's overblown portrayal of the Frankenstein Monster. This is countered, though, by Lon Chaney Jr.'s excellent performance in the role that made him a horror movie legend: the Wolf Man.

1943 B & W 73 minutes

FREAKS

★★★★

DIRECTOR: Tod Browning

CAST: Wallace Ford, Leila Hyams, Olga Baclanova, Henry Victor, Roscoe Ates, Harry Earles, Daisy Earles, Daisy Hilton, Violet Hilton, Rose Dione, Edward Brophy, Matt McHugh, Rardion, Johnny Eck, Martha the Armless Wonder

This legendary "horror" film by fabled director Tod Browning is perhaps the most unusual film ever made and certainly one of the most unsettling. Based on Tod Robbins's *Spurs*, this is the story of a circus midget who falls in love with a statuesque trapeze artist and nearly becomes her victim as she attempts to poison him for his money. Incensed by her betrayal and near murder of their little friend, the armless, legless, pinheaded "freaks" exact their revenge on the cold-blooded woman and her strong-man lover in one of the most horrifying sequences ever filmed.

1932 B & W 64 minutes

FRENZY

★★★★½

DIRECTOR: Alfred Hitchcock

CAST: Jon Finch, Barry Foster, Barbara Leigh-Hunt, Anna Massey, Alec McCowen

Frenzy makes a return to one of Hitchcock's favorite themes: that of a man accused of a murder he did not commit and all but trapped by the circumstantial evidence. Alfred Hitchcock described a scene from his movie by saying: "There's a body of a murdered girl that has fallen off of a potato truck. She falls out of a sack of potatoes in which the murderer stuffed her. This follows a scene in which the murderer has escaped, leaving the body hidden in the truck. Due to the braking of the truck, the body was shot out. The most significant thing about the whole scene is how it improved the taste of the potatoes." The master's wry sense of humor is evident in this description just as much as it is in his structuring of shock sequences in his films. Rated R.

1972 116 minutes

FRIDAY THE 13TH

★½

DIRECTOR: Sean S. Cunningham

CAST: Betsy Palmer, Harry Crosby, Adrienne King

In *Friday the 13th* the accent is on gore rather than entertainment. The victims are introduced only to be graphically mutilated. They are totally without personality, and therefore we feel no sympathy for them. What's worse, the grisly murders are experienced vicariously by the audience. Sean S. Cunningham, the producer-director, uses a subjective camera in the stabbing scenes, which, essentially, makes the viewer the killer. The camera moves in on the screaming, pleading victim, "looks down" at the knife, and then plunges it into chest, ear, or eyeball. Now that's sick. Rated R.

1980 95 minutes

FRIDAY THE 13TH, PART II

★

DIRECTOR: Steve Miner

CAST: Amy Steel, John Furey, Adrienne King, Betsy Palmer

This sequel to the box-office hit of the same name is essentially the *Psycho* shower scene repeated *ad nauseum* (literally!) but without any of the elements that made Hitchcock's film a horror classic. Because the murders are very gruesome, most viewers will be as disgusted as they are scared. Rated R.

1981 87 minutes

FRIDAY THE 13TH, PART III

★

DIRECTOR: Steve Miner
CAST: Dana Kimmel, Paul Kratka, Tracie Savage, Jeffrey Rogers, Catherine Parks, Larry Zerner

More gruesome axe, knife, and meat cleaver murders occur at sunny Crystal Lake. For the theatrical release, the blood, gore, and guts were in excellent 3-D (the only reason this thoroughly disgusting film rated two stars). So instead of covering your eyes during a particularly horrific scene, all you had to do was remove the glasses. Not a bad idea. But the video isn't in 3-D, so we suggest you avoid this trash altogether. Rated R for obvious reasons.

1982 96 minutes

FRIDAY THE 13TH—THE FINAL CHAPTER

DIRECTOR: Joseph Zito
CAST: Kimberly Beck, Corey Feldman, Peter Barton, Joan Freeman, Alan Hayes

More gruesome and nauseating axe, knife, and meat cleaver murders occur at sunny Crystal Lake. The producers promise it will be "The Final Chapter" of this blood, gore, and guts series, which tends to disgust and revolt more often than shock and scare. That turns out to be a cheat. The story does bring, as advertised, "the end of Jason," but the ending still leaves room for a sequel. And what if it makes money? Will there be a *Friday the 13th—The Final Chapter Part II*? The mind boggles—and the stomach churns. Rated R for gore, violence, nudity, sex, profanity, and sheer tastelessness.

1984 90 minutes

FRIDAY THE 13TH, PART V—A NEW BEGINNING

DIRECTOR: Danny Steinmann
CAST: Jean Shepherd, Shavar Ross, Melanie Kinnaman, Richard Young

Well, they did it. The producers promised *Friday the 13th—The Final Chapter* would be the last of its kind. They lied. So we get more disgusting trash. Rated R for graphic violence and simulated sex.

1985 92 minutes

FRIDAY THE 13TH PART VI: JASON LIVES

★★

DIRECTOR: Tom McLoughlin
CAST: Thom Mathews, Jennifer Cooke, David Kagen

It may be hard to believe, but this fifth sequel to the unmemorable *Friday the 13th* is actually better than all those that preceded it. After all, what can you say about a film that features Arnold Horshack (Ron Palillo) of TV's *Welcome Back Kotter* as the first victim of the immortal, maniacal Jason Voorhees? Of course this thing is loaded with violence, but it is also nicely buffered by good comedy bits and one-liners. For instance, when Jason is stalking a group of young children, one turns to the other and says: "So, what *were* you going to be when you grew up?" Moments like this let us know that the people responsible for this stuff have their tongues planted very firmly in cheek, thus making the movie a (sort-of) black comedy and, as such, quite palatable for those who are game. Rated R for language and violence.

1986 85 minutes

FRIGHT NIGHT

★★★★½

DIRECTOR: Tom Holland

CAST: Chris Sarandon, William Ragsdale, Roddy McDowall, Amanda Bearse, Stephen Geoffreys

Charley Brewster (William Ragsdale) is a fairly normal teenager save one thing: He's convinced his new next-door neighbor, Jerry Dandrige (Chris Sarandon), is a vampire—and he is! So Charley enlists the aid of former screen vampire hunter Peter Vincent (Roddy McDowall), and the result is a screamingly funny horror spoof. It's the most fun you've had being scared since *Ghostbusters*. Rated R for nudity, profanity, violence, blood, and gore.

1985 105 minutes

FROGS

★★

DIRECTOR: George McCowan

CAST: Ray Milland, Sam Elliott, Joan Van Ark

In this fair horror film, Ray Milland has killed frogs, so frogs come to kill his family. Milland accurately imitates Walter Brennan, and the whole cast dies convincingly. The film is no asset to the argument that horror flicks are good cinema. Rated PG.

1972 91 minutes

FROM BEYOND

★★½

DIRECTOR: Stuart Gordon

CAST: Jeffrey Combs, Barbara Crampton, Ken Foree, Ted Sorel, Carolyn Purdy-Gordon, Bunny Summers, Bruce McGuire

A lecherous scientist and his assistant create a machine that stimulates a gland in the brain that allows one to see into another dimension. The problem is that the experiment has two side effects. One: It causes strange things to happen in the brain. Two: Creatures that live in the other dimension can see into ours. Worse, they tend to be hungry. It turns out that the scientist is decapitated by one of the unworldly beasts, and his assistant is accused of the killing. With a police officer and psychiatrist, the assistant tries to prove his innocence and sanity by recreating the experiment. Then the fun begins—with better-than-average special effects, scary-looking monsters, and suspenseful horror. Made by the creators of *Reanimator*, it's the same type of film, although a little tamer. Recommended for horror and gore fans. Not rated, but contains graphic violence and brief nudity.

1986 89 minutes

FUNHOUSE, THE

★★½

DIRECTOR: Tobe Hooper

CAST: Elizabeth Berridge, Cooper Huckabee, Miles Chapin, Largo Woodruff, Sylvia Miles

Looking for a watchable modern horror film? Then welcome to *The Funhouse*. This film about a group of teens trapped in the carnival attraction of the title proves that buckets of blood and severed limbs aren't essential elements to movie terror. Rated R.

1981 96 minutes

FURY, THE

★★★★

DIRECTOR: Brian De Palma

CAST: Kirk Douglas, Andrew Stevens, Amy Irving, Fiona Lewis, John Cassavetes, Charles Durning, Gordon Jump

The Fury is a riveting and totally unpredictable film experience. It is a contemporary terror tale that avoids the archaic religion-versus-evil syndrome and utilizes instead the average-man-against-the-unknown approach that made Hitchcock's suspense films so effective. This time it is Peter (Kirk Douglas), battling against a supersecret government agency. They have attempted to kill him and have succeeded in kidnapping his son Robin (Andrew Stevens), who has unusual psychic powers. Peter once worked for the agency, so he knows their methods and uses them to avoid being captured or killed as he struggles to locate and free his son. In his search, he finds Gillian (Amy Irving), who has powers similar to those of Robin and is in danger of being abducted by the agency herself. She achieves a psychic connection with Robin and leads his father to him. That's only the beginning. Rated R.

1978 118 minutes

FUTURE-KILL

🦃

DIRECTOR: Ronald W. Moore

CAST: Edwin Neal, Marilyn Burns, Gabriel Folse, Wade Reese, Barton Faulks, Rob Rowley, Craig Kannet, Jeffrey Scott

Thoroughly rotten film about some obnoxious frat boys who get stuck on the wrong side of town and run into a gang of punks—one of whom has been exposed to radiation. This is as cheap as B movies get. Rated R for profanity, nudity, and gallons of gore.

1984 83 minutes

GASLIGHT

★★★★

DIRECTOR: George Cukor

CAST: Ingrid Bergman, Joseph Cotten, Charles Boyer

Ingrid Bergman won her first Academy Award as the innocent young bride who, unfortunately, marries Charles Boyer. Boyer is trying to persuade her she is going insane. He, you see, is trying to find some hidden jewelry, and the only way to do so is to make Bergman think she's crazy. Many consider this the definitive psychological thriller.

1944 B & W 114 minutes

GATE, THE

★★

DIRECTOR: Tibor Takacs

CAST: Stephen Dorff, Louis Tripp, Christa Denton

A film that insists that children shouldn't play heavy metal records with satanic messages. The kids in this film do and so unlock a gate to an ancient netherworld with an ancient evil more powerful than the devil. They are pursued through the house by creepy little creatures, the corpse of a child-molesting handyman, and other vile nastiness. When the lord of evil shows up, the kids find they must learn the lesson of friendship and love. Though not very scary, this film exhibits a good sense of humor and outstanding special effects. Rated PG-13 for mild violence and profanity.

1987 85 minutes

GHIDRAH, THE THREE-HEADED MONSTER

★★★

DIRECTOR: Inoshiro Honda

CAST: Yosuke Natsuki, Yuriko Hoshi, Hiroshi Koizumi, Emi Ito

A giant egg from outer space crashes into Japan and hatches the colossal three-headed flying monster of the title. It takes the combined forces of Godzilla, Rodan, and Mothra to save Tokyo from Ghidrah's rampage of destruction. Good Japanese monster movie is marred only by dumb subplot of evil agent out to kidnap a Martian princess. Fast-forward these boring scenes, as they really slow the action.

1965 85 minutes

GHOST STORY

★

DIRECTOR: John Irvin

CAST: John Houseman, Douglas Fairbanks Jr., Melvyn Douglas, Fred Astaire, Alice Krige, Craig Wasson, Patricia Neal

Ghost stories are supposed to be scary, aren't they? Then what happened here? This film, based on the best-selling novel by Peter Straub, is about as frightening as an episode of "Sesame Street," and much less interesting. Indeed, the only horrifying thing about *Ghost Story* is the shameless waste of its distinguished cast. Rated R because of shock scenes involving rotting corpses and violence.

1981 110 minutes

GHOUL, THE

★★½

DIRECTOR: Freddie Francis

CAST: Peter Cushing, John Hurt, Gwen Watford

"Stay out of the garden, dear, there's a flesh-eating monster living there." One of Peter Cushing's many horror films. No gore, but not boring, either. Rated R.

1975 88 minutes

GHOULIES

🦃

DIRECTOR: Luca Bercovici

CAST: Peter Liapis, Lisa Pelikan, Keith Joe Dick, John Nance

The ad for this low-budget horror film featured a gruesome little reptilian creature—in a jumpsuit, no less—poking his head out of a toilet under the tag line, "They'll get you in the end." Could the movie be as tasteless as its promotion? Yes! Rated PG-13 for violence and sexual innuendo.

1985 87 minutes

GODZILLA, KING OF THE MONSTERS

★★★½

DIRECTOR: Inoshiro Honda (original version)—Terry Morse (U.S. version)

CAST: Raymond Burr, Takashi Shimura

First, and by far the best, film featuring the four-hundred-foot monstrosity that was later reduced to a superhero. Here he's all death and destruction, and this movie really works, thanks to some expert photographic effects and weird music. Ignore all subsequent efforts; this is the *real* Godzilla. Originally filmed in 1954 and in color, scenes of Raymond Burr looking up, reacting, etc., were added for American release two years later but were accidentally shot in black and white. So the entire U.S. version had to be released that way, though actually it does add to the atmosphere and serves to make the film that much more nightmarish.

1956 B & W 80 minutes

GODZILLA VS. MONSTER ZERO

★★★

DIRECTOR: Inoshiro Honda

CAST: Nick Adams, Akira Takarada

Pretty good monster movie has an alien civilization "borrowing" Godzilla and Rodan to help defeat the hometown menace Monster Zero (known previously and since as Ghidrah). After massive destruction on their planet, the wily aliens decide to transport the three leviathans to Earth to continue the battle, at *our* expense. Great special effects, as usual, but poor dubbing hurts the scenes with human actors. Originally called simply *Monster Zero*, the title was apparently changed to help video rentals.

1966 90 minutes

GODZILLA VS. MOTHRA

★★★

DIRECTOR: Inoshiro Honda
CAST: Akira Takarada, Yuriko Hoshi, Hiroshi Koisumi

Fine Godzilla movie pits the "king of the monsters" against arch-enemy Mothra for its first half, later has him taking on twin caterpillars recently hatched from the moth's giant egg that had been incubating on a nearby beach. Excellent battle scenes in this one, with Godzilla's first appearance a doozy. As is the case with another Paramount release, *Godzilla vs. Monster Zero*, the title of this film was altered for video also. Originally known as *Godzilla vs. the Thing*.

1964 90 minutes

GODZILLA VS. THE SEA MONSTER

★

DIRECTOR: Jun Fukuda
CAST: Not Credited

Godzilla must tackle a giant, rotten-looking crab monster that can throw boulders in this weak entry in the series. Boring as all-get-out, mainly because our hero doesn't even appear until the film is half over. You'll have hit the rewind button long before that.

1966 85 minutes

GODZILLA 1985

DIRECTORS: Kohji Hashimoto, R. J. Kizer
CAST: Raymond Burr, Keiji Kobayashi, Ken Tanaka, Yasuka Sawaguchi

Once again, the giant Japanese lizard tramples cars and crushes tall buildings in his search for radioactive nutrition. Raymond Burr, who co-starred with the lizard in his 1956 debut film, *Godzilla*, returns to suffer even more on-screen embarrassment. What was okay in the 1950s and '60s in the giant-monster genre is totally out of place today, as a sci-fi flick even with more sophisticated special effects. Rated PG for gore.

1985 91 minutes

GORATH

½

DIRECTOR: Inoshiro Honda
CAST: Not Credited

An out-of-control planet headed for Earth is the subject of this Japanese science-fiction flick. Low-grade production with cheesy special effects by the usually exceptional Eiji Tsuburaya, boosted by some ridiculous dialogue and post-dubbing.

1964 77 minutes

GORGO

★★★½

DIRECTOR: Eugene Lourie
CAST: Bill Travers, William Sylvester, Vincent Winter, Martin Benson

Unpretentious thriller from England has a dinosaur-type monster captured and put on display in London's Piccadilly Circus, only to have its towering two-hundred-foot parent destroy half the city looking for it. Brisk pacing and well-executed effects propel this film into the must-see category. Sure-handed direction by Eugene Lourie.

1961 76 minutes

GORGON, THE

★★★

DIRECTOR: Terence Fisher
CAST: Peter Cushing, Christopher Lee, Richard Pasco, Barbara Shelley

Peter Cushing and Christopher Lee take on a Medusa-headed monster in this British Hammer Films chiller. A good one for horror buffs.

1964 83 minutes

GOTHIC

★★

DIRECTOR: Ken Russell

CAST: Gabriel Byrne, Julian Sands, Natasha Richardson, Myriam Cyr, Timothy Spall

Director Ken Russell returns to his favorite subject—the tortured artist—for this look at what may have happened that spooky evening in 1816 when Lord Byron, poet Percy Shelley, his fiancé Mary, her stepsister Claire, and Byron's ex-lover Dr. Polidori spent the evening together, attempting to scare each other. What the viewer gets is the usual Russell bag of tricks: insane hallucinations, group sex, scenes of gruesome murders, and much, much more. Unfortunately, this seems like a rerun of several past Russell films with nothing new or interesting added. As a horror film, this one really disappoints; for the hardcore Russell fans only. Rated R.

1986 90 minutes

GRADUATION DAY

★

DIRECTOR: Herb Freed

CAST: Christopher George, Patch MacKenzie, E. Danny Murphy, Michael Pataki, E. J. Peaker

A high-school runner dies during a competition. Soon someone begins killing all her teammates. Christopher George, as the coach, becomes a suspect along with the principal and the victim's sister. The only plus in this blood-and-guts flick is the surprising twist at the end. Plenty of violence in this one. Rated R.

1981 96 minutes

GRAVE OF THE VAMPIRE

★½

DIRECTOR: John Hayes

CAST: William Smith, Michael Pataki

Although it's far from the classic it's reputed to be, this film was groundbreaking for its day. The story involves a vampire who interrupts a couple's first date, killing the boyfriend and raping the girl. She eventually gives birth to a baby bloodsucker who grows up to search for his father and discover his birthright.

1972 95 minutes

GRIZZLY

★★

DIRECTOR: William Girdler

CAST: Christopher George, Andrew Prine, Richard Jaeckel, Joan McCall

Another "nature runs amok" film with Christopher George going up against an eighteen-foot killer bear this time out. Some taut action, but the movie has no style or pizzazz. Rated PG for violence.

1976 92 minutes

GUARDIAN OF THE ABYSS

★½

DIRECTOR: Don Sharp

CAST: Ray Lonnen, Rosalyn Landor, John Carson, Paul Darrow

Uneventful devil-worship flick from England; the kind that winds up on the late late show. An antiques broker buys a mirror that is actually a window to hell. Few surprises and an anticlimactic ending. Not rated, but the equivalent of a PG for some sex.

1985 50 minutes

HALLOWEEN

★★★★½

DIRECTOR: John Carpenter

CAST: Jamie Lee Curtis, Donald Pleasence, Nancy Loomis, P. J. Soles, Charles Cyphers, Kyle Richards

Considered the most successful independently made film of all time (having grossed over $40 million at the box office), this is a surprisingly tasteful and enjoyable slasher film. Director John Carpenter puts the accent on suspense and atmosphere rather than blood, gore, and guts, as in other films of this kind. In addition, fine performances are given by the cast—with Jamie Lee Curtis (her debut) and Donald Pleasence, a veteran British character actor, the stand-outs. The story revolves around the escape of a soulless maniac who returns to the town where he murdered his sister to kill again. Rated R for violence, profanity, and nudity.

1978 93 minutes

HALLOWEEN II

★★★½

DIRECTOR: Rick Rosenthal
CAST: Jamie Lee Curtis, Donald Pleasence, Charles Cyphers, Jeffrey Kramer, Lance Guest, Pamela Susan Shoop

This respectable sequel picks up where the original left off: with the boogeyman on the prowl and Jamie Lee Curtis running for her life. Rated R because of violence and nudity.

1981 92 minutes

HALLOWEEN III: SEASON OF THE WITCH

★★½

DIRECTOR: Tommy Lee Wallace
CAST: Tom Atkins, Stacey Nelkin, Dan O'Herlihy, Ralph Strait, Michael Currie

A maniacal mask manufacturer in Northern California provides kiddies with devilishly designed pumpkin masks. Not a true sequel to the gruesome *Halloween* twosome, but still watchable. Rated R.

1983 96 minutes

HAND, THE

DIRECTOR: Oliver Stone
CAST: Michael Caine, Andrea Marcovicci, Annie McEnroe, Bruce McGill

Thumbs down on this dull film. It's the story of a successful cartoonist (Michael Caine) whose life is shattered when he loses his drawing hand in a car accident. Pretty soon he begins to think that the missing hand has a life of its own. Too bad this film doesn't have a life of its own. Rated R.

1981 104 minutes

HAPPY BIRTHDAY TO ME

★

DIRECTOR: J. Lee Thompson
CAST: Melissa Sue Anderson, Glenn Ford, Tracy Bergman, Jack Blum, Matt Craven

After surviving a tragic car accident that killed her mother, a young woman (Melissa Sue Anderson) suffers recurrent blackouts. During these lapses of consciousness, other—more popular and more intelligent—students at her exclusive prep school are murdered in bizarre and vicious ways. Does she or doesn't she? Only her psychiatrist (Glenn Ford) knows for sure. Despite a few fresh splashes of brutality packaged in a psychological mystery framework, it's more than evident that story coherence and credibility have taken a back seat to all the bloodletting. Rated R.

1981 108 minutes

HATCHET FOR THE HONEYMOON

DIRECTOR: Mario Bava
CAST: Stephen Forsythe, Dagmar Lassander, Laura Betti

The man who brought you such substandard chillers as *Beyond the Door 2*, *Blood and Black Lace*, and *The House of Exorcism* strikes again with another forgettable fright flick. This one is about a psychotic killer fashion mogul who hacks up brides with a . . . guess what. The dialogue comes close to being black comedy, but the tone of this wretched little number is too earnest. Too bad. It is good for a couple of laughs, thanks to the poorly dubbed voices. Rated PG for violence.

1974 90 minutes

HAUNTED STRANGLER, THE

★★★½

DIRECTOR: Robert Day

CAST: Boris Karloff, Anthony Dawson, Elizabeth Allan

Boris Karloff is well cast in this effective story of a writer who develops the homicidal tendencies of a long-dead killer he's been writing about. Gripping horror film.

1958 B & W 81 minutes

HE KNOWS YOU'RE ALONE

[turkey]

DIRECTOR: Armand Mastroianni

CAST: Don Scardino, Caitlin O'Heany, Elizabeth Kemp, Tom Rolfing, Tom Hanks, Patsy Pease, Joseph Leon, James Rebhorn, James Carroll

There's a killer (Tom Rolfing) on the loose, specializing in brides-to-be. His current target for dismemberment is pretty Amy (Caitlin O'Henry), who can't decide whether to marry her male-chauvinist fiancé, Phil (James Carroll), or return to her former admirer, Marvin (Don Scardino), a lively lad who works in the morgue and is given to playing practical jokes. While stalking his special prey, the killer keeps his knife sharp by decimating the population of Staten Island. Rated R.

1981 94 minutes

HE WALKED BY NIGHT

★★★★½

DIRECTOR: Alfred L. Werker

CAST: Richard Basehart, Scott Brady, Jack Webb, Roy Roberts, Whit Bissell

Richard Basehart is superb in this documentary-style drama as a killer stalked by methodical policemen. A little-known cinematic gem, it's first-rate in every department and reportedly inspired Jack Webb to create *Dragnet*.

1948 B & W 79 minutes

HEARSE, THE

[turkey]

DIRECTOR: George Bowers

CAST: Trish Van Devere, Joseph Cotten, David Gautreaux, Donald Hotton, Med Flory

This film is about a satanic pact between an old woman and her lover. When Jane (Trish Van Devere) discovers this pact in her aunt's diary, the house starts shaking . . . literally. She tells the story to her own mysterious suitor, Tom (but we know who he really is, don't we?), who has an unusually high interest in the matter. What does Satan want with Jane? This film fails to answer that question. In some scenes he tries to kill her and in others he tries to possess her. This film is not only confusing; it's dull as well. Rated PG.

1980 100 minutes

HELL NIGHT

★

DIRECTOR: Tom Desimone

CAST: Linda Blair, Vincent Van Patten, Peter Barton, Jenny Neumann

Linda Blair (*The Exorcist*) returns to the genre that spawned her film career in this poor low-budget horror flick about fraternity and sorority pledges spending the night in a mansion "haunted" by a crazed killer. Rated R.

1981 101 minutes

HIDEOUS SUN DEMON, THE

★

DIRECTOR: Robert Clarke

CAST: Robert Clarke, Patricia Manning, Nan Peterson, Patrick Whyte, Fred La Porta, Bill Hampton

Everyone who saw this horror film as a kid when it was originally released probably remembers it as one of the scariest movies ever made. But look again—it's dreadful and just plain silly. Robert Clarke directed this and also stars as the scientist turned into a lizardlike monster by radiation.

1959 B & W 74 minutes

HILLS HAVE EYES, THE

DIRECTOR: Wes Craven

CAST: Susan Lamer, Robert Houston, Virginia Vincent, Russ Grieve, Dee Wallace Stone

The first scenes of this horror film reek of cheapness, and it gets worse. Foolish city folk have inherited a silver mine and are stopping on their way to California to check it out. The old-timer warns them to stay on the main road and head straight for California: "There ain't been no silver in them hills for years and you don't want to see what is out there." Naturally, they go out to find their fortune and the car breaks down. That's when a ghoulish family comes crawling out of the rocks. Rated R for violence and profanity.

1977 89 minutes

HITCHER, THE

★★★½

DIRECTOR: Robert Harmon

CAST: Rutger Hauer, C. Thomas Howell, Jeffrey Demunn, Jennifer Jason Leigh

C. Thomas Howell plays Jim Halsey, a young, squeamish California-bound motorist who picks up a hitchhiker, played by Rutger Hauer, somewhere in the barren Northwest. What transpires in the following ninety-six minutes is action that will leave you physically and emotionally drained. *The Hitcher* has all of the unflinching horror of a Wes Craven film and the kinetic power of a George Miller movie. If you thought *The Terminator* was too violent, this one will redefine the word for you. Rated R for profanity and extreme violence. Viewer discretion is strongly advised.

1986 96 minutes

HOLOCAUST 2000

★

DIRECTOR: Alberto De Martino

CAST: Kirk Douglas, Agnosta Belli, Simon Ward, Anthony Quayle

This is a shameless ripoff of *The Omen*. The Antichrist plans to destroy the world, using nuclear reactors. This movie stinks. Rated R.

1978 96 minutes

HOMEBODIES

★★★

DIRECTOR: Larry Yust

CAST: Douglas Fowley, Ruth McDevitt, Francis Fuller, Ian Wolfe, Bill Hansen, Paula Trueman

A cast of aging screen veterans liven up this offbeat thriller about a group of senior citizens who turn into a hit squad when faced with eviction. Director Larry Yust keeps things moving at a lively pace and even manages a few bizarre twists in the final scenes. Rated PG for violence, language.

1974 96 minutes

HONEYMOON

★★★½

DIRECTOR: Patrick Jamain
CAST: Nathalie Baye, John Shea, Richard Berry, Peter Donat

A Frenchwoman (Nathalie Baye) goes on what appears to be a carefree New York vacation with her boyfriend (Richard Berry). However, he is busted for smuggling cocaine, and she is set for deportation. Unwilling to leave her lover alone in jail in a foreign land, she goes to an agency that arranges marriages of convenience. She is assured that she will never see her new American "husband"—only to have him show up and refuse to leave her alone. Baye is first-rate as the hapless heroine, and John Shea is both chilling and poignant as her unhinged husband. Rated R for profanity, nudity, simulated sex, and violence.

1987 98 minutes

HONEYMOON KILLERS, THE

★★★

DIRECTOR: Leonard Kastle
CAST: Tony Lo Bianco, Shirley Stoler, Mary Jane Higby, Doris Roberts

Grim story of a smooth-talking Lothario and his obese lover who befriend and murder vulnerable older women for their money is based on the infamous "lonely-hearts killers" of the 1940s and 1950s. Tony LoBianco is fine as the slimy, egotistical woman hunter and Shirley Stoler gives a rich performance as the jealous woman who covets her glib conspirator-lover but allows him to woo other lonely women for profit. Not for the squeamish, but a solid entry in the growing file of true-crime films.

1970 108 minutes

HORROR EXPRESS

★★★

DIRECTOR: Eugenio Martin
CAST: Peter Cushing, Christopher Lee, Telly Savalas

Director Eugenio Martin creates a neat shocker about a prehistoric man-like creature terrorizing a trans-Siberian train when he is awakened from his centuries-old tomb. Lively cast includes veterans Christopher Lee and Peter Cushing as well as a pre-Kojak Telly Savalas in the role of a crazed Prussian officer intent on killing the thing. Break out the Jiffy Pop and enjoy. The original title: *Panic on the Trans-Siberian Express*. Rated R.

1972 88 minutes

HORROR HOSPITAL

★★

DIRECTOR: Anthony Balch
CAST: Michael Gough, Robert Askwith, Dennis Price, Skip Martin

A crazy doctor (Michael Gough) performing gruesome brain experiments at a remote English hospital runs into trouble when a nosy young couple checks in and begins snooping around. Slow-moving gorefest features a hammy performance by Michael Gough in a typical lunatic role which became his trademark in the late 1960s and early 1970s. Watch it if you must. Rated R for violence and blood.

1973 84 minutes

HORROR OF DRACULA

★★★★½

DIRECTOR: Terence Fisher
CAST: Christopher Lee, Peter Cushing, Michael Gough, Melissa Stribling, Miles Malleson

This is the one that launched Hammer Films' popular "Dracula" series, featuring Christopher Lee in the first—and best—of his many appearances as the Count and Peter Cushing as his archnemesis Van Helsing. A stylish, exciting reworking of Bram Stoker's classic story of a bloodthirsty vampire on the prowl from Transylvania to London and back again. Genuinely scary film, with a hell of an ending, too.

1958 82 minutes

HORROR OF FRANKENSTEIN

★★★★

DIRECTOR: Jimmy Sangster

CAST: Ralph Bates, Kate O'Mara, Graham Jones, Veronica Carlson, Dennis Price

Young medical student, fed up with school, decides to drop out and continue his studies alone. So what if his name just happens to be Frankenstein and he just happens to be making a monster? Good entry in the series has many ghoulish sequences, along with some welcome touches of humor. Recommended. Rated R.

1970 95 minutes

HOUSE

★★½

DIRECTOR: Steve Miner

CAST: William Katt, George Wendt, Kay Lenz, Richard Moll

A comedy-thriller about an author who moves into an old mansion left to him by an aunt who committed suicide. He's looking for solitude, but instead he finds an assortment of slimy monsters. The cast is good, but the creatures look phony, the shocks are predicatable, and the comedy is clumsy, crippling the suspense. In short, the structure of this house is rotten. Rated R for violence and profanity.

1986 93 minutes

HOUSE OF EXORCISM, THE

DIRECTORS: Mickey Lion, Mario Bava

CAST: Telly Savalas, Robert Alda, Elke Sommer

Early in this incomprehensible film, one of the characters prophetically proclaims, "It's awful." That it is. It looks as if the producers took a cheap horror film from Italy and added scenes of exorcism, including the now-standard cursing and vomiting, to update and commercialize it. They bear no apparent relationship to the rest of the film. Rated R for profanity, nudity, sex, gore, and violence.

1975 93 minutes

HOUSE OF SEVEN CORPSES, THE

★★½

DIRECTOR: Paul Harrison

CAST: John Ireland, Faith Domergue, John Carradine

Veteran cast almost saves this minor yarn about the grisly events that happen to the members of a film crew shooting a horror movie in a foreboding old mansion. Semi-entertaining nonsense. Rated PG.

1973 90 minutes

HOUSE OF THE DEAD

DIRECTOR: Knute Allmendinger

CAST: John Erickson, Charles Aidman, Bernard Fox, Ivor Francis

A young man stranded in a haunted house finds he is not alone. Don't ask why anyone would watch or enjoy this bomb. Rotten, rotten, rotten.

1980 90 minutes

HOUSE OF THE LONG SHADOWS

★★★

DIRECTOR: Pete Walker

CAST: Vincent Price, John Carradine, Christopher Lee, Desi Arnaz Jr., Peter Cushing

This is the good old-fashioned–type horror film that doesn't rely on blood and gore to give the viewer a scare. This gothic thriller is a great choice for horror fans who still like to use their imaginations. Rated PG.

1984 102 minutes

HOUSE OF WAX

★★★½

DIRECTOR: André De Toth

CAST: Vincent Price, Phyllis Kirk, Carolyn Jones

Vincent Price stars as a demented sculptor who, after losing the use of his hands in a fire, turns to murder to continue his work in this above-average horror film. A remake of the 1933 *Mystery of the Wax Museum*, *House of Wax* was long thought to be inferior to the original, which until three years ago was considered a lost film. The discovery of a print of *Mystery* brought about a reevaluation of both and the general agreement of the superiority of the Price version, which was also the first film to be made in 3-D by a major studio.

1953 88 minutes

HOUSE ON HAUNTED HILL

★★★

DIRECTOR: William Castle

CAST: Vincent Price, Carol Ohmart, Richard Long, Elisha Cook Jr., Carolyn Craig, Alan Marshal

Vincent Price is at his most relaxed and confident in this fun fright flick about the wealthy owner of a creepy old fortress who offers a group a fortune if they can survive a night there. Humorous at times, deadly serious at others. Robb White's intriguing script is well acted by the ensemble cast, with Elisha Cook Jr. outstanding as the one who knows the old house's secrets.

1958 B & W 75 minutes

HOUSE ON SORORITY ROW

🦃

DIRECTOR: Mark Rosman

CAST: Eileen Davidson, Kathryn McNeil, Robin Meloy

In this low-budget horror film, a group of college girls take over their sorority and kills the house mother. While the house mother may be down, she's not out—at least not out of the picture—as she comes back from the dead to wreak havoc. Rated R.

1983 90 minutes

HOUSE THAT BLED TO DEATH, THE

★★

DIRECTOR: Tom Clegg

CAST: Nicolas Ball, Rachel Davies, Brian Crouchen, Bat Maynard

Marginally scary horror film about a house that is possessed. Possessed by what or who? Don't ask us—the film refuses to give up the reason for all the blood that keeps shooting out of the pipes, or the various bloody members that show up in the fridge now and then. Not rated, but would probably merit a PG for violence and gore.

1985 50 minutes

HOUSE THAT DRIPPED BLOOD, THE

★★★½

DIRECTOR: Peter John Duffell

CAST: John Bennett, Christopher Lee, Peter Cushing, Denholm Elliott, Jon Pertwee, Ingrid Pitt

All-star horror-anthology high jinks adapted from the stories of Robert Bloch. It's not quite on a par with the pioneering British release *Dead of Night*, but it'll do. Best segment: A horror star (Jon Pertwee) discovers a vampire's cape and finds himself becoming a little too convincing in the role of a bloodsucker. Rated PG.

1970 102 minutes

HOUSE WHERE EVIL DWELLS, THE

★★

DIRECTOR: Kevin O'Connor
CAST: Edward Albert, Susan George, Doug McClure

Depressing little horror romp with a Japanese background. In a savagely violent opening, a young samurai swordsman discovers the amorous activities of his less-than-faithful wife, and a gory fight ensues wherein everyone is either beheaded or commits hara-kiri. This traps some really angry spirits in the house, which Edward Albert and Susan George move into centuries later. Pretty soon things go a lot more than bump in the night. Occasionally a quite interesting little ghost story, but it is marred by too much gruesome violence and some really sad nude scenes with an overweight Doug McClure and the always ready-to-peel Susan George, and the sleepwalking Edward Albert. Rated R for nudity, violence, language.

1985 91 minutes

HOWLING, THE

★★★★

DIRECTOR: Joe Dante
CAST: Dee Wallace Stone, Christopher Stone, Patrick Macnee, Dennis Dugan, Slim Pickens, John Carradine

The Howling has everything—every spooky scene you've ever seen, every horror movie cliché that's ever been overspoken, and every guaranteed-to-make-'em jump, out-of-the-dark surprise that Hollywood ever came up with for its scary movies. It also has the best special effects since *Alien* and some really off-the-wall humor, which makes this shocker truly bizarre. Rated R for gruesome adult horror.

1981 91 minutes

HOWLING II . . . YOUR SISTER IS A WEREWOLF

DIRECTOR: Philippe Mora
CAST: Christopher Lee, Reb Brown, Annie McEnroe, Sybil Danning, Marsha A. Hunt

Poor follow-up to *The Howling* concerns the plight of Ben White (Reb Brown, best remembered for the title role in *Yor, the Hunter from the Future*) to uncover and destroy the colony of werewolves that infected his sister. Fortunately, he has help in the person of Christopher Lee (who's great at keeping a straight face) as a professor who leads Ben to the wolves' sacred temple in Transylvania. An awful sequel; even Sybil Danning as the Leader of the Pack can't save it. Mediocre on all counts, with a video transfer that is so dark that the viewer is left mystified half the time as to what is going on. Skip this one—it doesn't even rate as a comedy. Rated R for nudity, blood, and gore.

1984 91 minutes

HUMAN MONSTER, THE (DARK EYES OF LONDON)

★★★

DIRECTOR: Walter Summers
CAST: Bela Lugosi, Hugh Williams, Greta Gynt, Edmon Ryan, Wilfred Walter

Creaky but sometimes clever suspense thriller about a humanitarian (Bela Lugosi) who may not be as philanthropic as he seems. Strange murders have been occurring in the vicinity of his charitable facility. This preposterous Edgar Wallace story has its moments.

1939 B & W 73 minutes

HUMANOIDS FROM THE DEEP

★★★

DIRECTOR: Barbara Peters
CAST: Doug McClure, Ann Turkel, Vic Morrow

As in *Jaws*, beachgoers are terrified by water beasts in this science-fiction film. This time, it's underwater vegetable monsters who attack seaside frolickers. This is a never-a-dull-moment thriller. Rated R.

1980 80 minutes

HUMONGOUS

★

DIRECTOR: Paul Lynch

CAST: Janet Julian, David Wallace

The title is the best thing about this dumb thriller. Rated R.

1981 93 minutes

HUNCHBACK OF NOTRE DAME, THE (ORIGINAL)

★★★★½

DIRECTOR: Wallace Worsley

CAST: Lon Chaney Sr., Patsy Ruth Miller, Ernest Torrence

This is the original silent classic. Although it has been remade, with varying degrees of success, in the sound era, nothing can touch the Lon Chaney version in screen spectacle or in the athletic excellence of moviedom's "man of a thousand faces." Chaney somehow conveys the tragic poignance of Victor Hugo's deformed bell ringer, from under layers of make-up. This film manages to hold up so well today, modern audiences don't even notice the lack of sound. A musical score has been added.

1923 B & W 108 minutes

HUNCHBACK OF NOTRE DAME, THE (REMAKE)

★★★★½

DIRECTOR: William Dieterle

CAST: Charles Laughton, Thomas Mitchell, Maureen O'Hara, Edmond O'Brien

In this horror classic, Charles Laughton gives a tour-de-force performance as the deformed bell-ringer who comes to the aid of a pretty gypsy (Maureen O'Hara). Cedric Hardwicke, as the hunchback's evil master, Thomas Mitchell, and Edmond O'Brien also give strong performances in this remake of the Lon Chaney silent film.

1939 B & W 117 minutes

HUNGER, THE

★

DIRECTOR: Tony Scott

CAST: Catherine Deneuve, David Bowie, Susan Sarandon, Cliff DeYoung

Arty and visually striking yet cold, this kinky sci-fi/horror film, directed by Tony Scott (brother of *Alien* director Ridley Scott), features French actress Catherine Deneuve as a seductive vampire. Her centuries-old boyfriend (David Bowie) is about to disintegrate, so she picks a new lover (Susan Sarandon). In the old-time vampire movies, you felt something for the victims—and maybe even the monster. As you watch this beautifully photographed but sluggish film, the only thing you feel is the urge to be somewhere else. Rated R for blood, gore, profanity, nudity, and sex.

1983 94 minutes

HUSH . . . HUSH, SWEET CHARLOTTE

★★★

DIRECTOR: Robert Aldrich

CAST: Bette Davis, Olivia De Havilland, Joseph Cotten, Agnes Moorehead, Cecil Kellaway, Mary Astor, Bruce Dern

Originally planned as a sequel to *What Ever Happened to Baby Jane?*, reuniting stars of that movie, Bette Davis and Joan Crawford, this effort was filmed with Bette opposite her old Warner Bros. cellmate—Olivia De Havilland. (Both walked out on what they felt were unfair contracts at the studio.) This time they're on opposite sides of the magnolia bush, with Olivia trying to drive poor Bette, who's not all there to begin with, mad.

1965 B & W 133 minutes

I CONFESS

★★★

DIRECTOR: Alfred Hitchcock

CAST: Montgomery Clift, Karl Malden, Anne Baxter, Brian Aherne, O. E. Haas, Dolly Haas

Alfred Hitchcock's method direction clashes with Montgomery Clift's method acting, and the result falls short of the Master of Suspense's best work. In spite of such shortcomings, this is the film that best reflects many of Hitch's puritanical ethics. Clift stars as a priest who takes confession from a man who—coincidentally—killed a blackmailer who knew of Clift's pre-vows relationship with Baxter. (Whew!) Karl Malden, as a police investigator, demonstrates where Peter Falk got a lot of his ideas for Columbo. Moody and atmospheric, but the notion of dual guilt never quite comes off.

1953 B & W 95 minutes

I DISMEMBER MAMA

★

DIRECTOR: Paul Leder

CAST: Zooey Hall, Geri Reischl, Greg Mullavey

Great title—horrible movie. Mama's boy escapes from institution and goes on a "purifying" spree. In a sick plot turn, he falls in love with an 11-year-old girl after carving up her mother. A low-budget bore. Too tame for gore fans, too silly for anyone else. Rated R for violence and nudity.

1972 86 minutes

I SPIT ON YOUR GRAVE

DIRECTOR: Meir Zarchi

CAST: Camille Keaton, Epon Tabor, Richard Pace, Anthony Nichols

After being brutally raped by a gang of thugs (one of whom is retarded), a young woman takes sadistic revenge. An utterly reprehensible motion picture with shockingly misplaced values. It seems to take more joy in presenting its heroine's degradation than her victory. She is repeatedly raped and tortured. When the tables finally turn, she proves to be just as vicious as her attackers. The scene where she robs a man of his offending "weapon" is one of the most appalling moments in cinema history. This is, beyond a doubt, one of the most tasteless, irresponsible, and disturbing movies ever made. Regardless of how much you may enjoy "bad" films, you will hate yourself for watching this one. The cassette box claims the movie is rated R; however, most videotapes of this title contain the longer X-rated version. Rated R or X.

1981 88 minutes

I WALKED WITH A ZOMBIE

★★★★½

DIRECTOR: Jacques Tourneur

CAST: Frances Dee, Tom Conway, James Ellison, Edith Barrett, James Bell

Director Jacques Tourneur made this classic horror film, involving voodoo and black magic, on an island in the Pacific. One of the best of its kind, this is a great Val Lewton production. Get the video and get ready to enjoy a great film.

1943 B & W 69 minutes

IMPULSE

★★

DIRECTOR: Graham Baker

CAST: Tim Matheson, Meg Tilly, Hume Cronyn

This mildly interesting thriller takes place in a town where the inhabitants find they have increasing difficulties in controlling their urges. Starring Meg Tilly (*The Big Chill*) and Tim Matheson (*Animal House*), the film attempts to tie up its plot in a hasty, unconvincing final ten minutes. Rated R for profanity and violence.

1984 91 minutes

IN THE SHADOW OF KILIMANJARO

★

DIRECTOR: Raju Patel

CAST: John Rhys-Davies, Timothy Bottoms, Irene Miracle, Michelle Carey, Leonard Trolley, Patty Foley

This is the gory but supposedly true story of what happened in Kenya when ninety thousand baboons went on a killing spree because of the 1984 drought. They were hungry, and people were the only readily available source of food. Rated R for violence and gore.

1986 97 minutes

INCUBUS, THE

DIRECTOR: John Hough

CAST: John Cassavetes, Kerrie Keane, Helen Hughes, John Ireland

About a spate of sex murders in a small town, this is a vile and mean-spirited film, a nightmare of bad taste and burdensome plotting, and a depressing example of movie-making at its most prurient. Rated R for all manner of gruesome goings-on.

1982 90 minutes

INDESTRUCTIBLE MAN

DIRECTOR: Jack Pollexfen

CAST: Lon Chaney Jr., Marian Carr, Ross Elliott, Casey Adams

Lon Chaney looks uncomfortable in the title role of an electrocuted man brought back to life who seeks revenge on the old gang who betrayed him. Nothing new has been added to the worn-out story, unless you want to count the awful narration, which makes this passable thriller seem utterly ridiculous at times.

1956 B & W 70 minutes

INITIATION, THE

DIRECTORS: Larry Stewart, Vera Miles, Clu Gulager, James Read, Marilyn Kagan, Daphne Zuniga

A particularly gruesome story involving psychotic terror and lots of blood and gore. In a quest to rid herself of a recurring nightmare, a young coed becomes involved in a bloody reality, unlocking a twisted past that was blotted from her memory at a young age. Rated R.

1984 97 minutes

INITIATION OF SARAH, THE

DIRECTOR: Robert Day

CAST: Kay Lenz, Shelley Winters, Kathryn Crosby, Morgan Brittany, Tony Bill

Adequate TV movie features Kay Lenz as a young college girl being victimized by other students during initiation, and her subsequent revenge upon acquiring supernatural powers. Hokey thriller should have been better, judging from the cast.

1978 100 minutes

INTERNECINE PROJECT, THE

★★★

DIRECTOR: Ken Hughes

CAST: James Coburn, Lee Grant, Harry Andrews, Ian Hendry, Michael Jayston, Christiane Kruger, Keenan Wynn

Ken Hughes, the director of *Chitty Chitty Bang Bang*, attempts a Hitchcock-style thriller. The results are mixed; the acting is good and the story is intriguing, but the screenplay drags and Hughes spends too much time tinkering with Hitchcock imagery and doesn't bother to pick up the pace. James Coburn plays an ambitious business tycoon who finds he has to kill four associates to meet a business agreement. The fashion in which he does this proves to be interesting. Worth a look for the trick ending. Rated PG for violence, partial nudity, and a little profanity.

1974 89 minutes

INVISIBLE GHOST

★

DIRECTOR: Joseph H. Lewis
CAST: Bela Lugosi, Polly Ann Young, John McGuire, Betty Compson, Jack Mulhall

This low-budget Monogram programmer features Bela Lugosi as an unwitting murderer, used by his supposedly dead wife to further her schemes—much the same as Lugosi himself was killed in films by overexposure in exploitative poverty row productions like this. Short on thrills, but look for silent cowboy hero Jack Mulhall in a supporting role as well as pretty Betty Compson, costar of *Of Mice and Men* in 1940. If the choice is given, go for a zombie movie.

1941 B & W 64 minutes

INVISIBLE MAN, THE

★★★★½

DIRECTOR: James Whale
CAST: Claude Rains, Gloria Stuart, William Harrigan, Una O'Connor, Henry Travers, E. E. Clive, Dwight Frye

Claude Rains goes unseen until the finish in his screen debut. He plays Jack Griffin, the title character in H. G. Wells's famous story of a scientist who creates an invisibility serum—with the side effect of driving a person slowly insane. Frightening film could initially be mistaken for a comedy, with large chunks of humor in the first half, turning deadly serious thereafter. Kudos to special effects man John P. Fulton and Universal for making us believe what we're *not* seeing in this acknowledged classic of the genre.

1933 B & W 71 minutes

INVISIBLE RAY, THE

★★★

DIRECTOR: Lambert Hillyer
CAST: Boris Karloff, Bela Lugosi, Frances Drake, Frank Lawton

Boris Karloff and Bela Lugosi are teamed in this interesting story. A brilliant research scientist (Karloff), experimenting in Africa, is contaminated by a hunk of radioactive meteor landing nearby and soon discovers that his mere touch can kill. Neat Universal thriller features first-rate effects and good ensemble acting, but it is hampered by a lame romantic subplot given too much screen time. At least Bela Lugosi gets to play the good guy for a change.

1936 B & W 81 minutes

ISLAND, THE

★½

DIRECTOR: Michael Ritchie
CAST: Michael Caine, David Warner, Angela Punch McGregor

Dreadful horror-adventure movie featuring Michael Caine as a reporter investigating the mysterious disappearances of pleasure crafts and their owners in an area of the Caribbean. At the beginning of the film, when author Peter "Jaws" Benchley's explanation for these documented disappearances is still a mystery, *The Island* is quite suspenseful and frightening. But when Caine discovers that the force behind the phenomenon is a band of pirates who have remained untouched by progress for three centuries, all impact is lost. In fact, if the movie wasn't so gruesome and gory, it would be funny. But it's just sick. Rated R.

1980 113 minutes

ISLAND CLAWS

★★

DIRECTOR: Hernan Cardenas
CAST: Robert Lansing, Barry Nelson, Steve Hanks, Nita Talbot

As science-fiction/horror thrillers go, this one is about average. *Attack of the Killer Crabs* would have been a more appropriate title, though. Dr. McNeal (Barry Nelson) is a scientist who is experimenting to make larger crabs as a food source. All goes well until a multitude of crabs (along with one giant crab) go berserk and begin attacking people in the nearby fishing village. Robert Lansing, as Moody the bar owner, delivers the best performance among many mediocre ones. The special effects were developed by Glen Robinson, who also did them for the 1976 version of *King Kong*. Rated PG for violence and gore.

1980 91 minutes

ISLE OF THE DEAD

★★★½

DIRECTOR: Mark Robson
CAST: Boris Karloff, Ellen Drew, Jason Robards Sr.

Atmospheric goings-on dominate this typically tasteful horror study from producer Val Lewton. A group of people are stranded on a Greek island during a quarantine. Star Boris Karloff is, as usual, outstanding.

1945 B & W 72 minutes

IT CAME FROM BENEATH THE SEA

★★★★

DIRECTOR: Robert Gordon
CAST: Kenneth Tobey, Faith Domergue, Donald Curtis, Ian Keith, Chuck Griffiths

Ray Harryhausen's powerhouse special effects light up the screen in this story of a giant octopus from the depths of the Pacific that causes massive destruction along the North American coast as it makes its way toward San Francisco. A little talky at times, but the brilliantly achieved effects make this a must-see movie even on the small screen; don't miss the now classic attack on the Golden Gate Bridge.

1955 B & W 80 minutes

IT LIVES AGAIN

★★★

DIRECTOR: Larry Cohen
CAST: Frederic Forrest, Kathleen Lloyd, John Ryan, John Marley, Andrew Duggan

In an effort to outdo the original *It's Alive!*, this film has three mutated babies on the loose, and everybody in a panic. Doesn't quite measure up to its predecessor, but still successful due to another fine make-up job on the monsters by Rick Baker, and some nice directorial touches by Larry Cohen, who helmed both projects. Rated R.

1978 91 minutes

IT'S ALIVE!

★★★½

DIRECTOR: Larry Cohen
CAST: John Ryan, Sharon Farrell, Andrew Duggan, Guy Stockwell, Michael Ansara

This camp classic about a mutated baby with a thirst for human blood has to be seen to be believed. Convincing effects work by Rick Baker and a fantastic score by Bernard Herrmann make this film one to remember. Rated PG.

1974 91 minutes

JACK THE RIPPER

★★

DIRECTOR: Jess (Jesus) Franco

CAST: Klaus Kinski, Josephine Chaplin

Klaus Kinski plays Jack the Ripper, and Josephine Chaplin is Cynthia, the Scotland Yard inspector's girlfriend. Jack the Ripper is terrorizing London by killing women and disposing of their bodies in the Thames River. When Cynthia (Chaplin) tries to help her boyfriend capture Jack, she puts herself in danger. Rated R for violence and nudity.

1979 82 minutes

JAWS

★★★★★

DIRECTOR: Steven Spielberg

CAST: Roy Scheider, Robert Shaw, Richard Dreyfuss, Lorraine Gary, Murray Hamilton

A young Steven Spielberg (27 at the time) directed this 1975 scare masterpiece based on the Peter Benchley novel. A large shark is terrorizing the tourists at the local beach. The eerie music by John Williams heightens the tension to underscore the shark's presence and scare the audience right out of their seats. Roy Scheider, Robert Shaw, and Richard Dreyfuss offer outstanding performances. Rated PG.

1975 124 minutes

JAWS 2

★★★

DIRECTOR: Jeannot Szwarc

CAST: Roy Scheider, Lorraine Gary, Murray Hamilton, Jeffrey Kramer

Even though it's a sequel, *Jaws 2* delivers. It has all the thrills, chills, shocks, and screams that could be desired. The story can best be described as *Close Encounters of the Third Kind* meets *Jaws*. Police chief Martin Brody (Roy Scheider) believes there's a shark in the waters off Amity again, but his wife and employers think he's crazy. Rated PG.

1978 120 minutes

JAWS 3

★★½

DIRECTOR: Joe Alves

CAST: Louis Gossett Jr., Dennis Quaid, Bess Armstrong, Simon MacCorkindale

Just when you thought it was safe to watch a video movie, this second sequel to Steven Spielberg's megabucks box-office hit rears its ugly head. Among those marked for lunch in this soggy, unexciting sequel are Louis Gossett Jr., Dennis Quaid, and Bess Armstrong (*High Road to China*). They look bored. You'll be bored. Rated PG for profanity, gore, and violence.

1983 97 minutes

JAWS THE REVENGE

DIRECTOR: Joseph Sargent

CAST: Lorraine Gary, Lance Guest, Michael Caine, Mario Van Peebles, Karen Young, Judith Barsi

This third sequel is lowest-common-denominator filmmaking, a by-the-numbers effort so routine that every agonizing, boring moment feels like a death sentence. The rabid Great White isn't the only thing fishy about this film; poor editing strongly suggests it was cut down severely, as if all concerned expected brevity to help things along. It doesn't. Lorraine Gary returns as Mom Brody, who inanely blames the *same animal*—conveniently forgetting all the others which were blown up and electrocuted—when her now-grown son becomes fish-food at the beginning of this film. Just what've we got here . . . Jason the shark? Gary tries to make us believe she's the toughest grandma in the Bahamas when she later tackles the monster by her lonesome; the idiocy of this plot development simply caps a script which passes beyond ludicrous in the first five minutes. Even Michael Caine can't bring any class to this vapid mess. Rated PG for violence, brief gore.

1987 89 minutes

JENNIFER

★★

DIRECTOR: Brice Mack

CAST: Lisa Pelikan, Bert Convy, Nina Foch, Amy Johnston, John Gavin, Wesley Eure, Jeff Corey, Louise Hoven, Ray Underwood

A carbon copy of *Carrie*—but with snakes. Jennifer is a sweet, innocent child on a "poor-kids scholarship" at an uppity school for rich girls. She is tormented by one particularly sadistic girl and her cohorts until she is harassed into a frenzy. What's the catch? Jennifer was raised by a cult of religious fanatics who believe that God has given her the power to command reptiles. Not particularly scary. Rated PG for brief nudity and violence.

1978 90 minutes

JESSE JAMES MEETS FRANKENSTEIN'S DAUGHTER

DIRECTOR: William Beaudine

CAST: John Lupton, Estelita, Cal Bolder, Jim Davis

At last! The one we've all been wating for! The one they said couldn't be made! Well, they were almost right. From the director of *Bela Lugosi Meets a Brooklyn Gorilla* comes a film that *shouldn't* have been made. The feeble plot pits hero Jesse James against the evil daughter of the infamous doctor of the title. Watch if you must.

1966 88 minutes

JIGSAW MAN, THE

★★★★

DIRECTOR: Freddie Francis

CAST: Michael Caine, Laurence Olivier, Susan George, Robert Powell, Charles Gray

In this suspense film, Michael Caine plays Sir Philip Kimberly, a British secret agent who has defected, under orders, to Russia. Before leaving, he discovered a list of Soviet spies operating in England and hid it. After forty years, he returns to England in order to get the list with spies from both countries hot on his trail. This is a wonderfully entertaining puzzle of a movie that keeps you guessing throughout. Caine is reunited with his *Sleuth* co-star, Laurence Olivier, who plays his chief nemesis. Rated PG for violence and profanity.

1984 90 minutes

JUNIOR

DIRECTOR: Jim Henley

CAST: Suzanne Delaurentis, Linda Singer, Jeremy Ratchford, Michael McKenever

We can't figure out what's more despicable about this film—its exploitation of women or its shameless theft of ideas from *Psycho* and *The Texas Chainsaw Massacre.* Two hardened female ex-cons (Suzanne Delaurentis and Linda Singer) try to build a marina on a lake. They get hassled by the locals, who can't party on the old dock now that the two women have bought the place. But their troubles get even worse when Junior (Jeremy Ratchford) gets the okay from his demented mother to go ahead and kill the two. Of course, this doesn't stop our two heroines from stripping down to nothing for some skinny-dipping once in a while. Not rated, but contains violence, nudity, and profanity.

1984 80 minutes

KEEP, THE

★½

DIRECTOR: Michael Mann

CAST: Ian McKellen, Alberta Watson, Scott Glenn, Jurgen Prochnow

This is a visually impressive but otherwise flat and disappointing horror film set during World War II. Ian McKellen and Alberta Watson play Jewish prisoners freed by the Nazis when a centuries-old presence awakens in an old castle. After an impressive beginning with good special effects, this ends up being no more than an interesting curio. Rated R for nudity, sex, and violence.

1983 96 minutes

KEEPER, THE

DIRECTOR: T. Y. Drake

CAST: Christopher Lee, Tell Schreiber, Sally Gray

You'd probably be more entertained by watching commercials on TV. Bad, bad, bad. Christopher Lee plays the title role of the owner of an insane asylum who preys on the wealthy families of his charges. Rated R.

1984 96 minutes

KIDNAPPING OF THE PRESIDENT, THE

★★★★

DIRECTOR: George Mendeluk

CAST: William Shatner, Hal Holbrook, Van Johnson, Ava Gardner

As the title implies, terrorists kidnap the president and hold him hostage in this excellent action thriller. Hal Holbrook plays the feisty president, who is locked up in an armored truck and wired to explode at the slightest touch. William Shatner portrays a secret service agent who finds himself in charge of the crisis and unprepared for the situation. Van Johnson is the crooked vice president being asked by Holbrook to resign. As acting head of state, he ultimately holds the president's life in his hands, leading to a suspenseful twist in the hostage crisis. The acting is excellent, the suspense taut, and the direction tightly paced. You can't go wrong with this one.

1979 120 minutes

KILLER INSIDE ME, THE

★★★

DIRECTOR: Burt Kennedy

CAST: Stacy Keach, Susan Tyrrell, Tisha Sterling, Keenan Wynn, Charles McGraw, John Dehner, Pepe Serna, Royal Dano, John Carradine, Don Stroud

Stacy Keach plays a schizophrenic sheriff in a small town. The psychological angle to the killings that occur in the town have been expressed in cinematic clichés and Keach's performance is not up to his usual standard. Still, a tightly woven plot offers the viewer plenty of surprises. Rated R for violence and profanity.

1975 99 minutes

KILLING HOUR, THE

★½

DIRECTOR: Armand Mastroianni

CAST: Perry King, Elizabeth Kemp, Norman Parker, Kenneth McMillan

Elizabeth Kemp (*He Knows You're Alone*) plays a clairvoyant art student who, through her drawings, becomes involved in a series of murders. The story is a blatant ripoff of *The Eyes of Laura Mars*. With that said, suspense is achieved during the last fifteen minutes of the film. Unfortunately, the viewer must suffer through the first hour, which moves at a snail's pace, to make sense of the climax. Rated R for violence, nudity, and profanity.

1984 97 minutes

KINDRED, THE

DIRECTORS: Jeffrey Obrow, Stephen Carpenter

CAST: David Allen Brooks, Amanda Pays, Rod Steiger, Kim Hunter

A senseless script and an unsatisfactory ending mar this derivative horror film, which steals its creature from *Alien* and its plot from any one of a hundred run-of-the razor slasher flicks. Rod Steiger, Kim Hunter, and Amanda Pays give strong performances in this story about a genetics experiment gone awry. Rated R for profanity, violence, and gore.

1987 95 minutes

KING KONG (ORIGINAL)

★★★★★

DIRECTORS: Merian C. Cooper, Ernest B. Schoedsack

CAST: Robert Armstrong, Fay Wray, Bruce Cabot, Frank Reicher, Noble Johnson

This classic was one of early sound film's most spectacular successes. The movie, about the giant ape who is captured on a prehistoric island and proceeds to tear New York City apart until his final stand on the Empire State Building, is the stuff of which legends are made. It utilized every possible form of special effect, some of which are still secret. Its marriage of sound, music, image, energy, pace, and excitement made *King Kong* stand as a landmark film and a testament to the genius of its creators.

1933 B & W 100 minutes

KING KONG (REMAKE)

★★

DIRECTOR: John Guillermin

CAST: Jeff Bridges, Jessica Lange, Charles Grodin

This remake, starring Jeff Bridges and Jessica Lange, is a pale imitation of the 1933 classic. For kids only. Rated PG for violence.

1976 135 minutes

KING KONG LIVES

DIRECTOR: John Guillermin

CAST: Brian Kerwin, Linda Hamilton, John Ashton, Peter Michael Goetz

A moronic sequel to director John Guillermin's regrettable 1976 remake of *King Kong*, this features Brian Kerwin and Linda Hamilton as human witnesses to the romance of the resuscitated Kong and his new love, Lady Kong. Rated PG-13 for violence.

1986 105 minutes

KING OF THE ZOMBIES

DIRECTOR: Jean Yarbrough

CAST: Dick Purcell, Joan Woodbury, Henry Victor, Mantan Moreland, John Archer

Typical mad scientist–zombie movie with evil genius attempting to create an invulnerable army of mindless slaves to further the cause of evil. Thinly veiled Nazis in this limp entry are inevitably overcome by the forces of good, who adhere to the code of the bad zombie movie: it must take place on a phony tropical island, it must involve Nazis of some sort, it must look cheap, and it must have Manton Moreland in there somewhere. Jean Yarbrough has to join the ranks of the great low-budget directors for the steady stream of grade D clinkers that Monogram Studios loosed upon a monster-glutted public in the 1940s.

1941 B & W 67 minutes

KINGDOM OF THE SPIDERS

★★★

DIRECTOR: John (Bud) Cardos

CAST: William Shatner, Tiffany Bolling, Woody Strode

William Shatner stars in this unsuspenseful thriller with lurid special effects. The title tells it all. Rated PG.

1977 94 minutes

KISS OF THE TARANTULA

★

DIRECTOR: Chris Munger

CAST: Suzanne Ling, Eric Mason, Herman Wallner, Patricia Landon

Boring, unpleasant story of an unhinged girl who obliterates her enemies with the help of some eight-legged friends. Rated PG for mild gore.

1972 85 minutes

LADY FRANKENSTEIN

½

DIRECTOR: Mel Welles

CAST: Joseph Cotten, Mickey Hargitay, Paul Whiteman, Sarah Bey

Bottom-rung horror film with Joseph Cotten ill-used as Baron Frankenstein attempting once again to create life in yet another silly-looking assemblage of spare parts. The twist to this one is that the Baron's daughter, Sarah Bey, takes over the duties and does her best to animate the lump on the operating table. Nothing new here—even the gore is listless. Rated R for violence.

1971 84 minutes

LADY IN A CAGE

★★★★

DIRECTOR: Walter Grauman

CAST: Olivia De Havilland, James Caan, Ann Sothern

Superb shocker may finally get the recognition it deserves, thanks to home video. Olivia De Havilland is terrorized by a gang of punks when she becomes trapped in an elevator in her home. Good acting, especially by a young James Caan, and excellent photography help make this film really something special. Very violent at times.

1964 B & W 93 minutes

LADY VANISHES, THE (ORIGINAL)

★★★★★

DIRECTOR: Alfred Hitchcock

CAST: Margaret Lockwood, Michael Redgrave, May Whitty

Along with *The Thirty-nine Steps*, this is the most admired film from Alfred Hitchcock's early directorial career. The comedy-suspense thriller centers around a group of British "types" on a train trip from England to central Europe. A young woman (Margaret Lockwood) seeks the aid of a fellow passenger (Michael Redgrave) in an attempt to locate a charming old lady (May Whitty) she had met earlier on the train and now is apparently missing. Something is amiss. Not all the travelers are who they appear to be. Great fun in the Hitchcock tradition.

1938 B & W 97 minutes

LADY VANISHES, THE

★½

DIRECTOR: Anthony Page

CAST: Elliott Gould, Cybill Shepherd, Angela Lansbury, Herbert Lom, Arthur Lowe, Ian Carmichael

A better title for this remake of the classic Alfred Hitchcock suspense film might be *The Plot Vanishes*. All sense and suspense is virtually cast aside as Elliott Gould and Cybill Shepherd cavort through a series of "comedy" scenes with some fine supporting players: Angela Lansbury, Herbert Lom, and Ian Carmichael. It is easy to find oneself pondering the movie that might have been while watching this misfire. But there is no need to wonder—the brilliant original is also available on video. Rated PG.

1979 95 minutes

LAST HORROR FILM, THE

DIRECTOR: David Winters
CAST: Caroline Munro, Joe Spinell, Judd Hamilton

Mama's boy obsessed with a horror movie actress goes on a killing spree at the Cannes Film Festival. This one is really sick. Even gore fans may find it overwhelming. It's unpleasant, unrelenting, and an embarrassment to everyone involved. Rated R for violence.

1984 87 minutes

LAST HOUSE ON THE LEFT

DIRECTOR: Wes Craven
CAST: David Hess, Lucy Grantham, Sandra Cassel, Marc Sheffler, Jeramie Rain

This is a sick slasher movie in which two teenage girls are tortured and killed by a sadistic trio. Later, one of the girls' parents take revenge. This movie will probably turn your stomach and keep you awake at night. Graphic torture and humiliation scenes rate this one an R at best.

1972 91 minutes

LAST WAVE, THE

★★★

DIRECTOR: Peter Weir
CAST: Richard Chamberlain, Olivia Hamnett

In this suspenseful, fascinating film, directed by Australia's Peter Weir (*Gallipoli*; *Picnic at Hanging Rock*), Richard Chamberlain plays a lawyer defending a group of aborigines on trial for murder. His investigation into the incident leads to a frightening series of apocalyptic visions. It's not quite a horror film. However, it is often quite scary. Superbly made, it's a real treat for movie buffs. Rated PG.

1977 106 minutes

LEGACY, THE

★★

DIRECTOR: Richard Marquand
CAST: Katharine Ross, Sam Elliott, John Standing, Roger Daltrey

A young American couple (Katharine Ross and Sam Elliott) staying at a mysterious English mansion discover that the woman has been chosen as the mate for some sort of ugly, demonic creature upstairs. The bulk of the action surrounds their attempts to escape from this bizarre "legacy." Could be enjoyable if you're in the right mood. Rated R for violence and language.

1979 100 minutes

LEGEND OF BOGGY CREEK

★★

DIRECTOR: Charles B. Pierce
CAST: Willie E. Smith, John P. Nixon, John W. Gates, Jeff Crabtree, Buddy Crabtree

One of the better "mystery of" docudramas, which were the rage of the early 1970s, this supposedly true story focuses on a monster that lurks in the swamps of Arkansas. Included are interviews with people who have come in contact with the creature and reenactments of said encounters. Rated PG.

1972 95 minutes

LEGEND OF HELL HOUSE, THE

★★★½

DIRECTOR: John Hough
CAST: Roddy McDowall, Pamela Franklin, Gayle Hunnicutt, Clive Revill

Richard Matheson's riveting suspense tale of a group of researchers attempting to survive a week in a haunted house in order to try to solve the mystery of the many deaths that have occurred there. Jarring at times, with very inventive camera shots and a great cast headed by Roddy McDowall as the only survivor of a previous investigation. Rated PG for violence, tense situations.

1973 95 minutes

LEOPARD MAN, THE

★★★½

DIRECTOR: Jacques Tourneur
CAST: Dennis O'Keefe, Isabel Jewell

This Val Lewton–produced thriller depicts the havoc and killing that begin when a leopard (used for publicity) escapes and terrorizes a New Mexico village.

1943 B & W 59 minutes

LET'S SCARE JESSICA TO DEATH

★★

DIRECTOR: John Hancock
CAST: Zohra Lampert, Barton Heyman, Gretchen Corbett

A young woman staying with some odd people out in the country witnesses all sorts of strange things, like ghosts and bloodstained corpses. Is it real, or some kind of elaborate hoax? The title tells it all in this disjointed terror tale, though it does contain a few spooky scenes. Rated PG.

1971 89 minutes

LIFT, THE

★★★

DIRECTOR: Dick Maas
CAST: Huub Stapel, Willeke van Ammelrooy, Josie van Dalam

An inquisitive mechanic (Huub Stapel) discovers that an elevator is possessed by some dark power and is killing the people who ride in it. The authorities don't believe him, and he alone is left to battle the unholy force. Competent acting and good production values lend considerable suspense to this dubbed-to-English German production, despite an unusual premise. Definitely worth watching for horror film fans.

1985 95 minutes

LINK

★★½

DIRECTOR: Richard Franklin
CAST: Terence Stamp, Elizabeth Shue, Steven Pinner, Richard Garnett, David O'Hara, Kevin Lloyd

In this reasonably suspenseful shocker, a student (Elizabeth Shue) takes a job with an eccentric anthropology professor (Terence Stamp) and finds herself menaced by a powerful, intelligent ape named Link. The story leaves a number of questions unanswered, but the film can be praised for taking the old cliché of an ape being on the loose and making it surprisingly effective. Rated R for profanity, brief nudity, and violence.

1986 103 minutes

LIPSTICK

DIRECTOR: Lamont Johnson
CAST: Margaux Hemingway, Mariel Hemingway, Anne Bancroft, Perry King, Chris Sarandon

This film proved that acting was not the career for model Margaux

Hemingway. In it, both she and her little sister (Mariel Hemingway) are sexually molested by a composer. When Margaux gets no justice in court, she takes matters into her own hands. Rated R.

1976 89 minutes

LITTLE GIRL WHO LIVES DOWN THE LANE, THE

★★★½

DIRECTOR: Nicolas Gessner
CAST: Jodie Foster, Martin Sheen, Alexis Smith

The Little Girl Who Lives Down the Lane is a remarkably subdued film from a genre that has existed primarily on gore, violence, and audience manipulation. Whatever shocks and suspense *Little Girl* has—and there is an atmosphere throughout that rivals a good, scary book by the fireside—are achieved through genuine skill on the part of author/screenwriter Laird Koenig and director Nicolas Gessner. Jodie Foster gives an absorbingly realistic performance in the title role. Martin Sheen is the child molester who menaces her. It's a well-acted chiller. Rated PG.

1976 94 minutes

LITTLE SHOP OF HORRORS, THE

★★★★

DIRECTOR: Roger Corman
CAST: Jonathan Haze, Mel Welles, Jackie Joseph, Jack Nicholson, Dick Miller

Dynamite Roger Corman superquickie about a meek florist shop employee (Jonathan Haze) who inadvertently creates a ferocious man-eating plant. This horror-comedy was filmed in two days and is one of the funniest ever made.

1960 B & W 72 minutes

LODGER, THE

★★★★

DIRECTOR: Alfred Hitchcock
CAST: Ivor Novello, Malcolm Keen, June, Marie Ault, Arthur Chesney

Alfred Hitchcock's first signature thriller remains a timeless piece of wonder, showcasing the unique visual and stylistic tricks that would mark Hitchcock's work for years to come. Ivor Novello stars as a man who checks into a boardinghouse and becomes the object of scrutiny when a series of murders plague the area. A local detective (Malcolm Keen) becomes jealous when his girlfriend develops an interest in Novello, who, as a result, becomes the primary suspect. The story builds to a suspenseful climax, with an angry mob chasing Novello through London's fog-enshrouded streets. Watch also for a clever point-of-view shot of Novello pacing in his room; as the other people contemplate the stranger in their midst, the camera looks up and through a "ceiling" made of glass. Aside from this film's genuine quality, it's significant historically since it's the only one of Hitchcock's few silent films to survive intact. Unrated; adult themes. Silent.

1926 B & W 75 minutes

LONG WEEKEND

★★★½

DIRECTOR: Colin Eggleston
CAST: John Hargreaves, Briony Behets

This Australian film is a must-see for environmentalists. We are introduced to a couple who carelessly starts a forest fire, runs over a kangaroo, senselessly destroys a tree, shoots animals for the sport of it, and breaks an eagle's egg. This is all part of their weekend away from the city. It becomes interesting when nature avenges itself on the unsuspecting couple. The two characters learn too late that one should respect the balance in one's natural habitat. Unrated, this contains obscenities, nudity, and gore.

1986 95 minutes

LOST BOYS, THE

★★★

DIRECTOR: Joel Schumacher

CAST: Jason Patric, Dianne Wiest, Corey Haim, Barnard Hughes, Edward Herrmann, Kiefer Sutherland, Jami Gertz, Corey Feldman, Jamison Newlander

In this vampire variation on *Peter Pan*, director Joel Schumacher seems more interested in pretty shots and fancy costumes than atmosphere and plot. The story has Jason Patric falling in with a group of hip bloodsuckers led by Kiefer Sutherland, who uses pretty Jami Gertz to lure Patric into becoming one of the undead. Their new disciple's younger brother (Corey Haim) joins up with a wacky pair of teenage vampire hunters (Corey Feldman and Jamison Newlander) and, of course, the final scenes are composed of a battle between good and evil. The acting is top-notch—even the adult actors (Dianne Wiest, Barnard Hughes and Edward Herrmann) get in some good licks—but *The Lost Boys* comes very close to being a casualty of style over substance. Rated R for violence, suggested sex and profanity.

1987 94 minutes

LOVE BUTCHER

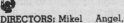

DIRECTORS: Mikel Angel, Don Jones

CAST: Erik Stern, Kay Neer, Robin Sherwood

A series of grisly murders of young women are committed by a deranged psycho. Pretty original, huh? Poorly conceived thriller doesn't even rate a turkey. Rated R.

1983 84 minutes

LOVE FROM A STRANGER

★★★

DIRECTOR: Richard Whorf

CAST: Sylvia Sidney, John Hodiak, John Howard, Isobel Elsom, Ernest Cossart

Just-married woman suspects her new husband is a murderer and that she will be his next victim in this suspense thriller in the vein of *Suspicion*.

1947 B & W 81 minutes

LOVELY BUT DEADLY

DIRECTOR: David Sheldon

CAST: Lucinda Dooling, John Randolph, Mel Novak, Marie Windsor, Mark Holden, Susan Mechsner, Michael O'Leary, Rick Moser

A teen-age boy dies by drowning in the ocean while under the influence of illegal drugs. Soon afterward, a teen-age girl appears, beating up pushers and giving them heavy doses of their own dope. When it's discovered that she's the older sister (nicknamed Lovely) of the boy who drowned, the drug suppliers call in the mob to get rid of this martial-arts supergirl. From that contrived point, this piece of low-budget tripe goes further than downhill. Rated PG and contains some profanity and brief nudity.

1981 88 minutes

LUST FOR A VAMPIRE

★★★

DIRECTOR: Jimmy Sangster

CAST: Suzanna Leigh, Michael Johnson, Yvette Stensgaard, Ralph Bates, Barbara Jefford

All-girls school turns out to be a haven for vampires, with a visiting writer (Michael Johnson) falling in love with one of the undead students (Yutte Stensgaard). Atmospheric blending of chills and fleshy eroticism combined with a terrific ending. American version was retitled *To Love a Vampire* and severely edited. This is the original English version, and not for kids or the squeamish. Rated R.

1970 95 minutes

MAGIC

★★★½

DIRECTOR: Richard Attenborough

CAST: Anthony Hopkins, Burgess Meredith, Ed Lauter, Ann-Margret

Magic will make your skin crawl. The slow descent into madness of the main character, Corky (Anthony Hopkins), a ventriloquist-magician, is the most disturbing study in terror to hit the screens since *Psycho*. Rated R.

1978 106 minutes

MANHATTAN PROJECT, THE

★★★

DIRECTOR: Marshall Brickman

CAST: John Lithgow, Christopher Collet, Cynthia Nixon, Jill Eikenberry

This contemporary comedy-adventure-thriller concerns a high-school youth (Christopher Collet) who, with the aid of his idealistic girlfriend (Cynthia Nixon), steals some plutonium and makes his own nuclear bomb. Though the film is sometimes far-fetched, there's a pleasing balance of humor and suspense. Director Marshall Brickman doesn't hit the audience over the head with his anti-nuke message. John Lithgow gives an endearing performance as the scientist who has tunnel vision when it comes to his work. Rated PG for violence.

1986 115 minutes

MAN THEY COULD NOT HANG, THE

★★★

DIRECTOR: Nick Grindé

CAST: Boris Karloff, Lorna Gray, Robert Wilcox, Roger Pryor

Boris Karloff's fine performance carries this fast-paced tale of a scientist executed for murder, brought back to life, and his bizarre plan of revenge on the judge and jury who convicted him. Guaranteed to hold the attention.

1939 B & W 72 minutes

MAN WHO HAUNTED HIMSELF, THE

★★★½

DIRECTOR: Basil Deardon

CAST: Roger Moore, Hildegard Neil, Alastair Mackenzie, Hugh Mackenzie

Freaky melodrama about a car crash with unexpected side effects. Recovering from the wreck, a man (Roger Moore) begins to question his sanity when it appears that his exact double has assumed his position in the world. Imaginative film keeps the viewer involved from start to finish as we follow Moore in his attempt to solve the puzzle. Rated PG.

1970 94 minutes

MAN WHO KNEW TOO MUCH, THE (ORIGINAL)

★★★★★

DIRECTOR: Alfred Hitchcock

CAST: Leslie Banks, Peter Lorre, Edna Best, Nova Pilbeam

The remake with James Stewart can't hold a candle (or even a shakily held flashlight) to this superb suspense film about a man (Leslie Banks) who stumbles onto a conspiracy and then is forced into action when his child is kidnapped to ensure his silence. This is Hitchcock at his best, with Peter Lorre in fine fettle as the sneering villain.

1934 B & W 83 minutes

MAN WHO KNEW TOO MUCH, THE (REMAKE)

★★★

DIRECTOR: Alfred Hitchcock

CAST: James Stewart, Doris Day, Carolyn Jones

James Stewart and Doris Day star in this fairly entertaining Alfred Hitchcock suspense thriller as a married couple who take a vacation trip to Africa and become involved in international intrigue when they happen on the scene of a murder. The dying victim whispers an important political secret into Stewart's ear. The villains then kidnap the couple's 10-year-old son to ensure the safekeeping of the secret, which involves an assassination. It's no match for the original, but the director's fans no doubt will enjoy it.

1955 120 minutes

MAN WITH TWO HEADS

DIRECTOR: Scott Williams

This semi-remake of *Dr. Jekyll & Mr. Hyde* is loaded with gore and guts. Another piece of slime that has nothing going for it. Rated R.

1982 80 minutes

MANIAC

DIRECTOR: Dwain Esper

CAST: Bill Woods, Horace Carpenter, Ted Edwards

An early independent exploitation film about a crazed actor who assumes the identity of a mad doctor. (Not a very sensible swap, but what do you expect? He's crazy!) The lunatic suffers from every mental illness under the sun, so title cards defining his diseases are displayed with annoying regularity (a gimmick meant to add relevancy to a film that most certainly would have been banned). If you thought *Reefer Madness* was a hoot, check this one out. It's got nudity, animal mutilation, schizophrenic delusions, dog fights (literal), cat fights (figurative), hypodermic attacks, and psychotic fits. *Maniac* is a kitsch classic, and an absolute scream.

1934 B & W 67 minutes

MANIAC

★★★

DIRECTOR: Michael Carreras

CAST: Kerwin Mathews, Nadia Gray, Donald Houston, Justine Lord

Spooky mystery film about a madman on the loose in France, with Kerwin Mathews perfect as an American artist whose vacation there turns out to be anything but. Chilling atmosphere.

1962 B & W 86 minutes

MANIAC

DIRECTOR: William Lustig

CAST: Joe Spinell, Caroline Munro, Gail Lawrence, Kelly Piper, Rita Montone, Tom Savini

For maniacs only. A plethora of shootings, stabbings, decapitations, and scalpings sadistically depicted in graphic detail will send even those with strong stomachs rushing out for airsick bags. Rated R for every excess imaginable.

1980 87 minutes

MANITOU, THE

DIRECTOR: William Girdler

CAST: Tony Curtis, Susan Strasberg, Michael Ansara, Ann Sothern, Burgess Meredith, Stella Stevens

Hilariously hokey film about a woman (Susan Strasberg) who by some strange trick of chance, is growing an ancient Indian out of her neck! It's apparently supposed to be scary, but wait until you see the birth scene. You'll be rolling on the floor in a puddle of tears! Oh well, one can only hope the stars were well paid for their efforts. Rated PG for foul language.

1978 104 minutes

MARK OF THE VAMPIRE

★★★½

DIRECTOR: Tod Browning

CAST: Lionel Barrymore, Elizabeth Allan, Bela Lugosi, Lionel Atwill, Carol Borland, Holmes Herbert

MGM's atmospheric version of *Dracula*, utilizing the same director and star. This time, though, it's Count Mora (Bela Lugosi) terrorizing the residents of an old estate along with his ghoulish daughter (Carol Borland). Lionel Barrymore is the believer who tries to put an end to their nocturnal activities.

1935 B & W 61 minutes

MARNIE

★★★½

DIRECTOR: Alfred Hitchcock

CAST: Sean Connery, Tippi Hedren, Diane Baker, Martin Gabel, Bruce Dern

Unsung Alfred Hitchcock film about a strange young woman (Tippi Hedren) who isn't at all what she appears to be, and Sean Connery as the man determined to get under the surface and find out what makes her tick. Compelling if overlong, confusing as well, but in the best Hitchcock tradition, with striking compositions and matte paintings, as well as another great Bernard Herrmann score. Video transfer is superb, too.

1964 129 minutes

MARTIN

★★★

DIRECTOR: George A. Romero

CAST: John Amplas, Lincoln Maazel, Christine Forrest, Elyane Nadeau

Director George Romero (of *Dawn of the Dead* and *Night of the Living Dead*) creates a good chiller with a lot of bloodcurdling power about a young man who thinks he's a vampire. This is very well done. Rated R.

1978 95 minutes

MARY, MARY, BLOODY MARY

★★

DIRECTOR: Juan Lopez Moctezuma

CAST: Cristina Ferrare, David Young, Helena Rojo, John Carradine

A bloody and grisly film depicting the horror of vampirism and mass murder. A beautiful vampire and artist, Mary (Cristina Ferrare), goes to Mexico to fulfill her need for blood. Her practices bring an investigation of the bloody murders. The arrival of her like-minded father brings the film to a head. This film is rated R for nudity, violence, and gore.

1987 95 minutes

MASQUE OF THE RED DEATH, THE

★★★

DIRECTOR: Roger Corman

CAST: Vincent Price, Hazel Court, Jane Asher, David Weston, Patrick Magee

The combination of Roger Corman, Edgar Allan Poe, and Vincent Price meant first-rate (though low-budget) horror films in the early 1960s. This was one of the best. Price is deliciously villainous. The period sets and costumes are more impressive than usual. The cinematography of Nicolas Roeg is a big plus. The film is stylish and eerie. The plague has never been so entertaining.

1964 86 minutes

MASSACRE AT CENTRAL HIGH

★★★

DIRECTOR: Renee Daalder

CAST: Andrew Stevens, Kimberly Beck, Derrel Maury, Robert Carradine

Low-budget production has a teenager exacting his own brand of revenge on a tough gang who are making things hard for the students at a local high school. This violent drama has a lot going for it, except for some goofy dialogue and wooden performances. Otherwise, nicely done. Rated R.

1976 85 minutes

MAUSOLEUM

★½

DIRECTORS: Jerry Zimmerman, Michael Franzese

CAST: Bobbie Bresee, Marjoe Gortner

Exorcist V, anyone? Actually, this is a reasonably spooky supernatural shocker about a rich, sexy housewife (Bobbie Bresee) who wreaks devastation on assorted victims because of a demonic possession dating back to 1682. Evangelist-turned-actor Marjoe Gortner (remember him?) plays her timid husband. Rated R.

1983 96 minutes

MAXIMUM OVERDRIVE

DIRECTOR: Stephen King

CAST: Emilio Estevez, Pat Hingle, Laura Harrington, Yeardley Smith, John Short, Ellen McElduff, J. C. Quinn

As "Dirty Harry" Callahan has said, "A man needs to know his own limitations," and author Stephen King should have realized that his were restricted to the written word. This boring, turgid, chaotic mess, loosely based on King's short story "Trucks," is a waste from start to finish. As a director, King hasn't the faintest idea how to elicit good performances from his cast, and the picture is paced abysmally. Violence and gore were toned down after the film was threatened with an X rating, but what remains is pretty vile. Do we really need to watch Little Leaguers get crushed? As if that weren't unpleasant enough, King fills in some of the many gaps with crude bathroom humor. Absoulutely unwatchable. Rated R for violence.

1986 97 minutes

MAZES AND MONSTERS

½

DIRECTOR: Steven H. Stern

CAST: Tom Hanks, Chris Makepeace, Wendy Crewson, David Wallace, Lloyd Bochner, Peter Donat, Louise Sorel, Susan Strasberg

There's really no reason why one should rent a made-for-TV movie unless it's of exceptional quality (e.g., *Sybil*). Bad theatrical films are bad enough, but poor television is too depressing even to talk about. *Mazes and Monsters*, a TV movie, isn't bottom of the barrel, but it's close. This film portrays the lives of several college students whose interest in a Dungeons and Dragons type of role-playing game becomes hazardous. The familiar faces of Tom Hanks, Chris Makepeace, and others are only that—familiar faces. If you're into this sword-and-sorcery stuff, rent *Ladyhawks* instead.

1982 103 minutes

MICROWAVE MASSACRE

DIRECTOR: Wayne Betwick

CAST: Jackie Vernon

The title says it all. Lounge comedian Jackie Vernon makes his movie debut in this pile of sludge about a henpecked husband who does away with his wife and feeds her to his mysterious microwave. Once he starts, there is no stopping, and he gets hooked on murder as a form of sexual gratification. Sound hilarious? This film is basically an attempt at black comedy, and watching it is as much fun as being at a funeral. Rated R for violence, nudity, gore, and profanity.

1979 75 minutes

MIDNIGHT

★

DIRECTOR: John Russo
CAST: Lawrence Tierney, Melanie Verlin, John Amplas, Greg Besnak, John Hall, Charles Jackson, Robin Walsh

On their way to Florida, two college guys and a female hitchiker end up in a southern town plagued by racial prejudice and a family of Satan worshipers. That may sound like an interesting premise, but, unfortunately, what unfolds is a muddled mess of sadism and vain attempts at social commentary. As the story progresses, the two men are murdered in cold blood by two police officers. Then they chase the girl to the home of the satanists, who practice human sacrifice. This film isn't horrifying; in fact, it's actually painful to watch. Even splatter fans will be disappointed. Rated R for violence and profanity.

1980 91 minutes

MIND SNATCHERS, THE

★★★

DIRECTOR: Bernard Girard
CAST: Christopher Walken, Ronny Cox, Joss Ackland, Ralph Meeker

Christopher Walken (*The Deer Hunter*, *The Dead Zone*) plays a nihilistic U.S. soldier in West Germany who is admitted to a mental institution. He finds out later the hospital is actually a laboratory where a German scientist is testing a new form of psychological control. Like *One Flew Over the Cukoo's Nest*, this film deals with the philosophical and moral issues of psychological treatment versus the freethinking human mind. Walken's performance is excellent and the idea is an interesting one, but the film moves a bit slowly. Rated PG for violence and profanity.

1972 94 minutes

MONSTER CLUB, THE

★★★½

DIRECTOR: Roy Ward Baker
CAST: Vincent Price, John Carradine, Donald Pleasence, Stuart Whitman, Britt Ekland, Simon Ward

Better-than-average series of horror tales by Ronald Chetwynd-Hayes linked by a sinister nightclub where the guys 'n' ghouls can hang out. All the stories keep tongue firmly in cheek and involve imaginary creatures of mixed parentage, such as a "shadmonk," borne of a vampire and werewolf. The best scenes take place inside the nightspot; particularly memorable is a stripper who peels off clothes—and then skin—to reveal the bare bones underneath. Now *that's* a striptease! Rated PG for violence.

1981 97 minutes

MONSTER DOG

DIRECTOR: Clyde Anderson
CAST: Alice Cooper, Victoria Vera

Alice Cooper's music video, shown in the first five minutes of the film, is the only part of this release worth watching. This incoherent attempt to make a werewolf film using a pack of tail-wagging, playful German shepherds with poorly dubbed growls hasn't enough gore to please slasher-flick fans and no plot with which to entertain fans of classical horror. The title is a perfect review. Unrated, the film has violence.

1986 88 minutes

MONSTER FROM GREEN HELL

★★

DIRECTOR: Kenneth Crane
CAST: Jim Davis, Robert E. Griffin, Barbara Turner, Eduardo Ciannelli

Giant rubber wasps on the rampage in Africa. Our heroes battle a lethargic script to the death. In an attempt to revive the audience, the last reel of the movie was filmed in color. Big deal.

1957 B & W 71 minutes

MONSTER FROM THE OCEAN FLOOR, THE

★

DIRECTOR: Wyott Ordung
CAST: Anne Kimball, Stuart Wade, Dick Pinner, Jack Hayes, Wyott Ordung

A legendary sea monster is discovered off the coast of Mexico. The first film produced by Roger Corman, the director of such low-budget classics as *Little Shop of Horrors, Bucket of Blood,* and *The Wild Angels*. He made the movie in six days, on a budget of only $12,000. You can tell. It's slow moving, endlessly talky, and the monster is almost impossible to see. But the picture made a profit of over $100,000 and started Corman's career.

1954 B & W 64 minutes

MONSTER MAKER, THE

★½

DIRECTOR: Sam Newfield
CAST: J. Carroll Naish, Ralph Morgan, Wanda McKay, Sam Flint, Glenn Strange

A scientist conducting experiments in glandular research accidentally injects a pianist with a serum that causes his body to grow abnormally large, especially his hands. Low-budget thriller revamps the old gland-operation theme but does very little with it this time around. Future Frankenstein Glenn Strange plays the monster in this one, and sometimes monster J. Carroll Naish gets a chance to play the scientist who should have let things alone. PRC Studios was famous for the threadbare quality of its product, and this pseudo–science fiction film is no exception.

1944 B & W 64 minutes

MOON OF THE WOLF

★★

DIRECTOR: Daniel Petrie
CAST: David Janssen, Barbara Rush, Bradford Dillman, John Beradino

Another ABC Movie of the Week makes it to video. Disappointing yarn of the search for a werewolf on the loose in Louisiana. Good acting by the leads, but there's not enough action or excitement to sustain interest.

1972 73 minutes

MORNING AFTER, THE

★★★½

DIRECTOR: Sidney Lumet
CAST: Jane Fonda, Jeff Bridges, Raul Julia, Diane Salinger, Richard Foronjy

An alcoholic ex–movie star (Jane Fonda) wakes up one morning in bed next to a dead man and is unable to remember what happened the night before. Fonda is terrific as the heroine-victim, and Jeff Bridges gives a typically solid performance as the ex-cop who comes to her aid. The result is an enjoyable thriller in the style of *Jagged Edge*. It may not be a materpiece of the genre, but it is a good choice for an evening of undemanding, forget-your-cares video viewing. Rated R for profanity, violence, and sex.

1986 103 minutes

MORTUARY

DIRECTOR: Howard Avedis
CAST: Christopher George, Lynda Day George

Christopher George and Lynda Day George are featured in this low-budget horror flick; one of the sickest entries in what has come to be called the knife-kill genre. All the standard "commercial" elements of profanity, gore, nudity, blood, and sex have been thrown together into a presentation that leaves one with little hope for the human race. Rated R for the aforementioned elements.

1984 91 minutes

MOST DANGEROUS GAME, THE

★★★½

DIRECTORS: Ernest B. Shoedsack, Irving Pichel
CAST: Joel McCrea, Fay Wray, Leslie Banks, Robert Armstrong

This sister production to *King Kong* utilizes the same sets, same technical staff, and most of the same cast to tell the story of Count Zaroff, the insane ruler of a secret island who spends his time hunting the victims of the ships that he wrecks. Filmed and acted in a grand fashion, this is the epitome of the classic pulp magazine story, although this story was originally published in a "slick" magazine and won an O. Henry award as best short story of the year. Filmed many times since and used as a theme for countless television plots, this original is still the standard to measure all the others by. Non-stop action for sixty-three tight minutes.

1932 B & W 63 minutes

MOTEL HELL

★★½

DIRECTOR: Kevin Connor
CAST: Rory Calhoun, Nancy Parsons, Paul Linke, Nina Axelrod, Elaine Joyce, Wolfman Jack

"It takes all kinds of critters to make Farmer Vincent Fritters!" Ahem! This above average horror-comedy stars Rory Calhoun (who overplays grandly) as a nice ol' farmer who has struck gold with his dried pork treats. What the public doesn't know—and, frankly, wouldn't *want* to know—is that his secret ingredient happens to be human flesh. A variety of attractive victims, male and female, wind up in his "fattening grounds" before the entire scheme collapses. Wait until half an hour after meals before viewing. Rated R for violence.

1980 102 minutes

MULTIPLE MANIACS

DIRECTOR: John Waters
CAST: Divine, Mink Stole, Paul Swift, Cookie Mueller, David Lochary, Mary Vivian Pearce, Edith Massey

A homage to gore king Herschell Gordon Lewis's *Two Thousand Maniacs*, *Multiple Maniacs* is director John Waters's favorite film. You can expect plenty of bad taste in this black-and-white movie, which trashes Christianity (Divine is seduced in a Catholic church) and just about any other established and respected institution that crosses Waters's viewfinder. In this film even the transvestite Divine seems harmless compared with the host of other deviants and degenerates who roam the landscapes looking for trouble. Unrated, but the equivalent of an X, due to sex, violence, and gore.

1971 B & W 70 minutes

MUMMY, THE (ORIGINAL)

★★★★

DIRECTOR: Karl Freund

CAST: Boris Karloff, Zita Johann, David Manners, Edward Van Sloan

First-rate horror thriller about an Egyptian mummy returning to life after 3,700 years. Boris Karloff plays the title role in one of his very best performances. Superb makeup, dialogue, atmosphere, and direction make this one of the best horror films using technique (rather than blood and guts) to terrify its audience. Despite its age, this all-time classic has lost none of its power.

1932 B & W 73 minutes

MUMMY, THE (REMAKE)

★★★½

DIRECTOR: Terence Fisher

CAST: Peter Cushing, Christopher Lee, Yvonne Furneaux, Eddie Byrne

Excellent updating of the "mummy" legend from Hammer Films. Christopher Lee is terrifying as the ancient Egyptian awakened from his centuries-old sleep to take revenge on those who desecrated the tomb of his beloved princess. Well-photographed, atmospheric production is high-quality entertainment.

1959 88 minutes

MURDER

★★★

DIRECTOR: Alfred Hitchcock

CAST: Herbert Marshall, Norah Baring, Phyllis Konstam, Edward Chapman

An early Alfred Hitchcock thriller, and a good one, although it shows its age. Herbert Marshall, a producer-director, is selected to serve on a murder-trial jury. He believes the accused, an aspiring actress, is innocent of the crime and takes it upon himself to apprehend the real killer.

1930 B & W 92 minutes

MURDER BY PHONE

★★★

DIRECTOR: Michael Anderson

CAST: Richard Chamberlain, John Houseman

In this okay shocker, Richard Chamberlain, the star of TV's *Shogun* and *The Thorn Birds*, is cast as an environmentalist whose lecture engagement in New York City turns out to be an opportunity to investigate the gruesome death of one of his students, who picked up a phone one day and was zapped by an extremely powerful charge of electricity. The circumstances of her death are being kept secret by "the phone company" and Chamberlain, a one-time 1960s radical, must resort to his old "rock-the-establishment" methods in order to solve the mystery. Rated R.

1980 79 minutes

MURDER BY TELEVISION

★½

DIRECTOR: Clifford Sanforth

CAST: Bela Lugosi, June Collyer, George Meeker, Hattie McDaniel, Huntley Gordon

Bela Lugosi plays dual roles as an inventor and a killer in this low-budget murder mystery. Television was still something out of *Science and Invention* back in 1935, so it was fair game as a contrivance used to commit the crime. Slow and creaky, only the pedestrian use of television and the presence of one-dimensional Bela Lugosi and future Oscar-winner Hattie McDaniel make this one worth more than a cursory glance.

1935 B & W 60 minutes

MURDER IN TEXAS

★★★★

DIRECTOR: Billy Hale
CAST: Farrah Fawcett, Sam Elliott, Katharine Ross, Andy Griffith, Bill Dana

Absorbing TV docudrama based on a true story. *Mask* star Sam Elliott is Dr. John Hill, a prominent plastic surgeon accused of murdering his socialite wife. At times a gripping study of psychopathic behavior. Good performances all around, including Farrah Fawcett and Andy Griffith, who reaped an Emmy nomination.

1983 200 minutes

MURDERS IN THE RUE MORGUE

★★

DIRECTOR: Gordon Hessler
CAST: Jason Robards, Herbert Lom, Michael Dunn, Lilli Palmer, Christine Kaufmann, Adolfo Celi

Members of a horror theatre troupe in nineteenth-century Paris are dispatched systematically by a mysterious fiend. Good cast, nice atmosphere, but confusing and altogether too artsy for its own good. Rated PG.

1971 87 minutes

MUTANT

★★½

DIRECTOR: John "Bud" Cardos
CAST: Bo Hopkins, Wings Hauser, Jody Medford, Jennifer Warren, Cary Guffey, Lee Montgomery

An incredibly frustrating film that displays well-crafted mood and tension during the first half and then lapses into the idiocy of yet another *Night of the Living Dead* ripoff. Wings Hauser lands in a small southern town, meets up with cute schoolteacher/barmaid Jody Medford (it's a *very* small town), and encounters decent folk who mutate into flesh-eaters after exposure to toxic waste. Bo Hopkins does we!l as a sheriff who takes occasional refuge in a bottle, and the atmosphere in the near-empty town is quite eerie for the first hour. The payoff, however, fails to equal the delivery. Too bad; this could—and should—have been much better. Rated R for violence.

1983 100 minutes

MY BLOODY VALENTINE

★½

DIRECTOR: George Mihalka
CAST: Paul Kelman, Lori Hallier, Neil Affleck

Candy boxes stuffed with bloody human hearts signal the return of a legendary murderous coal miner to Valentine Bluffs. Another variation on the *Halloween* holiday horror formula, this film provides a few doses of excitement and a tidal wave of killings. Unfortunately, it relies more on manipulative shocks than suspense for its impact. Rated R.

1981 91 minutes

MY SISTER, MY LOVE

★★★

DIRECTOR: Karen Arthur
CAST: Carol Kane, Lee Grant, Will Geer, James Olson

Offbeat story concerns two loving, but unbalanced, sisters who eliminate anyone who tries to come between them. Good acting all around and a perverse sense of style are just two elements that make this movie click. Alternate title—*The Mafu Cage*. Rated R.

1979 99 minutes

MYSTERY OF THE WAX MUSEUM

★★½

DIRECTOR: Michael Curtiz
CAST: Lionel Atwill, Fay Wray, Glenda Farrell, Frank McHugh, Allen Vincent

Dated but interesting tale of a crippled, crazed sculptor (the ever-dependable Lionel Atwill) who murders people and displays them in his museum as his own wax creations. Humorous subplot really curbs the attention, but stick with it. One of the earliest color films, it is often shown on television in black and white.

1933 77 minutes

NAKED FACE, THE

★★★½

DIRECTOR: Bryan Forbes

CAST: Roger Moore, Rod Steiger, Elliott Gould, Art Carney, Anne Archer

A psychiatrist (Roger Moore) finds himself the target of murder in this enjoyable suspense film. Only trouble is the police think he's the killer, as the first attempt on his life results in the death of a patient who had borrowed his raincoat. One of the investigators (Rod Steiger) is still mad about the psychiatrist's having testified in a case that involved the death of a policeman and helping the killer obtain an insanity plea. So the detective is unwilling to believe the psychiatrist is innocent and works overtime to get him. He's not the only one, and the other fellow is playing for keeps. Rated R for violence, gore, and profanity.

1984 98 minutes

NESTING, THE

★★

DIRECTOR: Armand Weston

CAST: Robin Groves, Christopher Loomis, Michael David Lally, John Carradine, Gloria Grahame

Tolerable haunted house film about a writer (Robin Groves) who rents a house in the country so as to get some peace and quiet. But guess what. You got it—the house is plagued with undead spirits who seek revenge for their untimely deaths many years ago. The final scene doesn't make a whole lot of sense, but then neither does the purely gratuitous nude scene. Rated R for nudity and violence.

1980 104 minutes

NEW KIDS, THE

DIRECTOR: Sean S. Cunningham

CAST: Shannon Presby, Lori Loughlin, James Spader

In this horror film, directed by gore specialist Sean S. Cunningham (*Friday the 13th*), two easygoing kids try to make friends at a new high school. Their attempt is thwarted by the town bully, who is angry because they refuse to bow to his superiority. This brings acts of violence from both sides. This theme was handled with greater intelligence, imagination, and taste in Tony Bill's *My Bodyguard*. In comparison, *The New Kids* is exploitative teen trash. Rated R for profanity, nudity, and violence.

1985 96 minutes

NIGHT CREATURE

DIRECTOR: Lee Madden

CAST: Donald Pleasence, Nancy Kwan, Ross Hagen, Lesly Fine, Jennifer Rhodes

Grade Z film has Donald Pleasence playing a half-crazed adventurer who captures a killer leopard and brings the creature to his private island. He then decides to release the leopard so that the two of them can have a showdown. Nancy Kwan plays his daughter who is trapped on the island along with her husband and child. Rated PG for language.

1978 83 minutes

NIGHT GALLERY

★★★

DIRECTORS: Boris Sagal, Steven Spielberg, Barry Shear

CAST: Roddy McDowall, Joan Crawford, Richard Kiley

Pilot for the TV series. Three tales of terror by Rod Serling told with style and flair. Segment one is the best, with Roddy McDowall eager to get his hands on an inheritance. Segment two features Joan Crawford as a blind woman with a yearning to see. Segment three, involving a paranoid war fugitive, is the least of the three. All in all, though, very entertaining and way above par for a made-for-TV movie.

1969 98 minutes

NIGHT OF THE CREEPS

★★★½

DIRECTOR: Fred Dekker

CAST: Jason Lively, Steve Marchall, Jill Whitlow, Tom Atkins, Dick Miller

A film derived from virtually every horror movie ever made, this does a wonderful job paying homage to the genre. The story involves an alien organism that lands on Earth in 1958 and immediately infects someone. Some thirty years later when this contaminated individual is accidentally released from cryogenic freeze, he wanders into a college town spreading these organisms in some rather disgusting ways. There are some great visual effects, lots of chills and suspense and a whole lot of humor. Horror enthusiasts will have a blast and the average film viewer should have a good time as well. Not rated, but contains graphic violence, brief nudity, and some profanity.

1986 89 minutes

NIGHT OF THE DEMON

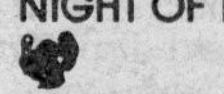

DIRECTOR: James C. Wasson

CAST: Michael Cutt, Jay Allen, Robert Collings, Jodi Lazarus

This is a boring little bomb of a movie with an intriguing title and nothing else. Not to be confused with the 1958 classic *Curse of the Demon*.

1983 97 minutes

NIGHT OF THE GHOULS

★

DIRECTOR: Edward D. Wood Jr.

CAST: Kenne Duncan, Criswell

From the director of *Plan 9 from Outer Space* and *Glen or Glenda* comes a film so bad it was never released. Not nearly as enjoyably bad as Edward Woods's other work, but definitely worth a look, for movie buffs. For the record, two young innocents stumble upon a haunted house (filled with some very tiresome bad actors).

1958 B & W 75 minutes

NIGHT OF THE HOWLING BEAST

DIRECTOR: M. I. Bonns

CAST: Paul Naschy, Grace Mills, Gil Vidal, Silvia Solar

One of the all-time worst! Paul Naschy stars in this mess as a guy who has a slight problem whenever the full moon rises. Lon Chaney Jr. and Universal Pictures did it better—much better. Rated R.

1984 87 minutes

NIGHT OF THE HUNTER

★★★★½

DIRECTOR: Charles Laughton

CAST: Robert Mitchum, Shelley Winters, Lillian Gish, James Gleason

Absolutely the finest film from star Robert Mitchum, who is cast as a suave, smooth-talking—and absolutely evil—preacher determined to catch and kill his stepchildren. Charles Laughton turned director for this macabre, nightmarish drama, and it was the only time he would step on that side of the camera. The entire film is eerie, exquisitely beautiful, and occasionally surreal; watch for the graceful, haunting shot of the children's freshly killed mother. The story loses steam during a rather syrupy conclusion, but everything else is simply masterful. Excellent screenplay by James Agee from Davis Grubb's equally mesmerizing novel. Unrated, but not suitable for younger viewers.

1955 B & W 93 minutes

NIGHT OF THE LIVING DEAD

★★★★

DIRECTOR: George A. Romero
CAST: Duane Jones, Judith O'Dea, Keith Wayne

This gruesome low-budget horror film still packs a punch for those who like to be frightened out of their wits. It is an unrelenting shock fest laced with touches of black humor that deserves its cult status.

1968 B & W 96 minutes

NIGHT OF THE ZOMBIES

DIRECTOR: Vincent Dawn
CAST: Frank Garfield, Margit Newton

A low-budget horror film about the dead coming back to life à la George Romero's *Night of the Living Dead* and about feasting on the living, this is a thoroughly disgusting motion picture. It's just one long cannibal feast—who needs this kind of trash? Rated R for violence and gore.

1983 101 minutes

NIGHT STALKER, THE

★★★★

DIRECTOR: John Llewellyn Moxey
CAST: Darren McGavin, Carol Lynley, Claude Akins

A superb made-for-television chiller about a modern-day vampire stalking the streets of Las Vegas. Richard Matheson's teleplay is tight and suspenseful, with Darren McGavin fine as the intrepid reporter on the bloodsucker's trail.

1971 73 minutes

NIGHT VISITOR, THE

★

DIRECTOR: Laslo Benedek
CAST: Liv Ullmann, Trevor Howard, Andrew Keir, Max von Sydow

Director Laslo Benedek and Max von Sydow wasted their skills on this film about a mental patient out for revenge. It is slow-moving and confusing. Keep plenty of No-Doz on hand. Rated PG.

1970 106 minutes

NIGHT WARNING

★★

DIRECTOR: William Asher
CAST: Jimmy McNichol, Bo Svenson, Susan Tyrrell

As in many gory movies, the victims and near-victims have a convenient and unbelievable way of hanging around despite clear indications they are about to get it. Consequently, *Night Warning*, in spite of good performances by stars Jimmy McNichol, Bo Svenson, and Susan Tyrrell, is an unremarkable splatter film. Rated R for violence and gore.

1982 96 minutes

NIGHT WATCH

★★

DIRECTOR: Brian G. Hutton
CAST: Elizabeth Taylor, Laurence Harvey, Billie Whitelaw, Robert Lang, Tony Britton

In this so-so suspense thriller, Elizabeth Taylor stars as a wealthy widow recovering from a nervous breakdown. From her window, she seems to witness a number of ghoulish goings-on. But does she? The operative phrase here after a while is "Who cares?" It's too predictable and slow-moving to be effective, but Taylor does get to wear some great clothes. Rated PG.

1973 98 minutes

NIGHTCOMERS, THE

★★½

DIRECTOR: Michael Winner
CAST: Marlon Brando, Stephanie Beacham, Thora Hird, Harry Andrews, Verna Harvey, Christopher Ellis, Anna Palk

Strange prequel to *The Turn of the Screw*, this uneven effort contains some fine acting and boasts some truly eerie scenes, but is hampered by Michael Winner's loose direction and a nebulous storyline. Marlon Brando is in good form as the mysterious catalyst, and Harry Andrews is fine as usual, but this murky melodrama still lacks the solid story and cohesiveness that could have made it a true chiller. Interesting but flawed. Rated R.

1971 96 minutes

NIGHTMARE IN WAX (CRIMES IN THE WAX MUSEUM)

★½

DIRECTOR: Bud Townsend
CAST: Cameron Mitchell, Anne Helm, Scott Brady

Cameron Mitchell plays a disfigured ex–makeup man running a wax museum in Hollywood. His idea of a good time is to inject movie stars with a formula that turns them into statues. Low-grade, barely watchable mess with an unsatisfying ending. Rated PG.

1969 91 minutes

NIGHTMARE ON ELM STREET, A

★★★★

DIRECTOR: Wes Craven
CAST: John Saxon, Ronee Blakley, Heather Langenkamp, Robert Englund

Wes Craven (*The Hills Have Eyes*; *Swamp Thing*) directed this clever shocker about a group of teenagers afflicted with the same bad dreams. Horror movie buffs, take note. Rated R for nudity, violence, and profanity.

1985 91 minutes

NIGHTMARE ON ELM STREET PART 2: FREDDY'S REVENGE, A

★

DIRECTOR: Jack Sholder
CAST: Mark Patton, Kim Myers, Clu Gulager, Hope Lange

The only thing this substandard horror film has in common with its far superior predecessor is the title and gruesome old Freddy Krueger. Outside of the obvious, it is dull and lacks the tension the first one had. Another teen exploitation film. Ugh! Rated R for nudity, language, and gore, gore, gore.

1985 83 minutes

NIGHTMARE ON ELM STREET PART III: THE DREAM WARRIORS

★★

DIRECTOR: Chuck Russell
CAST: Robert Englund, Heather Langenkamp, Patricia Arquette, Craig Wasson

Freddy is at it again, forcing his way into the dreams of unsuspecting teen-age girls and twisting those dreams into demented nightmares. This one is only slightly better than the second entry, but it does have some good laughs, albeit unintentional ones. Rated R.

1987 97 minutes

NIGHTMARE WEEKEND

DIRECTOR: H. Sala
CAST: Debbie Laster, Debra Hunter, Lori Lewis, Dale Miokiff, Andrea Thompson, Nick James

An incomprehensible film about a scientist who invents a computer system that can transform solid inorganic objects into deadly weapons. The computer is run by a hand puppet that is in love with the scientist's daughter, and is always using the computer to protect her from the male population of the town. While all this is going on, the scientist's financial partner is trying to sell the computer's secrets to international spies. The other subplots are about teen-age kids (who look about forty). Rated R for graphic violence and nudity.

1985 88 minutes

NIGHTMARES

DIRECTOR: Joseph Sargent
CAST: Cristina Raines, Emilio Estevez, Lance Henriksen, Timothy James

Four everyday situations are twisted into tales of terror in this mostly mediocre horror film in the style of *Twilight Zone—the Movie* and *Creepshow.* Number one features Cristina Raines as a nicotine addict who goes out for a carton of cigarettes even though there's a slasher stalking the neighborhood. It's just ho-hum. Two has a video game whiz-kid (Emilio Estevez) taking on a super-powered arcade attraction. This one's kinda dumb. In three, a retread of Steven Spielberg's *Duel*, a priest (Lance Henriksen) is pursued by a pickup from hell. Only number four, "Night of the Rats," features any real chills—and those are nearly nullified by the bargain-basement special effects. Rated R for violence and profanity.

1983 99 minutes

NIGHTWING

DIRECTOR: Arthur Hiller
CAST: David Warner, Kathryn Harrold, Nick Mancuso, Strother Martin

Absolutely laughable tale, derived from an abysmal Martin Cruz Smith novel, about a flock (herd? pack?) of vampire bats—the real ones, not the two-legged cousins that prey on nubile young women—terrorizing a small community. David Warner has never looked worse than as this deranged vampire-bat killer, and he spouts ludicrous lines that actually make him wince. Ambitious production values couldn't do a thing to save this turkey . . . er, this rabid bat. Rated PG.

1979 105 minutes

NOMADS

DIRECTOR: John McTiernan
CAST: Lesley-Anne Down, Pierce Brosnan, Anna-Maria Monticelli, Adam Ant, Jose Cotton, Mary Woronov

In this thought-provoking and chilling shocker, Pierce Brosnan is a French anthropologist who discovers a secret society of malevolent ghosts living in modern-day Los Angeles. In doing so, he incurs their wrath and endangers the life of a doctor (Lesley-Anne Down) fated to share his terrifying experiences. Those who appreciate original movie fare will want to give this one a look.

Rated R for profanity, nudity, and violence.

1986 95 minutes

NORTH BY NORTHWEST

★★★★★

DIRECTOR: Alfred Hitchcock

CAST: Cary Grant, Eva Marie Saint, James Mason, Martin Landau

Cary Grant and Eva Marie Saint star in this classic thriller by the master himself, Alfred Hitchcock, who plays (or preys) on the senses and keeps the action at a feverish pitch. The story is typical Hitchcock fare—a matter of mistaken identity embroils a man in espionage and murder. Fans can rejoice at the chance to experience one of the most exciting scenes ever filmed—a manhunt scaling the heights of Mount Rushmore—by one of the most imitated directors of our time.

1959 136 minutes

NOTORIOUS

★★★★½

DIRECTOR: Alfred Hitchcock

CAST: Cary Grant, Ingrid Bergman, Claude Rains, Louis Calhern

Notorious is among the finest Alfred Hitchcock romantic thrillers. Cary Grant, as an American agent, and Ingrid Bergman, as the "notorious" daughter of a convicted traitor, join forces to seek out Nazis in postwar Rio. Claude Rains gives one of his greatest performances—at times touching as the mommy's boy who has been betrayed by the woman he adores and at other times chillingly dangerous as the head of Nazi activities in Argentina.

1946 B & W 101 minutes

NUMBER 17

★★½

DIRECTOR: Alfred Hitchock

CAST: Leon M. Lion, Anne Grey, John Stuart, Donald Calthrop, Barry Jones, Garry Marsh

Seldom-seen thriller from Alfred Hitchcock is a humorous departure from his later more obsessive films, but it still maintains his wry touches and unusual characters. Once again an unsuspecting innocent (in this case, a hobo) accidentally comes across something that places him in jeopardy (a gang of jewel thieves) and winds up being chased all over the countryside. Rather inept miniatures and special effects can't spoil the locomotive and bus chase that highlights this British film, and the performances by a cast largely unknown to contemporary American audiences are just right. Although prints that run 64 minutes exist, this was originally released at a length of 83 minutes.

1932 B & W 83 minutes

OBLONG BOX, THE

★★½

DIRECTOR: Gordon Hessler

CAST: Vincent Price, Christopher Lee, Rubert Davies, Uta Levka, Sally Geeson, Alister Williamson

This little gothic horror is nothing to shiver about. Although it is taken from an Edgar Allan Poe short story, it can't escape the clichés of its genre: grave robbers, screaming women (with close-up shots of their widening eyes), lots of cleavage, and of course, the hero's bride-to-be, who is unaware of her betrothed's wrongdoings. Sound familiar? Rated R (but more like a PG by today's standards) for simulated sex and violence.

1969 91 minutes

OBSESSION

★★★★

DIRECTOR: Brian De Palma

CAST: Cliff Robertson, Genevieve Bujold, John Lithgow

This is director Brian De Palma's tour de force. Cliff Robertson, Genevieve Bujold, and John Lithgow transcend normal film acting. Bernard Herrmann scores again, his music as effective as that in *Taxi Driver*. In fact, the script, about a widower who meets his former wife's exact double, was written by Paul Schrader (in collaboration with De Palma), who also wrote the latter film. Critics enthusiastically compare this with prime Hitchcock, and it more than qualifies. Rated PG.

1976 98 minutes

OCTAMAN

★½

DIRECTOR: Harry Essex
CAST: Kerwin Matthews, Pier Angeli, Jeff Morrow, Norman Fields

Dull low-budget effort with a group of vacationers under attack by a funny-looking walking octopus-man created by a very young Rick Baker, who has since gone on to much bigger and better things. Rated PG for mild violence.

1971 90 minutes

OF UNKNOWN ORIGIN

★★½

DIRECTOR: George Dan Cosmatos
CAST: Peter Weller, Jennifer Dale, Lawrence Dane

Flashes of unintentional humor enliven this shocker, about a suburban family terrorized in their home by a monstrous rat. Contains some inventive photography and effects, but mediocre acting and forgettable music keep this film well away from "classic" status. Bring on the exterminator! Rated R.

1983 88 minutes

OMEN, THE

★★★★

DIRECTOR: Richard Donner
CAST: Gregory Peck, Lee Remick, Billie Whitelaw, David Warner

This, first of a series of movies about the return to Earth of the devil, is a real chiller. In the form of a young boy, Damien, Satan sets about reestablishing his rule over man. A series of bizarre deaths point to the boy. His stepfather (Gregory Peck), the American ambassador to England, suspects something is amiss, and his attempts to delve into the boy's past set the stage for a startling climax. Rated R.

1976 111 minutes

ONE DARK NIGHT

★★½

DIRECTOR: Tom McLoughlin
CAST: Meg Tilly, Adam West, Robin Evans, Elizabeth Daily

Meg Tilly, from *Agnes of God*, and Adam "Batman" West star in this story of a young woman (Tilly) who is menaced by an energy-draining ghost. Rated R.

1983 89 minutes

ONE FRIGHTENED NIGHT

★★

DIRECTOR: Christy Cabanne
CAST: Wallace Ford, Mary Carlisle, Hedda Hopper, Charlie Grapewin

A stormy night, a spooky mansion, an eccentric millionaire, and a group of people stranded together was about all it used to take to make a scary movie. This is one of dozens of similar films released in the 1930s and early 1940s. A good cast and some witty dialogue help, but there's only so much that can be done with this kind of mystery. Future scandalmonger Hedda Hopper has a role, and great character actor Charlie Grapewin (*The Wizard of Oz, The Grapes of Wrath*) plays the old coot with the loot that starts this story moving.

1935 B & W 69 minutes

ORCA

★★★½

DIRECTOR: Michael Anderson

CAST: Richard Harris, Keenan Wynn, Will Sampson, Bo Derek, Robert Carradine, Charlotte Rampling

It is not the summertime tourists we see slaughtered in this thought-provoking tale but rather a mammal of the sea with a brain larger than that of a human. Where *Jaws* was an exaggerated horror story, *Orca* is based on the tragic truth. Motivated by profit, Richard Harris and his crew go out with a huge net and find a family of whales. He misses the male and harpoons the female, who dies and aborts, leaving her huge mate to wreak havoc on the tiny seaport. Rated PG.

1977 92 minutes

PACK, THE

★★

DIRECTOR: Robert Clouse

CAST: Joe Don Baker, Hope Alexander Willis, Richard B. Shull, R. G. Armstrong

Slightly above average horror film about a pack of dogs that goes wild and tries to kill two families. Rated R.

1977 99 minutes

PARASITE

★★½

DIRECTOR: Charles Band

CAST: Robert Glaudini, Demi Moore, Luca Bercovici, Vivian Blaine

If director Charles Band intended a film that would sicken its audience, he succeeded with this futuristic monster movie. Memorable scenes include parasites bursting through the stomach of one victim and the face of another. The film's use of special effects makes it all the more gory. Luckily, the plot isn't as predictable as that of most horror films, so at least it's suspenseful. However, *Parasite* may be too much for kids. Rated R.

1982 85 minutes

PATRICK

★★½

DIRECTOR: Richard Franklin

CAST: Susan Penhaligon, Robert Helpmann

This film revolves around Patrick, who has been in a coma for four years. He is confined to a hospital, but after a new nurse comes to work on his floor he begins to exhibit psychic powers. He begins by sending her messages on a nearby typewriter but gets violent when he perceives certain people as his enemies. This Australian film is similar to many other films that use the highly developed psychic power as a theme. The dubbing of this film does more damage than it probably deserves. (The director, Richard Franklin, went on to direct *Psycho II*.) Some violence, but nothing extremely bloody. Rated PG.

1979 96 minutes

PEEPING TOM

★★★½

DIRECTOR: Michael Powell

CAST: Carl Boehm, Moira Shearer, Anna Massey

Carl Boehm gives a chilling performance as a lethal psychopath who photographs his victims as they are dying. This film outraged both critics and viewers alike when it was first released, and rarely has been revived since. Not for all tastes, to be sure, but if you're adventurous, give this one a try. Rated R.

1960 109 minutes

PHANTASM

★★½

DIRECTOR: Don Coscarelli

CAST: Michael Baldwin, Bill Thornbury, Reggie Bannister, Kathy Lester

This strange mixture of horror and science-fiction, while not an outstanding film by any account, does provide viewers with several thrills and unexpected twists. If you like to jump out of your seat, watch this alone with all the lights out. R-rated after scenes were cut from the original X-rated 1979 version.

1979 87 minutes

PHANTOM CREEPS, THE

★★½

DIRECTORS: Ford Beebe, Saul A. Goodkind

CAST: Bela Lugosi, Robert Kent, Regis Toomey, Dorothy Arnold

This Saturday-afternoon crowd-pleaser features a crazed scientist, a giant robot, an invisibility belt, and a meteorite fragment that can render an entire army immobile—just about anything a kid can ask for in a serial. There's a stalwart hero and a snoopy newspaper reporter thrown in for good measure, but it's the evil Dr. Alex Zorka (Bela Lugosi hamming it up) and his giant robot and wild inventions that rivet everyone's attention in this Universal chapter play. Lugosi is once again teamed with his nemesis from *Dracula*, Edward Van Sloan as Chief Jarvis, and they do their best for twelve episodes to do each other in. Not as slick as the Republic serials, but great fun.

1939 B & W 12 Chapters

PHANTOM OF THE OPERA

★★★★★

DIRECTOR: Rupert Julian

CAST: Lon Chaney Sr., Mary Philbin, Norman Kerry, Snitz Edwards

Classic silent horror with Lon Chaney in his most poignant and gruesome role combined with theater organ accompaniment. Sounds like a prescription for an old-fashioned good time, doesn't it? That's right. This 1925 sample of Chaney's brilliance—he was truly the "man of a thousand faces"—still has enough power to send chills up your spine and tug at your heart. But aren't these old-time melodramas pretty corny? Sure—and that's part of the fun. Enjoy.

1925 B & W 79 minutes

PHANTOM OF THE OPERA, THE

★★★

DIRECTOR: Arthur Lubin

CAST: Claude Rains, Susanna Foster, Nelson Eddy, Edgar Barrier, Miles Mander, Hume Cronyn

Overabundance of singing hurts this otherwise good remake of the 1925 Lon Chaney silent. The well-known story concerns a Paris opera house being terrorized by a disfigured composer (Claude Rains) whose best works have been stolen. Acting is great, production values are high, but that singing has got to go! Director Arthur Lubin is best known for the *Francis, the Talking Mule* series of the 1950s.

1943 92 minutes

PICTURE OF DORIAN GRAY, THE

★★★★

DIRECTOR: Albert Lewin

CAST: George Sanders, Hurd Hatfield, Donna Reed, Angela Lansbury, Peter Lawford

The classic adaptation of Oscar Wilde's famous novel, this features Hurd Hatfield giving a nicely restrained performance in the title role of a young man whose portrait ages while he remains eternally youthful. Though talky and slow-moving, this film nevertheless keeps you glued to the screen for its nearly two-hour running time, generating a chilling atmosphere and a foreboding sense of horror. A few key scenes shot in Technicolor for effect.

1945 B & W 110 minutes

PIECES

🦃

DIRECTOR: Juan Piquer Simon
CAST: Christopher George, Lynda Day George, Edmund Purdom

Christopher George and Lynda Day George, who were fast becoming the Lunt and Fontane of sicko horror flicks, star in this movie, which promises, "You don't have to go to Texas for a chainsaw massacre!" Sounds lovely. While not rated by the MPAA, the picture would probably qualify for an X rating.

1983 85 minutes

PIRANHA

★★★

DIRECTOR: Joe Dante
CAST: Bradford Dillman, Kevin McCarthy, Heather Menzies, Keenan Wynn

Director Joe Dante (*Gremlins*) and writer John Sayles (*Return of the Secaucus 7*; *Brother from Another Planet*) sent up *Jaws* in this nifty, gag-filled 1978 horror film. Full of scares and chuckles, with stars Bradford Dillman, Kevin McCarthy, and Heather Menzies. Rated R.

1978 92 minutes

PIRANHA PART TWO: THE SPAWNING

★

DIRECTOR: James Cameron
CAST: Tricia O'Neil, Steve Marachuk, Lance Henriksen, Leslie Graves

Sorry sequel to *Piranha* by the man who would later grace us with *The Terminator*. A mutated strain of piranha (with the ability to fly, no less) launches an air and sea tirade of violence against a group of vacationers at a tropical resort. Interesting idea poorly executed. The action bogs down time and time again to make way for "character development," leading to extreme boredom. Best sequence is the opening credits, with bizarre visuals and ominous music that trick the viewer into thinking this is going to be a great movie. No such luck. Rated R for mild gore.

1981 88 minutes

PIT AND THE PENDULUM, THE

★★★

DIRECTOR: Roger Corman
CAST: Vincent Price, John Kerr, Barbara Steele, Luana Anders, Anthony Carbong

More stylish, low-budget Edgar Allan Poe–inspired terror with star Vincent Price and director Roger Corman reteaming for this release. This is for fans of the series only.

1961 80 minutes

PLAY MISTY FOR ME

★★★★

DIRECTOR: Clint Eastwood
CAST: Clint Eastwood, Jessica Walter, Donna Mills, John Larch, Irene Hervey

A suspenseful shocker in which director-star Clint Eastwood, playing a disc jockey, is stalked by a crazed "fan" (Jessica Walter). It puts goosebumps on your goosebumps and marked an auspicious directorial debut for the squinty-eyed star. Rated R.

1971 102 minutes

PLUMBER, THE

★★★½

DIRECTOR: Peter Weir

CAST: Ivar Kants, Judy Morris, Robert Coleby

A slightly unhinged plumber completely destroys a young couple's bathroom and begins to terrorize the woman of the house during his visits to make the repairs. A very black comedy-horror-film from the director of *Witness*. Originally made for Australian television, this one is worth your attention. No rating (contains some strong language).

1980 76 minutes

POLTERGEIST

★★★★★

DIRECTOR: Tobe Hopper

CAST: Craig T. Nelson, JoBeth Williams, Beatrice Straight, Dominique Dunne

The ultimate screen ghost story, *Poltergeist* is guaranteed to raise goosepimples while keeping viewers marvelously entertained. What *The Haunting* and *The Legend of Hell House* attempted, this Steven Spielberg production achieves—and then some. Though directed by Tobe Hooper (*Texas Chainsaw Massacre*), it definitely bears the Spielberg stamp. A sort of *Close Encounters* of the supernatural, it's a scary story about the plight of a suburban family whose home suddenly becomes a house of horrors. Rated PG for tense situations.

1982 114 minutes

POLTERGEIST II: THE OTHERSIDE

★★

DIRECTOR: Brian Gibson

CAST: JoBeth Williams, Craig T. Nelson, Heather O'Rourke, Oliver Robins, Zelda Rubinstein, Will Sampson, Julian Beck, Geraldine Fitzgerald

Mere months (screen time) after their last film adventure, the stalwart Freeling family is up to its eyeballs in spooks again—although the ghosts stay backstage while another collection of effects parades before the audience. Coherence and common sense aren't in much evidence, and—in the real world—the Freeling adults probably could be charged with child endangerment. Although Julian Beck is a uniquely ghoulish villain, and Will Sampson lends credibility to the notion of "good Native American magic," the whole project collapses under its own weight. Some truly fine design work by H. R. Giger is all but unnoticed, due to poor editing. Rated PG-13 for intensity and violence.

1986 90 minutes

POWER, THE

★½

DIRECTORS: Jeffrey Obrow, Stephen Carpenter

CAST: Susan Stokey, Warren Lincoln, Lisa Erickson

Although the creators of this low-budget horror flick deserve a certain amount of credit for trying to make more than just another stab-'em, slash-'em horror gore fest, this is nowhere near a classic. It has a nearly incomprehensible story in which a centuries-old Aztec idol that holds the culture's forces of evil is unearthed by some youngsters, who must face the consequences. Teenagers who like to be scared and don't care too much about plot, performance, and directorial execution might enjoy it. For the rest of us, however, *The Power* is just more of the same old thing. Rated R for profanity, violence, and gore.

1980 87 minutes

PREMATURE BURIAL, THE

★★★

DIRECTOR: Roger Corman
CAST: Ray Milland, Hazel Court, Richard Ney, Heather Angel

A medical student's paranoia about being buried alive causes his worst fears to come true. Roger Corman's only Poe-derived film without Vincent Price. Although eventually released by A.I.P., the movie was originally produced for Pathè Distribution, which couldn't acquire Price, due to his contract with A.I.P. Film has the usual lush Corman atmosphere but is less ambitious and more stagey than his other Poe translations. Lacking Price's playful and hammy acting style, it all seems too serious.

1962 81 minutes

PREY, THE

★

DIRECTOR: Edwin Scott Brown
CAST: Debbie Thurseon, Steve Bond, Lori Lethin, Robert Wald, Gayle Gannes, Philip Wenckus, Jackson Bostwick, Jackie Coogan

Run-of-the-mill horror flick complete with young, attractive adults having sex before they get slaughtered (Horror Film Cliché No. 398) and a lot of scenes shot from the monster's point of view as he closes in on his prey (Horror Film Cliché No. 279) accompanied by a loud heartbeat (Horror Film Cliché No. 194). Six young hikers go up into the woods, where they run into a ghoul who hunts them down and has them for dinner. Yum. Rated R for sex, nudity, and violence.

1980 80 minutes

PROM NIGHT

★★

DIRECTOR: Paul Lynch
CAST: Jamie Lee Curtis, Leslie Nielsen, Casey Stevens

This okay slasher flick has a group of high-school students being systematically slaughtered as payment for the accidental death of one of their friends when they were all children. Watchable enough, though Leslie Nielsen looks as if he's about to break up while delivering his rather absurd dialogue. Rated R.

1980 92 minutes

PROPHECY

★

DIRECTOR: John Frankenheimer
CAST: Talia Shire, Robert Foxworth, Armand Assante, Richard Dysart, Victoria Racimo

A dumb ecological-horror thriller with laughable special effects. Rated PG.

1979 95 minutes

PSYCHIC KILLER

★

DIRECTOR: Raymond Danton
CAST: Jim Hutton, Paul Burke, Julie Adams, Nehemiah Persoff, Neville Brand, Aldo Ray, Della Reese

This is a completely ordinary thriller about a man who acquires psychic powers in a mental institution and then utilizes them for revenge. *Psychic Killer* doesn't take itself seriously and that's a plus, but it's not funny or shocking enough or sufficiently engrossing. Rated PG.

1975 89 minutes

PSYCHO

★★★★★

DIRECTOR: Alfred Hitchcock
CAST: Janet Leigh, Anthony Perkins, Vera Miles, John Gavin, John McIntire, Simon Oakland, John Anderson, Frank Albertson, Patricia Hitchcock

The quintessential shocker, which started a whole genre of films about psychotic killers enacting mayhem on innocent victims, still holds up well today. If all you can remember about this film is its famous murder of Janet Leigh in the shower, you might want to give it a second look. Anthony Perkins's performance and the ease with which Hitchcock maneuvers your emotions make *Psycho* far superior to the numerous films that tried to duplicate it.

1960 B & W 109 minutes

PSYCHO II

★★★

DIRECTOR: Richard Franklin
CAST: Anthony Perkins, Vera Miles, Meg Tilly, Robert Loggia, Dennis Franz, Hugh Gillin

Picking up where Alfred Hitchcock's original left off, this sequel begins with Norman Bates (Anthony Perkins) being declared sane after twenty-two years in an asylum. Old Normie goes right back to the Bates Motel, and strange things begin to happen. Directed with exquisite taste and respect for the old master by Richard Franklin. It's suspenseful, scary, and funny. Rated R for nudity, profanity, and violence.

1983 113 minutes

PSYCHO III

★★

DIRECTOR: Anthony Perkins
CAST: Anthony Perkins, Diana Scarwid, Jeff Fahey, Roberta Maxwell, Hugh Gillin, Lee Garlington, Robert Alan Browne

Second follow-up to *Psycho* works mainly because actor-director Anthony Perkins understands poor Norman Bates inside and out. Although lensed beautifully by Bruce Surtees and infused with a deliciously macabre wit, the film fails in the most critical area: creating suspense. There are no mysteries in Charles Edward Pogue's script, and grisly humor cannot mask that missing ingredient. Many of the camera angles, bits of dialogue, and plot points fondly echo Alfred Hitchcock's original, but it's impossible to create tension when everything is so straightforward. The film concludes with a chaotic plot summation that reduces the picture to the level of a mindless soap opera. Rated R for gory violence.

1986 93 minutes

PSYCHO SISTERS

★★★★

DIRECTOR: Reginald LeBorg
CAST: Susan Strasberg, Faith Domergue, Charles Knox Robinson

After her husband is killed, a woman goes to stay with her sister—her sister that has only recently emerged from an insane asylum and is still hearing their dead mother's voice. This film is a classic of the early 1970s horror/gore/exploitation cycle, and it reminds one of Hammer, A.I.P., and the best of Roger Corman. Do not expect too much, and make sure you break out plenty of popcorn and soda when sitting down to watch it. Rated PG for mild violence.

1972 76 minutes

PSYCHOMANIA

★★½

DIRECTOR: Don Sharp
CAST: George Sanders, Nicky Henson, Mary Larkin, Patrick Holt, Beryl Reid

This British-made film may better be called *Motorcycle-Mania*, because it's about a motorcycle gang. They call themselves the "Living Dead" gang, because they committed a group suicide and only came back to life through a pact with the devil. As the undead, they terrorize and murder people who are unfortunate enough to encounter them. The film moves slowly and is a little dull. Includes lots of violence. Rated R.

1971 95 minutes

PSYCHOS IN LOVE

★★½

DIRECTOR: Gorman Bechard

CAST: Carmine Capobianco, Debi Thibeault, Frank Stewart, Cecilia Wilde, Donna Davidge

This film is an *Eating Raoul*–style horror comedy. Joe is a bar owner who has no trouble meeting women and getting dates. The problem is that he is a psychopath who ends up killing them—generally when he finds out they like grapes! Then he meets Kate. She hates grapes and, coincidentally, is a psychotic killer. Their love blossoms, but their drains block up due to the disposal of their victims. No problem. The plumber turns out to be a cannibal. Crazy, sick, bizarre? Yes, but not without quite a few laughs if you like this type of humor. This made-for-video movie has lots of gore and nudity.

1985 88 minutes

PUMA MAN, THE

½

DIRECTOR: Alberto DeMartino

CAST: Donald Pleasence, Sydne Rome, Walter George Alton

Humorless Italian junk about a man given extraordinary powers to fight evil. Low-budget and low-brow, with insulting special effects. Thankfully, the movie was never released in the U.S.

1980 80 minutes

Q

★★★★

DIRECTOR: Larry Cohen

CAST: Michael Moriarty, David Carradine, Candy Clark, Richard Roundtree, John Capordice, James Dixon, Malachy McCourt

This is an old-fashioned giant monster film. The stop-motion animation is excellent, the acting (done tongue-in-cheek) is perfect, and the moments of humor are well worth waiting for. The story revolves around the arrival of a giant flying lizard in New York City. A series of ritualistic murders follows and points to the monster being Quetzelcoatl (the flying serpent god of the Aztecs). An ex-junkie stumbles upon the nest and blackmails the city for millions for the nest's location. Rated R.

1982 93 minutes

QUEST, THE

★½

DIRECTOR: Brian Trenchard-Smith

CAST: Henry Thomas, Tany Barry, Rachel Friend, Tamsin West, John Ewart, Dennis Miller, Katy Manning

Henry Thomas plays a young boy living in Australia who has reason to believe that a monster lives in a small lake not far from his home. One man has already allegedly been killed by looking into the eyes of the beast. So Thomas sets out to prove the creature's existence—or to expose it as a fraud. Though slow, this film has decent acting, funny moments, and some suspense. It also shows much of the beautiful Australian countryside. Adults may not get too excited, but children will find this film lots of fun. Rated PG.

1985 94 minutes

RABID

★★

DIRECTOR: David Cronenberg

CAST: Marilyn Chambers, Frank Moore, Joe Silver, Patricia Gage, Susan Roman

This horror flick has become a cult favorite despite many repulsive scenes. In it, porn queen Marilyn Chambers lives on human blood after a motorcycle accident operation. For fans of director David Cronenberg only. Rated R.

1977 90 minutes

RACE WITH THE DEVIL

★★

DIRECTOR: Jack Starrett
CAST: Warren Oates, Peter Fonda, Loretta Swit, Lara Parker

Good cast and exciting chase sequences can't save this muddled yarn. It's about two couples who accidentally intrude on a witches' sacrificial ceremony while on a vacation that literally becomes "hell on Earth" when they're discovered observing the proceedings. Rated PG for violence.

1975 88 minutes

RAGGEDY MAN

★★★½

DIRECTOR: Jack Fisk
CAST: Sissy Spacek, Eric Roberts, William Sanderson, Tracy Walter, Sam Shepard, Henry Thomas, Carey Hollis Jr.

Sissy Spacek gives another outstanding performance as a World War II divorcée trying to raise two sons and improve their lives in a small Texas Gulf Coast town. *Raggedy Man* is a curious mixture of styles. It begins as a character study and ends like a horror film. But it works. Rated PG for nudity and violence.

1981 94 minutes

RATS ARE COMING!, THE WEREWOLVES ARE HERE!, THE

★

DIRECTOR: Andy Milligan
CAST: Hope Stansbury, Jackie Skarvellis

England is besieged by a pack of werewolves in the 1800s. Boring horror film was made on shoestring budget, and it shows. Also featured in this nonsense are the pets of one of the werewolves' daughters—killer rats! Good title, bad movie. Rated R.

1972 92 minutes

RAVEN, THE

★★★★

DIRECTOR: Louis Friedlander
CAST: Boris Karloff, Bela Lugosi, Irene Ware, Lester Matthews, Samuel S. Hinds

Solid Universal Pictures horror thriller casts Bela Lugosi as a mad scientist who is obsessed with the writings of Edgar Allan Poe. Boris Karloff is the hapless fugitive Lugosi deforms in order to carry out his evil schemes. Unlike many of the 1930s horror classics, this one has retained its suspense and drama. Director Louis Friedlander, who later changed his name to Lew Landers, keeps things moving at a good pace and gets fine performances from those kings of terror, Karloff and Lugosi. This film is available on a double-feature video cassette with *Black Cat*.

1935 B & W 62 minutes

RAVEN, THE

★★★★

DIRECTOR: Roger Corman
CAST: Boris Karloff, Vincent Price, Peter Lorre, Jack Nicholson, Hazel Court, Olive Sturgess

The best of the Roger Corman–directed Edgar Allan Poe adaptations, this release benefits from a humorous screenplay by Richard Matheson and tongue-in-cheek portrayals by Boris Karloff, Vincent Price, and Peter Lorre. Look for Jack Nicholson in an early role as Lorre's mincing son.

1963 86 minutes

RAZORBACK

★★★½

DIRECTOR: Russell Mulcahy
CAST: Gregory Harrison

This Australian film, concerning a giant pig that is terrorizing a small

Aussie village, surprises the viewer by turning into a great little film. The special effects, photography, editing, and acting are great. Rated R.

1983 95 minutes

RE-ANIMATOR

★★★★

DIRECTOR: Stuart Gordon

CAST: Bruce Abbott, Barbara Crampton, David Gale, Robert Sampson, Jeffrey Combs

Stylishly grotesque and gory filming of H. P. Lovecraft's "Herbert West, Reanimator" hits the mark where all previous efforts to put this master storyteller on celluloid have failed. From the opening credits (stolen from Bernard Herrmann's intensely riveting score from the original *Psycho*) this film moves in a rhythmic cadence toward its inevitable conclusion, uniting the principals and the audience in a grim blood bath that is horrifying yet so outrageous that it evokes as many nervous laughs and giggles as screams. This is Grand Guignol in the classic sense as we follow brilliant young medical student Herbert West in his deranged efforts to bring the dead back to life to prove that he's not just another crackpot. Some outrageous scenes highlight this terror entry and, although very well done, it's not for the squeamish.

1985 86 minutes

REAR WINDOW

★★★★★

DIRECTOR: Alfred Hitchcock

CAST: James Stewart, Raymond Burr, Grace Kelly, Wendell Corey, Thelma Ritter, Judith Evelyn

James Stewart plays a magazine photographer who, confined to a wheelchair because of a broken leg, seeks diversion in watching his neighbors, often with a telephoto lens. He soon becomes convinced that one neighbor (Raymond Burr) has murdered his spouse and dismembered the body. One of the director's best, *Rear Window* will keep you fascinated and laughing right up until the edge-of-your-seat climax.

1954 112 minutes

RED HOUSE, THE

★★★½

DIRECTOR: Delmer Daves

CAST: Edward G. Robinson, Lon McCallister, Allene Roberts, Julie London, Judith Anderson, Rory Calhoun, Ona Munson

A gripping suspense melodrama enhanced by a musical score by Miklos Rozsa. Edward G. Robinson employs Rory Calhoun to keep the curious away from the decaying old house of the title deep in the woods near his farm. But his niece and a young hired hand *must* learn the secret. Allene Roberts is endearing as the niece, with Lon McCallister just right as the "hand" who loves her. Robinson is excellent as the guilt-ridden uncle who harbors a secret too horrible to tell!

1947 B & W 100 minutes

REFLECTIONS OF MURDER

★★★

DIRECTOR: John Badham

CAST: Tuesday Weld, Joan Hackett, Sam Waterston

A wife and a mistress set out to kill their abusive mate. They set up a foolproof trap to lure him to his death. The "accident" that kills him leads to more terror and horror than either women expected. A TV-movie version of the French classic *Diabolique*.

1987 98 minutes

REINCARNATION OF PETER PROUD, THE

★★

DIRECTOR: J. Lee Thompson

CAST: Michael Sarrazin, Jennifer O'Neill, Margot Kidder, Cornelia Sharpe

Laughably melodramatic tale of bewildered Michael Sarrazin, who—through dream research—recalls having been murdered in a previous life. Much to the dismay of girlfriend Cornelia Sharpe (bad, as always), he returns to the scene of the crime and falls in love with "his" daughter. Unfortunately, "his" former wife, Margot Kidder, isn't about to sit still for such rubbish. Turgid direction, contrived plot, adapted by Max Erlich from his not-much-better book. Rated R for considerable nudity.

1975 104 minutes

RETURN OF THE ALIEN'S DEADLY SPAWN, THE

★★

DIRECTOR: Douglas McKeown

CAST: Charles George Hildebrandt, Tom De Franco, Jean Tafler, Karen Tigue

Blood-filled horror film about alien creatures from outer space who kill and destroy anyone and everything that gets in their way. Lots of gore, ripped flesh, and off-the-wall humor. For people who like sick movies. Rated R for violence, profanity, and gore.

1984 90 minutes

RETURN OF THE FLY, THE

★★★

DIRECTOR: Edward L. Bernds

CAST: Vincent Price, Brett Halsey, David Frankham

In this fine sequel to *The Fly*, the son of the original insect makes the same mistake as his father . . . with identical results. Effective film benefits from stark black-and-white photography and solid effects. Watch out for the guinea pig scene!

1959 B & W 80 minutes

RETURN OF THE LIVING DEAD, THE

★★★★

DIRECTOR: Dan O'Bannon

CAST: Clu Gulager, James Karen, Don Calfa, Thom Mathews

Extremely gory horror film produced with a great deal of style and ample amounts of comedy as well. The residents of a small New Orleans cemetery are brought back to life after accidental exposure to a strange chemical, and they're hungry . . . for human brains. It's up to the employees of the nearby Uneeda Medical Supply warehouse, along with a gang of punks, to discover a way of stopping the creatures before we're all turned into lunch. While it's all tongue-in-cheek for the most part, there are still many horrifying moments as this clever movie manages to sustain a perfect balance between absolute hilarity and sheer terror throughout. The only drawback, as stated, is that it's as gruesome as can be. Viewers who are the least bit squeamish are advised to stay clear; all others—hang on! Rated R for violence, gore, nudity, and language.

1985 91 minutes

RETURN OF THE VAMPIRE, THE

★★★

DIRECTORS: Lew Landers, Kurt Neumann

CAST: Bela Lugosi, Frieda Inescort, Nina Foch, Miles Mander, Roland Varno, Matt Willis

Set during World War II, this surprisingly good vampire tale has the supposedly destroyed fiend, Armand Tesla (Bela Lugosi), unearthed by a German bombing raid on London to resume his reign of terror after twenty-three years of undead sleep. Exceptional production is marked by offbeat camera work, strong characters, and believable dialogue by screenwriter Griffin Jay. Also noteworthy is Columbia's use of a pristine print for this release, and the hi-fi sound is incredibly clean.

1943 B & W 69 minutes

RETURN TO HORROR HIGH

DIRECTOR: Bill Froechlich
CAST: Vince Edwards, Alex Rocco, Brendan Hughes, Scott Jacoby, Lori Lethin, Philip McKeon

A group of filmmakers go back to a high school where a series of murders took place eight years previous. The confusing screenplay was probably meant to tease the viewer by slyly going from the mock death scenes of the movie the filmmakers are creating to the bloody reality that lurks just around the corner. The ending proves to be even more frustrating. Rated R for sex, nudity, profanity, and violence.

1987 95 minutes

REVENGE

DIRECTOR: Jud Taylor
CAST: Shelley Winters, Stuart Whitman, Bradford Dillman, Roger Perry

Made for television, this has Shelley Winters out for—you guessed it—revenge for her daughter's rape. Not as bad as it could have been.

1971 78 minutes

REVENGE OF THE DEAD

DIRECTOR: Pupi Avati
CAST: Gabriele Lavia, Anne Canovas

Talky Italian film with misleading title. It's not part of George Romero's series, or even a bad imitation. It's an incredibly dull movie. Impossible to tell what it's about or why it was made. Rated R for violence and profanity.

1984 98 minutes

REVENGE OF THE ZOMBIES

DIRECTOR: Steve Sekely
CAST: John Carradine, Robert Lowery, Gale Storm, Veda Ann Borg, Mantan Moreland, Mauritz Hugo, Bob Steele

As soon as the Hollywood backlot native walks across the foggy bog in baggy underwear and begins to wail "Whoooooo," you know this is going to be one of those films. And it sure is, with mad scientist John Carradine, his zombie wife Veda Ann Borg (in her best role), do-gooders Gale Storm and Robert Lowery, and "feets do yo' stuff" Mantan Moreland aiding/escaping zombies and Nazis in this low budget howler.

1943 B & W 61 minutes

RIPPER, THE

DIRECTOR: Christopher Lewis
CAST: Tom Schreier, Wade Tower, Mona VanPernis, Andrea Adams

In this poorly filmed modernization of the Jack the Ripper legend, a college professer finds a ring, originally belonging to the nineteenth-century killer, which when worn turns him into—yes, you guessed it—Jack the Ripper. Amateurish throughout, this film has nothing to recommend it, even to die-hard fans of the genre.

1985 104 minutes

ROAD GAMES

★★½

DIRECTOR: Richard Franklin
CAST: Stacy Keach, Jamie Lee Curtis, Marion Howard, Grant Page, Bill Stacey

An elusive latter-day Jack the Ripper is loose in Australia. He cruises desolate areas in a mysterious, customized van, picking up female hitchhikers and then raping, killing, and dismembering them. Even though director Richard Franklin (*Psycho II*) actually studied under Alfred Hitchcock at USC's renowned film school, he doesn't show any of his mentor's ability here. While it has its moments, *Road Games* is essentially a thriller without any thrills. Rated PG.

1981 100 minutes

ROBOT MONSTER

DIRECTOR: Phil Tucker
CAST: George Nader, Gregory Moffett, Claudia Barrett, Selena Royle, John Mylong

Take a desolate-looking canyon outside of Los Angeles, borrow Lawrence Welk's bubble machine, and add a typical family on an outing and a man dressed in a gorilla suit wearing a diving helmet, and you have a serious competitor for the worst film of all time. This absurd drama of the last days of Earth and its conquest by robot gorillas has long been considered the most inept of all science-fiction films and shares the same closet space with *Plan 9 from Outer Space*, *Bride of the Monster*, and *Mesa of the Lost Women*. A must-see for all fans of truly terrible films.

1953 B & W 63 minutes

ROLLERCOASTER

★★★★½

DIRECTOR: James Goldstone
CAST: George Segal, Richard Widmark, Timothy Bottoms, Susan Strasberg, Henry Fonda

Fast-paced suspense film about an extortionist (Timothy Bottoms) blowing up rides in some of the nation's most famous amusement parks, and the efforts of a county safety inspector (George Segal) and an FBI agent (Richard Widmark) to nab him. Very well done, this much-maligned film has great action, crisp dialogue, and a brilliant, nail-biting climax seamlessly combined to provide a first-class entertainment. Rated PG for language and violence.

1977 119 minutes

ROPE

★★★★½

DIRECTOR: Alfred Hitchcock
CAST: James Stewart, John Dall, Farley Granger, Cedric Hardwicke

This recently resurrected Alfred Hitchcock film is based in part on the famous Leopold-Loeb thrill-murder case in Chicago in the 1920s. In it, the two killers divulge clues to their horrific escapade at a dinner party, to the growing suspicion of the other guests. It's one of Hitchcock's best.

1948 80 minutes

ROSEMARY'S BABY

★★★★

DIRECTOR: Roman Polanski
CAST: Mia Farrow, John Cassavetes, Ruth Gordon, Ralph Bellamy, Elisha Cook Jr., Maurice Evans, Patsy Kelly

This is the first movie to open up the subject of the modern-day practice of the occult. Mia Farrow is a young woman forced by her husband (John Cassavetes) into an unholy arrangement with a group of devil-worshipers. The suspense is sustained as she is made aware that those friendly people around her are not what they seem. Ruth Gordon is priceless in her Oscar-winning role as one of the seemingly normal neighbors. Rated R.

1968 136 minutes

RUBY

★★

DIRECTOR: Curtis Harrington
CAST: Piper Laurie, Stuart Whitman, Roger Davis, Janit Baldwin

A sleazy drive-in movie theater is the setting for this unexciting horror film about a young girl possessed by the homicidal ghost of a dead gangster. Rated R for gore.

1977 84 minutes

RUDE AWAKENING

★★½

DIRECTOR: Peter Sasdy
CAST: Denholm Elliott, James Laurenson, Pat Heywood

In another of Elvira's "Thriller Video" series, and one of the best, a real estate broker finds himself sucked into dreams that seem like reality; or is it the other way around? It sounds standard, but it's better than you would think. Definitely worth a look.

1982 60 minutes

RUN STRANGER RUN

★★★½

DIRECTOR: Darren McGavin
CAST: Patricia Neal, Cloris Leachman, Ron Howard, Bobby Darin

Ron Howard plays a teenager searching for his biological parents in a seaside town. Once there, he discovers that some of the town inhabitants have been disappearing. Unfortunately, the disappearances are closely linked to his past. Cloris Leachman plays Howard's real mother, and Bobby Darin is her boyfriend. Patricia Neal turns out to be Howard's aunt, and her family strongly resembles the Munsters. Overall, this film keeps viewer interest without dwelling on the slash-'em-up theme. Rated PG for gore.

1973 92 minutes

SABOTAGE

★★★

DIRECTOR: Alfred Hitchcock
CAST: Sylvia Sidney, Oscar Homolka, John Loder, Desmond Tester, Joyce Barbour

One of the first of Alfred Hitchcock's characteristic thrillers. London's being terrorized by an unknown bomber, and movie theater cashier Sylvia Sidney begins to fear that her husband (Oscar Homolka), who owns the theater, is behind it all. Hitch was still experimenting, and his use of shadows and sound effects betrays the influence of German silent films. The master director made one of his few artistic mistakes here: Sidney's young son, told to deliver a package—which, unknown to him, contains a bomb—by a certain hour, wastes time with youthful distractions and draws out the suspense to an unbelievable degree, until—BOOM!—he's killed when the bomb goes off. Audiences never forgave Hitch for that one.

1936 B & W 76 minutes

SABOTEUR

★★★★½

DIRECTOR: Alfred Hitchcock
CAST: Robert Cummings, Priscilla Lane, Norman Lloyd, Otto Kruger

Outstanding Alfred Hitchcock film about a World War II factory worker (Robert Cummings) turned fugitive after he's unjustly accused of sabotage. The briskly paced story follows his efforts to elude police while he tries to unmask the real culprit. Hitchcock is in top form in this first-rate thriller. A humdinger of a climax.

1942 B & W 108 minutes

SALEM'S LOT

★★★★

DIRECTOR: Tobe Hooper

CAST: David Soul, James Mason, Reggie Nalder, Lance Kerwin, Elisha Cook Jr., Ed Flanders

This story of vampires in modern-day New England is one of the better adaptations of Stephen King's novels on film. Some real chills go along with an intelligent script in what was originally a two-part TV movie. Be prepared for some frightening scenes.

1979 112 minutes

SATAN'S SCHOOL FOR GIRLS

★★½

DIRECTOR: David Lowell Rich

CAST: Pamela Franklin, Kate Jackson, Roy Thinnes, Cheryl Ladd

Originally made as an ABC Movie of the Week, this decent shocker concerns a series of apparent "suicides" at a prominent girls' school, but we all know better. Interesting story has good acting and some creepy atmosphere, but the typical TV ending falls flat.

1973 74 minutes

SATURDAY THE 14TH

★

DIRECTOR: Howard R. Cohen

CAST: Richard Benjamin, Paula Prentiss, Jeffrey Tambor, Rosemary DeCamp

Richard Benjamin and Paula Prentiss (who are husband and wife in real life) star in this low-budget horror comedy about a family that moves into a haunted house. Thanks to the curiosity of their son, Billy, they find themselves at the mercy of the Book of Evil and its onslaught of terrors. The jokes are tired, the monsters insipid, and the plot weak. It's a good horror movie for kids who don't really want to be scared. Rated PG.

1981 75 minutes

SAVAGE ATTRACTION

★★★★

DIRECTOR: Frank Shields

CAST: Kerry Mack, Ralph Schicha, Judy Nunn, Clare Binney

A psychotic German, Walter, becomes sadistically obsessed with a lovely Australian girl, Christine, in this bizarre but true tale. He uses both mental and physical cruelty to keep her with him. The suspense is never lacking as viewers continually wonder, What will he do to her next? Rated R for sex, sadism, nudity, and violence.

1983 93 minutes

SAVAGE WEEKEND

★

DIRECTOR: John Mason Kirby

CAST: Christopher Allport, James Doerr, Marilyn Hamlin, William Sanderson

Several couples head out from the big city into the backwoods to watch a boat being built, but they are killed off one by one. The only reason this movie earns any stars is for talented actor William Sanderson's performance as a demented lunatic who may or may not be the killer in this very drab, boring thriller. The sequences with him are interesting, but the rest of this film looks as if it were made by high-schoolers. Rated R for nudity, simulated sex, violence.

1979 88 minutes

SAVAGES

★★★

DIRECTOR: Lee H. Katzin

CAST: Andy Griffith, Sam Bottoms, Noah Beery Jr., James Best

Man hunts man! Sam Bottoms is guiding Andy Griffith on a hunt in the desert when Griffith goes bananas and begins a savage, relentless pursuit of Bottoms. A sandy rendition of the famous short story, "The Most Dangerous Game." Thrilling, suspenseful, intriguing to watch. Made for TV.

1974 78 minutes

SCALPEL

★

DIRECTOR: John Grissmer

CAST: Robert Lansing, Judith Chapman, Arlen Dean Snyder, David Scarroll, Sandy Martin

Robert Lansing is a cunning, unscrupulous plastic surgeon who transforms a young accident victim into the spitting image of his missing daughter to pull an inheritance swindle. A rather dull melodrama sinks to deplorable depths when it uses graphic, repulsive scenes of surgery. Rated R.

1976 96 minutes

SCANNERS

★★★½

DIRECTOR: David Cronenberg

CAST: Jennifer O'Neill, Patrick McGoohan, Stephen Lack, Lawrence Dane

From its first shocking scene—in which a character's head explodes, spewing blood, flesh, and bone all over—*Scanners* poses a challenge to its viewers: How much can you take? Shock specialist David Cronenberg (*The Brood* and *Rabid*) wrote and directed this potent film, about a bloody war among a group of people with formidable extrasensory powers. If feeling decidedly queasy after being shocked and nauseated by watching a movie is your idea of a good time, then don't miss it. But remember: You have been warned. Rated R.

1981 102 minutes

SCARED TO DEATH

★★

DIRECTOR: Christy Cabanne

CAST: Bela Lugosi, Douglas Fowley, Joyce Compton, George Zucco, Nat Pendleton

This tepid thriller is noteworthy primarily because it is Bela Lugosi's only color film, not for the lukewarm story about a woman who dies without a traceable cause. Plenty of hocus-pocus, red herrings, and hypnosis in this also-ran horror film directed by Christy Cabanne, a silent film pioneer.

1946 65 minutes

SCARS OF DRACULA

★★★

DIRECTOR: Roy Ward Baker

CAST: Christopher Lee, Dennis Waterman, Jenny Hanley, Christopher Matthews

A young couple searching for the husband's brother follow the trail to Dracula's castle, and soon regret it. Compares well with other films in the series, thanks primarily to Christopher Lee's dynamite portrayal of the Count, and the first-rate direction of horror veteran Roy Ward Baker. Rated R.

1970 94 minutes

SCHIZOID

★½

DIRECTOR: David Paulsen

CAST: Klaus Kinski, Mariana Hill, Craig Wasson, Christopher Lloyd

This is an unimaginative slasher flick with typically gory special effects. Not for the squeamish. Rated R.

1980 91 minutes

SCREAM AND SCREAM AGAIN

★★★½

DIRECTOR: Gordon Hessler

CAST: Vincent Price, Peter Cushing, Christopher Lee, Alfred

Marks, Judy Huxtable, Christopher Matthews, Michael Gothard, Marshall Jones

A top-notch cast propels in this chilling, suspenseful story of a crazed scientist (Vincent Price) attempting to create a race of superbeings while a baffled police force copes with a series of brutal murders that may or may not be related. Complex film benefits from polished performances by some horror greats, who look very comfortable in their respective roles. Based on the novel *The Disoriented Man*, by Peter Saxon. Rated PG for violence, language, brief nudity.

1970 95 minutes

SCREAM FOR HELP

DIRECTOR: Michael Winner
CAST: Rachel Kelly, David Brooks, Marie Master, Rocco Sisto, Lolita Lorre, Sandra Clark, Corey Parker

A frustratingly simple and poorly acted suspense thriller about a teen-age girl whose stepfather is trying to kill her and her mother. Of course, no one believes her, even when the evidence is abundantly clear. The characters meander through the story, acting insensitively and unrealistically. From beginning to end, the film treats us to needless sex scenes and unnecessary foul language. There are a few suspenseful moments near the end, but not enough to recommend this waste of time. Rated R for sex, nudity, profanity, and violence.

1986 95 minutes

SCREAM GREATS, VOL. 1

★★★

DIRECTOR: Damon Santostefano

The first in a projected series by *Starlog Magazine*. A documentary on horror effects master Tom Savini. Gory highlights are featured from many of his movies, including *Friday the 13th*, *Creepshow*, and *Dawn of the Dead*. Savini shows his secrets, explains his techniques, and tries to justify what he does for a living. Funny, disgusting, and fascinating, but too talky for repeat viewing. Unrated, contains massive but clinical gore.

1986 60 minutes

SCREAMERS

DIRECTORS: Sergio Martino, Dan T. Miller
CAST: Claudio Cassinelli, Richard Johnson, Joseph Cotten

Just what we needed, another low-budget horror film. Claudio Cassinelli, who is reportedly Italy's most popular male star, finds himself stranded on an uncharted island and at the mercy of a mad doctor (Richard Johnson), a crazy inventor (Joseph Cotten), and a bunch of underpaid extras in native costumes. Rated R.

1979 90 minutes

SEANCE ON A WET AFTERNOON

★★★★½

DIRECTOR: Bryan Forbes
CAST: Kim Stanley, Richard Attenborough, Patrick Magee, Nanette Newman

This is an absolutely fabulous movie. An unbalanced medium (Kim Stanley) involves her meek husband (Richard Attenborough) in a kidnapping scheme that brings about their downfall. Brilliant acting by all, working from a superb script. No rating, but some intense sequences.

1964 B & W 115 minutes

SEASON OF THE WITCH

★

DIRECTOR: George A. Romero
CAST: Jan White, Ray Lane, Anne Muffly, Joedda McClain, Bill Thunhurst

A somewhat slow-moving tale of an aging woman who is unable to cope with the disappointments of her daily routine. She seeks an answer to her boredom and disillusionment in witchcraft with disastrous results. Slim on plot as well as on dialogue. Also known as *Hungry Wives*. Rated R.

1972 90 minutes

SEDUCTION, THE

DIRECTOR: David Schmoeller
CAST: Morgan Fairchild, Andrew Stevens, Vince Edwards, Michael Sarrazin

This is a silly suspense film about a lady newscaster (Morgan Fairchild) stalked by an unbalanced admirer (Andrew Stevens) patched together from *The Fan* and all those Brian De Palma movies combining implausible menace with soapy eroticism. Rated R for nudity, sex, and violence.

1982 104 minutes

SEE NO EVIL

DIRECTOR: Richard Fleischer
CAST: Mia Farrow, Dorothy Alison, Robin Bailey

Chilling, suspenseful yarn follows a young blind woman (Mia Farrow) as she tries to escape the clutches of a ruthless killer who has done away with her entire family at their quiet country farm. Mia Farrow is very convincing as the maniac's next target, and there are enough shocks along the way to please the most hardened horror fan. Rated PG for tense moments.

1971 90 minutes

SENDER, THE

★★★

DIRECTOR: Roger Christian
CAST: Kathryn Harrold, Shirley Knight, Paul Freeman

Roger Christian, winner of Oscars for best set direction (*Star Wars*) and best short subject (*The Dollar Bottom*), makes his directorial debut with this horror film, which features bleeding mirrors and rats coming out of people's mouths. Rated R.

1982 91 minutes

SENTINEL, THE

DIRECTOR: Michael Winner
CAST: Chris Sarandon, Cristina Raines, Martin Balsam, John Carradine, José Ferrer, Ava Gardner, Arthur Kennedy, Burgess Meredith, Sylvia Miles, Deborah Raffin, Eli Wallach

Michael Winner once again causes the stomach to churn and the throat to gag. This is a dismal genre piece about a woman (Cristina Raines) who unknowingly moves into an apartment building over the gates of hell. *The Sentinel* doesn't have much suspense, nor does it deliver many shocks. Instead, it has a sort of nauseating relentlessness, which builds slowly to a nightmarish climax. Rated R for nudity, profanity, and violence.

1977 93 minutes

SEVERED ARM, THE

★★½

CAST: Paul Carr, Deborah Walley, Marvin Kaplan

Before being rescued from a cave-in, a group of trapped mine explorers cut off the arm of one of the men as food for the others. Many years later, the survivors of the expedition find are systematically slaughtered by an unseen psychopath. This low-budget independent production is fairly suspenseful, though the acting is often listless and the gore a bit excessive. Rated R.

1973 86 minutes

SHADOW PLAY

★

DIRECTOR: Susan Shadburne
CAST: Dee Wallace Stone, Cloris Leachman, Ron Kuhlman, Delia Salvi, Barry Laws

Described as a romantic mystery by its makers, this pitiful excuse for a movie presents Dee Wallace Stone as a Manhattan playwright who is obsessed by the tragic death of her fiancé seven years earlier. Indeed, she becomes possessed by his ghost, which inspires her to write awful lines of poetry ("I can still feel your taste on my tongue, and I will graze until morning."). Yuck and double yuck. Rated R for profanity, sex, and, violence.

1986 101 minutes

SHINING, THE

★★½

DIRECTOR: Stanley Kubrick
CAST: Jack Nicholson, Shelley Duvall, Scatman Crothers

A struggling writer (Jack Nicholson) accepts a position as the caretaker of a large summer resort hotel during the winter season. The longer he and his family spend in the hotel, the more Nicholson becomes possessed by it. Considering the talent involved, this is a major disappointment. Director Stanley Kubrick keeps things at a snail's pace, and Nicholson's performance approaches high camp. Rated R for violence and language.

1980 146 minutes

SHOCK

★★★

DIRECTOR: Alfred Werker
CAST: Vincent Price, Lynn Bari, Reed Hadley, Pierre Watkins, Frank Latimore

Highly effective thriller features Vincent Price in an early performance as a murderer—in this case he's a psychiatrist who murders his wife and is then forced to silence a witness through drugs and hypnosis. This minor classic provided the framework for many subsequent suspense movies. Price is fiendishly suave and gives a good glimpse of the style that would make him America's greatest horror star in the late 1950s and 1960s.

1946 B & W 70 minutes

SHOCK WAVES (DEATH CORPS)

★½

DIRECTOR: Ken Wiederhorn
CAST: Peter Cushing, Brooke Adams, John Carradine, Fred Buch

Vacationers stumble upon a crazed ex-Nazi controlling an army of underwater zombies. It's just as stupid as it sounds. The sopping-wet zombies wear full dress uniforms, perky little swimming goggles, and a stunning complement of seaweed accessories. They're a riot. Rated PG.

1977 86 minutes

SHOUT, THE

★★★

DIRECTOR: Jerzy Skolimowski
CAST: Alan Bates, Susannah York, John Hurt, Robert Stephens, Tim Curry

Enigmatic British chiller about a wanderer's chilling effect on an unsuspecting couple. He possesses the ancient power to kill people by screaming. Well made, with an excellent cast. The film may be too offbeat for some viewers. Rated R.

1979 87 minutes

SILENT NIGHT, DEADLY NIGHT

★

DIRECTOR: Charles E. Sellier Jr.
CAST: Lilyan Chauvin, Gilmer McCormick, Robert Brian Wilson, Toni Nero

This is the one that caused such a commotion among parents' groups for its depiction of Santa Claus as a homicidal killer. It was pulled from release just a week into its theatrical run, only to resurface on video. It will serve to satisfy the curiosity of those who want to see what all the fuss was about. What they'll find is no more than another routine slasher flick. A kid sees his parents slaughtered by a hitchhiker in a Santa Claus suit and is, understandably, haunted by the memory for years. Ten years later, while working as a stock boy at a toy store, he is asked to dress up as St. Nick for Christmas, which sends him off the deep end and out on a killing spree. Fortunately, this occurs late in the film, and the tormented youth (not to mention the poor viewer) is soon put out of his misery. No rating, but contains gobs of nudity and violent bloodshed.

1984 92 minutes

SILENT PARTNER, THE

★★★★½

DIRECTOR: Daryl Duke
CAST: Elliott Gould, Christopher Plummer, Susannah York, John Candy

This suspense thriller is what they call a sleeper. It's an absolutely riveting tale about a bank teller (Elliott Gould) who, knowing of a robbery in advance, pulls a switch on a psychotic criminal (Christopher Plummer) and might not live to regret it. A Canadian production inventively directed by Daryl Duke, *Silent Partner* is a real find for movie buffs. But be forewarned; it has a couple of truly unsettling scenes of violence. Rated R.

1978 103 minutes

SILENT SCREAM

★★½

DIRECTOR: Denny Harris
CAST: Yvonne De Carlo, Barbara Steele, Avery Schreiber, Rebecca Balding

This is a well-done shock film with a semi-coherent plot and enough thrills to satisfy the teens. Rated R.

1980 87 minutes

SILVER BULLET

★★★★

DIRECTOR: Daniel Attias
CAST: Gary Busey, Everett McGill, Corey Haim, Megan Follows, James Gammon, Robin Groves, Leon Russom

A superior Stephen King horror film, this release moves like the projectile after which it was named. From the opening scene, in which a railroad worker (gloriously played by that underrated character actor James Gammon) meets his gruesome demise at the claws of a werewolf, to the final confrontation between our heroes (Gary Busey and Corey Haim) and the hairy beast, it's an edge-of-your-seat winner. King, who adapted the screenplay from his novelette *Cycle of the Werewolf*, balances the terror with nice touches of humor; as things get very grisly at times, this offers a much-appreciated respite. Although a bit too gory in parts, *Silver Bullet* remains good, old tell-me-a-scary-story fun. Rated R for violence and gore.

1985 90 minutes

SINS OF DORIAN GRAY, THE

★½

DIRECTOR: Tony Maylam
CAST: Anthony Perkins, Belinda Bauer, Joseph Bottoms, Olga Karlatos, Michael Ironside, Caroline Yeager

This modern-day version of Oscar Wildes famous horror tale, with a portrait of dear old Dorian in female form, manages to disappoint at nearly every turn. Only the plot—about a beautiful woman who sells her soul for eternal youth and then watches a video screen test of herself age and decay—manages to fascinate. But then one could truly enjoy Wilde's tale by watching the far superior *The Picture of Dorian Gray* with Hurd Hatfield. Made for television.

1983 98 minutes

SISTERS

★★★★½

DIRECTOR: Brian De Palma
CAST: Margot Kidder, Charles Durning, Jennifer Salt, Barnard Hughes

A terrifying tale of two twin sisters (Margot Kidder), this is arguably Brian De Palma's best film to date. One is normal; the other is a dangerous psychopath. It's an extremely effective thriller on all levels. Charles Durning and Jennifer Salt give the stand-out performances in this release, which is not for the faint-hearted. Rated R for violence, nudity, and language.

1973 93 minutes

SKULLDUGGERY

★

DIRECTOR: Ota Richter
CAST: Thom Haverstock, Wendy Crewson, David Calderisi, David Main, Clark Johnson, Geordie Johnson

Thom Haverstock plays a costume store employee who inherits a satanic curse that sends him on a killing rampage. The soundtrack hints at black comedy and the board game motifs suggest the whole story is like a game, but these messages are not handled with enough skill to give the embellishments meaning of any worth to the viewer. Too odd to be taken seriously as a horror flick and not odd enough to be interesting. Terrible attempts at humor, too. Leave this one on the shelf for the Dungeons and Dragons freaks and devil worshipers. Not rated, but would earn a PG for sex, violence, and profanity.

1983 95 minutes

SLEEPAWAY CAMP

DIRECTOR: Robert Hiltzik
CAST: Mike Kellin, Katherine Kamhi, Paul DeAngelo

This bloody, disgusting film, written and directed by Robert Hiltzik, is one that will make you appreciate the fast-forward feature on your VCR. The story—and we use the term loosely—just doesn't wash, no matter how you look at it. One more vehicle for blood, gore, and violence, it doesn't even rate dollar day at your favorite video rental outlet!

1983 88 minutes

SLITHIS

★★

DIRECTOR: Stephen Traxler
CAST: Alan Blanchard, Judy Motulsky, Mello Alexandria, Dennis Lee Falt

Okay horror tale of a gruesome monster, derived from garbage and radiation in Southern California, and his reign of terror in and around the L.A. area. While earnestly done, the film just can't overcome its budget restrictions.

Actual on-screen title: *Spawn of the Slithis*. Rated PG.

1978 92 minutes

SLUMBER PARTY MASSACRE

★

DIRECTOR: Amy Jones
CAST: Michele Michaels, Robin Stille, Michael Villella, Debra Deliso, Andree Monore, Gina Mari, Jennifer Meyers

A typical exploitation film about a mass murderer who has escaped from a mental hospital and is killing young girls with a power drill. He follows a group of friends home from school and, under the cover of darkness, invades their slumber party. In between the bloodletting, the girls find enough time to disrobe, take showers, and have sex with their boyfriends. The acting is atrocious, the writing insipid, and the direction uninspired. Rated R for nudity and graphic violence.

1982 77 minutes

SNOW CREATURE, THE

★½

DIRECTOR: W. Lee Wilder
CAST: Paul Langton, Leslie Denison, Teru Shimade, Rollin Moriyana

Bargain-basement abominable snowman movie is one of the weakest of the batch that hit American theaters in the mid-1950s, but it did have one different gimmick: the yeti is captured and brought to Los Angeles. In the best tradition of captured snowmen, this one escapes and wreaks minor havoc on the terror-stricken metropolis before it is subdued. A cast of unknowns almost succeed in making this film bad enough to be funny, but it never really rises about its own ineptness.

1954 B & W 70 minutes

SNOWBEAST

DIRECTOR: Herb Wallerstein
CAST: Bo Svenson, Yvette Mimieux, Robert Logan, Clint Walker, Sylvia Sidney

Hokey white sasquatch/abominable snowman makes life miserable on the slopes for Bo Svenson and Yvette Mimieux's ski resort during a winter festival. Big Clint Walker and 1930s movie star Sylvia Sidney almost make this predictable comic-book thriller worth watching, but it's too poor to be a passable horror film and not bad enough to be funny. Obviously made for television, this tame monster movie is a low-priority rent at best.

1977 100 minutes

SOLE SURVIVOR

DIRECTOR: Thom Eberhardt
CAST: Anita Skinner, Kurt Johnson, Robin Davidson, Caren Larkey

A gory remake of a fine English suspense thriller of the same title —about the lone survivor of an airplane crash, haunted by the ghosts of those who died in the tragedy. A psychic tries to help this haunted woman by keeping the ghosts from killing her. Although there are some chills, this version pales in comparison to its predecessor. Fans of the supernatural will undoubtedly find this film entertaining, but you'd be better off tracking down the original with Robert Powell and Jenny Agutter. Rated R for sexual situations and violence.

1985 85 minutes

SON OF BLOB (BEWARE! THE BLOB)

DIRECTOR: Larry Hagman
CAST: Robert Walker, Richard Stahl, Godfrey Cambridge,

Carol Lynley, Larry Hagman, Cindy Williams, Shelley Berman, Marlene Clark, Gerrit Graham, Dick Van Patten

Larry Hagman made this sequel to *The Blob* in his low period between "I Dream of Jeannie" and "Dallas." It looks like he just got some friends together and decided to have some fun. The result is rather lame, but so was the original. Check out the opening titles, though . . . very strange. Rated PG.

1972 88 minutes

SON OF GODZILLA

★★

DIRECTOR: Jun Fukuda

CAST: Tadao Takashima, Akira Kubo, Bibari Maeda, Kenji Sahara

Juvenile production has the cute offspring of one of Japan's biggest stars taking on all sorts of crazy-looking monsters, with a little help from Dad. Good special effects and miniature sets make this at least watchable, but the story is just too goofy for its own good. Recommended viewing age: 2 and under. Rated PG.

1969 86 minutes

SON OF KONG, THE

★★½

DIRECTOR: Ernest B. Schoedsack

CAST: Robert Armstrong, Helen Mack, Victor Wong, John Marston, Frank Reicher, Lee Kohlmar

To cash in on the phenomenal success of *King Kong*, the producers hastily rushed this sequel into production using virtually the same cast and crew. This time out, Carl Denham (Robert Armstrong) returns to Skull Island in search of a lost treasure only to find King Kong's easygoing son trapped in a pool of quicksand. Denham saves the twelve-foot albino gorilla, who becomes his protector, and they continue the search together. Considering the pace at which this kiddy-oriented film was produced, the results are quite good. The special effects of Willis O'Brien are first-rate, as always, the acting is fine; but the script is weak and contains too much silliness.

1933 B & W 70 minutes

SORRY, WRONG NUMBER

★★★★

DIRECTOR: Anatole Litvak

CAST: Barbara Stanwyck, Burt Lancaster, Wendell Corey, Ed Begley Sr., Ann Richards

Slick cinema adaptation, by the author herself, of Lucille Fletcher's famed radio drama. Barbara Stanwyck is superb—and received an Oscar nomination—as an invalid who, due to those "crossed wires" so beloved in fiction, overhears two men plotting the murder of a woman. Gradually Stanwyck realizes that she is the target. Burt Lancaster is fine as her spineless husband. The bulk of the story takes place via imaginative flashbacks, so pay attention. Great finale.

1948 B & W 89 minutes

SPASMS

DIRECTOR: William Fruet

CAST: Peter Fonda, Oliver Reed, Kerrie Keane, Al Waxman, Marilyn Lightstone, George Bloomfield

An ancient snake monster transforms a number of people into mutants in this dud. How many of these lame, cheap, and trashy horror films are they gonna make? Forget it. Rated R.

1982 92 minutes

SPECIAL EFFECTS

★

DIRECTOR: Larry Cohen

CAST: Zoe Tamerlis, Eric Bogosian, Brad Rum, Kevin O'Connor

Low-budget, rather sick horror film about a film director (Eric Bogosian) who, in a fit of rage, murders a would-be actress (Zoe Tamerlis) and attempts to pin the rap on her holier-than-thou husband (Brad Rum). The director commits the act because his victim happens to mention his failure with a big special-effects picture. Writer-director Larry Cohen made a film called *Q*, which had special effects and did not get much box-office play (although it is entertaining). One can understand, therefore, where Cohen got the idea, but not why he made such an ugly, repulsive film. The acting—except by Kevin O'Connor as a starstruck cop—is poor, and the photography very grainy and dark. Only for Cohen fans. Unrated, the film has nudity and violence.

1984 90 minutes

SPELLBOUND

★★★★

DIRECTOR: Alfred Hitchcock
CAST: Ingrid Bergman, Gregory Peck, Leo G. Carroll, John Emery, Michael Chekhov, Wallace Ford, Rhonda Fleming, Bill Goodwin

There is little we can say about the plot of *Spellbound* without giving away any of the suspense in this Alfred Hitchcock thriller. Hitchcock said in his usual, understated manner that *Spellbound* "is just another manhunt story wrapped up in pseudo-psychoanalysis." The story is more than just another manhunt story; of that we can assure you. We can divulge that Ingrid Bergman plays the psychiatrist, Gregory Peck is the patient, and Salvador Dalí provides the nightmare sequences. The eerie musical score heightened the drama and won an Oscar for Miklos Rozsa.

1945 B & W 111 minutes

SPHINX

★★

DIRECTOR: Franklin J. Schaffner
CAST: Lesley-Anne Down, Frank Langella, Maurice Ronet, John Gielgud

This is a watchable film . . . but not a good one. Taken from the tedious novel by Robin Cook (*Coma*), it concerns the plight of an Egyptologist (Lesley-Anne Down) who inadvertently runs afoul of the underworld. Directed by Franklin J. Schaffner (*Patton*), this movie has a few suspenseful moments, but because of a ridiculously contrived plot, the best we can say about it is that it's better than the book. Rated PG.

1981 117 minutes

SPIRAL STAIRCASE, THE

★★★★

DIRECTOR: Robert Siodmak
CAST: George Brent, Dorothy McGuire, Ethel Barrymore, Kent Smith, Elsa Lanchester, Sara Allgood

Dorothy McGuire gives what some call the performance of her career as a mute servant in a hackle-raising household harboring a killer. Watch this one late at night, but not alone.

1946 B & W 83 minutes

SPIRIT OF THE DEAD

★★★½

DIRECTOR: Peter Newbrook
CAST: Robert Stephens, Robert Powell, Jane Lapotaire

Originally titled *The Asphyx*, slightly edited for videocassette. Interesting tale of a scientist who discovers the spirit of death possessed by all creatures. If the spirit is trapped, its owner becomes immortal. Well-made British film with sincere performances. Rated PG for mild violence.

1972 82 minutes

SPLATTER UNIVERSITY

DIRECTOR: Richard W. Haris
CAST: Francine Forbes, Ric Randig, Dick Biel, Suzy Collins

Typical slasher film featuring students having sex and then getting hacked to pieces. The school halls run red enough to thrill any splatter fan. Those who don't care for exploitative violence, or have weak stomachs, will more than likely be offended. Rated R for profanity, brief nudity, and violence.

1985 78 minutes

SQUIRM

DIRECTOR: Jeff Lieberman
CAST: Don Scardino, Patricia Pearcy

Ugly, disgusting horror film has hordes of killer worms attacking a small town. Only serves to nauseate. Rated PG.

1976 92 minutes

STAGE FRIGHT

DIRECTOR: Alfred Hitchcock
CAST: Marlene Dietrich, Jane Wyman, Michael Wilding, Alastair Sim, Richard Todd, Kay Walsh, Patricia Hitchcock

Master director Alfred Hitchcock cheats with this one, the only time he deliberately misleads his audience. As a result, the drama loses most of its impact at the climax. Drama student Jane Wyman spies on actress Marlene Dietrich to prove she murdered her husband. Alastair Sim steals his moments as Wyman's protective parent, but most of the other moments go to the hypnotic Dietrich. Watch for Patricia Hitchcock (yes, the director's daughter) in a small, but very pleasant, part.

1950 B & W 110 minutes

STANLEY

DIRECTOR: William Grefe
CAST: Chris Robinson, Alex Rocco, Susan Carroll, Steve Alaimo

A crazy Vietnam vet (Chris Robinson) uses an army of deadly snakes to destroy his enemies in this watchable, though rather grim, horror yarn. Rated PG for violence and unpleasant situations.

1972 106 minutes

STEPFATHER, THE

★★★★

DIRECTOR: Joseph Ruben
CAST: Terry O'Quinn, Shelley Hack, Jill Schoelen, Charles Lanyer, Stephen Shellen

In the 1950s and 1960s, television shows like *Father Knows Best* and the *Donna Reed Show* portrayed a kind of squeaky-clean American life where any problem could be solved in thirty minutes. The title character in this film firmly believes in that way of living. In fact, Jerry Blake (Terry O'Quinn) is so relentlessly cheerful that his stepdaughter, Stephanie Maine (Jill Schoelen), complains to a friend, "It's just like living with Ward Cleaver." Little does she know that the accent should be on the cleaver. Jerry, you see, has one character flaw: He's a raving maniac. If the members of his family do not live up to his expectations, he kills them and moves on to a new set of "loved ones." Suspense novelist Donald E. Westlake adds some nice—and welcome—touches of dark humor to the story by Carolyn Lefcourt and Brian Garfield, which was partly based on a true story. The result is a thriller of a chiller. Rated R for violence, profanity, and brief nudity.

1987 90 minutes

STEPHEN KING'S NIGHT SHIFT COLLECTION

★

DIRECTORS: Frank Durabont, Jeffrey C. Schiro

CAST: Michael Cornelison, Dee Croxton, Brion Libby, Michael Reid, Bert Linder, Mindy Silverman

In this so-called collection, featuring two short-story adaptations from Stephen King's book, *Night Shift*, we see again how hard it is to bring King's writing to the screen. Not that these filmmakers don't try. In fact, they come close in the first story, "The Lady in the Room," about a son and his terminally ill mother coming to terms with her impending death. This story will surely choke you up, if not bring tears to your eyes. However, in the second feature, director Schiro ruins one of King's most frightening stories, "The Boogey Man." In this, the Boogey Man is blamed for the crib deaths and fatal accidents that happen to children. They've rewritten, rather than adapted, this once horrifying yarn. It has poor acting and poor direction. Although this film has its moments, do yourself a favor: check *Night Shift* out of the library and *read* the stories.

1986 61 minutes

STILL OF THE NIGHT

★★★½

DIRECTOR: Robert Benton

CAST: Roy Scheider, Meryl Streep, Jessica Tandy, Joe Grifasi, Sara Botsford

In this well-crafted thriller by writer-director Robert Benton (*Kramer vs. Kramer*), a psychiatrist (Roy Scheider) falls in love with an art curator (Meryl Streep) who may have killed one of his patients and may be after him next. If you like being scared out of your wits, you won't want to miss it. Rated PG for violence and adult themes.

1982 91 minutes

STRAIT-JACKET

★★★½

DIRECTOR: William Castle

CAST: Joan Crawford, Diane Baker, Leif Erickson, George Kennedy

Chilling vehicle for Joan Crawford as a convicted axe murderess returning home after twenty years in an insane asylum, where it appears she was restored to sanity. But was she? Genuinely frightening film features one of Joan's most powerful, as well as restrained, performances. George Kennedy is almost as good in an early role as a farm hand.

1964 B & W 89 minutes

STRANGE BEHAVIOR

★★★½

DIRECTOR: Michael Laughlin

CAST: Michael Murphy, Marc McClure, Dan Shor, Fiona Lewis, Louise Fletcher, Arthur Dignam

Michael Murphy stars as the small-town police chief, John Brady, of Galesburg, Illinois, who suddenly finds himself inundated by unexplained knife murders. At least one of the murders was committed by the mild-mannered Oliver (Marc McClure), close friend of Brady's son, Pete (Dan Shor). But why? Perhaps it's the result of his participation in the experiments conducted by the Galesburg College Psychology Department, presided over by Professor Gwen Parkinson (Fiona Lewis). He's been getting a hundred dollars a day to participate in a series of secret experiments. To Pete, this sounds like a great way to raise money for his college tuition. And the terror builds. In all, this release is a true treat for horror movie fans and other viewers with a yen for something spooky. Rated R.

1981 98 minutes

STRANGENESS, THE

★

DIRECTOR: David Michael Hillman
CAST: Dan Lunham, Terri Berland

Extremely low-budget horror film shot mostly in the dark. The Gold Spike Mine is haunted by a creature from down deep inside the earth. Who of the wimpish cast will dare to challenge this "strangeness?" This film is not worth watching to find out. Unrated.

1985 90 minutes

STRANGER, THE

★★★★

DIRECTOR: Orson Welles
CAST: Orson Welles, Edward G. Robinson, Loretta Young, Richard Long, Martha Wentworth

Nazi war criminal (Orson Welles) assumes a new identity in a Midwestern town following World War II, unaware that a government agent (Edward G. Robinson) is tailing him. Extremely well done film, holds the viewer's interest from start to finish.

1946 B & W 95 minutes

STRANGER IS WATCHING, A

★

DIRECTOR: Sean S. Cunningham
CAST: Kate Mulgrew, Rip Torn, James Naughton, Shawn Von Schreiber

A psychotic killer kidnaps two young ladies and keeps them prisoner in the catacombs beneath Grand Central Station. This commuter's nightmare is directed by Sean S. Cunningham (*Friday the 13th*) and is an ugly, dimly lit suspenser for horror buffs only. Rated R.

1982 92 minutes

STRANGERS ON A TRAIN

★★★★★

DIRECTOR: Alfred Hitchcock
CAST: Farley Granger, Robert Walker, Ruth Roman, Leo G. Carroll, Patricia Hitchcock, Marion Lorne

Imagine yourself on a train, bus, or some other form of public transport. An eccentric stranger approaches you and proposes to commit a heinous crime for you, a crime you may have secretly been wishing for. In exchange you must commit a crime for him. This is the situation that confronts a tennis pro (Farley Granger) in what remains today one of the most discussed and analyzed of all of Alfred Hitchcock's films. *Strangers on a Train* was made during the height of Hitchcock's most creative period, the early 1950s. When you add a marvelous performance by Robert Walker as the stranger, you have one of the most satisfying Hitchcock thrillers ever.

1951 B & W 101 minutes

STRANGLER OF THE SWAMP

★★

DIRECTOR: Frank Wisbar
CAST: Rosemary La Planche, Robert Barrat, Blake Edwards, Charles Middleton, Effie Parnell, Frank Conlan, Nolan Leary

Ghostly revenge story about a ferry man who was unjustly lynched and who hangs his murderers one by one is atmospheric and eerie but bogged down by a cheap budget and an unnecessary love story. Future director Blake Edwards plays one of the young lovers and Robert Barrat lends his considerable presence to this impoverished production, but it is serial star Charles Middleton as the ghost who steals the show. Considered a minor classic among fantasy fans, this low-budget thriller has many interesting elements.

1946 B & W 60 minutes

STRAW DOGS

★★★★

DIRECTOR: Sam Peckinpah

CAST: Dustin Hoffman, Susan George, Peter Vaughn, T. P. McKenna, Peter Arne, David Warner

An American intellectual mathematician (played brilliantly by Dustin Hoffman) takes a wife (Susan George) and returns to her ancestral village on the coast of England. Her former boyfriends become jealous, resentful, and desirous of her. She taunts them with her wealth and power, and soon she is viciously raped. When Hoffman takes in the local village idiot who is suspected of killing and molesting a young girl, their house is put under siege by the incensed locals. He defends his house with a ferocity. The highly charged sequences of carnage in the conclusion make this a controversial film. Rated R.

1971 113 minutes

STUDENT BODIES

★★½

DIRECTOR: Mickey Rose

CAST: Kristin Ritter, Matthew Goldsby, Richard Brando, Joe Flood, Joe Talarowski

This comedy-horror release has something extra, because it is a parody of the blood-and-guts horror films. Rated R.

1981 86 minutes

STUFF, THE

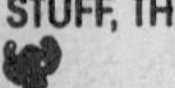

DIRECTOR: Larry Cohen

CAST: Michael Moriarty, Andrea Marcovicci, Garrett Morris, Paul Sorvino, Danny Aiello

A scrumptious, creamy dessert devours from within all those who eat it in this not funny and not scary horror-comedy. It's as flat as month-old whipped cream and just as enjoyable. Rated R for gore and profanity.

1985 93 minutes

SUSPICION

★★★★

DIRECTOR: Alfred Hitchcock

CAST: Joan Fontaine, Cary Grant, Cedric Hardwicke, Nigel Bruce, May Whitty, Isabel Jeans

Alfred Hitchcock had a problem. He had an excellent script: A timid woman gradually unnerved by apprehension. Bits of evidence lead her to believe that her charming husband is a killer and that she is the intended victim. He had the perfect "timid woman," Joan Fontaine, who played a similar role in *Rebecca* and eventually won a Best Actress Oscar for her performance in *Suspicion*. He had the most charming of all Hollywood actors, Cary Grant. So what's the problem? Studio executives would not think of allowing their charming Cary to play a killer. How Hitchcock effectively managed to make Grant threatening, yet keep his "image" intact and still build up the subtle suspense for which he is famous, is here for you to see.

1941 B & W 99 minutes

SVENGALI

★★★★

DIRECTOR: Archie Mayo

CAST: John Barrymore, Marian Marsh, Donald Crisp, Carmel Myers, Bramwell Fletcher

In case you don't know, John Barrymore was Drew Barrymore's grandfather. This film is adapted from the George Du Maurier novel that put Svengali into the language as one who controls another. Barrymore, a fine stage actor and excellent in his early films, of which this is a notable example, plays Svengali, a demonic artist obsessed with Trilby, a young artist's model. Under his hynotic influence, she becomes a singer who obeys his every command. John Barrymore's make-up is grotesque, his voice magnificent. Bizarre sets and arresting visual effects make this a surrealistic delight.

1931 B & W 76 minutes

SWAMP THING

★½

DIRECTOR: Wes Craven
CAST: Louis Jourdan, Adrienne Barbeau, Ray Wise, David Hess, Nicholas Worth

Kids will love this movie, about a monster-hero—part plant, part scientist—who takes on a super-villain (Louis Jourdan) and saves heroine Adrienne Barbeau. But adults will no doubt find it too corny and sloppily made for their tastes. *Swamp Thing* was based on the popular 1972 comic book of the same name. Rated PG, it has some tomato-paste violence and brief nudity.

1982 91 minutes

SWARM, THE

DIRECTOR: Irwin Allen
CAST: Michael Caine, Katharine Ross, Richard Widmark, Henry Fonda, Olivia De Havilland, Richard Chamberlain, Fred MacMurray

"Irwin Allen is still 'Lost in Space,'" science-fiction author Ray Bradbury once said of the notorious television and film producer who also fathered *The Poseidon Adventure* and *The Towering Inferno*. And there is no better proof of Allen's ineptitude than this dreadful, self-directed killer-bee ripoff of Alfred Hitchcock's *The Birds*. It wastes the talents of a top-flight cast. Rated PG.

1978 116 minutes

TALES FROM THE CRYPT

★★★½

DIRECTOR: Freddie Francis
CAST: Peter Cushing, Joan Collins, Ralph Richardson

Excellent anthology has five people gathered in a mysterious cave where the keeper (Ralph Richardson) foretells their futures, one by one, in gruesome fashion. Director Freddie Francis keeps things moving at a brisk pace, and the performances are uniformly fine, most notably Peter Cushing's in one of the better segments—*Poetic Justice*. Don't miss it. Rated PG.

1972 92 minutes

TALES OF TERROR

★★★

DIRECTOR: Roger Corman
CAST: Vincent Price, Basil Rathbone, Peter Lorre, Debra Paget

An uneven anthology of horror stories adapted from the works of Edgar Allan Poe. Directed by cult favorite Roger Corman, it does have a few moments.

1962 90 minutes

TARGETS

★★★★★

DIRECTOR: Peter Bogdanovich
CAST: Tim O'Kelly, Boris Karloff, Nancy Hsueh, James Brown, Peter Bogdanovich

The stunning film-making debut of critic-turned-director Peter Bogdanovich juxtaposes real-life terror, in the form of an unhinged mass murderer (Tim O'Kelly), with its comparatively subdued and safe screen counterpart, as represented by the scare films of Byron Orlock (Boris Karloff in a brilliant final bow). This rarely seen release is nothing short of a masterpiece. Rated PG.

1968 90 minutes

TEEN WOLF

★

DIRECTOR: Rod Daniel

CAST: Michael J. Fox, James Hampton, Scott Paulin, Susan Ursitti, Jerry Levine

Pitifully bad film about a teenager (Michael J. Fox) who discovers he has the ability to change into a werewolf, making him a hit at high school when he carries their losing basketball team to the championships. It's the same old story, even considering the "wolf" angle, with the usual cliché-ridden plot and "be yourself" message at the end. Boring and tiresome. Rated PG for mild language.

1985 95 minutes

TENANT, THE

★★★

DIRECTOR: Roman Polanski

CAST: Roman Polanski, Melvyn Douglas, Shelley Winters

Roman Polanski is superb in this flawed cryptic thriller about a bumbling Polish expatriate in France who leases an apartment owned previously by a young woman who committed suicide. Increasingly, Polanski believes the apartment's tenants conspired demonically to destroy the woman and are attempting to do the same to him. Supporting are Melvyn Douglas as the building's owner and Shelley Winters as the irascible concierge. Rated R.

1976 125 minutes

TENTACLES

DIRECTOR: Ovidio Assonitis (Oliver Hellman)

CAST: John Huston, Shelley Winters, Henry Fonda, Bo Hopkins, Cesare Danova

Rotten monster movie from Italy about a phony-looking octopus attacking and devouring some famous Hollywood stars, who should all be ashamed of themselves for appearing in this sleaze. Unbelievably poor. You want an octopus movie? Try *It Came from Beneath the Sea*. Rated PG.

1977 90 minutes

TERMINAL CHOICE

★★

DIRECTOR: Sheldon Larry

CAST: Joe Spano, Diane Venora, David McCallum, Robert Joy, Don Francks, Nicholas Campbell, Ellen Barkin

If it's blood you want, you'll get your money's worth with this one—by the gallons! There's some real tension in this film about a hospital that has a staff that secretly bets on the mortality of its patients—not exactly family entertainment. And when the hero of the day is an alcoholic doctor who has a history of accidentally killing patients by performing unnecessary operations under the influence, well, you know the cast of characters aren't a bunch of Ben Caseys. Rated R for sex, nudity, language, and plenty o'gore.

1984 98 minutes

TERMINAL MAN, THE

★★

DIRECTOR: Mike Hodges

CAST: George Segal, Joan Hackett, Jill Clayburgh

A dreary adaptation of the crackling novel by Michael Crichton, although George Segal tries hard to improve the film's quality. He stars as a paranoid psychotic who undergoes experimental surgery designed to quell his violent impulses; unfortunately (and quite predictably), he becomes even worse. What's missing is the credibility that Crichton himself, in films he later directed, manages to inject into a story of this type. Most of the cast doesn't seem to believe in what's taking place; as a result, we don't, either. Rated R for violence.

1974 104 minutes

TERROR, THE

DIRECTOR: Roger Corman
CAST: Boris Karloff, Jack Nicholson, Sandra Knight

This is an incomprehensible sludge of mismatched horror scenes even Boris Karloff can't save, but he does better than a miscast Jack Nicholson in this forgettable Roger Corman loser, which was shot in three days and shows it.

1963 81 minutes

TERROR AT THE RED WOLF INN

★★★

DIRECTOR: Bud Townsend
CAST: Linda Gillin, Arthur Space, John Neilson, Mary Jackson, Michael Macready

This is a sometimes ghoulishly funny horror comedy about a college student who is chosen as the winner of a free vacation at an inn owned by a sweet old couple. She is delighted with how they pamper her and serve up huge, delicious meals three times a day. What she doesn't know is the main course at these meals is the previous winner of the "contest" and that she is simply being fattened up for the kill. Not all of the film's scenes work, but we guarantee it will give you the willies and the sillies. Rated R. (Also known as *The Folks at the Red Wolf Inn* and *Terror House*.)

1972 98 minutes

TERROR IN THE AISLES

★★★

DIRECTOR: Andrew Kuehn
CAST: Donald Pleasence, Nancy Allen

Donald Pleasence (*Halloween*) and Nancy Allen (*Carrie*) host this basically enjoyable compilation film of the most graphic scenes from seventy-five horror films. Rated R for violence, profanity, nudity, and suggested sex.

1984 82 minutes

TERROR IN THE HAUNTED HOUSE

★★★

DIRECTOR: Harold Daniels
CAST: Gerald Mohr, Cathy O'Donnell

Although the title of this movie makes it sound as if it's a horror film, it is actually a psychological thriller along the Hitchcock line. It is the story of a young newlywed woman who has a recurring nightmare about a house she has never seen. She fears that something in the attic will kill her. The terror starts when her new husband takes her from Switzerland, where she has been since childhood, to the United States and . . . the house in her horrid dream. This video is an average 1950s B movie with a somewhat predictable outcome and no real terror for the viewer. The added "Psycho-Rama" effects are more of an annoyance than anything else.

1958 90 minutes

TERROR IN THE WAX MUSEUM

★

DIRECTOR: Georg Fenady
CAST: Ray Milland, Broderick Crawford, Elsa Lanchester, Maurice Evans, Shani Wallis, John Carradine, Louis Hayward, Patric Knowles

The all-star cast from yesteryear looks like a sort of Hollywood wax museum. Their fans will suffer through this unsuspenseful murder mystery. It belongs in a museum—of missed opportunities. With a cast like this, it should have at least been fun. Rated PG.

1973 93 minutes

TERROR OF MECHAGODZILLA

★★

DIRECTOR: Ishiro Honda
CAST: Katsuhiko Sasaki, Tomoko Ai

Another outlandish Godzilla epic from the 1970s with the big guy battling his own robot double, Mechagodzilla. Nothing special, but a lot of flashy effects and explosions help to make this an adequate time-passer, and, as always, the kids will love it. Rated G.

1978 89 minutes

TERROR ON THE 40TH FLOOR

★★

DIRECTOR: Jerry Jameson
CAST: John Forsythe, Joseph Campanella, Don Meredith

A typical disaster film, this deals with a skyscraper fire that traps a group of office workers on the top floor. In the face of impending death, they recount their lives. Unrated.

1974 100 minutes

TEXAS CHAINSAW MASSACRE, THE

★★½

DIRECTOR: Tobe Hooper
CAST: Marilyn Burns, Gunnar Hansen, Ed Neal

This, the first film about a cannibalistic maniac by horror specialist Tobe Hooper (*Funhouse*), went pretty much unnoticed in its original release. That's probably because it sounds like the run-of-the-mill drive-in exploitation fare. While it was made on a very low budget, it nevertheless has been hailed as a ground-breaking genre work by critics and film buffs and became a cult classic. Be forewarned if you intend to see it: you need a strong stomach. Rated R for blood and gore.

1974 83 minutes

TEXAS CHAINSAW MASSACRE 2, THE

★★★

DIRECTOR: Tobe Hooper
CAST: Dennis Hopper, Caroline Williams, Jim Siedow, Bill Johnson, Phil Keller

Leatherface is back! In fact, so is most of the family in this maniacal sequel to *The Texas Chainsaw Massacre*. Dennis Hopper stars as a retired lawman out to avenge the gruesome murder of his nephew, and Caroline Williams plays the disc jockey who helps him locate the butchers. Once they do, this film becomes an unrelenting exercise in stark terror and very black comedy, and in scene after scene it asks: can you take it? Unrated, but loaded with repulsive gore. Recommended for those with strong stomachs.

1986 112 minutes

THEATER OF BLOOD

★★★★

DIRECTOR: Douglas Hickox
CAST: Vincent Price, Diana Rigg, Robert Morley

Deliciously morbid horror-comedy about a Shakespearean actor (Vincent Price) who, angered by the thrashing he receives from a series of critics, decides to kill them in uniquely outlandish ways. He turns to the Bard for inspiration, and each perceived foe is eliminated in a manner drawn from one of Shakespeare's plays, such as losing a critical "pound of flesh." Although similar in tone to his two *Dr. Phibes* films, Price benefits here from better production values. We hope he finds *this* review sufficiently kind, as several plays still remain unused... Rated R for violence.

1973 104 minutes

THEATRE OF DEATH

★★½

DIRECTOR: Samuel Gallu

CAST: Christopher Lee, Julian Glover, Lelia Goldoni, Jenny Till

Mildly interesting mystery succeeds mainly due to Christopher Lee's assured performance and some well-timed scares as a series of gruesome murders is committed in Paris with an apparent connection to the local theater company. Good title sequence deserves mention.

1967 90 minutes

THEY SAVED HITLER'S BRAIN

½

DIRECTOR: David Bradley

CAST: Walter Stocker, Audrey Caire, Carlos Rivas, John Holland, Marshall Reed, Nestor Paiva, Dani Lynn

This bargain-basement bomb is actually a used movie since a major portion of it was lifted from an entirely different film made ten years earlier, edited together with new footage and given a snappy new title to attract the drive-in crowd. The story of a girl whose pursuit of her kidnapped scientist father leads her to an island teeming with Nazis is secondary to the question of *why* anybody would bother to save Hitler's brain and why anyone in their right mind would get involved in a mess like this. This film has a certain reputation among bad film aficionados, but if you are looking for a straight horror film or some sort of a war film, you're out of luck. Fun to watch if you know what you're getting into.

1963 B & W minutes

THIRD MAN, THE

★★★★★

DIRECTOR: Carol Reed

CAST: Joseph Cotten, Orson Welles, Alida Valli, Trevor Howard

Considered by many to be the greatest suspense film of all time, this classic inevitably turns up on every best-film list. It rivals any Hitchcock thriller as being the ultimate masterpiece of film suspense. A writer (Joseph Cotten) discovers an old friend he thought dead to be the head of a vicious European black market organization. Unfortunately for him, that information makes him a marked man.

1949 B & W 104 minutes

13 GHOSTS

★★★

DIRECTOR: William Castle

CAST: Charles Herbert, Donald Woods, Martin Milner, Rosemary DeCamp, Jo Morrow, Margaret Hamilton

Light-hearted horror tale of an average family inheriting a haunted house complete with a creepy old housekeeper (Margaret Hamilton) who may also be a witch, and a secret fortune hidden somewhere in the place. William Castle directs with his customary style and flair. Pretty neat.

1960 B & W 88 minutes

THIRTY-NINE STEPS, THE

★★★★★

DIRECTOR: Alfred Hitchcock

CAST: Robert Donat, Madeleine Carroll, Lucie Mannheim

If one film could be held responsible for the career of Alfred Hitchcock, it's *The Thirty-nine Steps*. Hitchcock's early directing assignments were spent making B movies in England. He was assigned to direct what was intended to be another simple, low-budget spy-chase thriller, but to give Hitchcock a thriller was like giving Rembrandt a paintbrush. Using the style and technique that were to make him famous, he gained immediate audience sympathy for the plight of his central character, an innocent Canadian (Robert Donat) who while visiting England is implicated in the theft of national secrets and murder. The result was a big hit.

1935 B & W 87 minutes

THREAT, THE

★★★

DIRECTOR: Felix Feist

CAST: Charles McGraw, Michael O'Shea, Frank Conroy, Virginia Grey, Julie Bishop, Robert Shayne, Anthony Caruso, Don McGuire, Frank Richards

This underrated suspense feature packs every minute with tension as vengeance-minded Charles McGraw escapes from jail and kidnaps the police detective and district attorney as well as snatches a singer he thinks may have told on him for good measure. The police put the pressure on the kidnapper and he puts the squeze on his captives.

1949 B & W 65 minutes

TICKET OF LEAVE MAN, THE

★★

DIRECTOR: George King

CAST: Tod Slaughter, John Warwick, Marjorie Taylor

British horror star Tod Slaughter gleefully plays a maniacal killer who swindles rich philanthropists with a phony charity organization he has established. Slaughter, the original Sweeney Todd of the cinema, singlehandedly presided as Great Britain's unofficial hobgoblin during the 1930s and early 1940s. The majority of his films have been unavailable for years in America.

1937 B & W 71 minutes

TIGHTROPE

★★★★★

DIRECTOR: Richard Tuggle

CAST: Clint Eastwood, Genevieve Bujold, Dan Hedaya, Alison Eastwood, Jennifer Beck

A terrific, taut suspense thriller, this ranks with the best films in the genre. Written and directed by Richard Tuggle, *Tightrope* casts Clint Eastwood as Wes Block, homicide inspector for the New Orleans Police Department. His latest assignment is to track down a Jack the Ripper–style sex-murderer. This case hits disturbingly close to home in more ways than one. Rated R for violence, profanity, and sex.

1984 115 minutes

TIME WALKER

DIRECTOR: Tom Kennedy

CAST: Ben Murphy, Nina Axelrod, Kevin Brophy, Shari Belafonte-Harper

Imagine sitting through a movie that isn't all that great to begin with and, as the story seems to be building up to a pretty good climax, the words "To Be Continued" flash on the screen. Outrageous, you say? Well, that's exactly what happens at the end of this horror ripoff, which features Ben Murphy (*The Winds of War*) as an Egyptologist who accidentally brings an ancient mummy back to life. Avoid it. Rated PG for nudity, profanity, and violence.

1982 83 minutes

TO ALL A GOOD NIGHT

★★

DIRECTOR: David Hess

CAST: Jennifer Runyon, Forrest Swenson, Linda Gentille, William Lauer

In this typical slasher film, a group of young teen-age girls gets away from supervision, and the mad killer shows up with a sharp weapon. There is some build-up of terror and suspense. The camera work is good and the timing fair, adding up to a slightly above average film of its genre. Rated R; has nudity, violence, and profanity.

1983 90 minutes

TO CATCH A KING

★★

DIRECTOR: Clive Donner

CAST: Robert Wagner, Teri Garr, Horst Janson, Barbara Parkins

Made-for-cable spy thriller that fails to live up to its promising premise. In 1940, cunning Nazis plot to kidnap the Duke and Duchess of Windsor during the romantic couple's respite in Lisbon. Robert Wagner plays a café owner, a more debonair version of *Casablanca*'s Rick. Teri Garr is a nightclub singer. The film is neither convincing nor exciting.

1984 113 minutes

TO CATCH A THIEF

★★★★

DIRECTOR: Alfred Hitchcock

CAST: Cary Grant, Grace Kelly, John Williams, Jessie Royce Landis

John Robie (Cary Grant) is a retired cat burglar living in France in peaceful seclusion. When a sudden rash of jewel thefts hit the Riviera, he is naturally blamed. He sets out to clear himself, and the fun begins. This is certainly one of director Alfred Hitchcock's most amusing, if not one of his most gripping, films. The unbounded charm of Cary Grant and his co-star, Grace Kelly, coupled with Hitchcock's unique treatment of suspense, make the film consistently appealing.

1955 103 minutes

TO KILL A CLOWN

★

DIRECTOR: George Bloomfield

CAST: Alan Alda, Blythe Danner, Heath Lambert

A husband (Heath Lambert) and wife (Blythe Danner) move from the big city to a remote island in an effort to save their marriage. Their new landlord (Alan Alda) appears at first to be a pleasant sort of fellow, but as time goes on, he is revealed to be a maniac bent on their destruction. *To Kill a Clown* is an unnecessarily depressing and essentially uninvolving drama. Rated R for violence and profanity.

1983 82 minutes

TO THE DEVIL, A DAUGHTER

★★★½

DIRECTOR: Peter Sykes

CAST: Richard Widmark, Christopher Lee, Honor Blackman, Denholm Elliott, Michael Goodliffe, Eva Maria Meinke, Nastassja Kinski

Dennis Wheatley wrote a number of books on the occult. This film was based on one of them, and it is his influence that raises this above the average thriller. Director Peter Sykes has also left some of the horror to the imagination. This commendable practice has become a rarity in recent years as emphasis has been placed on gory, explicit death scenes. Another plus is in the acting. Richard Widmark gives an understated and effective performance as occult novelist John Verney, who finds himself pitted against real satanists. As the leader of the opposition, Christopher Lee is once again brilliantly menacing. Nastassja Kinski is appealingly waifish as the victim protégée of the cult. Rated R, the film contains nudity, profanity, and violence in small quantities.

1976 95 minutes

TOMB OF LIGEIA

★★★

DIRECTOR: Roger Corman

CAST: Vincent Price, Elizabeth Shepherd, John Westbrook, Oliver Johnson

A grieving widower is driven to madness by the curse of his dead wife. Filmed in England, this was Roger Corman's final Poe-inspired movie. The most subtle and atmospheric entry in the series, it was photographed by Nicolas Roeg on sets left over from *Becket*. The screenplay was by Robert Towne, who went on to write *Chinatown*.

1964 81 minutes

TOO SCARED TO SCREAM

DIRECTOR: Tony Lo Bianco

CAST: Mike Connors, Anne Archer, Leon Isaac Kennedy, Ian McShane

Pathetic "demented killer" movie features *Mannix*'s Mike Connors as a grizzled New York detective on the trail of a psychopath who's knocking off tenants at a posh Manhattan apartment building. No suspense, just tedium, in a film laced with bad acting, writing, photography, etc. Director Tony Lo Bianco should stick to acting. Rated R for nudity and gore.

1982 104 minutes

TOPAZ

★★★

DIRECTOR: Alfred Hitchcock

CAST: John Forsythe, Frederick Stafford, Dany Robin, John Vernon

Medium-to-rare Hitchcock suspense thriller about cloak-and-dagger intrigue concerning Russian involvement in Cuba and infiltration of the French government. Constant shift of scene keeps viewers on their toes. Rated PG.

1969 127 minutes

TORMENT

★★

DIRECTORS: Samson Aslanian, John Hopkins

CAST: Taylor Gilbert, William Witt, Eve Brenner

This low-budget slasher film starts off slow and, if it weren't for one interesting plot twist halfway through, would be an exercise in boredom. The story revolves around a middle-aged man who becomes a psychotic killer when he is rejected by a younger woman. R for violence and gore.

1986 90 minutes

TORN CURTAIN

★★★

DIRECTOR: Alfred Hitchcock

CAST: Paul Newman, Julie Andrews, Lila Kedrova, David Opatoshu

This just-okay film was directed by Alfred Hitchcock in 1966. Paul Newman plays an American scientist posing as a defector, with Julie Andrews as his secretary/lover. Somehow we aren't moved by the action or the characters.

1966 128 minutes

TORTURE CHAMBER OF BARON BLOOD, THE

★★

DIRECTOR: Mario Bava

CAST: Joseph Cotten, Elke Sommer, Massimo Girotti, Rada Rassimov

Boring Italian production is basically nonsense as a long-dead nobleman (Joseph Cotten) is inadvertently restored to life, only to (naturally) embark on a horrendous killing spree. Can he be stopped? Worth watching for Mario Bava's unique directorial style, but you can skip the rest. Originally titled *Baron Blood*. Rated R.

1972 90 minutes

TORTURE GARDEN

★★★

DIRECTOR: Freddie Francis

CAST: Burgess Meredith, Jack Palance, Beverly Adams, Peter Cushing, Maurice Denham, Robert Hutton, Barbara Ewing

A group of patrons at a carnival sideshow has their possible futures exposed to them by a screwball barker (Burgess Meredith) who exclaims, "I've promised you horror... and I intend to keep that promise." Which he more than does in this frightening film laced with plenty of shocks, plot twists, and intense situations. The video transfer features superb color as well, though the soundtrack is muted. Rated PG.

1968 93 minutes

TOUCH OF EVIL

★★★★½

DIRECTOR: Orson Welles

CAST: Orson Welles, Charlton Heston, Marlene Dietrich, Janet Leigh, Zsa Zsa Gabor

In 1958, director-actor Orson Welles proved that he was still a film-making genius, with this dark and disturbing masterpiece about crime and corruption in a border town.

1958 B & W 93 minutes

TOURIST TRAP

★

DIRECTOR: David Schmoeller

CAST: Chuck Connors, Joan Van Ness, Jocelyn Jones, Tanya Roberts

Another in the endless stream of psycho-hack films with a lot of stupid unpaid actors wondering where all these life-size dummies in Chuck Connors's basement museum have come from. Some scary moments, and Connors carries a lethal axe. With Tanya Roberts in her pre-*Sheena* days. Rated R for violence, gore, nudity, and profanity.

1979 83 minutes

TOWN THAT DREADED SUNDOWN, THE

★★★½

DIRECTOR: Charles B. Pierce

CAST: Ben Johnson, Andrew Prine, Jim Citty, Dawn Wells, Robert Aquino, Bud Davis

The fact that *The Town that Dreaded Sundown* is based on actual events makes this effective little film all the more chilling. The story takes place in the year 1946 in the small Texas–Arkansas border town of Texarkana. It begins in documentary style, with a narrator describing the post–World War II atmosphere, but soon gets to the unsettling business of the Phantom, a killer who terrorized the locals. Rated R for violence.

1977 90 minutes

TOXIC AVENGER, THE

★★★

DIRECTORS: Michael Herz, Samuel Weil

CAST: Mitchell Cohen, Andree Miranda, Jennifer Baptist

Just another "nerdy pool attendant tossed into a tub of toxic waste becomes mutant crimefighter" picture. Actually, this low-budget horror spoof has a number of inspired moments. If you are looking for sick humor and creative bloodshed, press play and enjoy. But the fun is somewhat hampered by the movie's forced style and all-too-obvious attempt to be an instant cult film. Rated R for violence.

1985 100 minutes

TRAP, THE

★★★

DIRECTOR: Norman Panama

CAST: Richard Widmark, Lee J. Cobb, Earl Holliman, Tina Louise, Carl Benton Reid, Lorne Greene, Peter Baldwin

Fast pace and taut suspense mark this thriller about as fine a gaggle of fleeing gangsters as ever menaced the innocent inhabitants of a small California desert town. Don't expect any dull spots as the tension mounts and the safety valve lets go. This is edge-of-chair stuff. It was in films such as this that Richard Widmark made his name praisingly hissable. Lee J. Cobb is not exactly lovable, either.

1958 84 minutes

TRICK OR TREAT

★★

DIRECTOR: Charles Martin Smith

CAST: Marc Price, Tony Fields, Lisa Orgolini, Doug Savant, Elaine Joyce, Gene Simmons, Ozzy Osbourne

Perhaps it was inevitable that someone would make a horror film about the supposed satanic messages found in heavy metal rock music. While not a classic of the genre, *Trick or Treat* is both clever and funny. Unfortunately, most of the better moments occur during the first half, leaving little for the viewer to enjoy later on. Marc Price's performance is one of the film's pluses. He's believable as the "metal head" who wreaks revenge on his tormentors with the help of a rock star from hell. Rated R for profanity, nudity, suggested sex, and violence.

1986 97 minutes

TRILOGY OF TERROR

★★½

DIRECTOR: Dan Curtis

CAST: Karen Black, Robert Burton, John Karlen

Karen Black stars in this trio of horror stories, the best of which is the final episode, about an ancient Indian doll coming to life and stalking Black. It's often very frightening, and well worth wading through the first two tales. This was originally made as an ABC Movie of the Week.

1974 78 minutes

TWICE-TOLD TALES

★★

DIRECTOR: Sidney Salkow

CAST: Vincent Price, Sebastian Cabot, Joyce Taylor, Brett Halsey, Beverly Garland, Mari Blanchard

With all his usual feeling, Vincent Price lurks, leers, and hams his nefarious way through a trilogy of nineteenth-century novelist Nathaniel Hawthorne's most vivid horror stories, including *The House of the Seven Gables*.

1963 119 minutes

TWILIGHT ZONE—THE MOVIE

★★★

DIRECTORS: Steven Spielberg, John Landis, Joe Dante, George Miller

CAST: Vic Morrow, Scatman Crothers, Kathleen Quinlan, John Lithgow, Dan Aykroyd, Albert Brooks

A generally enjoyable tribute to the 1960s television series created by Rod Serling, this film, directed by Steven Spielberg (*E.T.*), John Landis (*Trading Places*), Joe Dante (*The Howling*), and George Miller (*Road Warrior*), is broken into four parts. In Landis's segment, a bigot (Vic Morrow) walks out of a neighborhood bar to become the victim of Nazis, the Ku Klux Klan, and U.S. troops in Vietnam. Spielberg helmed the next story, about a stranger (Scatman Crothers) who transforms the elderly in a retirement home into the young at heart. In Dante's, a schoolteacher (Kathleen Quinlan) encounters a boy with strange, frightening powers. Miller, however, brings us the best: a tale about a white-knuckled air traveler (John Lithgow) who sees a gremlin doing strange things on the wing of a jet. Rated PG.

1983 102 minutes

TWINS OF EVIL

★★★

DIRECTOR: John Hough

CAST: Peter Cushing, Madeleine and Mary Collinson, Luan Peters, Dennis Price

Playboy magazine's first twin Playmates, Madeleine and Mary Collinson, were tapped for this British Hammer Films horror entry about a good girl and her evil, blood-sucking sister. Peter Cushing adds class to what should in theory have been a forgettable exploitation film but provides surprisingly enjoyable entertainment for genre buffs. Rated R for nudity, violence, and gore.

1972 85 minutes

UNCANNY, THE

★

DIRECTOR: Denis Heroux

CAST: Peter Cushing, Ray Milland, Susan Penhaligon, Joan Greenwood, Donald Pleasence, Samantha Eggar, John Vernon

A paranoid writer tells three tales of cat-related horror. He believes felines are trying to take over the world. Judging from this film, they're trying to bore us to death. Rated R.

1977 88 minutes

UNEARTHLY, THE

DIRECTOR: Brooke L. Peters

CAST: John Carradine, Allison Hayes, Myron Healey, Sally Todd

Mad scientist John Carradine goes back into the lab to torture more innocent victims. The real sufferers, however, are not his human experiments but the video viewers unfortunate enough to watch this mess.

1957 73 minutes

UNION STATION

★★★

DIRECTOR: Rudolph Mate

CAST: William Holden, Nancy Olson, Allene Roberts, Barry Fitzgerald, Lyle Bettger, Jan Sterling, Ralph Sanford, Herbert Heyes

A big, bustling railroad terminal is the backdrop of this suspense-thriller centering on the manhunt that ensues following the kidnapping of a blind girl for ransom. William Holden is the hero, Lyle Bettger is the villain, Allene Roberts is the victim. The plot's tired, but ace cinematographer-turned-director Rudolph Mate keeps everything moving fast and frantic to a climax guaranteed to make hearts pound and palms sweat.

1950 B & W 80 minutes

UNSEEN, THE

DIRECTOR: Peter Foleg

CAST: Barbara Bach, Sidney Lassick, Stephen Furst

This awful horror film should remain unseen. Rated R.

1981 89 minutes

VAMP

★★★

DIRECTOR: Richard Wenk

CAST: Chris Makepeace, Grace Jones, Robert Rusler, Sandy Baron, Gedde Watanabe, Dedee Pfeiffer

Effective comedy-shocker concerns a pair of college kids (Chris Makepeace and Robert Rusler) who, in order to make it into the best fraternity on campus, must find a stripper for a big party being thrown that night. With the help of the resident school oddball (Gedde Watanabe in an inspired portrayal), the guys head off on their sacred mission. Upon arriving at the After Dark Club, the trio quickly decide on the outrageous Katrina (Grace Jones) as their unanimous choice, little realizing that she is actually a vicious, bloodthirsty vampire in disguise. This visually impressive production features ghoulish special effects, realistic performances, and a dank atmosphere of certain doom as the boys soon discover there's no escape from this nightmare. Rated R for gore and brief nudity.

1986 93 minutes

VAMPIRE LOVERS, THE

★★★

DIRECTOR: Roy Ward Baker

CAST: Ingrid Pitt, Peter Cushing, Pippa Steele, Madeleine Smith, George Cole, Dawn Addams, Kate O'Mara

Hammer Films of England revitalized the Frankenstein and Dracula horror series in the late 1950s. The films made stars of Peter Cushing and Christopher Lee, and proved very popular with teen-agers in America, where Forrest J. Ackerman's *Famous Monsters of Filmland* magazine had nearly canonized creature features. But by 1971, when *Vampire Lovers* was released, Hammer's horrors had become passé. Even adding sex to the mix, as the studio did in this faithful screen version of Sheridan LeFanu's *Camilla*, didn't help much. Nonetheless, sexy Ingrid Pitt makes a voluptuous vampire, and her seductions of pretty female victims provide more than enough eroticism. Rated R for violence, nudity, suggested sex, and gore.

1971 88 minutes

VARAN, THE UNBELIEVABLE

★★½

DIRECTOR: Inoshiro Honda

CAST: Jerry Baerwitz, Myron Healey, Tsuruko Kobayashi

Another Godzilla ripoff with better-than-average effects.

1962 B & W 70 minutes

VAULT OF HORROR

★★

DIRECTOR: Roy Ward Baker

CAST: Daniel Massey, Anna Massey, Terry-Thomas, Glynis Johns, Curt Jurgens, Dawn Addams, Tom Baker, Denholm Elliott, Michael Craig, Edward Judd

British sequel to *Tales from the Crypt* boasts a fine cast and five short stories borrowed from the classic EC comics line of the early 1950s but delivers very little in the way of true chills and atmosphere. Not nearly as effective as the earlier five-story thriller *Dr. Terror's House of Horrors* and not as much fun as the most recent homage to the EC horror story, *Creepshow.* Rated R.

1973 87 minutes

VENOM

DIRECTOR: Piers Haggard
CAST: Nicol Williamson, Klaus Kinski, Susan George, Oliver Reed, Sterling Hayden, Sarah Miles

This combination horror film and police thriller doesn't really work as either. The plot centers on the bungled kidnapping of a 10-year-old scion of a wealthy London family. Police trap the kidnappers in the boy's home, in which, unknown to either the police or criminals, a vicious black mamba snake stalks victims and slithers through the ventilation ducts. It wastes fine cast and the viewer's time. Rated R for nudity and violence.

1982 98 minutes

VERTIGO

DIRECTOR: Alfred Hitchcock
CAST: James Stewart, Kim Novak, Barbara Bel Geddes

The first hour of this production is slow, gimmicky, and artificial. However, the rest of this suspense picture takes off at high speed. James Stewart stars as a San Francisco detective who has a fear of heights and is hired to shadow an old friend's wife (Kim Novak). He finds himself falling in love with her—then tragedy strikes.

1958 128 minutes

VIDEODROME

★★½

DIRECTOR: David Cronenberg
CAST: James Woods, Deborah Harry, Sonja Smits, Peter Dvorsky

Director David Cronenberg (*Scanners*; *Rabid*; and *The Brood*) strikes again with a clever, gory nightmare set in the world of television broadcasting. James Woods and Deborah Harry (of the rock group Blondie) star in this eerie, occasionally sickening horror film about the boss (Woods) of a cable TV station catering to the "subterranean market" who falls victim to his own TV set. Rated R for profanity, sex, nudity, violence, gore, and pure nausea.

1983 88 minutes

VILLAGE OF THE DAMNED

★★★★

DIRECTOR: Wolf Rilla
CAST: George Sanders, Barbara Shelley, Michael Gwynne

A science-fiction thriller about twelve strangely emotionless children all born at the same time in a small village in England. Sanders plays their teacher, who tries to stop their plans for conquest. This excellent low-budget film provides chills for the viewer that many high-budgeted films fail to provide. The telepathic powers of the children are not overdone, and the horror comes from a well-written and well-acted script rather than blood and guts.

1960 B & W 78 minutes

VILLAGE OF THE GIANTS

DIRECTOR: Bert I. Gordon
CAST: Tommy Kirk, Beau Bridges, Ron Howard, Johnny Crawford, Toni Basil

Utterly ridiculous story of a gang of teenage misfits taking over a small town after they ingest a bizarre substance created by a 12-year-old named "Genius" and grow to gigantic heights. What makes this worth watching, though, are the famous faces of the many young stars-to-be. Some cool songs by the Beau Brummels also help keep things moving along. Be warned that the special effects are a joke.

1965 80 minutes

VISITING HOURS

DIRECTOR: Jean Claude Lord
CAST: Lee Grant, William Shatner, Linda Purl, Michael Ironside

Here's a Canadian production that actually forces the viewer to wallow in the degradation, humiliation, and mutilation of women. What Lee Grant, William Shatner, and Linda Purl are doing in such an awful picture is anybody's guess. Rated R for blood, gore, violence, and general unrelenting ugliness.

1982 103 minutes

W

★★★½

DIRECTOR: Richard Quine
CAST: Twiggy, Michael Witney, Eugene Roche, John Vernon, Dirk Benedict

Someone is trying to kill the Lewises, Katy (Twiggy) and Ben (Michael Witney). Each gets into a car and finds too late that it has been tampered with and nearly is killed in a head-long, high-speed crash. On each vehicle, the letter *W* is scrawled in the dust. Who could be after them? Katy knows, but she's afraid to tell. This is a highly involving, Hitchcockian thriller that will keep mystery lovers captivated as they pick up clues bit by bit. Rated PG.

1974 95 minutes

WAIT UNTIL DARK

★★★★

DIRECTOR: Terence Young
CAST: Audrey Hepburn, Alan Arkin, Richard Crenna, Efrem Zimbalist Jr.

Suspense abounds in this chiller about a blind housewife (Audrey Hepburn) who is being pursued by a gang of criminals. She has inadvertently gotten hold of a doll filled with heroin. Alan Arkin is especially frightening as the psychotic gang's mastermind who alternates between moments of deceptive charm and sudden violence in his attempt to separate Hepburn from the doll.

1967 108 minutes

WARNING SIGN

★★★

DIRECTOR: Hal Barwood
CAST: Sam Waterston, Kathleen Quinlan, Yaphet Kotto, Jeffrey De Munn, Richard Dysart, G. W. Bailey, Rick Rossovich

A sort of *The Andromeda Strain* meets *The Night of the Living Dead*, this is a passable science-fiction thriller about what happens when an accident occurs at a plant, producing a particularly virulent microbe for germ warfare. The screenplay, by director Hal Barwood and executive producer Matthew Robbins, occasionally strays into all-too-familiar territory, but the fine performances by Sam Waterston (best-actor nominee for *The Killing Fields*), Kathleen Quinlan (*I Never Promised You a Rose Garden*), Yaphet Kotto (*Alien*), and Jeffrey De Munn keep the viewer's interest. Rated R for violence and gore.

1985 99 minutes

WATCH ME WHEN I KILL

DIRECTOR: Anthony Bido
CAST: Richard Stewart, Sylvia Kramer

You've heard of the spaghetti western? Now here's the spaghetti slasher. Sylvia Kramer plays a woman who is witness to a murder and is now in danger of becoming one of the killer's next victims. Dubbed in English and stupid. Not rated; has violence and profanity.

1981 94 minutes

WATCHER IN THE WOODS, THE

★★

DIRECTOR: John Hough
CAST: Bette Davis, Lynn-Holly Johnson, Carroll Baker, David McCallum

This typical teenage gothic plot (family moves into old mansion and strange things begin to happen) is completely obscure and ends by defiantly refusing to explain itself. Rated PG because of minor violence.

1980 84 minutes

WHAT EVER HAPPENED TO BABY JANE?

★★★

DIRECTOR: Robert Aldrich
CAST: Bette Davis, Joan Crawford, Victor Buono

One of the last hurrahs of screen giants Bette Davis and Joan Crawford in a chillingly unpleasant tale of two aged sisters. Davis plays a former child movie star who spends her declining years dreaming of lost fame and tormenting her sister (Crawford). Victor Buono deserves special notice in a meaty supporting role.

1962 B & W 132 minutes

WHEN A STRANGER CALLS

★★★

DIRECTOR: Fred Walton
CAST: Carol Kane, Charles Durning, Colleen Dewhurst, Tony Beckley, Rachel Roberts, Ron O'Neal

A *Psycho II*–style atmosphere pervades this film when the murderer of two children returns after seven years to complete his crime.

1979 97 minutes

WHEN TIME RAN OUT!

★½

DIRECTOR: James Goldstone
CAST: Paul Newman, Jacqueline Bisset, William Holden, James Franciscus, Edward Albert, Red Buttons, Ernest Borgnine, Burgess Meredith, Valentine Cortese, Alex Karras, Barbara Carrera

This disastrous disaster film runs out of plot and characterization after the first few scenes. Time never seems to run out as we wait and wait for a volcano to erupt and put the all-star cast out of its misery. Producer Irwin Allen deserves to have a molten lava shampoo for inflicting this one on the public. Rated PG.

1980 121 minutes

WHITE PONGO (A.K.A. *BLOND GORILLA*)

DIRECTOR: Sam Newfield
CAST: Richard Fraser, Maria Wrixon, Lionel Royce, Al Ebon, Gordon Richards

Reverently referred to by fans of genre films as the worst of all crazed-gorilla/missing link jungle movies, this imbecilic waste features a no-star cast and a man in a frosted gorilla suit. Forget the nonsensical story about the rare White Pongo being an intelligent link between man and his jungle ancestors, because everyone knows that Pongo is just dying to get his chance to pick up Maria Wrixon and run around the underbrush with her. Just about as cheap and stupid as they come, this bottom-of-the-barrel disaster soiled many an unsuspecting screen before the word got around about what a stinker it was. This is to jungle films what *Robot Monster* is to science-fiction movies.

1945 B & W 74 minutes

WHITE ZOMBIE

★★★★

DIRECTOR: Victor Halperin
CAST: Bela Lugosi, Madge Bellamy, Robert Frazer, Brandon Hurst

This eerie little thriller is the consummate zombie film, with hordes of the walking dead doing the bidding of evil Bela Lugosi as their overseer and master. A damsel-in-distress story with a new twist, this independently produced gem features sets and production standards usually found in films by the major studios. A minor classic, with a stand-out role by Lugosi.

1932 B & W 73 minutes

WHO SLEW AUNTIE ROO?

★★

DIRECTOR: Curtis Harrington
CAST: Shelley Winters, Mark Lester, Chloe Franks, Ralph Richardson, Lionel Jeffries, Hugh Griffith

Ghoulish horror version of *Hansel and Gretel*, with Shelley Winters as the madwoman who lures two children (Mark Lester and Chloe Franks) into her evil clutches. Rated R for violence.

1971 89 minutes

WICKER MAN, THE

★★★★½

DIRECTOR: Robin Hardy
CAST: Edward Woodward, Christopher Lee, Britt Ekland, Diane Cilento, Ingrid Pitt, Lindsay Kemp

To call this simply one of the finest horror films ever made would be a grave disservice. It has plenty of suspense and terror, to be sure, but there is also ample mystery, comedy, and eroticism. An anonymous letter that implies a missing girl has been murdered brings Sergeant Howie (Edward Woodward), of Scotland Yard, to Summerisle, an island off the coast of England. The islanders are anything but cooperative. Lord Summerisle (Christopher Lee), the ruler and religious leader of the island, seems to take it all as a joke, so Howie swears to find the truth. Rated R.

1973 95 minutes

WILLARD

★★½

DIRECTOR: Daniel Mann
CAST: Bruce Davison, Ernest Borgnine, Sondra Locke

This worked far better as a novel, although the film accurately follows the elements of Stephen Gilbert's *Ratman's Notebooks*. Bruce Davison plays a put-upon wimp who identifies more with rodents than people. When nasty Ernest Borgnine becomes too unpleasant, Davison decides to make him the bait in a better rattrap. Pretty cheesy stuff . . . but it was destined to get worse in the sequel, entitled *Ben*. Rated PG—mild violence.

1971 95 minutes

WINDOW, THE

★★★½

DIRECTOR: Ted Tetzlaff
CAST: Bobby Driscoll, Arthur Kennedy, Barbara Hale, Paul Stewart, Ruth Roman

This chilling drama about a young boy who witnesses a murder and finds himself unable to convince any authority figures of what he has seen is one of the classic nightmare films for children of the postwar period, a select group that also includes *Night of the Hunter* and *Invaders from Mars*. Bobby Driscoll (who earned a special Academy Award for this film) is kidnapped by the murderers and the film becomes one taut encounter after another as he appears to be on the verge of being saved only to fall back into the clutches of his captors. The climactic chase over high beams in an empty building is one of the most suspenseful crawls ever filmed, and Bobby Driscoll is a most believable and engaging child actor—used by Walt Disney in *Song of the South* and *So Dear to My Heart* as well as the voice for the animated *Peter Pan*.

1949 B & W 73 minutes

WITCHBOARD

★★

DIRECTOR: Kevin S. Tenney

CAST: Todd Allen, Tawny Kitaen, Stephen Nicholas, Kathleen Wilhoite, Burke Burns, Rose Marie

Some good moments buoy this horror film about a group of people who play with a Ouija board at a party and find themselves haunted into becoming murderers and victims. Rated R for profanity and violence.

1987 100 minutes

WITCHING, THE (NECROMANCY)

DIRECTOR: Bert I. Gordon

CAST: Orson Welles, Pamela Franklin, Michael Ontkean, Lee Purcell, Harvey Jason, Sue Bernard

Whenever he was making a movie just for the money, Orson Welles would disguise himself. In this piece of trash from director Bert I. Gordon, he wears both a false nose and a beard. But there can be no doubt that *Citizen Kane* himself is playing Cato, the head of a community whose one enterprise is the manufacture of occult toys. Cato, as it turns out, takes his witchcraft seriously and attempts to use it to bring his dead son back to life. To do so, he needs a willing sacrifice: Pamela Franklin, still haunted by debuting in *The Innocents*. Rated PG.

1972 82 minutes

WITCHING TIME

DIRECTOR: Don Leaver

CAST: Jon Finch, Patricia Quinn, Prunella Gee, Ian McCulloch

Another entry from "Thriller Video," hosted by TV's Elvira, "Mistress of the Dark." The owner of an English farmhouse is visited by a previous occupant, a seventeenth-century witch. Unfortunately for him, after three hundred years, the old gal is hot to trot. Nice production values, but it fails to conjure up the needed suspense. Originally filmed for the British television series *Hammer House of Horror*. Unrated; nudity edited out of the print used for this cassette.

1985 60 minutes

WIZARD OF GORE, THE

★½

DIRECTOR: Herschell Gordon Lewis

CAST: Ray Sager, Judy Clark, Wayne Raven

Herschell Gordon Lewis (*Blood Feast*) is at it again! Blood and guts galore as a sideshow magician takes the old "saw the girl in half" trick a bit too far. Disgusting. Rated R.

1982 80 minutes

WOLFEN

★★

DIRECTOR: Michael Wadleigh

CAST: Albert Finney, Diane Venora, Gregory Hines, Tom Noonan, Edward James Olmos, Dick O'Neill

The best features of this sluggish horror film are its innovative visual work and actors (Albert Finney, Diane Venora, and Gregory Hines), who make the most of an uneven script. Directed by Michael Wadleigh (*Woodstock*), *Wolfen* follows a sequence of mysterious murders that are sometimes disturbingly bloody. This explains the "R" rating.

1981 115 minutes

WRAITH, THE

★★

DIRECTOR: Mike Marvin

CAST: Charlie Sheen, Randy Quaid, Clint Howard, Griffin O'Neal

A small town in Arizona is visited by a spirit taking revenge on a gang of road pirates. Some nice car wrecks and explosions. Car buffs will like the "Wraith Mobile." It's sleek, eerie, and very impressive—at least until you notice the logo on the hood. Apparently, Chrysler is seeing to the automotive needs of the dark side. Its PG rating keeps the violence under control, but while the movie is literally bloodless, it is also figuratively bloodless. Just a typical shallow revenge picture without style, substance, or surprises. Rated PG.

1986 93 minutes

WRONG MAN, THE

★★★★

DIRECTOR: Alfred Hitchcock

CAST: Henry Fonda, Vera Miles, Anthony Quayle, Harold J. Stone, Nehemiah Persoff

In this frightening true-life tale, Henry Fonda plays a man falsely accused of robbery. Vera Miles is his wife, who can't handle the changes wrought in their lives by this gross injustice. Fonda is excellent.

1956 B & W 105 minutes

XTRO

½

DIRECTOR: Harry Davenport

CAST: Philip Sayer, Bernice Stegers, Maryam D'Abo, Danny Brainin, Simon Nash

Grotesquely slimy sci-fi/horror flick with an idiot plot—one that requires every character to behave like a jerk at all times—that revolves around a series of repulsive bladder effects. Average dad Philip Sayer is abducted by aliens; he returns three years later and, just to prove his love, infects his son, kills countless people, and turns the family *au pair* girl into an alien breeding chamber. Hard to decide which of the many "wet" effects is the worst; probable winner is Sayer's return as he bursts, full-grown, from the stomach of an "impregnated" woman. Sick, sick, sick. Rated R.

1982 84 minutes

ZERO BOYS, THE

★½

DIRECTOR: Nico Mastorakis

CAST: Daniel Hirsch, Kelli Maroney, Jared Moses, Nicole Rio, Tom Shell

A survival-game team of three college buddies, along with their girls, truck out to the backwoods for some serious partying and instead ride straight into a murderous game of hide-and-seek with a couple of homegrown psychotics. This movie has the current prerequisites of very sick killers, a lot of guns with a lot of lousy marksmanship, torture barns, mass graves, and stupid reasons for being alone so someone can kill you. Rated R.

1985 89 minutes

ZOMBIE

½

DIRECTOR: Lucio Fulci
CAST: Tisa Farrow, Ian McCulloch, Richard Johnson

Gruesome, gory, and ghastly unauthorized entry in George Romero's zombie series. Richard Johnson is a mad scientist who reanimates the dead; the flesh-eating stiffs can be destroyed only by bullets in the brain . . . a chore that Johnson embraces lovingly and director Lucio Fulci's camera repeats *ad nauseum*. Tisa Farrow (yes, Mia's sister) joins an ever-dwindling group of adventurers who meet their fates on this unnamed Caribbean island. Watch for the grand moment when a sliver of wood punctures the eyeball of one unlucky lass. She never blinks; bet you will! Rated X for gore and nudity.

1979 91 minutes

ZOMBIES OF MORA TAU

★

DIRECTOR: Edward Cahn
CAST: Gregg Palmer, Allison Hayes

Laughable, low-budget time-waster about zombies and sunken treasure. Shows how dull zombies were before *Night of the Living Dead*. Unrated, but timid enough for your aunt Sally.

1957 B & W 70 minutes

MUSICALS

ABSOLUTE BEGINNERS

★★★★

DIRECTOR: Julien Temple

CAST: Eddie O'Connell, Patsy Kensit, David Bowie, James Fox, Ray Davies, Anita Morris, Sade Adu, Mandy Rice Davies

Julien Temple has taken what he learned from rock videos (the Stones's "She Was Hot" and Bowie's "Jazzin' for Blue Jean"), TV movies (*It's All True*, with Orson Welles, Grace Jones, and Mel Brooks), and feature films (the Sex Pistols's *The Great Rock 'n' Roll Swindle*), and has rekineticized the movie musical for the 1980s. The likes of *Absolute Beginners* has not been seen in quite some time: daring, inventive, and original; riveting colors and vivid sounds. It is based on the cult novel by Colin MacInnes, who chronicled the musical and social scene in London during the pivotal summer of 1958. Occasionally the accents are too thick and the references too obscure for Americans, but the overall effect is an unequivocal high. Rated PG-13 for stylized, but rather intense, violence and some profanity.

1986 107 minutes

ALL THAT JAZZ

★★★★

DIRECTOR: Bob Fosse

CAST: Roy Scheider, Ann Reinking, Jessica Lange,

While it may not be what viewers expect from a musical, this story of a gifted choreographer, Joe Gideon (Roy Scheider, in his finest performance), who relentlessly drives himself to exhaustion is daring, imaginative, shocking, and visually stunning. The screenplay, co-written by director Bob Fosse with producer Robert Alan Arthur, tells of Gideon's rise from an ambitious young dancer in sleazy strip joints (in flashback) to the most respected director-choreographer on Broadway. But while his success is unquestioned, Gideon's private life is a shambles. His health is hampered by overwork, amphetamines, and alcohol. And he gives so much of himself to his work, he has precious little left over for those who love him. Rated R.

1979 123 minutes

AMADEUS

★★★★★

DIRECTOR: Milos Forman

CAST: Tom Hulce, F. Murray Abraham, Elizabeth Berridge

Peter Shaffer adapted his acclaimed stage play into what is certain to be an enduring screen work. F. Murray Abraham, who won an Oscar for his performance, gives a haunting portrayal of Antonio Salieri, the court composer for Hapsburg Emperor Joseph II. A second-rate musician, Salieri felt jealousy and admiration for the young musical genius Wolfgang Amadeus Mozart (Tom Hulce), who died at the age of thirty-five—perhaps by Salieri's hand. It's a stunning film full of great music, drama, and wit. Rated PG for mild violence.

1984 158 minutes

AMERICAN HOT WAX

★★★½

DIRECTOR: Floyd Mutrux

CAST: Tim McIntire, Fran Drescher, Jay Leno, John Lehne, Laraine Newman, Jeff Altman, Chuck Berry, Jerry Lee Lewis, Screamin' Jay Hawkins

Though facts may be in short supply in this bio-pic of pioneer rock disc jockey Alan Freed, abundant energy and spirit make this movie a winner. The incredible excitement caused by the birth of rock-'n-roll is captured here. Tim McIntire gives a remarkable performance, molding the driven Freed into a memorable hero. Rated PG.

1978 91 minutes

AMERICAN IN PARIS, AN

★★★★★

DIRECTOR: Vincente Minnelli

CAST: Gene Kelly, Leslie Caron, Nina Foch, Oscar Levant

One of Gene Kelly's classic musicals, this release features the hoofer as the free-spirited author of the title. The picture is a heady mixture of light entertainment and the music of George Gershwin.

1951 113 minutes

ANCHORS AWEIGH

★★★

DIRECTOR: George Sidney

CAST: Gene Kelly, Frank Sinatra, Kathryn Grayson, Dean Stockwell

A somewhat tedious and overlong dance film that is perked up by a few truly impressive numbers, none finer than Gene Kelly's duet with an animated Jerry the mouse (of Tom and Jerry fame). Kelly and Frank Sinatra play a couple of sailors on leave, but most of their inane antics make one wonder if they've taken leave of their senses. While films of this type are supposed to be fluffy, this one suffers from an excess of emptiness. Rabid MGM musical fans will adore it, anyway; newcomers are advised to try another entry in the Kelly canon. Unrated; suitable for family viewing.

1945 140 minutes

ANNIE

★★★★

DIRECTOR: John Huston

CAST: Albert Finney, Carol Burnett, Bernadette Peters, Edward Herrmann, Aileen Quinn

A sparkling $40 million movie musical based on the Broadway production of the long-running comic strip *Little Orphan Annie.* Ten-year-old Aileen Quinn is just fine in the title role. Rated PG for brief profanity.

1982 128 minutes

BABES IN ARMS

★★★

DIRECTOR: Busby Berkeley
CAST: Mickey Rooney, Judy Garland, June Preisser, Douglas McPhail, Guy Kibbee, Charles Winninger, Henry Hull, Margaret Hamilton

Richard Rodgers and Lorenz Hart wrote the Broadway musical from which this film was taken—although most of the songs they wrote are absent. But never mind; Mickey and Judy sing, dance, and prance up a storm as the kids in town put on a show! If the tune "Good Morning" seems familiar, it's because you know it from the later, classic *Singin' in the Rain*.

1939 B & W 96 minutes

BACK TO THE BEACH

★

DIRECTOR: Lyndall Hobbs
CAST: Frankie Avalon, Annette Funicello, Connie Stevens, Lori Laughlin

The Big Kahuna (Frankie Avalon) now sells cars and the busty Mouseketeer (Annette Funicello) pushes beach party flicks. Annette and Frankie are married, in their 40's, live in Ohio, and have two children with behavioral problems. The pressures of selling Fords has convinced Frankie that a Hawaiian vacation is in order to rekindle fond memories and romance. A wipe out in terms of plot, dialogue, and acting. Cameo appearances by Don Adams, Bob Denver, and Pee-Wee Herman add interest. Rated PG for language.

1987 88 minutes

BAND WAGON, THE

★★★★

DIRECTOR: Vincente Minnelli
CAST: Fred Astaire, Cyd Charisse, Jack Buchanan, Nanette Fabray, Oscar Levant

One of Vincente Minnelli's best grand-scale musicals and one of Fred Astaire's most endearing roles. He plays a Hollywood has-been who decides to try his luck on stage. The story has a behind-the-scenes approach that blossoms into another "Let's put on a show!" extravaganza. Watch for the slick dance sequence that lampoons Mickey Spillane. Best of all, this is the film that gave us *That's Entertainment*. Lots of fun. Unrated—family fare.

1953 112 minutes

BARKLEYS OF BROADWAY, THE

★★★

DIRECTOR: Charles Walters
CAST: Fred Astaire, Ginger Rogers, Oscar Levant

As a film team, Ginger Rogers and Fred Astaire parted in 1939. This final pairing, the result of Judy Garland's inability to make the picture, does not favorably compare with earlier efforts. Rogers's dancing prowess had declined. She keeps up, but Astaire shines brilliantly in comparison. Harry Warren's score, while augmented by a great George Gershwin number, is not up to snuff. Nevertheless, the film was a critical and commercial hit.

1949 109 minutes

BEACH BLANKET BINGO

★★½

DIRECTOR: William Asher
CAST: Frankie Avalon, Annette Funicello, Paul Lynde, Harvey Lembeck, Don Rickles, Linda Evans, Jody McCrea,

Marta Kristen, John Ashley, Deborah Walley, Buster Keaton

The fifth in the series, and the last true "Beach Party" film. Basically, it's the same old stuff: stars on their way up (Linda Evans) or on their way down (Buster Keaton) or at their peak (Frankie and Annette), spouting silly dialogue and singing through echo chambers. But it's one of the best of the series, whether you're laughing with it or at it. Enjoyable for those who lived through that era, but don't be surprised if your kids wonder what the attraction is. Unrated.

1965 98 minutes

BEACH BOYS: AN AMERICAN BAND, THE

★★★

DIRECTOR: Malcolm Leo
CAST: The Beach Boys, Al Jardine, Bruce Johnston, Mike Love

Even the most fervent fans of the country's number-one surf group are likely to be a bit disappointed by this "authorized biography," directed by Malcolm Leo (*This Is Elvis*). It skims the surface of the band's troubled but ultimately triumphant history and only occasionally catches a wave. The disturbing problems of the Beach Boys' "genius" songwriter, Brian Wilson, who spent three years in bed because, in his words, he "got hold of all these drugs, and they messed me up," and his younger brother, drummer-singer-songwriter Dennis, who drowned in 1983 and was prevented from playing with the group in later years because of drinking and drug use, are glossed over. We are left wanting to know more and, more important, why. Still, there is much for Beach Boys fans to enjoy here, more than forty songs from their twenty-five-year career. Rated G.

1984 90 minutes

BEACH PARTY

★★½

DIRECTOR: William Asher
CAST: Bob Cummings, Dorothy Malone, Frankie Avalon, Annette Funicello, Harvey Lembeck, Jody McCrea, John Ashley, Morey Amsterdam

Bob Cummings, a bearded, sheltered anthropologist, studies the wild dating and mating habits of beach-bound teens. He ends up courting Annette Funicello to make Frankie Avalon jealous. This orgy of silly 1960s slapstick is intermittently fun to watch. Cummings has his moments, as does Harvey Lembeck, as the biker Eric Von Zipper. Nostalgia is the primary appeal here.

1963 101 minutes

BEAT STREET

★½

DIRECTOR: Stan Lathan
CAST: Rae Dawn Chong, Guy Davis, Robert Taylor, Jon Chardiet

Even though it has better production values and a stronger storyline than *Breakin'*, the low-budget movie about break dancing that preceded it, *Breakin'* is the better film. That's only because the emphasis in *Breakin'* is placed squarely where it belongs: on the amazing abilities of today's break dancers. Not so in this release, where the hackneyed plot, about kids breaking into show biz, and just-okay acting by Rae Dawn Chong (*Quest For Fire*), Guy Davis (son of Ossie Davis and Ruby Dee), and Jon Chardiet overpower the dancing and undermine the picture's excitement. Rated PG for profanity and violence.

1984 106 minutes

BELLE OF NEW YORK, THE

★★

DIRECTOR: Charles Walters
CAST: Fred Astaire, Vera-Ellen, Marjorie Main, Lisa Ferraday, Alice Pearce, Keenan Wynn, Percy Helton

A fantasy set at the turn of the century, this frothy film was a box office failure about which, in his autobiography, Fred Astaire snaps: "The less said about it the better . . ." His fans were greatly disappointed, though Vera-Ellen made an attractive co-star. Harry Warren's score—assembled from earlier hits—is terrific, though none of the songs have survived as standards.

1952 82 minutes

BELLS ARE RINGING

★★

DIRECTOR: Vincente Minnelli
CAST: Judy Holliday, Dean Martin, Fred Clark, Eddie Foy Jr.

This filmed version of the Broadway musical pits answering-service operator Judy Holliday against Dean Martin in an on-again, off-again love circle. Nothing new or exciting story-wise here, but Fred Clark and Eddie Foy ham it up enough to hold your interest. Look for Jean Stapleton in an early role. Judy Holliday's last film.

1960 127 minutes

BEST FOOT FORWARD

★★★

DIRECTOR: Edward Buzzell
CAST: Lucille Ball, William Gaxton, Virginia Weidler, Tommy Dix, June Allyson, Nancy Walker, Gloria DeHaven

Film star Lucille Ball accepts military cadet Tommy Dix's invitation to his school's annual dance. The film introduced June Allyson and Nancy Walker and gave numerous high schools a fight song by adapting its biggest hit, "Buckle Down, Winsocki." Wholesome family fun.

1943 95 minutes

BEST LITTLE WHOREHOUSE IN TEXAS, THE

★★★½

DIRECTOR: Colin Higgins
CAST: Burt Reynolds, Dolly Parton, Dom De Luise, Charles Durning

Dolly Parton and Burt Reynolds in a so-so version of the Broadway play, whose title explains all. Rated R for nudity, profanity, and sexual situations.

1982 114 minutes

BIKINI BEACH

★★

DIRECTOR: William Asher
CAST: Frankie Avalon, Annette Funicello, Keenan Wynn, Don Rickles

This silly film captures Frankie Avalon and Annette Funicello in their best swim attire. There are lots of girls in bikinis and some drag-racing for an added diversion. A group of kids who always hang out at the beach try to prevent a man from closing it. Ho-hum.

1964 100 minutes

BLUE HAWAII

★★★½

DIRECTOR: Norman Taurog
CAST: Elvis Presley, John Blackman, Angela Lansbury, Iris Adrian

In this enjoyable Elvis Presley flick, the star plays a returning soldier who works with tourists against his mom's (Angela Lansbury) wishes.

1962 101 minutes

BODY ROCK

DIRECTOR: Marcelo Epstein
CAST: Lorenzo Lamas, Vicki Frederick, Cameron Dye, Ray Sharkey

A boring pop musical, this features Lorenzo Lamas as a youngster from the South Bronx who sees the break-dancing subculture as his ticket to the big time. Rated PG-13.

1984 93 minutes

BREAKIN'

★½

DIRECTOR: Joel Silberg
CAST: Lucinda Dickey, Adolfo Quinones, Michael Chambers, Ben Lokey

If it weren't for the acting, direction, and plot, this would be a terrific little movie. The dancing scenes are wonderful. As a whole, *Breakin'* is pretty lame. Sort of *Flashdance* meets street break-dancing, the film would have us believe that jazz dancer Kelly (Lucinda Dickey) could hook up with street dancers Ozone ("Shabba-Do") and Turbo ("Boogaloo Shrimp") to win dance contests and finally break (no pun intended) into big-time show biz. No way. She's no match for them. Anyone watching *Breakin'* would know director Joel Silberg was only fakin'. But my, oh, my, those crazy dancin' feet—they almost make this movie worth sitting through. Rated PG for profanity and violence.

1984 90 minutes

BREAKIN' 2 ELECTRIC BOOGALOO

★★½

DIRECTOR: Sam Firstenberg
CAST: Lucinda Dickey, Adolfo Quinones, Michael Chambers

This sometimes exhilarating break-dancing movie is a follow-up to *Breakin'*, which grossed $38 million, and it's better than the original. This time, instead of trying to break into show business, Kelly (Lucinda Dickey), Ozone (Adolfo "Shabba-Doo" Quinones), and Turbo (Michael "Boogaloo Shrimp" Chambers) have to "put on a show" to save a local arts center for children. The result is generally an entertaining contemporary musical. Rated PG for brief violence and suggested sex.

1984 90 minutes

BREAKING GLASS

★★½

DIRECTOR: Brian Gibson
CAST: Phil Daniels, Hazel O'Connor, Jon Finch, Jonathan Pryce

British film about a New Wave singer's rise to the top, at the expense of personal relationships. Hazel O'Connor's heavy music isn't for all tastes, and the plot line is as old as film itself, but the actors are sincere, and the film contains some striking visual imagery. Rated PG.

1980 104 minutes

BRIGADOON

★★★★

DIRECTOR: Vincente Minnelli
CAST: Gene Kelly, Van Johnson, Cyd Charisse, Elaine Stewart, Barry Jones, Hugh Laing

This enchanting musical stars Van Johnson and Gene Kelly as two Americans who discover Brigadoon, a Scottish village with a lifespan of only one day for every hundred years. In the village, Kelly meets Cyd Charisse, and they naturally dance up a storm.

1954 108 minutes

BRING ON THE NIGHT

★

DIRECTOR: Michael Apted
CAST: Sting, Omar Hakim, Darryl Jones, Kenny Kirkland, Branford Marsalis

Obnoxious, self-serving documentary about popular rock star Sting (formerly of The Police) and the formation of his new band. The first three-quarters of the film features nothing more than a few rehearsal sessions and far too much of Sting talking about Sting, followed by a live concert finale which is intercut with unnecessary scenes of his son being born. Strictly for die-hard fans, this movie earns its one star for the dynamic performances of the Police classic "Roxanne." Rated PG-13 for the birth scene.

1985 97 minutes

BROADWAY MELODY OF 1936

★★★

DIRECTOR: Roy Del Ruth
CAST: Jack Benny, Eleanor Powell, Robert Taylor, Una Merkel, Buddy Ebsen

Backstage musical comedy. Obnoxious gossip columnist Jack Benny tries to use dancer Eleanor Powell to harass producer Robert Taylor. Forget the plot and enjoy the singing and dancing—including Taylor's rendition of "I've Got a Feelin' You're Foolin'," the only time he sang on-screen in his own voice.

1935 B & W 110 minutes

BROADWAY MELODY OF 1938

★★½

DIRECTOR: Roy Del Ruth
CAST: Robert Taylor, Eleanor Powell, George Murphy, Binnie Barnes, Sophie Tucker, Judy Garland, Buddy Ebsen, Willie Howard, Billy Gilbert

Fifteen-year-old Judy Garland stops the show and steals it in this tuneful musical anthology when she sings the now legendary "Dear Mr. Gable" version of "You Made Me Love You." The finale stretches credibility until it snaps as Eleanor Powell, in top hat and tails, dances with a division of chorus boys before a neon skyline. It's all sauce without substance, with a song to remember. The 1936 and 1940 editions are better by far.

1937 B & W 110 minutes

BYE BYE BIRDIE

★★★

DIRECTOR: George Sidney
CAST: Dick Van Dyke, Ann-Margret, Janet Leigh, Paul Lynde, Bobby Rydell

A rock star's approaching appearance in a small town turns several lives upside down in this pleasant musical comedy. Based on the successful Broadway play, this is pretty lightweight stuff, but a likable cast and good production numbers make it worthwhile. No rating; okay for the whole family.

1963 112 minutes

CABARET

★★★★½

DIRECTOR: Bob Fosse
CAST: Liza Minnelli, Michael York, Helmut Griem, Joel Grey

This classic musical-drama takes place in Germany in 1931. The Nazi party has not yet assumed complete controll and the local cabaret unfolds the story of two young lovers, the ensuing mood of the country, and the universal touch of humanity. Everything is handled with taste—bisexual encounters, the horrors of the Nazi regime, and the bawdy entertainment of the nightclub. "Host" Joel Grey is brilliant. Michael York and Liza Minnelli are first-rate. So is the movie. Rated PG.

1972 128 minutes

CALAMITY JANE

★★★

DIRECTOR: David Butler
CAST: Doris Day, Howard Keel, Allyn Ann McLerie, Phillip Carey

A legend of the Old West set to music for Doris Day, who mends her rootin', tootin' ways in order to lasso Howard Keel. The song "Secret Love" copped an Oscar. Cute 'n' perky. But then, what Doris Day film ain't?

1953 101 minutes

CAMELOT

★★★

DIRECTOR: Joshua Logan
CAST: Richard Harris, Vanessa Redgrave, Franco Nero, David Hemmings, Lionel Jeffries

The legend of King Arthur and the Round Table—from the first meeting of Arthur (Richard Harris) and Guinevere (Vanessa Redgrave) to the affair between Guinevere and Lancelot (Franco Nero), and finally the fall of Camelot—is brought to life in this enjoyable musical.

1967 178 minutes

CAN'T STOP THE MUSIC

DIRECTOR: Nancy Walker
CAST: The Village People, Valerie Perrine, Bruce Jenner, Steve Guttenberg, Paul Sand, Tammy Grimes, June Havoc, Jack Weston, Barbara Rush, Leigh Taylor-Young

Despite the positive-thinking title, the music of the Village People ("Macho Man," "YMCA") was stopped cold by this basically awful movie musical about the world of show biz. The only thing happy about this irrepressibly sunny groaner are the members of the featured musical group, which has completely slipped into obscurity. Rated PG.

1980 118 minutes

CAREFREE

★★★

DIRECTOR: Mark Sandrich
CAST: Fred Astaire, Ginger Rogers, Ralph Bellamy, Jack Carson

In this blend of music, slapstick situations, and romantic byplay, Ginger Rogers is a crazy, mixed-up girl-child who goes to psychiatrist Fred Astaire for counsel. His treatment results in her falling in love with him. While trying to stop this, he falls in love with her. Of course they dance! All along the way! Ralph Bellamy is the sap Ginger cannot decide about. "Change Partners" is the best-known of the Irving Berlin songs dotting the landscape. It's more a Rogers film than an Astaire film, and more screwball comedy than musical.

1938 B & W 80 minutes

CHORUS LINE, A

★★★★

DIRECTOR: Richard Attenborough
CAST: Michael Douglas, Alyson Reed, Terence Mann, Audrey Landers, Michael Belvins, Yamil Borges, Jan Gan Boyd, Sharon Brown, Gregg Burge, Janet Jones, Michelle Johnston, Pam Klinger, Cameron English, Tony Fields, Nicole Fosse, Vicki Frederick

The screen version of Michael Bennett's hit Broadway musical allows the viewer to experience the anxiety, struggle, and triumph of a group of dancers auditioning for a stage production. Director Richard Attenborough blends big production numbers with intimate moments as gracefully as he did the panorama and character development in *Gandhi*. The songs are not the kind one hums afterward. However, they do convey the feelings and personalities of the characters, a more important function in this film. In the story, a group of would-be Broadway hoofers strut their stuff for a demanding choreographer (Michael Douglas), who chooses from among them for his chorus line. Rated PG for profanity and sexual descriptions.

1985 120 minutes

CINDERFELLA

★

DIRECTOR: Frank Tashlin

CAST: Jerry Lewis, Anna Maria Alberghetti, Ed Wynn

This musical version of the oft-told fairy tale has little to recommend it. Adapted for the talents of star Jerry Lewis, it has no laughs to speak of and will only appeal to his fans.

1960 91 minutes

CLAMBAKE

★★★

DIRECTOR: Arthur H. Nadel

CAST: Elvis Presley, Shelley Fabares, Will Hutchins, Bill Bixby, Gary Merrill, James Gregory

This typical Elvis Presley musical romance has a *Prince and the Pauper* scenario. Elvis, an oil baron's son, trades places with Will Hutchins, a penniless water ski instructor, in order to find a girl who'll love him for himself and not his money. When Elvis falls for a gold-digging Shelley Fabares, he must compete with Bill Bixby, the playboy speedboat racer. There's a nice scene in which Elvis gives a frightened little girl confidence in herself. Although dated, this film still provides entertainment for Elvis fans.

1967 100 minutes

COAL MINER'S DAUGHTER

★★★★½

DIRECTOR: Michael Apted

CAST: Sissy Spacek, Tommy Lee Jones, Beverly D'Angelo, Levon Helm

Sissy Spacek gives a superb, totally believable performance in this film biography of country singer Loretta Lynn. The title role takes Spacek from Lynn's impoverished Appalachian childhood through marriage at thirteen up to her mid-thirties and reign as the "First Lady of Country Music." Directed with documentarylike credibility by Michael Apted. Rated PG.

1980 125 minutes

COLOR ME BARBRA

★★

DIRECTOR: Dwight Hemion

CAST: Barbra Streisand

Color Me Barbra, Streisand's second TV special, doesn't hold a candle to her first, *My Name Is Barbra*. The song selections can't compare and the skits aren't nearly as funny. The musical jaunt through the Philadelphia museum seems a bit flat and the "Funny Face" number she does with zoo animals is just plain silly. The brief "The Minute Waltz" is fun, and her at-the-mike performance of "Any Place I Hang My Hat Is Home" will blow your socks off, but otherwise this isn't topflight Streisand.

1966 60 minutes

COMEBACK

★★★½

DIRECTOR: Christel Buschmann

CAST: Eric Burdon

Real-life rock singer Eric Burdon (lead singer of the Animals) stars in this rock-'n-roll drama. Burdon plays a part that mirrors his own life: that of a white blues singer trying to get back on top. He has several obstacles to overcome: a huge debt to record companies, a wacky wife who goes on binges, and a manager who keeps giving him drugs. At one point Burdon refuses some cocaine offered by the latter, saying, "You know, anyone who's ever been managed by you is either dead or dying." The businessman replies that Burdon would be worth more to him dead. "When you're dead, you're great," he says in a phrase that evokes the posthumous fame of Jimi Hendrix, Janis Joplin, and Jim Morrison. Unrated.

1982 96 minutes

COMPLEAT BEATLES, THE

★★★★

DIRECTOR: Patrick Montgomery
CAST: Malcolm McDowell, The Beatles

Even experts on the life and times of the Fab Four are likely to find something new and enlightening in *The Compleat Beatles*. Furthermore, while not a consistent work, this film provides something of interest for fans and nonfans. Narrated by Malcolm McDowell, it focuses not only on the careers of John Lennon, Paul McCartney, George Harrison, and Ringo Starr but also on the era that made and molded them. Unrated.

1982 119 minutes

CROSSOVER DREAMS

★★★★

DIRECTOR: Leon Ichaso
CAST: Reuben Blades, Shawn Elliot, Elizabeth Peña, Tom Signorelli, Frank Robles

Reuben Blades plays a popular Latino musician who tries his talents at the big time. The price he pays for his efforts is high. And while this may all sound like one big movie cliché, it's now time to add that the cast put in performances that redefine the story, giving this trite tale a bite that will surprise the viewer, who may expect nothing but music and laughs. *Crossover Dreams* does not have an MPAA rating, but would probably be a PG for sex and profanity.

1985 85 minutes

CROSSROADS

★★★½

DIRECTOR: Walter Hill
CAST: Ralph Macchio, Joe Seneca, Jami Gertz, Joe Morton, Robert Judd, Steve Vai, Dennis Lipscomb, Harry Carey Jr.

A superb blues score by guitarist Ry Cooder (featuring the inspired harmonica playing of Sonny Terry) highlights this enjoyable fantasy about an ambitious young bluesman (Ralph Macchio) who "goes down to the crossroads," in the words of Robert Johnson, to make a deal with the devil for fame and fortune. Joe Seneca costars as the veteran blues singer and harp player Willie Brown, who takes Macchio on his journey. In some ways, this is just a music-oriented version of *The Karate Kid*, but this will bother only some viewers. Most will enjoy the performances, the story, and the music in this all-too-rare big-screen celebration of the blues and its mythology. Rated R for profanity, suggested sex, and violence.

1986 105 minutes

DAMES

★★★

DIRECTOR: Ray Enright
CAST: Joan Blondell, Dick Powell, Ruby Keeler, ZaSu Pitts, Guy Kibbee, Hugh Herbert

Music, songs, dancing, great Busby Berkeley production numbers. Plot? Know the one about backing a Broadway musical? But, gee, it's fun to see and hear Joan Blondell, Dick Powell, Ruby Keeler, ZaSu Pitts, Guy Kibbee, and Hugh "Woo-woo" Herbert again.

1934 B & W 90 minutes

DAMN YANKEES

★★★½

DIRECTORS: George Abbott, Stanley Donen

CAST: Gwen Verdon, Ray Walston, Tab Hunter

A torrid, wiggling vamp teams with a sly, hissing Devil to frame the Yankees by turning a middle-aged baseball fan into a wunderkind and planting him on the team. Gwen Verdon is sensational as the temptress Lola, who gets whatever she wants. Hollywood called on her to reprise her role in the original Broadway musical hit. Lots of pep and zing in this one.

1958 110 minutes

DAMSEL IN DISTRESS, A

★★★

DIRECTOR: George Stevens

CAST: Fred Astaire, Joan Fontaine, Gracie Allen, George Burns, Constance Collier, Reginald Gardiner

By choice, Fred Astaire made this one without Ginger, who complemented him, but with Joan Fontaine—then a beginner—who did not, and who could not dance. Fred's an American popular composer in stuffy London. He mistakenly thinks heiress Joan is a chorus girl. The best sequence in this last Gershwin film musical has Fred, George, and Gracie romping through a fun house. It won choreographer Hermes Pan an Oscar, but falls far short of making the film a winner. Vintage Astaire, however.

1937 B & W 98 minutes

DANCING LADY

★★★

DIRECTOR: Robert Z. Leonard

CAST: Joan Crawford, Clark Gable, Fred Astaire, Winnie Lightner, Franchot Tone, May Robson, Grant Mitchell, Sterling Holloway, Ted Healy, The Three Stooges

Joan Crawford goes from burlesque dancer to Broadway star in this backstage drama set to music. A good film, this was also one of her early moneymakers. Fred Astaire made his screen debut in one dance number. Against Crawford's powerful performance, costar Clark Gable is an also-ran.

1933 B & W 94 minutes

DANGEROUS WHEN WET

★★

DIRECTOR: Charles Walter

CAST: Esther Williams, Fernando Lamas, Jack Carson, Charlotte Greenwood, Denise Darcel

Fame and fortune await she who swims the English Channel. Esther Williams plays a cornfed wholesome who goes for it, Fernando Lamas cheers her on. Semi-sour Jack Carson and high-kicking Charlotte Greenwood clown. Good music and a novel underwater Tom and Jerry cartoon sequence.

1953 95 minutes

DIVINE MADNESS

★★★½

DIRECTOR: Michael Ritchie

CAST: Bette Midler

Here's the sassy, unpredictable Bette Midler as captured in concert by director Michael Ritchie (*Bad News Bears*). Some of it is great; some of it is not. It helps if you're a Midler fan. Rated R for profanity.

1980 95 minutes

DON'T LOOK BACK

★★★

DIRECTOR: D. A. Pennebaker
CAST: Bob Dylan, Joan Baez, Donovan, Alan Price

A documentary account directed by D. A. Pennebaker of folk singer/poet ("guitarist," he calls himself) Bob Dylan on a 1965 tour of England. The tedium of travel and pressures of performing are eased by relaxing moments with fellow travelers Joan Baez, Alan Price, and (briefly) Donovan. Shot in striking black and white, with excellent sound quality, *Don't Look Back* has not been exhibited in about a decade. Unrated, it contains some vulgarity.

1967 B & W 96 minutes

DOUBLE TROUBLE

★½

DIRECTOR: Norman Taurog
CAST: Elvis Presley, Annette Day

Typical Elvis Presley musical. This time he plays a rock-'n-roll singer touring England. When a teenage heiress (whose life is constantly threatened) falls for him, he gets caught up in the action. Lots of Elvis songs, the most popular of which is "Long Legged Girls."

1967 92 minutes

DU BARRY WAS A LADY

★★½

DIRECTOR: Roy Del Ruth
CAST: Red Skelton, Lucille Ball, Gene Kelly, Zero Mostel, Virginia O'Brien, Donald Meek, Louise Beavers, Tommy Dorsey, George Givot

Despite the incredible collection of talent showcased in this film, the result is a slow-moving adaptation of a popular stage hit minus most of the music that made it popular in the first place. Set in the court of Louis XIV, this musical romp gives Red Skelton a chance to mug and Gene Kelly a chance to dance, while Lucille Ball and the other gals traipse about in a continuous change of costumes. Tommy Dorsey and the boys liven this one up to a point, but it's still a filmed stage play and forced to conform to stage conventions. Not a bad film, but not as good as the cast would indicate.

1943 101 minutes

EASTER PARADE

★★★★

DIRECTOR: Charles Walters
CAST: Judy Garland, Fred Astaire, Peter Lawford, Jules Munshin, Ann Miller

Judy Garland and Fred Astaire team up for this thoroughly enjoyable musical. Irving Berlin provided the songs for the story, about Astaire trying to forget ex-dance partner Ann Miller as he rises to the top with Garland. The result is an always watchable—and repeatable—treat. Gene Kelly was originally set to co-star, but he broke an ankle on the eve of production. To avert potential disaster, MGM talked Astaire out of a two-year retirement, and in addition to producing a classic picture, the company gave Astaire's career a new boost, adding thirty more illustrious years to its glow.

1948 103 minutes

EASY TO LOVE

★★½

DIRECTOR: Charles Walters
CAST: Esther Williams, Tony Martin, Van Johnson, Carroll Baker, John Bromfield

Tony Martin and Van Johnson vie for the love of mermaid Esther Williams in this most lavish of her numerous water spectacles. A toe-curling, high-speed sequence performed on water skis tops the Busby Berkeley numbers staged in lush Cypress Gardens at Winter Haven, Florida. It was Mae West who remarked: "Wet, Esther Williams can act; dry, she can't."

1953 96 minutes

EDDIE AND THE CRUISERS

★★★½

DIRECTOR: Martin Davidson

CAST: Tom Berenger, Michael Pare, Ellen Barkin

Long after his death, rock-'n-roll singer Eddie Wilson's (Michael Pare) songs become popular all over again. This revives interest in a long-shelved concept album. The tape for it has been stolen, and it's up to Wilson's one-time song writing collaborator (Tom Berenger) to find them. Only trouble is, other people want the tapes, too, and they may be willing to kill to get them. This isn't one of the great rock-'n-roll movies, but it's not terrible, either. The songs are great! Rated PG.

1983 92 minutes

ELEPHANT PARTS

★★★½

DIRECTOR: William Dear

CAST: Mike Nesmith, Jonathan Nesmith, Bill Martin, Diane Owen

Mike Nesmith, formerly of The Monkees, is surprisingly versatile and talented in this video record. He sings five songs; especially memorable is "Tonight Is Magic," which dramatizes the romance of a roller-skating waitress at a hamburger stand. Between songs, Nesmith presents several funny spoofs. Unrated, but deals with drugs and adult topics comparable with a PG.

1981 60 minutes

FABULOUS DORSEYS, THE

★★

DIRECTOR: Alfred E. Green

CAST: Tommy Dorsey, Jimmy Dorsey, Janet Blair, William Lundigan, Paul Whiteman

A mildly musical, plotless dual biography of the Dorsey brothers as they fight their way to the top while fighting with each other, trombone and clarinet at the ready. Janet Blair is cute, William Lundigan is personable, and Paul "Pops" Whiteman is along for the ride.

1947 B & W 88 minutes

FAME

★★★½

DIRECTOR: Alan Parker

CAST: Irene Cara, Lee Curreri, Eddie Barth, Laura Dean, Paul McCrane, Barry Miller, Gene Anthony Ray, Maureen Teefy

In generations past, the ambitions of the young generally ranged from growing up to be president to becoming a doctor or a nurse or perhaps even a lawyer or a fireman. But today nearly everybody wants to be a star. *Fame* addresses that contemporary dream in a most charming and lively fashion. By focusing on the aspirations, struggles, and personal lives of a group of talented and ambitious students at New York City's High School of the Performing Arts, it manages to say something about all of us and the age we live in. Rated R.

1980 130 minutes

FAST FORWARD

★★★

DIRECTOR: Sidney Poitier

CAST: John Scott Clough, Don Franklin, Tamara Mark, Gretchen Palmer

An obvious attempt to capitalize on the success of *Fame*, *Flash-*

dance, and *Footloose* (if only in name), this is an undisguised variation on the cliché of "let's put on a show so we can make it in show biz." In other words, it's *Breakin' 3*—only this time from the Midwest. In it, eight high-school kids from Sandusky, Ohio, journey to the big city of New York for a promised audition. *Fast Forward* is a bubbly bit of fluff that relies on sheer energy to patch up its plot and make up for the lack of an inspired score. In general, it works. Rated PG.

1985 100 minutes

FIDDLER ON THE ROOF

★★★★

DIRECTOR: Norman Jewison
CAST: Topol, Norman Crane, Leonard Frey, Molly Picon, Paul Mann, Rosalind Harris, Isaac Stern

A lavishly mounted musical, this 1979 screen adaptation of the long-running Broadway hit, based on the stories of Sholem Aleichem, works remarkably well. This is primarily thanks to Topol's immensely likable portrayal of Tevye, the proud but put-upon father clinging desperately to the old values in a changing world. The score of Sheldon Harnick and Jerry Bock (featuring such songs as "If I Were a Rich Man" and "Sunrise, Sunset") is a delight. Isaac Stern is the rooftop fiddler. Rated G.

1971 181 minutes

FINIAN'S RAINBOW

★★½

DIRECTOR: Francis Coppola
CAST: Fred Astaire, Petula Clark, Tommy Steele, Keenan Wynn, Barbara Hancock, Don Francks

Those who believe Fred Astaire can do no wrong haven't seen this little oddity. Francis Coppola's heavy direction is totally inappropriate for a musical—a genre with which he clearly was not comfortable—and the story's concerns about racial progress, which were outdated when the film first appeared, are positively embarrassing now. The mix of Irish leprechauns and the American deep South is an uneasy vehicle for demonstrating the injustices of bigotry. Rated G.

1968 145 minutes

FIRST NUDIE MUSICAL, THE

★★★

DIRECTOR: Mark Haggard
CAST: Bruce Kimmel, Stephen Nathan, Cindy Williams, Diana Canova

A struggling young director saves the studio by producing the world's first pornographic movie musical à la Busby Berkeley. Pleasant but extremely crude little romp. Bruce Kimmel and Cindy Williams make a cute couple who act as if it's all nothing more than just harmless fun. At times it is. The score includes such memorable ditties as "Four Dancing Dildos out on a Spree!" and "Butch Dyke" (and that's a tango!). Not as bad as it sounds, but definitely for the very open-minded, and that's being generous. Rated R for nudity, profanity, and sex.

1979 100 minutes

FLASHDANCE

★★★

DIRECTOR: Adrian Lyne
CAST: Jennifer Beals, Michael Nouri, Lilia Skala

Director Adrian Lyne explodes images on the screen with eye-popping regularity while the spare screenplay centers on the ambitions of Alex Owens (Jennifer Beals), a welder who dreams of making the big time as a dancer. Alex finds this goal difficult to attain—until contractor Nick Hur-ley (Michael Nouri) decides to help. Rated R for nudity, profanity, and implied sex.

1983 96 minutes

FLOWER DRUM SONG

★★

DIRECTOR: Henry Koster

CAST: Jack Soo, Nancy Kwan, Benson Fong, Miyoshi Umeki, Juanita Hall, James Shigeta, Kam Tong, Reiko Sato

Set in San Francisco's colorful Chinatown, this Rogers and Hammerstein musical rings sour. It has its bright moments, but the score is largely second-rate. Whistled "Chop Suey" or hummed "I Enjoy Being A Girl" lately? The plot is conventional: a modern son's views versus those of an old-fashioned father. Ingredients include the usual Oriental cliché of an arranged marriage. Casting a pall over all is the obvious condescension displayed toward Chinese-Americans and the Bay City's Grant Avenue community. Moreover, the film is entirely too long.

1962 131 minutes

FLYING DOWN TO RIO

★★½

DIRECTOR: Thornton Freeland

CAST: Dolores Del Rio, Ginger Rogers, Fred Astaire

We're sure the joy of watching Fred Astaire and Ginger Rogers dance is the only thing that has prevented the negatives of this embarrassing movie from being burned. The ludicrous plot centers around an attempt to keep a Rio hotel afloat. The climactic dance number, in which chorus girls perform on airplane wings, is so corny it has now passed into the realm of camp humor.

1933 B & W 89 minutes

FOLLOW THE FLEET

★★★★

DIRECTOR: Mark Sandrich

CAST: Fred Astaire, Ginger Rogers, Randolph Scott, Harriet Hilliard, Betty Grable

In this musical Fred Astaire and Ginger Rogers are at their best, as a dance team separated by World War II. However, sailor Astaire still has time to romance Rogers while shipmate Randolph Scott gives the same treatment to her screen sister Harriet Hilliard (a.k.a. Harriet—Mrs. Ozzie—Nelson). Look for Lucille Ball in a small part.

1936 B & W 110 minutes

FOOTLIGHT PARADE

★★★½

DIRECTOR: Lloyd Bacon

CAST: James Cagney, Ruby Keeler, Joan Blondell, Dick Powell, Guy Kibbee, Hugh Herbert, Frank McHugh

Brash and cocksure James Cagney is a hustling stage director bent upon continually topping himself with Busby Berkeley–type musical numbers, which, not surprisingly, are directed by Busby Berkeley. Another grand-scale musical from the early days of sound films.

1933 B & W 100 minutes

FOOTLOOSE

★★★★

DIRECTOR: Herbert Ross

CAST: Kevin Bacon, Lori Singer, John Lithgow, Dianne Wiest, Christopher Penn

A highly entertaining film that combines the rock beat exuberance of *Flashdance* and *Risky Business* with an entertaining—and even touching—story. This features Kevin Bacon (*Diner*) as a Chicago boy who finds himself transplanted to a small rural town where rock music and dancing are banned—until he decides to do something about it. Rated PG for slight profanity and brief violence.

1984 107 minutes

42ND STREET

★★★★

DIRECTOR: Lloyd Bacon

CAST: Dick Powell, Ruby Keeler, Ginger Rogers, Warner Baxter, Una Merkel

Every understudy's dream is to get a big chance and rise to stardom. Such is the premise of *42nd Street*. This Depression-era musical of 1933 is lifted above cliché by its vitality and sincerity. Ruby Keeler plays the youngster with a dream, and Dick Powell is the romantic interest. Busby Berkeley began his illustrious choreographic career by staging the elaborate dance numbers.

1933 B & W 98 minutes

FRANKIE AND JOHNNY

★★★

DIRECTOR: Frederick de Cordova

CAST: Elvis Presley, Donna Douglas, Sue Ane Langdon, Harry Morgan, Nancy Kovack, Audrey Christie

As the song goes, Elvis, as a Mississippi riverboat singer-gambler, betrays his lady (Donna Douglas) with his roving heart. He easily captures the attention of beautiful young ladies but must suffer the consequences of his actions. Elvis fans won't be disappointed with this musical love story.

1966 87 minutes

FRENCH LINE, THE

★★

DIRECTOR: Lloyd Bacon

CAST: Jane Russell, Gilbert Roland, Mary McCarty, Craig Stevens, Steven Geray, Arthur Hunnicutt

This is a dull musical with forgettable songs. Ultrarich heroine Jane Russell can't find true love. She masquerades as a fashion model during a voyage on the French Line's luxury ship, *Liberté*, hoping her money won't show while she snags a man. Despite presenting Miss Russell in 3-D, the film was a bust.

1954 102 minutes

FROM MAO TO MOZART

★★★★½

DIRECTOR: Murray Lerner

CAST: Isaac Stern, David Golub, Tan Shuzhen

Violinist Isaac Stern's concert tour of Red China is the subject of this warm and perceptive Academy Award–winning documentary. Stern is seen playing with mainland Chinese orchestras and working with students who are all but incapable of understanding Western music. Beautifully photographed, this is a must for those interested in Stern, violin music, teaching, or a glimpse of mainland China not otherwise available. Unrated.

1980 88 minutes

FUN IN ACAPULCO

★★½

DIRECTOR: Richard Thorpe

CAST: Elvis Presley, Ursula Andress, Paul Lukas, Alejandro Rey, Elsa Cardenas

Beautiful Acapulco sets the stage for this sun-filled Elvis Presley musical. This time he's a lifeguard by day and a singer by night at a fancy beachfront resort. Typical of Elvis's films, this one never lacks romance.

1963 97 minutes

FUNNY FACE

★★★½

DIRECTOR: Stanley Donen

CAST: Fred Astaire, Audrey Hepburn, Kay Thompson, Michel Auclair, Ruta Lee

One of the best of Fred Astaire's later pictures. This time he's a fashion photographer who discovers naive Audrey Hepburn and turns her into a sensation. Typical fairy-tale plot, enlivened by Astaire's usual charm and a good score based on the works of George Gershwin. Kay Thompson has a good supporting part as a feisty magazine editor. Good fun. Unrated family fare.

1957 103 minutes

FUNNY GIRL

★★★★

DIRECTOR: William Wyler
CAST: Barbra Streisand, Omar Sharif, Walter Pidgeon, Kay Medford

The early years of Ziegfeld Follies star Fanny Brice was the inspiration for a superb stage musical. Barbra Streisand recreated her Broadway triumph in as stunning a movie debut in 1968 as Hollywood ever witnessed. She sings, roller-skates, cracks jokes, and tugs at your heart in a tour-de-force performance. Even though Streisand alone is reason enough to watch this classic, the costumes and sets go a long way in capturing an authentic flavor of the 1920s. Omar Sharif's cool sexuality is in perfect contrast to the fluttery Brice/Streisand. Rated G.

1968 155 minutes

FUNNY LADY

★★★

DIRECTOR: Herbert Ross
CAST: Barbra Streisand, James Caan, Omar Sharif, Ben Vereen

The sequel to Barbra Streisand's *Funny Girl* is not quite up to the original, but still worth seeing. We follow comedienne Fanny Brice after she became a stage luminary only to continue her misfortunes in private life. James Caan plays her second husband, producer Billy Rose, and Omar Sharif returns in his role of Fanny's first love. But Streisand's performance and a few of the musical numbers carry the day.

1975 149 minutes

GAY DIVORCEE, THE

★★★★

DIRECTOR: Mark Sandrich
CAST: Fred Astaire, Ginger Rogers, Edward Everett Horton, Alice Brady, Erik Rhodes, Eric Blore, Betty Grable

This delightful musical farce was the only Fred Astaire/Ginger Rogers film to be nominated for a best-picture Oscar. The outstanding score includes "Night and Day" and "The Continental." Edward Everett Horton heads the supporting cast, which, as usual, manages to add some comic touches to the wisp of a plot. After all, the fairy-tale nature of an Astaire/Rogers picture has only one essential, and that's a glistening dance floor.

1934 B & W 107 minutes

G.I. BLUES

★★★½

DIRECTOR: Norman Taurog
CAST: Elvis Presley, Juliet Prowse

Juliet Prowse improves this otherwise average Elvis Presley film. The action takes place in Germany, where Elvis makes a bet with his G.I. buddies he can date the aloof Prowse, who plays a nightclub dancer.

1960 104 minutes

GIGI

★★★★

DIRECTOR: Vincente Minnelli
CAST: Leslie Caron, Maurice Chevalier, Louis Jourdan, Hermione Gingold, Jacques Bergerac, Eva Gabor

Maurice Chevalier plays guardian to lovely Leslie Caron, who is coming of age in France in the early 1900s. Louis Jourdan plays her romantic interest.

1959 116 minutes

GIMME SHELTER

★★★★

DIRECTORS: David Maysles, Albert Maysles, Charlotte Zwerin

CAST: The Rolling Stones, Bill Wyman, Charlie Watts, Melvin Belli

This documentary chronicles the events leading up to and including the now infamous free Rolling Stones concert in 1969 at the Altamont Speedway outside San Francisco. It's the dark side of Woodstock, with many unforgettable scenes, including the actual murder of a spectator by the Hell's Angels in front of the stage as the Stones are playing. Mick Jagger's facial expressions tell all. Thought by many to have brought the curtain down on the flower-powered 1960s, the event on file is a must-see. Rated R for violence, language, and scenes of drug use.

1970 91 minutes

GIRL CRAZY

★★★

DIRECTORS: Busby Berkeley, Norman Taurog

CAST: Mickey Rooney, Judy Garland, June Allyson, Rags Ragland, Guy Kibbee, Gil Stratton, Nancy Walker, Henry O'Neill

Girls are driving the ever-ebullient Mickey Rooney bonkers. His family sends him to a small southwestern college, hoping the "craze" will fade, but he meets Judy Garland, and away we go into another happy kids-give-a-show musical with glorious George and Ira Gershwin tunes. It's all based on the 1930 Broadway hit, first filmed with Wheeler and Woolsey in 1932 and dully rehashed in 1965 as *When the Boys Meet the Girls*.

1943 B & W 99 minutes

GIRLS! GIRLS! GIRLS!

★★

DIRECTOR: Norman Taurog

CAST: Elvis Presley, Stella Stevens, Benson Fong, Laurel Goodwin, Jeremy Slate

In this musical comedy, Elvis Presley is chased by an endless array of beautiful girls. Sounds like the ideal situation? Not for poor Elvis as he tries to choose just one.

1962 105 minutes

GIVE MY REGARDS TO BROAD STREET

★★

DIRECTOR: Peter Webb

CAST: Paul McCartney, Ringo Starr, Barbara Bach, Linda McCartney

Paul McCartney has openly admitted he "wants to fill the world with silly love songs," which is fine, because he does them so well. However, now it seems he wants to do the same with silly movies. McCartney wrote and stars in the odd, but not really offensive, combination of great rock music and a truly insipid story as a rock singer who loses the master tapes for his album and finds his future seriously threatened. If the album isn't found by midnight, a sinister-looking fellow will then be able to take over his record company. Forget the story and enjoy the songs. Rated PG for mild violence.

1984 108 minutes

GLENN MILLER STORY, THE

★★★½

DIRECTOR: Anthony Mann

CAST: James Stewart, June Allyson, Charles Drake, Harry Morgan, Frances Langford, Gene Krupa, Louis Armstrong

Follows the life story of famous trombonist and bandleader Glenn Miller, who disappeared in a plane during World War II. Jimmy Stewart delivers a convincing portrayal of the popular bandleader whose music had all of America tapping its feet. Miller's music is the highlight of the film, with guest appearances by Louis Armstrong and Gene Krupa.

1954 116 minutes

GOLD DIGGERS OF 1933

★★★★

DIRECTOR: Mervyn LeRoy
CAST: Joan Blondell, Ruby Keeler, Dick Powell, Aline MacMahon, Ginger Rogers, Sterling Holloway

This typical 1930s song-and-dance musical revolves around a Broadway show. Notable tunes include: "We're in the Money," sung by Ginger Rogers; "Forgotten Man," sung by Joan Blondell; and "Shadow Waltz," by the chorus girls. Enjoyable fare if you like nostalgic musicals.

1933 B & W 96 minutes

GOLDWYN FOLLIES, THE

DIRECTOR: George Marshall
CAST: Adolphe Menjou, Andrea Leeds, Kenny Baker, The Ritz Brothers, Vera Zorina, Edgar Bergen and Charlie McCarthy

Goldwyn's folly is a better title for this turkey. The cast must have been standing around doing nothing on contract, and someone said, "Hey, let's make a movie! Adolphe, you be a producer. Andrea can be the wholesome ingenue. The Ritz Brothers can act zany, Zorina can dance, Edgar can do his thing, and Kenny can sing and sing and sing." And so they all did, darn it!

1938 120 minutes

GOOD NEWS

★★★

DIRECTOR: Charles Walters
CAST: June Allyson, Peter Lawford, Patricia Marshall, Joan McCracken, Mel Torme

Football hero Peter Lawford resists the class vamp and wins the big game and the campus cutie who loves him in this quintessential musical of college life. The plot's got a beard, the dialogue is painfully trite and trying, but energy and exuberance abound in the musical numbers. Set in the 1920s, it's fun to watch, if only as a nostalgic curiosity.

1948 95 minutes

GOSPEL

★★★★

DIRECTORS: David Levick, Frederick A. Rizenberg
CAST: Mighty Clouds of Joy, Clark Sisters, Walter Hawkins and the Hawkins Family, Shirley Caesar, Rev. James Cleveland

Featuring many of the top stars of black gospel music, this is a joyous, spirit-lifting music documentary that contains the highlights of a five-and-a-half-hour concert filmed in June 1981 at Oakland Paramount Theater. The spirited performances might even make a believer out of you—that is, if you aren't already. Rated G.

1982 92 minutes

GRATEFUL DEAD MOVIE, THE

★★★½

DIRECTORS: Jerry Garcia, Leon Gast
CAST: Grateful Dead

Deadheads will undoubtedly love this combination of backstage, concert, and animated psychedelic scenes. Supervised by Dead lead guitarist-vocalist Jerry Garcia, it's a laughable look at the mechanics and magic of rock. But the uninitiated and unconverted may find it tedious after a while.

1976 131 minutes

GREASE

★★

DIRECTOR: Randal Kleiser

CAST: John Travolta, Olivia Newton-John, Stockard Channing, Jeff Conaway, Didi Conn, Eve Arden, Sid Caesar

After they meet and enjoy a tender summer romance, John Travolta and Olivia Newton-John tearfully part. Surprisingly, they are reunited when she becomes the new girl at his high school. Around his friends, he must play Mr. Tough-Guy, and her goody-two-shoes image doesn't quite fit in. Some laughs, but quite a few yawns. Rated PG.

1978 110 minutes

GREASE 2

★★★

DIRECTOR: Patricia Birch

CAST: Maxwell Caufield, Michelle Pfeiffer, Adrian Zmed, Lorna Luft, Didi Conn

A sequel to the most successful screen musical of all time, *Grease 2* takes us back to Rydell High for more 1950s adolescent angst. *Grease* stars John Travolta and Olivia Newton-John have apparently graduated, leaving it up to Maxwell Caufield and Michelle Pfeiffer to lead the rockin' and romancin' in and out of the classroom. Choreographer-director Patricia Birch obviously didn't take it too seriously and keeps things moving at a fast pace, throwing in comedy, action, and musical numbers whenever things threaten to become dull. The result is a fun little movie that seems to work almost in spite of itself. Rated PG for suggestive gestures and lyrics.

1982 115 minutes

GREAT CARUSO, THE

★★★★

DIRECTOR: Richard Thorpe

CAST: Mario Lanza, Ann Blyth, Dorothy Kirsten, Jarmila Novatna

A number of factual liberties are taken in this lavish screen biography of the great Italian tenor, but no matter. Mario Lanza's voice is magnificent; Ann Blyth and Dorothy Kirsten sing like birds. Devotees of music will love the arias.

1950 109 minutes

GUYS AND DOLLS

DIRECTOR: Joseph L. Mankiewicz

CAST: Marlon Brando, Frank Sinatra, Jean Simmons, Vivian Blaine, Stubby Kaye, Veda Ann Borg

This passable musical stars Marlon Brando and Frank Sinatra as New York gamblers with a gangsterlike aura. Brando and Sinatra bet on whether or not a lovely Salvation Army soldier (Jean Simmons) is date bait.

1955 150 minutes

GYPSY

★★★

DIRECTOR: Mervyn LeRoy

CAST: Natalie Wood, Rosalind Russell, Karl Malden

The story of the backstage mother has been told so often it has become a stereotype. *Gypsy* tries to surpass this hackneyed situation with an energetic musical score and a story about real people. In this case, the characters are stripper Gypsy Rose Lee and her backstage mother supreme, Rose. The music is excellent, but the characters are weakly defined.

They end up very little removed from caricature.

1962 149 minutes

HAIR

★★★★

DIRECTOR: Milos Forman

CAST: Treat Williams, John Savage, Beverly D'Angelo, Annie Golden, Cheryl Barnes, Charlotte Rae

Neglected adaptation of the hit Broadway play about 1960s unrest deserved far better than it received at the box office. John Savage is the uptight Midwesterner who pals up with a group of (shudder) hippies celebrating the Age of Aquarius. Grand musical moments, due to Twyla Tharp's impressive choreography; particularly droll is Treat Williams's rendition of the title song at an upper-crust dinner party. However dated some of the concepts, the final role-reversal retains considerable emotional impact. Rated PG for nudity.

1979 121 minutes

HAPPY GO LOVELY

★★★

DIRECTOR: Bruce Humberstone

CAST: David Niven, Vera-Ellen, Cesar Romero

Perky Vera-Ellen is a dancing darling in this lightweight musical with a very tired plot about a producer who hires a chorus girl with the idea that her boyfriend has money to invest in his show. It's all cute, but nothing startling.

1951 87 minutes

HARD DAY'S NIGHT, A

★★★★★

DIRECTOR: Richard Lester

CAST: The Beatles, Wilfred Brambell, Victor Spinetti, Anna Quayle

Put simply, this is the greatest rock-'n-roll movie ever made. Scripted by Alan Owen as a sort of "day in the life of the Beatles," it's fast-paced, funny, and full of great Lennon-McCartney songs. Even more than twenty years after its release, it continues to delight several generations of viewers. That is in no small way due to the inspired direction of Richard Lester (*The Three Musketeers*; *Superman II*)—and, of course, the charisma of John Lennon, Paul McCartney, George Harrison, and Ringo Starr.

1964 B & W 85 minutes

HARD TO HOLD

★½

DIRECTOR: Larry Peerce

CAST: Rick Springfield, Janet Eilber, Patti Hansen, Albert Salmi

In this highly forgettable, mostly mediocre film, directed by Larry Peerce (*The Other Side of the Mountain*), Rick Springfield—we'll pause for screams from his fans here—makes his screen debut as—what else?—a sexy rock star. The former regular on the TV soap "General Hospital" and singer of such hits as "Jessie's Girl" and "Love Somebody" plays James "Jamie" Roberts, a music superstar who has everything except the one thing he really wants: the woman (Janet Eilber) he loves. Poor baby. The first half-hour, which is light and funny, is quite good, but from there it goes decidedly downhill, into sappy soap opera, making *Hard to Hold* hard to watch. Rated PG for brief nudity and profanity.

1984 93 minutes

HARDER THEY COME, THE

★★★★

DIRECTOR: Perry Henzell

CAST: Jimmy Cliff, Janet Barkley, Carl Bradshaw, Ras Daniel Hartman, Bobby Charlton

Made in Jamaica by Jamaicans, this film has become an underground cult classic. In it, a rural boy comes to the big city to become a singer. There, he is forced into a life of crime. Rated R.

1973 98 minutes

HARUM SCARUM

★½

DIRECTOR: Gene Nelson

CAST: Elvis Presley, Mary Ann Mobley, Fran Jeffries, Michael Ansara

Unbelievable tale of a movie star (Elvis Presley) who is kidnapped during a promotional tour of the Middle East.

1965 86 minutes

HARVEY GIRLS, THE

★★★

DIRECTOR: Vincente Minnelli

CAST: Judy Garland, John Hodiak, Ray Bolger, Preston Foster, Virginia O'Brien, Angela Lansbury, Marjorie Main, Chill Wills, Cyd Charisse, Kenny Baker

Rousing fun marks this big, bustling musical, which is loosely tied to the development of pioneer railroad-station restaurant-eur Fred Harvey's string of eateries along the Santa Fe right-of-way. Judy Garland is the innocent who goes West to grow up, Angela Lansbury is the wise bad girl, and John Hodiak is the requisite gambler. The songs and the way they're sung are great.

1945 104 minutes

HEAD

★★★

DIRECTOR: Bob Rafelson

CAST: Micky Dolenz, David Jones, Michael Nesmith, Peter Tork, Teri Garr, Vito Scotti, Timothy Carey, Logan Ramsey

They get the funniest looks from everyone they meet. And it's no wonder. This film is truly bizarre. The Monkees were hurtled to fame in the aftershock of the Beatles' success. Their ingratiating series was accused of imitating *A Hard Day's Night*, but their innovative feature-film debut, *Head*, was ahead of its time. A free-form product of the psychedelic era, it's vastly more entertaining than the Beatles' *Magical Mystery Tour*. Though the music here is far from the Monkees' most commercial, there's enough freshness and exuberance in the visuals to carry the film. The fact that it was written by Jack Nicholson and Bob Rafelson, as well as its featuring offbeat cameos by the likes of Frank Zappa, Sonny Liston, Victor Mature, and Annette Funicello, has contributed to making this one a cult favorite. Classic Hollywood film clips add to the fun. Watch for a young Teri Garr, billed as Terry Garr.

1968 86 minutes

HELLO, DOLLY!

★

DIRECTOR: Gene Kelly

CAST: Barbra Streisand, Walter Matthau, Michael Crawford, E. J. Peaker, Marianne McAndrew

A multimillion-dollar disaster, this 1969 "spectacular" features a miscast Barbra Streisand as an intrepid matchmaker. Streisand's co-star, Walter Matthau, has commented she is one of the few performers with whom he never wants to work again—and that has nothing to do with the box-office failure of this awkward musical, directed by Gene Kelly. Rated G.

1969 146 minutes

HELP!

★★★★

DIRECTOR: Richard Lester

CAST: The Beatles, Leo McKern, Eleanor Bron, Victor Spinetti

Though neither as inventive nor as charming as *A Hard Day's Night*, this second collaboration between director Richard Lester and the Fab Four has enough energy, fun, and memorable songs to make it worth viewing again and again. The slim plot has a bizarre religious cult trying to retrieve a sacrificial ring from Ringo. From the reverberating opening chord of the title tune, the movie sweeps you up in its irresistibly zesty spirit.

1965 90 minutes

HIGH SOCIETY

★★★½

DIRECTOR: Charles Walters
CAST: Bing Crosby, Frank Sinatra, Grace Kelly, Louis Armstrong

The outstanding cast in this film is reason enough to watch this enjoyable musical remake of *The Philadelphia Story.* The film moves at a leisurely pace, helped by some nice songs by Cole Porter.

1956 107 minutes

HOLIDAY INN

★★★★

DIRECTOR: Mark Sandrich
CAST: Bing Crosby, Fred Astaire, Marjorie Reynolds, Virginia Dale, Rosemary Clooney

Irving Berlin's music and the delightful teaming of Bing Crosby and Fred Astaire are the high points of this wartime musical. The timeless renditions of "White Christmas" and "Easter Parade" more than make up for a script that at best could be called fluff.

1942 B & W 101 minutes

HOLLYWOOD HOTEL

★★

DIRECTOR: Busby Berkeley
CAST: Dick Powell, Rosemary Lane, Lola Lane, Ted Healy, Alan Mowbray, Frances Langford, Hugh Herbert, Louella Parsons, Glenda Farrell, Edgar Kennedy

Saxophonist Dick Powell wins a talent contest, gets a film contract, but gets the boot because he won't cozy up to bitchy star Lola Lane, preferring her sister instead. Hired to voice-double nonsinging Alan Mowbray, he finally works his way upward when Mowbray is kept off Louella Parsons's "Hollywood Hotel" radio program. Powell appears, sings, and the truth comes out. Songs by Johnny Mercer and Richard Whiting, including "Hooray for Hollywood," help bolster this otherwise average musical mishmash. Glenda Farrell wisecracks; Edgar Kennedy blusters. Louella Parsons simpers and fawns.

1937 B & W 109 minutes

HONEYSUCKLE ROSE

★★½

DIRECTOR: Jerry Schatzberg
CAST: Willie Nelson, Dyan Cannon, Amy Irving, Slim Pickens

For his first starring role, country singer Willie Nelson is saddled with a rather stodgy film that all but sinks in the mire of its unimaginative handling and sappy story. As a result, *Honeysuckle Rose* is something only his devoted fans will love, and even then with a bit of effort. Rated PG.

1980 119 minutes

HOW TO STUFF A WILD BIKINI

★★

DIRECTOR: William Asher
CAST: Frankie Avalon, Annette Funicello, Dwayne Hickman, Mickey Rooney, Buster Keaton

It's no surprise to see Frankie Avalon and Annette Funicello together in this beach party film. Dwayne Hickman (TV's Dobie

Gillis) tries his hand at romancing Annette in this one. Not much plot, but lots of crazy (sometimes funny) things are going on (including a motorcycle race).

1965 90 minutes

I DO! I DO!

★★★★

DIRECTOR: Gower Champion
CAST: Lee Remick, Hal Linden

Lee Remick and Hal Linden step into the parts originally created on Broadway by Mary Martin and Robert Preston in this video of a performance taped before an audience. The play is the musical version of *The Fourposter*, and deals with the marriage of Michael to Agnes—from the night before their wedding to the day when they leave their home of forty years. The song that made the pop charts from this one is the beautiful "My Cup Runneth Over." In an age when music videos are too-common fare, it's nice to have one for people over the age and IQ of 12. Solid entertainment.

1982 116 minutes

IDOLMAKER, THE

★★★★

DIRECTOR: Taylor Hackford
CAST: Ray Sharkey, Tovah Feldshuh, Peter Gallagher, Maureen McCormick

This superior rock-'n-roll drama stands with a handful of pictures —*The Buddy Holly Story* and *American Hot Wax* among them —as one of the few to capture the excitement of rock music while still offering something in the way of a decent plot and characterization. Ray Sharkey is excellent as a songwriter-manager who pulls, pushes, punches, and plunders his way to the top of the music world. The score, by Jeff Barry, is topnotch. Rated PG.

1980 119 minutes

IN SEARCH OF THE WOW WOW WIBBLE WOGGLE WAZZLE WOODLE WOO!

★★★★

DIRECTOR: Barry Caillier
CAST: Tim Noah

An infectiously scored, engagingly staged musical, featuring Tim Noah in what is virtually a one-man show. The talented Noah is assisted by a company of Muppet-like soft-sculpture creatures, such as Musty Moldy Melvin and Greasy Grimy Gerty. A celebration of the imagination, this film will appeal to the child in everyone. Rated G.

1985 55 minutes

IN THE GOOD OLD SUMMERTIME

★★★

DIRECTOR: Robert Z. Leonard
CAST: Judy Garland, Van Johnson, S. Z. Sakall, Buster Keaton, Spring Byington

Despite its title, most of the action of this remake of the classic romantic comedy *The Shop Around the Corner* takes place in winter. Judy Garland and Van Johnson work in the same music store. They dislike each other, but are unknowingly secret pen pals who have much in common. Truth wins out, but by the time it does, love has struck. Lovely setting, some fine old tunes, but cutseypie. Buster Keaton is wasted as comic relief.

1949 102 minutes

INVITATION TO THE DANCE

★★★

DIRECTOR: Gene Kelly
CAST: Gene Kelly, Igor Youskevitch, Claire Sombert, David Paltenghi, Claude Bessy, Tommy Rall, Carol Haney, Daphne Dale

Strictly for lovers of the dance, this film tells three stories entirely by the art. It sort of drags until Gene Kelly appears in a live action-cartoon sequence about "Sinbad" of Arabian Nights fame.

1957 93 minutes

IT HAPPPENED AT THE WORLD'S FAIR

★★½

DIRECTOR: Norman Taurog

CAST: Elvis Presley, Joan O' Brien, Gary Lockwood, Yvonne Craig

Adorable tyke plays matchmaker for Elvis Presley and Joan O'Brien at Seattle Worlds's Fair. It's a breezy romantic comedy with bouncy songs. Elvis hadn't yet reached the point where he was just going through the motions. He seems to be having fun and you will, too.

1963 105 minutes

IT'S ALWAYS FAIR WEATHER

★★★

DIRECTORS: Gene Kelly, Stanley Donen

CAST: Gene Kelly, Dan Dailey, Michael Kidd, Cyd Charisse, Dolores Gray, David Burns

World War II buddies Gene Kelly, Dan Dailey, and Michael Kidd meet a decade after discharge and find they no longer have anything in common and actively dislike one another. Enter romance, reconciliation ploys, and attempted exploitation of their reunion on televison. In between are exuberant, clever musical dance sequences involving ashcan lids, roller skates, and boxers in a gym. Don't be surprised to realize it recalls *On the Town*.

1955 102 minutes

JAILHOUSE ROCK

★★★★

DIRECTOR: Richard Thorpe

CAST: Elvis Presley, Mickey Shaughnessy, Dean Jones, Judy Tyler

Quite possibly Elvis Presley's best as far as musical sequences go, this 1957 film is still burdened by a sappy plot. Good-hearted Presley gets stuck in the slammer, only to hook up with a conniving manager (Mickey Shaughnessy). Forget the plot and enjoy the great rock-'n-roll songs.

1957 B & W 96 minutes

JANIS

★★★

DIRECTORS: Howard Alk, Seaton Findlay

CAST: Documentary

The most comprehensive documentary study of flower-child Janis Joplin, this is filled with poignant memories and electrifying performances. The powerful and tragic singer sought love and acceptance but walked a path that brought her to despair and finally a junkie's death. Interviews with the lady herself as well as friends and fellow musicians are interspersed with a variety of different concert appearances that portray Janis at the top of her form. Rated R for language.

1974 96 minutes

JAZZ SINGER, THE

★

DIRECTOR: Richard Fleischer

CAST: Neil Diamond, Laurence Olivier, Lucie Arnaz

After completing this film, in which Neil Diamond plays the title role, Laurence Olivier called it "the worst piece of garbage" that he'd ever been associated with. We'll buy that. Diamond is a total non-actor, showing all the finesse of a comatose bill collector. Only Lucie Arnaz shines, as a sexy show business manager, in this film about a fifth-generation Jewish cantor who leaves his wife, father, and synagogue to become a big rock-'n-roll star. It's a mushy mishmash that only Diamond's most devoted fans will love. Rated PG.

1980 115 minutes

JESUS CHRIST SUPERSTAR

★★★½

DIRECTOR: Norman Jewison

CAST: Ted Neeley, Carl Anderson, Yvonne Elliman

Believe it or not, this could be the ancestor of such rock videos as Michael Jackson's "Thriller." The movie illustrates segments of Jesus Christ's later life by staging sets and drama to go along with the soundtrack. This will not offer any religious experiences in the traditional sense, but is interesting nonetheless. Rated G.

1973 103 minutes

JOLSON SINGS AGAIN

★★½

DIRECTOR: Henry Levine

CAST: Larry Parks, Barbara Hale, William Demarest, Bill Goodwin, Ludwig Donath, Myron McCormick

Most sequels do not measure up. This continuation of *The Jolson Story*, while watchable, is no exception. Larry Parks again does the great and incomparable Al Jolson to a turn; Jolson himself again sings his unforgettable standards. But the film, trumped up to cash in, hasn't the class, charm, or swagger of the original. "Jolie," however, sings up a storm.

1949 96 minutes

JOLSON STORY, THE

★★★★

DIRECTOR: Alfred E. Green

CAST: Larry Parks, William Demarest, Evelyn Keyes, Bill Goodwin, Ludwig Donath, Scotty Beckett

The show business life story of vaudeville and Broadway stage great Al Jolson gets all-stops-out treatment in this fast-paced, tuneful film. Larry Parks acts and lip-syncs the hard-driving entertainer to a T. Jolson himself dubbed the singing. Crammed with all his famous numbers: "Swanee," "April Showers," "Mammy," etc. This one's a winner.

1946 128 minutes

JUMBO

★½

DIRECTOR: Charles Walters

CAST: Doris Day, Stephen Boyd, Jimmy Durante, Martha Raye, Dean Jagger

A big-budget circus-locale musical that all but flopped, despite Rodgers and Hart songs, William Daniels photography, a Sidney Sheldon script from a Hecht and MacArthur story, and a cast that should have known better. Honestly, it's not worth sitting through to hear Jimmy Durante's enduring line, "Elephant? What elephant?"

1962 125 minutes

KID MILLIONS

★★

DIRECTOR: Roy Del Ruth

CAST: Eddie Cantor, Ethel Merman, Ann Sothern, George Murphy, Warren Hymer

The fifth of six elaborate musicals produced with Eddie Cantor by Samuel Goldwyn. Banjo Eyes inherits a fortune and becomes the mark for a parade of con artists. Lavish Busby Berkeley musical numbers help to salvage an otherwise inane plot. Goldwyn Girl Lucille Ball is discernible in the chorus. An engaging sequence set in an ice cream factory is in early three-color pastel Technicolor.

1934 B & W 90 minutes

KIDS ARE ALRIGHT, THE

★★★½

DIRECTOR: Jeff Stein

CAST: The Who, Ringo Starr, Steve Martin, Tom Smothers

More a documentary detailing the career of British rock group the Who than an entertainment, this film by Jeff Stein still manages to capture the essence of the trend-setting band and, in doing so, the spirit of rock-'n-roll. Rated PG.

1979 108 minutes

KING AND I, THE

★★★★½

DIRECTOR: Walter Lang

CAST: Yul Brynner, Deborah Kerr, Rita Moreno

Yul Brynner and Deborah Kerr star in this superb 1956 Rodgers and Hammerstein musicalization of *Anna and the King of Siam*. Kerr is the widowed teacher who first clashes, then falls in love with, the King (Brynner). The songs include "Hello, Young Lovers," "Getting to Know You," and "Shall We Dance?" (Kerr's singing was dubbed by Marni Nixon.)

1956 133 minutes

KING CREOLE

★★★★

DIRECTOR: Michael Curtiz

CAST: Elvis Presley, Carolyn Jones, Dolores Hart, Dean Jagger, Walter Matthau

A surprisingly strong Elvis Presley vehicle, this musical, set in New Orleans, benefits by strong direction from Michael Curtiz (*Casablanca*).

1958 116 minutes

KING OF JAZZ, THE

★★★

DIRECTOR: John Murray Anderson

CAST: Paul Whiteman and His Orchestra, John Boles, The Rhythm Boys (Bing Crosby, Al Rinker, Harry Barris)

Lavish big-budget musical revue chock-full of big production numbers and great songs. Shot in early two-color Technicolor. Imaginative settings and photography make this last of the all-star extravaganzas most impressive. Clever cartoon sequence opens the show.

1930 93 minutes

KISMET

★★½

DIRECTOR: Vincente Minnelli

CAST: Howard Keel, Ann Blyth, Monty Woolley, Vic Damone, Dolores Gray

The Borodin-based Arabian Nights fantasy, a hit on Broadway, is stylishly staged and ripe with "Baubles, Bangles, and Beads" and Dolores Gray's show-stopping "Bagdad." Sadly, however, the shift to film loses the snap and crackle despite great singing by Howard Keel, Vic Damone, and Ann Blyth. The earlier (1944) Ronald Colman version is more fun and half a star better.

1955 113 minutes

KISS ME KATE

★★★

DIRECTOR: George Sidney

CAST: Howard Keel, Katherine Grayson, Keenan Wynn, James Whitmore, Ann Miller, Tommy Rall, Bobby Van, Bob Fosee

That which is Shakespeare's *Taming of the Shrew* in the original is deftly rendered by Cole Porter, scripter Dorothy Kingsley, and George Sidney's graceful direction, by way of some fine performances by Howard Keel and Katherine Grayson as a married pair whose on-stage and off-stage lives mingle. Keenan Wynn and James Whitmore play as engaging a duo of low comic gangster types as ever brushed up on their Shakespeare.

1953 109 minutes

KNICKERBOCKER HOLIDAY

★★

DIRECTOR: Harry Brown

CAST: Nelson Eddy, Charles Coburn, Shelley Winters, Chester Conklin, Constance Dowling, Percy Kilbride

A plodding, lackluster rendition of the Kurt Weill/Maxwell Anderson musical about Peter Stuyvesant and Dutch New York. The best song, "September Song," was originally sung by Walter Huston. Unfortunately, he's not in the film.

1944 B & W 85 minutes

KOYAANISQATSI

★★★★

DIRECTOR: Godfrey Reggio

The title is a Hopi Indian word meaning "crazy life, life in turmoil, life disintegrating, life out of balance, a state of life that calls for another way of living." In keeping with this, director Godfrey Reggio contrasts scenes of nature to the hectic life of the city. There is no plot or dialogue. Instead, the accent is on the artistic cinematography, by Ron Fricke, and the score, by Philip Glass. It's a feast for the eyes and ears. No MPAA rating.

1983 87 minutes

KRUSH GROOVE

★½

DIRECTOR: Michael Schultz

CAST: Blair Underwood, Sheila E., Kurtis Blow, The Fat Boys, Run DMC

Lame rap musical featuring several performances by well-known artists and not much more. Blair Underwood plays the owner of Krush Groove Records, a small, struggling recoring company whose clients include Run DMC and Kurtis Blow. Unable to raise money for the pressing of their records, Underwood loses his acts to a rival record company. Of course, they all return to help him when he needs them. The film is a little more than a series of musical numbers staged with very little imagination. Rated R.

1985 95 minutes

LA BAMBA

★★★½

DIRECTOR: Luis Valdez

CAST: Lou Diamond Phillips, Rosana DeSoto, Esai Morales, Danielle von Zerneck, Elizabeth Peña

At the age of seventeen, with three huge hits under his belt, Ritchie Valens joined Buddy Holly and the Big Bopper on an ill-fated airplane ride that killed all three and left rock-'n-roll bereft of some giant talent. In this biography, *Zoot Suit* writer-director Luis Valdez achieves a fine blend of a 1950s hard-hitting rock-'n-roll tale and a good clean soap opera that only gets mawkish when dealing with the Valens brothers' sibling rivalry. Sweet-faced Lou Diamond Phillips makes an impressive debut as the determined Valens who went on to become America's first Latino singing star. Rosana DeSoto gives a vigorous performance as Valens's mother and staunchest supporter. Los Lobos does an outstanding job of covering the hits "Donna," "Come On Let's Go," and "La Bamba." Rated PG-13 for language.

1987 108 minutes

LADY SINGS THE BLUES

★★★½

DIRECTOR: Sidney J. Furie

CAST: Diana Ross, Billy Dee Williams, Richard Pryor

Former Supremes lead singer Diana Ross made a dynamic screen debut in this screen biography of another singing great, Billie Holiday, whose career was thwarted by drug addiction. Rated R.

1972 144 minutes

LAST WALTZ, THE

★★★★

DIRECTOR: Martin Scorsese

CAST: The Band, Bob Dylan, Neil Young, Joni Mitchell, Van Morrison, Eric Clapton, Neil Diamond, Muddy Waters

Director Martin Scorsese's (*Taxi Driver*) superb documentary of the Band's final concert appearance. With guest stars such as Eric Clapton, Joni Mitchell, Neil Young, Van Morrison, Muddy Waters, Paul Butterfield, and more, it's an unforgettable celebration of American music. Rated PG.

1978 117 minutes

LES GIRLS

★★★★

DIRECTOR: George Cukor

CAST: Gene Kelly, Kay Kendall, Taina Elg, Mitzi Gaynor, Jacques Bergerac

Gene Kelly is charming, Mitzi Gaynor is funny, Taina Elg is funnier, Kay Kendall is funniest in this tale of a libel suit over a published memoir. Three conflicting accounts of what was and wasn't emerge in flashback from the courtroom. A nifty, witty, wholly entertaining film with Cole Porter music and stylish direction by George Cukor. C'est magnifique!

1957 114 minutes

LET IT BE

★★★½

DIRECTOR: Michael Lindsay-Hogg

CAST: The Beatles

The last days of the Beatles are chronicled in this *cinéma vérité* production, which was originally meant to be just a documentary on the recording of an album. What emerges, however, is a portrait of four men who have outgrown their images and, sadly, one another. There are moments of abandon, in which they recapture the old magic—especially in the rooftop concert climax—but overall, the movie makes it obvious that the Beatles would never get back to where they once belonged. Rated G.

1970 80 minutes

LET'S SPEND THE NIGHT TOGETHER

★★★½

DIRECTOR: Hal Ashby

CAST: The Rolling Stones

In this documentary, directed by Hal Ashby (*Being There*; *Harold and Maude*), the Rolling Stones —Mick Jagger, Keith Richard, Bill Wyman, Charlie Watts, Ron Wood, and Ian Stewart—are seen rockin' and rollin' in footage shot during the band's 1981 American tour. It's a little too long—but Stone fans and hard-core rockers should love it. Rated PG for suggestive lyrics and behavior.

1982 94 minutes

LISZTOMANIA

DIRECTOR: Ken Russell

CAST: Roger Daltrey, Sara Kestleman, Paul Nicholas, Fiona Lewis, Ringo Starr

Ken Russell lets his lurid imagination run sickeningly wild in this hokey "screen biography" on the life of composer Franz Liszt (played by Roger Daltrey, lead singer for the rock group the Who). The director's fans will revel in this onslaught of bad taste and outrageousness, but those not lobotomized will want to avoid it. Rated R.

1975 105 minutes

LITTLE NIGHT MUSIC, A

★★½

DIRECTOR: Harold Prince
CAST: Elizabeth Taylor, Diana Rigg, Lesley-Anne Down

Based on Ingmar Bergman's comedy about sexual liaisons at a country mansion, this musical version doesn't quite come to life. Rated PG.

1978 124 minutes

LITTLE SHOP OF HORRORS

★★★★½

DIRECTOR: Frank Oz
CAST: Rick Moranis, Ellen Greene, Vincent Gardenia, Steve Martin, Jim Belushi, John Candy, Bill Murray, Christopher Guest

This totally bent musical-horror-comedy was based on director Roger Corman's bizarre horror cheapie from 1961. Rick Moranis is wonderful as the schnook who finds and cares for a man-eating plant set on conquering the world. Ellen Greene is delightfully dumb as the object of Moranis's affections, and Vincent Gardenia has a plum part as his greedy boss. In addition, Steve Martin, Bill Murray, John Candy, Jim Belushi, and Christopher Guest drop in for some hilarious comedy bits. It's outrageous, weird, and even a little sick on one hand, and uproariously funny, marvelously acted, spectacularly staged, and tuneful on the other. In other words, a classic of modern cinema. Rated PG-13 for violence.

1986 90 minutes

LOVING YOU

DIRECTOR: Hal Kanter
CAST: Elvis Presley, Lizabeth Scott, Wendell Corey, Dolores Hart

This better-than-average Elvis Presley vehicle features him as a small-town country boy who makes good when his singing ability is discovered. It has a bit of romance but the main attraction is Elvis singing his rock-'n-roll songs, including the title tune.

1957 101 minutes

MAGICAL MYSTERY TOUR

★½

DIRECTOR: The Beatles
CAST: The Beatles, Bonzo Dog Band, Mal Evans, Mike McGear

This is a tour by bus and by mind. Unfortunately, the minds involved must have been distorted at the time that the film was made. It is about as much fun as bus tour of Fresno during a heat wave. Occasional bursts of wit and imagination come through, but mostly this chunk of psychedelic pretension is a crashing bore. Songs include "Fool on the Hill," "I Am the Walrus," and "Strawberry Fields Forever."

1967 60 minutes

MAME

DIRECTOR: Gene Saks
CAST: Lucille Ball, Robert Preston, Jane Connell, Beatrice Arthur

You won't love Lucy in this one. Or Robert Preston, either. It's Roz Russell's boffo *Auntie Mame* with music, and the notes are all sour. Rated PG.

1974 131 minutes

MAN OF LA MANCHA

DIRECTOR: Arthur Hiller
CAST: Peter O'Toole, Sophia Loren, James Coco, Harry Andrews

For those who loved the hit Broadway musical and those who heard about it and looked forward to this film, this is a shameful and outrageous letdown. This is what happens when Hollywood thinks it can do better than a hundred-percent successful stage original. Rated G.

1972 130 minutes

MAYTIME

★★★

DIRECTOR: Robert Z. Leonard

CAST: Jeanette MacDonald, Nelson Eddy, John Barrymore, Herman Bing, Sig Ruman

A curio of the past. A penniless tenor meets and falls in love with an opera star suffering in a loveless marriage to her adoring and jealous teacher and mentor. The hands Fate deals are not pat. See if you can tell that John Barrymore is reading his lines from idiot boards off camera. This film is one of the Eddy/MacDonald duo's best.

1937 B & W 132 minutes

MEET ME IN ST. LOUIS

★★★★

DIRECTOR: Vincente Minnelli

CAST: Judy Garland, Margaret O'Brien, Tom Drake

Here's a fun-filled entertainment package made at the MGM studios during the heyday of their musicals. This nostalgic look at a family in St. Louis before the 1903 World's Fair dwells on the tension when the father announces an impending transfer to New York. Judy Garland's songs remain fresh and enjoyable today.

1944 112 minutes

METROPOLIS (MUSICAL VERSION)

★★★★★

DIRECTOR: Fritz Lang (and Giorgio Moroder)

CAST: Brigitte Helm, Alfred Abel, Gustav Froelich

Fritz Lang's 1926 silent science-fiction classic has been enhanced with special individual coloring and tints, recently recovered scenes, storyboards and stills. The rock score, supervised by Giorgio Moroder, features Pat Benatar, Bonnie Tyler, Loverboy, Billy Squier, Adam Ant, Freddie Mercury, Jon Anderson, and Cycle V. A modern screen triumph.

1984 120 minutes

MILLION DOLLAR MERMAID

★★

DIRECTOR: Mervyn LeRoy

CAST: Esther Williams, Victor Mature, Walter Pidgeon, David Brian, Jesse White

Esther William swims through her role as famous early distaff aquatic star Annette Kellerman, who pioneered one-piece suits and vaudeville tank acts. Victor Mature woos her in this highly fictionalized film biography. The Busby Berkeley production numbers are a highlight.

1952 115 minutes

MRS. BROWN YOU'VE GOT A LOVELY DAUGHTER

★★

DIRECTOR: Saul Swimmer

CAST: Herman's Hermits, Stanley Holloway

England's Herman's Hermits star in this film, named after one of their hit songs. The limited plot revolves around the group acquiring a greyhound and deciding to race it. Caution: Only for hardcore Herman's Hermits fans! Rated G.

1968 110 minutes

MURDER AT THE VANITIES

★★★½

DIRECTOR: Mitchell Leisen

CAST: Jack Oakie, Kitty Carlisle, Victor McLaglen, Carl Brisson, Donald Meek, Gail Patrick, Toby Wing, Jessie Ralph, Duke Ellington, Ann Sheridan

A musical whodunit, this blend of comedy and mystery finds tenacious Victor McLaglen embroiled in a murder investigation at Earl Carroll's Vanities, a popular and long-running variety show of the 1930s and 1940s. Musical numbers and novelty acts pop up between clues in this stylish oddity, ably directed by Paramount's reliable Mitchell Leisen, a highly capable and underrated comedy craftsman. Jack Oakie is fast and loose, and he and McLaglen get top support from character greats such as Donald Meek and Gail Patrick. Duke Ellington makes a special cameo appearance and the first rate songs and production numbers include "Sweet Marijuana" and "Tea for Two." Lots of fun for fans of comedy, detection, and night-club entertainment, this square peg is reminiscent of other Paramount peculiars such as *International House* and *Million Dollar Legs*.

1934 B & W 89 minutes

MUSIC MAN, THE

★★★★½

DIRECTOR: Morton Da Costa
CAST: Robert Preston, Shirley Jones, Buddy Hackett, Ronny Howard, Paul Ford, Hermione Gingold

They sure don't make musicals like this anymore, a smashing adaptation of Meredith Willson's Broadway hit. Robert Preston reprises the role of his life as a smooth-talkin' salesman who cajoles the parents of River City, Iowa, into purchasing band instruments and uniforms for their children. Rarely has a single musical produced so many recognizable, toe-tapping songs, including "Trouble" and "Seventy-six Trombones." A few new songs were added to this film version, but the spirit and excitement of the play remain intact.

1962 151 minutes

MY FAIR LADY

★★★★½

DIRECTOR: George Cukor
CAST: Rex Harrison, Audrey Hepburn, Stanley Holloway

Pygmalion, the timeless George Bernard Shaw play, has been a smashing success in every form in which it has been presented. This Oscar-winning 1964 movie musical adaptation is no exception. Rex Harrison, as Professor Henry Higgins, is the perfect example of British class snobbishness. Higgins accepts a bet that he can't take a cockney guttersnipe and transform her into a socially acceptable lady. Audrey Hepburn gives a fine performance as his subject, Eliza Doolittle (with Marni Nixon supplying the singing).

1964 170 minutes

MY NAME IS BARBRA

★★★★

DIRECTOR: Dwight Hemion
CAST: Barbra Streisand

Barbra Streisand fans have a real treasure awaiting them in *My Name Is Barbra*. Shown in 1965, shot in black and white, and featuring no guests, it was Streisand's first television special. It's a wonderful opportunity to see this exceptional performer that early in her career. There are a couple of really good musical-comedy skits, including "I'm Five," where she gives Lily Tomlin's Edith Ann a run for her money, and a segment where she sings down-and-out songs while parading through Bergdorf Goodman in ritzy clothes. And it's great finally to be able to watch Streisand sing some of the older tunes, to see the naughtiness in her eyes as she sings "How Does the Wine Taste" and "Lover, Come Back to Me." Viewers will also be treated to

knockout versions of "When the Sun Comes Out" and "My Man."
1965 60 minutes

NEPTUNE'S DAUGHTER

★★½

DIRECTOR: Edward Buzzell

CAST: Esther Williams, Red Skelton, Keenan Wynn, Ricardo Montalban, Betty Garrett, Mel Blanc, Mike Mazurki, Ted de Corsia, Xavier Cugat

Big-budgeted aquatic musical from MGM studios has Esther Williams playing a (what else?) swimsuit designer on holiday in South America floating in and out of danger with Red Skelton. Esther takes a back seat to the incredible waterworks and never-ending parade of arresting character actors (and voices) like Mel Blanc, Mike Mazurki, Ted de Corsica, and young Ricardo Montalban. The plot isn't too important to this film as long as you can keep in time with Xavier Cugat's mamba beat and not lose your place in the conga line. Harmless, enjoyable nonsense.
1949 93 minutes

NEVER STEAL ANYTHING SMALL

★★½

DIRECTOR: Charles Lederer

CAST: James Cagney, Shirley Jones, Roger Smith, Cara Williams, Nehemiah Persoff, Royal Dano, Horace MacMahon

Unbelievable musical comedy-drama about a goodhearted union labor leader is saved by the dynamic James Cagney, who was always enough to make even the most hackneyed story worth watching. Supported by the lovely Shirley Jones and a fine cast of top charcter actors, Cagney manages to pull this movie off where a lesser talent would have foundered. Certainly not one of the great or near-great films, this tuneful comedy-drama is still entertaining enough to stand on its own merits and offers another look at the incomparable Cagney.
1959 94 minutes

NEW YORK, NEW YORK

★★★½

DIRECTOR: Martin Scorsese

CAST: Robert De Niro, Liza Minnelli, Lionel Stander, Georgie Auld, Mary Kay Place

This is a difficult film to warm to, but worth it. Robert De Niro gives a splendid performance as an egomaniacal saxophonist who woos sweet-natured singer Liza Minnelli. The songs (especially the title tune) are great, and those with a taste for something different in musicals will find it rewarding. Rated PG.
1977 163 minutes

NO NUKES

★★★½

DIRECTORS: Julian Schlossberg, Danny Goldberg, Anthony Potenza

CAST: Jackson Browne, Crosby, Stills, and Nash, The Doobie Brothers, John Hall, Gil Scott-Heron, Bonnie Raitt, Carly Simon, Bruce Springsteen, James Taylor, Jessie Colin Young

Entertaining record of the MUSE concerts presented for five nights at Madison Square Garden to benefit the anti-nuclear movement. Your enjoyment will depend greatly on appreciation of the artists involved, but the rare footage of Bruce Springsteen in concert is electrifying and shouldn't be missed. While the picture is grainy, the stereo soundtrack is excellent. Rated PG for profanity.
1980 103 minutes

OKLAHOMA!

★★★★

DIRECTOR: Fred Zinnemann
CAST: Shirley Jones, Gordon MacRae, Rod Steiger, Eddie Albert

This movie adaptation of Rodgers and Hammerstein's Broadway musical stars Shirley Jones as a country girl (Laurie) who is courted by Curly, a cowboy (Gordon MacRae). Rod Steiger plays a villainous Jud, who also pursues Laurie. A very entertaining musical, it features great tunes like "Oh, What a Beautiful Mornin'" and "Oklahoma!"

1956 145 minutes

OLD CURIOSITY SHOP, THE

★★★

DIRECTOR: Michael Tuchner
CAST: Anthony Newley, David Hemmings, David Warner, Michael Hordern, Jill Bennett, Sarah Jane Varley

This enjoyable British-made follow-up to *Scrooge*, the successful musical adaptation of Charles Dickens' *A Christmas Carol*, adds tunes to the author's *The Old Curiosity Shop* and casts songwriter-singer Anthony Newley as the title villain. Rated PG.

1975 118 minutes

OLIVER

★★★★★

DIRECTOR: Carol Reed
CAST: Ron Moody, Oliver Reed, Hugh Griffith, Shani Wallis, Mark Lester, Jack Wild

Charles Dickens never was such fun. *Oliver Twist* has become a luxurious musical and multiple Oscar-winner (including best picture). Lionel Bart's songs are not as instrusive as those found in average musicals. Mark Lester is the angelic Oliver, whose adventures begin one mealtime when he pleads, "Please, sir, I want some more." Jack Wild is an impish Artful Dodger, and Ron Moody steals the show as the scoundrel Fagin. Then there's Oliver Reed, whose narrow-eyed menace prevents the tale from becoming *too* sugar-coated. Lester is the perfect star; you'd rather die than watch him suffer . . . and Dickens always includes a lot of suffering. A must-see. Rated G—suitable for family viewing.

1968 153 minutes

ON A CLEAR DAY, YOU CAN SEE FOREVER

★

DIRECTOR: Vincente Minnelli
CAST: Barbra Streisand, Yves Montand, Bob Newhart, Larry Blyden, Jack Nicholson

Crashing, thudding bore of a musical about a psychiatrist (Yves Montand) who discovers that one of his patients (Barbra Streisand) has lived a former life and can recall it under hypnosis. The flashbacks to nineteenth-century England provide work for the costume and set designers, but neither century contains characters who matter a whit to the viewer. Pompous screenplay filled with its own importance intrerrupted by vacuous songs. A poor epitaph for the classic Hollywood musical. Rated PG for violence.

1970 129 minutes

ON THE TOWN

★★★★

DIRECTORS: Gene Kelly, Stanley Donen
CAST: Gene Kelly, Frank Sinatra, Ann Miller, Vera-Ellen

This is a classic boy-meets-girl, boy-loses-girl fable set to music. Three sailors are on a twenty-four-hour leave and find themselves (for the first time) in the big city of New York. They seek romance and adventure during their leave—and find it.

1949 98 minutes

ONE FROM THE HEART

★★

DIRECTOR: Francis Coppola

CAST: Teri Garr, Frederic Forrest, Raul Julia, Nastassja Kinski, Harry Dean Stanton, Allen Goorwitz, Luana Anders

This Francis Coppola film is a ballet of graceful and complex camera movements occupying magnificent sets—but the characters get lost in the process. Teri Garr and Frederic Forrest play a couple flirting with two strangers (Raul Julia and Nastassja Kinski), but they fade away in the flash and fizz. Rated R.

1982 100 minutes

ONE TRICK PONY

★★★½

DIRECTOR: Robert M. Young

CAST: Paul Simon, Lou Reed, Rip Torn, Blair Brown, Joan Hackett, Sam and Dave, The B-52's, Tiny Tim, The Lovin' Spoonful

This good little movie looks at life on the road with a has-been rock star. Paul Simon is surprisingly effective as the rock star who finds both his popularity slipping and his marriage falling apart. Rated R for nudity.

1980 98 minutes

OTELLO

★★★★★

DIRECTOR: Franco Zeffirelli

CAST: Placido Domingo, Katia Ricciarelli, Justino Diaz, Petra Malakova, Urbano Barberini

As with his screen version of *La Traviata*, Franco Zeffirelli's *Otello* is a masterpiece of filmed opera. In fact, it may well be the best such motion picture ever made. Placido Domingo is brilliant in the title role, both as an actor and a singer. And he gets able support from Katia Ricciarelli as Desdemona and Justino Diaz as Iago. Verdi and Shakespeare would be pleased. Rated PG for stylized violence.

1987 122 minutes

PAGAN LOVE SONG

★½

DIRECTOR: Robert Alton

CAST: Esther Williams, Howard Keel, Minna Gombell, Rita Moreno

Watered-down love story about American schoolteacher Howard Keel who falls for native girl Esther Williams is just another excuse for singing, swimming, and studio-bound rehash of a tired old plot line. Basically an excuse to make an Esther Williams film with a time-tested script, this dull entry is for fans of soggy musicals and Esther Williams only.

1950 76 minutes

PAINT YOUR WAGON

★★

DIRECTOR: Joshua Logan

CAST: Clint Eastwood, Lee Marvin, Jean Seberg, Harve Presnell, John Mitchum

Clint Eastwood and Lee Marvin play partners during the California gold rush era. They share everything, including a mail-order bride (Jean Seberg), in this hapless musical. Adapted from a hit Broadway play and given the big-budget treatment, this film never gets off the ground. The major blame should go to the script writers for not caring enough about the characterizations to put any effort into their development. Rated PG.

1969 166 minutes

PARADISE HAWAIIAN STYLE

★★½

DIRECTOR: Michael Moore
CAST: Elvis Presley, Suzanna Leigh

Elvis Presley returns to Hawaii after his 1962 film, *Blue Hawaii*. This time he plays a pilot who makes time for romance while setting up a charter plane service. Some laughs and lots of Elvis's songs add to the Hawaiian beauty to make this enjoyable to watch.

1966 91 minutes

PENNIES FROM HEAVEN

★★★½

DIRECTOR: Herbert Ross
CAST: Steve Martin, Bernadette Peters, Jessica Harper

Steve Martin and Bernadette Peters star in this depressingly downbeat musical (which still has its moments), directed by Herbert Ross (*The Turning Point* and *Play It Again, Sam*). The production numbers are fabulous, but the dreary storyline—with Martin as a down-and-out song-plugger in Depression-era Chicago—may disappoint fans of the genre. Rated R for profanity and sexual situations.

1981 107 minutes

PETE KELLEY'S BLUES

★★½

DIRECTOR: Jack Webb
CAST: Jack Webb, Janet Leigh, Edmond O'Brien, Jayne Mansfield, Lee Marvin, Peggy Lee, Ella Fitzgerald, Martin Milner, Andy Devine

Guys, gals, gangsters, gin, and gut-bucket Dixieland jazz are done to a turn in this ultrarealistic re-creation of how it was in Kansas City and across the river in the Roaring Twenties. Sultry saloon singer Peggy Lee copped an Oscar nomination for her acting. Color hurt the mood. The film would be better in black and white.

1955 95 minutes

PHANTOM OF THE PARADISE

★★

DIRECTOR: Brian De Palma
CAST: Paul Williams, William Finley, Jessica Harper

Before he became obsessed with Hitchcock *hommages* and ultraviolent blood baths, director Brian De Palma did this odd little blend of Faust and *Phantom of the Opera*. William Finley sells his soul to Paul Williams and learns the dangers of achieving fame too quickly. Wildly erratic, with tedious dialogue alternating with droll visual bits (such as a poke at the shower scene in *Psycho*). Although the scathing attack on the music industry is occasionally interesting, the picture finally turns into a mess. Rated PG—mild violence.

1974 92 minutes

PINK FLOYD THE WALL

★½

DIRECTOR: Alan Parker
CAST: Bob Geldof, Christine Hargreaves, Bob Hoskins

For all its apparent intent, this visually impressive film, which has very little dialogue but, rather, uses garish visual images to the accompaniment of the British rock band's music, ends up being more of a celebration of insanity and inhumanity than an indictment of it as intended. Every conceivable kind of violence—even rape—is splashed on the screen to a pulsating rock beat. Seldom has a more bleak, negative, and just plain irresponsible work been foisted on the movie-going public. Written by Pink Floyd singer-songwriter Roger Waters and directed by Alan Parker (*Fame* and

Shoot the Moon). Rated R for nudity, profanity, violence, and gore.
1982 99 minutes

PIRATE, THE
★★★

DIRECTOR: Vincente Minnelli
CAST: Gene Kelly, Judy Garland, Walter Slezak, Gladys Cooper, Reginald Owen

Technicolor musical winner with Gene Kelly and Judy Garland in top form.
1948 102 minutes

PIRATE MOVIE, THE
★★

DIRECTOR: Ken Annakin
CAST: Christopher Atkins, Kristy McNichol, Ted Hamilton, Bill Kerr

This rock-'n-roll adaptation of Gilbert and Sullivan's *The Pirates of Penzance* is passable entertainment for the family. It's especially appropriate for teenagers, since the hero and heroine are Christopher Atkins (*The Blue Lagoon*) and Kristy McNichol. Expect a lot of music, a lot of swashbuckling, and a little sappy romance. Directed by Ken Annakin (*Swiss Family Robinson*), this film is rated PG for slight profanity and sexual innuendo (making it more fun for the parents).
1982 99 minutes

PIRATES OF PENZANCE, THE
★★★★

DIRECTOR: Wilford Leach
CAST: Angela Lansbury, Kevin Kline, Linda Ronstadt, Rex Smith, George Ross

In this film, directed by Wilford Leach, Angela Lansbury, Kevin Kline, rock superstar Linda Ronstadt, Rex Smith, and George Ross re-create the roles they originated in the Tony-winning Broadway adaptation of the Gilbert and Sullivan show. Stylized sets and takeoffs of Busby Berkeley camera setups give *Pirates* a true cinematic quality. Add to that outstanding work by the principals, some nice bits of slapstick comedy, and you have an enjoyable film for the entire family. Rated G.
1983 112 minutes

PRIVATE BUCKAROO
★★

DIRECTOR: Edward Cline
CAST: The Andrews Sisters, Joe E. Lewis, Dick Foran, Jennifer Holt, Donald O'Connor, Peggy Ryan, Harry James

Showcase vehicle for Patty, LaVerne, and Maxene, the Andrews Sisters, who decide to put on a show for soldiers. The Donald O'Connor/Peggy Ryan duo stands out.
1942 B & W 68 minutes

PURPLE RAIN
★★½

DIRECTOR: Albert Magnoli
CAST: Prince, Apollonia, Morris Day, Olga Karlatos, The Revolution

In his first movie, pop star Prince plays a struggling young musician searching for self-awareness and love while trying to break into the rock charts. The film unsuccessfully straddles the line between a concert release and a story-telling production. As it is, the music is great, but the plot leaves a lot to be desired. Rated R for nudity, suggested sex, and profanity.
1984 113 minutes

QUADROPHENIA
★★★½

DIRECTOR: Franc Roddam
CAST: Phil Daniels, Mark ingett, Phillip Davis, Leslie Ash, Garry Cooper, Sting

Based on the Who's rock opera, this is the story of a teenager growing up in the early 1960s and the decisions he is forced to make on the path to adulthood. The backdrop for the tale is London, and the focus is on the conflict between two English youth cults, the Rockers, a typical "bike gang" outfit, and the Mods, who also ride bikes but are more "responsible" types, holding jobs that provide the money they spend on sharp clothes and drugs. The gangs hate each other, primarily because of their differences in style, and the movie's failure to establish the reason for this tension is its one major flaw. Rated R because the language is rough, the violence graphic, and both sex and masturbation are represented.

1979 115 minutes

RAPPIN'

★½

DIRECTOR: Joel Silberg

CAST: Mario van Peebles, Tasia Valenza, Charles Flohe, Melvin Plowden

Rap songs get the *Breakin'* treatment in this uninspired formula musical. Once again, a street performer (rap singer Mario van Peebles) takes on the baddies and still has time to make it in show biz. Dumb stuff. Rated PG for profanity.

1985 92 minutes

RED SHOES, THE

★★★★

DIRECTOR: Michael Powell

CAST: Moira Shearer, Anton Walbrook

Fascinating backstage look at the world of ballet manages to overcome its unoriginal, often trite, plot. A ballerina (Moira Shearer) is urged by her forceful and single-minded impresario (Anton Walbrook) to give up a romantic involvement in favor of her career, with tragic consequences. Good acting and fine camera work save this film from its overlong standard story.

1948 133 minutes

ROCK, PRETTY BABY

★★

DIRECTOR: Richard Bartlett

CAST: John Saxon, Sal Mineo, Rod McKuen, Luana Patten, Edward Platt, Fay Wray, Shelley Fabares

John Saxon plays Jimmy Daley, 18-year-old leader of a struggling rock-'n-roll combo whose life is complicated by his doctor father who wants him to go into the medical profession and a difficult first-love relationship with Luana Patten. So laughably awful in spots that it becomes almost enjoyable, the film also has the onscreen talents of Rod McKuen, as well as a vintage but forgettable soundtrack by McKuen, Henry Mancini, Bobby Troup, and others.

1957 B & W 89 minutes

ROCK, ROCK, ROCK

★★

DIRECTOR: Will Price

CAST: Tuesday Weld, Teddy Randazzo, Alan Freed, Frankie Lymon and the Teenagers, Chuck Berry, The Flamingos, The Johnny Burnette Trio

If you love Tuesday Weld, fifties rock, or entertainingly terrible movies, this nostalgic blast from the past is for you. The plot is so flimsy, "Dobie Gillis" would have rejected it. But watching a young Weld lip-synch to songs actually sung by Connie Francis is a wonderful treat.

1956 B & W 83 minutes

ROMAN SCANDALS

★★★

DIRECTOR: Frank Tuttle
CAST: Eddie Cantor, Ruth Etting, Alan Mowbray, Edward Arnold

Old Banjo Eyes dreams himself back to ancient Rome and a string of low-comedy situations. Busby Berkeley staged the requisite musical numbers, including one censor-baiting stanza featuring semi-nude chorus girls, Goldwyn Girl Lucille Ball among them.

1933 B & W 92 minutes

ROSE, THE

★★★★

DIRECTOR: Mark Rydell
CAST: Bette Midler, Alan Bates, Frederic Forrest, Harry Dean Stanton

Bette Midler stars as a Janis Joplin–like rock siner who falls prey to the loneliness and temptations of superstardom. Mark Rydell (*On Golden Pond*) directed this character study, which features memorable supporting performances by Alan Bates and Frederic Forrest, and a first-rate rock score. Rated R.

1979 134 minutes

ROSE MARIE

DIRECTOR: W. S. Van Dyke
CAST: Nelson Eddy, Jeanette MacDonald, James Stewart, Alan Mowbray

If you enjoy MGM's perennial songbirds Nelson Eddy and Jeanette MacDonald, you might have fun with this musical romp into the Canadian Rockies. Unintentionally funny dialogue is created by the wooden way Eddy delivers it.

1936 B & W 110 minutes

ROUND MIDNIGHT

★★★★½

DIRECTOR: Bertrand Tavernier
CAST: Dexter Gordon, François Cluzet, Gabrielle Hacker, Sandra Reaves-Phillips, Lonette McKee, Christine Pascal, Hrbie Hancock

French director Bertrand Tavernier's ode to American jazz is a long overdue celebration of that great American music and a tribute to its brilliant exponents. It tells a semifictionized story of a friendship between a self-destructive, be-bop tenor saxophonist (Dexter Gordon) and Francis (François Cluzet), an avid French fan of the jazzman's music. Herbie Hancock won an Oscar for his score, which features some of jazz's finest instrumentalists. Rated R.

1986 133 minutes

ROUSTABOUT

★★½

DIRECTOR: John Rich
CAST: Barbara Stanwyck, Elvis Presley, Leif Erickson, Sue Ane Langdon

Barbara Stanwyck, as the carnival owner, upgrades this typical Elvis Presley picture. In this release, Presley is a young wanderer who finds a home in the carnival as a singer. Naturally, Elvis combines romance with hard work on the midway.

1964 101 minutes

ROYAL WEDDING

★★★

DIRECTOR: Stanley Donen
CAST: Fred Astaire, Jane Powell, Sarah Churchill, Peter Lawford, Keenan Wynn

Brother and sister Fred Astaire and Jane Powell are performing in London when Princess Elizabeth marries Philip, and manage to find their own true loves while royalty ties the knot.

1951 92 minutes

RUNNING OUT OF LUCK

★★★

DIRECTOR: Julien Temple

CAST: Mick Jagger, Rae Dawn Chong, Dennis Hopper, Jerry Hall

Video film built around Mick Jagger's solo album, *She's the Boss*, has Jagger and Jerry Hall going to Rio to shoot a musical video being directed by Dennis Hopper. After an evening shoot, Jagger is mugged, thrown into the back of a meat wagon, abandoned in the Brazilian jungle, and taken prisoner by an oversexed banana plantation owner. He finally escapes back to Rio with the aid of prostitute Rae Dawn Chong. If this all sounds pretty hokey, that's because it is. But it is great fun to watch Jagger spoof himself. Musical highlights include "She's the Boss" and "Just Another Night."

1987 80 minutes

RUTLES, THE (A.K.A. ALL YOU NEED IS CASH)

★★★★

DIRECTORS: Eric Idle, Gary Weiss

CAST: Eric Idle, Neil Innes, Ricky Fataar, John Halsey, Mick Jagger, Paul Simon, George Harrison, John Belushi, Dan Aykroyd, Gilda Radner

Superb spoof of the Beatles has ex–Monty Python member Eric Idle in a dual role as a television reporter and one of the Rutles, whose songs include "Cheese and Onions" and "Doubleback Alley." It's great stuff for fans of the Fab Four—with cameos from rock stars (including Beatle George Harrison) and members of *Saturday Night Live's* Not Ready for Prime-Time Players. Neil Innes did a terrific job on the music and gets a solid assist from Ricky Fataar, one-time member of South African, Beatles sound-alike The Flame and the Beach Boys.

1978 78 minutes

SGT. PEPPER'S LONELY HEARTS CLUB BAND

(turkey symbol)

DIRECTOR: Michael Schultz

CAST: The Bee Gees, Peter Frampton, Donald Pleasence, George Burns

Universally panned musical featuring the Bee Gees, Peter Frampton, etc., performing songs from the Beatles' famous album as they try to save the small town of Heartland from the rule of the evil Mr. Mustard. Rated PG.

1978 111 minutes

SATURDAY NIGHT FEVER

★★★★

DIRECTOR: John Badham

CAST: John Travolta, Donna Pescow, Karen Lynn Gorney

From the first notes of "Stayin' Alive" by the Bee Gees over the opening credits, it is obvious that *Saturday Night Fever* is more than just another youth exploitation film. It is *Rebel Without a Cause* for the 1970s, an encapsulization of the era's moral and social attitudes combined with realistic dialogue and effective dramatic situations. The story revolves around Tony Manero (John Travolta), disco dancer supreme. He is the epitome of cool, and crowds part at the local nightclub when he and his friends make for the dance floor. With his styled hair, floral bodyshirt, skin-tight pants, and platform shoes, he redefined American masculinity in the 1970s. Rated R for profanity, violence, partial nudity, and simulated sex.

1977 119 minutes

SAY AMEN, SOMEBODY

★★★★

DIRECTOR: George T. Nierenberg
CAST: Thomas A. Dorsey, Willie Mae Ford Smith, Sallie Martin

This is a joyful documentary about gospel singers Thomas A. Dorsey and Willie Mae Ford Smith. Two dozen gospel songs make this modest film a treat for the ears as well as the eyes and soul. Rated G.

1982 100 minutes

SCROOGE

★★★

DIRECTOR: Ronald Neame
CAST: Albert Finney, Alec Guinness, Edith Evans, Kenneth More, Michael Medwin, Laurence Naismith, Kay Walsh

Tuneful retelling of Charles Dickens's classic *A Christmas Carol* may not be the best acted, but it's certainly the liveliest. Albert Finney paints old curmudgeon Ebeneezer Scrooge with a broad brush, but he makes his character come alive just as he embodied Daddy Warbucks in *Annie*. Decent attempt to translate a stage musical to the screen but nowhere near as popular as the earlier Dickens success, *Oliver*. This is a nice companion piece for the earlier (1935) version of *Scrooge* as well as the classic 1951 version of *A Christmas Carol*, both nonmusicals. Rated G.

1970 118 minutes

SECOND CHORUS

★★★

DIRECTOR: H. C. Potter
CAST: Paulette Goddard, Fred Astaire, Burgess Meredith, Charlie Butterworth, Artie Shaw and his orchestra

Rival trumpet players Fred Astaire and Burgess Meredith vie for the affections of Paulette Goddard, who works for Artie Shaw. The two want into Shaw's orchestra and make a comic mess of Goddard's attempts to help them. Charlie Butterworth, in a typical more-money-than-brains role, brings order out of the chaos by backing a Shaw concert.

1940 B & W 83 minutes

SEVEN BRIDES FOR SEVEN BROTHERS

★★★★★

DIRECTOR: Stanley Donen
CAST: Howard Keel, Jane Powell, Russ Tamblyn, Julie Newmar

Delightful musical. Howard Keel takes Jane Powell as his wife. The fun begins when his six younger brothers decide they want to get married, too . . . immediately!

1954 108 minutes

1776

★★★★

DIRECTOR: Peter H. Hunt
CAST: William Daniels, Howard da Silva, Ken Howard, Blythe Danner

Broadway's hit musical about the founding of the nation is brought to the screen almost intact. Original cast members William Daniels, as John Adams, and Howard da Silva, as Benjamin Franklin, shine anew in this unique piece. Rated G.

1972 141 minutes

SHALL WE DANCE?

★★★★½

DIRECTOR: Mark Sandrich
CAST: Fred Astaire, Ginger Rogers, Eric Blore, Edward Everett Horton

Fred Astaire and Ginger Rogers team up (as usual) as dance partners in this musical comedy. The only twist is they must pretend to be married in order to get the job. Great songs include "Let's Call the Whole Thing Off."

1937 B & W 116 minutes

SHOW BOAT

★★★½

DIRECTOR: George Sidney

CAST: Kathryn Grayson, Howard Keel, Ava Gardner, Joe E. Brown, Agnes Moorehead, Marge and Gower Champion

This watchable musical depicts life and love on a Mississippi showboat during the early 1900s. Kathryn Grayson, Howard Keel, and Ava Gardner try but can't get any real sparks flying.

1951 107 minutes

SILK STOCKINGS

★★★

DIRECTOR: Rouben Mamoulian

CAST: Fred Astaire, Cyd Charisse, Janis Paige, Peter Lorre, Barrie Chase

In this remake, Greta Garbo's classic *Ninotchka* is given the Cole Porter musical treatment with a degree of success. Fred Astaire is a Hollywood producer who educates a Russian agent in the seductive allure of capitalism. Cyd Charisse plays the Garbo role.

1957 117 minutes

SINGIN' IN THE RAIN

★★★★★

DIRECTORS: Gene Kelly, Stanley Donen

CAST: Gene Kelly, Debbie Reynolds, Donald O'Connor, Jean Hagen, Cyd Charisse, Madge Blake, Rita Moreno

In the history of movie musicals, no single scene is more fondly remembered than Gene Kelly's song-and-dance routine to the title song of *Singin' in the Rain*. This picture has more to it than Kelly's well-choreographed splash through a wet city street. It has an interesting plot based on the panic that overran Hollywood during its conversion to sound. It has other show-stopping original tunes, such as "You Were Meant for Me" and "All I Do Is Dream about You." Last, it includes some excellent performances by Debbie Reynolds, Donald O'Connor, and Jean Hagen. So if you're expecting only to see Gene Kelly get his feet wet, be prepared for a whole lot more.

1952 102 minutes

SKY'S THE LIMIT, THE

★★★★

DIRECTOR: Edward H. Griffith

CAST: Fred Astaire, Joan Leslie, Robert Benchley, Elizabeth Patterson, Clarence Kolb, Robert Ryan, Richard Davis, Peter Lawford, Eric Blore

This rare blend of comedy and the dramatic uncertainty of human relationships under stress is more than just another Fred Astaire musical. He plays a Flying Tiger ace, on leave, who meets and falls in love with magazine photographer Joan Leslie, but nixes anything permanent. Both audiences and critics misjudged this film when it debuted, seeing it as light diversion rather than incisive comment on war and its effect on people.

1943 B & W 89 minutes

SMILIN' THROUGH

★★

DIRECTOR: Frank Borzage

CAST: Jeanette MacDonald, Gene Raymond, Brian Aherne, Ian Hunter

If you can believe it, an orphaned and brave Jeanette MacDonald falls in love with the son of a murderer. Directed and played for tear value. Best thing to come out of the picture was Jeannette's marriage to Gene Raymond.

1941 100 minutes

SOMETHING TO SING ABOUT

★★

DIRECTOR: Walter Schertzinger
CAST: James Cagney, William Frawley, Evelyn Daw, Gene Lockhart

Even the great talents of James Cagney can't lift this low-budget musical above the level of mediocrity. In it, he plays a New York bandleader who tests his mettle in Hollywood.

1937 B & W 93 minutes

SONG OF NORWAY

DIRECTOR: Andrew L. Stone
CAST: Florence Henderson, Torval Maurstad, Christina Schollin, Edward G. Robinson, Robert Morley

If he were not dead, Norwegian composer Edvard Grieg would expire upon seeing this insult to his life and career. Talk about butchering what was an engaging, tuneful stage musical! Pass the cranberry sauce. Rated G.

1970 142 minutes

SONG REMAINS THE SAME, THE

★★★

DIRECTORS: Peter Clifton, Joe Massot
CAST: Led Zeppelin, Peter Grant

If any band is truly responsible for the genre of "heavy metal" music, it is Led Zeppelin. In *Song*, Zeppelin proves this claim by performing smashing versions of such hits as "Rock-'n-Roll," "Whole Lotta Love," "Stairway to Heaven," and "Since I've Been Loving You." Although this movie is a must for Led Zeppelin fans, the untrained ear may find numbers such as the twenty-three-minute version of "Dazed and Confused" a bit tedious. Rated PG.

1976 136 minutes

SONG TO REMEMBER, A

★★★

DIRECTOR: Charles Vidor
CAST: Cornel Wilde, Merle Oberon, Paul Muni, George Coulouris, Nina Foch, Sig Arno, Stephen Bekassy

The music is superb, but the plot of this Chopin biography is as frail as the composer's health is purported to have been. Cornel Wilde received an Oscar nomination as the ill-fated tubercular Chopin, and Merle Oberon is resolute but vulnerable in the role of his lover, the emancipated trouser-wearing French female novelist George Sand. Paul Muni supports as Chopin's mentor; George Coulouris suffers genius as the piano baron Louis Playel in whose Paris concert hall the composer performs his greatest works as death steadily encroaches.

1945 113 minutes

SONGWRITER

★★★★

DIRECTOR: Alan Rudolph
CAST: Willie Nelson, Kris Kristofferson, Lesley Ann Warren, Melinda Dillon, Rip Torn

Wonderfully wacky and entertaining wish-fulfillment by top country stars Willie Nelson and Kris Kristofferson, who play—what else?—top country stars who take on the recording industry and win. Lesley Ann Warren, who also worked with director Alan Rudolph in the equally memorable *Choose Me*, is Nelson's protégée, and Melinda Dillon plays his loving but intolerant-of-his-life-style wife. Rip Torn is a sleazy yet somehow likable concert promoter. The actors are all excellent, and the film, despite its far-fetched premise, is a delight. Rated R for profanity, nudity, and brief violence.

1984 100 minutes

SOUND OF MUSIC, THE

★★★★½

DIRECTOR: Robert Wise

CAST: Julie Andrews, Christopher Plummer, Eleanor Parker

Winner of the Academy Award for best picture, this musical has it all: comedy, romance, suspense, and sadness. Julie Andrews plays the spunky Maria, who doesn't fit in at the convent. When she is sent to live with a large family as their governess, she falls in love with and marries her handsome boss, Baron Von Trapp (Christopher Plummer). Problems arise when the Nazi invasion of Austria forces the family to flee.

1965 174 minutes

SOUTH PACIFIC

★★★

DIRECTOR: Joshua Logan

CAST: Mitzi Gaynor, Rossano Brazzi, Ray Walston, John Kerr

This extremely long film, adapted from the famous Broadway play about sailors during World War II, seems dated and is slow going for the most part. Fans of Rodgers and Hammerstein will no doubt appreciate this one more than others.

1958 171 minutes

SPARKLE

★★★

DIRECTOR: Sam O'Steen

CAST: Irene Cara, Dorian Harewood, Lonette McKee

Largely forgotten but immensely appealing study of a Supremes–like girl group's rise to fame in the 1960s Motown era. A chance to see some of today's more popular black stars at an earlier stage. Lots of good musical numbers from Curtis Mayfield and the luscious Lonette McKee (*The Cotton Club*). Affectionate at times but marred by some cloying sentimentality. Nevertheless, check this one out. Rated PG for profanity and nudity.

1976 100 minutes

SPEEDWAY

★★

DIRECTOR: Norman Taurog

CAST: Elvis Presley, Nancy Sinatra, Bill Bixby, Gale Gordon

Elvis Presley plays a generous stock-car driver who confronts a seemingly heartless IRS agent (Nancy Sinatra). Not surprisingly, she melts in this unremarkable musical. Rated G.

1968 94 minutes

STAGE STRUCK

★★

DIRECTOR: Busby Berkeley

CAST: Joan Blondell, Dick Powell, Warren William, Frank McHugh, Jeanne Madden, Carol Hughes, Hobart Cavanaugh, Spring Byington

A no-talent singer-dancer, Joan Blondell, makes a bid for Broadway by financing a show for herself. She hires Dick Powell to direct. They clash, fall in love, clash, and depend on good old suave Warren William to smooth it all out. Not that anyone should care too much. Below par.

1936 B & W 86 minutes

STARSTRUCK

★★★½

DIRECTOR: Gillian Armstrong

CAST: Jo Kennedy, Ross O'Donovan, Pat Evison, Margo Lee, Max Cullen

For this movie, about a 17-year-old (Jo Kennedy) who wants to be a star and goes after it at top speed, director Gillian Armstrong (*My Brilliant Career*) has taken the "let's put on a show!" plot and turned it into an affable punk-rock movie. Rated PG for nudity and profanity.

1982 95 minutes

STAYING ALIVE

★

DIRECTOR: Sylvester Stallone
CAST: John Travolta, Cynthia Rhodes, Finola Hughes, Steve Inwood

This sequel to the gutsy, effective *Saturday Night Fever* is a slick, commercial near-ripoff. Six years have passed since Tony Manero (John Travolta) was king of the local disco, and he now attempts to break into the competitive life of Broadway dancing. For fans only. Rated PG for language and suggested sex.

1983 96 minutes

STOP MAKING SENSE

★★★★

DIRECTOR: Jonathan Demme
CAST: Talking Heads

Jonathan Demme's *Stop Making Sense* has been called a "star vehicle." Filmed over a three-night period in December 1983 at Hollywood's Pantages Theater, Demme (*Melvin and Howard*) and cinematographer Jordan Croneweth (*Blade Runner*) concentrate on the rock group Talking Heads. The movie is a straight recording of a Talking Heads concert that offers the movie audience front-row-center seats. It offers great fun for the band's fans. Rated PG for suggestive lyrics.

1984 88 minutes

STORY OF VERNON AND IRENE CASTLE, THE

★★★★

DIRECTOR: H. C. Potter
CAST: Fred Astaire, Ginger Rogers, Edna May Oliver, Walter Brennan, Lew Fields

Another fine film with the flying footsies of Fred Astaire and the always lovely Ginger Rogers.

1939 B & W 93 minutes

SUMMER STOCK

★★★

DIRECTOR: Charles Walters
CAST: July Garland, Gene Kelly, Eddie Bracken, Gloria DeHaven, Phil Silvers, Hans Conried, Marjorie Main

An echo of the Mickey Rooney–Judy Garland talented-kids let's-give-a-show films, this likeable musical is built around troupe of ambitious performers, led by Gene Kelly, who invade farmer Judy Garland's barn. Love blooms, music blooms, dancing blooms, and the whole blooming film somehow makes it. Judy's "Get Happy" number, filmed long after the movie was completed and spliced in to add needed flash, is inspired.

1950 109 minutes

SUNDAY IN THE PARK WITH GEORGE

★★★★★

DIRECTOR: James Lapine
CAST: Mandy Patinkin, Bernadette Peters, Barbara Byrne, Charles Kimbrough

This is a taped version of a performance of one of the most honored musicals of the 1980s. A Pulitzer Prize winner, the entire play is a fabrication of plot and characters based on the Georges Seurat painting, "Sunday Afternoon on the Island of La Grande Jatte."

The painting comes to life, and each of the figures has a story to tell, all centered around Seurat, who is played expertly by Mandy Patinkin. Bernadette Peters plays Dot, the artist's mistress—but only in the first act. In act two, the nineteenth century is left behind to make way for the world of high-tech art, including lasers. Peters plays Dot's daughter at the age of ninety, while Patinkin plays her grandson. Sounds complicated, but it's expertly handled. Stephen Sondheim's music and lyrics were never better.

1986 147 minutes

SWEENEY TODD: THE DEMON BARBER OF FLEET STREET

★★★★★

DIRECTOR: Harold Prince

CAST: Angela Lansbury, George Hearn, Cris Grownendal, Sara Woods, Edmund Lyndeck, Calvin Remsberg

One of the joys of video is that more than theatrical films can be viewed in the home. Such is the case with *Sweeny Todd*. This is not a film, but rather an eight-camera video of a Broadway musical taped during a performance before a theater audience. And what a musical it is , this 1979 Tony Award Winner! George Hearn is terrifying as Sweeney Todd, the barber who seeks revenge on the English judicial system by slashing the throats of the unfortunate who wind up in his tonsorial chair. Angela Lansbury is spooky as Mrs. Lovett, who finds a use for Todd's leftovers by baking them into meat pies for sale in her shop. The music and lyrics are by Stephen Sondheim, and they are among his most brilliant creations. While the show is not rated, care should be taken because of the graphic depiction of the slashings.

1982 150 minutes

SWEET DREAMS

★★★★½

DIRECTOR: Karel Reisz

CAST: Jessica Lange, Ed Harris, Ann Wedgeworth, David Clennon, Gary Basraba, John Goodman, Bruce Kirby, P. J. Soles, James Staley

Jessica Lange (*Frances*, *Tootsie*) is Patsy Cline, one of the greatest country-and-western singers of all time, in this film that is much more than a response to the popularity of *Coal Miner's Daughter*. Lange's performance is flawless right down to the singing, where she perfectly mouths Clines's voice. Ed Harris (*The Right Stuff*, *Under Fire*) is equally brilliant as Cline's "good ol' boy" husband. The film's only weak point is that it rarely confronts the singer's impact on the music world or how she dealt with her popularity. Rated PG for profanity and sex.

1985 115 minutes

SWING TIME

★★★★½

DIRECTOR: George Stevens

CAST: Ginger Rogers, Fred Astaire, Betty Furness, Victor Moore, Helen Broderick

Fred Astaire is a gambler trying to save up enough money to marry the girl he left behind (Betty Furness). By the time he's saved the money, he and Ginger Rogers are madly in love with each other.

1936 B & W 105 minutes

SYMPATHY FOR THE DEVIL

½

DIRECTOR: Jean-Luc Godard

CAST: The Rolling Stones

Several uncompleted sessions on the title song and documentary-style footage of black guerrillas with machine guns and white women in slips seem to be all that compose this boring film from internationally acclaimed director Jean-Luc Godard. Not recommended for the music fan who expects some concert footage, but an evening's diversion for anyone with enough patience to try and figure out what's going on and what it all means. Beware of the longer version of this tedium, entitled *One Plus One*.

1970 92 minutes

TAKE ME OUT TO THE BALL GAME

★★★

DIRECTOR: Busby Berkeley
CAST: Gene Kelly, Frank Sinatra, Esther Williams, Betty Garrett, Jules Munshin

Don't expect to see the usual Berkeley extravaganza in this one; this is just a run-of-the-mill musical. It does preview things to come, however: most of the leads for *On the Town* (1949) appear here. The film was actually a public screen test to see how well Gene Kelly and Stanley Donen worked together. Their partnership gave us *Singing in the Rain* (1952), and *Ball Game* falls far short of that. It does contain some entertaining musical numbers, such as "O'Brien to Ryan to Goldberg," and the lovely Esther Williams, sans swimming pool.

1949 93 minutes

TAKING MY TURN

★★

DIRECTOR: Robert H. Livingston
CAST: Margaret Whiting, Marni Nixon, Sheila Smith, Cissy Houston

This is a videotape of an actual off-Broadway musical. Unfortunately, you had to be there to really enjoy it. Sort of *A Chorus Line* for the Geritol generation, this features aging actors lamenting the way times have changed and how it feels to grow old. Their song-and-dance routines are good, but for the most part this is pretty depressing.

1984 90 minutes

TELEVISION PARTS HOME COMPANION

★★★

DIRECTORS: William Dear, Alan Myerson
CAST: Mike Nesmith, Joe Allain, Jim Cox, Bill Martin

This is more of Mike Nesmith's *Elephant Parts* style of variety-show entertainment. Again, he has hilarious skits and mock commercials, as well as choreographed stories to accompany his songs. His ballads include "Drive the El Dorado to the Moon," "The Voyage of the Kona Tike," "Homecoming," "Chow Mein and Bowling," "Fred and Ginger, I'll Remember You," and "Total Control."

1984 40 minutes

THANK GOD IT'S FRIDAY

★★

DIRECTOR: Robert Klane
CAST: Donna Summer, The Commodores, Ray Vitte, Debra Winger, Jeff Goldblum

This film is episodic and light in mood and features a cast primarily of newcomers. The best-known performers on screen are Donna Summer and the Commodores. Summer plays an aspiring singer who pesters a club's master of ceremonies and disc jockey, Bobby Speed (Ray Vitte), to let her sing. The Commodores have a brief dramatic appearance and spend the bulk of their screen time doing what they do best: performing their hits. Rated PG.

1978 90 minutes

THANK YOUR LUCKY STARS

★★★½

DIRECTOR: David Butler

CAST: Eddie Cantor, Dennis Morgan, Joan Leslie, Bette Davis, Olivia de Havilland, Ida Lupino, Ann Sheridan, Humphrey Bogart, Errol Flynn, John Garfield

Practically nonexistent plot—involving banjo-eyed Eddie Cantor as a cab driver and the organizer of this gala affair—takes a back seat to the wonderful array of Warner Bros. talent gathered together for the first and only time in one film. Bette Davis and Errol Flynn perform musical numbers with Flynn disguised behind a handlebar moustache and Bette singing "They're Either Too Young or Too Old." John Garfield and Humphrey Bogart aren't spared a guest appearance, and they seem to be good sports about it. Basically a studio effort to display as many stars as possible in one film, this is an enjoyable collection of vignettes and skits and is one of the brightest of the all-star productions. Lots of fun for film fans and buffs and a perfect example of the type of control the studios exerted over those performers bound to them.

1943 B & W 127 minutes

THAT WAS ROCK

★★★★★

DIRECTORS: Steve Binder, Larry Peerce

CAST: The Rolling Stones, Chuck Berry, Tina Turner, Marvin Gaye, The Supremes, Smokey Robinson and the Miracles, James Brown, Ray Charles, Gerry and the Pacemakers, The Ronettes

Compilation of two previous films, *The T.A.M.I. Show* and *The Big T.N.T. Show*, which were originally shot on videotape in the mid-1960s. It's black and white, but color inserts have been added, featuring Chuck Berry giving cursory introductions to each act. The video is muddy, the simulated stereo is annoying, and the audience nearly drowns out the performers, but it's one of the best collections of rock-'n-roll and R&B talent you will ever see. Unrated.

1984 92 minutes

THAT'S DANCING

★★★★

DIRECTOR: Jack Haley Jr.

CAST: Mikhail Baryshnikov, Ray Bolger, Sammy Davis Jr., Gene Kelly, Liza Minnelli

This is a glorious celebration of dance on film. From ballet to breakin', from Fred Astaire to Busby Berkeley, from James Cagney (in *Yankee Doodle Dandy*) to Marine Jahan (Jennifer Beals's stand-in in *Flashdance*), this one has it all. *That's Dancing* contains the best scenes from fifty years of musicals. All the dumb plot devices that are concocted to get the performers from one music segment to another are gone. That leaves all the high points. Mikhail Baryshnikov, Ray Bolger, Sammy Davis Jr., Gene Kelly, and Liza Minnelli host this superb compilation. Rated G.

1985 105 minutes

THAT'S ENTERTAINMENT

★★★★★

DIRECTOR: Jack Haley

CAST: Judy Garland, Fred Astaire, Frank Sinatra, Gene Kelly, Esther Williams

That's Entertainment is a feast of screen highlights. Culled from twenty-nine years of MGM classics, this release truly has something for everybody. Unlike films that rely on the continuity of story for their impact, it is an episodic collection of bits and pieces.

Taken from Metro-Goldwyn-Mayer's glory days when it boasted "more stars than there are in heaven," nearly every sequence is a showstopper. Rated G.

1974 135 minutes

THAT'S ENTERTAINMENT PART II

★★★★

DIRECTOR: Gene Kelly
CAST: Gene Kelly, Fred Astaire

More wonderful scenes from the history of MGM highlight this compilation, hosted by director Gene Kelly and Fred Astaire. It's a real treat for film buffs. Rated G.

1976 132 minutes

THERE'S NO BUSINESS LIKE SHOW BUSINESS

★★

DIRECTOR: Walter Lang
CAST: Ethel Merman, Dan Dailey, Marilyn Monroe, Donald O'Connor, Johnnie Ray, Mitzi Gaynor, Hugh O'Brian, Frank McHugh

Even the strength of the cast can't save this marginally entertaining musical-comedy about a show-biz family. Irving Berlin's tunes and Monroe's scenes are the only redeeming qualities in this one.

1954 117 minutes

THEY SHALL HAVE MUSIC

★★★

DIRECTOR: Archie Mayo
CAST: Jascha Heifetz, Joel McCrea, Andrea Leeds, Walter Brennan, Marjorie Main, Porter Hall

Good cast and great music help the appeal of this attempt to make concert violinist Jascha Heifetz a film star. Simple plot has a group of poor kids convincing him to play a benefit and save Walter Brennan's music school in the slums.

1939 B & W 101 minutes

THIS IS ELVIS

★★★★

DIRECTORS: Malcolm Leo, Andrew Solt
CAST: Elvis Presley, David Scott, Paul Boensh III

Even if you're not an Elvis Presley fan, this film may make you cry. At the very least, you will find it powerful as well as touching. *This Is Elvis* blends film footage of the "real" Elvis with other portions, played by convincing stand-ins. The result is a warm, nostalgic, funny, and tragic portrait of a man who touched the hearts and lives of young and old throughout the world. To many, he is still the King of rock-'n-roll —and this film explains why. Rated PG because of slight profanity.

1981 101 minutes

THIS IS THE ARMY

★★★

DIRECTOR: Michael Curtiz
CAST: George Murphy, Joan Leslie, Ronald Reagan, George Tobias, Alan Hale, Joe Louis, Kate Smith, Irving Berlin, Frances Langford, Charles Butterworth

Hoofer (later U.S. Senator) George Murphy portrays Ronald Reagan's father in this musical mélange penned by Irving Berlin to raise funds for Army Emergency Relief during World War II. It's a star-studded, rousing show of songs and skits from start to finish, but practically plotless.

1943 121 minutes

THOROUGHLY MODERN MILLIE

★★★

DIRECTOR: George Roy Hill
CAST: Julie Andrews, Mary Tyler Moore, Carol Channing,

James Fox, Beatrice Lillie, John Saxon, Pat Morita, Jack Soo

First-rate music characterizing America's jazz age dominates this hairbrained-plotted, slapstick-punctuated spoof of the 1920s, complete with villains, a bordello, and a cooing flapper so smitten with her stuffed-shirt boss that she can't see her boyfriend for beans. It's toe-tapping entertainment, but, like Sam's pants, a tad too long.

1967 138 minutes

THOUSANDS CHEER

★★★

DIRECTOR: George Sidney
CAST: John Boles, Kathryn Grayson, Mickey Rooney, Judy Garland, Gene Kelly, Red Skelton, Lucille Ball, Ann Sothern, Eleanor Powell, Frank Morgan, Lena Horne, Virginia O'Brien

The typical story about someone (in this case John Boles as an army officer) putting together a talent show for some good cause gets a major shot in the arm by the appearances of top MGM performers, including Mickey Rooney, Judy Garland, and Gene Kelly. Terrific cast in cameo performances make this musical worth the watch, and top comics Red Skelton, Lucille Ball, and Ann Sothern do their best to keep things moving. Not as famous as many MGM musicals, but castwise the match for *any* studio extravaganza. Overlong, but catching Lena Horne is worth the wait.

1943 126 minutes

THREE LITTLE WORDS

★★½

DIRECTOR: Richard Thorpe
CAST: Fred Astaire, Red Skelton, Vera-Ellen, Gloria De Haven, Arlene Dahl, Debbie Reynolds, Keenan Wynn, Harry Barris

That this is supposedly Fred Astaire's favorite among his numerous films says little for his taste. He and Red Skelton thoroughly enjoyed playing ace songwriters Bert Kalmar and Harry Ruby in this semi-accurate bio-pic, but, overall, the film lacks lustre—though it did well at the box office. Astaire dances, of course, and Vera-Ellen keeps pace with him, but the choreography is uninspired. The score was stitched together from songs written between 1912 and 1931, not all of them Kalmar-Ruby products.

1950 102 minutes

TICKLE ME

★★

DIRECTOR: Norman Taurog
CAST: Elvis Presley, Jocelyn Lane, Julie Adams, Jack Mullaney, Merry Anders

The plot falls below that found in a standard Elvis vehicle in this unfunny comedy-musical, which has Elvis working and singing at an all-female health ranch. Viewers seeking thought-provoking entertainment should avoid this mindless piece of fluff.

1965 90 minutes

TILL THE CLOUDS ROLL BY

★★½

DIRECTOR: Richard Whorf
CAST: Robert Walker, Van Heflin, Judy Garland, Lucille Bremer

Biography of songwriter Jerome Kern is a barrage of MGM talent that includes Judy Garland, Frank Sinatra, Lena Horne, Dinah Shore, Kathryn Grayson, and many more in short, tuneful vignettes that tie this all-out effort together. Not too bad as musical bio-pics go, but singing talent is definitely the star in this production—if you're following the story, the film seems too long; if you're just enjoying the segments, it's about long enough. Typical top-quality job by postwar MGM studio.

1946 137 minutes

TIMES SQUARE

★½

DIRECTOR: Alan Moyle

CAST: Tim Curry, Robin Johnson, Trini Alvarado, Peter Coffield

A totally unbelievable story involving two New York teens who hang out in Times Square. Film generates no energy at all. Rated R for profanity and subject matter.

1980 111 minutes

TOAST OF NEW ORLEANS

★★½

DIRECTOR: Norman Taurog

CAST: Kathryn Grayson, Mario Lanza, Thomas Mitchell, David Niven, J. Carrol Naish, Rita Moreno

Don't look for too much plot in this colorful showcase for the considerable vocal talent of the late Mario Lanza. Aided and abetted by the engaging soprano of Kathryn Grayson, Lanza sings up a storm. "Be My Love" was the film's and record stores' big number.

1950 97 minutes

TOMMY

★★½

DIRECTOR: Ken Russell

CAST: Roger Daltrey, Ann-Margret, Jack Nicholson, Oliver Reed, Elton John, Tina Turner

In bringing the Who's groundbreaking rock opera to the screen, director Ken Russell (*Women in Love* and *Altered States*) let his penchant for bad taste and garishness run wild. The result is an outragious movie about a deaf, dumb, and blind boy who rises to prominence as a "Pinball Wizard" and then becomes the new Messiah. The Who's lead singer, Roger Daltrey, plays the title role. Rated PG.

1975 111 minutes

TOP HAT

★★★★★

DIRECTOR: Mark Sandrich

CAST: Fred Astaire, Ginger Rogers, Edward Everett Horton, Eric Blore, Helen Broderick

Top Hat is the most delightful and enduring of the Fred Astaire–Ginger Rogers musicals of the 1930s. This movie has an agreeable wisp of a plot and amusing, if dated, comedy dialogue. It is handled by an expert team of supporting comics: Edward Everett Horton, Eric Blore, and Helen Broderick. Irving Berlin's score includes: "Cheek to Cheek" and "Isn't It a Lovely Day?" as well as the title number. Astaire and Rogers were at the peak of their careers in this classic musical.

1935 B & W 99 minutes

200 MOTELS

DIRECTOR: Frank Zappa

CAST: Tony Palmer, Frank Zappa and the Mothers of Invention, Theodore Bikel, Ringo Starr, Keith Moon

Indulgent full-length video is the kind of garish, free-association assault one would expect from the unconventional and downright bizarre Frank Zappa and the Mothers of Invention. Shot on videotape and edited to Zappa's specifications as a companion piece to the album of the same name, this episodic collage scores some laughs and has a few high points (including an X-rated animated sequence), but remains essentially an oddity and a staple for the midnight-movie crowd. Rated R.

1971 98 minutes

UNSINKABLE MOLLY BROWN, THE

★★★

DIRECTOR: Charles Waters

CAST: Debbie Reynolds, Harve Presnell, Ed Begley, Hermione Baddeley, Jack Kruschen

Noisy, big-budget version of hit Broadway musical has Debbie Reynolds at her spunkiest as the tuneful gal from Colorado who survives the sinking of the *Titanic* and lives to sing about it. High-stepping dance numbers and the performances and songs by Reynolds and Harve Presnell as the object of her affections make this a favorite with musicals fans, but it does drag a bit for the casual viewer at 128 minutes. One of the last of the old-time, overblown studio musical entertainments.

1964 128 minutes

VIDEO REWIND: THE ROLLING STONES GREAT VIDEO HITS

★★★★

DIRECTOR: Julien Temple

CAST: The Rolling Stones

This is a real score for lovers of the Rolling Stones or lovers of rock video in general. Mick Jagger and Bill Wyman take us on a tour of a "rock" museum, using flashbacks as a showcase for the band's videos. Included along with the videos are vintage clips of the Stones in concert. Highlights feature the uncensored versions of "She Was Hot" and "Neighbors." Only gripe is the sound quality, which (though acceptable) could have been much cleaner and sharper. Unrated.

1984 60 minutes

VIVA LAS VEGAS

★★

DIRECTOR: George Sidney

CAST: Elvis Presley, Ann-Margret, Cesare Danova, William Demarest, Jack Carter

In this romantic musical, Elvis Presley plays a race car driver who also sings. Ann-Margret is a casino dancer who becomes jealous when her father becomes interested in Elvis's race car. Eventually Elvis and Ann-Margret get together, which comes as no surprise to any viewer who didn't fall asleep within the first ten minutes of the film.

1964 86 minutes

WAGNER

★★★

DIRECTOR: Tony Palmer

CAST: Richard Burton, Vanessa Redgrave, Gemma Craven, Laszlo Galff, Sir John Gielgud, Sir Ralph Richardson, Sir Laurence Olivier, Marthe Keller, Ekkehardt Schall, Ronald Pickup

There are some who believe the great composers of Western music have not been justly served in cinema: Ken Russell's *Lisztomania* and *Mahler* have been deemed too weird, even if their namesakes did lead interesting lives, and some feel the cackling of Tom Hulce in *Amadeus* undercut Mozart's genius. In the case of *Wagner*, the filmmakers have delivered a highly stylized epic drama without resorting to camp or vulgarity. Unfortunately, Richard Burton's Wagner comes off as one-dimensional. This five-hour film gives you an idea of what the greatest opera composer may have been like, but it will not explain his behavior, and the legendary supporting cast, although credible, is not up to reputation. The first half of the movie centers on Wagner's efforts in the aborted German revolution of 1848–49 and artistic struggle during his subsequent exile. The second half focuses on the creation of his masterwork, *The Ring*, and hints at the composer's profound influence on a Germany entering the twentieth century. Not rated, but equal to an R for violence, profanity, sex, and nudity.

1982 300 minutes

WASN'T THAT A TIME!

★★★★★

DIRECTOR: Jim Brown

CAST: The Weavers: Pete Seeger, Lee Hays, Ronnie Gilbert, Fred Hellerman; with Arlo Guthrie, Don McLean, Holly Near, Mary Travers, Harry Reasoner, Studs Turkel

This is a folk music documentary about the Weavers' last reunion, as narrated wryly by group member Lee Hays. What really sets this apart from all the rest is the wealth of superb archival footage, all used in the proper proportion and sequence. The finale is the final reunion concert, and what a glorious and joyful event that was. Rated G.

1981 78 minutes

WEST SIDE STORY

★★★★★

DIRECTORS: Robert Wise, Jerome Robbins

CAST: Natalie Wood, Richard Beymer, Rita Moreno, George Chakiris

The Romeo-and-Juliet theme (with Richard Beymer and Natalie Wood in the lead roles) is updated to 1950s New York and given an endearing music score. The story of rival white and Puerto Rican youth gangs first appeared as a hit Broadway musical. None of the brilliance of the play was lost in its transformation to the screen. It received Oscars for best picture and its supporting players, Rita Moreno and George Chakiris. (Wood's vocals were dubbed by Marni Nixon.)

1961 151 minutes

WHITE CHRISTMAS

★★★

DIRECTOR: Michael Curtiz

CAST: Bing Crosby, Danny Kaye, Vera-Ellen, Rosemary Clooney

This attempt to capitalize on the title tune is an inferior remake of 1942's *Holiday Inn* (in which the song "White Christmas" first appeared). It's another in that long line of let's-put-on-a-show stories, with the last several reels showcasing the singing, dancing, and mugging talents of the cast. Entertaining and undemanding, but the format had begun to outwear its welcome.

1954 120 minutes

WHOOPEE

★★½

DIRECTOR: Thornton Freeland

CAST: Eddie Cantor, Eleanor Hunt, Paul Gregory, Ethel Shutta

The first of six Eddie Cantor musical films of the 1930s, this one's a two-color draft of his 1928 Broadway hit of the same name. The big-eyed comic plays a super-hypochondriac on an Arizona dude rance. Cowpokes and chorines abound. Busby Berkeley production numbers make it palatable. Nostalgia note: look for a nubile 14-year-old Betty Grable singing and dancing as things get under way.

1930 B & W 93 minutes

WIZ, THE

★

DIRECTOR: Sidney Lumet

CAST: Diana Ross, Richard Pryor, Michael Jackson, Nipsey Russell, Ted Ross, Mabel

King, Theresa Merritt, Thelma Carpenter, Lena Horne

Ineffective updating of *The Wizard of Oz* with an all-black cast, including Diana Ross (who is too old for the part), Richard Pryor, and Michael Jackson. Adapted from a successful Broadway play, this Sidney Lumet–directed picture should have been better. Rated G.

1978 133 minutes

WIZARD OF OZ, THE

★★★★★

DIRECTOR: Victor Fleming

CAST: Judy Garland, Ray Bolger, Bert Lahr, Jack Haley, Frank Morgan, Billie Burke, Margaret Hamilton, Charley Grapewin, Clara Blandick, The Singer Midgets

The all-time classic for children of all ages, this MGM release, directed by Victor Fleming (*Gone with the Wind*) and based on the story by L. Frank Baum, takes us "off to see the wizard . . . the wonderful wizard of Oz." Sometimes "there's no place like home" for watching great movies!

1939 101 minutes

WOODSTOCK

★★★½

DIRECTOR: Michael Wadleigh

CAST: Country Joe and the Fish, Jimi Hendrix, Jefferson Airplane, Ten Years After

Woodstock is probably, along with *Gimme Shelter*, the most important film documentation of the late 1960s counterculture in the United States. The bulk of the film consists of footage of the bands and various other performers who played at the festival. There are some great split-screen sequences and some imaginative interviews that make the film quite enjoyable today. Well worth viewing. Rated PG.

1970 184 minutes

WORDS AND MUSIC

★★½

DIRECTOR: Norman Taurog

CAST: Mickey Rooney, Tom Drake, June Allyson, Betty Garrett, Judy Garland, Gene Kelly, Ann Sothern, Vera-Ellen, Cyd Charisse, Allyn Ann McLerie, Mel Torme, Janet Leigh, Perry Como

Fictionalized biography of the song-writing team of Richard Rogers and Lorenz Hart, dwelling mostly on the short and tormented life of the latter, played to excess by Mickey Rooney. Tom Drake is a dull Rogers. As long as there's music, song, and dance, everything is great. The rest should have been silence.

1948 119 minutes

X, THE UNHEARD MUSIC

★★★½

DIRECTOR: W. T. Morgan

CAST: John Doe, Exene Cervenka, Billy Zoom, D. J. Bonebrake

Los Angeles's best early punk band, X, is chronicled through old haunts, tracking the movers and the music of the time in this fine documentary. The film, like the band, has a clear awareness of the times, a sense of the history of music, and a humorous perception of it all.

1985 84 minutes

XANADU

★★½

DIRECTOR: Robert Greenwald

CAST: Olivia Newton-John, Gene Kelly, Michael Beck, James Sloyan, Dimitri Arliss, Katie Hanley, Sandahl Bergman

This musical lacks inspiration and storyline. It is basically a full-length video that includes some good numbers by Olivia Newton-John and Gene Kelly. The rock groups the Tubes and the Electric Light Orchestra are also featured. See it for the musical entertainment, not for the story. Rated PG.

1980 88 minutes

YANKEE DOODLE DANDY

★★★★★

DIRECTOR: Michael Curtiz
CAST: James Cagney, Joan Leslie, Walter Huston, Irene Manning, Rosemary DeCamp, Richard Whorf, Jeanne Cagney

Magnetic James Cagney, stepping out of his gangster roles, gives a magnificent strutting performance in the life story of dancing vaudevillian George M. Cohan. An outstanding show-business story with unassuming but effective production.

1942 B & W 126 minutes

YELLOW SUBMARINE

★★★★

DIRECTOR: George Dunning
CAST: Animated

Clever cartoon versions of John, Paul, George, and Ringo journey into Pepperland to save it from the Blue Meanies in this delightful blend of psychedelic animation and topflight Beatles music. "All You Need Is Love," "When I'm 64," "Lucy in the Sky with Diamonds," and "Yellow Submarine" provide the background and power the action in a film that epitomized the flower generation.

1968 85 minutes

YENTL

★★½

DIRECTOR: Barbra Streisand
CAST: Barbra Streisand, Mandy Patinkin, Amy Irving, Nehemiah Persoff, Steven Hill

Barbra Streisand, who also produced, co-scripted, and directed, stars as a woman who must disguise herself as a man in order to pursue an education among Orthodox Jews in turn-of-the-century eastern Europe. The story in this dramatic musical—based on Isaac Bashevis Singer's *Yentl, the Yeshiva Boy*—is well-handled, but the songs, by Michel Legrand and Alan and Marilyn Bergman, are uninspired. What's worse, they all sound the same. Still, *Yentl* is, overall, a watchable work. Rated PG for brief nudity.

1983 134 minutes

YES, GIORGIO

★★

DIRECTOR: Franklin J. Schaffner
CAST: Luciano Pavarotti, Kathryn Harrold, Eddie Albert, Paolo Barboni, James Hong, Beulah Quo

In this old-fashioned star vehicle, Luciano Pavarotti makes a less-than-memorable screen debut as Giorgio Fini, a macho Italian tenor who meets a pretty Boston throat specialist (Kathryn Harrold) when his voice suddenly fails him during a rehearsal. They fall in love and the viewer falls asleep. Rated PG for adult themes.

1982 110 minutes

YOU WERE NEVER LOVELIER

★★★★

DIRECTOR: William Seiter
CAST: Fred Astaire, Rita Hayworth, Adolphe Menjou, Leslie Brooks, Adele Mara

In this interesting story, Fred Astaire goes stepping about with the most glamorous of all the stars—Rita Hayworth. This film's worth seeing twice.

1942 B & W 97 minutes

YOU'LL NEVER GET RICH

★★★½

DIRECTOR: Sidney Lanfield
CAST: Fred Astaire, Rita Hayworth, John Hubbard, Robert

Benchley, Osa Massen, Frieda Inescort, Guinn Williams

This musical-comedy has play producer Fred Astaire getting drafted right before his big show. Somehow he manages to serve his country and put the show on while romancing Rita Hayworth.

1941 B & W 88 minutes

YOUNG MAN WITH A HORN

★★★½

DIRECTOR: Michael Curtiz
CAST: Kirk Douglas, Lauren Bacall, Doris Day, Hoagy Carmichael, Juano Hernandez

Michael Curtiz (*Casablanca*) directed this interesting dramatic portrayal of a young horn player who fights to fill his need for music. Story becomes too melodramatic as Kirk Douglas becomes trapped in a romantic web between Lauren Bacall and Doris Day. Based on the life of Bix Beiderbecke. Hornwork by Harry James.

1950 B & W 112 minutes

ZIEGFELD FOLLIES

★★★

DIRECTOR: Vincent Minnelli
CAST: Fred Astaire, Lucille Ball, William Powell, Judy Garland, Fanny Brice, Lena Horne, Red Skelton, Victor Moore, Virginia O'Brien, Cyd Charisse, Gene Kelly, Edward Arnold, Esther Williams

MGM tries to imitate a Ziegfeld-style stage show. Don't get confused; this is not the Oscar-winning *The Great Ziegfeld* (with William Powell). The Ziegfeld name is merely a contrivance to provide some unified method of showcasing some of its stars.

1946 110 minutes

ZIGGY STARDUST AND THE SPIDERS FROM MARS

[turkey]

DIRECTOR: D. A. Pennebaker
CAST: David Bowie

Only the most devoted David Bowie fans will enjoy this documentary, filmed July 3, 1973, at London's Hammersmith Odeon Theatre during the English singer-songwriter's last live performance as an androgynous king (or queen, for that matter) with orange hair, black eyeshadow, and a spacesuit of glitter. Even they will probably be disappointed by this flat, uninspired, and overlong rock documentary by D. A. Pennebaker (*Monterey Pop*; *Don't Look Back*). Featured are such songs as "Space Oddity," "Suffragette City," "Cracked Actor," "Changes," "All the Young Dudes," and "Oh!" Rated PG for suggestive lyrics and stage movements.

1982 90 minutes

ADVENTURES OF BUCKAROO BANZAI, THE

★★★★

DIRECTOR: W. D. Richter
CAST: Peter Weller, John Lithgow, Ellen Barkin, Jeff Goldblum

Here's the wildest, wackiest science-fiction film ever to hit the screen. Peter Weller plays Buckaroo Banzai, a skilled neurosurgeon and physicist who becomes bored with his scientific and medical work and embarks on a career as a rock star and two-fisted defender of justice. This offbeat genre film is great fun for those who love highly original, laugh-filled, and action-packed entertainment; a silly movie for smart people. Rated PG.

1984 103 minutes

ADVENTURES OF HERCULES, THE

DIRECTOR: Lewis Coates
CAST: Lou Ferrigno, Milly Carlucci, Sonia Viviani, Wiliam Berger

This is the sequel to *Hercules*, the 1983 bomb with Lou "the Hulk" Ferrigno. But while you could argue that the first Ferrigno folly was a laughfest, one can only comment that this tiresome piece of junk would only benefit insomniacs. Rated PG for violence (yes, even *that* can be boring).

1984 89 minutes

AFTER THE FALL OF NEW YORK

DIRECTOR: Martin Dolman
CAST: Michael Sopkiw, Valentine Monnier, Anna Kanakis, Roman Geer, Vincent Scalondro

Dumb, dubbed, and dreadful Italian-made ripoff of the "Mad Max" series, with Michael Sopkiw as a two-fisted, post-apocalypse hero whose job is to save the human race by finding the last normal woman (she's been freeze-dried) and getting her pregnant. Not much to root for here. Rated R for violence, gore, and profanity.

1983 91 minutes

ALIEN

★★★★½

DIRECTOR: Ridley Scott
CAST: Tom Skerritt, Sigourney Weaver, John Hurt, Ian Holm, Harry Dean Stanton, Yaphet Kotto, Veronica Cartwright

A superb cinematic combination of science-fiction and horror, this is a heart-pounding, visually astounding shocker. The players are all excellent as the crew of a futuristic cargo ship that picks up an unwanted passenger: an alien that lives on human flesh and continually changes form. Rated R.

1979 116 minutes

ALIEN FACTOR, THE

★★★

DIRECTOR: Don Dohler
CAST: Don Leifert, Tom Griffith

As an amateur film, this is pretty decent. The cast and production crew are one and the same. There are four aliens on the planet Earth. Only one alien is good, and the Earthlings have a hard time figuring out which one is on their side. Rated PG.

1977 82 minutes

ALIEN PREDATORS

★½

DIRECTOR: Deran Sarafian
CAST: Dennis Christopher, Martin Hewit, Lynn-Holly Johnson

In this muddled cross between *Invasion of the Body Snatchers* and *Alien*, we see three young American adventurers who stumble into an alien invasion in a small Spanish town. The aliens have destroyed the original inhabitants and taken the bodies. The heroic three must then escape the horror of this town. Rated R for violence and gore.

1986 92 minutes

ALIEN WARRIOR

DIRECTOR: Edward Hunt
CAST: Brett Clark, Pamela Saunders, Reggie DeMorton, Nelson Anderson, Norman Bud

In this unwatchable film, a father on another planet sends his only remaining son (Brett Clark) to Earth to protect its people and confront the ultimate evil, who happens to be a pimp. If this story sounds at all familiar, it's because the only thing missing in this comic-book ripoff—besides an original idea—is Kryptonite. Although the hero isn't invulnerable, he may as well be. The only power he's lacking is the ability to act. In fact, the entire cast appears devoid of talent. If you decide to watch this film, it's recommended that you view it in fast-forward. Rated R for nudity, violence, and profanity.

1985 100 minutes

ALIENS

★★★★½

DIRECTOR: James Cameron
CAST: Sigourney Weaver, Carrie Henn, Michael Biehn, Paul Reiser, Lance Henriksen, Jenette Goldstein

Ridley Scott's *Alien* may have been a tough act to follow, but writer-director James Cameron, who performed similar chores on the deft and exciting *Terminator*, is up to the job. Fifty-seven years have passed during Warrant Officer Ripley's (Sigourney Weaver) deep-space sleep; when she wakes, nobody believes her story, and the planet Acheron—where the crew of the ill-fated *Nostromo* first encountered the nasty extraterrestrial—has, meanwhile, been colonized. Then, to everybody's surprise except Ripley's, contact is lost with the colonists. Weaver breathes fire into Ripley, who's one of the best female leads created in years, and Cameron keeps everything bouncing at an absolutely frantic pace. Equal to, although different than, the original. Rated R for considerable violence and profanity.

1986 137 minutes

ALPHA INCIDENT, THE

★★

DIRECTOR: Bill Rebane
CAST: Ralph Meeker, Stafford Morgan, Carol Irene Newell

A deadly organism from Mars, an attempted government cover-up, a radiation leak, panic, and havoc. Okay, if you like this sort of now-tired thing. Rated PG.

1977 84 minutes

ALTERED STATES

★★★½

DIRECTOR: Ken Russell
CAST: William Hurt, Blair Brown, Bob Balaban, Charles Haid, Drew Barrymore

At times in *Altered States*, you can't help but be swept along... and almost overwhelmed. In those moments, it becomes more than just a movie—it's a mindblower. William Hurt, Blair Brown, Bob Balaban, and Charles Haid star in this suspenseful film as scientists involved in the potentially dangerous exploration of the mind. Rated R for nudity, profanity, violence, and sex.

1980 102 minutes

ANDROID

★★★★

DIRECTOR: Aaron Lipstadt
CAST: Klaus Kinski, Don Opper, Brie Howard, Kendra Kirchner

A highly enjoyable, exciting, and funny tongue-in-cheek sci-fi adventure, this takes place on a space station where a mad scientist, Dr. Daniel (played by a surprisingly subdued and effective Klaus Kinski), is trying to create the perfect android. As a group of criminal castaways arrives at the station, the doctor's current robot assistant, Max 404 (Dan Opper), learns it is about to be replaced by a buxom new female model and decides it is time to rebel. Rated PG for nudity, violence, and profanity.

1982 80 minutes

ANDROMEDA STRAIN, THE

★★★★

DIRECTOR: Robert Wise
CAST: Arthur Hill, David Wayne, James Olson, Kate Reid, Paula Kelly

A powerful, tense science-fiction thriller, this film focuses on a team of scientists attempting to isolate a deadly virus while racing against time and the possibility of nuclear war. Though not as flashy as other entries in the genre, it's highly effective. Rated G.

1971 130 minutes

ANGRY RED PLANET, THE

★★½

DIRECTOR: Ib Melchior
CAST: Gerald Mohr, Nora Hayden, Les Tremayne, Jack Kruschen

Entertaining (if unoriginal) science-fiction tale of an expedition to Mars running into all sorts of alien terrors, most notable of which is a terrifying kind of giant mouse/spider hybrid. A fun film, though it takes forever to get to the action, and the viewer might be tempted to hit the "scan" button more than once.

1959 83 minutes

ANNA TO THE INFINITE POWER

★★★★

DIRECTOR: Robert Wiemer
CAST: Martha Byrne, Dina Merrill, Mark Patton, Donna Mitch-

ell, Jack Ryland, Loretta Devine, Jack Gilford

Is individuality determined purely by genetic code, or by some other factor beyond the control of science? This film explores the dimensions of that question via the struggles of a brilliant, troubled child—who is also the unwitting subject of a scientific experiment to establish her own identity. It also poses other questions, such as, What makes us who we are, and how much can we change? This kind of deep-think is not easy to explore on celluloid, but director Robert Weimer and his cast succeed in near brilliant fashion.

1982 107 minutes

AT THE EARTH'S CORE

★★½

DIRECTOR: Kevin Connor

CAST: Doug McClure, Peter Cushing, Caroline Munro, Cy Grant, Sean Lynch, Godfrey James

At the Earth's Core, an Edgar Rice Burroughs adaptation, benefits enormously from an inspired performance by British horror film stalwart Peter Cushing. He even manages to make Doug McClure look good occasionally. It's mostly for the kiddies, but we found ourselves clutching the arm of the chair a couple of times at the height of suspense. Rated PG.

1976 90 minutes

ATOMIC SUBMARINE, THE

★★★

DIRECTOR: Spencer Bennet

CAST: Arthur Franz, Dick Foran, Brett Halsey, Tom Conway, Bob Steele, Victor Varconi, Joi Lansing

Solid little thriller about U.S. atomic submarine and its encounter with an alien flying saucer in the Arctic suffers from budgetary limitations (and excess use of stock footage, a common ailment of 1950s science-fiction films), but benefits from a decent script, good direction, and an effective and thoroughly believable cast of fine character actors, including many former B-movie and series film stars. Even the smaller roles are taken by familiar faces with engaging personalities, like Sid Melton, and this adds to the believability of an otherwise threadbare and overused storyline. Veteran serial director Spencer Bennet did a good job on this one, and producer Alex Gordon (who at one time worked closely with the incredible Edward D. Wood Jr. and designed the "special effects" for *Bride of the Monster*) finally sunk his time and money into a project that most fans of low-budget monster films consider to be his best effort. Entertaining and effective without being too stupid or taking itself too seriously, this is decent fare for fantasy fans and one of the better "flying saucer" films to come out of the UFO-crazed 1950s.

1959 B & W 72 minutes

ATOR: THE FIGHTING EAGLE

DIRECTOR: David Hills

CAST: Miles O'Keeffe, Sabrina Siani, Warren Hillman

A low-budget stupid sword-and-sorcery flick with Miles O'Keeffe, from Bo Derek's *Tarzan, the Ape Man*. Rated PG for violence and nudity.

1983 98 minutes

AURORA ENCOUNTER

★★★½

DIRECTOR: Jim McCullough Sr.

CAST: Jack Elam, Peter Brown, Carol Bagdasarian, Dottie West

Here's one of few science fiction films that can be enjoyed by the whole family. Jack Elam is outstanding in a story about a small

Texas town visited by aliens in the late 1800s. Rated PG.

1985 90 minutes

BABY . . . SECRET OF THE LOST LEGEND

★★½

DIRECTOR: B.W.L. Norton

CAST: William Katt, Sean Young, Patrick McGoohan, Julian Fellowes

Set on the Ivory Coast of West Africa, this Disney story offers more than a cute fable about the discovery of a family of brontosauri. Nudity, violence, and a hint of sex represent Disney's attempt to appeal to a wider audience. The special effects of the ancient critters make the show worth watching. Rated PG primarily for the violence.

1985 90 minutes

BACK TO THE FUTURE

★★★★½

DIRECTOR: Robert Zemeckis

CAST: Michael J. Fox, Christopher Lloyd, Lea Thompson, Crispin Glover, Thomas F. Wilson

This delightful Steven Spielberg production, directed by Robert Zemeckis (*Romancing the Stone*), features Michael J. Fox as a teenager who is zapped back in time courtesy of a souped-up Delorean modified by mad scientist Christopher Lloyd. Once there, Fox meets his parents as teenagers, an act that could result in disaster. The first fifteen minutes of this film are pretty bad (thus its less-than-five-star rating), but once Fox gets back to where he doesn't belong, it's terrific entertainment. Rated PG for brief violence and profanity.

1985 116 minutes

BAMBOO SAUCER (a.k.a. COLLISION COURSE)

★★½

DIRECTOR: Frank Telford

CAST: Dan Duryea, John Ericson, Lois Nettleton, Bob Hastings, Nan Leslie

America and the U.S.S.R. compete with each other as they investigate reports of a UFO crash in the People's Republic of China. More concerned with plot and substance than special effects, this low-budget effort is thought-provoking and succeeds where a more gimmicky, less suspenseful approach would have failed. Film and television veteran Dan Duryea made his last appearance professionally in this film. The film received little theater play when originally released.

1968 100 minutes

BARBARELLA

★★½

DIRECTOR: Roger Vadim

CAST: Jane Fonda, John Phillip Law, Anita Pallenberg, Milo O'Shea

Futuristic fantasy has Jane Fonda in the title role of a space beauty being drooled over by various male creatures on a strange planet. Drags at times, but Jane's fans won't want to miss it. Rated PG for partial nudity, sexual content.

1968 98 minutes

BARBARIAN QUEEN

DIRECTOR: Hector Oliver

CAST: Lana Clarkson, Latta Shea, Frank Zagarino, Dawn Dunlap

Another one of those lame fantasy flicks à la *Yor*, the *Conan* films, and Lou Ferigno's *Hercules* films. Stupid and exploitative, this one is about a group of women who survive an attack on their village only to band together to defeat the raiders. Save your money. Although not rated, *Barbarian Queen* has lots of nudity, sex, and violence, and would qualify for an R rating under MPAA standards.

1985 75 minutes

BATTLE BEYOND THE STARS

★★★★

DIRECTOR: Jimmy T. Murakami

CAST: Richard Thomas, John Saxon, Robert Vaughn

Here's something different: a space fantasy-comedy. Richard Thomas stars in this funny and often exciting movie as an emissary from a peaceful planet desperately searching for champions to save it from destruction and domination by an evil warlord. It's *Star Wars* meets *The Magnificent Seven*, with fine tongue-in-cheek performances by George Peppard, Robert Vaughn (playing the same role he had in the western), and John Saxon. Rated PG.

1980 104 minutes

BATTLE FOR THE PLANET OF THE APES

★★

DIRECTOR: J. Lee Thompson

CAST: Roddy McDowall, Severn Darden, John Huston, Claude Akins, Paul Williams

Events come full circle in this final *Apes* film, with simian Roddy McDowall attempting peaceful coexistence with conquered humanity. Naturally, not everybody plays along with such a plan, and an impending nuclear threat adds little tension to a story whose outcome is known. Extensive use of stock footage from previous films must have helped this cheapie clean up at the box office. Although the series would have no further big-screen life, it next fell into the purgatory of a short-lived—and awful—network television series. Rated PG for violence.

1973 92 minutes

BATTLESTAR GALACTICA

★★

DIRECTOR: Richard A. Colla

CAST: Lorne Greene, Richard Hatch, Dirk Benedict, Lew Ayres, Jane Seymour

This film, adapted from the television series, opens with the preparation for a peace treaty by President Adar (Lew Ayres). He has arranged to end a thousand years of war between mankind and the subhuman Cylons. Events go downhill from there. It's seventh-rate *Star Wars*, as are the other "films" in this video series. Rated PG.

1978 125 minutes

BEASTMASTER, THE

★★★½

DIRECTOR: Don Coscarelli

CAST: Marc Singer, Tanya Roberts, Rip Torn, John Amos, Rod Loomis

A young medieval warrior (Marc Singer) who possesses the ability to communicate psychically with animals takes revenge—with the help of a slave (Tanya Roberts) and a master warrior (John Amos)—on the evil sorcerer (Rip Torn). It's fun for kids of all ages. Rated PG for violence, gore, and brief nudity.

1982 118 minutes

BENEATH THE PLANET OF THE APES

★★½

DIRECTOR: Ted Post

CAST: Charlton Heston, James Franciscus, Maurice Evans, Kim Hunter, Linda Harrison, James Gregory

Charlton Heston let himself get sucked into this sequel to *Planet of the Apes*. Astronaut James Franciscus—sent to find out what happened to the first team sent to the planet—has more than simians to contend with; he also discovers a race of u-g-l-y mutants that worships an atomic bomb, since it made them what they are. . . . Some of the original's energy remains, but this unpleasant sequel goes nowhere fast. Those who feel that nothing can happen after the world is destroyed need to check into the next entry, *Escape from the Planet of the Apes*. Rated PG for violence.

1970 95 minutes

BEYOND TOMORROW

★★½

DIRECTOR: A. Edward Sutherland

CAST: Jean Parker, Richard Carlson, Helen Vinson, Charles Winninger, Harry Carey, C. Aubrey Smith, Maria Ouspenskaya, Rod La Rocque

Sudden success goes to singer Richard Carlson's head. He switches his affections from fiancée Jean Parker to captivating stage star Helen Vinson. To see that right is done, three ghosts return from the grave and change his troubled mind. An interesting premise on paper, the film fails to live up to its possibilities.

1940 B & W 84 minutes

BLACK HOLE, THE

★

DIRECTOR: Gary Nelson

CAST: Maximilian Schell, Anthony Perkins, Robert Forster, Joseph Bottoms, Yvette Mimieux, Ernest Borgnine

Let's hear it for *Herbie Goes to Outer Space*! Boooooo! Only the splendid special effects make this sappy science-fiction dud from the Disney Studios bearable. Complete with a cute little robot (á la *Star Wars*) and a colorful crew (like "Star Trek"), it's an uninspired collection of space movie clichés. Rated PG.

1979 97 minutes

BLADE RUNNER

★★★★½

DIRECTOR: Ridley Scott

CAST: Harrison Ford, Rutger Hauer, Sean Young, Daryl Hannah, Edward James Olmos, M. Emmet Walsh

A genuine science-fiction film, this Ridley Scott (*Alien*) production is daring, thought-provoking, and visually impressive. Harrison Ford stars as a futuristic Philip Marlowe trying to find and kill the world's remaining rebel androids in 2817 Los Angeles. *Blade Runner* may not be for everyone, but those who appreciate something of substance will find it worthwhile. Rated PG for brief nudity and violence.

1982 118 minutes

BOY AND HIS DOG, A

★★★★½

DIRECTOR: L. Q. Jones

CAST: Don Johnson, Suzanne Benton, Jason Robards Jr.

Looking for intelligence and biting humor in a science-fiction satire? Try this Hugo Award–winning screen adaptation of Harlan Ellison's novel, which focuses on the adventures of a young scavenger (Don Johnson, of television's *Miami Vice*) and his telepathic dog as they roam the earth circa 2024 after a nuclear holocaust. It's funny, poignant, thought-provoking, and—especially at the conclusion—surprising. Rated R for violence, sexual references, and nudity.

1976 87 minutes

BRAIN FROM PLANET AROUS, THE

★★★

DIRECTOR: Nathan Juran

CAST: John Agar, Joyce Meadows, Robert Fuller

Great little film is much better than the plot or title would suggest. Giant brain from outer space takes over John Agar's body in an attempt to conquer the world. Not far behind is another brain that inhabits the body of Agar's dog and tries to prevent it. Good stuff.

1958 B & W 70 minutes

BRAIN THAT WOULDN'T DIE, THE

★★

DIRECTOR: Joseph Green

CAST: Herb Evers, Virginia Leith, Adele Lamont

Only the most dedicated science-fiction fans will enjoy this story, which revolves around a doctor who experiments with human limbs. When his fiancée is decapitated in a car accident, he saves her head and searches for the perfect body to go with it. There is some violence and plenty of blood.

1963 B & W 81 minutes

BRAINSTORM

★★★½

DIRECTOR: Douglas Trumbull

CAST: Christopher Walken, Natalie Wood, Louise Fletcher

Christopher Walken and Natalie Wood star in this sci-fi thriller about an invention that can read and record physical, emotional, and intellectual sensations as they are experienced by an individual and allow them to be re-experienced by another human being. The machine's potential for good—increasing communication and mutual understanding—is impressive. But what happens if it's used for evil? Rated PG for nudity and profanity.

1983 106 minutes

BROTHER FROM ANOTHER PLANET, THE

★★★★

DIRECTOR: John Sayles

CAST: Joe Morton, Darryl Edwards, Steve James

In this comic fantasy, directed by John Sayles (*Return of the Secaucus 7*), a dark-skinned extraterrestrial (Joe Morton) on the lam from alien cops crash-lands his spaceship in New York harbor, staggers ashore on Ellis Island, then makes his way to Harlem. As the Ellis Island opening suggests, this release is, like *Moscow on the Hudson*, about what it means to be an immigrant in America. Yet Sayles has more on his mind than "America the Beautiful," and that's what makes this alternately poignant, hilarious, and sobering study of our country so impressive. Unrated, the film has profanity and violence.

1984 110 minutes

BUCK ROGERS: DESTINATION SATURN (A.K.A. PLANET OUTLAWS)

★★½

DIRECTORS: Ford Beebe, Saul Goodkind

CAST: Buster Crabbe, Constance Moore, Jackie Moran, Jack Mulhall, Anthony Warde, C. Montague Shaw, Philip Ahn

Edited-down version of the popular serial loses much of the continuity of the twelve-episode chapter play but still proves to be great fun as ideal hero Buster Crabbe enthusiastically goes after the vile Killer Kan in an effort to help the oppressed people of future Earth. Although the film appears quaint today, and the special effects are laughable, this comic-strip adaptation was, along with the *Flash Gordon* serials, state-of-the-art space fodder for the imaginative youth of pre–World War II America.

1939 B & W 91 minutes

BUCK ROGERS IN THE 25TH CENTURY

★★

DIRECTOR: Daniel Haller
CAST: Gil Gerard, Erin Gray, Pamela Hensley, Tim O'Connor, Henry Silva, Felix Silla

Updating of the Buck Rogers legend finds Buck (Gil Gerard), after years of suspended animation, awakened in a future society under attack by the power-mad Princess Ardala (Pamela Hensley). Of course, it's up to our hero to save the day, with the help of a female fighter pilot (Erin Gray) and a dopey robot named Twiki (Felix Silla, with the voice of Mel Blanc). Substandard space fare was originally made as a TV pilot for the recent series but was released theatrically instead. Rated PG for two off-color words.

1979 89 minutes

CAPRICORN ONE

★★★★

DIRECTOR: Peter Hyams
CAST: Elliott Gould, James Brolin, Hal Holbrook, Sam Waterston, Karen Black, O. J. Simpson, Telly Savalas

Peter Hyams, who also directed *2010*, made his first big impression at the box office with this exciting and suspenseful release. In this story, a space flight to Mars is aborted. However, to save face, the government stages a mock flight to the red planet in a television studio, with astronauts James Brolin, Sam Waterston, and O. J. Simpson pretending to be in outer space and landing on another planet. Everything goes well. It all looks convincing on the TV screen. Then the news is released by the Pentagon that the ship crashed upon re-entry and all aboard were killed, which puts the lives of the astronauts in danger. Elliott Gould co-stars as a newspaper reporter on the track of the truth in this highly recommended nail-biter. Rated PG.

1978 124 minutes

CAPTIVE PLANET

DIRECTOR: Al Bradley
CAST: Sharon Baker, Chris Avran, Anthony Newcastle, Yarti Somer

Earth is once again besieged by alien invaders in this very missable movie. There may have been an interesting idea at the heart of this film, but it was lost in wooden acting, poor script, and unimaginative, budget-priced special effects.

1986 105 minutes

CARS THAT ATE PARIS, THE (CARS THAT EAT PEOPLE, THE)

★★★★

DIRECTOR: Peter Weir
CAST: John Meillon, Terry Camilleri, Kevin Miles

One of the first signs that Australian New Wave would bring a flood of brilliant films. This one, by perhaps the greatest director from Down Under, Peter Weir (*Witness*, *Picnic at Hanging Rock*, *The Last Wave*), is a black comedy about a small outback village plagued by driverless cars that come out by night. Weird, to be sure, but worth a look. Rated PG.

1975 90 minutes

CAT WOMEN OF THE MOON

DIRECTOR: Arthur Hilton
CAST: Sonny Tufts, Marie Windsor, Victor Jory

Another ludicrous entry in the travel-to-a-planet-of-barely-dressed-women subgenre which so fascinated makers of cheap, grade Z flicks in the 1950s. This one doesn't even qualify as camp entertainment; it's simply terrible. Avoid at all costs.

1954 64 minutes

CAVE GIRL

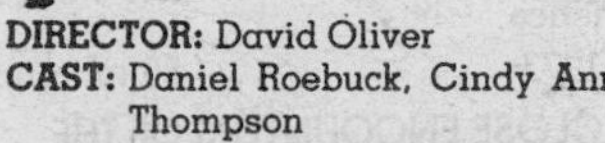

DIRECTOR: David Oliver
CAST: Daniel Roebuck, Cindy Ann Thompson

Yet another insult to the intelligence of the video-viewing public. This one is about a high-school student (who looks more like he is ready for his ten-year reunion) who gets lost in a cave during a field trip and pops up in prehistoric times. There he finds a beautiful woman with long blonde hair and pearly-white teeth. (It would seem that there were hairdressers and toothpaste back then.) Of course, he just has to have sex with her! And the first English words our hero teaches the Neanderthal nymphet are not suitable for this publication. Rated R for sex, nudity, and profanity.

1985 85 minutes

CHARLY

★★★★

DIRECTOR: Ralph Nelson
CAST: Cliff Robertson, Claire Bloom, Lilia Skala, Dick Van Patten, Leon Janney

Cliff Robertson won the best-actor Oscar for his role in this excellent science-fiction film as a retarded man turned into a genius through scientific experiments. Claire Bloom is also excellent as the caseworker who becomes his friend. Rated PG.

1968 103 minutes

CITY LIMITS

DIRECTOR: Aaron Lipstadt
CAST: Darrell Larson, John Stockwell, Kim Cattrall, Rae Dawn Chong, Robby Benson, James Earl Jones

Another in the endless parade of life-after-the-apocalypse, *Mad Max* ripoff films. In this dud, we have two rival youth gangs fighting it out for control of a big city. Most of the action involves gang members beating each other with chains and clubs while riding motorcycles in dark alleys. The acting talent of such stars as Rae Dawn Chong and James Earl Jones is thrown away, and the costumes all the characters wear are ridiculous beyond belief. Rated PG-13 for brief nudity, violence, and language.

1984 85 minutes

CLAN OF THE CAVE BEAR

★½

DIRECTOR: Michael Chapman
CAST: Daryl Hannah, Pamela Reed, Thomas G. Waites, John Doolittle

In this dreadfully dumb adaptation of Jean M. Auel's best-selling fantasy novel, Daryl Hannah plays a Cro-Magnon child who is grudgingly adopted by a tribe of Neanderthals, who, with a few exceptions, fear she is a dark spirit intent on destroying them. *Quest for Fire* did the cave man story best, and Hannah was better off in films like *Splash* and *Legal Eagles*. Even fans of the book will be disappointed. Rated R.

1986 100 minutes

CLASH OF THE TITANS

★★½

DIRECTOR: Desmond Davis
CAST: Laurence Olivier, Harry Hamlin, Judi Bowker, Bur-

gess Meredith, Maggie Smith

Despite its spectacular special effects and great possibilities, *Clash of the Titans* is not the film it could have been. The story is the retelling of a Greek myth in which Perseus (Harry Hamlin), the son of Zeus (Laurence Olivier), mounts his flying horse, Pegasus, and fights for the hand of Andromeda (Judi Bowker) against an onslaught of mythological monsters. Plagued by corny situations and stilted dialogue, only the visual wonders by special-effects wizard Ray Harryhausen make this movie worth seeing. Rated PG for violence and gore.

1981 118 minutes

CLOCKWORK ORANGE, A

★★★★

DIRECTOR: Stanley Kubrick
CAST: Malcolm McDowell, Patrick Magee, Adrienne Corri, Aubrey Morris, James Marcus

Not for every taste, this stylized, "ultraviolent" black comedy by director Stanley Kubrick is as funny as it was prophetic. This film (which was adapted from the Anthony Burgess novel) chillingly presaged the British punk movement of the 1970s and the early '80s. Malcolm McDowell stars as the number-one "malchick," Alex, who leads his "droogs" through "a bit of the old ultraviolence" for a real "horror show." Rated R.

1971 137 minutes

CLONES, THE

★★½

DIRECTORS: Paul Hunt, Lamar Card
CAST: Michael Greene, Bruce Bennett, Gregory Sierra, John Barrymore Jr., Angelo Rossito.

In a sinister plot to control the weather, several government scientists are duplicated and placed in strategic meteorological stations. Of course, this scheme is discovered by one of the "good" scientists, who is marked for extermination from that point on. Basically silly film is made watchable by the believable performances of Michael Greene and Gregory Sierra, and there's a terrific roller coaster–chase finale. Rated PG for language and violence.

1973 86 minutes

CLOSE ENCOUNTERS OF THE THIRD KIND

★★★★

DIRECTOR: Steven Spielberg
CAST: Richard Dreyfuss, Francois Truffaut, Teri Garr, Melinda Dillon

This is director Steven Spielberg's enchanting, pre-*E.T.* vision of an extraterrestrial visit to Earth. The movie goes against many long-nurtured conceptions about space aliens. The humans, such as Richard Dreyfuss, act more bizarre than the non-threatening childlike visitors. Spielberg never surrenders his role as storyteller to the distractions of special effects. That is one reason why his films are better received than most films of the genre. Rated PG.

1977 132 minutes

COCOON

★★★★★

DIRECTOR: Ron Howard
CAST: Don Ameche, Wilford Brimley, Hume Cronyn, Brian Dennehy, Jack Gilford, Steve Guttenberg, Barret Oliver, Maureen Stapleton, Jessica Tandy, Gwen Verdon, Tahnee Welch

Chalk up another winner for actor-turned-director Ron Howard. As with *Splash* and *Night Shift* before it, *Cocoon* is a splendid entertainment. The story in this science-fiction film revolves around a group of people in a retirement home who find what they believe is the fountain of youth. Only trouble is the magic place belongs to a group of extraterrestrials, who may or may not be friendly. Rated PG-13 for suggested sex, brief nudity, and light profanity.

1985 118 minutes

COMPANY OF WOLVES, THE

★★★½

DIRECTOR: Neil Jordan

CAST: Angela Lansbury, David Warner, Sarah Patterson, Micha Bergese

Neither a horror film nor a fantasy for the kiddies, this dark, psychologically oriented rendering of the "Little Red Riding Hood" story is for thinking viewers only. Angela Lansbury stars as Grandmother, who turns the dreams of her granddaughter (Sarah Patterson) into tales of spooky terror. Artistically made by director Neil Jordan, this movie deserves to be seen. Rated R for violence and gore.

1985 95 minutes

CONAN THE BARBARIAN

★★½

DIRECTOR: John Milius

CAST: Arnold Schwarzenegger, Sandahl Bergman, James Earl Jones, Gerry Lopez, Mako

Featuring Arnold Schwarzenegger in the title role, this $19 million sword-and-sorcery epic is just as corny, raunchy, sexist, and unbelievably brutal as the original tales by Robert E. Howard. Therefore, it seems likely Conan fans will be delighted. Yes, it's often unintentionally hilarious and dumb. In other words, it's an old-fashioned B movie on a grand scale—and basically enjoyable because of it. Rated R for nudity, profanity, sex, and violence.

1982 129 minutes

CONAN THE DESTROYER

★★★

DIRECTOR: Richard Fleischer

CAST: Arnold Schwarzenegger, Grace Jones, Wilt Chamberlain, Tracey Walter

Thank goodness the creators of this sequel to *Conan the Barbarian* didn't take themselves as seriously as their predecessors, and the result is a lightweight, violent movie that works quite well. Once again, we're back in the Hyborean Age—a pre-history, mythical time created by Robert E. Howard—where we find Conan (Arnold Schwarzenegger) besting beasts and bloodthirsty battlers at every turn with the help of his sidekick (Tracey Walter), a wizard (Mako), a staff-wielding thief (androgynous Grace Jones), and a giant warrior (Wilt Chamberlain) as they take a virgin princess (Olivia D'Abo) on a perilous mission to find a sacred stone. Rated PG for violence.

1984 103 minutes

CONQUEST OF THE PLANET OF THE APES

★★

DIRECTOR: J. Lee Thompson

CAST: Roddy McDowall, Ricardo Montalban, Don Murray, Severn Darden

Having been rescued by Ricardo Montalban at the end of his previous film adventure, simian Roddy McDowall matures and leads his fellow apes—now domesticated—in a freedom revolt that sets the stage for the events in the very first film. Very melodramatic and formulaic, with few clichés left unused. Unfortunately, the well was to be emptied once more, with *Battle for the Planet of the Apes*. Rated PG for violence.

1972 87 minutes

CREATION OF THE HUMANOIDS

★★

DIRECTOR: Wesley E. Barry
CAST: Don Megowan, Francis McCann, Erica Elliot

Don Megowan (a stuntman who once played *The Creature from the Black Lagoon*) stars in this futuristic parable about human prejudice toward robots. He plays a cop who is paranoid about the development of near-perfect androids, fearing they will eventually take over the world. It's bad enough that the machines are smarter and more productive than humans, but when his sister falls in love with one, Megowan vows to spill oil and strip gears. This is a low-budget, clunky vision of the future that is long on talk, short on action, and hard to take seriously. The postured performances, stilted dialogue, and sparse sets give it the look of a high school play.

1962 75 minutes

CREATURE

🦃

DIRECTOR: William Malone
CAST: Stan Ivar, Wendy Schaal, Klaus Kinski, Marie Laurin, Lyman Ward, Robert Jaffe

An insulting-to-the-intelligence ripoff of *Alien*, this film features the reawakening of human-devouring life on one of Jupiter's moons. Rated R for gore and violence.

1985 97 minutes

CREATURE FROM THE HAUNTED SEA, THE

★½

DIRECTOR: Roger Corman
CAST: Anthony Carbone, Betsy Jones-Moreland, Edward Wain, Edmundo Rivera Alvarez, Robert Beam

A muddled horror-comedy about a Bogart-type crook planning to steal a treasure with the help of a mythical sea monster. After shooting *The Battle of Blood Island* and *The Last Woman on Earth* in Puerto Rico, director Roger Corman decided to make another movie with the same cast. So he called up writer Charles Griffith and told him he had six days to come up with a script. Griffith agreed, but took his revenge by creating an enormously complex character that Corman himself would have to play since there were more roles in the script than actors available on location. Corman managed to avoid the challenge, though, by promoting Robert Beam from boom man to actor. The movie is about what you'd expect, all things considered.

1960 B & W 60 minutes

CYBORG: THE SIX MILLION DOLLAR MAN

★★★

DIRECTOR: Richard Irving
CAST: Lee Majors, Darren McGavin, Martin Balsam, Barbara Anderson

Pilot for the long-running ABC series is more serious and subdued than the episodes to follow. Col. Steve Austin (Lee Majors), flying an experimental jet that malfunctions, winds up in the hospital minus his left eye, right arm, and both legs. This gives the military the perfect opportunity to attempt a practical application of "cybornetics" they've been working with, turning the crippled pilot into a superman by giving him powerful robotic limbs capable of almost limitless strength. Unlike the subsequent series, this film is basically a human drama with dashes of sci-fi thrown in. Very good. High marks as well to MCA for the impeccable color and sound on this laserdisc.

1973 73 minutes

D.A.R.Y.L.

★★★★

DIRECTOR: Simon Wince
CAST: Barret Oliver, Mary Beth Hurt, Michael McKean, Josef Sommer

In this delightful science-fiction film, Barret Oliver (from *The NeverEnding Story*) stars as a boy adopted by Mary Beth Hurt and Michael McKean (*This Is Spinal Tap*). He turns out to be a perfect little fellow . . . maybe a little too perfect. *D.A.R.Y.L.* is a film the whole family can enjoy: an entertaining cinematic gem that will have viewers recommending it to their friends. Rated PG for violence and light profanity.

1985 99 minutes

DAGORA, THE SPACE MONSTER

★½

DIRECTOR: Inoshiro Honda
CAST: Yosuke Natsuki

From the folks who brought you *Godzilla*. A cache of gems stolen by Japanese gangsters is ripped off by a giant, flying, diamond-eating jellyfish. Probably a true story.

1964 80 minutes

DALEKS—INVASION EARTH 2150 A.D.

★★★

DIRECTOR: Gordon Flemyng
CAST: Peter Cushing, Bernard Cribbins, Andrew Keir, Ray Brooks, Jill Curzon, Roberta Tovey

The always watchable Peter Cushing revives his distinctive interpretation of the ever-popular Dr. Who in this honorable sequel to *Dr. Who and the Daleks*. This time, the title creatures are attempting to take over Earth.

1966 84 minutes

DAMNATION ALLEY

★★

DIRECTOR: Jack Smight
CAST: Jan-Michael Vincent, George Peppard, Dominique Sanda, Jackie Earle Haley, Paul Winfield

The nuclear holocaust movie, which disappeared after its heyday in the 1950s, was revived by *Damnation Alley*, complete with giant mutations and roaming survivors. While it's not a bad movie, it's not particularly good, either. The laser effects are awful. The film has its moments, and considering the outdated premise, that's quite an accomplishment. Rated PG, no violence, sex, or profanity.

1977 91 minutes

DARK CRYSTAL, THE

★★★★

DIRECTORS: Jim Henson, Frank Oz
CAST: Animation

Jim Henson of "The Muppets" fame created this lavish fantasy tale in the style of J.R.R. Tolkien (*The Lord of the Rings*), using the movie magic that brought E.T. and Yoda (*The Empire Strikes Back*) to life. It's a delight for children of all ages. Rated PG, the film has scenes that may be too strong for the younger set.

1983 93 minutes

DARK STAR

★★★½

DIRECTOR: John Carpenter
CAST: Dan O'Bannon, Brian Narelle, Dre Pahich

This is one of the strangest sci-fi films you are likely to run across. Four astronauts have been in space entirely too long as they seek and destroy unstable planets.

Director John Carpenter's first film is very funny in spurts and always crazy enough to hold the viewer's attention. Rated PG because of language.

1974 83 minutes

DAY AFTER, THE

★★★★

DIRECTOR: Nicholas Meyer

CAST: Jason Robards Jr., JoBeth Williams, Steve Guttenberg, John Cullum, John Lithgow

This excellent made-for-TV movie special received much advance publicity because of its timely topic: the effects of a nuclear war. Jason Robards plays a hospital doctor who treats many of the victims after the nuclear attack. Steve Guttenberg also stars, as a college student, and John Lithgow is a college professor.

1983 120 minutes

DAY OF THE DOLPHIN, THE

★★★

DIRECTOR: Mike Nichols

CAST: George C. Scott, Trish Van Devere, Paul Sorvino, Fritz Weaver

Fine film centering on a research scientist (George C. Scott) who teaches a pair of dolphins to speak, and how they're kidnapped and used in an assassination attempt. Rated PG for language.

1973 104 minutes

DAY OF THE TRIFFIDS, THE

★★★½

DIRECTOR: Steve Sekely

CAST: Howard Keel, Nicole Maurey, Janette Scott, Kieron Moore, Mervyn Johns

"Dallas" fans may be surprised to see Miss Ellie's husband, Clayton Farlow (Howard Keel), in a science-fiction flick. This British film has "triffids"—alien plants—arriving on Earth during a meteor shower. The shower blinds most of the Earth's people. Then the plants grow, begin walking, and eat humans. This one will grow on you.

1963 95 minutes

DAY THE EARTH CAUGHT FIRE, THE

★★★★

DIRECTOR: Val Guest

CAST: Edward Judd, Janet Munro, Leo McKern, Michael Goodliffe

Veteran director Val Guest helmed this near-classic film concerning the fate of the Earth following simultaneous nuclear explosions at both poles, sending the planet on a collision course with the sun. Incredibly realistic production is thought-provoking and more than a little unsettling, with Edward Judd perfectly cast as an Everyman caught up in the mass panic and hysteria as a frantic populace desperately searches for an answer.

1962 B & W 99 minutes

DAY THE EARTH STOOD STILL, THE

★★★★

DIRECTOR: Robert Wise

CAST: Michael Rennie, Patricia Neal, Hugh Marlowe, Sam Jaffe, Billy Gray

The Day the Earth Stood Still is one of the better science-fiction films. Even though some of the space gimmicks are campy and not up to today's standards of special effects, the film holds up well because of a good adult script and creditable performances by Michael Rennie and Patricia Neal. Rennie plays a man from another planet who visits Earth and does not receive what could be called a warm welcome.

1951 B & W 92 minutes

DEAD END DRIVE IN

★★

DIRECTOR: Brian Trenchard-Smith

CAST: Ned Manning, Natalie McCurry, Peter Whitford, Dave Gibson, Sande Ullingston, Ollie Hall, Wilbur Wilde

It's the year 1990. After widespread economic collapse, the world is in chaos. There are gangs on the streets: tow-truck drivers fight for the privilege to take away wrecked vehicles; and there are still drive-in theatres. The Dead-End Drive-In is, in fact, a relocation camp for the undesirable element that the authorities no longer wish to deal with. By looking at this microcosm of society, the film makes some powerful statements about social unrest, racial prejudice, and the looming threat of the police state. Rated R for language, violence, and nudity.

1986 92 minutes

DEADLY HARVEST

🦃

DIRECTOR: Timothy Bond

CAST: Clint Walker, Nehemiah Persoff, Kim Cattrall, David Brown, Jim Henshaw, Gary Davies

Mankind's unrelenting industrialization of arable land and subsequent cold winters (and summers!) wreak havoc with America's ecological system, slinging society into barbarism. Clint Walker sleepwalks through the lead role, leaving little room for any spontaneity in this sappy futuristic thriller. A laughable score adds to the reasons no one would want to watch this badly produced film. One especially disturbing scene finds a father secretly poisoning his family at the dinner table. For no one. Rated PG.

1976 86 minutes

DEATH RACE 2000

★★★

DIRECTOR: Paul Bartel

CAST: David Carradine, Sylvester Stallone, Louisa Moritz, Mary Woronov, Don Steele, Joyce Jameson, Fred Grandy

Futuristic look at what has become our national sport: road racing where points are accumulated for killing people with the race cars. David Carradine and Sylvester Stallone star in this tongue-in-cheek sci-fi action film. Does have plenty of gore but always has the audience smiling. Stallone is a howl as one of the competitors. Rated R—violence, nudity, language, sex.

1975 78 minutes

DEATH WATCH

★★★★

DIRECTOR: Bertrand Tavernier

CAST: Romy Schneider, Harvey Keitel, Harry Dean Stanton, Max von Sydow

A thought-provoking look at the power and the misuse of the media in a future society. Harvey Keitel has a camera implanted in his brain. A television producer (Harry Dean Stanton) uses Keitel to film a documentary of a terminally ill woman (Romy Schneider) without her knowledge. Suspenseful science-fiction drama. Rated R for profanity and suggested sex.

1980 117 minutes

DEATHSPORT

★★

DIRECTORS: Henry Suso, Allan Arkush

CAST: David Carradine, Claudia Jennings, Richard Lynch

Not really a sequel to *Deathrace 2000*, but cut from the same cloth. Both are low-budget action films centered around futuristic no-holds-barred road races. The first film, though, was a lot more fun. Rated R for violence and nudity.

1978 82 minutes

DEATHSTALKER

DIRECTOR: John Watson
CAST: Robert Hill, Barbi Benton, Lana Clarkson, Victor Bo

Mixing sex, sadism, and stupidity for a nearly unbearable movie experience, director John Watson (an obvious pseudonym) has created a thoroughly disgusting exploitation flick. A muscle-bound warrior (Robert Hill) attempts to save a beautiful princess (Barbi Benton) from an evil wizard. If the plot sounds familiar, it should. It's an unabashed ripoff of *Star Wars*. The only difference is that in George Lucas's far superior space fantasy, Carrie Fisher didn't have every stitch of her clothing torn off every fifteen minutes. However, for Benton, that's the extent of her "acting." Shame on her. Rated R for nudity, profanity, sex, simulated rape, and violence.

1984 80 minutes

DEFCON 4

★★½

DIRECTOR: Paul Donovan
CAST: Maury Chaykin, Kate Lynch, Tim Choate, Lenore Zann, Keven King, John Walsch

The first half of this film contains special effects the equal of any in modern science fiction, an intelligent script, and excellent acting by the three leads as astronauts in an orbiting space station that is part of an anti-nuclear war defense system. The tensions between the three (Maury Chaykin, Kate Lynch, and Tim Choate) are extremely well done. Global nuclear war breaks out, and lacking the signal to strike back, they wait and watch. In the second half of the film, they return to Earth, and the film becomes one more post-holocaust yawn. The overall impression is that perhaps the filmmakers ran out of time or money or both. Had the film maintained the quality of the first half throughout, it would have been a four-star film. Rated R for language and violence.

1985 85 minutes

DEMON (GOD TOLD ME TO)

★★★½

DIRECTOR: Larry Cohen
CAST: Tony Lo Bianco, Sandy Dennis, Sylvia Sidney, Deborah Raffin, Sam Levene, Mike Kellin

A minor masterpiece, this horror and mystery opens with several mass murders. A sniper picks off pedestrians on the street below from a watertower, a grocer suddenly attacks his customers with a knife, and a policeman marching in a St. Patrick's Day parade begins firing at spectators and participants. The only thing that connects all these incidents is they are committed by pleasant, smiling people who explain their acts by saying, "God told me to." Rated R for nudity, profanity, and violence.

1977 95 minutes

DEMON SEED

★★★

DIRECTOR: Donald Cammell
CAST: Julie Christie, Fritz Weaver, Gerrit Graham, Lisa Lu

Good, but not great, science-fiction film about a super-intelligent computer designed by scientist Fritz Weaver to solve problems beyond the scope of man. The computer, however, has other ideas: It wants to study and experiment on the strange Earth species known as man. Weaver's wife (Julie Christie) becomes its unwilling guinea pig and, eventually, mate. Rated R.

1977 94 minutes

DESTINATION MOON

★★★½

DIRECTOR: Irving Pichel
CAST: Warner Anderson, John Archer, Tom Powers, Dick Wesson

This story involves the first American spaceship to land on the moon. Even though the sets are dated today, they were what scientists expected to find when people did land on the moon. This film boasts the classic pointed spaceship and bubble helmets on the space travelers, but it is still great fun for fans of the genre. The film has George Pal as producer and Robert Heinlein as one of its screenwriters.

1950 91 minutes

DOC SAVAGE... THE MAN OF BRONZE

★★★

DIRECTOR: Michael Anderson
CAST: Ron Ely, Pamela Hensley, Darrell Zwerling, Michael Miller, Paul Wexler, Paul Gleason

Perfectly acceptable—although campy—first appearance by the famed hero of pulp novels, Doc Savage. In these days of post-*Raiders of the Lost Ark* action epics, this seems a reasonable entry in the genre. Ron Ely makes a suitable Doc Savage, complete with torn shirt and deadpan delivery. One of the best straight lines occurs when Doc compliments costar Pamela Hensley: "Mona . . . you're a brick." Paul Wexler is delightfully overbearing as the villain. Special effects and set design are minimal, a true shame since this is the last film produced by science-fiction pioneer George Pal. Rated PG—some violence.

1975 100 minutes

DR. STRANGE

★★

DIRECTOR: Philip DeGuere
CAST: Peter Hooten, Clyde Kusatsu, Jessica Walter, Eddie Benton, Philip Sterling, John Mills

Another Marvel Comics superhero comes to life in *Dr. Strange, Master of the Mystic Arts*. Dr. Strange is chosen by the guardian of the spirit world to protect Earth from the evil villainess (Jessica Walter) who is set on invading Earth. The adventures of our hero are high on magic and sorcery and a fair rendition of the comic book hero.

1978 94 minutes

DR. WHO AND THE DALEKS

★★★

DIRECTOR: Gordon Flemyng
CAST: Peter Cushing, Roy Castle, Jennie Linden, Roberta Tovey, Barrie Ingham

In this feature film derived from —but not faithful to—the long-running BBC television series, an eccentric old scientist (Peter Cushing) takes his friends on a trip through space and time. They end up on a planet that has been devastated by nuclear war and must help a peace-loving people fight the Daleks, a race of warmongering mutants who have encased their fragile bodies in robot shells. This juvenile science-fiction adventure should please youngsters. Rated G.

1965 83 minutes

DR. WHO: REVENGE OF THE CYBERMEN

★★★

DIRECTOR: Michael E. Briant
CAST: Tom Baker, Elizabeth Sladen, Ian Marter

This is the first video from the popular British TV series and stars the fourth Dr. Who, Tom Baker. In this film, the evil Cybermen attempt to destroy the planet Voga, which is made of solid gold, the only item that can kill them. Of course, Dr. Who is there to save the day. A good introduction to *Dr. Who*, the longest-running science-fiction TV series.

1986 92 minutes

DONOVAN'S BRAIN

★★★

DIRECTOR: Felix Feist
CAST: Lew Ayres, Nancy Davis, Gene Evans, Steve Brodie

After his death in a plane crash, a powerful business magnate has his brain removed by a research scientist (Lew Ayres) who hopes to communicate with the organ by feeding it electricity. Before you know it, the brain is in control, forcing the doctor to obey its ever-increasing demands. Creditable acting and tight pacing keep the film from becoming an 83-minute comedy sketch, which so often happens with "brain" movies.

1953 B & W 83 minutes

DRAGONSLAYER

★★½

DIRECTOR: Matthew Robbins
CAST: Peter MacNicol, Catlin Clarke, Ralph Richardson

Peter MacNicol plays a sorcerer's apprentice who, to save a damsel in distress, must face a fearsome fire-breathing dragon in this tale of romance and medieval magic. While the special effects are spectacular, the rest of the film doesn't quite live up to them. It's slow, and often too corny for older viewers. Rated PG for violence.

1981 110 minutes

DREAMCHILD

★★★★

DIRECTOR: Gavin Millar
CAST: Coral Browne, Peter Gallagher, Ian Holm, Jane Asher, Nicola Cowper, Caris Coffman, Amelia Shankey

Some of those familiar with *Alice's Adventures in Wonderland* may be surprised to learn that there was a real Alice. Author Lewis Carroll, whose real name was Rev. Charles Dodgson, first told his fanciful stories to 10-year-old Alice Liddel on a summer boat ride down the River Isis on July 1, 1862. In 1932, at the age of 80, Alice (then the widow Hargreaves) went to New York City to participate in a Columbia University tribute to Carroll on the one hundredth anniversary of his birth. From these facts, director Gavin Millar and writer Dennis Potter have fashioned this rich and thought-provoking film. Rated PG for adult subject matter.

1986 94 minutes

DREAMSCAPE

★★★★

DIRECTOR: Joseph Ruben
CAST: Dennis Quaid, Max von Sydow, Christopher Plummer, Eddie Albert, Kate Capshaw

If you can go along with its intriguing but far-fetched premise—that trained psychics can enter other people's nightmares and put an end to them—this film will reward you with top-flight special effects, thrills, chills, and surprises. But if you're one of those people who get hung up on realism, this is one release you probably should skip. Bizarre as it sounds, however, *Dreamscape* definitely has its moments of high tension and excitement. Rated PG-13 for suggested sex, violence, and profanity.

1984 99 minutes

DUNE

★½

DIRECTOR: David Lynch
CAST: Sting, Kyle MacLachlan, Max von Sydow, Jurgen Prochnow, Sean Young, Kenneth McMillan, Richard Jordan

The only good thing about the movie version of *Dune* is it makes one want to read (or reread) the book. Otherwise, it's a $47 million mess. Writer-director David Lynch (*The Elephant Man*) touches on most of the elements and events in Frank Herbert's celebrated five-hundred-page science-fiction novel and adequately explores none. The result is a study in viewer frustration. Rated PG-13 for gore, suggested sex, and violence.

1984 145 minutes

DUNGEONMASTER, THE

★

DIRECTORS: Rosemarie Turko, John Buechler, Charles Band David Allen, Steve Ford, Peter Manoogian, Ted Nicolaou
CAST: Jeffrey Byron, Richard Moll, Leslie Wing, Blackie Lawless, Danny Dick

This could be a movie sci-fi-fantasy buffs might put on their guilty pleasures list. It's corny, it's bad, it's simplistic, and, if you don't take it seriously, it's fun. A computer genius (Jeffrey Byron) and his girlfriend (Leslie Wing) are whisked away to a limbo world that borders the gates of hell. There, bored, evil magician Richard Moll challenges them to seven contests. Lose one and they forfeit their souls. The challenges aren't much to write about; some are over before you realize they've even started. But this movie is generally painless and harmless; it's a Saturday-afternoon matinee-style adventure for youngsters. Rated PG-13 for mild violence.

1985 73 minutes

EARTH VS. THE FLYING SAUCERS

★★★★

DIRECTOR: Fred F. Sears
CAST: Hugh Marlowe, Joan Taylor, Donald Curtis, Morris Ankrum, Thomas B. Henry

Stunning special effects by Ray Harryhausen enhance this familiar 1950s plot about an invasion from outer space. After misinterpreting a message for peace from the initially easygoing aliens, the military opens fire—and then all hell breaks loose! While the film loses much of its visual power on the small screen, Fred F. Sears's smooth direction, as well as solid performances all around, elevate this to near classic status. Great finale, too.

1956 B & W 83 minutes

EAT AND RUN

★

DIRECTOR: Christopher Hunt
CAST: Ron Silver, R. L. Ryan, Sharon Schlarth

This science-fiction spoof is about a four-hundred pound alien named Murry Creature (R. L. Ryan) who eats Italian—the people, not the food. A law-and-order detective (Ron Silver) is trying to stop him, but the world doesn't seem to care. This film may appeal to the cult-movie crowd, but is not for everyone. Rated R for nudity.

1986 85 minutes

ELIMINATORS, THE

DIRECTOR: Peter Manoogian
CAST: Andrew Prine, Denise Crosby, Patrick Reynolds, Conan Lee, Roy Dotrice

The makers of *The Eliminators* got so carried away with time travel, Cyborgs, mad scientists, kung fu, and fantastic weapons that they forgot to use a plot and a script. There's too much going on and not enough development of characters. A mad scientist creates the perfect weapon, the "Mandroid," which turns against him when the scientist uses it for evil purposes. Rated PG.

1986 95 minutes

EMBRYO

★★½

DIRECTOR: Ralph Nelson

CAST: Rock Hudson, Barbara Carrera, Diane Ladd

Rock Hudson plays a scientist who succeeds in developing a fetus into a full-grown woman in record time. But something isn't quite right. Adequate thriller with a good ending. Rated PG.

1976 104 minutes

EMPEROR'S NEW CLOTHES, THE

★★

DIRECTOR: Peter Medak

CAST: Alan Arkin, Art Carney, Dick Shawn, Timothy Dalton (narrator)

Lavishly costumed (as one might expect from such a title), this *Faerie Tale Theatre* production presents a narcissistic king (Dick Shawn) whose vanity eventually makes him the laughingstock of his country. Alan Arkin and Art Carney have to deliver some painfully banal lines—in modern argot and out of sync with the story's time and setting.

1984 54 minutes

EMPIRE OF THE ANTS

★½

DIRECTOR: Bert I. Gordon

CAST: Joan Collins, Robert Lansing, Albert Salmi, Robert Pine

H. G. Wells must somersault in his grave every time somebody watches this insulting adaptation of one of his more intriguing sci-fi stories. Director Bert I. Gordon really hit bottom with this, a laughable blend of Joan Collins's terrible acting and giant hypnotic insects. This isn't good enough even to be considered camp. An embarrassment for all. Rated PG for violence.

1977 90 minutes

EMPIRE STRIKES BACK, THE

★★★★★

DIRECTOR: Irvin Kershner

CAST: Billy Dee Williams, Harrison Ford, Carrie Fisher, Mark Hamill, Anthony Daniels, Dave Prowse, James Earl Jones (voice)

In George Lucas's follow-up to *Star Wars*, Billy Dee Williams joins Mark Hamill (Luke Skywalker), Harrison Ford (Han Solo), Carrie Fisher (Princess Leia), and the gang in their fight against the forces of the Empire led by Darth Vader (Dave Prowse/James Earl Jones). It's more action-packed fun in that faraway galaxy a long time ago. It's also that rarity of rarities: a superior sequel. It has more plot, more characterization, more special effects—in fact, more of everything than the original. Don't miss it. Rated PG.

1980 124 minutes

ENCOUNTER WITH THE UNKNOWN

★★★½

DIRECTOR: Harry Thomason

CAST: Rod Serling, Rosie Holotik, Gene Ross

Rod Serling narrates a series of true events in psychic phenomena. The episodes are based on studies made by Dr. Jonathan Rankin between 1949 and 1970. Each deals with a person's encounter with the unknown or supernatural. Rated PG.

1973 90 minutes

END OF THE WORLD

DIRECTOR: John Hayes
CAST: Christopher Lee, Sue Lyon, Lew Ayres, Dean Jagger, MacDonald Carey

Impressive cast founders in this film about aliens plotting to destroy the Earth while disguised as religious figures. Laughably bad movie might be good for a few, if only it weren't so slowly paced. Rated PG.

1977 87 minutes

ENDANGERED SPECIES

★★★½

DIRECTOR: Alan Rudolph
CAST: Robert Urich, JoBeth Williams, Paul Dooley, Hoyt Axton

Everything about this science-fiction suspense thriller is very real—that's why it works so well. The story deals with bizarre incidents involving cattle mutilation and is based on fact. In it, a country sheriff (JoBeth Williams, of *Poltergeist*) and a hard-boiled New York detective (Robert Urich) join forces to find out who or what is responsible. Could it be a satanic cult? UFOs? Or something even more frightening? The answer puts both their lives in danger. Rated R for discreetly handled nudity, violence, gore, and profanity.

1982 97 minutes

ENDGAME

DIRECTOR: Steven Benson
CAST: Al Cliver, Moira Chen, George Eastman, Jack Davis, Al Yamanouchi, Gus Stone, Mario Pedone, Gordon Mitchell

Ho-hum, another *Road Warrior* ripoff—this one complete with mutants who communicate via telepathy. Well, at least they don't look as stupid as the rest of the cast, who suffer the dreaded post-production humiliation of bad dubbing. Not rated, but the equivalent of a PG-13 for violence, gore, and partial nudity.

1985 98 minutes

ENEMY MINE

★½

DIRECTOR: Wolfgang Petersen
CAST: Dennis Quaid, Louis Gossett Jr., Brion James, Richard Marcus, Carolyn McCormick, Bumper Robinson, Jim Mapp, Lance Kerwin

A sort of science-fiction composite retelling of *The Defiant Ones* and *Hell in the Pacific*, this film by Wolfgang Petersen (*The NeverEnding Story, Das Boot*) is a good idea gone bad—a would-be outer-space epic that manages to disappoint on nearly every level. The story details what happens when two futuristic foes, an Earthman (Dennis Quaid) and a reptilian alien (Louis Gossett Jr.), are stranded on a hostile planet and forced to rely on each other for survival. The heart of the film is the supposed mutual understanding that grows between the two central characters. The actors do their best, but, apart from a few nice scenes, their relationship fails to convince because everything happens much too quickly. Perhaps Petersen wanted to get on with the more original elements in the story. This is commendable, but results in disaster. Later in the film there is a plot twist (which would be unfair to give away) by which the viewer is expected to be fascinated and touched, but the result is only mildly interesting. *Enemy Mine* should have been a terrific motion picture given the talent involved. As it is, this release will be best appreciated by youngsters and the most devout sci-fi buffs. Rated PG-13 for violence and profanity.

1985 108 minutes

ESCAPE FROM THE PLANET OF THE APES

★★★

DIRECTOR: Don Taylor
CAST: Roddy McDowall, Kim Hunter, Eric Braeden, Bradford Dillman, William Windom, Ricardo Montalban

Escaping the nuclear destruction of their own world and time, intelligent simians Roddy McDowall and Kim Hunter arrive on ours. This third *Apes* entry makes wonderful use of the *Strangers in a Strange Land* theme, which turns ugly all too quickly as humanity extends its own sort of warmth and decides to destroy the apes to prevent them from breeding. At this point, producer Arthur P. Jacobs knew he had something going, so the door is left open for subsequent films. Next would be *Conquest of the Planet of the Apes*. Rated PG for violence.

1971 98 minutes

ESCAPE 2000

DIRECTOR: Brian Trenchard-Smith
CAST: Steve Railsback, Olivia Hussey, Michael Craig, Carmen Duncan, Roger Ward

A nauseating science-fiction film from Britain, this consists of a series of close-ups of people in the throes of death—garrotings, bludgeonings, gut-stabbings, shoulder-slashings, and assorted thrashings. Yuck! Rated R for—you guessed it—violence and gore.

1981 92 minutes

ESCAPES

★★★

DIRECTOR: David Steensland
CAST: Vincent Price, Michael Patton-Hall, John Mitchum, Todd Fulton, Jerry Grisham, Ken Thorley

Low-budget anthology in the *Twilight Zone* vein, featuring six stories of the bizarre and done with great style by director David Steensland. Top honors go to "A Little Fishy," a grimly funny tale, and "Who's There?" a neat yarn about an escaped laboratory experiment and a Sunday jogger. While these two may be the best, the film never fails to entertain.

1985 71 minutes

EXCALIBUR

★★★★

DIRECTOR: John Boorman
CAST: Nicol Williamson, Nigel Terry, Helen Mirren, Nicholas Clay, Cherie Lunghi, Corin Redgrave, Paul Geoffrey

Swords cross and magic abounds in this spectacular, highly enjoyable version of the Arthurian legend. A gritty, realistic view of the rise to power of King Arthur, the forbidden love of Queen Guinevere and Sir Lancelot and the quest of the Knights of the Round Table for the holy grail. *Excalibur* is highlighted by lush photography and fine performances by the British cast—with Nicol Williamson especially memorable as Merlin the magician. Rated R.

1981 140 minutes

EXPLORERS

★★★½

DIRECTOR: Joe Dante
CAST: Ethan Hawke, River Phoenix, Jason Presson, Dick Miller, Robert Picardo

The young and the young at heart are certain to have a grand time watching *Explorers*. It's a just-for-fun fantasy about three kids (Ethan Hawke, River Phoenix, and Jason Presson) who literally share the same dream and soon find themselves taking off on the greatest adventure of all: a journey through outer space. Once there, they meet the most surprising—and entertaining—alien creatures ever to be in a movie. Directed by Joe Dante (*Gremlins*; *The Howling*), it's not a film for everyone. But if you love wacky, unpredictable humor, don't miss it. Rated PG for minor violence and light profanity.

1985 109 minutes

EXTERMINATORS OF THE YEAR 3000

★

DIRECTOR: Jules Harrison
CAST: Robert Jannucci, Alicia Moro, Alan Collins, Edvardo Fajardo, Fred Harris, Beryl Cunningham, Lucas Venantini

Geroge Miller should call his lawyer. This one rips off his *The Road Warrior* almost to the letter. The only major difference is that instead of a gas shortage, the world suffers a drought. A group of good guys and a group of bad guys fight it out, and a loner gets caught between the two. The action scenes, which are the bread and butter of these kind of films, are poorly directed and contain some wholly impossible incidents. Rated R for violence and profanity.

1983 101 minutes

FAHRENHEIT 451

★★★★

DIRECTOR: François Truffaut
CAST: Oskar Werner, Julie Christie, Cyril Cusack, Anton Diffring, Alex Scott

Still the best adaptation of a Ray Bradbury book to hit the screen (big or small). Oskar Werner is properly troubled as a futuristic "fireman" responsible for the destruction of books, who begins to wonder about the necessity of his work. This is director François Truffaut's first English-language film, and he treats the subject of language and literature with a dignity not found in most Americans. Wonderfully moody and quite faithful to the tone of the book; the conclusion, Truffaut's own invention, is particularly poignant. Unrated—family fare.

1967 111 minutes

FANTASTIC PLANET

★★★

DIRECTOR: René Laloux
CAST: Animated

This French-Czechoslovakian production is an animated metaphor concerning the class struggles—and, eventually, war—between two races on an alien planet. Lovely animation and a non-preachy approach to the story combine to produce a fine little film that makes its points and sticks in the memory. Short, but sincere and effective. Voices of Barry Bostwick, Nora Heflin. Rated PG—intense subject matter, some violence.

1973 71 minutes

FANTASTIC VOYAGE

★★★

DIRECTOR: Richard Fleischer
CAST: Stephen Boyd, Raquel Welch, Edmond O'Brien, Donald Pleasence, Arthur O'Connell, William Redfield, Arthur Kennedy

Scientists Stephen Boyd, Raquel Welch, Edmond O'Brien, Donald Pleasence, and Arthur O'Connell journey into inner space—the human body—by being shrunk to microscopic size. They then are threatened by the system's natural defenses. This Richard Fleischer film still packs an unusually potent punch.

1966 100 minutes

FANTASY ISLAND

★★½

DIRECTOR: Richard Lang

CAST: Ricardo Montalban, Bill Bixby, Sandra Dee, Peter Lawford, Carol Lynley, Hugh O'Brian

Dreams and fantasies come true and then some on a mysterious millionaire's island paradise in this sub-average TV-er that spawned the hit series. Yawn.

1977 100 minutes

FINAL COUNTDOWN, THE

★★½

DIRECTOR: Don Taylor

CAST: Kirk Douglas, Martin Sheen, Katharine Ross

Far-fetched but passable story about an aircraft carrier traveling backward in time to just before the start of World War II. The crew must then decide whether or not to change the course of history. Some good special effects and performances by the leads manage to keep this one afloat. Rated PG.

1980 104 minutes

FIRE AND ICE

★★★★

DIRECTOR: Ralph Bakshi

CAST: Animated

This animated film is geared more to adults than children. Sword and sorcery fantasy keeps the action moving and the viewer interested to the point you may forget the characters aren't real. The plot begins with evil sorcerer Nekron planning world domination. It thickens when he kidnaps the princess, Teegra, to force her father to turn his kingdom over to him as his daughter's ransom. Rated PG.

1983 81 minutes

FIRST SPACESHIP ON VENUS

★

DIRECTOR: Kurt Maetzig

CAST: Yoko Tani, Oldrich Lukes, Ignacy Machowski

Low-budget, lackluster German science-fiction plants an international crew of astronauts on Venus with poor special effects and worse dialogue. There are some interesting questions raised in this "let's proceed with caution" story, but not enough to merit it a spot in the science fiction hall of fame.

1960 78 minutes

FLASH GORDON

★★★

DIRECTOR: Mike Hodges

CAST: Sam J. Jones, Topol, Max von Sydow, Melody Anderson

If you don't take it seriously, this campy film based on the classic Alex Raymond comic strip of the 1930s is a real hoot. Sam Jones, as Flash, and Melody Anderson, as Dale Arden, race through the intentionally hokey special effects to do battle with Max von Sydow, who makes an excellent Ming the Merciless. Rated PG.

1980 110 minutes

FLASH GORDON: MARS ATTACKS THE WORLD (A.K.A. TRIP TO MARS; DEADLY RAY FROM MARS, THE)

★★½

DIRECTORS: Ford Beebe, Robert Hill

CAST: Buster Crabbe, Jean Rogers, Charles Middleton, Frank Shannon, Donald Kerr, Beatrice Roberts

In this edited version of the second Flash Gordon serial, Buster Crabbe and the gang head out to Mars to put a halt to a ray that is drawing nitrogen away from the Earth. Of course, Ming the Merciless is behind it all. Hokey but fun, even trimmed of almost half its running time, this space romp from simpler times is worth a watch just for the character acting, including Charles Middleton as the greatest of all serial scoundrels.

1938 B & W 99 minutes

FLASH GORDON: ROCKETSHIP (A.K.A. SPACESHIP TO THE UNKNOWN; PERILS FROM PLANET MONGO)

★★★

DIRECTOR: Frederick Stephani
CAST: Buster Crabbe, Jean Rogers, Frank Shannon, Charles Middleton, Priscilla Lawson, John Kipson, Richard Alexander, James Pierce

This original feature version of the first *Flash Gordon* serial is one of the best reedited chapter plays ever released. Boyish Buster Crabbe is the perfect Flash Gordon; Jean Rogers is one of the loveliest of all serial queens; and classic character heavy Charles Middleton becomes the embodiment of malevolent villainy as the infamous Ming the Merciless. Although this condensed version is well worth the watch, it might inspire you to watch all thirteen chapters in their entirety, which is how they were intended to be viewed.

1936 B & W 97 minutes

FLIGHT OF THE NAVIGATOR

★★★

DIRECTOR: Randal Kleiser
CAST: Joey Kramer, Veronica Cartwright, Cliff De Young, Sarah Jessica Parker, Howard Hessman, Matt Adler

This all-ages Disney delight concerns a youngster (Joey Kramer) who has the unique ability to communicate with machines and uses this to help a UFO find its way home. *Flight of the Navigator* has something for everyone. Kids will love its crazy creatures, special effects, and action-packed conclusion, while parents will appreciate its nice balance of sense and nonsense. Rated PG for mild cussing.

1986 90 minutes

FOOD OF THE GODS

DIRECTOR: Bert I. Gorden
CAST: Marjoe Gortner, Ida Lupino, Pamela Franklin, Ralph Meeker

H. G. Wells's story is thrashed in this typical Bert I. Gordon bomb. After ingesting an unknown substance, various animals become giant and threaten the occupants of a remote mountain cabin. Fakey special effects might have been acceptable in the 1950s, but they just don't cut it today. Rated PG for violence.

1976 88 minutes

FORBIDDEN PLANET

★★★★½

DIRECTOR: Fred McLeod Wilcox
CAST: Walter Pidgeon, Anne Francis, Leslie Nielsen, Jack Kelly

This is the most highly regarded sci-fi film of the 1950s. Its special-effects breakthroughs are rather tame today, but its story remains interesting. As a space mission from Earth lands on the Planet Altair-4 in the year 2200, they encounter a doctor (Walter Pidgeon) and his daughter (Anne Francis) who are all that remain from a previous colonization attempt. It soon becomes apparent that some unseen force on the planet does not bid them welcome.

1956 98 minutes

FORBIDDEN ZONE

DIRECTOR: Richard Elfman
CAST: Herve Villechaize, Susan Tyrrell, Marie-Pascale Elfman, Viva

Absurd "cult" film has Herve Villechaize as the ruler of a bizarre kingdom located in the "Sixth Dimension." A sort-of comedy, this should be avoided by all means. Rated R for nudity and adult content.

1980 B & W 76 minutes

4D MAN

★★★

DIRECTOR: Irvin S. Yeaworth Jr.
CAST: Robert Lansing, Lee Meriwether, James Congdon, Robert Strauss, Patty Duke

A scientist (Robert Lansing) learns of a method of moving through objects (walls, doors, bank vaults, etc.), without realizing the terrible consequences, which eventually lead to madness and murder. Eerie sci-fi film hampered only by an often brash music score by Ralph Carmichael. Still, quite spine-tingling. From the director of *The Blob*.

1959 85 minutes

FROM THE EARTH TO THE MOON

★★★

DIRECTOR: Byron Haskin
CAST: Joseph Cotten, George Sanders, Debra Paget, Don Dubbins

Entertaining tale based on Jules Verne's story of a turn-of-the-century trip to the Moon led by Joseph Cotten and sabotaged by George Sanders.

1958 100 minutes

FUTUREWORLD

★★★

DIRECTOR: Richard T. Heffron
CAST: Peter Fonda, Blythe Danner, Arthur Hill, Yul Brynner, Stuart Margolin, John Ryan

An amusement park of the future caters to any adult fantasy. Lifelike androids carry out your every whim. A fun place, right? Not so, as reporter Peter Fonda finds out in this sequel to "Westworld." Something is amiss. The androids are acting independent of how they were programmed. This is okay escapist fare. Rated PG.

1976 104 minutes

GALAXINA

★

DIRECTOR: William Sachs
CAST: Avery Schreiber, Dorothy R. Stratten, Stephen Macht, James David Hinton

See Captain Cornelius Butt (Avery Schreiber), of the spaceship *Infinity*, consume a raw egg and regurgitate a rubbery creature that later calls him "Mommy." Visit an inter-galactic saloon that serves humans (they're on the menu, not the guest list). And be amazed, then disgusted and bored by the general tackiness and idiocy of this low-budget space spoof. In this story, about a valuable space stone and a romance between a space cop and a robot, there are some funny moments, but not enough to make watching this movie worthwhile. Rated R.

1980 95 minutes

GALAXY OF TERROR

★★½

DIRECTOR: B. D. Clark
CAST: Erin Moran, Edward Albert, Ray Walston

The science-fiction film has certainly come a long way. Even the low-budget ones aren't as bad as they used to be. Take this movie, which was also known as *Planet of Horrors*, in which the crew of a spaceship sent to rescue a crash survivor finds itself facing one horror after another on a barren planet. This chiller wastes no time in getting to the thrills. Rated R because of profanity, nudity, and violence.

1981 82 minutes

GAMMA PEOPLE, THE

★½

DIRECTOR: John Gilling
CAST: Paul Douglas, Eva Bartok, Leslie Phillips, Walter Rilla

Weak science-fiction tale about the children of the middle European country of Gudavia being transformed into homicidal monsters or geniuses by the all-powerful dictator Dr. Boronski (Walter Rilla). Even considering the year it was made, acting and effects just aren't up to snuff.

1956 B & W 79 minutes

GLEN AND RANDA

★★★

DIRECTOR: Jim McBride
CAST: Steven Curry, Shelley Plimpton, Woodrow Chambliss, Garry Goodrow

As with all cult films, *Glen and Randa* will not appeal to everyone. The film, at times thought-provoking, is both depressing and satirical. Two young people, Glen (Steve Curry) and Randa (Shelley Plimpton), set out on a search for knowledge across post-holocaust America. Rated R for sex, nudity, and violence.

1986 94 minutes

GOLDEN VOYAGE OF SINBAD, THE

★★★★

DIRECTOR: Gordon Hessler
CAST: John Phillip Law, Tom Baker, Caroline Munro, Douglas Wilmer, Gregoire Aslan, John Garfield Jr.

This first-rate Arabian Nights adventure pits Captain Sinbad (John Phillip Law) against the evil Prince Koura (Tom Baker) for possession of a magical amulet with amazing powers. This is a superb fantasy, with some truly incredible effects by master animator Ray Harryhausen. Miklos Rozsa's excellent musical score greatly enhances the overall atmosphere of mystery present throughout the film. The battle scene with a six-armed sword-wielding bronze goddess is a knockout! Only drawback is RCA/Columbia's poor audio transfer to home video, resulting in an uninvolving "canned" sound quality. Nevertheless, this is a beautiful piece of film-making, and one not to be missed. Rated G.

1974 105 minutes

GOLDENGIRL

(turkey)

DIRECTOR: Joseph Sargent
CAST: Susan Anton, James Coburn, Curt Jurgens, Robert Culp, Leslie Caron, Jessica Walter

This modern retread of *Frankenstein* fails on all counts. Scientist Curt Jurgens turns Susan Anton into a super-athlete for Olympic glory. Acting, writing, and direction are terrible; the splicing between genuine Olympic footage and storyline fiction is equally lame. Anton—justifiably—must not have been too thrilled by this acting debut, because she's not been that noticeable since. Beware of a longer, television version: A boring film made even more interminable. Rated PG.

1979 104 minutes

GREMLINS

★★★★

DIRECTOR: Joe Dante
CAST: Zach Galligan, Phoebe Cates, Hoyt Axton, Frances Lee McCain, Polly Holliday, Glynn Turman, Dick Miller, Keye Luke, Scott Brady

This "Steven Spielberg Presentation" is a highly original, unpredictable, frantically paced, and just plain wacky movie. It's one part *E.T.—The Extra-Terrestrial*, one part scary/funny horror film (à la director Joe Dante's last picture, *The Howling*), one part

Muppet movie, and one part Bugs Bunny/Warner Bros. cartoon. Sound strange? You got it. In the story, Billy Peltzer (Zach Galligan) gets a cute little pet from his inventor-father (Hoyt Axton) for Christmas. But there's a catch. When Billy's father purchased the creature from a Chinese antique dealer, the latter told him, "Keep them away from water. Don't ever get them wet. Keep them out of light. They hate bright light. It will kill them. But the most important thing," he added ominously, "the thing you must never forget—no matter how much they cry, no matter how much they beg—never, never feed them after midnight." Rated PG for profanity and stylized violence.

1984 111 minutes

GROUNDSTAR CONSPIRACY, THE

★★★½

DIRECTOR: Lamont Johnson

CAST: George Peppard, Michael Sarrazin, Christine Belford

This nifty thriller has gone unrecognized for years. The story, with its commentaries on personal identity and blind loyalty, is more reminiscent of work usually done by the British in this genre. George Peppard stars as a government investigator sent to uncover the security leak that led to the destruction of a vital—and secret—space laboratory, and the amnesia-stricken Michael Sarrazin is his only lead. The clever plot and excellent character interactions build a surprising climax. Rated PG.

1972 103 minutes

HANDS OF STEEL

★

DIRECTOR: Martin Dolman

CAST: Daniel Greene, Janet Agren, Claudio Cassinelli, George Eastman, Robert Ben, Pat Monti, Donald O'Brien, Frank Walden, Amy Werba, John Saxon

A low-budget science-fiction yarn based in the near future. The plot revolves around a Cyborg (half man, half machine) that is hired to kill the only scientist left to give mankind a chance. The Cyborg must then decide whether or not to kill this man, and if he does not, how to stop others bent on the same job. Rated R for nudity and violence.

1986 94 minutes

HANGAR 18

🦃

DIRECTOR: James L. Conway

CAST: Darren McGavin, Robert Vaughn, Gary Collins, Joseph Campanella, James Hampton

The story revolves around an alien spaceship that is accidentally disabled by a U.S. satellite. Two astronauts (Gary Collins and James Hampton) in a nearby rocket witness the accident—a fellow astronaut is decapitated during the event—and, when they return to Earth, are blamed for the death of their partner. Rated PG.

1980 93 minutes

HARRY AND THE HENDERSONS

★★★½

DIRECTOR: William Dear

CAST: John Lithgow, Melinda Dillon, Don Ameche, Lainie Kazan, David Suchet, Margaret Langrick, Joshua Rudoy, M. Emmet Walsh, John Bloom, Kevin Peter Hall

For pure, mindless video-viewing fun, few films can top *Harry and the Hendersons*—that is, if it is taken in the right spirit. A sort of a shaggy *E.T.* story, it focuses on the plight of a family (headed by John Lithgow and Melinda Dillon) that just happens to run into

Bigfoot one day. Because they are in their car at the time, this causes a few complications. These continue to mount after the Hendersons decide to take the big fellow home with them. It's silly, outrageously sentimental, and a gentle poke in the ribs of Steven Spielberg, whose Amblin Productions financed the film. Rated PG for profanity and violence.

1987 110 minutes

HAUNTING PASSION, THE

DIRECTOR: John Korty
CAST: Jane Seymour, Gerald McRaney, Millie Perkins, Ruth Nelson, Paul Rossilli

An uneven made-for-TV supernatural romance in which a ghost seduces a housewife. Jane Seymour and the rest of the cast do the best they can with the bad romance novel dialogue they're given. There are a few chills, but more often than not, it falls short of the mark.

1983 98 minutes

HEADLESS HORSEMAN, THE

DIRECTOR: Edward Venturini
CAST: Will Rogers, Lois Meredith, Ben Hendricks Jr., Mary Foy, Charles Graham

The time-honored (but worn) story of lanky Yankee schoolmaster Icabod Crane's rube-ish efforts to wed wealthy Katrina Van Tassel, and his defeat by rival Brom Bones and the phantom headless horseman. Will Rogers looks the part of the homespun Crane and gives a fair impression of the character. Silent.

1922 B & W 52 minutes

HELLSTROM CHRONICLE, THE

DIRECTOR: Walon Green
CAST: Lawrence Pressman

This 1971 pseudo-documentary features fantastic close-up cinematography of insects and their ilk underpinning a storyline by Dr. Hellstrom (Lawrence Pressman), which contends the critters are taking over and we humans had better wise up before it's too late. Despite the dumb premise, *The Hellstrom Chronicle* remains a captivating film. Rated G.

1971 90 minutes

HERCULES

DIRECTOR: Lewis Coates
CAST: Lou Ferrigno, Sybil Danning, Brad Harris, Rosanna Podesta

Following the beefy footsteps of Conan, Ator, and Yor comes Lou Ferrigno (formerly TV's "The Incredible Hulk") as the most famous muscle man of them all, in this cheap and dreadful venture into Greek mythology. It was inevitable, but did it have to be so awful? Rated PG for violence.

1983 98 minutes

HERCULES UNCHAINED

★★

DIRECTOR: Pietro Francisci
CAST: Steve Reeves, Sylva Koscina, Primo Carnera, Sylvia Lopez

When the god of muscles sets his little mind on something, don't get in his way! In this one, he's out to rescue his lady fair. It's a silly but diverting adventure. Steve Reeves is still the best Hercules on film, dubbed voice and all.

1960 101 minutes

HIGHLANDER

★★

DIRECTOR: Russell Mulcahy
CAST: Christopher Lambert, Clancy Brown, Sean Connery

A sixteenth-century Scottish clansman discovers he is one of a small group of immortals destined to fight each other through the centuries. The last survivor will be rewarded with a valuable power. The movie climaxes in a fierce battle atop a skyscraper in modern-day Manhattan. Made by a pioneer music video director, the film is visually stunning, though sometimes distractingly so. If you're a style freak, you might enjoy it. If you prefer substance, watch out. The jumps in time are confusing, the film takes forty-five minutes to relay its basic plot, and the music by Queen is annoying and inappropriate. The movie is a treat for the eyes, but you'll owe your brain an apology. Rated R for violence.

1986 110 minutes

HOWARD THE DUCK

★

DIRECTOR: Willard Huyck
CAST: Lea Thompson, Jeffrey Jones, Tim Robbins, Ed Gale, Chip Zien, Tim Rose, Steve Sleap, Peter Baird

It requires truly monumental talent to botch the film debut of a character as clever as Steve Gerber's *Howard the Duck*, but writer-director Willard Huyck and writer-producer Gloria Katz—the same team that made a special-effects puppet of Indiana Jones in *The Temple of Doom*—managed to lay an extremely rotten egg. The potential for wry commentary expressed by a stranger in a strange land (handled so well by, say, Malcolm McDowell's H. G. Wells in *Time After Time*) is sacrificed on the megabudgetary altar: sensible plot and characterization are replaced with bigger and louder explosions, car wrecks, slimy monster makeup, more car wrecks, inane acting, and even more car wrecks. Unwisely rated PG, considering some smarmy sex scenes and frightening monster makeup.

1986 111 minutes

I MARRIED A MONSTER FROM OUTER SPACE

★★★

DIRECTOR: Gene Fowler
CAST: Tom Tryon, Gloria Talbott, Ken Lynch, Maxie Rosenbloom

The story is about aliens who duplicate their bodies in the form of Earth men in hopes of repopulating their planet. One Earth woman who unknowingly marries one of the aliens discovers the secret, but can't get anyone to believe her. This film is different in that it doesn't have a bunch of rampaging monsters running amok destroying Earth cities or trying to conquer our planet. They just want to preserve their race. The film does have a certain flair.

1958 B & W 78 minutes

I MARRIED A WITCH

★★★½

DIRECTOR: René Clair
CAST: Veronica Lake, Fredric March, Cecil Kellaway, Robert Benchley

The whimsy of humorist Thorne Smith (the author of *Topper*) shows its age, but watching Veronica Lake and Fredric March perform together is a treat in this very, very pre-"Bewitched" farce. Look for Susan Hayward in a small role.

1942 B & W 76 minutes

ICE PIRATES

★★★½

DIRECTOR: Stewart Raffill
CAST: Robert Urich, Mary Crosby, John Matuszak, Anjelica Huston, John Carradine

Essentially a pirate movie set in outer space, this entertaining and often funny sci-fi film takes place countless years from now, when the universe has run out of water. The evil Templars control what few millions of gallons still remain and ship them between the outposts of their far-flung empire. Their only enemies are a race of pirates (led by Robert Urich) who prowl the space lanes in fast little ships and specialize in boarding the Templar vessels and stealing the water. Rated PG for violence, profanity, scatological humor, and suggested sex.

1984 91 minutes

ICEMAN

★★★½

DIRECTOR: Fred Schepisi

CAST: Timothy Hutton, Lindsay Crouse, John Lone, Josef Sommer

Timothy Hutton stars in this often gripping and always watchable movie as an anthropologist who is part of an arctic exploration team that discovers the body of a prehistoric man (John Lone), who has been frozen forty thousand years. To their surprise, the scientists (who include Lindsay Crouse) discover the man is still alive. The question of what to do with this piece of living human history comes up, and Hutton finds himself defending the creature from those who want to poke, prod, and even dissect their terrified subject. Rated PG for violence and profanity.

1984 99 minutes

ILLUSTRATED MAN, THE

★½

DIRECTOR: Jack Smight

CAST: Rod Steiger, Claire Bloom, Robert Drivas

Ponderous, dull, and overly talky adaptation of the work of Ray Bradbury. It is lifelessly paced by director Jack Smight, who doesn't know the first thing about the awe and wonder that should accompany fantasy. The principals—Rod Steiger, Claire Bloom, and Robert Drivas—take multiple roles in a series of stories; the best (which isn't saying much) is the rendition of "The Veldt," a futuristic tale of spoiled children and a homicidal playroom. Ultimately, though, this is just one more disappointing failure to translate Bradbury's prose into pictures. Rated PG for violence, partial nudity.

1969 103 minutes

INCREDIBLE HULK, THE

★★½

DIRECTOR: Kenneth Johnson

CAST: Bill Bixby, Susan Sullivan, Lou Ferrigno, Jack Colvin, Charles Siebert

Bill Bixby is sincere in the role of Dr. Bob Banner, a scientist whose experiments with gamma rays result in his being transformed into a huge green creature (Lou Ferrigno) whenever something angers him. Pilot for the series is a lot of fun, with better production values than most TV efforts. Based on the Marvel Comics character.

1977 100 minutes

INCREDIBLE MELTING MAN, THE

★★★

DIRECTOR: William Sachs

CAST: Alex Rebar, Burr DeBenning, Myron Healey, Ann Sweeney

Superb make-up by Rick Baker highlights this story of an astronaut (Alex Rebar) who contracts a strange ailment that results in his turning into a gooey, melting mess upon his return to Earth. Wild stuff. Rated R for terminal grossness.

1978 86 minutes

INCREDIBLE SHRINKING MAN, THE

★★★★

DIRECTOR: Jack Arnold
CAST: Grant Williams, Randy Stuart, Paul Langton, April Kent

Good special effects as a man (Grant Williams), exposed to a strange radioactive mist, finds himself becoming smaller . . . and smaller . . . and smaller. Well-mounted thriller from Universal with many memorable scenes, including the classic showdown with an ordinary house spider. Top-flight entertainment.

1957 B & W 81 minutes

INDIANA JONES AND THE TEMPLE OF DOOM

★★★★

DIRECTOR: Steven Spielberg
CAST: Harrison Ford, Kate Capshaw, Ke Huy Quan, Amrish Puri

This sequel is almost as good as the original, *Raiders of the Lost Ark*. The story takes place before the events of *Raiders* with its two-fisted, whip-wielding hero, Dr. Indiana Jones (Harrison Ford) performing feats of derring-do in Singapore and India circa 1935. Parents may want to see this fast-paced and sometimes scary film before allowing their kids to watch it. Rated PG for profanity and violence.

1984 118 minutes

INFRA-MAN

★★½

DIRECTOR: Hua-Shan
CAST: Wang Hsieh, Lie Hsiu-Hsien

Mainly for kids, this *Ultraman* ripoff, about a giant superhero protecting the Earth from a bunch of crazy-looking monsters, still manages to succeed, despite the lame acting and hokey special effects. Ridiculous but enjoyable. Rated PG.

1976 92 minutes

INNERSPACE

★★★★

DIRECTOR: Joe Dante
CAST: Dennis Quaid, Martin Short, Meg Ryan, Kevin McCarthy, Fiona Lewis, Henry Gibson, John Hora, Robert Picardo, Wendy Schaal, William Schallert, Harold Sylvester

Get this storyline: Dennis Quaid is a rebel astronaut who is miniaturized in order to be injected into the body of a rabbit. Just at the big moment, the scientific laboratory in which the experiment is to take place is invaded by spies. So the chief scientist escapes with the syringe carrying Quaid and ends up injecting him into the body of hypochrondriac Martin Short. Sound weird? It is. Sound funny? We thought so. Only Joe Dante could make a silly movie like this work so well, but he does get some hilarious help from the remarkable Martin Short. Rated PG for profanity and violence.

1987 130 minutes

INTRUDER WITHIN, THE

(turkey)

DIRECTOR: Peter Carter
CAST: Chad Everett, Joseph Bottoms, Jennifer Warren

Cheesy ripoff of Ridley Scott's classic *Alien*. Action takes place on an ocean oil-drilling rig instead of commercial spacecraft.

1981 100 minutes

INVADERS FROM MARS (ORIGINAL)

★★★★

DIRECTOR: William Cameron Menzies
CAST: Helena Carter, Jimmy Hunt, Leif Erickson, Arthur Franz

Everybody remembers this one. Kid sees a flying saucer land in a nearby field, only nobody will believe him. Some really weird visuals throughout this minor sci-fi classic.

1953 78 minutes

INVADERS FROM MARS (REMAKE)

★★★

DIRECTOR: Tobe Hooper

CAST: Karen Black, Hunter Carson, Timothy Bottoms, Laraine Newman, James Karen, Louise Fletcher, Bud Cort

Screenwriters Dan O'Bannon and Don Jakoby and director Tobe Hooper have done fairly well with their remake of William Cameron Menzies's 1953 science-fiction classic. This version retains the kid's-eye point of view, the kid in this case played by Hunter Carson, in his first role after *Paris, Texas*. He wakes one night in time to see a spaceship land in the sand pit behind his house; thereafter, everybody who visits the site comes back . . . changed. Soon the boy has the help of only his junior-high-school nurse, played a bit too broadly by Karen Black. Hooper maintains the tone of the original; this *Invaders from Mars* feels like a 1950s movie made with 1980s production values. Rated PG-13 for rather intense situations and ugly beasties.

1986 94 minutes

INVASION OF THE ANIMAL PEOPLE

½

DIRECTORS: Virgil Vogel, Jerry Warren

CAST: Robert Burton, Barbara Wilson, Sten Gester, Bengt Bomgren, John Carradine (narrator)

This inept foreign science-fiction clinker is a borderline turkey, but lacks the presence of a John Agar to mire it firmly in the annals of truly terrible films. Nonsense about extraterrestrial visitors who assume various forms is as stale as a year-old cracker and just about as appealing.

1962 B & W 73 minutes

INVASION OF THE BEE GIRLS

★★★

DIRECTOR: Denis Sanders

CAST: Victoria Vetri, William Smith, Cliff Osmond, Anitra Ford

Enjoyable film about strange female invaders doing weird things to the male population of a small town in California. Plot is not too important in this wacky sci-fi spoof. Not for kids. Rated PG.

1973 85 minutes

INVASION OF THE BODY SNATCHERS (ORIGINAL)

★★★★★

DIRECTOR: Don Siegel

CAST: Kevin McCarthy, Dana Wynter, Carolyn Jones, King Donovan

Quite possibly the most frightening film ever made, this stars Kevin McCarthy as a small-town doctor who discovers his patients, family, and friends are being taken over by cold, emotionless human-duplicating pods from outer space. Not many films can be considered truly disturbing, but this one more than qualifies. Coming from the B-movie science-fiction boom of the 1950s, it has emerged as a cinema classic that can bring nightmares to the young and old.

1956 B & W 80 minutes

INVASION OF THE BODY SNATCHERS (REMAKE)

★★★★

DIRECTOR: Phil Kaufman

CAST: Donald Sutherland, Brooke Adams, Leonard Nimoy, Jeff Goldblum, Veronica Cartwright

Excellent semi-sequel to Don Siegel's 1956 classic of the same name, with Donald Sutherland fine in the role originally created by Kevin McCarthy (who has a cameo here). This time the story takes place in San Francisco, with mysterious "seeds" from outer space duplicating—then destroying—San Francisco Bay Area residents at an alarming rate. Very suspenseful, with Philip Kaufman's sure direction and a truly bizarre musical score by Denny Zeitlin adding to the feeling of paranoia this film creates. It is well worth your time. Rated PG.

1978 115 minutes

INVASION UFO

★

DIRECTORS: Gerry Anderson, Dave Lane, David Tomblin
CAST: Ed Bishop, George Sewell, Michael Billington

Strictly for fans of the short-lived science-fiction TV series, whose title explains all. Others will find the story trite, the acting second-rate, and the special effects primitive by today's standards.

1980 97 minutes

ISLAND AT THE TOP OF THE WORLD, THE

★★★

DIRECTOR: Robert Stevenson
CAST: David Hartman, Mako, Donald Sinden

A rich man ventures into the Arctic in search of his son. Unbelievably, he finds a Viking kingdom. This is Disney director Robert Stevenson's second attempt (*In Search of the Castaways* was number one) to re-create a Jules Verne classic. Rated G.

1974 93 minutes

ISLAND OF DR. MOREAU, THE

★★

DIRECTOR: William Witney
CAST: Burt Lancaster, Michael York, Barbara Carrera, Richard Basehart

Remake of 1933's *Island of Lost Souls* isn't nearly as good. Burt Lancaster develops process of turning animals into half-humans on a desolate tropical island. Watchable only for Burt's sturdy performance and Richard Basehart's portrayal of one of the beasts. Rated PG.

1977 104 minutes

IT CAME FROM OUTER SPACE

★★★★

DIRECTOR: Jack Arnold
CAST: Richard Carlson, Barbara Rush, Charles Drake

Science-fiction author Ray Bradbury wrote the screenplay for this surprisingly effective 3-D chiller from the 1950s about creatures from outer space taking over the bodies of Earthlings. It was the first film to use this theme and still holds up today.

1953 B & W 81 minutes

JASON AND THE ARGONAUTS

★★★★

DIRECTOR: Don Chaffey
CAST: Todd Armstrong, Gary Raymond, Honor Blackman

The captivating special effects by master Ray Harryhausen are the actual stars of this movie. This is the telling of the famous myth of Jason (Todd Armstrong), his crew of derring-doers, and their search for the "Golden Fleece." We are treated to some spectacular creations, including the battle with the skeleton army and the conquest of the multi-headed Hydra. Good entertainment for all ages.

1963 104 minutes

JOURNEY TO THE CENTER OF THE EARTH

★★★½

DIRECTOR: Henry Levin
CAST: James Mason, Pat Boone, Arlene Dahl, Diane Baker

This Jules Verne story was impressive when first released, but it looks pretty silly these days. However, James Mason is always fascinating to watch, production values are high, and kids should enjoy its innocent fun.

1959 12 chapters

JOURNEY TO THE CENTER OF TIME

★★½

DIRECTOR: David L. Hewitt
CAST: Scott Brady, Gigi Perreau, Anthony Eisley, Abraham Sofaer, Lyle Waggoner

A group of scientists working on a time-travel device are accidentally propelled five thousand years into the future following an equipment malfunction. Once there, they discover an alien civilization (headed by a young Lyle Waggoner) attempting to take over the world. Low-budget film features passable special effects, but the dialogue and acting are subpar.

1967 82 minutes

KING OF THE ROCKETMEN

★★★

DIRECTOR: Fred Bannon
CAST: Tristram Coffin, Mae Clarke, Dale Van Sickel, Tom Steele

This chapter-play precursor to the "Commando Cody" television series has longtime baddie Tristram Coffin joining the good guys for a change. Strapping on his flying suit, he does battle with evil conspirators. Good fun for serial fans, with highly implausible last-minute escapes.

1949 B & W 12 chapters

KRONOS

★★★

DIRECTOR: Kurt Neumann
CAST: Jeff Morrow, Barbara Lawrence

Jeff Morrow stars in this alien invasion film. In it, a giant, featureless robot is sent to Earth to test Earth's potential for supplying energy to an alien civilization. The robot absorbs all forms of energy and grows as it feeds. The scientists must find a way to destroy the giant before it reaches the high-population areas of Southern California. Although this film's special effects are nothing by today's film-making standards, this picture is one of the best from a decade dominated by giant monsters and alien invaders.

1957 B & W 78 minutes

KRULL

★½

DIRECTOR: Peter Yates
CAST: Ken Marshall, Freddie Jones, Lisette Anthony

In this poor sci-fi/sword-and-sorcery film, a young man (Ken Marshall of TV's "Marco Polo") is called upon by an old wizard (Freddie Jones) to take up an ancient weapon and do battle with a master of evil to save a beautiful princess (Lisette Anthony). Sound familiar? It should. It's an obvious and unimaginative ripoff of *Star Wars*. That said, the movie may not be a total loss. Younger kids might enjoy it. Most adults, however, will find *Krull* to be hopelessy dull. Rated PG for violence.

1983 117 minutes

LABYRINTH

★★★

DIRECTOR: Jim Henson
CAST: David Bowie, Jennifer Connelly, Toby Froud

A charming fantasy that combines live actors with another impressive collection of Jim Henson's Muppets. Jennifer Connelly stars as a young girl who wishes for the Goblin King (David Bowie) to kidnap her baby brother; when that idle desire is granted, she must journey to an enchanted land and solve a giant maze in order to rescue her little brother. The visuals and set design are quite impressive, particularly a chamber based on a famed drawing by M. C. Escher. The performers, alas, aren't up to that standard, although Bowie does reasonably well as the sly Goblin King. Rated PG for mild violence.

1986 101 minutes

LAND THAT TIME FORGOT, THE

★★

DIRECTOR: Kevin Connor
CAST: Doug McClure, Susan Penhaligon, John McEnery

Poor Edgar Rice Burroughs, his wonderful adventure books for kids rarely got the right screen treatment. This British production tries hard, but the cheesy special effects eventually do it in. A sequel, *The People That Time Forgot*, fared no better. Rated PG.

1975 90 minutes

LASERBLAST

★★

DIRECTOR: Michael Raye
CAST: Kim Milford, Cheryl Smith, Roddy McDowall, Keenan Wynn, Ron Masak

Dreadful low-budget film with some excellent special effects by David Allen. Story concerns a young man who accidentally lays his hands on an alien ray-gun and all sorts of bizarre things begin to happen. Plodding sci-fi only comes to life when the monsters are on screen, but they make it worth a look for buffs. Rated PG.

1978 90 minutes

LAST CHASE, THE

★★½

DIRECTOR: Martyn Burke
CAST: Lee Majors, Chris Makepeace, Burgess Meredith, Alexandra Stewart, Diane D'Aquila, George Touliatos, Ben Gordon, Harvey Atkin

Made at the end of the OPEC oil crisis, this film assumes the crisis only got worse until there was a civil war in America and the eastern states banned all cars and planes. Lee Majors (*The Six Million Dollar Man*) plays an aged race car driver who flees New York to California with a runaway (Chris Makepeace). Burgess Meredith is an old fighter pilot who is ordered to kill the fleeing rebels. Confusing at times, and the Orwellian touches have been done so often that all the scare has left them. Not rated, but the equivalent of a PG for sex and profanity.

1980 106 minutes

LAST DAYS OF MAN ON EARTH, THE

★★★½

DIRECTOR: Robert Fuest
CAST: Jon Finch, Sterling Hayden, Patrick Magee, Jenny Runacre, Hugh Griffith

Kinetic adaptation of Michael Moorcock's weird little novel *The Final Programme*, the first of his adventures featuring Jerry Cornelius. Jon Finch plays Jerry as a smart-assed James Bond, and the prize he fights for is a microfilm containing the secret to self-replicating beings... highly useful in case of nuclear war. Finch encounters a variety of oddball characters, none stranger than Jenny Runacre, an enigmatic adversary who absorbs her lovers. Full of ideas and reasonably well executed, although the longer British version (89 minutes) is superior to the American release. Rated R for violence and sex.

1973 73 minutes

LAST MAN ON EARTH, THE

★★★

DIRECTOR: Sidney Salkow

CAST: Vincent Price, Franca Bettoia, Emma Danieli, Giacomo Rossi-Stuart

In this nightmarish tale, a scientist (Vincent Price) is a bit late in developing a serum to stem the tide of a plague epidemic. He becomes the last man on Earth and lives in fear of the walking dead, who crave his blood. This paranoid horror film (based on Richard Matheson's *I Am Legend*) is more chilling than its higher-budget remake, *The Omega Man*.

1964 B & W 86 minutes

LAST STARFIGHTER, THE

★★★★

DIRECTOR: Nick Castle

CAST: Lance Guest, Robert Preston, Dan O'Herlihy, Catherine Mary Stewart, Barbara Bosson, Norman Snow

In this enjoyable comedy/science-fiction film, a young man (Lance Guest) beats a video game called the Starfighter and soon finds himself recruited by an alien (Robert Preston) to do battle in outer space. Thanks to its witty dialogue and hilarious situations, this hybrid is a viewing delight. Rated PG for violence and profanity.

1984 100 minutes

LAST UNICORN, THE

★★★½

DIRECTOR: Arthur Rankin Jr.

CAST: Animated

The voices of Alan Arkin, Jeff Bridges, Mia Farrow, Tammy Grimes, Angela Lansbury, and Christopher Lee are among those featured in this well-told feature-length cartoon from the Rankin-Bass company. As they proved with their television adaptation of J.R.R. Tolkien's *The Hobbit*, Arthur Rankin Jr. and Jules Bass know how to do a good story justice when telling it, but take too many shortcuts in their animation. Rated G.

1982 88 minutes

LEGEND

DIRECTOR: Ridley Scott

CAST: Tom Cruise, Tim Curry, Mia Sara, David Bennent, Billy Barty

Director Ridley Scott, always slick at creating the critical visual verisimilitude of otherworldly fantasies, strikes out completely with this one. *Legend* is a sad triumph of style over substance, a gorgeously-lensed but absolutely empty fantasy. Tom Cruise simply looks embarrassed as a forest-living lad who joins a quest to save a unicorn, keeper of his world's Light, from the evil entity who prefers to plunge the land into eternal Darkness. As that malevolent entity, Tim Curry looks properly scary; he's the only player even remotely comfortable with his character. The script is filled with witless and inane dialogue, attempts at juvenile humor which contrast horribly to Scott's darker tone. If you must watch this, turn the sound off. Rated PG for mild violence.

1986 89 minutes

LIFEFORCE

★

DIRECTOR: Tobe Hooper

CAST: Steven Railsback, Peter Firth, Mathilda May, Frank Finlay, Michael Gothard

In this disappointing and disjointed science-fiction/horror film by director Tobe Hooper (*Poltergeist*), ancient vampires from outer space return to Earth via

Halley's Comet to feed on human souls. Rated R for violence, gore, nudity, profanity, and suggested sex.

1985 96 minutes

LIFESPAN

DIRECTOR: Alexander Whitelaw
CAST: Klaus Kinski, Hiram Keller, Tina Aumont, Fons Rademakers, Lyda Polak

This Dutch-made science-fiction film is so slow you'll feel it takes a lifetime to watch. A young scientist tries to discover the secret of a long-life formula that belonged to a dead colleague. Along the way, he becomes involved with the deceased's girlfriend. There's nothing to recommend this plodding sci-fi attempt—certainly not the acting or plot. Unrated, it does have nudity and simulated sex.

1974 85 minutes

LIQUID SKY

★★★½

DIRECTOR: Slava Tsukerman
CAST: Anne Carlisle, Paula E. Sheppard

Here's a release that's the first of its kind: a punk-rock science-fiction movie. It's as much about alienation as aliens. An alien spaceship lands on Earth in search of chemicals produced in the body during sex. One of the aliens enters the life of a new-wave fashion model and feeds off her lovers, most of whom she's more than happy to see dead. *Liquid Sky* certainly can't be called boring. Producer-director-co-writer Slava Tsukerman, a Russian emigrée, alternately shocks and amuses us with this unusual, stark, and ugly—but somehow fitting—look at an American subculture. Still, we feel compelled to add: Watch at your own risk. Rated R for profanity, violence, rape, and suggested sex.

1983 112 minutes

LOGAN'S RUN

★★★

DIRECTOR: Michael Anderson
CAST: Michael York, Jenny Agutter, Peter Ustinov, Richard Jordan

Popular sci-fi film concerning a futuristic society where people are only allowed to live to the age of 30, and a policeman nearing the limit who searches desperately for a way to avoid mandatory extermination. Nice production is enhanced immeasurably by outlandish sets and beautiful, imaginative miniatures. Only real problem is the video's length. While only two hours, it somehow feels like three, causing the viewer to shift in his seat several times toward the climax. Rated PG.

1976 120 minutes

LOOKER

DIRECTOR: Michael Crichton
CAST: Albert Finney, James Coburn, Susan Dey, Leigh Taylor-Young

Writer-director Michael Crichton describes this movie as "a thriller about television commercials," but it's really a fairly simple-minded suspense film. Plastic surgeon Albert Finney discovers a plot by evil mastermind James Coburn to clone models for television commercials. This is fiction? Rated PG because of nudity and violence.

1981 94 minutes

LORD OF THE RINGS, THE

★

DIRECTOR: Ralph Bakshi
CAST: Animated

J.R.R. Tolkien's beloved epic fantasy is all but trashed in this animated film, directed by Ralph Bakshi (*Fritz the Cat*). It deals with the first half of the trilogy, in which Frodo Baggins takes up the Ring of Power in order to save his fellow hobbits and all of Middle Earth from the forces of evil. The movie suffers from too much gore and cut-rate animation techniques, spoiling what should have been a cinematic event. Rated PG.

1978 133 minutes

LOST WORLD, THE

★★★★

DIRECTOR: Harry Hoyt
CAST: Bessie Love, Lewis Stone, Wallace Beery, Loyd Hughes

Silent version of Arthur Conan Doyle's classic story of Professor Challenger and his expedition to a desolate plateau roaming with prehistoric beasts. The movie climaxes with a brontosaurus running amuck in London. An ambitious production, interesting as film history and quite entertaining, considering its age. The special effects by Willis O'Brien are actually superior to the 1960 remake. A few years later, the basic story and O'Brien's skills were used again in *King Kong*.

1925 B & W 60 minutes

MAD MAX

★★★½

DIRECTOR: George Miller
CAST: Mel Gibson, Joanne Samuel, Hugh Keays-Byrne, Tim Burns, Roger Ward

The most successful Australian film of all time ($100 million in worldwide rentals), this exciting sci-fi adventure features Mel Gibson (*The Bounty*) as a fast-driving cop who has to take on a gang of crazies in the dangerous world of the future. Rated R.

1979 93 minutes

MAD MAX BEYOND THUNDERDOME

★★★★½

DIRECTORS: George Miller, George Ogilvie
CAST: Mel Gibson, Tina Turner, Helen Buday, Frank Thring, Bruce Spence

Mad Max is back—and he's angrier than ever. Those who enjoyed *Road Warrior* will find more of the same—and then some—in director George Miller's third postapocalypse, action-packed adventure film. This time the resourceful futuristic warrior (Mel Gibson) begrudgingly confronts what is left of civilization (as run by evil ruler Tina Turner) and fulfills a prophecy by—again, begrudgingly—leading a group of children out of the death-dealing desert. Miller chose this time to concentrate solely on the action scenes and hired another director, George Ogilvie, to work with the actors. The result is the best film in the series. Rated PG-13 for violence and profanity.

1985 109 minutes

MAKING CONTACT

★★

DIRECTOR: Roland Emerich
CAST: Joshua Morell, Eve Kryll, Tammy Shields, Jan Zierold, Barbara Klein, Jerry Hall, Sean Johnson

After his father dies, a little boy begins to exhibit telekinetic powers and begins giving life to his favorite toys. Then he starts to talk to his father on the phone. Telling his classmates about this leads to ridicule, so with only his toys and a little girl who believes his stories, they set out on a frightening adventure. They find an old house and inside they discover a fifty-year-old ventriloquist's dummy. The boy takes the dummy home and the trouble starts. The dummy comes to life and begins trying to destroy the boy's toys and threatens his mother and friends. Only it's not just threats that are on the dummy's mind; it's murder. Obviously aimed at children, this film isn't bad. In fact it's quite imaginative, although some parts may be too frightening for younger viewers.

1985 82 minutes

MAN CALLED RAGE, A

DIRECTOR: Anthony Richmond
CAST: Conrad Nichols, Stelio Candel

In this dreadful, dubbed, Italian science-fiction flick, Rage, a Mad Max–type of character, leads a team to find uranium deposits that are vital to the survival of the human race. While searching for the uranium, Rage is followed by an evil band bent on stopping him. Rated PG for violence.

1987 90 minutes

MAN FROM BEYOND, THE

★★★

DIRECTOR: Burton King
CAST: Harry Houdini, Jane Connelly, Arthur Maude, Albert Tavernier, Erwin Connelly, Frank Montgomery, Luis Alberni, Nita Naldi

Legendary escape artist Harry Houdini wrote and starred in this timeless story of a man encased in a block of ice for one hundred years who is discovered, thawed out, and thrust into twentieth-century life. The concept of someone preserved over the ages and loosed upon an alien society in search of a former love has been the subject of books and stories from sources as divergent as Edgar Rice Burroughs and Henry James, but this was the first time the subject was dealt with in a feature film. While the special effects lack sophistication to today's audiences and the acting seems pretty broad, this is still worth watching for its place in cinema history as a fantasy masterpiece and one of the few existing examples of Houdini's film work. Thanks to film archivists and collectors Houdini still lives on film and tape and may well be the yardstick used to measure magicians for the next sixty years. Silent.

1921 B & W 50 minutes

MAN WHO COULD WORK MIRACLES, THE

★★★½

DIRECTOR: Lothar Mendes
CAST: Roland Young, Ralph Richardson, Joan Gardner, George Zucco

A timid department store clerk steps out of a British pub one evening and suddenly finds he possesses the power to do whatever he desires. Roland Young is matchless as the clerk, and is supported by a first-rate cast in this captivating fantasy film based on a story by H. G. Wells.

1937 B & W 82 minutes

MAN WHO FELL TO EARTH, THE

★★★★

DIRECTOR: Nicolas Roeg
CAST: David Bowie, Rip Torn, Candy Clark, Buck Henry

Nicolas Roeg (*Performance*; *Don't Look Now*) directed this moody, cerebral science-fiction thriller about an alien (David Bowie) who becomes trapped on our planet. Its occasional ambiguities are overpowered by sheer mind-tugging bizarreness and directorial brilliance. Rated R.

1976 140 minutes

MAN WHO SAW TOMORROW, THE

★★★½

DIRECTOR: Robert Guenette
CAST: Orson Welles (narrator)

Orson Welles narrates and appears in this fascinating dramatization of the prophecies of sixteenth-century poet, physician, and psychic Michel de Nostradamus. Through a combination of clips from old movies, newsreels, and newly shot footage, it focuses on the man who, more than four hundred years ago, predicted the French Revolution, the rise and fall of Napoleon, the discoveries of Louis Pasteur, World War II, and Adolf Hitler's reign of terror, among many other startling things. It may be just a matter of interpretation in some cases, but the fact remains that Nostradamus was astonishingly accurate and, in some cases, actually cited names and dates. His prediction for the future is equally amazing—and, sometimes, terrifying. Rated PG.

1981 90 minutes

MAROONED

DIRECTOR: John Sturges
CAST: Gregory Peck, Richard Crenna, David Janssen, Gene Hackman, James Franciscus, Lee Grant

The special effects are the only thing this bomb has going for it. Several dollars' worth of Hollywood acting talent is wasted in this tale of three astronauts unable to return to Earth and the ensuing rescue attempt. Rated PG.

1969 134 minutes

MASTER OF THE WORLD

★★★

DIRECTOR: William Witney
CAST: Vincent Price, Charles Bronson, Henry Hull, Mary Webster

Jules Verne's tale brought excitingly to the screen. Vincent Price plays a self-proclaimed god trying to end all war by flying around the world in a giant airship, armed to the teeth, blowing ships from the water, etc. Lots of fun.

1961 104 minutes

MEGAFORCE

DIRECTOR: Hal Needham
CAST: Barry Bostwick, Michael Beck, Persis Khambatta, Henry Silva

Director Hal Needham (*Cannonball Run*; *The Villain*) makes us groan and gag with his biggest dud ever. This deadly dull sci-fi adventure is about a rapid-deployment defense unit that galvanizes into action whenever and wherever freedom is threatened. But rather than gasps, their exploits produce only yawns. PG for no discernible reason.

1982 99 minutes

METALSTORM: THE DESTRUCTION OF JARED-SYN

DIRECTOR: Charles Band
CAST: Jeffrey Byron, Mike Preston, Tim Thomerson, Kelly Preston

Charles Band, who was responsible for such forgettable turkeys as *Laserblast*, *End of the World*, and *Parasite*, directed this dud. In it, Jeffrey Byron plays an outer space ranger who, in order to save a barren planet, takes on the powerful villain of the title, Jared-Syn (Mike Preston). Even the title is a cheat. The bad guy gets away at the end—leaving it wide open for a sequel. The mind boggles. Rated PG for violence.

1983 84 minutes

METEOR

★

DIRECTOR: Ronald Neame
CAST: Sean Connery, Natalie Wood, Karl Malden, Brian Keith, Henry Fonda

In this disaster film, which wastes an all-star cast, a comet strikes an asteroid, and sends a huge chunk of rock hurtling on a collision course with Earth. The United States and the U.S.S.R. must join forces to deflect the destructive mass, but the viewer wonders why they bother. Rated PG.

1979 103 minutes

METROPOLIS

★★★★★

DIRECTOR: Fritz Lang

CAST: Brigitte Helm, Alfred Abel, Gustav Froelich

Fritz Lang's 1926 creation embodies the fine difference between classic and masterpiece. Using some of the most innovative camerawork in film of any time, it's also an uncannily accurate projection of futuristic society. It is a silent screen triumph.

1926 B & W 120 minutes

MIDSUMMER NIGHT'S DREAM, A

★★★★

DIRECTOR: Max Reinhardt

CAST: James Cagney, Olivia De Havilland, Dick Powell, Mickey Rooney

Warner Bros. rolled out many of its big-name contract stars during the studio's heyday for this engrossing rendition of Shakespeare's classic comedy. Enchantment is the key element in this fairy-tale story of the misadventures of a group of mythical mischief-makers.

1935 B & W 117 minutes

MIGHTY JOE YOUNG

★★★½

DIRECTOR: Ernest B. Schoedsack

CAST: Terry Moore, Ben Johnson, Robert Armstrong, Frank McHugh

In this timeless fantasy from the creator of *King Kong* (Willis O'Brien with his young apprentice, Ray Harryhausen), the story follows the discovery of a twelve-foot gorilla in Africa by a fast-talking, money-hungry night-club owner (Robert Armstrong), who schemes to bring the animal back to Hollywood. Things go along reasonably well until a trio of drunks sneaks backstage and gets the star attraction drunk, which causes the big guy to go on a rampage through the club. *Mighty Joe Young* has been described as a *King Kong* for kids, and, in a way, it is; but the special effects are extremely well-done (which prompted an Oscar), and the story is paced so well that this movie is a pleasure.

1949 B & W 94 minutes

MISFITS OF SCIENCE

★★½

DIRECTOR: James D. Parriott

CAST: Dean Paul Martin, Kevin Peter Hall, Mark Thomas Miller, Courteney Cox, Jennifer Holmes, Eric Christmas, Larry Linville, Edward Winter

Dean Paul Martin stars as the ringleader of a group of individuals possessing unique abilities. He rallies them together to combine their powers of mind control, cryogenics, electric energy, and size manipulation to save the world from a terrible neutron cannon developed by the government. No rating. This was the first installment in the failed television series.

1986 96 minutes

MOTHRA

★★★

DIRECTOR: Inoshiro Honda

CAST: Lee Kresel, Franky Sakai, Hiroshi Koizumi

Two six-inch-tall princesses are taken from their island home to perform in a Tokyo nightclub. A native tribe prays for the return of the princesses, and their prayers hatch a giant egg, releasing a giant caterpillar. The caterpillar goes to Tokyo searching for the princesses and turns into a giant moth while wrecking the city. Although the story may sound corny, this is one of the best of the giant-monster movies to come out of Japan. The special effects of the miniature girls and the giant insect are very good, and there are no people in costumes stomping miniature buildings. Even the tune the princesses sing when calling Mothra is catchy.

1962 100 minutes

MY SCIENCE PROJECT

★

DIRECTOR: Jonathan R. Betuel

CAST: John Stockwell, Danielle Von Zerneck, Fisher Stevens, Dennis Hopper, Raphael Sharge, Richard Masur

You could see it coming: First there was *Real Genius*, which brilliantly turned the military industrial complex into a popcorn machine; then came *Weird Science*, a weird but funny film. Now the fast-buck artists come out of the woodwork. This little piece of exploitation sports some of the most obnoxious characters ever to plague the video monitor. Rated PG for profanity.

1985 94 minutes

MYSTERIANS, THE

★★½

DIRECTOR: Inoshiro Honda

CAST: Kenji Sahara, Yumi Shirakawa

An alien civilization attempts takeover of Earth after its home planet is destroyed. Massive destruction from the director of *Godzilla*. Quaint Japanese-style special effects look pretty silly these days, but the film can be fun if seen in the right spirit.

1959 85 minutes

MYSTERIOUS ISLAND

★★★★

DIRECTOR: Cy Endfield

CAST: Michael Craig, Joan Greenwood, Michael Callan, Gary Merrill, Herbert Lom

Fantasy adventure based on Jules Verne's novel about a group of Civil War prisoners who escape by balloon and land on an uncharted island in the Pacific, where they must fight to stay alive against incredible odds, including a monster crab, colossal bees, and an unstable volcano on the verge of eruption. With fantastic effects work by Ray Harryhausen and a breathtaking Bernard Herrmann score. Topnotch entertainment.

1961 101 minutes

NEPTUNE FACTOR, THE

★

DIRECTOR: Daniel Petrie

CAST: Ben Gazzara, Yvette Mimieux, Walter Pidgeon, Ernest Borgnine

Ben Gazzara stars as the commander of an experimental deep-sea submarine. He is called in to rescue an aquatic research team trapped in the remains of their lab on the ocean floor. Why they built it in the middle of a quake zone is the first in a series of dumb plot ideas that include bad special effects to make regular-size fish seem like "deep sea giants." Rated G.

1973 94 minutes

NEVERENDING STORY, THE

★★★★

DIRECTOR: Wolfgang Petersen

CAST: Barrett Oliver, Noah Hathaway, Tami Stronach

The imagination is truly a wondrous thing, and when it's sparked by a truly magical movie such as *The NeverEnding Story*, it can leave the young and the young at heart with a warm glow. This is a superb fantasy about a sensitive

10-year-old boy named Bastian (Barrett Oliver) who takes refuge in the pages of a fairy tale. In reading it, he's swept off to a land of startlingly strange creatures and heroic adventure where a young warrior, Atreyu (Noah Hathaway), does battle with the Nothing, a force that threatens to obliterate the land of mankind's hope and dreams—and only he has the power to save the day. Rated PG for slight profanity.

1984 92 minutes

NIGHT OF THE COMET

★★★½

DIRECTOR: Thom Eberhardt
CAST: Geoffrey Lewis, Mary Woronov, Catherine Mary Stewart

The passage of the comet, which last visited Earth 65 million years ago, when the dinosaurs disappeared, wipes out all but a few people on our planet. The survivors, mostly young adults, are hunted by a pair of baddies, played by Geoffrey Lewis and Mary Woronov (of *Eating Raoul*). The deadly duo, who were partially exposed to the comet's rays, drain the blood from those they capture in the hopes of coming up with a serum that will prevent them from becoming disfigured monsters. It all adds up to a zesty low-budget spoof of science-fiction movies. Rated PG-13.

1984 94 minutes

1984 (ORIGINAL)

★★★

DIRECTOR: Michael Anderson
CAST: Edmond O'Brien, Jan Sterling, Michael Redgrave, Donald Pleasence

Workmanlike adaptation of George Orwell's famous novel that, in spite of a good stab at Winston Smith by Edmond O'Brien, just doesn't capture the misery and desolation of the book. Frankly, this plays more like a postwar polemic than a drama, and great liberties have been taken with the storyline, particularly with the conclusion. Although made in Great Britain, it almost glows with the sanitized look of a product from Hollywood. The definitive version was yet to come (see next entry). Unrated; suitable for family viewing.

1955 B & W 91 minutes

1984 (REMAKE)

★★★★½

DIRECTOR: Michael Radford
CAST: John Hurt, Richard Burton, Suzanna Hamilton, Cyril Cusack

A stunning adaptation of George Orwell's novel, which captures every mote of bleak despair found within those pages. John Hurt, who's made a career of characters down on their luck, looks positively emaciated as the forlorn Winston Smith, the tragic figure who dares to fall in love in a totalitarian society where emotions are outlawed. Richard Burton, in his last film role, makes a grand interrogator: stiff, shrewd, and formal. Orwell's society under the watchful gaze of Big Brother has been rendered with meticulous attention to detail. This is one of the great, unsung science-fiction films, and it quite appropriately came out in its title year. Rated R for nudity and adult themes.

1984 123 minutes

1990: THE BRONX WARRIORS

DIRECTOR: Enzo G. Castellari
CAST: Vic Morrow, Christopher Connelly, Mark Gregory

Near the end of the 1980s, the Bronx is abandoned by law enforcement and becomes a kind of no man's land ruled by motorcycle gangs. Vic Morrow plays a lone wolf cop who tries to clean up the town but instead delivers some horribly tasteless lines about human decapitation. Obviously inspired by *Escape from New York* and *The Warriors*, it is a prime example of bad writing, acting, and direction. Rated R for violence and language.

1983 89 minutes

OMEGA MAN, THE

★★★½

DIRECTOR: Boris Sagal

CAST: Charlton Heston, Anthony Zerbe, Rosalind Cash

Chartlon Heston does a last-man-on-Earth number in this free adaptation of Richard Matheson's *I Am Legend*. The novel's vampirism has been toned down, but Chuck still is holed up in his high-rise mansion by night, and killing robed (and sleeping) zombies by day. Although this is no more faithful to Matheson's work than 1964's *The Last Man on Earth*, *The Omega Man* has enough throat-grabbing suspense to keep it moving. It's also one of Rosalind Cash's best roles. Rated PG —considerable violence.

1971 98 minutes

ON THE BEACH

★★★★

DIRECTOR: Stanley Kramer

CAST: Gregory Peck, Ava Gardner, Fred Astaire, Anthony Perkins

The effect of a nuclear holocaust on a group of people in Australia makes for engrossing drama in this film. Gregory Peck is a submarine commander who ups anchor and goes looking for survivors as a radioactive cloud slowly descends upon this apparently last human enclave. Director Stanley Kramer is a bit heavy-handed in his moralizing and the romance between Peck and Ava Gardner is distracting, yet the film remains a powerful anti-war statement.

1959 B & W 133 minutes

ONE MILLION B.C.

★★

DIRECTORS: Hal Roach, Hal Roach Jr.

CAST: Victor Mature, Carole Landis, Lon Chaney Jr., Mano Clark

D. W. Griffith reportedly directed parts of this prehistoric-age picture before producer Hal Roach and his son took over. Victor Mature, Carole Landis, and Lon Chaney Jr. try hard—and there are some good moments—but the result is a pretty dumb fantasy film. A remake in 1966 with Raquel Welch had better special effects but was thwarted by the same silly story and no acting to speak of.

1940 B & W 80 minutes

OUTER LIMITS, THE (TELEVISION SERIES)

★★★½

DIRECTORS: Byron Haskin, Laslo Benedek

CAST: Cliff Robertson, Donald Pleasence, Sidney Blackmer, James Hong, William O. Douglas Jr.

This well-remembered example of early television science fiction finally makes the transition to video. Assisted by the "control voice" that explained that there was "nothing wrong with your television set," this short-lived (1 1/2 years) series produced some fine morality plays that generally rewarded those with noble aspirations and condemned those with more evil, petty inclinations. Quite a few noted writers, including fantasist Harlan Ellison, cut their teeth on this program; with literate and absorbing scripts, the episodes hold up quite well today. Best among those released thus far is "The Galaxy Being," the series pilot that stars Cliff Robertson as a signal technician who beams in more than the local news on evening. Probably the only example of *film-noir* science fiction, this black and white series is a genuine pleasure to the eyes. Suitable for family viewing, although a bit intense for the small fry.

1964 B & W 52 minutes

OUTLAND

★★★★

DIRECTOR: Peter Hyams

CAST: Sean Connery, Peter Boyle, Frances Sternhagen

Sean Connery stars as the two-fisted marshal in this thoroughly enjoyable outer-space remake of *High Noon* directed by Peter Hyams (*Capricorn One*). Much of the credit for that goes to Connery. As he has proved in many pictures, he is one of the few actors today who can play a fully credible adventure hero. And *Outland*, a movie that never takes itself too seriously, makes the most of this. Rated R.

1981 109 minutes

PEOPLE, THE

★★

DIRECTOR: John Korty

CAST: William Shatner, Dan O'Herlihy, Diane Varsi, Kim Darby

This TV movie is a fair interpretation of the science-fiction stories of Zenna Henderson about a group of psychically talented aliens whose home world has been destroyed and who must survive on Earth. Sheriff William Shatner and schoolteacher Kim Darby, both humans who come to know and interact with the aliens, are guilty of overacting, and Diane Varsi, one of "the People," is colorless. The script gives Henderson's subtle themes a heavy-handed and unbalanced treatment.

1971 74 minutes

PEOPLE THAT TIME FORGOT, THE

★

DIRECTOR: Kevin Conner

CAST: Doug McClure, Patrick Wayne, Sarah Douglas, Thorley Walters

Edgar Rice Burroughs probably would have been outraged by this and its companion piece, *The Land That Time Forgot*. Doug McClure gets rescued by friend Patrick Wayne from a fate worse than death on a strange island circa 1919. Laughable rubber-suited monsters mix it up with ludicrous wire-controlled beasties. Strictly for the under-five set. Rated PG.

1977 90 minutes

PHASE IV

★★★½

DIRECTOR: Saul Bass

CAST: Nigel Davenport, Michael Murphy, Lynne Frederick

An interesting sci-fi mood piece from 1973 about scientists (Nigel Davenport, Michael Murphy) attempting to outwit super-intelligent mutant ants. Good effects and fine acting. Rated PG.

1974 86 minutes

PHILADELPHIA EXPERIMENT, THE

★★★½

DIRECTOR: Stewart Raffill

CAST: Michael Pare, Nancy Allen, Bobby DiCicco, Eric Christmas

Reportedly based on a true incident during World War II involving an anti-radar experiment that caused a naval battleship to disappear in Virginia, this entertaining science-fiction film stars Michael Pare (*Streets of Fire*) as a sailor on that ship. But instead of ending up in Virginia, he finds himself in the modern world of 1984. Nancy

Allen (*Dressed to Kill*; *Carrie*) co-stars as the woman who befriends Pare after his disorienting journey through time. The latter has its cataclysmic side-effects: a time warp that threatens to destroy the world. Rated PG for violence and profanity.

1984 102 minutes

PLAGUE DOGS, THE

★★★★½

DIRECTOR: Martin Rosen
CAST: Animated

This animated film is definitely *not* for children. It is a powerfully disturbing film which makes an unforgettable statement about animal rights. In it, two dogs escape from an experimental veterinary lab in which they had both been subjected to cruel and senseless operations and tests. Once free, the joy they feel is short-lived as they are hunted by both the "white coats" (lab doctors) and the nearby sheep owners. The animation team of *Watership Down*—Tony Guy and Colin White—does an excellent job while avoiding the darling Disney-type animation that would negate the torment that these animals undergo. Although this film is not rated, we do not recommend it for children under twelve.

1984 99 minutes

PLAN 9 FROM OUTER SPACE

DIRECTOR: Edward D. Wood Jr.
CAST: Bela Lugosi, Gregory Walcott, Tom Keene, Duke Moore, Mona McKinnon

Ever seen a movie that was so bad it was funny? Well, this low-budget 1950s program is considered to be the very worst picture ever made, and it's hilarious. Written and directed by Edward D. Wood, it's a ponderous science-fiction cheapie that attempts to deliver an anti-war message as well as thrills and chills. It does neither. The acting is atrocious, the sets are made of cardboard (and often bumped into by the stars), the dialogue incredibly moronic, and the film-making technique execrable. Even worse, Bela Lugosi is top-billed even though he died three months before the film was made. Undaunted, Wood used silent home-movie footage of the once great horror film star. Get the idea?

1959 B & W 79 minutes

PLANET OF THE APES

★★★★

DIRECTOR: Franklin J. Schaffner
CAST: Charlton Heston, Kim Hunter, Roddy McDowall, Maurice Evans

Here is the first and best of the "Planet of the Apes" sci-fi series. Four American astronauts crash on a far-off planet and discover a culture where evolution has gone awry. The dominant form of primates are apes and gorillas. Man is reduced to a beast of burden. Much of the social comment is cutesy and forced, but this remains an enjoyable fantasy. Rated PG for violence.

1968 112 minutes

PREDATOR

★★★★½

DIRECTOR: John McTiernan
CAST: Arnold Schwarzenegger, Carl Weathers, Elpidia Carrillo, Bill Duke, Jesse Ventura, Sonny Landham, Richard Chaves, R. G. Armstrong, Kevin Peter Hall

Sort of an earthbound *Alien*, *Predator* stars Arnold Schwarzenegger as a commando out to terminate a kill-crazy creature in a Latin American jungle. Although it sounds derivative, this film contains a number of inventive moments and delivers a pulse-pounding tale. Director John McTiernan keeps things rolling like a downhill rollercoaster while screenwriters Jim and John Thomas have added some welcome and effective bits of comedy to their thrill-packed storyline. Rated R for profanity and violence.

1987 107 minutes

PREHISTORIC WOMEN

DIRECTOR: Gregg Tallas
CAST: Laurette Luez, Allan Nixon, Joan Shawlee

One of the worst films ever made. A tribe of female bimbos runs into a tribe of male bimbos, and they bore each other to death. Among the astounding thrills: a stock-footage bird and a one-elephant stampede. The movie was shot silent with grunts and groans presumably dubbed by specialists in that sort of thing. A minimum-wage narrator babbles incessantly from beginning to end. If you can watch this one without hitting the scan button, you are a very troubled person.

1950 74 minutes

PRISONER, THE (TELEVISION SERIES)

★★★★

DIRECTORS: Patrick McGoohan, David Tomblin, Don Chaffey, Pat Jackson
CAST: Patrick McGoohan, Angelo Muscat, Leo McKern, Peter Bowles, Nigel Stock, Peter Wyngarde

Probably the finest science-fiction series ever created for television, this summer-replacement show (it stood in for The Jackie Gleason Show) was the brainchild of star Patrick McGoohan, who intended it to be an oblique follow-up to his successful *Danger Man* and *Secret Agent* series. The main character (McGoohan), whose name never is given—although he is believed to be *Secret Agent's* John Drake—abruptly resigns from a sensitive Intelligence position without explanation. He is abducted and awakens one morning in a mysterious community known only as The Village (actually Portmerion, in North Wales). Now called "Number Six"—every resident is known only by a number, never by a name—this new prisoner tries to escape while matching wits with a series of Number Twos (each is replaced as he or she fails), who desire to know just why he resigned. McGoohan conceived the show as a limited series of seventeen episodes; it therefore was the *first* television miniseries. Superior episodes are "The Arrival," wherein the Prisoner is abducted and learns about his new surroundings; "The Chimes of Big Ben," which details his first complicated escape scheme; "Schizoid Man," wherein the Prisoner is brainwashed into a new identity and confronts another person claiming to be Number Six; "Many Happy Returns," wherein the Prisoner wakes one morning to find The Village completely deserted; "Living in Harmony," an episode never shown on American television, which finds the Prisoner replaying a weird parody of his life in a western setting; "The Girl Who Was Death," another parody, this time of supersecret agents; and "Once Upon a Time" and "Fallout," the two-parter that brings the story to a close. Once seen, this series never is forgotten; some of its ideas and visuals are absolutely hypnotic. Aside from McGoohan, the only continuing character is Angelo Muscat's enigmatic butler, who serves the ever-changing Number Twos. Do not miss.

1968 52 minutes

PROJECT MOON BASE

★★

DIRECTOR: Richard Talmadge
CAST: Ross Ford, Donna Martell, Hayden Rorke, James Craven

Futuristic story (set in far-off 1970!) chronicles the fate of an expedition that leaves a space station orbiting Earth and heads for the moon. Made by independent producer Robert Lippert, this dull space story was co-authored by the esteemed Robert E. Heinlein, but it doesn't reflect his touch. More documentary-style future fact than adventure, this lacks the special effects wizardry of a Geroge Pal production and the presence of any known performers. Director Richard Talmadge was a former silent-screen stunt star who turned to directing halfway through his career.

1953 B & W 53 minutes

PROJECT X

★½

DIRECTOR: Jonathan Kaplan
CAST: Matthew Broderick, Helen Hunt, Bill Sadler, Johnny Ray McGhee, Jonathan Stark, Robin Gammell, Stephen Lang

A misguided attempt to turn a serious issue—the abuse of research animals—into a mainstream comedy-drama. Matthew Broderick is an Air Force misfit who winds up assigned to a secret project involving chimpanzees and air-flight simulators. What Broderick initially assumes to be computer-controlled coordination studies turns out to be much more deadly. When the story most desperately needs its grim and somber tone, director Jonathan Kaplan descends into the mindless slapstick of monkey antics; instead of the Marx Brothers, we get a trio of chimps dubbed Goofy, Goliath, and Razzbery. In a lighter film these well-trained animals (most particularly a lambent-eyed fellow named Virgil) would be appreciated for their cuteness and comic relief; here, the juxtaposition of moods trivializes the story's central issue. The result, alas, is often tasteless. Rated PG for intensity of theme.

1987 108 minutes

QUATERMASS CONCLUSION, THE

★★

DIRECTOR: Piers Haggard
CAST: John Mills, Simon MacCorkindale, Barbara Kellerman, Brewster Mason, Margaret Tyzack

It's sad to see a great premise destroyed by bad editing and sloppy script continuity. Of course, the fact that this film is an edited-down version of a British miniseries may be the cause. Why didn't they release the whole series on video? In the strange future world of the story, society seems to be suffering a terrible case of inertia. The world's teen population is committing mass suicide, and only Dr. Quatermass (John Mills), genius scientist, can save them.

1979 105 minutes

QUEST FOR FIRE

★★★★½

DIRECTOR: Jean-Jacques Annaud
CAST: Everett McGill, Rae Dawn Chong, Ron Perlman, Nameer Radi

In this movie, about the attempt to learn the secret of making fire by a tribe of primitive men, director Jean-Jacques Annaud (*Black and White in Color*) and screenwriter Gerard Brach (*Tess*) have achieved what once seemed to be impossible: a first-rate, compelling film about the dawn of man.

Rated R for violence, gore, nudity, and semi-explicit sex.

1981 97 minutes

QUIET EARTH, THE

★★★★

DIRECTOR: Geoffrey Murphy

CAST: Bruno Lawrence, Alison Routledge, Peter Smith

First-rate science-fiction thriller from New Zealand. A scientific researcher (Bruno Lawrence) wakes one morning and discovers that all living beings—people and animals—have vanished. Fearful that the world-encircling energy grid on which he'd been working may have been responsible, he sets out to find other people. Intelligent and absorbing adaptation of the book by Craig Harrison. The film concludes with an apocalyptic image that rivals the final moments of *2001* for sheer power and perverse ambiguity. Do not miss. Rated R for nudity and sexual situations.

1985 91 minutes

QUINTET

★★½

DIRECTOR: Robert Altman

CAST: Paul Newman, Fernando Rey, Bibi Andersson

This is about as pessimistic a view of the future as one is likely to see. Director Robert Altman has fashioned a very murky, hard-to-follow film, concerning the ultimate game of death, set against the background of a frozen post-nuclear wasteland. An intriguing idea, but Altman doesn't pull this one off. Rated R.

1979 110 minutes

RADIOACTIVE DREAMS

★★★

DIRECTOR: Albert F. Pyun

CAST: John Stockwell, Michael Dudikoff, George Kennedy, Don Murray, Michele Little, Norbert Weiser, Lisa Blount

This one has a little bit of everything: action, adventure, science fiction, fantasy, and an excellent score. Essentially a spoof, the story begins in a postapocalypse fallout shelter where two boys, who read 1930s detective novels and think the stories are real have lived most of their lives. They set out to find some "dames" and end up in the middle of a gang war with a mutant surfer, hippie cannibals, and biker women. The film will not appeal to everyone, but it is great fun for fans of the offbeat. Rated R for nudity and violence.

1984 94 minutes

RAIDERS OF THE LOST ARK

★★★★★

DIRECTOR: Steven Spielberg

CAST: Harrison Ford, Karen Allen, Wolf Kahler, Paul Freeman, Ronald Lacey, John Rhys-Davies, Denholm Elliott

For sheer spirit-lifting entertainment, you can't do better than this film, by director Steven Spielberg (*E.T.*) and writer-producer George Lucas (*Star Wars*). Harrison Ford stars as Indiana Jones, the roughest, toughest, and most unpredictable hero to grace the silver screen, who risks life and limb against a set of the nastiest villains you've ever seen. It's all to save the world—what else? Rated PG for violence and gore.

1981 115 minutes

RESURRECTION OF ZACHARY WHEELER, THE

★★

DIRECTOR: Bob Wynn

CAST: Bradford Dillman, Angie Dickinson, Leslie Nielsen

Disappointing science-fiction/mystery has a well-known senator (Bradford Dillman) taken to a bizarre out-of-the-way treatment center in New Mexico after a serious car accident, and an investigation of the incident by an intrepid reporter (Leslie Nielsen). Confusing movie. Rated G.

1971 100 minutes

RETURN OF THE JEDI

★★★★★

DIRECTOR: Richard Marquand

CAST: Mark Hamill, Harrison Ford, Carrie Fisher, Billy Dee Williams, Dave Prowse, Peter Mayhew, Anthony Daniels, James Earl Jones

This third film in the "Star Wars" series more than fulfills the viewer's expectations. The story centers on the all-out attempt by the Rebel forces—led by Luke Skywalker (Mark Hamill), Han Solo (Harrison Ford), Princess Leia (Carrie Fisher), and Lando Calrissian (Billy Dee Williams)—to turn back the tidal wave of interplanetary domination by the evil Galactic Empire and its forces, led by Darth Vader (Dave Prowse—with the voice of James Earl Jones). A marvelous movie, this George Lucas production has thrills, chills, laughs, and eye-popping wonders galore. Rated PG.

1983 133 minutes

RIDING WITH DEATH

★★

DIRECTORS: Alan J. Levi, Don McDougall

CAST: Ben Murphy, Katherine Crawford, Richard Dysart, William Sylvester, Andrew Prine, John Milford, Alan Oppenheimer, Smith Evans, Don Galloway

A film with spies, invisible men, and a ruthless inventor. This made-for-TV movie is a science-fiction adventure with lots of action. A revolutionary new fuel is to be transported across country under the protection of an invisible government agent. The fuel is a fraud and is set to explode while in transit, killing all concerned.

1976 97 minutes

RIP VAN WINKLE

★★½

DIRECTOR: Francis Ford Coppola

CAST: Harry Dean Stanton, Talia Shire, Ed Begley Jr., Mark Blankfield, Tim Conway, Hunter Carson

This episode of *Faerie Tale Theatre* will probably not grab most viewers. Francis Ford Coppola does not seem suited to directing fantasies. The story remains basically unchanged as Rip falls asleep for twenty years in the Catskill Mountains only to awaken as an old man.

1985 60 minutes

ROAD WARRIOR, THE

★★★★

DIRECTOR: George Miller

CAST: Mel Gibson, Bruce Spence, Vernon Wells, Mike Preston, Virginia Hay, Emil Minty, Kjell Nilsson

A sequel to *Mad Max*, the most successful Australian film of all time ($100 million in worldwide rentals), this exciting science-fiction adventure features Mel Gibson (*Gallipoli*) as a fast-driving, cynical Robin Hood in the desolate, dangerous, post-apocalypse world of the future. Good fun! Rated R for violence, nudity, and profanity.

1981 94 minutes

ROBIN HOOD AND THE SORCERER

★★★★

DIRECTOR: Ian Sharp

CAST: Michael Praed, Anthony Valentine, Nickolas Grace

Robin Hood, a BBC TV series, is beautifully done with fine acting, costumes, and script. The story in this first episode shows how Robin was chosen by Herne the

Hunter (king of the Drudic gods) to protect the fearful subjects of England. Both inventive and entertaining, this is one for fantasy buffs.

1986 115 minutes

ROBIN HOOD: THE SWORDS OF WAYLAND

★★★★

DIRECTOR: Robert Young
CAST: Michael Praed, Rula Lenska, Nickolas Grace

The second of the *Robin Hood* series from the BBC is as good as the first, if not better. The acting again is first-rate. This adventure pits Robin against the forces of darkness represented by the sorceress Morgwyn of Ravenscar (Rula Lenska). The story twists and turns as the sorceress gathers the seven swords of Wayland, one of which is in Robin's hands. A must-see for fantasy fans.

1986 105 minutes

ROBIN HOOD: HERNE'S SON

★★★

DIRECTOR: Robert Young
CAST: Jason Connery, Oliver Cotton, George Baker, Michael Craig, Nickolas Grace

The third in this series from the BBC begins with the death of Robin of Locksley and the choosing of Robert of Hunnington (Jason Connery) as his successor by Herne the Hunter. The refusal of the new Robin to serve leads to the breakup of the band, followed by the abduction of Maid Marion. The new Robin must then unite his followers and save his love. The result is a most enjoyable fantasy.

1986 101 minutes

ROBOCOP

★★★★½

DIRECTOR: Paul Verhoeven
CAST: Peter Weller, Nancy Allen, Dan O'Herlihy, Ronny Cox, Kurtwood Smith, Miguel Ferrer

RoboCop is the ultimate superhero movie. A stylish and stylized copy thriller set in the far future, it concerns a mortally wounded policeman (Peter Weller) who is melded with a machine to become the ultimate defender of justice, RoboCop. One word of warning: this is an extremely violent motion picture. Dutch director Paul Verhoeven pulls out all the stops for his first English-language production, and the result is a roller-coaster ride of thrills, chills, gasps, and laughs. Rated R for violence, profanity, and brief nudity.

1987 96 minutes

ROCKETSHIP X-M

★★½

DIRECTOR: Kurt Neumann
CAST: Lloyd Bridges, Hugh O'Brian, Noah Beery Jr., Osa Massen, John Emery

A rocket heading for the moon is knocked off course by a meteor storm and is forced to land on Mars. The crewmen find Mars to be very inhospitable, as it has been devastated by atomic war and has mutated creatures inhabiting the planet. While the story is weak and the acting only passable, this is one of the first of the science-fiction films that dominated the 1950s.

1950 B & W 77 minutes

RODAN

★★½

DIRECTOR: Inoshiro Honda
CAST: Kenji Sawara, Yumi Shirakawa, Akihiko Hirato, Ako Kobori

Giant-monster silliness from Japan—a hit in 1957, when special effects were far less sophisticated . . . as were we.

1957 72 minutes

ROLLERBALL

★★★★

DIRECTOR: Norman Jewison
CAST: James Caan, John Houseman, Maud Adams, Ralph Richardson, John Beck

Vastly underappreciated science-fiction film makes a strong statement about the effects of violence on society. The futuristic setting envisions a world controlled by business corporations; with no wars or other aggressive activities, the public gets its release in rollerball, a violent combination of basketball, ice hockey, and roller derby. James Caan is a top rollerball champ who refuses to quit the game in spite of threats from industrialist John Houseman, who perceives that Caan may turn into a public folk hero. The moody, classical soundtrack includes Bach's eerie *Toccata in D minor*. Do not miss. Rated R for violence.

1975 128 minutes

ROLLERBLADE

DIRECTOR: Donald G. Jackson
CAST: Suzanne Solari, Jeff Hutchinson, Shaun Michelle

Imagine a poor ripoff of *Mad Max* meeting *Kansas City Bomber* and *Red Sonja*. Now, remove any and all redeeming qualities and add a religious order whose icon is the classic smiling face. You then have an idea of how bad this movie is. Filmed without sound and then completely overdubbed with stilted dialogue, this film features gratuitous female nudity and such nifty special effects as slow-motion roller-skate chases. This film has the appearance of a weekend filming party among a group of friends—none of whom has any talent. If you enjoy laughing at ineptitude, this may be worth a rental.

1986 88 minutes

RUNAWAY

★★★

DIRECTOR: Michael Crichton
CAST: Tom Selleck, Cynthia Rhodes, Gene Simmons, Kirstie Alley

Tom Selleck (of television's "Magnum, P.I.") is top-billed in this release as a futuristic cop trying to track down a bunch of killer robots controlled by the evil villain (Gene Simmons, from the rock band KISS). It's a cinematic comic book and, although meant to be a thriller, never really gets the viewer involved in the story except for fleeting moments. At best, it's just an enjoyable time-passer. Rated PG for violence and profanity.

1984 99 minutes

SANTA CLAUS CONQUERS THE MARTIANS

DIRECTOR: Nicholas Webster
CAST: John Call, Leonard Hicks

Sounds like a classic, doesn't it? Well, guess again. This film, about a bunch of aliens abducting St. Nick because they don't have one of their own, is actually pretty slow, and not much really happens, though Pia Zadora does show off her acting skills as one of the younger residents of the red planet.

1964 80 minutes

SATURN 3

★★★

DIRECTOR: Stanley Donen
CAST: Kirk Douglas, Farrah Fawcett, Harvey Keitel

Although this space shocker is endowed with a goodly amount of thrills, chills, and surprises, there's very little else to it. The premise is very basic, and the screenplay (by Martin Amis) supplies just the barest embellishments. The story takes place in the distant future on the Eden-like space station Titan, which is located deep beneath the surface of one of Saturn's moons. It is happily inhabited by two chemists (Kirk Douglas and Farrah Fawcett) who are working on developing new forms of food for a starving Earth. Their idyllic existence is thrown into turmoil when a strangely hostile newcomer (Harvey Keitel) arrives from Earth, bringing orders to speed up production. In doing his part toward achieving this goal, creating a superpowered, highly intelligent robot, Keitel unleashes a terror that threatens to destroy them all. Rated R.

1980 88 minutes

7 FACES OF DR. LAO

★★★★

DIRECTOR: George Pal
CAST: Tony Randall, Barbara Eden, Arthur O'Connell

A first-rate fantasy taken from Charles Finney's classic story, "The Circus of Dr. Lao." Tony Randall plays multiple roles as a mysterious Chinese gentleman and his many strange circus side show creatures. Magical doings bring good fortune to a deserving few and work against those with less than pure motives. Fabulous make-up and special effects, surrounded by a heartwarming story. Perfect for all ages, one of the few films to capture the wonder and sinister overtones of a traveling circus.

1964 100 minutes

7TH VOYAGE OF SINBAD, THE

★★★★

DIRECTOR: Nathan Juran
CAST: Kerwin Mathews, Kathryn Grant, Torin Thatcher

Kerwin Mathews is Sinbad in this fantasy. Kathryn Grant (who later married Bing Crosby) plays the beautiful Princess. Sinbad battles an evil magician who has reduced the Princess, who is also Sinbad's fiancée, to six inches in height. Our hero must battle a sword-wielding skeleton, a roc (giant bird), and other dangers to restore his bride-to-be to her normal size. This film contains some of the best stop-motion animation ever created by the master in that craft, Ray Harryhausen. His giant cyclops is fabulous and worth viewing alone.

1958 87 minutes

SHE

★★½

DIRECTOR: G. B. Samuelson
CAST: Betty Blythe, Carlyle Blackwell, Mary Odette

Statuesque vamp Betty Blythe portrays the ageless Queen Ayesha (She) to perfection in this seventh and final silent version of adventure novelist H. Rider Haggard's fantasy about a lost tribe and a flame of eternal life in darkest Africa. Early American matinee idol Carlyle Blackwell plays the explorer who finds her secret queendom. Filmed in London and Berlin. Silent, with background music.

1925 B & W 77 minutes

SHE

(turkey)

DIRECTOR: Avi Nesher
CAST: Sandahl Bergman, Quin Kessler, David Goss, Harrison Muller, Gordon Mitchell, David Brandon

Another one of those films that try to sell the viewer the idea of a woman warrior, a female Conan (*Barbarian Queen*, *Red Sonja*, etc.). All these films end up being are excuses for showing some skin. This one is no exception. Sandahl Bergman (*Conan the Barbarian*, *Red Sonja*) is She, the leader of a postapocalyptic nation that looks upon men as second-class citizens. Nevertheless, She defies her country's wishes by helping a man defeat a gang of mutants. Not rated, but would be an R for violence and nudity.

1983 90 minutes

SHORT CIRCUIT

★★★★

DIRECTOR: John Badham

CAST: Ally Sheedy, Steve Guttenberg, Fisher Stevens, Austin Pendleton, G. W. Bailey

In this enjoyable sci-fi comedy-adventure, a sophisticated robot, Number Five, is zapped by lightning during a storm and comes alive (à la Frankenstein's monster) to the shock of his creator (Steve Guttenberg). Created as the ultimate war weapon, the mechanical man learns the value of life from an animal lover (Ally Sheedy) and sets off on his own—with the military in hot pursuit. The young and the young at heart should delight in this entertaining movie with a gentle message. Rated PG for profanity and violence.

1986 95 minutes

SILENT RUNNING

★★★★

DIRECTOR: Douglas Trumbull

CAST: Bruce Dern, Cliff Potts, Ron Rifkin

True science-fiction is most entertaining when it is not just glittering special effects and is, instead, accompanied by a well-developed plot and worthwhile message. This is such a picture. Bruce Dern is in charge of a futuristic space station that is entrusted with the last living remnants of Earth's botanical heritage. His efforts to preserve those trees and plants in spite of an order to destroy them makes for thoughtful movie-making. Rated G.

1971 89 minutes

SINBAD AND THE EYE OF THE TIGER

★★½

DIRECTOR: Sam Wanamaker

CAST: Patrick Wayne, Jane Seymour, Damian Thomas, Margaret Whiting, Patrick Troughton, Taryn Power

The story, what there is of it, has Sinbad (Patrick Wayne) sailing into a seaport, seeking the hand of Princess Farah (Jane Seymour) and permission from her brother, Prince Kassim (Damian Thomas), to wed. Kassim is next in line for Caliph but has been turned into a baboon by his wicked stepmother, Queen Zenobia (Margaret Whiting). In order to marry his princess, Sinbad must sail to a distant isle to find Melanthius (Patrick Troughton), the only wizard capable of breaking the spell. *Sinbad and the Eye of the Tiger* is not a terrible movie (children will love it), but it just provides more evidence that any film needs a good script and all the movie tricks in the world cannot disguise a bad one. Rated G.

1977 113 minutes

SLAUGHTERHOUSE FIVE

★★★★

DIRECTOR: George Roy Hill

CAST: Michael Sacks, Valerie Perrine, Eugene Roche, John Dehner, Holly Near

This film, based on Kurt Vonnegut's novel, centers around the activities of Billy Pilgrim, who has come unstuck in time. This enables, or forces, him to jump back and forth among different periods in his life and even experience two separate time/space incidents simultaneously. In portraying Billy Pilgrim, Michael Sacks is fascinatingly young and old. His face and physique seem to change with every switch. Even his motivations seem less adult when he is youthful in the wartime portions.

Valerie Perrine, as an often topless starlet, has a body that is pleasant to see, as well as acting talent. Her portions are intended to be humorous, and they do succeed. With so few lines, she manages to add grace to a role that, in other hands, might simply be silly or even revolting. Rated R.

1972 104 minutes

SOLARBABIES

DIRECTOR: Alan Johnson
CAST: Richard Jordan, Jami Gertz, Jason Patric, Charles Durning, Lukas Haas

In the far future, a group of sports teens (who play a hard-top variation of ice hockey on roller skates) join forces with a mystical force (which looks like a dining-room fixture) to wrest control of the world's water source from an evil empire. *Solarbabies* contains not one decent performance or moment of interest. But it should be preserved—as an example of how not to make a movie. Rated PG-13 for violence.

1986 94 minutes

SOMETHING WICKED THIS WAY COMES

★★★

DIRECTOR: Jack Clayton
CAST: Jason Robards Jr., Jonathan Pryce, Pam Grier, Shawn Carson

Ray Bradbury's classic fantasy novel has been fashioned into a good, but not great, movie by the Walt Disney Studios. Jason Robards stars as the town librarian whose task it is to save his family and friends from the evil temptations of Mr. Dark (Jonathan Pryce) and his Pandemonium Carnival. It's an old-fashioned, even gentle, tale of the supernatural; a gothic *Wizard of Oz* that seems likely to be best appreciated by pre-teens. It is just strong enough to be scary, while not so brutal as to cause nightmares. Rated PG for scenes of suspense and slight gore.

1983 94 minutes

SOMEWHERE IN TIME

★★★

DIRECTOR: Jeannot Szwarc
CAST: Christopher Reeve, Jane Seymour, Christopher Plummer, Bill Erwin, Teresa Wright

This gentle, old-fashioned film directed by Jeannot Szwarc (*Jaws 2*) celebrates tender passions with great style and atmosphere. Szwarc takes the time to develop his characters and luxuriate in the moment. Today's desensitized and jaded viewer may have a little trouble adjusting to this movie's simple charms, but it's well worth the effort. The story does have a bit of a twist to it—instead of the lovers having to overcome such mundane obstacles as dissenting parents, terminal illness, or other "great tragedies," in the screenplay by Richard Matheson, they must overcome time itself. Rated PG.

1980 103 minutes

SORCERESS

DIRECTOR: Brian Stuart
CAST: Leigh and Lynette Harris

Even if you like swords, sorcery, demons, and dragons, you probably still won't like this film. Though the story—about twin girls who are bestowed with the power of sorcery and the fighting skills of the masters—is fairly entertaining, it winds up looking something like "Charlie's Angels Return to the Dark Ages." Leigh and Lynette Harris's dumb-blonde characterizations make the film too silly and cheap for most viewers' tastes. Rated R for nudity and simulated sex.

1982 83 minutes

SOYLENT GREEN

★★★

DIRECTOR: Richard Fleischer
CAST: Charlton Heston, Edward G. Robinson, Joseph Cotten, Chuck Connors

In this watchable science-fiction flick, the year is 2022, and New York City is grossly overcrowded with a population of 40 million. Food is so scarce the government creates a product, Soylent Green, for people to eat. Heston plays the policeman who discovers what it's made of. There is some violence. Rated PG.

1973 97 minutes

SPACE RAIDERS

★★★½

DIRECTOR: Howard R. Cohen
CAST: Vince Edwards, David Mendenhall

In this low-budget sci-fi flick from B-movie king Roger Corman, a 10-year-old boy (David Mendenhall) is kidnapped by a group of space pirates led by Vince Edwards (once television's "Ben Casey"), who becomes his mentor. It's an entertaining adventure film which not-too-young-youngsters will enjoy. Rated PG for profanity and violence.

1983 82 minutes

SPACECAMP

★★★

DIRECTOR: Harry Winer
CAST: Kate Capshaw, Lea Thompson, Tom Skerritt, Kelly Preston, Tate Donovan, Leaf Phoenix

Kate Capshaw is a reluctant instructor at the U.S. Space Camp in Alabama. She and her independent charges—four teens and a younger child—board a real space shuttle and are accidentally launched on a perilous journey. With an attractive cast, impressive special effects, and a noble heart, the movie captures an adventurous pioneer spirit that should inspire the astronauts of the future. The cute robot and precocious Leaf Phoenix make this one especially entertaining for kids. Rated PG for suspense.

1986 104 minutes

SPACEHUNTER: ADVENTURES IN THE FORBIDDEN ZONE

DIRECTOR: Lamont Johnson
CAST: Peter Strauss, Molly Ringwald, Ernie Hudson, Andrea Marcovicci, Michael Ironside, Beeson Carroll

The grade-Z science-fiction flick is not dead; it just costs $12 million to make today. The kiddies undoubtedly will love this movie. Adults, however, will find it disappointing. The story is a compendium of cornball clichés and groan-worthy dialogue. Peter Strauss plays a futuristic hero who takes on an army of militant humanoids on a plague-infested planet in order to save a group of marooned women. Molly Ringwald co-stars as a babbling outer-space Valley Girl. Rated PG for violence.

1983 90 minutes

STAR CRASH

★

DIRECTOR: Lewis Coates
CAST: Caroline Munro, Christopher Plummer, Joe Spinell, Marjoe Gortner, David Hasselhoff

A vapid science-fiction space opera with but one redeeming quality: the scanty costumes worn by Caroline Munro as heroine Stella Star. An unbelievable waste of talent, most particularly Christopher Plummer, who seems embarrassed by the whole thing.

Cheap special effects and a cheaper plot. Perfect for those with four-year-old mentalities. Rated PG—some violence.

1979 92 minutes

STAR CRYSTAL

DIRECTOR: Lance Lindsay
CAST: Juston Campbell, Faye Bolt, John W. Smith

In this second-rate *Alien* ripoff, two astronauts encounter a rock containing a monster that feeds on and destroys humans. This one may please die-hard science-fiction fans, but there are much better genre films on video. Rated R for nudity and violence.

1986 93 minutes

STAR TREK: THE MENAGERIE

★★★★

DIRECTOR: Marc Daniels
CAST: William Shatner, Leonard Nimoy, Jeffrey Hunter, Susan Oliver, DeForest Kelley, James Doohan, Nichelle Nichols, George Takei

Yes, we know. This wasn't originally a theatrical or even made-for-TV movie. However, it was, prior to the release of *Star Trek II: The Wrath of Khan*, the best thing the series, created by Gene Roddenberry, ever wrought. We also feel it constitutes a bona fide movie in its video form. Combining the original "Star Trek" pilot, which starred Jeffrey Hunter (*The Searchers*) as the space-adventuring captain, with new footage featuring the show's eventual stars (William Shatner, Leonard Nimoy, DeForest Kelley, etc.), it tells a fascinating story of how Spock (Nimoy) risks his reputation and career to bring comfort to his former commander on a planet capable of fulfilling any fantasy. It's science-fiction entertainment of the first order.

1967 100 minutes

STAR TREK—THE MOTION PICTURE

★★½

DIRECTOR: Robert Wise
CAST: William Shatner, Leonard Nimoy, DeForest Kelley, James Doohan, Nichelle Nichols, George Takei, Walter Koenig

Even though it reunites the cast (William Shatner, Leonard Nimoy, DeForest Kelley, James Doohan, Nichelle Nichols, George Takei, etc.) of the popular television series and was directed by Robert Wise, who made one of the best science-fiction films of all time (*The Day the Earth Stood Still*), this $35 million film is a real hit-and-miss affair. Fans of the series may find much to love, but others will be bewildered—and sometimes bored—by the overemphasis on special effects (especially in the needless protracted opening scenes of the starship *Enterprise*) and the underemphasis on characterization (one of the series's pluses). Rated G.

1979 132 minutes

STAR TREK II: THE WRATH OF KHAN

★★★★

DIRECTOR: Nicholas Meyer
CAST: William Shatner, Leonard Nimoy, DeForest Kelley, Ricardo Montalban, James Doohan, George Takei, Nichelle Nichols, Walter Koenig

James T. Kirk (William Shatner), Mr. Spock (Leonard Nimoy), Doc "Bones" McCoy (DeForest Kelley) and the entire crew of the Starship *Enterprise* once more "boldly go where no man has gone before" in this "Star Trek" adventure. It's no *Gone with the Wind*—or even *Raiders of the Lost Ark*. But it is fun to watch, and Trekkies are sure to love it. Even non-fans will most likely find it enjoyable. As Khan, Ricardo Montalban reprises his supervillain role from the 1967 "Space Seed" episode of the television series. Rated PG for violence and gore.

1982 113 minutes

STAR TREK III: THE SEARCH FOR SPOCK

★★★★½

DIRECTOR: Leonard Nimoy
CAST: Leonard Nimoy, William Shatner, DeForest Kelley, James Doohan, George Takei, Nichelle Nichols, Walter Koenig

In this thrill-packed release, the crew of the U.S.S. *Enterprise* goes looking for their lost shipmate, Spock (Leonard Nimoy), who appeared to give his life to save his friends—at the end of *Star Trek II: The Wrath of Khan*. But is he dead? Finding out may be one of the most entertaining things you ever do in front of a TV set. Rated PG.

1984 105 minutes

STAR TREK IV: THE VOYAGE HOME

★★★★½

DIRECTOR: Leonard Nimoy
CAST: William Shatner, Leonard Nimoy, DeForest Kelley, James Doohan, George Takei, Walter Koenig, Nichelle Nichols, Catharine Hicks

After the leaden heaviness of the previous film, all concerned make a success of this entry in the *Trek* saga, by returning to those elements that made the original TV series so popular: character interaction, deft humor, and time travel. Our stalwart heroes journey back to Earth in their "borrowed" enemy spacecraft just in time to witness a new tragedy in the making: an alien deep-space probe is disrupting our planet's atmosphere by broadcasting a message that nobody understands. When Spock identifies the "language" as that of the humpback whale, extinct in the twenty-third century, Kirk leads his crew back to the twentieth century in an attempt to locate two of the great mammals and utilize them for translation duty. Charming and light-hearted, though rated PG for somewhat intense themes.

1986 119 minutes

STAR TREK (TELEVISION SERIES)

★★★½

DIRECTOR: Marc Daniels, Joseph Pevney, James Goldstone, Gerd Oswald, Vince McEveety
CAST: William Shatner, Leonard Nimoy, Deforest Kelley, George Takei, Walter Koenig, Nichelle Nichols, Majel Barrett, Grace Lee Whitney, James Doohan

These are the voyages of the Starship *Enterprise*. Her original five-year mission was given short shrift by television executives who pulled the plug after a mere three years from late 1966 to mid-1969, and then watched in horror as fans turned it into the single most popular television series ever made. Beginning in 1979, it begat a successful film series, and the end is nowhere in sight. Paramount has reissued the original shows on tapes made from 35-mm masters, and the *Enterprise* and her crew never have looked lovelier. Superior episodes are "The City on the Edge of Forever," scripted by fantasist Harlan Ellison, wherein Captain Kirk (William Shatner), Mr. Spock (Leonard Nimoy), and Dr. McCoy (DeForest Kelley) travel back in time to the Depression-era United States; "The Trouble with Tribbles," which concerns a shipboard "invasion" by little fluff balls with voracious appetites;

"Court Martial," which finds Kirk brought to trial for allegedly killing a crew member; "Shore Leave," scripted by science-fiction writer Theodore Sturgeon, which concerns a wacky planet that causes any person's secret fantasies to be brought to actual life; "A Piece of the Action," which sends the *Enterprise* to a planet that patterned its development on old Earth gangster stories; "Amok Time," also scripted by Sturgeon, which concerns Vulcan mating rituals and Mr. Spock's re turn to his home planet; "Menagerie," a two-parter that incorporates the program's original pilot, "The Cage," initially rejected for being "too cerebral for television;" "Balance of Terror," which introduces the Romulans and concerns what might turn into an interstellar war; "Space Seed," which introduces the evil Khan (Ricardo Montalban) and sets up the events later resolved in the second big-screen film; "Wolf in the Fold," scripted by horror writer Robert Bloch, which postulates that Jack the Ripper was a malevolent force that never died and has now invaded the *Enterprise*; and "Where No Man Has Gone Before," wherein two members of the *Enterprise* crew suddenly acquire incredible mental abilities at the expense of their humanity. Inferior episodes (those to be avoided at all costs) include "The Way to Eden," an embarrassment concerning space-faring hippies; "Spock's Brain," wherein the first officer's brain is kidnapped (!); "And the Children Shall Lead," a ludicrous mess featuring a cameo appearance by attorney Melvin Belli; "Plato's Stepchildren," wherein the *Enterprise* officers are turned into human puppets for the amusement of psychokinetic aliens; and "The Lights of Zetar," wherein Mr. Scott (James Doohan) has an embarrassing affair with a young woman whose mind is taken over by aliens.

1966–1969 50 minutes each

STAR TREK: THE CAGE

★★★★

DIRECTOR: Robert Butler

CAST: Jeffrey Hunter, Leonard Nimoy, Majel Barrett, John Hoyt, Susan Oliver

This is the first pilot episode of the *Star Trek* television series, initially rejected by NBC for being "too cerebral" and "too good for TV." Fortunately, NBC was sufficiently impressed to order a second pilot ("Where No Man Has Gone Before") that earned the series its airdate; that "too cerebral" pilot was later incorporated into a two-parter ("The Menagerie"), which went on to win all sorts of genre awards. Now restored to its original form, this is the only recorded story of Captain Christopher Pike (Jeffrey Hunter) and his quite different *Enterprise* crew. The biggest howl is Leonard Nimoy's early interpretation of Mr. Spock, who emotes all over the place and behaves in a very un-Vulcan-like manner. The plot concerns a planet of aliens who entrap various forms of animal life in their interplanetary "zoo." They decide that Pike would make a good companion for their human female. Unrated; suitable for family viewing.

1964 65 minutes

STAR WARS

★★★★★

DIRECTOR: George Lucas

CAST: Mark Hamill, Harrison Ford, Carrie Fisher, Alec Guinness, Peter Cushing, Anthony Daniels, Kenny Baker

May the Force be with you! Writer-director George Lucas blended the best of vintage pulp science-fiction, old-fashioned cliffhangers, comic books, and classic fantasy to come up with the ultimate adventure "a long time ago in a galaxy far, far away." Rated PG.

1977 121 minutes

STARFLIGHT ONE

★

DIRECTOR: Jerry Jameson
CAST: Lee Majors, Hal Linden, Lauren Hutton, Ray Milland, Gail Strickland, George Di Cenzo, Tess Harper, Terry Kiser, Robert Webber

Airport '82? A new supersonic jet experiences catastrophies, one after the other, and the action becomes split between the heroic people on board and the nervous ground crew looking at the little green bleeps on the radar screen. We get to know many of the characters and their troubled personal lives through a story as old as the Spirit of St. Louis and as effective as a DC-10. All the actors in this all-star line-up phone in their performances in the grand tradition of disaster films.

1982 115 minutes

STARMAN

★★★★

DIRECTOR: John Carpenter
CAST: Jeff Bridges, Karen Allen, Charles Martin Smith, Richard Jaeckel

John Carpenter (*Halloween*; *The Thing*) directed this release, which is more of a romance than a space opera or a science-fiction thriller. Jeff Bridges stars as an alien who falls in love with Earthling, Karen Allen (of *Raiders of the Lost Ark* fame). *Starman* is best described as a fairy tale for adults, but the kiddies undoubtedly will enjoy it, too. Rated PG-13 for suggested sex, violence, and profanity.

1984 115 minutes

STRANGE INVADERS

★★★★

DIRECTOR: Michael Laughlin
CAST: Paul LeMat, Diana Scarwid, Nancy Allen, Louise Fletcher, Michael Lerner, Kenneth Tobey, June Lockhart

A splendid tribute/parody of 1950s science-fiction movies, this film begins in 1958, with buglike aliens taking over a farm town called Centerville, Illinois. The story then jumps to New York City, twenty-five years later, where a college professor (Paul LeMat) is suddenly running off to Illinois after his ex-wife (Diana Scarwid), who has disappeared during a visit to Centerville. She left their daughter with him in New York, but she hasn't returned, and the phone lines in Centerville are dead. *Strange Invaders* is everything you always hoped the sci-fi flicks of the 1950s would be and so often weren't. Rated PG for violence.

1983 94 minutes

STRYKER

★

DIRECTOR: Cirio Santiago
CAST: Steve Sandor, Andria Savio, William Osterander

A low-budget futuristic action thriller à la *Spacehunter* and *Road Warrior*, the story here deals with a soldier of fortune (Steve Sandor) attempting to wrest a group of warrior women from the clutches of an evil tribe. Rated R.

1983 86 minutes

SUPER FUZZ

★★½

DIRECTOR: Sergio Corbucci
CAST: Terence Hill, Ernest Borgnine, Joanne Dru, Marc Lawrence, Julie Gordon, Lee Sandman

For adults, this is a silly, mindless film . . . but it's great fun for the kids. Terence Hill stars as Dave Speed, a police officer with supernatural powers that enable him to walk on water, intuitively sense when and where crimes are being committed, and the like. He and his ornery, befuddled partner (Ernest Borgnine) make an amusing team. Director Sergio Corbucci (*Odds and Evens*) maintains a lively pace. Rated PG apparently because of one scene involving provocatively dressed go-go dancers.

1981 94 minutes

SUPERGIRL

★★½

DIRECTOR: Jeannot Swarc

CAST: Faye Dunaway, Peter O'Toole, Helen Slater, Mia Farrow, Brenda Vaccaro, Simon Ward, Peter Cook, Hart Bochner

Helen Slater makes a respectable film debut as Superman's cousin in this screen comic book, which should delight the kiddies and occasionally tickle the adults. The stellar supporting cast doesn't seem to take it seriously, so why should we? Only the occasional lines of dialogue that border on blasphemy (although meant to be funny) might make this PG-rated release a questionable choice for some viewers, both young and old.

1984 105 minutes

SUPERMAN—THE SERIAL

★★½

DIRECTORS: Spencer Bennett, Thomas Carr

CAST: Kirk Alyn, Noel Neill, Tommy Bond, Carol Forman, Pierre Watkin, George Meeker, Charles King, Charles Quigley, Herbert Rawlinson

The first live-action Superman serial was one of the highest grossing of all chapter plays ever made, as well as Columbia's most prestigious effort in that field. Made for the notoriously tightfisted Sam Katzman, this serial and its sequel, *Atom Man vs. Superman*, followed the adage of all low-budget filmmakers: Make the first three chapters good enough to hook the distributors, and the hell with the rest of it. Wavy-haired serial and B-movie hero Kirk Alyn played the man of steel in both Columbia serials, encountering physical discomfort and embarrassing moments as he manfully strove to bring life to a story that centered around a female crime czar known as the Spider Lady and her plans to rule or ruin Earth through a reducer ray. Superman's origin is fairly faithfully re-created and his weakness to Kryptonite is depicted for the first time on film. But the film relies on inept flying sequences and the by-now classic relationship between Clark Kent and Lois Lane for the bulk of its action.

1948 B & W 15 chapters

SUPERMAN AND THE MOLE MAN

★★

DIRECTOR: Lee Sholem

CAST: George Reeves, Phyllis Coates, Jeff Corey, Walter Reed, J. Farrell MacDonald, Stanley Andrews, Frank Reicher, Byron Foulger

The first feature film starring the Man of Steel is considered a curiosity now, but when originally released it was intended as a means to present a film with the current "watch the skies, they might be friendly" attitude as well as to cash in on the success of the two Superman serials produced in 1948 and 1950. George Reeves here dons the tights and cape that he was to be identified with for the rest of his life. This story concerns a huge oil well that drills too far and yields fuzzy midgets from inside the Earth. (The mole men

—midgets in suits—have some sort of high-tech vacuum-cleaner ray.) This film led to the famous television series and was subsequently shown as a two-part episode.

1951 B & W 67 minutes

SUPERMAN

★★★½

DIRECTOR: Richard Donner

CAST: Christopher Reeve, Margot Kidder, Jackie Cooper, Marc McClure, Marlon Brando, Glenn Ford

After a somewhat overblown introduction, which encompasses the end of Krypton and Clark Kent's adolescence in Smallville, this film takes off to provide some great moments as Superman swings into action. The *Daily Planet* scenes are blessed with fast-paced dialogue and wit, and the action scenes are thrilling. Christopher Reeve is the consummate Superman. The distinction between the personalities of Kent and the Man of Steel are created with laudable believability. Margot Kidder's Lois Lane and Jackie Cooper's Perry White transcend all that has gone before. The action is complemented by fine tongue-in-cheek comedy. Rated PG.

1978 143 minutes

SUPERMAN II

★★★★

DIRECTOR: Richard Lester

CAST: Margot Kidder, Christopher Reeve, Gene Hackman, Ned Beatty, Jackie Cooper

Even better than the original, this terrific adventure of the Man of Steel includes a full-fledged—and beautifully handled—romance between Lois Lane (Margot Kidder) and Superman (Christopher Reeve) and a spectacular battle that pits our hero against three supervillains (during which the city of Metropolis is almost completely destroyed). Rated PG.

1980 127 minutes

SUPERMAN III

★★

DIRECTOR: Richard Lester

CAST: Christopher Reeve, Richard Pryor, Robert Vaughn, Annette O'Toole, Jackie Cooper, Marc McClure, Annie Ross, Pamela Stephenson

If it weren't for Christopher Reeve's excellent performance in the title role, *Superman III* would be a major disappointment. You would think the combination of Superman, Richard Pryor, and director Richard Lester (*A Hard Day's Night* and *The Three Musketeers*) would make for spectacular entertainment. It doesn't. The story features a subdued Pryor as a computer whiz who is hired by bad guy Robert Vaughn to do dastardly deeds with his magic programming. While it isn't awful, *Superman III* is definitely the least of the screen adventures of the Man of Steel. Rated PG.

1983 125 minutes

SUPERMAN IV: THE QUEST FOR PEACE

★½

DIRECTOR: Sidney J. Furie

CAST: Christopher Reeve, Gene Hackman, Margot Kidder, Jackie Cooper, Mariel Hemingway, Jon Cryer, Marc McClure, Sam Wanamaker, Mark Pillow

A well-intentioned plot about Superman (Christopher Reeve) attempting to rid the Earth of nuclear weapons cannot save this overlong, over-wrought, confusing and sometimes downright dull third sequel. Gene Hackman, as the humorously villainous Lex Luthor, tries hard to add some life to the proceedings--as do other series regulars Margot Kidder,

Jackie Cooper, and Marc McClure--but the uninspired direction by Sidney J. Furie and some hasty, last-minute chopping of the movie from two hours to 90 minutes make it unbearable. Worst part: an agonizingly stiff performance by Mariel Hemingway as the spoiled daughter of a sleazy publisher (Sam Wanamaker) out to take over the *Daily Planet*. Rated PG for violence.

1987 90 minutes

SWORD AND THE SORCERER, THE

★★

DIRECTOR: Albert Pyun

CAST: Lee Horsley, Kathleen Beller, Simon MacCorkindale, George Maharis, Richard Lynch, Richard Moll

But for the derring-do and bits of comedy provided by star Lee Horsley, this film would be a complete waste of time and talent. About a soldier of fortune (Horsley, star of television's "Matt Houston") who rescues a damsel in distress (Kathleen Beller) and her brother (Simon MacCorkindale) from an evil king and his powerful wizard, it was directed by Albert Pyun, who apprenticed under the great Japanese filmmaker Akira Kurosawa. Apparently, Pyun was able to pick up Kurosawa's visual sense, but not his gift for story-telling. Rated R because of nudity, violence, gore, and sexual references.

1982 100 minutes

TENTH VICTIM, THE

★★★½

DIRECTOR: Elio Petri

CAST: Marcello Mastroianni, Ursula Andress, Elsa Martinelli, Massimo Serato

A weird little science-fiction film that has achieved minor cult status, thanks to droll performances from Marcello Mastroianni and Ursula Andress and an intriguing plot taken from the novel by Robert Sheckley. The setting is the near future, and pop culture has embraced an assassination game that is played for keeps: ten participants start the hunt against one another, and the sequential elimination of opponents results in one winner. Unlike the paint pellets found in contemporary games, though, the ammo is live... and the losers aren't. Very imaginative; watch for a rather explosive bra. Unrated, contains sexual situations.

1965 92 minutes

TERMINATOR, THE

★★★½

DIRECTOR: James Cameron

CAST: Arnold Schwarzenegger, Linda Hamilton, Michael Biehn

In this science-fiction/time-travel adventure, Arnold Schwarzenegger (*Conan*) stars as a cyborg (part man, part machine) sent from the future to present-day Los Angeles to murder a woman (Linda Hamilton). Her offspring will play an important part in the world from which the killer came. Michael Biehn is the rebel soldier sent to thwart Schwarzenegger's plans. The film starts off like a shot out of a cannon. Fast-paced action fills the screen for the first twenty minutes. After that, it lurches along in fits and starts. Nevertheless, it is essentially an enjoyable, old-fashioned B movie. Rated R for nudity, simulated sex, violence, and profanity.

1984 108 minutes

TESTAMENT

★★★★★

DIRECTOR: Lynne Littman

CAST: Jane Alexander, William Devane, Ross Harris, Roxanna Zal, Lukas Haas, Lila Kedrova, Leon Ames, Mako

In its own quiet, unspectacular way, this film tells a simple story about what happens to one family when World War III begins and ends in a matter of minutes. Jane Alexander is superb as the mother attempting to cope with the unthinkable, and this fine movie is one you won't soon forget. Rated PG.

1983 90 minutes

THEM!

★★★★

DIRECTOR: Gordon Douglas

CAST: Edmund Gwenn, James Arness, James Whitmore, Fess Parker

Classic 1950s sci-fi about colossal mutant ants, at large in a New Mexico desert, threatening to take over the world. Frightening special effects and lightning pace make this a supercharged entertainment, with Edmund Gwenn delivering a standout performance as the scientist who foretells the danger. Great.

1954 B & W 94 minutes

THEY CAME FROM BEYOND SPACE

★★★

DIRECTOR: Freddie Francis

CAST: Robert Hutton, Jennifer Jayne, Zia Mohyeddin, Bernard Kay, Michael Gough

Enjoyable tale of formless aliens landing in Cornwall and taking over the minds and bodies of a group of scientists in an effort to preserve their dissipating race. Robert Hutton plays the one man who can't be controlled due to a metal plate in his skull. Before long, chaos ensues. A fun film, complemented by a beautiful video transfer. Based on *The Gods Hate Kansas* by Joseph Millard.

1967 86 minutes

THIEF OF BAGHDAD, THE

★★★★★

DIRECTORS: Ludwig Berger, Tom Whelan, Michael Powell

CAST: Sabu, John Justin, June Duprez, Rex Ingram

Alexander Korda's 1940 version of *The Thief of Baghdad* is a thing of wonder, the screen embodiment of the charm and imagination of the Arabian Nights. With its flying carpets, giant genies, magic spells, and evil wizards, *Thief of Baghdad* ranks as one of the finest fantasy films of all time. John Justin plays a young king, Ahmad, who is duped by his Grand Vizier, Jaffar, and loses his throne. June Duprez is the beautiful princess for whom he yearns and, of course, Jaffer kidnaps. With the aid of a colossal genie (excellently played by Rex Ingram) and other magical devices, Ahmad must do battle with Jaffar in a rousing fairy tale of good versus evil.

1940 106 minutes

THIEF OF BAGHDAD, THE

★★★½

DIRECTOR: Raoul Walsh

CAST: Douglas Fairbanks Sr., Julanne Johnson, Anna May Wong, Sojin

The first—and second best—of four spectacular versions of this classic Arabian Nights–ish fantasy adventure of derring-do with magically flying carpets, giant genies, and crafty evil sorcery. The now fabled Douglas Fairbanks is the thief, Julanne Johnson the beautiful princess he carries away on an airborne rug. Of all silent epics, this one is rated the most imaginative. Mr. Fairbanks is incredible, every flip proving him the superb athlete his legion of fans made king of Hollywood in the 1920s.

The sets rival everything filmed before and since. Silent.

1924 B & W 140 minutes

THING, THE

★★★★

DIRECTOR: John Carpenter

CAST: Kurt Russell, Wilford Brimley, Richard Dysart

The modern master of fright, John Carpenter (*Halloween*), has created a movie so terrifying, it'll crawl right up your leg. Rather than a remake, this updated version of Howard Hawks's 1951 science-fiction horror classic is closer to a sequel, with Kurt Russell and his crew arriving at the Antarctic encampment after the chameleonlike creature from outer space has finished off its inhabitants. It's good ol' "tell me a scary story" fun. Rated R for profanity and gore.

1982 108 minutes

THING (FROM ANOTHER WORLD), THE

★★★★★

DIRECTOR: Christian Nyby (Howard Hawks)

CAST: Kenneth Tobey, Margaret Sheridan, James Arness

A highly entertaining film, this was based on John W. Campbell's story "Who Goes There?" about a hostile visitor from space at large at an army radar station in the Arctic. Considered by many to be a classic, this relies on the unseen rather than the seen for its power, and as such it is almost unbearably suspenseful. Tight direction, deliberate pacing—not to mention exceptional performances by the entire cast—make this a viewing must. James Arness, in an early role, plays the monster.

1951 B & W 87 minutes

THINGS TO COME

★★★★

DIRECTOR: William Cameron Menzies

CAST: Raymond Massey, Cedric Hardwicke, Ralph Richardson

The world of the future as viewed from the perspective of the 1930s, this is an interesting screen curio based on the book by H. G. Wells. Special effects have come a long way since then, but sci-fi fans will still enjoy the spectacular sets in this honorable, thoughtful production.

1936 B & W 92 minutes

THIS ISLAND EARTH

★★★

DIRECTOR: Joseph M. Newman

CAST: Jeff Morrow, Rex Reason, Faith Domergue

A fine 1950s sci-fi flick about scientists kidnapped by aliens to help them save their planet, this has good make-up and effects for the era.

1955 86 minutes

THRESHOLD

★★

DIRECTOR: Richard Pearce

CAST: Donald Sutherland, John Marley, Jeff Goldblum, Michael Lerner

Donald Sutherland stars in this film about the first artificial-heart transplant. Made before Barney Clark was the first recipient of such an organ, this Canadian film went from science-fiction to real-life drama during the period when it was being prepared for release. Rated PG.

1981 106 minutes

THX 1138

★★★½

DIRECTOR: George Lucas

CAST: Robert Duvall, Donald Pleasence, Maggie McOmie

Science-fiction and movie buffs may want to rent this moody, atmospheric picture, starring Robert Duvall and Donald Pleasence, to see an example of the type of work director George Lucas was doing pre–*Star Wars*. It was the fabulously successful filmmaker's first. Interesting. Rated PG.

1971 88 minutes

TIME AFTER TIME

★★★★

DIRECTOR: Nicholas Meyer
CAST: Malcolm McDowell, David Warner, Mary Steenburgen

Nicholas Meyer, who wrote *The Seven-Per-Cent Solution* and went on to helm *Star Trek II: The Wrath of Khan*, also adapted and directed this 1979 release. In it, H. G. Wells (Malcolm McDowell) pursues Jack the Ripper (David Warner) into modern-day San Francisco via a time machine. Co-starring Mary Steenburgen, it's an enjoyable pastiche that has quite a few nice moments. Rated PG.

1979 112 minutes

TIME BANDITS

★★★★

DIRECTOR: Terry Gilliam
CAST: Sean Connery, Shelley Duvall, Ralph Richardson, Ian Holm, David Warner, John Cleese, Michael Palin

Anyone with a sense of adventure will find a lot to like about this delightful tale of a boy and six dwarves—no, this isn't *Snow White*—who travel back in time via a map that charts a course through holes in the fabric of the universe. Rated PG for violence and adult themes.

1981 110 minutes

TIME MACHINE, THE

★★★★

DIRECTOR: George Pal
CAST: Rod Taylor, Yvette Mimieux, Alan Young, Sebastian Cabot

Science-fiction need not always be thought-provoking to be entertaining; *Star Wars* proves that. *The Time Machine* won an Oscar for its special effects, but it is best remembered for its appealing story. Rod Taylor plays a scientist in the early 1900s who invents a device that can transport him within the dimensions of time. He goes forward past three world wars and into the year 802,701, where he encounters a world very different from the one he left. This movie has all the elements that make up a classic in science-fiction. It's adapted from a novel by H. G. Wells, and it's directed by the king of 1950s and '60s sci-fi, George Pal.

1960 103 minutes

TIME TRAVELERS, THE

★★½

DIRECTOR: Ib Melchior
CAST: Preston Foster, Philip Carey, Merry Anders, Steven Franken, John Hoyt, Joan Woodbury

Imaginative story of scientists who plunge into a time corridor to rescue a colleague and find themselves stuck in the wreckage of the Earth of the future. Similar in many respects to other survival-after-nuclear-holocaust films, this entertaining film boasts vicious mutants, intelligent survivors who live under the surface of Earth, and a trick ending that is unique and intriguing. This is a superior science-fiction movie.

1964 82 minutes

TRANCERS

DIRECTOR: Charles Band
CAST: Tim Thomerson, Helen Hunt, Michael Stefani, Art Le Fleur, Telma Hopkins, Richard Herd, Anne Seymour

Reprehensible ripoff of *Blade Runner* and *The Terminator* with none of the style or suspense of either. Tim Thomerson (*Fade to Black*, *Volunteers*) is Jack Death, a police officer in the 2280s who is sent into the past to bring back a violent cult leader who escaped into the twentieth century to cut off the bloodlines of his twenty-third-century leaders. Rated PG-13 for profanity and lots of violence.

1985 76 minutes

TRANSATLANTIC TUNNEL

★★½

DIRECTOR: Maurice Elvey
CAST: Richard Dix, Leslie Banks, Madge Evans, C. Aubrey Smith, George Arliss, Walter Huston, Helen Vinson

A truly splendid cast still manages to get bogged down a bit in this heavy-handed account of the building of a passageway under the Atlantic Ocean. Besides the fifty-foot radium drill used for digging the tunnel, this competitor to *Things to Come* boasts transatlantic airplane flights, international television broadcasts, and rooftop airports. Despite a screenplay by Curt Siodmak, this British production just didn't manage to pull it together enough to earn the status accorded H. G. Wells' classic. Richard Dix plays the stalwart engineer who can get the job done and Walter Huston plays the president of the United States.

1935 B & W 90 minutes

TRIPODS

★★½

DIRECTORS: Groham Theakston, Christopher Barry
CAST: John Shackley, Jim Baker, Ceri Seel, Roderick Horn, Jeremy Young, Pamela Salem, Charlotte Long, Richard Wordsworth

Though a bit hard to follow because it is a compilation of episodes from the middle of a BBC science-fiction TV series, *Tripods* is an interesting release about a young man's attempts to escape programming by alien conquerors of Earth in the far future. Once free, our hero decides to join the rebel forces and fight to free the Earth.

1984 150 minutes

TROLL

DIRECTOR: John Buechler
CAST: Noah Hathaway, Michael Moriarty, Shelley Hack, Jenny Beck, June Lockhart, Anne Lockhart, Sonny Bono, Brad Hall, Phil Fondacaro

Michael Moriarty, who deserves better, plays the head of a family beseiged by evil little creatures in this horrendous horror film. If your children have been misbehaving lately, make them watch this piece of garbage. They'll be on their best behavior for months afterward for fear you might make them watch it again. But be sure to be out of the room when it's playing. This film, about a troll who lives in a laundry room and attempts to take over the world, is much harder for adults to watch than it is for kids. Rated PG-13 for profanity, violence, and gore.

1986 95 minutes

TRON

★★★

DIRECTOR: Steven Lisberger
CAST: Jeff Bridges, David Warner, Bruce Boxleitner, Cindy Morgan, Barnard Hughes

An enjoyable, if somewhat lightheaded, piece of escapism, this science-fiction adventure concerns a computer genius (Jeff Bridges) who suspects evil doings by a corporate executive (David Warner). During his investigation, Bridges is zapped into another dimension and finds himself a player in a gladiatorial video game. Most of the action takes place inside the system, with dazzling computer-generated special effects dominating the screen. While the story direction and dialogue are weak, *Tron* has enough action and surprises to keep youngsters entertained. Rated PG for computer-simulated violence.

1982 96 minutes

2001: A SPACE ODYSSEY

★★★★★

DIRECTOR: Stanley Kubrick
CAST: Keir Dullea, William Sylvester, Gary Lockwood

There's no denying the visual magnificence of this highly overrated science-fiction epic. Ponderous, ambiguous, and arty, it's nevertheless considered a classic of the genre by many film buffs. The set design, costumes, cinematography, and Oscar-winning special effects combine to create unforgettable imagery. Rated G.

1968 139 minutes

2010

★★★★

DIRECTOR: Peter Hyams
CAST: Roy Scheider, John Lithgow, Helen Mirren, Bob Balaban, Keir Dullea

The exciting sequel to the epic 1968 version of Arthur C. Clarke's *2001: A Space Odyssey*, this stars Roy Scheider, John Lithgow, Helen Mirren, Bob Balaban, and Keir Dullea (reprising the role he played in the original) as participants in a joint American-Russian space mission. We finally find out what really happened to astronaut Dave Bowman (Dullea); the computer, HAL 9000; and the spaceship, *Discovery*, near the planet Jupiter. Rated PG.

1984 116 minutes

TWO WORLDS OF JENNIE LOGAN, THE

DIRECTOR: Frank DeFelitta
CAST: Lindsay Wagner, Marc Singer, Linda Gray, Alan Feinstein, Irene Tedrow, Henry Wilcoxon

A young woman in a troubled marriage finds an old dress in her new house. When she dons this aged garment, she is magically transported one hundred years into the past. There she meets and falls in love with a handsome young man with a horrible destiny she must try to prevent. Made for TV, this standard prime-time soap opera has some moments for romance fans, but the rest of us will be bored by bad acting and lack of suspense.

1979 99 minutes

ULTIMATE WARRIOR, THE

★★½

DIRECTOR: Robert Clouse
CAST: Yul Brynner, Max Von Sydow, Joanna Miles, William Smith, Stephen McHattie

The payoff doesn't match the promise of the premise in this less-than-thrilling science-fiction thriller. In the not-so-distant future, ragged residents of devastated New York City battle vicious gangs. Initially intriguing, the film stumbles to a ludicrous conclusion. Rated R.

1975 94 minutes

UNDERSEA KINGDOM

★★½

DIRECTORS: B. Reeves "Breezy" Eason, Joseph Kane

CAST: Ray "Crash" Corrigan, Lois Wilde, Monte Blue, William Farnum, Lee Van Atta, Smiley Burnette, Lon Chaney Jr., Lane Chandler, Jack Mulhall

"Crash" Corrigan plays himself in this science-fiction serial of the 1930s as he attempts to thwart the evil plans of Sharad and his followers, who live under the ocean in the ancient city of Atlantis. Filled with gadgetry, robots, and futuristic machines, this cliffhanger was extremely popular with young audiences, running second only to Universal's *Flash Gordon*. Familiar faces peer out of practically every frame of this film, and it's still a lot of fun today as the U.S. Navy and its champion, the undefeated Corrigan, take on Sharad and his funny-helmeted henchmen (including a young Lon Chaney Jr.).

1936 B & W 12 chapters

UNKNOWN WORLD

★½

DIRECTOR: Terrel O. Morse

CAST: Victor Killian, Bruce Kellogg, Marilyn Nash, Otto Waldis, George Baxter

Low-budget science-fiction story about an inventor who builds a drill capable of exploring inner Earth seems to borrow from Edgar Rice Burroughs' *Pellucidar* series, but it is actually closer to the nuclear-holocaust films of the postwar period. The purpose of the driving drill is to find a spot inside the Earth that will be safe from radioactive fallout, but when such a place is discovered, it contains risks of its own. Short on thrills, this effort uses extensive footage of Carlsbad Caverns to simulate the interior of our planet.

1950 B & W 74 minutes

VINDICATOR

★½

DIRECTOR: Jean Claude Lord

CAST: Teri Austin, Richard Cox, Pam Grier, Maury Chaykin, Linda Mason-Green, Denis Simpson, Stephen Mendel

A comic-bookish story about a scientist who is blown up by his evil employers and put back together using Cybornetic systems and a nearly indestructible futuristic space suit. Empowered with superhuman strength, he tries to protect his wife from corporate hit men and takes vengeance on those responsible for his predicament. Overall, it's a pretty typical story with some thrills and a fair amount of action and graphic violence. It is not recommended for younger children. Rated R for violence, adult language, and brief nudity.

1984 92 minutes

VOYAGE TO THE BOTTOM OF THE SEA

★★★

DIRECTOR: Irwin Allen

CAST: Walter Pidgeon, Joan Fontaine, Robert Sterling, Barbara Eden, Michael Ansara, Peter Lorre, Frankie Avalon, Henry Daniell

An atomic submarine rushes to save Earth from destruction by a burning radiation belt. Intrigue, adventure, and hokey fun, with a low-level all-star cast. Much better than the subsequent television show. Unrated, the film has mild violence.

1961 105 minutes

WAR OF THE WORLDS, THE

★★★★

DIRECTOR: Byron Haskin
CAST: Gene Barry, Les Tremayne, Ann Robinson

This science-fiction film stars Gene Barry as a scientist who is among the first Earthlings to witness the Martian invasion of Earth. The film is an updated version of H. G. Wells's classic story, with the action heightened by excellent special effects.

1953 85 minutes

WARGAMES

★★★★½

DIRECTOR: John Badham
CAST: Matthew Broderick, Dabney Coleman, Ally Sheedy, John Wood, Barry Corbin

Here's a terrific family movie that will have viewers on the edge of their seats from beginning to end. A young computer whiz (Matthew Broderick, from *Max Dugan Returns*) who thinks he's hooking into a game manufacturer's computer to get the scoop on its latest line accidentally starts World War III when he decides to "play" a selection titled "Global Thermonuclear Warfare." Though the movie contains almost no violence or any other sensationalistic content (apart from a wee bit of vulgar language), it still grips the viewer. This is the way movies should always be made. Rated PG.

1983 114 minutes

WARLORDS OF THE 21ST CENTURY

★★

DIRECTOR: Harley Cockliss
CAST: James Wainwright, Annie McEnroe, Michael Beck

If you've got time on your hands and want to see a movie that doesn't provoke, titillate, or stimulate, then *Warlords* is perfect. Set after the global apocalypse, a cold-blooded killer leads his band of roving outlaws in a siege against a peaceful community, only to face his comeuppance by an equally cold-blooded mystery man. James Wainwright as the villain, Annie McEnroe as the virtuous heroine, and Michael Beck (who achieved notoriety in that terrible musical *Xanadu*) give what they can to a predictable, uninspired script that has all the earmarks of a good old-fashioned shoot-'em-up without the action to back it up. Rated R for violence.

1982 91 minutes

WARRIOR AND THE SORCERESS, THE

[turkey symbol]

DIRECTOR: John Broderick
CAST: David Carradine, Luke Askew, Maria Socas

Why does David Carradine do films like this? In this sword-and-sorcery version of *A Fistful of Dollars*, two warring houses on opposite sides of a well in the middle of a desert both seek to control the well and destroy the other house. Carradine plays a "Dark Warrior" who arrives and pits the houses against each other while getting paid for it. Production values may seem high, and the photography has a certain comic-book flashiness, but poor David Carradine—he just can't make his Clint Eastwood imitation last—not even for eighty-one minutes. Rated R for gore and nudity.

1984 81 minutes

WARRIORS OF THE WIND

★★★★

DIRECTOR: Tokuma Shoten Pub. Co. Ltd.
CAST: Animated

This movie-length Japanese animated feature easily ranks with the best of American animated films. The characters are believable, the action is convincing, and the plot delivers the positive message that not everything good is beautiful and that ugliness, like true beauty, may take more than looking to be seen. Definitely not for the kiddies only.

1984 95 minutes

WATERSHIP DOWN

★★★★

DIRECTOR: Martin Rosen
CAST: Animated

Although it's a full-length cartoon about the adventures of a group of rabbits, you'll find no cutesy, Disney-styled Thumpers à la *Bambi*. The film has its lighter moments—and they are delightful—but the main thrust of the story is danger and courage. About the odyssey that a small group of rabbits undertakes after one of them has a vision of evil things coming to destroy their homes, this bears little resemblance to the melodramatic Disney children-oriented fare. However, their arduous journey is full of surprises and rewards. Rated PG.

1978 92 minutes

WAVELENGTH

★★★★

DIRECTOR: Mike Gray
CAST: Robert Carradine, Cherie Currie, Keenan Wynn

You've seen it all many times before in science-fiction movies of wide-ranging quality: the innocent visitors from outer space, the callous government officials who see them as guinea pigs instead of guests, the handful of compassionate Earthlings, even the race to the mother ship. But rarely has the plot been used so effectively. The film is both touching and exciting. Keenan Wynn gives a particularly affecting performance. Rated PG.

1983 87 minutes

WESTWORLD

★★★★

DIRECTOR: Michael Crichton
CAST: Yul Brynner, Richard Benjamin, James Brolin, Norman Bartold

This is another science-fiction yarn from the author (Michael Crichton) of *The Andromeda Strain*. The film concerns an expensive world for well-to-do vacationers. They can live out their fantasies in the Old West or King Arthur's Court with the aid of programmed robots repaired nightly by scientists so they can be "killed" the next day by tourists. Richard Benjamin and. James Brolin are tourists who come up against a rebellious robot (Yul Brynner). Rated PG.

1973 88 minutes

WHEN WORLDS COLLIDE

★★

DIRECTOR: Rudolph Maté
CAST: Richard Derr, Barbara Rush, Peter Hanson, Larry Keating, John Hoyt

Interesting end-of-the-world sci-fi fable from George Pal has dated badly since its original release in 1951. Final scene of Earth pilgrims landing on the planet and walking into an obvious superimposed painting is laughable today, but many of the other Oscar-winning effects are still quite convincing.

1951 81 minutes

WHERE THE RIVER RUNS BLACK

★★★½

DIRECTOR: Christopher Cain
CAST: Charles Durning, Peter Horton, Ajay Naidu, Conchata Ferrell, Alessandro Rabelo

About a primitive child who is snatched from his home in the

Amazon rain forest and brought into the modern world of corruption and violence, this fantasy unfolds like dream. Sumptuous images, courtesy of Juan Ruiz-Anchia's superb cinematography, fill the screen as its eerie, fanciful, and finally suspenseful tale is told. Director Christopher Cain paces his film in a hypnotic rhythm. The result is sort of a *Black Stallion* for older viewers. Rated PG for violence and suggested sex.

1986 105 minutes

WILD IN THE STREETS

★★

DIRECTOR: Barry Shear

CAST: Christopher Jones, Shelley Winters, Hal Holbrook, Diane Varsi, Ed Begley Jr., Millie Perkins, Richard Pryor, Bert Freed

Ridiculous what-if? film about future America when youth runs the show, the voting age is lowered to 14, and a rock singer involved in drug selling sits as president in the White House. All the old folks are locked up and "cool" becomes the order of the day for hip young America. This dated daydream of the 1960s was considered lame at the time of its release, but has gathered a following over the years. Early appearance by Hal Holbrook and a young Richard Pryor spice up this film, but at best it's just okay. Rated PG.

1968 97 minutes

WIRED TO KILL

★

DIRECTOR: Franky Schaeffer

CAST: Emily Longstreth, Deven Holescher, Merritt Buttrick, Kristina David, Dorothy Patterson, Tom Lister Jr., Frank Collison

The year is 1998, and 120 million Americans are dead from a killer plague. The country has been split into quarantine areas, where the survivors are victimized by violent street gangs of demented, drug-crazed youth. There are far too many plot flaws and inconsistencies in this film to make it believable. For example, our hero is a teen-age electronics whiz, who hopes he'll get his music recorded by the major studios; but industry seems all but defunct. Of course, the boy's dreams of glory fade when punks invade his home, kill his grandmother, maim his mother, and steal his girlfriend. Rated R for violence and raw language.

1986 90 minutes

WITHOUT WARNING

DIRECTOR: Greydon Clark

CAST: Jack Palance, Martin Landau, Cameron Mitchell, Larry Storch, Sue Ane Langdon

A cast of Hollywood veterans battle with an intergalactic alien hunter (a rubber-faced leftover from the "Outer Limits" television series) and his hungry pets in this awful low-budget science-fiction effort. Guess who ends up as lunch. Moreover, who cares? You won't—after the first ten minutes. Rated R.

1980 89 minutes

WIZARD OF MARS, THE

★½

DIRECTOR: David Hewitt

CAST: John Carradine, Vic McGee, Roger Gentry, Jerry Rannow

Low-budget interplanetary version of *The Wizard of Oz* finds a rocketship full of earthlings on the planet Mars where magic and fantasy are the prevalent forces. Written, directed, and produced by David Hewitt, with technical assistance from famed science-fiction-fantasy expert Forrest J. Ackerman, this labor of love is clever, but it doesn't really compare to major science-fiction or fantasy films. If it weren't for the presence of John Carradine, this film might have gone a long time without release, and at that it played in only the smallest houses and remotest drive-ins.

1964 81 minutes

WIZARDS

★★★

DIRECTOR: Ralph Bakshi
CAST: Animated

Director-animator Ralph Bakshi's cost-cutting corners, which had not been that evident in his *Fritz the Cat* films, become a bit too noticeable in this charming little tale of ultimate good versus ultimate evil. Our hero is an aged wizard who relies on magic for his good-deed doing; his evil doppelgänger resorts to the horrors of technology in a battle to wrest control of the universe. The conflict builds well until its climax, which (sadly) negates the premise of the entire battle. Many felt cheated by this one, with good cause. Early storyboard sequences were beautifully rendered by comic-book artist Mike Ploog. Rated PG for occasionally graphic violence.

1977 81 minutes

X (MAN WITH THE X-RAY EYES, THE)

★★★

DIRECTOR: Roger Corman
CAST: Ray Milland, Diana Van Der Vlis, Harold J. Stone, John Hoyt, Don Rickles

Intriguing, offbeat tale of a scientist (Ray Milland) who discovers a drug that gives him the power to see through objects. He has a great time at first, but soon becomes addicted and begins seeing more and more, until . . . This fine production is highly enjoyable, with a surprisingly effective role by comedian Don Rickles as a carnival barker. Not one penny of the low budget is wasted.

1963 80 minutes

YOR: THE HUNTER FROM THE FUTURE

DIRECTOR: Anthony M. Dawson
CAST: Reb Brown, Corinne Clery, John Steiner, Carole Andre, Alan Collins

In the glorious tradition of *Plan 9 from Outer Space* and *Robot Monster* comes *Yor, the Hunter from the Future*, a movie so incredibly awful that it's hilarious. In it, a mighty warrior (Reb Brown) attempts to discover his true identity on a planet trapped in a time warp where the past and the future collide. You'll howl at the pitiful "acting" of beefcake star Reb Brown. You'll guffaw at the unbelievable situations. You'll groan out loud at the insipid dialogue. In other words, it's a real hoot. Rated PG for violence and profanity.

1983 88 minutes

ZARDOZ

DIRECTOR: John Boorman
CAST: Sean Connery, Charlotte Rampling

Sorry sci-fi about a strange society of the future and Sean Connery's attempts to free the people from the evil rulers. Murky plot is hard to follow, and the viewer soon loses interest. Good photography is all but lost on the home screen, leaving nothing but Connery running around in a diaper for two hours. Rated R.

1974 105 minutes

ZONE TROOPERS

★

DIRECTOR: Danny Bilson
CAST: Tim Thomerson, Timothy Van Patten, Art La Fleur, Biff Manard, William Paulson

This is a dumb comic-book tale about an American troop in World War II lost behind German lines. Eventually, soldiers encounter space aliens who have crash-landed in the woods. Rated PG for mild violence.

1985 86 minutes

WESTERNS

ABILENE TOWN
★★★

DIRECTOR: Edwin L. Marin
CAST: Randolph Scott, Ann Dvorak, Rhonda Fleming, Lloyd Bridges, Edgar Buchanan

Cattlemen and homesteaders are at loggerheads in the 1870s in this fast-paced shoot-'em-up. Randolph Scott is the trusty tall man with the star who tries to sort it all out. Edgar Buchanan is sly, as always.

1946 B & W 89 minutes

AGAINST A CROOKED SKY
★★

DIRECTOR: Earl Bellamy
CAST: Richard Boone, Clint Ritchie, Henry Wilcoxon, Stewart Peterson

Nothing new in this familiar tale of a boy searching for his sister, who has been kidnapped by Indians. No more than just another inferior reworking of John Ford's classic western *The Searchers*. For fans who watch anything with a horse and a saddle. Rated PG for violence.

1975 89 minutes

ALAMO, THE
★★★½

DIRECTOR: John Wayne
CAST: John Wayne, Richard Widmark, Frankie Avalon, Richard Boone, Chill Wills, Laurence Harvey

This western, directed by and starring John Wayne, may have seemed overlong when originally released. But today it's the answer to a Duke-deprived fan's dream. Of course, there's the expected mushy flag-waving here and there. However, once Davy Crockett (Wayne), Jim Bowie (Richard Widmark), Will Travis (Laurence Harvey), and their respective followers team up to take on Santa Ana's forces, it's a humdinger of a period war movie.

1960 161 minutes

ALAMO: 13 DAYS TO GLORY, THE
★½

DIRECTOR: Burt Kennedy
CAST: James Arness, Brian Keith, Lorne Greene, Alex Baldwin, Jim Metzler, Gene Evans, Kathleen York

Television movie based on the famous battle of the Alamo during Texas's bid for independence from Mexico. With such a surefire topic, it would seem impossible not to turn out an exciting piece of moviemaking. Sadly, this is not the case. Scenes from John Wayne's superior film *The Alamo* are intercut with the action taking place inside the wall. Brian Keith as Davy Crockett, James Arness as Jim Bowie, and Alex Baldwin as Colonel Travis are all miscast. Director Burt Kennedy, responsible for some of John Wayne's lesser vehicles, fails to bring any excitement or originality to this distinctive bit of American history.

1987 150 minutes

ALLEGHENY UPRISING

★★★

DIRECTOR: William A. Seiter
CAST: John Wayne, Claire Trevor, George Sanders, Moroni Olsen, Chill Wills, Brian Donlevy

John Wayne and Claire Trevor were reteamed the same year of their co-starring triumph in 1939's *Stagecoach* for this potboiler set in the pre-Revolutionary American colonies, but the results were hardly as auspicious. Still, it's a decent time-passer and features Brian Donlevy in one of his better villain roles.

1939 B & W 81 minutes

ALONG CAME JONES

★★★★

DIRECTOR: Stuart Heisler
CAST: Gary Cooper, Loretta Young, Dan Duryea

Highly watchable comic western with Gary Cooper as an innocent cowboy who's mistaken for an infamous outlaw. Both lawmen and the real outlaw (Dan Duryea) pursue him.

1945 B & W 90 minutes

ALONG THE GREAT DIVIDE

★★½

DIRECTOR: Raoul Walsh
CAST: Kirk Douglas, John Agar, Walter Brennan, Virginia Mayo

With his usual determination and grit, lawman Kirk Douglas fights a sandstorm to capture an escaped criminal and return him to justice. The pace is slow, but the scenery is grand.

1951 B & W 88 minutes

ALVAREZ KELLY

★★

DIRECTOR: Edward Dmytryk
CAST: William Holden, Richard Widmark, Janice Rule, Patrick O'Neal, Victoria Shaw

Edward Dymtryk unimaginatively directed this plodding western starring William Holden as a cattle driver supplying beef to the Yankees. He is kidnapped by Confederate officer Richard Widmark, who wants him to steal that much-needed food supply for the South. Dull.

1966 116 minutes

AMERICAN EMPIRE

★★★

DIRECTOR: William McGann
CAST: Richard Dix, Frances Gifford, Preston Foster, Leo Carrillo, Guinn Williams

A formula film featuring the now standard grand opening, dramatic problem-posing center, and slambang breathtaking climax, but a good, entertaining western nonetheless. Friends and Civil War veterans Richard Dix and Preston Foster team to found a cattle empire in Texas. Villain Leo Carrillo makes most of the trouble the pair encounter. Fans of the genre will love it.

1942 B & W 82 minutes

AMERICANO, THE

★★½

DIRECTOR: William Castle
CAST: Glenn Ford, Cesar Romero, Frank Lovejoy, Abbe Lane

Texas cowboy Glenn Ford gets embroiled with a bunch of Brazilian bad guys in this way-south-of-the-border western. A change of scenery is commendable, but a familiar plot makes this film all but pedestrian. As always, however, Frank Lovejoy is refreshing in his wry way.

1954 85 minutes

ANGEL AND THE BADMAN

★★★★

DIRECTOR: James Edward Grant
CAST: John Wayne, Gail Russell, Harry Carey, Irene Rich, Bruce Cabot

A fine low-budget western with John Wayne as a gunman who sees the light through the love of Quaker girl Gail Russell. Harry Carey and Bruce Cabot also are memorable in this thoughtful action film directed by longtime Wayne screenwriter James Edward Grant.

1947 B & W 100 minutes

APACHE

★★

DIRECTOR: Robert Aldrich
CAST: Burt Lancaster, Jean Peters, Charles Bronson (Buchinsky), John Dehner, Monte Blue

Moralistic message western features Burt Lancaster as an idealistic warrior who resents yet understands the encroachment of the whites and refuses to live on government reservations. Lancaster hams it up as the noble savage who eludes his pursuers while imparting bits of wisdom intended to make them (and the audience) feel guilty. Strangely typical of early-to-mid-1950s Hollywood westerns, this entry is long on conscience and short on action. Charles Bronson appears under his original screen name in one of his many ethnic American roles, this time as an Indian, joining the pantheon of immigrants-cum-natives that includes Anthony Caruso and Michael Ansara.

1954 91 minutes

APPALOOSA, THE

★★

DIRECTOR: Sidney J. Furie
CAST: Marlon Brando, John Saxon, Anjanette Comer, Frank Silvera, Alex Montoya

This slight, often boring western follows Marlon Brando's attempts to recover an appaloosa horse stolen by a Mexican bandit. Brando's brooding, method-acting approach to the character only makes things worse in an already slow-moving film.

1966 98 minutes

BAD COMPANY

★★★★

DIRECTOR: Robert Benton
CAST: Jeff Bridges, Barry Brown, Jim Davis, David Huddleston, John Savage, Jerry Houser, Geoffrey Lewis

This is a much underrated Civil War–era western. The cultured Barry Brown and the street-wise Jeff Bridges team up as robbers. Charming performances by the leads and an intriguing, intelligent script by Robert Benton and David Newman make this well worth watching. Benton's vision of the West is a captivating blend of romance and realism. The late Jim Davis (of television's "Dallas") was given one of his rare opportunities to shine on the big screen in this offbeat gem, which was—along with *The Shootist*, *The Outlaw Josey Wales*, and *The Culpepper Cattle Company*—one of the few important westerns made in the 1970s. Rated R.

1972 94 minutes

BAD MAN'S RIVER

★★★

DIRECTOR: Gene Martin

CAST: Lee Van Cleef, Gina Lollobrigida, James Mason

A humorous western about the "dreaded" King gang, which robbed banks along the Texas and Mexican borders. A Mexican revolutionary offers them a million dollars to blow up the arsenal used by the Mexican army, which the gang does, only to find that they have been double-crossed. A fun western in the old tradition.

1959 96 minutes

BADMAN'S TERRITORY

★★★

DIRECTOR: Tim Whelan

CAST: Randolph Scott, Ann Richards, George "Gabby" Hayes, Ray Collins, Chief Thundercloud

Staunch and true marshal combats saddle scum when they flee across the border into territory beyond the government's reach. Good watching.

1946 B & W 97 minutes

BALLAD OF CABLE HOGUE, THE

★★★★½

DIRECTOR: Sam Peckinpah

CAST: Jason Robards, Stella Stevens, Strother Martin, L. Q. Jones, David Warner

Many critics found it quite fashionable to refer continually to Sam Peckinpah's films as excercises in violence and mayhem. There was a tender side to his work, which can be found in *Junior Bonner*, *Ride the High Country*, and *The Ballad of Cable Hogue*. Jason Robards has one of his finest roles as Hogue, a loner who discovers water in the desert and becomes a successful entrepreneur by opening a stagecoach stopover. Peckinpah's deft eye for period detail and outstanding acting by all involved make this one a winner. Rated R.

1970 121 minutes

BALLAD OF GREGORIO CORTEZ, THE

★★★★½

DIRECTOR: Robert M. Young

CAST: Edward James Olmos, James Gammon, Tom Bower, Alan Vint, Timothy Scott, Barry Corbin

This superb independent production tells the powerful story of one man's courage, pain, tragedy, and heartbreak—all of which come as the result of a simple misunderstanding. Edward James Olmos ("Miami Vice") gives a haunting portrayal of the title character, who becomes a fugitive through no fault of his own. Tom Bower and James Gammon lend solid support in this outstanding work solidly directed by Robert M. Young. Rated PG for violence.

1982 99 minutes

BANDOLERO!

★★★

DIRECTOR: Andrew V. McLaglen

CAST: James Stewart, Dean Martin, Raquel Welch, Will Geer, George Kennedy, Andrew Prine

Escape south of the border with outlaw brothers James Stewart and Dean Martin (if you can buy this), who ride just a few furlongs ahead of the law (George Kennedy), taking Raquel Welch along as hostage.

1968 106 minutes

BARBAROSA

★★★★

DIRECTOR: Fred Schepisi

CAST: Willie Nelson, Gary Busey, Isela Vega, Gilbert Roland,

Danny de la Paz, George Voskovec

This action-packed western stars Willie Nelson and Gary Busey as a pair of outcasts on the run. Australian director Fred Schepisi has created an exciting, funny movie that combines the scenic majesty of the great John Ford westerns (*Stagecoach*; *She Wore a Yellow Ribbon*; *The Searchers*; etc.) with the light touch of George Roy Hill's *Butch Cassidy and the Sundance Kid*. As a result, *Barbarosa* is everything devotees of the shoot-'em-up could ask for. If you've got a weakness for sagebrush, saddles, and shootouts, you won't want to miss it. Rated PG for violence.

1982 90 minutes

BELLS OF CORONADO

★★½

DIRECTOR: William Witney

CAST: Roy Rogers, Dale Evans, Pat Brady, Grant Withers, Leo Cleary, Clifton Young, Trigger

Former hero Grant Withers (*Jungle Jim* in the serial of the same name) takes time out from the character roles he played in John Ford films and heads an evil gang of foreign agents out to smuggle uranium to unfriendly powers. Roy Rogers plays a modern-day heroic insurance agent who, with the aid of Dale and Trigger and in spite of bumbling Pat Brady, is able to thwart the heavies and prevent them from flying the precious materials out of the country. Comic-book story is full of fast riding and action that carries it safely through any critical assaults (at least until the whole thing is over and you can catch your breath and say, "What?"). Color adds a lot to these later Rogers films.

1950 67 minutes

BELLS OF ROSARITA

★★½

DIRECTOR: Frank McDonald

CAST: Roy Rogers, Dale Evans, Gabby Hayes, Bob Nolan and the Sons of the Pioneers, Don "Red" Barry, Allan "Rocky" Lane, Sunset Carson, "Wild Bill" Elliott, Bob Livingston

Movie cowboy Roy Rogers enlists the aid of Republic Studios's top western stars in order to save Gabby Hayes and Dale Evans's circus. Chock full of tunes, this decent programmer offers unique behind-the scenes shots of films in production as well as providing the added bonus of six box-office champions for the price of one. All of the guest stars have their own brief action sequences and get to show their stuff as they round up the bad guys. This is a fun B western and a nice introduction to the reel heroes of Saturday afternoons all across America in the 1940s. Cantankerous Gabby Hayes is always a treat to watch.

1945 B & W 54 minutes

BEND OF THE RIVER

★★★★

DIRECTOR: Anthony Mann

CAST: James Stewart, Arthur Kennedy, Rock Hudson, Julia Adams

James Stewart and director Anthony Mann teamed up during the early 1950s to make a series of exceptional westerns that helped the genre return to popularity. This one deals with Stewart leading a wagon train across the country and his dealings with ex-friend Arthur Kennedy, who hijacks their supplies. Superior western fare in every sense.

1952 91 minutes

BETWEEN GOD, THE DEVIL AND A WINCHESTER

DIRECTOR: Dario Silvester
CAST: Richard Harrison, Gilbert Roland, Dominique Boschero

Because of films like this one Spain now rivals Italy in making rotten westerns. A treasure is stolen from a church in Texas and a band of outlaws and a holy man go on the trail to find it. Guaranteed to net only horselaughs thanks to the dubbed dialogue. Not rated, but the equivalent of a PG for violence.

1972 98 minutes

BIG COUNTRY

DIRECTOR: William Wyler
CAST: Gregory Peck, Jean Simmons, Charlton Heston, Carroll Baker, Burl Ives, Charles Bickford

Big-budget western pits Gregory Peck and Charlton Heston as adversaries in an ongoing feud between rival cowmen Burl Ives and Charles Bickford. Basically low-key film presents Jean Simmons as a schoolmarm and Carroll Baker as Bickford's daughter. The two of them provide the love interest and get the boys' blood boiling enough to inspire a knock-down, drag-out fight between Peck and Heston. This would-be epic looks good but lacks the punch and plot of the best and most famous westerns. One of Charlton Heston's higher-grade roles, and one of his better performances. Sprawling and overlong.

1958 163 minutes

BIG JAKE

★★★

DIRECTOR: George Sherman
CAST: John Wayne, Richard Boone, Maureen O'Hara, Patrick Wayne, Chris Mitchum, Bobby Vinton, Bruce Cabot

Big John Wayne takes up the trail of a gang of no-goods who kidnapped his grandson and shot up Maureen O'Hara's homestead and hired hands. Aided by second-generation movie "stars" Patrick Wayne and Chris Mitchum (Robert Mitchum's son), the Duke pursues Richard Boone and his henchmen to their hideout and deals harshly with them when they continue to exclaim, "I heard you were dead." Boone gives the Duke a strong and believable foe. One wishes there had been more scenes with Wayne and Maureen O'Hara together in this film, their last together.

1971 110 minutes

BIG SHOW, THE

DIRECTOR: Mack V. Wright
CAST: Gene Autry, Smiley Burnette, Kay Hughes, Sally Payne, William Newell, Max Terhune

Big-budget Gene Autry series film benefits from location shooting and the musical talent that appears on the show, including young Leonard Slye (soon to be known as Roy Rogers), with the Sons of the Pioneers. Autry plays a double role as a spoiled movie cowboy and the look-alike stunt man who steps into his boots when the star has a tantrum. Even Smiley Burnette's hamming can't sabotage this enjoyable western, and the music's a definite plus.

1936 B & W 70 minutes

BIG SKY, THE

★★

DIRECTOR: Howard Hawks
CAST: Kirk Douglas, Arthur Hunnicutt, Dewey Martin

Even the normally reliable director Howard Hawks can't enliven this average tale of early-day fur trappers on an expedition up the Missouri River. Action was

Hawks's forte, and there just isn't enough to sustain the viewer's interest. Plenty of beautiful scenery, but that's about it.

1952 B & W 122 minutes

BIG SOMBRERO, THE

★★½

DIRECTOR: Frank McDonald

CAST: Gene Autry, Elena Verdugo, Stephen Dunne, George J. Lewis, Vera Marshe, William Edmunds, Martin Garralaga, Gene Roth, Bob Cason

An impoverished Gene Autry comes to the aid of Elena Verdugo and saves her from land swindlers as well as a money-grubbing fiancé in this south-of-the-border tale. Filmed in Cinecolor with a largely Mexican cast, this is more of a musical than a horse opera and takes full advantage of the color process to inflict one garish production number after another on what must have been a grumbling adolescent audience in the late 1940s.

1949 77 minutes

BILLY THE KID RETURNS

★★½

DIRECTOR: Joseph Kane

CAST: Roy Rogers, Smiley Burnette, Lynne Roberts, Morgan Wallace, Fred Kohler, Trigger

Groomed to take over as Gene Autry's replacement in Republic's singing cowboy series, Roy Rogers made such an impact in his first starring role *Under Western Skies* that the studio decided to continue him in a series of his own. In this, his second featured lead, Rogers plays a look-alike to the dead Billy the Kid and restores the tranquillity of Lincoln County after subduing the criminal element.

1938 B & W 58 minutes

BITE THE BULLET

★★★★½

DIRECTOR: Richard Brooks

CAST: Gene Hackman, James Coburn, Candice Bergen, Ben Johnson, Jan-Michael Vincent, Dabney Coleman, Ian Bannen

A six-hundred-mile horse race is the subject of this magnificent adventure, an epic in every sense of the word. Made during Gene Hackman's busiest—and best—period, this intriguing character study allows equal understanding of the many contestants. The photography, by Harry Stradling Jr., is nothing short of magnificent. Particularly spectacular is a seamless shot when one horse passes another: the faltering animal moves only in slow motion, but the approaching horse thunders up at regular speed . . . then passes in slow motion . . . then roars off at full speed. A real sleeper, hardly noticed during its theatrical release. Rated PG.

1975 131 minutes

BLOOD ON THE MOON

★★★½

DIRECTOR: Robert Wise

CAST: Robert Mitchum, Barbara Bel Geddes, Robert Preston

Robert Mitchum is in top form in this western concerning cattle ranchers trying to terminate homesteaders on rangeland. This atmospheric film has much to offer.

1948 B & W 88 minutes

BLOODY TRAIL

🦃

DIRECTOR: Richard Robinson

CAST: Paul Harper, Rance Howard, John Mitchum, Ricki Richardson, Hagen Smith, Eve York

One of the worst movies you are likely to ever see—if you dare.

This western has no plot, just an ex–Union soldier wandering through the recently defeated South meeting up with angry African tribesmen(?), stubborn Confederates, and women who are ready to show off some skin. The fillmmakers must have been deaf; you can clearly hear a bulldozer in the background of one scene. Rated R for sex, nudity, profanity, and violence.

1972 91 minutes

BLUE CANADIAN ROCKIES

★½

DIRECTOR: George Archainbaud

CAST: Gene Autry, Pat Buttram, Gail Davis, Carolina Cotton, Ross Ford, Tom London, John Merton, Don Beddoe, Gene Roth, Cass County Boys, David Garcia

Processed stock footage of Canada forms the backdrop for this weak story about a young girl's strong-willed ambitions and her father's efforts to save her and her dreams from tragedy. Gene Autry and his pal Pat Buttram help both parties and expose the inevitable villains, as well as helping preserve a wild-game preserve. Spunky Gail Davis (TV's Annie Oakley) brightens this one up.

1952 B & W 58 minutes

BLUE STEEL

★★★

DIRECTOR: Robert N. Bradbury

CAST: John Wayne, Eleanor Hunt, George "Gabby" Hayes, Ed Peil, Yakima Canutt, George Cleveland

Fun but undistinguished B western with a very young John Wayne as a cowpoke who saves a town from extinction when he reveals a secret known only to an outlaw gang: there's gold in them thar hills.

1934 B & W 60 minutes

BOLD CABALLERO, THE

★★½

DIRECTOR: Wells Root

CAST: Robert Livingston, Heather Angel, Sig Rumann, Robert Warwick, Charles Stevens, Slim Whitaker

This little-known color film is the first sound Zorro movie and an early effort from Republic Studios, better known for their action-filled serials. Robert Livingston plays the masked avenger who sweeps tyranny out of his part of California, while clearing himself from a murder charge. An oddity in many ways, this movie was one of a handful of films produced by Burroughs/Tarzan Enterprises, a short-lived film venture set up by Edgar Rice Burroughs to film accurate versions of his books and other stories he admired, among them Johnston McCulley's *The Curse of Capistrano*, the original Zorro story.

1936 69 minutes

BONANZA (TELEVISION SERIES)

★★★

DIRECTORS: Edward Ludwig, William F. Claxton, Robert Gordon, Don McDougal

CAST: Lorne Greene, Pernell Roberts, Dan Blocker, Michael Landon, Victor Sen Yung

This western series dominated the Sunday-night ratings for over a decade. It's the story of patriarch Ben Cartwright (Lorne Greene) and his three sons, all from different mothers. Adam (Pernell Roberts) is suave and mature. Hoss (Dan Blocker) is a big man with a bigger heart. Little Joe (Michael Landon) is earnest and hot-tempered. Together they make the Ponderosa the most prosperous ranch in the Comstock Lode country. Week after week, the Cartwrights, noble gents that they were, used their position, their money, their fists, and their guns to help those in distress. Frequently, they'd take time out for romance. Volume I includes the pilot episode, "A Rose for Lotta," as well as "The Underdog," guest-starring Charles Bronson. Volume II features James Coburn in "The Dark Gate" and DeForest Kelley in "Honor of Cochise."

1959–1973 120 minutes

BOOTS AND SADDLES

★★

DIRECTOR: Joseph Kane
CAST: Gene Autry, Smiley Burnette, Ray Hould, Judith Allen, Guy Usher, John Ward, Gordon (William) Elliott, Chris-Pin Martin, Frankie Marvin, Bud Osborne

An English tenderfoot learns his lessons in the "code of the West" from no-nonsense Gene Autry and his not-so-subtle sidekick Smiley Burnette in this standard story of a foreigner who inherits a working ranch. No real suprises in this one, but a good cast of character actors (including the future "Wild Bill" Elliott) make this worth watching. Gene provides the tunes, and Smiley is responsible for the intentional humor in this film.

1937 B & W 59 minutes

BORDER PHANTOM

★★½

DIRECTOR: S. Roy Luby
CAST: Bob Steele, Harley Wood, Don Barclay, Karl Hackett, Miki Morita, Perry Murdock

Most film buffs will know Bob Steele for his memorable performances as the jealous husband in the original *Of Mice and Men* and as Canino, the brutal killer, in Howard Hawk's *The Big Sleep*. But "Battling Bob," as he was known to juvenile audiences of the 1930s and '40s, was most prolific as a fast-draw star of numerous B westerns. Although *Border Phantom*, like all B westerns, looks pretty creaky today, it's entertaining, thanks to Steele's energetic performance and an intriguing premise, which involves mysterious murders and slavery.

1937 B & W 59 minutes

BORROWED TROUBLE

★★

DIRECTOR: George Archainbaud
CAST: William Boyd, Andy Clyde, Rand Brooks, Elaine Riley, John Kellogg, Helen Chapman, John Parrish, Cliff Clark, Herbert Rawlinson, Don Haggerty

Hopalong Cassidy and his pals get bogged down in this comedy-drama about a town gone to seed and the outspoken (and obnoxious) school-teacher who wants to run the bad element out and restore her idea of a real community. Cutesy at times and light on the action, this one is perked up occasionally by the dialogue.

1948 B & W 58 minutes

BREAKHEART PASS

★★★

DIRECTOR: Tom Gries
CAST: Charles Bronson, Ben Johnson, Ed Lauter, Richard Crenna, Charles Durning, Jill Ireland, John Mitchum

Charles Bronson is a government agent on the trail of gun runners in the Old West. Most of the action of this modest western takes place aboard a train, so the excited pitch needed to fully sustain viewers' interest is never reached. Rated PG—some violence, rough language.

1976 95 minutes

BRONCO BILLY

★★★

DIRECTOR: Clint Eastwood

CAST: Clint Eastwood, Sondra Locke, Geoffrey Lewis, Scatman Crothers, Sam Bottoms, Bill McKinney, Dan Vadis

This warm-hearted character study centers around Clint Eastwood as the owner of a run-down Wild West show. Bronco Billy is an anachronism, a throwback to the values of the Old West. The crew (well played by Scatman Crothers, Sam Bottoms, Bill McKinney, and Dan Vadis) is loyal even though payday rarely comes. In the story, Antoinette Lily (Sondra Locke) is deserted on her honeymoon by her husband (Geoffrey Lewis). Desperate, Lily agrees to join the show as Billy's assistant until they reach the next town and she can phone for help, and that's when the lightweight tale takes a romantic turn. Rated PG.

1980 119 minutes

BUCK AND THE PREACHER

★★½

DIRECTOR: Sidney Poitier

CAST: Sidney Poitier, Harry Belafonte, Ruby Dee, Cameron Mitchell

Harry Belafonte and director Sidney Poitier play two escaped slaves heading west. On the way, they meet up with "bad guy" Cameron Mitchell and lovely Ruby Dee. So-so western. Rated PG.

1972 102 minutes

BUCKSKIN FRONTIER

★★★

DIRECTOR: Lesley Selander

CAST: Richard Dix, Jane Wyatt, Lee J. Cobb, Albert Dekker, Joe Sawyer, Victor Jory, Lola Lane

Railroad representative Richard Dix and freight line owner Lee J. Cobb fight over business and a crucial mountain pass in this big-budget, fast-action western. As usual, veteran heavies Joe Sawyer and Victor Jory make trouble.

1943 B & W 82 minutes

BUFFALO BILL AND THE INDIANS

★★★

DIRECTOR: Robert Altman

CAST: Paul Newman, Joel Grey, Kevin McCarthy, Burt Lancaster, Harvey Keitel, Geraldine Chaplin, Will Sampson

In this offbeat western, Paul Newman, Burt Lancaster, Harvey Keitel, Geraldine Chaplin, Joel Grey, Kevin McCarthy, and Will Sampson are fascinating as they interact like jazz musicians jamming on the theme of distorted history and the delusion of celebrity. The last fifteen minutes seem almost unnecessary, and some of the points are hammered home with a twenty-pound sledge, but the overall effect of this American period piece is that of ambling virtuosity and group dedication to the theme. Rated PG.

1976 120 minutes

BULLDOG COURAGE

★★½

DIRECTOR: Sam Newfield

CAST: Tim McCoy, Joan Woodbury, Paul Fix, Eddie Buzzard, John Cowell, Karl Hackett, John Elliott, Eddie Cobb

Tim McCoy is excellent in the dual role of father and son in this slow-paced series western. When Slim Braddock (McCoy) is killed, it's up to his son, Tim (McCoy), to avenge his death after a period of several years. In a bit of miscalculation, McCoy repeats word for word a comedy bit delivered earlier in the story by Paul Fix as a dynamiter named Bailey. It's fun to watch McCoy do it, but boring to hear the dialogue repeated.

This was one of McCoy's last starring films.

1935 B & W 66 minutes

BULLWHIP

★★½

DIRECTOR: Harmon Jones

CAST: Rhonda Fleming, Guy Madison, James Griffith, Don Beddoe

In this agreeable movie, Guy Madison avoids the hangin' tree by agreeing to marry a fiery half-breed (Rhonda Fleming). If the plot sounds familiar, it should. Jack Nicholson used a similar one in *Goin' South*.

1958 80 minutes

BUTCH CASSIDY AND THE SUNDANCE KID

★★★★½

DIRECTOR: George Roy Hill

CAST: Paul Newman, Robert Redford, Katharine Ross

George Roy Hill directed this gentle western spoof featuring personal-best performances by Paul Newman, Robert Redford, and Katharine Ross. A spectacular box-office success, and deservedly so, the release deftly combines action with comedy. Rated PG.

1969 112 minutes

BUTCH AND SUNDANCE: THE EARLY DAYS

★★

DIRECTOR: Richard Lester

CAST: William Katt, Tom Berenger, Brian Dennehy, John Schuck, Jeff Corey

Director Richard Lester has made better films (see *A Hard Day's Night* and *Superman II*), and because his usual film is a comedy, this outing is especially disappointing. Nearly all of the jokes fall flat despite a screenplay that hints at the original film with Paul Newman and Robert Redford. There are some action scenes that could have fit in with the original, but for the most part *Butch and Sundance: The Early Days* is a pale companion to the classic that inspired it. Rated PG for some mildly crude language and (very little) violence.

1979 111 minutes

CAHILL—US MARSHAL

★★½

DIRECTOR: Andrew V. McLaglen

CAST: John Wayne, George Kennedy, Gary Grimes, Neville Brand

John Wayne was still making B westerns in the 1970s—to the disappointment of those who (rightly) expected better. Although still enjoyable, this film about a lawman (Wayne) whose son (Gary Grimes) becomes a bank robber is routine at best. Still, the performances by the Duke and George Kennedy (as the chief baddie) do bring pleasure. Rated PG.

1973 103 minutes

CALAMITY JANE

★★★★

DIRECTOR: James Goldstone

CAST: Jane Alexander, Frederic Forrest, David Hemmings, Ken Kercheval, Talia Balsam

Director James Goldstone provides more than just the story of Annie Oakley, which is fascinating in itself as a tale of one of America's first feminists. His unglamorous production and straightforward storytelling give a true feeling of the Old West. Jane Alexander, in an Emmy-nominated performance, shows the many sides of this spirited lady. A made-for-TV movie.

1984 100 minutes

CALIFORNIA GOLD RUSH

★

DIRECTOR: Jack B. Hively
CAST: Robert Hays, John Dehner, Ken Curtis, Henry Jones, Don Haggerty

The writer Bret Harte (Robert Hays) is in the right place at the right time to chronicle the Gold Rush days of California from Sutter's Fort. Harte tells the story of the discovery, the people who came to find the gold, and the greed, violence, and corruption that came with them. Rated PG.

1985 100 minutes

CALL OF THE CANYON

★★

DIRECTOR: Joseph Santley
CAST: Gene Autry, Smiley Burnette, Sons of the Pioneers, Ruth Terry, Thurston Hall, Marc Lawrence, Joseph Strauch Jr., Eddy Waller, Budd Buster

Confusing story about meat swindling (meat swindling?) puts Gene and his Radio Ranch right in the middle of a cattle stampede and local beef thieves as the boys try to help songstress Ruth Terry put her act across the airwaves from Mr. Autry's personal frontier. The Sons of the Pioneers provide some of the sounds, and hammy Thurston Hall and menacing Marc Lawrence perk things up.

1942 B & W 71 minutes

CAPTAIN APACHE

★½

DIRECTOR: Alexander Singer
CAST: Lee Van Cleef, Stuart Whitman, Carroll Baker, Percy Herbert

Muddled western has Lee Van Cleef in title role gunning down dozens of one-dimensional characters who cross his path or appear likely to. Clichés and stock situations and characters inhabit this low-level entry. Violent, gruesome in spots. Rated PG for violence.

1971 94 minutes

CAT BALLOU

★★★

DIRECTOR: Elliot Silverstein
CAST: Jane Fonda, Lee Marvin, Michael Callan, Jay C. Flippen

In this offbeat, uneven but fun comedy/western, Jane Fonda plays Cat, a former schoolteacher out to avenge her father's death. Michael Callan is her main romantic interest. Lee Marvin outshines all with his Oscar-winning performance in the dual roles of the drunken hired gun and his evil look-alike.

1965 96 minutes

CATTLE QUEEN OF MONTANA

★★

DIRECTOR: Allan Dwan
CAST: Barbara Stanwyck, Ronald Reagan, Gene Evans, Jack Elam

Barbara Stanwyck gives a strong performance in this otherwise routine western. Plot revolves around Stanwyck trying to protect her farm from land grabbers, who also murdered her father. Meanwhile, the Indians are out to wipe out everybody. Ronald Reagan is typically lackluster. For Stanwyck fans only.

1954 88 minutes

CHEYENNE AUTUMN

★★★½

DIRECTOR: John Ford
CAST: Richard Widmark, Karl Malden, Carroll Baker, James Stewart, Edward G. Robinson, Ricardo Montalban

John Ford strays away from his traditional glorification of western mythology to bring this story of the mistreatment of the American Indian. His standard heroes, the

U.S. cavalry, are placed in the role of the villains as they try to stop a group of desperate Cheyenne Indians from migrating back to their Wyoming homeland from a barren reservation in Oklahoma. The Indians take on heroic proportions as they face numerous obstacles to their exodus. This movie is uniformly well acted, and as with any John Ford western, the scenery is breathtaking.

1964 160 minutes

CHINO

DIRECTOR: John Sturges
CAST: Charles Bronson, Jill Ireland, Vincent Van Patten

A surprisingly low-key Charles Bronson western about a horse breeder who attempts to live a peaceful life. The film was trimmed of much of its violence, and all that's left is an above-average performance by Bronson and an adequate one by his wife, Jill Ireland, as Chino's love interest. Rated PG.

1973 98 minutes

CHISUM

★★★½

DIRECTOR: Andrew V. McLaglen
CAST: John Wayne, Forrest Tucker, Christopher George, Ben Johnson, Patric Knowles, Bruce Cabot, Glenn Corbett, Geoffrey Duel

The best of the John Wayne westerns directed by Andrew V. McLaglen, this sprawling epic centers around the revenge sought by Billy the Kid (Geoffrey Duel) after his mentor (Patric Knowles) is murdered by the corrupt, land-grabbing bad guys. Forrest Tucker, Bruce Cabot, Ben Johnson, Christopher George, and Glenn Corbett are also seen in nice character bits. Everyone is in top form. Rated G.

1970 111 minutes

CIRCUS WORLD

★

DIRECTOR: Henry Hathaway
CAST: John Wayne, Rita Hayworth, Claudia Cardinale, John Smith, Lloyd Nolan, Richard Conte

Even the presence of John Wayne can't help this sappy soap opera set under the big top. It's a Cinerama extravaganza that does not survive the transfer to videotape (less than a third of the three-screen picture remains). But that's okay—the story is dreadful.

1964 135 minutes

COLORADO

★★

DIRECTOR: Joseph Kane
CAST: Roy Rogers, George "Gabby" Hayes, Pauline Moore, Milburn Stone, Hal Taliaferro, Maude Eberene, Vester Pegg, Fred Burns, Jay Novello

Roy Rogers and "Gabby" Hayes settle comfortably into what became a profitable and highly successful series in this routine shoot-'em-up about the two riders who aid the embattled homesteaders and clean up the territory for decent folk. Not too imaginative, but enjoyable.

1940 B & W 54 minutes

COMANCHEROS, THE

★★★★

DIRECTOR: Michael Curtiz
CAST: John Wayne, Stuart Whitman, Lee Marvin, Ina Balin, Bruce Cabot, Nehemiah Persoff

Big John Wayne is the laconic Texas Ranger assigned to bring in dandy gambler Stuart Whitman for murder. Along the way,

Wayne bests bad guy Lee Marvin, and Whitman proves himself a hero by helping the big guy take on the ruthless gun- and liquor-running villains of the title, led by Nehemiah Persoff. Director Michael Curtiz (*Casablanca*) died during production, and Wayne completed the film. It's a fine western with lots of nice moments.

1961 107 minutes

COMES A HORSEMAN

★★★★

DIRECTOR: Alan J. Pakula

CAST: Jane Fonda, James Caan, Jason Robards Jr., George Grizzard, Richard Farnsworth, Jim Davis

Dark, somber, but haunting western set in the 1940s about the efforts of a would-be land baron (Jason Robards Jr.) to cheat his long-suffering neighbor (Jane Fonda) out of her land. She fights back with the help of a World War II veteran (James Caan) and a crusty old-timer (Richard Farnsworth, in the role that netted him a best-supporting-actor Oscar nomination after thirty years as a bit player and stunt man in the movies). When Robards and Fonda are facing each other down, *Comes a Horseman* is more of a psychological western. However, Caan's two-fisted cowhand adds some terrific moments of action, and Farnsworth—in a sort of updated Gabby Hayes part—adds some wry humor and heart. Rated PG for violence.

1978 118 minutes

COW TOWN

★★½

DIRECTOR: John English

CAST: Gene Autry, Gail Davis, Harry Shannon, Jock Mahoney, Harry Harvey, Steve Darrell, Sandy Sanders, Ralph Sanford, Bud Osborne, Ted Mapes

Later Gene Autry film about rustlers and range wars lacks Smiley Burnette but boasts Jock Mahoney (future Range Rider and Tarzan) as well as TV's Annie Oakley, Gail Davis. Action and stunts as well as a good crew of familiar faces make this, Gene's seventy-second film as himself, better than many of his earlier efforts. Grazing rights, stampedes, gunplay, and a song or two (or three) are packed into the film.

1950 B & W 70 minutes

COWBOYS, THE

★★★★½

DIRECTOR: Mark Rydell

CAST: John Wayne, Roscoe Lee Browne, Bruce Dern, Colleen Dewhurst, Slim Pickens

Along with Don Siegel's *The Shootist*, this is the best of John Wayne's latter-day westerns. The Duke plays a rancher whose wranglers get gold fever. He's forced to recruit a bunch of green kids in order to take his cattle to market. Bruce Dern is on hand as Longhair, the outlaw leader who fights our hero in one of the genre's most memorable (and violent) scenes. After the sequence was shot, Wayne remarked to Dern that he was going to be hated by most Americans for his on-screen actions. "Yeah," said Dern, "but they'll love me in Berkeley." A classic. Rated PG.

1972 128 minutes

CROSSFIRE

DIRECTORS: Robert Conrad, Alfredo Zacarias

CAST: Robert Conrad, Jan-Michael Vincent, Manuel Lopez Ochoa, Roy Jenson

Insufferable western about three outlaws who are saved from execution by a gang of Mexican freedom fighters. The fugitives end up banding together with the rebels to fight the Spanish in the Mexican Revolution. Robert Conrad puts in a good performance. But as a director, he's better off selling flashlight batteries.

1986 82 minutes

CULPEPPER CATTLE CO., THE

★★★★

DIRECTOR: Dick Richards
CAST: Gary Grimes, Billy "Green" Bush, Luke Askew, Bo Hopkins, Geoffrey Lewis, Wayne Sutherlin, Royal Dano, John McLiam, Matt Clark, Anthony James, Jerry Gatlin, Gregory Sierra, Raymond Guth, Charles Martin Smith

A strong supporting cast of character actors makes this coming-of-age story set in the Old West into a real treat for fans of shoot-'em-ups. Gary Grimes is a 16-year-old farm boy who dreams of becoming a cowboy, something which the cowboys cannot quite understand. "Cowboying is something you do when you can't do nothin' else," he is told. But this doesn't stop him from signing on as the "Little Mary" (cook's helper) on an arduous cattle drive. Billy "Green" Bush is terrific as the tough-minded trail boss Culpepper. Luke Askew has the best role of his career as the soft-spoken gunman who befriends the young hero. And Geoffrey Lewis nearly steals the whole movie as a near-psychotic outlaw with a deadly obsession for his pearl-handled guns. A sort of *Red River* meets *The Wild Bunch*, this generally underrated western is being released uncut on video, a complete form in which it hasn't been seen since its release to theaters over a decade ago. Bravo! Rated R for violence.

1972 92 minutes

DAKOTA

★★½

DIRECTOR: Joseph Kane
CAST: John Wayne, Vera Hruba Ralston, Walter Brennan, Ward Bond

Any western with John Wayne, Walter Brennan, and Ward Bond has to be a winner, right? Wrong. This substandard film may be interesting to see for their performances, but you also have to put up with the incredibly untalented Vera Ralston (she was the wife of Republic Studio head Herbert Yates). It's almost worth it.

1945 B & W 82 minutes

DAKOTA INCIDENT

★★½

DIRECTOR: Lewis R. Foster
CAST: Dale Robertson, Linda Darnell, John Lund

It's a fight to the finish in this fairly good western as the Indians attack a stagecoach rolling through Dakota Territory in those thrilling days of yesteryear.

1956 88 minutes

DANGEROUS VENTURE

★★½

DIRECTOR: George Archainbaud
CAST: William Boyd, Andy Clyde, Rand Brooks, Fritz Leiber, Douglas Evans, Harry Cording, Betty Alexander, Francis McDonald, Patricia Tate, Ken Tobey

This better-than-average Hopalong Cassidy adventure finds our heroes searching for Aztec ruins in the Southwest and encountering hostile renegades and unscrupulous fortune hunters. Character greats Fritz Leiber, Harry Cording, and Richard Alexander (all veterans of serials and horror films) contribute to the quality of this film, and future monster fighter Kenneth Tobey (*The Thing*) makes an early appearance, as well. This movie was originally released in a fifty-nine-minute version.

1947 B & W 55 minutes

DANIEL BOONE

★★★

DIRECTOR: David Howard

CAST: George O'Brien, Heather Angel, John Carradine, Ralph Forbes, Clarence Muse, Harry Cording

Action-packed story of the early American frontier features rugged outdoor star George O'Brien in the title role and evil John Carradine as a renegade who aids the marauding Indians, a role similar to the one he reprised for John Ford in *Drums Along the Mohawk*. Not as well-known as contemporaneous frontier films like *Last of the Mohicans*, *Allegheny Uprising*, and *Northwest Passage*, this rousing film is great schoolboy adventure stuff. The movies mentioned here are a unique grouping of films about the history of America before the Revolutionary War, and among them have provided the bulk of the action footage used in subsequent movies with the same theme.

1936 B & W 77 minutes

DARK COMMAND

★★★★½

DIRECTOR: Raoul Walsh

CAST: John Wayne, Claire Trevor, Walter Pidgeon, Roy Rogers, Gabby Hayes

Raoul Walsh, who directed John Wayne's first big western, *The Big Trail*, was reunited with the star after the latter's triumph in *Stagecoach* for this dynamic shoot-'em-up. Walter Pidgeon is Quantrill, a once-honest man who goes renegade and forms Quantrill's Raiders. It's up to the Duke, with help from his *Stagecoach* co-star Claire Trevor, Roy Rogers, and Gabby Hayes, to set things right.

1940 B & W 94 minutes

DAWN ON THE GREAT DIVIDE

★★★

DIRECTOR: Howard Bretherton

CAST: Buck Jones, Raymond Hatton, Rex Bell, Mona Barrie, Harry Woods, Robert Frazer, Robert Lowery, Christine MacIntyre, Betty Blythe, Tristram Coffin, Jan Wiley, Dennis Moore, Roy Barcroft, Silver

When Tim McCoy bid his final "So Long, Rough Riders" in 1942's *West of the Law*, it brought an end to the famous series. However, producer Scott Dunlap still had Buck Jones and Raymond Hatton under contract, so he reteamed them with former B-western series star Rex Bell in *Dawn on the Great Divide* that same year. With a bigger budget than usual and a story with more plot twists than the average B western, the result was a good shoot-'em'-up in the series vein. Jones, of course, dominates as the two-fisted leader of a wagon train who takes on Indians, bad guys, and corrupt officials with equal aplomb. (Bell, unfortunately, is not so lucky. In fact, one suspects that he made enemies of the director and producer, who use takes that show him stumbling over lines and missing the holster with his gun.) Nevertheless, this is an enjoyable film and an important one historically. It was the last movie made by Jones, who died heroically trying to save lives during a fire at Boston's Coconut Grove on November 28, 1942.

1942 B & W 63 minutes

DAWN RIDER

★★

DIRECTOR: Robert N. Bradbury

CAST: John Wayne, Marion Burns, Yakima Canutt, Reed

Howes, Denny Meadows, Bert Dillard

John Wayne is out for revenge in this formula B western with no budget to speak of. His loving father is killed during a robbery, and it's up to a gangly, slightly stilted Wayne to get the bad guys.

1935 B & W 56 minutes

DEAD DON'T DREAM, THE

★★

DIRECTOR: George Archainbaud
CAST: William Boyd, Andy Clyde, Rand Brooks, John Parrish, Leonard Penn, Mary Tucker, Francis McDonald, Richard Alexander, Stanley Andrews, Don Haggerty

Hopalong Cassidy's partner Lucky finally decides to tie the knot, but his wedding plans are dashed when his fiancée's father is murdered before the ceremony. When Hoppy tries to get to the bottom of this mystery, he comes under suspicion and has to clear his own name as well as uncover the killers. Skulking desperadoes and mysterious goings on in an old mine add to the tension in this later entry in the Hopalong Cassidy series. Originally released at sixty-two minutes.

1948 B & W 55 minutes

DEADLY COMPANIONS, THE

★★½

DIRECTOR: Sam Peckinpah
CAST: Brian Keith, Maureen O'Hara, Chill Wills, Steve Cochran

When gunfighter Brian Keith accidentally kills the son of dance-hall hostess (Maureen O'Hara), he attempts to make amends by escorting her through hostile Indian territory. A less than grade-A western made notable because it was director Sam Peckinpah's first feature. Peckinpah fared much better the following year with *Ride the High Country.*

1961 90 minutes

DEATH RIDES A HORSE

(turkey)

DIRECTOR: Giulio Petroni
CAST: Lee Van Cleef, John Phillip Law, Mario Brega, Anthony Dawson, Luigi Pistilli

Needlessly tedious "spaghetti" western about a young boy who witnesses the butchery of his family and then grows up to be John Phillip Law so he can take his revenge. He and Lee Van Cleef spend most of the film saving and running from each other, all in the interests of those ludicrous gunfighters' codes. Wonderful dialogue, all badly dubbed: "This certainly is a surprise," says one victim as Van Cleef shows up. "Was it a good surprise," says the other, "or a bad surprise?" The picture's length results from weighty exchanges like that, triple takes, and pauses so pregnant they could give birth. Even Ennio Morricone's score is below par. Rated PG for violence.

1969 114 minutes

DEERSLAYER, THE

★★½

DIRECTOR: Dick Friedenberg
CAST: Steve Forrest, John Anderson, Ned Romero, Joan Prather, Betty Ann Carr

Made-for-T.V. movie, based on James Fenimore Cooper's classic, *The Deerslayer* is a film of adventure in early America. The heroes, Hawkeye (Steve Forrest) and Chingachgook (Ned Romero), attempt to save a Mohican princess and avenge the death of Chingachgook's son.

1978 98 minutes

DESERT TRAIL

★★

DIRECTOR: Robert N. Bradbury
CAST: John Wayne, Mary Kornman, Paul Fix, Edward Chandler, Lafe McKee, Henry Hull, Al Ferguson

Rodeo fans might like this standard B western about a big-time bronc rider (John Wayne) who fights on the side of justice, but others may want to ride in the opposite direction.

1935 B & W 54 minutes

DESPERATE WOMEN

DIRECTOR: Earl Bellamy
CAST: Dan Haggerty, Susan Saint James, Ronee Blakley, Ann Dusenberry, Susan Myers, Randy Powell

Three convicted women crossing a desert on their way to prison meet up with an ol' softy (Dan Haggerty) who takes them under his wing after the convicts' guards die of water poisoning. The comedy in this film is too sickly sweet to laugh over—the singing narrator should be strung up—and the action isn't fast enough to engage the John Wayne in us all. This film has no MPAA rating, and the little violence displayed would hardly be shocking to youngsters. Not a rotten film, but you might forget you even saw it when you're rewinding the thing.

1978 98 minutes

DESTRY RIDES AGAIN

★★★★

DIRECTOR: George Marshall
CAST: James Stewart, Marlene Dietrich, Brian Donlevy, Misha Auer, Una Merkel

Destry's plot may seem a trifle clichéd, but it is the classic western that copycats imitate. The story of a mild-mannered citizen who finds himself grudgingly forced to stand up against the bad guys may seem familiar, especially with Jimmy Stewart in the lead. But this is the original. It was also Stewart's first try at a genre that was to prove so important in his career. In this film, he's the deputy sheriff of the frontier town of Bottleneck. The baddies are headquartered in the local saloon, whose seductive chanteuse (Marlene Dietrich) is caught between her attraction for the deputy and her revulsion for his job. Dietrich's softened performance is a far cry from her standard icy vamps and is one of the joys of her long career.

1939 B & W 95 minutes

DEVIL'S PLAYGROUND

DIRECTOR: George Archainbaud
CAST: William Boyd, Andy Clyde, Rand Brooks, Elaine Riley, Robert Elliot, Joseph J. Greene, Francis McDonald, Ned Young, Earle Hodgins, John George

This so-so entry in the long-running Hopalong Cassidy series was the first to be produced by star William Boyd for his own company. Basically a mystery with supernatural overtones, the plot concerns crooked politicians, rumors of gold, and a forbidding, rugged area that holds the secrets to strange goings on in the adjoining valley. Rand Brooks as Lucky Jenkins joins saddle pals Hoppy and California for the first time in this film.

1946 B & W 65 minutes

DJANGO

DIRECTOR: Sergio Corbucci
CAST: Franco Nero, Loredana Nusciak

This spaghetti western lacks convincing performances. A border town is about to explode, and the stranger, Django (Franco Nero), lights the fuse. The battle of guns and wits between the stranger and the leaders of two rival gangs is a rousing end to a poor but action-filled movie.

1965 90 minutes

DODGE CITY

★★★★

DIRECTOR: Michael Curtiz

CAST: Errol Flynn, Olivia De Havilland, Ann Sheridan, Bruce Cabot, Alan Hale, Ward Bond

Swashbuckler Errol Flynn sets aside his sword for a pair of six-guns to clean up the wild, untamed frontier city of the title. The best of Flynn's westerns, this release is beautifully photographed in color with an all-star supporting cast.

1939 105 minutes

DON Q, SON OF ZORRO

★★★½

DIRECTOR: Donald Crisp

CAST: Douglas Fairbanks Sr., Mary Astor, Jack McDonald, Donald Crisp, Stell DeLantei, Warner Oland, Jean Hersholt, Albert MacQuarrie, Lottie Pickford

Derring-do in old California as the inimitable Douglas Fairbanks fights evildoers and greedy oppressors while saving ladylove Mary Astor from a fate worse than death. Oscar-winning actor Donald Crisp directed this adventure, and, as usual, Douglas Fairbanks painstakingly created stunts and action sequences guaranteed to keep audiences on the edge of their seats. Well-mounted, inventive, and fast-paced, this is one of a highly successful series of historical adventure films that earned Fairbanks his well-deserved reputation as the king of swashbuckling movies and the most athletic of all major stars. Silent.

1925 B & W 111 minutes

DONNER PASS: THE ROAD TO SURVIVAL

★★

DIRECTOR: James L. Conway

CAST: Robert Fuller, Diane McBain, Andrew Prine, John Anderson, Michael Callan

This fair retelling of the true story of the Donner party is based on historical accounts and tells of the snowstorm that traps the party and the physical hardship and starvation that lead to the infamous conclusion.

1978 98 minutes

DOWN DAKOTA WAY

★★½

DIRECTOR: William Witney

CAST: Roy Rogers, Dale Evans, Pat Brady, Monte Montana, Elizabeth Risdon, Roy Barcroft, Trigger

Roy Rogers takes a harder line with the bad guys in this film, tracking down the no-goods responsible for the death of his friend, a veterinarian who could finger the man responsible for flooding the market with diseased meat. Director William Witney rises above the confines of the ordinary Roy Rogers singing western and almost elevates it to the status of the "adult" westerns gaining popularity at that time. Dale is as perky as ever, and Pat Brady is the comic relief, which every studio felt was essential for audience acceptance.

1949 67 minutes

DOWN MEXICO WAY

★★

DIRECTOR: Joseph Santley

CAST: Gene Autry, Smiley Burnette, Fay McKenzie, Harold Huber, Sidney Blackmer,

Duncan Renaldo, Joe Sawyer, Paul Fix

Bland Gene Autry and his oafish sidekick Smiley Burnette head south and find themselves embroiled in trouble when they come up against a gang of thieves. An impressive cast of familiar character actors from movies and early television make this otherwise routine programmer worthy of note—any one of the supporting members of this cast had more charisma than former yodeling telegrapher Autry, one of the most unwarranted box-office champions of all time.

1941 B & W 78 minutes

DRAW

★★½

DIRECTOR: Steven Hillard Stern
CAST: James Coburn, Kirk Douglas

This western should have been cause for celebration among the starving fans of the genre; unfortunately, such is not the case. Kirk Douglas and James Coburn play outlaw and lawman respectively. Both appear on a collision course for a gunfight but, alas, what we are treated to is a trick ending. Lots of missed chances in this one. Made for HBO cable television.

1984 98 minutes

DRUM BEAT

★★½

DIRECTOR: Delmer Daves
CAST: Alan Ladd, Audrey Dalton, Marisa Pavan, Robert Keith, Anthony Caruso, Warner Anderson, Elisha Cook Jr., Charles Bronson, Richard Gaines

Indian fighter Alan Ladd is detailed to ensure peace with marauding Modocs on the California-Oregon border in 1869. His chief adversary, in beads and buckskins, is Charles Bronson. Modoc maiden Marisa Pavan loves the hero, but the code dictates he settle for Audrey Dalton. As usual, white man speaks with forked tongue, but everything ends well.

1954 111 minutes

DUCHESS AND THE DIRTWATER FOX, THE

★

DIRECTOR: Melvin Frank
CAST: George Segal, Goldie Hawn, Conrad Janis, Thayer David

This western/comedy romp never clicks. George Segal and Goldie Hawn labor so hard to get a laugh it's almost painful to watch. There isn't much of a story behind them, just a frontier hooker and a saddle tramp trying to make a buck in the Old West. It gets tedious real fast. Rated PG.

1976 103 minutes

DUEL IN THE SUN

★★★

DIRECTOR: King Vidor
CAST: Jennifer Jones, Gregory Peck, Joseph Cotten, Lionel Barrymore, Walter Huston, Lillian Gish, Harry Carey, Tilly Losch

This sprawling, brawling western has land baron Lionel Barrymore's sons, unbroken, short-fused Gregory Peck and solid-citizen Joseph Cotten, vying for the hand of hot-blooded, half-breed Jennifer Jones. Peck and Jones take a lusty love-hate relationship to the max in the steaming desert. A near epic with a great musical score. Orson Welles narrates the panoramic opening in Red Rock country.

1946 130 minutes

EL DORADO

★★★★½

DIRECTOR: Howard Hawks
CAST: John Wayne, Robert Mitchum, James Caan, Arthur Hunnicutt, Edward Asner,

Michele Carey, Christopher George, Charlene Holt, Jim Davis, Paul Fix, R. G. Armstrong, Johnny Crawford

The poster for this 1967 release proclaimed it to be, "The big one with the big two!" And so it is. While some may argue that it is just a rehash of director Howard Hawks's *Rio Bravo*, western-movie buffs know it to be one of the best-acted and best-directed of all the screen's shoot-'em-ups. Few stars could match John Wayne's ability to dominate a scene—and one of those few, Robert Mitchum, co-stars in this tale of a land war between bad, bad Edward Asner and family man R. G. Armstrong. Mitchum plays the drunk and Wayne is the gunfighter with whom he forms an uneasy alliance. Arthur Hunnicutt is the grizzled old-timer, and James Caan is the knife-throwing youth. It's basically an upscale B western with some of the best scenes ever to be found in a cowboy movie.

1967 126 minutes

ELFEGO BACA: SIX GUN LAW

★★½

DIRECTOR: Christian Nyby

CAST: Robert Loggia, James Dunn, Lynn Bari, James Drury, Jay C. Flippen, Kenneth Tobey, Annette Funicello, Patric Knowles, Audrey Dalton

Two-fisted lawyer Elfego Baca is charismatically portrayed by top actor Robert Loggia in this compilation of episodes from "Walt Disney Presents" originally aired from 1958 to 1962. Defending justice in Tombstone, Arizona, Elfego Baca fights for the lives of an Englishman framed for murder and a rancher charged with bank robbery. Wiry Robert Loggia later achieved minor cult status with his television show "T.H.E. CAT" and has been seen more recently in popular and critical successes *Jagged Edge*, *An Officer and a Gentleman*, and *Prizzi's Honor*.

1962 77 minutes

FALSE COLORS

★★½

DIRECTOR: George Archainbaud

CAST: William Boyd, Andy Clyde, Jimmy Rogers, Tom Seidel, Claudia Drake, Douglas Dumbrille, Robert Mitchum, Glenn Strange, Roy Barcroft, Tom London

Typical entry in the Hopalong Cassidy series places Hoppy on the side of the innocent people who are being terrorized and murdered by ace heavy Douglas Dumbrille, who wants their property and water rights. Supported by a fine cast of character actors, including a young Robert Mitchum and future Frankenstein Glenn Strange, this film introduced Jimmy Rogers (son of the great Will Rogers) as Hoppy's hot-tempered young sidekick. Rogers was to appear in six films with William Boyd and Andy Clyde before being replaced by Rand Brooks. Look for veteran western actors Roy Barcroft and Tom London in supporting roles.

1943 B & W 65 minutes

FALSE PARADISE

★★

DIRECTOR: George Archainbaud

CAST: William Boyd, Andy Clyde, Rand Brooks, Joel Friedkin, Elaine Riley, Kenneth MacDonald, Don Haggerty, Cliff Clark, Richard Alexander

Straight-shooting Hopalong Cassidy comes to the aid of a girl in peril and finds himself inveigled in yet another situation involving crooked ranch owners and false mining claims. Sometimes it's oil, sometimes it's gold, this time it's silver that drives the local riffraff into a frenzy and gives Hoppy,

California, and Lucky a chance to do their good deed for the week. Second-to-last film in the long-running series and the last in which William Boyd wore his traditional black outfit.

1948 B & W 59 minutes

FAR COUNTRY, THE

★★★½

DIRECTOR: Anthony Mann

CAST: James Stewart, Ruth Roman, Walter Brennan, Corinne Calvet, John McIntire, Jay C. Flippen, Steve Brodie, Harry Morgan, John Doucette, Royal Dano, Jack Elam, Robert J. Wilke

James Stewart is a tough-minded cattleman intent on establishing himself in Alaska during the Klondike gold rush of 1896. Taking a herd from Oregon to the beef-starved region, he plans to care for just himself and sidekick Walter Brennan. However, he cannot escape his commitment to the community of man. He learns this while taking on female business rival Ruth Roman, a self-appointed, Judge Roy Bean–style lawman (John McIntire), and the elements in the rugged high country. Borden Chase penned this semisequel to his *Red River*, with Stewart playing a variation on Montgomery Clift's character from that 1948 release and Brennan repeating his crusty old-timer. The result is fine western fare.

1955 97 minutes

FARGO EXPRESS

★★

DIRECTOR: Alan James

CAST: Ken Maynard, Helen Mack, Paul Fix, Roy Stewart, William Desmond, Jack Rockwell

When Helen Mack's brother (Paul Fix) is accused of a crime he didn't commit, Ken Maynard attempts to clear his name by impersonating him at another robbery. Strange plot, dumb western. Maynard gets plenty of opportunities to show off his riding skills, but even his fans will be scratching their heads over the illogical story.

1933 B & W 61 minutes

FIGHTING CARAVANS

★★★½

DIRECTORS: Otto Brower, David Burton

CAST: Gary Cooper, Lily Damita, Ernest Torrence, Eugene Pallette, Charles Winninger, Tully Marshall, Frank Campeau

Despite the title, this is a Zane Grey western—and a good one, full of intrigue, action, and, for leavening, a smattering of comedy. Lanky, taciturn Gary Cooper, wanted by the law, avoids arrest by conning a wagon train girl to pose as his wife. Romance blooms as the train treks west, into the sights of hostile Indians. Circle the wagons!

1931 B & W 80 minutes

FIGHTING KENTUCKIAN, THE

★★★

DIRECTOR: George Waggner

CAST: John Wayne, Vera Hruba Ralston, Philip Dorn, Oliver Hardy, Mark Windsor

Worth seeing if only for the rare and wonderful on-screen combination of John Wayne and Oliver Hardy, this period adventure casts the duo as frontiersmen who come to the aid of the homesteading Napoleonic French, in danger of being tricked out of their lands by the bad guys. If only Vera Hruba Ralston weren't the Duke's love interest, this could have been a real winner.

1949 B & W 100 minutes

FISTFUL OF DOLLARS, A

★★★

DIRECTOR: Sergio Leone
CAST: Clint Eastwood, Mario Brega, Gian Maria Volonté

Clint Eastwood parlayed his multi-year stint on television's "Rawhide" into international fame with this film, a slick remake of Akira Kurosawa's *Yojimbo*. *Fistful* started the genre of spaghetti westerns. What most people don't realize is that both films are adaptations of Dashiell Hammett's *Red Harvest*. As in the book and samurai film, Eastwood's laconic "man with no name" blows into a town nearly blown apart by two feuding families; after considerable manipulation by all concerned, he moves on down the road. Poor dubbing doesn't hurt much, since ol' Clint doesn't have that many lines. Superlative soundtrack by Ennio Morricone adds greatly to the story tension.

1964 96 minutes

FISTFUL OF DYNAMITE, A

★★★

DIRECTOR: Sergio Leone
CAST: Rod Steiger, James Coburn, Maria Monti, Romolo Valli

After his success with Clint Eastwood's Man with No Name westerns, Italian director Sergio Leone made this sprawling, excessive film set during the Mexican Revolution. A thief, played by Rod Steiger, is drawn into the revolution by Irish mercenary James Coburn. Soon both are blowing up everything in sight and singlehandedly winning the war. As in all of Leone's films there are endless close-ups of the characters' eyes. The action, once it gets going, is big and loud. Cut down from the 158-minute version known as *Duck You Sucker*. Rated PG.

1972 121 minutes

FLAMING FRONTIER

★★

DIRECTORS: Ray Taylor, Alan James
CAST: Johnny Mack Brown, Eleanor Hansen, Ralph Bowman, Charles Middleton, James Blaine, Charles Stevens, John Rutherford, Chief Thundercloud

Former football favorite Johnny Mack Brown rides into a long career as a western star in this fifteen-episode Universal serial. He plays Tex Houston, famous Indian scout. During the course of this Saturday matinee thriller Tex rescues Mary Grant several times, saves her brother and his gold mine, fights Indians and unscrupulous white men, and raises clouds of dust as he gallops from one hair-raising adventure to another without mussing his hair. Pretty standard western serial, full of familiar faces such as Charles "Ming the Merciless" Middleton and Chief Thundercloud, "Tonto" to the Lone Ranger in the serials.

1938 B & W 15 chapters

FLAMING STAR

★★★★

DIRECTOR: Don Siegel
CAST: Elvis Presley, Barbara Eden, Steve Forrest, Dolores Del Rio, John McIntire

A solid western directed by Don Siegel (*Dirty Harry*), this features Elvis Presley in a remarkably effective performance as a half-breed Indian who must choose sides when his mother's people go on the warpath.

1960 101 minutes

FOR A FEW DOLLARS MORE

★★½

DIRECTOR: Sergio Leone
CAST: Clint Eastwood, Lee Van Cleef, Gian Maria Volonte, Klaus Kinski, Mario Brega, Jose Egger

Plot-heavy and overlong sequel to *A Fistful of Dollars* finds Clint Eastwood's "man with no name" partnered with shifty Lee Van Cleef, with both in pursuit of badder guy Gian Maria Volonte. Sergio Leone's quick-cut back-and-forth direction began to seem pretentious this time around (an approach that proved more successful in the next entry, *The Good the Bad and the Ugly*). Ennio Morricone's superb soundtrack is, if anything, better than ever. Eastwood has his hands full, but the story contains few surprises. Fans will enjoy this, but everybody else will find it tedious.

1965 130 minutes

FORBIDDEN TRAIL

★★★½

DIRECTOR: Lambert Hillyer

CAST: Buck Jones, Barbara Weeks, Mary Carr, George Cooper, Frank Rice, Al Smith, Frank LaRue

In this superior series western, one of several Buck Jones made for Columbia Pictures in the 1930s, the star and Al Smith play a couple of happy-go-luckly cowboys who find themselves in the middle of a range war. Jones, usually the stalwart, square-jawed defender of justice, takes a comedic approach to his part, and the results are quite pleasing. Frank Rice, who was one of Jones's best saddle pals, has a plum role as the town sheriff.

1932 B & W 71 minutes

FORT APACHE

★★★★½

DIRECTOR: John Ford

CAST: John Wayne, Henry Fonda, Shirley Temple, Ward Bond, John Agar, George O'Brien

The first entry in director John Ford's celebrated cavalry trilogy (which also includes *She Wore a Yellow Ribbon* and *Rio Grande*), this western stars Henry Fonda as a post commandant who decides to make a name for himself by starting a war with the Apaches, against the advice of an experienced soldier (John Wayne). Great film.

1948 B & W 127 minutes

FOUR RODE OUT

DIRECTOR: John Peyser

CAST: Pernell Roberts, Sue Lyon, Julian Mateos, Leslie Nielsen, Maria Martin, Leonard Bell

Pernell Roberts plays a U.S. marshall in pursuit of a Mexican bank robber. Accompanied by the bandit's girlfriend and a slimy and unlikable Pinkerton agent (Leslie Nielsen), Roberts and company set out across the desert toward Mexico, perhaps never to return. This film is bad with a capital *B*. No one turns in an even half-way decent performance, and to make matters worse, we have to listen to Janis Ian singing horrible folk songs every fifteen minutes. You may want to ride out rather than watch this waste of film.

1968 90 minutes

FRISCO KID, THE

★★★

DIRECTOR: Robert Aldrich

CAST: Gene Wilder, Harrison Ford, William Smith, Raymond Bieri, Penny Peyser

Gene Wilder and Harrison Ford make a surprisingly effective and funny team as a rabbi and outlaw, respectively, making their way to San Francisco. Originally started by director Dick Richards (*The Culpepper Cattle Company*), this release was completed by Robert Aldrich and features fine support by William Smith and Ramon Bieri as a couple of nasty outlaws. Good fun. Rated PG.

1979 122 minutes

FRONTIER PONY EXPRESS

★★½

DIRECTOR: Joseph Kane
CAST: Roy Rogers, Mary Hart (Lynne Roberts), Raymond Hatton, Edward Keane, Monte Blue, Noble Johnson, George (Letz) Montgomery, Charles King, Bud Osborne, Fred Burns, Ernie Adams, Jack O'Shea, Jack Kirk

Good action-packed western finds Roy Rogers (in one of his early starring roles) coming to the aid of Pony Express riders who have been preyed on by robbers. Grizzled Raymond Hatton plays the ornery old varmint, and former and future cowboy stars Monte Blue, Charles King, and George Montgomery help raise the dust and trample the cactus.

1939 B & W 54 minutes

FRONTIERSMAN, THE

★★

DIRECTOR: Lesley Selander
CAST: William Boyd, George "Gabby" Hayes, Russell Hayden, Evelyn Venable, Roy Barcroft, William Duncan

Hopalong Cassidy (William Boyd) and his pals (George "Gabby" Hayes and Russell Hayden) take a break from upholding the law to help a schoolteacher (Evelyn Venable) educate a passel of young 'uns. The boys attending the school are played by the St. Brendans Boys' Choir, and there are, as a result, a number of forgettable musical numbers. Hoppy does end up going after a band of rustlers (led by venerable character actor Roy Barcroft), thus adding some welcome moments of action to an otherwise lethargic outing.

1938 B & W 58 minutes

GENTLE SAVAGE

★★★½

DIRECTOR: Sean MacGregor
CAST: William Smith, Gene Evans, Barbara Luna, Joe Flynn

In this well-paced western William Smith portrays an American Indian framed for the rape and beating of a white girl in a small town. The girl's stepfather, who actually committed the crime, incites the townsmen to go after the innocent man. When the townsmen kill the hapless fellow's brother, the American Indian community retaliates. Rated R for violence.

1978 85 minutes

GIT ALONG, LITTLE DOGIES

★★

DIRECTOR: Joseph Kane
CAST: Gene Autry, Smiley Burnette, Judith Allen, Weldon Heyburn, William Farnum, Willie Fung, Carleton Young, Will Ahearn, Gladys Ahearn, Frankie Marvin, Maple City Four, The Cabin Kids, Lynton Brent, Monte Montague

Typical of Gene Autry's prewar films, this thin story of a spoiled, willful girl who is eventually tamed and socialized by the silver-voiced cowboy is heavy on the music and singing stars. It also has some of the familiar faces that popped up in films from all different studios during the 1930s. Look for silent film star William Farnum and rodeo rider Monte Montague in supporting roles.

1937 B & W 60 minutes

GOIN' SOUTH

★★★

DIRECTOR: Jack Nicholson
CAST: Jack Nicholson, Mary Steenburgen, John Belushi

Star Jack Nicholson also directed this odd little western tale of an outlaw (Nicholson) saved from the gallows by a spinster (Mary Steenburgen). The catch is he must marry her and work on her farm. Lots of attempts at comedy, but only a few work. Look for John Belushi in a small role as a Mexican cowboy. Rated PG; some violence and language.

1978 109 minutes

GOLDEN STALLION, THE

★★½

DIRECTOR: William Witney

CAST: Roy Rogers, Dale Evans, Estelita Rodriguez, Pat Brady, Douglas Evans, Frank Fenton, Trigger, Trigger Jr.

This offbeat entry to the Roy Rogers series places the emphasis on Trigger and his efforts to save a cute Palomino mare from a life of crime. It seems this poor horse is innocently involved in diamond smuggling and is protected by Trigger, who kills one of the villains who has been mistreating her. Our human hero Roy takes the blame for the killing, but he in turn is aided by Trigger Jr., making it a family affair. Absolute hooey but fun to watch, and exciting for the kids and animal lovers in the audience.

1949 67 minutes

GONE WITH THE WEST (AKA BRONCO BUSTERS)

★

DIRECTOR: Bernard Gerard

CAST: James Caan, Stephanie Powers, Aldo Ray, Barbara Werle, Robert Walker Jr., Sammy Davis Jr., Michael Conrad

With this excellent cast, one would expect more, but this is a confusing and vague tale about an Old West ex-con on the vengeance trail. From the seemingly truncated beginning, this silly oater offers little more dialogue than "Huh?" and "Yeh!" A jazz-soul soundtrack accompanies most of the action, making the production even more off the wall.

1972 92 minutes

GOOD THE BAD AND THE UGLY, THE

★★★★

DIRECTOR: Sergio Leone

CAST: Clint Eastwood, Eli Wallach, Lee Van Cleef

The best of Italian director Sergio Leone's spaghetti westerns with Clint Eastwood, this release features the latter in the dubiously "good" role, with Lee Van Cleef as "the bad" and Eli Wallach as "the ugly." All three are after a cache of gold hidden in a Confederate army camp. For Leone fans, it's full of what made his movies so memorable. Others might find it a bit long, but no one can deny its sense of style.

1966 161 minutes

GRAND CANYON TRAIL

★★

DIRECTOR: William Witney

CAST: Roy Rogers, Jane Frazee, Andy Devine, Robert Livingston, Roy Barcroft, Charles Coleman, Trigger

Roy Rogers is saddled with what he thinks is a useless mine, and former serial hero Robert Livingston just about succeeds in swindling him out of what is actually a bonanza in silver. Fast-paced and almost tongue-in-cheek, this enjoyable entry benefits from a solid cast, including wheezing Andy Devine and perennial favorite Roy Barcroft. The Sons of the Pioneers are replaced by the Riders of the Purple Sage in the vocals department for this one.

1948 B & W 67 minutes

GREAT SCOUT AND CATHOUSE THURSDAY, THE

★★★

DIRECTOR: Don Taylor

CAST: Lee Marvin, Oliver Reed, Elizabeth Ashley, Robert Culp, Strother Martin, Kay Lenz

Eccentric western comedy involving a variety of get-rich-quick schemes concocted by an amusing band of rogues. Oliver Reed steals the show as a wacky American Indian whose double-crosses usually backfire. Not much plot and considerable silliness, but fun nonetheless. Rated PG for sexual situations.

1976 102 minutes

GREY FOX, THE

★★★★★

DIRECTOR: Phillip Borsos

CAST: Richard Farnsworth, Jackie Burroughs, Wayne Robson, Ken Pogue, Timothy Webber

Richard Farnsworth (*Comes a Horseman*) stars in this marvelously entertaining Canadian feature as the gentleman bandit Bill Miner who, as the movie poster proclaimed, "on June 17, 1901, after thirty-three years in San Quentin Prison for robbing stagecoaches, was released into the twentieth century." As directed by Phillip Borsos, it is highly reminiscent of the great westerns of John Ford. In other words, it's first-rate in every sense—a classic. Rated PG for brief violence.

1982 92 minutes

GUN FURY

★★★

DIRECTOR: Raoul Walsh

CAST: Rock Hudson, Donna Reed, Lee Marvin, Phil Carey, Neville Brand

Donna Reed is kidnapped. Rock Hudson chases the badmen and saves her from a fate worse than death in Arizona's mesmerizing Red Rock country. Villainy abounds.

1953 83 minutes

GUNDOWN AT SANDOVAL

★★★

DIRECTOR: Harry Keller

CAST: Tom Tryon, Dan Duryea, Beverly Garland, Lyle Bettger, Harry Carey Jr.

Texas John Slaughter faces overwhelming odds when he vows to avenge a friend's death and goes against the inhabitants of Sandoval, an infamous outlaw hideout. Dan Duryea is as nasty as ever as the overlord of the outlaws, and murderous Lyle Bettger and Beverly Garland make a fine pair as the leaders of the gang that killed Slaughter's friend. Harry Carey Jr. plays friend and ally to Tom Tryon's Texas Ranger. Featuring lots of hard riding and gunplay, this Disney television show was originally shown in Europe as a feature film.

1959 72 minutes

GUNFIGHT AT THE O.K. CORRAL

★★★★

DIRECTOR: John Sturges

CAST: Burt Lancaster, Kirk Douglas, Rhonda Fleming, Jo Van Fleet, John Ireland, Lee Van Cleef, Frank Faylen

The Wyatt Earp–Doc Holliday legend got another going-over in this rather good western. Burt Lancaster and Kirk Douglas portray these larger-than-life gunfighters, who shoot it out with the nefarious Clanton family in 1881 Tombstone. The movie effectively builds up its tension until the climactic gunfight.

1957 122 minutes

GUNMAN FROM BODIE

★★★½

DIRECTOR: Spencer G. Bennett

CAST: Buck Jones, Tim McCoy, Raymond Hatton, Christine

MacIntyre, Dave O'Brien, Frank LaRue, Wilbur Mack, John Merton, Charles King, Silver

The best of the many trio series westerns of the 1930s and '40s, "The Rough Riders" teamed two of the genre's most charismatic stars, Buck Jones and Tim McCoy, with one of the best sidekicks in the business, Raymond Hatton. Jones and McCoy had each made a number of notable westerns since debuting in the 1920s—both having done their best work at Columbia in the 1930s—before joining forces for the first Rough Riders film, *Arizona Bound*, in 1941. The second film in the series, *Gunman from Bodie*, is considered by most aficionados to be the best, and we agree. The plot, about a trio of marshals who set out to capture a gang of cattle thieves, may be old and worn-out, but the sheer star power and personality of Jones, McCoy, and Hatton make this formula B western a first-rate example of its kind.

1941 B & W 60 minutes

HANG 'EM HIGH

★★★

DIRECTOR: Ted Post
CAST: Clint Eastwood, Inger Stevens, Ed Begley Sr., Pat Hingle, Arlene Golonka, Ben Johnson

Clint Eastwood's first stateside spaghetti western is a good one, with the star out to get the vigilantes who tried to hang him for a murder he didn't commit. Pat Hingle is the hangin' judge who gives Clint his license to hunt, and Ben Johnson is the marshal who saves his life. Ed Begley Sr. is memorable as the leader of the vigilantes. Rated PG.

1968 114 minutes

HARLEM RIDES THE RANGE

★★½

DIRECTOR: Richard Kahn
CAST: Herbert Jeffrey (Jeffries), Lucius Brooks, Artie Young, F. E. Miller, Spencer Williams, Clarence Brooks

Uninspired oater is one of a handful of westerns made by black producers and directors for a black audience spread throughout the United States in the late 1930s and early 1940s. Not too different from its white counterparts, this low-budget horse opera from Hollywood Pictures has its own hero, evil heavy, saloon action, showdown, and inane comedy relief. Stale plot about stolen mine rights (to a radium mine this time) is secondary to the limited action and uniqueness of seeing an all-black cast in what has traditionally been the territory of white actors and actresses. Nothing special but worth a look. Spencer Williams of television's "Amos and Andy" show co-wrote the script for this film and plays a featured role.

1939 B & W 58 minutes

HARRY TRACY

★★★½

DIRECTOR: William A. Graham
CAST: Bruce Dern, Helen Shaver, Michael C. Gwynne, Gordon Lightfoot

Bruce Dern plays the title role in this surprisingly amiable little western, with the star as the last of a gentlemanly outlaw breed. Although he's a crafty character, Harry always seems to get caught. His mind is all too often on other things—in particular, a well-to-do woman (Helen Shaver). Dern gives his most likable portrayal in this Canadian-made film, and those who love shoot-'em-ups will find it to be an enjoyable timepasser. Rated PG.

1982 100 minutes

HATFIELDS AND THE MCCOYS, THE

★★½

DIRECTOR: Clyde Ware

CAST: Jack Palance, Steve Forrest, Richard Hatch, Joan Caulfield

The great American legend of backwoods feuding long celebrated in song and story. Jack Palance and Steve Forrest make the most of portraying the clan patriarchs. The feud was reason enough to leave the hills and head west in the 1880s. A guy could get killed for saying hello to the wrong face!

1975 74 minutes

HEART OF THE GOLDEN WEST

★★½

DIRECTOR: Joseph Kane

CAST: Roy Rogers, Smiley Burnette, George "Gabby" Hayes, Ruth Terry, Bob Nolan and the Sons of the Pioneers, Trigger

This modern-day adventure pits Roy Rogers and his fellow ranchers against cheating city slickers intent on defrauding the cowboys and putting them out of business. This film is a throwback to the earlier Gene Autry films in that the musical production numbers take precedence over the action; the increased budget granted this horse opera is evident in the singing segments rather than in more elaborate stunts and chases. Roy gets Smiley Burnett *and* Gabby Hayes in this one, and he's hard-pressed to make an impression when wedged between these two scene-stealers. Enjoyable western hokum.

1942 B & W 65 minutes

HEART OF THE RIO GRANDE

★★

DIRECTOR: William Morgan

CAST: Gene Autry, Smiley Burnette, Fay McKenzie, Edith Fellows, Pierre Watkins, Jimmy Wakely Trio, Gloria Gardner, Gladis Gardner, Budd Buster, Frankie Marvin

Gene Autry and the gang sing some sense into a snooty, spoiled rich girl and manage to bring her and her too busy father back together again. Standard story is given standard, simple-minded treatment, but it's the extras (like the Jimmy Wakely Trio) and the character parts that make this sort of programmer fun. After four more films like this, Gene would heed his country's call and join the air force, leaving the prairie wide open for Roy Rogers.

1942 B & W 70 minutes

HEARTLAND

★★★★

DIRECTOR: Richard Pearce

CAST: Conchata Ferrell, Rip Torn, Lilia Skala, Megan Folsom

This is an excellent and deceptively simple story of a widow (Conchata Ferrell) who settled, with her daughter and a homesteader (Rip Torn), in turn-of-the-century Wyoming. The film deals with the complex problems of surviving in nature and society. It's well worth watching. Rated PG.

1979 96 minutes

HEAVEN'S GATE

★★★

DIRECTOR: Michael Cimino

CAST: Kris Kristofferson, Christopher Walken, Isabelle Huppert, John Hurt, Sam Waterston, Brad Dourif, Jeff Bridges, Joseph Cotten

Written and directed by Michael Cimino (*The Deer Hunter*), this $36 million epic western about the land wars in Wyoming, between the cattle barons and immigrant farmers, is awkward and overlong but at least makes sense in the complete video version. The beautiful cinematography and painstaking period recreation add much to its high quality. Too bad it's not the great film it should have been. Rated R for nudity, sex, and violence.

1980 219 minutes

HELLBENDERS, THE

DIRECTOR: Sergio Corbucci

CAST: Joseph Cotten, Norma Bengel, Julian Mateos, Gino Pernice, Angel Aranda, Al Mulock

Joseph Cotten fans will weep at this badly overdubbed spaghetti western set in the post–Civil war era. It's the story of a washed-out Confederate and his band of sons who call themselves "The Hellbenders." In this overly long film, they are pursued across the barren landscape with stolen currency that Cotten plans to use to reorganize the Confederacy. Sappy dialogue and unlikable characters. Rated PG.

1967 92 minutes

HELLER IN PINK TIGHTS

★★½

DIRECTOR: George Cukor

CAST: Sophia Loren, Anthony Quinn, Margaret O'Brien, Edmund Lowe, Steve Forrest, Eileen Heckart, Ramon Navarro

The career of legendary nineteenth-century actress and love goddess Adah Issacs Menken inspired this odd film about a ragtag theatrical troupe wandering the West in the 1880s. Colorful but air-filled, it offers a busty blonde Sophia Loren with lusty Tony Quinn fending off belligerent townfolk, creditors, distrustful sheriffs, and ever-essential Indians while serving up a hash of gunslinging, backstage humor, burlesque, and rewritten dramatic history. Western novelist Louis L'Amour is blamed for the story.

1960 100 minutes

HELLFIRE

★★★½

DIRECTOR: R. G. Springsteen

CAST: William Elliott, Marie Windsor, Forrest Tucker, Jim Davis, Grant Withers, Paul Fix, Denver Pyle

Solid, offbeat western in which a ne'er-do-well gambler, William ("Wild Bill") Elliott, is shoved onto the path of righteousness when a preacher saves his life. Our hero, fast with his fists and his six-guns, devotes himself to the "peaceful" pursuit of raising funds to build a church, his rescuer's dying wish. To do so, he decides to talk a lady outlaw (Marie Windsor) into turning herself in so he can collect the reward money. Meanwhile, a lawman (Forrest Tucker) and a gang of cutthroats (led by Jim Davis) are on their trail. A bit preachy at times, *Hellfire* still packs a solid wallop of entertainment. Western buffs have favorably compared it with William S. Hart's classic silent shoot-'em-ups. It may not be a classic, but it is good fun.

1949 79 minutes

HELL TOWN

★★★½

DIRECTOR: Charles Barton

CAST: John Wayne, Marsha Hunt, Johnny Mack Brown, Alan Ladd, James Craig, Monte Blue, Lucien Littlefield

Here's a real find for fans of John Wayne, a pre-*Stagecoach* western of good quality. Stepping up from his low-budget programmers for studios like Republic and Monogram, the Duke was cast in this, the last of Paramount's series of films based on the stories of Zane Grey. He plays a happy-go-lucky cowhand who falls in with rustlers much to the chagrin of his serious-minded relative, lawman Johnny Mack Brown. A strong supporting cast helps things along, and the result is an enjoyable genre piece. Also known as *Born to the West*.

1938 B & W 50 minutes

HIGH NOON

★★★★★

DIRECTOR: Fred Zinnemann

CAST: Gary Cooper, Grace Kelly, Lloyd Bridges, Thomas Mitchell, Katy Jurado, Otto Kruger, Lon Chaney Jr.

Gary Cooper won his second Oscar for his role of the abandoned lawman in this classic western. It's the sheriff's wedding day, and the head of an outlaw band, who has sworn vengeance against him, is due to arrive in town at high noon. When Cooper turns to his fellow townspeople for help, no one comes forward. The suspense of this movie keeps snowballing as the clock ticks ever closer to noon.

1952 B & W 85 minutes

HIGH NOON, PART TWO

DIRECTOR: Jerry Jameson

CAST: Lee Majors, David Carradine, J. A. Preston, Pernell Roberts, M. Emmet Walsh, Katherine Cannon, Michael Pataki

This is a poor attempt at a sequel. It begins in much the same way as the original, with a man standing against impossible odds. The difference is the actors and the director. Lee Majors is not believable as the hero, a strong man with a very human fear. The film also lacks the suspense of the original. Add to this a weak script, and you have a very forgettable film—despite an impressive supporting cast.

1980 100 minutes

HIGH PLAINS DRIFTER

★★★

DIRECTOR: Clint Eastwood

CAST: Clint Eastwood, Verna Bloom, Marianna Hill, Mitchell Ryan, Jack Ging, Geoffrey Lewis, Anthony James, John Mitchum

Star-director Clint Eastwood tried to revive the soggy spaghetti-western genre one last time, with watchable results. The tale is almost horrific as Eastwood comes to a frontier town just in time to make sure its sleazy citizens are all but wiped out by a trio of revenge-seeking outlaws. Although atmospheric, it's also confusing and sometimes just downright nasty. Not great, but not bad either. Rated R for violence, profanity, and suggested sex.

1973 105 minutes

HILLS OF UTAH, THE

★★½

DIRECTOR: John English

CAST: Gene Autry, Pat Buttram, Elaine Riley, Onslow Stevens, Donna Martell, Harry Lauter, Tom London, Kenne Duncan, Denver Pyle, William Fawcett, Sandy Sanders, Teddy Infuhr, Lee Morgan, Billy Griffith

Harking back to a classic theme, Gene returns to the town where his father was killed and manages to settle a local feud as well as uncover the truth about his father's murder. Even with Pat Buttram, this is somber for a Gene Autry film. Great character actors and second leads Tom London, Harry Lauter, and Denver Pyle enchance this film.

1951 B & W 70 minutes

HIRED HAND, THE

★★★½

DIRECTOR: Peter Fonda

CAST: Peter Fonda, Warren Oates, Verna Bloom, Severn Darden, Robert Pratt

This low-key western follows two drifters, Peter Fonda and Warren Oates, as they return to Fonda's farm and the wife, Verna Bloom, he deserted seven years earlier. While working on the farm, Fonda and Bloom begin to rekindle their relationship, only to have it interrupted when Fonda must go to the aid of Oates, who is being held prisoner in a small town. Beautiful cinematography and fine performances, especially by the late Warren Oates, add greatly to this worthy entry in the genre. Rated R.

1971 93 minutes

HIS NAME WAS KING

★½

DIRECTOR: Don Reynolds

CAST: Richard Harrison, Klaus Kinski, Anne Pushin, John Silver, Lorenzo Finschi, Lucio Zarini

Spaghetti western about a bounty hunter named King (Richard Harrison) who tracks down a ring of gunrunners near the Mexican border. Plenty of action, but like most westerns from Italy, the bad guys are so bad that their psychotic behavior, coupled with stupid voice dubbing, comes off too close to comedy to be taken seriously. Klaus Kinski (*Fitzcarraldo*) plays a lawman and friend of King. Not rated, but equal to a PG for violence, sex, and profanity.

1983 90 minutes

HOMBRE

★★★★

DIRECTOR: Martin Ritt

CAST: Paul Newman, Fredric March, Richard Boone, Diane Cilento, Cameron Mitchell, Barbara Rush, Martin Balsam

Paul Newman gives a superb performance as a white man raised by Indians who is enticed into helping a stagecoach full of settlers make its way across treacherous country. Richard Boone is the baddie who makes this chore difficult, but the racism Newman encounters in this Martin Ritt film provides the real—and thought-provoking—thrust.

1967 111 minutes

HOPPY'S HOLIDAY

★★

DIRECTOR: George Archainbaud

CAST: William Boyd, Andy Clyde, Rand Brooks, Andrew Tombes, Jeff Corey, Mary Ware, Leonard Penn, Donald Kirke, Hollis Bane, Gil Patric, Frank Henry

A weak entry in the last of twelve Hopalong Cassidy films produced by William Boyd after he had purchased the rights to the character from former producer Harry "Pop" Sherman, this movie pits Hoppy and the Bar-20 cowboys against mechanized bank robbers. Programmers in the true sense of the term, these films did little more than keep Hopalong Cassidy's image alive and in front of America's children on Saturday afternoons. It worked out well because Boyd was able to insinuate himself into a wider audience than ever dreamed possible through the magic medium of early television.

1947 B & W 60 minutes

HORSE SOLDIERS, THE

★★★★

DIRECTOR: John Ford

CAST: John Wayne, William Holden, Constance Towers, Hoot Gibson

Based on a true incident during the Civil War, this is a minor, but enjoyable, John Ford cavalry outing. John Wayne and William Holden play well-matched adversaries in the Union Army.

1959 119 minutes

HOW THE WEST WAS WON

★★★½

DIRECTORS: John Ford, Henry Hathaway, George Marshall

CAST: Gregory Peck, Henry Fonda, James Stewart, John Wayne, Debbie Reynolds, Walter Brennan, Karl Malden, Richard Widmark, Robert Preston, George Peppard

Any western that stars John Wayne, James Stewart, Henry Fonda, Gregory Peck, Walter Brennan, Richard Widmark, and Robert Preston is at least worth a glimpse. Sadly, this 1962 epic doesn't hold up that well on video because it was released on the three-screen Cinerama process. Much of the grandeur of the original version is lost. But shoot-'em-up fans won't want to miss a chance to see many of the genre's greats in one motion picture.

1962 155 minutes

IN OLD CALIFORNIA

★★★

DIRECTOR: William McGann

CAST: John Wayne, Helen Parrish, Patsy Kelly

John Wayne plays a mild-mannered dentist in the Old West. Good viewing for fans.

1942 B & W 88 minutes

IN OLD CHEYENNE

★

DIRECTOR: Stuart Paton

CAST: Rex Lease, Dorothy Gulliver, Harry Woods, Jay Hunt, Harry Todd

Forgotten low-budget star Rex Lease takes a backseat to a smart stallion in this predictable old creaker. Rustler Harry Woods has been getting some unexpected help in his work from a rogue horse who opens all the local corrals and lets the mares loose, guiding them to his mountain hideout to become part of his harem. Hero Rex Lease and the villainous Woods eventually find out where the stock has disappeared to and they fight to settle things once and for all. Primitive and cheaply produced; the animal footage remains about the best part of this shoot-'em-up.

1931 B & W 60 minutes

INVITATION TO A GUNFIGHTER

★★

DIRECTOR: Richard Wilson

CAST: Yul Brynner, George Segal, Janice Rule, Pat Hingle

Studio-slick western is short on action and long on dialogue as a hired professional killer comes to town and changes the balance of power. Everybody gets a chance to emote in this gabfest—which helps, since the story is so slim. Typical of a Stanley Kramer message film but not quite as heavy-handed as most.

1964 92 minutes

JEREMIAH JOHNSON

★★★★

DIRECTOR: Sydney Pollack

CAST: Robert Redford, Will Geer, Stefan Gierasch, Allyn Ann McLerie, Charles Tyner

Robert Redford plays Johnson, a simple man who has no taste for cities. We see him as he grows from his first feeble attempts at survival to a hunter who has quickened his senses with wild meat and vegetation—a man who is a part of the wildlife of the mountains. *Jeremiah Johnson* gives a sense of humanness to a genre that had, up until its release, spent most of its history reworking the same myths. Here's an exciting new myth, and a slice of life to boot! Rated PG.

1972 107 minutes

JESSE JAMES

★★★½

DIRECTOR: Henry King

CAST: Tyrone Power, Henry Fonda, Nancy Kelly, Randolph Scott, Henry Hull, Jane Darwell, Brian Donlevy, Donald Meek, John Carradine, Slim Summerville, J. Edward Bromberg

Tyrone Power is Jesse and Henry Fonda is Frank in this legend-gilting account of the life and misdeeds of Missouri's most famous outlaw. Bending history, the film paints Jesse as a peaceful man driven to a life of crime by heartless big business in the form of a railroad, and a loving husband and father murdered for profit by a coward. Audiences ate it all up, and still do.

1939 105 minutes

JESSE JAMES AT BAY

★★½

DIRECTOR: Joseph Kane

CAST: Roy Rogers, George "Gabby" Hayes, Sally Payne, Pierre Watkin, Gale Storm, Roy Barcroft, Trigger

History-twistin' Republic Studios casts box-office smash Roy Rogers as a fictionalized Jesse James who rides not against the railroads, but against one evil bunch misrepresenting the railroad and stealing the land of poor, honest farmers. Just as entertaining as any of Rogers's pre-WWII films, but a top contender for *the* most far-fetched, fallacious frontier foolishness ever filmed. Hokum of the highest order, but fun to watch and full of familiar faces, including a perky young Gale Storm and the prolific Roy Barcroft.

1941 B & W 56 minutes

JOE KIDD

★★★½

DIRECTOR: John Sturges

CAST: Clint Eastwood, Robert Duvall, John Saxon, Don Stroud

While not exactly a thrill-a-minute movie, this western has a number of memorable moments. Director John Sturges (*The Magnificent Seven*) has been better, but Clint Eastwood and Robert Duvall are at the peak of their respective forms in this story of a gunman (Eastwood) hired by a cattle baron (Duvall) to track down some Mexican-Americans who are fighting back because they've been cheated out of their land. Rated PG.

1972 88 minutes

JOHNNY GUITAR

★★★½

DIRECTOR: Nicholas Ray

CAST: Joan Crawford, Mercedes McCambridge, Sterling Hayden, Scott Brady, Ward Bond, Ernest Borgnine, John Carradine

A positively weird western, this Nicholas Ray film features the ultimate role reversal. Bar owner Joan Crawford and landowner Mercedes McCambridge shoot it out while their gun-toting boyfriends (Sterling Hayden and Scott Brady) look on.

1954 110 minutes

JORY

★★★

DIRECTOR: Jorge Fons

CAST: Robby Benson, John Marley, B. J. Thomas, Linda Purl, Claudio Brook, Patricia Aspillaga, Brad Dexter, Ben Baker, Todd Martin

A surprisingly sensitive film for the genre finds Robby Benson, in his first film role, as a 15-year-old boy who must learn to go it alone in the Wild West after his father is senselessly murdered. B. J. Thomas is unexpectedly charming in his role as a gunslinger who tries to help the boy adapt to the environment. While remaining exciting and suspenseful, the film takes time to make commentary about manhood and machismo in an adult, thoughtful manner. Rated PG.

1972 97 minutes

JUBAL

★★★½

DIRECTOR: Delmer Daves
CAST: Glenn Ford, Ernest Borgnine, Valerie French, Rod Steiger, Charles Bronson, Noah Beery Jr., Felicia Farr

Adult western finds drifter Jubal Troop (Glenn Ford) enmeshed in just about everybody's problems when he signs on with rancher Ernest Borgnine. Beautifully photographed and well acted by a fine cast, this tale of jealousy and the revenge of a woman scorned has been likened to *Othello* by film critics, but, whatever the inspiration, this film is standout entertainment for western drama fans. Ford solidifies his character as the decent, capable loner (a role he would play with distinction until the 1970s), and Rod Steiger provides all the brooding menace he can muster as Borgnine's frustrated hired hand. Look for character favorites Charles Bronson and Noah Beery Jr. in prominent parts.

1956 101 minutes

JUNIOR BONNER

★★★

DIRECTOR: Sam Peckinpah
CAST: Steve McQueen, Robert Preston, Ida Lupino, Ben Johnson, Joe Don Baker

A rodeo "has-been," Steve McQueen, returns home for one last rousing performance in front of the home folks. McQueen is quite good as the soft-spoken cowboy who tries to make peace with his family. Robert Preston is a real scene-stealer as his hard-drinking carouser of a father. Rated PG.

1972 103 minutes

KANSAN, THE

★★½

DIRECTOR: George Archainbaud
CAST: Richard Dix, Jane Wyatt, Victor Jory, Albert Dekker, Eugene Pallette, Robert Armstrong

Tough, two-fisted Richard Dix sets his jaw and routs the baddies in a wide-open prairie town but must then contend with a corrupt official in this routine western, the third to pair him with Jane Wyatt and heavies Victor Jory and Albert Dekker.

1943 B & W 79 minutes

KANSAS PACIFIC

★★½

DIRECTOR: Ray Nazarro
CAST: Sterling Hayden, Eve Miller, Barton MacLane, Douglas Fowley, Myron Healey, Clayton Moore, Reed Hadley

Railroad drama set in pre–Civil War days has rangy Sterling Hayden romancing Eve Miller and battling pro-Confederate saboteurs intent on hindering construction of the Kansas Pacific Railroad. Decent actioner features top heavy Barton Maclane, versatile Myron Healey, and moonlighting Lone Ranger, Clayton Moore.

1953 73 minutes

KENTUCKIAN, THE

★★★

DIRECTOR: Burt Lancaster

CAST: Burt Lancaster, Diana Lynn, Dianne Foster, Walter Matthau, John Carradine, Una Merkel

Pushing west in the 1820s, Burt Lancaster bucks all odds to reach Texas and begin a new life. A good mix of history, adventure, romance, and comedy make this one worth a family watching.

1955 104 minutes

KING OF THE BULLWHIP

★★½

DIRECTOR: Ron Ormond

CAST: Lash LaRue, Al St. John, Jack Holt, Dennis Moore, Tom Neal, Anne Gwynne

Looking every bit like Humphrey Bogart's twin brother in a black hat, Lash LaRue was the whip-wielding westerner in a series of low budget shoot-'em-ups in the 1950s. This, his first for a major distributor, was one of his better efforts. Lash and his sidekick Al St. John must go undercover when a bandit pretends to be our hero while robbing a bank.

1951 60 minutes

KIT CARSON

★★★½

DIRECTOR: George B. Seitz

CAST: Jon Hall, Dana Andrews, Lynn Bari

This lively western about the two-fisted frontiersman gave Jon Hall one of his best roles. Good action scenes.

1940 B & W 97 minutes

LADY FROM LOUISIANA

★★

DIRECTOR: Bernard Vorhaus

CAST: John Wayne, Ray Middleton, Osa Massen

John Wayne is a crusading lawyer in this middling Republic period piece.

1941 B & W 82 minutes

LADY TAKES A CHANCE, A

★★★

DIRECTOR: William A. Seiter

CAST: Jean Arthur, John Wayne, Phil Silvers, Charles Winninger, Grady Sutton, Hans Conreid, Grant Withers, Mary Field

John Wayne is a rough-'n'-ready, not the marrying kind, rodeo star. Jean Arthur is an innocent girl from New York City out West. He falls off a horse into her lap, she falls for him, and the chase is on. Played for comedy, and well done, this one's *It Happened One Night* with spurs, a prairie moon, and the obligatory campfire scene.

1943 B & W 86 minutes

LAST COMMAND, THE

★★½

DIRECTOR: Frank Lloyd

CAST: Sterling Hayden, Richard Carlson, Anna Maria Alberghetti, Ernest Borgnine, Arthur Hunnicutt, Jim Davis, J. Carrol Naish

This is a watchable western about the famed last stand at the Alamo during Texas's fight for independence from Mexico. Jim Bowie (Sterling Hayden), Davy Crockett (Arthur Hunnicutt), and Colonel Travis (Richard Carlson) are portrayed in a more realistic manner than they were in John Wayne's *The Alamo*, but the story is still mostly hokum. There are some exciting battle scenes and solid direction. This film is not rated, but note that it contains some violent scenes.

1955 110 minutes

LAST GUN, THE

★

DIRECTOR: Serge Bergone
CAST: Cameron Mitchell, Frank Wolff, Celina Celly, Carl Moher, Kitty Karver

In this Italian western dubbed into English, a gunfighter tired of killing hangs up his pistols and settles down in a small town. Outlaws appear and he must protect the townspeople by putting on his guns. The story is classic. The acting and directing are not.

1964 98 minutes

LAST OF THE MOHICANS, THE

★★★★

DIRECTOR: George B. Seitz
CAST: Randolph Scott, Binnie Barnes, Heather Angel, Robert Barrat, Philip Reed, Henry Wilcoxon, Bruce Cabot

Blood, thunder, and interracial romance during the French and Indian War are brought to life from James Fenimore Cooper's novel. Randolph Scott is the intrepid Hawkeye; Robert Barrat is the noble Chingachgook; Binnie Barnes is Alice Monroe. The star-crossed lovers are Philip Reed, as Uncas, the title character, and Heather Angel, as Cora Monroe. Bruce Cabot plays the villainous Magua.

1936 B & W 100 minutes

LAST OF THE MOHICANS

★★½

DIRECTOR: James L. Conway
CAST: Steve Forrest, Ned Romero, Andrew Prine, Robert Tessler

In this TV film based on James Fenimore Cooper's classic, a small party headed for a fort is deserted by their guide and must turn to Hawkeye and Chingachgook to bring them to safety. When two of the party are captured, our heroes must rescue them and battle the leader of the Indians.

1985 97 minutes

LAST OF THE PONY RIDERS

★½

DIRECTOR: George Archainbaud
CAST: Gene Autry, Smiley Burnette, Buzz Henry, Harry Hines, Johnny Downs, Dick Jones, Gregg Barton, Arthur Space, Howard Wright, Harry Mackin

Gene Autry's last feature film is a limp addition to a genre—the series western—on its last legs. Reunited with his old sidekick Smiley Burnette for his last six films, Autry ended his nineteen-year film career with this lackluster mediocrity, his ninety-third film.

1953 B & W 80 minutes

LAST RIDE OF THE DALTON BOYS, THE

★★½

DIRECTOR: Dan Curtis
CAST: Jack Palance, Larry Wilcox, Dale Robertson, Bo Hopkins, Cliff Potts

When two former Dalton Gang train robbers are reunited in Hollywood in 1934, they relive the early days of the Dalton Gang as they share a bottle of whiskey. This western plays up the Daltons' poverty while steering clear of any bloodthirsty image of the boys. It is Jack Palance, as the detective hired by the railroad company, who comes out looking like the villain. Rated PG for violence.

1979 146 minutes

LAW RIDES AGAIN, THE

🦃

DIRECTOR: Alan James
CAST: Ken Maynard, Hoot Gibson, Betty Miles, Jack LaRue, Kenneth Harlan, Chief Thundercloud

Dismal low-budget entry in the "Trail Blazers" series has one-time cowboy greats Ken Maynard and Hoot Gibson bluffing their way through a formula story about lawmen catching a crooked Indian agent (Kenneth Harlan) with the unwitting help of an outlaw (Jack LaRue). Maynard by this time was overweight and uninterested in giving anything approximating a believable performance. Gibson tries hard but cannot add much to his scenes with Maynard, who forgets his lines and throws his co-star for an obvious loop on a number of occasions.

1943 B & W 58 minutes

LAWLESS FRONTIER

★★½

DIRECTOR: Robert N. Bradbury

CAST: John Wayne, Sheila Terry, George "Gabby" Hayes, Earl Dwire, Yakima Canutt, Jack Rockwell

A Mexican bandit (Earl Dwire) manages to evade the blame for a series of crimes he's committed because the sheriff is sure that John Wayne is the culprit. The Duke, of course, traps the bad guy and clears his good name in this predictable B western notable for an early appearance of Gabby Hayes as the sidekick character he was to play in hundreds of subsequent shoot-'em-ups.

1935 B & W 59 minutes

LAWLESS RANGE

★★

DIRECTOR: Robert N. Bradbury

CAST: John Wayne, Sheila Manners, Earl Dwire, Frank McGlynn Jr., Jack Curtis, Yakima Canutt

In this low, low budget early John Wayne western, a banker attempts to drive out the local ranchers and get his hands on some rich gold mines. Wayne, sent by the governor, soon sets things aright.

1935 B & W 59 minutes

LAWMAN IS BORN, A

★★½

DIRECTOR: Sam Newfield

CAST: Johnny Mack Brown, Iris Meredith, Al St. John, Warner Richmond, Dick Curtis, Charles King

Former football star Johnny Mack Brown made his biggest impression by playing the title role in the 1930 version of *Billy the Kid* opposite Wallace Beery as Pat Garrett. This led to a series of B westerns, of which *A Lawman Is Born* is one of the better entries. As in so many of these films, Brown is a two-fisted good guy who foils the nefarious plans of an outlaw gang. This time, the baddies are after land (as opposed to the alternate formulas of cattle, money, gold, or horses). It's fun for fans, with former silent star (and nephew of Fatty Arbuckle) Al St. John doing the comedy sidekick honors.

1937 B & W 58 minutes

LEATHER BURNERS, THE

★★½

DIRECTOR: Joseph E. Henabery

CAST: William Boyd, Andy Clyde, Victor Jory, Bobby Larson, George Givot, Robert Mitchum

In this oddball series western, Hopalong Cassidy (William Boyd) and his sidekick, California (Andy Clyde), are framed for murder by a calculating cattle rustler (Victor Jory). It's up to a junior detective (Bobby Larson) to prove our heroes' innocence in time to allow them to participate in the final showdown. This was Robert Mitchum's third appearance in the series.

1943 B & W 58 minutes

LEFT-HANDED GUN, THE

★★★

DIRECTOR: Arthur Penn
CAST: Paul Newman, Lita Milan, John Dehner, Hurd Hatfield

First film by director Arthur Penn (*Bonnie and Clyde*) follows the life of Billy the Kid (Paul Newman) after a group of his friends have been murdered and he seeks vengeance for their deaths. Paul Newman's use of method acting is a bit obvious.

1958 B & W 102 minutes

LEGEND OF THE LONE RANGER, THE

DIRECTOR: William A. Fraker
CAST: Klinton Spilsbury, Michael Horse, Jason Robards Jr.

Let your children watch *The Legend of the Lone Ranger*, but don't bother to watch it yourself. While kids will undoubtedly love what the advertising blurbs said was "the untold story of the man behind the mask and the legend behind the man," adults—after the first hour of this often corny, slow-paced western—will probably be falling asleep or, at least, daydreaming. Rated PG.

1981 98 minutes

LEGEND OF WALKS FAR WOMAN, THE

DIRECTOR: Mel Manski
CAST: Raquel Welch, Bradford Dillman, George Clutsei, Nick Mancuso, Elroy Phil Casados, Nick Ramos

Badly miscast Raquel Welch portrays an Indian heroine facing the perils of the Indian versus white man's culture clash. Her story leads to the climactic battle at Little Big Horn. Not even the scenery is enough to maintain interest.

1982 150 minutes

LIFE AND TIMES OF JUDGE ROY BEAN, THE

★★★

DIRECTOR: John Huston
CAST: Paul Newman, Stacy Keach, Victoria Principal, Jacqueline Bisset, Ava Gardner

Weird western with Paul Newman as the fabled hanging judge. It has some interesting set-pieces among the strangeness. Stacy Keach is outstanding as Bad Bob. Rated PG.

1972 120 minutes

LITTLE BIG MAN

★★★★

DIRECTOR: Arthur Penn
CAST: Dustin Hoffman, Chief Dan George, Faye Dunaway, Martin Balsam, Jeff Corey, Richard Mulligan

Dustin Hoffman gives a bravura performance as Jack Crabbe, a 121-year-old survivor of Custer's last stand. An offbeat western/comedy, this film chronicles, in flashback, Crabbe's numerous adventures in the Old West. It's a remarkable film in more ways than one, with special mention deserved by Dick Smith for the marvelous make-up he created for Hoffman as the elderly Crabbe. Rated PG.

1970 150 minutes

LONE RANGER, THE

★★★½

DIRECTOR: Stuart Heisler
CAST: Clayton Moore, Jay Silverheels, Lyle Bettger, Bonita Granville

The first color feature film based on the legend of the Lone Ranger is a treat for the kids and not too tough for the adults to sit through. Clayton Moore and Jay Silverheels reprise their television roles and find themselves battling white settlers, led by an evil Lyle Bettger, and the much put-upon

Indians, riled up by a surly Michael Ansara. Simple and straightforward, this film is a natural for a rainy afternoon and guaranteed to keep everyone's attention and is in no small way aided by the sincerity and credence lent it by Moore and Silverheels, the definitive Lone Ranger and Tonto.

1956 86 minutes

LONELY ARE THE BRAVE

★★★★

DIRECTOR: David Miller

CAST: Kirk Douglas, Walter Matthau, Gena Rowlands

A "little" Hollywood western set in modern times has a lot to offer those who can endure its heavy-handed message. Kirk Douglas is just right as the cowboy out of step with his times. His attempts to escape from jail on horseback in contrast to the mechanized attempts to catch him by a modern police force are handled well.

1962 B & W 107 minutes

LONELY MAN, THE

★★★

DIRECTOR: Henry Levin

CAST: Jack Palance, Anthony Perkins, Neville Brand, Robert Middleton, Elisha Cook Jr., Lee Van Cleef, Elaine Aiken

Interesting, but not exciting, this tautly directed oater is about a gunfighter, bent on reforming, who returns to his family after a seventeen-year hiatus. A brooding Jack Palance is the gunfighter. He is not warmly welcomed home by his deserted son, brooding Anthony Perkins. Two of a kind, the pair square off in a contest of wills and emotions. Hulking Robert Middleton, delightfully sleazy Elisha Cook Jr., veteran heavy Lee Van Cleef, and everybody's favorite saddle tramp Neville Brand add to the solid acting that makes this tired story worth the watching.

1957 B & W 87 minutes

LONG RIDERS, THE

★★★½

DIRECTOR: Walter Hill

CAST: David, Keith, and Robert Carradine; Stacy and James Keach; Nicholas and Christopher Guest; Dennis and Randy Quaid

Fans of westerns will probably enjoy this release. However, this film about the James-Younger Gang has a few deficiencies, which prevent it from being a completely satisfying shoot-'em-up. Director Walter Hill uses a sort of story-telling shorthand in which character development and plot complexity are ignored in favor of lots of action. This is partly offset by the casting of brothers—David, Keith, and Robert Carradine as the Youngers; Stacy and James Keach as the Jameses; Nicholas and Christopher Guest as the Fords; and Dennis and Randy Quaid as the Millers—in the roles. While it sounds like a gimmick, it actually works and adds a much-needed dimension of character to the picture. Rated R for violence.

1980 100 minutes

LOVE ME TENDER

★★★

DIRECTOR: Robert D. Webb

CAST: Elvis Presley, Debra Paget, Richard Egan

This western drama takes place in Texas after the Civil War, with Elvis and his brother fighting over Debra Paget. The most distinguishing characteristic of this movie is the fact that it was Elvis's first film. Elvis fans will, of course, enjoy his singing the ballad "Love Me Tender."

1956 B & W 89 minutes

LUCKY TEXAN

★★★

DIRECTOR: Robert N. Bradbury
CAST: John Wayne, Barbara Sheldon, George "Gabby" Hayes, Lloyd Whitlock, Yakima Canutt, Earl Dwire, Edward Parker

Gold miners John Wayne and "Gabby" Hayes strike it rich. But before they can cash in their claim, Hayes is falsely accused of robbery and murder. Of course, the Duke rides to his aid. Creaky, but fun for fans.

1934 B & W 56 minutes

LUSTY MEN, THE

★★★★

DIRECTOR: Nicholas Ray
CAST: Robert Mitchum, Susan Hayward, Arthur Kennedy

The world of rodeo cowboys is explored in this well-made film directed by cult favorite Nicholas Ray. Robert Mitchum has one of his best roles as a broken-down ex–rodeo star who gets a second chance at the big money by tutoring an egotistical newcomer on the circuit, well played by Arthur Kennedy.

1952 B & W 113 minutes

MACHO CALLAHAN

★★★

DIRECTOR: Bernard L. Kowalski
CAST: David Janssen, Jean Seberg, Lee J. Cobb, James Booth, David Carradine, Bo Hopkins

David Janssen convincingly portrays Macho Callahan, a man hardened by his confinement in a horrid Confederate prison camp. When he kills a man (David Carradine) over a bottle of champagne, the man's bride (Jean Seberg) seeks revenge. Bo Hopkins plays a shy young man with a crush on Seberg. Lee J. Cobb is the gambler responsible for Callahan's imprisonment. The opening scenes take place in the prison camp and are graphically horrifying. It is this painful introduction into Callahan's past that keeps us spellbound and compelled to stay with him to the bitter end. Rated R for violence and gore.

1970 99 minutes

MACKENNA'S GOLD

★★

DIRECTOR: J. Lee Thompson
CAST: Gregory Peck, Omar Sharif, Telly Savalas, Julie Newmar, Lee J. Cobb

Disappointing "big" western follows search for gold in a big canyon. Impressive cast cannot overcome poor script and uninspired direction.

1969 128 minutes

MAGNIFICENT SEVEN, THE

★★★★

DIRECTOR: John Sturges
CAST: Yul Brynner, Steve McQueen, Charles Bronson, James Coburn, Eli Wallach, Robert Vaughn

Japanese director Akira Kurosawa's *The Seven Samurai* served as the inspiration for this enjoyable western, directed by John Sturges (*The Great Escape*). It's the rousing tale of how a group of American gunfighters come to the aid of a village of Mexican farmers plagued by bandits. A fine shoot-'em-up.

1960 126 minutes

MAJOR DUNDEE

★★★

DIRECTOR: Sam Peckinpah
CAST: Charlton Heston, Richard Harris, James Coburn, Jim Hutton, Warren Oates, Ben Johnson

This is a flawed but watchable western directed with typical verve by master filmmaker Sam

Peckinpah. The plot follows a group of Confederate prisoners who volunteer to go into Mexico and track down a band of rampaging Apache Indians. Charlton Heston plays the Union officer who must lead the sullen southern soldiers into battle. An outstanding cast, impressive action scenes and beautiful photography give this film the usual Peckinpah trademark of excitement. Columbia's decision to edit the film resulted in incoherencies in the story.

1965 124 minutes

MAN ALONE, A

★★★

DIRECTOR: Ray Milland
CAST: Ray Milland, Mary Murphy, Ward Bond, Raymond Burr, Lee Van Cleef

Ray Milland's first directorial effort finds him hiding from a lynch mob in a small western town. And who is he hiding with? The sheriff's daughter! Not too bad, as westerns go.

1955 96 minutes

MAN AND BOY

★★½

DIRECTOR: E. W. Swackhamer
CAST: Bill Cosby, Gloria Foster, George Spell, Leif Erickson, Yaphet Kotto, Douglas Turner Ward, John Anderson, Henry Silva, Dub Taylor

Bill Cosby seems out of place in this post–Civil War story set on the Arizona frontier. Cosby and his family try to make a go of it by homesteading on the prairie. The story provides ample opportunity for some Cosbyesque explanations about the facts of life and the black experience of that period. Rated G.

1971 98 minutes

MAN CALLED HORSE, A

★★★

DIRECTOR: Elliot Silverstein
CAST: Richard Harris, Judith Anderson, Jean Gascon, Manu Tupou, Corinna Tsopei, Dub Taylor

Richard Harris (in one of his best roles) portrays an English aristocrat who's enslaved and treated like a pack animal by Sioux Indians in the Dakotas. He loses his veneer of sophistication and finds the core of his manhood. This strong film offers an unusually realistic depiction of American Indian life. Rated PG.

1970 114 minutes

MAN FROM MUSIC MOUNTAIN

★★

DIRECTOR: Joseph Kane
CAST: Gene Autry, Smiley Burnette, Carol Hughes, Sally Payne, Ivan Miller, Edward Cassidy, Polly Jenkins and her Plowboys, Frankie Marvin, Earl Dwire

Warbling Gene Autry and his simple-minded sidekick Smiley Burnette stymie the efforts of a swindler in this routine series film. Worthless mining stock and gullible townfolk are the ingredients in this warmed-over oater, twenty-sixth in the interminable ninety-three films in the Gene Autry series. More than enough tunes and good ol' country humor; a fair sampling of the majority of Autry's movies.

1938 B & W 54 minutes

MAN FROM UTAH, THE

★

DIRECTOR: Robert N. Bradbury
CAST: John Wayne, Polly Ann Young, George "Gabby" Hayes, Yakima Canutt, George Cleveland

Low, low budget western with a very young John Wayne as a lawman going undercover to catch some crooks using a rodeo to bilk unsuspecting cowboys. The rodeo footage was used over and over again by the film company, Monogram Pictures, in similar films. The best part is the dialogue, with such classic lines as "I'm gonna cloud up and rain all over you" and "Yeah? You and what army?"

1934 B & W 57 minutes

MAN OF THE FRONTIER, (RED RIVER VALLEY)

★★½

DIRECTOR: B. Reeves "Breezy" Eason

CAST: Gene Autry, Smiley Burnette, Frances Grant, Boothe Howard, Jack Kennedy, Champion, Sam Flint, George Chesebro, Charles King, Frank LaRue, Hank Bell

This early entry in the Gene Autry series features Gene as an undercover agent out to stop a gang bent on sabotaging construction of a much-needed dam. Disguised as a ditch digger, our hero teamed with his famous mount Champion for the first time. This is Autry's eighth film and his fifth at Republic Studios as the genial singing cowboy, and it contains enough action and good stunting to satisfy any western fan due in no small part to veteran serial and adventure director "Breezy" Eason and his fast-paced style. Very enjoyable, and a nice example of the kind of film Autry could make but didn't have to after a while.

1936 B & W 60 minutes

MAN WHO LOVED CAT DANCING, THE

★

DIRECTOR: Richard C. Sarafian

CAST: Burt Reynolds, Sarah Miles, George Hamilton, Lee J. Cobb, Jack Warden

Don't waste your time on this uninspired western. Burt Reynolds is wasted in this tale of a train robber who kidnaps a prim Sarah Miles and falls in love with her. Rated PG.

1973 114 minutes

MAN WHO SHOT LIBERTY VALANCE, THE

★★★★★

DIRECTOR: John Ford

CAST: John Wayne, James Stewart, Vera Miles, Lee Marvin, Edmond O'Brien, Woody Strode, Andy Devine

This release was director John Ford's last great western. It's a bittersweet farewell to a genre he created and defined. The interplay of John Wayne, James Stewart, and Lee Marvin is inspired. Wayne replays his role of the western man of action, this time with a twist. Stewart's part could well be called *Mr Smith Goes to Shinbone* it draws so much on his most famous image. Marvin has a field day as the meanest, nastiest, no-account outlaw that ever stalked the West. Combined with Ford's visual sense and belief in sparse dialogue, as well as fine ensemble playing in supporting roles, it adds up to a highly satisfying film.

1962 B & W 122 minutes

MAN WITHOUT A STAR

★★★

DIRECTOR: King Vidor

CAST: Kirk Douglas, Jeanne Crain, Claire Trevor, Richard Boone, Jack Elam, Mara Corday

With charm, fists, and guns, foreman Kirk Douglas swaggers through this stock story of rival ranchers. Jeanne Crain is his beautiful boss; Claire Trevor is, as usual, a big-hearted saloon hostess. Richard Boone and Jack Elam are in fine character.

1955 89 minutes

MANHATTAN MERRY-GO-ROUND

★★½

DIRECTOR: Charles F. Riesner
CAST: Gene Autry, Phil Regan, Leo Carrillo, Ann Dvorak, Tamara Geva, Ted Lewis, Cab Calloway and the Cotton Club Orchestra, Joe DiMaggio, Louis Prima, Henry Armetta, Max Terhune, Smiley Burnette, Jimmy Gleason

Incredible line-up of popular performers and celebrities is the main attraction of this catch-all production about a gangster who takes over a recording company. Basically a collection of performances strung together by a romantic thread, this oddity runs the gamut from Gene Autry's country crooning to the jivin' gyrations of legendary Cab Calloway. Even Joe DiMaggio makes a rare film appearance in a featured spot, and the comedy is handled by thick-accented Henry Armetta and ranch-house buffoons Smiley Burnette and Max Terhune. Definitely different and a showcase production typical of most studios that jammed as many names as possible into a film with the hope of garnering the widest possible audience.

1938 B & W 80 minutes

MARAUDERS

★★

DIRECTOR: George Archainbaud
CAST: William Boyd, Andy Clyde, Rand Brooks, Ian Wolfe, Dorinda Clifton, Mary Newton, Harry Cording, Earle Hodgins, Dick Bailey

Hopalong Cassidy and his two sidekicks take refuge in an abandoned church one rainy night and find themselves embroiled in a battle between a pious clegyman and mean-spirited Harry Cording, whose gang of thugs are intent on tearing the church down. This later effort by William Boyd still packs the good-natured humor and action of the earlier entries, but the story is routinely predictable. Fine character actor Ian Wolfe humbles it up as the man of the cloth.

1947 B & W 63 minutes

MASSACRE AT FORT HOLMAN (REASON TO LIVE...A REASON TO DIE, A)

★½

DIRECTOR: Tonino Valerii
CAST: James Coburn, Telly Savalas, Bud Spencer, Ralph Goodwin, Joseph Mitchell

Spaghetti western of marginal interest. Eight condemned men led by James Coburn, who plays a traitor to the Union Army in the Civil War, get a chance to redeem themselves by overtaking a rebel fort. Sound familar? *The Dirty Dozen, Kelly's Heroes*? Telly Savalas is the Confederate enemy he must defeat. Like most westerns of this sort, there is plenty of action, but that alone can't help the worn-out plot or western clichés. Rated PG for violence and profanity.

1984 90 minutes

MAVERICK QUEEN, THE

★★★

DIRECTOR: Joseph Kane
CAST: Barbara Stanwyck, Barry Sullivan, Scott Brady, Mary Murphy, Wallace Ford

Sparks erupt when a Pinkerton detective works undercover at a Wyoming gambling hotel that is a hangout for an outlaw gang. Barbara Stanwyck is cast aptly as the beauty who owns the hotel and is caught between her jealous lover and her love for the lawman.

1955 90 minutes

MCCABE AND MRS. MILLER

★★★★

DIRECTOR: Robert Altman

CAST: Warren Beatty, Julie Christie, Shelley Duvall, Keith Carradine

Life in the turn-of-the-century Northwest is given a first-class treatment in director Robert Altman's visually perfect comedy-drama. Sparkling performances are turned in by Warren Beatty, as a small-town wheeler-dealer, and Julie Christie, as a whore with a heart that beats to the jingle of gold and silver coins. Rated R.

1971 121 minutes

MEANEST MEN IN THE WEST, THE

DIRECTORS: Samuel Fuller, Charles S. Dubin

CAST: Charles Bronson, Lee Marvin, Lee J. Cobb, James Drury, Albert Salmi, Charles Grodin

Beware! This is the biggest ripoff ever to hit the video store shelves. It consists of two episodes of the 1960s television series *The Virginian* edited together so it appears that Charles Bronson and Lee Marvin are starring in a western together. In actuality, they were guest stars on two different episodes and never shared a scene. But that didn't stop some bozo from trying to make it look as if they did—with ludicrous results. We'll bet even the most devoted fans of the stars won't be able to watch this turkey all the way through.

1962 92 minutes

MELODY RANCH

★★½

DIRECTOR: Joseph Santley

CAST: Gene Autry, Jimmy Durante, Ann Miller, Barton MacLane, George "Gabby" Hayes, Vera Vague, Champion, Joe Sawyer, Bob Wills Orchestra, Tom London

It's hard to fathom what was going on in the minds of studio executives and the creative forces at Republic Studios in 1940, but somewhere along the line they decided to team Gene Autry with Jimmy Durante and Ann Miller, replace Smiley Burnette with Gabby Hayes and pretend nothing was different. Venerable heavy Barton MacLane provides the menace as a local gangster intent on running honorary sheriff Gene Autry out of town, but there isn't enough action to qualify this bigger-budgeted series entry as anything other than a curio and perhaps a failed effort to expand Autry's base of popularity.

1940 B & W 80 minutes

MELODY TRAIL

★★½

DIRECTOR: Joseph Kane

CAST: Gene Autry, Smiley Burnette, Ann Rutherford, Wade Boteler, Alan Bridge, Willy Castello, Marie Quillan, Fern Emmett, Gertrude Messinger, Ione Reed

The fifth Gene Autry–Smiley Burnette film is a pleasant story about a rodeo rider (Gene) who loses his winnings and is forced to work for a rancher with a romantic daughter. Needless to say, our hero manages to stop the omnipresent rustlers and save his boss's ranch as well as extricate himself from the clutches of the clinging female and escape to ever faithful and hopelessly inept Smiley Burnette.

1935 B & W 60 minutes

MIRACLE RIDER, THE

★★½

DIRECTORS: Armand Schaefer, B. Reeves "Breezy" Eason

CAST: Tom Mix, Jean Gale, Charles Middleton, Jason Robards, Edward Hearn, Robert Frazer, Ernie Adams, Wally Wales, Bob Kortmn

Tom Mix plays a Texas Ranger and friend of the Indian in this pseudoscience-fiction serial. Charles Middleton plays Zaroff, leader of a gang who preys on the superstitions of the Indians in order to scare them off their reservation. Although slow at times, this chapter play was the last time out for number-one action star Tom Mix, who had broken bones in front of the camera for twenty-five years. After this, Mix retired from the screen and concentrated on his circus and personal appearances.

1935 B & W 15 chapters

MISSOURI BREAKS, THE

★★

DIRECTOR: Arthur Penn

CAST: Marlon Brando, Jack Nicholson, Kathleen Lloyd, Harry Dean Stanton

For all its potential, this western really lets you down. The teaming of Marlon Brando and Jack Nicholson was looked upon with great anticipation when the film was announced. Nicholson is acceptable as the outlaw trying to make a clean start. Brando, on the other hand, is inconsistent as a relentless bounty hunter who's tracking Nicholson. The choppy script and the on-again, off-again, Brando performance subtract greatly from the impact of what could have been a good film. Rated PG.

1976 126 minutes

MR. HORN

★★★

DIRECTOR: Jack Starrett

CAST: David Carradine, Richard Widmark, Karen Black, Richard Masur, Jeremy Slate, Pat McCormick, Jack Starrett

William Goldman's version of the Tom Horn story lacks the screenwriter's usual light touch (as best evidenced in *Butch Cassidy and the Sundance Kid*). But this is perhaps because Goldman is more interested in debunking a western myth in this made-for-television product than promoting one. Whatever the reason, *Mr. Horn* is a bittersweet, near melancholy chronicle of the exploits of Horn (David Carradine), who is shown first as an idealistic young man helping an old-timer (Richard Widmark) track down Geronimo and later as a cynical gunman hired to eliminate some rustlers. His story ends, as did Steve McQueen's less successful *Tom Horn*, with the title character being framed and hanged for murder.

1979 200 minutes

MOHAWK

★½

DIRECTOR: Kurt Neumann

CAST: Scott Brady, Rita Gam, Neville Brand, Lori Nelson, Allison Hayes, Ted De Corsica

Cornball story about love between settler Scott Brady and Indian Rita Gam and their efforts to bring their people together must have been inspired by access to footage from John Ford's classic *Drums Along the Mohawk*, which was shot in Technicolor and has been used in dozens of early frontier films. Don't look for any of the cast in the best parts of the picture; they were all filmed more than fifteen years before this mediocrity was made. Not really bad, but filled with Hollywood clichés, typical flowery Hollywood Indian dialogue, and more New York Indians than you can shake a stick at.

1956 79 minutes

MONTE WALSH

★★★½

DIRECTOR: William Fraker

CAST: Lee Marvin, Jack Palance, Jeanne Moreau, Mitchell Ryan, Jim Davis

Sad but satisfying western about a couple of saddle pals (Lee Marvin, Jack Palance) attempting to make the transition to a new age and century. Cinematographer William Fraker made an impressive directorial debut with this fine film. Rated R for violence.

1970 106 minutes

MORE WILD WILD WEST

★★½

DIRECTOR: Burt Kennedy

CAST: Robert Conrad, Ross Martin, Jonathan Winters, Harry Morgan, René Auberjonois, Liz Torres, Victor Buono, Dr. Joyce Brothers, Emma Samms

This TV movie is a pale reminder of the irresistible original series. The Old West's most invincible Secret Service agents, James West and Artemus Gordon, again come out of retirement, this time to rescue the world from an invisibility plot. Jonathan Winters hams it up as the villainous Albert Paradine II. There's too much silly comedy, not enough excitement. Time for West and Gordon to retire permanently.

1980 94 minutes

MOUNTAIN MEN, THE

★

DIRECTOR: Richard Lang

CAST: Charlton Heston, Brian Keith, Victoria Racimo, Stephen Macht

A buddy movie about two bickering fur trappers who get involved in Indian uprisings and so on, this dull and overly violent film wastes the talents of its stars, Charlton Heston and Brian Keith. The few moments of enjoyment provided by the leads do not make up for the tedium of sitting through this disappointment. Rated R.

1980 102 minutes

MY DARLING CLEMENTINE

★★★★½

DIRECTOR: John Ford

CAST: Henry Fonda, Victor Mature, Walter Brennan, Linda Darnell, Ward Bond, Tim Holt

The epic struggle between good and evil is wrapped up in this classic retelling of the shootout at the O.K. Corral, between the Earps and the lawless Clanton family. Henry Fonda gives his Wyatt Earp a feeling of believability, perfectly matched by Walter Brennan's riveting portrayal of villainy as the head of the Clanton gang. The best part of this movie remains the phenomenal black-and-white cinematography. When director John Ford trained his cameras on his beloved Monument Valley, he created some of the most beautiful visual images ever put on film.

1946 B & W 97 minutes

MY NAME IS NOBODY

★★★½

DIRECTOR: Tonino Valerii

CAST: Henry Fonda, Terence Hill, Leo Gordon, Geoffrey Lewis

This is a delightful spoof of the Clint Eastwood spaghetti westerns. Terence Hill is a gunfighter who worships old-timer Henry Fonda, who merely wishes to go away and retire. Hill has the devil in his eyes and Fonda is really very funny with his dry manner. It appears that everyone is having fun in this movie, right down to the musical score and the typical long silences. Rated PG.

1974 115 minutes

MY PAL TRIGGER

★★★½

DIRECTOR: Frank McDonald

CAST: Roy Rogers, George "Gabby" Hayes, Dale Evans, Jack Holt, LeRoy Mason, Roy Barcroft, Trigger

One of the most fondly remembered and perhaps the best of all the Roy Rogers movies, this gentle story centers on Roy's attempts to mate his mare with a superb golden stallion. Villain Jack Holt is responsible for the death of the mare, and Roy is blamed and incarcerated. The foal grows into the great horse Trigger and is able to clear Roy's name as well as save "Gabby" Hayes's ranch, and they all settle down to a happy life together. Charming and lovingly directed, this is a fine film for the whole family and one of the highlights of the long Roy Rogers series.

1946 B & W 79 minutes

MYSTERY MOUNTAIN

★★

DIRECTORS: Otto Brewer, B. Reeves "Breezy" Eason

CAST: Ken Maynard, Verna Hillie, Edmund Cobb, Sid Saylor, Gene Autry, Bob Kortman, Tom London, George Chesebro, Lafe McKee, Smiley Burnette, Wally Wales, Art Mix, Philo McCullough

Cowboy great Ken Maynard stars in his only serial, the story of the mysterious master of disguise known as the "Rattler," who lives to wreck trains. Mascot Studios retooled their earlier John Wayne serial *Hurricane Express* and made it into a western adventure to showcase Maynard's famous riding skills. Ironically, John Wayne once starred in a series of westerns that were sound remakes of some of Ken Maynard's best silent films. Gene Autry and his silly sidekick Smiley Burnette make their second screen appearance in this chapter play, and Gene would go on to star in the next vehicle planned for Maynard, the phenomenally successful *Phantom Empire*, released the following year.

1934 B & W 12 chapters

NAKED IN THE SUN

★★½

DIRECTOR: R. John Hugh

CAST: James Craig, Barton MacLane, Lita Milan, Tony Hunter

Osceola (James Craig), war chief of the Seminole Indians, must battle unscrupulous whites, the United States Government, and his own tribe in order to live in dignity. One of many films of the 1950s that dealt with the American Indian as a noble, persecuted people. This is well-acted and effective in evoking audience sympathy, although it suffers from some script difficulties and slow pacing. Easily as enjoyable as some of the more famous "adult" westerns of the same vintage.

1957 79 minutes

NAKED SPUR, THE

★★★★½

DIRECTOR: Anthony Mann

CAST: James Stewart, Janet Leigh, Robert Ryan, Ralph Meeker, Millard Mitchell

Superb western finds bounty hunter James Stewart chasing bad guy Robert Ryan through the Rockies. Once captured, Ryan attempts to cause trouble between Stewart and his sidekicks. This is one of the many collaborations between Stewart and director Anthony Mann during the 1950s. Such great westerns as *Bend in the*

River, *Winchester '73*, and *The Naked Spur* were the result of this partnership, films that were rivaled perhaps only by the John Ford–John Wayne westerns of the late 1940s and early 1950s.

1953 91 minutes

NARROW TRAIL, THE

★★★

DIRECTOR: Lambert Hillyer

CAST: William S. Hart, Fritz the Horse

"Better a painted pony than a painted woman" was the slogan selling this above-average western about a cowboy's love for his horse. One of famous early-western star William S. Hart's many pictures, this one was something of a paean to his great horse, Fritz, the Tony and Trigger of his day. Like all Hart films, this one is marked by his scrupulous attention to authenticity of setting, scenery, and costume. Silent.

1917 B & W 56 minutes

'NEATH ARIZONA SKIES

★★½

DIRECTOR: Henry Frazer

CAST: John Wayne, Sheila Terry, Jay Wilsey, Yakima Canutt, John Rockwell, George "Gabby" Hayes

Formula B western has John Wayne as the protector of the heir to rich oil lands, a little Indian girl. Of course, the baddies try to kidnap her and the Duke rides to the rescue. Low-budget and predictable.

1934 B & W 57 minutes

NEVADA SMITH

★★★

DIRECTOR: Henry Hathaway

CAST: Steve McQueen, Karl Malden, Brian Keith, Arthur Kennedy, Suzanne Pleshette, Raf Vallone, Pat Hingle, Howard da Silva, Martin Landau

Steve McQueen, in the title role, is butcher's-freezer-cold, calculating, and merciless in this hard-hitting, gripping western. The focus is on a senseless, vicious double murder and the revenge taken by the son of the innocent victims. Story and characters are excerpted from a section of Harold Robbins's sensational novel *The Carpetbaggers* not used in the 1964 film.

1966 135 minutes

NEW FRONTIER

★★½

DIRECTOR: Carl Pierson

CAST: John Wayne, Muriel Evans, Mary McLaren, Murdock McQuarrie, Warner Richmond, Sam Flint, Earl Dwire

In a familiar plot, John Wayne is the son of a murdered sheriff out to find the baddies who did the dirty deed. Creaky but fun for fans.

1935 B & W 59 minutes

NIGHT OF THE GRIZZLY, THE

★★½

DIRECTOR: Joseph Pevney

CAST: Clint Walker, Martha Hyer, Ron Ely, Jack Elam

In order to maintain a peaceful standing in the rugged Old West, big Clint Walker must fight all the local bad guys (who should have known better) as well as a giant grizzly bear who moves in and out of camera range on a wheeled dolly. Nice outdoor sets and some good characterization help this no-frills family story, which culminates in the inevitable confrontation between Walker and the grizzly. Plenty of familiar faces among the character actors in this outdoor opus.

1966 102 minutes

NIGHT RIDERS, THE

★★½

DIRECTOR: George Sherman

CAST: John Wayne, Ray "Crash" Corrigan, Max Terhune, Doreen McKay, Ruth Rogers, Tom Tyler, Kermit Maynard

The Three Mesquiteers (John Wayne, Ray Corrigan, and Max Terhune) make like Zorro by donning cape and mask to foil a villain's attempt to enforce a phony Spanish land grant. Good formula western fun.

1939 B & W 58 minutes

NIGHT STAGE TO GALVESTON

★★

DIRECTOR: George Archainbaud

CAST: Gene Autry, Pat Buttram, Virginia Huston, Robert Livingston, Frank Sully, Thurston Hall, Clayton Moore, Harry Cording, Dick Alexander

Old-fashioned actioner set in post–Civil War South finds Gene Autry and his buddy Pat Buttram working for a crusading newspaperman who intends to expose corruption in the ranks of the Texas Rangers. Brimming with character actors from serials, westerns, and films of all kinds (including Lone Rangers Robert Livingston and Clayton Moore), this otherwise routine story is easy to watch and not too hard to forget. Shorter than most Autry films.

1952 B & W 61 minutes

NINE LIVES OF ELFEGO BACA, THE

★★★

DIRECTOR: Norman Foster

CAST: Robert Loggia, Robert F. Simon, Lisa Montell, Nestor Paiva, Leonard Strong, Charles Maxwell

Robert Loggia, as the long-lived hero of the Old West, faces one of his most harrowing perils as he confronts scores of gunmen determined to perforate him with lead and take away all of his lives. Dodging bullets and defeating the bad guys is all in a day's work for the lucky law enforcer and he comes through the gunsmoke with his integrity and body intact. Released theatrically in Europe, this topnotch Disney entry was originally shown in two parts on television as part of Disney's revolving western stories. Lots of action and fun for the whole family. Loggia is a good choice for the charismatic lead. Rated G.

1958 78 minutes

NORTH OF THE GREAT DIVIDE

★½

DIRECTOR: William Witney

CAST: Roy Rogers, Penny Edwards, Gordon Jones, Roy Barcroft, the Riders of the Purple Sage, Trigger

No-good Roy Barcroft is at it again, this time as a greedy salmon cannery owner who overfishes the waters and forces the local Indians to go hungry or turn to a life of crime. Roy Rogers plays a variation on his government agent identity but lacks the familiar support of Dale Evans, "Gabby" Hayes, or even Pat Brady in this lesser entry to the popular series.

1950 67 minutes

NORTH TO ALASKA

★★★★

DIRECTOR: Henry Hathaway

CAST: John Wayne, Stewart Granger, Capucine, Fabian, Ernie Kovacs

Rather than a typical John Wayne western, this is a John Wayne northern. It's a rough-and-tumble romantic comedy directed by Henry Hathaway. Delightfully tongue-in-cheek, it presents the Duke at his two-fisted best.

1960 122 minutes

OKLAHOMA KID, THE

★★★

DIRECTOR: Lloyd Bacon

CAST: James Cagney, Humphrey Bogart, Rosemary Lane, Donald Crisp, Charles Middleton, Ward Bond, Harvey Stephens

This big-budget Warner Brothers western inevitably elicits the simple question, "Why?" Why did Warner's choose to pool some of their top talent and put them in a routine oater about a feared gunman's revenge against the low-down snakes who hanged his innocent father and eventually kill his brother? Why did the powers-that-be decide to take James Cagney and Humphrey Bogart out of the contemporary gangster and social dramas that they excelled at and saddle them with monikers like "The Oklahoma Kid" and "Whip McCord?" Whatever the reasons were, these two screen legends, like the professionals they were, made the best of a silly situation and contributed broad, near-comic performances to put this trite story in proper perspective. "Cagney looked like a mushroom under a huge western hat, " Bogart said later, and Bogart played the epitome of the saloon slime, dressed in black and oozing menace. Definitely one of the oddest of all major sagebrush sagas, this film boasts a great cast of familiar characters as well as a musical interlude with Cagney singing "I Don't Want to Play in Your Yard" to the accompaniment of a honky-tonk piano and pair of six-shooters. We still don't have a clue why this film was made, but it's a competent curio that's fun and worth the watch.

1939 B & W 85 minutes

OKLAHOMAN, THE

★★

DIRECTOR: Francis D. Lyon

CAST: Joel McCrea, Barbara Hale, Brad Dexter, Douglas Dick, Verna Felton

Run-of-the-trail western with Joel McCrea riding point to protect the rights of an outcast Indian against white-eyed crooks.

1957 80 minutes

OLD BARN DANCE, THE

★½

DIRECTOR: Joseph Kane

CAST: Gene Autry, Smiley Burnette, Helen Valkis, Sammy McKim, Ivan Miller, Dick Weston (Roy Rogers), Champion

Typical Gene Autry hooey features the former railroad telegrapher as —what else?— a singing cowboy. He croons over the radio for a tractor company that's putting horse-dependent farmers and ranchers out of business. True to the code of the B-western star, Gene and his sidekick (Smiley Burnette) expose the tractor big shots as crooks. Important mainly as the film that introduced former singer Leonard Slye as Dick Weston. Soon after, young Dick Weston became Roy Rogers, the undisputed King of the Cowboys for the next fifteen years.

1938 B & W 60 minutes

OLD CORRAL, THE

★★★

DIRECTOR: Joseph Kane

CAST: Gene Autry, Smiley Burnette, Hope Manning, Roy Rogers, Sons of the Pioneers, Champion, Lon Chaney Jr., Buddy Roosevelt

Early Gene Autry film finds the spud-shaped singer fighting East coast gangsters who have invaded the frontier in search of a girl who knows too much. Future cowboy great Roy Rogers appears with the Sons of the Pioneer's to pick a few tunes, and former cowboy star Buddy Roosevelt makes an appearance in a supporting role.

1936 B & W 56 minutes

ON THE OLD SPANISH TRAIL

★½

DIRECTOR: William Witney

CAST: Roy Rogers, Tito Guizar, Jane Frazee, Andy Devine, Estelita Rodriguez, Charles McGraw

This odd collaboration of Republic Studios contract players finds Roy Rogers sharing the screen with Tito Guizar and Estelita Rodriguez as they take on villainous Charles McGraw and his cohorts. Gone are Dale Evans, "Gabby" Hayes, and most of the familiar elements in Rogers's homey series films, although Andy Devine adds some weight to the cast.

1947 75 minutes

ON TOP OF OLD SMOKY

★½

DIRECTOR: George Archainbaud

CAST: Gene Autry, Smiley Burnette, Gail Davis, Sheila Ryan, Kenne Duncan, Grandon Rhodes, Robert Bice, Cass County Boys, Jack Gargan

Gene Autry is reunited with old saddle pal Smiley Burnette in this familiar story of a singing cowpoke (Autry) who is mistaken for a Texas Ranger with a price on his head. Gene manages to dodge lead, inflict the audience with a few songs, and bring the bad guys to justice before the last reel ends. This is the eighty-ninth film in the long-running series and was originally released in an eighty-nine minute version.

1953 B & W 59 minutes

ONCE UPON A TIME IN THE WEST

★★★★★

DIRECTOR: Sergio Leone

CAST: Claudia Cardinale, Henry Fonda, Charles Bronson, Jason Robards, Jack Elam, Woody Strode, Lionel Stander

This superb film is the only spaghetti western that can be called a classic. A mythic tale about the coming of the railroad and the exacting of revenge with larger-than-life characters, it is a work on a par with the best by great American western film directors: John Ford, Howard Hawks, Sam Peckinpah, and Anthony Mann. Like Peckinpah's *The Wild Bunch*, it has a fervent—and well-deserved—cult following in America. Rated PG.

1969 165 minutes

ONE-EYED JACKS

★★★★

DIRECTOR: Marlon Brando

CAST: Marlon Brando, Karl Malden, Katy Jurado, Ben Johnson, Slim Pickens, Elisha Cook Jr.

Star Marlon Brando took over the reins of directing this western from Stanley Kubrick midway through production, and the result is a terrific entry in the genre. Superb supporting performances by Karl Malden, Katy Jurado, Ben Johnson, and Slim Pickens help this beautifully photographed film about an outlaw seeking revenge on a double-dealing former partner.

1961 141 minutes

100 RIFLES

★★

DIRECTOR: Tom Gries

CAST: Burt Reynolds, Raquel Welch, Jim Brown, Fernando Lamas, Dan O'Herlihy

The picture stirred controversy over guerrilla leader Raquel Welch's inter-racial love scene with deputy Jim Brown. But at this point, who cares? We're left with a so-so western yarn. Burt Reynolds, as a gun runner, has a rare opportunity to outact his co-stars. Rated R.

1969 110 minutes

OUTCAST, THE

★★

DIRECTOR: William Witney

CAST: John Derek, Joan Evans, Jim Davis

Before he became disenchanted with acting and turned to still photography, John Derek made a number of mostly mediocre films, this one among them. In this standard western, he fights to win his rightful inheritance. Justice prevails, of course, but you know that going in.

1954 90 minutes

OUTLAW, THE

★★

DIRECTORS: Howard Hughes, Howard Hawks

CAST: Jane Russell, Walter Huston, Thomas Mitchell, Jack Buetel

This once-notorious western now seems almost laughable. Jane Russell keeps her best attributes forward, but one wonders what Walter Huston and Thomas Mitchell are doing in this film. Only for those who want to know what all the fuss was about.

1943 103 minutes

OUTLAW JOSEY WALES, THE

★★★★½

DIRECTOR: Clint Eastwood

CAST: Clint Eastwood, Sondra Locke, Chief Dan George, William McKinney, John Vernon, John Mitchum, John Russell

This western, a masterpiece of characterization and action, is Clint Eastwood's best film as both an actor and director. With it, he took his place as one of the finest western film directors. Like the James Stewart/Anthony Mann collaborations of the 1950s, it focuses on a cowboy bent on bloody revenge. Josey Wales (Eastwood) is a farmer whose family is murdered by "Red Legs," a band of pillaging cutthroats who have allied themselves with the Union Army. Wales joins the Confederacy to avenge their deaths. After the war, everyone in his troop surrenders to the victorious Union except Wales. They are then murdered by Red Legs after being promised amnesty and he again becomes the hunter . . . and the hunted. Rated PG.

1976 135 minutes

PAINTED DESERT, THE

★★½

DIRECTOR: Howard Higgin

CAST: William Boyd, Helen Twelvetrees, William Farnum, J. Farrell MacDonald, Clark Gable

The future Hopalong Cassidy, William Boyd, plays a foundling who grows up on the other side of the range from his lady love and must decide between the family feud and the cattle or Helen Twelvetrees and the cattle. Silent greats, J. Farrell MacDonald and William Farnum play the rival parents locked in eternal conflict over range rights, and Clark Gable plays the dark cloud that is menacing the future of these two nice kids. Not as brisk and action-packed as the programmer westerns of the same period, but enthusiastically acted and worth the viewing just to watch a young Clark Gable, who was already on his rapid way up at MGM and wouldn't play a cowboy again until he was a star.

1931 B & W 75 minutes

PAINTED STALLION, THE

★★

DIRECTORS: William Witney, Ray Taylor

CAST: Ray Corrigan, Hoot Gibson, Sammy McKim, Jack Perrin, Hal Taliaferro, Duncan Renaldo, LeRoy Mason, Yakima Canutt

This history-bending serial finds Kit Carson, Davy Crockett, and Jim Bowie coming to the aid of Hoot Gibson as he leads a wagon train to Santa Fe. The former Mexican governor of Santa Fe doesn't want to allow the white settlers to take over his territory, so he uses every means at his disposal to stop the wagon train. But every time there is danger a mysterious female on a painted stallion shoots a whistling arrow to alert the Americans. Lots of action and plot reversals highlight this chapter play. Future Cisco Kid Duncan Renaldo plays one of the heavies.

1937 B & W 12 chapters

PALE RIDER

★★★½

DIRECTOR: Clint Eastwood

CAST: Clint Eastwood, Michael Moriarty, Carrie Snodgress, Christopher Penn, Richard Dysart, Richard Kiel, John Russell

Star-producer-director Clint Eastwood donned six-guns and a Stetson for the first time since the classic *The Outlaw Josey Wales* (1976) for this enjoyable western. The star is a mysterious avenger who comes to the aid of embattled gold prospectors in the Old West. *Pale Rider* is somewhat similar to Eastwood's 1973 *High Plains Drifter* in theme. Only this time he appears to have been sent from heaven rather than hell to right the usual wrongs. There is a welcome amount of humor in the newer film and the kind of action-oriented catharsis that prevented the 1973 release from being a first-rate entertainment. That said, *Pale Rider* is unlikely to be remembered as a milestone in the genre, even though it is well worth watching for fans. Rated R for violence and profanity.

1985 113 minutes

PALS OF THE SADDLE

★★½

DIRECTOR: George Sherman

CAST: John Wayne, Ray "Crash" Corrigan, Max Terhune, Doreen McKay, Frank Milan, Jack Kirk

The Three Mesquiteers (John Wayne, Ray Corrigan, and Max Terhune) help a woman government agent (Doreen McKay) trap a munitions ring in this enjoyable B western series entry.

1938 B & W 60 minutes

PANCHO VILLA

★★

DIRECTOR: Eugenio Martin

CAST: Telly Savalas, Clint Walker, Chuck Connors, Anne Francis

Telly Savalas plays the famous bandit to the hilt and beyond. Clint Walker runs guns for him. Chuck Connors postures as a stiff and stuffy military type. You'll soon see why the title role forever belongs to Wallace Beery. It all builds to a rousing head-on train wreck. Rated R.

1972 92 minutes

PARADISE CANYON

★★

DIRECTOR: Carl Pierson

CAST: John Wayne, Marion Burns, Yakima Canutt, Reed Howes, Peggy Murdock

A very young and sometimes awkward John Wayne stars in this low, low budget western as an undercover agent on the trail of counterfeiters (led by Yakima Canutt). For staunch Wayne and western fans only.

1935 B & W 59 minutes

PAT GARRETT AND BILLY THE KID

★★½

DIRECTOR: Sam Peckinpah

CAST: James Coburn, Kris Kristofferson, Bob Dylan, Jason Robards Jr., Rita Coolidge

This is an interesting but flawed western. James Coburn, as Pat, and Kris Kristofferson, as Billy, are good as the title characters, and director Sam Peckinpah creates some fine action scenes. However, Bob Dylan is pitifully inept in an anachronistic supporting role as Alias, and the film simply fails to jell overall. Rated R.

1973 106 minutes

PHANTOM OF THE WEST

★★

DIRECTOR: D. Ross Lederman

CAST: Tom Tyler, William Desmond, Tom Santschi, Dorothy Gulliver, Joe Bonomo, Tom Dugan, Kermit Maynard, Philo McCullough

This early sound serial featured a whole gallery of suspects that were just suspicious enough to be the mysterious Phantom, scourge of the territory. Tom Tyler is looking for his father's murderer as well as disproving rumors that he is the hooded villain. And if that's not enough, there's a gang of singing vigilantes who are shaking up the locals in their search for the Phantom and his gang. Primitive but virile, this chapter play stars a host of silent and sound adventure-film favorites, including the best known of all silent stuntmen, Joe Bonomo, and Ken Maynard's brother, Kermit. At ten episodes, *Phantom of the West* stands as one of the shortest serials ever released.

1931 B & W 10 chapters

PONY EXPRESS

★★★

DIRECTOR: Jerry Hopper

CAST: Charlton Heston, Rhonda Fleming, Jan Sterling, Forrest Tucker

Bigger than they were in life, western legends Buffalo Bill Cody and Wild Bill Hickok battle stagecoach station owners and Sioux Indians to establish the short-lived but glamorous Pony Express mail route between St. Joseph, Missouri, and Sacramento, Califorina, in the early 1860s. Rousing good action for the historical western fan who doesn't check every fact.

1953 101 minutes

POWDERSMOKE RANGE

★★½

DIRECTOR: Wallace Fox

CAST: Harry Carey Sr., Hoot Gibson, Bob Steele, Tom Tyler, Guinn "Big Boy" Williams, William Farnum, William Desmond, "Boots" Mallory, Art Mix, Wally Wales, Buffalo Bill Jr.

Despite its impressive all-star cast of western players, *Powdersmoke Range* is just an average B western. Its significance lies in it being the first film to feature Willim Colt MacDonald's Three Mesquiteers. Harry Carey, Hoot Gibson, and Guinn "Big Boy" Williams play the roles that were later claimed by Robert Livingston, Ray "Crash" Corrigan, and Max Terhune in the longest-running of the trio westerns. In eight entries in the series, John Wayne took over the role first played by Carey in this pioneering effort, which was called "The Greatest Roundup of Western Stars in History" and "The Barnum and Bailey of Westerns" on the publicity material released by RKO Pictures.

1935 71 minutes

PRAIRIE MOON

★★

DIRECTOR: Ralph Straub

CAST: Gene Autry, Smiley Burnette, Shirley Deane, Tommy Ryan, David Gorcey, Walter Tetley, Stanley Andrews, William Pawley, Tom London, Bud Osborne

Well-worn story about a promise to a dying man is shifted to Gene Autry's west and puts him in a position to care for a gangster's three children on his ranch. The kids are city-tough and cause no end of trouble, but by the end they have reformed (naturally) and help Gene and Smiley bring in a gang of rustlers. No real surprises, but familiar faces like David Gorcey and Stanley Andrews (the Old Ranger on *Death Valley Days*) make this tolerable viewing.

1938 B & W 58 minutes

PROUD REBEL, THE

★★★½

DIRECTOR: Michael Curtiz

CAST: Alan Ladd, Olivia De Havilland, David Ladd, Dean Jagger, Henry Hull

A post–Civil War sentimental drama about a Confederate veteran searching for a doctor who can cure his mute son, with father and son playing father and son. The principals in this one are excellent, the chemistry great. Well worth the watching, this was the ill-fated Alan Ladd's last "class" film.

1958 103 minutes

PURSUED

★★★

DIRECTOR: Raoul Walsh

CAST: Robert Mitchum, Judith Anderson, Dean Jagger, Harry Carey Jr., Alan Hale

A cowboy, Robert Mitchum, searches for the murderer of his father in this taut, atmospheric western. The entire cast is very good, and famed action director Raoul Walsh keeps things moving along at a brisk pace.

1947 B & W 101 minutes

QUICK AND THE DEAD, THE

★★★★½

DIRECTOR: Robert Day

CAST: Sam Elliott, Kate Capshaw, Tom Conti, Matt Clark, Kenny Morrison

This made-for-HBO western is the third in a trilogy of high-class shoot-'em-ups adapted from the stories by Louis L'Amour for star Sam Elliott. Like *The Sacketts* and *The Shadow Riders* before it, *The Quick and the Dead* is the answer to a cowboy-movie buff's prayers. Elliott is the consummate western hero of the 1980s and he is marvelous as a grizzled frontiersman who comes to the aid of a family (headed by Tom Conti and Kate Capshaw) making its way across the American wilderness. Elliott, of course, falls in love with Capshaw, and Conti has a hard time deciding whom to protect his wife from, the forthright-in-his-intentions Elliott or the grungy gang led by Matt Clark. The viewer, on the other hand, has no trouble making up his mind; this is one outstanding western.

1987 90 minutes

RACHEL AND THE STRANGER

★★★½

DIRECTOR: Norman Foster

CAST: William Holden, Loretta Young, Robert Mitchum

The leisurely-paced western is made easier to watch by a fine cast. William Holden's love for his wife Loretta Young finally comes to full blossom only after she is wooed by stranger Robert Mitchum. A nice story done with charm and class.

1948 B & W 93 minutes

RADIO RANCH (MEN WITH STEEL FACES, PHANTOM EMPIRE)

★★½

DIRECTORS: Otto Brewers, B. Reeves "Breezy" Eason

CAST: Gene Autry, Frankie Darro, Betsy King Ross, Dorothy Christy, Smiley Burnette, Wheeler Oakman

Condensed version of popular science-fiction serial *Phantom Empire*, this feature-length film sketchily tells the story of Gene Autry and his fight against scientists who want his Radio Ranch for the precious ore it contains, and his strange adventures in the underground city of Murania. This was Gene Autry's first leading role, and the success of the serial (also available on cassette) prompted the studio (Mascot recently merged to form Republic Studios) to rerelease it when Gene continued to be a success in a series of western movies. Running about one-third the length of the original serial, this version takes less time to view but doesn't make quite as much sense as the twelve-chapter serial.

1940 B & W 80 minutes

RANCHO NOTORIOUS

★★★½

DIRECTOR: Fritz Lang

CAST: Marlene Dietrich, Arthur Kennedy, Mel Ferrer, Lloyd Gough, William Frawley, Gloria Henry, Jack Elam, George Reeves

Brooding revenge western is a curio of the 1950s, one of those films that appears to mean something more than what the action implies. Carried out with style by a cast of capable second leads and bolstered by offbeat characters like Jack Elam and William Frawley, this film, while not a great western, is fun to watch and a treat for Marlene Dietrich fans. The great German director Fritz Lang, famous for foreign classics like *Metropolis* and *M* as well as the American films *Fury* and *Scarlet Street*, brings an interesting touch to this revered American art form, his second western.(*The Return of Frank James*, with Henry Fonda, was his first.) Not completely successful, but not too bad if you ignore the theme song.

1952 89 minutes

RANDY RIDES ALONE

★★★

DIRECTOR: Henry Frazer

CAST: John Wayne, Alberta Vaughan, George "Gabby" Hayes, Earl Dwire, Yakima Canutt

John Wayne stars in this enjoyable B western as a lawman who goes undercover to catch a gang that has been robbing an express office. The opening is particularly good.

1934 B & W 60 minutes

RARE BREED, THE

★★★

DIRECTOR: Andrew V. McLaglen

CAST: James Stewart, Maureen O'Hara, Brian Keith, Juliet Mills, Jack Elam, Ben Johnson

This is a generally rewarding western. Jimmy Stewart is a Texas cattle rancher who grudgingly assists an Englishwoman's (Maureen O'Hara) attempts to introduce a new line of short-horned cattle to the Texan range. The story is quite original and holds one's interest throughout.

1966 108 minutes

RAWHIDE

★★

DIRECTOR: Ray Taylor

CAST: Smith Ballew, Lou Gehrig, Lafe McKee, Evalyn Knapp, Arthur Loft

Lou Gehrig in a western? Yes, the Pride of the Yankees make one sagebrush adventure in support of former bandleader Smith Ballew, one of the least-remembered of all singing cowboys. Gehrig plays a rancher at constant odds with the badmen of the territory and Ballew plays the two-fisted young lawyer who helps to organize the honest folk in their battle against thieves and murderers. Ballew is a rather bland lead, but the presence of Gehrig alone makes this one worth a watch.

1938 B & W 58 minutes

RED RIVER

★★★★★

DIRECTOR: Howard Hawks

CAST: John Wayne, Montgomery Clift, Walter Brennan, Joanne Dru, John Ireland, Paul Fox, Coleen Gray, Noah Beery Jr., Harry Carey, Harry Carey Jr.

After seeing this western, directed by Howard Hawks, John Ford remarked, "I didn't know the big lug could act." The "big lug" he was referring to was the picture's star, John Wayne, whom Ford had brought to stardom in 1939's *Stagecoach*. This shoot-'em-up adaptation of *Mutiny on the Bounty* definitely features Wayne at his best in the role of a tough rancher making a historic cattle drive. The ending is a little unbelievable, but if you can accept or ignore it, the result is a classic cowboy picture.

1948 B & W 133 minutes

RED SUN

★★★½

DIRECTOR: Terence Young

CAST: Charles Bronson, Alain Delon, Toshiro Mifune, Ursula Andress, Capucine

Rambling pseudo–spaghetti western has an interesting premise but ultimately wastes the considerable talents of the great Japanese actor Toshiro Mifune and hands Charles Bronson another of those supporting-character roles that he underplays into a leading role just by staying away from the nonsense going on. Dashing Alain Delon has his hands full with beautiful Ursula Andress and steamy Capucine while stoic Mifune as a samurai warrior a long way from home calmly endures the humiliation required for him to collect his check and go back home. The action sequences in this overlong Italian/French/Spanish co-production are effective. Rated PG.

1972 112 minutes

RETURN OF A MAN CALLED HORSE, THE

★★★

DIRECTOR: Irvin Kershner

CAST: Richard Harris, Gale Sondergaard, Geoffrey Lewis, Bill Lucking, Jorge Luke, Enrique Lucero

The Return of a Man Called Horse is every bit as good as its predecessor, *A Man Called Horse*. Both films present an honest, and sometimes shocking, glimpse at the culture of the American Indian. The first film chronicled the events that change John Morgan (Richard Harris) from gentleman to warrior. To escape boredom, he arranges a hunt in the untamed wilderness of America. Everyone on the expedition is killed, except Morgan, who is taken as a slave by the Sioux Yellow Hand tribe and becomes a warrior. The new film picks up with a bored and unhappy Morgan deciding to return to America. Rated PG for violence.

1976 129 minutes

RETURN OF FRANK JAMES, THE

★★★

DIRECTOR: Fritz Lang

CAST: Henry Fonda, Gene Tierney, Donald Meek, John Carradine, Jackie Cooper, J. Edward Bromberg, Henry Hull

Gene Tierney made her film debut in this inevitable sequel to *Jesse James* (1939). Henry Fonda reprises his role as brother Frank and attempts to avenge Jesse's death at the hands of "dirty little coward" Bob Ford, played by John Carradine. Thanks to Fonda's fine acting and Fritz Lang's sensitive direction, what could have been a pale ripoff is an enjoyable western.

1940 92 minutes

RETURN OF THE BADMEN

★★★

DIRECTOR: Ray Enright

CAST: Randolph Scott, Ann Jeffreys, Robert Ryan, George "Gabby" Hayes, Lex Barker

Randolph Scott has his hands full in this routine western. No sooner does he settle down in Oklahoma than he must slap leather with Billy the Kid, the Dalton Gang, the Younger Brothers, and the Sundance Kid. As the latter, Robert Ryan shore ain't the appealing gunhand who rode with Butch Cassidy.

1948 B & W 90 minutes

RETURN OF THE SEVEN

★★½

DIRECTOR: Burt Kennedy

CAST: Yul Brynner, Robert Fuller, Warren Oates, Claude Akins, Emilio Fernandez, Jordan Christopher

This drab, inferior sequel to *The Magnificent Seven* follows Yul Brynner doing what he does best, getting six Yankee gunfighters fool enough to take on scores of Mexican bandits for no pay at all. Once again, the peasants of a small Mexican village being terrorized by bandits call on Brynner to help them. Nothing new whatsoever, simply another case against Hollywood's habit of following successful films with sequels. This mishmash was followed by *Guns of the Magnificent Seven*.

1966 96 minutes

RIDE IN THE WHIRLWIND

★½

DIRECTOR: Monte Hellman

CAST: Jack Nicholson, Cameron Mitchell, Millie Perkins, Harry Dean Stanton, Rupert Crosse, Tom Filer, Katherine Squire

Throwaway western with good cast of characters goes nowhere in the muddled story of three riders wrongfully pursued by an unrelenting posse. This sister production to *The Shooting* appears to have lost the toss on the editing and uses variations of the same camera shots over and over. A young Jack Nicholson also worked on the story and production end of this minor cult film.

1965 83 minutes

RIDE THE HIGH COUNTRY

★★★★½

DIRECTOR: Sam Peckinpah

CAST: Joel McCrea, Randolph Scott, Warren Oates, R. G. Armstrong, Mariette Hartley, John Anderson, James Drury, L. Q. Jones, Edgar Buchanan

Joel McCrea and Randolph Scott play two old-time gunslingers who team up to guard a gold shipment. McCrea just wants to do a good job so he can "enter (his) house justified." Scott, on the other hand, cares nothing for noble purpose and tries to steal the gold. From that point on, they are friends no longer. The result is a picture so good that McCrea and Scott decided to retire after making it—both wanted to go out with a winner and indeed did.

1962 94 minutes

RIDE THE MAN DOWN

★★

DIRECTOR: Joseph Kane

CAST: Brian Donlevy, Rod Cameron, Ella Raines, Chill Wills, Jack LaRue

A traditional western shot in the traditional manner. While waiting for its new owners to arrive, a ranch manager fights to keep the property out of the greedy hands of land grabbers. Jack LaRue plays a stinker, as usual.

1952 90 minutes

RIDE, RANGER, RIDE

★★

DIRECTOR: Joseph Kane

CAST: Gene Autry, Smiley Burnette, Kay Hughes, Monte Blue, Max Terhune, Chief Thundercloud, Iron Eyes Cody

Gene Autry, star graduate of the bland school of acting, plays the riding ranger in the title as he averts trouble with hostile Indians and patches things up between the red man and the settlers. A whole group of identifiable Indian character actors heighten this film, including the original Tonto, Chief Thundercloud, and the ageless Iron Eyes Cody.

1936 B & W 63 minutes

RIDERS OF DEATH VALLEY

★★★½

DIRECTORS: Ford Beebe, Ray Taylor

CAST: Dick Foran, Buck Jones, Leo Carrillo, Charles Bickford, Lon Chaney Jr., Noah Beery Jr., Guinn "Big Boy" Williams, Monte Blue, Glenn Strange

Somehow three-time Oscar nominee Charles Bickford ended up in a serial for Universal in 1941, but he couldn't have picked a better serial to play in. Dick Foran and his pals Buck Jones and Leo Carrillo head a group of men organized to police the mining districts and to fight it out with the thieves and murderers that flocked to the gold claims. Charles Bickford, as Wolf Reade, is the man who intends to take away all the gold. This serial provided true-life hero Buck Jones with yet another opportunity to prove what an engagingly solid figure he was, and had been for almost twenty years. One year after this fast-paced, humorous serial was released Buck Jones died in the tragic Cocoanut Grove fire.

1941 B & W 15 chapters

RIDERS OF DESTINY

★★★

DIRECTOR: Robert N. Bradbury

CAST: John Wayne, Cecilia Parker, George "Gabby" Hayes, Forrest Taylor, Al St. John, Heinie Conklin, Earl Dwire

The earliest low, low budget John Wayne B western available on tape, this casts an extremely young-looking Duke as Singin' Sandy, an undercover agent out to help ranchers regain their water rights. Fun for fans of the star.

1933 B & W 50 minutes

RIDERS OF THE DEADLINE

★★

DIRECTOR: Lesley Selander

CAST: William Boyd, Andy Clyde, Jimmy Rogers, Richard Crane, Frances Woodward, William Halligan, Robert Mitchum, Jim Bannon, Herbert Rawlinson, Monte Montana, Earl Hodgins, Bill

Beckford, Pierce Lyden, Tony Warde

Hopalong Cassidy pretends to befriend a smuggler in order to smoke out the real boss of the bad guys, who turns out to be an unsuspected pillar of the community, the local banker. Silent star Herbert Rawlinson, Jim Bannon (future Red Ryder), and soon-to-be major star Robert Mitchum take a hand in this one. Routine stuff, but better than the later films in the series and superior to many programmers of the time.

1943 B & W 70 minutes

RIDERS OF THE ROCKIES

★★½

DIRECTOR: Robert N. Bradbury

CAST: Tex Ritter, Louise Stanley, Charles King, Snub Pollard, Yakima Canutt, Horace Murphy

Entertaining Tex Ritter western finds the two-fisted singer joining a gang of rustlers in order to get the goods on them. Silent comedian Snub Pollard plays his comic sidekick and Charles King plays the man who has to face Ritter in a long, violent fight. One of Ritter's best westerns.

1937 B & W 56 minutes

RIDERS OF THE WHISTLING PINES

★½

DIRECTOR: John English

CAST: Gene Autry, Patricia White, Jimmy Lloyd, Douglass Dumbrille, Clayton Moore, Jason Robards Sr., Leon Weaver, Lane Chandler, Britt Wood

Even a fine cast of former and future cowboy stars as well as highly regarded character actors can't make a Gene Autry western much more than passable. As usual, our bland hero comes to the aid of a female in danger of being cheated out of her rightful property, and, true to the code of the western series film, the infinitely more interesting villains fold up and lose to the overweight yodeler.

1949 B & W 70 minutes

RIDIN' ON A RAINBOW

★½

DIRECTOR: Lew Landers

CAST: Gene Autry, Smiley Burnette, Mary Lee, Byron Foulger, Ed Cassidy, Forrest Taylor, Tom London, Ralf Harolde

Slow-moving, song-laden programmer spends too much time on a showboat focusing on Mary Lee (who also appeared opposite Roy Rogers) and ignores the sagebrush, cacti, and hoofbeats demanded by a largely adolescent audience. There's a pretty fair chase and roundup of bank robbers at the climax, but there are too many tunes in the middle for most action fans (even Autry fans!). Not one of the best of a generally mediocre bunch of westerns.

1941 B & W 79 minutes

RIO BRAVO

★★★★½

DIRECTOR: Howard Hawks

CAST: John Wayne, Walter Brennan, Ward Bond, Ricky Nelson, Dean Martin, John Russell, Claude Akins, Angie Dickinson, Bob Steele

A super-western, with John Wayne, Walter Brennan, Ward Bond, Ricky Nelson (aping Montgomery Clift's performance in *Red River*), and the scene-stealing Dean Martin taking on cattle baron John Russell, who's out to get his kill-crazy brother (Claude Akins) out of jail. Only Angie Dickinson is bothersome, as the Duke's too-talkative love interest, in this big-screen takeoff of the popular TV series of the era ("Maverick," "Cheyenne," "Sugarfoot," "Lawman," "Wagon Train," etc.)

1959 141 minutes

RIO CONCHOS

★★★

DIRECTOR: Gordon Douglas

CAST: Richard Boone, Stuart Whitman, Tony Franciosa, Edmond O'Brien, Jim Brown

Rip-roaring western action ignites this briskly paced yarn set in post–Civil War Texas. Richard Boone and his macho buddies try to get rich with a shipment of stolen rifles. Boone gives a wry performance. Stuart Whitman is rugged. Jim Brown, making his film debut, fits in nicely. And that entertaining character actor Edmond O'Brien is a delight in a colorful role.

1964 107 minutes

RIO GRANDE

★★★★

DIRECTOR: John Ford

CAST: John Wayne, Maureen O'Hara, Claude Jarman Jr., Ben Johnson, Harry Carey Jr., Victor McLaglen, Chill Wills, J. Carrol Naish

The last entry in director John Ford's celebrated cavalry trilogy (which also includes *Ford Apache* and *She Wore a Yellow Ribbon*), this stars John Wayne as a company commander coping with renegade Indians and a willful wife (Maureen O'Hara), who wants to take their soldier son (Claude Jarman Jr.) home.

1950 B & W 105 minutes

RIO LOBO

★★★

DIRECTOR: Howard Hawks

CAST: John Wayne, Jack Elam, Jorge Rivero, Jennifer O'Neill, Chris Mitchum, Mike Henry

Neither star John Wayne nor director Howard Hawks was exactly at the peak of his powers when this second reworking of *Rio Bravo* (the first being *El Dorado*) was released. If one adjusts the normally high expectations he or she would have for a western made by these two giants, *Rio Lobo* is a fun show. Jack Elam is terrific in a delightful supporting role. Rated G.

1970 114 minutes

ROARING GUNS

★★★

DIRECTOR: Sam Newfield

CAST: Tim McCoy, Rosalinda Price, Wheeler Oakman, Rex Lease, John Elliott, Karl Hackett, Dick Alexander

A ruthless cattle baron attempts to drive out the independent ranchers while using a phony feud with his main competitor as a cover-up. It's up to steely-eyed Tim McCoy to set things aright in this low-budget but enjoyable series western.

1936 B & W 66 minutes

ROBIN HOOD OF TEXAS

★★

DIRECTOR: Lesley Selander

CAST: Gene Autry, Lynne Roberts, Sterling Holloway, Adele Mara, James Cardwell, John Kellogg, James Flavin, Stanley Andrews, Edmund Cobb

More of a detective story than a formula western, Gene Autry's last film for Republic Studios finds him accused of bank robbery and keeping one step ahead of the law in order to clear his name. Better than many of his films and one of the best of his post-WWII movies, with a nicely turned story and more action and fisticuffs than most of Autry's productions.

1947 B & W 71 minutes

ROOSTER COGBURN

★★★½

DIRECTOR: Stuart Millar

CAST: John Wayne, Katharine Hepburn, Richard Jordan, Anthony Zerbe, Strother Martin, John McIntire

Okay, so this sequel to *True Grit* is only *The African Queen* reworked, with John Wayne playing the Humphrey Bogart part opposite the incomparable Katharine Hepburn, but we like—no, love—it. Watching these two professionals playing off each other is what movie-watching is all about. The plot? Well, it's not much, but the scenes with Wayne and Hepburn are, as indicated, priceless. Rated PG.

1975 107 minutes

ROOTIN' TOOTIN' RHYTHM

★½

DIRECTOR: Mack V. Wright

CAST: Gene Autry, Smiley Burnette, Armida, Monte Blue, Hal Taliaferro (Wally Wales), Al Clauser and his Oklahoma Outlaws, Ann Pendleton, Charles King

Gene Autry and his bumbling sidekick Smiley Burnette settle a range dispute and restore the peace to the prairie in this unimaginative programmer. The best thing about this one are the appearances by former cowboy greats Wally Wales and Monte Blue and veteran heavy Charles King. Too many songs and too much Smiley.

1938 B & W 55 minutes

ROUGH RIDERS' ROUNDUP

★★½

DIRECTOR: Joseph Kane

CAST: Roy Rogers, Mary Hart, Raymond Hatton, Eddie Acuff, William Pawley, George Meeker, Trigger

The accent is more on action than music in this early Roy Rogers western about the Rough Riders reuniting to rid the range of an outlaw gang. Raymond Hatton is along to add some first-rate sidekickery (and it is interesting to note that Hatton would team up with cowboy greats Buck Jones and Tim McCoy two years later for the Rough Riders series). In all, it's better than most of the Rogers vehicles that followed.

1939 B & W 58 minutes

ROUND-UP TIME IN TEXAS

★½

DIRECTOR: Joseph Kane

CAST: Gene Autry, Smiley Burnette, Maxine Doyle, LeRoy Mason, The Cabin Kids, Dick Wessel, Frankie Marvin

Gene Autry brings his usual air of contained energy to this fairly early entry in the long-running series Republic inflicted on unsuspecting children for over fifteen years. Filled with blank stares, lame humor, bland tunes, and insipid plot developments, this typical Autry programmer does have a good heavy in LeRoy Mason.

1937 B & W 58 minutes

RUN OF THE ARROW

★★★

DIRECTOR: Samuel Fuller

CAST: Rod Steiger, Brian Keith, Ralph Meeker, Sarita Montiel, Tim McCoy, Jay C. Flippen, Charles Bronson

One of the strangest of all adult westerns of the 1950s, this film tells the story of a man who joins the Sioux tribe after the Civil War rather than accept the reality of the South's defeat. Rod Steiger does a good job in a difficult role, and the sympathetic tone of the story was the only reason famed western authority and Indian activist Tim McCoy joined the venture after a fifteen-year hiatus from moviemaking. While not entirely successful, this thought-provoking film is well worth watching. Charles Bronson has a supporting role as one of the Indians, and a young Angie Dickinson dubbed the voice for female lead Sarita Montiel.

1957 85 minutes

RUSTLER'S VALLEY

★★

DIRECTOR: Nate Watt

CAST: William Boyd, George "Gabby" Hayes, Russell Hayden, Lee J. Cobb, Morris Ankrum, Muriel Evans

William Boyd as Hopalong Cassidy helps a rancher save his range while putting a stop to a villainous lawyer who is squeezing the locals dry with his thieving and legal shenanigans. "Gabby" Hayes and Russell Hayden lend support as Hoppy's saddle pals and future stage and screen star Lee J. Cobb rounds out his first year in films as the lawless lawyer.

1937 B & W 60 minutes

RUTHLESS FOUR, THE

★

DIRECTOR: Giorgio Capitani

CAST: Van Heflin, Gilbert Roland, Klaus Kinski, George Hilton

This spaghetti western could have been a lot worse, but that's no reason to watch it. Van Heflin plays a prospector who strikes gold, only to have to split the fortune with three other men less honest than he. This movie has some good shoot-'em-up scenes and a few surprises, but for the most part, it's quite dull.

1969 96 minutes

SACKETTS, THE

★★★★

DIRECTOR: Robert Totten

CAST: Sam Elliott, Tom Selleck, Glenn Ford, Ben Johnson, Ruth Roman, Gilbert Roland

Fine made-for-TV western adapted from two novels by Louis L'Amour, *The Daybreakers* and *The Sacketts*. Sam Elliott, Tom Selleck, Glenn Ford, and Ben Johnson are terrific in the lead roles, and there's plenty of action.

1979 200 minutes

SACRED GROUND

★★★½●

DIRECTOR: Charles B. Pierce

CAST: Tim McIntire, Jack Elam, Serene Hedin

Inter-racial marriage between a white mountain man and an Apache woman is further complicated when they have their child on the ancient burial grounds of another Indian tribe. The couple's romance and the trials they endure should hold viewer interest. Rated PG.

1983 100 minutes

SAGA OF DEATH VALLEY

★★½

DIRECTOR: Joseph Kane

CAST: Roy Rogers, George "Gabby" Hayes, Donald Barry, Frank M. Thomas, Doris Day, Jack Ingram, Hal Taliaferro, Lew Kelly, Lane Chandler, Jimmy Wakely

Early Roy Rogers film finds him fighting a gang of outlaws led by a desperado who turns out to be his own brother! The hidden identity or look-a-like theme was a common one for Roy's films of the late 1930s, but this well-produced western isn't lacking in action and excitement. "Gabby" Hayes is always a treat to watch, and Don Barry (future Red Ryder) is fine as Roy's outlaw brother. Familiar westerners Hal Taliaferro and Lane Chandler texture this one, and future singing cowboy favorite Jimmy Wakely plays a role.

1939 B & W 56 minutes

SAGEBRUSH TRAIL

★★★

DIRECTOR: Armand Schaefer
CAST: John Wayne, Nancy Shubert, Lane Chandler, Yakima Canutt, Wally Wales, Art Mix, Robert Burns, Earl Dwire

Big John Wayne, almost before he was shaving, is sent to prison for a murder he didn't commit. Naturally, our hero breaks out of the big house to clear his name. In a nice twist, he becomes friends—unknowingly—with the killer, who dies bravely in a climactic shootout. Good B western.

1933 B & W 58 minutes

SAGINAW TRAIL

★½

DIRECTOR: George Archainbaud
CAST: Gene Autry, Connie Marshall, Smiley Burnette, Eugene Borden, Ralph Reed, Henry Blair, Myron Healey, Billy Wilkerson

Similar in plot to a half dozen or more previous Gene Autry films, the only thing that's as tired as the story is Smiley Burnette, resurrected to co-star in the last six titles in the series. Overall, this is a pretty tame ending to a pretty lame run of ninety-three movies. As an actor, Gene Autry was a fair singer. Mercifully short at 56 minutes.

1953 B & W 56 minutes

SANTA FE STAMPEDE

★★½

DIRECTOR: George Sherman
CAST: John Wayne, Ray "Crash" Corrigan, Max Terhune, June Martel, William Farnum, LeRoy Mason

The Three Mesquiteers (John Wayne, Ray Corrigan, and Max Terhune) ride to the rescue of an old friend (William Farnum) who strikes it rich with a gold mine. A villain (LeRoy Mason) is trying to steal his claim. Lightweight western with plenty of action.

1938 B & W 58 minutes

SANTA FE TRAIL

★★★½

DIRECTOR: Michael Curtiz
CAST: Errol Flynn, Alan Hale, Olivia De Havilland, Ronald Reagan, Raymond Massey, Ward Bond, Van Heflin

Errol Flynn, Alan Hale, and Olivia De Havilland save this muddled western, with Ronald Reagan as one of Flynn's soldier buddies who go after John Brown (Raymond Massey).

1940 B & W 110 minutes

SANTEE

★★½

DIRECTOR: Gary Nelson
CAST: Glenn Ford, Dana Wynter, Michael Burns, Robert Donner, Jay Silverheels, Harry Townes, John Larch, Robert Wilke

Bounty hunter with a heart (Glenn Ford) loses his son and adopts the son of an outlaw he kills. A fine variety of old western hands add zip to this otherwise average oater. As usual, Ford turns in a solid performance. PG.

1973 93 minutes

SEARCHERS, THE

★★★★★

DIRECTOR: John Ford
CAST: John Wayne, Natalie Wood, Jeffrey Hunter, Ward Bond, Vera Miles, Harry Carey Jr., Lana Wood

John Ford is without a doubt the most celebrated director of westerns, and *The Searchers* is considered by many to be his masterpiece. In it, he and his favorite actor, John Wayne, reached the peak of their long and successful screen collaboration. This thoughtful film follows Ethan

Edwards (Wayne), an embittered Indian-hating, ex–Confederate soldier as he leads the search for his niece (Natalie Wood), who was kidnapped years earlier by Indians. As time goes on, we begin to wonder whether Edwards is out to save the girl or kill her.

1956 119 minutes

SHALAKO

DIRECTOR: Edward Dmytryk

CAST: Sean Connery, Brigitte Bardot, Stephen Boyd, Jack Hawkins, Honor Blackman, Woody Strode

Here's an awful British western about European immigrants Sean Connery, Brigitte Bardot, Stephen Boyd, Jack Hawkins, and Honor Blackman menaced by Apaches in the Old West. Ugh!

1968 113 minutes

SHANE

★★★★★

DIRECTOR: George Stevens

CAST: Alan Ladd, Jean Arthur, Jack Palance, Van Heflin, Ben Johnson, Elisha Cook Jr.

Shane is surely among the best westerns ever made. Alan Ladd plays the title role, the mysterious stranger who emerges to help a group of homesteaders in their struggle against the cattlemen.

1953 118 minutes

SHE WORE A YELLOW RIBBON

★★★★★

DIRECTOR: John Ford

CAST: John Wayne, Ben Johnson, Victor McLaglen, Harry Carey Jr., Mildred Natwick

Lest we forget, John Wayne was one of the screen's greatest actors. The Duke gave what was arguably his greatest performance in this gorgeous color western made by John Ford. As the aging Captain Nathan Brittles, Wayne plays a man set to retire but unwilling to leave his command at a time of impending war with the Apaches. The Ford stock company was never better: Ben Johnson, Victor McLaglen, Harry Carey Jr., and Mildred Natwick are all excellent. As a result, this is one of the great westerns.

1949 103 minutes

SHENANDOAH

★★★★

DIRECTOR: Andrew V. McLaglen

CAST: James Stewart, Doug McClure, Glenn Corbett, Patrick Wayne, Katharine Ross, George Kennedy, Strother Martin

James Stewart gives a superb performance in this, director Andrew V. McLaglen's best western. Stewart plays a patriarch determined to keep his family out of the Civil War. He ultimately fails and is forced into action to save his children from the ravages of war. It's an emotionally moving, powerful tale.

1965 105 minutes

SHINE ON HARVEST MOON

★★

DIRECTOR: Joseph Kane

CAST: Roy Rogers, Mary Hart (Lynne Roberts), Lulu Belle and Scotty, Stanley Andrews, William Farnum, Frank Jacquet, Pat Henning, David Sharpe

Roy Rogers rides to the rescue once again as he aids the forces of law and order and brings a gang of robbers to justice while clearing an old man's name. Early entry in the series boasts silent great William Farnum and character actor Stanley Andrews (The Old Ranger from *Death Valley Days*) as well as ace stunt man David Sharpe. Unfortunately, this film also showcases Lulu Bell and Scotty and gives us Mary Hart instead of Dale Evans, still years away from her fortunate teaming with the "King of the Cowboys."

1938 B & W 60 minutes

SHOOTING, THE

★★★

DIRECTOR: Monte Hellman

CAST: Warren Oates, Millie Perkins, Will Hutchins, Jack Nicholson

This early Jack Nicholson vehicle, directed by cult figure Monte Hellman, is a moody western about revenge and murder. An interesting entry into the genre, it may not be everyone's cup of tea. No rating; has some violence.

1967 82 minutes

SHOOTIST, THE

★★★★½

DIRECTOR: Don Siegel

CAST: John Wayne, Lauren Bacall, James Stewart, Ron Howard, Richard Boone, Hugh O'Brian, John Carradine, Harry Morgan, Scatman Crothers

The Shootist is a special film in many ways. Historically, it is John Wayne's final film. Cinematically, it stands on its own as an intelligent tribute to the passing of the era known as the "Wild West." Wayne's masterful performance is touching and bitterly ironic as well. He plays a famous gunfighter dying of cancer and seeking a place to die in peace, only to become a victim of his own reputation. Little did Wayne or the audience know he was, literally, dying of cancer. Rated PG.

1976 99 minutes

SHOWDOWN AT BOOT HILL

★★½

DIRECTOR: Gene Fowler Jr.

CAST: Charles Bronson, Robert Hutton, John Carradine, Carole Matthews, Paul Maxey, Thomas B. Henry

Stone-faced Charles Bronson does some impressive work as a lawman who finds that the criminal he has killed in the line of duty is actually a respected citizen in another community. The outraged citizenry of the town where he takes the body refuse to identify it and therefore cause Bronson to lose the reward money as well as to rethink his actions and the effects that they have had. This thoughtful little western is a pleasant watch, especially with veteran scene stealer John Carradine on the set.

1958 B & W 71 minutes

SILENT CONFLICT

★★

DIRECTOR: George Archainbaud

CAST: William Boyd, Andy Clyde, Rand Brooks, Virginia Belmont, Earl Hodgins, James Harrison, Forbes Murray, Herbert Rawlinson, Richard Alexander

A traveling charlatan hypnotizes and drugs Lucky into stealing money and trying to kill Hoppy and California. The same rocks, same shack, and same backgrounds found in all these later Hopalong Cassidy films get familiar to the viewer after a while, but what is different about this entry into the thirteen-year series is that Hoppy actually walks around in pajamas!

1948 B & W 61 minutes

SILVER QUEEN

★★

DIRECTOR: Lloyd Bacon

CAST: George Brent, Priscilla Lane, Bruce Cabot, Lynne Overman, Eugene Pallette, Quinn Williams

Young and devoted daughter Priscilla Lane is determined to uphold her family's honor and pay her father's debts. She does so by gambling in San Francisco, where she develops a reputation as a real sharpie.

1942 B & W 81 minutes

SILVERADO

★★★★

DIRECTOR: Lawrence Kasdan

CAST: Kevin Kline, Scott Glenn, Kevin Costner, Danny Glover, Rosanna Arquette, John Cleese, Brian Dennehy, Linda Hunt, Jeff Goldblum

Imagine a movie with the nonstop thrills of *Raiders of the Lost Ark*, the wisecracking humor of *Ghostbusters*, and the valiant heroes of the *Star Wars* series set in the Old West. This should give you a fairly good idea how entertaining this new-style western is. Directed by Lawrence Kasdan (*The Big Chill*; *Body Heat*), it tells the story of four strangers—Scott Glenn, Kevin Kline, Kevin Costner, and Danny Glover—who ride side by side to clean up the town of Silverado. Excitement, laughs, thrills, and chills abound in this marvelous movie. Even those who don't ordinarily like westerns are sure to enjoy it. Rated PG-13 for violence and profanity.

1985 133 minutes

SINGING BUCKAROO

★★

DIRECTOR: Tom Gibson

CAST: Fred Scott, William Faversham, Victoria Vinton, Cliff Nazarro, Howard Hill, Dick Curtis

Lesser-known western hero Fred Scott yodels the range for fly-by-night Spectrum Studios in this hard-ridin' horse opera about a frontier knight who pounds the prairie to help an innocent girl pursued and eventually kidnapped by villains intent on relieving her of her money. Nothing special but full of action interrupted by a few tunes. Average low budget musical western; mercifully short at less than one hour long.

1937 B & W 50 minutes

SINISTER JOURNEY

★★

DIRECTOR: George Archainbaud

CAST: William Boyd, Andy Clyde, Rand Brooks, Elaine Riley, John Kellogg, Don Haggerty, Stanley Andrews, Harry Strang, John Butler, Herbert Rawlinson

Coming to the aid of an old friend, Hoppy and his saddle pals find themselves involved in a mystery on a west-bound railroad. Standard Hopalong Cassidy film, doesn't have the punch of the earlier ones but is still worth the watch even though Hoppy doesn't wear his world-famous black outfit. This is the sixty-third in a series that was to dominate television in the late 1940s and early 1950s.

1948 B & W 58 minutes

SIOUX CITY SUE

★★

DIRECTOR: Frank McDonald

CAST: Gene Autry, Lynne Roberts, Sterling Holloway, Richard Lane, Pierre Watkins, Minerva Urecal, Kenne Duncan, Tristram Coffin, Tex Terry

Gene Autry's first film after World War II finds him in Hollywood, where he tries his luck in the movie business. Originally intended as the voice of an animated donkey, Autry wins the leading role in the picture when the big shots hear him stretch his tonsils. Rampaging rustlers throw a monkey wrench into the proceedings and provide Gene with an opportunity to show his stuff on the ground and on horseback. The inimitable Sterling Holloway leads a great cast of veteran actors and actresses.

1946 B & W 69 minutes

SKIN GAME

★★★★

DIRECTOR: Paul Bogart
CAST: James Garner, Louis Gossett Jr., Susan Clark, Edward Asner, Andrew Duggan

Perceptive social comedy/drama set during the slave era. James Garner and Louis Gossett Jr. are a pair of con artists; Garner "sells" Gossett to unsuspecting slave owners and later helps break him free. The fleecing continues until they meet up with evil Edward Asner, who catches on to the act . . . then the story takes a chilling turn toward realism. Susan Clark has a grand supporting part as another amiable bandit. Excellent on all levels. Rated PG for light violence.

1971 102 minutes

SMITH!

★★★

DIRECTOR: Michael O'Herlihy
CAST: Glenn Ford, Nancy Olson, Dean Jagger, Keenan Wynn, Warren Oates, Chief Dan George

A fine cast and sensitive screenplay distinguish this story of a strong man's efforts to secure a fair trial for an Indian accused of murder. Glenn Ford is believably rugged and righteous as he struggles with prejudice and ignorance in America's Southwest, and Chief Dan George is highly effective as the stoic focal point of the territory's rage. Great character actors Dean Jagger, Keenan Wynn, and Warren Oates help to make this offbeat Disney film memorable and a cut above the studio's productions of the same period. Good fare for the whole family. Rated G.

1969 101 minutes

SOLDIER BLUE

★★½

DIRECTOR: Ralph Nelson
CAST: Candice Bergen, Peter Strauss, John Anderson, Donald Pleasence

An extremely violent film that looks at the mistreatment of Indians at the hands of the U.S. Cavalry. This familiar subject has fared much better in films such as *Little Big Man*. Final attack is an exercise in excessive gore and violence. Rated R.

1970 112 minutes

SONG OF NEVADA

★★½

DIRECTOR: Joseph Kane
CAST: Roy Rogers, Dale Evans, Mary Lee, Bob Nolan and the Sons of the Pioneers, Lloyd Corrigan, Thurston Hall, John Eldredge, Forrest Taylor, George Meeker, Emmett Vogan, LeRoy Mason, Kenne Duncan, Si Jenks, Jack O'Shea

Roy, Dale, and the boys at the ranch come to the aid of an innocent girl who has become prey of a crook and his henchmen. This tuneful, hard-riding horse opera is chock-full of former cowboys and familiar faces and was intended to get the blood tingling and the toes tapping. It's typical of Roy's mid-1940s movies.

1944 B & W 75 minutes

SONG OF TEXAS

★★½

DIRECTOR: Joseph Kane
CAST: Roy Rogers, Sheila Ryan, Barton MacLane, Pat Brady, Harry Shannon, Arline Judge, Bob Nolan and the Sons of the Pioneers, Hal Taliaferro, Yakima Canutt, Tom London, Forrest Taylor, Eve March, Trigger

Roy Rogers and his friendly cowpokes help a former champion cowboy overcome his alcoholism and regain his self-esteem as well as corralling the bad guys and putting them in the pokey. Peopled with familiar faces like Tom London and Hal Taliaferro, this film also features great villain Barton MacLane and rodeo and stunt legend Yakima Canutt. Ignore Pat Brady and enjoy the action and even the songs in this entertaining western, one of the last of Roy's outings. Originally released at sixty-nine minutes.

1953 B & W 54 minutes

SONG OF THE GRINGO

★★

DIRECTOR: John P. McCarthy
CAST: Tex Ritter, Monte Blue, Fuzzy Knight, Joan Woodbury, Al Jennings, Warner Richmond

Tex Ritter's first western for Grand National is a low-budget shoot-'em-up with the singing cowboy as a deputy sheriff bent on cleaning out a gang of ruthless claim-jumpers. Former train robber and badman Al Jennings plays the role of the judge; legend has it that he imparted some of his skill with a gun to newcomer Ritter. Ritter's films for Grand National lack the pacing and budget that other studios added to their product, but character actors such as Fuzzy Knight and Yakima Canutt compensate for any shortcomings.

1936 B & W 62 minutes

SONS OF KATIE ELDER, THE

★★★

DIRECTOR: Henry Hathaway
CAST: John Wayne, Dean Martin, Earl Holliman, Michael Anderson Jr., James Gregory, George Kennedy, Martha Hyer, Jeremy Slate, Paul Fix

John Wayne stars in this entertaining film about four brothers reunited after the death of their mother and forced to fight to hold onto their land. Although this western rarely goes beyond the predictable, it's better than no Duke at all. There's plenty of action and roughhouse comedy.

1965 112 minutes

SOUTH OF THE BORDER

★★½

DIRECTOR: George Sherman
CAST: Gene Autry, Smiley Burnette, Lupita Tovar, Duncan Renaldo, June Storey, Mary Lee, William Farnum, Frank Reicher, Alan Edwards, Rex Lease, Reed Howes, Charles King, Hal Price, Dick Botiller, Claire DuBrey

Gene and Smiley mosey on down to Mexico as government operatives in order to quell a rebellion engineered by foreign powers who wish to control that country's oil resources. This patriotic film contains some good action scenes and boasts a fine cast of former cowboy favorites (William Farnum, Rex Lease, Charles King), as well as future Cisco Kid, Duncan Renaldo. Pretty good Gene Autry, directed by George Sherman of Hopalong Cassidy fame.

1939 B & W 71 minutes

SPIRIT OF THE WEST

★★

DIRECTOR: Otto Brower
CAST: Hoot Gibson, Doris Hill, Lafe McKee, Hooper Atchley, George Mendoza, Walter Perry, Tiny Sanford, Al Bridge

This entertaining but primitive western employs a tired old gimick that Hoot Gibson had used in previous films—that of a tough hombre who masquerades as a silly fool in order to help the gal in distress and bring the greedy, land-grabbing varmints to justice. Gibson was a real rodeo star and one of the most capable and best loved of the silent cowboy stars, but his sound films never recaptured the magic or audiences of his earlier efforts, and, like George O'Brien, Antonio Moreno, and Francis Ford, he ended up playing character bits in John Ford films.

1932 B & W 60 minutes

SPOILERS, THE

★★★★

DIRECTOR: Ray Enright
CAST: Marlene Dietrich, Randolph Scott, John Wayne, Harry Carey Sr., Russell Simpson, George Cleveland

John Wayne is a miner who strikes gold in Nome, Alaska. An unscrupulous gold commissioner (Randolph Scott) and his cronies plot to steal the rich claim. But the Duke, his partner (Harry Carey), and their backer (Marlene Dietrich) have other ideas. This was the fourth of five screen versions of Rex Beach's novel. The first, in 1914, created a sensation with its spectacular (for its time) climactic fistfight, and each remake attempted to outdo it. The Wayne-Scott battle royal still stands as the best and helps make this action-filled "northern" a real winner.

1942 87 minutes

SPRINGTIME IN THE SIERRAS

★★

DIRECTOR: William Witney
CAST: Roy Rogers, Jane Frazee, Andy Devine, Stephanie Bachelor, Roy Barcroft, Hal Landon

Beady-eyed Roy Rogers sets his sights on stopping evil Stephanie Bachelor and her hulking henchman Roy Barcroft from shooting game animals out of season. There's more action than story in this fast-paced series entry, and the tone is sober and more in keeping with the adult westerns emerging from many of the studios. Andy Devine provides the comic relief and Jane Frazee tries to take the Dale Evans role and make it her own.

1947 75 minutes

STAGECOACH

★★★★★

DIRECTOR: John Ford
CAST: John Wayne, Claire Trevor, Thomas Mitchell, John Carradine, Donald Meek, Andy Devine, George Barcroft, Tim Holt

John Ford utilized the "*Grand Hotel* formula" of placing a group of unrelated characters together in some common setting or dangerous situation. A stagecoach trip across the Old West provides the common setting and plenty of shared danger. Riding together with the mysterious Ringo Kid (John Wayne) is a grand assortment of some of Hollywood's best character actors, including Claire Trevor, Thomas Mitchell, John Carradine, Donald Meek, and Andy Devine. *Stagecoach* was Wayne's first big starring vehicle.

1939 B & W 99 minutes

STAR PACKER, THE

★★★

DIRECTOR: Robert N. Bradbury
CAST: John Wayne, Verna Hillie, George "Gabby" Hayes, Yakima Canutt, Earl Dwire, George Cleveland

The Shadow and his band of outlaws have a group of ranchers cowed until John Wayne rides into town and turns the tables on the baddies. A good B western that will be best appreciated by Wayne fans.

1934 B & W 60 minutes

STATION WEST

★★★

DIRECTOR: Sidney Lanfield
CAST: Dick Powell, Jane Greer, Tom Powers, Raymond Burr, Agnes Moorehead, Burl Ives, Regis Toomey, Steve Brodie, Guinn "Big Boy" Williams

An army undercover agent (Dick Powell) attempts to find out who is responsible for a rash of gold robberies, eventually falling in love with the ringleader (Jane Greer). This sturdy western boasts a fine supporting cast, good location cinematography, and nice action scenes. The one major drawback is that it takes the viewer only twenty minutes or so to figure out who's behind the robberies while Powell stumbles over clues for more than an hour.

1948 92 minutes

STRAIGHT TO HELL

DIRECTOR: Alex Cox
CAST: Sy Richardson, Jo Strummer, Dick Rude, Courtney Love, Dennis Hopper, Elvis Costello

Maybe—and we do mean maybe—you will find something of interest in this self-indulgent western spoof, but only if you've drunk as much tequila as the performers in the movie seem to have. Director Alex Cox, who specializes in punk cinema, such as *Repo Man* and *Sid and Nancy*, has gathered together musicians and actors for an extended in-joke that has something to do with bank robbers and thugs shooting at each other in a desert town. The only cast members who manage to be entertaining, Elvis Costello and Dennis Hopper, have little more than cameo appearances.

1987 86 minutes

STRANGE GAMBLE

★★

DIRECTOR: George Archainbaud
CAST: William Boyd, Andy Clyde, Rand Brooks, Elaine Riley, Joan Barton, James Craven, Herbert Rawlinson, Alberto Morin, Lee Tung Foo, Joel Friedkin

The crooked "boss" of a small town steals valuable mining rights from a drunken customer and leaves his sick sister without any money or place to stay. Hoppy and his pals intervene and encounter gunplay and fast riding as they attempt to return to the victim her rightful fortune. Hopalong Cassidy eschews his usual somber black and dresses like a dude in this one—he resembles Sky King. The bad element in town can't figure Hoppy out, either, and reckons he's a rival gunman come to cut in on the easy pickings. This is the sixty-sixth and last film in the thirteen-year run of the Hopalong Cassidy series.

1948 B & W 61 minutes

STRANGER AND THE GUNFIGHTER, THE

★★½

DIRECTOR: Anthony Dawson
CAST: Lee Van Cleef, Lo Lieh, Patty Shepard

The world may never be ready for this improbable mix, a tongue-in-cheek spaghetti western by way of a standard kung-fu chop-chop flick. Lee Van Cleef, as another of his weary gunslingers, teams with martial arts master Lo Lieh to find a missing treasure. The only map is in sections, each of which is tattooed on the rather delicate backsides of various comely wenches. A classic this isn't, but the fast action and camp humor make it watchable. Rated PG for violence.

1976 107 minutes

SUNSET SERENADE

★★½

DIRECTOR: Joseph Kane

CAST: Roy Rogers, George "Gabby" Hayes, Helen Parrish, Onslow Stevens, Joan Woodbury, Frank M. Thomas, Bob Nolan and the Sons of the Pioneers, Roy Barcroft, Jack Kirk, Dick Wessell, Rex Lease, Jack Ingram, Budd Buster

Beady-eyed Roy Rogers and his ornery sidekick "Gabby" Hayes thwart the plans of a couple of no-goods who aim to murder the heir to a ranch and take it over for themselves. Bob Nolan and the boys sing up a storm and dosome hard ridin' as well while character great Roy Barcroft and sagebrush veterans Rex Lease and Budd Buster give this oft-told story an element of class and authenticity. Enjoyable enough and not too demanding.

1942 B & W 58 minutes

SUPPORT YOUR LOCAL SHERIFF!

★★★★½

DIRECTOR: Burt Kennedy

CAST: James Garner, Joan Hackett, Walter Brennan, Harry Morgan, Jack Elam, Bruce Dern, Henry Jones

The time-honored backbone of the industry, the western, takes a real ribbing in this all-stops-out send-up. If it can be parodied, it is—in spades. James Garner is great as a gambler "just passing through" who gets roped into being sheriff and tames a lawless mining town against all odds, including an inept deputy, fem-lib mayor's daughter, and snide gunman. A very funny picture. Rated G.

1969 93 minutes

SUSANNA PASS

★½

DIRECTOR: William Witney

CAST: Roy Rogers, Dale Evans, Estelita Rodriguez, Martin Garralaga, Robert Emmett Keane, Lucien Littlefield, Douglas Fowley, David Sharpe, Foy Willing and the Riders of the Purple Sage, Trigger

Another variation on the crooked newspaper publisher theme, this minor effort again teams Roy Rogers and Dale Evans, the "King and Queen of the Westerns," with "Cuban Fireball" Estelita Rodriguez. Too many tunes and production numbers, as well as Republic Studios' vain effort to promote their south-of-the-border discovery, detract from the action in this film. Famous stunt man David Sharpe has a role in this one as well as performing the leaps and fights he was famous for. Filmed in Trucolor.

1949 67 minutes

TALL IN THE SADDLE

★★★★

DIRECTOR: Edwin L. Marin

CAST: John Wayne, George "Gabby" Hayes, Ward Bond, Ella Raines

A first-rate B western that combines mystery with shoot-'em-up action. John Wayne is wrongly accused of murder and must find the real culprit. Helping him is Gabby Hayes, and hindering is Ward Bond.

1944 B & W 87 minutes

TALL MEN, THE

★★

DIRECTOR: Raoul Walsh

CAST: Clark Gable, Jane Russell, Robert Ryan, Cameron Mitchell, Mae Marsh

Confederate army veterans Clark Gable and Cameron Mitchell join cattle baron Robert Ryan to drive his herd to market through Indian country. All three fancy Jane Russell, brawl for her favor, along with fighting Indians and the fickle elements.

1955 122 minutes

TELL THEM WILLIE BOY IS HERE

★★★

DIRECTOR: Abraham Polonsky

CAST: Robert Redford, Robert Blake, Katharine Ross

Robert Redford is a southwestern sheriff in the early days of this country. He is pursuing an Indian (Robert Blake) who is fleeing to avoid arrest. The story is elevated from a standard western chase by the dignity and concern shown to the Indian's viewpoint. Rated PG.

1969 96 minutes

TENNESSEE'S PARTNER

★★½

DIRECTOR: Allan Dwan

CAST: John Payne, Ronald Reagan, Rhonda Fleming, Coleen Gray

Allan Dwan directed this minor western featuring Ronald Reagan as a stranger who steps into the middle of a fight between gamblers and ends up befriending one (John Payne). This is one of Payne's better roles. He plays a bad guy who gets turned around by Reagan. Good little drama; better than the title suggests.

1955 87 minutes

TERROR OF TINY TOWN, THE

DIRECTOR: Sam Newfield

CAST: Billy Curtis, Yvonne Moray, Little Billy, John Bambury

The definitive all-midget western, with action, gunplay, romance, and a happy ending to boot. Just about as odd as they come, this turkey is an entertaining, if mysterious bad movie. One keeps asking, "Why did they do this? Are they serious?" Well, they did it, and whether they were serious or not, this little film is one of a kind.

1938 B & W 63 minutes

TEXAS

★★★

DIRECTOR: George Marshall

CAST: William Holden, Glenn Ford, Claire Trevor, George Barcroft, Edgar Buchanan, Raymond Hatton

Friends William Holden and Glenn Ford are rivals for the affections of Claire Trevor in this lively, action-jammed western pitting cattleman against cattle rustler in the sprawling land of Sam Houston. It might have been an epic, but a cost-conscious producer kept a tight rein. Good, though! And no one could play a good-hearted, trail-wise girl like Claire Trevor. Not even Dietrich or Stanwyck.

1941 B & W 93 minutes

TEXAS JOHN SLAUGHTER: GERONIMO'S REVENGE

★★½

DIRECTOR: James Neilson

CAST: Tom Tryon, Darryl Hickman, Betty Lynn, Brian Corcoran, Adeline Harris, Annette Gorman, Harry Carey Jr.

Peace-loving Texas John Slaughter is forced to take up arms against his Apache friends when renegade Geronimo goes on the warpath. Full of action and filmed in authentic-looking locations, this feature is composed of episodes originally broadcast on the popular television show *Walt Disney Presents*. Texas John Slaughter was a minor phenomenon, like the wildly popular Davy Crockett before him, and spawned a number of merchandising products, such as guns, hats, holsters, and comic books.

1960 77 minutes

TEXAS JOHN SLAUGHTER: STAMPEDE AT BITTER CREEK

★★½

DIRECTOR: Harry Keller
CAST: Tom Tyron, Harry Carey Jr., Adeline Harris, Annette Gorman, Betty Lynn, Stephen McNally, Grant Williams, Sidney Blackmer, Bill Williams

Former Texas Ranger John Slaughter is falsely accused of rustling as he attempts to drive his cattle into New Mexico despite threats from a rival rancher and his hired gun. Tom Tryon is ruggedly heroic as Texas John Slaughter in this Disney adventure western culled from episodes originally featured on *Walt Disney Presents* from 1958 to 1962.

1962 52 minutes

TEXAS JOHN SLAUGHTER: WILD TIMES

★★½

DIRECTOR: Harry Keller
CAST: Tom Tryon, Harry Carey Jr., Adeline Harris, Annette Gorman, Betty Lynn, Brian Corcoran, Robert Middleton

This film is a compilation of episodes from the popular series starring future best-selling author Tom Tryon as the lawman-turned-rancher. Handsomely photographed and well acted, these shows were originally released theatrically in Europe and, thanks to the video revolution, are available once again. Western veteran Harry Carey Jr. plays a continuing role in this series, as he did for the earlier daytime serial *Spin and Marty.*

1962 77 minutes

TEXAS LADY

★★

DIRECTOR: Tim Whelan
CAST: Claudette Colbert, Barry Sullivan, John Litel

An out-of-her-element Claudette Colbert is a crusading newspaper editor in the Old West. If you're a western fan, you'll like it.

1955 86 minutes

TEXAS TERROR

★★½

DIRECTOR: Robert N. Bradbury
CAST: John Wayne, Lucille Brown, LeRoy Mason, George "Gabby" Hayes, Buffalo Bill Jr., Yakima Canutt

John Wayne hangs up his guns (for a while) in this Lone Star western about a lawman falsely accused of the death of his friend. After the usual plot machinations and clues, Wayne finds the real culprits and gets a chance to do some hard ridin' and fancy sluggin'. Great characters, as usual, include stunt artist Yakima Canutt, silent cowboy star Buffalo Bill Jr., and the incomparable George "Gabby" Hayes.

1935 B & W 58 minutes

THERE WAS A CROOKED MAN

★★★½

DIRECTOR: Joseph L. Mankiewicz
CAST: Kirk Douglas, Henry Fonda, Hume Cronyn, Warren Oates, Burgess Meredith, Arthur O'Connell, Martin Gabel, Alan Hale, Lee Grant, John Randolph, Barbara Rhoades

Crooked-as-they-come Kirk Douglas bides and does his time harried by holier-than-thou Arizona prison warden Henry Fonda, who has more than redemption on his mind. A good plot and clever casting make this oater well worth the watching. And, yes, rattlesnakes do make good watchdogs. Rated R.

1970 123 minutes

THEY CALL ME TRINITY

★★½

DIRECTOR: E. B. Clucher

CAST: Terence Hill, Bud Spencer, Farley Granger

This western comedy can be best described as an Italian *Blazing Saddles*. Terence Hill and Bud Spencer team up as half-brothers trying to protect a colony from cattle rustlers and a shady sheriff. Rated G.

1971 109 minutes

THEY DIED WITH THEIR BOOTS ON

★★★★

DIRECTOR: Raoul Walsh

CAST: Errol Flynn, Olivia De Havilland, Arthur Kennedy, Gene Lockhart, Anthony Quinn, Sydney Greenstreet

Errol Flynn gives a first-rate performance as General George Custer in this Warner Bros. classic directed by Raoul Walsh. The superb supporting cast adds to this western epic.

1941 B & W 138 minutes

THREE FACES WEST

★★★

DIRECTOR: Bernard Vorhaus

CAST: John Wayne, Charles Coburn, Sigrid Gurie, Spencer Charters

John Wayne is the leader of a group of Dust Bowl farmers attempting to survive in this surprisingly watchable Republic release. Sigrid Gurie and Charles Coburn co-star as the European immigrants who show them what courage means.

1940 B & W 79 minutes

3:10 TO YUMA

★★★★

DIRECTOR: Delmer Daves

CAST: Glenn Ford, Van Heflin, Felicia Farr, Leora Dana, Henry Jones, Richard Jaeckel, Robert Emhardt

This first-rate adult western draws its riveting drama and power from the interaction of well-drawn characters rather than gun-blazing action. A farmer (Van Heflin) captures a notorious gunman (Glenn Ford) and, while waiting for the train to take them to Yuma prison, must hole up in a hotel and overcome the killer's numerous ploys to gain his freedom. This well-acted movie recalls the classic *High Noon*.

1957 B & W 92 minutes

TIN STAR, THE

★★★★

DIRECTOR: Anthony Mann

CAST: Henry Fonda, Anthony Perkins, Betsy Palmer, John McIntire, Michel Ray, Neville Brand, Mary Webster, Lee Van Cleef

Solid Anthony Mann–directed "adult" western has Anthony Perkins as the inexperienced sheriff of a wild-and-woolly town seeking the help of hardened gunfighter Henry Fonda. Although it contains some unconvincing moments, *The Tin Star* succeeds overall thanks to the skilled playing of its cast and Mann's typically tough style of storytelling. The film served as the inspiration for Fonda's 1960s television series, *The Deputy*. Dudley Nichols co-scripted.

1957 B & W 93 minutes

TOM HORN

★★½

DIRECTOR: William Wiard

CAST: Steve McQueen, Richard Farnsworth, Billy Green

Bush, Slim Pickens, Elisha Cook Jr.

Steve McQueen doesn't give a great performance in his next-to-last motion picture, about the last days of a real-life Wyoming bounty hunter, nor does director William Wiard craft a memorable western. But this 1980 release does have its moments—most of them provided by supporting players Richard Farnsworth (*The Grey Fox*), Billy Green Bush (*The Culpepper Cattle Company*), the late Slim Pickens, and the always reliable Elisha Cook. Rated R.

1980 98 minutes

TRAIL BEYOND, THE

★★½

DIRECTOR: Robert N. Bradbury
CAST: John Wayne, Verna Hillie, Noah Beery Sr., Irish Lancaster, Noah Beery Jr., Robert Frazer, Earl Dwire

Once again, John Wayne rides to the rescue in a low-budget western from the 1930s. It's pretty typical stuff as the Duke fights outlaws who are attempting to steal a gold mine. But this B western has lots of action and a rare appearance of father and son actors Noah Beery Sr. and Noah Beery Jr.

1934 B & W 55 minutes

TRAIL OF ROBIN HOOD

★★★

DIRECTOR: William Witney
CAST: Roy Rogers, Penny Edwards, Gordon Jones, Jack Holt, Emory Parnell, Clifton Young, Rex Allen, Allan "Rocky" Lane, Monte Hale, Kermit Maynard, Tom Keene, Ray "Crash" Corrigan, William Farnum, George Chesebro

This star-studded oddity finds Roy Rogers and a handful of contemporary western heroes aiding screen great Jack Holt (playing himself) in his effort to provide Christmas trees to needy families in time for the holidays. A pleasant yuletide gift to the children of America from Republic Studios, this warm-hearted film gives us nine sagebrush stars and former six-gun toters as well as reuniting near-legendary heavy George Chesebro with Jack Holt, one of the finest of all action stars and the father of 1950s hero Tim Holt. This ensemble film (like the previous *Bells of Rosarita*, etc.) gave the studio a chance to show off their contract stars. Enjoyable film for all ages and a special treat for fans of the genre. One of Roy's strangest films.

1950 67 minutes

TRAIL STREET

★★★

DIRECTOR: Ray Enright
CAST: Randolph Scott, Robert Ryan, Anne Jeffreys, George "Gabby" Hayes, Steve Brodie, Madge Meredith

Randolph Scott plays Bat Masterson in this well-acted story of conflicting western philosophies as Robert Ryan defends the farmers against gambler Steve Brodie and the cattle-rancher faction. "Gabby" Hayes lends some levity to this otherwise dramatic adult western, and Anne Jeffreys plays the saloon girl who must choose between Scott and Brodie. Skillful repackaging of a familiar story, this was a coup for both Scott and Ryan and they would both continue to make intelligent, compelling westerns for years to come.

1947 B & W 84 minutes

TRAIN ROBBERS, THE

★★½

DIRECTOR: Burt Kennedy
CAST: John Wayne, Ben Johnson, Ann-Margret, Rod Taylor, Ricardo Montalban

This is a typical example of John Wayne's films during his last decade of work. A good cast and an interesting idea go to waste at the hands of a second-rate director. Burt Kennedy and fellow director Andrew V. McLaglen were at the helm during most of Wayne's westerns throughout the 1970s, and neither could do him justice. This is no exception. Wayne and Ben Johnson join Ann-Margret in a search for a lost train and gold. Some nice moments but generally unsatisfying. For hard-core Wayne fans only. Rated PG for violence, but nothing extreme.

1973 92 minutes

TRAITOR, THE

★★½

DIRECTOR: Sam Newfield

CAST: Tim McCoy, Frances Grant, Wally Wales, J. Frank Glendon, Karl Hackett, Jack Rockwell

Marshal Tim McCoy goes undercover to catch a gang of cutthroats. He succeeds in his plan of joining the outlaws, but his life is in constant danger. This routine western features a game performance by McCoy, but the story is too typical and the direction is plodding.

1936 B & W 56 minutes

TRAMPLERS, THE

★½

DIRECTOR: Albert Band

CAST: Gordon Scott, Joseph Cotten, James Mitchum, Ilaria Occhini, Franco Nero

Gordon Scott returns from the Civil War to find his father (Joseph Cotten) trying to preserve the prewar South by burning out settlers and starting mass lynchings. Scott and his younger brother (James Mitchum), unable to abide his fathers actions, leave and join up with their father's enemies. In typical spaghetti western fashion, the film ends with the big shootout. Hard-core western fans may enjoy this film, but all others will not find much entertainment.

1966 105 minutes

TREASURE OF PANCHO VILLA, THE

★

DIRECTOR: George Sherman

CAST: Rory Calhoun, Shelley Winters, Gilbert Roland, Joseph Calleia

The legendary Mexican bandit has long been a film subject. This slow account of his exploits does little for his reputation and appeal as a colorful character of history. Only a good cast keeps it from being dubbed a bomb.

1955 96 minutes

TRIGGER, JR.

★★★

DIRECTOR: William Witney

CAST: Roy Rogers, Dale Evans, Pat Brady, Gordon Jones, Grant Withers, Peter Miles, George Cleveland, Frank Fenton, I. Stanford Jolley, Stanley Andrews, Foy Willing and the Riders of the Purple Stage, The Raynor Lehr Circus

This Trucolor Roy Rogers film has everything going for it in the form of plot, songs, character actors, and hard ridin'. Roy, Dale, and the gang battle an unscrupulous gang of blackmailers as well as teaching a young boy to overcome his fear of horses, particularly Trigger and his son, Trigger Jr. There's even a circus to prompt some tunes from Roy and Dale and their backup ranch hands.

1950 68 minutes

TRINITY IS STILL MY NAME

★★

DIRECTOR: E. B. Clucher
CAST: Bud Spencer, Terence Hill, Harry Carey Jr.

In this comedy sequel to *They Call Me Trinity*, Bud Spencer and Terence Hill again team up as the unlikely heroes of an Italian western. Rated G.

1972 117 minutes

TRIUMPHS OF A MAN CALLED HORSE

★½

DIRECTOR: John Hough
CAST: Richard Harris, Michael Beck, Ana De Sade

Richard Harris has his third go-round in the title role as John Morgan, an English nobleman who was captured by the Sioux in 1825 and eventually became their leader. Unlike its excellent predecessors, *A Man Called Horse* and *Return of a Man Called Horse*, *Triumphs* is cornball, cliché, and badly directed, by Englishman John Hough. In a real cheat, Harris is killed off in the first third of the film. That leaves the way clear for his gun-slinging son, Koda (Michael Beck), to take over the leadership of the tribe and battle the greedy gold prospectors invading their land. Yawn. Rated PG for violence and implied sex.

1983 86 minutes

TROUBLE IN TEXAS

★★½

DIRECTOR: Robert N. Bradbury
CAST: Tex Ritter, Rita Cansino (Hayworth), Earl Dwire, Yakima Canutt, Charles King, Dick Palmer

Two-fisted singing rodeo cowboy Tex Ritter investigates crooked rodeo contests and seeks the identity of the men responsible for the death of his brother. Future glamor girl Rita Hayworth appears on screen for the last time under her real name as an undercover agent who assists Ritter and his salty sidekick Earl Dwire. The dean of stuntmen, Yakima Canutt, plays one of the principal heavies. Filled with good stunts and furious fighting, this series entry features some memorable tunes, including the mournful "Rodeo Song." Directed by the seasoned Robert N. Bradbury, who was responsible for many of John Wayne's early films, this oater boasts a wild chase on a dynamite-laden wagon for a finale, a stunt that Yakima Canutt perfected and would be put to use in subsequent films.

1937 B & W 53 minutes

TRUE GRIT

★★★★

DIRECTOR: Henry Hathaway
CAST: John Wayne, Kim Darby, Robert Duvall, Glen Campbell

John Wayne finally won his best-actor Oscar for his 1969 portrayal of a boozy marshal helping a tough-minded girl (Kim Darby) track down her father's killers. Well-directed by Henry Hathaway, it's still not one of the Duke's classics—although it does have many good scenes, the best of which is the final shootout between Wayne's Rooster Cogburn and chief baddie, Ned Pepper (Robert Duvall). Rated G.

1969 128 minutes

TUMBLEWEEDS

★★★½

DIRECTORS: Wiliam S. Hart, King Baggott
CAST: William S. Hart, Barbara Bedford, J. Gordon Russell, Richard B. Neil, Lucien Littlefield, Jack Murphy, Lillian Leighton, George Marion

One of silent films greatest action sequences, the Oklahoma Land Rush along the Cherokee Strip, highlights this prestigious western, famed cowboy star William S. Hart's final film. He retired to write novels. This version, which was introduced with a prologue spoken by Hart—his only venture into sound film—was released in 1939. Silent, with musical score.

1925 B & W 114 minutes

TWILIGHT IN THE SIERRAS

★★

DIRECTOR: William Witney

CAST: Roy Rogers, Dale Evans, Estelita Rodriguez, Pat Brady, Russ Vincent, George Meeker, Fred Kohler Jr., House Peters Jr., Edward Keane, Pierce Lyden, Bob Burns, Foy Willing and the Riders of the Purple Sage

Roy Rogers and his sweetheart Dale Evans are weighed down by Estelita Rodriguez and moronic comedy relief Pat Brady in this story about state parole officer Roy and his two-fisted battles with a group of counterfeiters. Not as good as most of the series, this one runs a long (for a Roy Rogers) sixty-seven minutes and was filmed in Trucolor.

1950 67 minutes

TWO MULES FOR SISTER SARA

★★★

DIRECTOR: Don Siegel

CAST: Clint Eastwood, Shirley MacLaine, Manolo Fabregas

Clint Eastwood returns in his role of the Man with No Name (originated in Sergio Leone's Italian spaghetti westerns: *A Fistful of Dollars; For a Few Dollars More*; etc.), and Shirley MacLaine is an unlikely nun in this entertaining comedy-western. Rated PG.

1970 105 minutes

TWO RODE TOGETHER

★★★

DIRECTOR: John Ford

CAST: James Stewart, Richard Widmark, Shirley Jones, John McIntire, Woody Strode, Linda Cristal, Andy Devine, Henry Brandon, Mae Marsh, Anna Lee, Ken Curtis, John Qualen, Harry Carey Jr., Willis Bouchey, Jeanette Nolan, Paul Birch, Olive Carey, Ford Rainey

In this variation of *The Searchers*, director John Ford explores the anguish of settlers over the children they have lost to Indian raiding parties and the racial prejudice that arises when one boy, now a full-blown warrior, is returned to his "people." It is not a fully effective film, but it does have its moments. Ford attempts to use his style of broad comedy to balance the harsher aspects of the story with only marginal success. What does work is the relationship between the two protagonists, a cynical sheriff (James Stewart) and his friend, a career officer (Richard Widmark) in the cavalry. Like John Wayne's Ethan Edwards in *The Searchers*, Stewart's character is a hardened man. The difference between them is that Wayne was out for revenge while Stewart wants only money. This casts him, and the film itself, in an unsympathetic light that is never quite overcome.

1961 109 minutes

UNDEFEATED, THE

★★

DIRECTOR: Andrew V. McLaglen

CAST: John Wayne, Rock Hudson, Bruce Cabot, Ben Johnson, Antonio Aguilar, Harry Carey Jr., Lee Meriwether, Marian McCargo, John Agar, Roman Gabriel, Merlin Olsen, Paul Fix, Royal Dano, Dub Taylor, Pedro Armendariz Jr., Jan-Michael Vincent, Gregg Palmer

Lumbering large-scale western has Yankee colonel John Wayne forming an uneasy alliance with Confederate colonel Rock Hudson to sell wild horses to the French in Mexico during the war between Maximilian and Juarez. This film has little to recommend it—even to die-hard Wayne fans. The story is silly, and the direction is confused. Even the action is minimal. Rated PG.

1969 119 minutes

UNDER CALIFORNIA STARS

★★½

DIRECTOR: William Witney

CAST: Roy Rogers, Jane Frazee, Andy Devine, Michael Chapin, Wade Crosby, House Peters Jr., Steve Clark, Bob Nolan and the Sons of the Pioneers

Trigger, the "Smartest Horse in the Movies," is the victim of a horsenapping plot in this Roy Rogers oater. A gang of no-goods decide to stop trapping and selling regular wild horses and set their sights on the golden stallion, much to Roy's dismay. With the help of wheezing Andy Devine and Bob Nolan and his singing cowpokes, Roy saves his prized palomino and brings the culprits to justice.

1948 71 minutes

UNEXPECTED GUEST

★★

DIRECTOR: George Archainbaud

CAST: William Boyd, Andy Clyde, Rand Brooks, Una O'Connor, John Parrish, Earle Hodgins, Robert B. Williams, Patricia Tate, Ned Young, Joel Friedkin

Hopalong Cassidy comes to the aid of his saddle pal and comic relief California (Andy Clyde) after they discover that someone is trying to murder the cantankerous old cuss and all of his relatives. Hoppy gets to the bottom of things and uncovers a plot that revolves around an inheritance due the family.

1947 B & W 59 minutes

UNFORGIVEN, THE

★★★½

DIRECTOR: John Huston

CAST: Burt Lancaster, Audrey Hepburn, Audie Murphy, John Saxon, Charles Bickford, Lillian Gish, Doug McClure, Joseph Wiseman, Albert Salmi

This tough Texas saga is filled with pride, prejudice, and passion. Audrey Hepburn, as a troubled half-breed, is at the center of the turmoil. In addition to some intriguing relationships, the movie provides plenty of thrills with intense cowboy versus Indian action scenes. The cast is uniformly excellent.

1960 125 minutes

VALLEY OF FIRE

★★

DIRECTOR: John English

CAST: Gene Autry, Pat Buttram Gail Davis, Russell Hayden, Riley Hall, Terry Frost, Gregg Barton, Harry Lauter, Margie Liszt, Victor Sen Yung

Gene Autry's bland personality, flashing fists, and spontaneous burst of song are more then enough to tame a wide-open town. After dispersing or recruiting the bad elements in town, Gene plays matchmaker and, along with comic relief Pat Buttram, delivers a flock of females just dying to marry up with smelly prospectors and settle down in greasy tents. Pretty good fun and peopled with cowboy (and cowgirl) favorites from films and television.

1951 B & W 63 minutes

VENGEANCE VALLEY

★★

DIRECTOR: Richard Thorpe

CAST: Burt Lancaster, Robert Walker, Joanne Dru, Ray Collins, John Ireland, Sally Forrest

Slow-moving story of no-good cattle heir Robert Walker and his protective foster brother Burt Lancaster lacks suspense and doesn't have enough action. Nicely acted and well cast, this overblown drama can't compare with the superior westerns from Anthony Mann, Budd Boetticher, and Samuel Fuller that would help to redefine the genre during the 1950s. This was one of Robert Walker's last films before his premature death.

1951 83 minutes

VERA CRUZ

★★★

DIRECTOR: Robert Aldrich

CAST: Gary Cooper, Burt Lancaster, Denise Darcel, Ernest Borgnine

Two American soldiers of fortune find themselves in different camps during one of the many Mexican revolutions of the 1800s. Gary Cooper is the good guy, but Burt Lancaster steals every scene as the smiling, black-dressed baddie. The plot is pretty basic but holds your interest until the traditional climactic gunfight.

1954 94 minutes

VIGILANTES ARE COMING!

★★½

DIRECTORS: Mack V. Wright, Ray Taylor

CAST: Robert Livingston, Kay Hughes, Guinn "Big Boy" Williams, Raymond Hatton, Fred Kohler, William Farnum, Bob Kortman, Ray Corrigan, Yakima Canutt

This early Republic serial features Robert Livingston in a story suspiciously similar to the Zorro legend; a young man returns to 1840s California and finds that an evil despot has taken his family's lands so he dons a mask and robe and finds the oppressor under the name of The Eagle. Action-packed and with impressive stunts.

1936 B & W 12 chapters

VILLA RIDES

★★

DIRECTOR: Buzz Kulik

CAST: Yul Brynner, Robert Mitchum, Charles Bronson, Herbert Lom, Jill Ireland, Alexander Knox, Fernando Rey

Uneven rehash of the Pancho Villa legend ignores the wealth of the real story and becomes yet another comic-book adventure of the lethal yet patriotic bandit-hero and the gringo he comes to depend on and grudgingly respect. Yul Brynner puts on some hair and steps under the same sombrero worn on different occasions by Wallace Beery and Telly Savalas and brings about the same understanding to the role. Robert Mitchum reprises his character from Richard Fleischer's *Bandido* and is always interesting to watch even when he's laid back—the same goes for Charles Bronson, who plays another of his enigmatic, dangerous characters. Good cast, but this ill-fated production doesn't deliver what it should, and film buffs will always chalk it up to the fact that Sam Peckinpah's screenplay was tampered with and his direct involvement with the project limited. There are still some good films to be made about the United States' "war" with Mexico and Villa in the second decade of this century, but unfortunately, this isn't one of them.

1968 125 minutes

VIRGINIAN, THE

★★★★

DIRECTOR: Victor Fleming

CAST: Gary Cooper, Walter Huston, Mary Brian, Richard Arlen, Eugene Pallette, Chester Conklin, Helen Ware, Jack Pennick

"If you want to call me that—smile!" Although a bit slow in parts, this early western still impresses today. Gary Cooper (with a drawl helped along by coach Randolph Scott) is terrific in the title role as a fun-loving but tough ranch foreman who has to face the worst task of his life when a friend (Richard Arlen) falls in with an outlaw (Walter Huston). Huston, in his first film, plays the role of Trampas with an air of easygoing menace. Mary Brian is the schoolteacher who wins our hero's heart, while Eugene Pallette and Chester Conklin do the sidekick honors. It's a classic.

1929 B & W 90 minutes

WAGONMASTER

★★★★½

DIRECTOR: John Ford

CAST: Ben Johnson, Ward Bond, Harry Carey Jr., Joanne Dru, James Arness

John Ford was unquestionably the greatest director of westerns. This release ranks with the best of Ford's work. The only reason we can fathom for its being ignored is the absence of a big-name star. Yet Bond, who plays the elder in this story of a Mormon congregation migrating west, became a star, thanks to the popular television series it inspired: "Wagon Train." And Johnson, who won the best-supporting-actor Oscar in 1971 for *The Last Picture Show*, is excellent in his first starring role. Thanks to them and Ford's genius, *Wagonmaster* is a first-rate western.

1950 B & W 86 minutes

WANTED: DEAD OR ALIVE (TELEVISION SERIES)

★★★½

DIRECTORS: Thomas Carr, Richard Donner

CAST: Steve McQueen, Wright King

The public was first captivated by Steve McQueen's cool, tough, intense persona with this topnotch western series. McQueen plays dedicated bounty hunter Josh Randall, who travels the country searching for outlaws with his "Mare's Leg," a sawed-off rifle, strapped to his side. Often, Randall found himself in the role of protector of the downtrodden. Among the beneficiaries of his courage were troubled children, persecuted Indians, desperate wives, a Japanese geisha girl, and even a pet ewe named Baa-Baa. Though there was occasionally room for sentiment, romance, or humor, the key ingredients were taut stories and violent action. Among the guest stars were Victor Jory, Jay Silverheels, Martin Landau, Michael Landon, Nick Adams, Jay North, James Best, Mala Powers, Beverly Garland, Susan Oliver, Noah Beery, Warren Oates, DeForest Kelley, and Mary Tyler Moore. In a recurring role, Wright King played Jason Nichols, Randall's ingenuous partner. The first video releases feature "Reunion for Revenge" with James Coburn and Ralph Meeker and "Medicine Man" with J. Pat O'Malley and Cloris Leachman.

1958–1961 Colorized 30 minutes

WAR OF THE WILDCATS

★★★

DIRECTOR: Albert S. Rogell

CAST: John Wayne, Martha Scott, Albert Dekker, George "Gabby" Hayes, Sidney Blackmer, Dale Evans

Big John Wayne takes on bad guy Albert Dekker in this story of oil drillers at the turn of the century. "Gabby" Hayes adds a vintage touch to this standard-formula Republic feature.

1943 B & W 102 minutes

WAR WAGON, THE

★★★

DIRECTOR: Burt Kennedy
CAST: John Wayne, Kirk Douglas, Howard Keel, Keenan Wynn

While not John Wayne at his best, this western, co-starring Kirk Douglas and directed by Burt Kennedy, does have plenty of laughs and action. Its guaranteed to keep fans of the Duke and shoot-'em-ups pleasantly entertained.

1967 101 minutes

WARLOCK

★★★

DIRECTOR: Edward Dmytryk
CAST: Henry Fonda, Richard Widmark, Anthony Quinn, Dorothy Malone

Even a high-voltage cast cannot energize this slow-paced "adult" western. Lack of action hurts this film, which concentrates on psychological homosexual aspects of the relationship between gunfighter Henry Fonda and gambler Anthony Quinn. Richard Widmark is all but lost in the background as the town sheriff.

1959 121 minutes

WATERHOLE 3

★★★

DIRECTOR: William Graham
CAST: James Coburn, Carroll O'Connor, Margaret Blye, Bruce Dern, Claude Akins, Joan Blondell, James Whitmore

This amusing western-comedy follows the misadventures of three Confederate soldiers, led by James Coburn, who rob the Union army of a fortune in gold and bury it by a waterhole in the desert. Director William Graham keeps things moving along, but one suspects producer Blake Edwards was pulling the strings behind the scenes. At the time of its release, Coburn was at the height of his popularity and easily carries this mildly diverting film with his considerable talents.

1967 95 minutes

WEST OF THE DIVIDE

★★★

DIRECTOR: Robert N. Bradbury
CAST: John Wayne, Virginia Brown Faire, George "Gabby" Hayes, Lloyd Whitlock, Yakima Canutt, Earl Dwire

John Wayne is on the trail of his father's murderer (again) in this standard B western, which has the slight twist of having the Duke also searching for his younger brother, who has been missing since dear old Dad took the fatal bullet. Looks as if it was made in a day—and probably was. Good stunt work, though.

1934 B & W 54 minutes

WESTERNER, THE

★★★★

DIRECTOR: William Wyler
CAST: Gary Cooper, Walter Brennan, Forrest Tucker, Chill Wills, Dana Andrews, Tom Tyler, Fred Stone, Doris Davenport

The plot revolves around earnest settlers being run off their land. But the heart of this classic yarn rests in the complex relationship that entwines Judge Roy Bean (Walter Brennan) and a lanky stranger (Gary Cooper). Bean is a fascinating character, burdened with a strange sense of morality and an obsession for actress Lily Langtree. Brennan won an Oscar for his portrayal. Cooper is at his laconic best. And director William Wyler gives the film a haunting, lyrical quality.

1940 B & W 100 minutes

WHEEL OF FORTUNE

★★½

DIRECTOR: John H. Auer
CAST: John Wayne, Frances Dee, Ward Bond

John Wayne in a screwball comedy? Yep. Also titled *A Man Betrayed*, the surprise is that this low-budget production is watchable.

1941 B & W 83 minutes

WHEN A MAN RIDES ALONE

★★

DIRECTOR: J. P. McGowan
CAST: Tom Tyler, Alan Bridge

Whenever John Wayne needed a formidable screen opponent, Tom Tyler was a good choice. John Ford used the deep-voiced, steely-eyed Tyler to portray Luke Plummer, the Ringo Kid's enemy, in *Stagecoach* (1939). Tyler also drew down on the Duke in Howard Hawk's *Red River* (1948) and played a heroic soldier who sang the title tune in Ford's *She Wore a Yellow Ribbon* (1949). But mostly, Tyler was a star of B westerns like this none too original entry about a Robin Hood–style good guy thwarting a crooked mine owner. Tyler became one of the Three Mesquiteers (with Bob Steele) toward the end of that popular series and is perhaps best known today as the star of the superhero serial *The Adventures of Captain Marvel* and as the title monster in *The Mummy's Hand*.

1933 B & W 60 minutes

WHEN THE LEGENDS DIE

★★★½

DIRECTOR: Stuart Millar
CAST: Richard Widmark, Frederic Forrest

A young Ute Indian is taken from his home in the Colorado Rockies after his parents die. In the modern white world he is taught the "new ways." His extraordinary riding abilities make him a target for exploitation as Red Dillon (Richard Widmark) trains him as a rodeo bronco rider, then proceeds to cash in on his protégé's success. A touching story that finds Widmark in one of his better roles and introduces a young Frederic Forrest. Rated PG for some mild profanity.

1972 105 minutes

WILD BUNCH, THE

★★★★½

DIRECTOR: Sam Peckinpah
CAST: William Holden, Ernest Borgnine, Robert Ryan, Ben Johnson, Edmond O'Brien, Warren Oates, Strother Martin, L. Q. Jones, Emilio Fernandez

The Wild Bunch, a classic western, was brilliantly directed by Sam Peckinpah. He created a whole new approach to violence in this landmark film about men making a last stand. It is without a doubt Peckinpah's greatest film and is bursting with action, vibrant characters, and memorable dialogue. Good acting, too, by a first-rate cast. Rated R.

1969 145 minutes

WILD ROVERS, THE

★★★★

DIRECTOR: Blake Edwards
CAST: William Holden, Ryan O'Neal, Karl Malden, Tom Skerritt, Lynn Carlin, Joe Don Baker, Moses Gunn

Sadly overlooked western tells the story of two cowboys, William Holden and Ryan O'Neal, running from the law after robbing a bank. Holden is perfect as the older and not so wiser of the two, and O'Neal gives one of his best performances as the young partner. Rich in texture and smoothly directed by Blake Edwards, *The Wild Rovers* is a must-see for fans of the genre. Rated PG.

1971 109 minutes

WILD TIMES

★★★

DIRECTOR: Richard Compton

CAST: Sam Elliott, Ben Johnson, Timothy Scott, Harry Carey Jr., Bruce Boxleitner, Penny Peyser, Dennis Hopper, Cameron Mitchell, Pat Hingle, Gene Evans, Leif Erickson, Trish Stewart

A two-cassette western originally made for television. Sam Elliott plays sharp-shooter High Cardiff, whose life is anything but easy as he makes his way across the Old West. This could have been helped by some trimming.

1980 200 minutes

WILD WILD WEST REVISITED, THE

★★★

DIRECTOR: Burt Kennedy

CAST: Robert Conrad, Ross Martin, Paul Williams, Harry Morgan, René Auberjonois, Robert Shields, Lorene Yarnell

That diminutive genius, Miguelito Loveless, has a new plan for world domination. He's cloning heads of state. It's worked in England, Spain, and Russia. The United States and President Cleveland could be next. Those legendary agents James West and Artemus Gordon are called out of retirement to save the day. This revival of the sixties series is breezily entertaining. There's plenty of action and humor. Robert Conrad and Ross Martin have a good time poking fun at their characters. In the role of the evil Loveless, Paul Williams is no match for the late Michael Dunn, but he gets by. This made-for-TV movie is filled with old gimmicks, but most of them still work.

1979 95 minutes

WINCHESTER .73

★★★★

DIRECTOR: Anthony Mann

CAST: James Stewart, Shelley Winters, Dan Duryea, Stephen McNally, Will Geer, Rock Hudson, Tony Curtis, John McIntire

Cowboy James Stewart acquires the latest iron from the East, a Winchester .73 rifle, loses it to a thief, and pursues the prized weapon as it passes from hand to hand. He finally corners the original thief on a precipice. Responsible for renewing the popularity of the western as film fare, this oater is simple, brisk-paced, direct, action-packed, tongue-in-cheek, mean, sweaty, suspenseful, and entirely entertaining.

1950 B & W 92 minutes

WINDS OF THE WASTELAND

★★★

DIRECTOR: Mack V. Wright

CAST: John Wayne, Phyllis Fraser, Yakima Canutt, Lane Chandler, Sam Flint, Lew Kelly, Bob Kortman

Big John Wayne is the head of a stagecoach company that competes for a government mail contract in the days after the pony express. Better than most B westerns made by the Duke, because he was beginning to show more polish and confidence, but still no classic.

1936 B & W 57 minutes

WINDWALKER

★★★★

DIRECTOR: Keith Merril

CAST: Trevor Howard, Nick Ramus, James Remar, Serene Hedin, Dusty Iron, Wing McCrea

Trevor Howard plays the title role in this superb film which spans three generations of a Cheyenne Indian family. It refutes the unwritten rule that family entertainment has to be bland and predictable and is proof that films don't need to include sensationalism to hold the attention of modern filmgoers. *Windwalker* has all the joy, drama, and excitement you could ever ask for in a motion picture. Rated PG.

1980 108 minutes

WINNING OF THE WEST

★★

DIRECTOR: George Archainbaud
CAST: Gene Autry, Smiley Burnette, Gail Davis, Robert Livingston, Richard Crane, House Peters Jr., Gregg Barton, George Chesebro, Eddie Parker

Smiley Burnette was reunited with Gene Autry in this film. With the exception of one film in 1951, Gene and Smiley were not to be teamed for eleven years, and it's fitting that these two old-timers should ride off into the sunset in each other's company. The plot line? Same old stuff about a brave newspaper publisher who wants to stop corruption and lawlessness and enlists the aid of no-nonsense Gene and all-nonsense Smiley. Former stars Robert Livingston and House Peters Jr., as well as veteran stunt performers Gregg Barton and Eddie Parker, make this one interesting to watch. Perky Gail Davis reprises her role as somebody's daughter who has a yen for Gene but loses him to Smiley and Champion.

1953 B & W 57 minutes

YELLOW ROSE OF TEXAS

DIRECTOR: Joseph Kane
CAST: Roy Rogers, Dale Evans, George Cleveland, Harry Shannon, Grant Withers, Bob Nolan and the Sons of the Pioneers, Hal Taliaferro, Tom London, Dick Botiller, Rex Lease, Jack O'Shea

Roy Rogers plays an undercover insurance agent out to clear the name of an old man who has been accused of aiding a stage robbery. Dale Evans and the Sons of the Pioneers give Roy a hand, and Grant Withers evils it up as the ruthless heavy. Former Cowboy stars Rex Lease and Hal Taliaferro join veteran character actors like Tom London to make this an enjoyable but standard Republic programmer. Originally released at sixty-nine minutes.

1944 B & W 55 minutes

YUMA

★★½

DIRECTOR: Ted Post
CAST: Clint Walker, Barry Sullivan, Edgar Buchanan, Kathryn Hays, Peter Mark Richman, Morgan Woodward

Big Clint Walker fights most of the rowdy elements of a tough town and has to expose a plan to undermine his authority as a lawman in this enjoyable made-for-television western. Walker plays the soft-spoken but capable town marshal with his usual good nature and dignity and the badmen eventually come to realize what the audience knew all along. He is not the man to cross or challenge. Better than the usual made-for-TV fare, this is one of director Ted Post's better efforts and one of only a handful of films that the former "Cheyenne Bodie" starred in. Not a great film, but fun for western fans and a treat for those who consider Clint Walker a charismatic action star.

1970 73 minutes

ZACHARIAH

★★½

DIRECTOR: George England

CAST: John Rubinstein, Pat Quinn, Don Johnson, Country Joe and the Fish, Doug Kershaw, New York Rock Ensemble, Elvin Jones, James Gang, Dick Van Patten

Forget the storyline in this midnight movie western and sit back and enjoy the music and the images. Television performers, a variety of musicians and actors, (including a youthful Don Johnson), populate this minor cult favorite and take every opportunity to be cool and break into song. There are tunes for most tastes and the fast-moving nature of the film makes it a good choice for company or a party.

1971 93 minutes

ZORRO RIDES AGAIN

★★★

DIRECTORS: William Whitney, John English

CAST: John Carroll, Helen Christian, Reed Howes, Duncan Renaldo, Noah Beery Sr., Richard Alexander, Nigel de Brulier, Bob Kortman, Tom London

A modern-day Zorro, played by future major-studio leading man John Carroll, lends his hand to a railway under siege by ruthless Noah Beery Sr., one of the cinema's greatest heavies. Beery and his henchman El Lobo (Richard Alexander) make life miserable for the railway's owners and their workers; their constant harassment keeps Zorro on his toes. A great cast keeps this serial moving at a rapid clip.

1937 B & W 12 chapters

ZORRO'S BLACK WHIP

★★

DIRECTORS: Spencer Bennett, Wallace Grissell

CAST: George J. Lewis, Linda Stirling, Lucien Littlefield, Francis McDonald, Hal Taliaferro, John Merton, Tom London, Jack Kirk, Jay Kirby

Zorro never makes an appearance in this serial, but lovely-yet-lethal action star Linda Stirling dons a black outfit and becomes the Black Whip, riding in the hoofprints of her crusading father, who was killed for his just beliefs. After several setbacks, the lovely heroine and her boyfriend (George J. Lewis) help the good people of Idaho thwart the greedy plans of a meanie (Francis McDonald) who stands in the way of statehood for the territory.

1944 B & W 12 chapters

ZORRO'S FIGHTING LEGION

★★★

DIRECTORS: William Witney, John English

CAST: Reed Hadley, Sheila Darcy, William Corson, Edmund Cobb, C. Montague Shaw, Budd Buster, Carleton Young, James Pierce, Charles King

Quality serial places Reed Hadley (as Zorro) at the helm of a determined band of patriotic ranchers eager to ensure safe passage of the gold shipments needed to continue Juarez's rule. Zorro faces danger from corrupt officials as well as marauding Yaqui Indians. Reed Hadley has an aristocratic air and a superb speaking voice; he made an excellent hero in his only lead in a serial. He later played Red Ryder on radio and in film and made a successful transition to television with *Racket Squad.*

1939 B & W 12 chapters

CAST INDEX

DIRECTOR INDEX

Family Viewing

Alphabetical Listing of Movies

ABOUT THE AUTHORS

Mick Martin is the film critic for the *Sacramento Union* newspaper, host/producer of "Mick Martin's Entertainment Showcase" on television in Sacramento, film critic for KZAP radio, a contributing editor for Tower Records' *Pulse!* magazine, and a songwriter.

Marsha Porter, author of several short stories and a teacher's handbook, holds a master's degree in educational administration. Currently, she does freelance editing and is an English instructor in Sacramento. Formerly, she was a newspaper advisor and collegiate actress.